The Concise Dictionary of Classical Hebrew

The Concise Dictionary of Classical Hebrew

David J.A. Clines
Editor

David Stec and Jacqueline C.R. de Roo
Research Associates

Sheffield
Sheffield Phoenix Press

2009

Published by Sheffield Phoenix Press Ltd
Department of Biblical Studies, University of Sheffield,
45 Victoria Street, Sheffield S3 7QB, England

for Dictionary of Classical Hebrew Ltd

Typeset by the Hebrew Dictionary Project
University of Sheffield
and
printed by Lightning Source

British Library Cataloguing in Publication Data

Concise Dictionary of Classical Hebrew.
I. Clines, David J. A.
492.43

ISBN 978-1-906055-78-3 hardback
ISBN 978-1-906055-79-0 paperback

INTRODUCTION

The *Concise Dictionary of Classical Hebrew* (*CDCH*) is an abridgment of the eight-volume *Dictionary of Classical Hebrew* (*DCH*). It is about one-tenth the length of the full *Dictionary of Classical Hebrew*, and is designed to be a manageable reference work of value to students and scholars alike.

The *Dictionary of Classical Hebrew*, the first volume of which appeared in 1993, was the first dictionary of the Classical Hebrew language ever to be published. Unlike other dictionaries of the ancient Hebrew language, which cover only the texts of the Hebrew Bible, either exclusively or principally, *DCH* records the language of all texts written in Hebrew from the earliest times down to the end of the second century CE. That is to say, it includes not only the words used in the Hebrew Bible, but also those found in the Hebrew Book of Ben Sira (Ecclesiasticus), the Dead Sea Scrolls, and all the ancient Hebrew inscriptions.

Nevertheless, while *DCH* provides an invaluable resource for scholarly research, its exhaustive analysis of the evidence for the ancient Hebrew language makes it somewhat forbidding to students and even to many scholars. The *Concise Dictionary of Classical Hebrew* presents all that is most essential about *DCH* in a clear, concise and easy to use form. It includes all the words found in *DCH*, with the exception only of a very small number of non-biblical words based on uncertain or doubtful readings in the original sources. It is more than a mere abridgment of *DCH*, being a considered revision of the analysis of meanings, especially in the earlier volumes.

In general, the difference between the two dictionaries lies in the length of the treatment of each individual word. In the *Dictionary of Classical Hebrew*, every occurrence of every word (except a few of the very most common) is cited, and, in the case of verbs, all the nouns that serve as the subjects or objects of the verb are mentioned, while, in the case of nouns, all the verbs of which the noun is the subject or object are mentioned. In this way, the *Dictionary* provides a rich resource for the study of the use of words in the Hebrew language. The *Concise Dictionary* cannot of course include all this information, though very many subjects and objects are mentioned, but most other elements of the full *Dictionary* are present.

Unlike most other dictionaries of Hebrew, which are (with the notable exception of Ludwig Koehler's *Lexicon in Veteris Testamenti libros* of 1953) mainly revisions of earlier dictionaries, *DCH* represents an entirely fresh re-examination of the ancient Hebrew texts, original analyses of the meanings of all the words, and independent structures of the individual articles.

It is a feature of the *CDCH* that all the Hebrew cited is followed immediately by an English translation, so that the *Dictionary* is intelligible to users with only an elementary knowledge of the language.

1. *Elements of an Article*

What follows is a description of the normal layout of an article about a word in the *Concise Dictionary of Classical Hebrew.*

1. *Headword* (or, lemma). Like most other Hebrew dictionaries, in the *Concise Dictionary of Classical Hebrew* the headword of each article, if it is a verb, is not vocalized, and if it is a noun or some other part of speech, it is vocalized. If the form used as the headword does not occur in any of our extant texts, it is enclosed in square brackets. If the word is not found in the standard lexicon of Brown–Driver–Briggs (BDB), either because it occurs in a Hebrew text unknown to BDB (like the Dead Sea Scrolls) or because the word has been proposed by a modern scholar and is not yet universally accepted by other scholars, it is prefixed with an asterisk (*).

2. *Statistics.* Next comes a notation of the number of occurrences of the word in each of the four corpora of ancient Hebrew: the Bible, Ben Sira, the Dead Sea Scrolls, and the Inscriptions. Thus the notation $_{334.5.13.32}$ means that the word occurs 334 times in the Bible, 5 times in Ben Sira, 13 times in the Dead Sea Scrolls and 32 times in the Hebrew Inscriptions. If there is only one number in the statistics, the word occurs only in the Hebrew Bible, and if the notation is, for example, $_{0.0.7}$, it means that it occurs only in the Dead Sea Scrolls, and that 7 times. In the case of verbs, occurrence statistics are also given for each of the voices (or, *binyanim*).

3. *Part of speech.* For an explanation of the abbreviations showing the part of speech (and the grammatical gender of a word, when appropriate), see the List of Abbreviations. The gender of a noun appears in square brackets (e.g. pr.n.[m.]) if it only presumed and there is no textual evidence for it.

4. *Morphology.* There follow representative forms in which the word appears, e.g., in the case of verbs, the form for the imperfect, and in the case of nouns, forms of the plural and forms with suffixes. When a form is attested only in a corpus other than the Hebrew Bible, the abbreviation Si, Q or I (for Ben Sira, Qumran or Inscriptions) is prefixed to the form.

5. *Structure of the article.* The meanings or senses of every word appear in bold. Complementary information, such as an explanation of the terms used for the meanings or of the contexts in which the word appears, follows the meanings, in Roman type. In the case of a verb, the article is divided according to the voices (or, *binyanim*) in which the verb is used, in the order qal, niphal, piel, pual, hiphil, hophal, hithpael (other, less frequent, voices are also listed). Within each voice, the main senses of the word appear in bold letters, and are numbered, 1, 2, 3, etc., sometimes being subdivided as 1a, b, c, etc. In the case of a noun, the article is divided according to the main senses of the word, numbered in bold as in the case of the verbs.

6. *Citations.* No attempt is made to give a comprehensive list of citations (as in *DCH*), but there is usually at least one reference given to a text in which the word in the sense cited is used. Citations are made from all the four corpora of texts covered in the Dictionary.

7. *Emendations.* Many important proposed emendations of the text are included in the Dictionary. It is not implied that a given emendation should either be adopted or rejected; the Dictionary simply states the consequences of adopting particular emendations.

8. *Index references.* At the end of articles on verbs, an arrow (→) points to nouns that are 'derived' from the verb. At the end of articles on nouns, an arrow points to the verb from which the noun is 'derived', if it is known. When nouns do not have a verb from which they are derived, but are similar to another noun, the notation 'cf.' follows the arrow. When verbs or nouns have byforms (i.e. forms spelled differently) these also are registered with 'cf.' after the arrow.

2. *'New Words'*
The 'new words' in *DCH* and *CDCH*, marked with an asterisk (*) to the left of the headword, are those words that do not appear in the standard Hebrew–English lexicon of Brown–Driver–Briggs (BDB) of 1906. The great majority of these more than 3300 'new words' do not appear in any other Hebrew dictionary. They are of two types:

1. Words not found in the Bible but occurring in classical Hebrew texts outside the Bible (Ben Sira, the Dead Sea Scrolls, or the Hebrew Inscriptions); there are about 1200 such words. The occurrence statistics for these words will show zero occurrences in the first position (e.g. 0.5.13.3), signifying that the word does not occur in the Bible but does occur in other Classical Hebrew texts. Such words are not registered in other Hebrew dictionaries since those dictionaries usually restrict themselves to the Hebrew of the Bible.

2. Words proposed by modern scholars, more than 2100 in number. Especially in the twentieth century, many new proposals have been made for the meaning of Hebrew words, sometimes on the basis of similar words in cognate languages like Arabic, Akkadian and Ugaritic, and sometimes on the basis of a new consideration of the Hebrew evidence. Many of these proposals have not yet gained the approval of the mainstream of scholarly opinion, and many of them are mutually exclusive. Users of the Dictionary should be aware of the tentative nature of such proposed words and of the fact that the occurrences of such words have traditionally been explained otherwise; nevertheless, it is salutary to be reminded, on almost every page of the *CDCH*, that our knowledge of the ancient Hebrew language is not entirely assured and that the meanings of some thousands of words remain debated. The complete *DCH* contains a full Bibliography of the scholarly literature concerning such words. For an example of such 'new words', readers may consult the Dictionary under the word דבר. The verb is attested in over 1100 places as the normal word for 'speak'; but no fewer than seven other words spelled דבר and meaning 'destroy', 'turn the back', 'drive out', 'carry away', 'manage', 'follow', and 'have descendants' have now also been proposed as occurring in twenty-seven of the passages where the usual דבר I has traditionally been seen.

3. *Proper Nouns*

Included in *CDCH*, as in *DCH*, are all the proper nouns, i.e. personal names, place names and the like, that are found in the Hebrew texts covered for the *Dictionary*. Proper names are not, strictly speaking, part of the vocabulary of a language, but is customary for Hebrew dictionaries to include them—a practice that at least has the benefit of registering a standard English form for each name. The transliteration system used in the RSV and NRSV has been adopted here, and names not occurring in the Hebrew Bible have been normalized according to the same system. Unlike *DCH*, in which different persons of the same name are distinguished, and in which some encyclopaedic information about the persons is given, *CDCH* shows only the total number of occurrences for each name. No emended forms are included.

4. *Sources*

The following sources of the four corpora of classical Hebrew texts that have been used for this *Dictionary* are these:

1. For the Hebrew Bible, the edition of the Hebrew Bible that has been used is *Biblia hebraica stuttgartensia* (ed. K. Elliger and W. Rudolph; Stuttgart: Deutsche Bibelstiftung, 1967). Both the text of the Bible itself and the text of the critical apparatus have been used as source texts for this *Dictionary*.

2. For Ben Sira, the primary text for this *Dictionary* is that published in *The Book of Ben Sira: Text, Concordance and an Analysis of the Vocabulary* (Jerusalem: The Academy of the Hebrew Language and the Shrine of the Book, 1973).

3. For the Dead Sea Scrolls, a complete list of the manuscripts consulted is printed in *The Dictionary of Classical Hebrew*, VI, pp. 15-35. For some of the larger manuscripts from Cave 1 and also the main Temple Scroll (11QT) and the Damascus Document (CD) we have used the software Accordance 5.6.

4. For the Inscriptions, the basic resource has been the two volumes of Graham I. Davies, *Ancient Hebrew Inscriptions: Corpus and Concordance* (Cambridge: Cambridge University Press, 1991, 2004).

5. *Other Differences between* DCH *and* CDCH
The full *Dictionary of Classical Hebrew* contains a number of other features not mentioned above that have not been included in *The Concise Dictionary of Classical Hebrew* for reasons of space.

1. List of words under each letter of the alphabet arranged by frequency of occurrence.
2. List of sources outside the Hebrew Bible for the texts studied in the Dictionary.
3. Bibliography of scholarly literature on individual words (including especially those marked with an asterisk as 'new words' in *CDCH*).
4. English–Hebrew index of words contained in each volume of the Dictionary.

While the *Concise Dictionary of Classical Hebrew* is complete in itself, for further information the user is recommended to consult the fuller *Dictionary of Classical Hebrew*.

6. *Acknowledgments*
The abridgment and revision of *DCH* that has resulted in the present volume was carried out by David M. Stec, who was responsible for the letters aleph, gimel–waw, heth, lamed, nun and taw, and by Jacqueline C.R. de Roo, who was responsible for the letters beth, zayin, teth–kaph, mem, samekh, pe–qoph and sin. David Stec and Jacqueline de Roo were jointly responsible for ayin, resh and shin. David Clines proofread the volume and made appropriate editorial interventions.

DJAC
21 October, 2009

ABBREVIATIONS AND SIGNS

TEXTS

Gn Ex Lv Nm Dt Jos Jg 1 S 2 S 1 K 2 K Is Jr Ezk Ho Jl Am Ob Jon Mc Na Hb Zp Hg Zc Ml Ps Jb Pr Ru Ca Ec Lm Est Dn Ezr Ne 1 C 2 C

SIGNS

+ = the following is used in association with the preceding
|| = parallel with
:: = in opposition to
§ = section
* A 'new' word, i.e. not in BDB.
→ = the following are related words

ABBREVIATIONS

abbrev. = abbreviation, abbreviated
abs. = absolute, used absolutely
accus. = accusative (may sometimes be used interchangeably with obj.)
act. = active
adj. = adjective
adv. = adverb, adverbial, adverbially
AHL = Academy of the Hebrew Language
alw. = always
appar. = apparently
architect. = architectural
art. = article
assoc. = associated, association
attrib. -= attributive, attributively
BHS = *Biblia hebraica stuttgartensia*
cf. = compare, see also
cohort. = cohortative
coll. = collective, used collectively
conj. = conjunction
consec. = consecutive
cp = cpmmon plural
cs = common singular
cstr. = construct
def. = definite
del. = delete
demonstr. = demonstrative
descr. = describing, description
du. = dual
ellip. = ellipsis
em., *see* if em., or em.
esp. = especially
exc. = except
f., fem. = feminine
fin. = finite
fr. = fragment
freq. = frequently
fs = feminine singular
gent. = gentilic
Gnz = Genizah fragment, manuscript
hi. = hiphil
ho. = hophal
hothp. = hothpael
htp. = hithpael
htpal. = hithpalel
htpalp. = hithpalpel
htpilp. = hithpilpel
htpo. = hithpoel, hithpoal
htpol. = hithpolal, hithpolel
I = inscription
ident. = to be identified

if em. = the foregoing results from an emendation
impers. = impersonal
impf. = imperfect
impv. = imperative
indef. = indefinite
inf. = infinitive
ins. = insert
inscr. = inscription
intens. = intensive
interj. = interjection
intrans. = intransitive
interrog. = interrogative
juss. = jussive
Kh. = Khirbet
Kt = ketiv
L = Codex Leningradensis B19 A, text of *BHS*
lit. = literally
m., masc. = masculine
mg = marginal, sublinear, supralinear reading
mpl = masculine plural
ms = manuscript; (in morphology) masculine singular
MT = Masoretic Text
n. = noun
neg. = negative
ni. = niphal
nom. cl. = noun clause
ntp. = nithpael
nu. = nuphal (ni. mixed with pu.)
obj. = object
Occ = Occidental
oft. = often
opp. = opposite of, as opposed to
or em. = the foregoing will not be the case if the following emendation is accepted
orig. = originally
ost. = ostracon
pal. = palel
part. = particle
pass. = passive
perh. = perhaps
pf. = perfect
pi. = piel
pilp. = pilpel
pl. = plural
pl.n. = place name
po. = poel, poal,
pol. = polal, polel
polp. = polpal
pred. = predicative, predicatively
prep. = preposition, prepositional
pr.n. = personal name
prob. = probably
pron. = pronoun
pronom. = pronominal
ptc. = participle
pu. = pual
pulp. = pulpal
Q = Qumran
Qr = qere
ref(s). = reference(s)
rel. = relative
Sam = Samaritan
sf. = suffix
sg. = singular
Si = Ben Sira
sim. = similar, similarly
specif. = specific, specifially
subj. = subject
syn. = synonymous
t = times
trans. = transitive
usu. = usually
var(s). = variant(s)
vb. = verb
voc. = vocative
Y. = Yhwh

א

אָב 1215.20.84 n.m.—cstr. אֲבִי; sf. אָבִי, אֲבִיכֶם; pl. abs. אָבוֹת; cstr. אֲבוֹת; sf. אֲבוֹתַי—**1a.** usu. **father** Gn 2$_{24}$ 19$_{31}$. **b.** sometimes, esp. in pl., **parent** Ex 20$_{5}$ Pr 17$_{6}$. **2a. ancestor** Dt 26$_{5}$; usu. pl. Dt 10$_{22}$ Jr 3$_{18}$. **b. founding father, ancestor** of city, nation or group Gn 4$_{21}$ 19$_{38}$ 1 C 8$_{29}$. **3. father figure,** as protector, counsellor, etc., אָב לְפַרְעֹה *a father to Pharaoh* Gn 45$_{8}$, אָב ... לָאֶבְיוֹנִים *a father ... to the poor* Jb 29$_{16}$; God as father, Is 63$_{16}$; אָבִי *my father* in address, as term of respect 2 K 2$_{12}$. **4.** בֵּית(־)אָב **father's house(hold), phratry,** as kinship and perh. military unit Gn 46$_{31}$ 1 C 5$_{24}$. **5.** רָאשֵׁי (הָ)אָבוֹת **heads of fathers' households** Nm 36$_{1}$ Ne 12$_{22}$, רָאשִׁים לְאָבוֹת in same sense Ne 11$_{13}$, נְשִׂיאֵי הָאָבוֹת *the princes of fathers' households* 1 K 8$_{1}$||2 C 5$_{2}$, שָׂרֵי(־)הָאָבוֹת in same sense Ezr 8$_{29}$.

[אֵב] 2.0.2 n.m.—sf. אִבּוֹ; pl. cstr. אִבֵּי—**greenness** of plants Jb 8$_{12}$ Ca 6$_{11}$ 4QSD 7$_{14}$. → cf. אָבִיב *ear (of cereal).*

אֹב, see אוֹב I *ghost,* II *wineskin.*

*[אבא] 0.0.0.3 pr.n.m. **Abba.**

*[אבבעל] 0.0.0.1 pr.n.m. **Abibaal.**

[אֲבִגַיִל], see אֲבִיגַיִל *Abigail.*

אֲבַגְתָא 1 pr.n.m. **Abagtha.**

אבד 184.11.46 vb.—**Qal** 117.6.35 Pf. אָבַד, אָבָדְתָּ; impf. יֹאבַד (יֹאבֵד); ptc. אוֹבֵד, cstr. אֹבַד, אוֹבֶדֶת, אוֹבְדִים; pass. Si אבוד; inf. abs. אָבֹד; cstr. אֲבֹד (אֲבָדְךָ, אֲבָדְךְ) אֲבָדָם—**1a. perish, die, be destroyed, disappear,** oft. as divine judgment; of persons, nations Nm 16$_{33}$ (+ מִתּוֹךְ *from among*) 21$_{29}$ Dt 28$_{20}$ (+ מִפְּנֵי *on account of*) Jos 23$_{13}$ (+ מֵעַל *from upon*) Jon 1$_{14}$ (+ בְּ *on account of*) Mc 7$_{2}$ (+ מִן *from*) Jb 4$_{20}$, lion Jb 4$_{11}$ (+ מִבְּלִי טֶרֶף *for lack of prey*). **b. be about to die,** אֲרַמִּי אֹבֵד *an Aramaean on the point of death* Dt 26$_{5}$. **2. be destroyed, perish,** of earth and heavens Ps 102$_{27}$, weapons 2 S 1$_{27}$. **3. cease, vanish, fade away,** of hope Ezk 19$_{5}$, remembrance Ps 9$_{7}$, wisdom Is 29$_{14}$, wealth Ec 5$_{13}$. **4. be lost, stray,** of sheep Ps 119$_{176}$; כל האובד *any missing thing* CD 9$_{10}$.

Pi. 41.5.8 Pf. אִבַּד, אִבַּדְתָּ; impf. יְאַבֵּד; ptc. מְאַבְּדִים; inf. abs. אַבֵּד; cstr. אַבֵּד (אַבְּדֵנִי)—**1. destroy, kill persons,** nations Dt 8$_{20}$ (+ מִפְּנֵי *from before*) 11$_{4}$ Ezk 28$_{16}$ (+ מִתּוֹךְ *from among*) Ps 21$_{11}$ (+ מִן *from*), images of gods Nm 33$_{52}$, cult places Dt 12$_{2}$, bars of city gates Lm 2$_{9}$, good Ec 9$_{18}$. **2. lose** sheep Jr 23$_{1}$, **waste** wealth Pr 29$_{3}$.

Hi. 26.0.3 Pf. הֶאֱבַדְתָּ; impf. אֹבִידָה; ptc. מַאֲבִיד; inf. הַאֲבִיד—**destroy, kill** persons Lv 23$_{30}$ (+ מִקֶּרֶב *from among*) Dt 28$_{51}$ Ezk 25$_{7}$ (+ מִן *from*), name Dt 7$_{24}$ (+ מִתַּחַת *from under*), animals Ezk 32$_{13}$ (+ מֵעַל *from beside*), images of gods Ezk 30$_{13}$, hope Jb 14$_{19}$.

→ אֹבֵד *destruction,* אֲבֵדָה *lost object,* אֲבַדּוֹן *Abaddon,* אַבְדָן *destruction.*

אֹבֵד 2 n.[m.] **destruction** Nm 24$_{20.24}$. → אבד *perish.*

אֲבֵדָה 4.0.1 n.f. **lost object**—cstr. אֲבֵדַת—Ex 22$_{8}$. → אבד *perish.*

[אֲבַדֹּה], see אֲבַדּוֹן *destruction.*

אֲבַדּוֹ, see אֲבַדּוֹן *destruction.*

אֲבַדּוֹן 6.0.8 n.f.—אֲבַדּוֹ (Kt אבדה); pl. Q אבדונים; cstr. Q אבדוני—**destruction,** in ref. to death or abode of the dead, **Abaddon** Ps 88$_{12}$ Pr 15$_{11}$. → אבד *perish.*

אַבְדָן 2.0.2 n.[m.]—cstr. אָבְדַן—**destruction** Est 8$_{6}$ 9$_{5}$ 4QpsEzek[c] 1$_{2}$. → אבד *perish.*

אבה 54.3.2 vb.—**Qal** 54.3.2 Pf. אָבָה, אָבִיתִי; impf. יֹאבֶה; ptc. אֹבִים—**1. be willing** (usu. with neg. part.), followed by לְ + inf. cstr. Gn 24$_{5}$, inf. cstr. (without לְ) Dt 2$_{30}$, inf. abs. Is 42$_{24}$; abs. Jg 11$_{17}$. **2. consent to, accept,** followed by לְ Dt 13$_{9}$; with accus. Pr 1$_{25}$.

[אֵבֶה] 1 n.[m.] **reed,** אֳנִיּוֹת אֵבֶה *ships (made) of reed* Jb 9$_{26}$.

[אבוגיל], see אֲבִיגַיִל *Abigail.*

אֲבוֹי 1 interj. **alas** (or perh. noun, **discomfort**) Pr 23$_{29}$.

אֵבוּס 3 n.m.—cstr. אֵבוּס; sf. אֲבוּסֶךָ—**trough for feeding,** or perh. **stall for sleeping** Is 1$_{3}$ Jb 39$_{9}$ Pr 14$_{4}$. → אבס *fatten.*

אֹבוֹת, see אוֹב I *ghost,* II *wineskin.*

*[אָבוֹת] 0.0.3 n.f. **intercession,** אוחזי אבות *ones who hold,* i.e. make, *intercession* 1QS 2_9, מלאך אבות *angel of intercession* 4QPrEnosh 2_1.

[אִבְחָה] 1 n.f.—cstr. אִבְחַת—**slaughter** Ezk 21_{20} (or em. טִבְחַת or טֶבַח in same sense).

[אֲבַטִּיחַ] 1 n.[m.]—pl. אֲבַטִּחִים—**melon,** perh. **watermelon** (*Citrullus vulgaris*) Nm 11_5.

אָבִי 1 interj. **if only** (perh. var. of בִּי *pray,* or impf. ביה *entreat*) Jb 34_{36}; perh. 1 S 24_{12} 2 K 5_{13}.

אֲבִי *Abi,* see אֲבִיָּה *Abijah.*

אֲבִיאֵל 3 pr.n.m. **Abiel.**

אֲבִיאָסָף, see אֶבְיָסָף *Ebiasaph.*

אָבִיב 9.0.2 n.m.—pl. Q אביבות—**1. ear (of cereal)** Lv 2_{14}, specif. barley Ex 9_{31}. **2. Abib,** as month of first ears, ident. with later Nisan Ex 13_4. → אֵב cf. *greenness.*

אֲבִיגַיִל 17.0.0.2 pr.n.f. **Abigail,** also as אֲבִיגַל **Abigail.**

אֲבִידָן 5 pr.n.m. **Abidan.**

אֲבִידָע 2 pr.n.m. **Abida.**

אֲבִיָּה 26.0.4.7 pr.n.m.&f. **Abijah.**

אֲבִיָּהוּ, see אֲבִיָּה *Abijah.*

אֲבִיהוּא 12 pr.n.m. **Abihu.**

אֲבִיהוּד 1 pr.n.m. **Abihud.**

אֲבִיהַיִל 2 pr.n.f. **Abihail.**

אֲבִיו, see אֲבִיָּה. *Abijah.*

אֶבְיוֹן 61.3.27 adj.—sf. אֶבְיוֹנְךָ; pl. אֶבְיוֹנִים; cstr. אֶבְיוֹנֵי; sf. אֶבְיוֹנֶיהָ—**1. poor, needy,** esp. assoc. with dependence on divine help, adj. of man Ps 109_{16}, hired worker Dt 24_{14}, brother Dt 15_7. **2.** as noun, **poor one, needy one** Is 29_{19} Ps 40_{18} Si 13_{20}.

אֲבִיּוֹנָה 1 n.f. **caper-berry** (perh. *Capparis spinosa*) Ec 12_5.

*אביחי 0.0.0.1 pr.n.m. **Abihai.**

אֲבִיחַיִל 4 pr.n.m.&f. **Abihail.**

אֲבִיחַל, see אֲבִיחַיִל *Abihail.*

אֲבִיטוּב 1 pr.n.m. **Abitub.**

[אֲבִיטַל] 2 pr.n.f. **Abital.**

אֲבִיָּם 5 pr.n.m. **Abijam.**

אֲבִימָאֵל 2 pr.n.m. **Abimael.**

אֲבִימֶלֶךְ 67 pr.n.m. **Abimelech.**

אֲבִינָדָב 13 pr.n.m. **Abinadab.**

אֲבִינֹעַם 4 pr.n.m. **Abinoam.**

אֲבִינֵר, see אַבְנֵר *Abner.*

אֶבְיָסָף 4 pr.n.m. **Ebiasaph,** also as אֲבִיאָסָף **Abiasaph.**

אֲבִיעֶזֶר 7 pr.n.m. **Abiezer.**

[אֲבִיעֶזְרִי] 3 gent. **Abiezrite.**

אֲבִי־עַלְבוֹן 1 pr.n.m. **Abi-albon.**

[אָבִיר] 6.1 adj.—cstr. אֲבִיר—**mighty,** alw. as noun, **mighty (one),** with ref. to Y., אֲבִיר יַעֲקֹב *mighty one of Jacob* Gn 49_{24}, יִשְׂרָאֵל *of Israel* Is 1_{24}. → cf. אַבִּיר *mighty.*

אַבִּיר 17.2 adj.—כְּאַבִּיר; cstr. אַבִּיר; pl. אַבִּירִים; cstr. אַבִּירֵי; sf. אַבִּירָיו—**mighty,** alw. as noun, **1. mighty (one), hero,** appar. of angels Ps 78_{25}; usu. of humans Jb 24_{22}, specif. **chief** of herdsmen 1 S 21_8. **2.** mighty animal, **a. bull** Is 34_7. **b. stallion** Jg 5_{22}. → cf. אָבִיר *mighty.*

אֲבִירָם 11.1 pr.n.m. **Abiram.**

אֲבִישַׁג 5 pr.n.f. **Abishag.**

אֲבִישׁוּעַ 5 pr.n.m. **Abishua.**

אֲבִישׁוּר 2 pr.n.m. **Abishur.**

אֲבִישַׁי 25.0.2 pr.n.m. **Abishai.**

אֲבִישָׁלוֹם, see אַבְשָׁלוֹם *Absalom.*

אֶבְיָתָר 30 pr.n.m. **Abiathar.**

אבך 1 vb.—**Htp.** 1 Impf. + waw וַיִּתְאַבְּכוּ—**swirl, billow,** as plume of smoke Is 9_{17}.

אבל I 39.1.5 vb.—**Qal** 18.0.1 Pf. אָבַל; impf. תֶּאֱבַל—**mourn, grieve,** of persons Is 19_8, earth Is 24_4, gates Is 3_{26}.

Hi. 2 Pf. הֶאֱבַלְתִּי; + waw וַיַּאֲבֶל־—**1.** abs., **cause mourning,** subj. Y. Ezk 31_{15}. **2.** with accus., **cause to mourn,** subj. Y. Lm 2_8.

Htp. 19.1.4 Pf. הִתְאַבֵּל; impf. יִתְאַבֵּל; + waw וַיִּתְאַבֵּל; impv. Si הִתְאַבְּלִי, התאבל; ptc. מִתְאַבֵּל, מִתְאַבֶּלֶת, מִתְאַבְּלִים—**1. be in mourning** Gn 37_{34} (+ עַל *for* son). **2. lament** 1 S 15_{35} (+ אֶל *for* Saul) Is 66_{10} (+ עַל *over* Jerusalem) Ezr 10_6 (+ עַל *on account of* sin). **3. behave as a mourner** 2 S 14_2.

→ אָבֵל *mourning,* אֵבֶל *mourning.*

*אבל II 8 vb.—**Qal** 8 Pf. אָבַל; impf. תֶּאֱבַל—**be dry, be dried up,** of earth Is 24_4, pastures Am 1_2, new wine Is 24_7.

*אבל III 1 vb.—**Hi.** 1 Pf. הֶאֱבַלְתִּי—**shut** the abyss Ezk 31_{15}.

אָבֵל I 8.2.4 adj.—cstr. אֲבֵל־; pl. אֲבֵלִים, pl. אֲבֵלוֹת; cstr. אֲבֵלֵי; sf. אֲבֵלָיו—**mourning,** as noun, **mourner** Gn

37$_{35}$; אֲבֶל־אֵם *one mourning a mother* Ps 35$_{14}$. → אבל *mourn*.

אָבֵל II 13 pl.n. **Abel,** אָבֵל בֵּית־מַעֲכָה **Abel-beth-maachah,** אָבֵל מָיִם **Abel-maim,** אָבֵל הַגְּדוֹלָה **Abel-hagedolah** or **Great Abel,** אָבֵל מְחוֹלָה **Abel-meholah,** אָבֵל הַשִּׁטִּים **Abel-shittim,** אָבֵל כְּרָמִים **Abel-keramim,** אָבֵל מִצְרַיִם **Abel-mizraim.**

אֵבֶל 24.1.10 n.m.—cstr. אֵבֶל; sf. אֶבְלָם; pl. sf. Q אבליהמה—**mourning, (ritual** or **period of) mourning,** אֵבֶל יָחִיד *mourning of,* i.e. for, *an only child* Jr 6$_{26}$, יְמֵי אֵבֶל *days of mourning* Gn 27$_{41}$. → אבל *mourn*.

אֲבָל 11.1.1 adv.—1. adversative, **however** Dn 10$_{7}$. 2. emphatic, **indeed** Gn 42$_{21}$. 3. as interj., **alas** 2 S 14$_{5}$.

אֻבָל, see אוּבָל *river*.

*אבמעץ 0.0.0.2 pr.n.m. **Abmaaz.**

אֶבֶן 277.8.34 n.f.—אָבֶן; cstr. אֶבֶן; sf. אַבְנוֹ; pl. אֲבָנִים; cstr. אַבְנֵי; sf. אֲבָנָיו, אַבְנֵיהֶם—**1. stone, a.** as material: for building Gn 11$_{3}$, images of gods Dt 4$_{28}$. **b.** large stones: as memorial Gn 28$_{18}$, covering entrance to well Gn 29$_{2}$. **c.** small stones, as memorial cairn Gn 31$_{46}$. **d.** as weapon Ex 21$_{18}$ 1 S 17$_{40}$. **e.** engraved for tables of the law Ex 24$_{12}$. **f.** as ore producing iron and copper Dt 8$_{9}$. **g.** as symbol: of stillness Ex 15$_{16}$, commonness 1 K 10$_{27}$||2 C 1$_{15}$, strength Jb 6$_{12}$, hardness Jb 38$_{30}$; Y. as **Rock** of Israel Gn 49$_{24}$. **2. precious stone,** with adj. יְקָר *precious* 2 S 12$_{30}$||1 C 20$_{2}$; אֶבֶן־חֵן lit. 'stone of grace' Pr 17$_{8}$, אַבְנֵי־חֵפֶץ lit. 'stones of delight' Is 54$_{12}$; אֶבֶן־סַפִּיר *stone of sapphire* Ezk 1$_{26}$. **3a. weight,** אֶבֶן שְׁלֵמָה *a full weight* Pr 11$_{1}$, אֶבֶן הַמֶּלֶךְ *weight of the king,* i.e. the royal standard weight 2 S 14$_{26}$, אַבְנֵי־צֶדֶק *weights of righteousness,* i.e. true weights Lv 19$_{36}$, אֶבֶן מִרְמָה *of deceit,* i.e. fraudulent weights Mc 6$_{11}$, אֶבֶן וָאֶבֶן *weight and weight,* i.e. diverse (fraudulent) weights Dt 25$_{13}$. **b. plummet** Is 34$_{11}$. **4. hailstone,** אֶבֶן בָּרָד *hailstone* Is 30$_{30}$, אַבְנֵי אֶלְגָּבִישׁ *hailstones* Ezk 13$_{11}$, אֲבָנִים גְּדֹלוֹת *great stones* Jos 10$_{11}$. **5.** named stones, **a.** אֶבֶן בֹּהַן *stone of Bohan* Jos 15$_{6}$. **b.** אֶבֶן הַזֹּחֶלֶת *stone of Zoheleth* (or perh. *serpent's stone*) 1 K 1$_{9}$. **c.** אֶבֶן הָעֶזֶר *Ebenezer,* i.e. the stone (called) Help 1 S 5$_{1}$. **d.** הָאֶבֶן הָאָזֶל *the stone of Ezel* 1 S 20$_{19}$. → cf. אבן *stone,* מַאֲבָן *ballista.*

[אֹבֶן] 2.0.1 n.[m.]—du. אָבְנָיִם—**stone,** du., **pair of stones,** as potter's wheel Jr 18$_{3}$, perh. as birth stool Ex 1$_{16}$. → cf. אֶבֶן *stone.*

[אֲבָנָה] 2 K 5$_{12}$(Kt), see אֲמָנָה II *Amana.*

אַבְנֵט 9.0.2 n.[m.]—cstr. אַבְנֵט; sf. אַבְנֵטְךָ; pl. אַבְנֵטִים—**girdle,** usu. of priest Ex 28$_{4}$; also of royal officer Is 22$_{21}$.

[אבנעם], see אֲבִינֹעַם *Abinoam.*

אַבְנֵר 63.0.0.1 pr.n.m. **Abner.**

אבס 2 vb.—**Qal** 2 Ptc. pass. אֲבוּסִים, אָבוּס—pass. **be fattened,** or perh. **be kept in stall;** of fatted fowl 1 K 5$_{3}$, ox Pr 15$_{17}$. → אֵבוּס *trough,* מַאֲבוּס *granary.*

[אֲבַעְבֻּעָה] 2 n.f.—pl. אֲבַעְבֻּעֹת—**blister** Ex 9$_{9.10}$.

*[אֲבִעֶזֶר] 0.0.0.2 pl.n. **Abiezer.**

[אֶבֶץ] 1 pl.n. **Ebez.**

אִבְצָן 2 pr.n.m. **Ibzan.**

אבק 2 vb.—**Ni.** 2 + waw וַיֵּאָבֵק; inf. הֵאָבְקוֹ—**wrestle** Gn 32$_{25.26}$ (+ עִם *with*).

אָבָק 6.0.1 n.m.—cstr. אֲבַק; sf. אֲבָקָם—**dust, powder** Dt 28$_{24}$ Is 29$_{5}$. → cf. אֲבָקָה *powder.*

[אֲבָקָה] 1 n.f.—cstr. אַבְקַת—**powder,** used in perfume Ca 3$_{6}$. → cf. אָבָק *dust.*

אבר 1 vb.—**Hi.** 1 Impf. יַאֲבֶר־—**fly,** or perh. **grow wings,** of hawk Jb 39$_{26}$. → אֵבֶר *wings,* אֶבְרָה *wing.*

אֵבֶר 3.0.1 n.[m.]—1. sg. coll., **wings, wingfeathers** Is 40$_{31}$ Ps 55$_{7}$ Ezk 17$_{3}$. 2. pl., **limbs, members,** of sacrificial animal perh. Si 7$_{31}$ 11QT 24$_{8}$ (ארביה appar. for אבריה). → אבר *fly.*

אֶבְרָה 4 n.f.—sf. אֶבְרָתוֹ; pl. sf. אֶבְרוֹתֶיהָ—**wing** of bird Dt 32$_{11}$, of Y. as bird Ps 91$_{4}$. → אבר *fly.*

אַבְרָהָם 175.3.15 pr.n.m. **Abraham.**

*אבריהו 0.0.0.1 pr.n.m. **Abraiah.**

אַבְרֵךְ 1 appar. interj. perh. **bow down** or **hail, minister,** cried before Joseph Gn 41$_{43}$.

אַבְרָם 61.0.2 pr.n.m. **Abram.**

אַבְשַׁי, see אֲבִישַׁי *Abishai.*

אַבְשָׁלוֹם 111.0.2 pr.n.m. **Absalom,** also as אֲבִישָׁלוֹם **Abishalom.**

*אבשעל 0.0.0.1 pr.n.m. **Abshaal.**

אֹבֹת I 4 pl.n.—**Oboth.**

אֹבֹת II, see אוֹב I *ghost.*

אָגֵא 1 pr.n.m. **Agee.**

אֲגַג 8 pr.n.m. **Agag.**

אֲגָגִי 5 gent. **Agagite.**

*אגד 0.0.1 vb.—**Qal** 0.0.1 Inf. אגוד—**(un)bind** 5QRègle 2$_{7}$. → אֲגֻדָּה *bond.*

אֲגֻדָּה 4 n.f.—cstr. אֲגֻדַּת; sf. אֲגֻדָּתוֹ; pl. cstr. אֲגֻדּוֹת—**1. bond,** tying one to bar of yoke Is 58$_{6}$. **2. bunch** of hyssop Ex 12$_{22}$. **3. band, troop** 2 S 2$_{25}$. **4.** perh. **vault** of heavens Am 9$_{6}$. → אגד *bind.*

אֱגוֹז 1 n.[m.] **nut,** perh. specif. **walnut (tree)** (*Juglans regia*) Ca 6$_{11}$.

אָגוּר 1 pr.n.m. **Agur.**

[אֲגוֹרָה] 1 n.f.—cstr. אֲגוֹרַת—**payment,** or perh. **piece, coin** of silver 1 S 2$_{36}$.

[אַגְזָרִי] Is 13$_{9}$(1QIsa^{a}), var. of אַכְזָרִי *cruel.*

[אֶגֶל] 1.0.1 n.[m]—pl. cstr. אֶגְלֵי—**drop** of dew Jb 38$_{28}$ 4QBer^{a} 3$_{5}$.

אֶגְלַיִם 1 pl.n. **Eglaim.**

*[אגם] vb. **Qal, seethe,** דּוּד נָפוּחַ וְאֹגֵם *a boiling and seething pot* Jb 41$_{12}$ (if em. אַגְמֹן appar. *[burning] rushes*).

אֲגַם I 9.0.1 n.[m.]—cstr. אֲגַם; pl. אֲגַמִּים; cstr. אַגְמֵי; sf. אַגְמֵיהֶם—**pool** Ex 7$_{19}$, perh. **swamp** Jr 51$_{32}$. → cf. אַגְמוֹן *rush.*

*[אֲגַם] II 1 n.[m.] **bulwark** Jr 51$_{32}$.

[אָגֵם] 1 adj. **distressed,** אַגְמֵי־נָפֶשׁ *distressed of soul* Is 19$_{10}$.

אַגְמוֹן 5 n.[m.]—**rush** Is 9$_{13}$, used as barb Jb 40$_{26}$. → cf. אֲגַם *pool.*

אַגְמֹן, see אַגְמוֹן *rush.*

[אַגָּן] 3.0.0.1 n.[m.]—cstr. אַגַּן; pl. אַגָּנוֹת—**bowl,** or perh. **goblet** Ex 24$_{6}$ Is 22$_{24}$ Arad ost. 1$_{10}$; navel descr. as round bowl Ca 7$_{3}$.

[אֲגַף] I 7.0.1 n.[m.]—pl. cstr. Q אגפי; sf. אֲגַפָּיו—**troop, division** of army Ezk 12$_{14}$.

*[אֲגַף] II 0.0.1 n.[m.]—pl. cstr. אגפי—**(river) bank** 1QH 11$_{29}$.

אגר 3 vb.—**Qal** 3 Pf. אָגְרָה; impf. תֶּאֱגֹר; ptc. אֹגֵר—**gather** food Pr 6$_{8}$; obj. omitted Dt 28$_{39}$ Pr 10$_{5}$. → מָגוֹר III *storage pit,* מְגוּרָה I *granary,* מַמְּגוּרָה *granary.*

[אֶגְרוֹף], see אֶגְרֹף *fist.*

[אֲגַרְטָל] 2 n.m.—pl. cstr. אֲגַרְטְלֵי—**basket,** cultic vessel, perh. in shape of basket Ezr 1$_{9}$.

אֶגְרֹף 2.0.1 n.[m.]—cstr. אֶגְרֹף (1QIsa^{a} גורף)—**fist,** or perh. **club** Ex 21$_{18}$ Is 58$_{4}$ CD 11$_{6}$. → (?) גרף *sweep.*

אִגֶּרֶת 10 n.f.—cstr. אִגֶּרֶת; pl. אִגְּרוֹת; cstr. אִגְּרוֹת; sf. אִגְּרֹתֵיהֶם—**letter,** alw. of an official nature, אִגֶּרֶת הַפּוּרִים *letter of,* i.e. concerning, *Purim* Est 9$_{29}$, אִגְּרוֹת הַמֶּלֶךְ *letters of,* i.e. from, *the king* Ne 2$_{9}$.

אֵד 2 n.m.—sf. אֵדוֹ—**stream,** or perh. **mist** Gn 2$_{6}$ Jb 36$_{27}$.

אדב 1 vb.—**Qal, be sick,** ptc. as noun, **one who is sick** Si 7$_{35}$ (if em. אוהב *friend* to אודב).

Hi. 1 Inf. לַאֲדִיב—**sicken** 1 S 2$_{33}$.

אַדְבְּאֵל 2 pr.n.m. **Adbeel.**

אֲדַד 1 pr.n.m. **Adad.**

אִדּוֹ 2 pr.n.m. **Iddo.**

אֱדוֹם 100.0.1.2 pr.n.m. (& f.) **Edom.**

[אֱדוֹמִי], see אֲדֹמִי *Edomite.*

אָדוֹן 334.5.13.32 n.m.—cstr. אֲדוֹן; sf. אֲדֹנִי (וְ/בְּ/לַאדֹנִי); pl. אֲדֹנִים; cstr. אֲדֹנֵי; sf. אֲדֹנָיו (לְ/כַּאדֹנָיו)—**1a.** usu. **lord, master** (human), superior of other persons; suffixed forms (exc. אֲדֹנִי *my master*) usu. pl., even when in ref. to single individual (e.g. אֲדֹנֶיךָ *your master* Gn 44$_{8}$); אֲדֹנִי *sir* oft. as term of polite address 1 S 22$_{12}$. **b. husband** Gn 18$_{12}$. **c.** perh. **employer** Si 42$_{3}$. **d. owner** of hill 1 K 16$_{24}$. **2. Lord** (divine), אֲדֹנֵי הָאֲדֹנִים *Lord of lords* Dt 10$_{17}$, אֲדוֹן כָּל־הָאָרֶץ *Lord of all the earth* Jos 3$_{11}$, אדון לכול רוח *Lord of every spirit* 1QH 18$_{8}$, הָאָדֹן י׳ *the Lord, Y.* Ex 23$_{17}$, י׳ אֲדֹנֵינוּ *Y., our Lord* Ps 8$_{2}$. → cf. אֲדֹנָי *my Lord.*

אַדּוֹן, see אַדָּן *Addan.*

אֲדוֹנִירָם, see אֲדֹנִירָם *Adoniram.*

אֲדוֹרַיִם 1.0.1 pl.n. **Adoraim.**

אֹדוֹת, see אוֹדָה *cause.*

[אַדַּי] pr.n.m. **Addai.**

אַדִּיר 28.3.7 adj.—sf. אַדִּירוֹ; f.s. אַדֶּרֶת; m.pl. אַדִּירִים; cstr. אַדִּירֵי; sf. אַדִּירָיו—**1.** as attrib. adj., **majestic, mighty,** of water Ex 15$_{10}$, cedar Ezk 17$_{23}$, sound of trumpet Si 50$_{16}$, king Ps 136$_{18}$, nation Ezk 32$_{18}$, gods 1 S 4$_{8}$. **2.** as pred. adj. or noun, **majestic (one), mighty (one),** of Y. Is 33$_{21}$, name of Y. Ps 8$_{2}$, humans Jg 5$_{13}$, trees Is 10$_{34}$. → אדר *be majestic.*

אֲדַלְיָא 1 pr.n.m. **Adalia.**

אדם 10 vb.—**Qal** 1 Pf. אָדְמוּ—**be red,** of bones Lm 4$_{7}$ (+ מִן redder *than*).

Pu. 7 Ptc. מְאָדָּמִים, מְאָדָּם—**be made red,** of rams' skins Ex 25₅||35₇, shield Na 2₄.

Hi. 1 Impf. יַאְדִּימוּ—**be red,** of sin Is 1₁₈ (+ כַּ *as scarlet*).

Htp. 1 Impf. יִתְאַדָּם—**be red,** of wine Pr 23₃₁.

→ אָדוֹם *red,* אֲדַמְדָּם *reddish,* אַדְמֹנִי *ruddy,* אֹדֶם *ruby,* אָדָם I *human being,* III *earth,* אֲדָמָה I *earth,* III *blood.*

אָדָם I 548.31.101.2 n.m.—cstr. Q אדם—**1.** coll., **humanity, human beings, people** (as distinct from God or animals), persons in general (without regard to sex), human race as a whole, וַיִּבְרָא אֱלֹהִים אֶת־הָאָדָם בְּצַלְמוֹ *and God created humanity in his image* Gn 1₂₇, מָה־אָדָם *what is humanity?* Ps 144₃, אָדָם כַּיֶּלֶק מִלֵּאתִיךְ *I have filled you (with) people (numerous) as locusts* Jr 51₁₄, מֵאָדָם עַד־בְּהֵמָה *from humanity to beasts,* i.e. both humans and beasts Gn 6₇. **2a.** individual, **human being, person,** whether a particular person or a typical human, אָדָם יְלוּד אִשָּׁה *a human being, one born of a woman* Jb 14₁, הבל אדם בגויתו *a mere breath is a person in one's body* Si 41₁₁, אַתָּה אָדָם וְלֹא־אֵל *you are a human being, not God* Ezk 28₂, לֹא לְאָדָם דַּרְכּוֹ *not to a person is one's way,* i.e. one does not control one's own destiny Jr 10₂₃. **b.** with art., **the human,** i.e. Adam, in Gn 2–3, וַיְהִי הָאָדָם לְנֶפֶשׁ חַיָּה *and the human became a living being* Gn 2₇. **3a.** בֶּן־אָדָם **son of humanity,** individual **human being,** (1) in Ezk, alw. as voc. in address to prophet, 'O son of humanity' Ezk 2₁. (2) outside Ezk, לֹא אִישׁ אֵל ... וּבֶן־אָדָם *God is not a man ... nor a human being* Nm 23₁₉, אֱנוֹשׁ רִמָּה וּבֶן־אָדָם תּוֹלֵעָה *a mortal (who is) a maggot, and the son of humanity (who is) a worm* Jb 25₆. **b.** בְּנֵי(־)אָדָם **sons of humans, persons,** לִבּוֹת בְּנֵי־אָדָם *the hearts of humans* Pr 15₁₁. **c.** בְּנוֹת אָדָם **daughters of humans, women,** יָבֹאוּ בְּנֵי הָאֱלֹהִים אֶל־בְּנוֹת הָאָדָם *the sons of God went to the daughters of humans* Gn 6₄.

→ אדם *be red.*

***אָדָם** II 1 n.[m.] **leather** Ho 11₄.

***אָדָם** III 6 n.m. **earth,** עֵין אָדָם *surface of the earth* Zc 9₁; Gn 16₁₂ Jr 32₂₀ Zc 13₅ Jb 36₂₈ Pr 30₁₄.

אָדָם IV 9.1.8 pr.n.m. **Adam.** → אדם *be red.*

אָדָם V 1 pl.n. **Adam.** → אדם *be red.*

אָדֹם 9.0.1 adj.—אָדוֹם, f.s. אֲדֻמָּה; m.pl. אֲדֻמִּים—**1. red, brown,** of horse Zc 1₈, (complexion of) lover Ca 5₁₀. **2.** as noun, **red, brown stuff,** of stew Gn 25₃₀. → אדם *be red.*

אֹדֶם 3.1 n.[f.]—Si אודם—**ruby, sardius,** or sim. (semi-) precious stone Ex 28₁₇||39₁₀. → אדם *be red.*

אֱדֹם I, see אֱדוֹם *Edom,* עֹבֵד אֱדֹם *Obed-edom.*

***[אֱדֹם]** II n.m. **edom,** name of food requested by Esau Gn 25₃₀.₃₀ (both if em. הָאֹדֶם *the brown stuff*).

אֲדַמְדָּם 6 adj.—f.s. אֲדַמְדֶּמֶת; f.pl. אֲדַמְדַּמֹּת—**reddish,** of diseased area of flesh, לְבָנָה אֲדַמְדֶּמֶת *reddish-white* Lv 13₂₄; disease in garment, יְרַקְרַק אוֹ אֲדַמְדָּם *greenish or reddish* Lv 13₄₉. → אדם *be red.*

אֲדָמָה I 225.1.11 n.f.—cstr. אַדְמַת; sf. אַדְמָתִי, אַדְמַתְכֶם; pl. אֲדָמוֹת—**1. land, ground,** in contrast to water, etc., esp. as productive, **clay, soil, earth,** אַדְמַת־עָפָר *ground of dust,* i.e. dusty ground Dn 12₂, אַדְמַת־קֹדֶשׁ *ground of holiness,* i.e. holy ground Ex 3₅, פְּנֵי הָאֲדָמָה *surface of the ground* Gn 8₈, מִזְבַּח אֲדָמָה *altar of earth* Ex 20₂₄, חַרְשֵׂי אֲדָמָה *potsherds of clay* Is 45₉, פְּרִי הָאֲדָמָה *fruit of the ground,* Gn 4₃. **2a.** area of **land, territory,** אַדְמַת יִשְׂרָאֵל *land of Israel* Ezk 7₂, הָאֲדָמָה אֲשֶׁר נָתַתָּה לָנוּ *the land that you have given us* Dt 26₁₅, וְיָשְׁבוּ עַל־אַדְמָתָם *and they shall dwell in their (own) land* Jr 23₈, אֲדָמָה טְמֵאָה *an unclean land* Am 7₁₇. **b.** smaller (owned) area, **plot, farmland,** אַדְמַת מִצְרַיִם *farmland of Egypt* Gn 47₂₀. **3. the earth, world,** מַלְכֵי הָאֲדָמָה *kings of the earth* Is 24₂₁. → אדם *be red.*

אֲדָמָה II 4 pl.n. **Adamah.**

***[אֲדָמָה]** III 1 n.[m.] **blood,** אַדְמָתוֹ עַמּוֹ *blood of his people* Dt 32₄₃. → אדם *be red.*

אַדְמָה 5 pl.n. **Admah.**

אַדְמוֹנִי 3 adj. **ruddy**—of Esau Gn 25₂₅. → אדם *be red.*

אֲדֹמִי 12.0.0.1 gent. **Edomite.**

אֲדָמִי הַנֶּקֶב 1 pl.n. **Adami-nekeb.**

אֲדֻמִּים 2 pl.n. **Adummim.**

אַדְמֹנִי, see אַדְמוֹנִי *ruddy.*

אַדְמָתָא 1 pr.n.m. **Admatha.**

[אֶדֶן] 57 n.m.—אֶדֶן; pl. אֲדָנִים; cstr. אַדְנֵי; sf. אֲדָנָיו—**base,** supporting pillars Ca 5₁₅, esp. pillars of tabernacle and its courts Ex 26₂₅||36₃₀ 38₃₁; base of the earth Jb 38₆.

אַדָּן 2 pl.n. **Addan,** also as אַדּוֹן **Addon.**

אדני, see אֲדֹנִיָּהוּ *Adonijah.*

אֲדֹנָי 425.6.52 pr.n.m.—אֲדֹנָי (Q אדוני, לַאדֹנָי/בְּ/וְ)—**1. my Lord, Adonai,** as name of Y., and term of address to Y. Gn 18_3 Ex 4_{10} Ps 16_2; אֲדֹנָי הָאֱלֹהִים *my Lord God* Dn 9_3, אֲדֹנָי ״ *Y. my Lord* Hb 3_{19}. **2.** followed by ״ (Qr אֱלֹהִים *God*), **my Lord Y.** Dt 3_{24} Jos 7_7; אֲדֹנָי ״ צְבָאוֹת *my Lord Y. of hosts* Is 3_{15}. → cf. אָדוֹן *lord.*

אֲדֹנִי בֶזֶק 3 pr.n.m. **Adoni-bezek.**

אֲדֹנִיָּה, see אֲדֹנִיָּהוּ *Adonijah.*

אֲדֹנִיָּהוּ 26.0.0.7 pr.n.m. **Adonijah.**

*[**אדניחי**] 0.0.0.1 pr.n.m. **Adonihai.**

אֲדֹנִי־צֶדֶק 2 pr.n.m. **Adoni-zedek.**

אֲדֹנִיקָם 3 pr.n.m. **Adonikam.**

אֲדֹנִירָם 2 pr.n.m. **Adoniram.**

אדר 4.3 vb.—**Ni.** 3.2 Impf. Si יאדר; ptc. נֶאְדָּר (cstr. (נֶאְדָּרֵי), Si נאדרה—**be majestic, be exalted,** of Y. Ex 15_{11}, Esau Gn $27_{40(Sam)}$, rainbow Si $43_{11(B)}$.

Hi. Pf. 1.1 Q האדיר; impf. יַאְדִּיר; impv. Si האדר—**make glorious** Y.'s law Is 42_{21}, hand of Y. Si $33_{7(B)}$.

→ אַדִּיר *majestic,* אֶדֶר *majesty,* אַדֶּרֶת *majesty.*

אֶדֶר 2.0.1 n.[m.]—cstr. אֶדֶר—**majesty, magnificence** of garment Mc 2_8, pillar 4QapPsB 31_7, price Zc 11_{13}. → אדר *be majestic.*

אֲדָר 8 pr.n.[m.] **Adar,** final month of Babylonian-based calendar = February/March Est 3_7.

אַדָּר I 1 pr.n.m. **Addar.**

אַדָּר II 2 pl.n. **Addar.**

[**אֲדַרְכּוֹן**], see דַּרְכְּמוֹן *daric.*

אֲדֹרָם 2 pr.n.m. **Adoram.**

אַדְרַמֶּלֶךְ 3 pr.n.m. **Adrammelech.**

אֶדְרֶעִי 8 pl.n. **Edrei.**

אַדֶּרֶת 12 n.f.—אַדֶּרֶת; cstr. אַדֶּרֶת; sf. אַדַּרְתּוֹ—**1. majesty** of vine Ezk 17_8. **2. cloak, coat,** worn by king Jon 3_6, prophet 1 K 19_{13}; made of hair Gn 25_{25}. → אדר *be majestic.*

***אדשׁ** 1 vb. (appar. byform of דּוּשׁ)—**Qal** Inf. אָדוֹשׁ—**thresh** Is 28_{28}.

*[**אַדְשָׁךְ**] 0.0.1 n.[m.]—pl. אדשכים—**rafter,** or perh. **doorway** 11QT 41_{16}.

***אדתא** 0.0.0.1 pr.n.f. **Adatha.**

אהב 208.40.58 vb.—**Qal** 191.37.58 Pf. אָהֵב, אָהַבְתָּ; impf. יֶאֱהַב, תֶּאֱהָבוּ (תֶּאֱהָבוּן, תֶּאֱהָבוּ); + waw וָאֹהַב; impv. אֱהַב (Q אהבים, אֱהָבוּ; ptc. אֹהֵב (אֹהֲבִי) אֹהֶבֶת (אֹהַבְתִּי), אהוב), אֹהֲבֵי־; ptc. pass. אָהוּב, אֲהוּבָה; inf. אֱהֹב (אַהֲבָה) אַהֲבַת, (אַהֲבָם)—**1. love** another human, in family Gn 22_2, as friend, neighbour Lv 19_{18}, sexually Gn 24_{67}. **2. love** humans, of Y. Dt 4_{37}. **3. love** a deity: Y. Ex 20_6||Dt 5_{10}, name of Y. Ps 5_{12}, other gods Jr 2_{25} 8_2. **4. like, love** tasty food Gn 27_4, money Ec 5_9, good Am 5_{15}, wisdom Pr 8_{17}, law Ps 119_{97}, evil Ps 52_5, violence Ps 11_5, sleep Pr 20_{13}. **5.** ptc. as noun, **friend, lover** of other human Ps 38_{12}, Y. Is 41_8.

Ni. 1.2 Impf., Si תאהב; ptc. הַנֶּאֱהָבִים—**be loved** 2 S 1_{23} Si 3_{17} 7_{35}.

Pi. 16 Ptc. מְאַהֲבַי (מְאַהֲבֶיהָ, מְאַהֲבַיִךְ)—**love** (or ptc. as noun, **lover**), as a friend Zc 13_6, sexually Jr 22_{20}.

Hi. 0.1 Impv. האהב—**cause to be loved, endear,** האהב לנפשך לעדה *endear yourself to the assembly* Si 4_7.

→ אַהֲבָה *love,* אֹהַב *display of love,* אַהַב *loved one.*

[**אֹהַב**] 2 n.[m.]—sf. אֹהָבָם; pl. אֳהָבִים—**display of love** Pr 7_{18} Ho 9_{10}. → אהב *love.*

[**אַהַב**] 2.1 n.[m.]—pl. אֲהָבִים; sf. Si אהביה—**loved one, lover** Ho 8_9 Pr 5_{19} Si 9_8. → אהב *love.*

אַהֲבָה I 40.2.17 n.f.—cstr. אַהֲבַת; sf. אַהֲבָתִי—**love, 1.** among humans, **a.** friendship, loyalty, affection 1 S 20_{17} Ps 109_4. **b.** sexual love 2 S 13_{15} Jr 2_{33}. **2.** between deity and humans, **a.** of Y. for his people Is 63_9 Jr 31_3. **b.** of people for Y. Jr 2_2. → אהב *love.*

*[**אַהֲבָה**] II 2 n.[f.] **leather** Ho 11_4 Ca 3_{10}.

אֹהַד 2 pr.n.m. **Ohad.**

אֲהָהּ 15 interj. **alas,** אֲהָהּ אֲדֹנָי ״ *alas, my Lord Y.* Jos 7_7, אֲהָהּ לַיּוֹם *alas for the day* Jl 1_{15}.

אַהֲוָא 3 pl.n. **Ahava.**

אֵהוּד 9.0.0.1 pr.n.m. **Ehud.**

אהל I 3.0.1 vb.—**Qal** 2 Impf. + waw וַיֶּאֱהַל—**move tent** Gn $13_{12.18}$.

Pi. 1.0.1 Impf. יַהֵל (= יְאַהֵל), Q תאהל (perh. Qal)—**pitch tent, establish dwelling place** Is 13_{20} 4QWiles 1_7.

→ אֹהֶל I *tent.*

אהל II 1 vb.—**Hi.** 1 Impf. יַאֲהִיל—**shine,** of moon Jb 25_5.

אֹהֶל I 345.2.12 n.m.—+ ה of direction הָאֹהֱלָה; cstr. אֹהֶל; sf. אָהֳלִי; pl. אֹהָלִים (בָּאֳהָלִים); cstr. אָהֳלֵי; sf. אֹהָלָיו, אָהֳלֵיכֶם

—**1. tent** of person Gn 9_{21}; in heavens, as dwelling place for sun Ps 19_5. **2. tent** of sanctuary of Y., **tabernacle,** oft. with ref. to outer covering of מִשְׁכָּן *tabernacle* Ex 26_7||36_{14}, or to מִשְׁכָּן itself Ps 78_{60}, **a.** in wilderness, אֹהֶל מוֹעֵד *tent of meeting* Ex 27_{21}, אֹהֶל הָעֵדֻת *tent of the testimony* Nm 9_{15}. **b.** in Jerusalem 2 S 6_{17}||1 C 16_1, Shiloh Jos 18_1, Gibeon 2 C 1_3. → אהל *pitch tent.*

אֹהֶל II 1.0.0.1 pr.n.m. **Ohel.**

[אָהָל] 4 n.[m].—pl. אֲהָלִים, אֲהָלוֹת—**aloe, aloe wood** (perh. *Aloexylon agallochum* or *Aquilaria agallocha*), used for perfume Nm 24_6 Ps 45_9 Pr 7_{17} Ca 4_{14}.

אָהֳלָה 5 pr.n.f. **Oholah.**

אֲהָלוֹת, see אָהָל *Aloe.*

אָהֳלִיאָב 5 pr.n.m. **Oholiab.**

אָהֳלִיבָמָה 8 pr.n.f.&m. **Oholibamah.**

אֲהָלִים, see אָהָל *Aloe.*

אַהֲרֹן 347.5.38 pr.n.m. **Aaron.**

אוֹ 320.2.84 conj.—**or, 1.** expressing alternatives, without clear preference for either, עַל־יָמִין אוֹ עַל־שְׂמֹאל *to the right or to the left* Gn 24_{49}. **2. rather, or rather,** expressing preference, יָמִים אוֹ עָשׂוֹר *(a few) days or ten* Gn 24_{55}. **3.** אוֹ ... אוֹ **either ... or** Lv 5_1. **4.** אִם ... אוֹ **whether ... or** Lv 15_{23}. **5.** הֲ ... אוֹ **is ... or?,** הֲטוֹב ... אוֹ *is it better ... or?* Jg 18_{19}. **6. or if,** introducing a sentence אוֹ־בֵן יִגָּח *or if he gore a son* Ex 21_{31}.

אוּאֵל 1 pr.n.m. **Uel.**

אוֹב I 16.2.3 n.[m.]—pl. אֹבוֹת—**ghost,** in contexts of divination Lv 19_{31} 1 S 28_7; perh. **medium, necromancer,** i.e. one who consults a ghost 1 S 28_3.

*[אוֹב] II 1 n.m.—pl. אֹבוֹת—**wineskin** Jb 32_{19}.

אוֹבִיל 1 pr.n.m. **Obil.**

[אוּבָל] 3 n.[m.]—אֻבַל; cstr. אוּבַל—**river, stream, canal,** or perh. **tower** Dn $8_{3.2.6}$.

אוגמן, see אַגְמוֹן *rush.*

אוּד 3 n.m.—pl. אוּדִים—**firebrand** Is 7_4 Am 4_{11} Zc 3_2.

[אוֹדָה] 11 n.f.—pl. אֹדוֹת; cstr. אֹדוֹת; sf. אדוֹתֶיךָ—**cause, matter, 1.** עַל אוֹדֹת as prep., **a. about, concerning, with regard to** Gn 21_{25} Jos 14_6. **b. on account of, because of** Ex 18_8 Nm 13_{24}. **2.** עַל־אֹדוֹת אֲשֶׁר as conj., **because** Jr 3_8.

[אוֹדוֹת], see אוֹדָה *cause, matter.*

[אוֹדֶם], see אֹדֶם *ruby.*

אוֹדֹת, see אוֹדָה *cause, matter.*

אוה I 26.3.6 vb.—**Pi.** 11.2.3 Pf. אִוָּה, אִוִּיתִיךָ; impf. תְּאַוֶּה; ptc. Si מאויה—**desire, yearn for,** subj. Y. Ps 132_{13}, soul (נֶפֶשׁ), in ref. to Y. Jb 23_{13}, humans Dt 12_{20}; with accus. Y. Is 26_9, Zion Ps 132_{13}, evil Pr 21_{10}; with לְ of obj. wealth 1QS 10_{19}.

Htp. 15.1.3 Pf. הִתְאַוִּיתִי, הִתְאַוָּה; impf. יִתְאַוֶּה, יִתְאָו (יִתְאָו); + ptc. מִתְאַוִּים, מִתְאַוָּה—**desire, crave,** subj. alw. humans; with accus. property Dt 5_{21}, beauty Ps 45_{12}; לְ of obj. delicacies Pr 23_3; בְּ of obj. 1QS 9_{25}; אַל־תִּתְאָיו לִהְיוֹת אִתָּם *do not desire to be with them* Pr $24_{1(Qr)}$.

→ אַוָּה *desire,* תַּאֲוָה *desire,* מַאֲוַי *desire.*

אוה II 1 vb.—**Htp.** 1 Pf. + waw וְהִתְאַוִּיתֶם—**mark out** border of land Nm 34_{10}. → cf. perh. אוֹת *sign.*

[אַוָּה] 7.0.1 n.f.—cstr. אַוַּת; sf. אַוָּתִי—**desire,** בְּכָל־אַוַּת נַפְשְׁךָ *with all the desire of your soul,* i.e. as much as, or, whenever, you desire Dt 12_5. → אוה I *desire.*

אוּזַי 1 pr.n.m. **Uzai.**

אוּזָל 2 pr.n.m **Uzal.**

*[אוט] 0.0.8 n.[m.]—cstr. אוט; sf. אוטו—perh. **storehouse** 4QInstr[b] 2.2_{12} 4QInstr[d] 126.2_2.

*אוטרפלוס 0.0.1 pr.n.m. **Eutrapelos.**

אוֹי 24.0.2 interj.—**woe, 1.** abs., אוֹי מִי יִחְיֶה מִשֻּׂמוֹ אֵל *woe!, who will live when God places it?* Nm 24_{23}. **2.** lamenting one's own situation, אוֹי־לִי *woe to me* Is 6_5. **3.** announcing disaster for others, אוֹי לְרָשָׁע *woe to the wicked one* Is 3_{11}. → cf. אוֹיָה *woe.*

אֱוִי 2 pr.n.m. **Evi.**

אוֹיֵב *enemy,* see איב.

אוֹיָה 1 interj. **woe** Ps 120_5. → cf. אוֹי *woe.*

אֱוִיל I 26.4.4 adj.—cstr. אֱוִיל; pl. אֱוִילִים; cstr. Q אוילי—**1. foolish,** as attrib. adj. of a man Pr 29_9, descendants Si 41_5. **2.** usu. as pred. adj. or noun, **foolish (one), fool,** אֱוִיל הַנָּבִיא *the prophet is a fool* Ho 9_7, אֱוִיל שְׂפָתַיִם *one foolish of lips* Pr 10_8. → cf. אֱוִלִי *foolish,* אִוֶּלֶת *folly.*

*[אֱוִיל] II 1 n.[m.] **leader,** אולי הָאָרֶץ *leaders of the country* 2 K $24_{15(Kt)}$ (unless from אול II; Qr אֵילֵי, from אַיִל I).

אֱוִיל מְרֹדַךְ 2 pr.n.m. **Evil-merodach.**

[אוּל] I 1 n.[m.]—sf. אוּלָם—**body,** or perh. **belly** Ps 73_4.

*[אוּל] II n.[m.] **leader,** אולי הָאָרֶץ *leaders of the coun-*

try 2 K 24$_{15}$(Kt) (unless from אֱוִיל II; Qr אֵילֵי, from אַיִל I).

אֱוִלִי 1 adj. **foolish,** of shepherd Zc 11$_{15}$. → cf. אֱוִיל *foolish*.

אוּלַי I 45 adv.—אֻלַי—**1.** usu. **perhaps, supposing that, what if?** Gn 16$_{2}$ 18$_{24}$. **2. if** Jos 14$_{12}$. **3. unless** Nm 22$_{33}$.

[אוּלַי] II 2 pl.n. **Ulai.**

אוּלָם I 19.1 conj. **however, although** (usu. וְאוּלָם) Gn 28$_{19}$ 48$_{19}$; perh. also **(but) indeed** Ex 9$_{16}$ Jb 5$_{8}$.

אוּלָם II 49.0.4 n.m.—אֻלָם; cstr. אוּלָם; sf. Kt אלמו (אילמו); pl. אֵלַמּוֹת; cstr. אֵלַמֵּי; sf. Qr אֵלַמָּיו (forms in Ezk 40$_{16-36}$ as if from אֵילָם)—**porch, hall, portico** of temple 1 K 7$_{21}$ Ezk 40$_{8}$, palace 1 K 7$_{6}$.

אוּלָם III 4 pr.n.m. **Ulam.**

אִוֶּלֶת 25.5.5 n.f.—cstr. אִוֶּלֶת; sf. אִוַּלְתּוֹ—**folly,** assoc. with indiscipline Pr 5$_{23}$, shortness of temper Pr 14$_{17}$, rashness of speech Pr 18$_{13}$. → cf. אֱוִיל *foolish,* אֱוִלִי *foolish*.

[אוֹמֶץ], see אֹמֶץ *might*.

אוֹמָר 3 pr.n.m. **Omar.**

אוֹמֶר, see אֹמֶר *word*.

אָוֶן I 80.2.6 n.m.—sf. אוֹנוֹ; pl. Si אונים—**1. misfortune, trouble** Ps 55$_{11}$ Jb 5$_{6}$. **2. iniquity, evil, sin** Is 55$_{7}$ Ps 36$_{4}$. **3.** בֵּית אָוֶן **house of iniquity,** appar. as dysphemism for בֵּית אֵל *Bethel,* lit. 'house of God' Ho 4$_{15}$. **4.** פֹּעֲלֵי אָוֶן **evildoers** (אָוֶן = *harm, iniquity*) Is 31$_{2}$.

אָוֶן II, see בֵּית אָוֶן *Beth-aven*.

אוֹן I 13.1.2 n.m.—sf. אוֹנוֹ, אוֹנִי; pl. אוֹנִים—**1. strength** Ho 12$_{4}$ Jb 40$_{16}$; רֵאשִׁית אוֹנִי *first of my strength,* i.e. my firstborn Gn 49$_{3}$. **2. wealth** Ho 12$_{9}$.

אוֹן II 1 pr.n.m. **On.**

אוֹן III 3 pl.n. **On.**

[אוֹן] IV, see אֹנָה *distress*.

אוֹנוֹ 5 pl.n. **Ono.**

אוֹנִי, see אֹנָה *distress*.

אוֹנִיָּה, see אֳנִיָּה *ship*.

אוֹנִים, see אָוֶן I *iniquity,* אוֹן I *strength*.

אוֹנָם 4 pr.n.m. **Onam.**

אוֹנָן 8 pr.n.m. **Onan.**

*** [אוֹנֶס]** 0.1 n.[m.] **force** Si 20$_{4}$(B). → אנס *force*.

אוּפָז 2 pl.n. **Uphaz.**

אוֹפִיר I 12.1.2.1 pl.n. **Ophir.**

אוֹפִיר II 2 pr.n.m. **Ophir.**

אוֹפָן 35.1.8 n.m.—אֹפָן; cstr. אוֹפַן; pl. אוֹפַנִּים; cstr. אוֹפַנֵּי; sf. אוֹפַנֵּיהֶם—**wheel** of chariot Ex 14$_{25}$, base of laver 1 K 7$_{30}$, in Ezekiel's vision Ezk 1$_{15}$.

[אוֹפֶן], see אֹפֶן *occasion*.

אוֹפִר, see אוֹפִיר II *Ophir*.

אוץ 10.3.4 vb.—**Qal** 8.1.3 Pf. אַצְתִּי, אָץ; ptc. אָצִים, אָץ—**1a.** usu. **urge oneself on, hasten, be impatient** Jos 10$_{13}$; + בְּ *with* feet Pr 19$_{2}$, words Pr 29$_{20}$. **b.** perh. **urge on, hasten another,** with ellip. of obj. Ex 5$_{13}$. **2.** of space, **be narrow** Jos 17$_{15}$; of time, **be short** 1QM 18$_{12}$.

Hi. 2.2.1 Impf. תָּאִיצוּ; + waw וַיָּאִיצוּ—**be impatient, hasten**—Gn 19$_{15}$ Is 22$_{4}$ Si 7$_{17}$.

אוֹצָר 80.9.12 n.m.—cstr. אוֹצַר; sf. אוֹצָרוֹ; pl. אוֹצָרוֹת; cstr. אוֹצְרוֹת; sf. אוֹצְרוֹתָיו—**1. treasure** (oft. pl.), consisting of valuables in temple, palace 1 K 14$_{26}$||2 C 12$_{9}$, private wealth Si 40$_{18}$, stores of food and drink 2 C 11$_{11}$. **2. treasury, storehouse** (oft. sg.), of temple, palace 1 K 15$_{18}$||2 C 16$_{2}$; for private wealth Pr 8$_{21}$, food Ne 13$_{12}$; heaven as storehouse of wind, rain, etc. Dt 28$_{12}$ Jr 10$_{13}$. → אצר *store up*.

*** [אוֹצָרָה]** 0.0.1 n.f.—אצרה—**treasure** 3QTr 1$_{10}$. → אצר *store up*.

אור 43.3.30.2 vb.—**Qal** 6.1.1 Pf. אוֹר, אֹרוּ; + waw וַתָּאֹרְנָה; impv. אוֹרִי; ptc. אוֹר—**1. be light, bright, shine,** of morning Gn 44$_{3}$, eyes 1 S 14$_{27}$(Qr), face Si 13$_{26}$, Zion Is 60$_{1}$, sons of righteousness 1QM 1$_{8}$; וְאוֹר לָכֶם *and (when) it is light,* i.e. day breaks, *for you* 1 S 29$_{10}$. **2.** ptc. as adj., **enlightened,** רוח נבונה ואורה *an understanding and enlightened spirit* 11QPs^{a} 27$_{4}$.

Ni. 3 Impf. + waw וַיֵּאֹר; ptc. נָאוֹר; inf. לֵאוֹר (= לְהֵאוֹר)—**be light, bright, shine,** of Y. Ps 76$_{5}$, human Jb 33$_{30}$; וַיֵּאֹר לָהֶם *and (when) it was light,* i.e. day broke, *for them* 2 S 23$_{2}$.

Hi. 34.2.29.2 Pf. הֵאִירָה; impf. יָאִיר (יָאֵר); + waw וַיָּאֶר; impv. הָאֵר (הָאִירָה); ptc. מֵאִיר, מְאִירַת, מְאִירוֹת; inf. הָאִיר—**1. give light, shine,** of heavenly luminaries Gn 1$_{15}$, lamp Ex 25$_{37}$, blade 1QM 5$_{10}$, pillar of fire Ex 13$_{21}$, night Ps 139$_{12}$. **2. cause light to shine** 1QH 17$_{27}$. **3. light up, illuminate** night Ex 14$_{20}$, world Ps 77$_{19}$, way Ne 9$_{12}$. **4. kindle** fire, lamp Ml 1$_{10}$ Ps 18$_{29}$. **5a.**

enlighten, make shine covenant 1QM 17$_{7}$, heart 1QS 2$_{3}$, knowledge 4QShirShabb^{d} 1.2$_{35}$. **b. give enlightenment** Ps 119$_{130}$. **6.** with obj. פָּנִים **make one's face shine, a. show favour** Nm 6$_{25}$. **b. be cheerful** Si 32$_{11}$. **c. make cheerful** Ec 8$_{1}$. **d. enlighten,** i.e. teach 1QH 12$_{27}$. **7.** with obj. עֵינַיִם, **enlighten the eyes,** i.e. revive Ps 13$_{4}$.

→ אוֹר *light*, אוֹרָה *light*, אוּר I *fire*, מָאוֹר *luminary*, מְאוּרָה I *light-hole*, III *fiery coals*, IV *eye*, נָאוֹר *shining one*.

אוֹר 115.8.116 n.m. (& f.)—cstr. אוֹר; sf. אוֹרוֹ; pl. אוֹרִים—**1. light (of day),** by contrast with darkness Gn 1$_{3}$. **2. luminaries,** sun, moon, stars Is 60$_{19}$ Ps 136$_{7}$. **3. light** given by luminaries Is 13$_{10}$. **4. dawn** Ne 8$_{3}$. **5. lightning** Jb 36$_{30}$. **6. light,** from other sources: lamp Jr 25$_{10}$, fire Ps 78$_{14}$, arrows Hb 3$_{11}$. **7. light,** as representing goodness, hope, salvation, justice, etc. Is 2$_{5}$ Mc 7$_{8}$ Ps 27$_{1}$; esp. at Qumran 1QH 14$_{17}$ 1QM 17$_{6}$ 1QS 3$_{7}$; בני אור *sons of light* 1QM 1$_{1}$, גורל *lot of* 1QM 13$_{9}$, דרכי *ways of* 1QS 3$_{3}$, רוחות *spirits of* 1QS 3$_{25}$. → אור *be light.*

אוּר I 6.0.2 n.m.—cstr. אוּר; pl. אֻרִים—**1. fire** Is 31$_{9}$. **2a. light** Is 50$_{11}$. **b.** pl. appar. **region of light, east** Is 24$_{15}$. → אור *be light.*

אוּר II 1 pr.n.m. **Ur.**

אוּר III pl.n. 4.0.1 **Ur.**

אוֹרָה 3.0.1 n.f.—cstr. Q אורת; pl. אוֹרֹת—**1. light, a.** as opposed to darkness Ps 139$_{12}$. **b.** representing revival, success Is 26$_{19}$ Est 8$_{16}$. **2.** mental, spiritual **illumination** 1QS 11$_{3}$. → אור *be light.*

[אֻוֵרָה], see אֻרְוָה *stall.*

אוּרִי 8 pr.n.m. **Uri.**

אוּרִיאֵל 4 pr.n.m. **Uriel.**

אוּרִיָּה 39.0.1.11 pr.n.m. **Uriah.**

אוּרִיָּהוּ, see אוּרִיָּה *Uriah.*

אוריו, see אוּרִיָּה *Uriah.*

אוּרִים 7.0.3 n.m.pl.—sf. אוּרֶיךָ—**Urim,** perh. lit. 'curses', objects in high priest's breastplate, appar. used in divination (usu. + תֻּמִּים *Thummim*, lit. 'perfections') Ex 28$_{30}$. → (?) ארר *curse.*

אורנה, see אֲרַוְנָה *Araunah.*

*[אוֹרְתּוֹם] 0.0.5 n.[m.]—אורתם—**perfect light,** lit. 'light of perfection' 1QH 12$_{23}$ 21$_{14}$ 4QWorks 1$_{5}$ 4QShir Shabb^{d} 1.1$_{45}$ 1.2$_{1}$. → cf. אור *light* + תֹּם *perfection.*

[אוֹשׁ], from אשׁ *foundation.*

אות 4.0.2 vb.—**Ni.** 4.0.2 Impf. נֵאוֹת, יֵאֹתוּ (נֵאוֹתָה)—**1. agree, consent** Gn 34$_{15}$ (+ לְ *with, to* someone) 2 K 12$_{8}$ (+ לְבִלְתִּי קְחַת־ *not to take*). **2. share, associate with** (עִם) someone CD 20$_{7}$.

אוֹת 79.6.84.1 n.m. (& f.)—אֹת; cstr. אוֹת; pl. אֹתוֹת; cstr. אֹתוֹת; sf. אֹתוֹתָיו—**1. sign,** as **a.** reminder, memorial, of rainbow Gn 9$_{12}$, circumcision Gn 17$_{11}$, sabbath Ex 31$_{13}$, redemption of firstborn Ex 13$_{16}$, stones Jos 4$_{6}$. **b.** token, proof Ex 3$_{12}$ Dt 13$_{2}$. **c.** portent of the future Is 20$_{3}$ Jr 10$_{2}$. **d.** miraculous event Ex 4$_{8}$. **e.** as marker of seasons Gn 1$_{14}$; in ref. to year in which vernal equinox coincides with new moon 4QOtot 5$_{3}$. **f.** mark of identification, on Cain Gn 4$_{15}$. **g.** evidence, character Jb 21$_{29}$ 1QS 3$_{14}$. **h.** code, relating to signals Lachish ost. 4$_{11}$. **2. standard, ensign** of a military unit Nm 2$_{2}$ 1QM 3$_{13}$. → perh. אוה II *mark out.*

אָז 144.3.36.2 adv.—אֱזַי—**1.** temporal, **then, at that time, a.** of past time Gn 4$_{26}$. **b.** of future time Lv 26$_{34}$. **2.** logical, **a. if so, in that case** Jos 1$_{8}$. **b. therefore** Jr 22$_{15}$. **c. then,** introducing apodosis after conditional clause, אִם ... אָז *if ... then* Is 58$_{14}$, כִּי ... אָז *when ... then* Gn 49$_{4}$, לוּלֵא ... כִּי אָז *if not ... then* 2 S 2$_{27}$, אַחֲלֵי ... אָז *would that ... then* 2 K 5$_{3}$. **4.** מֵאָז, **a.** as adv., **from of old,** usu. of distant past Is 44$_{8}$; of nearer past 2 S 15$_{34}$. **b.** as conj., **since,** with pf. Gn 39$_{5}$, inf. Ex 4$_{10}$. **c.** as prep. **since, from** Ru 2$_{7}$.

אֶזְבַּי 1 pr.n.m. **Ezbai.**

***אזה** 0.0.0.2 pl.n. **Azzah.**

אֵזוֹב 10.0.2 n.m.—אֵזֹב—**hyssop** (perh. *Origanum maru* or *Majorana syriaca*), aromatic plant used in purification Ex 12$_{22}$.

אֵזוֹר 14.2.2 n.m. **girdle,** short waist-cloth of linen Jr 13$_{1}$, leather 2 K 1$_{8}$. → אזר *gird.*

אֱזַי, see אָז.

אַזְכָּרָה 7.2.1 n.f.—sf. אַזְכָּרָתָהּ—**token offering,** handful of fine flour, oil, and incense, taken from grain offering Lv 2$_{2}$, sin offering Lv 5$_{12}$. → זכר I *remember.*

אזל I 5 vb.—**Qal** Pf. אָזַל, אָזְלַת, אָזְלוּ; impf. תֵּזֵלִי; ptc. אֹזֵל—**go (away), be gone,** of person Pr 20$_{14}$, hand, i.e. strength Dt 32_{36}, food 1 S 9_{7}, water Jb 14_{11}. → cf. עֲזָאזֵל III *scapegoat.*

***אזל** II 1 vb.—**Pu.** Ptc. מְאוּזָל—**be woven,** ptc. as noun, **woven material** Ezk 27_{19}.

[**אֶזֶל**], see אֶבֶן *stone,* §5d.

אזן I 41.3.9 vb.—**Hi.** 41.3.9 Pf. הֶאֱזִין; impf. יַאֲזִין, אָזִין; + waw וְהֶאֱזִין; impv. הַאֲזִינָה, הַאֲזִינוּ, הַאֲזִינִי, הַאֲזִינָה; ptc. מֵזִין (Si מאזין); inf. Si האזין—**hear, listen (to)** Gn 4_{23}, oft. **obey** Ex 15_{26}. **a.** with accus. word Gn 4_{23}, law Is 1_{10}, prayer Ps 17_{1}. **b.** with prep. לְ *to* person Jb 34_{2}, message Ex 15_{26}; אֶל *to* person Dt 1_{45}, message Ps 143_{1}; עַד *to* person Nm 23_{18}. → אֹזֶן *ear.*

אזן II 1 vb.—**Pi.** 1 Pf. אִזֵּן—**weigh** proverbs Ec 12_{9}. → מֹאזְנַיִם *scales.*

אֹזֶן 187.10.27 n.f.—cstr. אֹזֶן; sf. אָזְנוֹ; du. אָזְנַיִם; cstr. אָזְנֵי; sf. אָזְנָיו—**ear, 1.** as physical organ, of human Ex 29_{20}, dog Pr 26_{17}. **2.** as organ of hearing, of Y. 1 S 8_{21}, human Ex 11_{2}; גלה אֹזֶן *uncover the ear* of someone, i.e. reveal to someone 1 S 9_{15}. → אזן *hear.*

[**אָזֵן**] 1 n.[m.]—sf. אֲזֵנֶךָ—**tool, weapon,** perh. coll. Dt 23_{14}.

אֻזֵּן שֶׁאֱרָה 1 pl.n. **Uzzen-sheerah.**

אַזְנוֹת תָּבוֹר 1 pl.n. **Aznoth-tabor.**

אָזְנִי I 1 pr.n.m. **Ozni.**

אָזְנִי II 1 gent. **Oznite.**

אֲזַנְיָה 1 pr.n.m. **Azaniah.**

[**אָזִק**] 2 n.[m.]—pl. הָ/בָּאזִקִּים—**manacle** Jr $40_{1.4}$. → cf. זִק *fetter.*

אזר 16.1.4 vb.—**Qal** 6.0.1 Pf. אָזְרוּ; impf. תֶּאְזֹר, יַאַזְרֵנִי; impv. אֱזָר־; ptc. pass. אָזוּר—**1a. gird oneself,** for battle, dispute, etc. 1 S 24 Jb 38_{3}. **b.** pass. **be girded** with belt (אֵזוֹר) 2 K 1_{8}. **2. bind, be tight around** someone, of clothing Jb 30_{18}.

Ni. 1 Ptc. נֶאְזָר—**be girded** with (בְּ) might, of Y. Ps 65_{7}.

Pi. 6.1 Impf. אֲאַזֶּרְךָ; + waw וַתְּאַזְּרֵנִי (וַתְּזְרֵנִי); ptc. מְאַזְּרֵי, מְאַזְּרֵנִי—**1. gird oneself,** with sparks Is 50_{11}. **2.** with double accus., **gird** someone **with strength** 2 S 22_{40}||18_{40} (+ לְ *for* battle), joy Ps 30_{12}. **3. envelop** someone Is 45_{5}.

Htp. 3.0.3 Pf. הִתְאַזָּר; impf. Q יתאזר; impv. הִתְאַזְּרוּ; ptc. Q מתאזרים; inf. cstr. Q התאזר—**gird oneself,** for battle, etc., of Y. Ps 93_{1} (+ עֹז *[with] strength*), army of Belial 1QM 1_{13}, distant places Is 8_{9}.

→ אֵזוֹר *belt.*

אֶזְרוֹעַ 2.0.3 n.f.—sf. אֶזְרֹעִי—**1. arm,** perh. specif. **forearm** of human Jb 31_{22}, Y. Jr 32_{21}. **2. leg, foreleg** of sacrificial animal 11QT 20_{16}. → cf. זְרוֹעַ *arm.*

אֶזְרָח 18.0.2 n.m.—cstr. אֶזְרַח—**1. native inhabitant, citizen of Israel,** as opposed to sojourner (גֵּר) Ex 12_{19}. **2. plant, tree,** growing in its native place, אֶזְרָח רַעֲנָן *a leafy tree* Ps 37_{35}.

אֶזְרָחִי 3 gent. **Ezrahite.**

אָח I 628.10.51.5 n.m.—cstr. אֲחִי; sf. אָחִיו (אֲחִיהוּ), אֲחִיהֶם; pl. אַחִים; cstr. אֲחֵי; sf. אַחַי (אֶחָי), אַחֶיךָ, אֶחָיו, אֲחֵיהֶם—**1a.** usu. **brother** Gn 24_{55}, including half-brother Jg 11_{3}. **b.** coll., **brother tribe, nation,** of Israel/Judah in relation to Edom Nm 20_{14}. **2a. nephew** Gn 14_{14}. **b. cousin** 1 C 23_{22}. **c.** other close relative, **kinsman** Nm 27_{4}; אח תלוי *a dependent relative* Si 7_{18}. **3. kinsman,** i.e. fellow member of group, esp. a tribe or nation, **a.** of Israelites Gn 31_{23} Ex 2_{11} Jr 34_{9}, including females Dt 15_{12}. **b.** of non-Israelites Gn 19_{7} Jr 49_{10}. **4.** without emphasis on consanguinity, **fellow** Dt 19_{18} Ps 22_{23}; אִישׁ ... אָחִיו *a man ... his fellow,* i.e. one ... another Gn 13_{11}. **5. colleague,** fellow member of group, institution, etc. Ne 4_{17} Si 10_{20}; of priests Lv 21_{10}, Levites Nm 8_{26}, members of religious group 1QS 6_{10}, soldiers Dt 20_{8}, reapers Meṣad Ḥashavyahu ost. 1_{10}. **6.** in voc., **my brother(s),** as polite or official form of address Gn 29_{4} 2 S 20_{9}. **7. partner,** of inanimate objects: faces of cherubim Ex 25_{20}||37_{9} (אִישׁ אֶל־אָחִיו *the one facing the other*), scales of Behemoth Jb 41_{9} (אִישׁ־בְּאָחִיהוּ cleaving *one to the other*). → cf. אַחֲוָה *brotherhood,* אָחוֹת *sister.*

אָח II 3 interj. **alas** Ezk 6_{11} 18_{10} 21_{20}.

אָח III 3 n.f. **brazier** Jr $36_{22.23.23}$.

[**אֹחַ**] 1.0.1 n.[m.]—pl. אֹחִים—**owl** Is 13_{21} 4QShir[a] 1_{5}.

***אחא** 0.0.0.8 pr.n.m. **Aha.**

אַחְאָב 93.0.2.8 pr.n.m. **Ahab.**

***אחאמה** 0.0.0.2 pr.n.m. **Ahamah.**

אֶחָב, see אַחְאָב *Ahab.*

אַחְבָּן 1 pr.n.m. **Ahban.**

אחד 1 vb.—**Htp.** 1 Impv. הִתְאַחֲדִי—**be united,** of sword of Y. Ezk 21_{21} (mss הִתְאַחֲרִי *turn to the rear;* or em. הִתְחַדִּי *sharpen yourself*). → אֶחָד *one.*

אֶחָד $970.13.151$ adj.—m.s. אֶחָד (חַד, אֶחָד); cstr. אַחַד; pl. אֲחָדִים; f.s. אַחַת (אֶחָת); cstr. אַחַת—**1a.** as adj. of quantity, **one (whole), single, same,** of ram Lv 16_5, flesh Gn 2_{24}, place Gn 1_9, measurement Ex 26_2||36_9, language Gn 11_1; פַּעַם אַחַת *one time,* i.e. once Jos 6_{14}, כְּאִישׁ אֶחָד *as one man,* i.e. with one accord Jg 20_1, פֶּה אֶחָד *(with) a single mouth,* i.e. with one accord Jos 9_2, דְּבָרִים אֲחָדִים *(with the) same words* Gn 11_1, אַחַת הִיא *it is one,* i.e. all the same Jb 9_{22}. **b.** as adj. of quality, **unique, singular,** of Y. Dt 6_4, nation 2 S 7_{23}||1 C 17_{21}. **c.** as particularizing adj., **a certain, a(n),** of man Gn 42_{11}, people Est 3_8, city 2 S 12_1; יוֹם־אֶחָד *one day,* i.e. some day (in the future) 1 S 27_1, יָמִים אֲחָדִים *some days, a few days* Gn 27_{44}. **2.** as noun. **a.** almost as indef. art., אַחַד, or אֶחָד מִן **(any)one of, a(n),** with pl. or coll. noun, people Gn 26_{10}, tribe Gn 49_{16}, servant 2 K 3_{11}, city Dt 4_{42}; אַחַד מִמֶּנּוּ *one of us* Gn 3_{22}, אַחַת מֵאֵלֶּה *one of these* Lv 5_4. **b. one (of us, you, them),** with ref. to one of a known group, oft. of two Lv 5_7 2 S 12_1. **c. a person alone, a single individual** Dt 32_{30} Ezk 33_{24}; עַד־אֶחָד not *unto one,* not *a single one* Ex 9_7, גַּם־אֶחָד not *even one* 2 S 17_{12}. **d.** אַחַת, **a single thing, just one thing** Ps 27_4. **e.** אַחַת, **one time, once** Ps 89_{36}; אַחַת בַּשָּׁנָה *once a year* Ex 30_{10}. **3a.** as adj., **each,** of man 2 K 15_{20}, ox Nm 15_{11}, bowl Nm 7_{85}. **b.** as noun, **each one,** with ref. to persons Ex 16_{22}, heavenly beings Is 6_2. **4. (as) one, united, a single unit,** וְהָיָה הַמִּשְׁכָּן אֶחָד *and the tabernacle shall be a single unit* Ex 26_6||36_{13}, מוּצָק אֶחָד *cast as one,* i.e. alike 1 K 7_{37}, כְּאֶחָד *as one, united* Is 65_{25}. **5.** as ordinal number, **a.** as adj., **first** (oft. + שֵׁנִי *second*), of camp Gn 32_9, woman 1 K 3_{17}, lamb Nm 28_4, stone Ex 28_{10}; בְּאֶחָד לַחֹדֶשׁ *on the first (day) of the month* Gn 8_5, בִּשְׁנַת אַחַת לְ *in the first year of (the reign of)* Dn 9_1. **b.** as noun, **first one, former,** שֵׁם הָאֶחָד *the name of the first one* Gn 2_{11}. **6.** in **other numbers,** אַחַד עָשָׂר *eleven* Gn 32_{23}, var. אַחַת עֶשְׂרֵה 2 K 9_{29}; אֶחָד/אַחַת וְעֶשְׂרִים *twenty-one* Ex 12_{18} 11QT 31_{10}, var. עֶשְׂרִים וְאֶחָד Hg 2_1, etc.; אַחַת וְשֵׁשׁ־מֵאוֹת *six hundred and one* Gn 8_{13}. → אחד *be united;* cf. חַד II *one.*

אָחוּ 3 n.m. **reed**—coll. Gn $41_{2.18}$ Jb 8_{11}.

אֵהוּד 1 pr.n. **Ehud.**

אַחֲוָה I 1 n.f. **brotherhood,** between Judah and Israel Zc 11_{14}. → cf. אָח *brother.*

[**אַחֲוָה**] II $1.0.1$ n.f.—sf. אַחֲוָתִי—**declaration** Jb 13_{17}. → חוה I *declare.*

אֲחוֹחַ 1 pr.n.m. **Ahoah.**

אֲחוֹחִי, see אֲחֹחִי II *Ahohite.*

אֲחוּמַי 1 pr.n.m. **Ahumai.**

אָחוֹר $51.3.7$ n.[m.]—pl. cstr. אַחֲרֵי; sf. אֲחֹרָיו, אֲחֹרֵיהֶם—**rear part, 1.** as adv. of direction, **backwards,** with סוג ni. *turn* 2 S 1_{22}, הלך *go* Jr 15_6, נפל *fall* Gn 49_{17}. **2a.** as adv. of position, **at the rear** Ezk 2_{10} (פָּנִים וְאָחוֹר *at the front and back*) Ps 139_5 (אָחוֹר וָקֶדֶם *behind and in front*). **b.** with prefixed prep., (1) מֵאָחוֹר **from the rear** 2 S 10_9 (+ מִפָּנִים *from the front*), perh. **from the west** Is 9_{11} (+ מִקֶּדֶם *from the east*). (2) בְּאָחוֹר **at the back** Pr 29_{11}. (3) לְאָחוֹר **to the rear** Ps 114_3. **3.** as adv. of time, לְאָחוֹר **in the future** Is 41_{23}. **4.** as pl. noun, **rear parts, back** of Y. Ex 33_{23}, humans Ezk 8_{16}, tabernacle Ex 26_{12}. → אחר *delay.*

אָחוֹת $114.0.10$ n.f.—cstr. אֲחוֹת; sf. אֲחֹתִי; pl. Q אחיות; cstr. Q אחיות; sf. אַחְיוֹתַי, אֲחוֹתֵךְ, אַחְיוֹתַיִךְ (אֲחוֹתֵךְ), אַחְיוֹתֵיהֶם—**1.** usu. **sister,** Gn 4_{22}, also half-sister 2 S 13, kinswoman Gn 24_{60}, country or city depicted as woman Jr 3 Ezk 16 23; term of endearment to lover Ca 4-5. **2. partner,** lit. 'sister', אִשָּׁה אֶל־אֲחֹתָהּ *each one to its partner,* with ref. to curtain Ex 26_3, loop Ex 26_5, wing Ezk 1_9. → cf. אָח *brother.*

אחז $67.3.12$ vb.—**Qal** $58.2.11$ Pf. אָחַז; impf. יֹאחֵז; + waw וַיֹּאחֶז (וַיֶּאֱחֹז, וָאֹחֵז (וָאֹחֲזָה)); impv. אֱחֹז, אֶחֱזוּ־, אֶחֱזוּ־; ptc. אֹחֵז, אֹחֶזֶת; ptc. pass. אָחוּז, אֲחוּזִים, אֲחֻזֵי; inf. אֱחֹז, לֶאֱחֹז/בְּ—**1a. hold, seize, grasp,** subj. Y. Ps 73_{23}, person Ex 4_4, lion Is 5_{29}, hand Gn 25_{26}, trap Jb 18_9, writhing Ex 15_{14}; with accus. person Jg 1_6, prey Is 5_{29}; בְּ of obj. heel Gn 25_{26}, horn of altar 1 K 1_5, justice Dt 32_{41}. **b. be able to hold, handle** spear and shield 2 C 25_5. **c. hold to, persist in** way, i.e. behaviour Jb 17_9. **2. fasten** gates **securely** Ne 7_3. **3.** pass. **a. be held, be taken,** of bird Ec 9_{12}, fabric Est 1_6, warrior Ca 3_8 (אֲחֻזֵי חֶרֶב *held of,* i.e. holding, *a sword*). **b.** as noun (1) sg., **selection** Nm 31_{30}. (2) pl., **support** for side-chambers of temple Ezk 41$_6$.

Ni. 7.1.1 Pf. נֶאֱחַז; + waw וַיֵּאָחֲזוּ; impv. הֵאָחֲזוּ; ptc. נֶאֱחָזִים—**1a. be held, trapped,** of humans CD 2$_{18}$ (+ בְּ *through* stubbornness), ram Gn 22$_{13}$ (+ בְּ *in* thicket, *by* horns), fish Ec 9$_{12}$ (+ בְּ *in* net). **b. be set, held in place,** of jewels Si 50$_9$. **2. hold property** Gn 34$_{10}$.

Pi. 1 Ptc. מְאַחֵז—**cover surface of throne** Jb 26$_9$.

Ho. 1 Ptc. מָאֳחָזִים—**be held, be attached,** of steps 2 C 9$_{18}$ (+ לְ *to* throne).

→ אֲחֻזָּה *possession.*

אָחָז 41.0.0.4 pr.n.m. **Ahaz.**

אֲחֻזָּה 66.0.4 n.f.—cstr. אֲחֻזַּת; sf. אֲחֻזָּתוֹ, אֲחֻזַּתְכֶם—**possession, inheritance, property,** in ref. to small area or plot of land Lv 25$_{10}$, Levitical cities Lv 25$_{32}$, Canaan as promised land Gn 17$_8$, Y. as possession of priests Ezk 44$_{28}$, non-Israelite purchased as slave Lv 25$_{45}$; אֲחֻזַּת קֶבֶר *possession of a grave,* i.e. land for it Gn 23$_4$; שְׂדֵה אֲחֻזָּתוֹ *field of his (inherited) possession,* i.e. owned by him Lv 27$_{16}$. → אחז *hold.*

אַחְזַי 1.0.0.1 pr.n.m. **Ahzai.**

אֲחַזְיָה, see אֲחַזְיָהוּ *Ahaziah.*

אֲחַזְיָהוּ 37.0.0.2 pr.n.m. **Ahaziah.**

אֲחֻזָּם 1 pr.n.m. **Ahuzzam.**

***אחזור** 0.0.1 pl.n. **Hazor.**

אֲחֻזַּת 1 pr.n.m. **Ahuzzath.**

אֲחוֹחִי I 1 pr.n.m. **Ahohi.**

אֲחוֹחִי II 4 gent. **Ahohite.**

אֵחִי 1 pr.n.m. **Ehi.**

אֲחִי 2.0.0.1 pr.n.m. **Ahi.**

***אחיאל** 0.0.0.1 pr.n.m. **Ahiel.**

אֲחִיאָם 2 pr.n.m. **Ahiam.**

אֲחִיָּה 24.0.0.6 pr.n.m. **Ahijah.**

אֲחִיָּהוּ, see אֲחִיָּה *Ahijah.*

אֲחִיהוּד 1 pr.n.m. **Ahihud.**

אַחְיוֹ 6.0.0.1 pr.n.m. **Ahio.**

***[אֲחִיּוֹת]** 0.0.1 pr.n.m. **Ahijoth.**

אֲחִיחֻד 1 pr.n.m. **Ahihud.**

אֲחִיטוּב 15 pr.n.m. **Ahitub.**

אֲחִילוּד 5 pr.n.m. **Ahilud.**

אחימה, see אחמא *Ahima.*

אֲחִימוֹת 1 pr.n.m. **Ahimoth.**

אֲחִימֶלֶךְ 17.0.0.18 pr.n.m. **Ahimelech.**

אֲחִימַן 4.0.0.1 pr.n.m. **Ahiman.**

אֲחִימַעַץ 15 pr.n.m. **Ahimaaz.**

אַחְיָן 1 pr.n.m. **Ahian.**

אֲחִינָדָב 1 pr.n.m. **Ahinadab.**

אֲחִינֹעַם 7.0.0.1 pr.n.f. **Ahinoam.**

אֲחִיסָמָךְ 3 pr.n.m. **Ahisamach.**

אֲחִיעֶזֶר 6 pr.n.m. **Ahiezer.**

אֲחִיקָם 20.0.0.8 pr.n.m. **Ahikam.**

אֲחִירָם 1 pr.n.m. **Ahiram.**

אֲחִירָמִי 1 gent. **Ahiramite.**

אֲחִירַע 5 pr.n.m. **Ahira.**

[אֲחִישַׁחַר] 1 pr.n.m. **Ahishahar.**

אֲחִישָׁר 1 pr.n.m. **Ahishar.**

אֲחִיתֹפֶל 20 pr.n.m. **Ahithophel.**

***אחך** 0.0.0.1 pr.n.m. **Ahicha.**

אַחְלָב 1 pl.n. **Ahlab.**

אַחֲלַי 2 interj.—אַחֲלֵי—**if only** 2 K 5$_3$ Ps 119$_5$.

[אַחְלַי] 2 pr.n.m.&f. **Ahlai.**

אַחְלָמָה 2 n.[f.] **amethyst, jasper,** or sim. stone, in Aaron's breastplate Ex 28$_{19}$||39$_{12}$.

***אחמא** 0.0.0.5 pr.n.m. **Ahima.**

אחמלך, see אֲחִימֶלֶךְ *Ahimelech.*

אחנעם, see אֲחִינֹעַם *Ahinoam.*

אֲחַסְבַּי 1 pr.n.m. **Ahasbai.**

אחקם, see אֲחִיקָם *Ahikam.*

אחר 17.6.9.1 vb.—**Qal** 1 + waw וָאֵחַר—**stay behind, delay** (intrans.) Gn 32$_5$.

Pi. 15.3.4.1 Pf. אֵחַר, אֵחֲרוּ; impf. יְאַחֵר; ptc. מְאַחֲרִים; cstr. מְאַחֲרֵי—**1.** intrans., **stay behind, delay,** of Y. Dt 7$_{10}$, human Arad ost. 2$_6$, salvation Is 46$_{13}$. **2.** trans., **detain, delay** person Gn 24$_{56}$, produce Ex 22$_{28}$. **3. be slow, late to, hold back from,** with inf. + לְ of עשׂה *do* Gn 34$_{19}$, שׁלם pi. *repay* Dt 23$_{22}$.

Hi. 1 + waw Qr וַיּוֹחֶר (Kt וייחר, perh. Qal, Pi., or Hi.)—intrans., **stay behind, delay** 2 S 20$_5$ (+ מִן *beyond* appointed time).

Htp. 0.3.5 Impf. Q יתאחר; ptc. Si מתאחר; inf. Q התאחר—**1.** intrans., **delay, be late, hold back, be held back from** (מִן) Si 7$_{34}$ 1QS 1$_{14}$. **2. turn to the rear,** of sword Ezk 21$_{21(mss)}$ (L הִתְאַחֲדִי *do it all at once*).

→ אָחוֹר *behind,* אַחֵר *other,* אַחְרָאִי *guarantor,* אַחֲרוֹן

latter, אַחֲרֵי *after,* אַחֲרִית *end,* אֲחֹרַנִּית *backwards.*

אַחַר 96.9.87.1 prep. 1. of time, a. as prep., **after, following** event Gn 15$_{1}$, flood Gn 9$_{28}$, jubilee Lv 25$_{15}$. **b.** as conj., **after,** preceding inf. Jr 40$_{1}$, fin. verb Jr 41$_{16}$; אַחַר אֲשֶׁר preceding fin. verb Ezk 40$_{1}$. **2.** of place, **a. behind, to the rear of, after** a person or thing; with verb הלך *go* Gn 37$_{17}$, עבר *pass* 1QS 2$_{20}$, עמד *stand* Ca 2$_{9}$. **b.** מֵאַחַר **from behind** the flock, with verb לקח *take* 2 S 7$_{8}$. **3.** of personal relationship, **a. after, in support of** Y. 1 S 12$_{14}$, human 1 S 11$_{7}$, sin 2 K 13$_{2}$; with verb היה *be* 1 S 12$_{14}$, הלך *go* 2 K 13$_{2}$, יצא *go out* 1 S 11$_{7}$. **b.** מֵאַחַר **from after** Y., with verb סוג ni. *turn aside* Is 59$_{13}$. **4. besides** Ne 5$_{15}$. **5. according to** Si 35$_{17(B)}$. **6a.** as adv. of time, **afterwards, then** Gn 10$_{18}$. **b.** אַחַר כֵּן **afterwards** Lv 14$_{36}$. **c.** אַחַר זֶה **after this** 2 C 32$_{9}$. **7.** as adv. of space, **behind** Gn 22$_{13}$. → אחר *delay*.

אַחֵר I 166.5.24 adj.—f.s. אַחֶרֶת, m.pl. אֲחֵרִים (אֲחֵרִין), f.pl. אֲחֵרוֹת—**1.** of contrast, **another, other, different,** of god Ex 20$_{3}$, people Dt 28$_{32}$, tongue Is 28$_{11}$, spirit Nm 14$_{24}$, name Is 65$_{15}$, place Nm 23$_{13}$, way 1 K 13$_{10}$. **2.** of similarity, **a. another, other, additional,** of man 2 S 18$_{26}$, dream Gn 37$_{9}$, scroll Jr 36$_{28}$, day Gn 8$_{10}$. **b.** with art., **the next, the second, the other,** of day 2 K 6$_{29}$, woman 1 K 3$_{22}$, side Ezk 40$_{40}$. **3.** as noun, **another one,** of sword 1 S 21$_{10}$, person Pr 25$_{9}$. → אחר *delay*.

אַחֵר II 1 pr.n.m. **Aher.**

*[אַחֲרָאי] 0.0.1 n.m. **guarantor** Mur 30 2$_{24}$. → אחר *delay*.

אַחֲרוֹן 51.2.18 adj.—אַחֲרֹן, f.s. אַחֲרוֹנָה; pl. אַחֲרוֹנִים, f.pl. Q אחרונות—**1a. last, latter,** as adj. of word 2 S 23$_{1}$, deed 1 C 29$_{29}$, day Is 30$_{8}$, time 1QpHab 7$_{7}$, generation Dt 29$_{21}$. **b.** as noun, **last one, latter one** Is 44$_{6}$. **2a. western,** as adj. of sea Dt 11$_{24}$. **b.** as noun, **one from the west** Jb 18$_{20}$. **3.** אַחֲרוֹנָה as adv., **afterwards, at the last,** alw. with prep.: בָּאַחֲרֹנָה Dt 13$_{10}$, לָאַחֲרֹנָה Nm 2$_{31}$, כָּאַחֲרֹנָה Dn 11$_{29}$. → אחר *delay*.

אַחֲרַח 1 pr.n.m. **Aharah.**

אַחַרְחֵל 1 pr.n.m. **Aharhel.**

אַחֲרֵי 619.13.44 prep.—in form, אַחֲרֵי is pl. cstr. of אַחַר; sf. אַחֲרֵיהֶם, אַחֲרָיו—**1a.** of time, (1) as prep., **after** event Gn 22$_{20}$, plague Nm 25$_{19}$. (2) as conj., **after,** preceding inf. cstr. Gn 5$_{4}$, fin. verb 1 S 5$_{9}$; אַחֲרֵי אֲשֶׁר preceding fin. verb Dt 24$_{4}$. **b. after (the death, reign, end of)** Jg 12$_{8}$ 1 K 1$_{13}$; מֵאַחֲרֵי in same sense Dt 29$_{21}$ Ec 10$_{14}$. **c. (which comes) after,** זַרְעֲךָ אַחֲרֶיךָ *your seed after you* Gn 17$_{7}$. **d. after (he had done),** אַחֲרָיו הֶחֱזִיק נְחֶמְיָה *after him Nehemiah repaired* Ne 3$_{16}$. **e.** אַחֲרֵי־כֵן **afterward** Lv 16$_{26}$. **2a.** of place, **after, (approaching) towards the rear of,** with verb of motion הלך *go* Gn 24$_{5}$, בוא *come* Ex 14$_{17}$; רדף *pursue* Gn 31$_{23}$; מֵאַחֲרֵי in same sense Gn 19$_{26}$ Ex 14$_{19}$. **b.** without implied motion towards, **at the back of, behind, after,** with verb שׁמע *hear* Ezk 3$_{12}$, חנה *encamp* Nm 3$_{23}$; מֵאַחֲרֵי in same sense Ex 14$_{19}$ Is 30$_{21}$. **c.** of greater distance, **beyond** Jg 18$_{12}$. **3.** perh. of status, **after, junior to** 2 S 23$_{11}$. **4. behind, in support of** Y. Nm 14$_{24}$, humans Ex 23$_{2}$. **5. in accordance with** stubbornness of heart Jr 3$_{17}$. **6.** as conj., **because, seeing that** Gn 41$_{39}$; אַחֲרֵי אֲשֶׁר in same sense Jg 11$_{36}$. **7.** מֵאַחֲרֵי **from behind, (away) from (following),** with verb שׁוב *turn* intrans. Nm 14$_{43}$, לקח *take* Am 7$_{15}$. **8.** אַחֲרֵי as noun, **back parts, rear,** בְּאַחֲרֵי הַחֲנִית he struck him *with (the) back of the spear* 2 S 2$_{23}$, מֵאַחֲרָיו the spear protruded *from his back* 2 S 2$_{23}$. → אחר *delay*.

אַחֲרֵי 1 adv. **afterwards** Pr 28$_{23}$. → אחר *delay*.

אַחֲרִית 61.15.34 n.f.—cstr. אַחֲרִית; sf. אַחֲרִיתוֹ—**1.** of place, **end, edge,** אַחֲרִית יָם *end of the sea* Ps 139$_{9}$. **2.** of time, **consequence, end, result, future,** אַחֲרִית דָּבָר *end of a matter* Ec 7$_{8}$, אַחֲרִיתוֹ עֲדֵי אֹבֵד *his end is to destruction* Nm 24$_{20}$; אַחֲרִית הַיָּמִים *the end of the days,* i.e. the latter days, the future Gn 49$_{1}$. **3.** of position, status, **last,** אַחֲרִית גּוֹיִם *the last of the nations* Jr 50$_{12}$. **4.** of persons, **a. descendants, posterity** Ps 37$_{37}$. **b. remnant** Ezk 23$_{15}$. → אחר *delay*.

אֲחֹרַנִּית 7 adv. **backwards** Gn 9$_{23}$. → אחר *delay*.

[אֲחַשְׁדַּרְפָּן] 4 n.m.—pl. אֲחַשְׁדַּרְפְּנִים; cstr. אֲחַשְׁדַּרְפְּנֵי—**satrap** Est 3$_{12}$.

אֲחַשְׁוֵרוֹשׁ 31 pr.n.m. **Ahasuerus.**

אֲחַשְׁוֵרֹשׁ, see אֲחַשְׁוֵרוֹשׁ *Ahasuerus.*

אֲחַשְׁתָּרִי 1 pr.n.m. **Ahashtari.**

[אֲחַשְׁתְּרָן] 2 adj. **royal,** רֹכְבֵי הָרֶכֶשׁ הָאֲחַשְׁתְּרָנִים appar. *riders of the royal steeds* Est 8$_{10.14}$.

*אחתמלך 0.0.0.1 pr.n.f. **Ahathmelech.**

אַט 5 n.[m.]—Q אוט; sf. אִטִּי—**gentleness, a.** with prep., לְאַט *according to,* or *with, gentleness,* i.e. gently Is 8$_{6}$, slowly Gn 33$_{14}$; לְאַט־לִי לַנַּעַר *(deal) gently, for my sake, with the lad* 2 S 18$_{5}$. **b.** without prep. (but in same sense) 1 K 21$_{27}$.

אָטָד 4 n.m. **bramble** (perh. *Lycaeum europaeum*) Jg 9$_{14}$ Ps 58$_{10}$.

[אֵטוּן] 1 n.[m.]—cstr. אֵטוּן—**linen,** from Egypt Pr 7$_{16}$.

[אִטִּי] 1 n.m. **ghost**—pl. אִטִּים (sg. perh. אַט or אִט)—Is 19$_{3}$.

אטם 8.0.1 vb.—**Qal** 7.0.1 Ptc. אֹטֵם; ptc. pass. אֲטֻמוֹת, אֲטֻמִים—**a. block** ear Is 33$_{15}$ (+ מִשְּׁמֹעַ דָּמִים *from hearing [about] bloodshed*), **shut** lip Pr 17$_{28}$. **b.** pass. perh. **be recessed,** of window 1 K 6$_{4}$.

Hi. 1 Impf. יַאְטֵם—**block** ear Ps 58$_{5}$.

אטר 1 vb.—**Qal** 1 Impf. תֶּאְטַר—**shut** mouth Ps 69$_{16}$. → אִטֵּר *shut.*

אָטֵר 5 pr.n.m. **Ater.**

אִטֵּר 2 adj. **shut,** אִטֵּר יַד־יְמִינוֹ *shut in respect of his right hand,* i.e. left-handed, or perh. ambidextrous Jg 3$_{15}$. → אטר *shut.*

אֵי 41.1 interrog. adv.—sf. אַיֶּכָּה, אֵיוֹ—**where?, 1a.** in nom. cl., **where is?,** אֵי הֶבֶל *where is Abel?* Gn 4$_{9}$; אֵיוֹ *where is he?* Ex 2$_{20}$. **b.** אֵי לְזֹאת **where for this,** i.e. **how?** Jr 5$_{7}$. **2a.** אֵי־זֶה with verb, **whither?, in which direction?** 1 K 22$_{24}$; in nom. cl., **where is?** 1 S 9$_{18}$. **b. what?, which?** Ec 2$_{3}$ 11$_{6}$. **3.** אֵי־מִזֶּה, **a. whence?** 2 S 1$_{3}$. **b. from which?,** אֵי־מִזֶּה עִיר אַתָּה *from which town are you?* 2 S 15$_{2}$. → cf. אֵיפֹה *where?*

אִי I 36.1.2 n.m. (& f.)—cstr. אִי; pl. אִיִּים (אִיִּן); cstr. אִיֵּי—**island, coast, coastland** (distinction difficult), אִי כַפְתּוֹר *island of Caphtor* Jr 47$_{4}$, יֹשֵׁב הָאִי *dweller(s) of,* i.e. in, *the coastland* Is 20$_{6}$, אִיִּים רַבִּים *many islands* Ps 97$_{1}$.

[אִי] II 3 n.m.—pl. אִיִּים—**jackal,** or sim. animal Is 13$_{22}$ 34$_{14}$ Jr 50$_{39}$.

אִי III 1 adv. **not,** אִי־נָקִי *(one who is) not innocent* Jb 22$_{30}$.

אִי IV 2 interj. **alas,** אִילוֹ *alas for him* Ec 4$_{10}$, אִי־לָךְ *alas for you* Ec 10$_{16}$.

איב 283.5.70 vb.—**Qal** 283.5.70 + waw וְאָיַבְתִּי; ptc. masc. אוֹיֵב (אֹיֵב); sf. אוֹיִבְךָ (אֹיִבְךָ); pl. אוֹיְבִים; cstr. אוֹיְבֵי; sf. אוֹיְבָיו; ptc. fem. sf. אֹיַבְתִּי—**1. be an enemy to, be at enmity with,** וְאָיַבְתִּי אֶת־אֹיְבֶיךָ *and I* (Y.) *shall be an enemy to your enemies* Ex 23$_{22}$. **2.** ptc. as noun, **enemy** of Israel Jg 2$_{18}$, foreign people Jr 49$_{37}$, king 1 S 14$_{47}$, Y. Jg 5$_{31}$; personal enemy of individual Ex 23$_{4}$. → אֵיבָה *enmity.*

אֵיבָה 5.0.2 n.f.—cstr. אֵיבַת—**enmity** of Philistines towards Israel Ezk 25$_{15}$; between killer and victim Nm 35$_{21}$, truth and iniquity 1QS 4$_{17}$. → איב *be an enemy.*

אֵיד 24 n.m.—cstr. אֵיד; sf. אֵידוֹ—**disaster, calamity,** for Israel Jr 18$_{17}$, wicked person Jb 21$_{30}$. → cf. מְאֹד II *calamity.*

אַיָּה I 3 n.f. **falcon,** or other bird of prey Lv 11$_{14}$||Dt 14$_{13}$ Jb 28$_{7}$.

אַיָּה II 6 pr.n.m. **Aiah.**

אַיֵּה 46 interrog. adv. **where?,** alw. in nom. cl., **where is?, where are?** Gn 18$_{9}$ Jg 6$_{13}$; אַיֵּה אֵפוֹא *where, then?* Jg 9$_{38}$. → cf. אֵי *where?*

אִיּוֹב 58.1 pr.n.m. **Job.**

אִיזֶבֶל 22.0.1 pr.n.f. **Jezebel.**

אייר, see אִיָּר *Iyyar.*

אֵיךְ 61.0.3 interrog. adv. **how?, 1.** introducing rhetorical question, **how is it possible that?, surely it is not possible that?,** אֵיךְ אֶעֱשֶׂה הָרָעָה הַגְּדֹלָה הַזֹּאת *how can I do this great evil?* Gn 39$_{9}$. **2.** introducing simple question, **how?, by what method?,** אֵיךְ אַתֶּם נוֹעָצִים לְהָשִׁיב *how do you advise me to answer?* 1 K 12$_{6}$||2 C 10$_{6}$. **3.** as interj., **how terribly!,** אֵיךְ נָפְלוּ גִבּוֹרִים *how are the mighty fallen!* 2 S 1$_{19}$. → cf. אֵיכָה *how?,* אֵיכָכָה *how?*

אִי־כָבוֹד 2 pr.n.m. **Ichabod.**

אֵיכָה 18.0.9 interrog. adv.—אֵיכֹה—**how?, where?, 1.** introducing rhetorical question, **how is it possible that?, surely it is not possible that?** Ps 73$_{11}$. **2.** introducing simple question, **how?, by what method?** Jg 20$_{3}$. **3.** as interj., **how terribly!** Lm 1$_{1}$. **4a. where?** Ca 1$_{7}$. **b.** in nom. cl., **where is?** 2 K 6$_{13}$. → cf. אֵיךְ *how?*

אֵיכֹה, see אֵיכָה *how?.*

אֵיכָכָה 4.2.4 interrog. adv.—אֵיכָכָה—**how?, 1.** introducing rhetorical question, **how is it possible that?, surely it is not possible that?** Est 8$_{6}$. **2.** as conj., how much more Si $10_{31(B)}$. → cf. אֵיךְ *how?*

אַיִל I 182.0.38 n.m.—אַיִל; cstr. אֵיל; pl. אֵילִים (אֵלִים); cstr. אֵילֵי—**1. ram** Gn 31_{38}; oft. as sacrifice Lv 8_{18}. **2. leader** of nation Ex 15_{15} Ezk 17_{13}.

אַיִל II 22 n.[m.]—cstr. אֵיל; sf. Kt אילו (אֵלו), pl. אֵילִים; sf. Qr אֵילָיו (אֵלָיו), אֵלֵיהֶמָה—**pillar,** projection in wall, supporting frame or post of door 1 K 6_{31}, window Ezk 40_{16}, gateway Ezk 40_{24}.

אֱיָל 1 n.[m.] **help,** or perh. **strength** Ps 88_5. → cf. אֱיָלוּת *help.*

אַיָּל 11.0.2 n.m. (& f.)—pl. אַיָּלִים—**deer** Dt 12_{15}. → cf. אַיָּלָה *hind.*

אַיָּלָה 11 n.f.—abs. אַיֶּלֶת; cstr. אַיֶּלֶת; pl. אַיָּלוֹת; cstr. אַיְלוֹת—**hind,** proverbial for agility 2 S 22_{34}||Ps 18_{34}, tenderness Pr 5_{19}. → cf. אַיָּל *deer.*

אִילוֹ, see אִי IV *alas.*

[אִילוּ], see אִלּוּ *if.*

אַיָּלוֹן 10 pl.n. **Aijalon.**

אֵילוֹן I 6.0.0.1 pr.n.m. **Elon.**

אֵילוֹן II 1 pl.n. **Elon.**

אֵילוֹן בֵּית חָנָן 1 pl.n. **Elon-beth-hanan.**

אֵילוֹת, see אֵילַת *Elath.*

[אֱיָלוּת] 1 n.f.—sf. אֱיָלוּתִי—**help,** or perh. **strength** Ps 22_{20}. → cf. אֱיָל *help.*

אֵילִים, see אַיִל I *ram,* II *pillar,* אֵלָה *terebinth.*

[אֵילָם], see אוּלָם II *porch.*

אֵילֹן, see אֵילוֹן I *Elon.*

*__[אִילָן]__ 0.0.1 n.[m.] **tree,** coll. 5/6ḤevBA 46_9.

אֵיל פָּארָן 1 pl.n. **El-paran.**

אֵילַת 8 pl.n. **Elath.**

אַיֶּלֶת, see אַיָּלָה *hind.*

אָיֹם 3 adj.—f.s. אֲיֻמָּה—**terrible,** of nation Hb 1_7, female lover Ca $6_{4.10}$. → cf. אֵימָה *terror.*

אֵימָה 16.2.4 n.f.—אֵימָתָה; cstr. אֵימַת; sf. אֵימָתוֹ, אֵימַתְכֶם; pl. אֵימִים; cstr. אֵימוֹת; sf. אֲמֶיךָ—**1. (feeling of) terror, dread** Ex 15_{16} Ps 55_5. **2a. (source of) terror, terror** Jb 41_6 Pr 20_2. **b. image of deity, perh.** as source of terror Jr 50_{38}. → אָיֹם *terrible.*

אֲיֻמָּה, from אָיֹם *terrible.*

אֵימִים, from אֵמִים *Emim.*

אַיִן I 790.55.228.3 neg. part.—אֵין; cstr. אֵין; sf. אֵינֶנִּי, אֵינְךָ, אֵינֶךָּ, 3ms אֵינֶנּוּ, אֵינֶנָּה, 1cp אֵינֶנּוּ, אֵינְכֶם, אֵינָם—**not, 1a. there is not (present),** אֵין אִישׁ *there was no man* Ex 2_{12}; in circumstantial clause, שְׁבִי־לָאָרֶץ אֵין־כִּסֵּא *sit on the ground, there being no,* i.e. without, *throne* Is 47_1. **b. there is not,** i.e. **has ceased to be, vanished, died,** בְּטֶרֶם אֵלֵךְ וְאֵינֶנִּי *before I go and am no more* Ps 39_{14}. **c. there is none,** מְבַקְשִׁים מַיִם וָאַיִן *seeking water but there is none* Is 41_{17}. **d.** אַיִן as whole clause, **no, there is not** Jg 4_{20}. **2a. there is no one who, nothing that,** followed by ptc., אֵין רֹאֶה *there is no one who sees* Ex 22_9. **b. there is no one who is, nothing that is,** followed by adj., אֵין־קָדוֹשׁ כַּי׳ *there is no one holy like Y.* 1 S 2_2. **3. there is no one, nothing,** אֵין כַּי׳ *there is no one like Y.* Ex 8_6. **4. is not,** in neg. nom. cl., **a.** predicate continued by prep. phrase, esp. אֵין לְ **there is not,** i.e. there does not belong, to, שָׁדַיִם אֵין לָהּ *she does not have breasts* Ca 8_8, אֵין אַחִים לְאָבִיו *his father does not have brothers* Nm 27_{11}; אֵין בְּ **there is not in,** אֵין־בִּי כֹחַ *there is not in me strength,* i.e. I have none Is 50_2, אֵין־יִרְאַת אֱלֹהִים בַּמָּקוֹם הַזֶּה *there is no fear of God in this place* Gn 20_{11}. **b.** predicate continued by adj., הַבְּהֵמָה אֲשֶׁר אֵינֶנָּה טְהֹרָה *the animals that are not clean* Gn 7_8. **c.** predicate continued by ptc., תֶּבֶן אֵין נִתָּן לַעֲבָדֶיךָ *no straw is given to your servants* Ex 5_{16}; אַיִן suffixed subject pron. and ptc., תְּמוּנָה אֵינְכֶם רֹאִים *you saw no form* Dt 4_{12}. **5.** אַיִן with prefixed prep., introducing **a.** final clause, **so that there is not, (so that it is) without, beyond, (1)** מֵאַיִן, וְהַאֲבַדְתִּיךְ מֵאֵין יוֹשֵׁב *and I shall destroy you so that there is not one inhabitant* Zp 2_5. **(2)** לְאַיִן, וַיִּפֹּל מִכּוּשִׁים לְאֵין לָהֶם מִחְיָה *and the Cushites fell so that there was not to them survival,* i.e. they had no survivors 2 C 14_{12}. **(3)** עַד־אֵין, נִפְלָאוֹת עַד־אֵין מִסְפָּר *wonders until there is no number,* i.e. beyond number Jb 5_9. **b.** causal clause, **because there is not, through lack of, (1)** מֵאַיִן, תִּבְאַשׁ דְּגָתָם מֵאֵין מַיִם *their fish stinks because there is not water* Is 50_2. **(2)** בְּאַיִן, הוּא יָמוּת בְּאֵין מוּסָר *he dies through lack of discipline* Pr 5_{23}. **c.** circumstantial clause, **while there is not, without there being, (1)** בְּאַיִן, אַנְשֵׁי־חֶסֶד נֶאֱסָפִים בְּאֵין מֵבִין *faithful people are taken away without anyone understanding (why)* Is 57_1. **(2)** לְאַיִן, פגריהם לאין קובר *corpses with no one to bury (them)* 1QM 11_1. **6.** אֵין לְ + inf. cstr. **it is not**

possible, permitted to, one cannot, may not, need not, מִמֶּנּוּ אֵין לִגְרֹעַ *it is not possible to diminish it* Ec 3_{14}. **7.** (וְ)אִם־אַיִן **(and) if not, otherwise,** הָבָה־לִּי בָנִים וְאִם־אַיִן מֵתָה אָנֹכִי *give me children, otherwise I am dead* Gn 30_{1}. **8.** perh. as abstract noun, **nothing(ness), vanity** Is 40_{23} 41_{24}.

אַיִן II 18.1 interrog. adv. **where?**, alw. מֵאַיִן **whence?**, **1.** with verb, מֵאַיִן בָּאתֶם *whence have you come?* Gn 42_{7}. **2.** in nom. cl., **whence is/are?**, מֵאַיִן אַתֶּם *whence are you?* Gn 29_{4}.

*איעדה 0.0.0.1 pr.n. **Iadah.**

אִיעֶזֶר 1 pr.n.m. **Iezer.**

אִיעֶזְרִי 1 gent. **Iezrite.**

אֵיפָה 41.1.3 n.f.—אֵפָה; cstr. אֵיפַת—**1. ephah,** unit of dry measure (about 40 litres); = ten omers Ex 16_{36}; one tenth of a homer, and equal to liquid measure bath Ezk 45_{11}. **2. ephah container, measure** Zc 5_{6}.

אֵיפֹה 10.0.1 interrog. adv. **where?**, **1.** with verb, אֵיפֹה לִקַּטְתְּ *where did you glean?* Ru 2_{19}. **2.** in nom. cl., **where is/are?**, אֵיפֹה הוּא *where is he?* 2 S 9_{4}. → אֵי *where?* + פֹּה *here.*

*[אִיָּר] 0.0.3 pr.n.m.—אייר—**Iyyar,** second month of postexilic calendar, previously called Ziv, April/May GnzPs 2_{7}.

אִישׁ I 2179.86.466.9 n.m.—cstr. אִישׁ; sf. אִישׁוֹ; pl. אֲנָשִׁים, אִישִׁים; cstr. אַנְשֵׁי; sf. אֲנָשָׁיו, אַנְשֵׁיהֶם—**1a.** usu. **man, person,** oft. without contextual emphasis on gender, כָּאִישׁ גְּבוּרָתוֹ *as is the man so is his strength* Jg 8_{21}, אִישׁ בְּחֶטְאוֹ יוּמָת *a man shall be put to death for his own sin* 2 K $14_{6(Qr)}$||2 C 25_{4}, וַיֵּאָסְפוּ כָל־הָעָם כְּאִישׁ אֶחָד *and all the people gathered together as one man* Ne 8_{1}, אֶרֶץ לֹא־אִישׁ *a land where there is no man* Jb 38_{26}. **b.** distributively, **each, anyone,** וַיֹּאמְרוּ אִישׁ אֶל־רֵעֵהוּ *and each said to the other,* lit. 'a man to his fellow' Gn 11_{3}, לֹא תוֹנוּ אִישׁ אֶת־עֲמִיתוֹ *you shall not oppress one another,* lit. 'a man his fellow' Lv 25_{17}, וַיִּפָּרְדוּ אִישׁ מֵעַל אָחִיו *and they were separated, each from the other,* lit. 'a man from his brother' Gn 13_{11}, וַיֵּלְכוּ כָל־הָעָם אִישׁ לְבֵיתוֹ *and all the people went, each to his house* 1 C 16_{43}, אִישׁ אִישׁ כִּי יִהְיֶה זָב מִבְּשָׂרוֹ *when anyone has a discharge from his flesh* Lv 15_{2}, לַעֲשׂוֹת כִּרְצוֹן אִישׁ־וָאִישׁ *to do according to the wish of each* Est 1_{8}; used of gods 2 K 18_{33}||Is 36_{18}, cherubim Ezk 10_{22}, scales of behemoth Jb 41_{9}. **2. one, someone,** sim. to indef. pron., esp. in neg. clauses, אִישׁ מִמֶּנּוּ אֶת־קִבְרוֹ לֹא־יִכְלֶה מִמְּךָ *none of us will withhold his sepulchre from you* Gn 23_{6}, לֹא־יַחְמֹד אִישׁ אֶת־אַרְצְךָ *no one will desire your land* Ex 34_{24}, לֹא־הִנִּיחַ לְאִישׁ לְעָשְׁקָם *he allowed no one to oppress them* 1 C 16_{21}. **3. man, husband,** as distinct from woman, הָאֲנָשִׁים עַל־הַנָּשִׁים *the men as well as the women* Ex 35_{22}, אִישׁ אוֹ אִשָּׁה *man or woman* Lv 13_{29}, אִישׁ ... אִשְׁתּוֹ *a man ... his wife* Gn 2_{24}, אִישׁ נָעֳמִי *the husband of Naomi* Ru 1_{3}. **4. man, person (as belonging),** אִישׁ יִשְׂרָאֵל *Israelite(s)* Dt 27_{14}, אַנְשֵׁי הָעִיר *men of the city* Gn 19_{4}, אִישׁ מִלְחָמָה *man of war,* i.e. warrior Jos 17_{1}, אַנְשֵׁי הַצָּבָא *men of the army* Nm 31_{21}, אִישׁ אֱלֹהִים *man of God,* i.e. prophet 1 S 2_{27}. **5. servant, member of retinue,** alw. pl., הָאֲנָשִׁים אֲשֶׁר אִתּוֹ *the men who were with him* Gn 24_{32}, אַנְשֵׁי דָוִד *the men of David* 1 S 23_{3}, הַמֶּלֶךְ וַאֲנָשָׁיו *the king and his men* 2 S 5_{6}. **6a. mortal,** as distinct from God, אֵל אָנֹכִי וְלֹא־אִישׁ *I am God and not man* Ho 11_{9}, שָׂרִיתָ עִם־אֱלֹהִים וְעִם־אֲנָשִׁים *you have striven with God and with men* Gn 32_{29}, אֱלֹהִים וַאֲנָשִׁים *gods and men* Jg 9_{9}. **b. human being,** as distinct from animals, אִם־בְּהֵמָה אִם־אִישׁ *whether beast or human* Ex 19_{13}, אָנֹכִי תוֹלַעַת וְלֹא־אִישׁ *I am a worm and not a man* Ps 22_{7}. **7. male animal,** מִן־הַבְּהֵמָה ... אִישׁ וְאִשְׁתּוֹ *from the beasts ... a male and his mate* Gn 7_{2}. → cf. אִישׁוֹן *pupil.*

אִישׁ־בֹּשֶׁת 11 pr.n.m. **Ish-bosheth.**

אִישְׁהוֹד 1 pr.n.m. **Ishhod.**

[אִישׁוֹן] 4.1.3 n.[m.] **pupil,** אִישׁוֹן עֵינוֹ *pupil of his eye* Dt 32_{10}, אִישׁוֹן לַיְלָה *pupil,* i.e. very middle, *of night* Pr 7_{9}. → cf. אִישׁ *man.*

אִישׁ־טוֹב 2 pr.n.m. **Ishtob.**

אִישַׁי, see יִשַׁי *Jesse.*

אִיתוֹן 1 n.m.—Kt יאתון—**entrance** Ezk 40_{15}.

אִיתַי, see אִתַּי *Ittai.*

אִיתִיאֵל 3 pr.n.m. **Ithiel.**

אִיתָמָר 21.0.2 pr.n.m. **Ithamar.**

אֵיתָן I 14.1.1 adj.—אֵתָן; sf. אֵיתָנוֹ; pl. אֵיתָנִים—**a.** as pred. adj. or noun, **continuous (one), continuity, perennial (one), eternal (one), eternity, reliable (one), reliability,** נְוֵה אֵיתָן *pasture of continuity* or *dwelling* *place of an eternal one* Jr 49$_{19}$, נַהֲרוֹת אֵיתָן *rivers of continuity*, i.e. continuously flowing Ps 74$_{15}$. **b.** perh. as attrib. adj. of stream Dt 21$_{4}$, nation Jr 5$_{15}$. **c.** as pr. n.m. **Ethanim,** 7th month of pre-exilic calendar, later known as Tishri, September/October 1 K 8$_{2}$.

אֵיתָן II 8 pr.n.m. **Ethan.**

אַךְ 164.10.1 adv. **1.** asseverative **surely, certainly, indeed,** אַךְ הִנֵּה אִשְׁתְּךָ *surely she is your wife* Gn 26$_{9}$, אַךְ בָּךְ אֵל *surely God is with you* Is 45$_{14}$. **2a.** restrictive **only, except,** וְעוֹד לוֹ אַךְ הַמְּלוּכָה *what else is there for him except the kingdom?* 1 S 18$_{8}$, אַךְ הֶבֶל בְּנֵי־אָדָם *human beings are only a breath* Ps 62$_{10}$. **b.** אַךְ הַפַּעַם **only this time,** i.e. **once more** Gn 18$_{32}$. **3a.** adversative **however, but, yet,** אַךְ לֹא בַת־אִמִּי *but* she is *not my mother's daughter* Gn 20$_{12}$. **b.** אַךְ אִם **but if,** אַךְ אִם־אַתָּה לוּ שְׁמָעֵנִי *but if you will, hear me* Gn 23$_{13}$. **4.** restrictive in temporal sequence **hardly, just when,** וַיְהִי אַךְ יָצֹא יָצָא יַעֲקֹב *and just when Jacob had gone out* Gn 27$_{30}$.

אַכַּד 1 pl.n. **Accad.**

אַכְזָב 2 adj. **deceptive,** as noun, **deceptive one,** of stream Jr 15$_{18}$. → כזב *lie.*

אַכְזִיב 4 pl.n. **Achzib.**

אַכְזָר 4 adj.—**1. cruel, fierce,** of poison Dt 32$_{33}$, person Jb 41$_{2}$. **2.** as noun, **cruel one,** of Y. Jb 30$_{21}$, Zion Lm 4$_{3}$. → cf. אַכְזָרִי *cruel*, אַכְזְרִיּוּת *cruelty.*

אַכְזָרִי 8.4.2 adj.—f.s. Q אכזוריה—**1. cruel,** of messenger Pr 17$_{11}$, nation Jr 6$_{23}$, day of Y. Is 13$_{9}$. **2.** as noun, **a. cruel one** Jr 30$_{14}$. **b. cruelty** Si 13$_{12}$. → cf. אַכְזָר *cruel.*

[אַכְזְרִיּוּת] 1 n.[m.] **cruelty** Pr 27$_{4}$. → cf. אַכְזָר *cruel.*

אֲכִילָה 1 n.f. **meal** 1 K 19$_{8}$. → אכל *eat.*

אָכִישׁ 21 pr.n.m. **Achish.**

אכל 816.10.140 vb.—**Qal** 746.9.134 Pf. אָכַל; impf. יֹאכַל (יֹאכֶל), יֹאכְלוּ (יוֹכְלוּ, יֹאכְלוּן, יֹאכֵלוּ); + waw וַיֹּאכַל (וַיֹּאכֶל); impv. אִכְלוּ (אֱכֹלוּ, אֱכָלֻהוּ), אֱכוֹל (אֱכָל־, אִכְלָה); ptc. אֹכֵל, אֹכְלָה (אֹכֵלָה), אֹכֶלֶת, אֹכְלִים, אֹכְלֵי; inf. abs. אָכֹל; cstr. אֲכֹל (אֱכֹל, אֱכָל־, אָכְלוֹ)—**1. eat food,** subj. usu. humans Gn 2$_{16}$, also animals Gn 37$_{20}$, birds Gn 40$_{17}$. **2. destroy, devour,** subj. fire Ex 24$_{17}$, sword Dt 32$_{42}$, wrath Ex 15$_{7}$, zeal Ps 69$_{10}$, persons Dt 7$_{16}$; obj. tree Ezk 21$_{3}$, stubble Is 5$_{24}$, land Dt 32$_{22}$, tent Jb 15$_{34}$, persons Dt 7$_{16}$, wickedness 1QM 11$_{10}$. **3. use, use up, enjoy** money, wealth Gn 31$_{15}$ Is 61$_{6}$, strength Ho 7$_{9}$. **4. experience** consequences of actions Is 3$_{10}$ Ho 10$_{13}$.

Ni. 45.0.4 Impf. יֵאָכֵל; ptc. נֶאֱכֶלֶת; inf. הֵאָכֹל—**1. be eaten,** of food in general Gn 6$_{21}$, unleavened bread Ex 13$_{7}$, fruit Lv 19$_{23}$, flesh Ex 21$_{28}$, animal Lv 11$_{47}$. **2. be destroyed, devoured,** of grain Ex 22$_{5}$, earth Zp 1$_{18}$, persons Ezk 23$_{25}$ (+ בְּ *by* fire).

Pu. 5 Pf. אֻכְּלוּ; impf. תְּאֻכְּלוּ; ptc. אֻכָּל—**be destroyed,** of bush Ex 3$_{2}$, gate Ne 2$_{3}$ (+ בְּ *by* fire), persons Is 1$_{20}$ (+ חֶרֶב *[by the] sword*).

Hi. 20.1.2 Pf. הֶאֱכַלְתִּי; impf. אוֹכִיל, יַאֲכִלֵנוּ; + waw וְהַאֲכַלְתִּי; impv. הַאֲכִלֵהוּ, הַאֲכִילֵהוּ; ptc. מַאֲכִיל; inf. הָכִיל—**1. feed** someone, **a.** with accus. of recipient and food: bread Ex 16$_{32}$, manna Dt 8$_{3}$, flesh Nm 11$_{4}$; **force to eat** own flesh Is 49$_{26}$. **b.** with accus. of recipient only 2 C 28$_{15}$. **2. destroy,** of sword Ezk 21$_{33}$ (but perh. כול hi. *contain*). **3. cause to enjoy** inheritance Is 58$_{14}$.

→ אֹכֶל *food*, אָכְלָה *food*, מַאֲכָל *food*, מַכֹּלֶת *food*, אֲכִילָה *meal*, מַאֲכֹלֶת *fuel*, מַאֲכֶלֶת *knife.*

אֹכֶל 43.2.7 n.m.—cstr. אֹכֶל; sf. אָכְלוֹ—**food,** as produce, harvest Gn 41$_{35}$, sacrificial offering Ml 1$_{12}$, prey of lion Ps 104$_{21}$. → אכל *eat.*

אֻכָל 1 pr.n.m. **Ucal.**

אָכְלָה 18.0.1 n.f.—or inf.; alw. לְאָכְלָה; Q לאוכלה—**1.** usu. **food,** consisting of plants Gn 1$_{29}$, manna Ex 16$_{15}$, animals Gn 9$_{3}$. **2. fuel** for fire Ezk 15$_{4}$. → אכל *eat.*

אָכֵן 19 part. **1.** emphatic, **indeed, surely,** אָכֵן יֵשׁ י׳ בַּמָּקוֹם הַזֶּה *surely Y. is in this place* Gn 28$_{16}$. **2.** adversative, **however, nonetheless,** אָכֵן מִשְׁפָּטִי אֶת־י׳ *nonetheless, my judgment is with Y.* Is 49$_{4}$.

*__[אַכְסַדְרָן]__ 0.0.1 n.[m.] **vestibule** 3QTr 11$_{3}$.

אכף 1 vb.—**Qal** 1 Pf. אָכַף—**press, urge on** Pr 16$_{26}$. → אֶכֶף *pressure*, אַכְפָּה *pressure.*

[אֶכֶף] 1 n.m.—sf. אַכְפִּי—**pressure,** or perh. **hand** Jb 33$_{7}$. → אכף *press.*

*__[אַכְפָּה]__ 0.1 n.[f.] **pressure,** caused by enemies Si 46$_{5}$. → אכף *press.*

אִכָּר 7.0.1 n.m.—pl. אִכָּרִים, sf. אִכָּרֵיכֶם—**farmer** Is 61$_{5}$.

אַכְשָׁף 3 pl.n. **Achshaph.**

אַל 725.249.206.2 adv.—**1.** expressing desire that an action will not occur, **let not, may it** (etc.) **not**, or prohibiting an action, **do not, you** (etc.) **are not to, 1a.** usu. with impf., juss., or cohort. verb, and usu. with verb immediately following, אַל־תִּירָא *do not fear* Gn 15_1, אַל־יַעַל כָּל־הָעָם *let not all the people go up* Jos 7_3, אַל־אֵבֹשָׁה *let me not be put to shame* Jr 17_{18}, אַל־נַקְשִׁיבָה אֶל־כָּל־דְּבָרָיו *let us not pay attention to any of his words* Jr 18_{18}; with word intervening between אַל and verb, אַל־בְּאַפְּךָ תוֹכִיחֵנִי *do not rebuke me in your anger* Ps 6_2; oft. אַל־נָא *do not, please* Gn 13_8. **b.** with other forms of verb: pf. 1 S 27_{10}, inf. Si $39_{34(B)}$, impv. CD 11_9. **c.** without verb following, אַל־נָא *no!, not* Gn 19_{18}, אַל *no!* 2 K 3_{13}; דִּרְשׁוּ־טוֹב וְאַל־רָע *seek good, not evil* Am 5_{14}; אַל before person addressed, אַל בְּנִי *no, my son* 2 S 13_{25}. **2.** as neg. part., **let there not be,** אַל־טַל וְאַל־מָטָר עֲלֵיכֶם *let there not be dew and let there not be rain upon you* 2 S 1_{21}, אַל־דֳּמִי־לָךְ *let there not be silence for you* Ps 83_2. **3.** as noun, **nothing,** וְיָשֵׂם לְאַל מִלָּתִי *and he will make my word as nought* Jb 24_{25}.

אֵל I 240.64.501.2 n.m.—sf. אֵלִי; pl. אֵלִים; cstr. Q אלי—**1a. god,** אֵל אַחֵר *another god* Ex 34_{14}, אֵל נֵכָר *a foreign god* Dt 32_{12}, אֵל זָר *a strange god* Ps 44_{21}, לֹא־אֵל *a non-god* Dt 32_{21}; freq. in pl., oft. as constituting divine/angelic assembly, מִי־כָמֹכָה בָּאֵלִם *who is like you among the gods?* Ex 15_{11}, עדת אלים *council of gods* 1QM 1_{10}, אֵל אֵלִים *God of gods* Dn 11_{36}, בְּנֵי אֵלִים *sons of gods* Ps 29_1, אלי רום *gods of height,* i.e. most exalted gods 4QShirShabb[d] 1.1_{33}. **b. image of a god** Is 44_{10} 46_6. **c.** as pr.n., **El,** in אֵל בְּרִית *El-Berith* Jg 9_{46}. **2. God, a.** of patriarchs, usu. with divine name or adj.: עֶלְיוֹן *Most High* Gn 14_{18}, רֳאִי *seeing* Gn 16_{13}, שַׁדַּי *Shaddai* Gn 17_1, עוֹלָם *eternal* Gn 21_{33}, בֵּית־אֵל *Bethel* Gn 31_{13}; אֵל אָבִיךָ *God of your father* Gn 49_{25}. **b.** of Israel, (1) oft. with divine name or adj., שַׁדַּי *Shaddai* Ezk 10_5, עֶלְיוֹן *Most High* Ps 78_{35}, ״ *Y.* Is 42_5, אֱלֹהִים ״ *God Y.* Jos 22_{22}. (2) as cstr., אֵל יִשְׂרָאֵל *God of Israel* Ps 68_{36}, הַשָּׁמָיִם *of the heavens* Ps 136_{26}, אֵלִים *of gods* Dn 11_{36}, הַכָּבוֹד *of glory* Ps 29_3, אֱמוּנָה *of faithfulness* Dt 32_4, דֵּעוֹת *of knowledge* 1 S 2_3, נְקָמוֹת *of vengeance* Ps 94_1. (3) with attrib. adj., אֶחָד *one* Ml 2_{10}, חַי *living* Jos 3_{10}, קָדוֹשׁ *holy* Is 5_{16}, צַדִּיק *righteous* Is 45_{21}, קַנָּא *jealous* Ex 20_5, רַחוּם וְחַנּוּן *compassionate and merciful* Ex 34_6, גָּדוֹל *great* Dt 7_{21}, גִּבּוֹר *mighty* Dt 10_{17}. **c.** as element in name, עִמָּנוּ אֵל *Immanuel,* i.e. *God is with us* Is 7_{14}, אֵל אֱלֹהֵי יִשְׂרָאֵל *El-Elohe-Israel* Gn 33_{20} (name of altar).

*[אֵל] II 5.2.1 n.m. **power,** יֶשׁ־לְאֵל יָדִי *there is according to the power of my hand,* i.e. *I have the power* Gn 31_{29}, אֵין לְאֵל יָדֵנוּ *there is not according to the power of our hand,* i.e. *we are powerless* Ne 5_5.

אֵל III, see אַיִל I *ram.*

אֵל IV, see אַיִל II *pillar.*

[אֵל] V, see אֵלָה I *terebinth.*

אֵל VI, see אֵלֶּה *these.*

אֶל 5464.81.229.33 prep.—usu. אֶל־ (אֱלֵי); sf. אֵלַי (אֵלָי), אֵלָיו, אֲלֵיהֶם (אֲלֵהֶם) אֱלֵימוֹ, Q (אליהמה)—**1a. to,** of movement, usu. horizontal, where goal is reached, **into,** + בוא *come* Gn 6_{20}, hi. *bring* Gn 2_{19}, שׁלח *send* Gn 32_4; with adj., קָרוֹב אֶל־ *near(est) to* Ex 12_4. **b. towards, in the direction of,** where contact is not made, + ירא hi. *shoot* at 2 S 11_{24}, פרשׂ *stretch* hands Ex 9_{29}, נסע *set out* Nm 10_{29}; in nom. cl., of eyes toward Y. Ps 25_{15}. **2. on(to), into,** expressing vertical motion. **a.** downward, + נפל *fall* Jos 5_{14}, שׂים *place* 1 S 6_{11}. **b.** upward, + עלה ni. *raise oneself* Ezk 9_3, רכב hi. *mount* 2 S 6_3. **3a.** of perceptual and verbal acts and dispositions of one person **to(wards)** another person, place, etc., + אמר *say* Gn 3_1, שׁמע *listen* Gn 21_{17}, ידע htp. *make oneself known* Gn 45_1, יטב hi. *be pleasing* 1 S 20_{13}. **b. addressed to, intended for,** + כתב ni. *be written* Est 3_{12}; תְּפִלָּתוֹ אֶל־אֱלֹהָיו *his prayer to his God* 2 C 33_{18}. **4. above, over,** without contact, + פרשׂ *stretch* wings 1 K 8_7. **5a. at, in, on, by, in the vicinity of,** etc., with no clear sense of movement towards, + היה *be (situated)* Jos 15_7, חנה *encamp* Jos 11_5, אכל *eat* Ezk 18_6. **b. alongside, next to,** + קבר *bury* Gn 49_{29}; in nom. cl. 2 K 11_{14}. **c. in the presence of, before,** + חרשׁ hi. *be silent* Is 41_1, עמד *stand* 2 K 5_{25}. **6. against,** + לחם ni. *fight* Jr 1_{19}, קום *rise up* Gn 4_8, קשׁר htp. *conspire* 2 K 9_{14}, רגז htp. *rage* 2 K 19_{27}||Is 37_{28}. **7. about, concerning,** + אמר *say* 2 K 19_{32}||Is 37_3, דרשׁ *ask* 1 K 14_5, כתב pass. *be written* Jr 51_{60}, אבל htp. *lament* for 1 S 15_{35}; דְּבַר־יי ... אֶל־ *Y.'s message ... concerning* Jr

47$_1$. **8. due to, because of,** + קוט ni. *be loathsome* because of evil Ezk 6$_9$, טול ho. *be cast down* at sight of Jb 41$_1$; אֶל־חִנָּם *for nothing, in vain* Ezk 6$_{10}$. **9. in aid of, in support of, on behalf of,** + עור *rouse oneself* Ps 7$_7$, פתח *open* mouth Pr 31$_8$. **10a. over, in charge of,** + מלך hi. *make king* 2 S 2$_9$, פקד *appoint* Jr 49$_{19}$= 50$_{44}$. **b. under (the charge of),** + עזב *leave* work Jb 39$_{11}$. **11. of, belonging to,** הַלְּשָׁכוֹת ... אֶל־הַכֹּהֲנִים *the chambers ... belonging to the priests* Ezk 46$_{19}$. **12. for (the benefit of),** + בקע hi. *conquer* territory Is 7$_6$, גרע *limit* wisdom Jb 15$_8$. **13. as well as, in addition to,** + הרג *kill* Jos 13$_{22}$, לקח *take* wife Lv 18$_{18}$. **14. (in comparison) to,** + דמה *be comparable* to Ezk 31$_2$, pi. *compare* with Is 40$_{18}$. **15.** perh. **to the tune,** in headings to psalms, אֶל־שֹׁשַׁנִּים *to 'Shoshanim' (roses)* Ps 80$_1$. **16. to the point of,** + שמח *rejoice* to the point of joy, i.e. exceedingly Ho 9$_1$. **17.** perh. **with, by means of,** אל לשונך אל תרגל *with your tongue, do not slander* Si 5$_{14}$. **18.** followed by other particles, etc., אֶל־אַחֲרֵי **behind, to the rear of** 2 S 5$_{23}$, אֶל־בֵּין **in between, among** Ezk 31$_{10}$, אֶל־מִבֵּית לְ **to within, behind** Lv 16$_{15}$ 2 K 11$_{15}$, אֶל־מוּל **in front of** Ex 34$_3$, אֶל־מוּל פְּנֵי **in front of** Ex 26$_9$, אֶל־מִחוּץ לְ **(to) outside** Lv 4$_{12}$, אֶל־פְּנֵי **in front of, opposite** Ex 23$_{17}$, אֶל־תּוֹךְ **inside, into the middle of** Ex 14$_{23}$, אֶל־תַּחַת **beneath** Jg 6$_{19}$ Ezk 10$_2$ (אֶל־תַּחַת לְ), **instead of** Lv 14$_{42}$, אֶל־נֹכַח פְּנֵי **toward the front of** Nm 19$_4$, אֶל־מִנֶּגֶב **to the south of** Jos 15$_3$, אֶל־יַד **under the charge of** Est 2$_3$, **alongside, next to** 2 S 14$_{30}$.

אֱלָא 1.0.0.2 pr.n.m. **Ela.**

*אלאמר 0.0.0.1 pr.n.m. **Eleamar.**

*אלבא 0.0.0.1 pr.n.m. **Elba.**

אֶלְגָּבִישׁ 3.0.1 n.[m.] **hail** Ezk 13$_{11}$. → cf. גָּבִישׁ *crystal.*

[אַלְגּוּם], see אַלְמֻג *almug.*

[אַלְגֻּם], see אַלְמֻג *almug.*

אֶלְדָּד 3 pr.n.m. **Eldad,** also as אֱלִידָד **Elidad.**

אֶלְדָּעָה 2 pr.n.m. **Eldaah.**

אלה I 6.0.1 vb.—**Qal** 3 Pf. אָלִית; inf. abs. אָלֹה, אָלוֹת—**1. utter a curse** Jg 17$_2$, perh. **swear an oath** Ho 10$_4$. **2.** inf. abs. as noun, **cursing** Ho 4$_2$.

Hi. 3.0.1 Impf. + waw וַיֹּאֶל; inf. cstr. הַאֲלֹתוֹ—**invoke a curse** on another 1 S 14$_{24}$.

→ אָלָה *curse,* תַּאֲלָה *curse.*

אלה II 1 vb.—**Qal** 1 Impv. אֱלִי—**mourn** Jl 1$_8$.

אָלָה 37.1.8 n.f.—sf. אָלָתוֹ; pl. אָלוֹת (אָלֹת), cstr. אָלוֹת—**1. curse, imprecation,** קוֹל אָלָה *sound of a curse* Lv 5$_1$, שְׁבֻעַת אָלָה *oath of curse,* i.e. of self-imprecation Nm 5$_{21}$, against unknown evil-doer CD 9$_{12}$. **2. stipulation** of covenant, expressed as curse Dt 29$_{20}$; perh. **covenant** Gn 26$_{28}$. **3. anathema,** i.e. object of curse Nm 5$_{21}$. → אלה *curse.*

אֵלָה I 17 n.f.—pl. אֵילִים; cstr. אֵילֵי; sf. אֵלֵיהֶם—**terebinth** Gn 35$_4$ 2 S 18$_9$; assoc. with foreign worship Ezk 6$_{13}$. → cf. אַלָּה *terebinth.*

אֵלָה II 13 pr.n.m. **Elah.**

*[אֵלָה] 0.0.2 adv. **only,** [אין פליט] להן אלה אחי *there was to them no survivor, only my colleague* Mur 45$_8$.

אַלָּה 1 n.[f.] **terebinth** Jos 24$_{26}$. → cf. אֵלָה *terebinth.*

אֵלֶּה 755.17.139.1 demonstr. pron. pl.m.&f. and adj.—אֵל, Si אילו, Q, I אלו—**1.** as pron., **these, those, such,** in ref. to things, persons, etc., as subj. of verb, מַדּוּעַ קְרָאֻנִי אֵלֶּה *why have these things befallen me?* Jr 13$_{22}$; as obj. of verb, זְכָר־אֵלֶּה *remember these things* Is 44$_{21}$; in nom. cl., אֵלֶּה הָאֲנָשִׁים *these are the men* Ezk 11$_2$. **2.** as demonstr. adj., **these,** (1) הָאֵלֶּה qualifying determined noun, הַדְּבָרִים הָאֵלֶּה *these things* Gn 15$_1$. (2) אֵלֶּה qualifying suffixed pl. noun, עֲבָדֶיךָ אֵלֶּה *these your servants* 1 K 10$_8$||2 C 9$_7$.

אֱלָהַ, see אֱלוֹהַּ.

*[אֱלָהוּת] 0.0.3 n.[f.]—cstr. אלוהות; sf. אלוהותו—**divinity,** אלוהות כבודו *divinity of his glory,* i.e. his glorious divinity 4QShirShabb[d] 1.1$_{33}$. → cf. אֱלֹהִים *God.*

אֱלֹהִים 2603.29.213.3 n.m.pl.—בֵּאלֹהִים/כֵּ/לֵ/וֵ,בֵּאלֹהִים (sim. in cstr. & sf.); cstr. אֱלֹהֵי; sf. אֱלֹהָיו, אֱלֹהֵיהֶם—**1. God,** in ref. to Y., י׳ אֱלֹהֶיךָ הוּא הָאֱלֹהִים *Y. your God—he is God* Dt 7$_9$; י׳ אֱלֹהֵי יִשְׂרָאֵל *Y., God of Israel* Ex 5$_1$, י׳ אֱלֹהֵי צְבָאוֹת *Y., God of hosts* 2 S 5$_{10}$, י׳ אֱלֹהֵי אֲבֹתֵיכֶם *Y., God of your ancestors* Ex 3$_{15}$, אֱלֹהֵי הַשָּׁמַיִם *God of heaven* Gn 24$_3$, י׳ הָאֱלֹהִים *Y. the God* Gn 2$_4$, אֱלֹהִים חַיִּים *living God* Dt 5$_{26}$. **2a. other god(s)** Ps 86$_8$; אֱלֹהֵי נֵכָר *gods of foreignness,* i.e. foreign gods Jos 24$_{20}$, אֱלֹהֵי הַגּוֹיִם *gods of the nations* Dt 29$_{17}$, אֱלֹהִים אֲחֵרִים *other gods* Ex 20$_3$. **b. (images of) other gods** Gn 31$_{30}$ 1 C 14$_{12}$; אֱלֹהֵי מַסֵּכָה *gods of metal* Ex 34$_{17}$, אֱלֹהִים מַעֲשֵׂה יְדֵי אָדָם עֵץ

וָאֶבֶן *gods, the work of human hands—wood and stone* Dt 4$_{28}$. **3a. divine being, god, deity,** in general, אלוהים נוראי כוח *divine beings, terrifying in strength* 11QShirShabb 8$_4$, אֱלֹהִים וַאֲנָשִׁים *gods and people* Jg 9$_9$, לֹא אֱלֹהִים *non-gods* 2 K 19$_{18}$||Is 37$_{19}$, בְּנֵי הָאֱלֹהִים *sons of the gods* Gn 6$_2$. **b. god,** i.e. **ghost** 1 S 28$_{13}$. → cf. אֱלוֹהַּ *God,* אֱלֹהוּת *divinity.*

[אֱלוֹ], see אֱלֹהַּ.

אִלּוּ 2 conj. **(even) if** Ec 6$_6$ Est 7$_4$. → cf. אִלּוּלֵי *if not.*

*[אֲלְוָא] 0.0.1 n.[m.]—לאה—**aloe,** כלי דמ[ע] לאה *vessels of resin of aloes* 3QTr 11$_{14}$.

אֱלוֹהַּ 57.1.5 n.m.—L אֱלוֹהַּ; cstr. אֱלוֹהַּ; sf. לֶאלהוֹ—**1.** usu. **God,** in ref. to Y. Dt 32$_{15}$ Jb 3$_4$; אֱלוֹהַּ יַעֲקֹב *God of Jacob* Ps 114$_7$. **2. other god,** אֱלוֹהַּ נֵכָר *god of foreignness,* i.e. foreign god Dn 11$_{39}$, אֱלוֹהַּ כָּל־גּוֹי וּמַמְלָכָה *god of any nation or kingdom* 2 C 32$_{15}$(L). → cf. אֱלֹהִים *God.*

[אֱלוֹהִים], see אֱלֹהִים *God.*

אֱלוּל I 1.0.2 pr.n.[m.] **Elul,** sixth month of postexilic Jewish calendar, August/September Ne 6$_{15}$ Mur 29 1$_{1.9}$.

[אֱלוּל] II, see אֱלִיל *worthlessness.*

*[אִלּוּלֵי] 0.0.1 conj.—אללי—**if not** MurEpBeth-Mashiko 5. → cf. אִלּוּ *(even) if.*

אֵלוֹן I 10.0.1 n.[m.]—cstr. אֵלוֹן; pl. cstr. אֵלוֹנֵי—**terebinth,** אֵלוֹן מוֹרֶה *terebinth of Moreh* or *of (the) teacher* Gn 12$_6$, אֵלֹנֵי מַמְרֵא *terebinths of Mamre* Gn 13$_{18}$.

אֵלוֹן II, see אֵילוֹן I *Elon.*

אַלּוֹן I 9 n.m.—cstr. אַלּוֹן; pl. אַלּוֹנִים; cstr. אַלּוֹנֵי—**oak,** or other large **tree,** אַלּוֹן בָּכוּת *Allon-bacuth,* lit. 'oak of weeping' Gn 35$_8$, אַלּוֹנֵי בָשָׁן *oaks of Bashan* Zc 11$_2$.

אַלּוֹן II 1 pr.n.m. **Allon.**

אַלּוּף I 60 n.m.—אַלֻּף; pl. אַלֻּפִים; cstr. אַלּוּפֵי; sf. אַלּוּפֵיהֶם—**chief** of Edom Gn 36$_{43}$||1 C 1$_{54}$, the Horites Gn 36$_{21}$, Judah Zc 12$_5$.

[אַלּוּף] II 1.1 n.m.—pl. sf. אַלּוּפֵינוּ—**ox** Si 38$_{25}$, pl. **cattle** Ps 144$_{14}$. → cf. אֶלֶף II *cattle.*

אַלּוּף III 8 adj.—cstr. אַלּוּף; sf. אַלּוּפִי; pl. אַלֻּפִים—**1. obedient,** of lamb Jr 11$_{19}$. **2.** as noun, **companion, friend** Jr 3$_4$. → אלף *learn.*

*[אִלּוּף] n.[m.] **instruction,** אִלּוּף נְעוּרֶיהָ *instruction of her youth* Pr 2$_{17}$ (if em. אַלּוּף *companion of*). → אלף *learn.*

אָלוּשׁ 2 pl.n. **Alush.**

אֵלוֹת, see אֵילַת *Elath.*

אֶלְזָבָד 2 pr.n.m. **Elzabad.**

*אלזכר 0.0.0.3 pr.n.m. **Elzachar.**

אלח 3 vb.—**Ni.** 3 Pf. נֶאֱלָחוּ; ptc. נֶאֱלָח—**be (morally) corrupt** Ps 14$_3$||53$_4$ Jb 15$_{16}$.

אֶלְחָנָן 4.0.0.2 pr.n.m. **Elhanan.**

אֱלִיאָב 21 pr.n.m. **Eliab.**

אֱלִיאֵל 10 pr.n.m. **Eliel.**

*אליאר 0.0.0.3 pr.n.m. **Eljair.**

אֱלִיאָתָה 2 pr.n.m. **Eliathah.**

*אליבר 0.0.0.1 pr.n.m. **Elibar.**

אֱלִידָד, see אֶלְדָּד *Eldad.*

אֶלְיָדָע 4 pr.n.m. **Eliada.**

אַלְיָה 5.0.1 n.f. **fat tail** of sacrificial ram Ex 29$_{22}$||Lv 8$_{25}$.

אֵלִיָּה, see אֵלִיָּהוּ *Elijah.*

אֵלִיָּהוּ 71.1.0.6 pr.n.m. **Elijah.**

אֱלִיהוּ, see אֱלִיהוּא *Elihu.*

אֱלִיהוּא 11 pr.n.m. **Elihu.**

אֶלְיְהוֹעֵינַי, see אֶלְיוֹעֵינַי *Elioenai.*

אֶלְיוֹעֵינַי 7 pr.n.m. **Elioenai.**

אֶלְיוֹעֵנַי, see אֶלְיוֹעֵינַי *Elioenai.*

אֶלְיַחְבָּא 2 pr.n.m. **Eliahba.**

אֱלִיחֹרֶף 1 pr.n.m. **Elihoreph.**

אֱלִיל 20.1.3 n.m.—אֱלִל; pl. abs. אֱלִילִים; cstr. אֱלִילֵי; sf. אֱלִילֶיהָ—**1. worthlessness, worthless thing,** אליל בעוף דברה *a worthless thing among winged creatures is the bee* Si 11$_3$, רֹעִי הָאֱלִיל *the shepherd of worthlessness,* i.e. worthless shepherd Zc 11$_{17}$. **2. worthless gods, images of deities,** אֱלִילֵי מִצְרַיִם *images of Egypt* Is 19$_1$, אֱלִילִים אִלְּמִים *dumb images* Hb 2$_{18}$.

אֱלִימֶלֶךְ 6 pr.n.m. **Elimelech.**

אֱלִיסמך, see אלסמך *Elisamach.*

אֶלְיָסָף 6 pr.n.m. **Eliasaph.**

אֱליעז, see אלעז *Eliaz.*

אֱלִיעֶזֶר 14.0.5 pr.n.m. **Eliezer.**

אֱלִיעָם 2.0.0.1 pr.n.m. **Eliam.**

אֶלְיְעֵנַי 1 pr.n.m. **Elienai.**

אֱלִיפַז 15 pr.n.m. **Eliphaz.**

אֱלִיפַל 1 pr.n.m. **Eliphal.**

אֱלִיפְלֵהוּ 2 pr.n.m. **Elipheleh.**

אֱלִיפֶלֶט 9.0.0.1 pr.n.m. **Eliphelet,** also as [אֶלְפֶּלֶט] **Elpelet.**

אֱלִיצוּר 5.0.0.1 pr.n.m. **Elizur.**

אֱלִיצָפָן 6 pr.n.m. **Elizaphan,** also as אֶלְצָפָן **Elzaphan.**

אֱלִיקָא 1 pr.n.m. **Elika.**

אֶלְיָקִים 12.0.0.6 pr.n.m. **Eliakim.**

אליקם, see אֶלְיָקִים *Eliakim.*

*אלירב 0.0.0.1 pr.n. **Elirab.**

אלירם, see אלרם *Eliram.*

אלישב, see אֶלְיָשִׁיב *Eliashib.*

אֱלִישֶׁבַע 1 pr.n.f. **Elisheba.**

אֱלִישָׁה 3 pr.n.m. **Elishah.**

אֱלִישׁוּעַ 2 pr.n.m. **Elishua.**

אֶלְיָשִׁיב 17.0.1.21 pr.n.m. **Eliashib.**

אֱלִישָׁמָע 17.0.0.13 pr.n.m. **Elishama.**

אֱלִישָׁע 58.0.1.5 pr.n.m. **Elisha.**

אֱלִישָׁפָט 1 pr.n.m. **Elishaphat.**

אֱלִיָּתָה, see אֱלִיאָתָה *Eliathah.*

*[אֲלַכְסָא] 0.0.1 pr.n.[m.] **Alexander.**

אֱלִל, see אֱלִיל *worthlessness.*

אַלְלַי 2 interj.—אַלְלַי—**alas,** אַלְלַי לִי *alas for me* Mc 7₁ Jb 10₁₅.

[אִלְלֵי], see אִלּוּלֵי *if not.*

אלם I 8.0.6 vb.—**Ni.** 8.0.6 Pf. נֶאֱלַמְתִּי, נֶאֶלְמָה; impf. תֵּאָלֵם, תֵּאָלַמְנָה; ptc. Q נאלם—**be dumb, be silent,** of person Ezk 3₂₆, ewe Is 53₇, lips Ps 31₁₉. → אֵלֶם *silence,* אִלֵּם *dumb.*

אלם II 1 vb.—**Pi.** 1 Ptc. מְאַלְּמִים—**bind sheaves** Gn 37₇. → אֲלֻמָּה *sheaf.*

אֵלֶם 2 n.[m.] **silence** Ps 56₁ (or em. אֵלִ[י]ם *mighty ones* or *terebinths*) 58₂ (or em. אֵלִ[י]ם *leaders* or *gods*). → אלם *be dumb.*

אִלֵּם 6.0.1 adj.—pl. אִלְּמִים—**1. dumb,** of person Ex 4₁₁, dog Is 56₁₀, image of a god Hb 2₁₈. **2.** as noun, **dumb one** Is 35₆. → אלם *be dumb.*

אֵלָם, see אולם II *porch.*

[אֵלָם], see אולם II *porch.*

*אלמא 0.0.3 pr.n.m. **Alma.**

[אַלְמֹג] 6 n.[m.].—pl. אַלְגּוּמִּים, אַלְמֻגִּים—**almug,** sweet-smelling sandalwood tree, as precious commodity, alw. עֲצֵי אַלְמֻגִּים/אַלְגּוּמִּים *timbers of almug/algum* 1 K 10₁₁||2 C 9₁₀.

[אֲלֻמָּה] 5 n.f.—sf. אֲלֻמָּתִי; pl. אֲלֻמִּים; sf. אֲלֻמֹּתָיו—**sheaf** Gn 37₇ Ps 126₆. → אלם *bind.*

[אַלְמוּג], see אַלְמֹג *almug.*

אַלְמוֹדָד 2 pr.n.m. **Almodad.**

אַלַּמֶּלֶךְ 1 pl.n. **Allammelech.**

אַלְמָן 1 adj. **widowed** (or perh. n.m. **widower**) Jr 51₅. → cf. אַלְמָנָה *widow.*

אַלְמֹן 1 n.[m]. **widowhood** Is 47₉. → cf. אַלְמָנָה *widow.*

אַלְמָנָה 56.2.2 n.f.—pl. אַלְמָנוֹת; sf. אַלְמְנוֹתָיו—**1. widow,** אִשָּׁה אַלְמָנָה *a woman, a widow* 1 K 7₁₄; oft. הַגֵּר וְהַיָּתוֹם וְהָאַלְמָנָה (and vars.) *the sojourner, the fatherless and the widow* Dt 14₂₉. **2. widowhood** Is 47₉₍1QIsaᵃ₎ (MT אַלְמֹן *widowhood*). → cf. אַלְמָן *widowed,* אַלְמֹן *widowhood,* אַלְמָנוּת *widowhood.*

[אַלְמָנוּת] 4 n.f.—cstr. אַלְמְנוּת; sf. אַלְמְנוּתָהּ, אַלְמְנוּתַיִךְ—**widowhood** Gn 38₁₄.₁₉ 2 S 20₃ Is 54₄. → cf. אַלְמָן *widowed.*

אַלְמֹנִי 3 adj.—**1. such and such,** מְקוֹם פְּלֹנִי אַלְמֹנִי *such and such a place* 1 S 21₃ 2 K 6₈. **2.** of person, פְּלֹנִי אַלְמֹנִי **so and so** Ru 4₁.

*אלמתן I 0.0.0.1 pl.n. **Elmattan.**

אֵלֹן, see אֵילוֹן I *Elon.*

אֵלֹנִי 1 gent. **Elonite.**

[אֶלְנַעַם] 1 pr.n.m. **Elnaam.**

אֶלְנָתָן 7.0.0.9 pr.n.m. **Elnathan.**

*אלסמך 0.0.0.3 pr.n.m. **Elisamach.**

*אלסמכי 0.0.0.1 pr.n.m. **Elsamchi.**

אֶלָּסָר 2 pl.n. **Ellasar.**

אֶלְעָד 1 pr.n.m. **Elead.**

אֶלְעָדָה 1.0.0.1 pr.n.m. **Eleadah.**

אֶלְעוּזַי 1 pr.n.m. **Eluzai.**

*אלעז 0.0.0.8 pr.n.m. **Eliaz.**

אֶלְעָזָר 72.3.27.2 pr.n.m. **Eleazar.**

אֶלְעָלֵא, see אֶלְעָלֵה *Elealeh.*

אֶלְעָלֵה 5 pl.n. **Elealeh.**

*אלעש 0.0.0.1 pr.n.m. **Eleash.**

אֶלְעָשָׂה 6 pr.n.m. **El(e)asah.**

אלף I 4 vb.—**Qal** 1 Impf. תֶּאֱלַף—**learn, become acquainted with ways** Pr 22₂₅.

Pi. 3 Impf. אֲאַלֶּפְךָ, יְאַלֵּף; ptc. מַלְּפֵנוּ—**teach,** יְאַלֵּף עֲוֹנְךָ פִיךָ *your iniquity teaches your mouth* Jb 15₅, אֲאַלֶּפְךָ חָכְמָה *I will teach you wisdom* Jb 33₃₃, מַלְּפֵנוּ

מִבַּהֲמוֹת אָרֶץ Y. *who teaches us more than the beasts of the earth* Jb 35_{11}.
→ אַלּוּף III *obedient*, אִלּוּף *instruction*.

אלף II $_1$ vb.—**Hi.** $_1$ Ptc. מַאֲלִיפוֹת—**be** or **produce a thousand,** of flocks Ps 144_{13}. → אֶלֶף I *thousand*.

*[אָלֶף] 0.0.2 n.[m.] **aleph,** the Hebrew letter CD 15_1.

[אַלֻּף], see אַלּוּף I *chief*, III *tame*.

אֶלֶף I $_{496.6.45.4}$ n.m.—אֶלֶף; sf. אַלְפִּי; du. אַלְפַּיִם; pl. אֲלָפִים; cstr. אַלְפֵי; sf. אֲלָפָיו, אַלְפֵיכֶם—**1. thousand,** as numeral or part of numeral, אֶלֶף כֶּסֶף *a thousand (pieces) of silver* Gn 20_{16}, עֶשְׂרִים וְשִׁבְעָה אֶלֶף אִישׁ *twenty-seven thousand men* 1 K 20_{30}. **2. unit of a thousand men,** usu. in military context, שַׂר־הָאֶלֶף *commander of the thousand* 1 S 17_{18}. → אלף II *be a thousand*.

[אֶלֶף] II $_8$ n.m.—אֶלֶף; pl. אֲלָפִים; sf. אֲלָפֶיךָ—**cattle** Dt 7_{13}. → cf. אַלּוּף II *cattle*.

*אֶלֶף III $_{13.0.2}$ n.m.—sf. אַלְפִּי; pl. אֲלָפִים; cstr. אַלְפֵי; sf. אַלְפֵיכֶם—**clan** of Judah 1 S 23_{23}, Manasseh Jg 6_{15}, Israel Jos 22_{14}.

אֶלֶף IV, see צֵלַע *Zela*.

[אֱלִפֶלֶט], see אֱלִיפֶלֶט *Eliphelet*.

[אֶלְפַּעַל] $_3$ pr.n.m. **Elpaal.**

אלץ $_1$ vb.—**Pi.** $_1$ Impf. + waw sf. וַתְּאַלְצֵהוּ—**press, urge** Jg 16_{16}.

אֶלְצָפָן, see אֱלִיצָפָן *Elizaphan*.

אַלְקוּם $_1$ perh. n.[m.] (var. of אֱלֹהִים) **God** Pr 30_{31} (mss אַל־קוּם appar. against whom *no one stands*).

אֶלְקָנָה $_{19}$ pr.n.m. **Elkanah.**

אֶלְקֹשִׁי $_1$ gent. **Elkoshite.**

*אלרם 0.0.0.3 pr.n.m. **Eliram.**

אלשב, see אֶלְיָשִׁיב *Eliashib*.

*אלשגב 0.0.0.1 pr.n.f. **Elsagab.**

אלשמע, see אֱלִישָׁמָע *Elishama*.

אֵלַת, see אֵילַת *Elath*.

אֶלְתּוֹלַד $_2$ pl.n. **Eltolad.**

אֶלְתְּקֵא $_2$ pl.n. **Elteke,** also as אֶלְתְּקֵה **Eltekeh.**

אֶלְתְּקֵה, see אֶלְתְּקֵא *Elteke*.

אֶלְתְּקֹן $_1$ pl.n. **Eltekon.**

אִם $_{1071.68.125.6}$ conj.—Q יאאם—**1.** as conditional part., **if,** introducing protasis (which usu. precedes apodosis), generally expressing fulfilled or fulfillable conditions, sometimes virtually equivalent to **when, a.** with pf. in protasis, אִם־חָכַמְתָּ חָכַמְתָּ לָּךְ *if you have become wise, you have become wise for yourself* Pr 9_{12}. **b.** with impf. in protasis, אִם־שׁוֹב תָּשׁוּב בְּשָׁלוֹם לֹא־דִבֶּר י׳ בִּי *if you indeed return in safety, Y. has not spoken through me* 1 K 22_{28}, אִם־יְחַיֻּנוּ נִחְיֶה *if they let us live, we shall live* 2 K 7_4. **c.** with inf. in protasis Jb 9_{27}. **d.** with ptc. in protasis Dt 5_{25}. **e.** with nom. cl. in protasis 1 S 20_8. **2a.** in oaths, following imprecatory formula (here and in §2b אִם is used with neg. oath, אִם־לֹא with positive), חָלִילָה לִּי אִם־אַצְדִּיק אֶתְכֶם *far be it from me, if I should declare you just* Jb 27_5, חַיֶּךָ וְחֵי נַפְשֶׁךָ אִם־אֶעֱשֶׂה אֶת־הַדָּבָר הַזֶּה *as you live, and as your soul lives, if I do,* i.e. I will not do, *this thing* 2 S 11_{11}. **b.** as asseverative part., **surely, certainly (not),** replacing imprecatory formula, אִם־יִרְאֶה אִישׁ בָּאֲנָשִׁים הָאֵלֶּה *surely not one of these men will see* Dt 1_{35}, אִם־לֹא אֲשִׁיתְךָ מִדְבָּר *surely I shall make you a desert* Jr 22_6. **3.** as interrog. part., **is it the case that?, a.** introducing interrog. sentence, אִם־כְּחֹמֶר הַיֹּצֵר יֵחָשֵׁב *shall the potter be reckoned as the clay?* Is 29_{16}; הַאִם as emphatic interrog., הַאִם תַּמְנוּ לִגְוֹעַ *shall we ever stop dying?* Nm 17_{28}. **b.** after clause beginning הֲ *is it the case that?*, to introduce another question, **or,** הֲמָלֹךְ תִּמְלֹךְ עָלֵינוּ אִם־מָשׁוֹל תִּמְשֹׁל בָּנוּ *will you indeed reign over us, or will you indeed govern us?* Gn 37_8. **4.** אִם as disjunctive part., **either, or,** אִם ... אִם *either ... or* Lv 3_1; אוֹ ... אִם *either ... or* Ex 21_{32}. **5.** as concessive part., **even though, even if,** אִם־אֶצְדָּק פִּי יַרְשִׁיעֵנִי *even though I were in the right, my mouth would condemn me* Jb 9_{20}. **6.** as desiderative part., **if only, would that,** הַיּוֹם אִם־בְּקֹלוֹ תִשְׁמָעוּ *if only you would listen to his voice today* Ps 95_7. **7.** עַד אִם **until,** אֶשְׁאָב עַד אִם־כִּלּוּ לִשְׁתֹּת *I shall draw water until they have finished drinking* Gn 24_{19}; עַד אֲשֶׁר אִם in same sense Gn 28_{15}. **8a.** כִּי(־)אִם, **but rather, except, unless, but only,** לֹא יַעֲקֹב יֵאָמֵר עוֹד שִׁמְךָ כִּי אִם־יִשְׂרָאֵל *your name no longer will be called Jacob, but rather Israel* Gn 32_{29}, לֹא אֲשַׁלֵּחֲךָ כִּי אִם־בֵּרַכְתָּנִי *I shall not release you unless you bless me* Gn 32_{27}. **b.** בִּלְתִּי אִם **except, unless,** לֹא נִשְׁאַר לִפְנֵי אֲדֹנִי בִּלְתִּי אִם־גְּוִיָּתֵנוּ *there is nothing left before my lord except for our bodies* Gn 47_{18}, הֲיֵלְכוּ שְׁנַיִם יַחְדָּו בִּלְתִּי אִם־נוֹעָדוּ *do two walk together, unless they have arranged it?* Am 3_3.

אֵם 220.9.23 n.f.—cstr. אֵם; sf. אִמּוֹ; pl. sf. אִמֹּתָם—**1a.** usu. human **mother** of children Gn 2$_{24}$ Ex 2$_{8}$. **b.** אֵם כָּל־חָי *mother of all living things,* as descr. of Eve Gn 3$_{20}$, of the earth Si 40$_{1(B)}$. **c.** Deborah as אֵם בְּיִשְׂרָאֵל *a mother in Israel* Jg 5$_{7}$. **d.** descr. of nation or city Is 50$_{1}$ Jr 50$_{12}$ Ezk 16$_{3}$. **2. mother** of animal Ex 23$_{19}$, bird Dt 22$_{6}$. **3. junction,** אֶל־אֵם הַדֶּרֶךְ בְּרֹאשׁ שְׁנֵי הַדְּרָכִים *at the junction of the road, at the head of the two roads* Ezk 21$_{26}$.

[אַמָּא], see אַמָּה III *conduit.*

אָמָה 56.0.8.2 n.f.—cstr. I אמת; sf. אֲמָתוֹ; pl. אֲמָהוֹת; cstr. אַמְהוֹת־; sf. אַמְהֹתָיו—**1. female servant, maid, female slave** Gn 20$_{17}$ 30$_{3}$, as sold Ex 21$_{7}$. **2.** אֲמָתְךָ **your maidservant,** in self-deprecatory address 1 S 25$_{24}$. **3. female official** (corresponding to עֶבֶד *official*) Governor Seal 18.

אַמָּה I 246.0.124.3 n.f.—Q אמת; cstr. אַמַּת; du. אַמָּתַיִם; pl. אַמּוֹת—**1. cubit, ell,** length of forearm as unit of measure, אַמַּת־אִישׁ *cubit of a man,* i.e. ordinary cubit Dt 3$_{11}$, אַמּוֹת בַּמִּדָּה הָרִאשׁוֹנָה *cubits by the former measure* 2 C 3$_{3}$, אַמָּה אַמָּה וָטֹפַח *a* (royal, long) *cubit was a cubit and a handbreadth* Ezk 43$_{13}$. **2. general measure,** בָּא קִצֵּךְ אַמַּת בִּצְעֵךְ *your end has come, the measure* (lit. 'cubit') *of your extortion* Jr 51$_{13}$. **3. forearm** of Y., אַמָּתִי הִיא סְמָכָתְנִי *my forearm supported me* Is 63$_{5}$ (if em. חֲמָתִי *my wrath*).

[אַמָּה] II 1 n.[f.]—pl. cstr. אַמּוֹת—**doorpost, pivot,** or perh. **foundation** of door Is 6$_{4}$.

***[אַמָּה] III** 0.0.5 n.f.—אמא; cstr. אמת—**conduit** 3QTr 5$_{1}$.

אַמָּה IV 1 pl.n. **Ammah.**

אַמָּה V, see מֶתֶג הָאַמָּה *Metheg-ammah.*

[אֻמָּה] 3.0.4 n.f.—pl. אֻמִּים, אֻמּוֹת; appar. cstr. אֻמּוֹת; sf. אֻמֹּתָם—**people, nation** Ps 117$_{1}$; **tribe** Gn 25$_{16}$.

אָמוֹן I 1 n.m. **confidant** Pr 8$_{30}$. → אמן I *be trustworthy.*

אָמוֹן II 1 n.m. **multitude** Jr 52$_{15}$ (||2 K 25$_{11}$ הָמוֹן *multitude*).

אָמוֹן III 17 pr.n.m. **Amon.**

אָמוֹן IV 2 pr.n.m. **Amon,** Egyptian god, assoc. with No (Thebes) Jr 46$_{25}$ Na 3$_{8}$.

[אֵמוּן], see אֵמֻן I *faithfulness,* II *faithful.*

אֱמוּנָה 49.5.11 n.f.—אֱמֻנָה (Q אימונה); cstr. אֱמוּנַת־; sf. אֱמוּנָתוֹ; pl. אֱמוּנוֹת—**1. faithfulness, trustworthiness, reliability, a.** of humans 1 S 26$_{33}$ Is 11$_{5}$. **b.** of Y. Dt 32$_{4}$ Ps 36$_{6}$. **c.** of Y.'s commandments Ps 119$_{86}$. **d.** of hands, **steadiness** Ex 17$_{12}$. **2. office of trust,** given to Levites 1 C 9$_{22}$. → אמן I *be trustworthy.*

אָמוֹץ 13.0.2.2 pr.n.m. **Amoz.**

אָמִי 1 pr.n.m. **Ami.**

***אמיה** 0.0.0.1 pr.n.f. **Ammia.**

אֵמִים 3 gent. **Emim.**

אֲמִינוֹן, see אַמְנוֹן *Amnon.*

אַמִּיץ 6.1.1 adj.—אַמִּץ; cstr. אַמִּיץ־—**mighty,** alw. pred., or as noun, **mighty (one),** of Y. Is 40$_{26}$, human Am 2$_{16}$, conspiracy of Absalom 2 S 15$_{12}$. → אמץ *be strong.*

אָמִיר 2 n.m. **branch,** of tree Is 17$_{6}$.

אמל I 16 vb.—**Qal** 1 Ptc. pass. אֲמֻלָה—pass. **be enfeebled,** of heart Ezk 16$_{30}$.

Pulal 15 Pf. אֻמְלַל, אֻמְלְלוּ (אֻמְלָלוּ)—**languish,** of earth Is 24$_{4}$, vine Is 16$_{8}$, gate Jr 14$_{2}$, person 1 S 2$_{5}$.

→ אֻמְלַל *languishing,* אֲמֵלָל *feeble;* cf. מלל I *wither.*

***אמל II** 1 vb.—**Qal** 1 Ptc. אֲמֻלָה—**be feverish, hot,** of anger Ezk 16$_{30}$.

***אמליוס** 0.0.2 pr.n.m. **Aemilius.**

אֻמְלַל 1 adj. **languishing,** of person Ps 6$_{3}$. → אמל *be feeble.*

[אֲמֵלָל] 1 adj.—pl. אֲמֵלָלִים—**feeble,** of Jews Ne 3$_{34}$. → אמל *be feeble.*

***[אמם]** vb. **Qal, lead the way**—Is 60$_{4}$ (if em. תֵּאָמַנָה *they will be carried* [אמן II, ni.] to תְּאַמֶּינָה *they will lead the way*).

אֲמָם 1 pl.n. **Amam.**

אמן I 97.18.35 vb.—**Ni.** 45.10.20 Pf. נֶאֱמַן, נֶאֶמְנוּ (נֶאֱמָנוּ); impf. יֵאָמֵן (יֵאָמֶן:); ptc. נֶאֱמָן, נֶאֱמָנָה (נֶאֱמֶנֶת), נֶאֱמָנִים, נֶאֶמְנֵי, נֶאֱמָנוֹת—**1. be trustworthy, faithful, reliable,** of Y. Is 49$_{7}$, person 1 S 22$_{14}$, heart Ne 9$_{8}$. **2. be declared reliable,** of witness CD 10$_{2}$. **3. be entrusted with** (בְּ) house of Y. Nu 12$_{7}$, **be attested as** (לְ) prophet 1 S 3$_{20}$. **4. be firm, lasting, established,** of persons Is 7$_{9}$, kingdom 2 S 7$_{16}$, covenant Ps 89$_{29}$. **5. prove trustworthy, be fulfilled,** of word Gn 42$_{20}$, prophet Si 36$_{21}$. **6.** ptc. as adj., **a. trustworthy, faithful, reliable,** of Y. Dt 7$_{9}$, priest 1 S 2$_{35}$, witness Is 8$_{2}$, city Is 1$_{21}$. **b. firm, enduring, established,** of house 1 S 2$_{35}$, loyalty Is 55$_{3}$, affliction Dt 28$_{59}$. **7.** ptc. as a noun, **a. trustworthy one, faithful one** Ps 101$_{6}$. **b. trustworthi-**

ness 4QOrd^a 2$_9$. **c. certainty** Ho 5$_9$. **8.** fem. ptc. as adv., **faithfully** 1QH 20$_{12}$.

Pi. 0.0.2 Pf. Q אמנתה; ptc. Q מאמנת—**1. establish covenant** 4QBark^c 1$_4$. **2. trust in** (בְּ) deeds of Y. 1QS 4$_3$.

Hi. 52.8.12 Pf. הֶאֱמִין; impf. יַאֲמִין (יַאֲמֵן); + waw וַיַּאֲמֵן; impv. הַאֲמִינוּ; ptc. מַאֲמִין—**1a. believe, trust** someone, with accus. Jg 11$_{20}$, לְ of obj. Gn 45$_{26}$, בְּ of obj. Ex 14$_{31}$; something, with לְ of obj. Ex 4$_8$, בְּ of obj. Ps 78$_{32}$; Y., with בְּ of obj. Gn 15$_6$. **b. believe, trust that,** (1) with כִּי *that* Ex 4$_5$. (2) with inf. Ps 27$_{13}$. **c. believe, have faith,** abs. Ex 4$_{31}$. **2. have assurance of, confidence in,** one's life continuing Dt 28$_{66}$. **3. stand still,** of horse Jb 39$_{24}$.

Htp. 0.0.1 Impf. אתאמן—**show oneself trustworthy** 4QapJoshua^b 18$_7$ (+ בְּ *with* words).

→ אֹמֶן *faithfulness,* אֱמוּנָה *faithfulness,* אֵמֻן *faithfulness,* אֵמֻן *faithful,* אֱמֶת *truth,* אָמֵן *Amen,* אָמְנָה *indeed,* אָמְנָם *indeed,* אֻמְנָם *indeed,* אֹמְנָה *doorpost,* אֲמָנָה *agreement,* אָמוֹן *confidant,* נֶאֱמָנוּת *trustworthiness,* הֵמוּתָה *faithfulness.*

אמן II 9.1.6 vb.—**Qal** 8.1.6 Ptc. אֹמֵן, אֹמֶנֶת (אֹמַנְתּוֹ), אֹמְנִים; ptc. pass. אֱמֻנִים—**1a.** ptc. as noun, **guardian, foster parent, (wet-)nurse** Nm 11$_{12}$ 2 S 4$_4$. **b.** pass. ptc. as noun, **foster child** Pr 8$_{30}$ (if em. אָמוֹן *confidant*). **2a. foster, bring up** Est 2$_7$. **b.** pass. **be brought up, be trained,** of person Lm 4$_5$, animal Si 7$_{22}$. **3.** inf., **fostering, being fostered** Est 2$_{20}$ (if em. אָמְנָה *fosterage* to אָמְנָהּ *her fostering*).

Ni. 1 Impf. תֵּאָמַנָה—**be carried** (as infant by nurse) Is 60$_4$ (or em. תְּאַמֵּנָה *they will lead the way,* from אמם).

→ אָמְנָה II *fosterage.*

אָמָן 1 n.m. **artisan** Ca 7$_2$.

אָמֵן 30.0.35.1 adv.—**1. amen, truly,** solemn formula of confirmation, oft. אָמֵן אָמֵן *Amen, amen,* in affirmation of oath or curse Nm 5$_{22}$ Dt 27$_{15}$, blessing or doxology Ps 89$_{53}$ Ne 8$_6$, other words 1 K 1$_{36}$. **2.** as noun, **Amen,** אֱלֹהֵי אָמֵן *the God of Amen* Is 65$_{16}$. → אמן I *be trustworthy.*

אָמֹן, see אָמוֹן III *Amon.*

*[**אָמֹן**] n.m. **army** Jr 52$_{15}$ (if em. אָמוֹן *multitude*).

אֹמֶן 1 n.m. **faithfulness,** אֱמוּנָה אֹמֶן *faithfulness (and more) faithfulness* Is 25$_1$. → אמן I *be trustworthy.*

אֵמֻן I 5.0.2 n.[m.]—pl. אֱמוּנִים (אֱמֻנִים)—**faithfulness** Dt 32$_{20}$ Pr 20$_6$. → אמן I *be trustworthy.*

[**אָמֻן**] II 3.1.2 adj.—(or [אָמוּן], qal ptc. pass. of אמן) Si אמן (אמון); pl. אֱמֻנִים; cstr. אֱמוּנֵי—**1. reliable, trustworthy** Si 37$_{13}$. **2.** as noun, **faithful, trustworthy person** Ps 12$_2$. → אמן I *be trustworthy.*

אֲמָנָה I 2.0.2 n.f.—sf. Q אמנתם—**agreement, covenant, pledge** Ne 10$_1$ 11$_{23}$ CD 20$_{12}$. → אמן I *be trustworthy.*

אֲמָנָה II 2 pl.n. **Amana.**

אָמְנָה I 2 adv. **truly** Gn 20$_{12}$ Jos 7$_{20}$. → אמן I *be trustworthy.*

אָמְנָה II 1 n.f. **fosterage** Est 2$_{20}$ (or em. אָמְנָהּ *her fostering,* i.e. אמן II inf.). → אמן II *foster.*

[**אֹמְנָה**] 1 n.f.—pl. אֹמְנוֹת—**doorpost** 2 K 18$_{16}$. → אמן I *be trustworthy.*

אַמְנוֹן 28 pr.n.m. **Amnon.**

אָמְנָם 9 adv. **truly** 2 K 19$_{17}$||Is 37$_{18}$. → אמן I *be trustworthy.*

אֻמְנָם 5 adv. **truly,** הַאֻמְנָם *is it true that?* Nm 22$_{37}$, הַאַף אֻמְנָם *is it indeed true (that)?* Gn 18$_{13}$. → אמן I *be trustworthy.*

אֲמִנוֹן, see אַמְנוֹן *Amnon.*

אמץ 41.3.7.1 vb.—**Qal** 16.0.2 Pf. אָמְצוּ; impf. יֶאֱמַץ; + waw וַיֶּאֶמְצוּ; impv. אֱמַץ (אֱמָץ), אִמְצוּ—**1a. be stronger than** (מִן) Gn 25$_{23}$. **b. prevail** 2 C 13$_{18}$. **2. be courageous,** חֲזַק וֶאֱמָץ *be strong and courageous* Jos 1$_6$.

Pi. 19.3.4.1 Pf. אִמֵּץ; impf. יְאַמֵּץ, תְּאַמְּצֵנוּ; + waw וַיְאַמֵּץ (וַיְאַמֶּץ־); impv. אַמֵּץ, אַמְּצוּ; ptc. מְאַמֶּץ־, Q מאמצת; inf. אַמְּצוּ—**1a. strengthen, make strong** (physically), feeble knees Is 35$_3$, temple 2 C 24$_{13}$, heaven Pr 8$_{28}$, **make secure** person 2 C 11$_{17}$. **b. strengthen, encourage** (mentally or spiritually) person Dt 3$_{28}$, heart 1QM 1$_{14}$. **c.** with obj. כֹּחַ, **retain strength** Am 2$_{14}$. **2.** with obj. לֵבָב, **harden heart** Dt 2$_{30}$. **3. let grow strong, nurture** tree Is 44$_{14}$.

Hi. 2 Impf. יַאֲמִץ (perh. Qal)—**exhibit strength, courage,** of heart Ps 27$_{14}$.

Htp. 4.0.1 Pf. הִתְאַמֵּץ; + waw וַיִּתְאַמְּצוּ; impv. Q התאמצו; ptc. מִתְאַמֶּצֶת—**1. exert oneself, be determined** Ru 1$_{18}$ (+ לָלֶכֶת *to go*) 4QapMes 2.2$_3$ (+ בעבדתו *in his* *service*). **2. press hard upon** (עַל) someone 2 C 13$_{7}$. → אֹמֶץ *strength*, אַמְצָה *strength*, מַאֲמָץ *strength*, אַמִּיץ *mighty*.

[אָמֹץ] I 2 adj.—pl. אֲמֻצִּים—**dappled,** of horses Zc 6$_{3.7}$.

[אָמֹץ] II, see אָמוֹץ *Amoz*.

[אַמִּץ], see אַמִּיץ *mighty*.

אֹמֶץ 1.1.6 n.[m].—cstr. Q, Si אומץ (Q אמוץ)—**might** Jb 17$_{9}$ 1QM 14$_{7}$. → אמץ *be strong*.

אַמְצָה 1 n.f. **might** Zc 12$_{5}$. → אמץ *be strong*.

אַמְצִי 2 pr.n.m. **Amzi.**

אֲמַצְיָה, see אֲמַצְיָהוּ *Amaziah*.

אֲמַצְיָהוּ 40 pr.n.m. **Amaziah.**

*[**אֶמְצַע**] 0.0.2 n.m.—sf. אמצעו, אמצען—**middle** 3QTr 4$_{7}$ 11QT 30$_{9}$.

אמר 5311.28.281.9 vb.—**Qal** 5286.27.279.9 Pf. אָמַר; impf. יֹאמַר, יֹאמְרוּ (יֹאמֵרוּ, Q יומרו, יואמרו); + waw וַיֹּאמֶר (וַיֹּאמַר), וָאֹמַר (וָאֹמְרָה); impv. אֱמֹר (אֱמָר־), אִמְרִי; ptc. אֹמֵר, אֹמֶרֶת, אֹמְרִים, אֹמְרוֹת (אֹמְרָה); ptc. pass. אָמוּר; inf. abs. אָמֹר; cstr. אֱמֹר (אֱמָר־), לֵאמֹר, כֶּאֱמֹר, בֶּ/אֱמֹר, אָמְרִי, אָמְרְךָ)—**1. say, a.** followed by or following direct speech, וַיֹּאמֶר אֱלֹהִים יְהִי אוֹר *and God said, Let there be light* Gn 1$_{3}$, oft. לֵאמֹר *saying* introduces direct speech Gn 2$_{16}$; with כִּי introducing direct speech Gn 21$_{30}$; oft. preceded by כֹּה *thus*, esp. כֹּה אָמַר י׳ *thus said Y.* Ex 4$_{22}$. **b.** rarely, introducing indirect speech, אִמְרִי־נָא אֲחֹתִי אָתְּ *say, please, that you are my sister* Gn 12$_{13}$. **c.** with obj., **say, utter, recite** word Pr 1$_{21}$, reviling Ezk 35$_{12}$, ordinance Dt 17$_{11}$. Preps.: לְ *to* Gn 1$_{28}$, *concerning* Gn 20$_{13}$; אֶל *to* Gn 3$_{1}$, *concerning* 2 K 19$_{32}$=Is 37$_{33}$; עַל *concerning* Jr 11$_{21}$, *against* Ezk 35$_{12}$; לִפְנֵי *in the presence of* Dt 26$_{5}$; לְעֵינֵי *in the sight of* Dt 31$_{7}$. **2. answer, reply** 2 K 8$_{12}$, **respond to** (אֶל) Jr 28$_{5}$. **3.** with no words of speech following, **speak** (= דבר pi.) Gn 4$_{8}$. **4. speak of, mention** someone Gn 43$_{29}$, someone's merits Ne 6$_{19}$; **declare** Y.'s fidelity and salvation Ps 40$_{11}$. **5. command, order, tell** someone to do something, לְכָל־יִשְׂרָאֵל אָמַר הַמֶּלֶךְ הָעוֹלָה *the king commanded the sacrifice for all Israel* 2 C 29$_{24}$; with waw consec. + verb, וָאֹמְרָה וַיְטַהֲרוּ *and I commanded that they cleanse* Ne 13$_{9}$; with כִּי *that*, וַיֹּאמֶר כִּי־יְשֻׁבוּן *and he commanded that they return* from wickedness Jb 36$_{10}$; with אֲשֶׁר *that*, וָאֹמְרָה אֲשֶׁר לֹא יִפְתָּחוּם *and I commanded that they should not open them* Ne 13$_{19}$; with לְ *to* + inf., וַיֹּאמֶר לִיהוּדָה לִדְרוֹשׁ אֶת־י׳ *and he commanded Judah to seek Y.* 2 C 14$_{3}$. **6. promise,** אָמַר י׳ לְהַרְבּוֹת אֶת־יִשְׂרָאֵל *Y. had promised to increase Israel* 1 C 27$_{23}$. **7a. think, say to oneself,** וַיֹּאמַר אָכֵן נוֹדַע הַדָּבָר *and he thought, The matter is definitely known* Ex 2$_{14}$. **b.** אמר בְּלִבּוֹ **say in one's heart, think** Gn 17$_{17}$, sim. Dt 7$_{17}$ (בִּלְבָבְךָ). **c.** אמר אֶל־לִבּוֹ **say to one's heart, think** Gn 8$_{21}$. **d.** with לְ + inf. of other verb, **think, propose, threaten** to do something Dt 9$_{25}$ 1 K 5$_{19}$

Ni. 21.1.2 Pf. נֶאֱמַר; impf. יֵאָמֵר (יֵאָמַר, יֵאָמֶר); + waw וַיֵּאָמֵר—**1. be called, named,** subj. name Gn 32$_{29}$; יֵאָמֵר לָכֶם *it will be called to you*, i.e. you shall be called Is 61$_{6}$. **2. be said of, concerning** (לְ) Nm 23$_{23}$. **3. be said (to), be told (to)** someone, followed by direct speech Jr 16$_{14}$; with לְ *to* Jos 2$_{2}$, אֶל *to* Ezk 13$_{12}$. **4. be recounted,** of vision Dn 8$_{26}$, praise Si 15$_{10(A)}$. **5.** perh. **be mentioned, cited,** of place name Gn 22$_{14}$, Wisdom 11QPs^a^ 18$_{11}$.

Hi. 2 Pf. הֶאֱמַרְתָּ, הֶאֱמִירְךָ—with לְ + inf. of other verb, **proclaim** someone to be, **vow, bid** to do something Dt 26$_{17.18}$.

Htp. 2 Impf. יִתְאַמְּרוּ, תִּתְיַמָּרוּ—**boast, speak self-regardingly** Is 61$_{6}$ (+ בְּ *concerning*) Ps 94$_{4}$.

→ אֹמֶר *word*, אִמְרָה *word*, מַאֲמָר *word*.

אֹמֶר 55.5.11 n.m.—cstr. Si אומר; sf. אִמְרוֹ; pl. אֲמָרִים; cstr. אִמְרֵי; sf. אִמְרֵיכֶם, אֲמָרַי (suffixed forms in sg. and all plurals vocalized as if abs. were אֵמֶר)—**word,** sometimes perh. **command,** or as coll. **speech,** אומר אלהים *command of God* Si 42$_{15(B)}$, אִמְרֵי י׳ *words of Y.* Jos 24$_{27}$, אֱמֶת *of truth* Pr 22$_{21}$, שֶׁקֶר *of falsehood* Is 32$_{7}$. → אמר *say*.

[אֵמֶר], see אֹמֶר *word*.

אִמֵּר I 2 pl.n. **Immer.**

אִמֵּר II 8.0.4 pr.n.m. **Immer.**

[אֶמְרָה], see אִמְרָה *word*.

[אִמְרָה] 37.1.4 n.f.—cstr. אִמְרַת; sf. אִמְרָתִי, אִמְרָתוֹ (אִמְרָתוֹ); pl. אֲמָרוֹת; cstr. אִמְרוֹת—**word** of (usu.) Y. 2 S 22$_{31}$||Ps 18$_{31}$ Is 5$_{24}$, humans Gn 4$_{23}$ Ps 17$_{6}$. → אמר *say*.

אֱמֹרִי 86.0.3 gent. **Amorite.**

אִמְרִי 2 pr.n.m. **Imri.**

אֲמַרְיָה 16.0.0.9 pr.n.m. **Amariah.**

אֲמַרְיָ֫הוּ, see אֲמַרְיָה *Amariah.*

אמריו, see אֲמַרְיָה *Amariah.*

אַמְרָפֶל 2 pr.n.m. **Amraphel.**

אֶמֶשׁ 5.0.1.1 n.[m.]—אֶ֫מֶשׁ—**1.** as adv., **last night** Gn 19$_{34}$; perh. less specif., **yesterday** Lachish ost. 3$_{6}$. **2.** noun, **evening, twilight** Jb 30$_{3}$.

אֱמֶת 127.7.204 n.f.—cstr. אֱמֶת; sf. אֲמִתְּךָ (אֲמִתֶּךָ), אֲמִתּוֹ—**1. reliability, dependability, trustworthiness, faithfulness, constancy,** as attribute of Y. Ps 57$_{11}$||108$_{5}$, humans Ho 4$_{1}$; חֶסֶד וֶאֱמֶת *loyalty and reliability* Gn 24$_{49}$. **2. stability** of political conditions 2 K 20$_{19}$||Is 39$_{8}$. **3a. truth, correctness** of words, statements, etc. Gn 42$_{16}$; אמת חוקי אל *truth of God's statutes* 1QS 1$_{12}$, אל אמת *God of truth* 1QH 7$_{25}$, דֶּרֶךְ אֱמֶת *way of truth,* i.e. right way Gn 24$_{48}$. **b.** as adv., **truthfully** Jr 23$_{28}$. **4. sincerity, honesty** of motives, עִבְדוּ אֹתוֹ בְּתָמִים וּבֶאֱמֶת *serve him with integrity and sincerity* Jos 24$_{14}$. **5a. genuineness, reality** of a thing, זֶרַע אֱמֶת *seed of genuineness,* i.e. genuine seed Jr 2$_{21}$, אֱלֹהִים אֱמֶת *God, genuineness,* i.e. genuine God Jr 10$_{10}$. **b.** as adv., **really** Dt 13$_{15}$. → אמן I *be trustworthy.*

[אַמְתַּחַת] 15 n.f.—cstr. אַמְתַּחַת; sf. אַמְתַּחְתּוֹ; pl. cstr. אַמְתְּחֹת; sf. אַמְתְּחֹתֵיכֶם—**sack** Gn 42$_{27}$. → מתח *spread out.*

אֲמִתַּי 2 pr.n.m. **Amittai.**

אָן 42 interrog. adv.—+ ה- of direction אָ֫נָה, אָנָה—**1. where?, whither?, a.** אָן 1 S 10$_{14}$. **b.** אָנָה Gn 16$_{8}$ Dt 1$_{28}$; אָנֶה וְאָנָה *(to) anywhere at all* 1 K 2$_{36}$. **2.** מֵאָן **whence?** 2 K 5$_{25(Kt)}$ (Qr, mss מֵאַיִן *whence?*). **3.** עַד־אָנָה **how long?** Ex 16$_{28}$, var. עַד־אָן Jb 8$_{2}$.

אָן, see און III *On.*

אָנָּא 13.0.2 interj.—אָנָּה—addressee usu. Y., **1. oh!,** expressing sorrow, etc., at past action Ex 32$_{31}$. **2.** perh. **please,** with verb expressing action desired Gn 50$_{17}$.

אנה I 2 vb.—**Qal** 2 Pf. + waw וְאָנוּ; ptc. אוֹנִים—**mourn** Is 3$_{26}$ 19$_{8}$. → אָנֶה *distress,* אֲנִיָּה *mourning,* תַּאֲנִיָּה *mourning.*

אנה II 4.1 vb.—**Pi.** 1.1 Pf. אִנָּה; impf. Si יאננה—**allow to happen, allow to come,** הָאֱלֹהִים אִנָּה לְיָדוֹ *God allows (him) to come into his hand* Ex 21$_{13}$, לא יאננה ליראו *he does not allow it* (evil) *to happen to those who fear him* Si 15$_{13}$.

Pu. 2 Impf. תְאֻנֶּה, יְאֻנֶּה—**happen, come,** of evil Ps 91$_{10}$ (+ אֶל *to* person) Pr 12$_{21}$ (+ לְ *to* person).

Htp. 1 Ptc. מִתְאַנֶּה—**seek occasion** to cause trouble 2 K 5$_{7}$.

→ תֹּאֲנָה *season.*

אָ֫נָה, see אָן *where?*

אָ֫נָּה, see אָנָּא *oh!, please.*

אָ֫נָה, see אָן *where?*

[אָנֶה], or [און] IV, or [אוֹנִי/אֹנִי] 3.0.2 n.m.—sf. אֹנִי (אוֹנִי), Q אונמה; pl. אוֹנִים—**distress, mourning, weariness,** בֶּן־אוֹנִי *son of my distress* Gn 35$_{18}$, לֶחֶם אוֹנִים *bread of mourning* Ho 9$_{4}$. → אנה I *mourn.*

[אָנוּ] 1.0.17 pron. **we,** with verb 1QLitPr 3.1$_{6}$, ptc. Jr 42$_{6(Kt)}$; in nom. cl. 4QD^{a} 11$_{13}$. → cf. אֲנַחְנוּ *we,* נַחְנוּ *we.*

אֱנוֹשׁ I 42.19.25 n.m.—Q אינוש; cstr. אֱנוֹשׁ—**1.** individual **man, person, human being,** usu. without ref. to gender, כֹּל אֱנוֹשׁ שְׁלוֹמִי *every man of my peace,* i.e. all my friends Jr 20$_{10}$, לב אנוש *heart of a person* Si 13$_{25}$, אֱנוֹשׁ כְּעֶרְכִּי *a person of my own rank,* lit. 'according to my valuation' Ps 55$_{14}$. **2.** frail **mortal,** בֶּן־אֱנוֹשׁ *son of a mortal* Ps 144$_{3}$, יְמֵי *days of* Jb 10$_{5}$; אֱנוֹשׁ מִן־הָאָרֶץ *a mortal from the earth* Ps 10$_{18}$, אֱנוֹשׁ רִמָּה *a mortal (who is) a maggot* Jb 25$_{6}$. **3.** coll. **people, humankind** Ps 90$_{3}$; חֶרְפַּת אֱנוֹשׁ *reproach of people* Is 51$_{7}$.

אֱנוֹשׁ II 7.1 pr.n.m. **Enosh.**

אנח 12.3.3 vb.—**Ni.** 12.0.2 Pf. נֶאֶנְחָה; impf. יֵאָנַח; impv. הֵאָנַח; ptc. נֶאֱנָח, נֶאֱנָחָה, נֶאֱנָחִים—**sigh, groan** Ex 2$_{23}$ (+ מִן *on account of*) Ezk 9$_{4}$ (+ עַל *on account of*).

Htp. 0.3.1 Impf. Si יתאנח; ptc. Si מתאנח, Q מתאנחים—**sigh, groan** Si 12$_{12}$ 25$_{18}$ 11QT 59$_{5}$ (+ מִפְּנֵי *on account of*).

→ אֲנָחָה *sigh;* cf. נוח II *sigh.*

אֲנָחָה 11.4.8 n.f.—sf. אנחתי, אַנְחָתָה; pl. sf. אַנְחֹתַי—**sigh, sighing, groaning** Jr 45$_{3}$ Is 35$_{10}$. → אנח *sigh.*

אֲנַחְנוּ 104.0.11 pron.—אֲנָ֫חְנוּ—**we,** with verb Gn 44$_{9}$, ptc. Gn 19$_{13}$, in nom. cl. Gn 29$_{4}$. → cf. אָנוּ *we,* נַחְנוּ *we.*

אֲנָחֲרַת 1 pl.n. **Anaharath.**

***אני** 0.0.0.1 pr.n.m. **Ani.**

אֳנִי, see אָנֶה *distress.*

אֲנִי 871.4.103.1 pron.—אָ֫נִי (BHS אָנִי), Q אניא—**I,** with verb Gn 14$_{23}$, ptc. Gn 9$_{12}$, in nom. cl. Gn 17$_{1}$; גַּם־אֲנִי *I too* Ex 6$_{5}$, אַף־אֲנִי *even I* Gn 40$_{16}$, אֲנִי ... אֲנִי *I ... I* for emphasis

Gn 37$_{30}$, אֲנִי *as for me,* when not functioning as subj. Gn 17$_{4}$. → cf. אָנֹכִי *I.*

אֳנִי 7 n.m.&f. **fleet** 1 K 9$_{26}$; אֳנִי־שַׁיִט *fleet of,* i.e. driven by, *oar(s)* Is 33$_{21}$. → cf. אֳנִיָּה *ship.*

אֳנִיָּה 20.0.4 n.f.—Q אוניה; pl. אֳנִיּוֹת; cstr. אֳנִיּוֹת; sf. אֳנִיּוֹתֵיהֶם —**ship,** אֳנִיּוֹת סוֹחֵר *ships of a merchant* Pr 31$_{14}$, תַּרְשִׁישׁ *of Tarshish* 1 K 22$_{49}$, אֵבֶה *of papyrus* Jb 9$_{26}$. → cf. אֳנִי *fleet.*

אֲנִיָּה 2 n.f. **mourning,** תַּאֲנִיָּה וַאֲנִיָּה *lamentation and mourning* Is 29$_{2}$ Lm 2$_{5}$. → אנה I *mourn.*

*__אניהו__ 0.0.0.3 pr.n.m. **Oniah.**

*__[אָנִין]__ 0.0.1 n.[m.]—sf. אנינם—perh. **sighing** 1QH fr. 5$_{8}$. → אנן *sigh.*

אֲנִיעָם 1 pr.n.m. **Aniam.**

אֲנָךְ 4 n.[m.]—**lead,** used as weight in plumbline Am 7$_{7.8.8}$; חוֹמַת אֲנָךְ *wall of lead,* perh. built with a plumbline Am 7$_{7}$.

אָנֹכִי 359.0.32 pron.—אָנֹכִי—**I,** freq. of Y., with verb Gn 19$_{19}$, ptc. Gn 7$_{4}$, in nom. cl. Gn 24$_{34}$; גַּם אָנֹכִי *I too* Gn 20$_{6}$, אָנֹכִי *as for me,* when not functioning as subj. Gn 24$_{27}$. → cf. אֲנִי *I.*

אנן 2.1 vb.—**Htpo.** 2.1 Impf. יִתְאוֹנֵן (Si יתונן); ptc. מִתְאֹנְנִים —**complain** Nm 11$_{1}$ Lm 3$_{39}$ Si 10$_{25(A)}$. → אָנִין *sighing,* מָנוֹן III *pained.*

אנס 1.1.1 vb.—**Qal** 1.0.1 Ptc. אֹנֵס; ptc. pass. Q אנוס—**1.** abs., **force** (to drink or not to drink) Est 1$_{8}$. **2.** pass. **be forced,** i.e. taken by force CD 16$_{13}$.

Ni. 0.1 Pf. נאנסתה—**be forced** Si 34$_{21(B)}$ (+ במטעמים *with,* i.e. to eat, *delicacies*).

→ אוֹנֶס *force.*

אנף 14.1.1 vb.—**Qal** 8 Pf. אָנַפְתָּ; impf. יֶאֱנַף—**be angry,** of Y. 1 K 8$_{46}$||2 C 6$_{36}$ (+ בְּ *with*).

Htp. 6.1.1 Pf. הִתְאַנַּף; impf. Q תתאנף; + waw וַיִּתְאַנַּף—**be angry,** of Y. Dt 1$_{37}$ (+ בְּ *with,* בִּגְלַל *on account of*) 4$_{21}$ (+ עַל־דִּבְרֵי *on account of*).

→ אַף II *nose.*

אֲנָפָה 2 n.f. **heron,** or other unclean bird Lv 11$_{19}$||Dt 14$_{18}$.

אנק 4.0.1 vb.—**Qal** 2 Impf. יֶאֱנֹק; inf. אֱנֹק—**groan** Jr 51$_{52}$ Ezk 26$_{15}$.

Ni. 2.0.1 Impv. הֵאָנֵק, ptc. נֶאֱנָקִים—**groan,** in mourning Ezk 9$_{4}$ (+ עַל *concerning*) 24$_{17}$.

→ אֲנָקָה *groan(ing).*

אֲנָקָה I 4.1 n.f.—cstr. אֶנְקַת—**groan(ing)** Ps 12$_{6}$. → אנק *groan.*

אֲנָקָה II 1 n.f. perh. **gecko** (*Hemidactylus turcicus*)—Lv 11$_{30}$.

אנשׁ 9.0.4 vb.—**Qal** 8.0.4 Ptc. pass. אָנוּשׁ (אָנֻשׁ), אֲנוּשָׁה—**be weak,** pass. ptc. as adj., **incurable,** of pain Is 17$_{11}$, wound Jr 15$_{18}$, heart Jr 17$_{9}$.

Ni. 1 Impf. + waw וַיֵּאָנַשׁ—**be incurable,** of child 2 S 12$_{15}$.

אֱנֹשׁ, see אֱנוֹשׁ *person.*

*__אנתיכוס__ 0.0.1 pr.n.m. **Antiochus.**

אָסָא 58 pr.n.m. **Asa.**

אָסוּךְ 1 n.m. **jar,** or other vessel 2 K 4$_{2}$. → סוך I *anoint.*

אָסוֹן 5.3 n.m. **harm,** as subj. of היה *be* Ex 21$_{22}$, קרא *meet,* i.e. befall Gn 42$_{4}$, נגע *strike* Si 34$_{22}$.

אֵסוּר 3 n.m.—pl. אֱסוּרִים; sf. אֱסוּרָיו—**bond, fetter** Jg 15$_{14}$ Ec 7$_{26}$; בֵּית הָאֵסוּר *house of (the) fetter(s),* i.e. prison Jr 37$_{15}$. → אסר *bind.*

*__אסטאן__ 0.0.1 n.[m.] **portico** 3QTr 11$_{2}$.

אָסִיף 2.0.0.1 n.[m.]—אָסִף—**harvest, ingathering** Ex 23$_{16}$ 34$_{22}$ Gezer Calendar$_{1}$. → אסף *gather.*

אָסִיר 13.0.1 n.m.—pl. אֲסִירִים; cstr. אֲסִירֵי; sf. אֲסִירָיו—**prisoner** Gn 39$_{22}$; אֲסִירֵי הַתִּקְוָה *prisoners of hope,* i.e. waiting in hope Zc 9$_{12}$. → אסר *bind.*

אַסִּיר I 4 n.m.—אַסִּר—**prisoner** 1 C 3$_{17}$; coll. Is 10$_{4}$ 24$_{22}$ 42$_{7}$. → אסר *bind.*

אַסִּיר II 4 pr.n.m. **Assir.**

*__אסם__ 0.0.0.2 vb.—**Qal** 0.0.0.2 Pf. אסם—**store (harvest)** Meṣad Ḥashavyahu ost. 1$_{5.6}$. → אָסָם *storehouse.*

[אָסָם] 2.0.1 n.m.—pl. sf. אֲסָמֶיךָ (Q אסמיכה)—**storehouse** Dt 28$_{8}$ Pr 3$_{10}$ 4QInstr^{d} 103.2$_{3}$. → אסם *store.*

אַסְנָה 1 pr.n.m. **Asnah.**

אָסְנַת 3 pr.n.f. **Asenath.**

אסף 200.7.29 vb.—**Qal** 104.2.11 Pf. אָסַף; impf. יֶאֱסֹף (יַאַסְפֵנִי), תַּאַסְפִי, אֶאֱסֹף (אֹסְפָה); + waw וַיֶּאֱסֹף; impv. אֱסֹף (אֶסְפָה), אִסְפִי, אִסְפוּ; ptc. אֹסֵף; ptc. pass. אֲסֻפֵי; inf. abs. אָסֹף; cstr. אֱסֹף (אָסְפְּךָ)—**1a. gather people together** Nm 21$_{23}$. **b. gather in, bring back** an individual to a larger group Jos 20$_{4}$, to ancestors in death 2 K 22$_{20}$|| 2 C 34$_{28}$. **c. collect, gather up** quails Nm 11$_{32}$, ashes Nm 19$_{9}$, money 2 K 22$_{4}$||2 C 34$_{9}$; **harvest** produce Ex

23_{10}. **2. take away, remove** hand 1 S 14_{19}, breath Ps 104_{29}, peace Jr 16_{5}, reproach Gn 30_{23}. Preps. (§§1–2): לְ *to* person Ps 50_{5}, place 2 C 29_{4}; אֶל *to* person Gn 6_{21}, place Gn 42_{17}; מִן *from* Ex 23_{16}; מֵאֵת *from* Jr 26_{5}. **3. bring up the rear, act as rearguard** Is 58_{8}. **4.** pass. **be gathered in,** אֲסֻפֵי רָעָב *ones gathered in of,* i.e. killed by, *famine* Ezk 34_{29}.

Ni. 81.5.18 Pf. נֶאֱסַף, נֶאֶסְפוּ; impf. יֵאָסֵף; + waw וַיֵּאָסֵף (וַיֵּאָסֶף); impv. הֵאָסֵף, הֵאָסְפִי, הֵאָסְפוּ; ptc. נֶאֱסָף, נֶאֱסָפִים; inf. abs. הֵאָסֹף; cstr. הֵאָסֵף—**1a. be gathered to** (אֶל) **ancestors, in death** Gn 25_{8}, to graves 2 K 22_{20}||2 C 34_{28}. **2a. be gathered, brought together,** of livestock Gn 29_{7}, Israel Is 49_{5}, water 2 S 14_{14}. **b. be taken away, removed,** of person Is 57_{1}, grass Pr 27_{25}, joy Is 16_{10}. **c. be brought into, return to** a place, of person Nm 11_{30}, beasts Ps 104_{22}, sword Jr 47_{6}, light 1QS 10_{1}. **3. gather** (intrans.), **come together** Gn 49_{1} Jg 16_{23}, esp. for war Gn 34_{30}. Preps. (§§2–3): אֶל *to, around* a person Ex 32_{26}, *(in)to* a place Lv 26_{25}, *against* Jg 20_{11}; עַל *against* Mc 4_{11}; מִן *from* Jg 20_{14}.

Pi. 8 Ptc. מְאַסֵּף (מְאַסִּפְכֶם, מְאַסְּפָיו)—**1. gather** harvest Is 62_{9}, dead bodies Jr 9_{21}. **2. take in** guest Jg 19_{15}. **3a. bring up the rear, act as rearguard** Nm 10_{25}. **b.** ptc. as noun, **rearguard** Jos 6_{9}.

Pu. 5 + waw וְאֻסַּף, וְאֻסְּפוּ; ptc. מְאֻסָּף—**be gathered together,** of persons Ezk 38_{12} (+ מִן *from*) Ho 10_{10} (+ עַל *against*), wealth Zc 14_{14}.

Htp. 1 Inf. הִתְאַסֵּף—**assemble** (intrans.) Dt 33_{5}.

→ אָסִף *harvest,* אָסֹף *storehouse,* אָסִיף *ingathering,* אֲסֵפָה *gathering,* אֲסֻפָּה *collection,* אֲסַפְסֻף *rabble,* מַאֲסָף *gathering,* מַסֹּרֶת *collecting point.*

אָסָף 46.0.0.1 pr.n.m. **Asaph.**

אָסִף, see אָסִיף *harvest.*

[אָסֹף] 3.0.1 n.[m.]—sf. Q אספיו; pl. אֲסֻפִּים; cstr. אֲסֻפֵּי—**storehouse,** or perh. **threshold** Ne 12_{25} 1 C $26_{15.17}$ 11QT 49_{13}. → אסף *gather.*

אֹסֶף 3 n.m.—cstr. אֹסֶף; pl. cstr. אָסְפֵּי—**1. harvest, picking** Is 32_{10} Mc 7_{1}. **2. swarm** of locusts Is 33_{4}. → אסף *gather.*

אֲסֵפָה 1 n.f. **gathering** of prisoners Is 24_{22}. → אסף *gather.*

[אֲסֻפָּה] 1 n.f.—pl. אֲסֻפּוֹת—**collection** of proverbs Ec 12_{11}. → אסף *gather.*

***אספי** 0.0.0.1 pr.n.m. **Aspi.**

[אֲסַפְסוּף], see אֲסַפְסֻף *rabble.*

[אֲסַפְסֻף] 1.0.1 n.[m.]—Q אספסוף; with art. הָאסַפְסֻף—**rabble** Nm 11_{4} 4QMidrEschat[b] 9_{4}. → אסף *gather.*

אַסְפָּתָא 1 pr.n.m. **Aspatha.**

אסר 72.0.13 vb.—**Qal** 65.0.10 Pf. אָסְרָה, אֲסַרְתֶּם; impf. יֶאְסֹר, נֶאֶסָרְךָ, יַאַסְרוּנִי, + waw וַיֶּאְסֹר (וַיֶּאֱסֹר, וַיַּאַסְרֵהוּ); impv. אֱסֹר, אִסְרוּ; ptc. אֹסְרִי, Q אוסרים; ptc. pass. אָסוּר, אֲסוּרִים, אֲסֻרוֹת; inf. abs. אָסֹר; cstr. אֱסוֹר (לֶאְסֹר, אָסְרָם, אֱסָרְךָ)—**1a. bind, tie up** someone, as prisoner Gn 42_{24} Jg 16_{7} (+ בְּ *with* cord). **b.** pass. **be bound, tied up,** as prisoner Jr 40_{1} (+ בְּ *with* fetters). **2a. imprison** someone 2 K 17_{4}. **b.** pass. **be imprisoned** Gn 39_{20}. **c.** pass. ptc. as noun, **prisoner** Is 49_{9}; בֵּית הָאֲסוּרִים *the house of prisoners,* i.e. prison Jg $16_{21(Qr)}$. **3a. tether** animal Gn 49_{11} (+ לְ *to* vine) 11QT 34_{6} (+ אֶל *to* ring). **b.** pass. **be tethered** 2 K 7_{10}. **4a. harness** animal 1 S 6_{7} (+ בְּ *to* cart) Jr 46_{4}. **b. prepare** chariot Gn 46_{29}. **5. join battle** 1 K 20_{14}. **6a. tie** girdle Jb 12_{18} (+ בְּ *around* loins). **b.** pass. **be bound, girded,** of sword Ne 4_{12} (+ עַל *at* loins). 7. **vow,** lit. 'bind an oath to oneself (עַל־נֶפֶשׁ)' Nm 30_{3}.

Ni. 5.0.3 Pf. Q נאסרתי; impf. יֵאָסֵר; impv. הֵאָסְרוּ—**1. be bound, tied up,** of person Jg 16_{6} (+ בְּ *with*). **2. stay in prison** Gn 42_{16}. **3. consist of,** על אלף איש תסאר המערכה *the battle-line consists of a thousand men* 1QM 5_{3}.

Pu. 2 Pf. אֻסְּרוּ (אֻסָּרוּ)—**be captured** Is $22_{3.3}$.

→ אֵסוּר *bond,* אָסִיר *prisoner,* אַסִּיר I *prisoner,* אִסָּר *vow,* מוֹסֵר *bond,* אֵסוּר I *bond,* מָסֹרֶת I *bond.*

אֹסֵר, see אָסִיר I *prisoner.*

אִסָּר 11.0.8 n.m.—cstr. אִסַּר; sf. אֱסָרָהּ; pl. Q אסרים; sf. אֱסָרֶיהָ (sf. forms vocalized as if from אֱסָר)—**vow,** a promise that binds one Nm 30_{3}. → אסר *bind.*

אֵסַר־חַדֹּן 3 pr.n.m. **Esarhaddon.**

אֶסְתֵּר 55 pr.n.f. **Esther.**

***[אִסְתְּרָא]** 0.0.1 n.[f.]—pl. אסתרין—**stater,** coin of high value 3QTr 9_{3}.

אַף I 134.4.24 conj.—**1. also, and, moreover, a.** usu. introducing second or third clause or noun Lv 26_{39}. **b.** before pron., e.g. אַף־אֲנִי *even I* Gn 40_{16}. **2.** emphatic part., **really, indeed** Gn 18_{13} (+ אָמְנָם *truly*) Am 2_{11}. **3.** specifying, **even** Ps 68_{19}. **4.** of consequence, **so, therefore** Is 43_{19}. **5. nonetheless, even so** Lv 26_{44}. **6.** אַף כִּי, **a. moreover** Ezk 23_{40}. **b. indeed** Gn 3_{1}. **c. how much more** Dt 31_{27}. **d. how much less** Ezk 15_{5}. **e. how then?** Jb 9_{14}.

אַף II 277.12.71 n.m.—אַף־; cstr. אַף; sf. אַפִּי; du. אַפַּיִם (אַפַּיִם); cstr. אַפֵּי; sf. אַפָּיו—**1. anger,** וַיִּחַר־אַף י׳ בְּמֹשֶׁה *and the anger of Y. was inflamed against Moses* Ex 4_{14}; חֲרוֹן אַף *inflammation of anger* of Y. Ex 32_{12}, sim. חֳרִי־אַף Ex 11_{8}; אֶרֶךְ אַפַּיִם *(one) long of,* i.e. slow to, *anger* Ex 34_{6}, קְצַר־אַפַּיִם *(one) short of anger,* i.e. impatient Pr 14_{17}. **2. nose,** du. **nostrils** of Y. 2 S 22_{16}||Ps 18_{16}, human Gn 2_{7}, animal Pr 11_{22}. **3.** du. **face** of person Si 41_{21}(B); זֵעַת אַפַּיִם *sweat of face* Gn 3_{19}; וַיִּשְׁתַּחוּ אַפַּיִם אָרְצָה *and he bowed with (his) face toward the ground* Gn 19_{1}. → אנף *be angry.*

אפד 2 vb.—**Qal** 2 + waw וַיֶּאְפֹּד; וְאָפַדְתָּ—**dress in ephod** Ex 29_{5}||Lv 8_{7}. → אֵפֹד I *ephod.*

אֵפֹד I 52.1.2 n.m.—אֵפוֹד; cstr. אֲפֻדַּת, sf. אֲפֻדָּתוֹ; pl. Q אפודת; sf. Q אפודיהם (cstr., sf., and pl. as if from [אֲפֻדָּה])—**1. ephod,** priestly garment, **a.** costly tunic for Aaron Ex 25_{7}||35_{9}. **b.** simpler vestment, אֵפוֹד בָּד *ephod of linen* 1 S 2_{18}. **2.** perh. **oracle,** for divination, kept in local shrine 1 S 23_{9}; אֵפוֹד וּתְרָפִים *an ephod and teraphim* Jg 17_{5}. → אפד *dress in ephod.*

אֵפֹד II 1 pr.n.m. **Ephod.**

[אֲפֻדָּה], see אֵפֹד I *ephod.*

[אַפֶּדֶן] 1 n.[m.] **palace,** אָהֳלֵי אַפַּדְנוֹ *tents of his palace,* i.e. his royal pavilion Dn 11_{45}(mss) (L אָהֳלֵי).

אפה 25 vb.—**Qal** 22 Pf. אָפָה, אָפִיתִי; impf. יֹאפוּ; + waw וַתֹּפֵהוּ; impv. אֵפוּ; ptc. אֹפֶה (אֹפֵהֶם), אֹפִים, אֹפוֹת—**1. bake** bread, etc. Lv 26_{26} 1 S 28_{24}. **2.** ptc. as noun, **baker** Gn 40_{2}.

Ni. 3 Impf. תֵּאָפֶה—**be baked,** of meal offering Lv 6_{10}, bread Lv 23_{17}.

→ מַאֲפֶה *baked food.*

אֵפָה, see אֵיפָה *ephah.*

אֵפוֹ, see אֵפוֹא *then.*

אֵפוֹא 15 part.—אֵפוֹ—**then, therefore, 1.** with interrog., מָה *what?* Gn 27_{37}, מִי *who?* Gn 27_{33}, אַיֵּה *where?* Jg 9_{38}. **2.** in commands, wishes, עֲשֶׂה זֹאת אֵפוֹא *do this, then* Pr 6_{3}. **3.** in conditional sentence with אִם *if,* אִם־כֵּן אֵפוֹא זֹאת עֲשׂוּ *if so, then do this* Gn 43_{11}.

אֵפוֹד, see אֵפֹד I *ephod.*

אֲפִיחַ 1 pr.n.m. **Aphiah.**

[אָפִיל] 1 adj.—pl. f. אֲפִילֹת—**late,** of crops Ex 9_{32}.

אַפַּיִם I, see אַף II *anger, nose.*

אַפַּיִם II 2 pr.n.m. **Appaim.**

[אָפִיק] I 18.1.2 n.m.—cstr. אֲפִיק; pl. אֲפִיקִים; cstr. אֲפִיקֵי; sf. אֲפִיקָיו—**1. channel** for water, in valley, etc. Jl 1_{20} Jb 6_{15}. **2a. tube,** Behemoth's bones as 'tubes of bronze' Jb 40_{18}. **b. furrow,** grooves between Leviathan's scales as 'furrows of shields' Jb 41_{7}. → אפק *be strong.*

[אָפִיק] II 1 adj. pl. אֲפִיקִים—**mighty,** as noun, **mighty one** Jb 12_{21}. → אפק *be strong.*

אֲפִיק, see אֲפֵק *Aphek.*

אֹפִיר, see אוֹפִיר I *Ophir.*

***[אפך]** 0.0.2 vb. (alternative form of הפך)—**Qal** 0.0.2 + waw ויופכו—**1.** trans., **turn** water **into** (לְ) blood 4Q ParGenEx 3_{7}. **2.** perh. intrans., **turn,** i.e. **be turned back** 4QapLamB$_{4}$.

אֹפֶל 9.0.1 n.m. **darkness** Is 29_{18}. → cf. אֲפֵלָה *darkness,* מַאֲפֵל *darkness,* מַאְפֵּלְיָה *deep darkness,* אָפֵל *dark.*

אָפֵל 1 adj. **dark,** perh. as noun, **darkness,** of day of Y. Am 5_{20}. → cf. אֹפֶל *darkness.*

אֲפֵלָה 10.0.5 n.f.—cstr. Q אפלת; sf. אֲפֵלָתֵךְ; pl. אֲפֵלוֹת; cstr. Q אפלות—**darkness, gloom,** חֹשֶׁךְ־אֲפֵלָה *darkness of gloom,* i.e. deepest darkness Ex 10_{22}, יוֹם חֹשֶׁךְ וַאֲפֵלָה *day of darkness and gloom* Jl 2_{2}. → cf. אֹפֶל *darkness.*

***אפלי** 0.0.0.1 pr.n.m. perh. **Aphulai.**

אֶפְלָל 2 pr.n.m. **Ephlal.**

[אֹפֶן] 1.1 n.[m.]—Si du./pl. אופנים; sf. אָפְנָיו—**(appropriate) occasion** Pr 25_{11} Si 50_{27}.

אפס 5.1 vb.—**Qal** 5.1 Pf. אָפֵס; ptc. Si אפס—**cease,** of person Is 16_{4}, silver Gn 47_{15}, loyalty Ps 77_{9}. → אֶפֶס *end,* אֹפֶס *ankle.*

אֶפֶס 43.4.10 n.m.—אַפְסִי; pl. cstr. אַפְסֵי; sf. Q אפסיו—**1. end, limit,** אַפְסֵי־אָרֶץ *ends of the earth* Dt 33_{17}. **2a.** as noun, **nothing(ness), worthlessness** Is 41_{29}. **b.** בְּאֶפֶס **without** (lit. 'in there not being', or 'with nothingness of'), + noun, תִּקְוָה *hope* Jb 7_{6}, לְאֹם *people* Pr 14_{28}. **3.** as neg. part., **there is not, there is no one,**

אֶפֶס כָּמוֹנִי *there is no one like me* Is 46_{9}. **4a.** as adv., **only** Nm 22_{35}. **b.** in conj., אֶפֶס כִּי **except that** Nm 13_{28}. → אפס *cease.*

אֶפֶס דַּמִּים 1 pl.n. **Ephes-dammim.**

[אֹפֶס] 1 n.m. **ankle,** du. מֵי אָפְסָיִם *waters of ankles,* i.e. ankle-deep water Ezk 47_{3}. → אפס *cease.*

[אֶפַע], see אֶפְעֶה I *viper,* II *nothing.*

אֶפְעֶה I 3 n.[m.]—1QIsaª אפע—**viper** (perh. *Echis colorata*) Is 30_{6} 59_{5} Jb 20_{16}.

[אֶפְעֶה] II 1.0.4 n.[m.]—אֶפַע—**nothing, worthlessness,** פָּעָלְכֶם מֵאָפַע *your work is of nothing,* i.e. worthless Is 41_{24}, הרית אפעה *one pregnant of,* i.e. with/by, *nothing* 1QH 11_{12}.

אפף 5.0.2 vb.—**Qal** 5.0.2 Pf. אָפְפוּ (אֲפָפוּנִי)—**surround,** of waters Jon 2_{6}, breakers/cords of death 2 S 22_{5}||Ps 18_{5}, evil Ps 40_{13}.

***אפצח** 0.0.0.2 pr.n. **Ephezach.**

אפק 7.1.3 vb.—**Htp.** 7.1.3 Pf. הִתְאַפְּקוּ; impf. יִתְאַפַּק; + waw וָאֶתְאַפַּק; inf. הִתְאַפֵּק—**1. force oneself** 1 S 13_{12}. **2. restrain oneself** (from tears, anger, etc.) Gn 43_{31} Is 42_{14} 1QH 6_{9} (+ עַל *against* acts of wickedness). → אָפִיק I *channel,* II *mighty.*

אֲפֵק 9 pl.n. **Aphek,** also as אֲפִיק **Aphik.**

אֲפֵקָה 1 pl.n. **Aphekah.**

אֵפֶר 22.3.6 n.[m.] **dust, ash(es),** אֵפֶר תַּחַת כַּפּוֹת רַגְלֵיכֶם *dust under the soles of your feet* Ml 3_{21}, אֵפֶר הַפָּרָה *ashes of the heifer* Nm 19_{9}, עָפָר וָאֵפֶר *dust and ashes* Gn 18_{27}, שַׂק וָאֵפֶר *sackcloth and ashes* Is 58_{5}.

אֲפֵר 2 n.[m.] **covering,** over eyes, as disguise 1 K $20_{38.41}$.

[אֹפֵר], see אוֹפִיר I *Ophir.*

[אֶפְרֹחַ] I 4.0.2 n.m.—pl. אֶפְרֹחִים; sf. אֶפְרֹחֶיהָ—**nestling** Dt 22_{6}. → פרח I *sprout.*

***[אֶפְרֹחַ]** II 0.0.0.8 pr.n.m. **Ephroah.**

אַפִּרְיוֹן 1 n.[m.] **palanquin** Ca 3_{9}.

אֶפְרַיִם I 180.2.11 pr.n.m. **Ephraim.**

אֶפְרַיִם II 1 pl.n. **Ephraim.**

אֶפְרָת, see אֶפְרָתָה I, II *Ephrathah.*

אֶפְרָתָה I 3 pr.n.f. **Ephrathah.**

אֶפְרָתָה II 8 pl.n. **Ephrathah.**

אֶפְרָתִי 5 gent. **Ephrathite.**

אֶצְבּוֹן 2 pr.n.m. **Ezbon.**

אֶצְבַּע 31.0.10 n.f.—cstr. אֶצְבַּע; sf. אֶצְבָּעוֹ; pl. אֶצְבָּעוֹת (אַצְבְּעוֹת); cstr. אֶצְבְּעוֹת; sf. אֶצְבְּעוֹתַי—**1. finger,** esp. forefinger Ex 29_{12}, used in measurement Jr 52_{21}; אֶצְבַּע אֱלֹהִים *finger of God* Ex 8_{15}. **2. toe** 2 S 21_{20}.

[אָצִיל] I 1 n.[m.]—pl. sf. אֲצִילֶיהָ—**side, edge** of earth Is 41_{9}. → אצל I *withhold.*

[אָצִיל] II 1 n.[m.]—pl. cstr. אֲצִילֵי—**leader** Ex 24_{11}.

[אַצִּיל] 3.1 n.[f.]—appar. + ה- of direction אַצִּילָה; pl. cstr. אַצִּילֵי, אֲצִלוֹת—**1a. joint** of arms (יָדַיִם), i.e. armpit Jr 38_{12}, perh. wrist Ezk 13_{18}. **b. elbow** Si 41_{19}. **2.** perh. **joint, edge** of foundations of temple side-chambers Ezk 41_{8}. → (?) אצל *withhold.*

אצל I 5.3 vb.—**Qal** 4 Pf. אָצַלְתִּי; + waw וַיָּאצֶל (perh. hi.)—**withhold** things desired Ec 2_{10}; **set aside** blessing Gn 27_{36}, spirit Nm 11_{17}.

Ni. 1.3 Pf. נֶאֱצַל; ptc. Si נאצל—**1. be set aside,** of persons Si 46_{8}. **2.** ptc. appar. as adj., **poor** (i.e. from whom wealth is withheld), of man Si 13_{17}. **3.** perh. **be recessed,** of upper chambers Ezk 42_{6}.

→ אֵצֶל *beside,* אָצִיל I *side,* (?) אַצִּיל *joint.*

***אצל** II 0.1 vb.—**Ni.** 0.1 Pf. נצל—**make an alliance,** עשיר אל רש נאצל *does a rich man make an alliance with a poor man?* Si 13_{17} (if em. איש *man* to רש).

אֵצֶל 61.2.24 prep.—sf. אֶצְלוֹ, Q הצלכם (Q אצלכן), אֶצְלָם (Q אצלן)—**1.** prep. **beside, with, near** Gn 39_{10}. **2.** מֵאֵצֶל **from beside, from near, beside** 1 S 17_{30}. → אצל I *withhold.*

אָצֵל 6 pr.n.m. **Azel.**

אָצַל 1 pl.n. **Azal.**

אֲצַלְיָהוּ 2.0.0.2 pr.n.m. **Azaliah.**

אֹצֶם 2 pr.n.m. **Ozem.**

אֶצְעָדָה 2 n.f. **bracelet**—Nm 31_{50} 2 S 1_{10}.

אצר 5 vb.—**Qal** 3 Pf. אָצְרוּ; ptc. אוֹצְרִים—**store up** treasure 2 K 20_{17}||Is 39_{6}, violence and robbery Am 3_{10}.

Ni. 1 Impf. יֵאָצֵר—**be stored up,** of profit Is 23_{18}.

Hi. 1 + waw וָאוֹצְרָה—**appoint as treasurer** Ne 13_{13}.

→ אוֹצָר *treasure,* אוֹצָרָה *treasure.*

אֵצֶר 5 pr.n.m. **Ezer.**

[אֹצָרָה], see אוֹצָרָה *treasure.*

אֶקְדָּח 1 n.[m.] perh. **beryl,** or **red granite** Is 54_{12}. → קדח *kindle.*

אַקּוֹ 1 n.m. **wild goat** (perh. *Capra aegagrus*) Dt 14_{5}.

אֹר, see יְאֹר *Nile.*

[אֲרָא] 1.0.0.1 pr.n.m. **Ara.**

אֲרָא, see אֲרָא *Ara.*

אראיל, see אֲרִיאֵל III *altar hearth.*

*[אַרְאֵל] n.m. **hero** 2 S 23$_{20}$||1 C 11$_{22}$ (if em. אֲרִ[י]אֵל *Ariel* to אַרְאֵלֵי *heroes of*) Is 33$_{7}$ (if em. אֵרָאֶלָם perh. *I shall appear to them* to אַרְאֵלִים *heroes*).

אַרְאֵל, see אֲרִיאֵל I *Ariel.*

אַרְאֵלִי I 2 pr.n.m. **Areli.**

אַרְאֵלִי II 1 gent. **Arelite.**

אֶרְאֶלָּם, see ראה *see*, אַרְאֵל *hero*, אֲרִיאֵלִי I *Arielite*, II *priest*.

ארב 41.4.6 vb.—**Qal** 38.4.5 Pf. אָרְבוּ; impf. יֶאֱרֹב, יֶאֶרְבוּ; + waw וַיֶּאֱרֹב (וַיָּרֶב), וַיֶּאֶרְבוּ; וַאֲרִב; נֶאֶרְבָה, (Q יורבו); impv. אֱרֹב; ptc. אֹרֵב, אֹרְבִים; inf. אֱרָב־—**1. ambush, lie in wait, a.** with prep., לְ *for* Dt 19$_{11}$; עַל *against* Jg 9$_{34}$. **b.** with accus., **lie in wait for** blood Pr 12$_{6}$. **c.** with inf., **lie in wait (to do)** Ps 10$_{9}$. **2.** ptc. as noun, **one lying in wait, ambush,** usu. sg. coll. Jos 8$_{2}$.

Pi. 2.0.1 Ptc. מְאָרְבִים—ptc. as noun, **one lying in wait, ambush** Jg 9$_{25}$.

Hi. 1 + waw וַיָּרֶב—**lie in wait** 1 S 15$_{5}$.

→ אֹרֶב *ambush*, אֶרֶב *lying in wait*, מַאֲרָב *ambush*.

[ארב] 11QT 24$_{8}$, see אֵבֶר *wing*, §2.

אֲרַב 1 pl.n. **Arab.**

[אֶרֶב] 2 n.[m.]—אֶרֶב—**1. place of lying in wait, lair** Jb 37$_{8}$. **2.** perh. **(act of) lying in wait** Jb 38$_{40}$. → ארב *wait in ambush.*

אֹרֵב, see ארב, Qal §2.

[אֹרֶב] 2 n.[m.]—sf. אָרְבּוֹ, אָרְבָּם—**1. ambush,** planned against neighbour Jr 9$_{7}$. **2. intrigue, conspiracy** Ho 7$_{6}$. → ארב *wait in ambush.*

אַרְבֵאל, see בֵּית אַרְבֵאל *Beth-arbel.*

אַרְבֶּה 24.1.2 n.m. **locust** (perh. *Schistocerca gregaria*), an edible species, usu. coll. Ex 10$_{4}$. → רבה *be many.*

[אָרְבָּה] 1 n.f. perh. **skill,** אָרְבּוֹת יָדָיו *skill of his hands* Is 25$_{11}$.

אֲרֻבָּה 9.0.2 n.f.—pl. אֲרֻבּוֹת; cstr. אֲרֻבּוֹת; sf. אֲרֻבֹּתֵיהֶם—**window,** through which smoke escapes Ho 13$_{3}$, in dovecotes Is 60$_{8}$, in sky, through which rain pours Gn 7$_{11}$.

אֲרֻבּוֹת 1 pl.n. **Arubboth.**

אַרְבִּי 1 gent. **Arbite.**

אַרְבַּע I 324.1.97.2 n.m.&f.—m. (with f. nouns) אַרְבַּע; cstr. אַרְבַּע; f. (with m. nouns) אַרְבָּעָה; cstr. אַרְבַּעַת; sf. אַרְבַּעְתָּם; du. אַרְבַּעְתָּיִם—**1. four,** אַרְבַּע טַבְּעֹת זָהָב *four rings of gold* Ex 25$_{12}$||37$_{3}$, אַרְבָּעָה מְלָכִים *four kings* Gn 14$_{9}$, אַרְבַּעַת יָמִים *four days* Jg 11$_{40}$. **2.** as ordinal numeral, **fourth,** בִּשְׁנַת אַרְבַּע *in the fourth year* Zc 7$_{1}$, בְּאַרְבָּעָה לַחֹדֶשׁ *on the fourth (day) of the month* Zc 7$_{1}$. **3.** du. **fourfold,** used adverbially of שׁלם pi. *pay* 2 S 12$_{6}$. **4. four (parts of moon's surface)** 4QAstrCrypt 2$_{21}$. **5.** as constituent of a larger number, אַרְבַּע עֶשְׂרֵה *fourteen* 2 C 13$_{21}$, var. אַרְבָּעָה עָשָׂר 1 C 25$_{5}$; עֶשְׂרִים וְאַרְבַּע *twenty-four* 1 K 15$_{33}$, var. עֶשְׂרִים וְאַרְבָּעָה; אַרְבַּע מֵאוֹת *four hundred* Gn 15$_{13}$, אַרְבַּעַת אֲלָפִים *four thousand* 1 S 4$_{2}$. → רבע I *make square.*

אַרְבַּע II 3 pr.n.m. **Arba.**

אַרְבָּעִים 135.0.20 n.m.&f. pl.—Q רבעים, ארבעין, אבעים—**1a. forty,** אַרְבָּעִים יוֹם *forty days* Gn 7$_{4}$. **b.** as constituent of a larger number, אַרְבָּעִים וְאַחַת *forty-one* 1 K 15$_{10}$. **2.** as ordinal numeral, **fortieth,** בְּאַרְבָּעִים שָׁנָה *in the fortieth year* Dt 1$_{3}$, var. בִּשְׁנַת הָאַרְבָּעִים Nm 33$_{38}$. → רבע I *make square.*

ארג 14.1.2 vb.—**Qal** 13.1.2 Impf. תַּאַרְגִי, יֶאֱרֹגוּ (Q יירגו); ptc. אֹרֵג, אֹרְגִים, אֹרְגוֹת—**1. weave** plait of hair Jg 16$_{13}$, spider's web Is 59$_{5}$. **2.** ptc. as noun, **weaver** Ex 28$_{32}$||39$_{22}$. → אֶרֶג *loom*, אֹרֶג *cloth.*

*[אֹרֶג] n.[m.] **cloth** Is 38$_{12}$ (if em. קִפַּדְתִּי כָאֹרֵג *I have rolled up as a weaver* to קִפַּדְתָּ כְאֹרֶג *you have rolled up* my life *as cloth*). → ארג *weave.*

אֶרֶג 2 n.[m.]—אֶרֶג—**shuttle** of loom Jg 16$_{14}$ Jb 7$_{6}$. → ארג *weave.* → ארג *weave.*

*[אַרְגָּב] n.[m.] **mound** 1 S 20$_{19}$ (if em. הָאֶבֶן *the stone*) 20$_{41}$ (if em. הַנֶּגֶב *the south*).

אַרְגֹּב I 1 pr.n.m. **Argob.**

אַרְגֹּב II 4 pl.n. **Argob.**

אַרְגְּוָן, see אַרְגָּמָן *purple.*

אַרְגַּז 3 n.m. **box,** or perh. **saddlebag** 1 S 6$_{8.11.15}$.

אַרְגָּמָן 39.1.5 n.m.—Q ארגמון, ארגון—אַרְגְּוָן—**purple** thread, cloth, etc., oft. תְּכֵלֶת וְאַרְגָּמָן וְתוֹלַעַת שָׁנִי (and vars.) *blue and purple and scarlet (material)* Ex 25$_{4}$||35$_{6}$.

אַרְדְּ 2 pr.n.m. **Ard.**

אַרְדּוֹן 1 pr.n.m. **Ardon.**

אַרְדִּי 1 gent. **Ardite.**

אֲרִדַי 1 pr.n.m. **Aridai.**

ארה 2 vb.—**Qal** 2 Pf. אָרִיתִי—**pluck** vine Ps 80$_{13}$, myrrh Ca 5$_1$.

[אֹרָה] 1 n.[f.]—pl. אֹרֹת—**mallow** (perh. *Malva rotundifolia*), wild plant with medicinal properties 2 K 4$_{39}$.

אֲרוֹד 1 pr.n.m. **Arod.**

אַרְוַד 2 pl.n. **Arvad.**

אֲרוֹדִי I 1 pr.n.m. **Arodi.**

אֲרוֹדִי II 1 gent. **Arodite.**

אַרְוָדִי 2 gent. **Arvadite.**

[אֻרְוָה] 4 n.f.—pl. אֻרְוֹת (אֻוּרוֹת); cstr. אֻרְוֹת (אֻרְיוֹת)—**stall,** for horses, etc. 1 K 5$_6$||2 C 9$_{25}$.

[אָרוּז] 1 adj. **secure,** בַּחֲבָלִים חֲבֻשִׁים וַאֲרֻזִים fabrics *bound with cords and (made) secure* Ezk 27$_{24}$.

אֲרוּכָה 6 n.f.—אֲרֻכָה; cstr. אֲרֻכַת; sf. אֲרֻכָתְךָ—**1. healing** Is 58$_8$. **2. repair** of building Ne 4$_1$ 2 C 24$_{13}$. → ארך *be long.*

[אֲרוּמָה] 1 pl.n. **Arumah.**

אָרוֹן 201.0.3.2 n.m. (& f.)—הָאָרֹן; cstr. אֲרוֹן; sf. 3mpl I ארונן; pl. I ארונות—**1.** usu. **ark of covenant,** אֲרוֹן הָאֱלֹהִים *ark of God* 1 S 4$_{13}$, '' *of Y.* Jos 3$_{13}$, הַבְּרִית *of the covenant* Jos 3$_6$, הָעֵדוּת *of the testimony* Ex 26$_{33}$. **2. coffer,** chest for money 2 K 12$_{10}$||2 C 24$_8$. **3. coffin** Gn 50$_{26}$.

אֲרַוְנָה 21 pr.n.m. **Araunah,** also as אָרְנָן **Ornan.**

אֶרֶז 73.1.11 n.m.—אָרֶז; cstr. אֶרֶז; pl. אֲרָזִים; cstr. אַרְזֵי; sf. אֲרָזָיו—usu. **cedar** of Lebanon, but sometimes a species of juniper (*oxycedrus* or *phoenicia*); esp. cedar tree Jg 9$_{15}$, oft. in ref. to height Am 2$_9$; also cut cedar 2 S 5$_{11}$||1 C 14$_1$, cedar wood 1 K 6$_{18}$. → cf. אַרְזָה *cedar work.*

אַרְזָה 1 n.f. **cedarwork** Zp 2$_{14}$. → cf. אֶרֶז *cedar.*

ארח 6.2.2 vb.—**Qal** 6.1 + waw וְאָרַח; ptc. אֹרֵחַ, אֹרְחִים; inf. Q ארוח (אָרְחִי)—**1. journey, go** Jb 34$_8$. **2.** ptc. as noun, **wanderer, traveller** 2 S 12$_4$.

Hi. 0.1 Impf. יאריח—of moon, **set seasons on journey** Si 43$_{6(M)}$.

→ אֹרַח *way,* אֹרְחָה *caravan,* אֲרֻחָה *provisions.*

אָרַח 4 pr.n.m. **Arah.**

אֹרַח 59.4.4 n.m.—cstr. אֹרַח; sf. אָרְחוֹ; pl. אֳרָחוֹת; cstr. אָרְחוֹת; sf. אֹרְחֹתָיו, אָרְחוֹתָם (אָרְחֹתֵיהֶם)—**1. path, way, a.** for traveller Gn 49$_{17}$. **b.** course of movement, route taken by traveller Jl 2$_7$. **2. way,** action viewed ethically: God's ways as taught to humans Is 2$_3$||Mc 4$_2$, way of justice Is 40$_{14}$. **3. way,** life viewed as a path Ps 142$_4$; way of, i.e. leading to, life Ps 16$_{11}$. **4. way, manner** of women, i.e. menstruation Gn 18$_{11}$. **5. embankment, earthwork,** for siege Jb 30$_{12}$. **6. traveller** Jb 31$_{32}$. **7. caravan** Jg 5$_6$. → ארח *journey.*

[אֹרְחָה] 2 n.f.—cstr. אֹרְחַת; pl. cstr. אֹרְחוֹת—**caravan** Gn 37$_{25}$ Is 21$_{13}$. → ארח *journey.*

אֲרֻחָה 6 n.f.—cstr. אֲרֻחַת; sf. אֲרֻחָתוֹ—**ration of food** 2 K 25$_{30}$||Jr 52$_{34}$. → ארח *journey.*

אֲרִי 35.1.3 n.m.—pl. אֲרָיוֹת (אֲרָיִים)—**1.** usu. **lion** Nm 23$_{24}$. **2.** in representations, **lion-relief,** etc. 1 K 7$_{29}$. → cf. אַרְיֵה *lion.*

אֲרִי, see אוּרִי *Uri.*

*אֲרִיאֵל I 3 pr.n.m. **Ariel.**

אֲרִיאֵל II 5 pl.n. **Ariel.**

*אֲרִיאֵל III 3 n.[m.]—הַרְאֵל, Kt אראיל—**altar hearth** Ezk 43$_{15.15.16}$.

*[אֲרִיאֵלִי] n.m. **priest,** i.e. person connected with altar hearth (אֲרִיאֵל III) 2 S 23$_{20}$||1 C 11$_{22}$ (if em. אֲר[י]אֵל *Ariel* to אֲר[י]אֵלֵי *priests of* Moab) Is 33$_7$ (if em. אֶרְאֶלָּם perh. *I shall appear to them* to אֲרִאֵלִים *priests*).

אֲרִידָתָא 1 pr.n.m. **Aridatha.**

אַרְיֵה I 45.1 n.m. **lion** Gn 49$_9$. → cf. אֲרִי *lion.*

אַרְיֵה II 1 pr.n.m. **Arieh.**

[אֻרְיָה], see אֻרְוָה *stall.*

אריהו, see אוּרִיָּה *Uriah.*

אריו, see אוּרִיָּה *Uriah.*

אַרְיוֹךְ 2 pr.n.m. **Arioch.**

אֻרִים, see אוּר I *fire,* §2b.

אֲרִיסַי 1 pr.n.m. **Arisai.**

ארך 34.2.5 vb.—**Qal** 3.0.1 Pf. אָרְכוּ; impf. Q יארוך, יַאַרְכוּ; + waw וַתֶּאֱרַכְנָה—**last long, grow long,** of days Gn 26$_8$, branches Ezk 31$_5$.

Hi. 31.2.4 Pf. הֶאֱרִיךְ; impf. יַאֲרִיךְ; + waw וְהַאֲרַכְתָּ; impv. Si האריך, הַאֲרִיכִי, Q האריכו; ptc. מַאֲרִיךְ; inf. abs. Si האריך; cstr. הַאֲרִיךְ—**1. prolong** one's days Dt 4$_{26}$, days of another 1 K 3$_{14}$. **2a. be long,** of pole 1 K 8$_8$|| 2 C 5$_9$. **b. last long, endure,** of days Ex 20$_{12}$, wicked person Ec 7$_{15}$. **3. hold back, postpone** anger Is 48$_9$. **4. extend, stretch out** hand Si 33$_{7(Bmg)}$, tongue, i.e.

speak Is 57$_4$; **lengthen** rope Is 54$_2$.
→ אָרֹךְ *long,* אֹרֶךְ *length,* אֲרוּכָה *restoration.*

[אָרֵךְ], see אָרֹךְ *long.*

[אָרֹךְ] 18.1.11 adj.—cstr. אֶרֶךְ; f.s. אֲרֻכָּה; m.pl. Q ארוכים; cstr. Q ארוכי; f.pl. Q ארוכות—**1.** abs. **long,** as adj. of person 4QCrypt 2.1$_3$, shields 1QM 9$_{12}$ (ארוכים שלוש אמות *three cubits long*), war 2 S 3$_1$, dimension Jb 11$_9$ (+ מִן longer *than*), exile Jr 29$_{28}$. **2.** cstr., **a.** as adj., **long of,** אֶרֶךְ אַפַּיִם *long of,* i.e. slow to, *anger* (of Y.) Ex 34$_6$, ארוכי רוח *long of,* i.e. able to sustain, *breath* (of warhorses) 1QM 6$_{12}$, אֶרֶךְ הָאֵבֶר *long of wings,* i.e. with long wings Ezk 17$_3$. **b.** as noun, **one long of,** אֶרֶךְ אַפַּיִם *one long of,* i.e. slow to, *anger* Pr 14$_{29}$, אֶרֶךְ־רוּחַ *one long of spirit,* i.e. patient Ec 7$_8$. → ארך *be long.*

אֹרֶךְ 95.1.20 n.[m.]—cstr. אֹרֶךְ (Q אורך, Q ארוך); sf. אָרְכּוֹ (Q אורכו)—**length** of ark Gn 6$_{15}$, days, i.e. long life Ps 21$_5$, anger (אַפַּיִם), i.e. restraint Pr 25$_{15}$. → ארך *be long.*

אֶרֶךְ 1 pl.n. **Erech.**

אַרְכִּי 6 gent. **Archite.**

אֲרָם 143.0.3 pr.n.m. **Aram;** also in compound names, **Aram-naharaim,** i.e. **Aram of Mesopotamia, Aram-zobah, Aram-Damascus, Aram-maacah, Aram Beth-rehob, Paddan-aram.** → cf. אֲרָמִית *in Aramaic.*

אַרְמוֹן 32.0.2 n.m.—cstr. אַרְמוֹן; pl. אַרְמְנוֹת; cstr. אַרְמְנוֹת; sf. אַרְמְנֹתָיו—**fortress,** אַרְמוֹן בֵּית־הַמֶּלֶךְ *fortress of the house of the king,* i.e. palace citadel 1 K 16$_{18}$, אַרְמְנוֹת יְרוּשָׁלִָם *fortresses of Jerusalem* Jr 17$_{27}$.

אֲרַמִּי 13 gent. **Aramaean.**

אֲרָמִית 5 adv. **in Aramaic** 2 K 18$_{26}$||Is 36$_{11}$. → cf. אֲרָם *Aram.*

*ארמל 0.0.1 vb.—**Htp.** 0.0.1 Pf. התארמלה—**become a widow** 4QD^f 3$_{12}$.

אַרְמֹנִי 1 pr.n.m. **Armoni.**

אֲרָן 2 pr.n.m. **Aran.**

אֹרֶן I 1 n.[m.] **laurel,** a type of tree Is 44$_{14}$.

אֹרֶן II 1 pr.n.m. **Oren.**

אַרְנֶבֶת 2 n.f. **hare** Lv 11$_6$||Dt 14$_7$.

אַרְנוֹן 25 pl.n. **Arnon.**

ארניה, see אֲרַוְנָה *Araunah.*

אַרְנָן 1 pr.n. **Arnan.**

אַרְנֹן, see אַרְנוֹן *Arnon.*

אָרְנָן, see אֲרַוְנָה *Araunah.*

ארס, see ארשׁ *desire.*

*[אַרְעִיבוֹת] n.f.pl. **juniper cedar** 4QJub^d 21$_{12}$ (ו[א]רעיבו[ת]).

אַרְפַּד 6 pl.n. **Arpad.**

אַרְפַּכְשַׁד 9.0.1 pr.n.m. **Arpachshad.**

*[ארץ] vb.—**Hi. fertilize** 2 S 23$_4$ (if em. מִמָּטָר דֶּשֶׁא מֵאֶרֶץ appar. *after,* or, *because of, rain, grass is,* i.e. sprouts, *from the soil* to מָטָר דֶּשֶׁא מַאֲרִץ *rain fertilizes the grass*).

אֶרֶץ 2504.24.224.3 n.f. (& m.)—אֶרֶץ (הָאָרֶץ/בְּאֶרֶץ/לְ/וְ/כְּ); + ה- of direction אַרְצָה (אָרְצָה); cstr. אֶרֶץ; sf. אַרְצִי; pl. אֲרָצוֹת; cstr. אַרְצוֹת; sf. אַרְצֹתָם—**1. land, territory, a.** usu. as possessed by people, nation, לְזַרְעֲךָ אֶתֵּן אֶת־הָאָרֶץ הַזֹּאת *to your descendants I will give this land* Gn 12$_7$, וִירִשְׁתֶּם אֶת־הָאָרֶץ הַטּוֹבָה הַזֹּאת *and you shall take possession of this good land* Dt 4$_{22}$, אֶרֶץ מִצְרַיִם *land of Egypt* Gn 13$_{10}$. **b.** plot or estate of land, אֶרֶץ אַרְבַּע מֵאֹת שֶׁקֶל־כֶּסֶף *a piece of land worth four hundred shekels of silver* Gn 23$_{15}$. **c.** region within a country, אֶרֶץ הַגָּלִיל *land of Galilee* 1 K 9$_{11}$. **d.** particular type of terrain, אֶרֶץ צִיָּה *land of dryness, parched land* Is 41$_{18}$, אֶרֶץ הָרִים וּבְקָעֹת *land (full) of mountains and valleys* Dt 11$_{11}$. **e.** הָאָרֶץ *the land,* in ref. to land of Judah or Israel 1 K 4$_{19}$ 2 K 3$_{27}$, inhabitants of the land 1 S 14$_{25}$. **2. earth, world,** לַי׳ הָאָרֶץ *the earth is Y.'s* Ex 9$_{29}$; שָׁמַיִם וָאָרֶץ *heaven and earth* Gn 14$_{19}$, מוֹסְדֵי אֶרֶץ *foundations of (the) earth* Is 24$_{18}$, אַפְסֵי־אָרֶץ *ends of (the) earth* Dt 33$_{17}$, מַמְלְכוֹת הָאָרֶץ *kingdoms of the earth* Dt 28$_{25}$, כָּל־הָאָרֶץ *all the earth,* i.e. its inhabitants Gn 9$_{19}$. **3a. ground,** עַל־כָּל־הָאָרֶץ הָיָה טָל *on all the ground there was dew* Jg 6$_{40}$, וַיִּשְׁתַּחוּ אָרְצָה *and he bowed to the ground* Gn 18$_2$. **b. soil,** with emphasis on composition and productivity of ground, כָּאָרֶץ תּוֹצִיא צִמְחָהּ *as the soil yields its growth* Is 61$_{11}$, אֶרֶץ לֹא זְרוּעָה *soil that is not sown* Jr 2$_2$, פְּרִי הָאָרֶץ *produce of the soil* Nm 13$_{20}$.

אַרְצָא 1 pr.n.m. **Arza.**

*ארצטון 0.0.1 pr.n.m. **Ariston.**

ארר 63.0.23.6 vb.—**Qal** 54.0.21.6 Pf. אֲרוֹתִיהָ; impf. תָּאֹר; impv. אֹרוּ, אָרָה־; ptc. אֹרְרֵי; ptc. pass. אָרוּר, אֲרוּרָה, אֲרוּרִים, Q ארורי; inf. אָרוֹר—**1. curse,** subj. Y. Gn 12$_3$, humans Ex 22:27; obj. usu. person, also blessing Ml 2:2. **2a.** pass. ptc., as adj., **cursed, accursed,** of Belial 1QM 13:4, Cain Gn 4:11, snake Gn 3:14, earth Gn 3:17, fruit Dt 28:18. **b.** as noun, **accursed one** 2 K 9:34.

Ni. 1.0.1 Pf. Q נארותה; ptc. נֵאָרִים—**suffer curse** Ml 3:9 (+ בְּ *with* curse) 1Q26 1:6 (+ בְּ *in respect of* produce).

Pi. 7 Pf. אֵרְרָהּ; ptc. מְאָרְרִים—**1. curse,** subj. Y. Gn 5:29, humans CD 20:8; obj. person CD 20:8, earth Gn 5:29. **2.** as technical term in ordeal, **effect curse,** of bitter waters Nm 5:18.

Ho. 1.0.1 Impf. יוּאַר—**suffer curse** Nm 22:6 CD 12:22.

→ מְאֵרָה *I curse,* אֲרָרָה *curse,* (?) אורים *Urim.*

* [אֲרָרָה] 0.0.5 n.[f.]—pl. cstr. ארורות—**curse** 4QDe 5:15 4QBéat 15:4. → ארר *curse.*

אֲרָרַט 4 pl.n. **Ararat.**

[אֲרָרִי], see הֲרָרִי *Hararite.*

ארשׂ 11.0.2 vb.—**Pi.** 6 Pf. אֵרַשְׂתִּי ,אֵרַשׂ; impf. תְּאָרֵשׂ—**betroth oneself to** woman, **take** woman **as one's betrothed** Dt 20:7 2 S 3:14 (+ לְ *to* oneself, בְּ *for the price of*); of Y. taking Israel Ho 2:21.

Pu. 5.0.2 Pf. אֹרָשָׂה; ptc. מְאֹרָשָׂה—of young woman, **be betrothed** Ex 22:15 Dt 22:23 (+ לְ *to* a man).

→ אֲרֶשֶׁת *desire.*

[אֲרֶשֶׁת] 1 n.f. **desire,** אֲרֶשֶׁת שְׂפָתָיו *desire of,* i.e. expressed through, *his lips* Ps 21:3. → ארשׁ *desire.*

אֹרֶת, see אֹרָה *mallow.*

אַרְתַּחְשַׁסְתְּ 9 pr.n.m. **Artaxerxes.**

אֲשַׂרְאֵל 1 pr.n.m. **Asarel.**

אֲשַׂרְאֵלָה 1 pr.n.m. **Asarelah.**

אַשְׂרִיאֵל 3 pr.n.m. **Asriel.**

אַשְׂרִיאֵלִי 1 gent. **Asrielite.**

אֵשׁ I 379.17.49 n.f.&m.—cstr. אֵשׁ; sf. אִשּׁוֹ ,אֶשְׁכֶם ,אִשָּׁם (Kt אשתם); pl. Si אשות—**fire, 1.** supernatural fire, assoc. with theophany of Y. Ex 24:17, burning bush Ex 3:2, heavenly being Ezk 8:2; עַמּוּד אֵשׁ *pillar of fire* Ex 13:21. **2.** fire of sacrifice Lv 1:7, in censer Lv 10:1. **3.** destructive fire Dt 13:17, in capital punishment Lv 20:14. **4a.** fire for cleansing metal booty Nm 31:23. **b.** for preparation of metal object Ex 32:24. **5.** domestic fire Ex 35:3, for preparing food Ex 12:8. **6.** fire in symbolic assoc. with anger of Y. Dt 32:22, jealousy Ezk 36:5, prophetic inspiration Jr 20:9. → cf. אִשֶּׁה *fire offering.*

* **[אֵשׁ]** II 2 n.[m.] **triviality,** יגע ... בְּדֵי־אֵשׁ *toil ... for the sake of triviality* Jr 51:58 Hb 2:13.

אִשׁ 3 part.—אִישׁ—**there is/are** 2 S 14:19 Mc 6:10 Pr 18:24.

* **[אֹשׁ]** 0.0.10 n.m.—pl. cstr. אושי; sf. אושיהם—**foundation** of wall 1QH 11:13, clay 1QH 11:30. → אשׁשׁ *be firm.*

***אשא** 0.0.0.8 pr.n.m. **Isha.**

אַשְׁבֵּל 3 pr.n.m. **Ashbel.**

אַשְׁבֵּלִי 1 gent. **Ashbelite.**

אֶשְׁבָּן 2 pr.n.m. **Eshban.**

אַשְׁבֵּעַ, see בֵּית אַשְׁבֵּעַ *Beth-ashbea.*

[אֶשְׁבַּעַל] 2 pr.n.m. **Eshbaal.**

[אֶשֶׁד] 7 n.f.—cstr. אֶשֶׁד; pl. אֲשֵׁדוֹת; cstr. אַשְׁדּוֹת—**slope,** אֶשֶׁד הַנְּחָלִים *slope of the valleys* Nm 21:15, אַשְׁדֹּת הַפִּסְגָּה *slopes of Pisgah* Dt 3:17.

אַשְׁדּוֹד 17 pl.n. **Ashdod.**

אַשְׁדּוֹדִי 6 gent. **Ashdodite.**

אשדת Dt 33:2(Kt), see אֵשׁ *I fire* and דָּת *law.*

אִשָּׁה 782.42.57.7 n.f.—אֵשֶׁת; cstr. אֵשֶׁת; sf. אִשְׁתִּי, אִשְׁתְּךָ, (אֶשְׁתְּךָ, אִשְׁתֶּךָ); pl. נָשִׁים; cstr. נְשֵׁי (אשת); sf. נָשָׁיו—**1. wife,** legitimate sexual partner of a man, אֵשֶׁת נֹחַ *wife of Noah* Gn 7:13, חַוָּה אִשְׁתּוֹ *Eve his wife* Gn 4:1; לקח לו לְאִשָּׁה *take for him(self) as a wife* Gn 25:20, נתן לו לְאִשָּׁה *give to him as a wife* Gn 16:3, היה לו לְאִשָּׁה *become to him as a wife, become his wife* Gn 24:67. **2a. woman,** ... אִישׁ ... אוֹ אִשָּׁה *a man ... or ... a woman* Ex 21:28, מֵאִישׁ וְעַד־אִשָּׁה *from man to woman,* i.e. both man and woman Jos 6:21, אִשָּׁה יָפָה *beautiful woman* Pr 11:22, אִשָּׁה יִשְׂרְאֵלִית *Israelite woman* Lv 24:10, אִשָּׁה זָרָה *strange,* or *foreign, woman* Pr 2:16, אִשָּׁה־אַלְמָנָה *woman* who is *a widow* 2 S 14:5, בֵּית הַנָּשִׁים *house of the women,* i.e. harem Est 2:3. **b.** used distributively, **each woman,** אִשָּׁה ... רְעוּתָהּ *each woman ... her neighbour* Ex 11:2, שֹׁבְנָה אִשָּׁה *return, each one (of you)* Ru 1:8. **3a. female animal,** in ark, תִּקַּח־לְךָ ... אִישׁ וְאִשְׁתּוֹ *you shall take ... a male and its mate* Gn 7:2. **b.** used distributively, **each animal,** דַּיּוֹת אִשָּׁה רְעוּתָהּ *(female) buzzards—each one with her neighbour* Is 34:15. **4.** of inanimate objects, used distributively, **each thing,** אִשָּׁה אֶל־אֲחֹתָהּ *each one to its partner* (lit. 'sister'), with ref. to curtain Ex 26:3, wing Ezk 1:9.

אִשֶּׁה 65.3.8 n.m.—cstr. אִשֵּׁה; pl. cstr. אִשֵּׁי; sf. אִשַּׁי (אִשַּׁי)—**fire offering,** i.e. offering made by fire, אִשֶּׁה הוּא לַי״ *it* *is a fire offering to Y.* Ex 29₂₅, אִשֵּׁי י׳ *fire offerings of Y.* Lv 2₃, אִשֵּׁה רֵיחַ(־)נִיחֹחַ *fire offering of pleasing odour* Lv 1₁₃. → cf. אֵשׁ *fire.*

אשויתיה, see אָשְׁיָה *tower.*

[אֱשׁוּן] 1 n.[m.]—cstr. אֱשׁוּן—**beginning** of darkness Pr 20₂₀(Qr) (Kt אִישׁוֹן *pupil,* i.e. middle, *of*).

אַשּׁוּר 150.1.5 pl.n. **Assyria.**

אַשּׁוּרִי 1 gent. **Ashurite,** or perh. **Assyrian.**

אַשּׁוּרִם 1 pr.n.m. **Asshurim.**

אַשְׁחוּר 2.0.0.2 pr.n.m. **Ashhur.**

אשחר, see אַשְׁחוּר *Ashhur.*

אשיה, see אשיהו *Ashiah.*

[אָשְׁיָה] 1 n.f.—pl. sf. Qr אָשְׁיוֹתֶיהָ (Kt אשויתיה)—**tower** Jr 50₁₅.

***אשיהו** 0.0.0.9 pr.n.m. **Ashiah.**

***[אָשִׁיחַ]** 0.1.4 n.m.—cstr. Q אשיח—**reservoir, cistern** Si 50₃ 3QTr 5₆ 7₄ 10₅ 11₁₂. → שׁוח *sink down.*

אֲשִׁימָא 1 pr.n.f. **Ashima.**

אֲשֵׁירָה, from אֲשֵׁרָה *Asherah.*

***[אָשִׁישׁ]** 1.0.5 n.m.—pl. Q אשישים; cstr. אֲשִׁישֵׁי; sf. Q אשישיהם—**adult** 1QpHab 6₁₁.

אֲשִׁישָׁה 4 n.f.—pl. אֲשִׁישׁוֹת, cstr. אֲשִׁישֵׁי—**raisin cake** 2 S 6₁₉ Ho 3₁.

[אֶשֶׁךְ] 1 n.[m.]—אֶשֶׁךְ—**testicle** Lv 21₂₀. → שׁכה *have large testicles.*

אֶשְׁכּוֹל I 9 n.m.—cstr. אֶשְׁכּוֹל; pl. אַשְׁכֹּלוֹת; cstr. אַשְׁכְּלוֹת; sf. אַשְׁכְּלֹתֶיהָ—**cluster,** usu. of grapes Gn 40₁₀, also of henna blossom Ca 1₁₄.

[אֶשְׁכּוֹל] II 2 pr.n.m. **Eshcol.**

אֶשְׁכּוֹל III 4 pl.n. **Eshcol.**

אַשְׁכְּנַז 3 pr.n.m. **Ashkenaz.**

אֶשְׁכָּר 2.0.0.1 n.[m.]—sf. אֶשְׁכָּרֵךְ—**payment, tribute** Ezk 27₁₅ Ps 72₁₀.

אֶשֶׁל 3 n.[m.]—mss אֵשֶׁל—**tamarisk,** a type of tree Gn 21₃₃.

אשם 36.1.8 vb.—**Qal** 34.1.7 Pf. אָשֵׁם (אָשַׁם), אָשְׁמוּ; impf. יֶאְשַׁם, יֶאְשְׁמוּ (יֶאְשָׁמוּ); inf. abs. אָשׁוֹם; cstr. לְאַשְׁמָה—**1a.** usu. **be guilty, incur guilt, trespass** Jr 50₇, esp. in respect of infringements of holiness Lv 4₁₃. **b.** with obj. אַשְׁמָה, **be guilty of wickedness** 11QT 59₉. **2. be accounted guilty** Is 24₆. **3. acknowledge guilt** Ho 5₁₅.

Ni. 1 Pf. נֶאְשָׁמוּ—**be accounted guilty,** of flocks of sheep Jl 1₁₈ (or = נָשַׁמּוּ *they are made desolate*).

Hi. 1.0.1 Impv. הַאֲשִׁימֵם; inf. Q האשים—**1. punish,** of Y., obj. the wicked Ps 5₁₁. **2. make guilty, wicked,** of Belial leading humanity astray 1QM 13₁₁.

→ אָשָׁם *guilt,* אַשְׁמָה *guilt,* אָשֵׁם *guilty.*

אָשָׁם 46.0.5 n.m.—sf. אֲשָׁמוֹ; pl. sf. אֲשָׁמָיו—**1.** usu. **guilt offering, trespass offering,** usu. of animal (but also golden haemorrhoids and mice 1 S 6₄.₁₇, soul of servant of Y. Is 53₁₀), as reparation, esp. for violation of vow or contact with uncleanness, אֵיל הָאָשָׁם *ram of the guilt offering* Lv 5₁₆, כֶּסֶף אָשָׁם *money of,* i.e. to purchase, *guilt offering* 2 K 12₁₇. **2. guilt, wickedness, wicked deed** Gn 26₁₀ Jr 51₅. **3. stolen item,** the possession of which incurs guilt CD 9₁₃. → אשם *be guilty.*

אָשֵׁם 3.0.2 adj.—pl. אֲשֵׁמִים (Q אשימים)—pred., or as noun, **guilty (one)** Gn 42₂₁ (+ עַל *concerning*) 2 S 14₁₃ CD 1₉. → אשם *be guilty.*

אַשְׁמָה 19.1.78 n.f.—cstr. אַשְׁמַת; sf. אַשְׁמָתוֹ; pl. אֲשָׁמוֹת; cstr. Q אשמות; sf. אַשְׁמוֹתַי—**1. guilt** Lv 4₃; עֲוֹן אַשְׁמָה *iniquity of,* i.e. resulting in, *guilt* Lv 22₁₆. **2. wickedness, wicked deed** Ps 69₆ 1QH 23₁₂; יצר אשמה *inclination of,* i.e. towards, *wickedness* CD 2₁₆. **3.** perh. **guilt offering** Lv 5₂₄. → אשם *be guilty.*

אַשְׁמוּרָה 7.1.1 n.f.—אַשְׁמֹרֶת; cstr. אַשְׁמֹרֶת; sf. Si אשמורתם; pl. אַשְׁמֻרוֹת; cstr. Q אשמורי; sf. Si אשמרותם—**watch,** period of night, אַשְׁמֹרֶת הַבֹּקֶר *watch of the morning* Ex 14₂₄, הָאַשְׁמֹרֶת הַתִּיכוֹנָה *the middle watch* Jg 7₁. → שׁמר *keep.*

[אַשְׁמָן] 1 adj.—pl. אַשְׁמַנִּים (1QIsaᵃ אשמונים)—**healthy,** as noun, **healthy one** Is 59₁₀. → שׁמן *be fat.*

[אַשְׁמֹרֶת], see אַשְׁמוּרָה *watch.*

***אשנא** 0.0.0.2 pr.n.m. **Ashna.**

אֶשְׁנָב 2.1 n.m.—sf. אֶשְׁנַבִּי—**window** Jg 5₂₈ Pr 7₆ Si 42₁₁(B).

אַשְׁנָה 2 pl.n. **Ashnah.**

אֶשְׁעָן 1 pl.n. **Eshan.**

[אַשָּׁף] 2 n.m.—pl. אַשָּׁפִים—**conjuror,** perh. specif. exorcist Dn 1₂₀ 2₂.

אַשְׁפָּה 6.0.1.1 n.f.—Q אשפא; sf. אַשְׁפָּתוֹ; pl. perh. I אשפת—**quiver** Is 22₆ Jb 39₂₃; בְּנֵי אַשְׁפָּתוֹ *sons of his quiver,* i.e. arrows Lm 3₁₃.

אַשְׁפְּנַז 1 pr.n.m. **Ashpenaz.**

אֶשְׁפָּר 2 n.[m.] **date cake** 2 S 6$_{19}$||1 C 16$_{3}$.

אַשְׁפֹּת 6.0.2 n.[m.]—אַשְׁפּוֹת; pl. אַשְׁפַּתּוֹת (Q אשפותות)—**1. midden, ash heap** 1 S 2$_{8}$ Lm 4$_{5}$. **2.** in name of gate of Jerusalem, שַׁעַר הָאַשְׁפֹּת *gate of ashes, Dung Gate* Ne 2$_{13}$. → שׁפת *set on fire.*

אַשְׁקְלוֹן 12 pl.n. **Ashkelon.**

אֶשְׁקְלוֹנִי 1 gent. **Ashkelonite.**

אשׁר I 7.1 vb.—**Qal** 1 Impv. אִשְׁרוּ—**go forward** Pr 9$_{6}$.

Pi. 5.1 Pf. אִשְּׁרוּ; impf. תְּאַשֵּׁר; impv. אַשֵּׁר, אַשְּׁרוּ; ptc. מְאַשְּׁרֵי—**1.** as Qal, **go forward** Pr 4$_{14}$. **2a. lead, direct** Pr 23$_{19}$ Si 4$_{18}$. **b.** ptc. as noun, **leader** Is 3$_{12}$ 9$_{15}$. **3. correct** Is 1$_{17}$.

Pu. 1 Ptc. מְאֻשָּׁרָיו—ptc. as noun, **one who is led** Is 9$_{15}$.

→ אֲשֻׁר *step,* (?) תְּאַשּׁוּר *cypress.*

אשׁר II 9.5 vb.—**Pi.** 7.4 Pf. אִשְּׁרוּ; impf. יְאַשְּׁרוּהוּ; ptc. מְאַשְּׁרִים—**1. pronounce happy, blessed, deem successful** Gn 30$_{13}$. **2. make happy** Si 25$_{23}$.

Pu. 2.1 Impf. Kt יאשר (Si יאושר); + waw Qr וְאֻשַּׁר; ptc. מְאֻשָּׁר—**be pronounced happy, blessed** Ps 41$_{3}$.

→ אֹשֶׁר *happiness,* אַשְׁרֵי *happy.*

אָשֵׁר 43.0.5 pr.n.m. **Asher.**

אֲשֶׁר 5495.57.944.29 part. of relation, **which, that, who**—(invariable as to number, gender, and case), **1.** as pron. introducing rel. clause, **which, that, who(m), a.** as subj. of rel. clause, הָאֲדָמָה אֲשֶׁר פָּצְתָה אֶת־פִּיהָ *the earth that opened its mouth* Gn 4$_{11}$. **b.** as obj. of rel. clause, הָאָדָם אֲשֶׁר יָצָר *the human being whom he had formed* Gn 2$_{8}$. **2.** as neither subj. nor obj. of rel. clause; connection with antecedent is made by suffixed prep. or adv., הָאֲדָמָה אֲשֶׁר־הֵם עָלֶיהָ *the ground that they are upon* (lit. 'upon it') Ex 8$_{17}$, הַמָּקוֹם אֲשֶׁר־אַתָּה שָׁם *the place where you are* Gn 13$_{14}$, הָאָרֶץ אֲשֶׁר־גַּרְתָּה בָּהּ *the land in which you stayed* Gn 21$_{23}$; אֲשֶׁר meaning **where, when,** חֹרֵב אֲשֶׁר כָּרַת י׳ *Horeb where Y. made (a covenant)* 1 K 8$_{9}$||2 C 5$_{10}$, עֵת אֲשֶׁר שָׁלַט הָאָדָם בְּאָדָם *a time when one person dominates another* Ec 8$_{9}$. **3.** as noun, **that which, what, the one who(m), whatever,** etc., without explicit antecedent, **a.** as subj. of verb, אֶהְיֶה אֲשֶׁר אֶהְיֶה *I am what I am* Ex 3$_{14}$. **b.** as obj. of verb, אֲשֶׁר יִרְאֶה יַגִּיד *what he sees he will announce* Is 21$_{6}$. **c.** as subj. of nom. cl., אֲשֶׁר עַל־הַבָּיִת *(the one) who is over the household* Gn 43$_{16}$. **d.** referring to a pron. or pronom. sf., אֲשֶׁר יִמָּצֵא אִתּוֹ יִהְיֶה־לִּי עָבֶד *the one with whom it is found will be my slave* Gn 44$_{10}$. **e.** prefixed by prep., עִם אֲשֶׁר תִּמְצָא אֶת־אֱלֹהֶיךָ לֹא יִחְיֶה *whoever you find your gods with will not live* Gn 31$_{32}$. **f. the place which, where, wherever,** בַּאֲשֶׁר הוּא־שָׁם *in the place where he is* Gn 21$_{17}$. **g. the manner in which, how,** יֶתֶר דִּבְרֵי יָרָבְעָם אֲשֶׁר נִלְחַם וַאֲשֶׁר מָלָךְ *the rest of the words about Jeroboam—how he fought and how he reigned* 1 K 14$_{19}$. **4.** as conj., introducing **a.** object-clause, **(the extent) that, how (much),** (1) אֲשֶׁר, רָאִיתָ אֲשֶׁר נְשָׂאֲךָ י׳ אֱלֹהֶיךָ *you have seen how Y. your God has carried you* Dt 1$_{31}$. (2) אֵת אֲשֶׁר, יָדַעְתָּ אֵת אֲשֶׁר עֲבַדְתִּיךָ *you know how I served you* Gn 30$_{29}$. **b.** final clause, **so that, in order that,** (1) אֲשֶׁר, מִי י׳ אֲשֶׁר אֶשְׁמַע בְּקֹלוֹ *who is Y., that I should listen to his voice?* Ex 5$_{2}$. (2) לְמַעַן אֲשֶׁר Gn 18$_{19}$. **c.** causal clause, **because, for,** (1) אֲשֶׁר alone, נָתַן אֱלֹהִים שְׂכָרִי אֲשֶׁר־נָתַתִּי שִׁפְחָתִי לְאִישִׁי *God has given (me) my hire because I gave my maid to my husband* Gn 30$_{18}$. (2) various compounds: אֲשֶׁר עַל־כֵּן Jb 34$_{27}$, עַל אֲשֶׁר Dt 29$_{24}$, יַעַן אֲשֶׁר Gn 22$_{16}$, בַּאֲשֶׁר Gn 39$_{9}$, עַל־דְּבַר אֲשֶׁר Dt 22$_{24}$, עֵקֶב אֲשֶׁר Gn 22$_{18}$, מִפְּנֵי אֲשֶׁר Ex 19$_{18}$, מֵאֲשֶׁר Is 43$_{4}$, עַל־אוֹדוֹת אֲשֶׁר Jr 3$_{8}$, כְּפִי אֲשֶׁר Ml 2$_{9}$, בְּשֶׁל אֲשֶׁר Ec 8$_{17}$ (unless אֲשֶׁר = *although*). **d.** temporal clause, (1) אֲשֶׁר **when** Jos 4$_{21}$. (2) עַד אֲשֶׁר **until** Ex 32$_{20}$. **e.** conditional clause, **if** Nm 5$_{29}$. **f.** comparative clause, **(just) as** Jr 33$_{22}$. **g.** perh. concessive clause, **although,** (1) אֲשֶׁר Est 4$_{16}$. (2) אֲשֶׁר אִם Jb 9$_{15}$. **5.** כַּאֲשֶׁר, introducing **a.** (usu.) comparative clause, **in the way that, (just) as,** less oft., **as though,** כַּאֲשֶׁר דִּבֶּר אֵלָיו י׳ *as Y. had said to him* Gn 12$_{4}$, כאשר לא היו היו *they have become as though they had never existed* Si 44$_{9}$, כַּאֲשֶׁר כָּתוּב *as (it is) written* 1 K 21$_{11}$; oft. כַּאֲשֶׁר ... כֵּן *as ... so* Ex 1$_{12}$; also כֵּן ... כַּאֲשֶׁר *so ... as* Gn 18$_{5}$. **b.** temporal clause, **when, after,** כַּאֲשֶׁר כִּלָּה *when he had finished* Gn 18$_{33}$. **c.** conditional clause, **if,** כַּאֲשֶׁר אָבַדְתִּי אָבָדְתִּי *if I perish, I perish* Est 4$_{16}$. **d.** causal clause, **because,** כַּאֲשֶׁר אֵינָם יֹדְעִים *because they do not know* 2 K 17$_{26}$. **6.** אַחַר/אַחֲרֵי אֲשֶׁר, introducing **a.** temporal clause, **after** Dt 24$_{4}$ Ezk 40$_{1}$. **b.** causal clause, **because, seeing that** 2 S 19$_{31}$.

7. תַּחַת אֲשֶׁר, a. introducing causal clause, **because of** Nm 25_{13}. b. + היה *be*, **instead of being** Ezk 36_{34}. 8. בַּעֲבוּר אֲשֶׁר, introducing **a.** final clause, **so that** Gn 27_{10}. **b.** causal clause, **because** CD 1_{18}. → cf. מֵאֲשֶׁר *that which*, -שֶׁ *which*.

[אָשֶׁר], see אַשְׁרֵי *happy*.

[אֹשֶׁר] 1.1 n.[m.] **happiness**, בְּאָשְׁרִי *in my happiness*, i.e. how happy I am Gn 30_{13}, אשר ראך ומת *happiness*, i.e. happy, *is the one that sees you and dies* Si 48_{11}. → אשר II *be happy*.

[אָשֻׁר] 10 n.f.—sf. אַשֻּׁרִי (as if from אֲשֻׁר), אֲשֻׁרוֹ; pl. אֲשֻׁרִים; sf. אֲשֻׁרֵי, אֲשֻׁרֵינוּ אֲשֻׁרֵינוּ [as if from אֲשֻׁר])—**1.** usu. **step** Ps 17_{5}. **2. track,** left by footstep of Y. Jb 23_{11}. → אשר I *go forward*.

אֲשַׂרְאֵלָה, see אֲשַׂרְאֵלָה *Asarelah*.

אֲשֵׁרָה 40.0.1.6 [pr.] n.f.—אֲשֵׁירָה; sf. I אשרתה; pl. אֲשֵׁרִים (אֲשֵׁרוֹת); sf. אֲשֵׁרֶיךָ—**Asherah, 1.** Canaanite goddess, נְבִיאֵי הָאֲשֵׁרָה *prophets of Asherah* 1 K 18_{19}. **2.** wooden pole or tree representing Asherah Ex 34_{13} Dt 16_{21}.

*__[אָשׁוּת]__ n.f. **mole** Ps 58_{9} (if em. אֵשֶׁת *woman* to וְאֶשֶׁת *and [as] a mole*).

*__אשרחי__ 0.0.0.1 pr.n.m. **Asherahi.**

אָשֵׁרִי 1 gent. **Asherite.**

אַשְׁרֵי 45.9.11 interj.—sf. אַשְׁרֶיךָ, אַשְׁרָיו, אַשְׁרֵיךְ (אַשְׁרֵהוּ)—**happy, blessed is/are** (lit. 'happiness, blessedness of', pl. cstr. of אֶשֶׁר), followed by **a.** noun 1 K 10_{8}||2 C 9_{7}. **b.** pronom. sf. Dt 33_{29}. **c.** ptc. Is 30_{18}. **d.** -שֶׁ *(one) who*, Ps 137_{8}. **e.** verb, without rel., אַשְׁרֵי תִּבְחַר וּתְקָרֵב *blessed is the one whom you choose and bring near* Ps 65_{5}. → אשר II *be happy*.

אשש 1 vb.—Htpo. 1 Impv. הִתְאֹשָׁשׁוּ—**make firm** in mind, or perh. **experience grief** Is 46_{8}. → אשׁ *foundation*.

אֵשֶׁת, see אִשָּׁה *woman*.

אֶשְׁתָּאוֹל, see אֶשְׁתָּאֹל *Eshtaol*.

אֶשְׁתָּאֹל 7 pl.n. **Eshtaol.**

אֶשְׁתָּאֻלִי 1 gent. **Eshtaolite.**

אֶשְׁתּוֹן 2 pr.n.m. **Eshton.**

אשתם Jr 6_{29}(Kt), see אֵשׁ I *fire* and תמם *be completed*.

אֶשְׁתְּמֹה, see אֶשְׁתְּמֹעַ I *Eshtemoa*.

אֶשְׁתְּמֹעַ I 4 pl.n. **Eshtemoa,** also as אֶשְׁתְּמֹה **Eshtemoh.**

אֶשְׁתְּמֹעַ II 2 pr.n.m. **Eshtemoa.**

[אַתְּ], see אַתָּה *you*.

אַתְּ 60.0.2 pron.—אַתְּ, mss, Sam, Kt אתי—**you** (fem. sg.) Gn 12_{11}.

אֵת I 10898.55.866.33 **object-marker**—אֶת־ (אֶת, אֵת; in Bar-Kochba letters, etc. normal form is ת, for both אֵת and -אֶת־הַ, usu. prefixed to object); with sf. אֹתִי (אֹתִי), אוֹתוֹ ,(אֹתְךָ) אוֹתְךָ ,(אֹתָכָה ,אֹתָךְ ,אוֹתָךְ ,אֹתְכָה ,אֹתָךְ) אוֹתָךְ, אוֹתְכֶם) אֶתְכֶם ,(אֹתָנוּ) אוֹתָנוּ ,(אֹתָהּ) אוֹתָהּ ,(אתה I ;אֹתוֹ), אֹתָן (אותמה Q ,אֶתְהֶם ,אוֹתְהֶם ,אֹתָם) אוֹתָם ,(אתכמה Q (אֶתְהֶן ,אוֹתְהֶן ,אֹתָנָה ,אוֹתָנָה)—**1.** with **determined direct object. a.** with **definite article,** בָּרָא אֱלֹהִים אֵת הַשָּׁמַיִם וְאֵת הָאָרֶץ *God created the heavens and the earth* Gn 1_{1}. **b.** with **suffixed pronoun,** וַיִּתֵּן אֹתָם אֱלֹהִים *and God placed them* Gn 1_{17}. **c.** with **suffixed noun,** אֶת־קֹלְךָ שָׁמַעְתִּי *I heard your voice* Gn 3_{10}. **d.** with **name** of person, place, etc., וְהָאָדָם יָדַע אֶת־חַוָּה *and the human knew Eve* Gn 4_{1}. **e.** with (determined) **construct chain,** וַיִּשְׁמְעוּ אֶת־קוֹל י׳ *and they heard the sound of Y.* Gn 3_{8}. **f.** with **demonstrative pronoun,** etc., אֶת־זֶה *this one* (masc.) Gn 29_{33}, אֶת־זֹאת *this one* (fem.) Gn 29_{27}, אֶת־אֵלֶּה *these ones* Gn 46_{18}, אֶת־מִי *whom?* Jos 24_{15}. **2.** אֵת before syntactically **undetermined direct object,** נָתַתִּי לָכֶם אֶת־כֹּל *I have given you everything* Gn 9_{3}, כִּי־יִגַּח שׁוֹר אֶת־אִישׁ אוֹ אֶת־אִשָּׁה *if an ox gores a man or a woman* Ex 21_{28}. **3a.** אֵת before **indirect object,** הַגֵּד אֶת־בֵּית־יִשְׂרָאֵל אֶת־הַבַּיִת *describe the temple to the house of Israel* Ezk 43_{10}. **b.** אֵת before **accusative of respect,** חָלָה אֶת־רַגְלָיו *he was diseased in his feet* 1 K 15_{23}. **c.** with **object of time,** וּזְרַעְתֶּם אֵת הַשָּׁנָה הַשְּׁמִינִת *and you are to sow the eighth year* Lv 25_{22}. **d.** (1) מלא אֵת **be full of** Jr 6_{11}. (2) שׂבע אֵת **be satisfied with** Jr 31_{14}. **4a.** אֵת before **subject of active verb,** אֵת כָּל־הָרָעָה הַזֹּאת בָּאָה *all this trouble has come* Dn 9_{13}. **b.** אֵת before **subject or predicate of nom. cl.,** אֶת־כָּל־אֵלֶּה אַנְשֵׁי־חָיִל *all these were warriors* Jg 20_{44}. **c.** אֵת before **subject of passive verb,** וַיִּוָּלֵד לַחֲנוֹךְ אֶת־עִירָד *and to Enoch was born Irad* Gn 4_{18}. **5.** as **resumptive** or **emphatic particle,** וְהִבִּיטוּ אֵלַי אֵת אֲשֶׁר־דָּקָרוּ *and they will look at me—the one that they have stabbed* Zc 12_{10}, וַתִּרְאֵהוּ אֶת־הַיֶּלֶד *and she saw him—the boy* Ex 2_{6}.

אֵת II 931.7.41.9 prep.—אֶת־; with sf. (forms oft. as though from אֵת I, i.e. אִתִּי, אִתְּךָ, אִתְּכֶם, etc.) אִתִּי, אִתָּךְ (אִתְּךָ), אִתְּךָ (מֵאִתְּךָ), אִתּוֹ, אִתָּהּ, אִתָּנוּ, אִתְּכֶם, אִתָּם—**1. (together, along) with, and,** joining two nouns (or noun and pronoun, two pronouns, etc.), a. each having similar semantic role in relation to verb, וַיְהִי אֱלֹהִים אֶת־הַנַּעַר *and God was with the lad* Gn 21_{20}, וַיֵּלֶךְ אִתּוֹ לוֹט *and Lot went with him* Gn 12_{4}. **b.** in nom. cl., הָעָם אֲשֶׁר־אִתּוֹ *the people who are with him* Gn 32_{8}, אֶת־צְנוּעִים חָכְמָה *wisdom is with the modest* Pr 11_{2}. **2. with, to,** linking verb (+ object noun) to additional noun, וַיְדַבֵּר אִתּוֹ אֱלֹהִים *and God spoke to him* Gn 17_{3}, כָּרַתִּי אִתְּךָ בְּרִית וְאֶת־יִשְׂרָאֵל *I have made a covenant with you and with Israel* Ex 34_{27}. **3. under the control of, in the care of, at the disposal of,** אֲשֶׁר יִהְיֶה לְךָ אֶת־אָחִיךָ *whatever you possess (that is) under the control of,* i.e. lent to, *your brother* Dt 15_{3}, נָתַתִּי אִתּוֹ אֵת אָהֳלִיאָב *I have put Oholiab at his disposal* Ex 31_{6}, שִׁלְחָה הַנַּעַר אִתִּי *send the lad in my care* Gn 43_{8}. **4a. in the presence of, near to, before,** וַיִּתְהַלֵּךְ חֲנוֹךְ אֶת־הָאֱלֹהִים *and Enoch walked in the presence of God* Gn 5_{22}, פְּשָׁעֵינוּ אִתָּנוּ *our sins are before us* Is 59_{12}, עֶצְיוֹן־גֶּבֶר אֲשֶׁר אֶת־אֵלוֹת *Ezion-geber which is near Eloth* 1 K 9_{26}. **b.** usu. אֶת־פְּנֵי **in the presence of, in front of, before,** יֵשְׁבוּ יְשָׁרִים אֶת־פָּנֶיךָ *the upright shall dwell in your presence* Ps 140_{14}, וַיִּחַן אֶת־פְּנֵי הָעִיר *and he encamped before the city* Gn 33_{18}. **5. in contention with, against,** with verb לחם ni. *fight* Jos 10_{25}, ריב *contend* Nm 20_{13}, שׁפט ni. *enter judgment* 1 S 12_{7}. **6a.** instrumental, **by (means of), with,** קָנִיתִי אִישׁ אֶת־יי *I have acquired a person by means of Y.* Gn 4_{1}. **b. without, apart from,** לֹא־יָדַע אִתּוֹ מְאוּמָה *he did not know anything without him* Gn 39_{6}. **7a.** מֵאֵת **from being with, away from, from,** וַיֵּלְכוּ מֵאִתּוֹ בְּשָׁלוֹם *and they went from him in peace* Gn 26_{31}, הָעָם הַשֹּׁאֲלִים מֵאִתּוֹ מֶלֶךְ *the people who were asking a king from him* 1 S 8_{10}. **b.** מֵאֵת פְּנֵי **(away) from the presence of, from before,** וַיְגָרֶשׁ אֹתָם מֵאֵת פְּנֵי פַרְעֹה *and he drove them out of the presence of Pharaoh* Ex 10_{11}, שְׂאוּ אֶת־אֲחֵיכֶם מֵאֵת פְּנֵי־הַקֹּדֶשׁ *carry your brothers from before the sanctuary* Lv 10_{14}.

[אֵת] III 5 n.[m.]—sf. אִתּוֹ; pl. אִתִּים (אֵתִים); sf. אִתֵּיכֶם—1. agricultural cutting instrument, perh. **ploughshare** 1 S 13_{20}. **2.** perh. **axehead** 2 K 6_{5} (unless אֵת obj.-marker introducing subj.).

אֹת, see אוֹת *sign.*

אֶתְבַּעַל 1 pr.n.m. **Ethbaal.**

אתה 21.1 vb.—**Qal** 21.1 Pf. אָתָה, אָתָנוּ; impf. תֵּאתֶה, יֶאֱתֶה, וַיֶּאֱתָיוּ; + waw וַיֵּתֵא (וַיֵּאתֶ, וַיֶּאֱתָיֻנִי), וַיֶּאֱתָיוּן; impv. אֵתָיוּ, ptc. אֹתִיּוֹת—**1. come,** of Y. Dt 33_{2} (+ מִן *from*), human Is 41_{25}, beasts Is 56_{9}, years Jb 16_{22}, disaster Pr 1_{27}. **2.** fem. ptc. pl. as noun, **that which is to come** Is 41_{23}.
Hi. Impv. הֵתָיוּ (Q האתיו)—**bring** Is 21_{14}.

אַתָּה 744.7.163.1 pron.—אַתָּה (אַתָּה), I, Q, Kt את—**you** (masc. sg.), with verb Gn 3_{15}, ptc. Gn 13_{15}, in nom. cl. Gn 3_{19}; אַתָּה לְבַדֶּךָ *you alone* Nm 11_{17}, גַּם־אַתָּה *you too* Gn 24_{44}; אַתָּה *as for you,* when not functioning as subj. Gn 49_{8}.

אָתוֹן 34 n.f.—sf. אֲתֹנוֹ; pl. אֲתֹנוֹת—**she-ass** Gn 12_{16} Nm 22_{21} (חֲמוֹר is *he-ass, donkey*).

[אַתּוּק], see אַתִּיק *ledge.*

[אַתִּי], see אַתְּ *you.*

אִתַּי 9 pr.n.m. **Ittai.**

[אֹתִיָּה], see אתה *come.*

אַתִּיק 5 n.m.—pl. אַתִּיקִים; sf. Qr אַתִּיקֶיהָא (Kt אתוקיהא)—**ledge, gallery** Ezk $41_{15.16}$ $42_{3.5}$.

אַתֶּם 279.0.12 pron.—Q אתמה, אתן—**you** (masc. pl.; appar. fem. at Ezk 13_{20}), with verb Gn 9_{7}, ptc. Ex 5_{17}, in nom. cl. Ex 33_{5}; גַּם־אַתֶּם *you too* Nm 18_{28}; אַתֶּם *as for you,* when not functioning as subj. Jos 23_{9}.

אֵתָם 4 pl.n. **Etham.**

אֶתְמוֹל 31.2 n.[m.]—אֶתְמוֹל, אִתְּמוֹל, תְּמוֹל, תְּמֹל—usu. with שִׁלְשׁוֹם *a third (day),* i.e. the day before yesterday, appar. in same sense as אֶתְמוֹל alone, **1. past, previous time,** perh. specif. **yesterday,** לו אתמול ולך היום *he has the past, you have today* Si 38_{22}; יוֹם אֶתְמוֹל *a day of previous time, yesterday* Ps 90_{4}; מִתְּמוֹל שִׁלְשׁוֹם *from a previous time* Ex 21_{29}. **2.** as adv., **previously,** perh. specif. **yesterday,** גַּם־תְּמוֹל גַּם־הַיּוֹם *both previously and today* 1 S 20_{27}, גַּם־תְּמוֹל גַּם־שִׁלְשֹׁם *both previously and before* 2 S 3_{17}, כִּתְמוֹל שִׁלְשׁוֹם *as previously* Gn 31_{2}.

אֵתָן, see אֵיתָן I *continuous.*

אַתֵּן, see אַתֶּם *you* (masc. pl.), אַתֵּנָה *you* (fem. pl.).

אַתֵּנָה 5 pron.—אַתֵּן—**you** (fem. pl.) Gn 31_{6} Ezk $13_{11.20}$

$34_{17.31}$.

אֶתְנָה, see אֶתְנַן I *fee*.

אֶתְנִי 1 pr.n.m. **Ethni.**

אֶתָנִים, see אֵיתָן I *continuous*.

אֶתְנַן I 12 n.m.—אֶתְנַן, אֶתְנָה; cstr. אֶתְנַן; sf. אֶתְנַנָּהּ (אֶתְנַנָּה); pl. sf. אֶתְנַנֶּיהָ—**fee,** paid to prostitute Dt 23_{19}, paid by prostitute Ezk 16_{34}. → נתן *give*.

[אֶתְנַן] II 1 pr.n.m. **Ethnan.**

אֲתָרִים 1 pl.n. **Atharim.**

ב

בְּ $15722.6015.c.4500.99$ prep.—before indef. noun בְּ; before def. noun, בַּ, בָּ, or בֶּ, i.e. with vowel of art. ה (and following dagesh, etc.), which is normally replaced by בּ; with sf. בִּי (ביא Q), בּוֹ (בוא Q), בְּךָ (בכי Q), בָּךְ (בְּכָה, בָּךְ), בָּהּ (בהא Q), בָּנוּ, בָּכֶם (בכמה Q), בָּהֶם/בָּם (בָּהֵמָּה), בָּהֶן (בָּהֵנָּה, בָּהֶן)—**1a.** of place, **in, inside, within, among, into, on, onto, upon, through, by, at,** הַכְּנַעֲנִי אָז בָּאָרֶץ *the Canaanite was then in the land* Gn 12_6, הִתְהַלֵּךְ בָּאָרֶץ *walk through the land* Gn 13_{17}, וַיַּעַל עֹלֹת בַּמִּזְבֵּחַ *and he offered burnt offerings on the altar* Gn 8_{20}, וְהֵפִיץ י״ אֶתְכֶם בָּעַמִּים *and Y. will scatter you among the nations* Dt 4_{27}. **b.** of time, **in, on, at, during, throughout,** בְּרֵאשִׁית *in the beginning* Gn 1_1, בַּיּוֹם הַשְּׁבִיעִי *on the seventh day* Gn 2_2. **c.** as conj., **when, whenever, if,** בְּגַלְּחוֹ אֶת־רֹאשׁוֹ *when he shaved his head* 2 S 14_{26}, בְּאָמְרִי לָרָשָׁע מוֹת תָּמוּת *if I say to the wicked (one), you will surely die* Ezk 3_{18}. **2.** of accompaniment, **in (a state of), with,** בְּעֶצֶב *in sorrow* Gn 3_{16}. **3.** of cause, **on account of, because of, for,** אִישׁ בְּחֶטְאוֹ יוּמָתוּ *each will be put to death for his own sin* Dt 24_{16}. **4.** of instrument, **by (means of), with, through,** בָּאֵשׁ תִּשָּׂרֵף *it will be burnt with fire* Lv 13_{52}. **5.** of agent, **by, through,** עַם נוֹשַׁע בַּי״ *a people saved by Y.* Dt 33_{29}. **6.** partitive, **(any) of, (some) of, from (among),** בַּל־אֶלְחַם בְּמַנְעַמֵּיהֶם *I do not eat of their delicacies* Ps 141_4. **7.** of essence, **(having the same nature) as, (sharing) in, (consisting) of,** בָּאֵשׁ י״ יָבוֹא *Y. comes as fire* Is 66_{15}, עֲלִלוֹת בְּרֶשַׁע *deeds consisting of wickedness* Ps 141_4. **8.** of comparison, **(more) than,** אֵין־טוֹב בָּאָדָם שֶׁיֹּאכַל וְשָׁתָה *there is no one among humans happier than the person who eats and drinks* Ec 2_{24}. **9. according to, in accordance with,** בְּמִסְפָּר בְּמִשְׁקָל *according to number, according to weight* Ezr 8_{34}. **10.** of price, **at the cost of, as the price of, at the risk of, (in exchange) for,** אֶקְנֶה מֵאוֹתְךָ בִּמְחִיר *I shall buy from you at a price* 2 S 24_{24}, הָאֲנָשִׁים הַהֹלְכִים בְּנַפְשׁוֹתָם *the men who went at the risk of their own lives* 2 S 23_{17}. **11. despite,** אִם־בְּזֹאת לֹא תִשְׁמְעוּ לִי *if despite this you do not obey me* Lv 26_{27}. **12. in respect of, concerning, about,** יָשִׂיחוּ בִי *they talk about me* Ps 69_{13}. **13. against,** וְנִלְחַם־בָּנוּ *and he will fight against us* Ex 1_{10}. **14. over, in charge of,** אֵין מֶלֶךְ בְּיִשְׂרָאֵל *there was no king over Israel* Jg 18_1. **15. from,** וַיִּקְרָא בְּסֵפֶר *and he read from the book of* the law Ne 8_{18}. **16. after,** בְּרֹב הַיָּמִים תִּמְצָאֶנּוּ *after many days you will find it* Ec 11_1. **17. to, with,** הֲרַק אַךְ־בְּמֹשֶׁה דִּבֶּר *did he only speak with Moses?* Nm 12_2. **18.** introducing obj., וְהֶחֱזַקְתָּ בּוֹ *and you are to hold him* Lv 25_{35}. → cf. בִּגְלַל *on account of*, בַּעֲבוּר *on account of*, בְּמוֹ *in*.

בַּאֲדָא, see בַּעֲרָא *Baara*.

בִּאָה $1.0.13$ n.f.—Q ביאה; cstr. Q ביאת—**1. arrival** of priestly course 4QMishA 1_3. **2. entrance** Ezk 8_5. → בוא *come*.

באר $3.0.3$ vb.—**Pi.** $3.0.3$ Pf. בֵּאֵר; impv. בָּאֵר—**explain, clarify** law Dt 1_5, vision Hb 2_2.

בְּאֵר I $37.0.13$ n.f.—cstr. בְּאֵר; sf. בְּאֵרֶךָ; pl. בְּאֵרֹת (בארות Q, בירות Q)—**1. well** Gn 26_{18}. **2. pit** Ps 55_{24}. **3. cistern** 2 S 17_{19}.

[בְּאֵר] II 2 pl.n. **Beer.**

בְּאֹר, see בּוֹר I *pit*.

בְּאֵר אֵילִים 1 pl.n. **Beer-elim.**

בְּאֵרָא 1 pr.n.m. **Beera.**

בְּאֵרָה 1 pr.n.m. **Beerah.**

בְּאֵרוֹת 5 pl.n. **Beeroth.**

בְּאֵרִי 2 pr.n.m. **Beeri.**

*[**בְּאֵרַיִם**] 0.0.0.1 pl.n. **Beeraim.**

בְּאֵר לַחַי רֹאִי 3 pl.n. **Beer-lahai-roi.**

בְּאֵר שֶׁבַע 34.0.1.1 pl.n. **Beer-sheba.**

בְּאֵרֹת, see בְּאֵרוֹת *Beeroth.*

בְּאֵרֹת בְּנֵי־יַעֲקָן 1 pl.n. **Beeroth Bene-jaakan.**

בְּאֵרֹתִי 6 gent. **Beerothite.**

באשׁ I 20.1.1 vb.—**Qal** 7.1.1 Impf. תִּבְאַשׁ; ptc. pass. בְּאֻשִׁים —**1. stink,** of water, food, etc. Ex 16_{20}. **2.** pass. ptc. pl. as noun, **stinking (ones),** of fruit Is 5_{2}.

Ni. 3 Pf. נִבְאַשׁ—**be odious, make oneself odious** 2 S 16_{21}.

Hi. 9 Pf. הִבְאַשְׁתֶּם; impf. יַבְאִישׁ—**1. make odious,** obj. person Gn 34_{30} (+ בְּ *to*), smell Ex 5_{21} (+ בְּעֵינֵי *in the sight of*). **b. make oneself odious** 1 S 27_{12} (+ בְּ *to*). **2. stink, fester,** of food Ex 16_{24}, wound Ps 38_{6}.

Htp. 1 Pf. הִתְבָּאֲשׁוּ—**be odious, make oneself odious** 1 C 19_{6}.

→ בְּאֹשׁ *stink,* בָּאְשָׁה *stinkweed.*

***באשׁ** II 1 vb.—**Hi.** 1 Impf. יַבְאִישׁ—**act humbly** Pr 13_{5}.

[**בְּאֹשׁ**] 3 n.m.—cstr. בְּאֹשׁ; sf. בָּאְשׁוֹ—**stink** Am 4_{10}. → באשׁ *stink.*

בָּאְשָׁה 1 n.f. **stinkweed** Jb 31_{40}. → באשׁ *stink.*

בַּאֲשֶׁר, see אֲשֶׁר *which, that, who.*

[**בָּבָה**] 1 n.f.—cstr. בָּבַת—**apple, pupil** of eye Zc 2_{12}.

בֵּבַי 6 pr.n.m. **Bebai.**

בָּבֶל 261.0.10 pl.n. **Babylon.**

***בַּג** 1 n.[m.] **share** Ezk 25_{7}.

בגד 49.2.14 vb.—**Qal** 49.2.14 Pf. בָּגְדָה; impf. יִבְגֹּד, תִּבְגְּדוּ; ptc. בֹּגֵד, בֹּגֵדָה, בֹּגְדִים, בֹּגְדֵי; inf. abs. בָּגוֹד; cstr. בְּגֹד (בְּגְדוֹ)—**1. betray,** with בְּ of obj. Y. Ho 5_{7}, human Jg 9_{23}. **2.** ptc. as noun, **traitor** Si $16_{4(B)}$. → בֶּגֶד II *treachery,* בָּגוֹד *treacherous,* בֹּגְדָה *treachery.*

*[**בָּגָד**] 0.0.0.1 pr.n.[m.] **Bagad.**

בֶּגֶד I 215.8.42.3 n.m.—בֶּגֶד; cstr. בֶּגֶד; sf. בִּגְדִי; pl. בְּגָדִים; cstr. בִּגְדֵי; sf. בְּגָדַי, בִּגְדֵיכֶם—**garment** of linen Gn 41_{42}, mourning 2 S 14_{2}, salvation Is 61_{10}; **cloth,** as cover of tabernacle Nm 4_{6}.

בֶּגֶד II 2 n.[m.] **treachery** Is 24_{16} Jr 12_{1}. → בגד *betray.*

[**בֹּגְדָה**] 1 n.f.—pl. בֹּגְדוֹת—**treachery** Zp 3_{4}. → בגד *betray.*

[**בָּגוֹד**] 2 adj.—f.s. בָּגוֹדָה—**treacherous** Jr $3_{7.10}$. → בגד *betray.*

בִּגְוַי 5 pr.n.m. **Bigvai.**

בִּגְלַל 10.4.2 part.—sf. בִּגְלָלֵךְ, בִּגְלַלְכֶם—**on account (of)** Dt 15_{10}. → cf. בְּ *in.*

בִּגְתָא 1 pr.n.m. **Bigtha.**

בִּגְתָן 2 pr.n.m. **Bigthan.**

בִּגְתָנָא, see בִּגְתָן.

בַּד I 23.0.5 n.[m.]—pl. בַּדִּים—**linen, linen garment** Lv 16_{23}.

בַּד II 45.0.3 n.m.—pl. בַּדִּים (Q בדין); cstr. בַּדֵּי; sf. בַּדָּיו—**1. part, proportion** of spices Ex 30_{34}. **2. limb** of body Jb 18_{13}. **3. branch** of vine Ezk 17_{6}. **4. pole** for carrying ark Nm 4_{6}, table Ex 35_{13}. **5. bar** of Sheol Jb 17_{16}.

[**בַּד**] III 5 n.m.—pl. בַּדִּים; sf. בַּדָּיו—**1. boast, prattle** Is 16_{6} Jr 48_{30} Jb 11_{3}. **2. boaster, prattler,** perh. specif. **diviner** Jr 50_{36}.

בַּד IV, see לְבַד *alone, besides.*

בַּד V 2 n.[m.]—pl. בַּדִּים—**diviner** Is 44_{25}.

***בַּד** VI 3 n.[m.]—pl. בַּדִּים—**power** of Moab Is 16_{6}, Leviathan Jb 41_{4}.

בדא 2 vb.—**Qal** 2 Pf. בָּדָא; ptc. sf. בּוֹדָאם—**devise** things out of (מִן) one's own mind Ne 6_{8}.

בדד I 3.1 vb.—**Qal** 3.1 Ptc. בּוֹדֵד—**be alone, be separate,** of person Si 12_{9}, animal Ho 8_{9}. → בַּד II *part,* בָּדָד *solitude.*

***בדד** II 1 vb.—**Qal** 1 Ptc. בּוֹדֵד—**moan,** of bird Ps 102_{8}.

בָּדָד 11.0.4 n.[m.] **solitude,** oft. with שׁכן *dwell,* **1.** with prep., לְבָדָד **in solitude, alone** Mc 7_{14}. **2.** as adv., **in solitude, alone** Lv 13_{46}. → בדד I *be alone.*

בְּדַד 2 pr.n.m. **Bedad.**

[**בְּדָיָה**], see בְּדָיָהוּ *Bedaiah.*

בֵּדְיָה 1 pr.n.m. **Bedeiah.**

*[**בְּדָיָהוּ**] 0.0.0.3 pr.n.m. **Bedaiah.**

[**בְּדְיוֹ**], see בְּדָיָהוּ *Bedaiah.*

*[**בְּדִיחֶבֶל**] 0.0.0.3 pr.n.[m.] **Badichebel.**

בְּדִיל 6.0.1 n.[m.]—pl. sf. בְּדִילָיִךְ—**tin,** representative of **alloy** produced in refining silver Is 1_{25}, used as plummet Zc 4_{10}; perh. **antinomy** Ezk 22_{18}. → בדל *be separate.*

בדל 42.2.55 vb.—**Ni.** 10.1.14 Pf. נִבְדְּלוּ; impf. יִבָּדֵל; impv.

הִבָּדְלוּ; ptc. נִבְדָּל; inf. Q הבדל—**be separated, separate oneself, withdraw** from (מִן) others Ezr 9_1, uncleanness Ezr 6_{21}; **defect to** (אֶל) someone 1 C 12_9.

Hi. 32.1.32 Pf. הִבְדַּלְתִּי, הִבְדִּיל; impf. יַבְדִּיל; + waw וַיַּבְדֵּל; ptc. מַבְדִּיל; inf. abs. הַבְדֵּל; cstr. הַבְדִּיל—**1. separate, make a separation, distinguish between** (בֵּין ... וּבֵין) one thing and another Gn 1_4 Lv 11_{47}; of iniquities separating between (בֵּין ... לְבֵין) people and Y. Is 59_2. **2. separate, set apart** people Lv 20_{24} (+ מִן *from*) Nm 8_{14} (+ מִתּוֹךְ *from among*), cities Dt 4_{41}. **3. sever** bird offered in sacrifice Lv 1_{17}.

Ho. 0.0.9 Pf. Q הובדל—**be separated** from (מִן) community meal 1QS 7_3.

→ בָּדָל *piece*, מִבְדָּלָה *enclave*.

[בָּדָל] 1 n.[m.]—cstr. בְּדַל—**piece** of an ear Am 3_{12}. → בדל *be separate*.

בְּדֹלַח 2 n.[m.] **bdellium**, an aromatic gum Gn 2_{12}.

בְּדָן I 2 pr.n.m. **Bedan**.

*[בְּדָן] II 0.0.15 n.[m.]—pl. cstr. בדני (אבדני)—**form, figure, decoration**, בדני להבת אש *forms of flames of fire* 4QShirShabb[d] 1.2_9, בדני אלוהים *figures of gods* 4QShirShabb[f] 14.1_6, בדני ריקמה *variegated decorations* 1QM 5_9.

בדק I 1 vb.—**Qal** 1 Inf. בְּדוֹק—**repair** temple 2 C 34_{10}. → בֶּדֶק *breach*.

*בדק II 1 vb.—**Qal** 1 Inf. בְּדוֹק—**examine** temple 2 C 34_{10}.

[בֶּדֶק] 10 n.m.—cstr. בֶּדֶק; sf. בִּדְקֵךְ—**breach**, in temple 2 K 12_6, ship Ezk 27_9. → בדק I *repair*.

בִּדְקַר 1 pr.n.m. **Bidkar**.

בֹּהוּ 3.0.1 n.[m.] **emptiness**, תֹּהוּ וָבֹהוּ *formlessness and emptiness* Gn 1_2, אַבְנֵי בֹהוּ *stones*, i.e. plummets, *of emptiness* Is 34_{11}.

[בְּהוֹן], see בֹּהֶן *thumb, big toe*.

בַּהַט 1 n.[m.] **porphyry**, or other precious stone Est 1_6.

בָּהִיר 1 adj. **bright**, or perh. **obscured**, בָּהִיר הוּא בַּשְּׁחָקִים *it* (light of sun) *is bright in*, or *obscured by*, *the clouds* Jb 37_{21}.

בהל 39.0.5 vb.—**Ni.** 24.0.2 Pf. נִבְהֲלָה; impf. תִּבָּהֵל; ptc. נִבְהָל, נִבְהָלָה—**1a. be dismayed, feel panic**, in defeat, etc., by (בְּ) Y.'s wrath Ps 90_7, at presence of (מִפְּנֵי) person Gn 45_3. **b.** ptc. as adj., (1) **terrified**, of person Ps 30_8. (2) **terrifying**, of destruction Zp 1_{18}. **2. tremble**, of part of body Ezk 7_{27}. **3. be in haste, hasten, a.** from presence of (מִפְּנֵי) person Ec 8_3. **b. after** (לְ) wealth Pr 28_{22}.

Pi. 10 Impf. יְבַהֲלֻהוּ; ptc. מְבַהֲלִים; inf. בַּהֲלָם—**1. terrify** someone, subj. Y. Ps 2_5, people Ezr $4_{4(Qr)}$, dread Jb 22_{10}, report Dn 11_{44}. **2a. be in haste** to speak Ec 5_1, to give Est 2_9, to become angry Ec 7_9. **b. hasten** someone 2 C 35_{21}.

Pu. 2 Ptc. מְבֹהָלִים—**1. be in haste**, of runner Est 8_{14}. **2. be gained in haste**, of inheritance Pr $20_{21(Qr)}$.

Hi. 3 Pf. הִבְהִילֻנִי; + waw וַיַּבְהִלוּ—**1. terrify** someone Jb 23_{16}. **2. hasten** someone 2 C 26_{20}.

Htp. 0.0.3 Impf. יתבהלו; ptc. מתבהלת—**1. be eager** to suckle 4QTNaph $1_{5.5}$. **2. hasten**, of days 4QpsEzek[a] 3_1.

→ בֶּהָלָה *dismay*.

בֶּהָלָה 4.0.1 n.f.—Sam בחלה; pl. בֶּהָלוֹת—**dismay, terror**, usu. as punishment from Y. Lv 26_{16}. → בהל *dismay*.

בְּהֵמָה 190.1.25 n.f.—cstr. בֶּהֱמַת; sf. בְּהֶמְתּוֹ; pl. בְּהֵמוֹת; cstr. בַּהֲמוֹת—**beast**, (non-human) **animal**, oft. coll., as distinct from birds, fish, creeping animals, and also from humans Gn 1_{26} 1 K 5_{13}; as livestock Nm 3_{41}, beast of burden Ne 2_{12}, food Dt 14_4, sacrifice Gn 8_{20}; בֶּהֱמַת הָאָרֶץ *beast(s) of the earth* Dt 28_{26}, בַּהֲמוֹת שָׂדֶה *beasts of (the) field* Jl 1_{20}, יַעַר *of (the) forest* Mc 5_7. → cf. בְּהֵמוֹת *Behemoth*.

בְּהֵמוֹת 1 pr.n.m. **Behemoth**, 'the beast', i.e. prob. **hippopotamus** Jb 40_{15}. → cf. בְּהֵמָה *beast*.

[בֹּהֶן] 16.0.1 n.[f.]—Q בוהן; cstr. בֹּהֶן; pl. בְּהֹנוֹת—**thumb, big toe**, בֹּהֶן יָדוֹ *thumb of his hand* Lv 8_{23}, בֹּהֶן רַגְלוֹ *big toe of his foot* Lv 8_{23}.

בֹּהַן 2 pr.n.m. **Bohan**.

בֹּהַק 1 n.m. **lesion** on skin Lv 13_{39}.

*[בהר] vb.—**shine, Hi., illuminate**, of woman Ca 8_5 (if em. מִן־הַמִּדְבָּר *from the desert* to מַבְהִירָה *illuminate*). → בָּהִיר *bright*, בַּהֶרֶת *spot*.

בַּהֶרֶת 12 n.f.—pl. בֶּהָרֹת—**spot** on skin Lv 13_2. → בהר *shine*.

בוא 2565.10.357.6 vb.—**Qal** 1992.5.277.6 Pf. בָּא, בָּאתָ; impf. יָבוֹא; impv. בֹּא, בֹּאִי, בֹּאוּ; ptc. בָּא, בָּאִים, בָּאוֹת; inf. בּוֹא (בֹּאִי)—**1.** usu. **come**, of person Gn 16_8, Y. in theophany Ex 19$_{9}$, prayer before Y. Ps 88$_{3}$, pain to a person Is 66$_{7}$, glory Is 60$_{13}$; also **come back** Gn 8$_{11}$ Jg 19$_{26}$. **2.** oft. appar. **go,** אַנְשֵׁי הַצָּבָא הַבָּאִים לַמִּלְחָמָה *men of war who had gone to battle* Nm 31$_{21}$, אֳנִיָּה בָּאָה תַרְשִׁישׁ *a ship going to Tarshish* Jon 1$_{3(mss)}$; sometimes **go away** Jg 6$_{19}$. **3. come in, enter** a place Jos 6$_{1}$; **penetrate** a woman, i.e. have sexual relations with her Gn 6$_{4}$; **come into** days, i.e. be advanced in age Gn 24$_{1}$. **4.** of event, prophecy, promise, sign, wonder, etc., **come about, come to pass** Dt 13$_{3}$ Jos 21$_{45}$; of disaster, **come upon, befall** Jb 21$_{17}$. **5.** of inanimate thing, **be brought** Gn 43$_{23}$. **6.** of sun, **set** Jos 8$_{29}$. **7.** in ref. to inception of action, hence, **begin,** וַיָּבֹא אַבְרָהָם לִסְפֹּד לְשָׂרָה *and Abraham began to mourn for Sarah* Gn 23$_{2}$. Preps.: בְּ *with* weapons 1 S 17$_{45}$, desire Dt 18$_{6}$, weeping, Jr 31$_{9}$; כְּ *as, like* thief Jl 2$_{9}$, bird Pr 26$_{2}$, rain Ho 6$_{3}$; לְ *to* person 2 S 12$_{4}$, place 1 S 9$_{12}$; אֶל *to, into* Y. Gn 18$_{21}$, person Jr 40$_{10}$, place Ru 4$_{11}$; עַד *unto* Y. Is 45$_{24}$, person 1 K 2$_{28}$, place Nm 13$_{23}$; עַל *against* person 2 S 17$_{12}$; מִן *from* person 2 C 19$_{10}$, place Is 49$_{12}$; עִם *with* person Est 5$_{14}$; אֵת *with* person Ca 4$_{8}$; אַחֲרֵי *after* person Ec 2$_{12}$; לִפְנֵי *before, in the presence of* Y. Ps 88$_{3}$, person Nm 27$_{17}$; ה- of direction, *to* place 2 S 24$_{6}$.

Hi. 549.5.73 Pf. הֵבִיא, הֵבֵאתָ; impf. יָבִיא; + waw וַיָּבֵא; impv. הָבֵא, הָבִיאָה, הָבִיאִי, הָבִיאוּ; ptc. מֵבִיא, מְבִיאִים; inf. הָבִיא (הֲבִיאָם)—**1. bring (near)** person Gn 39$_{14}$, food 1 K 17$_{6}$, garment Est 6$_{8}$, knowledge 1QS 1$_{11}$. **2. bring (in)** person Ca 2$_{4}$, animal Gn 6$_{10}$, tithe Ml 3$_{10}$. **3. cause** sun **to set** Am 8$_{9}$. **4. bring about** a state of affairs Jr 40$_{3}$. Preps.: לְ *to* Y. Lv 2$_{8}$, person Ezr 8$_{17}$, *(in)to* place Jl 4$_{5}$; אֶל *to* Y. Ex 18$_{19}$, person Jos 7$_{23}$, *(in)to* place Gn 29$_{13}$; עַל *upon, against* person Ezk 29$_{8}$; bring about *for* person Gn 18$_{19}$; מִן *from* place Ezr 3$_{7}$; ה- of direction, *to* place 1 S 5$_{1}$.

Ho. 24.0.7 Pf. הוּבָא; impf. יוּבָא; ptc. מוּבָא, מוּבָאִים, מוּבָאוֹת—**1. be brought (near),** of person Lv 14$_{2}$ (+ אֶל *to* person) Jr 27$_{22}$ (+ בָּבֶלָה *to Babylon*) Ps 45$_{15}$ (+ לְ *to* person), thing Gn 33$_{11}$ (+ לְ *to* person). **2. be brought (in),** of money 2 C 34$_{9}$ (+ בֵּית־אֱלֹהִים *[into] the house of God*). **3. be put into** (בְּ) something Ex 27$_{7}$.

→ בִּאָה *entrance,* מָבוֹא *entrance,* מוּבָא *entrance,* תְּבוּאָה *produce.*

*בּוֹגְדִים 1 n.m. **fraud** Pr 23$_{28}$.

בוז 14.2.7 vb.—**Qal** 14.2.7 Pf. בַּז, בָּזָה, בָּזוּ; impf. יָבוּז; ptc. בָּז; inf. בּוֹז—**despise, scorn, belittle, a.** with accus. person Pr 23$_{22}$, wisdom, discipline Pr 1$_{7}$. **b.** with לְ of obj. person 2 K 19$_{21}$. → בּוּז *contempt,* בּוּזָה *contempt.*

בּוּז I 11.1.9 n.m.—cstr. בּוּז—**contempt,** הַבּוּז לִגְאֵיוֹנִים *the contempt of the proud* Ps 123$_{4}$. → בוז *despise.*

בּוּז II 2 pr.n.m. **Buz.**

בּוּז III 1 pl.n. **Buz.**

בּוּזָה 1 n.[f.] **(object of) contempt** Ne 3$_{36}$. → בוז *despise.*

בּוּזִי I 1.0.0.1 pr.n.m. **Buzi.**

בּוּזִי II 2 gent. **Buzite.**

*[בּוֹט] 0.0.0.1 pr.n.[m.] **Bot.**

בַּוַּי 1 pr.n.m. **Bavvai.**

בוך 3 vb.—**Ni.** 3 Pf. נָבוֹכָה; ptc. נְבֻכִים—**be confused, dumbfounded, pressed, distressed,** of person Ex 14$_{3}$, animal Jl 1$_{18}$. → מְבוּכָה *confusion.*

בּוּל I 2 n.[m.]—cstr. בּוּל—**1. produce** Jb 40$_{20}$ (unless §2). **2. tribute,** or perh. **beasts** Jb 40$_{20}$. **3. block, lump** Is 44$_{19}$.

בּוּל II 1 n.[m.] **Bul,** in Canaanite calendar, month of autumn rains 1 K 6$_{38}$.

*[בּוּן] 0.0.0.1 pr.n.[m.] **Bun.**

בּוּנָה 1 pr.n.m. **Bunah.**

בּוּנִי, see בֻּנִּי *Bunni.*

בוס 12 vb.—**Qal** 7 Impf. יָבוּס; ptc. בּוֹסִים—**trample** someone, of Y. Is 63$_{6}$, warrior Zc 10$_{5}$.

Pol. 2 Pf. בּוֹסְסוּ—**trample** sanctuary Is 63$_{18}$, field Jr 12$_{10}$.

Ho. 1 Ptc. מוּבָס—**be trampled,** of corpse Is 14$_{19}$.

Htpol. 2 Ptc. מִתְבּוֹסֶסֶת—**be drenched** with (בְּ) blood, of Jerusalem Ezk 16$_{6}$.

→ מְבוּסָה *subjugation,* תְּבוּסָה *downfall.*

*בוע 0.0.1 vb.—**Hi.** 0.0.1 Impf. יַבִּיעוּ—**spring forth** 1QH 16$_{18}$.

*[בּוֹעַ] 0.0.0.1 pr.n.[m.] **Boa.**

*בוץ vb.—**Qal, run ahead,** of messengers Ezk 30$_{9}$ (if em. בַּצִּים *in ships* to בָּצִים *running ahead*).

בּוּץ 8 n.[m.]—בֻּץ—**byssus, fine linen** Est 8$_{15}$.

בּוֹצֵץ 1 pl.n. **Bozez.**

בוקא, see בּוּקָה *emptiness.*

בוקה 1.0.1 n.f.—Q בוקא—appar. **emptiness** Na 2:11. → cf. מְבוּקָה *void.*

בור 1 vb.—**Qal** 1 Inf. בּוּר—**explain** something, of heart Ec 9:1.

בּוֹר 70.0.17 n.m.—בּר (בּאר); pl. בֹּרוֹת—**1. pit, hole** Gn 37:20 Ex 21:33; מַקֶּבֶת בּוֹר *excavation of a pit,* i.e. quarry Is 51:1. **2. cistern, well** Lv 11:36 Dt 6:11. **3. pit, dungeon,** בֵּית הַבּוֹר *house of the dungeon* Ex 12:29. **4. grave, underworld,** esp. for wicked Is 14:15; מעמקי בור *depths of (the) underworld* 4QWiles 1:6.

בּוֹר הַסִּרָה 1 pl.n. **Borsirah.**

*****[**בּוֹרִין**] 1 n.[m.]—sf. בּוֹרֶיךָ—**health** Ec 12:1.

בּוֹר־עָשָׁן 1 pl.n. **Borashan.**

בוש I 128.12.4 vb.—**Qal** 95.10.3 Pf. בּוֹשׁ, בֹּשְׁתִּי, בֹּושׁוּ; impf. יֵבוֹשׁ, יֵבֹשׁוּ; impv. בּוֹשִׁי, בֹּושׁוּ; ptc. בּוֹשִׁים; inf. בּוֹשׁ—**1a.** abs., **be ashamed, be put to shame, feel shame** Is 49:23 Jr 6:15; עַד־בֹּשׁ *until shame was felt,* i.e. to the point of embarrassment 2 K 8:11. **b.** with accus. בֹּשֶׁת, **be utterly put to shame** Is 42:17. **2. be ashamed of, be put to shame through** someone or something, with מִן Is 1:29 Si 41:17; בְּ Ps 69:7. **3.** with inf., **be ashamed** to do something Ezr 8:22.

Pi. 0.1 Impf. חבייש—**dishonour** old person Si 8:6.

Pol. 2 Pf. בֹּשֵׁשׁ—**be delayed,** of person Ex 32:1, chariot Jg 5:28.

Hi. A 11.1.1 Pf. הֱבִישׁוֹתָ; impf. תְּבִישֵׁנִי; ptc. מֵבִישׁ, מְבִישָׁה—**1. put to shame, bring shame to** someone Pr 29:15; let someone **be put to shame** Ps 119:31. **2. act shamefully** Pr 17:2.

Hi. B 19 (unless from יבשׁ II) Pf. הֹבִישׁ, הֹבַשְׁתָּ; impv. הֹבִישׁוּ—**1.** as Qal, **be ashamed, be put to shame** Jr 8:9. **2. act shamefully** Ho 2:7. **3.** of joy, **fail** from (מִן) humans Jl 1:12. **4. put to shame** 2 S 19:6.

Htpol. 1 Impf. יִתְבֹּשָׁשׁוּ—appar. **be ashamed of one another** Gn 2:25.

→ בּוּשָׁה I *shame,* בַּיִשׁ *decorous,* בָּשְׁנָה *shame,* בֹּשֶׁת *shame,* מְבוּשִׁים *genitals.*

* **בוש** II vb. **Qal, scatter,** וַיּוֹחִילוּ עַד־בּוֹשׁ *and they waited until (their wits) were scattered* Jg 3:25 (if em. וַיָּחִילוּ *and they writhed*).

* **בוש** III 2 vb.—**Pol.** 2 Pf. בֹּשֵׁשׁ—**be slow, hesitant,** of person Ex 32:1, chariot Jg 5:28.

בּוּשָׁה I 4 n.f. **shame** Ezk 7:18. → בושׁ *be ashamed.*

* **בּוּשָׁה** II 1 n.f. **dryness** Ps 89:46.

בַּז 24.0.5 n.[m.]—sf. בִּזָּהּ—**spoil** Is 10:6. → בזז *plunder.*

בזא 2 vb.—**Qal** 2 Pf. בָּזְאוּ—**divide,** or **wash away** land, of river Is 18:2.

*[**בָּזָא**] I 0.0.1 n.m.—pl. cstr. בזאי—**mockery** 1QH 16:14.

בזה 43.5.9 vb.—**Qal** 32.5.7 Pf. בָּזָה (Q בזא), בָּזִינוּ; impf. תִּבְזֶה (Si חבז); + waw וַיִּבֶז; ptc. בּוֹזֶה; pass. בְּזוּי—**1a. despise** (accus.) Y. 2 S 12:10, person 1 S 17:42, word of Y. Nm 15:31, holiness Ezk 22:8, request Si 4:4. **b. feel contempt for** (לְ) someone 2 S 6:16||1 C 15:29. **2.** pass., **be despised,** of person Ps 22:7 (בְּזוּי עָם *despised of,* i.e. by, *people*), wisdom Ec 9:16.

Ni. 10.0.1 Ptc. נִבְזֶה; inf. הִבָּזוֹת—**be despised, contemptible,** of person Is 53:3, food Ml 1:12.

Hi. 1.0.1 Inf. הַבְזוֹת—**demean** someone Est 1:17 CD 9:4.

→ בִּזָּיוֹן *contempt.*

בִּזָּה 10 n.f. **booty** Dn 11:24. → בזז *plunder.*

בזז 43.0.3 vb.—**Qal** 39.0.3 Pf. בָּזַזְנוּ (בָּזוֹנוּ); impf. יָבֹזּוּ; impv. בֹּזּוּ; ptc. בֹּזְזִים; pass. בְּזוּזִ; inf. בֹּז—**1. plunder** people Is 17:14, city Gn 34:27. **2a. take as spoil** persons and livestock Dt 20:14, silver and gold Na 2:10. **b.** with accus. בַּז, **take spoil** Is 33:23. **3.** pass., **be plundered,** of people Is 42:22. **4.** inf. as noun, **spoil** Est 3:13.

Ni. 3 Impf. תִּבּוֹז; + waw וְנָבֹזּוּ—**be plundered, despoiled,** of earth Is 24:3, fortress Am 3:11.

Pu. 1 (or **Qal pass.**) Pf. בֻּזָּזוּ—**be plundered,** of treasure Jr 50:37.

→ בַּז *booty,* בִּזָּה *booty.*

בִּזָּיוֹן 1 n.[m.] **contempt** Est 1:18. → בזה *despise.*

בִּזְיוֹתְיָה 1 pl.n. **Biziothiah.**

בָּזָק 1 n.[m.] **lightning** Ezk 1:14.

בֶּזֶק 3 pl.n. **Bezek.**

בזר 2.0.3 vb.—**Qal** 1 Impf. יִבְזוֹר—**scatter** spoil, wealth Dn 11:24.

Pi. 1.0.3 Pf. בִּזַּר—of Y., **scatter** people Ps 68:31.

→ cf. פזר I *scatter.*

בִּזְּתָא 1 pr.n.m. **Biztha.**

בָּחוֹן 1 n.[m.] **assayer,** or perh. **watchtower** Jr 6:27. → בחן *test.*

[**בַּחוּן**] 1 n.m.—sf. Qr בַּחוּנָיו (Kt בחיניו)—**watchtower,** or siege tower Is 23$_{13}$. → cf. בַּחַן *watchtower*, בֹּחַן II *fortress*.

בָּחוּר 48.1 n.m.—pl. בַּחוּרִים; cstr. בַּחוּרֵי; sf. בַּחוּרֵי—**young man** (distinction from בָּחוּר [pass. ptc. of בחר] *chosen one* not alw. clear; cf. Ps 89$_{20}$), בַּחוּרֵי יִשְׂרָאֵל *young men of Israel* Ps 78$_{31}$, חֶמֶד *of*, i.e. who evoke, *desire* Ezk 23$_6$. → בחר I *choose*.

[בְּחוּרוֹת], see בְּחוּרִים *youth*.

בַּחוּרִים 5 pl.n. **Bahurim.**

[בְּחוּרִים] 3 n.m.pl.—sf. בְּחוּרוֹתֶךָ; בְּחֻרָיו—**youth** Ec 11$_9$. → בחר I *choose*.

[בַּחוּרְמִי], see בַּחֲרוּמִי *Baharumite*.

[בַּחִין], see בַּחוּן *watchtower*.

בָּחִיר 13.1.32 n.m.—cstr. בְּחִיר; sf. בְּחִירִי; pl. sf. בְּחִירָיו—**elect, chosen,** alw. by Y., בְּחִיר יי *elect of Y.* 2 S 21$_6$, בחירי אל *chosen ones of God* 1QpHab 10$_{13}$, שמים *of heaven* 1QM 12$_5$, ישראל *of Israel* CD 4$_3$. → בחר I *choose*.

בחל I 1 vb.—**Qal** 1 Pf. בָּחֲלָה—**reject, abhor** (בְּ of obj.) someone Zc 11$_8$.

***בחל** II 1 vb.—**Pu.** 1 Ptc. Kt מבחלת—appar. **be gained by greed,** of inheritance Pr 20$_{21(Kt)}$ (Qr בהל pu. *be gained in haste*).

[בַּחָלָה], see בֶּהָלָה *dismay, terror*.

בחן 29.1.25 vb.—**Qal** 25.1.21 Pf. בָּחַנְתָּ; impf. יִבְחַן, יִבְחָנוּ; impv. בְּחָנֵנִי, בְּחָנוּנִי; ptc. בֹּחֵן; inf. בְּחֹן—**1.** of Y., **test, examine** person Ps 26$_2$, heart, mind Jr 11$_{20}$. **2.** of person, **a. test, tempt** Y. Ps 95$_9$. **b. test** metal **by melting** Zc 13$_9$. **3.** of ear, **test, try** words Jb 12$_{11}$.

Ni. 3.0.4 Impf. יִבָּחֲנוּ—**be tested,** of person Jb 34$_{36}$ 1QS 9$_2$, word Gn 42$_{16}$.

Pu. 1 Pf. בֹּחַן—**be tested,** perh. of sword Ezk 21$_{18}$. → בֹּחַן I *testing*, בָּחוֹן *assayer*.

בַּחַן 1 n.[m.] **watchtower** Is 32$_{14}$. → cf. בַּחוּן *watchtower*, בֹּחַן II *fortress*.

בֹּחַן I 1.0.3 n.[m.] **testing,** אֶבֶן בֹּחַן *stone of testing* Is 28$_{16}$. → בחן *test*.

***בֹּחַן** II 1.0.3 n.[m.] **fortress,** אֶבֶן בֹּחַן *stone of a fortress*, i.e. massive stone Is 28$_{16}$, חומת הבחן *wall of the fortress* 1QS 8$_7$. → cf. בַּחוּן *watchtower*, בַּחַן *watchtower*.

***בֹּחַן** III 1.0.3 n.[m.] **granite,** אֶבֶן בֹּחַן *stone of granite* Is 28$_{16}$.

בחר I 172.9.74 vb.—**Qal** 164.5.73 Pf. בָּחַר; impf. יִבְחַר; impv. בְּחַר, בַּחֲרוּ; ptc. בֹּחֵר; pass. בָּחוּר, בְּחוּרֵי; inf. abs. בָּחוֹר; cstr. בְּחֹר—**1.** with either accus. or בְּ of obj., **a.** subj. Y., **choose, elect** Abram Ne 9$_7$, David 1 S 10$_{24}$, Israel Dt 7$_7$, place for his sanctuary Dt 12$_5$ (+ מִן *from among* tribes). **b.** subj. humans, **choose** Y. Jos 24$_{22}$, precepts of Y. Ps 119$_{173}$, king 1 S 12$_{13}$, life Dt 30$_{19}$, good Is 7$_{15}$. **2a.** subj. Y., **test, try** his people Is 48$_{10(MT)}$ (1QIsa[a] בחן *test*). **b.** subj. humans, **test, discern (for oneself)** what is right Jb 34$_4$. **3.** pass. **be chosen,** of chariotry Ex 14$_7$, warrior Jg 20$_{15}$; בְּחוּרֵי יִשְׂרָאֵל *chosen ones of Israel* 2 S 10$_{9(Qr)}$.

Ni. 7.4.1 Pf. נִבְחַר—**be chosen,** of person Si 34$_{16}$, gold Pr 8$_{10}$, death Jr 8$_3$ (+ מִן *more than* life).

Pu. 1 Impf. Kt יבחר (unless ni.)—**be chosen,** of person Ec 9$_{4(Kt)}$ (Qr חבר pu. *be joined*).

→ בָּחוּר *youth*, בְּחוּרִים *youth*, בָּחִיר *elect*, מִבְחָר *choice*, מִבְחוֹר *choice*.

***בחר** II 2 vb.—**Qal** 1 Ptc. בֹּחֵר—**associate** with (לְ) someone 1 S 20$_{30}$.

Pu. 1 Impf. יְבֻחַר—**be joined** to (אֶל) the living Ec 9$_4$.

***בחר** III 1 vb.—**Ni.** 1 Ptc. נִבְחָר—**be refined,** of silver Pr 10$_{20}$.

Pu., be tested, עַל־זֶה בֻּחַרְתָּ מֵעֹנִי *for this reason you have been tested by affliction* Jb 36$_{21}$ (if em. בָּחַרְתָּ *you have chosen*).

בַּחֲרוּמִי 1 gent. **Baharumite.**

בטא 3.1 vb.—**Qal** 1.1 Ptc. בּוֹטֶה—**speak impetuously** Ps 12$_{18}$ Si 5$_{13(A)}$.

Pi. 2 + waw וַיְבַטֵּא; inf. בַּטֵּא—**speak impetuously** Lv 5$_4$ Ps 106$_{33}$.

→ מִבְטָא *impetuous utterance*.

בטה, see בטא *speak impetuously*.

בטח I 120.12.11 vb.—**Qal** 115.10.10 Pf. בָּטַח, בָּטַחְתִּי; impf. יִבְטַח; impv. בְּטַח, בִּטְחוּ; ptc. בֹּטֵחַ, בֹּטְחִים; ptc. pass. בָּטוּחַ; inf. abs. בָּטוֹחַ; cstr. בְּטֹחַ (בִּטְחֵךְ)—**1. trust** in (בְּ) Y. Zp 3$_2$, human Jr 46$_{25}$, one's heart Pr 28$_{26}$, wealth Pr 11$_{28}$; in (אֶל) Y. 2 K 18$_{22}$, humans Jg 20$_{36}$, words Jr 7$_4$; in (עַל) Y. Ps 31$_{15}$, human Jr 9$_3$, wealth Ps 49$_7$. **2.** abs., **have confidence,** of humans Pr 28$_1$, Behemoth Jb 40$_{23}$.

Hi. 5.2.1 Pf. הִבְטַחְתַּ; impf. יַבְטַח; ptc. מַבְטִיחִי—**1. cause**

someone **to trust** in (אֶל) Y. 2 K 18₃₀||Is 36₁₅; in (עַל) falsehood Jr 28₁₅. **2. inspire** someone **with confidence** Ps 22₁₀.

→ בֶּטַח *security,* בִּטְחָה *confidence,* בִּטָּחוֹן *confidence,* בַּטֻּחוֹת *security,* מִבְטָח *trust,* מִבְטָחָה *confidence.*

*בטח II ₃ vb.—**Qal** ₂ Impf. יִבְטַח; ptc. בּוֹטֵחַ—**1. fall down,** of person Jr 12₅. **2. lie down,** of Behemoth Jb 40₂₃.

Hi. ₁ Ptc. מַבְטִיחִי—of Y., **lay** child on (עַל) mother's breasts Ps 22₁₀.

בֶּטַח I ₄₂.₁.₆ n.[m.] **security** Lv 25₁₈. → בטח I *trust.*

בֶּטַח II ₁ pl.n. **Betah.**

בִּטְחָה ₁ n.f. **confidence** Is 30₁₅. → בטח I *trust.*

[בַּטֻּחָה] I ₁ n.f.—pl. בַּטֻּחוֹת—**retreat** Jb 12₆.

* [בַּטֻּחָה] II ₁ n.f.—pl. בַּטֻּחוֹת—**valley** Jb 12₆.

בִּטָּחוֹן ₃ n.m. **confidence** 2 K 18₁₉||Is 36₄, perh. **hope** for the living Ec 9₄. → בטח I *trust.*

בַּטֻּחוֹת ₁ n.f. **security** Jb 12₆. → בטח I *trust.*

בטל ₁ vb.—**Qal** ₁ Pf. בָּטְלוּ—**be idle, cease,** of teeth Ec 12₃.

*[בטן] vb. **Pi., be pregnant,** מִלֵּדָה וּמִבֶּטֶן וּמֵהֵרָיוֹן *without birth, without pregnancy, without conception* Ho 9₁₁ (if em. מִבֶּטֶן *without womb*). → בֶּטֶן I *womb.*

בֶּטֶן I ₇₂.₁.₁₁ n.f.—בֶּטֶן; cstr. בֶּטֶן; sf. בִּטְנִי—**1.** usu. **womb** of woman Ps 22₁₁, but also **abdomen, stomach, belly, innards, body** of man Jg 3₂₁, woman Ca 7₃, beast Jb 40₁₆, **depths** of Sheol Jon 2₃. **2.** architect., appar. **bulge supporting capital,** or as decoration in capital's lower part 1 K 7₂₀. **3. thigh piece,** i.e. garment to protect belly, or perh. **curve of scimitar** 1QM 5₁₃. → בטן *be pregnant.*

בֶּטֶן II ₁ pl.n. **Beten.**

בְּטֹנִים ₁ pl.n. **Betonim.**

[בָּטְנָה] ₁ n.[m.]—pl. בָּטְנִים—**pistachio** Gn 43₁₁.

בִּי ₁₂ interj. **please,** in addressing superior, בִּי אֲדֹנִי *please, my lord* Gn 43₂₀; in addressing Y., בִּי אֲדֹנָי *please, my Lord* Ex 4₁₀.

[בִּיאָה], see בִּאָה.

*[בִּיבָא] ₀.₀.₁ n.f. **conduit** 3QTr 12₈.

בין ₁₇₀.₃₁.₁₃₁ vb.—**Qal** ₆₃.₀.₂₀ Pf. בִּינֹתִי, בַּנְתָּה; impf. יָבִין (יָבֵן); + waw וַיָּבֶן; impv. בִּין, בִּינָה, בִּינוּ; ptc. בָּנִים; inf. בִּין—**1. perceive, discern, recognize, notice,** with accus. Pr 7₇; לְ of obj. Jb 9₁₁. **2. understand, comprehend, a.** with accus. Pr 2₉ 20₂₄. **b.** abs. Ps 82₅ Pr 29₁₉. **c.** with כִּי *that* 1 S 3₈. **3. consider, give heed (to),** with accus. Dt 32₇ Ps 5₂; obj. introduced by prep. לְ Ps 73₁₇, בְּ CD 1₁, אֶל Ps 28₈, עַל Dn 11₃₀. **4.** ptc. as noun, **one who is wise** Jr 49₇.

Ni. ₂₂.₆.₉ Pf. נְבוֹנֹתִי; ptc. נָבוֹן—**1. be intelligent, discerning,** of person Gn 41₃₃ Pr 17₂₈, mind 1 K 3₁₂. **2.** ptc. as noun, **intelligent one** Pr 10₁₃.

Pol. ₁.₀.₃ Impf. יְבוֹנְנֵהוּ; ptc. Q מבונן—**1. apply understanding, be learned,** or perh. **instruct, give understanding,** כהן מבונן בספר ההגי *a priest learned,* or perh. *instructing, in the book of meditation* CD 13₂. **2. care, show consideration for** someone Dt 32₁₀.

Hi. ₆₂.₁₄.₆₅ Pf. הֵבִין, הֲבִינֹתֶם; impf. יָבִין, Si תבן; impv. הָבֵן, הָבִינוּ; ptc. מֵבִין; inf. הָבִין—**1.** as qal, **a. discern** (accus.) something 1 C 28₉, between (בֵּין ... לְ) things 1 K 3₉. **b. understand, comprehend** something Is 28₁₉ Pr 1₆; abs. Is 29₁₆. **c. consider, give heed to,** with obj. introduced by אֶל Ps 33₁₅; abs. Dn 8₅. **2a. cause** someone **to understand** something, **explain** something **to** someone, with double accus. Is 28₉; with accus. of thing + לְ *to* person Jb 6₂₄. **b. give** someone **understanding,** with accus. Ps 119₃₄; לְ of obj. Dn 11₃₃. **3.** ptc. as noun, **one who understands** or **causes to understand, expert** Pr 8₉ 1 C 15₂₂; מֵבִין עִם־תַּלְמִיד *expert with pupil* 1 C 25₈.

Htpol. ₂₂.₁₁.₃₄ Pf. הִתְבּוֹנָן; impf. אֶתְבּוֹנָן; + waw וַתִּתְבֹּנֵן; impv. הִתְבּוֹנֵן, הִתְבּוֹנְנוּ—**1. consider, examine, look (at), a.** with accus. Ps 119₉₅ Jb 37₁₄. **b.** obj. introduced by prep. בְּ Jr 30₂₄ Si 9₅, אֶל 1 K 3₂₁, עַל Jb 31₁, עַד Jb 32₁₂. **c.** abs. Jr 2₁₀ Jb 11₁₁. **2a.** with accus., **understand** Jb 26₁₄. **b.** with cognate accus. (בִּינָה) and בְּ of obj., **understand clearly** Jr 23₂₀. **3.** abs., **have understanding** Ps 119₁₀₀.

→ בִּין I *understanding,* בִּינָה *understanding,* מְבִינָה *understanding,* תְּבוּנָה *understanding.*

בֵּין ₄₀₃.₁₁.₃₉ prep.—בֵּינוֹת; sf. בֵּינִי, בֵּינוֹ, בֵּינֵינוּ (בֵּינוֹתֵינוּ), בֵּינֵיכֶם, בֵּינֵיהֶם (בֵּינוֹתָם)—**between, among, 1.** without sf., **a.** with pl. noun, כְּשׁוֹשַׁנָּה בֵּין הַחוֹחִים כֵּן רַעְיָתִי בֵּין הַבָּנוֹת *like a lily among thorns, so is my darling among the maidens* Ca 2₂. **b.** with sg. noun, (1) בֵּין ... וּבֵין,

וַיַּעֲמֹד בֵּין־הַמֵּתִים וּבֵין הַחַיִּים *and he stood between the dead and the living* Nm 17_{13}. (2) מִשְׁפַּט אֱמֶת ,בֵּין ... לְ יַעֲשֶׂה בֵּין אִישׁ לְאִישׁ *he judges fairly between man and man* Ezk 18_8. **2.** with sf., **a.** pl., יְהוָה יִהְיֶה שֹׁמֵעַ בֵּינוֹתֵינוּ *Y. himself will be a witness between us* Jg 11_{10}. **b.** sg., וְאֶתְּנָה בְרִיתִי בֵּינִי וּבֵינֶךָ *and I will establish my covenant between me and you* Gn 17_2. **3.** compounds, **a.** מִבֵּין **from among, from between** Ezk 37_{21}. **b.** אֶל־בֵּין **in between** Ezk 31_{14}. **c.** מִבֵּינוֹת לְ **from among, from between** Ezk 10_6. **d.** אֶל־בֵּינוֹת לְ **to the inside** Ezk 10_2. **e.** מִבֵּינוֹת **among** 4QShirShabb[d] 1.2_6.

→ cf. בֵּנַיִם *interval*, בֵּינָה *inward part*.

*[בִּין] I 0.0.1 n.m. **understanding** 4QShirShabb[d] 1.1_{37}. → בין *understand*.

*[בִּין] II n.[m.] **area, field,** וְצָמְחוּ כְּבִין חָצִיר *and they will spring up like a field of grass* Is 44_4 (if em. בְּבֵין *among*; mss, 1QIsa[a] כבין).

*[בֵּינָה] n.f. **inward part,** רוּחַ בֵּינָתִי *spirit of my inward parts* Jb 20_3 (if em. מִבִּינָתִי *from my understanding*). → cf. בֵּין *between*.

בִּינָה 37.4.76 n.f.—cstr. בִּינַת; sf. בִּינָתִי ,בִּינַתְכֶם; pl. בִּינוֹת, Q בנות—**understanding** Dt 4_6 Pr 23_{23}; personified Pr 7_4. → בין *understand*.

[בֵּנַיִם], see בֵּנַיִם *interval*.

[בֵּיצָה] 6.0.3 n.f.—pl. בֵּיצִים; cstr. בֵּיצֵי; sf. בֵּיצֶיהָ—**egg** of bird Dt 22_6, viper Is 59_5.

בִּיר, see בּוֹר I *pit*.

בִּירָה 16 n.f. **1. fortress** Est 1_2 Ne 7_2. **2. temple** of Jerusalem 1 C 29_1.

[בִּירָנִית] 2 n.f.—pl. בִּירָנִיּוֹת—**fortress, fortified place** 2 C 17_{12} 27_4.

*[בַּיָּשׁ] 0.2 adj.—בייש; f.s. ביישה—**decorous,** of wife Si 26_{15}. → בושׁ I *be ashamed*.

*[בֵּישָׁנִי] 0.0.0.4 gent. **Beshanite.**

*בית 0.0.1 vb.—**Qal** 0.0.1 Impf. תבית (unless hi.)—**dwell** perh. 1QH fr. 5_4.

Hi. 0.0.1 Impf. תבית (unless qal)—**cause to dwell,** obj. spirits of wickedness 1QH fr. 5_4.

בַּיִת 2034.25.161.15 n.m.—בָּיִת; + ה- of direction (בַּיְתָה) בַּיְתָה; cstr. בֵּית (בֵּיתָה); sf. בֵּיתִי ,בֵּיתָם; pl. בָּתִּים; cstr. בָּתֵּי; sf. בָּתֶּיךָ ,בָּתֵּיהֶם (בָּתֵּימוֹ)—**1. household, family,** בֵּית אָבִי *household of my father* Gn 20_{13}. **2. house** as physical structure, including courtyard, etc. 1 S 25_1, **estate,** i.e. property left in inheritance Jg 11_2, **palace** 2 S 7_1, **temple** of Y. 1 K 6_1, **quarters,** part of house, palace, etc., בֵּית הַנָּשִׁים *women's quarters*, i.e. harem Est 2_3. **3. place** of graves Ne 2_3. **4.** spider's **web** Jb 8_{14}, bird's **nest** Ps 84_4, badger's **sett** Pr 30_{26}, wild ass's **terrain** Jb 39_6. **5. container,** בָּתֵּי הַנֶּפֶשׁ *containers of perfume* Is 3_{20}. **6. body,** בָּתֵּי־חֹמֶר *houses of clay*, i.e. human bodies Jb 4_{19}. **7. the inside, a.** as prep., מִבֵּית לְ **within** Ex 26_{33}, אֶל־מִבֵּית לְ **within** Lv 16_{15}. **b.** as adv., (1) מִבַּיִת **on the inside** Gn 6_{14}. (2) בַּיְתָה **inwards** Ex 28_{26}||39_{19}.

בֵּית 3.1 prep. **between, among** Ezk 41_9 Jb 8_{17} Pr 8_2 Si 42_{12} (unless all four בֵּית *house of*).

בֵּית אָוֶן 4 pl.n. **Beth-aven.**

בֵּית־אֵל 70.0.3 pl.n. **Bethel.**

[בֵּית־אֱלִי] 1 gent. **Bethelite.**

*[בֵּית־אֲמָם] 0.0.0.1 pl.n. **Beth-amam.**

[בֵּית־אֵצֶל] 1 pl.n. **Beth-ezel.**

בֵּית אַרְבֵאל 1 pl.n. **Beth-arbel.**

*בֵּית אַשְׁבֵּעַ 1 pl. **Beth-ashbea.**

*[בֵּית אֶשְׁדָּתִין] 0.0.1 pl. n. **Beth-eshdathin.**

בֵּית בַּעַל מְעוֹן 1 pl.n. **Beth-baal-meon.**

בֵּית בִּרְאִי 1 pl.n. **Beth-biri.**

בֵּית בָּרָה 2 pl.n. **Beth-barah.**

בֵּית־גָּדֵר 1 pl.n. **Beth-gader.**

בֵּית גָּמוּל 1 pl.n. **Beth-gamul.**

[בֵּית דִּבְלָתָיִם] 1 pl.n. **Beth-diblathaim.**

בֵּית דָּגוֹן 2 pl.n. **Beth-dagon.**

בֵּית הַגִּלְגָּל 1 pl.n. **Beth ha-gilgal.**

[בֵּית הַגָּן] 1 pl.n. **Beth-haggan.**

בֵּית הַיְשִׁמוֹת 4 pl.n. **Beth-jeshimoth.**

בֵּית הַכֶּרֶם 2 pl.n. **Beth-haccherem.**

*[בֵּית הַמָּרָה] 0.0.1 pl.n. **Beth-hammarah.**

בֵּית הַמֶּרְחָק 1 pl.n. **Beth-merhak.**

בֵּית הָעֵמֶק 1 pl.n. **Beth-emek.**

בֵּית הָעֲרָבָה 3 pl.n. **Beth-arabah.**

בֵּית הָרָם 1 pl.n. **Beth-haram.**

בֵּית הָרָן 1 pl.n. **Beth-haran.**

*[בֵּית־הָרָפִד] 0.0.0.1 pl.n. **Beth-haraphid.**

בֵּית הַשִּׁטָּה 1 pl.n. **Beth-shittah.**

בֵּית חָגְלָה 3 pl.n. **Beth-hoglah.**

בֵּית חוֹרוֹן 14.0.1.1 pl.n. **Beth-horon.**
בֵּית חָנָן, see אֵילוֹן בֵּית חָנָן *Elon-beth-hanan.*
*[**בֵּית הַקּוֹץ**] 0.0.1 pl.n. **Beth-hakkoz.**
[**בֵּית כָּר**] 1 pl.n. **Beth-car.**
בֵּית לְבָאוֹת 1 pl.n. **Beth-lebaoth.**
בֵּית לֶחֶם 41 pl.n. **Bethlehem.**
[**בֵּית־לַחְמִי**] 4 gent. **Bethlehemite.**
בֵּית לְעַפְרָה 1 pl.n. **Beth-le-aphrah.**
בֵּית מִלּוֹא 3 pl.n. **Beth-millo.**
בֵּית מְעוֹן 1 pl.n. **Beth-meon.**
בֵּית מַרְכָּבוֹת 2 pl.n. **Beth-marcaboth.**
בִּיתָן 3.1 n.[m.]—cstr. בִּיתַן—**palace** Est 1₅.
בֵּית נִמְרָה 2 pl.n. **Beth-nimrah.**
בֵּית־עַזְמָוֶת 1 pl.n. **Beth-azmaveth.**
בֵּית־עֲנוֹת 1 pl.n. **Beth-anoth.**
בֵּית עֲנָת 3 pl.n. **Beth-anath.**
בֵּית־עֵקֶד הָרֹעִים 2 pl.n. **Beth-eked-haroim.**
[**בֵּית פֶּלֶט**] 2 pl.n. **Beth-pelet.**
בֵּית פְּעוֹר 4 pl.n. **Beth-peor.**
בֵּית פַּצֵּץ 1 pl.n. **Beth-pazzez.**
בֵּית־צוּר 4 pl.n. **Beth-zur.**
*[**בֵּית צִפּוֹר**] 0.0.1 pl.n. **Beth-zippor.**
בֵּית־רְחוֹב 1 pl.n. **Beth-rehob.**
בֵּית רָפָא 1 pr.n.m. **Beth-rapha.**
בֵּית־שְׁאָן 9 pl.n. **Beth-shean.**
*[**בֵּית שֶׁם**] 0.0.1 pl.n. **Beth-sham.**
בֵּית שֶׁמֶשׁ 21 pl.n. **Beth-shemesh.**
[**בֵּית־שִׁמְשִׁי**] 2 gent. **Beth-shemeshite.**
בֵּית שַׁן, see בֵּית־שְׁאָן *Beth-shean.*
*[**בֵּית תָּמָר**] 0.0.1 pl.n. **Beth-tamar.**
בֵּית תַּפּוּחַ 1 pl.n. **Beth-tappuah.**
בָּכָא 5 n.[m.]—pl. בְּכָאִים—**balsam,** or perh. **aspen tree** 2 S 5₂₄.
בכה 114.2.7 vb.—**Qal** 112.2.7 Pf. בָּכִיתִי, בָּכָה; impf. תִּבְכֶּה, יִבְכְּיוּן, תִּבְכּוּ + waw וַיֵּבְךְּ; impv. בְּכֶינָה, בְּכוּ; ptc. בֹּכֶה, בֹּכִים, בּוֹכִיָּה; inf. abs. (בָּכוֹ) בָּכֹה; cstr. לִבְכּוֹת—**1. weep** in grief, humiliation, penitence, relief, etc. Gn 21₁₆ Jg 11₃₇ (+ עַל *for* young womanhood) Jr 22₁₀ (+ לְ *for* someone) Ezr 10₁; with cognate accus. (בְּכִי), **weep bitterly** Jg 21₂. **2.** with accus., **bewail** deceased person Gn 23₂, killing fire of Y. Lv 10₆.

Pi. 2 Ptc. מְבַכּוֹת—**1. weep, mourn for** (עַל) children Jr 31₁₅. **2.** with accus., **bewail, mourn for** Tammuz Ezk 8₁₄.

→ בֶּכֶה *weeping,* בְּכִי *weeping,* בְּכִית *weeping.*

בֶּכֶה 1 n.[m.] **weeping** Ezr 10₁. → בכה *weep.*

בְּכוֹר 122.1.25 n.m.—בְּכֹר; sf. בְּכוֹרִי; pl. cstr. בְּכֹרוֹת, בְּכוֹרֵי; sf. בְּכוֹרֵיהֶם—**1. firstborn offspring,** both human and animal Ex 11₅. **2. firstborn** of Y., i.e. Israel Ex 4₂₂. **3.** בְּכוֹרֵי דַלִּים **firstborn of the poor,** i.e. the poorest Is 14₃₀. **4.** בְּכוֹר מָוֶת **firstborn of death,** i.e. most deadly disease Jb 18₁₃. → בכר *be early.*

בִּכּוּרָה 4 n.f.—pl. בִּכּוּרוֹת—**early fig** Jr 24₂. → בכר *be early.*

בִּכּוּרִים 17.0.4 n.m.pl. **firstfruits,** first portion of cereal and fruit crops, offered to God Ex 23₁₆ Ne 10₃₆. → בכר *be early.*

בְּכוֹרַת 1 pr.n.m. **Bechorath.**

בָּכוּת, see אַלּוֹן I *oak.*

*[**בָּכִי**] 0.0.0.2 pr.n.[m.] **Bachi.**

בְּכִי 29.1.4 n.m.—בֶּכִי; cstr. בְּכִי; sf. בִּכְיִי—**1. weeping, lamentation, tears** Gn 45₂ Est 4₃. **2. trickling, flowing of streams** Jb 28₁₁. → בכה *weep.*

בְּכִירָה 6 n.f. **firstborn daughter** Gn 19₃₁. → בכר *be early.*

[**בְּכִית**] 1.0.0.1 n.f.—sf. בְּכִיתוֹ—**weeping** Gn 50₄. → בכה *weep.*

בכר 4.0.1 vb.—**Pi.** 2 Impf. יְבַכֵּר; inf. בַּכֵּר—**1. produce new fruit,** of tree Ezk 47₁₂. **2. regard as firstborn, treat preferentially, favour** Dt 21₁₆.

Pu. 1 Impf. יְבֻכַּר—**belong as firstborn to** (לְ) Y. Lv 27₂₆.

Hi. 1.0.1 Ptc. מַבְכִּירָה—fem. ptc. as noun, **woman giving birth for first time** Jr 4₃₁.

→ בְּכוֹר *firstborn,* בְּכִירָה *firstborn daughter,* בֵּכֶר I *young he-camel,* בִּכְרָה *young she-camel,* בְּכֹרָה *firstborn's privilege,* בִּכּוּרָה *early fig,* בִּכּוּרִים *first fruits.*

[**בֵּכֶר**] I 1 n.m.—pl. cstr. בִּכְרֵי—**young he-camel** Is 60₆. → בכר *be early.*

בֶּכֶר II 5 pr.n.m. **Becher.**

בְּכֹר, see בְּכוֹר *firstborn.*

בְּכֹרָה 10.1.1 n.f.—sf. בְּכֹרָתִי—**firstborn's privilege** Gn 25₃₁. → בכר *be early.*

בִּכְרָה 1 n.f. **young she-camel** Jr 2₂₃. → בכר *be early.*

בֹּכְרוּ 2 pr.n.m. **Bocheru.**

בִּכְרִי 8 pr.n.m. **Bichri.**

בִּכְרִי 1 gent. **Becherite.**

בַּל I 69.2.15 adv. **not,** followed by **1.** verb, impf. Ps 21_{12}, pf. Ps 10_{11}, inf. Ps 32_{9}. **2.** adj. Pr 24_{23}. **3.** noun Si 35_{4}. **4.** prep. in nom. cl. Pr 23_{7}.

***בַּל** II 9 part. **indeed, surely,** וּבַל־יִפְּלוּ יֹשְׁבֵי תֵבֵל *and surely the inhabitants of the earth have fallen* Is 26_{18}. → cf. בֶּלֶת *not, no,* בִּלְתִּי *not.*

בֵּל 3 pr.n.m. **Bel,** Babylonian deity Is 46_{1}.

בַּלְאֲדָן 2 pr.n.m. **Baladan.**

בֵּלְאשַׁצַּר 1 pr.n.m. **Belshazzar.**

בלג I 4 vb.—**Hi.** 4 Impf. אַבְלִיגָה—**1. make oneself shine, be cheerful** Ps 39_{14}. **2. make shine, cause** destruction **to appear** Am 5_{9}. → (?) מַבְלָגָה *cunning simile,* מַבְלִיגִית *cheerfulness.*

***בלג** II 1 vb.—**Hi.** 1 Ptc. הַמַּבְלִיג—**send destruction** Am 5_{9}.

בִּלְגָּה 3 pr.n.m. **Bilgah.**

בִּלְגַּי 1.0.0.5 pr.n.m. **Bilgai.**

בִּלְדַּד 5 pr.n.m. **Bildad.**

בלה 16.1 vb.—**Qal** 11.1 Pf. בָּלוּ, בָּלְתָה; impf. יִבְלֶה; inf. בְּלֹתִי—**be worn out, wear oneself out,** of mantle Dt 8_{4} (+ מֵעַל *from upon*), old woman Gn 18_{12}, creation, earth, heaven Ps 102_{27} (+ כְּ *as* garment).

Pi. 5 Pf. בִּלָּה; impf. יְבַלּוּ—**1. wear out, trouble** people 1 C 17_{9}. **2. consume, use to the full** one's days in (בְּ) prosperity Jb 21_{13}(Kt) (Qr כלה pi.).

→ בָּלֶה *worn,* בְּלוֹי *rag,* תַּבְלִית *destruction.*

[בלה] 1 vb.—**Pi.** 1 Ptc. Kt מבלהים (Qr מְבַהֲלִים)—**frighten** people from building (לִבְנוֹת) Ezr 4_{4}(Kt). → בַּלָּהָה *terror.*

בָּלָה 1 pl.n. **Balah.**

[בָּלֶה] 5 adj.—f.s. בָּלָה; m.pl. בָּלִים—**1. worn,** of sandal Jos 9_{5}. **2.** fem. as noun, **worn out woman** Ezk 23_{43}. → בלה *be worn out.*

***[בְּלָה]** 0.0.1 n.f. **mixing, confusion** of tongue 1QM 10_{14}. → בלל *mix.*

בַּלָּהָה 10 n.f.—pl. בַּלָּהוֹת; cstr. בַּלְהוֹת—**terror, calamity** Ps 73_{19}. → בלה *frighten.*

בִּלְהָה I 10.0.6 pr.n.f. **Bilhah.**

בִּלְהָה II 1 pl.n. **Bilhah.**

בִּלְהָן 4 pr.n.m. **Bilhan.**

***[בְּלוֹ]** n.[m.] **gift** Ne 5_{15} (if em. בְּלֶחֶם *for bread* to בְּלוֹ לֶחֶם *gift of bread*).

[בְּלוֹי] 3 n.[m.] **rag,** בְּלוֹיֵ מְלָחִים *rags of old clothes* Jr 38_{11}. → בלה *be worn out.*

***[בַּלַּט]** 0.0.0.1 pr.n.m. appar. short form of סַנְבַלַּט **Sanballat.**

בֵּלְטְשַׁאצַּר 2 pr.n.m. **Belteshazzar.**

בְּלִי I 57.0.7 n.[m.] **1. nothingness,** שַׁחַת בְּלִי *pit of nothingness* Is 38_{17}. **2.** adv., **a.** בְּלִי **without,** זַךְ אֲנִי בְּלִי פָשַׁע *pure am I, without sin* Jb 33_{9}. **b.** compounds, (1) בִּבְלִי **without** Dt 19_{4}. (2) לִבְלִי **without** Jb 38_{41}, **beyond** Is 5_{14}. (3) מִבְּלִי **for lack of** Jb 24_{8}.

***בְּלִי** II 1 n.[m.] **rottenness,** שַׁחַת בְּלִי *pit of rottenness* Is 38_{17}.

בְּלִיל 3 n.m. **fodder** Is 30_{24}. → בלל *mix.*

בְּלִיַּעַל 27.1.77 n.m. **1. worthlessness, wickedness,** אִישׁ בְּלִיַּעַל *man of worthlessness* Pr 16_{27}. **2.** perh. **worthless one, wicked one,** of person 2 S 23_{6}, thought Dt 15_{9}. **3. Belial,** a demon, מצודות בליעל *nets of Belial* CD 4_{15}, ממשלת *dominion of* 1QS 1_{18}.

בלל 43.0.4 vb.—**Qal** 42.0.4 Pf. בָּלַל, בַּלֹּתִי; impf. נָבְלָה; + waw Qr וַיָּבָל (Kt ויבול); ptc. pass. בְּלוּלָה—**1a.** usu. pass., **be mixed, moistened with** (בְּ) oil, of flour Ex 29_{40}. **b.** act., **mix, confuse** language Gn 11_{7}. **2. feed, give fodder to** (לְ) ass Jg 19_{21}.

Htpo. 1 Impf. יִתְבּוֹלָל—perh. **mix oneself, associate with** (בְּ) Gentile nations Ho 7_{8}.

→ בְּלִיל *fodder,* שַׁבְּלוּל *snail,* בְּלָה *confusion,* מַבְלֵל *mixed herbs,* תֶּבֶל *perversion,* תְּבַלֻּל *confusion.*

בלם 1 vb.—**Qal** 1 Inf. בְּלוֹם—**bind, restrain** horse or mule with (בְּ) bridle Ps 32_{9}.

בלס 1 vb.—**Qal** 1 Ptc. בּוֹלֵס—**tend figs,** בּוֹלֵס שִׁקְמִים *tender of sycamore figs* Am 7_{14}.

בלע I 42.0.13 vb.—**Qal** 20.0.1 Pf. בָּלַע, בְּלָעוּנוּ; impf. תִּבְלָעֵהוּ; + waw וַיִּבְלַע; inf. בְּלַע—**swallow, devour, engulf, a.** obj. person(s); subj. people Ps 124_{3}, fish Jon 2_{1}, earth Nm 16_{30}, the deep Ps 69_{16}. **b.** obj. food Ho 8_{7}, wealth Jb 20_{15}.

Pi. 21.0.11 Pf. בִּלַּע; impf. יְבַלַּע; impv. בַּלַּע; ptc. מְבַלְּעֵךְ; inf. בַּלַּע (בַּלְּעוֹ, בַּלַּע)—**1. swallow, devour, destroy, a.** obj. person(s); subj. people Ps 35_{25}, lips Ec 10_{12}. **b.**

obj. habitations; subj. Y. Lm 2_{2}. **2.** ptc. as noun, **destroyer** 1QH 17_{8}.

Pu. 1 Impf. יְבֻלַּע—**be devoured,** פֶּן־יְבֻלַּע לַמֶּלֶךְ וּלְכָל־הָעָם *lest it be devoured in respect of the king and all the people,* i.e. lest they be destroyed 2 S 17_{16}.

Htp. 0.0.1 Impf. Q תתבלע—**be consumed by** (בְּ) possessions 4QInstr^{b} 2.3_{8}.

→ בֶּלַע I *swallowing.*

בלע II 7.0.1 vb.—**Ni.** 2 Pf. נִבְלַע—**be confused,** of persons Is 28_{7} (+ מִן *by* wine) Ho 8_{8}.

Pi. 2 Pf. בִּלְּעוּ; impf. אֲבַלֵּעַ—**confuse** course of paths Is 3_{12}, plans Is 19_{3}.

Pu. 2 Impf. יְבֻלַּע; ptc. מְבֻלָּעִים—**be confused,** of persons Is 9_{15} Jb 37_{20}.

Htp. 1.0.1 Impf. תִּתְבַּלָּע—**be confused,** of wisdom Ps 107_{27} 1QH 11_{14}.

בלע III 3 vb.—**Pi.** 1 Impf. יְבַלַּע—**communicate** evil, subj. mouth Pr 19_{28}.

Pu. 2 Impf. יְבֻלַּע—**be communicated,** פֶּן־יְבֻלַּע לַמֶּלֶךְ וּלְכָל־הָעָם *lest it be communicated to the king and all the people* 2 S 17_{16}.

***בלע** IV 12 vb.—**Ni.** 1 Pf. נִבְלְעוּ—**be struck by** (מִן) wine Is 28_{7}.

Pi. 8 Pf. בִּלַּעֲנוּהוּ; impf. יְבַלַּע—**afflict** person Ps 35_{25} Jb 2_{3}, plans Is 19_{3}.

Pu. 3 Impf. יְבֻלַּע—**be afflicted,** of person Jb 37_{20}; subj. impersonal, פֶּן־יְבֻלַּע לַמֶּלֶךְ וּלְכָל־הָעָם *lest it be afflicted in respect of the king and all the people,* i.e. lest disaster befall them 2 S 17_{16}.

→ בֶּלַע II *slander.*

[בֶּלַע] I 2 n.[m.]—בֶּלַע; sf. בִּלְעוֹ—**1. devouring, destruction,** דִּבְרֵי־בָלַע *words of destruction* Ps 52_{6}. **2. food** Jr 51_{44}. → בלע I *swallow.*

***[בֶּלַע]** II 1 n.[m.] **slander,** דִּבְרֵי בֶלַע *words of slander* Ps 52_{6}. → בלע IV *touch, strike.*

בֶּלַע III 12 pr.n.m. **Bela.**

בֶּלַע IV 2 pl.n. **Bela.**

[בִּלְעֲדֵי] 17.0.1 part.—בִּלְעֲדֵי (sf. בִּלְעָדַי ,בִּלְעָדֶיךָ); מִבַּלְעֲדֵי (sf. מִבַּלְעָדַי)—**1.** בִּלְעֲדֵי **apart from,** בִּלְעֲדֵי אֶחֱזֶה הֹרֵנִי *teach me (about matters) apart from (those that) I see* Jb 34_{32}. **2.** בִּלְעָדָי, appar. as interj., **not me,** i.e. **it is not through me** Gn 41_{16}. **3.** מִבַּלְעֲדֵי **apart from, without the consent of,** הֲיֵשׁ אֱלוֹהַּ מִבַּלְעָדַי *is there a God apart from me?* Is 44_{8}, מִבַּלְעֲדֵי אֲנָשֵׁינוּ *without our husbands' approval* Jr 44_{19}. → בַּל *not* + עַד *unto.*

בַּלְעִי 1 gent. **Belaite.**

בִּלְעָם I 60.0.1 pr.n.m. **Balaam.**

בִּלְעָם II 1 pl.n. **Bileam.**

[בִּלְעָן] 1 pr.n.m. **Bilean.**

בלק 2 vb.—**Qal** (or perh. **Po.**) 1 Ptc. בּוֹלְקָהּ—of Y., **devastate** land Is 24_{1}.

Pu. 1 Ptc. מְבֻלָּקָה—ptc. as noun, **devastation** Na 2_{11}.

בָּלָק 43 pr.n.m. **Balak.**

בִּלְשָׁן 2 pr.n.m. **Bilshan.**

***[בֵּלְת]** part. **not, no,** בֵּלְת כָּרַע תַּחַת אַסִּיר *no! one crouches among the prisoner(s)* Is 10_{4} (if em. בִּלְתִּי *not*). → cf. בַּל *not.*

בִּלְתִּי 111.1.16 adv.—sf. בִּלְתֶּךָ—**1a.** בִּלְתִּי **not,** בִּלְתִּי טָהוֹר הוּא *he is not clean* 1 S 20_{26}. **b.** compounds, (1) לְבִלְתִּי **not to, in order not to, so that not,** נִשְׁבַּעְנוּ בַי״ לְבִלְתִּי תֵּת־לָהֶם מִבְּנוֹתֵינוּ *we have sworn by Y. not to give any of our daughters to them* Jg 21_{7}. (2) מִבִּלְתִּי **because not,** מִבִּלְתִּי יְכֹלֶת י״ לְהָבִיא אֶת־הָעָם הַזֶּה אֶל־הָאָרֶץ *because Y. was not able to bring this people into the land ...* he slaughtered them Nm 14_{16}. (3) עַד־בִּלְתִּי **until not,** עַד־בִּלְתִּי שָׁמַיִם *until there are no heavens* Jb 14_{12}, וַיַּכּוּ אוֹתָם עַד־בִּלְתִּי הִשְׁאִיר־לוֹ שָׂרִיד *and they struck them, until no survivor was left to them* Jos 8_{22}. **2a.** בִּלְתִּי (1) **apart from,** אֵין בִּלְתֶּךָ *there is none apart from you* 1 S 2_{2}. (2) **unless,** לֹא־תִרְאוּ פָנַי בִּלְתִּי אֲחִיכֶם אִתְּכֶם *do not look at my face, unless your brother is with you* Gn 43_{3}. **b.** compound, בִּלְתִּי אִם (1) **apart from** Gn 47_{18}. (2) **unless** Am 3_{3}. → cf. בַּל *not.*

בָּמָה I 103.0.5 n.f.—+ ה- of direction בָּמָתָה; pl. בָּמוֹת; cstr. בָּמוֹת (Kt במותי), בָּמֳתֵי; sf. בָּמוֹתָם ,בָּמוֹתַי (בָּמוֹתֵימוֹ)—**1.** usu. **high place, platform,** as site of worship, בָּמוֹת הַבַּעַל *high places of Baal* Jr 19_{5}. **2. hill, height,** בָּמוֹת אַרְנֹן *heights of the Arnon* Nm 21_{28}. **3. top,** בָּמֳתֵי עָב *tops of the clouds* Is 14_{14}. **4. back,** בָּמֳתֵי יָם *back(s) of the sea* Jb 9_{8}, אַתָּה עַל־בָּמוֹתֵימוֹ תִדְרֹךְ *you will tread on their* (enemies') *backs* Dt 33_{29}.

***בָּמָה** II n.f. **1. back,** בָּמֳתֵי עָב *backs of cloud(s)* Is 14_{14} (if em. בָּמֳתֵי *high places of*). **2. beast,** בָּמָה נֶחְשַׁב הוּא

humanity *is reckoned a beast* Is 2$_{22}$ (if em. בַּמָּה *at what?*).

בִּמְהָל 1 pr.n.m. **Bimhal.**

בְּמוֹ 9 prep. **in, at, through, by (means of), with,** תֵּלֵךְ בְּמוֹ־אֵשׁ *you walk through fire* Is 43$_2$, אֲאַמִּצְכֶם בְּמוֹ־פִי *I would encourage you with my mouth* Jb 16$_5$. → cf. בְּ *in.*

בָּמוֹת 2 pl.n. **Bamoth.**

בָּמוֹת בַּעַל 2 pl.n. **Bamoth-baal.**

בֵּן I 4889.77.421.386 n.m.—cstr. בֶּן (בִּן ,בֶּן); sf. בְּנִי; pl. בָּנִים; cstr. בְּנֵי; sf. בָּנַי—**1a. son,** and (usu. in pl.) **child, descendant,** (1) of individual, בְּנֵי יִצְחָק *sons of Isaac* 1 C 1$_{34}$, רָחֵל *of Rachel* Gn 35$_{24}$; explicitly including women, בְּנֵי עַמְרָם אַהֲרֹן וּמֹשֶׁה וּמִרְיָם *the children of Amram were Aaron and Moses and Miriam* 1 C 5$_{29}$. (2) of nation as a whole, בְּנֵי יִשְׂרָאֵל *sons of Israel,* i.e. Israelites Lv 1$_2$, also in ref. to territory of a nation, גְּבוּל בְּנֵי עַמּוֹן *boundary of the Ammonites* Nm 21$_{24}$. (3) human offspring in general, בְּנֵי אָדָם *(sons of) human beings* Ps 11$_4$. **b.** בְּנִי **my son,** as term of affection or in address to younger person, e.g. Eli to Samuel 1 S 3$_6$; בִּנְךָ **your son,** in self-deference 2 K 8$_9$. **2. male offspring, young** of animals, בֶּן־בָּקָר *son of cattle,* i.e. calf Gn 18$_7$, בְּנֵי עֹרֵב *sons of raven,* i.e. young ravens Ps 147$_9$. **3.** בְּנֵי־הָאֱלֹהִים **sons of the gods,** i.e. divine beings Gn 6$_4$ Jb 1$_6$, בני שמים **sons of heaven,** i.e. angels 1QS 4$_{22}$. **4. product of** material, **that which emerges from** object, בְּנֵי רֶשֶׁף *sons of flame,* i.e. sparks Jb 5$_7$, בֶּן־קָשֶׁת *son of a bow,* i.e. arrow Jb 41$_{20}$. **5. one who is numbered among, follower, disciple** of the prophets 2 K 2$_5$, Wisdom Si 4$_{11}$. **6a. one possessing the characteristics of,** בֶּן־הַמְרַצֵּחַ *(son of a) murderer* 2 K 6$_{32}$. **b. possessor of, one characterized by,** בֶּן־אַרְבָּעִים שָׁנָה *son of forty years,* i.e. forty year old man Gn 25$_{20}$, בֶּן־בְּלִיַּעַל *son of worthlessness,* i.e. wicked man 1 S 25$_{17}$, בְּנֵי־חָיִל *sons of valour,* i.e. warriors Dt 3$_{18}$; at Qumran, בני אור *sons of light,* i.e. members of Qumran community 1QM 1$_1$, חושך *of darkness,* i.e. those outside the community under influence of Belial 1QM 1$_1$.

בֵּן II 1 pr.n.m. **Ben.**

בֶּן־אֲבִינָדָב 1 pr.n.m. **Ben-abinadab.**

בֶּן־אוֹנִי 1 pr.n.m. **Ben-oni.**

בֶּן־גֶּבֶר 1 pr.n.m. **Ben-geber.**

בֶּן־דֶּקֶר 1 pr.n.m. **Ben-deker.**

בנה I 373.4.33 vb.—**Qal** 343.4.31 Pf. בָּנִיתָ ,בָּנָה; impf. יִבְנֶה; + waw וַיִּבֶן; impv. בְּנֵה ,בְּנוּ; ptc. בֹּנֶה ,בֹּנִים; ptc. pass. בָּנוּי, בְּנוּיָה ,בְּנוּיִם; inf. abs. בָּנֹה; cstr. בְּנוֹת—**1a. build, rebuild** city Jg 1$_{26}$, house Dt 8$_{12}$; with double accus., **build** altar **with** stone 1 K 18$_{32}$. **b. fashion** rib Gn 2$_{22}$. **c. create** suffering Si 38$_{18}$. **d. establish** family, descendants Ru 4$_{11}$, the wicked Ps 28$_5$. **e. edify** soul 11QPs^a 24$_5$. **2.** pass., **be built,** of Jerusalem Ps 122$_3$, altar Jg 6$_{28}$. **3.** ptc. as noun, **builder** 1 K 5$_{32}$.

Ni. 30.0.2 Pf. נִבְנוּ; impf. יִבָּנֶה—**1. be (re)built,** of city Is 44$_{26}$, ruin Ezk 36$_{10}$. **2. be (re)established,** of Job Jb 22$_{23}$. **3. become mother of sons** Gn 16$_2$.

→ בִּנְיָה *building,* בִּנְיָן *structure,* מִבְנֶה *structure,* מַבְנִית I *structure,* תַּבְנִית *structure.*

***בנה** II 1 vb.—**Ni.** 1 Impf. תִּבָּנֶה—**show oneself good, mend one's ways,** אִם־תָּשׁוּב עַד־שַׁדַּי תִּבָּנֶה *if you return to Shaddai (and) mend your ways* Jb 22$_{23}$.

בֶּן־הֲדַד 25 pr.n.m. **Ben-hadad.**

בֶּן־הִנֹּם, see גֵּיא בֶן־הִנֹּם *Valley of Ben-hinnom, Gehinnom, Gehenna.*

בִּנּוֹ 2 pr.n.m. **Beno.**

בִּנּוּי 7 pr.n.m. **Binnui.**

בֶּן־זוֹחֵת 1 pr.n.m. **Ben-zoheth.**

בֶּן־חוּר 2 pr.n.m. **Ben-hur.**

בֶּן־חַיִל 1 pr.n.m. **Ben-hail.**

בֶּן־חָנָן 1 pr.n.m. **Ben-hanan.**

בֶּן־חֶסֶד 1 pr.n.m. **Ben-hesed.**

בָּנִי 15 pr.n.m. **Bani.**

בְּנָי 1 pr.n.m. **Benai.**

בֻּנִּי 3 pr.n.m. **Bunni.**

בְּנֵי־בְרַק 1 pl.n. **Bene-berak.**

בְּנָיָה, see בְּנָיָהוּ *Benaiah.*

בִּנְיָה 1 n.[f.] **building,** in ref. to temple or part thereof Ezk 41$_{13}$. → בנה I *build.*

בְּנָיָהוּ 42.0.0.21 pr.n.m. **Benaiah.**

בְּנֵי־יַעֲקָן 2 pl.n. **Bene-jaakan.**

***בֵּנַיִם** 2.0.19 n.[m.]du.—Q בינים—**interval,** אִישׁ הַבֵּנַיִם *man of the interval,* appar. champion, 1 S 17$_4$, אנשי הבנים *men of the interval,* perh. skirmishers 1QM 3$_1$.

→ cf. בֵּין *between*.

בֶּן־יְמִינִי 9 gent. **Benjaminite.**

בִּנְיָמִן 166.0.2 pr.n.m. **Benjamin.**

בִּנְיָן 7.0.1 n.m. **structure, building** Ezk 41$_{12}$; in ref. to wall around temple Ezk 40$_{5}$. → בנה I *build*.

בְּנִינוּ 1 pr.n.m. **Beninu.**

*[בֶּנְסָמַרְנֵר] 0.0.0.1 pr.n.m. **Ben-samarner.**

בִּנְעָא 2 pr.n.m. **Binea.**

*[בֶּנְעֲנָת] 0.0.0.1 pr.n.m. **Ben-anath.**

*[בֶּן־רַבָּה] II 0.0.1 pr.n.m. **Ben-rabbah.**

בְּסוֹדְיָה 1 pr.n.m. **Besodeiah.**

בֵּסַי 2.0.0.2 pr.n.m. **Besai.**

*[בסר] vb. **Pi., accuse,** ptc. as noun, **accuser** Is 41$_{27}$ (if em. בשׂר pi. *announce*).

בֹּסֶר 5.0.1 n.m.—sf. בִּסְרוֹ—**unripe grape** Is 18$_{5}$.

בַּעֲבוּר 49.10.4 prep.—בַּעֲבָר; sf. בַּעֲבוּרִי—**1.** as prep., **a.** usu. **on account of, because of, for the sake of,** אֲרוּרָה הָאֲדָמָה בַּעֲבוּרֶךָ *cursed is the ground because of you* Gn 3$_{17}$, לֹא אַשְׁחִית בַּעֲבוּר הָעֲשָׂרָה *I will not destroy (the city) for the sake of the ten* Gn 18$_{32}$. **b. for the price of** Am 2$_{6}$. **2.** as conj., **so that, in order that, a.** בַּעֲבוּר with impf. Gn 27$_{4}$, inf. 2 S 18$_{18}$. **b.** בַּעֲבָר אֲשֶׁר with impf. Gn 27$_{10}$. **c.** לְבַעֲבוּר with inf. Ex 20$_{20}$. → cf. בְּ *in* + עֲבוּר II *in order that*.

[בַּעַד] I 105.3.4 prep.—מִבַּעַד; cstr. בְּעַד; sf. בַּעֲדִי (בַּעֲדֵנִי)—**1. behind, after, around, over, through, on behalf of, for the sake of, because of, in place of, for,** בְּרִחֶיהָ בַעֲדִי *her bars are (closed) behind me* Jon 2$_{7}$, אַתָּה י׳ מָגֵן בַּעֲדִי *you are a shield around me* Ps 3$_{4}$, וַיַּשְׁקֵף ... בְּעַד הַחַלּוֹן *and he looked out ... through the window* Gn 26$_{8}$, יִתְפַּלֵּל בַּעַדְךָ *he will pray for you* Gn 20$_{7}$, עוֹר בְּעַד־עוֹר *skin for skin* Jb 2$_{4}$. **2.** מִבַּעַד לְ **from behind,** מִבַּעַד לְצַמָּתֵךְ *from behind your veil* Ca 4$_{1}$.

*בַּעַד II n.[m.] **price,** בְּעַד־אִשָּׁה זוֹנָה *price of a prostitute* Pr 6$_{26}$ (if em. בְּעַד *through*).

*[בַּעְדְּאֵל] 0.0.0.1 pr.n.[m.] **Beadel.**

*[בַּעֲדְיָהוּ] 0.0.0.2 pr.n.m. **Baadiah.**

בעה I 2 vb.—**Qal** 1 Impf. תִּבְעֶה—**cause water to boil,** of fire Is 64$_{1}$.

Ni. 1 Ptc. נִבְעֶה—**be swollen, bulge,** of breach in wall Is 30$_{13}$.

בעה II 3 vb.—**Qal** 2 Impf. תִּבְעָיוּן; impv. בְּעָיוּ—**inquire** Is 21$_{12}$.

Ni. 1 Pf. נִבְעוּ—**be sought,** of hoard Ob$_{6}$.

*בעה III 1 vb.—**Qal** 1 Impf. Sam יבעה—**graze** field, of beast Ex 22$_{4}$(Sam).

בְּעוֹר 10 pr.n.m. **Beor.**

[בְּעוּתִ] 2 n.m.—pl. cstr. בִּעוּתֵי; sf. בִּעוּתֶיךָ—**terror** Ps 88$_{17}$ Jb 6$_{4}$. → בעת *terrify*.

בֹּעַז 24 pr.n.m. **Boaz.**

בעט I 2 vb.—**Qal** 2 Impf. תִּבְעֲטוּ—**kick** against (בְּ) sacrifice 1 S 2$_{29}$.

*בעט II 2 vb.—**Qal** 2 Impf. תִּבְעֲטוּ—**despise** (בְּ of obj.) sacrifice 1 S 2$_{29}$.

[בְּעִיר] 6 n.m.—sf. בְּעִירָם—**beast,** alw. coll., beasts of burden Gn 45$_{17}$, livestock Nm 20$_{4}$. → בער III *be brutish*.

בעל I 16.0.6 vb.—**Qal** 14.0.6 Pf. בָּעַל, בְּעָלוֹ; impf. יִבְעַל; ptc. בֹּעֲלַיִךְ; ptc. pass. בְּעוּלָה; inf. Q בעל—**1.** act., **a.** usu. **marry, take woman as sexual partner** Dt 21$_{13}$. **b. be lord, rule over** (בְּ) Jr 31$_{32}$. **2.** pass., **a. be married,** of woman Gn 20$_{3}$ (בְּעֻלַת בָּעַל *married of,* i.e. to, *a husband*). **b.** appar. **be accustomed** to hearing noise, of horse 1QM 6$_{13}$.

Ni. 2 Impf. תִּבָּעֵל—**be married,** of unloved woman Pr 30$_{23}$, land Is 62$_{4}$.

→ בַּעַל I *lord*, בַּעֲלָה *lady*.

*בעל II 1 vb.—**Qal** 1 Ptc. בֹּעֲלַיִךְ—**do, make,** ptc. as noun, **creator** Is 54$_{5}$. → cf. פעל *do*.

בַּעַל I 160.17.16.1 n.m.—בָּעַל; cstr. בַּעַל (בְּעַל־, בַּעַל־); sf. בַּעְלִי; pl. בְּעָלִים; cstr. בַּעֲלֵי; sf. בְּעָלֶיהָ—**1a.** pl. **lords, rulers** of nations Is 16$_{8}$, of city, perh. **citizens, landowners** Jos 24$_{11}$ Jg 9$_{51}$. **b. husband** of woman Ex 21$_{3}$. **c. owner** of ox Ex 21$_{28}$, house Ex 22$_{7}$. **d. possessor** of dreams, i.e. dreamer Gn 37$_{19}$, of legal case Ex 24$_{14}$, anger Pr 29$_{22}$, wisdom Ec 7$_{12}$. **2.** הַבַּעַל **the lord,** effectively as pr.n.m. **Baal,** נְבִיאֵי הַבַּעַל *prophets of Baal* 1 K 18$_{19}$; הַבְּעָלִים **the lords, (the) baalim,** deities regarded as enemies of Y., מִזְבְּחוֹת הַבְּעָלִים *altars of the baalim* 2 C 34$_{4}$. → בעל I *be lord*.

בַּעַל II 3 pr.n.m. **Baal.**

*[בַּעֲלָא] 0.0.0.5 pr.n.[m.] **Baala.**

בַּעַל בְּרִית 2 pr.n.m. **Baal-berith,** Canaanite deity Jg 8$_{33}$.

בַּ֫עַל גָּד 3 pl.n. **Baal-gad.**

בַּעֲלָה I 4.1.1 n.f.—cstr. בַּעֲלַת—**1. lady, (wife of) owner** of house 1 K 17_{17}. **2. possessor of occult skills** Na 3_4. → בעל I *be lord.*

בַּעֲלָה II 5 pl.n. **Baalah.**

בַּעַל הָמוֹן 1 pl.n. **Baal-hamon.**

בְּעָלוֹת 2 pl.n. **Bealoth.**

בַּ֫עַל זְבוּב 4 pr.n.m. **Baal-zebub,** Canaanite deity 2 K 1_2.

*[בַּעַל־זָמַר] 0.0.0.1 pr.n.m. **Baal-zamar.**

בַּ֫עַל חָנָן 5.0.0.1 pr.n.m. **Baal-hanan.**

בַּ֫עַל חָצוֹר 1 pl.n. **Baal-hazor.**

בַּ֫עַל חֶרְמוֹן 2 pl.n. **Baal-hermon.**

בְּעֶלְיָדָע 1 pr.n.m. **Beeliada.**

בְּעַלְיָה 1 pr.n.m. **Bealiah.**

בַּעֲלֵי יְהוּדָה 1 pl.n. **Baale-jehudah.**

בַּעֲלִיס 1 pr.n.m. **Baalis.**

בַּ֫עַל מְעוֹן 3 pl.n. **Baal-meon.**

*[בַּעַלְמְעֹנִי] 0.0.0.1 pr.n.[m.] **Baalmeoni.**

*[בַּעַלְנָתָן] 0.0.0.2 pr.n.[m.] **Baal-nathan.**

*[בַּעַלְעֲזָכָר] 0.0.0.1 pr.n.[m.] **Baala-zachar.**

בַּ֫עַל פְּעוֹר 6 pr.n.m. **Baal-peor,** Canaanite deity Nm 25_3.

בַּ֫עַל פְּרָצִים 4 pl.n. **Baal-perazim.**

בַּ֫עַל צְפוֹן 3 pl.n. **Baal-zephon.**

בַּ֫עַל שָׁלִשָׁה 1 pl.n. **Baal-shalishah.**

בַּעֲלָת 3 pl.n. **Baalath.**

בַּעֲלַת בְּאֵר 1 pl.n. **Baalath-beer.**

בַּ֫עַל תָּמָר 1 pl.n. **Baal-tamar.**

בְּעֹן 1 pl.n. **Beon.**

בַּעֲנָא 3 pr.n.m. **Baana.**

בַּעֲנָה 9 pr.n.m. **Baanah.**

בער I 58.5.23 vb.—**Qal** 43.4.18 Pf. בָּעֲרָה; impf. יִבְעַר; ptc. בֹּעֵר, בֹּעֵרָה (בֹּעֶרֶת, בֹּעֵרָה), בֹּעֲרוֹת—**1a.** usu. intrans., **burn, blaze,** of Y., וַיִּבְעַר בְּיַעֲקֹב כְּאֵשׁ לֶהָבָה *and he has burned against Jacob like a flaming fire* Lm 2_3, of anger of Y. Is 30_{27}, fire Nm 11_1, wickedness Is 9_{17}, mountain Dt 4_{11} (+ בְּ *with* fire). **b. be burned,** of bush Ex 3_3. **2.** trans., **burn** forest, of fire Ps 83_{15}.

Ni. 0.0.1 Impf. תבער—**be consumed** by (בְּ) fire 4Q Instr^b 2.34.

Pi. 8.1.1 Pf. בִּעַרְתִּיהָ; impf. תְּבַעֲרוּ; ptc. מְבַעֲרִים; inf. בָּעֵר (בַּעֵר)—**1. kindle** fire Ex 35_3. **2. light** lamp 2 C 4_{20}. **3. burn** wood Lv 6_5.

Pu. 1 Ptc. מְבֹעֶרֶת—**burn,** of brazier Jr 36_{22}.

Hi. 6.0.3 Impf. תַּבְעִיר; + waw וַיַּבְעֵר; וְהִבְעַרְתִּי; ptc. מַבְעִר—**1. kindle fire** Ex 22_5. **2. light lamp** 11QT 22_1. **3. burn, sacrifice** child 2 C 28_3.

→ בְּעֵרָה *fire,* מַבְעֵרָה *burning.*

בער II 28.1.6 vb.—**Pi.** 26.0.6 Pf. בִּעֵר, בִּעַרְתָּ; impf. יְבַעֵר; inf. בָּעֵר—**1. remove evil from among** (מִקֶּרֶב) **nation** Dt 13_6, **destroy** images of gods, etc. 2 K 23_{24}. **2. destructively pursue after** (אַחֲרֵי) Ahab, of Y. 1 K 21_{21}.

Pu. 0.1 Impf. יבוער—**be grazed,** or **be destroyed,** of vineyard Si 36_{30}.

Hi. 2 Impf. ־יַבְעֶר; ptc. מַבְעִיר—**1. destructively pursue** after (אַחֲרֵי) house of Baasha 1 K 16_3. **2. allow field to be grazed** Ex 22_4.

בער III 7 vb.—**Qal** 3 Impf. יִבְעֲרוּ; ptc. בֹּעֲרִים—**be brutish, foolish** Ezk 21_{36}.

Ni. 4 Pf. נִבְעֲרוּ—**be foolish, be shown as foolish** Jr 10_{21}.

→ בְּעִיר *beast,* בַּעַר *fool.*

*בער IV 3 vb.—**Pi.** 3 Pf. בִּעַרְתֶּם; inf. בָּעֵר—**destroy, pillage** vineyard Is 3_{14} 5_5, land Is 6_{13}.

בַּ֫עַר 5 n.m. **fool** Ps 49_{11}. → בער III *be brutish.*

בַּעֲרָא 1.0.0.1 pr.n.f. **Baara.**

בְּעֵרָה 1 n.f. **fire** Ex 22_5. → בער *burn.*

בַּעֲשֵׂיָה 1 pr.n.m. **Baaseiah.**

בַּעְשָׁא 28 pr.n.m. **Baasha.**

בְּעֶשְׁתְּרָה 1 pl.n. **Beeshterah.**

בעת 16.0.4 vb.—**Ni.** 3.0.3 Pf. נִבְעַתִּי—**be terrified** Dn 8_{17} 1 C 21_{30} (+ מִפְּנֵי *[because] of*).

Pi. 13.0.1 Pf. בִּעֲתַתְנִי; impf. יְבַעֲתוּנִי; ptc. מְבַעֶתֶת—**terrify, overwhelm** someone, of Y. Jb 7_{14}, Y.'s terror Jb 9_{34}, evil spirit 1 S 16_{14}, stream 2 S 22_5||Ps 18_5.

→ בְּעָתָה *terror,* בִּעוּת *terror.*

בְּעָתָה 2 n.f. **terror** Jr 8_{15}. → בעת *terrify.*

בֹּץ 1.0.1 n.[m.] **mud,** or perh. **marsh** or **silt** Jr 38_{22}. → cf. בִּצָּה *marsh.*

[בֵּצָה], see בֵּיצָה *egg.*

בִּצָּה 3 n.f.—pl. sf. Qr בִּצֹּאתָיו—**marsh** Ezk 47_{11}. → cf. בֹּץ *mud.*

[בֵּצָי] 3 pr.n.m. **Bezai.**

בָּצִיר I 7 n.m.—cstr. בְּצִיר—**grape harvest** Jg 8_2. → בצר

I *harvest*.

בָּצִיר II 1 adj. **fortified,** יַעַר הַבָּצִיר appar. *forest of the fortified (one)*, i.e. fortress-like forest Zc 11₂(Qr). → בצר I *be fortified.*

[בָּצָל] I 1 n.[m.]—pl. בְּצָלִים—**onion** Nm 11₅.

*[בָּצָל] II 0.0.0.1 pr.n.m. **Bazal.**

בְּצַלְאֵל 9 pr.n.m. **Bezaleel.**

בַּצְלוּת 2 pr.n.m. **Bazluth.**

בַּצְלִית, see בַּצְלוּת *Bazluth.*

בצע I 16.2 vb.—**Qal** 10.2 Impf. יִבְצַע; impv. בִּצְעָם; ptc. בּוֹצֵעַ; inf. בְּצֹעַ (בִּצְעֵךְ)—**1.** with obj. בֶּצַע, **extort, make (unjust gain)** Jr 6₁₃. **2. cut off** tops of pillars Am 9₁. **3.** appar. **deviate** Jl 2₈.

Pi. 6 Pf. בִּצַּע; impf. יְבַצַּע—oft. of Y., **1. cut off person** Is 38₁₂ (+ מִן *from*). **2. accomplish, complete work** Is 10₁₂. **3.** appar. **make unjust gain from neighbours** by (בְּ) extortion Ezk 22₁₂.

→ בֶּצַע I *profit.*

*בצע II 0.2 vb.—**Qal** 0.2 Ptc. בוצע—**slander** Si 11₂₉.₃₀.

בֶּצַע I 23.1.8 n.m.—בָּצַע; sf. בִּצְעָם—**profit** Gn 37₂₆, usu. specif. **unjust gain, extortion** Ex 18₂₁. → בצע I *cut off.*

*[בֶּצַע] II 0.1 n.m. **blemish** Si 7₆.

בצק 2 vb.—**Qal** 2 Pf. בָּצֵקָה—**be swollen,** of feet Dt 8₄. → בָּצֵק *dough.*

בָּצֵק 5.0.0.1 n.[m.]—sf. בְּצֵקוֹ—**dough** Ex 12₃₄. → בצק *swell.*

*[בִּצְקְלוֹן] n.[m.] **plant, ear of corn,** בִּצְקְלֹן כַּרְמִלּוֹ *plant(s) of his vineyard* 2 K 4₄₂ (if em. כַּרְמֶל בְּצִקְלֹנוֹ *fresh produce in his wallet* or *in its stalk*).

בָּצְקַת 2 pl.n. **Bozkath.**

בצר I 38.2 vb.—**Qal** 34.1 Impf. יִבְצֹר; ptc. בֹּצְרִים, בּוֹצֵר; ptc. pass. בְּצוּרָה, בְּצוּרוֹת—**1a. harvest grapes** Lv 25₅, vineyard Dt 24₂₁. **b.** ptc. as noun, **harvester of grapes** Ob 5. **2.** of Y., **restrain** spirit of rulers Ps 76₁₃. **3.** pass., **be fortified, inaccessible,** of city Nm 13₂₈, wall Dt 28₅₂.

Ni. 2.1 Impf. יִבָּצֵר—**be cut off, withheld** from (מִן) someone, of food Si 37₂₀, plan Jb 42₂.

Pi. 2 Impf. תְּבַצֵּר—**fortify, make inaccessible** wall Is 22₁₀, height Jr 51₅₃.

→ בִּצָּרוֹן *stronghold,* בָּצִיר II *fortified,* מִבְצָר *Vintager,* מִבְצָר I *fortification,* בָּצִיר I *grape harvest,* בַּצָּרָה *drought,* בַּצֹּרֶת *drought,* בֶּצֶר I *gold,* בְּצַר *gold.*

*[בצר] II vb. **Pi., test,** ptc. as noun, **assayer** Jr 6₂₇ (if em. מִבְצָר *fortification* to מְבַצֵּר *assayer*).

[בֶּצֶר] I 2 n.[m.]—pl. sf. בְּצָרֶיךָ—**gold** Jb 22₂₄.₂₅. → בצר I *cut.*

בֶּצֶר II 3 pl.n. **Bezer.**

בֶּצֶר III 1.0.0.1 pr.n.m. **Bezer.**

[בְּצַר] 1 n.[m.]—בְּצָר—**gold** Jb 36₁₉. → בצר I *cut.*

בָּצְרָה 10 pl.n. **Bozrah.**

בַּצָּרָה 2 n.f. **drought** Ps 9₁₀ 10₁. → בצר I *cut.*

בִּצָּרוֹן 1 n.[m.] **stronghold,** unless pl.n. **Bizzaron** Zc 9₁₂. → בצר I *cut.*

בַּצֹּרֶת 2.1 n.f.—pl. בַּצָּרוֹת—**drought** Jr 14₁ 17₈. → בצר I *cut.*

בַּקְבֻּק I 3 n.[m.] **jug** Jr 19₁.

[בַּקְבֻּק] II 2 pr.n.m. **Bakbuk.**

בַּקְבֻּקְיָה 3 pr.n.m. **Bakbukiah.**

בַּקְבַּקַּר 1 pr.n.m. **Bakbakkar.**

בֻּקִּי 5.0.0.1 pr.n.m. **Bukki.**

בֻּקִּיָּהוּ 2 pr.n.m. **Bukkiah.**

[בָּקִיעַ] 2 n.[m.]—pl. בְּקִיעִים—**fissure,** in city Is 22₉, house Am 6₁₁. → בקע I *split.*

בקע I 51.1.4 vb.—**Qal** 16.1 Pf. בָּקַע, בָּקַעְתָּ; + waw וַיִּבְקַע; impv. בִּקְעֻהוּ; ptc. בֹּוקֵעַ; inf. בִּקְעָם—**1a. split** wood Ec 10₉. **b. divide** sea Ex 14₁₆. **c. tear** shoulder Ezk 29₇. **d. split open** pregnant woman Am 1₁₃. **2. breach the defences of, invade** Judah 2 C 21₁₇. **3. hatch eggs** Is 34₁₅ (if em. בְּצִלָּהּ *in her shade* to בֵּצֶיהָ *her eggs*).

Ni. 15.0.4 Pf. נִבְקַע; impf. יִבָּקַע (יִבָּקֵעַ); inf. הִבָּקַע—**1. be split,** of ground Nm 16₃₁, mountain Zc 14₄, cloud Jb 26₈, womb Jb 32₁₉. **2. be broken into,** i.e. be captured, of city 2 K 25₄. **3. break out,** of light Is 58₈. **4. be hatched, hatch out,** of crushed egg Is 59₅.

Pi. 12 Pf. בִּקַּע; impf. תְּבַקַּע (תְּבַקֵּעַ); + waw וַיְבַקְּעוּ—**1a. split, cut up** wood Gn 22₃. **b. carve out** channels in (בְּ) rocks Jb 28₁₀. **c. rip open** pregnant woman 2 K 8₁₂. **d. tear apart** child 2 K 2₂₄. **e. strike** loins of child Si 30₁₂. **2. hatch** eggs Is 59₅.

Pu. 3 Impf. יְבֻקָּעוּ; ptc. מְבֻקָּעָה—**1. be split open,** of wineskin Jos 9₄, pregnant woman Ho 14₁. **2. be breached,** of city Ezk 26₁₀.

Hi. 2 Impf. נִבְקָעֶנָּה; inf. הַבְקִיעַ—**1. break (a way) through to** (אֶל) someone 2 K 3₂₆. **2. invade** land Is 7₆.

Ho. 1 Pf. הָבְקְעָה—**be invaded,** of city Jr 39₂.

Htp. 2 Pf. הִתְבַּקְּעוּ; impf. יִתְבַּקָּעוּ—**be split open,** of valley Mc 1₄, wineskin Jos 9₁₃.

→ בֶּקַע *half a shekel,* בִּקְעָה *valley,* בָּקִיעַ *fissure,* מִבְקָע *cleavage;* cf. פֶּקַע II *blast.*

*בקע II 1 vb.—**Hi.** 1 Impf. נִבְקִעֶנָּה—**make come over** to (אֶל) one's side, obj. Judah Is 7₆.

*בקע III 1 vb.—**Qal** 1 Inf. בִּקְעָם—**break into sandy plateau** Am 1₁₃.

בֶּקַע 2.0.0.2 n.[m.] **half a shekel** Gn 24₂₂. → בקע I *split.*

בִּקְעָה 21.0.2 n.f.—cstr. בִּקְעַת; pl. בְּקָעוֹת—**valley,** oft. broad, **plain** Gn 11₂; אֶרֶץ הָרִים וּבְקָעֹת *a land of hills and valleys* Dt 11₁₁. → בקע I *split.*

בקק I 8 vb.—**Qal** 4 Pf. בָּקְקוּם; + waw וּבַקֹּתִי; ptc. בֹּקְקִים—**devastate, ruin, make useless** earth Is 24₁, plans Jr 19₇.

Ni. 3 Pf. נָבְקָה; impf. תִּבּוֹק; inf. הִבּוֹק—**be devastated,** of earth Is 24₃, spirit of the Egyptians Is 19₃.

Po. 1 Impf. וִיבֹקְקוּ—**devastate** land Jr 51₂.

בקק II 1 vb.—**Qal** 1 Ptc. בּוֹקֵק—**flourish, be widespread,** of vine Ho 10₁.

בקר I 7.1.9 vb.—**Pi.** 7.1.9 Impf. יְבַקֵּר; + waw וּבִקַּרְתִּים; ptc. Q מבקר; inf. לְבַקֵּר—**1. seek sheep** Ezk 34₁₁, to distinguish between (לְ ... בֵּין) good and bad things Lv 27₃₃, **examine** young woman (for proof of virginity) 4Q Ord[a] 2₈, **look at** (לְ) hair Lv 13₃₆; abs., **inquire** Si 11₇, **consider** Pr 20₂₅. **2.** ptc. as noun, **inspector, overseer** CD 14₈. → בַּקָּרָה *seeking,* בִּקֹּרֶת *inquiry.*

בקר II 1 vb.—**Qal** 1 Ptc. בּוֹקֵר—**shepherd,** ptc. as noun, **herdsman** Ho 7₁₄. → בָּקָר *cattle.*

בָּקָר 183.0.11 n.m. (& f.)—sf. בְּקָרוֹ; pl. בְּקָרִים; sf. בְּקָרֵינוּ—**1.** usu. coll., **cattle,** specif. **herd of cows** Gn 33₁₃, **livestock,** including bulls, rams, goats Nm 7₈₇. **2.** as unitary noun, **head of cattle, cow, bull** Ex 21₃₇; בֶּן־בָּקָר **calf, bullock** Gn 18₇. **3. images of oxen** 1 K 7₂₅||2 C 4₄. → בקר II *shepherd.*

בֹּקֶר 214.4.19.3 n.m.—pl. בְּקָרִים—**morning,** בַּבֹּקֶר כִּזְרֹחַ הַשֶּׁמֶשׁ *in the morning, as the sun rises* Jg 9₃₃, מִן־הַבֹּקֶר עַד־הָעֶרֶב *from the morning until the evening* Ex 18₁₃, כָּל־הַלַּיְלָה עַד־הַבֹּקֶר *all the night, until the morning* Jg 19₂₅.

בְּקֶרֶב, see קֶרֶב *midst.*

[בַּקָּרָה] 1 n.f. **seeking,** כְּבַקָּרַת רֹעֶה עֶדְרוֹ *as a shepherd's seeking of his flock* Ezk 34₁₂. → בקר I *seek.*

בִּקֹּרֶת 1 n.f. **inquiry** Lv 19₂₀. → בקר I *seek.*

בקשׁ I 225.15.29.2 vb.—**Pi.** 222.15.29.2 Pf. בִּקֵּשׁ (בִּקֶּשׁ־), בִּקַּשְׁתִּי, בִּקְשׁוּ; impf. יְבַקֵּשׁ, יְבַקְשׁוּ (יְבַקְשׁוּ); + waw וַיְבַקְשֵׁהוּ; impv. בַּקֵּשׁ, בַּקְשׁוּ (בַּקְּשׁוּ); ptc. מְבַקֵּשׁ, מְבַקְשִׁים; inf. בַּקֵּשׁ (בַּקְשׁוֹ)—**1. seek (to find)** persons Gn 37₁₆, lost asses 1 S 9₃; abs., **make a search** Jg 6₂₉. **2. seek (to obtain), require** authority from (מִן) Y. Si 7₄, vision from prophet Ezk 7₂₆, someone's life (נֶפֶשׁ) Ex 4₁₉, harm Nm 35₂₃. **3. seek (to do something),** with inf. Ex 4₂₄, more oft. לְ + inf. Ex 2₁₅. **4. seek** Y. Dt 4₂₉, face of Y. Ps 27₈, word of Y. Am 8₁₂. **5a. ask for, request** something, with accus. Est 2₁₅, עַל *for* Ne 2₄. **b. entreat, beseech** Y. or person (מִן of obj.) **for** (עַל) something Est 7₇ Ezr 8₂₃.

Pu. 3 Impf. יְבֻקַּשׁ; + waw וּתְבֻקְשִׁי—**be sought,** of Tyre Ezk 26₂₁, iniquity Jr 50₂₀, matter Est 2₂₃.

→ בַּקָּשָׁה *request.*

*בקשׁ II 5.1 vb.—**Pi.** 5.1 Impf. יְבַקֵּשׁ, יְבַקְשׁוּ; inf. בַּקֵּשׁ—**magnify** name of Y. Ps 83₁₇, **make much of** prayer Dn 9₃, the persecuted Si 5₁ (subj. Y.).

*[בִּקֵּשׁ] 0.0.0.1 pr.n.m. **Bikkesh.**

[בַּקָּשָׁה] 6.0.3 n.m.—sf. בַּקָּשָׁתִי—**request** Est 5₃. → בקשׁ I *seek.*

בַּר I 14 n.m.—בָּר—**grain** Jl 2₂₄.

בַּר II 4.0.39.4 n.m.—cstr. בַּר; sf. בְּרִי—**son** Pr 31₂. → cf. בָּרָה *daughter.*

בַּר III 6 adj.—f.s. בָּרָה; m.pl. cstr. בָּרֵי—**1. pure,** of commandment of Y. Ps 19₉, woman Ca 6₉, man Jb 11₄. **2.** as noun, **pure one,** בַּר־לֵבָב *one pure of heart* Ps 24₄.

[בַּר] IV 1 n.[m.]—בָּר—**field** Jb 39₄.

[בֹּר] I 5.0.2 n.m.—cstr. בֹּר (Q בור); sf. בֹּרִי—**cleanness** of hands 2 S 22₂₁.

בֹּר II 2 n.[m.] **soap,** or cleansing agent used in or instead of soap, e.g. **lye, potash** Jb 9₃₀. → cf. בֹּרִית *soap.*

בֹּר III, see בּוֹר *pit.*

ברא I 48.11.41 vb.—**Qal** 38.7.38 Pf. בָּרָא, בָּרָאתָ; impf. יִבְרָא; impv. בְּרָא; ptc. בֹּרֵא; inf. בְּרֹא—alw. of Y., **create** heavens and earth Gn 1₁, day and night Jr 33₂₅, animals

Gn 1$_{21}$, human being Gn 1$_{27}$.

Ni. 10.4.3 Pf. נִבְרֵאת; impf. יִבָּרֵאוּן; ptc. נִבְרָא; inf. הִבָּרְאָךְ—**be created,** of earth and heaven Gn 2$_{4}$, people Ps 102$_{19}$, miracles Ex 34$_{10}$.

→ בְּרִיאָה *creation.*

ברא II 2 vb.—**Hi.** 1 Inf. הַבְרִיאֲכֶם—**fatten** oneself with (מִן) sacrificial meat 1 S 2$_{29}$.

Ni. 1 Impf. יִבָּרֵאוּן—perh. **be made fat, healthy,** of works of Y. Ps 104$_{30}$.

→ בָּרִיא *fat.*

*ברא III 5 vb.—**Pi.** 5 + waw וּבֵרֵאתָ; inf. בָּרֵא—**cut down** women Ezk 23$_{47}$, forest Jos 17$_{15}$, **cut out** sign Ezk 21$_{24}$.

ברא IV, see ברה *eat.*

*[בָּרָא] 0.0.0.1 pr.n.[m.] **Bara.**

בְּרֹאדַךְ בַּלְאֲדָן 1 pr.n.m. **Berodach-baladan.**

בְּרָאיָה 1 pr.n.m. **Beraiah.**

[בַּרְבּוּר] 1 n.m.—pl. בַּרְבֻּרִים—**goose,** or perh. **chicken** or **cuckoo** 1 K 5$_{3}$.

ברד 1 vb.—**Qal** 1 + waw וּבָרַד—**rain hail** Is 32$_{19}$. → בָּרָד *hail.*

בָּרָד 29.4.1 n.m. **hail** Ex 9$_{18}$; אַבְנֵי הַבָּרָד *stones of hail* Jos 10$_{11}$. → ברד *rain hail.*

[בָּרֹד] 4 adj.—pl. בְּרֻדִּים—**mottled,** of horse Zc 6$_{3}$, he-goat Gn 31$_{10}$.

[בֶּרֶד] I 1 pl.n. **Bered.**

בֶּרֶד II 1 pr.n.m. **Bered.**

ברה I 6 vb.—**Qal** 3 Pf. בָּרָה (בָּרָא); impf. אֶבְרֶה—**eat** bread 2 S 12$_{17}$; without obj. 2 S 13$_{6}$ (+ מִיַּד *from the hand of*).

Pi. 1 Inf. בָּרוֹת—inf. as noun, **food** Lm 4$_{10}$.

Hi. 2 Impf. תַּבְרֵנִי; inf. הַבְרוֹת—with double accus., **feed** bread to someone 2 S 13$_{5}$.

→ בִּרְיָה *food,* בָּרוּת *food.*

*ברה II 1 vb.—**Qal** 1 Impv. בְּרוּ—**choose, appoint** someone **as representative** 1 S 17$_{8}$.

*ברה III 1 vb.—**Qal** 1 Impv. בְּרוּ—**commission** someone 1 S 17$_{8}$.

*[בָּרָה] 0.0.1 n.f. **daughter**—cstr. ברת—Mur 30 2$_{33}$. → cf. בַּר *son.*

*[בִּרָה] 3 n.f. **double-hour,** measure of distance, c. 11 km, בְּעוֹד כִּבְרַת־אֶרֶץ לָבֹא אֶפְרָתָה *when there was still about a double-hour of distance to go to Ephrath* Gn 48$_{7}$.

בָּרוּךְ 26.0.0.3 pr.n.m. **Baruch.**

בְּרוֹשׁ 20.0.2 n.m.—pl. בְּרוֹשִׁים; sf. בְּרֹשָׁיו—**1. juniper** Ezk 27$_{5}$. **2.** perh. **spear shaft** Na 2$_{4}$ (or em. פָּרָשׁ *rider*). → cf. בְּרוֹת *juniper.*

[בָּרוּת] 1 n.f.—sf. בָּרוּתִי—**food** Ps 69$_{22}$. → ברה I *eat.*

[בְּרוֹת] 1 n.[f.]—pl. בְּרוֹתִים—**juniper** Ca 1$_{17}$(Qr). → cf. בְּרוֹשׁ *juniper.*

בֵּרוֹתָה 1 pl.n. **Berothah.**

[בִּרְזַיִת] 1 pl.n. **Birzaith.**

בַּרְזֶל 76.2 n.m. **iron,** חָרַשׁ בַּרְזֶל *artisan of,* i.e. in, *iron* Is 44$_{12}$, נֵשֶׁק *weapon of* Jb 20$_{24}$, מֹטוֹת *yokes of* Jr 28$_{13}$. → cf. פַּרְזֶל *iron,* פִּרְזוֹן II *iron.*

בַּרְזִלַּי 11 pr.n.m. **Barzillai.**

ברח I 65.1.5 vb.—**Qal** 59.1.5 Pf. בָּרַח; impf. יִבְרַח; impv. בְּרַח, בִּרְחוּ; ptc. בֹּרֵחַ, בֹּרַחַת; inf. abs. בָּרוֹחַ; cstr. בְּרֹחַ (בָּרְחוֹ)—**1.** usu. **flee, make haste,** from (מִן) land 2 S 19$_{10}$, people Is 48$_{20}$; from before (מִפְּנֵי) someone Gn 35$_{1}$; אֶל *to* someone 1 S 23$_{6}$, land Am 7$_{12}$; אַחֲרֵי *after* someone 1 S 22$_{20}$; abs. Ex 14$_{5}$. **2. run,** of bar Ex 36$_{33}$ (+ בְּתוֹךְ *through*).

Hi. 6 Pf. הִבְרִיחוּ; impf. יַבְרִיחַ; ptc. מַבְרִחַ—**1. expel, put to flight** people 1 C 8$_{13}$, Leviathan Jb 41$_{20}$. **2. run,** of bar Ex 26$_{28}$.

→ בָּרִחַ I *fugitive,* מִבְרָח I *fugitive,* בְּרִיחַ *bar.*

*ברח II 1 vb.—**Hi.** 1 Impf. יַבְרִיחֶנּוּ—**wound** Leviathan Jb 41$_{20}$.

בָּרִחַ, see בָּרִיחַ I *fugitive,* II *evil,* III *dangerous,* IV *primaeval.*

בַּרְחֻמִי 1 gent. **Barhumite.**

בֵּרִי I 1 pr.n.m. **Beri.**

[בֵּרִי] II 1 gent. **Berite.**

בָּרִיא 14 adj.—Q ברי; f.s. בְּרִיאָה; m.pl. בְּרִאִים; cstr. בְּרִיאֵי; f.pl. בְּרִיאוֹת—**fat, fleshy,** i.e. nourished, healthy, of person Jg 3$_{17}$, cattle Gn 41$_{2}$ (בְּרִיאֹת בָּשָׂר *fat of flesh*), ear of grain Gn 41$_{5}$. → ברא II *be fat.*

בְּרִיאָה 1.1.16 n.f.—Q בריה; pl. cstr. Q בריאות; sf. Q בריאותיו—**1. creation,** יום הבריאה *day of creation* 4QpsJub[a] 1$_{7}$. **2. creature,** בריאות הבשר *creatures of flesh* 4QBer[b] 3$_{2}$. → ברא I *create.*

בִּרְיָה 3 n.f. **food** 2 S 13$_{5.7.10}$. → ברה I *eat.*

[בָּרִיחַ] I 4 n.m. and adj.—בָּרִחַ; pl. בְּרִיחִים—**1. fugitive**

Is 15$_{5}$. **2.** adj. **fleeing, swift,** of serpent Is 27$_{1}$. → ברח I *run*.

*בָּרִיחַ II 2 adj. **evil,** לִוְיָתָן נָחָשׁ בָּרִחַ *Leviathan the evil serpent* Is 27$_{1}$.

*בָּרִיחַ III 2 adj. **dangerous,** לִוְיָתָן נָחָשׁ בָּרִחַ *Leviathan the dangerous serpent* Is 27$_{1}$.

*בָּרִיחַ IV 2 adj. **primaeval,** לִוְיָתָן נָחָשׁ בָּרִחַ *Leviathan the primaeval serpent* Is 27$_{1}$.

בָּרִיחַ V 1 pr.n.m. **Bariah.**

בְּרִיחַ 40.1.5 n.m.—cstr. בְּרִיחַ; pl. בְּרִיחִים; cstr. בְּרִיחֵי; sf. בְּרִיחָיו—**bar, pole** of wood, joining frames of tabernacle Ex 26$_{26}$||36$_{31}$; **bar** of city gate Dt 3$_{5}$ Ps 147$_{14}$, made of iron Is 45$_{2}$. → ברח I *flee*.

בְּרִיעָה 11 pr.n.m. **Beriah.**

בְּרִיעִי 1 gent. **Beriite.**

בְּרִית I 285.10.156 n.f.—cstr. בְּרִית; sf. בְּרִתִי; pl. sf. Si בריתיך—**covenant, agreement,** or **obligation** between individuals Gn 31$_{44}$, groups Ps 83$_{6}$, ruler and subjects 2 S 5$_{3}$, Y. and individual Gn 9$_{9}$, Y. and Israel Ex 19$_{5}$; כרת בְּרִית אֵת *cut,* i.e. make, *a covenant with* someone Gn 15$_{18}$, vars. with עִם *with* Gn 26$_{28}$, בֵּין ... וּבֵין *between ... and* 2 K 11$_{17}$||2 C 23$_{16}$; קום בְּרִית אֵת hi. *establish a covenant with* Gn 6$_{18}$, בוא בִּבְרִית אֵת *enter into a covenant with* Ezk 16$_{8}$, באי הברית *those who enter the covenant* 1QS 2$_{18}$; סֵפֶר הַבְּרִית *book of the covenant* Ex 24$_{7}$, אֲרוֹן *ark of* Jos 3$_{6}$, דַּם־ *blood of* Ex 24$_{8}$.

*בְּרִית II 1 n.[f.] **fetter,** וְהֵבֵאתִי אֶתְכֶם בְּמָסֹרֶת הַבְּרִית *and I shall bring you into the bondage (?) of the fetter* Ezk 20$_{37}$.

*בְּרִית III 1 n.[f.] **splendour,** וְאֶתֶּנְךָ לִבְרִית עָם *and I shall make you the splendour of the people* Is 42$_{6}$.

בֹּרִית 2 n.f. **soap,** or other cleansing agent, e.g. **lye, potash** Jr 2$_{22}$ Ml 3$_{2}$. → cf. בֹּר *soap*.

ברך I 327.14.190.16 vb.—**Qal** 71.1.59.7 Ptc. pass. בָּרוּךְ, בְּרוּכָה, בָּרוּךְ, בְּרוּכִים, בְּרוּכֵי—only pass., **be blessed,** of Y. Ezr 7$_{27}$, person Ru 2$_{20}$ (+ לְ *by* Y.), animal Dt 28$_{4}$, fruit Dt 28$_{4}$, day Jr 20$_{14}$.

Ni. 3.0.3 + waw וְנִבְרְכוּ—**be blessed** by (בְּ) Abram, of family Gn 12$_{3}$.

Pi. 233.12.123.9 Pf. בֵּרַךְ (בֵּרֵךְ); impf. יְבָרְכוּ; + waw וַיְבָרֶךְ; וּבֵרַכְתָּ; impv. בָּרֵךְ, בָּרְכִי, בָּרְכוּ; ptc. מְבָרֵךְ; inf. abs. בָּרֵךְ (בָּרוֹךְ); cstr. בָּרֵךְ (בָּרְכוֹ)—**1.** usu. **bless,** subj. Y. Gn 12$_{2}$, priest Lv 9$_{22}$, king 1 K 8$_{55}$, Israelites Dt 8$_{10}$; obj. Y. Jg 5$_{2}$, Y.'s name Ps 96$_{2}$, person Ru 2$_{4}$, abode Pr 3$_{33}$, sabbath day Ex 20$_{11}$. **2.** rarely, **curse** God, king 1 K 21$_{10}$ Jb 1$_{5}$.

Pu. 13.1 Impf. יְבֹרַךְ; ptc. מְבֹרָךְ—**be blessed,** of name of Y. Ps 113$_{2}$, person Ps 128$_{4}$, land Dt 33$_{13}$.

Hi. 0.0.3 Pf. הברכנו; inf. הברך—**bless** Y. 1QS 10$_{6}$, firstfruits 1QS 6$_{5}$ (בְּ of obj.).

Htp. 7.0.2 Pf. הִתְבָּרְכוּ; impf. יִתְבָּרֵךְ; ptc. מִתְבָּרֵךְ—**1. bless oneself** by (בְּ) Y., of nations Jr 4$_{2}$. **2. be blessed,** of Y. GnzPs 4$_{11}$.

→ בְּרָכָה *blessing*.

*ברך II 2 vb.—**Pi.** 1 Pf. בֵּרֵךְ—**strengthen** sons Ps 147$_{13}$.

Htp. 1 **strengthen oneself in** (בְּ) one's heart Dt 29$_{18}$.

ברך III 3 vb.—**Qal** 2 Impf. נִבְרְכָה; + waw וַיִּבְרַךְ—**kneel** upon (עַל) knees 2 C 6$_{13}$, before (לִפְנֵי) Y. Ps 95$_{6}$.

Hi. 1 + waw וַיַּבְרֵךְ—**make** camel **kneel** Gn 24$_{11}$.

→ בֶּרֶךְ *knee*.

בֶּרֶךְ 25.1.3 n.f.—du. בִּרְכַּיִם; cstr. בִּרְכֵּי; sf. בִּרְכַּי—**knee,** כרע עַל־בִּרְכַּיִם *kneel on the knees* Jg 7$_{5}$, פִּק בִּרְכַּיִם *shaking of knees* Na 2$_{11}$. → ברך III *kneel*.

בַּרַכְאֵל 2 pr.n.m. **Barachel.**

בְּרָכָה I 69.12.30.2 n.f.—cstr. בִּרְכַּת; sf. בִּרְכָתִי; pl. בְּרָכוֹת; cstr. בִּרְכוֹת; sf. בִּרְכוֹתֵיכֶם—**1. blessing,** from Y. Ml 3$_{10}$. **2. gift,** from human Gn 33$_{11}$. **3. source of blessing,** in ref. to Abraham Gn 12$_{2}$. **4. pronouncement of blessing,** by parent upon child Gn 49$_{28}$. **5. praise** of Y. Ne 9$_{5}$. **6. covenant, peace treaty** 2 K 18$_{31}$. → ברך I *bless*.

בְּרָכָה II 1.0.0.1 pr.n.m. **Beracah.**

בְּרֵכָה 17.0.0.1 n.f. **pool**—cstr. בְּרֵכַת; pl. בְּרֵכוֹת—2 S 2$_{13}$ 2 K 18$_{17}$.

*[בַּרְכִּי] 0.0.0.1 pr.n.[m.] **Barchi.**

בֶּרֶכְיָה 11.0.0.7 pr.n.m. **Berechiah.**

בְּרֹמִים 1 n.[m.] **multi-coloured cloth,** גִּנְזֵי בְּרֹמִים perh. *carpets of multi-coloured material* Ezk 27$_{24}$.

בֶּרַע 1 pr.n.m. **Bera.**

בְּרֵעָה, see בְּרִיעָה *Beriah*.

ברק 1.0.1 vb.—**Qal** 1 Impv. בְּרוֹק—**flash lightning** Ps 144$_{6}$. → בָּרָק I *lightning*, בַּרְקָה *flash*, (?) בַּרְקָן *briar*.

בָּרָק I 21.3.2 n.m.—cstr. בְּרַק; pl. בְּרָקִים; sf. בְּרָקָיו—**1.**

lightning Ex 19_{16} Ps 77_{19}. **2. flash** of sword Dt 32_{41}. → ברק *flash.*

בָּרָק II 13 pr.n.m. **Barak.**

בְּרַק, see בְּנֵי־בְרַק *Bene-berak.*

***[בַּרְקָה]** 0.0.1 n.[f.]—cstr. ברקת—**flash** of spear 1QM 6_2. → ברק *flash.*

בַּרְקוֹס 2 pr.n.m. **Barkos.**

[בַּרְקָן] 2 n.[m.]—pl. בַּרְקֳנִים—**briar** Jg $8_{7.17}$. → (?) ברק *flash.*

בָּרֶקֶת 2 n.[f.] **emerald,** or other precious green stone Ex 28_{17}||39_{10}. → cf. בָּרְקַת *emerald.*

בָּרְקַת 1 n.[f.] **emerald,** or other precious green stone Ezk 28_{13}. → cf. בָּרֶקֶת *emerald.*

ברר I 16.2.17 vb.—**Qal** 7.0.5 + waw וּבָרוֹתִי; ptc. בְּרוּרָה, בָּרוּר; inf. בָּרֻם) בּוּר)—**cleanse, purify** knowledge 1QS 1_{12}, sinner, of Y. Ezk 20_{38}. **2.** pass. ptc. as adj., **purified,** of lips Zp 3_9, knowledge Jb 33_3.

Ni. 3.0.2 Impv. הִבָּרוּ; ptc. נָבָר—**1. purify oneself** Is 52_{11}. **2.** ptc. as noun, **pure one** 2 S 22_{27}||Ps 18_{27}.

Pi. 1.0.4 Inf. בָּרֵר—**purify** deeds 1QS 4_{20}.

Hi. 2.2.6 Pf. Si הברותי; impv. Si הבר—**clean, refine** arrow Jr 51_{11}, face Si $38_{10(Bmg)}$.

Htp. 3 Impf. יִתְבָּרְרוּ—**behave purely,** of Y. 2 S 22_{27}, human Dn 12_{10}.

ברר II 3.0.6 vb.—**Qal** 2.0.6 Impf. Q תבר; + waw Q ובררו; ptc. בְּרוּרִים—**1. select warriors** 11QT 57_5 (+ מִן *from*). **2a.** pass. **be chosen,** as judges CD 10_4 (+ מִן *from among*). **b.** pass. ptc. as noun, **chosen one** 1 C 16_{41}.

Hi. 1 Inf. הָבַר—**sift,** of wind Jr 4_{11}.

ברר III 2 vb.—**Qal** 1 Ptc. בָּרוּר—pass. **be sharpened,** of arrow Is 49_2.

Hi. 1 Pf. הָבֵרוּ— **sharpen** arrow Jr 51_{11}.

בִּרְשַׁע 1 pr.n.m. **Birsha.**

בֵּרֹתַי 1 pl.n. **Berothai.**

בֵּרֹתִי, see בְּאֵרֹתִי *Beerothite.*

בְּרִתִי, see בְּרִית *covenant.*

בְּשׂוֹר 3 pl.n. **Besor.**

בְּשׂוֹרָה 6 n.f.—בְּשֹׂרָה—**news** 2 S 18_{22}. → בשׂר I *announce news.*

בֹּשֶׂם 30 n.m.—בֶּשֶׂם; sf. בְּשָׂמִי; pl. בְּשָׂמִים; sf. בְּשָׂמָיו—**1. spice, perfume** Ex 25_6||35_8. **2. balsam tree** Ca 5_{13}.

בָּשְׂמַת 7 pr.n.f. **Basemath.**

בשׂר I 24.0.6 vb.—**Pi.** 23.0.6 Pf. בִּשַּׂר; impf. תְּבַשֵּׂר; impv. בַּשְּׂרוּ; ptc. מְבַשֵּׂר, מְבַשֶּׂרֶת, מְבַשְּׂרוֹת; inf. בַּשֵּׂר—**1a. announce news to** (accus.) someone Jr 20_{15}. **b. announce salvation** Ps 96_2||1 C 16_{23}. **2.** ptc. as noun, **messenger** Is 52_7.

Htp. 1 Impf. יִתְבַּשֵּׂר—**receive news** 2 S 18_{31}.

→ בְּשׂוֹרָה *news.*

***בשׂר** II 1 vb.—**Pi.** 1 Ptc. מְבַשֵּׂר—ptc. as noun, **one who refutes,** i.e. an advocate Is 41_{27}.

בָּשָׂר 270.16.64 n.m.—cstr. בְּשַׂר; sf. בְּשָׂרִי; pl. בְּשָׂרִים—**1. flesh,** as substance of body Gn 2_{21}. **2. body** of person Ex 30_{32}, in contrast to spirit or soul Is 10_{18} 31_3. **3. creature** in general Gn 9_{11}. **4. human being** Jb 34_{15}, in contrast to Y. Gn 6_3. **5. relative** Lv 18_6. **6. animal** other than human being Gn 8_{17}. **7. meat** Ex 12_8. **8. genitals** of man or ass Ex 28_{42} Ezk 23_{20}.

בשׁל 30.1.4 vb.—**Qal** 2.1.2 Pf. בָּשַׁל; inf. Si בשול—**1. be boiled,** of bone Ezk 24_5. **2. be ripe,** of grape Si 51_{15}.

Pi. 23.0.2 Pf. בִּשְּׁלָם; impf. תְּבַשְּׁלוּ; impv. בַּשֵּׁל, בַּשְּׁלוּ; ptc. מְבַשְּׁלִים; inf. בַּשֵּׁל—**boil, cook stew** 2 K 4_{38}, sacrifices Ezk 46_{24}, children Lm 4_{10}; by, with (בְּ) fire 2 C 35_{13}, in (בְּ) milk Ex 23_{19}.

Pu. 4 Pf. בֻּשָּׁלָה; impf. תְּבֻשַּׁל; ptc. מְבֻשָּׁל—**be boiled, be cooked** in (בְּ) water, of meat Ex 12_9.

Hi. 1 Pf. הִבְשִׁילוּ—**become ripe,** of clusters of grapes Gn 40_{10}.

→ בָּשֵׁל *boiled,* מְבַשְּׁלוֹת *hearths.*

בָּשֵׁל 2 adj. **boiled**—f.s. בְּשֵׁלָה—of sacrificial animal Ex 12_9. → בשׁל *boil.*

בִּשְׁלָם 1 pr.n.[m.] **Bishlam.**

בָּשָׁן I 59 pl.n. **Bashan.**

***בָּשָׁן** II 2 n.m. **snake** Dt 33_{22} Ps 68_{23}.

בָּשְׁנָה 1 n.f. **shame** Ho 10_6. → בושׁ I *be ashamed.*

[בֵּשָׁנִי], see בֵּישָׁנִי *Beshanite.*

בשׁס 1 vb.—**Po.** 1 Inf. בּוֹשַׁסְכֶם—**trample on** (עַל) the poor Am 5_{11}.

בֹּשֶׁת 30.7.6 n.f.—cstr. בֹּשֶׁת; sf. בָּשְׁתָּם—**1. shame,** בֹּשֶׁת עֶרְוַת אִמֶּךָ *shame of your mother's genitals* 1 S 20_{30}, בושת על פנים *shame is upon the face* 1QH 13_{35}, בשת משאת עון *shame (worthy) of burden of guilt* Si 4_{21}. **2. Shame,** name of a deity, perh. in ref. to (or scribal emendation of) בַּעַל *Baal* Jr 11_{13}. → בושׁ I *be ashamed.*

בַּת I 584.6.28.16 n.f.—sf. בִּתִּי; pl. בָּנוֹת; cstr. בְּנוֹת; sf. בְּנֹתָם— 1. usu. **daughter** of humans Gn 5₄ 29₁₆. 2. **female young** of animals Lv 14₁₀; specif. בַּת יַעֲנָה **(young of) ostrich,** or perh. **eagle owl** Lv 11₁₆||Dt 14₁₅. 3. **possessor of, a.** years of life, אִם־שָׂרָה הֲבַת־תִּשְׁעִים שָׁנָה תֵּלֵד *can Sarah, a possessor of ninety years,* i.e. at the age of ninety, *bear a child?* Gn 17₁₇. **b.** steps, שֵׁן בַּת־אֲשֻׁרִים *ivory, daughter of steps,* i.e. inlaid ivory Ezk 27₆. 4. **daughter,** as personification of city, land or people, בַּת־צִיּוֹן *daughter of Zion* Is 1₈, בַּת־עַמִּי *daughter of my people* Is 22₄. 5. **environ, village,** as daughter of a larger town, or perh. **fortification, fortified place,** usu. וּבְנֹתֶיהָ *and its villages,* preceded by pl.n. Jos 15₄₅ Jr 49₂. 6. perh. **branch** of tree Gn 49₂₂. 7. **one who is, one who is numbered among,** בְּנוֹת הַשִּׁיר *daughters of (the) song,* i.e. songs Ec 12₄. 8. **one having the form of,** בַּת־גְּדוּד *daughter of a troop,* i.e. (as) a single troop Mc 4₁₄. 9. **pupil** of eye Ps 17₈.

בַּת II 13.0.1.2 n.f. (& m.)—cstr. בַּת; pl. בַּתִּים—**bath,** liquid measure, equivalent to the dry measure, an ephah, c. 22 litres, and a tenth of a homer or kor Ezk 45₁₄.

*****[בַּת]** III 0.0.0.3 pr.n. **Bat,** appar. short form of בגבת **Bagabat.**

בַּת־גַּלִּים 1 pl.n. **Bath-gallim.**

בָּתָה 1 n.f. **destruction** Is 5₆.

[בַּתָּה] 1 n.f. **precipice,** נַחֲלֵי הַבַּתּוֹת *valleys of the precipices* Is 7₁₉.

בְּתוּאֵל I 9 pr.n.m. **Bethuel.**

בְּתוּאֵל II 1 pl.n. **Bethuel.**

בְּתוֹךְ, see תָּוֶךְ *middle.*

[בְּתוּל] 10.2.1 n.f.—cstr. Q בתול; pl. cstr. בְּתוּלֵי; sf. בְּתוּלֶיהָ—**young womanhood,** in ref. to period of **adolescence,** דַּדֵּי בְּתוּלֶיהָ *breasts of her young womanhood,* i.e. her young woman's breasts Ezk 23₈; sometimes **virginity,** esp. in connection with marriageability, בְּתוּלִים לַנַּעֲרָה *(tokens of) the virginity of the girl* Dt 22₂₀. → cf. בְּתוּלָה *young woman.*

בְּתוּל 1 pl.n. **Bethul.**

בְּתוּלָה 50.2.4 n.f.—cstr. בְּתוּלַת; pl. בְּתוּלוֹת; cstr. בְּתוּלֹת; sf. בְּתוּלֹתַי—**young woman,** esp. as marriageable, sometimes specif. **virgin,** נַעֲרָה בְתוּלָה אֲשֶׁר לֹא־יָדְעָה אִישׁ לְמִשְׁכַּב זָכָר *a girl, a young woman who had not known a man by lying with a male* Jg 21₁₂; rarely of married woman, אֱלִי כִּבְתוּלָה חֲגֻרַת־שַׂק עַל־בַּעַל נְעוּרֶיהָ *mourn like a young woman in sackcloth grieving for the husband of her youth* Jl 1₈; in personification, בְּתוּלַת יִשְׂרָאֵל *young woman (of) Israel,* i.e. Israel itself Jr 18₁₃. → cf. בְּתוּל *young womanhood.*

*****[בַּתּוּק]** n.[m.] **massacre** Ezk 7₂₃ (if em. רַתּוֹק *chain*). → בתק *massacre.*

בִּתְיָה 1 pr.n.f. **Bithiah.**

בתק 1 vb.—**Pi.** 1 + waw וּבִתְּקוּךְ—**massacre** prostitutes with (בְּ) sword Ezk 16₄₀. → בַּתּוּק *massacre.*

בתר 2 vb.—**Qal** 1 Pf. בָּתַר—**cut** birds **in two** Gn 15₁₀.

Pi. 1 + waw וַיְבַתֵּר—**cut** sacrificial animals **in two** Gn 15₁₀.

→ בֶּתֶר *part,* בִּתְרוֹן *gorge.*

בֶּתֶר I 3 n.m.—sf. בִּתְרוֹ; pl. cstr. בִּתְרֵי, sf. בְּתָרָיו—**part, piece** of sacrificial animal Gn 15₁₀ Jr 34₁₈.₁₉. → בתר *cut in two.*

[בֶּתֶר] II 1 n.m. **gorge,** הָרֵי בָתֶר *mountains of gorge(s)* Ca 2₁₇.

בַּת־רַבִּים 1 pl.n. **Bath-rabbim.**

בִּתְרוֹן 1 n.[m.] **morning,** or perh. **gorge,** or pl.n. **Bithron,** near Mahanaim 2 S 2₂₉. → בתר *cut in two.*

בַּת־שֶׁבַע 11 pr.n.f. **Bathsheba.**

בַּת־שׁוּעַ 3 pr.n.f. **Bath-shua.**

ג

גֵּא 1 adj. **proud** Is 16₆. → גאה *arise.*

גאה 7.1 vb.—**Qal** 7.1 Pf. גָּאָה; impf. יִגְאֶה; inf. גָּאֹה—**arise, be exalted,** of Y. Ex 15₁, dust and ashes, i.e. humans Si 10₉, water Ezk 47₅, reed Jb 8₁₁. → גֵּא *proud,* גֵּאֶה

proud, גֵּאָה *pride,* גַּאֲוָה *pride,* גָּאוֹן *pride,* גֵּאוּת *pride,* גֵּוָה *pride.*

גֵּאָה 1 n.f. **pride** Pr 8$_{13}$. → גאה *arise.*

גֵּאֶה 9.2.1 adj.—pl. גֵּאִים; cstr. Qr גֵּאֵי—**1. proud** Jr 48$_{29}$. **2.** as noun, **proud one** Is 2$_{12}$ Ps 94$_{2}$. → גאה *arise.*

גְּאוּאֵל 1 pr.n.m. **Geuel.**

גַּאֲוָה 19.6.2 n.f.—cstr. גַּאֲוַת; sf. גַּאֲוָתוֹ—**1. pride, haughtiness** Is 9$_{8}$. **2. majesty** of Y. Dt 33$_{26}$, Moab Is 16$_{6}$. **3. rising up** of the sea Ps 46$_{4}$. → גאה *arise.*

גְּאוּלָּה, see גְּאֻלָּה *redemption.*

[גְּאוּלִים], see גאל I *redeem,* §1c.

גָּאוֹן 49.3.1 n.m.—cstr. גְּאוֹן; sf. גְּאוֹנוֹ; pl. sf. גְּאוֹנַיִךְ—**1. pride, majesty, magnificence** of Y. Ex 15$_{7}$, Jacob Am 6$_{8}$, waves Jb 38$_{11}$, Jordan, i.e. perh. lush growth Jr 12$_{5}$. **2. pride, arrogance** Jb 35$_{12}$ Pr 8$_{13}$. → גאה *arise.*

גֵּאוּת 8.0.3 n.f.—**1. pride, arrogance** Ps 17$_{10}$. **2a. majesty** of Y. Is 26$_{10}$. **b. majestic things** Is 12$_{5}$. **3. swelling up** of sea Ps 89$_{10}$, **billowing** of smoke Is 9$_{17}$. → גאה *arise.*

[גַּאֲיוֹן], see גֵּאֶה *proud,* cstr.

גאל I 103.3.13.1 vb.—**Qal** 95.3.13.1 Pf. גָּאַל; impf. יִגְאַל; impv. גְּאַל; ptc. גֹּאֵל; ptc. pass. גְּאוּלִים; inf. abs. גָּאֹל; cstr. גְּאוֹל (גָּאֳלֵךְ)—**1a.** of humans, **redeem,** i.e. pay redemption price for dispossessed relative Lv 25$_{48}$, relative's property Lv 25$_{25}$, offering made to Y. Lv 27$_{13}$; **reclaim** day of birth Jb 3$_{5}$. **b.** ptc. as noun, **redeemer, avenger** of relative's lost property or blood Lv 25$_{25}$ Dt 19$_{6}$. **c.** pass. ptc. as noun, **one who is redeemed** Is 62$_{12}$; perh. **redemption** Is 63$_{4}$. **2a.** of Y., **rescue** Israel Is 43$_{1}$, individual Ps 119$_{154}$, one's life Ps 69$_{19}$; with prep. מִן *from* Gn 48$_{16}$; מִיַּד *from (the hand/power of)* Ps 106$_{10}$. **b.** ptc. as noun, **redeemer, saviour** Is 41$_{14}$ Ps 19$_{15}$.

Ni. 8 Impf. יִגָּאֵל; + waw וְנִגְאַל—**1.** usu. **be redeemed,** i.e. bought back, of property Lv 25$_{30}$, person Lv 25$_{54}$, first-born beast Lv 27$_{27}$; of Jerusalem by Y. Is 52$_{3}$. **2. redeem oneself** Lv 25$_{49}$.

→ גְּאֻלָּה *redemption.*

גאל II 11.0.6 vb.—**Ni./Nufal** (Ni. mixed with Pu.) 3 Pf. נְגֹאֲלוּ; ptc. נְגֹאָלָה—**be defiled,** of city Zp 3$_{1}$, hand Is 59$_{3}$ (+ בְּ *by* blood).

Pi. 1.0.3 Pf. גֵּאַלְנוּךָ—**defile** Y. Ml 1$_{7}$, sanctuary 11QT 47$_{13}$.

Pu. 4.0.1 Pf. גֹּאֲלוּ; + waw וַיְגֹאֲלוּ; ptc. מְגֹאָל—**be defiled,** of food Ml 1$_{7}$, persons Ezr 2$_{62}$||Ne 7$_{64}$ (+ מִן *from* priesthood, i.e. disqualified from it).

Hi. 1 Pf. אֶגְאָלְתִּי—**defile,** i.e. **stain** clothing (with blood) Is 63$_{3}$ (1QIsa^{a,b} pi.).

Htp. 2.0.2 Impf. יִתְגָּאַל; inf. Q התגאל—**defile oneself** with (בְּ) food and wine Dn 1$_{8}$, blood 1QM 9$_{8}$.

→ גֹּאַל *defilement,* תְּגֹאֶלֶת *defilement.*

[גֹּאַל] 1.0.2 n.[m.]—pl. Q גולים (corrected to גואלים); cstr. גָּאֳלֵי (Q גואולי)—**defilement, stain** Ne 13$_{29}$ 1QS 3$_{2}$ CD 12$_{16}$. → גאל II *defile.*

גְּאֻלָּה 14.0.7.2 n.f.—גְּאוּלָה; cstr. גְּאֻלַּת; sf. גְּאֻלָּתוֹ—**1. redemption,** i.e. price of redemption Lv 25$_{26}$, right of redemption Jr 32$_{8}$. **2. redemption,** i.e. **deliverance** of Israel Mur 22 1$_{1}$. → גאל I *redeem.*

*[**גְּאַלְיָהוּ**] 0.0.0.5 pr.n.m. **Gealiah.**

גַּב I 12 n.m.—cstr. גַּב, sf. גַּבִּי; pl. cstr. גַּבֹּת, גַּבֵּי; sf. גַּבֵּיכֶם—**1. back, body** of person Ps 129$_{3}$. **2. brow** of eye Lv 14$_{9}$. **3. rim, felloe** of wheel Ezk 1$_{18}$. **4. boss** of shield Jb 15$_{26}$. **6.** appar. **mound, platform** for altar, worship Ezk 16$_{24}$ 43$_{13}$.

*[**גַּב**] II 2 n.[m.]—cstr. גַּבֵּי; sf. גַּבֵּיכֶם—**response** Jb 13$_{12}$.

*[**גַּב**] III 2 n.[m.]—cstr. גַּבֵּי; sf. גַּבֵּיכֶם—**fabrication** Jb 13$_{12}$.

[גֵּב] I 6 n.[m.]—pl. גֵּבִים—**1. ditch, stowage-tank** for irrigation 2 K 3$_{16}$ Jr 14$_{3}$. **2. coffer,** rectangular grid in ceiling 1 K 6$_{9}$.

[גֵּב] II 1 n.[m.]—pl. גֵּבִים (sg. perh. גֵּבֶה, not גֵּב)—**locust** Is 33$_{4}$.

גֶּבֶא 2.0.1. n.m.—pl. sf. גְּבָאָיו—**cistern,** or perh. **swamp, puddle** Is 30$_{14}$ Ezk 47$_{11}$ CD 10$_{12}$.

גבה 34.0.4 vb.—**Qal** 24.0.1 Pf. גָּבַהּ, גָּבַהְתָּ; impf. יִגְבַּהּ; inf. גָּבְהָה, גֹּבַהּ—**1. be high,** of heaven Is 55$_{9}$ (+ מִן higher *than* the earth), person 1 S 10$_{23}$. **2. be exalted,** of Y. Is 5$_{16}$, servant of Y. Is 52$_{13}$. **3. be proud, be haughty,** of women Is 3$_{16}$, heart Ezk 28$_{2}$.

Hi. 10.0.3 Pf. הִגְבַּהְתִּי; impf. יַגְבִּיהַּ; ptc. מַגְבִּיהַּ; inf. הַגְבֵּהַּ—**1. make high, raise** wall 2 C 33$_{14}$, the lowly Ezk 21$_{31}$, a request Is 7$_{11}$. **2. raise oneself,** of Y. Ps 113$_{5}$; **fly upward,** of sparks Jb 5$_{7}$, eagle Jb 39$_{27}$.

→ גָּבֹהַּ I *high,* גֹּבַהּ *height,* גַּבְהוּת *pride,* גָּבְהָן *proud.*

גָּבֹהַּ I 40.0.3 adj.—cstr. גְּבַהּ (גְּבֹהַּ); f.s. גְּבֹהָה; m.pl. גְּבֹהִים, f.pl. גְּבֹהוֹת—**1. high, tall,** of mountain Gn 7_{19}, tree Ezk 17_{24}, tower Is 2_{15}. **2.** as noun, **a. haughty one, proud one** Is 5_{15}. **b. high-ranking one** Ec 5_{7}. **c. height** of stature 1 S 16_{7}. **3.** as adv., **proudly, haughtily** 1 S 2_{3}. → גבה *be high.*

***גָּבֹהַּ** II 3 n.m.—pl. גְּבֹהִים—**collector** Ec 5_{7}.

[**גֹּבָה**], see גֹּב II *locust.*

גֹּבַהּ 17.1.17.1 n.m.—cstr. גֹּבַהּ; sf. גָּבְהוֹ; pl. cstr. גָּבְהֵי—**1. height** of person 1 S 17_{4}, cedars Am 2_{9}, building 2 C 3_{4}. **2. exaltation** Jb 40_{10}. **3. pride, haughtiness** Jr 48_{29} Pr 16_{18}. → גבה *be high.*

[**גַּבְהוּת**] 2.0.2 n.f.—cstr. גַּבְהוּת—**pride, haughtiness** Is $2_{11.17}$ 4QHod^a^ 7.2_{8} CD 1_{15}. → גבה *be high.*

*[**גַּבְהָן**] 0.1 adj. **proud** Si 4_{29}. → גבה *be high.*

גְּבוּל I 240.0.40 n.m.—גְּבֻל; cstr. גְּבוּל; sf. גְּבוּלוֹ; pl. sf. גְּבוּלַיִךְ—**1. border, boundary,** usu. of nation, tribe Nm 21_{13} Jos 13_{23}, also of private property Jos 24_{30}, the sea Jr 5_{22}; **barrier** before chambers Ezk 40_{12}; **rim** of altar Ezk 43_{13}. **2. boundary marker** Dt 19_{14}. **3. territory (within boundary)** Ex 7_{27} Nm 20_{17}. → גבל I *border.*

***גְּבוּל** II 6 n.m.—cstr. גְּבוּל—**mountain, hill-country** 1 S 10_{2} 13_{18} Ezk $11_{10.11}$ Ps 78_{54} 105_{33}.

גְּבוּלָה 10.0.6 n.f.—sf. גְּבֻלָתוֹ; pl. גְּבֻלוֹת; cstr. גְּבוּלוֹת; sf. גְּבוּלֹתֶיהָ—**1. border, boundary,** of nation or tribe Nm 34_{2} Jos 18_{20}, field Is 28_{25}. **2. boundary marker** Jb 24_{2}. **3. territory** of city Nm 32_{33}. → גבל I *border.*

גִּבּוֹר 159.5.46 adj.—גִּבֹּר; cstr. גִּבּוֹר; sf. גִּבּוֹרָם; pl. גִּבּוֹרִים; cstr. גִּבּוֹרֵי; sf. גִּבֹּרָיו—**1. mighty,** as attrib. adj. of God Dt 10_{17}, man 1 S 14_{52}. **2.** as pred. adj. or noun, **mighty (one),** oft. specif. **warrior,** גִּבּוֹר חַיִל *mighty one of valour, warrior* Jg 11_{1}, הַגִּבֹּרִים אֲשֶׁר לְדָוִד *the warriors who belonged to David* 2 S 23_{8}, גִּבֹּר־צַיִד *mighty one of hunting* Gn 10_{9}, י׳ גִּבּוֹר מִלְחָמָה *Y., mighty of,* i.e. in, *war* Ps 24_{8}. → גבר *be mighty.*

*[**גִּבּוֹר**] 0.1 n.[m]—sf. גבורם—**might** Si $44_{3(Bmg)}$ (B גְּבוּרָה *might*). → גבר *be mighty.*

*[**גִּבּוֹרָה**] 2 n.f.—cstr. גבורת—**heroine** Is $47_{5(1QIsa^a)}$ (MT גְּבֶרֶת, from גְּבִירָה *lady*). → גבר *be mighty.*

גְּבוּרָה 61.13.101 n.f.—cstr. גְּבוּרַת; sf. גְּבוּרָתוֹ, גְּבוּרַתְכֶם; pl. גְּבוּרוֹת (גְּבֻרוֹת); cstr. גְּבוּרוֹת; sf. גְּבוּרֹתֶיךָ—**1. might, strength** of Y. Ps 21_{14}, human Jg 8_{21} Ps 90_{10} (pl.), horse Jb 39_{19}, Leviathan Jb 41_{4} (pl.), sun Jg 5_{31}. **2. mighty deeds, a.** sg., of king 1 K 15_{23}. **b.** pl., of Y. Dt 3_{24}. → גבר *be mighty.*

גִּבֵּחַ I 1 adj. **bald (of forehead)** Lv 13_{41}. → cf. גַּבַּחַת *baldness.*

*[**גִּבֵּחַ**] II 0.0.0.1 pr.n.[m.] **Gibbeah.**

גַּבַּחַת 4 n.f.—sf. גַּבַּחְתּוֹ—**1. baldness (of forehead)** Lv 13_{42}. **2. outer** (or visible) **side** of cloth Lv 13_{55}. → cf. גִּבֵּחַ *bald.*

גַּבַּי 1 pr.n.[m.] **Gabbai.**

גֹּבַי 2 n.m.—גֹּבָי—**(swarm of) locusts** Am 7_{1} Na 3_{17}.

גֵּבִים 1 pl.n. **Gebim.**

גְּבִינָה 1 n.f. **cheese** Jb 10_{10}.

גָּבִיעַ 14 n.m.—cstr. גְּבִיעַ; sf. גְּבִיעִי; pl. גְּבִעִים; sf. גְּבִיעֶיהָ—**cup** of Joseph Gn 44_{2}, **bowl** for drinking wine Jr 35_{5}; **cup** of candelabrum Ex 25_{31}‖37_{17}.

גְּבִיר 2 n.m. **lord** Gn 27_{37}. → גבר *be mighty.*

גְּבִירָה 15.1 n.f.—גְּבֶרֶת; cstr. גְּבֶרֶת; sf. גְּבִרְתִּי—**1. lady, mistress** of servant Gn 16_{4}, subservient kingdoms Is 47_{5}. **2. queen,** wife of Pharaoh 1 K 11_{19}. **3. queen mother** 1 K 15_{13}‖2 C 15_{16}. → גבר *be mighty.*

גָּבִישׁ 1 n.m. **(rock) crystal** Jb 28_{18}. → cf. אֶלְגָּבִישׁ *hail.*

גבל I 5.0.2 vb.—**Qal** 3.0.1 Pf. גָּבְלוּ; impf. יִגְבֹּל־—**1. border on, form border with** place Jos 18_{20} Zc 9_{2} (בְּ of obj.). **2.** with obj. גְּבוּל, **set border** Dt 19_{14}.

Hi. 2.0.1 + waw וְהִגְבַּלְתָּ; impv. הַגְבֵּל—**circumscribe, set bounds for** people Ex 19_{12} (+ סָבִיב *around*), mountain Ex 19_{23}.

→ גְּבוּל I *border,* גְּבוּלָה *border.*

*[**גבל**] II 0.0.5 vb.—**Qal** Ptc. pass. Sam גְּבֻלוֹת—**pass. be forged,** of chain Ex $28_{22(Sam)}$‖$39_{15(Sam)}$ (MT גַּבְלֻת *twisting*).

Pu. 0.0.5 Ptc. Q מגבל—**1. be forged,** of chain Ex 28_{14} (if em. מְגֻבָּלֹת *chains,* to מְגֻבָּלֹת). **2. be kneaded** (unless noun מְגֻבָּל *kneading*), of person 1QH 11_{24} (+ בְּ *with* water) 1QS 11_{21} (+ מִן *from* dust).

→ גְּבֻלוֹת *welding,* מְגֻבָּלֹת *forged work,* (?) מְגֻבָּל *kneading.*

גְּבַל 1 pl.n. **Gebal.**

גֶּבָל 1 pl.n. **Gebal.**

גִּבְלִי 2 gent. **Gebalite.**

גַּבְלֻת 2 n.f. **twisting,** or **welding** Ex 28_{22}‖39_{15}. → גבל II *forge.*

גִּבֵּן 1 adj. **hunchbacked** Lv 21$_{20}$. → cf. גַּבְנֹן *peak.*

[גַּבְנֹן] 2 n.[m.]—pl. גַּבְנֻנִּים—**peak** Ps 68$_{16.17}$. → cf. גִּבֵּן *hunchbacked.*

גֶּבַע 19.0.0.1 pl.n. **Geba.**

*[גֹּבַע] 1 appar. n.[m.]—cstr. Gnz גבע—**exultation** Pr 16$_{5(Gnz)}$ (MT גְּבַהּ *exalted [one] of* heart).

גִּבְעָא 1 pr.n.[m.] **Gibea.**

גִּבְעָה I 64.0.4 n.f.—cstr. גִּבְעַת; sf. גִּבְעָתִי; pl. גְּבָעוֹת; cstr. גִּבְעוֹת; sf. גִּבְעוֹתֶיךָ—**hill** Ex 17$_9$, as place of worship Dt 12$_2$; named hills: hill of (or Gibeath-) Ammah 2 S 2$_{24}$, Hachilah 1 S 23$_{19}$, God (or Gibeath-elohim) 1 S 10$_5$, Moreh (or the teacher) Jg 7$_1$, Araloth (or the foreskins) Jos 5$_3$. → cf. מִגְבָּעָה I *headdress,* II *hilly place.*

גִּבְעָה II 46 pl.n. **Gibeah.**

גִּבְעוֹן 37.0.0.28 pl.n. **Gibeon.**

גִּבְעֹנִי 8 gent. **Gibeonite.**

גִּבְעֹל 1 n.[m.] **bud** Ex 9$_{31}$.

גִּבְעַת 1 pl.n. **Gibeath.**

גִּבְעַת אַמָּה, see גִּבְעָה I *hill* and אַמָּה IV *Ammah.*

גִּבְעַת בִּנְיָמִין, see גִּבְעָה II *Gibeah.*

גִּבְעַת הָאֱלֹהִים, see גִּבְעָה I *hill* and אֱלֹהִים *God.*

גִּבְעַת הַחֲכִילָה, see גִּבְעָה I *hill.*

גִּבְעַת הַמּוֹרֶה, see גִּבְעָה I *hill* and ירה III *teach.*

גִּבְעַת הָעֲרָלוֹת, see גִּבְעָה I *hill* and ערל *regard as foreskin.*

גִּבְעָתִי 1 gent. **Gibeathite.**

גִּבְעַת שָׁאוּל, see גִּבְעָה II *Gibeah* and שָׁאוּל *Saul.*

גבר 25.5.41 vb.—**Qal** 17.3.13 Pf. גָּבַר, גָּבְרוּ (גָּבֵרוּ); impf. יִגְבַּר—**be mighty, prevail,** of persons 1 S 2$_9$ (+ בְּ *by means of* strength) 2 S 1$_{23}$ (+ מִן *[more] than*) 11$_{23}$ (+ עַל *against, over*) 1 C 5$_2$ (+ בְּ *[more] than*), water Gn 7$_{18}$.

Pi. 3.0.5 Pf. גִּבַּרְתִּי; impf. יְגַבֵּר—**1. make someone mighty** Zc 10$_6$. **2.** with obj. חַיִל, **exert strength** Ec 10$_{10}$.

Hi. 2.1.16 Pf. Q הגברתה; impf. נַגְבִּיר; + waw וְהִגְבִּיר; inf. Q הגבירכה—**1. be mighty, prevail,** of persons Ps 12$_5$ (+ לְ *by [means of]* tongue). **2. make oneself great, display might,** of Y. 1QH 12$_8$ (+ בְּ *through* someone). **3. strengthen** light 1QM 13$_{15}$, tongue 1QH 16$_{35}$; **enforce** covenant Dn 9$_{27}$.

Htp. 3.2.7 Impf. יִתְגַּבָּר—**1. display might, prevail** against (עַל), of Y. Is 42$_{13}$, humans CD 20$_{33}$. **2. display arrogance, vaunt oneself,** of humans Jb 15$_{25}$ (+ אֶל *against*) 36$_9$ CD 8$_7$ (+ לְ *for* or *with* wealth).

→ גְּבוּרָה *might,* גְּבוּר *might,* גִּבּוֹר *mighty,* גְּבוֹרָה *heroine,* גֶּבֶר *man,* גְּבִיר *lord,* גְּבִירָה *lady.*

גֶּבֶר I 66.8.22 n.m.—גְּבַר (Ps 18$_{26}$), גָּבֶר; pl. גְּבָרִים—**1.** usu. **man, as distinct from woman** Jr 31$_{22}$, from God Jb 4$_{17}$; assoc. with strength Jb 38$_3$. **2.** perh. as indef. pron., **one** Jb 34$_9$; distributive, **each one** Jl 2$_8$. → גבר *be mighty.*

גֶּבֶר II 1.0.0.1 pr.n.m. **Geber.**

גִּבָּר 1 pl.n. **Gibbar.**

גַּבְרִיאֵל 2.0.4 pr.n.m. **Gabriel.**

גְּבֶרֶת, see גְּבִירָה *lady.*

גִּבְּתוֹן 6 pl.n. **Gibbethon.**

גָּג 30.0.8 n.m.—+ ה- of direction גָּגָה; cstr. גַּג; sf. גַּגּוֹ; pl. גַּגּוֹת; cstr. גַּגּוֹת; sf. גַּגּוֹתֶיהָ—**1. roof** of house Dt 22$_8$, tower Jg 9$_{51}$, gatehouse 2 S 18$_{24}$; as place of worship 2 K 23$_{12}$. **2. cover** of incense altar Ex 30$_3$||37$_{26}$.

*[גַּגִּי] 0.0.0.1 pr.n.[m.] **Gagi.**

גָּד 69.0.6 pr.n.m. **Gad.**

גַּד I 2 n.m. **coriander** Ex 16$_{31}$ Nm 11$_7$.

גַּד II 2 n.[m.]—גָּד—**good fortune** Gn 30$_{11}$; perh. name of god (of good fortune), **Gad** Is 65$_{11}$.

*[גַּדָּא] 0.0.0.1 pr.n.[m.] **Gadda.**

גִּדְגָּד, see חֹר הַגִּדְגָּד *Hor-hagidgad.*

גֻּדְגֹּדָה 2 pl.n. **Gudgodah,** or **Gudgod.**

גדד I 2.0.1 vb.—**Qal** 1.0.1 Impf. יָגוֹדּוּ—**band together** Ps 94$_{21}$ (+ עַל *against*).

Htpo. 1 Impf. יִתְגּוֹדָדוּ—**roam about, come as a troop** Jr 5$_7$ (+ בֵּית *[at] house* of prostitute).

→ גְּדוּד I *troop.*

גדד II 6.0.2 vb.—**Pol.** 0.0.1 Ptc. גודד—**cut** days and years 4QpsEzek^a 4$_4$.

Htpo. 6.0.1 Impf. יִתְגֹּדֵד; ptc. מִתְגֹּדְדִים—**lacerate oneself** Dt 14$_1$ 1 K 18$_{28}$. → גְּדוּד II *furrow,* III *wall,* גְּדוּדָה *incision.*

גָּדָה 4.0.3 n.f.—pl. sf. גְּדוֹתָיו (Kt גדיתיו)—**bank (of river)** Jos 3$_{15}$.

גַּדָּה, see חֲצַר גַּדָּה *Hazar-gaddah.*

גְּדוּד I 33.2.10 n.m.—pl. גְּדוּדִים; cstr. גְּדוּדֵי; sf. גְּדוּדָיו—**troop,** marauding band 1 S 30$_8$, army Jb 29$_{25}$; pl. units of army 1 C 7_4, troops of Y. Jb 19_{12}. → גדד I *band together*.

[גְּדוּד] II 1 n.[m.]—pl. cstr. גְּדוּדֶיהָ—**furrow** Ps 65_{11}. → גדד II *cut*.

*[גְּדוּד] III 2 n.m. **wall** 2 S 22_{30}||Ps 18_{30}. → גדד II *cut*.

[גְּדוּדָה] 1 n.[f.]—pl. גְּדֻדֹת—**incision** Jr 48_{37}. → גדד II *cut*.

גָּדוֹל 528.10.105.24 adj.—cstr. גְּדוֹל (גְּדָל־); sf. גְּדוֹלָם; f.s. גְּדוֹלָה; m.pl. גְּדוֹלִים, cstr. גְּדֹלֵי; sf. גְּדֹלָיו; f.pl. גְּדֹלוֹת—**1. great,** in ref. to **a.** importance of Y. Jr 10_6, his works Ps 111_2, name Jos 7_9, goodness Ne 9_{25}, compassion Is 54_7; Y. as גְּדֹל הָעֵצָה *great of,* i.e. in, *counsel* Jr 32_{19}, גְּדָל־חָסֶד *great of,* i.e. in, *loyalty* Ps 145_8; importance of person 2 K 5_1. **b.** magnitude of sea Nm 34_6, wilderness Dt 1_{19}, population Gn 12_2, wealth 1 S 17_{25}. **c.** intensity of fear Dt 4_{34}, sin Gn 20_9, rain 1 K 18_{45}, sound Gn 39_{14}. **d.** age Gn 27_1. **2.** as noun, **a. great one,** of important person Pr 25_6, older person Gn 29_{16}; מִקָּטֹן וְעַד־גָּדוֹל *from small unto great,* i.e. both of them Gn 19_{11}. **b.** fem. pl. **great things** Dt 10_{21}. **c. greatness** of Y.'s arm Ex 15_{16}, goodness 1QH 18_{16}. → גדל I *be great*.

גְּדוּלָּה 12.1.4 n.f.—גְּדֻלָּה; cstr. גְּדֻלַּת; sf. גְּדוּלָּתוֹ; pl. גְּדֻלּוֹת—**greatness,** attribute of Y. 1 C 29_{11}, human Est 1_4; **great deed(s)** of Y. 2 S 7_{21}||1 C 17_{19}. → גדל I *be great*.

[גִּדּוּף] 3.0.5 n.m.—pl. גִּדּוּפִים; cstr. גִּדּוּפֵי; sf. גִּדֻּפֹתָם—**reproach, reviling** Is 43_{28} Zp 2_8 1QS 4_{11}. → גדף *revile*.

גִּדּוּפָה 1.0.1 n.f.—sf. Q גדופתם—**1. (object of) reproach** Ezk 5_{15}. **2. reviling** 1QH 10_{35}. → גדף *revile*.

גְּדוֹר I 4 pr.n.m. **Gedor.**

גְּדוֹר II 3 pl.n. **Gedor.**

גָּדִי I 2 pr.n.m. **Gadi.**

גָּדִי II 16 gent. **Gadite.**

גַּדִּי 1.0.0.1 pr.n.m. **Gaddi.**

גְּדִי 16.1 n.m.—cstr. גְּדִי; pl. גְּדָיִים; cstr. גְּדָיֵי—**kid** Gn 38_{17}. → cf. גְּדִיָּה *female kid*.

[גְּדִיָּה] 1.0.1 n.f.—pl. sf. גְּדִיֹּתַיִךְ—**female kid** Ca 1_8 11QPs[a] 28_4. → cf. גְּדִי *kid*.

גַּדִּיאֵל 1 pr.n.m. **Gaddiel.**

*[גַּדִּיָּהוּ] 0.0.0.20 pr.n.m. **Gaddiah.**

[גדיו], see גַּדִּיָּהוּ *Gaddiah*.

[גְּדִיל] 2.0.4 n.[m.]—pl. גְּדִלִים—**1. tassel** of garment Dt 22_{12}. **2. festoon** of chainwork on capital of pillar 1 K 7_{17}. → גדל II *weave*.

*[גְּדִילָה] n.[f.] **distortion** Ps 12_4 (if em. גְּדֹלוֹת *great things* to גְּדִילוֹת). → גדל II *weave*.

גָּדִישׁ I 3 n.m. **shock (of grain)** Ex 22_5.

גָּדִישׁ II 1 n.[m.] **burial mound** Jb 21_{32}.

גדל I 115.2.22.1 vb.—**Qal** 51.1.3 Pf. גָּדַל (גְּדֵלַנִי); impf. יִגְדַּל; ptc. גְּדֵלֵי, גָּדֵל—**1. be great, become great,** in wealth Gn 24_{35} 26_{13} (וַיֵּלֶךְ הָלוֹךְ וְגָדֵל *and he became ever greater*), importance Gn 41_{40}, intensity (of outcry) Gn 19_{13}, value 1 S 26_{24}; of Y. 2 S 7_{22}. **2. grow up, become older** Gn 21_8.

Pi. 25.1.9.1 Pf. גִּדֵּל (גִּדַּל), גִּדְּלָה; impf. יְגַדֵּל; + waw וַיְגַדֵּל; impv. גַּדְּלוּ; ptc. מְגַדְּלִים; inf. גַּדֵּל (גַּדְּלָם)—**1. make great, magnify, exalt** Y. (in praise) Ps 34_4 (לְ of obj.), person Jos 3_7, name Gn 12_2, throne 1 K 1_{37} (+ מִן *[more] than*). **2. bring up, educate** children 2 K 10_6. **3. grow** hair Nm 6_5, tree Is 44_{14}.

Pu. 1 Ptc. מְגֻדָּלִים—**be grown,** of plants Ps 144_{12}.

Hi. 34.0.8 Pf. הִגְדִּיל; impf. יַגְדִּיל; ptc. מַגְדִּיל; inf. הַגְדִּיל—**1.** trans., **increase, enlarge** joy Is 9_2, loyalty Gn 19_{19}, works Ec 2_4, shekel Am 8_5; **magnify** law of Y. Is 42_{21}. **2.** intrans., **a.** הִגְדִּיל לַעֲשׂוֹת **act mightily,** of. Y. Jl 2_{21}. **b. act boastfully, magnify oneself** Jr 48_{26} (+ עַל *against* Y.) Lm 1_9.

Htp. 4.0.2 Impf. יִתְגַּדֵּל (יִתְגַּדָּל); + waw וְהִתְגַּדִּלְתִּי—**magnify oneself, display strength,** of Y. Ezk 38_{23}, king Dn 11_{36} (+ עַל *above,* i.e. more than), saw Is 10_{15} (+ עַל *against*).

→ גֹּדֶל *greatness,* גָּדוֹל *great,* גְּדוּלָּה *greatness,* מִגְדָּל I *tower,* II *magnification,* מִגְדּוֹל I *tower,* נִגְדָּל *fortified city*.

*גדל II 1 vb.—**Hi.** 1 Pf. הִגְדִּיל—**weave** slander Ps 41_{10} (if em. עָקֵב *heel* to עָקֹב *slander*). → גְּדִיל *tassel,* גְּדִילָה *distortion*.

גָּדֵל, see גדל I *be great*.

[גְּדִל], see גְּדִיל *tassel*.

גִּדֵּל 4.0.0.2 pr.n.m. **Giddel.**

גֹּדֶל 13.1.6 n.m.—sf. גָּדְלוֹ (גָּדְלוֹ)—**1. greatness** of Y. Dt 3_{24}, his loyalty Nm 14_{19}; of Pharaoh Ezk 31_2, tree Ezk 31_7. **2.** גֹּדֶל לֵבָב **greatness of heart,** i.e. **arrogance**

Is 9₈. → גדל I *be great*.

גְּדֻלָּה, see גְּדוּלָּה *greatness*.

גְּדַלְיָה, see גְּדַלְיָהוּ *Gedaliah*.

גְּדַלְיָהוּ 32.0.0.10 pr.n.m. **Gedaliah.**

גִּדַּלְתִּי 2 pr.n.m. **Giddalti.**

גדע 22.3.1 vb.—**Qal** 5.3.1 Pf. גָּדַע; + waw וָאֶגְדַּע; ptc. pass. גְּדוּעִים, גְּדוּעָה; inf. Si גדוע—**1a. hew off** person 4QMª 8.1₈, arm 1 S 2₃₁, horn Lm 2₃. **b. break** staff Zc 11₁₀. **2.** pass., **be hewn down,** of tree Is 10₃₃.

Ni. 7 Pf. נִגְדַּע, נִגְדְּעָה—**be hewn off, hewn down** of tribe Jg 21₆, horn Jr 48₂₅, peg Is 22₂₅, incense altar Ezk 6₆.

Pi. 9 Pf. גִּדַּע (גִּדֵּעַ); impf. אֲגַדֵּעַ; + waw וַיְגַדַּע—**hew off, hew down** Asherah Dt 7₅, horn Ps 75₁₁, iron bar Is 45₂.

Pu. 1 Pf. גֻּדָּעוּ—**be hewn down,** of tree Is 9₉.

גִּדְעוֹן 35 pr.n.m. **Gideon.**

גִּדְעוֹנִי, see גִּדְעֹנִי *Gideoni*.

גִּדְעֹם 1 pl.n. **Gidom.**

גִּדְעֹנִי 5 pr.n.m. **Gideoni.**

גדף 7.2.4 vb.—**Pi.** 7.2.4 Pf. גִּדְּפוּ, גִּדַּפְתָּ; impf. Si יגדף; ptc. מְגַדֵּף—**revile, blaspheme** Y. 2 K 19₆||Is 37₆; without obj. Ps 44₁₇. → גְּדוּפָה *reproach*, גִּדּוּף *reproach*, גַּדְּפָן *blasphemer*, מְגַדְּפָה *blasphemy*.

*[גַּדְּפָן] 0.0.2 n.m. **blasphemer** 4QapJerCᵇ 2.2₈ 4QapJer Cᵈ 8.2₉. → גדף *revile*.

גדר 10.0.1 vb.—**Qal** 10.0.1 Pf. גָּדַר; + waw וַתִּגְדְּרוּ; ptc. גֹּדֵר, גֹּדְרִים—**1.** with obj., **a. build wall** Ezk 13₅. **b. block** way Jb 19₈. **c. repair** breach Is 58₁₂. **2.** without obj., **build wall** Lm 3₇. **3.** ptc. as noun, **mason** 2 K 12₁₃. → גָּדֵר *wall*, גְּדֵרָה *wall*, גֶּדֶרֶת *wall*.

גָּדֵר 14.1.2.19 n.m.—cstr. גֶּדֶר; sf. גְּדֵרוֹ; pl. sf. גְּדֵרֶיהָ—**1. wall, fence** of vineyard Is 5₅, temple buildings Ezk 42₇, city Ps 80₁₃. **2. vineyard** (as enclosed by wall) appar. Gibeon jar handle inscr. 1. → גדר *build wall*.

גֶּדֶר 1 pl.n. **Geder.**

גְּדֹר, see גְּדוֹר I, II *Gedor*.

גְּדֵרָה I 8 n.f.—pl. גְּדֵרוֹת; cstr. גִּדְרוֹת; sf. גְּדֵרֹתָיו—**wall, fence** Na 3₁₇; of city Ps 89₄₁, sheep-fold (lit. 'walls of the flock') Nm 32₁₆. → גדר *build wall*.

גְּדֵרָה II 2 pl.n. **Gederah.**

גְּדֵרוֹת 2 pl.n. **Gederoth.**

גְּדֵרִי 1 gent. **Gederite.**

גְּדֶרֶת 1 n.f. **wall** of temple Ezk 42₁₂. → גדר *build wall*.

גְּדֵרָתִי 1 gent. **Gederathite.**

[**גְּדֵרֹתַיִם**] 1 pl.n. **Gederothaim.**

גֵּה 1 (?) demonstr. pron. **this** Ezk 47₁₃ (mss זֶה *this*).

גהה 1.1 vb.—**Qal** 1 Impf. יִגְהֶה—**be healed,** of wound Ho 5₁₃ (or em. hi. *heal* wound).

Hi. 0.1 Impf. Si יגהה—**heal** eye Si 43₁₈₍B₎, wound Ho 5₁₃ (if em.).

→ גֵּהָה *healing*.

גֵּהָה I 1 n.f. **healing** Pr 17₂₂. → גהה *heal*.

***גֵּהָה** II 1 n.f. **face** Pr 17₂₂.

גהר 3 vb.—**Qal** 3 + waw וַיִּגְהַר—**bend down, crouch** 1 K 18₄₂ 2 K 4₃₄.₃₅.

***גֵּו** 1 n.[m.] **voice,** מִן־גֵּו *with a shout* Jb 30₅ (if em. גֵּו from *society*).

[**גֵּו**] 3.0.1 n.[m.]—sf. גֵּוֶךָ—**back,** שלך אַחֲרֵי גֵו hi. *cast behind one's back*, i.e. ignore 1 K 14₉. → cf. גֵּו *back*, גֵּוָה *back*.

[**גֵּו**] I 6 n.[m.]—cstr. גֵּו; sf. גֵּוִי—**back,** as beaten Is 50₆; שלך אַחֲרֵי גו hi. *cast behind one's back*, i.e. disregard, sins Is 38₁₇. → cf. גֵּו *back*.

***גֵּו** II 1 n.[m.] **society** Jb 30₅.

גּוֹאֵל *redeemer*, see גאל I, Qal §§1b, 2b.

גּוֹב I 2 pl.n. **Gob.**

גֹּב 1 n.[m.] **locust** Na 3₁₇ (or del.).

גּוֹג 12.0.1 pr.n.m. **Gog.**

גוד 3.0.1 vb.—**Qal** Impf. יָגֻד (יְגוּדֶנּוּ)—**attack,** or perh. **troop (against)** Gn 49₁₉ Hb 3₁₆ 4QMª 11.1₁₇.

*[**גּוּדָל**] 0.0.1 n.m. **thumb,** as unit of measure 1QM 5₁₃.

גֵּוָה I 1 n.f. **back, body** Jb 20₂₅ (or em. גֵּוֹה *his back*). → cf. גֵּו *back*.

גֵּוָה II 3.0.2 n.f. **pride** Jr 13₁₇. → גאה *arise*.

גוז 2 vb.—**Qal** 2 Pf. גָּז; + waw וַיָּגָז—**1. pass over,** of quails Nm 11₃₁ (or em. וַיָּגָז, i.e. hi.). **2. pass away,** of days Ps 90₁₀.

Hi., bring quails from (מִן) sea, of wind Nm 11₃₁ (if em. qal).

גוֹזָל 2 n.m.—pl. sf. גּוֹזָלָיו—**fledgling** Gn 15₉ Dt 32₁₁.

גּוֹזָן 5 pl.n. **Gozan.**

*[**גְּוִי**] 0.1 n.m.—sf. גויו—**body** Si 10₉. → cf. גְּוִיָּה *body*.

גּוֹי I 556.15.91 n.m.—cstr. גּוֹי; sf. גּוֹיֶךָ; pl. גּוֹיִם; cstr. גּוֹיֵי (גּוֹיִ);

sf. Qr גּוֹיֵךְ, גּוֹיֵהֶם—**1. nation, people,** usu. non-Israelite Gn 15$_{14}$, but also of Israel Ex 19$_{6}$, Judah Jr 5$_{9}$, descendants of Abram Gn 12$_{2}$; כֹּל גּוֹיֵי אֶרֶץ *all the nations of (the) earth* Gn 18$_{18}$, מַמְלְכוֹת הַגּוֹיִם *kingdoms of the nations* Hg 2$_{22}$, אֱלֹהֵי הַגּוֹיִם *gods of the nations* 2 K 18$_{33}$||Is 36$_{18}$. **2. swarm** of locusts Jl 1$_{6}$.

*גּוֹי II 1 n.[m.] **field,** חַיְתוֹ־גוֹי *beasts of the field* Zp 2$_{14}$.

גְּוִיָּה 13.7.13 n.f.—cstr. גְּוִיַּת; sf. גְּוִיָּתוֹ; pl. גְּוִיּוֹת; sf. גְּוִיֹּתֵיהֶם, גְּוִיֹּתֵיהֶנָה—**1. (living) body** of heavenly beings Ezk 1$_{11}$. **2. (dead) body, corpse** 1 S 31$_{10}$, **carcass** of animal Jg 14$_{8}$. **3.** perh. **person, self** Gn 47$_{18}$. → cf. גֵּו *body.*

גּוֹיִם 3 pr.n.m. **Goiim.**

*[גְּוִיעַ] 0.1 n.[m.]—sf. גויעם—**death** Si 38$_{16}$(Bmg). → גוע *expire.*

*[גְּוִיעָה] 0.1 n.f.—sf. גויעתם—**death** Si 38$_{16}$(B). → גוע *expire.*

גּוֹלָה *exile(s),* see גלה I, Qal §2c.

*[גּוּלֹת] 0.0.1 pl.n. **Guloth.**

גּוֹלָן 4 pl.n. **Golan.**

גּוּמָּץ 1 n.m. **pit** Ec 10$_{8}$.

גּוּנִי I 4 pr.n.m. **Guni.**

גּוּנִי II 1 gent. **Gunite.**

גוע 24.8.1 vb.—**Qal** 24.8.1 Pf. גָּוַע, גָּוְעוּ; impf. יִגְוַע; ptc. גֹּוֵעַ; inf. abs. Si גוע; cstr. גְּוֹעַ (גְּוֹעַ)—**1. expire, die** Gn 6$_{17}$ 25$_{8}$ (וַיִּגְוַע וַיָּמָת *and he expired and died*). **2. gasp** Ps 88$_{16}$. **3.** ptc. as noun, **one who is dead** Si 48$_{5}$. → גְּוִיעַ *death,* גְּוִיעָה *death.*

גוף 1 vb.—**Hi.** 1 Impf. יָגִיפוּ—**close** door Ne 7$_{3}$.

[גּוּפָה] 2 n.f.—cstr. גּוּפַת; pl. גּוּפֹת—**(dead) body, corpse** 1 C 10$_{12.12}$.

גור I 81.2.7 vb.—**Qal** 80.2.6 Pf. גָּר, גַּרְתִּי; impf. יָגוּר (יְגֻרְךָ), אָגוּרָה; + waw וַיָּגָר; impv. גּוּר, גּוּרִי; ptc. גָּר, גָּרֶת, גָּרִים; inf. גּוּר—**1.** usu. intrans., **a. sojourn, take up residence (as a resident alien)** Gn 12$_{10}$ (+ שָׁם *there*) 20$_{1}$ (+ בְּ *in*) 32$_{5}$ (+ עִם *with*) Ex 12$_{48}$ (+ אֵת *with*) 12$_{49}$ (+ בְּתוֹךְ *among*). **b. dwell, stay** Jr 43$_{5}$; of wolf dwelling with (עִם) lamb Is 11$_{6}$. **2.** trans., **a. inhabit, dwell in** house Ex 3$_{22}$ (גָּרַת בֵּיתָהּ *she who sojourns of,* i.e. in, *her house*). **b. dwell with** Y. Ps 5$_{5}$, fire Is 33$_{14}$, ships Jg 5$_{17}$.

Htpol. 1.0.1 Ptc. מִתְגּוֹרֵר—**sojourn, stay** 1 K 17$_{20}$ (+ עִם *with*).

→ גֵּר *sojourner,* גֵּרוּת *lodging place,* מָגוֹר I *sojourning.*

גור II 6.0.2 vb.—**Qal** 6.0.2 Pf. גָּר; impf. יָגוּר; inf. גּוֹר—**1. attack someone** 1QH 15$_{12}$; יָגוּרוּ מִלְחָמוֹת *they attack (with) wars* Ps 140$_{3}$. **2. show hostility** Is 54$_{15}$ (+ אֵת *against*) Ps 59$_{4}$ (+ עַל *against*).

גור III 10.3.2 vb.—**Qal** 10.3.2 Impf. תָּגוּר; + waw וַיָּגָר; impv. Si גּוּרוּ, גור—**1.** usu. intrans., **a. be afraid** of someone, with מִן Dt 18$_{22}$, מִפְּנֵי Nm 22$_{3}$. **b. be in awe** of (מִן) Y. Ps 22$_{24}$. **2.** trans., **fear** provocation Dt 32$_{27}$. → מָגוֹר II *fear,* מְגוּרָה *(object of) fear;* cf. יגר *fear.*

[גּוֹר], see גּוּר I *cub.*

גּוּר I 9 n.m.—pl. cstr. גּוּרֵי (mss גּוּרֵי); sf. גּוּרֶיהָ, גֻּרוֹתָיו—**cub,** usu. of lion Gn 49$_{9}$, also of jackal Lm 4$_{3}$.

גּוּר II 1 pl.n. **Gur.**

*[גּוּר] III 0.0.0.1 pr.n.m. **Gur.**

גּוּר־בַּעַל 1 pl.n. **Gur-baal.**

גּוֹרָל 77.3.78 n.m.—cstr. גּוֹרַל; sf. גּוֹרָלוֹ; pl. גּוֹרָלוֹת—**1. lot,** cast to assign territory Nm 26$_{55}$, duty 1 C 24$_{5}$; to dispose of people Jl 4$_{3}$, property Ps 22$_{19}$; to select goat Lv 16$_{8}$, determine guilty person Jon 1$_{7}$. **2.** the assigned portion itself, גֹּרַל נַחֲלָתֵנוּ *lot of our inheritance* Nm 36$_{3}$, עָרֵי גּוֹרָלָם *cities of their lot* Jos 21$_{20}$; in ref. to destiny of persons Is 17$_{14}$, rank 1QS 1$_{10}$. **3.** company of people belonging to portion, specif. lot of God 1QM 13$_{5}$, truth 1QM 13$_{12}$, Belial 1QM 1$_{5}$, darkness 1QM 1$_{11}$.

[גּוּשׁ] 1.0.1 n.[m.]—cstr. Qr גּוּשׁ, Kt גִּישׁ—coll., **scabs** of dust, i.e. dirty scabs; or perh. **clods** of earth Jb 7$_{5}$.

גֵּז 4.0.1 n.[m.]—cstr. גֵּז; pl. cstr. גִּזֵּי—**1. fleece, wool** of sheep Dt 18$_{4}$ Jb 31$_{20}$. **2. reaping** of crops Am 7$_{1}$. **3. mown field** Ps 72$_{6}$. → גזז *shear.*

[גִּזְבָּר] 1 n.m.—גִּזְבָּר—**treasurer** Ezr 1$_{8}$.

גזה 1 vb.—**Qal** 1 Ptc. גּוֹזִי—**sever** someone from womb Ps 71$_{6}$. → גָּזִית *cutting.*

גִּזָּה 7 n.f.—cstr. גִּזַּת—**fleece** Jg 6$_{37}$. → גזז *shear.*

גִּזוֹנִי 1 gent. **Gizonite.**

גזז 15.0.1 vb.—**Qal** 14.0.1 Impf. תָּגֹז; + waw וַיָּגָז; impv. גֹּזִּי (גָּזִי); ptc. גֹּזֵז, גֹּזְזִים; inf. גֹּז—**1.** usu. **shear** sheep Gn 31$_{19}$; also **shave** head of man Jb 1$_{20}$, **cut** hair of woman Jr 7$_{29}$. **2.** ptc. as noun, **(sheep)shearer** Gn 38$_{12}$.

Ni. 1 Pf. נָגֹזּוּ—**be cut off,** of persons Na 1$_{12}$.

→ גֵּז *shearing,* גִּזָּה *fleece.*

גָּזֵז 2 pr.n.m. **Gazez.**

גָּזִית 11.0.2 n.f. **cutting,** אַבְנֵי גָזִית *stones of cutting,* i.e. hewn stones 1 K 5_{31}; without אַבְנֵי, **hewn stones** Ex 20_{25}. → גזה *cut.*

גזל 30.0.11 vb.—**Qal** 29.0.9 Pf. גָּזַל; impf. תִּגְזֹל (תִּגְזָל־); ptc. גֹּזֵל, גֹּזְלֵי; ptc. pass. גָּזוּל; inf. גְּזֹל—**1. a. rob** someone Pr 28_{24}. **b. seize** flock Jb 24_2, field Mc 2_2, plunder (גְּזֵלָה) Lv 5_{23}. **c. snatch away** orphan from (מִן) breast Jb 24_9, skin from upon (מֵעַל) people Mc 3_2, water Jb 24_{19}. **2.** pass., **a.** of person, **be robbed** Dt 28_{29}. **b.** of what is taken, **be seized** Dt 28_{31} (+ מִלְּפְנֵי *from [before]*) Ml 1_{13}.

Ni. 1.0.2 + waw וְנִגְזְלָה—**be snatched away,** of sleep Pr 4_{16}.

→ גָּזֵל *robbery,* גֵּזֶל *robbery,* גְּזֵלָה *plunder.*

גָּזֵל 4.2 n.[m.] **robbery** Lv 5_{21}; object of robbery, **plunder** Ezk 22_{29}. → גזל *rob.*

[גֵּזֶל] 2 n.[m.]—cstr. גֵּזֶל (perh. cstr. of גָּזֵל)—**robbery,** i.e. misappropriation, of judgment Ec 5_7; object of robbery, **plunder** Ezk 18_{18}. → גזל *rob.*

גְּזֵלָה 6 n.f.—cstr. גְּזֵלַת; pl. גְּזֵלוֹת—**plunder,** thing seized Lv 5_{23}. → גזל *rob.*

גָּזָם 3 n.m. **locust,** appar. in early stage, i.e. **grub, caterpillar,** coll. Jl 1_4.

גַּזָּם 2 pr.n.m. **Gazzam.**

[גֶּזַע] 3.0.5 n.m.—sf. גִּזְעוֹ—**stump** of tree Jb 14_8, Jesse Is 11_1; **stem** Is 40_{24}.

גזר I 13 vb.—**Qal** 7 Pf. גָּזַר; impf. תִּגְזַר־; + waw וַיִּגְזֹר; impv. גִּזְרוּ (גְּזֹרוּ); ptc. גֹּזֵר—**1. cut in two, separate** child 1 K 3_{25}, sea Ps 136_{13}, **cut down** tree 2 K 6_4. **2. decide, decree** Jb 22_{28}. **3.** appar. **snatch, devour** Is 9_{19}.

Ni. 6 Pf. נִגְזַר, נִגְזַרְתִּי—**1.** usu. **be cut off** Is 53_8 (+ מִן *from*) Ezk 37_{11}. **2. be decided, decreed** Est 2_1 (+ עַל *against*).

→ גֶּזֶר *piece,* גְּזֵרָה *isolation,* גִּזְרָה *cut,* מַגְזֵרָה *axe.*

*גזר II 4 vb.—**Qal** 1 Pf. גָּזַר—**disappear,** of flock Hb 3_{17} (+ מִן *from* fold).

Ni. 3 Pf. נִגְזַר, נִגְזַרְתִּי—**disappear,** of persons, abs. Lm 3_{54}; + מִן *from* land Is 53_8, house 2 C 26_{21}.

[גָּזֵר], see גְּזֵרָה *isolation.*

[גֶּזֶר] I 2 n.[m.]—pl. גְּזָרִים—**piece** of sacrificed beasts Gn 15_{17}, Sea of Reeds Ps 136_{13}. → גזר I *cut.*

גֶּזֶר II 15.0.1.1 pl.n. **Gezer.**

גְּזֵרָה 1 n.f. **isolation,** אֶרֶץ גְּזֵרָה *land of isolation* (unless *isolated,* or *infertile, land,* from גָּזֵר adj.) Lv 16_{22}. → גזר I *cut.*

גִּזְרָה 8 n.f.—גִּזְרָתָם—**1. cut, form** of human body Lm 4_7. **2.** adjoining **space,** separating temple from outside Ezk 41_{12}. → גזר I *cut.*

גִּזְרִי 1 gent. **Gizrite.**

גחה 1 vb.—**Qal** 1 Ptc. גֹּחִי—**extract** child from (מִן) womb Ps 22_{10}.

גָּחוֹן 2 n.m.—sf. גְּחֹנְךָ—**chest** of reptile Gn 3_{14} Lv 11_{42}.

גִּחוֹן, see גִּיחוֹן *Gihon.*

גֵּחֲזִי, see גֵּיחֲזִי *Gehazi.*

[גָּחָל], [גַּחַל], see גַּחֶלֶת *coal.*

גַּחֶלֶת 18.1.4 n.f.—sf. גַּחַלְתִּי; pl. גֶּחָלִים; cstr. גַּחֲלֵי; sf. גֶּחָלָיו (pl. forms perh. from sg. גַּחַל or גָּחָל)—**(live) coal, ember,** גַּחֲלֵי־אֵשׁ *coals of fire* Lv 16_{12}, גַּחֲלֵי רְתָמִים *coals (consisting) of broomwood* Ps 120_4.

גַּחַם 1.0.0.1 pr.n.[m.] **Gaham.**

גַּחַר 2 pr.n.m. **Gahar.**

גַּיְא I 33.0.4 n.m. (& f.)—גַּי, גֵּיא, גָּיְא, גֵּיא, גַּיְא; cstr. גֵּיא (גֵּי); pl. גֵּאָיוֹת; sf. גֵּאוֹתֶיךָ—**valley** Nm 21_{20}; גֵּיא חִזָּיוֹן *valley of vision* Is 22_1, הַהֲרֵגָה *of slaughter* Jr 7_{32}, צַלְמָוֶת *of the shadow of death* Ps 23_4.

גַּיְא II 1 pl.n. **Gai.**

גֵּיא בֶן־הִנֹּם 13 pl.n. **Valley of Ben-hinnom, Gehinnom, or Gehenna.**

גֵּי(א) הִנֹּם, see גֵּיא בֶן־הִנֹּם *Valley of Ben-hinnom.*

גֵּיא חֲרָשִׁים 2 pl.n. **Ge-harashim.**

גֵּיא־מֶלַח 5 pl.n. **Ge-melah, Valley of Melah,** or **Valley of Salt.**

גֵּיא צְפָתָה 1 pl.n. **Ge-zephathah,** or **Valley of Zephathah /Zaphath.**

[גִּיד] 7.0.7 n.m.—cstr. גִּיד; pl. גִּידִים; cstr. גִּידֵי—**sinew, muscle, tendon** Gn 32_{33} Ezk 37_6.

גֵּי הַחֲרָשִׁים, see גֵּיא חֲרָשִׁים *Ge-harashim.*

*[גֵּי הַסְּכָכָא] 0.0.1 pl.n. **Ge-sekaka,** or **Valley of Sekaka.**

גֵּי הַצְּבֹעִים 1 pl.n. **Ge-hazzeboim, Valley of Zeboim,** or **Valley of the Jackals.**

גיח 5.0.1 vb.—**Qal** 3.0.1 Impf. יָגִיחַ; impv. גֹּחִי; inf. גִּיחוֹ—**burst out,** of sea Jb 38_8 (+ מִן *from* womb), Jordan Jb

40$_{23}$, Zion (perh. with waters of childbirth) Mc 4$_{10}$.

Hi. 2 + waw וַתָּגַח; ptc. מֵגִיחַ—**burst out,** of army in ambush Jg 20$_{33}$, Pharaoh as dragon in river Ezk 32$_{2}$.

גִּיחַ 1 pl.n. **Giah.**

גִּיחוֹן 6 pl.n. **Gihon.**

גֵּיחֲזִי 12.0.1 pr.n.m. **Gehazi.**

גֵּי יִפְתַּח־אֵל 2 pl.n. **Ge-iphtahel,** or **Valley of Iphtahel.**

גִּיל I 45.1.20 vb.—**Qal** 45.1.18 Pf. גַּלְתִּי; impf. יָגִיל (יָגֵל), יָגִילוּ (יְגִילוּן), תְּגֵלְנָה; + waw וַיָּגֶל; impv. גִּילוּ, גִּילִי; inf. גִּיל—**rejoice, shout in exultation,** abs. Is 49$_{13}$; with בְּ *in* Y. Is 41$_{16}$, salvation Ps 9$_{15}$; עַל *over* Zion Zp 3$_{17}$.

Hi. 0.0.2 Impv. Q הגלנה—**rejoice,** abs. 1QM 12$_{13}$.

→ גִּיל *rejoicing,* גִּילָה *rejoicing.*

*גִּיל II 1 vb.—**Qal** 1 Impv. גִּילוּ—**live** Ps 2$_{11}$ (+ בְּ *in* trembling). → גִּיל II *life.*

*גִּיל III 1 vb.—**Qal** 1 Impv. גִּילוּ—**worship** Ps 2$_{11}$ (+ בְּ *with* trembling). → גִּיל III *worship.*

*גִּיל IV 2 vb.—**Qal** 2 Impf. יָגִילוּ; impv. גִּילוּ—**be afraid** for (עַל) honour Ho 10$_{5}$, **fear with** (בְּ) trembling Ps 2$_{11}$.

גִּיל I 8.2.2 n.[m.] **rejoicing** Is 16$_{10}$. → גיל I *rejoice.*

*גִּיל II 2 n.[m.]—sf. גִּילִי, גִּילְכֶם—**1. life** Ps 43$_{4}$. **2. stage in life, age** Dn 1$_{10}$. → גיל II *live.*

*גִּיל III 1 n.[m.]—sf. גִּילִי—**worship** Ps 43$_{4}$. → גיל III *worship.*

גִּילָה 2.0.2 n.f.—cstr. גִּילַת; pl. cstr. Q גילות—**rejoicing** Is 35$_{2}$. → גיל I *rejoice.*

גִּילֹנִי, see גִּלֹנִי *Gilonite.*

גִּינַת 2 pr.n.[m.] **Ginath.**

גִּישׁ, see גּוּשׁ *scab.*

גֵּישָׁן 1 pr.n.m. **Geshan.**

גַּל I 18.0.1 n.m.—גַּל, pl. גַּלִּים—**1. heap** of stones Ho 12$_{12}$. **2.** stones piled up as memorial, **cairn** Gn 31$_{46}$. **3. heap of ruins** 2 K 19$_{25}$||Is 37$_{26}$. → גלל I *roll.*

גַּל II 15.0.5 n.m.—pl. גַּלִּים; cstr. גַּלֵּי; sf. גַּלָּיו—**wave** of sea Is 48$_{18}$. → גלל I *roll.*

*גַּל III 1 n.m. **spring** Ca 4$_{12(L)}$ (mss גַּן *garden*).

[גֵּל] 3 n.[m.]—sf. גֶּלְלוֹ; pl. cstr. גֶּלְלֵי—**dung,** גֶּלְלֵי צֵאת הָאָדָם *dung(s) of effluent of humans* Ezk 4$_{12}$. → גלל II *be foul.*

[גֹּל], see גֻּלָּה *bowl.*

[גַּלָּב] 1 n.[m.]—pl. גַּלָּבִים—**barber** Ezk 5$_{1}$.

גִּלְבֹּעַ 8 pl.n. **Gilboa.**

*[גַּלְגּוּלָה] 0.0.4 pr.n.[m.] **Galgula.**

גַּלְגַּל I 12.1.4 n.m.—cstr. גַּלְגַּל; pl. sf. גַּלְגִּלָּיו—**1. wheel** of cart Is 28$_{28}$, chariot Is 5$_{28}$; appar. coll., **wheelwork** Ezk 10$_{2.6}$; perh. **paddle wheel** at well Ec 12$_{6}$. **2.** perh. **whirlwind** Is 17$_{13}$ Ps 83$_{14}$. **3. orbit of sun** CD 10$_{15}$. → גלל I *roll.*

*גַּלְגַּל II 2 n.[m.] **tumbleweed** Is 17$_{13}$ Ps 83$_{14}$. → גלל I *roll.*

*גַּלְגַּל III n.[m.] **water-pitcher** Ec 12$_{6}$.

גִּלְגָּל I 40 pl.n. **Gilgal.**

*[גִּלְגָּל] II 0.0.0.1 pr.n.m. **Gilgal.**

גֻּלְגֹּלֶת 12 n.f.—sf. גֻּלְגָּלְתּוֹ; pl. sf. גֻּלְגְּלֹתָם—**1. skull** Jg 9$_{53}$. **2. person,** for purposes of counting Ex 16$_{16}$ Nm 1$_{2}$. → גלל I *roll.*

[גֶּלֶד] 1 n.m.—sf. גִּלְדִּי—**skin** Jb 16$_{15}$.

גלה 229.10.89 vb.—**Qal** 92.0.29 Pf. גָּלָה; impf. יִגְלֶה (יִגֶל); + waw וַיִּגֶל; impv. גְּלֵה; ptc. גֹּלֶה, גֹּלָה, גֹּלִים; pass. גָּלוּי; inf. abs. גָּלֹה; cstr. גְּלוֹת—**1a. uncover** ear, i.e. inform 1 S 9$_{15}$, **reveal secret** Am 3$_{7}$ (+ אֶל *to*). **b.** pass., **be issued,** of copy of document Est 3$_{14}$ (+ לְ *to*). **c.** pass. ptc. as noun, **opened one,** in ref. to copy of deed of sale Jr 32$_{11}$. **2a.** usu. **be exiled, go into exile** Jg 18$_{30}$ 2 K 17$_{23}$ (+ מֵעַל *from [upon]*) Ezk 12$_{3}$ (+ מִן ... אֶל *from ... to*); also **depart, disappear,** of glory 1 S 4$_{21}$, grass Pr 27$_{25}$. **b.** ptc. as unitary noun, **exile,** i.e. one who goes into exile, masc. Am 6$_{7}$, fem. Is 49$_{21}$. **c.** fem. ptc. as coll. noun, **exile(s), diaspora** Jr 29$_{1}$; as abstract noun, **(state of) exile** Jr 29$_{16}$.

Ni. 32.1.39 Pf. נִגְלָה; impf. יִגָּלֶה, תִּגָּלֶה (תִּגָּל); + waw וַתִּגָּלֶה; impv. הִגָּלוּ; ptc. נִגְלָה, נִגְלֹת; inf. abs. נִגְלֹה; cstr. הִגָּלוֹת, נִגְלוֹת—**1a. reveal oneself,** of Y. Gn 35$_{7}$ (+ אֶל *to*). **b. be revealed,** of word of Y. 1 S 3$_{7}$ (+ אֶל *to*), glory of Y. Is 40$_{5}$. **c. uncover oneself** 2 S 6$_{20}$. **d. be uncovered,** of nakedness Ex 20$_{26}$, foundations 2 S 22$_{16}$||Ps 18$_{16}$, transgressions Ezk 21$_{29}$. **e. be removed,** of dwelling Is 38$_{12}$ (+ מִן *from*). **2.** ptc. as noun, **revealed matter** 1QS 5$_{12}$.

Pi. 56.7.18 Pf. גִּלָּה, גִּלִּיתִי (גִּלֵּיתִי); impf. יְגַלֶּה, תְּגַלֶּה (תְּגַלֶּה, תְּגַל); + waw וַיְגַל; impv. גַּל, גַּלִּי; ptc. מְגַלֶּה; inf. גַּלּוֹת—**1. uncover, expose** nakedness Lv 18$_{6}$, foundations Mc 1$_{6}$, eyes, i.e. open them Nm 22$_{31}$, veil, i.e.

remove it Is 47_{2}. **2. reveal, disclose** secret Pr 11_{13}, peace and truth Jr 33_{16} (+ לְ *to*); **make known** cause Jr 20_{12} (+ אֶל *to*).

Pu. 2.1.2 Pf. גֻּלְּתָה; ptc. מְגֻלָּה—**1. be revealed, be uncovered,** of reproof Pr 27_{5}, deeds Si 16_{15}. **2. be exiled** Na 2_{8}.

Hi. 38.0.2 Pf. הִגְלִיתָ, הֶגְלָה; + waw וַיֶּגֶל (וַיַּגְלֵם); inf. הַגְלוֹת (הַגְלוֹתָם, בְּגַלוֹתוֹ)—**(take into) exile** 2 K 15_{29} (+ אַשּׁוּרָה *to Assyria*) 2 K 17_{28} (+ מִן *from* Samaria) Am 5_{27} (+ מֵהָלְאָה לְ *beyond* Damascus) 2 C 36_{20} (+ אֶל *to Babylon*).

Ho. 7 Pf. הָגְלָה, הָגְלְתָה (הָגְלַת); ptc. מָגְלִים—**be exiled** Jr 40_{1} (+ בָּבֶלָה *to Babylon*) Est 2_{6} (+ מִן *from* Jerusalem) 1 C 9_{1} (+ לְ *to* Babylon).

Htp. 2.1 Impf. Si יתגלה; + waw וַיִּתְגַּל; inf. הִתְגַּלּוֹת—**1. uncover oneself** Gn 9_{21}. **2. reveal oneself, be revealed,** of person Si 12_{15} (+ לְ *to*), heart Pr 18_{2}.

→ גִּלָּיוֹן I *tablet*, II mirror, III *papyrus garment*, גָּלוּת *diaspora*.

גִּלֹה 2 pl.n. **Giloh.**

גֻּלָּה 14.0.1 n.f.—cstr. גֻּלַּת; sf. גֻּלָּה (appar. from abs. גֹּל); pl. גֻּלּוֹת; cstr. גֻּלֹּת—**1. bowl** Ec 12_{6}, of lamp, i.e. receptacle for oil Zc 4_{2}. **2.** bowl-shaped lower part of capital 1 K 7_{41}||2 C 4_{12}. **3. spring** Jos 15_{19}||Jg 1_{15}, or perh. pl.n. **(Upper, Lower) Gulloth** Jos $15_{19.19}$||Jg $1_{15.15}$. → גלל I *roll.*

[גִּלּוּל] 48.1.7 n.m.—pl. גִּלּוּלִים; cstr. גִּלּוּלֵי; sf. גִּלּוּלָיו—**image (of god),** sg. Si 30_{18}; elsewhere alw. pl. 1 K 15_{12} Ezk 6_{4}. → גלל I *roll.*

[גְּלוֹם] 1 n.[m.]—pl. cstr. גְּלוֹמֵי—perh. **cloak** Ezk 27_{24}. → גלם *wrap.*

גלון, see גּוֹלָן *Golan.*

גָּלוּת 15.0.3 n.f.—cstr. גָּלוּת; sf. גָּלוּתִי—**1. diaspora, exiles** Jr 24_{5}. **2. (state of) exile** Ezk 33_{21}. → גלה *reveal.*

גלח 23.0.3 vb.—**Pi.** 18.0.3 Pf. גִּלַּח (גִּלְּחוֹ); impf. יְגַלַּח (יְגַלֵּחַ); inf. גַּלְּחוֹ—**1. shave** person 1 C 19_{4}, head Nm 6_{9}, hair Lv 14_{8}. **2. shave oneself** Gn 41_{14}.

Pu. 3 Pf. גֻּלַּח, גֻּלַּחְתִּי; ptc. מְגֻלְּחֵי—**be shaved,** of person Jg 16_{17}, hair Jg 16_{22}; מְגֻלְּחֵי זָקָן *shaved of beard* Jr 41_{5}.

Htp. 2 Pf. הִתְגַּלָּח; inf. הִתְגַּלְּחוֹ—**shave oneself** Lv 13_{33}.

גִּלָּיוֹן I 1 n.m.—**tablet,** for writing upon Is 8_{1}. → גלה *reveal.*

[גִּלָּיוֹן] II 1 n.[m].—pl. גִּלְיֹנִים—**mirror** Is 3_{23}. → גלה *reveal.*

***[גִּלָּיוֹן]** III 1 n.[m].—pl. גִּלְיֹנִים—**papyrus garment** Is 3_{23}. → גלה *reveal.*

[גָּלִיל] I 2 adj.—pl. גְּלִילִים—**hinged,** of doorleaf 1 K 6_{34}. → גלל I *roll.*

[גָּלִיל] II 2 n.m.—pl. cstr. גְּלִילֵי—**rod,** supporting hangings Est 1_{6}, descr. of hands Ca 5_{14}. → גלל I *roll.*

גָּלִיל III 6 pl.n. **Galilee.**

***[גָּלִיל]** IV 0.0.1 n.[m.] **encircling,** גליל כפים *encircling of flanks*, i.e. pincer movement 1QM 9_{10}.

[גְּלִילָה] 5 n.f.—pl. cstr. גְּלִילוֹת—**district, territory, environ(s)** of the Philistines Jos 13_{2}, the Jordan Jos 22_{10}. → גלל I *roll.*

גְּלִילוֹת 1 pl.n. **Geliloth.**

***[גְּלִילִי]** 0.0.1 gent. **Galilaean.**

גַּלִּים 2 pl.n. **Gallim.**

***[גָּלִין]** n.[m.] **garment** Is 3_{23} (if em. הַגִּלְיֹנִים *the papyrus garments* to הַגְּלִינִים).

גָּלְיַת 6.1.2 pr.n.m. **Goliath.**

גלל I 18.2.12 vb.—**Qal** 11.1 Pf. גַּל, גַּלּוֹתִי, גָּלְלוּ; + waw וַיָּגֶל; impv. גֹּל, גֹּלּוּ; ptc. גֹּלֵל—**1. roll, roll away** stone from (מֵעַל) mouth of well Gn 29_{3}, reproach from person Jos 5_{9}. **2a. roll,** i.e. **commit** deeds to (אֶל) Y. Pr 16_{3}. **b.** גלל **roll oneself to** (אֶל), i.e. **rely on** Y. Ps 22_{9}.

Ni. 2 Pf. נָגֹלּוּ; impf. יִגַּל—**1. be rolled up,** of heavens, as document Is 34_{4}. **2. flow,** of justice, as water Am 5_{24}.

Poal 1.0.1 Ptc. מְגוֹלָלָה—**be rolled,** of mantle, in (בְּ) blood Is 9_{4}.

Htpo. 2.1.11 Pf. Q התגוללתי; impf. Q יתגוללו; ptc. מִתְגֹּלֵל; inf. הִתְגֹּלֵל—**1. roll oneself upon** (עַל), i.e. **seek occasion against** Gn 43_{18}. **2. roll oneself about, wallow** in (בְּ) blood 2 S 20_{12}, iniquity Si 12_{14}, guilt 1QH 14_{22}.

Pilp. 1 + waw וְגִלְגַּלְתִּיךָ—**roll** mountain from (מִן) rocks Jr 51_{25}.

Htpalp. 1 Pf. הִתְגַּלְגָּלוּ—**keep rolling on,** of rabble Jb 30_{14}.

→ גַּל I *heap*, II *wave*, גִּלּוּל *idol*, גָּלִיל I *hinged*, II *rod*,

גְּלִילָה *district*, גֻּלָּה *bowl*, גַּלְגַּל I *wheel*, II *tumbleweed*, גֻּלְגֹּלֶת *skull*, מְגִלָּה *scroll*.

*גלל II 0.1.14 vb.—**Poal** 0.0.3 Ptc. מגולל—**be defiled**, of person 1QH 22_4.

Htpo. 0.1.11 Pf. Q התגוללה—**defile oneself, be defiled**, of world 1QS 4_{19} (+ בְּ *in* ways of wickedness), persons CD 3_{17} (+ בְּ *with* transgressions).

→ גֵּל *dung*, גָּלָל II *dung*.

גָּלָל I 3 pr.n.m. **Galal**.

גָּלָל II 2 n.[m.]—pl. גְּלָלִים—**dung** 1 K 14_{10} Zp 1_{17}. → גלל II *be foul*.

גָּלָל III, see בִּגְלַל *on account of*.

גִּלֲלַי 1 pr.n.m. **Gilalai**.

גלם 1 vb.—**Qal** 1 + waw וַיִּגְלֹם—**wrap (up)** cloak 2 K 2_8. → גֹּלֶם *embryo*, גְּלוֹם *cloak*.

[גֹּלֶם] 1 n.[m.]—sf. גָּלְמִי—**embryo** Ps 139_{16}. → גלם *wrap*.

גַּלְמוּד 4 adj.—f.s. גַּלְמוּדָה—**barren, hard**, of Zion (as woman) Is 49_{21}, night Jb 3_7, hunger Jb 30_3.

גִּלֹנִי 2 gent. **Gilonite**.

גלע 3.0.1 vb.—**Pi.** 0.0.1 Inf. גלעם—**split open** olives 4QHarv $1_{7(mg)}$.

Htp. Impf. יִתְגַּלָּע; inf. הִתְגַּלַּע—**burst out**, of person Pr 18_1 (+ בְּ *against*) 20_3, dispute Pr 17_{14}.

גַּלְעֵד 2 pl.n. **Galed**.

גִּלְעָד I 86.0.1 pl.n. **Gilead**.

גִּלְעָד II 14 pr.n.m. **Gilead**.

גִּלְעָדִי 11 gent. **Gileadite**.

גלשׁ 2 vb.—**Qal** 2 Pf. גָּלְשׁוּ—**flow**, or **leap** from (מִן) Mount Gilead, of goats Ca 4_1 6_5.

גֻּלֹּת, see גֻּלָּה *bowl*.

גַּם I 771.49.44.1 adv.—**1.** usu. **also, too, as well, likewise,** immediately followed by noun Gn 38_{22}, verb Gn 30_6, pron. Gn 27_{31}, prep. Gn 3_6, adv. Gn 40_{15}; oft. repeated, **both ... and** Gn 24_{25}, **(n)either ... (n)or** 1 S 28_{15} 1 K 3_{26}. **2. even,** גַּם־צִפּוֹר מָצְאָה בַיִת *even the sparrow has found a home* Ps 84_3, אֵין גַּם־אֶחָד *there is not even one* Ps 14_3. **3.** גַּם כִּי **even though,** גַּם כִּי־תַרְבּוּ תְפִלָּה אֵינֶנִּי שֹׁמֵעַ *even though you increase your prayers, I shall not listen* Is 1_{15}.

*גַּם II 10 adv. **aloud, loudly,** וַיָּשֻׁבוּ וַיִּבְכּוּ גַּם בְּנֵי יִשְׂרָאֵל *and the Israelites again wept loudly* Nm 11_4.

גמא 2 vb.—**Pi.** 1 Impf. יְגַמֶּא־—**swallow** the ground, of galloping horse Jb 39_{24}.

Hi. 1 Impv. הַגְמִיאִינִי—**allow to swallow** Gn 24_{17}.

גֹּמֶא 4 n.m. **reed,** תֵּבַת גֹּמֶא *chest of reed(s)* Ex 2_3, כְּלֵי־ *vessels of* Is 18_2.

גֹּמֶד 1 n.[m.] **gomed**, perh. short cubit Jg 3_{16}.

[גַּמָּדִי] 1 gent. **Gammadite.**

גָּמוּל 1.0.33 pr.n.m. **Gamul.**

גְּמוּל 19.1.18 n.m.—cstr. גְּמוּל; sf. גְּמֻלוֹ; pl. sf. גמוליו—**1. recompense, requital** of God Is 35_4; שִׁלֵּם גְּמוּל לְ pi. *render recompense to* someone Is 66_6, sim. שׁוּב גְּמוּל לְ hi. Ps 28_4. **2. dealing,** גְּמוּל יָדָיו *dealing of his hands*, i.e. his deeds Jg 9_{16}. **3. benefit** of Y. Ps 103_2. → גמל *repay*.

גְּמוּלָה 3.1 n.f. **recompense,** אֵל גְּמֻלוֹת *God of recompense(s)* Jr 51_{56}. → גמל *repay*.

גִּמְזוֹ 1 pl.n. **Gimzo.**

*[גְּמִילוּת] 0.1 n.[f.]—cstr. גמילות—**recompense** Si 37_{11} (Bmg, D). → גמל *repay*.

גמל 37.2.7 vb.—**Qal** 34.2.7 Pf. גָּמַל; impf. תִּגְמֹל; + waw וַיִּגְמֹל; impv. גְּמֹל; ptc. גֹּמֵל, גֹּמְלִים; ptc. pass. גָּמוּל; inf. גְּמָלָה—**1a. repay** someone (with) something, with double accus. Gn 50_{15} 2 S 19_{37}; (less oft.) with accus. of thing + לְ *to* person Dt 32_6 Ps 137_8. **b. deal generously** with (עַל) Ps 13_6. **2a. wean** child 1 S 1_{23}. **b.** pass. ptc. as noun, **weaned child** Ps 131_2; גְּמוּלֵי מֵחָלָב *ones weaned from milk* Is 28_9. **3a.** intrans., **ripen, become mature,** of grapes Is 18_5. **b.** trans., **ripen, produce** almonds Nm 17_{23}.

Ni. 3 Impf. יִגָּמֵל; + waw וַיִּגָּמַל; inf. הִגָּמֵל—**be weaned** Gn 21_8.

→ גְּמוּל *recompense*, גְּמוּלָה *recompense*, גְּמִילוּת *recompense*, תַּגְמוּל *recompense*.

גָּמָל 54 n.m. (& f.) **camel**—pl. גְּמַלִּים; cstr. גְּמַלֵּי; sf. גְּמַלָּיו—Gn 12_{16}; fem. Gn 32_{16}.

גְּמַלִּי 1 pr.n.m. **Gemalli.**

גַּמְלִיאֵל 5 pr.n.m. **Gamaliel.**

*[גמליָהו] 0.0.0.3 pr.n.m. **Gemaliah.**

*גמם 1 vb.—**Qal** 1 Pf. גַּם—**be ended, pass,** of night Is 21_{12}.

גמר I 5.1 vb.—**Qal** 5.1 Pf. גָּמַר; impf. יִגְמֹר (יִגְמָר־); ptc. גֹּמֵר—**1. be ended,** of person Ps 12_2, word Ps 77_9. **2. accomplish one's purpose,** of Y. Ps 57_3 (+ עַל *for*)

138_8 (+ בְּעַד *for*). **3. bring to an end, destroy** Si 43_4. → גֹּמֶר *completion*.

*גמר II 2 vb.—**Qal** 2 Impf. יִגְמֹר; ptc. גֹּמֵר—**avenge** someone, with עַל of obj. Ps 57_3, בְּעַד of obj. Ps 138_8.

Ni. be avenged, of evil Ps 7_{10} (if em. יִגְמָר *let it come to an end* to יִגְמֶר).

* [גֹּמֶר] 0.0.2 n.m. **completion,** גמר הקץ *completion of the age* 1QpHab 7_2. → גמר I *be ended.*

גֹּמֶר 6.0.0.1 pr.n.m.&f. **Gomer.**

גְּמַרְיָה, see גְּמַרְיָהוּ *Gemariah.*

גְּמַרְיָהוּ 5.0.0.8 pr.n.m. **Gemariah.**

* [גְּמְרִיּוּת] 0.0.1 n.f. appar. **glowingness** 4QCryptic 2.1_1.

גַּן 41.0.5 n.m. (& f.)—גָּן; cstr. גַּן; sf. גַּנּוֹ; pl. גַּנִּים—**garden,** in Eden Gn 2_{15}, at king's house 2 K 21_{18}; for vegetables Dt 11_{10}, fruit Ca 4_{16}, spices Ca 5_1. → גנן *cover.*

גנב I 40.0.3 vb.—**Qal** 31.0.3 Pf. גָּנַבְתָּ; impf. יִגְנֹב; inf. גְּנֹב; ptc. גֹּנֵב; ptc. pass. גְּנֻבְתִי, גָּנוּב—**1a. steal** something Gn 31_{30} 44_8 (+ מִן *from*); specif. **kidnap** person Ex 21_{16}, **rescue** child secretly 2 K 11_2||2 C 22_{11} (+ מִתּוֹךְ *from among*), **appropriate** someone 2 S 19_{42}, **sweep away,** of wind Jb 21_{18}. **b.** גנב לֵב **steal heart,** i.e. **deceive** Gn 31_{20}; without לֵב Gn 31_{27}. **2.** pass. **be stolen** Gn 30_{33}. **3.** inf. abs. as noun, **theft** Ho 4_2.

Ni. 1 Impf. יִגָּנֵב—**be stolen** Ex 22_{11} (+ מֵעִמּוֹ).

Pi. 2 Impf. יְגַנֵּב; ptc. מְגַנְּבֵי—**steal** hearts 2 S 15_6, words of Y. Jr 23_{30} (+ מֵאֵת *from*).

Pu. 4 Pf. גֻּנַּב; impf. יְגֻנַּב; inf. abs. גֻּנֹּב—**1. be stolen,** of person Gn 40_{15} (+ מִן *from*), money or goods Ex 22_6 (+ מִן). **2. be taken stealthily,** of word Jb 4_{12} (+ אֶל *to*).

Htp. 2 Impf. יִתְגַּנֵּב—**go stealthily** 2 S 19_4.

→ גַּנָּב *thief,* גְּנֵבָה *stolen object.*

*גנב II 1 vb.—**Pu.** 1 Impf. יְגֻנַּב—**be hurled,** of word Jb 4_{12} (+ אֶל *upon*).

גַּנָּב 17.1 n.m.—pl. גַּנָּבִים—**thief** Ex 22_1. → גנב I *steal.*

גְּנֵבָה 2 n.f.—sf. גְּנֵבָתוֹ—**stolen object** Ex $22_{2.3}$. → גנב I *steal.*

גְּנֻבַת 2 pr.n.m. **Genubath.**

גַּנָּה 16.0.2 n.f.—cstr. גִּנַּת, גִּנָּתוֹ; pl. גַּנּוֹת; sf. גַּנּוֹתֵיכֶם—**garden** Nm 24_6; at palace Est 1_5, as place of non-Yahwistic worship Is 1_{29}. → גנן *cover.*

* [גִּנָּה] n.[f.] **protection,** הַגְּדֶרֶת הַגִּנָּה *the wall, the protection,* i.e. the protecting wall Ezk 42_{12} (if em. הַגְּדֶרֶת הֲגִינָה *[?] the suitable wall*).

[גֶּנֶז] I 2 n.[m.]—cstr. גִּנְזֵי—**treasury** Est 3_9 4_7. → גַּנְזַךְ *treasury.*

[גֶּנֶז] II 1 n.[m.]—cstr. גִּנְזֵי—**carpet,** or perh. **(treasure) chest** (as גֶּנֶז I) Ezk 27_{24}.

[גַּנְזַךְ] 1 n.[m.]—pl. sf. גַּנְזַכָּיו—**treasury** 1 C 28_{11}. → גֶּנֶז *treasury.*

גנן 8 vb.—**Qal** 8 Pf. גַּנּוֹתִי; impf. יָגֵן; inf. גָּנוֹן—**cover, protect** Jerusalem or its people, subj. alw. Y.; with obj. introduced by עַל 2 K 20_6||Is 38_6, אֶל 2 K 19_{34}, בְּעַד Zc 12_8. → גַּן *garden,* גַּנָּה *garden,* מָגֵן I *shield,* II *protection,* מְגִנָּה *covering.*

גִּנְּתוֹי 1 pr.n.m. **Ginnethoi.**

גִּנְּתוֹן 2 pr.n.m. **Ginnethon.**

* [גִּנְּתֵל] 0.0.0.1 perh. pr.n.m. **Ginnethel.**

* [גַּעְגַּע] 0.1 interj. **nonsense!** Si 13_{22}.

געה 2 vb.—**Qal** 2 Impf. יִגְעֶה; inf. גְּעוֹ (mss גְּעֹה)—**low,** of cow 1 S 6_{12}, ox Jb 6_5.

[גֹּעָה] 1 pl.n. **Goah.**

געל 10.1.11 vb.—**Qal** 8.0.10 Pf. גָּעֲלָה; impf. תִּגְעַל; ptc. גֹּעֶלֶת—**abhor, reject** persons Lv 26_{11} Jr 14_{19} (בְּ of obj.), statutes Lv 26_{43}.

Ni. 1.1.1 Pf. נִגְעַל; impf. Si תגעל—**be abhorred, rejected,** of person Si 34_{16}, shield 2 S 1_{21}.

Hi. 1 Impf. יַגְעִל—**cause mate to abhor,** or **show abhorrence,** of bull Jb 21_{10}.

→ גֹּעַל *abhorrence.*

גַּעַל 9 pr.n.m. **Gaal.**

גֹּעַל 1 n.m.—cstr. גֹּעַל—**abhorrence** Ezk 16_5. → געל *abhor.*

* [גַּעֲלִי] 0.0.0.3 pr.n.m. **Gaali.**

גער 14.0.5 vb.—**Qal** 14.0.5 Pf. גָּעַרְתָּ; impf. יִגְעַר; impv. גְּעַר; ptc. גּוֹעֵר; inf. גְּעָר־—**1. rebuke,** with accus. nations Ps 9_6, beasts Ps 68_{31}; with בְּ of obj. person Gn 37_{10}, sea Na 1_4, Satan Zc 3_2. **2. drive away** spirits of destruction 1QM 14_{10}.

Htp. be rebuked Pr 28_4 (if em. גרה htp. *fight*).

→ גְּעָרָה *rebuke,* מִגְעֶרֶת I *rebuke.*

גְּעָרָה 15.1.1 n.f.—cstr. גַּעֲרַת; sf. גַּעֲרָתִי—**1. rebuke,** given by Y. 2 S 22_{16}||Ps 18_{16}, human Pr 13_1. **2. shout, threat,** in battle Is 30_{17}. → גער *rebuke.*

געש 9 vb.—**Qal** 2 + waw וַתִּגְעַשׁ—**quake,** or perh. **heave,**

vomit, of earth 2 S $22_{8(Kt)}$||Ps 18_{8}.

Pu. 1 Impf. יְגֹעֲשׁוּ—**be in turmoil,** of people Jb 34_{20}.

Htp. 4 Impf. יִתְגָּעֲשׁוּ—**quake, be in turmoil,** of earth 2 S $22_{8(Qr)}$||Ps $18_{8(mss)}$, waves Jr 5_{22}.

Htpo. 2 Impf. יִתְגֹּעֲשׁוּ; + waw וְהִתְגֹּעֲשׁוּ—**be put in turmoil,** of waters Jr 46_{8}, perh. **vomit,** of nations Jr 25_{16}.

גַּעַשׁ 4 pl.n. **Gaash.**

גַּעְתָּם 3 pr.n.m. **Gatam.**

[גַּף] I 1 n.m.—pl. cstr. גַּפֵּי—perh. **summit** Pr 9_{3}.

גַּף II 3 n.m. **body,** בְּגַפּוֹ *with his body,* i.e. on his own Ex 21_{3}.

*[גִּפָּה] 0.1 n.f. **bank,** גפת נחל *bank of river* Si $40_{16(B)}$ (M גפות pl.).

גֶּפֶן I 55.0.3 n.f. (& m.)—גֶּפֶן; sf. גַּפְנוֹ; pl. גְּפָנִים—**vine** Gn 40_{9}, representing Israel Ps 80_{9}; גֶּפֶן הַיַּיִן *vine of the wine,* i.e. grapevine Nm 6_{4}, גֶּפֶן שָׂדֶה *vine of (the) field,* i.e. wild vine 2 K 4_{39}.

*גֶּפֶן II 1 n.[m.] **saddle** Gn 49_{11}.

גֹּפֶר 1 n.[m.] **gopher,** or perh. **cypress,** wood for construction of ark Gn 6_{14}.

גָּפְרִית 7.0.3 n.f. **brimstone** Gn 19_{24}.

גֵּר 92.1.10 n.m.—sf. גֵּרוֹ; pl. גֵּרִים—**sojourner, resident alien** Gn 15_{13}, as distinct from אֶזְרָח *native* Ex 12_{19}; oft. mentioned in connection with oppression Ex 22_{20} Jr 7_{6}. → גור I *sojourn.*

גִּר 1 n.[m.] **chalk** Is 27_{9}.

גֵּרָא 9.0.0.2 pr.n.m. **Gera.**

גָּרָב 3 n.[m.] perh. **eczema** Lv 21_{20} 22_{22} Dt 28_{27}.

גָּרֵב I 2 pr.n.m. **Gareb.**

גָּרֵב II 1 pl.n. **Gareb.**

[גַּרְגַּר] 1.1.4 n.m.—Si גרגר; pl. גַּרְגְּרִים—**berry,** i.e. olive Is 17_{6}, grape 4QD[b] 6_{2}.

*[גַּרְגְּרָן] 0.1 n.m. **glutton** Si $34_{16(Bmg)}$.

[גַּרְגֶּרֶת] 4.1 n.f.—pl. גַּרְגְּרוֹת; sf. גַּרְגְּרוֹתֶיךָ—**1. neck** Pr 1_{9} $3_{3.22}$ 6_{21}. **2. throat** Si 36_{23}.

גִּרְגָּשִׁי 7.0.1 gent. **Girgashite.**

גרד 1.0.1 vb.—**Qal** 0.0.1 Impf. Q יגרודו—**scrape, rub** floor, etc. 11QT 49_{12}.

Htp. 1 Inf. הִתְגָּרֵד—**scrape oneself, scratch oneself** with (בְּ) sherd Jb 2_{8}.

גרה 14 vb.—**Pi.** 3 Impf. יְגָרֶה—**provoke** contention Pr 15_{18}.

Htp. 11 Pf. הִתְגָּרִית; impf. יִתְגָּרֶה; impv. הִתְגָּר—**1. contend with, fight against** (בְּ) Dt 2_{5}. **2. provoke** (בְּ of obj.) trouble 2 K 14_{10}||2 C 25_{19}. **3a.** without obj., **get ready for war, push forward** Dn 11_{10}. **b. wage war** (לְ of obj.) Dn 11_{25}.

→ תִּגְרָה *hostility,* תִּגָּר *contention.*

גֵּרָה I 10 n.f. **cud** Lv 11_{3}||Dt 14_{6}. → גרר I *drag.*

גֵּרָה II 5.0.1.10 n.f. **gerah,** twentieth of a shekel Ex 30_{13}.

גָּרוֹן 8.1 n.m.—sf. גְּרוֹנִי—**1. throat,** as organ of speech Is 58_{1}, of swallowing Si 34_{12}; as feeling thirst Jr 2_{25}. **2. neck** Ezk 16_{11}.

[גְּרוּשָׁה] 1 n.f.—pl. sf. גְּרֻשֹׁתֵיכֶם—**(act of) expulsion** Ezk 45_{9}. → גרשׁ I *expel.*

[גֵּרוּת] 1 n.f. **lodging place,** גֵּרוּת כִּמְהָם *lodging place of Chimham* Jr $41_{17(Qr)}$ (or pl.n. *Geruth-chimham*). → גור I *sojourn.*

גרז I 1 vb.—**Ni.** 1 Pf. נִגְרַזְתִּי—**be cut off** Ps 31_{23} (+ מִנֶּגֶד *from before*). → גַּרְזֶן *axe.*

*גרז II 1 vb.—**Ni.** 1 Pf. נִגְרַזְתִּי—**disappear** Ps 31_{23} (+ מִנֶּגֶד *from before*).

[גִּרְזִי] 1 S 27_{8}, see גִּזְרִי *Gizrite.*

גְּרִזִים 4.0.1 pl.n. **Gerizim.**

גַּרְזֶן 4.0.0.3 n.m. **axe,** for cutting wood Dt 19_{5}; **pickaxe,** for breaking through rock Siloam tunnel inscr.$_{2}$; **adze,** for cutting stone 1 K 6_{7}. → גרז I *cut.*

*[גֵּרִי] 0.0.0.1 pr.n.[m.] **Geri.**

*[גְּרִיָּהוּ] 0.0.0.1 pr.n.m. **Gerijah.**

*[גָּרִים] adj. **strong,** of ass Gn $49_{14(Sam)}$. → גרם I *break bones.*

*[גָּרִיס] 0.0.2 pr.n.m. **Garis.**

[גרל] vb. **Qal, cast lot** Zp $2_{8.10}$ (if em. גדל hi. *magnify* in both). → גּוֹרָל *lot.*

גרם I 3 vb.—**Qal** 2 Pf. גָּרְמוּ—**break, gnaw bones** Zp 3_{3}.

Pi. 2 Impf. תְּגָרֵמִי ,יְגָרֵם—**crush,** or **tear out** bones Nm 24_{8}, **gnaw** sherds Ezk 23_{34}.

→ גֶּרֶם I *bone,* גָּרִים *strong.*

*גרם II 1 vb.—**Qal** 1 Pf. גָּרְמוּ—**set aside** until (לְ) morning Zp 3_{3}.

[גֶּרֶם] I 5.0.1 n.[m.]—גֶּרֶם; cstr. גֶּרֶם; pl. sf. גְּרָמָיו—**1. bone** Jb 40_{18}, coll. Pr 17_{22}; חֲמֹר גָּרֶם *ass of (strong) bone(s)* Gn 49_{14}. **2. self,** גֶּרֶם הַמַּעֲלוֹת *the steps themselves,* i.e.

the bare steps, or *the bone*, i.e. surface, *of the steps* 2 K 9_{13}. → גרם I *break bones.*

*[גֶּ֫רֶם] II 1 n.[m.]—cstr. גֶּ֫רֶם—**top of steps, i.e. landing** 2 K 9_{13}.

גַּרְמִי 1 gent. **Garmite.**

גֹּ֫רֶן 34.0.5 n.f.—+ ה- of direction גֹּ֫רְנָה; cstr. גֹּ֫רֶן; sf. גָּרְנִי, pl. גְּרָנוֹת; cstr. גָּרְנוֹת—**1. threshing floor** Nm 15_{20} Dt 15_{14}. **2. open space,** at entrance of city gate 1 K 22_{10}||2 C 18_{9}. → cf. מִגְרוֹן II *threshing floor,* מְגֹרֶן *threshing.*

גֹּ֫רֶן הָאָטָד 2 pl.n. **Goren-ha-atad.**

גֹּ֫רֶן כִּידֹן 1 pl.n. **Goren-chidon** (unless *threshing floor of Chidon*).

גֹּ֫רֶן נָכוֹן 1 pl.n. **Goren-nacon** (unless *threshing floor of Nacon*).

גרס 2 vb.—**Qal** 1 Pf. גָּרְסָה—**be crushed** with longing Ps 119_{20}.

Hi. 1 + waw וַיַּגְרֵס—**crush, grind** teeth Lm 3_{16}.

→ cf. גֶּ֫רֶשׂ *grits.*

גרע I 22.1.2 vb.—**Qal** 14.1.2 Pf. Si גרע; impf. יִגְרַע; ptc. pass. גְּרוּעָה; inf. גְּרֹעַ—**1a. diminish, reduce** clothing and conjugal rights Ex 21_{10}. **b. diminish** from (מִן) quota of bricks Ex 5_8, word, i.e. commandment Dt 4_2. **2a. withdraw** eyes from (מִן) Jb 36_7. **b.** abs., perh. **withdraw one's favour** Ezk 5_{11}. **3. restrain, limit** wisdom Jb 15_8 (+ אֶל *to* oneself), meditation Jb 15_4. **4.** pass. **a. be diminished,** i.e. **shorn,** of beard Is 15_2. **b.** perh. **be recessed,** of foundation 4Q365a 3_2.

Ni. 7 Impf. (יִגָּרַע) יִגָּרַע; + waw וְנִגְרַע; ptc. נִגְרָע—**1. be diminished, reduced** from (מִן) work Ex 5_{11}, value Lv 27_{18}. **2. be withdrawn,** of name Nm 27_4 (+ מִתּוֹךְ *from among*), inheritance Nm 36_3 (+ מִן *from*). **3. be restrained** Nm 9_7 (+ לְבִלְתִּי הַקְרִב *from offering*).

Pi. 1 Impf. יְגָרַע—**withdraw,** i.e. **draw up** drops of water Jb 36_{27}.

→ מִגְרָעָה *recess.*

*גרע II 1 vb.—**Pi.** 1 Impf. יְגָרַע—perh. **distil,** or **suck in** drops of water Jb 36_{27}.

גרף 1 vb.—**Qal** 1 Pf. גְּרָפָם—**sweep away,** of river Jg 5_{21}. → מְגְרַף *shovel,* מֶגְרָפָה I *shovel,* II *flood-water,* (?) אֶגְרֹף *fist.*

*[גֵּר פֶּ֫לַע] 0.0.1 pl.n. **Ger-pela.**

גרר I 4.0.1 vb.—**Qal** 3.0.1 Impf. יָגֹר, יְגֹרֵהוּ—**1. drag (away)** fish with (בְּ) net Hb 1_{15}, **sweep (away)** violence Pr 21_7. **2. ruminate, chew** cud Lv 11_7.

Poal 1 Ptc. מְגֹרָרוֹת—**be sawn,** of stone 1 K 7_9 (+ בְּ *with* saw).

→ גֵּרָה *cud,* מְגֵרָה *saw.*

*גרר II 1 vb.—**Htpol.** Impf. יִתְגּוֹרָרוּ—**fornicate** Ho 7_{14} (+ עַל *[in exchange] for*).

גְּרָר 10 pl.n. **Gerar.**

[גֶּ֫רֶשׂ] 2 n.[m.]—cstr. גֶּ֫רֶשׂ; sf. גִּרְשָׂהּ—**grits,** crushed new grain Lv $2_{14.16}$. → cf. גרס *be crushed.*

גרשׁ I 45.0.2 vb.—**Qal** 7.0.1 Ptc. גֹּרֵשׁ; pass. גְּרוּשָׁה; inf. מְגָרְשָׁהּ—**1.** of Y., **expel** peoples from before (מִפְּנֵי) Israel Ex 34_{11}. **2a.** pass., **be divorced,** of woman Lv 21_7 (+ מִן *from* man). **b.** pass. ptc. fem. as noun, **divorced woman** Lv 21_{14}.

Ni. 1 Pf. נִגְרַשְׁתִּי—**be expelled** from before (מִנֶּגֶד) eyes Jon 2_5.

Pi. 35.0.1 Pf. גֵּרַשְׁתָּ; impf. יְגָרֵשׁ; + waw וַיְגָרֶשׁ; impv. גָּרֵשׁ; inf. גָּרֵשׁ—**expel, drive out** Israel from (מִן) Egypt Ex 6_1, Canaanites from before (מִפְּנֵי) Israel Ex 23_{29}, Aaron and Moses from presence of (מֵאֵת פְּנֵי) Pharaoh Ex 10_{11}, Cain from upon surface of (מֵעַל פְּנֵי) ground Gn 4_{14}, Abiathar from being (מִהְיוֹת) priest 1 K 2_{27}.

Pu. 2 Pf. גֹּרְשׁוּ; impf. יְגֹרָשׁוּ—**be expelled,** of Israelites from (מִן) Egypt Ex 12_{39}, outcasts from (מִן) society Jb 30_5.

→ גֶּ֫רֶשׁ *yield,* מִגְרָשׁ I *pasture,* II *driven wave,* גְּרוּשָׁה *expulsion.*

*[גרשׁ] II 3.0.3 vb.—**Qal** 1.0.2 Pf. Q גרשו; + waw וַיִּגְרְשׁוּ; ptc. Q גורשי—of water, **churn up** slime and mud Is 57_{20}.

Ni. 2 + waw וְנִגְרְשָׁה; ptc. נִגְרָשׁ—**be churned up,** of sea Is 57_{20}, land Am 8_8.

Hi. 0.0.1 Impf. יגרישו—of waves, **churn up** slime and mud 1QH 10_{13}.

Htp. 1 Impf. יתגרשו—**be churned up** into slime and mud Is 57_{20}(1QIsa[a]).

[גֶּ֫רֶשׁ] 1 n.[m.]—cstr. גֶּ֫רֶשׁ—**yield** Dt 33_{14}. → גרשׁ I *expel.*

גֵּרְשׁוֹם, see גֵּרְשׁוֹן *Gershon.*

גֵּרְשׁוֹן 31 pr.n.m. **Gershon,** also as גֵּרְשׁוֹם **Gershom.**

גֵּרְשֹׁם, see גֵּרְשׁוֹן *Gershon.*

גֵּרְשֻׁנִּי 13 gent. **Gershonite.**

גְּשׁוּר 9 pl.n. **Geshur.**

גְּשׁוּרִי 6 gent. **Geshurite.**

גשׁם 1 vb.—**Pu. be rained upon** Ezk 22_{24} (if em. גִּשְׁמָהּ *its rain* to גֻּשְׁמָה *it will be rained upon*).

Hi. 1 Ptc. מַגְשִׁמִים—**cause to rain** Jr 14_{22}.

→ גֶּשֶׁם *rain,* גֹּשֶׁם *rain.*

גֶּשֶׁם I 35.0.6 n.m.—גָּשֶׁם; cstr. גֶּשֶׁם; pl. גְּשָׁמִים; cstr. גִּשְׁמֵי; sf. גִּשְׁמֵיכֶם—**rain** Gn 7_{12}; גֶּשֶׁם יוֹרֶה וּמַלְקוֹשׁ *the rain, the early rain and the latter rain* Jr $5_{24(Qr)}$. → גשׁם *rain.*

גֶּשֶׁם II 3 pr.n.m. **Geshem.**

[גֹּשֶׁם] 1 n.[m.]—sf. גֻּשְׁמָהּ—**rain** Ezk 22_{24} (or em. גֻּשְּׁמָה *it will* not *be rained upon*). → גשׁם *rain.*

גַּשְׁמוּ 1 pr.n.m. **Gashmu.**

*[גַּשְׁמִי] 0.0.0.1 pr.n.[m.] **Gashmi.**

גֹּשֶׁן 15 pl.n. **Goshen.**

גִּשְׁפָּא 1 pr.n.m. **Gishpa.**

*גֶּשֶׁר 0.0.1 n.m. **bridge** 4QapMes 5.2_{12}.

גשׁשׁ 2.0.2 vb.—**Pi.** 2.0.2 Impf. נְגַשְׁשָׁה (נְגַשֲּׁשָׁה); ptc. Q מגששים—**grope for wall,** like blind person Is 59_{10}.

גַּת I 5.0.3 n.f.—pl. גִּתּוֹת—**1. winepress** Is 63_2 Lm 1_{15}. **2. threshing floor** Jg 6_{11}.

גַּת II 33.0.0.1 pl.n. **Gath.**

[גַּת חֵפֶר] 2 pl.n. **Gath-hepher.**

גִּתִּי 10.0.1 gent. **Gittite.**

[גִּתַּיִם] 2 pl.n. **Gittaim.**

גִּתִּית 3 n.f. **gittith,** in psalm titles, perh. an instrument or melody assoc. with (musician from) Gath or with winepress Ps 8_1 81_1 84_1.

*[גַּת־פֶּרַח] 0.0.0.1 pl.n. **Gath-perah.**

גֶּתֶר 2 pr.n.m. **Gether.**

גַּת־רִמּוֹן 4 pl.n. **Gath-rimmon.**

ד

דאב 3.1.1 vb.—**Qal** 3.0.1 Pf. דָּאֲבָה; inf. דַּאֲבָה—**be dry, languish,** of people Jr 31_{12}, soul Jr 31_{25}, eye Ps 88_{10} (+ מִן *on account of* affliction).

Hi. 0.1 Impf. תדאיב—**cause to languish** Si 4_1.

→ דְּאָבָה *dismay,* דְּאָבוֹן *languishing.*

דְּאָבָה 1 n.f. **dismay** Jb 41_{14} (or em. דְּבָאָה or דֹּבֶא *strength*). → דאב *languish.*

[דְּאָבוֹן] 1.0.2 n.[m.]—cstr. דַּאֲבוֹן—**languishing** of soul Dt 28_{65}. → דאב *languish.*

דאג 7.3.4 vb.—**Qal** 7.3.3 Pf. דָּאַג; impf. אֶדְאַג, יִדְאַג; impv. Si דאג; ptc. דֹּאֵג, דֹּאֲגִים—**1.** intrans., **a. be anxious** 1 S 9_5 (+ לְ *concerning*) Jr 42_{16} (+ מִן *concerning*). **b. be attentive to, care for** (לְ) someone Si 35_1 50_4. **2.** trans., **fear** someone Is 57_{11}.

Hi. 0.0.1 Impf. תדאיגי—**be anxious** 4QJub[h] 35_{17}.

→ דְּאָגָה *anxiety.*

דָּאג, see דָּג *fish.*

דֹּאֵג 6 pr.n.m. **Doeg.**

דְּאָגָה 6.5 n.f.—cstr. Si דאגת; sf. Si דאגתו—**anxiety, concern, fear** Jos 22_{24} Si 34_1. → דאג *be anxious.*

דאה 4.0.1 vb.—**Qal** 4.0.1 Impf. יִדְאֶה; + waw וַיֵּדֶא—**fly, dart,** of eagle Dt 28_{49}, Y. Ps 18_{11}. → דָּאָה *kite,* דַּיָּה *kite.*

דָּאָה 1 n.f. **kite** Lv 11_{14}. → דאה *fly.*

דְּאֹר, see דּוֹר VI *Dor.*

דֹּב 12.3 n.m. (& f.)—דּוֹב; pl. דֻּבִּים—**bear** 1 S 17_{34}.

[דֹּבֶא] 1 n.[m.]—sf. דָּבְאֶךָ—**strength** Dt 33_{25}.

*[דְּבָאָה] n.m. **strength** Jb 41_{14} (if em. דְּאָבָה *dismay*).

דבב 1.0.1 vb.—**Qal** 1.0.1 ptc. דּוֹבֵב; inf. abs. Q דבוב—**1.** of wine, **glide over lips** Ca 7_{10}. **2. perh. spread an evil report** 4QsapDidA 1_3. → (?) דִּבָּה *evil report.*

דִּבָּה 9.5.1 n.m.—cstr. דִּבַּת; sf. דִּבָּתָם—**evil report, gossip, defamation,** דִּבַּת־הָאָרֶץ *evil report of,* i.e. about, *the land* Nm 13_{32}, רַבִּים *of,* i.e. by, *many* Jr 20_{10}. → (?) דבב *glide over.*

דְּבוֹרָה I 4.1.1 n.f.—pl. דְּבוֹרִים—**bee** Jg 14_8.

דְּבוֹרָה II 10.0.1 pr.n.f. **Deborah.**

דִּבְיוֹנִים 1 n.[m.] **dove's dung** 2 K $6_{25(Qr,\ mss)}$ (Kt חרי יונים in same sense; mss חריונים).

דְּבִיר I 16.2.23 n.m.—Q דיבר (3QTr 2_3); cstr. דְּבִיר; pl. Q דבירי—**1. inner sanctuary** of temple 1 K 8_6||2 C 5_7, pl. 4QShirShabb[f] 14$_{7}$. **2. room** of cave 3QTr 2$_{3}$.

דְּבִיר II 13 pl.n. **Debir.**

דְּבִיר III 1 pr.n.m. **Debir.**

דְּבֵלָה 5 n.f.—cstr. דְּבֶלֶת; pl. דְּבֵלִים—**fig-cake, lump** of pressed figs 1 S 25$_{18}$, as poultice 2 K 20$_{7}$||Is 38$_{21}$.

[דִּבְלָה] 1 pl.n. **Diblah.**

[דִּבְלַיִם] 1 pr.n.m. **Diblaim.**

דִּבְלָתַיִם, see בֵּית דִּבְלָתַיִם *Beth-diblathaim*, עַלְמֹן דִּבְלָתָיְמָה *Almon-diblathaim*.

דבק 54.4.15 vb.—**Qal** 39.2.13 Pf. דָּבַק (דָּבֵק), דָּבְקוּ (דָּבֵקוּ); impf. יִדְבַּק; inf. דָּבְקָה (Q דבוק)—**1a. cling, stick, hold fast** to something, with לְ *to* Ps 102$_{6}$, בְּ *to* Ezk 29$_{4}$, אֶל *to* 2 S 23$_{10}$. **b. stick together,** of folds of flesh Jb 41$_{15}$. **2. cling, adhere,** in devotion, with בְּ *to* Y. Dt 10$_{20}$, human Gn 2$_{24}$, testimonies Ps 119$_{31}$; אַחֲרֵי *after* Y. Ps 63$_{9}$. **3. keep close, pursue closely,** with עִם *to* someone Ru 2$_{8}$; אַחֲרֵי *after* someone Jr 42$_{16}$. **4.** of misfortune, **overtake** someone Gn 19$_{19}$.

Ni. 0.1 Pf. נדבק; ptc. נדבק—**be joined, join oneself to** (בְּ) wealth Si 34$_{10}$.

Pu. 2 Impf. יְדֻבָּקוּ—**be joined, stick fast together,** of clod of earth Jb 38$_{38}$, scale of Leviathan Jb 41$_{9}$.

Hi. 12.1.2 Pf. הִדְבַּקְתִּי; impf. יַדְבֵּק, אַדְבִּיק; + waw וַיַּדְבֵּק, וַיַּדְבִּיקוּ (וַיַּדְבְּקוּ)—**1. cause to cling, cause to adhere,** with בְּ *to* Dt 28$_{21}$ Ezk 29$_{4}$, אֶל *to* Jr 13$_{11}$ Ezk 3$_{26}$. **2. pursue closely** after (אַחֲרֵי) someone Jg 20$_{45}$. **3. overtake** someone Gn 31$_{23}$.

Ho. 1 Ptc. מֻדְבָּק—**be caused to adhere** Ps 22$_{16}$.

→ דָּבֵק *clinging*, דֶּבֶק *joining*.

דָּבֵק 3 adj.—דָּבֵק, דְּבֵקָה, דְּבֵקִים—**clinging, holding fast, joining** of wing to (לְ) wing 2 C 3$_{12}$, Israelites to (בְּ) Y., friend closer than (מִן) a brother Pr 18$_{24}$. → דבק *cling*.

דֶּבֶק 3.0.1 n.m.—pl. דְּבָקִים; cstr. Q דבקי—**1. joining, soldering** of image Is 41$_{7}$. **2. joint, appendage** of armour 1 K 22$_{34}$||2 C 18$_{33}$. **3.** perh. **tessera** 4QShirShabb[f] 19$_{5}$. → דבק *cling*.

דבר I 1140.9.120.1 vb.—**Qal** 42.2.3 Ptc. דֹּבֵר, דֹּבְרִים; pass. דָּבֻר; inf. דַּבְּרֵךְ—**speak,** oft. frequentative, alw. (exc. Ps 51$_{6}$ Pr 25$_{11}$) act. ptc.; abs. Nm 32$_{27}$; with accus. truth Ps 15$_{2}$, peace Ps 28$_{3}$, lies Ps 5$_{7}$, word Jr 28$_{7}$; prep. לְ *to* Est 10$_{3}$; אֶל *to* Gn 16$_{13}$; עַל *to, concerning* Jr 32$_{42}$, *against* Ps 31$_{19}$; עִם *with* Ps 28$_{3}$.

Ni. 4 Pf. נִדְבְּרוּ, נִדְבַּרְנוּ; ptc. נִדְבָּרִים—**1a. speak with** (אֵת) **one another** Ml 13$_{16}$. **b. speak** Ezk 33$_{20}$ (+ בְּ *concerning*) Ml 3$_{13}$ (+ עַל *against*). **2. be spoken,** of parables and riddles 4QMyst[b] 1.2$_{1}$ (unless pi.).

Pi. 1089.7.117.1 Pf. דִּבֶּר (דִּבַּר), דִּבְּרוּ (דִּבֵּרוּ); impf. יְדַבֵּר (יְדַבֶּר־), יְדַבְּרוּ (יְדַבֵּרוּ); + waw וַיְדַבֵּר; impv. דַּבֵּר (דַּבֶּר־), דַּבְּרִי, דַּבְּרוּ; ptc. מְדַבֵּר, מְדַבֶּרֶת; inf. דַּבֵּר (דַּבֶּר־, דַּבְּרוֹ)—**speak, say,** sometimes with more specif. meanings, e.g. **tell** Lv 23$_{44}$, **command** Gn 12$_{4}$, **promise** Gn 18$_{19}$, **specify** Gn 23$_{16}$, **plan** Ex 32$_{14}$, **pronounce** Jg 12$_{6}$. **a.** abs. Gn 24$_{15}$. **b.** with accus. word Gn 44$_{6}$, statute Lv 10$_{11}$, truth 1 K 22$_{16}$||2 C 18$_{15}$, good Nm 10$_{29}$, wisdom Ps 49$_{4}$, evil 1 K 22$_{23}$||2 C 18$_{22}$, apostasy Dt 13$_{6}$, lies Jg 16$_{10}$, folly Is 32$_{6}$. **c.** adv. uses: דבר קָשׁוֹת *speak harshly* Gn 42$_{7}$, טֹבוֹת *kindly* 2 K 25$_{28}$||Jr 52$_{32}$, צָחוֹת *clearly* Is 32$_{4}$, גְּבֹהָה גְבֹהָה *proudly* 1 S 2$_{3}$, פָּנִים אֶל־פָּנִים *face to face* Ex 33$_{11}$, אֲרָמִית *in Aramaic* 2 K 18$_{26}$||Is 36$_{11}$. **d.** with prep. לְ *to* Gn 24$_{7}$, *concerning* Ezk 44$_{5}$; בְּ *with, in* Dt 18$_{22}$, *by (means of), with* Ps 39$_{4}$, *concerning* Dt 3$_{26}$; בְּיַד *by means of, through* Ex 9$_{35}$; כְּ *according to* Gn 32$_{20}$; אֶל *to* Gn 8$_{15}$, *concerning* Jr 51$_{62}$; *against* Jr 36$_{31}$; עַל *concerning* 1 K 14$_{2}$, *against* Jr 25$_{13}$; אֵת *with* Gn 17$_{3}$; עִם *with* Gn 31$_{24}$. **e.** followed by לֵאמֹר to introduce direct speech Gn 8$_{15}$, a fin. form of אמר to introduce direct speech Gn 18$_{29}$.

Pu. 2 Pf. Si דבר (Q דובר); impf. יְדֻבַּר; ptc. מְדֻבָּר—**be spoken,** בַּיּוֹם שֶׁיְּדֻבַּר־בָּהּ *on the day when she* (our sister) *is spoken for?*, lit. 'it is spoken for her' Ca 8$_{8}$, נִכְבָּדוֹת מְדֻבָּר בָּךְ *glorious things are spoken of you* Ps 87$_{3}$, חזון דבר בשמך *the vision spoken in your name* Si 36$_{20}$, חזון דובר עליך *a vision spoken about you* 11QPs[a] 22$_{14}$.

Htp. 3 Ptc. מִדַּבֵּר—**speak, a.** with accus. word 2 S 14$_{13}$. **b.** with prep. אֶל *to* Nm 7$_{89}$.

→ דָּבָר *word*, דִּבֵּר *speech*, דַּבֶּרֶת *word*, דִּבְרָה *cause*, מִדְבָּר II *mouth*.

***דבר** II 5 vb.—**Pi.** 3 Impf. יְדַבֵּר; inf. דַּבֵּר—**destroy** Is 32$_{7}$ Pr 21$_{28}$ 2 C 22$_{10}$.

Pu. be destroyed Pr 21$_{28}$ (if em. יְדַבֵּר *will speak*).

Hi. 2 Impf. יַדְבֵּר; + waw וַיַּדְבֵּר—**subdue** Ps 18$_{48}$ 47$_{4}$.

***דבר** III 7 vb.—**Pi.** 7 Impf. תְּדַבֵּר; + waw וַיְדַבְּרוּ; inf.

דַּבְּרוֹ—**turn the back** Gn 34$_{13}$ Jr 31$_{20}$ Ps 50$_{20}$ 75$_{6}$ 78$_{19}$ Jb 19$_{18}$ Ca 5$_{6}$.

***דבר IV** $_{7.1}$ vb.—**Pi.** $_{5}$ Impf. יְדַבֵּר; ptc. מְדַבֵּר; inf. דַּבֵּר—**1. drive out, pursue** Ps 2$_{5}$ 127$_{5}$ 2 C 22$_{10}$. **2.** ptc. as noun, **pursuer, persecutor** Lm 5$_{9}$ (if em. הַמִּדְבָּר *the steppe*).

Pu. $_{0.1}$ Impf. ptc. מדבר—**be persecuted** Si 13$_{22}$.

Hi. $_{2}$ Impf. + waw וַיַּדְבֵּר—**drive out** Ps 18$_{48}$ 47$_{4}$.

***דבר V** vb.—**Htp. be carried away** Ps 116$_{10}$ (if em. אֲדַבֵּר *I shall speak* to אֶדַּבֵּר).

***דבר VI** $_{6}$ vb.—**Pi.** $_{6}$ Pf. דִּבֵּר, דִּבַּרְתִּי; impv. דַּבְּרוּ (דַּבְּרוּ); ptc. מְדַבֵּר; inf. דַּבֵּר—**manage** Jg 19$_{30}$ Is 8$_{10}$ 46$_{11}$ 58$_{13}$ Est 1$_{22}$ 7$_{9}$.

***דבר VII** $_{1}$ vb.—**Pi.** $_{1}$ Inf. דַּבְּרוֹ—**follow** Ca 5$_{6}$.

***[דבר] VIII** $_{1}$ vb.—**Pi.** $_{1}$ Impf. יְדַבֵּר—**have descendants** Pr 21$_{28}$.

דָּבָר $_{1442.38.221.11}$ n.m. (f. Si 43$_{29}$)—cstr. דְּבַר; sf. דְּבָרוֹ; pl. דְּבָרִים; cstr. דִּבְרֵי; sf. דְּבָרָיו, דִּבְרֵיהֶם—**1. word, speech;** in some contexts with more specif. meanings, e.g. **report** 2 S 11$_{18}$, **request** 2 S 14$_{15}$, **promise** 1 K 2$_{4}$, **command** Est 1$_{12}$, **commission** Gn 24$_{33}$, **thought** Dt 15$_{9}$, **theme** Ps 45$_{2}$, **sentence, verdict** Dt 17$_{9}$, **accusation** CD 9$_{3}$. **a.** of human beings, דְּבַר מֹשֶׁה *word of Moses* Ex 8$_{9}$, דִּבְרֵי שָׁלוֹם וֶאֱמֶת *words of peace and truth* Est 9$_{30}$, אִישׁ דְּבָרִים *man of words,* i.e. eloquent man Ex 4$_{10}$. **b.** of Y., דְּבַר־יי *word of Y.* Gn 15$_{1}$, כָּל־הַדְּבָרִים אֲשֶׁר־דִּבֶּר יי אֶל־מֹשֶׁה *all the words which Y. had spoken to Moses* Ex 4$_{30}$, הַדָּבָר אֲשֶׁר הָיָה אֶל־יִרְמְיָהוּ מֵאֵת יי *the word that came to Jeremiah from Y.* Jr 7$_{1}$; with ref. to commandment, statute Ex 20$_{1}$ 24$_{3}$. **c.** of heavens Ps 19$_{4}$. **d.** of wisdom Pr 1$_{23}$. **2. thing, a. matter, affair, cause, case,** וַיִּשָּׁבַע לוֹ עַל־הַדָּבָר הַזֶּה *and he swore to him concerning this matter* Gn 24$_{9}$; דְּבַר־פְּעוֹר *matter of Peor* Nm 25$_{18}$, דִּבְרֵי עוֹלָה וָזָבַח *matters of burnt offering and sacrifice* Jr 7$_{22}$, דְּבַר יוֹם בְּיוֹמוֹ *the thing of a day for its day,* i.e. what is appropriate or due each day Ex 5$_{13}$; with ref. to legal case, cause, דִּבְרֵי רִיבֹת *cases of contention,* i.e. contentious cases Dt 17$_{8}$, דִּבְרֵי צַדִּיקִים *causes of righteous persons* Ex 23$_{8}$; עַל־דְּבַר **because of (the matter of), on account of** (cf. also §4) Gn 12$_{17}$ 43$_{18}$ Dt 4$_{21}$. **b. deed,** (1) of humans Gn 24$_{66}$; דִּבְרֵי שְׁלֹמֹה *deeds of Solomon* 1 K 11$_{41}$, דְּבַר הַנְּבָלָה *deed of folly* Jg 19$_{24}$. (2) of Y. 2 K 20$_{9}$||Is 38$_{7}$; דִּבְרֵי נִפְלְאוֹתֶיךָ *deeds of your wonders,* i.e. your wonderful deeds Ps 145$_{5}$. **c. event,** דִּבְרֵי הַיָּמִים *events of the days,* i.e. chronicles 1 K 14$_{19}$, אַחַר הַדְּבָרִים הָאֵלֶּה *after these things* Gn 22$_{1}$, הֲנִהְיָה כַּדָּבָר הַגָּדוֹל הַזֶּה *has such a great thing as this ever happened?* Dt 4$_{32}$. **d. something, anything,** הֲיִפָּלֵא מֵיי דָּבָר *is anything too hard for Y.?* Gn 18$_{14}$, לֹא אוּכַל לַעֲשׂוֹת דָּבָר *I cannot do anything* Gn 19$_{22}$, לֹא חָסַרְתָּ דָּבָר *you have not lacked anything* Dt 2$_{7}$, כָּל־דָּבָר *anything, everything* Lv 5$_{2}$. **3. way, manner,** דבר הנקבה *manner of the boring through* Siloam inscr.$_{1}$, דְּבַר הַשְּׁמִטָּה *manner of the release* Dt 15$_{2}$. **4. reason, cause** (cf. also §2a), זֶה דְּבַר־הַמַּס *this is the reason of,* i.e. for, *the forced labour* 1 K 9$_{15}$, זֶה הַדָּבָר אֲשֶׁר־הֵרִים יָד בַּמֶּלֶךְ *this is the reason why he lifted up (his) hand against the king* 1 K 11$_{27}$. → דבר I *speak.*

דֶּבֶר I $_{49.1.3}$ n.m.—דֶּבֶר; pl. sf. דְּבָרֶיךָ—**pestilence, plague,** usu. among humans Ex 5$_{3}$ Lv 26$_{25}$, also animals Ex 9$_{3}$.

***דֶּבֶר II** $_{1}$ n.[m.] **violence,** דֶּבֶר הַוּוֹת *violence of the winds* Ps 91$_{3}$.

דְּבִר, see דְּבִיר II *Debir.*

דִּבֵּר $_{1}$ n.[m.] **speech** Jr 5$_{13}$ (ms הַדָּבָר *the word*). → דבר I *speak.*

[דֹּבֶר] $_{2}$ n.[m.]—sf. דָּבְרוֹ—**pasture** Is 5$_{17}$ Mc 2$_{12}$. → cf. מִדְבָּר *steppe.*

[דִּבְרָה] $_{5}$ n.f.—cstr. דִּבְרַת (דִּבְרָתִי, mss דִּבְרָתוֹ); sf. דִּבְרָתִי—**1. legal case,** or perh. **speech** Jb 5$_{8}$. **2. manner,** עַל־דִּבְרָתִי מַלְכִּי־צֶדֶק *according to the manner of Melchizedek* Ps 110$_{4}$. **3a.** עַל־דִּבְרַת, **because of, on account of** Ec 3$_{18}$ 8$_{2}$. **b.** עַל־דִּבְרַת שֶׁ־, **in order that** Ec 7$_{14}$. → דבר I *speak.*

[דֹּבְרָה] $_{1}$ n.f.—pl. דֹּבְרוֹת—**raft** 1 K 5$_{23}$.

דְּבֹרָה, see דְּבוֹרָה II *Deborah.*

דִּבְרִי $_{1}$ pr.n.m. **Dibri.**

דָּבְרַת $_{3}$ pl.n. **Daberath.**

[דַּבֶּרֶת] $_{1}$ n.f.—pl. sf. דִּבְּרֹתֶיךָ—**word** Dt 33$_{3}$. → דבר I *speak.*

דְּבַשׁ $_{54.3.6}$ n.m.—דְּבַשׁ; sf. דִּבְשִׁי—**honey,** אֶרֶץ זָבַת חָלָב וּדְבָשׁ *a land flowing with milk and honey* Ex 3$_{8}$.

דַּבֶּשֶׁת I $_{1}$ n.f.—cstr. דַּבֶּשֶׁת—**hump (of camel)** Is 30$_{6}$.

דַּבֶּשֶׁת II $_{1}$ pl.n. **Dabbesheth.**

דָּג 19.0.6 n.m.—דָּאג; pl. דָּגִים; cstr. דְּגֵי—**fish,** as coll. only Ne 13_{16}; דְּגֵי הַיָּם *fishes of the sea* Gn 9_2, שַׁעַר הַדָּגִים *fish Gate* Zp 1_{10}. → דיג *fish;* cf. דָּגָה *fish.*

דגה 1 vb.—**Qal** 1 Impf. יִדְגּוּ—**increase** Gn 48_{16}.

דָּגָה 15.0.1 n.f.—cstr. דְּגַת; sf. דְּגָתָם—**fish,** as coll. (exc. Jon 2_2), דְּגַת הַיָּם *fish of the sea* Gn 1_{26}. → דיג *fish;* cf. דָּג *fish.*

דָּגוֹן 13 pr.n.m. **Dagon,** Philistine deity 1 S 5_2.

דגל I 4 vb.—**Qal** 2 Impf. נִדְגֹּל; ptc. pass. דָּגוּל—**1. lift banners** Ps 20_6. **2.** pass. **be raised as a standard,** i.e. **be conspicuous, prominent,** of male lover Ca 5_{10}.

Ni. 2 **be bannered**—Ptc. נִדְגָּלוֹת—ptc. as noun, **bannered troops** Ca $6_{4.10}$.

→ דֶּגֶל I *standard.*

***דגל** II 4 vb.—**Qal** 2 Impf. נִדְגֹּל; ptc. pass. דָּגוּל—**1.** pass. **be seen, be outstanding, be remarkable,** of male lover Ca 5_{10}. **2. wait upon** name of Y. Ps 20_6.

Ni. 2 Ptc. נִדְגָּלוֹת—Ptc. as noun, **(admirable) sight** Ca $6_{4.10}$.

***דגל** III vb. Qal, **lie** Si 5_{14} (if em.). → דִּגֵּל *falsehood,* דִּגְּלוּת *falsehood.*

דֶּגֶל I 14.0.26 n.m.—cstr. דֶּגֶל; sf. דִּגְלוֹ; pl. Q דגלים; cstr. Q דגלי; sf. דִּגְלֵיהֶם—**1. standard, banner** Nm 1_{52}, perh. with ref. to division of tribe Nm 2_3. **2. battalion, company (of troops),** דגלי אל *battalions of God* 1QM 3_6, הבינים *of infantry,* lit. 'of the space between' 1QM 6_1. → דגל I *raise standard.*

***דֶּגֶל** II n.[m.]—sf. דִּגְלוֹ—**glance** Ca 2_4.

***דִּגֵּל** n.[m.] **falsehood** Ps 15_3 (if em. רָגַל *he slanders*). → דגל III *lie.*

***דִּגְּלוּת** n.f. **falsehood** Ps 12_4 (if em. גְּדֹלוֹת *great things*). → דגל III *lie.*

דָּגָן 39.0.15 n.m.—cstr. דְּגַן; sf. דְּגָנְךָ—**corn, grain** of cereals Dt 7_{13}.

דגר 2 vb.—**Qal** 2 Pf. דָּגַר, דָּגְרָה—**incubate (eggs), brood** Is 34_{15} Jr 17_{11}.

[דַּד] 4 n.m.—du. cstr. דַּדֵּי; sf. דַּדֶּיהָ—**breast, teat, nipple** Ezk 23_3.

דֹּד, see דּוֹד *beloved.*

דדה 2 vb.—**Htp.** 2 Impf. אֶדַּדֶּה (אֶדַּדֵּם)—**1.** perh. **go** Is 38_{15}. **2.** perh. **lead in procession** Ps 42_5.

[דֹּדָה], see דּוֹדָה *(paternal) aunt.*

דֹּדוֹ, see דּוֹדוֹ *Dodo.*

דֹּדָוָהוּ 1 pr.n.m. **Dodavahu.**

***דֹּדִיָּהוּ** 0.0.0.1 pr.n.m. **Dodiah.**

דְּדָן 11 pr.n.m. & pl.n. **Dedan.**

[דְּדָנִי] 1 gent. **Dedanite.**

דֹּדָנִים 1 pr.n.m. **Dodanim.**

***[דהה]** I vb. **fear** Is 44_8 (if em. תִּרְהוּ *be afraid* to תִּדְהוּ [qal] or תִּדָּהוּ [ni.]).

***דהה** II vb. **Pilp., roll stones** Is 11_8 (if em. יָדוֹ הָדָה *will stretch out his hand* to יְדַהְדֵּה).

דהם 1.0.0.1 vb.—**Ni.** 1.0.0.1 Impf. I תדהם; ptc. נִדְהָם—**1. be astonished, dumbfounded** Jr 14_9. **2. keep silent** Meṣad Ḥashavyahu ost. 1_{14}.

דהר I 1 vb.—**Qal** 1 Ptc. דֹּהֵר—**gallop,** or perh. **neigh,** of horse Na 3_2. → דַּהֲרָה *galloping.*

***דהר** II vb. **Pi., race chariot,** מִדַּהֲרִים דַּהֲרוֹת אַבִּירָיו *their stallions ran chariot races* Jg 5_{22} (if em. מִדַּהֲרוֹת *from chariot-races*).

[דַּהֲרָה] I 2 n.f.—pl. abs. דַּהֲרוֹת; cstr. דַּהֲרוֹת—**galloping** of stallions Jg 5_{22}.

***[דַּהֲרָה]** II 1 n.f.—pl. דַּהֲרוֹת—**chariot-race** Jg 5_{22}.

דוב 1 vb.—**Hi.** 1 Ptc. מְדִיבֹת—**cause soul to pine away,** of diseases Lv 26_{16}. → cf. מַדְהֵב I *distress,* מַדְהֵבָה I *distress.*

דּוֹב, see דֹּב *bear.*

[דַּוָּג] 2 n.m.—pl. דַּוָּגִים—**fisher** Jr $16_{16(Kt)}$ (Qr דַּיָּגִים) Ezk 47_{10}. → דיג *fish.*

דּוּגָה 1 n.f. **fishing,** סִירוֹת דּוּגָה *fish-hooks* Am 4_2. → דיג *fish.*

דָּוִד 1023.7.23 pr.n.m. **David.**

דּוֹד 61.1 n.m.—cstr. דּוֹד; sf. דּוֹדוֹ; pl. דּוֹדִים; sf. דֹּדֶיךָ—**1. beloved, lover** Is 5_1 Ca 1_{13}; perh. **friend** Si 40_{20}. **2. (paternal) uncle** Lv 10_4. **3.** perh. **Philistine governor, prefect** 1 S $10_{14.15}$. **4.** pl. **love** Ezk 16_8 Pr 7_{18} Ca 1_2.

דּוּד 8.0.1 n.m.—pl. abs. דּוּדִים (דְּוָדִים); cstr. דּוּדָאֵי—**1. pot, kettle,** for cooking 1 S 2_{14}. **2. basket** 2 K 10_7 Jr 24_1.

דּוּדָאִים 6 n.m.—pl. cstr. דּוּדָאֵי—**mandrakes** (*Atropa mandragora* or *Mandragora officinarum*) Gn 30_{14} Ca 7_{14}.

[דּוֹדָה] 3 n.f.—sf. דֹּדָתוֹ, דֹּדָתְךָ—**(paternal) aunt, father's**

brother's wife Lv 18$_{14}$, father's sister Ex 6$_{20}$ Lv 20$_{20}$.

דּוֹדוֹ 5 pr.n.m. **Dodo.**

דּוֹדַי 1 pr.n.m. **Dodai.**

דוה 1.0.1.1 vb.—**Qal** 1.0.1.1 Pf. I דוה; Inf. דְּוֹתָהּ—**1. be faint** Lachish ost. 3$_{7}$. **2. menstruate,** נִדַּת דְּוֹתָהּ *impurity of her menstruation* Lv 12$_{2}$. → דָּוֶה *faint,* דַּוָּי *faint,* דְּוַי *sickness,* מַדְוֶה *illness,* דְּוֹן *grief,* דְּוָיָה *grief.*

דָּוֶה 5.1.2 adj.—f.s. דָּוָה (Q דאוה)—**1. faint, sad,** of Zion Lm 1$_{13}$, heart Lm 5$_{17}$. **2. menstruous,** of woman Lv 20$_{18}$. **3.** as noun, **a. menstruous woman** Lv 15$_{33}$. **b.** perh. **garment stained by menstruation** Is 30$_{22}$. **c. sickness** 4QJub[h] 35$_{7}$. → דוה *be faint.*

דוח I 3 vb.—**Hi.** 3 Impf. יָדִיחַ—**cleanse, wash** burnt offering Ezk 40$_{38}$, bloodstain Is 4$_{4}$.

דוח II 1 vb.—**Hi.** 1 Pf. Kt הדיחנו (Qr הֱדִיחָנִי)—**vomit** Jr 51$_{34}$ (or em. הִדִּיחָנִי *he has thrust me out,* from נדח hi.).

[דַּוָּי] 3 adj.—דַּוָּי—**faint,** of heart Is 1$_{5}$ Jr 8$_{18}$ Lm 1$_{22}$. → דוה *be faint.*

[דְּוַי] 2 n.[m.] **sickness,** דְּוֵי לַחְמִי *sickness of my food* Jb 6$_{7}$, עֶרֶשׂ דְּוָי *bed of sickness* Ps 41$_{4}$. → דוה *be faint.*

***דְּוִי** 1 n.[m.] **echo, sound,** הֵמָּה כִּדְוִי לַחְמִי *my bowels rumble,* or *fade away, like an echo* Jb 6$_{7}$ (if em.), דֵּי שֹׁפָר *sound of the trumpet* Jb 39$_{25}$.

[דּוֹיֵג], see דֹּאֵג *Doeg.*

דָּוִיד, see דָּוִד *David.*

***[דְּוָיָה]** 0.0.1 n.f.—דוויה—**grief** GnzPs 4$_{2}$. → דוה *be faint.*

דוך 1.1 vb.—**Qal** 1 Pf. דָּכוּ—**crush, pound** manna in mortar Nm 11$_{8}$.

Pulp. 0.1 Ptc. מְדֻכְדָּךְ—ptc. as noun, **crushed, oppressed (one)** Si 4$_{4}$.

→ מְדֹכָה *mortar;* cf. דכא *crush,* דָּכָה *crush,* דכך *crush.*

דּוּכִי, see דֳּכִי II *cleanness.*

דּוּכִיפַת 2 n.f. **hoopoe,** a bird Lv 11$_{19}$ Dt 14$_{18}$.

***[דום]** vb.—**Qal** (alw. if em. דמם I *be silent*), **stand still, cease, wait,** of sun Jos 10$_{12.13}$, person 1 S 14$_{9}$ Jr 8$_{14}$ Ezk 24$_{17}$ Ps 35$_{15}$ 37$_{7}$ Jb 29$_{21}$, bowels Jb 30$_{27}$, sword Jr 47$_{6}$, glory Ps 30$_{13}$, tears La 2$_{18}$.

Hi., cause to wait Jr 8$_{14}$ (if em. דמם IV hi. *cause to perish*).

דּוּמָה I 2.0.1 n.f. **silence,** as place or state of the dead Ps 94$_{17}$ 115$_{17}$ 4QWiles 1$_{7}$. → דמם I *be silent.*

דּוּמָה II 2 pr.n.m. **Dumah.**

דּוּמָה III 1 pl.n. **Dumah.**

דּוּמִיָּה I 4 n.f.—דֻּמִיָּה—**silence** Ps 22$_{3}$; נֶאֱלַמְתִּי דוּמִיָּה *I was dumb (in) silence* Ps 39$_{3}$. → דמה III *be silent.*

***דּוּמִיָּה II** 3 n.f. **response, satisfaction** Ps 22$_{3}$ 39$_{3}$ 62$_{2}$.

דּוּמָם 3 n.[m.]—**1. silence,** אֶבֶן דּוּמָם *stone of silence* Hb 2$_{19}$. **2.** as adv., **in silence** Is 47$_{5}$ Lm 3$_{26}$. → דמם III *be silent.*

דּוּמֶשֶׂק, see דַּמֶּשֶׂק *Damascus.*

דון I 1 vb.—**Qal** 1 Impf. יָדוֹן—**remain, abide,** of Y.'s spirit Gn 6$_{3}$ (+ בְּ *in* humans).

***דון II** 2 vb.—**Qal** 2 Impf. יָדִין; impv. דִּין—**be lowly** Gn 49$_{16}$ Jb 35$_{14}$.

***דון III** 1 vb.—**Hi.** 1 Impf. יָדִין—**enrich, feed** Jb 36$_{31}$.

***דון IV** 3 vb.—**Qal** 3 Pf. דָּנַנִּי; impf. יָדוֹן, יָדִין—**be close to,** with accus. Gn 49$_{16}$, בְּ *to* Gn 6$_{3}$ 30$_{6}$.

***[דְּוֹן]** 0.0.1 n.[m.]—sf. דוני—**grief, sorrow** 4QpsEzek[a] 4$_{1}$. → דוה *be faint.*

דּוּן 1 n.[m.] **judgment,** לְמַעַן תֵּדְעוּן שַׁדּוּן *that you may know that there is a judgment* Jb 19$_{29(Qr)}$ (Kt שדין; or em. יֵשׁ דַּיָּן *there is a judge*). → דין I *judge.*

דּוֹנַג 4.0.5 n.m.—דּוֹנָג—**wax,** in comparisons with melting of heart Ps 22$_{15}$, the wicked Ps 68$_{3}$, mountains Mc 1$_{4}$.

***דוסתס** 0.0.5 pr.n.m. **Dositheus.**

***דוע** 1 vb.—**Qal** 1 Impf. יָדְעוּן—**flow with goodwill,** of lips Pr 10$_{32}$.

***דוף** 2 vb.—**Hi.** 2 Pf. הדיפו; inf. הדיף—**thrust, drive out** Dt 6$_{19(Sam)}$ 9$_{4(Sam)}$ (both MT הדף *thrust*).

דוץ 1.0.1 vb.—**Qal** 1.0.1 Impf. תָּדוּץ; impv. Q דוצי—**dance, leap** Jb 41$_{14}$, **leap for joy** 4QTobit[e] 7.1$_{1}$.

***[דוק]** vb.—**Hi., muster, inspect** Gn 14$_{14}$ (if em. וַיָּרֶק *and he poured out* to וַיָּדֶק).

***[דּוֹק]** 0.0.1 pl.n. **Dok.**

***[דּוּקָה]** 0.0.16 n.f.—דוקו, דוקוה—**new moon,** in calendrical tables 4QCalMishB 1$_{6}$ 4QCalMishC 4$_{8}$.

דור I 1.4.4 vb.—**Qal** 1.4.4 Impf. Q ידור; ptc. Si דר; ptc. pass. Si דור; inf. דּוּר—**dwell,** of person Ps 84$_{11}$, spirit of Y. 4QCommGenA 1$_{2}$ (=Gn 6$_{3}$ יָדוֹן *remain*). → דּוֹר IV *dwelling,* דִּירָה *dwelling,* מָדוֹר *dwelling place.*

דור II 1 vb.—**Qal** 1 Impv. (or inf. abs.?) דּוּר—**heap up** wood Ezk 24$_{5}$ (if em. הָעֲצָמִים *the bones* to הָעֵצִים *the wood*). → מְדוּרָה *pile.*

*[דַּוָּר] 0.1 n.[m.] **governor,** דורי ארץ *governors of the earth* Si 44₃.

דּוֹר I 166.10.78 n.m.—דֹּר; cstr. דּוֹר; sf. דּוֹרוֹ; pl. דּוֹרִים, דֹּרוֹת; cstr. דּוֹרוֹת (Q דורי); sf. דֹּרֹתָם (Q דוריהם, Q דורותיהמה)—**1. generation,** a stage in the desecent of people from a common ancestor, דּוֹר רְבִיעִי *the fourth generation* Gn 15₁₆, אֶלֶף דּוֹר *a thousand generations* Dt 7₉, לְדֹרֹתֵיכֶם *throughout your generations* Gn 17₁₂, לְדוֹר וָדוֹר *throughout all generations* Ps 10₆, דֹּרֹת עוֹלָם *generations of eternity* Gn 9₁₂. **2. group, community** of the righteous Ps 14₅, those who seek Y. Ps 24₆, those under the wrath of Y. Jr 7₂₉.

*דּוֹר II 15 n.m.—sf. דּוֹרוֹ; cstr. דּוֹר—**assembly, council, group** Is 38₁₂ 53₈ Jr 2₃₁ Ps 22₃₁ 49₂₀ 95₁₀.

*דּוֹר III 2.0.1 n.m.—cstr. דּוֹר; pl. sf. Q דורותם—**fate, appointed destiny** Is 53₈ Ps 24₆(Qr) 1QS 3₁₄.

*דּוֹר IV 1 n.m.—sf. דּוֹרִי—**dwelling** Is 38₁₂. → דור I *dwell.*

*דּוֹר V 2 n.m. **circle, circular motion (of nature)** Ec 1₄.

דּוֹר VI 7.0.0.1 pl.n. **Dor.**

*דּוֹר VII n.m. **circular wall** 2 S 5₉ (if em. דָּוִד *David*).

דּוּר I 1 n.[m.] **ball,** כַּדּוּר *like a ball* Is 22₁₈ (unless כַּדּוּר is *ball*).

*דּוּר II 2 n.[m.] **city wall** Is 22₁₈ 29₃.

דּוּשׁ 16.1.3 vb.—**Qal** 13.0.3 Impf. תָּדוּשׁ, יְדוּשֶׁנּוּ; + waw וְדַשְׁתִּי; impv. דּוֹשִׁי; ptc. דָּשׁ; inf. דּוּשׁ (דִּישׁוֹ, דּוּשָׁם)—**thresh, tread, trample** Gilead Am 1₃ (+ בְּ *with* threshing sledge), nation Hb 3₁₂, wheat 1 C 21₂₀, egg Jb 39₁₅, flesh Jg 8₇ (+ אֶת *with* thorns and briars).

Ni. 2.1 Pf. + waw וְנָדוֹשׁ; ptc. Si נודשים; inf. הִדּוּשׁ—**be trampled down,** of Moab, as straw-heap Is 25₁₀.

Ho. 1 Impf. יוּדַשׁ—**be threshed,** of black cumin Is 28₂₇ (+ בְּ *with* threshing sledge).

→ דַּיִשׁ *threshing,* מְדֻשָׁה *threshing.*

דחה 7.1.3 vb.—**Qal** 4.0.3 Pf. דְּחִיתַנִי; ptc. דּוֹחֶה; ptc. pass. דְּחוּיָה; inf. abs. דָּחֹה (mss דָּחֹה), cstr. דְּחוֹת—**1. push, thrust** Ps 35₅ 118₁₃ 140₅. **2.** pass. ptc. as adj., **pushed in, tottering,** of fence Ps 62₄.

Ni. 2.1 Impf. יִדָּחֶה; ptc. Si נדחה—**be pushed, thrust down,** of person Pr 14₃₂.

Pu. 1 Pf. דֹּחוּ—**be thrust down,** of person Ps 36₁₂.

→ דְּחִי *stumbling,* מִדְחֶה *downfall.*

דחח 1 vb.—**Ni.** 1 Impf. יִדַּחוּ—**be pushed, thrust down** Jr 23₁₂ (mss יִדָּחוּ, from דחה).

[דְּחִי] 2 n.[m.]—דֶּחִי—**stumbling** Ps 56₁₄ 116₈. → דחה *push.*

דֹּחַן 1 n.m. **millet** Ezk 4₉.

דחף 4.1 vb.—**Qal** 2.1 Pf. Si. רחפם; ptc. pass. דְּחוּפִים—**1. drive away** Si 36₁₂. **2.** pass. **be in haste** Est 3₁₅ 8₁₄.

Ni. 2 Pf. נִדְחַף—**hasten oneself, hurry** Est 6₁₂ 2 C 26₂₀.

→ מַדְחֵפָה *thrust.*

דחק 2.0.1 vb.—**Qal** 2 Impf. יִדְחָקוּן; ptc. דֹּחֲקֵיהֶם—**1. press oneself upon, jostle** Jl 2₈. **2. oppress** Jg 2₁₈.

Pi. 0.0.1 Ptc. מדחק—**rush, hurry** 4QJub[h] 37₂₄.

דַּי I 39.4.9 n.m.—דַּי (Si דיי); cstr. דֵּי; sf. דַּיָּם—**1. sufficiency, enough,** דֵּי חֲלֵב עִזִּים *sufficiency of goat's milk* Pr 27₂₇, דֵּי שֶׂה *sufficiency of a lamb,* i.e. enough to buy a lamb Lv 5₇, בְּרָכָה עַד־בְּלִי־דָי *blessing until there is not sufficiency,* i.e. inexhaustibly abundant blessing Ml 3₁₀. **2.** as compound prep., **a.** בְּדֵי (1) **sufficient for** Na 2₁₃. (2) **(in exchange) for** Jr 51₅₈. (3) **as often as,** בְּדֵי שֹׁפָר *as often as the trumpet (sounds)* Jb 39₂₅. **b.** כְּדֵי (1) **sufficient for** Lv 25₂₆. (2) **according to, in proportion to** Dt 25₂. (3) כְּדֵי כֵן **in like measure, proportionately** Si 11₁₁ (vocalized כְּדֵי) 13₉. **c.** מִדֵּי **as often as,** with inf. cstr., 1 S 1₇, fin. verb Jr 20₈; מִדֵּי שָׁנָה בְּשָׁנָה *as often as there was a year,* i.e. from year to year 1 S 7₁₆.

*[דַּי] II n.f. **hand,** לֹא כֵן בְּדָיו *no-truth is in his hands* Is 16₆ Jr 48₃₀ (both if em. בַּדָּיו *his idle talk*).

דִּיבוֹן 11 pl.n. **Dibon.**

דיג 1 vb.—**Qal** 1 Pf. דִּיגוּם; ptc. pl. 1QIsa[a] דגים—**fish for, catch** Is 19₈(1QIsa[a]) Jr 16₁₆. → דָּג *fish,* דָּגָה *fish,* דַּיָּג *fisher,* דַּוָּג *fisher,* דּוּגָה *fishing.*

[דַּיָּג] 2.0.1 n.m.—pl. Qr דַּיָּגִים—**fisher** Is 19₈ Jr 16₁₆ 1QH 13₈. → דיג *fish.*

דַּיָּה 2 n.f.—pl. דַּיּוֹת—**kite** Dt 14₁₃ Is 34₁₅. → דאה *fly.*

דְּיוֹ 1 n.m. **ink** Jr 36₁₈.

*דיונטס 0.0.1 pr.n.m. **Dionytas.**

דִּי זָהָב 1 pl.n. **Dizahab.**

דִּימוֹן 2 pl.n. **Dimon.**

דִּימוֹנָה 1 pl.n. **Dimonah.**

דין I $_{23.0.2}$ vb.—**Qal** $_{22.0.2}$ Pf. דָּן; impf. תָּדִין; impv. דִּין, דִּינוּ; ptc. דָּן; inf. דִּין—**1. judge, pass judgment upon,** of Y. judging nations Gn 15$_{14}$ Ps 9$_{9}$ (+ בְּ *with* equity). **2a. judge, vindicate, plead (cause) of** poor and weak, subj. Y. Dt 32$_{36}$, humans Jr 22$_{16}$ Ps 72$_{2}$ (+ בְּ *with* righteousness, justice); obj. person(s) Dt 32$_{36}$ Ps 72$_{2}$, cause Jr 5$_{28}$. **b.** with obj. מִשְׁפָּט, **execute justice** Jr 21$_{12}$. **3. judge,** i.e. **govern** people, of Y. Jb 36$_{31}$, humans Zc 3$_{7}$. **4. contend** with (עִם) someone Ec 6$_{10}$.

Ni. $_{1}$ Ptc. נָדוֹן—**dispute, argue** 2 S 19$_{10}$.

→ דִּין I *judgment,* דּוֹן *judgment,* דַּיָּן *judge,* מָדוֹן *strife,* מְדָיָן II *strife,* מְדִינָה I *province,* II *place of judgment,* III *prefect.*

*דין II $_{1}$ vb.—**Qal** $_{1}$ Impv. דִּין—**humble oneself** before (לִפְנֵי) Y. Jb 35$_{14}$.

דַּיָּן $_{2.0.3}$ n.m.—cstr. דַּיַּן (Q דיין)—**judge,** in ref. to Y. 1 S 24$_{16}$ Ps 68$_{6}$ 11QPs^{a} 24$_{6}$. → דין I *judge.*

דִּין I $_{20.5.2}$ n.[m.]—sf. דִּינִי—**1. judgment, justice,** דִּין־רָשָׁע *judgment of,* i.e. on, *the wicked* Jb 36$_{17}$, כִּסֵּא דִין *throne of judgment* Pr 20$_{8}$. **2. cause, plea, case** Jr 5$_{28}$. **3. strife** Pr 22$_{10}$. → דין I *judge.*

*דִּין II $_{1}$ n.m. **food,** דִּין רָשָׁע *food of the wicked* Jb 36$_{17}$.

דִּינָה $_{8}$ pr.n.f. **Dinah.**

*[דִּינָר] $_{0.0.3}$ n.m.—pl. דינרין—**denar,** coin and unit of currency 5/6ḤevBA 44$_{20}$.

דִּיפַת $_{1}$ pr.n.m. **Diphath.**

דָּיֵק $_{6}$ n.m. **siege wall, tower** 2 K 25$_{1}$||Jr 52$_{4}$.

*[דִּירָה] n.f.—**dwelling, lodge,** דירת בית המשכב *lodge of the banqueting hall,* or perh. *of the graveyard* 3QTr 11$_{16}$. → דור I *dwell.*

דַּיִשׁ $_{1}$ n.m. **threshing** Lv 26$_{5}$. → דושׁ *thresh.*

דִּישׁוֹן I $_{1}$ n.[m.] **ibex,** or perh. **pygarg** Dt 14$_{5}$.

דִּישׁוֹן II $_{7}$ pr.n.m. **Dishon.**

דִּישָׁן $_{5}$ pr.n.m. **Dishan.**

דַּךְ $_{4.1.2}$ adj.—דָּךְ; pl. Q דכים; sf. דַּכָּיו—**1. crushed,** of bone GnzPs 2$_{7}$. **2.** as noun, **crushed, oppressed (one)** Ps 9$_{10}$. → דכה *crush.*

דכא $_{18.1.2}$ vb.—**Ni.** $_{1.1.1}$ Pf. mss נִדְכֵּאתִי; ptc. נִדְכָּאִים—**1. be crushed, oppressed** Si 11$_{5}$. **2.** ptc. as noun, **contrite one** Is 57$_{15}$.

Pi. $_{11.0.1}$ Pf. דִּכָּא, דִּכְּאתָ; impf. תְּדַכֵּא; inf. דַּכֵּא (דַּכְּאוֹ)—**crush** someone Is 3$_{15}$.

Pu. $_{4}$ Pf. דֻּכְּאוּ; impf. יְדֻכָּא; ptc. מְדֻכָּא—**1. be crushed,** of person Is 53$_{5}$. **2. humble oneself** Jr 44$_{10}$.

Htp. $_{2}$ Impf. יִדַּכְּאוּ (יִדַּכָּאוּ)—**be crushed,** of person Jb 5$_{4}$.

→ דַּכָּא I *crushed,* II *crushing;* cf. דוך *crush,* דכה *crush,* דכך *crush.*

דַּכָּא I $_{3.1}$ adj.—pl. cstr. דַּכְּאֵי—**crushed,** alw. as noun, **1. crushed one, contrite one** Is 57$_{15}$; דַּכְּאֵי־רוּחַ *crushed ones of,* i.e. in, *spirit* Ps 34$_{19}$. **2. dust** Ps 90$_{3}$. → דכא *crush.*

דַּכָּא II $_{1}$ n.[m.] **crushing,** פְּצוּעַ־דַּכָּא *one wounded of,* i.e. by, *crushing (testicles)* Dt 23$_{2}$. → דכא *crush.*

דכה $_{5.0.2}$ vb.—**Qal** $_{1}$ Impf. Qr יִדְכֶּה; + waw Kt ודכה—**be crushed,** of person Ps 10$_{1}$.

Ni. $_{2.0.2}$ Pf. נִדְכֵּיתִי; ptc. נִדְכֶּה—**1. be crushed,** of person Ps 38$_{9}$. **2. be contrite,** of heart Ps 51$_{19}$.

Pi. $_{2}$ Pf. דִּכִּיתָ—**crush, break** someone Ps 44$_{20}$, bones Ps 51$_{10}$.

→ דַּךְ *crushed,* דֳּכִי *pounding;* cf. דכא *crush,* דכך *crush.*

*[דִּכּוּי] n.[m.] **acquittal** Pr 26$_{28}$ (if em. דַּכָּיו *its crushed ones*).

[דֳּכִי] I $_{1}$ n.[m.]—sf. דָּכְיָם—**pounding** of ocean waves Ps 93$_{3}$. → דכה *crush.*

*[דֳּכִי] II $_{0.0.1}$ n.m.—דוכי—**cleanness, purity** 1QS 3$_{9}$. → cf. זכך *be pure.*

*דכך vb.—**Ni. be crushed,** of grass Ps 58$_{8}$ (if em.). → cf. דכא *crush,* דכך *crush.*

דַּל I $_{48.12.7}$ adj.—דָּל; m.pl. דַּלִּים, f.pl. דַּלּוֹת—**1. poor, weak, thin,** of cow Gn 41$_{19}$, people Jr 39$_{10}$, clan Jg 6$_{15}$; **dejected,** of person 2 S 13$_{4}$. **2.** as noun, **poor (one)** Jb 34$_{28}$. → דלל I *be low.*

[דַּל] II or [דֶּל] $_{1}$ n.[m.]—cstr. דַּל—**door** of lips Ps 141$_{3}$. → דלת *have doors.*

*[דַּל] III $_{0.0.0.1}$ pr.n.m. **Dal.**

דלג $_{5.1.3}$ vb.—**Qal** $_{1.0.1}$ Ptc. דּוֹלֵג—**1. leap over** (עַל) threshold Zp 1$_{9}$. **2. leap over** (עַל), i.e. **omit,** statute 4QShirShabb^{f} 23.1$_{10}$.

Pi. $_{4.1.2}$ Impf. אֲדַלֶּג־, יְדַלֵּג; ptc. מְדַלֵּג—**1. leap,** like (כְּ) deer Is 35$_{6}$, upon (עַל) mountains Ca 2$_{8}$, from (מִן) city to (אֶל) city Si 36$_{31}$. **2.** with accus., **leap over** wall 2 S 22$_{30}$||Ps 18$_{30}$.

דלה I $_{5.0.1}$ vb.—**Qal** $_{4.0.1}$ Pf. דָּלָה; impf. יִדְלֶנָּה; inf. abs. דָּלֹה—**1. draw water** Ex 2_{16}. **2. draw out** counsel, like water Pr 20_5.

Pi. $_1$ Pf. דִּלִּיתָנִי—**draw up,** i.e. rescue Ps 30_2.

→ דְּלִי *bucket.*

דלה II $_{1.0.1}$ vb.—**Qal** Pf. דַּלְיוּ—**hang down,** of legs from lame person Pr 26_7.

Ho. Ptc. מודלים—**be hung,** ptc. as noun, **vine creepers** Mur 29_{11}.

→ (?) דָּלִית *branch;* cf. דלל II *hang down.*

[דָּלָה] Is 26_{20}, see דֶּלֶת *door.*

[דַּלָּה] I $_5$ n.f.—cstr. דַּלַּת; pl. cstr. דַּלּוֹת—**the poor, insignificant,** דַּלַּת עַם־הָאָרֶץ *the poor one(s),* i.e. poorest, *of the people of the land* 2 K 24_{14}. → דלל I *be low.*

דַּלָּה II $_2$ n.f.—cstr. דַּלַּת—**1. hair** Ca 7_6. **2. thrum,** threads of warp in loom Is 38_{12}. → דלל II *hang down.*

*[דַּלּוּי] $_{0.0.1}$ pr.n.m. **Dallui.**

*[דַּלּוּת] $_{0.2}$ n.f.—sf. דלותו—**poverty** Si $10_{31.31}$. → דלל I *be low.*

דלח $_3$ vb.—**Qal** Impf. תִּדְלַחֵם; + waw וַתִּדְלַח—**make turbid, stir up** water Ezk $32_{2.13.13}$.

דלי, see דְּלָיָהוּ *Delaiah.*

דְּלִי $_2$ n.[m.]—du. sf. דָּלְיָו—**bucket** Nm 24_7 Is 40_{15}. → דלה I *draw water.*

דְּלָיָה, see דְּלָיָהוּ *Delaiah.*

דְּלָיָהוּ $_{7.0.1.6}$ pr.n.m. **Delaiah.**

דליו, see דְּלָיָהוּ *Delaiah.*

דְּלִילָה $_6$ pr.n.f. **Delilah.**

[דָּלִית] $_{8.0.5}$ n.f—sf. Q דליתו; pl. sf. דָּלִיּוֹתָיו—**branch(es), tendril** of olive Jr 11_{16}, cedar Ezk 17_{23}, vine Ezk 17_6. → (?) דלה II *hang down.*

דלל I $_{7.0.2}$ vb.—**Qal** $_{7.0.1}$ Pf. דַּלּוֹתִי ,דַּלְלוּ (דַּלּוּ); impf. יִדַּל; inf. Q דל—**be low, brought low, diminished,** of persons Jg 6_6 Ps 116_6.

Po. $_{0.0.1}$ Impf. ידולל—**bring low** 4QBéat 15_3.

→ דַּל I *poor,* דַּלָּה I *the poor,* דַּלּוּת *poverty.*

דלל II $_1$ vb.—**Qal** $_1$ Pf. דַּלּוּ—**hang down, dangle,** of miners in shaft Jb 28_4.

→ דַּלָּה II *hair, thrum,* (?) דָּלִית *branch;* cf. דלה II *hang down.*

*__דלל__ III $_1$ vb.—**Qal** $_1$ Pf. דַּלּוּ—**be raised,** of eyes Is 38_{14} (+ לְ *toward* heaven).

דִּלְעָן $_1$ pl.n. **Dilean.**

*__דלף__ I $_2$ vb.—**Qal** $_2$ Pf. דָּלְפָה—**be sleepless, wait sleeplessly** Jb 16_{20} (+ אֶל *for* Y.) Ps 119_{28} (+ מִן *on account of* grief).

דלף II $_2$ vb.—**Qal** $_2$ Impf. יִדְלֹף—**1. drip, leak,** of house Ec 10_{18}. **2. shed tears,** of eyes Jb 16_{20} (+ אֶל *to* Y.). → דֶּלֶף *dripping.*

*__דלף__ III $_2$ vb.—**Qal** $_2$ Pf. דָּלְפָה; impf. יִדְלֹף—**collapse** Ps 119_{28} Ec 10_{18}.

*__דלף__ IV $_1$ vb.—**Qal** $_1$ Pf. דָּלְפָה—**be oppressed, downcast** Ps 119_{28}.

דֶּלֶף $_2$ n.m. **dripping** Pr 19_{13} 27_{15}. → דלף II *drip.*

דַּלְפוֹן $_1$ pr.n.m. **Dalphon.**

דלק I $_{5.1}$ vb.—**Qal** $_3$ Pf. דָּלְקוּ; ptc. דֹּלְקִים—**burn,** intrans. Ps 7_{14}, of lips Pr 26_{23}; perh. trans. Ob $_{18}$.

Hi. $_{2.1}$ Impf. יַדְלִיקֵם; impv. הַדְלֵק—**1. kindle** a fire Ezk 24_{10}. **2.** of sun, **set ablaze** mountains Si $43_{4(B)}$. **3.** of wine, **inflame** someone Is 5_{11}.

→ דֶּלֶק *burning,* דַּלֶּקֶת *inflammation.*

דלק II $_4$ vb.—**Qal** $_4$ Pf. דָּלַקְתָּ; impf. יִדְלַק; inf. דְּלֹק—**pursue, chase,** with accus. Lm 4_{19} Ps 10_2; אַחֲרֵי *after* Gn 31_{36} 1 S 17_{53}.

*__דלק__ III $_2$ vb.—**Qal** $_2$ Ptc. דֹּלְקִים—**be sharp,** of arrows Ps 7_{14}, lips Pr 26_{23}.

*__דלק__ IV $_1$ vb.—**Qal** $_1$ Ptc. דֹּלְקִים—**pour forth** Pr 26_{23}.

*[דֶּלֶק] $_{0.0.1}$ n.[m.]—cstr. דלק—**burning** 1QM 17_1. → דלק I *burn.*

דַּלֶּקֶת $_1$ n.f. **inflammation** Dt 28_{22}. → דלק I *burn.*

*__דלת__ $_{0.0.1}$ vb.—**Pu.** $_{0.0.1}$ Ptc. מדולתים—**have doors** 11QT 33_{13}. → דַּל II *door,* דֶּלֶת *door.*

*[דָּלֶת] $_{0.0.1}$ n.f. **daleth,** the fourth Hebrew letter CD 15_1.

דֶּלֶת $_{87.1.14.1}$ n.f.—דָּלֶת; sf. Qr דַּלְתֵךְ (as if from דָּלָה [Is 26_{20}]), דַּלְתּוֹ; du. דְּלָתַיִם; cstr. דַּלְתֵי; sf. דְּלָתֶיךָ; pl. דְּלָתוֹת; cstr. דַּלְתוֹת; sf. דַּלְתֹתָיו—**1. door** of house Gn 19_6, room Jg 3_{23}, heaven Ps 78_{23}, sea Jb 38_8, pit 1QH 11_{18}, womb Jb 3_{10}, face, i.e. jaw, of Leviathan Jb 41_6. **2. gate** of city Dt 3_5. **3. lid** of chest 2 K 12_{10}. **4. leaf,** i.e. hinged (folding) section, of door Ezk 41_{24}. **5. column** of text Jr 36_{23} perh. Lachish ost. 4_3 (or דֶּלֶת = hinged writing tablet). → דלת *have doors.*

*[דְּלָתְיָהוּ] $_{0.0.0.1}$ pr.n.m. **Delethiah.**

דָּם 360.7.43 n.m.—cstr. דַּם; sf. דָּמוֹ, דִּמְכֶם; pl. דָּמִים; cstr. דְּמֵי; sf. דָּמָיו, דְּמֵיהֶם—**1. blood, a.** as life of human or animal, and prohibited as food Gn 94 Lv 1710.11. **b.** of humans, from wound 1 K 2235, in blood vessel 4QDg 1.16a, menstruation Lv 1519. **c.** of animals Gn 3731, used in ritual Lv 15. **d.** of grapes, i.e. juice Gn 4911. **e.** water turned into blood Ex 49. **f.** portent in heaven Jl 33. **2. bloodshed, blood** as shed by violence (sg. or pl.) Gn 410 96; דַּם חָלָל *blood of the slain one* Dt 3242, דְּמֵי מִלְחָמָה *blood of*, i.e. shed in, *war* 1 K 25, דָּם נָקִי *innocent blood*, i.e. shed of an innocent person Dt 1910, אִישׁ דָּמִים *man of blood* 2 S 168, גֹּאֵל הַדָּם *avenger of blood* Nm 3519, דָּבָר לַמִּשְׁפָּט בֵּין־דָּם לְדָם *a case for decision between one kind of bloodshed and another* Dt 178. **3. bloodguilt** Lv 174 Dt 1910 Ps 5116; דָּמִים לוֹ *there is bloodguilt to him* Ex 222, דָּמָיו בּוֹ *his bloodguilt is upon him* Lv 209.

דמה I 31.3.20 vb.—**Qal** 13.3.18 Pf. דָּמָה, דָּמִיתָ; impf. יִדְמֶה; impv. דְּמֵה; ptc. דּוֹמֶה—**1. be like, comparable with, resemble, a.** with comparison indicated by לְ Ps 897, בְּ 4QMa 11.117, אֶל Ezk 312 (+ בְּ *in* greatness). **b.** abs. Is 465. **2. be fitting,** לְךָ דֻמִיָּה תְהִלָּה *praise befits you* Ps 652 (if em. דֻּמִיָּה *silence*). **3. be adequate** Jr 1417.

Ni. 3.0.1 Pf. נִדְמֵיתָ—**liken oneself to, be like,** with accus. Ezk 322.

Pi. 14 Pf. דִּמָּה, דִּמִּיתִי; impf. יְדַמֶּה, תְּדַמְּיוּן (תְּדַמְּיוּנִי)—**1a. liken, compare** someone **to,** with comparison indicated by לְ Is 465, אֶל Is 4018. **b. use similitudes, parables,** of Y. Ho 1211 (+ בְּיַד *through* prophets). **2. a. think, imagine, intend,** with (1) inf. cstr. Nm 3356. (2) כֵּן *so* Is 107. (3) כַּאֲשֶׁר *as* Is 1424. (4) לְ *against, concerning* 2 S 215. **b.** with accus., **think about, consider** Ps 4810. **c. think that** Ps 5021.

Htp. 1.0.1 Pf. Q הדמה; impf. אֶדַּמֶּה—**make oneself like,** with comparison indicated by לְ Is 1414, בְּ 4QMa 11.116.

→ דְּמוּת I *likeness*, דְּמִין *likeness*.

דמה II 2 vb.—**Qal** 2 Impf. תִּדְמֶה, תִּדְמֶינָה—**cease (from weeping),** of eyes Jr 1417 Lm 349.

***דמה III** 0.0.2 vb.—**Qal** 0.0.1 Impf. ידמה—**wait silently, be inactive** 4QInstrd 5511.

Ni. Pf. נדמו—0.0.1 **be silent, keep silent at** (בְּ) rebuke 1QpHab 510.

→ דּוּמִיָּה *silence*, דּוּמָם *silence*, דֳּמִי I *silence*, דֻּמָה I *one silenced*; cf. דמם I *be silent*.

***דמה IV** 17.0.1 vb.—**Qal** 4 Pf. דָּמִיתִי—**destroy** Jr 62 Ho 45.

Ni. 13.0.1 נִדְמָה, נִדְמֵיתָ; ptc. נִדְמֶה; inf. abs. נִדְמֹה—**be destroyed, cut off,** of city Is 151, people Ho 46, beasts Ps 4913.

→ cf. דמם IV *destroy*.

דֻּמָה I 1 n.f. **one silenced,** of Tyre Ezk 2732. → דמה III *be silent*.

***דֻּמָה II** 1 n.f. **fortress,** of Tyre Ezk 2732.

דְּמוּת I 25.0.6 n.f.—cstr. דְּמוּת; sf. דְּמוּתוֹ—**1a. likeness, appearance, form** of God Gn 51, human Ezk 15. **b. image, figure** of oxen 2 C 43. **c. plan, model** of altar 2 K 1610. **2.** adv., **in the likeness of** Is 134 Ps 585 (כִּדְמוּת). → דמה I *be like*.

***[דְּמוּת] II** 1 n.f.—cstr. דְּמוּת—**midst** Ezk 113. → cf. דְּמִי *half*.

***[דְּמִי]** 0.0.1 n.[m.]pl. **value** 1QMyst 1.28.

דְּמִי 1 n.[m.]—cstr. דְּמִי—**half, midst** of days Is 3810. → cf. דְּמוּת II *midst*.

דֳּמִי I 3 n.[m.] **silence, rest** Is 626.7; אַל־דֳּמִי־לָךְ *let there be no silence to you* Ps 832. → דמה III *be silent*.

***[דֶּמִי] II** 1 n.[m.]—pl. דָּמִים—**1. tear** Ps 5116. **2. mourning** Is 3810 (if em. בִּדְמִי *in the midst of*). → דמם II *weep*.

דֻּמִיָּה, see דּוּמִיָּה *silence*.

[דְּמִין] 1.1.1 n.f.—sf. דִּמְינוֹ; pl. Si דמיונות, Q דמיונים—**1a. likeness** Ps 1712. **b. spectacle** 1QM 613. **2. imagination, thought** Si 324. → דמה I *be like*.

***דמך** 0.1 vb.—**Qal** 0.1 Impf. תִּדְמוֹךְ—**sleep** Si 94.

***[דָּמְלָא]** 0.0.0.4 pr.n.m. **Domla.**

***[דָּמְלְיָהוּ]** 0.0.0.4 pr.n.m. **Domliah.**

דמם I 30.0.1 vb.—**Qal** 29.0.1 Pf. דַּמּוּ; impf. יִדֹּם, תִּדַּמִּי, יִדְּמוּ; + waw וָאֶדֹּם; impv. דּוֹם, דֹּמִּי, דֹּמּוּ—**1. be silent,** i.e. hold one's peace Lv 103, wait silently Ps 377; be silent in death Ps 3118. **2. be still, stand still,** of sun Jos 1012, sword Jr 476; of persons, out of dread Ex 1516 (+ כְּ *as* stone), to wait for someone 1 S 149. **3. cease activity** Ps 3515 Jb 3027.

Po. 1 Pf. דּוֹמַמְתִּי—**quieten, still** one's soul Ps 1312.

→ דּוּמָם *silence*; cf. דמה III *be silent*.

*דמם II $_{6}$ vb.—**Qal** $_{5}$ Impv. דֹּמּוּ, דֹּם; inf. דְּמִי—**weep, lament** Is 23$_{2}$ Ezk 24$_{17}$ Am 5$_{13}$ Ps 4$_{5}$ La 2$_{10}$.

Hi. $_{1}$ Pf. הֲדִמָּנוּ—**cause to weep** Jr 8$_{14}$.

→ דֳּמִי II *tear*.

*דמם III $_{6}$ vb.—**Qal** $_{6}$ Impf. יִדְּמוּ, יִדֹּם; impv. דֹּם, דֹּמּוּ—**moan, whisper** Is 23$_{2}$ Ezk 24$_{17}$ Am 5$_{13}$ Ps 4$_{5}$ La 2$_{10}$ La 3$_{28}$. → דְּמָמָה *whisper*.

*דמם IV $_{13}$ vb.—**Qal** $_{6}$ Ptc. דָּמִים—**maltreat**, ptc. as noun, **1. wicked thing** Is 33$_{1}$. **2. wickedness**, אַנְשֵׁי־דָמִים *men of wickedness* Ps 26$_{9}$ 55$_{24}$ 59$_{3}$ 139$_{19}$, אִישׁ־ *man of* Ps 5$_{7}$.

Ni. $_{6}$ Pf. נָדַמּוּ; impf. יִדְּמוּ (יִדֶּמוּ); pf. + waw וְנָדַמּוּ—**be destroyed, cut off** 1 S 2$_{9}$ 25$_{37}$ Jr 8$_{14}$ 49$_{26}$=50$_{30}$ 51$_{6}$.

Hi. $_{1}$ Pf. הֲדִמָּנוּ—**cause to perish, destroy** Jr 8$_{14}$.

→ cf. דמה IV *destroy*.

*דמם V $_{1}$ vb.—**Pol.** $_{1}$ Pf. דוֹמַמְתִּי—**level** one's soul Ps 131$_{2}$.

דְּמָמָה $_{3.0.9}$ n.f.—cstr. Q דממת; sf. Q דממתך—**1. whisper, sighing, (low) rumbling**, קוֹל דְּמָמָה דַקָּה *a sound, a thin whisper* 1 K 19$_{12}$, דְּמָמָה וָקוֹל *a whisper and a voice*, i.e. a whispering voice Jb 4$_{16}$, דממת ברך *whisper of blessing* 4QShirShabb^{f} 20.2$_{12}$. **2.** perh. **silence, calm** of sea 1QH 14$_{23}$. → דמם III *moan, whisper*.

דֹּמֶן $_{6.0.3}$ n.m.—**dung**, as descr. of corpses, דֹּמֶן עַל־פְּנֵי הָאֲדָמָה *dung upon the surface of the ground* Jr 8$_{2}$. → cf. מַדְמֵנָה I *dung-pit*.

דִּמְנָה $_{1}$ pl.n. **Dimnah.**

דמע $_{2.2}$ vb.—**Qal** $_{2.1}$ Impf. תִּדְמַע; inf. abs. דָּמֹעַ—**weep**, abs. Jr 13$_{17}$; with accus. דִּמְעָה *tears* Si 34$_{13(B)}$.

Hi. $_{0.1}$ Impf. ידמיע—**shed tears** Si 12$_{16}$.

→ דִּמְעָה *tears*, (?) דֶּמַע *juice*.

[דֶּמַע] $_{1.0.14}$ n.[m.]—cstr. Q דמע; sf. דִּמְעֲךָ—**tithe, best part**, specif. **juice**, i.e. wine or oil Ex 22$_{28}$, **resin** of fir tree 3QTr 11$_{4}$; כלי דמע *tithe vessels* 3QTr 1$_{9}$. → (?) דמע *weep*.

דִּמְעָה $_{23.4.2}$ n.f.—cstr. דִּמְעַת; sf. דִּמְעָתִי; pl. abs. דְּמָעוֹת—**tears**, usu. sg. as coll. 2 K 20$_{5}$||Is 38$_{5}$; pl. Lm 2$_{11}$. → דמע *weep*.

דַּמֶּשֶׂק $_{45.0.6}$ pl.n. **Damascus.**

דְּמֶשֶׁק $_{1}$ n.[m.]—cstr. דְּמֶשֶׁק—perh. **damask**, or **part of a bed** Am 3$_{12}$.

*דַּן I $_{1}$ n.[m.] **cask**, וְדַנֵּי יַיִן *and casks of wine* Ezk 27$_{19}$ (if em. וְדָן וְיָוָן *Vedan and Javan*).

דָּן II $_{47.0.6}$ pr.n.m. **Dan.**

דָּן III $_{22}$ pl.n. **Dan.**

דנאל, see דָּנִיֵּאל *Daniel*.

*[דנב] vb. **Pi.**, **rout**, יְדַנֵּב גּוֹיִם *he routs nations* Ps 110$_{6}$ (if em. יָדִין בַּגּוֹיִם *he judges among the nations*).

דַּנָּה $_{1}$ pl.n. **Dannah.**

דִּנְהָבָה $_{2}$ pl.n. **Dinhabah.**

דָּנִי $_{5}$ gent. **Danite.**

דָּנִיֵּאל $_{29.0.2}$ pr.n.m. **Daniel.**

*דנן I $_{1}$ vb.—**Qal** $_{1}$ Impf. יָדוֹן—**be strong** Gn 6$_{3}$.

*דנן II $_{1}$ vb.—**Qal** $_{1}$ Impf. יָדוֹן—**answer for, protect** Gn 6$_{3}$.

[דֵּעַ] I $_{5.1}$ n.[m.]—sf. דֵּעִי; pl. abs. דֵּעִים—**knowledge, opinion** of human Jb 32$_{6}$, Y. Jb 37$_{16}$. → ידע I *know*.

*[דֵּעַ] II $_{6.1}$ n.[m.]—sf. דֵּעִי; pl. דֵּעִים, דֵּעוֹת—**word, speech** of human Jb 32$_{6}$, Y. Jb 36$_{4}$.

*דעה I vb.—**Qal, ask, desire** Ho 6$_{3}$ Pr 10$_{32}$ 24$_{14}$ 29$_{7}$ (all four, if em.). → דַּעַת II *lawsuit*.

*דעה II vb.—**Pi., pull down** Ezk 19$_{7}$ 74$_{5}$ (both, if em.).

דֵּעָה $_{6.1.32}$ n.f.—pl. דֵּעוֹת—**knowledge** Is 28$_{9}$; אֵל דֵּעוֹת *God of knowledge* 1 S 2$_{3}$; with verbal force, **knowing** Is 11$_{9}$. → ידע I *know*.

דְּעוּאֵל $_{4}$ pr.n.m. **Deuel.**

דעך I $_{9.1}$ vb.—**Qal** $_{7}$ Pf. דָּעֲכוּ; impf. יִדְעַךְ (יִדְעָךְ)—**be extinguished, go out**, of army Is 43$_{17}$ (+ כְּ *as* wick), lamp Jb 18$_{6}$.

Ni. $_{1.1}$ Pf. נִדְעֲכוּ—**1. be dried up, disappear**, of wadi Jb 6$_{17}$. **2. be withered**, of reed Si 40$_{16}$.

Pu. $_{1}$ Pf. דֹּעֲכוּ—**be extinguished**, of nation Ps 118$_{12}$.

*דעך II $_{1}$ vb.—**Po.** $_{1}$ Pf. דֹּעֲכוּ—**attack** Ps 118$_{12}$.

דַּעַת I $_{90.6.130}$ n.f. (m. at Pr 2$_{10}$ 14$_{6}$)—דָּעַת; cstr. דַּעַת; sf. דַּעְתּוֹ—**knowledge, discernment, understanding**, דַּעַת אֱלֹהִים *knowledge of God* Ho 4$_{1}$, רזי דעת *mysteries of knowledge* 1QS 4$_{6}$, חָכְמָה וָדַעַת *wisdom and knowledge* Ec 1$_{16}$, בְּלִי דַעַת *without knowledge*, i.e. unintentionally Dt 4$_{42}$; with verbal force, **knowing**, עֵץ הַדַּעַת טוֹב וָרָע *tree of knowing good and evil* Gn 2$_{9}$. → ידע I *know*.

*[דַּעַת] II $_{2}$ n.f.—דַּעַת—**lawsuit, claim** Pr 22$_{12}$ 29$_{7}$. →

דעה I *ask*.

*[דֵּעַת] III 2 n.f.—דֵּעַת—**friend** Pr 22$_{12}$; דֵּעַת מְזִמּוֹת *friend of Discretion* Pr 8$_{12}$.

*[דֵּעַת] IV 1 n.f.—דֵּעַת—**humiliation, punishment** Dn 12$_{4}$. → ידע II *humiliate*.

*[דֵּעַת] V 1 n.f.—sf. דַּעְתּוֹ—**sweat** Is 53$_{11}$. → ידע V *sweat*.

[דֳּפִי] 1.1 n.[m.]—דָּפִי—**blemish, fault** Ps 50$_{20}$ Si 44$_{19(Bmg)}$ (B מום *blemish*).

דפק 3 vb.—**Qal** 2 + waw וּדְפָקוּם; ptc. דּוֹפֵק—**1. beat, drive** cattle **excessively** Gn 33$_{13}$. **2. knock (at door)** Ca 5$_{2}$.

Htp. 1 Ptc. מִתְדַּפְּקִים—**hurl oneself, beat at door** Jg 19$_{22}$.

דָּפְקָה 2 pl.n. **Dophkah.**

דַּק 14.0.5 adj.—דַּק, f.s. דַּקָּה; f.pl. דַּקּוֹת; cstr. דַּקּוֹת—**1a. thin,** of ear (of grain) Gn 41$_{7}$, cow Gn 41$_{3}$, hair Lv 13$_{30}$. **b. small, fine,** of incense Lv 16$_{12}$, dust Is 29$_{5}$. **c. faint,** of whisper 1 K 19$_{12}$. **2.** as noun, **a. thin (one),** of man Lv 21$_{20}$. **b. fine (thing),** of dust Is 40$_{15}$, manna Ex 16$_{14}$. → דקק *crush*.

דֹּק 1 n.[m.] **curtain** Is 40$_{22}$. → דקק *crush*.

*[דֶּקֶל] I 0.0.3 n.m.—pl. דקלים—**date palm** 5/6ḤevBA 46$_{4.4.6}$.

*[דֶּקֶל] II 0.0.1 n.m. **battalion,** דקלי או[ר] *battalions of light* 4QPrQuot 51$_{8}$ (perh. error for דגלי).

דִּקְלָה 2 pr.n.m. **Diklah.**

*דקם 0.0.1 vb.—perh. **Pi.** 0.0.1 + waw וידקמום—**beat, stun** CD 8$_{4}$ (or em. וידבקם *and it shall cling to them*, or וידבק מום *and the defect shall cling*).

דקק 13.0.2 vb.—**Qal** 4 Pf. דַּק (דָּק); impf. תָּדֹק—**1. crush** grain Is 28$_{28}$, mountain Is 41$_{15}$. **2. be fine, pulverized,** of image of calf Ex 32$_{20}$.

Hi. 8 Pf. הֵדַק; impf. אֲדִקֵּם; + waw וַיָּדֶק, וְהֵדַקּוֹת; inf. abs. הָדֵק, cstr. הָדֵק—**pulverize** enemies 2 S 22$_{43}$, incense Ex 30$_{36}$, Asherah 2 K 23$_{6}$||2 C 34$_{4}$ (+ לְ *to* dust).

Ho. 1 Impf. יוּדַק—**be crushed,** of grain Is 28$_{28}$.

Polp. 0.0.2 Ptc. מדוקדק—**be minutely treated, set out exactly, defined** CD 16$_{2.3}$.

→ דַּק *thin*, דֹּק *curtain*.

דקר 11 vb.—**Qal** 7 Pf. דְּקָרוּ; + waw וַיִּדְקֹר; impv. דָּקְרֵנִי—**pierce, thrust through** Nm 25$_{8}$ 1 S 31$_{4}$||1 C 10$_{4}$ (+ בְּ *with* sword).

Ni. 1 Impf. יִדָּקֵר—**be thrust through** Is 13$_{15}$.

Pu. 3 Ptc. מְדֻקָּרִים—**1. be pierced, wounded** Jr 37$_{10}$ 51$_{4}$. **2. be debarred from, deprived of** (מִן) produce Lm 4$_{9}$.

→ מַדְקָרָה *piercing*.

דֶּקֶר, see בֶּן־דֶּקֶר *Ben-deker*.

דַּר 1 n.[m.] **pearl, mother of pearl** Est 1$_{6}$.

דֵּרָאוֹן 2 n.m.—cstr. דִּרְאוֹן—**abhorrence** Dn 12$_{2}$; **object of abhorrence** Is 66$_{24}$.

[דָּרְבוֹן], see דָּרְבָן *goad*.

דָּרְבָן 2 n.[m.]—pl. דָּרְבֹנוֹת—**goad** 1 S 13$_{21}$ Ec 12$_{11}$.

*[דֶּרֶג] n.[m.] **way** Ho 2$_{8}$ (if em. גְּדֵרָהּ *her fence* to דְּרָגֶיהָ *her ways*). → cf. דֶּרֶךְ I *way*.

דַּרְדַּע 1 pr.n.m. **Darda.**

דַּרְדַּר 2.0.2 n.[m.] **thistles,** as coll. Gn 3$_{18}$ Ho 10$_{8}$ 1QH 16$_{25}$.

דָּרוֹם 17.0.10 n.m.—**1. the south** Dt 33$_{23}$. **2. south wind** Jb 37$_{17}$. → cf. דָּרוֹמִי *south*.

*[דָּרוֹמִי] 0.0.2 adj. **south, southern**—דרומית—of corner 3QTr 3$_{1}$ 11$_{2}$. → cf. דָּרוֹם *south*.

דְּרוֹר I 7.0.2 n.[m.] **release, liberty,** in jubilee year Lv 25$_{10}$; for slaves Jr 34$_{8}$, captives Is 61$_{1}$.

דְּרוֹר II 2 n.f. **swallow,** a bird Pr 26$_{2}$ Ps 84$_{4}$.

*דְּרוֹר III 1 n.[m.] **flowing,** מָר־דְּרוֹר *myrrh of flowing*, perh. as solidified drops Ex 30$_{23}$.

*דְּרוֹר IV 1 n.[m.] **continuity,** מָר־דְּרוֹר *myrrh of continuity*, i.e. solid myrrh Ex 30$_{23}$.

דָּרוֹשׁ Ezr 10$_{16}$, see דרשׁ *seek*, qal (inf.).

דָּרְיָוֶשׁ 10 pr.n.m. **Darius.**

דרך I 63.6.9 vb.—**Qal** 50.2.8 Pf. דָּרַךְ; impf. יִדְרֹךְ; ptc. דֹּרֵךְ, דֹּרְכִים; ptc. pass. דְּרוּכָה, דְּרֻכוֹת—**1a. tread, trample, march, advance,** subj. Y. Am 4$_{13}$, humans Dt 11$_{25}$, foot Jos 14$_{9}$, star Nm 24$_{17}$; obj. path Jb 22$_{15}$; prep. בְּ *in, on* Dt 1$_{36}$; עַל *upon* Dt 33$_{29}$. **b.** ptc. as noun, **traveller** Si 42$_{3(M)}$. **2. tread,** i.e. **press,** subj. Y. Lm 1$_{15}$, humans Jg 9$_{27}$; obj. grapes Am 9$_{13}$, winepress Jb 24$_{11}$, olives Mc 6$_{15}$, nations Is 63$_{3}$. **3a.** with obj. קֶשֶׁת, **tread,** i.e. **bend,** the bow Ps 7$_{13}$. **b.** pass. **be trodden,** i.e. **bent,** of קֶשֶׁת *bow* Is 5$_{28}$, *arc* (a battle formation) 1QM 9$_{11}$.

Hi. 13.4.1 Pf. הִדְרַכְתִּיךָ; impf. יַדְרֵךְ (יַדְרִכֵנִי); + waw וַיַּדְרְכוּ, וַיַּדְרִיכֵם; impv. הַדְרִיכֵנִי; ptc. מַדְרִיכְךָ; inf. Si, Q הדריכם—**1. tread, trample,** subj. humans Jg 20$_{43}$, beasts Jb 28$_{8}$; obj. persons Jg 20$_{43}$, path Jb 28$_{8}$. **2a. cause to tread, lead,** subj. Y. Is 42$_{16}$, human CD 1$_{11}$, wisdom Pr 4$_{11}$; obj. alw. person; prep. בְּ *in* path Is 42$_{16}$, *with, in* truth Ps 25$_{5}$; עַל *upon* high place Hb 3$_{19}$. **b. allow to trample** Si 9$_{2}$. **3. reach, attain to, obtain** wisdom Si 15$_{1.7}$. **4. tread,** i.e. **bend** tongue, as a bow Jr 9$_{2}$.

→ דֶּרֶךְ I *way*, III *treading (of grapes)*, מִדְרָךְ *treading-place*, מִדְרוֹךְ *treading place*; cf. דֶּרֶג *way*.

*דרך II 5 vb.—**Qal** 4 Pf. דָּרַכְתָּ, דָּרְכוּ; impf. יִדְרֹךְ—**aim, direct** arrow Ps 58$_{8}$ 64$_{4}$, horse Hb 3$_{15}$, work Pr 8$_{22}$.

Hi. 1 Impf. + waw וַיַּדְרְכוּ—**aim** tongue, as a bow Jr 9$_{2}$.

*דרך III 2.1 vb.—**Qal** 2.1 Pf. דָּרַךְ; ptc. דֹּרְכֵי—**1a. prevail** Nm 24$_{17}$. **b. persecute** Lm 3$_{11}$. **2.** ptc. as noun, **master** Si 42$_{3(M)}$ (B אדון *master*). → דֶּרֶךְ II *power*.

דֶּרֶךְ I 706.21.190 n.m. (& f.)—דָּרֶךְ; cstr. דֶּרֶךְ; sf. דַּרְכּוֹ; du. דְּרָכַיִם; pl. דְּרָכִים; cstr. דַּרְכֵי; sf. דְּרָכָיו, דַּרְכֵיהֶם—**1. way, path, road, passage** Gn 38$_{16}$; with ref. to route Nm 21$_{1}$, way to(wards), direction Gn 3$_{24}$ Nm 14$_{25}$, way ahead or space Nm 22$_{26}$, course in movement, taken by camel Jr 2$_{23}$, lightning Jb 28$_{26}$, Y. in storm Na 1$_{3}$, ship on sea Pr 30$_{19}$. **2. way,** i.e. **journey** Gn 19$_{2}$ Jos 9$_{11}$; of a specif. period of time Gn 30$_{36}$, of a great distance Nm 9$_{10}$. **3. way,** i.e. **venture, mission, errand** Gn 24$_{21}$. **4. way,** i.e. **manner** of all the earth Gn 19$_{31}$, women (i.e. menstruation) Gn 31$_{35}$, the ant Pr 6$_{6}$. **5. way, a.** of human beings, i.e. (1) course of life, conduct, morality Gn 6$_{12}$ Ex 18$_{20}$, leading to life or death Jr 21$_{8}$. (2) fate, as consequence of course of life Ps 49$_{14}$. **b.** of Y., (1) commandments Gn 18$_{19}$. (2) activity Dt 32$_{4}$. **c.** of spirits of light and darkness, who determine human conduct 1QS 4$_{15}$. **d.** of wisdom Pr 3$_{17}$. → דרך I *tread*.

*דֶּרֶךְ II 11 n.[m.]—cstr. דֶּרֶךְ; sf. דַּרְכּוֹ, pl. cstr. דַּרְכֵי; sf. דְּרָכַיִךְ—**power, substance** of humans Ho 10$_{13}$ Jr 3$_{13}$ Pr 31$_{3}$, Y. Ps 67$_{3}$ 110$_{7}$ (if em.) 119$_{37}$ 138$_{5}$ Jb 26$_{14}$ 36$_{23}$ 40$_{19}$ Pr 8$_{22}$ 19$_{16}$; the 'Power of Beersheba' Am 8$_{14}$. → דרך III *prevail*.

*דֶּרֶךְ III 1 n.[m.] **treading (of grapes)** 1 K 18$_{27}$. → דרך I *tread*.

[דַּרְכְּמוֹן] 6 n.[m.]—pl. דַּרְכְּמוֹנִים (אֲדַרְכֹנִים)—**daric,** Persian gold coin weighing c. 8 gm Ezr 2$_{69}$ Ne 7$_{69}$.

[דַּרְכְּמוֹן], see דַּרְכְּמוֹן *daric*.

דַּרְמֶשֶׂק, see דַּמֶּשֶׂק *Damascus*.

דָּרַע 1 pr.n.m. **Dara.**

דַּרְקוֹן 2 pr.n.m. **Darkon.**

דרשׁ 164.9.107 vb.—**Qal** 155.9.106 Pf. דָּרַשׁ; impf. יִדְרֹשׁ; impv. דִּרְשׁוּ, (דורשם Q) דִּרְשׁ־; ptc. דֹּרֵשׁ, דֹּרְשֵׁי; ptc. pass. דְּרוּשָׁה, דְּרוּשִׁים; inf. abs. דָּרוֹשׁ, cstr. דְּרֹשׁ (דָּרְשׁוֹ, דְּרָשׁ־)—**1. seek (in worship, commitment)** Y. Dt 4$_{29}$ (+ בְּ *with* all heart) Am 5$_{4}$, other gods Dt 12$_{30}$ (לְ of obj.) Jr 8$_{2}$. **2.** דרשׁ אֶל **resort, turn to** a place for religious purposes Dt 12$_{5}$. **3. consult, inquire of, seek guidance of,** with accus. Y. Gn 25$_{22}$, ark of Y. 1 C 13$_{3}$, word of Y. 1 K 22$_{5}$||2 C 18$_{4}$; with prep. בְּ *of* Baal-zebub 2 K 1$_{1}$, מֵאֵת *of* prophet 1 K 22$_{7}$||2 C 18$_{6}$, מֵעִם *of* Ahijah 1 K 14$_{5}$, אֶל *of* the dead, familiar spirit Dt 18$_{11}$ Is 8$_{19}$. **4. inquire (concerning), investigate** thing Lv 10$_{16}$, person CD 15$_{11}$; with prep. לְ *concerning* 2 S 11$_{3}$, עַל of obj. and *concerning* 2 C 31$_{9}$; without obj. or prep. Dt 17$_{4}$ (+ הֵיטֵב *diligently*). **5. seek, look for** something Pr 31$_{13}$. **6a. require, demand** something Ezk 20$_{40}$, of someone to do something, with מֵעִם *of* Dt 23$_{22}$, מִן *of* Mc 6$_{8}$, עַל *of* 2 C 24$_{6}$. **b. require (a reckoning), avenge** bloodshed Gn 9$_{5}$ (+ מִיַּד *of*), failure to heed words Dt 18$_{19}$ (+ מֵעִם *of*). **7a. seek with interest, be intent on, study, interpret** law Ezr 7$_{10}$, justice Is 1$_{17}$, good Am 5$_{14}$, evil Pr 11$_{27}$. **b.** pass. **be studied,** of works of Y. Ps 111$_{2}$. **8a. care for, care about,** with accus. land Dt 11$_{12}$, person Jr 30$_{14}$; prep. לְ *for, about* person Ps 142$_{5}$. **b.** pass. דְּרוּשָׁה **'Cared for'**, as name of city Is 62$_{12}$.

Ni. 9.0.1 Pf. נִדְרַשְׁתִּי, נִדְרָשׁוּ; impf. אִדָּרֵשׁ; inf. abs. אִדְּרֹשׁ; ptc. נִדְרָשׁ—**1a. (let oneself) be inquired of, sought,** of Y. Is 65$_{5}$ Ezk 14$_{3}$ (+ לְ *by*), Samuel Si 46$_{20}$. **b. inquire of, seek** someone 1QH 12$_{24}$ (לְ of obj.). **2. be required,** of blood Gn 42$_{22}$. **3. be sought out,** of persons 1 C 26$_{31}$.

→ מִדְרָשׁ *study*.

*[דַּרְשְׁיָהוּ] 0.0.0.2 pr.n.m. **Darshiah.**

דשׁא 2 vb.—**Qal** 1 Pf. דָּשְׁאוּ—**sprout,** of pastures Jl 2$_{22}$.

Hi. 1 Impf. תַּדְשֵׁא—**cause to sprout** Gn 1$_{11}$.

→ דֶּשֶׁא I *grass*.

דֶּשֶׁא I 14.0.2 n.m. **grass,** (cultivated) vegetation in general Gn 1:11, food of animals Jr 14:5, second crop, growing after חָצִיר *grass* Pr 27:25. → דשא *sprout.*

*[**דֶּשֶׁא**] II 0.0.1 n.[m.] **ashes,** דשא [ה]מזבח *ashes of the altar* 4QMMT B31 (perh. error for דשן).

דשן I 9.4.9 vb.—**Qal** 1 + waw וְדָשֵׁן—**be fat,** of Israel Dt 31:20.

Pi. 3.3.1 Pf. דִּשַּׁנְתָּ; impf. תְּדַשֶּׁן; ptc. Q מדשן; inf. Si דשן—**1. make fat,** i.e. **a. anoint** head Ps 23:5. **b. refresh** bones Pr 15:30. **c. bring joy** Si 26:2 (+ לְ *to*). **d.** offer sacrifice (obj. altar) 11QPsa 18:9. **2. regard** burnt offering **as fat,** i.e. acceptable Ps 20:4.

Pu. 4 Impf. יְדֻשָּׁן—**be made fat, saturated,** of dust Is 34:7, person (through prosperity) Pr 11:25.

Htp. 0.1.8 Pf. Q התדשנו (or hothpaal); + waw Q והדשנתם (or hothpaal); Q וידשנו (or qal); impv. Si הדשן (or ni.); inf. Q הדשן (or ni.)—**make oneself fat, be satisfied** Si 14:11 1QH 18:26 (+ מִן *from* land) 1QM 2:5 1QS 10:15 (+ בְּ *with* produce).

Hothpaal 1 Pf. הֻדַּשְּׁנָה—**make oneself fat, be satiated,** of sword Is 34:6 (+ מִן *with* fat).

→ דָּשֵׁן *fat,* דֶּשֶׁן *fat,* דֶּשֶׁן *fatness.*

דשן II 2 vb.—**Pi.** 2 + waw וְדִשְּׁנוּ; inf. דַּשְּׁנוֹ—**clear altar of ashes** Ex 27:3 Nm 4:13. → דֶּשֶׁן II *ashes.*

דָּשֵׁן 3 adj.—pl. דְּשֵׁנִים; cstr. דִּשְׁנֵי—**1. fat,** of grain Is 30:23, person Ps 92:15. **2.** as noun, **vigorous one** Ps 22:30. → דשן I *be fat.*

דֶּשֶׁן I 7.1.1 n.m.—דֶּשֶׁן; sf. דִּשְׁנִי—**fat, fatness, oil** Jg 9:9 Is 55:2 Ps 63:6. → דשן I *be fat.*

דֶּשֶׁן II 8 n.m.—דֶּשֶׁן—**ashes** of sacrificial victims Lv 1:16 1 K 13:3. → דשן II *clear of ashes.*

*__דֶּשֶׁן__ III 2 n.[m.]—pl. cstr. דִּשְׁנֵי—**what is hidden,** i.e. the dead (as buried) Ps 22:30 Jr 31:40.

*[**דֶּשֶׁן**] IV 1 n.[m.]—pl. cstr. דִּשְׁנֵי—**nomad** Ps 22:30.

*[**דֹּשֶׁן**] 1 n.[m.] **fatness** Ps 127:2 (if em. שֵׁנָא *sleep [?]*). → דשן I *be fat.*

*[**דָּשָׁץ**] 0.0.0.1 pr.n.[m.] **Dashaz.**

דָּת 22 n.f.—cstr. דָּת; sf. דָּתוֹ; pl. cstr. דָּתֵי; sf. דָּתֵיהֶם—**1. decree, edict** Est 2:8 Ezr 8:36. **2. law,** דָּתֵי פָרַס־וּמָדַי *laws of the Persians and Medes* Est 1:19, דָּת הַנָּשִׁים *law of,* i.e. concerning, *the women* Est 2:12.

דָּתָן 10.1 pr.n.m. **Dathan.**

דֹּתָן 3 pl.n. **Dothan.**

ה

הַ 30359.113.c.4000.c.150 art.—**the,** alw. with dagesh in following consonant, exc. (1) in the sequences הַיְ and הַמְ (excluding הַיְהִ, הַיְעַ, הַמְּהֻ, הַמְּעַ, and הַמְּרַ) or (2) before הַ, חָ, חֶ, and עַ (but not עָ), where הַ is replaced by הֶ, and (3) before א, הֹ, ר, and עָ, where הַ is replaced by הָ; in following combinations, first vowel of noun in its undetermined form is changed when art. is attached: (עַם) הָעָם, (חַג) הֶחָג, (הַר) הָהָר, (אֶרֶץ) הָאָרֶץ, (אֲרוֹן) הָאָרוֹן, (פַּר) הַפָּר; after prefixed prepositions לְ *to,* בְּ *in,* כְּ *as,* ה is usu. elided; מֵהַ־ *from the* is oft. used instead of מִן־הַ. **1.** as art., **the,** prefixed to noun, הַשָּׁמַיִם *the heavens* Gn 1:1. **2.** as rel. pron. (sometimes incorporating antecedent), (the one) **that, which, who, a.** with ptc., לַיי׳ הַנִּרְאֶה אֵלָיו *to Y., who had appeared to him* Gn 12:7. **b.** rarely with indicative verb, כֹּל הַהִקְדִּישׁ שְׁמוּאֵל *all that Samuel had consecrated* 1 C 26:28. **3.** as voc., **O,** הַמֶּלֶךְ *O king* 1 S 17:55. **4.** as demonstr. adj. in expressions of time, **this,** הַיּוֹם *this day, today* Gn 4:14, הַפַּעַם *this time, now* Gn 18:32.

הֲ 746.8.34.2 interrog. part.—**is?, are?, am?, was?, were?, has?, have?, had?, does?, do?, did?,** הֲ before non-gutturals (and ר); הַ before consonant with shewa or hatef (but הֶחֳדַלְתִּי, and sometimes with dagesh in following letter: הַגְּמוּל, הַכְּתֹנֶת, הַבְּדֶרֶךְ, הַלְּבֶן, הַרְּאִיתֶם) or before ע, ח, ה, א (but הֶ before עָ, חָ, הָ, אָ). **1.** הֲ (etc.), prefixed to pf. Jl 1:2, impf. 2 K 7:2, inf. abs. Gn 37:10, inf. cstr. Jg 9:2, ptc. Gn 4:9, pron. Is 66:9, Jr 8:19, adj. Nm 13:19, prep. Gn 17:17, part. Jg 14:3; question with הֲ followed by another with אִם *is?* Gn 17$_{17}$, אִם־לֹא *or is not?* Ex 16$_{4}$, אוֹ *or is?* Ec 2$_{19}$. **2.** הֲלֹא, הֲלוֹא *is it not?*, oft. rhetorical, followed by pf. 1 K 1$_{11}$, impf. 2 S 3$_{38}$, inf. abs. Nm 22$_{37}$, inf. cstr. Jg 14$_{15}$, ptc. Pr 24$_{12}$, pron. Is 45$_{21}$, noun Jg 4$_{14}$, adj. Nm 14$_{3}$, prep. Gn 34$_{23}$, adv. Hb 2$_{7}$, part. Gn 4$_{7}$.

הֵא 2 interj. **behold** Gn 47$_{23}$ Ezk 16$_{43}$.

הֶאָח 12.1 interj. **aha,** expression of satisfaction or joy, usu. in response to another's misfortune Is 44$_{16}$ Ezk 25$_{3}$ Ps 35$_{21}$.

*[הֶאֱמָן] 0.0.0.1 pr.n.m. **Heman.**

הָאֲרָרִי, see הֲרָרִי *Hararite.*

הַב I, see יהב *give.*

הַב II **elephant (?),** see שֶׁנְהַבִּים *ivory.*

*[הֲבָאִיָה] 0.0.2 n.f.—הבאה—**produce** 5/6ḤevBA 45$_{17}$ 5/6ḤevBA 46$_{6}$.

*הַבָּה n.f. **flowering plant** Is 27$_{6}$ (if em. הַבָּאִים *those coming*).

*[הַבְהַב] 0.0.1 n.[m.] **1. passion** Pr 30$_{15}$ (if em. הַב הַב *Give, give!*) Ho 8$_{13}$ (if em. הַבְהָבַי *my gifts*). **2. greed** 4QsapHymnA 2$_{1}$.

[הַבְהָב] 1 n.m. perh. **gift,** זִבְחֵי הַבְהָבַי *sacrifices of my gifts,* i.e. given to me Hos 8$_{13}$. → יהב *give.*

*הֱבוֹ 1 n.[m.] **passion** Ho 4$_{18}$.

הבל 5 vb.—**Qal** 4 Impf. תֶּהְבָּלוּ; + waw וַיֶּהְבָּלוּ—**be vain, act vainly,** וַיֵּלְכוּ אַחֲרֵי הַהֶבֶל וַיֶּהְבָּלוּ *and they went after vanity and became vain* 2 K 17$_{15}$, לָמָּה־זֶּה הֶבֶל תֶּהְבָּלוּ *why do you become vain with vanity?,* i.e. act altogether vainly Jb 27$_{12}$.

Hi. 1 Ptc. מַהְבִּלִים—**cause to become vain** Jr 23$_{16}$. → הֶבֶל I *vanity.*

הֶבֶל I 73.2.10 n.m.—הֶבֶל; cstr. הֲבֵל; sf. הֶבְלוֹ; pl. הֲבָלִים; cstr. הַבְלֵי; sf. הַבְלֵיהֶם—**1. vanity, worthlessness,** הֲבֵל הֲבָלִים *vanity of vanities* Ec 1$_{2}$, חַיֵּי הֶבְלוֹ *life of his vanity,* i.e. his vain life Ec 6$_{12}$, מעשי הבל *deeds of vanity,* i.e. vain deeds 1QS 5$_{19}$. **2. image,** הַבְלֵי הַגּוֹיִם *images of the nations* Jr 14$_{22}$, שָׁוְא *of vanity,* i.e. vain images Jon 2$_{9}$. **3. breath,** הֶבֶל כָּל־אָדָם *every human being is a (mere) breath* Ps 39$_{12}$. → הבל *be vain.*

הֶבֶל II 8.0.1 pr.n.m. **Abel.**

הָבְנִים 1 n.[m.]pl.—Kt הובנים—**ebony** Ezk 27$_{15}$.

הבר I 1 vb.—**Qal** 1 Pf. Kt הברו; ptc. Qr הֹבְרֵי (1QIsa[a] הוברי)—**divide the heavens,** of astrologers Is 47$_{13}$.

*הבר II 1 vb.—**Qal** 1 Pf. Kt הברו; ptc. Qr הֹבְרֵי (1QIsa[a] הוברי)—**worship** the heavens Is 47$_{13}$.

הֵגֶא, see הֵגַי *Hegai.*

*[הֲגָבָה] 0.0.0.1 pr.n.m. **Hagabah.**

הַגְּדוֹלִים 1 pr.n.m. **Haggedolim.**

הגה I 25.3.10 vb.—**Qal** 23.3.10 Pf. הָגִיתִי; impf. יֶהְגֶּה; inf. abs. הָגֹה, cstr. Q הגות—**1a. growl,** of lion Is 31$_{4}$. **b. moan,** as dove Is 38$_{14}$. **2. moan, groan,** in mourning Is 16$_{7}$ (+ לְ *for*) Jr 48$_{31}$ (+ אֶל *for*). **3. utter, speak** righteousness Ps 35$_{28}$, wisdom Ps 37$_{30}$, truth Pr 8$_{7}$, deceit Jb 27$_{4}$. **4a. meditate on** (בְּ) Y. Ps 63$_{7}$, law Ps 1$_{2}$, wisdom Si 14$_{20}$, mystery 4QInstr[d] 43$_{4}$. **b.** with inf., **consider** how to do something Pr 15$_{28}$. **5. imagine, plot** vanity Ps 2$_{1}$, terror Is 38$_{13}$.

Po. 1 Inf. abs. הֹגוֹ—**utter** words of falsehood Is 59$_{13}$ (or em. qal).

Hi. 1 Ptc. מַהְגִּים—**mutter,** of familiar spirit Is 8$_{19}$.

→ הֶגֶה *sigh,* הִגָּיוֹן *music,* הָגוּת *meditation,* הֶגִי *meditation.*

הגה II 3 vb.—**Qal** 3 Pf. הָגָה; inf. abs. הָגוֹ—**remove** person Pr 25$_{5}$, dross from (מִן) silver Pr 25$_{4}$.

*הגה III 0.1 vb.—**Qal** 0.1 impf. Si יהגה (Bmg; M יהג)—**dazzle** Si 43$_{18(Bmg, M)}$ (B נהה *heal*).

הֶגֶה 3 n.m.—**1. sigh** Ps 90$_{9}$. **2. moaning** Ezk 2$_{10}$. **3. rumbling (of thunder)** Jb 37$_{2}$. → הגה I *moan.*

[הָגוּת] 1 n.f.—cstr. הָגוּת—**meditation** Ps 49$_{4}$. → הגה I *meditate.*

הגוי, see הֶגִי *meditation.*

*[הֶגִי] 0.0.7 n.[m.]—הגוי; cstr. הגי—**meditation** 1QH 19$_{2}$; ספר ההגי *the book of meditation* (unless *Hagi* is name of book) CD 10$_{6}$, חזון ההגוי לספר זכרון *vision of the meditation of the book of memorial* 4QInstr[c] 1.1$_{16}$. → הגה I *meditate.*

הֵגַי 4 pr.n.m. **Hegai.**

[הָגִיג] 2 n.m.—sf. הֲגִיגִי—**murmuring,** in prayer Ps 5$_{2}$; **musing** Ps 39$_{4}$.

הִגָּיוֹן 4 n.m.—cstr. הִגְיוֹן; sf. הֶגְיוֹנָם—**1a. music** Ps 92$_{4}$. **b. higgaion,** appar. musical technical term Ps 9$_{17}$. **2. meditation, talk** Ps 19$_{15}$ Lm 3$_{62}$. → הגה I *moan.*

[הָגִין] 1 adj. **suitable,** הַגְּדֶרֶת הַגִּינָה appar. *the suitable wall* Ezk 42$_{12}$. → הגן *be suitable.*

*[הגן] vb.—**Qal, be suitable** Si 40$_{23}$ (if em. ינהגו *lead*

[?] to יהגנו). → הָגִין *suitable.*

*[הגר] vb.—**Hi., leave alone** Ps 59₁₂ (if em. תַּהַרְגֵם *slay them* to תְּהַגְּרֵם).

הָגָר 12 pr.n.f. **Hagar.**

הַגְרִי I 5 gent. **Hagrite.**

הַגְרִי II 1 pr.n.m. **Hagri.**

הֵד I 1 n.[m.] **(joyful) shout** Ezk 7₇.

*הֵד II 1 n.[m.] **thunderclap** Ezk 7₇ Am 4₁₃ (if em. הָרִים *mountains* to הֵדִים).

הֲדַד 12 pr.n.m. **Hadad.**

הֲדַדְעֶזֶר 21 pr.n.m. **Hadadezer,** also as הֲדַרְעֶזֶר **Hadarezer.**

הֲדַד־רִמּוֹן 1 pl.n. **Hadad-rimmon.**

הדה 1 vb.—**Qal** 1 Pf. הָדָה—**stretch out** hand Is 11₈.

הֹדּוּ 1 pl.n. **India.**

הֲדוּרִים 1 n.[m.]pl. **mountainous land** Is 45₂.

הֲדוֹרָם 4 pr.n.m. **Hadoram.**

הִדַּי 1 pr.n.m. **Hiddai.**

הֹדַיְוָהוּ, see הוֹדַוְיָה *Hodaviah.*

הדך 1 vb.—**Qal** 1 Impv. הֲדֹךְ—**tread down** Jb 40₁₂.

*[הדם] vb.—**Qal, dismember,** הֹדֵם חֲזִיר *one who dismembers a pig* Is 66₃ (if em. דַּם *blood of*).

הֲדֹם 6.0.2 n.m.—pl. cstr. Q הדומי—**footstool** of Y. Is 66₁, king Ps 110₁.

הֲדַס 6 n.m.—pl. הֲדַסִּים—**myrtle (tree)** (*Myrtus communis*) Is 41₁₉.

הֲדַסָּה 1 pr.n.f. **Hadassah.**

הדף 11.4.1 vb.—**Qal** 11.4.1 Pf. הֲדָפוֹ; impf. יֶהְדֹּף (יֶהְדְּפֵם); inf. הֲדֹף (הֲדָפָה)—**1. thrust, push** someone Nm 35₂₀. **2. push (away), drive out** someone from (מִן) office Is 22₁₉, from light to (אֶל) darkness Jb 18₁₈.

הדר 6.5.5 vb.—**Qal** 4.2.2 Pf. הָדַרְתָּ; impf. תֶּהְדַּר; pass ptc. הָדוּר—**1. honour** Lv 19₃₂; i.e. **show partiality to** Ex 23₃. **2.** pass. **be adorned, made glorious** in (בְּ) one's clothing Is 63₁.

Ni. 1.3.3 Pf. נֶהְדָּרוּ—**be honoured, be glorious** Lm 5₁₂.

Htp. 1 Impf. תִּתְהַדַּר—**claim honour,** before (לִפְנֵי) king Pr 25₆.

→ הָדָר *honour,* הֲדָרָה *adornment.*

הָדָר 31.3.34 n.m.—cstr. הֲדַר (הֶדֶר); sf. הֲדָרִי; pl. cstr. הַדְרֵי—**1. honour, splendour, majesty,** הוֹד וְהָדָר פָּעֳלוֹ *his (Y.'s) work is splendour and majesty* Ps 111₃, עֹז־וְהָדָר לְבוּשָׁהּ *strength and honour are her* (woman's) *clothing* Pr 31₂₅, מדת הדר *garment of honour* 1QS 4₈, רוחי הדר *spirits of splendour* 4QShirShabb[f] 14.1₆. **2. adornment,** הֲדַר זְקֵנִים שֵׂיבָה *the adornment of old men is grey hair* Pr 20₂₉. → הדר *honour.*

הֲדַר 1 pr.n.m. **Hadar.**

[הֲדָרָה] I 5 n.f. **adornment,** הַדְרַת־קֹדֶשׁ *adornment of holiness,* i.e. holy adornment Ps 29₂. → הדר *honour.*

*[הֲדָרָה] II 3 n.f. **(divine) appearance,** הַדְרַת־קֹדֶשׁ *(his) holy theophany* Ps 29₂.

הֲדֹרָם, see הֲדוֹרָם *Hadoram.*

הֲדַרְעֶזֶר, see הֲדַדְעֶזֶר *Hadadezer.*

הָהּ 1 interj. **alas** Ezk 30₂.

הוֹ 2 interj. **alas** Am 5₁₆.₁₆. → cf. הוֹי *alas.*

הוא I, see הוה II *fall.*

הוא II, see הוה I *be.*

הִוא, see הִיא *she.*

הוא 1386.49.347.3 pron.—Q הואה, Q הו—**1. he, it,** with verb Gn 3₁₅, ptc. Gn 31₂₀, in nom. cl. Gn 2₁₉; resumptive of non-subj. sf., עָלָיו גַּם־הוּא *upon him too* 1 S 19₂₃. **2.** הַהוּא, as demonstr. adj., **that,** הָאִישׁ הַהוּא *that man* Lv 17₉, בַּיּוֹם הַהוּא *on that day* Gn 15₁₈.

*הוב 0.0.1 vb. (appar. error for חוב)—**Qal** 0.0.1 Pf. הבו—**be guilty** CD 3₁₀.

הוֹד I 24.10.20 n.m.—cstr. הוֹד; sf. הוֹדוֹ—**splendour, majesty, beauty** of Y. Hb 3₃, human king Ps 21₆, snorting of horse Jb 39₂₀, natural phenomena Is 30₃₀ Si 43₉; in ref. to authority of Moses Nm 27₂₀, human vigour Pr 5₉, physical appearance of person Dn 10₈.

הוֹד II 1 pr.n.m. **Hod.**

*[הוֹדָאָה] 0.0.2 n.f. **(song of) thanksgiving** GnzPs 2₁₃.₁₅. → ידה I *give thanks.*

[הוֹדָה] 1.1.15 n.f.—pl. הֹדוֹת; cstr. Q הודות (Q הודי); sf. Q הודותם—**(song of) thanksgiving, praise, confession** (perh. hi. inf. ידה), הודות אל *thanksgivings of,* i.e. to, *God* 1QM 4₁₄, הודי פלא *thanksgiving of wonder,* i.e. wondrous thanksgiving 4QShirShabb[f] 3.2₁₁, שִׁיר־תְּהִלָּה וְהֹדוֹת *song of praise and thanksgiving* Ne 12₄₆. → ידה I *give thanks.*

הוֹדְוָה 1 pr.n.m. **Hodevah.**

הוֹדַוְיָה 4.0.0.3 pr.n.m. **Hodaviah.**

הוֹדַוְיָהוּ, see הוֹדַוְיָה *Hodaviah.*

הוֹדְיָה, see הוֹדְוָה *Hodevah.*

הוֹדִיָּה 6.0.0.4 pr.n.m. **Hodiah.**

הוה I 5 vb.—**Qal** 5 Impf. יְהוּא; impv. הֱוֵי, הֱוֵה; ptc. הֹוֶה—**be, become,** הֱוֵה גְבִיר לְאַחֶיךָ *be a lord to your brothers* Gn 27$_{29}$. → cf. היה *be.*

הוה II 1 vb.—**Qal** 1 Impv. הֱוֵא—**fall,** of snow Jb 37$_{6}$ (+ אֶרֶץ *[to the] earth*). → הֹוָה II *destruction,* הֹוָה *disaster.*

[הַוָּה] I 3.0.1 n.f.—cstr. הַוַּת—**desire** Mc 7$_{3}$ Pr 10$_{3}$.

הַוָּה II 13.0.21 n.f.—sf. הַוָּתוֹ; pl. הַוּוֹת—**1. destruction, ruin,** הַוֹּת לְאָבִיו בֵּן כְּסִיל *a foolish son is ruin to his father* Pr 19$_{13}$, רוח הוות *spirit of destruction* 1QH 15$_{11}$. **2. wickedness** of heart 1QH 13$_{26}$. → הוה II *fall.*

*__[הַוָּה] III__ 15 n.f.—cstr. הַוַּת, sf. הַוָּתוֹ; pl. הַוּוֹת; cstr. הַוּוֹת—**wind, bluster, boast,** קִרְבָּם הַוּוֹת *their insides are (full of) wind, bluster* Ps 5$_{10}$, הַוֹּת לְאָבִיו בֵּן כְּסִיל *a foolish son is an ill wind to his father* Pr 19$_{13}$, לְשׁוֹן הַוֹּת *boastful tongue* Pr 17$_{4}$.

*__[הַוָּה] IV__ 16 n.f.—cstr. הַוַּת, sf. הַוָּתוֹ; pl. הַוּוֹת; cstr. הַוּוֹת—**evil word,** קִרְבָּם הַוּוֹת *their inward part is evil words* Ps 5$_{10}$, לְשׁוֹן הַוֹּת *tongue of evil words* Pr 17$_{4}$.

*__[הָוָה]__ n.f. **word** Jb 6$_{30}$ (if em. הַוּוֹת *[?] destruction* to הָוֹת *words*).

הֹוָה 3 n.f. **disaster** Is 47$_{11}$ Ezk 7$_{26}$. → הוה II *fall.*

הוֹהָם 1 pr.n.m. **Hoham.**

הוֹי 51.2.9 interj. **alas,** הוֹי הוֹי וְנֻסוּ *alas, alas, (and) flee* Zc 2$_{10}$, הוֹי אָחִי *alas, my brother* 1 K 13$_{30}$, הוֹי לִמְתַפְּרוֹת *alas to the women who sew* Ezk 13$_{18}$. → cf. הוֹ *alas.*

[הוֹלֵל] 4.0.3 n.[m.]—pl. הוֹלֵלוֹת—**1. madness** Ec 1$_{17}$ 2$_{12}$. **2. folly, delusion** 1QH 10$_{36}$ 12$_{8.20}$. → הלל III *be foolish.*

הוֹלֵלוּת 1 n.f. **madness** Ec 10$_{13}$. → הלל III *be foolish.*

הום 6.1 vb. (byform of המם)—**Qal** 1 + waw וְהָמָם—**discomfit, confuse** Dt 7$_{23}$.

Ni. 3 + waw וַתֵּהֹם—**be in a stir, be in uproar,** of land 1 S 4$_{5}$, city 1 K 1$_{45}$.

Hi. 2.1 Impf. אָרִימָה, תְּהִימֶנָה; impv. Si ההם—**1. be disquieted** Ps 55$_{3}$. **2. make noise,** like flock of sheep Mc 2$_{12}$. **3. make mourning noisy** Si 38$_{17(Bmg)}$.

→ מְהוּמָה *discomfiture.*

הוֹמָם 1 pr.n.m. **Homam.**

הון I 1 vb.—**Hi.** 1 + waw וַתָּהִינוּ—**1. regard as easy** Dt 1$_{41}$. **2. make easy, alleviate** Jb 30$_{24}$ (if em. לָהֶן *appar. to them* to לְהֹן *for alleviation*). → הוֹן *wealth.*

*__הון II__ 1 vb.—**Qal** 1 Impf. + waw וַתָּהִינוּ—**put on armour** Dt 1$_{41}$.

הוֹן 26.5.67 n.m.—sf. הוֹנוֹ; pl. sf. הוֹנָיִךְ—**1. wealth, property,** הוֹן וָעֹשֶׁר *wealth and riches* Ps 112$_{3}$. **2. sufficiency,** as exclamation, **enough!** Pr 30$_{15}$. → הון I *be easy.*

*__[הור]__ vb.—**Qal, pull down,** אֲחֵרִים הָרוּ *they have destroyed others* Ps 16$_{4}$ (if em. אַחֵר מָהָרוּ *they hasten after another [? god]*).

*__[הוֹר]__ n.[m.] **mountain,** הוֹרֵי עַד *mountains of eternity,* i.e. eternal mountains Gn 49$_{26}$.

*__[הוֹרָה]__ 0.0.1 n.f.—pl. cstr. הורות—**teaching** 4QShir Shabb^{a} 1.1$_{17}$. → ירה III *teach.*

*__[הוֹרָיָה]__ 0.0.2 n.f.—sf. הריתי—**teaching** 4QM^{a} 11.1$_{16}$ 4QHod^{e} 1$_{3}$. → ירה III *teach.*

*__[הוּרָרַט]__ 0.0.2 pl.n. **Hurarat.**

הוֹשָׁמָע 1 pr.n.m. **Hoshama.**

הוֹשֵׁעַ 16.0.1.1 pr.n.m. **Hos(h)ea.**

הוֹשַׁעְיָה 3.0.0.16 pr.n.m. **Hoshaiah.**

הות I 1 vb.—**Pol.** 1 Impf. תְּהוֹתְתוּ—**attack, rush in against** (עַל) Ps 62$_{4}$.

*__הות II__ 1 vb.—**Pol.** 1 Impf. תְּהוֹתְתוּ—**threaten** Ps 62$_{4}$.

הוֹתִיר 2 pr.n.m. **Hothir.**

הזה 1 vb.—**Qal** 1 Ptc. הֹזִים—**dream, rave,** of guards as inactive dogs Is 56$_{10}$.

*__[הַזָּיָה]__ n.f. **sprinkling,** מימי ה[ז]יה *waters of sprinkling* 4QRitPurB 1.12$_{6(mg)}$. → נזה I *sprinkle.*

*__[הֶטֶל] I__ 0.0.3 n.[m.]—cstr. הטל—**throwing** 1QM 8$_{15}$ 16$_{5}$ 1QM 17$_{12}$. → טול hi. *throw.*

*__[הֶטֶל] II__ 0.0.3 n.[m.]—cstr. הטל—**troop (of soldiers)** 1QM 8$_{15}$ 16$_{5}$ 1QM 17$_{12}$.

הִי 1 n.[m.] **woe** Ezk 2$_{10}$. → היה II *wail.*

הִיא 484.10.103. pron.—Kt הוא, Si הי, Q היאה—**1. she, it,** with verb Gn 3$_{12(Qr)}$, ptc. Jos 2$_{15}$, in nom. cl. 1 K 3$_{27}$. **2.** הַהִיא, as demonstr. adj., **that,** בָּעֵת הַהִיא *at that time* Jos 5$_{2}$.

הֵידָד I 7 n.m. **shout(ing), cry,** in battle Is 16$_{9}$, of joy at treading of grapes Is 16$_{10}$.

*__הֵידָד II__ 7 n.m.—**1. thunderstorm** Is 16$_{9}$. **2. stormtroop** Is 16$_{10}$.

הֻיְּדוֹת 1 n.f.pl. **(songs of) praise** Ne 12$_{8}$.

→ ידה hi. *give thanks.*

היה I $3548.61.570.9$ vb.—**Qal** $3527.59.514.9$ Pf. הָיָה, הֱיִיתֶם; impf. יִהְיֶה (יְהִי ,יֶהִי); + waw וַיְהִי (וַיֶּהִי), וָאֶהְיֶה; impv. הֱיֵה (וֶהְיֵה), הֱיִי ,הֱיוּ (וִהְיוּ); ptc. הוֹיָה; inf. abs. הָיֹה (הָיוֹ); cstr. הֱיוֹת (מִ/הֱיוֹת/ בִּ/לִ), הֱיוֹתְךָ (מִ/לִהְיוֹתְךָ)—**1. be, become, exist,** וַיְהִי רָעָב בָּאָרֶץ *and there was a famine in the land* Gn 12_{10}, הָיִיתָ מִשְׂגָּב לִי *you have been a refuge to me* Ps 59_{17}, אֲנִי קֹהֶלֶת הָיִיתִי מֶלֶךְ עַל־יִשְׂרָאֵל בִּירוּשָׁלָםִ *I, Koheleth, was king over Israel in Jerusalem* Ec 1_{12}, וְאַתֶּם תִּהְיוּ נְקִיִּם *you shall be innocent* Gn 44_{10}, וְהָיוּ כְּלוֹא הָיוּ *and they will be as though they had not been* Ob16, מַה־שֶּׁהָיָה הוּא שֶׁיִּהְיֶה *what has been is what will be* Ec 1_9, מֵעֵת הֱיוֹתָהּ שָׁם אָנִי *since the time when it came to be I have been there* Is 48_{16}; of Israel's relation with Y., וְהָיִיתִי לָכֶם לֵאלֹהִים וְאַתֶּם תִּהְיוּ־לִי לְעָם *and I shall be to you as a God, and you shall be to me as a people* Lv 26_{12}; of woman in marriage, וַתְּהִי לִי לְאִשָּׁה *and she became to me as a wife* Gn 20_{12}. **2a. be, happen, occur, come to pass,** esp. with impersonal subj., followed (rarely preceded) by clause or phrase indicating time, place, etc. (the subsequent narrative being continued by another verb), וַיְהִי כְּבוֹא אַבְרָם מִצְרָיְמָה *and it came to pass, when Abram had come to Egypt* Gn 12_{14}, וַיְהִי כַּאֲשֶׁר־בָּא יוֹסֵף אֶל־אֶחָיו *and it came to pass, when Joseph had come to his brothers* Gn 37_{23}, וַיְהִי הַשֶּׁמֶשׁ בָּאָה *and it came to pass, (when) the sun had gone down* Gn 15_{17}, וַיְהִי אַחַר הַדְּבָרִים הָאֵלֶּה *and it came to pass after these things* Gn 22_1, וַיְהִי־כֵן *and it was so* Gn 1_7, וְהָיָה אִם־שָׁמוֹעַ תִּשְׁמַע בְּקוֹל י׳ *and it shall be, if you obey the voice of Y.* Dt 28_1, וְהָיָה בַּיּוֹם הַהוּא *and it shall be on that day* Is 7_{18}. **b.** ptc. as noun, **the present, (present) event, (present) existence,** i.e. that which exists, those that exist, מאל הדעות כול הווה ונהייה *from the God of knowledge is every present and future event* 1QS 3_{15}, רז נהיה והווא *mystery of future and present existence/events* 1QS 11_4, הוי עד *that which exists of eternity,* i.e. for ever MasShir Shabb 1_2, sim. הוי עולמים CD 2_{10}. **3.** with ptc. of another verb, expressing continuous state, וּמֹשֶׁה הָיָה רֹעֶה אֶת־צֹאן יִתְרוֹ *and Moses was tending the flock of Jethro* Ex 3_1, וְהַנַּעַר הָיָה מְשָׁרֵת אֶת־י׳ *and the lad was ministering to Y.* 1 S 2_{11}.

Ni. $21.2.56$ Pf. נִהְיָה, נִהְיֵיתָ; ptc. נִהְיָה, Q נהיית, Q נהיי, Si, Q נהיות—**1a. happen, occur, come to pass, be realized,** אֵיכָה נִהְיְתָה הָרָעָה הַזֹּאת *how has this evil thing happened?* Jg 20_3, הֲנִהְיָה כַּדָּבָר הַגָּדוֹל הַזֶּה *has such a great thing as this happened?* Dt 4_{32}, לֹא נִהְיְתָה ... כָּזֹאת *nothing like this ... has happened* Jg 19_{30}, הִנֵּה בָאָה וְנִהְיָתָה *behold, it is coming and will happen* Ezk 21_{12}. **b.** ptc. as noun, **the future, (future) event, (future) existence,** i.e. that which/those that will exist, נהיה עולם *existence of,* i.e. for, *eternity* 4QInstr[d] 69.2_7, נהיות עולם *events of eternity* CD 13_8, var. נהיי עולמים 1QM 17_5, רז נהיה *mystery of existence/the future* 1QMyst 1.1_3, קץ נהיה *end time of the future* 1QS 10_5. **2. become, exist,** הַיּוֹם הַזֶּה נִהְיֵיתָ לְעָם *today you will become a people* Dt 27_9. **3. be finished, exhausted,** of person Dn 8_{27}; **be gone,** of sleep Dn 2_1.

→ cf. הוה I *be.*

*היה II $_1$ vb.—**Qal** $_1$ Pf. הָיוּ—**go up** Ezk 7_{16}.

*היה III $_3$ vb.—**Qal** $_3$ Pf. הָיִינוּ; impf. תְּהֱיֶינָה; + waw וָאֶהְיֶה—**wail** Is 16_2 26_{17} Ps 102_8. → הִי *woe.*

*היה IV $_{11}$ vb.—**Qal** $_9$ Pf. הָיָה; impf. תְּהִיֶה; + waw וַתְּהִי, וַנִּהְיֶה; inf. לִהְיוֹת—**fall,** of soldiers 2 S 11_{23} (+ עַל *upon* enemy), sword Ezk 21_{17} (+ בְּ *upon* people), rain Jr 3_3.

Ni. $_2$ Pf. נִהְיֵיתִי—**fall,** of person Dn 8_{27}, sleep Dn 2_1.

Hi. make to fall 1 K 11_{15} (if em. בְּהִיּוֹת *when he was*).

[הַיָּה], see הַוָּה II *destruction.*

הֵיךְ $2.0.1$ interrog. adv.—Q היככה—**how?,** introducing rhetorical question Dn 10_{17} 1 C 13_{12} 4QpsEzek[a] 2_3. → cf. אֵיךְ *how?*

היככה, see הֵיךְ *how?.*

הֵיכָל $80.5.15$ n.m.—cstr. הֵיכַל; sf. הֵיכָלוֹ; pl. הֵיכָלוֹת; cstr. הֵיכְלֵי; sf. Q הֵיכְלֵיכֶם, היכלותיך—**1. palace,** of Ahab 1 K 21_1, king of Babylon 2 K 20_{18}||Is 39_7. **2. temple,** in Shilo 1 S 1_9, Jerusalem 2 K 18_{16}, the heavenly temple of Y. 2 S 22_7||Ps 18_7. **3. hall, nave** of temple in Jerusalem, between the אוּלָם *porch* and דְּבִיר *inner sanctuary* 1 K 6_3.

*[הֵיכָן] $0.0.1$ interrog. adv.—**where?** 4QapJerC[a] 17_4.

*[הֵילָל] n.m. **morning-star, crescent moon** Is 14_{12} (if em. הֵילֵל *shining one*).

הֵילֵל $_1$ n.m. **shining one,** in ref. to king of Babylon,

הֵילֵל בֶּן־שָׁחַר *shining one, son of dawn* Is 14_{12}. → הלל II *shine*.

הֵימָם 1 pr.n.m. **Hemam.**

הֵימָן 17 pr.n.m. **Heman.**

*[**הֵימֵן**] 0.0.6 prep.—sf. הימנו, המך—**1.** of direction, **from** Mur 24 B_{13}. **2.** of comparison, **than,** יתר הימנו *more than it* 5/6ḤevBA 44_{23}. → cf. מִן *from.*

*[**הֵיָן**] adj. **rash,** as noun, **rash one** Hb 2_5 (if em. הַיַּיִן *wine*).

הִין 22.0.9.1 n.m.—pl. Q הינים—**hin,** unit of liquid measure, about 6 litres, as measure of oil Ex 29_{40}, wine Ex 29_{40}, water Ezk 4_{11}.

*[**הָכָה**] 0.0.1 adv. **here, now** Mur 24 D_{15}.

*__הַכּוֹס__ 0.0.0.1 pr.n.m. **Hakkos.**

*__הָכֵן__ 2 adv. **here** Jos 3_{17} (unless inf. of כון hi. *establish*) Is $40_{7(1QIsa^a)}$ (MT אָכֵן *surely*).

*__הָכֵף__ 2 part. (deictic ה + modal כ + demonstr. פ) **indeed** Jg $8_{6.15}$.

הכר 1 vb.—**Qal (or Hi.)** 1 Impf. תַּהְכְּרוּ—**wonder at** Jb 19_3.

[**הַכָּרָה**] 1 n.f. **recognition,** הַכָּרַת פְּנֵיהֶם *recognition of their face,* i.e. their partiality Is 3_9 (1QIsa[a] הכרות). → נכר I hi. *recognize.*

הלא 1 vb.—**Ni.** 1 Ptc. נַהֲלָאָה—**be far removed,** ptc. as noun, **far removed one,** of straying sheep Mc 4_7. → הָלְאָה *onwards.*

הָלְאָה 16 adv.—**1.** of place, **a. there, yonder,** גֶּשׁ־הָלְאָה *approach there,* i.e. stand back Gn 19_9, זְרֵה־הָלְאָה *scatter yonder* Nm 17_2. **b. beyond, further,** (1) וָהָלְאָה *and beyond,* מֵעֵבֶר לַיַּרְדֵּן וָהָלְאָה *on the other side of the Jordan and beyond* Nm 32_{19}, מִמְּךָ וָהָלְאָה *from you and beyond,* i.e. beyond you 1 S 20_{22}. (2) מֵהָלְאָה לְ *beyond* Gn 35_{21}. **2.** of time, **onwards,** מִן־הַיּוֹם ... וָהָלְאָה *from the day ... and onwards* Nm 15_{23}. → הלא *be far removed.*

*[**הָלְוֹן**] 0.0.2 demonstr. adj. (common pl.)—**these** 5/6 ḤevBA $44_{17.18}$.

[**הִלּוּל**] 2.0.1 n.[m.]—Q הלל; pl. הִלּוּלִים—**praise,** festival at vintage Jg 9_{27}, fruit from trees in fourth year as offering of praise Lv 19_{24}, praise in assembly of gods 4QShirShabb[f] 14_3. → הלל I *praise.*

הַלָּז 7 demonstr. pron. and adj. (common sg.)—**1.** as noun, **that one,** Dn 8_{16}. **2.** as attrib. adj., **that, yonder,** הַסֶּלַע הַלָּז *that rock* Jg 6_{20}. → cf. הַלָּזֶה *that,* הַלֵּזוּ *that,* זֶה *this.*

הַלָּזֶה 2 demonstr. adj. (masc. sg.)—**that,** הָאִישׁ־הַלָּזֶה *that man* Gn 24_{65}. → cf. הַלָּז *that,* הַלֵּזוּ *that,* זֶה *this.*

הַלֵּזוּ 1 demonstr. adj. (fem. sg.) **that**—הָאָרֶץ הַלֵּזוּ *that land* Ezk 36_{35}. → cf. הַלָּז *that,* הַלָּזֶה *that,* זֶה *this.*

[**הֵלִיךְ**] 1.0.2 n.[m.]—sf. Q הליכמה; pl. sf. הֲלִיכַי—**step,** or **foot** Jb 29_6 4QInstr[d] 127_4. → הלך *go.*

[**הֲלִיכָה**] 6 n.f.—sf. Qr הֲלִיכָתָם; pl. cstr. הֲלִיכוֹת; sf. הֲלִיכוֹתֶיךָ—**1. going, way** Na 2_6, i.e. conduct Pr 31_{27}. **2. procession** Ps 68_{25}. **3. caravan** Jb 6_{19}. **4. orbit (of stars)** Hb 3_6. → הלך *go.*

הלך 1549.15.224.1 vb.—**Qal** 1413.11.136.1 Pf. הָלַךְ, הֲלַכְתֶּם; impf. יֵלֵךְ (יַהֲלֹךְ ,יֵלֶךְ ,יֵלֶךְ־) + waw וַיֵּלֶךְ (וַיֵּלַךְ ,וַתֵּלֶךְ (וַתְּהַלַּךְ)); impv. לֵךְ (לֶךְ־ ,לְכָה ,לֵכָה ,Q הלך ,Si הלוך), לְכִי (לְכִי), לְכוּ (לְכוּ ,הִלְכוּ ,לֵכְנָה); ptc. הֹלֵךְ ,הֹלֶכֶת (הֹלְכָה), הֹלְכִים; inf. abs. הָלֹךְ; cstr. לֶכֶת (לֶכֶת ,לְכְתּוֹ ,הֲלֹךְ (הֲלָךְ־)) —**1. go, come, walk, proceed,** of humans Gn 22_6, Y. Ex 13_{21}, animals Ex 10_{26} Lv 11_{27}, serpent (on belly) Gn 3_{14}. **2. go away, depart,** of Y. Gn 18_{33}, humans Gn 34_{17}, i.e. **die** 2 C 21_{20}. **3. go,** in more specif. senses, according to context: of water, **flow** 1 K 18_{35}; of ark, **float** Gn 7_{18}; of ship, **sail** 1 K 22_{49}; of plant, **grow** Jr 12_2; of wind, **blow** Ec 1_6. **4.** with ref. to living moral or religious life, **go, walk,** in law of Y. Ex 16_4, in ways of Y. Dt 8_6, ways of kings of Israel 2 K 16_3; go after other gods Dt 6_{14}, sins of Jeroboam 2 K 13_2.

With adv. accus., (1) *to, into* named place 2 S 13_{38}, land Jg 1_{26}, steppe Dt 1_{19}, house 2 S 13_7. (2) *for (a specified period of)* days Ex 15_{22}, years Jos 5_6. (3) *in, with* righteousness Is 33_{15}, perfection Ps 2_7, crookedness Pr 6_{12}, darkness Jb 29_3. (4) *as a* blameless one Ps 15_2, slanderer Lv 19_{16}.

Preps.: לְ *to* place 1 S 8_{22}; בְּ *in, into, through* Gn 24_{65} Ex 3_{18} 1 K 18_5; *in (accordance with), with* statutes, etc. 1 K 6_{12}, integrity 1 K 9_4, sins 1 K 15_3, stubbornness Jr 7_{24}; מִן *from* Gn 12_1; אֶל *to* person Gn 26_1, place Gn 24_{10}; עַד *as far as, to* Jg 19_{18}; עַל *upon, over* Gn 7_{18} Jos 4_{18}; אֵת *with* Gn 12_4; עִם *with* Nm 22_{39}; לִפְנֵי *before* 1 K 2_4; אַחֲרֵי *after* 1 K 14_8; אַחַר *after* 2 K 23_3; ה- of direction, *to(wards)* Gn 11_{31}.

הלך expressing continuity, progression, וַיֵּלֶךְ הָלוֹךְ וְאָכֹל *and he went on, eating as he went* Jg 14$_9$, וַיֵּלֶךְ הָלוֹךְ וְקָרֵב *and he came nearer and nearer* 2 S 18$_{25}$, דָּוִד הֹלֵךְ וְחָזֵק וּבֵית שָׁאוּל הֹלְכִים וְדַלִּים *David became stronger and stronger, and the house of Saul became weaker and weaker* 2 S 3$_1$.

הלך impv. as an introductory word, *go/come, do,* לְכָה נַשְׁקֶה אֶת־אָבִינוּ יַיִן *come, let us make our father drink wine* Gn 19$_{32}$, לְכִי אִיעָצֵךְ נָא עֵצָה *come, let me give you counsel* 1 K 1$_{12}$.

Ni. $_1$ Pf. נֶהֱלָכְתִּי—**be gone, fade away,** כְּצֵל־כִּנְטוֹתוֹ נֶהֱלָכְתִּי *as a shadow when it stretches out I am gone* Ps 109$_{23}$.

Pi. $_{25.3.6}$ Pf. הִלַּכְתִּי; impf. יְהַלֵּךְ; impv. הַלֵּךְ; ptc. מְהַלֵּךְ, מְהַלְּכִים—**1. go, walk, go about,** of Y. Ps 104$_3$, human 1 K 21$_{27}$, animals Lm 5$_{18}$, ships Ps 104$_{26}$, righteousness Ps 85$_{14}$. **2. flow,** of spring Ps 104$_{10}$.

Hi. $_{46.0.1}$ Pf. הוֹלִיךְ; impf. יוֹלִיךְ (יוֹלֵךְ); + waw וַיֹּלֶךְ (וַיּוֹלִכֵנִי, וַיֹּלַךְ); impv. הוֹלֵךְ, הֵילִיכִי (Ex 2$_9$), הֹלִיכוּ; ptc. מוֹלִיךְ, מוֹלִכוֹת; inf. הֹלִיכוֹ—**1. lead, bring, take** someone Dt 8$_2$ 2 K 6$_{19}$. **2. bring, take, carry** child Ex 2$_9$, object Zc 5$_{10}$, utterance Ec 10$_{20}$, shame 2 S 13$_{13}$. **3. cause to walk** upright (קוֹמְמִיּוּת) Lv 26$_{13}$, **cause** arm **to go** Is 63$_{12}$, **cause** sea **to go back** Ex 14$_{21}$, **cause** river **to flow** Ezk 32$_{14}$. Preps.: לְ *at* right hand Is 63$_{12}$; בְּ *in, through* steppe Dt 8$_2$, land Jos 24$_3$; אֶל *to* person 2 K 6$_{19}$, place Ezk 43$_1$.

Htp. $_{64.2.81}$ Pf. הִתְהַלַּכְתִּי; impf. יִתְהַלֵּךְ (יִתְהַלֶּךְ־, יִתְהַלָּךְ); + waw וַיִּתְהַלֵּךְ; impv. הִתְהַלֵּךְ, הִתְהַלְּכוּ; ptc. מִתְהַלֵּךְ, מִתְהַלֶּכֶת, מִתְהַלְּכִים; inf. הִתְהַלֵּךְ (Q לתהלך)—**1. go, walk, go about, go to and fro,** of Y. Gn 3$_8$, Satan Jb 1$_7$, human Gn 13$_{17}$, horses Zc 6$_7$, arrows, i.e. lightning Ps 77$_{18}$. **2. walk, go,** i.e. live in a particular way: with (אֶת) Y. Gn 5$_{22}$; before (לִפְנֵי) Y. in (בְּ) faithfulness 2 K 20$_3$||Is 38$_3$; with (בְּ) integrity of heart Ps 101$_2$, in accordance with (בְּ) statutes 1QS 9$_{12}$. **3. walk before** (לִפְנֵי), i.e. act as leader of 1 S 12$_2$. **4. go down, flow down** smoothly (בְּמֵישָׁרִים), of wine Pr 23$_{31}$.

→ הֵלֶךְ *traveller,* הָלִיךְ *step,* הֲלָכָה *walking,* הֲלִיכָה *going,* מַהֲלָךְ *journey,* מַהֲלֶכֶת *gait,* תַּהֲלֻכָה *procession.*

הֵלֶךְ $_2$ n.m.—cstr. הֵלֶךְ—**1. traveller** 2 S 12$_4$. **2. flowing** of honey 1 S 14$_{26}$. → הלך *go.*

*[הֲלָכָה] $_{0.0.1}$ n.f. **walking,** הלכת תמים *walking of,* i.e. in, *perfection* 1QS 3$_9$. → הלך *go.*

*[הֶלְכּוֹס] $_{0.0.1}$ pr.n.m. **Helkos.**

הלל I $_{146.7.73}$ vb.—**Pi.** $_{113.6.63}$ Pf. הִלֵּל, הִלַּלְתִּיךָ; impf. יְהַלֵּל, אֲהַלֵּל (אֲהַלְלָה), יְהַלֶּל־; + waw וַיְהַלְלוּ; impv. הַלְלִי, הַלְלוּ; ptc. מְהַלְלִים; inf. abs. הַלֵּל; cstr. הַלֵּל—**1. praise, extol** Y. Jr 20$_{13}$ 1 C 16$_4$ (לְ of obj.), name of Y. Jl 2$_{26}$; הַלְלוּיָהּ *praise Y.* Ps 106$_1$, vars. הַלְלוּ־יָהּ Ps 104$_{35}$, הַלְלוּ יָהּ Ps 111$_1$. **2. praise** a person Gn 12$_{15}$ (+ אֶל *to*) Si 44$_1$. **3. boast** in (בְּ) Y. Ps 44$_9$; concerning (עַל) desire Ps 10$_3$.

Pu. $_{10.2}$ Pf. הוּלָּלוּ; impf. יְהֻלַּל־; ptc. מְהֻלָּל—**1. be praised, renowned,** of person Pr 12$_8$, city Ezk 26$_{17}$. **2.** ptc. **be praiseworthy,** of Y. Ps 48$_2$, name of Y. Ps 113$_3$.

Htp. $_{23.1.8}$ Impf. יִתְהַלֵּל (יִתְהַלָּל); impv. הִתְהַלְלוּ; ptc. מִתְהַלֵּל, מִתְהַלְלִים; inf. cstr. הִתְהַלֵּל—**1. boast of, glory, gloat** in (בְּ) Y. Ps 34$_3$, name of Y. Ps 105$_3$||1 C 16$_{10}$, image of god Ps 97$_7$, wisdom, might, riches Jr 9$_{22}$. **2. be praised,** of woman Pr 31$_{30}$.

→ הִלּוּל *praise,* מַהֲלָל *praise,* תְּהִלָּה I *praise.*

הלל II $_{4.1}$ vb.—**Pi.** Impf. Si יהלל—**cause face to shine** Si 36$_{27}$(Bmg).

Hi. $_4$ Impf. יָהֵל, תָּהֵל, יָהֵלּוּ; inf. בְּהִלּוֹ—**1. shine,** of lamp Jb 29$_3$, light, i.e. sun Jb 31$_{26}$. **2. cause light to shine,** of stars Is 13$_{10}$, sneezing of Leviathan Jb 41$_{10}$.

→ הֵילֵל *shining one.*

הלל III $_{15.0.5}$ vb.—**Qal** $_{4.0.1}$ Impf. תָּהֹלּוּ; ptc. הוֹלְלִים—**act foolishly, insanely;** perh. **boast** (cf. הלל II htp.) Ps 5$_6$ 73$_3$ 75$_5$.

Poel $_{4.0.1}$ Impf. יְהוֹלֵל; ptc. מְהוֹלְלִי; inf. Q הולל—**1. make foolish, make a fool of** someone Is 44$_{25}$. **2. mock** deeds 1QH 12$_{17}$.

Poal $_1$ Ptc. מְהוֹלָל—**be mad,** of laughter Ec 2$_2$.

Htpo. $_{6.0.3}$ Pf. הִתְהֹלָלוּ; impf. יִתְהוֹלְלוּ (יִתְהֹלָלוּ); + waw וַיִּתְהֹלֵל; impv. הִתְהֹלְלוּ—**1. act like a mad one, feign madness** 1 S 21$_{14}$ Jr 25$_{16}$. **2. dash about madly,** of chariot Jr 46$_9$.

→ הוֹלֵל *madness,* הוֹלֵלוֹת *madness,* תָּהֳלָה *error,* תּוֹלָל II *mocker.*

הִלֵּל $_{2.0.4}$ pr.n.m. **Hillel.**

*[הַלָּלוּ] $_{0.0.3}$ demonstr. pron. (common pl.)—+ object marker תהללו—**these** 5/6ḤevBA 45$_{24}$ 5/6ḤevBA 46$_{4.9}$.

הַלְלוּיָהּ, see הלל I *praise*.

הלם 8 vb.—**Qal** Pf. הָלְמָה; impf. יַהַלְמוּן, יֶהֶלְמֻנִי; ptc. הוֹלֵם; ptc. pass. הֲלוּמֵי—**1. hammer, strike** anvil Is 41_{17}, carvings Ps 74_{6}, person Jg 5_{26} Ps 141_{5}. **2.** without obj., **beat**, of horses' hooves Jg 5_{22}. **3.** pass. **be struck**, i.e. overcome, with wine Is 28_{1}. → הַלְמוּת *hammer*, מַהֲלֻמוֹת *beatings*.

הֲלֹם 12 adv.—**1a. hither** Ex 3_{5} Jg 18_{3}. **b.** הֲלֹם וַהֲלֹם **hither and thither** 1 S 14_{16} (if em. וַהֲלֹם). **2. here** Jg 20_{7}. **3.** עַד־הֲלֹם **thus far** 2 S 7_{18}||1 C 17_{16}.

הֶלֶם 1 pr.n.m. **Helem.**

הַלְמוּת 1 n.f.—cstr. הַלְמוּת—**hammer** Jg 5_{26}. → הלם *hammer*.

הָם 1 pl.n. **Ham.**

הֵם I 237.3.52 pron. **1. they** (masc.), **a.** with verb Gn 14_{24}, ptc. Gn 34_{22}, in nom. cl. Gn 48_{9}; with prefixed prep., כָּהֵם *such as them, the like of them* 2 S 24_{3}. **2.** הָהֵם as demonstr. adj., **those,** בַּיָּמִים הָהֵם *in those days* Gn 6_{4}. → cf. הֵמָּה I *they* (masc.).

*__הֵם__ II 3 part. **behold** Dt $33_{3.17}$. → הֵמָּה II *behold.*

*[הֹם] n.[m.] **discomfiture** Ps 90_{10} (if em. בָּהֶם *in them* to בְּהֹם *in discomfiture*). → המם I *discomfit.*

הַמְּדָתָא 5 pr.n.m. **Hammedatha.**

המה I 34.2.12 vb.—**Qal** 34.2.12 Pf. הָמוּ; impf. יֶהֱמֶה, יֶהֱמוּ (יֶהֱמָיוּן); + waw וַתֶּהֱמִי; ptc. הֹמֶה, הוֹמָה (הֹמִיָּה), הֹמוֹת (הֹמִיּוֹת); inf. הֲמוֹת—**1a. be in tumult, commotion, turmoil, uproar,** of city, people, etc. 1 K 1_{41} Is 17_{12}. **b.** ptc. as noun, **bustling streets** Pr 1_{21}. **2. be boisterous,** of foolish woman Pr 9_{13}, (effects of) strong drink Pr 20_{1}. **3. roar,** of sea and its waves Is 51_{15} Ps 46_{4}. **4. murmur, moan, stir,** of heart, soul, etc. Is 16_{11} Jr 4_{19} Ps 42_{6}, person Ps 55_{18}. **5. make a noise,** i.e. **growl, howl, moan,** etc., as bears Is 59_{11}, doves Ezk 7_{16}, dog Ps 59_{7}. **6. thunder,** of clouds 1QH 11_{13}. **7.** trans., **make dispute noisy,** on the lyre 1QH 13_{29}. → הָמוֹן *tumult*, הֶמְיָה *sound*, הֶמֶה *multitude*.

*[המה] II vb. **waste away,** of bowels Jb 6_{7} (if em. הֵמָּה *they* to הָמָה).

הֵמָּה I 284.1.95. pron. **1. they** (masc.), with verb Jos 1_{15}, ptc. Nm 14_{27}, in nom. cl. Gn 6_{4}; with prefixed prep., לָהֵמָּה *to/for them* Jr 14_{16}; בָּהֵמָּה *in them* Ex 36_{1}, *by (means of) them* Ex 30_{4}; כָּהֵמָּה *like them, such as them* Jr 36_{32}; מֵהֵמָּה *on account of them* Jr 10_{2}, *(more than) them* Ec 12_{12}. **2.** הָהֵמָּה, as demonstr. adj., **those,** הָאֲנָשִׁים הָהֵמָּה *those men* Nm 9_{7}. → cf. הֵם I *they* (masc.).

*__הֵמָּה__ II 2 part. **behold** Ho 6_{7} Ps 48_{6}. → הֵם II *behold.*

[הֶמֶה] 1 n.m.—sf. הֱמֵהֶם—**multitude,** or perh. **tumult,** or **wealth** Ezk 7_{11}. → המה I *make a noise.*

הֲמוּלָּה, see הֲמֻלָּה *roaring.*

הָמוֹן 81.5.53 n.m. (f. at Jb 31_{34})—cstr. הֲמוֹן; sf. הֲמוֹנוֹ; pl. הֲמוֹנִים; cstr. Q המוני; sf. הֲמוֹנֶיהָ—**1. tumult, commotion, (up)roar, noise,** made by crowd 1 S 14_{19} Is 17_{12}, songs Ezk 26_{13}, rain 1 K 18_{41}, chariot wheels Jr 47_{3}. **2. multitude, crowd** Gn 17_{4}; of army Jg 4_{7}. **3. abundance, wealth** Is 60_{5} Ezk 29_{19}; **abundance** of compassion 1QH 12_{36}. → המה I *make a noise.*

הֲמוֹנָה 1 pl.n. **Hamonah.**

*[הֲמוּתָה] n.f. **faithfulness** Ps 116_{15} (if em. הַמָּוְתָה *[?] the death*). → אמן *be trustworthy.*

[הֶמְיָה] 1 n.f.—cstr. הֶמְיַת—**1. sound, music** of harp; or perh. **multitude, stream,** of corpses Is 14_{11}. **2. wailing** of child Pr 19_{18} (if em. הֲמִיתוֹ *putting him to death* to הֶמְיָתוֹ *his wailing*). **3.** pl. **riotous places** Pr 1_{21} (if em. הֹמִיּוֹת *bustling streets* to הֶמְיוֹת). → המה I *make a noise.*

*[הֶמְיָה] n.f. **whimpering** Pr 19_{18} (if em. הֲמִיתוֹ *his killing* to הֶמְיָתוֹ *his whimpering*).

*[הָמִיר] 1 n.[m.] **throat,** הָמִיר אֶרֶץ *throat of the underworld* Ps 46_{3}.

הֲמֻלָּה 2 n.f.—הֲמוּלָּה—**roaring,** of tree being set on fire Jr 11_{16}, beating of wings compared with noise of crowd Ezk 1_{24}.

המם I 13.1.1 vb. (byform of הום)—**Qal** 13.1.1 Pf. Qr הֲמָמַנִי; impf. תְּהֻמֵּם; + waw וַיָּהָם, וַהֲמֹּתִי; Qr וַיָּהֹם; inf. הֻמָּם—**1. discomfit, rout, confuse** army, etc., subj. Y. Ex 14_{24} Dt 2_{15} (+ מִקֶּרֶב *from among*) Jos 10_{10} (+ לִפְנֵי *before*), human Jr 51_{34}. **2. drive** cart wheel in threshing, or perh. intrans. **move noisily,** of wheel Is 28_{28}. → הֹם *discomfiture.*

*__המם__ II 1 vb.—**Qal** 1 Pf. Qr הֲמָמַנִי—**drain, suck out** Jr 51_{34}.

המן 1 vb.—**Qal** 1 Inf. הֲמָנְכֶם—**be turbulent, rage** Ezk 5_{7}.

הָמָן 54 pr.n.m. **Haman.**

*[המס] vb. **cogitate** Jb 21₂₇ (if em. תַּחְמֹסוּ *you wrong* to תַּהְמֹסוּ).

[הֶמֶס] 1 n.[m.]—pl. הֲמָסִים—**brushwood** Is 64₁.

*[הַמָּרָה] n.f. **snarling,** וּבְהַמְּרוֹתָם תִּלְאֶין עֵינָי *and my eyes are wearied by their snarling* Jb 17₂ (if em. תָּלַן עֵינִי *my eye dwells*).

*[הֲמֹרָה] n.f. **slime-pit** Jb 17₂ (if em. וּבְהַמְּרוֹתָם *[?] and by their bitterness* [מרה hi. inf.] to וּבְהֲמֹרוֹתָם *and in the twin slime-pits*).

הֵן I 99.1.4.2 interj.—**behold,** with pf. verb Gn 3₂₂, impf. verb Gn 30₃₄, nom. cl. Gn 27₁₁; sometimes **if,** esp. when clause introduced by הֵן is followed by question functioning as apodosis of conditional sentence Ex 8₂₂ Jr 2₁₀ Hg 2₁₂; appar. **all right,** i.e. I accept what you say Gn 30₃₄. → cf. הִנֵּה *behold.*

[הֵן] II 20 pron.—**they** (fem.), only with prefixed prep., לָהֵן *on account of them* Ru 1₁₃ (unless *therefore*); בָּהֵן *in them* Gn 19₂₉, *by (means of), with them* Lv 11₂₁, *(in exchange) for them* Gn 30₂₉; כָּהֵן *the like of them, such things* Ezk 18₁₄, מֵהֵן *more than they* Ezk 16₄₇. → cf. הֵנָּה I *they* (fem.).

*הנה 0.1.1 vb.—**Ni.** 0.1.1 Impf. Q יהנו; ptc. Si נהנה—**enjoy, profit from** Si 30₁₉ Mur 22 1₆.

הֵנָּה I 49.0.2 pron.—**1. they** (fem.), **these,** with verb Gn 33₆, in nom. cl. Gn 41₂₆; with prefixed prep., כָּהֵנָּה *things like this, such things* Gn 41₁₉; אַחַת מֵהֵנָּה *one of them* Lv 4₂. **2.** as demonstr. adj., **these,** מְעַט הַצֹּאן הָהֵנָּה *these few sheep* 1 S 17₂₈. → cf. הֵן II *they* (fem.).

הֵנָּה II 50.1.5. adv. **here, hither** Gn 15₁₆ Jos 2₂ Pr 25₇; הֵנָּה וְהֵנָּה *hither and thither* Jos 8₂₀, מִמְּךָ וָהֵנָּה *from you and over there,* i.e. on this side of you 1 S 20₂₁, דֶּרֶךְ הֵנָּה *the way of here,* i.e. in this direction Jr 50₅, עַד־הֵנָּה *up to here, thus far* (in place or time) Gn 15₁₆ 2 K 8₇.

הִנֵּה 1057.0.35.5 interj.—sf. הִנְנִי (הִנֶּנִּי), הִנּוֹ, הִנָּם—**1.** without pronom. sf., **a.** usu. **behold,** followed by verb Gn 1₂₉, noun or pron. as subj. of ptc. Gn 24₁₅ 25₃₂, nom. cl. Gn 16₆. **b.** followed by noun, **there is, there was, there will be,** etc. Gn 8₁₁ 18₁₀ 24₆₃, **here is, here are** Gn 12₁₉ 22₇; and even, in place of suffixed form, **I am, he is, they are,** etc. Gn 18₉ 24₃₀ 1 K 21₁₈. **c. if, when** clause introduced by הִנֵּה is followed by question functioning as apodosis of conditional sentence Ex 3₁₃ Dt 13₁₅. **d. when,** when following clause is introduced by waw consec. 1 K 20₃₆. **2.** with pronom. suffix, **a. behold,** the suffix providing subj. of a following ptc. Gn 6₁₃ 20₃, pass. ptc. Jos 7₂₁, pred. adj. Gn 16₁₁, nom. cl. Gn 44₁₆. **b. here am I, here we are,** esp. in response to a call Gn 22₁ 1 S 3₄. → cf. הֵן I *behold.*

הֲנָחָה 1 n.f. **giving of rest,** i.e. **remission of taxes** or **holiday** Est 2₁₈. → נוח I *rest.*

*[הֲנִיפָה] 0.0.1 n.f. **waving,** יום הניפת העומר *day of the waving of the omer* 11QT 18₁₀. → נוף I hi. *wave.*

הִנֹּם, see גֵּיא בֶן־הִנֹּם *Valley of Ben-hinnom.*

*[הֲנָמַי] 0.0.0.1 pr.n.m. **Hanamai.**

הֵנַע 3 pl.n. **Hena.**

*[הֵנֶף] 0.0.11 n.[m.] **waving,** הנף העמר *waving of the sheaf* 4QCalMishA 4.4₈. → נוף I hi. *wave.*

הֲנָפָה, see נוף I hi. *wave.*

הַס 6 interj.—הָס—**hush!, be silent!** Jg 3₁₉; הַס מִפְּנֵי *be silent before* Y. Zp 1₇. → הסה *be silent.*

הסה 2.0.1 vb.—**Pi.** 1 Impv. הַסּוּ—**be silent** Ne 8₁₁.

Hi. 1.0.1 + waw וַיַּהַס; inf. Q להס—**1. silence** people Nm 13₃₀. **2. be silent** 1QH 18₁₅.

→ הַס *be silent!*

הָסוּרִים, see אסר *bind.*

[הֲפֻגָה] 1 n.f.—pl. הֲפֻגוֹת—**cessation, respite,** for weeping of eye Lm 3₄₉. → פוג *grow numb.*

*[הפה] vb.—**Pu., be counted as fair,** of hateful words Si 13₂₂ (מ[ה]ופין).

הפך 94.13.18 vb.—**Qal** 55.7.10 Pf. הָפַךְ, הֲפַכְתֶּם; impf. יַהֲפֹךְ, אֶהֱפֹךְ, יַהַפְכוּ; + waw וַיַּהֲפֹךְ (וַיַּהֲפָךְ־, וַיַּהַפְכֵהוּ); impv. הֲפֹךְ; ptc. הֹפֵךְ, הֹפְכִים; pass. ptc. הֲפוּכָה, Si הפוכות; inf. abs. הָפוֹךְ; cstr. הֲפֹךְ (הָפְכִּי, הַפְכָה)—**1a.** trans., **turn, turn round, pervert, subvert** person Si 11₃₃ (+ מִן *from* covenant), back of neck Jos 7₈, hand Lm 3₃, heart 1 S 10₉, wind Ex 10₁₉, tent Jg 7₁₃ (+ לְמַעְלָה *upwards,* i.e. upside down), dish 2 K 21₁₃ (+ עַל־פָּנֶיהָ *on its face,* i.e. upside down), word Jr 23₃₆. **b.** pass. **be turned,** of cake Ho 7₈. **2. turn,** i.e. **change, transform** skin Jr 13₂₃, hair Lv 13₁₀ (+ לָבָן *white*), rock Ps 114₈ (+ אֲגַם *[into a] pool*), יָם *sea* Ps 66₆ (+ לְ *into* dry land), קְלָלָה *curse* Dt 23₆ (+ לְ *into* blessing). **3. overthrow, destroy, devastate** city Gn 19₂₁, land Jb 12₁₅, chariots and riders Hg 2₂₂, the wicked Pr 12₇. **4.** intrans., **turn,**

turn round, turn back, of Y. 4QpsEzek^{b} 1.2$_{6}$ (+ עַל *to* remnant), humans 1 S 25$_{12}$ (+ לְ *to* way) 2 K 5$_{26}$ (+ מֵעַל *from [upon]* chariot). **5.** intrans., **turn,** i.e. **change,** of hair Lv 13$_{3}$ (+ לָבָן *white*).

Ni. $_{34.7.7}$ Pf. נֶהְפַּךְ, נֶהְפְּכוּ (נֶהֶפְכוּ); impf. יֵהָפֵךְ; ptc. נֶהְפָּךְ, נֶהְפֶּכֶת; inf. abs. נַהֲפוֹךְ—**1. turn (oneself),** intrans., **turn back, be turned over (to), come (upon)** someone, of persons Jos 8$_{20}$ (+ אֶל *upon*) Jb 19$_{19}$ (+ בְּ *against*), pain 1 S 4$_{19}$ (+ עַל *upon*), abundance Is 60$_{5}$ (+ עַל *over [to]*), inheritance Lm 5$_{2}$ (+ לְ *to*). **2. turn,** i.e. **change (oneself), be turned,** i.e. **a. be changed,** of Y. Is 63$_{10}$ (+ לְ *into* enemy), hair Lv 13$_{25}$ (+ לָבָן *white*), water Ex 7$_{17}$ (+ לְ *into* blood). **b. be reversed** Est 9$_{1}$. **c. be perverse** Pr 17$_{20}$ (+ בְּ *with* tongue). **3. be turned over, overthrown,** of Nineveh Jon 3$_{4}$. **4.** perh. **be turned,** i.e. **set,** of sapphire Si 35$_{5(\mathrm{Bmg})}$ (+ בְּ *in* chain).

Ho. $_{1}$ Pf. הָהְפַּךְ—**be turned,** of terror Jb 30$_{15}$ (+ עַל *upon* someone).

Htp. $_{4.0.1}$ Impf. תִּתְהַפֵּךְ; ptc. מִתְהַפֵּךְ, מִתְהַפֶּכֶת—**1. turn one way and another, turn over and over,** of sword Gn 3$_{24}$, cloud Jb 37$_{12}$ (+ בְּ *by* guidance); **tumble,** of loaf Jg 7$_{13}$ (+ בְּ *into* camp). **2. transform oneself,** of earth Jb 38$_{14}$ (+ כְּ *as* clay).

→ הֵפֶךְ *the contrary,* הֲפֵכָה *overthrow,* הֲפַכְפַּךְ *crooked,* מַהְפָּךְ *turning,* מַהְפֵּכָה *overthrow,* מַהְפֶּכֶת *stocks,* תַּהְפֻּכֹת *perversity.*

הֵפֶךְ $_{3}$ n.m.—הֵפֶךְ; sf. הַפְכְּכֶם—**1. the contrary, opposite** Ezk 16$_{34}$. **2. perversity,** as exclamation Is 29$_{16}$. → הפך *turn.*

הֲפֵכָה $_{1}$ n.f. **overthrow** Gn 19$_{29}$. → הפך *turn.*

הֲפַכְפַּךְ $_{1}$ adj. **crooked,** of way Pr 21$_{8}$. → הפך *turn.*

*[הֵפֶץ] $_{0.0.1}$ n.[m.] (appar. error for חֵפֶץ)—cstr. הפץ—**pleasure, will** 1QS 6$_{11}$.

[הצל] MurEpBarC^{a}4, see אֵצֶל *beside.*

הַצָּלָה $_{1}$ n.f. **deliverance** Est 4$_{14}$. → נצל hi. *deliver.*

*[הִצִּלְיָהוּ] $_{0.0.0.12}$ pr.n.m. **Hizziliah.**

הַצְלֶלְפּוֹנִי $_{1}$ pr.n.f. **Hazzelelponi.**

הֹצֶן $_{1}$ n.[m.] perh. **arms, weapons** Ezk 23$_{24}$.

הַקּוֹץ $_{3}$ pr.n.m. **Hakkoz.**

הַקָּטָן $_{1}$ pr.n.m. **Hakkatan.**

הַר I $_{559.4.33.1}$ n.m.—בָּהָר/בְּ, + ה- of direction הָהָרָה (הֶרָה Gn 14$_{10}$); cstr. הַר; sf. הַרְרִי (הֲרָרִי), הַרְכֶם, הַרְרָם; pl. הָרִים; cstr. הָרֵי (הַרְרֵי); sf. הָרַי, הָרָיו, הֲרָרֶיהָ—**1. mountain, hill** Gn 22$_{2}$ Ex 3$_{12}$; הַר י׳ *mountain of Y.* Gn 22$_{14}$, הַקֹּדֶשׁ *of holiness,* i.e. holy mountain Is 27$_{13}$; oft. of particular mountains, הַר סִינַי *Mount* (lit. 'mountain of') *Sinai* Ex 19$_{11}$, הַר צִיּוֹן *Mount Zion* 2 K 19$_{31}$, הֹר הָהָר *Mount Hor,* lit. 'Hor the mountain' Nm 20$_{22}$. **2a.** sg., **hill-country, mountainous region** Nm 13$_{17}$ Jos 13$_{6}$; of Judah Jos 21$_{11}$, Gilead Gn 31$_{21}$, Seir Gn 36$_{8}$. **b.** pl., **mountains, hills** of Judah 2 C 21$_{11}$, Samaria Jr 31$_{5}$.

*[הַר] II $_{1}$ n.[f.]—pl. cstr. הָרוֹת—**stony tract, plain** Am 1$_{13}$.

הֹר $_{12}$ pl.n. **Hor.**

הָרָא $_{1}$ pl.n. **Hara.**

הַרְאֵל, see אֲרִיאֵל III *altar hearth.*

הַרְבֵּה *much, many,* see רבה I, hi. §6.

*__הָרַבָּה__ $_{1}$ pl.n. **Harabbah.**

הרג $_{167.1.14}$ vb.—**Qal** $_{162.1.13}$ Pf. הָרַג, הָרַגְתִּי; impf. יַהֲרֹג (יַהַרְגֵנִי, יַהֲרָג־), אֶהֱרֹג (אֶהַרְגָה); + waw וַיַּהַרְגֵהוּ, וָאֶהֶרְגֵהוּ; impv. הֲרֹג (הָרְגֵנִי), הִרְגוּ (הַרְגוּ); ptc. הֹרֵג; ptc. pass. הֲרוּגִים, הֲרֻגֶיהָ; inf. abs. הָרֹג; cstr. הֲרֹג (הָרְגֵנִי, הָרְגָךְ, הָרְגוֹ)—**1. kill, slay,** in murder, assassination, etc. Gn 4$_{8}$ Jg 9$_{5}$, oft. as retribution, punishment Ex 2$_{15}$ 2 S 3$_{30}$ (לְ of obj.), in judicial punishment Lv 20$_{16}$, in battle, conquest Jos 8$_{24}$ 2 K 8$_{12}$; of Y. killing, usu. in punishment, judgment Gn 20$_{4}$ Ex 4$_{23}$ Am 2$_{3}$; of killing by animals 2 K 17$_{25}$ Jb 20$_{16}$; of killing animals Lv 20$_{15}$ Nm 22$_{29}$, destruction of vines in storm Ps 78$_{47}$. **2.** pass. ptc. as noun, **slain one** Is 10$_{4}$ Ezk 37$_{9}$.

Ni. $_{3.0.1}$ Impf. יֵהָרֵג, תֵּהָרַגְנָה; inf. בֵּהָרֵג—**be killed, slain** Ezk 26$_{6.15}$ Lm 2$_{20}$.

Pu. $_{2}$ Pf. הֹרַג, הֹרַגְנוּ—**be killed, slain** Is 27$_{7}$ Ps 44$_{23}$.

→ הֶרֶג *slaughter,* הֲרֵגָה *slaughter.*

הֶרֶג $_{5}$ n.m.—cstr. הֶרֶג—**slaughter** Is 27$_{7}$ 30$_{25}$. → הרג *kill.*

הֲרֵגָה $_{5.0.1}$ n.f. **slaughter** Jr 7$_{32}$ 12$_{3}$. → הרג *kill.*

הרה $_{43.0.3}$ vb.—**Qal** $_{41.0.3}$ Pf. הָרִיתִי; impf. תַּהֲרוּ; + waw וַתַּהַר, וַתַּהֲרֶין; ptc. הוֹרִי, הוֹרָתִי; inf. abs. הָרֹה (הָרוֹ)—**1. conceive, be(come) pregnant** Gn 4$_{1}$ 38$_{18}$ (+ לְ *by*) 19$_{36}$ (+ מִן *by*). **2.** with obj., **conceive, be pregnant with** a child Nm 11$_{12}$ Ho 2$_{7}$, chaff Is 33$_{11}$, trouble Is 59$_{4}$; חֶדֶר הוֹרָתִי *chamber of her who conceived me* Ca 3$_{4}$.

Pu. 1 Pf. הֹרָה—**be conceived** Jb 3_{3}.

Po. 1 Inf. abs. הֹרוֹ—**conceive, devise** words Is 59_{13} (but perh. Qal pass. *be conceived, devised*).

→ הָרָה *pregnant*, הֵרוֹן I *pregnancy*, הֵרָיוֹן *conception*.

[הָרֶה] 15.0.8 adj.—f.s. הָרָה (Q הריה), cstr. הָרַת (Q הרית); f.pl. cstr. הָרוֹת; sf. הָרוֹתֶיהָ, הָרִיּוֹתָיו—**1. pregnant,** of אִשָּׁה *woman* Ex 21_{22}, הָעַלְמָה *young woman* Is 7_{14}; לְאִישׁ ... אָנֹכִי הָרָה *... I am pregnant ... by (the) man* Gn 38_{25}. **2.** as noun, **pregnant (one),** הָרוֹת הַגִּלְעָד *pregnant ones of Gilead* Am 1_{13}, הרית גבר *pregnant one of,* i.e. with/by, *man* 1QH 11_{9}, כור הריה *crucible,* i.e. womb, *of (the) pregnant one* 1QH 11_{8}. → הרה *conceive*.

*[הֵרוֹדִיס] 0.0.3 pl.n. **Herodium.**

הָרוּם 1 pr.n.m. **Harum.**

*[הֵרוֹן] 1 n.[m.]—sf. הֵרֹנֵךְ—**(sexual) desire** Gn 3_{16}. → הרר *desire*.

[הֵרוֹן] I 1 n.[m.]—sf. הֵרֹנֵךְ—**pregnancy** Gn 3_{16}. → הרה *conceive*.

*[הֵרוֹן] II 1 n.[m.]—sf. הֵרֹנֵךְ—**trembling** Gn 3_{16}.

הֲרֹרִי 1 gent. **Harorite.**

הַר־חֶרֶס 1 pl.n. **Har-heres.**

[הָרִיָּה], see הָרָה *pregnant*.

*[הַרְיָהוּ] 0.0.0.1 pr.n.m. **Hariah.**

הֵרָיוֹן 2 n.[m.]—sf. Sam הֵרָיוֹנֵךְ—**conception** Gn $3_{16(Sam)}$ Ho 9_{11} Ru 4_{13}. → הרה *conceive*.

[הֲרִיסָה] 1.1 n.f.—pl. sf. הֲרִסֹתָיו—**ruin** Am 9_{11} Si 49_{13}. → הרס *tear down*.

[הֲרִיסוּת] 1 n.f.—sf. הֲרִסֻתֵךְ—**overthrow, ruin** Is 49_{19}. → הרס *tear down*.

הָרָם Jos 13_{27}, see בַּיִת *house*.

הֹרָם 1 pr.n.m. **Horam.**

[הַרְמוֹן] 1 n.[m.]—+ ה- of direction הַרְמוֹנָה—**high place** (or pl.n. **Harmon**) Am 4_{3}.

הָרַמִּים 2 C 22_{5}, see אֲרַמִּי *Aramaean*.

הָרָן 7 pr.n.m. **Haran.**

*[הֵרֶן] n.[m.] **pledge** Jb 34_{32} (if em. הֹרֵנִי *teach me* to הֵרְנִי *my pledge*).

הרס 43.1.1 vb.—**Qal** 30.1 Pf. הָרַס; impf. יֶהֱרֹס (יֶהֶרְסֵם), (יֶהֶרְסוֹ) יֶהֶרְסוּ, אֶהֱרֹס; impv. הֲרֹס־ (הָרְסָה); ptc. הֹרֵס; ptc. pass. הָרוּס; inf. הֲרֹס—**1. tear down, break down, break away, overthrow** Israelites Jr 24_{6}, person Is 22_{19} (+ מִן *from* office), city 2 S 11_{25}, altar Jg 6_{25}, walls Ezk 26_{12}. **2. break** teeth in mouth Ps 58_{7}. **3.** intrans., **break through** Ex $19_{21.24}$.

Ni. 10 Pf. נֶהֶרְסוּ, נֶהֱרָסָה; impf. יֵהָרֵס; ptc. נֶהֱרָסוֹת—**be torn down, overthrown,** of mountains Ezk 38_{20}, cities Ezk 36_{35}, foundations Ezk 30_{4}.

Pi. 3 תְּהָרְסֵם; ptc. מְהָרְסַיִךְ; inf. abs. הָרֵס—**tear down, overthrow** Israel Is 49_{17}, (images of) gods Ex 23_{24}.

→ הֶרֶס *destruction*, הֲרִיסָה *ruin*, הֲרִיסוּת *overthrow*.

הֶרֶס 1 n.[m.] **destruction,** עִיר הַהֶרֶס *city of destruction* Is 19_{18} (mss, 1QIsa^{a} הַחֶרֶס *of the sun*, perh. Heliopolis). → הרס *tear down*.

*[הֻרְקָנוֹס] 0.0.1 pr.n.m. **Hyrcanus.**

*[הרר] vb. **Pi., desire** Ps 76_{5} (if em. מֵהַרְרֵי *than the mountains of* to מְהֹרְרֵי *those who lusted after*).

Hi., desire Ps 68_{17} (if em. הָהָר *the mountain* to הֶהֱר *which he desired*).

הֲרָרִי 5 gent. **Hararite.**

הָשֵׁם 1 pr.n.m. **Hashem.**

[הַשְׁמָעוּת] 1 n.f.—**causing to hear,** הַשְׁמָעוּת אָזְנַיִם *causing of ears to hear,* by bringing news Ezk 24_{26}. → שׁמע *hear*.

הָשְׁפּוֹת Ne 3_{13}, see אַשְׁפֹּת *refuse heap*.

*[הִשְׁתַּחֲוֹת] 0.0.0.1 n.f.pl. (or htpal. inf. of שׁחה)—**prostration,** for prayer CD 11_{22}. → שׁחה htpal. *prostrate oneself*.

*[הִשְׁתַּעֲנוּת] 0.1 n.f. **support** Si $44_{8(B)}$. → שׁען *support oneself*.

[הִתּוּךְ] 1 n.[m.]—cstr. הִתּוּךְ—**melting** Ezk 22_{22}. → נתך *pour out*.

הִתְחַבְּרוּת 1 n.f. (or htp. inf. of חבר)—**making an alliance** Dn 11_{23}. → חבר I *be joined*.

הֲתָךְ 4 pr.n.m. **Hathach.**

התל 1.2 vb.—**Pi.** 1.2 + waw וַיְהַתֵּל—**mock,** with בְּ of obj. 1 K 18_{27} Si 11_{4} 13_{7}. → הֲתֻלִּים *mockery*, מַהֲתַלָּה *deception*; מְהוֹתָלָה *deception*; cf. תלל I *mock*.

הֲתֻלִים 1 n.[m.]pl. **mockery** Jb 17_{2}. → התל *mock*.

ו

וְ I $_{51035.1575.c.10000.c.160}$ conj.—וּ (before a consonant other than ׳ vocalized with simple shewa, and before ב, ו, and מ with any vowel; exceptions include -וְיְ [not -וּיְ], וָ/וֶ/וַ ,(וֶחְיֵה ,וֶהְיֵה) (before consonants with composite shewa), וָ (sometimes before stress-bearing syllable), וַ (before impf. waw consec. forms, oft. with dagesh in first consonant of verb), וֵאלֹהִים ,וַאדֹנָי etc., וִהְיִיתֶם ,וַי״ etc.—**1a. and,** conjoining two nouns, verbs, etc., בָּרָא אֱלֹהִים אֵת הַשָּׁמַיִם וְאֵת הָאָרֶץ *God created the heavens and the earth* Gn 1_{1}, עָפָר וָאֵפֶר *dust and ashes* Gn 18_{27}, חֲגֹר … וְקַח *gird … and take* 2 K 9_{1}. **b.** in lists, between each word or phrase, צָפֹנָה וָנֶגְבָּה וָקֵדְמָה וָיָמָּה *northward and southward and eastward and westward* Gn 13_{14}. **c.** in lists, before the last item(s), בַּמִּקְנֶה בַּכֶּסֶף וּבַזָּהָב *in cattle, in silver, and in gold* Gn 13_{2}. **d.** וְ … וְ **both … and,** וְקֹר וָחֹם וְקַיִץ וָחֹרֶף וְיוֹם וָלַיְלָה *both cold and heat, both summer and winter, both day and night* Gn 8_{22}. **e. upon, after,** linking repeated nouns in distributive structures, דּוֹר־וָדוֹר *generation after generation,* i.e. each generation Dt 32_{7}. **f. and another, and a different,** linking repeated nouns in a non-distributive structure, אֵיפָה וְאֵיפָה גְּדוֹלָה וּקְטַנָּה *one ephah and another ephah, one big and one small* Dt 25_{14}. **g.** linking two words as representative parts of a whole, שָׁלוֹם וָשֶׁקֶט *peace and quiet,* i.e. complete tranquillity 1 C 22_{9}. **h. of,** etc., linking one word to another in a modifying role, חֶסֶד וֶאֱמֶת *loyalty of truth,* i.e. genuine loyalty Gn 24_{49}, וַיְנַסּוּ וַיַּמְרוּ *and they tested and rebelled,* i.e. they rebelliously tested Ps 78_{56}. **2.** disjunctive, **or,** מַכֵּה אָבִיו וְאִמּוֹ *one who strikes father or mother* Ex 21_{15}. **3. together with, in the company of,** הָאִשָּׁה וִילָדֶיהָ תִּהְיֶה לַאדֹנֶיהָ *the woman with her children will belong to her lord* Ex 21_{4}. **4. but, on the contrary,** הוּא יְשׁוּפְךָ רֹאשׁ וְאַתָּה תְּשׁוּפֶנּוּ עָקֵב *he will crush you (in your) head but you will crush him (in his) heel* Gn 3_{15}. **5.** perh. **and especially, in particular,** מִכַּף כָּל־אֹיְבָיו וּמִכַּף שָׁאוּל *from the hand of all his enemies, and especially from the hand of Saul* 2 S 22_{1}||Ps $18_{1(mss)}$. **6.** explanatory, **that is,** בִּכְלִי הָרֹעִים אֲשֶׁר־לוֹ וּבַיַּלְקוּט *into the shepherd's instrument he had with him, that is, into the pouch* 1 S 17_{40}, אַלְמָנָה אָנִי וַיָּמָת אִישִׁי *I am a widow—(that is) my husband has died* 2 S 14_{5}. **7. (and, but) as for,** וְאַתֶּם לֹא־עָמַד אִישׁ בִּפְנֵיכֶם *(and) as for you, no man could stand against you* Jos 23_{9}. **8. so, in that case,** וַתֹּאמַרְןָ אִישׁ מִצְרִי הִצִּילָנוּ … : וַיֹּאמֶר … וְאַיּוֹ *and they said, An Egyptian man saved us … And he said …, So where is he?* Ex 2_{19}. **9. when, even though,** הוֹאַלְתִּי לְדַבֵּר … וְאָנֹכִי עָפָר וָאֵפֶר *I have undertaken to speak … even though I am dust and ashes* Gn 18_{27}. **10. for, because,** הָבָה־לָּנוּ עֶזְרָת מִצָּר וְשָׁוְא תְּשׁוּעַת אָדָם *give us help from (the) adversary, for vain is the salvation of human beings* Ps 60_{13}. **11. (so) that,** הֶרֶף וְאַגִּידָה לְּךָ *stop, that I might tell you* 1 S 15_{16}. **12. likewise, just as, just like** (sometimes with ellip. of verb), הַדֶּלֶת תִּסּוֹב עַל־צִירָהּ וְעָצֵל עַל־מִטָּתוֹ *the door turns on its hinge just like the idler on his bed* Pr 26_{14}. **13a. waw** consecutive or conversive, typically prefixed to pf. following impf. without וְ, or to an impf. following a pf. without וְ (although waw consec. with impf. oft. introduces a new narrative unit), וַיֹּאמֶר אֱלֹהִים יְהִי אוֹר וַיְהִי אוֹר *and God said, Let there be light, and there was light* Gn 1_{3}, וְאֵד יַעֲלֶה מִן־הָאָרֶץ וְהִשְׁקָה *and a mist used to go up from the earth and would water* the earth's surface Gn 2_{6}, כִּי־שָׁמַעְתָּ לְקוֹל אִשְׁתֶּךָ וַתֹּאכַל *because you have listened to the voice of your wife and eaten* Gn 3_{17}. **b. then,** in conditional and other sentences, אִם־אֶמְצָא … וְנָשָׂאתִי *if I find … then I shall forgive* Gn 18_{26}, אִם־יָשַׁבְנוּ פֹה וָמָתְנוּ *if we stay here, then we shall die* 2 K 7_{4}. **14. if,** וְיֵשׁ י״ עִמָּנוּ *if Y. is with us* Jg 6_{13}. **15.** appar. used redundantly, עֶרֶב וִידַעְתֶּם *by evening (and) you shall know* Ex 16_{6}. **16.** oft. **now, now then,** introducing new topic or new aspect of current topic, וְשָׂרַי אֵשֶׁת אַבְרָם לֹא יָלְדָה לוֹ *now Sarai, Abram's wife had borne him no children* Gn 16_{1}.

ו

*וְ II 1 voc. part.—O, וְאֵל אֲדֹנָי אֶתְחַנָּן *O El, my Lord, I plead for mercy* Ps 30₉ (if em. וְאֶל *and to*).

וְדָן 1 pl.n. **Vedan.**

וָהֵב 1 pl.n. **Waheb.**

[וָו] 13 n.[m.]—pl. וָוִים; cstr. וָוֵי; sf. וָוֵיהֶם—**hook,** or, **nail,** in tent of meeting Ex 26₃₂.

*וזן 2 vb.—**Hi.** 2 Impf. אָזִין; ptc. מֵזִין—**weigh up, ponder on,** שֶׁקֶר מֵזִין עַל־לְשׁוֹן הַוֹּת *(?) a lie ponders on a tongue of evil words* Pr 17₄, אָזִין עַד־תְּבוּנֹתֵיכֶם *I pondered on your wise sayings* Jb 32₁₁.

וָזָר 1 adj. **guilty**—אִישׁ וָזָר *a guilty man* Pr 21₈.

וַיְזָתָא 1 pr.n.m. **Vaizatha.**

וָלָד 1.0.2 n.[m.]—**1. child** Gn 11₃₀. **2. foetus** of animal 4QMMT B36.37. → ילד *give birth.*

וַנְיָה 1 pr.n.m. **Vaniah.**

וָפְסִי 1 pr.n.m. **Vophsi.**

*[ושׁב] vb. **Qal, dwell,** וְשַׁבְתִּי בְּבֵית־י׳ *I shall dwell in the house of Y.* Ps 23₆ (if em. וְשַׁבְתִּי *and I shall return* to).

וַשְׁנִי 1 pr.n.m. **Vashni.**

וַשְׁתִּי 10 pr.n.f. **Vashti.**

*[וָתִיק] 0.1 adj. **experienced,** איש ותיק *an experienced man* Si 36₂₅.

ז

זְאֵב I 7.2.1 n.m.—Q זב; pl. זְאֵבִים; cstr. זְאֵבֵי—**wolf,** זְאֵב עֲרָבוֹת *wolf of [the] steppe(s)* Jr 5₆.

זְאֵב II 6 pr.n.m. **Zeeb.**

זֹאת 600.4.67.4 demonstr. pron. sg. f. & adj.—Kt זאתה, Q זואת, זאות, זות—**1.** as pred. adj. or pron., **this (one),** זֹאת אִשְׁתּוֹ *this is his wife* Gn 12₁₂, also **such (a one)** Is 23₇, oft. with neuter or indeterminate ref., esp. in מַה־זֹּאת עָשִׂית *what is this you have done?* Gn 3₁₃; also **the other (one),** וְזֹאת אֹמֶרֶת *but the other one said...* 1 K 3₂₆; in ref. to time, **at that time, then,** וַיְחִי אִיּוֹב אַחֲרֵי־זֹאת מֵאָה וְאַרְבָּעִים שָׁנָה *and afterwards, Job lived one hundred and forty years* Jb 42₁₆. **2.** as attrib. adj., **this,** הַמִּשְׁפָּחָה הַזֹּאת *this clan* Mc 2₃. **3.** as adv., **thus,** נִקְּפוּ זֹאת *they will strike off,* perh. flay, *thus* Jb 19₂₆.

זבד 1.1 vb.—**Qal** 1.1 Pf. זְבָדַנִי; impv. Si זבדה—**1.** with double accus., **endow** someone **with, give** someone **a gift** (זֵבֶד) Gn 30₂₅. **2. give** one's daughter to (אֶל) a man ([ג]בר) Si 7₂₅(C). → זֵבֶד *gift.*

זָבָד 8 pr.n.m. **Zabad.**

זֵבֶד 1.2 n.m. **gift** Gn 30₂₀. → זבד *endow.*

זַבְדִּי 7 pr.n.m. **Zabdi.**

זַבְדִּיאֵל 2 pr.n.m. **Zabdiel.**

זְבַדְיָה 9.0.0.1 pr.n.m. **Zebadiah.**

זְבַדְיָהוּ, see זְבַדְיָה *Zebadiah.*

[זְבַדְיוֹ], see זְבַדְיָה *Zebadiah.*

זְבוּב 2 n.m.—pl. cstr. זְבוּבֵי—**fly** Ec 10₁.

זָבוּד 2 pr.n.m. **Zabud.**

זְבוּדָּה 1 pr.n.f. **Zebuddah.**

[זְבוּל], see זְבֻל I *dwelling place,* II *dais.*

[זְבוּלוּן], see זְבוּלֻן *Zebulun.*

זְבוּלֻן 45.0.3 pr.n.m. **Zebulun.**

זְבוּלֹנִי 3 gent. **Zebulunite.**

זבח 134.0.27 vb.—**Qal** 112.0.25 Pf. זָבַחְתִּי, זָבַח; impf. תִּזְבַּח; impv. זְבַח, זִבְחוּ; ptc. זֹבֵחַ, זֹבְחִים; inf. זְבֹחַ (זְבֹחַ)—**1a. offer a sacrifice** (זֶבַח) Gn 31₅₄, peace offerings Dt 27₇, thanksgiving Ps 50₁₄. **b. offer in sacrifice, slaughter** animal **for sacrifice** Dt 17₁ 1 C 15₂₆. **c.** abs., **offer sacrifice** Ex 3₁₈. Preps.: לְ *to* Y. Dt 17₁, Dagon Jg 16₂₃; לִפְנֵי *before* Y. Lv 9₄. **2. slaughter** beast for non-sacrificial eating 1 S 28₂₄. **3. kill** human being, perh. as sacrifice 1 K 13₂.

Pi. 22.0.2 Pf. זִבַּח; impf. יְזַבֵּחַ; ptc. מְזַבֵּחַ, מְזַבְּחִים; inf. זַבֵּחַ—**1a. offer** a sacrifice to (לְ) Y. 2 C 30₂₂. **b. sacrifice** animal (to Y.) 1 K 8₅||2 C 5₆. **c.** abs., **offer sacrifice** to (לְ) non-Israelite gods 1 K 11₈. **2.** appar. **capture for sacrifice** by means of (לְ) net Hb 1₁₆.

→ זֶבַח *sacrifice,* מִזְבֵּחַ *altar.*

זֶבַח I 162.1.26 n.m.—sf. זִבְחֲכֶם; pl. זְבָחִים; cstr. זִבְחֵי—**sacrifice, religious offering** in general, oft. defined by assoc. term, זֶבַח־פֶּסַח *sacrifice of passover* Ex 12₂₇,

תּוֹדָה *of thanksgiving* Lv 22$_{29}$, etc., usu. as offered to Y., but also to non-Israelite gods Ex 34$_{15}$ Is 57$_{7}$, **1.** object sacrificed Lv 3$_{1}$. **2.** less oft. act or ceremony of sacrificing 1 S 16$_{3}$. → זבח *sacrifice.*

זֶבַח II $_{12}$ pr.n.m. **Zebah.**

זַבַּי $_{2}$ pr.n.m. **Zabbai.**

[זְבִידָה] $_{1}$ pr.n.f. **Zebidah.**

זְבִינָא $_{1}$ pr.n.m. **Zebina.**

*** [זְבִינוּת]** $_{0.0.1}$ n.f.—זבנות—**purchase** MurEpBeth-Mashiko4.

זבל I $_{1}$ vb.—**Qal** $_{1}$ Impf. יִזְבְּלֵנִי—**exalt, honour** wife Gn 30$_{20}$.

***זבל** II vb. **dwell** Gn 49$_{13}$ (if em. שׁכן *dwell*). → זְבֻל I *dwelling place,* מִזְבָּל *dwelling.*

***זבל** III vb. **Qal, rule (over)** Ob$_{20}$ (if em. גָּלֻת הַחֵל־הַזֶּה לִבְנֵי יִשְׂרָאֵל אֲשֶׁר *the diaspora of this fortress of the sons of Israel, which* to גָּלֻת בְּנֵי יִשְׂרָאֵל אֲשֶׁר בַּחֲלַח יִזְבְּלוּ *the diaspora of the sons of Israel who are in Halah will rule*).

זְבֻל I $_{5.0.8}$ n.[m.]—+ ה- of direction זְבֻלָה—**dwelling place** of Y. 1 K 8$_{13}$||2 C 6$_{2}$ Is 63$_{15}$, sun and moon Hb 3$_{11}$. → זבל II *dwell.*

*** [זְבֻל]** II $_{1}$ n.[m.] **dais,** יָרֵחַ עָמַד זְבֻלֹה *(the) moon stood (on) his dais* Hb 3$_{11}$ (if em. זְבֻלָה *in [its] dwelling place*).

זְבֻל III $_{6}$ pr.n.m. **Zebul.**

זְבֻלוּן, see זְבוּלֻן *Zebulun.*

זָג $_{1}$ n.m. perh. **skin,** or **seed** of grape, or **tip** of vine shoot Nm 6$_{4}$.

זֵד $_{15.4.2}$ adj.—pl. זֵדִים—**1. presumptuous, arrogant, impudent,** of man Jr 43$_{2}$. **2.** as noun, **a. presumptuous one** Ml 3$_{19}$. **b.** perh. **presumptuous deed** or **thought,** i.e. **sin** Ps 19$_{14}$. → זיד *be presumptuous.*

*** [זְדָה]** $_{0.0.0.1}$ n.f. **fissure,** or perh. **overlap, contact, narrowing, turbulence, echo, excitement** Siloam tunnel inscr.3.

זָדוֹן $_{11.11.9}$ n.m.—cstr. זְדוֹן; sf. זְדֹנְךָ—**1. presumptuousness, arrogance, impudence,** זְדוֹן לִבֶּךָ *presumptuousness of your heart* Jr 49$_{16}$. **2. presumptuous person** Jr 50$_{31.32}$. → זיד *be presumptuous.*

זֶה $_{1173.21.193.13}$ demonstr. pron. sg. (sometimes pl.) m. (rarely f.) & adj.—Q זא, I perh. ז—**1.** pred. adj. or pron., **this (one), such (a one),** זֶה סֵפֶר תּוֹלְדֹת אָדָם *this is the record of the generations of Adam* Gn 5$_{1}$, with neuter or indeterminate ref., גַּם־זֶה הָבֶל *this also is vanity* Ec 2$_{19}$; **this place, here,** נָסְעוּ מִזֶּה *they have gone from here* Gn 37$_{17}$. **2.** combined rel. pron. with antecedent, **that which, what, the one(s) who, (s)he who(m), etc.,** רְאֵה זֶה מָצָאתִי *see what I have found* Ec 7$_{27}$. **3.** rel. pron., **that, which,** בְּרִיתִי וְעֵדֹתִי זֶה אֲלַמְּדֵם *my covenant and my testimony, which I shall teach them* Ps 132$_{12}$(Gnz, ms, 11QPs^{a}). **4. one that is of, possessor of, lord of,** י׳ זֶה סִינַי *Y., the lord of Sinai* Jg 5$_{5}$. **5.** attrib. adj., usu. **this,** הָעָם־הַזֶּה *this people* Ex 3$_{21}$, also **such and such, a certain,** דָּוִד בֶּן־אִישׁ אֶפְרָתִי הַזֶּה *David was the son of a certain Ephrathite* 1 S 17$_{12}$, **these,** זֶה יָמִים רַבִּים *these many days* Jos 22$_{3}$. **6.** אֵי־זֶה **whither?, in which direction?** 1 K 22$_{24}$. **7.** אֵי־זֶה **what?** Ec 2$_{3}$, **which?** Ec 11$_{6(L)}$. **8.** אֵי־מִזֶּה **whence?** Gn 16$_{8}$. **9.** אֵי־מִזֶּה **from which?** 2 S 15$_{2}$. **10.** לָמָּה(־)זֶּה **why?** Ex 2$_{20}$. **11.** מַה־זֶּה usu. **why?** Jg 18$_{24}$, perh. also **what?** 1 S 10$_{11}$, **how?** Gn 27$_{20}$. **12.** מִזֶּה ... וּמִזֶּה **over here ... and over there, on this side ... and on that side** Nm 22$_{24}$. → cf. זוֹ *this,* הַלָּז *that,* הַלָּזֶה *that,* הַלֵּזוּ *that.*

זֹה $_{11.1}$ demonstr. pron. sg. f. **this (one),** זֹה מַתַּת אֱלֹהִים הִיא *this is a gift of God* Ec 5$_{18}$.

זָהָב I $_{387.10.40.2}$ n.m.—cstr. זְהַב; sf. זְהָבִי—**1. gold,** זָהָב טָהוֹר *pure gold* Ex 25$_{11}$, נֶזֶם זָהָב *(nose) ring of gold* Gn 24$_{22}$, כִּכַּר *talent of* 2 S 12$_{30}$. **2.** appar. **object made of gold** 1 C 29$_{2b.5b}$.

***זָהָב** II $_{1}$ n.[m.] **spice,** or **incense** Is 60$_{6}$.

*** [זָהִיר]** $_{0.4}$ adj. **1. cautious, prudent** Si 13$_{13}$. **2.** as interj., **beware** Si 11$_{34}$. → זהר I *warn.*

*** [זְהִירָה]** $_{0.1}$ n.f.—sf. זהירתו—**brightness** Si 43$_{8(B)}$. → זהר II *be bright.*

זהל, see זחל *crawl.*

זהם $_{1}$ vb.—**Pi.** $_{1}$ + waw וְזִהֲמַתּוּ—**abhor** bread Jb 33$_{20}$.

[זַהַם] $_{1}$ pr.n.m. **Zaham.**

זהר I $_{21.2.2}$ vb.—**Ni.** $_{8.2.1}$ Pf. נִזְהַר; impv. הִזָּהֵר; ptc. נִזְהָר; inf. הִזָּהֵר—**be warned, be careful** Ec 12$_{12}$.

Hi. $_{13.0.2}$ Pf. הִזְהַרְתָּ; impf. יַזְהִרוּ; inf. הַזְהִיר—**1. warn** someone 2 K 6$_{10}$ Ezk 3$_{18}$ (+ מִן *concerning*). **2.** with double accus., **teach** people statutes Ex 18$_{20}$.

→ זָהִיר *careful.*

זהר II 1.2 vb.—**Qal** 0.1 Ptc. זהרת—**shine,** of sun Si 42$_{16(M)}$ (+ עַל *upon*).

Hi. 1.1 Impf. יַזְהִרוּ; ptc. Si מזהיר—**shine,** of light Si 43$_{9(B)}$, wise one Dn 12$_3$.

→ זֹהַר *brightness,* זְהִירָה *brightness.*

זֹהַר 2.0.2 n.m. **brightness, brilliance, splendour,** זֹהַר הָרָקִיעַ *brightness of the firmament* Dn 12$_3$, זהרי הוד *brilliance of splendour* 4QBer^a 1$_3$. → זהר II *be bright.*

זִו I 2 pr.n.m. **Ziv,** second month of pre-exilic calendar, April/May, corresponding to Babylonian month of Iyyar 1 K 6$_1$.

זִו II, see זִיו II *splendour.*

זוֹ 4.0.0.1 demonstr. pron. sg. f. & adj.—I זוא—**1.** adj., **this,** שְׁבֻעָתֵךְ הַזּוֹ *this oath of yours* Jos 2$_{17}$ (if em. זֶה *this*). **2.** pron., **this (one),** זוֹ מַתַּת אֱלֹהִים הִיא *this is a gift of God* Ec 5$_{18(Gnz)}$. **3.** as rel. pron., **that, which,** בְּרִיתִי וְעֵדֹתִי זוֹ אֲלַמְּדֵם *my covenant and my testimony, which I shall teach them* Ps 132$_{12}$.

זוּ 14.0.3 part. of relation, **1.** relative pron., **which, that, who(m),** עַם־זוּ גָּאָלְתָּ *a people that you redeemed* Ex 15$_{13}$. **2.** combined rel. pron. and antecedent, **that which,** זו כחו לאלהו *that which is his strength (belongs) to his god* Hb 1$_{11}$.

זוב 41.2.9 vb.—**Qal** 40.1.9 Pf. זָב; impf. יָזוּב; ptc. זָב—**1.** of land, **flow, run,** אֶרֶץ זָבַת חָלָב וּדְבָשׁ *a land flowing with milk and honey* Ex 3$_8$. **2.** of water, **flow, gush** Is 48$_{21}$. **3.** of person, **pine away,** because of hunger Lm 4$_9$. **4a. have a discharge,** of woman (menstruation) Lv 15$_{19}$, man (venereal disease) Lv 15$_2$. **b.** ptc. as noun, **one who has a discharge** Lv 15$_{32}$.

Hi. 1.1 Pf. 1QIsa^a הזיב—**cause to flow,** obj. water Is 48$_{21(1QIsa^a)}$, tears Si 38$_{16}$.

→ זוֹב *discharge.*

זוֹב 13.0.8 n.m.—sf. זוֹבָהּ—**discharge,** from man (venereal disease) Lv 15$_2$, woman (menstrual and other bleeding) Lv 15$_{19.25}$. → זוב *flow.*

***זוג** 0.0.1 vb.—**Htp.** 0.0.1 Pf. הזדוגא—appar. **be held together,** of stone 3QTr 10$_9$.

זוד, see זיד *be presumptuous.*

*[**זוּז**] 0.0.3 n.[m.]—pl. זוזין—**zuz,** silver coin worth a quarter of a shekel (tetradrachma), half a half-shekel (didrachma), or six oboli (meah) Mur 30 2$_{21}$ 5/6Ḥev BA 46$_8$; abbrev. ז on weight from Lachish (Weight 13).

[**זוּזִי**] 1 gent. **Zuzite.**

***זוח** I 0.1 vb.—**Qal** 0.1 Impf. תזוח—**be moved, depart,** of person Si 8$_{11}$.

***זוח** II 0.1 vb.—**Qal** 0.1 Impf. תזוח—**be proud** Si 8$_{11}$.

*[**זוֹחֶלְזָלָף**] 0.0.1 perh. pr.n.m. **Zohelzalaph.**

זוֹחֵת 2 pr.n.m. **Zoheth.**

[**זָוִית**] 2 n.f.—pl. זָוִיֹּת—**corner** of altar Zc 9$_{15}$, **cornerstone** Ps 144$_{12}$.

זול I 1 vb.—**Qal** 1 Ptc. זָלִים—**spend** gold Is 46$_6$.

***זול** II vb. **cease** Ho 7$_{16}$ (if em. זוֹ לַעְגָּם *this is their mockery* to וְזָל לַעְגָּם *and their mockery will cease*).

זוּלַת 16.2.11 prep.—זוּלָתִי; sf. זוּלָתְךָ, זוּלָתִי—**apart from,** אֵין־זָר אִתָּנוּ בַּבַּיִת זוּלָתִי שְׁתַּיִם־אֲנַחְנוּ בַּבָּיִת *no stranger was with us in the house apart from the two of us in the house* 1 K 3$_{18}$.

זון 1 vb. **Qal, feed** people, of Y. Jb 36$_{31}$ (if em. דין *judge*).

Ho. 1 Kt Occ מוזנים—**be well fed,** of horse Jr 5$_8$.

→ מָזוֹן *food.*

*[**זוֹנוּת**] 0.0.3 n.f. **fornication,** perh. with ref. to unlawful marriages 4QMMT B$_{75}$. → זנה I *prostitute oneself.*

זוע I 3.3.7 vb.—**Qal** 2.2.2 Pf. זָע; impf. יָזֻעוּ—**1. tremble,** of person Est 5$_9$ (+ מִן *on account of*). **2. flicker,** of eye Si 34$_{13(B)}$ (+ מִפְּנֵי *on account of*).

Pilp. 1.0.1 Ptc. מְזַעְזְעֶיךָ—**terrify** someone Hb 2$_7$.

Hi. 0.2 Impf. תזיע; ptc. מזיע—**1.** appar. **flicker,** of eye Si 34$_{13(Bmg)}$. **2. shed** tears Si 34$_{13(Bmg)}$. **3.** appar. **be greedy** Si 37$_{30(Bmg, D)}$.

Htpalp. 0.0.4 Impf. תתזעזע—**be shaken,** of foundation 1QS 8$_8$, way 1QS 11$_4$.

→ זְוָעָה *trembling,* זַעֲוָה *trembling,* זִיעַ *trembling.*

***זוע** II 1 vb.—**Qal** 1 Pf. זָע—**stand aside** Est 5$_9$ (+ מִן *on account of*).

זְוָעָה 6 n.f.—Qr זַעֲוָה—**1. trembling** Is 28$_{19}$. **2. cause of trembling,** i.e. something terrible Dt 28$_{25(mss, Sam)}$. → זוע I *tremble.*

זוֹעָן 1 pr.n.m. **Zoan.**

זור I 77.12.11 vb.—**Qal** 74.11.10 Pf. זָרָה, זָרוּ; ptc. זָר, זָרִים—**1. be strange,** of Y.'s work Is 28$_{21}$, **be estranged** from (מִן) womb Ps 58$_4$, person Jb 19$_{13}$. **2.** ptc. as adj., **foreign,** and hence, sometimes, **forbidden,** of woman

Pr 2_{16}, gods Ps 44_{21}. **3.** ptc. as noun, **a. stranger, foreigner,** in ref. to a **non-Israelite,** oft. as enemy Is 1_7. **b. unfamiliar, unrelated person** 1 K 3_{18}. **c. lay Israelite,** i.e. one who is not a priest or Levite Lv 22_{10}. **d. foreign woman,** perh. **woman to whom one is not married** Pr 5_3. **e. alien god** Jr 2_{25}. **f. strange thing** Ho 8_{12}.

Ni. 2.0.1 Pf. נָזֹרוּ—**become estranged,** from (מִן) covenant 1QH 4_{19}, from (מֵעַל) Y. Ezk 14_5.

Ho. 1.1 Ptc. מוּזָר—ptc. as noun, **stranger** Ps 69_9.

→ זָרוּת *strangeness.*

זור II 3 vb.—**Qal** 3 Impf. תְּזוּרֶהָ; + waw וַיָּזַר; ptc. pass. זוּרֶה—**1. squeeze** fleece Jg 6_{38}. **2a. crush** eggs Jb 39_{15}. **b.** pass. ptc. as noun, **crushed one,** in ref. to crushed egg Is 59_5. **3. flow,** of water Jr 18_{14}. → מָזוֹר I *wound,* III *running sore,* IV *trap;* cf. זרר II *squeeze.*

זור III 1.1 vb.—**Qal** 1 Pf. זָרָה—**be abhorrent to** (לְ) wife, of husband's breath Jb 19_{17}.

Ho. 0.1 Ptc. מוזר—ptc. as adj., **abhorrent,** of master Si $4_{30(A)}$.

→ זָרָא *abhorrence,* זוּרֶה *rotten egg.*

***זור IV** 5.0.1 vb.—**Qal** 3 Pf. זָרוּ (זרו)—**depart** from (מִן) someone Jb 19_{13}, one's desire Ps 78_{30}.

Ni. 2.0.1 Pf. נָזֹרוּ (Q נזורו)—**depart** from (מִן) covenant 1QH 12_{19}, from (מֵעַל) Y. Ezk 14_5.

***זוּרֶה** 1 n.[f.] **rotten egg** Is 59_5. → זור III *be abhorrent.*

זָזָא 1 pr.n.m. **Zaza.**

זחח 2 vb.—**Ni.** 2 Impf. יִזַּח—**be detached** from (מֵעַל) ephod, of breastpiece Ex 28_{28}||39_{21}.

*[זחט] 0.0.0.1 perh. pr.n.m. **Zahat.**

זחל I 2.0.2 vb.—**Qal** 2.0.2 Ptc. זֹחֲלֵי—**crawl,** ptc. as noun, **crawling thing,** in ref. to snake Dt 32_{24} Mc 7_{17}.

זחל II 1 vb.—**Qal** 1 Pf. זָחַלְתִּי—intrans., **fear** Jb 32_6.

זֹחֶלֶת 1 pl.n. **Zoheleth.**

זיד 9.2.3 vb.—**Qal** 2 Pf. זָדוּ, זָדָה—**be presumptuous, be arrogant, be impudent,** towards (אֶל) Y. Jr 50_{29}, against (עַל) Israel Ex 18_{11}.

Hi. 7.2.3 Pf. הֵזִידוּ; impf. יָזִיד; + waw וַיָּזֶד; ptc. Si מזיד—**1.** as qal, **be presumptuous,** etc., **display presumptuousness,** against (עַל) people Ne 9_{10}. **2. boil, seethe** stew Gn 25_{29}.

→ זֵד *presumptuous,* זָדוֹן *presumptuousness,* זֵידָה *presumptuousness,* זֵידוֹן *seething,* נָזִיד *pottage.*

*[זֵידָה] 0.0.2 n.f.—pl. זידות—**presumptuousness** 1Q29 13_4 14_1. → זיד *be presumptuous.*

[זֵידוֹן] 1 adj.—pl. זֵידוֹנִים—**seething,** of water Ps 124_5. → זיד *be presumptuous.*

[זִיו] I, see זִו I *Ziv.*

*זִיו II 2.0.2 n.m. **splendour, brightness,** זיו שָׂדַי *splendour of the field* Ps $50_{11(mss)}$, כבוד זוך *glory of your splendour* 1QNoah 13_1.

זִיז I 2 n.m.—cstr. זִיז—**moving thing(s),** i.e. **animal(s),** perh. **locust(s)** Ps 50_{11} 80_{14}.

זִיז II 1.0.1 n.[m.]—cstr. זִיז—**teat** Is 66_{11}.

זִיזָא 3 pr.n.m. **Ziza.**

זִיזָה 1 pr.n.m. **Zizah.**

*[זִימְיָא] 0.0.1 n.f.—זימו—**penalty** Mur 45_7.

זִינָא 1 pr.n.m. **Zina.**

*[זִיעַ] I 0.0.1 n.[m.] **trembling** GnzPs 4_2. → זוע I *tremble.*

זִיעַ II 1 pr.n.m. **Zia.**

זִיף I 9.0.0.5 pl.n. **Ziph.**

זִיף II 1 pr.n.m. **Ziph.**

זִיפָה 1 pr.n. **Ziphah.**

[זִיפִי] 3 gent. **Ziphite.**

[זִיקָה] 2.1.1 n.f.—pl. זִיקוֹת—**flaming arrow, firebrand** Is 50_{11} CD 5_{13}, i.e. **lightning flash** Si $43_{13(M)}$.

זַיִת 38.1.4 n.m.—זָיִת; cstr. זֵית; sf. זֵיתְךָ; pl. זֵיתִים; sf. זֵיתֵיכֶם—**1.** usu. **olive tree** Jg 9_8, or **olive grove** Jos 24_{13}. **2. olive(s),** i.e. fruit of olive tree Ex 27_{20}.

זֵיתָן 1 pr.n.m. **Zethan.**

זַךְ 11.0.1 adj.—f.s. זַכָּה—**pure, 1.** of unadulterated substances, frankincense Ex 30_{34}, olive oil Ex 27_{20}. **2.** of righteous person, זַךְ אֲנִי בְּלִי פָשַׁע *I am pure, without sin* Jb 33_9. → זכך *be pure.*

*[זַכָּא] 0.0.0.1 pr.n. **Zacca.**

זכה 8.0.5 vb.—**Qal** 4.0.2 Impf. יִזְכֶּה—**be morally pure, worthy, justified,** of Y. Mc 6_{11}, human Jb 15_{14}.

Pi. 3 Pf. זִכִּיתִי; impf. יְזַכֶּה—**purify** one's heart Ps 73_{13}, way Ps 119_9.

Htp. 1.0.3 Impv. הִזַּכּוּ—**1. purify oneself** Is 1_{16}. **2.** of deeds, **be cleansed** from (מִן) evil 1QS 8_{18}.

*[זָכֶה] adj. **pure,** as noun, **unblemished beast,** suitable for sacrifice Ml 1_{14} (if em. זָכָר *male*).

זְכוֹכִית 1 n.f. **glass** Jb 28_{17}. → זכך *be pure.*

זָכוּר 1 adj. **mindful,** of Y. Ps 103$_{14}$.

זַכּוּר 10.0.0.12 pr.n.m. **Zaccur.**

[זָכוּר] 4.0.2 n.m.—sf. זְכוּרְךָ—**male,** coll. Ex 23$_{17}$. → cf. זָכָר *male.*

זַכַּי 4 pr.n.m. **Zaccai.**

זכך 4.0.2 vb.—**Qal** 3.0.1 Pf. זַכּוּ—**be pure, clean,** of person Lm 4$_7$ (+ מִן purer *than* snow), heavens Jb 15$_{15}$ (+ בְּ *in* eyes of Y.).

Hi. 1.0.1 Pf. הֲזִכּוֹתִי, Q הזכו—**clean, purify** one's hands Jb 9$_{30}$, way 1QS 9$_9$.

→ זַךְ *pure,* זְכוֹכִית *glass.*

זכר I 231.20.43.1 vb.—**Qal** 171.17.34.1 Pf. זָכַר, זְכַרְתַּנִי; impf. יִזְכֹּר; impv. זְכֹר (זָכְרָה), זִכְרוּ (זָכְרוּ); ptc. זֹכְרֵי; ptc. pass. זָכוּר; inf. abs. זָכֹר; cstr. זְכֹר (זָכְרֵנוּ)—**1. remember, call to mind, recall** experiences, dreams Gn 42$_9$. **2. remember, be faithful to** covenant (subj. Y.) Ex 2$_{24}$, Y.'s commandments (subj. human) Nm 15$_{39}$. **3. remember, take into consideration, think of** someone (subj. Y.) Gn 8$_1$. **4. make mention of** (בְּ) ark of covenant Jr 3$_{16}$. **5.** perh. **muster** mighty ones Na 2$_6$. **6.** pass. ptc. as adj., **mindful,** זָכוּר כִּי־עָפָר אֲנָחְנוּ *he is mindful that we are dust* Ps 103$_{14}$.

Ni. 20.1.3 Impf. יִזָּכֵר; ptc. נִזְכָּרִים; inf. הִזָּכֶרְכֶם—**1. be remembered,** of person Jb 24$_{20}$. **2. be mentioned,** of person's name Jr 11$_{19}$. **3. be remembered, commemorated,** of holy days Est 9$_{28}$.

Hi. 40.2.6 Pf. הִזְכִּיר; impf. יַזְכִּיר; impv. הַזְכִּירֵנִי, הַזְכִּירוּ; ptc. מַזְכִּיר, מַזְכֶּרֶת, מַזְכִּרִים; inf. הַזְכִּיר—**1. remind** someone Is 43$_{26}$. **2. keep** name **in remembrance** 2 S 18$_{18}$. **3. mention** person to (אֶל) someone Gn 40$_{14}$. **4. invoke** (בְּ of obj.) name of Y. Ps 20$_8$. **5. announce, proclaim,** הַזְכִּירוּ כִּי נִשְׂגָּב שְׁמוֹ *proclaim that his name is exalted* Is 12$_4$. **6. offer** frankincense **(as) token offering** Is 66$_3$. **7.** ptc. as noun, **recorder,** royal functionary 2 K 18$_{18}$.

→ זִכָּרוֹן *memorial,* אַזְכָּרָה *token offering,* זֵכֶר I *remembrance.*

***זכר II** 1 **Hi.** 1 Impf. נַזְכִּיר—**display strength** Ps 20$_8$.

***זכר III** 7 vb.—**Qal** 2 Impf. יִזְכֹּר—**boast about** (בְּ) ark Jr 3$_{16}$.

Ni. 1 Impf. יִזָּכְרוּ—**boast about** (בְּ) names of the Baalim Ho 2$_{19}$.

Hi. 4 Impf. יַזְכִּירוּ—**boast about** (בְּ) names of foreign gods Jos 23$_7$.

זָכָר 80.2.10 adj.—pl. זְכָרִים—**1. male,** of person Jos 17$_2$, animal Lv 4$_{23}$. **2.** as noun, **male person** Is 66$_7$, animal Lv 1$_3$, god Dt 4$_{16}$. → cf. זָכוּר *male.*

זֵכֶר I 23.10.8 n.m.—cstr. זֵכֶר; sf. זִכְרִי—**1. remembrance, memory** of person Ps 112$_6$, Y. Ps 6$_6$, Y.'s deeds Ps 111$_4$, holy days Est 9$_{28}$. **2.** as || of שֵׁם *name,* **memorial** of the righteous Pr 10$_7$, Y. Ex 3$_{15}$. → זכר I *remember.*

[זֶכֶר] II 1 pr.n.m. **Zecher.**

זִכָּרוֹן 24.2.29 n.m.—cstr. זִכְרוֹן; sf. זִכְרוֹנֵךְ; pl. זִכְרֹנוֹת; sf. זִכְרֹנֵיכֶם—**1.** usu. **memorial,** וְהָיוּ הָאֲבָנִים הָאֵלֶּה לְזִכָּרוֹן *and these stones shall serve as a memorial* Jos 4$_7$. **2. (act of) remembering,** אֵין זִכְרוֹן לָרִאשֹׁנִים *there is no remembrance of former (things)* Ec 1$_{11}$. **3. (act of) reminding,** זִכְרֹנֵיכֶם מִשְׁלֵי־אֵפֶר *your reminders are proverbs of ashes* Jb 13$_{12}$. → זכר I *remember.*

זִכְרִי 12.0.0.1 pr.n.m. **Zichri.**

***[זְכַרְיאֵל]** 0.0.1 pr.n. **Zechariel.**

זְכַרְיָה 41.0.5.5 pr.n.m. **Zechariah.**

זְכַרְיָהוּ, see זְכַרְיָה *Zechariah.*

[זְכַרְיוֹ], see זְכַרְיָה *Zechariah.*

זֻלּוּת 1 n.f. **worthlessness** Ps 12$_9$. → זלל I *be worthless.*

[זַלְזַל] 1 n.[m.]—pl. זַלְזַלִּים—**shoot** of vine Is 18$_5$.

זלל I 2.0.1 vb.—**Qal** 1.0.1 Ptc. זוֹלֵל—**1.** ptc. as adj., **worthless,** of Jerusalem Lm 1$_{11}$. **2.** ptc. as noun, **worthlessness** Jr 15$_{19}$.

Hi. 1 Pf. הִזִּילוּהָ—**despise, regard** Jerusalem **as worthless** Lm 1$_8$.

→ זֻלּוּת *worthlessness.*

***זלל II** 4.1 **Qal** 4.1 Ptc. זוֹלֵל—**be gluttonous,** ptc. as noun, **glutton** Dt 21$_{20}$.

זלל III 2 vb.—**Ni.** 2 Pf. נָזֹלּוּ—**quake,** of mountain Is 63$_{19}$.

זַלְעָפָה 3.1.2 n.f.—pl. זַלְעָפוֹת; cstr. זַלְעֲפוֹת—**raging** Ps 119$_{53}$; זַלְעֲפוֹת רָעָב *ragings of famine* Lm 5$_{10}$, צפון *of north (wind)* Si 43$_{17(B)}$.

זִלְפָּה I 7.0.2 pr.n.f. **Zilpah.**

***זִלְפָּה II** 0.0.1 pl.n. **Zilpah.**

זִמָּה I 29.2.10 n.f.—cstr. זִמַּת; sf. זִמָּתֵךְ, זִמָּתְכֵנָה; pl. זִמּוֹת; sf. זִמֹּתַי—**1. wickedness** Ho 6$_9$, specif. in ref. to fornication or incest Lv 18$_{17}$ Jr 13$_{27}$. **2. plan, planning, de-**

vice Jb 17_{11}; usu. with evil intent Is 32_7, זמות בליעל *devices of Belial* 1QH 12_{13}. → זמם *plan*.

זִמָּה II ₃ pr.n.m. **Zimmah.**

*[זִמָּה] III $_1$ n.f.—sf. זִמֹּתַי—**cord** Jb 17_{11}.

זְמוֹרָה I $_5$ n.f.—cstr. זְמֹרַת; pl. sf. זְמֹרֵיהֶם—**branch** of vine Nm 13_{23}; assoc. with non-Israelite cult Is 17_{10} Ezk 8_{17}. → זמר II *prune*.

*זְמוֹרָה II $_1$ n.f. **stench** Ezk 8_{17}.

*זְמוֹרָה III $_1$ n.f. **band of toughs** Ezk 8_{17}.

*[זְמוֹרָה] IV $_1$ n.[f.]—pl. sf. זְמֹרֵיהֶם—**warrior** Na 2_3.

[זַמְזֻמִּי] $_1$ gent. **Zamzummite.**

זָמִיר I $_{7.0.2}$ n.m.—cstr. זְמִיר; pl. זְמִרוֹת—**song, singing,** זְמִרוֹת יִשְׂרָאֵל *songs of Israel* 2 S 23_1, עֵת הַזָּמִיר *time of singing (of birds)* Ca 2_{12}. → זמר I pi. *sing*.

זָמִיר II $_{1.0.0.1}$ n.m.—I זמר—**pruning,** עֵת הַזָּמִיר *time of pruning* Ca 2_{12}. → זמר II *prune*.

*[זָמִיר] III $_1$ n.[m.] **guardian,** נְעִים זְמִרוֹת יִשְׂרָאֵל *the beloved of the guardian(s) of Israel* 2 S 23_1.

זְמִירָה $_1$ pr.n.m. **Zemirah.**

זמם $_{13.1.11}$ vb.—**Qal** $_{13.1.11}$ Pf. זָמַמְתִּי, זַמֹּתָ; impf. Q יזום, יָזֹמּוּ; ptc. זֹמֵם; inf. Q זום (זַמֹּתִי)—**1a.** of Y., **plan, intend, determine** Lm 2_{17}; with inf. Zc $8_{14.15}$. **b.** of humans, with evil intent, **plan, devise, plot against** (לְ) someone Ps 37_{12}; with inf. Ps 31_{14}. **2.** appar. **make plans for** (accus.) field Pr 31_{16}. → זָמָם *plan*, זִמָּה *plan*, מְזִמָּה *plan*.

[זָמָם] $_1$ n.[m.]—sf. זְמָמוֹ—**plan** Ps 140_9. → זמם *plan*.

זמן $_3$ vb.—**Pu.** $_3$ Ptc. מְזֻמָּנִים—**be set,** of time Ezr 10_{14}. → זְמָן *(set) time*.

זְמָן $_{4.2.5}$ n.m.—pl. sf. זְמַנֵּיהֶם—**(set) time,** לַכֹּל זְמָן *for everything there is a time* Ec 3_1. → זמן *set time*.

זמר I $_{45.0.13}$ vb.—**Pi.** $_{45.0.13}$ Impf. יְזַמֶּרְךָ; impv. זַמְּרוּ; inf. זַמֵּר (זַמְּרָה)—**1. sing (praise) to** (לְ) Y. Jg 5_3; abs. Ps 98_4. **2. praise** Y. Is 12_5. **3. sing** hymn Ps 47_8. → זֶמֶר *song (of praise)*, זָמִיר I *song*, זִמְרָה I *song*, מִזְמוֹר *melody*, מְזַמֶּרֶת II *musical instrument*.

זמר II $_{3.0.1}$ vb.—**Qal** $_{2.0.1}$ Impf. תִּזְמֹר—**prune** vineyard Lv 25_3.

Ni. $_1$ Impf. יִזָּמֵר—**be pruned,** of vineyard Is 5_6.

→ זָמִיר II *pruning*, זְמוֹרָה I *branch*, זִמְרָה II *choice products*, מַזְמֵרָה *pruning-knife*, (?) מְזַמֶּרֶת I *snuffer*.

[זָמָר], see בַּעַל־זָמָר *Baal-zamar*.

*[זֶמֶר] I $_{0.0.3}$ n.[m.]—pl. cstr. זמרי—**song (of praise)** 4QShirShabb[d] 1.1_6. → זמר I *sing*.

[זֶמֶר] II $_1$ n.[m.]—זֶמֶר—perh. **mountain sheep** Dt 14_5.

[זְמֹרָה], see זְמוֹרָה I *branch*.

זִמְרָה I $_{7.0.4}$ n.f.—זִמְרָת; cstr. זִמְרַת; sf. Q זמרתה; pl. Q זמרות—**1. song,** זמרות פלא *songs of wonder* 4QShir Shabb[d] 1.1_{40}. **2. melody,** זִמְרַת נְבָלֶיךָ *melody of your harps* Am 5_{23}. → זמר I *sing*.

[זִמְרָה] II $_1$ n.f.—cstr. זִמְרַת—**choice produce** of the land Gn 43_{11}. → זמר *prune*.

*[זִמְרָה] III $_3$ n.f.—זִמְרָת; sf. mss, Sam זִמְרָתִי—**refuge,** עָזִּי וְזִמְרָת יָהּ *Y. is my strength and (my) refuge* Ex 15_2 Is 12_2 Ps 118_{14}.

*[זִמְרָה] IV $_3$ n.f.—זִמְרָת; sf. mss, Sam זִמְרָתִי—**warrior,** עָזִּי וְזִמְרָת יָהּ *Y. is my protector and warrior* Ex 15_2 Is 12_2 Ps 118_{14}.

זִמְרוֹן $_1$ pr.n.m. **Zimron.**

זִמְרִי I $_{14}$ pr.n.m. **Zimri.**

זִמְרִי II $_1$ gent. **Zimrite.**

*[זְמַרְיָה] $_{0.0.0.1}$ pr.n.m. **Zemariah.**

[זְמַרְיָהוּ], see זְמַרְיָה *Zemariah*.

זִמְרָן $_2$ pr.n.m. **Zimran.**

זַן $_{3.2}$ n.[m.]—pl. זְנִים—**kind, sort,** מִזַּן אֶל־זַן *from kind to kind*, i.e. all kinds (of food) Ps 144_{13}, זני מרכבה *kinds of chariot* Si 49_8.

זנב $_2$ vb.—**Pi.** $_2$ + waw וַיְזַנֵּב; וְזִנַּבְתֶּם—**cut off rear, attack** enemy **from behind,** perh. **massacre rearguard,** or **cut off retreat** Dt 25_{18} Jos 10_{19}. → זָנָב *tail*.

זָנָב $_{11.0.2}$ n.m.—sf. זְנָבוֹ; pl. זְנָבוֹת; cstr. זַנְבוֹת—**tail** of snake Ex 4_4, fox Jg 15_4, hippopotamus Jb 40_{17}; in ref. to stump of firebrand Is 7_4, people of low status Is 9_{13}, king ruled by enemies 11QT 59_{21}. → זנב *have tail*.

זנה I $_{60.2.5}$ vb.—**Qal** $_{51.2.5}$ Pf. זָנְתָה, זָנוּ; impf. תִּזְנֶה; + waw וַתִּזֶן (וַתִּזְנֶה); ptc. זֹנָה, זוֹנָה, זֹנִים; inf. abs. זָנֹה; cstr. זְנוֹת—**1.** of woman, **a. be** or **act as a prostitute,** of wife Ho 2_7, Israel personified Jr 3_1. **b. fornicate** Dt 22_{21}. **2.** of man, **fornicate** Nm 25_1. **3.** זנה אַחֲרֵי **whore after,** i.e. seek for illicit sex, in ref. to worship of foreign gods Ex 34_{15}, demons Lv 17_7, abominations Ezk 20_{30}. **4.** ptc. as noun (alw. fem.) Gn 34_{31}; oft. אִשָּׁה זוֹנָה *a woman, a prostitute* Lv 21_7.

Pu. $_1$ Pf. זוּנָּה—appar. **be prostituted** Ezk 16_{34}.

Hi. 8 Pf. הִזְנְתָה, הִזְנוּ; + waw וַיֶּזֶן, וַתַּזְנֶה; inf. abs. הַזְנֵה; cstr. הַזְנוֹת—**1.** as qal, **prostitute oneself, commit fornication** Ho 4:10. **2. prostitute, lead into prostitution** Lv 19:29, including religious infidelity 2 C 21:11; **cause to whore after** (אַחֲרֵי) foreign gods Ex 34:16.

→ זְנוּת *prostitution*, זוֹנוּת *prostitution*, זְנוּנִים *prostitution*, תַּזְנוּת *prostitution*.

***זנה II** 1 vb.—**Qal** 1 + waw וַתִּזְנֶה—**be angry** with (עַל), or **abhor** husband Jg 19:2.

זָנוֹחַ 5 pl.n. **Zanoah.**

[זָנוֹחַ־קַיִן] 1 pl.n. **Zanoah-Kain.**

זְנוּנִים 12.0.1 n.m.—cstr. זְנוּנֵי; sf. זְנוּנַיִךְ—**prostitution, fornication** Gn 38:24; also in ref. to religious infidelity Ho 4:12. → זנה I *prostitute oneself*.

זְנוּת 9.2.12 n.f.—sf. זְנוּתֵךְ, זְנוּתַיִךְ, זְנוּתֵיכֶם—**prostitution, fornication** Ho 4:11; also in ref. to religious infidelity Nm 14:33; appar. in ref. to illicit marriage or improper sexual acts 4QMMT B75 CD 4:20. → זנה I *prostitute oneself*.

***זנזח** 0.0.1 vb.—**Pi.** 0.0.1 Impf. תזנזח—of Y., **reject** someone 4QapPsB 46:6 (perh. error for זנח hi., i.e. תזניח).

זנח I 19.1.3 vb.—**Qal** 16.1 Pf. זָנַח, זָנַחְתָּ; impf. תִּזְנַח—of Y., **reject**, or perh. **be angry with** people Ps 60:3; of Israel, **reject** good Ho 8:3.

Hi. 3.0.3 Pf. הִזְנִיחַ; impf. יַזְנִיחֲךָ—**1. reject** someone (subj. Y.) 1 C 28:9, vessels (subj. human) 2 C 29:19. **2. exclude** someone from serving as priest (מִכַּהֵן) 2 C 11:14.

זנח II 1.0.1 vb.—**Hi.** 1.0.1 + waw וְהֶאֶזְנִיחוּ—**stink, be foul**, of river Is 19:6.

זָנֹחַ, see זָנוֹחַ *Zanoah*.

זנק 1 vb.—**Pi.** 1 Impf. יְזַנֵּק—**leap**, of lion's cub Dt 33:22.

***זעה** 1.0.1 vb.—**Pilp.** 1.0.1 Ptc. מְזַעְזְעֶיךָ—**bark at** someone Hb 2:7.

[זֵעָה] 1 n.f. **sweat**, זֵעַת אַפֶּיךָ *sweat of your face* Gn 3:19.

זַעֲוָה 6.0.3 n.f.—cstr. Q זעות—**trembling, cause of trembling**, i.e. something terrible, זַעֲוָה לְכֹל מַמְלְכוֹת הָאָרֶץ *a cause of trembling to all the kingdoms of the earth* Dt 28:25. → זוע I *tremble*.

זַעֲוָן 2 pr.n.m. **Zaavan.**

***[זַעֲטוּט]** 0.0.5 n.m. **lad** 1QM 7:3.

***[זָעִיר]** 0.1 adj.—pl. Si זעירים—**little**, as noun, **little one, inferior** Si 11:6. → cf. זְעֵיר I *a little*, צָעִיר I *a little*.

זְעֵיר I 5 n.[m.] **a little** Is 28:10.13; adv. **(for) a little (time)** Jb 36:2. → cf. זָעִיר *little*; מִזְעָר I *a little*.

***זְעֵיר II** 4 n.[m.] **servant** Is 28:10.13.

זעך 1 vb.—**Ni.** 1 Pf. נִזְעָכוּ—**be extinguished**, of days Jb 17:1.

זעם 12.3.11 vb.—**Qal** 11.1.11 Pf. זָעַם, זְעַמְתָּה; impf. אֶזְעֹם; impv. זֹעֲמָה; ptc. זֹעֵם; ptc. pass. זְעוּמָה—**1. be indignant, show indignation against, a.** with accus. enemy (subj. Y.) Is 66:14. **b.** with עַל *against* covenant (subj. human) Dn 11:30. **2. curse, denounce** Israel Nm 23:8, Belial 1QM 13:1. **3a.** pass., **be accursed**, of people of Belial's lot 1QS 2:7. **b.** pass. ptc. as noun, **cursed one**, זְעוּם י׳ *cursed one of Y.*, i.e. one cursed by Y. Pr 22:14.

Ni. 1 Ptc. נִזְעָמִים—**be made indignant**, of face Pr 25:23.

Hi. 0.2 Impf. יזעים; ptc. מזעים—appar. **make mountains indignant**, of Y. Si 43:16(B).

→ זַעַם *indignation*, זַעֲמָה *curse*.

זַעַם 22.2.2 n.m.—זָעַם; cstr. זַעַם; sf. זַעְמִי—**1.** usu. **indignation**, זַעַם־אַפּוֹ *indignation of his anger* Lm 2:6. **2.** perh. **cursing** or **stammering**, זַעַם לְשׁוֹנָם *cursing of their tongue* Ho 7:16. → זעם *be indignant*.

***[זַעֲמָה]** 0.0.1 n.f. **curse** 4QCurses 2:4. → זעם *be indignant*.

זעף I 5 vb.—**Qal** 5 Impf. יִזְעַף; inf. זַעְפּוֹ—**be angry, enraged** against (עַל) Y. Pr 19:3, with (עִם) priests 2 C 26:19. → זַעַף *anger*, זָעֵף *angry*.

***זעף II** 2 vb.—**Qal** 2 Ptc. זֹעֲפִים—**be thin, wretched-looking** Gn 40:6 Dn 1:10.

זַעַף 6.0.3 n.m.—cstr. זַעַף; sf. זַעְפּוֹ—**anger, raging**, of Y. Is 30:30, Kittim 1QpHab 3:12, sea Jon 1:15. → זעף I *be angry*.

זָעֵף 2 adj. **angry, upset** 1 K 20:43. → זעף I *be angry*.

זעק 71.0.11 vb.—**Qal** 58.0.10 Pf. זָעֲקוּ; impf. תִּזְעַק; impv. זְעַק, זַעֲקוּ; inf. זְעֹק (זַעֲקֵךְ)—**1.** usu. intrans., **cry, cry out (for help), a.** with אֶל *to* Y. Jg 3:9, gods Jon 1:5, human 2 S 19:29. **b.** with לְ *to* Y. 1 C 5:20. **c.** with עַל *against* someone Jb 31:38. **d.** abs. 1 S 4:13. **2.** rarely trans., **summon (for help)** Y. Ne 9:28, humans Jg 12:2.

Ni. 6 Pf. נִזְעָקוּ; + waw וַיִּזָּעֵק—**be called (together),**

be assembled, of people Jos 8_{16}.

Hi. 7.0.1 Impf. יַזְעִיקוּ; + waw וַיַּזְעֵק; impv. הַזְעֶק־; ptc. Q מזעיקים; inf. הַזְעִיק—**1.** trans., **cry out to, call together, summon** people, esp. for military service Jg 4_{13}. **2.** intrans., **a. cry out (for help)** Jb 35_9 11QT 59_6. **b. make proclamation** Jon 3_7.

→ זְעָקָה *cry*; cf. צעק *cry out*.

זְעָקָה 20.0.2 n.f.—cstr. זַעֲקַת; sf. זַעֲקָתִי—**1. cry of distress** or for help Pr 21_{13}. **2. outcry, clamour** Gn 18_{20}. → זעק *cry*.

[זִיף], see זִיף I *Ziph*.

[זִפִי], see זִיפִי *Ziphite*.

זִפְרֹן 1 pl.n. **Ziphron.**

* **[זפת]** **Shaphel, make female lover as black as pitch,** of sun Ca 1_6 (if em. שֶׁזְּפָתְנִי *looked at me* to שֶׁזִּפְּתַתְנִי *made me black as pitch*). → זֶפֶת *pitch*.

זֶפֶת 3.1.1 n.f.—זֶפֶת—**pitch** Ex 2_3 Is 34_9. → זפת *make black as pitch*.

[זֵק] I 4.0.4 n.[m.]—pl. זִקִּים; cstr. Q זקי—**fetter** Is 45_{14} 1QH 13_{37}. → cf. אָזֵק *manacle*.

[זֵק] II 1.1.2 n.[m.]—pl. זִקִּים—**flaming arrow, firebrand** Pr 26_{18}.

זקן 20.1.1 vb.—**Qal** 18.0.1 Pf. זָקַן, זָקַנְתִּי; + waw וַיִּזְקַן—**be old, grow old** Gn 18_{13}; זָקַנְתִּי מִהְיוֹת לְאִישׁ *I am too old to belong to a man* Ru 1_{12}.

Hi. 2.1 Impf. יַזְקִין, Si חזקין—**1. grow old,** of person Pr 22_6, root Jb 14_8. **2. make old,** of anxiety Si 30_{24}.

→ זָקֵן I *old*, זֹקֶן *old age*, זִקְנָה *old age*, זְקֻנִים *old age*.

זָקָן 19.0.3 n.m. (& f.)—cstr. זְקַן; sf. זְקָנִי, זְקַנְכֶם—**1. beard** of man, שְׂעַר ... זְקָנִי *hair ... of my beard* Ezr 9_3, of animal 1 S 17_{35}. **2.** perh. **chin** Lv 13_{29}.

זָקֵן I 186.2.30 adj.—cstr. זְקַן—**1. old, elderly,** אֲבִיכֶם הַזָּקֵן *your elderly father* Gn 43_{27}. **2.** as noun, **a. old one, elderly one,** הֲדַר זְקֵנִים שֵׂיבָה *grey hair is the splendour of old men* Pr 20_{29}. **b. elder,** i.e. leading member of community, זִקְנֵי יִשְׂרָאֵל *elders of Israel* Ex 3_{16}. → זקן *be old*.

* **[זָקֵן]** II 0.0.0.1 pr.n.m. **Zaken.**

זֹקֶן 1 n.[m.] **old age** Gn 48_{10}. → זקן *be old*.

זִקְנָה 6 n.f.—cstr. זִקְנַת; sf. זִקְנָתוֹ—**old age** 1 K 11_4. → זקן *be old*.

זְקֻנִים 4 n.[m.]pl. **old age** Gn 44_{20}. → זקן *be old*.

זקף 2.0.3 vb.—**Qal** 2.0.3 Impf. Q יזקוף; ptc. זֹקֵף—**1.** of Y., **raise** someone, with accus. Ps 146_8; לְ of obj. Ps 145_{14}. **2.** appar. **raise oneself, stand erect** 1QS 7_{11}.

* **[זָקֵף]** adj. **startling,** of man 1 S 28_{14} (if em. זָקֵן *old*).

זקק 7.0.6 vb.—**Qal** 2 Impf. יָזֹקּוּ—**refine, distil** gold Jb 28_1, rain Jb 36_{27}.

Pi. 1.0.2 Impf. Q יזקק; + waw וְזִקַּק—**refine, purify** remnant 1QH 14_8, sons of Levi Ml 3_3 (+ כְּ *like* gold and silver).

Pu. 4.0.4 Ptc. מְזֻקָּק—**be refined, purified,** of metal Ps 12_7, wine by settling of lees Is 25_6, perh. person from sin 4QShir[b] 35_2.

[זֵר] 10.1 n.m.—cstr. זֵר (Si זיר); sf. זֵרוֹ—**1. border,** around ark Ex 25_{11}||37_2, table Ex 25_{24}||37_{11}, altar Ex 30_3||37_{26}. **2.** appar. **setting** in item of jewellery Si $35_{5(Bmg)}$.

זָרָא 1.2 n.[f.]—Sam, Si זרה—**abhorrence, nausea, disgusting thing** Nm 11_{20} Si 37_{30}. → זור III *be abhorrent*.

זרב 1 vb.—**Pu.** 1 Impf. יְזֹרְבוּ—**be scorched, be dried up,** or perh. **be in spate,** of wadi Jb 6_{17}.

* **[זֶרֶב]** 0.0.1 n.[m.] perh. **gutter** or **ossuary** or **lining** 3QTr 9_8.

זְרֻבָּבֶל 21 pr.n.m. **Zerubbabel.**

זֶרֶד 4 pl.n. **Zered.**

זרה I 39.2.5 vb.—**Qal** 11.2.1 Impf. תִּזְרֶה; + waw וַיִּזֶר; impv. זְרֵה; ptc. זֹרֶה; inf. זְרוֹת—**1. scatter** dust of golden calf Ex 32_{20}, fire Nm 17_2. **2. winnow** threshing floor Ru 3_2, people Jr 15_7 (+ בְּ *with* fork). **3.** appar. **vomit** Si 37_{29} (Bmg).

Ni. 2 + waw וַיִּזָּרוּ—**be scattered,** of Israelites Ezk 36_{19}.

Pi. 24.0.4 Pf. זֵרוּ, זֵרִיתָ; impf. אֱזָרֶה; ptc. מְזָרֶה, מְזָרִים; inf. זָרוֹת (זָרוֹתָם)—**1. scatter, disperse, spread** Israel Lv 26_{33} (+ בְּ *among* nations), knowledge Pr 15_7. **2.** pl. ptc. (מְזָרִים) as noun, **scatterers,** appar. in ref. to **north wind(s)** Jb 37_9. **3. winnow, sift** person's way Ps 139_3, evil Pr 20_8.

Pu. 2 Impf. יְזֹרֶה; ptc. מְזֹרָה—**be scattered, be sprinkled, be strewn,** of brimstone Jb 18_{15} (+ עַל *upon* habitation), net Pr 1_{17}.

→ מִזְרֶה *winnowing fork*.

***זרה** II 2 vb.—**Pi.** 2 Pf. זֵרִיתָ—**measure, discern** person's way, (subj. Y.) Ps 139_3, evil, (subj. king) Pr 20_8. →

זֶרֶת *span.*

[זָרָה] I, see זָרָא *abhorrence.*

זָרָה II, see זור I *be strange.*

זֵרוּעַ 2 n.[m.] **sowing, thing sown** Is 61$_{11}$. → זרע *sow.*

זְרוֹעַ 91.1.5.2 n.f. (& m.)—cstr. זְרוֹעַ (זְרֹעַ); sf. זְרוֹעִי; pl. זְרֹעִים (זְרוֹעוֹת); cstr. זְרֹעֵי; sf. זְרֹעָיו זְרוֹעֹתָיו), זְרוֹעֹתֵיכֶם—**1. arm,** perh. specif. **forearm** 2 S 1$_{10}$; **shoulder** 2 K 9$_{24}$; **wrist** Gn 49$_{24}$. **2. leg, shoulder** of animal Nm 6$_{19}$. **3. arm** of God Ex 15$_{16}$. **4. arm,** assoc. with physical power Is 33$_{2}$ Jb 22$_{8}$; perh. **army** Ezk 17$_{9}$. → cf. אֶזְרוֹעַ *arm.*

*זָרוּת 1 n.f. **strangeness,** perh. in ref. to prostitution Pr 22$_{14(mss)}$. → זור I *be strange.*

*זרז 0.1 vb.—**Pi.** 0.1 Impv. or inf. זריז—**strengthen** right hand, subj. Y. Si 33$_{7(Bmg)}$.

[זַרְזִיף] 1 n.[m.] **sprinkling,** זַרְזִיף אָרֶץ *a sprinkling of the earth* Ps 72$_{6}$.

[זַרְזִיר] 1 appar. adj. **strong, girded,** as noun, זַרְזִיר מָתְנַיִם *one strong/girded of loins,* perh. greyhound or cockerel Pr 30$_{31}$.

זרח 18.0.1.1 vb.—**Qal** 18.0.1.1 Pf. זָרַח, זָרְחָה; impf. יִזְרַח; ptc. זוֹרֵחַ; inf. זְרֹחַ—1. usu. **arise, (start to) shine,** of sun Jb 9$_{7}$, light Is 58$_{10}$, Y. Dt 33$_{2}$ (+ לְ *upon* Israelites). **2. appear, emerge,** of leprosy 2 C 26$_{19}$. → זֶרַח I *shining,* מִזְרָח *east,* מִזְרָחִי *eastern.*

[זֶרַח] I 1 n.m. **shining,** נֹגַהּ זַרְחֵךְ *brightness of your shining* Is 60$_{3}$. → זרח *arise.*

זֶרַח II 21.0.0.1 pr.n.m. **Zerah.**

זַרְחִי 6 gent. **Zerahite.**

זְרַחְיָה 5.0.0.1 pr.n.m. **Zerahiah.**

זרם I 2.0.1 vb.—**Qal** 1 Pf. זְרַמְתָּם—of Y., **overwhelm** people Ps 90$_{5}$.

Po. 1.0.1 Pf. זֹרְמוּ—of clouds, **pour** rain Hb 3$_{10}$.

→ זֶרֶם *downpour,* זִרְמָה *ejaculate.*

*זרם II 1 vb.—**Qal** 1 זְרַמְתָּם—of Y., **destroy, put an end to, stop** people Ps 90$_{5}$.

זֶרֶם 9.0.5 n.m.—זֶרֶם—**downpour, rainstorm,** זֶרֶם מַיִם *downpour of water(s)* Hb 3$_{10}$, בָּרָד *of hail* Is 28$_{2}$. → זרם I *pour.*

[זִרְמָה] 2 n.f. **ejaculate,** זִרְמַת סוּסִים זִרְמָתָם *their ejaculate is the ejaculate of horses* Ezk 23$_{20}$. → זרם I *pour.*

זרע 56.2.5 vb.—**Qal** 46.1.4 Pf. זָרַע, זְרַעְתִּיהָ; impf. תִּזְרַע; impv. זְרַע, זִרְעוּ; ptc. זֹרֵעַ, זֹרְעִים; ptc. pass. זָרוּעַ, זְרוּעָה; inf. זְרֹעַ—1a. usu. **sow,** (1) abs. Gn 26$_{12}$. (2) with accus. of land, field, etc. Ex 23$_{10}$ Lv 19$_{19}$. (3) with accus. of seed, etc. Lv 26$_{16}$ Jr 12$_{13}$, righteousness Pr 11$_{18}$, trouble Jb 4$_{8}$. (4) with double accus., **sow** field, etc. **with** something Lv 19$_{19}$. **b.** ptc. as noun, **sower** Jr 50$_{16}$. **c.** pass., **be sown,** of land Jr 2$_{2}$, light Ps 97$_{11}$. **2. bear (seed),** of tree, plant Gn 1$_{29}$.

Ni. 6.0.1 Impf. יִזָּרַע (יִזָּרֵעַ); + waw וְנִזְרְעָה—**1. be sown,** of **a.** seed Lv 11$_{37}$. **b.** ground Dt 21$_{4}$. **2. be able to retain (husband's) seed,** of woman Nm 5$_{28}$.

Pu. 1 Pf. זֹרָעוּ—**be sown,** of ruler Is 40$_{24}$.

Hi. 3.1 Impf. תַּזְרִיעַ; ptc. מַזְרִיעַ—**1. produce seed,** of plant Gn 1$_{11}$. **2. conceive,** of woman Lv 12$_{2}$.

→ זֶרַע *seed,* זֵרוּעַ *sowing,* זֵרֹעַ *vegetable,* זֵרְעֹן *vegetable,* מִזְרָע *place of sowing.*

[זֵרֹעַ] 1.0.1 n.[m.]—pl. זֵרֹעִים—**vegetable** Dn 1$_{12}$. → זרע *sow.*

זֶרַע 229.15.49.2 n.m.—זָרַע; cstr. זֶרַע (זְרַע); sf. זַרְעִי; pl. sf. זַרְעֵיכֶם—**1. seed,** for sowing Gn 47$_{23}$. **2.** human seed, i.e. **semen** Lv 15$_{16}$. **3.** produce of seed, **a. grain** Nm 20$_{5}$. **b. offspring,** usu. coll., and usu. of humans Gn 12$_{7}$, rarely of animals Gn 7$_{3}$; in ref. to a single (human) offspring Gn 4$_{25}$. **4.** perh. **seed time,** זֶרַע וְקָצִיר *seed time and harvest* Gn 8$_{22}$. → זרע *sow.*

זְרֹעַ, see זְרוֹעַ *arm.*

[זֵרְעֹן] 2 n.[m.]—זֵרְעֹנִים—**vegetable** Dn 1$_{16}$. → זרע *sow.*

*[זרף] vb. **Hi. or Pilp., sprinkle,** Ps 72$_{6}$ (if em. זַרְזִיף *sprinkling* to יַזְרִיפוּ [hi.] or זַרְזְפוּ [pilp.] showers *[that] sprinkle* the earth).

זרק I 35.0.5 vb.—**Qal** 33.0.5 Pf. זָרַק, זָרְקָה; impf. יִזְרֹק; + waw וַיִּזְרֹק; impv. זְרֹק; ptc. זֹרֵק, זֹרְקִים; inf. זְרֹק—**1. scatter, sprinkle, toss** dust upon (עַל) head Jb 2$_{12}$, water upon someone Ezk 36$_{25}$, blood upon altar Lv 1$_{5}$. **2.** perh. **be profuse,** of grey hair Ho 7$_{9}$.

Pu. 2 Pf. זֹרַק—**be sprinkled** upon (עַל) person, of water Nm 19$_{13}$.

→ מִזְרָק *bowl,* זֶרֶק *javelin.*

*זרק II 1 vb.—**Qal** 1 Pf. זָרְקָה—**creep up,** of grey hair Ho 7$_{9}$.

*[זֶרֶק] 0.0.4 n.m.—pl. cstr. זרקות—appar. **javelin** 1QM 6$_{2}$. → זרק I *scatter.*

זרר I 1 vb.—**Po.** 1 + waw וַיְזוֹרֵר—**sneeze** 2 K 4$_{35}$.

*זרר II 1 vb.—**Qal pass.** 1 Pf. זֹרוּ—**be squeezed,** of wound Is 1_6. → cf. זור II *squeeze.*

זֶרֶשׁ 4 pr.n.f. **Zeresh.**

זֶרֶת 7.0.1 n.f.—זֶרֶת; sf. Q זרתו—**1. span, handbreadth,** as a measurement of length, half a cubit, 8 to 10 inches Ex 28_{16}. **2.** perh. **outstretched hand** Is 40_{12}. → זרה II *measure.*

זַתּוּא 4 pr.n.m. **Zattu.**

זֵתָם 2 pr.n.m. **Zetham.**

זֵתַר 1 pr.n.m. **Zethar.**

ח

[חֹב] 1 n.[m.]—sf. חֻבִּי—**fold of garment** Jb 31_{33}.

חבא 34.0.8 vb.—**Ni.** 16 Pf. נֶחְבָּא, נֶחְבֵּאתָ, נַחְבְּאָה, נַחְבְּתֶם; impf. תֵּחָבֵא; ptc. נֶחְבָּא, נֶחְבָּאִים; inf. הֵחָבֵא—**1. hide oneself** Gn 3_{10}. **2. be hidden,** of person Jb 5_{21} (+ בְּ *from*), voice, i.e. be hushed Jb 29_{10}.

Pi. 0.0.2 Pf. חבא; + waw וחבא—**hide truth** 1QH 17_{24} 1QS 4_6 (לְ of obj.).

Pu. 1.0.2 Pf. חֻבָּאוּ; ptc. Q מחובאים—**1. keep oneself hidden,** of person Jb 24_4. **2. be hidden,** of trees 1QH 16_6.

Hi. 6.0.1 Pf. הֶחְבִּיאַנִי, הֶחְבִּיאָה, הֶחְבִּאַתָּה (הֶחְבְּאַתָה); + waw וַיַּחְבִּיאֵם—**hide,** or **keep** someone **hidden** Jos 6_{17} Is 49_2.

Ho. 1 Pf. הָחְבָּאוּ—**be kept hidden,** of people Is 42_{22}.

Htp. 10 Pf. הִתְחַבְּאוּ; impf. יִתְחַבֵּא, יִתְחַבְּאוּ (יִתְחַבָּאוּ); ptc. מִתְחַבֵּא, מִתְחַבְּאִים—**keep oneself hidden** Gn 3_8 1 S 13_6.

→ חֶבְיוֹן *hiding,* מַחֲבֵא *hiding place,* מַחֲבֹא *hiding place;* cf. חבה *hide.*

*[חֻבָּא] 0.0.0.1 pr.n.m. **Hubba.**

חבב I 1.2.2 vb.—**Qal** 1 Ptc. חֹבֵב—**love people,** of Y. Dt 33_3.

Pi. 0.2.2 Impv. Si חביב (Si חבב)—**love someone** Si $7_{21(A)}$ (+ כְּ *as* oneself).

→ חָבִיב *beloved.*

*חבב II 1 vb.—**Qal** 1 Ptc. חֹבֵב—**be pure,** ptc. as noun, **pure one** Dt 33_3.

חֹבָב 2 pr.n.m. **Hobab.**

חבה 5.0.2 vb.—**Qal** 1.0.2 Pf. Q חבתה (or חבא pi.); impv. חֲבִי—**1. hide law** 1QH 13_{11}, **mystery** 1QH 13_{25}. **2. hide oneself** Is 26_{20}.

Ni. 4 + waw וְנֶחְבָּה, וְנֶחְבֵּתֶם (or חבא ni.); inf. הֵחָבֵה (or חבא ni.)—**hide oneself** 1 K 22_{25}.

→ cf. חבא *hide.*

חֻבָּה 1 pr.n.m. **Hubbah.**

חָבוֹר 3 pl.n. **Habor.**

*[חִבּוּר] 0.0.1 n.[m.]—cstr. חבור—**community, company** CD 12_8. → חבר I *join.*

חַבּוּרָה 7 n.f.—sf. חַבֻּרָתוֹ; pl. cstr. חַבֻּרוֹת; sf. חַבּוּרֹתָי—**blow, wound** Ex 21_{25}; חַבֻּרוֹת פֶּצַע *blows of,* i.e. that cause, *wounds* Pr 20_{30}.

חבט I 5.1 vb.—**Qal** 4.1 Impf. יַחְבֹּט; ptc. חֹבֵט—**beat, beat out olive tree** Dt 24_{20}, **wheat** Jg 6_{11}, **complaint** Si 32_{17} (Bmg).

Ni. 1 Impf. יֻחְבַּט—**be beaten out,** of cumin Is 28_{27} (+ בְּ *with* rod).

*חבט II 0.1 vb.—**Qal** 0.1 Impf. תחבט—**pour (out) complaint** Si $32_{17(Bmg)}$.

*[חֶבִי] n.[m.] **hiding, secret** Jb 31_{33} (if em. בְּחֻבִּי *in my bosom*).

*[חָבִיב] 0.0.1 adj. **beloved,** as noun, **beloved one** 4Q NarrC$_{11}$. → חבב *love.*

חֲבַיָּה, see חֳבַיָּה *Hobaiah.*

חֳבַיָּה 2 pr.n.m. **Hobaiah.**

[חֶבְיוֹן] 1 n.[m.]—cstr. חֶבְיוֹן—**hiding,** or perh. **veil of** Y.'s **power** Hb 3_4. → חבא *hide.*

חֲבִילָה, see חֲכִילָה *Hachilah.*

חבל I 13 vb.—**Qal** 12 Pf. חָבַל; impf. יַחְבֹּל, תַּחְבֹּל (תַּחֲבֹל), יַחְבְּלוּ (יַחְבֹּלוּ); impv. חֲבְלֵהוּ; ptc. חֹבֵל; ptc. pass. חֲבֻלִים; inf. abs חָבֹל—**1a. take in pledge, hold in pledge** garment Ex 22_{25}, millstone Dt 24_6. **b.** pass. **be taken in pledge,** of garment Am 2_8. **2. take a pledge** from (accus.) someone Jb 22$_{6}$, **impose (the giving of) a pledge upon** (עַל) someone Jb 24$_{9}$. **3. hold liable for pledge given** Pr 20$_{16}$.

Ni. 1 Impf. יֵחָבֵל—**have a pledge taken,** i.e. become a debtor Pr 13$_{13}$.

→ חֲבֹל *pledge*, חֲבֹלָה *pledge*.

חבל II 11.1.3 vb.—**Qal** 3 Pf. חָבַלְנוּ; impf. אֶחְבֹּל; ptc. pass. Si חבולי; inf. חֲבֹל—**1. act corruptly** Ne 1$_{7}$ (+ לְ *against* Y.). **2.** pass. **be corrupted,** חבולי זהב *corrupted of,* i.e. by, *gold* Si 34$_{6(B)}$.

Ni. Impf. יֵחָבֵל—**ruin oneself** Pr 13$_{13}$.

Pi. 6.0.3 Impf. תְּחַבֵּל; + waw וְחִבֵּל; ptc. מְחַבְּלִים; inf. חַבֵּל—**ruin** someone Is 32$_{7}$, **destroy** something Is 13$_{5}$ Ca 2$_{15}$, **corrupt** one's spirit 4QInstr[b] 2.3$_{6}$.

Pu. 2 + waw וְחֻבַּל—**be destroyed, be broken,** of yoke Is 10$_{27}$, one's spirit Jb 17$_{1}$.

→ חֶבֶל II *destruction*, חַבָּל *wrongdoer*.

חבל III 3 vb.—**Pi.** 3 Pf. חִבְּלָה (חִבְּלַתְךָ); impf. יְחַבֶּל־—**be pregnant with, in labour with, give birth to** a child Ca 8$_{5}$, iniquity Ps 7$_{15}$. → חֵבֶל *labour pains*.

חבל IV 1.1 vb.—**Qal** 1.1 Impf. יַחְבְּלוּ; pass. ptc. Si חבולי—**1. bind** ox Jb 24$_{3}$. **2.** pass. **be bound,** חבולי זהב *bound of,* i.e. to, *gold* Si 34$_{6(B)}$.

→ חֶבֶל I *rope*, חֶבְלָה *rope*, חִבֵּל *mast*, חֹבֵל *sailor*, חֹבְלִים *union*, תַּחְבֻּלָה *guidance*.

*[חַבָּל] n.m. **wrongdoer** Ps 140$_{6}$ (if em. חֲבָלִים *ropes* to חַבָּלִים) Jb 21$_{17}$ (if em. חֲבָלִים *destruction* to חַבָּלִים). → חבל II *act corruptly*.

חֲבֹל 3 n.[m.] **pledge,** item taken in pledge for debt Ezk 18$_{12}$. → חבל I *take in pledge*.

חֵבֶל 9.0.8 n.m.—pl. חֲבָלִים; cstr. חֶבְלֵי; sf. חֲבָלֶיהָ, חֶבְלֵיהֶם—**1. labour pains** of one giving birth Ho 13$_{13}$, of Sheol 1QH 11$_{9}$. **2. foetus** Jb 39$_{3}$. → חבל III *be pregnant*.

חֶבֶל I 51.0.3 n.m. (f. at Zp 2$_{6}$)—mss חָבֶל; cstr. חֶבֶל; sf. חַבְלוֹ; pl. חֲבָלִים; cstr. חַבְלֵי (חֶבְלֵי); sf. חֲבָלָיו—**1. rope, cord** Jos 2$_{15}$, of tent Is 33$_{20}$, ship's tackle Is 33$_{23}$, snare Jb 18$_{10}$; as **measuring line** 2 S 8$_{2}$. **2. territory, region** Dt 32$_{9}$, **(allotted) portion** Dt 32$_{9}$. **3. band of** prophets 2 S 10$_{5}$, perh. **herd** of goats or hinds Jb 39$_{3}$. → חבל IV *bind*.

חֶבֶל II 2.0.5 n.m.—pl. חֲבָלִים—**destruction** Mc 2$_{10}$ Jb 21$_{17}$ CD 2$_{6}$. → חבל II *act corruptly*.

*[חֶבֶל] III n.[m.]—**mountain** Pr 23$_{34}$ (if em. חִבֵּל *mast*).

חִבֵּל 1 n.[m.] **mast,** or perh. **tackle, rigging** Pr 23$_{34}$. → חבל IV *bind*.

חֹבֵל 5 n.m. **sailor, pilot**—pl. cstr. חֹבְלֵי; sf. חֹבְלַיִךְ—Ezk 27$_{29}$; רַב הַחֹבֵל *chief of the sailors*, i.e. captain Jon 1$_{6}$. → חבל IV *bind*.

*[חֶבְלָה] 0.1 n.f.—sf. חבלתה—**rope** Si 6$_{29}$. → חבל IV *bind*.

[חֲבֹלָה] 1 n.f.—sf. חֲבֹלָתוֹ—**pledge** Ezk 18$_{7}$. → חבל I *take in pledge*.

*[חַבָּלִי] 0.0.0.1 pr.n. **Habbali.**

חֹבְלִים 2 n.[m.] **union,** name given to a staff Zc 11$_{7.14}$. → חבל IV *bind*.

[חֲבַצֶּלֶת] 2 n.f.—חֲבַצֶּלֶת; cstr. חֲבַצֶּלֶת—**asphodel,** a flowering plant, or perh. **meadow saffron** or **narcissus** Is 35$_{1}$ Ca 2$_{1}$.

חֲבַצִּנְיָה 1 pr.n.m. **Habazziniah.**

חבק 13.1 vb.—**Qal** 2 Ptc. חֹבֵק, חֹבֶקֶת; inf. חֲבוֹק—**1. embrace** 2 K 4$_{16}$. **2. fold** hands, in idleness Ec 4$_{5}$.

Pi. 11.1 Pf. חִבְּקוּ; impf. תְּחַבֵּק; + waw וַיְחַבֵּק (וַיְחַבֶּק־); inf. חַבֵּק—**embrace** a person Gn 29$_{13}$ (לְ of obj.) 33$_{4}$, rock Jb 24$_{8}$, wisdom Pr 4$_{8}$; abs. Ec 3$_{5}$.

→ חִבֻּק *folding*.

[חִבֻּק] 2 n.[m.]—cstr. חִבֻּק—**folding** of hands Pr 6$_{10}$=24$_{33}$. → חבק *embrace*.

חֲבַקּוּק 2.0.1 pr.n.m. **Habakkuk.**

חבר I 31.10.9 vb.—**Qal** 13.4.3 Pf. חָבְרוּ; impf. יְחָבְרְךָ (Ps 94$_{20}$, or pu.); ptc. חֹבֵר; ptc. pass. cstr. חֲבוּר—**1a.** intrans., **join,** i.e. **be joined (together),** of two things joined together: wings Ezk 1$_{9}$, curtains Ex 26$_{3}$. **b. join together,** of kings Gn 14$_{3}$. **c. ally oneself with** (אֶל) Si 12$_{14}$. **d.** pass. **be joined to** images Ho 4$_{7}$ (חֲבוּר עֲצַבִּים). **2. cast spell** (חֶבֶר) Dt 18$_{11}$, in charming snakes Ps 58$_{6}$.

Pi. 9.1.1 Pf. חִבַּר; + waw וַיְחַבֵּר; impv. Si חברה; inf. חַבֵּר—**1. join (together), couple** curtains Ex 26$_{6}$||36$_{13}$ (+ בְּ *with* hooks), tent Ex 26$_{11}$||36$_{18}$. **2. join,** i.e. **bring** someone **into alliance** with (עִם) 2 C 20$_{36}$. **3. join** daughter **in marriage** to (אֶל) Si 7$_{25(A)}$.

Pu. 4.2.1 Pf. חֻבַּר; impf. Qr יְחֻבַּר; ptc. Q מחברת—**1. be joined (together), attached,** of ephod Ex 28$_{7}$||39$_{4}$, city Ps 122$_{3}$ (+ לְ *to* itself). **2. be joined to, be allied**

with (אֶל) Ec 9₄(Qr) Si 13₁₆.

Hi. 1.0.1 Pf. Q החבירו; impf. אַחְבִּירָה—**join (together) an assembly** 11QPsᵃ 18₁, **words** Jb 16₄ (בְּ of obj.; + עַל *against*).

Htp. 4.3.2 Pf. אֶתְחַבַּר; impf. יִתְחַבָּרוּ; inf. הִתְחַבֶּרְךָ—**join oneself to** (אֶל) Si 13₂, **make an alliance with** (עִם) 2 C 20₃₅.

→ חִבּוּר *company*, חַבָּר *partner*, חָבֵר *companion*, חֶבְרָה *company*, חֹבֶרֶת *companion*, חֹבֶרֶת *series*, הִתְחַבְּרוּת *making an alliance*, מְחַבְּרָה *beam*, מַחְבֶּרֶת *join*.

*חבר II 3.1.2 vb.—**Qal** 2.1.1 Ptc. חֹבֵר—**mutter charm** (חֶבֶר) Dt 18₁₁ Ps 58₆; obj. omitted Si 12₁₃.

Hi. 1 Impf. אַחְבִּירָה—**harangue with** (בְּ) **words** Jb 16₄.

→ חֶבֶר II *noise, spell.*

*חבר III 1 vb.—**Hi.** 1 Impf. אַחְבִּירָה—**be brilliant in** (בְּ) **words** Jb 16₄. → חֲבַרְבֻּרָה *spot.*

*חבר IV 1 vb.—**Hi.** 1 Impf. אַחְבִּירָה—**heap up** (בְּ of obj.) **words** Jb 16₄.

[חַבָּר] 1 n.m.—pl. חַבָּרִים—**partner (in trade)** Jb 40₃₀. → חבר I *join.*

חָבֵר 12.3 n.m.—sf. חֲבֵרוֹ; pl. חֲבֵרִים; cstr. חַבְרֵי; sf. חֲבֵרָיו—**companion, associate,** חבר שלחן *companion of,* i.e. at, *a table* Si 6₁₀, חַבְרֵי גַּנָּבִים *companions of thieves* Is 1₂₃; with ref. to allied tribe, **confederate** Jg 20₁₁. → חבר I *join.*

חֶבֶר I 3.0.6.14 n.[m.]—חֶבֶר; cstr. חֶבֶר; sf. Q חברך; pl. חֲבָרִים—**1. company, association** of priests Ho 6₉; בֵּית חָבֶר *house of association,* i.e. shared house Pr 21₉. **2.** at Qumran and on coins, **community,** חבר היהודים *community of the Jews* Alexander Jannaeus Coin 14, בית החבר *house of the community* 4QDᵃ 10.1₁₀. → חבר I *join.*

חֶבֶר II 6.0.2 n.m.—חֶבֶר; pl. חֲבָרִים; sf. חֲבָרַיִךְ—**1. noise, tumult,** בֵּית חָבֶר *house of noise* Pr 21₉. **2. spell, charm, incantation** Dt 18₁₁ Is 47₉; for snakes Ps 58₆ 1QH 13₂₈. → חבר II *mutter.*

חֶבֶר III 11 pr.n.m. **Heber.**

[חֲבַרְבֻּרָה] 1 n.f.—pl. sf. חֲבַרְבֻּרֹתָיו—**spot, mark,** on leopard Jr 13₂₃. → חבר III *be brilliant.*

חֶבְרָה 1 n.f. **company,** וְאָרַח לְחֶבְרָה עִם־פֹּעֲלֵי אָוֶן *and he goes for company with evildoers* Jb 34₈. → חבר I *join.*

חֶבְרוֹן I 63.0.0.5 pl.n. **Hebron.**

חֶבְרוֹן II 8 pr.n.m. **Hebron.**

חֶבְרוֹנִי 6 gent. **Hebronite.**

חֶבְרִי 1 gent. **Heberite.**

[חֲבֶרֶת] 1.0.1 n.f.—sf. חֲבֶרְתְּךָ—**companion (in marriage),** i.e. wife Ml 2₁₄. → חבר I *join.*

[חֹבֶרֶת] 4 n.f.—חֹבֶרֶת—**series** of curtains joined together, or perh. **place of joining** of curtains Ex 26₄. → חבר I *join.*

*[חבשׁ] vb.—**Qal, inquire** Jb 34₁₇ (if em. חבשׁ *bind,* i.e. govern).

Pi., seek source of river Jb 28₁₁ (if em. חבשׁ pi. *dam up*).

חבשׁ 33.0.3 vb.—**Qal** 29.0.3 Pf. חֲבַשְׁתֶּם; impf. יַחֲבוֹשׁ, יֶחְבָּשׁ, (אֶחְבְּשָׁה) אֶחֱבֹשׁ, (יַחְבְּשֵׁנוּ), וַיַּחְבְּשׁוּ; + waw וַיַּחֲבֹשׁ (וַיַּחֲבָשׁ־) (וַיַּחַבְּשׁוּ); impv. חֲבֹשׁ, חִבְשׁוּ; ptc. חֹבֵשׁ; ptc. pass. חָבוּשׁ, חֲבוּשִׁים; inf. חֲבֹשׁ (חָבְשָׁה)—**1. bind up** wound Is 30₂₆, broken arm Ezk 30₂₁. **2a. tie around** headdress Ex 29₉. **b.** pass. **be wrapped around** (לְ) head Jon 2₆. **3a. saddle** ass Gn 22₃. **b.** pass. **be saddled,** of ass Jg 19₁₀. **4.** pass. **be twisted,** of rope Ezk 27₂₄. **5. fetter, imprison** Jb 40₁₃. **6.** perh. **govern** Jb 34₁₇.

Pi. 2 Pf. חִבֵּשׁ; ptc. מְחַבֵּשׁ—**1. bind up** wound Ps 147₃. **2. dam up** source of river Jb 28₁₁.

Pu. 2 Pf. חֻבָּשׁוּ, חֻבָּשָׁה—**be bound, be bandaged,** of wound Is 1₆, arm Ezk 30₂₁.

חֲבִתִּים 1 n.[m.]pl. **flat cakes** 1 C 9₃₁. → cf. מַחֲבַת *griddle.*

חַג 62.1.26 n.m.—cstr. חַג; sf. חַגִּי; pl. חַגִּים; sf. חַגַּיִךְ—**1. festival, feast** of passover Ex 34₂₅, unleavened bread Ex 23₁₅, weeks Ex 34₂₂, booths Lv 23₃₄. **2. festival offering** Ps 118₂₇. → חגג *celebrate festival.*

חָגָּא 1 n.[f.] **terror, (object of) dread** Is 19₁₇.

חָגָב I 5.0.2 n.m.—pl. חֲגָבִים—**locust, grasshopper,** an edible species of insect Lv 11₂₂.

חָגָב II 1.0.0.4 pr.n.m. **Hagab.**

חֲגָבָה 2 pr.n.m. **Hagabah.**

חגג 16.0.3 vb.—**Qal** 16.0.3 Pf. Q חגו; impf. תָּחֹג, תְּחֹגּוּ; + waw וְחַגֹּתֶם; impv. חָגִּי; ptc. חֹגְגִים, חוֹגֵג; inf. חֹג—**1a. celebrate festival,** with accus. חַג *feast* Lv 23₃₉, abs. Ex 5₁. **b. keep** a certain day **as a festival** Ex 12₁₄. **2. dance,** after victory 1 S 30₁₆. **3. reel, stagger,** of sailors in storm Ps 107$_{27}$. → חַג *feast*.

[חָגוּ] 3 n.m.—pl. cstr. חַגְוֵי—**cleft, cranny,** in rock Jr 49$_{16}$||Ob 3 Ca 2$_{14}$.

[חָגוֹר] 1 adj. **belted,** as noun, **belted one** Ezk 23$_{15}$. → חגר *gird*.

חֲגוֹר 3 n.[m.]—cstr. חֲגוֹר; sf. חֲגֹרוֹ—**belt, girdle** 1 S 18$_4$ Pr 31$_{24}$; חֲגוֹר חֶרֶב *a belt of,* i.e. with, *a sword* 2 S 20$_8$. → חגר *gird*.

חֲגוֹרָה 5 n.f.—חֲגֹרָה; sf. חֲגֹרָתוֹ; pl. חֲגֹרֹת—**1. belt** 2 S 18$_{11}$. **2. loincloth** Gn 3$_7$. → חגר *gird*.

חַגַּי 11.0.0.8 pr.n.m. **Haggai.**

חַגִּי I 2 pr.n.m. **Haggi.**

חַגִּי II 1 gent. **Haggite.**

חַגִּיָּה 1 pr.n.m. **Haggiah.**

חַגִּית 5.0.0.1 pr.n.f. **Haggith.**

חָגְלָה I 4 pr.n.f. **Hoglah.**

***[חָגְלָהוּ] II** 0.0.0.3 pl.n. **Hoglah.**

חגר 44.0.1 vb.—**Qal** 43.0.1 Pf. חָגְרָה; impf. יַחְגֹּר; impv. חֲגוֹר (חֲגוֹרָה), חִגְרִי, חִגְרוּ, חֲגֹרְנָה; ptc. חֹגֵר; ptc. pass. חָגוּר, חֲגֻרַת, חֲגוּרִים—**1. gird** someone **with** girdle Ex 29$_9$. **2. gird** one's loins 2 K 4$_{29}$. **3. gird oneself with, a.** with accus. girdle Ps 109$_{19}$, sackcloth 2 S 3$_{31}$, sword Jg 3$_{16}$, joy Ps 65$_{13}$. **b.** with prep. בְּ *with* girdle Lv 16$_4$, strength Pr 31$_{17}$. **4.** pass., **a. be girded,** of loins Ex 12$_{11}$. **b. be girded with,** חֲגוּר כְּלֵי מִלְחָמָה *girded with weapons of war* Jg 18$_{11}$, חֲגֻרַת־שַׂק *girded with sackcloth* Jl 1$_8$. → חָגוֹר *belted,* חֲגוֹר *belt,* חֲגוֹרָה *belt,* מַחֲגֹרֶת *robe*.

***[חִגֵּר]** 0.0.1 adj. **limping,** as noun, **limping one** 4QD^a 8.1$_8$.

חֲגֹרָה, see חֲגוֹרָה *belt*.

[חַד] I 4.0.7 adj.—חַדָּה—**1. sharp,** of sword Is 49$_2$, spear 1QH 13$_{10}$. **2. shrill,** of sound 1QM 8$_9$. → חדד *be sharp*.

חַד II 1 adj. **one,** as noun, **one (person),** חַד אֶת־אַחַד *one with another* Ezk 33$_{30}$. → אֶחָד *one*.

***[חַד]** n.[m.] **limit** Is 34$_{12}$ (if em. חֹרֶיהָ *her nobles* to חַדֶּיהָ *its limits*).

חדד 6.0.1 vb.—**Qal** 1.0.1 Pf. חַדּוּ—**be sharp,** i.e. **quick,** of horse Hb 1$_8$ (+ מִן quicker *than* wolf).

Hi. 2 Impf. יָחַד (יַחַד)—**sharpen,** בַּרְזֶל בְּבַרְזֶל יָחַד וְאִישׁ יַחַד פְּנֵי־רֵעֵהוּ *iron sharpens iron, and one man sharpens the face of another* Pr 27$_{17}$.

Ho. 3 Pf. הוּחַדָּה—**be sharpened,** of sword Ezk 21$_{14}$. → חַד I *sharp,* חַדּוּד *sharp*.

חֲדַד 2 pr.n.m. **Hadad.**

חדה I 3.1 vb.—**Qal** 2.1 Impf. יִחַדְּ—**rejoice** Ex 18$_9$ (+ עַל *on account of*) Jb 3$_6$.

Pi. 1 Impf. תְּחַדֵּהוּ—**make joyful** Ps 21$_7$ (+ בְּ *with* joy).

→ חֶדְוָה *joy*.

***חדה II** 4 vb.—**Qal** 3 Impf. יַחַד (יֶחַד)—**1. see** something Ps 33$_{15}$, **see (that)** Ps 49$_{11}$. **2. look at** (עַל) someone Jb 34$_{29}$.

Ni. 1 Impf. תֵּחַד—**appear in** (בְּ) congregation Gn 49$_6$.

[חַדּוּד] 1.0.1 adj. **sharp,** as noun, **1. sharp one,** חַדּוּדֵי חָרֶשׂ *sharp(est) ones of potsherd(s),* as descr. of scales of Leviathan Jb 41$_{22}$. **2. ray** of sun 1QNoah 3$_5$. → חדד *be sharp*.

חֶדְוָה 3 n.f.—cstr. חֶדְוַת—**joy** Ne 8$_{10}$ 1 C 16$_{27}$||Ps 96$_{6(mss)}$. → חדה I *rejoice*.

חָדִיד 3 pl.n. **Hadid.**

***[חֲדִיתָא]** 0.0.1 pl.n. **Haditha.**

חדל I 59.5.4 vb.—**Qal** 56.5.4 Pf. חָדַל, חָדְלוּ חָדֵלוּ (חָדֵלּוּ); impf. יֶחְדַּל; + waw וַיֶּחְדְּלוּ; impv. חֲדַל, חִדְלוּ חֲדָלוּ (חֲדֵלּוּ); inf. חֲדֹל—**1. cease, come to an end,** of thunder Ex 9$_{29}$, person from (מִקֶּרֶב) land Dt 15$_{11}$. **2. cease to do, leave off doing, refrain from doing** something, with inf. + לְ Gn 11$_8$, inf. without לְ Is 1$_{16}$, inf. + מִן 1 K 15$_{21}$||2 C 16$_5$; abs. Jg 15$_7$; חָדְלוּ רֹגֶז *they have ceased (from) raging* Jb 3$_{17}$. **3. cease from** (מִן), i.e. **leave** someone **alone, let be** Ex 14$_{12}$, **be unconcerned about** something 1 S 9$_5$.

Ho. 3 Pf. הֶחֳדַלְתִּי—**be made to leave off** fatness Jg 9$_9$, sweetness Jg 9$_{11}$, wine Jg 9$_{13}$.

→ חָדֵל *ceasing*.

***חדל II** 3 vb.—**Qal** 3 Pf. חָדְלוּ; impv. חֲדַל—**1. be fat** 1 S 2$_5$. **2. be successful** Pr 19$_{27}$ perh. 23$_4$.

חָדֵל 4 adj.—cstr. חֲדַל—**1. ceasing, transient,** of person Ps 39$_5$ 89$_{48(mss)}$. **2.** as noun, **one refusing** to hear Ezk 3$_{27}$. **3.** as noun, **one shunning,** or **one being shunned** by men (חֲדַל אִישִׁים) Is 53$_3$. → חדל I *cease*.

[חֶדֶל] 2 n.[m.]—חָדֶל—**1. world** Is 38$_{11}$ (mss חֶלֶד in same sense). **2. duration of life, lifespan** Ps 89$_{48(mss)}$ (L חֶלֶד in same sense).

[חַדְלַי] 1 pr.n.m. **Hadlai.**

חֵדֶק 2 n.[m.]—חֵדֶק—**briar, perh. nightshade** (*Solanum coagulans*) Mc 7$_{4}$ Pr 15$_{19}$.

חִדֶּקֶל 2 pl.n. **Tigris, Hiddekel.**

חדר I 1.1 vb.—**Qal** 1.1 Impf. Si אחדר; ptc. חֹדֶרֶת—**surround, encircle, perh. enter, penetrate deeply,** of sword Ezk 21$_{19}$ (לְ of obj. slain one), person Si 51$_{19(B)}$ (לְ of obj. wisdom). → חֶדֶר *chamber.*

*חדר II 0.1 vb.—**Qal** 0.1 Impf. אחדר—**remain, keep oneself for** (לְ) wisdom Si 51$_{19(B)}$.

חֲדַר 2 pr.n.m. **Hadar.**

חֶדֶר 38.1.15.2 n.m.—חֶדֶר; + ה- of direction הַחַדְרָה (הֶחָדְרָה); cstr. חֲדַר (חֶדֶר) חֲדַר; sf. חֶדְרוֹ; pl. חֲדָרִים; cstr. חַדְרֵי; sf. חֲדָרָיו—**chamber, room** Gn 43$_{30}$; חֶדֶר בְּחָדֶר *room in a room,* i.e. inner room 1 K 20$_{30}$, חֲדַר הַמִּטּוֹת *chamber of the beds* 2 K 11$_{2}$||2 C 22$_{11}$, מִשְׁכָּבוֹ *of his bed* 2 S 4$_{7}$; חַדְרֵי־מָוֶת *chambers of death,* i.e. Sheol Pr 7$_{27}$, תֵּמָן *of the south,* i.e. southern constellations Jb 9$_{9}$, בָּטֶן *of (the) belly,* i.e. innards of body Pr 18$_{8}$. → חדר I *surround.*

חַדְרָךְ 1 pl.n. **Hadrach.**

חדשׁ I 10.2.11 vb.—**Pi.** 9.1.7 Impf. תְּחַדֵּשׁ; + waw וַיְחַדֵּשׁ; וְחִדְּשׁוּ; impv. חַדֵּשׁ; inf. חַדֵּשׁ—**1. renew kingship** 1 S 11$_{14}$, face of ground Ps 104$_{30}$, days Lm 5$_{21}$. **2. repair city** Is 61$_{4}$, house of Y. 2 C 24$_{4}$. **3.** perh. **create, engender** right spirit Ps 51$_{12}$.

Htp. 1.1.4 Impf. תִּתְחַדֵּשׁ; ptc. Si מתחדשׁ; inf. Q התחדשׁ—**renew oneself,** of youth Ps 103$_{5}$ (+ כְּ *as* eagle), new moon Si 43$_{8}$.

→ חָדָשׁ *new,* חֹדֶשׁ *month.*

*[חדשׁ] II vb.—**Pi., attack,** ptc. as noun **invader** Ho 5$_{7}$ (if em. יֹאכְלֵם חֹדֶשׁ *the new moon will devour them* to יֹאכַל מְחַדֵּשׁ *an invader will consume*).

חָדָשׁ 53.3.26 adj.—f.s. חֲדָשָׁה; m.pl. חֲדָשִׁים; f.pl. Q חדשׁות—**1. new,** of king Ex 1$_{8}$, wineskin Jos 9$_{13}$, cart 1 S 6$_{7}$, song Is 42$_{10}$, covenant Jr 31$_{31}$, heavens and earth Is 65$_{17}$. **2.** as noun, **(the) new, new one, new thing,** of produce Lv 26$_{10}$, friend Si 9$_{10}$, coming events Is 42$_{9}$. → חדשׁ I *make new.*

חֹדֶשׁ I 281.2.87.8 n.m.—cstr. חֹדֶשׁ; sf. חָדְשׁוֹ; pl. חֳדָשִׁים (Q חודשׁים); cstr. חָדְשֵׁי; sf. חָדְשָׁיו, חָדְשֵׁיכֶם—**1. month** Gn 7$_{11}$; חֹדֶשׁ הָאָבִיב *month of Abib* Ex 13$_{4}$. **2.** beginning of month, **new moon,** and assoc. feast 1 S 20$_{5}$ 2 K 4$_{23}$; יוֹם הַחֹדֶשׁ *day of the new moon* Ezk 46$_{1}$, מָחֳרַת הַחֹדֶשׁ *morrow of,* i.e. day after, *the new moon* 1 S 20$_{27}$. **3. mating season** of female camel Jr 2$_{24}$. → חדשׁ *make new.*

חֹדֶשׁ II 1 pr.n.f. **Hodesh.**

חֲדָשָׁה 1 pl.n. **Hadashah.**

חָדְשִׁי, see תַּחְתִּים חָדְשִׁי *Tahtim-hodshi.*

חֲדַתָּה, see חָצוֹר חֲדַתָּה *Hazor-hadattah.*

חוב 1.1.3 vb.—**Qal** 0.0.2 Pf. חבו; + waw וחב—**be guilty** CD 3$_{10}$ 4QD^{a} 5.2$_{13}$ (+ בְּ *on account of*).

Pi. 1.1.1 + waw וְחִיַּבְתֶּם—**1. make guilty,** i.e. **endanger** head Dn 1$_{10}$, reward Si 11$_{18}$. **2. declare** garments **guilty,** i.e. **impure** 4QTohB^{a} 1$_{2}$.

→ חוֹב *debt,* חוֹבָה *condemnation,* חַיָּב *guilty.*

חוֹב 1 n.[m.] **debt** Ezk 18$_{7}$. → חוב *be guilty.*

חוֹבָה I 1 pl.n. **Hobah.**

*[חוֹבָה] II 0.0.1 n.f.—cstr. חובת—**condemnation,** or perh. **doom** of land 4QpIsa^{b} 2$_{1}$. → חוב *be guilty.*

חוג 1 vb.—**Qal** 1 Pf. חָג—**draw a circle upon** (עַל) face of waters Jb 26$_{10}$ (+ חֹק *[as] a boundary*). → חוּג *circle,* מְחוּגָה *compass,* מְחִיגָה *cause of reeling.*

חוּג 3.1.1 n.[m.]—cstr. חוּג—**circle,** in ref. to **horizon** Is 40$_{22}$ Pr 8$_{27}$ 1QM 10$_{13}$, **vault of heaven** Jb 22$_{14}$ Si 43$_{12}$. → חוג *draw a circle.*

חוד 4 vb.—**Qal** 4 Pf. חַדְתָּ; impf. אָחוּדָה; impv. חוּד (חוּדָה)—**propound a riddle** Jg 14$_{12}$ Ezk 17$_{2}$. → חִידָה *riddle.*

חוה I 6.2.1 vb.—**Pi.** 6.2 Impf. יְחַוֶּה; ptc. Si מחוה; inf. חַוֹּת—**1a. declare something** Ps 19$_{3}$. **b.** with double accus., **declare something to someone** Jb 32$_{6}$. **2. inform** someone Jb 15$_{17}$. → אַחֲוָה *declaration.*

*חוה II, see שׁחה htpal. *bow down.*

[חַוָּה] I 7 n.f.—pl. cstr. חַוֹּת; sf. חַוֹּתֵיהֶם—**tent village** Nm 32$_{41}$; חַוֹּת יָאִיר *tent villages of Jair,* usu. as pl.n. *Havvoth-jair* Nm 32$_{41}$.

חַוָּה II 2 pr.n.f. **Eve.**

*[חַוָּהיָהוּ] 0.0.0.1 pr.n.m. **Hivvahiah.**

[חוֹזֶה], see חזה I *seer.*

[חוֹזַי] 1 pr.n.m. **Hozai.**

חוֹחַ I 11 n.m.—pl. חוֹחִים—**1. thorn, briar, thistle** 2 K 14$_{9}$||2 C 25$_{18}$. **2. hook,** for Leviathan Jb 40$_{26}$, captives 2 C 33$_{11}$.

*[חוֹחַ] II 1 n.[m.]—pl. חֲוָחִים—**hole, crevice** 1 S 13$_{6}$.

[חוט] 1 vb.—**Hi.** 1 Impf. Sam^{mss} אחיטנה—**weigh out, account for torn animal** Gn 31_{39}(Sam^{mss}).

*[חוט] 0.0.1 n.[m.]—**tusk** of hippopotamus or elephant, שתין חטן *two tusks* 3QTr 9_{2}(Wolters) (Milik חפור *dig* two [cubits]).

חוט 7 n.m. **thread, cord** Gn 14_{23}; חוּט הַשָּׁנִי *thread of scarlet* Jos 2_{18}, הַחוּט הַמְשֻׁלָּשׁ *the three-ply cord* Ec 4_{12}.

*חוֹטֵא 2 n.[m.]—cstr. חוֹטֵא—**sin** Ec 9_{18}.

חִוִּי 25.0.1 gent. **Hivite.**

[חֲוִיל] 1 pr.n.m. **Havil.**

חֲוִילָה I 4 pr.n.m. **Havilah.**

חֲוִילָה II 5 pl.n. **Havilah.**

חול I 8.0.1 vb.—**Qal** 5 Pf. חָלוּ, חָלָה; impf. יָחוּל, יָחִלוּ; inf. חוּל—**1. whirl, move about,** of storm Jr 23_{19} (+ עַל *upon* head), sword Ho 11_{6} (+ בְּ *against* cities). **2. dance** Jg 21_{21}. **3. fall,** of bloodguilt 2 S 3_{29} (+ עַל *upon* head).

Pol. 2.0.1 Ptc. מְחֹלְלוֹת—fem. ptc. as noun, **dancer** Jg 23_{13}.

Htpol. 1 Ptc. מִתְחוֹלֵל—**whirl,** of tempest Jr 23_{19}.

→ מָחוֹל I *dance,* מְחֹלָה *dance,* מְחוֹלְלָה I *dance.*

*חול II 1 vb.—**Qal** Pf. חָלוּ—**be weak,** of hands Lm 4_{6}.

חול I 23.2.1 n.m. **sand,** oft. representing what is numerous, כְּחוֹל הַיָּם *as the sand of the sea* Gn 32_{13}.

חול II 1 n.[m.] **phoenix** Jb 29_{18}.

[חול] III, see חֹל *profaneness.*

חול 2.0.1 pr.n.m. **Hul.**

חום 4 adj. **brown,** colour of sheep Gn 30_{32}.

חוֹמָה 133.0.11 n.f.—חֹמָה; cstr. חוֹמַת; sf. חוֹמָתָהּ; du. חֹמֹתַיִם; pl. חוֹמוֹת; cstr. חוֹמוֹת; sf. חוֹמֹתַי—**wall** of city Lv 25_{29}, building Lm 2_{7}, around building Ezk 40_{5}; Y. as wall of fire Zc 2_{9}, prophet as wall of bronze Jr 15_{20}, waters of Red Sea as wall Ex 14_{22}.

*[חוֹנִי] 0.0.4 pr.n.m. **Honi.**

*[חוֹנָן] 0.0.0.1 pr.n.m. **Honan.**

חוס 24.0.2 vb.—**Qal** 24.0.2 Pf. חָסָה, חַסְתָּ; impf. יָחֹס (יָחוּס), אָחוּס; + waw וַתָּחָס; impv. חוּסָה—**1. pity, look with compassion upon, spare,** subj. eye Gn 45_{20}, Y. Jl 2_{17}, person Jr 21_{7}; with עַל *upon* or of obj. person Dt 7_{16}, plant Jon 4_{10}, possessions Gn 45_{20}. **2.** abs. **have pity,** of eye Dt 25_{12} Y. Jr 13_{14}.

חוף 7 n.[m.] **shore, coast,** חוֹף הַיָּם *shore of the sea* Dt 1_{7}, חוֹף אֳנִיּוֹת *of ships,* i.e. harbour Gn 49_{13}.

חוּפָם 1 pr.n.m. **Hupham.**

חוּפָמִי 1 gent. **Huphamite.**

[חוֹפֶשׁ], see חֹפֶשׁ II *freedom.*

*חוץ 1 vb.—**Polel** Ptc. חֹצֵץ—**1. be massed,** of locusts Pr 30_{27}. **2. strike up tune** Jg 5_{11} (if em. מְחַצְּצִים sound of *those distributing water* [חצץ pi.] to מְחֹצְצִים). → חוץ III *aloud.*

חוץ I 164.0.24 n.[m.]—cstr. חוּץ; pl. חוּצוֹת; cstr. חוּצוֹת; sf. חוּצֹתָיו; + ה- of direction חוּצָה—**1.** as noun, **a.** usu. **street,** חוּץ הָאֹפִים *the bakers' street* Jr 37_{21}, חוּצֹת אַשְׁקְלוֹן *streets of Ashkelon* 2 S 1_{20}. **b. open field, countryside** Ps 144_{13}. **c. (the) outside** Ezk 47_{2}. **d.** perh. **bazaar** 1 K 20_{34}. **2.** as adv., **a.** חוּץ **outside** Dt 23_{14}. **b.** הַחוּץ, הַחוּצָה, חוּצָה **(to the) outside** Gn 39_{12} Ex 12_{46} Jg 19_{25}; also הַחוּצָה **from or on, the outside** 1 K 8_{8}||2 C 5_{9}, **beyond** Nm 35_{4}. **c.** לַחוּץ, לְחוּצָה **(on the) outside, beyond** Ezk 42_{7} 2 C 32_{5}. **d.** בַּחוּץ **(on the) outside, outdoors** Gn 9_{22} Ex 21_{19}. **e.** מִחוּץ, מֵהַחוּץ, מִחוּצָה **(on the) outside** Gn 6_{14} Ezk 40_{40} 41_{25}. **f.** אֶל־הַחוּץ **(on the) outside** Ezk 41_{9}. **g.** אֶל־הַחוּצָה **(to) outside, abroad** Ezk 34_{21}. **3.** as prep., **a.** חוּץ לְ, חוּצָה לְ **outside** 2 C 33_{15} CD 10_{21}. **b.** חוּץ מִן, הוּצָה מִן **outside, apart from** Ec 2_{25} CD 11_{5}. **c.** לְחוּץ מִן **outside** 11QT 46_{5}. **d.** מִחוּץ לְ, מִחוּצָה לְ **outside** Gn 19_{16} Ezk 40_{44}. **e.** אֶל־מִחוּץ לְ **(to) outside** Lv 14_{40}. → cf. חִיצוֹן *outer.*

[חוּץ] II 1 pr.n.m. **Huz.**

*[חוּץ] III 1 adv.—+ ה- חֻצָה—**aloud** Is 33_{7}. → חוץ *be massed.*

*חוק 1 vb.—**Qal** 1 Inf. חוּקוֹ—**gather** foundations of earth Pr 8_{29}.

[חוֹק], see חֹק *statute.*

*[חוּק] 0.1 n.[m.] **circle,** in ref. to vault of heaven Si 43_{12}(B) (M חוּג *circle;* Bmg הוד *splendour*).

חוּקֹק 2 pl.n. **Hukok.**

חור I 2 vb.—**Qal** 2 Pf. 1QIsa^{a} חורו; impf. יֶחֱוָרוּ—**be white, pale,** of face Is 29_{22}, person Is 19_{9}(1QIsa^{a}). → חוּר II *white,* חוֹרִי *white stuff,* חֹרִי III *white bread.*

*חור II 1 vb.—**Qal** 1 Pf. חָרוּ—**become feeble, dwindle away,** of person Is 24_{6}.

*חור III 1 vb.—**Qal** 1.0.1 Impf. יֶחֱוָרוּ—**go to and fro,** of face Is 29_{22}.

חוֹר, see חֹר I *noble*, II *hole*.

חוּר I 14 pr.n.m. **Hur.**

חוּר II 2.0.1 n.[m.] **white,** colour of cloth Est 1_{6} 8_{15}, angelic beings 4QShirShabb[f] 23.2_{9}. → חור I *be white*.

[חוּר] III, see חֹר *hole*.

חוֹרֵב, see חֹרֵב *Horeb*.

*[חוֹרוֹן] 0.0.1 pl.n. **Horon.**

חוֹרִי, see חֹרִי I *Hori*.

[חוּרִי] 1 n.[m.]—חוּרָי—**white stuff** Is 19_{9}. → חור I *be white*.

חוּרַי 1 pr.n.m. **Hurai.**

חוּרִי 1 pr.n.m. **Huri.**

חוּרָם, see חִירָם *Hiram*.

חַוְרָן 2 pl.n. **Hauran.**

חוֹרֹנַיִם, see חֹרֹנַיִם *Horonaim*.

*[חוֹרָץ] 0.0.0.1 pr.n.m. **Horaz.**

חוש I 21.2.6 vb.—**Qal** 15.1.4 Pf. חָשׁ; impf. Q יחושו; + waw וַתָּחָשׁ; impv. חוּשָׁה; ptc. pass. חֻשִׁים; inf. חוּשִׁי—intrans., **hasten,** of Y. Ps 38_{23}, human 1 S 20_{38}, foot Jb 31_{5}, eagle Hb 1_{8} (+ לֶאֱכוֹל *to eat*), events Dt 32_{35}; prep. לְ *to* person Ps 70_{6}, *to, for* help Ps 22_{20}; עַל *to* deceit Jb 31_{5}.

Hi. 6.1.3 Pf. הֶחִישׁוּ; impf. יָחִישׁ (יָחִישָׁה); + waw וַתָּחַשׁ (unless qal); impv. Si החישׁ—**1.** intrans., **hasten,** of person Jg 20_{37}, sword 1QH 14_{29}, work Is 5_{19} (or §2). **2.** trans., **a. hasten work** Is 5_{19} (or §1), end Si 33_{10}, event Is 60_{22}. **b. seek refuge with haste** Ps 55_{9}. **3. give way, be dislodged** from (מִן) place, of foundations 1QS 8_{8}. → חִישׁ *quickly*.

חוש II 2 vb.—**Qal** 2 Impf. יָחוּשׁ; inf. חוּשִׁי—**1.** of person, **feel (pain),** or (if em. to יָחוּשׁוּ) of thoughts, **be painful** Jb 20_{2}. **2. feel joyful** Ec 2_{25}.

*חוש III 1 vb.—**Qal** 1 Impf. יָחוּשׁ—**be anxious** Ec 2_{25}.

*חוש IV 1 vb.—**Qal** 1 Impf. יָחוּשׁ—**be sated** Ec 2_{25}.

*חוש V 0.0.1 vb.—**Hi.** 0.0.1 Impf. Q יחישו—**cease,** perh. **be silent,** of sound 1QM 8_{11}.

חוּשָׁה 1 pr.n.m. **Hushah.**

חוּשַׁי 14 pr.n.m. **Hushai.**

חוּשִׁים 4 pr.n.m.&f. **Hushim.**

חוּשָׁם, see חֻשָׁם *Husham*.

[חוּשָׁתִי], see חֻשָׁתִי *Hushathite*.

*חות vb. **Qal, be bold** Is 8$_{9.9.9}$ (all three, if em. חֹתּוּ *be dismayed* [from חתת] to חוּתוּ *be bold*).

חוֹתָם I 14.4.2.2 n.m.—חֹתָם; cstr. mss חוֹתָם; sf. חֹתָמוֹ—**seal, signet ring** Gn 38_{18}; חֹמֶר חוֹתָם *clay of*, i.e. under, *the seal* Jb 38_{14}, פִּתּוּחֵי חֹתָם *engravings of a signet* Ex 28_{11} ||39_{6}. → חתם *seal*.

חוֹתָם II 2 pr.n.m. **Hotham.**

חֲזָאֵל 23 pr.n.m. **Hazael.**

חזה I 59.6.4 vb.—**Qal** Pf. חָזָה; impf. יֶחֱזֶה; impv. חֲזוּ, חֲזֵה; ptc. חֹזֶה, חֹזִים; inf. חֲזוֹת—**1. see, perceive,** subj. usu. humans, also Y. Si 15_{18}, eyes Is 33_{17}; obj. Y. Ex 24_{11}, human Pr 22_{29}, deeds of Y. Ps 46_{9}, vengeance Ps 58_{11}. **2. see (in prophecy)** vision Nm 24_{4}, word Is 2_{1} (+ עַל *concerning*), falsehood Ezk 13_{6}. **3.** with בְּ, **gaze upon (with gratification)** Mc 4_{11} Ps 27_{4}. **4. seek out, select** men from (מִן) people Ex 18_{21}. → חֹזֶה I *seer*, חָזֶה *vision*, חָזוֹן *vision*, חָזוּת *revelation*, חָזָה *vision*, חִזָּיוֹן *vision*, מַחֲזֶה *vision*, מֶחֱזָה *window*.

*חזה II 4 vb.—**Qal** 4 Pf. חָזוּ; impf. יֶחֱזֶה—**1. be opposite** stone heap Jb 8_{17}. **2. stand apart from** Y. Ex 24_{11} Ps 63_{3} Jb 36_{25} (בְּ of obj.).

*חזה III 1 vb.—**Qal** 1 Impf. אֶחֱזֶה—**be vile,** of person Jb 34_{32}.

[חָזָה] 1 n.f. **vision,** חֲזוֹת יֶעְדּוֹ הַחֹזֶה *visions of Iddo the seer*, as title of prophetic book 2 C 9_{29}. → חזה I *see*.

חָזֶה I 13.0.4 n.m.—cstr. חֲזֵה (Q חזי); pl. חָזוֹת—**breast** of sacrificial animal, as wave offering Ex 29_{27}.

*חָזֶה II 3 adj.—f.s. חָזִית, חָזוּת—**1. prominent, erect, protruding,** of יָד hand, i.e. penis Is 57_{8}, horn Dn 8_{5}. **2.** as noun, **protruding one,** of horn Dn 8_{8}.

חֹזֶה I 16.1.3 n.m.—cstr. חֹזֵה; pl. חֹזִים—**seer,** חֹזֵה דָוִד *seer of David* 2 S 24_{11}. → חזה I *see*.

חֹזֶה II 1 n.[m.] **agreement** Is 28_{15}.

חֲזָהאֵל, see חֲזָאֵל *Hazael*.

חֲזוֹ 1 pr.n.m. **Hazo.**

חָזוֹן I 35.2.11 n.m.—cstr. חֲזוֹן—**1. vision,** assoc. with **a.** prophecy, revelation 1 S 3_{1} Ezk 7_{26}, as false Jr 14_{14}. **b.** dreaming, חֲזוֹן לַיְלָה *vision of (the) night* Is 29_{7}. **2.** in title of prophetic book, **revelatory word, inspired saying** Is 1_{1}. → חזה I *see*.

*חָזוֹן II 1 n.m. **pact** Ezk 7_{13}.

*חָזוֹן III 1 n.[m.] **magistrate** Pr 29_{18}.

חָזוּת I 4.1 n.f.—cstr. חָזוּת—**1a. vision** of prophet Is 21_{2}

29$_{11}$. **b. (fleeting) glimpse** of Y.'s works Si 42$_{22}$(M). **2a. conspicuousness,** קֶרֶן חָזוּת *horn of conspicuousness,* i.e. conspicuous horn Dn 8$_5$. **b. conspicuous one,** of horn Dn 8$_8$. → חזה I *see.*

[חָזוּת] II 1 n.f. **agreement,** חָזוּתְכֶם אֶת־שְׁאוֹל *your agreement with Sheol* Is 28$_{18}$.

חֲזִיאֵל 1 pr.n.m. **Haziel.**

חֲזָיָה 1 pr.n.m. **Hazaiah.**

חֶזְיוֹן 1 pr.n.m. **Hezion.**

חִזָּיוֹן 9.0.1 n.m.—cstr. חֶזְיוֹן; sf. חֶזְיֹנוֹ; pl. חֶזְיֹנוֹת; cstr. חֶזְיֹנוֹת—**1. vision** Jl 3$_1$; assoc. with dreaming Jb 4$_{13}$. **2. revelation,** given to prophet 2 S 7$_{17}$. **3.** גֵּיא חִזָּיוֹן **valley of vision** Is 22$_1$. → חזה I *see.*

[חֲזִיז] I 3.2 n.[m.]—cstr. חֲזִיז; pl. חֲזִיזִים—**thundercloud** Zc 10$_1$; **thunderbolt, lightning,** חֲזִיז קֹלוֹת *lightning of thunder* Jb 28$_{26}$.

*[חֲזִיז] II 1 n.[m.]—pl. חֲזִיזִים—**dream** Zc 10$_1$.

חֲזִיר 7.0.1 n.m.—1QIsa^a חוזיר—**swine, wild boar** Lv 11$_7$ ||Dt 14$_8$ Is 65$_4$; חֲזִיר מִיַּעַר *wild boar from the forest* Ps 80$_{14}$.

חֵזִיר 2.0.11.1 pr.n.m. **Hezir.**

חזק I 293.13.91 vb.—**Qal** 84.1.18 Pf. חָזַק; impf. יֶחֱזַק (יֶחֱזָק), יֶחֶזְקוּ (יֶחְזְקוּ); + waw וַיֶּחֱזַק; impv. חֲזַק, חִזְקוּ; ptc. חָזֵק; inf. חָזְקָה (חֶזְקָה)—**1a. be (physically) strong,** of bonds Is 28$_{22}$. **b. be courageous** 2 S 13$_{28}$; חֲזַק וֶאֱמָץ *be strong and courageous* Jos 1$_7$. **c. be powerful** Jos 17$_{13}$; דָּוִד הֹלֵךְ וְחָזֵק *David became stronger and stronger* 2 S 3$_1$. **d. be firm,** of royal power 2 K 14$_5$; with inf., **be firm, be sure to do something** Jos 23$_6$; **be firm in, devoted to** (בְּ) law of Y. 2 C 31$_4$. **e. be urgent with** (עַל) someone Ex 12$_{33}$. **f. be stronger than, too strong for, prevail against** someone, with מִן 1 S 17$_{50}$ 2 S 13$_{14}$, אֶל 2 S 24$_4$, עַל Dn 11$_5$, בְּ Jg 19$_4$, accus. Jr 20$_7$. **g. recover (from sickness)** Is 39$_1$. **h. be severe,** of famine Gn 41$_{56}$. **i. be hard,** of heart Ex 7$_{13}$. **j. be loud,** of trumpet sound Ex 19$_{19}$. **2. be caught fast,** of head 2 S 18$_9$ (+ בְּ *in* branches of tree). **3.** trans., **strengthen** someone 2 C 28$_{20}$.

Pi. 64.4.28 Pf. חִזַּק; impf. אֲחַזֵּק; + waw וַיְחַזֵּק; impv. חַזֵּק, חַזְּקוּ, חַזְּקִי; ptc. מְחַזֵּק; inf. חַזֵּק—**1a. make strong, strengthen** someone Jg 3$_{12}$ (+ עַל *against*) 16$_{28}$. **b. encourage** someone Dt 1$_{38}$ 2 C 35$_2$ (+ לְ *in* service of temple); lit. 'strengthen the hands of' 1 S 23$_{16}$ (+ בְּ *in* God). **c. support, help** someone 2 C 29$_{34}$; lit. 'strengthen the hands of' Ezr 6$_{22}$ (+ בְּ *in* work). **2a. strengthen, reinforce** tent peg Is 54$_2$, fortifications Na 3$_{14}$. **b. repair** temple 2 C 34$_8$. **3. harden** heart Ex 4$_{21}$, **make** face **harder than** (מִן) rock Jr 5$_3$. **4a. hold firm** base of mast Is 33$_{23}$. **b. fasten** image of god Is 41$_7$. **c. bind** someone **with** girdle Is 22$_{21}$. **d. gird** loins Na 2$_2$. **5. hold to, grasp** covenant 1QS 5$_3$ (בְּ of obj.), counsel 4QpNah 3.3$_8$.

Pu. 0.1 Pf. חוזק—**be repaired,** of temple Si 50$_1$.

Hi. 117.6.31 Pf. הֶחֱזִיק, הֶחֱזַקְתִּי; impf. יַחֲזִיק, יַחֲזֵק (יַחֲזִק), אַחֲזִיק; + waw וַיַּחֲזֵק (וַיַּחֲזֶק־), וַיַּחֲזִיקוּ; impv. הַחֲזֵק, הַחֲזִיקִי, הַחֲזִיקוּ; ptc. מַחֲזִיק, מַחֲזֶקֶת; inf. הַחֲזִיק (Q לחזיק, הֶחֱזִיקִי)—**1. make strong, strengthen** arms Ezk 30$_{25}$, battle 2 S 11$_{25}$, watch Jr 51$_{12}$. **2. repair** ships Ezk 27$_9$, wall Ne 3$_4$ (obj. omitted). **3. urge** someone (בְּ of obj.) to do something 2 K 4$_8$. **4a. hold,** with בְּ of obj. 2 S 3$_{29}$, accus. Ne 4$_{11}$. **b. take hold of, grasp, seize,** with בְּ of obj. Gn 19$_{16}$, לְ of obj. 2 S 15$_5$, accus. Ps 35$_2$. **c. uphold, maintain, support,** with בְּ of obj. person Lv 25$_{35}$, work Ne 5$_{16}$. **d. retain,** with בְּ of obj. persons Jg 7$_8$, accus. anger Mc 7$_{18}$. **e. contain** 2 C 4$_5$. **5. join with** (עַל) someone Ne 10$_{30}$. **6.** abs., **a. become strong** 2 C 26$_8$. **b. prevail** Dn 11$_7$. **c. stand firm** Dn 11$_{32}$.

Htp. 27.2.13 Pf. הִתְחַזֵּק; impf. יִתְחַזֵּק, נִתְחַזְּקוּ; + waw וַיִּתְחַזֵּק (וַיִּתְחַזַּק); impv. הִתְחַזֵּק, הִתְחַזְּקוּ; ptc. מִתְחַזֵּק; inf. הִתְחַזֵּק—**1. strengthen oneself** 1 K 20$_{22}$; with בְּ *in* Y. 1 S 30$_6$; עַל *over* kingdom 2 C 1$_1$, *against* Israel 2 C 17$_1$. **2a. be strengthened** Dn 10$_{19}$. **b. find one's strength** Gn 48$_2$. **3. take courage** Jg 20$_{22}$; חֲזַק וְנִתְחַזַּק *be strong and let us take courage* 2 S 10$_{12}$. **4. act with strength, resolution** 2 C 32$_5$. **5. show oneself strong** before (לִפְנֵי), i.e. **withstand** 2 C 13$_7$. **6. hold fast with** (עִם), i.e. **support** 1 C 11$_{10}$.

→ חָזָק I *strong,* חֵזֶק *strength,* חֶזְקָה *strength,* חֹזֶק *strength,* חָזְקָה *strength.*

*חזק II 1 vb.—**Qal** 1 Pf. חֲזַקְתַּנִי—**outwit** Jr 20$_7$.

חָזָק I 57.3.7 adj.—f.s. חֲזָקָה; m.pl. חֲזָקִים; cstr. חִזְקֵי—**1a. strong, mighty,** of hand Ex 3$_{19}$, wind Ex 10$_{19}$, person Jos 14$_{11}$. **b. hard, firm,** of skies Jb 37$_{18}$, face Ezk 3$_8$, persons Ezk 2$_4$ (חִזְקֵי־לֵב *strong of heart,* i.e. obstinate).

c. severe, of carnage 1QM 1$_{9}$, illness 1 K 17$_{17}$, famine 1 K 18$_{2}$. **d. loud,** of trumpet sound Ex 19$_{16}$. **2.** as noun, **strong one, mighty one, a.** masc., of Y. Is 40$_{10}$, human Am 2$_{14}$. **b.** fem., of arm Ezk 30$_{22}$, sheep Ezk 34$_{16}$. → חזק I *be strong.*

*[חָזָק] II 0.0.0.1 pr.n.[m.] **Hazak.**

חָזָק, see חזק *be strong,* qal.

[חֵזֶק] 1 n.[m.]—חֶזְקִי—**strength** Ps 18$_{2}$. → חזק I *be strong.*

[חֹזֶק] 5.2.4 n.m.—cstr. חֹזֶק (Q חוזק); sf. חָזְקֵנוּ—**strength,** חֹזֶק יָד *strength of hand* Ex 13$_{3}$, חוזק מעמד *strength of standing,* i.e. to stand 1QM 14$_{6}$. → חזק I *be strong.*

חזקא, see חִזְקִיָּהוּ *Hezekiah.*

[חֶזְקָה] 4.0.3 n.f. (or חזק I inf.)—cstr. חֶזְקַת; sf. חֶזְקָתוֹ—**1. strength,** i.e. **being strong,** of king Dn 11$_{2}$. **2.** perh. **grasping** of hand Is 8$_{11}$. **3. right of tenure** 5/6ḤevBA 44$_{13.16}$. → חזק I *be strong.*

חָזְקָה 5 n.f. **strength, severity,** בְּחָזְקָה *with strength,* i.e. mightily Jon 3$_{8}$, by force, violently Jg 4$_{3}$ 1 S 2$_{16}$; *with severity,* i.e. severely Jg 8$_{1}$. → חזק I *be strong.*

חִזְקִי 1 pr.n.m. **Hizki.**

חִזְקִיָּה, see חִזְקִיָּהוּ *Hezekiah.*

חִזְקִיָּהוּ 125.2.3.4 pr.n.m. **Hezekiah,** also as יְחִזְקִיָּהוּ **Jehizkiah.**

*חזר 0.1.1 vb.—**Qal** 0.1.1 Ptc. חוזר—**turn around, revolve,** of wheel Si 36$_{5}$.

חָח 7 n.m.—sf. חַחִי; pl. חַחִים—**1. hook,** to lead away captives or animals 2 K 19$_{28}$||Is 37$_{29}$ Ezk 19$_{4}$. **2. brooch** Ex 35$_{22}$.

[חַט], see חוט *tusk.*

חטא 238.6.7 vb.—**Qal** 182.6.6 Pf. חָטָא, חָטָאתִי; impf. יֶחֱטָא; ptc. חֹטֵא (חֹטֶא), חֹטְאִים, חֹטֵאת; inf. חֲטֹא (חֲטוֹ, חֲטֹאתוֹ)—**1a. sin against, do wrong to, offend** a human, usu. with לְ *against, to* or of obj. Gn 20$_{9}$, also with בְּ Gn 42$_{22}$; abs. 1 S 26$_{21}$. **b. sin against** (לְ) Y. Gn 20$_{6}$; abs. Ex 20$_{20}$. **c.** ptc. as noun, **sinner** Pr 11$_{31}$. **2. incur (liability for)** sacrificial offering Lv 5$_{7}$. **3. endanger,** or **forfeit** life (נֶפֶשׁ) Hb 2$_{10}$ Pr 20$_{2}$. **4. miss, fail to attain** Pr 8$_{36}$; הַחוֹטֶא בֶּן־מֵאָה שָׁנָה *the one who fails to attain an age of a hundred years* Is 65$_{20}$.

Pi. 15 Pf. חִטְּאוּ; impf. תְּחַטְּאֵנִי; + waw וַיְחַטֵּא; ptc. מְחַטֵּא; inf. חַטֵּא—**1. cleanse from sin, purify** altar Lv 8$_{15}$, sanctuary Ezk 45$_{18}$, person Ps 51$_{9}$ (+ בְּ *with* hyssop). **2. offer as sin offering** a goat Lv 9$_{15}$, blood 2 C 29$_{24}$. **3. bear the loss of** a torn animal Gn 31$_{39}$.

Hi. 32.0.1 Pf. הֶחֱטִיא; impf. תַּחֲטִיא; ptc. מַחֲטִיאֵי; inf. הַחֲטִיא (לַחֲטִיא)—**1. cause to sin,** with accus. of person Ex 23$_{33}$ (+ לְ *against* Y.) Jr 32$_{35}$, of person and sin 2 K 17$_{21}$. **2. bring guilt upon** Dt 24$_{4}$. **3. declare guilty** with (בְּ) a word Is 29$_{21}$. **4. miss the target,** in slinging of stones Jg 20$_{16}$.

Htp. 9 Impf. יִתְחַטָּא, תִּתְחַטְּאוּ (תִּתְחַטָּאוּ)—**1. purify oneself, be purified (from sin)** Nm 8$_{21}$ 31$_{23}$ (+ בְּ *with* water). **2. withdraw oneself** Jb 41$_{17}$.

→ חֵטְא *sin,* חַטָּא *sinful,* חֲטָאָה *sin,* חַטָּאָה *sin,* חַטָּאת I *sin* חֶטְאָה *sin.*

[חַטָּא] 19.0.1 n.m. & adj.—f.s. חַטָּאָה; m.pl. חַטָּאִים; cstr. חַטָּאֵי; sf. חַטָּאֶיהָ—**1.** as noun, **sinner** Gn 13$_{13}$ (+ לי״ *against* Y.) 1 S 15$_{18}$. **2.** as adj., **sinful,** of man Nm 32$_{14}$, kingdom Am 9$_{8}$. → חטא *sin.*

חֵטְא 33.7.8 n.m.—Si חט, Q חוט/חיט; cstr. חֵטְא; sf. חֶטְאוֹ; pl. חֲטָאִים; cstr. חֲטָאֵי; sf. חֲטָאֵי, חֲטָאֵיכֶם—**1. sin, offence** against Y. Ps 51$_{11}$, human Gn 41$_{9}$; חֵטְא מִשְׁפַּט־מָוֶת *sin (worthy) of a sentence of death* Dt 21$_{22}$. **2. guilt of sin** Dt 15$_{9}$; as obj. of נשׂא *bear* Lv 19$_{17}$ (or §3). **3. punishment for sin** Ezk 23$_{49}$. → חטא *sin.*

*[חִטָּא] 0.0.3 pr.n.m. **Hitta.**

חֲטָאָה 8.0.8 n.f.—**1. sin,** חֲטָאָה גְדֹלָה *a great sin* Gn 20$_{9}$, מבנה החטאה *structure of sin,* as descr. of person 1QH 9$_{22}$. **2. sin offering** Ps 40$_{7}$. → חטא *sin.*

חַטָּאָה 2 n.f. **sin** Ex 34$_{7}$ Is 5$_{18}$. → חטא *sin.*

חֶטְאָה 1 n.f. (or inf. of חטא) **sin** Nm 15$_{28}$. → חטא *sin.*

חַטָּאת I 291.5.52 n.f.—חַטָּאת (חַטָּת); cstr. חַטַּאת; sf. חַטָּאתוֹ (Q חטתו), חַטַּאתְכֶם; pl. חַטָּאוֹת; cstr. חַטֹּאות; sf. חַטֹּאותֶיךָ (חַטֹּאתֶיךָ)—**1. sin,** against human Gn 31$_{36}$, Y. Lv 4$_{14}$. **2. guilt of sin** Gn 18$_{20}$ Jr 17$_{1}$. **3. punishment for sin** Zc 14$_{19}$. **4. purification from sin,** מֵי חַטָּאת *water of purification* Nm 8$_{7}$. **5. sin offering** Lv 4$_{8}$. **6.** appar. **sinner** Pr 13$_{6}$. → חטא *sin.*

*חַטָּאת II 1 n.f. **penury** Pr 10$_{16}$.

*חַטָּאת III 2 n.f.—sf. חַטָּאתִי—**step** Jb 14$_{16}$ Pr 13$_{6}$.

חטב 9 vb.—**Qal** 8 Impf. יַחְטְבוּ; ptc. חֹטֵב; inf. לַחְטֹב—**1. cut, hew** wood Dt 19$_{5}$. **2.** ptc. as noun, **hewer of wood** Dt 29$_{10}$.

Pu. 1 Ptc. מְחֻטָּבוֹת—**be cut, be carved,** of corner

pillars Ps 144$_{12}$.

[חֲטֻבוֹת] 1 n.f.pl.—cstr. חֲטֻבוֹת—**multicoloured cloth** Pr 7$_{16}$.

חִטָּה 30.0.13.5 n.f.—pl. חִטִּים (חִטִּין, Q חנטין); cstr. חִטֵּי—**wheat,** אֶרֶץ חִטָּה *land of wheat* Dt 8$_{8}$, חֵלֶב חִטָּה *fat of wheat,* i.e. finest wheat Ps 81$_{17}$; oft. pl. as coll., קְצִיר־חִטִּים *harvest of wheat* Gn 30$_{14}$; **ears of wheat** Jg 6$_{11}$, **wheat grain** 1 K 5$_{25}$.

חַטּוּשׁ 5.0.0.1 pr.n.m. **Hattush.**

חֲטִיטָא 2 pr.n.m. **Hatita.**

חַטִּיל 2 pr.n.m. **Hattil.**

חֲטִיפָא 2 pr.n.m. **Hatipha.**

חטם 1 vb.—**Qal** 1 Impf. אֶחֱטָם־—**restrain (anger),** with ellip. of obj. Is 48$_{9}$ (+ לְ *for*).

חטף 4 vb.—**Qal** 4 Impf. יַחְטֹף (יַחְטֹף); + waw וַחֲטַפְתֶּם; inf. חֲטוֹף—**seize, snatch away** someone Jg 21$_{21}$ Ps 10$_{9.9}$ Jb 9$_{12(mss)}$ (L חתף *snatch away*).

***חטר** 0.1 vb.—**Qal** 0.1 Ptc. חוטר (or from חֹטֶר *shoot*)—**cut one's support, i.e. neck** Si 30$_{35}$.

חֹטֶר 2.1.1 n.m.—cstr. חֹטֶר—**1. shoot** Is 11$_{1}$. **2. rod** Pr 14$_{3}$ Si 30$_{35}$.

חַטָּת, see חַטָּאת *sin.*

חַי I 249.16.52.2 adj.—חַי (Am 8$_{14}$ +), חָי; cstr. חֵי; sf. חַיֶּךָ; f.s. חַיָּה; m.pl. חַיִּים; f.pl. חַיּוֹת—**1.** as attrib. adj., **a. living,** of God Dt 5$_{26}$, soul (נֶפֶשׁ), i.e. creature Gn 1$_{20}$, child 1 K 3$_{25}$, goat Lv 16$_{20}$; כָּעֵת חַיָּה *as the living time,* i.e. at this time next year Gn 18$_{10}$. **b. running, fresh,** of water Gn 26$_{19}$. **c. raw,** of flesh Lv 13$_{10}$. **2.** as pred. adj., **alive, healthy, a.** of person Gn 43$_{7}$ Si 30$_{14}$ (חי בעצמו *alive in his body*). **b.** esp. in oaths, חַי־יי *(as) Y. is alive* Jg 8$_{19}$, חַי־אָנִי *(as) I* (Y.) *am alive* Nm 14$_{21}$, חֵי נַפְשְׁךָ *(as) your soul is alive* 1 S 1$_{26}$. **3.** as adv. accus., **alive,** תִּפְשׂוּם חַיִּים *capture them alive* 1 K 20$_{18}$. **4.** as noun, **living being, one that is alive,** חֵי־הָעוֹלָם *one that is alive of,* i.e. for, *eternity* Dn 12$_{7}$, אֵם כָּל־חָי *mother of every living being* Gn 3$_{20}$. → חיה I *live.*

חַי II 2 n.[m.]—sf. חַיַּי (חַיָּי)—**kinsfolk** 1 S 18$_{18}$ Ps 42$_{9}$. → חיה I *live.*

חִיאֵל 1 pr.n.m. **Hiel.**

***[חַיָּב]** 0.1.0.1 adj.—cstr. I חיב; pl. Si חייבים—**1. guilty** Si 8$_{5}$. **2. indebted** Frey 1286$_{19(AHL)}$. → חוב *be guilty.*

***[חִיד]** 0.0.1 n.[m.] (appar. error for יַחַד)—**community** 1QS 6$_{3}$.

חִידָה 17.2.4 n.f.—sf. חִידָתִי; pl. חִידוֹת; sf. חִידֹתָם (Si חידתיהם)—**1. riddle** Nm 12$_{8}$ Jg 14$_{12}$. **2. obscure saying, problem** Dn 8$_{23}$. → חוד *propound a riddle.*

חיה I 282.3.19 vb.—**Qal** 203.3.14 Pf. חָיָה (חַי, חָי, חָי), חָיוּ; impf. יִחְיֶה (יְחִי, יְחִי, וִיחִי, יֶחִי), תְּחִיוּ; + waw וַיְחִי (וַיְחִי, וַחִי, וַיֶּחִי), וְחָיָה; וַיְחִי, וַיֶּחִי (וְחִי), וִחְיִיתֶם; impv. חְיֵה, חֲיִי, וִחְיוּ; inf. abs. חָיֹה (חָיוֹ); cstr. לִחְיוֹת (חֲיוֹתָם)—**1. live, remain alive** Gn 3$_{22}$ (+ לְ *to* eternity, i.e. for ever) Ex 1$_{16}$ Lv 25$_{35}$ (+ עִם *with* someone) Dt 8$_{3}$ (+ עַל *by* bread, utterance of Y.) Lm 4$_{20}$ (+ בְּ *among* nations) Hb 2$_{4}$ (+ בְּ *by* faithfulness); for a specif. length of time Gn 5$_{3}$. **2. revive, recover** (intrans.), from weakness Jg 15$_{19}$, illness 2 K 1$_{2}$ (+ מִן *from*), death 2 K 13$_{21}$.

Pi. 56.0.4 Pf. חִיָּה, חִיִּיתֶם; impf. יְחַיֶּה, יְחַיּוּ; impv. חַיֵּנִי; ptc. מְחַיֶּה; inf. חַיּוֹת—**1. let live, keep alive** person Gn 12$_{12}$ Dt 6$_{24}$, animal 1 K 18$_{5}$. **2. cause to live, revive** person (from death) Ho 6$_{2}$ Ps 30$_{4}$ (+ מִן *from among* those who go down the pit) Jb 33$_{4}$, stones Ne 3$_{34}$; abs. 1 S 2$_{6}$. **3a. cause grain to grow** Ho 14$_{8}$. **b. rear** animal 2 S 12$_{3}$. **4. repair** city 1 C 11$_{8}$.

Hi. 22.0.1 Pf. הֶחֱיָה, הֶחֱיִיתִי, הַחֲיִתֶם; impv. הַחֲיֵנִי, הַחֲיוּ; inf. abs. הַחֲיֵה, cstr. הַחֲיוֹת—**1. let live, keep alive** person Nm 31$_{18}$ Jos 6$_{25}$, animal Gn 6$_{19}$. **2. cause to live, revive** person 2 K 8$_{1}$; abs. 2 K 5$_{7}$.

→ חַי I *living,* II *kinsfolk,* חַיָּה I *beast,* II *life,* חָיֶה *lively,* חַיִּים *life,* חִיּוּת *living,* מִחְיָה *preservation of life.*

***חיה II** vb.—**Ni. (or Ho.) be gathered, assemble,** אִיִּים יֵחָיוּ (or יְחָיוּ) מִשְּׂמֹאל *the islands will be gathered from the north* Nm 24$_{23}$ (if em. אוֹי מִי יִחְיֶה מִשֻּׂמוֹ אֵל *woe [to] whoever lives apart from God's appointing it*). → חַיָּה III *troop.*

חַיָּה I 96.3.23 n.f.—cstr. חַיַּת (חַיְתוֹ); sf. חַיָּתוֹ, חַיָּתָם; pl. חַיּוֹת—oft. coll., **1. beast(s), animal(s),** usu. wild, חַיַּת הָאָרֶץ *beast(s) of the earth* Gn 1$_{25}$, var. חַיְתוֹ אֶרֶץ Gn 1$_{24}$, חַיַּת הַשָּׂדֶה *beast(s) of the field* Gn 2$_{19}$, פְּרִיץ חַיּוֹת *ravenous one of (the) beasts* Is 35$_{9}$. **2. living being(s)** of Ezekiel's vision Ezk 1$_{5}$ 4QpsEzek^{a} 6$_{6}$. → חיה I *live.*

***[חַיָּה] II** 12.1.1 n.f.—cstr. חַיַּת; sf. חַיָּתוֹ—**1. life** Ezk 7$_{13}$ Jb 33$_{18}$ Si 51$_{6}$. **2. appetite** of young lions Jb 38$_{39}$. → חיה I *live.*

חַיָּה III 3 n.f.—cstr. חַיַּת; sf. חַיָּתְךָ—**1. troop, band** 2 S

23$_{13}$. 2. perh. **tribe** Ps 68$_{11}$. → חיה II *gather.*

*[חַיָּה] IV 1 n.f.—sf. חַיָּתְךָ—**dwelling place,** or perh. **land** Ps 68$_{11}$.

[חָיֶה] 1 adj.—f.pl. חָיוֹת—**lively, lifegiving,** of Hebrew women Ex 1$_{19}$. → חיה I *live.*

חַיּוּת I 1 n.f. **living,** אַלְמְנוּת חַיּוּת *widowhood of living,* i.e. life of widowhood 2 S 20$_{3}$. → חיה I *live.*

*חַיּוּת II 1 n.f. **shame,** אַלְמְנוּת חַיּוּת *widowhood of shame* 2 S 20$_{3}$.

חַיִּים I 147.41.57.2 n.m.pl.—חַיִּין; cstr. חַיֵּי; sf. חַיֵּי, חַיֶּיךָ (חַיָּךְ), 2fs חַיָּיְכִי (Q חייך), חַיָּיו, חַיֵּיהֶם—**1a. (physical) life,** נִשְׁמַת חַיִּים *breath of life* Gn 2$_{7}$. **b. (duration of) life, lifetime,** כָּל־יְמֵי חַיֶּיךָ *all the days of your life* Gn 3$_{14}$, יְמֵי שְׁנֵי־חַיֵּי אַבְרָהָם *the days of the years of the life of Abraham* Gn 25$_{7}$, בְּחַיֶּיהָ *in her lifetime,* i.e. while she is alive Lv 18$_{18}$. **c. (quality of) life,** דֶּרֶךְ הַחַיִּים *way of life* Jr 21$_{8}$, הַחַיִּים וְהַשָּׁלוֹם *life and peace* Ml 2$_{5}$, חַיִּים וָחֶסֶד *life and kindness* Jb 10$_{12}$. **d. everlasting life,** lit. 'life of everlastingness', חַיֵּי עוֹלָם Dn 12$_{2}$, חיי נצח CD 3$_{20}$. **2. livelihood** Pr 27$_{27}$. → חיה I *live.*

[חַיִּים] II, see חַיִּם *Haim.*

חיל I 46.3.3 vb.—**Qal** 30.1.1 Pf. חַלְתִּי, חָלָה; impf. תָּחִיל, יָחִילוּ, חִילוּ; + waw וַיָּחֶל, וַתָּחֶל, וַתָּחֹל (וַתָּחֹל); impv. חִילִי (חוּלִי), חִילוּ, (יְחִילוּן); ptc. חוֹלָה; inf. חוּל—**1. be in pain, be in labour** Is 66$_{7}$ Jr 4$_{31}$. **2. be in anguish, writhe, tremble,** of persons Dt 2$_{25}$ (+ מִפְּנֵי *on account of*) Jr 4$_{19}$ 1 C 10$_{3}$ (+ מִן *on account of*), heart Ps 55$_{5}$ (+ בְּקֶרֶב *within*), mountains Hb 3$_{10}$, earth Ps 96$_{9}$ (+ מִפְּנֵי *before* Y.).

Hi. 2.1.2 Impf. יָחִיל; inf. Q החיל—**1. cause steppe to tremble** Ps 29$_{8}$. **2. cause writhing (in childbirth)** 1QH 11$_{8}$.

Ho. 1 Impf. יוּחַל—**be brought to birth,** of land Is 66$_{8}$.

Polel 7 Impf. יְחוֹלֵל; ptc. מְחֹלֲלֵךְ; inf. חֹלֵל—**1. bring** hinds **into labour** Ps 29$_{9}$. **2. bring to birth** people Is 51$_{2}$, earth Ps 90$_{2}$, rain Pr 25$_{23}$.

Polal 4 Pf. חוֹלָלְתִּי; impf. יְחוֹלָלוּ—**1. be brought to birth** Jb 15$_{7}$ Ps 51$_{7}$ (+ בְּ *in* iniquity). **2. be brought to trembling** Jb 26$_{5}$.

Htpol. 1.1 Ptc. מִתְחוֹלֵל—**writhe in fear** Jb 15$_{20}$ Si 3$_{27}$.

Htpalp. 1 + waw וַתִּתְחַלְחַל—**writhe in fear** Est 4$_{4}$.

→ חִיל *pain,* חִילָה *pain,* חַלְחָלָה *anguish.*

*חיל II 5 vb.—**Qal** 3 Pf. חָלָה; + waw וַיָּחֶל, וַיָּחִילוּ—**wait** seven days Gn 8$_{10}$, until (עַד) ashamed Jg 3$_{25}$, for (לְ) good Mc 1$_{12}$.

Pol. 1 Impf. תְּחוֹלֵל—**wait for** (לְ) Y. Jb 35$_{14}$.

Htpol. 1 Impv. הִתְחוֹלֵל—**wait longingly for** (לְ) Y. Ps 37$_{7}$.

*חיל III 2 vb.—**Qal** 2 Impf. יָחִיל—**endure, prosper,** of way Ps 10$_{5}$, prosperity Jb 20$_{21}$. → חַיִל *power.*

*חיל IV 3.1 vb.—**Qal** 2 Pf. חָלוּ; ptc. חלה—**take heed** 1 S 22$_{8}$ (+ עַל *concerning*) Jr 5$_{3}$.

Htpol. 1.1 Ptc. מִתְחוֹלֵל—**boast** Jb 15$_{20}$ Si 3$_{27}$.

חַיִל 267.11.32.1 n.m.—חֵיל (חַיִל); cstr. חֵיל; sf. חֵילִי; pl. חֲיָלִים; sf. חֵילֵהֶם—**1a. power, might, strength** of humans, גִּבּוֹר חַיִל *mighty one of strength, warrior* Jg 11$_{1}$, אִישׁ חַיִל *man of might, warrior* Jg 3$_{29}$, בֶּן־חַיִל *son of might,* i.e. mighty man 1 S 14$_{52}$; of horse Ps 33$_{17}$. **b. ability,** אַנְשֵׁי־חַיִל *men of ability* Gn 47$_{6}$, אֵשֶׁת־חַיִל *wife of ability* Pr 12$_{4}$, גִּבּוֹרֵי חֵיל מְלֶאכֶת עֲבוֹדַת בֵּית־הָאֱלֹהִים *mighty ones of ability of,* i.e. those very able for, *the service of the house of God* 1 C 9$_{13}$. **2. property, wealth** Gn 34$_{29}$ Dt 8$_{18}$. **3. army** Ex 14$_{4}$ 1 S 17$_{20}$; חַיִל גָּדוֹל *a great army* 2 K 7$_{6}$. **4. upper classes** of Samaria Ne 3$_{34}$. → חיל III *endure.*

חֵיל, see חֵל *rampart,* חַיִל *power.*

חִיל 6 n.m. **pain, writhing, anguish** Ex 15$_{14}$; חִיל כַּיּוֹלֵדָה *pain like (that of) one giving birth* Jr 6$_{24}$. → חיל I *be in pain.*

*[חִילָא] 0.0.0.2 pr.n.m. **Hela.**

חִילָה 1 n.f. **pain, anguish** Jb 6$_{10}$. → חיל I *be in pain.*

חִילֵז 1 pl.n. **Hilez.**

חִילֵךְ 1 pl.n. **Helech.**

חֵילָם 2 pl.n. **Helam.**

חִילֵן, see חֵלֹן *Helon.*

חִילֵן 1 pl.n. **Hilen.**

*[חַיִּם] 0.0.0.2 pr.n.[m.] **Haim.**

*חין 1 vb.—**Qal pass.** or **Pu.** 1 Impf. יֻחַן (unless חנן ho. *be shown favour*)—**die** Is 26$_{10}$.

[חִין] 1 n.[m.]—cstr. חִין—**gracefulness** Jb 41$_{4}$. → חנן I *be gracious.*

חַיִץ 1.0.4 n.m.—Q חוץ—**wall** Ezk 13$_{10}$ CD 4$_{19}$.

חִיצוֹן 25.0.5.1 adj.—f.s. חִיצוֹנָה, I חיצונית—**1. outer, exter-**

nal, of gate Ezk 44$_1$, court Ezk 10$_5$, wall 2 C 33$_{14}$, valley 3QTr 8$_4$, work Ne 11$_{16}$. **2.** as noun, **outer one,** of room of temple 1 K 6$_{29}$, coffin Beth Shearim tomb inscr. 17$_1$. → cf. חוּץ *outside.*

חֵיק 38.1.7 n.m.—חֵק; cstr. חֵיק; sf. חֵיקוֹ—**1. fold** of garment above belt, i.e. **bosom,** of man Ex 4$_6$, woman Dt 28$_{56}$. **2. inner part of body** Jb 19$_{27}$. **3. hollow** of chariot 1 K 22$_{35}$. **4. channel or rim** around altar Ezk 43$_{13}$.

*[חִיר] 0.0.1 n.[m.]—sf. חירה—**den** of lion 4QpNah 3.1$_6$ (=Na 2$_{13}$ חֹרָיו *his hole).*

חִירָה I 2 pr.n.m. **Hirah.**

*[חִירָה] II 3.0.1 n.f.—Q חרה; pl. חִירֹת—**1. court** Ps 84$_{11}$ (if em. בָּחַרְתִּי *I chose* to בְּחִרָתִי *in my court).* **2. desert tract,** פִּי הַחִירֹת *mouth,* i.e. entrance, *of desert tracks* Ex 14$_2$ (or pl.n. *Pi-hahiroth).* **3.** perh. **rock** 3QTr 8$_4$.

חִירוֹם, see חִירָם *Hiram.*

חִירָם 33 pr.n.m. **Hiram,** also as חִירוֹם **Hirom,** חוּרָם **Huram.**

חִישׁ, see חושׁ I *hasten,* V *cease.*

חִישׁ 1 adv. **quickly** Ps 90$_{10}$. → חושׁ I *hasten.*

חֵךְ I 18.3.1 n.m.—Si חיך; sf. חִכִּי—**palate, roof of mouth, mouth,** in connection with taste Jb 12$_{11}$, speech Jb 31$_{30}$ Pr 8$_7$.

*חֵךְ II 1 n.[m.] **disposition**—Ca 5$_{16}$.

חכה 14.0.7 vb.—**Qal** 1.0.3 Ptc. חוֹכֵי—**wait for** (לְ) Y. Is 30$_{18}$.

Pi. 13.0.4 Pf. חִכָּה; impf. יְחַכֶּה; impv. חַכֵּה, חַכּוּ; ptc. מְחַכֶּה (מְחַכֵּה־); inf. חַכֵּי—**1. wait, a.** for (לְ) Y. Is 8$_{17}$, counsel Ps 106$_{13}$, death Jb 3$_{20}$; with accus. **wait for** someone Jb 32$_4$. **b.** until (עַד) light of morning 2 K 7$_9$. **c.** to be gracious Is 30$_{18}$. **d.** abs. Dn 12$_{12}$. **2. delay** (intrans.) 2 K 9$_3$. **3. lie in wait,** כְּחַכֵּי אִישׁ *as the lying in wait of,* i.e. for, *a man* Ho 6$_9$.

חַכָּה 3 n.f. **fish-hook** Is 19$_8$ Hb 1$_{15}$ Jb 40$_{25}$.

*[חָכוֹר] 0.0.5 n.[m.] **rent,** i.e. money paid as rent 5/6 ḤevBA 44$_{17}$, appar. land rented 5/6ḤevBA 45$_{10}$. → חכר I *rent.*

חֲכִילָה 3 pl.n. **Hachilah.**

*[חָכִיר] 0.0.3 n.[m.] **rent,** i.e. money paid as rent Mur 24 E$_{10}$. → חכר I *rent.*

*[חֲכִירוּת] 0.0.0.1 n.f. **rent,** i.e. money paid as rent Mur 24 E$_6$ (בחרתי; appar. for בחכרתי). → חכר I *rent.*

*[חֶכֶל] 0.0.0.1 pr.n.m. **Hechel.**

חֲכַלְיָה 2 pr.n.m. **Hacaliah.**

[חַכְלִילוּת] 1 n.f.—cstr. חַכְלִילוּת—**dullness,** or perh. **sparkle,** or **redness of eyes,** after drinking wine Pr 23$_{29}$.

[חַכְלִילִי] 1 adj.—cstr. חַכְלִילִי—**dull,** as noun, **dull (one),** or perh. **sparkling (one),** or **red (one)** of eyes, i.e. one who has dull/sparkling/red eyes Gn 49$_{12}$.

חכם 28.15.3 vb.—**Qal** 18.6.2 Pf. חָכַם; impf. יֶחְכַּם; impv. חֲכַם, חֲכָמוּ—**1. be wise** Dt 32$_{29}$ 1 K 5$_{11}$ (+ מִן wiser *than).* **2. become wise** Pr 8$_{33}$. **3. act wisely** Ex 2$_{19}$.

Ni. 0.3 Pf. נחכם—**be wise, show oneself wise** Si 37$_{19}$.

Pi. 3.1 Impf. יְחַכֵּם—**1. make** someone **wiser than** (מִן) Ps 119$_{98}$. **2. teach** someone **wisdom** Ps 105$_{22}$.

Pu. 2 Ptc. מְחֻכָּם—**be made wise** Ps 58$_6$ Pr 30$_{24}$.

Hi. 1.0.1 Ptc. מַחְכִּימַת—**make** someone **wise** Ps 19$_8$.

Htp. 2.5 Impf. נִתְחַכְּמָה, תִּתְחַכַּם—**1. make oneself wise** Ec 7$_{16}$. **2. deal wisely with** (לְ) people Ex 1$_{10}$.

→ חָכָם *wise,* חָכְמָה *wisdom,* חָכְמוֹת *wisdom.*

חָכָם 138.21.14 adj.—f.s. חֲכָמָה; cstr. m.s. חֲכַם, f.s. חַכְמַת; m.pl. חֲכָמִים; cstr. חַכְמֵי; sf. חֲכָמָיו; f.pl. חֲכָמוֹת; cstr. חַכְמוֹת—**1.** as adj., **wise,** i.e. **a. competent** in politics, administration Gn 41$_{33}$ 1 K 5$_{21}$. **b. astute** 2 S 13$_3$. **c. prudent** Dt 4$_6$. **d. skilful,** as artisan 2 C 2$_6$. **3.** as noun, **a. wise one, sage,** (1) learned class of Egypt Gn 41$_8$, Babylon Jr 50$_{35}$, Persia Est 1$_{13}$. (2) political advisers Is 19$_{11}$ Jr 18$_{18}$. (3) in religion and ethics Pr 1$_6$ 13$_{14}$. **b. skilled one,** as (1) **artisan** Jr 10$_9$. (2) **mourner** (fem.) Jr 9$_{16}$. → חכם *be wise.*

חָכְמָה 153.25.44 n.f.—Q חוכמא; cstr. חָכְמַת; sf. חָכְמָתִי, חָכְמַתְכֶם—**1. skill,** in technical work Ex 28$_3$ 1 K 7$_{14}$. **2.** personified **Wisdom** Jb 28$_{12}$ Pr 8$_1$. **3a. wisdom, good sense, insight** 2 S 20$_{22}$ Dn 1$_4$. **b.** religious, ethical **wisdom, prudence** Dt 4$_6$ Ps 111$_{10}$. **c. wisdom** of God 1 K 3$_{28}$. → חכם *be wise.*

חַכְמֹנִי I 2 pr.n.m. **Hachmoni.**

[חַכְמוֹנִי] II 1 gent. **Hachmonite.**

חָכְמוֹת 4.1 n.f.pl. **wisdom** Pr 24$_7$ Ps 49$_4$; personified **Wisdom** Pr 1$_{20}$ 9$_1$ Si 4$_{11}$. → חכם *be wise.*

*חכר I 0.0.10 vb.—**Qal** 0.0.9 Pf. חכרתי—**rent, lease** land from (מִן) someone 5/6ḤevBA 44$_6$ Mur 24 3$_6$.

Hi. 0.0.1 Pf. החכרתי—**let** land to (לְ) someone 5/6

ḤevBA 45$_7$.

→ חָכוֹר *rent*, חָכִיר *rent*, חֲכִירוּת *rent*.

*חכר II $_1$ vb.—Impf. mss תַּחְכְּרוּ—**oppress,** with לְ of obj. Jb 19$_3$(mss) (L הכר *wonder at*).

חֵל $_{9.0.3}$ n.m.—חֵיל; cstr. חֵל; sf. חֵילֵךְ—**1.** usu. **rampart, outer wall of defences** 2 S 20$_{15}$, or perh. space in front of city walls 1 K 21$_{23}$. **2. ditch around temple** 11QT 46$_9$. **3.** perh. **fortress** Ob$_{20}$.

חֹל $_{7.0.2}$ n.[m.]—Q חול—**profaneness, commonness,** as opposed to קֹדֶשׁ *holiness* Lv 10$_{10}$; לֶחֶם חֹל *bread of commonness,* i.e. common bread 1 S 21$_5$. → I חלל *profane*.

חלא I $_2$ vb.—**Qal** $_1$ + waw וַיֶּחֱלָא (mss וַיֶּחֱלֶא)—**become diseased** 2 C 16$_{12}$.

Hi. $_1$ Pf. הֶחֱלִי (unless חלה hi.)—**make ill** Is 53$_{10}$.

→ תַּחֲלֻאִים *diseases*.

*חלא II $_{0.1}$ vb.—**Pi., cleanse** city **of rust** Ezk 24$_{12}$ (if em. בְּאֵשׁ חֶלְאָתָהּ appar. *into a fire its rust [is to go]* to בְּאֵשׁ תְּחַלְּאֶהָ *by fire you shall cleanse it of rust*).

Hi. $_{0.1}$ Impf. יחליא—**show rust,** of evil Si 12$_{10}$ (+ כְּ *as* bronze).

→ חֶלְאָה *rust*.

*[חֵלֶא] $_{0.0.0.1}$ pr.n.[m.] **Hele.**

[חֶלְאָה] I $_5$ n.f.—sf. חֶלְאָתָהּ (חֶלְאָתָה)—**rust** Ezk 24$_6$. → II חלא *be rusty*.

חֶלְאָה II $_2$ pr.n.f. **Helah.**

חֲלָאִים, see חֲלִי I *ornament*.

חֶלְאמָה, see חֵילָם *Helam*.

חָלָב $_{44.2.3}$ n.m.—cstr. חֲלֵב; sf. חֲלָבִי—**1.** usu. **milk,** אֶרֶץ זָבַת חָלָב וּדְבַשׁ *a land flowing with milk and honey* Ex 3$_8$, טְלֵה חָלָב *lamb of milk,* i.e. suckling lamb 1 S 7$_9$. **2. cheese** 1 S 17$_{18}$.

חֵלֶב I $_{91.2.20}$ n.m.—cstr. חֵלֶב; sf. חֶלְבָּם (חֶלְבָּמוֹ); pl. חֲלָבִים; cstr. חֶלְבֵי; sf. חֶלְבֵהֶן—**1. fat, a.** of human body Jg 3$_{22}$. **b.** of beasts Dt 32$_{14}$, esp. offered as sacrifice Lv 3$_3$. **2. choicest, best part** of products of land Gn 45$_{18}$ Nm 18$_{12}$.

חֵלֶב II $_1$ pr.n.m. **Heleb.**

חֶלְבָּה $_1$ pl.n. **Helbah.**

חֶלְבּוֹן $_1$ pl.n. **Helbon.**

חֶלְבְּנָה $_1$ n.f. **galbanum,** gum used in incense Ex 30$_{34}$.

*[חלד] vb. **Qal, live** Ps 49$_9$ Jb 14$_6$ (both if em. חדל *cease*). → חָלֶד *everlasting*, חֶלֶד *duration of life*.

*[חָלֶד] adj. **everlasting** Ps 89$_{48}$ (if em. חֶלֶד *duration of life*). → חלד *live*.

חֵלֶד $_2$ pr.n.m. **Heled.**

חֶלֶד $_5$ n.[m.]—חָלֶד; sf. חֶלְדִּי—**1. duration of life, life-span** Ps 39$_6$. **2. world** Ps 49$_2$. → חלד *live*.

חֹלֶד $_{1.0.1}$ n.[m.]—Q חולד—**weasel** Lv 11$_{29}$ 11QT 50$_{20}$.

חֻלְדָּה $_2$ pr.n.f. **Huldah.**

חֶלְדַּי $_{2.0.0.2}$ pr.n.m. **Heldai.**

חלה I $_{59.0.5}$ vb.—**Qal** $_{38.0.2}$ Pf. חָלָה; + waw וַיָּחַל; ptc. חֹלֶה, חוֹלָה, חוֹלַת; inf. חֲלֹתוֹ—**1. be weak, be faint** Jg 16$_7$; חוֹלַת אַהֲבָה *faint of,* i.e. with, *love* Ca 2$_5$. **2a. be(come) ill, sick** Gn 48$_1$. **b.** with obj., **be ill with** illness (חֳלִי) 2 K 13$_{14}$, **be diseased in** feet 1 K 15$_{23}$. **3. feel pain, regret, be concerned** 1 S 22$_8$ (+ עַל *for*) Jr 5$_3$ Pr 23$_{35}$. **4.** ptc. as **a.** noun, **weak one, sick one,** of sheep Ezk 34$_4$, sacrificial animals Ml 1$_8$. **b.** adj., **grievous,** of evil Ec 5$_{12}$.

Ni. $_{10}$ Pf. נֶחֱלוּ, נֶחֱלֵיתִי; ptc. נַחֲלָה (נַחְלָה), נַחֲלוֹת—**1. be made weak, sick** Dn 8$_{27}$. **2. tire oneself out** Jr 12$_{13}$. **3. be concerned, grieved for** (עַל) Am 6$_6$. **4.** ptc. as **a.** noun, (1) **weak one,** of sheep Ezk 34$_4$. (2) **sickness** Is 17$_{11}$. **b.** adj., **severe, grievous,** of wound Jr 10$_{19}$.

Pi. $_1$ Pf. חִלָּה—**make sick,** תַּחֲלֻאֶיהָ אֲשֶׁר־חִלָּה י׳ בָּהּ *its* (the land's) *sicknesses with which Y. has made it sick* Dt 29$_{21}$.

Pu. $_1$ Pf. חֻלֵּיתָ—**be made weak** Is 14$_{10}$.

Hi. $_{3.0.3}$ Pf. הֶחֱלֵיתִי; ptc. מַחֲלָה—**1. make** the heart **sick** Pr 13$_{12}$. **2. make sore,** הֶחֱלֵיתִי הַכּוֹתֶךָ *I have made sore your striking,* i.e. stricken you sore Mc 6$_{13}$. **3. become sick with** the heat of wine Ho 7$_5$.

Ho. $_3$ Pf. הָחֳלֵיתִי—**be wounded** 1 K 22$_{34}$||2 C 18$_{33}$.

Htp. $_3$ + waw וַיִּתְחָל; impv. הִתְחָל; inf. הִתְחַלּוֹת—**1. make oneself ill** 2 S 13$_2$. **2. feign sickness** 2 S 13$_{5.6}$.

→ חֳלִי *sickness*, מַחֲלָה *sickness*, מַחֲלֶה *sickness*, מַחֲלוּיִם *sickness*, נְחִילוֹת II *sickness*.

חלה II $_{16.2.1}$ vb.—**Pi.** $_{16.2.1}$ Pf. חִלִּיתִי; impf. יְחַלּוּ; + waw וַיְחַל; impv. חַל, חַלּוּ; inf. חַלּוֹת—**appease, entreat the favour of,** with obj. פָּנִים lit. 'face' of Y. Ex 32$_{11}$ 1 S 13$_{12}$, humans Ps 45$_{13}$ (+ בְּ *with* a present) Jb 11$_{19}$.

*חלה III vb.—**Ni., be adorned** Pr 14$_{18}$ (if em. נֶחֱלוּ

they inherit folly to נֶחֱלוּ *they are adorned* [with] folly). → חֲלִי I *ornament.*

***חלה** IV 5 vb.—**Qal** 4 Pf. חָלִיתִי; ptc. חֹלֶה—**be concerned** 1 S 22$_{8}$ (+ עַל *for*) Is 57$_{10}$ Jr 5$_{3}$; **be aware** Pr 23$_{35}$.

Ni. 1 Pf. נֶחְלוּ—**be distressed** on account of (עַל) Am 6$_{6}$.

***חלה** V 20.2.1 vb.—**Qal** 2 Ptc. חוֹלָה—**1. be alone,** ptc. as adj., **unique,** of evil Ec 5$_{12.15}$. **2. be disengaged,** of right hand Ps 77$_{11}$ (if em. חַלּוֹתִי הִיא *it is my being wounded* to חָלְתָה *it is disengaged*). **3. desist from** (מִן) burden Ho 8$_{10}$ (if em. וַיָּחֵלּוּ *and they began* to וְיֶחֱלוּ *and they will desist.*

Ni. 1 Ptc. נַחְלָה—**be unprecedented,** of wound Na 3$_{19}$.

Pi. 16.2.1 Pf. חִלִּיתִי; impf. יְחַלּוּ; + waw וַיְחַל; impv. חַל, חַלּוּ; inf. חַלּוֹת—**make face unique,** i.e. secure favour for oneself alone, with obj. 'face' of Y. Ex 32$_{11}$ 1 S 13$_{12}$, humans Ps 45$_{13}$ (+ בְּ *with* a present) Jb 11$_{19}$.

Pu. 1 Pf. חֻלֵּיתָ—**be left alone,** i.e. removed from society Is 14$_{10}$.

Hi. 1 Pf. הֶחֱלֵיתִי—**make** wound **unique** Mc 6$_{13}$.

חַלָּה 14.0.4 n.f.—cstr. חַלַּת; pl. חַלּוֹת; cstr. חַלֹּת—**cake,** used in offerings, חַלַּת לֶחֶם *cake of bread* 2 S 6$_{19}$, מַצָּה *of unleavened bread* Lv 8$_{26}$.

*[**חִלּוּל**] 1 n.[m.]—pl. Sam חִלּוּלִים—**commonness, desanctification** of a vineyard by offering its firstfruits to Y., thereby allowing humans to consume its fruit Lv 19$_{24(Sam)}$ (MT הִלּוּלִים *praise*). → חלל I *be profaned.*

חֲלוֹם 65.2.5 n.m.—חֲלֹם; cstr. חֲלוֹם; sf. חֲלֹמוֹ; pl. חֲלֹמוֹת; cstr. חֲלוֹמוֹת; sf. חֲלֹמֹתָיו—**dream** Is 29$_{7}$; oft. with prophetic content Nm 12$_{6}$; חלם חֲלוֹם *have* (lit. 'dream') *a dream* Gn 37$_{5}$, בַּעַל הַחֲלֹמוֹת *the master of,* i.e. expert in, *dreams* Gn 37$_{19}$. → חלם I *dream.*

*[**חֲלוֹמָה**] n.f. **wise woman** Zc 10$_{2}$ (if em. חֲלֹמוֹת הַשָּׁוְא *dreams of falsehood* to הַחֲלֹמוֹת שָׁוְא *the wise women* speak *falsehood*) Jr 27$_{9}$ (if em. חֲלֹמֹתֵיכֶם *your dreams* to חֲלֹמֹתֵיכֶם *your wise women*).

חַלּוֹן 31.1.2 n.m.—cstr. חַלּוֹן; pl. חַלּוֹנִים, חַלּוֹנוֹת; cstr. חַלּוֹנֵי; sf. חַלּוֹנָיו—**window** Gn 8$_{6}$ Jos 2$_{15}$.

חֵלוֹן, see חלן *Helon.*

חֹלוֹן, see חלן *Holon.*

חֲלוֹף 1 n.m. **passing away,** or perh. **opposition,** or **foolishness** Pr 31$_{8}$. → חלף I *pass on.*

חָלוּץ, see חלץ II *equip (for war),* Qal §2.

חֲלוּשָׁה 1 n.f. **defeat,** perh. **defeated ones** Ex 32$_{18}$. → חלש I *defeat.*

[**חֲלַח**] 3 pl.n. **Halah.**

חַלְחוּל 1 pl.n. **Halhul.**

חַלְחָלָה 4.0.2 n.f. **anguish** Is 21$_{3}$ Ezk 30$_{4}$. → חיל I *be in pain.*

חלט 1 vb.—**Qal** (or perh. **Hi.**) 1 + waw וַיַּחְלְטוּ—**accept (words)** as convincing 1 K 20$_{33}$.

[**חֲלִי**] I 2 n.m.—cstr. חֲלִי; pl. חֲלָאִים—**ornament,** item of jewellery Pr 25$_{12}$ Ca 7$_{2}$. → חלה III *adorn.*

חֲלִי II 1 pl.n. **Hali.**

חֳלִי 24.3.3 n.m.—חֹלִי; sf. חָלְיוֹ; pl. חֳלָיִם (חֳלָיִים); sf. חֳלָיֵנוּ—**1.** usu. **sickness, illness** Dt 7$_{15}$ 1 K 17$_{17}$; חֳלִי לְאֵין מַרְפֵּא *an illness without cure* 2 C 21$_{18}$. **2. affliction** Jr 10$_{19}$ Ec 6$_{2}$. → חלה I *be weak.*

חליא, see חֶלְיָה *sediment.*

[**חֶלְיָה**] 1 n.f.—sf. חֶלְיָתָהּ—**jewellery** Ho 2$_{15}$.

*[**חֶלְיָה**] 0.0.1 n.f.—חליא—**sediment** at bottom of cistern, or perh. **(perforated) stone** covering top of cistern 3QTr 1$_{7}$.

*[**חַלְיוֹ**] 0.0.0.1 pr.n.[m.] **Hallio.**

חָלִיל 6.1.4 n.m.—cstr. Q חליל; pl. חֲלִלִים—**flute, pipe** 1 S 10$_{5}$ 1 K 1$_{40}$ 1QH 19$_{23}$. → חלל IV *play the flute;* cf. נְחִילוֹת I *flutes.*

חָלִילָה 21 interj.—חָלִלָה—**may it not be, 1.** חָלִילָה alone 1 S 14$_{45}$. **2.** חָלִילָה followed by **a.** לְ, חָלִילָה לִּי *far be it from me* 1 S 2$_{30}$. **b.** לְ and מִן, חָלִלָה לְּךָ מֵעֲשֹׂת *far be it from you to do* Gn 18$_{25}$, חָלִילָה לִּי מֵיְ׳ מִתִּתִּי *may Y. prevent me from giving* 1 K 21$_{3}$, חָלִלָה לָאֵל מֵרֶשַׁע *may any wickedness be far from God* Jb 34$_{10}$. **c.** לְ + אִם, חָלִילָה לִּי אִם־אֲבַלַּע *far be it from me to destroy* 2 S 20$_{20}$, חָלִילָה לִּי מֵיְ׳ אִם־אֶעֱשֶׂה *may Y. prevent me from doing* 1 S 24$_{7}$.

*[**חֲלִיפָא**] 0.0.2 pr.n.m. **Halipha.**

[**חֲלִיפָה**] I 12.1.3 n.f.—sf. חֲלִיפָתִי; pl. חֲלִיפוֹת; cstr. חֲלִיפוֹת—**1. change** of clothing Gn 45$_{22}$, way of life Ps 55$_{20}$. **2. relay** of forced labourers 1 K 5$_{28}$. **3. reserve** of troops 1QM 16$_{12}$. **4. relief** from hard service Jb 14$_{14}$. → חלף I *pass on.*

*[**חֲלִיפָה**] II 1 n.f.—pl. חֲלִיפוֹת—**(respect for) oath** Ps

55₂₀.

[חֲלִיצָה] 2 n.f.—sf. חֲלִצָתוֹ; pl. sf. חֲלִיצוֹתָם—**spoil,** stripped from body Jg 14₁₉ 2 S 2₂₁. → חלץ I *loosen.*

חֶלְכָה 3.0.5 adj.—חֶלְכָה; pl. Kt, Q חלכאים (Qr חֵיל כָּאִים appar. *army of dejected ones*); cstr. Q חילכיא—as noun, **1. wretched one, hapless one** Ps 10₈.₁₀.₁₄. **2. wicked one, tyrant** 1QH 11₂₅ 12₂₅ 4QapLamB₄.

חלל I 79.3.17 vb.—**Ni.** 10.2 Pf. נִחַל; impf. יֵחַל, תֵּחֵל; + waw וָאֵחַל, וְנִחַלְתְּ; inf. הֵחַל (הֵחַלּוֹ)—**1. be profaned,** of Y. Ezk 22₂₆, name of Y. Ezk 20₉, sanctuary Ezk 7₂₄. **2. profane, defile oneself** Lv 21₄.₉.

Pi. 66.1.12 Pf. חִלֵּל, חִלְּלוּ; impf. יְחַלֵּל, יְחַלְּלוּ; + waw וַתְּחַלְלֶהָ; ptc. מְחַלֵּל, מְחַלֶּלֶת, מְחַלְלִים (מְחַלְלֶיהָ); inf. חַלֵּל (חַלְּלוֹ)—**1. profane** Y. Ezk 13₁₉, name of Y. Lv 18₂₁, person Lv 19₂₉, land Jr 16₁₈, sanctuary Lv 21₁₂, couch 1 C 5₁, sabbath Ex 31₁₄. **2. make profane use of** vineyard Dt 20₆. **3. expel as profane from** (מִן) mountain of Y. Ezk 28₁₆.

Pu. 1 ptc. מְחֻלָּל—**be profaned,** of name of Y. Ezk 36₂₃.

Hi. 1.0.5 Pf. Q החל; impf. יַחֵל; inf. Q החל—**1. profane** sabbath CD 11₁₅, oil 1QM 9₈. **2. make word invalid** Nm 30₃.

→ חֹל *profaneness,* חָלָל II *profane,* חלול *commonness.*

*חלל II 54.0.12 vb.—**Hi.** 53.0.12 Pf. הֵחֵל, הֵחֵלָּה, הַחִלֹּתִי; impf. יָחֵל, תָּחֵלּוּ; + waw וַיָּחֶל, וַיָּחֵלּוּ, וַתְּחִלֶּינָה; impv. הָחֵל; ptc. מֵחֵל; inf. הָחֵל (הַחִלָּם)—**begin,** abs. Nm 17₁₁; followed by **a.** usu. inf. cstr., הֵחֵל הָאָדָם לָרֹב *human beings began to multiply* Gn 6₁. **b.** fin. verb, הָחֵל רָשׁ *begin, possess* Dt 2₂₄. **c.** inf. abs., הָחֵל וְכַלֵּה *beginning and ending,* i.e. from beginning to end 1 S 3₁₂. **d.** prep., בְּ *with* someone Gn 44₁₂, מִן *from* place Ezk 9₆.

Ho. 1 Pf. הוּחַל—**be begun,** הוּחַל לִקְרֹא *it was begun,* i.e. people began, *to call* Gn 4₂₆.

→ תְּחִלָּה *beginning.*

חלל III 8 vb.—**Qal** 2 Pf. חָלַל; inf. חַלּוֹתִי—**be pierced, wounded,** of person Ps 77₁₁, heart Ps 109₂₂.

Pi. 1.0.1 + waw Q ויחללהו; ptc. מְחַלְלֶיךָ—**pierce** someone Ezk 28₉.

Pu. 1 Ptc. מְחֻלָּלֵי—ptc. as noun, **pierced one,** מְחֻלְלֵי חֶרֶב *pierced ones of,* i.e. by, *the sword* Ezk 32₂₆.

Poel 4 Pf. חֹלְלָה; ptc. מְחוֹלֵל, מְחוֹלֶלֶת, ms מְחֹלְלֶיךָ—**pierce, wound** Is 51₉ Jb 26₁₃ Pr 26₁₀.

Poal 1 Ptc. מְחֹלָל—**be wounded** Is 53₅ (+ מִן *on account of*).

→ חָלָל I *slain one,* מְחִלָּה *hole,* מְחוֹלְלָה II *wound.*

חלל IV 2 vb.—**Qal** 1 Ptc. חֹלְלִים—**play the flute,** ptc. as noun, **flautist** Ps 87₇.

Pi. 1 Ptc. מְחַלְּלִים—**play the flute** 1 K 1₄₀.

→ חָלִיל *flute.*

*חלל V 1 vb.—**Qal** Pf. חָלַל—**tremble, be disturbed,** of heart Ps 109₂₂.

חָלָל I 91.1.41 n.m.—cstr. חֲלַל; pl. חֲלָלִים; cstr. חַלְלֵי; sf. חֲלָלָיו, חַלְלֵיהֶם—**1. one slain, one pierced** Dt 21₁; חַלְלֵי יי *ones slain of,* i.e. by, Y. Is 66₁₆, חֶרֶב *of,* i.e. by, *the sword* Is 22₂, רָעָב *of,* i.e. by, *famine* Lm 4₉. **2. one deflowered** Lv 21₇. **3.** pl. in 1QM perh. **carnage, massacre,** חללי אל *carnage of God* 1QM 4₇. → חלל III *be pierced.*

חָלָל II 4 adj.—f.s. חֲלָלָה; m.pl. cstr. חַלְלֵי—**1. profane,** of person Ezk 21₃₀. **2.** as noun, **a. profane one** Ezk 21₃₄. **b. defiled one,** of woman defiled sexually Lv 21₇.₁₄. → חלל I *profane.*

חָלִלָה, see חָלִילָה *may it not be.*

חלם I 26.0.5 vb.—**Qal** 26.0.4 Pf. חָלַם; impf. יַחֲלֹם, יַחֲלֹמוּן; + waw וַיַּחֲלֹמוּ; ptc. חֹלֵם—**1. dream** Is 29₈; oft. with accus. חֲלוֹם *dream* Gn 37₅. **2.** ptc. as noun, **dreamer,** חֹלֵם חֲלוֹם *dreamer of dream(s)* Dt 13₂.

Hi. 1 Ptc. מַחְלְמִים—**dream,** with accus. חֲלוֹם *dream* Jr 29₈.

→ חֲלוֹם *dream.*

חלם II 2.2.2 vb.—**Qal** 1 Impf. יַחְלְמוּ—**1. be healthy, strong,** of animals Jb 39₄. **2.** pass. ptc. as noun, **one who is sound** Ec 5₂ (if em. הַחֲלוֹם *the dream* to הֶחָלוּם).

Ni. 0.0.1 Impv. החלמי—**be sure, be confident** 4Q Jubg 25₁₀.

Hi. 1.2.1 Pf. Si החלים; impf. תַּחֲלִימֵנִי; inf. Q החלימם—**heal, make someone strong** Is 38₁₆ Si 15₂₀₍A₎ 49₁₀.

חֵלֶם 1 pr.n.m. **Helem.**

*[חֶלְמָה] I 0.0.1 n.f. **seamed robe** 4QTohB[b] 1.2₄.

*[חֶלְמָה] II 0.0.1 n.f. **clay** 4QTohB[b] 1.2₄.

חַלָּמוּת I 1 n.f. **mallow,** or **purslane,** plant with tasteless juice Jb 6₆.

*חַלָּמוּת II $_{1}$ n.f. **egg-yolk,** רִיר חַלָּמוּת *juice of egg-yolk,* i.e. white of egg Jb 6$_{6}$.

חַלָּמִישׁ $_{5.0.2}$ n.m.—cstr. חַלְּמִישׁ—**flint** Dt 8$_{15}$.

חֵלֹן $_{5}$ pr.n.m. **Helon.**

חֹלֹן $_{3.0.0.1}$ pl.n. **Holon.**

חלף I $_{28.5.4}$ vb.—**Qal** $_{15.4.3}$ Pf. חָלַף; impf. יַחֲלֹף; inf. חֲלֹף—**1a. pass on, pass by,** of Y. Jb 9$_{11}$, human 1 S 10$_{3}$ (+ מִשָּׁם וָהָלְאָה *from there and further*), spirit Jb 4$_{15}$, river Is 8$_{8}$, whirlwind Is 21$_{1}$. **b. pass away,** of images of god Is 2$_{18}$ (+ כָּלִיל *utterly*), heaven and earth Ps 102$_{27}$, rain Ca 2$_{11}$. **2. be renewed,** of grass Ps 90$_{5}$. **3.** trans., **a. pass by, elude** Y. Si 42$_{20}$. **b. transgress** statute Is 24$_{5}$. **c. exchange** goodness Si 42$_{25}$ (+ עַל *with*).

Pi. $_{2}$ + waw וַיְחַלֵּף—**change** garments Gn 41$_{14}$.

Hi. $_{10.1.1}$ Pf. הֶחֱלִף; impf. יַחֲלִיף; + waw וַתַּחֲלֵף; impv. הַחֲלִיפוּ—**1. change** wages Gn 31$_{7}$, garments Gn 35$_{2}$. **2. replace, substitute** beast Lv 27$_{10}$, cedars Is 9$_{9}$. **3. renew** strength Is 40$_{31}$, person 4QapMes 2.2$_{6}$ (+ בְּ *with* strength). **4.** intrans., **renew oneself, show newness,** of tree Jb 14$_{7}$, bow Jb 29$_{20}$.

→ חֲלוֹף *passing away,* חֵלֶף I *in return for,* חֲלִיפָה I *change,* מַחֲלָף I *knife,* II *censer,* מַחְלָפָה I *plait of hair.*

*חלף II $_{2.1}$ vb.—**Qal** $_{2.1}$ Pf. חָלְפָה; impf. תַּחֲלְפֵהוּ—**pierce through** person Jb 20$_{24}$, temple Jg 5$_{26}$, clouds Si 32$_{21}$ (Bmg). → (?) מַחְלָפָה II *copious hair.*

*חלף III $_{2}$ vb.—**Qal** $_{1}$ + waw חָלַף—**grow, sprout,** of grass Ps 90$_{6}$.

Hi. $_{1}$ Impf. יַחֲלִיף—**sprout,** of tree Jb 14$_{7}$.

חֵלֶף I $_{2.0.2}$ prep. **in return for** Nm 18$_{21.31}$.

חֵלֶף II $_{1}$ pl.n. **Heleph.**

*[חֲלַפְתָּא] $_{0.0.0.1}$ pr.n.m. **Halaphta.**

חלץ I $_{23.0.4}$ vb.—**Qal** $_{5}$ Pf. חָלַץ; impf. יַחֲלֹץ; ptc. pass. חֲלוּץ—**1. loosen, expose** breast Lm 4$_{3}$. **2a. take off** sandal from (מֵעַל) foot Dt 25. **b.** pass., **be taken off,** חֲלוּץ הַנָּעַל *one taken off of sandal,* i.e. whose sandal is taken off Dt 25$_{10}$. **3.** intrans., **withdraw from** (מִן) Ho 5$_{6}$.

Ni. $_{4}$ Impf. יֵחָלְצוּן (יֵחָלֵצוּ); ptc. נֶחֱלָץ—**be delivered** Ps 60$_{7}$ Pr 11$_{8}$ (+ מִן *from* distress) 11$_{9}$ (+ בְּ *by* knowledge).

Pi. $_{13.0.4}$ Pf. חִלֵּץ, חִלְּצוּ; impf. יְחַלֵּץ; + waw וָאֲחַלְּצָה; impv. חַלְּצָה (חַלְּצֵנִי)—**1. deliver** someone 2 S 22$_{20}$||Ps 18$_{20}$ Ps 116$_{8}$ (+ מִן *from*). **2. plunder** enemy Ps 7$_{5}$. **3. pull out** stones (from wall) Lv 14$_{40}$.

→ חֲלִיצָה I *spoil,* מַחֲלָצָה I *robe.*

חלץ II $_{21.0.2}$ vb.—**Qal** $_{17.0.2}$ Impf. Q יחלוצו; ptc. pass. חָלוּץ, חֲלוּצִים—**1. equip (for war), arm** 1QM 2$_{7.8}$. **2.** pass. ptc. as **a.** adj., **equipped (for war), armed** Nm 32$_{30}$. **b.** noun, **one equipped (for war), armed man,** coll. sg. Jos 6$_{13}$; pl., חֲלוּצֵי צָבָא *men equipped of,* i.e. for, *war* Nm 31$_{5}$.

Ni. $_{3.0.1}$ Impf. תֵּחָלְצוּ; impv. הֵחָלְצוּ—**be equipped, equip oneself** Nm 31$_{3}$ 32$_{17}$.

Hi. $_{2.0.1}$ Impf. יַחֲלִיץ—**make** bones **strong** Is 58$_{11}$.

חֶלֶץ $_{5.0.0.8}$ pr.n.m. **Helez.**

*[חֶלֶצְיָהוּ] $_{0.0.0.5}$ pr.n.m. **Heleziah.**

[חֲלָצַיִם] $_{10}$ n.[f.]du.—חֲלָצַיִם; sf. חֲלָצָיו—**loins,** בִּנְךָ הַיֹּצֵא מֵחֲלָצֶיךָ *your son who shall go out from your loins* 1 K 8$_{19}$||2 C 6$_{9}$, אֱזָר־נָא כְגֶבֶר חֲלָצֶיךָ *gird your loins like a man* Jb 38$_{3}$.

חלק I $_{56.10.9}$ vb.—**Qal** $_{17}$ Pf. חָלַק; impf. יַחֲלֹק, תַּחְלְקוּ; + waw וַיַּחְלְקוּ, וַיַּחְלְקֵם; impv. חִלְקוּ; ptc. חוֹלֵק; inf. חֲלֹק—**1a. allot, apportion** gods Dt 4$_{19}$ (+ לְ *to*), land Jos 14$_{5}$. **b. distribute (supplies)** Ne 13$_{13}$ (+ לְ *to*). **2a. divide, share** spoil Jos 22$_{8}$ (+ עִם *with*), land 2 S 19$_{30}$. **b. obtain a share of** spoil (obj. omitted) 1 S 30$_{24}$, inheritance Pr 17$_{2}$. **3. divide up, plunder** house of Y. 2 C 28$_{21}$. **4. divide** persons **into groups** 1 C 24$_{4.5}$. **5. assign** someone in charge of (עַל) 2 C 23$_{18}$.

Ni. $_{8.3.3}$ Pf. Si נחלק; impf. יֵחָלֵק (יֵחָלֶק); + waw וַיֵּחָלֵק—**1. divide oneself, deploy oneself** Gn 14$_{15}$ 1QM 18$_{4}$ (+ עַל *against*). **2. be divided,** of people into (לְ) two factions 1 K 16$_{21}$; of war, i.e. **be waged against** (עַל) 1QM 2$_{13.14}$. **3. be apportioned, allotted,** of land Nm 26$_{53}$ (+ בְּ *as* inheritance), praise Si 15$_{9}$ (+ לְ *to*), work Si 7$_{15}$. **4. be distributed, dispersed,** of light Jb 38$_{24}$.

Pi. $_{26.0.6}$ Pf. חִלְּקָם, חִלְּקוּ, חִלֵּק; impf. יְחַלֵּק, אֲחַלֵּק, אֲחַלֶּק־ (אֲחַלְּקָה); + waw וַיְחַלֶּק־; impv. חַלֵּק; inf. חַלֵּק (חַלְּקָם)—**1. divide up** spoil Gn 49$_{27}$, land Jl 4$_{2}$, garments Ps 22$_{19}$. **2. apportion** land Jos 13$_{7}$ (+ בְּ *as* inheritance, לְ *to* tribes), statute 1QS 10$_{25}$ (+ בְּ *with* line). **3. distribute** food 2 S 6$_{19}$ (+ לְ *to*). **4. scatter** people Gn 49$_{7}$.

Pu. $_{3}$ Pf. חֻלָּק; impf. תְּחֻלָּק—**be divided,** of land Am

7_{17} (+ בְּ *with* line), spoil Zc 14_{1}.

Hi. 1 Inf. חֲלֹק—**receive a share (of property)** Jr 37_{12}.

Htp. 1 + waw וְהִתְחַלְּקוּ—**divide land with one another** Jos 18_{5} (+ לְ *into* seven portions).

→ חֵלֶק I *portion*, חֶלְקָה I *plot (of land)*, חֲלֻקָּה *division*, מַחֲלֹקוֹת *distribution*, מַחֲלֹקֶת I *division*.

חלק **II** 10.0.2 vb.—**Qal** 2 Pf. חָלַק—**be smooth, slippery,** of curds, i.e. words Ps 55_{22}, heart (as false) Ho 10_{2}.

Hi. 8.0.2 Pf. הֶחֱלִיק; impf. יַחֲלִיקוּן; ptc. מַחֲלִיק—**1. make smooth,** in metal working Is 41_{7} (+ פַּטִּישׁ *[with] a hammer*). **2a. make smooth** one's speech in flattery, obj. tongue Ps 5_{10}, word Pr 2_{16}. **b. use flattery** Ps 36_{3} (+ אֶל *to* oneself) Pr 29_{5} (+ עַל *upon* someone).

→ חָלָק I *smooth*, חַלַּק *smooth*, חֵלֶק *smoothness*, חֶלְקָה II *smoothness*, חֲלַקְלַקּוֹת I *smoothness*, מַחֲלֻקֶת II *smoothness*.

*חלק **III** 2 vb.—**Pi.** 1 Pf. חִלְּקָם; impf. יְחַלֵּק—**destroy** persons Lm 4_{16} Jb 21_{17}. → חֲלָקוֹת *perdition*.

*חלק **IV** 1 vb.—**Ni.** 1 + waw וַיֵּחָלֵק—**draw round, encircle** Gn 14_{15} (+ עַל *around*).

*חלק **V** 1 vb.—**Qal** 1 Pf. חָלַק—**strip** temple, etc. 2 C 28_{21}.

*חלק **VI** 1 vb.—**Ni.** 1 Impf. יֵחָלֵק—**be created,** of light Jb 38_{24}.

*חלק **VII** 1 vb.—**Hi.** 1 Inf. חֲלֹק—**flee, escape** Jr 37_{12} (+ מִשָּׁם *from there*).

חָלָק **I** 10.0.14 adj.—f.pl. חֲלָקוֹת (חֲלָקוֹת), m.pl.cstr. חַלְּקֵי—**1a. smooth,** of man Gn 27_{11} (opp. hairy), palate Pr 5_{3} (+ מִן smoother *than* oil). **b. flattering,** of mouth Pr 26_{28}. **3.** as *noun*, **smooth one, a.** (masc. pl.) appar. **smooth stone** Is 57_{6}. **b.** (fem. pl.) **slippery places** Ps 73_{18}. **c.** (masc. sg.) **flattery,** or perh. **flatterer** Ezk 12_{24}. **d.** (fem. pl.) **smooth speech, flattery** Ps 12_{3} Dn 11_{32}. **e.** (fem. pl.) usu. at Qumran **smooth things, easy interpretations,** attributed to sectarians' opponents CD 1_{18} 1QH 10_{32}. → חלק II *be smooth*.

*חָלָק **II** 2 pl.n. **Halak.**

*[חָלָק] **III** 0.1 n.[m.] **creature**—Si 36_{13}.

[חַלַּק] 1 adj. **smooth,** as noun, **smooth one,** חַלְּקֵי־אֲבָנִים *smooth ones of stones*, i.e. smooth stones 1 S 17_{40}. → חלק II *be smooth*.

חֵלֶק **I** 66.6.7 n.m.—cstr. חֵלֶק; sf. חֶלְקוֹ; pl. חֲלָקִים; sf. חֶלְקֵיהֶם—**1a. portion, share,** of plunder Gn 14_{24}, food Lv 6_{10}, inheritance Gn 31_{14}. **b.** חֵלֶק בְּ **portion,** i.e. **right, interest, in** Y. Jos 22_{25}, David 2 S 20_{1}. **2. portion (of land),** as allotted territory Nm 18_{20}, land around city 2 K 9_{10}, land in general Am 7_{4}. **3. (one's) portion,** i.e. **a.** chosen lot Ps 50_{18}. **b.** possession; people as Y.'s portion Dt 32_{9}, Y. as people's portion Jr 10_{16}. **4. portion,** i.e. **reward,** for work Ec 2_{10}. → חלק I *divide*.

חֵלֶק **II** 2.0.0.4 pr.n.m. **Helek.**

*חֵלֶק **III** 0.0.0.3 pl.n. **Helek.**

[חֵלֶק] **IV** 1 n.[m.]—cstr. חֵלֶק—**smoothness** of speech, i.e. flattery Pr 7_{21}. → חלק II *be smooth*.

*[חִלְקָא] 0.0.0.1 pr.n.[m.] **Hilka.**

[חֲלֻקָּה] 1.0.1 n.f.—cstr. חֲלֻקַּת; pl. sf. Q חלוקותמה—**division, part** of father's house 2 C 35_{5}, army 4QM[a] 1_{6}. → חלק I *divide*.

חֶלְקָה **I** 23.0.1 n.f.—cstr. חֶלְקַת; sf. חֶלְקָתִי; pl. sf. Q חלקותיכה—**plot (of land), field** 2 S 14_{30} Am 4_{7}; חֶלְקַת הַשָּׂדֶה *plot of the field*, i.e. plot of land Gn 33_{19}. → חלק I *divide*.

[חֶלְקָה] **II** 2 n.f.—cstr. חֶלְקַת—**1. smooth part** of neck Gn 27_{16}. **2. smoothness** of tongue, i.e. flattery Pr 6_{24}. → חלק II *be smooth*.

*חֲלָקוֹת 1 n.f.pl. **perdition** Ps 73_{18}. → חלק III *destroy*.

חֲלַקּוֹת, see חָלָק I *smooth*.

[חֶלְקַי] 1 pr.n.m. **Helkai.**

חֶלְקִי **I** 1 gent. **Helekite.**

חֶלְקִי **II** 1 pr.n.m. **Helki.**

חִלְקִיָּה, see חִלְקִיָּהוּ *Hilkiah*.

חִלְקִיָּהוּ 34.0.1.16 pr.n.m. **Hilkiah.**

חֲלַקְלַקּוֹת **I** 4 n.f.pl.—**1. slipperiness, slippery places** Ps 35_{6} Jr 23_{12}. **2. smoothness (of speech), flattery, intrigue** Dn $11_{21.34}$. → חלק II *be smooth*.

*חֲלַקְלַקּוֹת **II** 1 n.f.pl. **darkness** Ps 35_{6}.

חֶלְקַת 2 pl.n. **Helkath.**

חֶלְקַת הַצֻּרִים 1 pl.n. **Helkath-hazzurim.**

*חלשׁ **I** 2 vb.—**Qal** 2 + waw וַיַּחֲלֹשׁ; ptc. חוֹלֵשׁ—**1. defeat** Ex 17_{13} (+ לְ *with* edge of sword). **2. inflict defeat upon** (עַל) Is 14_{12}.

חלשׁ **II** 1 vb.—**Qal** 1 + waw וַיֶּחֱלַשׁ—**be weak, powerless,** pass away Jb 14_{10}. → חָלַשׁ *weak.*

חַלָּשׁ 1 adj. **weak,** as noun, **weak one** Jl 4_{10}. → חלשׁ II *be weak.*

[חַם] 2.0.2 adj.—חַם; pl. חַמִּים—**1. hot,** of bread Jos 9_{12}, garment Jb 37_{17}. **2.** as noun, **hot water** 3QTr 10_{15}. → חמם *be warm.*

חָם I 12.0.3 pr.n.m. **Ham.**

חָם II 4 pl.n. **Ham.**

[חָם] III 4.1 n.m.—sf. חָמִיךְ—**father-in-law,** husband's father Gn $38_{13.25}$ 1 S $4_{19.21}$, wife's father Si 37_{10}.

חֹם 6.1.5.1 n.m.—Q חום; cstr. חֹם—**heat,** קֹר וָחֹם *cold and heat* Gn 8_{22}, לֶחֶם חֹם *bread of heat,* i.e. hot bread 1 S 21_7. → חמם *be warm.*

חֵמָא, see חֵמָה *anger.*

חֶמְאָה 11 n.f.—חֶמְָה; cstr. חֶמְאַת; pl. mss חֶמְאוֹת—**curd(s), butter** Gn 18_8 Dt 32_{14}. → cf. מַחְמָאֹת *curd-like things.*

חמד 21.3.8 vb.—**Qal** 16.2.5 Pf. חָמַד, חֲמַדְתֶּם; impf. יַחְמֹד, נֶחְמְדֵהוּ; + waw וָאֶחְמְדֵם; ptc. pass. חֲמוּדוֹ, חֲמוּדֵיהֶם—**1a. desire, covet** neighbour's wife and property Ex 20_{17}, gold and silver Dt 7_{25}. **b. delight in** scorning Pr 1_{22}; **find** person **pleasing** Is 53_2. **c. desire,** i.e. choose, mountain as (לְ) abode Ps 68_{17}. **2.** pass. ptc. as noun, **desirable thing,** of possessions, etc. Ps 39_{12}; **delightful thing,** of images of gods Is 44_9.

Ni. 4.1.3 Ptc. נֶחְמָד—ptc. as adj., **1. desirable,** of treasure Pr 21_{20}, tree Gn 2_9 (+ לְ *to* sight), ordinances Ps 19_{11} (+ מִן *[more] than* gold). **2. delightful,** of Y.'s works Si 42_{22}.

Pi. 1 Pf. חִמַּדְתִּי—**delight greatly in** (בְּ) Ca 2_3.

→ חֶמֶד *desire,* חֶמְדָּה *desire,* חֲמֻדוֹת *preciousness,* מַחְמָד *precious thing.*

חֶמֶד 6.0.2 n.[m.]—sf. Q חמדו—**desire, delight,** כַּרְמֵי־חֶמֶד *vineyards of delight,* i.e. delightful vineyards Am 5_{11}, בַּחוּרֵי חֶמֶד *youths of desire,* i.e. handsome youths Ezk 23_6. → חמד *desire.*

*[חֶמְדָּא] 0.0.0.1 pr.n.m. **Hemda.**

חֶמְדָּה 17.1.4 n.f.—cstr. חֶמְדַּת; sf. חֶמְדָּתִי—**1a. desire,** חֶמְדַּת יִשְׂרָאֵל *desire of Israel* 1 S 9_{20}. **b. (obj. of) desire,** חֶמְדַּת נָשִׁים *desire of,* i.e. one desired by, *women* Dn 11_{37}. **2. delight, beauty,** אֶרֶץ חֶמְדָּה *land of delight,* i.e. beautiful land Jr 3_{19}. **3. preciousness,** כְּלִי חֶמְדָּה *vessel of preciousness,* i.e. precious vessel Ho 13_{15}. → חמד *desire.*

חֲמֻדוֹת 9.1.1 n.f.pl.—cstr. חֲמֻדוֹת—**1a. preciousness,** אִישׁ־חֲמֻדוֹת *man of preciousness,* i.e. precious man Dn 10_{11}. **b. precious things** Dn 11_{38}, i.e. garments Gn 27_{15}. **2a. desirableness,** ארץ חמדות כל הארצות *land of desirableness of all the lands,* i.e. most desirable of all the lands 4QDiscourse 2.2_5. **b. desires,** חמודות רעה *desires of evil,* i.e. evil desires Si 5_2. → חמד *desire.*

חֲמֻדֹת, see חֲמֻדוֹת *preciousness.*

*חמה I 0.1 vb.—**Qal** 0.1 Pt. Si חמיך—**1. see, look upon with disdain** Si 37_{10}. **2. beware** Jb 36_{18} (if em. חֵמָה *wrath* to חֲמֵה).

*[חמה] II vb.—**Qal, 1. be hot** (alw. if em.), of storm Jr 23_{19}=30_{23}, wine Jr 25_{15}. **2. be inflamed with** (מִן) wine Ho 7_5. → cf. חמם *be hot,* יחם *be in heat.*

חַמָּה 6.1 n.f.—sf. חַמָּתוֹ—**1. heat of sun** Ps 19_7. **2. sun** Is 24_{23} Jb 30_{28}. → חמם *be warm.*

חֵמָה I 125.2.23 n.f.—חֵמָא; cstr. חֲמַת; sf. חֲמָתוֹ; pl. חֵמוֹת—**1. anger, wrath** of Y. Nm 25_{11}, human Gn 27_{44}. **2. heat** of fever caused by wine Ho 7_5. **3. poison, venom** of serpents Dt 32_{33}, humans Ps 58_5, arrows Jb 6_4. → חמם *be warm.*

*[חֵמָה] II 1 n.f.—pl. חֵמֹת—**family** Ps 76_{11} 1 C 2_{55} (if em. חַמַּת *Hammath*).

*[חֵמָה] III n.f. **protection** Jb 30_{28} (if em. חַמָּה *sun*).

חֵמָה IV, see חֶמְאָה *curd.*

חַמּוּאֵל 2 pr.n.m. **Hammuel.**

חֲמוּדוֹת, see חֲמֻדוֹת *preciousness.*

חֲמוּדֹת, see חֲמֻדוֹת *preciousness.*

חֲמוּטַל 3 pr.n.f. **Hamutal.**

חָמוּל 3 pr.n.m. **Hamul.**

חָמוּלִי 1 gent. **Hamulite.**

חַמּוֹן 2 pl.n. **Hammon.**

חָמוֹץ 2 n.m. **oppressor** Is 1_{17} 16_4(1QIsa[a]) (MT הַמֵּץ *the extortioner*). → חמץ II *oppress.*

[חָמוּץ] 1 adj. **crimson,** as noun, **crimson(-stained) one,** חֲמוּץ בְּגָדִים *one crimson of garments,* i.e. with crimson garments Is 63_1.

[חַמּוּק] 1 n.m. **curve,** חַמּוּקֵי יְרֵכַיִךְ *curves of your thighs* Ca 7_2.

חֲמוֹר I 96.1.5.1 n.m. (f. at 2 S 19_{27})—חֲמֹר; cstr. חֲמוֹר; sf.

חֲמֹרוֹ; pl. חֲמוֹרִים; sf. חֲמֹרֵינוּ—**ass** Gn 12_{16}; sg. coll. Gn 32_6.

חֲמוֹר II 13 pr.n.m. **Hamor.**

חֲמוֹר III 2 n.[m.]—du. חֲמֹרָתָיִם—**heap** Jg $15_{16.16}$.

[חֲמוּשׁ] *grouped in fifties,* see חמשׁ, qal.

[חָמוֹת] 11 n.f. **mother-in-law**—sf. חֲמוֹתָהּ—husband's mother Mc 7_6 Ru 1_{14}.

חֹמֶט 1.0.1 n.[m.] **lizard** Lv 11_{30} 11QT 50_{21}.

חֻמְטָה 1 pl.n. **Humtah.**

*[חֲמִיאֹהֶל] 0.0.0.1 pr.n.f. **Hamiohel.**

חֲמִיטַל 3 pr.n.f. **Hamital.**

*[חָמִיד] 0.1 n.[m.] **unreliable guide** Si 37_{10}.

*[חֲמִיעֲדָן] 0.0.0.1 pr.n.f. **Hamiadan.**

חָמִיץ 1 n.[m.]—1QIsa[a] חמץ—**sorrel, a herb** Is 30_{24}. → חמץ I *be sour.*

חֲמִישִׁי 34.0.33 adj. —חֲמִשִׁי; f.s. חֲמִישִׁית—**1. fifth,** of day Gn 1_{23}, month Nm 33_{38}, year Lv 19_{25}. **2.** as noun, **fifth (one),** in ref. to person 1 C 12_{11}, lot 1 C 24_9, battle standard 1QM 4_{10}, month Ezk 20_1, year 1QM 2_{11}. → חמשׁ *be five.*

[חֲמִישִׁית] 11.0.2 n.f.—cstr. חֲמִישִׁית; sf. חֲמִישִׁתוֹ; pl. sf. חֲמִשֹׁתָיו—**fifth (part)** of produce Gn 47_{24}, silver Lv 27_{15}, valuation Lv 5_{16}, principal Lv 5_{24}. → חמשׁ *be five.*

חמל 41.4.7 vb.—**Qal** 41 Pf. חָמַל, חֲמַלְתֶּם; impf. יַחְמֹל, תַּחְמְלוּ (תַּחְמֹלוּ); inf. חֶמְלָה—**spare, pity, have compassion upon, a.** with עַל *upon* or of obj. person Dt 13_9, animals 1 S 15_9, dwelling place 2 C 36_{15}. **b.** with אֶל of obj. person Is 9_{18}, arrows Jr 50_{14}. **c.** abs. 2 S 12_6. **d.** with inf., i.e. **be loath to do** 2 S 12_4. → חֶמְלָה *compassion,* מַחְמָל *(object of) compassion.*

*[חָמָל] 0.0.0.2 pr.n.m. **Hamal.**

[חֶמְלָה] 2 n.f.—cstr. חֶמְלַת; sf. חֶמְלָתוֹ—**compassion** of Y. Gn 19_{16} Is 63_9. → חמל *spare.*

חֶמְלָה, see חמל *spare* (inf.).

חמם 26 vb.—**Qal** 23 Pf. חַם, חַמּוֹתִי; impf. יֵחַם, יָחֹם (יֵחָם, יֵחַם), יֵחַמּוּ; + waw וַיִּחַם; inf. חֹם, חַמָּם (לַחְמָם)—**1. be,** or **become warm, hot,** of sun Ex 16_{21}, day Gn 18_1, pot Ezk 24_{11}, heart Dt 19_6; subj. impersonal 1 K 1_1 (+ לְ *to* someone). **2. warm oneself** Is 44_{15}.

Ni. 1 Ptc. נֵחָמִים—**inflame oneself** Is 57_5.

Pi. 1 Impf. תְּחַמֵּם—**keep eggs warm** Jb 39_{14}.

Htp. 1 Impf. יִתְחַמָּם—**warm oneself with** (מִן) fleece Jb 31_{20}.

→ חַם *hot,* חֹם *heat,* חַמָּה *heat; sun,* חֵמָה I *amger;* cf. יחם *be in heat,* חמה II *be hot.*

[חַמָּן] 8 n.m.—pl. חַמָּנִים; sf. חַמָּנֵיכֶם—**incense altar** Lv 26_{30} Is 17_8.

*[חַמּוֹן] 0.0.0.2 pr.n.m. **Hammon.**

חמס I 8.1.1 vb.—**Qal** 7.1.1 Pf. חָמְסוּ; impf. יַחְמֹס; ptc. חֹמֵס—**1. treat violently,** obj. person Jr 22_3, law Ezk 22_{26}. **2.** of vine, **drop** unripe grapes Jb 15_{33}. **3. do wrong** against (עַל) Jb 21_{27} (+ מְזִמּוֹת *[with] devices).*

Ni. 1 Pf. נֶחְמְסוּ—**suffer violence** Jr 13_{22}.

→ חָמָס *violence.*

*חמס II 1 vb.—**Qal** 1 תַּחְמֹסוּ—**devise** devices against (עַל) Jb 21_{27}.

*חמס III vb.—**Qal, make bare** Pr 26_6 (if em. חָמָס שֹׁתֶה *drinks violence* to חֹמֵס שָׁתוֹ *bares his buttocks).*

חָמָס 60.10.15 n.m.—cstr. חֲמַס; sf. חֲמָסוֹ; pl. חֲמָסִים—**violence, wrong,** חֲמָסוֹ *his violence,* i.e. that which he commits Ps 7_{17}, חֲמָסִי *my wrong,* i.e. the wrong done to me Gn 16_5, אִישׁ חָמָס *man of violence,* i.e. violent man Ps 18_{49}, עֵד חָמָס *witness of violence,* i.e. malicious witness Ex 23_1. → חמס I *be violent.*

חמץ I 4 vb.—**Qal** 3 Pf. חָמֵץ; impf. יֶחְמָץ; inf. sf. חֻמְצוֹ—**be leavened,** of dough Ex 12_{34}.

Htp. 1 Impf. יִתְחַמֵּץ—**be soured, embittered,** of heart Ps 73_{21}.

→ חָמֵץ *leavened,* חֹמֶץ *vinegar,* חָמִיץ *sorrel,* מַחְמֶצֶת *leavened thing.*

חמץ II 1 vb.—**Qal** 1 Ptc. חוֹמֵץ—**oppress,** ptc. as noun, **oppressor** Ps 71_4. → חָמוֹץ *oppressor.*

[חמץ] III vb.—**be red,** of foot Ps 68_{24} (if em. תִּמְחַץ appar. *you will shatter* to תֶּחְמַץ *it will be red).*

חָמֵץ 11.0.3 adj.—**1. leavened,** of bread Lv 7_{13}. **2.** as noun, **leavened thing, leaven** Ex 12_{15} Lv 2_{11}. → חמץ I *be sour.*

חֹמֶץ 6.0.1.1 n.m.—cstr. חֹמֶץ—**vinegar** Nm 6_3 Ps 69_{22} Ru 2_{14}. → חמץ I *be sour.*

חמק 2 vb.—**Qal** 1 Pf. חָמַק—intrans., **turn away** Ca 5_6.

Htp. 1 Impf. תִּתְחַמָּקִין—**turn hither and thither,** i.e. **waver** Jr 31_{22}.

חמר I 4.1 vb.—**Qal** 2 Pf. חָמַר; impf. יֶחְמְרוּ—**foam,** of water Ps 46_4, wine Ps 75_9.

Pealal 2 Pf. חֲמַרְמְרוּ (חֳמַרְמָרוּ)—**ferment,** of bowels Lm 1$_{20}$.

Hi. 0.1 Impf. יחמיר—**cause** bowels **to ferment** Si 4$_{2}$.

→ חֶמֶר *wine,* חמר III *foaming.*

חמר II 1 vb.—**Qal** 1 + waw וַתַּחְמְרָה—**cover with bitumen** Ex 2$_{3}$ (+ בַּחֵמָר וּבַזָּפֶת *with bitumen and with pitch*). → חֵמָר *bitumen.*

חמר III 1 vb.—**Pealal** 1 Pf. Kt חמרמרה, Qr חֳמַרְמְרוּ—**be reddened,** of face Jb 16$_{16}$ (+ מִן *on account of* weeping).

***חמר IV** vb.—**Qal, flay** Jg 15$_{16}$ (if em. חֲמוֹר חֲמֹרָתַיִם *a heap, two heaps* to חָמוֹר חֲמַרְתִּים *I have utterly flayed them*).

חֶמֶר 2.2 n.[m.] **wine** Dt 32$_{14}$. → חמר I *foam.*

חֵמָר 3 n.[m.] **bitumen** Gn 11$_{3}$ 14$_{10}$ Ex 2$_{3}$. → חמר II *cover with bitumen.*

חֹמֶר I 17.1.13 n.m.—cstr. חֹמֶר—**1. clay,** as material of vessels Is 29$_{16}$, the human body Jb 33$_{6}$ 1QH 9$_{21}$. **2. clay,** as substance in the earth, **mud** Is 10$_{6}$. **3. mortar** Gn 11$_{3}$ Ex 1$_{14}$.

חֹמֶר II 12.0.0.2 n.m.—cstr. חֹמֶר; pl. חֳמָרִים—**homer,** unit of dry measure (also liquid measure Arad ost. 2$_{5}$), about 400 litres, equal to ten ephahs, or ten baths of liquid measure Ezk 45$_{11}$.

*[**חֹמֶר**] **III** 2 n.[m.]—cstr. חֹמֶר—**1. foaming** of water Hb 3$_{15}$. **2. (fermenting) wine** Is 27$_{2(1QIsa^a)}$ (חומר; mss חֶמֶר *wine;* L חֶמֶד *desire*). → חמר I *foam.*

[**חֹמֶר**] **IV** 2 n.[m.]—pl. חֳמָרִם—**heap** Ex 8$_{10}$.

חַמְרָן 1 pr.n.m. **Hamran.**

חמשׁ 5 vb.—**Qal** 4 Ptc. pass. חֲמֻשִׁים—pass. **be grouped in fifties,** in battle-readiness, חֲמֻשִׁים עָלוּ *they went up grouped in fifties* Ex 13$_{18}$, קְצֵה הַחֲמֻשִׁים *end,* i.e. edge, *of those grouped in fifties* Jg 7$_{11}$.

Pi. 1 + waw וְחִמֵּשׁ—**take a fifth (part) of** (produce of) land Gn 41$_{34}$.

→ חָמֵשׁ *five,* חֲמִשִּׁים *fifty,* חֲמִישִׁי *fifth,* חֲמִישִׁית *fifth (part),* חֹמֶשׁ *fifth (part).*

חָמֵשׁ 344.0.34.2 n.m.&f. **five**—m. (with f. nouns) חָמֵשׁ; cstr. חֲמֵשׁ; f. (with m. nouns) חֲמִשָּׁה; cstr. חֲמֵשֶׁת—**1. five,** חָמֵשׁ אַמּוֹת *five cubits* Ex 27$_{1}$, חֲמִשָּׁה אֲנָשִׁים *five men* Gn 47$_{2}$, חֲמֵשֶׁת הַמְּלָכִים *the five kings* Jos 5$_{17}$. **2.** as ordinal numeral, **fifth,** בִּשְׁנַת חָמֵשׁ *in the fifth year* 2 K 8$_{16}$, בַּחֲמִשָּׁה לַחֹדֶשׁ *on the fifth day of the month* Ezk 1$_{2}$. **3.** with ellip. of noun, **a. five (persons)** Gn 18$_{28}$. **b. five (things)** 1 K 7$_{49}$ Is 17$_{6}$. **c. five (cubits)** 1 K 6$_{6}$. **4.** as constituent of a larger number, חֲמִשָּׁה עָשָׂר *fifteen* 2 S 9$_{10}$, vars. חֲמֵשֶׁת עָשָׂר 2 S 19$_{18}$, חֲמֵשׁ עֶשְׂרֵה Gn 7$_{20}$; עֶשְׂרִים וַחֲמִשָּׁה *twenty-five* Ezk 8$_{16}$, vars. עֶשְׂרִים וְחָמֵשׁ Ezk 40$_{13}$; חֲמֵשׁ וְעֶשְׂרִים Ezk 40$_{25}$, חֲמֵשׁ מֵאוֹת *five hundred* Gn 11$_{11}$, חֲמֵשֶׁת אֲלָפִים *five thousand* Jos 8$_{12}$. → חמשׁ *be five.*

חֹמֶשׁ I 1.0.2 n.[m.]—sf. Q חומשה; pl. Q חומשים—**fifth (part)** of produce Gn 47$_{26}$, redemption fee 4QD^{e} 2.2$_{10}$. → חמשׁ *be five.*

חֹמֶשׁ II 4 n.[m.] **abdomen** 2 S 2$_{23}$ 3$_{27}$ 20$_{10}$.

חֲמִשִׁי, see חֲמִישִׁי *fifth.*

חֲמִשִּׁים 165.0.30 n.m.&f.—sf. חֲמִשָּׁיו, חֲמִשֵּׁיהֶם—**1a. fifty,** חֲמִשִּׁים יוֹם *fifty days* Lv 23$_{16}$, חֲמִשִּׁים אַמָּה *fifty cubits* Gn 6$_{15}$. **b.** as constituent of a larger number, חֲמִשִּׁים וְחָמֵשׁ *fifty-five* 2 K 21$_{1}$, חֲמִשִּׁים אֶלֶף *fifty thousand* 1 C 5$_{21}$. **2.** as ordinal numeral, **fiftieth,** שְׁנַת הַחֲמִשִּׁים שָׁנָה *the fiftieth year* Lv 25$_{10}$. **3.** with ellip. of noun, **fifty (persons)** 2 K 1$_{9}$, **fifty (cubits)** Ex 27$_{18}$, **fifty (years)** 1QM 6$_{14}$. → חמשׁ *be five.*

חֲמֻשִׁים *grouped in fifties,* see חמשׁ, qal.

חַמַּת I 1 pr.n.m. **Hammath.**

חַמַּת II 1 pl.n. **Hammath.**

חֲמָת 36 pl.n. **Hamath.**

חֵמֶת 3 n.[m.]—cstr. חֵמַת—**skin (bottle)** Gn 21$_{14}$.

חַמֹּת דֹּאר 1 pl.n. **Hammoth-dor.**

חֲמָתִי 2 gent. **Hamathite.**

חֲמַת צוֹבָה 1 pl.n. **Hamath-zobah.**

חֵן I 69.11.3 n.m.—cstr. חֵן; sf. חִנּוֹ—**1. favour, grace,** with Y. Pr 3$_{34}$, humans Pr 22$_{1}$; מצא חֵן בְּעֵינֵי *find favour in the sight of* Gn 6$_{8}$, נתן חֵן בְּעֵינֵי *give favour in the sight of* Ex 3$_{21}$, נשׂא חֵן לִפְנֵי *bear favour before* Est 2$_{17}$. **2. charm, elegance,** of woman Pr 11$_{16}$, doe Pr 5$_{19}$, stone Pr 17$_{8}$, speech Ps 45$_{3}$. → חנן I *be gracious.*

חֵן II 1 pr.n.m. **Hen.**

***חנג** 0.1 vb.—**Htp.** 0.1 Impf. תתחנג (perh. error for ענג htp. *take delight*)—**dance** Si 37$_{29(Bmg, D)}$.

חֵנָדָד 4 pr.n.m. **Henadad.**

חנה I 143.3.7 vb.—**Qal** 143.3.7 Pf. חָנָה, חָנִיתִי; impf. תַּחֲנֶה; + waw וַיִּחַן, וַנַּחֲנֶה; impv. חֲנֵה, חֲנוּ; ptc. חֹנֶה, חֹנָה, חֹנִים; inf.

חֲנוֹת—**1. encamp,** of individual Gn 26_{17} (+ בְּ *in*) 33_{18} (+ אֶת־פְּנֵי *before*), Israelites at exodus Ex 14_{2} (+ לִפְנֵי *before*) 14_{9} (+ עַל *beside*), army Jos 10_{5} (+ עַל *against*), Y. Zc 9_{8} (+ לְ *at*), angel of Y. Ps 34_{8} (+ סָבִיב לְ *around*). **2. decline,** of day Jg 19_{9}. → מַחֲנֶה *camp,* תַּחֲנָה *encampment.*

*חנה II 1 vb.—**Pi.** 1 Inf. חַנּוֹת—**have compassion,** of Y. Ps 77_{10}.

חַנָּה 13.0.3.2 pr.n.f. **Hannah.**

חֲנוֹךְ I 16.1.2 pr.n.m. **Enoch.**

חֲנוֹךְ II 1 pl.n. **Enoch.**

חָנוּן 11 pr.n.m. **Hanun.**

חַנּוּן 13.0.2 adj. **gracious,** oft. + רַחוּם *compassionate;* of Y. Ex 34_{6} Jl 2_{13}; perh. of human Ps 112_{4}. → חנן I *be gracious.*

[חָנוּת] 1 n.f.—pl. חֲנֻיוֹת—**vault,** perh. **cellar** Jr 37_{16}.

חנט I 3 vb.—**Qal** 1 + waw וַיַּחַנְטוּ; inf. חֲנֹט—**embalm** Gn $50_{2.2.26}$. → חֲנֻטִים *embalming.*

חנט II 1 vb.—**Qal** 1 Pf. חָנְטָה—**make early figs ripe,** or perh. **red** Ca 2_{13}.

חֲנֻטִים 1 n.[m.]pl. **embalming** Gn 50_{3}. → חנט I *embalm.*

[חֹנִי], see חוֹנִי *Honi.*

*[חָנְיָא] 0.0.0.2 pr.n.m. **Honia.**

חַנִּיאֵל 2 pr.n.m. **Hanniel.**

[חָנְיָה], see חָנְיָא *Honia.*

*[חַנִּיָּהוּ] 0.0.0.1 pr.n.m. **Hanniah.**

חֲנֻיוֹת, see חָנוּת *vault.*

[חָנִיךְ] 1 n.[m.] **retainer** Gn 14_{14}. → חנך *dedicate.*

*[חָנִין] 0.0.4.1 pr.n.m. **Hanin.**

*[חֲנִינָא] 0.0.2 pr.n.m. **Hanina.**

חֲנִינָה 1.0.2 n.f. **grace, favour** Jr 16_{13}; אל הרחמים והחנינה *God of compassion and grace* 1QH 19_{29}. → חנן I *be gracious.*

חֲנִית 47.1.7 n.f.—cstr. חֲנִית; sf. חֲנִיתוֹ; pl. חֲנִיתִים; sf. חֲנִיתוֹתֵיהֶם—**spear** 1 S 13_{19}; עֵץ חֲנִית *wood,* i.e. shaft, *of a spear* 2 S 23_{7}, לַהֶבֶת חֲנִיתוֹ *flame,* i.e. head, *of his spear* 1 S 17_{7}, אַחֲרֵי הַחֲנִית *back,* i.e. butt, *of the spear* 2 S 2_{23}.

חנך 5 vb.—Pf. חֲנָכוֹ; + waw וַיַּחְנְכוּ; impv. חֲנֹךְ—**1. dedicate** (private) house Dt 20_{5}, temple 1 K 8_{63}‖ 2 C 7_{5}. **2. train** lad Pr 22_{6} (לְ of obj.). → חֲנֻכָּה *dedication,* חָנִיךְ *retainer.*

חֲנֻכָּה 8 n.f.—cstr. חֲנֻכַּת—**1. dedication** of altar Nm 7_{11}, temple Ps 30_{1}, wall of Jerusalem Ne 12_{27}. **2. dedication offering,** for altar Nm 7_{10}. → חנך *dedicate.*

חֲנֹכִי 1 gent. **Hanochite.**

חִנָּם 32.1.4 adv. **1. for nothing,** i.e. **a. without cause, needlessly, unjustly** 1 S 19_{5} Ps 35_{7}. **b. at no cost, gratis** Gn 29_{15} Ex 21_{2}. **c. in vain** Pr 1_{17} CD 6_{12}. **2.** as noun, **needlessness,** דְּמֵי חִנָּם *blood of needlessness,* i.e. innocent blood 1 K 2_{31}, קִלְלַת חִנָּם *curse of needlessness,* i.e. a curse without cause Pr 26_{2}. **3.** אֶל־חִנָּם **without cause, in vain** Ezk 6_{10}.

חֲנַמְאֵל 4 pr.n.m. **Hanamel.**

[חֲנָמַל] 1.0.1 n.[m.]—חֲנָמַל—perh. **frost,** or **flood** Ps 78_{47} 4QParGenEx 3_{10}.

*[חַנִּמֶּלֶךְ] 0.0.0.1 pr.n.[m.] **Hannimelech.**

חנן I 78.4.26.1 vb.—**Qal** 55.1.22 Pf. חָנַן (חַנַּנִי); impf. יָחֹן (יְחֻנֵּן, יְחָנְךָ, Q יחונך, יְחָנֵּנוּ); + waw וְחַנֹּתִי; וַיָּחָן (וַיְחָנֶּנּוּ), Q ותחון; impv. חָנֵּנִי, חָנֵּנִי; ptc. חוֹנֵן; inf. abs. חָנוֹן, cstr. חֶנְנָה (Q חֲנַנְכֶם, חונכה)—**1.** with accus. of recipient, **be gracious to, show favour to, spare,** subj. Y. Gn 33_{11}, humans Dt 7_{2}. **2.** with accus. of both thing given and recipient, **graciously give to** Gn 33_{5}. **3.** abs., **be generous** Ps 37_{21}.

Ni. 1 Pf. נֵחַנְתְּ—**be pitied** Jr 22_{23}.

Pi. 1 Impf. יְחַנֵּן—**make** voice **gracious** Pr 26_{25}.

Po. 2 Impf. יְחֹנֵנוּ; ptc. מְחוֹנֵן—**have pity on,** subj. humans Ps 102_{15} Pr 14_{21}.

Ho. (or Qal pass.) 2.2 Impf. יֻחַן—**be shown favour** Is 26_{10} Pr 21_{10} Si 12_{13}.

Htp. 17.1.4 Pf. הִתְחַנַּנְתִּי; impf. תִּתְחַנֵּן; + waw וַיִּתְחַנֵּן (וַיִּתְחַנֶּן־); inf. הִתְחַנֶּן־ (הִתְחַנְנוֹ)—**make supplication, implore favour,** + לְ *to* angel Ho 12_{5}, human Est 4_{8}; אֶל *to* Y. Dt 3_{23}, human Gn 42_{21}; לִפְנֵי *before* Y. 1 K 8_{59}.

→ חִין *gracefulness,* חֵן I *grace,* חֲנִינָה *grace, favour,* חַנּוּן *gracious,* תְּחִנָּה I *supplication,* תַּחֲנוּן *supplication.*

חנן II 1 vb.—**Qal** 1 + waw וְחַנֹּתִי—**be loathsome** Jb 19_{17} (+ לְ *to*).

חָנָן 12.0.0.11 pr.n.m. **Hanan.**

חֲנַנְאֵל I 4 pl.n. **Hananel.**

*חֲנַנְאֵל II 0.0.0.1 pr.n.m. **Hananel.**

*[חֲנָנָה] 0.0.0.1 pr.n.f. **Hananah.**

חֲנָנִי 12.0.0.1 pr.n.m. **Hanani.**

חֲנַנְיָה 28.0.3.33 pr.n.m. **Hananiah.**

חֲנַנְיָהוּ, see חֲנַנְיָה *Hananiah.*

חָנֵס 1.0.1 pl.n. **Hanes.**

חנף I 11 vb.—**Qal** 7 Pf. חָנְפָה, חָנְפוּ; impf. תֶּחֱנַף; inf. abs. חָנוֹף—**1. be polluted,** of land Is 24$_5$ (+ תַּחַת *on account of* inhabitants) Ps 106$_{38}$ (+ בְּ *with* blood). **2. be impious** Jr 23$_{11}$. **3. pollute** land Jr 3$_9$ (or em. hi.).

Hi. 4 Impf. יַחֲנִיף—**1. pollute** land Nm 35$_{33}$ Jr 3$_2$ (+ בְּ *with* fornication and evil). **2. profane** someone with (בְּ) flattery Dn 11$_{32}$.

→ חָנֵף *profane,* חֹנֶף *profaneness,* חֲנֻפָּה *impiousness.*

*[חנף] II vb.—**Pi., limp** Ps 35$_{16}$ (if em. בְּחַנְפֵי appar. *as profane ones of* to בְּחַנְפִי *when I limped*).

*[חנף] III 4 vb.—**Qal** 1 Pf. חָנְפָה—**suffer outrage,** of land Is 24$_5$ (+ תַּחַת *on account of* inhabitants).

Ni. suffer outrage, be violated (if em. qal)—of land Ps 106$_{38}$ (+ בְּ *with* blood), Zion Mc 4$_{11}$.

Hi. 3 Impf. יַחֲנִיף—**subject to outrage, violate** land Nm 35$_{33}$ Jr 3$_2$ (+ בְּ *with* fornication and evil).

חָנֵף I 13.3.1 adj.—pl. חֲנֵפִים; cstr. חַנְפֵי—**1. profane, impious,** of person Jb 34$_{30}$, nation Is 10$_6$. **2.** as noun, **profane one, impious one** Is 33$_{14}$ Jb 8$_{13}$. → חנף I *be polluted.*

*[חָנֵף] II 1 adj. **haughty,** as noun, **haughty one** Jb 36$_{13}$.

חֹנֶף 1.0.1 n.[m.] **profaneness** Is 32$_6$. → חנף I *be polluted.*

חֲנֻפָּה 1.0.1 n.f.—Q חנופה—**impiousness** Jr 23$_{15}$ 4QTestim 28. → חנף I *be polluted.*

חנק 2.0.1 vb.—**Ni.** 1 + waw וַיֵּחָנַק—**hang oneself** 2 S 17$_{23}$.

Pi. 1.0.1 Ptc. מְחַנֵּק—**strangle (prey),** of lion Na 2$_{13}$ (+ לְ *for* lioness).

→ מַחֲנָק *strangling.*

חַנָּתֹן 1 pl.n. **Hannathon.**

חסד I 2 vb.—**Htp.** 2 Impf. תִּתְחַסָּד—**show oneself loyal,** of Y. 2 S 22$_{26}$||Ps 18$_{26}$ (+ עִם *with*). → חֶסֶד I *loyalty,* חָסִיד *loyal.*

חסד II 1 vb.—**Pi.** 1 יְחַסֶּדְךָ—**bring shame upon, reproach** someone Pr 25$_{10}$. → חֶסֶד II *shame.*

חֶסֶד I 246.26.104.1 n.m.—חָסֶד; cstr. חֶסֶד; sf. חַסְדּוֹ; pl. חֲסָדִים; cstr. חַסְדֵי; sf. חֲסָדָיו—**loyalty, faithfulness, kindness, love, mercy,** pl. **mercies, (deeds of) kindness, a.** of Y. to humans Mc 7$_{20}$; חֶסֶד י׳ *mercy of Y.* Ps 33$_5$, אל החסדים *God of mercies* 1QM 14$_8$, רַב־חֶסֶד וֶאֱמֶת *great of mercy and faithfulness* Ex 34$_6$, רֹב חֲסָדָיו *abundance of his mercies* Is 63$_7$, לְעוֹלָם חַסְדּוֹ *his mercy is to eternity* Jr 33$_{11}$, חַסְדֵי דָוִד *mercies of,* i.e. shown to, *David* Is 55$_3$. **b.** of humans to Y. Ho 6$_4$; חֶסֶד נְעוּרַיִךְ *loyalty of your youth* Jr 2$_2$. **c.** between humans 1 S 20$_{15}$ 2 S 16$_{17}$; אִישׁ חֶסֶד *man of kindness* Pr 11$_{17}$, עָשָׂה חֶסֶד עִם *deal loyally with, show kindness to* Gn 21$_{23}$. **d.** of flesh, i.e. its **beauty** Is 40$_6$. → חסד I *be loyal.*

חֶסֶד II 2.1.1 n.m.—cstr. חֶסֶד; pl. Q חסדים—**shame, reproach** Pr 14$_{34}$ perh. 1QM 3$_6$; **shameful thing,** of incest Lv 20$_{17}$. → חסד II *be ashamed.*

חֶסֶד III, see בֶּן־חֶסֶד *Ben-hesed.*

*[חַסְדָּא] 0.0.0.1 pr.n.[m.] **Hasda.**

חַסְדָה, see חַסְרָה *Hasrah.*

חֲסַדְיָה 1.0.0.2 pr.n.m. **Hasadiah.**

*[חִסְדַּי] 0.0.0.2 pr.n.m. **Hisday.**

[חֲסַדְיָהוּ], see חֲסַדְיָה *Hasadiah.*

[חֲסִדִין], see מְצַד חֲסִידִין *Mezad-hasidin.*

חסה 37.2.3 vb.—**Qal** 37 Pf. חָסִיתִי, חָסוּ (חָסָיוּ); impf. יֶחֱסֶה, יֶחֱסוּ (יֶחֱסָיוּן); impv. חֲסוּ; ptc. חֹסֶה, חֹסִים; inf. חֲסוֹת (לַחְסוֹת)—**seek refuge, take refuge** in (בְּ) Y. 2 S 22$_3$||Ps 18$_3$, shade Jg 9$_{15}$; under (תַּחַת) wings of Y. Ps 91$_4$; from (מִן) one who rises up Ps 17$_7$, heat Si 14$_{27}$. → חָסוּת *refuge,* מַחְסֶה *shelter.*

חֹסָה I 4 pr.n.m. **Hosah.**

חֹסָה II 1 pl.n. **Hosah.**

חָסוּת 1 n.f. **refuge** Is 30$_3$. → חסה *seek refuge.*

חָסִיד 32.1.9 adj.—sf. חֲסִידְךָ; pl. חֲסִידִים; sf. חֲסִידָיו—**1a. loyal, godly,** of nation Ps 43$_1$, individual Ps 86$_2$. **b.** as noun, **loyal one, godly one** 1 S 2$_9$ Mc 7$_2$. **2. kind, merciful,** of Y. Jr 3$_{12}$ Ps 145$_{17}$. → חסד I *be loyal.*

חֲסִידָה 6 n.f. **stork** Lv 11$_{19}$||Dt 14$_{18}$.

חָסִיל 6.0.1 n.m. **locust** 1 K 8$_{37}$||2 C 6$_{28}$. → חסל *consume.*

חָסִין 1 adj. **strong**—of Y. Ps 89$_9$. → חסן *be strong.*

[חָסִיר], see חָסֵר *lacking.*

חסל 1 vb.—**Qal** 1 (or **Hi.**) Impf. יַחְסְלֶנּוּ—**consume,** of locust Dt 28$_{38}$. → חָסִיל *locust.*

[חָסָל], see חָסִיל *locust.*

חסם 2.1.1 vb.—**Qal** 2.1.1 Impf. תַּחְסֹם; ptc. חֹסֶמֶת—**1. block (the way of)** travellers Ezk 39$_{11}$. **2. dam** mountain Si 48$_{17}$. **3. muzzle** ox Dt 25$_4$. → מַחְסוֹם *muzzle.*

חסן 1 vb.—**Ni.** 1 Impf. יֵחָסֵן—**be secured, hoarded,** of gain Is 23_{18}. → חָסִין *strong,* חֹסֶן *wealth,* חָסֹן *strong.*

חָסֹן I 2 adj.—sf. 1QIsa[a] החסנכם—**1. strong,** of Amorite Am 2_9 (+ כָּאַלּוֹנִים *as the oaks*). **2.** as noun, **strong one** Is 1_{31}. → חסן *be strong.*

*__חָסֹן__ II n. m. **flax** Is 1_{31}.

חֹסֶן 5.0.2 n.m.—cstr. חֹסֶן; sf. 1QIsa[a] חסנכה—**1. wealth, abundance** Is 33_6 Jr 20_5. **2. strength** Is 1_{31}(1QIsa[a]). **3. stronghold** Ps 144_2 (if em. חַסְדִּי *my loyalty* to חָסְנִי *my stronghold*). → חסן *be strong.*

חסף 1 vb.—**Pualal** 1 Ptc. pass. מְחֻסְפָּס—**be scaly,** of manna, דַּק מְחֻסְפָּס *a fine, scaly, thing* Ex 16_{14}.

חסר 25.6.6 vb.—**Qal** 21.4.6 Pf. חָסֵר, חָסַרְתָּ; impf. יֶחְסַר, יַחְסְרוּ; ptc. חָסֵר; inf. abs. חָסוֹר—**1a.** trans., **lack, need** bread and water Ezk 4_{17}, nothing Dt 8_9. **b.** abs., **lack anything, be in need** Ps 23_1. **2.** intrans., **be lacking, fail,** of bread Is 51_{14}, wisdom Si 3_{25}. **3. diminish, abate,** of water Gn 8_3.

Pi. 2.2 Pf. Si חסרתו; + waw וַתְּחַסְּרֵהוּ; ptc. מְחַסֵּר—**1. cause to lack, deprive of** (מִן) Ec 4_8. **2. cause to be less than** (מִן) Ps 8_6. **3.** perh. **dishonour** Si 14_2.

Hi. 2 Pf. הֶחְסִיר; impf. יַחְסִיר—**1.** abs., **lack anything** Ex 16_{18}. **2. cause someone to lack something** Is 32_6.

→ חָסֵר *lacking,* חֶסֶר *want,* חֹסֶר *lack,* חֶסְרוֹן *deficiency,* מַחְסוֹר *need.*

חָסֵר 16.9.6.1 adj.—cstr. חֲסַר; f.s. Si חסירה; m.pl. cstr. Si חֲסֵרֵי—**1.** as attrib. adj. of person (נֶפֶשׁ) Si 4_2. **2.** as pred. adj. or noun, **(one) lacking (in),** חֲסַר־לֵב *(one) lacking of heart,* i.e. in sense Pr 6_{32}, לֶחֶם *of,* i.e. in, *bread* 2 S 3_{29}; חסר דינרין ששה עשר *lacking of,* i.e. minus, *sixteen denars* 5/6ḤevBA 44_{20}. → חסר *lack.*

חֶסֶר 2 n.m. **want, lack** Jb 30_3 Pr 28_{22}. → חסר *lack.*

[חֹסֶר] 3.3.2 n.[m.]—cstr. חֹסֶר (Q חוסר)—**lack, want, need** Dt 28_{48} Am 4_6 Si 34_4. → חסר *lack.*

חַסְרָה 1 pr.n.m. **Hasrah.**

חֶסְרוֹן 1 n.m. **deficiency** Ec 1_{15}. → חסר *lack.*

חַף 1 adj. **pure,** of person Jb 33_9.

חפא 1 vb.—**Pi.** 1 + waw וַיְחַפְּאוּ—**do things secretly against** (עַל) Y. 2 K 17_9.

חפה 12 vb.—**Qal** 6 Pf. חָפוּ; ptc. pass. חָפוּי, חֲפוּי—**1. cover, veil** head 2 S 15_{30}, face Est 7_8. **2.** pass. **be covered,** of head 2 S 15_{30}.

Ni. 1 Ptc. נֶחְפָּה—**be covered,** of wings of dove Ps 68_{14} (+ בְּ *with*).

Pi. 5 Pf. חִפָּה; + waw וַיְחַף—with double accus., **overlay something with** 2 C 3_5.

חֻפָּה I 3.1 n.f.—sf. חֻפָּתוֹ—**1. shelter, canopy** Is 4_5 Si 40_{27}. **2. chamber** of bride Jl 2_{16}, groom Ps 19_6. → חפף *cover.*

חֻפָּה II 1.0.9 pr.n.m. **Huppah.**

חפז 9.0.3 vb.—**Qal** 6.0.3 Impf. יַחְפּוֹז; inf. חָפְזִי—**make haste, hurry away, be alarmed** Dt 20_3 2 S 4_4 (+ לָנוּס *to flee*) Ps 31_{23}.

Ni. 4 Pf. נֶחְפָּזוּ; impf. יֵחָפֵזוּן; ptc. נֶחְפָּז; inf. הֵחָפְזָם—**hurry away** 1 S 23_{26} (+ לָלֶכֶת *to go*) Ps 48_6.

→ חִפָּזוֹן *haste.*

חִפָּזוֹן 3 n.m. **haste, hurried flight** Ex 12_{11} Dt 16_3 Is 52_{12}. → חפז *make haste.*

חֻפִּים 3 pr.n.m. **Huppim.**

חֹפֶן 6 n.m.—du. חָפְנַיִם; cstr. חָפְנֵי; sf. חָפְנָיו—**hollow of the hand** Pr 30_4; מְלֹא חָפְנַיִם *fulness of both hands,* i.e. two handfuls Ec 4_6.

חָפְנִי 5 pr.n.m. **Hophni.**

חפף 1 vb.—**Qal** 1 Ptc. חֹפֵף—**cover over** (עַל), i.e. **shelter,** of Y. Dt 33_{12}. → חֻפָּה *shelter;* cf. חפה *cover.*

*__[חֲפַפְיוֹ]__ 0.0.0.1 pr.n.[m.] **Haphaphiah.**

חפץ I 86.7.12 vb.—**Qal** 86.7.12 Pf. חָפֵץ, חָפַצְתִּי; impf. יַחְפֹּץ (יֶחְפָּץ), יַחְפְּצוּ (יֶחְפָּצוּ); impv. Si חפוץ; ptc. חָפֵץ; inf. חָפֹץ—**1. desire, delight (in), take pleasure (in), a.** with accus. sacrifice Ps 40_7, loyalty Ho 6_6, wickedness Ps 5_5. **b.** with בְּ *in* person 1 S 18_{22}, understanding Pr 18_2. **2. be willing, pleased (to do), a.** with inf. Jg 13_{23}. **b.** with fin. verb Is 42_{21}. **3.** abs., **be willing** Ca 2_7. → חֵפֶץ *desire.*

חפץ II 1 vb.—**Qal** 1 Impf. יַחְפֹּץ—**let tail hang** Jb 40_{17}.

חָפֵץ, see חפץ I *desire.*

חֵפֶץ 40.8.39 n.m.—cstr. חֵפֶץ; sf. חֶפְצוֹ; pl. חֲפָצִים; cstr. Si חפצי; sf. חֲפָצֶיךָ—**1. delight,** בְּתוֹרַת יי׳ חֶפְצוֹ *his delight is in the law of Y.* Ps 1_2; אֶרֶץ חֵפֶץ *land of delight,* i.e. delightful land Ml 3_{12}, אַבְנֵי־חֵפֶץ *stones of delight,* i.e. precious stones Is 54_{12}. **2. desire** 1 K 5_{24} Ps 107_{30}. **3. pleasure, will** of Y. Is 44_{28}. **4. affair, matter** Ec 3_1 5_7. → חפץ I *desire.*

חֶפְצִי־בָהּ 2 pr.n.f. **Hephzibah.**

חפר I 22.0.27 vb.—**Qal** 23.0.27.1 Pf. חָפַר, חָפְרוּ; impf. יַחְפְּרוּ; + waw וַיַּחְפֹּר; impv. Q חפור; ptc. חֹפֵר; inf. לַחְפֹּר—**1a. dig well** Gn 21$_{30}$, pit Ec 10$_{8}$. **b. dig in** (בְּ) place **for** specified number of cubits 3QTr 2$_{14}$. **c.** of horse, **paw in** (בְּ) valley Jb 30$_{21}$. **2. search out, explore** land Dt 1$_{22}$. **3. search for** death Jb 3$_{21}$, food Jb 39$_{29}$.

חפר II 17.1 vb.—**Qal** 13 Pf. חָפְרָה (חָפֵרָה); impf. יַחְפְּרוּ (יֶחְפָּרוּ)—**be ashamed, be confounded,** of persons Is 1$_{29}$ (+ מִן *on account of*), face Ps 34$_{6}$, moon Is 24$_{23}$.

Hi. 4.1.0 Pf. הֶחְפִּיר; impf. יַחְפִּיר; ptc. מַחְפִּיר, Si מחפרת—**1. be ashamed** Is 33$_{9}$ Is 54$_{4}$. **2. act shamefully, cause shame** Pr 13$_{5}$ 19$_{26}$.

*[**חפר**] III vb.—**Pu. be protected** Jb 11$_{18}$ (if em. וְחָפַרְתָּ appar. *and you will search* to וְחֻפַּרְתָּ).

חֵפֶר I 2 pl.n. **Hepher.**

חֵפֶר II 7.0.0.1 pr.n.m. **Hepher.**

חֶפְרִי 1 gent. **Hepherite.**

חֲפָרַיִם 1 pl.n. **Hapharaim.**

חָפְרַע 1 pr.n.m. **Hophra.**

[**חֲפַרְפָּרָה**] 1 n.f.—pl. לַחְפֹּר פֵּרוֹת; mss לַחֲפַרְפָּרוֹת (1QIsa[a] לחפרפרים)—**mole,** or perh. **shrew,** or **bat** Is 2$_{20}$.

חפשׂ I 23.0.2 vb.—**Qal** 4 Impf. נַחְפְּשָׂה, יַחְפְּשׂוּ; ptc. חֹפֵשׂ—**1. search out, examine** one's ways Lm 3$_{40}$. **2. search for understanding** Pr 2$_{4}$.

Ni. 1.0.2 Pf. נֶחְפְּשׂוּ; impf. Q יחפש—**1. be searched out** Ob$_{6}$. **2. let oneself be searched out,** i.e. **hide oneself** 1QH 16$_{29}$ (+ עִם *with*) 18$_{34}$ (+ בְּ *in*).

Pi. 8 Pf. חִפְּשׂוּ; impf. אֲחַפֵּשׂ; + waw וַיְחַפֵּשׂ; impv. חַפְּשׂוּ—**1. search for** person 1 S 23$_{23}$, thing (obj. omitted) Gn 31$_{35}$. **2. search through** house 1 K 20$_{6}$.

Pu. 2 Impf. יְחֻפַּשׂ; ptc. מְחֻפָּשׂ—**be searched for,** i.e. **hidden,** of person Pr 28$_{12}$.

Htp. 8 Pf. הִתְחַפֵּשׂ; impf. יִתְחַפֵּשׂ; inf. הִתְחַפֵּשׂ—**let oneself be searched for,** i.e. **disguise oneself** 1 S 28$_{8}$.

→ חֵפֶשׂ *plot,* מְחַפֵּשׂ *investigator.*

*__חפשׂ__ II 1 vb.—**Pu.** Impf. יְחֻפַּשׂ—**be prostrated** Pr 28$_{12}$.

חֵפֶשׂ 1 n.m. **plot,** or (if em. following word) **disguise** Ps 64$_{7}$. → חפשׂ I *search.*

חפשׁ 1.1 vb.—**Qal** 0.1 Inf. Si חפש—**be free with** (עִם) someone Si 13$_{11}$.

Pu. 1 Pf. חֻפְּשָׁה—**be freed,** of female servant Lv 19$_{20}$.

→ חֹפֶשׁ II *freedom,* חֻפְשָׁה *freedom,* חָפְשׁוּת *freedom,* חָפְשִׁי *free.*

חֹפֶשׁ I 1 n.m. **woven material,** for saddlecloths Ezk 27$_{20}$.

*[**חֹפֶשׁ**] II 0.1 n.m.—חופש—**freedom** Si 7$_{21}$. → חפשׁ *be free.*

*[**חֹפֶשׁ**] III 1 n.[m.]—sf. חָפְשִׁי—**prison** Ps 88$_{6}$.

חֻפְשָׁה 1 n.f. **freedom** Lv 19$_{20}$. → חפשׁ *be free.*

חָפְשׁוּת 2 n.f.—Qr חָפְשִׁית—**freedom,** i.e. separation (on account of leprosy), בֵּית הַחָפְשׁוּת *house of freedom* 2 K 15$_{5(mss)}$||2 C 26$_{21(Kt)}$. → חפשׁ *be free.*

חָפְשִׁי 17 adj.—pl. חָפְשִׁים—**1. free,** of slave Jb 3$_{19}$. **2.** as noun, **freed one** Ex 21$_{2}$. **3.** as adv. accus., **free, in freedom** Dt 15$_{12}$. → חפשׁ *free.*

חָפְשִׁית, see חָפְשׁוּת *freedom.*

חֵץ 53.1.5 n.m.—cstr. חֵץ; sf. חִצּוֹ; pl. חִצִּים; cstr. חִצֵּי; sf. חִצַּי, חִצֶּיךָ (חִצֶּיךָ)—**arrow, a.** usu. as weapon 2 K 19$_{32}$||Is 37$_{33}$; בַּעֲלֵי חִצִּים *masters of arrows,* i.e. archers Gn 49$_{23}$. **b.** as instrument of divination Ezk 21$_{26}$. **c.** perh. of lightning Ps 144$_{6}$. → cf. חֵצִי I *arrow.*

חצב I 25.1.1.4 vb.—**Qal** 22.1.1.3 Pf. חָצַב, חָצַבְתִּי; impf. תַּחְצֹב; ptc. חֹצֵב, חֹצְבִים; ptc. pass. חֲצוּבִים—**1a. hew out** cistern Jr 2$_{13}$, tomb Is 22$_{16}$. **b. quarry, mine** copper Dt 8$_{9}$. **c. hew, dress** stone 1 C 22$_{2}$. **2.** pass. **be hewn out,** of cistern Dt 6$_{11}$. **3.** ptc. as noun, **stonemason** 1 K 5$_{29}$. **4. strike down** Ho 6$_{5}$. **5. divide** flames of fire Ps 29$_{7}$.

Ni. 1 Impf. יֵחָצְבוּן—**be hewn, engraved** in (בְּ) rock Jb 19$_{24}$.

Pu. 1 Pf. חֻצַּבְתֶּם—**be hewn out** from rock Is 51$_{1}$.

Hi. 1 Ptc. מַחְצֶבֶת—**hew in pieces** Rahab Is 51$_{9}$.

→ מַחְצֵב *hewing,* חַצָּבִי *stonemason.*

*__חצב__ II 1 vb.—**Qal** 1 Ptc. חֹצֵב—**rake** flames of fire Ps 29$_{7}$.

*[**חַצָּבִי**] n.m. **stonemason** Ezr 2$_{57}$||Ne 7$_{59}$ (if em.). → חצב I *hew.*

*[**חֲצָד**] 0.0.1 n.m. **date,** perh. a particular variety, coll. 5/6ḤevBA 46$_{5}$.

*[**חֲצָד**] 0.0.1 n.m. **harvest** 5/6ḤevBA 46$_{5}$.

חצה I 14.0.2 vb.—**Qal** 11.0.2 Pf. חָצְתָה, חָצִיתָ; impf. יֶחֱצֶה; + waw וַיַּחַץ (וַיֶּחֱצֵם)—**1. divide** price Ex 21$_{35}$, people into (לְ) two companies Gn 32$_{8}$, children among (עַל)

women Gn 33$_{1}$, booty between (בֵּין) warriors Nm 31$_{27}$. **2. halve,** i.e. **live out half,** one's days Ps 55$_{24}$.

Ni. 4 Impf. יֵחָצוּ, תֵּחָץ—**be divided,** of water 2 K 2$_{8}$ (+ הֵנָּה וָהֵנָּה *to one side and the other*), people into (לְ) two kingdoms Ezk 37$_{22}$, kingdom to (לְ) four winds Dn 11$_{4}$.

→ חֲצוֹת *middle,* חֲצִי *half,* מֶחֱצָה *half,* מַחֲצִית *half.*

***חצה** II 1 vb.—**Qal** Impf. יֶחֱצֶה—**reach,** of stream Is 30$_{28}$ (+ עַד *to* neck).

חֲצֹצְרָה 29.1.51 n.f.—חֲצֹצְרָה; pl. חֲצֹצְרוֹת; cstr. חֲצֹצְרוֹת—**1. trumpet,** sounded during worship Ps 98$_{6}$, at coronation 2 K 11$_{14}$||2 C 23$_{13}$, in battle 1QM 3$_{1}$. **2. trumpeter** 2 K 11$_{14}$||2 C 23$_{13}$. → חצצר *sound trumpet.*

חָצוֹר I 16 pl.n. **Hazor.**

*[**חָצוֹר**] II adj. **green** Is 44$_{4}$ (if em. בְּבֵין חָצִיר *among grass* to כְּבִין חָצוֹר *like a green tamarisk*).

חָצוֹר חֲדַתָּה 1 pl.n. **Hazor-hadattah.**

חֲצוֹת 3 n.f.—cstr. חֲצוֹת—**middle** of the night Ex 11$_{4}$. → חצה I *divide.*

חֻצוֹת, see חוּץ *outside.*

חֲצִי 126.0.9.3 n.m.—cstr. חֲצִי (בַּ/לַחֲצִי, וַחֲצִי, חֵצִי); sf. חֶצְיוֹ—**1. half,** חֲצִי הָעָם *half of the people* 1 K 16$_{21}$; אַמָּה וָחֵצִי *one cubit and a half* Ex 25$_{10}$. **2. middle** of altar, i.e. halfway up it Ex 27$_{5}$, of the night Ex 12$_{29}$; **midst** of one's days Ps 102$_{25}$. → חצה I *divide.*

חֵצִי I 4 n.m. **arrow**—1 S 20$_{36}$. → cf. חֵץ *arrow.*

*[**חֶצְיִ**] II 0.0.0.2 pr.n.m. **Hezi.**

*[**חֶצְיִן**] n.[m.] **battle-axe** 2 S 23$_{8}$ (if em. עֲדִינוֹ הָעֶצְנִי [Qr] perh. *Adino the Eznite* to עֹרֵר חֶצְיִנוֹ *he brandished his battle-axe*).

חָצִיר I 18.1 n.m.—cstr. חֲצִיר—**grass** 1 K 18$_{5}$ Is 40$_{6}$.

***חָצִיר** II 3 n.[m.] **reed,** coll. Is 35$_{7}$ 44$_{4}$ Jb 8$_{12}$.

***חָצִיר** III 1 n.[m.] **leek,** coll. Nm 11$_{5}$.

חֹצֶן I 3 n.m.—sf. חִצְנִי, חָצְנוֹ—**fold (of garment)** Is 49$_{22}$ Ps 129$_{7}$ Ne 5$_{13}$.

חֹצֶן II 1 n.[m.] **war-horses,** coll. Ezk 23$_{24}$ (mss) (L הֹצֶן *arms*).

*[**חָצֹף**] 0.1 adj. **impudent,** as noun, **impudent one, impudence** Si 40$_{28(M)}$.

חצץ 3 vb.—**Qal** 1 Ptc. חֹצֵץ—intrans., **divide (into swarms),** of locusts Pr 30$_{27}$.

Pi. 1 Ptc. מְחַצְצִים—ptc. as noun, **one who distributes water** Jg 5$_{11}$.

Pu. 1 Pf. חֻצָּצוּ—**be cut off, be at an end** Jb 21$_{21}$. → חָצָץ *gravel.*

חָצָץ 2 n.m. **gravel** Pr 20$_{17}$ Lm 3$_{16}$. → חצץ *divide.*

חַצְצוֹן תָּמָר 2 pl.n. **Hazazon-tamar.**

חצצר 6 vb.—**Pi.** 1 Ptc. Kt מחצצרים (Qr מַחְצְרִים)—**sound trumpet** 2 C 5$_{13}$.

Hi. 5 Ptc. Kt מחצצרים (Qr מַחְצְרִים)—1 C 15$_{24}$. → חֲצֹצְרָה *trumpet.*

חֲצֹצְרָה, see חֲצוֹצְרָה *trumpet.*

חָצֵר 190.0.19 n.m.&f.—+ ה- of direction חָצֵרָה; cstr. חֲצַר; sf. חֲצֵרוֹ; pl. חֲצֵרִים, חֲצֵרוֹת; cstr. חַצְרֵי, חַצְרוֹת; sf. חֲצֵרַי, חֲצֵרוֹתַי, חֲצֵרֶיךָ, חַצְרוֹתָיו—**1. court, enclosure** of palace Est 1$_{5}$, tabernacle Ex 27$_{9}$, temple 1 K 6$_{36}$. **2. settlement, village** Gn 25$_{16}$, without wall Lv 25$_{31}$.

חֲצַר אַדָּר 1 pl.n. **Hazar-addar.**

*[**חֲצַר אֲסָם**] 0.0.0.1 pl.n. **Hazar-asam.**

חֲצַר גַּדָּה 1 pl.n. **Hazar-gaddah.**

חָצֵר הַתִּיכוֹן 1 pl.n. **Hazer-hatticon.**

חֶצְרוֹ 2 pr.n.m. **Hezro.**

חֶצְרוֹן I 16 pr.n.m. **Hezron.**

חֶצְרוֹן II 1 pl.n. **Hezron.**

חֶצְרוֹנִי 2 gent. **Hezronite.**

חֲצֵרוֹת 6.0.0.4 pl.n. **Hazeroth.**

חֶצְרַי 1 pr.n.m. **Hezrai.**

חֲצַרְמָוֶת 2 pr.n.m. **Hazarmaveth.**

חֲצַר סוּסָה, 2.0.0.1 pl.n. **Hazar-susa,** also as חֲצַר סוּסִים **Hazar-susim.**

חֲצַר עֵינוֹן 4 pl.n. **Hazar-enon,** also as חֲצַר עֵינָן **Hazar-enan.**

חֲצַר שׁוּעָל 4 pl.n. **Hazar-shual.**

חֹק 129.19.107 n.m.—cstr. חֹק (חָק־); sf. חֻקְּכֶם, חָקִּוֹ, חֻקּוֹ; pl. חֻקִּים; cstr. חֻקֵּי (חֻקְקֵי־, חוּקֵּי); sf. חֻקָּיו—**1.** usu. **statute, decree, law, rule, instruction,** issued by Y. Ex 18$_{16}$ Ps 119$_{83}$, Wisdom 4QBéat 2.2$_{1}$, human Gn 47$_{26}$; social **convention, custom** Jg 11$_{39}$. **2. institution,** arising from regular observance of statute Ex 12$_{24}$; and sim. legal or conventional **right** to, or expected **allocation** of, food Pr 30$_{8}$, sacrifice Lv 6$_{11}$, royal rights Si 47$_{11}$; oft. חָק־עוֹלָם *statute/due of everlastingness* Ex 29$_{28}$. **3. lot, appointed destiny** 1QH 15$_{34}$, in ref. to death Si 41$_{3}$, **appointed time** Jb 14$_{13}$. **4. law** in general Ezr 7₁₀; **law of nature** Jr 31₃₆. **5.** perh. **prescription** of Y. for person Jb 23₁₄. **6. boundary** of earth 1QM 10₁₂, sea Pr 8₂₉; **limit** of Sheol's appetite Is 5₁₄. **7.** perh. **metre** of psalms Si 44₅. → חקק *engrave.*

חקה 4.0.1 vb.—**Pu.** 3.0.1 Ptc. מְחֻקֶּה, Q cstr. מחקת—**1a. be carved, engraved** on (עַל) wall Ezk 8₁₀. **b.** ptc. as noun, **carved thing, engraving** 1 K 6₃₅ Ezk 23₁₄.

Htp. 1 Impf. תִּתְחַקֶּה—**engrave for oneself** on (עַל) soles of feet Jb 13₂₇.

→ cf. חקק *engrave.*

חֻקָּה 100.0.19 n.f.—cstr. חֻקַּת; pl. חֻקּוֹת; cstr. חֻקּוֹת; sf. חֻקֹּתָיו, חֻקְּתֵיהֶם (חֻקֹּתָם)—**1. statute, ordinance, law, decree,** issued by Y. Dt 6₂, oft. חֻקַּת עוֹלָם *statute of everlastingness,* i.e. everlasting statute Ex 12₁₄; as regulation for natural order, **fixed time, prescribed order** of heaven and earth Jr 33₂₅, sun 1QH 20₅, moon Jr 31₃₅, harvest Jr 5₂₄. **2. statute, custom** of humans Lv 18₃ 1 K 3₃. → חקק *engrave.*

חֲקוּפָא 2 pr.n.m. **Hakupha.**

חקק 19.1.19 vb.—**Qal** 9.0.11 Pf. חַקֹּתִיךָ; + waw וְחַקּוֹתָ; impv. חֻקָּה; ptc. חֹקְקִים, חֹקְקֵי; ptc. pass. חֲקֻקִים; inf. חוּקוֹ (חוּקוֹ)—**1a. engrave, inscribe** something on (עַל) book Is 30₈, brick Ezk 4₁. **b. draw, mark out** circle Pr 8₂₇ (+ עַל *on* face of deep), foundations of earth Pr 8₂₉. **2. cut out** dwelling place in (בְּ) rock Is 22₁₆. **3. decree** iniquitous decrees Is 10₁. **4.** pass., **a. be engraved, be drawn** of images Ezk 23₁₄ (+ בְּ *with* vermilion). **b. be decreed,** of visitation 4QInstr[c] 1.1₁₄, time of anger 4QD[a] 2.1₃ (+ לְ *for* people). **5.** ptc. as noun, **commander** Jg 5₉.

Pu. 1.0.2 Ptc. מְחֻקָּק—**1. be engraved,** of figures 4QShirShabb[f] 19₅ (+ סָבִיב לְ *around* brickwork). **2.** ptc. as noun, **decree** Pr 31₅.

Po. 8.1.6 Impf. יְחֹקְקוּ; ptc. מְחֹקֵק, מְחֹקְקִים—**1. decree** righteousness Pr 8₁₅. **2.** ptc. as noun, **a. commander** Dt 33₂₁. **b. commander's staff, sceptre** Gn 49₁₀.

Ho. 1 Impf. יֻחָקוּ—**be inscribed,** of words Jb 19₂₃ (+ בְּ *in* book).

→ חֹק *statute,* חֻקָּה *statute;* cf. חקה *engrave..*

חקר I 27.8.7 vb.—**Qal** 22.8.7 Pf. חֲקַרְתַּנִי; impf. יַחְקֹר (יַחֲקֹר־), אֶחְקֹר; impv. חִקְרוּ, חָקְרֵנִי; ptc. חוֹקֵר; inf. חֲקֹר (לַחְקֹר, חֲקֹרָה)—**1. search (out), explore** land Jg 18₂, a matter Pr 25₂; of Y. searching the heart Jr 17₁₀. **2a. investigate, examine** a legal case Jb 29₁₆, one's ways Lm 3₄₀; **cross-examine** someone Pr 18₁₇. **b.** abs., **make investigation** Dt 13₁₅. **3. try out** mixed wine Pr 23₃₀. **4. sound out** someone 1 S 20₁₂. **5. search for words** Jb 32₁₁.

Ni. 4 Pf. נֶחְקַר; impf. יֵחָקֵר—**be searched out, be ascertained,** of foundations of earth Jr 31₃₇, weight of bronze 1 K 7₄₇||2 C 4₁₈.

Pi. 1 Pf. חִקֵּר—**search out** proverbs Ec 12₉.

→ חֵקֶר *searching,* מֶחְקָר *depth,* מַחְקֶרֶת *searching out.*

*חקר II 1 vb.—**Qal** 1 Impf. יַחְקְרֶנּוּ—**despise** someone Pr 28₁₁.

חֵקֶר 12.2.11 n.m.—pl. cstr. חִקְרֵי—**1. searching (out),** חִקְרֵי־לֵב *searchings of heart* Jg 5₁₆, אֵין חֵקֶר *there is no searching,* i.e. it cannot be found Is 40₂₈. **2. (object of) searching out, depth** of ocean Jb 38₁₆, God Jb 11₇, hidden things Si 42₁₉. → חקר I *search.*

*[חִקָּר] 0.0.1 pl.n. **Hikkar.**

*[חַר] adj. **scorched,** of ground Jr 14₄ (if em. חַתָּה *it is dismayed* [חתת I] to הָחָרָה).

חֹר I 13.1 n.m.—pl. חֹרִים; cstr. חֹרֵי; sf. חֹרֶיהָ—**noble** 1 K 21₈.

חֹר II 7 n.[m.]—pl. חֹרִים; cstr. חֹרֵי; sf. חֹרָיו—**hole,** as hiding place 1 S 14₁₁, den of lions Na 2₁₃, socket of eye Zc 14₁₂; in wall Ezk 8₇, lid of chest 2 K 12₁₀.

[חֻר] 2 n.[m.]—cstr. חֻר; pl. חוּרִים—**hole** of snake Is 11₈; as hiding place of people Is 42₂₂.

*[חֲרָא] 0.0.1 adv.—לחרא (perh. = לְאַחֲרָא)—perh. **afterwards** 4QParGenEx 2₁₁.

[חֲרָא] 3 n.[m.]—cstr. Kt הרי; pl. sf. חראיהם (חריהם)—**dung** 2 K 18₂₇(Kt)||Is 36₁₂(Kt) (Qr צוֹאָתָם *their filth*); חרייונים *doves' dung,* perh. name of plant 2 K 6₂₅(Kt) (Qr דִּבְיוֹנִים *dove's dung*). → cf. מַחֲרָאָה *latrine.*

חרב I 37.1.6 vb.—**Qal** 15.1.1 Pf. חָרְבוּ; impf. יֶחֱרַב, יֶחֶרְבוּ; impv. חֲרָבִי, חָרְבוּ; inf. abs. חָרֹב—**1. be dry, dried up,** of water, surface of ground Gn 8₃, sea Ps 106₉. **2. be wasted away, desolate,** of nations Is 60₁₂, city Jr 26₉.

Ni. 2 Ptc. נֶחֱרֶבֶת, נֶחֱרָבוֹת—**be laid waste,** of city Ezk 26₁₉.

Pu. 2 Pf. חֹרָבוּ—**be dried up,** of cord Jg 16₇.

Hi. 13.0.5 Pf. הֶחֱרַבְתִּי ,הֶחֱרִיב; impf. אַחֲרִיב; + waw וְהַחֲרַבְתִּי; ptc. מַחֲרִיב ,מַחֲרֶבֶת; inf. Q להחריבה ,לחריב—**1. dry up** sea Is 50$_2$. **2. lay waste** land Jg 16$_{24}$, city Ezk 19$_7$.

Ho. 2 Pf. הָחֳרָבָה; ptc. מָחֳרָבוֹת—**be laid waste,** of Jerusalem Ezk 26$_2$.

→ חָרֵב *dry,* חֹרֶב *drought,* חָרָבָה *dry land,* חֲרָבוֹן *dry heat,* חָרְבָּה *waste,* חָרְבָּן *desolation.*

*חרב II 4 vb.—**Qal** 2 Impv. חֲרֹב ,חִרְבוּ—**destroy** persons, Jr 50$_{21}$, bull Jr 50$_{27}$.

Ni. 1 Pf. נֶחֶרְבוּ—**be destroyed,** of persons 2 K 3$_{23}$ (with ho. inf. abs.).

Ho. 1 Inf. abs. הָחֳרֵב—**be destroyed,** הָחֳרֵב נֶחֶרְבוּ *they must have been destroyed* 2 K 3$_{23}$ (or em. ni.).

→ חֶרֶב *sword,* חֲרִיבָה *ruin,* מַחֲרָב *laying waste.*

חָרֵב 10.0.2 adj.—f.s. חֲרֵבָה; pl. חֳרָבוֹת—**1. dry,** of grain offering Lv 7$_{10}$, morsel Pr 17$_1$. **2. devastated, in ruins,** of city Ezk 36$_{35}$, house, i.e. temple Hg 1$_4$. **3.** חֲרֵבָה as noun, **ruin** Ezk 26$_2$ (if em.). → חרב I *be dry.*

חֶרֶב 411.3.55 n.f.—חָרֶב; cstr. חֶרֶב sf. חַרְבּוֹ; pl. חֲרָבוֹת; cstr. חַרְבוֹת; sf. חַרְבוֹתָם ,חַרְבוֹתָיו (חַרְבֹתֵיהֶם)—**1.** usu. **sword** Gn 3$_{24}$; חַלְלֵי־חֶרֶב *slain ones of,* i.e. by, *the sword* Is 22$_2$, לְפִי־חֶרֶב *with the mouth,* i.e. edge, *of the sword* Jos 8$_{24}$; perh. also **dagger** Jg 3$_{16}$. **2. knife,** חַרְבוֹת צֻרִים *knives of flint,* for circumcision Jos 5$_2$; חֶרֶב חַדָּה *sharp knife,* for shaving Ezk 5$_1$. **3. tool,** for hewing stone Ex 20$_{25}$. → חרב II *destroy.*

חֹרֶב I 16.4 n.m.—sf. Si חרבו—**1a. dryness** of ground Jg 6$_{37}$. **b. drought** Hg 1$_{11}$. **c. heat, warmth** of sun Gn 31$_{40}$, fever Jb 30$_{30}$. **2. desolation** Is 61$_4$.

*חֹרֶב II 1 n.[m.] perh. **bustard,** large bird Zp 2$_{14}$.

חֹרֵב 17.1 pl.n. **Horeb.**

חָרְבָּה 41.1.3 n.f.—pl. חֳרָבוֹת; cstr. חָרְבוֹת; sf. חָרְבֹתָיו, חָרְבוֹתֵיהֶם—**waste, desolation, ruin,** of cities Lv 26$_{31}$, land Jr 7$_{34}$, temple Ezr 9$_9$. → חרב I *be dry.*

חָרָבָה 8.0.2 n.f. **dry land** Gn 7$_{22}$ Ex 14$_{21}$. → חרב I *be dry.*

*[חֶרְבָּה] 1 n.f.—pl. cstr. חֶרְבוֹת—**deceit** Ps 59$_8$.

[חֲרָבוֹן] 1 n.m.—pl. cstr. חַרְבֹנֵי—**dry heat** Ps 32$_4$. → חרב I *be dry.*

חַרְבוֹנָא 2 pr.n.m. **Harbona.**

*[חָרְבָּן] 0.0.2 n.[m.]—cstr. חרבן—**desolation** of land CD 5$_{20}$ 4QapJerC^e 1$_8$. → חרב I *be dry.*

חרג 1 vb.—**Qal** 1 Impf. יַחְרְגוּ—**come fearfully** Ps 18$_{46}$ (+ מִן *from* dungeon) Ps 18$_{46}$.

חַרְגֹּל 1.0.1 n.[m.] **locust,** an edible species Lv 11$_{22}$=11QT 48$_3$.

חרד I 39.0.2 vb.—**Qal** 30.0.1 Pf. חָרַד; impf. יֶחֱרַד ,יֶחֶרְדוּ (יֶחֶרְדוּ ,יִחְרְדוּ); impv. חִרְדוּ—**1. tremble, quake,** of person Gn 27$_{33}$ (+ חֲרָדָה גְּדֹלָה *[with] great trembling*) Ex 19$_{16}$, heart 1 S 28$_5$, mountain Ex 19$_{18}$. **2. go, come,** or **turn trembling** to (אֶל) Gn 42$_{28}$, after (אַחֲרֵי) 1 S 13$_7$, to meet (לִקְרַאת) 1 S 16$_4$, from (מִן) Ho 11$_{10}$. **3.** חרד הַחֲרָדָה **go to the trouble for** (אֶל) 2 K 4$_{13}$.

Hi. 16.0.1 Pf. הֶחֱרִיד; + waw וְהַחֲרַדְתִּי; ptc. מַחֲרִיד; inf. הַחֲרִיד—**startle, disturb, frighten** someone 2 S 17$_2$; oft. abs., וְאֵין מַחֲרִיד *and none shall frighten (you)* Lv 26$_6$.

→ חָרֵד *trembling,* חֲרָדָה I *trembling.*

*חרד II 1 vb.—**Qal** 1 Impf. יֶחֱרַד—**be angry** Gn 27$_{33}$ (+ חֲרָדָה גְּדֹלָה *[with] great anger*). → חֲרָדָה II *anger.*

*חרד III 5 vb.—**Qal** 3 Pf. חָרַדְתְּ, impf. יֶחֶרְדוּ—**1.** חרד הַחֲרָדָה **provide separate accommodation for** (אֶל) 2 K 4$_{13}$. **2. make haste from** (מִן) Ho 11$_{10.11}$.

Hi. 2 Pf. הֶחֱרִיד; + waw וְהַחֲרַדְתִּי—**1.** intrans., **disperse, scatter** Jg 8$_{12}$. **2.** trans., **separate, isolate** 2 S 17$_2$.

→ חֲרָדָה III *lodging.*

*חרד IV 1 vb.—**Hi.** 1 Inf. הַחֲרִיד—**re-unite** Zc 2$_4$. → חֲרָדָה IV *loincloth.*

חָרֵד 6 adj.—pl. חֲרֵדִים—**1. trembling,** of person Jg 7$_3$, heart 1 S 4$_{13}$. **2.** as noun, **one who trembles** at word, with עַל Is 66$_2$, אֶל Is 66$_5$, בְּ Ezr 9$_4$. → חרד I *tremble.*

חֲרֹד 1 pl.n. **Harod.**

חֲרָדָה I 9 n.f.—cstr. חֶרְדַּת; pl. חֲרָדוֹת—**1. trembling, fear,** חֶרְדַּת אֱלֹהִים *trembling of,* i.e. inspired by, *God* 1 S 14$_{15}$, חרד חֲרָדָה גְּדֹלָה *tremble [with] great trembling* Gn 27$_{33}$. **2. trouble, care** 2 K 4$_{13}$. → חרד I *tremble.*

*חֲרָדָה II 1 n. f. **anger,** חרד חֲרָדָה גְּדֹלָה *be angry [with] great anger* Gn 27$_{33}$. → חרד II *be angry.*

*חֲרָדָה III 1 n.f. **lodging, (separate) accommodation** 2 K 4$_{13}$. → חרד III *separate.*

*[חֲרָדָה] IV 1 n.f.—pl. חֲרָדוֹת—**loincloth** Ezk 26$_{16}$. → חרד IV *re-unite.*

חֲרָדָה V 2 pl.n. **Haradah.**

חֲרֹדִי 1 gent. **Harodite.**

חרה I 96.5.13 vb.—**Qal** 85.1.11 Pf. חָרָה; impf. יֶחֱרֶה (יִחַר); + waw וַיִּחַר; inf. חָרֹה, חֲרוֹת—**1.** intrans., **a. burn, be kindled,** subj. אַף *anger* of Y. Ex 4$_{14}$ (+ בְּ *against*), human Ex 32$_{19}$. **b. be angry,** with impersonal subj. and prep., (1) וַיִּחַר לוֹ *and he was angry,* lit. 'and it was kindled to him' (and vars.), of Y. Gn 18$_{30}$, human Gn 4$_{5}$. (2) אַל־יִחַר בְּעֵינֵי אֲדֹנִי *let not my lord be angry,* lit. 'let it not be kindled in the eyes of my lord' Gn 31$_{35}$. **2.** trans., **kindle,** הריתי נפשי בה *I kindled my soul,* i.e. desire, *for her* Si 51$_{19(11QPs^a)}$.

Ni. 3.2 Pf. נֶחֱרוּ; impf. Si תאחר; ptc. נֶחֱרִים—**be angry, incensed** against (בְּ) Is 41$_{11}$.

Hi. 2.0.1 Pf. הֶחֱרָה; + waw וַיַּחַר—**1.** intrans., **burn with zeal** Ne 3$_{20}$ (or del.). **2.** trans., **kindle anger against** (עַל) Jb 19$_{11}$.

Htp. 4.2.2 Impf. תִּתְחַר—**show oneself angry, be vexed** on account of (בְּ) Ps 37$_{1}$.

Tiphel 2 Impf. תְּתַחֲרֶה; ptc. מְתַחֲרֶה—**compete** Jr 12$_{5}$ (+ אֵת *with*) 22$_{15}$ (+ בְּ *in*).

→ חָרוֹן *burning,* חֳרִי *heat,* תַּחֲרָה *strife.*

***חרה** II 1 vb.—**Qal** 1 Pf. חָרוּ—**dwindle away** Is 24$_{6}$.

[חָרָה], see חִירָה *court.*

חֹר הַגִּדְגָּד 2 pl.n. **Hor-hagidgad.**

חַרְהֲיָה 1 pr.n.m. **Harhaiah.**

***[חֲרוּב]** 0.0.2 n.[m.]—pl. חרובים—**carob-tree** Mur 22 1$_{12}$.

***[חֲרוּבָה]** n.f.—**fortress** 3QTr 1$_{1(Allegro)}$ (others חֲרִיבָה *ruin* or חֹרֵיבָה *Horebbah*).

[חָרוּז] 1 n.m.—pl. חֲרוּזִים—**necklace** Ca 1$_{10}$.

חָרוּל 3.0.1 n.m.—pl. חֲרֻלִּים—**nettles,** or **thistles** Zp 2$_{9}$.

[חָרוּם] *split,* see חרם II, qal.

חֲרוּמַף 1 pr.n.m. **Harumaph.**

חָרוֹן 41.2.32 n.m.—cstr. חֲרוֹן; sf. חֲרוֹנוֹ; pl. cstr. Q חרוני; sf. חֲרוֹנֶיךָ—**1.** חֲרוֹן אַף **burning of anger** of Y. Ex 32$_{12}$. **2.** without אַף, **anger, wrath** (alw.) of Y. Ex 15$_{7}$; קץ חרון *time of wrath* CD 1$_{5}$. → חרה I *burn.*

חֹרֹנַיִם 4 pl.n. **Horonaim.**

חֲרוּפִי 1 gent. **Haruphite.**

חָרוּץ I 6.2 n.m. **gold** Zc 9$_{3}$ Ps 68$_{14}$ Pr 3$_{14}$.

***חָרוּץ** II 4 n.m.—pl. cstr. חֲרֻצוֹת—**threshing sledge** Is 28$_{27}$ Am 1$_{3}$. → חרץ *decide, sharpen.*

חָרוּץ III 1 n.m. **channel, moat** Dn 9$_{25}$. → חרץ *decide, sharpen.*

חָרוּץ IV 1 pr.n.m. **Haruz.**

חָרוּץ V 1 adj. **mutilated,** as noun, **mutilated one** Lv 22$_{22}$. → חרץ *decide, sharpen.*

חָרוּץ VI 5 adj.—pl. חָרוּצִים—**diligent,** as noun, **diligent one** Pr 10$_{4}$ 13$_{4}$. → חרץ *decide, sharpen.*

***חָרוּץ** VII 1 adj. **sickly,** of emaciation (כִּלָּיוֹן) Is 10$_{22}$.

חָרוּץ VIII, see חרץ *decide,* qal, §3.

חָרוּץ IX, see עֵמֶק חָרוּץ *Valley of Decision.*

***[חֵרוּת]** 0.0.1.17 n.f.—cstr. חרות I (חרת, חר)—**freedom** Bar-Kochba Revolt Year 2 Coins 176 194.

[חַרְחוּר] I 1.1.1 n.m.—חַרְחֻר—**1. burning fever** Dt 28$_{22}$. **2. heated strife** Si 40$_{9}$ 4QpNah 3.2$_{5}$. → חרר *burn.*

חַרְחוּר II 2 pr.n.m. **Harhur.**

חַרְחַיָה, see חַרְהֲיָה *Harhaiah.*

חַרְחַס 1 pr.n.m. **Harhas.**

חַרְחֻר, see חרחור I *burning.*

חֶרֶט 2.0.1 n.m. **stylus** Ex 32$_{4}$ Is 8$_{1}$ 1QM 12$_{3}$.

חַרְטֹם 11.0.1 n.m.—pl. חַרְטֻמִּים; cstr. חַרְטֻמֵּי—**magician, soothsayer,** or perh. **minister (of state)** of Egypt Gn 41$_{8}$, Babylon Dn 1$_{20}$.

[חֲרִי], see חֶרֶא *dung.*

חֹרִי I 3 pr.n.m. **Hori.**

חֹרִי II 7 gent. **Horite.**

חֹרִי III 1 n.[m.] **white bread** Gn 40$_{16}$. → חור I *be white.*

חֳרִי 6.1.1 n.m.—cstr. חֳרִי—**heat of anger** (אַף) Ex 11$_{8}$ Dt 29$_{23}$. → חרה I *burn.*

***[חֲרִיבָה]** n.f. **ruin** 3QTr 1$_{1(García Martínez)}$ (others חֲרוּבָה *fortress* or חֹרֵיבָה *Horebbah*). → חרב II *ruin.*

***[חֹרֵיבָה]** pl.n. **Horebbah.**

[חָרִיט] 2 n.m.—pl. חֲרִטִים—**purse,** or perh. **coat** 2 K 5$_{23}$ Is 3$_{22}$.

[חָרִים], see חָרִם *Harim.*

חריונים, see חֶרֶא *dung* and יוֹנָה *dove.*

חָרִיף 2 pr.n.m. **Hariph.**

חָרִיץ I 2 n.m.—pl. cstr. חֲרִיצֵי—**pickaxe** 2 S 12$_{31}$ 1 C 20$_{3}$. → חרץ *decide, sharpen.*

***[חָרִיץ]** II 0.0.1 n.[m.] **channel** 3QTr 5$_{8}$. → חרץ *decide, sharpen.*

[חָרִיץ] III 1 n.m.—pl. cstr. חֲרִצֵי—**slice of cheese** 1 S 17$_{18}$.

*[חָרִיץ] IV 0.1 n.[m.] **gold** Si 34₅(Bmg) (B חרוץ *gold*).

חָרִישׁ 3 n.m.—sf. חֲרִישׁוֹ—**1. ploughing** 1 S 8₁₂. **2. ploughing time** Gn 45₆ Ex 34₂₁. → חרשׁ I *plough*.

[חֲרִישִׁי] 1.0.1 adj.—f. s. חֲרִישִׁית—**1. sultry,** of wind Jon 4₈. **2.** as noun, **sultry wind** 1QH 15₅.

חרך 1 vb.—**Qal** 1 Impf. יַחֲרֹךְ—**roast** game Pr 12₂₇.

[חֲרַךְ] 1 n.m.—pl. חֲרַכִּים—**lattice (window)** Ca 2₉.

חרם I 51.1.9 vb.—**Hi.** 48.1.8 Pf. הֶחֱרַמְתִּי, הֶחֱרִים; impf. יַחֲרִם; + waw וְהַחֲרַמְתִּי, וַיַּחֲרֵם, וַיַּחֲרִימוּ; impv. הַחֲרִימוּ, הַחֲרֵם; inf. הַחֲרִים, הַחֲרֵם (הַחֲרִימָם)—**1.** usu. **devote to ban of destruction, destroy** land 2 K 19₁₁||Is 37₁₁, nation Dt 7₂, city Nm 21₂, beasts 1 S 15₉. **2. dedicate to** (לְ) Y., thereby excluding redemption Lv 27₂₈ Mc 4₁₃. → חֵרֶם *devoted object.*

חרם II 2 vb.—**Qal** 1 Ptc. חָרֻם—pass. ptc. as adj., **split, mutilated** (perh. specif. of nose), of אִישׁ *man* Lv 21₁₈.

Hi. 1 + waw וְהֶחֱרִים—**divide** tongue of sea Is 11₁₅.

→ חֵרֶם II *net.*

חָרִם 11.0.4 pr.n.m. **Harim.**

חֵרֶם I 29.2.7 n.m.—cstr. חֵרֶם; sf. חֶרְמִי—**1. devoted object, that which is banned,** i.e. excluded from profane use and devoted to Y. for destruction Dt 13₁₈ Jos 6₁₇, or religious use Lv 27₂₈. **2. ban, devotion** to destruction, אִישׁ־חֶרְמִי *man of my ban,* i.e. man whom I have devoted to destruction 1 K 20₄₂; to religious use Lv 27₂₁. → חרם I *destroy.*

חֵרֶם II 9.0.3 n.m.—sf. חֶרְמוֹ; pl. חֲרָמִים—**net,** for fishing Ezk 26₅, hunting Mc 7₂. → חרם II *split.*

חֳרֵם 1 pl.n. **Horem.**

חָרְמָה 9 pl.n. **Hormah.**

חֶרְמוֹן 14 pl.n. **Hermon.**

חֶרְמֵשׁ 2 n.[m.] **sickle** Dt 16₉ 23₂₆.

חָרָן I 10.0.7 pl.n. **Haran.**

חָרָן II 2 pr.n.m. **Haran.**

חַרְנֶפֶר 1 pr.n.m. **Harnepher.**

חֶרֶס I 2 n.m.—+ ה- of direction הַחַרְסָה—**sun** Jg 14₁₈ Jb 9₇.

[חֶרֶס] II 1 n.m.—חֶרֶס—**itch** Dt 28₆₇.

חֶרֶס III 1 pl.n. **Heres.**

חַרְסִית 1 n.f. **potsherd,** שַׁעַר הַחַרְסִית *gate of the potsherd* Jr 19₂(Qr) (Kt חרסות).

חרף I 39.3.2.1 vb.—**Qal** 4.0.0.1 Impf. יְחָרֵף; ptc. חֹרְפִי, חוֹרְפֶיךָ—**1. reproach, taunt,** Jb 27₆ (+ מִן *on account of*). **2.** ptc. as noun, **one who reproaches, taunts** Ps 119₄₂.

Pi. 35.3.2 Pf. חֵרֵף, חֵרַפְתָּ; impf. יְחָרֵף; + waw וַיְחָרֵף; ptc. מְחָרֵף; inf. חָרֵף (חָרְפָם)—**reproach, revile** Y. 2 K 19₄ ||Is 37₄, humans 1 S 17₂₅; עַם חֵרֵף נַפְשׁוֹ לָמוּת *a people who reproached their lives to the death,* i.e. put them at risk Jg 5₁₈.

→ חֶרְפָּה I *reproach.*

חרף II 1.1 vb.—**Qal** 1 Impf. תֶּחֱרָף—**spend winter,** of beasts Is 18₆.

Pi. 0.1 Impf. תחרף (תחריף)—**make** south wind **cold** Si 43₁₆.

→ חֹרֶף I *winter.*

*חרף III 1.0.1 vb.—**Qal** 0.0.1 Ptc. pass. חרופה—pass. **be designated,** of female servant 4QDᵉ 4₁₄.

Ni. 1 Pf. נֶחֱרֶפֶת—**be betrothed,** of female servant Lv 19₂₀ (+ לְ *to*).

חָרֵף 1.0.0.1 pr.n.m. **Hareph.**

*[חֶרֶף] 0.0.1 n.m. **catapult** 4QMᶜ₅.

חֹרֶף I 6.0.2 n.m. **winter** Gn 8₂₂. → חרף II *spend winter.*

*חֹרֶף II 1 n.[m.] **youth,** יְמֵי חָרְפִּי *days of my youth* Jb 29₄.

חֶרְפָּה I 73.9.13 n.f.—cstr. חֶרְפַּת; sf. חֶרְפָּתִי; pl. חֲרָפוֹת; cstr. חֶרְפּוֹת—**1. reproach, taunt** Is 51₇. **2. (condition of) reproach, shame, disgrace** Gn 30₂₃. **3. (object of) reproach** Jr 6₁₀. → חרף I *reproach.*

*חֶרְפָּה II 1 n.f. **knife** Jb 16₁₀.

חרץ 11.0.11 vb.—**Qal** 5.0.4 Pf. חָרַץ; impf. יֶחֱרַץ; ptc. pass. חָרוּץ, חֲרוּצִים; inf. Q חרוץ—**1a. decide,** i.e. pronounce, judgment 1 K 20₄₀. **b.** abs., **take decisive action** 2 S 5₂₄. **2. sharpen** tongue Jos 10₂₁. **3a.** pass. **be decided,** of destruction Is 10₂₂, days Jb 14₅; **be destined,** of priest 1QM 15₆ (+ לְ *for*). **b.** pass. ptc. as noun, **appointed one,** חרוצי מלחמה *ones appointed of,* i.e. *for, battle* 1QM 16₁₁.

Ni. 5.0.6 Ptc. נֶחֱרָצָה (נֶחֱרֶצֶת)—**1. be determined,** of desolation Dn 9₂₆, time of judgment 1QS 4₂₀. **2.** ptc. as noun, **that which is determined,** כָּלָה וְנֶחֱרָצָה *destruction and that which is determined,* i.e. determined destruction Is 10₂₃.

Pu. 0.0.1 Ptc. מחורץ—**be fluted,** of socket of javelin

1QM 5$_{9}$.

→ חָרוּץ II *threshing sledge*, III *channel*, V *mutilated*, VI *diligent*, חָרִיץ I *pickaxe*, II *channel*.

[חַרְצֻבָּה] 2.0.1 n.f.—pl. חַרְצֻבּוֹת—**1. fetter** of wickedness Is 58$_{6}$. **2. torment** Ps 73$_{4}$.

חַרְצָן 1 n.m.—pl. חַרְצַנִּים—**sour grape** Nm 6$_{4}$.

חרק I 5.0.3 vb.—**Qal** 5.0.3 Pf. חָרַק; impf. יַחֲרֹק; + waw וַיַּחַרְקוּ; ptc. חֹרֵק; inf. חָרֹק—**gnash** teeth Ps 35$_{16}$; with (בְּ) teeth at (עַל) someone Jb 16$_{9}$.

*חרק II vb.—**Ni. be broken,** of cord Ec 12$_{6}$ (if em. רחק ni. *be distant*).

חרר 10 vb.—**Qal** 3 Pf. חָרָה, חָרוּ—**1. burn, be scorched,** of persons Is 24$_{6}$, bones Jb 30$_{30}$ (+ מִן *on account of* heat). **2. glow,** of copper Ezk 24$_{11}$.

Ni. 6 Pf. נִחַר (נָחָר), נִחָרוּ; impf. יֵחָרוּ; + waw וַיֵּחָר—**1. be set aglow,** of wood Ezk 15$_{5}$, bones Ezk 24$_{10}$. **2. be hoarse,** of throat Ps 69$_{4}$.

Pilp. 1 Inf. חַרְחַר—**kindle** strife Pr 26$_{21}$.

→ חָרֵר *parched place*, חָרָר *dispute*, חַרְחוּר *burning fever*.

*[חָרָר] 0.0.1 n.[m.] **dispute** Mur 30 2$_{25}$. → חרר *burn*.

חָרֵר 1 n.m.—pl. חֲרֵרִים—**parched places, lava stretches** Jr 17$_{6}$. → חרר *burn*.

*חרשׁ 0.1 vb.—**Qal** 1 Impf. תחרש—**provoke** Si 8$_{2}$ (עַל of obj.).

חֶרֶשׂ 17.0.4 n.m.—חֶרֶשׂ; pl. cstr. חַרְשֵׂי; sf. חַרְשֶׂיהָ—**1. pottery, earthenware** Lv 6$_{21}$. **2. potsherd** Is 30$_{14}$.

חרשׁ I 27.4.3 vb.—**Qal** 24.2.3 Pf. חָרְשׁוּ, חֲרַשְׁתֶּם; impf. יַחֲרֹשׁ; ptc. חֹרֵשׁ, חֹרְשִׁים; ptc. pass. חֲרוּשָׁה; inf. חֲרֹשׁ—**1. plough,** usu. without obj. Dt 22$_{10}$ (+ בְּ *with* ox) Is 28$_{24}$; with obj. ploughing (חָרִישׁ) 1 S 8$_{12}$, wickedness Ho 10$_{13}$. **2. devise** good Pr 14$_{22}$, evil Pr 3$_{29}$. **3.** pass., **a. be engraved,** of sin Jr 17$_{1}$ (+ עַל *on* tablet). **b. be designated for** (לְ) battle 4QM[a] 10.2$_{13}$. **3.** ptc. as noun, **a. ploughman** Am 9$_{13}$. **b. artisan** 1 K 7$_{14}$.

Ni. 2 Impf. תֵּחָרֵשׁ—**be ploughed** Jr 26$_{18}$.

Hi. 1 Ptc. מַחֲרִישׁ—**plan, devise** evil against (עַל) 1 S 23$_{9}$.

→ חָרָשׁ *artisan*, חֲרֹשֶׁת *carving*, חָרִישׁ *ploughing*, מַחֲרֵשָׁה *ploughshare*, מַחֲרֵשָׁה *goad*, מַחֲרֹשׁ *scheming*.

חרשׁ II 47.5.3 vb.—**Qal** 7 Impf. יֶחֱרַשׁ—**1. be silent,** of Y. Ps 39$_{13}$ (+ אֶל *to* tears) 83$_{2}$. **2. be deaf,** of Y. Ps 28$_{1}$ (+ מִן *to* person), ear Mc 7$_{16}$.

Hi. 39.4.3 Pf. הֶחֱרִישׁ, הֶחֱרַשְׁתִּי; impf. יַחֲרִישׁ; impv. הַחֲרֵשׁ, הַחֲרִישִׁי, הַחֲרִישׁוּ; ptc. מַחֲרִישׁ, מַחֲרִשִׁים; inf. abs. הַחֲרֵשׁ—**1a. be silent, be still,** of Y. Is 42$_{14}$, humans Ex 14$_{14}$. **b. keep silent, hold one's peace,** of Y. Ps 50$_{21}$, humans Gn 34$_{5}$ Nm 30$_{5}$ (+ לְ *to* someone) Is 41$_{1}$ (+ אֶל *to* Y.). **c.** with מִן *from* someone, i.e. **cease speaking to** Jr 38$_{27}$, **cease activity for** 1 S 7$_{8}$. **2. make silent** Jb 11$_{3}$.

Htp. 1.1 Pf. Si התחרישו; + waw וַיִּתְחָרְשׁוּ—**keep still** Jg 16$_{2}$ Si 41$_{20}$(Bmg).

→ חֵרֵשׁ *deaf*, חֶרֶשׁ I *sorcery*, II *secretly*.

חָרָשׁ 37.1.6 n.m.—cstr. חָרַשׁ; pl. חָרָשִׁים (חֲרָשִׁים); cstr. חָרָשֵׁי—**artisan,** worker in stone Ex 28$_{11}$, wood 2 S 5$_{11}$, metal 1 S 13$_{19}$; maker of images of gods Is 45$_{16}$; one skilled in destruction Ezk 21$_{36}$. → חרשׁ I *plough*.

חֵרֵשׁ 9.0.3 adj.—pl. חֵרְשִׁים—**1. deaf,** of cobra Ps 58$_{5}$. **2.** as noun, **deaf one** Lv 19$_{14}$ Is 42$_{18}$. → חרשׁ II *be silent*.

חֶרֶשׁ I 1 n.m.—pl. חֲרָשִׁים—**sorcery, magic** Is 3$_{3}$. → חרשׁ II *be silent*.

חֶרֶשׁ II 1 adv. **secretly** Jos 2$_{1}$. → חרשׁ II *be silent*.

חֶרֶשׁ III 1 pr.n.m. **Heresh.**

חֹרֶשׁ I 3 n.m.—pl. חֳרָשִׁים—**wood, wood land** Is 17$_{9}$ Ezk 31$_{3}$ 2 C 27$_{4}$.

חֹרֶשׁ II 4 pl.n. **Horesh.**

חַרְשָׁא 2 pr.n.m. **Harsha.**

חֹרְשָׁה, see חֹרֶשׁ *Horesh.*

חֲרֹשֶׁת 4 n.f.—cstr. חֲרֹשֶׁת—**carving, cutting** of stone and wood Ex 31$_{5}$=35$_{33}$. → חרשׁ I *plough*.

חֲרֹשֶׁת הַגּוֹיִם 3 pl.n. **Harosheth-ha-goiim.**

חרת 1.1.12 vb.—**Qal** 1.1.12 Pf. Q חרת; impf. Q אחורתם; ptc. pass. חָרוּת—**1. engrave** covenant 1QM 12$_{3}$ (+ בְּ *with* stylus), statutes 4QShirShabb[a] 1.1$_{5}$. **2.** pass., **be engraved,** of writing Ex 32$_{16}$ (+ עַל *upon* tablet), stone Si 45$_{11}$, statute 1QS 10$_{6}$. → חֶרֶת *ink*.

חֶרֶת I 1 pl.n. **Hereth.**

*[חֶרֶת] II 0.0.1 n.f. **ink** 1QH 9$_{24}$. → חרת *engrave*.

חֲשׂוּפָא 2 pr.n.m. **Hasupha.**

חֲשׂוּפַי Is 20$_{4}$, see חשׂף I *make bare*, §3.

[חָשִׂיף] 1 n.m.—cstr. חֲשִׂפֵי—**little flock** of goats 1 K 20$_{27}$.

חשׂך I 28.3.1 vb.—**Qal** 26.2 Pf. חָשַׂךְ; impf. יַחְשֹׂךְ, אֶחְשֹׂךְ; + waw וָאֶחְשֹׂךְ; impv. חֲשֹׂךְ; ptc. חוֹשֵׂךְ—**1. withhold, hold** back, spare someone or something Gn 20$_6$ (+ מֵחֲטוֹ *from sinning*) 22$_{12}$ (+ מִן *from* Y.) Pr 13$_{24}$; abs. Pr 21$_{26}$. **2. reserve** something Jb 38$_{23}$ (+ לְ *for*). **3. restrain** someone 2 S 18$_{16}$, one's feet Jr 14$_{10}$, mouth Jb 7$_{11}$. **4. refrain, hold oneself back** Is 54$_2$. **5. be held back,** i.e. **fail to appear,** of day Ezk 30$_{18}$.

Ni. 2.1 Impf. יֵחָשֵׂךְ (יֵחָשֶׂךְ)—**1. be spared,** of person Jb 21$_{30}$ (+ לְ *at* day of calamity). **2. be held back,** i.e. **kept,** of straightness Si 9$_{17}$ (+ בְּ *by* the skilled). **3. be assuaged,** of pain Jb 16$_6$.

***חשׂך** II 1 vb.—**Qal** 1 Impf. יַחְשֹׂךְ—**be continuous, unceasing,** of movement of lips Jb 16$_5$.

*[**חֲשֵׂכָה**] n.f.—cstr. חֲשֵׂכַת—**abundance** of water Ps 18$_{12}$ (if em. חֶשְׁכַת־ *darkness of*).

חשׂף I 11.2 vb.—**Qal** 11.2 Pf. חָשַׂף; + waw וַיֶּחֱשֹׂף; impv. חֶשְׂפִּי־; ptc. pass. חֲשׂוּפָה, pl. cstr. חֲשׂוּפֵי; inf. חָשֹׂף (לַחְשֹׂף, Si חסוף)—**1a. make bare** arm Is 52$_{10}$, fig tree Jl 1$_7$. **b. strip off** train Is 47$_2$. **2. skim** water Is 30$_{14}$ (+ מִן *from* cistern), winepress Hg 2$_{16}$. **3.** pass. **be made bare, be stripped,** of arm Ezk 4$_7$, buttocks Is 20$_4$ (חֲשׂוּפֵי שֵׁת lit. 'bared of buttocks'). → מַחְשֹׂף *stripping.*

***חשׂף** II 2 vb.—**Qal** 2 Inf. לַחְשֹׂף—**scoop up** water Is 30$_{14}$ (+ מִן *from cistern*), liquid (from winepress) Hg 2$_{16}$.

חשׁב 123.10.55 vb.—**Qal** 65.8.25 Pf. חָשַׁב, חֲשַׁבְתֶּם; impf. יַחְשֹׁב (יַחְשְׁבוּ, יַחְשְׁבוּ, יַחֲשָׁב־); ptc. חֹשֵׁב, חֹשְׁבִים; inf. לַחְשֹׁב—**1a. think, consider** a person or thing to be something, (1) with accus. and לְ, Gn 38$_{15}$. (2) with double accus. Is 53$_4$. **b. regard** someone as (כְּ) Jb 19$_{11}$. **2a.** with double accus., **reckon** something to (לְ) someone as Gn 15$_6$. **b. impute** something to (לְ) someone 2 S 19$_{20}$. **3a. have regard for, value, esteem** something Is 13$_{17}$, someone Is 33$_8$. **b. take thought for, care for** (לְ) someone Ps 40$_{18}$. **4. plan, devise, intend** evil Gn 50$_{20}$ (+ עַל *against*), plans (מַחֲשָׁבוֹת) 2 S 14$_{14}$; (with inf.) to do something 1 S 18$_{25}$. **5a. invent, design** Ex 31$_4$ Am 6$_5$ (+ לְ *for* oneself). **b.** ptc. as noun, **designer, skilled person** Ex 26$_1$||36$_8$ 35$_{35}$.

Ni. 30.1.17 Pf. נֶחְשַׁב; impf. יֵחָשֵׁב; + waw וַתֵּחָשֵׁב; ptc. נֶחְשָׁב—**1. be thought of, be regarded, be considered** as (לְ) Is 29$_{17}$, as like (כְּ) Is 5$_{28}$, as being with (עִם) Ps 88$_5$, as classed according to (עַל) Lv 25$_{31}$; הֲלוֹא נָכְרִיּוֹת נֶחְשַׁבְנוּ לוֹ *are not we regarded by him as foreigners?* Gn 31$_{15}$. **2a. be counted, be reckoned** to (לְ) someone Lv 7$_{18}$ Nm 18$_{30}$ (+ כְּ *as*). **b. be accounted for** 2 K 22$_7$ (+ אֵת *with*, i.e. from). **3. be considered (as valuable)** 1 K 10$_{21}$||2 C 9$_{20}$.

Pi. 16.0.4 Pf. חִשַּׁב, חִשַּׁבְתִּי; impf. יְחַשֵּׁב; ptc. מְחַשֵּׁב—**1. think about, consider, be mindful of** someone Ps 144$_3$, something Ps 119$_{59}$; how to do something Ps 73$_{16}$. **2. devise, plan** evil Ho 7$_{15}$ (+ אֶל *against*); to do evil Pr 24$_8$. **3. be about to** Jon 1$_4$. **4a. calculate, reckon** years Lv 25$_{27}$, value Lv 27$_{18}$ (+ לְ *for*). **b. settle accounts with** 2 K 12$_{16}$.

Hi. 0.1.1 Impf. Q יחשיבוני—**count, esteem** oneself Si 7$_{16}$ (+ בְּ *with, among*), someone else 1QH 11$_6$.

Ho. 0.0.1 Pf. החשבו—**be counted, be reckoned** in (בְּ) covenant 1QS 5$_{11}$.

Htp. 1.0.7 Impf. יִתְחַשָּׁב—**1. reckon oneself** among (בְּ) Nm 23$_9$. **2. be reckoned** to (לְ) 4QpsJub^a 2.1$_8$, with (עִם) 4QAges^b 1$_3$.

→ חֵשֶׁב *girdle,* חֶשְׁבּוֹן I *reckoning,* חִשָּׁבוֹן *device,* מַחֲשָׁב I *design,* מַחֲשָׁבָה *thought.*

חֵשֶׁב 8.0.1 n.m.—cstr. חֵשֶׁב—**1. girdle, band** of ephod Ex 28$_8$||39$_5$. **2. artistry,** descr. of spirit's garments 4QShirShabb^f 23.2$_{10}$. → חשׁב *think.*

חַשְׁבַּדָּנָה 1 pr.n.m. **Hashbaddana.**

חֲשֻׁבָה 1 pr.n.m. **Hashubah.**

חֶשְׁבּוֹן I 3.5.2 n.m.—sf. Si חשבונך—**1. reckoning, sum** Ec 7$_{25}$. **2. thought** Ec 9$_{10}$. **3. conversation, expression of thought** Si 9$_{15}$. → חשׁב *think.*

חֶשְׁבּוֹן II 38 pl.n. **Heshbon.**

[**חִשָּׁבוֹן**] 2.0.1 n.m.—pl. חִשְּׁבֹנוֹת—**1. device** Ec 7$_{29}$. **2. war engine** 2 C 26$_{15}$. **3. scheme** 1QMyst 1.2$_2$. → חשׁב *think.*

חֲשַׁבְיָה 15 pr.n.m. **Hashabiah.**

חֲשַׁבְיָהוּ, see חֲשַׁבְיָה *Hashabiah.*

חֲשַׁבְנָה 1 pr.n.m. **Hashabnah.**

חשׁה 16.2.2 vb.—**Qal** 7.2.1 Pf. Si חשתה; impf. תֶּחֱשֶׁה; inf. חֲשׁוֹת—**be silent, keep silence,** of Y. Is 64$_{11}$, humans Is 62$_6$ 1QM 9$_1$ (+ מִן *from* sound of alarm, i.e. cease sounding it), waves Ps 107$_{29}$.

Hi. 9.0.1 Pf. הֶחֱשֵׁיתִי; impf. Q יחשו; impv. הַחֲשׁוּ; ptc. מַחְשִׁים, מַחְשֶׁה—**1. be silent,** of Y. Is 42$_{14}$, humans 2 K 2$_3$. **2. silence** someone Ne 8$_{11}$ (לְ of obj.), sound of alarm 1QM 16₉. 3. intrans., **delay** Jg 18₉ 1 K 22₃ (+ מִקַּחַת *from taking*).

חַשּׁוּב 5 pr.n.m. **Hasshub.**

חָשׁוּק 8 n.m.—sf. חֲשׁוּקֵיהֶם—**band,** ring or bar on pillars of tabernacle Ex 27₁₀. → חשׁק *cling to.*

[חִשֻּׁק] 1 n.m.—sf. חִשֻּׁקֵיהֶם—**spoke** of wheel 1 K 7₃₃.

[חִשֻּׁר] 1 n.m.—sf. חִשֻּׁרֵיהֶם—**hub** of wheel 1 K 7₃₃.

[חֻשַׁי], see חוּשַׁי *Hushai.*

חֲשֵׁיכָה, see חֲשֵׁכָה *darkness.*

חֻשִׁים, see חוּשִׁים *Hushim.*

חשׁך 17.0.1 vb.—**Qal** 11.0.1 Pf. חָשַׁךְ; impf. תֶּחְשַׁךְ, יֶחְשְׁכוּ—**1. be, become dark,** of land Ex 10₁₅, sun Is 13₁₀, appearance Lm 4₈ (+ מִן darker *than* soot). **2. be dim,** of eyes Ps 69₂₄ (+ מֵרְאוֹת *so as not to see*). **3. be gloomy,** of person Ec 12₃.

Hi. 6 Pf. הֶחְשִׁיךְ; impf. יַחְשִׁיךְ; + waw וַיַּחְשִׁךְ, וְהַחֲשַׁכְתִּי; ptc. מַחְשִׁיךְ—**1. make dark, darken** day Am 5₈ (+ לַיְלָה *[into] night*), counsel Jb 38₂, earth Am 8₉ (לְ of obj.). **2. be dark,** of darkness Ps 139₁₂ (+ מִן *from,* i.e. to, Y.).

→ חֹשֶׁךְ *darkness,* חֲשֵׁכָה *darkness,* חָשֹׁךְ *obscure,* מַחְשָׁךְ *dark place.*

*__[חָשָׂךְ]__ n.[m.] **thorn hedge** Jb 19₈ (if em. חֹשֶׁךְ *darkness*).

[חָשֹׁךְ] 1 adj.—pl. חֲשֻׁכִּים—**obscure,** as noun, **obscure one** Pr 22₂₉. → חשׁך *be dark.*

חֹשֶׁךְ 80.2.57 n.m.—cstr. חֹשֶׁךְ; sf. חָשְׁכִּי—**darkness** Gn 1₂; assoc. with distress Is 9₁, day of Y. Am 5₈, ignorance Jb 37₁₉, evil Pr 2₁₃; ממשלת חושך *dominion of darkness* 1QH 20₆, מלאך *angel of* 1QS 3₂₁, גורל *lot of* 1QM 1₁₁. → חשׁך *be dark.*

חֲשֵׁכָה 6 n.f.—חֲשֵׁיכָה; cstr. חֶשְׁכַת; pl. חֲשֵׁכִים—**darkness** Gn 15₁₂; assoc. with distress Is 8₂₂, ignorance Ps 82₅. → חשׁך *be dark.*

חשׁל 1 vb.—**Ni.** 1 Ptc. נֶחֱשָׁלִים—**lag behind** (אַחַר) someone Dt 25₁₈.

חָשֻׁם 5 pr.n.m. **Hashum.**

חֻשָׁם 4 pr.n.m. **Husham.**

חֶשְׁמוֹן 1 pl.n. **Heshmon.**

חַשְׁמַל 3.0.1 n.m.—הַחַשְׁמַלָה—**amber,** or perh. **bronze** Ezk 1₄.₂₇ 8₂.

[חַשְׁמַן] 1 n.m.—pl. חַשְׁמַנִּים—**envoy** Ps 68₃₂.

*__[חַשְׁמַן]__ 1 n.m.—pl. חַשְׁמַנִּים—**bronze,** or **red cloth** Ps 68₃₂.

חַשְׁמֹנָה 2 pl.n. **Hashmonah.**

חֹשֶׁן 25.2.2 n.m.—cstr. חֹשֶׁן; pl. cstr. Q חשני—**breastpiece, pouch,** worn by high priest, containing the Urim and Thummim Ex 25₇.

חשׁק 11.2.1 vb.—**Qal** 8.1.1 Pf. חָשַׁק—**1. desire, cling to, love,** with בְּ of obj. Y. Ps 91₁₄, woman Dt 21₁₁, wisdom Si 51₁₉₍B₎. **2.** with inf., **desire** to do 1 K 9₁₀||2 C 8₆. **3. lovingly deliver** soul from (מִן) pit Is 38₁₇.

Ni. 0.1 Ptc. נחשקת—**be desired, loved,** of woman Si 40₁₉.

Pi. 1 Pf. חִשַּׁק—**bind** capital Ex 38₂₈.

Pu. 2 Ptc. מְחֻשָּׁקִים—**be bound,** of pillars Ex 27₁₇||Ex 38₁₇ (+ כֶּסֶף *[with] silver*).

→ חָשׁוּק *band,* חֵשֶׁק *desire.*

חֵשֶׁק 4 n.m.—cstr. חֵשֶׁק; sf. חִשְׁקִי—**desire** 1 K 9₁; נֶשֶׁף חִשְׁקִי *twilight of my desire,* i.e. which I desire Is 21₄. → חשׁק *desire.*

[חִשֻּׁק], see חִשּׁוּק *spoke.*

[חָשֻׁק], see חָשׁוּק *band.*

[חִשֻּׁר], see חִשּׁוּר *hub.*

[חַשְׁרָה] 1 n.f.—cstr. חַשְׁרַת—**sieve, strainer** of water 2 S 22₁₂ (||Ps 18₁₂ חֶשְׁכַת־ *darkness of*).

חֲשַׁשׁ 2 n.m. **dried grass** Is 33₁₁.

חֻשָׁתִי 5 gent. **Hushathite.**

חַת I 2 n.m.—חַת; sf. חִתְּכֶם—**terror** Gn 9₂ Jb 41₂₅. → חתת *I be shattered.*

חַת II 2 adj.—pl. חַתִּים—**1. shattered, broken,** of bows 1 S 2₄. **2. dismayed,** of persons Jr 46₅. → חתת I *be shattered.*

חֵת 14 pr.n.m. **Heth.**

*__[חתא]__ vb.—**Qal pass., be destroyed** Hb 3₇ (if em. תַּחַת אָוֶן *instead of iniquity* to תֻּחַתְאָנָה *they were destroyed*).

Ni. be carried off Hb 3₇ (if em. תַּחַת אָוֶן *instead of iniquity* to תֻּחַתְאוּן *they were carried off*).

חתה I 4.0.1 vb.—**Qal** 4.0.1 Impf. יַחְתֶּה; ptc. חֹתֶה; inf. לַחְתּוֹת—**1. take (away), snatch** coal Pr 25₂₂, fire Is 30₁₄ (+ מִן *from* hearth). **2. destroy** person Ps 52₇. → מַחְתָּה *firepan.*

*__חתה II__ 3 vb.—**Qal** 3 Impf. יַחְתֶּה; ptc. חֹתֶה; inf. לַחְתּוֹת—

kindle fire Is 30_{14} Pr 6_{27}, coal Pr 25_{22}.

חִתָּה 1 n.f.—cstr. חִתַּת—**terror** Gn 35_5. → חתת I *be shattered.*

חִתּוּל 1 n.m. **bandage,** or **splint,** for broken arm Ezk 30_{21}. → חתל *wrap.*

חָתוּם, see חתם *seal,* qal §2.

[חַתְחַת] 1 n.m.–pl. חַתְחַתִּים—**terror** Ec 12_5. → חתת I *be shattered.*

חִתִּי 48.0.1 gent. **Hittite.**

* **[חֲתִים]** 2 n.[m.]—sf. חתימך—**signet ring** Gn $38_{18(Sam)}$ (MT חוֹתָם *signet ring*) $38_{25(Sam)}$ (MT חֹתֶמֶת *signet ring*). → חתם *seal.*

* **[חֲתִימָה]** 0.0.1 n.f. **seal** 4Q185 1.2_4. → חתם *seal.*

חִתִּית 8 n.f.—cstr. חִתִּית; sf. חִתִּיתִי—**terror** Ezk 27_{16} 32_{23}. → חתת I *be shattered.*

חתך 1.0.1 vb.—**Ni.** 1.0.1 Pf. נֶחְתַּךְ; + waw Q ויחתכו—**be determined,** of weeks Dn 9_{24} (+ עַל *concerning*), days 4QCommGenA 1.1_2 (+ עַד *until*).

חתל 2 vb.—**Pu.** 1 Pf. חֻתָּלְתְּ—**be swaddled** Ezk 16_4.

Ho. 1 Inf. הָחְתֵּל—**be swaddled** Ezk 16_4.

→ חִתּוּל *bandage,* חֲתֻלָּה *swaddling band.*

חֲתֻלָּה 1 n.f.—sf. חֲתֻלָּתוֹ—**swaddling band** Jb 38_9. → חתל *wrap.*

חֶתְלוֹן 2 pl.n. **Hethlon.**

חתם 28.0.12.2 vb.—**Qal** 23.0.12 Pf. Q חתמתה; impf. יַחְתֹּם; impv. חֲתֹם, חֲתֹמוּ; ptc. חוֹתֵם; ptc. pass. חֲתוּמִים, חָתוּם; inf. abs. חָתוֹם; cstr. לַחְתֹּם—**1. seal, set one's seal on, seal up** letter 1 K 21_8 (+ בְּ *with* seal), deed of sale Jr 32_{10}, (jar of) oil Arad ost. 17_6, teaching Is 8_{16}, stars Jb 9_7 (בְּעַד of obj.). **2a.** pass. **be sealed,** of book Is 29_{11}, transgression Jb 14_{17} (+ בְּ *in* bag), fountain Ca 4_{12}. **b.** pass. ptc. as noun, **sealed thing,** in ref. to copy of deed of sale Jr 32_{11}.

Ni. 2 Pf. נֶחְתָּם; inf. abs. נַחְתּוֹם—**be sealed,** of edict Est 3_{12} (+ בְּ *with* ring).

Pi. 1 Pf. חִתְּמוּ—**keep (house) sealed,** i.e. **shut** Jb 24_{16} (+ לְ *for* oneself).

Pu. 0.0.2 Pf. חותם—**be sealed,** of mystery 1QH 8_{11}.

Hi. 2 Pf. הֶחְתִּים—**be blocked,** of flesh, i.e. penis Lv 15_3 (+ מִן *[so as to be] without* discharge).

→ חוֹתָם I *seal,* חֲתִים *signet ring,* חֲתִימָה *seal,* חֹתֶמֶת *signet ring.*

חֹתָם, see חוֹתָם *seal.*

חֹתֶמֶת 1 n.f. **signet ring** Gn 38_{25}. → חתם *seal.*

חתן 11 vb.—**Htp.** 11 Pf. הִתְחַתַּנְתֶּם; impf. תִּתְחַתֵּן; impv. הִתְחַתְּנוּ, הִתְחַתֵּן; inf. הִתְחַתֵּן—of a man, **1. become related by marriage to, intermarry with,** with בְּ Dt 7_3, אֶת Gn 34_9. **2. become son-in-law of,** with בְּ 1 S 18_{21}, לְ 2 C 18_1, אֶת 1 K 3_1. → חֹתֵן *father-in-law,* חֹתֶנֶת *mother-in-law,* חָתָן *bridegroom,* חֲתֻנָּה *wedding.*

חָתָן 20 n.m.—cstr. חֲתַן; sf. חֲתָנוֹ; pl. sf. חֲתָנָיו—**1. bridegroom** Is 61_{10}; חֲתַן־דָּמִים *bridegroom of blood* Ex 4_{25}. **2. son-in-law,** i.e. **daughter's husband** Gn 19_{12}. **3. (male) relative by marriage** 2 K 8_{27}. → חתן *marry.*

חֹתֵן 21 n.m.—cstr. חֹתֵן; sf. חֹתְנוֹ, חֹתֶנְךָ—**father-in-law,** wife's father Ex 3_1. → חתן *marry.*

חֲתֻנָּה 1 n.f.—sf. חֲתֻנָּתוֹ—**wedding** Ca 3_{11}. → חתן *marry.*

[חֹתֶנֶת] 1 n.f.—sf. חֹתַנְתּוֹ—**mother-in-law** Dt 27_{23}. → חתן *marry.*

* **[חַתֻּס]** 0.0.0.1 pr.n.m. **Hattus.**

חתף 1.1.2 vb.—**Qal** 1.1.2 Impf. יַחְתֹּף; ptc. Si חותפו; inf. Q חתוף—**snatch away** person Si 15_{14}, simile (or poison) of serpents 4QHod^c^ 2_{10}; abs. Jb 9_{12} 1QH 13_{10}. → חֶתֶף *robber.*

חֶתֶף 1.2 n.m. **robber,** or perh. **robbery, prey** Pr 23_{28} Si $35_{21(B)}$ 50_4. → חתף *snatch away.*

חתר 8 vb.—**Qal** 8 Pf. חָתַר; impf. יַחְתְּרוּ; + waw וָאֶחְתֹּר; impv. חֲתָר־—**1. dig into, break through,** with accus. house Jb 24_{16}; prep. בְּ *into, through* wall Ezk 8_8, Sheol Am 9_2. **2. row** Jon 1_{13}. → מַחְתֶּרֶת *breaking in.*

חתת I 57.0.3 vb.—**Qal** 21 Pf. חַת, חַתּוּ (חָתּוּ, חָתּוּ); impv. חֹתּוּ—**be dismayed, terrified,** of persons 2 K 19_{26}||Is 37_{27}, ground Jr 14_4, stronghold Jr 48_1.

Ni. 29.0.1 Pf. נִחַת; impf. יֵחַת (יֵחָת), אֵחָתָּה, תֵּחַתּוּ (תֵּחָתּוּ)—**1. be shattered,** of Ephraim Is 7_8 (+ מִן *from [being]* a people), righteousness Is 51_6. **2. be terrified, dismayed,** of nation Is 30_{31} (+ מִן *on account of*), individual Jr 1_{17} (+ מִפְּנֵי *on account of*), horse Jb 39_{22}.

Pi. 2 Pf. חִתַּתְנִי, חִתְּתָה—**1. dismay** someone Jb 7_{14} (+ בְּ *with* dreams). **2.** appar. **be shattered,** of bow Jr 51_{56}.

Hi. 5.0.2 Pf. הֵחַתֹּתָ; impf. יָחֵת (יְחִתַּן, יְחִתֵּנִי), אַחְתְּךָ; + waw וְהַחִתֹּתִי—**1. shatter** staff Is 9_3. **2. dismay, terrify** nation Jr 49_{37} (+ לִפְנֵי *before* enemies), individual Jb

31_{34}. **3. let someone be dismayed** 1QH 10_{35}. → חַת I *terror*, II *shattered*, חִתָּה *terror*, חַתְחַת *terror*, חִתִּית *terror*, חֲתַת *terror*, מְחִתָּה *terror*.

***חתת** II 1 vb.—**Qal** 1 Pf. חָתָּה—**be parched, be dried up,** of ground Jr 14_4.

חֲתַת I 1 n.[m.] **terror** Jb 6_{21}. → חתת *be shattered*.

חֲתַת II 1 pr.n.m. **Hathath.**

ט

טאטא I 1 vb.—**Pilp.** 1 + waw וְטֵאטֵאתִיהָ—**sweep (away)** Babylon with (בְּ) broom Is 14_{23}. → מַטְאֲטֵא I *broom*.

***טאטא** II 0.0.1 vb.—**Polp.** 0.0.1 Inf. Q טואטאי—perh. **be muddied, sunk in mud,** בטואטאיי רגל[הם] perh. *when their foot is sunk in mud* 1QH 13_{21}. → טִיט *mud*.

טָבְאַל 1 pr.n.m. **Tabal.**

טָבְאֵל 1.0.0.1 pr.n.m. **Tabeel.**

***טבב** 1 vb.—**Qal** 1 Inf. טוֹב—**speak,** הֶחֱשֵׁיתִי מִטּוֹב *I refrained from speaking* Ps 39_3. → טִבָּה *word*, טוֹב IV *word*, טוּב II *word*, טוֹבָה II *word*.

*[**טִבָּה**] n.f. **word, report, rumour** Ne 6_{19} (if em. טוֹבֹתָיו *his good deeds* to טִבֹּתָיו *rumours about him*). → טבב *speak*.

טֹבָה, see טוֹבָה *goodness*.

[**טְבוּל**] 1 n.[m.]—pl. טְבוּלִים—**turban** Ezk 23_{15}.

[**טַבּוּר**] 2 n.[m.] **navel, centre,** טַבּוּר הָאָרֶץ *centre of the land*, perh. intersection of routes east of Shechem Jg 9_{37}, *middle of the world*, appar. Jerusalem Ezk 38_{12}.

טבח 11.0.3 vb.—**Qal** 11.0.3 Pf. טָבְחָה; impv. טְבֹחַ; ptc. Q טובחים; ptc. pass. טָבוּחַ; inf. טְבֹחַ—**1. slaughter** animal Ex 21_{37}, **kill human being** Lm 2_{21}. **2.** pass., **be slaughtered,** of shepherds Jr 25_{34}. → טַבָּח *cook*, טַבָּחָה *cook*, טֶבַח I *slaughter*, טִבְחָה *slaughter*, מַטְבֵּחַ *slaughterhouse*.

טַבָּח 32.0.1 n.m.—pl. טַבָּחִים—**1. cook** 1 S 9_{23}. **2. domestic servant,** שַׂר הַטַּבָּחִים *master of the domestic servants*, i.e. chief steward Gn 37_{36}. **3. (body)guard,** רַב־טַבָּחִים *captain of (the body)guard(s)* 2 K 25_8. → טבח *slaughter*.

טֶבַח, see טֶבַח I *slaughter*.

טֶבַח I 12 n.m.—L טָבַח; sf. טִבְחָהּ—**slaughter,** of beasts for food Pr 7_{22}, human beings in war, etc. Is 34_2. → טבח *slaughter*.

טֶבַח II 1 pr.n.[m.] **Tebah.**

טֶבַח III, see טִבְחַת *Tibhath*.

[**טַבָּחָה**] 1 n.f.—pl. טַבָּחוֹת—**cook** 1 S 8_{13}. → טבח *slaughter*.

טִבְחָה 3 n.f.—sf. טִבְחָתִי—**1. slaughter,** צֹאן לְטִבְחָה *flock for slaughter* Jr 12_3. **2. thing slaughtered, meat** 1 S 25_{11}. → טבח *slaughter*.

טִבְחַת 1 pl.n. **Tibhath.**

טְבִיָּה, see טוֹבִיָּה *Tobiah*.

[**טְבִיָּהוּ**], see טוֹבִיָּה *Tobiah*.

*[**טְבִילָה**] 0.0.1 n.f. **immersion,** ניקרת הטבילה *cave of immersion* 3QTr 1_{12}. → טבל *immerse*.

טבל 16.0.2 vb.—**Qal** 15.0.2 Impf. תִּטְבְּלֵנִי; + waw וַיִּטְבֹּל, וְטָבַל; ptc. טֹבֵל—**1. immerse, dip** finger in (בְּ) blood Lv 4_6, rod in (בְּ) honey 1 S 14_{27}; appar. **wet** finger with (מִן) blood Lv 4_{17}, oil Lv 14_{16}. **2. immerse oneself** in (בְּ) Jordan 2 K 5_{14}.

Ni. 1 Pf. נִטְבְּלוּ—appar. **touch (water),** of feet Jos 3_{15}.

→ טְבִילָה *immersion*.

טְבַלְיָהוּ 1 pr.n.m. **Tebaliah.**

טבע 10.0.2 vb.—**Qal** 6.0.1 Pf. טָבַעְתִּי; impf. אֶטְבְּעָה; + waw וַיִּטְבַּע—**sink, slip, fall,** of person into (בְּ) mud Jr 38_6, gates into ground Lm 2_9, stone into forehead 1 S 17_{49}.

Pi. 0.0.1 + waw Q וטבעת—of Y., **drown** enemy in (בְּ) the deep GnzPs 1_{24}.

Pu. 1 Pf. טֻבְּעוּ—**be drowned** in (בְּ) sea Ex 15_4.

Ho. 3 Pf. הָטְבְּעוּ—**1.** as qal, **sink** into (בְּ) mud, of feet Jr 38_{22}. **2.** perh. **be sunk, set, established,** of base of world Jb 38_6.

טַבָּעוֹת 2 pr.n.m. **Tabbaoth.**

טַבַּעַת 49.0.2 n.f.—sf. טַבַּעְתּוֹ; pl. טַבָּעוֹת; cstr. טַבְּעוֹת; sf. טַבְּעֹתֵיהֶם (טַבְּעֹתָם)—**ring, 1.** usu. as means of support for curtains, poles of ark, etc. Ex 25$_{15}$. **2a.** item of jewellery Ex 35$_{22}$. **b.** signet ring of king Est 3$_{12}$.

טַבְרִמֹּן 1 pr.n.m. **Tabrimmon.**

*[**טֹבְשָׁלֹם**] 0.0.0.3 pr.n.m. **Tob-shalom.**

טַבָּת 1 pl.n. **Tabbath.**

טֵבֵת 1 pr.n.[m.] **Tebeth,** tenth month of Babylonian-based calendar, corresponding to December/January Est 2$_{16}$.

טָהוֹר 95.0.48 adj.—טָהֹר; cstr. טְהוֹר (טְהָר־, Qr טְהָר־); f.s. טְהוֹרָה; m.pl. טְהוֹרִים; cstr. Q טהורי; f.pl. טְהֹרוֹת—**1a. (ritually) pure, purified, clean, cleansed,** of person Nm 19$_{9}$, animal Gn 7$_{2}$, place Lv 4$_{12}$. **b. pure, upright,** of words of Y. Ps 12$_{7}$, human heart Ps 51$_{12}$. **c. pure, solid,** of gold Ex 25$_{11}$. **d. (in a) fit (state),** of person 1 S 20$_{26}$. **e.** perh. **radiant,** of fear of Y. Ps 19$_{10}$. **2.** as noun, **pure, purified one, one who** or **something that is pure, purified,** טְהָר־לֵב *one who is pure of heart* Pr 22$_{11 (Qr)}$, מִי־יִתֵּן טָהוֹר מִטָּמֵא *who can produce a clean thing out of an unclean one?* Jb 14$_{4}$. → טהר *be pure.*

טהר 94.1.64 vb.—**Qal** 34.0.20 Pf. טָהַרְתִּי; impf. יִטְהַר; + waw וְטָהֵר; impv. טְהָר; inf. Q טהור—**1. be (regarded as) ritually pure, purified, cleansed** Lv 11$_{32}$ 12$_{7}$ (+ מִן *from* flow of blood). **2. be (regarded as) healed** 2 K 5$_{10}$. **3a. be (regarded as) pure, upright** Jb 4$_{17}$. **b. be purged** from (מִן) sin Pr 20$_{9}$.

Pi. 39.1.25 Pf. טִהַרְתִּיךָ; impf. אֲטַהֵר; + waw וְטִהֲרוּ ;וַיְטַהֲרוּ; impv. טַהֲרֵנִי; ptc. מְטַהֵר; inf. טַהֵר (טַהֲרוֹ)—**1a. purify, cleanse** someone or something from (מִן) uncleanness Lv 16$_{19}$ Ezk 36$_{25}$. **b. declare clean** person with skin disease Lv 13$_{13}$. **2.** esp. in Qumran literature, perh. **save, release, absolve** someone from (מִן) (or **fortify** against) sin 1QH 11$_{21}$ 1QS 4$_{21}$. **3. refine** precious metal Ml 3$_{3}$. **4. clear away, remove** clouds Jb 37$_{21}$, violence 11QPs^{a} 22$_{7}$.

Pu. 1 Ptc. מְטֹהָרָה—**be pure, purified,** of land Ezk 22$_{24}$.

Htp. 20.0.19 Pf. הִטַּהֲרוּ; impf. Q יטהר; + waw וְהִטֶּהָרוּ; וַיִּטַּהֲרוּ; ptc. מִטַּהֵר ,מִטַּהֲרִים; impv. הִטַּהֲרוּ; inf. Q הטהר—**1a. purify, cleanse oneself** Gn 35$_{2}$; **absolve oneself** from (מִן) iniquity 1QS 3$_{7}$. **b. be purified,** of land 4QapPsB 69$_{6}$. **2.** ptc. as noun, **one who undergoes or is required to undergo purification** Lv 14$_{4}$.

→ טָהוֹר *pure,* טְהָר *purity,* טֹהַר *purity,* טָהֳרָה *purity,* מִטְהָר *splendour.*

טָהֹר, see טָהוֹר *pure.*

[**טְהָר**] 1 n.[m.]—sf. טְהָרוֹ—**purity** Ps 89$_{45}$. → טהר *be pure.*

טֹהַר 3.1.16 n.[m.]—Q טוהר ,טהור; sf. טָהֳרָהּ (Q טוהרה)—**1. purity, clarity, splendour** Ex 24$_{10}$; אלי טוהר *gods,* i.e. angels, *of purity* 4QBer^{a} 7.1$_{6}$, לשון הטוהר *tongue of purity* 4QShirShabb^{a} 3.1$_{2}$. **2. (process of) purification,** e.g. after childbirth Lv 12$_{4}$. → טהר *be pure.*

טָהֳרָה 13.1.48 n.f.—Q טוהרה; cstr. טָהֳרַת; sf. טָהֳרָתוֹ—**1.** usu. **(process of) purification, purification ritual, period of purification** of man after discharge Lv 15$_{13}$, woman after childbirth Lv 12$_{4}$ (דְּמֵי טָהֳרָה *blood of,* i.e. requiring, *purification*), person with skin disease Lv 13$_{7}$; perh. **purification regulation(s)** 4QMMT B$_{13}$. **2. purity** 1QS 4$_{5}$; of animal hides 11QT 47$_{10}$. **3. (ritually) pure thing(s)** 11QT 49$_{21}$. **4. pure food,** i.e. meals of the elect, טהרת הרבים *pure food of the Many* 1QS 6$_{16}$. → טהר *be pure.*

טוב 113.6 vb.—**Qal** 106.5 (for most forms distinction from טוֹב adj. unclear) Pf. טוֹב ,טֹבוּ; inf. טוֹב—**1. be good, pleasing, appropriate, all right,** אִם־עַל־הַמֶּלֶךְ טוֹב *if it please the king* Est 1$_{19}$, אִם־כֹּה יֹאמַר טוֹב *if he says, 'It is good',* i.e. that's all right 1 S 20$_{7}$. **2. be good, happy, merry, in good spirits, healthy,** טוֹב לָךְ *it will be good for you,* i.e. you will feel better 1 S 16$_{16}$, טוֹב לֶב־הַמֶּלֶךְ בַּיָּיִן *the heart of the king was merry with wine* Est 1$_{10}$. **3. be worthwhile,** הֲטוֹב לְךָ כִּי־תַעֲשֹׁק *is it worthwhile for you to oppess?* Jb 10$_{3}$. **4.** טוֹב מִן **be better than** Jg 11$_{25}$.

Hi. 7.1 Pf. הֱטִיבֹתָ; + waw וְהֵטַבְנוּ; ptc. מֵטִיב (unless יטב hi. *do well*)—**1. be right, do well, act benevolently,** abs. Ps 119$_{68}$; with כִּי *that* 1 K 8$_{18}$||2 C 6$_{8}$, לְ + inf. 2 K 10$_{30}$. **2.** trans., **please** someone Si 26$_{13}$.

→ טוֹב I adj. *good,* II n.m. *good,* טוּב *good,* טוֹבָה *good,* טִיב *character;* cf. יטב *be good.*

טוֹב I 262.31.32.2 adj.—f.s. טוֹבָה; cstr. טוֹבַת; m.pl. טוֹבִים (טֹבִים); cstr. טוֹבֵי; f.pl. טֹבוֹת—**good,** distinction from

טוב vb. *be good* and טוֹב n.m. *good* oft. difficult, **1a.** (1) **attractive, good-looking,** of young woman, טֹבַת מַרְאֶה *good of appearance* Gn 24_{16}. (2) **well-fed, fat, healthy,** שֶׁבַע פָּרֹת הַטֹּבֹת *seven well-fed cows* Gn 41_{26}. (3) **well-finished, well-polished,** נְחֹשֶׁת מֻצְהָב טוֹבָה *well-finished bright bronze* Ezr 8_{27}. (4) **luxurious, good-quality,** אַדֶּרֶת שִׁנְעָר אַחַת טוֹבָה *a beautiful mantle from Shinar* Jos 7_{21}. **b.** (1) **prosperous, plentiful,** הַשָּׁנִים הַטֹּבֹת ... הָאֵלֶּה *these prosperous years* Gn 41_{35}. (2) **mature, ripe,** שֵׂיבָה טוֹבָה *ripe old age* Gn 15_{15}. **c.** (1) **festive,** יוֹם טוֹב *a feast day* 1 S 25_{8}. (2) **pleasing,** בְּשׂוֹרָה טוֹבָה *pleasing news* 2 S 18_{27}, עשׂה הַטּוֹב בְּעֵינֵי *do what is pleasing in the sight of* Gn 16_{6}. (3) **favourable,** הַדָּבָר הַטּוֹב *the favourable word,* i.e. promise Jr 33_{14}. **d.** (1) **good, just, virtuous,** אִישׁ טוֹב *a good man* Pr 14_{14}, ענות טוב *virtuous humility* 1QS 2_{24}. (2) **kind, well-disposed,** הָאֲנָשִׁים טֹבִים לָנוּ מְאֹד *the men were very kind to us* 1 S 25_{15}. (3) **happy, cheerful, content,** טוֹב־לֵב *a cheerful heart* Pr 15_{15}. **e. correct,** נֵדְעָה בֵינֵינוּ מַה־טּוֹב *let us determine among ourselves what is correct* Jb 34_{4}. **2.** as noun, **a. good person** Pr 2_{20}. **b. healthy beast** Lv 27_{10}. **3.** as adv., **favourably,** of פתר *interpret* Gn 40_{16}. → טוב *be good.*

טוֹב II n.[m.] 141.11.29.3 n.m. **good, 1. goodness, good thing(s), prosperity** Pr 23_{6} Jb 21_{13}. **2. well-being** Ps 122_{9} Ec 2_{24}. **3. good location, good place** Dt 23_{17} Est 2_{9}. **4. good news** 1 K 14_{2}. **5.** moral **goodness, good deeds** Ps 37_{27} Ec 7_{20}. → טוב *be good.*

טוֹב III 4 pl.n. **Tob.**

*טוֹב IV 2 n.[m.] **word** Jr 15_{11} Ho 14_{3}. → טבב *speak.*

*טוֹב V 2 n.[m.] **perfume,** יֵין הַטּוֹב *wine of perfume* Ca 7_{10}, שֶׁמֶן *oil of* 2 K 20_{13}.

*טוֹב VI 6 n.m. **rain** Dt 28_{12} Jr 5_{25} 17_{6} Ho 10_{1} Ps 4_{7} 85_{13}.

טוּב I 32.12.35 n.m.—sf. טוּבִי; pl. sf. Q טוביך—**good, 1. goods, property** Gn 45_{20}. **2a. health, prosperity, well-being** Jb 20_{21}. **b. prospering** Pr 11_{10}. **3. beauty** Ho 10_{11}. **4. happiness, joy** of heart Dt 28_{47}. **5. moral goodness, virtue** Si $42_{14(Bmg)}$. → טוב *be good.*

*טוּב II 1 n.[m.] **word** Ps 119_{66}. → טבב *speak.*

טוֹב אֲדֹנִיָּה 1 pr.n.m. **Tob-adonijah.**

טוֹבָה I 66.23.2 n.f.—טֹבָה; sf. טוֹבָתִי; pl. טֹבוֹת; sf. טוֹבֹתָיו—**good, 1a. prosperity** Si 6_{11}. **b. bounty** Ps 65_{12}. **c. happiness, pleasure, satisfaction** Lm 3_{17}. **2a. good news** 2 C 18_{7}. **b. kind, pleasant word,** דבר טובות pi. *speak kind words* Jr 12_{6}. **3a.** moral **good(ness), good deed(s)** GnzPs 1_{9}. **b. value, worth** of a friend Si 6_{15}. **4. (treaty of) friendship** Dt 23_{7}. → טוב *be good.*

*טוֹבָה II 1 n.f.—sf. טוֹבֹתָיו—**word** Ne 6_{19}. → טבב *speak.*

טוֹבִיָּה 18.0.0.4 pr.n.m. **Tobi(j)ah.**

טוֹבִיָּהוּ, see טוֹבִיָּה *Tobi(j)ah.*

טוה 2 vb.—**Qal** 2 Pf. טָווּ—**spin** goat-hair Ex 35_{26}; abs. 35_{25}.

→ מַטְוֶה *yarn,* טָוָה *cloth.*

[טָוָה] 2 n.f. **cloth** Ex $35_{25(Sam)}$. → טוה *spin.*

[טֹוהַר], see טֹהַר *purity.*

טוח 11.0.4 vb.—**Qal** 9.0.4 Pf. טָחוּ, טְחֹתֶם; ptc. טָחִים; ptc. pass. Q טוח; inf. טוּחַ—**1a. (re)plaster** infected house Lv 14_{42}. **b.** with double accus., **daub, plaster wall with** whitewash Ezk 13_{10}. **c.** perh. **decorate** walls of temple (with gold and silver) 1 C 29_{4}. **d. cover** face in (בְּ) shame 1QH 12_{23}. **2.** pass., appar. **be sealed with pitch,** of vessel CD 11_{9}.

Ni. 2 Inf. הִטּוֹחַ—**be re-covered, replastered,** of infected house Lv 14_{43}.

→ טִיחַ *plaster;* cf. טחח *be covered.*

[טוֹטֶפֶת] 3 n.f.—pl. טוֹטָפֹת (טֹטָפֹת)—**symbol, amulet, headband** Dt 6_{8}.

טול 14.0.2 vb.—**Hi.** 9.0.1 Pf. הֵטִיל; impf. אֲטִילְךָ; + waw וְהֵטַלְתִּי; וַיָּטֶל; impv. הֲטִילֻנִי—**1. fling, hurl** spear 1 S 18_{11}. **2. throw** Pharaoh onto (עַל־פְּנֵי) ground Ezk 32_{4}, things into (אֶל) sea Jon 1_{5}. **3.** of Y., **send wind upon** (אֶל) sea Jon 1_{4}. **4. eject, expel** person from (מֵעַל) land Jr 16_{13}.

Ho. 4.0.1 Pf. הוּטְלוּ; impf. יוּטַל—**1. be thrown down, fall** Ps 37_{24}. **2. throw oneself down** Jb 41_{1}. **3. be ejected, expelled** Jr 22_{28}. **4.** of lot, **be cast into** (בְּ) lap Pr 16_{33}.

Pilp. 1 Ptc. מְטַלְטֶלְךָ—of Y., **hurl,** or perh. **shake** someone Is 22_{17}.

→ טַלְטֵלָה *hurling* or *shaking,* הֵטֶל *throwing.*

טוּר I 26.0.1 n.m.—pl. טוּרִים; cstr. טוּרֵי—**1. row** of jewels Ex 28_{17}. **2. course** of stone or wood 1 K 7_{12}. **3. supporting wall, parapet** 3QTr 7_{15}. → cf. טִיר *wall,* טִירָה *row.*

*[טוּר] II 0.0.1 n.[m.] **rock** 3QTr 7_{15}.

טוש 1 vb.—**Qal** 1 Impf. יָטוּשׂ—**swoop** upon (עַל) food, of eagle Jb 9_{26}.

טחה 1 vb.—**Pal.** 1 Ptc. מְטַחֲוֵי—**shoot** bow, הַרְחֵק כִּמְטַחֲוֵי קֶשֶׁת *making distance, as those who shoot a bow,* i.e. at the distance of an archer from a target Gn 21_{16}.

טְחוֹן 1 n.[m.] **millstone** Lm 5_{13}. → טחן *grind.*

טֻחוֹת I 2 n.f. perh. **viscera, innards** Ps 51_8 Jb 38_{36}.

***טֻחוֹת** II 1 n.f. perh. **darkness** Ps 51_8.

***טֻחוֹת** III 1 n.f. perh. **ibis** Jb 38_{36}.

טחח 1 vb.—**Qal** 1 Pf. טַח—**be covered,** of eyes Is 44_{18} (+ מֵרְאוֹת *so as not to see*). → cf. טוח *cover.*

טחן 8 vb.—**Qal** 8 Pf. טָחֲנוּ; impf. תִּטְחַן; impv. טַחֲנִי; ptc. טוֹחֵן; inf. abs. טָחוֹן—**1a. grind** flour Is 47_2 Jb 31_{10}. **b. crush, pulverize** golden calf Dt 9_{21}. **2.** fem. ptc. as noun, **grinder,** in ref. to tooth Ec 12_3.

Ni., be ground, i.e. **be subjected to sexual intercourse,** of wife Jb 31_{10} (if em. תִּטְחַן *she will grind* for [לְ] another to תִּטָּחֵן *she will be ground* by another).

→ טְחוֹן *millstone,* טַחֲנָה *mill.*

טַחֲנָה 1 n.f. **mill** Ec 12_4. → טחן *grind.*

[טְחֹר] 8 n.m.—(usu. as Qr for Kt עפל *haemorrhoid*) pl. טְחֹרִים; cstr. טְחֹרֵי—**haemorrhoid, boil** Dt 28_{27}.

[טֹטֶפֶת], see טוֹטֶפֶת *symbol.*

***[טִיב]** 0.1 n.m. **character** of woman Si $42_{14(B, M)}$. → טוב *be good.*

טִיחַ 1 n.[m.] **plaster** Ezk 13_{12}. → טוח *cover.*

טִיט 13.0.5 n.m. **1. mud** Jr 38_6. **2. clay** for pottery Is 41_{25}, building work Na 3_{14}. → טאטא II *be muddied.*

***[טֵיף]** 0.0.1 n.[m.] **a little** 3QTr $11_{17(Wolters)}$.

***[טִיף]** 0.0.1 n.[m.] perh. **stand** for stove or **duct, channel, tank** 3QTr $7_{15(Allegro)}$.

***[טִיר]** 0.0.1 n.m. **wall,** or perh. **enclosure, encampment** 3QTr 7_{15} (others טור). → cf. טִירָה *encampment,* טוּר *row.*

[טִירָה] 7 n.f.—cstr. טִירַת; sf. טִירָתָם; pl. טִירוֹת; sf. טִירוֹתָם, טִירוֹתֵיהֶם—**1.** usu. **encampment, settlement** Gn 25_{16}. **2. battlement** Ca 8_9. **3.** appar. **row, course** of masonry, **wall** Ezk 46_{23}. → cf. טִיר *wall,* טוּר *row.*

טַל 31.1.4 n.m.—cstr. טַל; sf. טַלָּם—**dew** 2 S 1_{21}. → טלל III *give dew.*

טלא 8 vb.—**Qal** 7 Ptc. pass. טָלוּא—pass. ptc. as adj., **1a. spotted,** of goat Gn 30_{32}. **b.** as noun, **spotted kid** Gn 30_{39}. **2.** perh. **embroidered** or **colourful,** of high places Ezk 16_{16}.

Pu. 1 Ptc. מְטֻלָּאוֹת—ptc. as adj., **patched,** of shoes Jos 9_5.

טְלָאִים 1 pl.n. **Telaim.**

טָלֶה 3 n.m.—pl. טְלָאִים (Q טלים)—**lamb** Is 65_{25}.

טלטל, see טול *hurl,* pilp.

טַלְטֵלָה 1 n.f. **hurling** or **shaking** Is 22_{17}. → טול *hurl.*

טלל I 1 vb.—**Pi.** 1 + waw וִיטַלְלֶנּוּ—**cover, roof** gate Ne 3_{15}.

***[טלל]** II 1 vb.—**Hi.** 1 Ptc. 1QIsaᵃ מטלים—**cause to fall,** נתתי ... לחיי למטלים *I have given ... my cheeks to those who make me fall* Is $50_{6(1QIsa^a)}$ (MT מרט *pluck*).

***[טלל]** III vb. **Qal, give dew,** כָּלְאוּ שָׁמַיִם מִטַּל *(the) heavens have held back from giving dew* Hg 1_{10} (if em. מִטָּל *some dew*).

Hi., drip dew, מִמֶּגֶד שָׁמַיִם מֵטַל *by means of the bounty of the heavens dripping dew* Dt 33_{13} (if em. מִטָּל *on account of dew*).

→ טַל *dew.*

טֶלֶם I 1 pr.n.m. **Telem.**

טֶלֶם II 1 pl.n. **Telem.**

טַלְמוֹן 5 pr.n.m. **Talmon.**

טמא 162.0.57 vb.—**Qal** 77.0.23 Pf. טָמֵא; impf. יִטְמָא; inf. טָמְאָה—**be(come) impure, unclean, a.** of food Lv 11_{34}, object Lv 11_{32}. **b.** of person, because of contact with unclean animal Lv 22_5, emission of semen Lv 15_{16}, childbirth Lv 12_2; as consequence of sin Ps 106_{39}.

Ni. 18.0.1 Pf. נִטְמָא, נִטְמֵאת; + waw וְנִטְמֵתֶם; ptc. נִטְמְאִים—**defile oneself,** by eating unclean animals Lv 11_{43} (+ בְּ *by means of*), through prohibited sexual acts Nm 5_{13}, idolatry Jr 2_{23}.

Pi. 50.0.27 Pf. טִמֵּא (טִמָּה), טִמֵּאת; impf. תְּטַמֵּא; + waw וַיְטַמֵּא; impv. טַמְּאוּ; ptc. Q מטמא; inf. abs. טַמֵּא, cstr. טַמֵּא (טַמַּאֲכֶם, טַמְּאוֹ)—**1. make impure, make unclean, defile, desecrate** one's Nazirite head through contact with corpse Nm 6_9, another man's wife through adultery Ezk 18_6, the land through bloodshed Nm 35_{34}, the temple by non-Israelites Ps 79_1. **2. declare impure, unclean** person with leprosy Lv 13_3, infected garment Lv 13_{59}.

Pu. 1 Ptc. מְטֻמָּאָה—**be defiled,** of person Ezk 4_{14}.

Htp. 15.0.6 Impf. יִטַּמָּא—**defile oneself, be defiled,** through contact with unclean animals Lv 11_{24} (+ לְ *by means of*), with human corpse Nm 6_{7}, forbidden sexual acts Lv 18_{24} (+ בְּ *by means of*), idolatry Ezk 20_{7} (+ בְּ).

Hothp. 1 Pf. הֻטַּמָּאָה—**be defiled, made impure, unclean,** of wife Dt 24_{4}.

→ טָמֵא *impure,* טָמָא *impurity,* טֻמְאָה *impurity,* טָמְאָה *impurity;* cf. טמה *regard as unclean.*

טָמֵא 87.0.45 adj.—cstr. טְמֵא; f.s. טְמֵאָה; cstr. טְמֵאַת; m.pl. טְמֵאִים—**1. impure,** of person with leprosy Lv 13_{11}, menstruating woman Lv 15_{25}, animal Lv 5_{2}, open vessel Nm 19_{15}. **2.** as noun, **a.** masc., **impure one or thing, unclean one or thing** Is 52_{11} Jb 14_{4}. **b.** fem., **impure (city)** Ezk 22_{5}, **impure (woman)** Lv 15_{33}. → טמא *be impure.*

* **[טָמָא]** 0.0.3 n.[m.] **impurity, uncleanness, defilement** 1QS $5_{14.20}$ CD 4_{18}. → טמא *be impure.*

טֻמְאָה 1 n.f. **impurity** Mc 2_{10}. → טמא *be impure.*

טֻמְאָה 36.0.47 n.f.—cstr. טֻמְאַת; pl. cstr. טֻמְאוֹת—**impurity, uncleanness,** caused by menstruation Lv 18_{19}, discharge Lv 15_{3}, leprosy Lv 14_{19}, sin Lv 16_{16}. → טמא *be impure.*

טמה 1 vb.—**Ni.** 1 Pf. נִטְמִינוּ—**be regarded as unclean,** of person Jb 18_{3} (+ בְּעֵינֵי *in the sight of*). → cf. טמא *be unclean.*

טמם 1.1 vb.—**Ni.** 1 Pf. mss נִטַּמְּנוּ—**be stopped up,** i.e. **be stupid,** of person Jb $18_{3(mss)}$ (+ בְּעֵינֵי *in the sight of*).

Pilp. 0.1 Pf. טמטם—of Y., **stop up, fill in** footprint of nations Si 10_{16}.

טמן 31.4.3 vb.—**Qal** 28.2.3 Pf. טָמַן; + waw וַיִּטְמֹן; impv. טָמְנֵם; ptc. pass. טְמוּנִים, טְמוּנָה, טָמוּן; inf. טְמוֹן (טָמְנוֹ)—**1. conceal, hide** person Jos 2_{6}, (images of) gods Gn 35_{4}, trap Jr 18_{22}, iniquity Jb 31_{33}. **2a.** pass., **be concealed,** of silver, gold Jos 7_{21}, wisdom Si 41_{14}. **b.** pass. ptc. as noun, **concealed place** Jb 40_{13}.

Ni. 1 Impv. הִטָּמֵן—**conceal oneself,** of Israel Is 2_{10}.

Hi. 2.2 + waw וַיַּטְמִנוּ—**conceal** plunder 2 K 7_{8}, wisdom Si $41_{15(Bmg)}$, folly Si $41_{15(M)}$.

→ מַטְמוֹן *treasure,* מַטְמֹנָה I *treasure,* II *crypt,* מָטוֹן *hiding place.*

טֶנֶא 4.1.2 n.m.—sf. טַנְאֲךָ—**basket** Dt 26_{2}.

טנף 1 vb.—**Pi.** 1 Impf. אֲטַנְּפֵם—**soil, defile** feet Ca 5_{3}.

* **[טַס]** 0.1 n.m. **plate,** of gold Si $35_{5(F)}$.

טעה 1.0.2 vb.—**Qal** 0.0.2 Impf. Q יטעו—**stray, err** on account of (בְּ) vanity GnzPs 3_{18}.

Hi. 1 Pf. הִטְעוּ—**lead** people **astray** Ezk 13_{10}.

→ cf. תעה *err.*

טעם 11.3 vb.—**Qal** 11.3 Pf. טָעַם; impf. יִטְעַם; impv. טַעֲמוּ; inf. abs. טָעֹם—**1. taste** food Jb 12_{11}. **2. perceive,** טָעֲמָה כִּי־טוֹב סַחְרָהּ *she perceives that her merchandise is profitable* Pr 31_{18}. → טַעַם *taste,* מַטְעַם *savoury food.*

טַעַם 13.3 n.m.—טָעַם; sf. טַעְמוֹ—**1. taste** of cake Nm 11_{8}. **2. discernment** of elders Jb 12_{20}. **3. decree** of king Jon 3_{7}. → טעם *taste.*

טען I 1 vb.—**Pu.** 1 Ptc. מְטֹעֲנֵי—**be pierced** by the sword Is 14_{19}.

טען II 1 vb.—**Qal** 1 Impv. טַעֲנוּ—**load** beast Gn 45_{17}.

* **טעע** vb. **Pulp., be led astray, disturbed,** מטעטע מחזון נפשו *he who is disturbed by the vision of his soul,* i.e. mind Si 40_{6} (if em. מעט טע appar. *a little*).

טַף 42.0.6 n.m.—טַף; sf. טַפֵּנוּ—alw. coll., **children, infants** Gn 34_{29}. → טפף *walk carefully.*

טפח I 1 vb.—**Pi.** 1 Pf. טִפְּחָה—**extend** the skies Is 48_{13}. → טֶפַח *handbreadth,* מִטְפַּחַת *cloak.*

טפח II 1 vb.—**Pi.** 1 Pf. טִפַּחְתִּי—of Zion, **give birth to** child Lm 2_{22}. → טִפֻּחִים *birth.*

טֶפַח 9.0.2 n.m.—טֹפַח; pl. טְפָחוֹת—**1. handbreadth,** as unit of measure 1 K 7_{26}||2 C 4_{5}. **2. coping stone** 1 K 7_{9}. → טפח I *extend.*

טִפֻּחִים 1 n.[m.] perh. **birth,** עֹלְלֵי טִפֻּחִים *children of birth,* i.e. new-born children Lm 2_{20}. → טפח II *give birth.*

טפל 3.1 vb.—**Qal** 3.1 Pf. טָפְלוּ; + waw וַתִּטְפֹּל; ptc. טֹפְלֵי—**1. daub, smear** falsehood over (עַל) someone Ps 119_{69}. **2. plaster over** (עַל) iniquity Jb 14_{17}.

טִפְסָר 2 n.m.—טִפְסָר—**scribe (?), official** Jr 51_{27} Na 3_{17}.

טפף 1 vb.—**Qal** 1 Inf. טָפֹף—**walk carefully, walk with mincing gait** Is 3_{16}. → טַף *children.*

טפשׁ 1 vb.—**Qal** 1 Pf. טָפַשׁ—**be fat,** of heart of the arrogant Ps 119_{70}. → טפשׁ *foolish.*

* **[טִפֵּשׁ]** 0.1 adj.—f.s. טפשה—**foolish,** of woman Si 42_{6}

(Bmg). → טפשׁ *be fat.*
טָפַת 1 pr.n.f. **Taphath.**
*[טֹקַח] 0.0.0.1 pr.n. **Tekah.**
טרד 2.2.6 vb.—**Qal** 2.2.6 Pf. Si טרתי; ptc. טֹרֵד; ptc. pass. Q טרוד; inf. Si לטרד—**1.** intrans., **a. be persistent,** of person Si 35_{9}. **b. be continuous,** of dripping Pr 19_{13}. **2.** trans., appar. **continually arouse** soul Si 51_{20}(11QPs[a]). **3.** pass. ptc. as adj., **staccato,** קול חד טרוד *a shrill staccato sound* 1QM 8_{9}.
טרח 1 vb.—**Hi.** 1 Impf. יַטְרִיחַ—of Y., **burden** clouds with (בְּ) moisture Jb 37_{11}. → טֹרַח *burden.*
טֹרַח 2.0.1 n.m. **burden**—sf. טָרְחֲכֶם—Dt 1_{12} Is 1_{14}. → טרח *burden.*
טָרִי 2 adj.—f.s. טְרִיָּה—**fresh, raw,** of wound Is 1_{6}.
טֶרֶם 56.5.25.1 conj. (rarely, prep.)—Kt טרום—**1. before,** usu. with impf., וַיָּלִנוּ שָׁם טֶרֶם יַעֲבֹרוּ *and they lodged there before they crossed over* Jos 3_{1}; with pf. Gn 24_{15}. **2.** בְּטֶרֶם **before, a.** conj., usu. with impf., אַבְלִיגָה בְּטֶרֶם אֵלֵךְ וְאֵינֶנִּי *I shall be cheerful before I go and am no more* Ps 39_{14}; with pf. Pr 8_{25}, inf. 1QH 9_{11}. **b.** prep., כְּבִכּוּרָה בְּטֶרֶם קַיִץ *like an early fig before the harvest* Is 28_{4}. **3.** מִטֶּרֶם **before,** or perh. **as long as** or **immediately after, from the beginning of** Hg 2_{15}.
טרף 25.0.5 vb.—**Qal** 20.0.3 Pf. טָרַף; impf. יִטְרֹף; ptc. טֹרֵף; inf. abs. טָרֹף; cstr. טְרוֹף (לִטְרָף־)—**tear (apart), savage** prey (subj. wolf) Ezk 22_{27}, person (subj. enemy) Ps 7_{3} (+ כְּ *like* lion).
Ni. 2.0.1 Impf. יִטָּרֵף—**be torn,** of beast Ex 22_{12}, person Jr 5_{6}.
Pu. 2 Pf. טֹרַף—**be torn,** of person Gn 37_{33}.
Hi. 1.0.1 Impv. הַטְרִיפֵנִי—of Y., **feed** someone bread Pr 30_{8}.
→ טָרָף *fresh,* טֶרֶף *prey,* טְרֵפָה *savaged beast.*
טָרָף 2.0.1 adj.—pl. cstr. טַרְפֵּי—**1. fresh, freshly-plucked,** of olive leaf Gn 8_{11}. **2.** as noun, **fresh leaf** Ezk 17_{9}. → טרף *tear.*
טֶרֶף 22.1.10 n.m.—טָרֶף; sf. טַרְפּוֹ—**1.** usu. **prey** of ferocious beasts Gn 49_{9}. **2. food** of humans Ps 111_{5}, animals Jb 24_{5}. → טרף *tear.*
טְרֵפָה 9.0.1 n.f. **savaged beast,** one torn apart by other beasts Gn 31_{39}. → טרף *tear.*

י

יאב 1.0.3 vb.—**Qal** 1.0.3 Pf. יָאַבְתִּי—**desire, long for** (לְ) Y.'s commandments Ps 119_{131}.
יאה 1 vb.—**Qal** 1 Pf. יָאָתָה—**befit,** with לְ of obj. Jr 10_{7}.
יְאוֹר, see יְאֹר *Nile.*
*[יָאוּשׁ] 0.0.0.5 pr.n.m. **Jaush.**
*[יַאֲזַן] 0.0.0.2 pr.n.m. **Jaazan.**
יַאֲזַנְיָה 5.0.0.12 pr.n.m. **Jaazaniah.**
*[יַאֲחַץ] 0.0.0.1 pr.n.m. **Jaahaz.**
יָאִיר 12.0.0.1 pr.n.m. **Jair.**
יָאִירִי, see יָאִרִי *Jairite.*
יאל I 19.0.1 vb.—**Hi.** 19.0.1 Pf. הוֹאִיל, הוֹאַלְתָּ; impf. יֹאֵל; + waw וַיּוֹאֶל; impv. הוֹאֵל (הוֹאֶל־), הוֹאִילוּ—**1. be pleased, be willing** to do, with inf., וַיּוֹאֶל מֹשֶׁה לָשֶׁבֶת *and Moses was willing to stay* Ex 2_{21}; with fin. vb., לוּ הוֹאַלְנוּ וַנֵּשֶׁב *would that we had been willing to dwell* beyond the Jordan Jos 7_{7}. **2. undertake** to do, with inf. Gn 18_{27}, fin. vb. Dt 1_{5}. **3. be determined** to do, **persist** in doing, with inf. Jg 1_{27}, fin. vb. Ho 5_{11}.
יאל II 4.1.1 vb.—**Ni.** 4.1.1 Pf. נוֹאֲלוּ—**be foolish, become a fool** Nm 12_{11}.
יֹאֵל, see יוֹאֵל *Joel.*
יְאֹר 65.2.3 pl.n.—יְאוֹר; + article הַיְאֹר; sf. יְאֹרִי; pl. יְאֹרִים; cstr. יְאֹרֵי; sf. יְאֹרָיו—**1.** the river **Nile** Gn 41_{1}. **2.** pl., **(Nile-)streams,** i.e. the **branches** and **canals** of the lower Nile Ex 7_{19}. **3.** other **river, stream** Is 33_{21}. **4. channel,** i.e. **gallery,** of mine Jb 28_{10}.
יָאִרִי 1 gent. **Jairite.**
יאשׁ 6.1 vb.—**Ni.** 5 + waw וְנוֹאַשׁ; ptc. נוֹאָשׁ—**1. despair (of),** וְנוֹאַשׁ מִמֶּנִּי שָׁאוּל לְבַקְשֵׁנִי *and Saul will despair of me to seek me,* i.e. of seeking me 1 S 27_{1}. **2.** ptc. as

noun, **despairing one** Jb 6$_{26}$. 3. ptc. as interj., **desperate!, it is hopeless!** Is 57$_{10}$.

Pi. 1 inf. יַאֵשׁ—**cause** one's heart **to despair** Ec 2$_{20}$.

Pu. 0.1 Ptc. מְיוֹאָשׁ—**be in despair** Si 47$_{23}$.

[יָאשׁ], see יָאוּשׁ *Jaush*.

יֹאשׁ, see יוֹאָשׁ *Joash*.

יֹאשִׁיָּה, see יֹאשִׁיָּהוּ *Josiah*.

יֹאשִׁיָּהוּ 53.2 pr.n.m. **Josiah**.

יאתון, see אִיתוֹן *entrance*.

יְאָתְרַי 1 pr.n.m. **Jeatherai**.

יבב 1 vb.—**Pi.** 1 + waw וַתְּיַבֵּב—**cry aloud**, perh. **lament** Jg 5$_{28}$.

יְבוּל 13.1.1 n.m.—sf. יְבֻלָהּ—**1. produce** of the soil Jg 6$_4$. **2.** perh. **possessions** Jb 20$_{28}$. → יבל *bring*.

יְבוּס 4 pl.n. **Jebus**.

יְבוּסִי 41.0.2 gent. **Jebusite**.

יבושה, see יַבָּשָׁה *dry land*.

יִבְחָר 3 pr.n.m. **Ibhar**.

יָבִין 8 pr.n.m. **Jabin**.

יָבֵישׁ, see יָבֵשׁ II, III *Jabesh*.

יבל 18.0.1 vb.—**Hi.** 7.0.1 Impf. יוֹבִילֵנִי; impv. Q הובל—**1. bring, carry** gifts to (לְ) Y. Ps 68$_{30}$. **2.** of Y., **lead** people Jr 31$_9$.

Ho. 11 Impf. יוּבַל—**1. be brought**, of gifts Is 18$_7$ (+ לְ *to*). **2. be led**, of people Is 55$_{12}$.

→ יָבָל *stream*, יוּבַל I *stream*, יְבוּל *produce*, יַבֶּלֶת *running sore*.

[יָבָל] I 2.1 n.[m.]—pl. cstr. יִבְלֵי—**stream, watercourse** Is 30$_{25}$. → יבל *bring*; cf. מַבּוּל *flood*.

יָבָל II 1 pr.n.m. **Jabal**.

יִבְלְעָם 3 pl.n. **Ibleam**.

יַבֶּלֶת 1 n.f. **running sore**, or perh. **wart**, in animal Lv 22$_{22}$. → יבל *bring*.

יבם I 3 vb.—**Pi.** 3 + waw וְיַבְּמָהּ; impv. יַבֵּם; inf. יַבְּמִי—**marry sister-in-law** of deceased brother, **perform brother-in-law's duty** to widow Gn 38$_8$. → יָבָם *husband's brother*, יְבֶמֶת *sister-in-law*.

*יבם II vb.—**Qal, create**, אָדֹן יָבַם סִינַי בַּקֹּדֶשׁ *the Lord created Sinai as (his) sanctuary* Ps 68$_{18}$ (if em. אֲדֹנָי בָם סִינַי בַּקֹּדֶשׁ *my Lord is among them [at] Sinai, in holiness*).

[יָבָם] 2 n.m. **husband's brother**—sf. יְבָמָהּ—Dt 25$_{5.7}$. → יבם I *marry sister-in-law*.

[יְבֶמֶת] 5 n.f.—sf. יְבִמְתֵּךְ—**sister-in-law**, specif. **wife** (widow) of brother Dt 25$_{7.9}$, of husband's brother Ru 1$_{15}$. → יבם I *marry sister-in-law*.

יַבְנְאֵל 2 pl.n. **Jabneel**.

יַבְנֵה 1 pl.n. **Jabneh**.

יִבְנְיָה 1 pr.n.m. **Ibneiah**.

יִבְנִיָּה 1 pr.n.m. **Ibnijah**.

יְבֻסִי, see יְבוּסִי *Jebusite*.

יַבֹּק 7 pl.n. **Jabbok**.

יְבֶרֶכְיָהוּ 1 pr.n.m. **Jeberechiah**.

יִבְשָׂם 1 pr.n.m. **Ibsam**.

יבשׁ I 61.0.5 vb.—**Qal** 42.0.3 Pf. יָבֵשׁ; impf. יִיבַשׁ, תִּיבַשׁ; inf. abs. יָבוֹשׁ; cstr. יְבֹשׁ, יְבֹשֶׁת—**1. be dry**, of bread Jos 9$_5$; **be dried up**, of ground Am 4$_7$, human strength Ps 22$_{16}$ (+ כְּ *as* potsherd); **wither**, of grass Is 15$_6$, arm Zc 11$_{17}$. **2. dry up**, of water Gn 8$_7$.

Pi. 3.0.2 Impf. תְּיַבֵּשׁ; + waw וַיְיַבְּשֵׁהוּ—**1. make dry, make wither** shoots Jb 15$_{30}$, bones Pr 17$_{22}$. **2. dry up** sea Na 1$_4$.

Hi. 16 Pf. הוֹבִישׁ; impf. אוֹבִישׁ—**1.** trans., **a. make dry, make to wither** fruit Ezk 19$_{12}$, grass Is 42$_{15}$. **b. dry up** streams Is 44$_{27}$. **2.** intrans., **a. be dry, wither**, of grain Jl 1$_{17}$. **b. dry up**, of wine Jl 1$_{10}$, joy Jl 1$_{12}$ (+ מִן *from among* people).

→ יָבֵשׁ *dry*, יַבָּשָׁה *dry land*, יַבֶּשֶׁת *dry land*.

*יבשׁ II 18 vb.—**Hi.** 18 (unless from בושׁ I hi. B) Pf. הוֹבִישׁ, הֹבַשְׁתְּ—**1. be ashamed** Jr 8$_9$. **2. be put to shame** Jr 2$_{26}$. **3. act shamefully** Ho 2$_7$. **4. put to shame** one's followers 2 S 19$_6$.

יָבֵשׁ I 9.2.2 adj. **dry**, of bone Ezk 37$_4$, tree Is 56$_3$, spring Si 14$_{10}$, throat (נֶפֶשׁ) Nm 11$_6$. → יבשׁ I *be dry*.

יָבֵשׁ II 21 pl.n. **Jabesh**.

יָבֵשׁ III 3 pr.n.m. **Jabesh**.

יַבָּשָׁה 14.0.5 n.f.—Q יבושה—**dry land**, opp. sea Jon 1$_9$. → יבשׁ I *be dry*.

יַבֶּשֶׁת 2 n.f.—יַבֶּשֶׁת—**dry land** Ps 95$_5$. → יבשׁ I *be dry*.

יִגְאָל 3.0.0.1 pr.n.m. **Igal**.

יגב 2 vb.—**Qal** 2 Ptc. יֹגְבִים—**farm**, ptc. as noun, **farmer** 2 K 25$_{12}$. → יָגֵב *field*.

[יָגֵב] 1 n.[m.]—pl. יְגֵבִים—**field** Jr 39$_{10}$. → יגב *farm*.

יָגְבְּהָה 2 pl.n. **Jogbehah.**

יָגְבְּחָה, see יָגְבְּהָה *Jogbehah.*

יִגְדַּלְיָהוּ 1.0.0.1 pr.n.m. **Igdaliah.**

יגה I 9 vb.—**Ni.** 2 Ptc. נוּגוֹת ,נוּגַי—**be grieved** Lm 1$_4$.

Pi. 1 + waw וַיַּגֶּה—**grieve** someone Lm 3$_{33}$.

Hi. 6 Pf. הוֹגָה; impf. תּוֹגְיוּן; ptc. מוֹגַיִךְ—**1. grieve** someone Jb 19$_2$; abs. **cause grief** Lm 3$_{32}$. **2. cause to suffer** pain Lm 1$_{12}$.

→ יָגוֹן *grief,* תּוּגָה *grief.*

יגה II 1 vb.—**Hi.** 1 Pf. הֹגָה—**remove** slain person from (מִן) highway 2 S 20$_{13}$.

יָגוֹן 14.0.16 n.[m.]—sf. יְגוֹנָם—**grief, sorrow** Gn 42$_{38}$ Ps 31$_3$. → יגה I *be grieved.*

יָגוֹעַ 1 adj. **toiling** Ps 88$_{16(mss)}$ (L גֹּוֵעַ *expiring*). → יגע *be weary.*

יָגוֹר, see יגר *fear.*

יָגוּר 1 pl.n. **Jagur.**

[יָגִיעַ] 1.1 adj.—pl. cstr. יְגִיעֵי—**1. concerned (for),** אם תכשל יגיע אליך *if you stumble, (he is) concerned for you* Si 37$_{12(B)}$. **2.** as noun, **weary one** Jb 3$_{17}$. → יגע *be weary.*

[יְגִיעַ] 16.1.1 n.m.—sf. יְגִיעוֹ; pl. sf. יְגִיעֵי—**1. toil, labour** Gn 31$_{42}$. **2. product of labour, property** Dt 28$_{33}$ Ps 109$_{11}$. → יגע *be weary.*

[יְגִיעָה] 1 n.f. **wearying,** לַהַג הַרְבֵּה יְגִעַת בָּשָׂר *much study is a wearying of the flesh* Ec 12$_{12}$. → יגע *be weary.*

*[יגל] vb. **Qal, be afraid** Ho 10$_5$ (if em. יָגִילוּ *they rejoiced* [from גיל] to יָגֻ[ו]לוּ *they will be afraid*).

יָגְלִי 1 pr.n.m. **Jogli.**

*[יגן] vb. **Ni., be downcast** Ps 77$_7$ (if em. נְגִינָתִי *my song* to נוּגַנְתִּי *I am downcast*).

יגע 27.2.6 vb.—**Qal** 20.2.4 Pf. יָגַעְתָּ ,יָגַעְתְּ; impf. יִיגְעוּ ,תִּיגַע (יִגְעוּ)—**1. be weary, weary oneself** 2 S 23$_{10}$ Is 40$_{28}$ 43$_{22}$ (+ בְּ *because of*). **2. toil, labour** Jos 24$_{13}$ (+ בְּ *[in exchange] for*) Ps 49$_4$ (+ לְרִיק *in vain*).

Pi. 3 Pf. יִגַּע; impf. תְּיַגַּע—**1. make weary** Ec 10$_{15}$. **2. cause to toil** Jos 7$_3$. **3.** perh. **torture** someone with (בְּ) pike/dagger 2 S 5$_8$.

Hi. 4.0.2 Pf. הוֹגַעְתָּנִי; inf. Q לוגיע—**make** someone **weary** with (בְּ) something Is 43$_{23.34}$ Ml 2$_{17}$.

→ יָגִיעַ *weary,* יְגִיעַ *toil, product,* יָגָע *gain,* יָגֵעַ *weary,* יָגוֹעַ *toiling,* יְגִיעָה *wearying.*

יָגָע 1.0.1 n.[m.] **gain,** i.e. product of labour Jb 20$_{18}$. → יגע *be weary.*

יָגֵעַ 3 adj.—pl. יְגֵעִים—**1. weary,** of person Dt 25$_{18}$. **2. wearisome,** of things Ec 1$_8$. → יגע *be weary.*

יגר 7 vb.—**Qal** 7 Pf. יָגֹרְתִּי; ptc. יָגוֹר—**fear, be afraid of** something, with accus. Jb 9$_{28}$, מִפְּנֵי *(on account) of* Dt 9$_{19}$. → cf. גור III *fear.*

*[יָגָר] 0.0.3 n.[m.] **cairn** 3QTr 4$_{13}$ 6$_{14}$ 8$_8$.

יָד I 1634.52.379.6 n.f. (& m.)—cstr. יַד; sf. יָדָם ,יֶדְכֶם ,יָדִי; du. יָדַיִם; cstr. יְדֵי; sf. יְדֵיהֶם ,יָדַי; pl. יָדוֹת (יָדֹת); cstr. יְדוֹת; sf. יְדֹתָיו—**1. hand, a.** of human being Gn 3$_{22}$, image 1 S 5$_4$, personified object Hb 3$_{10}$; also **wrist, forearm,** צְמִידִים עַל־יָדֶיהָ *bracelets for her wrists* Gn 24$_{22}$, perh. **arm** Ec 7$_{26}$, **upper arm** Jr 38$_{12}$; perh. specif. **left hand** Jg 3$_{21}$. **b.** of Y., יַד־יי הָיְתָה־בָּם *the hand of Y. was against them* Ex 9$_3$. **2.** perh. **penis,** אָהַבְתְּ מִשְׁכָּבָם יָד חָזִית *you loved their bed(s), you gazed at (their) penis(es)* Is 57$_8$. **3. hand** as representing person, יָדִי עִמָּךְ *my hand will be with you,* i.e. I will help you 2 S 3$_{12}$, nation Jg 4$_{24}$, animal 1 S 17$_{37}$, object Ps 141$_9$; also בְּיַד **in the possession of** Ec 5$_{13}$, **by means of, through,** דְּבַר־יי אֶל־יִשְׂרָאֵל בְּיַד מַלְאָכִי *the word of Y. to Israel through Malachi* Ml 1$_1$. **4a. hand** as **(sphere of) power, rule, control,** מִיַּד שְׁאוֹל אֶפְדֵּם *I will deliver them from the power of Sheol* Ho 13$_{14}$, **grip,** i.e. hold on power 1 K 2$_{46}$, **authority,** תַּחַת יַד־פַּרְעֹה *under the authority of Pharaoh* Gn 41$_{35}$, **charge, custody, command,** בֵּית הַנָּשִׁים אֶל־יַד הֵגֶא *the harem in the custody of Hege* Est 2$_3$, pl. **directions** Ezr 3$_{10}$. **b. hand** as **power, strength, force,** בְּיָד חֲזָקָה *with a strong force* Nm 20$_{20}$, **courage,** וַיִּרְפּוּ יָדָיו *then his courage failed* 2 S 4$_1$. **5. sleight of hand, theft** Si 41$_{19}$. **6. bounty,** יַד הַמֶּלֶךְ *bounty of the king* Est 1$_7$. **7a. side** of gate 1 S 4$_{18}$, way Ps 140$_6$, city Ne 7$_4$; **side** of person, i.e. position next to him 1 S 19$_3$, position next in authority 1 C 23$_{28}$; **latrine** outside camp Dt 23$_{13}$; **region, direction,** מִיַּד כִּתִּים *from the region of Kittim* Nm 24$_{24}$. **b.** in compound prep., **beside,** (1) לְיַד Pr 8$_3$; (2) בְּיַד 2 C 7$_6$; (3) אֶל־יַד 2 S 14$_{30}$; (4) עַל־יְדֵי Ex 2$_5$, עַל־יַד Jg 11$_{26}$. **8.** pl., **(fractional) parts, portions, divisions** 2 S 19$_{44}$; **times (greater),** מַשְׂאַת בִּנְיָמִן מִמַּשְׂאֹת כֻּלָּם חָמֵשׁ יָדוֹת *Benjamin's portion was five times greater than any* *of their portions* Gn 43$_{34}$. 9. **monument,** מַצִּיב לוֹ יָד *he erected for himself a monument* 1 S 15$_{12}$. **10. tenon, peg,** in boards of tabernacle Ex 26$_{17}$. **11. axletree** of wheel 1 K 7$_{32}$. **12. stay, support** of stand 1 K 7$_{35}$; **arm rest** of throne 1 K 10$_{19}$. **13. handle** of pot Is 45$_{9}$; **hilt** of sword 1QM 5$_{14}$. **14.** perh. **flock** Jr 6$_{3}$. **15.** perh. **descendant** 2 S 18$_{18}$. **16.** perh. **signal** for order of battle 1QM 8$_{5}$.

*[יָד] II 4.0.2 n.[f.] **penis,** וינקו ידים על האבנים *and penises empty themselves,* i.e. ejaculate, *into the vaginas* Is 65$_{3}$(1QIsa^{a}), חַיַּת יָדֵךְ *life of your penis,* i.e. your sexual vigour Is 57$_{10}$.

*[יָד] III 7 n.[m.]—cstr. יַד; sf. יָדוֹ; pl. sf. יָדֶיהָ, יָדָיו—**1. love,** יַד יי *love of Y.* Is 66$_{14}$, מִיָּדָם *for the love of them,* i.e. for their sake Ps 16$_{4}$. **2. loved one,** יָדָיו *his loved ones* Jb 20$_{10}$. → cf. יְדִדוּת *loved one,* יָדִיד *beloved,* יְדִידֹת *love.*

יִדְאֲלָה 1 pl.n. **Idalah.**

יִדְבָּשׁ 1 pr.n.m. **Idbash.**

[ידד], see ידה II *throw.*

יְדִדוּת 1 n.f. **loved one,** יְדִדוּת נַפְשִׁי *loved one of my soul* Jr 12$_{7}$. → cf. יָד III *love.*

ידה I 110.17.40 vb.—**Hi.** 99.17.39 Pf. הוֹדִינוּ; impf. יוֹדֶה, יוֹדוּ; impv. הוֹדוּ; ptc. מוֹדֶה, מוֹדִים; inf. הֹדוֹת—**1a. praise** (accus.) Y. Ps 7$_{18}$, Judah Gn 49$_{8}$. **b. give praise to** (לְ) Y. Ps 100$_{4}$. **c.** perh. **thank** (accus.) Y. Is 38$_{19}$. **d. acclaim** Y., with accus. Ps 71$_{22}$, לְ of obj. Ps 6$_{6}$. **2. lead worship, act as choir** or **orchestra,** לְשָׁרֵת וּלְהֹדוֹת וּלְהַלֵּל בְּשַׁעֲרֵי מַחֲנוֹת יי *to minister, to lead worship and to give praise in the gates of the courts of Y.* 2 C 31$_{2}$. **3. confess (sin)** Ps 32$_{5}$ 1QS 1$_{24}$.

Htp. 11.0.1 + waw וַיִּתְוַדּוּ, וָאֶתְוַדֶּה; וְהִתְוַדָּה; ptc. מִתְוַדֶּה, מִתְוַדִּים; inf. הִתְוַדֹּתוֹ—**1. confess sin, a.** with accus. Lv 16$_{21}$. **b.** with עַל of obj. Ne 1$_{6}$. **2.** abs., **make confession** Ezr 10$_{1}$.

→ הוֹדָאָה *(song of) thanksgiving,* הוֹדָה *thanksgiving,* הֻיְּדוֹת *songs of praise,* תּוֹדָה *thanksgiving.*

ידה II 6.1 vb.—**Qal** 1.1 Impv. יְדוּ; ptc. Si יוֹדֵי—**1. shoot (arrow)** Jr 50$_{14}$. **2.** ptc. as noun, **one who casts lots** Si 14$_{15}$.

Pi. 5 Impf. יַדּוּ; inf. יַדּוֹת—**throw** stone Lm 3$_{53}$, **cast** lots Jl 4$_{3}$, appar. **throw down, cut off** horn of enemy Zc 2$_{4}$.

*[יְדָה] 2 n.[m.]—sf. יְדֵיהוּ—**voice** Hb 3$_{10}$.

יִדּוֹ 2.0.0.3 pr.n.m. **Iddo.**

יָדוֹן 1 pr.n.m. **Jadon.**

יַדּוּעַ 3.0.0.4 pr.n.m. **Jaddua.**

יְדוּתוּן 17 pr.n.m. **Jeduthun.**

יַדַּי 1 pr.n.m. **Jaddai.**

[יָדִיד] 8.0.8 adj.—cstr. יְדִיד; sf. יְדִידִי; pl. Q ידידים; sf. יְדִידֶיךָ; f.pl. יְדִידוֹת—**1.** as adj., **beloved,** of Y.'s dwelling place Ps 84$_{2}$. **2.** as noun, **beloved (one)** Is 5$_{1}$; יְדִיד יי *beloved of Y.* Dt 33$_{12}$. → cf. יָד III *love.*

יְדִידָה 1 pr.n.f. **Jedidah.**

יְדִידוּת, see יְדִידֹת *love.*

יְדִידְיָה 1 pr.n.m. **Jedidiah.**

יְדִידֹת 1 n.f. pl.—mss יְדִידוּת (יְדִידֹת)—**love,** שִׁיר יְדִידֹת *love song* Ps 45$_{1}$. → cf. יָד III *love.*

יְדִידֻת, see יְדִידֹת *love.*

יְדָיָה 2 pr.n.m. **Jedaiah.**

יְדִיעֲאֵל 6 pr.n.m. **Jediael.**

יְדִיתוּן, see יְדוּתוּן *Jeduthun.*

יִדְלָף 1 pr.n.m. **Jidlaph.**

*[יְדָנְיָהוּ] 0.0.0.2 pr.n.m. **Jedoniah.**

ידע I 948.28.261.5 vb.—**Qal** 822.24.204.5 Pf. יָדַע, יָדַעְתָּ; impf. יֵדַע (וַיֵּדַע), אֵדַע (אֵדְעָה); impv. דַּע, דְּעוּ; ptc. יֹדֵעַ, יֹדַעַת, יֹדְעִים; ptc. pass. cstr. יְדוּעַ, יְדוּעִים; inf. abs. יָדֹעַ; cstr. דַּעַת (דַּעְתִּי)—**1a.** with obj., **know, realize, be aware of, have knowledge of** something, לֹא יָדַעְתִּי יוֹם מוֹתִי *I do not know the day of my death* Gn 27$_{2}$. **b. know (that), realize (that), be aware (that),** וַיֵּדְעוּ כִּי עֵירֻמִּם הֵם *then they realized that they were naked* Gn 3$_{7}$, לְמַעַן אֲשֶׁר יֵדְעוּ אֲשֶׁר אֲנִי יי *that they might know that I am Y.* Ezk 20$_{26}$. **c.** abs., **know,** אֵין רֹאֶה וְאֵין יוֹדֵעַ *no one saw or knew* 1 S 26$_{12}$. **2. know, be familiar with, experience** something, אַנְשֵׁי אֳנִיּוֹת יֹדְעֵי הַיָּם *sailors who were familiar with the sea* 1 K 9$_{27}$. **3. know, be acquainted with,** יְדַעְתִּיךָ בְשֵׁם *I* (Y.) *know you by name* Ex 33$_{12}$, אֱלֹהִים אֲחֵרִים אֲשֶׁר לֹא־יְדַעְתֶּם *other gods whom you were not acquainted with* Dt 11$_{28}$. **4. know** someone **carnally, have sexual relations (with),** הָאָדָם יָדַע אֶת־חַוָּה *Adam had sexual relations with Eve* Gn 4$_{1}$; of homosexual relations Gn 19$_{5}$. **5. know, recognize, learn, perceive, understand,** הָאֵדַע בֵּין־טוֹב

לְרָע *can I know the difference between good and bad?* 2 S 19$_{36}$. 6. **know (how) to do, be skilful in, be knowledgeable about,** לֹא־יָדַעְתִּי דַּבֵּר *I do not know how to speak* Jr 1$_{6}$. 7. **know, find out, discover,** וְיָדַעַתְּ אֶת־הַמָּקוֹם אֲשֶׁר יִשְׁכַּב־שָׁם *and you will discover the place where he lies down* Ru 3$_{4}$. 8. **pay attention to, be concerned about,** לֹא־יָדַע אִתּוֹ מְאוּמָה *with him (in charge) he was not concerned about anything* Gn 39$_{6}$, אֶת־בָּנָיו לֹא יָדָע *he did not pay attention to his (own) children* Dt 33$_{9(Qr)}$. 9. **acknowledge,** פְּשָׁעַי אֲנִי אֵדָע *I acknowledge my sins* Ps 51$_{5}$. 10. perh. specif. **recognize (authority of),** לֹא יָדְעוּ אֶת־י״ *they did not recognize (the authority of) Y.* 1 S 2$_{12}$. 11. perh. **choose,** וְאַתָּה י״ יְדַעְתָּנִי *yet you Y. have chosen me* Jr 12$_{3}$. 12. pass., a. **be known** MurEpBeth-Mashiko$_{2}$. b. **be well known** or perh. **be experienced, be proved** Dt 1$_{13}$. 13. pass. ptc. as noun, a. **one who is known** Is 53$_{3}$. b. **one who is well known,** or perh. **one who is experienced** 1QSa 1$_{28}$.

Ni. 41.3.8 Pf. נוֹדַע; impf. יִוָּדַע (יִוָּדֵעַ); ptc. נוֹדָע; inf. הִוָּדְעִי—1. **be known, made known,** of person Pr 31$_{23}$, place Na 3$_{17}$, matter Est 2$_{22}$, sin Lv 4$_{14}$. 2. **make oneself known to** (לְ) someone Ex 6$_{3}$ (subj. Y.) Ru 3$_{3}$. 3. **be found out, discovered,** of people in hiding 1 S 22$_{6}$, sinner Pr 10$_{9}$, (secret of) strength Jg 16$_{9}$. 4. perh. **be made to know,** of person Jr 31$_{19}$.

Pi. 1 Pf. Qr יִדַּעְתָּ—**cause** the dawn **to know** its place Jb 38$_{12}$.

Pu. 8 Ptc. מְיֻדָּע—1. **be made known,** of Y.'s glorious deeds Is 12$_{5(Kt)}$. 2. ptc. as noun, **acquaintance, intimate friend** Ps 55$_{14}$; **kinsman** Ru 2$_{1(Kt)}$.

Po. 1 Pf. יוֹדַעְתִּי—**cause to know,** i.e. direct to (אֶל) a place 1 S 21$_{3}$.

Hi. 71.1.49 Pf. הוֹדַעְתָּ, הוֹדִיעַ; impf. יוֹדִיעַ, יֹדִיעוּ, נוֹדִיעָה; + waw וַיֹּדַע; impv. הוֹדַע (הוֹדִיעֵנִי), הוֹדִיעוּ; ptc. מוֹדִיעֲךָ, מוֹדִיעִים; inf. הוֹדִיעַ—1. **make known, declare** something Ezk 39$_{7}$ Ps 89$_{2}$. 2a. **make something known to** (לְ) someone Dt 4$_{9}$ Is 64$_{1}$. b. with double accus., **cause someone to know something, show, teach someone something** Ex 33$_{13}$ Ezk 20$_{11}$. 3. with בֵּין, perh. **distinguish between** Ezk 22$_{26}$.

Ho. 3 Pf. הוֹדַע; ptc. Qr מוּדַעַת—**be made known,** of Y.'s glorious deeds Is 12$_{5(Qr)}$, sin Lv 4$_{23}$.

Htp. 2 Impf. אֶתְוַדַּע; inf. הִתְוַדַּע—**make oneself known to** (אֶל) someone, of Y. Nm 12$_{6}$, person Gn 45$_{1}$.

→ דֵּעַ *knowledge,* דֵּעָה *knowledge,* דַּעַת I *knowledge,* יַדָּע *expert,* מַדָּע I *knowledge,* מֹדָע *kinsman,* מֹדַעַת *kin,* יִדְּעֹנִי *familiar spirit,* מַדּוּעַ *why?*

***ידע** II 29.1.1 vb.—**Qal** 22.1.1 Pf. יְדָעוּךָ; impf. יֵדַע (יֵיָדַע), תֵּדַע; ptc. pass. יְדוּעַ; inf. דַּעַת—1. **be quiet, be at rest** Jr 14$_{18}$; also **be submissive** Jb 21$_{19}$. 2. **be humiliated, humbled, reduced to submission** Ho 9$_{7}$. 3. **be submissive (as devotee) to** Y. Is 45$_{4}$. 4. **cause to be submissive, reduce to submission, humiliate** someone Ps 138$_{6}$. 5. pass. ptc. as noun, **one who is humbled** Is 53$_{3}$.

Ni. 6 Pf. נוֹדַע; impf. יִוָּדַע (יִוָּדֵעַ); inf. הִוָּדְעִי—1. **be made quiet, be made submissive** Jr 31$_{19}$. b. **be weakened,** of strength Jg 16$_{9}$. 2. **be granted rest** 1 S 6$_{3}$.

Hi. 1 + waw וַיֹּדַע—**make submissive, humiliate** people Jg 8$_{16}$.

→ דַּעַת IV *humiliation.*

***ידע** III 14 vb.—**Qal** 14 Impf. אֵדַע; + waw וַיֵּדַע; ptc. יוֹדֵעַ—**care about, care for,** usu. with accus. person Gn 18$_{19}$ Ps 144$_{3}$; with בְּ of obj. distress Ps 31$_{8}$.

***ידע** IV 8.1 vb.—**Qal** 5.1 Impf. יֵדְעוּ; + waw וַיֵּדַע; ptc. pass. cstr. יְדוּעַ—1. **punish,** subj. Y. Gn 18$_{21}$, person Si 7$_{20(A)}$. 2. **be punished** Ho 9$_{7}$. 3. pass. ptc. as noun, **one who is punished** Is 53$_{3}$.

Ni. 2 Impf. יִוָּדַע; inf. הִוָּדְעִי—**be punished** Jr 31$_{19}$.

Hi. 1 + waw וַיֹּדַע—**punish** Jg 8$_{16}$.

***ידע** V 4.1 vb.—**Qal** 2 Impf. יֵדְעוּן; inf. דַּעְתּוֹ—**flow with** what is pleasing, of lips of righteous Pr 10$_{32}$.

Ni. 2 Impf. יִוָּדֵעַ—**be caused to sweat** Pr 10$_{9}$.

Hi. 0.1 Impf. תדיע—**cause to sweat,** i.e. **vex** Si 12$_{1}$.

→ דַּעַת V *sweat;* cf. יֶזַע *sweat.*

***ידע** VI 3 vb.—**Qal** 3 Impf. נֵדְעָה, יֵדְעוּן; impv. דְּעָה—**seek, ask for, desire** wisdom Pr 24$_{14}$, acceptance Pr 10$_{32}$.

***ידע** VII 2 vb.—**Po.** 1 Pf. יוֹדַעְתִּי—**bid farewell, leave** 1 S 21$_{3}$.

Ni. 1 Pf. נוֹדַע—**take leave** 1 S 22$_{6}$.

***ידע** VIII 2 vb.—**Qal** 2 Pf. יָדַעְתִּי—**call** Jb 23$_{3}$; **call**

upon Y.'s name Ps 91$_{14}$.

*ידע IX 2 vb.—**Qal** 1 + waw וַיֵּדַע—**tear down, destroy** fortresses Ezk 19$_{7}$ (if em. אַלְמְנוֹתָיו appar. *his widows* to אַרְמְנוֹתֵיהֶם *their fortresses*).

Ni. 1 Impf. יִוָּדַע—**be torn down,** of temple Ps 74$_{5}$.

*ידע X 2 vb.—**Qal** 2 Pf. יָדַעְתָּ—**leave alone, neglect** suffering Ex 3$_{7}$, knowledgeable lips Pr 14$_{7}$.

*ידע XI 2 vb.—**Qal** 2 Pf. יָדַע—**wrap up** cake Ho 7$_{9.9}$.

*[ידע] XII vb. **Ni., be reconciled** Am 3$_{3}$ (if em. נוֹעָדוּ *they have made an appointment* to נוֹדָעוּ *they have been reconciled*).

*[ידע] XIII vb. **Hi., place** 1 K 8$_{12}$ (if ins. שֶׁמֶשׁ הוֹדִיעַ בַּשָּׁמַיִם *he placed the sun in the heavens*).

Ho., be placed, deposited, of baskets Jr 24$_{1}$ (if em. מוּעָדִים appar. *placed* [יעד ho.] to מוּדָעִים *placed*).

יָדָע 2 pr.n.m. **Jada.**

*[יָדָע] 0.0.1 adj. **expert,** as noun, הנבונים והידעים *the intelligent ones and the experts* 1QSa 1$_{28}$. → ידע I *know*.

יְדַעְיָה 11.0.13.12 pr.n.m. **Jedaiah.**

ידעיהו, see יְדַעְיָה *Jedaiah*.

ידעיו, see יְדַעְיָה *Jedaiah*.

יִדְּעֹנִי 11.0.3 n.m.—pl. יִדְּעֹנִים—**1. familiar spirit,** אוֹב וְיִדְּעֹנִי *ghost and familiar spirit* Dt 18$_{11}$. **2.** perh. **medium, necromancer** 1 S 28$_{3}$ CD 12$_{3}$. → ידע I *know*.

יָהּ 50.1.4.1 pr.n.m. **Yah,** form of divine name יהוה *Yhwh*, Ex 15$_{2}$; הַלְלוּ־יָהּ *praise Yah*, hallelujah Ps 104$_{35}$. → cf. יהוה *Yhwh*, יָהוּ *Yahu*.

יהב 33.1.1 vb.—**Qal** 33.1.1 Impv. הָבָה, הָבוּ—**1. give** something Gn 29$_{21}$ 47$_{15}$ (+ לְ *to* someone). **2. ascribe glory** to (לְ) Y. Ps 29$_{1}$. **3. set aside** someone for a specific task Jos 18$_{4}$. **4. place** soldier in front line (אֶל־מוּל פְּנֵי) of battle 2 S 11$_{15}$. **5.** as interj., **come!, come on!** Gn 11$_{3}$. → הַבְהַב *gift*, יְהָב *burden*.

[יְהָב] 1 n.[m.]—sf. יְהָבְךָ—**burden,** i.e. matter of concern, perh. **lot,** i.e. portion in life Ps 55$_{23}$. → יהב *give*.

יהד 1 vb.—**Htp.** 1 Ptc. מִתְיַהֲדִים—**become a Jew,** perh. **declare oneself to be a Jew** Est 8$_{17}$. → יְהוּדִי I *Jewish*.

יְהֻד 1.0.0.14 pl.n. **Jehud.**

[יַהְדַּי] 1 pr.n.m. **Jahdai.**

*[יָהוּ] 0.0.0.2 pr.n.m. **Yahu,** alternative form of divine names יהוה *Yhwh* and יָהּ *Yah* Kuntillet 'Ajrud add. inscr. 2. → cf. יהוה *Yhwh*, יָהּ *Yah*.

יֵהוּא 57.0.0.1 pr.n.m. **Jehu.**

יְהוּא, see הוה *be*.

*[יְהוֹאָב] 0.0.0.4 pr.n.m. **Jehoab.**

*[יְהוֹאָח] 0.0.0.2 pr.n.m. **Jehoah.**

יְהוֹאָחָז 20.0.0.1 pr.n.m. **Jehoahaz.**

*[יְהוֹאֵל] 0.0.0.1 pr.n.m. **Jehoel.**

יְהוֹאָשׁ 17 pr.n.m. **Jehoash.**

*[יְהוֹבָנָה] 0.0.0.2 pr.n.[m.] **Jehobanah.**

*[יְהוֹבַעַל] 0.0.0.1 pr.n.[m.] **Jehobaal.**

יהוד, see יְהֻד *Jehud*.

יְהוּדָה 806.3.59.13 pr.n.m. **Judah,** name of person or tribe.

יְהוּדִי I 82.0.1.4 gent. **Jewish,** oft. as pl. noun, **Judaeans, Jews** Est 3$_{10}$; יְהוּדִית as adv., **in Judaean,** i.e. Hebrew, the language of Judah Ne 13$_{24}$. → יהד *be a Jew*.

יְהוּדִי II 4 pr.n.m. **Jehudi.**

יְהוּדִית I 1 pr.n.f. **Judith.**

יְהוּדִית II, see יְהוּדִי *Jewish*.

יהוה 6828.66.181.32 pr.n.m.—L יְהוָה (Qr שְׁמָא *the Name*), sometimes יְהוִֹה (Qr אֲדֹנָי *my Lord*); אֲדֹנָי יְהוִה, rarely יְהוִה אֲדֹנָי (Qr אֲדֹנָי אֱלֹהִים *my Lord, God*); יְהוִה אֲדֹנָי (Qr אֱלֹהִים אֲדֹנָי *God ,my Lord*); prefixed forms מֵיְהוָה (Qr מִשְּׁמָא), rarely מִיהוָה, מֵיהוָה, וַ/בַּ/לַיהוָה, etc. (Qr, appar. וַ/בַּ/ לַאדֹנָי etc.); Si ייי, יי, י״י; Q ····—**Yhwh,** divine name, י׳ אֱלֹהִים *Y., God* Gn 2$_{4}$, י׳ צְבָאוֹת *Y. of hosts* 1 S 1$_{11}$. → cf. יָהּ *Yah*, יָהוּ *Yahu*.

יְהוֹזָבָד 4 pr.n.m. **Jehozabad.**

*[יְהוֹזָרַח] 0.0.0.2 pr.n.m. **Jehozarah.**

*[יְהוֹחַי] 0.0.0.1 pr.n.m. **Jehohai.**

*[יְהוֹחַיִל] 0.0.0.5 pr.n.m. **Jehohail.**

יְהוֹחָנָן 9.0.2.11 pr.n.m. **Jehohanan.**

יְהוֹיָדָע 51 pr.n.m. **Jehoiada.**

יְהוֹיָכִין 10 pr.n.m. **Jehoiachin.**

יְהוֹיָקִים 37 pr.n.m. **Jehoiakim.**

יְהוֹיָרִיב 2 pr.n.m. **Jehoiarib.**

*[יְהוֹיִשְׁמַע] 0.0.0.1 pr.n.f. **Jehoishma.**

יְהוּכַל 1.0.0.6 pr.n.m. **Jehucal.**

*[יְהוֹמָלֵךְ] 0.0.0.1 pr.n.m. **Jehomalach.**

יְהוֹנָדָב 8.0.0.1 pr.n.m. **Jehonadab.**

יְהוֹנָתָן 82.0.16.7 pr.n.m. **J(eh)onathan.**

יְהוֹסֵף 1.0.15.3 pr.n.m. **J(eh)oseph.**

יְהוֹעַדָּה 2 pr.n.m. **Jehoaddah.**

יְהוֹעַדָּן 2.0.0.1 pr.n.f. **Jehoaddan.**

יְהוֹעַדִּין, see יְהוֹעַדָּן *Jehoaddan.*

*[**יְהוֹעַז**] 0.0.0.3 pr.n.m. **Jehoaz.**

*[**יְהוֹעֶזֶר**] 0.0.0.3 pr.n.m. **Jehoezer.**

*[**יְהוֹעֱלִי**] 0.0.0.1 pr.n.[m.] **Jehoale.**

*[**יְהוֹעָנָה**] 0.0.0.1 pr.n.[m.] **Jehoanah.**

יְהוֹצָדָק 8 pr.n.m. **Jehozadak.**

*[**יְהוֹקִם**] 0.0.0.3 pr.n.[m.] **Jehokim.**

יְהוֹרָם 29.0.0.1 pr.n.m. **Jehoram.**

יְהוֹשַׁבְעַת 3 pr.n.f. **Jehoshabeath, Jehosheba.**

יְהוֹשֻׁעַ 218.1.1.4 pr.n.m. **J(eh)oshua.**

יְהוֹשָׁפָט 84 pr.n.m. **Jehoshaphat.**

יָהִיר 2 adj. **proud** Hb 2_{5} Pr 21_{24}.

יַהֵל, see אהל I *pitch tent.*

יְהַלֶּלְאֵל 2 pr.n.m. **Jehallelel.**

יָהֲלֹם 3 n.[m.]—mss יַהֲלֹם—perh. **onyx** Ex 28_{18}||39_{11} Ezk 28_{13}.

יַהַץ 9 pl.n. **Jahaz.**

יַהְצָה, יָהְצָה, see יַהַץ *Jahaz.*

יוֹאָב 145 pr.n.m. **Joab.**

יוֹאָח 11 pr.n.m. **Joah.**

יוֹאָחָז 4 pr.n.m. **Joahaz.**

יוֹאֵל 19.0.0.3 pr.n.m. **Joel.**

*[**יוֹאָמָן**] 0.0.0.1 pr.n.[m.] **Joaman.**

*[**יוֹאוֹר**] 0.0.0.1 pr.n.[m.] **Joor.**

יוֹאָשׁ 47 pr.n.m. **Joash.**

יוֹב 1 pr.n.m. **Job.**

יוֹבָב 9 pr.n.m. **Jobab.**

יוֹבֵל 27.0.25 n.m.—יֹבֵל; pl. יוֹבְלִים, Q יובלות; cstr. Q יובלי; sf. Q יובליהם—**1. ram, ram's horn,** קֶרֶן הַיּוֹבֵל *horn of the ram* Jos 6_{5}, שופרות היובל *trumpets of the ram's horn* 1QM 7_{14}. **2. Jubilee,** i.e. **(year of) remission,** the fiftieth year, inaugurated by blowing of ram's horn Lv 25_{10}; in the Book of Jubilees a period of seven weeks of years 4QJub[f] 23_{11}, ספר מחלקות העתים ליובליהם ובשבותיהם *book of the division of the times according to their jubilees and weeks* CD 16_{4}.

יוּבַל I 3.0.2 n.[m.] **stream** Jr 17_{8}; יובלי מים *streams of water* Is 30_{25}(1QIsa[a]). → יבל *bring.*

[**יוּבָל**] II 1 pr.n.m. **Jubal.**

*[**יוֹבָנָה**] 0.0.0.3 pr.n.[m.] **Jobanah.**

*[**יוֹד**] 0.0.1 n.[m.] **yodh, the tenth Hebrew letter, appar.** in ref. to Y., משפטי יוד *judgments of Yod,* i.e. Y. 4QShir[b] 10_{12} (or em. ידו of *his hand*).

*[**יוּדָן**] 0.0.0.1 pr.n.m. **Judan.**

יוֹזָבָד 11 pr.n.m. **Jozabad.**

יוֹזָכָר 1 pr.n.m. **Jozacar.**

*[**יוֹזָן**] 0.0.0.1 pr.n.m. **Jozan.**

יוֹחָא 2 pr.n.m. **Joha.**

יוֹחָנָן 24.1.3.2 pr.n.m. **Johanan.**

יוּטָּה, see יֻטָּה *Juttah.*

יוֹיָדָע 5 pr.n.m. **Joiada.**

יוֹיָכִין 1 pr.n.m. **Joiachin.**

יוֹיָקִים 4 pr.n.m. **Joiakim.**

יוֹיָרִיב 5.0.11 pr.n.m. **Joiarib.**

*[**יוֹיָשַׁע**] 0.0.0.1 pr.n.[m.] **Joiasha.**

יוֹכֶבֶד 2 pr.n.f. **Jochebed.**

יוּכַל 1 pr.n.m. **Jucal.**

*[**יוֹכִן**] 0.0.0.3 pr.n.[m.] **Jochin.**

יוֹם I 2268.56.525.15 n.m.—I ים; cstr. יוֹם (Q, I ים); sf. יוֹמוֹ; du. יוֹמַיִם; pl. יָמִים; + ה- of direction יָמִימָה; cstr. יְמֵי, יְמוֹת; sf. יָמַי, יְמֵיהֶם—**1. day,** opp. night, **daytime,** לַיְלָה וָיוֹם *by night and by day* 1 K 8_{29}, יוֹם אוֹר *daylight* Am 8_{9}, עוֹד הַיּוֹם גָּדוֹל *the day is still great,* i.e. it is still daylight Gn 29_{7}. **2. day of 24 hours,** שִׁבְעַת יָמִים *seven days* Gn 8_{10}. **3a. particular or recurring day** of celebration, commemoration, etc., יוֹם הַשַּׁבָּת *day of the sabbath* Ex 20_{8}, הַכִּפֻּרִים *of atonement* Lv 23_{27}. **b.** pl., **recurring days, period, season** in nature, יְמֵי נִדָּתָהּ *days of her impurity,* i.e. her menstrual period Lv 15_{25}, קַיִץ *of summer* Si 50_{8}, קָצִיר *of harvest* Jos 3_{15}. **4. day of Y.,** of judgment, etc., יוֹם י׳ *day of Y.* Jl 1_{15}, יוֹם עֶבְרַת י׳ *day of the wrath of Y.* Zp 1_{18}. **5. day as a particular point in time,** טוֹב ... יוֹם הַמָּוֶת מִיּוֹם הִוָּלְדוֹ *better is ... the day of death than the day of one's birth* Ec 7_{1}, יוֹם חֲתֻנָּתוֹ *day of his wedding* Ca 3_{11}. **6. day as part of a date,** בְּיוֹם אֶחָד לַחֹדֶשׁ *on the first day of the month* Hg 1_{1}. **7.** pl., **days of life, lifespan,** הֶבֶל יָמָי *my days are a breath* Jb 7_{16}, כָּל־יָמֶיךָ *all your days,* i.e. as long as you live Dt 12_{19}, מִיָּמָיו *since his days,* i.e. throughout his life 1 K 1_{6}. **8. day, time, a.** sg., כָּל־הַיּוֹם *all the time,* i.e. continually Gn 6_{5} Ps 140_{3} (כל יום). **b.** pl., כָּל־הַיָּמִים *all the time,* i.e. for ever, continually Dt 31_{13}.

9. pl., **year,** זֶבַח הַיָּמִים *sacrifice of the year,* i.e. yearly sacrifice 1 S 1_{21}, לַיָּמִים *per year* Jg 17_{10}, יָמִים לַיָּמִים *every year* 2 S 14_{26}, מִיָּמִים יָמִימָה *from year to year* Jg 21_{19}. Various idioms: יוֹם טוֹב *a good day,* i.e. a day of feasting Est 8_{17}, מַחֲצִית הַיּוֹם *half of the day,* i.e. mid-day Ne 8_{3}, הַיּוֹם *today* Dt 1_{10}, לִפְנֵי יוֹם *before today* Is 48_{7}, מִיּוֹם *from today,* i.e. henceforth Is 43_{13}, כַּיּוֹם *first of all* Gn 25_{31}, כְּהַיּוֹם *at about this day,* i.e. now 1 S 9_{13}, יוֹם אֶתְמוֹל *day of previous time,* i.e. yesterday Ps 90_{4}, יוֹם מָחֳרָת *day of the morrow,* i.e. the next day Nm 11_{32}, יוֹם מָחָר *day of the morrow,* i.e. in the future Gn 30_{33}, יוֹם וָיוֹם *day after day* Est 2_{11}, יוֹם בְּיוֹם *day after day* Ne 8_{18}, יוֹם יוֹם *daily* Pr 8_{30}, מִיּוֹם־לְיוֹם *from day to day* 1 C 16_{23}, יָמִים עַל־יָמִים *day upon day* 2 C 21_{15}, יוֹמַיִם *for two days* Ex 21_{21}, לִשְׁלֹשֶׁת יָמִים *every three days* Am 4_{4}, חֹדֶשׁ יָמִים *month of days,* i.e. a whole month Gn 29_{14}, הַיּוֹם שְׁלֹשָׁה *today three,* i.e. three days ago 1 S 30_{13}, בוא בַּיָּמִים *come into days,* i.e. become old Gn 18_{11}, אַחֲרִית הַיָּמִים *end of the days,* i.e. the end of time Dn 10_{14}, דִּבְרֵי הַיָּמִים *events of the days,* i.e. chronicles 1 K 14_{19}, תְּקֻפוֹת הַיָּמִים *the circuits of days,* i.e. the course of time 1 S 1_{20}, לְיָמִים מִיָּמִים *in the course of time* 2 C 21_{19}. → cf. יוֹמָם *by day.*

*יוֹם II 7.0.0.1 n.m. **wind, 1. storm,** רוּחַ הַיּוֹם *wind of the storm* Gn 3_{8}. **2. breath,** קְשֵׁה־יוֹם *one hard of,* i.e. with failing, *breath* Jb 30_{25}.

יוֹמָם 52.0.21 adv. **1. by day,** יוֹמָם וָלַיְלָה *by day and by night* Ex 13_{21}. **2.** appar. noun, **day(time)** Jr 15_{9}; מבוא יומם *coming of daytime* 1QH 20_{7}. → cf. יוֹם *day.*

יָוָן 12.0.3 pr.n.m. **Javan, Greece.**

יָוֵן 2 n.[m.] **mire**—cstr. יְוֵן—Ps 40_{3} 69_{3}.

יוֹנָדָב 8 pr.n.m. **Jonadab.**

יוֹנָה I 33.0.6 n.f.—cstr. יוֹנַת; sf. יוֹנָתִי; pl. יוֹנִים; cstr. יוֹנֵי—**1. dove, pigeon** Gn 8_{8} Lv 1_{14}. **2.** יוֹנָתִי **my dove,** term of affection for female lover Ca 2_{14}.

יוֹנָה II 19 pr.n.m. **Jonah.**

יוֹנָה III *oppressor,* see ינה *oppress.*

[יְוָנִי] 1 gent. **Greek.**

*[יְוָנִת] n.f. **Greek (language),** יְוָנִת אִיִּים *Greek of the* distant *coastlands* Ps 56_{1} (if em. יוֹנַת אֵלֶם *dove of silence*).

יוֹנָתָן 42.0.3.3 pr.n.m. **Jonathan.**

יוסה, see יוֹסֵי *Jose.*

*[יוֹסֵי] 0.0.1.1 pr.n.m. **Jose.**

יוֹסֵף 210.1.6.3 pr.n.m. **Joseph.**

יוֹסִפְיָה 1 pr.n.m. **Josiphiah.**

*[יוֹסְתֵּר] 0.0.0.1 pr.n.m. **Joster.**

יוֹעֵאלָה 1 pr.n.m. **Joelah.**

יוֹעֵד 1 pr.n.m. **Joed.**

יוֹעֶזֶר 1.0.0.2 pr.n.m. **Joezer.**

*[יוֹעֲלְיָהוּ] 0.0.0.2 pr.n.m. **Joiliah.**

יוֹעָשׁ 2 pr.n.m. **Joash.**

*[יוֹעָשָׂה] 0.0.0.2 pr.n.m. **Joasah.**

יוֹצָדָק 4 pr.n.m. **Jozadak.**

יוֹקִים 1.0.0.1 pr.n.m. **Jokim.**

יוֹרֶא I, see ירה II, ho. *be given drink.*

יוֹרֶא II, see יוֹרֶה I *early rain.*

יוֹרָה 1 pr.n.m. **Jorah.**

יוֹרֶה 3.0.2 n.[m.]—Sam יוֹרֶא—**early rain,** from end of October to beginning of December Dt 11_{14}. → ירה II *water.*

יוֹרַי 1 pr.n.m. **Jorai.**

יוֹרָם 20 pr.n.m. **Joram.**

יוּשַׁב חֶסֶד 1 pr.n.m. **Jushab-hesed.**

יוֹשַׁבְיָה, see יוֹשַׁוְיָה *Joshaviah.*

יוֹשִׁבְיָה 1 pr.n.m. **Joshibiah.**

יוֹשָׁה 1 pr.n.m. **Joshah.**

יוֹשַׁוְיָה 1 pr.n.m. **Joshaviah.**

יוֹשָׁפָט 2 pr.n.m. **Joshaphat.**

יוֹתָם 24 pr.n.m. **Jotham.**

יושר, see יֹשֶׁר *uprightness.*

יוֹתֵר 9.5.2.1 n.m.—יֹתֵר—**1. remainder, surplus** 1 S 15_{15}. **2. excess, abundance** of wealth Si 10_{27}; חיי יותר *life of abundance* Si $40_{18(Bmg, M)}$. **3. advantage, superiority,** כִּי מַה־יּוֹתֵר לֶחָכָם *for what advantage does the wise one have?* Ec 6_{8}. **4.** as adv., **a. excessively, too (much)** Ec 7_{16}. **b.** יוֹתֵר מִן (1) **more than** Est 6_{6}. (2) **too much for, beyond,** אל תערב יתר ממך *do not stand surety too much for you,* i.e. beyond your means Si 8_{13}. **c.** -יוֹתֵר שֶׁ **besides** Ec 12_{9}. → יתר *exceed.*

*[יְזֶבֶל] 0.0.0.1 pr.n.[f.] **Jezebel.**

יזואל, see יְזִיאֵל *Jeziel.*

[יְזִיאֵל] 1 pr.n.m. **Jeziel.**

יִזִּיָּה 1 pr.n.m. **Izziah.**

יָזִיז 1 pr.n.m. **Jaziz.**

יִזְלִיאָה 1 pr.n.m. **Izliah.**

יזן 1 vb.—**Pu.** 1 Ptc. מְיֻזָּנִים—appar. **be aroused sexually, be on heat,** of horse Jr 5_8.

[יְזַנְיָה], see יְזַנְיָהוּ *Jezaniah.*

יְזַנְיָהוּ 2 pr.n.m. **Jezaniah.**

[יֶזַע] 1 n.[m.]—יֶזַע—**sweat,** i.e. clothes that cause sweat Ezk 44_{18}. → cf. ידע V *sweat.*

יִזְרָח 1 gent. **Izrahite.**

יִזְרַחְיָה 3 pr.n.m. **Izrahiah.**

יִזְרְעֶאל I 2 pr.n.m. **Jezreel.**

יִזְרְעֶאל II 34 pl.n. **Jezreel.**

יִזְרְעֵאלִי 13 gent. **Jezreelite.**

[יְחֻבָּה], see יְחֻבָּה *Jehubbah.*

[יְחֻבָּה] 1 pr.n.m. **Jehubbah.**

יחד 3.1.10 vb.—**Qal** 2.1 Impf. תֵּחַד—**be united, come together, join with** person(s), with בְּ Gn 49_6, אֶת Is 14_{20}, עִם Si 34_{14}(Bmg).

Ni. 0.0.7 Impf. יוחד; inf. להוחד, ליחד—**be united, join with** (לְ) Qumran congregation 1QS 5_{20}, with (בְּ) Qumran council 1QS 1_8, with (עִם) wife 4QInstr[b] 2.4_5.

Pi. 1 Impv. יַחֵד—**unite heart,** יַחֵד לְבָבִי לְיִרְאָה שְׁמֶךָ *unite my heart,* i.e. give me an undivided heart, *to fear your name* Ps 86_{11}.

Hi. 0.0.2 Inf. להחיד—**be united, join with** (לְ) Y. 4QWorks 1_2, with (עִם) sons of heaven 1QH fr. 2.1_{10}.

Htp. 0.0.1 Impf. תתיחד—perh. **be declared as one,** תתיחד מלכי מפי כל משרתך *may your unity be declared, O my king, from the mouth of each of your servants* GnzPs 4_{12}.

→ יַחַד *unity,* יַחְדָּו *together,* יָחִיד *only.*

יַחַד 45.1.168 n.[m.]—יַחַד—**1. unity** 1 C 12_{18}; יחד כול אנשי סודי *unity of all the men of my counsel* 1QH 6_{18}. **2. community,** esp. Qumran community, אנשי היחד *men of the community* 1QS 5_1. **3.** as adv., **(all) together,** in ref. to **a.** proximity or unity, יַחַד שִׁבְטֵי יִשְׂרָאֵל *the tribes of Israel were together* Dt 33_5. **b.** inclusiveness or entirety, i.e. **both ... and, (both/all) alike, both/all (of them, etc.),** יַחַד עָשִׁיר וְאֶבְיוֹן *both rich and poor* Ps 49_3. **c.** exclusivity, i.e. **alone,** אֲנַחְנוּ יַחַד נִבְנֶה *we alone will build (it)* Ezr 4_3. **d.** degree, i.e. **altogether, utterly, entirely,** יַחַד נִכְמְרוּ נִחוּמָי *my tenderness is entirely stirred* Ho 11_8; with neg., **at all,** יַחַד לֹא יְרוֹמֵם *he does not raise (them) up at all* Ho 11_7. **e.** time, (1) **at the same time,** אֶשֹּׁם וְאֶשְׁאַף יָחַד *I will gasp and pant at the same time* Is 42_{14}. (2) **at once,** יִגְוַע כָּל־בָּשָׂר יָחַד *all flesh would expire at once* Jb 34_{15}. **f.** association, יַחַד **together,** מלאכי קודש עם צבאותם יחד *angels of holiness together with their armies* 1QM 7_6. → יחד *be united.*

יַחְדָּו 98.4.6 adv.—יַחְדָּיו—**together,** in ref. to, **1.** proximity or unity, **(all) together, as one,** יַחְדָּו הֵמָּה עַל־יְהוּדָה *together they are against Judah* Is 9_{20}. **2.** inclusiveness or entirety, i.e. **both ... and, (both/all) alike, both/all (of them, etc.),** הַטָּמֵא וְהַטָּהוֹר יַחְדָּו יֹאכְלֶנּוּ *the unclean and the clean alike shall eat of it* Dt 12_{22}. **3.** exclusivity, i.e. **alone,** אֲנַחְנוּ יַחְדָּו *we were alone* 1 K 3_{18}. **4.** degree, i.e. **altogether, utterly,** פֹּשְׁעִים נִשְׁמְדוּ יַחְדָּו *transgressors shall be utterly destroyed* Ps 37_{38}. **5.** association, **together,** לֹא־תַחֲרֹשׁ בְּשׁוֹר־וּבַחֲמֹר יַחְדָּו *you shall not plough with an ox and an ass together* Dt 22_{10}. **6.** (almost) contemporaneous activity, modifying two verbs, **both,** יַחְדָּו אֶשְׁכְּבָה וְאִישָׁן *I both lie down and sleep* Ps 4_9. → יחד *be united.*

יַחְדּוֹ 1 pr.n.m. **Jahdo.**

יַחְדִּיאֵל 1 pr.n.m. **Jahdiel.**

יֶחְדְּיָהוּ 2 pr.n.m. **Jehdeiah.**

יחואל, see יְחִיאֵל *Jehiel.*

[יְחוֹעֵלִי]* 0.0.0.1 pr.n.[m.] **Jehoeli.**

[יַחֲזָא]* 0.0.0.1 pr.n.[m.] **Jahaza.**

יַחֲזִיאֵל 6 pr.n.m. **Jahaziel.**

יַחְזְיָה 1.0.0.1 pr.n.m. **Jahzeiah.**

יחזיהו, see יַחְזְיָה *Jahzeiah.*

[יְחָזָק]* 0.0.0.1 pr.n.[m.] **Johazak.**

יְחֶזְקֵאל 3.1.14 pr.n.m. **Ezekiel.**

יְחִזְקִיָּה, see חִזְקִיָּהוּ *Hezekiah.*

יְחִזְקִיָּהוּ, see חִזְקִיָּהוּ *Hezekiah.*

יַחְזֵרָה 1 pr.n.m. **Jahzerah.**

[יְחִי]* 0.0.0.1 pr.n.[m.] **Jehi.**

יְחִיאֵל 14 pr.n.m. **Jehiel.**

יְחִיאֵלִי 2 pr.n.m. **Jehieli.**

יָחִיד 12.0.7 adj.—sf. יְחִידְךָ; f.s. יְחִידָה; sf. יְחִידָתִי; m.pl. יְחִידִים; sf. Q יחידיהן—**1. only,** as noun, **only one,** in ref. to son Gn 22_2, daughter Jg 11_{34}; יְחִידָתִי **my only**

one, i.e. my life Ps 22_{21}. 2. **lonely, solitary,** a. יָחִיד וְעָנִי אָנִי *I am lonely and afflicted* Ps 25_{16}. b. as noun, **solitary one** Ps 68_7. 3. **unique,** מה הואה יחיד *how unique is he?* 4QInstr[c] 2.1$_6$. → יחד *be united.*

[יְחִיָּה] 1 pr.n.m. **Jehiah.**

יחיהו, see יְחִיָּה *Jehiah.*

יָחִיל 1 n.[m.] **waiting** Lm 3_{26}. → יחל I *wait.*

יחל I 41.0.7 vb.—**Ni.** 2 Pf. נוֹחָלָה; + waw וַיִּיָּחֶל—**wait,** וַיִּיָּחֶל עוֹד שִׁבְעַת יָמִים אֲחֵרִים *and he waited another seven days* Gn 8_{12}.

Pi. 24.0.5 Pf. יִחַלְנוּ, יִחֲלוּ; impf. אֲיַחֵלָה, יְיַחֵל; impv. יַחֵל; ptc. מְיַחֵל, מְיַחֲלִים—**1a. wait for, hope in,** with לְ *for, in* Y. Ps 31_{25}, human being Mc 5_6, healing CD 8_4; אֶל *for, in* Y. Ps 131_3. b. abs., **hope, have hope** Ps 71_{14}. 2. **cause** someone **to hope** Ps 119_{49}.

Hi. 15.0.2 Pf. הוֹחַלְתִּי; impf. אוֹחִיל, תּוֹחֵל; + waw וַיּוֹחֶל; impv. הוֹחִילִי—**wait for, hope in** (לְ) Y. Mc 7_7, Y.'s word Ps 130_5. 2. abs., **wait,** תּוֹחֵל שִׁבְעַת יָמִים *you shall wait seven days* 1 S 10_8.

→ יָחִיל *waiting,* תּוֹחֲלָה *hope,* תּוֹחֶלֶת *hope.*

*יחל II 4.1.1 vb.—**Ni.** 1.1 Pf. נוֹחָלָה; ptc. Si נוחל—**1. be desperate, uncertain,** of hope Ezk 19_5. 2. **wrestle** with (עִם) someone Si $37_{5(Bmg)}$.

Hi. 3 Pf. הוֹחַלְתִּי; impf. אוֹחִיל—**despair** Jb 32_{11} (+ לְ *on account of*) Lm 3_{21}.

Ho. 0.0.1 Ptc. Q מוחלה—**be sick** 11QM 1.2$_{12}$.

יַחְלְאֵל 2 pr.n.m. **Jahleel.**

יַחְלְאֵלִי 1 gent. **Jahleelite.**

יחם 6 vb.—**Qal** 2 + waw וַיֵּחַמְנָה, וַיֶּחֱמוּ—**be in heat, conceive,** of flock Gn $30_{38.39}$.

Pi. 4 Impf. יֶחֱמַתְנִי; inf. cstr. יַחֵם (יַחְמֵנָה)—**conceive,** of woman Ps 51_7, flock Gn 30_{41}.

→ cf. חמם *be warm,* חמה II *be hot.*

יַחְמוּר 2 n.[m.] **roebuck** Dt 14_5 1 K 5_3.

יַחְמַי 1 pr.n.m. **Jahmai.**

*[יְחָמָל] 0.0.0.1 pr.n.[m.] **Johamal.**

*[יַחְמַלְיָהוּ] 0.0.0.2 pr.n.[m.] **Jahmaliah.**

*יחן 0.1 vb.—**Qal** 0.1 Impf. ייחן—**dwell** Si 4_{15}.

*[יֹחָן] 0.0.0.1 pr.n.[m.] **Johan.**

*[יֹחָנֵה] 0.0.1 pr.n.m. **Jannes.**

*[יְחָנֵנִי] 0.0.0.1 pr.n.[m.] **Jehonneni.**

יָחֵף 5 adj. **barefoot,** used predicatively with הלך *go* 2 S 15_{30}.

יַחְצְאֵל 3 pr.n.m. **Jahzeel.**

יַחְצְאֵלִי 1 gent. **Jahzeelite.**

יַחְצָה, see יַחַץ *Jahaz.*

יַחֲצִיאֵל, see יַחְצְאֵל *Jahzeel.*

יחר, see אחר *delay.*

יחשׂ 20 vb.—**Htp.** 20 Pf. הִתְיַחֲשׂוּ; ptc. מִתְיַחְשִׂים; inf. הִתְיַחֵשׂ (הִתְיַחְשָׂם)—**1. be genealogically registered, register oneself, be enrolled** Ne 7_5. 2. inf. as noun, a. **(genealogical) registration** 2 C 31_{17}. b. **registered person** 2 C 31_{19}. 3. ptc. pl. as noun, perh. as title of document, **those who are registered** Ezr 2_{62}. → יַחַשׂ *genealogy.*

יַחַשׂ 1.0.3 n.[m.]—Q יחוש (Q יחוס); pl. Q יחשים—**genealogy, (genealogical) registration,** סֵפֶר הַיַּחַשׂ *document of registration* Ne 7_5. → יחשׂ *register.*

יַחַת 8 pr.n.m. **Jahath.**

יטב 114.8.2.1 vb.—**Qal** 44.0.1 Impf. יִיטַב (יִטַב)—**1.** subj. impers., **go well for** (לְ) someone Gn 12_{13} Ru 3_1. **2.** of word, matter, etc., **be pleasing,** usu. with בְּעֵינֵי *in the sight of* Gn 34_{18} Lv 10_{19}; also with לְ *to* Ps 69_{32} (+ מִן *more* pleasing *than*), לִפְנֵי *before* Est 5_{14}. **3.** of person, **find favour,** with בְּעֵינֵי *in the sight of* Est 2_4, לִפְנֵי *before* Ne 2_5. **4.** of heart, **be glad, merry** Ru 3_7. **5.** יטב מִן **be (in a) better (position) than,** הֲתֵיטְבִי מִנֹּא אָמוֹן *are you (in a) better (position) than No-amon?* Na 3_8.

Hi. 70.8.1.1 Pf. הֵיטַבְתָּ, הֵיטִיב; impf. יֵיטִיב (יֵיטִב, יֵיטִיב, יֵיטֵב); impv. הֵיטִיבָה, הֵיטִיבוּ; ptc. מֵיטִיב, מֵיטִיבִים; inf. abs. הֵיטֵב; cstr. הֵיטִיב—**1a. do good to, deal well with, act benevolently toward** someone, with לְ *to* Gn 12_{16}, עִם *with* Gn 32_{10}. b. with accus., **benefit** person Jb 24_{21}, nation Jr 18_{10}. **2.** ethically, abs., **do good, do right,** לִמְדוּ הֵיטֵב *learn to do right* Is 1_{17}. **3. prosper,** וְיוֹדֻךָ כִּי־תֵיטִיב לָךְ *and they praise you when you prosper* Ps 49_{19}. **4. be good, pleasing,** יֵיטַב אֶל־אָבִי אֶת־הָרָעָה עָלֶיךָ *it is pleasing to my father to do you harm* 1 S 20_{13}. **5. make good,** i.e. **improve** knowledge Pr 15_2, **amend** one's ways, deeds Jr 7_3, **direct** one's way Jr 2_{33}, **beautify** head 2 K 9_{30}, **dress** lamp Ex 30_7; **make better, greater than** (מִן) 1 K 1_{47}. **6. make glad, merry** one's heart Jg 19_{22}, countenance

Pr 15₁₃. **7a. do well, do thoroughly, be skilful,** מֵטִב נַגֵּן *(he) plays music skilfully* Ezk 33₃₂. **b.** inf. abs. הֵיטֵב as adv., **well, thoroughly, utterly** Dt 9₂₁ 13₁₅.

→ מֵיטָב *best;* cf. טוב *be good.*

יָטְבָה 1 pl.n. **Jotbah.**

יָטְבָתָה 3 pl.n. **Jotbathah.**

יֻטָּה 2 pl.n. **Juttah.**

יְטוּר 3 pr.n.m. **Jetur.**

יטשׁ* 2 vb.—**Qal** 2 + waw וַיִּטְּשֵׁהוּ, וַתִּטֹּשׁ—**1. clash,** i.e. be joined with a clash, of battle 1 S 4₂. **2. dash** cedar Ezk 31₁₂.

יַיִן 141.17.17.31 n.m.—יָיִן; sf. יֵינוֹ—**1. wine** Gn 9₂₁; יין חדש *new wine* 11QT 19₁₄, יין ישן *old wine* Samaria ost. 5₃, יֵין הָרֶקַח *spiced wine* Ca 8₂(Gnz), חֹמֶץ יַיִן *vinegar made from wine* Nm 6₃. **2. wine-induced stupor** Gn 9₂₄.

יכה* 1 vb.—**Ho.** 1 Impf. תֻּכּוּ—**crouch** Dt 33₃.

יְכָונְיָה, see יְכָנְיָה *Jeconiah.*

יכח 59.2.37 vb.—**Ni.** 3.1 Impf. נִוָּכְחָה; ptc. נוֹכָח, נֹכַחַת—**1a. be justified** Gn 20₁₆ (+ אֵת perh. *in the presence of* all). **b.** appar. **be acquitted** Jb 23₇ (+ עִם *with,* i.e. by, Y.). **2. be adjudged, be understood** Si 6₂₂(B) (+ לְ *by* many). **3. reason together** Is 1₁₈.

Hi. 54.1.36 Pf. הוֹכִיחַ, הוֹכַחְתָּ; impf. יוֹכִיחַ (יוכח); + waw וַיּוֹכַח; impv. הוֹכַח; ptc. מוֹכִיחַ; inf. abs. הוֹכֵחַ; cstr. הוֹכִיחַ—**1a. reprove** someone, (1) with accus., subj. Y. Jb 22₄, person Gn 21₂₅. (2) with לְ of obj. Pr 9₇. **b. argue** against (אֶל) God Jb 13₃. **c. correct** words Jb 6₂₆. **2a. give justice to** (לְ) people Is 2₄. **b. administer justice** 1 C 12₁₈. **c. decide by** (לְ) what one hears Is 11₃. **d. declare, acknowledge (as just)** Y.'s judgment 1QS 10₁₁. **e. plead, defend oneself** with regard to (עַל) sin 1QH 9₂₅. **3. appoint** wife for (לְ) someone, of Y. Gn 24₄₄. **4.** ptc. as noun, **one who reproves, arbiter** Am 5₁₀. **5.** inf. appar. as noun, **reproof, rebuke,** וּמַה־יּוֹכִיחַ הוֹכֵחַ מִכֶּם *but how does reproof from you reprove?* Jb 6₂₅.

Ho. 1 Pf. הוּכַח—**be reproved by** (בְּ) pain Jb 33₁₉.

Htp. 1.0.1 Impf. יִתְוַכָּח; inf. Q התוכח—**1. argue with** (עִם) Israel, of Y. Mc 6₂. **2.** inf. as noun, **argument, controversy** 4QapPsB 76₁₀.

→ תּוֹכֵחָה *reproof,* תּוֹכַחַת *reproof.*

יכיליה, see יְכָלְיָהוּ *Jecoliah.*

יָכִין 8.0.6 pr.n.m. **Jachin.**

יָכִינִי 1 gent. **Jachinite.**

יכל 207.4.19.1 vb.—**Qal** 207.4.19.1 Pf. יָכֹל (יָכוֹל), יָכֹלְתִּי; impf. יוּכַל; + waw וַיָּכָל, וַיְכָלְתְּ; inf. abs. יָכֹל (יָכוֹל); cstr. יְכֹלֶת—**1. be able** to do something, in ref. to **a.** physical ability, לוֹא אוּכַל לָקוּם מִפָּנֶיךָ כִּי־דֶרֶךְ נָשִׁים לִי *I am not able to stand up before you, because the way of women is upon me,* i.e. I am having my period Gn 31₃₅, מַיִם רַבִּים לֹא יוּכְלוּ לְכַבּוֹת אֶת־הָאַהֲבָה *vast floods cannot quench love* Ca 8₇. **b.** what is permitted by custom or law, לֹא נוּכַל לַעֲשׂוֹת הַדָּבָר הַזֶּה ... כִּי־חֶרְפָּה הִוא לָנוּ *we are not able to do this ..., because it is a disgrace among us* Gn 34₁₄. **c.** will, הַבִּיט אֶל־עָמָל לֹא תוּכָל *you cannot countenance,* i.e. tolerate, *wrongdoing* Hb 1₁₃. **2. be capable of, attain,** יָדַעְתִּי כִּי־כֹל תּוּכָל *I know that you are capable of everything* Jb 42₂(Qr). **3. endure, a.** trans., obj. person Ps 101₅, thing Is 1₁₃. **b.** intrans. Est 8₆. **4a. prevail, succeed,** of Y. Jr 20₇, Israel Jr 3₅. **b. prevail against** (לְ) someone Jg 16₅. **c. overcome** (accus.) enemy Ps 13₅.

יְכָלְיָה, see יְכָלְיָהוּ *Jecoliah.*

יְכָלְיָהוּ 2 pr.n.f. **Jecoliah.**

יְכָנְיָה 7.0.0.1 pr.n.m. **Jeconiah.**

יְכָנְיָהוּ, see יְכָנְיָה *Jeconiah.*

ילד 495.7.39 vb.—**Qal** 241.3.23 Pf. יָלַד, יְלִדְתַּנִי; impf. יֵלֵד, תֵּלֵד; + waw 3fs וַתֵּלֶד; ptc. יֹלֵד, יֹלֶדֶת, יֹלַדְתְּ (יוֹלֵדָה, יֹלֵדָה), יֹלְדוֹת; ptc. pass. יָלוּד, יְלוּדִים; inf. abs. יָלֹד; cstr. לֶדֶת, לָלֶדֶת, לְלִדְתָּהּ (לְלֵדָה)—**1a. bear, give birth to,** usu. of woman bearing child Gn 3₁₆ 4₂₅ 16₁ (+ לְ *to* husband); also of animals bearing young Gn 30₃₉; of bird, **lay (eggs),** קֹרֵא דָגַר וְלֹא יָלָד *a partridge incubating what she did not lay* Jr 17₁₁. **b. give birth to, bring forth** wind, i.e. nothing (subj. Israel) Is 26₁₈, iniquity (subj. the wicked) Jb 15₃₅. **c.** of day, **produce** events Pr 27₁. **d. issue** statute Zp 2₂. **e.** perh. **be born,** עֵת לָלֶדֶת וְעֵת לָמוּת *a time to be born, and a time to die* Ec 3₂. **2. beget,** of father Gn 4₁₈, eponymous ancestor Gn 10₁₅, Y. as father Ps 2₇. **3.** ptc. as noun, **one who bears,** חֶבְלֵי יוֹלֵדָה *labour pains of one who bears (a child)* Ho 13₁₃. **4a.** pass., **be born,** הואה המולד אשר הוא ילוד עליו *this is the birthday on which he was born* 4QCrypt 1.2₈. **b.** pass. ptc. as noun, one who is born, child 1 K 3₂₆ Jb 14₁.

Ni. 36.2.8 Pf. נוֹלַד; impf. יִוָּלֵד; ptc. נוֹלָד, נוֹלָדִים; inf. הִוָּלֵד (הִוָּלְדוֹ)—**1. be born,** usu. of person Gn 4₁₈ (+ לְ to father); of nation Is 66₈, animal Lv 22₂₇. **2.** perh. **become,** אִישׁ נָבוּב יִלָּבֵב וְעַיִר פֶּרֶא אָדָם יִוָּלֵד *a hollow man will get understanding, when a wild ass becomes a man* Jb 11₁₂. **2.** ptc. as noun, **one who is born** Ezr 10₃.

Nu. 2 Pf. נוּלְּדוּ—**be born,** of persons 1 C 3₅.

Pi. 10.0.1 Impf. Q יילד; ptc. מְיַלֶּדֶת, מְיַלְּדֹת; inf. יַלֶּדְכֶן—**1. assist in delivery,** obj. woman Ex 1₁₆, animal CD 11₁₃. **2.** ptc. as noun, **midwife** Gn 35₁₇.

Pu. 27 Pf. יֻלַּד; ptc. יוּלָּד (unless **Qal Pass.**)—**1. be born,** of person Gn 4₂₄ (+ לְ *to* father). **2. be descended (from),** גַּם־הוּא יֻלַּד לְהָרָפָה *he also was descended from the giants* 2 S 21₂₀. **3. come into being,** of mountains Ps 90₂.

Hi. 176.2.7 Pf. הוֹלִיד, הוֹלַדְתְּ; impf. יוֹלִיד; + waw וַיּוֹלֶד; ptc. מוֹלִיד, מוֹלִדִים; inf. abs. הוֹלֵיד; cstr. הוֹלִידוֹ—**1a. beget,** of father begetting child Gn 5₄ 1 C 8₉ (+ מִן *by* wife). **b.** of Y., **bring about birth** Is 66₉. **2. bring forth** iniquity Is 59₄.

Ho. 3 Inf. הֻלֶּדֶת—**be born,** יוֹם הוּלֶּדֶת אֹתָךְ *day of your birth* Ezk 16₄.

Htp. 1 + waw וַיִּתְיַלְדוּ—**register genealogy** according to (עַל) clan Nm 1₁₈.

→ יֶלֶד *child,* וָלָד *child,* יַלְדָּה *girl,* יִלּוֹד *born,* יָלִיד *born,* יַלְדוּת *youth,* לֵדָה *birth,* מוֹלָד *birth,* מוֹלֶדֶת *offspring,* תּוֹלֵדוֹת *generations.*

יֶלֶד 89.2.4 n.m.—יָלֶד; pl. יְלָדִים; cstr. יַלְדֵי; sf. יְלָדָיו, יַלְדֵיהֶן—**1a. male child** Ex 1₁₇; as distinct from יַלְדָּה *girl* Jl 4₃. **b. youth, young man** 1 K 12₈‖2 C 10₈ Dn 1₄. **c. unborn child, foetus** Ex 21₂₂. **2. young** of birds and wild animals Jb 38₄₁ 39₃. → ילד *give birth.*

יַלְדָּה 3.0.1 n.f.—pl. יְלָדוֹת—**girl,** as child Zc 8₅, of marriageable age Gn 34₄. → ילד *give birth.*

יַלְדוּת 3 n.f.—sf. יַלְדוּתֶיךָ (יַלְדֻתֶיךָ)—**1. youth,** as period of life Ec 11₉.₁₀. **2. young men** Ps 110₃. → ילד *give birth.*

ילה 1 vb.—**Qal** 1 + waw וַתֵּלַהּ—**be anxious, distressed** on account of (מִפְּנֵי) famine, of land Gn 47₁₃.

יִלּוֹד 6 adj.—pl. יִלּוֹדִים—**born,** of people Jos 5₅ (+ בְּ *in* place), son 2 S 12₁₄ (+ לְ *to* someone). → ילד *give birth.*

יָלוֹן 1 pr.n.m. **Jalon.**

[יָלִיד] 13 adj.—cstr. יְלִיד; pl. יְלִידֵי—**born,** as noun, **1. one (who is) born,** יְלִיד בַּיִת *one born of,* i.e. to, *a household,* i.e. home-born slave Gn 17₁₂. **2. descendant** of Anak Nm 13₂₂, the Rephaim 1 C 20₄. → ילד *give birth.*

ילל 27.0.2 vb.—**Hi.** 27.0.2 Impf. יְיֵלִיל; + waw וְהֵילַל; impv. הֵילִילוּ, הֵילֵל—**howl, wail, lament,** of persons Jl 1₁₁ (+ עַל *over, for*), tree Zc 11₂, gate Is 14₃₁, ship Is 23₁. → יְלֵל *howling,* יְלָלָה *howling,* (?) תּוֹלָל *tormentor.*

יְלֵל 1 n.[m.] **howling,** יְלֵל יְשִׁמֹן *howling of,* i.e. heard in, *the wilderness* Dt 32₁₀. → ילל *howl.*

יְלָלָה 5 n.f.—cstr. יִלְלַת; sf. יִלְלָתָהּ—**howling** Is 15₈. → ילל *howl.*

יָלַע, see לעע *be rash.*

יַלֶּפֶת 2 n.f. **scab,** disqualifying priests from serving Lv 21₂₀, animals from being sacrificed Lv 22₂₂.

יֶלֶק 9 n.m. **locust,** coll. Jl 1₄.

יַלְקוּט 1 n.[m.] **pouch,** carried by shepherd 1 S 17₄₀. → לקט *gather.*

יָם 392.2.35 n.m.—cstr. יָם (יַם); + ה- of direction יָמָּה; sf. יַמָּהּ; pl. יַמִּים—**1. sea,** in general, opp. land, sky Gn 1₂₆; perh. personified as a deity, **Yam,** הֲיָם־אָנִי אִם־תַּנִּין *am I Yam or the sea monster?* Jb 7₁₂. **2.** particular **sea, a.** הַיָּם הַגָּדוֹל *the Great Sea,* i.e. Mediterranean Sea Nm 34₆, also called הַיָּם הָאַחֲרוֹן *the Western Sea* Dt 11₂₄, and יַם פְּלִשְׁתִּים *Sea of the Philistines* Ex 23₃₁; as the direction, **west,** יָמָּה *to(wards) the west* Gn 13₁₄, פְּאַת־יָם *western side* Ex 27₁₂. **b.** יָם הַמֶּלַח *Sea of Salt,* i.e. Dead Sea Gn 14₃, also called יָם הָעֲרָבָה *Sea of the Arabah* Dt 3₁₇, הַיָּם הַקַּדְמוֹנִי *the Eastern Sea* Zc 14₈. **c.** יַם־סוּף *Sea of Reeds,* perh. Red Sea Ex 13₁₈. **d.** יָם־כִּנֶּרֶת *Sea of Chinnereth,* i.e. Sea of Galilee Nm 34₁₁ Jos 12₃ (כִּנְרוֹת *Chinneroth*). **3. basin** in temple, יָם הַנְּחֹשֶׁת *basin of bronze* 2 K 25₁₃. **4. tank, vat** 3QTr 10₈.

יְמוּאֵל 2 pr.n.m. **Jemuel.**

[יְמוֹנִי], see יְמָנִי *right.*

יְמִימָה 1 pr.n.f. **Jemimah.**

יָמִין I 139.3.26.1 n.f.—cstr. יְמִין; sf. יְמִינִי—**1.** oft. **right, right-hand side,** אַל־תָּסוּר מִמֶּנּוּ יָמִין וּשְׂמֹאול *do not deviate from it* (the law) *to the right or to the left* Jos 1₇, הַיָּמִין

שׁוֹק *thigh of the right-hand side,* i.e. right thigh Ex 29$_{22}$||Lv 8$_{25}$. **2.** perh. specif. **south,** מִימִין הַיְשִׁימוֹן *to the south of Jeshimon* 1 S 23$_{19}$, צָפוֹן וְיָמִין *north and south* Ps 89$_{13}$. **3. right hand, a.** of human being Gn 48$_{13}$. **b.** of Y. Is 41$_{10}$. → ימן *go to right;* cf. יְמָנִי *right.*

יָמִין II $_{6}$ pr.n.m. **Jamin.**

*[יָמִין] III $_{1}$ adj. **propitious,** וּשְׁמָהּ יָמִין יִקָּרֵא the north is a harsh wind *but its name is called propitious* Pr 27$_{16}$ (if em. וְשֶׁמֶן יְמִינוֹ יִקְרָא whoever encloses a contentious woman encloses the wind *and his right hand encounters oil*).

*[יָמִין] IV $_{2}$ n.[m.] **oath,** יְמִינָם יְמִין שָׁקֶר *their oath is an oath of deceit* Ps 144$_{8.11}$.

יָמִינִי $_{1}$ gent. **Jaminite.**

יְמִינִי I $_{4}$ gent. **Benjaminite.**

[יְמִינִי] II, see יְמָנִי *right.*

יַמְלֵךְ $_{1}$ pr.n.m. **Jamlech.**

יֵמִם $_{1}$ n.[m.] perh. **hot spring(s)** or **mule(s)** or **marsh fish(es)** or **snake(s)** Gn 36$_{24}$.

ימן $_{5}$ vb.—**Hi.** $_{5}$ Impf. תַּאֲמִינוּ, אֵימִינָה; impv. הֵימִינוּ; ptc. מַיְמִינִים; inf. הֵמִין—**1. go to right (side), stay on right (side)** Gn 13$_{9}$. **2. be right-handed** 1 C 12$_{2}$. → יָמִין I *right (side),* יְמָנִי *right,* תֵּימָן I *south.*

יִמְנָה $_{5}$ pr.n.m. **Imnah.**

יְמָנִי $_{33.0.2}$ adj.—Kt ימוני, ימיני; f.s. יְמָנִית—**1a. right,** רַגְלוֹ הַיְמָנִית *his right foot* Lv 14$_{14}$. **b. southern,** הָעַמּוּד הַיְמָנִי *the southern column* 1 K 7$_{21}$. **2.** as noun, **a. right-hand one** 1 C 3$_{17(Qr)}$. **b. southern one** 2 C 4$_{10}$. → ימן *go to right.*

יִמְנָע $_{1}$ pr.n.m. **Imna.**

ימר I, see אמר htp. *boast.*

ימר II, see מור hi. *exchange.*

יִמְרָה $_{1}$ pr.n.m. **Imrah.**

ימשׁ $_{1}$ vb.—**Hi.** $_{1}$ Impv. הֲיִמִשֵׁנִי—**let** Samson **feel** pillars Jg 16$_{26}$. → cf. משׁשׁ I *feel,* מושׁ II *feel.*

ינה $_{19.0.3}$ vb.—**Qal** $_{5}$ Impf. נִינָם; ptc. f.s. יוֹנָה—**1. oppress, treat violently** Ps 74$_{8}$. **2.** ptc. as noun, **oppressor** Jr 25$_{38}$.

Hi. $_{14.0.3}$ Pf. הוֹנָה, Q הוניתה, הוֹנוּ; impf. יוֹנֶה, תּוֹנוּ; ptc. מוֹנַיִךְ; inf. הוֹנָתָם—**oppress** people Ezk 45$_{8}$, widow Jr 22$_{3}$, poor Ezk 18$_{12}$.

→ מַתָּנָה II *violence.*

יָנוֹחַ $_{3}$ pl.n. **Janoah.**

יָנוּם $_{1}$ pl.n. **Janum.**

[יְנִיקָה] $_{1}$ n.f. **shoot,** רֹאשׁ יְנִיקוֹתָיו *head of its shoots,* i.e. topmost twigs Ezk 17$_{4}$. → ינק *suck.*

ינק $_{31.0.4}$ vb.—**Qal** $_{16.0.3}$ Impf. יִינָק; + waw וַתִּינָקִי; ptc. יוֹנֵק, יֹנְקִים, יוֹנְקֵיו; inf. Q לינוק—**1. suck breast** Ca 8$_{1}$, milk Is 60$_{16}$. **2.** masc. ptc., יוֹנֵק, as noun, **a. (male) infant, suckling child** Jl 2$_{16}$. **b. shoot** Is 53$_{2}$. **3.** fem. ptc., יֹנֶקֶת, as noun, **shoot** Ho 14$_{7}$.

Hi. $_{15.0.1}$ Pf. הֵינִיקָה; impf. תֵּינִק; + waw וַיֵּנִקֵהוּ; impv. הֵינִקֵהוּ; ptc. מֵינִיקוֹת, (מֵינִקְתּוֹ) מֵינֶקֶת; inf. הֵינִיק—**1. suckle** child (subj. woman) Gn 21$_{7}$, cub (subj. jackal) Lm 4$_{3}$. **2.** with double accus., **feed** Israel **with** honey and oil (subj. Y.) Dt 32$_{13}$. **3.** fem. ptc., מֵינֶקֶת, as noun, **(wet-) nurse** Gn 35$_{8}$.

→ יְנִיקָה *shoot.*

יַנְשׁוּף $_{3}$ n.m.—יַנְשׁוֹף—perh. **screech owl,** unclean bird Lv 11$_{17}$. → נשׁף *blow.*

יסד I $_{41.2.16}$ vb.—**Qal** $_{19.1.11}$ Pf. יְסַדְתָּ, (יְסָדָהּ) יָסַד; ptc. יֹסֵד; inf. יְסוֹד (יְסֹדוֹ, יְסֹד)—**1. establish, found** heavens and earth Ps 89$_{12}$, land Is 23$_{13}$, temple Ezr 3$_{12}$, person 1QH 13$_{9}$, Y.'s commandments Ps 119$_{152}$. **2. educate** people Si 10$_{1}$. **3. accumulate** heaps 2 C 31$_{7}$.

Ni. $_{2.0.2}$ Impf. תִּוָּסֵד; inf. הִוָּסְדָהּ—**be established,** of temple Is 44$_{28}$, Egypt Ex 9$_{18}$.

Pi. $_{10.1.3}$ Pf. יִסַּד, יִסְּדָהּ; impf. Si. תיסד—**1. establish** Zion Is 14$_{32}$. **2.** perh. **re-establish, repair** temple Ezr 3$_{10}$. **3. ordain** gatekeepers 1 C 9$_{22}$. **4. decree,** כֵּן יִסַּד הַמֶּלֶךְ *thus the king had decreed* Est 1$_{8}$.

Pu. $_{7}$ Pf. יֻסַּד; ptc. מְיֻסָּד—**1a. be established, be set,** of pillars Ca 5$_{15}$. **b.** perh. **be re-established, be repaired,** of temple Hg 2$_{18}$. **2.** ptc. as noun, **foundation** of stones 1 K 7$_{10}$.

Ho. $_{3}$ Ptc. מוּסָד; inf. הוּסַד—**be established,** מוּסָד מוּסָּד *a (well-)established foundation* Is 28$_{16}$.

→ יְסֹד *establishment,* יְסוֹד *foundation,* יְסוּדָה *foundation,* מוֹסָד *foundation,* מוּסָד *foundation,* מוֹסָדָה *foundation,* מַסָּד *foundation,* סוֹד II *foundation.*

יסד II $_{2}$ vb.—**Ni.** $_{2}$ Pf. נוֹסְדוּ; inf. הִוָּסְדָם—**conspire** against (עַל) Ps 2$_{2}$ 31$_{14}$.

[יְסֹד] $_{1}$ n.m. **establishment** Ezr 7$_{9}$. → יסד I *establish.*

יְסוֹד 20.1.22 n.m.—Q ישוד; sf. יְסֹדוֹ; pl. Q יסודים, יסודות; cstr. Si, Q יסודי; sf. יְסוֹדֹתֶיהָ—**1a. foundation, base** of altar Ex 29_{12}, the world Si 16_{19}. **b. re-establishment, repair** of temple 2 C 24_{27}. **2a. founding principle** of covenant CD 10_{6}. **b. authority** of the community 1QS 7_{17}. **c.** perh. **pillar** of congregation 1QSa 1_{12}. **3.** perh. **thigh** Hb 3_{13}. → יסד I *establish.*

יְסוּדָה 1 n.f. **foundation** Ps 87_{1}. → יסד I *establish.*

[יָסוּר] 1 n.[m.]—cstr./sf. Kt יסורי—**one who departs,** יסורי בָּאָרֶץ יִכָּתֵבוּ perh. *those who depart from me will be inscribed in the (under)world* or *those who depart of the land,* i.e. those in the land who depart, *will be inscribed* Jr 17_{13}(Kt) (Qr וְסוּרַי *and those who depart from me*). → סור I *turn aside.*

יִסּוֹר 1.1.10 n.[m.]—pl. Q יסורים; cstr. Q יסורי—**1. reprover** or **one who is to be disciplined** Job 40_{3}. **2.** appar. **punishment, pain, torture, chastisement** 1QH 4_{22}. **3. instruction, precept** 1QS 3_{1} CD 7_{5}. → יסר I *discipline.*

יִסְכָּה 1 pr.n.f. **Iscah.**

יִסְמַכְיָהוּ 1 pr.n.m. **Ismachiah.**

יסף 215.5.42 vb.—**Qal** 34.0.3 Pf. יָסַף, יָסְפוּ; impv. סְפוּ; ptc. יוֹסֵף, יֹסְפִים—**1a. add** evil to (עַל) one's sins 1 S 12_{19}, a fifth part to a valuation Lv 27_{13}. **b. increase** joy Is 29_{19} (+ בְּ *on account of* Y.). **c. regenerate** roots, of remnant 2 K 19_{30}||Is 37_{31}. **2.** as auxiliary verb, **a. do again,** לֹא־יָסַף עוֹד מַלְאַךְ יי לְהֵרָאֹה אֶל־מָנוֹחַ *the angel of Y. never appeared again to Manoah* Jg 13_{21}. **b. continue, go on to do,** אִם ... לֹא תִשְׁמְעוּ לִי וְיָסַפְתִּי לְיַסְּרָה אֶתְכֶם *if ... you do not listen to me, then I will go on to discipline you* Lv 26_{18}.

Ni. 6.1.7 Pf. נוֹסַף; ptc. נוֹסָף—**1. be added to** (עַל) inheritance Nm 36_{3}, words Jr 36_{32}. **2. join (oneself)** to (לְ) community 1QS 8_{19}; to (עַל) enemies Ex 1_{10}. **3.** ptc. as noun, **something additional,** of punishment Is 15_{9}.

Hi. 174.4.30 Pf. הוֹסַפְתִּי, הֹסִיף; impf. יוֹסִיף (יֹסֵף); + waw וַיֹּסֶף; ptc. מוֹסִיפִים; inf. הוֹסִיף (Q לוסיף)—**1a. add** son to (לְ) someone Gn 30_{24}; years to (עַל) someone's life 2 K 20_{6}||Is 38_{5}. **b. increase, multiply** the faithless Pr 23_{28} (+ בְּ *among*), wealth 1QpHab 6_{1}, pain Ec 1_{18}. **c. gain** wisdom Pr 1_{5}. **d. exceed,** הוֹסַפְתָּ חָכְמָה וָטוֹב אֶל־הַשְּׁמוּעָה *in wisdom and wealth you have (far) exceeded the report* 1 K 10_{7}. **e. use** hand **again** Is 11_{11}. **f. give further cause for wrath** Ne 13_{18} (+ עַל *against*). **2.** as auxiliary verb, **a. do again,** רַק אַל־יֹסֵף פַּרְעֹה הָתֵל *only let not Pharaoh act deceitfully again* Ex 8_{25}. **b. continue to do,** לֹא־תֹסֵף תֵּת־כֹּחָהּ לָךְ *it* (the ground) *will no longer yield its produce to you* Gn 4_{12}. **c. do more,** וַיּוֹסִפוּ עוֹד שְׂנֹא אֹתוֹ *then they hated him all the more* Gn 37_{5}. **d. happen again,** וְהָיְתָה צְעָקָה ... אֲשֶׁר כָּמֹהוּ לֹא נִהְיָתָה וְכָמֹהוּ לֹא תֹסִף *then there will be wailing ... such as has never been or will ever be again* Ex 11_{6}.

Ho. 1.0.2 Impf. יוּסַף—**be added,** וּמַה־יֹּסִף לָךְ *and what will be added to you?* Ps 120_{3}(ms) (L יֹסִיף [hi.] what *will he add?*).

*[יָסֹף] 0.0.0.1 pr.n.m. **Jasoph.**

יסר I 44.4.19 vb.—**Qal** 5 Impf. אֶסֳּרֵם, יִסְּרֵנִי; ptc. יֹסֵר; inf. יָסֹר—**1.** of Y., **a. discipline** nations Ps 94_{10}, scoffer Pr 9_{7}. **b. warn** prophet Is 8_{11} (+ מִלֶּכֶת *from walking*). **2. instruct, train** in (בְּ) music 1 C 15_{22}.

Ni. 5.1.1 Impf. אִוָּסֵר, יִוָּסֵר; impv. הִוָּסְרוּ—**1. be disciplined** Pr 29_{19} (+ בְּ *by* words). **2. accept rebuke** Jr 6_{8}. **3. become wise** Si 6_{33}.

Pi. 32.3.8 Pf. יִסַּר; impf. יְיַסֵּר; impv. יַסֵּר; ptc. מְיַסֶּרְךָ; inf. יַסֵּר—**1. discipline, chastise** Lv 26_{18} (+ עַל *on account of* sins; subj. Y.) 1 K 12_{11}||2 C 10_{11} (+ בְּ *with* whips). **2. warn, admonish,** יִסְּרוּנִי כִלְיוֹתָי *my conscience admonishes me* Ps 16_{7}. **3. instruct, train** Jb 4_{3}.

Hi. 1 Impf. אַיְסִרֵם (mss אַיְסִירֵם)—perh. **punish** Ho 7_{12}.

Htp. 0.0.5 Pf. התיסר, התוסרו; ptc. מתיסרים; inf. לתיסר—**be instructed** in (בְּ) judgments 1QS 9_{10}, interpretation of law CD 4_{8}.

Ntp. 1 + waw וְנִוַּסְּרוּ—**accept discipline** Ezk 23_{48}.

→ יִסּוֹר *reprover, punishment,* מוּסָר *discipline,* מֹסָר *discipline,* מֹסֶרֶת *chastisement.*

*יסר II 2 vb.—**Pi.** 2 Pf. יִסַּרְתָּ—**strengthen** people Jb 4_{3}, arms of people Ho 7_{15}.

יָע 9 n.m.—pl. יָעִים; sf. יָעָיו—**fire-shovel,** for cleaning altar Ex 27_{3}. → יעה *sweep together.*

יַעְבֵּץ I 1 pl.n. **Jabez.**

יַעְבֵּץ II 3 pr.n.m. **Jabez.**

יעד 29.0.16 vb.—**Qal** 5.0.3 Pf. יְעָדוֹ (יְעָדָהּ); impf. יִיעָדֶנָּה—**1. appoint** time 2 S 20₅, day 1QM 13₁₄ (+ לְ *for* oneself; of Y.). **2. designate wife for** (לְ) son Ex 21₉.

Ni. 19.0.11 Pf. נוֹעַדְתִּי ,נוֹעֲדוּ; impf. אִוָּעֵד; + waw וַיִּוָּעֲדוּ; ptc. נוֹעָדִים—**1. have appointment with** (לְ) someone, of Y. Ex 25₂₂. **2. make an appointment,** of two people Am 3₃. **3. gather oneself** for battle Jos 11₅, to (אֶל) someone Nm 10₃, against (עַל) Y. Nm 14₃₅. **4.** ptc. as noun, **comrade** 1QH 13₂₃.

Hi. 3.0.1 Impf. יֹעִדֵנִי—**summon** Jr 49₁₉ Jb 9₁₉.

Ho. 2.0.1 Ptc. מוּעָדִים—**1. be designated,** לביאים מועדים לבני אשמה *lions who are designated for children of guilt* 1QH 13₇. **2. be placed** before (לִפְנֵי) temple, of baskets Jr 24₁.

→ עֵדָה I *congregation,* מוֹעֵד I *appointed time,* מוֹעָד I *rank,* מוֹעָדָה *appointment.*

יַעְדָּה 2 pr.n.m. **Jadah.**

[יֶעְדּוֹ] 1 pr.n.m. **Iddo.**

יעדי, see יֶעְדּוֹ *Iddo.*

יעה 1 vb.—**Qal** 1 + waw וְיָעָה—**sweep together, sweep away** refuge of lies Is 28₁₇. → יָעֶה *fire-shovel.*

יְעוּאֵל 1 pr.n.m. **Jeuel.**

יְעוּץ 1 pr.n.m. **Jeuz.**

יְעוּר, see יָעִיר *Jair.*

יְעוֹרִים, see יַעַר *wood.*

יְעוּשׁ 9 pr.n.m. **Jeush.**

יעז 1 vb.—**Ni.** 1 ptc. נוֹעָז—**be insolent** Is 33₁₉. → מָעוֹז *arrogance.*

יַעֲזִיאֵל 1 pr.n.m. **Jaaziel.**

יַעֲזִיָּהוּ 2 pr.n.m. **Jaaziah.**

יַעְזֵיר 13 pl.n. **Jazer.**

יעט 1 vb.—**Qal** 1 Impf. יְעָטָנִי—**cover,** of Y., מְעִיל צְדָקָה יְעָטָנִי *he has covered me with a robe of righteousness* Is 61₁₀. → cf. עטה *wrap.*

יְעִיאֵל 13 pr.n.m. **Jeiel.**

יָעִיר 1 pr.n.m. **Jair.**

יְעִישׁ, see יְעוּשׁ *Jeush.*

יַעְכָּן 1 pr.n.m. **Jachan.**

יעל 23.3.3 vb.—**Hi.** 23.3.3 Pf. הוֹעִיל; impf. יוֹעִיל; ptc. מוֹעִיל; inf. abs. הוֹעֵל; cstr. הוֹעִיל—**1a.** with obj., **avail** someone, of deeds Is 57₁₂. **b.** abs., **be of avail, be of use,** of words Jr 7₈, wealth Pr 10₂, useless objects, perh. images 1 S 12₂₁. **2. profit, get advantage,** אוּלַי תּוּכְלִי הוֹעִיל *perhaps you will be able to profit* Is 47₁₂. → תּוֹעֶלֶת *profit,* תּוֹעֵלָה *profit.*

יָעֵל I 3 n.m.—pl. יְעֵלִים; cstr. יַעֲלֵי—**wild (he-)goat** Ps 104₁₈ Jb 39₁. → cf. יַעֲלָה *wild she-goat.*

יָעֵל II 6 pr.n.f. **Jael.**

[יַעֲלָה] 1 n.f. **wild she-goat,** יַעֲלַת־חֵן *she-goat of grace,* as descr. of graceful woman Pr 5₁₉. → cf. יָעֵל *wild (he-) goat.*

יַעֲלָה 2 pr.n.m. **Jaalah.**

יַעְלָם 4 pr.n.m. **Jalam.**

[יָעֵן] I 1 n.[m.] **ostrich,** יְעֵנִים בַּמִּדְבָּר *ostriches in the steppe* Lm 4₃₍Qr₎.

[יָעֵן] II 1 n.[m.] **bedouin,** members of a nomadic tribe, יְעֵנִים בַּמִּדְבָּר *bedouin in the steppe* Lm 4₃₍Qr₎.

יַ֫עַן I 96.0.3 conj. **1.** יַעַן as conj. of cause, **because, since,** וְנָתַתִּי אֶת־הָאָרֶץ שְׁמָמָה יַעַן מָעֲלוּ מַעַל *and I will make the land desolate, because they have acted faithlessly* Ezk 15₈. **2.** יַעַן as prep., **on account of,** וְעָשִׂיתִי בָךְ אֵת אֲשֶׁר לֹא־עָשִׂיתִי ... יַעַן כָּל־תּוֹעֲבֹתָיִךְ *and on account of all your abominations, ... I will do among you what I have never done* Ezk 5₉. **3.** יַעַן אֲשֶׁר as conj. of cause, **because, since,** הוּא יִרְאֶנָּה ... יַעַן אֲשֶׁר מִלֵּא אַחֲרֵי י׳ *he will see it* (i.e. the promised land), *because he remained loyal to Y.* Dt 1₃₆; also **inasmuch as** 1 K 8₁₈. **4.** יַעַן אֲשֶׁר as final conj., **so that,** פָּנָיו יְכַסֶּה יַעַן אֲשֶׁר לֹא־יִרְאֶה *he will cover his face so that he does not see* Ezk 12₁₂. **5.** יַעַן כִּי as conj. of cause, **because, since,** יַעַן כִּי־נִכְנַע מִפָּנַי לֹא־אָבִיא הָרָעָה בְּיָמָיו *because he has humbled himself before me, I will not bring the disaster in his lifetime* 1 K 21₂₉.

יַ֫עַן II 1 pl.n. **Jaan.**

יַעֲנָה I 8 n.f. **desert,** alw. בַּת הַיַּעֲנָה *daughter of the desert,* i.e. **ostrich** or **eagle owl** Lv 11₁₆.

יַעֲנָה II 8 n.f. **greed,** alw. בַּת הַיַּעֲנָה *daughter of greed,* i.e. **ostrich** or **eagle owl** Lv 11₁₆.

יַעְנַי 1 pr.n.m. **Janai.**

יעף I 9 vb.—**Qal** 8 Pf. יָעֲפוּ; impf. יִיעַף, יִעֲפוּ—**be weary, weary oneself** Is 40₃₀ Hb 2₁₃ (+ בְּדֵי־רִיק *for nothing*).

Ho. 1 Ptc. מֻעָף (mss מוּעָף)—**be wearied,** of Daniel Dn 9₂₁.

→ יָעֵף *weary,* יְעָף *weariness;* cf. עיף I *be weary.*

***יעף** II 1 vb.—**Ho.** 1 Ptc. מֻעָף (mss מוּעָף)—**be swift,** of Gabriel Dn 9$_{21}$. → יְעָף *flying.*

יָעֵף 4 adj.—pl. יְעֵפִים—**1. weary** Jg 8$_{15}$. **2.** as noun, **weary one** 2 S 16$_{2}$. → יעף I *be weary.*

יְעָף I 1 n.m. **weariness** Dn 9$_{21}$. → יעף I *be weary.*

***יְעָף** II 1 n.m. **flying** Dn 9$_{21}$. → יעף II *be swift.*

***[יַעְפּוּר]** 0.0.1 pl.n. **Jaapur.**

יעץ 80.4.6 vb.—**Qal** 57.3.3 Pf. יָעַץ, יָעֲצוּ; impf. אִיעָצָה; ptc. יוֹעֵץ (יֹעֲצֵךְ), יֹעֲצוֹ, יוֹעֲצִים, יֹעֲצֵי, יֹעֲצָיו; ptc. pass. יְעוּצָה—**1a. advise, counsel** someone Ex 18$_{19}$. **b.** with cognate accus. (עֵצָה), **give** someone **advice, counsel** 1 K 1$_{12}$; with cognate accus. only 2 S 16$_{23}$. **2. devise** something, **a.** with accus. noble action Is 32$_{8}$, evil Is 7$_{5}$ (+ עַל *against* someone). **b.** with cognate accus., שִׁמְעוּ עֲצַת־י״ אֲשֶׁר יָעַץ אֶל־אֱדוֹם *hear what Y. has devised against Edom* Jr 49$_{20}$. **3.** ptc. as noun, **counsellor** Mc 4$_{9}$.

Ni. 22.1.2 Pf. נוֹעֲצוּ; impf. יִוָּעֲצוּ; + waw וַיִּוָּעַץ; ptc. נוֹעָץ, נוֹעָצִים; inf. Q להיעץ—**1. take counsel together** 1 K 12$_{6}$||2 C 10$_{6}$ (+ אֶת *with*) 1 C 13$_{1}$ (+ עִם *with*) 2 C 20$_{21}$ (+ אֶל *with*); **decide together** 2 C 30$_{2}$. **2. advise (after consultation)** 1 K 12$_{6}$||2 C 10$_{6}$. **3.** ptc. as noun, **one who seeks advice** Pr 13$_{10}$.

Htp. 1.0.1 Impf. יִתְיָעֲצוּ; ptc. Q מתיעצים—**take counsel against** (עַל) someone Ps 83$_{4}$.

→ עֵצָה I *counsel,* מוֹעֵצָה I *plan.*

יעק, see עוק *be hindered.*

יַעֲקֹב 350.6.39 pr.n.m.—יַעֲקוֹב—**Jacob, 1.** 215.1.29 patriarch, son of Isaac and father of tribes of Israel Gn 25$_{26}$. **2.** 135.5.7 people claiming Jacob (§1) as their ancestor, sometimes || Israel Nm 23$_{7}$. **3.** other persons 0.0.3 Mur EpBeth-Mashiko3.10.13.

יַעֲקֹבָה 1 pr.n.m. **Jaakobah.**

יַעֲקָן 1 pr.n.m. **Jaakan.**

יַעַר I 57.0.5 n.m.—יָעַר; + ־ה of direction יַעְרָה; sf. יַעְרוֹ; pl. יְעָרִים—**1. wood, forest** in general Dt 19$_{5}$ Is 7$_{2}$. **2.** particular **forest,** e.g. יַעַר חָרֶת *forest of Hereth* 1 S 22$_{5}$. **3. thickets,** הַר הַבַּיִת לְבָמוֹת יָעַר *the temple mount will become a mound of,* i.e. overgrown with, *thickets* Mc 3$_{12}$.

[יַעַר] II 1 n.m.—sf. יַעְרִי—**honeycomb** Ca 5$_{1}$. → cf. יַעְרָה I *honeycomb.*

יַעַר III 1 pl.n. **Jaar.**

[יַעְרָה] I 1 n.f. **honeycomb,** יַעְרַת הַדְּבָשׁ *comb of the honey* 1 S 14$_{27}$. → cf. יַעַר II *honeycomb.*

***[יַעְרָה]** II 1 n.f.—pl. יְעָרוֹת—**kid** Ps 29$_{9}$.

יַעְרָה 2 pr.n.m. **Jarah.**

יַעְרֵי אֹרְגִים 1 pr.n.m. **Jaare-oregim.**

יַעֲרֶשְׁיָה 1 pr.n.m. **Jareshiah.**

***[יעש]** 0.0.0.1 pr.n.m. **Jaas.**

יַעֲשָׂו 1 pr.n.m. **Jaasu.**

יַעֲשִׂיאֵל 2 pr.n.m. **Jaasiel.**

יִפְדְיָה 1 pr.n.m. **Iphdeiah.**

יפה 8.5.1 vb.—**Qal** 5.4.1 Pf. יָפִית, יָפוּ; + waw וַיִּיף, וְתִיפִי; ptc. Si יפה, Si יפים—**1. be beautiful,** of loved one Ca 7$_{7}$, cedar Ezk 31$_{7}$. **2. be befitting,** of words Si 35$_{5}$.

Pi. 1 + waw וַיְיַפֵּהוּ—**decorate, make** tree or image **beautiful with** (בְּ) silver and gold Jr 10$_{4}$.

Ho. 0.1 Ptc. מ[ו]ה[ו]פין—**be regarded as beautiful,** of words Si 13$_{22}$.

Htp. 1 Impf. תִּתְיַפִּי—**make oneself beautiful** Jr 4$_{30}$.

Pealal 1 Pf. יָפְיָפִיתָ—**be fair,** of king Ps 45$_{2}$ (+ מִן *fairer than*).

→ יָפֶה *beautiful,* יְפֵה־פִיָּה *handsome,* יֳפִי *beauty,* (?) יפות *harmony.*

יָפֶה 42.0.4 adj.—cstr. יְפֵה; f.s. יָפָה; cstr. יְפַת; sf. יָפָתִי; f.pl. יָפוֹת; cstr. יְפוֹת—**1. fair, attractive, beautiful,** of young woman 1 K 1$_{3}$, wheat Mur 24 B$_{16}$. **2.** as noun, **fair (one),** הַיָּפָה בַּנָּשִׁים *O (most) beautiful one among women* Ca 5$_{9}$. → יפה *be beautiful.*

יְפֵה־פִיָּה 1 adj.—mss יְפֵיפִיָּה—**handsome,** of heifer Jr 46$_{20}$. → יפה *be beautiful.*

יָפוֹ 4 pl.n. **Joppa.**

***[יפות]** 0.0.1 **harmony,** דורש בתורה ... על יפות perh. *explaining the Torah ... in harmony* 1QS 6$_{7}$ (or em. חליפות *[in] turns*). → (?) יפה *be beautiful.*

יפח 1 vb.—**Htp.** 1 Impf. תִּתְיַפֵּחַ—**gasp for breath** Jr 4$_{31}$. → יָפֵחַ I *breathing out.*

[יָפֵחַ] I 1 adj. **breathing out,** as noun, **one breathing out,** יְפֵחַ חָמָס *one breathing out violence* Ps 27$_{12}$. → יפח *gasp for breath.*

***יָפֵחַ** II 8 n.m. **witness,** יָפִיחַ כְּזָבִים *witness of lies,* i.e. false witness Pr 6$_{19}$. → פוח II *testify.*

*[יָפְטַר] 0.0.0.1 pr.n.m. **Jophtar.**

יְפִי 19.2.5 n.m. **beauty**—(יֹפִי) יוֹפִי—cstr. יְפִי; sf. יָפְיֵךְ, יָפְיוֹ; pl. Q יפים—of woman Is 3$_{24}$, tree Ezk 31$_{8}$, wisdom Ezk 28$_{7}$. → יפה *be beautiful.*

*[יְפַיָּהוּ] 0.0.0.1 pr.n.m. **Jephaiah.**

יָפִיחַ, see יָפֵחַ II *witness.*

יָפִיעַ I 4 pr.n.m. **Japhia.**

יָפִיעַ II 1 pl.n. **Japhia.**

יְפֵיפִיָּה, see יְפֵה־פִיָּה *handsome.*

יַפְלֵט 3 pr.n.m. **Japhlet.**

יַפְלֵטִי 1 gent. **Japhletite.**

יְפֻנֶּה 16.1 pr.n.m. **Jephunneh.**

יפע 8.2.32 vb.—**Hi.** 8.2.32 Pf. הוֹפִיעַ; impf. Si יופיע, תּוֹפַע; impv. הוֹפִיעָה; ptc. Si מופיע; inf. Q הופע (Q הופיע)—**1. shine (forth),** of light Jb 37$_{15}$ (unless §3), sun Si 43$_{2}$ (M), truth 1QH 19$_{26}$. **2. appear (in radiance),** of Y. Ps 94$_{1}$; **be evident,** of deeds CD 20$_{3}$. **3. cause light to shine,** of Y. Jb 37$_{15}$ (unless §1). → יִפְעָה *splendour.*

[יִפְעָה] I 2 n.f.—sf. יִפְעָתֶךָ—**splendour** Ezk 28$_{7.17}$. → יפע *shine forth.*

*[יִפְעָה] II 2 n.f.—sf. יִפְעָתֶךָ—**arrogance** Ezk 28$_{7.17}$.

*[יָפְקַד] 0.0.0.1 pr.n.m. **Jophkad.**

*יפר 1 vb.—**Hi.** 1 Impf. אוֹפִיר—**esteem,** אָדָם מִכֶּתֶם אוֹפִיר *a human being I shall esteem more than fine gold* Is 13$_{12}$.

*[יִפְרַעְיוֹ] 0.0.0.1 pr.n.[m.] **Iphraio.**

יֶפֶת 11.0.2 pr.n.m. **Japheth.**

יִפְתָּח I 29 pr.n.m. **Jephthah.**

יִפְתָּח II 1 pl.n. **Iphtah.**

יִפְתַּח־אֵל, see גֵּי יִפְתַּח־אֵל *Ge-Iphtahel.*

יצא I 1067.20.156.1 vb.—**Qal** 785.14.120.1 Pf. יָצָא, יָצָאתָ; impf. יֵצֵא, אֵצְאָה; impv. צֵא (צְאָה), צְאִי, צְאוּ, צֶאינָה; ptc. יֹצֵא, יֹצֵאת, יֹצְאִי, יֹצְאִים, יֹצְאֹת; inf. abs. יָצֹא; cstr. צֵאת (צֵאתִי)—**1.** of human, Y. or animal, **a. go out (from), come out (of), leave** a place, (1) intrans., צֵא מִן־הַתֵּבָה *come out of the ark!* Gn 8$_{16}$, וַתֵּצֶאנָה שְׁתַּיִם דֻּבִּים מִן־הַיַּעַר *then two female bears came out of the woods* 2 K 2$_{24}$. (2) trans., יָצְאוּ אֶת־הָעִיר *they had left the city* Gn 44$_{4}$. **b. depart (from)** Y., וַיֵּצֵא קַיִן מִלִּפְנֵי י׳ *then Cain departed from the presence of Y.* Gn 4$_{16}$. **c. set out,** וַיֵּצְאוּ לָלֶכֶת אַרְצָה כְּנַעַן *then they set out to go to the land of Canaan* Gn 12$_{5}$. **d. march out,** י׳ כַּגִּבּוֹר יֵצֵא *Y. will march out like a warrior* Is 42$_{13}$. **e. get out, escape,** וַיִּלָּכֵד יוֹנָתָן וְשָׁאוּל וְהָעָם יָצָאוּ *then Jonathan and Saul were taken, but the people escaped* 1 S 14$_{41}$. **f. surrender,** וַיֵּצֵא ... עַל־מֶלֶךְ בָּבֶל *then he surrendered ... to the king of Babylon* 2 K 24$_{12}$. **g. be descended,** מֵאֵלֶּה יָצְאוּ הַצָּרְעָתִי *from these descended the Zorathites* 1 C 2$_{53}$. **2.** of bodily elements, **a.** of semen, **come out, be discharged,** תֵּצֵא מִמֶּנּוּ שִׁכְבַת־זֶרַע *(an emission of) semen comes out of him* Lv 15$_{32}$. **b.** of foetus, **come out early, abort,** וְנָגְפוּ אִשָּׁה הָרָה וְיָצְאוּ יְלָדֶיהָ *and they strike a pregnant woman and (as a result) her foetuses come out early* Ex 21$_{22}$. **c.** of intestines, **prolapse,** יֵצְאוּ מֵעֶיךָ מִן־הַחֹלִי *your intestines prolapse because of the disease* 2 C 21$_{15}$. **d.** of breath, **expire,** בְּצֵאת נַפְשָׁהּ *when her breath expired,* i.e. when she was dying Gn 35$_{18}$. **e.** of hand, **strike out,** יָצְאָה בִי יַד־י׳ *the hand of Y. has struck out against me* Ru 1$_{13}$. **3.** of natural phenomena, **a.** of root, **grow (out of),** וְיָצָא חֹטֶר מִגֵּזַע יִשָׁי *yet a shoot will grow out of the stump of Jesse* Is 11$_{1}$. **b.** of river, **flow (out),** נָהָר יֹצֵא מֵעֵדֶן לְהַשְׁקוֹת אֶת־הַגָּן *a river flowed (out) from Eden to water the garden* Gn 2$_{10}$. **c.** of stars, **come out, appear,** עַד צֵאת הַכּוֹכָבִים *until the stars appeared* Ne 4$_{15}$. **d.** of sun, **rise,** כְּצֵאת הַשֶּׁמֶשׁ בִּגְבֻרָתוֹ *like the sun rising in might* Jg 5$_{31}$. **4.** of lot, **fall,** וַיֵּצֵא הַגּוֹרָל לִבְנֵי יוֹסֵף *and the lot fell on the descendants of Joseph* Jos 16$_{1}$. **5.** of part of building, **project, protrude,** הַמִּגְדָּל הַיּוֹצֵא מִבֵּית הַמֶּלֶךְ הָעֶלְיוֹן *the tower projecting from the upper palace* Ne 3$_{25}$. **6.** of border, **stretch,** וְיָצָא אֶל־מִנֶּגֶב *and it stretched to the south* Jos 15$_{3}$. **7.** of expenditure, **be outlaid, spent,** כֹּל אֲשֶׁר־יֵצֵא עַל־הַבַּיִת לְחָזְקָה *everything that is spent on the repairs of the temple* 2 K 12$_{13}$. **8.** of land sold, **be released,** i.e. be returned to previous owner, וְיָצָא בַּיֹּבֵל *and in the year of jubilee it shall be released* Lv 25$_{28}$. **9.** of word, **be uttered,** יָצָא מִפִּי צְדָקָה דָּבָר *a word has been uttered from my mouth in (all) integrity* Is 45$_{23}$. **10.** of wrath, **break out,** תֵּצֵא כָאֵשׁ חֲמָתִי *my wrath will break out like fire* Jr 4$_{4}$. **11.** of vindication, **come, originate (from),** מִלְּפָנֶיךָ מִשְׁפָּטִי יֵצֵא *my vindication will come from you* Ps 17$_{2}$. **12.** of contention, **depart, cease,** גָּרֵשׁ לֵץ וְיֵצֵא מָדוֹן *expel the scoffer and contention ceases* Pr 22$_{10}$.

Hi. 277.6.36 Pf. הוֹצִיא, הוֹצֵאתִי; impf. יוֹצִיא (יֹצֵא), תּוֹצֵא; + waw וַיּוֹצֵא (וַיֹּצֵא, וַיּוֹצִיא); impv. הוֹצֵא (הוֹצִיא, הוֹצִיאָה), הוֹצִיאוּ, הוֹצִיאִי; ptc. מוֹצִיא (מוֹצֵא), מוֹצִיאִים, מוֹצִאֵי; inf. cstr. הוֹצִיא (הוֹצִיאוֹ)—**1a. bring out, lead out** person, וַיּוֹצֵא אֹתוֹ הַחוּצָה *then he brought him outside* Gn 15_{5}, הוֹצִיאוּ אֶת־בְּנֵי יִשְׂרָאֵל מֵאֶרֶץ מִצְרַיִם *lead out the Israelites from the land of Egypt!* Ex 6_{26}; animal Nm 19_{3}. **b. cause** someone **to withdraw,** הוֹצִיאוּ כָל־אִישׁ מֵעָלָי *have everyone withdraw from me!* Gn 45_{1}. **c. cause to leave home, marry off** daughter Si 7_{25}. **d. send away** foreign wives and children Ezr 10_{3}. **2. carry out** object, וַיֹּצֵא אֶת־הָאֲשֵׁרָה מִבֵּית י׳ *he also carried the Asherah out of the temple of Y.* 2 K 23_{6}. **3a. draw (out)** sword, וְהוֹצֵאתִי חַרְבִּי מִתַּעְרָהּ *and I will draw my sword from its sheath* Ezk 21_{8}. **b. draw back** one's hand Ex 4_{6}. **4a. pay out** money, וַיּוֹצִיאֻהוּ לְחָרָשֵׁי הָעֵץ *and they paid it out to the carpenters* 2 K 12_{12}. **b. exact** money 2 K 15_{20}. **5a. bring (out)** bad report Nm 13_{32}. **b. utter** words Jb 8_{10}. **6a.** of grass, **produce** vegetation Gn 1_{12}. **b.** of person, (1) **produce** water **miraculously,** וְהוֹצֵאתָ לָהֶם מַיִם מִן־הַסֶּלַע *thus you will produce water for them from the rock* Nm 20_{8}. (2) **forge** weapon Is 54_{16}. **7.** of Y.'s actions, **a.** in individual's life, (1) **bring out** of difficult situation, **free** person, מִמְּצוּקוֹתַי הוֹצִיאֵנִי *free me from my distresses* Ps 25_{17}. (2) **release, free** person's feet from (מִן) snare Ps 25_{15}. **b.** in nation's history, **bring about** Israel's vindication Jr 51_{10}. **c.** in nature, (1) **bring forth** wind Jr 10_{13}. (2) **cause** food **to grow (out)** of (מִן) the earth Ps 104_{14}. (3) **cause** heavenly luminaries **to appear** Is 40_{26}.

Ho. 5 Pf. הוּצָאָה; ptc. מוּצָאִים, מוּצֵאת—**1. be brought out,** of person Gn 38_{25}. **2.** perh. **be caused to flow out,** of waters Ezk 47_{8} (+ אֶל־הַיָּמָה *into the sea*).

→ יָצִיא *coming out,* יְצִיאָה *outlet,* מוֹצָא I *going out,* מוֹצָאָה *origin,* תּוֹצָאָה *extremity,* צֶאֱצָא *offspring.*

*יצא II 3 vb.—**Qal** 3 + waw וַיֵּצֵא—**shine, flash,** of vessel Pr 25_{4}, anger Jr 4_{4}.

יצב 48.7.27 vb.—**Htp.** 48.7.27 Pf. הִתְיַצְּבוּ; impf. יִתְיַצֵּב (יִתְיַצָּב); + waw וַיִּתְיַצֵּב, וַתֵּתַצַּב; impv. הִתְיַצֵּב (הִתְיַצְּבָה), הִתְיַצְּבוּ; inf. הִתְיַצֵּב—**1. stand, station oneself** Ex 2_{4} (+ מֵרָחֹק *at a distance*) 1 S 3_{10} 2 S 18_{13} (+ מִנֶּגֶד *aloof*). **2. present oneself, a.** before (לִפְנֵי) Y. Jos 24_{1}. **b.** to (עַל) Y. Zc 6_{5}. **3a. take one's position** in preparation for battle Jr 46_{14}. **b. take one's stand** in an argument Jb 33_{5}. **c. stand up in defiance,** (1) before (לִפְנֵי) leader Jos 1_{5}. (2) against (בִּפְנֵי) nation Dt 7_{24}.

יצג 16.1 vb.—**Hi.** 15 Pf. הִצַּגְתִּיו; impf. אַצִּיגָה; + waw וַיַּצֵּג (וַיַּצֵּג), וַיַּצִּיגוּ; impv. הַצִּיגוּ; ptc. מַצִּיג; inf. הַצֵּג—**1. place** object on (בְּ) threshing floor Jg 6_{37}, in (בְּ) trough Gn 30_{38}, inside (בְּתוֹךְ) tent 1 C 16_{1}, beside (אֵצֶל) idol 1 S 5_{2}. **2a. set** person **apart** (לְבָד) Jg 7_{5}. **b. station** servants with (עִם) someone Gn 33_{15}. **c. present** person before (לִפְנֵי) Pharaoh Gn 47_{2}. **3. set** sole of foot on (עַל) ground Dt 28_{56}. **4. establish** justice Am 5_{15}. **5a. make (into),** וְהִצִּגַנִי לִמְשֹׁל עַמִּים *and he made me a byword of the peoples* Jb 17_{6}. **b. make (as),** וְהִצַּגְתִּיהָ כְּיוֹם הִוָּלְדָהּ *and I will make her as in the day she was born* Ho 2_{5}.

Ho. 1.1 Impf. יֻצַּג; ptc. Si מצגת—**be placed,** of wave-offering Si 30_{18} (+ לִפְנֵי *before* image). **2. be left behind,** of herds Ex 10_{24}.

*יצד vb. **Pi., fasten,** וּבַמַּקָּבוֹת יְיַצְּדֵהוּ *and with hammers he fastens it* (image) Is 44_{12} (if em. יְצָרֵהוּ *he shapes it*).

*יצה 2 vb.—**Pi.** 2 + waw וַיְצַו; impv. צַו—**give last injunctions (to), 1.** with accus. son 1 K 2_{1}. **2.** with לְ *to* household 2 K 20_{1}. → cf. צוה pi. *command.*

יִצְהָר I 23.1.12 n.m.—sf. יִצְהָרֶךָ—**fresh oil,** זֵית יִצְהָר *olive(s) of fresh oil* 2 K 18_{32}, בְנֵי־הַיִּצְהָר *sons of the new oil,* i.e. anointed ones Zc 4_{14}. → צהר I *press out oil.*

יִצְהָר II 9 pr.n.m. **Izhar.**

יִצְהָרִי 4 gent. **Izharite.**

יָצוּעַ I 5.3.3 n.m.—sf. יְצוּעִי; pl. cstr. יְצוּעֵי; sf. יְצוּעַי—**couch, bed** Gn 49_{4}; עֶרֶשׂ יְצוּעָי *couch of my bed* Ps 132_{3}, יצועי שחת *couches of corruption* 4QWiles 1_{5}. → יצע *spread.*

יָצוּעַ II, see יָצִיעַ *terrace.*

*[יָצוּר] 0.1 n.m.—sf. יצוריו—**creature** Si 34_{19}(Bmg). → יצר *form.*

יִצְחָק 112.2.13 pr.n.m. **Isaac.**

[יִצְחָר] 1 pr.n.m. **Izhar.**

יָצִיא 1 adj. **coming out,** as noun, מִיצִיאֵי מֵעָיו *from among the ones coming forth of his genitals,* i.e. his very own sons 2 C 32_{21}(Qr). → יצא I *go out.*

*[יְצִיאָה] 0.0.1 n.f. **outlet,** על פי יציאת המים *by the mouth of the water outlet* 3QTr 7₁₄. → יצא I *go out.*

[יָצִיעַ] 3 n.m.&f.—Qr יָצוּעַ, Kt יציע—lower projecting **storey** or **terrace** of temple 1 K 6₅.₆.₁₀. → יצע *spread out.*

יָצַל, see אָצַל *take away.*

יצע 4.1.2 vb.—**Hi.** 2.1.2 Pf. Q הוצעת; impf. יַצִּיעַ, Si חצע, אַצִּיעָה—**1. extend, spread out as couch** sackcloth and ashes Is 58₅. **2. spread a couch,** וְאַצִּיעָה שְׁאוֹל *and (if) I should spread a couch (in) Sheol* Ps 139₈.

Ho. 2 Impf. יֻצַּע—**be spread out as a couch,** of sackcloth and ashes Est 4₃, maggots Is 14₁₁.

→ יָצוּעַ I *couch,* יָצִיעַ *terrace,* מַצָּע *couch.*

יצק 55.3.6 vb.—**Qal** 42.1.1 Pf. יָצַק; impf. אֶצֹּק; + waw וַיִּצֹק (וַיִּצָק), וַיִּצְקוּ ,וַתִּצֹק; impv. יְצֹק (צַק); ptc. pass. יָצוּק, יְצוּקִים ,יְצֻקוֹת; inf. צֶקֶת—**1a. pour out** water 1 K 18₃₄ (+ עַל *upon*), oil 2 K 9₆ (+ אֶל *upon*). **b.** of Y., **bestow** spirit Is 44₃ (+ עַל *upon*). **2. cast** metal object Ex 25₁₂. **3.** intrans., **flow, pour,** of blood 1 K 22₃₅, dust Jb 38₃₈ (+ לְ *into* a mass). **4. issue** statute Si 16₂₂. **5.** pass., **a. be cast,** of metal object 1 K 7₂₄. **b. be firm,** of heart of Leviathan Jb 41₁₆.

Hi. 4 + waw וַיַּצִּקוּ; ptc. מוֹצֶקֶת—**1. set down** ark 2 S 15₂₄. **2. place, display** precious objects before (לִפְנֵי) Y. Jos 7₂₃.

Ho. 9.2.5 Pf. הוּצַק; impf. יוּצַק; ptc. מוּצָק, Q מוצקות—**1a. be poured out,** of oil Lv 21₁₀ (+ עַל *upon*). **b. be bestowed,** of grace Ps 45₃ (+ בְּ *upon* lips). **2. be cast,** of metal object 1 K 7₁₆. **3. be washed away,** of foundation Jb 22₁₆. **4.** ptc. as noun, מוצקות **streams of liquid** 4QMMT B₅₅.

→ יְצֻקָה *casting,* מוּצָק I *casting,* מוּצֶקֶת *cast pipe.*

יְצֻקָה 1 n.f. **casting** 1 K 7₂₄. → יצק *pour out.*

יצר 63.11.17 vb.—**Qal** 60.3.14 Pf. יָצַר ,יָצַרְתָּ; impf. יִצְּרֵהוּ, אֶצָּרְךָ; + waw וַיִּצֶר; ptc. יוֹצֵר, pl. יוֹצְרִים ,יֹצְרֵי; inf. Q ליצור—**1. form, fashion, create, shape, a.** subj. human; obj. image of god Is 44₁₂. **b.** subj. Y.; obj. earth Is 45₁₈, mountains Am 4₁₃, human being Gn 2₇ (+ עָפָר מִן־הָאֲדָמָה *[out of] dust from the ground*), human breath Zc 12₁, human heart Ps 33₁₅. **2. frame, devise, plan, a.** subj. human; obj. mischief Ps 94₂₀. **b.** subj. Y.; obj. event 2 K 19₂₅||Is 37₂₆. **3.** ptc. as noun, **one who forms, creator, potter,** אֲנַחְנוּ הַחֹמֶר וְאַתָּה יֹצְרֵנוּ *we are the clay and you are our potter* Is 64₇.

Ni. 1.8.1 Pf. נוֹצַר—**be formed, created,** of human being Si 36₁₀ (+ מִן *from* dust), god Is 43₁₀, darkness Si 11₁₆ (+ לְ *for* transgressors).

Pu. 1.0.1 Pf. יֻצָּרוּ; ptc. Q יוצר—**1. be devised, ordained,** of days Ps 139₁₆. **2.** ptc. as noun, **that which is formed, created,** יוצר יד *that which is formed by the hand* or *created by the penis* 1QS 11₂₂.

Ho. 1.0.1 Impf. יוּצַר—**be formed,** of weapon Is 54₁₇ (+ עַל *against*).

→ יֵצֶר I *creature,* יֵצֶר *inclination,* יְצוּר *creature,* יְצֻרִים *bodily members.*

יֵצֶר I 9.2.66 n.m.—sf. יִצְרוֹ; cstr. Q יצרי—**1. thing formed, a. creature, human being** Is 29₁₆; יצר חמר *creature of clay* 1QH 12₂₉. **b. image** of god Hb 2₁₈. **2. formation, constitution** of human being Ps 103₁₄. **3a. thinking, devising** of the human heart Gn 8₂₁. **b.** perh. **inclination, instinct** of human being Si 15₁₄; יצר רע *evil inclination* 11QPs[a] 19₁₆. **c. character** of a person 1QJub[b] 35₉. → יצר *form.*

יֵצֶר II 3 pr.n.m. **Jezer.**

*[יֵצֶר] 0.0.1 n.m.—יוצר—**inclination** 4QParGenEx 1₁₂. → יצר *form.*

יִצְרִי I 1 gent. **Jezerite.**

יִצְרִי II 1 pr.n.m. **Izri.**

יְצֻרִים 1 n.m.—sf. יְצֻרַי—**bodily members** Jb 17₇. → יצר *form.*

יצת 30.2 vb.—**Qal** 4 Impf. יִצַּתוּ; + waw וַתִּצַּת—**1. be kindled** with (בְּ) fire, of gates Jr 51₅₈. **2.** with בְּ of obj., **kindle, burn up** thickets, of wickedness as fire Is 9₁₇.

Ni. 8.1 Pf. נִצְּתָה—**1. be burned up,** of land Jr 9₁₁, gates (+ בְּ *with* fire). **2. be kindled against** (בְּ) Israel, of Y.'s anger 2 K 22₁₃.

Hi. 18.1 Pf. הִצִּית ,הִצַּתִּי; impf. תַּצִּיתוּ; + waw וַיַּצֶּת־; ptc. מַצִּית—**1. kindle a fire** Lm 4₁₁. **2. burn** city with (בְּ) fire Jos 8₈.

*[יָצִת] 0.0.0.7 pl.n. **Jazith.**

יֶקֶב 16.0.1 n.m.—יָקֶב; sf. יִקְבֶךָ; pl. יְקָבִים; cstr. יִקְבֵי—**1. trough** or **channel** dug in rock, receptacle of juice trodden out in the wine-press Is 5₂. **2. wine-press** Is

16$_{10}$.

יְקַבְצְאֵל 1 pl.n. **Jekabzeel.**

יקד 8.1.1 vb.—**Qal** 3.1 Impf. יֵקַד; + waw וַתִּיקַד; ptc. יֹקֶדֶת—**be kindled, burn,** of fire Dt 32$_{22}$.

Ho. 5.0.1 Impf. תּוּקַד—**be kindled, be kept burning,** of fire Lv 6$_2$.

→ יְקֹד *conflagration,* יָקוּד *hearth,* מוֹקֵד *hearth,* מוֹקְדָה *hearth.*

יְקֹד 2 n.m. **conflagration** Is 10$_{16}$. → יקד *be kindled.*

יָקְדְעָם 1 pl.n. **Jokdeam.**

יָקֶה 1 pr.n.m. **Jakeh.**

[יְקָהָה] 2 n.f. **obedience,** יִקְּהַת עַמִּים *obedience of the peoples* Gn 49$_{10}$, אֵם *of,* i.e. due to, *a mother* Pr 30$_{17}$ (לִיקֲּהַת).

יָקוּד 1 n.m. **hearth** Is 30$_{14}$. → יקד *be kindled.*

יָקוֹט 1 n.m. perh. **gossamer** Jb 8$_{14}$. → קוט II *break.*

יְקוּם 3.1.3 n.m. **living form** Gn 7$_4$. → קום *arise.*

יָקוֹשׁ 1 n.[m.] **(game) hunter,** פַּח יָקוֹשׁ *a hunter's trap* Ho 9$_8$. → יקשׁ *trap.*

יָקוּשׁ 3.0.1 n.[m.]—pl. יְקוּשִׁים—**(game) hunter** Jr 5$_{26}$ Ps 91$_3$ Pr 6$_5$. → יקשׁ *trap.*

יְקוּתִיאֵל 1 pr.n.m. **Jekuthiel.**

*יקח 2 vb.—**Pi.** 2 Impf. תְּקַחֵךְ—**embolden,** מַה־יִּקָּחֲךָ לִבֶּךָ *why has your heart emboldened you?* Jb 15$_{12}$; Pr 6$_{25}$.

יָקְטָן 6 pr.n.m. **Joktan.**

יָקִים 2.0.9 pr.n.m. **Jakim.**

*[יְקִימְיָהוּ] 0.0.0.1 pr.n.m. **Jakimiah.**

יַקִּיר 1 adj. **precious,** of son Jr 31$_{20}$. → יקר *be precious.*

יְקַמְיָה 3.0.0.13 pr.n.m. **Jekamiah.**

יְקַמְעָם 2 pr.n.m. **Jekameam.**

יָקְמְעָם 2 pl.n. **Jokmeam.**

יָקְנְעָם 3 pl.n. **Jokneam.**

יקע 8 vb.—**Qal** 4 Impf. תֵּקַע—**1. be alienated** from (מִן) someone, subj. one's soul (נֶפֶשׁ) Jr 6$_8$. **2. be dislocated,** of socket of thigh joint Gn 32$_{26}$.

Hi. 3 Pf. הוֹקַעֲנוּם; + waw וְהוֹקִיעוּם; impv. הוֹקַע—**expose** someone **with broken limbs** 2 S 21$_6$ (+ לְ *to* Y.).

Ho. 1 Ptc. מוּקָעִים—**be exposed with broken limbs** 2 S 21$_{13}$.

→ cf. נקע *recoil.*

יקץ 11 vb.—**Qal** 11 Impf. יִיקַץ; + waw וַיִּיקַץ (וַיִּקַץ, וַיִּקֶץ)—**awake, be active,** of Y. Ps 78$_{65}$; of human being, from (מִן) sleep Jg 16$_{14}$, wine Gn 9$_{24}$. → cf. קִיץ *awake.*

יקר 11.1 vb.—**Qal** 9 Pf. יָקְרָה; impf. יֵיקַר (יֵקַר); + waw וַיֵּיקַר—**1. be precious, valued, honoured,** of life 1 S 26$_{21}$ (+ בְּעֵינֵי *in the sight of*), person's name 1 S 18$_{30}$, Y.'s thoughts Ps 139$_{17}$. **2. be costly,** of ransom for life Ps 49$_9$.

Hi. 2.1 Impf. אוֹקִיר; impv. הֹקַר—**1. make** human beings **rare,** of Y. Is 13$_{12}$ (+ מִן rarer *than* gold). **2.** perh. **make foot heavy,** i.e. **stay away from** (מִן) neighbour's house Pr 25$_{17}$. **3. honour** the downtrodden Si 12$_5$.

→ יָקָר I *precious,* יְקָר *preciousness,* יַקִּיר *precious.*

יָקָר I 36.1.7 adj.—cstr. יְקַר; pl. יְקָרִים; f.s. יְקָרָה; cstr. יִקְרַת; pl. יְקָרוֹת—**1a. precious,** of life Pr 6$_{26}$. **b. choice, costly,** of stones 1 K 5$_{31}$. **c.** perh. **weighty,** יָקָר מֵחָכְמָה מִכָּבוֹד סִכְלוּת מְעָט *a little folly is more weighty than wisdom (and) honour* Ec 10$_1$. **d. rare,** of word of Y. 1 S 3$_1$. **2.** ptc. as noun, **a. precious one,** בְּנוֹת מְלָכִים בְּיִקְּרוֹתֶיךָ *daughters of kings are among your precious ones* Ps 45$_{10}$. **b. splendour, beauty,** יָרֵחַ יָקָר הֹלֵךְ *the moon moving about (in) splendour* Jb 31$_{26}$, כִּיקַר כָּרִים *like the beauty of the pastures* Ps 37$_{20}$. → יקר *be precious.*

*[יָקָר] II 1 adj. **split,** אֲבָנִים יְקָרוֹת *split stones* 1 K 5$_{31}$.

יְקָר 17 n.m.—cstr. יְקַר; sf. יְקָרוֹ—**1a. preciousness,** כְּלִי יְקָר *precious jewel* Pr 20$_{15}$. **b. price,** אֶדֶר הַיְקָר *handsome price* Zc 11$_{13}$. **c.** coll., **prized belongings** Jr 20$_5$. **2. honour, respect,** כָּל־הַנָּשִׁים יִתְּנוּ יְקָר לְבַעְלֵיהֶן *all women will give honour to their husbands* Est 1$_{20}$. → יקר *be precious.*

יקשׁ 8.6 vb.—**Qal** 3 Pf. יָקֹשְׁתִּי—**set a trap, 1.** without obj., of Y., יָקֹשְׁתִּי לָךְ *I set a trap for you* Jr 50$_{24}$. **2.** with obj., פַּח יָקְשׁוּ לִי *the trap they have set for me* Ps 141$_9$.

Ni. 4.6 Pf. נוֹקַשְׁתְּ; impf. תִּוָּקֵשׁ; ptc. Si נוקשׁ—**be trapped,** alw. of person Dt 7$_{25}$ Pr 6$_2$.

Pu. 1 Ptc. יוּקָשִׁים—**be caught,** of person Ec 9$_{12}$.

→ יָקוֹשׁ *(game) hunter,* יָקוּשׁ *(game) hunter,* מוֹקֵשׁ I *snare;* cf. נקשׁ II *ensnare,* קושׁ *lay snare.*

יָקְשָׁן 4 pr.n.m. **Jokshan.**

יָקְתְאֵל 2 pl.n. **Joktheel.**

ירא I 378.13.62 vb.—**Qal** 328.9.36 Pf. יָרֵא, יָרֵאתִי; impf. יִירָא (יִרָאֶךָּ); + waw וַיִּירָא (וַיִּרָא); impv. יְרָא, יְרְאוּ; ptc. יָרֵא,

cstr. יְרֵא, pl. יְרֵאִים, cstr. יִרְאֵי, sf. יְרֵאֶיךָ, f. cstr. יִרְאַת; inf. cstr. יִרְאָה (יְרֹא, לְרֹא, יִרְאָתוֹ)—**1. be afraid, fear, be fearful, a.** abs., of person Gn 18_{15}, heart Ps 27_{3}, animal Jl 2_{22}, land Jl 2_{21}. **b.** with inf. cstr., **be afraid of (doing), fear (to do),** יָרֵא לָשֶׁבֶת בְּצוֹעַר *he was afraid to stay in Zoar* Gn 19_{30}, וָאִירָא מֵחַוֹּת דֵּעִי אֶתְכֶם *so I was afraid of declaring my opinion to you* Jb 32_{6}. **c.** with accus., **be afraid of, fear** something Ezk 11_{8}, someone 1 K 1_{51}, sometimes Y. (but usu. §2) Jb 9_{35}. **d.** with prep., **be afraid, fear** on account of (מִן or מִפְּנֵי or מִלִּפְנֵי or בְּ) someone or something Dt 5_{5} 1 S 18_{12} Jr 51_{46} Ps 119_{120}. **2. fear,** or perh. **revere** Y. Jon 1_{9}, Y.'s name and glory Ps 102_{16}, Y.'s sanctuary Lv 19_{30}, other gods Jg 6_{10}, person Jos 4_{14}; with preps. מִן or מִפְּנֵי or מִלִּפְנֵי Lv 19_{14} Hg 1_{12} Ec 3_{14}; abs. Jr 44_{10}. **3.** ptc. as noun, **one who fears** Y. Ps 25_{12}, Y.'s name Ml 3_{20}, commandment Pr 13_{13}.

Ni. 45.4.17 Pf. נוֹרָא; impf. תִּוָּרֵא; ptc. נוֹרָא, נוֹרָאָה, נוֹרָאוֹת (נוֹרְאֹתֶיךָ)—**1. be feared, revered,** perh. **make oneself feared,** of Y. Ps 76_{13}. **2.** ptc. as adj., **a. dreadful,** of steppe Dt 1_{19}. **b. feared, dreaded,** of people Is 18_{7}. **c. fear-inspiring, inspiring reverence, awesome,** הָאֵל הַגָּדוֹל וְהַנּוֹרָא *the great and awesome God* Ne 1_{5}, אלוהים נוראי כוח *gods awesome of strength,* i.e. whose strength is awesome 11QShirShabb 5_{3}. **3.** ptc. as noun, **a.** masc., **awesome one** or **thing,** perh. אל הנוראים *God of the awesome ones/things* 4QInstr[d] 43_{1}. **b.** fem. pl., **awesome deeds** Dt 10_{21}. **4.** ptc. as adv., **awesomely,** נוֹרָאוֹת נִפְלֵיתִי *I am awesomely made* Ps 139_{14}.

Pi. 5.0.9 Pf. יִרְאֻנִי; ptc. מְיָרְאִים; inf. יָרְאֵנִי—alw. of person, **1. cause fear** 8QHymn 1_{1}. **2. make** someone **afraid** 2 C 32_{18}. **3. cause** Y. **to be feared** 4QShir[b] 35_{6}.

→ יִרְאָה *fear,* מוֹרָא I *fear.*

*ירא II 2 vb.—**Qal** 2 Impf. תֵּרֶא; impv. רְאוּ—**drink deeply (of),** אַל־תֵּרֶא יָיִן *do not drink deeply of wine* Pr 23_{31}; abs. Ps 34_{9}.

יִרְאָה 44.8.5 n.f.—cstr. יִרְאַת; sf. יִרְאָתִי,—**1. fear** of someone or something, **dread, terror,** יִרְאָה לָהֶם *terror was to them,* i.e. they inspired terror Ezk 1_{18}, יִרְאַת שָׁמִיר וָשָׁיִת *fear of briars and thorns* Is 7_{25}. **2. fear** of Y., perh. **reverence, devotion** Is 11_{2} Ps 111_{10}. **3.** perh. **one who fears** Y. 2 S 23_{3}. → ירא *fear.*

יִרְאוֹן 1 pl.n. **Iron,** or **Yiron.**

*[יִרְאִוִּיָּהוּ] 0.0.0.1 pr.n.m. **Irivvijah.**

יִרְאִיָּה 2 pr.n.m. **Irijah.**

*יָרֵב 2 adj. **great,** of king Ho 5_{13}. → cf. רבב *be great.*

יְרֻבַּעַל 14.0.0.1 pr.n.m. **Jerubbaal.**

יָרָבְעָם 104.1.0.3 pr.n.m. **Jeroboam.**

יְרֻבֶּשֶׁת 1 pr.n.m. **Jerubbesheth.**

ירד I 379.8.31.2 vb.—**Qal** 306.7.26.2 Pf. יָרַד, יָרַדְתִּי (רַד); impf. יֵרֵד, תֵּרֵד (תֵּרֶד, תֵּרֶד); + waw וַיֵּרֶד (וַיֵּרַד); impv. רֵד (רְדָה), רְדָה, רְדוּ, רְדִי; ptc. יוֹרֵד, יֹרֶדֶת (יֹרְדָה), יוֹרְדִים, יוֹרְדֵי, יוֹרְדוֹת; inf. abs. יָרֹד; cstr. רֶדֶת (רִדְתִּי)—**1.** of person, **a. go down, come down, descend,** בְּרֶדֶת מֹשֶׁה מֵהַר סִינַי *when Moses came down from Mount Sinai* Ex 34_{29}. **b. step down,** וַיֵּרֶד מֵעֲשֹׂת הַחַטָּאת *then he stepped down after offering the sin offering* Lv 9_{22}. **c. dismount,** וַתֵּרֶד מֵעַל הַחֲמוֹר *and she dismounted from the ass* 1 S 25_{23}. **d. fall,** וְיָרְדוּ סוּסִים וְרֹכְבֵיהֶם אִישׁ בְּחֶרֶב אָחִיו *and horses and their riders will fall, each by the sword of his brother* Hg 2_{22}. **e. sink,** לְקִצְבֵי הָרִים יָרַדְתִּי *I sank to the foundations of the mountains* Jon 2_{7}. **f.** appar. **go up** into mountainous country, but perh. **go south, go down country,** וַיֵּרֶד הַסֶּלַע *then he went up,* or *south, into the rocky region* 1 S 23_{25}. **g. roam** upon mountains, וְיָרַדְתִּי עַל־הֶהָרִים וְאֶבְכֶּה עַל־בְּתוּלַי *then I will roam upon the mountains and bewail my virginity* Jg 11_{37}. **h. travel, sail** the sea, יוֹרְדֵי הַיָּם בָּאֳנִיּוֹת *those who go down to,* i.e. travel, *the sea in ships* Ps 107_{23}. **i. be present,** לֹא־יֵרֵד עִמָּנוּ בַּמִּלְחָמָה *he must not be present with us in battle* 1 S 29_{4}. **2.** of Y. in theophany, **come down** from heaven to earth, וַיֵּרֶד י׳ בֶּעָנָן *then Y. came down in a cloud* Nm 11_{25}. **3.** of bird, **swoop down,** וַיֵּרֶד הָעַיִט עַל־הַפְּגָרִים *then birds of prey swooped down on the carcasses* Gn 15_{11}. **4a.** of hail, **fall** Ex 9_{19}. **b.** of wall, **fall down** Dt 28_{52}. **c.** of city, **fall,** i.e. be captured Dt 20_{20}. **d.** of forest, **be felled** Zc 11_{2}. **5a.** of liquid, **flow down,** of water Jos 3_{13} (+ מִלְמָעְלָה *from above,* i.e. downstream), oil Ps 133_{2}, tears Si 32_{18} (+ עַל *on* cheek). **b.** of eyes, **(over)flow with tears,** תֵּרַדְנָה עֵינַי דִּמְעָה *let my eyes flow with tears* Jr 14_{17}. **6a.** of boundary, **go downward** Nm 34_{12} (+

הַיַּרְדֵּנָה *to the Jordan*). **b.** of way, **lead down,** דַּרְכֵי שְׁאוֹל ... יֹרְדוֹת אֶל־חַדְרֵי־מָוֶת *the ways of Sheol ... leading down to the chambers of death* Pr 7_{27}. **7.** of shadow, **decline** Is 38_{8}. **8.** of day(light), **draw to a close, be over** Jg 19_{11}.

Hi. 67.1.4 Pf. הוֹרִד, הוֹרַדְתָּנוּ, הוֹרִידוּ; impf. אוֹרִיד, תּוֹרֵד; + waw וַיּוֹרֶד, וַיּוֹרִדוּ; impv. הוֹרֵד (הוֹרִדֵהוּ), הוֹרִידִי, הוֹרִידוּ; ptc. מוֹרִיד; inf. הוֹרִיד—**1a. take down, bring down, lead down** someone to (אֶל) a person Gn 44_{21}, place Jg 7_{4}. **b. let down** someone through (בְּעַד) window 1 S 19_{12}. **c. pull down** someone from (מִן) height Jr 49_{16}. **d. bring down** someone's grey head to Sheol (שְׁאוֹלָה) Gn 42_{38}. **2a. carry down** present Gn 43_{11}. **b. lower** pitcher Gn 24_{18}, sack Gn 44_{11}. **c. take off** jewellery Ex 33_{5}. **3. bow** head Lm 2_{10}. **4. let flow down** saliva 1 S 21_{14}, tears Lm 2_{18}. **5.** of Y., **a. make** streams **flow down** Ps 78_{16}. **b. send down** rain Ezk 34_{26}. **c. subdue** people in (בְּ) anger Ps 56_{8}. **d. hurl** people's glory to (לְ) the ground Is 63_{6}. **e. cast down** into Sheol, מוֹרִיד שְׁאוֹל וַיָּעַל *Y. casts down into Sheol and raises up* 1 S 2_{6}.

Ho. 6.0.1 Pf. הוּרַד; impf. תּוּרַד—**1. be brought down,** of person Gn 39_{1}. **2. be taken down, apart,** of tabernacle Nm 10_{17}. **3. be laid low,** of pride Zc 10_{11}.

→ יְרִידָה *descent,* מוֹרָד *slope.*

***ירד** II 1 vb.—**Hi.** 1 Impf. + waw וְהוֹרַדְתִּי—**cause fugitives to appear** Is 43_{14}.

יֶרֶד 7 pr.n.m. **Jared.**

יַרְדֵּן I 181.0.3 pl.n. **Jordan.**

***יַרְדֵּן** II 1 n.m. **river** Jb 40_{23}.

ירה I 29.0.6 vb.—**Qal** 13.0.1 Pf. יָרָה, יָרִיתִי; + waw וַנִּירָם; impv. יְרֵה; ptc. יֹרֶה, יוֹרִים; inf. abs. יָרֹה; cstr. לִירוֹת (לִירוֹא)—**1a. cast** lot Jos 18_{6}. **b.** of Y., **throw** enemy into (בְּ) sea Ex 15_{4}. **c. overthrow** enemy Nm 21_{30}. **2a. erect** pillar Gn 31_{51}. **b. lay** cornerstone Jb 38_{6}. **3a. shoot** arrow, with accus. 1 S 20_{36}, בְּ of obj. 2 C 26_{15}. **b.** with ellip., **shoot** at (לְ) someone Ps 11_{2}. **4.** ptc. as noun, **archer** 2 C 35_{23}.

Ni. 1 Impf. יִיָּרֶה—**be shot,** of person Ex 19_{13}.

Hi. 15.0.5 Pf. הוֹרָנִי; impf. יוֹרֶה, אוֹרֶה, יֹרוּ; + waw וַיֹּור; ptc. מוֹרֶה, מוֹרִים—**1. cast** lot for (עַל) someone 4Qp Nah 3.4_{2}. **2.** of Y., **throw** someone into (לְ) mud Jb 30_{19}. **3. shoot** arrow 1 S 20_{20}. **4.** ptc. as noun, **archer** 2 S 11_{24}.

→ מוֹרֶה *archer.*

ירה II 3 vb.—**Hi.** 2 Impf. יוֹרֶה—**1.** of rain, water, **rain** upon earth Ho 6_{3}. **2.** of Y., **cause** righteousness **to rain down** for (לְ) Israel Ho 10_{12}.

Ho. 1 Impf. יוֹרֶא (mss יוֹרֶה)—**be given drink,** of person Pr 11_{25}.

→ יוֹרֶה *early rain,* מוֹרֶה I *early rain;* cf. רוה *water.*

ירה III 45.0.30 vb.—**Qal** 0.0.3 Ptc. יורה, יוריהם—**teach,** ptc. as noun, **teacher** CD 3_{8} 20_{14}; יורה הצדק *the teacher of righteousness* CD 6_{11}.

Hi. 45.0.27 Pf. הוֹרֵיתִיךָ, הוֹרָהוּ; impf. יוֹרֶה, תֹּרְךָ; impv. הוֹרֵנִי, הוֹרוּנִי; ptc. מוֹרֶה, מוֹרֶיךָ; inf. הוֹרוֹת—**1. teach,** with **a.** double accus., אֶת־מִי יוֹרֶה דֵעָה *whom will he teach knowledge?* Is 28_{9}. **b.** accus. of person, subj. Y., אַתָּה הוֹרֵתָנִי *you yourself have taught me* Ps 119_{102}, subj. beast Jb 12_{7}, earth Jb 12_{8}. **c.** accus. of person + בְּ, אוֹרֶה אֶתְכֶם בְּיַד־אֵל *I will teach you concerning the power of God* Jb 27_{11}. **d.** accus. of thing, נָבִיא מוֹרֶה־שֶׁקֶר *a prophet who teaches lies* Is 9_{14}. **e.** obj. of thing + לְ, יוֹרוּ מִשְׁפָּטֶיךָ לְיַעֲקֹב *they will teach your ordinances to Jacob* Dt 33_{10}. **2. show** the way, subj. oft. Y., with **a.** double accus., הוֹרֵנִי י׳ דַּרְכֶּךָ *show me your way, O Y.* Ps 27_{11}. **b.** accus. of person + בְּ, יוֹרֶה חַטָּאִים בַּדָּרֶךְ *he shows sinners the way* Ps 25_{8}. **c.** accus. of person + אֶל, תּוֹרֵם אֶל־הַדֶּרֶךְ הַטּוֹבָה *you have shown them the proper way* 2 C 6_{27}. **d.** ellip., לְהוֹרֹת לְפָנָיו גֹּשְׁנָה *to show (before) him (the way) to Goshen* Gn 46_{28}. **3a. point out, show** something, וַיּוֹרֵהוּ י׳ עֵץ *then Y. pointed out to him a piece of wood* Ex 15_{25}. **b. point** with (בְּ) one's fingers Pr 6_{13}. **4.** ptc. as noun, **teacher,** מורה הצדק *the teacher of righteousness* 1QpHab 1_{13}.

→ הוֹרָה *teaching,* הוֹרָיָה *teaching,* מוֹרָה III *muzzle,* מָרָה I *instruction,* תּוֹרָה *law.*

***ירה** IV 2 vb.—**Hi.** 2 Pf. הֹרֵתִיךָ; impf. תּוֹרֵם—**lead** someone in(to) the right way, with בְּ Pr 4_{11}, אֶל 2 C 6_{27}.

***ירה** 1 vb.—**Qal** 1 Impf. תִּרְהוּ—**be terrified** Is 44_{8}. → cf. ירע *tremble.*

יְרוּאֵל 1 pl.n. **Jeruel.**

יָרוֹחַ 1 pr.n.m. **Jaroah.**

***יָרוּם** 6 adj. **1. elevated, raised,** of rock Ps 61_{3}, head Ps

276. 2. **exalted,** of Y. Ps 1847||2 S 2247, Y.'s servant Is 5213. 3. **arrogant,** of heart Dn 1112(Kt). → רום *be exalted.*

יָרוֹק 1.0.1 n.m. **green plants** Jb 398. → cf. יָרָק *herbage.*

יְרוּשָׁא 2 pr.n.f. **Jerusha.**

יְרוּשָׁלַםִ 641.2.29.5 pl.n. **Jerusalem.**

יָרֵחַ 27.2.1 n.m.—sf. וִירֵחֵךְ—**moon** Gn 379. → cf. יֶרַח *month.*

יֶרַח I 12.0.4.9 n.m.—pl. יְרָחִים; cstr. יַרְחֵי—**month** Ex 22; יֶרַח יָמִים *month of days,* i.e. a full month Dt 2113. → cf. יָרֵחַ *moon.*

יֶרַח II 2 pr.n.m. **Jerah.**

יְרֵחוֹ, see יְרִיחוֹ *Jericho.*

יְרֹחָם 10 pr.n.m. **Jeroham.**

יְרַחְמְאֵל 8.0.0.1 pr.n.m. **Jerahmeel.**

יְרַחְמְאֵלִי 2 gent. **Jerahmeelite.**

יַרְחָע 2 pr.n.m. **Jarha.**

ירט 2 vb.—**Qal** 2 Pf. יָרַט; impf. יִרְטֵנִי—1. of way, **be precipitate, be steep** Nm 2232. 2. of Y., **thrust** person into (עַל) hands of wicked Jb 1611.

יְרִיאֵל 1 pr.n.m. **Jeriel.**

[יָרִיב] I 3 n.[m.]—sf. יְרִיבֶךָ; pl. sf. יְרִיבָי—**adversary** Is 4925 Ps 351. → ריב *contend.*

יָרִיב II 3 pr.n.m. **Jarib.**

יְרִיבַי 1 pr.n.m. **Jeribai.**

*[יְרִידָה] 0.0.1 n.f.—sf. ירידתו—**descent** 3QTr 101. → ירד I *go down.*

יְרִיָּה, see יְרִיָּהוּ *Jeriah.*

יְרִיָּהוּ 3 pr.n.m. **Jeriah.**

יְרִיחֹה, see יְרִיחוֹ *Jericho.*

יְרִיחוֹ 58.0.3 pl.n. **Jericho.**

יְרֵימוֹת, see יְרִימוֹת *Jerimoth.*

יְרִימוֹת 7.0.0.1 pr.n.m. **Jerimoth.**

יְרִיעָה 54.0.1 n.f.—pl. יְרִיעוֹת; sf. יְרִיעֹתַי, יְרִיעוֹתֵיהֶם—**curtain** of tent Is 542, specif. of tabernacle Ex 261||368. → ירע *tremble.*

יְרִיעוֹת 1 pr.n.f. **Jerioth.**

יָרֵךְ 34.0.1 n.f.—cstr. יֶרֶךְ; sf. יְרֵכְךָ; du. יְרֵכַיִם; sf. יְרֵכַיִךְ—1a. **thigh, hip, hip joint,** (1) of human being, חַמּוּקֵי יְרֵכַיִךְ *curves of your hips* Ca 72. (2) of animal, כַּף הַיָּרֵךְ *socket of the hip joint* Gn 3233. b. perh. **genitals,** יֹצְאֵי יְרֵכוֹ *those coming out of his genitals,* i.e. his children Gn 4626. 2. **side,** יֶרֶךְ הַמִּשְׁכָּן צָפֹנָה *north side of the tabernacle* Ex 4022. 3. **base** of lampstand Ex 2531. 4. **deepest place, hollow, recess** of cistern or vault 3QTr 17. → cf. יְרֵכָה *flank.*

יְרֵכָה 28.0.1.1 n.f.—sf. יַרְכָתוֹ; du. יַרְכָתַיִם; cstr. יַרְכְּתֵי—1. sg., **side, distant border** of Zebulun Gn 4913. 2. du., a. **sides, remotest parts** of the earth Jr 622, the north Is 1413. b. **innermost parts** of cave 1 S 244, house Am 610, ship Jon 15. c. **depths** of the pit Is 1415. → cf. יָרֵךְ *thigh.*

*ירם 6 vb.—**Qal** 6 Impf. + waw וַנִּירָם; ptc. pass. יָרוּם—1. **become high, exalted,** וַנִּירָם אָבַד חֶשְׁבּוֹן *and we became exalted, but Heshbon passed away* Nm 2130. 2. pass., a. **be raised, elevated,** of rock Ps 613, head Ps 276. b. **be exalted,** of Y. Ps 1847, servant of Y. Is 5213. c. **be arrogant,** of heart Dn 1112(Kt). → cf. רום *be high.*

יָרָם, see יוֹרָם *Joram.*

יַרְמוּת 7 pl.n. **Jarmuth.**

יְרָמוֹת, see יְרֵמוֹת *Jeremoth.*

יְרֵמוֹת 6 pr.n.m. **Jeremoth.**

יְרֵמַי 1.0.0.1 pr.n.m. **Jeremai.**

יִרְמְיָה, see יִרְמְיָהוּ *Jeremiah.*

יִרְמְיָהוּ 144.1.7.12 pr.n.m. **Jeremiah.**

ירע 1 vb.—**Qal** 1 Pf. יָרְעָה—**tremble, be faint-hearted** Is 154. → יְרִיעָה *curtain;* cf. ירה *be terrified.*

יִרְפְּאֵל 1 pl.n. **Irpeel.**

ירק 3.0.1 vb.—**Qal** 3.0.1 Pf. יָרַק; + waw וְיָרְקָה; inf. abs. יָרֹק—**spit** in (בְּ) person's face Nm 1214 Dt 259.

יָרָק 5 n.m. coll., **herbage, vegetables,** וִירַק דֶּשֶׁא *and green shoots of grass* 2 K 1926||Is 3727, גַּן הַיָּרָק *garden of vegetables* Dt 1110. → cf. יֶרֶק *grass, plants,* יְרַקְרַק *greenish,* יָרוֹק *green plants,* יֵרָקוֹן *mildew.*

יֶרֶק 6.0.4 n.m. **grass, plants** Gn 130; יֶרֶק הַשָּׂדֶה *grass of the field* Nm 224. → cf. יָרָק *herbage.*

יַרְקוֹן 1 pl.n. **Jarkon.**

יֵרָקוֹן 6.0.1 n.m. 1. disease of grain, **rust or mildew** 1 K 837. 2. **paleness** of face Jr 306. → cf. יָרָק *herbage.*

יָרְקְעָם 1 pr.n.m. **Jorkeam.**

יְרַקְרַק 3 adj.—f. pl. יְרַקְרַקֹּת—1. **greenish,** of wound Lv 1349. 2. perh. as noun, **leaf,** אֶבְרוֹתֶיהָ בִּירַקְרַק חָרוּץ *her wings are (covered) with leaf of gold* Ps 6814. → cf. יָרָק

herbage.

ירש I 230.5.32 vb.—**Qal** 160.1.18 Pf. יָרַשׁ, יָרְשׁוּ; impf. יִירַשׁ (יִרַשׁ); + waw וְיָרַשְׁתָּ (וִירִשְׁתָּהּ), וִירִשְׁתֶּם, וַיִּרָשׁוּךָ; impv. רֵשׁ, רְשׁוּ, יְרָשָׁה, רִשְׁתּוֹ; ptc. יוֹרֵשׁ, יֹרֶשֶׁת, יֹרְשִׁים, יוֹרְשִׁים; inf. רֶשֶׁת (רֶשֶׁת), רִשְׁתּוֹ, יְרֵשָׁנוּ)—**1a. take possession of** land, property of others Nm 21$_{35}$ 1 K 21$_{15}$ Ne 9$_{25}$; subj. animals Is 34$_{11}$. **b. inherit** property Nm 36$_{8}$, specif. non-Israelite slaves as property Lv 25$_{46}$. **2. inherit from, be heir of** (accus.) someone Gn 15$_{4}$. **3a. dispossess** people, nation Dt 2$_{12}$ 11$_{23}$. **b. make** someone **poor** Jg 14$_{15}$. **4.** ptc. as noun, **a. heir** Jr 49$_{1}$. **b. conqueror** Mc 1$_{15}$.

Ni. 4 Impf. יִוָּרֵשׁ—**be deprived of property, become poor** Pr 30$_{9}$.

Pi. 1 Impf. יְיָרֵשׁ—subj. cricket, **take possession of,** i.e. devour, fruit Dt 28$_{42}$.

Hi. 65.4.14 Pf. הוֹרִישׁ, הוֹרַשְׁתָּ; impf. יוֹרִישׁ (יוֹרִשֶׁנּוּ), אוֹרִישׁ; + waw וַיּוֹרֶשׁ (וַיֹּרִשֵׁם); ptc. מוֹרִישׁ; inf. abs. הוֹרֵשׁ; cstr. הוֹרִישׁ—**1a. cause to possess,** יְרֻשָּׁתְךָ אֲשֶׁר הוֹרַשְׁתָּנוּ *your possession which you* (Y.) *caused us to possess* 2 C 20$_{11}$. **b.** subj. Y., **make inherit** (consequences of) sin Jb 13$_{26}$. **2. hold land as a possession** Nm 14$_{24}$. **3a. dispossess** people, nation Nm 32$_{39}$ Dt 7$_{17}$. **b. drive out** nation Ex 34$_{24}$ (+ מִפְּנֵי *[from] before* Israelites). **c. subdue** people Ex 15$_{9}$. **d. make poor,** ״ מוֹרִישׁ וּמַעֲשִׁיר *Y. makes poor and makes rich* 1 S 2$_{7}$. **4. empty out,** חַיִל בָּלַע וַיְקִאֶנּוּ מִבִּטְנוֹ יֹרִשֶׁנּוּ אֵל *riches he swallows and vomits; God empties it out of his stomach* Jb 20$_{15}$.

→ מוֹרָשׁ *possession,* יְרֵשָׁה *possession,* רֶשֶׁת *net,* יְרֻשָּׁה I *possession,* מוֹרָשָׁה *possession.*

***ירש** II 1 vb.—**Qal** 1 Impf. תִּירוֹשׁ—**press (grapes)** Mc 6$_{15}$. → תִּירוֹשׁ *new wine.*

יְרֵשָׁה 2.0.1 n.f. **possession,** acquired by conquest Nm 24$_{18}$. → ירשׁ I *take possession of.*

יְרֻשָּׁה 14 n.f.—cstr. יְרֻשַּׁת; sf. יְרֻשָּׁתְךָ—**possession,** acquired by conquest, אֶרֶץ יְרֻשָּׁתוֹ *land of his possession* Dt 2$_{12}$; also in connection with family property, מִשְׁפַּט הַיְרֻשָּׁה *the right of possession* Jr 32$_{8}$. → ירשׁ I *take possession of.*

*[**יָרֹת**] 0.0.0.2 pl.n. **Jaroth.**

יִשְׂחָק, see יִצְחָק *Isaac.*

יְשִׂימִאֵל 1 pr.n.m. **Jesimiel.**

יִשְׂרָאֵל 2512.21.354.22 pr.n.m. **Israel, 1.** patriarch, orig. named Jacob 1 C 1$_{34}$. **2.** nation regarding §1 as its eponymous ancestor, ״ אֱלֹהֵי יִשְׂרָאֵל *Y., God of Israel* Ex 5$_{1}$. → cf. יִשְׂרְאֵלִי *Israelite.*

יְשַׂרְאֵלָה 1 pr.n.m. **Jesharelah.**

יִשְׂרְאֵלִי 5 gent. **Israelite.** → cf. יִשְׂרָאֵל *Israel.*

יִשָּׂשכָר 43.0.5 pr.n.m. **Issachar.**

יֵשׁ 138.45.22 part.—יֶשׁ־; sf. יֶשְׁכֶם, יֶשְׁנוֹ—**1. (there) is,** as part., linking a subj. to a complement (*X is*), e.g. ״ יֵשׁ בַּמָּקוֹם הַזֶּה *Y. is in this place* Gn 28$_{16}$, or as the complement of an indef. subj. (*there is X*), e.g. יֶשׁ־שֶׁבֶר בְּמִצְרָיִם *there is grain in Egypt* Gn 42$_{1}$, יֶשׁ־לָנוּ אָב זָקֵן *there is to us,* i.e. we have, *an elderly father* Gn 44$_{20}$. **2.** as noun, **property** Pr 8$_{21}$; מחלקת נחלה ויש *distribution of inheritance and property* Si 43$_{3(M)}$. **3.** יֵשׁ אֲשֶׁר appar. as conditional conj., **if, whenever,** יֵשׁ אֲשֶׁר יִהְיֶה הֶעָנָן ... עַל־הַמִּשְׁכָּן *whenever the cloud rested ... over the tabernacle* Nm 9$_{20}$.

[**יִשְׁאָל**] 1.0.0.1 pr.n.m. **Ishal.**

ישׁב 1085.20.82.1 vb.—**Qal** 1036.13.80.1 Pf. יָשַׁב, יָשַׁבְתָּ; impf. יֵשֵׁב (יֵשֶׁב) וַיֵּשֶׁב (וַיֵּשֶׁב); + waw וַיֵּשֶׁב; impv. שֵׁב (שֶׁב־) שְׁבָה, שְׁבוּ, (שֵׁבוּ); ptc. יֹשֵׁב (יֹשְׁבֵי) יֹשֶׁבֶת, יֹשְׁבִים, יֹשְׁבֵי, יֹשְׁבָיו, יֹשֶׁבֶת; inf. abs. יָשׁוֹב; cstr. שֶׁבֶת—**1. sit,** הוּא־יֹשֵׁב בַּעֲלִיַּת הַמְּקֵרָה *he was sitting in the cool upper chamber* Jg 3$_{20}$. **2. sit down,** וַתֵּשֶׁב בְּפֶתַח עֵינַיִם *then she sat down at the gate of Enaim* Gn 38$_{14}$. **3. sit on throne, be enthroned,** ״ צְבָאוֹת יֹשֵׁב הַכְּרֻבִים *Y. of hosts enthroned on the cherubim* 1 S 4$_{4}$. **4. lie down, rest,** שָׁוְא לָכֶם מַשְׁכִּימֵי קוּם מְאַחֲרֵי־שֶׁבֶת *it is in vain that you rise up early and go late to rest* Ps 127$_{2}$. **5. remain, stay,** of person, שְׁבוּ אִישׁ תַּחְתָּיו *let everyone remain where he is* Ex 16$_{29}$; of object, וַיֵּשֶׁב אֲרוֹן ״ בֵּית עֹבֵד אֱדֹם *and the ark of Y. remained in the house of Obed-edom* 2 S 6$_{11}$. **6. dwell,** וִישַׁבְתֶּם עַל־הָאָרֶץ לָבֶטַח *and you shall dwell in the land securely* Lv 25$_{18}$, אָנֹכִי יוֹשֵׁב בְּבֵית אֲרָזִים *I dwell in a house of cedar* 2 S 7$_{2}$||1 C 17$_{1}$. **7. settle,** וַיֵּשֶׁב בְּאֶרֶץ־נוֹד *and he settled in the land of Nod* Gn 4$_{16}$. **8. be inhabited, populated,** of land Jr 50$_{13}$, city Zc 2$_{8}$. **9. be set,** of eye, as jewel Ca 5$_{12}$; of teeth 4QCrypt 2.1$_{3}$. **10. be established, stand, endure,** of throne Ps 122$_{5}$. **11.** perh. **sit in worship** Ps 23$_{6}$. **12. wait for** (לְ) someone Ex 24$_{14}$. **13.** ptc. as noun, **inhabitant,** oft.

coll., יֹשֵׁב הָאָרֶץ *inhabitant(s) of the land* Gn 34$_{30}$, also pl. יֹשְׁבֵי הָאָרֶץ Ex 23$_{31}$; fem. coll., יוֹשֶׁבֶת צִיּוֹן *inhabitant(s) of Zion* Is 12$_{6}$.

Ni. 8.2 Pf. נוֹשָׁבָה; ptc. נוֹשֶׁבֶת—**1. be inhabited,** of city Jr 22$_{6}$. **2.** perh. **be habitable,** of land Ex 16$_{35}$. **3.** fem. ptc. as noun, **inhabited one,** of city Ezk 26$_{17}$, world Si 43$_{4}$.

Pi. 1 + waw וְיִשְּׁבוּ—**establish** settlements Ezk 25$_{4}$.

Hi. 38.5.2 Pf. הוֹשַׁבְתִּי, הֹשִׁיב; impf. יוֹשִׁיבוּ, אוֹשִׁיבְךָ; + waw (וַיּוֹשֶׁב) וַיֹּשֶׁב, וַתֹּשִׁיבוּ; impv. הוֹשִׁיבוּ, הוֹשֵׁב; ptc. מוֹשִׁיב; inf. הוֹשִׁיב—**1. cause to sit, allow to sit, place** person 1 S 2$_{8}$. **2. accommodate, cause to dwell, (re)settle** people 2 K 17$_{6}$. **3.** of Y., **cause to be inhabited, populate** cities Ezk 36$_{33}$. **4. cause to remain, leave** men at (בְּ) wadi 1 S 30$_{21}$. **5. marry** a woman Ezr 10$_{2}$.

Ho. 2 Pf. הוּשַׁבְתֶּם; impf. תּוּשַׁב—**1. be made to dwell,** of person Is 5$_{8}$. **2. be inhabited,** of city Is 44$_{26}$.

→ שֶׁבֶת *seat,* מוֹשָׁב *seat,* מוֹשֶׁבֶת *dwelling,* יְשִׁיבָה *sitting,* תּוֹשָׁב *sojourner,* שִׁיבָה *stay,* שׁוּבָה II *stillness.*

יֶשֶׁבְאָב 1.0.6 pr.n.m. **Jeshebeab.**

יֹשֵׁב בַּשֶּׁבֶת 1 pr.n.m. **Josheb-basshebeth.**

יִשְׁבָּח 1 pr.n.m. **Ishbah.**

יִשְׁבִּי 1 pr.n.m. **Ishbi.**

יָשֻׁבִי לֶחֶם 1 pr.n.m. **Jashubi-lehem.**

יָשָׁבְעָם 3 pr.n.m. **Jashobeam.**

יִשְׁבָּק 2 pr.n.m. **Ishbak.**

יָשְׁבְּקָשָׁה 2 pr.n.m. **Joshbekashah.**

יָשׁוּב I 3.0.0.1 pr.n.m. **Jashub.**

*[יָשׁוּב] II 0.0.0.1 pl.n. **Jashub.**

יָשׁוּבִי 1 gent. **Jashubite.**

יִשְׁוָה 2 pr.n.m. **Ishvah.**

יְשׁוֹחָיָה 1 pr.n.m. **Jeshohaiah.**

יִשְׁוִי I 4 pr.n.m. **Ishvi.**

יִשְׁוִי II 1 gent. **Ishvite.**

יֵשׁוּעַ I 27.2.15 pr.n.m. **Jeshua, Joshua.**

יֵשׁוּעַ II 1 pl.n. **Jeshua.**

יְשׁוּעָה 78.1.22 n.f.—יְשׁוּעָתָה; cstr. יְשׁוּעַת; sf. יְשׁוּעָתִי; pl. יְשׁוּעוֹת (יְשֻׁעוֹת)—**1a. salvation, deliverance,** usu. brought by Y. Ex 14$_{13}$ Ps 147||53$_{7}$; also by human 2 S 10$_{11}$. **b.** perh. in pl. sometimes **saviour,** יְשׁוּעוֹת ... י׳ מְשִׁיחוֹ *Y. is ... the saviour of his anointed one* Ps 28$_{8}$. **2. victory,** brought by Y. Is 52$_{7}$, by human 1 S 14$_{45}$. **3. prosperity,** כְּעָב עָבְרָה יְשֻׁעָתִי *my prosperity passed away like a cloud* Jb 30$_{15}$. → ישׁע *save.*

*[יְשׁוּר] 0.0.1 n.m. **uprightness,** ישור לבבי *uprightness of my heart* 1QS 11$_{2}$. → ישׁר *be straight.*

[יֶשַׁח] 1 n.m.—sf. יֶשְׁחֲךָ—perh. **dysentery, faeces,** or perh. **semen** Mc 6$_{14}$.

ישׁט 3.4 vb.—**Hi.** 3.3 Impf. יוֹשִׁיט; + waw וַיּוֹשֶׁט; impv. Si הושיט—**extend, hold out** sceptre Est 4$_{11}$, hand Si 7$_{32}$.

Ho. 0.1 Ptc. מושטת—**be stretched out,** of hand Si 43$_{1}$.

יִשַׁי 41.1.4 pr.n.m. **Jesse.**

[יָשִׁיב] 1 pr.n.m. **Jashib.**

*[יְשִׁיבָה] 0.1 n.f.—sf. ישיבתי—**sitting** of teacher, i.e. **teaching,** perh. **academy** Si 51$_{29}$. → ישׁב *sit.*

יִשִּׁיָּה 7 pr.n.m. **Isshiah.**

יִשִּׁיָּהוּ, see יִשִּׁיָּה *Isshiah.*

יְשִׁימוֹן I 7 n.m.—יְשִׁמוֹן (יְשִׁמֹן, יְשִׁימֹן)—**desert, steppe** Ps 107$_{4}$.→ ישׁם *be desolate.*

יְשִׁימוֹן II 6 pl.n. **Jeshimon.**

[יְשִׁימָה] 1 n.f.—pl. Kt ישימות—**desolation** Ps 55$_{16}$. → ישׁם *be desolate.*

יְשִׁימוֹת, see בֵּית יְשִׁימוֹת *Beth-jeshimoth.*

יָשִׁישׁ 4.2 adj.—pl. יְשִׁישִׁים—**1. aged,** of person Si 8$_{5}$. **2.** as noun, **aged one** Jb 15$_{10}$. → cf. יָשֵׁשׁ *aged.*

יְשִׁישַׁי 1 pr.n.m. **Jeshishai.**

ישׁם 4 vb.—**Qal** 4 Impf. תֵּשַׁם, תִּישַׁמְנָה—**be desolate,** of land Gn 47$_{19}$. → יְשִׁמָה *desolation,* יְשִׁימוֹן *desert;* cf. שׁמם *be desolate.*

יִשְׁמָא 1 pr.n.m. **Ishma.**

יִשְׁמָעֵאל 48.0.1.20 pr.n.m. **Ishmael.**

יִשְׁמְעֵאלִי 8 gent. **Ishmaelite.**

יִשְׁמַעְיָה, see יִשְׁמַעְיָהוּ *Ishmaiah.*

יִשְׁמַעְיָהוּ 2 pr.n.m. **Ishmaiah.**

יִשְׁמְעֵלִי, see יִשְׁמְעֵאלִי *Ishmaelite.*

יִשְׁמְרַי 1 pr.n.m. **Ishmerai.**

ישׁן I 16.1.2 vb.—**Qal** 15.1.2 Pf. יָשַׁנְתִּי, יָשְׁנוּ; impf. אִישָׁן, יִשְׁנוּ; + waw וַיִּישָׁן; ptc. יָשֵׁן; inf. לִישׁוֹן—**be asleep, sleep, go to sleep,** of person Jb 3$_{13}$, sheep Ezk 34$_{25}$, Y. Ps 44$_{24}$.

Pi. 1 + waw וַתְּיַשְּׁנֵהוּ—**cause** person **to fall asleep** Jg 16$_{19}$.

→ יָשֵׁן *asleep*, שֵׁנָה *sleep*, יְשֵׁנָה *sleep*.

ישׁן II 3.2.1 vb.—**Qal** 0.1 Pf. ישׁן—**become old,** of wine Si 9_{10}.

Ni. 3.0.1 Pf. נוֹשַׁנְתֶּם; ptc. נוֹשָׁן—**1. become old,** of person Dt 4_{25}, grain Lv 26_{10}. **2. become advanced,** of disease Lv 13_{11}.

Htp. 0.1 Impv. התישן—**make oneself old** Si 11_{20}.

→ יָשָׁן *old*.

יָשָׁן 8.1.0.14 adj.—f.s. יְשָׁנָה; m.pl. יְשָׁנִים—**1. old,** of gate Ne 3_{6}, produce Lv 25_{22}, wine Samaria ost. 5_{3}, friend Si 9_{10}. **2.** as noun, **old food** Lv 26_{10}. → ישׁן II *become old*.

יָשֵׁן I 9 adj.—f.s. יְשֵׁנָה; m.pl. יְשֵׁנִים; cstr. יְשֵׁנֵי—**1. asleep** 1 S 26_{7}. **2.** as noun, **one who is asleep** Ca 7_{10}; in ref. to the dead Dn 12_{2}. → ישׁן I *sleep*.

יָשֵׁן II 1 pr.n.m. **Jashen.**

יְשָׁנָה 1 pl.n. **Jeshanah.**

*[**יְשִׁנָה**] 0.1 n.f.—ישינה—**sleep** Si 34_{20}. → ישׁן I *sleep*.

ישׁע 205.7.37.3 vb.—**Ni.** 21.1.3 Pf. נוֹשַׁע; impf. יִוָּשֵׁעַ; impv. הִוָּשְׁעוּ; ptc. נוֹשָׁע; inf. Si הושע—**1. be saved,** עַם נוֹשַׁע בַּי׳ *a people saved by Y.* Dt 33_{29}, וְנוֹשַׁעְתֶּם מֵאֹיְבֵיכֶם *and you shall be saved from your enemies* Nm 10_{9}. **2. be victorious,** גִּבּוֹר לֹא־יִנָּצֵל בְּרָב־כֹּחַ *a warrior is not victorious through his great strength* Ps 33_{16}.

Hi. 184.6.34.3 Pf. הוֹשִׁיעַ, הוֹשַׁעְתָּ; impf. יוֹשִׁיעַ (יֹשַׁע, יְהוֹשִׁיעַ); + waw וַיּוֹשַׁע; impv. הוֹשַׁע (הוֹשִׁיעֵנִי, הוֹשִׁיעָה); ptc. מוֹשִׁיעַ, pl. מוֹשִׁיעִים; inf. abs. הוֹשֵׁעַ; cstr. הוֹשִׁיעַ—**1. deliver, a.** subj. Y. Jr 31_{7}; + מִן *from* distress Ps 107_{13}, מִיַּד *from the hand of* enemy Ex 14_{30}, בְּיַד *by the hand of* Jg 6_{36}. **b.** subj. human, + מִיַּד *from the hand of* Jg 2_{18}. **2. save from** (מִן) backsliding, subj. Y. Ezk 37_{23}. **3. bring victory to** (לְ) someone, subj. Y. 1 C 18_{6}; וַתּוֹשַׁע לוֹ זְרֹעוֹ *and his* (Y.'s) *own arm brought him victory* Is 59_{16}. **4.** ptc. as noun, **saviour, deliverer,** in ref. to Y. Is 49_{26}, human Jg 3_{9}.

→ יֵשַׁע *salvation*, יֵשַׁע *salvation*, יְשׁוּעָה *salvation*, שׁוֹעַ II *noble*, מוֹשָׁעָה *salvation*, תְּשׁוּעָה *salvation*.

יֵשַׁע 36.2.11.3 n.m.—יָשַׁע; sf. יִשְׁעִי—**1. salvation,** brought by Y., יֵשַׁע עַמֶּךָ *salvation of your people* Hb 3_{13}, אֱלֹהֵי יִשְׁעִי *God of my salvation* Mc 7_{7}. **2. victory,** גְּבֻרוֹת יֵשַׁע יְמִינוֹ *mighty victories of his right hand* Ps 20_{7}. **3. prosperity** Jb 5_{4}. → ישׁע *save*.

*[**יֹשַׁע**] 1 n.m.—sf. יֹשַׁעֲכֶם—**salvation** Is 35_{4}. → ישׁע *save*.

*[**יֵשׁוּעָא**] 0.0.0.1 pr.n.m. **Jeshua.**

יִשְׁעִי 5 pr.n.m. **Ishi.**

יְשַׁעְיָהוּ 39.1.5.12 pr.n.m. **Isaiah, Jeshaiah.**

יְשֻׁעָתָה, see יְשׁוּעָה *salvation*.

יָשְׁפֵה 3 n.m. **jasper,** a gemstone, or perh. a kind of **quartz** Ex 28_{20}.

יִשְׁפָּה 1 pr.n.m. **Ispah.**

יִשְׁפָּן 1 pr.n.m. **Ishpan.**

*[**יִשְׁפָּט**] 0.0.0.1 pr.n.m. **Ishpat.**

ישׁר 25.1.11 vb.—**Qal** 13.1.1 Pf. יָשַׁר, יָשְׁרוּ; impf. יִישַׁר; + waw וַיִּישַׁר—**1. be pleasing** in the sight of (בְּעֵינֵי) someone, of woman Jg 14_{3}, matter 1 S 18_{20}. **2. be upright,** לֹא־יָשְׁרָה נַפְשׁוֹ בּוֹ *his soul is not upright within him* Hb 2_{4}. **3. go straight,** וַיִּשַּׁרְנָה הַפָּרוֹת בַּדֶּרֶךְ *then the cows went straight ahead* (lit. *in the way*) 1 S 6_{12}.

Pi. 9.0.8 Pf. יִשַּׁרְתִּי; impf. יְיַשֵּׁר; + waw וַיְּשַׁרֵם (Kt ויישרם); impv. יַשְּׁרוּ; ptc. מְיַשְּׁרִים—**1. level** paths Pr 3_{6}. **2. channel** waters 2 C 32_{30}. **3.** of Y., **direct** someone's steps 1QH 15_{14}. **4. go straight on** one's way Pr 9_{15}. **5. keep** precepts **precisely** Ps 119_{128}.

Pu. 1.0.1 Pf. Q יושר; ptc. מְיֻשָּׁר—**1. be evenly hammered,** of gold 1 K 6_{35}. **2. be pleasing** in the sight of (בְּעֵינֵי) Y. GnzPs 3_{3}.

Hi. 2.0.1 Impf. יַיְשִׁרוּ; impv. הַיְשַׁר—**1. make** path **straight** Ps 5_{9}. **2.** of eyelids, **look straight ahead** Pr 4_{25}.

→ יֹשֶׁר *uprightness*, יָשָׁר *aright*, יֹשֶׁר *uprightness*, יְשָׁרָה *uprightness*, מֵישָׁרִים I *righteousness*, III *smoothness*, IV *gullet*, מִישׁוֹר *plain*.

יָשָׁר 118.1.31 adj.—cstr. יְשַׁר; f.s. יְשָׁרָה; m.pl. יְשָׁרִים; cstr. יִשְׁרֵי; f.pl. יְשָׁרוֹת—**1a. right, pleasing,** of lifestyle, דֶּרֶךְ אֱוִיל יָשָׁר בְּעֵינָיו *the way of a fool seems right in his (own) eyes* Pr 12_{15}. **b. upright,** of Y. Ps 25_{8}, person Jb 8_{6}. **c. undivided,** of heart 2 K 10_{15}. **d. straight,** of foot Ezk 1_{7}. **e. stretched,** of wings Ezk 1_{23}. **f. level,** of road Jr 31_{9}. **2.** as noun, **a. that which is right,** וַיַּעַשׂ הַיָּשָׁר בְּעֵינֵי י׳ *and he did that which was right in the eyes of Y.* 2 C 34_{2}; כָּל־הַיְשָׁרָה *all that is right* Mc 3_{9}. **b. upright person,** צִדְקַת יְשָׁרִים *righteousness of the upright* Pr 11_{6}. → ישׁר *be straight*.

יֵשֶׁר 1 pr.n.m. **Jesher.**

יֹשֶׁר 14.4.7 n.m.—sf. יָשְׁרוֹ—**uprightness, rectitude, integrity, honesty,** יֹשֶׁר לֵבָב *integrity of heart* Ps 119$_{7}$, אָרְחוֹת יֹשֶׁר *paths of rectitude* Pr 2$_{13}$, אִמְרֵי־יֹשֶׁר *words of honesty* Jb 6$_{25}$. → ישר *be straight.*

יְשָׁרָה 1.0.1 n.f. **uprightness** of heart 1 K 3$_{6}$. → ישר *be straight.*

יְשֻׁרוּן 4.1 pr.n.m. **Jeshurun.**

יָשֵׁשׁ 1 adj. **aged,** as noun, **aged one** 2 C 36$_{17}$. → cf. יָשִׁישׁ *aged.*

יָתֵד 24.0.1 n.f.—cstr. יְתַד (יְתֶד); pl. יְתֵדוֹת; cstr. יִתְדוֹת; sf. יְתֵדֹתָיו—**1a. tent-pin,** of metal Ex 27$_{19}$. **b. hanging peg,** of wood Ezk 15$_{3}$. **c. stake, secure hold** in holy place Ezr 9$_{8}$. **d. support,** in ref. to leader Zc 10$_{4}$. **2a. digging stick** Dt 23$_{14}$. **b. beating stick** for weft on loom Jg 16$_{14}$.

יָתוֹם 42.2.4 n.m.—pl. יְתוֹמִים; sf. יְתֹמָיו—**orphan,** i.e. one who is fatherless, כָּל־אַלְמָנָה וְיָתוֹם *every widow and fatherless child* Ex 22$_{21}$.

*[יְתוּר] 1 n.[m.] **outcrop(s),** יְתוּר הָרִים *the outcrops of the mountains* Jb 39$_{8}$. → יתר *exceed.*

יַתִּיר 4 pl.n. **Jattir.**

יִתְלָה 1 pl.n. **Ithlah.**

*[יָתָם] 0.0.0.2 pr.n.m. **Jathum.**

יִתְמָה 1 pr.n.m. **Ithmah.**

*[יתן] I vb. **Qal, be constant** Is 33$_{16}$ (if em. נִתָּן bread *will be given* to יִתַּן *will be constant*) Pr 12$_{12}$ (if em. יִתֵּן *he will give* root to יִתַּן the root *will be constant*).

*[יתן] II vb. **Qal, give, cause to be,** אֹיְבַי יָתַתָּה לִּי עֹרֶף *you gave me my enemies (as) a neck,* i.e. you made them flee from me 2 S 22$_{41}$ (if em. תַּתָּה, from נתן *give*). → cf. נתן *give.*

*[יֹתֵן] 0.0.0.1 pr.n.m. **Jothen.**

יַתְנִיאֵל 1 pr.n.m. **Jathniel.**

יִתְנָן 1 pl.n. **Ithnan.**

יתר 105.2.18 vb.—**Ni.** 82.0.10 Pf. נוֹתַר, נוֹתְרוּ; impf. יִוָּתֵר (יִוָּתֶר); ptc. נוֹתָר, נוֹתֶרֶת, נוֹתָרִים, נוֹתָרוֹת—**1a. be left, remain,** of tribe Jos 18$_{2}$, survivor Ezk 14$_{22}$, plants Ex 10$_{15}$. **b. be left** alone, וַיִּוָּתֵר יַעֲקֹב לְבַדּוֹ *then Jacob was left alone* Gn 32$_{25}$. **2.** ptc. as noun, **a. that which is left over** of (מִן) offering Lv 2$_{3}$. **b. remaining one,** i.e. person Jg 21$_{7}$, animal Gn 30$_{36}$.

Hi. 23.2.8 Pf. הוֹתִיר; impf. יוֹתִיר (יוֹתֵר), נוֹתַר; impv. הוֹתֵר; ptc. Q מותר; inf. abs. הוֹתֵר; cstr. הוֹתִיר—**1a.** trans., **leave over, leave behind,** אֵת כָּל־פְּרִי הָעֵץ אֲשֶׁר הוֹתִיר הַבָּרָד *all the fruit of the trees that the hail had left* Ex 10$_{15}$, לוּלֵי יי צְבָאוֹת הוֹתִיר לָנוּ שָׂרִיד *unless Y. of hosts had left us a remnant* Is 1$_{9}$. **b.** abs., of Y., **leave a remnant** Ezk 6$_{8}$. **2. have food left over** Ru 2$_{18}$. **3. give abundantly, enrich,** וְהוֹתִרְךָ יי לְטוֹבָה *and Y. will give you abounding prosperity* Dt 28$_{11}$. **4. have pre-eminence** Gn 49$_{4}$.

→ יְתוּר *outcrop,* יֶתֶר I *remainder,* II *cord,* יָתֵר *more,* יִתְרָה *abundance,* יוֹתֵר *remainder,* יֹתֶרֶת *appendage,* יִתְרוֹן *profit,* מוֹתָר *abundance.*

יֶתֶר, see יַתִּיר *Jattir.*

*[יָתֵר] 0.3.2 adv.—Q יתיר—**1. (even) more** Si 10$_{31}$. **2.** substantivized, **more or one who has more,** אל תערב יתר ממך *do not pledge more than you have* or *do not stand surety for one who is greater than you* Si 8$_{13}$. → יתר *exceed.*

יֶתֶר I 96.1.1.2 n.m.—pl. יְתָרִים—**1a. remainder, rest** of food Ex 23$_{11}$, vessels Jr 27$_{19}$. **b. remnant,** i.e. of Israel Zp 2$_{9}$. **2.** perh. **totality, all, majority** of the Rephaim Dt 3$_{11}$. **3. excess, abundance,** שְׂפַת־יֶתֶר *lips of excess,* i.e. arrogant speech Pr 17$_{7}$; used adverbially, מְשַׁלֵּם עַל־יֶתֶר עֹשֵׂה גַאֲוָה *he requites abundantly him who acts haughtily* Ps 31$_{24}$, וַתִּגְדַּל־יֶתֶר *and it grew exceedingly great* Dn 8$_{9}$. **4. pre-eminence** of honour and power Gn 49$_{3}$. **5.** perh. **wealth** Hb 2$_{8}$. → יתר *be left.*

יֶתֶר II 6.1 n.m.—sf. יִתְרָם; pl. יְתָרִים—**1. cord, sinews,** for binding Jg 16$_{7}$. **2. tent rope** Jb 4$_{21}$. **3. bow-string** Ps 11$_{2}$. → יתר *be left;* cf. מֵיתָר *cord.*

יֶתֶר III 9 pr.n.m. **Jether.**

יֹתֵר, see יוֹתֵר *remainder.*

יִתְרָא 1.0.1 pr.n.m. **Ithra.**

יִתְרָה 2 n.f.—cstr. יִתְרַת—**abundance** Is 15$_{7}$ Jr 48$_{36}$. → יתר *be left.*

יִתְרוֹ 9 pr.n.m. **Jethro.**

יִתְרוֹן 10 n.m. **profit, benefit, advantage,** מַה־יִּתְרוֹן לָאָדָם *what profit is there to a human being?* Ec 1$_{3}$, יִתְרוֹן דַּעַת *advantage of knowledge* Ec 7$_{12}$. → יתר *be left.*

יִתְרִי 3 gent. **Ithrite.**

יִתְרָן 3 pr.n.m. **Ithran.**

יִתְרְעָם 2 pr.n.m. **Ithream.**

יֹתֶ֫רֶת 11.0.1 n.f.—יוֹתֶרֶת—**appendage, lobe, or fatty mass** at opening of liver of sacrificial animal Ex 29_{22}.
→ יתר *exceed.*

יְתֵת 2 pr.n.m. **Jetheth.**

כ

כְּ 2471.c.155.c.550.17 prep.—1. כְּ usu. before any consonant other than א, ה, ח, or ע; 2. כָּא֫, כֶּא֫, כַּא֫, before א, ה, ח, or ע; exceptions כֵּאלֹהִים, כַּי׳, כַּאדֹנָי, כַּאבִּיר; 3. with demonstr. pron., כָּזֶה, כָּאֵלֶּה, כָּהֵמָּה; 4. with sf., כָּכֶם (כָּכֵם), כָּהֶם (כָּהֵם, כָּהֵמָּה), כָּהֵן (כָּהֵנָּה); other sfs. are attached to כְּמוֹ—**1. as, like,** comparing, הֲכַיּוֹצֵר הַזֶּה לֹא אוּכַל לַעֲשׂוֹת *can I not act like this potter?* Jr 18_{6}. **2. as ... so,** indicating equivalence, כִּשְׁמוֹ כֶּן־הוּא *as is his name, so is he* 1 S 25_{25}, כָּמוֹנִי כָמוֹךָ *I am as you are* 1 K 22_{4}. **3.** indicating approximate number, **around, about, approximately,** כְּשֵׁשׁ־מֵאוֹת אֶלֶף *about 600,000* Ex 12_{37}. **4. in accordance with, after,** וַיִּקְרָא שֵׁם הָעִיר כְּשֵׁם בְּנוֹ חֲנוֹךְ *he called the name of the city after the name of his son Enoch* Gn 4_{17}. **5.** indicating time, **at, when, as,** usu. with inf. cstr., כְּבוֹא אַבְרָם מִצְרָיְמָה *when Abram came into Egypt* Gn 12_{14}; with noun, הִנְנִי מַמְטִיר כָּעֵת מָחָר *tomorrow at (about) this time I shall cause it to rain* Ex 9_{18}. **6.** perh. possessive, **of,** אֹרַח כַּנָּשִׁים *the way of women* Gn 18_{11}. → cf. כְּמוֹ *as,* כְּמוֹת *like.*

כאב 8.2 vb.—**Qal** 4.1 Impf. יִכְאַב; ptc. כֹּאֵב, כֹּאֲבִים—**be in pain** Gn 34_{25} Ps 69_{30}.

Hi. 4.1 Pf. הִכְאַבְתִּיו; impf. יַכְאִיב; ptc. מַכְאִיב—**1. hurt, a.** with obj. feelings, subj. person Si 4_{3}. **b.** abs., subj. Y. Jb 5_{18}, thorn Ezk 28_{24}. **2. ruin** field with (בְּ) stones 2 K 3_{19}.

→ כְּאֵב *pain,* מַכְאוֹב *pain.*

כְּאֵב 6.4.2 n.m.—sf. כְּאֵבִי—**pain** Is 65_{14}. → כאב *hurt.*

כאה 3.0.2 vb.—**Ni.** 2.0.2 + waw וְנִכְאָה; ptc. נִכְאֵה—**be discouraged** Dn 11_{30}. **2.** ptc. as noun, **downcast one** Ps 109_{16}.

Hi. 1 Inf. הַכְאוֹת—**discourage** hearts Ezk 13_{22}.

*[**כָּאוֹר**] 0.0.1 adj.—כאורה—**repulsive** 4QpNah 3.3_{2}. → כאר II *be repulsive.*

*[**כאף**] 0.2 vb.—**Pi.** 0.1 Impv. כיף—**bow head** Si 30_{12}.

Hi. 0.1 Impv. הכאף—**bow head** Si 4_{7}.

כאר I 1 vb.—**Qal** 1 Pf. mss כָּאֲרוּ (L כָּאֲרִי *like a lion*)—**bind** hands and feet Ps $22_{17(mss)}$.

***כאר II** 1.0.1 vb.—**Qal** 1 Pf. mss כָּאֲרוּ—**be repulsive,** of hands and feet Ps $22_{17(mss)}$.

Pi. 0.0.1 + waw וכארום—**consider** someone **repulsive** 4QpNah 3.3_{4}.

Po., mutilate hands and feet Ps $22_{17(mss)}$ (if em. כָּאֲרוּ *they are repulsive* to כֹּאֲרוּ *they mutilated*).

→ כָּאוֹר *repulsive.*

כַּאֲשֶׁר, see אֲשֶׁר *which.*

כבד 113.23.56.1 vb.—**Qal** 23.0.1 Pf. כָּבֵד (כָּבַד); impf. יִכְבַּד; impv. Q כבוד—**1a. be heavy,** of battle Jg 20_{34}, labour Ex 5_{9}, burden of sin Ps 38_{5}. **b. be heavily laden** (with cargo), of Tyre Ezk 27_{25}. **c. weigh, rest heavily** upon (אֶל) someone, of Y.'s hand 1 S 5_{6}; upon (עַל) earth, of sin Is 24_{20}. **d. be grave,** of sin Gn 18_{20}. **2a. be stubborn,** of heart Ex 9_{7}. **b. be dull** (to hear), of ear Is 59_{1}. **c. be dim,** of eyes Gn 48_{10}. **3a. be honoured,** of person Jb 14_{21}. **b. be glorified,** of Y. Is 66_{5}. **4.** appar. **honour** parents 4QInstr[b] 2.3_{15}.

Ni. 30.10.33 Pf. נִכְבַּד; impf. אֶכָּבֵד; impv. הִכָּבֵד; ptc. נִכְבָּד, נִכְבָּדִים, נִכְבַּדֵּי, נִכְבָּדֶיהָ, נִכְבָּדוֹת; inf. הִכָּבְדִי—**1. be respected, be distinguished,** of person Gn 34_{19}. **2a. gain glory (for oneself)** through (בְּ) people, of Y. Ex 14_{4}. **b. be glorious,** of name of Y. Dt 28_{58}. **3. abound,** מַעְיָנוֹת נִכְבַּדֵּי־מָיִם *springs abounding with water* Pr 8_{24}. **4.** ptc. as noun, **honourable one** Is 23_{8}. **5.** ptc. fem. pl. as noun, **glorious things** Ps 87_{3}.

Pi. 38.6.20.1 Pf. כִּבַּדְתָּנִי; impf. יְכַבֵּד; impv. כַּבֵּד, כַּבְּדוּהוּ; ptc. מְכַבֵּד, מְכַבְּדוֹ; inf. כַּבֵּד—**1a. make honourable, honour** parents Ex 20_{12}, Y. Ps 91_{15}, sabbath Is 58_{13}. **b.**

perh. specif. **honour person with banquet, fête** Ps 15$_4$. **2. make** one's heart **dull, insensitive** 1 S 6$_6$. **3. cleanse** house 11QT 49$_{11}$.

Pu. 3 Impf. יְכֻבַּד; ptc. מְכֻבָּד—**1. be honoured,** of person Pr 13$_{18}$, holy day Is 58$_{13}$. **2.** perh. **be enriched,** of person Pr 13$_{18}$.

Hi. 17.3.1 Pf. הִכְבִּיד; + waw וַיַּכְבֵּד; impv. Si הכבד; ptc. מַכְבִּיד; inf. הַכְבֵּד—**1.** let yoke **weigh heavily** upon (עַל) people Is 47$_6$. **2a. harden** someone's heart (subj. Y.) Ex 10$_1$, one's own heart Ex 8$_{11}$. **b. make** someone's ears **unresponsive** Is 6$_{10}$. **3a. bring honour to** nation Jr 30$_{19}$. **b. glorify** law GnzPs 4$_6$. **4.** perh. **multiply** nation Jr 30$_{19}$.

Htp. 2.5.1 Impv. הִתְכַּבֵּד—**1. multiply (oneself)** like (כְּ) locusts Na 3$_{15}$. **2. put on airs** Pr 12$_9$. **3.** perh. **be fêted** Pr 12$_9$.

→ כָּבֵד I *heavy,* II *liver,* כֹּבֶד *heaviness,* כִּבּוּד *hardness,* כְּבֵדֻת *heaviness,* כָּבוֹד *glory,* כְּבוּדָּה *wealth.*

כָּבֵד I 41.5.4 adj.—cstr. כְּבַד (כְּבֶד); pl. כְּבֵדִים; cstr. כִּבְדֵי—**1a. heavy,** of person 1 S 4$_{18}$; כְּבַד לָשׁוֹן *heavy of tongue,* i.e. slow of speech Ex 4$_{10}$. **b. massive,** of rock Is 32$_2$. **c. dense,** of cloud Ex 19$_{16}$. **d. numerous,** of people 1 K 3$_9$. **e. rich,** of person Gn 13$_2$. **f. severe,** of famine Gn 12$_{10}$. **g. burdensome,** of task Ex 18$_{18}$. **h. weary,** of hands Ex 17$_{12}$. **i. obstinate,** of heart Ex 7$_{14}$. **j. deep, profound,** of mourning Gn 50$_{10}$. **2.** as adv., **in great numbers** Ex 10$_{14}$. → כבד *be heavy.*

כָּבֵד II 14.0.3 n.m.—sf. כְּבֵדוֹ—**liver** of animal Lv 3$_4$, consulted in divination Ezk 21$_{26}$; of person, as seat of emotion Lm 2$_{11}$. → כבד *be heavy.*

כֹּבֶד 4 n.m. **1. heaviness** of stone Pr 27$_3$. **2.** perh. **denseness** of clouds Is 30$_{27}$. **3. mass** of corpses Na 3$_3$. **4. fierceness** of battle Is 21$_{15}$. → כבד *be heavy.*

כְּבֵדֻת 1 n.f. **heaviness, awkwardness** Ex 14$_{25}$. → כבד *be heavy.*

כבה 24.2.2 vb.—**Qal** 14.0.1 Pf. כָּבוּ; impf. יִכְבֶּה—**be extinguished, quenched,** of fire Lv 6$_5$, wrath of Y. Jr 7$_{20}$.

Pi. 10.2.1 Pf. כִּבּוּ; impf. יְכַבֶּנָּה; ptc. מְכַבֶּה; inf. כַּבּוֹת—**extinguish, quench** fire Si 51$_4$, love Ca 8$_7$.

→ כָּבָה *dimness.*

*[**כָּבָה**] 0.1 n.f. **dimness,** כבות אש *dimness of a fire* Si 51$_4$. → כבה *be extinguished.*

כָּבוֹד 199.33.315 n.m. (rarely f.)—cstr. כְּבוֹד; sf. כְּבֹדוֹ—**1. glory, majesty** of Y. Dt 5$_{24}$. **2. honour, reputation** of person Hb 2$_{16}$. **3. splendour** of temple Hg 2$_3$, throne Is 22$_{23}$. **4. wealth** Gn 31$_1$. **5.** appar. **soul, inner being** Gn 49$_6$. → כבד *be heavy.*

*[**כִּבּוּד**] 0.0.2 n.[m.]—כיבוד—**hardness** of heart 1QS 4$_{11}$, **dullness** of ear, i.e. hearing 1QS 4$_{11}$. → כבד *be heavy.*

כְּבוּדָּה 3 n.f. **wealth, property** Jg 18$_{21}$ Ezk 23$_{41}$ Ps 45$_{14}$. → כבד *be heavy.*

כָּבוּל 2 pl.n. **Cabul.**

כַּבּוֹן 1 pl.n. **Cabbon.**

*[**כִּבּוּס**] 0.0.1 n.[m.] **washing,** טמא כבוס *unclean one of washing,* i.e. unclean person with washed garments CD 11$_{22}$. → כבס *wash.*

כָּבִיר 2 n.m.—cstr. כְּבִיר—**braided article,** perh. **cushion** or **quilt,** made from goats' hair 1 S 19$_{13.16}$. → cf. כְּבָרָה I *sieve,* מַכְבֵּר *cover,* מִכְבָּר *grating.*

כַּבִּיר 10.0.1 adj.—m.pl. כַּבִּירִים; f.pl. Q כבירות—**1. strong, powerful,** of Y. Jb 36$_5$, people Is 16$_{14}$, wind Jb 8$_2$, water Is 17$_{12}$. **2.** as noun, **Mighty One,** or perh. **Aged One,** as title of Y. Jb 34$_{17}$. → כבר *multiply.*

כֶּבֶל 2.0.2 n.m.—pl. Q כבלים; cstr. כַּבְלֵי—**fetter** Ps 105$_{18}$ 149$_8$.

*[**כַּבְלוּלָה**] 0.0.2 pr.n.[f.] **Cablulah.**

כבס 48.0.30 vb.—**Qal** 3 Ptc. כּוֹבֵס—ptc. as noun, **fuller,** שְׂדֵה כוֹבֵס *field of the fuller* Is 7$_3$.

Pi. 41.0.29 Pf. כִּבֵּס (כִּבֶּס), כִּבַּסְתֶּם; impf. יְכַבֵּס; impv. כַּבְּסִי, כַּבְּסֵנִי; ptc. מְכַבְּסִים—**1. wash, launder** clothes Lv 11$_{25}$. **2. clean** doorposts 11QT 49$_{13}$. **3.** of Y., **cleanse, purify** person from (מִן) iniquity Ps 51$_4$.

Pu. 2 Pf. כֻּבַּס—**be washed** with (בְּ) water, of clothes Lv 15$_{17}$.

Htp. 0.0.1 Impf. יתכבסו—**be washed,** of clothes 11QT 49$_{16}$.

Hothp. 2 Pf. הֻכַּבַּס—**be washed,** of clothes Lv 13$_{55}$.

→ כִּבּוּס *washing.*

כבר 3.0.1 vb.—**Hi.** 2.0.1 Pf. Q הכביר; impf. יַכְבִּר; ptc. מַכְבִּיר—**1. multiply** words Jb 35$_{16}$. **2.** perh. ptc. as noun, **abundance** Jb 36$_{31}$.

Pi. 1 Inf. כַּבִּר—inf. as adv., **thoroughly** Is 1$_{25}$.

→ כַּבִּיר *strong.*

כְּבָר I 9.0.2 adv. **1. already, long ago** Ec 9$_{7}$. **2.** as prep., בִּשְׁכְּבָר **during** Ec 2$_{16}$.

כְּבָר II 8.0.2 pl.n. **Chebar.**

כְּבָרָה I 1 n.f. **sieve** Am 9$_{9}$. → cf. כָּבִיר *braided article,* מָכְבֵּר *cover,* מִכְבָּר *grating.*

[כִּבְרָה] II 3 n.f.—cstr. כִּבְרַת—**stretch (of land),** i.e. distance Gn 48$_{7}$.

כֶּבֶשׂ 107.1.23 n.m.—pl. כְּבָשִׂים; sf. כְּבָשַׂי—**ram,** male sheep, perh. young **lamb,** as distinct from אַיִל *ram,* male adult sheep Ezk 46$_{6}$, and from כִּבְשָׂה *ewe,* female adult sheep; usu. sacrificial animal Lv 14$_{10}$. → cf. כִּבְשָׂה *ewe.*

כִּבְשָׂה 8 n.f.—כַּבְשָׂה; cstr. כִּבְשַׂת; pl. כְּבָשֹׂת; cstr. כִּבְשׂת—**ewe,** female sheep, perh. young **ewe lamb** 2 S 12$_{3}$. → cf. כֶּבֶשׂ *ram.*

כבשׁ 14.0.2 vb.—**Qal** 8.0.1 Impf. יִכְבֹּשׁ; + waw וְכִבְשׁוּ; כִּבְשֻׁהָ; ptc. כֹּבְשִׁים; inf. כְּבוֹשׁ—**1. make** slaves **subservient** Jr 34$_{11(Qr)}$. **2. rape** woman Est 7$_{8}$. **3. dominate** the earth Gn 1$_{28}$. **4.** of Y., **subdue** sin Mc 7$_{19}$.

Ni. 5.0.1 Pf. נִכְבְּשָׁה; ptc. נִכְבָּשׁוֹת—**1.** of land, **be subdued before** (לִפְנֵי) Israelites, i.e. be under their control Jos 18$_{1}$. **2.** of daughters, **be enslaved,** or perh. **raped** Ne 5$_{5}$.

Pi. 1 Pf. כִּבֵּשׁ—**subdue** nations 2 S 8$_{11}$.

Hi. 1 + waw וַיַּכְבִּישׁוּם—**subjugate** slaves Jr 34$_{11(Kt)}$. → כֶּבֶשׁ *footstool,* כִּבְשָׁן *furnace.*

כֶּבֶשׁ 1 n.m. **footstool** 2 C 9$_{18}$. → כבשׁ *subdue.*

כִּבְשָׁן 4.1.1 n.m. **kiln, furnace** Gn 19$_{28}$. → כבשׁ *subdue.*

*כבת vb. **Ni., be humbled** Jr 17$_{13}$ (if em. יִכָּתֵבוּ *they will be inscribed* to יִכָּבֵתוּ *they will be humbled*).

כַּד 18.0.0.1 n.f.—sf. כַּדֵּךְ; pl. כַּדִּים—**jar** as container for water Gn 24$_{14}$, flour 1 K 17$_{12}$, etc., perh. **goblet** in silver 3QTr 2$_{11}$ (others בַּד silver *bar*).

כַּדּוּר 2 n.m. **1. ball, skein,** of yarn Is 22$_{18}$. **2. circle** Is 29$_{3}$.

כַּדְכֹּד 2 n.m. **agate,** a semi-precious stone Is 54$_{12}$.

*כדם 1 n.f. **Qal** 1 Ptc. pass. כְּדֻמָה—pass., **be held captive or be anchored,** of Tyre Ezk 27$_{32}$.

כְּדָרְלָעֹמֶר 5 pr.n.m. **Chedorlaomer.**

כֹּה 582 adv. **1.** usu. of manner, **so, thus, in this way,** כֹּה אָמַר הָאֱלֹהִים *thus God said* 2 C 24$_{20}$. **2.** of place or direction, **a. (over) here,** שִׂים כֹּה *put (it) here* Gn 31$_{37}$. **b.** כֹּה ... כֹּה **on this side, ... on that side** Nm 11$_{31}$. **3.** as compound adv., **a.** בְּכֹה **in this way** 1 K 22$_{20}$. **b.** עַד־כֹּה **until now** Jos 17$_{14}$.

כהה I 8 vb.—**Qal** 5 Pf. כָּהֲתָה; impf. יִכְהֶה; + waw וַתֵּכַהּ; inf. כָּהֹה—**1. be dim,** of eyes Gn 27$_{1}$. **2. be weak,** of person Is 42$_{4}$.

Pi. 3 Pf. כִּהֲתָה, כֵּהָה—**1. be colourless,** of spots on skin Lv 13$_{6}$. **2. be disheartened,** of spirit Ezk 21$_{12}$. → כֵּהֶה *dim,* כֵּהָה *lessening.*

כהה II 1 vb.—**Pi.** 1 Pf. כִּהָה—**rebuke, restrain** (בְּ of obj.) son 1 S 3$_{13}$.

*כהה III 0.0.1 vb.—**Qal** 0.0.1 Impf. יכהו—**be blunt,** of weapon 1QM 17$_{1}$.

כֵּהָה 1 n.f. **lessening,** assuaging of wound Na 3$_{19}$. → כהה I *be weak.*

כֵּהֶה 7.0.1 adj.—f.s. כֵּהָה; pl. כֵּהוֹת—**1a. dim,** of wick Is 42$_{3}$. **b. dull, colourless,** of spot Lv 13$_{39}$. **c. drooping,** of spirit Is 61$_{3}$. **2.** as noun, כהה עינים **one dim of eyes,** i.e. with poor eyesight CD 15$_{16}$. → כהה I *be dim.*

כהן 23.3.1 vb.—**Pi.** 23.3.1 Pf. כִּהֵן; impf. יְכַהֵן; כַּהֵן (כַּהֲנוֹ)—**1. be priest, serve as priest** Ex 31$_{10}$ Lv 7$_{35}$ (+ לְ *to* Y.). **2.** perh. **consecrate,** or **parade like a priest, flaunt** clothing, כְּחָתָן יְכַהֵן פְּאֵר *like a bridegroom, who consecrates,* or *flaunts, a turban* Is 61$_{10}$. → כֹּהֵן *priest,* כְּהֻנָּה *priesthood.*

כֹּהֵן 752.4.181.21 n.m. **priest, 1.** Israelite cultic official of Y., offering sacrifice and making atonement Lv 14$_{19}$, sounding trumpet Jos 6$_{4}$, making judicial decisions Ml 2$_{8}$; הַכֹּהֵן הַגָּדוֹל *the high priest* Jos 20$_{6}$, הַכֹּהֲנִים וְהַלְוִיִּם *the priests and the Levites* 1 K 8$_{4}$, כֹּהֲנֵי יי *priests of Y.* 1 S 22$_{17}$, כֹּהֵן לְדָוִד *priest of David* 2 S 20$_{26}$, מַמְלֶכֶת כֹּהֲנִים *kingdom of,* i.e. consisting of, *priests* Ex 19$_{6}$. **2.** priest of other gods Gn 41$_{50}$; כֹּהֵן הַבַּעַל *priest of Baal* 2 K 11$_{18}$. → כהן *be priest.*

כְּהֻנָּה 14.1.12 n.f.—cstr. כְּהֻנַּת; pl. כְּהֻנּוֹת—**priesthood** Jos 18$_{7}$. → כהן *be priest.*

כּוּב 1 pl.n. **Cub.**

כּוֹבַע 6 n.m.—cstr. כּוֹבַע; pl. כּוֹבָעִים—**helmet** 1 S 17$_{5}$ Ezk 27$_{10}$. → cf. קוֹבַע *helmet.*

כוה 2.1 vb.—**Ni.** 2.1 Impf. תִּכָּוֶה—**be burned, scorched,** of people Is 43$_{2}$, feet Pr 6$_{28}$. → כְּוִיָּה *burn,* כִּי III *burn,* מִכְוָה *burn.*

[כּוֹזְבָא], see כֹּזְבָא *Cozeba.*

כּוֹחַ, see כֹּחַ *strength*.

כְּוִיָּה 2 n.f. **burn** Ex 21$_{25}$. → כוה *burn*.

* [כּוּךְ] n.[m.] **crypt** 3QTr 12$_{2}$ (others בור *cistern*).

כּוֹכָב 37.2.12 n.m.—cstr. כּוֹכַב; pl. כּוֹכָבִים; cstr. כּוֹכְבֵי; sf. כּוֹכְבֵיהֶם—**1. star** Gn 22$_{17}$. **2.** perh. **royal ensign** Am 5$_{26}$.

* [כּוֹכָבָה] 0.0.1 pl.n. **Cochaba.**

כּוּל 37.7.8.4 vb.—**Qal** 1.0.1.4 Pf. כָּל; impf. Q יכול—**lay hold of, measure** dust Is 40$_{12}$.

Pilp. 23.4.3 Pf. כִּלְכֵּל; impf. יְכַלְכֵּל; ptc. מְכַלְכֵּל; inf. כַּלְכֵּל—**1. sustain, provide for** someone Gn 50$_{21}$. **2. endure** illness Pr 18$_{14}$. **3. manage affairs** Ps 112$_{5}$ (or §4). **4. measure** words Ps 112$_{5}$. **5.** of heavens, **contain** Y. 2 C 2$_{5}$.

Polp. 1 Pf. כָּלְכְּלוּ—**be provisioned,** of Israelite army 1 K 20$_{27}$.

Hi. 12.0.3 Pf. Q הכיל; impf. יָכִיל; inf. הָכִיל—**1a.** of cistern, **contain water** Jr 2$_{13}$. **b.** of altar, **hold** offering 1 K 8$_{64}$. **2.** of people, **endure** words of prophet Am 7$_{10}$, anger of Y. Jr 10$_{10}$.

Htpalp. 0.2.1 Impf. Si יתכלכל, Q יתכלכלו—**1. stand before** (לִפְנֵי), i.e. **withstand** heat Si 43$_{3(B)}$. **2. restrain oneself** Si 12$_{15}$.

Htpol. 0.1 Impf. יתכולל—**stand before** (לִפְנֵי), i.e. **withstand** heat Si 43$_{3(M)}$.

→ כּל III *measure,* מִיכָל II *collection.*

כּוּמָז 2.1 n.m. **ornament,** for woman's neck and breast Ex 35$_{22}$.

כּוּן 217.18.101 vb.—**Ni.** 65.7.29 Pf. נָכוֹנָה; impf. יִכֹּנוּ; impv. הִכּוֹן, הִכּוֹנוּ; ptc. נָכוֹן, נְכוֹנָה, נְכֹנִים; inf. Q הכון (Q הנכון)—**1a. be firm,** of breasts Ezk 16$_{7}$. **b. stand firm,** of mountain Is 2$_{2}$, world Ps 93$_{1}$. **c. be established, be set up** on (עַל) pillars, of temple Jg 16$_{26}$. **c. be established, be secure,** of person 1 S 20$_{31}$, kingdom 1 S 20$_{31}$. **2. be determined,** of matter Gn 41$_{32}$ (+ מֵעִם *by* Y.) Dt 13$_{15}$. **3. be well organized, well executed, properly accomplished,** of work 2 C 8$_{16}$, service in temple 2 C 29$_{35}$. **4. be ready,** of person Ex 19$_{11}$. **5. be steadfast,** of spirit Ps 51$_{12}$. **6. be right,** לֹא נָכוֹן לַעֲשׂוֹת כֵּן *it would not be right to do this* Ex 8$_{22}$. **7.** ptc. as noun, **a.** masc., **certainty,** וַיֵּדַע כִּי־בָא שָׁאוּל אֶל־נָכוֹן *and he learned of a certainty that Saul had arrived* 1 S 26$_{4}$. **b.** fem., **that which is right, the truth** Jb 42$_{7}$.

Polel 30.1.5 Pf. כּוֹנֵן, כּוֹנַנְתָּ; impf. יְכוֹנֵן; impv. כּוֹנֵן (כּוֹנְנֵהוּ); ptc. Si מכונן—**1.** oft. of Y., **establish, found** heaven Pr 3$_{19}$, earth Is 45$_{18}$, kingdom 2 S 7$_{13}$, city Ps 48$_{9}$ 107$_{36}$. **2. fit** arrow to (עַל) bow-string Ps 11$_{2}$. **3.** of Y., **appoint** people 2 S 7$_{24}$. **4.** of Y., **make** someone's steps **steady** Ps 40$_{3}$. **5.** of Y., **make** work **prosper** Ps 90$_{17}$. **6.** of Y., **form** child in (בְּ) womb Jb 31$_{15}$.

Polal 2.1 Pf. כּוֹנָנוּ—**1. be prepared,** of stones Ezk 28$_{13}$. **2. be made steady** by (מִן) Y., of person's steps Ps 37$_{23}$.

Hi. 110.8.62 Pf. הֵכִין, הֲכִינוֹתָה; impf. יָכִין; + waw וַיָּכֶן; impv. הָכֵן, הָכִינוּ; ptc. מֵכִין; inf. הָכִין—**1a. make ready, prepare** sacrifice Zp 1$_{7}$, present Gn 43$_{25}$, provisions Jos 1$_{11}$, net Ps 57$_{7}$, weapons Ps 7$_{14}$, ambush Jr 51$_{12}$, place Ex 23$_{20}$. **b.** with לְ + 'reflexive' suffix, **get oneself ready, prepare oneself** Jr 46$_{14}$. **2.** of Y., **provide, a.** with obj., rain for (לְ) earth Ps 147$_{8}$. **b.** without obj., for (לְ) needy Ps 68$_{11}$. **3a.** of Y., **make** mountains **stand firm** Ps 65$_{7}$. **b.** of Y., **establish** world Jr 10$_{12}$, kingdom 1 S 13$_{13}$. **c.** of Y., **set** luminary **in place** Ps 74$_{16}$. **d. set up** altar on (עַל) its site Ezr 3$_{3}$. **4.** of Y., **strengthen** heart Ps 10$_{17}$. **5. direct, a.** one's face toward (אֶל) city Ezk 4$_{3}$. **b.** one's own steps Jr 10$_{23}$, person's steps, of Y. Pr 16$_{9}$. **c.** one's heart to (אֶל) Y. 1 S 7$_{3}$. **6.** of Y., **appoint** person as (לְ) king 2 S 5$_{12}$. **7.** ptc. as noun, **one who ordains,** of Y., מכין טובי *one who ordains my good* 1QS 10$_{12}$.

Ho. 6.1.4 Pf. הוּכַן; impf. Q תוכן; ptc. מוּכָן, מוּכָנִים—**1. be made ready, prepared** for (לְ) someone or something, of Topheth Is 30$_{33}$, horse Pr 21$_{31}$. **2. be proper,** fit for (לְ) bride, of man 4QD^{f} 3$_{9}$. **3a. be established,** of throne Is 16$_{5}$. **b. be set up,** of screen Na 2$_{6}$.

Htpol. 4.0.1 Impf. יִתְכּוֹנֵן, יִכּוֹנָנוּ—**1. be established, founded,** of city Nm 21$_{27}$, house Pr 24$_{3}$. **2. form oneself in battle array** Ps 59$_{5}$.

→ כֵּן II *correct,* מָכוֹן *place,* מְכוֹנָה *base,* תְּכוּנָה *place.*

[כַּוָּן] 2 n.m.—pl. כַּוָּנִים—**cake,** as offering Jr 7$_{18}$ 44$_{19}$.

כּוּן 1 pl.n. **Cun.**

* [כּוֹנָנָה] 0.0.1 n.f.—cstr. pl. Q כוננות—**bowl,** altar vessel of silver 11QT 33$_{14}$.

כּוֹנַנְיָהוּ, see כָּנַנְיָהוּ *Conaniah.*

כּוֹס I 31.0.7 n.f.—sf. כּוֹסִי; pl. כּוֹסוֹת—**cup,** for wine Jr 35$_{5}$; cup of Y.'s judgment Ps 75$_{9}$, blessing Ps 23$_{5}$.

כּוֹס II 3 n.m. perh. **tawny owl,** unclean bird Lv 11$_{17}$.

*[כּוֹסְבָא] 0.0.10 pr.n.m. **Cosiba.**

כור 1 vb.—**Qal** 1 Pf. mss כָּרוּ (L כָּאֲרִי *like a lion*)—perh. **bind** hands and feet Ps 22$_{17(mss)}$.

כּוּר 9.2.11 n.m. **1. smelting-pot, furnace,** כּוּר הַבַּרְזֶל *furnace of iron* Dt 4$_{20}$. **2. crucible** of conception, **womb,** כור הריה *womb of pregnant woman* 1QH 11$_{8}$. → cf. כִּיר *cooking-furnace.*

*[כּוֹר] 0.0.0.1 pl.n. **Chor.**

כּוֹר עָשָׁן 1 pl.n. **Chor-ashan.**

כּוֹרֶשׁ 16 pr.n.m. **Cyrus.**

כּוּשׁ 30.0.2 pr.n.m. **Cush.**

כּוּשִׁי I 24 gent. **Cushite.**

כּוּשִׁי II 2 pr.n.m. **Cushi.**

כּוּשָׁן 1 gent. **Cushan.**

כּוּשַׁן רִשְׁעָתַיִם 4 pr.n.m. **Cushan-rishathaim.**

כּוֹשָׁרוֹת I 1 n.f.pl. **prosperity** Ps 68$_{7}$.

*כּוֹשָׁרוֹת II 1 n.f.pl. perh. **skill, music** Ps 68$_{7}$.

*כּוֹשָׁרוֹת III 1 n.f.pl. **Cosharoth,** Canaanite goddesses of conception and childbirth Ps 68$_{7}$.

כּוּת 2 pl.n. **Cuth.**

כּוֹתֶרֶת, see כֹּתֶרֶת *capital.*

כזב 16.1.4 vb.—**Qal** 1 Ptc. כֹּזֵב—**lie** Ps 116$_{11}$.

Ni. 2 Pf. נִכְזָבָה—**1. be false,** of hope Jb 41$_{1}$. **2. be declared a liar** Pr 30$_{6}$.

Pi. 12.1.4 Pf. כִּזֵּב; impf. יְכַזֵּב; ptc. Q מכזבים; inf. כַּזֶּבְכֶם—**1a. lie to** (לְ) someone, of Y. Ps 89$_{36}$, person Ps 78$_{36}$. **b.** with בְּ of obj., **deceive** someone 2 K 4$_{16}$. **2. prove false,** of vision Hb 2$_{3}$. **3. fail,** of waters of spring Is 58$_{11}$.

Hi. 1 Impf. יַכְזִיבֵנִי—**make someone a liar** Jb 24$_{25}$. → אַכְזָב *deceitful,* כָּזָב *lie.*

כָּזָב 31.5.18 n.m.—pl. כְּזָבִים; sf. כִּזְבֵיהֶם—**lie, falsehood,** אִישׁ כָּזָב *man of a lie,* i.e. liar Pr 19$_{22}$. → כזב *lie.*

כֹּזֵבָא 1.0.1 pl.n. **Cozeba.**

כָּזְבִּי 2 pr.n.f. **Cozbi.**

כְּזִיב I 1 pl.n. **Chezib.**

*כְּזִיב II 1 n.[m.] **menopause** Gn 38$_{5}$.

כֹּחַ I 125.11.94 n.m.—כּוֹחַ; sf. כֹּחִי, כֹּחֲךָ—**1a. strength** of human being, e.g. Samson Jg 16$_{5}$. **b. ability** of human being Ec 9$_{10}$. **c. power** of king 2 C 13$_{20}$, nation Dn 8$_{22}$. **d. power, might** of Y. Ex 9$_{16}$, angels Ps 103$_{20}$. **2. produce** of ground Gn 4$_{12}$. **3. wealth** Pr 5$_{10}$.

כֹּחַ II 1.0.1 n.[m.] **lizard** Lv 11$_{30}$.

*כֹּחַ III 1 n.m. **suppuration, festering** Jb 30$_{18}$.

כחד 32.0.5 vb.—**Ni.** 10.0.2 Pf. נִכְחַד; impf. יִכָּחֵד; ptc. נִכְחֶדֶת, נִכְחָדוֹת—**1. be hidden** from (מִן) someone, of matter 2 S 18$_{13}$; from Y., of guilty deeds Ps 69$_{6}$, Israel Ho 5$_{3}$. **2. be effaced,** of city Jb 15$_{28}$, person Ex 9$_{15}$ (+ מִן *from* earth).

Pi. 16.0.2 Pf. כִּחֲדְתִּי, כִּחֵד; impf. תְּכַחֲדִי, תְּכַחֵד—**1. hide information** asked for, **a.** with obj., אַל־תְּכַחֵד מִמֶּנִּי דָּבָר *do not hide anything from me* Jr 38$_{14}$. **b.** oft. with ellip., אַל־תְּכַחֵד מִמֶּנִּי *do not hide anything from me* Jos 7$_{19}$. **2. keep hidden, fail to speak of** Y.'s love and loyalty Ps 40$_{11}$.

Hi. 6.0.1 Pf. הִכְחַדְתִּיו; impf. יַכְחִידֶנָּה; + waw וַיַּכְחֵד, וְאַכְחִיד; inf. הַכְחִיד—**1. efface, destroy** people, of Y. Ex 23$_{23}$, angel 2 C 32$_{21}$, humans Ps 83$_{5}$. **2. conceal evil** Jb 20$_{12}$.

כחל 1 vb.—**Qal** 1 Pf. כָּחַלְתְּ—**paint (eyes)** Ezk 23$_{40}$. → כָּחֹל *blue.*

*[כָּחֹל] 0.0.0.1 adj. **blue,** יין כחל *blue,* i.e. dark, *wine* Hebron jar inscr. 1. → כחל *paint (eyes).*

*[כֹּחֵל] 0.0.0.1 pl.n. **Cohel.**

*[כָּחְלִת] 0.0.4 pl.n. **Cohlith.**

*כחס 0.0.1 vb.—**Pi.** 0.0.1 Impf. יכחס—**lie** 1QS 7$_{3}$. → cf. כחשׁ *lie.*

כחשׁ 22.2.2 vb.—**Qal** 1 Pf. כָּחַשׁ—**be lean, without** (מִן) **fat,** or **be exhausted** of fat Ps 109$_{24}$.

Ni. 1 Impf. יִכָּחֲשׁוּ—**cringe before** (לְ) someone, perh. **feign obedience** Dt 33$_{29}$.

Pi. 19.2.2 Pf. כִּחֵשׁ (כִּחֶשׁ); impf. יְכַחֵשׁ (יְכַחֶשׁ); inf. כַּחֵשׁ—**1a. lie,** וַתְּכַחֵשׁ שָׂרָה לֵאמֹר לֹא צָחַקְתִּי *then Sarah lied, saying, 'I did not laugh'* Gn 18$_{15}$. **b. deal deceitfully** with (בְּ) neighbour Lv 5$_{21}$. **c.** appar. **betray** companion Si 37$_{6(Bmg)}$. **d. be unfaithful** to (לְ) Y. Jb 31$_{28}$. **e.** abs., perh. **conceal** Jos 7$_{11}$. **2.** as Ni., **cringe before** (לְ) someone, perh. **feign obedience** Ps 18$_{45}$. **3. fail, be exhausted,** of wine Ho 9$_{2}$, produce of olive Hb 3$_{17}$. **4.** inf. as noun, **lying** Ho 4$_{2}$.

Htp. 1 Impf. יִתְכַּחֲשׁוּ—**cringe before** (לְ) someone 2 S 22$_{45}$.

→ כחשׁ *lie,* כֶּחָשׁ *untruthful;* cf. כחס *lie.*

כַּחַשׁ 6.2.4 n.m.—כַּחַשׁ; sf. כַּחֲשִׁי; pl. sf. כַּחֲשֵׁיהֶם—**1. lie, deceit** Ho 10$_{13}$ 1QS 4$_{9}$. **2. emaciation, sickliness** Jb 16$_{8}$. → כחשׁ *be lean.*

[כֶּחָשׁ] 1.0.1 adj.—pl. כֶּחָשִׁים—**untruthful** Is 30$_{9}$. → כחשׁ *lie.*

כִּי I 4488.156.898.10 conj.—Q כיא—**1.** introducing causal clause, **for, because,** לְזֹאת יִקָּרֵא אִשָּׁה כִּי מֵאִישׁ לֻקֳחָה־זֹּאת *this one shall be called Woman because she was taken from a man* Gn 2$_{23}$. **2.** introducing 'obj.' clause, **that,** ואדעה כיא בידו משפט כול חי *and I know that in his hand is the judgment of every living being* 1QS 10$_{16}$. **3.** perh. as rel. part., **that, which, who,** תבל כיא להתגוללה בדרכי רשע *the world, which has polluted itself by ways of wickedness* 1QS 4$_{19}$. **4.** introducing purpose clause, **so that,** מַה־תִּתֶּן־לִי כִּי תָבוֹא אֵלָי *what will you give me, so that you may come to me?* Gn 38$_{16}$. **5.** introducing conditional or temporal clause, **if, when,** כִּי תִקְנֶה עֶבֶד עִבְרִי שֵׁשׁ שָׁנִים יַעֲבֹד *when you buy a Hebrew slave, he shall serve six years* Ex 21$_{2}$. **6.** introducing concessive clause, **although,** לֹא־נָחָם אֱלֹהִים דֶּרֶךְ אֶרֶץ פְּלִשְׁתִּים כִּי קָרוֹב הוּא *God did not lead them by way of the land of the Philistines, although it was near* Ex 13$_{17}$. **7.** כִּי עַתָּה or כִּי אָז **then (by) now,** כִּי לוּלֵא הִתְמַהְמָהְנוּ כִּי־עַתָּה שַׁבְנוּ זֶה פַעֲמָיִם *for if we had not delayed, then by now we would have returned twice* Gn 43$_{10}$. **8.** introducing adversative clause, **(but) rather, yet, nonetheless, except,** לֹא מְרַגְּלִים אַתֶּם כִּי כֵנִים אַתֶּם *you are not spies; rather, you are honest men* Gn 42$_{34}$. **9.** as emphatic part., **surely, indeed; now, then, in fact, namely; how!,** כִּי שִׂיחַ וְכִי־שִׂיג לוֹ וְכִי־דֶרֶךְ לוֹ *surely he is meditating or busy or on a journey* 1 K 18$_{27}$. **10.** as part. of consequence, **so, therefore,** כִּי יַעַן אֲשֶׁר עָשִׂיתָ אֶת־הַדָּבָר הַזֶּה ... ׃ כִּי־בָרֵךְ אֲבָרֶכְךָ *for because you have done this thing ..., therefore I shall indeed bless you* Gn 22$_{17}$. **11.** כִּי ... כֵּן perh. as ... so, כִּי־גָבְהוּ שָׁמַיִם מֵאָרֶץ כֵּן גָּבְהוּ דְרָכַי מִדַּרְכֵיכֶם perh. *as the heavens are higher than the earth so are my ways higher than your ways* Is 55$_{9}$. **12.** as interrog. part., כִּי הָאָדָם עֵץ הַשָּׂדֶה *are the trees of the field human beings?* Dt 20$_{19}$. **13.** appar. as prep., **a. despite** Jr 11$_{15}$. **b. on account of** 2 C 22$_{6}$. **14.** compounds, **a.** כִּי אִם (1) **(but) rather** Gn 32$_{29}$. (2) **apart from** Jos 14$_{4}$. (3) **otherwise** 1 K 20$_{6}$. (4) **surely** 1QM 11$_{1}$. (5) **for if, but if** Ex 8$_{17}$. **b.** אַף כִּי (1) **how much more (if)** Dt 31$_{27}$. (2) **how much less (if)** Ezk 15$_{5}$. **c.** גַּם כִּי **even though** Is 1$_{15}$. **d.** כִּי־עַל־כֵּן **since** Gn 18$_{5}$. **e.** עַל כִּי **because** Dt 31$_{17}$. **f.** תַּחַת כִּי **because** Pr 1$_{29}$. **g.** עֵקֶב כִּי **because** 2 S 12$_{10}$. **h.** יַעַן כִּי **because** 1 K 13$_{21}$. **i.** עַד כִּי **until** 2 C 26$_{15}$. **j.** אֶפֶס כִּי **except that** Nm 13$_{28}$. **k.** אַךְ כִּי **but** 1 S 8$_{9}$. **l.** אִם־לֹא כִּי **unless** Dt 32$_{30}$.

*כִּי II 1 n.m. perh. **vulture** Jb 39$_{27}$.

כִּי III 1 n.m. **burn** Is 3$_{24}$. → כוה *burn.*

כִּיבוּד, see כָּבוּד *hardness.*

[כִּיד] I 1 n.[m.]—sf. כִּידוֹ—**misfortune** Jb 21$_{20}$.

*[כִּיד] II 1 n.[m.]—sf. כִּידוֹ—**cup** Jb 21$_{20}$.

[כִּידוֹד] I 1 n.m. **spark,** כִּידוֹדֵי אֵשׁ *sparks of a fire* Jb 41$_{11}$.

*[כִּידוֹד] II 1 n.m. **son,** כִּידוֹדֵי אֵשׁ *sons of fire* Jb 41$_{11}$.

כִּידוֹן 9.1 n.m.—כִּידֹן—**javelin** or **short curved sword** (as כִּידֹן) 1 S 17$_{6}$.

כִּידוֹר 1 n.[m.] perh. **attack** Jb 15$_{24}$.

*[כִּידָן] 0.0.5 n.m.—pl. כידנים—**(Spanish) sword** (*gladius*) 1QM 5$_{12}$.

כִּידֹן 1 pr.n.m. **Chidon.**

כִּיּוּן I 1.0.2 pr.n.m. **Kiyyun.**

*כִּיּוּן II 1.0.2 n.[m.] **pedestal** or **palanquin,** כִּיּוּן צַלְמֵיכֶם *pedestal of your images* Am 5$_{26}$.

כִּיּוֹר 23.0.10 n.m.—כִּיֹּר; pl. כִּיֹּרוֹת (כִּיֹּרִים)—**1. bronze bowl, basin for washing,** i.e. **laver** Ex 30$_{18}$. **2. pot** for cooking 1 S 2$_{14}$. **3.** movable **hearth** or **brazier** Zc 12$_{6}$. **4.** bronze **platform** for king in court of temple 2 C 6$_{13}$.

*[כִּיּוּר] 0.0.2 n.[m.] **panelling, eaves** of gate to temple court, כיור ארז *panelling of cedar* 11QT 36$_{10}$.

כִּילַי 1 n.m. **villain** Is 32$_{5}$. → נכל *be crafty.*

[כֵּילַף] 1 n.f.—pl. כֵּילַפֹּת—**crowbar** Ps 74$_{6}$.

כִּימָה 3 n.f. **Pleiades** Am 5$_{8}$.

*[כִּיִּן] n.[m.] **vagina** Am 5$_{26}$ (if em. כִּיּוּן *Kiyyun* or *pedestal*).

כִּיס 5.2.2 n.m.—cstr. כִּיס—**1. bag** of stones Mc 6$_{11}$. **2. purse** Pr 1$_{14}$ (unless §3) Si 35$_{5}$ 4QInstr[b] 2.2$_{4}$. **3. lot, destiny** Pr 1$_{14}$.

[כִּיר] 1.0.1 n.m.—du. כִּירַיִם—**cooking-furnace** Lv 11$_{35}$. → cf. כּוּר *smelting pot.*

כִּיר, see כִּיּוֹר *pot.*

*[כִּירְגָּר] 0.0.1 n.[m.] perh. **cistern** 3QTr 10$_{3}$.

כִּישׁוֹר 1 n.[m.] **spindle,** or perh. **spinning whorl** or **distaff** Pr 31$_{19}$.

כָּכָה 37.3.11 adv.—Si כך—**1.** adv., usu. of manner, **so, thus, in this way,** מַדּוּעַ אַתָּה כָּכָה דַּל *why are you so dejected?* 2 S 13$_{4}$, ככה רוחב ואורך לכול רוחותיה *thus shall be the width and length of all its sides* 11QT 38$_{13}$. **2.** עַל־כָּכָה **concerning such a matter** Est 9$_{26}$. **3.** לְעֻמַּת כָּכָה **in accordance with this, accordingly** Mur 30 1$_{6}$.

כִּכָּר I 13 n.f. **district,** sometimes perh. specif. **valley,** כִּכַּר הַיַּרְדֵּן *district of the Jordan* Gn 13$_{10}$.

כִּכָּר II 55.0.47 n.f.—cstr. כִּכַּר; du. כִּכָּרַיִם; pl. כִּכָּרִים; cstr. כִּכְּרֵי (כִּכְּרוֹת)—**1. talent,** i.e. **disc** of gold or silver as unit of weight or value Est 3$_{9}$. **2. lead disc** or **cover** Zc 5$_{7}$. **3. loaf of bread** Jg 8$_{5}$.

כֹּל I 5408.145.2540.15 n.m.—כּוֹל; cstr. כֹּל (כָּל־); sf. כֻּלּוֹ, כֻּלְּךָ, כּוּלָּם—**1.** in abs. or with pron. suffix or followed by אֲשֶׁר or ptc. (sometimes with art. -הַ), **all, everyone, everything, everywhere, wherever, whenever, the total, the whole,** הַכֹּל עֲבָדֶיךָ *all are your servants* Ps 119$_{91}$, דעת כולם *knowledge of all of them* 1QS 8$_{9}$, לא הכל לכל טוב *not everything is good for everyone* Si 37$_{28(B)}$, כֹּל־אֲשֶׁר תִּפְנֶה שָׁם *everywhere you turn* 1 K 2$_{3}$, הכל ככרין שש מאות *the total is six hundred talents* 3QTr 12$_{7}$. **2.** in cstr., as first element (*nomen regens*) (usu. כָּל־), **all (of), every, each (of), the whole of,** immediately before noun (abs., cstr., sg., pl.) or adj. as noun, כָּל־יְמֵי חַיֶּיךָ *all the days of your life* Gn 3$_{14}$, כֹּל עֵץ־הַגָּן *every tree of the garden* Gn 2$_{16}$, בְּכָל־לְבָבְךָ *with your whole heart* Dt 4$_{29}$, כָּל־טָהוֹר *everyone who is pure* Lv 7$_{19}$. → כלל *perfect.*

*כֹּל II 1 n.[m.] **mallow** or another plant Jb 24$_{24}$.

*כֹּל III 1 n.[m.] **measure** Pr 28$_{5}$. → כול *measure.*

כלא 17.0.1 vb.—**Qal** 14.0.1 Pf. כָּלְאָה, כְּלָתַנִי, כָּלוּ; impf. יִכְלֶה, אֶכְלָא; impv. כְּלָאֵם; ptc. pass. כָּלֻא; inf. לִכְלוֹא—**1a. withhold** something from (מִן) someone, obj. burial place Gn 23$_{6}$, compassion Ps 40$_{12}$. **b.** of earth, **fail to yield** produce Hg 1$_{10}$. **2a. restrain** wind or spirit Ec 8$_{8}$, someone from (מִן) bloodguilt 1 S 25$_{33}$. **b. hold back** one's feet from (מִן) evil way Ps 119$_{101}$. **3. imprison** someone Jr 32$_{3}$. **4.** pass., **be kept imprisoned** Jr 32$_{2}$.

Ni. 3 + waw וַיִּכָּלֵא—**1. be held back** from (מִן) sky, of rain Gn 8$_{2}$. **2. be restrained,** of people Ex 36$_{6}$.

→ כֶּלֶא I *confinement,* כְּלִיא *confinement,* מִכְלָא *fold,* כְּלָאָה *fold.*

כֶּלֶא I 10 n.m.—sf. כִּלְאוֹ; pl. כְּלָאִים—**confinement, imprisonment,** בֵּית כֶּלֶא *the house of imprisonment,* i.e. prison 2 K 17$_{4}$. → כלא *restrain.*

*[כֶּלֶא] II n.[m.] **both,** כֶּלֶא אוֹיְבָיו *both of his adversaries* Ps 89$_{43}$ (if em. כָּל־ *all*).

כֶּלֶא 1 n.m. **all** Ezk 36$_{5}$ (or em. כֻּלָּהּ *all of it*). → כלל *be complete.*

כִּלְאָב 1 pr.n.m. **Chileab.**

*[כְּלָאָה] 0.0.1 n.f.—pl. כלאת—**fold, enclosure** Mur 30 1$_{3}$. → כלא *restrain.*

כִּלְאַיִם 4.0.5 n.m.du.—כִּלְאָיִם—**1.** in ref. to forbidden intermixing, **two kinds** of cattle, seed, cloth Lv 19$_{19}$. **2. mixed kinds** of judges 4QMixedKinds 1$_{2}$, unsuitable marriage partners 4QD[d] 9$_{2}$.

כָּלֵב I 34.2.0.1 pr.n.m. **Caleb.**

כָּלֵב II 2 pl.n. **Caleb.**

*[כַּלָּב] n.m. **hunter** Ps 22$_{17}$ (if em. כֶּלֶב *dog*).

כֶּלֶב I 32.3.2.3 n.m.—כָּלֶב; pl. כְּלָבִים; cstr. כַּלְבֵי; sf. כְּלָבֶיךָ—**1. dog** 1 K 14$_{11}$. **2.** perh. **devotee** of god Dt 23$_{19}$.

*כֶּלֶב II 8.0.0.3 n.m. **servant,** רֹאשׁ כֶּלֶב *head of a servant,* i.e. chief slave 2 S 3$_{8}$; sometimes **temple servant, hierodule** Dt 23$_{19}$.

כָּלִבִּי 1 gent. **Calebite.**

כלה 206.6.37 vb.—**Qal** 63.0.8 Pf. כָּלָה, כָּלִיתִי, כָּלוּ; impf. יִכְלֶה, (יִכֶל), תִּכְלֶה, יִכְלוּ; + waw וַתֵּכֶל; ptc. כָּלוֹת; inf. כְּלוֹת—**1a. come to an end,** of period of time Gn 41$_{53}$, anger of Y. Is 10$_{25}$. **b. be finished, completed,** of work Ex 39$_{32}$, temple 1 K 6$_{38}$. **c. be fulfilled,** of word of Y. Ezr 1$_{1}$. **2. be used up, consumed,** of water Gn 21$_{15}$, jar of flour 1 K 17$_{14}$. **3a. disappear, vanish,** of grass Is 15$_{6}$. **b. perish,** of person Is 1$_{28}$. **4. fail,** of human strength Ps 71$_{9}$, body and mind Ps 73$_{26}$, eyes Ps 69$_{4}$. **5. be determined** by (מֵעִם) someone, of evil 1 S 20$_{7}$.

Pi. 141.6.29 Pf. כִּלָּה, כִּלִּיתָ, כִּלֵּיתִי, כִּלּוּ; impf. יְכַלֶּה, יְכַלּוּ;

+ waw וַיְכַל; impv. כַּלּוּ; ptc. מְכַלָּה, מְכַלּוֹת; inf. abs. כַּלֵּה, cstr. כַּלּוֹת—**1a. finish,** (1) with obj., work Gn 2_{2}. (2) with inf., כִּלָּה לְדַבֵּר אֶל־אַבְרָהָם *he finished speaking to Abraham* Gn 18_{33}. **b. end (with),** וַיְחַפֵּשׂ בַּגָּדוֹל הֵחֵל וּבַקָּטֹן כִּלָּה *then he searched, beginning with the oldest and ending with the youngest* Gn 44_{12}. **2. use up** arrows on (בְּ) people Dt 32_{23}. **3a. consume, ravage** land, of famine Gn 41_{30}. **b. destroy** people Ex 32_{10}. **4. make eyes pine** 1 S 2_{33}.

Pu. 2 Pf. כֻּלּוּ; + waw וַיְכֻלּוּ—**1. be completed, finished,** of sky, earth, stars Gn 2_{1}. **2. be ended,** of prayers Ps 72_{20}.

→ כָּלֶה *longing,* כָּלָה *destruction,* כִּלָּיוֹן *annihilation,* מִכְלוֹת *perfection,* תִּכְלָה *perfection,* תַּכְלִית *completeness.*

כָּלֶה 1 adj.—f.pl. כָּלוֹת—**longing,** of eyes Dt 28_{32}. → כלה *be complete.*

כָּלָה 22.2.46 n.f. **1. destruction,** כָּלָה וְנֶחֱרָצָה *destruction and that which is determined,* i.e. determined destruction Is 10_{23}, כלת אל *destruction of,* i.e. by, *God* 1QM 4_{12}. **2.** as adv., **completely,** כָּלָה גָּרֵשׁ יְגָרֵשׁ אֶתְכֶם מִזֶּה *he will drive you out of here completely* Ex 11_{1}. → כלה *be complete.*

כַּלָּה 34.0.1 n.f.—sf. כַּלָּתָהּ; pl. sf. כַּלֹּתֶיךָ—**1. daughter-in-law,** רוּת ... כַּלָּתָהּ עִמָּהּ *Ruth ... her daughter-in-law was with her* Ru 1_{22}. **2. bride, young wife,** מַה־יָּפוּ דֹדַיִךְ אֲחֹתִי כַלָּה *how beautiful is your love, my sister, (my) bride* Ca 4_{10}. → cf. כְּלוּלֹת *betrothal.*

[כְּלֻהַי] 1 pr.n.m. **Cheluhi.**

כְּלוּא 2 n.[m.] **confinement,** בֵּית הַכְּלוּא *house of confinement,* i.e. prison Jr $37_{4(Qr)}$ $52_{31(Qr)}$. → כלא *restrain.*

כְּלוּב I 3.2 n.m. **1. basket,** for fruit Am 8_{1}. **2. bird-cage** Jr 5_{27}.

כְּלוּב II 2 pr.n.m. **Chelub.**

כְּלוּבָי 1 pr.n.m. **Chelubai.**

כְּלוּהוּ 1 pr.n.m. **Cheluhi.**

כְּלוּלֹת 1 n.f.pl.—sf. כְּלוּלֹתָיִךְ—**betrothal** Jr 2_{2}. → cf. כַּלָּה *bride.*

כֶּלַח* I 2 n.m.—כֶּלַח—**old age** Jb 5_{26} 30_{2}.

כֶּלַח II 2 n.m.—כֶּלַח—**vigour** Jb 5_{26} 30_{2}.

כֶּלַח III 2 pl.n. **Calah.**

כָּל־חֹזֶה 2 pr.n.m. **Col-hozeh.**

כְּלִי 324.8.65 n.m.—כֶּלִי; sf. כֶּלְיְךָ; pl. כֵּלִים; cstr. כְּלֵי; sf. כֵּלַי, כְּלֵיהֶם—**1.** in general, **object, article, thing,** oft. pl., **a. goods, belongings,** כְּלֵי־בֵיתֶךָ *your household goods* Gn 31_{37}. **b. baggage** 1 S 17_{22}. **c. furnishings** of tabernacle Ex 25_{9}. **2a. vessel, container, pot, cup,** of clay or bronze, for boiling Lv 6_{21}; of gold, for drinking 1 K 10_{21}. **b. sack, bag,** for grain Gn 42_{25}, used by shepherd 1 S 17_{40}. **3a. utensil,** such as flesh hook, scraper Nm 4_{14}. **b.** pl., **equipment** for chariots 1 S 8_{12}. **c.** pl., **gear,** i.e. **yokes** of oxen 2 S 24_{22}. **d. weapon,** כְּלֵי מִלְחָמָה *weapons of war* Jg 18_{11}; **object used as weapon,** of iron Nm 35_{16}, wood Nm 35_{18}. **e. musical instrument,** כְּלֵי נְבָלִים *instruments (consisting) of harps* 1 C 16_{5}. **4. jewelry,** of silver or gold Gn 24_{53}. **5. clothing,** made of animal skin Lv 13_{49}, worn by man Dt 22_{5}. **6. boat, ship,** of papyrus Is 18_{2}. **7. idea, tactic, plan,** כֵּלַי כֵּלָיו רָעִים *as for a villain, his plans are evil* Is 32_{7}. **8.** perh. **device, mechanism,** as descr. of sun and moon Si $43_{2(M).8}$. **9.** perh. **(military) signal** Si 43_{8} (unless §3d or §8). **10.** perh. **body of human** 1 S 21_{6}.

כֵּלַי 1 n.m. **villain** Is 32_{7}. → כִּילַי *villain.*

[כְּלִיא] 2 n.[m.] **confinement,** בֵּית הכליא *house of confinement,* i.e. prison Jr $37_{4(Kt)}$ $52_{31(Kt)}$ (Qr הַכְּלוּא). → כלא *restrain.*

[כִּלְיָה] 31.0.10 n.f.—pl. כְּלָיוֹת (כְּלָיֹת); cstr. כִּלְיוֹת; sf. כִּלְיוֹתַי, כִּלְיוֹתֵיהֶם—**kidney,** alw. pl., **1.** of animal Lv 8_{16}. **2a.** of human Jb 16_{13}. **b.** as seat of human conscience, joy, grief., etc. Pr 23_{16}. **3.** choicest part of wheat Dt 32_{14}.

כִּלָּיוֹן 2.0.1 n.m.—cstr. כִּלְיוֹן—**1. destruction** Is 10_{22}. **2. failure** of eyes Dt 28_{65}. → כלה *be complete.*

כִּלְיוֹן 3 pr.n.m. **Chilion.**

כָּלִיל I 15.3.4 adj.—cstr. כְּלִיל, f.s. cstr. כְּלִילַת—**1. whole,** עוֹלָה כָּלִיל *whole burnt offering* 1 S 7_{9}. **2.** as noun, **a. complete one,** כְּלִיל תְּכֵלֶת *complete one of purple wool,* i.e. completely of purple wool Ex 28_{31}, כְּלִיל הָעִיר *totality of the city* Jg 20_{40}. **b. whole burnt offering** Dt 33_{10}. **c. perfect one,** כְּלִילַת יֹפִי *perfect one of beauty,* i.e. perfect in beauty Ezk 27_{3}. **3.** adv., **completely,** הָאֱלִילִים כָּלִיל יַחֲלֹף *the idols will completely disappear* Is 2_{18}. → כלל *perfect.*

[כָּלִיל]* II 0.1.2 n.[m.] **crown** 1QS 4_{7}.

[כְּלִילָה]* 1 n.f.—cstr. כְּלִילַת—**crown** Lm 2_{15}.

כַּלְכֹּל 2.0.0.1 pr.n.m. **Calcol.**

*[**כַּלְכֹּלְיָהוּ**] 0.0.0.1 pr.n.m. **Calcoliah.**

כלל 2 vb.—**Qal** 2 Pf. כָּלְלוּ—**perfect** beauty Ezk $27_{4.11}$. → כֹּל *all,* כָּלָא *all,* כָּלִיל I *whole,* כָּלָל *total,* מִכְלוֹל *perfection,* מִכְלָל *perfection,* מַכְלֻל *ornate robe.*

*[**כְּלָל**] I 0.0.1 n.[m.] **total,** כלל חלליהם *total of their slain ones* 4QpNah 3.2_6. → כלל *perfect.*

כְּלָל II 1 pr.n.m. **Chelal.**

כלם I 38.5.1 vb.—**Ni.** 26.3.1 Pf. נִכְלַמְתִּי; impf. תִּכָּלֵם; impv. הִכָּלְמוּ; ptc. נִכְלָמִים ,נִכְלָם; inf. הִכָּלֵם—**1. be humiliated, be put to shame** Nm 12_{14}.

Hi. 10.2 Pf. הִכְלַמְנוּ; impf. יַכְלִים; ptc. מַכְלִים; inf. הַכְלִים —**1. humiliate, shame** someone, subj. human Jb 19_3, Y. Ps 44_{10}. **2. abuse** woman Ru 2_{15}. 3. appar. **feel ashamed** Jr 6_{15}.

Ho. 2 Pf. הָכְלַמְנוּ—**1. be ashamed** Jr 14_3. **2. suffer harm** 1 S 25_{15}.

→ כְּלִמָּה *insult,* כְּלִמּוּת *disgrace.*

*[**כלם**] II 1 vb.—**Hi.** 1 Ptc. מַכְלִים—**speak,** perh. specif. **speak with authority** Jg 18_7. → כְּלִמָּה II *speech.*

*[**כָּלֵם**] 0.0.0.1 pr.n.m. **Chalem.**

כִּלְמַד 1 pl.n. **Chilmad.**

כְּלִמָּה I 30.0.4 n.f.—cstr. כְּלִמַּת; sf. כְּלִמָּתִי; pl. כְּלִמּוֹת—**insult, reproach, disgrace** Ezk 34_{29}. → כלם I *humiliate.*

*[**כְּלִמָּה**] II 1 n.f.—pl. כְּלִמּוֹת—**speech** Mc 2_6. → כלם II *speak.*

כְּלִמּוּת 1 n.f. **disgrace** Jr 23_{40}. → כלם I *humiliate.*

כַּלְנֵה 3 pl.n. **Calneh.**

כַּלְנוֹ, see כַּלְנֵה *Calneh.*

כמה 1 vb.—**Qal** 1 Pf. כָּמַהּ—**long, yearn for** (לְ) Y. Ps 63_2.

כַּמָּה, see מָה *what.*

כַּמֶּה, see מָה *what.*

כִּמְהָם I 3 pr.n.m. **Chimham.**

כִּמְהָם II 1 pl.n. **Chimham.**

כִּמְהָן, see כִּמְהָם *Chimham.*

כְּמוֹ 140.7.17 prep. (byform form of כְּ)—sf. כָּמֹנִי—**1.** without suffix, **as, like,** comparing, כֻּלָּם ... כְּמוֹ תַנּוּר *they are all ... like a heated oven* Ho 7_4. **2.** other uses, **a. when,** וּכְמוֹ הַשַּׁחַר עָלָה *(and) when morning dawned* Gn 19_{15}. **b. now,** כְּמוֹ עַתָּה *as it is now* Ezk 16_{57}. **c. whether,** כְּמוֹ חַי כְּמוֹ־חָרוֹן *whether alive,* i.e. green, *or ablaze* Ps 58_{10}. **3.** כְּמוֹ with suffix and neg. part., **(none) like,** כִּי־אֵין כָּמוֹךָ *for there is none like you* 2 S 7_{22}. **4.** כְּמוֹ with suffix, **as,** expressing equivalence, כָּמוֹךָ כְמוֹהֶם *as you are so were they* Jg 8_{18}. → cf. כְּ *as,* כְּמוֹת *like.*

כְּמוֹהָם, see כִּמְהָם II *Chimham.*

כְּמוֹשׁ 8.0.0.2 pr.n.m. **Chemosh.**

*[**כְּמוֹת**] 0.0.1 prep. **like, with suffix,** מי כמותו *who is like him?* GnzPs 4_8. → cf. כְּ *like,* כְּמוֹ *like.*

כְּמִישׁ, see כְּמוֹשׁ *Chemosh.*

כַּמֹּן 3 n.m. **cummin,** a spicy herb Is 28_{25}.

כמס 1 vb.—**Qal** 1 Ptc. pass. כָּמֻס—pass. **be stored up** Dt 32_{34}.

כמר 4 vb.—**Ni.** 4 Pf. נִכְמְרוּ—**1. grow warm,** of compassion Gn 43_{30} (+ אֶל *for*) 1K 3_{26} (+ עַל *for*) Ho 11_8. **2. burn** like (כְּ) oven, of skin Lm 5_{10}.

כֹּמֶר 3 n.m.—pl. כְּמָרִים—**priest** of non-Israelite deity 2 K 23_5 Ho 10_5 Zp 1_4.

*[**כַּמְרִיר**] 0.1 n.[m.] **darkness, eclipse** Jb 3_5 (if em. כִּמְרִירֵי *as the bitter things of*) Si $11_{4(B,\ D)}$.

*[**כָּן**] 0.0.1 adv. here MurEpJonathan4.

כֵּן I 567.56.97.1 adv.—כֶּן־—**1.** adv. of manner, **so, thus, such, in this way, in the same way, accordingly, that is what ... is like,** כְּמוֹת זֶה כֵּן מוֹת זֶה *as one dies, so dies the other* Ec 3_{19}, כֵּן דּוֹדִי *that is what my beloved is like* Ca 2_3; oft. almost as noun, **this (thing), that (thing),** etc., וְאַתָּה לֹא כֵן נָתַן לְךָ י׳ אֱלֹהֶיךָ *but for you, Y. your God has not permitted such things* Dt 18_{14}. **2.** perh. adv. of quantity, **in such quantity, so much, so many,** לֹא בָא־כֵן עֲצֵי אַלְמֻגִּים *timbers of almug had not come in such quantity* 1 K 10_{12}; **in sufficient quantity,** לֹא־מָצְאוּ לָהֶם כֵּן *they did not find* (women) *for themselves in sufficient quantity* Jg 21_{14}; **(the more ...) the more,** הֵמָּה רָאוּ כֵּן תָּמָהוּ *(the more) they saw, the more they were amazed* Ps 48_6. **3.** adv. of time, **then,** כְּבֹאֲכֶם הָעִיר כֵּן תִּמְצְאוּן אֹתוֹ *as (soon as) you enter the city, then you will find him* 1 S 9_{13}. **4.** appar. **also, too** Na 1_{12}. **5.** כֵּן ... כֵּן **as ... so** 4Q185 1.2_{14}. **6.** appar. prep., **as, like** Jg 5_{15}. **7.** compounded with preceding prep., as adv. or conj., **a.** אַחַר כֵּן **afterwards** Lv 14_{36}. **b.** אַחֲרֵי־כֵן **afterwards** Jg 16_4. **c.** בְּכֵן **then, afterwards** Est 4_{16}. **d.** בַּעֲבוּר כֵּן **because of**

this, therefore Si 51_{21}. **e.** כְּדֵי כֵן **in like measure, proportionately** Si 13_{9}. **f.** לָכֵן **therefore,** see לָכֵן. **g.** עַד־כֵּן **unto this, still** Ne 2_{16}. **h.** עַל־כֵּן **therefore, because of this, that is why** Gn 26_{33}. **i.** כִּי־עַל־כֵּן **because, seeing that, inasmuch as** Nm 10_{31}. **j.** אֲשֶׁר עַל־כֵּן **because** Jb 34_{27}.

כֵּן II 12.0.1 adj.—pl. כֵּנִים—usu. indeclinable, **1a. right, correct, true,** of boasting Jr 48_{30}; מקצת דברינו כן *some of our practices are correct* 4QMMT C_{30}. **b.** as adv., **rightly, correctly** Ex 10_{29} Jg 12_{6}. **2a. (morally) right,** דְּבָרִים אֲשֶׁר לֹא־כֵן *things that were not right* 2 K 17_{9}. **b.** as noun, **(what is) right** Is 10_{7} Ec 8_{10}. **3. honest (person)** Gn 42_{11}. → כון *be firm.*

כֵּן III 13 n.m.—sf. כַּנּוֹ—**1.** usu. **stand, base** for basin (כִּיּוֹר) of tabernacle, and other objects Ex 30_{18} 1 K $7_{29.31}$. **2. (in) place (of)** Dn 11_{7}. **3. socket** of mast Is 33_{23}.

כֵּן IV 7.1.1 n.[m.]—pl. כִּנִּים (כִּנָּם)—**louse, maggot, gnat, mosquito** Ex 8_{12}.

[כֵּן] V 5 n.[m.]—sf. כַּנִּי—**position, place, status, office** Gn 40_{13}.

*[כַּנָּא] 0.0.1 n.[f.] **base** perh. 3QTr 6_{7}.

*[כֵּנֵד] **jug** Ps 33_{7} (if em. כַּנֵּד *like a heap*).

כנה 4.3.1 vb.—**Pi.** 4.3 Pf. Si כיניתה; impf. יְכַנֶּה—**grant title, give honorary name to,** with accus. of recipient Is 45_{4}, אֶל *to* Jb 32_{21}.

Pu. 0.0.1 Pf. Q כונו—**be named** 4QNetin 1_{2}.

כַּנָּה 1 n.f. **stock** of vine Ps 80_{16}.

כַּנֵּה 1 pl.n. **Canneh.**

כִּנּוֹר 42 n.m.—sf. כִּנֹּרִי; pl. כִּנֹּרוֹת; sf. כִּנּוֹרֶיךָ—**lyre, harp** Is 5_{12}.

כָּנְיָהוּ 3.0.0.2 pr.n.m. **Coniah.**

[כִּנִּיּוֹם], see כֵּן V *louse.*

כַּנְלֹתְךָ, see נלה *obtain.*

כִּנָּם 2 n.[m.] **vermin** Ex $8_{13.14}$.

כְּנָנִי 1 pr.n.m. **Chenani.**

כְּנַנְיָה 3 pr.n.m. **Chenaniah.**

כְּנַנְיָהוּ, see כְּנַנְיָה *Chenaniah.*

כָּנַנְיָהוּ 3 pr.n.m. **Conaniah.**

כנס 11.0.4 vb.—**Qal** 7.0.4 Pf. כָּנַסְתִּי; impv. כְּנוֹס; ptc. כֹּנֵס, Q כונסים; inf. כְּנוֹס—**1a. collect** portions of harvest Ne 12_{44}. **b. amass** silver, gold Ec 2_{8}. **2. gather** Jews Est 4_{16}.

Pi. 3 + waw וְכִנַּסְתִּי; impf. יְכַנֵּס—**gather, assemble** Israel Ezk 22_{21}.

Htp. 1 Inf. הִתְכַּנֵּס—**wrap oneself** Is 28_{20}.

→ מִכְנָסַיִם *breeches,* כְּנֶסֶת *congregation.*

*[כְּנֶסֶת] 0.0.2 n.f. **congregation** 4QpNah 3.3_{7}. → כנס *gather.*

כנע 36.5.15 vb.—**Ni.** 25.1.5 Pf. נִכְנַע; impf. יִכָּנַע; impv. Si היכנע, ptc. Q ניכנעים; inf. Q הכנע (הִכָּנְעוֹ)—**1. be humble(d), humble oneself,** of heart Lv 26_{41}, person 2 C 33_{23} (+ מִלִּפְנֵי *before* Y.). **2. be subdued under** (תַּחַת) foreign power, of nation Jg 3_{30}. **3. be overcome,** of wickedness 1QM 1_{6}. **4.** ptc. as noun, **oppressed one** 1QS 10_{26}.

Hi. 11.4.10 Pf. הִכְנִיעַ; impf. אַכְנִיעַ; + waw וַיַּכְנַע (וַיַּכְנִיעֵם)—**1. humble** proud person Jb 40_{12}, heart Ps 107_{12}. **2. subdue** nation Dt 9_{3} (+ לִפְנֵי *before* Israel; subj. Y.) 2 S 8_{1}||1 C 18_{1}.

[כִּנְעָה] 1 n.f.—sf. כִּנְעָתֵךְ—**bundle** Jr 10_{17}.

כְּנַעַן I 9.0.1 pr.n.m. **Canaan.**

כְּנַעַן II 84.0.5 pl.n. **Canaan.**

כְּנַעַן III 1 n.m. **merchant** Ho 12_{8}. → cf. כְּנַעֲנִי II *merchant.*

[כִּנְעָן] 1 n.m.—pl. sf. כִּנְעָנֶיהָ—**merchant** Is 23_{8}.

כְּנַעֲנָה 5 pr.n.m. **Chenanah.**

כְּנַעֲנִי I 73.0.3 gent. **Canaanite.**

כְּנַעֲנִי II 3 n.m.—pl. כְּנַעֲנִים—**merchant** Zc 14_{21}. → cf. כְּנַעַן III *merchant.*

כנף I 1 vb.—**Ni.** 1 Impf. יִכָּנֵף—**hide oneself** Is 30_{20}. → כָּנָף *wing.*

*כנף II 1 vb.—**Qal** 1 Pf. כָּנְפָה—of vine, **bend,** or perh. **gather its roots** Ezk $17_{7(mss)}$ (L כפן *stretch hungrily*).

כָּנָף 109.1.19 n.f.—cstr. כְּנַף; sf. כְּנָפִי; du. כְּנָפַיִם; pl. cstr. כַּנְפוֹת (כַּנְפֵי); sf. כְּנָפֶיךָ—**1a. wing** of bird Gn 1_{21}, insect 11QT 48_{5}, cherubim 1 K 6_{24}, seraphim Is 6_{2}, wind 2 S 22_{11}, dawn Ps 139_{9}. **b. winged creature** Gn 7_{14}. **2. skirt, hem, edge** of garment Ru 3_{9}. **3. flank** of army 1QM 9_{11}. **4. corner, end** of world Is 11_{12}. → כנף *hide.*

כִּנְּרוֹת 3 pl.n. **Chinneroth.**

כִּנֶּרֶת 4 pl.n. **Chinnereth.**

[כְּנָת] 1 n.m.—pl. sf. כְּנָוֹתָיו—**associate** Ezr $4_{7(Qr)}$.

כֵּס, see כִּסֵּא *throne.*

כֶּסֶא 2 n.m.—כֶּסֶה—**full moon** Pr 7$_{20}$.

כִּסֵּא 135.4.21 n.m.—כִּסֵּה; cstr. כִּסֵּא (כֵּס); sf. כִּסְאֲךָ; pl. כִּסְאוֹת; sf. כִּסְאוֹתָם—**1. throne,** of king Gn 41$_{40}$, messiah Zc 6$_{13}$, Y. in heaven Ps 11$_4$; oft. in ref. to power, authority of king 2 S 3$_{10}$. **2. jurisdiction** of governor Ne 3$_7$. **3. seat, chair** 2 K 4$_{10}$.

*[כֹּסֶא] 0.0.0.1 pr.n.m. **Choseh.**

כסה 156.6.19 vb.—**Qal** 3 Ptc. כֹּסֶה; pass. כְּסוּי—**1. conceal** knowledge Pr 12$_{23}$, dishonour Pr 12$_{16}$. **2.** pass., **be covered, forgiven,** of sin Ps 32$_1$.

Ni. 2.1.3 Pf. נִכְסְתָה; impf. Q תכסה; inf. הִכָּסוֹת—**be covered, hidden,** of sun Si 43$_2$, blood Ezk 24$_8$, Babylon Jr 51$_{42}$ (+ בְּ *by* waves).

Pi. 135.3.16 Pf. כִּסָּה, כִּסִּיתָ, כִּסּוּ; impf. יְכַסֶּה, תְּכַסִּי; + waw וַיְכַס; impv. כַּסֻּנוּ; ptc. מְכַסֶּה, מְכַסִּים; inf. כַּסּוֹת—**1a. cover** nakedness Gn 9$_{23}$, one's face Gn 38$_{15}$. **b. cover oneself, clothe oneself with** (בְּ) veil Gn 38$_{14}$, cloak Dt 22$_{12}$. **2a. cover up, conceal** blood Gn 37$_{26}$. **b. hide** one's plans from (מִן) someone Gn 18$_{17}$. **3a.** of floods, **spread over, overwhelm** army Ex 15$_5$. **b.** of cherubim, **spread (wings)** over (עַל) ark 2 C 5$_8$. **c.** of disease, **spread over, break out over** skin Lv 13$_{12}$. **4. cover over** (עַל) sin, **forgive** Ne 3$_{37}$. **5.** perh. **uncover, reveal,** פִּי רְשָׁעִים יְכַסֶּה חָמָס *the mouth of the wicked reveals violence* Pr 10$_{11}$.

Pu. 7.2 Pf. כֻּסּוּ; impf. יְכֻסֶּה; + waw וַיְכֻסּוּ; ptc. מְכֻסִּים—**1a. be covered (by water),** of mountains Gn 7$_{19}$. **b. be covered** in (בְּ) darkness Ec 6$_4$. **c.** with accus., **be covered with** shade Ps 80$_{11}$. **2. be clothed in** (בְּ) sackcloth 1 C 21$_{16}$.

Htp. 9 Impf. יִתְכַּסּוּ; + waw וַיִּתְכַּס; ptc. מִתְכַּסֶּה, מִתְכַּסִּים—**1. clothe oneself with** (בְּ) mantle 1 K 11$_{29}$, with (accus.) sackcloth Jon 3$_8$; abs. Gn 24$_{65}$. **2. be concealed** by (בְּ) deception, of hatred Pr 26$_{26}$.

→ כְּסוּי *covering,* כְּסוּת *covering,* מִכְסֶה *covering,* מְכַסֶּה *covering.*

כֶּסֶה, see כֶּסֶא *full moon.*

כִּסֵּה, see כִּסֵּא *throne.*

[כָּסוּי] 2 n.m. **covering,** כְּסוּי עוֹר *covering of skin* Nm 4$_{6.14}$. → כסה *cover.*

כְּסוּת 8.0.1 n.f.—sf. כְּסוּתוֹ—**1. clothing** Ex 21$_{10}$ Dt 22$_{12}$. **2. covering** of eyes Gn 20$_{16}$, Abaddon Jb 26$_6$. → כסה *cover.*

כסח 2 vb.—**Qal** 2 Ptc. pass. כְּסוּחָה—pass. **be cut off, cut down,** of thorn-bush Is 33$_{12}$, vine Ps 80$_{17}$.

*[כֵּסְיָה] 1 n.f. **great throne** Ex 17$_{16}$ (L כֵּס יָהּ *throne of* Y.).

כְּסִיל I 70.7.1 n.m.—pl. כְּסִילִים—**fool,** enjoys doing wrong Pr 10$_{23}$, spreads slander Pr 10$_{18}$, delays paying vow Ec 5$_3$, gives full vent to anger Pr 29$_{11}$. → כסל *be foolish.*

כְּסִיל II 4.0.1 pr.n.m.—pl. Q כסילים; sf. כְּסִילֵיהֶם—**Orion** Am 5$_8$; pl. **stars (of Orion)** Is 13$_{10}$.

כְּסִיל III 1 pl.n. **Chesil.**

כְּסִילוּת 1 n.f. **stupidity,** אֵשֶׁת כְּסִילוּת *woman of stupidity* or *Lady Folly* Pr 9$_{13}$. → כסל *be foolish.*

כסל 1 vb.—**Qal** 1 Impf. יִכְסָלוּ—**be foolish, stupid** Jr 10$_8$. → כְּסִיל I *fool,* כְּסִילוּת *stupidity,* כֶּסֶל I *stupidity,* כִּסְלָה *stupidity.*

כֶּסֶל I 6.0.1 n.m.—sf. כִּסְלִי—**1. stupidity** Ec 7$_{25}$. **2. confidence** Jb 31$_{24}$. → כסל *be foolish.*

כֶּסֶל II 7.1.3 n.m.—כֶּסֶל; pl. כְּסָלִים; sf. כְּסָלַי—**thigh** of sacrificial animal Lv 3$_4$, person Ps 38$_8$.

*[כְּסַלְאָ] 0.0.0.2 pr.n.m. **Choselah.**

כִּסְלָה 2 n.f.—sf. כִּסְלָתֶךָ—**stupidity, confidence** Jb 4$_6$. → כסל *be foolish.*

כִּסְלֵו 2.0.1 pr.n.[m.] **Chislev,** ninth month of Babylonian-based calendar = November/December Zc 7$_1$.

כְּסָלוֹן 1 pl.n. **Chesalon.**

כִּסְלוֹן 1 pr.n.m. **Chislon.**

[כַּסְלֻחִי] 2 gent. **Casluhite.**

כִּסְלֹת תָּבוֹר 1 pl.n. **Chisloth-tabor.**

כסם 2.0.1 vb.—**Qal** 2 Impf. יִכְסְמוּ; inf. abs. כָּסוֹם—**clip** head, i.e. hair Ezk 44$_{20}$.

Pi. 0.0.1 + waw ויכסמוהו—**tear off, ravage,** of wild boar (חזן[ירים]) 4QAdmonPar 2.3$_6$.

→ כֻּסֶּמֶת *spelt.*

כֻּסְּמִים, see כֻּסֶּמֶת *spelt.*

כֻּסֶּמֶת 3 n.f.—pl. כֻּסְּמִים—**spelt,** a species of wheat Ex 9$_{32}$. → כסם *clip.*

כסס 1 vb.—**Qal** 1 Impf. תָּכֹסּוּ—**reckon, count,** אִישׁ לְפִי אָכְלוֹ תָּכֹסּוּ עַל־הַשֶּׂה *each according to his eating you shall reckon for the lamb* Ex 12$_4$. → מֶכֶס *tribute,* מִכְסָה *number.*

כסף I 6 vb.—**Qal** 2 Impf. יִכְסוֹף—**1. be eager** to tear, of lion Ps 17$_{12}$. **2. long for** (לְ) a creature, of Y. Jb 14$_{15}$.

Ni. 4 Pf. נִכְסַפְתָּה; ptc. נִכְסָף; inf. abs. נִכְסוֹף—**1. long for** (לְ) something Gn 31$_{30}$ Ps 84$_{3}$. **2. be ashamed** Zp 2$_{1}$.

*כסף II 1 vb. **be ashamed,** הַגּוֹי לֹא נִכְסָף *O nation that is not ashamed* Zp 2$_{1}$. → כֶּסֶף II *disappointment,* כֹּסֶף *disappointment.*

כֶּסֶף I 403.4.49.6 n.m.—כֶּסֶף; sf. כַּסְפִּי; pl. sf. כַּסְפֵּיהֶם—**1. (refined) silver, money,** גְּבִיעַ הַכֶּסֶף *cup of silver* Gn 44$_{2}$, אֱלֹהֵי כֶסֶף *gods of silver* Ex 20$_{23}$, שֶׁקֶל־כֶּסֶף *shekel of silver* Gn 23$_{15}$. **2. silver ore,** הָגוֹ סִיגִים מִכָּסֶף *remove dross from silver* Pr 25$_{4}$.

*[כֶּסֶף] II 1 n.[m.]—sf. כַּסְפָּם—**disappointment** Ho 9$_{6}$ (or em. כֹּסְפָּם [from כֹּסֶף] in same sense). → כסף II *be ashamed.*

*[כֶּסֶף] III 1 n.[m.]—כֶּסֶף—**food** Is 55$_{1}$.

*[כֹּסֶף] n.[m.] **disappointment,** מַחְמַד לְכֹסְפָּם *that which they desire results in disappointment* Ho 9$_{6}$ (if em. מַחְמַד לְכַסְפָּם *their treasures of silver*). → כסף II *be ashamed.*

כָּסִפְיָא 2 pl.n. **Casiphia.**

*[כָּסֵר] 0.0.0.1 pl.n. **Caser.**

כֶּסֶת 2 n.f.—pl. כְּסָתוֹת; sf. כִּסְּתוֹתֵיכֶנָה—**band,** for magical purposes Ezk 13$_{18.20}$.

כעס 54.1.3 vb.—**Qal** 6 Pf. כָּעַס; impf. אֶכְעַס; inf. כְּעוֹס—**be angry, vexed,** of Y. Ezk 16$_{42}$, person Ps 112$_{10}$ 2 C 16$_{10}$ (+ אֶל *towards* someone).

Pi. 2 Pf. כִּעֲסוּנִי—**provoke (to anger)** Y. Dt 32$_{21}$, person 1 S 1$_{6}$.

Hi. 46.1.3 Pf. הִכְעַסְתָּ; impf. אַכְעִיסֵם; + waw וַיַּכְעֵס; ptc. מַכְעִיסִים; inf. הַכְעִיס—**1. vex, provoke to anger** Y. 1 K 16$_{2}$ (+ בְּ *with* sins), person 1 S 1$_{7}$. **2.** subj. Y., **trouble** human heart Ezk 32$_{9}$.

→ כַּעַס *anger,* כַּעַשׂ *vexation.*

כַּעַס 21.1.4 n.m.—כַּעַס; sf. כַּעְסִי; pl. כְּעָסִים—**1.** of human, **a. vexation,** caused by bad treatment 1 S 1$_{16}$. **b. grief,** בְּרֹב חָכְמָה רָב־כָּעַס *with much wisdom comes much grief* Ec 1$_{18}$. **2. anger** of Y. Ps 85$_{5}$. **3. provocation, taunt** of enemy Dt 32$_{27}$. → כעס *be vexed;* cf. כַּעַשׂ *vexation.*

*[כער] 0.2 vb.—**Pu.** 0.2 Ptc. מכוערין—**be ugly, repulsive,** of word Si 13$_{22}$, person Si 11$_{2(A)}$ (+ בְּ *in* appearance).

כַּעַשׂ 4 n.m.—כַּעַשׂ; sf. כַּעְשִׂי—**vexation** Jb 6$_{2}$. → כעס *be vexed;* cf. כַּעַס *vexation.*

כַּף I 192.2.17 n.f.—כַּף; sf. כַּפִּי; du. כַּפַּיִם; cstr. כַּפֵּי; sf. כַּפַּי; pl. כַּפּוֹת; sf. כַּפֹּתָיו—**1a.** usu. **hand, palm,** entire hand Dt 25$_{12}$, palm as distinct from hand, כַּפּוֹת יָדָיו *palms of his hands* 1 S 5$_{4}$. **b. power, domination, grip,** כַּף־מִדְיָן *power of Midian* Jg 6$_{13}$. **c. foot** of animal Lv 11$_{27}$. **d.** perh. fingerless **stump** of hand 2 K 9$_{35}$. **e. sole** of foot, human Dt 2$_{5}$, divine Ezk 43$_{7}$, animal Gn 8$_{9}$. **2. ladle, spoon** or perh. **saucer, dish,** as cultic object Nm 7$_{86}$. **3. socket** of hip joint Gn 32$_{33}$. **4. hollow** of sling 1 S 25$_{29}$. **5. handle** of bolt Ca 5$_{5}$. **6.** perh. **wing, flank** of army 1QM 9$_{10}$. **7. handful** 1 K 17$_{12}$. **8.** perh. **basin** of drain 3QTr 9$_{11(Allegro)}$. → כפף *bend.*

*[כַּף] II 4 n.f.—sf. כַּפִּי; pl. sf. כַּפָּיו—**skirt** Ex 33$_{22}$ Is 33$_{15}$ Ps 129$_{7}$ 139$_{5}$.

כֵּף I 2 n.m.—pl. כֵּפִים—**rock** or **mountain top** Jr 4$_{29}$ Jb 30$_{6}$.

*[כַּף] II n.[m.] **edge,** perh. read כף הביב *edge of the drain* 3QTr 9$_{11}$.

*[כִּפָּא] 0.0.1 pl.n. **Kippa.**

כפה 1.0.1 vb.—**Qal** 1.0.1 Pf. Q כפיתה; impf. יִכְפֶּה—**subdue** anger, subj. gift Pr 21$_{14}$.

כִּפָּה 4.0.1 n.f.—כִּפָּה; sf. כִּפָּתוֹ; pl. cstr. כִּפֹּת; sf. Q כפותיו—**branch,** usu. of palm tree Lv 23$_{40}$. → כפף *bend.*

כְּפוֹר I 9 n.m.—pl. cstr. כְּפוֹרֵי—**bowl** of silver or gold Ezr 1$_{10}$.

כְּפוֹר II 3.2 n.m.—cstr. כְּפֹר—**hoar frost** Jb 38$_{29}$.→ כפר *cover.*

כְּפִי 11.1.6 prep.—sf. כְּפִיךָ—lit. *according to the mouth of,* **1.** as prep., **a. in accordance with, in proportion to,** כְּפִי נִדְרוֹ אֲשֶׁר יִדֹּר כֵּן יַעֲשֶׂה *in accordance with the vow that he has taken, so shall he act* Nm 6$_{21}$. **b. as, like,** הֵן־אֲנִי כְפִיךָ לָאֵל *behold, I am like you before God* Jb 33$_{6}$. **2.** as conj., **in such a way that, so that** Zc 2$_{4}$. **3.** כְּפִי אֲשֶׁר **because** Ml 2$_{9}$. → כְּ *as* + פֶּה *mouth.*

כָּפִיס 1.0.3 n.m. **beam, rafter** Hb 2$_{11}$ 1QH 14$_{26}$.

כְּפִיר I 31.1.4 n.m.—pl. כְּפִרִים; sf. כְּפִירַיִךְ—**young lion** Jg 14$_{5}$.

*[כְּפִיר] II 1 n.m.—pl. sf. כְּפִרֶיהָ—**copper vessel** Ezk 38$_{13}$.

כְּפִירָה 4 pl.n. **Chephirah.**

כְּפִירִים 1 pl.n. **Chephirim.**

כפל 5.0.1 vb.—**Qal** 4.0.1 Impf. Q יכפלו; + waw וְכָפַלְתָּ; ptc. pass. כָּפוּל—**1. double (over), fold** curtain Ex 26$_{9}$. **2.** pass., **be folded,** of breastpiece Ex 39$_{9}$.

Ni. 1 Impf. תִּכָּפֵל—**be doubled, used a second time,** of sword Ezk 21$_{19}$.

→ כֶּפֶל *double.*

כֶּפֶל 3.1 n.[m.]—du. כִּפְלַיִם—**1. double (amount)** Si 26$_{1}$. 2. perh. **equivalent (amount)** Is 40$_{2}$. → כפל *be double.*

כפן 1 vb.—**Qal** 1 Pf. כָּפְנָה—of vine, **stretch out** roots **hungrily** toward (עַל) eagle Ezk 17$_{7}$. → כָּפָן *hunger.*

כָּפָן 2 n.[m.] **hunger** Jb 30$_{3}$. → כפן *be hungry.*

כפף 5.1 vb.—**Qal** 4.1 Pf. כָּפַף; impv. Si כיף; ptc. pass. כְּפוּפִים; inf. כֹּף—**1. bow down** head Is 58$_{5}$. **2. be bowed down,** of soul Ps 57$_{7}$. **3.** pass. ptc. as noun, **one who is bowed down** Ps 145$_{14}$.

Ni. 1 Impf. אִכַּף—**bow oneself down** to (לְ) Y. Mc 6$_{6}$.

→ כַּף I *palm (of hand),* כִּפָּה *branch.*

כפר 102.3.51 vb.—**Qal** 1 + waw וְכָפַרְתָּ—**cover over** ark with (בְּ) bitumen Gn 6$_{14}$.

Pi. 92.3.45 Pf. כִּפֶּר, כִּפַּרְתֶּם; impf. יְכַפֵּר, אֲכַפְּרָה; impv. כַּפֵּר; inf. כַּפֵּר (כַּפְּרִי, כַּפֶּרְךָ)—**1a.** of person, **atone, make atonement, make expiation, effect ransom,** oft. because of sin Lv 4$_{20}$, also **purify ritually** person with discharge, illness, etc. (with no notion of wrongdoing) Lv 15$_{15}$, (1) for (עַל) oneself by giving money Ex 30$_{15}$; for someone else by performing sacrificial rituals Lv 4$_{20}$, specif. before (לִפְנֵי) Y. Lv 14$_{18}$. (2) ritually, for (עַל) sin of someone else Lv 4$_{35}$. (3) vicariously, for (בְּעַד) sins of others Ex 32$_{30}$. (4) because of (מִן) sin Lv 16$_{34}$, discharge Lv 15$_{15}$. (5) with (בְּ) guilt offering Lv 7$_{7}$, with (עַל) goat for Azazel appar. Lv 16$_{10}$ (unless עַל *over*). **b.** of Y., (1) **forgive** sin, with accus. Ps 78$_{38}$, עַל of obj. Ps 79$_{9}$, בְּעַד of obj. 1QS 11$_{14}$. (2) **forgive** person, with לְ of obj. Dt 21$_{8}$, בְּעַד of obj. CD 2$_{5}$. **2. purify, purge** place, **a.** with accus. altar Lv 16$_{20}$, holy place Lv 16$_{20}$, sanctuary Lv 16$_{33}$, temple Ezk 45$_{20}$. **b.** with עַל of obj., altar Ex 29$_{37}$, holy place Lv 16$_{16}$ (+ מִן *from* uncleanness and transgressions). **3. cover** person's face, i.e. **pacify, appease** person Gn 32$_{21}$ (+ בְּ *with* present). **4. avert** anger Pr 16$_{14}$, disaster Is 47$_{11}$.

Pu. 7.0.5 Pf. כֻּפַּר; impf. יְכֻפַּר—**1. be atoned for,** of sin Is 6$_{7}$. **2. be covered,** i.e. **annulled,** of covenant Is 28$_{18}$.

Hi. 0.0.1 Pf. הכפרתה—perh. **make atonement** 4QPrFêtes^{c} 54$_{2}$.

Htp. 1 Impf. יִתְכַּפֵּר—**be atoned for** by (בְּ) sacrifice, of iniquity 1 S 3$_{14}$.

Ntp. 1 Pf. נִכַּפֵּר—**be atoned for,** of guilt of innocent blood Dt 21$_{8}$.

→ כְּפוֹר II *hoar frost,* כֹּפֶר I *ransom,* II *bitumen,* כִּפֻּר *atonement,* כַּפֹּרֶת *cover.*

[כָּפָר] 1.0.1 n.m.—pl. כְּפָרִים—**village** 1 C 27$_{25}$ 5/6ḤevBA 46$_{5}$.

[כִּפֻּר] 8.0.20 n.m.—Q כפור; pl. כִּפֻּרִים; cstr. Q כפורי—usu. pl. (sg. only at 4QRitPurA 8$_{4}$), **1. atonement,** חַטַּאת הַכִּפֻּרִים *sin offering of the atonement* Ex 30$_{10}$, כֶּסֶף *money of,* i.e. for Ex 30$_{16}$, יוֹם *day of* Lv 23$_{27}$. **2.** perh. **rite of atonement** 1QS 3$_{4}$. → כפר pi. *make atonement.*

כֹּפֶר I 13.1.6 n.m.—Q כופר; sf. כָּפְרְךָ—**1. ransom, redemption payment,** כֹּפֶר נֶפֶשׁ *ransom of,* i.e. for, *a life* Pr 13$_{8}$. **2. bribe** 1 S 12$_{3}$. → כפר pi. *make atonement.*

כֹּפֶר II 1 n.m. **bitumen, asphalt,** covering Noah's ark Gn 6$_{14}$. → כפר *cover.*

כֹּפֶר III 1 n.m. **village** 1 S 6$_{18}$.

כֹּפֶר IV 3 n.m.—pl. כְּפָרִים—**henna** (or perh. **cyprus**) **blossom** Ca 1$_{14}$.

כְּפַר הָעַמֹּנִי 1 pl.n. **Chephar-ammoni.**

*[כֻּפְרִי] I adj. **tarred,** כלין כופרין *tarred vessels* perh. 3QTr 10$_{11}$.

*[כִּפְּרִי] II adj. **expiatory,** כלין כופרין *expiatory vessels* perh. 3QTr 10$_{11}$.

כַּפֹּרֶת 26.0.2 n.f. **cover, lid** of ark of covenant, as base for cherubim Ex 25$_{17}$||37$_{6}$, **mercy seat, propitiatory** upon which ritual of day of atonement is performed Lv 16$_{13}$. → כפר *cover.*

כפשׁ 1 vb.—**Hi.** 1 Pf. הִכְפִּישַׁנִי—of Y., **(cause to) bend, make cower, trample** someone in (בְּ) ashes Lm 3$_{16}$.

כַּפְתּוֹר I 18 n.m.—כַּפְתֹּר; pl. sf. כַּפְתֹּרֶיהָ—**1. knob,**

ornament, on tabernacle lampstand Ex 25$_{31}$||37$_{17}$. **2. capital** of pillar Am 9$_{1}$.

כַּפְתּוֹר II $_{3}$ pl.n. **Caphtor.**

[כַּפְתֹּרִי] $_{3}$ gent. **Caphtorite.**

כַּר I $_{13}$ n.[m.]—pl. כָּרִים—**1. (young) ram** Dt 32$_{14}$. **2. battering ram** Ezk 4$_{2}$.

כַּר II $_{2}$ n.m.—pl. כָּרִים—**pasture** Is 30$_{23}$.

[כַּר] III $_{1}$ n.[m.] **saddle-basket** of camel Gn 31$_{34}$.

כֹּר $_{8.0.2}$ n.m.—pl. כֹּרִים (Q כורין)—**cor,** also known as omer, a measure of dry or liquid capacity, c. 200 litres, שְׁלֹשִׁים כֹּר סֹלֶת *thirty cors of flour* 1 K 5$_{2}$.

כרבל $_{1}$ vb.—**Pu.** $_{1}$ Ptc. מְכֻרְבָּל—**be wrapped in** (בְּ) robe 1 C 15$_{27}$.

כרה I $_{15.1.4}$ vb.—**Qal** $_{14.0.4}$ Pf. כָּרָה, כָּרִיתִי; impf. יִכְרֶה; ptc. כֹּרֶה; inf. Q כרות—**1. dig, excavate** well Gn 26$_{25}$, pit Pr 26$_{27}$, grave Gn 50$_{5}$. **2. open** ears Ps 40$_{7}$. **3.** perh. **pierce** hands and feet Ps 22$_{17(mss)}$. **4.** perh. **make deep** thoughts 4Q424 3$_{6}$.

Ni. $_{1.1}$ Impf. יִכָּרֶה—**be dug,** of pit Ps 94$_{13}$, reservoir Si 50$_{3}$.

→ כָּרָה *cistern,* מִכְרֶה I *pit.*

כרה II $_{4.0.1}$ vb.—**Qal** $_{4.0.1}$ Impf. יִכְרוּ; + waw וַיִּכְרֶה—**1. purchase** water Dt 2$_{6}$, woman with (בְּ) silver Ho 3$_{2}$. **2. bargain** over (עַל) friend Jb 6$_{27}$. **3.** perh. **acquire** thoughts 4Q424 3$_{6}$.

כרה III $_{3}$ vb.—**Qal** $_{2}$ Impf. יִכְרוּ; + waw וַיִּכְרֶה—**1.** with obj. כֵּרָה, **give feast** 2 K 6$_{23}$. **2. feast, feed on** (עַל) Leviathan Jb 40$_{30}$.

Hi. $_{1}$ Inf. mss לְהַכְרוֹת—**invite** someone **to eat** food 2 S 3$_{35(mss)}$.

→ כֵּרָה *feast.*

*כרה IV $_{1}$ vb.—**Qal** $_{1}$ Pf. mss כָּרוּ—**bind** hands and feet Ps 22$_{17(mss)}$.

*כרה V $_{1}$ vb.—**Qal** $_{1}$ Pf. mss כָּרוּ—**shrivel** hands and feet Ps 22$_{17(mss)}$.

[כָּרָה] $_{1}$ n.f.—pl. cstr. כְּרֹת—**cistern** Zp 2$_{6}$. → כרה I *dig.*

כֵּרָה $_{1}$ n.f. **feast** 2 K 6$_{23}$. → כרה III *feast.*

כְּרוּב I $_{91.0.5}$ n.m.—כְּרֻבִים; cstr. Q כרובי; sf. Q כרוביהם—**cherub,** supernatural winged creature, usu. with protective function, oft. pl., **1.** image of cherub, made of gold Ex 25$_{18}$||37$_{7}$, olive wood 1 K 6$_{23}$. **2.** throne of Y. 1 S 4$_{4}$. **3.** chariot of Y. 2 S 22$_{11}$||Ps 18$_{11}$. **4.** guard of garden of Eden Gn 3$_{24}$.

כְּרוּב II $_{2}$ pl.n. **Cherub.**

כָּרִי $_{2}$ gent. **Carite.**

כְּרִית $_{2}$ pl.n. **Cherith.**

כְּרִיתוּת $_{4}$ n.f. **divorce,** סֵפֶר כְּרִיתֻת *document of divorce* Dt 24$_{1}$. → כרת *cut.*

כַּרְכֹּב $_{2}$ n.m. **ledge** of altar Ex 27$_{5}$ 38$_{4}$.

כַּרְכֹּם $_{1}$ n.m. **saffron** Ca 4$_{14}$.

כַּרְכְּמִישׁ $_{3}$ pl.n. **Carchemish.**

כַּרְכַּס $_{1}$ pr.n.m. **Carcas.**

[כִּרְכָּרָה] $_{1}$ n.f.—pl. כִּרְכָּרוֹת—**dromedary** Is 66$_{20}$. → כרר *turn.*

כרם $_{5}$ vb.—**Qal** $_{5}$ Ptc. כֹּרְמִים, כֹּרְמֵיכֶם—**dress vines,** ptc. as noun, **vinedresser** Is 61$_{5}$. → כֶּרֶם *vineyard.*

כֶּרֶם I $_{91.1.4.10}$ n.m.—כֶּרֶם; sf. כַּרְמִי; pl. כְּרָמִים; cstr. כַּרְמֵי; sf. כַּרְמֵיכֶם, כְּרָמֶיהָ—**vineyard,** כְּרָמֵינוּ סְמָדַר *our vineyards are in blossom* Ca 2$_{15}$, כֶּרֶם י׳ צְבָאוֹת בֵּית יִשְׂרָאֵל *the vineyard of Y. of hosts is the house of Israel* Is 5$_{7}$. → כרם *dress vines.*

[כֶּרֶם] II $_{1}$ pl.n. **Cherem.**

כַּרְמִי I $_{8.0.0.2}$ pr.n.m. **Carmi.**

כַּרְמִי II $_{1}$ gent. **Carmite.**

כַּרְמִיל $_{3}$ n.m. **crimson** 2 C 2$_{6}$.

כַּרְמֶל I $_{13}$ n.m.—sf. כַּרְמִלּוֹ—**1. orchard, cultivated field, garden of fruit trees and vines** Is 16$_{10}$. **2. plantation** of trees 2 K 19$_{23}$||Is 37$_{24}$, **fruitful land** in general Jr 2$_{7}$.

כַּרְמֶל II $_{7.0.2}$ pl.n. **Carmel.**

כַּרְמֶל III $_{3}$ n.m. **fresh ears (of cereal),** prior to drying for making bread Lv 2$_{14}$.

כַּרְמְלִי $_{7}$ gent. **Carmelite.**

כְּרָן $_{2}$ pr.n.m. **Cheran.**

כרסם $_{1}$ vb.—**Pi.** $_{1}$ Impf. יְכַרְסְמֶנָּה—of wild boar, **tear off** vine Ps 80$_{14}$.

כרע $_{36.0.1}$ vb.—**Qal** $_{31.0.1}$ Pf. כָּרַע, כָּרְעוּ; impf. יִכְרַע; ptc. כֹּרְעִים, כֹּרֵעַ; inf. כְּרֹעַ—**1. crouch,** of Judah as lion's whelp Gn 49$_{9}$, woman in labour 1 S 4$_{19}$. **2. get down** on (עַל) one's knees Jg 7$_{5}$. **3a. kneel, bow down** before (לִפְנֵי) Y. Ps 95$_{6}$. **b.** of knee(s), **bend, bow down** to (לְ) Y. Is 45$_{23}$, Baal 1 K 19$_{18}$. **4. kneel** over (עַל) woman, for sexual intercourse Jb 31$_{10}$. **5a. collapse** in (בְּ) chariot 2 K 9$_{24}$, between (בֵּין) someone's feet Jg

5_{27}. **b.** of knees, **falter, give way** Jb 4_{4}. **6.** ptc. as noun, **prostrate one** 1QM 11_{13}.

Hi. 5 Pf. הִכְרִיעַ; impf. תַּכְרִיעַ; impv. הַכְרִיעֵנִי; inf. הַכְרֵעַ—**1.** of Y., **cause to bow down, bring** someone **down** 2 S 22_{40}||Ps 18_{40} (+ תַּחַת *under* someone) Ps 17_{13}. **2. throw** someone **into misery** Jg 11_{35}.

→ כֶּרַע *leg.*

[כֶּרַע] 9.0.3 n.[f.]—du. כְּרָעַיִם; pl. sf. כְּרָעָיו—**leg** of lamb Ex 12_{9}, of locust Lv 11_{21}. → כרע *bow down.*

כַּרְפַּס 1 n.[m.] **linen** Est 1_{6}.

כרר 3 vb.—**Pilp.** 3 Ptc. מְכַרְכֵּר—**dance** or **play** (with hands), i.e. **clap,** before (לִפְנֵי) Y. 2 S 6_{14}. → כִּרְכָּרוֹת *dromedary.*

כָּרֵשׂ 1.1 n.f.—sf. כְּרֵשׂוֹ—**stomach** Jr 51_{34}.

***[כַּרְשֹׁן]** 0.0.0.1 pr.n.m. **Carshon.**

כַּרְשְׁנָא 1 pr.n.m. **Carshena.**

כרת 288.6.53 vb.—**Qal** 135.2.17 Pf. כָּרַת, כָּרַתִּי; impf. יִכְרֹת; + waw וַיִּכְרֹת (וַיִּכְרָת־); impv. כְּרֹת (כְּרָת־), כִּרְתָה, כִּרְתוּ; ptc. כֹּרֵת, כֹּרְתִים; ptc. pass. כָּרוּת; inf. abs. כָּרוֹת; cstr. כְּרֹת (כְּרָת־, כָּרְתִי)—**1.** cut, i.e. **a. make covenant** (בְּרִית) Gn 21_{27}; + אֵת *with* Gn 15_{18}, עִם *with* Dt 4_{23}, לְ *with* Ps 89_{4}, בֵּין *between* 2 K 11_{17}, לִפְנֵי *before* Y. 1 S 23_{18}. **b.** without obj., **make covenant** 1 S 20_{16}. **c. give** word Hg 2_{5}. **d. inscribe** statute Si 44_{20}. **2a. cut down** tree Dt 19_{5}. **b. cut off** foreskin Ex 4_{25}, head 1 S 17_{51}. **c. cut, split** calf into (לְ) two Jr 34_{18}. **d. tear** garment 2 S 10_{4}. **e.** perh. **take, remove** vine from (מִן) place Nm 13_{23}. **f.** perh. **destroy** someone from (מִן) land Jr 50_{16}. **3.** pass. **be cut off,** of head and hands of Dagon 1 S 5_{4}. **4.** pass. ptc. as noun, **one who is mutilated,** i.e. genitally Dt 23_{2}.

Ni. 72.4.27 Pf. נִכְרַת, נִכְרַתָּ; impf. יִכָּרֵת; ptc. Q נכרתים; inf. הִכָּרֵת—**1a. be cut off,** of tongue Pr 10_{31}. **b. be cut down,** of tree Jb 14_{7}. **2a. be destroyed,** of creatures Gn 9_{11} (+ מִן *by* water), land Gn 41_{36} (+ בְּ *by* famine). **b. disappear,** of name of deceased Ru 4_{10} (+ מֵעִם *from among* brothers). **c. fail,** of hope Pr 23_{18}. **3. be blocked,** of waters of Jordan Jos 3_{13}. **4. be excommunicated** from (מִן) congregation of Israel Ex 12_{19}. **5.** appar. **be abrogated,** of covenant Si 50_{24}. **6. be made,** of covenant (implied), באות עולם נכרת עמו *with an eternal sign a covenant was made with him* (i.e. Noah) Si $44_{18(B)}$. **7.** perh. **be chewed,** of meat Nm 11_{33}.

Pu. 2 Pf. כֹּרְתָה, כֹּרַּת (unless both qal pass.)—**1. be cut off,** of navel cord Ezk 16_{4}. **2. be cut down,** of Asherah Jg 6_{28}.

Hi. 78.0.9 Pf. הִכְרִית, הִכְרַתִּי; impf. יַכְרִית (יַכְרֶת); + waw וַיַּכְרֵת; inf. הַכְרִית—**1a. cut off, destroy, kill,** (1) obj. persons, of Y. Dt 12_{29}, human Jos 11_{21} (+ מִן *from* hill country), sword Na 3_{15}, death Jr 9_{20} (+ מִן *from* streets). (2) obj. animals, of Y. Ezk 14_{13} (+ מִן *from* land), of beast Lv 26_{22}. **b.** of Y., **destroy** incense altars Mc 5_{12}, place Jr 51_{62}. **2.** of Y., **cut off** tongue Ps 12_{4}. **3. wipe out** person's name, memory from (מִן) earth, of humans Jos 7_{9}, Y. Ps 34_{17}. **4. remove** one's kindness from (מֵעִם) family 1 S 20_{15}.

Ho. 1 Pf. הָכְרַת—**be cut off, ended** from (מִן) temple, of cereal offering Jl 1_{9}.

→ כְּרִיתוּת *divorce,* כְּרֻתָה *beam,* מַכְרֵת *circumcision blade.*

***כְּרֻתוֹת** 3 n.f.pl. **beams** of cedar 1 K 6_{36}. → כרת *cut.*

כְּרֵתִי 10 gent. **Cherethite.**

כֶּשֶׂב 13.0.1 n.m. (byform of the more common כֶּבֶשׂ)—pl. כְּשָׂבִים—**sheep** Gn 30_{32}. → כִּשְׂבָּה *ewe.*

כִּשְׂבָּה 1 n.f. **ewe** Lv 5_{6}; more commonly כִּבְשָׂה. → כֶּשֶׂב *sheep.*

כֶּשֶׂד 1 pr.n.m. **Chesed.**

[כַּשְׂדִּי] 69.0.1.1 gent. **Chaldaean.**

כַּשְׂדִּים 7 pl.n. **Chaldaea.**

כשה 1 vb.—**Qal** 1 Pf. כָּשִׂיתָ—**be sated, gorged with food** Dt 32_{15}.

***[כשח]** vb. **Qal, be lame, disabled,** of right hand Ps 137_{5} (if em. תִּשְׁכַּח *may it forget* to תִּכְשַׁח *may it be disabled*).

***[כָּשַׁי]** 0.0.0.1 pr.n.m. **Cashai.**

כַּשִּׁיל 1 n.m. **axe** Ps 74_{6}. → כשל *stumble.*

***[כַּשִּׁיר]** adj. **skilful,** as noun, **skilful (player),** כַּשִּׁיר עֲגָבִים *a skilful player of love songs* Ezk 33_{32} (if em. כְּשִׁיר *as a song* of love).

כשל 62.8.24 vb.—**Qal** 29.3.12 Pf. כָּשַׁל, כָּשַׁלְתָּ; impf. Q יכשול, יִכְשְׁלוּ; ptc. כּוֹשֵׁל, כּוֹשְׁלוֹת; inf. כָּשׁוֹל—**1a.** abs., **stumble, stagger,** כָּשְׁלוּ וְנָפְלוּ *they stagger and fall* Jr 46_{6}. **b. stumble over** (בְּ) bodies Na $3_{3(Qr)}$, stumbling blocks Jr 6:21, sin Ho 14:2 (or בְּ *on account of*), over one another (אִישׁ־בְּאָחִיו) Lv 26:37. **c. fall backward** (אָחוֹר) Is 28:13. **2.** of knees, **totter, give way** Is 35:3. **3.** of strength, **fail** Ne 4:4. **4.** ptc. as noun, **one who stumbles** 1QM 14:5.

Ni. 23.4.2 Pf. נִכְשַׁל; impf. תִּכָּשֵׁל, יִכָּשֶׁל־; ptc. נִכְשָׁל, נִכְשָׁלִים; inf. הִכָּשְׁלָם—**1a.** abs., **stumble, stagger** Dn 11:19. **b. stumble** over or on account of (בְּ) sin Ho 5:5. **2. fall by** (בְּ) sword Dn 11:33. **3.** ptc. as noun, **feeble (one), tottering (one)** 1 S 2:4.

Pi. 1 Impf. תְּכַשְּׁלִי—**cause** nation **to stumble** Ezk 36:14(Kt).

Hi. 8.2.10 Pf. הִכְשִׁיל; impf. יַכְשִׁילוּ; ptc. Q מכשלת, מכשילים; inf. הַכְשִׁיל—**1. cause** people **to stumble** morally, of false gods Jr 18:15, spirits of Belial 1QS 3:24, priests Ml 2:8 (+ בְּ *by* teaching). **2.** of Y., **overthrow** king before (לִפְנֵי) enemy 2 C 25:8. **3.** of Y., **cause** someone's strength **to fail** Lm 1:14.

Ho. 1 Ptc. מֻכְשָׁלִים—**be overthrown** before (לִפְנֵי) Y. Jr 18:23.

→ כַּשִּׁיל *axe*, כִּשָּׁלוֹן *stumbling*, מִכְשׁוֹל *obstacle*, מַכְשֵׁלָה *ruin*.

כִּשָּׁלוֹן 1.1.1 n.m. **stumbling** Pr 16:18. → כשל *stumble*.

כשף 6.0.1 vb.—**Pi.** 6.0.1 Pf. כִּשֵּׁף; ptc. מְכַשֵּׁף, מְכַשֵּׁפָה, מְכַשְּׁפִים—**1. practise sorcery** 2 C 33:6. **2.** ptc. as noun, **sorcerer** Dt 18:10. → כַּשָּׁף *sorcerer*, כֶּשֶׁף *sorcery*.

כַּשָּׁף 1 n.m.—pl. sf. כַּשָּׁפֵיהֶם—**sorcerer** Jr 27:9. → כשף *practise sorcery*.

כֶּשֶׁף 6 n.m.—pl. כְּשָׁפִים—**sorcery** Mc 5:11. → כשף *practise sorcery*.

כשר 3.1 vb.—**Qal** 2.1 Pf. כָּשֵׁר; impf. mss יִכְשַׁר—**1.** of proposal, **be right** before (לִפְנֵי) king Est 8:5. **2.** of action, **succeed** Ec 11:6.

Hi. 1 Inf. הַכְשִׁיר—**be an advantage**, יִתְרוֹן הַכְשִׁיר חָכְמָה *wisdom is an advantage for bringing success* Ec 10:10.

→ כֹּשֶׁר *propriety*, כִּשְׁרוֹן *skill*.

* **[כֹּשֶׁר]** 0.0.3 n.[m.]—כושר—**propriety, rightness** 4QTobit[e] 1.2:3 4QInstr[c] 1.1:11. → כשר *be right*.

כִּשְׁרוֹן 3 n.m. **1. skill, skilfulness** Ec 2:21 4:4. **2. success** or **profit** Ec 5:10. → כשר *be right*.

כתב 225.1.130.6 vb.—**Qal** 207.1.121.6 Pf. כָּתַב, כָּתַבְתָּ; impf. אֶכְתֹּב (אֶכְתָּב־, אֶכְתֳּבֶנָּה); + waw וַיִּכְתֹּב (וַיִּכְתָּב־); impv. כְּתֹב (כְּתָב־, כְּתָבָהּ), כִּתְבוּ; ptc. כֹּתֵב, כֹּתְבִים, pass. כָּתוּב, כְּתוּבָה; inf. abs. כָּתוֹב; cstr. כְּתֹב (כָּתְבוֹ)—**1a. write** words on (אֶל) scroll Jr 36:2, letter to (אֶל) someone 2 S 11:14, bitter things against (עַל) someone Jb 13:26. **b. inscribe, incise, engrave** words upon (עַל) stone tablets Ex 34:1.28, inscription upon gold diadem Ex 39:30. **c. sign** (בְּ of obj.) document Jr 32:12. **2. register** people 1 C 24:6. **3.** pass., **a.** of words, deeds, etc., **be written, recorded** in document, with בְּ *in* Dt 28:58, עַל *in* 2 S 1:18. **b.** of stone tablets, **be inscribed with** (בְּ) finger of Y. Ex 31:18.

Ni. 17.0.8 Pf. Q נכתבו; impf. יִכָּתֵב; ptc. נִכְתָּב—**1. be written,** of document Ml 3:16, edict Est 8:8. **2.** of words, matters, **be written down in** (בְּ) document Jb 19:23 Est 2:23. **3. be recorded (as)** friend of Y. CD 3:3, member of community 1QS 7:21.

Pi. 1 Pf. כִּתְּבוּ—**keep writing** or **compose** iniquitous documents Is 10:1.

Hi. 0.0.1 Inf. הכתיב—**dictate** 4QJub[a] 1:27.

→ כְּתָב *document*, כְּתֹבֶת *writing*, מִכְתָּב *writing*.

כְּתָב 17.4.4 n.m.—cstr. כְּתָב; sf. כְּתָבָהּ—**1. document, letter, royal edict** Est 3:14. **2. register, enrolment** Ezk 13:9. **3. script, character, writing** Est 1:22. → כתב *write*.

כְּתֹבֶת 1.0.1 n.f. **writing, incision of tattoo** Lv 19:28. → כתב *write*.

[כִּתִּי] 8.0.35.11 gent. **Kittite.**

כִּתִּים, see כִּתִּי *Kittite*.

כָּתִית 5.0.1 adj. **beaten,** of oil Ex 27:20. → כתת *crush*.

[כֹּתֶל] 1.0.2 n.[m.]—sf. כָּתְלֵנוּ—**wall** Ca 2:9.

כִּתְלִישׁ 1 pl.n. **Chitlish.**

כתם 1 vb.—**Ni.** 1 Ptc. נִכְתָּם—**be stained** before (לִפְנֵי) Y., of iniquity Jr 2:22. → מִכְתָּם III *inscription*.

כֶּתֶם 9.1.3 n.m. **gold,** כֶּתֶם אוֹפִיר *gold of Ophir* Is 13:12, חֲלִי־כֶתֶם *ornament of gold* Pr 25:12. → מִכְתָּם IV *gold-lettered inscription*.

כֻּתֹּנֶת 29.1.2 n.f.—cstr. כְּתֹנֶת; sf. כֻּתָּנְתִּי; pl. כֻּתֳּנֹת (כָּתְנֹת); cstr. כָּתְנוֹת; sf. כָּתְנֹתָם—**tunic, long shirt-like garment** Gn 37:3, of skin Gn 3:21, linen Lv 16:4; כְּתֹנֶת יוֹסֵף *tunic of Joseph* Gn 37:31, כתונת אשה *tunic of a woman* 4QOrd[a] 2:7, כָּתְנֹת כֹּהֲנִים *tunics of the priests* Ezr 2:69.

כָּתֵף 67.0.0.1 n.f.—cstr. כֶּתֶף; sf. כְּתֵפִי; pl. כְּתֵפֹת; cstr. כִּתְפֹת; sf. כְּתֵיפָיו—**1. side, wall** of court of tabernacle Ex 27$_{14}$, temple 1 K 6$_{8}$. **2. shoulder, back** of person Nm 7$_{9}$, beast Is 30$_{6}$. **3. slope, hill** Ezk 25$_{9}$. **4. shoulder piece** of ephod Ex 28$_{7}$. **5. bracket, cross piece** at bottom of laver stand 1 K 7$_{30}$.

*[כָּתֵף] II 2 n.[m.]—pl. sf. כְּתֵפָיו (כְּתֵיפָיו)—**weapon** Dt 33$_{12}$ 1 S 17$_{6}$.

כֹּתֶף 1 n.m. **timbrel** Jb 21$_{12}$.

כתר I 1 vb.—**Pi.** 1 Impv. כַּתַּר—**be patient with** (לְ) someone Jb 36$_{2}$.

כתר II 4 vb.—**Pi.** 2 Pf. כִּתְּרוּנִי—**surround** someone Jg 20$_{43}$ Ps 22$_{13}$.

Hi. 2 Impf. יַכְתִּרוּ; ptc. מַכְתִּיר—**1. surround,** i.e. **hem in** someone Hb 1$_{4}$. **2. surround,** i.e. **gather around** (בְּ of obj.) someone Ps 142$_{8}$.

כתר III 1 vb.—**Hi.** 1 Impf. יַכְתִּרוּ—**be crowned,** עֲרוּמִים יַכְתִּרוּ דָעַת *the shrewd will be crowned with knowledge* Pr 14$_{18}$. → כֶּתֶר *crown,* כֹּתֶרֶת *capital.*

כֶּתֶר 3.0.1 n.m. **1. crown, turban** of Persian king and queen Est 1$_{11}$ 2$_{17}$. **2. crest** on head of horse Est 6$_{8}$. → כתר III *be crowned.*

כֹּתֶרֶת 24 n.f.—כּוֹתֶרֶת; pl. כֹּתָרוֹת—**1. capital** of column 1 K 7$_{16}$. **2.** round **crown piece** on stand for laver 1 K 7$_{31}$. → כתר III *be crowned.*

כתשׁ 1 vb.—**Qal** 1 Impf. תִּכְתּוֹשׁ—**pound** fool in (בְּ) mortar Pr 27$_{22}$. → מַכְתֵּשׁ I *mortar.*

כתת 17.0.3 vb.—**Qal** 5.0.2 Impf. אֶכּוֹת; + waw וָכְתּוֹתִי; impv. כֹּתּוּ; ptc. pass. כָּתוּת—**1a. beat, hammer** blade Jl 4$_{10}$ (+ לְ *into* sword). **b. crush** golden calf Dt 9$_{21}$, adversary Ps 89$_{24}$. **2.** pass., **a. be crushed,** of testicles Lv 22$_{24}$. **b. be smashed,** of jar Is 30$_{14}$.

Pi. 5 Pf. כִּתַּת—**1. beat, hammer** sword Is 2$_{4}$||Mc 4$_{3}$ (+ לְ *into* blade). **2. hammer into pieces, crush** images 2 C 34$_{7}$, land Zc 11$_{6}$.

Pu. 1 Pf. כֻּתְּתוּ—**be crushed,** of nation against (בְּ) nation 2 C 15$_{6}$.

Hi. 2 + waw וַיַּכְּתוּ—**crush** Israelites Dt 1$_{44}$.

Ho. 4.0.1 Impf. יֻכַּתּוּ—**be beaten, crushed,** of gate Is 24$_{12}$, warriors Jr 46$_{5}$.

→ כָּתִית *beaten,* מְכִתָּה *fragment.*

ל

לְ 18687.c.640.c.6000.926 prep.—**a.** vocalized לַאֲ, לֶאֱ, לָאֳ' before א, ה, ח, or ע (exc. לֵאלֹהִים, לֵאלֹהָיו, etc., לַאדֹנָי/לַיי׳); **b.** לִגְ before any other consonant; **c. usu.** לָ before tone syllable, (לָהֵנָּה, לָהֵן) לָהֶן, לָהֵמָּה; **d.** before a def. noun, לַ, לָ, or לֶ, i.e. with the vowel of the art. הַ; **e.** with sf., לִי, (לכה) לְךָ, (לְכִי) לָךְ, לוֹ (לְמוֹ), לָהּ (לְהּ), לָנוּ, לָכֶם (לכמה Q), (להמה Q), לָהֶם (לָמוֹ), (לָכֶנָּה) לכן Q, לָהֶן Q—**1.** of possession, **of, (belonging) to, pertaining to,** כָּל־אֲשֶׁר־לוֹ *everything that he has* Gn 24$_{36}$, כֹּל אֲשֶׁר אֵין־לוֹ סְנַפִּיר *whatever does not have fins* Lv 11$_{12}$, מִזְמוֹר לְאָסָף *a psalm of Asaph* Ps 73$_{1}$, אַל לַמְּלָכִים *it does not pertain to kings,* i.e. kings should not Pr 31$_{4}$. **2.** of direction, **to, towards,** וַתִּתֵּן גַּם־לְאִישָׁהּ *and she gave also to her husband* Gn 3$_{6}$, שַׁלְּחֻנִי לַאדֹנִי *send me to my master* Gn 24$_{54}$, שְׂאוּ לַשָּׁמַיִם עֵינֵיכֶם *lift your eyes towards the heavens* Is 51$_{6}$. **3a. (so) as (to be), into,** וּנְתַתִּיךָ לְגוֹיִם *and I will make you into nations* Gn 17$_{6}$, וּמְשַׁחְתּוֹ לְנָגִיד *and you will anoint him as a ruler* 1 S 9$_{16}$. **b. as, in the function of, in the capacity of,** וּקְשַׁרְתֶּם לְאוֹת *and you will bind (them) as a sign* Dt 6$_{8}$. **c.** היה לְ **be as,** i.e. **become, turn into,** וַיְהִי ... לְנֶפֶשׁ חַיָּה *and he became ... a living soul* Gn 2$_{7}$, וְהָיִיתִי לָהֶם לֵאלֹהִים *and I will be their God* Gn 17$_{8}$. **4.** of place, time, **at, by, on, along, over,** אִישׁ לְפֶתַח אָהֳלוֹ *each at the entrance of his tent* Nm 11$_{10}$, תִּהְיֶיןָ לְרֹאשׁ יוֹסֵף *they will be on Joseph's head* Gn 49$_{26}$, לִתְשׁוּבַת הַשָּׁנָה לְעֵת צֵאת *at the return of the year, the time when* kings *go forth* 2 S 11$_{1}$. **5.** of purpose, **a.** followed by noun, **for (the purpose of), to be used for,** סֹלֶת בְּלוּלָה בַשֶּׁמֶן לְמִנְחָה *flour mixed with oil for a cereal offering* Nm 7$_{79}$. **b.** followed by inf. cstr., **(in order) to, so as to,** וַיְשַׁלְּחֵהוּ ... לַעֲבֹד *and he sent him out ... to work* the ground Gn 3₂₃, וַיֵּצְאוּ לָלֶכֶת *and they went out to go* Gn 12₅. **c. for, in order to obtain,** וַיַּעֲלוּ ... לַמִּשְׁפָּט *and they went up ... for judgment* Jg 4₅. **6. about, concerning, with regard to, in respect of, as for, in relation to,** מִי אֵלֶּה לָךְ *what are these in relation to you?* Gn 33₅, כָּל־הַכָּתוּב לַחַיִּים *all who are recorded in respect of life* Is 4₃, לָמָּה זֶּה תִּשְׁאַל לִשְׁמִי *why do you ask about my name?* Gn 32₃₀, לַנְּבִאִים *concerning the prophets* Jr 23₉, לְיִשְׁמָעֵאל *as for Ishmael* Gn 17₂₀. **7.** of benefit, **to (the advantage/disadvantage of), for (the benefit, use, of), to be used by,** לֹא תִקַּח אִשָּׁה לִבְנִי *do not take a wife for my son* Gn 24₃₇, וַיֵּרַע לְמֹשֶׁה *and it went ill for Moses* Ps 106₃₆. **8.** לְ + 'reflexive' sf., restating subj., לֶךְ־לְךָ מֵאַרְצְךָ *go from your country* Gn 12₁. **9. in accordance with, corresponding to,** וְלֹא־לְמַרְאֵה עֵינָיו יִשְׁפּוֹט *and he will not judge (merely) in accordance with what he sees* Is 11₃, לְמִשְׁפְּחֹתֵיהֶם יָצְאוּ *they went out according to their families* Gn 8₁₉. **10.** specifying or emphasizing, **namely, even, that is to say,** הָרַג מְלָכִים עֲצוּמִים: לְסִיחוֹן ... וּלְעוֹג *he killed mighty kings, even Sihon ... and Og* Ps 135₁₁. **11. amounting to,** זָהָב טוֹב לְכִכָּרִים שֵׁשׁ מֵאוֹת *fine gold, amounting to 600 (talents)* 2 C 3₈. **12.** introducing obj., וְנָשָׂאתִי לְכָל־הַמָּקוֹם *I will forgive the whole place* Gn 18₂₆. **13.** in passive constructions, of agent, **by (the agency of),** נִדְרַשְׁתִּי לְלוֹא שָׁאָלוּ *I was (ready to be) sought by those who did not ask* Is 65₁. **14.** of cause, **on account of, for (the sake of), because of, at,** אַל־תִּבְכּוּ לְמֵת *do not weep for the dead* Jr 22₁₀, לְאַט־לִי *deal gently for my sake* with the lad 2 S 18₅, נָסוּ לְקֹלָם *they fled at their cry* Nm 16₃₄. **15.** of accompaniment, **with, in (a state of),** וְאִישׁ מָשַׁךְ בַּקֶּשֶׁת לְתֻמּוֹ *and a man drew a bow in his innocence*, i.e. at random 1 K 22₃₄, לָבֶטַח *in safety* Lv 26₅. **16.** of instrument, **by (means of), with,** לְפִי־חָרֶב *with the edge of the sword* Ex 17₁₃. **17. in the estimation of, before,** מָרְדֳּכַי ... גָּדוֹל לַיְּהוּדִים *Mordecai ... was great in the estimation of the Jews* Est 10₃, וָאֱהְיֶה תָמִים לוֹ *and I was blameless before him* 2 S 22₂₄. **18. against,** חָטָאנוּ לַי׳ *we have sinned against Y.* Dt 1₄₁. **19.** לְלֹא **without,** יָמִים רַבִּים לְיִשְׂרָאֵל לְלֹא אֱלֹהֵי אֱמֶת *Israel had many days without the true God* 2 C 15₃. **20.** perh. asseverative, emphatic, **indeed,** בַּת־עַמִּי לְאַכְזָר *the daughter of my people is indeed cruel* Lm 4₃. **21.** voc., **O,** הוי למות *alas, O death* Si 41₁(Bmg). **22.** perh. of direction, **from, since,** י׳ לַמַּבּוּל יָשָׁב *Y. has sat enthroned since the flood* Ps 29₁₀. **23.** לְ + inf. cstr. not expressing purpose (contrast §5b), **a.** following modal or auxiliary verb, etc., לֹא־יָכֹל יוֹסֵף לְהִתְאַפֵּק *Joseph could not control himself* Gn 45₁, חָדַלְנוּ לְקַטֵּר *we ceased to burn incense* Jr 44₁₈. **b.** with verb of quantity or quality, וַתֹּסֶף לָלֶדֶת *and she bore again* Gn 4₂, הִקְשִׁיתָ לִשְׁאוֹל *you have asked a hard thing* 2 K 2₁₀. **c.** expressing ability, sufficiency, כֵּן אֲדֹנִי הַמֶּלֶךְ לִשְׁמֹעַ הַטּוֹב *thus is my lord the king able to discern good* 2 S 14₁₇, חָלָה ... לָמוּת *he was sick (enough) ... to die* 2 K 20₁. **d.** functioning as ptc., noun, etc., וְהִנֵּה דְבַר־י׳ אֵלָיו לֵאמֹר *and behold the word of Y. came to him, saying* Gn 15₄. **e.** introducing object clause, מָה י׳ ... שֹׁאֵל מֵעִמָּךְ כִּי אִם־לְיִרְאָה *what does Y. ... ask of you except to fear?* Dt 10₁₂. → cf. לְמוֹ *to.*

*[לָא] n.[m.]—**strength,** יֶשׁ־לְאֵל יָדִי *there is strength to my hand*, i.e. I can Gn 31₂₉ (if em. יֶשׁ־לָא לְיָדִי, i.e. אֵל II *strength*). → לאה II *be strong.*

*[לָא] I adj. **hesitant** Jb 6₂₁ (if em. Kt לא *nothing*). → לאה I *be weary.*

לֹא I 5196.176.1092.9 neg. part.—לוֹא, לה (Dt 3₁₁ [mss לא]), Q לו)—**no(t), 1.** followed by pf., **a.** usu. introducing factual statement, לֹא הִמְטִיר י׳ אֱלֹהִים *Y. God had not caused it to rain* Gn 2₅. **b.** in statements implying consequence or cause, (1) וְלֹא **so that not, seeing that not,** הָיָה רְכוּשָׁם רָב וְלֹא יָכְלוּ לָשֶׁבֶת יַחְדָּו *their possessions were great so that they could not live together* Gn 13₆, יָדַעְתִּי כִּי־יְרֵא אֱלֹהִים אַתָּה וְלֹא חָשַׂכְתָּ אֶת־בִּנְךָ *I know that you fear God, seeing that you have not withheld your son* Gn 22₁₂. (2) בְּלֹא **so that not, seeing that not, unless** 1QH 16₁₀ 18₅. **c.** in adversative clauses, (1) וְלֹא **but not,** וָאֲדַבֵּר אֲלֵיכֶם וְלֹא שְׁמַעְתֶּם *and I spoke to you but you did not listen* Dt 1₄₃. (2) בְּלֹא **but not** 1QH 16₁₃. **d.** in question, preceded by interrog.: לָמָּה לֹא *why not?* Gn 12₁₈, מַדּוּעַ לֹא *why not?* Ex 5₁₄, הֲלֹא *did not?* Gn 20₅, אִם־לֹא *did not?* Jb 30₂₅; without introductory part. 2 S 19₄₄. **e.** in protasis of conditional sentence, (1) אִם־לֹא *if not* Gn 43$_9$. (2) אֲשֶׁר־לֹא *if not* Ex 21$_{13}$. (3) הִנֵּה לֹא *if not* Lv 13$_{32}$. **f.** in apodosis of conditional sentence 1 K 22$_{28}$||2 C 18$_{27}$. **g.** with inf. abs. and pf., הַצֵּל לֹא־הִצַּלְתָּ אֶת־עַמֶּךָ *you have by no means delivered your people* Ex 5$_{23}$. **2.** followed by impf., **a.** usu. in factual or descriptive statement or assurance, וְלֹא יִתְבֹּשָׁשׁוּ *and they were not ashamed* Gn 2$_{25}$, לֹא־אֹסִף לְקַלֵּל עוֹד אֶת־הָאֲדָמָה *I shall never again curse the ground* Gn 8$_{21}$. **b.** in statements of consequence or purpose, (1) וְלֹא **so that not, lest,** וְלֹא תֹאמַר אֲנִי הֶעֱשַׁרְתִּי אֶת־אַבְרָם *so that you may not say, I have made Abram rich* Gn 14$_{23}$, הַרְבָּה אַרְבֶּה אֶת־זַרְעֵךְ וְלֹא יִסָּפֵר מֵרֹב *I shall indeed multiply your seed so that it cannot be counted for multitude* Gn 16$_{10}$. (2) in other combinations meaning **so that not, lest:** אֲשֶׁר לֹא Gn 11$_7$, שֶׁלֹּא Ec 7$_{14}$, לְמַעַן לֹא Ezk 19$_9$, בְּלֹא Lm 4$_{14}$. **c.** וְלֹא in adversative clause, **but not,** וַאֲכַלְתֶּם וְלֹא תִשְׂבָּעוּ *and you will eat but not be satisfied* Lv 26$_{26}$. **d.** in prohibition, instruction, לֹא תֹאכְלוּ מִכֹּל עֵץ הַגָּן *you are not to eat of any tree in the garden* Gn 3$_1$, כָּל־מְלָאכָה לֹא־יֵעָשֶׂה *no work is to be done* Ex 12$_{16}$. **e.** אֲשֶׁר לֹא *not,* in prohibition, in Qumran texts, אשר לוא ילך איש בשרירות לבו *a man is not to go in the stubbornness of his heart* 1QS 5$_4$. **f.** in refusal, לֹא אָשׁוּב עִמָּךְ *I shall not return with you* 1 S 15$_{26}$. **g.** in question, usu. preceded by interrog. part.: לָמָּה/לָמָה לֹא *why not?* 1 S 1$_8$, מַדּוּעַ לֹא *why not?* Ex 3$_3$, הֲלֹא *do not?*, etc. (or in a clause introduced by interrog. -הֲ) Gn 18$_{25}$ Is 40$_{21}$, עַד־אָנָה לֹא *for how long not?*, i.e. how long until? Nm 14$_{11}$, מִי לֹא *who not?* Jr 10$_7$; without interrog. part. Ex 8$_{22}$. **h.** in protasis of conditional sentence, (1) אִם־לֹא *if not* Gn 24$_{41}$. (2) אוּלַי לֹא *suppose that not* Gn 24$_5$. (3) אֲשֶׁר לֹא *if* Zc 14$_{17}$. **i.** in apodosis of conditional sentence Ex 21$_{10}$. **j.** with inf. abs. and impf., לֹא־מוֹת תְּמֻתוּן *you will certainly not die* Gn 3$_4$, הַרְחֵק לֹא־תַרְחִיקוּ לָלֶכֶת *you are not to go a great distance* Ex 8$_{24}$. **3.** followed by ptc., לֹא מְבַקֵּשׁ רָעָתוֹ *he was not seeking his harm* Nm 35$_{23}$. **4.** with inf., **a.** לֹא, לֹא לְהַזְכִּיר בְּשֵׁם י׳ *one must not mention the name of Y.* Am 6$_{10}$. **b.** הֲלֹא **is it not?,** הֲלוֹא לָכֶם לָדַעַת *is it not for you to know?* Mc 3$_1$. **c.** בְּלֹא **without,** בְּלֹא רְאוֹת *without seeing* Nm 35$_{23}$. **5.** followed by nom. cl., לֹא מִזַּרְעֲךָ הוּא *he is not of your offspring* Gn 17$_{12}$, הֲלוֹא־אִישׁ אַתָּה *are you not a man?* 1 S 26$_{15}$. **6a.** לֹא with following noun, לֹא אֱלֹהַ *a non-god* Dt 32$_{17(L)}$, בֹּקֶר לֹא עָבוֹת *a morning without clouds* 2 S 23$_4$, גּוֹיִם לֹא מְעָט *nations not a few* Is 10$_7$. **b.** בְּלֹא **without, when it is not,** etc., בְּלֹא־אֵיבָה *without enmity* Nm 35$_{22}$, בְּלֹא עֶת־נִדָּתָהּ *when it is not the time of her impurity* Lv 15$_{25}$, בְּלוֹא לְשָׂבְעָה *(for that which is) without satiety* Is 55$_2$. **c.** לֹא with following adj. or adv., לֹא־טוֹב *not good* Ex 18$_{17}$, לֹא־כֵן *not so* Nm 12$_7$. **7.** לֹא as substantivized rel. part., **one who is not, one who has not,** etc. (cf. §6a), מֶה־עָזַרְתָּ לְלֹא־כֹחַ *how have you helped one who is without strength* Jb 26$_2$, נִמְצֵאתִי לְלֹא בִקְשֻׁנִי *I was found by those who did not seek me* Is 65$_1$. **8.** as noun, **nothing,** עַתָּה הֱיִיתֶם לֹא *now you have become nothing* Jb 6$_{21(Kt)}$ (Qr לוֹ *to him*). **9.** as interj., **no, it is not so,** לֹא־אֲדֹנִי שְׁמָעֵנִי *no, my lord, hear me* Gn 23$_{11}$. **10.** הֲלֹא **is it not the case that?, surely,** modifying an entire clause or sentence, הֲלֹא דַּרְכֵיכֶם לֹא יִתָּכֵנוּ *surely it is your ways that are not just* Ezk 18$_{25}$. **11.** אִם לֹא in oaths, etc. (thus may Y. do to me) **if (I do) not, truly, I swear that,** etc., כֹּה יַעֲשֶׂה־לִּי אֱלֹהִים וְכֹה יוֹסִיף אִם־לֹא שַׂר־צָבָא תִּהְיֶה *thus may God do to me and thus may he continue (to do) if you do not become commander of the army* 2 S 19$_{14}$, אִם־לֹא מִדְּאָגָה מִדָּבָר עָשִׂינוּ אֶת־זֹאת *truly, we did this out of concern for the matter* Jos 22$_{24}$, אִם־לֹא אֶל־בֵּית־אָבִי תֵּלֵךְ *I swear that you will go to my father's house* Gn 24$_{38}$.

*[לֹא] II 27 part. (perh. to be vocalized לָא or לְא)—**indeed,** לֹא־נָבִיא אָנֹכִי וְלֹא בֶן־נָבִיא אָנֹכִי *I am indeed a prophet but not the son of a prophet,* i.e. not a member of a prophetic guild Am 7$_{14}$; Ex 8$_{22}$ 1 S 20$_9$.

לָא, see לֹא II *indeed,* לוּ *if.*

לֹא דְבָר, see לוֹ דְבָר *Lo-debar.*

לאה I 19.1 vb.—**Qal** 3 Impf. תִּלְאֶה; + waw וַתֵּלֶא, וַיִּלְאוּ—**be weary,** i.e. **be weak** Gn 19$_{11}$ (+ מצא inf. too weak *to find*), **be impatient** Jb 4$_{2.5}$.

Ni. 10 Pf. נִלְאָה, נִלְאֵיתִי, נִלְאוּ—**1. weary oneself, languish** Is 16$_{12}$ (+ עַל *upon* high place) 47$_{13}$ (+ בְּ *with* multitude of counsels) Ps 68$_{10}$. **2.** with inf., **be weary** of doing, **be unable** to do Ex 7$_{18}$ Is 1$_{14}$ Jr 6$_{11}$.

Hi. 6 Pf. הֶלְאֵנִי, הֶלְאָת, הֶלְאֵיתִיךָ; impf. תַּלְאוּ; inf. הַלְאוֹת—**weary, wear out** Y. Is 7$_{13}$, human Jr 12$_5$.

→ תְּלָאָה *weariness*, לֵא *hesitant*.

*לאה II vb.—**Qal, 1. be strong,** לָאִיתִי אֵל וְאֻכָל *I am strong (with) strength and I succeed* Pr 30_1 (if em. לְאִיתִיאֵל *to Ithiel*). **2.** ptc. לֵא (alw. if em. לֹא *not*) as noun, **victor, omnipotent one** Ps 7_{13} Jb 13_{15} 14_4; as part of divine title, Shaddai **the omnipotent** Jb 24_1. → לֵא *strength*.

לֵאָה I 34.0.2 pr.n.f. **Leah.**

[לֵאָה] II, see אֲלְוָא *aloe*.

לְאוֹם, see לְאֹם *nation*.

לָאט, see לָט *secrecy*, לוט *wrap*.

לְאַט, see אַט *gentleness*.

לָאֵל 1 pr.n.m. **Lael.**

לְאֹם 38.0.6 n.m.—לְאוֹם; sf. לְאוּמִּי; pl. לְאֻמִּים—**nation, people** of Israel Is 51_4, Israel and Edom Gn 25_{23}; usu. of other nations Ps 7_8 67_5; people in general Pr 11_{26}.

לְאֻמִּים 1 pr.n.m. **Leummim.**

לֹא עַמִּי 2 pr.n.m. **Lo-ammi.**

[לֹא רֻחָמָה] 3 pr.n.f. **Lo-ruhamah.**

לֵב 599.60.166.1 n.m.—cstr. לֵב (לֶב־); sf. לִבּוֹ, לִבָּם (Q לבמה), לִבָּן (לִבְּהֶן); pl. לִבּוֹת; cstr. לִבּוֹת; sf. לִבּוֹתָם—**heart** (appar. not different in meaning from לֵבָב), **1. mind, thinking, intention, understanding,** intellectual processes, as responsible for, or ident. with **a.** thought, reason, knowledge, counsel, of humans Is 6_{10}, Y. Ps 33_{11}; לֵב לָדַעַת *a mind to know* Dt 29_3, לֵב חֹרֵשׁ מַחְשְׁבוֹת אָוֶן *a heart that devises plans of iniquity* Pr 6_{18}; אמר בְּלֵב *say in (one's) heart,* i.e. say or think to oneself Gn 17_{17}, sim. (in same sense) אמר אֶל־לֵב *say to (one's) heart* 1 S 27_1, דבר עַל־לֵב pi. *speak to (one's) heart* 1 S 1_{13}. **b.** wisdom, common sense 1 K 10_{24}||2 C 9_{23} 1QS 2_3; לֵב שֹׁמֵעַ *a listening heart,* i.e. understanding mind 1 K 3_9, חֲכַם־לֵב *wise of heart* Pr 10_8, חֲסַר־לֵב *lacking of,* i.e. in, *sense* Pr 6_{32}. **c.** attention, memory, of humans, שׂים לֵב *place the heart,* i.e. pay attention Ex 9_{21}, sim. שׁית לֵב Ex 7_{23}, נתן לֵב Pr 23_{26}; שׂים אֶל־לֵב *place to the heart,* i.e. bear in mind 2 S 13_{33}, sim. נתן אֶל־לֵב Ec 7_2, שׁוב אֶל־לֵב hi. 1 K 8_{47}, שׂים עַל־לֵב Is 42_{25}, נתן עַל־לֵב Si 50_{28}; עלה עַל־לֵב *come up into mind* Is 65_{17}; of Y. 1 K 9_3||2 C 7_{16}. **d.** ability, skill, חֲכַם־לֵב *wise of heart,* i.e. able Ex 31_6. **2. feelings,** of humans 2 S 14_1 Jr 20_9, דבר עַל־לֵב pi. *speak to the heart,* i.e. persuasively Gn 34_3; of Y. Gn 6_6. Esp. as sensitive to joy Ex 4_{14}, pain, grief, sadness Is 65_{14} Jr 8_{18}, weakness, anxiety, fear Gn 42_{28} Ezk 21_{12}, courage, strength 2 S 17_{10} Ps 27_{14}. **e.** anger Pr 19_3, contempt 2 S 6_{16}||1 C 15_{29}, jealousy Pr 23_{17}, conscience 1 S 24_6. **3. will, inclination, disposition, personality,** of humans Gn 6_5, Y. Lm 3_{33}; לֵב characterized as loyal, devoted 2 S 15_{13}, upright, pure Ps 7_{11} Pr 22_{11}, hard, stubborn Ex 4_{21} Jr 3_{17}, evil, godless Jr 4_{14} Jb 36_{13}, deceitful Jr 17_9, perverse Pr 11_{20}, uncircumcised Jr 9_{25}, hostile Ps 55_{22}, foolish Pr 12_{23}, arrogant, proud 2 K 14_{10}||2 C 25_{19} Pr 16_5. **4.** physical **heart, chest** of human Ex 28_{29} 2 K 9_{24}, Leviathan Jb 41_{16}. **5. middle, depth, height,** of sea Ex 15_8, heaven Dt 4_{11}, terebinth 2 S 18_{14}. → לבב I *think*; cf. לֵבָב *heart*.

לְבֹא חֲמָת, see לְבוֹא חֲמָת *Lebo-hamath*.

[לָבִא] 1 n.[m.]—pl. לְבָאִם—**lion** Ps 57_5. → cf. לָבִיא *lion*.

[לְבִאָה] 1 n.f.—pl. sf. לִבְאֹתָיו—**lion** (fem.) Na 2_{13}. → cf. לָבִיא *lion*.

לְבָאוֹת 1 pl.n. **Lebaoth.**

לבב I 3 vb.—**Ni.** 1 Impf. יִלָּבֵב—**gain understanding,** or perh. **lack understanding** Jb 11_{12}.

Pi. 2 Pf. לִבַּבְתִּנִי—**seduce, infatuate** Ca $4_{9.9}$ (+ בְּ *with* eyes, bead of necklace).

→ לֵב *heart*, לֵבָב *heart*.

לבב II 2 vb.—**Pi.** 1 Impf. תְּלַבֵּב—**bake cakes** 2 S $13_{6.8}$. → לְבִבָה *cake*.

*[לבב] III vb.—**Pi. cause to sprout, produce,** אִישׁ נָבוּב יְלַבְּבוֹ עָיִר *a man is an offspring that a donkey produces* Jb 11_{12} (if em. אִישׁ נָבוּב יִלָּבֵב וְעַיִר *a hollow[ed] man will gain, or lacks, understanding; and a donkey*).

לֵבָב 252.9.96.1 n.m.—cstr. לְבַב; sf. לְבָבוֹ, לְבַבְכֶם (Q לבבכמה); pl. לְבָבוֹת; sf. לִבְבֵהֶן—**heart** (appar. not different in meaning from לֵב), **1. mind, thinking, intention, understanding,** intellectual processes, as responsible for, or ident. with **a.** thought, reason, knowledge, counsel Dt 8_5 1 S 9_{19} Is 6_{10}; אמר בִּלְבָב *say in (one's) heart,* i.e. say or think to oneself Dt 7_{17}. **b.** wisdom, common sense Jb 12_3 Si 50_{23}; אַנְשֵׁי לֵבָב *men of heart,* i.e. understanding Jb 34_{10}, חֲכַם לֵבָב (of Y.) *wise of heart* Jb 9_4. **c.** attention, memory Dt 6_6 Ezk 3_{10};

שִׂים לְבָב *place*, i.e. apply, *the heart* Dt 32$_{46}$, שׁוּב אֶל־לְבָב hi. *turn*, i.e. lay, *to heart* Dt 4$_{39}$, שִׂים בְּלְבָב *place in*, i.e. take to, *heart* 1 S 21$_{13}$, עלה עַל־לְבָב *come up into mind* Jr 51$_{50}$. **2. feelings** Ps 62$_{9}$; esp. as sensitive to joy Dt 28$_{47}$, pain, grief, sadness 1 K 8$_{38}$ Ps 25$_{17}$, weakness, anxiety, fear Lv 26$_{36}$ Jos 2$_{11}$, courage, strength Ps 31$_{25}$ Dn 11$_{25}$, anger Dt 19$_{6}$, hatred Lv 19$_{17}$, desire Pr 6$_{25}$, conscience Jb 27$_{6}$. **3. will, inclination, disposition, personality,** of humans Dt 8$_{2}$, Y. 1 S 2$_{35}$; לְבָב *heart* characterized as loyal, devoted Dt 6$_{5}$, upright, pure Gn 20$_{5}$ Dt 9$_{5}$, penitent 2 K 22$_{19}$||2 C 34$_{27}$, arrogant, proud Dt 8$_{14}$ Ezk 28$_{5}$, stubborn, hard Dt 2$_{30}$, evil Ps 28$_{3}$, perverse Ps 101$_{4}$, uncircumcised Lv 26$_{41}$. **4.** physical **heart, chest** Na 2$_{8}$ 4QBark[d] 2.1$_{3}$. **5. middle** of sea Jon 2$_{4}$. → לבב I *think*; cf. לֵב *heart*.

[לְבִבָה] 3 n.f.—pl. לְבִבוֹת—**cake** 2 S 13$_{6.8.10}$. → לבב II *bake*.

לְבַד 156.2.18 adv. & prep.—לְבַד; sf. לְבַדּוֹ, לְבַדְּהֶן (לְבַדְּנָה)—**1.** לְבַד, **a.** as adv., **alone, only, on one's own** Gn 2$_{18}$ Ex 18$_{14}$ Ps 86$_{10}$. **b.** as prep., **besides, apart from** Dt 18$_{8}$. **2.** לְבַד בְּ as adv., **only, alone** Is 26$_{13}$. **3.** לְבַד מִן as prep., **besides, apart from** Dt 3$_{5}$. **4.** לְבַד עַל as prep., **besides, apart from** Ezr 1$_{6}$. **6a.** מִלְּבַד as prep., **besides, apart from** Gn 26$_{1}$. **b.** מִלְּבַד as adv., **alone, on one's own** 1 K 12$_{33(Kt)}$ (Qr מִלִּבּוֹ *from his [own] heart*). **7.** לְבַד מֵאֲשֶׁר as conj., **unless** Est 4$_{11}$.

[לַבָּה] 1 n.f.—cstr. לַבַּת—**flame** Ex 3$_{2}$.

*[לִבָּה] 1 n.f. **spirit,** or **anger,** מָה אֲמֻלָה לִבָּתֵךְ *how enfeebled is your spirit* Ezk 16$_{30}$ (or em. אֲמֻלָה to אֶמָּלֵא/ אִמָּלֵא *I am filled* with anger against you).

לְבוֹא חֲמָת 7 pl.n. **Lebo-hamath.**

לְבוֹנָה I 21.1.7 n.f.—לְבֹנָה; sf. לְבֹנָתָהּ—**frankincense,** ingredient of incense Ex 30$_{34}$, placed on cereal offering Lv 2$_{1}$, with bread of presence Lv 24$_{7}$; ingredient of perfume Ca 3$_{6}$, cleansing or deodorizing agent CD 11$_{4}$.

לְבוֹנָה II 3 pl.n. **Lebonah.**

לְבוּשׁ, see לבשׁ *dress*, qal §3.

לְבוּשׁ 31.0.2 n.m.—cstr. לְבוּשׁ; sf. לְבוּשִׁי; pl. sf. לְבֻשֵׁיהֶן—**garment, clothing** of man Gn 49$_{11}$, woman Ps 45$_{14}$, warrior 2 S 20$_{8}$, worshipper 2 K 10$_{22}$, king Est 6$_{8}$; skin of Leviathan Jb 41$_{5}$. → לבשׁ *dress*.

לבט 3.0.2 vb.—**Ni.** 3.0.2 Impf. יִלָּבֵט; inf. Q הלבט—**be ruined,** of person Ho 4$_{14}$ Pr 10$_{8.10}$ 1QH 10$_{19}$ (+ בְּ *on account of* error) 12$_{7}$ (+ בְּלֹא *without* understanding).

לָבִיא 11.0.1 n.[m.]—pl. Q לביאים—**lion** Gn 49$_{9}$. → cf. לְבָא *lion*, לְבִאָה *lion* (fem.), לְבִיָּא *lion* (fem.), לְבִיָּה *lion* (fem.).

לְבִיָּא 1 n.f. **lion** (fem.) Ezk 19$_{2}$. → cf. לָבִיא *lion*.

לְבִיָּה 4.0.1 n.f.—pl. sf. Q לביותיו—**lion** (fem.) Gn 49$_{9(Sam)}$ (MT לָבִיא) 4QpNah 3.1$_{4}$ (=Na 2$_{13}$ לִבְאֹתָיו, from לְבָאָה). → cf. לָבִיא *lion*.

לֻבִים, see לוּבִים *Libyans*.

לבן I 5.0.1 vb.—**Pu.** 0.0.1 Ptc. מלובן—**be whitened,** of iron 1QM 5$_{11}$ (+ כְּ *as* a mirror).

Hi. 4 Pf. הִלְבִּינוּ; impf. יַלְבִּינוּ; inf. לְהַלְבֵּן—**1. be white,** of person Ps 51$_{9}$ (+ מִן whiter *than* snow), tendril Jl 1$_{7}$, sin Is 1$_{18}$ (+ כְּ *as* snow). **2. whiten** someone Dn 11$_{35}$.

Htp. 1 Impf. יִתְלַבְּנוּ—**whiten oneself** Dn 12$_{10}$.

→ לָבָן I *white*, לֹבֶן *whiteness*, לְבָנָה I *moon*.

לבן II 3 vb.—**Qal** 3 Impf. נִלְבְּנָה; inf. לִלְבֹּן—**make bricks** Gn 11$_{3}$ Ex 5$_{7.14}$. → לְבֵנָה *brick*, מַלְבֵּן *brick mould*.

לָבָן I 29.0.4 adj.—cstr. לְבֶן־; f.s. לְבָנָה; m.pl. לְבָנִים, f.pl. לְבָנוֹת—**1a. white,** of spot Lv 13$_{4}$, horse Zc 1$_{8}$, iron 1QM 5$_{10}$, manna Ex 16$_{31}$, garment Ec 9$_{8}$. **b. bare, treeless,** of dust, i.e. land 5/6ḤevBA 44$_{12.15}$. **2.** as noun, **white(ness)** Gn 30$_{35}$, **white one** Zc 6$_{6}$. → לבן I *be white*.

לָבָן II 54.0.3 pr.n.m. **Laban.**

לָבָן III 1 pl.n. **Laban.**

לַבֵּן 1 perh. pr.n.[m.] **Labben.**

*[לֹבֶן] 0.1 n.[m.]—sf. (לבנה) לבנו—**whiteness** Si 43$_{18}$. → לבן I *be white*.

לִבְנָה 18 pl.n. **Libnah.**

לִבְנֶה 2 n.[m.] **storax tree** (*Styrax officinalis*), or **poplar** (*Populus alba*) Gn 30$_{37}$ Ho 4$_{13}$.

לְבָנָה I 3 n.f. **moon** Is 24$_{23}$ 30$_{26}$ Ca 6$_{10}$. → לבן I *be white.*

לְבָנָה II 2 pr.n.m. **Lebanah.**

לְבֵנָה 12.0.3 n.f.—cstr. לִבְנַת; pl. לְבֵנִים; cstr. Q לבני; sf. לִבְנֵיכֶם—**1. brick, tile** Gn 11$_{3}$ Ex 1$_{14}$ Is 65$_{3}$. **2.** perh. **paving stone** of sapphire Ex 24$_{10}$. → לבן II *make bricks*.

לְבֹנָה, see לְבוֹנָה I *frankincense*.

לְבָנוֹן 71.2.7 pl.n. **Lebanon.**

לִבְנִי I 5 pr.n.m. **Libni.**

לִבְנִי II 2 gent. **Libnite.**

לִבְנָת, see שִׁיחוֹר לִבְנָת *Shihor-libnath.*

לֵב קָמָי, see לֵב *heart.*

לבשׁ 112.6.13 vb.—**Qal** 76.2.12 Pf. לָבַשׁ (לָבֵשׁ); impf. יִלְבַּשׁ; impv. לְבַשׁ, לִבְשִׁי, לִבְשׁוּ; ptc. לֹבְשִׁים; ptc. pass. לָבוּשׁ, לְבוּשֵׁי; inf. abs. לָבוֹשׁ; cstr. לִלְבֹּשׁ—**1a. dress (oneself) in, wear** garment Gn 28$_{20}$ Est 6$_{8}$ (בְּ of obj.), armour Jr 46$_{4}$, strength Is 51$_{9}$, righteousness Ps 132$_{9}$, shame Ps 35$_{26}$, curse Ps 109$_{18}$. **b.** abs., **dress oneself** Hg 1$_{6}$. **2. clothe, envelop** someone, subj. spirit Jg 6$_{34}$, righteousness Jb 29$_{14}$. **3.** pass. **be dressed (in), wear, a.** abs., לָבֻשׁ בַּדִּים *dressed (in) linen* Ezk 9$_{2}$. **b.** cstr., לְבֻשׁ הַבַּדִּים *dressed of,* i.e. in, *linen* Ezk 9$_{11}$.

Pu. 4 Ptc. מְלֻבָּשִׁים—**be dressed (in), wear,** מְלֻבָּשִׁים בְּגָדִים *dressed in garments* 1 K 22$_{10}$||2 C 18$_{9}$.

Hi. 32.3.1 Pf. הִלְבִּישׁוּ; impf. תַּלְבִּישׁ; + waw וַיַּלְבֵּשׁ (וַיַּלְבִּשֵׁם); ptc. מַלְבִּשְׁכֶם; impv. הַלְבֵּשׁ; inf. הַלְבִּישׁ—**1a.** with double accus., **dress** someone **with** garment Gn 41$_{42}$, armour 1 S 17$_{38}$, skin and flesh Jb 10$_{11}$, salvation Ps 132$_{16}$, shame Ps 132$_{18}$. **b.** with accus. of person only, **dress** someone Gn 3$_{21}$. **2.** with accus. and prep., **put** clothing **on** (עַל) someone Gn 27$_{16}$.

Htp. 0.1 Inf. התלבשו—**dress oneself (in), wear** garment Si 50$_{11}$.

→ לְבוּשׁ *garment,* מַלְבּוּשׁ *garment,* תִּלְבֹּשֶׁת *garment.*

לְבֻשׁ, see לבשׁ *dress,* qal §3b.

לֹג 5.0.0.3 n.m.—cstr. לֹג—**log,** unit of liquid measure, perh. a sixth of a litre Lv 14$_{10}$.

לֹד 4 pl.n. **Lod.**

לִדְבִר 1 pl.n. **Lidbir.**

לֵדָה 4.0.1 n.f. **birth** 2 K 19$_{3}$||Is 37$_{3}$ Ho 9$_{11}$; אֵשֶׁת לֵדָה *woman of,* who is about to give, *birth* Jr 13$_{21}$. → ילד *give birth.*

לֹה, see לֹא *not.*

***להב** 1 vb.—**Qal** 1 Ptc. לוהבת—**blaze** Is 5$_{24(1QIsa^a)}$. → לַהַב *flame,* לֶהָבָה *flame,* לֶהָבָה *flame;* cf. להט I *blaze.*

לַהַב 12.0.8 n.m.—cstr. לַהַב; pl. לְהָבִים; cstr. לַהֲבֵי—**1. flame** Jg 13$_{20}$; לַהַב אֵשׁ *flame of fire* Is 29$_{6}$. **2. flash** of sword Na 3$_{3}$. **3. blade** of sword Jg 3$_{22}$. **4. point** of spear Jb 39$_{23}$. → להב *blaze.*

*[לֹהַב] 0.0.6 n.[m.]—להוב (להוב) לוהב; cstr. להוב—**1. point** of spear 1QM 5$_{7}$. **2.** perh. **flash** of (point of) spear 1QH 10$_{26}$. **3. flame,** שביבי להוב *flashes of flame* 1QH 11$_{30}$. → להב *blaze.*

לֶהָבָה 20.2.5 n.f.—cstr. לֶהָבַת; pl. לֶהָבוֹת; cstr. לַהֲבוֹת—**1. flame** Nm 21$_{28}$; לַהֲבוֹת אֵשׁ *flames of fire* Ps 29$_{7}$, אֵשׁ לֶהָבָה *fire of flame,* i.e. flaming fire Is 4$_{5}$. **2. point** of spear 1 S 17$_{7}$. → להב *blaze.*

[לְהָבִי] 2 gent. **Lehabite.**

לַהַג 1 n.[m.] **study** Ec 12$_{12}$.

[לַהַד] 1 pr.n.m. **Lahad.**

להה 1.2 vb.—**Htpalp.** 1.2 Ptc. מִתְלַהְלֵהַּ—ptc. as noun, **fool,** perh. specif. **madman** Pr 26$_{18}$, **irreligious one** Si 35$_{14.15}$.

להה 1 vb.—**Qal** 1 + waw וַתֵּלַהּ—**languish,** of land Gn 47$_{13}$ (+ מִפְּנֵי *on account of* famine).

להט I 10.2 vb.—**Qal** 1.1 Ptc. לֹהֵט, Si, Q לוהטת—**blaze,** of fire Ps 104$_{4}$.

Pi. 9.1 Pf. לִהֲטָה; impf. תְּלַהֵט—**set ablaze, burn,** subj. fire Dt 32$_{22}$, flame Jl 1$_{19}$, Y.'s anger Is 42$_{25}$, breath of Leviathan Jb 41$_{13}$; obj. Israel Is 42$_{25}$, the wicked Ps 106$_{18}$, foundations of mountains Dt 32$_{22}$, trees Jl 1$_{19}$, coals Jb 41$_{13}$; of woman setting lovers ablaze with (בְּ) fire Si 9$_{8}$.

→ לַהַט I *flame;* cf. להב *blaze.*

***להט II** 1 vb.—**Qal** 1 Ptc. לֹהֲטִים—perh. **devour,** or **bewitch,** of lions Ps 57$_{5}$. → לַהַט II *enchantment,* לָט *secret.*

[לַהַט] I 1.0.1 n.[m.]—cstr. לַהַט—**1.** perh. **blade** of sword Gn 3$_{24}$. **2. flame** of fire 1QH 16$_{12}$. → להט I *blaze.*

***[לַהַט] II** 4 n.[m.]—sf. לַהֲטֵיהֶם—**enchantment** Ex 7$_{11.22(Sam)}$ 8$_{3(Sam).14(Sam)}$ (MT לָט *enchantment* in all three). → להט II *bewitch.*

להם 2 vb.—**Htp.** 2 ptc. מִתְלַהֲמִים—ptc. as noun, **delicacies** Pr 18$_{8}$=26$_{22}$.

לָהֵן 2 conj. **therefore** Ru 1$_{13}$.

[לַהֲקָה] 1 n.f.—cstr. לַהֲקַת—**1. (senior) company** of prophets 1 S 19$_{20}$. **2. old age** of mother Pr 30$_{17}$ (if em. לִיקֲהַת *obedience of*).

לוּ 22 conj.—לוּא, mss לֹא, Sam לוי—**1.** usu. **if only,** introducing irreal condition; protasis with **a.** pf., לוּ הַחֲיִתֶם אוֹתָם לֹא הָרַגְתִּי אֶתְכֶם *if you had kept them alive, I would not kill you* Jg 8$_{19}$. **b.** impf., לוּ שָׁקוֹל יִשָּׁקֵל כַּעְשִׂי ... כִּי־עַתָּה מֵחוֹל יַמִּים יִכְבָּד *if my anger were weighed ... it would now be heavier than the sand of the seas*

Jb 6$_2$. **c.** ptc., לוּ עַמִּי שֹׁמֵעַ לִי ... כִּמְעַט אוֹיְבֵיהֶם אַכְנִיעַ *if only my people would listen to me, ... I would quickly subdue their enemies* Ps 81$_{14}$. **e.** nom. cl., לוּ יֶשׁ־חֶרֶב בְּיָדִי כִּי עַתָּה הֲרַגְתִּיךְ *if there were a sword in my hand, I would kill you now* Nm 22$_{29}$. **2. supposing, what if?, perhaps,** לוּ יִשְׂטְמֵנוּ יוֹסֵף *supposing Joseph holds it against us?* Gn 50$_{15}$. **3.** as exclamation, **if only, would that,** לוּ־מַתְנוּ בְּאֶרֶץ מִצְרַיִם *would that we had died in the land of Egypt!* Nm 14$_2$.

*[לָוְא] interj. **woe,** לָוְא אֲלֵיכֶם *woe to you* Lm 1$_{12}$ (if em. לוֹא *is it nothing* to you?).

לוֹא, see לֹא *not*.

לוֹא, see לוּ *if*.

לוֹא דְבָר, see לוֹ דְבָר *Lo-debar*.

*[לוּב] 0.0.1 pr.n.m. **Libya.**

[לוּבִי] 4 gent. **Libyan.**

לוּד 5.0.1 pr.n.m. **Lud.**

לוֹ דְבָר 3 pl.n. **Lo-debar.**

[לוּדִי] 3 gent. **Lydian.**

לוה I 14.3.3 vb.—**Qal** 5.0.3 Pf. לָוִינוּ; impf. תִּלְוֶה; ptc. לֹוֶה—**borrow** money Ne 5$_4$ (+ לְ *for*); abs. Dt 28$_{12}$.

Hi. 9.3 Impf. תַּלְוֶה, יַלְוְךָ; + waw וְהִלְוִיתָ; ptc. מַלְוֶה, cstr. מַלְוֵה—with accus. of recipient, **lend to** someone Ex 22$_{24}$ (+ accus. money) Dt 28$_{44}$; מַלְוֵה י״ *lender of,* i.e. to, Y. Pr 19$_{17}$.

לוה II 12.1.10 vb.—**Qal** 1.1 Impf. יִלְוֶנּוּ—**accompany, stay with** someone, of good Ec 8$_{15}$, name Si 41$_{12}$ (+ מִן *more than* treasures).

Ni. 11.0.10 Pf. נִלְוָה; impf. יִלָּוֶה, יִלָּווּ; ptc. נִלְוִים; inf. Q הלוות—**join, join oneself** to, **associate, be associated** with, **ally oneself** with, of husband to (אֶל) wife Gn 29$_{34}$, Israel to (אֶל) Y. Jr 50$_5$, Levites to (עַל) house of Aaron Nm 18$_2$, foreigners to (עַל) Israel Is 14$_1$, nation with (עִם) nation Ps 83$_9$.

לוז 5.1.4 vb.—**Qal** 1 Impf. יַלִּזוּ—**depart** from (מִן) sight Pr 3$_{21}$.

Ni. 4.1.1 Pf. Si נלוז; + waw Q וילוזו; ptc. נָלוֹז, נְלוֹז, pl. נְלוֹזִים—**1. depart, stray after** (אַחַר) wealth Si 34$_8$. **2. be devious** in (בְּ) one's ways Pr 2$_{15}$; נְלוֹז דְּרָכָיו *one devious of,* i.e. in, *one's ways* Pr 14$_2$. **3.** ptc. as noun, **perversity** Is 30$_{12}$.

Hi. 1.0.3 Impf. יַלִּיזוּ; inf. abs. Q הליז—**1. allow to depart** from (מִן) sight Pr 4$_{21}$. **2. be devious with** (בְּ) lips, i.e. in speech 4Q424 1$_9$. **3. mock, sneer at** (עַל) someone with (בְּ) unjust lips 1QH 13$_{24}$.

→ לָזוּת *perversity,* לוז *perversity.*

*[לוֹז] 0.0.1 n.[m.]—cstr. לוז—**perversity** 4Q424 1$_8$. → לוז *be devious.*

לוּז I 1 n.[m.]—**almond (tree)** (*Amygdalus communis*) Gn 30$_{37}$.

לוּז II 8 pl.n. **Luz.**

לוּחַ 43.0.5 n.m.—cstr. לוּחַ; pl. לֻחֹת; du. לֻחֹתַיִם; cstr. לֻחֹת—**1.** wooden or stone **tablet** for writing Ex 24$_{12}$ Is 30$_8$; tablet of heart Jr 17$_1$. **2.** wooden **board, plank** of altar Ex 27$_8$||38$_7$, door Ca 8$_9$, boat Ezk 27$_5$. **3.** bronze **plate** of washstand in temple 1 K 7$_{36}$.

לוּחִית 2.0.1 pl.n. **Luhith.**

לוֹחֵשׁ, or more prob. הַלּוֹחֵשׁ 2 pr.n.m. **Hallohesh.**

לוט 4 vb.—**Qal** 3 Pf. לָאט; ptc. לוֹט; ptc. pass. לוּטָה—**1. wrap, cover** one's face 2 S 19$_5$, **cover over** (עַל) people Is 25$_7$. **2.** pass. **be wrapped, be covered,** of sword 1 S 21$_{10}$ (+ בְּ *in* cloth).

Hi. 1 + waw וַיָּלֶט—**wrap** one's face in (בְּ) cloak 1 K 19$_{13}$.

→ לוֹט I *covering.*

לוֹט I 1 n.m.—**covering** Is 25$_7$. → לוט *wrap.*

לוֹט II 33.1 pr.n.m. **Lot.**

לוֹטָן 7 pr.n.m. **Lotan.**

לֵוִי I 58.1.23.5 pr.n.m. **Levi.**

לֵוִי II 296.0.36.2 gent.—pl. לְוִיִּם (Q לויים, Q לויאים); sf. לְוִיֵּנוּ—**Levite,** one belonging tribe of Levi Ex 4$_{14}$, usu. as cultic functionary, **1.** sg., **a.** individual Levite Dt 18$_6$. **b.** coll., מִשְׁפְּחֹת הַלֵּוִי *clans of the Levites* Ex 6$_{19}$. **2.** pl., מִשְׁפְּחֹת הַלְוִיִּם *clans of the Levites* Jos 21$_{27}$, בְּנֵי *sons of* 1 C 15$_{15}$.

[לִוְיָה] 2 n.f. **garland,** לִוְיַת חֵן *garland of grace* Pr 1$_9$ 4$_9$.

לִוְיָתָן 6.0.1 n.m. **Leviathan,** sea creature, as serpent Is 27$_1$, crocodile Jb 40$_{25}$, perh. whale Ps 104$_{26}$.

[לוּל] 1 n.[m.]—pl. לוּלִים—**step,** between storeys of temple 1 K 6$_8$.

לוּלֵא 14 conj.—לוּלֵי—**1.** as unreal conditional part., **if not, had not,** etc., **unless,** protasis with **a.** pf., לוּלֵא הִתְמַהְמָהְנוּ כִּי־עַתָּה שַׁבְנוּ זֶה פַעֲמָיִם *if we had not delayed, we could now have returned twice* Gn 43$_{10}$. **b.** impf.,

אָמַרְתִּי אַפְאֵיהֶם ... לוּלֵי כַּעַס אוֹיֵב אָגוּר *I might have said, I shall destroy them, ... if I had not feared the anger of the enemy* Dt 32$_{27}$. **c.** ptc. 2 K 3$_{14}$. **d.** nom. cl. Ps 94$_{17}$. **2.** perh. as emphatic adv., **indeed** Ps 27$_{13}$. **3.** לוּלֵי שֶׁ- **except that, unless** Ps 124$_{1}$.

*[לוּלָב] 0.0.1 n.[m.] **lulab**, palm-branch used for festive purposes 4QRitMar 99$_{2}$ ([לולבי]ם).

לון I 14.0.3 vb.—**Ni.** 8.0.2 Impf. Q ילון; + waw וַיִּלֹּנוּ—**murmur** against (עַל) Ex 15$_{24}$ 1QS 7$_{17}$.

Hi. 10.0.1 Pf. הֲלִינֹתֶם; impf. Qr תַּלִּינוּ; + waw וַיָּלֶן, Qr וַיַּלִּינוּ; ptc. מַלִּינִים—**1. murmur** against (עַל) Ex 16$_{2.8}$ (with accus. תְּלֻנָּה *murmuring*) Nm 14$_{27}$. **2. cause to murmur** against (עַל) Nm 14$_{36(Qr)}$.

→ תְּלֻנָּה *murmuring*.

לון II, see לין *pass night*.

לוע, see לעע I *be rash*, II *swallow*.

לוש 5 vb.—**Qal** 5 + waw Qr וַתָּלָשׁ (Kt ותלוש); impv. לוּשִׁי; ptc. לָשׁוֹת; inf. לוּשׁ—**knead** dough Jr 7$_{18}$. → מָלוֹשׁ *kneading trough*.

[לוּשׁ], see לַיִשׁ III *Laish*.

[לָז], see הַלָּז *that*.

[לָזֶה], see הַלָּזֶה *that*.

[לֵזוּ], see הַלֵּזוּ *that*.

[לָזוּת] 1 n.f.—cstr. לְזוּת—**perversity** Pr 4$_{24}$. → לוז *be devious*.

לַח 6.0.3 adj.—לַח, m.pl. לַחִים—**moist, fresh,** of grape Nm 6$_{3}$, tree Ezk 17$_{24}$, cord Jg 16$_{7}$, rod Gn 30$_{37}$. → cf. לֵחַ *moisture*, לֵחָה *liquid*.

[לֵחַ] 1.1 n.m.—sf. לֵחֹה—**1. moisture** of tear Si 34$_{13}$. **2. freshness, vigour** of person Dt 34$_{7}$. → cf. לח *moist*.

*[לֵחָה] 0.0.5 n.f.—cstr. לחת—**liquid, moisture** of dew 4QTohA 3.2$_{5}$, water 11QT 49$_{12}$. → cf. לח *moist*.

[לְחוּם] I 2 n.[m.]—sf. לְחֻמָם, לחומו—**flesh, body, bowel(s)** Zp 1$_{17}$ Jb 20$_{23}$.

*[לְחוּם] II 1 n.[m.]—sf. לחומו—**warfare,** or **anger** Jb 20$_{23}$. → לחם I *fight*.

לְחִי I 20.1.2 n.f.—לֶחִי; cstr. לְחִי; sf. לֶחֱיוֹ; du. לְחָיַיִם; cstr. לְחָיֵי; sf. לְחָיָו, לְחָיֵיהֶם—**1. jaw(bone)** of ass Jg 15$_{15}$, Leviathan Jb 40$_{26}$, human Is 30$_{28}$. **2. cheek** of human 1 K 22$_{24}$||2 C 18$_{23}$, sacrificial beast Dt 18$_{3}$.

[לְחִי] II 5 pl.n. **Lehi.**

*[לְחִי] III n.[m.] **curse** Dn 11$_{18}$ (if em. בִּלְתִּי *but rather* to בְּלְחִי *with a curse*).

*[לְחִי] IV n.[m.] **hip, buttock** Ca 5$_{13}$.

לַחַי רֹאִי, see בְּאֵר לַחַי רֹאִי *Beer-lahai-roi*.

לֻחִית, see לוּחִית *Luhith*.

לחך 6.0.2 vb.—**Qal** 1 Inf. לְחֹךְ—**lick up, eat** grass, of ox Nm 22$_{4}$.

Pi. 5.0.1 Pf. לִחֲכָה; impf. יְלַחֵכוּ (יְלַחֲכוּ)—**lick (up), eat,** of fire licking up water 1 K 18$_{38}$, enemies licking dust, in humiliation Ps 72$_{9}$, Israel licking land clean Nm 22$_{4}$.

לחם I 171.2.21 vb.—**Qal** 5.0.1 Impv. לְחַם; ptc. לֹחֵם—**1. fight** adversaries Ps 35$_{1}$. **2.** ptc. as noun, **adversary, warrior** Ps 35$_{1}$ 56$_{3}$. **3.** pass., **be embattled, battered,** לְחֻמֵי רֶשֶׁף *battered by plague* Dt 32$_{24}$.

Ni. 167.2.20 Pf. נִלְחַם; impf. יִלָּחֵם (יִלָּחֶם); + waw וַיִּלָּחֶם; impv. הִלָּחֵם (הִלָּחֶם), הִלָּחֲמוּ; ptc. נִלְחָם; inf. abs. נִלְחֹם; cstr. הִלָּחֵם (הִלָּחֶם, הִלָּחֲמוֹ)—**1. fight, wage war, enter battle, a. for, on behalf of,** with prep. לְ Ex 14$_{25}$, עַל Jg 9$_{17}$. **b. against, with,** with prep. בְּ Ex 1$_{10}$, אֶל Jr 1$_{19}$, עַל Dt 20$_{10}$, עִם Ex 17$_{8}$, אֵת Jos 24$_{8}$. **c.** abs. Dt 1$_{41}$. **d.** with יַחַד, **fight together** 1 S 17$_{10}$ 1QM 1$_{11}$. **2.** with accus., **a. fight battle** 1 S 8$_{20}$. **b. attack someone** Ps 109$_{3}$.

→ לחום II *warfare*, לֶחֶם II *war*, מִלְחָמָה I *war*, לָחֵם *warrior*.

לחם II 6 vb.—**Qal** 6 Pf. לָחֲמוּ; impf. תִּלְחַם; impv. לַחֲמוּ; ptc. לְחֻמֵי; inf. לְחוֹם—**1a. eat bread** Pr 4$_{17}$, some (בְּ) delicacies Ps 141$_{4}$. **b. dine with** (אֵת) someone Pr 23$_{1}$. **2.** pass., **be devoured,** לְחֻמֵי רֶשֶׁף *devoured of*, i.e. by, *plague* Dt 32$_{24}$. → לֶחֶם I *bread*.

לָחֶם 1 n.[m.] perh. **warrior** Jg 5$_{8}$. → לחם I *fight*.

לֶחֶם I 297.12.40.6 n.m. (f. at Gn 49$_{20}$ 1 S 10$_{4}$)—לָחֶם; cstr. לֶחֶם; sf. לַחְמוֹ—**1. bread,** as distinct from other foods Gn 25$_{34}$; כִּכַּר לֶחֶם *loaf of bread* Ex 29$_{23}$, חֲמִשָּׁה־לֶחֶם *five loaves of bread* 1 S 21$_{4}$, לֶחֶם הַפָּנִים *bread of the presence* Ex 35$_{13}$, מַטֵּה־לֶחֶם *staff of*, i.e. for holding, *bread* Lv 26$_{26}$. **2. food** in general, **a.** including bread, in meal Gn 3$_{19}$ Ex 2$_{20}$, offered in sacrifice Lv 3$_{11}$, as livelihood of priestly families Lv 22$_{7}$, payment for work 1 S 2$_{5}$, for prostitution Ho 2$_{7}$; אֶרֶץ לֶחֶם *land of bread* 2 K 18$_{32}$||Is 36$_{17}$, חֹסֶר לֶחֶם *lack of bread* Am 4$_{6}$. **b.** food other than bread: tears Ps 42$_{4}$, milk Pr 27$_{27}$, manna Ex 16$_{4}$. **c.** flesh of sacrificial victims Si 7$_{31}$. **d.** food of animals Ps 147_{9}. **e. fruit** of tree Jr 11_{19}. **3. meal** 1 S 20_{27}. **4. food allowance** Ne 5_{14}. **5. grain** for bread Is 28_{28}. → לחם II *eat.*

*[לֶחֶם] II 0.2 n.[m.] **war, fighting** Si 41_{19}; כלי לחם *weapons of war* Si 12_{5}. → לחם I *fight.*

לַחְמִי 1 pr.n.m. **Lahmi.**

לַחְמָם, see לַחְמָס *Lahmas.*

לַחְמָס 1 pl.n. **Lahmas.**

לחץ 19.0.1 vb.—**Qal** 18 Pf. לָחַץ; impf. יִלְחָצֵנִי; + waw וַתִּלְחַץ; ptc. לֹחֲצִים—**1. press, squeeze, push** people into hill country (הָהָרָה) Jg 1_{34}, person with (בְּ) door 2 K 6_{32}, foot against (אֶל) wall Nm 22_{25}. **2. oppress** someone Ex 3_{9} (+ לַחַץ *[with] oppression*) Ps 106_{42}.

Ni. 1.0.1 Pf. Q נחלץ; + waw וַתִּלָּחֵץ—**1. press oneself,** of ass Nm 22_{25} (+ אֶל *against* wall). **2. be forced, be under duress** CD 5_{15}.

→ לַחַץ *oppression.*

לַחַץ 12.0.1 n.m.—לָחַץ; cstr. לַחַץ; sf. לַחֲצֵנוּ—**oppression, distress** of, i.e. inflicted by, enemy Ps 42_{10}, of, i.e. inflicted on, Israel 2 K 13_{4}; לֶחֶם לַחַץ וּמַיִם לַחַץ *bread of oppression and water of oppression,* i.e. scant rations 1 K 22_{27}||2 C 18_{26}. → לחץ *squeeze.*

לחשׁ 3 vb.—**Pi.** 1 Ptc. מְלַחֲשִׁים—ptc. as noun, **(snake-) charmer** Ps 58_{6}.

Htp. 2 Impf. יִתְלַחֲשׁוּ; ptc. מִתְלַחֲשִׁים—**whisper together** 2 S 12_{19} Ps 41_{8} (+ עַל *concerning, against*).

→ לַחַשׁ *whisper.*

לַחַשׁ I 5.1 n.[m.]—לָחַשׁ; pl. לְחָשִׁים—**1. whisper** of enemy Si 12_{18}, perh. of prayer Is 26_{16}. **2. charming** of snakes Jr 8_{17}; **(magic) charms** Is 3_{3}. **3. amulet,** perh. of conch shells Is 3_{20}. → לחשׁ *whisper.*

*לַחַשׁ II 0.0.0.1 pr.n.[m.] **Lahash.**

לָט 7 n.[m.]—לָאט; sf. לָטֵיהֶם—**1. secrecy,** בַּלָּט *with, in secrecy,* i.e. secretly 1 S 18_{22}, var. בַּלָּאט Jg 4_{21}. **2. magic spell, enchantment** Ex 7_{22}.

לֹט 2 n.[m.] **myrrh,** gum, perh. of a species of cistus Gn 37_{25} 43_{11}.

לְטָאָה 1.0.1 n.f. **lizard** Lv 11_{30} 11QT 50_{20}.

לְטוּשִׁים 1 pr.n.m. **Letushim.**

לטשׁ 5.1 vb.—**Qal** 4.1 Impf. יִלְטוֹשׁ; ptc. לֹטֵשׁ; inf. לְטוֹשׁ—**sharpen, whet** ploughshare, etc. 1 S 13_{20}, sword Ps 7_{13}, eyes Jb 16_{9} (+ לְ *against*). **2.** ptc. as noun, **forger, smith** Gn 4_{22} Si 34_{26}.

Pu. 1 Ptc. מְלֻטָּשׁ—**be sharpened,** of razor Ps 52_{4}.

→ cf. נטשׁ III *be sharp.*

[לֹיָה] 3 n.f.—pl. לֹיוֹת—**spiral (border),** metal decoration on bases of lavers in temple 1 K 7_{29}.

לַיִל 8 n.m.—לֵיל; cstr. לֵיל—**night** Ex 12_{42} Is 16_{3} 21_{11}. → cf. לַיְלָה *night.*

לַיְלָה 227.1.57 n.m.—לָיְלָה; pl. לֵילוֹת; cstr. לֵילוֹת—**night** Gn 1_{5}; חֲצֹת הַלַּיְלָה *midnight* Ex 11_{4}, var. חֲצִי הַלַּיְלָה Ex 12_{29}; בַּלַּיְלָה *at night, in the night* Ps 42_{9}, בַּלַּיְלָה הַהוּא *(in) that night* Gn 19_{35}; adv. uses: הַלַּיְלָה *tonight* Gn 19_{5}, לַיְלָה *by night, in the night* Ex 40_{38}, יוֹמָם וָלַיְלָה *by day and by night* Ex 13_{21}, כָּל־הַלַּיְלָה *all the night* Ex 14_{21}, אַרְבָּעִים יוֹם וְאַרְבָּעִים לָיְלָה *(for) forty days and forty nights* Gn 7_{12}. → cf. לַיִל *night.*

לִילִית 1.0.1 pr.n.f.—pl. Q ליליות—**Lilith,** demon 4QShir[a] 1_{5}; or perh. n.f. **nightjar** Is 34_{14}.

לין 71.4.1.2 vb.—**Qal** 69.3.1 Pf. לָן, לָנוּ; impf. יָלִין, 3fs תָּלִין (תָּלַן), 2ms תָּלֶן (תָּלַן); + waw 3fs וַיָּלֶן ,וַיָּלִינוּ ;וַלָּנוּ ,וְלָנָה; impv. לִין, לִינִי, לִינוּ; ptc. לֵנִים; inf. לוּן (לִין)—**1. lodge, spend the night,** of person Gn 24_{23}, beast Jb 39_{9}, caravan Is 21_{13}, weeping Ps 30_{6}. **2. remain (overnight),** of corpse Dt 21_{23}, flesh of sacrifice Dt 16_{4}, wages of hired servant Lv 19_{13}. **3. dwell, remain,** of person Ps 49_{13} (+ בְּ *in* honour), error Jb 19_{4} (+ אֵת *with* someone), myrrh Ca 1_{13} (+ בֵּין *between* breasts).

Hi. 2 (unless Qal) Impf. יָלִין—**1. allow people to rest overnight** 2 S 17_{8}. **2. retain wages overnight** Lv 19_{3}.

Htpol. 2.1.1 Impf. יִתְלוֹנָן; impv. Q התלוננו—**dwell, abide,** of person Ps 91_{1}, eagle Jb 39_{28}.

→ מָלוֹן *lodging place,* מְלוּנָה *hut.*

ליץ 23.10.3 vb.—**Qal** 17.10.3 Pf. + waw וְלַצְתָּ; ptc. לֵץ, לֵצִים—**1.** abs., **scorn, scoff** Pr 9_{12}. **2.** ptc. as noun, **scorner, scoffer** Is 29_{20}.

Hi. 4 Pf. הֱלִיצֻנִי; impf. יָלִיץ—**scorn, deride, mock** someone Ps 119_{51} Pr 3_{34} (לְ of obj.), justice Pr 19_{28}.

Pol. 1 Ptc. לֹצְצִים—ptc. as noun, **scoffer** Ho 7_{5}.

Htpol. 1 Impf. תִּתְלוֹצָצוּ—**scoff** Is 28_{22}.

→ לָצוֹן *scorning,* מְלִיצָה I *mocking poem.*

לַיִשׁ I 3 n.m. **lion** Is 30_{6} Jb 4_{11} Pr 30_{30}.

לַיִשׁ II 4 pl.n. **Laish.**

לַיִשׁ III 2 pr.n.m. **Laish.**

לַיְשָׁה 1 pl.n. **Laishah.**

לכד 121.2.6 vb.—**Qal** 83.1.3 Pf. לָכַד; impf. יִלְכּוֹד; + waw וַיִּלְכֹּד (וַיִּלְכָּד־); impv. לִכְדוּ, לִכְדָה; ptc. לֹכֵד; inf. abs. לָכוֹד; cstr. לָכְדֵנִי—**1. capture, seize, catch, ensnare,** subj. Y. Jb 5₁₃, persons Nm 21₃₂, lion Am 3₄, trap Am 3₅, iniquity Pr 5₂₂; obj. cities Dt 2₃₄, land Jos 10₄₂, fortress Hb 1₁₀, persons Jg 7₂₅, foxes Jg 15₄. **2. take by lot** Jos 7₁₄.

Ni. 36.1.3 Pf. נִלְכַּד; impf. יִלָּכֵד (יִלָּכֶד); ptc. נִלְכָּד—**1. be captured, caught, ensnared,** of nation Jr 48₇, city 1 K 16₁₈, persons Jr 6₁₁, foot Ps 9₁₆; with prep. בְּ *by (means of), with, in* trap Is 24₁₈, rope Jb 36₈, words Pr 6₂. **2. be taken by lot** Jos 7₁₆.

Htp. 2 Impf. יִתְלַכְּדוּ (יִתְלַכָּדוּ)—**grasp one another, be compacted together,** of (frozen) face of deep Jb 38₃₀, scales of Leviathan Jb 41₉.

→ לֶכֶד *capture,* מַלְכֹּדֶת *snare.*

[לֶכֶד] 1 n.[m.]—לֶכֶד—**capture, being caught** Pr 3₂₆. → לכד *capture.*

לֵכָה 1 pr.n.m. **Lecah.**

*__[לְכוּשִׁי]__ 0.0.1 adj. **(Aleppo) pine,** of resin 3QTr 3₉.

לָכִישׁ 24.0.0.1 pl.n. **Lachish.**

[לָכֶם], see לָכֵן *therefore.*

לָכֵן 200.2 adv.—Si לכם—**1. therefore, thus, so, in that case, or and, now then** Ex 6₆ 1 K 14₁₀; יַעַן ... לָכֵן *because ... therefore* Nm 20₁₂, לָכֵן כֹּה אָמַר י׳ *therefore thus has Y. said* 2 K 1₄, לָכֵן שְׁמַע דְּבַר־י׳ *therefore hear the word of Y.* 1 K 22₁₉||2 C 18₁₈. **2. surely, assuredly** 1 S 28₂. → cf. לְ *for* + כֵּן *thus.*

[לֻלָאָה] 13 n.f.—cstr. לֻלְאֹת—**loop,** on edge of curtain Ex 26₄||36₁₁.

למד 86.10.26 vb.—**Qal** 24.4.5 Pf. לָמַד; impf. יִלְמַד; impv. לִמְדוּ; ptc. pass. לְמוּדֵי; inf. abs. לָמֹד; cstr. Q למוד (לְמֹדִי)—**1a. learn** something Dt 5₁ Is 26₉. **b.** with inf. cstr. of another verb, **learn to do something** Dt 4₁₀ Ezk 19₃, sim. inf. abs. Is 1₁₇. **2.** pass. **be trained,** לְמוּדֵי מִלְחָמָה *trained of,* i.e. in, *war* 1 C 5₁₈.

Pi. 57.6.17 Pf. לִמַּד; impf. יְלַמֵּד (יְלַמֶּד־); + waw וַיְלַמְּדוּ; impv. לַמֵּד, לַמְּדָנָה, לַמְּדֵנִי; ptc. מְלַמֵּד; inf. abs. לַמֵּד; cstr. לַמֵּד (לְלַמְּדָם)—**1. teach, train, a.** abs. 2 C 17₇. **b.** with accus. of person and thing taught Dt 4₅. **c.** with accus. of person only Jr 32₃₃. **d.** with accus. of person and inf., teach someone to do something Ps 143₁₀. **e.** with accus. and prep., teach, train hands for (לְ) war 1 S 22₃₅||Ps 18₃₅, something to (לְ) someone Jb 21₂₂, someone in (בְּ) path of justice Is 40₁₄, someone from (מִן) law Ps 94₁₂. **2.** ptc. as noun, **teacher** Ps 119₉₉. **3.** perh. **know, have sex with** Ca 8₂. **4.** perh. **practise (a battle song)** Ps 60₁.

Pu. 5.0.4 Pf. לֻמַּד; ptc. מְלֻמְּדֵי, מְלֻמָּדָה—**1. be trained, skilled,** מְלֻמְּדֵי מִלְחָמָה *trained of,* i.e. in, *war* Ca 3₈, עֶגְלָה מְלֻמָּדָה *a trained heifer* Ho 10₁₁. **2. be taught,** of commandment Is 29₁₃.

→ לִמֻּד *taught,* מַלְמָד *ox-goad,* תַּלְמוּד *teaching,* תַּלְמִיד *scholar.*

*__[לָמֶד]__ 0.0.1 n.[m.] **lamedh,** the twelfth Hebrew letter CD 15₁.

[לִמֻּד] 6.1.5 adj.—cstr. לִמֻּד; sf. Q למודו; pl. לִמּוּדִים; cstr. לִמֻּדֵי; sf. לִמּוּדָי—**taught,** as noun, **1. one used to,** לִמֻּד מִדְבָּר *one used to the steppe* Jr 2₂₄, לִמֻּדֵי הָרֵעַ *ones used to doing evil* Jr 13₂₃. **2. pupil, apprentice, student** Is 8₁₆ 1QH 15₁₀. **3. thing taught, teaching** Si 51₂₈ 4QBarkª 1.14. → למד *learn.*

לָמָה 178.10.2 interrog. adv.—לָמָּה usu. before א, ה, ע, alw. before יהוה, and at Ps 42₁₀ 43₂, also לָמָּה Jb 7₂₀, לָמֶה 1 S 1₈—**why?, for what reason?** Gn 4₆ Ex 2₁₃ Nm 11₁₁; sometimes perh. as neg. final conj., **lest** Gn 27₄₅ Ec 5₅. → cf. לְ *for* + מָה I *what?*

לְמוֹ 4 prep. (alternative form of לְ)—**to, for, as** Jb 27₁₄ Jb 29₂₁ 38₄₀ 40₄. → cf. לְ *to.*

לְמוּאל, see מוּל *front.*

לְמוֹאֵל, see לְמוּאֵל *Lemuel.*

לְמוּאֵל 2 pr.n.m. **Lemuel.**

לִמּוּד, see לִמֻּד *taught.*

לֶמֶךְ 11.0.1 pr.n.m. **Lamech.**

לְמַעַן 272.10.51 prep.—sf. לְמַעֲנִי, לְמַעַנְךָ—**1. for the sake of, on account of** Gn 18₂₄ Dt 3₂₆. **2.** as conj., **in order that, so that, a.** לְמַעַן, with inf. cstr. Gn 18₁₉ Ex 9₁₆, impf. Gn 12₁₃ Dt 4₁. **b.** לְמַעַן אֲשֶׁר, with impf. Gn 18₁₉ Dt 20₁₈.

לְנֶגֶד, see נֶגֶד *in front of.*

[לֹעַ] 1 n.[m.]—sf. לֹעֶךָ—**throat** Pr 23₂. → לעע II *swallow.*

לעב 1.1 vb.—**Hi.** 1 Ptc. מַלְעִבִים—**deride** someone (בְּ of obj.) 2 C 36$_{16}$.

Htp. 0.1 Impf. יתלעבך—**deride** someone Si 30$_{13(B)}$ (+ בְּ *with* folly).

לעג 18.2.1 vb.—**Qal** 12.2 Pf. לָעֲגָה; impf. יִלְעַג; ptc. לֹעֵג—**deride, mock (at),** obj. introduced by לְ 2 K 19$_{21}$||Is 37$_{22}$, עַל Si 34$_{22(Bmg)}$; abs. Jb 11$_{3}$.

Ni. 1 Ptc. cstr. נִלְעַג—ptc. as noun, **incomprehensible one,** נִלְעַג לָשׁוֹן *one incomprehensible of tongue,* i.e. speech Is 33$_{19}$.

Hi. 5.1.1 Impf. תַּלְעִיג; + waw וַיַּלְעַג; ptc. מַלְעִגִים—**deride, mock (at),** obj. introduced by לְ Ps 22$_{8}$, בְּ 2 C 30$_{10}$, עַל Ne 3$_{33}$; abs. Jb 21$_{3}$.

→ לַעַג *derision.*

[לָעֵג] 1 adj.—pl. cstr. לַעֲגֵי—**mocking;** as noun, **mocker** Ps 35$_{16}$. → לעג *deride.*

לַעַג 8.0.2 n.[m.]—cstr. לַעַג; sf. לַעְגָּם; pl. cstr. לַעֲגֵי—**1a. derision, mockery** Jb 34$_{7}$. **b. (object of) derision, mockery** Ps 44$_{14}$. **2.** pl. **stammering,** לַעֲגֵי שָׂפָה *stammering of speech* Is 28$_{11}$. → לעג *deride.*

לַעְדָּה 1 pr.n.m. **Laadah.**

לַעְדָּן 7 pr.n.m. **Ladan.**

לעז 1 vb.—**Qal** 1 Ptc. לֹעֵז—**speak a foreign language, be foreign** Ps 114$_{1}$.

לעט 1 vb.—**Qal, devour,** of lion Ps 57$_{5}$ (if em. להט *devour*).

Hi. 1 Impv. הַלְעִיטֵנִי—**allow to gulp down** Gn 25$_{30}$ (+ מִן *of* red stuff).

לַעִיר 2 pl.n. **Lair.**

לְעֻמַּת 31.2.10 prep.—Q לעומת; sf. לְעֻמָּתוֹ; pl. לְעֻמּוֹת—**1. close by, beside, alongside, parallel to** Ex 25$_{27}$||37$_{14}$ Lv 3$_{9}$, i.e. **as well as** Ec 7$_{14}$. **2. corresponding to, agreeing with, according to** Ezk 40$_{18}$ Ne 12$_{24}$. **3.** לעמת ככה **in accordance with this, accordingly** Mur 24 C$_{18}$. **4.** מִלְּעֻמַּת **close by** 1 K 7$_{20}$. **5.** כְּלְעֻמַּת שֶׁ- as conj., **as in accordance with (the way) that** Ec 5$_{15}$ (if em. כָּל־עֻמַּת *just as*).

לַעֲנָה 8.1.5 n.f. **wormwood** (perh. *Artemisia absinthium*), bitter plant Dt 29$_{17}$.

לעע I 2 vb.—**Qal** 2 Pf. לָעוּ; impf. יָלַע—**be rash,** of words Jb 6$_{3}$; **speak rashly** Pr 20$_{25}$.

לעע II 1.1 vb.—**Qal** 1 Impf. Si תלע; + waw וְלָעוּ—**swallow, gulp down,** abs. Ob$_{16}$ Si 34$_{17}$.

Pilp. **lap up** blood Jb 39$_{30}$ (if em. יְעַלְעוּ *they suck* [עלע pi.] to יְלַעְלְעוּ *they lap up*).

→ לֹעַ *throat.*

לְפִי 16.1.1 prep.—sf. לְפִיהֶן—**1. according to, in proportion to** Gn 47$_{12}$ Lv 25$_{51}$. **2.** as conj., **according as, when(ever),** with inf. cstr. Nm 9$_{17}$ Jr 29$_{10}$. → cf. לְ *to* + פֶּה *mouth.*

לַפִּיד 13.0.1 n.m.—cstr. לַפִּיד; pl. לַפִּידִים; cstr. לַפִּידֵי—**1. torch** Gn 15$_{17}$. **2. lightning** Ex 20$_{18}$.

לַפִּידוֹת 1 pr.n.m. **Lappidoth.**

[לִפְנַי] 1 adv.—לִפְנַי—**in front** 1 K 6$_{17}$ (or em. לִפְנֵי הַדְּבִיר *in front of the inner sanctuary*).

לִפְנֵי 1103.40.251.2 prep.—sf. לְפָנָיו, לִפְנֵיכֶם—**1.** לִפְנֵי **a. before, in front of, in the presence of,** usu. of place Gn 6$_{11}$ Ex 4$_{21}$ Lv 3$_{8}$, also of time Jos 10$_{14}$ Am 1$_{1}$, of seniority Gn 48$_{20}$. **b. against** Nm 16$_{2}$ Dt 31$_{21}$. **c. before,** as conj., with inf. cstr. Gn 13$_{10}$ 1 S 9$_{15}$. **2.** מִלִּפְנֵי, **a. from before, from the presence of,** usu. of place Gn 4$_{16}$ Ex 35$_{20}$ 1 K 8$_{54}$, also of time Ec 1$_{10}$. **b. on account of, (because) of** 1 S 8$_{18}$ 4QapLamB 1$_{6}$. **3.** עַל־לִפְנֵי **to the front of** Ezk 40$_{15}$. **4.** עַד לִפְנֵי **to the front of** Est 4$_{2}$. **5.** כִּי אִם־לִפְנֵי **except before,** i.e. **until, unless,** with inf. cstr. 2 S 3$_{13.35}$.

לְפָנִים I 21.3.7 adv.—**1. formerly, in time past** Dt 2$_{10}$ Jb 42$_{11}$. **2. first** (adv.) Si 4$_{17}$ 11$_{7}$. **3. forwards** Jr 7$_{24}$. **4.** מִלְּפָנִים **from of old** Is 41$_{26}$. **5.** לְמִלְּפָנִים **formerly, from of old** CD 3$_{19}$.

*[לְפָנִים] II 2 n.m. **predecessors** Ps 80$_{10}$ Jb 21$_{8}$.

*לפף vb.—**Pi.,** perh. **cling, wrap** 4Q517 67$_{1}$ (מלפפ[ן]).

לפת 3 vb.—**Qal** 1 + waw וַיִּלְפֹּת—**grasp** pillar, perh. with twisting motion Jg 16$_{29}$.

Ni. 2 Impf. יִלָּפְתוּ; + waw וַיִּלָּפֵת—**1. turn oneself over,** in bed Ru 3$_{8}$. **2.** intrans., **wind about, turn aside,** of caravans Jb 6$_{18}$ (+ דַּרְכָּם *[from] their path*).

לֵץ *scorner,* see ליץ, qal §2.

לָצוֹן 3.0.6 n.[m.] **scorning,** or **babbling** Pr 1$_{22}$; אַנְשֵׁי לָצוֹן *men of scorning* Is 28$_{14}$. → ליץ *scorn.*

לֹצְצִים *scoffers,* see ליץ, pol.

*[לָקָה] 0.1 n.f.—sf. לְקוֹתֶיהָ—**trap** Si 9$_{3}$.

לַקּוּם 1 pl.n. **Lakkum.**

לקח 965.16.91.7 vb.—**Qal** 938.12.88.6 Pf. לָקַח; impf. יִקַּח; impv. קַח (קָחֶנּוּ), קְחִי (לְקְחִי), קְחוּ (קָחֵהוּ, קָחוּ); ptc. לֹקֵחַ;

ptc. pass. לְקֻחִים; inf. abs. לָקוֹחַ; cstr. (לְ)קַחַת (קַחַת, קַחְתּוֹ)—**1a.** usu. **take** Gn 2$_{15}$ Ex 17$_{12}$. **b. receive** Gn 4$_{11}$ Nm 34$_{14}$. **c. accept** Jg 13$_{23}$ 1 S 2$_{15}$. **d. bring** Gn 15$_{9}$ 1 K 7$_{13}$. **e. place, set** Jg 19$_{28}$ 2 S 13$_{19}$. **f. seize, capture** Nm 21$_{25}$ Jos 11$_{16}$. **g. acquire, obtain, purchase** Ne 10$_{32}$ Si 8$_{9}$. **h. grasp,** i.e. **understand** 4QInstr[d] 77$_{4}$. Preps.: (1) לְ *to, for* oneself Gn 14$_{21}$ Ex 6$_{7}$, someone else Gn 15$_{9}$; *as, for (the purpose of being)* people Ex 6$_{7}$, sin offering Lv 9$_{2}$. (2) בְּ *in* hand Gn 22$_{6}$; *by (means of), with* finger Lv 4$_{25}$, force 1 S 2$_{16}$; *(in exchange) for* price 1 K 10$_{28}$||2 C 1$_{16}$. (3) מִן *from* person Gn 23$_{13}$, hand Gn 4$_{11}$, place Jr 13$_{7}$; *some of* Lv 4$_{5}$. (4) other preps.: מֵאֵת *from* Ex 25$_{3}$, מֵעִם *from* Ex 21$_{14}$, מֵעַל *from upon* Lv 16$_{12}$, אֶל *to* Gn 48$_{9}$, עַל *upon* 2 S 13$_{19}$, עִם *with* Jg 4$_{6}$, אֵת *with* Ex 17$_{5}$. **2. marry, take in,** or, **for, marriage, sexual intercourse, a.** usu. of woman being taken by man for (לְ) himself Gn 11$_{29}$ Dt 21$_{11}$ (+ לְאִשָּׁה *as a wife*). **b.** of man being taken by woman Gn 30$_{15}$ Ezk 16$_{32}$. **c.** of person who arranges marriage or obtains wife for (לְ) man Gn 21$_{21}$ (+ מִן *from*). **3.** ptc. as noun, **purchaser** Mur 22 2$_{11}$ 30 2$_{22}$.

Ni. 10.4.2.1 Pf. נִלְקַח; impf. אֶלָּקַח; + waw וַתִּלָּקַח; ptc. Si נלקח; inf. הִלָּקַח—**1. be taken (away), removed,** of person 2 K 2$_{9}$ (+ מֵעִם *from*), bread 1 S 21$_{7}$. **2. be captured,** of ark 1 S 4$_{11}$. **3. be taken, brought,** of person Est 2$_{8}$ (+ אֶל *to*). **4. be obtained,** of wisdom 4QBéat 2.3$_{2}$ (+ בְּ *[in exchange] for*). **5. be accepted,** or perh. **be understood,** of statute 4Q460 9.1$_{9}$ (+ לְ *by*).

Pu. 9.0.2 Pf. לֻקַּח, לֻקְּחוּ; ptc. לֻקָּח—**1. be taken** Gn 2$_{23}$ (+ מִן *from*), i.e. be stolen Jg 17$_{2}$ (+ לְ *with respect to,* i.e. from). **2. be taken away, be removed** 2 K 2$_{10}$ (+ מֵאֵת *from*) Jr 48$_{46}$ (+ בְּ *into* captivity). **3. be taken up** as a curse (קְלָלָה) Jr 29$_{22}$ (+ מִן *from*).

Ho. 6 Impf. יֻקַּח; + waw וַתֻּקַּח—**1. be taken** Is 49$_{24}$ (+ מִן *from*). **2. be brought** Gn 12$_{15}$ (+ בַּיִת *[to] house*) 18$_{4}$.

Htp. 2 Ptc. מִתְלַקַּחַת—**flash,** of fire (lightning) Ex 9$_{24}$ Ezk 1$_{4}$.

→ לֶקַח I *teaching,* II *acquisition,* מַלְקוֹחַ *booty,* מַלְקוֹחַיִם *jaws,* מֶלְקָחַיִם *tongs,* מִקָּח *taking,* מַקָּחָה *wares.*

לֶקַח I 9.3.4 n.m.—sf. לִקְחִי—**1. teaching, instruction, insight** Dt 32$_{2}$ Is 29$_{24}$ Pr 1$_{5}$. **2. persuasiveness** Pr 7$_{21}$ 16$_{21}$. → לקח *take.*

***[לֶקַח]** II 0.2 n.[m.]—sf. לקחו—**1. acquisition,** i.e. item received Si 42$_{7}$(B). **2. acceptance** Si 42$_{15}$. → לקח *take.*

לִקְחִי 1 pr.n.m. **Likhi.**

לקט 37.0.5 vb.—**Qal** 14.0.4 Pf. לָקְטוּ (לָקֵטוּ); impf. יִלְקְטוּ (יִלְקֹטוּן); impv. לִקְטוּ; inf. לְקֹט—**1. gather** manna Ex 16$_{4}$, lilies Ca 6$_{2}$, stones Gn 31$_{46}$. **2.** abs., **glean** Ru 2$_{8}$.

Pi. 21 Pf. לִקֵּטָה, לִקַּטְתְּ; impf. אֲלַקֳּטָה, תְּלַקֵּט; + waw וַיְלַקֵּט; ptc. מְלַקְּטִים, מְלַקֵּט; inf. לַקֵּט, וּלְקַטָּה—**1a. gather** fallen grapes Lv 19$_{10}$, gleanings (לֶקֶט) Lv 19$_{9}$, wood Jr 7$_{18}$, arrows 1 S 20$_{38}$. **b.** abs., **gather (scraps of food)** Jg 1$_{7}$. **2. glean** ears of grain Is 17$_{5}$; abs. Ru 2$_{2}$. **3. collect** money Gn 47$_{14}$ (+ בְּ *[in exchange] for* grain).

Pu. 1 Impf. תְּלֻקְּטוּ—**be gathered,** of people as grain Is 27$_{12}$ (+ לְאַחַד אֶחָד *one by one*).

Htp. 1 + waw וַיִּתְלַקְּטוּ—**assemble** (intrans.), of people Jg 11$_{3}$ (+ אֶל *to,* i.e. around).

→ לֶקֶט *gleaning,* יַלְקוּט *pouch,* מַלְקֹט *gleaning.*

[לֶקֶט] 2.0.1 n.[m.]—cstr. לֶקֶט—**gleaning,** i.e. thing (that may be) gleaned Lv 19$_{9}$ 23$_{22}$ 4QD[a] 6.3$_{5}$. → לקט *gather.*

לקק 7 vb.—**Qal** 5 Pf. לָקְקוּ; impf. יָלֹק, יָלֹקּוּ—**lick, lap,** of dogs licking blood 1 K 21$_{19}$, persons lapping water like dog Jg 7$_{5}$.

Pi. 2 Ptc. מְלַקְקִים—**lap,** of persons Jg 7$_{6.7}$.

לִקְרַאת, see קרא II *meet,* qal.

לקשׁ 1 vb.—**Qal** 1 Impf. יְלַקֵּשׁוּ—**glean** vineyard Jb 24$_{6}$. → לֶקֶשׁ *crop.*

לֶקֶשׁ 2.0.0.1 n.[m.]—לֶקֶשׁ—**crop, spring growth of grass** after latter rains Am 7$_{1}$ Gezer calendar$_{2}$. → לקשׁ *glean.*

[לְשַׁד] 2 n.m.—cstr. לְשַׁד; sf. לְשַׁדִּי—**1. cake, delicacy,** לְשַׁד הַשָּׁמֶן *cake of,* i.e. made with, *oil* Nm 11$_{8}$. **2. moisture,** i.e. strength, vigour Ps 32$_{4}$.

לָשׁוֹן 117.15.62 n.f. (& m.)—לָשׁוֹן; cstr. לְשׁוֹן (Si לשאון); sf. לְשׁוֹנוֹ; pl. לְשֹׁנוֹת; cstr. לְשֹׁנוֹת, Q לשוני; sf. Si לשוניך, לְשֹׁנֹתָם—**1. tongue, a.** of human Jg 7$_{5}$; as organ of speech (cf. §§2, 3) 2 S 23$_{2}$, representative of (speaking) person Is 45$_{23}$; כְּבַד לָשׁוֹן *heavy of tongue* Ex 4$_{10}$. **b.** of Y. Is 30$_{27}$. **c.** of animal: dog Ex 11$_{7}$, viper Jb 20$_{16}$. **2. words, speech** Is 3$_{8}$; specif. as soft Pr 25$_{15}$, pure Si 40$_{21}$, false Ps 109$_{2}$, destructive Pr 17$_{4}$; אִישׁ לָשׁוֹן *man of (unmea-*

sured) speech Ps 140$_{12}$, בַּעַל הַלָּשׁוֹן *possessor of speech,* i.e. snake charmer Ec 10$_{11}$. **3.** (foreign) **language** Gn 10$_{5}$ Jr 5$_{15}$; לְשׁוֹן עַם וָעָם *language of each people* Ne 13$_{24}$. **4. bay** of sea Jos 15$_{2}$ Is 11$_{15}$. **5. flame** of fire Is 5$_{24}$. **6. ray** of sun Si 43$_{4}$. **7. bar, ingot** of gold Jos 7$_{21}$. → לשן *slander.*

לִשְׁכָּה 47 n.f.—+ ה- of direction לִשְׁכָּתָה; cstr. לִשְׁכַּת; pl. לְשָׁכוֹת; cstr. לִשְׁכוֹת—**chamber, room, hall,** usu. part of a sanctuary 1 S 9$_{22}$ 2 K 23$_{11}$ Ne 10$_{38}$; also of secretary's room in royal palace Jr 36$_{12}$. → cf. נִשְׁכָּה *chamber.*

לֶשֶׁם I 2 n.[m.] **jacinth,** or perh. **pale carnelian,** (semi-) precious stone in Aaron's breastplate Ex 28$_{19}$||39$_{12}$.

לֶשֶׁם II 2 pl.n. **Leshem.**

לשן 2 vb.—**Hi.** 1 Impf. תַּלְשֵׁן—**slander** servant to (אֶל) master Pr 30$_{10}$.

Po. 1 Ptc. Qr מְלָשְׁנִי, Kt מלושני—**slander** neighbour in (בְּ) secret Ps 101$_{5}$.

sured) speech Ps 140$_{12}$, בַּעַל הַלָּשׁוֹן *possessor of speech,* i.e. snake charmer Ec 10$_{11}$. **3.** (foreign) **language** Gn 10$_{5}$ Jr 5$_{15}$; לְשׁוֹן עַם וָעָם *language of each people* Ne 13$_{24}$. **4. bay** of sea Jos 15$_{2}$ Is 11$_{15}$. **5. flame** of fire Is 5$_{24}$. **6. ray** of sun Si 43$_{4}$. **7. bar, ingot** of gold Jos 7$_{21}$. → לשן *slander.*

[לֶשַׁע] 1 pl.n. **Lasha.**

לַשָּׁרוֹן 1 pl.n. **Lasharon.**

לֵת, see ילד *give birth.*

[לֶתֶךְ] 1.0.1 n.[m.]—cstr. לֶתֶךְ—**lethech,** unit of dry measure, perh. half a homer Ho 3$_{2}$ Mur 24 E$_{12}$.

מ

***ם־** enclitic mem, part.—normally attached to end of word, without meaning; prob. vocalized *-ma* or *-mi* after consonant, *-m* after vowel; not recognized by MT, but vocalized as, e.g., pl. ending or suffix; mostly in poetry—**1.** at end of word, עָרֵי מָעֻזּוֹ *his strong cities* Is 17$_{9}$ (if em. עָרֵי־ם עֻזּוֹ), גְּמוּלֵי מֵחָלָב *those weaned from milk* Is 28$_{9}$ (if em. גְּמוּלֵי־ם חָלָב), יֵשׁ־אֱלֹהִים שֹׁפְטִים בָּאָרֶץ *there is a God who judges on earth* Ps 58$_{12}$ (if em. שֹׁפֵט־ם). **2.** rarely internal enclitic mem, יְנַחֲמֵנוּ *he will give us rest* Gn 5$_{29}$ (if em. to יְנַחֵ־מ־נוּ, from נוח *rest*).

[מֹאָב], see מוֹאָב *Moab.*

[מַאֲבוּס] 1 n.[m.]—pl. sf. מַאֲבֻסֶיהָ—**granary** or **cattle-pen** Jr 50$_{26}$. → אבס *fatten.*

***[מַאֲבָן]** 0.0.1 n.[m.] **ballista, catapult** 4QM^{c} 1$_{5}$. → cf. אֶבֶן *stone.*

***[מָאֵד]** I (or perh. vocalized מְאֹד) n.m. **Grand One, Almighty,** divine name, עַל־כָּל־הָאָרֶץ מָאֵד *the Grand One is over all the earth* Ps 97$_{9}$ (if em. מְאֹד *very*). → cf. מְאֹד *very.*

***[מָאֵד]** II (or perh. vocalized מְאֹד) n.f. **1. calamity,** perh. as name for Sheol Ps 6$_{4}$ (if em. מְאֹד *very*). **2.** (**object of**) **terror** Ps 31$_{12}$ (if em. מְאֹד *very*). → cf. אֵיד *disaster.*

***[מָאֹד]** I n.[m.] **burden,** הָיִיתִי ... לִשְׁכֵנַי מְאֹד *I have become ... to my neighbours a burden* Ps 31$_{12}$ (if em. מְאֹד *very*). → cf. אֵיד *disaster,* מְאֹד II *burden.*

***[מָאֹד]** II n.[m.] **nightfall,** תֵּרֵד מְאֹד *you shall go down (at) nightfall* 1 S 20$_{19}$ (if em. מְאֹד *very*).

מְאֹד I 299.10.30.1 adv.—Q מאוד, מאדה, מואדה, מאודה, מודה; sf. Q מודי, מְאֹדֶךָ—**1.** as adv., **a. very, very much, greatly,** כִּי־יָפָה הִיא מְאֹד *for she was very beautiful* Gn 12$_{14}$(Qr), וַיִּכָּנַע מְאֹד מִלִּפְנֵי אֱלֹהֵי אֲבֹתָיו *and he humbled himself greatly before the God of his ancestors* 2 C 33$_{12}$. **b. well, very well,** נַפְשִׁי יֹדַעַת מְאֹד *I know very well* Ps 139$_{14}$. **c. far away,** נֻסוּ נֻּדוּ מְאֹד *flee, wander far away* Jr 49$_{30}$. **d.** perh. **completely, utterly,** וַיִּמְאַס מְאֹד בְּיִשְׂרָאֵל *and he completely rejected Israel* Ps 78$_{59}$. **2.** as noun, **a. strength,** בְּכָל־מְאֹדֶךָ *with all your strength* Dt 6$_{5}$. **b.** appar. **property,** מאד המחנה *property of the camp* CD 9$_{11}$. **c.** idioms, (1) עַד־מְאֹד *unto greatness,* i.e. exceedingly Gn 27$_{33}$ 2 C 16$_{14}$ (עַד־לְמְאֹד). (2) בִּמְאֹד

מְאֹד perh. lit. *in the quality of greatness exceedingly,* i.e. very greatly, exceptionally Gn 17$_2$. → cf. מְאֹד I *Grand One.*

*מְאֹד II 1 n.[m.] **burden, object of distress** Ps 31$_{12}$. → cf. אֵיד *disaster,* מְאֹד I *burden.*

מְאֹד III, see מְאֹד I *Grand One.*

*מאה vb. **Pi., repeat a hundred times** Ps 22$_{26}$ (if em. מֵאִתְּךָ *from you* to מֵאִיתִיךָ *I will repeat to you a hundred times*). → מֵאָה *hundred,* מֵאַת *a hundred times.*

מֵאָה 581.3.63.3 n.m.&f.—cstr. מְאַת; pl. מֵאוֹת; du. מָאתַיִם—**hundred, 1.** מְאַת שָׁנָה *hundred years* Gn 11$_{10}$, מָאתַיִם שָׁנָה *two hundred years* Gn 11$_{23}$, מֵאָה פְעָמִים *hundred times* 2 S 24$_3$, שְׁלֹשׁ מֵאוֹת אַמָּה *three hundred cubits* Gn 6$_{15}$, מֵאָה וַעֲשָׂרָה הַזְּכָרִים *hundred and ten males* Ezr 8$_{12}$, מֵאָה אֶלֶף אֵילִים *one hundred thousand rams* 2 K 3$_4$. **2.** as military unit or unit of population, שָׂרֵי מֵאוֹת *princes of hundreds* Ex 18$_{21}$. **3.** without unit of measurement specified, אֶחָד נֶפֶשׁ מֵחֲמֵשׁ הַמֵּאוֹת *one person out of five hundred (warriors)* Nm 31$_{28}$. **4.** name of tower in Jerusalem, מִגְדַּל הַמֵּאָה *the Tower of the Hundred* Ne 3$_1$ 12$_{39}$. → מאה pi. *repeat a hundred times.*

[מַאֲוַי] 1 n.[m.]—pl. cstr. מַאֲוַיֵּי—**desire** Ps 140$_9$. → אוה I *desire.*

מְאוּם I 1.0.2 indef. pron. **anything, nothing,** לוא ידבק בידכה מאום מן החרם *nothing from the devoted objects shall cling to your hand* 11QT 55$_{11}$. → cf. מְאוּמָה *anything.*

מְאוּם II, see מוּם *blemish.*

מְאוּמָה 32.2.1.1 indef. pron.—L מְאוּמָה—**1. anything, nothing,** הַמֵּתִים אֵינָם יוֹדְעִים מְאוּמָה *the dead do not know anything* Ec 9$_5$. **2. anything, something,** רַצְתִּי אַחֲרָיו וְלָקַחְתִּי מֵאִתּוֹ מְאוּמָה *I will run after him, and take something from him* 2 K 5$_{20}$. → cf. מְאוּם I *anything.*

מָאוֹס 1 n.[m.] **refuse** Lm 3$_{45}$. → מאס I *reject.*

מָאוֹר 19.1.19 n.m.—מָאֹר; cstr. מְאוֹר; pl. מְאֹרֹת, Q מאורים; cstr. Q מאורות, מְאוֹרֵי—**1. luminary,** sun and moon Gn 1$_{14}$, stars 1QM 10$_{11}$. **2. light,** in general 1QM 13$_{10}$, of lamp Lv 24$_2$, countenance Ps 90$_8$, eyes Pr 15$_{30}$; Y. as a light 1QH 15$_{25}$. → אור *be light.*

[מְאוּרָה] I 1 n.f.—cstr. מְאוּרַת; pl. cstr. 1QIsa^a מאורות—**light-hole,** entrance to snake's den Is 11$_8$. → אור *be light.*

*[מְאוּרָה] II 1 n.f.—cstr. מְאוּרַת; pl. cstr. 1QIsa^a מאורות—**den** of snake Is 11$_8$.

*[מְאוּרָה] III 1 n.f.—cstr. מְאוּרַת; pl. cstr. 1QIsa^a מאורות—**fiery coals (?)** of snake Is 11$_8$. → (?) אור *be light.*

*[מְאוּרָה] IV 1 n.f.—cstr. מְאוּרַת; pl. cstr. 1QIsa^a מאורות—**eye** of snake Is 11$_8$. → אור *be light.*

*[מְאוּרָה] V 1 n.f.—cstr. מְאוּרַת; pl. cstr. 1QIsa^a מאורות—**young** of snake Is 11$_8$.

מֹאזְנַיִם 15.1.5 n.[m.]du.—Q מוזנים (Si, Q מזנים); cstr. מֹאזְנֵי—**balances, scales,** for weighing money Jr 32$_{10}$, hills Is 40$_{12}$, humans Ps 62$_{10}$; מֹאזְנֵי מִרְמָה *balances of deceit,* i.e. deceptive balances Ho 12$_8$. → אזן II *weigh.*

מֵאיוֹת, see מֵאָה *hundred.*

מַאֲכָל 30.6.8 n.m.—cstr. מַאֲכַל; sf. מַאֲכָלוֹ; pl. sf. Q מאכליהם—**food, nourishment,** in ref. to produce of trees Gn 2$_9$, honey Jg 14$_{14}$, grain Is 62$_8$, baked food Gn 40$_{17}$, meat Ps 44$_{12}$, food of ant Pr 6$_8$, human corpse as food for birds and animals Dt 28$_{26}$, wild asses as prey of lion Si 13$_{19}$. → אכל *eat.*

מַאֲכֶלֶת 4 n.f.—pl. מַאֲכָלוֹת—**knife** Gn 22$_6$. → אכל *eat.*

[מַאֲכֹלֶת] 2 n.f. **fuel,** perh. also **food** (as byform of מַאֲכָל *food*), מַאֲכֹלֶת אֵשׁ *fuel of,* i.e. for, *the fire* Is 9$_{4.18}$. → אכל *eat.*

מאמן, see מִיָּמִן *Miamun.*

[מַאֲמָץ] 1 n.[m.]—pl. cstr. מַאֲמַצֵּי—**exertion, power;** less prob., **wealth, expense** Jb 36$_{19}$. → אמץ *be strong.*

[מַאֲמָר] 3.2.6 n.m.—cstr. מַאֲמַר—**1. word** Si 3$_8$. **2. command** of king Est 1$_{15}$. → אמר *say.*

מאן 46.1.1 vb.—**Pi.** 46.1.1 Pf. מֵאֵן, מֵאַנְתָּ; impf. יְמָאֵן, יְמָאֲנוּ; ptc. מְאֵן, מְאֵנִים; inf. abs. מָאֵן—**1. refuse,** usu. followed by inf., וַיְמָאֵן לְהִתְנַחֵם *but he refused to be comforted* Gn 37$_{35}$; abs. Is 1$_{20}$. **2. act defiantly** Si 4$_{27}$.

מאס I 74.10.33 vb.—**Qal** 71.4.31 Pf. מָאַס, מָאֲסוּ; impf. יִמְאַס; ptc. מֹאֵס, מֹאֶסֶת; ptc. pass. Q מאוסי; inf. abs. מָאוֹס; cstr. מָאֳסָם—**1a. reject, spurn, despise,** (1) with accus. laws and covenant of Y. 2 K 17$_{15}$, discipline Jb 5$_{17}$, life Jb 9$_{21}$, Y. Nm 11$_{20}$ (subj. Israel), Israel Lv 26$_{44}$ (subj. Y.). (2) with בְּ of obj. laws of Y. Lv 26$_{15}$, promised land Nm 14$_{31}$, evil Is 7$_{15}$, Israel (subj. Y.) Ps 78$_{59}$. **b.** without obj., perh. **feel loathing, contempt, revulsion** Ps 89$_{39}$ Jb 34$_{33}$ 36$_5$ 42$_6$; perh. **loathe life** Jb 7$_{16}$. **c.** followed by inf., **refuse (to do something)** Jb 30$_1$. **2.** pass., **be** rejected, הם מאוסי אלוהי[ם] *they are rejected of,* i.e. by, *God* 4QLitB 2₅.

Ni. 3.6.1 Pf. Q נמאסתי; impf. תִּמָּאֵס; ptc. נִמְאָס—**be rejected, despised, reprobate,** of wife Is 54₆, silver Jr 6₃₀.

Pu. 0.0.1 Ptc. ממואסה—**be rejected,** of corner(-stone) GnzPs 1₁₈.

→ מָאוֹס *refuse.*

מאס II 5 vb.—**Qal** 3 Pf. מָאַסְתִּי—**1. waste away** Jb 42₆. **2.** perh. **cower** Jb 36₅.

Ni. 2 Impf. יִמָּאֲסוּ—**flow (away), run, vanish,** of skin Jb 7₅, the wicked Ps 58₈ (+ כְּ *like* water).

→ cf. מסס *melt,* מסה *melt.*

***מאס III** 1 vb.—**Ni.** 1 + waw וַיִּמָּאֵס—**discharge pus, fester,** of skin Jb 7₅.

***מאס IV** 1 vb.—**Ni.** 1 + waw וַיִּמָּאֵס—**gape open,** of skin Jb 7₅.

***מאס V** 2 vb.—**Qal** 1 Pf. מָאַסְתִּי—**err, transgress** Jb 7₁₆.

Ni. 1 Impf. יִמָּאֲסוּ—**err, transgress** Ps 58₈.

*[**מֹאָס**] 0.0.0.1 pr.n.[m.] **Maas.**

*[**מַאֲסָף**] 0.0.3 n.[m.] **1. gathering** of troops in battle 1QM 3₂. **2. swarm** of locusts Is 33₄ (if em. שְׁלַלְכֶם אֹסֶף *your booty, a swarm of* to שָׁלָל כְּמַאֲסַף *booty as a swarm of*). **3.** perh. **withdrawal** of troops from battle 1QM 7₁₃. → אסף *gather.*

[**מַאֲפֶה**] 1 n.[m.] **baked food,** מַאֲפֵה תַנּוּר *something baked of,* i.e. in, *the oven* Lv 2₄. → אפה *bake.*

*[**מַאֲפִילָה**] adj. **waterless, becoming parched late in the season; late in bearing produce,** of land Jr 2₃₁ (if em. מַאְפֵּלְיָה *deep darkness*).

מַאֲפֵל 1 n.[m.] **darkness** Jos 24₇. → cf. אֹפֶל *darkness,* מַאְפֵלָה *darkness,* מַאְפֵּלְיָה *deep darkness.*

*[**מַאְפֵלָה**] 0.0.1 n.f. **darkness** 4QJub^a 2₂. → cf. אֹפֶל *darkness.*

מַאְפֵּלְיָה 1 n.f. **deep darkness** Jr 2₃₁. → מַאֲפֵל *darkness* + יָהּ *Yah.*

מאר 4.0.4 vb. **Qal, feel hatred** Ps 71₁₀ (if em. אָמְרוּ *they say* to מָאֲרוּ *they feel hatred*).

Ni. 0.0.3 Ptc. Q נאמר—**be painful, malignant,** of plague 1QH 13₂₈.

Hi. 4.0.1 Ptc. מַמְאִיר, מַמְאֶרֶת—**1. cause pain,** of briar Ezk 28₂₄. **2. be malignant,** of leprosy Lv 13₅₁.

מַאְרָב 5.0.2 n.m.—cstr. מַאְרַב—**1. place of ambush** Jos 8₉. **2. people waiting in ambush** 2 C 13₁₃. **3. act of ambush** 1QM 3₂. → ארב I *ambush.*

מְאָרֵב, *one lying in wait,* see ארב I *ambush,* pi.

מְאֵרָה I 5 n.f.—cstr. מְאֵרַת; pl. מְאֵרוֹת—**curse** Dt 28₂₀ Ml 2₂ Pr 3₃₃. → ארר *curse.*

***מְאֵרָה II** 1 n.f. **starvation** Dt 28₂₀.

***מְאֵרָה III** 1 n.f. **twitching (of limbs)** Dt 28₂₀.

מאש, see מאס I *reject.*

*[**מָאַשׁ**] 0.0.0.2 pr.n.m. **Maash.**

*[**מְאַשֵּׁר**] n.[m.] **evergreen tree, cedar** Pr 3₁₈ (if em. מְאֻשָּׁר *one who is pronounced happy*). → אשר I *go forward;* cf. תְּאַשּׁוּר *box-tree.*

*[**מֵאֲשֶׁר**] n.m. **that which** Is 47₁₃ (if em. מֵאֲשֶׁר *from which*). → אֲשֶׁר *which.*

*[**מֵאַת**] adv. **a hundred times,** with שׁאל *ask* Ps 27₄ (if em. מֵאֵת *from*). → מאה pi. *repeat a hundred times.*

מֵאֵת, see מִן *from,* אֵת *with.*

מבא, see מָבוֹא *entrance.*

[**מִבְדָּלָה**] 1 n.f.—pl. מִבְדָּלוֹת—**enclave** Jos 16₉. → בדל *be separate.*

מָבוֹא 25.2.15 n.m.—cstr. מְבוֹא; sf. מְבוֹאוֹ; pl. cstr. מְבוֹאֹת, מְבוֹאֵי; sf. Si מבואיה—**1. entrance, entryway** of city Jg 1₂₄, building 2 K 11₁₆, sea, i.e. harbour Ezk 27₃, wisdom Si 14₂₂. **2. entering, (act of) entry,** sometimes perh. **those who enter** temple Ezk 44₅, city by force Ezk 26₁₀; **coming in,** in phrase 'going out and coming in', of one's activity as a whole 2 S 3₂₅(Kt); **coming (together)** of people Ezk 33₃₁; **coming, arrival** of light 1QH 20₄, day and night 1QS 10₁₀, seasons 1QS 10₃. **3.** as cstr. with שֶׁמֶשׁ or with sf. in ref. to שֶׁמֶשׁ, **going in, setting of sun, the west** Dt 11₃₀. → בוא *come.*

מְבוּכָה 2 n.f.—sf. מְבוּכָתָם—**confusion** Is 22₅. → בוך *be disturbed.*

מַבּוּל 13.1.7 n.m. **flood,** in time of Noah Gn 7₆; heavenly **flood,** i.e. water above the firmament Ps 29₁₀. → cf. יָבָל *stream.*

מְבוּנִים, see בין *understand,* hi.

מְבוּסָה 3 n.f. **trampling, subjugation** Is 22₅. → בוס *trample.*

מַבּוּעַ 3.0.3 n.[m.] **spring, (public) fountain** Ec 12₆; מַבּוּעֵי

מַיִם *springs of water* Is 35_{7}. → נבע I *gush.*

מְבוּקָה 1 n.f. **void, devastation** Na 2_{11}. → cf. בּוּקָה *emptiness.*

[מְבוּשִׁים] 1 n.[m.]pl.—sf. מְבֻשָׁיו—**genitals** of man Dt 25_{11}. → בושׁ I *be ashamed.*

מִבְחוֹר 2 n.m. **choice, choicest (one),** עִיר מִבְחוֹר *city of choice,* i.e. choice city 2 K 3_{19}, מִבְחוֹר בְּרֹשָׁיו *choicest of his junipers* 2 K 19_{23}. → בחר I *choose.*

[מִבְחָר] I 14 n.m. **choice, choicest (one[s]),** מִבְחַר שָׁלִשָׁיו *choicest of his officers* Ex 15_{4}, עַם מִבְחָרָיו *people of his choice ones,* i.e. his choice people (troops) Dn 11_{15}. → בחר I *choose.*

מִבְחָר II 1 pr.n.m. **Mibhar.**

[מַבָּט] 3 n.m.—sf. מַבָּטֵנוּ, מֶבָּטָהּ—**(object of) hope, expectation,** of Ethiopia as hope of Judah Is 20_{5}. → נבט *look.*

[מִבְטָא] 2 n.[m.] **impetuous utterance,** מִבְטָא שְׂפָתֶיהָ *impetuous utterance of her lips* Nm 30_{7}. → בטא *speak impetuously.*

מִבְטָח 16.0.3 n.m.—cstr. מִבְטַח; sf. מִבְטַחִי; pl. מִבְטָחִים; sf. מִבְטַחַיִךְ—**trust, confidence, security,** usu. of object of trust Ps 71_{5}; also of placing of trust Pr 22_{19}. → בטח I *trust.*

*[מִבְטָחָה] 0.0.1 n.f.—pl. מבטחות—**confidence** GnzPs 4_{2}. → בטח I *trust.*

*[מִבְטַחְיָהוּ] 0.0.0.3 pr.n.m. **Mibtahiah.**

מֵבִין *one who understands, expert,* see בין *understand,* hi.

*[מְבִינָה] 0.0.4 n.f.—sf. מבינתם; pl. מבינות; sf. מבינותו—**understanding** 4QInstr[c] 1.1_{11} 29.1_{7}. → בין *understand.*

*[מַבָּךְ] n.[m.] **source (of waters), fountain,** מַבְּכֵי נְהָרוֹת *sources of (the) rivers* Jb 28_{11} (if em. מִבְּכִי *without trickling*). → cf. נֶבֶךְ *spring;* נָבוֹךְ *spring.*

*[מַבֵּל] n.f. **fire** Jb 20_{23} (if em. עָלֵימוֹ בִּלְחוּמוֹ *upon him, on his flesh* to עָלָיו מַבֵּל חֲמָתוֹ *upon him the fire of his anger*).

*[מַבְלָגָה] 0.0.1 n.f.—pl. מבלגות—**cunning simile,** of serpents 4QHod[c] 2_{10}. → (?) בלג I *shine.*

[מַבְלִיגִית] 1 n.f.—sf. מַבְלִיגִיתִי—**cheerfulness** Jr 8_{18}. → בלג I *shine.*

*[מַבְלֵל] n.f. **mixed herbs** for use in exorcism Jb 18_{15} (if em. מִבְּלִי־לוֹ *without to him*). → בלל *mix.*

מְבֻלָּקָה *devastation,* see בלק *devastate.*

*[מָבָן] 0.0.0.1 pr.n.[m.] **Maban.**

[מִבְנֶה] 1.0.3 n.m. **structure,** מִבְנֵה־עִיר *structure of a city* Ezk 40_{2}. → בנה I *build.*

מְבֻנַּי 1 pr.n.m. **Mebunnai.**

*[מַבְנִית] I 0.0.11 n.f.—sf. מבניתי—**structure, building** of the heavenly sanctuary 4QShirShabb[d] 1.1_{41}, of a person, i.e. **body,** אושי מבניתי *foundations of my structure* 1QH 15_{4}. → בנה I *build.*

*[מַבְנִית] II n.f. **likeness** of idols Ho 13_{2} (if em. כִּתְבוּנָם *according to their understanding* to כְּמַבְנִית *according to the likeness*).

*[מַבָּע] 0.0.2 n.[m.] **flow of breath, utterance,** מבעי רוחות *flows of breath,* or perh. *utterances of (the) spirits* 1QH 9_{29}. → נבע *flow.*

*[מַבְעֵרָה] n.[f.] **burning** Jr 8_{13} (if em. וָאֶתֵּן לָהֶם יַעַבְרוּם *and I gave them [permission] to pass them* to וָאֶתְּנֵם לְמַבְעֵרָה *and I gave them for the purpose of burning*). → בער I *burn.*

מִבְצָר I 37.1.4 n.m.&f.—cstr. מִבְצַר; pl. מִבְצָרִים, מִבְצָרוֹת; cstr. מִבְצְרֵי; sf. מִבְצָרָיו, מִבְצְרֵיהֶם—**fortification, fortress, stronghold,** עִיר מִבְצָר *city of fortification,* i.e. fortified city 1 S 6_{18}. → בצר I *cut.*

מִבְצָר II 2 pr.n.m. **Mibzar.**

*[מְבַצֵּר] n.[m.] **the Vintager,** a star, also known as **Vendemiator** Am 5_{9} (הַמַּבְלִיג שֹׁד עַל־עָז וְשֹׁד עַל־מִבְצָר יָבוֹא *who makes the Bull to rise hard upon [the rising of] the She-goat and the Bull comes upon [the rising of] the Vintager;* if em. מִבְצָר *fortification* to מְבַצֵּר and שֹׁד *ruin* to שׁוֹר *bull* and עָז *strong* to עֵז *she-goat*). → I בצר *cut off.*

*[מִבְקָע] 0.0.1 n.[m.] **cleavage, rift,** מבקע תהומות *cleavage of the deeps* 1QM 10_{13}. → בקע I *split.*

[מִבְרָח] I 1 n.m.—pl. sf. Qr מִבְרָחָיו—**fugitive** Ezk 17_{21}. → ברח I *flee.*

*[מִבְרָח] II 1 n.m.—pl. sf. Qr מִבְרָחָיו—**hero, commander, court** or **military staff** Ezk 17_{21}.

*[מִבְרָח] III 1 n.m.—pl. sf. Qr מִבְרָחָיו—**picked man** Ezk 17_{21}.

מִבְשָׂם 3 pr.n.m. **Mibsam.**

מְבַשְּׁלוֹת 1 n.f.pl. **hearths** Ezk 46_{23}. → בשׁל *boil.*

מָג, see רַב־מָג *Rabmag.*

מַגְבִּישׁ I 1 pr.n.m. **Magbish.**

מַגְבִּישׁ II 1 pl.n. **Magbish.**

*[מִגְבָּל] 0.0.4 n.[m.] **kneading, thing kneaded,** alw. of person, אני ... מגבל המים *I am ... a thing kneaded with water* 1QH 9$_{21}$. → (?) גבל II *forge.*

מִגְבָּלֹת 1 n.f.pl. **forged work,** making braided chains Ex 28$_{14}$. → גבל II *forge.*

[מִגְבָּעָה] I 4.0.1 n.f.—pl. מִגְבָּעוֹת—**headdress, turban, headband,** of priest Ex 28$_{40}$. → cf. גִּבְעָה *hill.*

*[מִגְבָּעָה] II n.f. **hilly place** Jr 3$_{23}$ (if em. מִגְּבָעוֹת *from the hills* to מִגְבָּעוֹת *hilly places*). → cf. גִּבְעָה *hill.*

*מגד I 1 vb.—**Qal** 0.0.1 + waw ותמגדנו—of Y., **give** Israelites **into** (בְּ) **power** of sin Is 64$_{6}$(1QIsa^{a}) (MT וַתְּמוּגֵנוּ appar. *and you have caused us to melt*).

*[מגד] II vb. **Pi., make excellent, make abundant** Am 4$_{13}$ (if em. מַגִּיד לְאָדָם מַה־שֵּׂחוֹ *declaring to humans what is his thought* to מְמַגֵּד לְאֲדָמָה שִׂיחָהּ *making abundant its plants for the earth*). → מֶגֶד *choice produce,* מִגְדָּנוֹת *precious things.*

[מֶגֶד] 8 n.m.—pl. מְגָדִים—**excellence,** i.e. **choice produce** Ca 4$_{16}$. → מגד II *be excellent.*

מְגִדּוֹ 12 pl.n. **Megiddo.**

[מִגְדּוֹל] I 1 n.[m.] **tower** 2 S 22$_{51}$(Qr). → גדל *be great;* cf. מִגְדָּל *tower.*

מִגְדּוֹל II, see מִגְדֹּל *Migdol.*

מְגִדּוֹן, see מְגִדּוֹ *Megiddo.*

מַגְדִּיאֵל 2 pr.n.m. **Magdiel.**

מִגְדָּל I 48.0.13 n.m.—cstr. מִגְדַּל; pl. מִגְדָּלִים, מִגְדָּלוֹת; pl. cstr. מִגְדְּלוֹת; sf. מִגְדָּלֶיהָ, מִגְדְּלוֹתַיִךְ—**1. tower** Jr 31$_{38}$. **2. raised platform, pulpit** Ne 8$_{4}$. **3. raised bed** of garden, **bank** Ca 5$_{13}$ (or §4 or §5). **4. heap, pile (of coins)** Is 33$_{18}$. **5. chest, box** Ca 5$_{13}$. **6. high-ranking officer** Is 30$_{25}$. **7. tower,** as name of a battle formation 1QM 9$_{13}$. → גדל I *be great;* cf. מִגְדּוֹל *tower.*

*מִגְדָּל II 0.0.1 n.[m.] **magnification** 4QShirShabb^{d} 1.2$_{25}$. → גדל I *be great.*

מִגְדֹּל 6 pl.n. **Migdol.**

מִגְדַּל־אֵל 1 pl.n. **Migdal-el.**

מִגְדַּל־גָּד 1 pl.n. **Migdal-gad.**

מִגְדַּל־עֵדֶר 2 pl.n. **Migdal-eder.**

מִגְדָּנוֹת 4 n.f.pl.—מִגְדָּנֹת—**precious things** Gn 24$_{53}$. → מגד II *be excellent.*

*[מְגַדֵּפָה] 1 n.f.—pl. sf. מגדפותם—**blasphemy** Is 51$_{7}$(1QIsa^{a}) (ממגדפותם corrected from מגדפותם; MT מִגִּדֻּפֹתָם from גִּדּוּף). → גדף *revile.*

מָגוֹג 4.0.2 pr.n.m. **Magog.**

[מָגוֹר] I 11.1.3 n.[m.]—sf. מְגוּרָם; cstr. מְגוּרֵי; sf. מְגוּרָיו—**1. sojourning, dwelling** Gn 37$_{1}$. **2. sojourning place, dwelling place** Si 16$_{8}$ 1QS 6$_{2}$. → גור I *sojourn.*

מָגוֹר II 9.0.1 n.m.—pl. sf. מְגוּרַי—**fear, terror,** מָגוֹר מִסָּבִיב *terror all around* Jr 6$_{25}$; **(object of) terror** Jr 20$_{4}$. → גור III *fear.*

*[מָגוֹר] III 1 n.[m.]—sf. מְגוּרָם—**storage pit,** i.e. heart, mind Ps 55$_{16}$. → cf. מְגוּרָה I *granary.*

*[מָגוֹר] IV 1 n.[m.]—sf. מְגוּרָם—**throat** Ps 55$_{16}$. → cf. גָּרוֹן *neck, throat.*

[מְגוֹרָה] 3 n.f.—cstr. מְגוֹרַת; pl. sf. מְגוּרוֹתַי—**(object of) fear, dread** Ps 34$_{5}$. → גור III *fear.*

מְגוּרָה I 1 n.f. **granary,** or **grain pit, bin** Hg 2$_{19}$. → cf. אגר *gather;* cf. מָגוֹר III *storage pit.*

*מְגוּרָה II 2 n.f.—sf. מְגוּרָם—**furrow** Ps 55$_{16}$.

*[מְגוּרָה] III n.f. **pool** Jl 1$_{17}$ (if em. מַמְּגֻרוֹת *granaries* to מְגֻרוֹת *pools*).

*[מְגָזָה] 0.0.1 n.f. **ford,** מגזת הכוהן הגדול *ford of the high priest* 3QTr 6$_{14}$.

[מַגְזֵרָה] 1 n.f. **axe,** מַגְזְרֹת הַבַּרְזֶל *axes of iron* 2 S 12$_{31}$. → גזר I *cut.*

מַגִּיד, *messenger,* see נגד hi. *tell.*

מַגָּל 2 n.[m.] **sickle** Jl 4$_{13}$.

מְגִלָּה 21 n.f. **scroll** Jr 36$_{6}$; מְגִלַּת־סֵפֶר *scroll of writing* Jr 36$_{2}$. → גלל I *roll.*

[מְגַמָּה] 1 n.f. perh. **multitude, totality, massing,** מְגַמַּת פְּנֵיהֶם *multitude of their faces* Hb 1$_{9}$.

*מגן I 3.0.1 vb.—**Pi.** 3.0.1 Pf. מִגֵּן; impf. אֲמַגֶּנְךָּ—**1.** of Y., **deliver up, surrender** enemies into someone's power (בְּיַד) Gn 14$_{20}$. **2.** with double accus., **bestow crown upon** Pr 4$_{9}$. → מֶגֶן *gift,* מָגָן *benefactor.*

*מגן II vb. **beseech,** ptc. as noun, **beggar** Pr 6$_{11}$=24$_{34}$ (if em. כְּאִישׁ מָגֵן *as a man of a shield* to כְּאִישׁ מֹגֵן *as a beggar*). → מָגָן *beggar.*

*[מָגָן] (or perh. vocalized מָגֵן or מֹגֵן) 18 n.m.—cstr. מָגֵן; sf. מָגִנֵּי; pl. cstr. מָגִנֵּי—**benefactor, suzerain, general,** מָגֵן שָׁאוּל *the general of Saul* 2 S 1$_{21}$, כִּי לַי׳ מָגִנֵּנוּ *truly Y. is our Suzerain* Ps 89$_{19}$. → מגן I *bestow.*

*[מָגֵן] n.m. **beggar** Pr 6$_{11}$=24$_{34}$ (if em. כְּאִישׁ מָגֵן *as a man of a shield* to כְּאִישׁ מָגֵן *as a beggar*). → מגן II *beseech*.

מָגֵן I 60.2.14 n.m.&f.—pl. מָגִנִּים (מָגִנּוֹת); cstr. מָגִנֵּי—**1. shield, buckler,** used by warrior Jg 5$_8$, ornament in palace 1 K 10$_{17}$||2 C 9$_{16}$; Y. as shield Gn 15$_1$. **2. shield,** i.e. **scale,** of Leviathan Jb 41$_7$. → גנן *cover*.

*[מָגֵן] II 0.0.1 n.[m.] **protection** 1QH 14$_{27}$. → גנן *cover*.

*מָגֵן III 4 adj.—pl. cstr. מָגִנֵּי—**1. insolent** Pr 6$_{11}$. **2.** as noun, **insolent, bold, mighty one** Ps 47$_{10}$. → cf. מְגִנָּה II *shamelessness*.

*[מָגֵן] IV 0.0.0.6 pr.n.m. **Magen.**

*[מֶגֶן] 1 n.[m.]—pl. sf. מְגִנֶּיהָ—**gift, reward,** for drunkenness or prostitution Ho 4$_{18}$. → מגן I *deliver up*.

[מְגִנָּה] I 1 n.f. **covering,** מְגִנַּת־לֵב *covering of the heart* Lm 3$_{65}$. → גנן *cover*.

*[מְגִנָּה] II 1 n.f. **shamelessness,** מְגִנַּת־לֵב *shamelessness of the heart* Lm 3$_{65}$. → cf. מָגֵן III *insolent*.

*[מַגְנֵס] 0.0.1 pr.n.[m.] **Magnus.**

*[מַגָּע] 0.0.4 n.m.—sf. מגעו—**contact, one who has contact,** with person who has a discharge 4QTohA 1.1$_8$. → נגע I *touch*.

מִגְעֶרֶת I 1 n.f. **rebuke,** perh. **threat** Dt 28$_{20}$. → גער *rebuke*.

*מִגְעֶרֶת II 1 n.f. **dysentery** Dt 28$_{20}$.

מַגֵּפָה 26.1.3 n.f.—Q מגפא; cstr. מַגֵּפַת; pl. sf. מַגֵּפֹתַי—**1.** alw. sent by Y., **plague, pestilence** Nm 14$_{37}$, **stroke** Ezk 24$_{16}$. **2. slaughter, defeat** in battle 1 S 4$_{17}$. → נגף *strike*.

מַגְפִּיעָשׁ 1 pr.n.m. **Magpiash.**

מגר 2.0.2 vb.—**Qal** 1.0.1 Ptc. pass. מְגוּרֵי—pass. **be thrown, delivered up to** (אֶל) sword Ezk 21$_{17}$, **be cast down** with (עִם) sickness 1QH 16$_{26}$.

Pi. 1.0.1 Pf. מִגַּרְתָּה—of Y., **throw down** throne to (לְ) ground Ps 89$_{45}$.

מְגֵרָה 4 n.f.—pl. מְגֵרוֹת—**saw** 2 S 12$_{31}$. → גרר I *drag*.

מִגְרוֹן I 2 pl.n. **Migron.**

*מִגְרוֹן II 1 n.[m.] **threshing floor** 1 S 14$_2$. → cf. גֹּרֶן *threshing floor*.

*[מִגְרָן] 0.0.1 n.[m.] perh. **destruction, threshing** 4QpsHodA 1$_3$. → cf. גֹּרֶן *threshing floor*.

[מִגְרָעָה] 1 n.f.—pl. מִגְרָעוֹת—**recess, rebatement,** in wall 1 K 6$_6$. → גרע I *diminish*.

*[מַגְרֵף] n.m. **shovel** Am 6$_{10}$ (if em. וּמְסָרְפוֹ *and the one who burns him* to מַגְרֵפוֹ *his shovel*). → גרף *sweep away*.

[מֶגְרָפָה] I 1 n.f.—pl. sf. מֶגְרְפֹתֵיהֶם—**shovel, spade** Jl 1$_{17}$. → גרף *sweep away*.

*[מֶגְרָפָה] II 1 n.f.—pl. sf. מֶגְרְפֹתֵיהֶם—**floodwater, alluvial soil** Jl 1$_{17}$. → גרף *sweep away*.

*[מֶגְרָפָה] III 1 n.f.—pl. sf. מֶגְרְפֹתֵיהֶם—**dyke** Jl 1$_{17}$.

מִגְרָשׁ I 114 n.m.—cstr. מִגְרַשׁ; pl. מִגְרָשׁוֹת; cstr. מִגְרְשֵׁי; sf. מִגְרָשֶׁיהָ—**land outside city walls,** claimed as territory of city, or as exclusion or sacral zone Lv 25$_{34}$, oft used as pasture land Jos 14$_4$. → גרשׁ I *expel*.

*[מִגְרָשׁ] II 1 n.m.—pl. מִגְרָשׁוֹת—**driven wave** Ezk 27$_{28}$. → גרשׁ *expel*.

*[מַגָּשׁ] n.m. **offering** Ml 1$_{11}$ (if em. מֻגָּשׁ *brought near,* i.e. נגשׁ ho.). → נגשׁ *approach*.

[מַד] I 9 n.m.—sf. (מַדּוֹ) מִדּוֹ; pl. מִדִּין; sf. מַדָּיו—**1. (outer) garment, clothing** of priest Lv 6$_3$, warrior, perh. **under-garment** 2 S 10$_4$; perh. **armour** 1 S 17$_{38}$. **2. cloth, rug,** perh. as saddle Jg 5$_{10}$. → cf. מִדָּה II *garment*, מַדּוּ *garment*.

[מַד] II 3.0.1 n.[m.]—sf. מִדָּה; pl. sf. מִדַּיִךְ—**1. measure(ment)** Jb 11$_9$. **2. (great) stature,** אִישׁ מדין *man of (great) stature* 2 S 21$_{20(Kt)}$. → מדד *measure*.

מִדְבָּר I 271.2.16 n.m. **steppe, wilderness, desert,** dry Is 41$_{18}$, salty Jr 17$_6$, place of wild animals and birds Ml 1$_3$ Ps 102$_7$, largely uninhabited Ps 107$_4$, though having towns Jos 15$_{61}$; מִדְבַּר יְהוּדָה *steppe of Judah* Jg 1$_{16}$. → cf. דֹּבֶר *pasture*.

[מִדְבָּר] II 1 n.m. **mouth,** מִדְבָּרֵיךְ נָאוֶה *your mouth is beautiful* Ca 4$_3$. → דבר I *speak*.

מדד 53.0.8 vb.—**Qal** 43.0.7 Pf. מָדַד; impf. תָּמֹד, תָּמֹדּוּ; + waw וָאָמֹד, וַיָּמָד; ptc. Q מודד; inf. מֹד—**1. measure, a.** usu. length, distance, (1) with obj. length, width Ezk 40$_{20}$, temple Ezk 41$_{13}$. (2) without obj., וּמָדְדוּ אֶל־הֶעָרִים *and they will measure the distance to the cities* Dt 21$_2$. **b.** capacity, (1) with obj. water Is 40$_{12}$, (measure of) barley Ru 3$_{15}$. (2) without obj., וַיָּמֹדּוּ בָעֹמֶר *and they measured (it) by the omer* Ex 16$_{18}$. **2.** of Y., **measure out (recompense), reward** deeds Is 65$_7$.

Ni. 3.0.1 Impf. יִמַּד, יִמַּדּוּ—**be measured,** of heaven

Jr 31$_{37}$, sand Ho 2$_{1}$.

Pi. $_{5}$ Pf. מִדַּד; impf. אֲמַדֵּד—**1. measure** people 2 S 8$_{2}$, valley Ps 60$_{8}$. **2. extend, continue,** of evening Jb 7$_{4}$.

Po. $_{1}$ + waw וַיְמֹדֶד—of Y., **measure** earth Hb 3$_{6}$.

Htpo. $_{1}$ וַיִּתְמֹדֵד—**stretch oneself out upon** (עַל) child 1 K 17$_{21}$.

→ מַד II *measure,* מִדָּה I *measure,* מֵמַד *measurement,* (?) מוֹדָה *measure.*

מִדָּה I $_{54.0.27}$ n.f.—cstr. מִדַּת; pl. מִדּוֹת; sf. מִדּוֹתֶיהָ—**1. measure, measuring** of length, distance Jr 31$_{39}$, liquid Jb 28$_{25}$, truth 1QS 8$_{4}$. **2. measurement, size, extent,** of temple furnishings 1 K 7$_{37}$, one's days Ps 39$_{5}$. **3. (great) size, stature,** אַנְשֵׁי מִדּוֹת *men of (great) stature* Nm 13$_{32}$. **4. (measured) section, portion,** of temple area Ezk 45$_{3}$, knowledge 4QsapHymnA 1.1$_{1}$. → מדד *measure.*

*[מִדָּה] II $_{1.0.1}$ n.f.—pl. sf. מִדּוֹתָיו—**garment** Ps 133$_{2}$; מדת הדר *garment of splendour* 1QS 4$_{8}$. → cf. מַד I *garment,* מַדּוּ *garment.*

[מִדָּה] III $_{1.0.1}$ n.f. **tribute, tax** Ne 5$_{4}$ 4QWays[a] 2$_{3}$.

*[מַדְהֵב] I $_{0.0.2}$ n.[m.] **distress** 4QInstr[b] 2.2$_{14}$ CD 13$_{9}$. → cf. דוב *pine away;* מַדְהֵבָה I *distress.*

*[מַדְהֵב] II $_{0.0.2}$ n.[m.] **driven out person** 4QInstr[b] 2.2$_{14}$ CD 13$_{9}$. → cf. מַדְהֵבָה II *rout.*

*מַדְהֵבָה I $_{1.0.3}$ n.f. perh. **distress, calamity** Is 14$_{4}$ 1QH 11$_{25}$ 20$_{18}$ 4QInstr[d] 176$_{3}$. → cf. דוב *pine away;* מַדְהֵב I *distress,* II *driven out person.*

*מַדְהֵבָה II $_{1.0.3}$ n.f. **rout, defeat** Is 14$_{4}$ 1QH 11$_{25}$ 20$_{18}$ 4QInstr[d] 176$_{3}$. → cf. מַדְהֵב II *driven out person.*

[מַדּוּ] $_{2}$ n.m.—pl. sf. מַדְוֵיהֶם—**garment** 2 S 10$_{4}$||1 C 19$_{4}$. → cf. מַד I *garment,* מִדָּה II *garment.*

[מַדְוֶה] $_{2}$ n.m.—cstr. מַדְוֵה; pl. cstr. מַדְוֵי—**disease, plague** Dt 7$_{15}$ 28$_{60}$. → דוה *be faint.*

מַדּוּחִים I $_{1}$ n.[m.]pl. **enticement** Lm 2$_{14}$. → נדח I *thrust.*

*מַדּוּחִים II $_{1}$ n.[m.]pl. **false claims** Lm 2$_{14}$. → נדח I *thrust.*

*מַדּוּחִים III $_{1}$ n.[m.]pl. **folly** Lm 2$_{14}$.

מדוכה, see מְדֹכָה *mortar.*

מָדוֹן I $_{20.0.6}$ n.m.—pl. מְדָנִים—**1.** usu. **strife, contention, quarrelling,** אִישׁ מָדוֹן *man of strife* Jr 15$_{10}$. **2. (object of) strife** Ps 80$_{7}$. → דין I *judge.*

*מָדוֹן II $_{1}$ n.[m] **(object of) contempt** Ps 80$_{7}$.

מָדוֹן III $_{2}$ pl.n. **Madon.**

מַדּוּעַ $_{72.2.1}$ interrog. adv.—מַדֻּעַ—**why?,** either not distinct semantically from לָמָּה *why?*, or esp. with ref. to past events or present situations (לָמָּה being used esp. with ref. to future events or intentions), or else esp. with factual questions (לָמָּה being used esp. for reproach or complaint), מַדּוּעַ אַתָּה לְבַדֶּךָ *why are you alone?* 1 S 21$_{2}$. → ידע I *know.*

*[מָדוֹר] $_{0.0.5}$ n.[m.]—sf. מדורו—**dwelling place, station,** מדור חושך *dwelling place of darkness* 1QH 20$_{25}$. → דור I *dwell.*

מְדוּרָה $_{2}$ n.f.—מְדֻרָתָהּ—**pile** of wood, **pyre** Is 30$_{33}$ Ezk 24$_{9}$. → דור II *heap up.*

מִדְחֶה $_{1}$ n.m. **downfall, ruin,** caused by flattering speech Pr 26$_{28}$. → דחה *push.*

[מַדְחֵפָה] $_{1}$ n.f.—pl. מַדְחֵפֹת—**thrust, blow,** or perh. **haste,** or perh. **exile,** as name for the underworld Ps 140$_{12}$. → דחף *drive, hasten.*

מָדַי $_{15}$ pr.n.m. **Madai, Media.**

מָדַי $_{1}$ gent. **Mede.**

מַדַּי, see דַּי *sufficiency.*

מִדֵּי, see דַּי *sufficiency.*

מִדִּין $_{1}$ pl.n. **Middin.**

מִדְיָן I $_{59.0.3}$ pr.n.m. **Midian.**

[מִדְיָן] II $_{10}$ n.m. **strife, contention, quarrelling,** אִישׁ מִדְיָנִים *man of strife* Pr 26$_{21}$(Qr), מִדְיְנֵי אִשָּׁה *quarrelling of a wife* Pr 19$_{13}$. → דין I *judge.*

מְדִינָה I $_{54.0.1}$ n.f.—pl. מְדִינוֹת—**province, district,** or perh. sometimes **town,** of Israel 1 K 20$_{14}$, Persian empire Est 1$_{1}$, in general Ec 2$_{8}$. → דין I *judge.*

*מְדִינָה II $_{2}$ n.f.—pl. מְדִינוֹת—**place of judgment** Ec 2$_{8}$ 5$_{7}$. → דין I *judge.*

*[מְדִינָה] III $_{1}$ n.f.—pl. מְדִינוֹת—**prefect** Ec 2$_{8}$. → דין I *judge.*

מִדְיָנִי $_{8}$ gent. **Midianite.**

מְדֹכָה $_{1.0.1}$ n.f. **mortar** Nm 11$_{8}$. → דוך *crush.*

*[מְדָל] I n.m. **cloud,** מַר מִדְּל *drop of,* i.e. from, *a cloud* Is 40$_{15}$ (if em. מִדְּלִי *from a bucket*).

*[מְדָל] II n.m. **thunderbolt,** מַר מִדְּל *drop of,* i.e. from, *a thunderbolt* Is 40$_{15}$ (if em. מִדְּלִי *from a bucket*).

*[מַדְלֶי] n.[m.] **scales,** מַר מִדְּלִי *fine dust of the scales*

Is 40$_{15}$ (if em. מִדְּלִי *from a bucket*).

מַדְמֵן 1 pl.n. **Madmen.**

מַדְמַנָּה 2 pl.n. **Madmannah.**

מַדְמֵנָה I 1 n.f. **dung-pit** Is 25$_{10}$. → cf. דֹּמֶן *dung*.

מַדְמֵנָה II 1 pl.n. **Madmenah.**

מְדָן 2 pr.n.m. **Medan.**

מְדָנִים, see מִדְיָן I *Midian*, II *strife*.

מַדָּע I 6.2.5 n.m.—sf. מַדָּעֲךָ—**1. knowledge, understanding, intelligence** Dn 1$_4$; מדע תורה *knowledge of the law* 4QMMT C$_{28}$. **2. (place of) carnal knowledge,** i.e. bedroom Ec 10$_{20}$ (or §3). **3. mind, thought** Ec 10$_{20}$. → ידע I *know*.

*[מַדָּע] II 1 n.[m.]—sf. מַדָּעֲךָ—**repose** Ec 10$_{20}$. → ידע II *be quiet*.

*[מַדָּע] III 1 n.[m.]—sf. מַדָּעֲךָ—**friend** Ec 10$_{20}$.

*[מַדָּע] IV 1 n.[m.]—sf. מַדָּעֲךָ—**kinsman** Ec 10$_{20}$. → ידע I *know*.

*[מַדָּע] V 1 n.[m.]—sf. מַדָּעֲךָ—**messenger** Ec 10$_{20}$.

מֹדָע 2.0.2 n.m.—מוֹדָע; pl. sf. Q מודעי—**relative, kinsman,** מֹדָע לְאִישָׁהּ *a relative on her husband's side* Ru 2$_{1(Qr)}$, perh. **acquaintance** 1QH 12$_9$. → ידע I *know*.

[מֹדַעַת] 1 n.f.—sf. מֹדַעְתָּנוּ—**relative, kin** Ru 3$_2$. → ידע I *know*.

*[מֵדֶף] I 0.0.1 n.[m.] **trap, stone sealing a tomb** 3QTr 3$_{12}$.

*[מֵדֶף] II 0.0.1 n.[m.] **uncleanness** 3QTr 3$_{12}$.

[מַדְקָרָה] 1 n.f.—pl. cstr. מַדְקְרוֹת—**piercing, stab** of sword Pr 12$_{18}$. → דקר *pierce*.

*[מֶדֶר] n.[m.] **wet clay** Jb 37$_{17}$ (if em. מִדָּרוֹם *on account of the south wind* to מִדְּרָם *their wet clay*).

מַדְרֵגָה 2 n.f.—pl. מַדְרֵגוֹת—**steep place, cliff** Ca 2$_{14}$.

*[מִדְרוֹךְ] 0.0.1 n.[m.] **treading place** 4QJub^h 32$_{18}$. → דרך I *tread*.

[מִדְרָךְ] 1.0.1 n.[m.]—cstr. מִדְרַךְ—**treading place** Dt 2$_5$. → דרך I *tread*.

*[מִדְרָס] 0.0.1 n.[m.] **floor, treading place,** מדרס דבירי פלא *floor of the inner sanctuaries of wonder* 4QShir Shabb^f 19$_2$.

[מִדְרָשׁ] 2.1.7 n.[m.]—cstr. מִדְרַשׁ; sf. Si מדרשי—**1. study, inquiry, interpretation, midrash,** perh. **explanation, development** of existing data, מדרש התורה *study of the law* 1QS 8$_{15}$, מדרש מאשרי [ה]איש *midrash of 'Happy is the man'* 4QMidrEschat^a 3$_{14}$. **2. (written) discourse,** מִדְרַשׁ הַנָּבִיא *discourse of the prophet* Iddo 2 C 13$_{22}$. → דרשׁ *seek*.

[מְדֻשָּׁה] 1 n.f.—sf. מְדֻשָׁתִי—**threshing** Is 21$_{10}$. → דושׁ *thresh*.

מָה I 492.48.122 pron.—מַה־ (מַה, מֶה, מֶה־, מָה, Q מאה); usu. מַה־, with dagesh in following consonant—**1.** interrog., **what?, how?, why?,** מָה אַתָּה רֹאֶה *what are you seeing?* Jr 1$_{11}$, מָה אֶקֹּב לֹא קַבֹּה אֵל *how could I curse what God has not cursed?* Nm 23$_8$, מֶה לֹא־תִשָּׂא פִשְׁעִי *why do you not pardon my transgression?* Jb 7$_{21}$; oft. introducing rhetorical question, **of what importance/ value (is) ... ?,** מָה עַבְדֶּךָ *of what importance is your servant?* 2 S 9$_8$. **2.** as exclamation, **how (much, great, greatly, etc.)!,** מַה־גָּדְלוּ מַעֲשֶׂיךָ *how great are your deeds!* Ps 92$_6$. **3.** as combined existential and interrog. part., **what is there?, what is taking place?, what happens?,** לֹא יָדַעְתִּי מָה *I did not know what (was taking place)* 2 S 18$_{29}$ (or §7). **4.** appar. as combined interrog. and conditional part., **what if?,** מַה־יַּעַנְךָ אָבִיךָ קָשָׁה *what if your father gives you a harsh response?* 1 S 20$_{10}$. **5. what ails?, what need is there?,** מַה־בְּרִי *what ails my son?* Pr 31$_2$, מַה־שַּׁדַּי כִּי־נַעַבְדֶנּוּ *what need has the Almighty that we should serve him?* Jb 21$_{15}$. **6. how much?,** מַה־מִּנִּי יַהֲלֹךְ *how much of it will go away?* Jb 16$_6$. **7.** as indef. pron., **anything, something,** לֹא יָדַעְתִּי מָה *I did not know anything* 2 S 18$_{29}$ (or §3). **8.** appar. as combined rel. part. and antecedent, **what (ever),** מַה־אַתֶּם אֹמְרִים אֶעֱשֶׂה לָכֶם *whatever you say, I shall do for you* 2 S 21$_4$. **9.** -מַה־שֶּׁ **what(ever)** Ec 1$_9$. **10.** מָה אֲשֶׁר **what(ever)** 1QMyst 1.1$_4$. **11.** בַּמָּה **by what (means)?, how?** Ml 1$_2$. **12.** כַּמָּה **a. how many?** Gn 47$_8$. **b. how much?, how great?** Zc 2$_6$. **c. how long?** Ps 35$_{17}$. **d. how often?** Jb 21$_{17}$. **13.** עַד־כַּמֶּה **(unto) how many?** 1 K 22$_{16}$. **14.** לָמָּה **a. why?** Gn 12$_{19}$; see also לָמָּה *why?*. **b. lest** 4QD^a 5.2$_3$. **15.** שֶׁלָּמָּה **lest** CD 15$_{11}$. **16.** יַעַן מֶה **on account of what?, why?** Hg 1$_9$. **17.** עַד־מָה **until what (time)?, how long?** Ps 74$_9$. **18.** עַל־מָה **on account of what?, why?** Ps 89$_{48}$. **19.** תַּחַת מָה **on account of what?, why?** Jr 5$_{19}$. → cf. לָמָּה *why?*, מַתְּלָאָה *what a weariness!*

מָה II 15 neg. part. **1. not,** הִשְׁבַּעְתִּי אֶתְכֶם ... מַה־תָּעִירוּ וּמַה־

תְּעֹרְרוּ אֶת־הָאַהֲבָה *I adjure you ... that you do not awaken and do not arouse love* Ca 8₄. **2.** בְּלִי־מָה **absolute void** Jb 26₇.

מהה 9.3.3 vb. **Pilp., delay** perh. 1QM 11₁₈ (unless למהמה is from מְהוּמָה *discomfiture*).

Htpalp. 9.3.3 Pf. הִתְמַהְמָהְתִּי; impf. יִתְמַהְמָהּ; impv. הִתְמַהְמְהוּ; ptc. מִתְמַהְמֵהַּ; inf. הִתְמַהְמֵהַּ—**delay** (intrans.), **linger, wait,** of Y. Si 32₂₂, Israelites Is 29₉, spirit 4QShirShabb^f 23.1₁₁, vision Hb 2₃, death Si 14₁₂.

מְהוּמָה 12.1.6 n.f.—cstr. מְהוּמַת; pl. מהומות—**discomfiture, uproar, panic, disturbance,** מְהוּמַת־י׳ *discomfiture of Y.* Zc 14₁₃, מָוֶת *of death* 1 S 5₁₁. → הום *discomfit.*

מְהוּמָן 1 pr.n.m. **Mehuman.**

*[מְהוֹתָלָה] 0.0.1 n.f.—pl. מהותלות—perh. **deception** 4QBark^e 4.3₁. → התל *mock;* cf. מַהֲתַלָּה *deception.*

מְהֵיטַבְאֵל 3 pr.n.m.&f. **Mehetabel.**

מָהִיר I 1 adj. **quick,** as noun, **quick one,** מְהִר צֶדֶק *one quick of,* i.e. zealous for, *righteousness* Is 16₅. → מהר I *hasten.*

מָהִיר II 4 adj. **1. skilled, expert,** מָהִיר בְּתוֹרַת מֹשֶׁה *skilled in the law of Moses* Ezr 7₆. **2.** as noun, **one skilled,** מְהִר צֶדֶק *one skilled of,* i.e. in, *justice* Is 16₅.

מהל I 1 vb.—**Qal** 1 Ptc. pass. מָהוּל—pass. **be diluted** with (בְּ) water, of liquor Is 1₂₂.

*מהל II 0.0.1 vb.—**Qal** 0.0.1 Ptc. מוהלת—**circumcise,** of spirit 4QBéat 6.2₃. → cf. מול *circumcise,* מלל IV *circumcise.*

*מהל III 1 vb.—**Qal** 1 Ptc. pass. מָהוּל—pass. **be weakened** by (בְּ) water, of liquor Is 1₂₂.

[מַהֲלָךְ] 5.1 n.m.—cstr. מַהֲלַךְ; sf. מַהֲלָכְךָ; pl. מַהֲלְכִים—**1. journey** Ne 2₆, specif. **life-journey** Si 11₁₂. **2. passage** in temple buildings Ezk 42₄. **3.** pl. **(right of) access** Zc 3₇. → הלך *go.*

*[מַהֲלֶכֶת] 0.1 n.f. **gait** Si 42₅(M). → הלך *go.*

[מַהֲלָל] 1 n.[m.]—sf. מַהֲלָלוֹ—**praise, reputation** Pr 27₂₁. → הלל I *praise.*

מְהֻלָּל *praiseworthy,* see הלל I *praise,* pu.

מַהֲלַלְאֵל 7.0.1 pr.n.m. **Mahalalel.**

מַהֲלֻמוֹת 2 n.f.pl. **beatings** Pr 18₆ 19₂₉. → הלם *hammer.*

*מהם I 0.1 vb.—**Qal** 0.1 Pf. מהם—of furnace, **melt solid casting** Si 43₄(B).

*מהם II 0.1 vb.—**Htp.** 0.1 Impf. יתמהמה—**make oneself pleasant** Si 12₁₆.

מָהֵם, see מָה *what?,* הֵם *they.*

[מַהֲמֹרָה] 1.1 n.f.—pl. מַהֲמֹרוֹת—**pit,** perh. as filled with water, or as name for the underworld, or perh. **effusion** Ps 140₁₁ Si 12₁₆.

*[מַהְפָּךְ] 0.0.1 n.[m.]—pl. sf. מהפכיהם—**turning,** of gates or spirits 4QShirShabb^d 1.2₄. → הפך *turn.*

[מַהְפֵּכָה] 6 n.f. **overthrow,** מַהְפֵּכַת סְדֹם *overthrow of Sodom* Dt 29₂₂. → הפך *turn.*

מַהְפֶּכֶת 4 n.f. **stocks,** device for punishment, locking feet between bars of wood Jr 20₂; בֵּית הַמַּהְפֶּכֶת *house of the stocks* 2 C 16₁₀. → הפך *turn.*

מְהֻקְצָעוֹת 1 perh. n.f.pl. **corner rooms** Ezk 46₂₂. → קצע II *be the same size.*

מהר I 67.6.11 vb.—**Ni.** 4.1.6 Pf. נִמְהָרָה; ptc. נִמְהָר, נִמְהָרִים—**1a. act quickly** Si 50₁₇. **b.** of counsel, **be hurried (to destruction)** Jb 5₁₃. **2a.** ptc. as adj., **hasty, impetuous** Hb 1₆. **b.** ptc. as noun, **hasty one,** נִמְהֲרֵי־לֵב *ones hasty of mind,* i.e. anxious Is 35₄, נמהרי צדק *ones hasty of,* i.e. eager for, *righteousness* 1QH 13₂₁.

Pi. 63.4.5 Pf. מִהַר, מִהֲרָה; impf. יְמַהֵר; impv. מַהֵר (מַהֲרָה), מַהֲרוּ; ptc. מְמַהֵר (מַהֵר), מְמַהֲרוֹת; inf. מַהֵר—**1. hasten, come quickly, go quickly,** of Y. Is 5₁₉, warrior 1 C 12₉, day Zp 1₁₄, misfortune Jr 48₁₆. **2. hasten, act quickly, a.** מהר as auxiliary with another verb, **hastily, quickly,** וַתְּמַהֵר וַתֵּרֶד מֵעַל הַחֲמוֹר *then she quickly dismounted from the ass* 1 S 25₂₃. **b.** מהר alone, **act quickly** 2 C 24₅. **3.** trans., **a. bring someone quickly** Est 5₅. **b. prepare food quickly** Gn 18₆. **4.** ptc. as adj., **swift, keen,** of witness Ml 3₅.

Hi. 0.1 Ptc. ממהיר—**hasten** Si 42₅(B).

→ מָהִיר I *quick,* מַהֵר *quickly,* מְהֵרָה *haste.*

מהר II 3 vb.—**Qal** 3 Pf. מְהָרוּ; impf. יִמְהָרֶנָּה; inf. abs. מָהֹר—**acquire** (with bride-gift) young woman as (לְ) wife Ex 22₁₅. → מֹהַר *bride-gift.*

*מהר III 1 vb.—**Qal** 1 Pf. מָהָרוּ—**serve** another (god) Ps 16₄.

*מהר IV 1 vb.—**Ni.** 1 Pf. נִמְהָרָה—of counsel, **be betrayed** Jb 5₁₃.

מַהֵר 14.0.4 adv. **quickly,** pi. inf. abs. of מהר *hasten,* רִדְפוּ מַהֵר אַחֲרֵיהֶם *pursue them quickly* Jos 2₅. → מהר I *hasten.*

מֹהַר 3 n.[m.] **bride-gift,** מֹהַר הַבְּתוּלֹת *bride-gift of the young women* Ex 22₁₆. → מהר II *acquire.*

*[**מָהֵר**] n.[m.] **warrior,** in name *Maher-shalal-hash-baz* Is 8₁.₃ (both if em.).

מְהֵרָה 20.0.0.2 n.f. **1.** as noun, **haste, speed** Ec 4₁₂. **2.** as adv., **hastily, quickly, soon,** עֲלֵה אֵלֵינוּ מְהֵרָה *come up to us quickly* Jos 10₆. → מהר I *hasten.*

מַהֲרַי 3 pr.n.m. **Maharai.**

מַהֵר שָׁלָל חָשׁ בַּז 2 pr.n.m. **Maher-shalal-hash-baz.**

[**מַהֲתַלָּה**] 1.0.1 n.f.—pl. מַהֲתַלּוֹת—**deception** Is 30₁₀. → התל *mock;* cf. מְהוֹתָלָה *deception.*

*__מוֹ__ 6 n.[m.] **water,** מוֹ־נָחַל *water of a wadi* Jb 6₁₅, מוֹ־שָׁלֶג *water of snow,* i.e. snow-water Jb 9₃₀(Kt). → מַיִם *water,* מַיָּה *water.*

מוֹאָב 178.1.4.1 pr.n.m. (& f.) **Moab.**

מוֹאָבִי 16.0.2 gent. **Moabite.**

מוֹאל, see מוּל *front.*

מוֹבָא 2 n.[m.] **1. entrance** of temple Ezk 43₁₁. **2. coming in,** מוֹצָאָיו וּמוֹבָאָיו *its going out and its coming in,* referring to one's activity as a whole 2 S 3₂₅(Qr). → בוא *come.*

מוג I 17.1.7 vb.—**Qal** 4 Impf. תָּמוּג; + waw וַתָּמוֹג; inf. מוּג—**1.** intrans., **melt, faint,** of heart Ezk 21₂₀, earth Am 9₅. **2.** of Y., **cause** people **to melt** on account of (בְּיַד) sin Is 64₆.

Ni. 8.1.2 Pf. נָמוֹג; ptc. נְמוֹגִים—**1. melt away, faint, tremble,** of persons Ex 15₁₅, earth Ps 75₄, palace Na 2₇. **2.** ptc. as noun, **trembling one** 1QM 14₆.

Pol. 2 תְּמֹגְגֶנִּי—of Y., **dissipate, soften** person Jb 30₂₂, earth Ps 65₁₁ (+ בְּ *with* showers).

Htpol. 3.0.5 Pf. הִתְמֹגָגוּ; impf. תִּתְמוֹגָג—**melt away, dissolve,** of soul, i.e. courage Ps 107₂₆, hills Am 9₁₃.

*__מוג__ II 17.1.7 vb.—**Qal** 4 Impf. תָּמוּג; + waw וַתָּמוֹג; inf. מוּג—**1.** intrans., **waver,** of heart Ezk 21₂₀, earth Am 9₅. **2.** of Y., **cause** people **to waver** on account of (בְּיַד) sin Is 64₆ (or §3). **3.** of Y., perh. **turn away, depart from** people on account of (בְּיַד) sin Is 64₆.

Ni. 8.1.2 Pf. נָמוֹג; ptc. נְמוֹגִים—**1. waver,** of persons Ex 15₁₅, earth Ps 75₄, palace Na 2₇. **2.** ptc. as noun, **trembling one** 1QM 14₆.

Pol. 2 תְּמֹגְגֶנִּי—of Y., **cause to waver,** obj. person Jb 30₂₂, earth Ps 65₁₁ (+ בְּ *with* showers).

Htpol. 3.0.5 Pf. הִתְמֹגָגוּ; impf. תִּתְמוֹגָג—**waver,** of soul, i.e. courage Ps 107₂₆, hills Am 9₁₃.

מוד, see מיד *shake, convulse.*

[**מוֹד**] I *strength,* see מְאֹד *strength.*

*[**מוֹד**] II 0.0.1 n.[m.]—sf. מודי—**love** 11QPsᵃ 22₁.

*[**מוֹדָה**] n.f. perh. **measure** Judaean Hills ost. 1₃ (others מקדה *Makkedah*). → (?) מדד *measure.*

מוט 37.8.11 vb.—**Qal.** 12.2.3 Pf. מָטָה, מָטוּ; impf. תָּמוּט; ptc. מָטִים; ptc. pass. Si מוט; inf. abs. מוֹט; cstr. מוֹט—**1. totter, slip,** of person Pr 25₂₆, foot Dt 32₃₅. **2. shake,** of earth Is 24₁₉, mountains Ps 46₃, kingdom Ps 46₇, covenant Is 54₁₀. **3.** pass., **be made to slip,** of person Si 13₂₁.

Ni. 23.5.3 Pf. נָמוֹטּוּ; impf. יִמּוֹט; ptc. Si נמוט—**1. be shaken, be moved, move,** of world Ps 93₁, earth's foundations Ps 82₅, folds of crocodile's flesh Jb 41₁₅, idol Is 40₂₀, loyalty Si 40₁₇(B). **2. be made to slip,** of person Ps 13₅. **3. be made to drop** upon (עַל) people, of coals Ps 140₁₁(Qr).

Hi. 2.0.1 Impf. יָמִיטוּ—**1. let fall, drop,** perh. **dislodge** upon (עַל) someone coals Ps 140₁₁(Kt), trouble Ps 55₄. **2. shake, tremble,** of abyss 4QHymnB 1₄.

Pol. 0.0.1 Ptc. מוטטי—ptc. as noun, **one who totters** 11QPsᵃ 19₂.

Htpol. 1.1.3 Pf. הִתְמוֹטְטָה; impf. Q תתמוטט; ptc. Si מתמוטט—**1. stagger** away from (מִן) way of Y.'s heart 1QH 14₂₁. **2. be shaken,** of earth Is 24₁₉. **3.** ptc. as noun, **totterer,** perh. **capricious one** 4Q424 1₄ (מתמ[ו]טט).

→ מוֹט I *shaking.*

מוֹט I 3 n.[m.] **shaking, slipping** Ps 55₂₃. → מוט *totter.*

מוֹט II 4 n.[m.]—sf. מֹטֵהוּ—**1. pole,** for carrying cluster of grapes Nm 13₂₃. **2. frame,** for carrying cultic objects Nm 4₁₀.₁₂. **3. bar** of yoke Na 1₁₃.

*__מוֹט__ III 2 n.[m.] **Quagmire,** as name for the underworld Ps 66₉ 121₃.

מוֹטָה 12 n.f.—pl. מוֹטוֹת (מֹטֹת)—**1. bar** of yoke, **yoke** Lv 26₁₃ Jr 28₁₀. **2. pole,** for carrying ark 1 C 15₁₅.

*[**מוֹטַח**] n.[m.] **club,** מֹטַח תַּשְׁמִידֵם יי *with a club you annihilate them, O Y.* Lm 3₆₆ (if em. מִתַּחַת שְׁמֵי יי *from under the heavens of Y.*).

מוך 5.1 vb.—**Qal** 5.1 Impf. יָמוּךְ; + waw וּמָךְ; ptc. מָךְ—**1.**

become poor Lv 25$_{25}$. **2.** ptc. as noun, **poor one, downtrodden one** Si 12$_5$. → cf. מכך *be brought low.*

*[מוֹכֶן] 0.0.1 n.[m.] **locust,** coll. Is 51$_{6(1QIsa^b)}$ (MT כְּמוֹ־כֵן *like gnats,* or *like thus,* i.e. likewise).

מוּל I 30.0.8 vb.—**Qal** 12.0.7 Pf. מָלוֹ, מַל; + waw וּמַלְתָּה; וַיָּמָל; ptc. pass. מָלִים, מוּל; inf. Q מוּל—**1. circumcise flesh** of foreskin Gn 17$_{23}$, foreskin of heart Dt 10$_{16}$, heart Dt 30$_6$, son Gn 21$_4$. **2.** pass., **be circumcised,** of people Jos 5$_5$.

Ni. 18.0.1 Pf. נִמּוֹל; impf. יִמּוֹל; ptc. נִמֹּלִים; inf. abs. הִמּוֹל; cstr. הִמּוֹל—**be circumcised,** of male Gn 17$_{10}$, flesh of foreskin Lv 12$_3$.

→ מוּלָה *circumcision;* cf. מהל II *circumcise,* מלל IV *circumcise.*

*מוּל II 3 vb.—**Hi.** 3 Impf. אֲמִילַם—**fend off, drive away** nations Ps 118$_{10.11.12}$.

מוּל I 36.0.1 n.[m.]—מוּל (מואל); cstr. מוּל; sf. מֻלִי—**1.** as noun, **front,** מוּל מֶחֱזָה *front of window* 1 K 7$_5$. **2.** as prep., **a.** מוּל alone, **in front of, before, opposite** Dt 1$_1$. **b.** אֶל־מוּל **in front of, before** Jos 9$_1$. **c.** אֶל־מוּל פְּנֵי **in front of, at the front of** Nm 8$_2$. **d.** מִמּוּל **from the front of, from before, at the front of, (from) opposite** 2 S 5$_{23}$. **e.** מִמּוּל פְּנֵי **from the front of** Ex 28$_{27}$.

*[מוֹלָד] 0.0.11 n.[m.]—pl. מולדים; cstr. מולדי; sf. מולדיו—**1. birth, origin, source,** מולדי עת *births of time,* i.e. moments when a period of time begins 1QH 20$_8$. **2.** perh. also **one born, offspring,** מולדי עולה *offspring of injustice* 1QMyst 1.1$_5$. → ילד *give birth.*

מוֹלָדָה 4.0.0.1 pl.n. **Moladah.**

[מוֹלֶדֶת] 22 n.f.—sf. מוֹלַדְתּוֹ; pl. sf. מוֹלְדוֹתַיִךְ—**1. birth,** or perh. better **birthplace,** אֶרֶץ מוֹלַדְתִּי *land of my birth* Gn 24$_7$. **2. kindred,** אָבְדַן מוֹלַדְתִּי *destruction of my kindred* Est 8$_6$. **3. one born, offspring,** מוֹלֶדֶת אָבִיךָ *one born of your father* Lv 18$_{11}$. → ילד *give birth.*

[מוּלָה] 1 n.f.—pl. מולת—**circumcision** Ex 4$_{26}$. → מוּל I *circumcise.*

מוֹלִיד 1 pr.n.m. **Molid.**

מוּם 21.4.7 n.m.—מְאוּם (mss מָאוּם); sf. מוּמוֹ; pl. sf. Q מומיה—**1. physical blemish, defect, disfigurement, a.** in human Ca 4$_7$. **b.** in animal, unsuitable for sacrifice Nm 19$_2$. **2. moral blemish, defect** Jb 11$_{15}$.

מומכן, see מְמוּכָן *Memucan.*

[מוּסָב] 1 n.[m.] **enclosure,** מוּסַב־הַבַּיִת *enclosure of the house* Ezk 41$_7$. → סבב I *surround.*

[מוֹסָד] I 13.0.13 n.m.—pl. Q מוסדים, מוֹסָדוֹת; cstr. מוֹסְדוֹת, מוֹסְדֵי—**1. foundation,** מוסד אמת *foundation of truth* 1QS 5$_5$, מֹסְדֵי אָרֶץ *foundations of the earth* Mc 6$_2$. **2. ruins, remains,** מוֹסְדֵי דוֹר־וָדוֹר *remains of many generations* Is 58$_{12}$. → יסד I *establish.*

*[מוֹסָד] II 0.0.2 n.[m.] **council,** מוסדי אנשים *councils of men* 4QShirShabb^a 2$_2$. → cf. סוֹד *council.*

מוּסָד 2 n.m. **1. foundation,** פִּנַּת יִקְרַת מוּסָד *a precious cornerstone of a foundation* Is 28$_{16}$. **2. founding, laying of foundation,** מוּסַד בֵּית־י׳ *founding of the temple of Y.* 2 C 8$_{16}$. → יסד I *establish.*

מוּסָדָה 2 n.f.—pl. cstr. Qr מוּסְדוֹת—**1. foundation** Ezk 41$_{8(Qr)}$. **2. appointment** Is 30$_{32}$. → יסד I *establish.*

[מוּסָךְ] I 1 n.[m.]—cstr. Qr מוּסַךְ (Kt מיסך)—**covered way** 2 K 16$_{18}$. → סכך I *cover.*

*[מוּסָךְ] II 1 n.[m.]—cstr. Qr מוּסַךְ (Kt מיסך)—**fence, rampart** 2 K 16$_{18}$.

*[מוּסָךְ] III 1 n.[m.]—cstr. Qr מוּסַךְ (Kt מיסך)—**bench, divan** 2 K 16$_{18}$.

*[מוֹסֵר] I 1 n.[m.]—sf. מֹסְרָם—**bond** Jb 33$_{16}$.

*[מוּסָר] II 4 n.[m.]—cstr. מוּסַר; sf. מֻסָרָם—**basis, essence** Jr 10$_8$ Jb 33$_{16}$ Pr 7$_{22}$ 15$_{33}$.

[מוֹסֵר] 3.0.2 n.m.—pl. cstr. מוֹסְרֵי; sf. מוֹסְרֵיכֶם, מוֹסֵרֶי—**bond, fetter,** מוֹסְרֵי צַוָּארֵךְ *bonds of your neck* Is 52$_2$. → אסר *bind.*

מוּסָר 50.14.11 n.m.—cstr. מוּסַר; sf. מוּסָרִי, מֻסָרָם—**1. discipline, as instruction, training,** מוסר שכל *instruction of wisdom* Si 50$_{27}$. **2. discipline, as correction, chastisement,** שֵׁבֶט מוּסָר *rod of chastisement* Pr 22$_{15}$. **3. warning** Ezk 5$_{15}$. → יסר I *discipline.*

[מוֹסֵרָה] I 8 n.f.—pl. מוֹסֵרוֹת; cstr. מֹסְרוֹת; sf. מוֹסְרוֹתֶיךָ—**bond, fetter, thong** of yoke Jr 2$_{20}$ 27$_2$.

מוֹסֵרָה II 1 pl.n. **Moserah.**

[מוֹעָד] I 1 n.[m.]—pl. sf. מוֹעָדָיו—**place of assembly,** in army Is 14$_{31}$. → יעד *appoint.*

*[מוֹעָד] II 1 n.[m.]—pl. sf. מוֹעָדָיו—**horde** Is 14$_{31}$.

מוֹעֵד I 223.6.140 n.m.—מֹעֵד; sf. מוֹעֲדוֹ; pl. מוֹעֲדִים, מוֹעֲדוֹת; cstr. מֹעֲדֵי; sf. מוֹעֲדַי—**1. meeting, assembly,** אֹהֶל מוֹעֵד *tent of meeting* Ex 27$_{21}$, קְרִאֵי מוֹעֵד *summoned* *ones*, i.e. members, *of the assembly* Nm 16$_2$. **2. meeting place, appointed place,** מוֹעֲדֵי־אֵל *meeting places of God* Ps 74$_8$. **3. appointed time, due season,** מועד אל *appointed time of God* 1QM 1$_8$, מוֹעֵד קֵץ *appointed time of the end* Dn 8$_{19}$; oft. in general, **time, season,** מועד קציר *season of harvest* 1QS 10$_7$. **4. festival, (time of) appointed feast,** מועד שבת *festival of the sabbath* 4QRitPurB 33.4$_1$. **5. agreement, appointment,** perh. **appointed signal** Jg 20$_{38}$. → יעד *appoint*.

*[מוֹעֵד] II $_{0.1}$ adj. **fresh, tender,** as noun, **fresh figs** Si 50$_8$.

מוּעָדָה $_1$ n.f. **appointment,** עָרֵי הַמּוּעָדָה *cities of the appointment*, i.e. cities appointed (for refuge) Jos 20$_9$. → יעד *appoint*.

מוֹעַדְיָה $_1$ pr.n.m. **Moadiah.**

מוּעָף I $_1$ n.[m.] **darkness** Is 8$_{23}$. → עוף II *be dark*.

*מוּעָף II $_1$ n.[m.] **gleam, lustre** Is 8$_{23}$.

*מוּעָף III $_1$ n.[m.] **flight, escape** Is 8$_{23}$.

[מוֹעֵצָה] I $_7$ n.f.—pl. מֹעֵצוֹת; sf. מֹעֲצוֹתָם—**counsel, plan** Ps 5$_{11}$. → יעץ *advise*.

*[מוֹעֵצָה] II $_3$ n.f.—pl. מֹעֵצוֹת; sf. מֹעֲצוֹתֵיהֶם—**disobedience** Jr 7$_{24}$. → cf. מְעֵצָה *disobedience*.

מוּעָקָה I $_1$ n.f. **affliction, distress** Ps 66$_{11}$. → עוק I *press*.

*מוּעָקָה II $_1$ n.f. **ulcer** Ps 66$_{11}$.

מופעת, see מֵיפַעַת *Mephaath*.

מוֹפֵת $_{36.2.14}$ n.m.—sf. מוֹפֶתְכֶם; pl. מֹפְתִים; cstr. Q מופתי; sf. מוֹפְתַי—**1. wonder, sign, portent, miracle,** oft. of Y. Dt 6$_{22}$ Ps 105$_5$, also of humans 4QShir[b] 49.2$_5$; אַנְשֵׁי מוֹפֵת *men of*, i.e. as, *a sign* Zc 3$_8$. **2. target** of archers Ps 71$_7$.

מוֹץ, see מֹץ *chaff*.

מוֹצָא I n.m. $_{27.3.19.1}$—cstr. מֹצָא; sf. מוֹצָאֲךָ; pl. cstr. מוֹצָאֵי; sf. מוֹצָאָיו—**1. place of going out, a. exit, way out** of temple Ezk 43$_{11}$. **b. place of going out** of sun Ps 19$_7$, **the east** Ps 75$_7$. **c. source, spring** of water Is 58$_{11}$. **d. mine** Jb 28$_1$. **e. growing-place** Jb 38$_{27}$. **f. point of departure** Nm 33$_2$. **2. act of going out, a. going out, exit, departure,** of Y. Ho 6$_3$, person 2 S 3$_{25}$, word Dn 9$_{25}$, evening and morning 1QM 14$_{14}$. **b. export** of horses 1 K 10$_{28}$. **c. growth** of seed Si 37$_{11}$ (Bmg, D). **3. that which goes out, a. utterance** Dt 8$_3$. **b. one who goes out,** מוֹצָאֵי גוֹלָה *ones who go (out) into exile* Ezk 12$_4$. **c.** perh. **crop** Jb 38$_{27}$. → יצא *go out*.

מוֹצָא II $_5$ pr.n.m. **Moza.**

*[מוֹצָא] III $_1$ n.[m.]—pl. cstr. מוֹצָאֵי—**star, sparkler** Ps 65$_9$.

*מוֹצָא IV $_1$ n.[m.] **smelter** Jb 28$_1$.

[מוֹצָאָה] $_2$ n.f.—pl. Qr מוֹצָאוֹת; sf. מוֹצָאֹתָיו—**1. origin** Mc 5$_1$. **2. latrine** 2 K 10$_{27(Qr)}$. → יצא *go out*.

מוּצָק I $_{2.1}$ n.m. **1. casting** of metal 1 K 7$_{37}$. **2. solid mass** of dust Jb 38$_{38}$. → יצק *pour out*.

מוּצָק II $_3$ n.[m.] **1. constraint** Jb 36$_{16}$. **2. distress** Is 8$_{23}$. → צוק I *constrain*.

*מוּצָק III $_1$ n.[m.] **outpouring,** מוּצָק אַף *outpouring of (his) nostrils* Jb 37$_{10}$ (if em. מוּצָק : אַף).

מוּצָק IV *cast object, casting*, see יצק *pour out*, ho.

[מוּצֶקֶת] I $_2$ n.f.—sf. מֻצַקְתּוֹ; pl. מוּצָקוֹת—**1. casting** 2 C 4$_3$. **2. pipe,** of lamp Zc 4$_2$. → יצק *pour out*.

*[מוּצֶקֶת] II $_1$ n.f.—pl. מוּצָקוֹת—**cast metal** Zc 4$_2$.

מוק $_1$ vb.—**Hi.** $_1$ Impf. יָמִיקוּ—**mock** Ps 73$_8$.

מוֹקֵד $_2$ n.m.—pl. cstr. מוֹקְדֵי—**hearth, burning** Is 33$_{14}$. → יקד *be kindled*.

מוֹקְדָה $_1$ n.f. **hearth** of altar Lv 6$_2$. → יקד *be kindled*.

*[מוֹקִר] $_{0.0.0.1}$ pr.n.[m.] **Mokir.**

מוֹקֵשׁ I $_{27.3.6}$ n.m.—pl. מוֹקְשִׁים, Si מוקשת; cstr. מוֹקְשֵׁי, מֹקְשׁוֹת—**snare,** or specif. **striker,** part of trap that falls on its victim, or **bait, decoy,** for bird Am 3$_5$; in ref. to Y. Is 8$_{14}$, wife 1 S 18$_{21}$, wine Si 34$_{30(B)}$, death 2 S 22$_6$||Ps 18$_6$. → יקשׁ *trap*.

*מוֹקֵשׁ II $_1$ n.[m.] **boomerang** Am 3$_5$.

מור I $_{16.1.8}$ vb.—**Qal** $_1$ Ptc. מֵרִים—**obtain, acquire disgrace** Pr 3$_{35}$.

Ni. $_1$ Pf. נָמַר—**be changed,** of scent of wine Jr 48$_{11}$.

Hi. $_{14.1.8}$ Pf. הֵמִיר; impf. יָמִיר (יָמֵר, יָמֵר); inf. abs. הָמֵר; cstr. הָמִיר—**1a.** trans., **change** person 1QH 10$_{18}$. **b.** intrans., **change, alter,** of earth Ps 46$_3$. **2. exchange** beast for (בְּ) beast Lv 27$_{10}$, glory for shame Ho 4$_7$; abs. Ezk 48$_{14}$.

→ תְּמוּרָה *exchange*; cf. מרה II *change*.

[מור] II vb. **Ni., quake, shake,** of earth Ps 46$_3$ (if em. בְּהָמִיר *when it changes* to בְּהִמּוֹר *when it quakes*).

מוֹר, see מֹר *myrrh*.

מוֹרָא I $_{12.1.3}$ n.m.—מֹרָא (מוֹרָה); sf. מוֹרָאִי; pl. מוֹרָאִים—**1.**

fear, dread of Israelites Dt 11_{25}. **2. fear, reverence,** due to Y., אַיֵּה מוֹרָאִי *where is my reverence?* Ml 1_{6}. **3. (object of) fear, reverence** Is 8_{12}. **4. terror, terrible deed, fearful thing,** displaying power of Y. Dt 26_{8}. → ירא I *fear.*

מוֹרָא II, see מוֹרָה I *razor.*

מוֹרַג 3 n.m.—pl. מוֹרִגִּים—**threshing sledge** 2 S 24_{22}.

מוֹרָד I 5.0.1 n.[m.]—cstr. מוֹרַד—**1. descent, slope,** as geographical term Jos 10_{11}. **2. hanging,** מַעֲשֵׂה מוֹרָד *work of hanging,* perh. spiral or pendant work 1 K 7_{29}. → ירד I *go down.*

***מוֹרָד** II 1 n.[m.] **watering-place** Mc 1_{4}.

***מוֹרָד** III 1 n.[m.] **rivulet** Mc 1_{4}.

מוֹרָה I 3 n.m.—mss מורא—**razor** Jg 13_{5}. → ערה *be bare.*

מוֹרָה II, see מוֹרָא *fear.*

***מוֹרָה** III 1 n.f. **muzzle** Ps 9_{21}. → ירה III *teach.*

מוֹרֶה I 3 n.[m.] **early rain, from end of October to beginning of December** Jl 2_{23}. → ירה II *water.*

מוֹרֶה II 3 pl.n. **Moreh.**

מוֹרֶה III *teacher,* see ירה III *teach,* hi.

[מוֹרֶה] IV *archer,* see ירה I *throw,* hi.

מוֹרֶה V *rebel,* see מרה I *rebel.*

מוֹרִיָּה 2 pl.n. **Moriah.**

[מוֹרָשׁ] I 2 n.[m.]—cstr. מוֹרַשׁ; pl. sf. מוֹרָשֵׁיהֶם—**possession** Is 14_{23} Ob$_{17}$. → ירשׁ I *take possession of.*

[מוֹרָשׁ] II 1 n.[m.] **desire,** מוֹרָשֵׁי לְבָבִי *desires of my heart* Jb 17_{11}. → cf. אֲרֶשֶׁת *desire.*

***[מוֹרָשׁ]** III 1 n.[m.] **string,** מוֹרָשֵׁי לְבָבִי *strings of my heart* Jb 17_{11}.

מוֹרָשָׁה 9 n.f. **possession,** of land Ex 6_{8}, people Ezk 25_{4}, law Dt 33_{4}. → ירשׁ I *take possession of.*

מוֹרֶשֶׁת גַּת 1 pl.n. **Moresheth-gath.**

מוֹרַשְׁתִּי 2 gent. **Morashtite.**

מוּשׁ I, מִישׁ 20.4.13 vb.—**Qal** 18.4.13 Pf. מָשׁוּ; impf. יָמוּשׁ (יָמִישׁ)—**1a. depart** from (מִן) a place Jg 6_{18}, from within (מִתּוֹךְ) tent Ex 33_{11}. **b.** abs., **move,** of mountains Is 54_{10}. **c. be removed** from (מֵאֵת) Israelites, of Y.'s loyalty Is 54_{10}. **2. cease** from (מִן) yielding fruit, i.e. to yield fruit, of tree Jr 17_{8}. **3. be lacking, missing** from (מֵאֵת) the council of the community, of priest 1QS 6_{3}; from (מִן) mouth, of words Is 59_{21}. **4.** of Y., **remove** guilt Zc 3_{9}.

Hi. 3 Impf. יָמִישׁ—**1. remove,** i.e. free, one's neck Mc 2_{3}. **2. dismiss** commandment Jb 23_{12} (unless qal).

מוּשׁ II 3.0.1 vb.—**Qal** 1.0.1 + waw וַאֲמֻשְׁךָ—**feel** someone Gn 27_{21}.

Hi. 2 + waw יְמִישׁוּן; impv. Qr, mss הֲמִשֵׁנִי (Kt הימשני, i.e. ימשׁ hi.)—**1.** abs., **feel,** of idols Ps 115_{7}. **2. let** someone **feel** something Jg $16_{26(Qr,\ mss)}$.

→ cf. משׁשׁ *feel,* ימשׁ *touch.*

מוֹשָׁב 44.2.36 n.m.—cstr. מוֹשַׁב; sf. מוֹשָׁבִי; pl. Q מושבות; cstr. מוֹשְׁבֵי, Q משבות; sf. מוֹשְׁבוֹתֵיהֶם (מוֹשְׁבוֹתָם)—**1. seat, place of sitting,** at meal 1 S 20_{18}, as a throne Ezk 28_{2}. **2a. (sitting) company, assembly** of elders Ps 107_{32}. **b. session, (meeting of) assembly** of the Many 1QS 6_{8}. **3a. dwelling place** of person Ex 12_{20}, of Y., i.e. Zion Ps 132_{13}. **b. inhabited place** Ezk 34_{13}. **4. dwelling, habitation,** אֶרֶץ מוֹשְׁבֹתֵיכֶם *land of your dwelling* Nm 15_{2}. **5. (length of) time of dwelling** Ex 12_{40}. **6. those who dwell,** כֹּל מוֹשַׁב בֵּית־צִיבָא *all those who dwelt of,* i.e. in, *the house of Ziba* 2 S 9_{12}. **7. situation, position, office,** מושב כבוד *office of honour* Si 7_{4}. → ישׁב *sit.*

***[מוֹשָׁבָה]** n.f. **settlement, transportation** Lm 1_{7} (if em. מְשַׁבַּתֶּהָ *her inactivity* to מוֹשָׁבָתָהּ *her transportation*).

***[מוֹשֶׁבֶת]** 0.0.1 n.f. **dwelling** CD 11_{10}. → ישׁב *sit.*

מוּשִׁי I 8 pr.n.m. **Mushi.**

מוּשִׁי II 2 gent. **Mushite.**

מוֹשִׁיעַ *saviour, advocate,* see ישׁע *save,* hi.

[מוֹשָׁעָה] 1 n.f. **salvation,** אֵל לְמוֹשָׁעוֹת *a God of salvation* Ps 68_{21}. → ישׁע *save.*

מוּת 841.12.75.1 vb.—**Qal** 627.12.50.1 Pf. מֵת, מַתְנוּ; impf. יָמוּת; + waw וַיָּמָת (וַיָּמֹת); impv. מֻת; ptc. מֵת (מֵתוֹ), מֵתָה, מֵתִים, (מֵתֶיךָ), מֵתֵי; inf. abs. מוֹת; cstr. מוּת (מוֹת, מוֹתוֹ, מוּתֵנוּ)—**1.** intrans., **a. die, be dead,** of human being Gn 5_{5}, animal Is 50_{2}, tree-stump Jb 14_{8}, deities Ps 82_{7}. **b. be put to death** Ex 22_{18}. **c. perish,** of land Gn 47_{19}, wisdom Jb 12_{2}. **2.** trans., with cognate accus., **die a death,** תָּמֹת נַפְשִׁי מוֹת יְשָׁרִים *may I die the death of the upright* Nm 23_{10}, מְמוֹתֵי תַחֲלֻאִים יָמֻתוּ *they will die gruesome deaths* Jr 16_{4}. **3.** ptc., **a.** as noun, (1) **dead (one),** human being 1 K3_{22}, animal Ex 21_{34}. (2) מֵתִים **Death,** i.e. **place of death** Ps 88_{6}. **b.** as adj., **dead,** of human being Dt

25_6, corpse Is 37_{36}, dog 1 S 24_{15}. **4.** לַמּוּת as superlative, **very, exceedingly,** lit. 'to (the point of) death' Jg 16_{16} 2 K 20_1.

Pol. 9 Pf. מֹתֲתִי; impf. תְּמוֹתֵת; impv. מוֹתְתֵנִי; ptc. מְמוֹתֵת; inf. מוֹתֵת—**kill, put human being to death** Jg 9_{54}.

Hi. 138.0.10 Pf. הֵמִית, הֱמִתֶּם; impf. יָמִית; + waw וַיָּמֶת, וַיְמִיתוּ; impv. הָמִיתוּ, הֲמִיתֵנִי; ptc. מֵמִית, מְמִיתִים; inf. abs. הָמֵת; cstr. הָמִית (הֲמִיתוֹ)—**1. put to death, kill, slay, a.** obj. human being; subj. Y. Gn 18_{25}, human being Gn 37_{18} (in murder) Lv 20_4 (in execution), animal 1 K 13_{24}. **b.** obj. animal; subj. Y. Ps 105_{29}, human being 1 S 17_{35}. **2. cause the death of** someone 1 K 17_{18}.

Ho. 67.0.15 Pf. הוּמַת, הֻמְתוּ; impf. יוּמַת; ptc. מוּמָת, מוּמָתִים—**be put to death, killed,** of human being Lv 19_{20} (by execution) 2 K 11_2 (by murder), animal Lv 20_{16}.

→ מָוֶת *death,* מָמוֹת *death,* תְּמוּתָה *death.*

מָוֶת 155.23.30 n.m.—Si מוות; cstr. מוֹת; sf. מוֹתִי; pl. cstr. מוֹתֵי; sf. מֹתָיו—**death, 1.** event of death, מוֹת אַבְרָהָם *death of Abraham* Gn 25_{11}. **2.** state of death, פֶּן־אִישַׁן הַמָּוֶת *lest I sleep the sleep of death* Ps 13_4. **3.** manner of death, הַכְמוֹת נָבָל יָמוּת אַבְנֵר *should Abner have died the death of an outcast?* 2 S 3_{33}. **4.** death as **a.** deserved, אִישׁ מָוֶת *man of,* i.e. deserving, *death* 1 K 2_{26}. **b.** undeserved Pr 24_{11}. **5a.** death as suffering, destruction, specif. **plague** Jr 15_2. **b.** death as danger, premature end of life Jb 5_{20}. **6.** death as release from suffering Jb 3_{21}. **7.** death opp. life Dt 30_{15}. **8.** perh. as superlative, **a.** in cstr., חֶבְלֵי־מָוֶת *pains of death,* i.e. terrible pains Ps 18_5. **b.** with prep., חָרָה־לִי עַד־מָוֶת *I am angry unto death,* i.e. extremely angry Jon 4_9. **9.** death personified, as deity, **Death, Mot** 2 S 22||Ps 18_5. **10.** place of the dead Is 38_{18}. → מות *die;* cf. צַלְמָוֶת *shadow of death.*

מוֹתָר 3.0.1 n.m.—cstr. מוֹתַר; pl. sf. Q מותריכה—**abundance, profit, advantage** Pr 14_{23}. → יתר *exceed.*

[מַז], see מַזְדַּי *Mazdai.*

*[מֵז] 0.0.0.2 n.[m.] **extract,** מז צמקים *extract of,* i.e. wine or syrup made from, *raisins* Lachish inscr. 30. → cf. (?) מִיץ *pressing.*

מִזְבֵּחַ 400.3.46 n.m.—+ ה- of direction מִזְבֵּחָה; cstr. מִזְבַּח; sf. מִזְבְּחִי, מִזְבַּחֲךָ; pl. מִזְבְּחוֹת; sf. מִזְבְּחֹתֶיךָ—**altar, a.** usu. for sacrifice to Y., מִזְבַּח י׳ *altar of Y.* Lv 17_6, מִזְבֵּחַ לי׳ *an altar to Y.* Gn 8_{20}, מִזְבַּח הָעֹלָה *altar of burnt offering* Ex 30_{28}, הַקְּטֹרֶת *of incense* 1 C 6_{34}; made of wood Ex 27_1||38_1, earth Ex 20_{24}, stones Ex 20_{25}, bronze Ex 38_{30}; sometimes as place to seek sanctuary 1 K 1_{50}. **b.** for other gods: Baal Jg 6_{25}, host of heaven 2 K 21_5||2 C 33_5. → זבח *sacrifice.*

*[מִזְבָּל] n.[m.] **dwelling,** שְׁאוֹל מִזְּבֻל לוֹ *Sheol is his dwelling place* Ps 49_{15} (if em. מִזְּבֻל *without a dwelling place*). → זבל II *dwell.*

[מֶזֶג] 1 n.m.—מָזֶג—**mixed wine** Ca 7_3.

*[מַזְדַּי] 0.0.0.4 pr.n.m. **Mazdaeus.**

[מָזֶה] I 1 adj.—pl. cstr. מְזֵי—**sucked dry, emaciated** by famine Dt 32_{24}.

*[מָזֶה] II 1 adj.—pl. cstr. מְזֵי—**thin, weakened** by famine Dt 32_{24}.

*[מָזֶה] III n.m. **storeplace, repository,** מזה ברית *repository of the covenant* 1QH 13_9 (if em. מיה perh. *water*). → cf. מָזוּ *storehouse.*

מַזֶּה, see מָה *what,* זֶה *this.*

מִזָּה 3 pr.n.m. **Mizzah.**

*מִזֶּה 1 n.m. **spurt** of wine from cup of Y. Ps 75_9 (unless מִזֶּה *from this*). → נזה *spurt.*

[מָזוּ] 1 n.m.—pl. sf. מְזָוֵינוּ—**storehouse, granary** Ps 144_{13}. → cf. מָזֶה III *storeplace.*

מְזוּזָה 19.0.1 n.f.—cstr. מְזוּזַת; sf. מְזוּזָתִי; pl. מְזוּזֹת; sf. Q מזוזותיו—**doorpost, gatepost** of house Ex 12_7, palace 1 K 7_5, temple 1 S 1_9, city gate Jg 16_3.

מָזוֹן 2.0.1 n.[m.] **food, provisions** Gn 45_{23}. → זון *feed.*

מָזוֹר I 3.0.1 n.[m.]—sf. מְזֹרוֹ—**wound(s)** Ho 5_{13}. → זור II *squeeze.*

*מָזוֹר II 3.0.1 n.[m.]—sf. מְזֹרוֹ—**sore, ulcer, boil** Ho 5_{13}.

*מָזוֹר III 3.0.1 n.[m.] **running sore** Ho 5_{13}. → זור II *squeeze.*

*מָזוֹר IV 1 n.[m.] **trap, net, noose** Ob 7. → זור II *squeeze.*

*[מְזוֹרוֹת] I 0.0.1 n.[f.]pl. **rotten eggs** 1QH 10_{27}.

*[מַזּוֹרוֹת] II 0.0.1 n.[f.]pl. **catapults** 1QH 10_{27}.

*[מַזּוֹרוֹת] III 0.0.1 n.[f.]pl. **constellations** 1QH 10_{27}. → מַזָּרוֹת *Mazzaroth.*

*מזז 0.0.2 vb.—**Pu.** 0.0.2 ptc. ממוזזים—**be joined togeth-**

er, **blended,** of gold, silver, bronze 1QM $5_{5.8}$. → cf. (?) מסס *melt.*

*מֵזַח I 1 n.[m.] **shipyard** Is 23_{10} (or em. מָחוֹז *harbour*).

מֵזַח II 1 n.m. **girdle** Ps 109_{19}. → cf. מְזִיחַ *girdle.*

*מֵזַח III n.[m.] **impudence** (lit. **brow**) of the mighty Jb 12_{21} (if em. מְזִיחַ *girdle of*). → cf. מֵצַח *brow.*

[מְזִיחַ] 1 n.[m.] **girdle** Jb 12_{21}. → cf. מֵזַח II *girdle.*

מֵזִין, see אזן I *hear.*

*[מְזָל] 0.0.7 n.[m.] **flow** of lips, **utterance** 1QH 19_5. → נזל *flow.*

מַזְלֵג 2 n.m. **fork** 1 S $2_{13.14}$. → cf. מִזְלָגָה *fork.*

[מִזְלָגָה] 5.0.1 n.f.—pl. מִזְלָגוֹת; sf. מִזְלְגֹתָיו—**fork,** as sacrificial implement of altar Nm 4_{14}. → cf. מַזְלֵג *fork.*

*[מְזָלָה] n.f. **pit** Ps 12_9 (if em. כְּרֻם זֻלּוּת *when worthlessness is exalted* to כְּר מְזָלוֹת *digging* [= כָּרֹה inf. abs.] *pits*).

מַזָּלוֹת 1.0.2 n.[f.]pl. **planets,** or perh. **constellations** of the zodiac 2 K 23_5. → cf. מַזָּרוֹת *Mazzaroth.*

מְזִמָּה 19.3.16 n.f.—מְזִמָּתָה; cstr. Q מזמת; sf. מְזִמָּתוֹ; pl. מְזִמּוֹת; sf. מְזִמּוֹתָיו—**1. plan, purpose, intention, thinking,** esp. **private thoughts, a.** of Y., עַל־בָּבֶל מְזִמָּתוֹ *his plan is against Babylon* Jr 51_{11}. **b.** of human 1QH 17_{12}. **2. wicked plan, scheme, plot,** מזמות בליעל *wicked schemes of Belial* 1QH 10_{16}. **3. discretion, caginess,** אִישׁ מְזִמּוֹת *man of discretion* Pr 14_{17}. → זמם *plan.*

מִזְמוֹר 57.5.1 n.[m.] **1. psalm,** as designation in psalm titles, מִזְמוֹר לְדָוִד *a psalm of/to/for David* Ps 3_1. **2. psalm, song, music,** religious Si 44_5, at banquets Si 49_1. → זמר I *sing (praise).*

[מַזְמֵרָה] 4 n.f.—pl. מַזְמֵרוֹת; sf. מַזְמְרֹתֵיכֶם—**pruning knife** Jl 4_{10}. → זמר II *prune.*

[מְזַמֶּרֶת] I 5 n.f.—pl. מְזַמְּרוֹת—**snuffer,** or perh. **knife** to trim wick, as utensil in temple 1 K 7_{50}||2 C 4_{22}. → (?) זמר II *prune.*

*[מְזַמֶּרֶת] II 5 n.f.—pl. מְזַמְּרוֹת—**musical instrument** 1 K 7_{50}||2 C 4_{22}. → זמר I *sing (praise).*

*[מְזָנִים] 1 n.[m.]pl. **clouds,** שחק מזנים *rags of clouds,* i.e. ragged clouds Is $40_{15(1QIsa^a)}$ (MT מֹאזְנַיִם dust of *the scales*).

*[מְזַעְזֵעַ] I 1 n.m.—pl.sf. מְזַעְזְעֶיךָ—**one who reminds** Hb 2_7.

מְזַעְזֵעַ II *shaking,* see זוע I *shake.*

מְזַעְזֵעַ III *barking,* see זעה *bark.*

מִזְעָר I 4.3 n.[m.] **a little, a few,** of quantity, שְׁאָר מְעַט מִזְעָר *the remnant will be a little, a few,* i.e. very few Is 16_{14}; of time Is 10_{25}. → cf. זְעֵיר I *a little.*

מִזְעָר II, see מִצְעָר II *Mizar.*

מִזְקָא, see מִזְקָה *canal.*

*[מִזְקָה] 0.0.2 n.f.—מזקא; pl. מזקות—**canal, conduit** 3QTr 2_9 10_3.

*[מזר] vb. **Qal,** pass., **be spread out,** of net Pr 1_{17} (if em. מְזֹרָה *scattered* [זרה pu.] to מְזָרָה or מְזוּרָה *spread out*).

מִזְרֶה 2 n.[m.] **pitchfork,** for winnowing Is 30_{24}. → זרה I *scatter.*

מַזָּרוֹת 1 pr.n.m. **Mazzaroth,** star or constellation, prob. the Zodiac, perh. of the southern hemisphere, or perh. Venus, the Hyades, the boat of Arcturus, or n.f. pl. **constellations** (= מַזָּלוֹת) Jb 38_{32}. → cf. מְזוּרוֹת *constellations.*

מִזְרָח 74.0.29 n.[m.]—+ ה- of direction מִזְרָחָה; cstr. מִזְרַח (+ ה- of direction מִזְרְחָה); sf. Q מזרחו—**1.** as cstr. with שֶׁמֶשׁ, **(place of) rising** of the sun, **east** Jos 13_5. **2.** מִזְרָח alone, **sunrise, east, eastern side,** מִזְרַח הַיַּרְדֵּן *east of the Jordan* 1 C 6_{63}. → זרח *arise;* cf. מִזְרָחִי *eastern.*

*[מִזְרָחִי] 0.0.5 adj.—f.s. מזרחית—**eastern,** of gate 3QTr 2_7, corner 3QTr 3_5, tunnel 3QTr 4_{11}. → זרח *arise;* cf. מִזְרָח *east.*

*מְזָרִים I 1 n.[m.]pl. **press,** squeezing waters from the clouds Jb 37_9.

מְזָרִים II, see זרה I *scatter,* pi.

[מִזְרָע] 1 n.m.—cstr. מִזְרַע—**place of sowing** Is 19_7. → זרע *sow.*

מִזְרָק 32.0.5 n.m.—pl. מִזְרָקִים, מִזְרָקוֹת; cstr. מִזְרְקֵי; sf. מִזְרְקֹתָיו—**basin, bowl** of gold 2 C 4_8, silver Nm 7_{13}; usu. for use with blood at altar 11QT 23_{12}, מִזְרָקִים לִפְנֵי הַמִּזְבֵּחַ *basins before the altar* Zc 14_{20}; also as table utensil for wine Am 6_6. → זרק I *toss.*

[מֵחַ] 2 n.[m.] **fatling** of sheep, עֹלוֹת מֵחִים *burnt offerings of fatlings* Ps 66_{15}. → מחה III *be full of marrow.*

[מֹחַ] 1 n.m. **marrow** Jb 21_{24}. → מחה III *be full of marrow.*

מחא I 3 vb.—**Qal** 3 Impf. יִמְחֲאוּ—**clap** hands (כַּף or יָד),

in expression of triumph or approval, of person Ezk 25_6, tree Is 55_{12}, river Ps 98_8. → cf. מחה II *strike*.

*מחא II 0.0.1 vb. perh. **refuse,** מחא להרים [את הקודשים] perh. *one who refuses to offer the holy things* 4QDe 2.2_5.

*מחא III 1 vb.—**Hi.** 1 Inf. cstr. לְמְחוֹת—**destroy** kings Pr 31_3.

מחא IV, see מחה III *be full of marrow.*

מַחֲבֵא 1 n.[m.] **hiding place, shelter,** מַחֲבֵא־רוּחַ *hiding place of,* i.e. from, *the wind* Is 32_2. → חבא *hide.*

[מַחֲבֹא] 1 n.[m.]—pl. מַחֲבֹאִים—**hiding place** 1 S 23_{23}. → חבא *hide.*

*[מַחֲבָן] n.m. **fertile place** Nm 13_{19} (if em. מַחֲנִים *camps* to מַחֲבָנִים *fertile places*).

[מִחְבָּן] 1 n.[m.]—pl. Sam מִחְבָּנִים—**fertile land,** perh. **rotten land** Nm 13_{19}(Sam^{ms}) (MT מַחֲנִים *camps*).

[מְחַבְּרָה] 2 n.f.—pl. מְחַבְּרוֹת—**beam, brace, truss,** or perh. **clamp, coupling,** made of iron 1 C 22_3, wood 2 C 34_{11}. → חבר I *join.*

מַחְבֶּרֶת 10.0.2 n.f.—מַחְבֶּרֶת; sf. מֶחְבַּרְתּוֹ—**1. join, series** of curtains joined together Ex 36_{11}. **2. join,** i.e. **looped pattern** around edge of shield 1QM 5_5. **3. place of joining** of ephod Ex 28_{27}. → חבר I *join.*

מַחֲבַת 5 n.f. **1a. griddle, baking tray** Lv 2_5. **b. plate** of iron Ezk 4_3. **2. cake baked on griddle** 1 C 23_{29}. → cf. חֲבִתִּים *flat cakes.*

[מַחֲגֹרֶת] 1 n.f. **robe of sackcloth** Is 3_{24}. → חגר *gird.*

מחה I 34.4.5.2 vb.—**Qal** 22.2.3.2 Pf. מָחִיתָ, מָחָה; impf. יִמְחֶה; + waw וַיִּמַח; impv. מְחֵה; ptc. מֹחֶה; inf. abs. מָחֹה; cstr. מְחוֹת—**1. wipe clean** dish 2 K 21_{13}, mouth Pr 30_{20}, tears Is25_8, Jerusalem (subj. Y.) 2 K 21_{13}. **2a.** subj. oft. Y, **wipe out, obliterate, annihilate** humans Gn 6_7 (+ מֵעַל *from upon* face of earth), someone's name Dt 9_{14} (+ מִתַּחַת *from under* heavens), memory Ex 17_{14}, sin Ps 51_3. **b. waste away** the flesh, of falsehood Si 34_1.

Ni. 9.2.1 Impf. יִמָּחֶה (יִמַּח); + waw וְנִמְחוּ—**be wiped out, obliterated, annihilated,** of humans and animals Gn7_{23} (+ מִן *from* earth), name Dt 25_6 (+ מִן *from* Israel), work Ezk 6_6, sin Ps 109_{14}.

Hi. 3.0.1 Pf. Q המחיתה; impf. תֶּמַח; inf. לְמְחוֹת—**1.** of Y., **wipe out, blot out** sin Jr 18_{23}, good deeds Ne 13_{14}. **2. destroy, ruin** persons Pr 31_3.
→ תֶּמַח *wiping.*

מחה II 1 vb.—**Qal** 1 + waw וּמָחָה—of border, **strike against** (עַל), i.e. **reach** slope Nm 34_{11}. → מְחִי *thrust;* cf. מחא I *clap.*

מחה III 1 vb.—**Pu.** 1 Ptc. מְמֻחָיִם (Qr^{mss} מְמֻחָאִים)—**be full of marrow, flavoured with marrow,** of fatty food Is 25_6. → מֹחַ *marrow,* מֵחַ *fatling.*

*[מָחָה] 1 n.f.—pl. cstr. מְחוֹת—**female prophet** Pr 31_3.

מְחוּגָה 1 n.f. **compass,** or perh. **lathe for polishing** Is 44_{13}. → חוג *draw a circle.*

[מָחוֹז] 1.0.1 n.[m.]—cstr. מְחוֹז—**harbour, town** Ps 107_{30}.

מְחוּיָאֵל 2 pr.n.m. **Mehujael.**

[מַחֲוִי] 1 gent. **Mahavite.**

מָחוֹל I 6 n.m.—cstr. מְחוֹל; sf. מְחֹלֵנוּ—**dance, dancing** Jr 31_4. → חול I *whirl.*

מָחוֹל II 1 pr.n.m. **Mahol.**

*[מְחוֹלְלָה] I 0.0.1 n.f.—pl. מחוללות—**dance** 4QMg 7_5. → חול I *whirl.*

*[מְחוֹלְלָה] II 0.0.1 n.f.—pl. מחוללות—**wound** 4QMg 7_5. → חלל III *be pierced.*

*[מְחוֹת] 1 n.f.pl.—cstr. מְחוֹת—**full measure** Pr 31_3.

מַחֲזֶה 4 n.[m.]—cstr. מַחֲזֵה—**vision,** מַחֲזֵה שַׁדַּי *vision of the Almighty* Nm 24_4. → חזה I *see.*

מֶחֱזָה 4 n.f. **window** of palace 1 K 7_4. → חזה *see.*

מַחֲזִיאוֹת 2 pr.n.m. **Mahazioth.**

[מְחִי] 1 n.[m.]—cstr. מְחִי—**thrust** Ezk 26_9. → מחה II *strike.*

*[מְחִיגָה] n.f. **cause of reeling** 4QDiscourse 2.2_6 ([מחיג[ה]). → חוג *make a circle.*

מְחִידָא 2 pr.n.m. **Mehida.**

מִחְיָה 8.3.2 n.f.—cstr. מִחְיַת; sf. מִחְיָתֶךָ—**1. (preservation of) life,** in famine Gn 45_5, through work of physician Si 38_{14}. **2. sustenance, livelihood,** דאגת מחיה *anxiety of,* i.e. for, *livelihood* Si $34_{1.2}$. **3. reviving, recovery,** among postexilic community Ezr $9_{8.9}$. **4.** place of life, i.e. **patch of flesh,** or **formation of new flesh,** or perh. **rawness of flesh** Lv 13_{10}. **5.** coll., **living beings, survivors** 1QM 13_8. **6. materials for repair** Ezr 9_9. → חיה I *live.*

מְחִיָּיאֵל, see מְחוּיָאֵל *Mehujael.*

[מְחָיִם] *annihilated ones,* see מחה I *wipe out.*

מְחִיר I 15.4.11 n.m.—sf. מְחִירָהּ; pl. sf. מְחִירֵיהֶם—**1. price, cost, value,** מְחִיר שָׂדֶה *price of a field* Pr 27$_{26}$. **2. hire, wages,** מְחִיר כֶּלֶב *hire of a dog,* i.e. (temple) servant Dt 23$_{19}$. **3. money,** מְחִיר בְּיַד־כְּסִיל *money in the hand of a fool* Pr 17$_{16}$. → cf. מִמְחִיר *bargaining.*

מְחִיר II 1 pr.n.m. **Mehir.**

מְחִירָא, see מְחִידָא *Mehida.*

*__מחל__ 0.0.1 vb.—**Qal** 0.0.1 Pf. מחלת—of Y., **forgive sin** GnzPs 1$_{13}$.

מַחְלָה 5 pr.n.f. **Mahlah.**

מַחֲלָה 4.3 n.f. **sickness, disease** Ex 15$_{26}$. → חלה I *be weak;* cf. מַחֲלֶה *sickness.*

[**מַחֲלֶה**] 2.0.4 n.m.—cstr. מַחֲלֵה; sf. מַחֲלֵהוּ; pl. Q מחלים—**sickness, disease** Pr 18$_{14}$ 2 C 21$_{15}$. → חלה I *be weak;* cf. מַחֲלָה *sickness.*

[**מְחִלָּה**] 1.0.1 n.f.—pl. cstr. מְחִלּוֹת—**hole** Is 2$_{19}$. → חלל III *be pierced.*

[**מְחֹלָה**] 8 n.f.—pl. מְחֹלוֹת—**dance, dancing,** not necessarily in a ring, with music Jg 11$_{34}$, in worship Ex 15$_{20}$; מְחֹלַת הַמַּחֲנָיִם perh. *dance of,* i.e. in, *two lines* Ca 7$_{1}$. → חול I *whirl;* cf. מָחוֹל *dance,* מְחוֹלְלָה *dance.*

[**מַחֲלוּיִם**] 1 n.[m.]pl.—Kt מחליים—**sickness, suffering** 2 C 24$_{25}$. → חלה I *be weak.*

מַחְלוֹן 4 pr.n.m. **Mahlon.**

מַחְלִי I 12 pr.n.m. **Mahli.**

מַחְלִי II 2 gent. **Mahlite.**

[**מַחֲלָף**] I 1 n.m.—pl. מַחֲלָפִים—**knife** Ezr 1$_{9}$. → חלף I *pass.*

*[**מַחֲלָף**] II 1 n.m.—pl. מַחֲלָפִים—**censer** Ezr 1$_{9}$. → חלף I *pass.*

[**מַחְלָפָה**] I 2 n.f.—pl. cstr. מַחְלְפוֹת—**plait, lock of hair** Jg 16$_{13.19}$. → חלף I *pass.*

*[**מַחְלָפָה**] II 2 n.f.—pl. cstr. מַחְלְפוֹת—**copious hair, flowing locks** Jg 16$_{13.19}$. → (?) חלף II *pierce through.*

[**מַחֲלָצָה**] I 2 n.f.—pl. מַחֲלָצוֹת—**festive robe** of woman Is 3$_{22}$, high priest Zc 3$_{4}$. → חלץ I *loosen.*

*[**מַחֲלָצָה**] II 2 n.f.—pl. מַחֲלָצוֹת—**white garments** of woman Is 3$_{22}$, high priest Zc 3$_{4}$.

*[**מַחֲלָקוּת**] 0.1 n.f. **distribution** Si 41$_{21(Bmg)}$. → חלק I *divide.*

מַחֲלֹקֶת I 43.2.9 n.f.—sf. מַחֲלֻקְתּוֹ; pl. מַחְלְקוֹת; cstr. מַחְלְקוֹת; sf. מַחְלְקוֹתֵיהֶם, מַחְלְקֹתָם—**1. (tribal) division** of Israel Jos 11$_{23}$. **2. division, course** of priests and Levites 1 C 26$_{1}$. **3. (military) division** 1QM 2$_{10}$. **4. division** of time, **season,** ספר מחלקות העתים *book of the divisions of the times* CD 16$_{3}$. **5. division, allotment** of inheritance and property Si 42$_{3(M)}$. **6. part, portion, share** of land Ezk 48$_{29}$. **7.** in pl.n., סֶלַע הַמַּחְלְקוֹת **Rock of Divisions** 1 S 23$_{28}$. → חלק I *divide.*

[**מַחֲלֹקֶת**] II 1 n.f. **smoothness,** in pl.n. סֶלַע הַמַּחְלְקוֹת **Rock of Smoothness** 1 S 23$_{28}$. → חלק II *be smooth.*

מָחֲלַת I 2 n.[f.] **Mahalath,** musical term in psalm titles Ps 53$_{1}$ 88$_{1}$.

מָחֲלַת II 7 pr.n.f. **Mahalath.**

מַחֲלַת, see מָחֲלַת II, *Mahalath.*

מְחֹלָתִי 2 gent. **Meholathite.**

מַחְמָאֹת 1 n.f.pl. **curd-like things,** in ref. to smooth speech Ps 55$_{22}$. → חֶמְאָה *curd.*

[**מַחְמָד**] 13.4.2 n.m.—cstr. מַחְמַד; pl. מַחֲמַדִּים; cstr. מַחֲמַדֵּי; sf. מַחֲמַדֵּי—**(object of) desire, delight, pleasure, precious thing,** in ref. to children Ho 9$_{16}$, wife Ezk 24$_{16}$, male lover Ca 5$_{16}$, temple Ezk 24$_{21}$, idols GnzPs 2$_{21}$; מחמד עין *desirable thing of,* i.e. to, *the eye* Si 36$_{27}$. → חמד *desire.*

*__מַחְמַד__ 1 pl.n. **Machomades.**

[**מַחְמֹד**] 2 n.[m.]—pl. sf. מַחֲמֻדֶּיהָ—**precious thing** Lm 1$_{7}$. → חמד *desire.*

[**מַחְמָל**] 1 n.[m.] **(object of) compassion** or **longing,** מַחְמַל נַפְשְׁכֶם *compassion of your soul* Ezk 24$_{21}$. → חמל *spare.*

*[**מַחְמָם**] 0.0.0.1 pr.n.[m.] **Mahmam.**

מַחְמֶצֶת 2 n.f. **leavened thing,** sour-tasting Ex 12$_{19.20}$. → חמץ I *be leavened.*

*[**מַחֲנָה**] 1 n.f.—pl. מַחֲנוֹת—**mantlet,** shelter for besieging troops Ezk 4$_{2}$.

מַחֲנֶה 215.1.58 n.m.&f.—cstr. מַחֲנֵה; sf. מַחֲנֶךָ, מַחֲנֵהוּ; du. מַחֲנָיִם; pl. מַחֲנִים, מַחֲנוֹת; cstr. מַחֲנֹת, Q מחני; sf. מַחֲנֵיהֶם, Q מחנותם—**1. camp, encampment, a.** of Jacob Gn 32$_{22}$. **b.** of Israelites Ex 16$_{13}$. **c.** tabernacle and temple as camp of Levites 1 C 9$_{18}$, as camp of Y. 1 C 9$_{19}$. **2. camp,** in ref. to towns and settled communities, **a.** Jerusalem, ירושלים היאה מחנה הקדש *Jerusalem is the camp of holiness* 4QMMT B$_{60}$. **b.** town(s) outside Jerusalem 4QMMT B$_{30}$. **c.** community, settlement, as distinct from towns CD 12₂₃. **d.** of inhabitants of world GnzPs 2₁₈. **3a. (military) camp, (place of) encampment** of Israelites 1 S 4₆, Philistines 1 S 13₁₇. **b. army, host, force(s), armed troop** of Israelites Ex 14₁₉, Egyptians Ex 14₂₄. **4. camp, army, host** of Y. Jl 2₁₁. **5. company, group of people** 2 K 5₁₅; perh. **line of dancers** Ca 7₁. → חנה I *encamp.*

מַחֲנֵה־דָן 2 pl.n. **Mahaneh-dan.**

מַחֲנַיִם I 13 pl.n. **Mahanaim.**

*[מַחֲנַיִם] II 0.0.2 pr.n.m. **Mahanaim.**

מַחֲנָק 1 n.[m.] **1. strangling** Jb 7₁₅ (or §2). **2.** perh. **strangler,** an epithet of the death-god, וַתִּבְחַר מַחֲנָק נַפְשִׁי *and the Strangler has chosen my neck* Jb 7₁₅. → חנק *strangle.*

מַחְסֶה 20.0.3 n.m.—מַחְסֶה; cstr. מַחְסֵה (Q מחסי); sf. מַחְסִי (מַחְסִי), מַחְסֵהוּ—**(place of) shelter,** rather than **refuge** (מָנוֹס or מָעוֹז), **a.** for humans, from rain and storm Jb 24₈. **b.** rocks as shelter for animals Ps 104₁₈. **c.** Y. as shelter Ps 14₆. **d.** lies as shelter Is 28₁₅. → חסה *seek refuge.*

מַחְסוֹם 1 n.[m.] **muzzle,** for mouth of psalmist Ps 39₂. → חסם *block.*

מַחְסוֹר 13.1.22 n.[m.]—sf. מַחְסוֹרְךָ; pl. cstr. Q מחסורי; sf. מַחְסֹרֶיךָ—**lack, want, need, thing needed,** אֵין מַחְסוֹר לִירֵאָיו *those who fear him have no want* Ps 34₁₀, כָּל־מַחְסוֹרְךָ *all your need(s)* Jg 19₂₀. → חסר *lack.*

מַחְסֵיָה 2.0.0.10 pr.n.m. **Mahseiah.**

מחסיהו, see מַחְסֵיָה *Mahseiah.*

*[מְחַפֵּשׂ] n.m. **investigator,** as term for God Ps 64₇ (if em. חֵפֶשׂ מְחֻפָּשׂ וְקֶרֶב אִישׁ appar. *a plot is devised and the mind of a man* to חָפַשׂ מְחַפֵּשׂ קֶרֶב אִישׁ *the Investigator will search the mind of a man*). → חפשׂ I *search.*

מחץ I 14.1.2.1 vb.—**Qal** 14.1.2.1 Pf. מָחַץ, מָחַצְתָּ; impf. יִמְחַץ; impv. מְחַץ—**1.** oft. of Y., **strike through, wound, crush, shatter** nations 1QM 12₁₁, head Ps 110₆, crown Ps 68₂₂. **2.** perh. **plunge** feet into (בְּ) blood Ps 68₂₄. → מַחַץ *wound;* cf. מחק *crush.*

*מחץ II 1 vb.—**Qal** 1 Impf. תִּמְחַץ—**dip** feet in (בְּ) blood Ps 68₂₄.

*מחץ III 1 vb.—**Qal** 1 Impf. תִּמְחַץ—**run,** of feet to (בְּ) blood Ps 68₂₄.

[מַחַץ] 1.0.1 n.[m.] **wound,** מַחַץ מַכָּתוֹ *wound of,* i.e. from, *his blow* Is 30₂₆. → מחץ I *strike through.*

*מחצב vb. **Qal, smite,** הֲלוֹא אַתְּ־הִיא הַמֹּחֶצֶבֶת רַהַב *was it not you who smote Rahab?* Is 51₉ (if em. הַמַּחְצֶבֶת *who hewed*).

מַחְצֵב 3 n.[m.] **hewing,** אַבְנֵי מַחְצֵב *stones of hewing,* i.e. hewn stone 2 K 12₁₃. → חצב I *hew.*

מֶחֱצָה 2 n.f. **half,** מֶחֱצַת הָעֵדָה *half of,* i.e. (of spoils) belonging to, *the congregation* Nm 31₄₃. → חצה I *divide.*

[מַחֲצִית] 16.0.14 n.f. **1. half,** מחצית העם *half of the people* 11QT 58₁₀, מַחֲצִית הַשֶּׁקֶל *half a shekel* Ex30₁₃. **2. middle,** מַחֲצִית הַיּוֹם *middle of the day* Ne 8₃. → חצה I *divide.*

מחק 1 vb.—**Qal** 1 Pf. מָחֲקָה—**crush** head Jg 5₂₆. → cf. מחץ I *strike through, shatter.*

*[מֶחְקְקָה] n.f. **decree** of ruler Si 44₄(M) ([מחקק]תם).

[מֶחְקָר] 1.0.1 n.[m.] **1. depth,** or **recess,** as place to be searched out, מֶחְקְרֵי־אָרֶץ *depths of the earth* Ps 95₄. **2. searching out, study,** מחקר צדק *study of righteousness* 4QWays[a] 1a.2₃. → חקר I *search.*

*[מַחְקֶרֶת] 0.1 n.f.—pl. sf. מחקרותם—**searching out, study** Si 44₄(B). → חקר I *search.*

*[מחר] vb. **Qal, appraise, value,** ptc. as noun, **appraiser, valuer,** וְדָרְשׁוּ מֹחֵר בָּתֵּיהֶם *and let their houses be investigated by the appraiser* Ps 109₁₀ (if em. וְדָרְשׁוּ מֵחָרְבוֹתֵיהֶם *and let them seek from their ruins*).

מָחָר 52.2.1.2 n.[m.] **1. morrow, future,** יוֹם מָחָר *day of the morrow,* i.e. tomorrow, in the future Pr 27₁. **2.** as adv., **tomorrow, in the future** Ex 8₂₅; כָּעֵת מָחָר *(about) this time tomorrow* Ex 9₁₈, הַיּוֹם וּמָחָר *today and tomorrow* Ex 19₁₀. → cf. מָחֳרָת *morrow.*

[מַחֲרָאָה] 1 n.f.—pl. Kt מחראות—**latrine** or **rubbish dump** 2 K 10₂₇(Kt) (Qr מוֹצָאוֹת *latrines*). → cf. חֶרֶא *dung.*

*[מַחֲרָב] n.[m.] **laying waste** Jr 15₈ (if em. עַל־אֵם בָּחוּר *against the mother of a young man* to עַל־מַחֲרָב *for laying waste*). → חרב II *destroy.*

*[מַחֲרָשׁ] 0.0.1 n.[m.] **scheming, devising,** perh. lit. 'ploughing', בסאון רשע מחרשו *his scheming is in the filth of wickedness* 1QS 3₂. → חרשׁ I *plough.*

[מַחֲרֵשָׁה] 2 n.f.—sf. מַחֲרַשְׁתּוֹ; pl. מַחֲרֵשֹׁת—**ploughshare** 1 S 13₂₀.₂₁. → חרשׁ I *plough.*

*[מַחֲרֶשֶׁת] 1 n.f.—sf. מַחֲרַשְׁתּוֹ—**goad** 1 S 13₂₀. → חרשׁ I

plough.

מָחֳרָת 32.0.4 n.f. **morrow, next day**, oft. מִמָּחֳרָת *on the morrow, the next day* Gn 19_{34}, also לְמָחֳרָת in same sense Jon 4_{7}; יוֹם הַמָּחֳרָת *day of the morrow*, i.e. the next day Nm 11_{32}. → cf. מָחָר *morrow.*

[מַחְשֹׂף] 1.0.1 n.[m.] **stripping** of bark to expose wood Gn 30_{37}. → חשׂף I *make bare.*

*[מַחֲשָׁב] I 0.0.7 n.m.—pl. cstr. מחשבי—1. **(skilful) design, crafting** of spirits' garments 4QShirShabb^{f} 23.2$_{10}$, the heavens 4QHod^{a} 7.2$_{21}$. 2. **(skilfully crafted) furnishing, decoration** of inner sanctuary 4QShirShabb^{d} 1.2$_{13.14}$. → חשׁב *think.*

*[מַחֲשָׁב] II 0.0.2 n.m.—pl. cstr. מחשבי; pl. sf. מחשביה—pl. **network of fissures, depths** of abyss 1QH 11$_{32.33}$.

מַחֲשָׁבָה 56.4.73 n.f.—מַחֲשֶׁבֶת (מַחֲשֶׁבֶת); cstr. מַחֲשֶׁבֶת; pl. מַחֲשָׁבוֹת; cstr. מַחְשְׁבוֹת; sf. מַחְשְׁבוֹתַי—1. **thought, purpose, plan, scheme** of Y. Jr 18_{11}, spirits 1QM 13_{4}, humans Gn 6_{5}. 2. **device, (skilful) design, crafting** of tabernacle furnishings Ex 31_{4}, temple furnishings 2 C 2_{13}, treasury 1QH 9_{13}, war engines 2 C 26_{15} (מַחֲשֶׁבֶת חוֹשֵׁב *device of a [skilful] designer*); **skill** in design and making of weapons 1QM 5_{6}. → חשׁב *think.*

מַחְשָׁךְ 7.0.4 n.m.—pl. מַחֲשַׁכִּים; cstr. מַחֲשַׁכֵּי; sf. Q מחשכיהמה—**dark place, darkness**, as hiding place Is 29_{15}, place of dead Ps 88_{7}, the underworld 1QS 4_{13} (אשׁ מחשכים *fire of dark places*). → חשׁך *be dark.*

מַחַת 3 pr.n.m. **Mahath.**

מַחְתָּה 22.0.2 n.f.—sf. מַחְתָּתוֹ; pl. מַחְתּוֹת; sf. מַחְתֹּתָיו—1. **fire-pan**, utensil of altar, made of gold 1 K 7_{50}||2 C 4_{22}, bronze Ex 27_{3}. 2. **censer**, of bronze Nm 17_{4}. 3. **snuff-dish**, utensil of lampstand, of gold Ex 25_{38}. → חתה I *take, snatch.*

מְחִתָּה 11.0.1 n.f.—cstr. מְחִתַּת—1. **terror** Is 54_{14}; **(cause of) horror** Jr 48_{39}, **(cause of) dismay** Pr 21_{15}. 2. **ruin, cause of ruin,** פִּי־אֱוִיל מְחִתָּה קְרֹבָה *the mouth of a fool is an imminent ruin* Pr 10_{14}. → חתת I *be dismayed.*

מַחְתֶּרֶת 2 n.f. **breaking in, burglary** Jr 2_{34}. → חתר *dig.*

*[מַחְתּוֹשׁ] 0.0.1 pr.n.[m.] **Mahtosh.**

[מַטְאֲטֵא] I 1 n.[m.] **broom,** מַטְאֲטֵא הַשְׁמֵד *broom of destruction* Is 14_{23}. → טאטא I *sweep.*

*[מַטְאֲטֵא] II 1 n.[m.]—cstr. מַטְאֲטֵא—**means of destruction,** perh. **implement for pounding, crushing** Is 14_{23}.

מַטְבֵּחַ 1 n.[m.] **slaughter, place for slaughter,** or **means of slaughter** Is 14_{21}. → טבח *slaughter.*

מַטָּה 19.0.4 adv.—מָטָּה—1. מַטָּה, a. **downwards, lower** Dt 28_{43}. b. **beneath, below** Pr 15_{24}. 2. לְמַטָּה, a. **downwards** Ec 3_{21}. b. **beneath, below,** מוֹסְדֵי־אֶרֶץ לְמָטָּה *foundations of the earth beneath* Jr 31_{37}. c. לְמַטָּה מִן **less than,** חָשַׂכְתָּ לְמַטָּה מֵעֲוֹנֵנוּ *you have withheld (punishment) less than our iniquity (deserved)* Ezr 9_{13}. 3. מִלְּמַטָּה **(from) beneath, (from) below** Ex 26_{24}. → נטה *stretch out.*

*[מֻטֶּה] 1 adj.—pl. מֻטִּים—**reaching,** as noun, **one reaching, one approaching** Pr 24_{11}. → cf. מצא I *find*, §4a.

מַטֶּה I 252.4.19.2 n.m.—cstr. מַטֵּה; sf. מַטְּךָ, מַטֵּהוּ, מַטֶּךָ; pl. מַטּוֹת; sf. מַטָּיו, מַטּוֹתָם—1a. **staff, rod, stick,** usu. for support, מַטְּךָ אֲשֶׁר בְּיָדֶךָ *your staff that is in your hand* Gn 38_{18}; also for punishment Is 10_{5}, beating out cummin Is 28_{27}, holding bread Lv 26_{26}. b. **sceptre** Ps 110_{2}. c. **shaft** of arrow Hb 3_{9}. d. **stem** of vine Ezk 19_{11}. e. perh. **stalk** of grain Ps 105_{16}. 2. **tribe,** usu. one of twelve tribes of Israel, consisting of מִשְׁפָּחוֹת *clans* Jos 13_{15}, and equivalent to שֵׁבֶט *tribe* Nm 18_{2}; מַטֵּה אֶפְרַיִם *tribe of Ephraim* Jos 21_{5}, רָאשֵׁי הַמַּטּוֹת *heads of the tribes* Nm 30_{2}. → נטה *stretch out.*

*[מַטֶּה] II 2 n.[m.]pl.—cstr. מַטּוֹת; sf. מַטָּיו—**mace** Hb $3_{9.14}$.

מִטָּה 29.1 n.f.—cstr. מִטַּת; sf. מִטָּתִי; pl. מִטּוֹת; sf. Si מטותם—1. **bed, couch,** for resting at night Ps 6_{7}, in the day 2 S 4_{7}, in sickness Gn 47_{31}, for reclining at feasts Est 7_{8}. 2. prob. **litter, sedan,** for carrying a person Ca 3_{7}. 3. **bier,** for carrying a corpse 2 S 3_{31}. → נטה *stretch out.*

מֹטָה, see מוֹטָה *bar.*

[מֻטָּה] 1 n.f.—pl. cstr. מֻטּוֹת—**outspreading** of wings Is 8_{8}. → נטה *stretch out.*

מֻטֶּה 1.0.1 n.[m.] **injustice, perversity** Ezk 9_{9}. → נטה *stretch out.*

*[מִטְהָר] n.[m.] **splendour, lustre** or perh. **purity** Ps 89_{45} (if em. מִטְּהָרוֹ *some of his purity* to מִטְהָרוֹ *his splendour*). → טהר *be pure.*

*[מָטוּ] 2 n.[m.]—pl. cstr. מַטּוֹת; sf. מַטָּיו—**war, company** Hb $3_{9.14}$.

מַטְוֶה 1 n.[m.] **yarn** Ex 35₂₅. → טוה *spin.*

*[**מָטוֹן**] 0.0.1 n.[m.]—pl. cstr. מטוני—**hiding place** 1QH fr. 3₄. → טמן *conceal.*

[**מְטִיל**] I 1 n.[m.] **rod,** as descr. of bones of Behemoth, מְטִיל בַּרְזֶל *rod of iron* Jb 40₁₈.

*מְטִיל II 1 adj. **strong,** גְּרָמָיו כִּמְטִיל בַּרְזֶל *his limbs like strong iron* Jb 40₁₈.

*[**מְטִיל**] III 1 n.[m.]—pl. מטלים—**destroyer** Is 50₆(1QIsaᵃ) (MT מֹרְטִים *those who made smooth*).

מַטִּיף *preacher, teacher,* see נטף *drip.*

*[**מֶטֶל**] n.[m.] **trap,** as descr. of bones of Behemoth, מֶטֶל בַּרְזֶל *trap(s) of iron* Jb 40₁₈ (if em. מְטִיל *rod of*).

*מְטַל 2 n.[m.]—cstr. מְטַל—**dew** Hg 1₁₀; מְטַל הַשָּׁמַיִם *dew of heaven* Gn 27₂₈. → cf. טַל *dew.*

מַטְמוֹן I 5.1 n.[m.]—pl. מַטְמוֹנִים; cstr. מַטְמֻנֵי—**1. (hidden) treasure** Gn 43₂₃ Pr 2₄. **2. hidden store of food** Jr 41₈. → טמן *conceal.*

*[**מַטְמוֹן**] II n.[m.] **crypt,** for burial Jb 3₂₁ (if em. וַיַּחְפְּרֻהוּ מִמַּטְמוֹנִים appar. *and they dig for it more than [for] treasure* [מַטְמוֹן I] to וַיַּחְפְּרֻהוּם מַטְמוֹנִים *and they dig for themselves crypts*). → טמן *conceal.*

*[**מַטְמֹנֶת**] 0.1 n.f.—cstr. מטמנת—**treasure** Si 42₉(B). → טמן *conceal.*

מַטָּע 6.0.5 n.m.—cstr. מַטַּע; sf. מַטָּעָהּ; pl. cstr. מַטָּעֵי; sf. Qr מַטָּעַי—**1. (place of) planting, plantation** Ezk 31₄; מַטָּעֵי כָרֶם *places of planting of vineyards* Mc 1₆. **2. (object of) planting, plant,** מַטַּע י׳ *planting of Y.* Is 61₃. **3. (act of) planting,** נֵצֶר מַטָּעַי *shoot of my planting* Is 60₂₁(Qr). → נטע *plant,* מַטַּעַת *planting.*

[**מַטְעַם**] 8.6 n.[m.]—sf. Si מטעמו; pl. מַטְעַמִּים (Si מטעמים); cstr. Si מטעמי; sf. מַטְעַמּוֹתָיו—**delicacy, tasty dish** Gn 27₄. → טעם *taste.*

*מַטַּעַת 0.0.10 n.f. **1. (place of) planting, plantation** 1QH 16₉. **2. (object of) planting, plant,** descr. of community, מטעת עולם *everlasting plant* 1QS 8₅. → נטע *plant.*

מִטְפַּחַת 2 n.f.—pl. מִטְפָּחוֹת—**cloak** Ru 3₁₅. → טפח I *extend.*

מטר 17.0.1 vb.—**Ni.** 1 תִּמָּטֵר—**be rained upon,** of field Am 4₇.

Hi. 16.0.1 Pf. הִמְטִיר; impf. יַמְטֵר, תַּמְטִיר; ptc. מַמְטִיר; inf. הַמְטִיר—**1.** of Y., **cause it to rain rain, hailstones, burning sulphur on** (עַל) people Ezk 38₂₂. **2.** of clouds, **rain, drop rain** Is 5₆.

→ מָטָר *rain.*

מָטָר 38.2.4 n.m.—cstr. מְטַר; pl. cstr. מִטְרוֹת—**1. rain,** מְטַר הַשָּׁמַיִם *rain of heaven* Dt 11₁₁, אַרְצְךָ *of your land* Dt 28₁₂. **2. snowfall** Si 43₁₈. → מטר *rain.*

מַטָּרָא, see מַטָּרָה *target.*

מַטְרֵד 2 pr.n.f. **Matred.**

מַטָּרָה 16 n.f.—מַטָּרָא—**1. guard, watch,** חֲצַר הַמַּטָּרָה *court of the guard* Jr 32₂. **2. target** for archery 1 S 20₂₀. → נטר I *keep.*

מַטְרִי 1 gent. **Matrite.**

מִי 423.28.81.3 interrog. (& rel.) pron.—Q מיא—**1. who? whom? whose?,** usu. with ref. to identity, מִי אַתֶּם *who are you?* Jos 9₈, אֶת־מִי אֶשְׁלַח *whom shall I send?* Is 6₈, בַּת־מִי אַתְּ *whose daughter are you?* Gn 24₂₃. **2. who?,** with ref. to significance, almost **what?,** מִי י׳ אֲשֶׁר אֶשְׁמַע בְּקֹלוֹ *who is Y. that I should listen to his voice?* Ex 5₂. **3. which one(s)?,** out of several, אֶל־מִי מִקְּדֹשִׁים תִּפְנֶה *to which of the holy ones will you turn?* Jb 5₁. **4.** with inanimate noun, **what?,** מִי שְׁמֶךָ *what is your name?* Jg 13₁₇. **5.** as rel. pron., **who,** רְאוּ מִי הָלַךְ מֵעִמָּנוּ *see who has gone from us* 1 S 14₁₇. **6.** perh. indef. rel. pron., **whoever,** מִי־פֶתִי יָסֻר הֵנָּה *whoever is naïve, let him turn here* Pr 9₄. **7.** perh. **what!, what?, why?,** as colloquial, מִי אֲנַחֲמֵךְ *what? shall I comfort you?* Is 51₁₉.

[**מֵיאָה**], see מֵאָה *hundred.*

*[**מִיאָמִן**] 0.0.0.9 pr.n.m. **Miamun.**

[**מֵיאשָׁה**], see מֵישָׁא *Mesha.*

*מיד 1 vb.—**Pol.** 1 + waw וַיְמֹדֵד—of Y., **shake, convulse** earth Hb 3₆ (unless מדד *measure*).

מֵידְבָא 5 pl.n. **Medeba.**

מֵידָד 2 pr.n.m. **Medad.**

*[**מַיָה**] n.[f.] **water** perh. Lachish ost. 3₁₈ (others מִזֶּה *from here;* others מָזוֹ *provisions*). → cf. מַיִם *water.*

מֵי זָהָב I 2 pr.n. **Me-zahab.**

מֵי זָהָב II 2 pl.n. **Me-zahab.**

[**מֵיטָב**] 6 n.[m.] **best, best part,** מֵיטַב הָאָרֶץ *best of the land* Gn 47₆, הַצֹּאן *of the flock* 1 S 15₉. → יטב *be good.*

מִיכָא 4 pr.n.m. **Mica.**

מִיכָאֵל 13.0.4 pr.n.m. **Michael.**

מִיכָה 33.0.0.2 pr.n.m. **Micah.**

[מִיכָהוּ] 1 pr.n.m. **Micah.**

מִיכָיָה 4 pr.n.m. **Micaiah.**

מִיכָיְהוּ 2 pr.n.m.&f. **Micaiah.**

מִיכָיְהוּ 21.0.0.15 pr.n.m.**Micaiah.**

[מִיכָל] I 1 n.[m.] perh. **pool or stream,** מִיכַל הַמַּיִם *the water pool* 2 S 17₂₀.

*[מִיכָל] II 1 n.[m.] **collection, container, hoard,** מִיכַל הַמַּיִם *collection of waters* 2 S 17₂₀. → כול *contain.*

מִיכַל 18 pr.n.f. **Michal.**

*מיל 3 vb.—**Qal** 3 Impf. אֲמִילַם—**ward off** nations Ps 118₁₀.₁₁.₁₂.

מַיִם 580.9.168.3 n.m.—מָיִם; cstr. מֵי (מֵימֵי); sf. מֵימֶיךָ; + ה- of direction מַיְמָה—**1. water(s), a.** in nature, as sea-water Am 5₈, river-water Ex 2₁₀, spring-water 2 C 32₃, flood-water Gn 7₇, melted snow Jb 24₁₉, rain Jg 5₄, clouds Jr 10₁₃. **b.** for use, drinking Gn 21₁₄, cooking Ezk 24₃, washing 2 K 5₁₂, purifying: מֵי חַטָּאת *water of purification from sin* Nm 8₇, דוכי *of purity* 1QS 3₉, נִדָּה *of,* i.e. for removing, *impurity* Nm 19₉. **c.** cosmic waters Gn 1₂. **d.** as metaphor, for abundance Am 5₂₄, refreshment Is 32₂, weakness Jos 7₅, instability Gn 49₄. **e.** in place names, e.g. שַׁעַר הַמַּיִם *Water Gate* Ne 3₂₆. **2.** other liquids, **a. tears** Lm 1₁₆. **b. urine** 2 K 18₂₇(Qr). **c.** appar. **semen** Is 48₁. → cf. מוֹ *water,* מָיָה *water.*

מִיָּמִן 4.0.18 pr.n.m. **Mijamin.**

[מִין] 31.4.8 n.m.—sf. מִינוֹ (מִינֵהוּ); pl. sf. מִינֵהֶם—**1a.** usu. in classifications of fauna and flora, **kind, species** Gn 1₁₁; מין כל חי *every kind of living being* Si 43₂₅(B). **b. one's own kind,** מין כל בשר *each creature's own kind* Si 13₁₆. **2. kind, type, sort,** שלושת מיני הצדק *(the) three kinds of righteousness* CD 4₁₆.

[מֵיסָךְ], see מוּסָךְ I *covered way,* II *fence,* III *bench.*

[מֵיפַעַת] 3 pl.n. **Mephaath.**

*מיץ I 1 vb.—**Qal** 1 Ptc. מֵץ—**press, oppress,** ptc. as noun, **oppressor** Is 16₄. → מֵיץ *extortioner,* מִיץ I *pressure;* cf. מזז *extract.*

*מיץ II 1 vb.—**Qal** 1 Inf. מִיץ—**churn (milk), press, stir up,** מִיץ חָלָב *churning of milk* Pr 30₃₃. → מִיץ II *churning.*

[מֵיץ] 1 n.m.—מֵץ—**extortioner** Is 16₄. → מיץ I *press.*

[מִיץ] I 3 n.m. **pressure, pressing,** or perh. **squeezing** Pr 30₃₃. → מיץ I *press.*

*[מִיץ] II 3 n.m. **churning, pressing, stirring** Pr 30₃₃. → מיץ II *churn.*

*מיר 1 vb.—**Qal** 1 Ptc. מֵרִים—**procure** shame Pr 3₃₅.

[מֵירַב], see מֵרַב *Merab.*

*[מֵירָשׁ] n.m. **new wine** Pr 23₃₁ Ca 1₄ 7₁₀ (all if em. מֵישָׁרִים to מֵירָשִׁים). → cf. מֵישָׁרִים II (type of) *wine.*

מִישׁ, see מוּשׁ *depart.*

מֵישָׁא 1 pr.n.m. **Mesha.**

מִישָׁאֵל 7 pr.n.m. **Mishael.**

מִישׁוֹר, see מִישֹׁר *plain.*

מֵישַׁךְ 1 pr.n.m. **Meshach.**

מֵישַׁע 1 pr.n.m. **Mesha.**

מֵישָׁע 1 pr.n.m. **Mesha.**

מִישֹׁר 23.1.3 n.m.—מִישׁוֹר—**1. plain,** esp. **plateau, tableland** of Moab, between the Arnon and Heshbon Jos 13₉, of the Golan 1 K 20₂₃. **2. plain,** as place of safety and confidence Ps 26₁₂. **3. equity,** כִּי־תִשְׁפֹּט עַמִּים מִישׁוֹר *for you judge the peoples (with) equity* Ps 67₅. → ישׁר *go straight.*

מֵישָׁרִים I 16.0.1 n.m.pl. **1. righteousness,** אֲנִי מֵישָׁרִים אֶשְׁפֹּט *I will judge righteously* Ps 75₃. **2.** appar. **peace, friendship** Dn 11₆. → ישׁר *go straight.*

*מֵישָׁרִים II 3 n.m.pl. (a kind of) **wine** Pr 23₃₁ Ca 1₄ 7₁₀. → cf. מֵירָשׁ *new wine.*

*מֵישָׁרִים III 2 n.m.pl. **smoothness** Pr 23₃₁ Ca 7₁₀. → ישׁר *go straight.*

*מֵישָׁרִים IV 2 n.m.pl. **gullet** Pr 23₃₁ Ca 7₁₀. → ישׁר *go straight.*

[מֵיתָר] 9 n.[m.]—pl. sf. מֵיתָרֶיךָ—**1.** usu. **cord, rope** of tent Nm 3₂₆. **2.** appar. **string** of bow Ps 21₁₃. → cf. יֶתֶר II *cord.*

מָךְ *poor one,* see מוך *be low.*

*[מַכָּא] 0.0.0.2 pr.n.m. **Makka.**

מַכְאוֹב 16.3.5 n.m.—sf. מַכְאֹבִי; pl. מַכְאוֹבִים, מַכְאֹבוֹת; sf. מַכְאֹבָיו—**pain, suffering** Ex 3₇ Ps 69₂₇. → כאב *be in pain.*

מַכְבֵּנָה I 1 pr.n.[m.] **Machbenah.**

מַכְבֵּנָה II 1 pl.n. **Machbenah.**

מַכְבַּנַּי 1 pr.n.m. **Machbannai.**

מַכְבֵּר 1 n.[m.] **cover,** perh. of netted cloth 2 K 8₁₅. → cf. כָּבִיר *braided article,* כְּבָרָה *sieve,* מִכְבָּר *grating.*

מִכְבָּר 6.0.1 n.m.—cstr. מִכְבַּר—**grating, lattice-work** of bronze, around altar Ex 27$_4$||38$_4$. → cf. כָּבִיר *braided article,* כְּבָרָה *sieve,* מַכְבֵּר *cover.*

מַכָּה 48.4.15 n.f.—cstr. מַכַּת; sf. מַכָּתִי; pl. מַכִּים, מַכּוֹת; sf. מַכּוֹתֶיהָ—**1. stroke, blow, stripe,** מַכַּת אוֹיֵב *blow of an enemy* Jr 30$_{14}$. **2. wound,** דַּם־הַמַּכָּה *blood of the wound* 1 K 22$_{35}$. **3. plague,** מַכּוֹת הָאָרֶץ *plagues of the land* Dt 29$_{21}$. **4. defeat, slaughter,** מַכָּה בַּפְּלִשְׁתִּים *the slaughter among the Philistines* 1 S 14$_{30}$. → נכה hi. *strike.*

מִכְוָה 7 n.f.—cstr. מִכְוַת—**(scar of a) burn,** in skin, מִחְיַת הַמִּכְוָה *rawness of the burn* Lv 13$_{24}$. → כוה *burn.*

מָכוֹן 17.2.11 n.m.—cstr. מְכוֹן; sf. מְכוֹנִי; pl. Q מכונים; cstr. Q מכוני; sf. מְכוֹנֶיהָ—**1a. place** of Y.'s dwelling 1 K 8$_{39}$||2 C 6$_{30}$, **site** of Y.'s house Ezr 2$_{68}$, Mount Zion Is 4$_5$. **b. (dwelling) place** of distress 1QS 10$_{15}$. **c.** perh. **dwelling,** בית מכונים *house of dwelling* 4QInstr^d 178$_3$. **2. base, foundation** of Y.'s throne Ps 89$_{15}$, the earth Ps 104$_5$; net of wisdom as a strong foundation Si 6$_{29}$. → כון *be firm.*

מְכוֹנָה 25.2.2 n.f.—sf. מְכוֹנָתוֹ; pl. מְכֹנוֹת; sf. מְכוֹנֹתָיו—**1. base, stand** of laver in temple 1 K 7$_{27}$, ephah Zc 5$_{11}$, altar Ezr 3$_3$. **2. dwelling place, property, estate** Si 44$_6$. **3. foundation** of Sheol, מכונתו א[ש] *its foundation is fire* 4QBéat 15$_6$. → כון *be firm.*

[מְכוּרָה] 3 n.f.—sf. מְכוּרֹתָם—**origin,** אֶרֶץ מְכֻרוֹתַיִךְ *land of your origin* Ezk 21$_{35}$.

מָכִי 1.0.0.5 pr.n.m. **Machi.**

[מִכָיְהוּ], see מִיכָיְהוּ *Micaiah.*

מָכִיר 22.0.0.1 pr.n.m. **Machir.**

מָכִירִי 1 gent. **Machirite.**

מכך 3 vb.—**Qal** 1 + waw וַיָּמֹכּוּ—**be brought low, be humiliated, collapse,** on account of (בְּ) sin, of Israelites Ps 106$_{43}$.

Ni. 1 Impf. יִמַּךְ—**sag, sink,** on account of (בְּ) laziness, of roof-beam Ec 10$_{18}$.

Ho. 1 Pf. הֻמְּכוּ—**be brought low,** of wicked Jb 24$_{24}$. → cf. מוך *be low.*

[מִכַל], see מִיכַל *Michal.*

[מִכְלָא] 3 n.[m.]—מִכְלָה; pl. cstr. מִכְלְאֹת—**fold, enclosure,** for sheep Hb 3$_{17}$ Ps 78$_{70}$, goats Ps 50$_9$. → כלא *restrain.*

*[מִכְלְבֹת] n.f.pl. **tongs,** מִכְלְבֹת זָהָב *(pair of) golden tongs* 2 C 4$_{21}$ (if em. מִכְלוֹת זָהָב *perfection of gold*).

מִכְלָה, see מִכְלָא *fold.*

מִכְלוֹל 2.0.1 n.[m.] **perfection,** לְבֻשֵׁי מִכְלוֹל *those clothed of,* i.e. in, *perfection* Ezk 23$_{12}$, מכלול הדר *perfection of adornment* 1QSb 3$_{25}$. → כלל *perfect.*

[מִכְלוֹת] 1 n.f.pl. **perfection,** מִכְלוֹת זָהָב *perfection of gold,* i.e. purest gold 2 C 4$_{21}$. → כלה *be complete.*

[מִכְלָל] 1 n.[m.]—pl. מַכְלֻלִים—**ornate robe** Ezk 27$_{24}$. → כלל *perfect.*

[מִכְלָל] 1 n.[m.] **perfection,** מִכְלַל־יֹפִי *perfection of beauty* Ps 50$_2$. → כלל *perfect.*

מַכֹּלֶת 1 n.f. **food** 1 K 5$_{25}$. → אכל *eat.*

[מִכְמָן] 1 n.[m.] **treasure,** מִכְמַנֵּי הַזָּהָב וְהַכֶּסֶף *treasures of gold and silver* Dn 11$_{43}$.

מִכְמָס 11 pl.n. **Michmas.**

מִכְמָר 2 n.[m.]—pl. sf. מִכְמֹרָיו—**net** Ps 141$_{10}$; תּוֹא מִכְמָר *antelope of,* i.e. in, *a net* Is 51$_{20}$. → cf. מִכְמֹרֶת *net.*

מִכְמֹרֶת 3.0.2 n.f.—sf. מִכְמַרְתּוֹ—**net,** perh. specif. **fishing net** Hb 1$_{15}$. → cf. מִכְמָר *net.*

מִכְמָשׂ, see מִכְמָס *Michmas.*

מִכְמָשׁ, see מִכְמָס *Michmas.*

מִכְמְתָת 2 pl.n. **Michmethath.**

מַכְנַדְבַי 1 pr.n.m. **Machnadebai.**

מְכֹנָה 1 pl.n. **Meconah.**

[מִכְנָסַיִם] 5.1.1 n.m.du.—cstr. מִכְנְסֵי—**breeches,** linen undergarments of priests Ex 28$_{42}$. → כנס *gather.*

מֶכֶס 6.0.3.1 n.m.—cstr. מֶכֶס; sf. מִכְסָם—**tribute,** tax on spoil for cultic purposes Nm 31$_{41}$. → כסס *reckon.*

[מִכְסָה] 2.0.1 n.f.—cstr. מִכְסַת; pl. cstr. Sam מִכְסוֹת—**number** of persons Ex 12$_4$, **amount** of valuation Lv 27$_{23}$. → כסס *reckon.*

מִכְסֶה 16.0.1 n.m.—cstr. מִכְסֵה; sf. מִכְסֵהוּ—**covering** of skin, for tent of meeting Ex 26$_{14}$||36$_{19}$; covering of Noah's ark Gn 8$_{13}$. → כסה *cover.*

מְכַסֶּה 4 n.m.—pl. sf. מְכַסַּיִךְ—**covering,** of fatty tissue around internal organs Lv 9$_{19}$, worms covering the dead Is 14$_{11}$, awning of ship Ezk 27$_7$, clothing Is 23$_{18}$. → כסה *cover.*

מַכְפֵּלָה 6 pl.n. **Machpelah.**

מכר I 80.1.22 vb.—**Qal** 57.0.18 Pf. מָכַר; impf. יִמְכֹּר (יִמְכָּר־); impv. מִכְרָה, מִכְרִי; ptc. מֹכֵר, מֹכֶרֶת, מֹכְרִים; inf. abs. מָכֹר; cstr. לִמְכּוֹר (לְמִכְרָהּ, מִכְרָם).—**1. sell** clothing Pr 31$_{24}$, field Lv 27$_{20}$, animal Ex 21$_{35}$, daughter as (לְ) slave

Ex 21_7, birthright Gn 25_{31}, truth Pr 23_{23}. **2. deliver over** Israel into power of (בְּיַד) enemies (subj. Y.) Jg 2_{14}, person to (לְ) Sheol (subj. iniquities) 11QPsa 19_{10}. **3.** ptc. as noun, **trader** Ne 13_{20}.

Ni. 19.0.3 Pf. נִמְכַּר; impf. יִמָּכֵר; ptc. נִמְכָּרִים; inf. הִמָּכְרוֹ—**1. be sold,** of land Lv 25_{23}, animal Lv 27_{27}, person as slave Jr 34_{14}. **2. be delivered over,** of Israelites by Y. Is 52_3. **3. deliver up oneself, sell oneself** to (לְ) creditor Lv 25_{39}.

Hi. 0.0.1 Impf. תמכיר—**sell** one's honour for (בְּ) a price 4QInstr^b 2.2_{18}.

Htp. 4.1 Pf. הִתְמַכֶּר; + waw וַיִּתְמַכְּרוּ ;הִתְמַכֶּרְךָ—**1. deliver oneself** to do evil 1 K 21_{20}. **2. sell oneself** to (לְ) enemy as (לְ) slave Dt 28_{68}.

→ מֶכֶר *value,* מִמְכָּר *mortgaged property,* מִמְכֶּרֶת *sale,* מַכָּר I *business assessor,* III *sale.*

*מכר II 3.1 vb.—**Htp.** 3.1 Pf. הִתְמַכֵּר; + waw וַיִּתְמַכְּרוּ—**practise deceit, guile** 1 K $21_{20.25}$ 2 K 17_{17} Si 47_{25}. → מְכֵרָה IV *beguilement.*

*[מַכָּר] I 2 n.[m.]—sf. מַכָּרוֹ; pl. sf. מַכָּרֵיכֶם—**business assessor,** temple official valuing sacrificial animals and offerings 2 K $12_{6.8}$. → מכר I *sell.*

[מַכָּר] II 2 n.[m.]—sf. מַכָּרוֹ; pl. sf. מַכָּרֵיכֶם—**acquaintance** of priest, from whom money is received for repair of temple 2 K $12_{6.8}$. → נכר I *recognize.*

*[מַכָּר] III 2 n.[m.]—sf. מַכָּרוֹ; pl. sf. מַכָּרֵיכֶם—**sale** of offerings by priests to raise finance for repair of temple 2 K $12_{6.8}$. → מכר I *sell.*

מֶכֶר 3.0.9 n.m.—sf. מִכְרָם—**1. value, price** of water Nm 20_{19}, capable wife Pr 31_{10}. **2. mortgaged land, land sold** Mur 30 1_4, **merchandise** Ne 13_{16}. **3. sale** Mur 30 2_{24}. **4.** מֶכֶר עַל־הָאָבוֹת perh. **patrimony, inheritance from father** Dt 18_8. → מכר I *sell.*

[מִכְרֶה] I 1 n.m. **pit** or **mine,** מִכְרֵה־מֶלַח *pit of salt* Zp 2_9. → כרה I *dig.*

*[מִכְרֶה] II 1 n.m. **heap,** מִכְרֵה־מֶלַח *heap of salt* Zp 2_9.

*[מְכֵרָה] I 1 n.f.—pl. sf. מְכֵרֹתֵיהֶם—**counsel, plan** Gn 49_5.

*[מְכֵרָה] II 1 n.f.—pl. sf. מְכֵרֹתֵיהֶם—**weapon** Gn 49_5.

*[מְכֵרָה] III 1 n.f.—pl. sf. מְכֵרֹתֵיהֶם—**staff** Gn 49_5.

*[מְכֵרָה] IV 1 n.f.—pl. sf. מְכֵרֹתֵיהֶם—**beguilement** Gn 49_5. → מכר II *practise deceit.*

מִכְרִי 1 pr.n.m. **Michri.**

*[מְכֵרֶת] 1 n.f.—pl. sf. מְכֵרֹתֵיהֶם—**circumcision blade** Gn 49_5. → כרת *cut.*

מְכֵרָתִי 1 gent. **Mecherathite.**

מִכְשׁוֹל 14.2.12 n.m.—pl. מִכְשֹׁלִים—**stumbling block, (cause of) stumbling,** מִכְשׁוֹל עָוֹן *stumbling block of iniquity* Ezk 18_{30}; in ref. to Y., צוּר מִכְשׁוֹל *rock of,* i.e. that causes, *stumbling* Is 8_{14}. → כשׁל *stumble.*

*מכשׁל vb. **Hi.,** of Y., **bring down to destruction** Zp 1_3 (if em. וְהַמַּכְשֵׁלוֹת אֶת־הָרְשָׁעִים *and the stumbling blocks with the wicked* to וְהִמְכַּשַׁלְתִּי אֶת־הָרְשָׁעִים *and I will bring the wicked down to destruction*). → cf. מכך *sink,* כשׁל *stumble.*

מַכְשֵׁלָה 2 n.f.—pl. מַכְשֵׁלוֹת—**1. ruin** Is 3_6. **2. stumbling block** Zp 1_3. → כשׁל *stumble.*

מִכְתָּב 9.0.0.1 n.m. **1. writing, script,** מִכְתַּב אֱלֹהִים *writing of God* Ex 32_{16}. **2a. (piece of) writing, document,** i.e. composition Is 38_9, letter Arad ost. 40_{12}. **b. inscription** Ex 39_{30}. → כתב *write.*

[מְכִתָּה] 1 n.f.—sf. מְכִתָּתוֹ—**fragment(s)** of smashed pot Is 30_{14}. → כתת *crush.*

מִכְתָּם I 6 n.[m.] **Miktam,** particular kind of psalm Ps 16_1.

*מִכְתָּם II 6 n.[m.] **secret prayer** Ps 16_1.

*מִכְתָּם III 6 n.[m.] **inscription** on stone slab Ps 16_1. → כתם *stain.*

*מִכְתָּם IV 6 n.[m.] **gold-lettered inscription** Ps 16_1. → כֶּתֶם *gold.*

*מִכְתָּם V 6 n.[m.] **song sung to the capped reed pipe** Ps 16_1.

מַכְתֵּשׁ I 2 n.m. **1. mortar** Pr 27_{22}. **2. hollow,** geographical feature, perh. lit. 'molar tooth' Jg 15_{19}. → כתשׁ *pound.*

מַכְתֵּשׁ II 1 pl.n. **Machtesh.**

*[מֵל], [מֶל] n.[m.] **hair** Is 57_9 (if em. וַתָּשֻׁרִי *and you journeyed* to וַתְּשָׁרִי [qal] or וַתְּשָׁרִי [hi.] *and you abounded* (with oil) and em. לַמֶּלֶךְ *to the king* to לְמַלֵּךְ or לְמֶלְךָ *for your hair*).

מלא 250.9.46.2 vb.—**Qal** 101.2.22 Pf. מָלֵא ,מָלְאָה; impf. יִמְלְאוּ; impv. מִלְאוּ; ptc. מָלֵא ,מְלֵאִים; inf. מְלֹאת—**1a. be full,** of vessel 2 K 4_6, of Israelites Zc 9_{15} (+ כְּ *like* bowl). **b. be full of water, overflow,** of Jordan Jos 3_{15}. **c. be** fully set, determined to do evil, of heart Ec 8_{11}. **d. be satisfied,** השב נא את בגדי ואמלא *return my garment, and I will be satisfied* Meṣad Ḥashavyahu ost. 1_{12}. **2.** with accus. of material, **a. be full of, be filled with** grain Jl 2_{24}, violence Gn 6_{13}, cursing Ps 10_7, anger Jr 6_{11}. **b. have one's fill of, be sated with** blood (subj. sword of Y.) Is 34_6. **3a. be fulfilled, accomplished, completed,** of days Gn 25_{24}, military service Is 40_2. **b.** inf. as noun, **fulfilment** 4QShir^b 63.3_2. **4a. fill** earth (subj. humans) Gn 1_{28}, heaven and earth (subj. Y.) Jr 23_{24}, tabernacle (subj. glory of Y.) Ex 40_{34}. **b. fill** person, מְלָאוֹ לִבּוֹ לַעֲשׂוֹת כֵּן *his heart has filled him,* i.e. he dares, *to do such a thing* Est 7_5. **5. fill with, a.** double accus., jar with water 1 K 18_{34}, place with blood Jr 19_4. **b.** accus. + prep., omer with (מִן) manna Ex $16_{32(Sam)}$. **6.** obj. יָד, lit. 'fill the hand', **consecrate, ordain** oneself to (לְ) Y. Ex 32_{29}.

Ni. 36.1.4 Pf. נִמְלָא; impf. יִמָּלֵא—**1. be filled,** of land Ps $80_{10(mss)}$, temple 2 K 10_{21}. **2. be full of, filled with, a.** with accus. of material: rain Ec 11_3, praise Ps 71_8, anger Est 3_5, knowledge 1 K 7_{14}. **b.** with prep. מִן *of, with* Pharaoh's body Ezk 32_6. **3a. have one's fill, be satisfied,** of appetite Ec 6_7. **b. be sated with** (מִן) hearing (subj. ear) Ec 1_8. **4. be full in number, be complete,** of days Ex 7_{25}, army 1QM 5_3. **5. be fully** with (בְּ), i.e. **fully trust** wisdom Si 4_{17}. **6. be paid in full,** of recompense Jb 15_{32}. **7. arm oneself with** iron and shaft of spear 2 S 23_7.

Pi. 111.7.20.2 Pf. מִלֵּא (מִלָּא), מִלֵּאתָ; impf. יְמַלֵּא (יְמַלֶּה); impv. מַלֵּא, מַלְאוּ; ptc. מְמַלֵּא, מְמַלְאִים; inf. מַלֵּא (מַלְאָם), מַלֹּאות—**1a.** with accus. only of thing filled, **fill** skin bottle Jos 9_{13}, one's stomach Ezk 7_{19}, someone's mouth Ps 81_{11}, treasuries Pr 8_{21}. **b. fill with,** (1) with double accus., sack with food Gn 44_1, land with glory. 1QM 12_{12}, mouth with laughter Jb 8_{21}, person with spirit of wisdom Ex 28_3. (2) with accus. + prep., hand with (מִן) grain offering Lv 9_{17}, land with (בְּ) uncleanness Ezr 9_{11}. **2a. fulfil, accomplish, complete** word of Y. 1 K 2_{27}, number of days Ex 23_{26}, deeds 1QS 3_{16}. **b. confirm** someone's words 1 K 1_{14}. **3. fill in, set** precious stones Ex 31_5. **4a. fill bow, set (arrow)** to bowstring Zc 9_{13}. **b.** with obj. יָד, **fill hand** with (בְּ) bow, i.e. **draw** bow 2 K 9_{24}. **5.** with obj. יָד, **fill hand,** i.e. **ordain, consecrate as priest** Ex 28_{41}, **consecrate** altar Ezk 43_{26}, oneself to (לְ) Y. 1 C 29_5. **6. wholly follow** after (אַחֲרֵי) Y. Nm 14_{24}. **7. do fully,** as auxiliary verb of קרא *call,* i.e. call loudly Jr 4_5. **8. give** something **in full number** to (לְ) someone 1 S 18_{27}. **9. replenish, satisfy** person Jr 31_{25}, appetite Pr 6_{30}. **10. overflow** over (עַל) banks, of river 1 C 12_{16}. **11.** perh. privatively **empty (from)** stomach Jb 15_2. **12. assemble en masse,** קִרְאוּ מַלְאוּ *cry, assemble en masse* Jr 4_5 (or §7).

Pu. 1 Ptc. מְמֻלָּאִים—**be set with** (בְּ) precious stones Ca 5_{14}.

Htp. 1 Impf. יִתְמַלְּאוּן—**mass** (intrans.) against (עַל) person Jb 16_{10}.

→ מָלֵא *full,* מְלֹא *fulness,* מְלֵאָה *full produce,* מִלֻּאָה *setting,* מִלֻּא *consecration,* מִלֵּאת I *setting,* II *water-hole,* V *fulness,* מִלּוֹא I *citadel;* cf. מלה *be full.*

מָלֵא 64.6.10 adj.—Q מלה; cstr. מְלֵא; f.s. מְלֵאָה; cstr. מְלֵאַתִי; m.pl. מְלֵאִים; f.pl. מְלֵאוֹת—**1a. full,** of storehouse Ps 144_{13}, cistern 3QTr 2_1, sea Ec 1_7, ear of grain Gn 41_7, horse 1QM 6_{12}, moon Si 50_6, wind Jr 4_{12}, price Gn 23_9. **b.** as noun, **full one,** in ref. to vessel 2 K 4_4. **2. full of, a.** abs., גְּבִעִים מְלֵאִים יַיִן *bowls full of wine* Jr 35_5, לֵב בְּנֵי־הָאָדָם מָלֵא־רָע *the heart of humanity is full of evil* Ec 9_3. **b.** cstr., קִרְיָה ... מְלֵאֲתִי מִשְׁפָּט *city ... full of justice* Is 1_{21}. **c.** cstr. as noun, מְלֵא יָמִים *one full of days,* i.e. aged one Jr 6_{11}. **3. pregnant,** of woman 11QT 50_{10}, animal 11QT 52_5. **4.** as noun, **fulness** or **full one,** i.e. sea, מֵי מָלֵא *waters of fulness,* i.e. abundant waters Ps 73_{10}. **5.** as adv., (1) **fully,** קַשׁ יָבֵשׁ מָלֵא *straw that is fully dried* Na 1_{10}. (2) **loudly,** קָרְאוּ אַחֲרֶיךָ מָלֵא *they cry loudly after you* Jr 12_6. → מלא *be full.*

מִלֹא, see מִלּוֹא *citadel.*

[מִלֻּא] 15.0.1 n.m.—pl. מִלֻּאִים; sf. מִלֻּאֵיכֶם—**1a. consecration (to the priesthood)** Ex 29_{22} Lv 8_{33}. **b. consecration offering** Ex 29_{34}. **2. setting** of precious stones Ex 25_7||35_9. → מלא *be full.*

[מְלֹא] 38.0.6.1 n.m.—מְלֹא, מְלוֹ; sf. מְלֹאוֹ—**1. fulness,** i.e. **amount that fills,** מְלֹא כַּף *fulness of hand,* i.e. handful Ec 4_6. **2. fulness,** i.e. **that which fills, contents,** לִי תֵּבֵל וּמְלֹאָהּ *mine is the world and its fulness* Ps 50_{12}.

3. **multitude,** מְלֹא־הַגּוֹיִם *multitude of the nations* Gn 48₁₉. → מלא *fill.*

מְלֵאָה 3.0.3 n.f.—sf. מְלֵאָתְךָ—**full produce** Ex 22₂₈ Nm 18₂₇ Dt 22₉. → מלא *be full.*

[מִלֻּאָה] 3.1 n.f.—cstr. מִלֻּאַת; pl. sf. מִלּוּאֹתָם—**setting** of precious stone Ex 28₁₇. → מלא *be full.*

מַלְאָךְ 213.1.81 n.m.—cstr. מַלְאַךְ; sf. מַלְאָכִי; pl. מַלְאָכִים; cstr. מַלְאֲכֵי; sf. מַלְאָכָיו—**1. messenger,** sometimes with task other than conveying of message Jos 7₂₂ Ps 104₄, political envoy Jr 27₃, spy Jos 6₁₇; מַלְאַךְ י׳ *messenger of Y.*, in ref. to prophet Hg 1₁₃, priest Ml 2₇. **2. heavenly messenger, angel,** מַלְאַךְ אֱלֹהִים *angel of God*, as good 1 S 29₉, wise, discerning 2 S 14₁₇, powerful 2 S 19₂₈, מַלְאַךְ י׳ *angel of Y.*, as destructive 2 K 19₃₅, מלאך משטמה *angel of malevolence* 1QM 13₁₁, חושך *of darkness* 1QS 3₂₀. **2. salesman** Is 23₂(1QIsa^a). → cf. מַלְאָכוּת *message.*

מְלָאכָה 166.7.19.1 n.f.—cstr. מְלֶאכֶת; sf. מְלַאכְתְּךָ; pl. cstr. מַלְאֲכוֹת; sf. מַלְאֲכוֹתֶיךָ—**1a. work, task, deed** of Y., in creation Gn 2₂, judgment Jr 50₂₅; of humans, in farming 1 C 27₂₆, rebuilding temple Hg 1₁₄, preparing sacrifices 2 C 29₃₄, serving king Dn 8₂₇. **b. handiwork, craft,** מְלֶאכֶת חָרָשׁ *craft of an artisan* Ex 35₃₅. **c. business, trade,** עֹשֵׂי מְלָאכָה *traders* Ps 107₂₃. **2. (product of) work,** מְלֶאכֶת עוֹר *work (made) of skin* Lv 13₄₈. **3. use, purpose,** הֲיִצְלַח לִמְלָאכָה *is it good for any use?* Ezk 15₄. **4. property, object, livestock** Gn 33₁₄ Ex 22₇; מלאכת הרבים *property of the Many* 1QS 6₂₀.

[מַלְאָכוּת] 1 n.f.—cstr. מַלְאֲכוּת—**message** or perh. **messenger** of Y. Hg 1₁₃. → cf. מַלְאָךְ *messenger.*

מַלְאָכִי 1.0.0.1 pr.n.m. **Malachi.**

מלאכיה, see מַלְכִּיָּה *Malchi(j)ah.*

מְלֶאכֶת I, see מְלָאכָה *work.*

מְלֶאכֶת II, see מְלֶכֶת *queen.*

מִלֵּאת I 1 n.f. **setting** of eyes Ca 5₁₂. → מלא *be full.*

*מִלֵּאת II 1 n.f. **waterhole, pond** Ca 5₁₂. → מלא *be full.*

*מִלֵּאת III 1 n.f. **stream** Ca 5₁₂.

*מִלֵּאת IV 1 n.f. **pool** Ca 5₁₂.

*מִלֵּאת V 1 n.f. **fulness** Ca 5₁₂. → מלא *be full.*

מִלְּבַד, see לְבַד *alone.*

מַלְבּוּשׁ 8 n.m.—sf. מַלְבּוּשֶׁךָ; pl. sf. מַלְבּוּשָׁי—**garment, clothing** Is 63₃. → לבשׁ *dress.*

מַלְבֵּן 3 n.[m.] **1. brick mould** 2 S 12₃₁(Qr) (Kt מלכן). **2. brick pavement, terrace** or **quadrangle** Jr 43₉. → לבן II *make bricks.*

*[מלה] 0.0.3 vb.—**Qal** 0.0.3 Ptc. מלה—**be full,** ptc. as noun, **filled place,** i.e. terrace 3QTr 3₈.₁₁, cistern 3Q Tr 2₁. → cf. מלא *be full.*

מִלָּה 38.0.7 n.f.—sf. מִלָּתִי; pl. מִלִּים (מִלִּין); sf. מִלֶּיךָ—**1. word, speech** of Y. 2 S 23₂; usu. of humans Ps 139₄ Jb 4₂. **2.** derisive, **byword** Jb 30₉. → מלל II *speak.*

מְלוֹ, see מְלֹא *fulness.*

מִלּוֹא I 7.0.2 n.[m.]—מִלֹּא (Q מלה)—**1. citadel,** or as pl.n. **Millo,** הַמִּלּוֹא עִיר דָּוִד *the citadel in the city of David* 2 C 32₅. **2. mound** of earth, perh. **esplanade** or **terrace** 3QTr 3₈.₁₁. → מלא *fill.*

*מִלּוֹא II 7 pl.n. **Millo.**

מִלּוֹא III, see בֵּית מִלּוֹא *Beth-millo.*

מַלּוּחַ 1 n.[m.] **saltwort, mallow,** desert plant growing in salt marshes, *Mesembrianthum forskalii*, or **orache** *Atriplex halimus* Jb 30₄. → מלח I *salt.*

מַלּוּךְ 6 pr.n.m. **Malluch.**

מְלוּכָה I 24.0.4 n.f. **kingship, kingdom, royalty,** מִשְׁפַּט הַמְּלֻכָה *regulation(s) of the kingship* 1 S 10₂₅, זֶרַע הַמְּלוּכָה *offspring of royalty*, i.e. royal descendants Jr 41₁. → מלך I *be king.*

*מְלוּכָה II 4 n.f. **king** 2 S 12₂₆ Is 34₁₂ Ezk 16₁₃ Ps 22₂₉. → מלך I *be king.*

[מַלּוּכִי] 1 pr.n.m. **Malluchi.**

מָלוֹן 8.0.1 n.m. **lodging place** Gn 42₂₇; מְלוֹן אֹרְחִים *lodging place of travellers* Jr 9₁. → לין *lodge.*

מְלוּנָה 2 n.f. **hut,** for watching field at night Is 1₈ 24₂₀. → לין *lodge.*

מַלּוֹתִי 2 pr.n.m. **Mallothi.**

*[מָלוֹשׁ] 0.0.1 n.[m.] perh. **kneading trough** 4Q439 1.1₂. → לושׁ *knead.*

מלח I vb.—5.1.6 **Qal** 1.0.2 Impf. תִּמְלָח; ptc. Q מולחים—**salt, season with** (בְּ) salt, obj. grain offering Lv 2₁₃, meat 11QT 34₁₀.

Ni. 1 Pf. נִמְלָחוּ—**be grey, be dark** like (כְּ) smoke, of heavens Is 51₆.

Pu. 1.1.4 Ptc. מְמֻלָּח (Q ממולח)—**be salted, mixed with salt,** of incense Ex 30₃₅.

Ho. 2 Pf. הָמְלַחַתְּ; inf. abs. הָמְלֵחַ—**be rubbed with**

salt water, of Jerusalem as new born Ezk 16_4.
→ מַלּוּחַ *saltwort*, מְלֵחָה *salt land*.

מלח II 1.0.1 vb.—**Ni.** 1.0.1 Pf. נִמְלָחוּ; ptc. Q נמלח—**be dissipated, vanish,** of smoke 1QM 15_{10}, heavens like (כְּ) smoke Is 51_6. → מֶלַח II *frayed clothing*.

*מלח III 1 vb.—**Ni.** 1 Pf. נִמְלָחוּ—**be dark** like (כְּ) smoke, of heavens Is 51_6.

[מַלָּח] 4.0.2 n.m.—pl. מַלָּחִים; sf. מַלָּחַיִךְ—**mariner, sailor** Ezk 27_9.

מֶלַח I 28.3.4 n.m. **1. salt,** to season food Jb 6_6, added to offerings Lv 2_{13}; בְּרִית מֶלַח עוֹלָם *everlasting covenant of salt* Nm 18_{19}. **2. salt land** Si 39_{23}. → מלח I *salt*.

[מֶלַח] II 2 n.[m.]—pl. מְלָחִים—**frayed clothing, old clothing, rags** Jr $38_{11.12}$. → מלח II *be dissipated*.

מְלֵחָה 3.0.1 n.f. **salt land,** as unproductive Ps 107_{34}. → מלח I *salt*.

*[מְלָחִים] n.m. **cleverness,** אֵין מִשְׁלַחַת בִּמְלָחִם *there is no deliverance in cleverness* Ec 8_8 (if em. בַּמִּלְחָמָה *in war*).

מִלְחָמָה I 318.4.147 n.f.—cstr. מִלְחֶמֶת; sf. מִלְחַמְתְּךָ; pl. מִלְחָמוֹת; cstr. מִלְחֲמוֹת; sf. מִלְחֲמֹתָיו—**1.** usu. **war, battle, conflict** Gn 14_2; אִישׁ מִלְחָמָה *man of war* Jos 17_1, סֵפֶר מִלְחֲמֹת י׳ *the Book of the Wars of Y.* Nm 21_{14}, מלחמת שחקים *war of the clouds* 4QShirShabb^c 4_{10}. **2.** perh., by synecdoche, **weapons of war,** and perh. particular weapons, **lances** Ps 76_4. **3.** perh. **troops,** קַדְּשׁוּ מִלְחָמָה *consecrate the troops* Jl 4_9. → לחם I *fight*.

*[מִלְחָמָה] II 1 n.f. **adaptation, harmony, sistrum,** like Egyptian ivory or wood clappers or sistrum for beating time in music Is 30_{32}.

מלט I 95.4.10 vb.—**Qal** 0.0.2 Pf. מלטו—**escape, survive** during time of judgment CD 7_{21}.

Ni. 63.2.3 Pf. נִמְלַט; impf. יִמָּלֵט; impv. הִמָּלְטִי, הִמָּלֵט; ptc. נִמְלָט; inf. הִמָּלֵט—**1. escape from** (מִן) someone Ec 7_{26}, something 1 K 19_{17}. **2. flee to a place,** הָהָרָה הִמָּלֵט *flee to the hills!* Gn 19_{17}. **3. be delivered** (by Y.), אֵלֶיךָ זָעֲקוּ וְנִמְלָטוּ *to you they cried out and were delivered* Ps 22_6. **4a. slip away** 1 S 20_{29}. **b. slip in** 2 S 4_6.

Pi. 28.3.5 Pf. מִלֵּט (מִלְּטָנוּ); impf. יְמַלֵּט (יְמַלְּטֵהוּ); impv. מַלְּטָה, מַלְּטוּ; ptc. מְמַלֵּט, מְמַלְּטִים; inf. מַלֵּט—**1. deliver, save** people 2 S 19_{10} (+ מִן *from*), one's life (נֶפֶשׁ) 1 S 19_{11}, someone else's life 2 S 19_6 Ps 116_4 (subj. Y.). **2. leave** bones of deceased **undisturbed** 2 K 23_{18}. **3. lay eggs,** of snake Is 34_{15}.

Hi. 2.0.1 Pf. הִמְלִיטָה—**1. deliver, save,** of Y. Is 31_5. **2. give birth to, be delivered of** male Is 66_7.

Htp. 2 Impf. יִתְמַלָּטוּ—**1. escape,** of person Jb 19_{20}. **2. fly out,** of sparks Jb 41_{11}.

מלט II 1 vb.—**Htp.** 1 + waw וָאֶתְמַלְּטָה—**be bald on** (בְּ) skin of teeth Jb 19_{20}.

*מלט III 1 vb.—**Htp.** 1 + waw וָאֶתְמַלְּטָה—**bite oneself, gnaw oneself in** (בְּ) skin Jb 19_{20}.

*מלט IV 1 vb.—**Htp.** 1 + waw וָאֶתְמַלְּטָה—**cleave, stick to** (בְּ) skin of teeth Jb 19_{20}. → מֶלֶט *mortar*.

מֶלֶט 1 n.[m.] **mortar,** or **clay floor** Jr 43_9. → מלט IV *cleave*.

מְלַטְיָה 1 pr.n.m. **Melatiah.**

*[מְלִיָּהוּ] 0.0.0.2 pr.n.[m.] **Maliah.**

[מְלִיכוּ], see מַלּוּכִי *Malluchi*.

[מְלִילָה] 1.0.1 n.f.—pl. מְלִילֹת—**ear of corn** Dt 23_{26}. → מלל III *scrape*.

*מֵלִיץ I 5.1.14 n.m.—pl. cstr. מְלִיצֵי; sf. מְלִיצֶיךָ—**1. interpreter** Gn 42_{23}. **2. spokesperson, mediator** Jb 33_{23}, מליץ לעמך *a mediator for your people* 4QDiscourse 7_2. **3. envoy** 2 C 32_{31}. **4. official** Si 10_2. → cf. מְלִיצָה V *trope*.

*מֵלִיץ II 5.1.14 n.m.—pl. cstr. מְלִיצֵי—**1. one who speaks freely** Gn 42_{23}. **2. spokesperson** Is 43_{27}. **3. envoy** 2 C 32_{31}. **4. official** Si 10_2.

מְלִיצָה I 2.1 n.f. **mocking poem, figure** Hb 2_6 Pr 1_6 Si 47_{17}. → ליץ *scorn*.

*מְלִיצָה II 2.1 n.f. **allusive saying, slippery saying, enigma** Hb 2_6 Pr 1_6 Si 47_{17}. → מליץ *be smooth*.

*מְלִיצָה III 2.1 n.f. **sharp saying, obscure saying** Hb 2_6 Pr 1_6 Si 47_{17}.

*מְלִיצָה IV 2.1 n.f. **sweet saying** Hb 2_6 Pr 1_6 Si 47_{17}. → מליץ *be pleasant*.

*מְלִיצָה V 2.1 n.f. **trope, saying that puts things in different words** Hb 2_6 Pr 1_6 Si 47_{17}. → cf. מֵלִיץ I *interpreter*.

מלך I 347.1.8.1 vb.—**Qal** 297.1.7.1 Pf. מָלַךְ, מָלְכָה; impf. יִמְלֹךְ; + waw וַיִּמְלֹךְ (וַיִּמְלָךְ־); impv. מְלֹךְ־, מָלְכָה Qr, מָלְכִי Qr; ptc. מֹלֵךְ, מֹלֶכֶת; inf. abs. מָלֹךְ; cstr. מְלֹךְ (מָלְכוֹ)—**1a. be**

king, become king, of Y. Ps 93$_{1}$, human 1 S 24$_{21}$ 1 K 11$_{43}$||2 C 9$_{31}$ (+ תַּחַת *in place of*). **b. be queen** Est 2$_{4}$ (+ תַּחַת). **2. reign over** (עַל), of Y. Mc 4$_{7}$, human 1 K 11$_{25}$.

Hi. 49.0.1 Pf. הִמְלַכְתָּ, הִמְלִיךְ; impf. נַמְלִיךְ; + waw וַיַּמְלֵךְ, וַיַּמְלִיכוּ; ptc. מַמְלִיךְ; inf. הַמְלִיךְ—**1.** trans., **a. make** someone **king,** of Y. 1 S 15$_{35}$ (+ עַל *over*), humans 2 K 14$_{21}$||2 C 26$_{1}$ (+ תַּחַת *in place of*). **b. cause** someone **to reign** as (לְ) king, subj. Y. 1 S 15$_{11}$, humans Jg 9$_{6}$. **c. make** someone **queen** Est 2$_{17}$ (+ תַּחַת *in place of*). **2.** abs., **make kings,** הֵם הִמְלִיכוּ וְלֹא מִמֶּנִּי *they made kings, but without my sanction* Ho 8$_{4}$.

Ho. 1 Pf. הָמְלַךְ—**be made king** over (עַל) kingdom Dn 9$_{1}$.

→ מֶלֶךְ I *king,* מַלְכָּה *queen,* מְלֶכֶת *queen,* מֹלֶךְ II *kingdom,* מְלוּכָה I *kingship,* II *king,* מַלְכוּת *kingdom,* מַמְלָכָה *kingdom,* מַמְלָכוּת *kingdom,* מֹלֶכֶת *sororarch.*

מלך II 2 vb.—**Ni.** 1 + waw וַיִּמָּלֵךְ—**take counsel,** וַיִּמָּלֵךְ לִבִּי עָלַי *and my heart took counsel with me,* i.e. I considered (it) Ne 5$_{7}$.

Hi. 1 Pf. הִמְלִיכוּ—**seek counsel** through (מִן) Y. Ho 8$_{4}$.

→ מֹלֵךְ III *counsellor,* מֶלֶךְ III *counsel,* מְלָךְ *counsel.*

*מלך III 1 vb.—**Ni.** 1 + waw וַיִּמָּלֵךְ—**be torn away, be snatched,** וַיִּמָּלֵךְ לִבִּי עָלַי *and my heart was snatched from me,* i.e. I was beside myself Ne 5$_{7}$.

*מלך IV vb. **Qal, own,** ptc. as noun, **owner** Ec 1$_{12}$ (if em. מֶלֶךְ *king* to מֹלֵךְ).

מַלָּךְ *counsellor,* see מֹלֵךְ III *counsellor.*

מֶלֶךְ I 2518.16.130.70 n.m.—sf. מַלְכִּי; pl. מְלָכִים (מַלְכִין); cstr. מַלְכֵי; sf. מַלְכֵיהֶם, מְלָכֶיהָ—**king, ruler, 1.** usu. human, of Israel 1 S 15$_{1}$, Egypt Ex 1$_{8}$, Babylonian empire, descr. as מֶלֶךְ מְלָכִים *king of kings* Ezk 26$_{7}$. **2.** Y., מֶלֶךְ הַכָּבוֹד *king of glory* Ps 24$_{7}$, מֶלֶךְ כָּל־הָאָרֶץ *king of all the earth* Ps 47$_{8}$. **3.** Leviathan Jb 41$_{26}$. **4.** tree Jg 9$_{8}$. → מלך I *be king.*

מֶלֶךְ II 2 pr.n.m. **Melech.**

*[מֶלֶךְ] III 1 n.[m.]—pl. מְלָכִין—**counsel, advice** Pr 31$_{3}$. → מלך II *take counsel.*

מֹלֶךְ I 8 pr.n.[m.] **Molech.**

*מֹלֶךְ II 1 n.m.—pl. מְלָכִים—**kingdom** Ps 136$_{17}$. → מלך I *be king.*

*[מֹלֵךְ] III or [מַלָּךְ] n.m. **counsellor** Ec 1$_{12}$ (if em. מֶלֶךְ *king*). → מלך II *take counsel.*

*[מְלָךְ] 1 n.m.—pl. מְלָכִין—**counsel** Pr 31$_{3}$. → מלך II *take counsel.*

מלכא, see מַלְכָּה *queen.*

[מַלְכֹּדֶת] 1 n.f.—sf. מַלְכֻּדְתּוֹ—**snare** Jb 18$_{10}$. → לכד *capture.*

מַלְכָּה 35.0.1 n.f.—Q מלכא; cstr. מַלְכַּת; pl. מְלָכוֹת—**queen, 1.** usu. wife of non-Israelite king, אֶסְתֵּר הַמַּלְכָּה *Esther, the queen* Est 2$_{22}$; also of sovereign, מַלְכַּת־שְׁבָא *queen of Sheba* 1 K 10$_{1}$. **2.** wife of Israelite king Ca 6$_{8.9}$. → מלך I *be king.*

מִלְכָּה 11 pr.n.f. **Milcah.**

מַלְכוּת 91.2.47 n.f.—sf. מַלְכוּתִי; pl. mss מַלְכֻיּוֹת (L מַלְכֻיוֹת)—**1. kingdom, realm, kingship, rule, a.** usu. of human, מַלְכוּת שָׁאוּל *kingdom of Saul* 1 C 12$_{24}$. **b.** of Y. 1 C 28$_{5}$. **2a. royalty, royal status** Est 1$_{19}$. **b.** appar. **royal robes** Est 5$_{1}$. **3. (period of) reign,** תְּחִלַּת מַלְכוּתוֹ *beginning of his reign* Ezr 4$_{6}$. → מלך I *be king.*

*[מַלְכִּי] 0.0.0.1 pr.n.m. **Malchi.**

מַלְכִּיאֵל 3 pr.n.m. **Malchiel.**

מַלְכִּיאֵלִי 1 gent. **Malchielite.**

מַלְכִּיָּה 16.0.13.17 pr.n.m. **Malchi(j)ah.**

מַלְכִּיָּהוּ, see מַלְכִּיָּה *Malchi(j)ah.*

מַלְכִּי־צֶדֶק 2.0.3 pr.n.m. **Melchizedek.**

מַלְכִּירָם 1.0.0.2 pr.n.m. **Malchiram.**

*[מַלְכִּי־רֶשַׁע] 0.0.1 pr.n.m. **Melchiresha.**

מַלְכִּי־שׁוּעַ 5 pr.n.m. **Malchishua.**

מַלְכָּם 1 pr.n.m. **Malcam.**

מִלְכֹּם 3 pr.n.[m.] **Milcom.**

מלכן, see מַלְבֵּן *brick mould.*

*[מַלְכְּנֵר] 0.0.0.1 pr.n.[m.] **Malchiner.**

[מְלֶכֶת] 5 n.f. **queen,** מְלֶכֶת הַשָּׁמַיִם *the queen of heaven* Jr 7$_{18}$ 44$_{17.18.19.25}$ (all five mss מְלֶאכֶת). → מלך I *be king.*

*מֹלֶכֶת 1 n.f. **sororarch,** i.e. sister who rules 1 C 7$_{18}$ (unless הַמֹּלֶכֶת pr.n.f. *Hammolecheth*). → מלך I *be king.*

מלל I 6.0.1 vb.—**Qal** (unless **Ni.**) 4.0.1 Impf. יִמַּל—**wither, wilt, fade,** of branch Jb 18$_{16}$, human being Jb 14$_{2}$.

Po. 1 Impf. יְמוֹלֵל—**wither,** of grass Ps 90$_{6}$.

Htpo. 1 Impf. יִתְמֹלְלוּ—**wither,** of wicked Ps 58$_{8}$.

→ cf. אמל I *be feeble.*

מלל II 4.1.1 vb.—**Pi.** 4.1.1 Pf. מִלֵּל; impf. יְמַלֵּל—**1. speak, utter, declare knowledge** Jb 33₃, name of Y. 4QapPsA 1.1₇. **2. say to** (לְ) someone, מִי מִלֵּל לְאַבְרָהָם הֵינִיקָה בָנִים שָׂרָה *who would have said to Abraham that Sarah would suckle children!* Gn 21₇. → מִלָּה *word.*

מלל III 1 vb.—**Qal** 1 Ptc. מֹלֵל—**scrape** with (בְּ) feet, to make signs Pr 6₁₃. → מְלִילָה *ear of corn.*

מלל IV 4 vb.—**Qal** 1 Impv. מֹל—**circumcise** someone Jos 5₂.

Ni. 2 + waw וּנְמַלְתֶּם; + waw וַיִּמָּל—**1. be cut off,** of person Jb 14₂. **2. be circumcised** Gn 17₁₁.

Htpo. 1 Impf. יִתְמֹלָלוּ—**be cut off,** of the wicked Ps 58₈.

→ cf. מהל II *circumcise,* מול I *circumcise.*

מִלֲלַי 1 pr.n.m. **Milalai.**

[מַלְמָד] 1.1 n.[m.] **goad,** מַלְמַד הַבָּקָר *goad of (the) cattle* Jg 3₃₁. → למד *learn.*

מלץ 2 vb.—**Ni.** 2 Pf. נִמְלְצוּ—**be smooth, pleasant,** of Y.'s word(s) Ps 119₁₀₃, human words Jb 6₂₅₍ₘₛ₎. → מְלִיצָה II *allusive saying,* IV *sweet saying.*

מֶלְצַר 2 n.m. **guardian** Dn 1₁₁.₁₆.

מלק 2 vb.—**Qal** 2 + waw וּמָלַק—**pinch off, wring** head of bird Lv 1₁₅.

מַלְקוֹחַ 7 n.m. **spoil, booty** Nm 31₁₁. → לקח *take.*

[מַלְקוֹחַיִם] 1 n.[m.]du.—sf. מַלְקוֹחָי—**jaws** Ps 22₁₆. → לקח *take.*

מַלְקוֹשׁ 8.0.4 n.m. **latter rain,** from December to March Zc 10₁.

מֶלְקָחַיִם 6.0.1 n.[m.]du.—L מֶלְקָחַיִם; sf. מַלְקָחֶיהָ—**tongs,** to remove coal Is 6₆, as snuffers Ex 25₃₈. → לקח *take.*

*** [מַלְקֶט]** n.[m.] **gleaning,** מַלְקֶט שִׁבֳּלִים *gleaning of sheaves* Is 17₅ (if em. מְלַקֵּט *one gleaning*). → לקט *gather.*

*** [מָלָשׁ]** 0.0.0.2 pr.n.[m.] **Malash.**

*** [מַלְשֶׁנֶת]** n.f. **slander** Lm 3₆₁ (if em. מַחְשְׁבֹתָם *their schemes* to מַלְשֻׁנְתָם *their slander*).

מֶלְתָּחָה 1 n.f. **clothes store,** or **wardrobe,** or perh. **cloakroom** 2 K 10₂₂.

[מַלְתָּעוֹת] 1 n.f.pl.—pl. cstr. מַלְתְּעוֹת—**jaw-bone,** perh. **fangs** Ps 58₇. → (?) נתע *be broken;* cf. מְתַלְּעוֹת *jaw-bone.*

[מַמְּגוּרָה] 1 n.f.—pl. מַמְּגֻרוֹת—**granary, silo** Jl 1₁₇. → אגר *gather;* cf. מָגוֹר III *storage pit,* מְגוּרָה *granary.*

[מֵמַד] 1 n.[m.]—pl. sf. מְמַדֶּיהָ—**measurement** Jb 38₅. → מדד *measure.*

מְמוּכָן 3 pr.n.m. **Memucan.**

*** [מָמוֹן]** 0.1.4 n.[m.]—sf. Q ממונו—**wealth, property** 1QS 6₂.

[מָמוֹת] 2 n.[m.] **(manner of) death,** מְמוֹתֵי תַחֲלֻאִים *death of,* i.e. caused by, *diseases* Jr 16₄. → מות *die.*

מַמְזֵר 2.0.9 n.m.—pl. Q ממזרים—**bastard,** non-Judaean, excluded from assembly of Y. Dt 23₃, specif. Ashdodite Zc 9₆; later, appar. one born out of prohibited union 4QMMT B₃₉; their spirits mentioned with other evil spirits 4QShir[a] 1₅.

*** [מִמְחִיר]** n.[m.] **bargaining** Si 42₅₍M₎ ([מ]מחיר). → cf. מְחִיר *price.*

*** [מִמֶּךְ]** n.[m.] **sinkhole,** name for Sheol Am 3₁₁ (וְהוֹרִד מִמֵּךְ עֻזֵּךְ *and he will bring your strength down to the Sinkhole;* if em. מִמֵּךְ *from you*).

מִמְכָּר 10.2.1 n.m.—cstr. מִמְכַּר; pl. sf. מִמְכָּרָיו—**1. mortgaged property** Lv 25₁₄. **2. act of mortgaging** Lv 25₅₀. **3. value of mortgage** of inheritance Dt 18₈. **4. item for sale, wares, merchandise** Ne 13₂₀. → מכר I *sell.*

מִמְכֶּרֶת 1.0.2 n.f. **sale** or **transfer of possession,** מִמְכֶּרֶת עָבֶד *transfer of ownership of a slave* Lv 25₄₂. → מכר I *sell.*

מַמְלָכָה 117.3.26 n.f.—cstr. מַמְלֶכֶת (L מַמְלֶכֶת); pl. מַמְלָכוֹת; cstr. מַמְלְכוֹת—**1a. kingdom, realm** 2 S 3₂₈. **2. kingship, sovereignty** 1 S 24₂₁. **3. royalty,** זֶרַע הַמַּמְלָכָה *offspring of royalty,* i.e. royal family 2 K 11₁. **4. (period of) reign** Jr 28₁. **5.** perh. **king** Lm 2₂. → מלך I *be king.*

[מַמְלָכוּת] 9.0.1 n.f.—cstr. מַמְלְכוּת—**1. kingdom, realm** Jos 13₂₁. **2. kingship, sovereignty** Ho 1₄. **3. (period of) reign** Jr 26₁. → מלך I *be king.*

מֶמְסָךְ I 2 n.[m.] **(bowl of) mixed wine,** mixed with water, or perh. with spices or honey Pr 23₃₀. → מסך I *mix.*

*** מִמְסָךְ** II 1 n.[m.] **bowl, amphora** Pr 23₃₀. → מסך I *mix.*

מֶמֶר 1 n.[m.] **bitterness** Pr 17₂₅. → מרר I *be bitter.*

מַמְרֵא I 9.0.1 pl.n. **Mamre.**

מַמְרֵא II 2 pr.n.m. **Mamre.**

*[מַמְרֶה] n.m. **rebellion,** נַחֲלַת מַמְרֶה *inheritance of rebellion* Jb 20$_{29}$ (if em. אִמְרוֹ *his word*). → מרה I *rebel.*

מַמְרֹרִים 1 n.[m.]pl. **bitterness** Jb 9$_{18}$ (or em. מְמָרְרִים or בְּמְרֹרִים *with bitter things*, from מָרֹר). → מרר I *be bitter.*

מִמְשַׁח I 1 n.[m.] **anointing,** כְּרוּב מִמְשַׁח *anointed cherub* Ezk 28$_{14}$. → משׁח I *anoint.*

*מִמְשַׁח II 1 n.[m.] perh. **extension,** כְּרוּב מִמְשַׁח *cherub of extension*, i.e. with outstretched wings Ezk 28$_{14}$. → משׁח III *measure.*

*מִמְשַׁח III 1 n.[m.] **sparkling,** כְּרוּב מִמְשַׁח *sparkling cherub* Ezk 28$_{14}$.

מִמְשָׁל 3.0.12 n.[m.]—sf. Q ממשלו; pl. מִמְשָׁלִים—**1. dominion, rule,** קץ ממשל לכול אנשי גורלו *a period of dominion for all the men of his lot* 1QM 1$_5$. **2.** pl., **rulers,** הַמִּמְשָׁלִים לְבֵית אֲבִיהֶם *the rulers of their father's house* 1 C 26$_6$. → משׁל I *rule.*

מֶמְשָׁלָה 17.6.64 n.f.—sf. מֶמְשַׁלְתּוֹ, מֶמְשַׁלְתְּךָ; cstr. מֶמְשֶׁלֶת; pl. cstr. מֶמְשְׁלוֹת; sf. מֶמְשְׁלוֹתָיו—**1. dominion, rule, authority** of Y. Ps 145$_{13}$, Belial 1QM 14$_9$, angel 1QM 10$_{12}$, human 1 K 9$_{19}$, light 1QS 10$_1$, darkness 1QH 20$_6$, justice 11QMelch 2$_9$, evil 1QM 17$_5$. **2. (sphere of) dominion, realm** of Y., i.e. Israel Ps 114$_2$; of human ruler 2 K 20$_{13}$||Is 39$_2$. **3. military might** of Sennacherib 2 C 32$_9$. **4.** coll., perh. **subject(s)** of ruler Ps 103$_{22}$. → משׁל I *rule.*

[מִמְשָׁק] I 1 n.[m.]—cstr. מִמְשַׁק—**ground** Zp 2$_9$. → cf. מֶשֶׁק I *acquisition.*

*[מִמְשָׁק] II 1 n.[m.]—cstr. מִמְשַׁק—**place of possession** Zp 2$_9$.

*[מֶמְשָׁת] 0.0.0.5 pl.n. **Memshath.**

מַמְתַקִּים 2 n.[m.]pl. **sweetness, sweet things,** perh. specif. **sweet drink** Ca 5$_{16}$ Ne 8$_{10}$. → מתק I *be sweet.*

מָן I 14.0.1 n.m.—sf. מַנְךָ—**manna,** daily food of Israelites in desert, white like coriander seed, tasting like wafer made with honey Ex 16$_{31}$, or with oil Nm 11$_8$.

מָן II 1 perh. interrog. pron. **what?,** in ref. to manna, מָן הוּא *what is it?* Ex 16$_{15}$.

[מַן] I interrog. pron. **1. who?,** מַן־הוּא רָאָה הֲלִיכוֹתֶיךָ אֱלֹהִים *who is it who has seen your processions, O God?* Ps 68$_{24}$ (if em. מְנָהוּ : רָאוּ *his portion. They have seen*). **2. how many?,** מַן־הֵיכְלֵי שֵׁן *how many are (your) ivory palaces!* Ps 45$_9$ (if em. מִן *from*).

*[מַן] II n.m. **whoever,** מְחַץ מָתְנַיִם קָמָיו וּמְשַׂנְאָיו מַן־יְקוּמוּן *crush the loins of his opponents and of his enemies whoever rises up* Dt 33$_{11}$ (if em. מְשַׂנְאָיו מִן־יְקוּמוּן *of those who hate him, that they rise not again*).

[מֵן] I 2.1 n.[m.]—pl. מִנִּים—**string, stringed instrument** Ps 150$_4$.

[מֵן] II 1 n.[m.]—sf. מְנֵהוּ—**portion** Ps 68$_{24}$.

מִן 7717.59.c.1300.106 prep.—1a. before noun with art., מִן־ (מִן Ex 2$_7$), מֵ־; b. before non-guttural, usu. מִ־, with doubling of following consonant; rarely מִן־; c. before gutturals and ר, usu. מֵ־ (exceptions מִחוּץ, מחוּט, מִהְיוֹת, מִרְדֹּף, מְחוּצָה); d. before יְ, מִי־ assimilating יְ; e. before ״, מְ־. 2. rarer forms, מִנִּי, מִנֵּי (Is 30$_{11}$). 3. with suffix, מִנִּי (מִמֶּנִּי), מִכֶּם, מֵהֶן—**1.** of direction, **a. (away) from,** לָמָּה תַתְעֵנוּ ״ מִדְּרָכֶיךָ *why do you make us go astray, O Y., from your paths?* Is 63$_{17}$. **b. (positioned away) from, to, on, at; from (the side of), in (the direction of), to(wards),** מִכָּל־עֲבָרָיו *on all its sides* Jr 49$_{32}$, וַיִּסַּע לוֹט מִקֶּדֶם *and Lot journeyed eastwards* Gn 13$_{11}$. **c. from (out of), (from) out of,** ״ מִשָּׁמַיִם הִשְׁקִיף *Y. looked down from heaven* Ps 14$_2$. **d. in from the outside,** from the perspective of one who is inside, מַשְׁגִּיחַ מִן־הַחַלֹּנוֹת *gazing in from the windows* Ca 2$_9$. **e. (originating) from, of,** חֲזִיר מִיָּעַר *a wild boar from the forest* Ps 80$_{14}$. **f. from, (at the instigation) of, with (the sanction of),** הֵם הִמְלִיכוּ וְלֹא מִמֶּנִּי *they make kings, but not with my sanction* Ho 8$_4$. **g. starting from,** כִּי־יִהְיֶה בְךָ אֶבְיוֹן מֵאַחַד אַחֶיךָ *if there is a poor man among you, (starting) from one of your brothers* Dt 15$_7$. **2.** of time, **a. from, since,** מִבֶּטֶן אִמִּי אֵלִי אָתָּה *from the womb of my mother*, i.e. since I was born, *you have been my God* Ps 22$_{11}$. **b. after, at (the end of), beyond,** מִיָּמִים *after some days* Jg 14$_8$. **c. immediately after,** לָמָּה לֹּא מֵרֶחֶם אָמוּת *why did I not die immediately after (being in) the womb?* Jb 3$_{11}$. **3.** of source or origin, **(out) of, (made) from, (consisting) of,** נִסְכֵּיהֶם מִדָּם *their libations of blood* Ps 16$_4$. **4.** partitive, **a. (some) of, (one) of, (any) of, (none) of,** וַיָּמוּתוּ מֵעַבְדֵי הַמֶּלֶךְ *and some of the servants of the king died* 2 S 11$_{24}$. **b. (out) of, from (among),** שְׁנַיִם מִכֹּל *two of each* Gn 6$_{19}$. **5.** of comparison, **a. (more)** than, (better) than, (less) than, עַז מֵאֲרִי *stronger than a lion* Jg 14₁₈. **b. (more) than (all others),** i.e. most of all, גָּבֹהַּ מִכָּל־הָעָם *taller than any of the people* 1 S 9₂. **c. too much for,** רַב מִמְּךָ הַדָּרֶךְ *the journey will be too great for you* 1 K 19₇. **6.** privative, **a. without, for lack of, away from,** נִבְעַר כָּל־אָדָם מִדַּעַת *all humans are foolish (and) without knowledge* Jr 10₁₄. **b. from (being), from (doing), so as not to be, so as not to do, so that not,** אַל־תִּירָא מֵרְדָה מִצְרַיְמָה *do not be afraid of going down to Egypt* Gn 46₃. **7.** locative, **in, on,** קוֹל נְהִי נִשְׁמַע מִצִּיּוֹן *a sound of wailing is heard in Zion* Jr 9₁₈. **8.** of cause, **on account of, because of, for (reason of), through, at,** שְׂמַח מֵאֵשֶׁת נְעוּרֶךָ *rejoice on account of the wife of your youth* Pr 5₁₈. **9.** of agent, **by,** הָאָרֶץ תֵּעָזֵב מֵהֶם *the land will be abandoned by them* Lv 26₄₃. **10.** of instrument, **by (means of), with,** נִבְלְעוּ מִן־הַיַּיִן *they are confused by wine* Is 28₇. **11. in the estimation of, before,** וִהְיִיתֶם נְקִיִּים מֵיי *and you will be innocent in the estimation of Y.* Nm 32₂₂. **12.** perh. **against, (for protection) from,** מחזק עירו מצר *he who strengthened his city against the enemy* Si 50₄. **13.** מִמְּךָ and vars. as noun, **your offspring,** גָּלוּ מִמֵּךְ *your offspring shall go into exile* Mc 1₁₆. **14.** מִן in assoc. with other preps., מִזָּכָר עַד־נְקֵבָה *both male and female* Nm 5₃, מִטּוֹב עַד־רָע *either good or evil* Gn 31₂₄, מִיּוֹם־לְיוֹם *day after day* Ps 96₂.

מְנָאוֹת, see מְנָת *portion*.

[מַנְגִּינָה] 1 n.f.—sf. מַנְגִּינָתָם—**mocking song** Lm 3₆₃. → נגן *play a stringed instrument*.

מנה 28.3.4.2 vb.—**Qal** 12.1.1.2 Pf. מָנָה; impf. תִּמְנֶה; impv. מְנֵה; ptc. מוֹנֶה; inf. מְנוֹת—**1. count, number, a.** with accus. people 2 S 24₁, money 2 K 12₁₁, days Ps 90₁₂. **b.** with בְּ of obj. people 1 C 21₁₇. **2. muster** army 1 K 20₂₅. **3. appoint, assign** someone to (לְ) sword Is 65₁₂. **4. reckon as,** אין חייו למנות חיים *he should not reckon his life as life* Si 40₂₈(B).

Ni. 6.1.2 Pf. נִמְנָה; impf. יִמָּנֶה, יִמָּנוּ; inf. הִמָּנוֹת—**1. be counted, numbered,** of people 1 K 3₈, animals 1 K 8₅. **2. be counted as, reckoned as** from among (מִן) the elderly Si 8₆.

Pi. 9.1.1 Pf. מִנָּה, מִנּוּ; + waw וַיְמַן; impv. מַן—**1a. appoint** guardian over (עַל) someone Dn 1₁₁. **b.** of Y., **send** wind Jon 4₈. **2. apportion** food and drink Dn 1₁₀. **3. arrange payment (to oneself)** Mur 30 2₂₆.

Pu. 1 Ptc. מְמֻנִּים—**be appointed** over (עַל) vessels, wine, oil, etc. 1 C 9₂₉.

→ מָנָה *portion*, מָנָה II *portion*, מִנְיָן *number*, מֹנֶה *time*, מְנָת *portion*, (?) מְנִי *destiny*.

מָנָה I 12.2.4 n.f.—pl. מָנוֹת; sf. sf. מְנוֹתֶהָ—**1. portion, share** of food Est 2₉. **2. gift,** אשה [ט]ובה מנה *a good wife is a gift* Si 26₃. → מנה *count*.

*__מָנָה__ II 0.1 n.f. **fate,** אשה [ט]ובה מנה *a good wife is a fate* Si 26₃.

מָנֶה I 5.0.5 n.m.—pl. מָנִים (Q מנין)—**mina,** unit of weight for precious metals Ezr 2₆₉||Ne 7₇₀.

*__[מָנֶה]__ II 0.0.1 n.[m.] **portion** 4QShirShabb[d] 1.2₂₀. → מנה *count*.

[מֹנֶה] 2 n.[m.]—pl. מֹנִים—**time, occasion** Gn 31₇.₄₁. → מנה *count*.

מִנְהָג 2.0.1 n.[m.]—cstr. מִנְהַג—**1. driving** of chariot 2 K 9₂₀. **2. custom** of the law CD 19₃. → נהג I *drive*.

[מִנְהָרָה] I 1 n.f.—pl. מִנְהָרוֹת—**hollow place** Jg 6₂.

*__[מִנְהָרָה]__ II 1 n.f.—pl. מִנְהָרוֹת—**signal station** Jg 6₂. → נהר II *shine*.

*__[מָנוֹ]__ 0.0.1 pl.n. **Mano.**

[מָנוֹד] 1 n.[m.] **(object of) shaking,** מְנוֹד־רֹאשׁ *shaking of the head* Ps 44₁₅. → נוד I *sway*.

מָנוֹחַ I 7.2.9 n.m.—cstr. מְנוֹחַ; pl. sf. מְנוּחָיְכִי—**1a. resting place,** for exiles Dt 28₆₅, bird Gn 8₉. **b. home** acquired through marriage Ru 3₁. **2. rest,** for soul, i.e. self Ps 116₇; שבת מנוח *sabbath of rest* 1QM 2₉. **3. coming to rest** of ark 1 C 6₁₆. → נוח I *rest*.

מָנוֹחַ II 18.0.0.2 pr.n.m. **Manoah.**

מְנוּחָה 21.1.7 n.f.—מְנֻחָה; sf. מְנוּחָתִי; pl. מְנוּחֹת (מְנֻחוֹת)—**1a. resting place** of Israel Dt 12₉, word of Y. Zc 9₁. **b. home** acquired through marriage Ru 1₉. **c. royal seat** of Y. Is 66₁. **2. rest, refreshment, peace** Jr 45₃; מנוחות עד *eternal rest* 4QBéat 14.2₁₄. → נוח I *rest*.

[מִנְלֹה] n.m. **possessions** Jb 15₂₉ (if em. מִנְלָם perh. *their acquisitions* to מִנְלָם *their possessions*). → נִיל *acquire*; cf. מִנְלִים *possessions*.

מָנוֹן I 1.1 adj. **insolent,** or as noun, **insolent** or **disdainful one** Pr 29₂₁.

*מָנוֹן II 1 adj. **weak,** or as noun, **weak one, weakling** Pr 29₂₁.

*מָנוֹן III 1 adj. **pained,** אַחֲרִיתוֹ יִהְיֶה מָנוֹן *in the end he will be pained* Pr 29₂₁. → אנן *complain.*

*מָנוֹן adj. **weak,** as noun, **weak one, weakling** Pr 29₂₁ (if em. מָנוֹן).

מָנוֹס 8.0.4 n.m. **1. flight** Jr 46₅. **2. (place of) refuge, escape,** מְנוּסִי ... יי *Y. is ... my refuge* 2 S 22₃. → נוס I *flee.*

מְנוּסָה 2 n.f. **flight,** מְנֻסַת־חֶרֶב *flight of,* i.e. from, *the sword* Lv 26₃₆. → נוס I *flee.*

[מָנוֹר] 4 n.[m.] **weaver's beam, leash** or **heddle-rod,** מְנוֹר אֹרְגִים *beam of weavers* 1 S 17₇.

מְנוֹרָה 42.1.1 n.f.—מְנֹרָה; cstr. מְנוֹרַת; pl. מְנֹרוֹת; cstr. מְנֹרוֹת—**lampstand,** in tabernacle Nm 3₃₁, temple 1 C 28₁₅, private house 2 K 4₁₀. → cf. נִיר I *lamp,* נֵר I *lamp.*

[מִנְּזָר] I 1 n.[m.] **consecrated one, prince** Na 3₁₇. → נזר *consecrate oneself.*

*[מִנְּזָר] II 1 n.[m.] **guard** Na 3₁₇.

*[מִנְּזָר] III 1 n.[m.] **courtier, official** Na 3₁₇.

*[מִנְּזָר] IV 1 n.[m.] **exorcist, conjuror** Na 3₁₇.

מֻנָּח *free space,* see נוח I *rest,* Ho.

מִנְחָה 211.1.38 n.f.—cstr. מִנְחַת; sf. מִנְחָתִי; pl. sf. מִנְחֹתֵיכֶם—**1. gift, present,** מִנְחָה לְעֵשָׂו *a present for Esau* Gn 32₁₄. **2. tribute** 2 K 17₃. **3. offering** to Y., of meat or grain Gn 4₃.₄, specif. **grain offering** Lv 23₁₃.

[מִנְחָה] n.[m.] **complaint** Nm 16₁₅ (if em. מִנְחָתָם *their offering* to מִנְחָתָם *their complaint*). → נוח II *sigh.*

מְנֻחוֹת, see מָנַחְתִּי *Manahathite.*

מְנַחֵם I 8.0.1.23 pr.n.m. **Menahem.**

מָנַחַת I 2 pr.n.m. **Manahath.**

[מָנַחַת] II 1 pl.n. **Manahath.**

מָנַחְתִּי 1 gent. **Manahathite.**

מְנִי 1 n.[m.] **1. destiny** Ps 23₄ (if em. יְנַחֲמֻנִי *they comfort me* to יְנַחוּ מְנִי *they guide my destiny*). **2.** as pr.n. **Meni,** or **Destiny,** name of a god (of fate) Is 65₁₁. → (?) מנה *count.*

מִנִּי I 1 pl.n. **Minni.**

מִנִּי II, see מִן *from.*

מִנִּי III, see מֵן I *string.*

מְנָיוֹת, see מְנָת *portion.*

מִנְיָמִין 3 pr.n.m. **Miniamin.**

*[מִנְיָן] 0.0.1 n.[m.] **number** 4QapJerC[a] 5₂. → מנה *count.*

*[מָנֵיס] 0.0.1 pr.n.[m.] **Manes.**

מִנִּית I 2 pl.n. **Minnith.**

*מִנִּית II 1 n.[m.] **rice** Ezk 27₁₇.

[מִנְלֶה] 1 n.[m.]—sf. מִנְלָם—perh. **acquisition(s)** Jb 15₂₉. → נלה II *obtain.*

*[מְנָלִים] n.[m.]pl. **possessions** Jb 15₂₉ (if em. ... יִטֶּה מִנְלָם *their acquisitions ... will* not *spread* to יַטֶּה ... מְנָלִים *he shall* not *bring down ... [his] possessions*). → (?) נלה II *obtain;* cf. מָנוֹל *possessions.*

*מנן vb. **Hi., be disdainful, ungrateful,** of Israel Ezk 5₇ (if em. הֲמָנְכֶם *you are turbulent* [from המן] to הֲמִנֶּכֶם *you are disdainful,* inf. with sf.).

*[מָנֹס] 0.0.1 pl.n. **Manos.**

מנע 29.8.2 vb.—**Qal** 25.8.2 Pf. מָנַעְתִּי, מָנַע; impf. יִמְנַע; impv. מְנַע, מִנְעִי; ptc. מֹנֵעַ—**withhold, hold back, restrain,** אל תמנע ממני את שאלתי *do not withhold from me,* i.e. refuse, *my request* GnzPs 3₄, מְנָעֲנִי מֵהָרַע אֹתָךְ *he has held me back from harming you* 1 S 25₃₄, אַל־תִּמְנַע מִנַּעַר מוּסָר *do not withhold discipline from a child* Pr 23₁₃, מִנְעִי קוֹלֵךְ מִבֶּכִי *restrain your voice from weeping* Jr 31₁₆.

Ni. 4 Pf. נִמְנַע; impf. יִמָּנַע—**1. be withheld,** of showers Jr 3₃, light Jb 38₁₅ (+ מִן *from* the wicked). **2. hold oneself back, refrain,** אַל־נָא תִמָּנַע מֵהֲלֹךְ אֵלָי *do not hold yourself back from coming to me* Nm 22₁₆.

מַנְעוּל 6.0.2 n.[m.]—sf. מַנְעָלָיו (מַנְעוּלָיו)—**bolt,** of door of house Ca 5₅, city gate Ne 3₃, Sheol 4QBéat 15₇. → נעל I *lock.*

[מִנְעָל] 1 n.[m.]—pl. sf. מִנְעָלֶיךָ—**bolt** Dt 33₂₅. → נעל I *lock.*

[מַנְעַמִּים] 1 n.[m.]pl.—pl. sf. מַנְעַמֵּיהֶם—**delicacies** Ps 141₄. → נעם I *be pleasant.*

[מְנַעְנֵעַ] 1 n.[m.]—pl. מְנַעַנְעִים—**sistrum, sounding rattle** 2 S 6₅. → נוע I *tremble.*

[מְנַקִּית] 4.0.2 n.f.—pl. מְנַקִּיּוֹת; sf. מְנַקִּיֹּתָיו—**bowl,** for sacrificial use, of gold Ex 25₂₉||37₁₆. → (?) נקה I *be clean.*

*[מָנֹר] 0.0.0.1 pr.n.[m.] **Manor.**

מְנַשֶּׁה 146.0.9.4 pr.n.m. **Manasseh.**

מְנַשִּׁי 4 gent. **Manassite.**

[מְנָת] 9.0.2 n.f.—cstr. מְנָת; pl. cstr. מְנָיוֹת (מְנָאוֹת)—**portion, share,** מְנָיוֹת הַלְוִיִּם *portions of,* i.e. for, *the Levites* Ne

1310. → מנה *count*.

מָס 1.0.1 adj. **melting,** as noun, **one who melts, fails, despairs,** כול מסי לבב *all who are melting of heart,* i.e. whose courage is failing 1QM 106. → מסס *melt*.

מַס I 23.0.3.1 n.m.—pl. מִסִּים—**1. levy, (forced) labour,** מַס עֹבֵד perh. **state slavery** 1 K 921. **2. tax, taxation,** וַיָּשֶׂם ... מַס עַל־הָאָרֶץ *and he imposed ... a tax on the land* Est 101.

*__מַס__ II 1 n.[m.] **melting,** בַּחוּרָיו לָמַס יִהְיוּ *his youths will become as melting,* i.e. their limbs will weaken Is 318. → מסס *melt*.

מֵסַב 4.0.1 n.[m.]—sf. מְסִבּוֹ; pl. cstr. מְסִבֵּי, מְסִבּוֹת—**1. couch** (perh. **table**) Ca 112. **2.** pl., **surroundings, environs,** מְסִבֵּי יְרוּשָׁלַםִ *the environs of Jerusalem* 2 K 235. **3.** as adv., **all over, everywhere, throughout** 1 K 629. **4.** perh. as prep., **against,** רֹאשׁ מְסִבָּי *(if) a head is against me* Ps 14010. → סבב I *turn*.

[מְסִבָּה] 1.0.3 n.f.—pl. מְסִבּוֹת—**1. circle** Jb 3712. **2.** architectural, **(winding) staircase** 11QT 305. → סבב I *turn*.

*__[מַסְבָּלָא]__ 0.0.1 pr.n.m. **Masbala.**

מְסֻגָּב, see מִשְׂגָּב I *stronghold*.

מַסְגֵּר I 4 n.[m.] **smith, metalworker** 2 K 2414.16 Jr 241 292. → סגר II *smelt*.

*__מַסְגֵּר__ II 3.0.0.1 n.[m.] **prison** Is 2422 427 Ps 1428 Seal 857. → סגר I *close*.

*__מַסְגֵּר__ III 1 n.[m.] **women of the harem** Jr 241.

מִסְגֶּרֶת I 14 n.f.—sf. מִסְגַּרְתּוֹ; pl. מִסְגְּרוֹת; sf. מִסְגְּרֹתֶיהָ—**1. panel, inset** of temple stands 1 K 728. **2. rim, framework** of table for bread of presence Ex 2525||3712. → סגר I *shut*.

*__[מִסְגֶּרֶת]__ II 3 n.f.—pl. sf. מִסְגְּרֹתָם (מִסְגְּרוֹתֵיהֶם)—**stronghold, prison** 2 S 2246||Ps 1846(mss) Mc 717. → סגר I *shut*.

מַסָּד 1 n.[m.]—mss מֵסַד—**foundation** 1 K 79. → יסד I *establish*.

[מִסְדְּרוֹן] 1 n.[m.]—+ ה- of direction, הַמִּסְדְּרוֹנָה—**porch, lavatory** or **armoury,** perh. **air-shaft** Jg 323. → סדר *arrange*.

מסה 4 vb.—**Hi.** 4 Pf. הִמְסִיו; impf. אַמְסֶה, יַמְסֵם; + waw וַתֶּמֶס—**cause to melt, dissolve, cause to disintegrate, wash away** snow, ice Ps 14718, couch Ps 67, heart, i.e. **discourage** Jos 148. → cf. מאס II *flow away*, מסס *melt*.

מַסָּה I 4 n.f.—cstr. מַסַּת; pl. מַסּוֹת—**trial, testing** Dt 434. → נסה I *test*.

מַסָּה II 5 pl.n. **Massah.**

[מַסָּה] III 1 n.f.—cstr. מַסַּת—**despair** or **calamity** Jb 923. → מסס *melt*.

[מִסָּה] 1 n.f.—cstr. מִסַּת—perh. **sufficiency** or **proportion** or **measure** Dt 1610.

מַסְוֶה 3 n.[m.] **veil** Ex 3433.34.35. → cf. סוּת *garment*.

מְסוּכָה I 1 n.f. **hedge,** i.e. **obstacle** Mc 74. → סוך II *enclose*; cf. מְשׂוּכָה *hedge*.

[מְסוּכָה] II 1 n.f.—sf. מְסֻכָתֶךָ—**covering, decoration** Ezk 2813. → סכך I *cover*.

*__[מְסוֹלָל]__ 1 n.[m.] **road** Is 358(1QIsa[a]). → סלל *raise*.

מַסָּח I 1 appar. adv. **by turns** or **all around** 2 K 116.

*__מַסָּח__ II 1 n.[m.] **detachment, relief body of troops** 2 K 116.

[מִסְחָר] 1.0.1 n.[m.] **goods,** מִסְחַר הָרֹכְלִים *merchants' goods* 1 K 1015. → סחר I *go around*.

מסך I 5.0.1 vb.—**Qal** 5.0.1 Pf. מָסַךְ, מָסְכָה; inf. מְסֹךְ—**1. mix** wine, prob. with other liquids, herbs, honey, etc. Pr 92. **2.** of Y., **mix, mingle** spirit of distortion Is 1914. → מֶסֶךְ I *mixed wine*, II *bowl*, מִמְסָךְ I *mixed wine*, II *bowl*.

*__מסך__ II 2 vb.—**Qal** 2 Pf. מָסְכָה—**draw, pour** wine Pr 92, **drink** Ps 10210.

מָסָךְ 25.0.1 n.[m.]—cstr. מָסַךְ—**1. vertical screen, curtain,** מָסַךְ פֶּתַח הָאֹהֶל *screen of the entrance of the tent* Ex 3938. **2.** vertical screen as **border defence, bulwark** Is 228. **3.** horizontal screen, **covering,** perh. of cloth 2 S 1719, of cloud Ps 10539. → סכך I *cover*.

מֶסֶךְ I 1 n.[m.] **mixed wine, wine** mixed prob. with other liquids, herbs, honey, etc. Ps 759. → מסך I *mix*.

*__מֶסֶךְ__ II 1 n.[m.] **bowl** Ps 759. → מסך I *mix*.

מַסֵּכָה I 25 n.f.—cstr. מַסֵּכַת; pl. מַסֵּכוֹת; sf. מַסֵּכֹתָם—**image** of a deity, forged or cast, כָּל־צַלְמֵי מַסֵּכֹתָם *all their cast images* Nm 3352. → נסך I *pour*.

מַסֵּכָה II 2 n.f. **covering,** perh. specif. **veil, pall** Is 257, **sheet, blanket, counterpane** Is 2820. → נסך II *weave*.

*__מַסֵּכָה__ III 1 n.f. **libation,** to seal an alliance Is 301. → נסך I *pour*.

*__מַסֵּכָה__ IV 1 n.f. **scheme** Is 301. → נסך II *weave*.

*__[מְסָכָה]__ 0.0.1 n.f. **screen** 4QRP[c] 83 (= Ex 2636 מָסָךְ *screen*). → סכך I *cover*.

מִסְכֵּן 4.2 adj.—sf. Si מסכינך—**1. poor,** of child Ec 4₁₃, man Ec 9₁₅. **2.** as noun, **poor one, pauper** Ec 9₁₆. → סכן III *be poor;* cf. מִסְכֵּנֻת *poverty.*

מְסֻכָּן I *impoverished one* Is 40₂₀, see סכן III *be poor,* pu.

***מְסֻכָּן** II 1 n.[m.] **mulberry tree** or **wood** Is 40₂₀.

***מְסֻכָּן** III 1 n.[m.] **sisu tree** or **wood** Is 40₂₀.

מִסְכְּנוֹת I 7 n.f. **1.** appar. **supplies** of food or soldiers, עָרֵי מִסְכְּנוֹת *cities of supplies,* i.e. store, or garrison, cities Ex 1₁₁. **2. storehouses,** for produce 2 C 32₂₈. → סכן I *be of use.*

***מִסְכְּנוֹת** II 5 n.f. **forced labour,** עָרֵי מִסְכְּנוֹת *cities of,* i.e. built with, *forced labour* Ex 1₁₁.

***מִסְכְּנוֹת** III 1 n.f. **threshing place** 2 C 16₄.

מִסְכֵּנֻת 1 n.f. **poverty** Dt 8₉. → סכן III *be poor;* cf. מִסְכֵּן *poor.*

***[מְסַכְסְכָה]** 1 n.f. **covering** (of bed) Is 28₂₀(1QIsaᵃ). → סכך I *cover.*

[מַסֶּכֶת] 2 n.f.—מַסֶּכֶת—**web** or **warp** Jg 16₁₃.₁₄. → נסך II *weave.*

מְסִלָּה I 27.0.5 n.f.—cstr. מְסִלַּת; sf. מְסִלָּתוֹ; pl. מְסִלּוֹת; sf. מְסִלֹּתַי—**1.** usu. **(main) road, highway,** connecting cities or countries Is 11₁₆. **2. paved way,** within temple–palace complex 1 C 26₁₆; perh. wooden **ramp** 2 C 9₁₁. **3.** perh. **byway, beaten track** Nm 20₁₉. **4. file** of soldiers Jl 2₈; **course** of stars Jg 5₂₀. **5.** perh. **gate** 2 C 9₁₁. **6. way, behaviour, conduct,** מְסִלַּת יְשָׁרִים *way of the upright* Pr 16₁₇. → סלל *raise.*

***[מְסִלָּה]** II 1 n.f.—pl. מְסִלּוֹת—**high praise** Ps 84₆. → סלל *raise.*

***[מְסִלָּה]** III 3 n.f.—pl. מְסִלּוֹת—**gatehouse, gateway** 1 C 26₁₆.₁₈ 2 C 9₁₁.

מַסְלוּל 1 n.m. **road** between cities Is 35₈. → סלל *raise.*

***[מְסֶלַע]** 1 n.[m.] **rocky place** Nm 20₁₉(mss). → cf. סֶלַע *cliff.*

***[מְסַמָּא]** 0.0.1 n.f. **sealing stone** 3QTr 11₆.

[מַסְמֵר] 5.0.1 n.m.—pl. מַשְׂמְרוֹת, מַסְמְרוֹת, מַסְמְרִים, מַסְמְרִים, מַסְמְרוֹת—**1. nail,** of iron 1 C 22₃, gold 2 C 3₉. **2.** perh. **sceptre** Ec 12₁₁ (or §1). → סמר II *nail.*

מסס 23.1.15.1 vb.—**Qal** 3.0.1 Inf. מְסֹס (מְשׂוֹשׂ, Q מוס)—**melt,** במוס לבי *in the melting of my heart,* i.e. in my terror 1QH 10₂₈, **fade away, pine,** perh. **collapse,** כִּמְסֹס נֹסֵס *as the fading away* or *collapsing of one who is ill* Is 10₁₈.

Ni. 19.1.14.1 Pf. נָמַסּוּ; impf. יִמַּס; ptc. נָמֵס; inf. הִמֵּס—**1. melt, evaporate, dissolve, disappear,** of ice Si 3₁₅(C), manna Ex 16₂₁, one's heart Ps 22₁₅. **2.** appar. **be worthless,** of captured goods 1 S 15₉.

Hi. 2.0.4 Pf. הֵמַסּוּ—**melt** someone's heart, i.e. discourage, frighten one Dt 1₂₈.

→ מָס *melting,* מַס II *melting,* מַסָּה III *despair,* תֶּמֶס *melting;* cf. מאס II *flow away,* מסה *melt,* (?) מזז *be joined together,* משׂשׂ *melt.*

מַסָּע I 1 n.[m.] **quarry,** אֶבֶן־שְׁלֵמָה מַסָּע *whole stone(s), (of) a quarry,* i.e. perh. undressed 1 K 6₇. → נסע I *pull out* or II *travel.*

מַסָּע II 1 n.[m.] **missile, dart** or **arrow,** or other **weapon** Jb 41₁₈.

מַסַּע I 12.0.4 n.[m.]—pl. cstr. מַסְעֵי; pl. sf. מַסְעָיו—**journey, travel, stage of journey, start of journey,** מַסְעֵי בְנֵי־יִשְׂרָאֵל *the journeys of the Israelites* Nm 10₂₈. → נסע II *travel.*

***מַסַּע** II 1.0.2 n.[m.] **breaking** or **setting out from** camp Nm 10₂ 1QM 3₅ 1QSa 2₁₅. → נסע I *pull up, out.*

מִסְעָד I 1 n.[m.] **table, bench, banister,** or **support** 1 K 10₁₂. → סעד *support.*

***מִסְעָד** II 1 n.[m.] **step, ramp** 1 K 10₁₂. → סעד *support.*

***[מִסְעָר]** 0.1 n.f. **storm** Si 36₂(Bmg). → סער I *storm.*

מִסְפֵּד 16.1.3 n.m.—cstr. מִסְפַּד; sf. מִסְפְּדִי—**1. mourning, funeral rites** Gn 50₁₀. **2. wailing,** after calamity Ezk 27₃₁, before calamity Est 4₃. **3. wailing,** in contrition Is 22₁₂. → ספד *mourn.*

מִסְפּוֹא 5.1 n.m. **fodder,** for camels Gn 24₃₂, donkeys Jg 19₁₉.

[מִסְפָּחָה] 2 n.f.—pl. מִסְפָּחוֹת; sf. מִסְפְּחֹתֵיכֶם—**veil** or **headcovering, shawl** Ezk 13₁₈.₂₁.

מִסְפַּחַת 3 n.f. **scab,** perh. **rash** Lv 13₆.₇.₈. → cf. סַפַּחַת *scab,* שׂפח *cause a rash.*

מִסְפָּר I 133.11.20 n.m.—cstr. מִסְפַּר; sf. מִסְפָּרָם; pl. cstr. מִסְפְּרֵי—**1a.** usu. **number, total (number),** כֹּל מִסְפַּר רָאשֵׁי הָאָבוֹת ... אַלְפַּיִם וְשֵׁשׁ מֵאוֹת *the total number of the ancestral heads ... was two thousand six hundred* 2 C 26₁₂; with non-countable noun, **quantity, amount,** עֹלַת יוֹם בְּיוֹם בְּמִסְפָּר *the daily burnt offering in (its* *proper) quantity* Ezr 3₄. **b.** specif. **a certain** (agreed, conventional, etc.) **number** Dt 25₂. **c. report of number,** מִסְפַּר הַהֲרוּגִים *report of the number of those slain* Est 9₁₁. **d. final number, limit,** [לא] מספר לתשועתו *there is no limit to his salvation* Si 39₂₀. **e.** perh. **statement** or (alphabetic) **order** of names, etc. Nm 26₅₃. **2.** perh. as noun from ספר *count,* i.e. **counting, numbering,** מִסְפַּר בְּנֵי־לֵוִי *numbering of the Levites* 1 C 23₂₇. → ספר I *count.*

[מִסְפָּר] II ₃.₀.₂ n.[m.] **account, narrative,** מִסְפַּר הַחֲלוֹם *account of the dream* Jg 7₁₅. → ספר I *count.*

*[מִסְפָּר] III ₁ n.[m.]—cstr. מִסְפַּר—**border** Dt 32₈.

מִסְפָּר IV ₁.₀.₀.₁ pr.n.m. **Mispar.**

מִסְפֶּרֶת I ₁ pr.n. **Mispereth.**

*[מִסְפֶּרֶת] II ₀.₁ n.f.—sf. מספרתם—**scholarship** Si 44₄ (Bmg). → ספר *count.*

*מסר I ₁ vb.—**Ni.** ₁ + waw וַיִּמָּסְרוּ—**be counted, provided, conscripted,** of warrior Nm 31₅. → מָסֹרֶת III *number,* IV *division.*

*מסר II ₀.₀.₂ vb.—**Qal** ₀.₀.₁ + waw וימסור—**hand down, transmit** commandments CD 3₃.

Ni. ₀.₀.₁ Impf. ימסרו—**be handed over to** (לְ) sword CD 19₁₀(B).

→ מָסֹרֶת II *tradition.*

מסר III ₂ vb.—**Qal** ₁ Inf. לִמְסָר־—**offer,** i.e. commit, trespass against (בְּ) Y. Nm 31₁₆.

Ni. ₁ + waw וַיִּמָּסְרוּ—**be delivered up, offered,** of warrior Nm 31₅.

*מסר IV ₁ vb.—**Ni.** ₁ + waw וַיִּמָּסְרוּ—**be selected,** of warrior Nm 31₅.

*[מֹסָר] ₁ n.[m.]—sf. מֹסָרָם—**discipline** Jb 33₁₆. → יסר I *discipline.*

*[מִסְרָב] n.[m.] **obstinacy** Jr 13₁₇ (if em. בְּמִסְתָּרִים my soul will weep *in hidden places,* i.e. in secret, to בְּמִסְרָבִים if you do not listen *through [acts of] obstinacy*). → סרב *be obstinate.*

*[מִסָרֵף] I ₁ n.m.—sf. מְסָרְפוֹ—**maternal uncle** Am 6₁₀.

[מִסָרֵף] II ₁ n.m.—sf. מְסָרְפוֹ—**one who burns incense,** specif. **one charged with burning incense** for the dead Am 6₁₀. → סרף II pi. *burn.*

*[מִסְרָר] n.[m.] **stubbornness** Jr 13₁₇ (if em. בְּמִסְתָּרִים my soul will weep *in hidden places,* i.e. in secret, to בְּמִסְרָרִים if you do not listen *through stubbornness[es]).* → סרר I *be stubborn.*

מָסֹרֶת I ₁.₀.₁ n.f.—pl. sf. Q מסרותם—**1. bond,** מָסֹרֶת הַבְּרִית *bond of the covenant* Ezk 20₃₇. **2. conjunction** of sun and moon at the nodes of the moon 1QS 10₄. → אסר *bind.*

*מָסֹרֶת II ₁.₀.₁ n.f. **1. tradition,** מָסֹרֶת הַבְּרִית *tradition of the covenant* Ezk 20₃₇. **2. handing over, transmission** 1QS 10₄. → מסר II *hand down.*

*מָסֹרֶת III ₁ **number, muster-roll,** מָסֹרֶת הַבְּרִית *number of the covenant* Ezk 20₃₇. → מסר I *count.*

*[מָסֹרֶת] IV ₀.₀.₃ n.f.—pl. מסורות—**division, unit of army,** etc. 1QM 3₃. → מסר I *count.*

*[מָסֹרֶת] V ₀.₀.₁ n.f.—pl. מסורות—**command post** 1QM 3₃.

*[מַסֹּרֶת] ₀.₀.₁ n.f.—pl. מסורות—**collecting point** 1QM 3₃. → אסף *gather.*

מֹסֵרֹת pl.n. ₂ **Moseroth.**

*מֹסֶרֶת n.f. **chastisement,** מֹסֶרֶת הַבְּרִית *chastisement of the covenant* Ezk 20₃₇ (if em. מָסֹרֶת). → יסר I *discipline.*

מַסַּת, see מַסָּה *sufficiency.*

מִסְתּוֹר ₁ n.[m.] **shelter** Is 4₆. → סתר I *hide.*

[מַסְתֵּר] ₁ n.[m.]—cstr. מַסְתֵּר—**hiding** Is 53₃. → סתר I *hide.*

מִסְתָּר ₁₀.₁ n.[m.]—pl. מִסְתָּרִים; sf. מִסְתָּרָיו—**hidden place, hiding place, secret (place),** מַטְמֻנֵי מִסְתָּרִים *hoards of hidden places,* i.e. buried treasures Is 45₃; Wisdom's **secrets** Si 4₁₈. → סתר I *hide.*

[מַעְבָּד] I ₁.₁ n.[m.]—pl. sf. מַעְבָּדֵיהֶם—**deed** Jb 34₂₅. → עבד *work.*

*[מַעְבָּד] II ₁ n.[m.]—pl. sf. מַעְבָּדֵיהֶם—**path** Jb 34₂₅.

*[מַעֲבַדְיָה] ₀.₀.₀.₁ pr.n.[m.] **Maabadiah.**

[מַעֲבֶה] ₁.₀.₁ n.[m.]—cstr. מַעֲבֵה—**1. thickness,** i.e. depth, of (clay) soil, used as clay mould, earthen foundry 1 K 7₄₆. **2.** perh. **foundry,** המעבה של מנוס *the foundry of Manos* 3QTr 1₁₃. → עבה I *be thick.*

[מַעֲבָר] I ₃ n.[m.]—cstr. מַעֲבַר—**1a.** mountain **pass** of Michmas 1 S 13₂₃. **b. ford** of Jabbok Gn 32₂₃. **2. passing, stroke** Is 30₃₂. → עבר I *pass.*

*[מַעֲבָר] II ₁ n.[m.] **burning,** כֹּל מַעֲבַר מַטֵּה מוּסָדָה *every*

burning of a raised bed Is 30$_{32}$ (if em. מַטֶּה *rod* to מִטָּה *bed*).

מַעְבָּרָה 8 n.f.—pl. מַעְבְּרוֹת (מַעְבָּרֹת, מַעְבָּרוֹת)—**1.** perh. mountain **pass** of Michmas Is 10$_{29}$; **passageway,** i.e. **ravine,** near Michmas 1 S 14$_{4}$. **2. ford,** מַעְבְּרוֹת הַיַּרְדֵּן *fords of the Jordan* Jg 3$_{28}$. → עבר I *pass.*

[מַעְגָּל] I 11 n.m.—cstr. מַעְגַּל; pl. cstr. מַעְגְּלֵי; sf. מַעְגְּלֹתָיו—**track, course,** of life, behaviour, מַעְגַּל צַדִּיק *way of a righteous one* Is 26$_{7}$, טוֹב *of goodness* Pr 2$_{9}$. → (?) עֲגָלָה *cart.*

***[מַעְגָּל]** II 3 n.m.—+ ה- of direction מַעְגָּלָה—**encampment,** perh. as **ring of wagons** 1 S 17$_{20}$ 26$_{5.7}$. → עגל *round.*

***[מַעְגָּל]** III 1 n.m. **pasture,** מַעְגְּלֵי־צֶדֶק *pastures of righteousness* Ps 23$_{3}$.

***[מַעְגָּל]** IV 1 n.m.—pl. sf. מַעְגָּלֶיךָ—**cart, chariot** Ps 65$_{12}$. → cf. עֲגָלָה *cart.*

מעד 7 vb.—**Qal** 5 Pf. מָעֲדוּ; impf. תִּמְעַד—**slip, falter, give way,** of ankle 2 S 22$_{37}$, person Ps 26$_{1}$.

Pu. 1 Ptc. מוּעֶדֶת—**be out of joint, be sprained,** of foot Pr 25$_{19}$.

Hi. 1 Impv. הַמְעַד—**shake, put hip out of joint** Ps 69$_{24}$.

→ מַעֲדָן III *faltering step,* IV *reluctant,* מַעֲדַנִּית *hesitantly.*

מַעֲדַי 1 pr.n.m. **Maadai.**

מַעַדְיָה 2 pr.n.m. **Maadiah.**

[מַעֲדָן] I 4.0.1 n.[m.]—pl. מַעֲדַנִּים, מַעֲדַנֹּת—**1. delicious food, delicacy,** מַעֲדַנֵּי־מֶלֶךְ *a king's delicacies* Gn 49$_{20}$. **2.** perh. **delicateness** 1 S 15$_{32}$ (or §3). **3. delight** 1 S 15$_{32}$ Pr 29$_{17}$. → עדן *luxuriate.*

[מַעֲדָן] II 2 n.[f.]—pl. מַעֲדַנֹּת—**1. bond,** מַעֲדַנּוֹת כִּימָה *the bonds of the Pleiades,* i.e. that unite them in a single constellation Jb 38$_{31}$. **2. chain** 1 S 15$_{32}$. → ענד *bind.*

***[מַעֲדָן]** III 1 n.[f.]—pl. מַעֲדַנֹּת—**faltering step** 1 S 15$_{32}$. → מעד *shake.*

***[מַעֲדָן]** IV 1 n.[f.]—pl. מַעֲדַנֹּת—**reluctance,** as adv., **reluctantly** 1 S 15$_{32}$. → מעד *shake.*

***[מְעֻדָּנָה]** 0.0.0.1 pr.n.f. **Meuddanah.**

[מַעֲדַנִּית] adv. **hesitantly,** וַיֵּלֶךְ אֵלָיו אֲגַג מַעֲדַנֹּת *and Agag came towards him hesitantly* 1 S 15$_{32}$ (if em. מַעֲדַנֹּת *[in] chains*). → מעד *shake.*

***[מַעֲדֶנֶת]** 1 n.[f.] **company, chorus,** הַתְקַשֵּׁר מַעֲדַנּוֹת כִּימָה *can you control the company of the Pleiades?,* i.e. prevent their letting loose the spring rains Jb 38$_{31}$.

[מְעֻדֶּנֶת] n.f. **pampered woman** 1 S 15$_{32}$ (if em. מַעֲדַנֹּת *[in] chains* to מְעֻדֶּנֶת *[as] a pampered woman*). → עדן *luxuriate.*

מַעְדֵּר 1 n.[m.] **hoe** Is 7$_{25}$. → עדר II *hoe.*

[מָעָה] I 1.0.2 n.f.—pl. Q מעות, מעת; sf. מְעֹתָיו—**1. particle, grain** (of sand) Is 48$_{19}$. **2.** as name of coin of lowest value, **maah,** מעות שתין *two maahs* 3QTr 10$_{9}$ (others בעזת שתין *by two supports*).

***[מָעָה]** II 1 n.f.—pl. sf. מְעֹתָיו—**multitude** Is 48$_{19}$.

[מֵעֶה] 34.3.3.1 n.m.—du./pl. Si מעים; cstr. מְעֵי; sf. מֵעַי, מֵעֶיךָ, מֵעָיו (מְעוֹתָיו)—alw. du./pl., **belly, womb, gut(s), entrails, bowel(s), internal organs,** etc.; exact anatomical reference oft. uncertain, in general, **(the) inside, 1.** perh. **genitals** of man 2 S 7$_{12}$. **2. womb** of woman Gn 25$_{23}$. **3.** perh. **offspring,** תבא ברכה במעיו perh. *may blessing come to his offspring* Kfar Baram inscr.$_{2}$. **4. belly,** as organ of ingestion, of man Ezk 3$_{3}$, fish Jon 2$_{1}$. **5. internal organs,** of man 2 S 20$_{10}$. **6. inner person, self, a.** of human, seat of distress Jr 4$_{19}$. **b.** of Y., seat of compassion Is 63$_{15}$. **7. belly** as viewed externally, in descr. of male lover's body Ca 5$_{14}$.

מָעוֹג I 2 n.[m.] **1. loaf** or perh. **slice (of bread)** or **cake** 1 K 17$_{12}$. **2.** perh. **circle** Ps 35$_{16}$. → עוג I *bake (cake).*

***מָעוֹג** II 1 n.[m.] **provisions** 1 K 17$_{12}$. → (?) עוג *bake.*

***מָעוֹג** III 1 n.[m.] **round silo,** thus provisions kept in a silo 1 K 17$_{12}$.

***מָעוֹג** IV 1 n.[m.] **place to which one turns for provisions** 1 K 17$_{12}$.

***מָעוֹג** V 1 n.[m.] **lame person** Ps 35$_{16}$.

מָעוֹז I 34.1.9 n.m.—cstr. מָעוֹז; sf. מָעוּזִּי; pl. מָעֻזִּים—**(place of) refuge** or **protection,** oft. of Y., י׳ מָעוֹז־חַיַּי *Y. is the refuge, or protection, of my life* Ps 27$_{1}$, perh. of people Ps 60$_{9}$, of tree 1QH 16$_{24}$. → עוז *take refuge.*

***מָעוֹז** II 24.1.9 n.m.—pl. מָעֻזִּים; cstr. מָעוּזֵּי—**1. stronghold** Jg 6$_{26}$ Ezk 30$_{15}$; as descr. of Y. 2 S 22$_{33}$, way of Y. Pr 10$_{29}$. **2. strength** of Y. Is 27$_{5}$, army 1QH 18$_{23}$, body 1QH 16$_{32}$. → עזז *be strong.*

***[מָעוֹז]** 0.1 n.m. **arrogance** Si 10$_{12}$. → יעז *be insolent.*

*[מָעֹוזֶן] 1 n.[m.]—pl. sf. מָעֻזְנֶיהָ—**refuge** Is 23₁₁. → עוז *take refuge.*

*[מַעוּזְיָה] 0.0.8 pr.n.m. **Mauzzijah.**

*[מְעוּט] 0.1.1 n.[m.] **1. small thing,** בוזה מעוטים *one who despises small things* Si 19₁. **2. diminution,** מעוט האדם *diminution of humankind* 4QpIsa^c 4.2₈. → מעט I *be few.*

מָעוֹךְ 1 pr.n.m. **Maoch.**

מָעוֹן I 19.1.29 n.[m.]—cstr. מְעוֹן; sf. מְעוֹנוֹ; pl. cstr. Q מעוני; sf. Q מעוניהם—**dwelling place, abode, dwelling, place, home,** oft. of Y., מְעוֹן קָדְשְׁךָ ... הַשָּׁמַיִם *the dwelling place of your holiness ... the heavens* Dt 26₁₅; also of angels 4QShirShabb^a 2₅, wild animals Na 2₁₂, light 1QS 10₁. → עון *dwell.*

*מָעוֹן II 3 n.[m.] **help,** Y. as a help Ps 90₁ 91₉; צוּר מָעוֹן *a rock of help* Ps 71₃.

*מָעוֹן III 1 n.[m.] **reminder of sin** Ps 90₁. → עָוֹן *sin.*

מָעוֹן IV 5 pl.n. **Maon.**

מָעוֹן V 3 pr.n.m. **Maon.**

מְעוֹן, see בֵּית מְעוֹן *Beth-meon,* בֵּית בַּעַל מְעוֹן *Beth-baal-meon,* בַּעַל מְעוֹן *Baal-meon.*

[מְעוֹנָה] 9.4 n.f.—מְעֹנָה; sf. מְעוֹנָתוֹ; pl. מְעוֹנוֹת; sf. מְעוֹנֹתֵינוּ—**dwelling place, abode** of Y. Ps 76₃, Wisdom Si 14₂₇, darkness 1QH 20₇; **lair** of wild animals Am 3₄. → עון *dwell.*

[מְעוּנִי] 4 gent. **Maonite.**

מְעוֹנֹתַי 1 pr.n.m. **Meonothai.**

[מָעוּף] 1 n.[m.]—cstr. מְעוּף—**darkness** Is 8₂₂. → עוף II *be dark.*

[מָעוֹר] 1 n.[m.]—pl. sf. מְעוֹרֵיהֶם—**nakedness, pl. genitalia** Hb 2₁₅. → עור III *be laid bare.*

מַעַזְיָה 1 pr.n.m. **Maaziah.**

*[מַעֲזָן] 1 n.[m.]—pl. sf. מָעֻזְנֶיהָ—**market** Is 23₁₁.

מעט I 22.4.8 vb.—**Qal** 8.1.4 Pf. Q מעטו; impf. יִמְעַט; inf. מְעֹט—**be reduced, be diminished, be (too) few, be (too) small,** of humankind 4QpIsa^c 4.2₈, wealth Pr 13₁₁.

Pi. 1.2 Pf. מִעֲטוּ; impv. Si מעט—**1. become few** or perh. **reduce output** Ec 12₃. **2. withdraw** soul from (מִן) world's greatness Si 3₁₈. **3. make few,** כל לאמר ומעט הרבה *finish speaking and make few (words count for) many* Si 35₈.

Pu. 0.0.2 Ptc. מועט—ptc. as noun, **something reduced,** i.e. **a few, a little, a minimum,** עשרה אנשים למועט *ten men as a minimum* CD 13₁.

Hi. 13.1.2 Pf. Si המעיטם; impf. יַמְעִיט; ptc. מַמְעִיט—**1a. reduce people in number** Lv 26₂₂. **b. reduce** inheritance **in size** Nm 26₅₄. **2.** perh. **diminish** country **in power** Ezk 29₁₅. **3a. collect less** Ex 16₁₇. **b. pay less** Ex 30₁₅.

→ מְעַט *few,* מְעוּט *small thing,* מָעָט *small.*

*מעט II 1 vb.—**Pu.** 1 ptc. מְעֻטָּה—**be drawn (out), stretched,** בָּרָק מְעֻטָּה לְטָבַח *lightning drawn out for slaughter* Ezk 21₂₀.

[מָעָט] 1 adj. **small,** עֲשׂוּיָה לְבָרָק מְעֻטָּה לְטָבַח *(it is) made like lightning, small (enough) for slaughter* Ezk 21₂₀. → מעט I *be few.*

מְעַט 101.11.12 n.[m.]—מְעָט; pl. מְעַטִּים—**1a.** as noun, **(a) few, (a) little,** עִיר קְטַנָּה וַאֲנָשִׁים בָּהּ מְעָט *there was a small town and the people in it were few* Ec 9₁₄, מְעַט־שֶׁמֶן *a little oil* 1 K 17₁₂. **b.** as adv., **a little** Ps 8₆. **c.** as adv., **a little while,** קָצַפְתִּי מְּעָט *I was angry for a little while* Zc 1₁₅. **d.** as adv., מְעַט מְעַט **little by little** Ex 23₃₀. **e.** as pred. adj., **few, little,** יִהְיוּ דְבָרֶיךָ מְעַטִּים *let your words be few* Ec 5₁. **f.** appar. as indeclinable attrib. adj., **little, few,** שְׁאָר מְעַט מִזְעָר *a little, small, remnant* Is 16₁₄. **g.** adj. as noun, **little thing** Si 39₂₀. **2.** כִּמְעַט, **a. almost, nearly** Is 1₉. **b. just, hardly** Ps 2₁₂. **c. very soon** or **immediately** or **suddenly** Ps 81₁₅. **3.** עוֹד מְעַט **(in) yet a little while,** i.e. **soon** Jr 51₃₃. → מעט I *be few.*

[מַעֲטֶה] 1 n.[m.] **garment,** מַעֲטֵה תְהִלָּה *garment of praise* Is 61₃. → עטה I *wrap.*

[מַעֲטֶפֶת] 1 n.f.—pl. מַעֲטָפוֹת—**garment,** appar. **shawl** or **coat** Is 3₂₂. → עטף II *cover oneself.*

מָעַי 1 pr.n.m. **Maai.**

מְעִי I 1 n.[m.] **ruin** Is 17₁. → עוה *bend;* cf. עִי *ruin.*

מְעִי II, see מָעַי *Maai.*

מְעִיל 28.2.1 n.m.—sf. מְעִילוֹ—**robe, 1.** sacral vestment of high priest Aaron Ex 28₄, of David perh. as priest 1 C 15₂₇, of worshipper clothed by Y. Is 61₁₀ (מְעִיל צְדָקָה *robe of righteousness*). **2.** in non-sacral use, worn by man Jb 1₂₀, daughters of king 2 S 13₁₈.

מֵעִים, see מֵעֶה *belly, womb.*

מַעְיָן 23.1.15 n.[m.]—cstr. מַעְיַן (מַעְיְנוֹ); sf. מַעְיָנוֹ; pl. מַעְיָנוֹת, מַעְיָנִים; cstr. מַעְיְנֹת, מַעְיְנֵי; sf. מַעְיָנַי, מַעְיְנֹתֶיךָ—**1. spring, water source** 2 K 3$_{19}$; sometimes specif. of primordial waters, מַעְיְנֹת תְּהוֹם *springs of (the) abyss* Gn 7$_{11}$. **2. spring, spiritual source,** מעין קודש *spring of holiness* 1QS 10$_{12}$, כבוד *of glory* 1QS 11$_{7}$, דעת *of knowledge* 1Q36 12$_{2}$, אור *of light* 1QS 3$_{19}$, חיים *of life* 1QH 16$_{12}$, מַעַיְנֵי הַיְשׁוּעָה *springs of salvation* Is 12$_{3}$. → cf. עַיִן *spring.*

[מְעָיָן], see מַעְיָן *spring.*

[מְעִינִי] 2 gent. perh. **Minaean.**

מעך 3.0.2 vb.—**Qal** 2.0.2 Impf. Q ימעכו; ptc. מָעוּךְ, מְעוּכָה—1. appar. **press, squeeze** foodstuffs 4QTohA 3.1$_{7}$. 2. pass., **be pressed** in (בְּ) ground, of spear 1 S 26$_{7}$. 3. pass. ptc. as noun, perh. **animal that is pressed,** perh. in ref. to squeezing of testicles for castration Lv 22$_{24}$.

Pu. 1 Pf. מֹעֲכוּ—**be pressed,** of female breasts Ezk 23$_{3}$.

מַעֲכָה I 18 pr.n.m.&f. **Maacah.**

מַעֲכָה II 3 pl.n. **Maacah.**

מַעֲכָה III, see אָבֵל בֵּית־מַעֲכָה *Abel-beth-maacah.*

מַעֲכַת 1 pr.n.m. **Maacath.**

מַעֲכָתִי 8 gent. **Maacathite.**

מעל 35.0.10 vb.—**Qal** 35.0.10 Pf. מָעַל, מָעֲלוּ; impf. יִמְעַל, תִּמְעֹל; ptc. Q מועל; inf. abs. מָעוֹל; cstr. מְעָל־ (מַעַל, מָעֳלוֹ)—**sin, commit (sin), be sinful, transgress,** esp. **commit sacrilege,** as redressed by the אָשָׁם *guilt offering,* 1. with cognate obj., וְתִמְעֹל מַעַל בְּאִישָׁהּ *and she sinned against her husband* (i.e. by committing adultery) Nm 5$_{27}$. 2. without obj., אֲנַחְנוּ מָעַלְנוּ בֵּאלֹהֵינוּ *we (ourselves) have sinned against our God* Ezr 10$_{2}$. → מַעַל I *sin.*

מַעַל I 29.3.32 n.[m.]—sf. מַעֲלָם—**sin, sinning, sinfulness, transgression,** esp. **sacrilege,** as redressed by the אָשָׁם *guilt offering,* מַעַל בַּי׳ *sin against Y.* Lv 5$_{21}$, אשמת מעל *guilt of sin* 1QH 12$_{30}$, מעל ישראל *Israel's sinning* CD 20$_{23}$; perh. **deceit** Jb 21$_{34}$ Si 41$_{18}$. → מעל *sin.*

מַעַל II 141.2.32 n.[m.]—מָעַל־; + ה- of direction מַעְלָה (מָעְלָה)—**1.** as noun, **height,** מרומי מעל *heights of the height,* i.e. highest heavens Si 26$_{16}$. **2-14,** as adv. or prep., **2.** לְמַעְלָה **a. above, on top, on high, upwards,** עֲוֹנֹתֵינוּ רָבוּ לְמַעְלָה רֹאשׁ *our sins have increased upwards (towards the) head* Ezr 9$_{6}$. **b. upside down,** + הפך *turn* Jg 7$_{13}$. **c. exceedingly,** + רבה *be numerous* 1 C 23$_{17}$. **3.** לְמַעְלָה לְ **above,** + רום htpol. *be exalted* 4QConfess 3$_{6}$. **4.** מִלְמַעְלָה **above, on top,** עַל־רָאשֵׁיהֶם מִלְמָעְלָה *above their heads* Ezk 1$_{22}$. **5.** מִלְמַעְלָה מִן **above** 11QT 10$_{11}$ (מל[מ]עלה). **6.** perh. מִלְמַעְלָה לְ **above** 11QT 3$_{15}$. **7.** מִמַּעַל **above,** הַשָּׁמַיִם מִמַּעַל *the heavens above* Jr 4$_{28}$. **8.** מִמַּעְלָה **above** 4QShirShabb[f] 31$_{3}$. **9.** מַעְלָה **upwards, high(er),** יַעֲלֶה עָלֶיךָ מַעְלָה מָּעְלָה *he will rise above you, higher (and) higher* Dt 28$_{43}$. **10.** מַעְלָה לְ **above** 4QapJoshua[a] 6.2$_{5}$. **11.** מִמַּעַל לְ **above,** שְׂרָפִים עֹמְדִים מִמַּעַל לוֹ *the seraphim stood above him* (i.e. Y.) Is 6$_{2}$. **12.** מִן ... וָמָעְלָה **from ... and above/and over** Ex 30$_{14}$. **13.** מִן ... וּלְמַעְלָה **from ... and above/and over** Ezk 8$_{2}$. **14.** עַד־לְמַעְלָה **exceedingly** or perh. **from then on** 2 C 16$_{12}$. → עלה I *go up.*

מֹעַל I 1 n.[m.] **raising,** מֹעַל יְדֵיהֶם *raising of their hands* Ne 8$_{6}$. → עלה I *go up.*

[מֹעַל] II, see מַעַל *sin.*

מַעֲלָה I 47.0.8 n.f.—Q מעלהא; pl. מַעֲלוֹת; sf. Qr מַעֲלוֹתָיו (Kt מעלותו), מַעֲלֹתֶהוּ—**1. step** Ex 20$_{26}$; בית מעלות *building of steps,* i.e. staircase or stairwell 11QT 42$_{7}$. **2. stage, degree** of sundial Is 38$_{8}$. **3. upper room** or **roof** Am 9$_{6}$. **4.** (act of) **ascent,** i.e. **return from exile,** הַמַּעֲלָה מִבָּבֶל *the ascent from Babylon* Ezr 7$_{9}$. **5.** perh. title of Y., **Height** 1 C 17$_{17}$. → עלה I *go up.*

*__מַעֲלָה__ II 15.0.1 n.f. **extolment,** שִׁיר הַמַּעֲלוֹת *song of extolments* Ps 120$_{1}$ (unless מַעֲלָה I, *ascents*). → עלה I *go up.*

מָעְלָה, see מַעַל *height.*

מַעֲלֶה 19.1.1 n.m.—pl. sf. Qr מַעֲלָיו—**1. ascent, elevation, hill,** מַעֲלֵה הָעִיר *ascent of,* i.e. to, *the city* 1 S 9$_{11}$. **2.** geographical, pl.n. **Ascent,** e.g. מַעֲלֵה הֶחָרֶס *Ascent of Heres* Jg 8$_{13}$. **3. platform** Ne 9$_{4}$. → עלה I *go up.*

[מַעֲלִיל] 1 n.[m.]—pl. sf. Kt מעליליכם—**deed** Zc 1$_{4}$(Kt) (Qr מַעֲלָל *deed*). → עלל I *do.*

[מַעֲלָל] 41.0.4 n.m.—pl. מַעֲלָלִים; cstr. מַעַלְלֵי; sf. מַעֲלָלָיו—**deed, 1.** of human being, usu. evil Dt 28$_{20}$. **2.** of Y. Ps 77$_{12}$. → עלל I *do.*

מַעֲמָד 5.1.46 n.[m.]—cstr. מַעֲמַד; sf. מַעֲמָדָם—**1. place,**

[מַעֲקָשׁ] 1.0.1 n.[m.]—pl. מַעֲקַשִּׁים—**rough place** Is 42₁₆. → עקשׁ *twist.*

[מַעַר] 2 n.[m.]—cstr. מַעַר; sf. מַעְרֵךְ—**1. nakedness** of woman, or perh. specif. **pudenda** Na 3₅. **2. empty space, bare place** 1 K 7₃₆. → ערה *lay bare.*

מַעֲרָב I 14.0.15 n.[m.] **1. (the) west,** לַמַּעֲרָב *to the west* 1 C 7₂₈, מַעֲרָבָה *westward* 1 C 26₃₀, צפון המערב *the northwest* 11QT 46₁₄. **2. setting (of sun)** Is 45₆ (if em. מִמַּעֲרָבָה *in [the] west* to מִמַּעֲרָבָהּ *in its* [sun's] *setting*). → ערב IV *become evening.*

[מַעֲרָב] II 9 n.m.—sf. מַעֲרָבֵךְ; pl. sf. מַעֲרָבַיִךְ—**merchandise** Ezk 27₂₇. → ערב II *exchange* or V *offer.*

*מַעֲרָבָה 1 n.f. **west** Is 45₆. → ערב IV *become evening.*

*[מַעֲרָבִי] 0.0.5 adj.—f.s. מערבית—**western,** הצד המערבי *the western side* 3QTr 10₁₃, הפנא המערבית *the western corner* 3QTr 3₁₀. → ערב IV *become evening.*

[מַעֲרֶה] I 1 n.[m.] **empty space,** מַעֲרֵה־גָבַע *empty space of Geba* Jg 20₃₃. → ערה *lay bare;* cf. מְעָרָה II *empty space.*

*[מַעֲרֶה] II 1 n.[m.] **approaches, vicinity,** מַעֲרֵה־גָבַע *approaches to* or *vicinity of Geba* Jg 20₃₃.

מְעָרָה I 40.0.4 n.f.—Q מערא; cstr. מְעָרַת; pl. מְעָרוֹת—**1. cave,** temporary dwelling place Gn 19₃₀, military hiding place Jos 10₁₆, place of burial, acquisition Gn 23₉, treasury 3QTr 2₃; מְעָרוֹת צֻרִים *caves of rocks* Is 2₁₉, פֶּתַח הַמְּעָרָה *entrance of the cave* 1 K 19₁₃, יַרְכְּתֵי *recesses of* 1 S 24₄. **2.** perh. **cave country** 1 K 18₄.₁₃.

*[מְעָרָה] II 1 n.f.—pl. מְעָרוֹת—**empty space** Is 32₁₄. → ערה *lay bare;* cf. מַעֲרֶה I *empty space.*

מְעָרָה III 1 pl.n. **Mearah.**

[מַעֲרָךְ] 1 n.[m.] **disposition, arrangement,** מַעַרְכֵי־לֵב *dispositions of (the) heart* Pr 16₁. → ערך I *arrange.*

מַעֲרָכָה 20.2.63 n.f.—cstr. Q מערכת; pl. cstr. מַעַרְכוֹת; sf. Q מערכותמה—**1.** of persons, usu. of troops, **a. battle-line,** perh. sometimes **battle, army,** מַעַרְכוֹת פְּלִשְׁתִּים *battle-lines of (the) Philistines* 1 S 23₃, אֱלֹהִים חַיִּים *of the living God* 1 S 17₂₆. **b.** perh. **row** of worshippers or **array** of all humankind 1QS 10₁₄. **2. row** of lamps, נֵרֹת מַעֲרָכָה *lamps in due order* Ex 39₃₇. **3. row of array** of showbread Lv 24₆. **4.** appar. **row** of logs on altar, מערכות עליון *rows (of logs) of the Most High* Si 50₁₄. **5. ordered array of stones or level ground** or

מעמד מים יקרים *place of cold waters* Si 43₂₀₍B₎. **2. position,** מעמד איש אחר איש *position of (one) person after another* 1QM 5₄. **3. standing (up),** מעמד האיש השואל את עצת היחד *standing (up) of the person questioning the council of the community* 1QS 6₁₂. **4. (holding) office** Is 22₁₉; כול עונות מעמדמה *all the periods of their (holding) office* 4QBer^a 7.2₆. → עמד I *stand.*

מָעֳמָד 1 n.[m.] **standing ground, firm place** Ps 69₃. → עמד *stand.*

מַעֲמָסָה 1 n.f. **burden,** אֶבֶן מַעֲמָסָה *stone of burden,* i.e. heavy weight Zc 12₃. → עמס *load.*

[מַעֲמָק] 5.0.3 n.[m.]—pl. מַעֲמַקִּים; cstr. מַעֲמַקֵּי; sf. Q מעמקיה—**depth,** מַעֲמַקֵּי־יָם *depths of (the) sea* Is 51₁₀, תהום *of (the) abyss* 4QapJoseph^b 1₃₀. → עמק I *be deep.*

[מַעַן], see לְמַעַן *for the sake of.*

[מַעֲנָד] n.[f.] **bond, chain,** וַיֵּלֶךְ אֵלָיו אֲגַג מַעֲנַדֹּת *and Agag came towards him (in) chains* 1 S 15₃₂ (if em. מַעֲדַנֹּת). → ענד *bind.*

מַעֲנָה 2 n.f.—pl. sf. Kt מענותם—**furrow** or specif. **plough furrow,** area at end of field where plough is turned 1 S 14₁₄ Ps 129₃₍Kt₎. → (?) ענה IV *be occupied;* cf. מַעֲנִית IV *furrow.*

מַעֲנֶה I 7.3.7 n.m. **answer,** אֵין מַעֲנֵה אֱלֹהִים *there is no answer of,* i.e. from, *God* Mc 3₇. → ענה I *answer.*

*[מַעֲנֶה] II 1.2 n.[m.]—sf. מַעֲנֵהוּ—**purpose** Pr 16₄. → ענה IV *be occupied.*

[מַעֲנִית] 1 n.f.—pl. sf. Qr מַעֲנִיתָם—**furrow** Ps 129₃₍Qr₎. → (?) ענה IV *be occupied;* cf. מַעֲנָה *furrow.*

מעסר, see מַעֲשֵׂר *tenth, tithe.*

מַעַץ 1 pr.n.m. **Maaz.**

מַעֲצֵבָה 1 n.f. **(place of) pain** Is 50₁₁. → עצב I *hurt.*

מַעֲצָד 2 n.[m.] **axe, billhook** Jr 10₃. → עצד *cut.*

*[מַעֲצָדָה] n.f. **axe** Is 10₃₃ (if em. בְּמַעֲרָצָה *with terror,* i.e. frighteningly, to בְּמַעֲצָדָה *with an axe*). → עצד *cut.*

*[מַעֲצָה] n.f. **disobedience** Jr 7₂₄ (if em. בְּמֹעֵצוֹת *in counsels* to בְּמַעֲצוֹת *in disobedience[s]*). → cf. מוֹעֵצָה II *disobedience.*

מַעְצוֹר 1.1 n.[m.] **stopping, restraint, impediment** 1 S 14₆. → עצר I *restrain.*

מַעְצָר 1 n.[m.] **stopping, restraint, impediment** Pr 25₂₈. → עצר I *restrain.*

מַעֲקֶה 1.0.1 n.[m.] **parapet** Dt 22₈.

correct (building) procedure for building altar Jg 6_{26}. → ערך I *arrange.*

מַעֲרֶכֶת 9 n.f. **array, row (of showbread),** מַעֲרֶכֶת תָּמִיד *a row (of showbread) of continuity,* i.e. a continual offering of showbread 2 C 2_3. → ערך I *arrange.*

[מַעֲרֹם] 1.2 n.[m.]—pl. sf. מַעֲרֻמֵּיהֶם—**1. nakedness,** perh. specif. **pudenda** 2 C 28_{15} (or §2). **2. naked person** 2 C 28_{15}. **3.** perh. **secret** of abyss and heart Si 42_{18}. → עור III *be laid bare.*

*__[מַעֲרָף]__ 0.1 n.[m.] **drop (of rain),** מערף ענן *drop of cloud* Si 43_{22}. → ערף II *drip.*

*__[מַעֲרָץ]__ n.[m.] **terror,** הוּא מַעֲרַצְכֶם *he will be your terror,* i.e. the one who strikes terror into you Is 8_{13} (if em. מַעֲרִצְכֶם *the one who terrifies you*). → ערץ I *be terrified.*

מַעֲרָצָה 1 n.f. **terror** Is 10_{33}. → ערץ I *be terrified.*

מַעֲרָת 1 pl.n. **Maarath.**

מַעֲשֶׂה I 234.40.293 n.m.—cstr. מַעֲשֵׂה; sf. מַעֲשֶׂךָ, מַעֲשֵׂהוּ; pl. מַעֲשִׂים; cstr. מַעֲשֵׂי; sf. מַעֲשֶׂיךָ—**1a.** usu. **deed, action,** oft. of Y. Dt 3_{24}, מעשי אדון הכול *deeds of the Lord of all* 11QPs[a] 28_7; of woman Pr 31_{31}. **b.** coll., **deeds, activity, behaviour,** מַעֲשֵׂה הָאֱלֹהִים *activity of God* Ec 7_{13}. **c. product, produce, production, work, working, making, manufacture,** מַעֲשֵׂה אֹפֶה *product of a baker* Gn 40_{17}, מַעֲשֵׂה יְדֵי יוֹצֵר *work of a potter's hands* Lm 4_2, מַעֲשֵׂה־זַיִת *produce of the olive* Hb 3_{17}; **work (giving the appearance)** of a lotus 1 K 7_{19}; **work achieved, achievement,** פָּרַץ י׳ אֶת־מַעֲשֶׂיךָ *Y. will destroy the work you achieved* 2 C 20_{37}; **(process of) production,** מַעֲשֵׂה הַחֲבִתִּים *production of the flat cakes* 1 C 9_{31}; **construction, structure, composition, make-up, design** of a finished product, מַעֲשֵׂה הַמְּנֹרָה *structure of the lampstand* Nm 8_4. **d. labour, work(ing), task, occupation, trade, business,** שֵׁשֶׁת יְמֵי הַמַּעֲשֶׂה *six working days* Ezk 46_1, מַה־מַּעֲשֵׂיכֶם *what is your occupation?* Gn 46_{33}. **e. creation, creature, created being,** תמהי מעשהו *marvels of his creation* Si $43_{25(B)}$, בָּרְכוּ י׳ כָּל־מַעֲשָׂיו *bless Y., all his creatures* Ps 103_{22}. **f. object,** מַעֲשֵׂה תַּעְתֻּעִים *object of mockery* Jr 10_{15}, perh. cultic **apparatus** (coll.) 2 C 4_6. **g. (act of) sexual intercourse,** לעשות מעשה *to 'do the deed'* 4QD[f] 3_{11}. **h.** perh. **event, episode, story,** יוֹם הַמַּעֲשֶׂה *day of the event* 1 S 20_{19}, אֹמֵר אָנִי מַעֲשַׂי לְמֶלֶךְ *I tell my stories to the king* Ps 45_2. **2.** כְּמַעֲשֵׂה, as prep., **like (the construction of), as though it were,** מגני נחושת מרוקה כמעשה מראת פנים *shields of bronze, polished like a face mirror* 1QM 5_4. → עשׂה I *do.*

*__[מַעֲשֶׂה]__ II 2 n.m.—pl. sf. מַעֲשֶׂיךָ—**1. covering** Is 59_6. **2. cloud** Ps 104_{13}. → עשׂה III *cover.*

*__מַעֲשֶׂה__ III 1 n.m. **evening, evening feast,** יוֹם הַמַּעֲשֶׂה *day of the evening feast* 1 S 20_{19}.

*__[מַעֲשֶׂה]__ IV 1 n.m. **storehouse,** פְּרִי מַעֲשֶׂיךָ *supplies of your storehouses* Ps 104_{13}.

מַעֲשַׂי 1 pr.n.m. **Maasai.**

מַעֲשֵׂיָה 17.0.0.2 pr.n.m. **Maaseiah.**

מַעֲשֵׂיָהוּ 7.0.0.7 pr.n.m. **Maaseiah.**

מַעֲשֵׂר 32.1.10 n.m.—Q מעסר; cstr. מַעְשַׂר; pl. מַעַשְׂרוֹת; sf. מַעְשְׂרֹתֵיכֶם—**1. tenth,** מַעְשַׂר הַחֹמֶר *tenth of a homer* Ezk 45_{11}. **2. tithe,** tax for religious purposes, not necessarily of an exact tenth, כָּל־מַעְשַׂר תְּבוּאָתְךָ *full tithe of your produce* Dt 14_{28}. → עשׂר *take a tenth part;* cf. עֶשֶׂר *ten,* עָשָׂר *ten.*

[מַעֲשַׁקָּה] 2 n.f. **extortion,** בֶּצַע מַעֲשַׁקּוֹת *gain of,* i.e. from, *extortion(s)* Is 33_{15}. → עשׁק I *oppress.*

מֹף 1.0.2 pl.n. **Memphis.**

*__[מְפֹאָר]__ 0.0.1 n.m. **beauty, glory,** אדם מפאר עליון *humankind is the glory of the Most High* 11QPs[a] 18_7. → פאר I *adorn;* cf. תִּפְאָרָה *beauty.*

מְפִבֹשֶׁת, see מְפִיבֹשֶׁת *Mephibosheth.*

מִפְגָּע 1 n.[m.] **target for archery** Jb 7_{20}. → פגע *meet.*

[מַפָּח] 1.1 n.m. **expiring, breathing out,** מַפַּח־נָפֶשׁ *breathing out of life,* i.e. expiring in death Jb 11_{20}; מפח נפש *expiring of the soul,* i.e. heartache, disappointment Si $30_{12(B)}$. → נפח I *breathe.*

מַפֻּחַ 1 n.m. **bellows** Jr 6_{29}. → נפח I *breathe.*

מְפִיבֹשֶׁת 15.0.2 pr.n.m. **Mephibosheth.**

מֻפִּים I 1 pr.n.m. **Muppim.**

*__מֻפִּים__ II 1 n.[m.]pl. **defects in scribe's archetype** Gn 46_{21}.

מֵפִיץ I 1 n.[m.] **scatterer, disperser** Pr 25_{18}. → פוץ I *scatter.*

*__מֵפִיץ__ II 1 n.[m.] **club,** or perh. **hammer** Pr 25_{18}. → פוץ I *scatter;* cf. מַפֵּץ *hammer.*

[מַפָּל] 2 n.m. **1. refuse,** what is discarded, מַפַּל בַּר *refuse* *of the wheat* Am 8_{6}. **2. skin-fold** of Leviathan, מַפְּלֵי בְשָׂרוֹ *folds of its flesh* Jb 41_{15}. → נפל I *fall.*

[מִפְלָאָה] 1 n.f. **wondrous work,** מִפְלְאוֹת תְּמִים דֵּעִים *wondrous works of the one perfect of knowledge* Jb 37_{16}. → פלא *be wonderful.*

*[מִפְלָג] 0.0.9 n.[m.]—sf. מפלגו; pl. sf. מפלגיו—**1. division, class** of followers of good and evil spirits 1QS $4_{15.16}$. **2. channel (of water)** 1QH 16_{21} ([מפלגי]הם). **3. separation,** חוקי מפלגיה *boundaries of its separations* 1QM 10_{12}. **4. course** of wood between stone courses in wall 1QH 11_{30}. → פלג *be divided.*

[מִפְלַגָּה] 1.0.1 n.f.—pl. מִפְלַגּוֹת; sf. Q מפלגותם—**division** of lay family groups 2 C 35_{12}, of followers of good and evil spirits 1QS 4_{17}. → פלג *be divided.*

מַפָּלָה 3 n.f.—מַפֵּלָה—**ruin(s)** Is 23_{13} 25_{2}; מְעִי מַפָּלָה *heap of ruins* Is 17_{1}. → נפל I *fall*; cf. מַפֶּלֶת *downfall.*

מַפֵּלָה, see מַפָּלָה *ruin.*

מִפְלָט 1 n.[m.] **refuge,** ״ ... מִפְלָטִי *Y. is ... my refuge* 2 S 22_{2}. → פלט I *escape.*

מִפְלֶצֶת 4 n.f.—מִפְלֶצֶת; sf. מִפְלַצְתָּהּ—**horrible image,** made for Asherah 1 K 15_{13}. → פלץ *tremble.*

[מִפְלָשׂ] 1 n.[m.] **poising, balancing,** מִפְלְשֵׂי עָב *poising of the clouds* Jb 37_{16}. → פלס I *make level.*

[מַפֶּלֶת] 8.1 n.f.—sf. מַפַּלְתָּם—**1. downfall** of wicked Pr 29_{16}, Tyre Ezk 26_{15}; **fall of tree, in ref. to Pharaoh** Ezk 31_{16}. **2. felled tree trunk** Ezk 31_{13}. **3. carcass of lion** Jg 14_{8}. → נפל I *fall*; cf. מַפָּלָה *ruin.*

מִפְנֵי, see פָּנִים *face.*

[מִפְעָל] 3.2 n.[m.]—pl. cstr. מִפְעֲלוֹת; sf. מִפְעָלָיו—**deed, work** of Y. Ps 46_{9}, human Si $15_{19(A)}$. → פעל *do.*

מֵפַעַת, see מֵיפַעַת *Mephaath.*

[מַפָּץ] 1.0.2 n.[m.] **shattering,** כְּלִי מַפָּצוֹ *the weapons of his shattering,* i.e. his shattering weapon Ezk 9_{2}. → נפץ I *shatter.*

מַפֵּץ 1.0.1 n.[m.] **club,** or perh. **hammer** Jr 51_{20}. → נפץ I *shatter*; cf. מֵפִיץ II *club.*

מִפְקָד 5.2.0.1 n.[m.]—cstr. מִפְקַד—**1a. muster, counting, census,** מִפְקַד־הָעָם *muster of the people* 2 S 24_{9}, מפקד יד *counting of hand* Si $42_{7(Bmg)}$. **b.** שַׁעַר הַמִּפְקָד as pl.n. **Muster Gate** Ne 3_{31}. **2. appointed place,** or perh. **mustering place** Ezk 43_{21}. **3. appointment,** עת מפקד *appointed time* Si 35_{11} (or §4). **4. farewell,** עת מפקד *time of farewell* Si 35_{11}. **5. guard** T. 'Ira ost. 1_{1}. → פקד *visit.*

[מִפְרָץ] I 1 n.[m.]—pl. sf. מִפְרָצָיו—**landing place,** for ships Jg 5_{17}. → פרץ I *break through.*

*[מִפְרָץ] II 1 n.[m.]—pl. sf. מִפְרָצָיו—**wadi** Jg 5_{17}. → (?) פרץ *break through.*

[מַפְרֶקֶת] 1 n.f.—sf. מַפְרַקְתּוֹ—**neck** 1 S 4_{18}. → פרק *tear off.*

[מִפְרָשׂ] 2.0.2 n.[m.]—cstr. Q מפרשׂ; sf. מִפְרָשֵׂךְ; pl. cstr. מִפְרְשֵׂי—**1. spreading out, expanse** of clouds Jb 36_{29}. **2. place of spreading** 1QH fr. 3_{4}. **3. sail** Ezk 27_{7}. → פרשׂ I *spread.*

*[מִפְשָׂע] 0.0.1 n.[m.] **marching** 1QM 8_{7}. → פשׂע *march.*

מִפְשָׂעָה 1 n.f. **buttocks** 1 C 19_{4}.

מַפְתֵּחַ 3.1 n.m. **key** Jg 3_{25}; מַפְתֵּחַ בֵּית־דָּוִד *key of the house of David* Is 22_{22}. → פתח I *open.*

[מִפְתָּח] 1.0.1 n.[m.] **opening (up),** מִפְתַּח שְׂפָתַי *opening of my lips* Pr 8_{6}, מפתח חסדיו *opening up of his mercies* 1QS 10_{4}. → פתח I *open.*

מִפְתָּן 8 n.[m.]—cstr. מִפְתַּן—**threshold,** as viewed from inside a building (as contrasted with סַף) 1 S 5_{4} Ezk 9_{3}.

מֵץ, see מֵיץ *extortioner.*

מֹץ 8.0.1 n.m. **chaff,** מֹץ לִפְנֵי רוּחַ *chaff before the wind* Ps 35_{5}.

מצא I 457.33.66 vb.—**Qal** 308.27.34 Pf. מָצָא, מָצָאתָ; impf. יִמְצָא, תִּמְצֶאןָ; impv. מְצָא, מִצְאוּ, מְצֶאןָ; ptc. מֹצֵא (מֹצְאוֹ), מֹצֵאת, מֹצְאִים (מֹצְאֵיהֶם), מֹצְאֵי, מֹצְאוֹת; inf. מְצֹא (מֹצַאֲכֶם) —**1. find what is sought, missed:** thing Gn 26_{32}, person Ca 3_{1}, Y. Jr 29_{13}. **2a. find, meet, encounter** someone Gn 4_{14}. **b. befall, overtake** someone, subj. hardship Ex 18_{8}. **3a. find, discover, come across** something Gn 11_{2}. **b. find written,** ... וַיִּמְצְאוּ כָּתוּב בַּתּוֹרָה *and they found written in the law ...* Ne 8_{14}. **4a. find (one's way to),** i.e. **reach** Jb 3_{22}. **b.** of axe head, **hit** person Dt 19_{5}. **c.** of fire, **catch (hold of), spread to** thornbushes Ex 22_{5}. **5. find (out), discover, learn** answer to riddle Jg 14_{18}, mysteries of Y. Jb 11_{7}. **6. find out, detect** wrongdoing 1 S 29_{3}. **7a. find (to be so),** through examination, experience, וּמָצָאתָ אֶת־לְבָבוֹ נֶאֱמָן לְפָנֶיךָ *and you found his heart (to be) true to you* Ne 9_{8}. **b. find to be sound** Si 34_{22}. **8a. find,** i.e. **obtain, gain, achieve** booty Nm 31_{50}, wealth Pr 1_{13}, wisdom Pr 3$_{13}$, life Pr 21$_{21}$, rest Si 6$_{28}$; מצא חֵן בְּעֵינֵי *find favour in the sight of* Gn 6$_{8}$. **b. experience** distress and sorrow Ps 116$_{3}$. **9a. find (from one's resources),** i.e. **afford,** תְּנָה־נָּא אֵת אֲשֶׁר תִּמְצָא יָדְךָ לַעֲבָדֶיךָ *please, give to your servants whatever your hand finds,* i.e. whatever you can afford 1 S 25$_{8}$. **b. find sufficient,** לֹא־מָצְאוּ לָהֶם כֵּן *they did not find sufficient (women) for them* Jg 21$_{14}$. **c. find (possible to do),** עֲשֵׂה לְךָ אֲשֶׁר תִּמְצָא יָדֶךָ *do whatever your hand finds possible to do,* i.e. whatever you can 1 S 10$_{7}$. **d.** of wisdom, **provide** knowledge and discretion Pr 8$_{12}$. **10.** מצא אַחֲרֵי **find fault with,** לֹא יִמְצָא הָאָדָם אַחֲרָיו מְאוּמָה *humanity may find no fault with him* (Y.) Ec 7$_{14}$.

Ni. 142.7.32 Pf. נִמְצְאתִי, נִמְצָא; impf. יִמָּצֵא; ptc. נִמְצָא, נִמְצָאָה, נִמְצָאִים (נִמְצְאִים; נִמְצָאֶיךָ), נִמְצָאוֹת; inf. abs. הִמָּצֵא; cstr. הִמָּצְאוֹ—**1.** (of what is sought, missed, lost) **be found,** of thing 2 K 22$_{13}$, person Jos 10$_{17}$, Y. 1 C 28$_{9}$ (+ לְ *by* someone). **2. be found, encountered, met,** of human corpse Dt 21$_{1}$, words of Y. Jr 15$_{16}$. **3a. be present,** of person Dt 17$_{2}$, Y. Ps 46$_{2}$. **b. be (found), exist, remain,** of person 1 S 13$_{19}$ (+ בְּ *in* place), wisdom Pr 10$_{13}$ (+ בְּ *on* lips). **c. be found with** (אֵת), i.e. **in the possession of** someone 1 C 29$_{8}$. **d. be found (written),** נִמְצָא כָּתוּב בּוֹ אֲשֶׁר ... *in it was found written that* ... Ne 13$_{1}$. **4. be found,** i.e. **discovered, detected,** of thing stolen Ex 22$_{3}$, evil 1 K 1$_{52}$ (+ בְּ *in* person). **5. be caught, be captured, be seized,** of thief Ex 22$_{1}$. **6a. be found (to be so),** through examination, experience, לֹא נִמְצָא מִכֻּלָּם כְּדָנִיֵּאל *among them all none was found (to be) like Daniel* Dn 1$_{19}$. **b. be found to be correct,** of matter investigated Est 2$_{23}$. **7. be found (out),** through study, revelation, of wisdom 1QS 9$_{13}$. **8. be (found to be) sufficient,** לֹא־יִמָּצֵא לָנוּ הָהָר *the hill-country is not sufficient for us* Jos 17$_{16}$. **9. be gained,** of grey hair as crown of glory Pr 16$_{31}$ (+ בְּ *by* way of righteousness). **10a. be left over, survive,** of root Is 37$_{31(1QIsa^a)}$. **b.** perh. ptc. as noun, **survivor(s), refugee(s)** Dn 12$_{1}$ (or §3). **11. be reached,** of wisdom Jb 28$_{12}$.

Hi. 7 Pf. הִמְצִיאוּ, הִמְצִיתָךְ; impf. יַמְצִאֶנּוּ; ptc. מַמְצִיא—**1. cause to meet, deliver up** someone into hand of (בְּיַד) someone, subj. human 2 S 3$_{8}$, subj. Zc 11$_{6}$. **2.** of Y., **cause to befall, cause to overtake, cause to come,** כְּאֹרַח אִישׁ יַמְצִאֶנּוּ *according to a man's ways he will make it befall him* Jb 34$_{11}$. **3. bring, present** burnt offering to (אֶל) Aaron Lv 9$_{12}$.

→ cf. מְטָה *reaching*.

*מצא II 5 vb.—**Qal** 3 Pf. מָצְאוּ—**suffice, be sufficient,** of food for (לְ) Israelites Nm 11$_{22.22}$, wives for Benjaminites Jg 21$_{14}$.

Ni. 2 Impf. יִמָּצֵא—**be sufficient** for (לְ) people, of hill country as dwelling place Jos 17$_{16}$; also Zc 10$_{10}$.

*מצא III 2 vb.—**Ni.** 2 Impf. יִמָּצֵא—**be drained out, be drained dry,** of blood Lv 1$_{15(Sam)}$ 5$_{9(Sam)}$. → cf. מצה *drain*, מצץ *suck*.

מֹצָא, see מוֹצָא I *going out*.

מַצָּב 10.0.1 n.m.—cstr. מַצַּב; sf. מַצָּבְךָ—**1. standing place** Jos 4$_{3}$. **2. military post, garrison** 1 S 13$_{23}$. **3. position, office** Is 22$_{19}$. → נצב I *stand*.

מֻצָּב I 1 n.[m.] perh. **siege mound** Is 29$_{3}$. → נצב I *stand*.

מֻצָּב II, see נצב II *stand*, ho.

מַצָּבָה 1 n.f. **guard,** אַנְשֵׁי הַמַּצָּבָה *men of the guard* 1 S 14$_{12}$. → נצב I *stand*.

מַצֵּבָה 38.0.4 n.f.—מַצֶּבֶת; cstr. מַצֶּבֶת (מַצְּבַת); sf. מַצַּבְתָּהּ; pl. מַצֵּבוֹת; cstr. מַצְּבוֹת; sf. מַצְּבֹתֵיהֶם, מַצְּבוֹתָם—**1. pillar, memorial stone,** commemorating appearance of Y. Gn 28$_{18}$, making of covenant Gn 31$_{45}$; erected in Egypt to Y. Is 19$_{19}$; assoc. with cult of Canaanites Ex 23$_{24}$, with Baal 2 K 3$_{2}$; at Rachel's tomb Gn 35$_{20}$; erected by Absalom as personal memorial 2 S 18$_{18}$. **2.** appar. **stump** of tree Is 6$_{13}$. → נצב I *stand*.

מְצֹבָיָה 1 gent. **Mezobaite.**

מְצַד 11.0.1 n.f.—cstr. מְצַד; pl. מְצָדוֹת; cstr. מְצָדוֹת—**stronghold, mountain fastness,** מְצַד מִדְבָּרָה *stronghold of the steppe* 1 C 12$_{9}$, מְצָדוֹת עֵין־גֶּדִי *strongholds of En-gedi* 1 S 24$_{1}$, סְלָעִים *of rocks* Is 33$_{16}$.

מצה 7 vb.—**Qal** 4 Pf. מָצִית; impf. יִמְצוּ; + waw וַיִּמֶץ—**1. drain** cup Is 51$_{17}$. **2. wring out** water from (מִן) fleece Jg 6$_{38}$.

Ni. 3 Impf. יִמָּצֶה, יִמָּצוּ; + waw וְנִמְצָה—**be drained out,** of blood Lv 1$_{15}$, water Ps 73$_{10}$.

→ מְצִירוֹק *emission of spittle*; cf. מצא III *drain*, מצץ *suck*.

מֹצָה 1.0.0.1 pl.n. **Moza.**

מַצָּה I 53.0.4 n.f. **1. unleavened bread, cake,** flat, made of barley meal and water 1 S 28_{24}. **2.** חַג הַמַּצּוֹת **(festival of) Unleavened Bread,** seven days after Passover Ex 12_{15}.

מַצָּה II 3 n.f. **strife, contention** Pr 17_{19}. → נצה I *fight.*

[מִצְהָלָה] 2 n.f.—pl. cstr. מִצְהֲלוֹת; sf. מִצְהֲלוֹתַיִךְ—**neighing** of horses Jr 8_{16}, of adulterous Jerusalem Jr 13_{27}. → צהל I *neigh.*

[מָצוֹד] I 3 n.[m.]—cstr. מְצוֹד; sf. מְצוּדוֹ; pl. מְצוֹדִים—**net, snare** Pr 12_{12} Ec 7_{26}. → צוד I *hunt.*

[מָצוֹד] II 3.0.1 n. [m.]—cstr. מְצוֹד; sf. מְצוּדוֹ; pl. מְצוֹדִים—**1. stronghold,** מְצוֹד רָעִים *stronghold of evil ones* Pr 12_{12}. **2. watchtower** CD 4_{12}. **3. siegeworks,** מְצוֹדִים גְּדֹלִים *great siegeworks* Ec 9_{14}. → cf. מְצוּדָה II *stronghold,* מְצוּדָה II *stronghold.*

***[מָצוֹד]** n.[m.] **game,** מְצוֹד רֵעִים *game of friends* Pr 12_{12} (if em. מְצוֹד רָעִים *net/stronghold of evil ones*).

מְצוֹדָה I 2.1.3 n.f.—pl. מְצֹדוֹת—**net, snare** Ezk 19_{9} Ec 9_{12}; מצודות בליעל *nets of Belial* CD 4_{15}. → צוד I *hunt.*

[מְצוֹדָה] II 1 n.f.—sf. מְצֹדָתָהּ—**stronghold** Is 29_{7}. → cf. מָצוֹד II *stronghold,* מְצוּדָה II *stronghold.*

מְצוּדָה I 4 n.f.—sf. מְצוּדָתִי—**1. net** Ezk 12_{13}. **2. prey** Ezk 13_{21}. **3. eyrie,** dwelling place and lookout of bird of prey Jb 39_{28}. → צוד I *hunt.*

מְצוּדָה II 17.0.2 n.f.—cstr. מְצֻדַת; sf. מְצוּדָתִי; pl. מְצוּדוֹת—**1. stronghold, mountain fastness** 1 S 22_{4}; מְצֻדַת צִיּוֹן *stronghold of Zion* 2 S 5_{7}. **2. siegeworks** Is $29_{3(mss, 1QIsa^a)}$ (L מְצֻרֹת *siegeworks*). → cf. מָצוֹד II *stronghold,* מְצוֹדָה II *stronghold.*

***מְצוּדָה** III 1 n.f. **steppe, place of wandering** Ps 66_{11}.

מִצְוָה 181.9.45 n.f.—cstr. מִצְוַת; sf. מִצְוָתְךָ; pl. מִצְוֹת (מִצְווֹת); sf. מִצְוֹתַי (מִצְוֹתָי, Q מצוותיכ)—**1. command(ment)** of Y., **a.** sg., coll., הַתּוֹרָה וְהַמִּצְוָה *the law and the commandment(s)* Ex 24_{12}; particular command 1 S 13_{13}. **b.** pl., שֹׁמְרֵי מִצְוֹתָיו *those who keep his commandments* Ne 1_{5}. **2. commandment** of Wisdom Pr 2_{1}. **3a. command, order** of human, מִצְוַת הַמֶּלֶךְ *order of the king* Est 3_{3}. **b. obligation** of religious contribution Ne 10_{33}. **c.** perh. **due,** מִצְוַת הַלְוִיִּם *due of Levites* Ne 13_{5}. **d.** perh. **terms** of deed transferring property Jr 32_{11}. → צוה *command.*

[מְצוֹלָה], see מְצוּלָה *depth.*

מְצוּלָה 12.0.8 n.f.—מְצֻלָה; pl. מְצוֹלֹת (מְצֻלוֹת); cstr. מְצֻלוֹת (מְצוּלוֹת)—**1. depth, the deep,** perh. as a term for the underworld Ps 69_{3}; sg. the deep sea Jon 2_{4}; pl. **depths** of the sea Ps 68_{23}, the Nile Zc 10_{11}. **2.** perh. **hollow** Zc 1_{8}. → צלל II *sink.*

מָצוֹק 6.1 n.[m.] **distress, anguish** 1 S 22_{2}. → צוק I *distress.*

מָצוּק 2.1 n.[m.] **1. pillar,** מְצֻקֵי אֶרֶץ *pillars of the earth* 1 S 2_{8}. **2. solid casting** Si $43_{4(B)}$. → צוק II *pour out.*

מְצוּקָה 7.2.5 n.f.—pl. cstr. Si מְצוּקוֹת; sf. מְצוּקוֹתֵיהֶם (Q מצוקותיהמה, Q מצוקותם)—**distress, anguish, affliction** Zp 1_{15} Ps 107_{6}; מצוקות שלהבת *distress of,* i.e. caused by, *flame* Si 51_{4}. → צוק I *distress.*

מָצוֹר I 20.0.1 n.[m.]—cstr. מְצוֹר; sf. מְצוּרֵךְ; pl. mss מְצוּרִים—**1. siege** 2 K 24_{10} Ezk 4_{7}, perh. **distress** Dt 28_{53}. **2. siegeworks** Dt 20_{20}. → צור I *confine.*

מָצוֹר II 6.0.2 n.[m.] **1. fortification, fortress,** עִיר מָצוֹר *fortified city* Ps 31_{22}. **2. watchtower** Hb 2_{1}. → צור I *confine.*

***[מָצוֹר]** III 0.0.2 n.[m.] **creature(s), formation,** מצור ימים *creatures of the seas* 4QBer^{a} 5_{9}. → צור III *fashion.*

מָצוֹר IV 5 pl.n. **Egypt.**

***מָצוֹר** V 4 n.m. **whey,** i.e. glacier rivulets, יְאֹרֵי מָצוֹר *streams of whey* Is 19_{6}.

מְצוּרָה I 8 n.f.—pl. מְצֻרוֹת—**1. fortification,** עָרֵי מְצוּרָה *fortified cities* 2 C 14_{5}, var. עָרֵי מְצֻרוֹת 2 C 11_{10}. **2. siegeworks** Is 29_{3}. → צור I *confine.*

***[מְצוּרָה]** II n.f. **distress** Ps 66_{11} (if em. מְצוּדָה *net*).

[מַצּוּת] 1.1 n.f. **strife,** אַנְשֵׁי מַצֻּתֶךָ *men of your strife,* i.e. who strive with you Is 41_{12}. → נצה I *fight.*

***[מצח]** vb. **Qal,** of foot, **tread** through (בְּ) blood Ps 68_{24} (if em. תִּמְחַץ perh. *you will wound* to תִּמְצַח *it will tread*).

מֵצַח 13.1.1 n.m.—sf. מִצְחוֹ; pl. cstr. מִצְחוֹת—**forehead, brow** Ex 28_{38}. → cf. מֵזַח III *impudence, brow.*

[מִצְחָה] 1 n.f.—cstr. מִצְחַת—**greaves,** armour protecting the shins 1 S 17_{6}.

***[מְצִירוֹק]** 0.0.2 n.[m.] **emission of spittle,** i.e. of semen 1QS 11_{21} 4QShir^{b} 28_{3}. → מצה *drain* + רק *spittle.*

[מְצִלָּה] 1 n.f. **bell,** מְצִלּוֹת הַסּוּס *bells of the horse(s)* Zc 14_{20}. → צלל I *tingle.*

*[מִצְלַחַת] 0.1 n.f. **success** in physician's hand Si 38$_{13}$. → צלח II *prosper*.

מְצִלְתַּיִם 13 n.f.du. **cymbals** 1 C 15$_{16}$. → צלל *tingle*.

*[מָצָן] n.[m.] **place of thorns, the Thicket,** i.e. the underworld Jb 5$_{5}$ (if em. אֶל־מִצִּנִּים *to thorns* to perh. אֶל־מָצָנִים *to the Thicket*).

מִצְנֶפֶת 12.1.1 n.f.—מִצְנֶפֶת—**turban,** usu. of high priest, מִצְנֶפֶת בַּד *turban of linen* Lv 16$_{4}$; of king Ezk 21$_{31}$. → צנף *wind*.

מַצָּע 1 n.m. **couch** Is 28$_{20}$. → יצע *extend*.

[מִצְעָד] 3.0.9 n.[m.]—sf. Q מצעדם; pl. cstr. מִצְעֲדֵי; sf. מִצְעָדָיו—**1. step,** מִצְעֲדֵי־גֶבֶר *steps of a man* Ps 37$_{23}$. **2. heel** Dn 11$_{43}$. **3. flight,** i.e. descent, of arrow into the deep 1QH 11$_{17}$. → צעד *march*.

מִצְעָר I 5.2.2 n.m.—cstr. מִצְעַר—**1. small thing, small one,** of city Gn 19$_{20}$, beginning Jb 8$_{7}$. **2. a few,** מִצְעַר אֲנָשִׁים *a few men* 2 C 24$_{24}$. **3. a little while** Is 63$_{18}$. → צער *be insignificant*.

מִצְעָר II 1 pl.n. **Mizar.**

מִצְפָּה 40 pl.n. **Mizpah.**

מִצְפֶּה I 2.1 n.m. **watchtower,** הַמִּצְפֶּה לַמִּדְבָּר *the watchtower of,* i.e. overlooking, *the steppe* 2 C 20$_{24}$. → צפה I *keep watch*.

מִצְפֶּה II 6.0.1 pl.n. **Mizpeh.**

[מַצְפּוֹן] 1 n.[m.]—pl. sf. מַצְפֻּנָיו—**hidden treasure,** perh. **hiding place** Ob$_{6}$. → צפן *hide*.

מצץ 1 vb.—**Qal** 1 Impf. תָּמֹצּוּ—**suck, draw milk** Is 66$_{11}$. → cf. מצה *drain*.

מֻצָק *cast object, casting,* see יצק ho.

מֵצַר 3.0.2 n.[m.]—pl. מְצָרִים—**1. distress, torment,** מְצָרֵי שְׁאוֹל *torments of Sheol* Ps 116$_{3}$. **2. narrow place** 1QH 13$_{29}$. **3.** perh. **Confinement,** as name for the underworld Ps 118$_{5}$. → צרר I *bind, be narrow*.

*[מֶצֶר] 0.0.0.1 pr.n.m. **Mezer.**

[מַצָּרָה] I n.f. **watch** Na 2$_{2}$ (if em. מְצֻרָה *fortress*).

*[מַצָּרָה] II n.f. **guard-house** Ezk 19$_{9}$ (if em. בַּמְּצֹדוֹת *into the nets* to בַּמַּצָּרָה *into the guard-house*).

מִצְרִי I 30 gent. **Egyptian.**

*מִצְרִי II 0.0.0.2 pr.n.m. **Mizri.**

[מֻצְרִי] *Musri,* see מִצְרַיִם II *Mizraim*.

מִצְרַיִם I 674.0.34.2 pr.n.m. **Egypt.**

מִצְרַיִם II 7 pl.n. **Mizraim, Musri.**

אָבֵל מִצְרַיִם, *Abel-mizraim,* see אָבֵל II *Abel*.

מַצְרֵף 2.0.14 n.[m.]—pl. sf. Q מצרפיו (Q מצרפותיו)—**1. crucible** Pr 17$_{3}$; בחוני מצרף *ones tested of,* i.e. in, *a crucible* 1QM 17$_{1}$. **2. affliction, hardship, trial** 1QS 8$_{4}$. → צרף *refine*.

מַק 2 n.m.—מָק—**rottenness** or **stench** Is 3$_{24}$ 5$_{24}$. → מקק *rot*.

מַקֶּבֶת I 4 n.f.—pl. מַקָּבוֹת—**hammer** Jg 4$_{21}$. → נקב I *pierce*.

[מַקֶּבֶת] II 1 n.f. **excavation,** or perh. **fissure,** מַקֶּבֶת בּוֹר *excavation of a pit,* i.e. quarry Is 51$_{1}$. → נקב I *pierce*.

מַקֵּדָה 9.0.0.1 pl.n. **Makkedah.**

מִקְדָּשׁ 74.5.81 n.m.—cstr. מִקְדַּשׁ; sf. מִקְדָּשִׁי; pl. מִקְדָּשִׁים; cstr. מִקְדְּשֵׁי; sf. מִקְדָּשֵׁי, מִקְדְּשֵׁיכֶם, מִקְדְּשֵׁיהֶם—**1. sanctuary, sacred place** (but not Temple building, which is בֵּית הַמִּקְדָּשׁ *house of the sanctuary*), usu. belonging to Y., מִקְדְּשֵׁי בֵּית י״ *sacred places of the house of Y.* Jr 51$_{51}$, מקדש אדם *sanctuary of humans* 4QMidrEschat[a] 3$_{6}$. **2. holy things** Nm 10$_{21}$. **3. consecrated part** of offering Nm 18$_{29}$. → קדשׁ *be holy*.

*[מִקְדָּשׁ] 2 n.[m.]—sf. מִקְדָּשׁוֹ—**holiest part** Nm 18$_{29}$; מִקְדַּשׁ הַקֹּדֶשׁ *holiest part of the sanctuary* Lv 16$_{33}$. → קדשׁ *be holy*.

[מַקְהֵל] 2 n.[m.]—pl. מַקְהֵלִים, מַקְהֵלוֹת—**assembly** Ps 26$_{12}$ 68$_{27}$. → קהל *assemble*.

מַקְהֵלֹת 2 pl.n. **Makheloth.**

מִקְוֵא, see מִקְוֶה II *collection*.

מִקְוָה 1 n.f. **reservoir** Is 22$_{11}$. → קוה II *be collected*.

מִקְוֶה I 5.0.6 n.m.—cstr. מִקְוֵה—**1. hope,** אֵין מִקְוֶה *there is no hope* 1 C 29$_{15}$. **2.** of Y., **Hope,** מִקְוֵה יִשְׂרָאֵל *Hope of Israel* Jr 14$_{8}$. → קוה I *wait*.

[מִקְוֶה] II 7.5.9 n.m.—cstr. מִקְוֵה (מִקְוֵא; Q מקוי); pl. sf. Q מקויהם—**1a. collection of waters, reservoir, pool** Gn 1$_{10}$ Lv 11$_{36}$. **b.** of Y., **Fountain, Source,** מִקְוֵה יִשְׂרָאֵל *Fountain of Israel* Jr 14$_{8}$. **2. heap,** מקוי אפר *heap of ashes* 1QH fr. 3$_{6}$. **3. company,** מִקְוֵה סֹחֲרֵי הַמֶּלֶךְ *company of the king's merchants* 1 K 10$_{28}$. **4. droves** (of horses) 1 K 10$_{28}$. → קוה II *be collected*.

*מִקְוֶה III 2 n.m.—cstr. מִקְוֵה—**1. abode,** מִקְוֵה אֲבוֹתֵיהֶם *abode of their fathers* Jr 50$_{7}$. **2. abiding** 1 C 29$_{15}$.

מָקוֹם 401.10.65.4 n.m.&f.—cstr. מְקוֹם; sf. מְקוֹמִי; pl. מְקֹמוֹת (מְקוֹמֹת); sf. מְקוֹמֹתָם, מְקוֹמֹתֵיכֶם—**1. place, location,**

site, a. of city, מְקוֹם שְׁכֶם *site of Shechem* Gn 12$_{6}$. **b.** of land 1 S 12$_{8}$. **2. dwelling place, abode, home, a.** of human, שָׁב לִמְקֹמוֹ *he returned home* Gn 18$_{33}$. **b.** of Y. Is 26$_{21}$. **c.** of animal Ps 44$_{20}$. **3. sanctuary, sacred site, a.** of Y., הַמָּקוֹם אֲשֶׁר יִבְחַר *the sacred site he* (Y.) *would choose* Jos 9$_{27}$. **b.** of other gods Ezk 6$_{13}$. **4. space, room** Gn 24$_{23}$. **5. (plot of) land, property, estate, fief** 1 S 27$_{5}$. **6a. tomb** Jr 7$_{32}$. **b. Sheol** Ec 6$_{6}$. **7. place** for refuge Ex 21$_{13}$. **8. place, seat** at meal, וַיִּפָּקֵד מְקוֹם דָּוִד *but David's place was empty* 1 S 20$_{25}$. **9. site** of leprosy 2 K 5$_{11}$. **10a. position** Jos 8$_{19}$. **b. rightful place, normal position** Jos 4$_{18}$. **11. office, post** 1 K 20$_{24}$. **12. reason** Si 4$_{5}$. **13. opportunity** (to speak) Si 13$_{22}$. **14. direction** Ezk 10$_{11}$. **15. (the) place,** perh. as reverential periphrasis for Y. Est 4$_{14}$. **16.** מְקוֹם cstr. **(in) place of, instead of** Ho 2$_{1}$. → קום *arise.*

*[מְקוֹמָה] n.f. **opposition** Na 1$_{8}$ (כָּלָה יַעֲשֶׂה מְקוֹמָה *he will make a full end of opposition*; if em. מְקוֹמָהּ *its place*). → קום *arise.*

מָקוֹר I 18.2.39 n.m.—cstr. מְקוֹר; sf. מְקוֹרוֹ—**1a.** of eyes, **fount** of tears Jr 8$_{23}$. **b.** of reproductive organs, **source** of menstrual blood Lv 20$_{18}$, semen 1QM 7$_{6}$. **2.** human words as **source** of wisdom Pr 18$_{4}$, understanding as **fountain** of life Pr 16$_{22}$. **3.** of Y., **Source, Fountain,** מקור דעת *Source of knowledge* 1QS 10$_{12}$, מְקוֹר מַיִם־חַיִּים *Fountain of living waters* Jr 17$_{13}$. **4.** of wife, **fountain of pleasure** Pr 5$_{18}$ (or §1b). → קור *dig.*

*[מָקוֹר] II 2 n.[m.] **convocation,** מְקוֹר יִשְׂרָאֵל *convocation of Israel* Ps 68$_{27}$, חָכְמָה *of Wisdom* Pr 18$_{4}$.

[מִקָּח] 1.0.1 n.[m.] **1. taking,** מִקַּח־שֹׁחַד *taking of bribes* 2 C 19$_{7}$. **2. buying** CD 13$_{15}$. → לקח *take.*

[מַקָּחָה] 1 n.f.—pl. מַקָּחוֹת—**wares, merchandise** Ne 10$_{32}$. → לקח *take.*

[מִקְטָר] 1 n.[m.]—cstr. מִקְטַר—**place of burning,** מִזְבֵּחַ מִקְטַר קְטֹרֶת *an altar, a place of burning incense* Ex 30$_{1}$. → קטר I *burn incense.*

מֻקְטָר 1 n.m. **incense,** perh. **frankincense** Ml 1$_{11}$. → קטר I *burn incense.*

מִקְטֶרֶת 2.0.2 n.f.—sf. מִקְטַרְתּוֹ—**1. censer** Ezk 8$_{11}$. **2. incense** or **offering of incense,** מקטרת ניחוח *soothing incense* 1QM 2$_{5}$. → קטר I *burn incense.*

[מְקַטֶּרֶת] 1 n.f.—pl. מְקַטְּרוֹת—**incense altar** or perh. **utensils for smoke cult** 2 C 30$_{14}$. → קטר I *burn incense.*

מַקֵּל 18 n.m.&f.—cstr. מַקֵּל (מַקַּל); sf. מַקְלִי; pl. מַקְלוֹת—**1a. rod** of ruler Jr 48$_{17}$. **b. staff** of traveller Gn 32$_{11}$, shepherd 1 S 17$_{40}$. **c.** as weapon, **club** Ezk 39$_{9}$. **d. branch** of almond tree Jr 1$_{11}$. **2.** perh. **penis,** in supposed divination Ho 4$_{12}$.

מִקְלוֹת 4 pr.n.m. **Mikloth.**

מִקְלָט 20.0.1 n.[m.]—cstr. מִקְלַט; sf. מִקְלָטוֹ—**refuge, asylum,** מִקְלַט הָרֹצֵחַ *refuge of,* i.e. for, *the killer* Jos 21$_{13}$, עָרֵי מִקְלָט *cities of refuge* Nm 35$_{6}$.

*[מַקְלִיָּה] 0.0.1 pr.n.[m.] **Makliah.**

[מִקְלַעַת] 4 n.f.—pl. מִקְלְעוֹת—**carving** 1 K 6$_{29}$. → קלע II *carve.*

*[מְקִימְיָהוּ] 0.0.0.1 pr.n.m. **Mekimiah.**

*[מִקְמָשׁ] n.[m.] **pile,** מִקְמַשׁ חָרוּל *a heap of wild vetch* Zp 2$_{9}$ (if em. מִמְשַׁק *ground of*).

*[מֵקֶן] 0.0.0.1 pr.n.[m.] **Meken.**

מִקְנָה 15.1 n.f.—cstr. מִקְנַת; sf. מִקְנָתוֹ—**1. purchase, a. thing purchased,** e.g. field Lv 27$_{22}$. **b. person purchased,** מִקְנַת־כֶּסֶף *one purchased with money* Gn 17$_{12}$. **2. possession (though purchase)** Gn 23$_{18}$. **3. purchase price** Lv 25$_{51}$. → קנה *buy.*

מִקְנֶה 76.0.6 n.m.—cstr. מִקְנֵה; sf. מִקְנְךָ; pl. cstr. מִקְנֵי; sf. מִקְנֵיהֶם—**1. (possessions consisting of) cattle, livestock,** usu. of cows and sheep, but also camels, horses, asses Ex 9$_{3}$. **2. (purchased) property,** of field and tomb Gn 49$_{32}$, servants Jb 1$_{3}$. → קנה *buy.*

מִקְנֵיָהוּ 2.0.0.6 pr.n.m. **Mikneiah.**

מקניו, see מִקְנֵיָהוּ *Mikneiah.*

*[מִקְנְמֶלֶךְ] 0.0.0.2 pr.n.m. **Miknemelech.**

[מִקְסָם] 2 n.[m.] **divination,** מִקְסַם כָּזָב *lying divination* Ezk 13$_{7}$. → קסם *practise divination.*

מָקַץ 1 pl.n. **Makaz.**

מִקְצֹעַ 12.0.11 n.m.—pl. מִקְצֹעֹת; cstr. מִקְצֹעֹת, מִקְצוֹעֵי; sf. מִקְצְעוֹתָיו—**1. corner (piece)** of altar Ex 26$_{24}$. **2a. corner** of pool 3QTr 2$_{13}$. **b. (inner). corner, angle** of court Ezk 46$_{21}$. **3.** perh. pl.n. **the Angle,** corner in the wall of Jerusalem Ne 3$_{19}$. → קצע II *be of the same size.*

[מַקְצֻעָה] I 1 n.f.—pl. מַקְצֻעוֹת—**knife, scraping tool,** for shaping wood Is 44$_{13}$. → קצע I *scrape.*

*[מַקְצֻעָה] II 1 n.f.—pl. מַקְצֻעוֹת—**square,** for working with wood Is 44₁₃. → קצע II *be of the same size.*

מִקְצָת, see קָצָת *end.*

מקק 11 vb.—**Ni.** 9 Pf. נָמַקּוּ; impf. יִמַּקּוּ, תִּמַּק; ptc. נְמַקִּים—**1. rot, decay,** of host of heaven Is 34₄, eye, tongue Zc 14₁₂. **2. fester,** of wound Ps 38₆. **3. pine away** because of (בְּ) sin, of Israel Ezk 24₂₃.

Hi. 1 Inf. abs. הָמֵק—**cause flesh to rot,** of Y. Zc 14₁₂.

Perh. **Haphtil** 1 Impf. תַּמְתִּיק—**putrefy** in (בְּ) mouth, of evil Jb 20₁₂.

→ מַק *rottenness.*

מִקְרָא 23.0.14 n.m.—sf. Q מקראם; pl. cstr. מִקְרָאֵי; sf. מִקְרָאֶיהָ—**1a. convocation, assembly,** מִקְרָא־קֹדֶשׁ *a holy convocation* Lv 23₃. **b.** perh. **place of assembly** Is 4₅. **c. day of assembly** Is 1₁₃. **2.** as verbal noun, **assembling, summoning,** חצוצרות המקרא *trumpets of summoning* 1QM 7₁₃. **3. reading, what is read** Ne 8₈. → קרא I *call.*

*[מְקָרָה] 0.0.5 n.f.—sf. מקראה; cstr. מקרת; pl. sf. מקרותיו—**beam-work, rafter** 11QT 33₉. → קרה II *lay beams.*

מִקְרֶה 10.0.2 n.m.—cstr. מִקְרֶה (מקרה); sf. מִקְרֶהָ—**1. accident, chance,** מקרה לילה *accident of the night,* i.e. emission of semen 11QT 45₇, מִקְרֶה הוּא הָיָה לָנוּ *it has happened to us by chance* 1 S 6₉. **2. fate, fortune,** מִקְרֶה אֶחָד לָהֶם *they have the same fate* Ec 3₁₉. → קרה I *befall.*

*[מְקָרָה] n.f. **living room,** עֲלִיַּת הַמְּקָרָה *upper chamber of the living room* Jg 3₂₀ (if em. הַמְּקֵרָה *of coolness*).

מְקָרֶה 1 n.m. **beam-work, rafter,** of roof, ceiling Ec 10₁₈. → קרה *lay beams.*

מְקֵרָה 2 n.f. **coolness** or **cool place, summer palace,** חֲדַר הַמְּקֵרָה *the cool chamber* Jg 3₂₄. → קרר I *keep cool.*

*מְקַרְקַר 1 n.[m.] **echoing shout, echo sound,** מְקַרְקַר קִר *echoing sound of a clamour* Is 22₅.

*[מִקְרֶשׂ] n.[m.] **frame,** מִקְרֶשׂ עָרֶשׂ *frame of a bed* Am 3₁₂ (if em. דְּמֶשֶׁק appar. *damask of*). → קרשׂ *make framework.*

מִקְשָׁה I 9.1 n.f. **hammered work,** of cherubim Ex 25₁₈, lampstand Nm 8₄, trumpets Nm 10₂.

מִקְשָׁה II 2 n.f. **cucumber field** Jr 10₅. → cf. קִשֻּׁאָה *cucumber,* קִשּׁוּת *cucumber.*

מִקְשֶׁה 1 n.[m.] **locks of hair** Is 3₂₄.

מַר I 38.3.1 adj.—f.s. מָרָה; cstr. מָרַת; m.pl. מָרִים; cstr. מָרֵי—**1a. bitter,** of person, מַר־נֶפֶשׁ *bitter of soul,* i.e. embittered 1 S 22₂; of cry Est 4₁, day Am 8₁₀. **b. poisonous,** of word Ps 64₄. **2.** as adv., **bitterly, in bitterness,** מַר יִבְכָּיוּן *they weep bitterly* Is 33₇. **3.** as noun, **a. bitter one,** מָרֵי נָפֶשׁ *those bitter of soul* Jb 3₂₀. **b. bitterness, bitter thing,** מַר־הַמָּוֶת *bitterness of death* 1 S 15₃₂. **c.** perh. specif. **illness,** מֵי הַמָּרִים *waters of,* i.e. that (may) cause, *illness* Nm 5₂₄. → מרר I *be bitter.*

*מַר II 9 adj. **1. strong,** of person, מָרֵי נֶפֶשׁ *strong of soul,* i.e. tough Jg 18₂₅. **2.** as adv., **strengthened,** וָאֵלֵךְ מַר *and I went strengthened* Ezk 3₁₄.

מַר III 1 n.[m.] **drop** Is 40₁₅.

*מַר IV 1 n.[m.] **dust** Is 40₁₅.

*[מַר] V 2 n.[m.] **abortion,** מֵי הַמָּרִים *waters of,* i.e. that cause an, *abortion* Nm 5₁₈.

מֹר I 12 n.m.—מוֹר; cstr. מָר־; sf. מוֹרִי—**myrrh,** fragrant resin, used as perfume, שֶׁמֶן הַמֹּר *oil of myrrh* Est 2₁₂; as anointing oil for tabernacle furniture Ex 30₂₃.

*מֹר II n.[m.] **foam,** מֹר יָם *foam of the sea* Ho 11₄ (if em. מְרִימֵי *ones who raise,* i.e. רום hi.).

*מרא I 1.0.1 vb.—**Qal** 1 Ptc. מֹרְאָה—**be rebellious,** of city Zp 3₁.

Hi. 0.0.1 Impf. ימרא—**provoke** servant on (בְּ) sabbath CD 11₁₂.

→ cf. מרה I *be rebellious.*

מרא II 1 vb.—**Hi.** 1 Impf. תַּמְרִיא—of ostrich, **beat air** with wings, i.e. **flap wings,** or **strike ground with foot** Jb 39₁₈.

*[מרא] III vb.—**graze, feed on the fat of the land,** of calf Is 11₆ (if em. וּמְרִיא *and the fatling* to יִמְרְאוּ *they will graze;* cf. 1QIsa[a] ימרו). → מְרִיא *fatling.*

*מרא IV 1 vb.—**Hi.** 1 Impf. תַּמְרִיא—of ostrich, **act the man** Jb 39₁₈.

מָרָא 1 pr.n.f. **Mara.**

מְרֹאדַךְ בַּלְאֲדָן, see מְרֹדַךְ בַּלְאֲדָן *Merodach-baladan.*

מַרְאָה 12.0.6 n.f. **1. vision,** as means of revelation Nm 12₆; מַרְאוֹת אֱלֹהִים *visions of God* Ezk 1₁. **2. mirror** Ex 38₈; מראת פנים *face mirror* 1QM 5₅. → ראה *see.*

מַרְאֶה 103.6.22 n.m.—cstr. מַרְאֵה (Q מראי); sf. מַרְאֵהוּ; pl. cstr. Q מראי; sf. sg. or pl. מַרְאֵיהֶם—**1. appearance, visible form, figure, countenance,** מַרְאֵה כְּבוֹד י׳ *appearance of the glory of Y.* Ex 24_{17}, הַנֶּגַע *of the disease* Lv 13_3, אִישׁ מַרְאֶה *man of appearance,* i.e. handsome man 2 S $23_{21(Qr)}$. **2. (eye) sight, seeing,** כָּל־עֵץ נֶחְמָד לְמַרְאֶה *every tree that is pleasing to the sight,* i.e. to the eye Gn 2_9. **3a. sight, thing seen, spectacle,** מַרְאֵה עֵינֶיךָ *sight of your eyes,* i.e. that which your eyes see Dt 28_{34}. **b.** specif. **vision** Dn 8_{16}; מראה האלוהים *vision of God* 4QVisSam 1_5. → ראה *see.*

*[**מַרְאָה**] n.f. **edict,** מַרְאַת י׳ *edict of Y.* Ps 19_{10} (if em. עֵינָיִם: יִרְאַת *eyes. The fear of* to מַרְאַת עֵינָי: *my eyes. The edict of*).

[**מֻרְאָה**] or [**מֻרְאָה**] 2 n.f. **1. crissum,** area or feathers around the cloaca of bird, or perh. **crop,** pouchlike element of the gullet Lv 1_{16}. **2.** perh. **excrement** Zp 3_1.

מְרֹאוֹן, see שִׁמְרוֹן מְרֹאוֹן *Shimron-meron.*

מָרֵאשָׁה, see מָרֵשָׁה *Mareshah.*

[**מְרַאֲשׁוֹת**] 10 n.[f.]pl.—pl. cstr. מְרַאֲשֹׁתֵי; sf. מְרַאֲשֹׁתָיו—usu. **place of head** of one lying down, adv. **at the head of** 1 S 26_{12}; perh. **head support** Gn 28_{11}. → cf. ראשׁ I *head.*

מֵרַב 4.0.0.1 pr.n.f. **Merab.**

[**מַרְבָד**] 2 n.[m.]—pl. מַרְבַדִּים—**cover,** for couch Pr 7_{16}. → רבד *deck.*

מִרְבָּה 1 n.f. **much** Ezk 23_{32}. → רבה *be much.*

מַרְבֶּה 2 n.[m.] **abundance, 1.** as adv., **in abundance** Is 33_{23}. **2. increase,** מַרְבֵּה הַמִּשְׂרָה *increase of dominion* Is 9_6. → רבה I *be many.*

מַרְבִּית 5 n.f.—sf. מַרְבִּיתָם—**1. increase,** in ref. to descendants, כָּל־מַרְבִּית בֵּיתְךָ *all the increase of your house* 1 S 2_{33}. **2. interest,** perh. specif. on loan of food, **profit** Lv 25_{37}. **3a. majority** 1 C 12_{29}. **b. multitude** of people 2 C 30_{18}. **4. greatness** of wisdom 2 C 9_6. → רבה I *be many.*

מרבעל, see מְרִיב בַּעַל *Merib-baal.*

מַרְבֵּץ 2.0.1 n.[m.]—cstr. מַרְבַּץ—**resting place** of wild beasts Zp 2_{15}, sheep Ezk 25_5. → רבץ *lie down.*

מַרְבֵּק 4.1 n.[m.] **1. stall,** עֶגֶל־מַרְבֵּק *calf of the stall,* i.e. fatted calf 1 S 28_{24}. **2. fattening** Si 38_{26}.

מַרְגּוֹעַ 1 n.[m.] **(place of) rest** Jr 6_{16}. → רגע II *be at rest.*

[**מַרְגְּלוֹת**] 5 n.[f.]pl.—pl. sf. מַרְגְּלֹתָיו—**place of feet** of one lying down Ru 3_4, adv. **at the feet of** Ru 3_8; **feet** Dn 10_6. → רגל III *use the foot.*

*[**מַרְגָּלִית**] 0.0.1 n.f.—pl. מרגליות—**jewel** GnzPs 2_{29}.

מַרְגֵּמָה I 1 n.f. **sling** Pr 26_8. → רגם I *stone.*

***מַרְגֵּמָה** II 1 n.f. **heap of stones** Pr 26_8. → רגם I *stone.*

מַרְגֵּעָה n.f. **(place of) rest** Is 28_{12}. → רגע II *be at rest.*

מרד 25.2.4 vb.—**Qal** 25.2.4 Pf. מָרַדְתָּ, מָרַד; impf. תִּמְרְדוּ; + waw וַיִּמְרֹד (וַיִּמְרָד־); ptc. מֹרְדִים, מֹרְדֵי; inf. מְרֹד (מָרְדְכֶם)—**rebel, revolt, a.** against Y., with בְּ Nm 14_9; abs. Dn 9_5. **b.** against humans, with בְּ 2 K 24_1, עַל 2 K 24_1, accus. Jos 22_{19}; abs. Gn 14_4. **c.** מֹרְדֵי־אוֹר *those who rebel against the light* Jb 24_{13}. → מֶרֶד I *rebellion,* מַרְדּוּת I *rebelliousness.*

מֶרֶד I 1.0.1 n.[m.] **rebellion,** against Y. Jos 22_{22}. → מרד *rebel.*

מֶרֶד II 2 pr.n.m. **Mered.**

מַרְדּוּת I 1 n.f. **rebelliousness** 1 S 20_{30}. → מרד *rebel.*

*[**מַרְדּוּת**] II 0.2 n.f. **chastisement, discipline** Si 30_{33} $42_{8(Bmg)}$. → רדה I *rule.*

[**מְרֹדָךְ**] 1 pr.n.m. **Merodach.**

מְרֹדַךְ בַּלְאֲדָן 1 pr.n.m. **Merodach-baladan.**

מָרְדֳּכַי 60 pr.n.m. **Mordecai.**

*[**מִרְדָּף**] 0.0.4 n.[m.] **pursuit** 1QM 3_2. → רדף *pursue.*

מֻרְדָּף 1 n.[m.] **persecution** Is 14_6. → רדף *pursue.*

מרה I 45.5.13 vb.—**Qal** 23.2 Pf. מָרָה, מָרִיתִי; ptc. מֹרֶה, מֹרִים; inf. abs. מָרוֹ—**1. be rebellious** against (בְּ) Y. Ho 14_1. **2. disobey** Y. Jr 4_{17}, command Nm 20_{24}. **3.** ptc. as adj., **rebellious, disobedient,** בֵּן סוֹרֵר וּמוֹרֶה *a stubborn and rebellious son* Dt 21_{18}.

Hi. 22.3.13 Pf. הִמְרוּ; impf. יַמְרֶה; + waw וַיַּמְרוּ, וַתֶּמֶר; ptc. מַמְרִים; inf. לַמְרוֹת, הַמְרוֹתָם (Si המראה)—**1. defy, provoke** Y. Ps 78_{40}, spirit Ps 106_{33}, command Dt 1_{26}. **2. be rebellious** against (בְּ) Y. Ezk 20_8. **3.** perh. inf. as noun, **rebelliousness** Si $41_{2(Bmg)}$.

→ מַמְרֵה *rebellion,* מְרִי *rebellion,* מָרָה *disputed matter,* מָרוֹ *violent man;* cf. מרא I *be rebellious.*

***מרה** II 0.0.1 vb.—**Hi.** 0.0.1 Impf. תמר (תאמר)—**exchange** holy spirit for (בְּ) wealth 4QInstr[b] 2.2_6. → cf. מור I *change.*

מרה III **Htp., graze, feed,** of Israelites Is 61_6 (if em.

תִּתְיַמָּרוּ *you will boast* [אמר htp.] to תִּתְמָרוּ *you will graze*). → מְרִיא *fatling*.

*מרה IV 1 vb. **be strong,** מִי כָמֹהוּ מוֹרֶה *who is as powerful as he?* Jb 36$_{22}$ (or ירה ptc. *teacher*).

*[מָרָה] I 1 n.[f.] **instruction, revelation,** מֵי הַמָּרִים *waters of instruction* Nm 5$_{24}$. → ירה III *teach*.

מָרָה II 5 pl.n. **Marah.**

מָרָה III, see מָרָא *Mara*.

*[מָרֶה] 1 n.m. **disputed matter, contention,** מֵי הַמָּרִים *waters of contention* Nm 5$_{24}$. → מרה I *be rebellious*.

[מֹרָה] 2 n.f.—cstr. מֹרַת (מָרַת)—**bitterness,** מֹרַת רוּחַ *bitterness of spirit* Gn 26$_{35}$. → מרר I *be bitter*.

מֹרֶה, see מוֹרֶה *Moreh*.

*[מַרְהֵבָה] 1 n.f. **raging** or **onslaught** Is 14$_{4}$(1QIsa^{a}) (MT מַדְהֵבָה *distress*). → רהב *storm*.

*[מְרוֹ] 1 n.[m.]—with prosthetic aleph אִמְרוֹ—**violent man, oppressor** Jb 20$_{29}$. → מרה I *be rebellious*.

*[מְרוֹגֶלֶת] 0.0.1 n.f. **clothing for legs** 1QM 5$_{13}$. → רגל *use the foot*; cf. רֶגֶל *foot*.

[מָרוּד] 3.1 n.[m.]—sf. מְרוּדִי; pl. מְרוּדִים; sf. מְרוּדֶיהָ—**1. wandering, homelessness** Lm 3$_{19}$. **2. homeless one** Is 58$_{7}$. → רוד *wander*.

מֵרוֹז 1 pl.n. **Meroz.**

[מָרוֹחַ] 1 n.[m.] **crushing,** מְרוֹחַ אָשֶׁךְ *crushing of testicle* Lv 21$_{20}$. → מרח *rub*.

מָרוֹם 54.10.30 n.m.—cstr. מְרוֹם; pl. מְרוֹמִים (מְרֹמִים); cstr. מְרוֹמֵי; sf. מְרוֹמָיו—**1. height, elevated place, on high** Hb 2$_{9}$; מְרוֹם הָרִים *height of the mountains* 2 K 19$_{23}$. **2. height (of heaven), heaven, sky, on high** 2 S 22$_{17}$ ‖Ps 18$_{17}$; מרומי אל *heights of God* Si 43$_{9}$(B). **3a.** (of social status) **height, exaltation, on high** Ps 73$_{8}$. **b. height,** i.e. **most exalted one(s),** מְרוֹם עַם־הָאָרֶץ *height,* i.e. most exalted, *of the people of the earth* Is 24$_{4}$. **4. height,** as divine title, **Exalted One,** מְרוֹם־צִיּוֹן *Exalted One of Zion* Jr 31$_{12}$. **5.** as adv., **on high, upwards, haughtily,** + נשׂא *lift* eyes 2 K 19$_{22}$. → רום *be high*.

מֵרוֹם 2 pl.n. **Merom.**

מֵרוֹץ 1 n.[m.] race Ec 9$_{11}$. → רוץ *run*.

[מְרוּצָה] I 4 n.f.—cstr. מְרוּצַת (מְרֻצַת); sf. מְרוּצָתָם—**1. (mode of) running** 2 S 18$_{27}$. **2. course, way of life** Jr 23$_{10}$. → רוץ *run*.

מְרוּצָה II 1 n.f. **extortion** Jr 22$_{17}$. → רצץ *crush*.

[מְרוּקִים] 1.0.1 n.[m.]pl.—sf. מְרוּקֵיהֶם—**cosmetic treatment** Est 2$_{12}$. → מרק I *polish*.

מָרוֹר, see מָרֹר *bitter thing*.

מְרוֹרָה, see מְרֵרָה *bitter thing*.

מָרוֹת 1 pl.n. **Maroth.**

מַרְזֵחַ 2 n.m.—cstr. מִרְזַח—**1. feasting,** or perh. **place of feasting** or **group of those feasting** Am 6$_{7}$. **2. funeral meal** Jr 16$_{5}$.

מרח 1 vb.—**Qal** 1 Impf. יִמְרְחוּ—**rub** fig-cake on (עַל) boil Is 38$_{21}$. → מָרוֹחַ *crushing*.

מֶרְחָב 6.0.3 n.[m.]—cstr. mss מֶרְחַב; pl. cstr. מֶרְחֲבֵי—**1. broad place, a.** pasture for sheep Ho 4$_{16}$. **b.** perh. Y.'s heavenly dwelling Ps 118$_{5}$. **c.** perh. Sheol Ps 18$_{20}$. **2. expanse of land** Hb 1$_{6}$. **3. wide space** in heart 1QH 13$_{33}$. → רחב *be wide*.

מֶרְחָק 19.0.2 n.m.—pl. מֶרְחַקִּים (מֶרְחַקִּים); cstr. מֶרְחַקֵּי—**distance, distant place, afar,** אֶרֶץ מֶרְחָק *land of distance,* i.e. distant land Is 13$_{5}$, מֶרְחַקֵּי־אָרֶץ *distant places of the earth* Is 8$_{9}$, מִמֶּרְחָק *from afar* Is 10$_{3}$. → רחק *be distant*.

*[מַרְחֶשְׁוָן] 0.0.2 pr.n.[m.] **Marcheshvan,** eighth month of postexilic Jewish calendar, October/November Mur 22 1$_{1}$.

מַרְחֶשֶׁת 2 n.f. **pan,** perh. specif. with lid Lv 2$_{7}$. → רחשׁ *be astir*.

מרט 14 vb.—**Qal** 7 + waw וָאֶמְרְטָה; ptc. מֹרְטִים; pass. מְרוּטָה; inf. מָרְטָה—**1. polish** sword Ezk 21$_{16}$. **2a. pull out hair** of person Ne 13$_{25}$. **b. pull out some** (מִן) hair Ezr 9$_{3}$. **3.** pass., **a. be rubbed raw,** of shoulder Ezk 29$_{18}$. **b. be polished,** of sword Ezk 21$_{14}$.

Ni. 2 Impf. יִמָּרֵט—**lose hair,** of head Lv 13$_{40}$.

Pu. 5 Pf. מֹרָטָה; ptc. מְמֹרָט (מוֹרָט)—**1. be polished,** of bronze 1 K 7$_{45}$, sword Ezk 21$_{15}$. **2. be smooth-skinned,** of nation Is 18$_{2}$.

מְרִי 23 n.[m.]—מֶרִי; sf. מֶרְיְךָ, מִרְיָם—**1. rebellion, rebelliousness, defiance** 1 S 15$_{23}$. **2. rebellious one(s)** Ezk 2$_{7}$. → מרה *be rebellious*.

מְרִיא 8.0.1 n.[m.]—pl. מְרִיאִים; cstr. מְרִיאֵי; sf. מְרִיאֵיכֶם—**fatling** Am 5$_{22}$. → מרא III *graze*.

*[מָרִיב] n.[m]. **contention,** עַמְּךָ מְרִיבֵי הַכֹּהֵן *with you is my contention, O priest* Ho 4$_{4}$ (if em. עַמְּךָ כִּמְרִיבֵי כֹהֵן

appar. *your people are as those who contend with a priest*). → ריב *strive*.

מְרִיבָה I 2 n.f.—cstr. מְרִיבַת—**strife** Nm 27_{14}. → ריב *strive*.

מְרִיבָה II 11 pl.n. **Meribah.**

מְרִיב בַּעַל 4.0.0.1 pr.n.[m.] **Merib-baal.**

מְרִיבוֹת קָדֵשׁ 1 pl.n. **Meriboth-kadesh.**

מְרִיבַת קָדֵשׁ 3 pl.n. **Meribath-kadesh.**

מְרָיָה 1 pr.n.m. **Meraiah.**

מֹרִיָּה, see מוֹרִיָּה *Moriah*.

מְרָיוֹת 7 pr.n.m. **Meraioth.**

*מָרִים 5 n.m. **blessing,** מֵי מָרִים *waters of blessing* Nm 5_{18}.

*מְרִים I n.m. **desire,** מְרִים כְּסִילִים קָלוֹן *the desire of fools is shame(ful)* Pr 3_{35} (if em. כְּסִילִים מֵרִים קָלוֹן *fools exalt shame*).

מִרְיָם II 15.0.1 pr.n.f. **Miriam.**

*[מְרִירָה] n.f. **act of violence** Jb 13_{26} (if em. מְרֹרוֹת *bitter things* to מְרִרוֹת *acts of violence*). → מרר III *be strong*.

מְרִירוּת 1 n.f. **bitterness** Ezk 21_{11}. → מרר I *be bitter*.

מְרִירִי I 2.1 adj. **1. bitter,** of destruction, i.e. pestilence Dt 32_{24}. **2.** as noun, **a. bitter one** Si 11_4. **b. poisonous one,** מְרִירֵי יָם *Poisonous Ones of Yam* Jb 3_5 (if em. יוֹם *of the day*). → מרר I *be bitter*.

*[מְרִירִי] II 2 n.m.—pl. cstr. מְרִירֵי—**demon** Jb 3_5; name of a demon, **Meriri** Dt 32_{24}.

*מְרִירִי III 1 adj. **mighty,** of destruction Dt 32_{24}. → מרר III *be strong*.

מֹרֶךְ 1 n.[m.] **faintness, despair** Lv 26_{36}. → רכך *be tender*.

מֶרְכָּב 3 n.m. **means for riding,** such as **saddle** Lv 15_9; **seat** of litter Ca 3_{10}. **2. chariotry,** or perh. **chariot depot** 1 K 5_6. → רכב *ride*.

מֶרְכָּבָה 44.1.11 n.f.—cstr. מִרְכֶּבֶת; sf. מֶרְכַּבְתּוֹ; pl. מַרְכָּבוֹת; cstr. מַרְכְּבוֹת; sf. מַרְכְּבוֹתָיו—**chariot, chariotry, 1.** for war Ex 14_{25}. **2.** for transport Gn 46_{29}. **3.** in cult of sun 2 K 23_{11}. **4.** as bearing cherubim in temple 1 C 28_{18}. **5.** heavenly, for Y.'s battles Hb 3_8. → רכב *ride*.

[מַרְכֹּלֶת] 1 n.f.—sf. מַרְכֻּלְתֵּךְ—**market place** or **trading** Ezk 27_{24}. → רכל I *trade*.

מִרְמָה I 39.1.8 n.f.—pl. מִרְמוֹת—**1. deceit, treachery** Gn 27_{35}; אַבְנֵי מִרְמָה *fraudulent weights* Mc 6_{11}. **2.** perh. **self-deceit** or **disillusionment** Pr 14_8. **3.** perh. **slander** Ps 5_7. → רמה II *deceive*.

מִרְמָה II 1 pr.n.m. **Mirmah.**

מְרֵמוֹת 6.0.0.2 pr.n.m. **Meremoth.**

מִרְמָס 7.0.1 n.[m.] **trampling place, trampled ground** Is 5_5; מִרְמַס שֶׂה *trampling place of sheep* Is 7_{25}. → רמס *trample*.

*[מִרְמָשׂ] 0.0.1 n.[m.] **reptile** 4QRitMar 9_5. → רמשׂ *creep*.

מֵרֹנֹתִי 2 gent. **Meronothite.**

מֶרֶס 1 pr.n.m. **Meres.**

מַרְסְנָא 1 pr.n.m. **Marsena.**

מֵרַע, see רעע I *be evil*, Hi.

[מֵרֵעַ] 9 n.m.—sf. מֵרֵעֵהוּ (מֵרֵעֵהוּ); pl. מֵרֵעִים—**friend** Jg 14_{11}. → רעה II *associate with*.

*[מַרְעֶה] 1 n.m.—sf. מֵרֵעֵהוּ—**pasturage supervisor** Gn 26_{26}. → רעה I *pasture*.

מִרְעֶה 13 n.m.—cstr. מִרְעֵה; sf. מִרְעֵהוּ, מִרְעֵיכֶם—**pasture, grazing land** Gn 47_4 Is 32_{14}. → רעה I *pasture*.

[מַרְעִית] 10.1.4 n.f.—cstr. Si מרעית; sf. מַרְעִיתוֹ—**1. pasturing, shepherding,** צֹאן מַרְעִיתִי *sheep of my pasturing* Jr 23_1. **2. pasture, pasturage** Is 49_9. **3. flock** Jr 10_{21}. → רעה I *pasture*.

מַרְעֲלָה 1 pl.n. **Maralah.**

מַרְפֵּא I 15.2.9 n.m.—מַרְפֵּה—**healing, remedy, health** Pr 16_{24}; חֳלִי לְאֵין מַרְפֵּא *a disease for which there is no healing* 2 C 21_{18}. → רפא I *heal*.

*מַרְפֵּא II 3.1 n.m.—cstr. מַרְפֵּא—**1. calmness,** לֵב מַרְפֵּא *a calm disposition* Pr 14_{30}. **2. gentleness,** מַרְפֵּא לָשׁוֹן *gentle speech* Pr 15_4. → רפה *drop*.

מַרְפֵּה I, see מַרְפֵּא I *healing*.

מַרְפֵּה II, see מַרְפֵּה *relaxation*.

*[מַרְפֵּה] 2.0.1 n.m.—מַרְפֵּא, מַרְפֵּה—**relaxation, remission** Jr 8_{15} Ec 10_4 1QH 10_{26}. → רפה *drop*.

[מִרְפָּשׂ] 1 n.[m.]—cstr. מִרְפַּשׂ—**muddied waterhole** Ezk 34_{19}. → רפס *trample*.

מרץ I 4.0.2 vb.—**Ni.** 3.0.2 Pf. נִמְרְצוּ; ptc. נִמְרָץ, נִמְרֶצֶת—**be sickening, painful, grievous,** of labour pains 1QH 11_8, words Jb 6_{25}.

Hi. 1 Impf. יַמְרִיצְךָ—**sicken someone** Jb 16_3.

→ מֶרֶץ *agony*.

*מרץ II 4 vb.—**Ni.** 3 Pf. נִמְרְצוּ; ptc. נִמְרָץ, נִמְרֶצֶת—**be** forceful, difficult, of words Jb 6₂₅, curse 1 K 2₈, destruction Mc 2₁₀.

Hi. 1 Impf. יַמְרִיצְךָ—**provoke** someone Jb 16₃.

*מרץ III 2 vb.—**Ni.** 2 Pf. נִמְרְצוּ; ptc. נִמְרֶצֶת—**be victorious,** of words Jb 6₂₅, curse 1 K 2₈.

*[מֶרֶץ] 0.0.1 n.[m.] **agony,** חבלי מרץ *labour pains of agony* 1QH 11₁₁. → מרץ I *be sick.*

מְרֻצָתָם, see מְרוּצָה I *running.*

מַרְצֵעַ 2 n.[m.] **awl,** to pierce ear of slave Ex 21₆ Dt 15₁₇. → רצע *pierce.*

[מַרְצֶפֶת] 1 n.f. **pavement** or **plastered floor,** in temple, מַרְצֶפֶת אֲבָנִים *pavement of stones* 2 K 16₁₇. → רצף I *be inlaid.*

מרק I 4.0.1 vb.—**Qal** 2.0.1 Impv. מִרְקוּ; ptc. pass. מָרוּק—**1. polish** spear Jr 46₄. **2.** pass., **be polished,** of bronze 2 C 4₁₆.

Pu. 1 + waw וּמֹרַק—**be scoured,** of bronze vessel Lv 6₂₁.

Hi. 1 Impf. Kt תמריק—**cleanse away** (בְּ of obj.) evil Pr 20₃₀(Kt).

→ מְרוּקִים *cosmetic treatment,* תַּמְרוּק *cosmetic treatment.*

*מרק II 0.0.2 vb.—**Pi.** 0.0.2 Inf. מרק—**complete sale** Mur 30 1₅ 2₂₄.

מָרָק 3.0.1 n.[m.]—cstr. Qr מְרַק—**broth** Jg 6₁₉; מרק זבחם *broth of their sacrifices* 4QMMT B₈.

[מֶרְקָח] 1 n.[m.]—pl. מֶרְקָחִים—**perfume, spices** Ca 5₁₃. → רקח *mix ointment.*

מֶרְקָחָה 2 n.f. **pot of ointment** Jb 41₂₃, **spice** Ezk 24₁₀. → רקח *mix ointment.*

מִרְקַחַת 3.1 n.f. **ointment mixture** Ex 30₂₅ 1 C 9₃₀. → רקח *mix ointment.*

מרר I 16.2 vb.—**Qal** 6 Pf. מַר, מָרָה—**be bitter,** of strong drink Is 24₉, soul 1 S 30₆.

Pi. 3 Pf. אֲמָרֵר; + waw וַיְמָרְרֻהוּ—**1a. show bitterness by** (בְּ) weeping Is 22₄. **b. show bitterness to** (accus.) someone Gn 49₂₃. **2. make life bitter with** (בְּ) labour Ex 1₁₄.

Hi. 5.1 Pf. הֵמַר; impf. תַּמֵּר; inf. abs. הָמֵר—**1a. show bitterness against** (בְּ) Y. Ex 23₂₁. **b. show bitter grief** on account of (עַל) firstborn Zc 12₁₀. **2.** of Y., **a. make life bitter** Jb 27₂. **b. cause bitterness to** (לְ) someone Ru 1₂₀.

Htp. 0.1 Impv. התמרר—**show bitter grief** Si 38₁₆(B).

Htpalp. 2.1 Impf. יִתְמַרְמַר; impv. Si התמרמר—**1. be enraged** Dn 11₁₁. **2. show bitter grief** Si 38₁₆(Bmg).

→ מַר I *bitter,* מֹר *myrrh,* מֶמֶר *bitterness,* מֹרָה *bitterness,* מֹרֹר *bitter thing,* מְרִירוּת *bitterness,* מְרֵרָה *gall,* מְרֹרָה *bitter thing,* מַמְרֹרִים *bitterness,* תַּמְרוּר *bitterness,* מְרִירִי I *bitter.*

*מרר II 1 vb.—**Hi.** 1 Inf. הָמִיר—**flow,** of earth Ps 46₃.

*מרר III 4.1 vb. **Qal, be strong, harden** with (בְּ) counsel Ps 106₄₃ (if em. יַמְרוּ to יָמֹרוּ *they were strong*).

Ni. 0.1 Impv. המר—**strengthen oneself** Si 38₁₇.

Pi. 2 + waw וַיְמָרְרֻהוּ—**strengthen** someone Gn 49₂₃, life with (בְּ) labour Ex 1₁₄.

Htpalp. 2 Impf. יִתְמַרְמַר—**strengthen oneself** Dn 11₁₁.

→ מְרִירָה *act of violence,* מְרִירִי III *mighty,* מְרֹרָה *strong thing.*

[מָרֹר] 3.0.11 n.m.—pl. מְרֹרִים—**bitter thing, bitterness** Lm 3₁₅; אבל מרורים *bitter mourning* 1QH 19₁₉, perh. **bitter plague** 4QD[a] 3.4₂, **bitter herb** for passover meal Ex 12₈. → מרר I *be bitter.*

[מְרֵרָה] 1 n.f.—sf. מְרֵרָתִי—**gall** Jb 16₁₃. → מרר I *be bitter.*

[מְרֹרָה] I 4 n.f.—cstr. מְרוֹרַת; sf. מְרֹרָתִי; pl. מְרֹרוֹת—**1. bitter thing** Jb 13₂₆. **2. gall, bile** Jb 20₂₅. **3. poison, venom** of asps Jb 20₁₄. → מרר I *be bitter.*

*[מְרֹרָה] II 1 n.f.—pl. מְרֹרוֹת—**strong thing** Jb 13₂₆. → מרר III *be strong.*

מְרָרִי I 39.0.2 pr.n.m. **Merari.**

מְרָרִי II 1 gent. **Merarite.**

מָרֵשָׁה I 6 pl.n. **Mareshah.**

מָרֵשָׁה II 2 pr.n.m. **Mareshah.**

מִרְשַׁעַת 1 n.f. **wickedness,** i.e. wicked one 2 C 24₇. → רשע *act wickedly.*

מֹרַשְׁתִּי, see מוֹרַשְׁתִּי *Morashtite.*

מְרָתַיִם 1 pl.n. **Merathaim.**

מַשָּׂא I 37.4.14.1 n.m.—cstr. מַשָּׂא (משא, Si משוא); sf. מַשָּׂאוֹ, מַשַּׂאֲכֶם; pl. cstr. Q, Sam משאי—**1. load, burden,** carried by animal Ex 23₅, by humans Jr 17₂₁. **2. consignment, goods,** as contents of load Ne 13₁₅. **3. weight** carried by peg Is 22₂₅. **4. mental load** Si 51₂₆, **burden** of sin Ps 38$_5$. **5. assigned duty, responsibility, task** Nm 4$_{15}$. **6.** (as verbal noun of נשׂא *raise*), i.e. **raising, lifting up, transport(ing)** Nm 4$_{24}$; מַשֹּׂא פָנִים *raising of the face*, i.e. favouritism 1 C 19$_7$. **7.** perh. **exaltation,** משא אלוהים *exaltation of God* or *heavenly beings* 11Q ShirShabb 8$_6$. **8.** perh. **music** 1 C 15$_{22}$. **9.** perh. **tribute** 2 C 17$_{11}$. → נשׂא I *lift*.

מַשָּׂא II 29.1.4 n.m.—pl. cstr. Q משאי—**pronouncement, utterance, speech** 2 K 9$_{25}$; מַשָּׂא י׳ *pronouncement of Y.* Jr 23$_{33}$; specif. **utterance of praise** 11QShirShabb 10$_6$. → נשׂא I *lift*; cf. מַשְׂאֵת II *utterance*.

*[מַשָּׂא] III 1 n.[m.]—cstr. מַשָּׂא—**tribute** Ho 8$_{10}$. → נשׂא I *lift*.

מַשָּׂא IV 2 pr.n.m. **Massa.**

מַשֹּׂא, see מַשָּׂא I *burden*.

מַשָּׂאָה 1 n.f. **burden** Is 30$_{27}$. → נשׂא I *lift*.

*[מַשָּׂאָה] n.f. **smoke signal,** כֹּבֶד מַשָּׂאָה *heavy of a column of smoke*, i.e. a dense smoke signal Is 30$_{27}$ (if em. כֹּבֶד מַשָּׂאָה *[?] heavy is the burden*). → cf. מַשְׂאֵת III *smoke signal*.

מַשְׂאֵת I 12.2.1. n.f.—cstr. מַשְׂאַת; pl. מַשְׂאֹת; sf. מַשְׂאוֹתֵיכֶם—**1. gift** 2 S 11$_8$. **2. offering** to Y. Ezk 20$_{40}$. **3. tribute, tax** as given to ruler Am 5$_{11}$. **4.** perh. **raising** as verbal noun of נשׂא *raise* 1QM 18$_3$. **5.** perh. **burden** of reproach Zp 3$_{18}$, iniquity Si 4$_{21}$. → נשׂא I *lift*.

*[מַשְׂאֵת] II 1 n.f.—pl. cstr. מַשְׂאוֹת—**utterance** Lm 2$_{14}$. → cf. מַשָּׂא II *utterance*.

*מַשְׂאֵת III 3.0.0.1 n.f. **beacon, fire-signal,** מַשְׂאַת הֶעָשָׁן *signal of smoke* Jg 20$_{38}$, משאת לכש *beacons of Lachish* Lachish ost. 4$_{10}$. → נשׂא I *lift*.

[מַשְׂבָּלָה], see מַסְבָּלָא *Masbala*.

מִשְׂגָּב I 17.0.2 n.f.—cstr. מִשְׂגַּב; sf. מִשְׂגַּבִּי—**stronghold** Is 25$_{12}$; Y. as a stronghold Ps 59$_{10}$. → שׂגב *be high*.

מִשְׂגָּב II 1 pl.n. **Misgab.**

מַשֶּׂגֶת, see נשׂג I *reach*, hi. ptc.

*מַשֶּׂה 1 n.m. **place where sheep can be eaten** Ex 12$_4$.

[מַשּׂוֹא], see מַשָּׂא *burden*.

[מְשׂוּכָה] 1 n.f. **hedge,** מְשֻׂכַת חֵדֶק *hedge of briar* Pr 15$_{19}$. → שׂוך II *fence in*; cf. סוך II *enclose*, מְסוּכָה I *hedge*.

[מְשׂוּכָה] 1 n.f.—sf. מְשׂוּכָתוֹ—**hedge** of vineyard Is 5$_5$. → שׂכך *cover*.

*[מָשׂוֹר] 0.0.1 n.[m.] **measure,** [מ]שור במשורה perh. *measure by measure* 4QInstr[d] 1$_1$. → cf. מְשׂוּרָה *measure*.

מַשּׂוֹר 1 n.m. **saw** Is 10$_{15}$.

*[מְשׂוֹרָה] 2 n.f. **government, dominion** Is 9$_{5(1QIsa^a)}$. $_{6(1QIsa^a\ mg)}$ (MT מִשְׂרָה *government*). → שׂרר I *rule*.

מְשׂוּרָה 4.0.2 n.f. **measure** Ezk 4$_{11}$; specif. **capacity** Lv 19$_{35}$. → cf. מָשׂוֹר *measure*.

מָשׂוֹשׂ I 17 n.m.—cstr. מְשׂוֹשׂ; sf. מְשׂוֹשִׂי—**joy** Lm 5$_{15}$, appar. **joyful sound** Is 24$_8$, **joyful place** Is 32$_{14}$, perh. **object of joy** Ps 48$_3$. → שׂישׂ *rejoice*.

*[מָשׂוֹשׂ] II 1 n.m. **rottenness** Jb 8$_{19}$.

מִשְׂחָק 1 n.[m.] **(object of) laughter** Hb 1$_{10}$. → שׂחק *laugh*.

*[מִשְׂטָם] 0.0.1 n.[m]. **hostility** 4QRenEarth$_5$. → שׂטם *harass*.

מַשְׂטֵמָה I 2.0.14 n.f.—pl. Q משטמות—**hostility** Ho 9$_{7.8}$; מלאך משטמה *angel of hostility*, i.e. Belial 1QM 13$_{11}$. → שׂטם *harass*.

*מַשְׂטֵמָה II 2 **cord, noose, fetter, snare** Ho 9$_{7.8}$.

*מֵשִׂים 1 n.[m.] **attention,** ellip. for מֵשִׂים לֵב *setting to heart* Jb 4$_{20}$.

מַשְׂכִּיל I 14 n.[m.] **maskil,** usu. as (part of) title of psalm, perh. **psalm of success,** מַשְׂכִּיל לְדָוִד *a maskil of* or *for David* Ps 52$_1$. → שׂכל I *be wise*.

*מַשְׂכִּיל II 14 n.[m.] **responsive song** Ps 52$_1$. → שׂכל II *lay crosswise*.

*מַשְׂכִּיל III 14 n.[m.] **instructive** or **skilful song** Ps 52$_1$. → שׂכל I *be wise*.

מַשְׂכִּיל IV *instructor*, see שׂכל hi. *be intelligent*.

מַשְׂכִּית I 6.0.2 n.f.—sf. מַשְׂכִּיתוֹ; pl. cstr. מַשְׂכִּיּוֹת; sf. מַשְׂכִּיֹּתָם—**1. image,** perh. a **relief,** for cultic use, אֶבֶן מַשְׂכִּית *stone with an image* Lv 26$_1$. **2.** perh. **ornament** in silver Pr 25$_{11}$. **3. imagination, thought** Ps 73$_7$. → שׂכה *look out*.

*מַשְׂכִּית II 2 n.f.—pl. cstr. מַשְׂכִּיּוֹת—**desire** Lv 26$_1$ Ps 73$_7$.

[מַשְׂכֹּרֶת] 4.0.2 n.f.—sf. מַשְׂכֻּרְתִּי—**1.** general, **reward, recompense** Ru 2$_{12}$. **2.** specif. **wages** Gn 29$_{15}$. → שׂכר *hire*.

*[מִשְׂמָחָה] n.f.—pl. sf. משמחותם—**celebration** Si 44$_{4(B)}$ (others משמחותם *their watches*). → שׂמח *rejoice*.

[מַשְׂמֵר], see מַסְמֵר *nail*.

[מְשַׂנֵּא] *adversary*, see שׂנא, pi.

מִשְׁפָּח I 1 n.[m.] perh. **bloodshed** Is 5₇. → ספח II *pour out*.

*מִשְׁפָּח II 1 n.[m.] **legal infringement, breaking of law** Is 5₇.

מִשְׂרָה 2.0.5 n.f.—cstr. Q משרת—**government, dominion** Is 9₅; of Belial 1QM 13₄ Michael 1QM 17₆. → שׂרר I *rule*.

[מִשְׂרָפָה] 2 n.f.—pl. cstr. מִשְׂרְפוֹת—**burning,** in ref. to fires of destruction Is 33₁₂; appar. ceremonial fires of funeral, מִשְׂרְפוֹת אֲבוֹתֶיךָ *burnings (in honour) of your ancestors* Jr 34₅. → שׂרף *burn*.

מִשְׂרְפוֹת מַיִם 2 pl.n. **Misrephoth-maim.**

מַשְׂרֵקָה 2 pl.n. **Masrekah.**

מַשְׂרֵת 1.0.1 n.f. **pan** or **tray** 2 S 13₉; משרת אשמתו perh. *pan*, i.e. underworld fires, *of his punishment* 1QM 13₄.

*מָשַׁשׁ 1 vb.—**Qal** 1 Inf. מְשׁוֹשׂ—**melt, trickle,** of waters Is 8₆. → cf. מסס *melt*, מסה *melt*, מאס II *flow away*, (?) מזז *be joined together*.

מַשׁ I 2 pr.n.m. **Mash.**

*מַשׁ II n.[m.] **swamp** Jb 30₃ (if em. אֶמֶשׁ *twilight* to אוֹ מַשׁ *or swamp*).

*[מַשׁ] III 1 n.m.—sf. מַשָּׁם—**statue** 2 K 23₁₂.

*[משא] vb. **Qal, sweep away, destroy** vine Ezk 17₉ (if em. לְמַשְׂאוֹת *to lift* [נשׂא inf.] to לְמַשְׁאוֹת *to destroy*).

מַשָּׁא 3 n.m.—cstr. מַשָּׁא—**debt** Ne 5₁₀. → נשׁא I *lend*.

מֵשָׁא I 1 pl.n. **Mesha.**

מֵשָׁא II 1.0.1 pr.n.m. **Mesha.**

[מַשְׁאָב] 1 n.[m.]—מַשְׁאַבִּים—perh. **watering hole** Jg 5₁₁. → שׁאב *draw water*.

[מַשָּׁאָה] 2 n.f.—cstr. מַשַּׁאת; pl. מַשָּׁאוֹת—**debt** Dt 24₁₀ Pr 22₂₆. → נשׁא *lend*.

מְשׁוֹאָה 3.1.2 n.f.—מְשׁוֹאָה—**devastation** Jb 30₃.

[מַשָּׁאָה] 2 n.f.—pl. מַשּׁוּאוֹת; cstr. מַשְּׁאוֹת—**deception** Ps 74₃; perh. **underworld** Ps 73₁₈. → נשׁא II *be deluded*.

מַשָּׁאוֹן 1 n.[m.] **deception** Pr 26₂₆. → נשׁא *be deluded*.

מִשְׁאָל 2 pl.n. **Mishal.**

[מִשְׁאָלָה] 2.0.1 n.f.—pl. cstr. מִשְׁאֲלֹת; sf. מִשְׁאֲלוֹתֶיךָ—**request** Ps 20₆ 37₄. → שׁאל *ask*.

[מִשְׁאֶרֶת] 4 n.f.—sf. מִשְׁאַרְתֶּךָ; pl. sf. מִשְׁאֲרוֹתֶיךָ—**kneading trough** or **tray** Ex 12₃₄ Dt 28₅.

[מִשְׁבְּצָה] 9.0.1 n.f.—pl. מִשְׁבְּצוֹת—**setting** of stones and chains on ephod and breastplate, or perh. **chequerwork** or **plaiting,** מִשְׁבְּצוֹת זָהָב *settings of gold* Ex 28₁₁ ||39₆. → שׁבץ *weave with patterns*.

מַשְׁבֵּר 3.0.6 n.[m.]—cstr. מַשְׁבֵּר; pl. Q משברים; cstr. Q משברי—**mouth of cervix** 2 K 19₃||Is 37₃ Ho 13₁₃. → (?) שׁבר I *break*.

[מִשְׁבָּר] I 5.0.8 n.[m.]—pl. Q משברים; cstr. מִשְׁבְּרֵי; sf. מִשְׁבָּרֶיךָ—**1. surf, breaker** (wave), מִשְׁבְּרֵי־יָם *breakers of (the) sea* Ps 93₄. **2.** perh. **rage** Ps 88₈. → שׁבר I *break*.

[מִשְׁבָּר] II, see מַשְׁבֵּר *mouth of cervix*.

[מִשְׁבָּת] I 1 n.[m.]—pl. sf. מִשְׁבַּתֶּהָ—**cessation, inactivity** Lm 1₇. → שׁבת *cease*.

*[מִשְׁבָּת] II 1 n.[m.]—pl. sf. מִשְׁבַּתֶּהָ—**shattering** Lm 1₇.

*[מִשְׁגָּה] 0.0.3 n.f.—cstr. משגת; sf. משגתם; pl. sf. משגותם—**error** CD 3₅. → שׁגה *err*.

מִשְׁגֶּה 1.0.2 n.m. **mistake** Gn 43₁₂. → שׁגה *err*.

[מִשְׁגָּה] n.f. **mistake** Jb 19₄ (if em. מְשׁוּגָתִי to מִשְׁגָּתִי *my mistake*). → שׁגג *err*.

משׁה 3 vb.—**Qal** 1 Pf. מְשִׁיתִהוּ—**pull out** someone from (מִן) water Ex 2₁₀.

Hi. 2 Impf. יַמְשֵׁנִי—**pull out** someone from (מִן) water 2 S 22₁₇||Ps 18₁₇.

[מַשֶּׁה] 1.0.1 n.m. **loan, debt,** or perh. **part of patrimony,** מַשֵּׁה יָדוֹ *debt of his hand*, i.e. what is owed to a creditor Dt 15₂. → נשׁה I *lend*.

מֹשֶׁה 762.4.75 pr.n.m. **Moses.**

*[מָשׁוֹב] 0.0.11 n.[m.] **1. return, coming back, withdrawal** of troops, תהלת המשוב *hymn of the return (from battle)* 1QM 14₂. **2.** appar. **restoration,** משוב חיו *restoration of his life* 1QS 3₁. **3.** appar. **turning** 4QShirShabb[d] 1.1₃₉. → שׁוב *go back*.

מְשׁוֹבָב 1 pr.n.m. **Meshobab.**

[מְשׁוּבָה] I 12.2 n.f.—מְשֻׁבָה; cstr. מְשׁוּבַת; sf. מְשׁוּבָתִי; pl. sf. מְשֻׁבוֹתֵיהֶם—**1a. going back, apostasy, rebellion,** מְשֻׁבָה נִצַּחַת *persistent rebellion* Jr 8₅; pl., perh. **act of apostasy, rebellion** Jr 2₁₉. **b.** perh. **indecisiveness** or **aversion to instruction** Pr 1₃₂. **c.** perh. **illness** Ho 14₅. **2.** as descr. of (female) person, **one who goes back, rebel, apostate** Jr 3₆. **3. turning back, ability to turn back** (trans.) Si 43₂₃(Bmg). → שׁוב *go back*.

*[מְשׁוּבָה] II 1 n.f. **idleness,** מְשׁוּבַת פְּתָיִם *idleness of*

the naive Pr 1_{32}.

[מְשׁוּגָה] 1 n.f.—sf. מְשׁוּגָתִי—**mistake, error, inadvertent sin** Jb 19_4. → cf. שׁגה *err.*

מָשׁוֹט 1 n.[m.] **oar** Ezk 27_{29}. → שׁוט I *go about.*

מִשׁוֹט 1 n.[m.]—pl. sf. מִשּׁוֹטַיִךְ—**oar** Ezk 27_6. → שׁוט I *go about.*

*[מְשׁוּכִים] 0.0.2 pl.n. **Meshuchim.**

*[מְשׁוּלֶּמֶת] 0.0.0.1 pr.n.f. **Meshullemeth.**

[מְשׁוּסָּה] 1.0.1 n.f. **plunder** Is $42_{24(Kt)}$ 11QT 59_8. → שׂסס *plunder.*

מָשַׁח I 70.3.6 vb.—**Qal** 65.3.6 Pf. מָשַׁח (מְשַׁחֲךָ); impf. יִמְשַׁח; impv. מִשְׁחוּ, מִשְׁחוּהוּ; ptc. מֹשְׁחִים; ptc. pass. מָשׁוּחַ, מְשֻׁחִים; inf. abs. מָשׁוֹחַ; cstr. מְשֹׁחַ (מָשְׁחֲךָ, מָשְׁחוֹ), מָשְׁחָה—**1. anoint,** smear with oil, rather than pour (יצק) oil, usu. on head Ex 29_7, **a.** obj. person, as (לְ) king 2 S 12_7, priest 1 C 29_{22}, prophet 1 K 19_{16}. **b.** obj. sacrificial animal Ex 29_{36}, tabernacle Ex 40_9, pillar Gn 31_{13}. **2. smear** shield **with oil** Is 21_5. **3.** pass., **a. be anointed,** of king 2 S 3_{39}, priest Nm 3_3. **b. be smeared with** (בְּ) oil, of wafer Ex 29_2. **4.** ptc. as noun, **anointed one, 'messiah',** equivalent to מָשִׁיחַ *anointed one*) CD 12_{23}.

Ni. 5 Pf. נִמְשַׁח; inf. הִמָּשַׁח—**be anointed,** of priest Lv 6_{13}, altar Nm 7_{10}.

→ מָשִׁיחַ *anointed one,* מִשְׁחָה I *anointing,* מָשְׁחָה I *anointing,* מְשִׁיחָה *anointing,* מִמְשַׁח I *anointing.*

*מָשַׁח II 1 vb.—**Qal** 1 Pf משחתי—**mar** appearance of Y.'s servant Is $52_{14(1QIsa^a)}$.

*מָשַׁח III 0.0.2 vb.—**Qal** 0.0.2 Impv. משח—**measure** cubits 3QTr 7_6 9_1. → מֶשַׁח *distance,* מִשְׁחָה II *measurement,* מָשְׁחָה II *prescribed portion,* מִמְשַׁח II *extension.*

*[מֶשַׁח] 0.0.2 n.[m.] **distance** 3QTr 7_6 9_1. → משח III *measure.*

מִשְׁחָה I 23.0.1 n.f.—cstr. מִשְׁחַת; pl. sf. Q משחותיהם—**1. anointing,** שֶׁמֶן הַמִּשְׁחָה *the oil of anointing* Ex 25_6||35_8. **2. oil** 3QTr 12_{12}. → משח I *anoint.*

[מִשְׁחָה] II 2.0.1 n.f.—cstr. מִשְׁחַת; pl. sf. Q משחותיהם—**1. measurement** 3QTr 12_{12}. **2. prescribed portion** of priests from sacrifices Lv 7_{35}. → משח III *measure.*

*[מִשְׁחָה] III 2.0.1 n.f.—cstr. מִשְׁחַת—**consecrated portion** of priests from sacrifices Lv 7_{35}. → משח I *anoint.*

מָשְׁחָה I 2 n.f.—sf. מָשְׁחָתָם—**anointing** Ex 29_{29} 40_{15}. → משח I *anoint.*

מָשְׁחָה II 1 n.f. **prescribed portion** of priests from sacrifices Nm 18_8. → משח III *measure.*

*[מִשְׁחוֹר] n.[m.] **darkness** 1QH 13_{32} ([משחו[ר). → שׁחר I *be black.*

מַשְׁחִית I 10.0.2 n.[m.] **destruction, ruin** Pr 18_9. → שׁחת *destroy.*

מַשְׁחִית II *destroyer,* see שׁחת *destroy,* hi.

מִשְׁחָר I 1 n.[m.] **dawn** Ps 110_3. → שַׁחַר cf. *dawn.*

*מִשְׁחָר II 1 n.[m.] **radiance** Ps 110_3.

[מַשְׁחֵת] 1 n.[m.]—sf. מַשְׁחֵתוֹ—**destruction** Ezk 9_1. → שׁחת *destroy.*

[מִשְׁחַת] 1 n.f.—cstr. מִשְׁחַת—**disfigurement** Is 52_{14}. → שׁחת *destroy.*

מָשְׁחָת 2 n.[m.]—sf. מָשְׁחָתָם—**1. blemish** Lv 22_{25}. **2. blemished (sacrificial) animal** Ml 1_{14}. → שׁחת *destroy.*

מִשְׁטוֹחַ 1.0.1 n.[m.] **spreading place,** for net Ezk 47_{10}, priestly linen perh. 3QTr 7_{11} (others הַמִּשְׁמָרָה). → שׁטח *spread.*

[מִשְׁטָח] 2 n.[m.]—cstr. מִשְׁטַח—**spreading place,** for net Ezk $26_{5.14}$. → שׁטח *spread.*

[מִשְׁטָר] 1 n.[m.]—sf. מִשְׁטָרוֹ—**writing** in heavens, i.e. pattern of stars, or **ordinance(s)** by which they rule earth, or that **rule** Jb 38_{33}. → (?) שׁטר *rule.*

מֶשִׁי 2 n.[m.] **fine cloth,** prob. not silk Ezk $16_{10.13}$.

מֻשִׁי, see מוּשִׁי *Mushi.*

מְשֵׁיזַבְאֵל 3 pr.n.m. **Meshezabel.**

מָשִׁיחַ 39.1.23 n.m.—cstr. מְשִׁיחַ; sf. מְשִׁיחִי; pl. cstr. Q משיחי; sf. מְשִׁיחָי—**anointed one, 1.** in ref. to **king,** מְשִׁיחַ יי *Y.'s anointed one* 1 S 24_7. **2.** in ref. to **priest** Lv 4_3. **3.** in ref. to **prophet** Ps 105_{15}. **4.** in ref. to eschatological figure, **messiah,** royal or priestly, משיח הצדק *the messiah of righteousness* 4QCommGenA 5_3, אהרן וישראל *of Aaron and Israel* CD 19_{10}. → משח I *anoint.*

*[מְשִׁיחָה] 0.0.2 n.f.—cstr. משיחת—**anointing** 1QM 9_8. → משח I *anoint.*

*[מְשִׁיכָה] 0.0.1 n.f. **drawing (of water)** 4QHalakhahA 1_4. → משך *pull.*

*[מֵשִׁיר] n.[m.] **song,** מְשִׁירִי אֲהוֹדֶנּוּ *(with) my song I will praise him* Ps 28_7 (if em. מְשִׁירִי *with my song*). → שׁיר *sing;* cf. שִׁיר *song.*

מָשַׁךְ I 36.2.6 vb.—**Qal** 30.1.5 Pf. מָשַׁךְ, מְשַׁכְתִּיךְ; impf. יִמְשׁוֹךְ;

impv. מְשֹׁךְ (מָשְׁכֵנִי), מִשְׁכוּ; ptc. מֹשֵׁךְ, מֹשְׁכִים; inf. מְשֹׁךְ (מָשְׁכוֹ)—1. **drag, haul, pull (along, off, away),** מְשַׁכְתִּיךְ חָסֶד *I (Y.) have dragged you along (with) loyalty* Jr 31$_3$ (or §4), מֹשְׁכֵי הֶעָוֹן בְּחַבְלֵי הַשָּׁוְא *those who drag along sin with cords of falsehood* Is 5$_{18}$. 2. **pull, pull up** person Gn 37$_{28}$. 3. **pull out** lambs from flock Ex 12$_{21}$. 4. **prolong,** מְשַׁכְתִּיךְ חָסֶד *I (Y.) have prolonged to you loyalty* Jr 31$_3$. 5. **sow** seeds Am 9$_{13}$. 6. appar. **extend** hand, perh. **make common cause** with (אֵת) mockers Ho 7$_5$. 7. appar. **pull away,** i.e. **pervert** law Si 35$_{17}$. 8. **draw** water 4QHalakhahA 1$_3$. 9. with בְּ of obj., **draw** bow 1 K 22$_{34}$, **wield** spear Jg 5$_{14}$ (or §10 or §15). b. ptc. as noun, **archer** Is 66$_{19(ms)}$. 10. appar. **draw up, march** Jg 5$_{14}$. 11. appar. **draw, mislead** enemy Jg 4$_7$. 12. perh. **stimulate** body with (בְּ) wine Ec 2$_3$ (or §18). 13. **follow, trail behind** (אַחֲרֵי) evil one Jb 21$_{33}$. 14. perh. **be patient** Ne 9$_{30}$. 15. **hold** (בְּ of obj.) staff Jg 5$_{14}$. 16. of calf, **carry, bear** (בְּ of obj.) yoke Dt 21$_3$. 17. **lay out** person **for burial** with (עִם) wicked Ps 28$_3$. 18. **sustain** body with (בְּ) wine Ec 2$_3$.

Ni. 3.1.1 Impf. תִּמָּשֵׁךְ—1. **be delayed** or **be prolonged,** of days Is 13$_{22}$, word of Y. Ezk 12$_{25}$. 2. **be pulled away,** i.e. **disappear,** of human work Si 14$_{19}$.

Pu. 3 Ptc. מְמֻשָּׁךְ—1. appar. **be tall,** of people Is 18$_2$. 2. **be delayed,** of hope Pr 13$_{12}$.

→ מֶשֶׁךְ I *trail,* (?) II *(leather) pouch,* מְשִׁיכָה *drawing,* מֹשְׁכֶת *belt.*

*משך II 7 vb.—**Qal** 7 Pf. מָשַׁךְ; impf. יִמְשׁוֹךְ—**seize** Leviathan with (בְּ) hook Jb 40$_{25}$, someone together with (עִם) the wicked Ps 28$_3$. → (?) מֶשֶׁךְ II *(leather) pouch.*

*משך III 2 vb.—**Pu.** 2 Ptc. מְמֻשָּׁךְ—**be scented,** of people Is 18$_{2.7}$.

[מֶשֶׁךְ] I 2 n.[m.] 1. **trail** of seed Ps 126$_6$. 2. **acquisition,** as a drawing up, מֶשֶׁךְ חָכְמָה *acquisition of wisdom* Jb 28$_{18}$. → משך I *pull.*

*[מֶשֶׁךְ] II 2 n.[m.] **(leather) pouch, bag, bagful,** מֶשֶׁךְ־הַזָּרַע *bag of seed* Ps 126$_6$, מֶשֶׁךְ חָכְמָה appar. *bag(ful) of wisdom* Jb 28$_{18}$. → משך I *pull* or II *seize.*

*[מֶשֶׁךְ] III 1 n.[m.] **price** of wisdom Jb 28$_{18}$.

מֶשֶׁךְ IV 9 pl.n. **Meshech.**

מִשְׁכָּב 46.3.9 n.m.—cstr. מִשְׁכַּב; sf. מִשְׁכָּבִי, מִשְׁכַּבְכֶם; pl. cstr. מִשְׁכְּבֵי; sf. מִשְׁכְּבוֹתָם—1. **bed,** whether bedstead or mat and covers, **place to lie down,** חֲדַר מִשְׁכָּבְךָ *your bedroom* Ex 7$_{28}$. 2. **bedding** Lv 15$_4$. 3. specif. **marital bed** Ca 3$_1$, or as place of fornication Pr 7$_{17}$. 4. **sickbed** Jb 33$_{19}$; **deathbed** 1 K 1$_{47}$. 5. perh. **prayer mat** Ps 149$_5$; **place of lying down** in ecstasy or prayer Is 57$_8$. 6. **dining couch** 3QTr 11$_{16}$. 7. **bier** 2 C 16$_{14}$. 8. **grave** Is 57$_2$. 9. **lying (down),** in ref. to sexual relations, מִשְׁכַּב דֹּדִים *lying down of love,* i.e. love-making Ezk 23$_{17}$. → שׁכב *lie down.*

מִשְׁכָּן 139.0.6 n.m.—cstr. מִשְׁכַּן; sf. מִשְׁכָּנִי; pl. מִשְׁכָּנוֹת; cstr. מִשְׁכְּנוֹת (מִשְׁכְּנֵי); sf. מִשְׁכְּנוֹתֶיךָ, מִשְׁכְּנֹתָם (מִשְׁכְּנֵיהֶם)—1. oft. (tent) **Tabernacle** as **dwelling-place** of Y., נֹשְׂאֵי הַמִּשְׁכָּן *bearers of the tabernacle* Nm 10$_{17}$. 2. rarely, **small tabernacle,** within the Tabernacle proper Ex 26$_{13}$. 3. pl., **temple** as **dwelling place** of Y. Ps 43$_3$. 4. **dwelling, dwelling place, tent** of human Nm 16$_{24}$. 5. **grave,** viewed as a dwelling-place Is 22$_{16}$. 6. **dwelling** of wild ass Jb 39$_6$. → שׁכן *dwell.*

[מֹשֶׁכֶת] 1 n.f.—pl. cstr. מֹשְׁכוֹת—**belt** of Orion, less prob. **cord** by which he is dragged along Jb 38$_{31}$. → משך I *pull.*

מָשַׁל I 81.14.70 vb.—**Qal** 78.10.49 Pf. מָשַׁל, מָשַׁלְתָּ; impf. יִמְשֹׁל (יִמְשָׁל־, יִמְשׁוֹל); ptc. מֹשֵׁל, מֹשְׁלָה, Si מושלת, מֹשְׁלִים; impv. מְשָׁל־; inf. abs. מָשֹׁל; cstr. מְשֹׁל (מְשָׁל־)—1. **rule, dominate, (have) control, have charge,** a. usu. with בְּ *over* people (subj. Y. and human leader) Jg 8$_{23}$, sin Gn 4$_7$, one's temper Pr 16$_{32}$, day and night (subj. luminaries) Gn 1$_{18}$. b. less oft. with עַל *over* people Pr 28$_{15}$, אֶל *over* people Jr 33$_{26}$. c. abs. Pr 12$_{24}$. 2. **assume authority, presume,** לֹא־יִמְשֹׁל לְמָכְרָהּ *he must not presume to deliver her over or sell her* Ex 21$_8$. 3. **implement** rule Dn 11$_3$. 4. ptc. as noun, **ruler, one who controls** 1 K 5$_1$.

Pu. 0.1 Ptc. מושל—**be dominated** Si 41$_{2(Bmg)}$ (or qal).

Hi. 3.4.21 Pf. Q המשיל; impf. תַּמְשִׁילֵהוּ; inf. abs. הַמְשֵׁל—1. oft. of Y., **cause to rule, give dominion, control over** (בְּ) creation Ps 8$_7$, inheritance 4QInstr[b] 2.3$_{12}$. 2. of parent, **let child have its own way** Si 30$_{11}$. 3. of Moses, perh. **give** Aaron **responsibility** for (בְּ) legal affairs Si 45$_{17}$. 4. of Y., perh. **make person competent, skilful** with regard to (בְּ) craftsmanship 4QInstr[d] 81$_{15}$.

5. abs., **rule,** of Y. Jb 25$_{2}$.

→ מֹשֶׁל I *rule,* מִמְשָׁל *dominion,* מֶמְשָׁלָה *rule.*

משל II 18.2 vb.—**Qal** 10.2 Impf. יִמְשֹׁל; ptc. מֹשֵׁל, מֹשְׁלִים; impv. מְשֹׁל; inf. מְשֹׁל—**1a. tell, recite** proverb Ezk 18$_{2}$. **b.** ptc. as noun, **teller of proverbs, sage, bard** Ezk 16$_{44}$. **2.** perh. **be like,** אֶל־אִישֵׁךְ תְּשׁוּקָתֵךְ וְהוּא יִמְשָׁל־בָּךְ *your desire will be for your husband, and he will be like you* (in desire) Gn 3$_{16}$ (if not משל I).

Ni. 5 Pf. נִמְשַׁל—**1. be like(ned), be comparable** to (אֶל) king Is 14$_{10}$, with (עִם) one who goes down the pit Ps 28$_{1}$. **2. be as** (כְּ) beast Ps 49$_{13}$.

Pi. 1 Ptc. מְמַשֵּׁל—ptc. as noun, מְמַשֵּׁל מְשָׁלִים **teller of proverbs** Ezk 21$_{5}$.

Hi. 1 Impf. תַּמְשִׁלוּנִי—**liken, compare** Y. to (לְ) someone Is 46$_{5}$.

Htp. 1 + waw וָאֶתְמַשֵּׁל—**be(come) as** (כְּ) dust Jb 30$_{19}$.

→ מָשָׁל I *proverb,* מֹשֶׁל II *likeness.*

מָשָׁל I 39.5.2 n.m.—cstr. מְשַׁל; sf. מְשָׁלוֹ; pl. מְשָׁלִים; cstr. מִשְׁלֵי—**proverb, (proverbial) saying, maxim, parable, prediction, prophecy, didactic** or **moral verse** or **theme, discourse** Nm 23$_{7}$ 1 S 10$_{12}$; מִשְׁלֵי שְׁלֹמֹה *proverbs of Solomon* Pr 1$_{1}$. → משל II *be like.*

מָשָׁל II 1 pl.n. **Mashal.**

מֹשֶׁל I 2.2 n.[m.]—sf. מָשְׁלוֹ—**1. rule, government, dominion** Zc 9$_{10}$. **2.** perh. **mastery,** מושל אופנים *mastery of (different) situations* Si 50$_{27}$. → משל I *rule.*

מֹשֶׁל II 2.1 n.[m.]—cstr. מֹשֶׁל (Si מושל); sf. מָשְׁלוֹ—**1. like(ness)** Jb 41$_{25}$. **2.** perh. **uttering of proverbs, ability to utter proverbs** or **proverbial wisdom** Si 50$_{27}$. **3.** perh. **proverb** Jb 17$_{6}$. → משל II *be like.*

[מִשְׁלָח] 7.0.3 n.[m.]—cstr. מִשְׁלַח, sf. Q משלחם—**1a. extending, moving** of limbs 1QS 10$_{13}$. **b.** specif. **activity, enterprise** Dt 28$_{20}$. **2. grazing ground** of oxen Is 7$_{25}$. → שלח I *send.*

[מִשְׁלֹחַ] 3.0.5 n.[m.] **1. extending, giving, sending,** מִשְׁלוֹחַ מָנוֹת *sending of presents* Est 9$_{19}$. **2.** specif. **extending** of hand, i.e. **(military) attack** 1QM 1$_{1}$. **3. dominion** or **possession** Is 11$_{14}$. → שלח I *send.*

מִשְׁלַחַת 2.0.1 n.f.—pl. sf. Q משלחותיו—**1. undertaking** or perh. **mission** 4QShir[b] 16$_{2}$. **2.** perh. **sending (a replacement)** for oneself to battle, i.e. **deputation, substitution,** or **setting aside, laying down** of weapons, or **discharging** of oneself from battle Ec 8$_{8}$. **3.** perh. **sending, dispatching** of troop of angels, or **company** of angels Ps 78$_{49}$. → שלח I *send.*

מְשֻׁלָּם I 25.0.0.17 pr.n.m. **Meshullam.**

מְשִׁלֵּמוֹת 2 pr.n.[m.] **Meshillemoth.**

מְשֶׁלֶמְיָה 1 pr.n.m. **Meshelemiah.**

מְשֶׁלֶמְיָהוּ 3 pr.n.m. **Meshelemiah.**

מְשִׁלֵּמִית 1 pr.n.m. **Meshillemith.**

מְשֻׁלֶּמֶת 1.0.0.2 pr.n.f. **Meshullemeth.**

***מִשְׁלֹשׁ** 1 n.[m.] **triad,** מִשְׁלֹשׁ חֳדָשִׁים *triad of months* Gn 38$_{24}$. → שׁלשׁ *divide into three parts.*

***[מְשַׁם]** 0.0.1 n.[m.] perh. **desolation** GnzPs 3$_{18}$ (or em. מִשְׁגֶּה *error*). → שׁמם *be desolate.*

מְשַׁמָּה 7.0.1 n.f.—pl. מְשַׁמּוֹת—**1. (place of) devastation** Ezk 6$_{14}$. **2. horror** Ezk 5$_{15}$. → שׁמם *be desolate.*

[מַשְׁמָן] 1 n.[m.]—pl. מַשְׁמַנִּים—**rich food, delicacy** Ne 8$_{10}$. → שׁמן *be fat.*

[מִשְׁמָן] 6 n.m.—cstr. מִשְׁמַן; pl. cstr. מִשְׁמַנֵּי; sf. מִשְׁמַנָּיו—**1.** of body, **fat, fattest** or **healthiest part** Is 17$_{4}$. **2.** of person, **fat, healthy, sturdy, strong(est)** Ps 78$_{31}$. **3.** of crops, **choice produce** Gn 27$_{28}$. **4.** of land, **choice area,** i.e. **most fertile area** Gn 27$_{39}$. **5.** of province, perh. **best** or **strongest city** Dn 11$_{24}$. → שׁמן *be fat.*

מַשְׁמַנָּה, see מִשְׁמַנָּה *Mishmannah.*

מִשְׁמַנָּה 1 pr.n.m. **Mishmannah.**

[מִשְׁמָע] I 1.0.4 n.[m.] **hearing,** מִשְׁמַע אָזְנָיו *hearing of his ears* Is 11$_{3}$. → שׁמע *hear.*

מִשְׁמָע II 4 pr.n.m. **Mishma.**

[מִשְׁמַעַת] 4 n.f.—sf. מִשְׁמַעְתָּם—**1. hearing** 1 S 22$_{14}$. **2.** appar. **servant** or **vassal (nation)** Is 11$_{14}$. **3.** perh. **retinue, court,** or **bodyguard** 2 S 23$_{23}$||1 C 11$_{25}$. → שׁמע *hear.*

מִשְׁמָר I 22.1.6.1 n.m.—cstr. מִשְׁמַר; sf. מִשְׁמָרוֹ; pl. sf. מִשְׁמָרָיו—**1a. guard(ing), watch(ing)** Ezk 38$_{7}$. **b. custody, imprisonment** Gn 40$_{3}$ (or §3b). **2.** of person, **guard, sentry, lookout** Ne 4$_{3}$. **3a.** of object, **barrier** Jr 51$_{12}$. **b. prison** Gn 40$_{3}$. **4. protection,** משמר שלומכה *protection of,* i.e. afforded by, *your peace* 1QH 17$_{33}$. **5. (cultic) service** Ne 13$_{14}$. **6. (priestly) course, division** Ne 12$_{24}$. → שׁמר *keep.*

***מִשְׁמָר II** 1 n.m. **muzzle** Jb 7$_{12}$. → שׁמר *keep.*

*מִשְׁמָר III 1 n.m. **wakefulness** Jb 7:12. → שׁמר *keep.*

[מִשְׁמָרָה] 0.0.1 n.f. perh. **guardhouse** or **fortress** 3QTr 7:11. → שׁמר *keep.*

מִשְׁמֶרֶת 78.1.9 n.f.—מִשְׁמֶרֶת; sf. מִשְׁמַרְתִּי; pl. מִשְׁמָרוֹת; cstr. מִשְׁמְרוֹת; sf. sf. מִשְׁמְרוֹתָם (מִשְׁמְרוֹתֵיהֶם)—**1.** usu. priestly, **a. watch, vigil, guard, (religious) observance** Gn 26:5. **b. duty, guard-duty, shift** Ne 12:9. **2. division** of priests, Levites, or Israelites 1QM 2:2.3.4. **3. guardianship, custody** Nm 18:8. **4. something to keep watch over** Ex 12:6. **5. something reserved** (for later usage) Ex 16:23. **6. (duty of) protection,** מִשְׁמֶרֶת בֵּית־שָׁאוּל *protection of the household of Saul* 1 C 12:30. **7.** appar. **place of watching, (sentry) post** Is 21:8. → שׁמר *keep.*

*[מִשְׁמֵשׁ] 0.0.0.1 pr.n.m. **Meshammesh.**

*[מִשְׁנָה] n.f. **bladder,** זִרְמַת מִשְׁנָה *effusion of the bladder* Ps 90:5 (if em. זְרַמְתָּם שֵׁנָה *you overwhelm them, sleep*).

מִשְׁנֶה I 35.0.10 n.[m.]—cstr. מִשְׁנֵה; sf. מִשְׁנֵהוּ; pl. מִשְׁנִים; cstr. Q משני; sf. Q משניו—**1. second** in rank or importance, **deputy, second-in-command,** מִשְׁנֵה הַמֶּלֶךְ *the king's deputy* 2 C 28:7. **2. second child** or perh. **younger brother** 1 S 8:2. **3.** animal of the **second brood** 1 S 15:9. **4. copy, duplicate, equivalent** Dt 17:18. **5. second quarter** of Jerusalem, **the Mishneh** 2 K 22:14. **6. double (share), twice as much** Gn 43:12. → שׁנה II *repeat.*

*מִשְׁנֶה II 3 n.[m.] **equivalent,** מִשְׁנֵה עֲוֹנָם *equivalent of their iniquity* Jr 16:18.

*מִשְׁנֶה III 1 n.[m.] **the best (portion)** Is 61:7.

מְשִׁסָּה 6 n.f.—Q משיסה; pl. מְשִׁסּוֹת—**plunder** Hb 2:7. → שׁסס *plunder.*

מִשְׁעוֹל 1 n.[m.] **(narrow) pathway,** מִשְׁעוֹל הַכְּרָמִים *pathway through the vineyards* Nm 22:24. → cf. שֹׁעַל *hollow hand.*

מִשְׁעִי I 1 n.[f.] **cleansing** (of new-born child) Ezk 16:4. → שׁעע I *be smeared over.*

*מִשְׁעִי II 1 n.[f.] **rubbing** Ezk 16:4. → שׁעע I *be smeared over.*

*מִשְׁעִי III 1 n.[f.] **midwife** Ezk 16:4.

*מִשְׁעִי IV 1 n.[f.] **smoothness** Ezk 16:4. → שׁעע I *be smeared over.*

מִשְׁעָם 1 pr.n.m. **Misham.**

מַשְׁעֵן 1 n.[m.] **support, sustenance** Is 3:1. → שׁען *lean.*

מִשְׁעָן I 4.3.2 n.[m.]—cstr. מִשְׁעַן; sf. Q משעני—**1a. support, help,** of Y. 2 S 22:19. **b. staff,** הווא עולם משען ימיני *he who is eternal* (i.e. Y.) *is the staff of my right hand* 1QS 11:4. **2.** appar. **sustenance** Is 3:1. → שׁען *lean.*

*[מִשְׁעָן] II 0.0.0.1 pr.n.m. **Mishan.**

מַשְׁעֵנָה 1 n.f. **support, sustenance** Is 3:1. → שׁען *lean.*

מִשְׁעֶנֶת 11.0.7 n.f.—cstr. מִשְׁעֶנֶת; sf. מִשְׁעַנְתִּי; pl. sf. מִשְׁעֲנֹתָם—**1. stick, staff for walking** Ex 21:19, **digging well** Nm 21:18, **performing miracle** Jg 6:21. **2. support,** משענת אל *God's support* 1QM 4:13. → שׁען *lean.*

מִשְׁפָּחָה 304.2.22 n.f.—cstr. מִשְׁפַּחַת; sf. מִשְׁפַּחְתִּי; pl. מִשְׁפָּחוֹת; cstr. מִשְׁפְּחֹת; sf. מִשְׁפְּחֹתָיו—**1. clan,** מִשְׁפַּחַת אֱלִימֶלֶךְ *clan of Elimelech* Ru 2:1, משפחות אל *clans of God* 1QM 4:10. **2. species** Gn 8:19. **3. type** Jr 15:3.

מִשְׁפָּט 421.20.420 n.m.—cstr. מִשְׁפַּט; sf. מִשְׁפָּטִי; pl. מִשְׁפָּטִים (Q משפטות); cstr. מִשְׁפְּטֵי; sf. מִשְׁפָּטַי, מִשְׁפְּטֵיהֶם—**1. judgment, a. act of judgment,** לאל המשפט *to God is the judgment* 1QS 11:10. **b. sentence, decision,** מִשְׁפַּט־מָוֶת *sentence of death* Jr 26:11. **c. case to be judged, cause** 1 K 8:45‖2 C 6:35; משפט האוב *case of the medium* CD 12:3. **d. place** or **seat of judgment, court,** אֻלָם הַמִּשְׁפָּט *hall of judgment* 1 K 7:7. **e. execution of judgment,** רְצוּץ מִשְׁפָּט *broken by judgment* Ho 5:11. **2a. justice,** מִשְׁפַּט אֶבְיֹנְךָ *justice due to your poor* Ex 23:6. **b.** perh. **just one** Ps 37:28. **3. ordinance,** משפטי התורה *ordinances of the law* CD 14:8. **4. custom, manner,** מִשְׁפַּט הַכֹּהֲנִים *custom of the priests* 1 S 2:13. **b.** perh. **destiny** Jg 13:12. **c. rank** Si 38:16. **5. legal right, entitlement,** מִשְׁפַּט הַיְרֻשָּׁה *legal right of possession* Jr 32:8. **6. just measure, specification, proper measure, moderation, restraint, discretion,** כִּי לְכָל־חֵפֶץ יֵשׁ עֵת וּמִשְׁפָּט *for to every matter there is a time and a proper measure* Ec 8:6. → שׁפט *judge.*

מִשְׁפְּתַיִם I 2 n.[m.]du. **fire-places, ash-heaps** Gn 49:14 Jg 5:16. → שׁפת *set on fire.*

*מִשְׁפְּתַיִם II 2 n.[m.]du. **saddle-bags** of a mule Gn 49:14 Jg 5:16.

*מִשְׁפְּתַיִם III 2 n.[m.]du. **divided sheepfolds** Gn 49:14 Jg 5:16.

*מִשְׁפְּתַיִם IV 2 n.[m.]du. **double wall** Gn 49:14 Jg 5:16.

*מִשְׁפְּתַיִם V 2 n.[m.]du. **grazing places** Gn 49:14 Jg 5:16.

מֶשֶׁק I 1 n.[m.] **acquisition, possession** Gn 15_{2}. → cf. מִמְשָׁק I *ground*.

***מֶשֶׁק** II 1 n.[m.] **libation** Gn 15_{2}.

*[**מֶשֶׁק**] III 1 pr.n.f. **Meshek.**

[**מַשָּׁק**] I 1 n.[m.]—cstr. מַשַּׁק—**rushing about** or **infestation** or **assault** of locusts Is 33_{4}. → שׁקק I *rush about*.

*[**מַשָּׁק**] II 1 n.[m.]—cstr. מַשַּׁק—**swarm,** of locusts Is 33_{4}. → נשׁק II *be equipped*.

מַשְׁקֶה I 13 n.m.—cstr. מַשְׁקֵה; sf. מַשְׁקֵהוּ; pl. מַשְׁקִים; sf. מַשְׁקָיו—**1. cup-bearer** of king Gn 40_{1}. **2. office of cup-bearer** Gn 40_{21}. → שׁקה hi. *give a drink*.

מַשְׁקֶה II 6.1.10 n.m.—pl. cstr. Q משקי—**1. drink** 1 K 10_{21}. **2. irrigated land,** מַשְׁקֵה יִשְׂרָאֵל *irrigated land of Israel* Ezk 45_{15}. → שׁקה hi. *give a drink*.

מִשְׁקוֹל 1 n.[m.] **weight** Ezk 4_{10}. → שׁקל *weigh*.

מַשְׁקוֹף 3.0.6 n.m.—pl. sf. Q משקופיו—**lintel** Ex 12_{7}. → שׁקף *look down*.

מִשְׁקָל 49.3.17 n.m.—cstr. מִשְׁקַל; sf. מִשְׁקָלוֹ—**1.** usu. **weight, full weight** 1 K 7_{47}‖2 C 4_{18}. **2. value,** משקל איש ואיש *value of each man* 1QS 9_{12}. → שׁקל *weigh*.

[**מִשְׁקֶלֶת**] 2.0.2 n.f.—cstr. מִשְׁקֹלֶת—mason's **level** or **plumbline** Is 28_{17}. → שׁקל *weigh*.

[**מִשְׁקָע**] 1 n.[m.] **what is settled,** מִשְׁקַע־מַיִם *what is settled of the water*, i.e. clear water Ezk 34_{18}. → שׁקע *sink*.

[**מִשְׁרָה**] 1 n.f. **juice,** מִשְׁרַת עֲנָבִים *juice of grapes* Nm 6_{3}.

מִשְׁרָעִי 1 gent. **Mishraite.**

משׁשׁ I 10 vb.—**Qal** 3 Impf. יְמֻשֵּׁנִי—**feel** person Gn 27_{12}.
 Pi. 6 Pf. מִשַּׁשְׁתָּ; impf. יְמַשֵּׁשׁ; ptc. מְמַשֵּׁשׁ—**1. grope** Dt 28_{29} (+ בְּ in *darkness*). **2.** with accus., **search** tent **with hands** Gn 31_{34}.
 Hi. 1 Impf. יָמֵשׁ—**feel** darkness Ex 10_{21}.
 → cf. ימשׁ *touch*, מושׁ II *feel*.

***משׁשׁ** II 1.1 vb.—**Qal** 0.1 Impf. תמוש—**arrive,** of destruction Si $40_{10(Bmg)}$ (+ בַּעֲבוּר *on account of* the wicked).
 Hi. 1 Impf. יָמֵשׁ—**arrive,** of darkness Ex 10_{21}.

מִשְׁתֶּה 46.5 n.m.—cstr. מִשְׁתֵּה; pl. sf. מִשְׁתָּיו—**1. feast,** מִשְׁתֵּה הַיַּיִן *feast of wine* Est 5_{6}. **2. drink** Dn 1_{5}. → שׁתה I *drink*.

[**מַת**] I 22.2.2 n.m.—pl. מְתִים; cstr. מְתֵי; sf. מְתָיו—**man,** מְתֵי יִשְׂרָאֵל *men of Israel* Is 41_{14}.

*[**מַת**] II adv. **truly,** מַת אֵב אָנֹכִי אֶת־גְּאוֹן יַעֲקֹב *truly I am the foe of Jacob's pride* Am 6_{8} (if em. מְתָאֵב *loathing* to מַת אֵב, i.e. אֵב is stative ptc. of איב).

מֵת *dead one*, see מות *die*.

*[**מַת**] 1 n.m. **louse,** insect parasite on human hair, מְתֵי יִשְׂרָאֵל *lice of Israel* Is 41_{14}.

מַתְבֵּן 1 n.[m.] **heap of straw** Is 25_{10}. → cf. תֶּבֶן *straw*.

מֶתֶג 4 n.m.—sf. מִתְגִּי—**bridle,** or perh. **muzzle** 2 K 19_{28}.

מֶתֶג הָאַמָּה 1 appar. pl.n. **Metheg-ammah.**

מִתּוֹךְ, see תָּוֶךְ *midst*.

מָתוֹק 12.0.3 adj.—מְתוּקָה; pl. מְתוּקִים—**1. sweet,** of honey Pr 24_{13}, sleep Ec 5_{11}, light Ec 11_{7}. **2.** as noun, **sweet thing, sweetness** Is 5_{20}. → מתק I *be sweet*.

*[**מָתוֹר**] 0.0.1 n.[m.] **following after,** מתור שרירות לבו *following after the stubbornness of his heart* 1QS 3_{3} (others מתיר *going about*, i.e. תור hi. inf.). → תור *go about*.

מְתוּשָׁאֵל 2 pr.n.m. **Methushael.**

מְתוּשֶׁלַח 6.0.1 pr.n.m. **Methuselah.**

מתח 1 vb.—**Qal** 1 + waw וַיִּמְתָּחֵם—of Y., **spread out** heavens as (כְּ) tent Is 40_{22}. → אַמְתַּחַת *sack*, מְתָחָה *spreading out*.

***מְתָחָה** n.f. **spreading out** Dt 33_{27} (if em. וּמִתַּחַת *and beneath* to וּמְתָחַת *and the spreading [out] of*). → מתח *spread out*.

מָתַי 43.1.3 interrog. adv. **1. when?** Gn 30_{30}. **2.** עַד־מָתַי **how long?** Is 6_{11}. **3.** לְמָתַי **for when?** Ex 8_{5}. **4.** אַחֲרֵי מָתַי עֹד **how much longer?** Jr 13_{27}.

*[**מָתָךְ**] n.[m.] **intoxicating drink, wine,** מְסַפֵּחַ הַמָּתָךְ *of the outpouring of wine* Hb 2_{15} (if em. מְסַפֵּחַ חֲמָתְךָ *joining your anger*). → נתך *pour out*.

*[**מַתָּךְ**] 0.0.1 n.[m.] **outpouring,** מתך חמה *outpouring of anger* 1QH 11_{28}. → נתך *pour out*.

[**מַתְכֹּנֶת**] 5.1 n.f.—sf. מַתְכֻּנְתּוֹ—**measurement, specification, specified number** Ex 5_{8}. → תכן *weigh up*.

מַתְּלָאָה 1 interj. **what a weariness!** Ml 1_{13}. → מָה *what*, תְּלָאָה *weariness*.

*[**מְתִלָּה**] 1 n.f.—pl. מתלות—**deception** Is $30_{10(1QIsa^a)}$ (MT מַהֲתַלּוֹת *deceptions*). → תלל *mock, deceive*.

[**מְתַלְּעָה**] 3.0.1 n.f.—pl. cstr. מְתַלְּעוֹת; sf. מְתַלְּעוֹתָיו—**tooth** or **jaws, jawbone** Jl 1_{6}. → cf. מַלְתָּעוֹת *jawbone*.

מְתֹם 3 n.[m.] **1. well-being** Is 1_{6}. **2. entirety** Jg 20_{48}. →

תמם (?) *be complete.*

[מִתְמוֹטֵט] *totterer,* see מוט *totter,* htpol.

מַתָּן I 5.7 n.m.—sf. מַתָּנָם—**gift(s)** Pr 196. → נתן *give.*

מַתָּן II 2.0.0.19 pr.n.m. **Mattan.**

*[מֹתֶן] n.[m.] **strength** Ec 77 (if em. מַתָּנָה *gift* to מָתְנוֹ *his strength*).

מַתָּנָה I 17.3.3 n.f.—cstr. מַתְּנַת; sf. Si מתנתו; pl. מַתָּנוֹת; cstr. מַתְּנוֹת; sf. מַתְּנוֹתָם —**1. gift, offering** Ex 2838; **bribe** Pr 1527. **2. dedication** Nm 187. → נתן *give.*

*מַתָּנָה II 1 n.f. **violence** Ec 77. → ינה *oppress.*

מַתָּנָה III 2 pl.n. **Mattanah.**

*[מָתְנָה] n.f. **strength** Ec 77 (if em. מַתָּנָה *gift*).

מַתְּנַי 3 pr.n.m. **Mattenai.**

מִתְנִי 1 gent. **Mithnite.**

מַתַּנְיָה 16.0.0.16 pr.n.m. **Mattaniah.**

מַתַּנְיָהוּ, see מַתַּנְיָה *Mattaniah.*

מָתְנַיִם 47.3.6 n.m.du.—מָתְנַיִם; cstr. מָתְנֵי; sf. מָתְנָיו—**loins,** or perh. rather **musculature** linking upper part of body with lower Jr 1311.

מתק I 5.5.1 vb.—**Qal** 3.1.1 Pf. מָתְקוּ; impf. יִמְתְּקוּ—**be sweet, become sweet,** of water Ex 1525, life Si 4018.

Hi. 2.4 Pf. Si המתיקו; impf. תַּמְתִּיק; ptc. Si ממתיק—**cause sweetness, make sweet, pleasant,** תַּמְתִּיק בְּפִיו רָעָה *evil gives a sweet taste in his mouth* Jb 2012, יַחְדָּו נַמְתִּיק סוֹד *together we made our fellowship pleasant* Ps 5515.

→ מֶתֶק *sweetness,* מֹתֶק *sweetness,* מָתֹק *sweetness,* מָתוֹק *sweet,* מַמְתַקִּים *sweetness.*

*מתק II 2 vb.—**Qal** 2 Pf. מְתָקוֹ—**1.** of worm, **suck** corpse Jb 2420. **2.** of waters, **suckle** (לְ of obj.) the wicked Jb 2133.

*[מָתָק] 1 n.m.—sf. מְתָקוֹ—**sweetness, lover** Jb 2420. → מתק *be sweet.*

[מֶתֶק] or [מָתֶק] 2.0.1 n.m. **sweetness,** מֶתֶק שְׂפָתַיִם *sweetness of lips* Pr 1621, רֵעֵהוּ *of his friend* Pr 279. → מתק I *be sweet.*

[מֹתֶק] 1 n.[m.]—sf. מָתְקִי—**sweetness** Jg 911. → מתק I *be sweet.*

מִתְקָה 2 pl.n. **Mithkah.**

*[מִתְקָל] 0.0.1 n.m. **offence** 4QBéat 14.226. → תקל *stumble.*

מִתְרְדָת 2 pr.n.m. **Mithredath.**

[מַתָּת] 6.3 n.f.—מַתַּת—**gift,** מַתַּת אֱלֹהִים *gift of God* Ec 313. → נתן *give.*

מַתַּתָּה 1 pr.n.m. **Mattathah.**

מַתִּתְיָה 8.0.2.4 pr.n.m. **Mattithiah.**

מַתִּתְיָהוּ, see מַתִּתְיָה *Mattithiah.*

נ

נָא I 405.4.10.3 part. **please,** oft. linked with preceding word by maqqeph, and oft. with spelled נָּא when vowel precedes. Preceded by **1.** impv. Gn 1213. **2.** impf., juss. or cohort. Gn 1821 2628 4418 Jg 138. **3.** part., **a.** הִנֵּה־נָא **behold, please** Gn 1211. **b.** אַל־נָא **please let not, do not,** (1) followed by impf., juss. or cohort. Gn 138 2 S 1325. (2) אַל־נָא as interj., **please let it not be so!, Oh, no!** Gn 1918 3310. **c.** אִם־נָא **if now, please,** alw. in phrase אִם־נָא מָצָאתִי חֵן *if now I have found favour* Gn 183. **d.** אִם יֶשְׁךָ־נָּא **if you now, please** Gn 2442. **e.** אוֹי־נָא **woe now!** Jr 431. **f.** אַיֵּה־נָא **where now, please?** Ps 1152. **g.** נֶגְדָה־נָּא לְ **may it please be in the presence of!** Ps 11614.

נָא II 1 adj. **raw,** of meat Ex 129.

נֹא 5 pl.n. **No, Thebes.**

נֹאד 6 n.m.—cstr. נֹאד; sf. נֹאדְךָ; pl. cstr. נֹאדוֹת—**1. skin bottle, skin,** for wine Jos 94, milk Jg 419. **2.** perh. **parchment** for writing Ps 569. → cf. נֵד III *wineskin.*

נאה 3.1.1 vb.—**Qal** 0.1 Pf. נאתה—**be fitting,** of praise Si 159 (+ בְּ *in* mouth).

Pal. 3.0.1 Pf. נָאווּ ,נָאֲוָה—**1. be comely, beautiful,** of cheek Ca 110, feet Is 527. **2. befit,** of holiness, befitting (לְ of obj.) house of Y. Ps 935.

→ נָאֶה *fitting,* נָאָה *pleasant place,* נָאוֶה *comely, fit* ting; cf. נוה II *glorify*.

*[נָאָה] 12 n.f.—cstr. נְאוֹת—**pleasant place, oasis** (unless from נָוֶה *pasture*) Jr 9$_9$ Ps 83$_{13}$. → נאה *be fitting*.

*[נָאֶה] 0.2.1 adj.—f.s. Si נאה, m.pl. Si נאים—**fitting, suitable,** of fine words Si 35$_5$, beauty and strength GnzPs 3$_{24}$ (+ לְ *for* Y.). → נאה *be fitting*.

*[נָאהֲבַת] 0.0.0.1 pr.n.f. **Nahabath.**

*נאו 3 vb.—**Pi.** 3 Inf. נָאוָה—**praise** (unless from נָאוֶה *fitting*) Ps 33$_1$ 93$_5$ 147$_1$.

נָאוֶה 11.4 adj.—m.s. נָאוֶה, f.s. נָאוָה (נָוָה), cstr. נְוַת—**1a. comely, beautiful,** of woman Ca 1$_5$, countenance Ca 2$_{14}$. **b.** as noun, **comely one,** of Zion Jr 6$_2$. **2. fitting, suitable** (+ לְ *for, to* someone), of praise Ps 33$_1$, honour Pr 26$_1$, wealth Si 14$_3$. → נאה *be fitting*.

נִאוּפִים 2 n.[m.]pl.—sf. נִאֻפַיִךְ—**adultery,** prob. tokens of, or the urge to commit it Jr 13$_{27}$ Ezk 23$_{43}$. → נאף *commit adultery*.

*נָאוֹר 1 n.[m.] **Shining One,** in ref. to Y. Ps 76$_5$. → אור *be light*.

נְאוֹת, see נָוֶה *pasture*.

נאכר, see נֵכָר *foreignness*.

נאם 1 vb.—**Qal** 1 + waw וַיִּנְאֲמוּ—**utter a prophetic oracle** Jr 23$_{31}$. → נְאֻם *utterance*; cf. נום II *speak*.

[נְאֻם] 376.0.1 n.m.—cstr. נְאֻם—**utterance, oracle,** usu. of Y., given through prophet, נְאֻם י׳ *utterance of Y.* Gn 22$_{16}$; rarely of human Nm 24$_3$. → נאם *utter a prophetic oracle*.

*[נֶאֱמָנוּת] 0.0.3 n.f. **trustworthiness, assurance,** CD 7$_5$=19$_1$ 14$_2$ 4QOrd^a 2$_9$. → אמן *be trustworthy*.

נאף 31 vb.—**Qal** 16 Impf. יִנְאַף; ptc. נֹאֵף, נֹאֶפֶת, נֹאֲפוֹת; inf. abs. נָאֹף—**1. commit adultery (with),** of man with (accus.) woman Lv 20$_{10}$, Judah with wood and stone, i.e. worship images made of them Jr 3$_9$; abs. Ex 20$_{14}$||Dt 5$_{18}$. **2.** ptc. as noun, **adulterer, a.** masc. Lv 20$_{10}$. **b.** fem. Ezk 16$_{38}$. **3.** inf. abs. as noun, **(act of) adultery** Ho 4$_2$.

Pi. 15 Pf. נִאֵף, נִאֲפוּ; impf. תְּנָאַפְנָה; + waw וַיְנָאֲפוּ; ptc. מְנָאֵף, מְנָאֶפֶת, מְנָאֲפִים—**1. commit adultery (with),** of man with (accus.) woman Jr 29$_{23}$, woman with strangers Ezk 16$_{32}$, with images of gods, i.e. worship them Ezk 23$_{37}$. **2.** masc. ptc. as noun, **adulterer** Jr 9$_1$.

→ נִאוּפִים *adultery*, נַאֲפוּפִים *adultery*.

נֹאֵף *adulterer*, see נאף, qal §2; pi. §2.

[נַאֲפוּפִים] 1 n.[m.]pl.—sf. נַאֲפוּפֶיהָ—**adultery,** prob. tokens of it, such as gifts of jewellery Ho 2$_4$. → נאף *commit adultery*.

נאץ 24.1.13 vb.—**Qal** 8.1.9 Pf. נָאַץ; impf. יִנְאַץ, יִנְאָצוּן—**have contempt for, despise, spurn, disdain** persons Jr 33$_{24}$, counsel Ps 107$_{11}$, reproof Pr 1$_{30}$.

Pi. 15.0.4 Pf. נִאֵץ, נִאֲצוּ; impf. יְנָאֵץ; ptc. מְנַאֲצַי; inf. abs. נִאֵץ—**1. have contempt (for), revile, spurn** Y. Nm 14$_{11}$, name of Y. Ps 74$_{10}$, word of Y. Is 5$_{24}$, humans Is 60$_{14}$. **2.** perh. **cause someone to have contempt** 2 S 12$_{14}$.

Htpo. 1 Ptc. מִנֹּאָץ—**be treated with contempt, reviled,** of name of Y. Is 52$_5$.

→ נֶאָצָה *reviling*, נְאָצָה *disgrace*.

[נֶאָצָה] 3.0.2 n.f.—Q נצה; pl. נֶאָצוֹת; sf. נֶאָצוֹתֶיךָ—**reviling, blasphemy** Ezk 35$_{12}$ Ne 9$_{18.26}$ 4QTestim$_{28}$. → נאץ *have contempt*.

נְאָצָה 2 n.f. **disgrace** 2 K 19$_3$||Is 37$_3$. → נאץ *have contempt*.

נאק 2 vb.—**Qal** 2 Impf. יִנְאֲקוּ; + waw וְנָאַק—**groan** Ezk 30$_{24}$ (+ accus. נְאָקָה *groaning*) Jb 24$_{12}$. → נְאָקָה *groaning*.

[נְאָקָה] 4 n.f.—cstr. נַאֲקַת; sf. נַאֲקָתָם; pl. cstr. נַאֲקוֹת—**groaning, groan** Ex 2$_{24}$ 6$_5$ Jg 2$_{18}$ Ezk 30$_{24}$. → נאק *groan*.

נאר I 2 vb.—**Pi.** 2 Pf. נֵאֵר, נֵאַרְתָּה—**repudiate, spurn** covenant Ps 89$_{40}$, sanctuary Lm 2$_7$.

*נאר II 2 vb.—**Pi.** 2 Pf. נֵאֵר, נֵאַרְתָּה—**curse** covenant Ps 89$_{40}$, sanctuary Lm 2$_7$.

נֹב 7 pl.n. **Nob.**

נבא 115.0.9 vb.—**Qal** 0.0.3 Ptc. pass. Q נבואיו—pass. ptc. as noun, **thing prophesied, prophecy** GnzPs 2$_7$ 3$_{11}$ 4$_{17}$.

Ni. 87.0.6 Pf. נִבָּא, נִבֵּאתָ (נִבֵּיתָ); impf. יִנָּבֵא; impv. הִנָּבֵא; ptc. נִבָּא, נִבָּאִים (נִבְּאִים), נִבְּאֵי; inf. הִנָּבֵא (הִנָּבְאוֹ, הִנָּבְאֹתוֹ) —**prophesy, 1.** usu. of prophet giving word of Y. Jr 19$_{14}$ Am 3$_8$; with obj. דָּבָר *word* Jr 20$_1$. **2.** in ecstatic state 1 S 10$_{11}$, with music 1 C 25$_1$. **3.** of 'false' prophets 1 K 22$_{12}$||2 C 18$_{11}$ Jr 14$_{14}$ (obj. falsehood). **4.** of prophesying by (בְּ) Baal Jr 2$_8$. Preps.: לְ *to* Jr 14$_{16}$, *concerning* Jr 28$_8$; בְּ *in* name of Y. Jr 11$_{21}$, *with* falsehood Jr 5$_{31}$; אֶל *to* Am 7$_{15}$, *concerning* Ezk 13$_{16}$; עַל *against* Ezk 11$_4$, *concerning* Ezk 36$_{6}$, *to* Ezk 37$_{4}$.

Htp. 28 Pf. הִנַּבֵּאתִי, הִנַּבְּאוּ; impf. יִתְנַבֵּא; + waw וְהִתְנַבֵּיתָ; ptc. מִתְנַבֵּא; inf. הִתְנַבּוֹת—**1. prophesy, a.** of prophet giving word of Y. 1 K 22$_{8}$ (obj. good and evil) Jr 29$_{27}$. **b.** in ecstatic state Nm 11$_{25}$, with music 1 S 10$_{5}$. **c.** of 'false' prophets 1 K 22$_{10}$||2 C 18$_{9}$ Jr 14$_{14}$ (obj. vision, divination, deceit). **d.** of prophesying by (בְּ) Baal Jr 23$_{13}$. Preps.: לְ *to* Jr 29$_{27}$; בְּ *in* name of Y. Jr 26$_{20}$; מִן *out of* own heart Ezk 13$_{17}$; עַל *against* 2 C 20$_{37}$, *concerning* 1 K 22$_{8}$||2 C 18$_{7}$. **2. rave** 1 S 18$_{10}$.

→ נְבוּאָה *prophecy*, נָבִיא *prophet*, נְבִיאָה *prophet* (fem.).

נבב 4 vb.—**Qal** 4 Ptc. pass. נָבוּב; cstr. נְבוּב—pass. ptc. as adj., **hollow,** of pillar Jr 52$_{21}$, altar Ex 27$_{8}$||38$_{7}$, empty-minded man Jb 11$_{12}$.

נְבוֹ I 1 pr.n.m. **Nebo.**

נְבוֹ II 12.0.1 pl.n. **Nebo.**

נְבוֹ, see סַמְגַּר נְבוֹ *Samgar-nebo.*

[נָבוּא] *thing prophesied,* see נבא, qal.

נְבוּאָה 3.4.2 n.f.—cstr. נְבוּאַת; sf. Si נבואתם—**1. prophecy,** as word of Y. 2 C 15$_{8}$, false Ne 6$_{12}$, written 2 C 9$_{29}$. **2. giving of prophecy, office of prophet** Si 46$_{1}$. → נבא *prophesy.*

***[נָבוּב]** n.[m.] **offspring,** אִישׁ נָבוּב יְלַבְּבוֹ עַיִר *man is an offspring that an ass produces* Jb 11$_{12}$ (if em.). → נוב *bear fruit.*

נבוד 4QShirShabbc 8$_{5}$, see כָּבוֹד *glory.*

נְבוּזַרְאֲדָן 15.0.1 pr.n.m. **Nebuzaradan.**

***[נָבוֹךְ]** 0.0.1 n.[m.]—pl. cstr. נבוכי—**spring** 1QH 11$_{15}$. → נבך *pour out;* cf. מַבָּךְ *source.*

נְבוּכַדְנֶאצַּר *Nebuchadnezzar,* see נְבוּכַדְרֶאצַּר *Nebuchadrezzar.*

נְבוּכַדְרֶאצַּר 61.0.1 pr.n.m. **Nebuchadrezzar,** also (less accurately) as נְבוּכַדְנֶאצַּר **Nebuchadnezzar.**

נָבוֹן *intelligent one,* see בין ni.

נְבוּשַׁזְבָּן 1 pr.n.m. **Nebushazban.**

נָבוֹת 22 pr.n.m. **Naboth.**

נבח 1 vb.—**Qal** 1 Inf. לִנְבֹּחַ—**bark,** of dog Is 56$_{10}$.

נֹבַח I 1 pr.n.m. **Nobah.**

נֹבַח II 2 pl.n. **Nobah.**

נִבְחַז 1 pr.n.[m.] **Nibhaz.**

נִבְחַן, see נִבְחַז *Nibhaz.*

נבט 69.18.26 vb.—**Pi.** 1 + waw וְנִבַּט—**look at** (לְ) land Is 5$_{30}$.

Hi. 68.18.26 Pf. הִבִּיט, הִבַּטְתֶּם; impf. יַבִּיט; + waw וַיַּבֵּט; impv. הַבֵּט (הַבֶּט־, הַבִּיטָה), הַבִּיטוּ; ptc. מַבִּיט; inf. הַבִּיט—**1a. look,** abs. 1 S 17$_{42}$; with prep. אֶל *towards, at* Y. Ex 3$_{6}$, person 2 K 3$_{14}$, heaven Gn 15$_{5}$, serpent Nm 21$_{9}$, trouble Hb 1$_{13}$; מִן *from* heaven Is 63$_{15}$; עַל *on, at* nakedness Hb 2$_{15}$; אַחֲרֵי *behind* Gn 19$_{17}$. **b. look at, behold, see,** (1) with accus., Y. Nm 12$_{8}$, person Is 38$_{11}$, misfortune Nm 23$_{21}$. (2) with prep. בְּ *at* or of obj., light 1QS 3$_{7}$, glory 1QH 18$_{20}$, wisdom Si 51$_{21}$. **2a. consider, have regard,** abs. Ps 13$_{4}$. **b.** with prep., **have regard for** (לְ) covenant Ps 74$_{20}$; **pay attention to** (אֶל) appearance 1 S 16$_{7}$, commandments Ps 119$_{6}$. **c.** with accus., (1) **consider, have regard for** deeds of Y. Is 5$_{12}$, trouble and vexation Ps 10$_{14}$. (2) **regard favourably, accept graciously** persons Lm 4$_{16}$, peace offerings Am 5$_{22}$. **3. cause to be seen, display** light Si 43$_{1}$(Bmg) (subj. heaven).

→ מַבָּט *expectation.*

נְבָט 25.1.1 pr.n.m. **Nebat.**

***[נָבִי]** 0.0.0.3 pr.n.[m.] **Nabi.**

נָבִיא 325.5.44.2 n.m.—cstr. Q נביא; sf. נְבִיאֲךָ; pl. נְבִיאִים; cstr. נְבִיאֵי; sf. נְבִיאָיו—**prophet, 1.** of Y. Dt 18$_{15}$ 1 S 3$_{20}$; in ref. to ecstatic prophets Nm 11$_{29}$ 1 S 10$_{5}$, 'false' prophets Jr 14$_{14}$, Abraham Gn 20$_{7}$. **2.** of Asherah 1 K 18$_{19}$, Baal 1 K 18$_{19}$. **3.** Aaron as spokesman for Moses acting as a god Ex 7$_{1}$. → נבא *prophesy.*

נְבִיאָה 6.0.1 n.f. **prophet** (fem.), prophesying with song Ex 15$_{20}$, as judge Jg 4$_{4}$, giving word of Y. 2 K 22$_{14}$||2 C 34$_{22}$, opponent of Nehemiah Ne 6$_{14}$, wife of Isaiah Is 8$_{3}$. → נבא *prophesy.*

נְבָיוֹת 5 pr.n.m. **Nebaioth.**

***[נבך]** vb. **Qal, pour out** soul Ps 69$_{11}$ (if em. וָאֶבְכֶּה *and I wept* to וָאֶבְּכָה *and I poured out*).

Hi. cause to flow Ps 84$_{7}$ (if em. עֹבְרֵי בְּעֵמֶק הַבָּכָא *those who pass through the valley of Baca* to עִבְּרֵי בְּעֵמֶק הַבָּכָא *he caused brooks to flow in the valley*).

→ נֵבֶךְ I *spring;* cf. נבק *pour out.*

[נֵבֶךְ] I 1 n.[m.]—cstr. נִבְכֵי—**spring** Jb 38$_{16}$. → נבך *pour out;* cf. מַבָּךְ *source.*

***[נֵבֶךְ]** II 1 n.[m.]—cstr. נִבְכֵי—**sandy depths** Jb 38$_{16}$.

נבל I 20.1.2 vb.—**Qal** 20.1.2 Pf. נָבֵל; impf. יִבּוֹל; + waw וְנָבֵל;

ptc. נֹבֶלֶת ,נֹבֵל; inf. abs. נָבֹל; cstr. נְבֹל—**1. wither, fade, drop, decay, crumble away,** of flower Is 28₁, leaf Is 1₃₀, the wicked Ps 37₂, the world Is 24₄, mountain Jb 14₁₈. **2.** of persons, **wear oneself out** Ex 18₁₈, **lose heart** 2 S 22₄₆||Ps 18₄₆. → נְבֵלָה *corpse,* נֹבֶלֶת *withered fruit;* נַבְלוּת II *ruin;* cf. נפל II *wither.*

נבל II 5.1.1 vb.—**Qal** 1 Pf נָבַלְתָּ—**be foolish** Pr 30₃₂.

Pi. 4 Impf. תְּנַבֵּל; + waw וַיְנַבֵּל; ptc. מְנַבֵּל—**treat as a fool, spurn, dishonour** father Mc 7₆, city Na 3₆, rock of salvation Dt 32₁₅, throne of glory Jr 14₂₁.

Hi. 0.0.1 Inf. הביל—**make foolish** 4QWiles 1₁₅.

Htp. 0.1 Inf. Si התנבל—**act foolishly** Si 9₇.

→ נָבָל I *foolish,* (?) נַבְלוּת *lewdness.*

*נבל III 5.1.1 vb.—**Qal** 1 Pf. נָבַלְתָּ—**be sacrilegious** Pr 30₃₂.

Pi. 4 Impf. תְּנַבֵּל; + waw וַיְנַבֵּל; ptc. מְנַבֵּל—**treat with contempt, spurn, dishonour** Dt 32₁₅ Jr 14₂₁ Mc 7₆ Na 3₆.

Hi. 0.0.1 Inf. הביל—**dishonour** 4QWiles 1₁₅.

Htp. 0.1 Inf. התנבל—**act sacrilegiously** Si 9₇.

→ נָבָל II *outcast, sacrilegious,* נְבָלָה II *sacrilege,* (?) נַבְלוּת *lewdness.*

*נבל IV 5.1.1 vb.—**Qal** 1 Pf. נָבַלְתָּ—**act ignominiously** Pr 30₃₂.

Pi. 4 Impf. תְּנַבֵּל; + waw וַיְנַבֵּל; ptc. מְנַבֵּל—**treat ignominiously** Dt 32₁₅ Jr 14₂₁ Mc 7₆ Na 3₆.

Hi. 0.0.1 Inf. Q הביל—**dishonour, treat ignominiously** 4QWiles 1₁₅.

Htp. 0.1 Inf. התנבל—**act ignominiously** Si 9₇.

→ נָבָל IV *ignominious.*

נָבָל I 18.5.3 adj.—m.pl. נְבָלִים, f.pl. נְבָלוֹת—**1. foolish,** of people Dt 32₆, prophet Ezk 13₃, דָּבָר *word* 1QS 7₉. **2.** as noun, **fool, a.** masc. 2 S 3₃₃. **b.** fem. Jb 2₁₀. → נבל II *be foolish.*

*נָבָל II 18.5.3 adj.—m.pl. נְבָלִים, f.pl. נְבָלוֹת—**1. outcast, sacrilegious,** of people Dt 32₆, prophet Ezk 13₃, דָּבָר *word* 1QS 7₉. **2.** as noun, **outcast, sacrilegious person, a.** masc. 2 S 3₃₃. **b.** fem. Jb 2₁₀. → נבל III *treat with contempt.*

*נָבָל III 1.1 adj. **noble,** of nation Si 50₂₆; as explanation of name 1 S 25₂₅.

*נָבָל IV 18.5.3 adj.—m.pl. נְבָלִים, f.pl. נְבָלוֹת—**1. low-class, ignominious,** of people Dt 32₆, prophet Ezk 13₃, דָּבָר *word* 1QS 7₉. **2.** as noun, **low-class, ignominious person, a.** masc. 2 S 3₃₃. **b.** fem. Jb 2₁₀. → נבל IV *act ignominiously.*

נָבָל V 22 pr.n.m. **Nabal.**

נֵבֶל I 11.1.0.22 n.m.—cstr. נֵבֶל; pl. cstr. נִבְלֵי; sf. נִבְלֵיהֶם—**jar,** prob. an **amphora,** not a **leather bottle,** for storing wine 1 S 1₂₄, oil Samaria ost. 16₂; the clouds as 'jars of heaven' Jb 38₃₇.

נֵבֶל II 27.3.3 n.m.—נֵבֶל (נֶבֶל); cstr. נֵבֶל; pl. נְבָלִים; sf. נְבָלֶיךָ—**harp** 1 S 10₅.

*[נֵבֶל] III n.[m.] **young shoot, sprig** Is 28₄ (if em. נֹבֵל *fading*).

נְבָלָה 13 n.f. **sacrilege, outrage,** serious **disorderly conduct,** rather than **folly,** of sexual offence Gn 34₇, retaining devoted object Jos 7₁₅, impious speech Is 9₁₆, impious behaviour 1 S 25₂₅; **disgrace** Jb 42₈. → נבל III *be sacrilegious.*

נְבֵלָה 48.0.7 n.f.—cstr. נִבְלַת; sf. נִבְלָתוֹ ,נִבְלָתִי—**1. corpse** of humans, oft. coll. Dt 28₂₆ Is 5₂₅. **2. carcass** of animal Lv 5₂; that dies of itself Dt 14₂₁. **3. carcass** of idols, coll. Jr 16₁₈. → נבל I *wither.*

[נַבְלוּת] I 1.0.1 n.f.—sf. נַבְלֻתָהּ—**lewdness, shamelessness, sexual misconduct,** rather than **foolishness, degeneration** Ho 2₁₂ 1QS 10₂₂. → נבל II *be foolish* or III *be sacrilegious.*

*[נַבְלוּת] II 1 n.f.—sf. נַבְלֻתָהּ—**ruin, degeneration, withering away** Ho 2₁₂. → נבל I *wither.*

נְבַלָּט 1 pl.n. **Neballat.**

*נֹבֶלֶת I 1 n.f. **unripe fig(s),** or **withered fruit** Is 34₄. → נבל I *wither.*

נֹבֶלֶת II *withered,* see נבל I.

נבע I 10.6.7 vb.—**Qal** 1 Ptc. נֹבֵעַ—**gush,** of stream Pr 18₄.

Pi. 0.1 Pf. ניבע—**pour out, utter** proverbs, etc. Si 50₂₇.

Hi. 9.5.7 Pf. Si הביע; impf. יַבִּיעַ; impv. Q הביעו, Q הבענה; ptc. Si מביע—**1.** trans., **a. pour out** heat, of sun Si 43₂(B). **b.** usu. **pour out,** i.e. **spout, utter speech** Ps 19₃, folly Pr 15₂, evil Pr 15₂₈. **c.** perh. **belch** swords Ps 59₈. **2.** intrans., **a. gush out,** of stream 1QH 16₁₈. **b. burst out, shout** with joy 1QM 19₇. → מַבּוּעַ *spring,* מַבָּע *flow.*

*נבע II 1 vb.—**Hi.** 1 Impf. יַבִּיעַ—**cause ointment to ferment,** of dead flies Ec 10₁.

*נבק 1 vb.—**Qal** 1 + waw וְנָבְקָה—**1. pour, flow** (unless from בקק ni. *be devastated*), of spirit of Egypt Is 19₃. **2.** trans. **pour out** soul Ps 69₁₁ (if em. וָאֶבְכֶּה *and I wept* to וָאֶבְקָה *and I poured out*). → cf. נבך *pour out.*

*[נֶבֶשׁ] 0.0.0.1 n.[f.] (alternative form of נֶפֶשׁ)—sf. I נבשכם—**soul,** i.e. life Arad ost. 24₁₈.

נִבְשָׁן 1 pl.n. **Nibshan.**

נֶגֶב I 112.0.3 n.m.—cstr. נֶגֶב; + ה- of direction נֶגְבָּה—**1. south country, a. Negeb,** the region south of Judah 1 S 27₁₀. **b.** in ref. to Egypt Dn 11₅. **2. south,** נֶגֶב יְרוּשָׁלָם *south of Jerusalem* Zc 14₁₀, פְּאַת נֶגֶב *southern side* Ex 36₂₃ (||26₁₈ נֶגְבָּה), מִנֶּגֶב לְנַחַל *on the south of the wadi* Jos 15₇.

*נֶגֶב II 2 n.[m.] **provision** Is 30₆ Jr 13₁₉.

*[נֶגֶב] III 0.0.0.2 pr.n.[m.] **Negeb.**

*[נֶגְבִּי] 0.0.0.1 pr.n.m. **Negbi.**

נגד 371.7.32.1 vb.—**Hi.** 336.6.32 Pf. הִגִּיד; impf. יַגִּיד (יַגֵּד־); + waw וַיַּגֵּד (וַיַּגֶּד־), וָאַגִּיד; impv. הַגֵּד (הַגֶּד־), הַגִּידָה, הַגִּידוּ, הַגִּידִי; ptc. מַגִּיד, מַגֶּדֶת; inf. abs. הַגֵּד; cstr. הַגִּיד (Kt לניד)—**1a. tell, declare, announce, report, make known** word, matter Gn 44₂₄ 2 S 11₁₈, praise Is 42₁₂, vision 1 S 3₁₅, former things Is 41₂₂, secrets Jb 11₆, righteousness Ps 50₆, sins Is 3₉, vengeance Jr 50₂₈, distress Ps 142₃, one's people Est 2₁₀; with object clause introduced by כִּי *that* Gn 3₁₁, מָה *what?* Gn 29₁₅, מִי *who?* 1 K 1₂₀, אֵיפֹה *where?* Gn 37₁₆, לֵאמֹר *saying,* followed by direct speech Gn 45₂₆. Indirect obj. usu. introduced by לְ *to* Gn 3₁₁, rarely by אֶל *to* Ex 19₉, and rarely as accus. of person Dt 32₇. **b. explain, expound** to (לְ) someone, obj. riddle Jg 14₁₂, dream Dn 2₇. **2. inform against** someone Jr 20₁₀ Jb 17₅, **denounce** way, i.e. conduct, of person Jb 21₃₁ (+ עַל *to* face). **3.** perh. **invite** friends to (לְ) feast Jb 17₅. **4.** ptc. as noun, מַגִּיד **messenger** 2 S 15₁₃.

Ho. 35.1.0.1 Pf. הֻגַּד; + waw וַיֻּגַּד; inf. abs. הֻגֵּד—**be told, announced, reported,** subj. usu. impersonal Gn 22₂₀, vision Is 21₂, appointed time Si 14₁₂; thing told indicated as accus. Gn 27₄₂, as clause beginning with כִּי *that* Gn 31₂₂, לֵאמֹר *saying* Gn 22₂₀, direct speech 2 S 19₂; alw. with לְ *to* of person told.

→ נֶגֶד *in front of,* perh. נָגִיד *leader.*

נֶגֶד I 151.8.44 prep.—sf. נֶגְדּוֹ; ה- of direction נֶגְדָּה—**1.** נֶגֶד alone, **a. in front of, before, opposite** Ex 19₂ Ne 3₁₀. **b. before, in the presence of** Gn 31₃₂ Dt 31₁₁. **c. against** Jb 10₁₇, **over against** Ps 23₅. **d.** perh. **toward** Ps 52₁₁. **e.** with reflexive sf., **in front of oneself,** i.e. straight ahead Jos 6₅. **2.** נֶגְדָּה לְ **before, in the presence of** Ps 116₁₄. **3.** with prep., **a.** לְנֶגֶד (1) **in front of, before** Gn 33₁₂. (2) **before, in the presence of** Ps 39₂. (3) **opposite** Ne 12₉. (4) **against** Pr 21₃₀. (5) **comparable to** 1QH 20₃₁. (6) **over,** i.e. in charge of Ne 11₂₂. **b.** מִנֶּגֶד (1) **from before, away from (the presence of)** 1 S 26₂₀, **aloof from** Ps 38₁₂. (2) as adv., **in front, opposite, at a distance** Gn 21₁₆ Dt 32₅₂, **aloof** 2 S 18₁₃. **c.** מִנֶּגֶד לְ (1) **in front of, opposite** Jg 20₃₄. (2) **from before, from the presence of** Pr 14₇. **d.** כְּנֶגֶד (1) **corresponding to, fit for** Gn 2₁₈. (2) **before,** or perh. **in contrast with** GnzPs 1₉. **e.** עַד־נֶגֶד **as far as opposite** Ne 3₁₆. → נגד *tell.*

*[נֶגֶד] II 1 n.[m.]—sf. נֶגְדִּי—**blow, affliction** Jb 10₁₇.

*[נֶגֶד] III adj.—honest, pl. as noun, **honest things, forthright things** Pr 8₆ (if em. נְגִידִים *noble things* to נְגָדִים).

*[נִגְדָּל] n.[m.] **fortified city** Ca 6₄.₁₀ (both if em. כַּנִּדְגָּלוֹת *like bannered troops* [דגל ni. ptc.] to כְּנִגְדָּלוֹת). → גדל *be great.*

נגה 6.2 vb.—**Qal** 3 Pf. נָגַהּ; impf. יִגַּהּ—**shine,** of light Is 9₁ (+ עַל *upon*), flame Jb 18₅.

Hi. 3.2 Impf. יַגִּיהַּ—**1. give light to, brighten** darkness 2 S 22₂₉||Ps 18₂₉. **2. cause light to shine** Is 13₁₀, **cause wrath to blaze** against (עַל) Si 16₁₁.

→ נֹגַהּ I *brightness,* נְגֹהָה *brightness.*

נֹגַהּ I 19.0.7 n.f.—cstr. נֹגַהּ; sf. נָגְהָם—**brightness, shining, light** 2 S 22₁₃||Ps 18₁₃ Is 4₅. → נגה *shine.*

נֹגַהּ II 2 pr.n.m. **Nogah.**

[נְגֹהָה] 1 n.f.—pl. נְגֹהוֹת—**brightness** Is 59₉. → נגה *shine.*

נגח 11.0.3 vb.—**Qal** 4 Impf. יִגַּח—**gore,** of ox Ex 21₂₈.

Pi. 6.0.3 Impf. יְנַגַּח, נְנַגֵּחַ; ptc. מְנַגֵּחַ; inf. Q נגח—**gore, push** Dt 33₁₇ (+ בְּ *with* horns) Ps 44₆ (+ בְּ *with [help of]* Y.).

Htp. 1 Impf. יִתְנַגַּח—**join in combat** with (עִם) Dn 11₄₀.

→ נָגָח *prone to gore.*

נַגָּח $2.0.1$ adj. **prone to gore,** of ox Ex 21_{29}. → נגח *gore.*

נָגִיד $44.2.2$ n.m.—cstr. נְגִיד; pl. נְגִידִים; cstr. נְגִידֵי—**1. leader, prince, ruler, a.** in general Ps 76_{13}. **b.** king of Israel, נָגִיד עַל־עַמִּי יִשְׂרָאֵל *ruler over my people Israel* 1 S 9_{16}. **c.** prince of Tyre Ezk 28_{2}. **2. leader, commander, chief officer** of army 1 C 13_{1}, tribe 1 C 27_{16}, family 2 C 11_{22}; in fortress 2 C 11_{11}, palace 2 C 28_{7}, house of Y. Jr 20_{1}; נָגִיד עַל־הָאֹצָרוֹת *chief officer over the treasuries* 1 C 26_{24}. **3.** pl. **noble things** Pr 8_{6}. **4. Leader, Prince,** as title for God Ps 16_{8} (if em.). → (?) נגד hi. *tell.*

[נְגִינָה] $14.1.3$ n.f.—נְגִינַת; sf. נְגִינָתִי; pl. נְגִינוֹת; cstr. נְגִינוֹת; sf. נְגִינוֹתַי—**1. string music** Is 38_{20}; in psalm title Ps 4_{1}. **2. (mocking) song** Ps 69_{13} Jb 30_{9}. → נגן *play a stringed instrument.*

נגיע, see נֶגַע *stroke.*

נִגְלָה *revealed matter,* see גלה, ni.

נגן $15.1.1$ vb.—**Qal** $_{1}$ Ptc. נֹגְנִים—ptc. as noun, **musician** Ps 68_{26}.

Pi. $14.1.1$ Impf. יְנַגֵּן; ptc. מְנַגֵּן, Si מְנַגְּנוֹת; inf. נַגֵּן—**1. play (a stringed instrument)** 1 S 16_{16} Ezk 33_{32}. **2. accompany** song **with a stringed instrument** 11Q Ps[a] 27_{10}. **3.** ptc. as noun, **musician, a.** masc. 2 K 3_{15}. **b.** fem. Si 9_{4}.

→ נְגִינָה *string music.*

נֹגֵן *musician,* see נגן, qal.

נגע I $150.12.65$ vb.—**Qal** $107.3.51$ Pf. נָגַע; impf. יִגַּע, יִגְּעוּ; impv. גַּע; ptc. נֹגֵעַ, נֹגַעַת, נֹגְעִים, נֹגְעֹת; ptc. pass. נָגוּעַ; inf. נְגֹעַ, גַּעַת (נְגֹעוֹ, לִנְגֹּעַ)—**1a. touch** something Gn 3_{3}, someone sexually Gn 20_{6}, someone, causing harm Gn 26_{11}; **strike** Jb 1_{19}, with plague 1 S 6_{9}. Obj. rarely as accus. Gn 26_{29}; usu. introduced by בְּ Gn 26_{11}, also by אֶל Gn 20_{6}, עַל Is 6_{7}, לְ 4QS[d] 1_{7}. **b. reach, arrive (at), overtake,** with עַל of obj. Jg 20_{34}, אֶל of obj. Dn 9_{21}, עַד *as far as* Is 16_{8}. **c.** of time, **arrive** Ezr 3_{1}. **2.** pass. **a. be stricken, plagued** Is 53_{4} Ps 73_{14}. **b.** as noun, **one stricken, plagued** 4QWays[a] 2_{4}.

Ni. $_{1}$ + waw וַיִּנָּגְעוּ—**(pretend to) be defeated,** Jos 8_{15} (+ לִפְנֵי *before*).

Pi. $_{3}$ Pf. נִגְּעוּ; + waw וַיְנַגַּע—**strike, afflict (with plague, disease),** with accus. of person 2 K 15_{5} 2 C 26_{20}, of person and plague Gn 12_{17}.

Pu. $1.0.8$ Pf. Q נוגע; impf. יְנֻגָּעוּ; ptc. Q מנוגע—**be stricken, afflicted** Ps 73_{5} 1QSa 2_{5} (+ בְּ *in* flesh) 11QT 48_{14} (+ בְּ *with* leprosy, etc.).

Hi. $38.10.6$ Pf. הִגִּיעַ, הִגַּעְתָּ; impf. יַגִּיעַ; + waw וַיַּגַּע, וַיַּגִּיעוּ; ptc. מַגִּיעַ, מַגַּעַת; inf. הַגִּיעֵנוּ—**1. reach (as far as), extend to** Gn 28_{12} Is 8_{8} Ps 32_{6}, i.e. afford Lv 5_{7}, **reach, arrive (at), come, attain to, draw near** 1 S 14_{9} Is 30_{4} Ps 88_{4}, of time Ezk 7_{12}, **reach one's goal** Si 11_{10}, **reach an age** CD 15_{5}. With accus. Lv 5_{7}, לְ *to, at* Ps 88_{4}, אֶל *to* 1 S 14_{9}, עַד *to, as far as* Is 8_{8}, ה- of direction, *to* Gn 28_{12}. **2a. cause to touch, touch with,** thing touched introduced by לְ Ex 4_{25}, אֶל Ex 12_{22}, עַל Is 6_{7}, בְּ 4QOrd[b] 2.2_{1}. **b. cause to reach,** i.e. **extol** wisdom to (עַד) clouds Si 13_{23}, **cast down** city to (עַד) dust Is 26_{5}, wall to (אֶל) ground Ezk 13_{14}. **c. join, bring together** house to (בְּ) house Is 5_{8}. **d. bring near,** i.e. **offer** due sacrifice to (אֶל) Y. Si 50_{19}. **3. befall, happen to** (אֶל) Ec 8_{14}.

→ נֶגַע *stroke, plague,* מַגָּע *contact.*

***נגע II** $_{1}$ vb.—**Qal** $_{1}$ Inf. לִנְגוֹעַ—**rest** Jb 6_{7}.

***[נגע] III** vb. **Qal, sit** Ps 38_{12} (if em. מִנֶּגֶד נִגְעִי יַעֲמֹדוּ *they stand aloof from my plague* to מִנֶּגֶד נָגְעוּ *they sit aloof*).

נֶגַע $78.3.49$ n.m.—נָגַע; cstr. נֶגַע; sf. נִגְעִי; pl. נְגָעִים (Q נגיעים); cstr. נִגְעֵי (Q נגיעי); sf. Q נגיעי—**1. stroke, blow, assault,** in violent crime Dt 17_{8}, punishment 2 S 7_{14}. **2. plague, disease, affliction,** caused by Y. Gn 12_{17}; specif. skin disease Lv 13_{2}, in ref. to the diseased spot Lv 13_{6}, diseased person Lv 13_{4}; in cloth garment Lv 13_{47}, (walls of) house Lv 14_{34}. → נגע I *touch.*

נגף $49.0.13$ vb.—**Qal** $25.0.6$ Pf. נָגַף; impf. יִגֹּף; ptc. נֹגֵף; inf. abs. נָגֹף; cstr. לִנְגֹּף (נָגְפוֹ)—**1a. strike,** causing injury or death, of men striking woman Ex 21_{22}, ox striking ox Ex 21_{35}, person striking foot against (בְּ) stone Ps 91_{12}, Y. striking person 1 S 25_{38}. **b.** of Y., **plague** Ex 7_{27} (+ בְּ *with* frogs) 32_{35}; נגף מַגֵּפָה **strike** people **with plague** Zc 14_{12}. **2. strike down, defeat, rout** Jg 20_{35} (+ לִפְנֵי *before*). **3. stumble,** of foot Pr 3_{23}.

Ni. $23.0.6$ Pf. נִגַּף; impf. יִנָּגֵף; + waw וַיִּנָּגֶף; ptc. נִגָּף, נִגָּפִים; inf. abs. נִגּוֹף; cstr. הִנָּגֵף—**be defeated, routed** Lv 26_{17} (+ לִפְנֵי *before* enemies).

Htp. 1.0.1 Impf. יִתְנַגְּפוּ—**stumble,** of foot Jr 13_{16}.
→ נֶגֶף *striking,* מַגֵּפָה *plague.*

נֶגֶף 7.1.2 n.m.—נֶגֶף—**1a. striking,** אֶבֶן נֶגֶף *stone of striking,* i.e. which the foot strikes, causing stumbling Is 8_{14}. **b. obstacle,** against which one strikes the foot Si $35_{20(B)}$. **2. plague** Ex 12_{13}. → נגף *strike.*

נגר I 10.0.3 vb.—**Ni.** 4.0.1 Pf. נִגְּרָה; + waw Q וינגר; ptc. נִגָּרִים, נִגָּרוֹת—**1. be poured out, be spilt, flow,** of eye Lm 3_{49}, water 2 S 14_{14} (+ אַרְצָה *upon the ground*), heart 1QH 16_{32}. **2. be stretched out,** of hand Ps 77_3. **3.** fem. pl. ptc. as noun, **torrent** Jb 20_{28}.

Hi. 5.0.1 Impf. יַגִּירֵהוּ; + waw וַיַּגֵּר; וְהִגַּרְתִּי; impv. הַגִּרֵם; ptc. Q מגיר—**1a. pour** from (מִן) cup Ps 75_9. **b. pour down, hurl down** stones into (לְ) valley Mc 1_6. **2. deliver up** to power of (עַל־יְדֵי) sword Jr 18_{21}.

Ho. 1.0.1 Ptc. מֻגָּרִים—**be poured out,** of water Mc 1_4 (+ בְּ *on* slope).

*נגר II 3 vb.—**Pi.** 1 Pf. נִגְּרָה—**smite,** of hand Ps 77_3.

Hi. 2 Impf. יַגִּירֵהוּ; impv. הַגִּרֵם—**smite** with edge (עַל־יְדֵי) of sword Jr 18_{21}.

[נִגֶּרֶת] *torrent,* see נגר I, ni. §3.

נגשׂ 23.0.2 vb.—**Qal** 19.0.2 Pf. נָגַשׂ; impf. יִגֹּשׂ; ptc. נֹגֵשׂ, נֹגְשִׂים—**1. oppress** labourer Is 58_3. **2. exact (payment) from, be a creditor,** in connection with debts Dt 15_2 (accus. of person), tribute 2 K 23_{35} (accus. of person and thing exacted). **3.** ptc. as noun, **a. ruler, oppressor** Is 3_{12}. **b. taskmaster** Ex 3_7. **c. exactor (of tribute)** Dn 11_{20}. **d. (ass-)driver** Jb 39_7.

Ni. 4 Pf. נִגַּשׂ—**1. be hard pressed** 1 S 13_6. **2. be distressed** 1 S 14_{24}. **3. be oppressed** Is 53_7. **4. oppress one another** Is 3_5.

נֹגֵשׂ *oppressor, taskmaster,* etc., see נגשׂ, qal §3.

נגשׁ 125.4.31 vb.—**Qal** 68.0.7 Impf. יִגַּשׁ, יִגְּשׁוּ, יִגְּשׁוּ (יִגָּשׁוּ, יִגַּשְׁוּ); impv. גַּשׁ (גֶּשׁ־, גְּשָׁה), גְּשִׁי, גְּשׁוּ, גֹּשׁוּ (גֹּשׁוּ); inf. גֶּשֶׁת (גִּשְׁתּוֹ)—**1. draw near, approach, a.** abs. Gn 18_{23}; to (אֶל) someone Gn 43_{19}, for sexual purposes Ex 19_{15}. **b.** in legal contexts, to receive judgment Ex 24_{14}, to give judgment 1QSa 1_{13}, as legal opponent Is 50_8. **c.** of priest's approach to (אֶל) altar Ex 28_{43}. **d.** for (לְ) battle Jg 20_{23}. **2. be near to** (בְּ), of scales of crocodile Jb 41_{16}. **3. move away,** i.e. make room for (לְ) someone Is 49_{20}.

Ni. 17.0.8 Pf. נִגַּשׁ; ptc. נִגָּשִׁים; inf. Q הנגשו—**draw near, approach, a.** abs. Gn 33_7; to someone, with אֶל *to* 1 K 20_{13}, בְּ *to* Am 9_{13}. **b.** to (אֶל) place of judgment Dt 25_1. **c.** to (אֶל) Y., at Sinai Ex 19_{22}. **d.** for (לְ) battle 1 S 7_{10}.

Hi. 37.4.15 Pf. הִגִּישׁוּ; impf. יַגִּישׁ, יַגִּישׁוּ; + waw וַיַּגֶּשׁ (וַיַּגֶּשׁ, וַיַּגֶּשׁ־); impv. הַגִּישָׁה, הַגִּישׁוּ; ptc. מַגִּישׁ, מַגִּישִׁים; inf. Si הגיש (Q לניש, Si הגשת)—**1. bring near, present, bring, a.** bring a thing or person to someone, with לְ *to* 2 S 17_{29}, אֶל *to* 1 S 15_{32}, לִפְנֵי *before* 1 S 28_{25}. **b.** in cultic contexts, of offerings Ex 32_6 Lv 2_8 (+ אֶל *to* altar) Ml 1_7 (+ עַל *upon* altar). **c.** in legal contexts, of bringing evidence Is 41_{21} 45_{21}. **2.** perh. **draw** sword Jb 40_{19}.

Ho. 2.0.1 Pf. Q הוגשתי, הֻגְּשׁוּ; ptc. מֻגָּשׁ—**1. be brought near,** of feet to (לְ) fetters 2 S 3_{34}, person into (בְּ) community 1QH 6_{18}. **2. be offered,** of incense and offerings to (לְ) name of Y. Ml 1_{11}.

Htp. 1 Impv. הִתְנַגְּשׁוּ—**draw near** Is 45_{20} (+ יַחְדָּו *together*).
→ מַגָּשׁ *offering.*

נָד I *wanderer,* see נוד I *wander.*

נָד II *one grieving,* see נוד II *grieve.*

נֵד I 6.0.1 n.m.—cstr. נֵד—**heap, wall, dam, dike** of waters Ex 15_8 Jos $3_{13.16}$ Ps 78_{13}.

*נֵד II 1 n.[m.] **mist** Ex 15_8.

*נֵד III 2 n.m. **mud-bank** Jos $3_{13.16}$.

[נֹד] I 1 n.[m.]—sf. נֹדִי—**wandering** or **variability** of circumstances, thus **misery** Ps 56_9. → נוד *wander* or נדד I *flee.*

*[נֹד] II 1 n.[m.]—sf. נֹדִי—**grief, lament** Ps 56_9. → נוד II *grieve.*

*[נֹד] III n.[m.] **wineskin** Ex 15_8 (if em. נִצְּבוּ כְמוֹ־נֵד *they stood as a heap* to נִצְּבוּ כְּמוֹ נֹד *they swelled up like a wineskin*). → נֹאד *skin bottle.*

נדא 1 vb.—**Hi.** + waw Kt וידא (Qr, mss נדח hi. *drive away*)—**drive away** Israel 2 K 17_{21} (+ מֵאַחֲרֵי *from [following]* Y.).

נדב 17.1.14 vb.—**Qal** 3.1 Pf. נָדַב; impf. יִדְּבֶנּוּ—**impel, stir** someone, of heart Ex 25_2 35_{29} (+ לְהָבִיא *to bring*), spirit Ex 35_{21}.

Ni. 0.0.3 Ptc. נדבים—**offer oneself, volunteer** 1QS 1_7 (+ לעשות *to do*) 1_{11} (+ לְ *for* truth).

Pu. 0.0.1 Ptc. מנודבים—ptc. as noun, **one freely devoted** 4QapLamB 1_3.

Htp. 14.0.10 Pf. הִתְנַדַּבְתִּי; + waw וַיִּתְנַדְּבוּ; ptc. מִתְנַדֵּב; inf. הִתְנַדֵּב (־הִתְנַדֵּבָם, הִתְנַדֵּב)—**1. offer oneself, volunteer** (for war) Jg 5_2, to (לְ) Y. 2 C 17_{16}; with inf., **offer willingly** to do something Ne 11_2. **2. make a freewill offering** to (לְ) Y., with obj. נְדָבָה *freewill offering* Ezr 3_5, without obj. 1 C 29_9. **3. be given as a freewill offering** Ezr 1_6.

→ נְדָבָה *free will*, נָדִיב *willing*, נְדִיבָה *nobility*.

נָדָב 20 pr.n.m. **Nadab.**

נְדָבָה 26.0.13 n.f.—cstr. נִדְבַת; pl. נְדָבוֹת; cstr. נִדְבוֹת; sf. נִדְבֹתֶיךָ—**1a. free will, voluntariness, generosity,** אנשי נדבת מלחמה *men of the voluntariness of,* i.e. volunteers for, *battle* 1QM 7_5, גֶּשֶׁם נְדָבוֹת *rain of generosity,* i.e. abundant rain Ps 68_{10}. **b.** as adv., **freely, voluntarily, generously** Dt 23_{24} Ho 14_5. **2. freewill offering,** usu. of sacrificial offering Lv 7_{16}; of contributions for building and furnishing of sanctuary Ex 35_{29}. **3.** perh. **noble utterance** Ps 119_{108}. → נדב *impel.*

נְדַבְיָה 1.0.0.2 pr.n.m. **Nedabiah.**

נדביהו, see נְדַבְיָה *Nedabiah.*

***נִדְגָּלוֹת** I 2 n.f.pl. **admirable** or **conspicuous sights, heavenly phenomena,** perh. **stars** Ca $6_{4.10}$.

נִדְגָּלוֹת II *bannered troops,* see דגל I, ni.

נדד I 28.1.5 vb.—**Qal** 23.1.4 Pf. נָדְדוּ (נָדֵדוּ); impf. יִדּוֹד; + waw וַתִּדַּד; ptc. נוֹדֶדֶת, נֹדֵד; inf. נְדֹד—**1. flee, escape, depart,** of persons Is 21_{15} (+ מִפְּנֵי *from* sword), animals and birds Jr 9_9, sleep Gn 31_{40} (+ מִן *from* eyes). **2. wander about** Ho 9_{17} (+ בְּ *among* nations) Pr 27_8 (+ מִן *from* place) Jb 15_{23} (+ לְ *for* bread). **3. flutter** wings, as bird Is 10_{14}. **4.** ptc. as noun, **fugitive** Is 21_{14}.

Poal 1 + waw וְנוֹדֵד—**fly away,** of locusts Na 3_{17}.

Hi. 1 Impf. יְנִדֻּהוּ—**chase away, expel** someone from (מִן) world Jb 18_{18}.

Ho. 2 Impf. יֻדַּד; ptc. מֻנָד—**1. be chased away,** of person Jb 20_8. **2. be discarded,** of thorns 2 S 23_6.

Htpo. 1.0.1 Impf. יִתְנֹדֲדוּ—**flee away, recoil in horror** Ps 64_9.

→ (?) נֹד *wandering,* נְדֻדִים *restlessness,* נִדָּה II *flow of blood.*

***[נדד]** II vb. **Qal, be burned up,** of harvest Is 17_{11} (if em. נֵד *heap of* to נַד *it is burned up*).

***נדד** III 4 vb.—**Qal** 3 Impf. יִדֹּדוּן, אֶדַּדֶּה—**bow down, prostrate oneself** Is 38_{15} (unless דדה htp. *go*) Ps $68_{13.13}$.

Htpo. 1 יִתְנֹדֲדוּ—**be brought low** Ps 64_9.

נֹדֵד *fugitive,* see נדד I, qal §4.

נְדֻדִים 1 n.[m.]pl. **restlessness, tossings,** through sleeplessness Jb 7_4. → נדד I *flee.*

נדה I 2.1.1 vb.—**Pi.** 2 Ptc. מְנַדִּים, sf. מְנַדֵּיכֶם—**1. thrust aside, exclude** someone Is 66_5. **2. postpone** day Am 6_3 (לְ of obj.).

Pu. 0.0.1 Ptc. מנודה—**be excluded** 4QRitPurB 1.12_{17}.

Htp. 0.1 Impf. יתנדה—**distance oneself from** (מִן) someone Si 6_{11}.

***נדה** II 2 vb. **Qal Pass., be thrown, be hurled,** of persons, as (כְּ) stone Ex 15_{16} (if em. יִדְּמוּ *they are silent* [דמם] to יִדּוּ־ם *they are hurled* [qal pass., with enclitic mem]), into (לְ) Sheol Ps 31_{18} (if em. יִדְּמוּ to יִדּוּ־ם).

Pi. 1 Ptc. מְנַדִּים—**1. cast, fling** Ps 36_{12} (if em. תְּנִדֵנִי *let it* not *cause me to wander* [נוד hi.] to תְּנַדֵּנִי *let it* not *fling me*) Jb 18_{18} (if em. יְנִדֻּהוּ *they expel him* [נדד I hi.] to יְנַדֻּהוּ *they cast him*). **2. escape from** (לְ) day Am 6_3.

Hi. 1 + waw וַיַּדּוּ (unless from ידה pi. *throw*)—**fling** stone at (בְּ) someone Lm 3_{53}.

***נדה** III 2 vb.—**Pi.** 2 Ptc. מְנַדִּים, sf. מְנַדֵּיכֶם—**make impure, declare impure** person Is 66_5, day Am 6_3 (לְ of obj.). → נִדָּה I *impurity,* נִידָה I *impurity.*

נֵדֶה 1 n.m. **gift,** given to prostitute Ezk 16_{33}.

נִדָּה I 29.0.68 n.f.—cstr. נִדַּת; sf. נִדָּתָהּ; pl. Q נדות; cstr. Q נדות—**1. impurity,** in ref. to **a.** menstruation Lv 12_2; טְמֵאַת הַנִּדָּה *woman unclean (because) of impurity* Ezk 22_{10}, אִשָּׁה נִדָּה *a woman, impurity,* i.e. a menstruous woman Ezk 18_6. **b.** contact with corpse, מֵי נִדָּה *water of,* i.e. for removing, *impurity* Nm 19_9. **c.** prohibited marriage Lv 20_{21}. **d.** sexual intercourse CD 12_2. **e.** immorality, worship of images Ezr 9_{11}. **2. impure thing, abomination** Ezk 7_{19}, of cultic objects 2 C 29_5. → נדה III *make impure;* cf. נִידָה I *impurity.*

***נִדָּה** II 29.0.68 n.f.—cstr. נִדַּת; sf. נִדָּתָהּ; pl. Q נדות; cstr. Q נדות—**1. flow of blood,** causing ritual impurity, in ref. to **a.** menstruation Lv 12_2. **b.** contact with corpse Nm 19_9. **c.** prohibited marriage Lv 20_{21}. **d.** sexual intercourse CD 12_2. **e.** immorality, idolatry Ezr 9_{11}. **2. impure thing, abomination** Ezk 7_{19}, of cultic objects

2 C 29₅. → נדד I *flee.*

נדח I 55.3.15 vb.—**Qal** 2 impf. יִדַּח; inf. לִנְבֹּחַ—**1. thrust** axe against (עַל) tree Dt 20₁₉. **2. thrust away, banish** someone 2 S 14₁₄ (+ מִן *from*).

Ni. 24.1.8 Pf. נִדְּחָה; ptc. נִדְּחֵי, נִדָּחִים (נִדַּחַת) נִדָּחָה, נִדָּח), (נִדָּחַי)—**1. be thrust out, be driven away, be banished,** of persons Jr 40₁₂ 49₅ (+ לְפָנֵי *before* oneself, i.e. straight ahead), effective aid Jb 6₁₃ (+ מִן *from*). **2. go astray,** of animals Dt 22₁. **3. (allow oneself to) be drawn away, led astray** Dt 4₁₉. **4.** ptc. as noun, **a.** masc., **banished one(s), outcast(s)** Dt 30₄ Is 11₁₂. **b.** fem., (1) **banished one(s), outcast(s)** Jr 30₁₇ Mc 4₆. (2) **strayed one,** of sheep Ezk 34₄.

Pu. 1.0.1 Ptc. מְנֻדָּח—**1. be thrust,** אֲפֵלָה מְנֻדָּח *thrust (into) darkness* Is 8₂₂. **2.** ptc. as noun, **banished one, exile** 4QPrFêtes^c 12.1₁.

Hi. 27.2.6 Pf. הִדַּחְתִּי; impf. אַדִּיחֵם; + waw וַיַּדַּח, וַיַּדִּיחוּ; impv. הַדִּיחֵמוֹ; inf. הַדִּיחַ—**1. thrust** evil upon (עַל) someone 2 S 15₁₄. **2. thrust away, (cause to) turn aside, lead astray** persons from (מִן) way Dt 13₆, from (מֵעַל) Y. Dt 13₁₁, by means of (בְּ) smooth speech Pr 7₂₁. **3. chase away, scatter** flock Jr 23₂. **4. thrust out, drive away, banish** persons Jl 2₂₀ (+ אֶל *to*) 1QH 12₈ (+ מִן *from*), prosperity Si 8₁₉ (+ מֵעַל *from*).

Ho. 1 Ptc. מֻדָּח—**be chased away,** of gazelle Is 13₁₄.

→ מַדּוּחִים I *enticement,* II *false claims.*

***נדח** II 3 vb.—**Qal** 1 Inf. לִנְבֹּחַ—**wield** axe against (עַל) tree Dt 20₁₉.

Ni. 1 + waw וְנִדְּחָה—**be at work** with (בְּ) an axe Dt 19₅.

Hi. 1 + waw וְהִדִּיחַ—**impel** evil upon (עַל) someone 2 S 15₁₄.

***נדח** III 1 vb.—**Pu.** 1 Ptc. מְנֻדָּח—**be widespread,** of darkness Is 8₂₂.

נִדָּח *banished one(s),* see נדח I ni. §4a.

נִדַּחַת *banished one(s),* see נדח I ni. §4b.

נָדִיב 27.5.13 adj.—m.s. cstr. נְדִיב; f.s. נְדִיבָה; m.pl. נְדִיבִים; cstr. נְדִיבֵי; sf. נְדִיבֵמוֹ (Q נדיביהמה)—**1. willing,** of spirit Ps 51₁₄. **2.** as noun, **a. willing one,** נְדִיב לֵב *willing one of heart,* i.e. whose heart is willing Ex 35₂₂, כָּל־נָדִיב בַּחָכְמָה *every willing one who has a skill* 1 C 28₂₁. **b. noble (one), prince** Nm 21₁₈ 1 S 2₈. → נדב *impel.*

[נְדִיבָה] 3 n.f.—sf. נְדִבָתִי; pl. נְדִיבוֹת—**1. nobility, honour** Jb 30₁₅. **2. noble thing** Is 32₈.₈. → נדב *impel.*

[נָדָן] I 1 n.[m.]—sf. נְדָנָהּ—**sheath,** for sword 1 C 21₂₇.

[נָדָן] II 1 n.[m.]—pl. sf. נְדָנַיִךְ—**gift,** given by prostitute to lover Ezk 16₃₃.

נדף I 9.1.3 vb.—**Qal** 3.1.1 Impf. יִדְּפֶנּוּ, תִּנְדֹּף—**1. drive about, blow away** chaff Ps 1₄. **2. defeat, refute** someone Jb 32₁₃.

Ni. 6.0.2 Pf. נִדַּף; ptc. נִדָּף; inf. הִנָּדֵף—**be driven about, be blown away,** of leaf Lv 26₃₆, stubble Is 41₂, smoke Ps 68₃, vapour Pr 21₆.

***נדף** II 3 vb.—**Ni.** 3 Ptc. נִדָּף—**be dried up,** of leaf Lv 26₃₆, vapour Pr 21₆.

נדר 31.0.10 vb.—**Qal** 31 Pf. נָדַר; impf. יִדֹּר; + waw וַיִּדַּר; impv. נִדְרוּ; ptc. נֹדֵר; inf. לִנְדֹּר—**make a vow,** oft. with obj. נֶדֶר *vow* Gn 28₂₀ 31₁₃ (+ לְ *to* Y.) Nm 6₂ (+ לְהַזִּיר *to separate oneself*); without obj. Lv 27₈. → נֶדֶר *vow.*

נֶדֶר 60.0.12 n.m.—נֵדֶר; cstr. נֶדֶר (נְדֶר); sf. נִדְרִי; pl. נְדָרִים; sf. נִדְרֵיהֶם, נְדָרַי—**1. vow,** subj. of קום *stand* Nm 30₅; obj. of נדר *vow* Gn 28₂₀, עשׂה *do* Jg 11₃₉, שׁלם pi. *pay* Dt 23₂₂; נֶדֶר נָזִיר *vow of a Nazirite* Nm 6₂. **2. votive offering,** i.e. offering made in payment of a vow Lv 7₁₆. → נדר *make a vow.*

נֹהַּ 1 n.[m.] **pre-eminence** Ezk 7₁₁.

נהג I 30.4.3 vb.—**Qal** 20.4.3 Pf. נָהַג; impf. יִנְהַג, יְנַהֲגוּ; impv. נְהַג; ptc. נֹהֵג, נֹהֲגִים; pass. נְהוּגִים—**1. drive, lead (away), urge on** animals Gn 31₁₈ Is 11₆ (בְּ of obj.), cart 2 S 6₃, person Ca 8₂, captives Is 20₄, army to battle 1 C 20₁; of Y. leading Israel as (כְּ) flock Ps 80₂. **2. lead one's life, conduct oneself** Si 3₂₆. **3.** of heart, **give guidance** Ec 2₃. **4.** pass. **be led in procession** Is 60₁₁.

Pi. 10 Pf. נִהַג; impf. יְנַהֵג—**1. lead** people Is 49₁₀, **lead away,** as captives Gn 31₂₆. **2. drive on** wind Ex 10₁₃. **3. drive** chariot Ex 14₂₅.

Pu. be led away, into captivity Na 2₈ (if em. מְנֻהָגוֹת *lament,* i.e. נהג II pi.).

→ מִנְהָג *driving.*

נהג II 1 vb.—**Pi.** 1 Ptc. מְנַהֲגוֹת—**lament** Na 2₈ (or em. מְנֻהָגוֹת *led away,* i.e. נהג I pu.).

נהה I 3.1 vb.—**Qal** 2.1 + waw וְנָהָה; impv. נְהֵה—**lament, wail over** (עַל) Ezk 32₁₈; with accus. נְהִי *lamentation*

Mc 2₄, קִינָה *dirge* Si 38₁₆B).

Ni. 1 + waw וַיִּנָּהוּ—**lament** after (אַחֲרֵי) Y., i.e. follow him repentantly 1 S 7₂.

→ נְהִי *lamentation,* נְהִיָה I *lamentation,* נִי *wailing.*

*נהה II 1 vb.—**Ni.** 1 + waw וַיִּנָּהוּ—**follow after** (אַחֲרֵי) Y., i.e. adhere to him 1 S 7₂.

*נהה III 1 vb.—**Ni.** 1 + waw וַיִּנָּהוּ—**turn after** (אַחֲרֵי) Y. 1 S 7₂.

*[נָהוֹר] n.[m.] **light,** נה[ור]י אורים *lights of flames* 4QBer^a 1.2₃. → נהר II *shine.*

נְהִי 7.1 n.[m.]—נְהִי—**lamentation, wailing** Jr 9₉ Am 5₁₆. → נהה I *lament.*

*נְהִיָה I 1 n.f. **lamentation** Mc 2₄. → נהה I *lament*

נִהְיָה II *the future,* see היה I, ni.

נהל I 10.0.2 vb.—**Pi.** 9.0.2 Pf. נֵהַלְתָּ; impf. יְנַהֵל; ptc. מְנַהֵל; inf. Q נהל—**1a. lead, guide,** of Y. leading people Ex 15₁₃ (+ אֶל *to* abode) Is 49₁₀ (+ עַל *beside* springs), as sheep Is 40₁₁. **b. lead, carry on** (בְּ) asses 2 C 28₁₅. **2. supply, provide with** (בְּ) food Gn 47₁₇ (+ בְּ *in exchange for*). **3. give people rest,** of Y. 2 C 32₂₂ (+ מִסָּבִיב *on all sides*).

Htp. 1 Impf. אֶתְנַהֲלָה—**lead on, travel by stages** Gn 33₁₄.

*נהל II 10.0.2 vb.—**Pi.** 9.0.2 Pf. נֵהַלְתָּ; impf. יְנַהֵל; ptc. מְנַהֵל; inf. Q נהל—**give rest,** of Y. giving people rest Ex 15₁₃ (+ אֶל *at* abode) Is 49₁₀ (+ עַל *beside* springs) 2 C 32₂₂ (+ מִסָּבִיב *on all sides*); with human subj., give rest by means of (בְּ) food Gn 47₁₇, asses as transport 2 C 28₁₅.

Htp. 1 Impf. אֶתְנַהֲלָה—**continue on** Gn 33₁₄.

→ נַהֲלֹל I *watering place.*

*[נַהַל] 0.0.0.1 pr.n.[m.] **Nahal.**

נַהֲלָל 2 pl.n. **Nahalal.**

[נַהֲלֹל] I 1 n.[m.]—pl. נַהֲלֹלִים—**watering place** Is 7₁₉. → נהל II *give rest.*

*[נַהֲלֹל] II 1 n.[m.]—**thornbush**—pl. נַהֲלֹלִים—Is 7₁₉.

נַהֲלֹל III 1 pl.n. **Nahalol.**

נהם I 5 vb.—**Qal** 5 Impf. יִנְהֹם; + waw וְנָהַמְתָּ; ptc. נֹהֵם—**1. growl,** of lion Pr 28₁₅. **2. groan,** of persons Ezk 24₂₃. → נַהַם *growling,* נְהָמָה I *roaring.*

*[נהם] II vb.—**Pi.** or **Hi., put to sleep** Jb 11₂₀ (if em. מָנוֹס אָבַד מִנְהֶם *escape has perished from them* to מָנוֹס אִבֵּד מְנַהֵם/מַנְהִם *he who puts to sleep destroys their escape*). → cf. נום I *sleep.*

נַהַם 2 n.[m.] **growling** of lion, as descr. of king's wrath Pr 19₁₂ 20₂. → נהם I *growl.*

[נְהָמָה] I 2.0.1 n.f.—cstr. נַהֲמַת; sf. Q נהמתי—**1. roaring** of sea Is 5₃₀. **2. groaning** Ps 38₉ 1QH 18₃₃. → נהם I *growl.*

*נְהָמָה II 1 n.f.—cstr. נַהֲמַת—**yearning** of heart Ps 38₉.

נהק 2 vb.—**Qal** 2 Impf. יִנְהַק, יִנְהֲקוּ—**bray,** of wild ass Jb 6₅, outcasts Jb 30₇.

נהר I 3 vb.—**Qal** 3 Impf. יִנְהֲרוּ; + waw וְנָהֲרוּ—**flow, stream,** of nations Is 2₂ Jr 51₄₄ (both + אֶל *to*) Mc 4₁ (+ עַל *to*). → נָהָר I *river.*

נהר II 3.0.1 vb.—**Qal** 3 + waw וְנָהַרְתְּ, וְנָהֲרוּ—**shine, be radiant (with joy)** Is 60₅ Jr 31₁₂ Ps 34₆.

Hi. 0.0.1 Impf. יהיר (unless from אור hi.)—**cause stars to shine** 4QapPsB 1₅.

→ נָהוֹר *light,* נְהָרָה *light,* מִנְהָרָה *signal station.*

*נהר III 6 vb.—**Qal** 6 Impf. יִנְהֲרוּ; + waw וְנָהַרְתְּ, וְנָהֲרוּ—**1. be noisily excited** Is 60₅ Jr 31₁₂ Ps 34₆. **2. come in noisy excitement** Is 2₂ Jr 51₄₄ (both + אֶל *to*) Mc 4₁ (+ עַל *to*).

נָהָר I 119.2.11 n.m.—cstr. נְהַר; pl. נְהָרִים, נְהָרוֹת; cstr. נַהֲרֵי, נַהֲרוֹת; sf. נַהֲרוֹתֶיךָ—**1. river, stream** Gn 2₁₀ Nm 24₆; נְהַר־פְּרָת *river (of the) Euphrates* Gn 15₁₈, and oft. of Euphrates as הַנָּהָר *the river* Gn 31₂₁, or נָהָר *(the) river* Is 7₂₀; הַנָּהָר הַגָּדוֹל *the great river,* in ref. to Euphrates Gn 15₁₈, Tigris Dn 10₄. **2. flood, current** of sea Jon 2₄ Ps 93₃. → נהר I *flow.*

*[נָהָר] II n.[m.] **oil,** פְּלַגּוֹת נָהָר *streams of oil* Jb 20₁₇ (if em. נַהֲרֵי *rivers of*).

נְהָרָה 1.1 n.f. **light** Jb 3₄ Si 43₁(Bmg) (B הדרו *its splendour*). → נהר II *shine.*

נַהֲרַיִם, see אֲרָם *Aram,* §2a.

נוא 8.0.8 vb.—**Qal** 1 Impf. Kt תנואון—**restrain** Nm 32₇, see Hi. §2.

Hi. 8.0.8 Pf. הֵנִיא; impf. יָנִיא (יָנִי), Q יניאה, Q יאנה), Qr תְּנִיאוּן; inf. Q הניא—**1a. restrain, oppose,** woman in making of vow Nm 30₆. **b. annul, make ineffectual** oath made by woman CD 16₁₀. **2. discourage** the heart of someone Nm 32₇(Qr) (+ מֵעֲבֹר *from crossing over*) Nm 32₉ (+ לְבִלְתִּי־בֹא *from entering*). **3. hinder, frustrate** plans Ps 33₁₀. **4. refuse** oil Ps 141₅.

→ תְּנוּאָה *opposition.*

נוב 4.0.5 vb.—**Qal** 3 Impf. יָנוּב, יְנוּבוּן—**1. flow with wisdom** Pr 10$_{31}$. **2. be full of sap, prosper, bear fruit,** of the righteous Ps 92$_{15}$, wealth Ps 62$_{11}$.

Pol. 1.0.5 Impf. יְנוֹבֵב, ptc. Q מנובבם—**1. make flourish, cause to prosper,** obj. persons Zc 9$_{17}$. **2. produce fruit** (obj. פְּרִי), of land 11QM 1.2$_{10}$, tree 1QH 16$_{13}$.

→ נְבוֹב *offspring,* נוֹב I *fruit,* II *speech,* נִיב *fruit,* תְּנוּבָה *produce;* cf. נפף *sprinkle.*

[נוֹב] 1.2 n.[m.]—cstr. Kt נוב—**fruit** of lips, i.e. praise Is 57$_{19(Kt)}$; item of jewellery Si 35$_{5(Bmg)}$. → נוב *bear fruit.*

נובי, see נֵיבַי *Nebai.*

נוגות, see יגה I *be grieved.*

נוד I 24.2.1 vb.—**Qal** 18.2.1 Pf. נָדוּ; impf. יָנוּד, impv. נוּדִי, נֻדוּ; ptc. נָד; inf. נוּד—**1. sway,** of reed 1 K 14$_{15}$. **2a. wander, flee,** of humans and animals Jr 4$_{1}$ Jr 50$_{3}$, birds Pr 26$_{2}$. **b.** ptc. as noun, **wanderer** Gn 4$_{12}$. **3. shake head,** i.e. **show grief, sympathize for** (לְ) someone Jr 15$_{5}$.

Hi. 3.1 Impf. יָנִיד; inf. הָנִיד—**1. cause to wander, cause to flee** 2 K 21$_{8}$ (+ מִן *from*) Ps 36$_{12}$, i.e. make destitute Si 34$_{2(B)}$. **2. shake the head** Jr 18$_{16}$ (בְּ of obj.).

Htpol. 3 Impf. תִּתְנוֹדֵד; + waw וְהִתְנוֹדְדָה; ptc. מִתְנוֹדֵד—**1. sway, move to and fro,** of earth Is 24$_{20}$ (+ כְּ *as* hut). **2. shake the head,** in mockery Jr 48$_{27}$. **3. pity oneself** Jr 31$_{18}$.

→ נֹד I *wandering,* נִיד *shaking,* נִידָה II *shaking of head,* מָנוֹד *shaking.*

***נוד** II 1 vb.—**Qal** 1 Ptc. נוּד—ptc. as noun, **one grieving, lamenter** Ps 69$_{21}$. → נֹד II *grief.*

נוֹד 1 pl.n. **Nod.**

נוֹדָב 1 pr.n.m. **Nodab.**

נוה I 2 vb.—**Qal** 2 Impf. יִנְוֶה; ptc. נָוַת—**1. dwell, remain** Hb 2$_{5}$. **2.** fem. ptc. as noun, **(female) dweller, inhabitant** (unless from נָאוֶה *comely*) Ps 68$_{13}$. → נָוֶה *habitation,* נָוָה *pasture.*

נוה II 1.1 vb.—**Hi.** 1 Impf. אַנְוֵהוּ—**glorify,** or **beautify** Y. Ex 15$_{2}$.

Htp. 0.1 Impf. יתנוה—**boast** Si 13$_{3}$.

→ cf. נאה *be fitting, comely.*

***נוה** III 2 vb.—**Qal** 1 Impf. יִנְוֶה—**aim at, achieve, settle** Hb 2$_{5}$.

Hi. 1 Impf. אַנְוֵהוּ—**admire** Y. Ex 15$_{2}$.

[נָוָה] I 14 n.f.—cstr. נְוַת; pl. נְוֹת; cstr. נְאוֹת—**1. pasture, meadow,** נְאוֹת מִדְבָּר *pastures of the steppe* Jr 9$_{9}$. **2. habitation, abode** Lm 2$_{2}$; נְוַת צִדְקֶךָ *habitation of your righteousness,* i.e. your rightful habitation Jb 8$_{6}$. → נוה I *dwell.*

[נָוָה] II *(female) dweller,* see נוה I *dwell.*

נָוֶה I 32.1 n.m.—cstr. נְוֵה; sf. נָוְךָ, נָוֵהוּ, נְוֵהֶם—**1. habitation, abode** of Y. Ex 15$_{13}$, Israel Jr 10$_{25}$, jackals Is 34$_{13}$; in ref. to house Pr 21$_{20}$, city Is 27$_{10}$, land Jr 31$_{23}$. **2. pasture, grazing land, meadow,** for sheep 2 S 7$_{8}$ ||1 C 17$_{7}$, camels Ezk 25$_{5}$. → נוה I *dwell.*

***[נָוֶה]** II 0.0.0.1 pr.n.[m.] **Naveh.**

נוח I 142.17.14.1 vb.—**Qal** 33.10.2.1 Pf. נָחוּ, נַחְתִּי; impf. יָנוּחַ; + waw וַיָּנוּחוּ, וַיָּנַח, וַנָּחְנוּ; inf. abs. נוֹחַ; cstr. נוּחַ (נוֹחַ, נחה)—**1a. rest, settle down,** of person Pr 21$_{16}$ (+ בְּ *in*), animals and birds 2 S 21$_{10}$ (+ עַל *upon*), spirit Nm 11$_{25}$ (+ עַל), ark Nm 10$_{36}$. **b. rest upon** (עַל), i.e. form alliance with Is 7$_{2}$. **2. have rest, repose,** of Y. Ex 20$_{11}$, humans Dt 5$_{14}$ Est 9$_{22}$ (+ מִן *from*), animals Ex 23$_{12}$; subj. impersonal Jb 3$_{13}$ (+ לְ *to* someone). **3. cease (speaking)** 1 S 25$_{9}$. **4. wait quietly for** (לְ) Hb 3$_{16}$.

Hi. A. 33.2.4 Pf. הֵנִיחַ; impf. יָנִיחַ; + waw וַיָּנַח, וַהֲנִחֹתִי; impv. הָנִיחוּ; ptc. מֵנִיחַ; inf. הָנִיחַ (הָנִיחִי)—**1. cause to rest, give rest to,** usu. with לְ *to* or of obj., of Y. giving rest from (מִן) enemies Dt 12$_{10}$; with accus., of son giving rest to parent Pr 29$_{17}$. **2. pacify, satisfy anger** upon (בְּ) someone Ezk 5$_{13}$. **3. relieve** pain with (בְּ) medicine Si 38$_{7}$. **4. quieten, still, cause to cease,** obj. sound of alarm 1QM 17$_{14}$. **5.** (as Hi. B), **cause to rest upon, set down, lower, place** person Ezk 40$_{2}$ (+ אֶל *upon*), hand Ex 17$_{11}$, spirit Zc 6$_{8}$ (+ בְּ *in*), blessing Ezk 44$_{30}$ (+ אֶל).

Hi. B. 71.5.8 Pf. הִנִּיחַ, הִנִּיחוּ; impf. יַנִּיחַ; + waw וַיַּנַּח, וַיַּנִּיחוּ; impv. הַנַּח (הַנִּיחָה), הַנִּיחוּ; ptc. מַנִּיחַ; inf. הַנִּיחוֹ—**1. place, set down, lower, set aside** person Gn 2$_{15}$ (+ בְּ *in*) 1 K 13$_{29}$ (+ אֶל *upon*) Is 14$_{1}$ (+ עַל *upon*), image of god Is 46$_{7}$ (+ תַּחַת *beneath,* i.e. in its place), manna Ex 16$_{33}$ (+ לִפְנֵי *before*). **2. leave, leave behind, leave over, abandon** person Nm 32$_{15}$ (+ בְּ *in*) 2 S 20$_{3}$ (+

לִשְׁמֹר *to keep*) Jr 43_6 (+ אֵת *with*), (product of) toil Ec 2_{18} (+ לְ *to*), place Ec 10_4. **3a. let alone, allow to remain, leave undisturbed,** with accus. nation Jg 2_{23}; with לְ of obj. Y. Ex 32_{10}, human 2 S 16_{11}. **b. leave vessels unweighed** 1 K 7_{47}. **4. let go of** person Jg 16_{26}, hand Ec 7_{18}. **5.** with inf., **allow, permit** to do something Ps 105_{14} Ec 5_{11}.

Ho. A. 1 Pf. הוּנַח—**be given rest,** subj. impersonal Lm 5_5 (+ לְ *to*).

Ho. B. 5 + waw הֻנִּיחָה; ptc. מֻנָּח—**1. be placed, deposited,** of ephah Zc 5_{11} (+ עַל *upon*). **2a. be left free** Ezk 41_9. **b.** ptc. as noun, **free space, open space** Ezk 41_{11}.

→ נוֹחַ *resting place,* נוּחָה *rest,* נוֹחָה I *respite,* מָנוֹחַ I *resting place,* מְנוּחָה *resting place,* נִיחֹחַ *soothing,* נַחַת II *quietness,* הֲנָחָה *giving of rest.*

*נוח II 1 vb.—**Qal** 1 Impf. אָנוּחַ—**sigh** Hb 3_{16} (+ לְ *on account of*). → מִנְחָה *complaint;* cf. אנח *sigh.*

[נוֹחַ] 1.0.2 n.[m.]—sf. נוּחֶךָ—**1. resting place** of Y. 2 C 6_{41}. **2. softness, low pitch,** of trumpet signal to troops 1QM 8_7. → נוח I *rest.*

*[נוֹחָה] I n.f. **respite** Jg 20_{43} (if em. מְנוּחָה *[at] the resting place* to מְנוֹחָה *without respite*). → נוח I *rest;* cf. נוחה *rest.*

נוֹחָה II 1 pr.n.m.—**Nohah.**

*[נוּחָה] 0.1 n.f.—cstr. נוחת—**rest** Si 30_{17}. → נוח I *rest;* cf. נוֹחָה *respite.*

נוט 1 vb.—**Qal** 1 Impf. תָּנוּט—**shake, quake,** of the earth Ps 99_1.

*[נָוִי] 0.0.0.1 pr.n.m. **Navi.**

*[נוֹיָה] 0.0.0.1 pr.n.f. **Noijah.**

נוית, see נָיוֹת *Naioth.*

נוֹכֵל *deceitful one,* see נכל, qal.

נוכרי, see נָכְרִי *foreign.*

*[נָוֶל] n.m. **thread (of life)** Ezk 37_{11} (if em. נִגְזַרְנוּ לָנוּ *we have indeed been cut off* to נִגְזַר נָוְלֵנוּ *our thread has been cut off*).

נוּם I 6.1.4 vb.—**Qal** 6.1.4 Pf. נָמוּ; impf. יָנוּם; ptc. Q נָם; inf. נוּם—**be drowsy, fall asleep, slumber** Is 5_{27} Ps 76_6 (+ accus. שֵׁנָה *[with] sleep*). → נוֹם *sleep,* נוּמָה *drowsiness,* תְּנוּמָה *slumber;* cf. נהם II *sleep.*

*נוּם II vb. **Qal, speak** Is 41_{27} (if em. הִנֵּה הִנָּם *behold, behold them* to הִנְנִי נָם *behold, I am speaking*). → cf. נאם *utter oracle.*

*[נוֹם] n.[m.] **sleep,** בֶּן־הַנֹּם *son of sleep,* i.e. child about to be sacrificed (play on son of Hinnom) Jr 7_{32}. → נום I *be drowsy.*

נוּמָה 1.4 n.f. **drowsiness, slumber** Pr 23_{21} Si $34_{1.2}$. → נום I *be drowsy.*

*[נוֹמוֹס] 0.0.2 n.[m.]—**custom** (Greek νόμος) 5/6ḤevBA $46_{6.8}$.

נון, see נין *increase,* qal.

נוּן 30.1.1 pr.n.m. **Nun.**

נוס I 158.2.3 vb.—**Qal** 154.2.2 Pf. נָסְתִּי, נָס; impf. יָנוּס; + waw וַיָּנָס (וַיָּנֹס); impv. נֻסוּ; ptc. נָס; inf. abs. נֹס, cstr. נוּס—**1. flee (away), escape, go away,** of persons Gn 14_{10}, vigour Dt 34_7, sea Ps 114_3, shadow Ca 2_{17}; with prep. לְ *to* 1 S 4_{10}, אֶל *to* Nm 35_{32}, מִן *from* Zc 2_{10}, לִפְנֵי *before* Dt 28_7, מִפְּנֵי *from (before)* Ex 14_{25}, ה- of direction, *towards* Jg 20_{45}. **2.** ptc. as noun, **fugitive, escaped one** Jr 48_{45}.

Polel 1 Pf. נֹסְסָה—of wind, **drive on** (בְּ of obj.) river Is 59_{19}.

Hi. 5.0.1 Pf. הֵנִיס; impf. יָנִיסוּ; inf. הָנִיס—**1a. put to flight** Dt 32_{20}. **b. cause to flee (for safety)** Ex 9_{20} (+ אֶל *to*). **c. remove (to a safe place)** or perh. **conceal** Jg 6_{11} (+ מִפְּנֵי *from [before]*). **2. flee** Jg $7_{21(Kt)}$.

Htpol. 1 Inf. הִתְנוֹסֵס (unless from נסס htpo. *rally to the banner*)—**flee (for safety)** Ps 60_6 (+ מִפְּנֵי *from [before]*).

→ מָנוֹס *flight,* מְנוּסָה *flight,* נֵס III *means of flight,* נִיס *fugitive.*

*נוס II 1 vb.—**Qal** 1 Pf. נָסָה—**tremble** Is 10_{29}. → נֵס II *trembling;* cf. נסס III *sway.*

*נוס III 1 vb.—**Qal** 1 Pf. נָס—**dry up** Dt 34_7.

*נוס IV 1 vb.—**Qal** 1 Impf. יָנוּס—**swing, dangle** Is 30_{16} (+ עַל *upon* horse). → cf. נסס III *sway.*

נוע I 41.3.3 vb.—**Qal** 25.1 Pf. נָעוּ; impf. תָּנוּעַ; + waw וַיָּנַע; ptc. נָע; inf. abs. נוֹעַ; cstr. נוּעַ—**1. tremble, quiver, sway, swing to and fro, stagger,** of persons Ex 20_{18} Ps 107_{27} (+ כְּ *as* drunkard), olive tree Jg 9_9 (+ עַל *over* trees), doorpost Is 6_4 (+ מִן *at* voice), images of gods Is 19_1 (+ מִפְּנֵי *[from] before* Y.). **2. wander, roam,** or perh. **beg by going around as a suppliant,** in (בְּ) street

Lm 4₁₄, to (אֶל) city Am 4₈, from (מִן) sea to (עַד) sea Am 8₁₂. 3. ptc. as noun, **vagabond, wanderer** Gn 4₁₂.

Ni. 2 Impf. יִנּוֹעַ—**be shaken,** of fig tree Na 3₁₂, perh. grain with (בְּ) sieve Am 9₉.

Hi. 14.2.1 Pf. הֵנִיעָה; impf. יָנִיעַ (יָנַע); + waw וַהֲנִעוֹתִי; וַיְּנִעוּ; impv. הֲנִיעֵמוֹ—**1a. shake** head (in scorn) 2 K 19₂₁‖Is 37₂₂ (+ אַחֲרֵי *behind*) Lm 2₁₅ (+ עַל *at*), hand Zp 2₁₅, Israel Am 9₉ (+ בְּ *among* nations). **b. set** person **shaking** onto (עַל) hands and knees Dn 10₁₀. **2. disturb, move** bones 2 K 23₁₈. **3. cause** someone **to wander** Nm 32₁₃ (+ בְּ *in*) 2 S 15₂₀ (+ עִם *with*).

Htpol. 0.0.2 + waw ויתנועעו—**tremble,** of heart 4QDiscourse 2.2₇.

→ מְנַעַנְעַ *sistrum.*

*נוע II 5 vb.—**Qal** 5 Ptc. נָע; inf. נוּעַ—**1. be rootless, without support,** of tree Jg 9₉. **2.** ptc. as noun, **rootless person** Gn 4₁₂.

נוֹעַדְיָה 2 pr.n.m.&f. **Noadiah.**

נוף I 35.7.6.1 vb.—**Polel** 1 Impf. יְנֹפֵף—**wave hand, shake fist,** in hostility Is 10₃₂(Qr).

Hi. 33.7.6.1 Pf. הֵנִיף, הֵנַפְתָּ, הֲנִיפוֹתִי; impf. תָּנִיף; + waw וַיָּנֶף; impv. הָנִיפוּ; ptc. מֵנִיף; inf. הָנִיף (הֲנָפָה, הֲנִיפְכֶם)—**1. wield** tool Ex 20₂₅ (+ עַל *over*), javelin Si 46₂ (+ עַל *against*). **2a. wave** the hand, in healing 2 K 5₁₁ (+ אֶל *over*), hostility Zc 2₁₃ (+ עַל *over, against*), as signal Is 13₂. **b. stretch out** the hand, to do something 1QH 16₂₂. **3. wave** an offering, **a.** with accus. of thing waved before (לִפְנֵי) Y.: sheaf Lv 23₁₁, grain offering Nm 5₂₅. **b.** with accus. תְּנוּפָה *(as a) wave offering* and of thing waved, (1) before (לִפְנֵי) Y.: Levites Nm 8₁₁, lamb Lv 14₁₂, thigh Lv 9₂₁. (2) to (לְ) Y.: gold objects Ex 35₂₂. **4.** of Y., **shake to and fro, sift** nations with (בְּ) sieve Is 30₂₈, mountains Si 43₁₆(M).

Ho. 1 Pf. הוּנַף—**be waved,** of offering Ex 29₂₇.

→ נָפָה I *sieve,* הֶנֶף *waving,* הֲנִיפָה *waving,* תְּנוּפָה I *wave offering.*

*נוף II 2.1.4 vb.—**Qal** 1 Pf. נַפְתִּי—**sprinkle** bed **with** myrrh, etc. Pr 7₁₇.

Hi. 1.1.4 Pf. Q הניפותה; Impf. תָּנִיף—**sprinkle, shed** rain Ps 68₁₀, spirit 1QH 4₂₆ (+ עַל *upon*) 15₇ (+ בְּ *upon*).

→ cf. נפף *sprinkle.*

*[נוף] III vb. **Qal, bow down** Ps 88₁₆ (if em. אָפוּנָה perh. *I am helpless* to אָנוּפָה *I bow down*).

*נוף IV 20.0.1 vb.—**Hi.** 20.0.1 Pf. הֵנִיף; impf. יְנִיפֶנּוּ; + waw וְהֵנַפְתָּ; וַיָּנֶף; inf. הָנִיף (הֲנִיפְכֶם)—**declare superfluous, treat as a special contribution,** in presenting it at the altar, **a.** with accus. of thing presented before (לִפְנֵי) Y.: sheaf Lv 23₁₁, grain offering Nm 5₂₅. **b.** with accus. תְּנוּפָה *(as a) special contribution* and of thing presented, (1) before (לִפְנֵי) Y.: Levites Nm 8₁₁, lamb Lv 14₁₂, thigh Lv 9₂₁. (2) to (לְ) Y.: gold objects Ex 35₂₂.

→ תְּנוּפָה III *special contribution.*

נוף V 35.7.6.1 vb.—**Polel** 1 Impf. יְנֹפֵף—**raise hand,** in hostility Is 10₃₂(Qr).

Hi. 33.7.6.1 Pf. הֵנִיף, הֵנַפְתָּ, הֲנִיפוֹתִי; impf. תָּנִיף; + waw וַיָּנֶף; impv. הָנִיפוּ; ptc. מֵנִיף; inf. הָנִיף (הֲנָפָה, הֲנִיפְכֶם)—**1. raise, wield** tool Ex 20₂₅ (+ עַל *over*), javelin Si 46₂ (+ עַל *against*). **2a. raise** the hand, in healing 2 K 5₁₁ (+ אֶל *over*), hostility Zc 2₁₃ (+ עַל *over, against*), as signal Is 13₂. **b. stretch out** the hand, to do something 1QH 16₂₂. **3. raise, present** an offering , **a.** with accus. of thing presented before (לִפְנֵי) Y.: sheaf Lv 23₁₁, grain offering Nm 5₂₅. **b.** with accus. תְּנוּפָה *(as an) offering* and of thing presented, (1) before (לִפְנֵי) Y.: Levites Nm 8₁₁, lamb Lv 14₁₂, thigh Lv 9₂₁. (2) to (לְ) Y.: gold objects Ex 35₂₂.

Ho. 1 Pf. הוּנַף—**be presented,** of offering Ex 29₂₇.

→ נֶפֶת *height,* תְּנוּפָה II *raised offering.*

*נוף VI 1 vb.—**Hi.** 1 Impf. תָּנִיף—**deliver** rain **in large measure** Ps 68₁₀.

נוֹף I 1 n.[m.] **height,** יְפֵה נוֹף *fair of height* Ps 48₃.

נוֹף II 1 pl.n. **Memphis.**

*נוץ I 1 vb.—**Qal** 1 Pf. נָצוּ—**flee, go away** (unless from נצה III *fly* or IV *hasten*) Lm 4₁₅.

*נוץ II 1.0.1 vb.—**Pol.** 1.0.1 Ptc. נֹצְצִים—**sparkle** (unless from נצץ *sparkle*) Ezk 1₇. → cf. נצץ I *sparkle,* נסס II *sparkle.*

נוֹצָה 4 n.f.—sf. נֹצָתָהּ—**plumage, feathers** Lv 1₁₆ Ezk 17₃.

*[נוֹר] 0.1 n.[m.]—sf. נורה—**fire** of the sun Si 43₄. → ניר II *shine.*

נוש I 1 vb.—**Qal** 1 + waw וָאָנוּשָׁה—**be sick** Ps 69₂₁.

*נוש II vb.—**Qal** 1 + waw וָאָנוּשָׁה—**tremble** Ps 69₂₁.

*[נוֹתוֹס] 0.0.1 pr.n.m. **Nothos.**

נזה I 24.0.17 vb.—**Qal** 4 Impf. יַזֶּה (יִז); + waw וַיִּז—intrans., **spurt, spatter,** of (subj. מִן *some of*) blood Lv 6_{20} (+ עַל *upon*) 2 K 9_{33} (+ אֶל *upon*).

Hi. 20.0.16 Impf. יַזֶּה; + waw וַיַּז ,וְהִזָּה; impv. הַזֵּה; ptc. מַזֶּה; inf. Q הזות—**1. sprinkle, spatter** (obj. oft. מִן *some of* or implied by context) blood Lv 4_{17} (+ לִפְנֵי *before*), water Lv 14_{51} (+ אֶל *upon*), oil Lv 8_{11} (+ עַל *upon*), spirit 1QS 4_{21}. **2. sprinkle** nations Is 52_{15}, flesh with (בְּ) water 1QS 3_9.

Ho. 0.0.1 Pf. הוזו—**be sprinkled,** of skin, garments and vessels 4QD[f] 2_{11}.

→ מַזֶּה *spurt,* הַזָּיָה *sprinkling.*

נזה II 1 vb.—**Qal, leap to one's feet,** in respect Is 52_{15} (if em.; see Hi.).

Hi. 1 Impf. יַזֶּה—**cause to leap, startle** nations Is 52_{15} (or em. יָזֻו *they will leap,* i.e. qal).

נָזִיד 6 n.[m.]—cstr. נְזִיד—**pottage, stew** Gn 25_{29} 2 K 4_{38}; of lentils Gn 25_{34}. → זיד *boil.*

נָזִיר I 16.1 n.m.—cstr. נְזִיר; sf. נְזִירֶךָ; pl. נְזִרִים; sf. נְזִירֶיהָ—**1. consecrated one, prince** Gn 49_{26} Lm 4_7. **2. Nazirite,** one dedicated to Y. by vow that prescribes growing hair, avoiding contact with corpse, and abstaining from wine Nm 6_2 Jg 13_5. **3. untrimmed vine** Lv $25_{5.11}$. → נזר I *consecrate.*

*[נָזִיר] II 2 n.[m.]—cstr. נְזִיר—**accursed one,** of Joseph Gn 49_{26} Dt 33_{16}.

נזל 16.1.1 vb.—**Qal** 15.1.1 Pf. נָזְלוּ (נָזְלוֹ); impf. יִזַּל ,יִזְּלוּ; ptc. נוֹזְלִים—**1a. flow, trickle,** of water Nm 24_7. **b. distil,** of word Dt 32_2 (+ כְּ *as* dew). **c. waft,** of perfume Ca 4_{16}. **2.** trans., **flow with, pour out, rain down,** of eyelids with water Jr 9_{17}, clouds with rain Jb 36_{28}. **3.** ptc. as noun, **a. stream, flood** Ex 15_8 Is 44_3. **b.** perh. **irrigator,** נֵד נֹזְלִים *dike(s) of irrigators* Ex 15_8.

Hi. 1 Pf. הִזִּיל—**cause water to flow** from (מִן) rock Is 48_{21}.

→ מַזָּל *flow.*

נֶזֶם 17 n.m.—cstr. נֶזֶם; sf. נִזְמָהּ; pl. נְזָמִים; cstr. נִזְמֵי—**ring,** for nose Gn 24_{47}, ears Ex 32_2.

*נזף 0.1 vb.—**Hi.** 0.1 Impf. תַּזִּיף—**reprove, rebuke** Si 11_7.

[נֵזֶק] 1 n.[m.]—cstr. נֵזֶק—**injury,** or perh. **trouble** Est 7_4.

נזר I 10.0.7 vb.—**Ni.** 4.0.6 Pf. Q נזרו; impf. יִנָּזֵר; impv. Q הנזר; + waw וַיִּנָּזְרוּ; inf. abs. הִנָּזֵר; cstr. Q הנזור—**1. consecrate oneself** to (לְ) shame, i.e. Baal Ho 9_{10}. **2. separate oneself, abstain** from (מִן) people CD 8_8, wealth CD 6_{15}; from following (מֵאַחֲרֵי) Y. Ezk 14_7. **3. keep oneself away** from (מִן), i.e. **respect as sacred** holy things Lv 22_2. **4. fast** Zc 7_2.

Hi. 6.0.1 Impf. יַזִּיר; + waw וְהִזִּיר; inf. הַזִּיר—**1. consecrate oneself** to (לְ) Y. (as a Nazirite) Nm 6_2. **2. separate oneself, abstain** from (מִן) wine Nm 6_3, fornication CD 7_1. **3. consecrate, separate** someone from (מִן) uncleanness Lv 15_{31}, one's days to (לְ) Y. Nm 6_{12}.

→ נָזִיר I *consecrated one,* נֵזֶר I *consecration,* מִנְזָר I *consecrated one.*

*נזר II 1 vb.—**Hi.** 1 + waw וְהִזַּרְתֶּם—**guard, warn against** (מִן) uncleanness Lv 15_{31}.

נֵזֶר I 25.0.3 n.m.—cstr. נֵזֶר; sf. נִזְרוֹ—**1. consecration, separation, Naziriteship,** נֵזֶר אֱלֹהָיו *consecration of,* i.e. to, *his God* Nm 6_7, רֹאשׁ נִזְרוֹ *head of his consecration,* i.e. his consecrated head Nm 6_9. **2. hair (of consecration),** of Nazirite Nm 6_{19}, of woman, grown long Jr 7_{29}. **3. crown, diadem,** as a sign of consecration, of king 2 S 1_{10}, high priest Ex 29_6. → נזר I *consecrate.*

*נֵזֶר II 9.0.1 n.m.—cstr. נֵזֶר; sf. נִזְרוֹ—**flower,** on head of king 2 S 1_{10}, turban of high priest Ex 29_6.

נֹחַ 46.1.14 pr.n.m. **Noah.**

*[נחב] vb. **Ni., be lean, dry up,** of voice Jb 29_{10} (if em. נֶחְבָּאוּ *they were hidden* to נִחַב *it was dried up*).

נַחְבִּי 1 pr.n.m. **Nahbi.**

נחה I 39.0.1 vb.—**Qal** 11 Pf. נָחִיתָ; impv. נְחֵה—**lead, guide** someone (subj. usu. Y.) Gn 24_{27} (+ בְּ *in* way) 32_{34} (+ אֶל *to*) Ps 60_{11} (+ עַד *to*) 77_{21} (+ כְּ *as* flock).

Hi. 28.0.1 Pf. הִנְחַנִי; impf. תַּנְחֵה; inf. לְהַנְחֹתָם (לַנְחֹתָם)—**lead, guide, bring** someone (subj. oft. Y.) Gn 24_{48} (+ בְּ *in* way) Nm 23_7 (+ מִן *from*) Ps 107_{30} (+ אֶל *to*).

*נחה II 1 vb.—**Qal** 1 Pf. נָחָה—**support, stand by** Is 7_2 (+ עַל *beside*).

*נחה III 2 vb.—**Qal** 1 Pf. נָחָה—**incline towards** (עַל) Is 7_2.

Ni. 1 + waw וַיִּנָּהוּ—**follow after** (אַחֲרֵי) Y. 1 S 7₂.

Pi. aim bow 2 S 22₃₅||Ps 18₃₅ (if em. וְנִחֲתָה/וְנִחַת *and it lowers* [נחת pi.] to וְנִחַת *and it aims*), arrows at (בְּ) Ps 38₃ (if em. נִחֲתוּ *they sink* [נחת ni.] to נָחֲתָה *you aim*).

*נחה IV 1 vb.—**Qal** 1 Pf. נָחָה—**ally oneself** Is 7₂ (+ עַל *with*).

נַחוּם 1.0.0.27 pr.n.m. **Nahum.**

נְחוּם 1 pr.n.m. **Nehum.**

*[נִחוּמִים] I 1 n.[m.]pl.—sf. נִחוּמָי (unless from נִחֻמִים *compassion*)—**inward parts** Ho 11₈.

[נִחוּמִים] II, see נִחֻמִים *comfort.*

נָחוֹר 18 pr.n.m. **Nahor.**

נָחוּשׁ 1 n.[m.] **bronze** Jb 6₁₂. → cf. נְחוּשָׁה *copper,* נְחֹשֶׁת *copper.*

נְחוּשָׁה I 10.0.3 n.f.—נְחֻשָׁה—**1. copper** Jb 28₂. **2. bronze** bow 2 S 22₃₅||Ps 18₃₅, doors Is 45₂, tubes Jb 40₁₈. → cf. נָחוּשׁ *bronze,* נְחֹשֶׁת *copper.*

*נְחוּשָׁה II 1 n.f.—**enchantment,** קֶשֶׁת־נְחוּשָׁה *bow of enchantment,* i.e. enchanted bow 2 S 22₃₅||Ps 18₃₅. → נחשׁ I *practise divination.*

[נְחוּשֶׁת], see נְחֹשֶׁת *copper.*

נְחִילוֹת I 1 n.f.pl.—**flutes,** in psalm title Ps 5₁. → cf. חָלִיל *flute.*

*נְחִילוֹת II 1 n.f.pl.—**sickness,** in psalm title Ps 5₁. → חלה I *be sick.*

*נְחִילוֹת III 1 n.f.pl.—**inheritances,** in psalm title Ps 5₁. → נחל I *inherit.*

[נָחִיר] 1 n.[m.]—du. sf. נְחִירָיו—**nostril** of Leviathan Jb 41₁₂. → נחר I *snort.*

נחל I 59.7.34 vb.—**Qal** 30.4.17 Pf. נָחַלְתִּי; impf. יִנְחַל; + waw וַיִּנְחֲלוּ; ptc. Si נוחל; inf. נְחֹל—**1a. inherit, take possession of, hold as a possession** an inheritance (נַחֲלָה) Nm 18₂₃, land Ex 23₃₀, vanity Jr 16₁₉, honour Pr 3₃₅; of Y. inheriting Israel Ex 34₉. **b.** without obj., **have an inheritance** Nm 18₂₀. **2. divide, distribute** land **as an inheritance** Nm 34₁₇ (+ לְ *for* Israelites) Jos 19₄₉ (+ לְ *according to* borders).

Pi. 4 Pf. נִחַל; inf. נַחֵל—**1. allocate portions to,** with accus. of recipient Nm 34₂₉. **2. distribute** inheritance by (בְּ) lot Jos 19₅₁.

Hi. 17.2.16 Pf. הִנְחַלְתִּי; impf. יַנְחִיל; ptc. מַנְחִיל; inf. הַנְחִיל (הַנְחִילוֹ, הַנְחֵל)—**1. cause to inherit, give as an inheritance to,** with accus. of recipient and thing inherited: Israelites, land Dt 1₃₈, the poor, a seat of honour 1 S 2₈. **2. give an inheritance to,** with obj. of recipient Dt 32₈ Ezk 46₁₈ (+ מִן *out of* property). **3. leave land as an inheritance to** (לְ) 1 C 28₈. **4. allot** inheritance (נַחֲלָה) Is 49₈.

Ho. 1 Pf. הָנְחַלְתִּי—**be allotted, be made to inherit,** הָנְחַלְתִּי לִי יַרְחֵי־שָׁוְא *I am allotted months of emptiness* Jb 7₃.

Htp. 7.1.1 Impf. תִּתְנַחֲלוּ (תִּתְנַחֲלוּ); + waw וְהִתְנַחַלְתֶּם—**1a. inherit, take as a possession for oneself,** obj. inheritance (נַחֲלָה) Nm 32₁₈, land Nm 33₅₄ (+ בְּ *by* lot). **b.** without obj., **have an inheritance** Si 36₁₆. **2. divide, distribute** land **as an inheritance to** (לְ) Ezk 47₁₃. **3. pass on** slaves **as an inheritance to** (לְ) Lv 25₄₆.

→ נַחֲלָה I *inheritance,* נְחִילוֹת III *inheritances.*

*נחל II 4 vb.—**Qal** 1 Impf. תִּנְחַל—**sift** nations Ps 82₈ (בְּ of obj.).

Ni. 1 + waw וְנִחַלְתְּ (unless from חלל I ni. *be profaned*)—**be sifted,** of Jerusalem Ezk 22₁₆.

Pi. 1 Pf. נִחֲלוּ (unless from חלה I ni. *be made weak*) —**sift** Jr 12₁₃.

Hi. 1 Inf. הַנְחֵל—**sift, sprinkle (as through a sieve),** obj. nations Dt 32₈.

נַחַל I 139.3.17 n.m.—נַחַל; + ה- of direction נַחְלָה; cstr. נַחַל (נַחְלָה); du. נַחֲלַיִם; pl. נְחָלִים; cstr. נַחֲלֵי; sf. נְחָלֶיהָ—**1. wadi, river valley,** usu. with water only in rainy seasons Gn 26₁₉. **2. stream, river, torrent** Dt 9₂₁; נַחַל שׁוֹטֵף *an overflowing stream* Is 30₂₈, נַחֲלֵי מָיִם *streams of water* Dt 8₇. **3. grave trench** Jb 21₃₃. **4. mine shaft** Jb 28₄. **5. tunnel** Ne 2₁₅.

*[נַחַל] II 2 n.[m.]—נַחַל; pl. נְחָלִים—**date palm** Nm 24₆ Ca 6₁₁.

*נַחַל III 2 n.[m.]—pl. נְחָלִים—**tomb,** cut in rocks Is 57₅.₆.

*נַחַל IV 1 n.[m.] **(mine) shaft** Jb 28₄.

*נַחַל V 1 n.[m.]—נַחַל—**dust** Jb 21₃₃.

*נַחַל VI 1 n.[m.] **excavation, shaft** Jb 28₄.

נַחֲלָה I 222.12.77 n.f.—נַחֲלָת; cstr. נַחֲלַת; sf. נַחֲלָתוֹ, נַחֲלַתְכֶם; pl. נְחָלוֹת—**1. inheritance, possession,** inalienable hereditary **property,** of individual Jos 24₃₀ 1 K 21₃. **2.** land as inheritance of (tribes and families of) Israel

Nm 26_{53} Dt 4_{21}; as inheritance of Y. Jr 2_{7}. **3.** nations as inheritance of king Ps 2_{7}. **4.** Y. as inheritance of priests and Levites Nm 18_{20}. **5.** tithes and offerings as inheritance of Levites Nm 18_{21} Jos 13_{14}, priesthood as inheritance of Levites Jos 18_{7}. **6.** Israel as inheritance of Y. Dt 4_{20}. **7.** inheritance as one's portion, share of truth 1QS 4_{24}, the lot of light CD 13_{12}, one's lot from Y. Jb 20_{29}. → נחל I *inherit*.

*נַחֲלָה II 1 n.f. (unless from חלה I ni. *be made weak*) **wasting disease** Is 17_{11}.

*נַחֲלָה III 1 n.f. (unless from חלה I ni. *be made weak*) **destruction** Is 17_{11}.

נַחֲלָה IV 2 pl.n. **Nahalah.**

נַחֲלָה V *one who is weak*, see חלה I, ni.

נַחֲלִיאֵל 2 pl.n. **Nahaliel.**

נֶחֱלָמִי 3 gent. **Nehelamite.**

נַחֲלַת, see נַחֲלָה I *inheritance*.

נחם 108.3.18 vb.—**Ni.** 48.2.4 Pf. נִחַם (נִחָם); impf. יִנָּחֵם; + waw וַיִּנָּחֶם (וַיִּנָּחֵם); impv. הִנָּחֵם; ptc. נִחָם; inf. הִנָּחֵם—**1. regret, be sorry, repent, relent, a.** with prep., (1) עַל *of, concerning* evil Ex 32_{12}. (2) אֶל *of, concerning* evil 2 S 24_{16}. **b.** with כִּי *that* Gn 6_{6}. **c.** abs. 1 S 15_{29}. **2. be moved to pity, have compassion** on account of (מִן) something Jg 2_{18}; for, upon someone, with לְ Jg 21_{15}, אֶל Jg 21_{6}, עַל Ps 90_{13}. **3. comfort oneself, be comforted, be consoled, a.** with עַל *concerning, for* someone 2 S 13_{39}, evil Ezk 14_{22}, dust and ashes Jb 42_{6}. **b.** abs. Gn 24_{67}. **4. gain satisfaction (for oneself), avenge oneself** upon (מִן) enemies Is 1_{24}.

Pi. 51.1.12 Pf. נִחַם; impf. יְנַחֵם; + waw וַיְנַחֵם; ptc. מְנַחֵם; impv. נַחֲמוּ; inf. נַחֵם (נַחֲמוֹ)—**1. comfort, console** someone, **a.** with prep. מִן *from* work Gn 5_{29}; אֶל *for* dead one 2 S 10_{2}; עַל *for* dead one Jr 16_{7}, misfortune Jb 42_{11}. **b.** abs. Zc 10_{2}. **2.** perh. **vindicate** Ps 23_{4}. **3.** ptc. as noun, **comforter** 2 S 10_{3}||1 C 19_{3}.

Pu. 2 Pf. נֻחָמָה; impf. תְּנֻחָמוּ—**be comforted** Is 54_{11} 66_{13}.

Htp. 7.0.2 Impf. יִתְנֶחָם; + waw וָאֶתְנֶחָם; וְהִנֶּחָמְתִּי; ptc. מִתְנַחֵם; inf. הִתְנַחֵם—**1. (allow oneself to) be comforted** Gn 37_{35} Ps 119_{52}. **2. comfort oneself,** by plotting vengeance Gn 27_{42} (+ לְ *with respect to*); by taking vengeance Ezk 5_{13}. **3. repent** Nm 23_{19}. **4. have compassion upon** (עַל) Dt 32_{36}.

→ נֶחָמָה *comfort*, נִחֻמִים *comfort*, נֹחַם *compassion*, תַּנְחוּם *consolation*.

נַחַם 1 pr.n.m. **Naham.**

נֹחַם 1 n.m. **compassion,** or perh. **revenge** Ho 13_{14}. → נחם *comfort*.

[נֶחָמָה] 2 n.f.—sf. נֶחָמָתִי—**comfort, consolation** Ps 119_{50} Jb 6_{10}. → נחם *comfort*.

נְחֶמְיָה 8.1.0.14 pr.n.m. **Nehemiah.**

נחמיהו, see נְחֶמְיָה *Nehemiah*.

נִחֻמִים 3.0.1 n.[m.]pl.—sf. נִחוּמַי—**1. comfort** Is 57_{18}; דְּבָרִים נִחֻמִים *words, comfort,* i.e. comforting words Zc 1_{13}. **2. compassion** Ho 11_{8}. → נחם *comfort*.

נַחֲמָנִי 1 pr.n.m. **Nahamani.**

*נחן 1 vb.—**Pi.** 1 Pf. נֶחַנְתְּ (unless from חנן ni. *be pitied*)—**groan** Jr 22_{23}.

נַחְנוּ 6.0.0.1 pron.—נַחְנוּ—**we** (shorter form of אֲנַחְנוּ) Gn 42_{11} Lm 3_{42}. → cf. אֲנוּ *we*, אֲנַחְנוּ *we*.

נחץ I 1 vb.—**Qal** 1 Ptc. pass. נָחוּץ—pass. perh. **be urgent,** of king's business 1 S 21_{9}.

*נחץ II 1 vb.—**Qal** 1 Ptc. pass. נָחוּץ—pass. **be private,** of king's business 1 S 21_{9}.

*נחר I 2 vb.—**Qal** 1 Pf. נָחַר (unless from חרר ni. *be set aglow*)—**snort,** of bellows Jr 6_{29}.

Pi. 1 Pf. נִחֲרוּ (unless from חרה I ni. *be angry*)—**be angry** against (בְּ) Ca 1_{6}.

→ נַחַר *snorting*, נַחֲרָה *snorting*, נָחִיר *nostril*.

*נחר II 1 vb.—**Ni.** 1 Pf. נִחַר (unless from חרר ni. *be scorched*)—**be hoarse,** of throat Ps 69_{4}.

[נַחַר] 1 n.[m.]—sf. נַחְרוֹ—**snorting** of horse Jb 39_{20}. → נחר I *snort*.

[נַחֲרָה] 1 n.f.—cstr. נַחֲרַת—**snorting** of horses Jr 8_{16}. → נחר I *snort*.

נַחְרַי 2 pr.n.m. **Naharai.**

נחשׁ I 11.0.1 vb.—**Pi.** 11 Pf. נִחֵשׁ; impf. יְנַחֵשׁ; ptc. מְנַחֵשׁ, inf. abs. נַחֵשׁ—**1. practise divination** Gn 44_{5} (+ בְּ *by means of* cup). **2. learn by divination, observe omens** Gn 30_{27} 1 K 20_{33}. **3.** ptc. as noun, **diviner** Dt 18_{10}. → נַחַשׁ *divination*, נְחוּשָׁה II *enchantment*.

*נחשׁ II 1 vb.—**Pi** 1 Pf. נִחַשְׁתִּי—**become rich** Gn 30_{27}.

נַחַשׁ 2 n.[m.]—pl. נְחָשִׁים—**divination, augury, omen** Nm 23_{23} 24_{1}. → נחשׁ I *practise divination*.

נָחָשׁ I 31 n.m.—cstr. נְחַשׁ; pl. נְחָשִׁים—**serpent** Gn 3$_{1}$ Ex 4$_{3}$; in ref. to Leviathan Is 27$_{1}$.

נָחָשׁ II 9 pr.n.m. **Nahash.**

נָחָשׁ III, see עִיר נָחָשׁ *Irnahash.*

*[**נַחְשׁוֹל**] 0.0.1 n.[m.]—pl. cstr. נחשולי—**gale** 1QH 10$_{12}$.

נַחְשׁוֹן 10 pr.n.m. **Nahshon.**

*[**נַחְשִׁיר**] I 0.0.3 n.m. **carnage** 1QM 1$_{9.10.13}$.

*[**נַחְשִׁיר**] II 0.0.3 n.m. **hunting** 1QM 1$_{9.10.13}$.

*[**נַחְשִׁיר**] III 0.0.3 n.m. **fear, terror** 1QM 1$_{9.10.13}$.

נְחֹשֶׁת I 140.2.10 n.m.&f.—cstr. נְחֹשֶׁת; sf. נְחֻשְׁתִּי, נְחָשְׁתָּם; du. נְחֻשְׁתַּיִם—**1. copper,** as ore Dt 8$_{9}$. **2. copper, bronze,** as material Gn 4$_{22}$ 1 S 17$_{5}$. **3. bronze fetters** du. Jg 16$_{21}$; sg. Lm 3$_{7}$. **4.** perh. **money** Ezk 16$_{36}$. → cf. נָחוּשׁ *copper,* נְחוּשָׁה *copper.*

[**נְחֹשֶׁת**] II 1 n.[f.]—נְחָשְׁתֵּךְ—**indecency, lust** or **menstrual blood** of woman Ezk 16$_{36}$.

נְחֻשְׁתָּא 1 pr.n.f. **Nehushta.**

נְחֻשְׁתָּן 1 pr.n.m. **Nehushtan.**

נחת I 9 vb.—**Qal** 4 Impf. יֵחַת; + waw וַתִּנְחַת—**1. go down, descend,** of person Jb 21$_{13}$ (+ שְׁאוֹל *[to] Sheol*), hand Ps 38$_{3}$ (+ עַל *upon*). **2. go down, march** against (עַל) Jr 21$_{13}$. **3. sink deep,** of rebuke Pr 17$_{10}$.

Ni. 1 Pf. נִחֲתוּ—**sink, penetrate,** of arrow Ps 38$_{3}$ (+ בְּ *into*).

Pi. 3 + waw וְנִחַת; inf. abs. נַחֵת—**1. bend, stretch** a bow, or perh. **lower** bow into arms 2 S 22$_{35}$||Ps 18$_{35}$. **2. cause to sink, make smooth** furrows Ps 65$_{11}$.

Hi. 1 Impv. הַנְחַת—**bring down, launch into battle,** obj. warriors Jl 4$_{11}$.

→ נָחֵת *descending,* נַחַת I *descent.*

*****נחת** II 2 vb.—**Pi.** 2 + waw וְנִחַת—**make** arms **strong** for a bronze bow 2 S 22$_{35}$||Ps 18$_{35}$. → נַחַת III *strength.*

*****נחת** III 1 vb.—**Hi.** 1 Impv. הַנְחַת—**deport** Jl 4$_{11}$.

*****נחת** IV 2 vb.—**Pi.** 2 + waw וְנִחֲתָה, וְנִחַת—**fashion** arms into a bronze bow 2 S 22$_{35}$||Ps 18$_{35}$.

[**נָחֵת**] 1 adj.—pl. נְחִתִּים—**descending,** of Aramaeans 2 K 6$_{9}$. → נחת I *go down.*

[**נַחַת**] I 1 n.[m.]—cstr. נַחַת—**descent** of arm of Y. Is 30$_{30}$. → נחת I *go down.*

*****נַחַת** II 7.4 n.[f.]—נָחַת; cstr. נַחַת—**1. quietness, rest, calm, peace** Is 30$_{15}$ Pr 29$_{9}$ Ec 4$_{6}$. **2. that which rests (on table),** i.e. **spread,** or perh. **comfort (of table)** Jb 36$_{16}$. → נוח I *rest.*

*[**נַחַת**] III 1 n.[m.]—cstr. נַחַת—**strength** of arm of Y. Is 30$_{30}$. → נחת II *make strong.*

נַחַת IV 5 pr.n.m. **Nahath.**

*****נטב** 1 vb.—**Qal** 1 Inf. מְטוֹב (unless מִן *from* + טוֹב *good*)—**drop (word), speak** Ps 39$_{3}$.

Hi., drip, i.e. **dispense,** knowledge Pr 15$_{2}$ (if em. תֵּיטִיב *it makes good* [יטב hi.] to תַּטִּיב).

→ cf. נטף *drip.*

נטה 216.16.20.1 vb.—**Qal** 137.8.6 Pf. נָטָה, נָטִיתִי; impf. יִטֶּה (יֵט); + waw וַיֵּט (וַיֶּט־), וַיִּטּוּ; impv. נְטֵה; ptc. נֹטֶה; ptc. pass. נָטוּי, נְטוּיָה; inf. נְטוֹת—**1. stretch out, hold out, extend** hand Ex 7$_{5}$ (+ עַל *over, against*), sword Ezk 30$_{25}$ (+ אֶל *against*), javelin Jos 8$_{26}$ (בְּ of obj.), line 2 K 21$_{13}$, loyalty Gn 39$_{21}$ (+ אֶל *to*). **2a. spread out** canopy Jr 43$_{10}$ (+ עַל *over*), שָׁמַיִם heavens Is 40$_{22}$ (+ כְּ *as* curtain), rainbow Si 43$_{12}$. **b. pitch** tent Gn 12$_{8}$. **3.** intrans., **spread out, extend,** of slope Nm 21$_{15}$ (+ לְ *to*). **4a. bend, bow** shoulder Gn 49$_{15}$. **b. incline** heart Ps 119$_{112}$. **5.** intrans., **bend, bow,** of person Jg 16$_{30}$. **6.** intrans., **a. turn, incline,** of Y. Ps 40$_{2}$ (+ אֶל *to*), person 1 S 14$_{7}$ (+ לְ reflexive), heart Jg 9$_{3}$ (+ אַחֲרֵי *after*). **b. decline,** of day Jg 19$_{8}$, shadow 2 K 20$_{10}$. **c.** perh. **go down,** of person Si 9$_{9}$ (+ אֶל *to*). **7. turn aside, deviate,** of person Gn 38$_{16}$ (+ אֶל *to*) Nm 20$_{17}$ (+ יָמִין וּשְׂמאוֹל *[to the] right or left*), heart 1 K 11$_{9}$ (+ מֵעִם *from*), ass Nm 22$_{23}$ (+ מִן *from*). **8.** pass. **a.** (1) **be stretched out,** of hand Is 5$_{25}$, sword 1 C 21$_{16}$ (+ עַל *over*). (2) pass. ptc. as adj., **outstretched,** of arm Ex 6$_{6}$. **b. be spread out,** of day Ps 102$_{12}$, firmament Ezk 1$_{22}$ (+ עַל *over*). **c. be turned,** אֲנִי נְטוּי רַגְלָי *I was turned (with regard to) my feet,* i.e. I stumbled Ps 73$_{2}$. **d.** pass. ptc. as adj., **leaning,** of wall Ps 62$_{4}$.

Ni. 3 Pf. נִטָּיוּ; impf. יִנָּטֶה—**1. stretch oneself out, extend, lengthen,** of wadi Nm 24$_{6}$, shadow Jr 6$_{4}$. **2. be stretched out,** of line Zc 1$_{16}$ (+ עַל *over*).

Hi. 76.8.14.1 Pf. הִטָּה; impf. יַטֶּה, תַּטֶּה (תַּט); + waw וַיַּט, וָאַט; impv. הַטֵּה (הַט), הַטּוּ, הַטִּי; ptc. מַטֶּה; inf. הַטּוֹת—**1. stretch out, hold out, extend** hand Jr 6$_{12}$ (+ עַל *against*), loyalty Ezr 7$_{28}$ (+ לִפְנֵי *before*). **2a. spread out** curtain Is 54$_{2}$, sackcloth 2 S 21$_{10}$ (+ אֶל *upon*). **b. pitch** tent 2 S 16$_{22}$ (+ עַל *upon*). **3. turn, direct, take**

aside person 2 S 3_{27} (+ אֶל־תּוֹךְ *inside*), ass Nm 22_{23} (+ הַדֶּרֶךְ *[to the] way*), heart Pr 21_1 (+ עַל *to*), ark 1 C 13_{13} (+ אֶל *to*). **4. thrust away, turn away, thrust down** the poor Am 5_{12} (+ בְּ *in* gate) Is 10_2 (+ מִן *from* justice), reproof Si 35_{17}. **5. pervert** justice Ex 23_6. **6. incline** ear 2 K 19_{16}||Is 37_{17} Ps 17_6 (+ לְ *to*), heart Jos 24_{23} (+ אֶל *to*). **7a. persuade** person Pr 7_{21}, heart 2 S 19_{15}. **b. cause to deviate, lead astray** person Is 44_{20}, heart 1 K 11_2 (+ אַחֲרֵי *after* gods). **8.** intrans., **turn aside, deviate,** of person Is 30_{11} (+ מִן *from*) Pr 4_{27} (+ יָמִין וּשְׂמֹאול *[to] the right or left*). **9. bend, bow** shoulder Si 6_{25}, the heavens Ps 144_5. **10.** intrans., **bend down** Ho 11_4 (+ אֶל *to*), **stretch oneself out** Am 2_8 (+ אֵצֶל *beside*).

→ מַטָּה *downwards,* מַטֶּה I *staff,* מִטָּה *bed,* מֻטֶּה *outspreading,* מֻטֶּה *injustice.*

נָטוּעַ *thing planted,* see נטע, qal §3.

נְטוֹפָתִי, see נְטֹפָתִי *Netophathite.*

[נָטִיל] 1 adj.—**laden,** as noun, **one laden,** נְטִילֵי כֶסֶף *ones laden of,* i.e. with, *silver* Zp 1_{11}. → נטל *lift.*

[נָטִיעַ] 1 n.[m.]—pl. נְטִעִים—**plant** Ps 144_{12}. → נטע *plant.*

[נְטִיפָה] 2 n.f.—pl. נְטִיפוֹת—**pendant** Jg 8_{26} Is 3_{19}. → נטף *drip.*

[נְטִישָׁה] 3 n.f.—pl. נְטִישׁוֹת; sf. נְטִישֹׁתַיִךְ—**tendril** of vine Is 18_5 Jr 5_{10} 48_{32}. → נטשׁ I *leave.*

נטל 4.1.2.1 vb.—**Qal** 3.1.2.1 Pf. נָטַל; impf. יִטּוֹל; ptc. נוֹטֵל—**1. lift up** isles Is 40_{15}, rock and dust CD 11_{10}. **2. lay** yoke upon (עַל) Lm 3_{28}, something over (עַל) someone, i.e. offer 2 S 24_{12}. **3. take away** wheat MurEpBar C^b_{10}. **4. take** counsel Si $43_{8(B)}$. **5.** perh. **weigh** Arad ost. 60_1.

Pi. 1 + waw וַיְנַטְּלֵם—**lift up** people Is 63_9.

→ נָטִיל *laden,* נֵטֶל *weight.*

[נֵטֶל] 1 n.[m.]—cstr. נֵטֶל—**weight, burden** Pr 27_3. → נטל *lift.*

נטע 58.2.8 vb.—**Qal** 57.1.7 Pf. נָטַע; impf. יִטַּע; impv. נִטְעוּ; ptc. נוֹטֵעַ (נֹטֵעַ); ptc. pass. נָטוּעַ; inf. לִנְטֹעַ (לָטַעַת)—**1a. plant** tree Lv 19_{23}, garden Gn 2_8, ear Ps 94_9, law 4QDibHam^a 1.2_{13} (+ בְּ *in* heart). **b. transplant** vine Ps 80_9, people Ex 15_{17}. **c. replant** desolate place Ezk 36_{36}. **d.** with double accus., **plant** vineyard **with** vines Is 5_2. **e.** abs. Is 65_{22}. **2. pitch** tent Dn 11_{45}. **3a.** pass. **be planted, fixed,** of nail Ec 12_{11}. **b.** pass. ptc. as noun, **planted thing** Ec 3_2.

Ni. 1.1.1 Pf. נִטָּעוּ; impf. Si תנטע; ptc. Q נטעת—**be planted,** of rulers Is 40_2, vine 6QAllegory 1_6, righteousness Si $3_{14(A)}$.

→ נֶטַע I *plant,* נָטִיעַ *plant,* מַטָּע *planting,* מַטַּעַת *planting.*

[נֶטַע] I 4.4.3 n.[m.]—נֶטַע; cstr. נֶטַע; sf. נִטְעֵךְ; pl. cstr. נִטְעֵי—**1. plant, shoot** Is 17_{10} Jb 14_9. **2. plantation** Is 5_7. **3. (act of) planting** Is 17_{11}. → נטע *plant.*

*[נֶטַע] II n.[m.] **pavilion** Ps 144_{12} (if em. כִּנְטִעִים מְגֻדָּלִים *like plants full grown* to כִּנְטָעִים מִגְדָּלִים *like pavilions [and] towers*).

נְטָעִים 1 pl.n. **Netaim.**

נטף 18.0.8 vb.—**Qal** 9 Pf. נָטְפוּ; impf. תִּטֹּף; ptc. נֹטְפוֹת—**drip, drop, a.** trans., obj. water Jg 5_4, honey Pr 5_3, myrrh Ca 5_5. **b.** intrans., of word Jb 29_{22} (+ עַל *upon*).

Hi. 9.0.8 Pf. Impf. תַּטִּיף; + waw וְהִטִּיפוּ; impv. הַטֵּף; ptc. מַטִּיף; inf. abs. הטף—**1. drip** water of lies CD 1_{14} (+ לְ *onto*), sweet wine Am 9_{13}. **2a. preach, teach, prophesy,** with prep. לְ *to* someone Mc 2_{11}, *concerning* Mc 2_{11}; אֶל *against* Ezk $21_{2.7}$; עַל *against* Am 7_{16}. **b. preach to, teach** (accus.) people with (לְ) lies CD 19_{25}. **3.** ptc. as noun, **preacher, teacher** Mc 2_{11}; מטיף הכזב *preacher of lies* 1QpHab 10_9.

→ נָטָף *stacte,* נֶטֶף *drop,* נְטִיפָה *pendant;* cf. נטב *drop.*

נָטָף 1 n.[m.] **stacte,** a resin, ingredient of incense Ex 30_{34}. → נטף *drip.*

*[נָטֹף] 0.0.1 pl.n. **Natoph.**

[נֶטֶף] 1 n.[m.]—pl. cstr. נִטְפֵי—**drop** of water Jb 36_{27}. → נטף *drip.*

נְטִפָה, see נְטִיפָה *pendant.*

נְטֹפָה 2 pl.n. **Netophah.**

נְטֹפָתִי 11 gent. **Netophathite.**

נטר I 4.0.1 vb.—**Qal** 4.0.1 Pf. נָטַרְתִּי; ptc. נֹטְרִים, נֹטֵרָה—**keep, guard** fruit Ca 8_{12}, vineyard Ca $1_{6.6}$. → מַטָּרָה *guard;* cf. נצר I *keep.*

*נטר II 5.0.15 vb.—**Qal** 5.0.14 Impf. יִטּוֹר (יִנְטֹר), תִּטֹּר; ptc. נוֹטֵר; inf. Q נטור—**be angry,** with prep. לְ *against* Na 1_2; אֵת *with,* i.e. against Lv 19_{18}; בְּ *with* anger 1QS 10_{20}, *in, concerning* matter 4QD^a 10.2_1.

Ni. 0.0.1 Inf. abs. Q ניטור—**bear a grudge against**

(לְ) CD 8₅.

נטשׁ I 40.4.3 vb.—**Qal** 33.4.2 Pf. נָטַשׁ; impf. יִטּשׁ; impv. נְטוֹשׁ; ptc. pass. נְטֻשִׁים, נְטוּשָׁה—**1. leave** quails beside (עַל) camp Nm 11₃₁, sheep with (עַל) keeper 1 S 17₂₀. **2. forsake, abandon, cast away,** of Y. forsaking people Jg 6₁₃, his dwelling place Ps 78₆₀, loyalty Si 47₂₂; people forsaking Y. Dt 32₁₅, teaching of parents Pr 1₈. **3. leave** land **fallow** Ex 23₁₁. **4. forego, relinquish** crops of seventh year and debts Ne 10₃₂. **5. disregard** cry Si 32₁₇. **6. permit,** לֹא נְטַשְׁתַּנִי לְנַשֵּׁק *you did not permit me to kiss* Gn 31₂₈. 7. perh. **spread out,** of battle 1 S 4₂. **8.** pass. **a.** of persons, **be spread out** over (עַל־פְּנֵי) land 1 S 30₁₆. **b.** of sword, **be drawn** Is 21₁₅.

Ni. 6 Pf. נִטְּשָׁה; + waw וַיִּנָּטְשׁוּ—**1. be forsaken,** of Israel Am 5₂ (+ עַל *upon* land). **2. spread oneself out, be spread out,** of persons 2 S 5₁₈, shoot Is 16₈. **3. hang loose,** of rope Is 33₂₃.

Pu. 1 Pf. נֻטָּשׁ—**be forsaken,** of fortress Is 32₁₄.

→ נְטִישָׁה *tendril.*

*__נטשׁ__ II 3 vb.—**Qal** 3 + waw וַתִּטֹּשׁ—**1. dash to the ground,** obj. cedar Ezk 31₁₂.₁₂. **2. clash,** of battle 1 S 4₂.

*__נטשׁ__ III 2 vb.—**Qal** 2 + waw וַתִּטֹּשׁ; ptc. pass. נְטוּשָׁה—**1. be sharp,** of battle 1 S 4₂. **2.** pass. **be sharpened,** of sword Is 21₁₅. → cf. לטשׁ *sharpen.*

[נִי] 1 n.[m.]—sf. נִיהֶם—**wailing** Ezk 27₃₂ (mss בְּנֵיהֶם *their sons*). → נהה I *lament.*

[נִיב] I 2.1 n.[m.]—cstr. Qr נִיב; sf. נִיבוֹ—**fruit** of lips, i.e. praise Is 57₁₉(Qr), fruit of gold (item of jewellery) Si 35₅(B). → נוב *flow, bear fruit.*

*[נִיב] II 1 n.[m.]—cstr. Qr נִיב—**speech, utterance** Is 57₁₉(Qr). → נוב *flow, bear fruit.*

נֵיבַי 1 pr.n.m. **Nebai.**

[נִיד] 1 n.m.—cstr. נִיד—**shaking** of lips, in sympathy Jb 16₅. → נוד I *move to and fro.*

נִידָה I 1 n.f. **impurity,** i.e. impure thing Lm 1₈. → נדה III *make impure;* cf. נִדָּה I *impurity.*

*__נִידָה__ II 1 n.f. **shaking of head,** in derision Lm 1₈. → נוד I *move to and fro.*

נָיוֹת 6 pl.n. **Naioth.**

נִיחֹחַ 43.1.20 n.[m.]—נִיחֹחַ; cstr. Q ניחוח; sf. נִיחֹחִי, נִיחֹחֲכֶם; pl. sf. נִיחוֹחֵיהֶם—**1. soothing, pleasing, appeasement,** usu. רֵיחַ נִיחֹחַ *odour of soothing,* i.e. soothing odour, of sacrifice Gn 8₂₁ Ex 29₁₈. **2. pleasing odour** 4QapLamA 1.1₆, of righteousness 1QS 9₅. → נוח I *rest.*

*[נִיל] vb. **Qal, acquire** Ps 84₄ (if em. לָהּ *to her* to נָלָה *she has acquired*). → מָנוֹל *possession;* cf. נלה II *acquire.*

נִין 1 vb.—**Qal** 1 Impf. Kt ינין—**increase, have descendants** Ps 72₁₇(Kt) (Qr ni. יִנּוֹן in same sense; or vocalize יְנַיֵּן pi. *he shall have offspring*).

Ni. 1 Impf. Qr יִנּוֹן—see qal.

→ נִין *offspring.*

נִין 3.2 n.m.—sf. נִינִי—**offspring, posterity** Gn 21₂₃ Is 14₂₂ Jb 18₁₉ Si 41₅ 47₂₂. → נין *increase.*

נִינָם, see ינה *oppress,* qal.

נִינְוֵה 17 pl.n. **Nineveh.**

*[נִיס] 1 n.m. **fugitive** Jr 48₄₄(Kt) (Qr הַנָּס *the one who flees,* i.e. נוס qal ptc.). → נוס I *flee.*

נִיסָן 2 pr.n.[m.] **Nisan,** first month of postexilic calendar, previously called Abib, March/April Ne 2₁.

נִיצוֹץ 1.2 n.[m.]—Si נצוץ—**spark** Is 1₃₁ Si 11₃₂ 42₂₂. → נצץ I *sparkle.*

ניר I 3 vb.—**Qal** 3 Impv. נִירוּ; ptc. נֵר—**break up, till** untilled ground Jr 4₃ Ho 10₁₂. → נִיר II *untilled ground.*

*__ניר__ II vb.—**Qal, shine with** oil, of head Ps 141₅ (if em. יָנִי *let it not refuse* to יָנִיר *let it not shine*). → נִיר I *lamp;* cf. נֵר I *lamp,* נוּר *fire.*

נִיר I 5 n.[m.]—cstr. נִר—**lamp** 1 K 11₃₆ 15₄ 2 K 8₁₉||2 C 21₇. → ניר II *shine;* cf. נֵר I *lamp,* מְנוֹרָה *lampstand.*

נִיר II 7 n.[m.]—cstr. נִיר—**1. untilled ground** Jr 4₃ Ho 10₁₂, **tillage** Pr 13₂₃. **2.** perh. **field,** thus **dominion** 1 K 11₃₆ 15₄ 2 K 8₁₉||2 C 21₇. → ניר I *break up.*

*__נִיר__ III 1 n.[m.] **sign of power** 1 K 11₃₆.

*[נִיר] IV 1 n.[m.] **mark,** נִר רְשָׁעִים *mark of the wicked* Pr 21₄.

*__נִיר__ V 3 n.[m.] **dominion** 1 K 11₃₆ 15₄ 2 K 8₁₉||2 C 21₇.

*__נִיר__ VI 2 n.[m.] **new break, new beginning** 2 K 8₁₉||2 C 21₇.

[נִיר], see נֵר *lamp.*

נֵירָם, see ירם *be high.*

נכא I 1.0.1 vb.—**Qal** 0.0.1 + waw ויכא—**strike** 4QpsJub[a] 1₃.

Ni. 1 Pf. נִכְּאוּ—**be struck, scourged out** from (מִן)

the land Jb 30_{8}.

→ נָכָא *stricken*, נָכֵא *stricken*; cf. נכה *strike*.

*נכא II 1 vb.—**Ni.** 1 Pf. נִכְּאוּ—**be low** Jb 30_{8} (+ מִן lower *than* the land).

*נכא III 1 vb.—**Ni.** 1 Pf. נִכְּאוּ—**be put to flight** from (מִן) the land Jb 30_{8}.

[נָכָא] 1 adj.—pl. נְכָאִים—**stricken** Is 16_{7}. → נכא I *strike*.

[נָכֵא] 3.0.3 adj.—m. cstr. Q נכאה (Q נכאי), f. abs. נְכֵאָה, m.pl. Q נכאים, cstr. Q נכאי—**1. stricken, downcast,** of spirit Pr 17_{22}. **2.** as noun, **stricken one, lame one** 1QSa 2_{5}; **contrite one, downcast one** Is $66_{2(1QIsa^{a})}$. → נכא I *strike*.

נְכֹאת 2 n.f. **ladanum,** a spice, from resin of the cistus rose Gn 37_{25} 43_{1}.

נֶכֶד 3.2 n.m.—sf. נֶכְדִּי—**progeny, posterity** Gn 21_{23} Is 14_{22} Jb 18_{19} Si 41_{5} 47_{22}.

נכה 502.3.23.1 vb.—**Ni.** 1 + waw וְנִכָּה—**be struck** 2 S 11_{15}.

Pu. 2 Pf. נֻכּוּ, נֻכְּתָה—**be beaten down,** by hail Ex $9_{31.32}$.

Hi. 483.3.22.1 Pf. הִכֵּיתִי, הִכִּיתָ, הִכָּה; impf. יַכֶּה (יַךְ); + waw וַיַּכֶּה (וַיַּךְ); ptc. מַכֶּה; inf. abs. הַכֵּה; cstr. הַכּוֹת—**1a. strike, beat, beat down** a person, as act of violence Ex 2_{11}, in punishment Dt 25_{2}, with arrow shot from bow 1 K 22_{34}‖2 C 18_{33}; of striking a beast Nm 22_{23}, rock, with (בְּ) rod Nm 20_{11}, bow, from (מִן) hand Ezk 39_{3}; of Y. striking river Is 11_{15}, vines and fig trees Ps 105_{33}; of hail striking crops, people and animals Ex 9_{25}, sun, moon striking people Ps 121_{6}, one's conscience striking one 1 S 24_{5}. **b. thrust** fork into (בְּ) pot 1 S 2_{14}. **c. pin** someone to (בְּ) wall with (בְּ) spear 1 S 19_{10}. **d. clap** hands 2 K 11_{12}. **e. play** harp 4QS[d] 9_{8}. **f.** of plant, **strike roots** Ho 14_{6}. **g.** of roots, **penetrate** into (בְּ) rock 1QH 16_{23}. **2. strike fatally, kill,** in manslaughter, murder Gn 37_{21} Nm 35_{11} (+ בְּ *with* inadvertence), as vengeance, punishment 2 S 1_{15} 2 K 9_{7}, in warfare, conquest Dt 13_{16} (+ לְפִי־חֶרֶב *with the edge of the sword*) Jos 11_{10} (+ בְּ *with* sword); killing of beast Lv 24_{18}; beast killing humans 1 K 20_{36}, worm killing plant Jon 4_{7}. **3. attack, defeat, rout, destroy, subdue** Gn 14_{5} Jos 7_{3} 1 K 21_{21} (בְּ of obj.; + מַכָּה גְדוֹלָה *[with] a great defeat*); subduing waves of sea Zc 10_{11}. **4a. strike** someone with (בְּ) plague, etc. Nm 14_{12} Dt 28_{22}. **b. strike** someone, causing outbreak of tumours 1 S 5_{9}. **c. strike** land Ex 12_{13} (בְּ of obj.) Ml 3_{24} (+ חֵרֶם *[with a] ban of destruction*). **5.** of Y., **strike in punishment, strike for correction** Lv 26_{24} (+ עַל *for* sins) Jr 5_{3}.

Ho. 16.0.1 Pf. הֻכֵּיתִי, הֻכָּה; impf. תֻּכּוּ; + waw וַיֻּכּוּ; ptc. מֻכֶּה—**1. be beaten** Zc 13_{6}, as punishment Ex 5_{14}. **2. be struck fatally, be killed** Ex 22_{1}, as punishment Nm 25_{14}; מֻכֵּי־חֶרֶב *killed of,* i.e. by, *the sword,* in battle Jr 18_{21}. **3. be defeated** Ezk 33_{21}. **4. be struck with** (בְּ) haemorrhoids 1 S 5_{12}; of plant, **be struck, blighted,** causing withering Ho 9_{16}. **5. be struck,** as punishment, by Y. Is 1_{5} 53_{4}.

→ נָכֶה *lame; contrite,* נָכֶה *stricken,* נָכוֹן *blow,* מַכָּה *stroke*; cf. נכא I *strike*.

[נָכֶה] 3.0.1 adj.—cstr. נְכֵה (Q נכי)—**1. lame,** נְכֵה רַגְלַיִם *lame of,* i.e. in, *the feet* 2 S 4_{4}. **2. contrite, meek,** נְכֵה־רוּחַ *contrite of,* i.e. in, *spirit* Is 66_{2}. → נכה *strike*.

[נֵכֶה] 1 adj.—pl. נֵכִים—**stricken,** as noun, **stricken one** Ps 35_{15}. → נכה *strike*.

נְכֹה 8 pr.n.m. **Neco.**

נְכוֹ, see נְכֹה *Neco*.

נָכוֹן I 1 n.[m.] **blow,** or **push, thrust** Jb 12_{5}. → נכה *strike*.

נָכוֹן II 1 pr.n.m. **Nacon.**

נָכוֹן III *certainty,* see כון, ni. §2.

נֹכַח 25.5.3 n.[m.]—sf. נִכְחוֹ—**1.** נֹכַח, **a.** noun, **thing in front** Si $34_{16(Bmg)}$. **b.** usu. as prep., **in front of, before, opposite (to)** Ex 26_{35}‖40_{24} Jr 17_{16}. **2.** נֹכַח לְ **in front of, opposite** Jos 15_{7}. **3.** לְנֹכַח, **a. in front of** Gn 30_{38}. **b. for, on behalf of** Gn 25_{21}. **c.** as adv., **forward, straight ahead** Pr 4_{25}. **4.** אֶל־נֹכַח פְּנֵי **towards the front of** Nm 19_{4}. **5.** עַד־נֹכַח **as far as opposite** Jg 19_{10}. → cf. נָכֹחַ *straight*.

[נָכֹחַ] 8.2.2 adj.—sf. נְכֹחוֹ; f.s. נְכֹחָה; m.pl. נְכֹחִים; f.pl. נְכֹחוֹת—**1. straightforward, right,** of word Pr 24_{26}. **2.** as noun, **a. straightforward one, upright one,** 4QS[f] 5_{1}. **b. uprightness, rectitude,** masc. sg. Is 57_{2}, fem. sg. Is 59_{14}, fem. pl. Is 26_{10}. → cf. נֹכַח *front*.

נכל 4 vb.—**Qal** 1 Ptc. נוֹכֵל—ptc. as noun, **deceitful one, cheat** Ml 1_{14}.

Pi. 1 Pf. נִכְּלוּ—**deceive** Nm 25_{18} (לְ of obj.).

Htp. 2 + waw וַיִּתְנַכְּלוּ; inf. הִתְנַכֵּל—**act deceitfully**

against, deal craftily with, with accus. Gn 37$_{18}$, בְּ of obj. Ps 105$_{25}$.

→ נֵכֶל *deceitfulness*, כִּילַי *villain*.

[נֵכֶל] 1.0.1 n.[m.]—pl. sf. נִכְלֵיהֶם—**deceitfulness, craft** Nm 25$_{18}$ 1QpHab 3$_{5}$. → נכל *be deceitful*.

*[נְכָנְיָהוּ] 0.0.0.1 pr.n.[m.] **Neconiah.**

[נֶכֶס] 5.1.2 n.m.—pl. נְכָסִים; cstr. Si נכסי—**wealth, riches** Jos 22$_{8}$ Ec 5$_{18}$ 2 C 1$_{11}$ Si 5$_{8}$.

נכר I 40.4.16 vb.—**Ni.** 1.1 Pf. נִכְּרוּ; impf. Si ינכר—**be recognized** Lm 4$_{8}$ Si 11$_{28}$.

Pi. 2 Pf. נִכַּר; impf. תְּנַכְּרוּ—**recognize, have regard for** the noble Jb 34$_{19}$ (+ לִפְנֵי *before* the poor), signs Jb 21$_{29}$.

Hi. 38.3.16 Pf. הִכִּיר; impf. יַכִּיר; + waw וַאַכִּירָה, וַיַּכֵּר; impv. הַכֶּר־; ptc. מַכִּיר; inf. abs. הַכֵּר; cstr. הַכִּירֵנִי—**1. recognize** person or thing known Gn 27$_{23}$ 37$_{33}$ Jg 18$_{3}$, face, i.e. show partiality Dt 1$_{17}$. **2. be acquainted with, know** something Jb 24$_{13}$. **3. acknowledge** someone Dt 21$_{17}$. **4. pay attention to** someone Ps 142$_{5}$. **5. discern, understand, realize** Ne 6$_{12}$ 4QMMT C$_{20}$. **6. distinguish** one sound from (לְ) another Ezr 3$_{13}$. **7. observe, examine (in order to recognize)** Gn 37$_{32}$.

Htp. 1 Impf. יִתְנַכֶּר־—**make oneself known by** (בְּ) one's deeds Pr 20$_{11}$.

→ הַכָּרָה *recognition*, מַכָּר II *acquaintance*.

נכר II 7.2.1 vb.—**Ni.** 1.0.1 Impf. יִנָּכֵר; inf. Q הנכר—**act as a stranger, disguise oneself** Pr 26$_{24}$ (+ בְּ *with* lips).

Pi. 3.1 Pf. נִכַּר; impf. יְנַכְּרוּ—**1. misconstrue** Dt 32$_{27}$. **2. treat as strange, alienate** someone 1 S 23$_{7}$ (+ בְּ *into* the hand of), place Jr 19$_{4}$.

Htp. 3.1 + waw וַיִּתְנַכֵּר; ptc. מִתְנַכֵּרָה; inf. Si התנכר—**act as a stranger, disguise oneself** Gn 42$_{7}$ (+ אֶל *towards*) 1 K 14$_{5}$.

→ נֵכָר *foreignness*, נֵכֶר *misfortune*, נֹכֶר *misfortune*, נָכְרִי *foreign*.

*נכר III 2 vb.—**Qal** 1 + waw וָאֶכְּרֶהָ (unless from כרה II *purchase*)—**acquire, purchase** woman Ho 3$_{2}$ (+ לְ *for* oneself, בְּ *[in exchange] for*).

Pi. 1 Pf. נִכַּר—**sell** someone 1 S 23$_{7}$ (+ בְּ *into* the hand of).

*נכר IV 2 vb.—**Pi.** 1 Pf. נִכַּר—**remove** someone 1 S 23$_{7}$ (+ בְּ *into* the hand of).

Hi. 1 Impf. יַכִּיר—**repudiate** deeds Jb 34$_{25}$.

*נכר V 1 vb.—**Hi.** 1 Impf. יַכִּיר—**disapprove of deeds** Jb 34$_{25}$.

נֵכָר 36.1.12 n.[m.] **foreignness, strangeness,** אֱלֹהֵי נֵכָר *gods of foreignness*, i.e. foreign gods Jos 24$_{20}$, בֶּן־נֵכָר *son of foreignness*, i.e. foreigner Gn 17$_{12}$, כָּל־נֵכָר *all foreignness*, i.e. everything foreign Ne 13$_{30}$. → נכר II *be foreign*.

נֵכֶר 1 n.[m.] **misfortune** Jb 31$_{3}$. → נכר II *be foreign*.

[נֹכֶר] 1 n.[m.]—sf. נָכְרוֹ—**misfortune** Ob$_{12}$. → נכר II *be foreign*.

נָכְרִי 45.2.4 adj.—Q נוכרי; f.s. נָכְרִיָּה; m.pl. נָכְרִים; f.pl. נָכְרִיּוֹת—**1. foreign, alien, strange,** of people Ex 21$_{8}$, vine Jr 2$_{21}$, land Ex 2$_{22}$. **2.** as noun, **foreigner, alien, stranger, a.** masc. Dt 14$_{21}$; coll. Jg 19$_{12}$. **b.** fem. Ru 2$_{10}$. → נכר II *be foreign*.

[נְכֹת] 2 n.[f.] **treasure,** בֵּית נְכֹתֹה *house of his treasure* 2 K 20$_{13}$||Is 39$_{2}$.

נלה I 1 vb.—**Hi.** 1 Inf. כַּנְּלֹתְךָ—**finish** Is 33$_{1}$ (or em. with 1QIsa[a] כְּכַלֹּתְךָ *when you have finished*, i.e. כלה pi.).

*נלה II 1 vb.—**Hi.** 1 Inf. כַּנְּלֹתְךָ—**obtain, attain to,** כַּנְּלֹתְךָ לִבְגֹּד *when you have fully attained being treacherous* Is 33$_{1}$. → (?) מָנוֹל *possessions*, מִנְלָה *acquisition(s)*; cf. ניל *acquire*.

נִמְבְזָה, see בזה *despise*, ni.

*[נמה] 1 vb.—**Qal** Ptc. 1QIsa[a] הנומה (MT הִנֵּם *behold them*)—ptc. as noun, **one who brings tidings** Is 41$_{27(1QIsa^a)}$.

נִמְהָר *hasty one*, see מהר I, ni.

נְמוּאֵל 3 pr.n.m. **Nemuel.**

נְמוּאֵלִי 1 gent. **Nemuelite.**

[נָמוֹג] I *trembling one*, see מוג I, ni.

[נָמוֹג] II *wavering one*, see מוג II, ni.

*[נִמְטָר] 0.0.0.1 pr.n.[m.] **Nimtar.**

נְמָלָה 2 n.f.—pl. נְמָלִים—**ant** Pr 6$_{6}$ 30$_{25}$.

נָמֵר 6 n.m.—pl. נְמֵרִים—**leopard** Is 11$_{6}$ Jr 5$_{6}$ 13$_{23}$.

נִמְרֹד 4 pr.n.m. **Nimrod.**

נִמְרָה 1 pl.n. **Nimrah.**

נִמְרִים 2 pl.n. **Nimrim.**

*[נֶמֶשׁ] 0.0.0.3 pr.n.m. **Nemesh.**

נִמְשִׁי 5 pr.n.m. **Nimshi.**

*[נִמְשָׁר] 0.0.0.3 pr.n.m. **Nimshar.**

נָס *fugitive*, see נוס I, qal §2.

נֵס I 21.0.3 n.[m.]—cstr. נֵס; sf. נִסִּי—**1. standard, banner, flag, ensign,** as rallying point or signal Is 5$_{26}$, flag pole Is 30$_{17}$, pole for bronze serpent Nm 21$_{8}$, 'Y. is my standard' as name of altar Ex 17$_{15}$. **2. sail** of ship Is 33$_{23}$. **3. sign, warning** Nm 26$_{10}$. → נסס III *wave to and fro*, or V *rally to the banner*.

*נֵס II 1 n.[m.] **trembling** Is 31$_{9}$. → נוס II *tremble*.

*נֵס III 1 n.[m.] **(means of) flight** Ps 60$_{6}$. → נוס I *flee*.

נסא, see נשׂא *lift*, hi.

נְסִבָּה 1 n.f. **turn of affairs** 2 C 10$_{15}$. → סבב I *surround*.

*נסג 1 vb.—**Qal** 1 Impf. יַסֵּג (unless from סוג ni. *depart*) —**forge** Mc 2$_{6}$.

נסה I 36.1.4.1 vb.—**Pi.** 34.1.3.1 Pf. נִסָּה, נִסִּיתִי; impf. אֲנַסֶּה; + waw וַיְנַסּוּ, וַיְנַסֵּם; impv. נַס (נַסֵּנִי); ptc. מְנַסֶּה; inf. נַסּוֹת—**1a. test, try, prove,** of Y. testing humans Gn 22$_{1}$ Dt 8$_{2}$ (+ לָדַעַת *to know*) Jg 2$_{22}$ (+ בְּ *by* nations), humans testing Y. Ex 17$_{2}$, one person testing another 1 K 10$_{1}$ ||2 C 9$_{1}$ (+ בְּ *with* riddles). **b.** without obj., **make a test** Jg 6$_{39}$ (+ בְּ *with* fleece). **2.** (perh. ni.) **a.** with inf., **attempt to do something** Dt 4$_{34}$. **b. venture** a word to (אֶל) someone Jb 4$_{2}$. **3.** perh. **train (for military action), give experience (of war)** Ex 15$_{25}$ Jg 3$_{1}$.

Ni. 2 Pf. נִסָּה, נִסִּיתִי—**1. be trained (to wear armour)** 1 S 17$_{39}$. **2.** see Qal §2.

→ נִסּוּי *trial*, נִסָּיוֹן *test*, מַסָּה I *trial*.

נסה II *lift*, see נשׂא *lift*.

*[נִסּוּי] 0.2.4 n.[m.]—sf. Q נסויה; cstr. Q נסוי; pl. Q נסויים; sf. Q נסוייכה—**trial** Si 36$_{1}$ 4QTime 1.2$_{2}$ 4QDibHam[a] 1.5$_{18}$. → נסה I *test*.

נסח 4.2.0.1 vb.—**Qal** 3.1 Impf. יִסַּח (יִסָּחֲךָ), יִסְּחוּ—**1. tear away** person from (מִן) tent Ps 52$_{7}$, land Pr 2$_{22}$. **2. tear down** house Pr 15$_{25}$.

Ni. 1.1.0.1 + waw וְנִסַּחְתֶּם—**be torn away,** of Israelites from (מֵעַל) land Dt 28$_{63}$.

[נָסִיא], see נָשִׂיא I *prince*.

*[נִסָּיוֹן] 0.3 n.[m.]—pl. נסיונות—**test, trial** Si 4$_{17}$ 6$_{7}$ 13$_{11}$. → נסה I *test*.

[נָסִיךְ] I 1 n.[m.]—sf. נְסִיכָם—**libation** Dt 32$_{38}$. → נסך I *pour out*.

*[נָסִיךְ] II 1 n.[m.]—pl. sf. נְסִכֵיהֶם—**molten image** Dn 11$_{8}$. → נסך I *pour out*.

[נָסִיךְ] III 4.1 n.m.—pl. cstr. נְסִיכֵי; sf. נְסִיכֵמוֹ—**prince, leader** Jos 13$_{21}$ Ps 83$_{12}$. → נסך I *consecrate (with a libation)*.

נסך I 26.0.2 vb.—**Qal** 9.0.1 Pf. נָסַךְ; impf. יִסְּכוּ; inf. לִנְסֹךְ—**1. pour out** wine to (לְ) Y. Ho 9$_{4}$, libation on (עַל) altar Ex 30$_{9}$, spirit of deep sleep upon (עַל) people Is 29$_{10}$. **2. consecrate (with a libation), install** king Ps 2$_{6}$. **3. cast, forge** image of god Is 40$_{19}$.

Ni. 1 Pf. נִסַּכְתִּי—of wisdom, **be poured out,** i.e. emanate Pr 8$_{23}$.

Pi. 1.0.1 + waw וַיְנַסֵּךְ, Q וינסכוה—**pour out** water as a libation to (לְ) Y. 1 C 11$_{18}$.

Hi. 14 Pf. הִסִּכוּ; impf. אַסִּיךְ; + waw וַיַּסֵּךְ, וַיַּסִּיכוּ; impv. הַסֵּךְ; inf. abs. הַסֵּךְ; cstr. הַסֵּךְ—**pour out** libation upon (עַל) pillar Gn 35$_{14}$, to (לְ) Y. Nm 28$_{7}$.

Ho. 2 Impf. יֻסַּךְ—**be poured out** Ex 25$_{29}$||37$_{16}$.

→ נֶסֶךְ I *libation*, II *molten image*, נָסִיךְ I *libation*, II *molten image*, III *prince*, מַסֵּכָה I *image*.

נסך II 2 vb.—**Qal** 1 Ptc. pass. נְסוּכָה—pass. **be woven,** of covering Is 25$_{7}$.

Ni. 1 Pf. נִסַּכְתִּי—**be woven, fashioned,** of wisdom Pr 8$_{23}$.

→ מַסֵּכָה II *covering*, IV *scheme*, מַסֶּכֶת *web*.

נֶסֶךְ I 58.0.29.1 n.m.—נֶסֶךְ (נָסֶךְ); cstr. נֶסֶךְ; sf. נִסְכּוֹ; pl. נְסָכִים; sf. נִסְכֵּיהֶם, נִסְכֶּיהָ—**libation, drink offering** to Y. Gn 35$_{14}$, of wine Ex 29$_{40}$; to other gods Jr 7$_{18}$, of blood Ps 16$_{4}$. → נסך I *pour out*.

[נֶסֶךְ] II 4 n.m.—sf. נִסְכּוֹ; pl. sf. נִסְכֵּיהֶם—**molten image** Is 41$_{29}$ 48$_{5}$ Jr 10$_{14}$=51$_{17}$. → נסך I *pour out*.

נסס I 1 vb.—**Qal** 1 Ptc. נֹסֵס—**be sick** Is 10$_{18}$.

*נסס II 1 vb.—**Htpo.** 1 Ptc. מִתְנוֹסְסוֹת—**sparkle,** of jewels of crown Zc 9$_{16}$. → cf. נוץ II *sparkle*, נצץ I *sparkle*.

*נסס III 4 vb.—**Qal** 2 Ptc. נֹסֵס, נֹסְסָה—**1. pass to and fro,** of spirit of Y., upon (בְּ) river Is 59$_{19}$ (unless from נוס I pol. *drive on*). **2. stagger** Is 10$_{18}$.

Htpo. 2 Ptc. מִתְנוֹסְסוֹת; inf. הִתְנוֹסֵס—**sway, wave to and fro,** of standard Ps 60$_{6}$, jewels of crown Zc 9$_{16}$ (+ עַל *over* land).

→ cf. נוס II *tremble*, IV *swing*.

*נסס IV 1 vb.—**Qal** 1 Ptc. נֹסֵס—**suffer convulsions** Is 10$_{18}$.

*נסס V 1 vb.—**Htpo.** 1 Inf. הִתְנוֹסֵס—**rally to the ban-**

ner Ps 60$_6$. → נֵס *standard.*

***נסס** VI vb. **dry up,** of moisture Dt 34$_7$ (if em. נָס appar. *fled* to נָס).

נסע I $_5$ vb.—**Qal** $_3$ + waw וַיִּסַּע (וַיִּסָּעֵם)—**pull up, pull out** tent peg Is 33$_{20}$, doorpost Jg 16$_3$.

Ni. $_2$ Pf. נִסַּע—**be pulled up, removed,** of dwelling Is 38$_{12}$, cord Jb 4$_{21}$.

→ מַסָּע I *breaking* camp, (?) מַסָּע I *quarry.*

***נסע** II $_{141.0.2}$ vb.—**Qal** $_{133}$ Pf. נָסַע; impf. יִסַּע, יִסְעוּ (יִסָּעוּ); impv. סְעוּ; ptc. נֹסֵעַ; inf. abs. נָסוֹעַ; cstr. נְסֹעַ (נָסְעָם)—**travel, journey, move, go about,** of person Gn 12$_9$, wind Nm 11$_{31}$, pillar of cloud Ex 14$_{19}$, tabernacle Nm 15$_1$, ark Nm 10$_{33}$; with prep. לְ *according to,* i.e. in, stages Ex 17$_1$, מִן *from* Nm 33$_3$, אֶל *to* Nm 10$_{29}$, לִפְנֵי *before* Nm 10$_{33}$, אַחֲרֵי *after* Ex 14$_{10}$; with ה- of direction, *(to)wards* Gn 12$_9$.

Hi. $_{8.0.1}$ Impf. יַסַּע, תַּסִּיעַ; + waw וַיַּסִּעוּ; ptc. מַסִּיעַ; inf. Q לסיע (Q להסיע)—**1. lead out, bring out** people Ex 15$_{22}$ (+ מִן *from*), east wind Ps 78$_{26}$. **2. remove, move** vessel 2 K 4$_4$, boundary CD 1$_{16}$, hope Jb 19$_{10}$. **3. quarry** stone 1 K 5$_{31}$.

→ מַסָּע I *journey,* (?) מַסָּע *quarry.*

נסק, see שׂלק *burn.*

נִסְרֹךְ $_2$ pr.n.m. **Nisroch.**

נָע I *vagabond,* see נוע I, qal §3.

נָע II *rootless person,* see נוע II, qal §2.

נֵעָה $_1$ pl.n. **Neah.**

נֹעָה I $_4$ pr.n.f. **Noah.**

*[**נֹעָה**] II $_{0.0.0.2}$ pl.n. **Noah.**

[**נַעֲוָה**], see עוה *twist,* ni.

*[**נַעֲוָיָה**] $_{0.0.5}$ n.f.—cstr. נעוית; sf. נעויתי—**perversity** 1QS 5$_{24}$ 10$_{11}$ 11$_9$. → עוה *twist.*

נְעוּרִים $_{46.7.6}$ n.f.pl. **(time of) youth,** מִנְּעֻרָיו *from his youth* Gn 8$_{21}$, בִּנְעוּרֶיהָ *in her youth* Ezk 23$_8$; אֵשֶׁת נְעוּרֶיךָ *wife of your youth* Ml 2$_{14}$, חַטֹּאות נְעוּרַי *sins of my youth* Ps 25$_7$. → נער VII *be a youth.*

נְעִיאֵל $_1$ pl.n.—**Neiel.**

נָעִים I $_{13.0.1}$ adj.—cstr. נְעִים; m.pl. נְעִימִים; f.pl. נְעִמוֹת—**1. pleasant, delightful, lovely,** of person Ca 1$_{16}$, lyre Ps 81$_3$, word Pr 23$_8$, wealth Pr 24$_4$. **2.** as noun, **a. pleasant one,** of person 2 S 23$_1$. **b. pleasant place, delightful place** Ps 16$_6$. **c. pleasure, delight** Ps 16$_{11}$ Jb 36$_{11}$. → נעם I *be pleasant.*

נָעִים II $_2$ adj.—cstr. נְעִים—**1. musical, sweet sounding,** of lyre Ps 81$_3$. **2.** as noun, **sweet sounding one, singer** 2 S 23$_1$. → נעם II *sing.*

*[**נְעִימָה**] $_{0.1}$ n.f. **melody,** or perh. **pleasant sound,** made by bells on Aaron's robe Si 45$_9$. → נעם II *sing.*

נעל I $_6$ vb.—**Qal** $_6$ Pf. נָעַל; impv. נְעֹל; ptc. pass. נָעוּל, נְעֻלוֹת—**1. lock, bolt** door Jg 3$_{23}$ 2 S 13$_{17.18}$ (+ אַחֲרֵי *after*). **2.** pass. **be locked, bolted, sealed,** of door Jg 3$_{24}$, garden Ca 4$_{12}$. → מִנְעוּל *bolt,* מַנְעָל *bolt.*

נעל II $_2$ vb.—**Qal** $_1$ + waw וָאֶנְעָלֵךְ—**provide with sandals,** with accus. of person and material of sandals Ezk 16$_{10}$.

Hi. $_1$ + waw וַיַּנְעִלוּם—**provide with sandals,** with accus. of person 2 C 28$_{15}$.

→ נַעַל *sandal.*

נַעַל $_{22}$ n.f.—נָעַל; sf. נַעֲלִי; du. נַעֲלַיִם; pl. נְעָלִים, נְעָלוֹת; sf. נְעָלָיו, נַעֲלֵיכֶם—**sandal** Gn 14$_{23}$ Ex 3$_5$; removed when refusing to contract levirate marriage Dt 25$_9$ Ru 4$_7$. → נעל II *provide with sandals.*

*[**נַעֲלָם**] $_{1.1.1}$ n.[m.]—pl. נַעֲלָמִים (unless עלם ni. ptc. *ones who conceal themselves*)—**1. bribe** Am 2$_6$ 8$_6$ (both if em. נַעֲלַיִם *a pair of sandals*) Si 46$_{19}$. **2. one who takes bribes** Ps 26$_4$ 1QH 12$_{13}$. → עלם I *conceal.*

נעם I $_{8.4}$ vb.—**Qal** $_{8.3}$ Pf. נָעֵמָה, נָעַמְתָּ (נָעַמְתְּ); impf. יִנְעָם—**be pleasant, delightful, lovely, sweet,** of person 2 S 1$_{26}$ (+ לְ *to*), food Si 36$_{23(Bmg)}$ (+ מִן *[more] than*), word Ps 141$_6$, land Gn 49$_{15}$.

Hi. $_{0.1}$ Pf. הנעים—**make pleasant** sound of song Si 47$_{9(Bmg)}$.

→ נָעִים I *pleasant,* נֹעַם *pleasantness,* נַעֲמָנִים *pleasantness,* מַנְעַמִּים *delicacies.*

***נעם** II $_{0.1}$ vb.—**Hi.** $_{0.1}$ Pf. Si הנעים—**sing (with), make melodious** sound of song Si 47$_{9(Bmg)}$. → נָעִים II *musical sounding,* נְעִימָה *melody.*

[**נַעַם**] $_1$ pr.n.m. **Naam.**

נֹעַם $_{7.1}$ n.m.—cstr. נֹעַם—**pleasantness, kindness, loveliness** of Y. Ps 27$_4$, new wine Si 32$_6$; דַּרְכֵי־נֹעַם *ways of pleasantness* Pr 3$_{17}$, אִמְרֵי־ *words of* Pr 15$_{26}$; name given to staff Zc 11$_7$. → נעם I *be pleasant.*

*[**נַעַמְאֵל**] $_{0.0.0.1}$ pr.n.[m.] **Neamel.**

נַעֲמָה I $_4$ pr.n.f. **Naamah.**

נַעֲמָה II 1 pl.n. **Naamah.**

נַעֲמִי 1 gent. **Naamite.**

נָעֳמִי 21 pr.n.f. **Naomi.**

נַעֲמָן 16 pr.n.m. **Naaman.**

נַעֲמָנִים 1 n.[m.]pl.—**pleasantness,** נִטְעֵי נַעֲמָנִים *plants of pleasantness,* i.e. pleasant plants Is 17_{10}. → נעם I *be pleasant.*

נַעֲמָתִי 4 gent. **Naamathite.**

נַעֲצוּץ 2 n.[m.]—pl. נַעֲצוּצִים—**thornbush** Is 7_{19} 55_{13}.

נער I 1 vb.—**Qal** 1 Pf. נָעֲרוּ—**growl,** like (כְּ) lion Jr 51_{38}.

נער II 11.1 vb.—**Qal** 4 Pf. נָעַרְתִּי; ptc. נֹעֵר; ptc. pass. נָעוּר—**1. shake** hands Is 33_{15}, **shake out** fold of garment Ne 5_{13}, **shake off (leaves)** Is 33_9. 2. pass. **be shaken out,** of person Ne 5_{13}.

Ni. 3 Pf. נִנְעַרְתִּי; impf. יִנָּעֲרוּ, אִנָּעֵר—**1. shake oneself free** Jg 16_{20}. **2. be shaken off,** of person Ps 109_{23} (+ כְּ *as* locust) Jb 38_{13} (+ מִן *from* the earth).

Pi. 3.1 Pf. נִעֵר; impf. יְנַעֵר; + waw וַיְנַעֵר—**1. shake off, shake out** people into (בְּתוֹךְ) the sea Ex 14_{27}. **2. shake** someone **free from** (מִן) dust Si 11_{12}.

Htp. 1 Impv. הִתְנַעֲרִי—**shake oneself free from** (מִן) dust Is 52_2.

*נער III 11.1 vb.—**Qal** 4 Pf. נָעַרְתִּי; ptc. נֹעֵר; ptc. pass. נָעוּר—**1. strip, uncover, bare** hand Is 33_{15}, fold of garment Ne 5_{13}. **2.** pass. **be stripped bare,** of person Ne 5_{13}.

Ni. 3 Pf. נִנְעַרְתִּי; impf. יִנָּעֲרוּ, אִנָּעֵר—**1. be rid of,** Jg 16_{20}. **2. be stripped bare,** of person Ps 109_{23} (+ כְּ *as* locust) Jb 38_{13} (+ מִן *from* the earth).

Pi. 3.1 Pf. נִעֵר; impf. יְנַעֵר; + waw וַיְנַעֵר—**strip, uncover, bare persons** Ex 14_{27} Ps 136_{15} Si 11_{12}.

Htp. 1 Impv. הִתְנַעֲרִי—**bare oneself** of (מִן) dust Is 52_2.

→ נְעֹרֶת *tow;* cf. עור III *be bare,* ערה *be bare.*

*[נער] IV vb. Qal, **wander** Zc 11_{16} (if em. הַנַּעַר *the lad* to הַנֹּעֵר *the one who wanders*).

*[נער] V 1 vb.—**Qal** 1 Ptc. נֹעֵר—**be parched, be dry** Is 33_9.

*[נער] VI vb.—**Qal, vacillate** Zc 11_{16} (if em. הַנַּעַר *the lad* to הַנֹּעֵר *the one who vacillates*).

*[נער] VII 1 vb.—**Ni.** 1 Pf. נִנְעַרְתִּי—**lose one's youth** Ps 109_{23} (נִנְעַרְתִּי כִּי אֶרְבֶּה *I have lost my youth, truly I have aged;* if em. כָּאַרְבֶּה *as a locust*). → נַעַר *youth,* נַעֲרָה *young woman,* נֹעַר *(time of) youth,* נְעֻרוֹת *youth,* נְעֻרוֹת *youth.* → נְעוּרִים *(time of) youth.*

נַעַר 240.4.11.9 n.m.—נַעַר; cstr. נַעַר; sf. נַעֲרוֹ; pl. נְעָרִים; cstr. נַעֲרֵי; sf. נְעָרַי, נַעֲרֵיהֶם—**1. boy, lad, youth** Gn 21_{12} Jg 13_{24} 1 S 17_{33}, newborn 1 S 4_{21}, not yet weaned 1 S 1_{22}. **2. young man** Ex 24_5 Jos 6_{23}, aged seventeen Gn 37_2. **3. servant, attendant** Gn 18_7 Nm 22_{22}, **squire of king** 2 S 9_9, of prophet 1 K 18_{43}; as armour-bearer Jg 9_{54}. **4.** perh. **slave** Ho 11_1. → נער VII *be a youth.*

*[נֹעַר] n.m. **sparrow** Jb 40_{29} (if em. לְנַעֲרוֹתֶיךָ *for your young women* to כְּנֹעָר *as a sparrow*). → cf. נַעֲרָה II *sparrow,* נֹעָרָה *sparrow.*

נֹעַר 4.1 n.[m.] **(time of) youth** Ps 88_{16} Jb 33_{25} 36_{14} Pr 29_{21}. → נער VII *be a youth.*

נַעֲרָה I 63.1.11 n.f.—Kt נער; pl. נְעָרוֹת; cstr. נַעֲרוֹת; sf. נַעֲרֹתַי—**1. young woman, girl,** unmarried Gn 24_{14}, betrothed Dt 22_{23}, newly married Dt 22_{15}, secondary wife Jg 19_3, widow Ru 2_5. **2. maid, attendant, servant,** in service of woman Gn 24_{61}, wisdom Pr 9_3; gathering harvest Ru 2_8. → נער VII *be a youth.*

*[נַעֲרָה] II 1 n.f.—pl. sf. נַעֲרוֹתֶיךָ—**sparrow** Jb 40_{29}. → cf. נֹעַר *sparrow,* נֹעָרָה *sparrow.*

נַעֲרָה III 3 pr.n.f. **Naarah.**

[נַעֲרָה] IV 1 pl.n. **Naarah.**

*[נֹעָרָה] n.f. **sparrow** Jb 40_{29} (if em. לְנַעֲרוֹתֶיךָ *for your young women* to כְּנֹעָרוֹת *as the sparrows*). → cf. נֹעַר *sparrow,* נַעֲרָה II *sparrow.*

*[נַעֲרוּת] 0.3 n.f.—sf. נערותי—**(time of) youth** Si 30_{12} $51_{14(B).28}$. → נער VII *be a youth.*

[נְעֻרוֹת] 1 n.f.pl.—sf. נְעֻרֹתֵיהֶם—**(time of) youth** Jr 32_{30}. → נער VII *be a youth.*

נַעֲרַי 1 pr.n.m. **Naarai.**

נְעַרְיָה 3 pr.n.m. **Neariah.**

נַעֲרָן 1 pl.n. **Naaran.**

נְעֹרֶת 2 n.f. **tow,** coarse, flammable fibres of flax Jg 16_9 Is 1_{31}. → נער III *strip.*

נֹף 7 pl.n. **Memphis.**

נֶפֶג 4 pr.n.m. **Nepheg.**

[נָפָה] I 1 n.f.—cstr. נָפַת—**sieve** Is 30_{28}. → נוף I *wave.*

[נָפָה] II 3 n.f.—cstr. נָפַת; pl. cstr. נָפוֹת—**height, hill-country,** נָפוֹת דּוֹר *heights of Dor* (unless *Naphoth-*

dor) Jos 11_2. → cf. נוֹף I *height*.

*[נָפָה] III 4 n.f.—cstr. נָפַת; pl. cstr. נָפוֹת—**1. yoke, bridle** Is 30_{28}. **2. district,** נָפוֹת דּוֹר *districts of Dor* (unless *Naphoth-dor*) Jos 11_2.

[נְפוּסִים], see נְפִיסִים *Nephisim*.

[נָפוּץ] *dispersed one*, see נפץ II, qal §2.

[נְפוּשְׁסִים] 1 pr.n.m. **Nephushesim.**

נפח I 13.1.5 vb.—**Qal** 9.1.3 נָפַחְתִּי; + waw וַיִּפַּח; impv. פְּחִי; ptc. נֹפֵחַ; ptc. pass. נָפוּחַ; inf. לָפַחַת—**1. breathe, blow,** breath of life Gn 2_7 (+ בְּ *into* nostrils), sigh or (last) breath Jr 15_9. **2. blow, fan** fire, with accus. Ezk 22_{20} (+ עַל *upon*); בְּ of obj. Is 54_{16}. 3. ptc. as noun, **smith** 1QH 13_{16}. **4.** pass. **be blown, be fanned,** of pot placed on fire, thus made to boil Jr 1_{13}.

Ni. 1.0.1 Impf. ינפח; inf. Sam הנפח—**be blown, be fanned,** of furnace 4QInstr[b] 4_2, fire Nm $21_{30(Sam)}$.

Pu. 1.0.1 Pf. נֻפַּח; ptc.Q מנפח—**be blown, fanned,** of fire Jb 20_{26}.

Hi. 2 Pf. הִפַּחְתִּי, הִפַּחְתֶּם—**1. cause to breathe** sigh or (last) breath Jb 31_{39}. **2. sniff at** name of Y. (in contempt) Ml 1_{13}.

→ מַפָּח *expiring*, מַפֻּחַ *bellows*, תַּפּוּחַ *apple*.

*נפח II 1 vb.—**Hi.** 1 Pf. הִפַּחְתִּי—**beat, afflict** Jb 31_{39}.

נֹפַח 1 pl.n. **Nophah.**

נַפָּח *smith*, see נפח I, qal §3.

נְפִילִים, see נְפִלִים *giants*.

[נְפִישְׁסִים], see נְפוּשְׁסִים *Nephushesim*.

[נְפִיסִים] 1 pr.n.m. **Nephisim.**

נָפִישׁ 3 pr.n.m. **Naphish.**

נֹפֶךְ 4.1 n.[m.] **turquoise, garnet,** or other (semi-) precious stone, in Aaron's breastplate Ex 28_{18}||39_{11}, assoc. with wealth of Tyre Ezk 27_{16}.

נפל I 434.13.73 vb.—**Qal** 367.11.52 Pf. נָפַל; impf. יִפֹּל; + waw וַיִּפֹּל (וַיִּפָּל־); impv. נִפְלוּ; ptc. נֹפֵל, נֹפֶלֶת; inf. abs. נָפוֹל; cstr. נְפֹל (נָפְלוֹ, נִפְלוֹ)—**1a. fall,** of persons, oft. by accident Gn 49_{17} (+ אָחוֹר *backward*) Dt 22_8 (+ מִן *from* roof) 2 S 4_4 2 K 1_2 (+ בְּעַד *through* lattice), through violence 2 S 2_{16}; of beasts Ex 21_{33}, objects 1 S 26_{20} (+ אַרְצָה *to the ground*) 2 S 20_8 2 K 6_5 (+ אֶל *into* water). **b. fall (down), descend,** of hailstones Ezk 13_{11}, star Is 14_{12} (+ מִן *from* heaven), bird Am 3_5 (+ עַל *into* trap), wealth and people Ezk 27_{27} (+ בְּ into *sea*). **c. fall down, collapse, give way,** of wall Ezk 38_{20} (+ לְ *to* ground), tent Jg 7_{13}, house Jg 16_{30} (+ עַל *upon* someone), mountains Jb 14_{18}, tree Ec 11_3 (+ בְּ *towards* south). **d. fall, drop,** of countenance Gn 4_5. **2. fall,** i.e. **a.** die Ex 19_{21}, in warfare, conquest, by (לְ) sword Lv 26_7, by (בְּ) hand of someone 1 C 5_{10}. **b. come to ruin, experience calamity** Is 3_8. **3. fall (in exhaustion), collapse (through lack of strength)** 2 S 1_{10} Ps 118_{13}; **fail,** of courage 1 S 17_{32}. **4. fall away, waste away,** of thigh Nm 5_{21}. **5. be void,** i.e. not reckoned Nm 6_{12}, **fail (to be accomplished)** Jos 21_{45}. **6. be born** Is 26_{18}. **7. settle camp** alongside (עַל־פְּנֵי) Gn 25_{18}. **8a.** of lot, **fall** Jon 1_7 (+ עַל *upon*) 1 C 26_{14} (+ לְ *to*) CD 20_4 (+ בְּתוֹךְ *among*). **b.** of land, **fall (by lot), be allocated** Nm 34_2 (+ בְּ *as* inheritance) Jos 17_5. **9. turn out, happen** Ru 3_{18} Si 37_8 (+ אֶל *to*). **10. fall upon, come upon, a.** with עַל, of sleep Gn 15_{12}, dread Jos 2_9, disaster Is 47_{11}, hand of Y. Ezk 8_1. **b.** with בְּ, of word from Y. Is 9_7. **11. come before** (לִפְנֵי), i.e. **be accepted,** of supplication Jr 36_7. **12. fall upon,** i.e. attack, with עַל Jr 48_{32}; בְּ Jos 11_7. **13. fall into** (בְּ) the hand of Jg 15_{18}. **14. fall away, desert** 2 K 7_4 (+ אֶל *to*) Jr $37_{13.14}$ (+ עַל *to*). **15. alight, dismount,** from (מֵעַל) camel Gn 24_{64}, chariot 2 K 5_{21}. **16. fall down (deliberately), prostrate oneself, throw oneself down,** upon (עַל) sword 1 S 31_4||1 C 10_4, upon someone's neck in affection Gn 33_4, upon one's face in reverence Gn 17_3; before (לִפְנֵי) someone in respect Gn 44_{14} (+ אַרְצָה *to the ground*); **bend down** to help someone Si 12_{15}. **17. be prostrate, lying down, fallen down,** of person, on (עַל) couch Est 7_8, dead on ground Dt 21_1; of animal Dt 22_4, booth Am 9_{11}. **18. be inferior** to (מִן) Jb 12_3, **be low** in (בְּ) one's own sight Ne 6_{16}. **19.** ptc. as noun, **a. fallen one** 1QM 14_{11}. **b. deserter** Jr 39_9.

Pilel 1 + waw וְנִפְלַל—**fall,** by (בְּ) sword Ezk 28_{23}.

Hi. 61.2.18 Pf. הִפַּלְתִּי, הִפִּיל; impf. יַפִּיל; + waw וַיַּפֵּל, וַיַּפִּילוּ; impv. הַפִּילוּ, הַפִּלָה; ptc. מַפִּיל; inf. לִנְפֹּל לְהַפִּיל, Q הַפִּילְכֶם, לפיל—**1a. cause to fall, cause to drop,** obj. person, into (בְּ) pit Ps 140_{11}, thing, from (מִן) hand Ezk 30_{22}; **place among** (בְּ) nations Ps 106_{27}. **b. cause to fall down, cause to descend,** obj. birds Ps 78_{28}, stars Dn 8_{10} (+ אַרְצָה *to the ground*). **c. cause to fall**

down, cause to collapse, demolish wall 2 S 20_{15}, fell tree 2 K 3_{19}, **knock out** tooth Ex 21_{27}. **d. let countenance fall,** i.e. look in anger, upon (בְּ) Jr 3_{12}. **2. cause to fall, bring down,** i.e. cause to die Pr 7_{26}, by (בְּ) sword 2 K 19_7||Is 37_7, hand of 1 S 18_{25}. **3. cause to fall away, cause to waste away,** obj. thigh Nm 5_{22}. **4. let fall (to the ground), let fail** any of (מִן) one's words 1 S 3_{19}. **5. drop, abandon** any of (מִן) one's practices Jg 2_{19}. **6. give birth to, cause to be born** Is 26_{19}. **7. cast** stone upon (עַל) someone Nm 35_{23}, cedars into (עַל) fire Jr 22_7. **8a. cast lot** Jon 1_7; obj. omitted 1 S 14_{42} (+ בֵּין *between*). **b. throw in one's lot among** (בְּתוֹךְ), i.e. join together with Pr 1_{14}. **c. cause to fall (by lot), allocate** land as (בְּ) inheritance Jos 13_6 (+ לְ *to*). **9. cause to fall upon, cause to come upon** (עַל), obj. sleep Gn 2_{21}, terror Jr 15_8. **10. cause to fall before, present supplication** before (לִפְנֵי) Jr 38_{26} Dn 9_{18}. **11. cause someone to lie down** Dt 25_2. **12. debase, disgrace** oneself (accus.) in (בְּ) assembly Si 7_7.

Ho. 0.0.1 Pf. הוּפַל—**be caused to fall, be cast down** from (מִן) the truth 4QD[a] 5.2_{10}.

Htp. 5.0.2 Pf. הִתְנַפַּלְתִּי; + waw וָאֶתְנַפַּל; ptc. מִתְנַפֵּל; inf. הִתְנַפֵּל—**1. throw oneself upon** (עַל) someone Gn 43_{18}. **2. prostrate oneself, lie prostrate before** (לִפְנֵי) Y. Dt 9_{18}, house of Y. Ezr 10_1.

→ נְפִלִים *giants,* נֵפֶל *miscarriage,* מַפָּל *refuse,* מַפָּלָה *ruin,* מַפֶּלֶת *downfall.*

***נפל II** 1 vb.—**Qal** 1 Impf. יִפֹּל—**wither,** of person Pr 11_{28}. → cf. נבל I *wither.*

נֹפֵל *fallen one, deserter,* see נפל I, qal §19.

נֵפֶל 3 n.m.—נֵפֶל; cstr. נֵפֶל—**miscarriage** Ps 58_9 Jb 3_{16} Ec 6_3. → נפל I *fall.*

נִפְלָאוֹת *wonders,* see פלא, ni. §3.

נְפִלִים 3.0.1 n.m.pl.—נְפִילִים; cstr. Q נפילי—**giants, Nephilim,** antediluvians Gn 6_4, early inhabitants of Canaan Nm 13_{33}. → נפל I *fall.*

***נפת** 1.1 vb. **Qal, sprinkle** bed with spices Pr 7_{17} (if em. נַפְתִּי appar. *I have waved* [נוף I] to נַפֹּתִי *I have sprinkled*).

Hi. 1.1 Impf. תָּנִיף (unless נוף hi.)—**sprinkle** rain Ps 68_{10}, snow Si $43_{17(B)}$.

→ cf. נוף II *sprinkle,* נוב *be full of sap.*

נפץ I 18 vb.—**Qal** 2 Ptc. pass. נָפוּץ; inf. abs. נָפוֹץ—**1. shatter, smash** jar Jg 7_{19}. **2.** pass. **be shattered,** of pot Jr 22_{28}.

Pi. 15 Impf. תְּנַפְּצֵם; + waw וְנִפַּץ; inf. נַפֵּץ—**break up, shatter, smash to pieces** nations Ps 2_9 (+ כְּ *as* vessel), children Ps 137_9 (+ אֶל *against* rock), rafts 1 K 5_{23}, jars Jr 48_{12}.

Pu. 1 Ptc. מְנֻפָּצוֹת—**be smashed to pieces,** of chalk stone Is 27_9.

→ נֶפֶץ *cloudburst,* מַפָּץ *shattering,* מַפֵּץ *club.*

נפץ II 4.0.1 vb.—**Qal** 4.0.1 Pf. נָפַץ; ptc. pass. נְפֻצוֹת; inf. abs. Q נפוץ—**1.** intrans., **scatter, disperse,** of people Gn 9_{19} 1 S 13_{11} (+ מֵעַל *from*) Is 33_3. **2.** pass. ptc. as noun, **dispersed one** Is 11_{12}. → cf. פוץ *be scattered.*

נֶפֶץ 1.0.1 n.[m.] **cloudburst,** or **pattering of rain** Is 30_{30} 1QH 10_{27}. → נפץ I *shatter.*

נפשׁ 3 vb.—**Ni.** 3 + waw וַיִּנָּפַשׁ (וַיִּנָּפֵשׁ)—**be refreshed, refresh oneself** Ex 23_{12} 31_{17} 2 S 16_{14}. → נֶפֶשׁ I *soul.*

נֶפֶשׁ I 754.64.197.2 n.f.—נֶפֶשׁ; cstr. נֶפֶשׁ; sf. נַפְשִׁי; pl. נְפָשׁוֹת, נְפָשִׁים; cstr. נַפְשׁוֹת; sf. נַפְשֹׁתֵיכֶם, נַפְשֹׁתָם—**1. palate, throat, gullet** Nm 11_6 Is 5_{14}. **2. neck** Ps 105_{18}. **3. appetite, hunger, desire, wish** Ex 15_9 Jr 50_{19} Pr 6_{30}; עַזֵּי־נֶפֶשׁ dogs *strong of appetite,* i.e. with a strong appetite Is 56_{11}. **4. soul, heart, mind,** as seat of desire, will, feelings and emotions Lv 26_{11} (soul of Y.) Dt 6_5 Is 61_{10}, also of intellect Jos 23_{14}; צָרַת נַפְשׁוֹ *distress of his soul* Gn 42_{21}, תַּאֲוַת־נֶפֶשׁ *desire of the soul* Is 26_8. **5. breath, last breath, soul,** as inner being, נֶפֶשׁ בְּעָלֶיהָ *last breath of its owners* Jb 31_{39}, נֶפֶשׁ חַיָּה *breath of life* Gn 1_{30}, מַפַּח־נָפֶשׁ *expiring of the life* Jb 11_{20}. **6. life, soul,** as the vital self, הַדָּם הוּא הַנָּפֶשׁ *the blood is the life* Dt 12_{23}, נֶפֶשׁ תַּחַת נָפֶשׁ *a life shall be for a life* Lv 24_{18}, נֶפֶשׁ הָאָדָם *life of a human being* Gn 9_5, מְבַקְשֵׁי נַפְשָׁם *those who seek their life* Jr 19_7. **7. being, creature(s),** שֶׁרֶץ נֶפֶשׁ *swarms of creatures* Gn 1_{20}, כָּל־נֶפֶשׁ חַיָּה *every living creature* Gn 9_{12}. **8a. person, individual,** of either sex Gn 17_{14} 36_6. **b.** coll., **persons, people** Gn 46_{18}. **c.** perh. **deceased person, (dead) body,** נֶפֶשׁ אָדָם *dead body of a human being* Nm 9_6, נֶפֶשׁ מֵת *body of the dead* Nm 6_6, טְמֵא־נֶפֶשׁ *impure one of,* i.e. made unclean by, *a body* Lv 22_4. **d.** perh. specif. **slave**

Gn 12₅. **9a.** נֶפֶשׁ with pronom. sf., equivalent to personal pron., נַפְשִׁי **I, me** Gn 12₁₃ Ps 120₂, נַפְשְׁךָ **you** 1 S 1₂₆, נַפְשׁוֹ **he** Ps 25₁₃, etc. **b.** as reflexive pron., **oneself,** without pronom. sf. Nm 30₁₄; with pronom. sf., נַפְשִׁי **myself** Ps 35₁₃, נַפְשְׁךָ **yourself** Dt 4₉, נַפְשׁוֹ **himself** Ex 30₁₂, etc. **c.** as possessive pron.: נַפְשִׁי **my,** שֹׂטְנֵי נַפְשִׁי *my accusers* Ps 71₁₃; נַפְשׁוֹ **his,** שֹׁפְטֵי נַפְשׁוֹ *his judges,* i.e. those who condemn him Ps 109₃. **10. sepulchre, (funerary) monument** 3QTr 1₅. → נפשׁ *breathe.*

*נֶפֶשׁ II ₂ n.f.—sf. נַפְשֶׁךָ—**abundance** Is 58₁₀ Pr 6₂₆.

*נֶפֶשׁ III ₂ n.[m.]—נֶפֶשׁ—**perfume, odour,** עֲצַת־נֶפֶשׁ *tree of perfume,* i.e. odoriferous tree Pr 27₉, בָּתֵּי הַנֶּפֶשׁ *houses,* i.e. boxes, *of perfume* Is 3₂₀.

[נֹפֶת] ₁ n.f.—נֶפֶת—**height** Jos 17₁₁. → נוף V *raise.*

נֹפֶת ₆.₀.₁ n.m. **flowing honey** Pr 5₃ 24₁₃; נֹפֶת צוּפִים *flowing honey of,* i.e. from, *the honeycomb* Ps 19₁₁. → נוף II *sparkle.*

נֶפְתּוֹחַ ₂ pl.n. **Nephtoah.**

[נַפְתּוּלִים] ₁ n.[m.]pl.—**wrestlings,** נַפְתּוּלֵי אֱלֹהִים *wrestlings of God,* i.e. mighty wrestlings Gn 30₈. → פתל *twist.*

[נַפְתֻּחִי] ₂ gent. **Naphtuhite.**

נַפְתָּלִי ₅₁.₀.₇ pr.n.m. **Naphtali.**

[נֵץ] I ₁.₂.₁ n.f.—sf. נִצָּה—**blossom** Gn 40₁₀ Si 50₈ 51₁₅(11QPsᵃ) 1QH 18₃₂. → נצץ *sparkle;* cf. נִצָּה *blossom,* נִצָּץ *blossom.*

נֵץ II ₃ n.m. **hawk** Lv 11₁₆||Dt 14₁₅ Jb 39₂₆. → cf. נֹצָה II *hawk.*

נצא ₁ vb.—**Qal** ₁ Inf. abs. נָצֹא—**fly away** Jr 48₉. → cf. נצה III *fly.*

נצב I ₇₅.₀.₇ vb.—**Qal** ₀.₀.₁ Ptc. pass. נצובים—pass. **be stood, positioned** 4QapJerB 20₄.

Ni. ₅₁.₀.₂ Pf. נִצְּבָה; ptc. נִצָּב, נִצָּבָה (נִצֶּבֶת)—**1. stand, position oneself, stand upright,** of persons Gn 18₂ (+ עַל *beside*) Ex 5₂₀ (+ לִקְרָאתָם *to meet them*), sheaves Gn 37₇, floods Ex 15₈ (+ כְּמוֹ *as in* a heap). **2. present oneself to** (לְ) Y. Ex 34₂. **3. be set over** (עַל), i.e. in charge of Ru 2₅. **4. be set, stand firm,** of word of Y. Ps 119₈₉. **5.** perh. **be healthy** Zc 11₁₆. **6.** ptc. as noun, **a. head,** i.e. chief, over (עַל) 1 S 19₂₀. **b. governor, deputy, officer** 1 K 4₅.₇ (+ עַל *over*).

Hi. ₂₁.₀.₄ Pf. הִצִּיב, הִצַּבְתָּ; impf. יַצִּיב (יַצֵּב); + waw וַיַּצֵּב (וַיַּצִּבֵנִי, וַיַּצֶּב־); impv. הַצִּיבִי; ptc. מַצִּיב; inf. הַצִּיב—**1. cause to stand, set up, erect monument** 1 S 15₁₂ (+ לְ *for* oneself), altar Gn 33₂₀, door Jos 6₂₆. **2. set, place person** Ps 41₁₃ (+ לִפְנֵי *before*) Lm 3₁₂ (+ כְּ *as* a target), lamb Gn 21₂₈ (+ לְבַד *apart*). **3. fix, establish boundary** Dt 32₈. **4.** perh. **set straight, sharpen** goad 1 S 13₂₁.

Ho. ₃ Pf. הֻצַּב; ptc. מֻצָּב—**be set up, established** on the earth (אַרְצָה), of ladder Gn 28₁₂.

→ נִצָּב I *hilt,* II *image,* נְצִיב I *pillar,* מַצָּב *standing place,* מֻצָּב *siege mound,* מַצָּבָה *guard,* מַצֵּבָה *pillar.*

*נצב II ₁ vb.—**Ni.** ₁ Ptc. נִצָּבָה—**be weak, exhausted** Zc 11₁₆.

*נצב III ₁ vb.—**Ni.** ₁ Ptc. נִצָּב—**vanish, die** Ps 39₆.

נִצָּב I ₁ n.m. **hilt** of sword Jg 3₁₁. → נצב I *stand.*

*נִצָּב II ₁ n.[m.] **image, semblance** (unless ni. ptc.) Ps 39₆. → נצב I *stand.*

נִצָּב III *head, governor,* see נצב I, ni. §6.

נְצִבִי, see נְצִיב I *pillar.*

נצה I ₈.₂ vb.—**Ni.** ₅.₁ Impf. יִנָּצוּ; ptc. נִצִּים—**fight, quarrel** Ex 2₁₃ Dt 25₁₁ (+ יַחְדָּו *together*) Si 8₃ (+ עִם *with*).

Pi. ₀.₁ Impf. ינצה—perh. **set in motion** Si 43₅(Bmg).

Hi. ₃ Pf. הִצּוּ; inf. הַצּוֹתוֹ—**fight, strive against** (עַל) Nm 26₉, with (אֵת) Ps 60₂.

→ מַצָּה II *strife,* מַצּוּת *strife.*

*נצה II ₆ vb.—**Qal** ₁ Impf. תִּצֶּינָה— **go to ruin,** of cities Jr 4₇.

Ni. ₅ Pf. נִצְּתָה (unless יצת ni.); ptc. נִצִּים—**be in ruins, be ruined, be laid waste** Jr 2₁₅ 9₁₁ 46₁₉; גַּלִּים נִצִּים *ruined heaps* 2 K 19₂₅||Is 37₂₆.

נצה III ₁ vb.—**Qal** ₁ Pf. נָצוּ—**fly,** of exiles Lm 4₁₅. → cf. נצא *fly.*

*נצה IV ₁ vb.—**Qal** ₁ Pf. נָצוּ—**hasten,** of priests and prophets Lm 4₁₅.

*נצה V ₁ vb.—**Qal** ₁ Pf. נָצוּ—**be joined,** of exiles Lm 4₁₅.

נִצָּה ₂ n.f.—sf. נִצָּתוֹ—**blossom** of vine Is 18₅, olive Jb 15₃₃. → נצץ I *sparkle;* cf. נֵץ I *blossom,* נִצָּץ *blossom.*

נֹצָה I, see נוֹצָה *plumage.*

נֹצָה II ₁ n.f. **hawk** Jb 39₁₃. → cf. נֵץ II *hawk.*

*[נָצוּר] I ₁ n.[m.]—pl. נְצוּרִים—**secret place,** or perh. **watch-hut** Is 65₄. → נצר I *keep.*

*[נָצוֹר] II 1 n.[m.]—pl. נְצוּרִים—**mountain** Is 65_{4}.

נָצוֹר III *preserved one*, see נצר I *keep*.

נְצוּרָה *murmuring throng*, see נצר II.

נְצוּרִים *secret places*, see נצר I, qal §3c (2).

*נצח I 64.0.8 vb.—**Pi.** 64.0.8 Ptc. מְנַצֵּחַ; inf. נַצֵּחַ—**1a. oversee, supervise** work assoc. with temple Ezr 3_{8} (עַל of obj.), workers 2 C 2_{1} (עַל of obj.) 34_{13} (לְ of obj.). **b. lead music** 1 C 15_{21}. **c. direct slingers** 1QM 8_{1}, battle 1QM 8_{9}. **2.** ptc. as noun, **a. overseer, supervisor** 2 C 2_{17}. **b.** perh. **director of music,** or **famous one** Hb 3_{19} Ps 4_{1}.

*נצח II 0.5.1 vb.—**Qal** 0.3.1 (unless pi.) Pf. Si נצח; impf. Si ינצח—**shine, flash,** of lightning Si 35_{10}.

Pi. 0.2 Impf. ינצח—**cause to shine, make brilliant** Si $43_{5.13}$.

→ נֵצַח II *glory*.

נצח III 1 vb.—**Ni.** 1 Ptc. נִצַּחַת—ptc. as adj., **enduring, persistent,** of apostasy Jr 8_{5}. → נֵצַח I *endurance*.

*נצח IV 0.0.2 vb.—**Qal** 0.0.1 Pf. נצחו—**defeat** enemies 11QT 58_{11}.

Pi. 0.0.1 Inf. נצח—**be victorious over** (לְ) spirit 4Q Bark[c] 1.1_{1}.

Htp. 0.0.1 Ptc. מתנצחה—of battle, **be directed,** perh. **prevail against** (בְּ) 1QM 16_{9}.

→ נֵצַח III *victory*.

נֵצַח I 41.3.39.1 n.m.—נֶצַח; cstr. נֵצַח; pl. נְצָחִים—**1. endurance, everlastingness, endlessness,** מַשֻּׁאוֹת נֶצַח *ruins of everlastingness*, i.e. everlasting ruins Ps 74_{3}; לָנֶצַח *to everlastingness*, i.e. for ever 2 S 2_{26}, לְנֵצַח נְצָחִים *to everlastingness of everlastingnesses*, i.e. for ever and ever Is 34_{10}; נֶצַח without prep., *(to) everlastingness*, i.e. for ever Ps 16_{11}. **2. faithful one** of Israel 1 S 15_{29}. → נצח III *endure*.

*נֵצַח II 5.0.1 n.m.—cstr. נֵצַח; sf. נִצְחִי—**1. glory, eminence** Lm 3_{18} 1 C 29_{11}; נֵצַח יִשְׂרָאֵל *Glory of Israel*, as divine title 1 S 15_{29}. **2.** perh. **purification** of the heart 4QMidrEschat [b] 9_{9}. → נצח II *shine*.

*[נֵצַח] III 0.0.2 n.[m.]—cstr. נצח—**victory** 1QM 4_{13} 4Q Hod[a] 7.1_{16}. → נצח IV *conquer*.

[נֵצַח] IV 3 n.m.—sf. נִצְחָם, נִצְחִי—**juice** of grape, perh. as metonym, or metaphorical, for blood Is $63_{3.6}$ perh. Lm 3_{18}.

נְצִיב I 14.1.1 n.m.—cstr. נְצִיב; pl. נְצִיבִים; cstr. נְצִבֵי—**1. pillar** of salt Gn 19_{26}. **2. governor, deputy** 1 K 4_{19}. **3. garrison** of the Philistines 1 S 13_{3}. → נצב I *stand*.

נְצִיב II 1.0.0.2 pl.n. **Nezib.**

נְצִיחַ 2 pr.n.m. **Neziah.**

[נָצִיר] 1 adj.—pl. cstr. Kt נצירי—as noun, **preserved one** Is 49_{6}. → נצר *keep*.

נצל 213.7.34 vb.—**Ni.** 15.1.5 Pf. נִצַּלְנוּ; impf. יִנָּצֵל; impv. הִנָּצֵל; ptc. Q ניצל; inf. הִנָּצֵל—**be delivered, deliver oneself, escape,** abs. Gn 32_{31}; from (מִן) enemies Ps 69_{15}, hand, i.e. power, of evil Hb 2_{9}; from (מִפְּנֵי) king Is 20_{6}; (of slave) from (מֵעִם) master to (אֶל) someone else Dt 23_{16}.

Pi. 4 Impf. יְנַצְּלוּ; + waw וַיְנַצְּלוּ, וְנִצַּלְתֶּם—**1a. strip, plunder, spoil** someone Ex 3_{22} 12_{36}. **b. take spoil** for (לְ) oneself 2 C 20_{25}. **2.** obj. נֶפֶשׁ, **deliver oneself** Ezk 14_{14}.

Hi. 191.6.28 Pf. הִצִּיל, הִצַּלְתָּ; impf. יַצִּיל (יַצִּלֵם, יַצֶּל); + waw וַיַּצֵּל; impv. הַצֵּל (הַצִּילָה), הַצִּילוּ; ptc. מַצִּיל; inf. abs. הַצֵּל; cstr. הַצִּיל—**1. take away, snatch away** cattle Gn 31_{9}, riches from (מִן) someone Gn 31_{16}, word from mouth Ps 119_{43}. **2a. deliver, save, rescue** person from (מִן) the hand of someone Gn 32_{12}, from enemies Ps 59_{2}, distress 1 S 26_{14}; life from death Jos 2_{13}, foot from slipping Ps 56_{14}, sheep from mouth of predator 1 S 17_{35}; **secure** plot of land 2 S 23_{12}||1 C 11_{14}. **b. recover** cities Jg 11_{26}, territory from (מִן) hand of Philistines 1 S 7_{14}, property 1 S 30_{18}.

Ho. 2 Ptc. מֻצָּל—**be snatched, be rescued,** of brand from (מִן) fire Zc 3_{2}.

Htp. 1 + waw וַיִּתְנַצְּלוּ—**strip oneself of** ornaments Ex 33_{6}.

Maphul 0.0.1 Ptc. מצול—**be delivered** from (מִן) trouble 4QMMT C_{24}.

→ הַצָּלָה *deliverance*.

[נִצָּן] 1.0.1 n.[m.]—pl. נִצָּנִים; cstr. Q נצני—**blossom** Ca 2_{12} 4QBéat 2.3_{5}. → נצץ *sparkle*; cf. נֵץ *blossom*, נִצָּה *blossom*.

*[נֶצֶף] 0.0.0.2 n.[m.]—**nezeph,** weight of c. 10 grams Weights 31, 33.

*[נִצְפָּה] 0.0.1 n.f.—**caper bush,** or perh. **vine,** source of new wine 4QpsEzek[b] 1.2_{5}.

נצץ I $_{4.0.2}$ vb.—**Qal** $_{1}$ Ptc. נֹצְצִים—**sparkle,** of living beings Ezk 1_{7}.

Hi. $_{3.0.2}$ Pf. הֵנֵצוּ; impf. יָנֵאץ—**blossom, flourish,** of pomegranates Ca 6_{11} 7_{13}, almond tree Ec 12_{5}.

→ נֵץ I *blossom,* נִצָּה *blossom,* נִצָּן *blossom,* נִיצוֹץ *spark;* cf. נוץ II *sparkle,* נסס II *sparkle.*

***נצץ** II $_{1}$ vb.—**Hi.** $_{1}$ Impf. יָנֵאץ—**become dry,** of almond tree Ec 12_{5}.

נצר I $_{63.2.5}$ vb.—**Qal** $_{63.2.5}$ Pf. נָצְרוּ, נָצַרְתִּי; impf. יִצֹּר, יִצְּרוּ (יִנְצְרֵהוּ, יִצְּרוּנִי, יִנְצֹּרוּ); impv. נְצֹר (נִצְּרָה, נִצְרָהָ); ptc. נֹצֵר; ptc. pass. נָצוּר; inf. abs. נָצוֹר; cstr. לִנְצֹר—**1a. keep (safely), preserve, protect** someone Dt 32_{10} (+ כְּ *as* pupil of eye) Is 42_{6} Ps 32_{7} (+ מִן *from* distress). **b. watch, guard** vineyard Is 27_{3}, fortification Na 2_{2}, soul Pr 24_{12}, one's tongue from (מִן) evil Ps 34_{14}. **c. keep, observe** commandments Ps 78_{7}, wisdom Pr 3_{21}, loyalty Ex 34_{7} (+ לְ *for*). **2.** ptc. as noun, **a. watcher, sentry, guardian** Jr 31_{6}; Y. as נֹצֵר הָאָדָם *watcher of humans* Jb 7_{20}. **b. besieger** Jr 4_{16}. **3.** pass. **a. be wily,** of woman Pr 7_{10} (נְצֻרַת לֵב *wily of heart*). **b. be besieged,** of city Is 1_{8}. **c.** pass. ptc. as noun, (1) **preserved one** Ezk 6_{12}. (2) נְצוּרִים **secret places** Is 65_{4}. (3) נְצֻרוֹת **secret things, hidden things** Is 48_{6}.

→ נָצוּר I *secret place,* נָצִיר *preserved,* נִצְּרָה *seal;* cf. נטר I *keep.*

***נצר** II $_{4}$ vb.—**Qal** $_{4}$ Ptc. נֹצְרִים; ptc. pass. נְצוּרָה—**1.** ptc. as noun, **murmuring throng** Jr 4_{16} 31_{6}. **2.** pass. **a. be tumultuous,** of woman Pr 7_{10} (נְצֻרַת לֵב *tumultuous of heart*). **b. hum,** of city Is 1_{8}.

נֵצֶר I $_{4.1.6}$ n.m.—cstr. נֵצֶר; sf. Si נצרו—**shoot, branch(es)** Is 11_{1} Is 60_{21} 1QH 14_{15}.

***נֵצֶר** II $_{1}$ n.m. **putrefying matter** Is 14_{19}.

נֹצֵר *watcher, besieger,* see נצר I, qal §2.

***נִצְּרָה** $_{1}$ n.f. **seal** (unless נצר impv.) Ps 141_{3}. → נצר I *keep.*

נְצֻרוֹת *secret things,* see נצר I, §3c (3).

נֹצְרִים *murmuring throng,* see נצר II, §1.

***נצת** $_{29.2}$ vb. **kindle,** a possible alternative verb for the forms (exc. אֲצִיתֶנָּה at Is 27_{4}) analysed under יצת *kindle.*

נקב I $_{20}$ vb.—**Qal** $_{14}$ Pf. נָקַבְתָּ; impf. יִקֹּב־ (יִקְּבֻנּוּ), יִקְּבֻהוּ; + waw וַיִּקֹּב; impv. נָקְבָה; ptc. נֹקֵב; pass. נָקוּב; inf. נָקְבוֹ—**1a. pierce** hand 2 K 18_{21}||Is 36_{6}, cheek Jb 40_{26} (+ בְּ *with* hook). **b. bore** hole 2 K 12_{10}. **2. designate** name Is 62_{2}, wages Gn 30_{28}. **3. blaspheme** name of Y. Lv 24_{11}. **4.** pass. **a. be pierced,** i.e. have holes, of bag Hb 1_{6}. **b.** pass. ptc. as noun, **distinguished one** Am 6_{1}.

Ni. $_{6}$ Pf. נִקְּבוּ—**be designated** by (בְּ) name Nm 1_{17}.

→ נֶקֶב I *engraving,* II *pipe,* III *passage, mine,* IV *orifice,* נְקִבָה *boring through,* נְקֵבָה *female,* מַקֶּבֶת I *hammer,* II *excavation.*

***נקב** II $_{3}$ vb.—**Qal** $_{14}$ + waw וַיִּקֹּב; ptc. נֹקֵב; inf. נָקְבוֹ—**blaspheme** name of Y. Lv 24_{11}. → cf. קבב *curse.*

[נֶקֶב] I $_{1}$ n.[m.]—pl. sf. נְקָבֶיךָ—**engraving, socket, spangle, bead,** feature or item of jewellery Ezk 28_{13}. → נקב I *pierce.*

***[נֶקֶב]** II $_{1}$ n.[m.]—pl. sf. נְקָבֶיךָ—**pipe, flute,** as hollowed out Ezk 28_{13}. → נקב I *pierce.*

***נֶקֶב** III $_{2}$ n.[m.]—pl. sf. נְקָבֶיךָ—**passage, mine** Jos 19_{33} Ezk 28_{13}. → נקב I *pierce.*

***[נֶקֶב]** IV $_{1}$ n.[m.]—pl. sf. נְקָבֶיךָ—**orifice** of female or hermaphrodite body Ezk 28_{13}. → נקב I *pierce.*

נֶקֶב V, see אֲדָמִי הַנֶּקֶב *Adami-nekeb.*

***[נְקִבָה]** $_{0.0.0.3}$ n.f. **boring through, tunnelling** Siloam tunnel inscr.$_{1}$. → נקב I *pierce.*

נְקֵבָה $_{22.0.7}$ n.f. **female,** of humans Gn 1_{27}, animals Gn 6_{19}. → נקב I *pierce.*

נָקֹד $_{9}$ adj.—m.pl. נְקֻדִּים, f.pl. נְקֻדּוֹת—**1. speckled,** of sheep, goats Gn $30_{32.35}$. **2.** as noun, **speckled (kid)** Gn 30_{39}. → cf. נִקּוּד *spot,* נְקֻדָּה *bead.*

נֹקֵד I $_{2}$ n.m.—pl. נֹקְדִים—**sheep breeder, shepherd** 2 K 3_{4} Am 1_{1}.

***נֹקֵד** II $_{2}$ n.m.—pl. נֹקְדִים—**soothsayer, hepatoscoper** 2 K 3_{4} Am 1_{1}.

***נֹקֵד** III $_{2}$ n.m.—pl. נֹקְדִים—**cultic official** 2 K 3_{4} Am 1_{1}.

[נְקֻדָּה] $_{1}$ n.f.—pl. cstr. נְקֻדּוֹת—**bead,** perh. globular or drop-shaped Ca 1_{11}. → cf. נָקֹד *speckled,* נִקּוּד *spot.*

נִקֻּדִים, see נִקּוּד *crumb.*

נקה I $_{44.6.8.1}$ vb.—**Qal** $_{1}$ Inf. abs. נָקֹה—**be clear, exempt from punishment** Jr 49_{12}.

Ni. $_{25.6.5.1}$ Pf. נִקָּה; impf. יִנָּקֶה; impv. הִנָּקִי; inf. abs. הִנָּקֵה—**1. be cleaned out, emptied, banished** Is

326 Zc 53. **2. be free (from guilt), be blameless** of (מִן) iniquity Nm 531. **3. be clear, exempt from punishment** Jr 2529 Si 78 (+ בְּ *in respect of*). **4. be free, exempt** from (מִן) oath Gn 248. **5. be free (from harm)** from (מִן) water of bitterness Nm 519.

Pi. 18.0.3 Pf. נִקֵּיתִי; impf. יְנַקֶּה; impv. נַקֵּנִי; inf. abs. נַקֵּה—**1a. leave unpunished,** obj. person Ex 207||Dt 511, blood Jl 421. **b.** without obj., **remit punishment** Ex 347. **2. declare as innocent, acquit** someone of (מִן) iniquity Jb 1014, hidden faults Ps 1913.

→ נָקִי *clean,* נִקָּיוֹן *cleanness,* (?) מְנַקִּית *bowl.*

*נקה II 3 vb.—**Ni.** 1 + waw וְנִקְּתָה—**be poured out** Is 326.

Pi. 2 Pf. נִקֵּיתִי—**pour out** blood Jl 421.

[נָקוֹב] *distinguished one,* see נקב I, qal §4b.

[נִקֻּוד] 3 n.[m.]—pl. נִקֻּדִים—**1. crumb,** of stale bread, or perh. **spot, mould,** in bread Jos 95.12. **2. biscuit,** or **small pastry** 1 K 143. → cf. נָקֹד *speckled,* נְקֻדָּה *bead.*

נְקוֹדָא 4 pr.n.m. **Nekoda.**

*[נִקּוּף] 0.0.1 n.[m.]—cstr. נקוף—**gleaning, striking off (of olives)** 4QDe 3.215. → נקף I *strip off.*

נָקֹטָה, see קוט *feel loathing,* ni.

נָקִי 43.0.7 adj.—נָקִיא; cstr. נְקִי; m.pl. נְקִיִּם, f.pl. Q נקיות—**1. clean, pure,** of wheat Mur 24 B17. **2. free, exempt (from obligation),** of person, נָקִי מֵאָלָתִי *free from my oath* Gn 2441, נְקִיִּם מֵי׳ *free from,* i.e. in respect of, Y. Nm 3222. **3a. innocent, blameless, guiltless,** of person Gn 4410, blood Dt 1910. **b.** as noun, **clean one, innocent one, blameless one** Ex 237. → נקה I *be clean.*

נָקִיא, see נָקִי *clean.*

נִקָּיוֹן 5 n.[m.]—cstr. נִקְיוֹן—**1. cleanness** of teeth, as evidence of hunger Am 46. **2. innocence, purity** Ho 85 Ps 266; נִקְיֹן כַּפַּי *innocence of my hands* Gn 205. → נקה I *be clean.*

[נָקִיק] 3 n.[m.]—cstr. נְקִיק; pl. cstr. נְקִיקֵי—**cleft (of rock)** Is 719 Jr 134 1616.

*[נִקְלָה] 0.0.1 pr.n.m. **Niklah.**

נקם 35.1.18 vb.—**Qal** 13.0.18 Impf. יִקֹּם; + waw וּנְקָמֵנִי; impv. נְקֹם; ptc. נֹקֵם, נֹקֶמֶת; inf. abs. נָקֹם; cstr. נְקֹם—**avenge, take vengeance (upon), a.** without obj. Lv. 1918 Ps 998 (+ עַל *for* misdeeds). **b.** obj. person on whom vengeance is taken Jos 1013 Na 12 (לְ of obj.). **c.** obj. person for whom vengeance is taken 1 S 2413 (+ מִן *from,* i.e. upon, someone), blood Dt 3243. **d.** obj. נָקָם *vengeance* Lv 2625, נְקָמָה *vengeance* Nm 312 (+ מֵאֵת *from,* i.e. upon, someone).

Ni. 12.1 Pf. נִקְמוּ, נִקַּמְתִּי; impf. יִנָּקֵם, אִנָּקְמָה; impv. הִנָּקְמוּ, הִנָּקֵם; inf. הִנָּקֵם—**1. avenge oneself, take revenge,** with בְּ *upon* Jg 157, מִן *upon* 1 S 1424 Jr 1515 (+ לְ *for* oneself); with obj. נָקָם *vengeance* Jg 1628. **2. be avenged** Ex 2120.

Pi. 2 + waw וְנִקַּמְתִּי—**1. avenge** blood 2 K 97. **2.** with obj. נְקָמָה + sf., **take vengeance for** Jr 5136.

Ho. 3 Impf. יֻקַּם—**be avenged** Gn 424, perh. **suffer vengeance** Gn 415 Ex 2121.

Htp. 5 Impf. תִּתְנַקֵּם; ptc. מִתְנַקֵּם—**1. avenge oneself upon** (בְּ) Jr 59. **2.** ptc. as noun, **avenger** Ps 83.

→ נָקָם *vengeance,* נְקָמָה *vengeance.*

נָקָם 17.5.16 n.m.—cstr. נְקַם; pl. cstr. Si נקמי—**vengeance,** usu. of Y.; of humans Jg 1628; as obj. of נקם *take vengeance* Lv 2625, שׁוב hi. *bring* Dt 3241, לקח *take* Is 473, עשׂה *do* Mc 514; נקמי אויב *vengeance of,* i.e. upon, *the enemy* Si 461, נְקַם־בְּרִית *vengeance of,* i.e. for, *the covenant* Lv 2625. → נקם *avenge.*

נְקָמָה 27.1.10 n.f.—cstr. נִקְמַת; sf. נִקְמָתִי; pl. נְקָמוֹת—**vengeance,** usu. of Y.; of humans Nm 312; as obj. of נקם *take vengeance* Nm 312, נתן *give* 2 S 48, לקח *take* Jr 2010, עשׂה *do* Jg 1136; נִקְמַת י׳ *vengeance of* Y. Nm 313, נִקְמַת בְּנֵי *vengeance of,* i.e. for, *the sons of* Israel Nm 312. → נקם *avenge.*

*[נִקָּנֹר] 0.0.0.1 pr.n.m. **Nicanor.**

נקע 3 vb.—**Qal** 3 Pf. נָקְעָה—**recoil, be alienated** Ezk 2322 (+ מִן *from*) 2318 (+ מֵעַל *from*). → cf. יקע *be dislocated.*

נקף I 2.0.1 vb.—**Pi.** 2 Pf. נִקְּפוּ; + waw וְנִקַּף—**1. strip off** skin Jb 1926. **2. cut down thicket** Is 1034. → נֹקֶף *striking,* נקוף *gleaning.*

נקף II 18.3.1 vb.—**Qal** 1 Impf. יִנְקֹפוּ—of feast, **go around,** i.e. be celebrated in yearly cycle Is 291.

Hi. 17.3.1 Pf. הִקִּיף; impf. יַקִּיפוּ; + waw וַיַּקִּף, וַיַּקִּפוּ; impv. הַקִּיפוּהָ; ptc. מַקִּיפִים; inf. abs. הַקֵּף—**1a.** trans., **go around** city Jos 63, border Is 158. **b.** intrans., **complete a circle, come to a full end,** of feast day Jb

1$_{5}$. **2. encircle, encompass, surround** a person Ps 22$_{17}$ 88$_{18}$ (עַל of obj.), fortification 1QpHab 4$_{7}$, city 2 K 6$_{14}$ (עַל of obj.). **3. round off, trim** corner of back of the head Lv 19$_{27}$. → נִקְפָּה *rope*, תְּקוּפָה *going round.*

[נֹקֶף] 2.0.1 n.[m.]—cstr. נֹקֶף; sf. Q נקפה—**striking** of olive trees to harvest olives Is 17$_{6}$ 24$_{13}$, **gleaning (of olives)** 4QD^{e} 3.2$_{15}$. → נקף I *strike off.*

נִקְפָּה 1 n.f. **rope** Is 3$_{24}$. → נקף II *go round.*

נקר 6 vb.—**Qal** 2 Impf. יִקְּרוּהָ; inf. נְקוֹר—**1. gouge out** eye 1 S 11$_{2}$. **2. peck out eye** Pr 30$_{17}$.

Pi. 3 Pf. נִקַּר; impf. תְּנַקֵּר; + waw וַיְנַקְּרוּ—**1. gouge out** eyes Nm 16$_{14}$. **2. bore away** bones Jb 30$_{17}$ (+ מֵעַל *from upon*).

Pu. 1 Pf. נֻקַּרְתֶּם—**be dug**, מַקֶּבֶת בּוֹר נֻקַּרְתֶּם *the quarry-pit from which you were dug* Is 51$_{1}$.

→ נְקָרָה *crevice.*

[נְקָרָה] 2.0.1 n.f.—cstr. נִקְרַת (Q ניקרת); pl. cstr. נִקְרוֹת—**1. crevice, cleft** of rock Ex 33$_{22}$ Is 2$_{21}$. **2. cave** of immersion 3QTr 1$_{12}$. → נקר *bore.*

נקשׁ I 1.1 vb.—**Qal** 1.1 Ptc. נוֹקֵשׁ—**1. strike,** of pot striking pot Si 13$_{2}$ (בְּ of obj.).

Pi. 1 Impf. + waw וַיְנַקְשׁוּ—**harass, or revile** Ps 38$_{13}$.

*נקשׁ II 5.1 vb.—**Qal** 1.1 Ptc. נוֹקֵשׁ—**ensnare** someone Ps 9$_{17}$ (+ בְּ *with*).

Ni. 1. Impf. תִּנָּקֵשׁ—**be ensnared, lured** Dt 12$_{30}$ (+ אַחֲרֵי *after*) Si 41$_{2(B)}$ (+ בְּ *by means of*).

Pi. 2 Impf. יְנַקֵּשׁ; + waw וַיְנַקְשׁוּ—**1. ensnare,** i.e. seize (לְ of obj.) something Ps 109$_{1}$. **2. lay snares** Ps 38$_{13}$.

Htp. 1 Ptc. מִתְנַקֵּשׁ—**lay snare for** (בְּ) someone's life 1 S 28$_{9}$.

→ cf. יקשׁ *trap,* קושׁ *lay snare.*

נֵר I 44.3.2 n.m.—cstr. נֵר; sf. נֵרוֹ; pl. נֵרוֹת; sf. נֵרֹתֶיהָ—**lamp,** in tabernacle Ex 25$_{37}$||37$_{23}$, temple 1 K 7$_{49}$||2 C 4$_{21}$, tent Jb 18$_{6}$; word of Y. as a lamp Ps 119$_{105}$; lamp, in ref. to Y. 2 S 22$_{29}$, David 2 S 21$_{17}$. → cf. נִיר I *lamp,* מְנוֹרָה *lampstand.*

*[נֵר] II 1 n.[m.]—**mark,** נֵר רְשָׁעִים חַטָּאת *the mark of the wicked is sin* Pr 21$_{4(mss)}$ (L נִר *mark of*).

נֵר III 16 pr.n.m. **Ner.**

נָר, see נִיר I *lamp,* II *mark.*

נרא, see נֵרִיָּה *Neriah.*

נֵרְגַל 1 pr.n.m. **Nergal.**

נֵרְגַל שַׂר־אֶצֶר 2 pr.n.m. **Nergal-sharezer.**

נֵרְדְּ 3 n.m.—sf. נִרְדִּי; pl. נְרָדִים—**nard,** aromatic plant Ca 1$_{12}$ 4$_{13.14}$.

נרי, see נֵרִיָּה *Neriah.*

נֵרִיָּה 10.0.1.51 pr.n.m. **Neriah.**

נֵרִיָּהוּ, see נֵרִיָּה *Neriah.*

נריו, see נֵרִיָּה *Neriah.*

נשׂא I 659.27.68 vb.—**Qal** 601.25.58 Pf. נָשָׂא, נָשָׂאתָ, נְשָׂאתֶם; impf. יִשָּׂא; + waw וַיִּשָּׂא (וַיִּשָּׂאֵהוּ), וַתִּשֶּׂאנָה (וַתִּשֶּׂנָה); impv. נְשָׂא (נְסָה, שָׂא, שָׂאֵהוּ), שְׂאִי, שְׂאוּ (שָׂאוּנִי); ptc. נֹשֵׂא, נֹשְׂאֵת, נֹשְׂאִים; ptc. pass. נָשׂוּא (נְשׂוּי), נְשֻׂאִים; inf. abs. נָשׂא; cstr. נְשֹׂא (שְׂאֵת, לָשֵׂאת, שׂוֹא, מַשְּׂאוֹת, שְׂאֵתִי, נְשֹׂאִי)—**1a. lift up, take up, raise** person Ezk 3$_{12}$, sword Is 2$_{4}$||Mc 4$_{3}$ (+ אֶל *against*), ark Gn 7$_{17}$, **erect column** 11QMelch 3$_{10}$. **b. lift** face, (1) of someone else, i.e. **show partiality to, grant favour to, respect, accept** Gn 19$_{21}$ Lv 19$_{15}$. (2) one's own face to (אֶל), i.e. **look upwards** 2 K 9$_{32}$, **show favour** Nm 6$_{26}$, **show partiality** Si 32$_{16}$. **c.** (1) **lift** (one's own) head, i.e. **show defiance** Jg 8$_{28}$. (2) **lift** head of someone else, i.e. **grant favour to, exalt** Gn 40$_{13}$ Si 11$_{1}$, **pardon, free** from prison 2 K 25$_{27}$||Jr 52$_{31}$, **execute** Gn 40$_{19}$, **take census of, count** Ex 30$_{12}$. (3) **lift** number of, i.e. **count, list** Nm 3$_{40}$ 1 C 27$_{23}$. **d. lift** hand, to bless people Lv 9$_{22}$, swear oath Ex 6$_{8}$, show power Ps 10$_{12}$; in hostility 2 S 18$_{28}$ (+ בְּ *against*), prayer Ps 28$_{2}$ (+ אֶל *to*). **e. lift** foot, i.e. **set out** Gn 29$_{1}$. **f. lift** eyes, i.e. **look up** Gn 13$_{10}$. **g. lift** soul, i.e. **set heart, desire** Dt 24$_{15}$, perh. **flee for protection to** (אֶל) Y. Ps 25$_{1}$; **turn heart away from** (מִן), i.e. **forget about** Si 7$_{35}$. **h. lift** voice, in weeping Gn 21$_{16}$, exultation Is 24$_{14}$, to speak aloud Jg 9$_{7}$; with ellip. of קוֹל *voice,* **speak out, cry out** Is 42$_{2}$, **sing** Jb 21$_{12}$. **i. lift, take up,** i.e. **utter** name Ex 20$_{7}$||Dt 5$_{11}$, discourse Nm 23$_{7}$, prayer 2 K 19$_{4}$||Is 37$_{4}$. **2. carry, bear, transport** persons (viewed as a burden) Nm 11$_{12}$ 2 K 4$_{19}$ (+ אֶל *to*), spices Gn 37$_{25}$, ark Dt 10$_{8}$, weapons 1 S 16$_{21}$ (נֹשֵׂא כֵּלִים *armour-bearer*); **share a burden with** (אֵת) someone Ex 18$_{22}$, **help carry,** i.e. **ease** complaint Jb 7$_{13}$ (בְּ of obj.); perh. **wear** ephod 1 S 2$_{28}$. **3a. bear, suffer, endure** guilt, punishment Gn 4$_{13}$ Lv 19$_{17}$ (+ עַל *on account of*), sickness, i.e. affliction Jr 10$_{19}$, reproach Jr 15$_{15}$ (+ עַל *for the sake of*); **bear with** someone Jb 21_3. **b. suffer punishment for** sin Ezk 23_{49}. **4. forgive, pardon,** with (1) accus. sin Ex 10_{17}. (2) לְ of obj. people Nm 14_{19}, sin Ps 25_{18}. **5.** of land, **support, sustain** someone Gn 13_6. **6.** of unit of measure, **bear a capacity of, contain** Ezk 45_{11}. **7. take, take away, carry away** person 1 K 18_{12} (+ עַל *to*), gold and silver 1 C 18_{11} (+ מִן *from*). **8. receive, obtain** favour Est 2_9 (+ לִפְנֵי *before*) 2_{15} (+ בְּעֵינֵי *in the sight of*), blessing Ps 24_5 (+ מֵאֵת *from*). **9. take** woman **in marriage** for (לְ) oneself Ru 1_4, for one's sons Ezr 9_{12}. **10. bring, present** tribute 2 S 8_2||1 C 18_2, nation Dt 28_{49} (+ מִן *from*). **11. place** calamity in (בְּ) balances Jb 6_2. **12. bear, produce, yield** fruit Ezk 17_8, boughs Ezk 17_{23}. **13. carry out** business 1QSa 1_{20}. **14.** of heart, **a. stir, impel** Ex 35_{21}. **b. make presumptuous** 2 K 14_{10}||2 C 25_{19}. **15.** intrans., **a. rise up, heave,** of earth Na 1_5, waves Ps 89_{10}. **b. be exalted,** of Ephraim Ho 13_1. **c. arise, occur,** of strife and contention Hb 1_3. **16.** pass. **a.** נְשָׂא פָנִים (1) **be lifted of face,** i.e. **be favoured, respected** 2 K 5_1. (2) as noun, **honoured one, high-ranking one** Is 3_3. **b. be carried** since (מִן) birth Is 46_3. **c. be forgiven,** נְשֻׂא עָוֹן *forgiven of,* i.e. for, *iniquity* Is 33_{24}.

Ni. $_{34.2.4}$ Pf. נִשָּׂאת, נִשָּׂא; impv. (יִנָּשְׂאוּ, יִנָּשׂוּא) יִנָּשְׂאוּ, יִנָּשֵׂא; impv. הִנָּשְׂאוּ, הִנָּשֵׂא; ptc. (נִשֵּׂאת) נִשָּׂאָה, נִשָּׂא; inf. abs. נִשֹּׂאת; cstr. (הִנָּשְׂאָם) הִנָּשֵׂא—**1a. be lifted up, be raised up, be exalted, lift oneself up, rise,** of Y. Is 33_{10}, human Is 52_{13}, mountain Is 2_2||Mc 4_1 (+ מִן *[more] than*), kingdom 1 C 14_2 (+ לְמַעְלָה *on high*). **b.** ptc. as adj., (1) **lifted up, exalted,** of cedar Is 2_{13}, mountain Is 57_7, throne Is 6_1. (2) as noun, **that which is lifted up, lofty one, exalted one** Is 2_{12} 57_{15}. **2. be carried,** of persons Is 49_{22} (+ עַל *on* shoulder), table Ex 25_{28} (+ בְּ *with* pole). **3. be taken away, carried away,** of persons Dn 11_{12}, things 2 K 20_{17}||Is 39_6. **4. be beguiled, be enticed,** of heart Si 46_{11}.

Pi. $_{13}$ Pf. (נִשָּׂא) נִשֵּׂא; impf. יְנַשְּׂאוּהוּ; + waw וַיְנַשְּׂאֵם; impv. נַשְּׂאֵם; ptc. מְנַשְּׂאִים—**1a. lift up,** perh. **carry away** Am 4_2. **b. exalt** someone Est 3_1 5_{11} (+ עַל *above*), kingdom 2 S 5_{12}. **c. lift up** one's soul, i.e. **desire** Jr 22_{27}. **2. bear, carry** Is 63_9. **3. support, help** Ezr 8_{36}, **supply** with (בְּ) 1 K 9_{11}.

Hi. $_{2.0.3}$ Impf. Q ישיאנו; + waw וְהִשִּׂיאוּ—**1. cause** someone **to bear iniquity,** guilt Lv 22_{16}. **2. bring** something to (אֶל) 2 S 17_{13}.

Htp. $_{10.0.3}$ Impf. (תִּנַּשֵּׂא) תִּתְנַשֵּׂא, יִתְנַשֵּׂא, יִנַּשְּׂאוּ, תִּתְנַשְּׂאוּ (Q תתנסו); + waw וַיִּנַּשֵּׂא; ptc. מִתְנַשֵּׂא; inf. הִתְנַשֵּׂא—**lift oneself up, exalt oneself, be exalted,** of Y. 1 C 29_{11}, humans Nm 16_3 (+ עַל *above*), kingdom Nm 24_7.

→ נְשׂוּאָה *carried thing,* נָשִׂיא I *prince,* (?) II *mist,* III *one brought,* מַשָּׂא I *load,* II *utterance,* III *tribute,* מַשָּׂאָה *burden,* מַשְׂאֵת I *gift,* II *utterance,* III *beacon,* שְׂאֵת *exaltation,* שִׂיא *pride,* שׂוֹאָה *acquisition.*

* [נשׂא] II vb. **Hi., smoke, fume** Is 30_{27} (if em. כָּבֵד מַשָּׂאָה *heaviness of burden* to כָּבֵד מַשִּׂיאָה *[his] liver is fuming*).

נשׂג I $_{49.10.16}$ vb.—**Hi.** $_{49.10.16}$ Pf. הִשִּׂיגָה; impf. יַשִּׂיג (יַשֵּׂג); + waw וַיַּשֵּׂג (וַיַּשִּׂגֵם); ptc. מַשִּׂיג (מַשִּׂיגֵהוּ), מַשֶּׂגֶת; inf. abs. הַשֵּׂג—**1. reach, overtake, come upon,** subj. person Gn 31_{25}, blessing Dt 28_2, curse Dt 28_{15}, sword Jr 42_{16}, days Gn 47_9, threshing Lv 26_5. **2. reach,** i.e. **be able to afford, have sufficient, be sufficient,** subj. alw. hand; with accus. Lv 14_{22}, לְ of obj. Lv 5_{11}, בְּ of obj. Lv 14_{32}. **3. attain to, gain, obtain** path of life Pr 2_{19}, wisdom Si 6_{18}. **4. appreciate, understand, accept** word Si 12_{12}, discipline 1QS 6_{14}. **5.** perh. **arrive, come about,** of joy Is 35_{10}. **6. cause to reach, put** hand **to** (אֶל) mouth 1 S 14_{26}.

* [נשׂג] II $_1$ vb.—**Hi.** Ptc. מַשִּׂיגֵהוּ—**hunt** Leviathan with sword Jb 41_{18}.

נשׂה I, see נסה I *test.*

נשׂה II, see נשׂא *lift.*

[נְשׂוּאָה] $_1$ n.f.—pl. sf. נְשֻׂאֹתֵיכֶם—**carried thing,** in ref. to images of gods Is 46_1. → נשׂא I *lift.*

נָשִׂיא I $_{130.1.45.1}$ n.m.—Q נשי; cstr. נְשִׂיא (Q נשי, Q נסיא, Q נסי); pl. נְשִׂיאִים; cstr. נְשִׂיאֵי (Q נשיי); sf. נְשִׂיאֵיהֶם—**prince, chief, leader, a.** of or from nation or people Nm 25_{18} Ezk 30_{13}, the sea Ezk 26_{16}, the earth Ezk 39_{18}. **b.** of congregation of Israel Ex 16_{22}, tribes of Israel Nm 1_{16}, father's house Nm 3_{24}. **c.** specif. prince of the congregation 1QSb 5_{20}. **d.** particular rulers: Solomon 1 K 11_{34}, Simeon bar Cosiba Mur 24 B_3. **e.** Abraham as נְשִׂיא אֱלֹהִים *prince of God,* i.e. mighty prince Gn 23_6. **f.** angelic figures 4QShirShabb[d] 1.1_1. → נשׂא I *lift.*

[נָשִׂיא] II 4.0.1 n.[m.]—pl. נְשִׂאִים—**mist, vapour, cloud** Jr 10₁₃=51₁₆ Ps 135₇ Pr 25₁₄. → (?) נשׂא I *lift.*

*[נָשִׂיא] III 1 n.[m.] **one brought,** נְשִׂיא אֱלֹהִים *one brought of,* i.e. by, *God* Gn 23₆. → נשׂא I *lift.*

נשׂק, see שׂלק *burn.*

נשׁא I 5.0.1 vb.—**Qal** 5 + waw וְנָשָׁא; ptc. נֹשֶׁא, נֹשְׁאִים—**1. lend to** (בְּ) Ne 5₇. **2. borrow from** (בְּ) Is 24₂. **3. impose** an oath upon (בְּ) 1 K 8₃₁||2 C 6₂₂. **4.** ptc. as noun, **lender, creditor** 1 S 22₂.

Hi. 0.0.1 Pf. Q השאתה—perh. **lend to** (בְּ) 4Qpara Kings 109₁.

→ מַשָּׁא *debt,* מַשָּׁאָה *debt;* cf. נשׁה I *lend.*

נשׁא II 16.1 vb.—**Ni.** 1.1 Pf. נִשְּׁאוּ; impf. Si חנשה—**1. be deluded** Is 19₁₃. **2. be beguiled, be enticed** Si 42₁₀(Bmg).

Hi. 15 Pf. הִשִּׁיא, הִשֵּׁאתָ; impf. יַשִּׁיא; inf. abs. הַשֵּׁא—**1a. deceive, beguile** someone; with accus. 2 K 19₁₀||Is 37₁₀, לְ of obj. Jr 4₁₀, בְּ of obj. Ps 89₂₃. **b.** with obj. נֶפֶשׁ, **deceive oneself** Jr 37₉. **2.** intrans., **be deceitful** against (עַל) Ps 55₁₆(Qr).

→ מַשָּׁאָה *deception,* מַשָּׁאוֹן *deception.*

נשׁא III, see נשׁה II *forget.*

נֹשֶׁא *lender, creditor,* see נשׁא I, qal §4.

נשׁב 3.1.1 vb.—**Qal** 1.1.1 Pf. נָשְׁבָה; impf. Si ישוב—of wind, **blow upon** (בְּ) Is 40₁₇.

Hi. 2.1 Impf. יַשֵּׁב; + waw וַיַּשֵּׁב—**1. cause wind to blow** Ps 147₁₈. **2. frighten away** birds Gn 15₁₁.

→ cf. נשׁף *blow.*

נשׁה I 13.0.5 vb.—**Qal** 10.0.3 Pf. נָשִׁיתִי; ptc. נֹשֶׁה, נֹשִׁים—**1a. lend, be a creditor** to (בְּ) Dt 24₁₁. **b. lend** something to (בְּ) Ne 5₁₀.₁₁. **2.** ptc. as noun, **creditor** 2 K 4₁.

Hi. 3.0.2 Pf. הִשָּׁה; impf. יַשֶּׁה—**1. lend** to (בְּ) Dt 15₂. **2. lend** something to (בְּ), i.e. **cause** someone **to be indebted with** Dt 24₁₀ CD 10₁₈.

→ נְשִׁי *debt,* מַשֶּׁה *debt;* cf. נשׁא I *lend.*

נשׁה II 7.0.1 vb.—**Qal** 3 Pf. נָשִׁיתִי; inf. abs. נָשֹׁא—**forget** people Jr 23₃₉, good Lm 3₁₇.

Ni. 1 Pf. תִּנָּשֵׁנִי—**be forgotten,** לֹא תִנָּשֵׁנִי *you shall not be forgotten by me* Is 44₂₁.

Pi. 1 Pf. נַשַּׁנִי—**cause** someone **to forget** something Gn 41₅₁.

Hi. 2 Pf. הִשָּׁה; impf. יַשֶּׁה—**1. cause** ostrich **to forget wisdom** Jb 39₁₇. **2. cause to be forgotten, overlook** some of (מִן) one's guilt for (לְ) one Jb 11₆.

→ נְשִׁיָּה *forgetfulness.*

*נשׁה III 1 vb.—**Ni.** 1 Impf. תִּנָּשֵׁנִי—**be given up,** לֹא תִנָּשֵׁנִי *you shall not be given up by me* Is 44₂₁.

נשׁה IV, see נשׁא II *deceive.*

נָשֶׁה 1 n.[m.] **sciatic nerve,** in socket of hip Gn 32₃₃.

נֹשֶׁה *creditor,* see נשׁה I, qal §2.

[נְשִׁי] 1 n.[m.]—sf. Qr נִשְׁיֵךְ (Kt נשיכי)—**debt** 2 K 4₇. → נשׁה I *lend.*

נְשִׁיָּה 1 n.f. **forgetfulness,** אֶרֶץ נְשִׁיָּה *land of forgetfulness* Ps 88₁₃. → נשׁה II *forget.*

*[נָשִׁים] I n.m.pl. (byform of אֲנָשִׁים as pl. of אִישׁ *man*)—**men** Ps 2₁₂ (if em. נַשְּׁקוּ־בַר appar. *kiss the son* to נְשֵׁי קֶבֶר *men of the grave,* i.e. mortal men).

נָשִׁים II, see אִשָּׁה *woman.*

[נְשִׁיקָה] 2 n.f.—pl. cstr. נְשִׁיקוֹת—**kiss** Pr 27₆ Ca 1₂. → נשׁק I *kiss.*

נשׁך I 11.1 vb.—**Qal** 9 Pf. נָשַׁךְ; impf. יִשֹּׁךְ (יִשְּׁכֶנּוּ ,יִשָּׁךְ); ptc. נֹשֵׁךְ; ptc. pass. נָשׁוּךְ—**1. bite,** subj. serpent Gn 49₁₇, humans Mc 3₅ (+ בְּ *with* teeth), wine Pr 23₃₂ (+ כְּ *as* serpent). **2.** pass., **be bitten** Nm 21₈.

Pi. 2 + waw וַיְנַשְּׁכוּ—**bite,** subj. serpent Nm 21₆.

נשׁך II 5 vb.—**Qal** 2 Impf. יַשִּׁךְ; ptc. נֹשְׁכֶיךָ—**1. pay interest** Dt 23₂₀. **2.** ptc. as noun, **creditor,** or perh. **debtor** Hb 2₇.

Hi. 3 Impf. תַשִּׁיךְ—**lend on interest** (accus. נֶשֶׁךְ *interest*) to (לְ) Dt 23₂₀ 23₂₁.

→ נֶשֶׁךְ *interest.*

נֶשֶׁךְ 12 n.[m.]—cstr. נֶשֶׁךְ—**interest, usury,** on loan of money Ex 22₂₄, food Dt 23₂₀; נתן בְּנֶשֶׁךְ *give for,* i.e. lend at, *interest* Lv 25₃₇. → נשׁך II *pay interest.*

[נֹשֵׁךְ] *creditor,* see נשׁך II, qal §2.

נִשְׁכָּה 3.0.11 n.f. (alternative form of לִשְׁכָּה)—sf. נִשְׁכָּתוֹ; pl. נְשָׁכוֹת; sf. Q נשכותמה—**chamber, room** of individual Ne 3₃₀; for storage Ne 12₄₄. → cf. לִשְׁכָּה *chamber.*

נשׁל 7 vb.—**Qal** 6 Impf. יִשַּׁל; + waw וְנָשַׁל; impv. שַׁל—**1.** intrans., **slip off, drop off,** of olive Dt 28₄₀, axehead Dt 19₅ (+ מִן *from* handle). **2. remove, take off** sandal from (מֵעַל) foot Ex 3₅. **3. clear away** nations from before (מִפְּנֵי) Israel Dt 7₁.₂₂.

Pi. 1 + waw וַיְנַשֵּׁל—**clear away** Jews from (מִן) Elath 2 K 16_{6}.

נשׁם 1 vb.—**Qal** 1 Impf. אֶשֹּׁם—**pant, gasp,** as woman giving birth Is 42_{14}. → נְשָׁמָה *breath,* תִּנְשֶׁמֶת *chameleon, owl.*

נְשָׁמָה 24.2.5.1 n.f.—נִשְׁמַת; sf. נִשְׁמָתִי; pl. נְשָׁמוֹת—**1. breath** of humans and animals, as evidence of life Gn 7_{22} 1 K 17_{17}; נִשְׁמַת חַיִּים *breath of life* Gn 2_{7}. **2. breath** of God, Is 30_{33}; imparted to humans Jb 32_{8}. **3. person, soul,** כָּל־נְשָׁמָה *every breathing thing* Dt 20_{16}. → נשׁם *pant.*

נשׁף 2 vb.—**Qal** 2 Pf. נָשַׁף—**blow,** subj. Y. Ex 15_{10} (+ בְּ *with* wind) Is 40_{24} (+ בְּ *upon*). → נֶשֶׁף I *twilight,* יַנְשׁוּף *screech owl;* cf. נשׁב *blow.*

נֶשֶׁף I 12.1.1 n.[m.]—נֶשֶׁף; cstr. נֶשֶׁף; sf. נִשְׁפּוֹ—**1. twilight, a.** usu. of evening Is 5_{11}. **b.** of morning Ps 119_{147}. **2. darkness** in general Si 35_{16}. → נשׁף *blow.*

*[**נֶשֶׁף**] II 1 n.[m.] **trace, faint suspicion,** נֶשֶׁף חִשְׁקִי *trace of my desire* Is 21_{4}.

נשׁק I 31 vb.—**Qal** 25 Pf. נָשַׁק; impf. יִשַּׁק (יִשָּׁקֵנִי); + waw וַיִּשַּׁק; impv. שְׁקָה; inf. לִנְשֹׁק־—**1. kiss,** with accus. Gn 33_{4}, with לְ of obj. Gn 27_{26}. **2. kiss one another,** of righteousness and peace Ps 85_{11} (or em. ni. נִשָּׁקוּ).

Pi. 5 + waw וַיְנַשֵּׁק (וַיְנַשֶּׁק); impv. נַשְּׁקוּ; inf. נַשֵּׁק—**kiss,** with accus. Ps 2_{12}; usu. with לְ of obj. Gn 29_{13}.

Hi. 1 Ptc. מַשִּׁיקוֹת—**touch,** of wings Ezk 3_{13} (+ אֶל *against* each other).

→ נְשִׁיקָה *kiss.*

נשׁק II 3 vb.—**Qal** 3 Ptc. נֹשְׁקֵי—**be equipped, armed with,** נֹשְׁקֵי קֶשֶׁת *armed of,* i.e. with, *the bow* 1 C 21_{2} 2 C 17_{17}, sim. Ps 78_{9}. → נֶשֶׁק *weapons,* מַשָּׁק II *swarm.*

*__נשׁק__ III 2.0.1 vb.—**Qal** 1.0.1 Impf. יִשַּׁק—**be in order, stand side by side, submit oneself** according to (עַל) command Gn 41_{40} CD 13_{3}.

Hi. 1 Ptc. מַשִּׁיקוֹת—**keep in line,** of wings Ezk 3_{13} (+ אֶל *against* each other).

*__נשׁק__ IV 3 vb.—**Qal** 3 Impf. יִשַּׁק (יִשָּׁק); + waw וַתִּשַּׁק—**seal (the mouth, lips),** i.e. be silent, with accus. Pr 24_{26}, לְ of obj. Jb 31_{27}; obj. omitted Gn 41_{40} (+ עַל *according to* command).

*__נשׁק__ V 1 vb.—**Qal** 1 Impf. יִשַּׁק—**acquiesce, yield** at (עַל) command Gn 41_{40}.

נֶשֶׁק 10 n.[m.]—נֶשֶׁק (נָשֶׁק); cstr. נֶשֶׁק (נְשֶׁק)—**1. weapons, military equipment** 2 K 10_{2}. **2. armoury** Ne 3_{19}. **3. battle** Ps 140_{8}. → נשׁק II *be equipped with.*

*__נֶשֶׁק__ I 2 n.[m.] **perfume** 1 K 10_{25}||2 C 9_{24}.

נֶשֶׁק II, see נֶשֶׁק *weapons.*

*[**נַשָּׁר**] n.[m.] **herald** Ho 8_{1} (if em. כַּנֶּשֶׁר *as an eagle* to כְּנַשָּׁר *like a herald*) Jb 39_{25} (if em. שָׂרִים *princes* to נַשָּׁרִים *heralds*).

נֶשֶׁר 26.0.4 n.m.—נֶשֶׁר; pl. נְשָׁרִים; cstr. נִשְׁרֵי—**eagle** or **vulture** Ex 19_{4} Lv 11_{13}.

נשׁת 3 vb.—**Qal** 2 Pf. נָשַׁתָּה (נָשָׁתָּה)—**1. be parched** with (בְּ) thirst, of tongue Is 41_{17}. **2. be exhausted,** of might Jr 51_{30}.

Ni. 1 + waw וְנִשְּׁתוּ—**be dried up,** of water Is 19_{5} (+ מִן *from* sea).

נִשְׁתְּוָן 2 n.[m.] **letter** Ezr 4_{7} 7_{11}.

[**נָתוּק**] *animal that is torn,* see נתק, qal §3.

[**נָתוּשׁ**] *uprooted one,* see נתשׁ, qal §2.

נתח 9.0.1 vb.—**Pi.** 9.0.1 Pf. נִתַּח; impf. תְּנַתֵּחַ; + waw וַיְנַתַּח; ptc. Q מנתחים—**cut into pieces** (usu. + לִנְתָחִים *into pieces*) woman Jg 19_{29}, animal Ex 29_{17}. → נֵתַח *piece (of meat).*

נֵתַח 14.1.3 n.m.—pl. נְתָחִים; sf. נְתָחָיו—**piece (of meat),** usu. of sacrificial animal Ex 29_{17}; of woman Jg 19_{29}. → נתח *cut into pieces.*

נָתִיב 5.0.1 n.m.—cstr. נְתִיב; pl. cstr. Q נתיבי—**path** Ps 78_{50}. → cf. נְתִיבָה *path.*

נְתִיבָה I 21.0.10 n.f.—sf. נְתִיבָתִי; pl. נְתִיבוֹת; cstr. נְתִיבוֹת; sf. נְתִיבוֹתַי—**path** of wisdom Pr 3_{17}, justice Pr 8_{20}, the stars 1QH 9_{12}; הֹלְכֵי נְתִיבוֹת *those who walk in the paths,* i.e. travellers Jg 5_{6}. → cf. נָתִיב *path.*

*[**נְתִיבָה**] II 1 n.f. **ruin,** מְשֹׁבֵב נְתִיבוֹת *restorer of ruins* Is 58_{12}.

*[**נְתִבְיָהוּ**] 0.0.0.1 pr.n.m. **Nethibiah.**

[**נָתִין**] 17.0.1 n.m.—pl. נְתִינִים—alw. pl. **temple servants, Nethinim,** postexilic cultic functionaries Ezr 2_{43}||Ne 7_{46}. → (?) נתן *give.*

*[**נְתִיצָה**] n.f. **ruin,** מְשֹׁבֵב נְתִיצוֹת *restorer of ruins* Is 58_{12} (if em. נְתִיבוֹת *of paths*).

נתך 21.0.3 vb.—**Qal** 7 Impf. תִּתַּךְ—**pour out** (intrans.), **be poured out,** of wrath Jr 42_{18} (+ עַל *upon*) 2 C 12_{7} (+ בְּ *upon*), roaring Jb 3_{24} (+ כְּ *as* water).

Ni. 8.0.3 Pf. נִתַּךְ ,נִתְּכָה; impf. Q יִנתך; ptc. נִתֶּכֶת—**1. pour out** (intrans.), **be poured out,** of rain Ex 9$_{33}$ (+ אַרְצָה *onto the earth*), water 2 S 21$_{10}$ (+ עַל *upon*), wrath Jr 42$_{18}$ (+ עַל). **2. be melted,** of persons Ezk 22$_{21}$ (+ בְּתוֹךְ *within* Jerusalem, as furnace).

Hi. 5 Pf. הִתִּיכוּ; Impf. תַּתִּיכֵנִי; + waw וְהִתַּכְתִּי ,וַיַּתִּיכוּ; inf. הַנְתִּיךְ—**1. pour out** embryo like (כְּ) milk Jb 10$_{10}$, money 2 K 22$_{9}$||2 C 34$_{17}$. **2. melt** persons as metals Ezk 22$_{20}$.

Ho. 1 Impf. תֻּתְּכוּ—**be melted,** of persons within (בְּתוֹךְ) Jerusalem as furnace Ezk 22$_{22}$.

→ הִתּוּךְ *melting,* מִתָּךְ *outpouring,* מֶתֶךְ *intoxicating drink.*

נתן 2015.62.228.26 vb.—**Qal** 1924.58.214.26 Pf. נָתַן ,נָתַתִּי ,נָתַנּוּ; impf. יִתֵּן (יִתֶּן־) ,יִתְּנוּ ,אֶתֵּן (אֶתֶּן־) ,אֶתְּנָה; + waw וַיִּתֵּן (וַיִּתֶּן־) ,וָאֶתֵּן (וָאֶתֶּן־) ,וָאֶתְּנָה; impv. תֵּן (תֶּן־) ,תְּנָה ,תְּנִי (תְּנִי־) ,תְּנוּ; ptc. נֹתֵן ,נֹתְנִים; ptc. pass. נָתוּן ,נְתֻנִים; inf. abs. נָתוֹן; cstr. תֵּת ,תֶּת ,לָתֵת ,לָתֶת־ ,לְתִתֵּן ,תִּתָּם (נְתֹן)—**1. give, a. give (to), grant, bestow (upon), pay,** in various senses including, **a.** hand over, deliver up: items Ex 22$_{6}$, people Ex 23$_{31}$; of Y. giving up Israel Ho 11$_{8}$. **b.** bestow graciously Gn 24$_{35}$. **c.** supply, provide with Ex 5$_{7}$. **d.** serve, distribute, food 2 K 4$_{42}$, feed animal Gn 42$_{27}$. **e.** show favour Jr 16$_{13}$, grant mercy Gn 43$_{14}$, victory Jg 15$_{1}$, vengeance 2 S 4$_{8}$. **f.** grant a request 1 S 1$_{17}$, desire Ps 21$_{3}$. **g.** sell Gn 47$_{16}$, allow to purchase Gn 23$_{4}$. **h.** lend Lv 25$_{37}$, give in pledge Gn 38$_{18}$. **i.** render amount due Ex 5$_{18}$, as purchase price Gn 23$_{13}$, payment for goods 1 K 9$_{11}$, tribute 2 K 15$_{19}$. **j.** as reward Jg 16$_{5}$, recompense for deeds Jr 17$_{10}$. **k.** as gift Gn 24$_{53}$. **l.** as offering, to Y. Ex 22$_{28}$. **m.** as inheritance Gn 25$_{5}$. **n.** in marriage Ezr 9$_{12}$. **o.** give one's lying down, i.e. have sex Lv 18$_{20}$. **p.** cause hurt Pr 10$_{10}$, strife Pr 13$_{10}$. **q.** assign Nm 3$_{9}$. **r.** entrust Gn 39$_{4}$. **s.** ascribe 1 S 18$_{8}$, allege Ps 50$_{20}$. **t.** reveal, display Pr 23$_{31}$, show sign Dt 6$_{22}$, inform of 2 S 24$_{9}$||1 C 21$_{5}$. **u.** pay attention Lachish ost. 3$_{12}$. **v.** institute Ezk 20$_{12}$. **w.** yield, bear, produce Lv 25$_{19}$. Preps. include: (1) לְ *to* person Gn 13$_{15}$, sword Jr 15$_{9}$, death Ps 118$_{18}$; *as, for (the purpose of being)* wife Gn 29$_{28}$, possession Gn 17$_{8}$. (2) בְּ *into* the hand of Gn 27$_{17}$; *(in exchange) for* cattle Gn 47$_{16}$, money Gn 23$_{9}$, interest Lv 25$_{37}$; *with, in* faithfulness Is 61$_{8}$; *as, for (the purpose of being)* inheritance Nm 18$_{26}$; *against* person Ne 9$_{10}$. (3) כְּ *according to* ways 1 K 8$_{39}$||2 C 6$_{30}$. (4) מִן *(some) of* (as obj.) Jg 21$_{7}$; *from among, out of* tribes Jos 21$_{9}$, sacrifice Lv 7$_{32}$; *by (means of), through* person Gn 17$_{16}$. (5) אֶל *to* person Gn 21$_{14}$; *according to* command Jos 15$_{13}$. (6) עַל (bestow) *upon* person 1 C 29$_{25}$; (give) *into* the hand of 2 K 12$_{12}$; *according to* command Nm 3$_{51}$. (7) תַּחַת *under* sun Ec 8$_{15}$; *in place of, (in exchange) for* life Ex 21$_{23}$, vineyard 1 K 21$_{2}$. **2a.** מִי יִתֵּן **who will grant?,** i.e. **would that!, if only!,** מִי יִתֵּן בִּשְׁאוֹל תַּצְפִּנֵנִי *oh, that you would hide me in Sheol* Jb 14$_{13}$. **b.** מִי־יִתֶּן לִי **who will grant me?,** i.e. **oh, that I had!,** + מִי־יִתֶּן לִי אֵבֶר כַּיּוֹנָה *oh, that I had wings like a dove* Ps 55$_{7}$. **3. give out, sound out, utter** voice Gn 45$_{2}$ (+ בְּ *with* weeping) Jr 12$_{8}$ (בְּ of obj.), i.e. make proclamation 2 C 24$_{9}$. **4. place,** in various senses, including, **a. place, put, set** somewhere Gn 1$_{17}$, over, i.e. in charge of Gn 41$_{41}$, into someone's charge Gn 30$_{35}$; set one's mind to do something Ec 1$_{13}$, dread upon someone Dt 2$_{25}$, fire against, i.e. set fire to Ezk 30$_{8}$. **b. turn** shoulder Zc 7$_{11}$, face Dn 9$_{3}$, **stretch out** hand Gn 38$_{28}$, i.e. make terms with Lm 5$_{6}$, **shoot out** branches Ezk 36$_{8}$. **c. cast** lots Lv 16$_{8}$. **d. fasten** Ex 25$_{26}$, **set up** Ex 40$_{8}$. **e. spread** fear Ezk 30$_{13}$. **f. pour out** Nm 19$_{17}$. **g. impose** Dt 26$_{6}$. **h. afflict with, send against** Dt 7$_{15}$; **bring (punishment, guilt) upon** Jr 26$_{15}$. **i. appoint, assign** Ex 31$_{6}$. **j. make** covenant Gn 9$_{12}$, **establish** laws Lv 26$_{46}$. Preps. include: (1) לְ *for* Ezr 8$_{20}$. (2) בְּ *in* place Gn 1$_{17}$, hand, i.e. charge, of Gn 30$_{35}$; *against, upon* Ex 7$_{4}$; *by (means of), with* Ex 29$_{12}$. (3) מִן *(some) of* (as obj.) Lv 4$_{7}$. (4) אֶל *into* Lv 8$_{8}$, *upon* Ezk 21$_{34}$. (5) עַל *upon* Ex 29$_{12}$; *over,* i.e. in charge of Dt 17$_{15}$. (6) בְּתוֹךְ *within, among* Lv 26$_{11}$ 2 C 6$_{13}$. (7) בְּקֶרֶב *among* Dt 21$_{8}$. (8) בֵּין *between* Gn 9$_{12}$. (9) אֵצֶל *beside* 2 K 12$_{10}$. (10) לִפְנֵי *before* Gn 18$_{8}$. (11) תַּחַת *under* 1 K 5$_{17}$; *in place of* 1 K 2$_{35}$. **5a. make (into), cause to be, make as, appoint as** (1) with double accus. Gn 17$_{5}$, consisting of noun and adj. Ps 18$_{33}$. (2) with accus. + לְ *into, as* Gn 17$_{6}$, בְּ *as* Nm 21$_{29}$, כְּ *as* Lv 26$_{19}$. **b. make out as, take as,** with accus. + כְּ *as* Gn 42$_{30}$, לִפְנֵי *before,* i.e. as 1 S 1$_{16}$. **6. cause, make happen,** יִתֶּנְךָ יי נִגָּף *Y. will cause you to be defeated* Dt 28$_{25}$. **7.**

with inf., **allow, permit** to do something Ex 3₁₉. **8.** pass. **a. be given, be assigned, be appointed** to (לְ) Dt 28₃₂, over (בְּ) Ne 13₄, (in exchange) for (בְּ) Si 7₆, from among (מִתּוֹךְ) Nm 8₁₆. **b. be placed, be stationed** in (בְּ) 11QT 58₄.

Qal Pass. (unless **Ho.**) 8.1.1 Impf. יֻתַּן—**1. be given, be granted,** of person 2 S 21₆(Qr), land Nm 32₅, gold Jb 28₁₅. Preps.: לְ *to* someone Nm 32₅, *as* wife 1 K 2₂₁; לְפִי *according to* Nm 26₅₄; תַּחַת *in exchange for* Jb 28₁₅. **2. be placed,** of person 2 S 18₉ (+ בֵּין *between*), water Lv 11₃₈ (+ עַל *upon*).

Ni. 83.5.14 Pf. נִתְּנוּ ,(נִתְּנָה) נִתְּנָה, נִתַּן; impf. יִנָּתֵן (יִנָּתֶן־ ,יִנָּתֶן); + waw וַיִּנָּתְנוּ ;וְנִתַּתֶּם; ptc. נִתָּן; inf. abs. הִנָּתֹן; cstr. הִנָּתֵן—**1. be given, be granted, be bestowed (upon),** i.e. be handed over, delivered up Gn 9₂ 2 K 22₇, be assigned 2 C 2₁₃, (of decree) be issued Est 3₁₅, (of moral blemish) be found Si 44₁₉; be given in marriage Gn 38₁₄, as payment for service Ezk 16₃₄, to priests as due Lv 10₁₄. Preps. include: (1) לְ *to* someone Jos 24₃₃; *as* wife Gn 38₁₄, possession Ezk 11₁₅. (2) בְּ *into* the hand of Gn 9₂; *by (means of), with* Jr 32₃₆; *on account of* Ezr 9₇. (3) מִן *from (among)* Lv 10₁₄; *by* Ec 12₁₁. (4) מִפְּנֵי *on account of* Jr 32₂₄. **2.** מִי יִנָּתֵן **who will let it be granted?,** i.e. **would that it were granted!, if only!** 4QTestim₃ (=Dt 5₂₉ qal). **3.** of sound, **be given out, be uttered** Jr 51₅₅. **4. be placed, set in** (בְּ) Ezk 32₂₃, against (עַל) Dn 8₁₂, with (אֵת) Ezk 32₂₉, among (בְּתוֹךְ) Ezk 32₂₅. **5. be made into, be made like,** חָצִיר יִנָּתֵן *he is made like grass* Is 51₁₂. **6.** with inf., **be allowed, permitted** to do Est 9₁₃.

Ho. See Qal Pass.

→ (?) נָתִין *temple servant,* אֶתְנַן *fee,* מַתָּן I *gift,* מַתָּנָה I *gift,* מַתַּת *gift,* תְּתָה *giving out;* cf. יתן *give.*

נָתָן 42.1.0.6 pr.n.m. **Nathan.**

נְתַנְאֵל 14 pr.n.m. **Nethanel.**

נְתַנְיָה 20.0.0.7 pr.n.m. **Nethaniah.**

נְתַנְיָהוּ, see נְתַנְיָה *Nethaniah.*

נְתַן־מֶלֶךְ 1.0.0.1 pr.n.m. **Nathan-melech.**

נתס I 1 vb.—**Qal** 1 Pf. נָתְסוּ—**break up** path Jb 30₁₃. → cf. נתע I *break,* נתץ *pull down,* נתק *tear away,* נתשׁ *pluck up.*

*נתס II 1 vb.—**Qal** 1 Pf. נָתְסוּ—**place thorns (in)** path Jb 30₁₃.

נתע I 1.1 vb.—**Ni.** 1.1 Pf. נִתָּעוּ; impf. Si תנחע—**be broken,** of teeth Jb 4₁₀. → (?) מַלְתָּעוֹת *jawbone;* cf. נתס *break up,* נתץ *pull down,* נתק *tear away,* נתשׁ *pluck up.*

*נתע II 1 vb.—**Ni.** 1 נִתָּעוּ—**cease,** of roaring and teeth of lion Jb 4₁₀.

*נתע III 1—**Ni.** 1 נִתָּעוּ—**be pulled out, knocked out,** of teeth Jb 4₁₀.

נתץ 42.1.1 vb.—**Qal** 31.1.1 Pf. נָתַץ; impf. יִתֹּץ; + waw וַיִּתֹּץ, וַיִּתְּצוּ ,וַתִּתְּצוּ; impv. נְתֹץ; ptc. pass. נְתֻצִים; inf. לִנְתוֹץ—**1a. pull down, break down** altar Ex 34₁₃, house Lv 14₄₅, nation Jr 18₇. **b. break** teeth Ps 58₇. **2.** pass. **be pulled down,** of houses Jr 33₄.

Ni. 2 Pf. נִתְּצוּ—**be pulled down, ruined,** of city Jr 4₂₆, rocks Na 1₆ (+ מִן *by* or *on account of* Y.).

Pi. 7 Pf. נִתַּץ; + waw וַיְנַתֵּץ—**tear down** altar Dt 12₃, high place 2 C 31₁, wall 2 C 36₁₉.

Pu. 1 Pf. נֻתַּץ—**be torn down,** of altar Jg 6₂₈.

Ho. (unless **Qal Pass.**) 1 יֻתַּץ—**be broken up,** of oven, etc. Lv 11₃₅.

→ cf. נתס I *break up,* נתע I *break,* נתק *tear away,* נתשׁ *pluck up.*

נתק 27.0.3 vb.—**Qal** 3.0.1 Impf. Q יתקו ;אֶתְּקֶנְךָּ; + waw וּנְתַקְּנֻהוּ; ptc. pass. נָתוּק—**1. tear away, pull off** person (as signet ring) from (מִן) hand Jr 22₂₄. **2. draw, lure away** people from (מִן) city to (אֶל) highways Jg 20₃₂. **3.** pass. ptc. as noun, **animal that is torn** Lv 22₂₄.

Ni. 10.0.1 Pf. נִתְּקוּ ,נִתַּק; impf. יִנָּתֵק; + waw וַיִּנָּתְקוּ—**1. be torn apart, be snapped,** of cord Is 33₂₀. **2. be torn away,** of person, from (מִן) tent Jb 18₁₄. **3. be separated, be removed,** in metal smelting Jr 6₂₉. **4. be drawn, lured away** from (מִן) city Jos 8₁₆. **5. be lifted out** (from river) onto (אֶל) dry ground Jos 4₁₈.

Pi. 11.0.1 Pf. נִתַּקְתִּי ,נִתְּקוּ; impf. יְנַתֵּק; inf. Q נתק—**1. tear apart, snap, break** cord Jg 16₁₂ (+ מֵעַל *from upon* arm), bar of yoke Is 58₆, bond Jr 2₂₀. **2. tear out, pull up** roots Ezk 17₉, breasts Ezk 23₂₄.

Hi. 2 Impv. הַתִּקֵם; inf. הַתִּיקֵנוּ—**draw out, lure away** people from (מִן) city Jos 8₆, like (כְּ) sheep Jr 12₃.

Ho. 1 Pf. הָנְתְּקוּ—**be drawn, be lured away from** (מִן) city Jg 20₃₁.

→ נֶתֶק *scall;* cf. נתס *break up,* נתע I *break,* נתץ *pull down,* נתשׁ *pluck up.*

נתק נֶתֶק 14.0.4 n.m.—נֶתֶק—**scall,** itching disease of the scalp Lv 13$_{30}$; the person with the disease Lv 13$_{33}$. → נתק *tear away.*

נתר I 5.0.3 vb.—**Hi.** 5.0.3 Impf. יַתֵּר; + waw וַיַּתֵּר (וַיַּתִּירֵהוּ); ptc. מַתִּיר; inf. abs. הַתֵּר—**1. loosen** bonds Is 58$_{6}$; וַיַּתֵּר תְּמִים דַּרְכִּי perh. *and he has loosened my way safely,* i.e. made it safe 2 S 22$_{33(Qr)}$. **2. set free** prisoners Ps 146$_{7}$.

***נתר** II 3.0.1 vb.—**Qal** 1.0.1 Impf. יִתַּר; inf. Q לנתור—**spring, start up, leap,** of winged insects 11QT 48$_{5}$ (+ בְּ *with* legs, עַל *upon* earth), heart Jb 37$_{1}$ (+ מִן *from* its place).

Pi. 1 Inf. נַתֵּר—**leap,** of winged insects Lv 11$_{21}$ (+ בְּ *with* legs, עַל *upon* earth).

Hi. 1 + waw וַיַּתֵּר—**cause to leap, cause to start,** obj. nations Hb 3$_{6}$.

***נתר** III 2 vb.—**Hi.** 2 + waw וַיַּתֵּר; inf. הַתֵּר—**tear asunder** nations Hb 3$_{6}$, bonds Is 58$_{6}$.

*[**נתר**] IV 2 vb.—**Qal** 1 Impf. יִתַּר—**fall away** from (מִן) place Jb 37$_{1}$.

Hi. 1 Impf. יַתֵּר—**snatch away,** יַתֵּר יָדוֹ וִיבַצְּעֵנִי *would that he would snatch me away [with] his hand and cut me off* Jb 6$_{9}$.

*[**נתר**] V 1 vb.—**Pi.** 1 Inf. נַתֵּר—**hop, leap,** of winged insects Lv 11$_{21}$ (+ בְּ *with* legs, עַל *upon* earth).

נֶתֶר I 2 n.[m.]—נֶתֶר—**natron,** a form of sodium carbonate, used in making soap Jr 2$_{22}$ Pr 25$_{20}$.

*[**נֶתֶר**] II 1 n.[m.]—נֶתֶר—**wound** Pr 25$_{20}$.

נתשׁ 21.3.1 vb.—**Qal** 16.3.1 Pf. נָתַשְׁתָּ; impf. אֶתּוֹשׁ; + waw וְנָתַשׁ; וַיִּתְּשֵׁם; ptc. נֹתֵשׁ, pass. Q נתושים; inf. abs. נָתוֹשׁ; cstr. לִנְתוֹשׁ (נְתָשִׁי)—**1. pluck up, uproot** kingdom Jr 1$_{10}$, Israel from upon (מֵעַל) land 1 K 14$_{15}$, Asherah from among (מִקֶּרֶב) Israelites Mc 5$_{13}$. **2.** pass. ptc. as noun, **uprooted one, expelled one** 4QapMes 2.2$_{13}$.

Ni. 4 Impf. יִנָּתֵשׁ—**be plucked up, uprooted,** of kingdom Dn 11$_{4}$, Israelites Am 9$_{15}$ (+ מֵעַל *from upon* land).

Ho. 1 + waw וַתֻּתַּשׁ—**be plucked up, be uprooted,** of vine Ezk 19$_{12}$.

→ cf. נתס I *break up,* נתע I *break,* נתץ *pull down,* נתק *tear away.*

ס

ס, see סְאָה *seah.*

סְאָה 9.0.8.1 n.f.—du. סָאתַיִם; pl. סְאִים (Q סאין)—**1. seah,** unit of capacity, about 12 litres 1 K 18$_{32}$. **2.** ס abbrev. for סְאָה *seah,* City of David ost. 2$_{2}$.

*[**סָאוֹב**] 0.0.1 n.[m.] **filth** 4QBéat 21$_{6}$.

*[**סָאוֹן**] 0.0.1 n.[m.] **purpose** 1QS 3$_{2}$.

סְאוֹן I 1.0.2 n.m. **1. boot** Is 9$_{4}$. **2. tramping, steps (of boot)** 1QS 3$_{2}$. → סאן I *march.*

***סְאוֹן** II 1 n.m. **knot** Is 9$_{4}$. → סאן II *whirl.*

*[**סְאָל**] 0.0.0.1 pr.n.m. **Seal.**

סאן I 1 vb.—**Qal** 1 Ptc. סֹאֵן—**march, tread, trample,** of boot Is 9$_{4}$. → סְאוֹן I *boot.*

***סאן** II 1 vb.—**Qal** 1 Ptc. סֹאֵן—**whirl,** of knot Is 9$_{4}$. → סְאוֹן II *knot.*

סאסא I 1 vb.—**Pilp.** 1 Inf. cstr. סַאסְאָה—of Y., **drive away** Israelites Is 27$_{8}$.

***סאסא** II 1 vb.—**Pilp.** 1 Inf. cstr. סַאסְאָה—of Y., **shoo on Israelites** Is 27$_{8}$.

***סאסא** III 1 vb.—**Pilp.** 1 Inf. cstr. סַאסְאָה—of Y., **afflict** Israelites **with harm** Is 27$_{8}$.

***סַאסְאָה** I 1 n.f. **scare** Is 27$_{8}$.

***סַאסְאָה** II 1 n.f. **quarrel** Is 27$_{8}$.

סַאסְאָה III, see סאסא I *drive away.*

*[**סֹב**] 0.0.1 n.[m.]—pl. סבין—**gallery** 3QTr 11$_{8}$.

סבא 6.1 vb.—**Qal** 6.1 Impf. נִסְבְּאָה; ptc. סֹבֵא, סֹבְאֵי; ptc. pass. סְבוּאִים—**1a. drink excessively** Is 56$_{12}$. **2.** pass., **be intoxicated** Na 1$_{10}$. **3.** ptc. as noun, **drunkard** Si 18$_{33}$. → סֹבֶא *strong drink,* סָבָא I *drunkard.*

[סָבָא] I 1 n.[m.]—pl. Qr סָבָאִים—**drunkard** Ezk 23$_{42(Qr)}$. → סבא *drink excessively.*

*[סָבָא] II 2 n.[m.]—sf. סָבְאָם; pl. Qr סָבָאִים—**bindweed** Ezk 23$_{42(Qr)}$.

[סֹבֶא] 3 n.m.—sf. סָבְאָם—**strong drink** Is 1$_{22}$. → סבא *drink excessively.*

סְבָא 4.0.1 pr.n.m. **Seba.**

[סְבָאִי] 1 gent. **Sabaean.**

סבב I 162.6.13.1 vb.—**Qal** 90.4.9 Pf. סָבְבוּ, סַבֹּותִי, סָבַב; impf. יָסֹב; + waw וַיָּסָב; impv. סֹב, סֹבִּי, סֹבּוּ; ptc. סוֹבֵב; inf. סֹב (לִסְבֹב)—**1. surround** Behemoth, of poplars Jb 40$_{22}$, **encompass** Y. with (בְּ) deceit, of Ephraim Ho 12$_{1}$. **2. go around, circumnavigate** Zion Ps 48$_{13}$. **3.** intrans., **turn (around)** 1 S 15$_{27}$. **4.** trans., **turn away** inheritance Si 9$_{6}$ (unless §6). **5. turn, change, become** like (כְּ) steppe, of land Zc 14$_{10}$. **6. hand over** inheritance Si 9$_{6}$. **7. be handed over,** of inheritance Nm 36$_{7}$ (unless §3). **8. be responsible for** (בְּ) soul 1 S 22$_{22}$. **9. gather around** table to dine Si 35$_{1}$. **10. close a circle,** i.e. sit down to meal 1 S 16$_{11}$.

Ni. 20 Pf. נָסַבּוּ, (נָסְבָה) נָסֵבָּה; impf. יִסַּבּוּ—**1. surround** house Jg 19$_{22}$. **2. circle about, stretch (in a curved path),** of border Jos 15$_{3}$. **3. turn around,** of living being Ezk 1$_{9}$, wheel Ezk 10$_{16}$. **4. be turned over, handed over,** of possessions Jr 6$_{12}$.

Pi. 1.1 Impf. Si יסביב; inf. cstr. סַבֵּב—**1. cause to turn, change course** of events 2 S 14$_{20}$. **2. turn hither and thither** Si 36$_{31(C)}$.

Po. 12.0.1 Impf. יְסֹבְבֵנִי—**1. surround (protectively)** person Dt 32$_{10}$. **2. surround (threateningly)** city Ps 55$_{11}$. **3. gather around** Y. Ps 7$_{8}$. **4. walk around (in ritual procession)** altar Ps 26$_{6}$.

Hi. 33.1.2.1 Pf. הֵסֵב; impf. (נָסֵבָּה) נָסֵב; + waw וַהֲסִבֹּתִי; וַיַּסֵּב; impv. הָסֵב, הָסֵבִּי; ptc. מֵסֵב, מְסִבִּי; inf. cstr. לְהָסֵב—**1. cause** people **to wander around** Ex 13$_{18}$, **transport** ark 1 S 5$_{8}$. **2. cause to go around** ambush 2 C 13$_{13}$. **3. cause to turn,** obj. Israel 2 S 3$_{12}$, face Jg 18$_{23}$, heart Ezr 6$_{22}$. **4. cause to be turned over, hand over** kingdom 1 C 12$_{24}$. **5. change** name 2 K 23$_{34}$. **6. gather around** table to dine Si 34$_{16}$. **7.** ptc. as noun, **one who surrounds** (with evil intent) Ps 140$_{10}$.

Ho. 6.0.1 Impf. יוּסַב; ptc. מוּסַבּוֹת—**1. be encircled,** of stone Ex 28$_{11}$. **2. be caused to go round, be rolled,** of wheel Is 28$_{27}$. **3. be caused to turn,** of door Ezk 41$_{24}$. **4. be changed,** of name Nm 32$_{38}$.

→ מוּסָב *enclosure,* מֵסַב *surroundings,* מְסִבָּה *circle,* נְסִבָּה *turn of events,* סִבָּה *turn of events,* סָבִיב *vicinity,* סְבִיבָה *circuit,* תְּסִבָּה *going round.*

*סבב II 1 vb.—**Qal** 1 Impf. נָסֹב—**go away** 1 S 16$_{11}$.

סִבָּה 1 n.f. **turn of events** 1 K 12$_{15}$. → סבב I *surround.*

סָבִיב 335.8.38 n.m.&f.—cstr. סְבִיב; sf. Q סביבה; m.pl. cstr. סְבִיבֵי; sf. סְבִיבָיו; f.pl. סְבִיבוֹת; sf. סְבִיבוֹתַי—**1. surrounding area, vicinity** Nm 11$_{24}$, sometimes **inhabitants of vicinity** Jr 48$_{17}$. **2.** as adv., **a.** סָבִיב **around, round about** Ex 28$_{32}$. **b.** סָבִיב סָבִיב **all around** Ezk 40$_{5}$. **3.** as prep., סְבִיבוֹתָיו **round about him** Ps 18$_{12}$. → סבב I *surround.*

[סְבִיבָה] 1 n.f.—pl. sf. סְבִיבֹתָיו—**circuit** Ec 1$_{6}$. → סבב I *surround.*

סבך 2 vb.—**Qal** 1 Ptc. pass. סְבֻכִים—pass., **be entangled,** of people Na 1$_{10}$.

Pu. 1 Impf. יְסֻבָּכוּ—**be entangled,** of roots Jb 8$_{17}$.

→ סְבָךְ *thicket,* סֹבֶךְ *thicket.*

סְבָךְ 3 n.[m.]—pl. cstr. סִבְכֵי—**thicket** Gn 22$_{13}$. → סבך *entangle.*

[סֹבֶךְ] 2 n.[m.]—cstr. סְבַךְ; sf. סֻבְּכוֹ—**thicket** Ps 74$_{5}$. → סבך *entangle.*

סִבְּכַי 4.0.0.1 pr.n.m. **Sibbecai.**

סבל 9.0.2 vb.—**Qal** 7.0.1 Pf. סְבָלָם; impf. יִסְבֹּל; inf. סְבֹל—**1. bear** son 4QTobit^{e} 2$_{2}$, pain Is 53$_{4}$. **2.** of Y., **support (in old age)** Is 46$_{4}$.

Pi. 0.0.1 Impf. יסיבלו—**burden** 4QBéat 5$_{12}$.

Pu. 1.0.1 Ptc. מְסֻבָּלִים—**be burdened,** perh. **be pregnant,** of cows Ps 144$_{14}$.

Htp. 1 Impf. יִסְתַּבֵּל—**be weighed down,** of locust Ec 12$_{5}$.

→ סַבָּל I *burden-bearer,* II *burden,* סֵבֶל *burden,* סֹבֶל *burden,* סִבְלָה *burden.*

סַבָּל I 5 n.[m.]—pl. סַבָּלִים—**burden-bearer** Ne 4$_{4}$. → סבל *bear.*

*סַבָּל II 1 n.[m.] **burden** 1 K 5$_{29}$. → סבל *bear.*

סֵבֶל 3 n.[m.]—סֵבֶל; cstr. סֵבֶל—**1. forced labour** 1 K 11$_{28}$. **2. heavy load** Ps 81$_{7}$ (unless §3). **3. corvée basket** Ps 81$_{7}$. → סבל *bear.*

[סֹ֫בֶל] 3 n.m.—sf. סֻבֳּלוֹ—**burden** Is 9$_3$. → סבל *bear.*

[סִבְלָה] 6 n.f.—pl. cstr. סִבְלוֹת; sf. סִבְלֹתָם—**burden, arduous labour** Ex 6$_6$. → סבל *bear.*

סִבְלוֹת, see סִבְלָה *burden.*

סִבֹּ֫לֶת 1 n.f. **Sibboleth,** Ephraimite pronunciation of שִׁבֹּ֫לֶת *Shibboleth* Jg 12$_6$.

סִבְרַ֫יִם 1 pl.n. **Sibraim.**

סַבְתָּא 2 pr.n.m. **Sabtah.**

סַבְתָּה, see סַבְתָּא *Sabtah.*

סַבְתְּכָא 2 pr.n.m. **Sabteca.**

*סגב 0.0.1 vb. (byform of שׂגב)—**Ni.** 0.0.1 Ptc. נסגבה—**be high,** of wall 1QH 14$_{25}$.

סגד 4 vb.—**Qal** 4 Impf. יִסְגּוֹד—**bow down** Is 44$_{15}$.

*סגה 0.0.1 vb.—**Htp.** 0.0.1 Impf. [י]סתגון—**increase** 4Q523 3$_1$.

*סָגוּר I 8 n.m. **gold, thinly beaten out gold** 1 K 6$_{20}$.

*סָגוּר II 8 adj. **red (gold)** 1 K 6$_{20}$.

סָגוּר III **refined (gold),** see סגר II *refine.*

סְגוֹר I 1 n.m.—cstr. סְגוֹר—**1. enclosure, enclosing tissue** or **2. covering of stomach** Ho 13$_8$. → סגר I *shut.*

*סְגוֹר II 1 n.[m.] **gold** Jb 28$_{15}$. → סגר II *refine.*

סִגִים, see סִיג *dross.*

סְגֻלָּה 8.0.2 n.f.—cstr. סְגֻלַּת—**possession** Ex 19$_5$.

*סגן 0.0.1 vb.—**Qal** 0.0.1 Ptc. pass. סגונים—pass. ptc. as noun, **appointed one, official, ruler** GnzPs 2$_{12}$.

[סֶ֫גֶן] 17.0.1 n.m.—pl. סְגָנִים; sf. סְגָנֶיהָ—**ruler** Ezk 23$_{23}$. → סגן *appoint.*

סגר I 91.3.30 vb.—**Qal** 44.0.10 Pf. סָגַר, סָגַרְתְּ; impf. יִסְגֹּר; impv. סְגֹר, סִגְרוּ; ptc. סֹגֵר, סֹגֶרֶת; ptc. pass. סָגוּר; inf. סְגוֹר—**1.** trans., **shut** door Jg 3$_{23}$, mouth 1QH 13$_9$. **2a.** intrans., **shut,** of gate Jos 2$_5$. **b.** pass. ptc. **(be) shut,** of gate Ezk 44$_1$. **3.** of Y., **close up** flesh Gn 2$_{21}$ (unless §4). **4.** of flesh, **close up** in place of (תַּחַת) rib Gn 2$_{21}$. **5.** of Y., **lock up** behind (בַּעַד) Noah Gn 7$_{16}$. **6.** of steppe, **encroach against** (עַל) Israelites Ex 14$_3$. **7. repair** breach 1 K 11$_{27}$. **8.** ptc. as noun, **one who closes** Is 22$_{22}$. **9.** pass. ptc., זָהָב סָגוּר appar. **gold which is closed** 1 K 10$_{21}$.

Ni. 8.0.4 Pf. נִסְגַּר; impf. יִסָּגֵר; impv. הִסָּגֵר; inf. Q הסגר—**1. be shut,** of gate Is 45$_1$. **2. be shut away,** of person Nm 12$_{14}$. **3. shut oneself away** Ezk 3$_{24}$. **4. be closed in** 1 S 23$_7$. **5. be delivered up** CD 3$_{10}$.

Pi. 4 Pf. סִגַּר; impf. יְסַגֶּרְךָ—**deliver up** enemy 1 S 26$_8$.

Pu. 5.1 Pf. סֻגַּר; impf. Si 3fs תסוגר; ptc. מְסֻגֶּרֶת—**1. be shut,** of door Ec 12$_4$, throat Si 36$_{23}$(Bmg). **2. be shut away** in (עַל) prison Is 24$_{22}$. **3. be closed up,** of house Is 24$_{10}$.

Hi. 30.1.14 Pf. הִסְגִּיר, הִסְגַּרְתַּנִי; impf. יַסְגִּיר; + waw וַיַּסְגֵּר; ptc. Q מסגיר; inf. הַסְגִּיר (הַסְגִּירוֹ)—**1. shut away, quarantine** person with skin disease Lv 13$_{11}$. **2.** of Y., perh. **imprison** worshipper in Sheol Ps 31$_9$ (unless §4). **3. close up** house Lv 14$_{38}$. **4. deliver up** enemy 1QM 11$_{13}$. **5. seal** knowledge 4QMyst[a] 8$_9$. **6.** ptc. as noun, **one who closes** CD 6$_{12}$.

Ho. 0.0.2 Pf. הוסגרו—**be delivered up** to (לְ) sword CD 7$_{13}$.

Htpo. 0.1 Impf. יסתוגר—**seal oneself off** Si 38$_{15}$ (Bmg).

→ מַסְגֵּר II *prison,* מִסְגֶּרֶת I *panel,* II *prison,* סְגוֹר I *enclosure,* סְגֹר I *javelin,* II *lock,* סוּגַר *collar,* סָגָר or סֶ֫גֶר *socket;* cf. סכר I *shut.*

*סגר II vb. **Qal, 1.** pass., **be refined** Jb 28$_{15}$ (if em. סְגוֹר *gold* to זָהָב סָגוּר *refined gold*). **2.** ptc. pass. as noun, **refined thing** Jb 28$_{15}$ (if em. סְגוֹר *gold* to סָגוּר). → סְגוֹר II *gold,* מַסְגֵּר I *smith.*

*[סָגָר] or [סֶ֫גֶר] 0.0.3 n.m. **socket** 1QM 5$_7$. → סגר I *shut.*

*סְגֹר I 1.0.3 n.m. **javelin** Ps 35$_3$. → סגר I *shut.*

*סְגֹר II n.m. **lock** Jb 41$_7$ (if em. סָגוּר *closed* to סְגֹרוֹ *its lock*). → סגר I *shut.*

סַגְרִיר 1 n.[m.] **heavy rain** Pr 27$_{15}$.

סַד 2 n.[m.] **shackles,** rather than **stocks** Jb 13$_{27}$.

*סדד 1 vb.—**Qal** 1 Inf. סוֹד—with עַל of obj., of Y., **protect tent** Jb 29$_4$.

[סְדוֹם], see סְדֹם *Sodom.*

*[סִדּוּר] 0.0.1 n.[m.]—sf. סדורו—**arrangement,** perh. of showbread upon altar 1QS 11$_{21}$. → סדר *order.*

סָדִין 4 n.[m.]—pl. סְדִינִים—**linen garment,** perh. undergarment Jg 14$_{12}$.

*[סְדִירָה] n.f. **orderliness** Si 10$_1$ (if em. סרידה *net*). → סדר *order.*

סְדֹם 39.0.1 pl.n. **Sodom.**

*[סֶ֫דֶק] 0.0.1 n.[m.] **fissure** 3QTr 5$_5$.

*סדר 0.1.9 vb.—**Qal** 0.0.1 Ptc. pass. סדורים—pass., **be**

arranged, of battle formation 1QM 5_{4}.

Pi. 0.1.8 Pf. Q סדרו; impf. Q יסדרו—**arrange battalion** 1QM 5_{3}.

→ מִסְדְּרוֹן *porch,* סָדוֹר *arrangement,* סְדִירָה *orderliness,* סֵדֶר *order,* סְדֵרָה *row (of beams);* cf. שְׂדֵרָה *row.*

[סֵדֶר] I 1.0.17 n.[m.]—pl. סְדָרִים; cstr. Q סדרי; sf. Q סדריהם—**order,** esp. of battle formations 1QM 3_{1}. → סדר *arrange.*

*[סֵדֶר] II 1 n.[m.] **beam of light** Jb 10_{22}.

*[סְדֵרָה] 0.0.3 n.f.—pl. sf. סדרותיו—**row (of beams)** 11QShirShabb 1_{5}. → סדר *arrange;* cf. שְׂדֵרָה *row.*

*[סַדְרְיָהוּ] 0.0.0.1 pr.n.m. **Sadrijah.**

סַהַר 1 n.[m.] perh. **roundness** Ca 7_{3}.

סֹהַר 8.0.1 n.[m.] **enclosure** Gn 39_{20}.

סוֹא I 1 pr.n.m. **So.**

*סוֹא II 1 pl.n. **Sais.**

*סוֹא III 1 n.m.—cstr. סוֹא—**vizier** 2 K 17_{4}.

סוג I 24.1.18 vb.—**Qal** 3.0.1 Pf. סָג; impf. נָסוֹג; ptc. סוּג—**1. turn back, be unfaithful** Ps 80_{19}. **2.** ptc. as noun, **faithless one** Pr 14_{14}.

Ni. 14.1.7 Pf. נָסוֹג, נְסוּגֹתִי; impf. יִסֹּגוּ, יִסַּג; ptc. נְסוֹגִים; inf. abs. נָסוֹג; cstr. Q הסוגו—**1a. turn oneself away, flee** Jr 46_{5}. **b. be turned back** Ps 35_{4}. **2a. turn oneself away, be unfaithful** Is 59_{13}. **b.** ptc. as noun, **backslider** Zp 1_{6}. **3. depart,** of reproaches Mc 2_{6}.

Hi. 6.0.9 Impf. תַּסִּיג (תַּסֵּג); ptc. מַסִּיג; inf. Q הסיג—**1a. remove** border Dt 19_{14}. **b.** ptc. as noun, **one who removes** boundary Dt 27_{17}. **2.** abs., **carry away** Mc 6_{14}. **3.** of Y., **turn away** heart 4QMa 11.2_{15}.

Ho. 1.0.1 Pf. הֻסַּג; impf. Q תוסג—**be removed,** of justice Is 59_{14}.

→ סִיג *dross.*

סוג II 3.0.1 vb.—**Qal** 1 Ptc. pass. סוּגָה—pass., **be hedged in,** of heap of wheat Ca 7_{3}.

Hi. 1 Impf. תַּסֵּג—abs., **surround with fence** Mc 6_{14}.

Pilp. 1 Impf. תְּשַׂגְשֵׂגִי—**hedge in** plant Is 17_{11}.

Htpalp. 0.0.1 Impf. יתשגשגו—**be hedged in,** of tree 1QH 16_{9}.

[סוּג], see סִיג *dross.*

סוּגַר 1 n.[m.] **neck-collar** Ezk 19_{9}. → סגר I *shut.*

*סוד 0.5 vb.—**Qal or Ni. or Pi.** 0.1 Impf. תסוד—**give counsel** Si 7_{14}.

Htp. 0.4 Impf. תסתיד; impv. הסתייד—**take counsel** with (עִם) wise one Si 9_{14}.

→ סוֹד I *counsel.*

סוֹד I 21.9.83 n.[m.]—cstr. סוֹד; sf. סֹדָם; pl. Q סודות; cstr. Q סודי; sf. Q סודיהמה—**1. counsel** Jr 23_{18}. **2. secret** Pr 11_{13}. **3. company** Jr 6_{11}. **4. intimacy** Ps 25_{14}. **5. counsellor** 1QH 10_{10}. → סוד *give counsel.*

*[סוֹד] II 0.0.55 n.[m.]—cstr. סוד; sf. סודו; pl. סודות; cstr. סודי; sf. סודיהמה—**foundation** of truth 1QH 10_{10}, eternity 1QH 11_{21}. → יסד *establish.*

*[סוֹד] III n.m. **chieftaincy** Ps 25_{14} (LXX κραταίωμα).

*[סוֹד] IV 0.1 n.m. **melancholy** Si 40_{29}(B).

*סוֹד V n.[m.] **core of the heart** Ezk 13_{9} (Pesh *bgw* 'within').

סוֹדִי 1 pr.n.m. **Sodi.**

*[סוּחַ] I 0.0.2 n.[m.] **fir tree** 3QTr $11_{4.10}$.

סוּחַ II 1 pr.n.m. **Suah.**

סוּחָה I 2 n.f. **rubbish** Is 5_{25} Ps 80_{17}.

*סוּחָה II 1 n.f. **faeces** Is 5_{25}.

[סוֹחֵרָה], see סֹחֵרָה I *buckler,* II *enclosing wall,* III *protection.*

[סוֹחֶרֶת], see סֹחֶרֶת *black stone.*

סוֹטַי 2 pr.n.m. **Sotai.**

סוך I 10.0.1 vb.—**Qal** 9.0.1 Pf. סָכְתִּי; impf. תָּסוּךְ; + waw וַיָּסֶךְ—**1. anoint oneself (with), a.** obj., oil Mc 6_{15}. **b.** with (מִן) olive oil 11QT 22_{15}. **2. anoint** captives 2 C 28_{15}.

Qal Pass. (unless Ho.) 1 Impf. יִיסָךְ—of oil, **be poured upon** (עַל) flesh Ex 30_{32}.

→ אָסוּךְ *jar.*

סוך II 2.0.1 vb. (byform of שׂוך)—**Qal** (unless **Hi.**) 2.0.1 + waw וַיָּסֶךְ—**enclose** sea Jb 38_{8}. → מְסוּכָה I *hedge;* cf. שׂוך *fence in,* מְשׂוּכָה *hedge.*

*סוך III 2 vb.—**Pilp.** 2 Impf. יְסַכְסֵךְ—of Y., **stir up** enemy Is 9_{10} 19_{2}.

*סוּכָה n.f. **prickle,** a small mark or character Mc 7_{4} (if em. וַיְעַבְּתוּהָ ... יָשָׁר מִמְּסוּכָה *and they weave it together ... more upright than a hedge* to יְתָעֵב יָשְׁרָם מִסּוּכָה *he loathes ... their uprightness more than a prickle).*

סוֹכֵךְ, see סֹכֵךְ *screen.*

סוֹלְלָה, see סֹלְלָה *mound.*

[סוּלָם], see סֻלָּם I *ladder*.
*[סוּמָה] 0.1 n.f.—pl. cstr. סומות—**treasure** Si 41$_{12(Bmg)}$. → cf. סִימָה *treasure*.
סְוֵנֵה 2 pl.n. **Syene**.
*[סְוֵנִי] 0.0.1 gent. **Syenite**.
סוּס I 137.1.9.1 n.m.—cstr. סוּס; pl. סוּסִים; sf. סוּסַי—**horse** Gn 47$_{17}$; sg. coll., perh. **cavalry** Jos 11$_{4}$. → cf. סוּסָה *mare*.
סוּס II 2 n.[m.] **swift, swallow**, possibly **golden oriole** Is 38$_{14}$ Jr 8$_{7}$.
*[סָוָס] n.[m.] **courier** Est 8$_{10}$ (if em. בַּסּוּסִים *on the horses* to בַּסָּוָסִים *by the couriers*).
[סוּסָה] 1.0.0.1 n.f.—sf. סֻסָתִי—**mare** Ca 1$_{9}$. → cf. סוּס *horse*.
סוּסִי 1 pr.n.m. **Susi**.
*סוע 1 vb.—**Qal** 1 Ptc. סֹעָה—**sweep**, of wind Ps 55$_{9}$.
סוף 9.0.2 vb.—**Qal** 4.0.1 Pf. סָפוּ; impf. יָסוּף—**come to an end, perish**, of wicked Ps 73$_{19}$.

Ni. 0.0.1 Inf. הסוף—**be finished**, of grain Mur 45$_{3}$.

Hi. 4 Impf. אָסֵף (אֲסִיפֵם)—of Y., **bring to an end, destroy** creatures Zp 1$_{3}$.

Shaphel 1 + waw וַיְשַׁסֵּף—**bring to an end, destroy** person 1 S 15$_{33}$.

→ סוֹף *end*.

סוֹף 5.3.19 n.m.—cstr. סוֹף; sf. סֹפוֹ; pl. cstr. Q סופי—**1a. end** of time Ec 3$_{11}$. **b. death** Ec 7$_{2}$. **2. end** of place 2 C 20$_{16}$. **3. conclusion** Ec 12$_{13}$. **4. sum** of words GnzPs 2$_{11}$. → סוף *come to an end*.
סוּף I 28.0.2 n.m. **rushes**, יַם סוּף *Sea of Rushes* Ex 10$_{19}$, sometimes **reeds** Ex 2$_{3}$, perh. **kelp, seaweed** Jon 2$_{6}$.
סוּף II 1 pl.n. **Suph**.
סוּפָה I 15.1.1 n.f.—sf. סוּפָתְךָ; pl. סוּפוֹת; + ה- of direction סוּפָתָה—**storm-wind** Pr 10$_{25}$, perh. **cyclone** Is 5$_{28}$.
סוּפָה II 1 pl.n. **Suphah**.
סוֹפֶרֶת, see סֹפֶרֶת *Sophereth*.
סור I 321.9.54 vb.—**Qal** 159.6.36 Pf. סָר; impf. יָסוּר; + waw וַיָּסַר; impv. סוּר (סוּרָה), סוּרוּ; ptc. סָר, סָרָה, Q סרים, סרי; ptc. pass. סוּרָה, סוּרֵי; inf. abs. סוֹר; cstr. סוּר—**1a. turn aside, deviate** from (מִן) snare Pr 13$_{14}$, commandment Dt 17$_{20}$, Y. Jr 17$_{5}$. **b. neglect** commandment 2 C 8$_{15}$. **c.** pass., **be turned aside**, of Jerusalem Is 49$_{21}$. **d.** ptc. as noun, **one turning aside** from discretion Pr 11$_{22}$. **e.** pass. ptc. as noun, **one turned aside** from Y. Jr 17$_{13(Qr)}$. **2. depart** from (מִן) people Ex 8$_{7}$, Jerusalem Ezk 16$_{42}$. **3. depart, cease to do, repent** from (מִן) sin 2 K 3$_{3}$. **4. cease (to exist)**, of high place 1 K 15$_{14}$, guilt Is 6$_{7}$. **5. gain access to** (אֶל) hearing 1 S 22$_{14}$. **6.** perh. **intoxicate**, of strong drink Ho 4$_{18}$. **7.** perh. **remove** understanding CD 10$_{9}$. **8. escape** Jb 15$_{30}$.

Ni. with infixed-t (unless סתר I ni. *be hidden*) 6.1 Pf. נִסְתַּר; impf. תִּסָּתֵר—**1. turn aside** from (מִן) Y. Ps 38$_{10}$, heat Ps 19$_{7}$. **2.** of Y., **estrange oneself** Ps 89$_{47}$. **3.** ptc. fem. pl. as noun, **aberrations** Ps 19$_{13}$.

Pol. 1 Pf. סוֹרֵר—of Y., **divert** way Lm 3$_{11}$.

Hi. 134.2.17 Pf. הֵסִיר; impf. יָסִיר (יָסֵר); + waw וַיָּסַר; impv. הָסֵר (הָסִיר), הָסִירִי; ptc. מֵסִיר; inf. abs. הָסֵר; cstr. הָסִיר (הֲסִירָהּ)—**1. cause to turn aside** from (מִן) evil Pr 4$_{27}$, (away) from (following) (מֵאַחֲרֵי) Y. Dt 7$_{4}$. **2. remove** robe Ezk 26$_{16}$. **3. move** ark 2 S 6$_{10}$. **4. discard** Asherah 2 C 17$_{6}$. **5. ward off** sickness Dt 7$_{15}$. **6. neglect** (to do) something Jos 11$_{15}$. **7. desist** from (מִן) (doing) injustice Si 38$_{10(Bmg)}$. **8. cut off** head 1 S 17$_{46}$. **9. depose** king 1 K 20$_{24}$. **10. bring to an end** dominion 1QM 18$_{11}$ (ממןשולח).

Hi. with infixed-t (unless סתר hi. *hide*) 16 Pf. הִסְתִּיר; impf. יַסְתֵּר—oft. of Y., **turn away** one's face Is 8$_{17}$.

Ho. 5.0.1 Pf. הוּסַר; impf. יוּסַר; ptc. מוּסָר; מוּסָרִים—**be removed**, of fat Lv 4$_{31}$. **2. be turned away** from (מִן) Belial 11QMelch 2$_{22}$.

→ סוּר I *apostate*, סָרָה II *turning aside*, יָסוּר *one who departs*.

*סור II 1 vb.—**Qal** 1 Pf. סָר—**be corrupt** Ps 14$_{3}$. → סוּרִי *rotten*.
*סור III 1 vb.—**Pol.** 1 Pf. סוֹרֵר—of Y., **obstruct way with thorns** Lm 3$_{11}$.
*[סוּר] I 1 n.m.—pl. cstr. סוּרֵי—**apostate** Jr 2$_{21}$. → סור I *turn aside*.
סוּר II 1 pl.n. **Sur**.
*[סוּר] III 0.0.1 pl.n. **Sur**.
*[סוּרִי] adj. **stinking**, as noun, **rotten thing** Jr 2$_{21}$ (if em. אֵיךְ נֶהְפַּכְתְּ לִי סוּרֵי הַגֶּפֶן נָכְרִיָּה appar. *how you have changed for me, O apostates of the strange vine* to אֵיךְ נֶהְפַּכְתְּ לְסוּרִיָּה גֶּפֶן נָכְרִיָּה *how you have changed*

into a rotten thing, a strange vine). → סור II *be corrupt.*

*סוּרִים I 1 n.m. **entrails** Ec 4:14 (if em. הַסּוּרִים *the prisoners* to הַסּוּרִים *the entrails*).

סוּרִים II, see אסר *bind*, pass. ptc. *prisoner.*

*סוֹרְרִים 1 n.m.pl. **revolt** Jr 6:28. → סרר I *be stubborn.*

סות 18.0.1 vb.—**Hi.** 18.0.1 Pf. הֱסִיתְךָ; impf. יָסִית; + waw וַיָּסֶת (וַיְסִיתֵהוּ); ptc. מֵסִית—delocutive verb, **1. entice** to sin, of Satan 1 C 21:1, human being 1 K 21:25. **2. urge** to make a petition Jos 15:18. **3. provoke** someone to enmity against (בְּ) person, of Y. 1 S 26:19, Satan Jb 2:3, human being Jr 43:3. **4. persuade** by inspiring false hope 2 K 18:32. **5. draw away** soldiers from (מִן) someone, of Y. 2 C 18:31.

[סוּת] 1 n.[m.]—sf. סוּתֹה—**garment** Gn 49:11. → cf. מַסְוֶה *veil.*

סחב 5.1 vb.—**Qal** 5.1 Impf. יִסְחָבוּם; + waw וְסָחַבְנוּ; inf. abs. סָחוֹב; cstr. סְחֹב—**drag** body Jr 22:19, **tear** Judaeans like prey Jr 15:3, perh. **abuse** mother Si 3:16(C). → סְחָבָה *rag.*

[סְחָבָה] 2.0.0.1 n.f.—pl. סְחָבוֹת—**rag** Jr 38:11. → סחב *drag.*

סחה 1.1 vb.—**Pi.** 1.1 + waw וְסִחֵיתִי—**scrape off** dust Ezk 26:4, **sweep away** proud Si 10:17. → סְחִי *scrapings.*

סְחוֹרָה, see סְחֹרָה *merchandise.*

*סחט vb. **Ni.**, **be squeezed, pressed,** of olives 4QHarv 1:8 (יסח[ט]).

סְחִי 1 n.[m.] **scrapings** Lm 3:45. → סחה *scrape.*

*[סְחִיפָה] n.f. **downpour** Jb 14:19 (if em. סְפִיחֶיהָ *its aftergrowths*). → סחף *throw down.*

סָחִישׁ 1 n.[m.] **self-sown grain** 2 K 19:29. → cf. שָׁחִיס *self-sown grain.*

סחף 2 vb.—**Qal** 1 Ptc. סֹחֵף—**beat down,** of rain destroying crops Pr 28:3.

Ni. 1 Pf. נִסְחַף—**be thrown down,** of defeated Egyptians Jr 46:15.

→ סְחִיפָה *downpour.*

*סחק 0.0.1 vb. (byform of שחק)—**Qal** 0.0.1 Ptc. ס[ו]חק—**laugh** 4QD^a 10.2:12. → cf. שחק *laugh*, צחק *laugh.*

סחר I 21.1.2 vb.—**Qal** 20.1.2 Pf. סָחֲרוּ; impf. תִּסְחֲרוּ; impv. סְחָרוּהָ; ptc. סֹחֵר, סֹחֲרֵךְ, סֹחֲרִים; ptc. pass. 1QIsa^a סחורה—**1a. go around, travel around** land Gn 34:10. **b. wander** to (אֶל) land Jr 14:18. **2.** pass., **be encircled** Is 54:11(1QIsa^a). **3.** ptc. as noun, **trader** Gn 37:28, **trading syndicate** Ezk 27:15.

Pealal 1 Pf. סְחַרְחַר—**move about violently,** i.e. **palpitate,** of heart Ps 38:11.

→ מִסְחָר *goods*, סַחַר *profit*, (?) סֹחֵרָה I *buckler*, II *enclosing wall*, (?) סֹחֵרָה *protection*, סְחֹרָה *merchandise; commerce.*

*סחר II 1 vb.—**Pealal** 1 Pf. סְחַרְחַר—**burn with fever,** of heart Ps 38:11.

*סחר III 2 vb.—**Qal** 1 Ptc. סֹחֲרַיִךְ—ptc. as noun, **sorcerer** Is 47:15.

Pealal 1 Pf. סְחַרְחַר—**be bewitched,** of heart/mind Ps 38:11.

[סַחַר] 7 n.m.—cstr. סְחַר; sf. סַחְרָהּ—**1. profit** Pr 3:14. **2. merchandise** Pr 31:18 (unless §1). **3. mart** Is 23:3. → סחר I *go around.*

*סחרה 0.0.1 n.[f.] word in writing exercise, 4QExerCalC 1:2.

סֹחֵרָה I 1.0.1 n.f. **buckler** Ps 91:4. → (?) סחר I *go around.*

*סֹחֵרָה II 1.0.1 n.f. **enclosing wall** Ps 91:4. → סחר I *go around.*

*סֹחֵרָה III 1.0.1 n.f. **protection** Ps 91:4. → (?) סחר I *go around.*

[סְחֹרָה] 1 n.f.—cstr. סְחֹרַת—**1. merchandise** Ezk 27:15 (unless §2). **2. trading** Ezk 27:15. → סחר I *go around.*

[סֹחֶרֶת] 1 n.f.—סֹחָרֶת—**stone** Est 1:6.

[סֵט] I 1 n.[m.]—pl. סֵטִים—**apostate** Ps 101:3. → cf. שׂוּט *fall away*, שֵׂט *apostate.*

*[סֵט] II 1 n.[m.]—pl. סֵטִים—**image** Ps 101:3.

סֹטַי, see סוֹטַי *Sotai.*

*סיג vb. **consider** fortresses Ps 48:14 (if em. פַּסְּגוּ *pass between!* to פְּ־סִיגוּ *and consider!*).

סִיג 8 n.[m.]—Kt סוג; pl. סִיגִים; sf. סִיגַיִךְ—**dross** Is 1:22. → סוג I *turn back.*

*[סִיד] n.[m.] **lime or chalk** Jb 13:27 (if em. סַד *fetters*).

סִיוָן 1 pr.n.[m.] **Sivan,** third month of postexilic Jewish calendar, May/June Est 8:9.

*[סַיָּח] n.m. **young ass** Jb 30:7 (if em. שִׂיחִים *bushes* to סְיָחִים *young asses*).

סִיחוֹן 37.0.1 pr.n.m. **Sihon.**

סִיחֹן, see סִיחוֹן *Sihon.*

סִיךְ, see סוך I *anoint.*

*[סִילָא] 0.0.0.2 pr.n.m. **Sila.**

*[סִימָה] 0.2.3 n.f.—Si שִׂימָה; pl. Q סימות—treasure Si 41$_{14}$(Bmg, M). → cf. סוּמָה treasure.
*[סִימַי] 0.0.1 pr.n.m. Simai.
סִין I 4 pl.n. Sin.
סִין II 2 pl.n. Sin, Pelusium.
סִינַי 35.1.4 pl.n. Sinai.
סִינִי 3 gent. Sinite.
*סִינִים 1 pl.n. Sinim.
*סיס 0.0.1 vb.—Qal 0.0.1 + waw ויסיסו—rejoice CD 1$_{21}$.
סִיס, see סוּס II swift.
סִיסְרָא 21 pr.n.m. Sisera.
סִיעָא Sia, see סִיעֲהָא Siaha.
סִיעֲהָא 2 pr.n.m. Siaha.
סִיר I 30.1 n.m.&f.—pl. סִירוֹת; sf. סִירֹתָיו—pot, for cooking Ex 16$_{3}$, washing Ps 60$_{10}$, cultic use Ex 27$_{3}$.
[סִיר] II 5.0.2 n.m.&f.—pl. סִירִים; cstr. סִירוֹת—1. thorn Is 34$_{13}$. 2. hook Am 4$_{2}$ (unless §3). 3. harpoon Am 4$_{2}$.
*סִיר III n.[m.] prison Ec 7$_{6}$ (Symmachus δεσμωτήριον).
*[סִירָא] I 0.0.1 n.[f.] (timber of) white pine 3QTr 11$_{14}$.
*[סִירָא] II 0.3 pr.n.m. Sira.
[סִירָה], see סִיר I pot, II thorn.
*[סַךְ] I 1 n.[m.]—סָךְ—barrier Ps 42$_{5}$. → סכך I screen.
[סַךְ] II 1 n.[m.]—סָךְ—crowd Ps 42$_{5}$. → סכך II weave.
*[סֵךְ] n.[m.] (byform of שֵׂךְ) thorn Na 1$_{10}$ (if em. כְּסָבְאָם סְבוּאִים like those intoxicated [by] their strong drink to כְּסֵכִים סְבֻכִים as entwined thorns).
*[סֹךְ] I 2 n.[m.]—sf. סֻכּוֹ—shelter, dwelling place Ps 76$_{3}$. → סכך I screen; cf. שֹׂךְ booth.
[סֹךְ] II 2 n.[m.]—sf. סֻכּוֹ—thicket Ps 10$_{9}$. → סכך II weave.
*[סֻכָּה] 0.0.1 n.f.—pl. cstr. סכות—image CD 7$_{14}$.
סֻכָּה I 30.0.30 n.f.—Q סוכה; cstr. סֻכַּת; sf. סֻכָּתוֹ; pl. סֻכּוֹת; pl. sf. Q סוכותיהמה—1. booth, חַג הַסֻּכּוֹת festival of booths Lv 23$_{34}$. 2. canopy of Y. in heaven 2 S 22$_{12}$. 3. shelter to protect from heat Is 4$_{6}$. 4. perh. litter CD 7$_{15}$. → סכך I screen.
סֻכָּה II 1 n.f. thicket Jb 38$_{40}$. → סכך II weave.
סִכּוּת I 1.0.1 pr.n.m. Sikkuth.
*סִכּוּת II 1 n.f. shrine Am 5$_{26}$.
*סִכּוּת III 1 n.f. pole Am 5$_{26}$.
סֻכּוֹת 21.0.1 pl.n. Succoth.
סֻכּוֹת בְּנוֹת 1 pr.n.m. Succoth-benoth.
[סֻכִּי] 1 gent. Sukkite.

סְכִים, see שַׂר־סְכִים Sarsechim.
סכך I 16.0.2 vb.—Qal 11.0.1 Pf. סַכֹּתָה; impf. יְסֻכֵּהוּ; + waw וַיָּסֹכּוּ; impv. Q סכו; ptc. סֹכֵךְ, סֹכְכִים—1. cover, protect, a. with עַל or לְ of obj., + ark, of Moses Ex 40$_{3}$, + person's head, of Y. Ps 140$_{8}$. b. obj. Behemoth, of trees Jb 40$_{22}$. 2. cover (oneself) with (בְּ) anger Lm 3$_{43}$.
Hi. 5.0.1 Impf. יָסֵךְ; ptc. מֵסִיךְ; inf. abs. הָסֵךְ—1. cover, protect, a. with עַל or לְ of obj., + ark, of Moses Ex 40$_{21}$, + worshipper, of Y. Ps 91$_{4}$. 2. cover feet, i.e. evacuate bowels Jg 3$_{24}$.
→ מוּסָךְ I covered way, מְסוּכָה II covering, מָסָךְ screen, מְסָכָה screen, סַךְ I barrier, סֹךְ I shelter, סֻכָּה I shelter, סֹכֵךְ screen, מְסֻכְסֻכָה covering.
סכך II 2.0.1 vb.—Qal 1 Impf. תְּסֻכֵּנִי—of Y., weave embryo within (בְּ) womb Ps 139$_{13}$.
Po. 1.0.1 Impf. תְּסֹכְכֵנִי—1. of Y., weave embryo Jb 10$_{11}$. 2. of city, intertwine paths 4QapLamA 2$_{7}$.
→ סֹךְ II thicket, סַךְ II crowd, סֻכָּה II thicket.
*סכך III vb. Qal, cover, veil anger Lm 3$_{43}$ (if em. סַכֹּתָה בָאַף you have wrapped yourself with anger to סַכֹּתָה אַפֶּיךָ you have veiled your anger).
סֹכֵךְ 1 n.[m.] screen, siege works Na 2$_{6}$. → סכך I screen.
סְכָכָא, see סְכָכָה Secacah.
סְכָכָה 1.0.4 pl.n. Secacah.
סכל I 8.0.1 vb.—Ni. 4 Pf. נִסְכַּלְתָּ—act foolishly 2 S 24$_{10}$.
Pi. 2 Impf. יְשַׂכֵּל; impv. סַכֶּל—make foolish, make nonsense of knowledge of sage Is 44$_{25}$, frustrate counsel 2 S 15$_{31}$.
Hi. 2.0.1 Pf. הִסְכַּלְתָּ—act foolishly Gn 31$_{28}$.
→ סָכָל fool, סֶכֶל fool, סִכְלוּת folly.
*סכל II 0.0.1 vb. (byform of שׂכל)—Hi. 0.0.1 Impf. תסכילו—understand, consider Y.'s wonders 4QInstr^{c} 20$_{2}$.
סָכָל 7.1 n.m.—pl. סְכָלִים—1. as noun, fool Ec 10$_{3}$. 2. as adj., foolish, of son Jr 4$_{22}$, people Jr 5$_{21}$. → סכל I be foolish.
סֶכֶל 1 n.m. fool, perh. folly Ec 10$_{6}$. → סכל I be foolish.
סִכְלוּת 7.0.1 n.f.—שִׂכְלוּת; cstr. סִכְלוּת—folly Ec 10$_{1}$. → סכל I be foolish.
סכן I 12 vb.—Qal 8 Impf. יִסְכּוֹן; ptc. סֹכֵן, סֹכֶנֶת—1. be of use to, be profitable to someone Jb 34$_{9}$. 2. ptc. as noun, one who is of use, of David's companion 1 K 1$_{2}$.

Hi. 4 Pf. הִסְכַּנְתָּה; impv. הַסְכֶּן; inf. abs. הַסְכֵּן—**1.** + inf. עשׂה, **be accustomed to, be in the habit of doing** Nm 22$_{30}$. **2a. be familiar with** (עִם) Y. Jb 22$_{21}$. **b.** of Y., **know intimately** ways of person Ps 139$_3$.

→ מִסְכְּנוֹת I *supplies.*

*סכן II vb. **Pi., set up, erect,** ptc. as noun, **one who erects** Is 40$_{20}$ (if em. הַמְסֻכָּן תְּרוּמָה appar. *the impoverished one chooses [for] an offering to* הַמְסַכֵּן תְּמוּנָה *the one who erects an image*).

סכן III 1 vb.—**Pu.** 1 Ptc. מְסֻכָּן—ptc. as noun, **impoverished one** Is 40$_{20}$. → מִסְכֵּן *poor,* מְסֻכָּן I *impoverished one,* מִסְכֵּנֻת *poverty.*

*סכן IV 1 vb. **Pi., form,** ptc. as noun, **one who makes (a statue)** Is 40$_{20}$ (if em. הַמְסֻכָּן תְּרוּמָה perh. *the impoverished one chooses [for] an offering to* הַמְסַכֵּן תְּמוּנָה *the one who makes an image*).

Pu. 1 Ptc. מְסֻכָּן—ptc. as noun, **that which is formed, image, idol** Is 40$_{20}$.

*סכן V vb. **Pi., guard,** ptc. as noun, **one who guards** Is 40$_{20}$ (if em. הַמְסֻכָּן תְּרוּמָה perh. *the impoverished one chooses [for] an offering to* הַמְסַכֵּן תְּמוּנָה *the one who guards an image*).

סכן VI 6 vb.—**Qal** 5 Impf. יִסְכּוֹן—**run risk, incur danger,** מַה־יִּסְכָּן־לָךְ *how does that make you run a danger?* Jb 35$_3$.

Ni. 1 Impf. יִסָּכֶן—**run risk, incur danger with** (בְּ) wood Ec 10$_9$.

*סכן VII 1 vb.—**Ni.** 1 Impf. יִסָּכֶן—**cut oneself with** (בְּ) (splitting) logs Ec 10$_9$. → cf. שַׂכִּין *knife.*

*סכן VIII 1 vb.—**Hi.** 1 Impv. הַסְכֶּן—**agree with** (עִם) Y. Jb 22$_{21}$.

*סכן IX 1 vb.—**Hi.** 1 Pf. הִסְכַּנְתָּה—of Y., **rule** person's ways Ps 139$_3$.

*סכן X 1 vb.—**Hi.** 1 Impv. הַסְכֶּן—**be quiet, acquiesce with** (עִם) Y. Jb 22$_{21}$.

*סכן XI 3 vb.—**Qal** 2 Ptc. סֹכֶנֶת—ptc. as noun, **nurse** 1 K 1$_2$.

Ni. 1 Impf. יִסָּכֶן—**be careful with** (בְּ) wood Ec 10$_9$.

*סכן XII 1 vb.—**Pu.** 1 Ptc. מְסֻכָּן—ptc. as noun, **one who is acquainted with, connoisseur** Is 40$_{20}$.

*סֹכֶנֶת 2 n.f. **female official, attendant** 1 K 1$_{2.4}$.

סכסך, see סוך III *stir up.*

סכר I 3.0.1 vb. (byform of סגר)—**Qal** 0.0.1 Impv. סכר—with בְּ of obj., perh. **fortify** Bethel 4QapJoshua[b] 26$_2$.

Ni. 2 Impf. יִסָּכֵר—**be shut, closed,** of sources of flood waters Gn 8$_2$, mouths of liars Ps 63$_{12}$.

Pi. 1 + waw וְסִכַּרְתִּי—of Y., **shut up** Egyptians in (בְּ) hand of harsh master Is 19$_4$.

→ cf. סגר I *shut.*

סכר II 1 vb. (byform of שׂכר)—cstr. פִּתְרוֹן; sf. פִּתְרֹנוֹ; pl. פִּתְרֹנִים—**Qal** 1 Ptc. סֹכְרִים—**hire, bribe** counsellors against (עַל) Judaeans Ezr 4$_5$.

*סכר III 1 vb.—**Pi.** 1 + waw וְסִכַּרְתִּי—of Y., **hand over, deliver up** Egyptians into (בְּ) hand of harsh master Is 19$_4$.

סכת 1.1 vb. (byform of שׁקט)—**Ni.** 0.1 Pf. נסכתו—**be silent, quieten down,** perh. **be (respectfully) silent** Si 13$_{23}$.

Hi. 1 Impv. הַסְכֵּת—**remain silent** Dt 27$_9$.

סֻכֹּת, see סֻכּוֹת *Succoth.*

סַל 15.0.4 n.m.—cstr. סַל; pl. סַלִּים; cstr. סַלֵּי—**basket** Ex 29$_{23}$.

סלא 1.0.1 vb. (byform of סלה)—**Pu.** 1.0.1 Ptc. מְסֻלָּאִים—**be weighed, valued** as (בְּ) gold, of son of Zion Lm 4$_2$. → cf. סלה II *weigh.*

סַלָּא, see סַלּוּא *Salu.*

*[סִלָּא] 0.0.0.6 pr.n.m. **Sila.**

סִלָּא 1 pl.n. **Silla.**

סלד I 1 vb.—**Pi.** 1 + waw וַאֲסַלְּדָה—**spring up** Jb 6$_{10}$.

*סלד II 1 vb.—**Pi.** 1 + waw וַאֲסַלְּדָה—**jump (for joy)** Jb 6$_{10}$.

*סלד III 1 vb.—**Pi.** 1 + waw וַאֲסַלְּדָה—**recoil, tremble** Jb 6$_{10}$.

*סלד IV 1 vb.—**Pi.** 1 + waw וַאֲסַלְּדָה—**harden oneself** Jb 6$_{10}$.

סֶלֶד 2 pr.n.m. **Seled.**

סלה I 2.0.1 vb.—**Qal** 1 Pf. סָלִיתָ—of Y., **despise, consider worthless, regard as dross** those who go astray Ps 119$_{118}$.

Pi. 1 Pf. סִלָּה—of Y., **flout, reject, spurn, regard as dross** all warriors Lm 1$_{15}$.

Pu. 0.0.1 Pf. סולה—**be flouted, rejected, spurned** 4QsapDidB 2.14.

סלה II 2.0.1 vb. (byform of סלא)—**Pu.** 2.0.1 Impf. תְּסֻלֶּה—**be weighed, valued,** thus perh. **be bought,** with

(בְּ) gold Jb 28₁₆. → cf. סלא *weigh.*

סֶלָה 74.0.7.1 n.f. **selah,** perh. musical term Ps 3₃.

סַלּוּ, see סַלּוּא *Sallu.*

סָלוּא 1.0.1 pr.n.m. **Salu.**

סַלּוּא 3 pr.n.m. **Sallu.**

*[סַלּוֹן] I 1 n.m.—pl. סַלּוֹנִים—**blasphemer, traitor** Ezk 2₆.

[סַלּוֹן] II, see סִלּוֹן *briar.*

[סִלּוֹן] 2 n.m.—pl. סַלּוֹנִים—**briar, thorn** Ezk 28₂₄ 2₆.

סלח 46.2.13 vb.—**Qal** 33.2.9 Pf. סָלַחְתִּי; impf. אֶסְלוֹחַ—with לְ of obj., alw. of Y., **forgive, pardon** sin Ex 34₉, people 1 K 8₅₀.

Ni. 13.0.4 + waw וְנִסְלַח; inf. abs. Q נסלוח—**be forgiven, pardoned,** subj. sin + לְ of person, וְנִסְלַח לוֹ *and it will be forgiven him* Lv 4₃₁.

→ סַלָּח *ready to forgive,* סְלִיחָה *forgiveness.*

סַלָּח 1 adj. **ready to forgive, forgiving,** of Y. Ps 86₅. → סלח *forgive.*

סַלַּי 2 pr.n.m. **Sallai.**

סְלִיחָה 3.1.27 n.f.—pl. סְלִיחוֹת (סְלִחוֹת); sf. Q סליחותיכה—**forgiveness** Ps 130₄; pl. intens., **great forgiveness,** אֱלוֹהַּ סְלִיחוֹת *God of great forgiveness* Ne 9₁₇. → סלח *forgive.*

סַלְכָה 4 pl.n. **Salecah.**

סלל 12.2.1 vb.—**Qal** 10 + waw וַיָּסֹלּוּ; impv. סֹלּוּ (סָלּוּהָ); ptc. pass. סְלוּלָה—**1a. raise, lift up** road, as technical term for (re)building it Is 62₁₀. **b.** pass., **be raised up,** of road Pr 15₁₉. **2a. raise** rampart against (עַל) person Jb 19₁₂. **b. pile up** Babylonian corpses Jr 50₂₆. **3.** with לְ of obj., **exalt, praise** Y. Ps 68₅.

Ni. 0.0.1 + waw ונסלו—**be raised, exalted,** ונסלו להם לעולם *and they shall be exalted by them forever* 4QMidrEschat[b] 3₁₀(Allegro).

Pilp. 1 Impv. סַלְסְלֶהָ—**esteem highly, cherish** or **caress** wisdom Pr 4₈.

Htpol. 1.2 Impf. Si יסתוללו; ptc. מִסְתּוֹלֵל—**1a. exalt oneself, raise oneself up** against (בְּ) people Ex 9₁₇. **b. be arrogant, beg** Si 40₂₈(B). **2. be broken up, dug up,** of way Si 39₂₄.

→ מְסִלָּה I *road,* II *high praise,* מַסְלוּל *road,* מְסִלּוּל *road,* סֹלְלָה *mound.*

סֹלְלָה 11 n.f.—סוֹלְלָה; pl. סללות—**mound, earthworks,** against besieged city Jr 6₆. → סלל *raise.*

*[סָלֹם] 0.0.1 n.m. (byform of שָׁלוֹם) **peace, greetings** 5/6ḤevEp 1₂.

סֻלָּם I 1.0.1 n.m. **ladder** Gn 28₁₂.

***סֻלָּם** II 1 n.m. **staircase,** of ziggurat or tower Gn 28₁₂.

***סֻלָּם** III 1 n.m. **entrance way** Gn 28₁₂.

***סֻלָּם** IV 1 n.m. **door** (of heaven) Gn 28₁₂.

***סֻלָּם** V 1 n.m. **temple tower with steps, ziggurat** Gn 28₁₂.

*[סַלְמָה] 0.0.1 n.f. (byform of שַׂלְמָה)—pl. sf. סלמותמה—**garment** 11QT 49₁₈.

סלסל, see סלל *esteem highly.*

[סַלְסִלָּה] I 1 n.f. (byform of זַלְזַל)—pl. סַלְסִלּוֹת—**shoot, branch, tendril,** of vine Jr 6₉.

*[סַלְסִלָּה] II 1 n.f.—pl. סַלְסִלּוֹת—**basket,** for harvested grapes Jr 6₉.

סֶלַע I 51.2.13 n.m.—sf. סַלְעִי; pl. סְלָעִים—**1a. rock, cliff, crag,** oft. with opening, crevice or cave, חַגְוֵי הַסֶּלַע *clefts of the rock* Ca 2₁₄. **b. rocky region** 1 S 23₂₅. **c.** perh. **rocky ground, rocky surface** Am 6₁₂. **d. block of stone, boulder,** as altar Jg 6₂₀. **e.** perh. **large building stone** of fortress Is 33₁₆. **f.** coll., **small rocks, stones** CD 11₁₁. **g. tomb-chamber** Is 22₁₆. **h. stone cistern** CD 10₁₂. **i. headstone** 4QVisSam 3.2₃. **j. stone material,** only breakable by hammer Jr 23₂₉, חִזְּקוּ פְנֵיהֶם מִסֶּלַע *they made their faces harder than stone* Jr 5₃. **2a. rock** as **strong place, fortress,** in ref. to Y., י״ סַלְעִי *Y. is my rock* 2 S 22₂. **b. rock** as **foundation,** of Babylonian empire Jr 51₂₅, **firm place,** for standing Ps 40₃. → cf. מִסְלָע *rocky place.*

*[סֶלַע] II 0.0.5 n.f.—pl. סלעים (סלעין)—**sela (coin)** 5/6 ḤevBA 44₂₁.

סֶלַע III 8 pl.n. **Sela.**

***סֶלַע** IV 2 n.m.—sf. סַלְעוֹ—**(staff) officer** Is 31₉ Ps 141₆.

***סֶלַע הַמַּחְלְקוֹת** 1 pl.n. **Sela-hammahlekoth.**

סֶלַע הָרִמּוֹן, see סֶלַע רִמּוֹן *Sela-rimmon.*

סָלְעָם 1.0.1 n.m. **locust,** perh. **long-headed locust** or **bald locust,** permitted as food Lv 11₂₂.

סֶלַע עֵיטָם 2 pl.n. **Sela Etam.**

*[סֶלַע צִיּוֹן] 0.0.1 pl.n. **Sela Zion.**

סֶלַע רִמּוֹן 4 pl.n. **Sela-rimmon.**

סלף 7.2.1 vb.—**Pi.** 7.2.1 Impf. יְסַלֵּף; ptc. מְסַלֵּף—**1. twist,**

pervert wicked Pr 21_{12}. **2. subvert** cause Ex 23_8. 3. perh. **find fault** Si 11_7. → סֶלֶף *perversity.*

סֶלֶף 2 n.m.—cstr. סֶלֶף—**perversity, crookedness** Pr 11_3. → סלף *twist.*

סלק 1 vb.—**Qal** 1 Impf. אֶסַּק—**ascend,** אִם־אֶסַּק שָׁמַיִם *if I ascend (to) heaven* Ps 139_8.

סֹלֶת 53.0.9.1 n.f.—sf. סָלְתָּהּ—**semolina, choice wheat flour,** סֹלֶת חִטִּים *semolina (made) of wheat* Ex 29_2.

[סַם] 16.2.1 n.m.—pl. סַמִּים (Si שמים)—**1. spice** burnt on incense altar Lv 4_7. **2. herb** as natural remedy Si $38_{4(Bmg)}$.

*__[סִמְגַּר]__ 1 n.m. **official,** neo-Babylonian title of dignitary Jr 39_3.

*__[סַמְגָּר]__ pl.n. **Sin-magir** (if em. ־סַמְגַּר).

*__סַמְגַּר־נְבוֹ__ 1 pr.n.m. **Samgar-nebo.**

סְמָדַר I 3.0.0.1 n.m. **1. bud(s), blossom(s),** specif. of vine Ca 2_{15}. **2.** perh. **blossom-flavoured wine** Hazor inscr. 7.

*__[סְמָדַר]__ II 0.0.0.1 pr.n.m. **Semadar.**

*__סמה__ 0.0.1 vb.—**Qal** 0.0.1 Ptc. סומ[י]ם—ptc. as noun, **blind one** 4QMMT B_{49}.

סְמְחָה, see שִׂמְחָה *joy.*

סמך 48.5.22 vb.—**Qal** 41.5.19 Pf. סָמַךְ, סְמַכְתִּיהוּ; impf. יִסְמְכֵנִי; + waw וַיִּסְמֹךְ; ptc. סוֹמֵךְ, סֹמְכֵי; impv. סָמְכֵנִי; ptc. pass. סָמוּךְ, סְמוּכִים—**1a. support (with), sustain (with), uphold,** (1) with accus., רוּחַ נְדִיבָה תִסְמְכֵנִי *let a vigorous spirit sustain me* Ps 51_{14}. (2) with double accus., תִּירֹשׁ סְמַכְתִּיו *I have sustained him with new wine* Gn 27_{37}. (3) with accus. + prep. בְּ, סמכתני בעוזכה *you have supported me with your strength* 1QH 15_6. **b.** pass., **be supported, sustained,** of heart Ps 112_8, Y.'s commands Ps 111_8. **c.** ptc. as noun, **supporter, upholder** Ezk 30_6. **d.** pass. ptc. as adj., **supported, firm, steadfast,** of character 1QH 9_{35}. **e.** pass. ptc. as musical term, **sustained, drawn out,** of sound 1QM 8_7. **2a. lay hands upon** (עַל) sacrificial animal Lv 1_4, Levite Nm 8_{10}. **b.** of Y., **lay** or **set** glorious garments upon (עַל) prince 4QPrEnosh 1.2_8. **3a.** of Y.'s anger, **lean, lie heavily** against (עַל) worshipper Ps 88_8. **b. lay siege** to (אֶל) city Ezk 24_2. **4. lean** hand against (עַל) wall Am 5_{19}.

Ni. 6.0.3 Pf. נִסְמַכְתִּי; impf. יִסָּמֵךְ; inf. cstr. Q הסמך—**1. lean, rest (oneself)** on (עַל) pillars Jg 16_{29}. **2. rely** on (עַל) Y. Ps 71_6, word of king 2 C 32_8. **3.** pass., **be supported, firm,** of heart 4QBark[d] 2.1_{14}.

Pi. 1 Impv. סַמְּכוּנִי—**sustain** lover with (בְּ) raisin cakes Ca 2_5.

→ סֶמֶךְ *support*; cf. שְׂמִיכָה *covering.*

[סָמַךְ], see סְמַכְיָהוּ *Semachiah.*

*__[סֶמֶךְ]__ 0.1 n.m. **support, help** Si 13_{21}. → סמך *lean.*

[סְמַכִי], see סְמַכְיָהוּ *Semachiah.*

[סְמַכְיָה], see סְמַכְיָהוּ *Semachiah.*

סְמַכְיָהוּ 1.0.0.36 pr.n.m. **Semachiah.**

[סְמַכְיוֹ], see סְמַכְיָהוּ *Semachiah.*

סֶמֶל 5.0.1 n.m.—סֶמֶל; cstr. סֶמֶל—**image (of a deity), icon, statue,** פֶּסֶל הַסֶּמֶל *image of the statue* 2 C 33_7.

*__[סמל]__ 0.0.2 n.[m.] (byform of שְׂמֹאל) **left** 3QTr 1_{13} 10_6.

סמם, see שׂמם *paint the face.*

סמן 1 vb.—**Ni.** 1 Ptc. נִסְמָן—**be placed,** of crops being planted Is 28_{25}.

*__[סַמָּן]__ 0.0.1 n.m.—pl. סמנים—**spice, medicine** CD 11_{10}.

*__[סָמָע]__ 0.0.0.1 pr.n.m. **Sama.**

סמר I 2 vb.—**Qal** 1 Pf. סָמַר—of flesh, **tremble** because of (מִן) fear Ps 119_{120}.

Pi. 1 Impf. תְּסַמֵּר—of hair of body, **bristle, stand on end** Jb 4_{15}.

→ סָמָר *bristling,* (?) מַסְמֵר *nail.*

*__סמר__ II vb. **nail** Ps 119_{120} (LXX καθήλωσον *nail!*). → מַסְמֵר *nail.*

סָמָר 1 adj. **bristling,** of locust Jr 51_{27}. → סמר I *bristle.*

[סַן], abbrev. of סַנְבַלַּט *Sanballat.*

סנא, see שׂנא *hate.*

סְנָאָה I 3 pr.n.m. **Senaah.**

*__סְנָאָה__ II 3 pl.n. **Senaah.**

סַנְבַלַּט 10.0.0.6 pr.n.m. **Sanballat.**

סַנָּה, see קִרְיַת־סַנָּה *Kiriath-sannah.*

סֶנֶּה 1 pl.n. **Seneh.**

סְנֶה 6.1.1 n.m. **bush,** perh. specif. **senna,** 'burning bush' Ex 3_2.

סְנוּאָה, see סְנָאָה *Senaah.*

סַנְוֵרִים 3 n.m. **blindness** Gn 19_{11}.

סַנְחֵרִיב 13.1 pr.n.m. **Sennacherib.**

*__[סָנִיב]__ 0.0.0.1 pr.n.m. **Sanib.**

[סַנְסִן] 1 n.m.—pl. sf. סַנְסִנָּיו—**cluster, panicle** Ca 7_9.

סַנְסַנָּה 1 pl.n. **Sansannah.**

סַנְסִנָּה, see סַנְסַן *cluster.*

סְנַפִּיר 5 n.[m.] appar. **fins** Lv 11₉.

סָס 1.1 n.m. **moth,** or another cloth-eating insect Is 51₈.

סִסְמַי 2 pr.n.m. **Sismai.**

*[**סְעַגְיָהוּ**] 0.0.0.1 pr.n.m. **Seagiah.**

סעד 12 vb.—**Qal** 12 Impf. יִסְעָדֵנִי; + waw וְסָעַד; impv. סַעֲדוּ; impv. סְעָד, סַעֲדוּ; inf. cstr. סַעֲדָה—**1a.** of Y., **support, sustain, uphold** person Ps 20₃. **b.** of king, **maintain** throne Pr 20₂₈. **2. strengthen, give sustenance to** heart, of bread Ps 104₁₅, person Jg 19₈. → מִסְעָד I *table,* II *step,* סַעַד *support.*

*[**סַעַד**] 0.0.1 n.[m.]—sf. סעדך—**support, help** 4QapJer Cᵃ 17.2₇. → סעד *support.*

[**סְעָדָה**], see סְעַדְיָהוּ *Saadiah.*

[**סַעֲדְיָה**], see סְעַדְיָהוּ *Saadiah.*

*[**סַעֲדְיָהוּ**] 0.0.0.6 pr.n.m. **Saadiah.**

[**סַעֲדִיוּ**], see סְעַדְיָהוּ *Saadiah.*

סעה 1.0.1 vb.—**Qal** 1.0.1 Ptc. סֹעָה—ptc. as adj., **rushing,** of wind Ps 55₉.

[**סָעִיף**] I 4 n.[m.]—cstr. סְעִיף; pl. cstr. סְעִפֵי (1QIsaᵃ שעפי) —**cleft,** סְעִפֵי הַסְּלָעִים *clefts in the rocks,* i.e. caves Is 2₂₁. → סעף *divide.*

*[**סָעִיף**] II 2 n.[m.]—pl. sf. סְעִפֶּיהָ—**branch,** of tree Is 17₆ 27₁₀. → סעף *divide.*

*[**סָעִיף**] III 1 n.[m.] **projection,** סְעִפֵי הַסְּלָעִים *projections of the cliffs* Is 57₅ (1QIsaᵃ שעפי).

***סעל** vb. **Ni., be little, be paltry, be stunted,** of wing of ostrich Jb 39₁₃ (if em. נֶעֱלָסָה to נִסְעֲלָה *it is paltry*).

*[**סְעָלִי**] 0.0.0.1 pr.n.m. **Seali.**

סעף 1 vb.—**Pi.** 1 Ptc. מְסָעֵף—**cut, cut off** branch with (בְּ) axe Is 10₃₃. → סָעִיף I *cleft,* II *branch,* סֵעֵף *divided,* סְעַפָּה *branch,* סְעִפָּה I *division,* II *crutch,* III *choice,* סַרְעַפָּה *branch.*

[**סֵעֵף**] 1 adj.—pl. סֵעֲפִים—**divided,** as noun, **one who is double-minded, unsure** Ps 119₁₁₃. → סעף *divide.*

[**סְעַפָּה**] 2 n.f.—pl. sf. סעפתיו—**branch** Ezk 31₆.₈. → סעף *divide.*

[**סְעִפָּה**] I 1 n.f. **division,** שְׁתֵּי הַסְּעִפִּים *two contrary ideas* 1 K 18₂₁. → סעף *divide.*

*[**סְעִפָּה**] II 1 n.f. **crutch,** שְׁתֵּי הַסְּעִפִּים *two crutches* 1 K 18₂₁. → סעף *divide.*

*[**סְעִפָּה**] III 1 n.f. **choice,** שְׁתֵּי הַסְּעִפִּים *two choices* 1 K 18₂₁. → סעף *divide.*

סְעִפִּים, see סְעִפָּה I *division,* II *crutch,* III *choice.*

סער I 7.1.2 vb.—**Qal** 3.0.2 Impf. יִסְעָרוּ; ptc. סֹעֵר—**storm, rage,** of sea Jon 1₁₁.

Ni. 1 + waw וַיִּסָּעֵר—**be enraged, disquieted,** of heart 2 K 6₁₁.

Pi. 1 + waw וְאֵסָעֲרֵם—of Y., **blow away, disperse** Israel(ites) Zc 7₁₄.

Po. 1 Impf. יְסֹעֵר—**be tossed** or **driven by storm, be whisked away** from (מִן) threshing floor, of chaff Ho 13₃.

Pu. 1 Pf. סֹעֲרָה—**be tossed** or **driven by storm,** of afflicted one Is 54₁₁.

Hi. 0.1 Pf. הסערתה—**blow away,** thus **astound, astonish** people Si 47₁₇.

→ מִסְעָר *storm,* סַעַר *tempest,* סְעָרָה *storm-wind.*

***סער** II 0.1 vb. (byform of שׂער)—**Hi.** 0.1 Pf. הסערתה—**excite** people Si 47₁₇.

סַעַר 8.0.1 n.m. **tempest, storm,** oft. attacks by enemy Ps 55₉; perh. **tossing** (of waves) Jon 1₄. → סער I *storm;* cf. שַׂעַר II *storm.*

סְעָרָה 16.3.1 n.f.—cstr. סַעֲרַת; pl. סְעָרוֹת; cstr. סַעֲרוֹת—**storm-wind, strong wind,** סַעֲרַת י׳ *storm-wind of Y.* Jr 23₁₉, סַעֲרוֹת תֵּימָן *storm-winds of the south* Zc 9₁₄. → סער I *storm.*

[**סְעַרִי**], see סְעַרְיָהוּ *Seariah.*

*[**סְעַרְיָהוּ**] 0.0.0.3 pr.n.m. **Seariah.**

סַף I 7.0.1 n.m.—cstr. סַף; pl. סִפִּים, סִפּוֹת (סִפּוֹת); cstr. סִפּוֹת —**basin, dish, cup** 2 K 12₁₄.

סַף II 30.1.3 n.m.—cstr. סַף; sf. סִפִּי; pl. סִפִּים—**threshold,** viewed from inside of building, שֹׁמְרֵי הַסַּף *keepers of the threshold,* i.e. priests 2 K 12₁₀, palace guards Est 2₂₁, שֹׁעֲרֵי הַסִּפִּים *porters of the thresholds,* i.e. Levites 2 C 23₄. → ספף I *stand outside.*

סַף III 2 pr.n.m. **Saph.**

ספד 30 vb.—**Qal** 28 Impf. תִּסְפֹּד; + waw וְסָפְדוּ; impv. סִפְדוּ, סְפֹדְנָה; inf. abs. סָפוֹד; cstr. סְפוֹד (לִסְפֹּד)—**1a.** context of bereavement, **lament, mourn,** (1) for (לְ) someone Gn 23₂. (2) on account of (עַל) someone 2 S 1₁₂. (3) with cognate accus. מִסְפֵּד Gn 50₁₀. (4) abs. 1 K 13₂₉. **b.** ptc. as noun, **mourner, wailer** Ec 12₅. **2.** context of (impending) disaster, **lament, wail** on account of (עַל) fields Is 32_{12}.

Ni. 2 Impf. יִסָּפְדוּ—**be lamented, mourned,** of deceased Jr 16_{4}.

→ מִסְפֵּד *mourning*.

ספה I 16.2.3 vb.—**Qal** 7.0.1 Pf. סָפְתָה; impf. תִּסְפֶּה; + waw וְסָפוּ; inf. cstr. סְפוֹת—**1a. sweep away, wipe out, destroy** people, of Y. Gn 18_{24} (:: נשׂא *forgive*). **b. cut off, shave** beard Is 7_{20}. **2. be swept away, removed,** of animal Jr 12_{4}, house Am 3_{15}.

Ni. 9.2.2 Pf. Q נספיתה; impf. אֶסָּפֶה, תִּסָּפוּ—**1. be swept away, wiped out, destroyed,** of people 1 S 12_{25}, spirit 1QS 2_{14}. **2.** ptc. as noun, **one who is carried or swept away, captive** Is 13_{15}.

***ספה II** 3.0.1 vb. (byform of יסף)—**Qal** 2.0.1 Inf. cstr. סְפוֹת (סְפוֹת)—**increase, add,** סְפוֹת חַטָּאת עַל־חַטָּאת *to add sin to sin* Is 30_{1}.

Hi. 1 Impf. אַסְפֶּה—of Y., **increase, multiply,** אַסְפֶּה עָלֵימוֹ רָעוֹת *I shall increase against them evils* Dt 32_{23}.

***ספה III** 1 vb.—**Qal** 1 Inf. cstr. סְפוֹת—**satisfy, quench** thirst Dt 29_{18}.

***[סָפָה]** 0.0.1 n.f. (byform of שָׂפָה)—pl. ספות—**lip,** perh. **groove, fold** 1QM 5_{12}.

***[סָפָה]** 1 n.f.—pl. סַפּוֹת—**coverlet, bedding** 2 S 17_{28}.

סְפוּ, see יסף *add*.

***[סָפוּן]** 0.0.1 pr.n.m. **Saphun.**

***[סְפוּק]** 0.1 n.[m.] **abundance** of food Si 34_{12}. → ספק V *abound*.

סְפוֹרָה, see סְפֹרָה *literacy, art of writing*.

ספח I 5.0.1 vb.—**Qal** 1 Impv. סְפָחֵנִי—**attach, join, assign** person to (אֶל) priestly office 1 S 2_{36}.

Ni. 1 + waw וְנִסְפְּחוּ—**attach oneself, join oneself** to (עַל) house of Jacob Is 14_{1}.

Pi. 1 Ptc. מְסַפֵּחַ—with double accus., **associate** someone **with** anger, thus **cause** him **to share** anger Hb 2_{15}.

Pu. 1 Impf. יְסֻפָּחוּ—**join, huddle together** Jb 30_{7}.

Htp. 1.0.1 Inf. cstr. הִסְתַּפֵּחַ (Q השתפח)—**1. attach, join oneself** to (לְ) house of Judah CD 4_{11}. **2. partake in** (בְּ) Y.'s inheritance 1 S 26_{19}.

→ סָפִיחַ I *aftergrowth*.

***ספח II** 1 vb.—**Pi.** 1 Ptc. מְסַפֵּחַ—**pour out** anger Hb 2_{15}. → מִשְׂפָּח I *bloodshed*, סֶפַח *outpouring*, סָפִיחַ II *outpouring*.

***[סֶפַח]** n.[m.] **outpouring** Hb 2_{15} (if em. מַשְׁקֵה רֵעֵהוּ מְסַפֵּחַ חֲמָתְךָ *one who causes his friend to drink, causing [him] to share your anger* to מַשְׁקֵה רֵעֵהוּ שֵׁכָר מִסֶּפַח חֲמָתְךָ *one who gives strong drink to his neighbour from the outpouring of your anger*).

→ ספח II *pour out*.

סַפַּחַת 2.0.4 n.f.—Q שפחת—**scab,** perh. of secondary benign stage of skin disorder Lv 13_{2}. → cf. מִסְפַּחַת *scab*; cf. שׂפח *make a scab*.

סְפִי, see סַף III *Saph*.

סָפִיחַ I 5.0.1 n.[m.]—Q שפיח; cstr. סְפִיחַ; pl. sf. סְפִיחֶיהָ—**aftergrowth,** grain that grows without cultivation, סְפִיחַ קְצִירְךָ *aftergrowth of your harvest* Lv 25_{5}. → ספח I *attach*.

[סָפִיחַ] II 1 n.[m.]—pl. sf. סְפִיחֶיהָ—**outpouring** of rain, **torrent, rainstorm** Jb 14_{19}. → ספח II *pour out*.

סְפִינָה I 1.0.2 n.f.—Q שפינא; pl. Q שפינת—**ship, boat** Jon 1_{5}.

***סְפִינָה II** 1 n.f. **hold** of ship, **storeroom** Jon 1_{5}. → ספן I *cover*.

***[סָפִיר]** n.m. **envoy, agent** 2 K 20_{12}||Is 39_{1} (if em. סְפָרִים *letters* to סְפִירִים *envoys*).

סַפִּיר 11.2.1 n.[m.]—pl. סַפִּירִים—**lapis lazuli,** a blue semi-precious stone Ex 24_{10}.

סֵפֶל 2 n.[m.] **(large) bowl** Jg 5_{25} 6_{38}.

ספן I 6.0.1 vb. (byform of שׂפן)—**Qal** 6.0.1 + waw וַיִּסְפֹּן; ptc. pass. סָפוּן, סְפוּנִים—**1. panel, roof** temple **with beams and planks** 1 K 6_{9}. **2.** pass., **a. be panelled, roofed,** of house 1 K 7_{3}. **b. be covered, preserved, reserved,** of plot of land Dt 33_{21}. → סְפִינָה II *hold* of ship, סִפֻּן *ceiling*.

***ספן II** 5 vb.—**Qal** 5 + waw וַיִּסְפֹּן; ptc. pass. סָפוּן, סְפוּנִים—**1. honour** temple 1 K 6_{9} (+ גֵּבִים וּשְׂדֵרֹת בָּאֲרָזִים *with beams and planks of cedar*). **2.** pass., **be honourable, be (made) majestic,** of house Hg 1_{4}.

סִפֻּן 1 n.[m.] **ceiling,** of temple 1 K 6_{15}. → ספן I *cover*.

***[סַפְסַג] I** n.[m.] **glaze** Ezk 22_{18} (if em. סִגִים כֶּסֶף *dross, silver* to כְּסַפְסַגִּים *like glaze*).

***[סַפְסַג] II** n.[m.] **bowl** Pr 26_{23} (if em. כֶּסֶף סִיגִים מְצֻפֶּה עַל־חָרֶשׂ appar. *silver of dross laid over earthenware* to כְּסַפְסָג מְצֻפֶּה עַל־חָרֶשׂ *like a bowl laid over earthenware*).

סַפְסִיג, see סַפְסָג I *glaze*.

ספף I 1.0.1 vb.—**Htpol.** 1.0.1 Inf. cstr. הִסְתּוֹפֵף—**stand outside, be shut out, be excluded,** of worshipper Ps 84₁₁. → סַף II *threshold*.

*ספף II, **burn** Nm 21₁₄ (LXX ἐφλόγισεν *set on fire*).

ספק I 6 vb. (byform of שׂפק)—**Qal** 6 Pf. סָפְקָם; impf. יִסְפּוֹק; impv. סְפֹק—**1.** in derision or anger, **clap** hands **together** Nm 24₁₀, against (עַל) Jerusalem Lm 2₁₅; with ellip. Jb 34₃₇. **2.** in distress, **slap, beat** or **strike** hand upon (עַל) thigh Jr 31₁₉, against (אֶל) thigh Ezk 21₁₇. **3.** as punishment, of Y., **strike** person Jb 34₂₆. → סֶפֶק I *clap*.

*ספק II 1 vb.—**Qal** 1 Impf. יִסְפּוֹק—**doubt** transgression Jb 34₃₇.

*ספק III 1 vb.—**Qal** 1 + waw וְסָפַק—**wallow, splash around** in (בְּ) vomit Jr 48₂₆.

*ספק IV 2 vb.—**Qal** 2 Impf. יִסְפּוֹק; + waw וְסָפַק—**spew out, vomit** Jr 48₂₆ Jb 34₃₇.

*ספק V 1.5 vb. (byform of שׂפק)—**Qal** 1.2 Pf. Si ספקה; impf. יִסְפּוֹק—**1. be abundant in provision,** of Y. Si 39₃₃, wisdom Si 15₁₈. **2. multiply** transgression Jb 34₃₇.

Pi. 0.1 Ptc. מספק—**cause to be abundant, increase** wound, of abundance of wine Si 34₃₀.

Hi. 0.2 Pf. Si הספיקו; impf. יספיק—**be sufficient, be able,** of Y. Si 39₁₆.

→ סֶפֶק II *abundance*.

*ספק VI 1 vb.—**Qal** 1 Impf. יִסְפּוֹק—**be shameless** Jb 34₃₇.

[סֶפֶק] I 1 n.[m.]—סֶפֶק—**scoffing, scorning** Jb 36₁₈. → ספק I *clap*.

*[סֶפֶק] II 1 n.[m.] (byform of שֶׂפֶק)—סֶפֶק—**abundance** Jb 36₁₈. → ספק V *abound*.

*[סֶפֶק] III 1 n.[m.]—סֶפֶק—**chastisement** Jb 36₁₈.

*[סֶפֶק] IV 1 n.[m.]—סֶפֶק—**meanness** Jb 36₁₈.

ספר I 161.8.80.13 vb.—**Qal** 81.2.15.13 Pf. סָפַר (סְפָרָם); impf. יִסְפֹּר; impv. סְפֹר, סִפְרוּ; ptc. סֹפֵר, סֹפְרִים, סֹפְרֵי; inf. cstr. לִסְפֹּר—**1a. count, number, reckon** stars Gn 15₅, days Lv 15₂₈, persons, thus **take census** 2 C 2₁₆. **b. take into account, consider** person's misery Ps 56₉. **c. set aside (specific number of)** people as burden-bearers 2 C 2₁. **d. survey** houses Is 22₁₀. **2.** ptc. as noun, **one who counts, a. scribe, scholar,** as copying the Law Jr 8₈. **b. (military) officer, commander** of army 2 K 25₁₉. **c. (civil) officer, official, administrator** Est 3₁₂. **d.** perh. specif. **tribute** or **tax collector** Is 33₁₈. **e. one who is counting** days of impurity, i.e. one who is impure 4QTohA 1.1₇.

Ni. 8.0.1 Impf. יִסָּפֵר—**be counted, numbered,** of people 1 K 3₈, sand Gn 32₁₃ (both לֹא־יִסָּפֵר מֵרֹב *it is or they are too numerous to be counted*).

Pi. 67.6.62 Pf. סִפַּרְתִּי; impf. אֲסַפֵּר; impv. סַפֵּר (סַפְּרָה), סַפְּרוּ; ptc. מְסַפֵּר, מְסַפְּרִים, Q מספרה; inf. cstr. סַפֵּר—**1a.** trans., **recount, describe** Y.'s deeds Jr 51₁₀, content of dream Gn 37₉, **reveal** Y.'s secret 1Q30 4₁, **impart** knowledge 1QS 10₂₄, **tell of, inform about** daughter's defects 4QD[f] 3₈, **recite** statutes Ps 119₁₃, **confess** sins Ezk 12₁₆, **utter** curse Ps 59₁₃. **b.** intrans., **speak** CD 9₄. **2a.** in idiom 'tell Y.'s name', thus **declare** or **announce** Y.'s virtues Ps 22₂₃. **b.** in idiom '**declare** (song of) praise', thus **sing** or **recite** praise Si 44₁₅. **3a. count, number** bones Ps 22₁₈, clouds Jb 38₃₇. **b.** of Y., **take into account, consider, appraise** wisdom Jb 28₂₇.

Pu. 5.0.2 Pf. סֻפַּר; impf. יְסֻפַּר—**be told, described,** Y.'s faithfulness Ps 88₁₂.

→ מִסְפָּר I *number*, II *account*, מִסְפֶּרֶת II *scholarship*, סֵפֶר I *document*, סְפָר I *census*, סִפְרָה *document*, סְפֹרָה I *number*, II *literacy*, III *scroll*, סֹפֶרֶת I *office of scribe*.

*ספר II 1 vb.—**Pi.** 1 Impf. יְסַפֵּר—**disperse** clouds Jb 38₃₇.

*ספר III 1 vb.—**Pi.** 1 Impf. יְסַפֵּר—**beautify** clouds Jb 38₃₇.

*ספר IV 1 vb.—**Pi.** 1 + waw וַיְסַפְּרָהּ—**probe** wisdom Jb 28₂₇.

*[ספר] V vb. **Pi.**, of Y., **cut off** life Is 38₁₂ (if em. קִפַּדְתִּי כָאֹרֵג חַיַּי *I have rolled up, like a weaver, my life* to סִפַּרְתָּ כָאֹרֵג חַיַּי *you have cut off my life like a weaver*). → סַפָּר *barber*.

*סַפָּר n.m. **barber,** תַּעַר הַסַּפָּר *knife of the barber* Jr 36₂₃ (if em. הַסֹּפֵר *the scribe* to הַסַּפָּר). → ספר V *cut off*.

סֵפֶר I 185.0.60.15 n.m.—pl. סְפָרִים—**1. document, record,**

rarely **book,** literary composition, i.e. סֵפֶר הַבְּרִית *document of the covenant* Ex 24_7, הַתּוֹרָה *of the law* Jos 1_8, כְּרִיתֻת *of divorce* Dt 24_1, **register** or **roll** with names Dn 12_1, **gazetteer** Jos 18_9, **textbook** Ec 12_{12}, specif. **scroll** Jr 36_2; pl. perh. **Scriptures** Dn 9_2. **2. letter** Jr 29_{25}, specif. **written order** Est 1_{22}, **diplomatic correspondence** 2 K 5_5, **epistle** to exiles Jr 29_1, **letter of propaganda** 2 C 32_{17}. **3. literature,** יוֹדֵעַ הַסֵּפֶר *one who knows the literature,* i.e. is literate Is $29_{11(Kt)}$. → ספר I *count.*

*סֶפֶר II 3 n.m. **bronze** Ex 17_{14} Is 30_8 Jb 19_{23}.

*[סֶפֶר] III 0.0.0.2 pl.n. **Sepher.**

סְפָר I 1 n.[m.] **census** 2 C 2_{16}. → ספר I *count.*

*[סְפָר] II 1 n.[m.]—+ ה- of direction סְפָרָה—**border country** Gn 10_{30}.

[סְפָר] III 1 pl.n. **Sephar.**

סְפָרַד 1 pl.n. **Sepharad.**

[סִפְרָה] I 1.1 n.f.—sf. סִפְרָתֶךָ—**document, scroll,** of Y.'s record Ps 56_9; **learning** Si 44_4. → ספר I *count.*

*[סִפְרָה] II 1 n.f.—sf. סִפְרָתֶךָ—**bag** Ps 56_9. → cf. סֹפֶרֶת II *leather preparers.*

[סְפֹרָה] I 1.0.1 n.f.—pl. סְפֹרוֹת—pl., **numbers** or **sum** Ps 71_{15}, perh. **calculations** 4QInstr[d] 148.2_7. → ספר I *count.*

*[סְפֹרָה] II 1.1.1 n.f.—sf. Si ספרתם; pl. סְפֹרוֹת—sg., **literacy** Si 44_4; pl., **art of writing** or **scribal craft** Ps 71_{15} 4QInstr[d] 148.2_7. → ספר I *count.*

*[סְפֹרָה] III 1 n.f.—pl. סְפֹרוֹת—**scroll** Ps 71_{15}. → ספר I *count.*

[סְפַרְוִי] 1 gent. **Sepharvite.**

סְפַרְוַיִם 6 pl.n. **Sepharvaim.**

*[סִפְרִי] 1 gent. **Sophrite.**

*סֹפְרִים 1 pl.n. **Sophrim.**

*סֹפֶרֶת I 2 n.[f.]—סוֹפֶרֶת—**office of scribe, scribe** Ezr 2_{55}||Ne 7_{57}. → ספר I *count.*

*סֹפֶרֶת II 2 n.[f.]—סוֹפֶרֶת—**leather preparers** Ezr 2_{55} ||Ne 7_{57}. → cf. סִפְרָה II *bag.*

סֹפֶרֶת III 2 pr.n.m. **Sophereth.**

*[סַק] 0.0.0.2 pl.n. **Saq.**

סקל 22.0.4 vb.—**Qal** 12.0.4 Impf. יִסְקְלֻנוּ; + waw וּסְקָלֻהוּ; impv. סִקְלֻהוּ; inf. abs. סָקוֹל; cstr. סָקְלוֹ—**stone person,** outside legal process Ex 17_4, **execute person with** (בְּ) stones Jos 7_{25}.

Ni. 4 Impf. יִסָּקֵל—**be stoned, be executed by means of stoning,** of person and animal Ex 19_{13}.

Pi. 4 + waw וַיְסַקֵּל (וַיְסַקְּלֵהוּ); impv. סַקְּלוּ—**1. stone, pelt** person with (בְּ) stones 2 S 16_6. **2. clear place of stones** Is 5_2.

Pu. 2 Pf. סֻקַּל—**be stoned,** of person 1 K $21_{14.15}$.

סַר 3 adj.—f. סָרָה—**sullen, ill-tempered,** of person 1 K 21_4, spirit 1 K 21_5. → סרר I *be stubborn.*

*סרב 0.1 vb.—**Pi.** 0.1 Impf. תסרב—**be thorny,** i.e. **obstinate, arrogant** with (עִם) God Si 4_{25}. → סָרָב *thorn,* מִסְרָב *obstinacy.*

[סָרָב] I 1.1 n.m.—pl. סָרָבִים—**thorn** or another **stinging plant** Ezk 2_6. → סרב *be thorny.*

*[סָרָב] II 1.1 adj.—pl. סָרָבִים—**obstinate** Ezk 2_6.

סַרְגוֹן 1 pr.n.m. **Sargon.**

סֶרֶד 2 pr.n.m. **Sered.**

סַרְדִּי 1 gent. **Seredite.**

*סרה 1 vb. (byform of סרר)—**Qal** 1 Ptc. סורה—**be stubborn, rebellious** Is $65_{2(1QIsa^a)}$.

*סָרָה I 7.1.9 n.f. **1. rebellion** against religious or ethical instruction or duty Jr 28_{16}. **2. falsehood** Dt 19_{16}. **3. obstinacy** Is 1_5. → סרר I *be rebellious.*

סָרָה II 8.1.9 n.f. **turning aside, 1. apostasy** Jr 28_{16}. **2. wrongdoing** in general Dt 19_{16}. **3. cessation of action** Is 14_6 (unless §4). **4. deviation** Is 14_6. → סור I *turn aside.*

סִרָה, see בּוֹר הַסִּרָה *Borsirah.*

סרח I 7 vb.—**Qal** 6 Impf. תִּסְרַח; ptc. סֹרַחַת; ptc. pass. סְרוּחַ, סְרוּחִים—**1.** trans., **a. leave curtain hanging free** over (עַל) back of tabernacle Ex 26_{12} (unless §2). **b.** pass., of curtain, **be left hanging free** over (עַל) sides of tabernacle Ex 26_{13}. **c.** pass. ptc. as noun, (1) **one left hanging free** of turban, i.e. whose turban hangs free Ezk 23_{15}. (2) **one who lounges around** Am $6_{4.7}$. **2.** intrans., **a.** of curtain, **be free, hang free** over (עַל) back of tabernacle Ex 26_{12}. **b.** ptc. as adj., **free, freely growing,** of vine Ezk 17_6.

Ni. 1 Pf. נִסְרְחָה—**be free, be at large,** thus **depart,** of wisdom Jr 49_7.

→ סֶרַח I *free part.*

*סרח II 1.1 vb.—**Qal** 0.1 Ptc. סרח—**rot, stink,** of name

Si 42₁₁(Bmg).

Ni. ₁ Pf. נִסְרְחָה—**be rotten,** of wisdom Jr 49₇.

[סֶ֫רַח] I ₁ n.m.—cstr. סֶ֫רַח—**free part,** of curtain Ex 26₁₂. → סרח I *free.*

סֶ֫רַח II, see תִּמְנַת־סֶרַח *Timnath-serah.*

*סרט ₀.₀.₀.₁ vb.—**Qal** ₀.₀.₀.₁ Ptc. סרט—perh. **tear, rip** rags in mourning City of David jar inscr. 2₁.

סֹרִי, see סוּרִי *stinking.*

*[סְרִידָה] ₀.₁ n.f. **net,** ממשלת מבין סרידה appar. *the rule of an understanding person is a net* Si 10₁ (but prob. סרידה is error for סדירה *orderliness* or סדורה *well ordered,* i.e. סדר pass.).

*[סְרָיָה] ₀.₀.₀.₁ pr.n.m. **Seraiah.**

[סִרְיוֹן] ₂ n.[m.] (byform of שִׁרְיוֹן)—sf. סִרְיֹנוֹ; pl. סִרְיֹנֹת—**armour, coat of mail** Jr 46₄.

סָרִיס I ₄₅ n.m.—cstr. סְרִיס; pl. סָרִיסִים; cstr. סָרִיסֵי (סְרִיסֵי); sf. סָרִיסָיו—**1. high official,** סְרִיס פַּרְעֹה *official of Pharaoh* Gn 37₃₆, סָרִיסֵי הַמֶּלֶךְ *officials of the king* Est 2₂₁. **2.** rarely **eunuch,** castrated male Is 56₃.

*[סָרִיס] II ₂ n.m. **guardian,** סְרִיס פַּרְעֹה *guardian of Pharaoh* Gn 37₃₆ 39₁.

*סָרִיס III ₄₅ n.m.—cstr. סְרִיס; pl. סָרִיסִים; cstr. סָרִיסֵי (סְרִיסֵי); sf. סָרִיסָיו—**majordomo, seneschal,** סְרִיס פַּרְעֹה *majordomo of Pharaoh* Gn 37₃₆, רַב־סָרִיס *chief seneschal* Jr 39₃.

*סרך ₀.₀.₄ vb.—**Qal** ₀.₀.₃ Impf. יסרוכו; ptc. סורכי—**1a. arrange, organize** things 1QM 2₆. **b.** ptc. as noun, **one who arranges, one who organizes, commissioner** 1QM 7₁. **2. rank** priests after (אַחַר) high priest, i.e. arrange in order, hierarchically 1QM 2₁.

Pi. ₀.₀.₁ Inf. cstr. סרך—**muster** every man 4QWays[b] 1.1₃.

→ סֶרֶךְ *rule, order.*

*[סֶ֫רֶךְ] ₀.₀.₅₄ n.m.—cstr. סרך; sf. סרכו—**1. rule** or **body of regulations** for a community, סרך התורה *rule of the law* CD 7₈; in military context, **army-regulations, rule(s) for battle** 1QM 5₃. **2a. religious order** abiding by such a rule, סרך היחד *religious order of the Community* 1QS 1₁₆. **b. military organization, army,** alw. in context of Qumran eschatological battle 1QM 3₃. **3a. order, sequence,** of battle formations 1QM 5₄. **b. rank, hierarchical order,** in sectarian membership 1QS 6₂₂. **4. list, (army-)register** 1QM 4₆. **5. (good) order,** of teeth 4QCrypt 2.1₃. **6. rule, charge** 1QM 6₁₀. → סרך *arrange.*

[סֶ֫רֶן] I ₂₁.₁ n.m.—pl. סְרָנִים; cstr. סַרְנֵי; sf. סַרְנֵיכֶם—**lord, governor, ruler,** סַרְנֵי פְלִשְׁתִּים *lords of the Philistines* Jg 3₃.

[סֶ֫רֶן] II ₁ n.[m.]—pl. cstr. סַרְנֵי—**axle,** on base of laver in temple 1 K 7₃₀.

[סַרְעַפָּה] ₁ n.f.—pl. sf. סַרְעַפֹּתָיו—**branch, bough** Ezk 31₅. → סעף *divide.*

*סרף I ₁ **Pi.** ₁ Ptc. מְסָרְפוֹ—**anoint** corpse **with spices** Am 6₁₀.

*סרף II ₁.₀.₁ (byform of שׂרף)—**Qal** ₀.₀.₁ Ptc. סורף—**burn** cow 4QMMT B₁₄.

Pi. ₁ Ptc. מְסָרְפוֹ—**burn, cremate** corpse Am 6₁₀.

→ מְסָרֵף II *one who burns incense.*

סרף III, see מְסָרֵף I *maternal uncle.*

*סִרְפַּד ₁ n.[m.]—סרפוד—**thorn** or **nettle** Is 55₁₃(1QIsa[a]).

סרר I ₁₇.₀.₈ vb.—**Qal** ₁₇.₀.₈ Pf. סָרַר; ptc. סוֹרֵר, סֹרֵרָה, סֹרֶרֶת, סוֹרְרִים—**be stubborn, rebellious,** of son Dt 21₁₈, woman Pr 7₁₁, heart Jr 5₂₃, beast CD 11₇. → סָרָה I *rebellion, falsehood,* סַר *sullen,* סוֹרְרִים *revolt;* cf. סרה *be stubborn.*

*סרר II ₁ vb.—**Qal** ₁ Ptc. סוֹרֵר—of Y., **make** person's way **thorny, difficult** Lm 3₁₁.

*סרר III ₁ vb.—**Qal** ₁ Ptc. סֹרֶרֶת—**meditate, scheme,** of woman Pr 7₁₁.

סרר IV, see יסר *instruct.*

סרר V, see שׂרר *rule.*

סתו, see סְתָיו *winter.*

סְתוּר ₁ pr.n.m. **Sethur.**

סְתָיו ₁ n.m.—Kt סתו—**winter,** rainy season, from mid October to mid May Ca 2₁₁.

סתם ₁₄.₁.₄ vb.—**Qal** ₁₁.₁.₂ Pf. סָתַם; impf. יִסְתְּמוּ; impv. סְתֹם; ptc. Q סותם; ptc. pass. סָתוּם, סְתֻמִים; inf. סְתוֹם—**1. stop up** water 2 C 32₃. **2.** of Y., **shut out** prayer Lm 3₈(mss). **3. seal up, keep secret, conceal** vision Dn 8₂₆, word Dn 12₄. **4a.** pass., **be stopped up, sealed up, closed,** of mouth Si 30₁₈, word Dn 12₉, floor 3QTr 1₇. **b.** pass. ptc. as noun, **secret, secrecy** Ezk 28₃; perh. **closed place,** i.e. heart Ps 51₈.

Ni. ₁.₀.₂ Inf. הִסָּתֵם—**1. be stopped up, be closed,**

of breach Ne 4_1, valley Zc $14_{5(mss)}$. **2. be kept secret** 4QMyst[a] $3c_2$.

Pi. 2 Pf. סִתְּמוּם; + waw וַיְסַתְּמוּם—**stop up** well Gn 26_{15}. → cf. שׂתם *shut out.*

*[סֹתֶמָךְ] 0.0.0.1 pr.n.m. **Sothemech.**

סתר I 81.10.44 vb. **Qal**, see Pi.

Ni. 30.6.21 Pf. נִסְתַּרְתָּ; impf. יִסָּתֵר; impv. הִסָּתֵר; ptc. נִסְתָּרוֹת, נִסְתָּרִים, נִסְתָּר; inf. הִסָּתֵר—**1. hide oneself,** of Y. Ps 89_{47}, from before (מִנֶּגֶד) Y.'s sight, of human being Am 9_3. **2. be hidden, concealed,** from (מִן) Y., of Israel's way Is 40_{27}, from (מִן) humanity, of wisdom and knowledge 1QS 11_6. **3. be undiscovered, undetected,** of unfaithful wife Nm 5_{13}. **4.** reciprocal, **be separated, absent,** of a man from (מִן) his fellow, i.e. from one another Gn 31_{49}. **5.** ptc. fem. pl. as noun, **hidden things, secret things,** i.e. sins or perh. **sins unknowingly committed** Ps 19_{13}, **hidden deeds** 4QRitPurB 34.5_3.

Pi. 1.0.4 (sometimes perh. qal) Pf. Q סתרת; impv. סַתְּרִי—**hide, conceal** spring of understanding 1QH 13_{26}.

Pu. 1.2.3 Pf. Q סותר; ptc. Si מסותר, מְסֻתֶּרֶת—**be hidden, concealed,** of teacher 11QMelch 2_5 ([סתר[ו), face 4QapJerC[b] 2.2_9, treasure Si $41_{14(Bmg, M)}$, love Pr 27_5.

Hi. 44.1.16 Pf. הִסְתִּיר; impf. יַסְתִּיר (יַסְתֵּר); + waw וַיַּסְתֵּר; impv. הַסְתֵּר; ptc. מַסְתִּיר; inf. cstr. לְסַתִּיר; abs. הַסְתֵּר—**1. hide, conceal** person, of Y. Jr 36_{26}, from before (מִפְּנֵי) murderess, of human being 2 K 11_2, one's plan from (מִן) Y. Is 29_{15}. **2a.** specif. **hide one's face** (oft. from [מִן] someone), usu. of Y., withdrawing his favour Is 64_6, not paying attention Ps 13_2, of human, out of shame or reverence Ex 3_6. **b.** of sins, **hide Y.'s face** from (מִן) people Is 59_2. **3.** of Y., perh. **hide oneself** Is 57_{17} (unless §2a, with ellip.).

Ho. 0.1.1 Ptc. Si מוסתר—**be hidden,** of treasure Si $41_{14(B)}$.

Htp. 5 Impf. תִּסְתַּתֵּר; ptc. מִסְתַּתֵּר—**hide oneself,** of Y. Is 45_{15}, David 1 S 23_{19}, understanding Is 29_{14}.

→ סֵתֶר I *hiding place,* סִתְרָה I *protection,* מִסְתָּר *hiding place,* מַסְתּוֹר *shelter,* מַסְתֵּר *hiding.*

*סתר II 1 vb.—**Ni.** 1 Impf. יִסָּתֵר—**be pulled down, destroyed,** of human being Pr 28_{28}.

סֵתֶר I 35.1.9 n.[m.]—cstr. סֵתֶר; sf. סִתְרִי; pl. סְתָרִים—**1a. hiding place, secret place, shelter, refuge,** סֵתֶר עֶלְיוֹן *shelter of the Most High* Ps 91_1. **b.** specif. **Sheol as secret place** Is 45_{19}. **2. covering, cover,** of darkness hiding Y. Ps 18_{12}, **veil** Jb 24_{15}. **3. secrecy, secret,** דְּבַר־סֵתֶר *secret message* Jg 3_{19}. → סתר I *hide.*

*סֵתֶר II 2 n.[m.]—cstr. סֵתֶר—**cleft, fissure** 1 S 25_{20} Ca 2_{14}.

*סֵתֶר III 2 n.[m.] **veil** Jb 22_{14} 24_{15}.

*סֵתֶר IV 2 n.[m.]—cstr. סֵתֶר—**side** 1 S 25_{20} Jb 13_{10}.

סִתְרָה I 1 n.f. **protection** Dt 32_{38}. → סתר I *hide.*

*[סִתְרָה] II 0.0.0.1 pr.n.[m]. **Sithrah.**

סִתְרִי 1 pr.n.m. **Sithri.**

ע

עאף, see עיף *be weary.*

עָב I 31.4.4 n.m.—cstr. עָב (עֲב); pl. עָבִים, עָבוֹת; cstr. עָבֵי; sf. עָבָיו—**1. cloud,** producing rain Jg 5_4, giving shade Is 25_5; as high Jb 20_6, chariot of Y. Ps 104_3. **2. thickness, density, mass,** עַב הֶעָנָן *thickness of the cloud* Ex 19_9. **3. thicket** Jr 4_{29}. → עוב II *be cloudy.*

[עָב] II 3 n.[m.]—cstr. עָב; pl. עֻבִּים—**canopy, projecting roof** of palace 1 K 7_6, temple Ezk $41_{25.26}$.

*עָב III 2 n.[m.]—cstr. עָב; pl. עֻבִּים—**gate** of temple Ezk $41_{25.26}$.

*עָב IV 1 n.[m.] **entrance gate** of palace 1 K 7_6.

עבד I 290.9.58 vb.—**Qal** 271.7.53 Pf. עָבַד; impf. יַעֲבֹד, יַעַבְדוּ; impv. עֲבֹד (עִבְדוּ), עִבְדוּ (עָבְדֵהוּ); ptc. עֹבֵד, עֹבְדִים; inf. עֲבֹד (עָבְדוֹ)—**1a.** without obj., **work, labour** Ex 20_9||Dt 5_{13}. **b.** עבד עֲבֹדָה **perform work** Is 28_{21} Ezk 29_{18} (+ עַל *against*). **2. till the ground** Gn 2_5, **cultivate garden**

Gn 2₁₅, vineyard Dt 28₃₉. **3. serve, work for, a.** as worker, labourer Gn 29₁₅ 30₂₆ (+ בְּ *[in exchange] for*). **b.** as slave, forced labourer Gn 15₁₃; specif. מַס־עֹבֵד **serving levy,** i.e. forced labour gang Gn 49₁₅. **c.** as one sold into slavery, bonded labourer Ex 21₂. **d.** in voluntary servitude Ex 21₆. **4a. serve,** i.e. **be subservient to, be subject to** nation or king, with accus. Jr 25₁₁; לְ *to* 1 S 4₉. **b. serve** king, as a subject 1 K 12₄||2 C 10₄. **5a. serve (in religious sense), worship** Y. Dt 6₁₃, other gods and their images Ex 23₃₃ Dt 4₂₈ Jg 2₁₃ (לְ of obj.), heavenly bodies Dt 4₁₉. **b. perform service** (in the cult), **do the service** (of the tent of meeting), accus. עֲבֹדָה *service* Ex 13₅ Nm 3₇, אֹהֶל *tent* Nm 8₁₅. **6. do, perform** Nm 4₂₆ Si 10₂₆(A) (B עשׂה *do*). **7. impose labour upon, make work as slave,** with accus. עֲבֹדָה *labour* and בְּ *upon* or of obj. Ex 1₁₄ Lv 25₃₉; with בְּ only Jr 30₈. **8.** ptc. as noun, **a. worker, labourer** Is 19₉ Ec 5₁₁. **b. worshipper** of Baal 2 K 10₁₉, images of gods Ps 97₇.

Ni. 4.0.1 Pf. נֶעֱבַד; impf. יֵעָבֵד—**1. be tilled, be cultivated,** of land Ezk 36₃₄, field Ec 5₈ (or §2). **2.** perh. **be served,** of king Ec 5₈ (+ לְ *by* field).

Pu. (unless Qal Pass.) 2.0.1 Pf. עֻבַּד—**1. be worked,** subj. impersonal Dt 21₃ (+ בְּ *with* heifer). **2. be made to serve,** הָעֲבֹדָה הַקָּשָׁה אֲשֶׁר עֻבַּד־בָּךְ *the hard labour with which it was made to be served by you,* i.e. which you were made to serve Is 14₃.

Hi. 8.2.3 Pf. הֶעֱבִיד; + waw וַיַּעֲבֵד, וַיַּעֲבִדוּ; impv. Si העבד; ptc. מַעֲבִדִים; inf. הַעֲבִיד—**1a. make,** i.e. cause to, **work,** as slaves, forced labourers Ex 1₁₃ (+ בְּ *with* severity). **b. make army work with hard labour** (accus. עֲבֹדָה גְדֹלָה) Ezk 29₁₈. **2. burden** someone with (בְּ) something Is 43₂₃.₂₄. **3. make people serve** their enemies Jr 17₄. **4. make someone serve, worship** Y. 2 C 34₃₃.

Ho. (unless Qal) 4 Impf. נָעָבְדֵם, תָעָבְדֵם—**allow oneself to serve** gods, images Ex 20₅||Dt 5₉ Ex 23₂₄.

→ עֶבֶד I *slave,* עֲבָד *deed,* עֲבֹדָה *labour,* עֲבֻדָּה I *service,* II *cattle,* עַבְדוּת *servitude,* מַעְבָּד I *deed.*

*עבד II 3 vb.—**Qal** 3 Ptc. עֹבֵד—**endure, be perpetual,** of levy, i.e. forced labour Gn 49₁₅ Jos 16₁₀ 1 K 9₂₁.

[עֲבָד] 1 n.[m.]—pl. sf. עֲבָדֵיהֶם—**1. deed, work** Ec 9₁. **2. (product of) work,** עֲבָדֵי י׳ *works of Y.* (if em. עַבְדֵי *servants of*) Ps 113₁. → עבד I *work.*

עֶבֶד I 802.13.78.58 n.m.—עָבֶד; cstr. עֶבֶד; sf. עַבְדִּי; pl. עֲבָדִים; cstr. עַבְדֵי; sf. עֲבָדַי, עַבְדֵיהֶם—**1. slave, servant** of household or person Gn 24₂ 39₁₇, obtained by purchase Ex 21₂, taken by creditor 2 K 4₁. **2. slave,** as forced labourer, captive Gn 43₁₈; specif. Israel as slaves in Egypt Dt 5₁₅, described as בֵּית עֲבָדִים *house of slaves* Ex 13₃. **3. servant** of king, in ref. to officials, courtiers, soldiers, etc. Gn 20₈ 1 S 8₁₄ 2 K 24₁₀, labourers 1 K 5₂₀||2 C 2₇, loyal subjects 1 K 12₇||2 C 10₇. **4. servant** of Y., **a.** sg., in ref. to (1) particular individuals: Abraham Gn 26₂₄, David 2 S 3₁₈, Moses Ex 14₃₁. (2) Israel Is 41₈. (3) worshipper Ps 116₁₆. **b.** pl., in ref. to followers of Y. 1 K 8₂₃||2 C 6₁₄. **5. servant, slave,** one in subject or subordinate position, **a.** individuals Gn 50₁₈. **b.** nation or people Jos 9₈ 1 S 17₉, bearing tribute to superior nation 2 S 8₂||1 C 18₂. **c. vassal,** subordinate ruler 1 S 27₁₂. **6. servant,** as descr. of king in relation to his people 1 K 12₇. **7.** in polite address, (1) as self-effacement, equivalent to a first-pers. pron., עַבְדְּךָ **your servant** Gn 18₃, עַבְדּוֹ **his servant** Gn 33₁₄, etc. (2) in ref. to a third party, עַבְדְּךָ **your servant** Gn 43₂₈, עַבְדּוֹ **his servant** 1 S 19₄. → עבד I *work.*

עֶבֶד II 6 pr.n.m. **Ebed.**

עֹבֵד, see עוֹבֵד *Obed.*

עַבְדָּא 2.0.0.6 pr.n.m. **Abda.**

עֹבֵד אֱדוֹם, see עֹבֵד אֱדֹם *Obed-edom.*

עֹבֵד אֱדֹם 20 pr.n.m. **Obed-edom.**

עַבְדְּאֵל 1.0.0.2 pr.n.m. **Abdeel.**

עֲבֹדָה 145.3.62.1 n.f.—עֲבוֹדָה; cstr. עֲבֹדַת; sf. עֲבֹדָתִי, עֲבֹדַתְכֶם—**1a. work, labour,** in cultivating plants Ps 104₁₄, tilling the land 1 C 27₂₆, constructing tabernacle Ex 35₂₄, besieging city Ezk 29₁₈. **b. (enforced) labour, servitude** Ex 1₁₄. **2. work,** more generally, i.e. **a. deed, activity, service (of a particular cause),** of righteousness 1QH 14₁₉, truth 1QpHab 7₁₁, wickedness 4QInstr[b] 1₁₀; **work** of Y. in judgment Is 28₂₁; **(effect of) work** Is 32₁₇. **b. function, task, duty** of humans 1QH 9₁₆, meteors and lightning 1QH 9₁₂. **3. service,** rendered to king 1 C 26₃₀; by Nethinim to Levites Ezr 8₂₀; military service 1QM 2₉. **4. (sacred) service, (sacred) task,** in tabernacle Ex 27₁₉, temple Ne 10₃₃; performed by Levites Ex 38₂₁, priests Nm 18₇, follower of Y. 1QH 10₃₃; in ref. to passover Ex 12₂₅. → עבד I *work.*

עֲבֻדָּה I 2.1 n.f.—sf. Si עבודתך—**service,** i.e. **(body of) servants, household** Gn 26₁₄ Jb 1₃ Si 4₃₀(C). → עבד I *work.*

*עֲבֻדָּה II 2 n.f. **cattle** Gn 26₁₄ Jb 1₃. → עבד I *work.*

עַבְדּוֹן I 6 pr.n.m. **Abdon.**

עַבְדּוֹן II 3 pl.n. **Abdon.**

[עַבְדוּת] 3 n.f.—sf. עַבְדֻתֵנוּ—**servitude, bondage** Ezr 9₈.₉ Ne 9₁₇. → עבד I *work.*

עַבְדִּי 3.0.0.15 pr.n.m. **Abdi.**

עַבְדִּיאֵל 1 pr.n.m. **Abdiel.**

עֹבַדְיָה 20.0.1.12 pr.n.m. **Obadiah.**

עֹבַדְיָהוּ, see עֹבַדְיָה *Obadiah.*

עבדיו, see עֹבַדְיָה *Obadiah.*

*[עַבְדִּירֵחַ] 0.0.0.1 pr.n.[m.] **Abdireah.**

עֶבֶד־מֶלֶךְ 6 pr.n.m. **Ebed-melech.**

עֲבֵד נְגוֹ 1 pr.n.m. **Abednego.**

*[עַבְדִּשַּׁחַר] 0.0.0.1 pr.n.[m.] **Abdishahar.**

עבה I 3.1.1 vb.—**Qal** 3 Pf. עָבָה, עָבִיתָ—**be thick,** of Jeshurun Dt 32₁₅, little finger 1 K 12₁₀||2 C 10₁₀ (+ מִן thicker *than* loins).

Pi. 0.1 Impf. תעבה—**make thick,** i.e. **increase** strength Si 6₂.

Pu. 0.0.1 Ptc. מעבא—**be made thick,** ptc. as adj. **thick,** בשוא המעבא *in the thick ruin* 3QTr 1₁₃.

→ עֳבִי *thickness,* מַעֲבֶה *thickness;* cf. עוב I *be thick.*

*עבה II 0.0.1 vb.—**Pu.** 0.0.1 Ptc. מעבא—**be made waterproof,** ptc. as adj. **waterproof,** בשיח המעבא *in the waterproof cistern* 3QTr 1₁₃.

*[עָבָה] n.f. **fatness,** תֶּלֶם עָבֹת *furrow of fatness,* i.e. fertile furrow Jb 39₁₀ (if em. עֲבֹתוֹ in the furrow *[with] his rope*).

עֲבוֹט 4 n.[m.]—sf. עֲבֹטוֹ—**pledge,** item taken as security for loan Dt 24₁₀. → עבט I *give a pledge.*

[עָבוּר] I 2.0.0.2 n.[m.]—I עבר; cstr. עֲבוּר—**produce** Jos 5₁₁.₁₂; perh. specif. **corn, grain** Arad ost. 31₁₀.

*[עָבוּר] II 0.1 conj. **1.** עָבוּר alone, **in order that, so that** Si 3₈. **2.** בַּעֲבוּר as compound prep., see בַּעֲבוּר *on account of.*

*[עִבּוּרָה] 0.0.1 n.f.—sf. עוּבורתמה—**pregnancy,** or perh. **produce, grain** 4QInstr[d] 2₁₁₃. → עבר I *pass* or IV *impregnate.*

עֲבוֹת, see עֲבֹת I *cord,* II *branch.*

עבט I 6 vb.—**Qal** 2 Impf. תַּעֲבֹט; inf. cstr. עֲבֹט—**1. give a pledge, borrow (on security)** Dt 15₆. **2. accept a pledge** (accus. עֲבוֹט) Dt 24₁₀.

Pi. 1 Impf. יְעַבְּטוּן—**change** one's path, of locusts Jl 2₇.

Hi. 3 Impf. תַּעֲבִיטֶנּוּ; + waw הַעֲבַטְתָּ; inf. abs. הַעֲבֵט—**cause to give a pledge, lend (on security) to,** accus. of one to whom lent Dt 15₆, and of thing lent Dt 15₈.

→ עֲבוֹט *pledge,* עַבְטִיט *pledge.*

*עבט II 1 vb.—**Pi.** 1 Impf. יְעַבְּטוּן—**lose (one's way),** of locusts Jl 2₇.

*עבט III 1 vb.—**Pi.** 1 Impf. יְעַבְּטוּן—**break line (from one's paths),** of locusts Jl 2₇.

עַבְטִיט 1 n.[m.] **pledge,** item taken as security for loan Hb 2₆. → עבט I *give a pledge.*

[עֳבִי] 5.0.1 n.[m.]—cstr. עֳבִי (Q עובִי); sf. עָבְיוֹ—**1. thickness** of sea of bronze 1 K 7₂₆||2 C 4₅, pillar Jr 52₂₁, bosses of shield Jb 15₂₆. **2. compactness** of ground, used as mould for casting metal 2 C 4₁₇. → עבה I *be thick.*

עבר I 547.4.63.2 vb.—**Qal** 464.3.57.2 Pf. עָבַר, עֲבַרְתֶּם; impf. יַעֲבֹר, יַעַבְרוּ; impv. עֲבֹר, עִבְרִי (עֲבֹרִי), עִבְרוּ; ptc. עֹבֵר, עֹבְרִים; inf. cstr. עֲבֹר (עָבְרִי); abs. עָבוֹר—**pass,** in various senses, **1.** with obj. of place, thing or person passed, **a. pass over, cross** river Gn 31₂₁, boundary Ps 104₉. **b. pass through** territory Jg 11₂₉, river Is 47₂. **c. pass by, go past, pass beyond** Gn 32₃₂, subj. boundary Jos 15₃; **overtake** someone 2 S 18₂₃. **d. pass away from** Jr 8₁₃. **e. pass along** way Is 35₈. **f. pass over,** i.e. **overcome,** subj. wine Jr 23₉, **pass over (the head),** i.e. **overwhelm,** subj. iniquity Ps 38₅. **g. pass beyond the bound with, go to excess with** evil deeds Jr 5₂₈. **h. overstep, transgress** command Nm 14₄₁, law Is 24₅, covenant Dt 17₂. **2.** without obj. of place, thing or person passed (but sometimes with accus. of direction or destination), **a. pass over, cross over** Ex 15₁₆ Nm 32₇ (+ אֶל *to*) Dt 3₁₈ (+ חֲלוּצִים *armed*)

3$_{21}$ (+ שָׁמָּה *[to] there*); specif. **trample over** Is 51$_{23}$; of water, **flow over** (עַל) Is 54$_{9}$; of wind, **blow over** (בְּ) Ps 103$_{16}$. **b. pass over to** Is 45$_{14}$ (+ עַל *to*) Am 5$_{5}$ (+ accus.); specif. **pass over to** (עַל) numbered ones, i.e. be numbered among them Ex 30$_{13}$. **c. pass through** (בְּ) Gn 12$_{6}$. **d. pass between** (בֵּין) Gn 15$_{17}$, **pass among** (בְּתוֹךְ) Jb 15$_{19}$. **e. pass under** (תַּחַת) Lv 27$_{32}$. **f. pass along, pass in** (בְּ) way Jos 3$_{4}$. **g. pass around,** specif. כֶּסֶף עֹבֵר לַסֹּחֵר *money passing around,* i.e. valid currency, *of the merchant* Gn 23$_{16}$. **h. pass by, go past** Gn 18$_{3}$ (+ מֵעַל *[from] beside*) 37$_{28}$; specif. **be past, be over,** of mourning 2 S 11$_{27}$. **i. pass away,** i.e. **cease (to exist), vanish, perish** Na 1$_{12}$ Ps 144$_{4}$; of law, obligation, **become invalid, be abrogated** Est 1$_{19}$ 9$_{27}$; of festival, **cease (to be observed)** Est 9$_{28}$. **j. pass on, go on, move forward** Gn 33$_{3}$ (+ לִפְנֵי *before*) Jos 10$_{34}$ (+ מִן *from*). **k. pass on to, come over, come upon** (עַל) Nm 5$_{14}$. **l. pass into, enter into** (בְּ) covenant Dt 29$_{11}$. **m. pass over** (עַל) offence, i.e. **overlook, pardon** Mc 7$_{18}$; **pass by** (לְ) offender, i.e. **forgive, spare** Am 7$_{8}$. **n. transgress,** abs. Ps 17$_{3}$; + עַל *against* 1QH 20$_{24}$. **o. flow, be liquid,** of myrrh Ca 5$_{5}$.

Ni. $_{1}$ Impf. יֵעָבֵר—**be able to be passed through,** of stream Ezk 47$_{5}$.

Pi. $_{2}$ Pf. עִבַּר; + waw וַיְעַבֵּר—**1. draw across** 1 K 6$_{21}$ (בְּ of obj.). **2. impregnate,** of bull Jb 21$_{10}$.

Hi. $_{80.1.6}$ Pf. הֶעֱבִיר ,הֶעֱבַרְתָּ ,הֶעֱבַרְתִּי; impf. יַעֲבִיר; + waw וְהַעֲבַרְתָּ ,וַיַּעֲבֵר ,וַיַּעֲבִירוּ; impv. הַעֲבֵר ,הַעֲבִירֻנִי; ptc. מַעֲבִיר; inf. cstr. הַעֲבִיר (לַעֲבִיר) ,הַעֲבִירוֹ; abs. הַעֲבִיר—**1. cause to pass over** (עַל) Gn 8$_{1}$; with double accus., **send across, bring across** Gn 32$_{24}$ 2 S 19$_{16}$. **2. cause to pass through, bring through** (בְּ) Nm 31$_{23}$, **let pass through** Dt 2$_{30}$, **cause to pass through(out)** (בְּ), specif. of proclamation Ex 36$_{6}$, trumpet blast Lv 25$_{9}$, **spread about** report 1 S 2$_{24}$. **3. cause to pass by** 1 S 16$_{9}$ Ezk 37$_{2}$ (+ עַל *beside*), **cause to pass before** Ex 33$_{19}$ (עַל־פְּנֵי) 1 S 16$_{8}$ (לִפְנֵי), **let pass by** Jr 46$_{17}$, **cause to pass beyond** 1 S 20$_{36}$. **4. cause to pass under** (תַּחַת) Ezk 20$_{37}$. **5. cause to pass on to, bring to** (אֶל) Ezk 46$_{21}$. **6. cause to pass on,** i.e. **put to work** 2 S 12$_{31}$ (+ בְּ *with* brickmould). **7. make (property) over to, allow (property) to pass to** (לְ) Nm 27$_{7}$, **transfer (ownership of)** Ezk 48$_{14(Qr)}$. **8. cause to pass away, take away, remove** 2 S 3$_{10}$ (+ מִן *from*) Zc 3$_{4}$ (+ מֵעַל *from [upon]*) 2 C 35$_{23}$, **turn away** eyes from (מִן) seeing Ps 119$_{37}$. **9a. set apart, devote,** firstborn of beasts to (לְ) Y. Ex 13$_{12}$. **b. cause child to pass through** (בְּ) **fire,** as offering Dt 18$_{10}$, **devote, offer** child to (לְ) to Molech Lv 18$_{21}$. **10. overstep, transgress** covenant CD 1$_{20}$.

→ עֵבֶר I *side,* עֲבָרָה *ford,* עֶבְרָה I *overflowing,* II *ferry,* מַעֲבָר I *pass,* מַעְבָּרָה *pass,* עָבָר *pregnant,* עִבּוּרָה *pregnancy.*

עבר II $_{8.2.1}$ vb.—**Htp.** $_{8.2.1}$ Pf. הִתְעַבָּרְתָּ ,הִתְעַבֵּר; + waw וַיִּתְעַבֵּר (וַיִּתְעַבָּר); ptc. מִתְעַבֵּר—**1a. be angry, become enraged,** abs. Ps 78$_{21}$; with בְּ *with* Dt 3$_{26}$, עִם *with* Ps 89$_{39}$, עַל *on account of* Pr 26$_{17}$. **b. pretend to be angry** with (בְּ) Si 13$_{7}$. **2. incite to anger, infuriate** Pr 20$_{2}$. **3. be arrogant, be headstrong** Pr 14$_{16}$ Si 16$_{8}$ (+ בְּ *with* pride). → עֶבְרָה II *rancour, indignation.*

***עבר** III $_{1.4}$ vb.—**Htp.** $_{1.4}$ Impf. Si יתעבר; ptc. מִתְעַבֵּר—**delay, procrastinate, be negligent** Pr 14$_{16}$, in repentance Si 5$_{7}$, almsgiving Si 7$_{10}$, prayer Si 38$_{9}$.

***עבר** IV $_{1}$ vb.—**Pi.** $_{1}$ Pf. עִבַּר—**impregnate,** of bull Jb 21$_{10}$.

Pu. be crossed, i.e. **mated** Dt 21$_{3}$ (if em. עֻבַּר *it has not been worked* [עבד pu.] to עֻבַּר).

→ (?) עִבּוּרָה *pregnancy,* עָבָר *pregnant.*

עֵבֶר I $_{90.0.10}$ n.m.—cstr. עֵבֶר; sf. עֶבְרוֹ; pl. עֲבָרִים; cstr. עֶבְרֵי; sf. עֶבְרֵיהֶם ,עֲבָרָיו—**1a. side, edge** of ephod Ex 28$_{26}$||39$_{19}$, sword 1QM 5$_{12}$, ravine Jr 48$_{22}$. **b. (one) side (as opposed to another)** 1 S 14$_{4}$ 1QM 6$_{9}$. **c. (one's own) side, direction,** מִכָּל־עֲבָרָיו *on all his sides* 1 K 5$_{4}$, אֶל־עֵבֶר פָּנָיו *to the side of his face,* i.e. straight ahead of him Ezk 1$_{9}$. **2. other side, region beyond,** from the standpoint of the speaker, whether east Dt 4$_{41}$, or west Jos 5$_{1}$; מֵעֵבֶר לַיַּרְדֵּן *on the other side of/ beyond the Jordan* Nm 32$_{19}$, בְּעֵבֶר הַנָּהָר *beyond the river (Euphrates)* Jos 24$_{4}$. → עבר I *pass.*

עֵבֶר II $_{15}$ pr.n.m. **Eber.**

*[עָבָר[ה $_{0.0.2}$ adj.—f.s. עברה—**1. pregnant,** [חיה עבר[ה *a pregnant beast* 4QD^{e} 2.2$_{15}$. **2.** as noun, **pregnant beast** 4QMMT B$_{38}$. → עבר I *pass* or IV *impregnate.*

עֲבָרָה I 2 n.f.—pl. cstr. mss עַבְרוֹת—**ford** 2 S 15₂₈(Kt) 17₁₆(mss) 19₁₉. → עבר I *pass.*

*__עֲבָרָה__ II 1 n.f. **ferry, raft** 2 S 19₁₉. → עבר I *pass.*

[עֶבְרָה] I 3 n.f.—cstr. עֶבְרַת; sf. עֶבְרָתוֹ—**overflowing, excess, arrogance** of Moab Is 16₆ Jr 48₃₀, the proud Pr 21₂₄. → עבר I *pass.*

*__עֶבְרָה__ II 31.2.16 n.f.—cstr. עֶבְרַת; sf. עֶבְרָתִי; pl. עֲבָרוֹת; cstr. עֶבְרוֹת (עַבְרוֹת)—**rancour, indignation,** usu. of Y. Is 9₁₈; of Edom Am 1₁₁, king Pr 14₃₅; אֵשׁ עֶבְרָתִי *fire of my indignation* Ezk 21₃₆, יוֹם עֶבְרָה *day of indignation* Zp 1₁₅. → עבר II *be angry.*

עִבְרִי I 34 gent. **Hebrew.**

עִבְרִי II 1 pr.n.m. **Ibri.**

עֲבָרִים 5 pl.n. **Abarim.**

עֶבְרֹן 1 pl.n. **Ebron.**

עַבְרֹנָה 2 pl.n. **Abronah.**

עבשׁ 1 vb.—**Qal** 1 Pf. עָבְשׁוּ—**shrivel,** of grain Jl 1₁₇.

עבת 1 vb.—**Pi.** 1 + waw וַיְעַבְּתוּהָ—**twist, weave together** Mc 7₃. → עֲבֹת I *cord,* II *branch,* עָבֹת *leafy.*

עָבֹת 4 adj.—f.s. עֲבֻתָּה—**leafy, thick with foliage,** of tree Lv 23₄₀, terebinth Ezk 6₁₃. → עבת *twist.*

עֲבֹת I 19.0.2 n.m.&f.—cstr. עֲבוֹת; sf. עֲבֹתוֹ; pl. עֲבֹתִים, עֲבֹתֹת; cstr. עֲבֹתֹת, Q עבותי; sf. עֲבֹתֵימוֹ—**1. cord, rope** Jg 15₁₃; מַעֲשֵׂה עֲבֹת *work of,* i.e. like, *cord* Ex 28₁₄||39₁₅. **2.** perh. **yoke** Ps 2₃. → עבת *twist.*

*__[עֲבֹת]__ II 5 n.[m.]—pl. עֲבֹתִים—**branch, thick foliage** Ezk 19₁₁ 31₃ Ps 118₂₇. → cf. עָבוֹת *leafy.*

עֹג, see עוֹג *Og.*

עגב 7 vb.—**Qal** 7 Pf. עָגְבָה (עָגֶבָה); + waw וַתַּעְגַּב (וַתַּעְגְּבָה); ptc. עֹגְבִים—**1. lust after** (עַל) Ezk 23₅. **2.** ptc. as noun, **lover** Jr 4₃₀. → עֲגָבָה *lustfulness,* עֲגָבִים *lust.*

[עֲגָבָה] 1 n.f.—sf. עַגְבָתָהּ—**lustfulness** Ezk 23₁₁. → עגב *lust.*

עֲגָבִים 2 n.[m.]pl. **lust, love** Ezk 33₃₁.₃₂. → עגב *lust.*

עֻגָה 7 n.f.—cstr. עֻגַת; pl. עֻגוֹת; cstr. עֻגֹת—**cake, (round) loaf** Gn 18₆; made of barley Ezk 4₁₂, manna Nm 11₈; unleavened Ex 12₃₉. → עוג I *bake.*

עָגוֹל, see עָגֹל *round.*

עָגוּר 2 n.[m.] **crane,** or perh. **swallow, short-footed thrush, golden oriole, wryneck** Is 38₁₄ Jr 8₇.

עָגִיל 2 n.[m.]—pl. עֲגִילִים—**earring** Nm 31₅₀ Ezk 16₁₂.

*__[עֲגִילָה]__ n.f. **round (shield)** Ps 46₁₀ (if em. עֲגָלוֹת *wagons* to עֲגִלוֹת). → cf. עֶגְלָה II *roundness,* עָגֹל *round.*

עָגֹל 7 adj.—עָגוֹל; f.pl. עֲגֻלּוֹת—**round, rounded,** of head, i.e. top, of throne 1 K 10₁₉, mouth, i.e. opening, of stand 1 K 7₃₁. → cf. עֲגִילָה *round (shield),* עֶגְלָה II *roundness,* מַעְגָּל II *encampment.*

עֵגֶל I 35.0.3 n.m.—cstr. עֵגֶל; sf. עֶגְלְךָ; pl. עֲגָלִים; cstr. עֶגְלֵי—**1. male calf, young bull** Lv 9₂; עֵגֶל מַרְבֵּק *calf of the stall,* i.e. fatted calf 1 S 28₂₄. **2. (image of) calf,** as cultic object Ex 32₄; עֶגְלֵי זָהָב *calves of gold* 1 K 12₂₈.

*__[עֵגֶל]__ II 0.0.1 n.[m.] **larva,** עגלי הדבורים *the larvae of the bees* CD 12₁₂.

עֲגָלָה 25 n.f.—sf. עֶגְלָתוֹ; pl. עֲגָלוֹת; cstr. עֶגְלֹת—**wagon, cart** Gn 45₁₉ 1 S 6₇. → cf. מַעְגָּל IV *cart,* (?) מַעְגָּל I *track.*

עֶגְלָה I 12.0.4 n.f.—cstr. עֶגְלַת; sf. עֶגְלָתִי; pl. cstr. עֶגְלוֹת—**heifer, female calf, young cow** Gn 15₉; עֶגְלַת בָּקָר *heifer of the herd* Dt 21₃.

*__[עֶגְלָה]__ II 0.0.1 n.f. **roundness,** מגני עגלה *shields of roundness,* i.e. round shields 1QM 6₁₅. → cf. עֲגִילָה *round (shield),* עָגֹל *round,* מַעְגָּל II *encampment.*

עֶגְלָה III 2 pr.n.f. **Eglah.**

עֶגְלוֹן I 8 pl.n. **Eglon.**

עֶגְלוֹן II 5 pr.n.m. **Eglon.**

*__[עֶגְלִיָּה]__ 0.0.0.1 pr.n.[m.] **Egeliah.**

עֶגְלַיִם, see עֵין עֶגְלַיִם *En-eglaim.*

*__[עֶגְלָתַיִן]__ 0.0.1 pl.n. **Eglathain.**

עֶגְלַת שְׁלִשִׁיָּה 2 pl.n. **Eglath-shelishiyah.**

עגם 1 vb.—**Qal** 1 Pf. עָגְמָה—**be grieved for** (לְ) the poor Jb 30₂₅.

עגן 1 vb.—**Ni.** 1 Impf. תֵּעָגֵנָה—**shut oneself off from** marriage, of woman Ru 1₁₃.

*__עד__ 1 vb. (contraction of יעד)—**Qal** 1 Pf. עַד—**command, order,** עַד־יָרֵחַ וְלֹא יַאֲהִיל *he commands the moon and it does not shine* Jb 25₅.

*__[עַד]__ I 1 n.[m.]—pl. sf. עָדַי—**promise, contract** Gn 31₄₄ (if em. לְעֵד *as a witness* to לְעַד *as a contract*) Nm 23₁₈ Is 33₈ (if em. עָרִים *cities* to עֲדִים *promises*).

*__[עַד]__ II 1 n.[m.]—pl. sf. עָדַי—**admonition, oath, treaty** Nm 23₁₈. → עוד IV *admonish.*

עַד I 1264.42.312.4 prep.—עֲדֵי; sf. עָדַי, עֲדֵיכֶם—**1.** of place, direction, **a. unto, as far as, to** Gn 11₃₁; sometimes implying **up to and including,** (לְ)מִדָּן וְעַד־בְּאֵר שֶׁבַע

from Dan to Beer-sheba, i.e. all Israel Jg 20₁. **b. at, near, by** Gn 13₁₂. **2.** of time, **a.** usu. **unto, until, to** Gn 26₃₃ Ex 12₁₀; עַד־עוֹלָם *unto everlastingness*, i.e. for ever Gn 13₁₅. **b. before, by (the arrival of)** Jg 6₃₁. **c. for (the duration of)** 11QT 63₁₄, **for only** Jb 20₅. **d. during** Si 12₁₅. **3.** of degree or extent, **a. (even) unto, as far as** Jon 4₉ Dn 8₁₀; **as much as, as many as, (for) a total of** 2 K 4₃₅ Est 5₃. **b.** with neg., **(not) even, (not) so much as** Dt 2₅. **c. (even) like** Na 1₁₀. **4.** of range of objects, **a. even, including** Lv 11₄₂. **b.** עַד ... עַד **even down to ... and, including both ... and** Nm 8₄. **c.** (וְ)עַד ... (לְ)מִן of range or class of objects, (1) **from ... to, both ... and,** מֵאָדָם וְעַד־בְּהֵמָה *both humans and beasts* Ex 9₂₅. (2) **either ... or, neither ... nor, whether ... or,** מִטּוֹב עַד־רָע *either good or evil* Gn 31₂₄. **5.** compound prepositions include: **a.** עַד־לְ (1) **as far as, right up to** 2 C 14₁₂. (2) **until** Ezr 9₄. (3) **until (there was)** 1 C 12₂₃. **b.** עַד מִן (1) **as far as (from)** Is 57₉. (2) **until after** Lv 23₁₆. **c.** עַד־נֹכַח **as far as opposite** Jg 20₄₃. **6.** compound adverbs include: **a.** עַד־הֵנָּה (1) of place, **(up to) here, thus far** Jr 51₆₄. (2) of time, **until now, hitherto, thus far** 1 S 7₁₂. **b.** עַד־עַתָּה **until now** Gn 46₃₄. **c.** עַד־כֹּה **here, this place, yonder** Gn 22₅. **d.** עַד־מְאֹד **unto greatness, i.e. exceedingly, completely** 1 S 11₁₅ Ps 38₉. **e.** עַד־לְמַעְלָה **exceedingly** 2 C 26₈. **f.** עַד־כַּלֵּה **unto making complete** (pi. inf. abs. of כלה), i.e. **completely, utterly** 2 K 13₁₇. **g.** עַד־מָתַי **until when, i.e. how long?** Is 6₁₁. **h.** עַד־אָנָה **how long?** Ex 16₂₈. **i.** עַד־מָה **until what (time?), how long?** Ps 74₉. **8.** as conjunction, **a. until** Gn 34₅ Dt 7₂₃. **b. before, by when** Gn 48₅ 2 K 16₁₁. **c. while, while still** 1 S 14₁₉ Jon 4₂. **9.** compound conjunctions include: **a.** עַד־לְ (1) **until** 1 K 18₂₉. (2) **as far as, to the point of (doing)** 2 C 32₂₄. **b.** עַד אֲשֶׁר **until** 2 K 17₂₀. **c.** עַד אֲשֶׁר אִם **until** Gn 28₁₅. **d.** עַד שֶׁ- (1) **until** Ca 2₁₇. (2) **when, while** Ca 1₁₂ 3₄. **e.** עַד אִם **until** Gn 24₁₉. **f.** עַד כִּי **until** Gn 26₁₃. **g.** עַד לֹא (1) **before, while not (yet)** Pr 8₂₆. (2) **so that not, but not** Is 47₇. **h.** עַד אֲשֶׁר לֹא (1) **until not** 2 S 17₁₃. (2) **before** Ec 12₁. **i.** עַד־אֵין **until (there is) no** Ps 40₁₃. **j.** עַד־בְּלִי **until the absence of** Ps 72₇. **k.** עַד־בִּלְתִּי **until not** Nm 21₃₅.

עַד II 47.6.77 n.m.—לָעַד, וָעֶד; pl. cstr. Q עדי—**1. perpetuity, everlastingness, eternity,** usu. of future time, הַרְרֵי־עַד *mountains of everlastingness*, i.e. everlasting mountains Hb 3₆, עוֹלְמֵי עַד *everlastingness of perpetuity*, i.e. for ever and ever Is 45₁₇, לָעַד *to perpetuity*, i.e. perpetually, for ever Is 64₈, לְעוֹלָם וָעֶד *to everlastingness and perpetuity*, i.e. for ever and ever Ps 9₆, לכול עדי עולמים *to all perpetuity of everlastingness*, i.e. for ever and ever 1QS 4₁, עֲדֵי־עַד *unto perpetuity*, i.e. for ever Is 26₄, מִנִּי־עַד *from perpetuity*, i.e. from the earliest times Jb 20₄. **2. Everlasting One,** עַד־מְאֹד *Everlasting Grand One* Ps 119₈ (if em. עַד־מְאֹד *unto greatness*, i.e. exceedingly).

עַד III 4 n.[m.]—cstr. עַד—**1. booty, prey** Gn 49₂₇ Is 33₂₃. **2. food** 1 S 2₅ (if em. חָדֵלּוּ עַד־ *they have ceased; even* to חָדְלוּ עַד *they have grown fat with food*) Jb 14₆ (if em. וְיֶחְדָּל עַד *that he may cease, until* to וְיֶחְדַּל עַד *that he may be filled with food*).

*[עַד] IV 3.0.3 n.[m.]—cstr. Q עד—**1. (full) number, (full) amount** Is 64₈ Jr 11₁₄ (unless בְּעַד *on account of*); עַד־שְׁנוֹתֶיךָ *number of your years* Ezk 22₄. **2. (minimum) number, quorum** 1QSa 2₂₂ CD 10₄ 13₁.

*עַד V 11 n.m.—cstr. עַד—**throne, throne room,** עַד־אֱדוֹם *throne of Edom* Ps 60₁₁||108₁₁, עוֹלָם *of everlastingness*, i.e. everlasting throne 2 S 7₁₆||1 C 17₁₄, גְּבֶרֶת עַד *queen of, i.e. on, the throne* Is 47₇. → cf. עֶדֶת *enthronement.*

*עַד VI 40.1 n.f.—cstr. עַד—**1. time, duration,** עַד רָעָתָם *time of their trouble* Jr 11₁₄. **2.** used as adv., **at the time of, at the time when, for the time when,** עַד־זִקְנָה וְשֵׂיבָה *at the time of old age and grey hair* Ps 71₁₈, עַד בְּלִי־דָי *at the time when there is not sufficiency* Ml 3₁₀. **3.** as conj., **a.** עַד **when** Gn 27₄₅. **b.** עַד אֲשֶׁר **at the time when** Ps 112₈. **c.** עַד שֶׁ- **at the time when** Ca 1₁₂.

*[עַד] VII 6 n.[m.]—cstr. עַד—**1. extent, reaches** Nm 21₂₄ Dt 2₅ Jb 38₁₈. **2. wide realm** Is 9₅ Ps 147₁₅.

*עַד VIII 6 prep. **near** Gn 13₁₂ 38₁ Nm 21₃₀ Dt 2₂₃ Jg 4₁₁ Ps 118₂₇.

עַד IX, see עד *command.*

עֵד 69.0.40.1 n.m.—Q עיד; cstr. עֵד; sf. עֵדִי; pl. עֵדִים; cstr. עֵדֵי; sf. עֵדַי, עֵדֵיהֶם—**1. witness,** i.e. one who witnesses something or bears witness, **a.** humans, oft. in judicial context Ex 23_{1} Dt 17_{6}; to transfer of property Ru 4_{9}, signature of document Jr 32_{10}; Israelites as witnesses of Y. Is 43_{10}. **b.** Y. Gn 31_{50} 1 S 12_{5}. **2. (act of bearing) witness, witness (borne), testimony** Ex 20_{16}||Dt 5_{20}. **3. (object as) witness, testimony, evidence,** in ref. to heap of stones Gn 31_{48}, altar Jos 22_{27}, song Dt 31_{19}. עֵד אֱמֶת *witness of truth,* i.e. true witness Jr 42_{5}, עֵד שֶׁקֶר *witness of falsehood,* i.e. false witness Dt 19_{18}, עֵד בֵּין *a witness between* Gn 31_{44}, עֵד בְּ *a witness against* Dt 31_{19}, עֵד כִּי *a witness that* 1 S 12_{5}. → עוד I *bear witness.*

עֹד, see עוֹד I *still, again,* II *continuance.*

עִדֹּא, see עִדּוֹ *Iddo.*

*[**עֶדֶב**] n.[m.] **lot** Pr 12_{9} (if em. עֶבֶד *servant*).

*[**עדד**] 2 vb.—**Po.** 2 Impf. יְעוֹדֵד; ptc. מְעוֹדֵד—**comfort, reassure** someone Ps 146_{9} 147_{6}.

Htpo., rejoice Jb 31_{29} (if em. הִתְעֹרַרְתִּי *I was excited* [עור htpol.] to הִתְעֹדַדְתִּי *I rejoiced*).

עֹדֵד 3.0.0.1 pr.n.m. **Oded.**

עדה I 2 vb.—**Qal** 1 Pf. עָדָה—**pass over** (עַל) path Jb 28_{8}.

Hi. 1 Ptc. מַעֲדֶה—**remove garment** Pr 25_{20}.

עדה II 8.0.2 vb.—**Qal** 9.0.2 Pf. עָדִית; impf. תַּעְדֶּה, תַּעְדִּי; + waw וַתַּעַד; impv. עֲדֵה, Q עדינה—**1. adorn oneself with** jewels Is 61_{10}, ornaments (עֲדִי) Jr 4_{30}, pride and exaltation Jb 40_{10}. **2.** with double accus., **adorn** someone **with** ornaments (עֲדִי) Ezk 16_{11}. → עֲדִי *ornaments,* עֶדְיָה II *ornament,* (?) עִדּוּי *delight,* (?) עִדּוּן *delight.*

עָדָה 8.0.0.1 pr.n.f. **Adah.**

עֵדָה I 149.10.102 n.f.—cstr. עֲדַת; sf. עֲדָתִי—**1. company, band** of Korah Nm 16_{5}, evildoers Ps 22_{17}, the righteous Ps 1_{5}. **2a. congregation, assembly** of peoples Ps 7_{8}, princes Si 7_{14}, of the gate, i.e. court Si $42_{11(Bmg)}$. **b. congregation, assembly, community** of Israel, esp. at the exodus and settlement of the land Ex 12_{3} Jos 18_{1}. **c. congregation, community** of Qumran 1QSa 2_{21}, as elect 4QpIsa[d] 1_{3}, holy 1QS 5_{20}. **d. congregation, assembly** of opponents of the Qumran community, referred to as Belial 1QH 10_{22}, traitors CD 1_{12}, bastards 4QShir[b] 2.2_{3}, seekers of smooth things 1QH 10_{32}. **e. (divine) congregation, assembly, council,** עֲדַת אֵל *congregation of (the) god(s)* Ps 82_{1}, עדת בני שמים *congregation of the sons of heaven* 1QH 11_{22}, המלך *of the king* 4QShirShabb[d] 1.2_{24}. **3a. swarm** of bees Jg 14_{8}. **b. herd** of bulls Ps 68_{31}. → יעד *appoint.*

[**עֵדָה**] II 22.1.1 n.f. (& perh. m.)—pl. עֵדֹת; cstr. Q עידות; sf. עֵדֹתַי, עֵדֹתֶיךָ—**testimony, law** of Y., alw. pl. Dt 4_{45} Ps 119_{2}. → עוד I *bear witness.*

עֵדָה III 4 n.f. **witness,** in ref. to pillar Gn 31_{52}, stone Jos 24_{27}, acceptance of lambs Gn 21_{30}. → עוד I *bear witness.*

*[**עֵדָה**] IV 1 n.f.—pl. sf. עֵדֹתֶיךָ—**throne, kingship, royal installation** Ps 93_{5}.

[**עִדָּה**] 1 n.[f.] **menstruation,** בֶּגֶד עִדִּים *garment of,* i.e. stained by *menstruation* Is 64_{5}.

עִדּוֹ 8 pr.n.m. **Iddo.**

עִדּוֹא, see עִדּוֹ *Iddo.*

*[**עִדּוּי**] I 0.1 n.[m.] **delight** Si 34_{28}. → (?) עדה II *adorn.*

*[**עִדּוּי**] II 0.1 n.[m.] **nourishment** Si 34_{28}.

*[**עִדּוּן**] n.[m.] **delight** Si 34_{28} (if em. עדוי *delight*). → (?) עדה II *adorn.*

עֵדוּת 61.3.8 n.f.—עֵדֻת; cstr. עֵדוּת; pl. cstr. Q עדוות (עדייות); sf. עֵדוֹתֶיךָ—**1. testimony, witness,** perh. **treaty,** לֻחֹת הָעֵדֻת *tablets of the testimony* Ex 31_{18}, אֲרוֹן *ark of* Ex 26_{34}, מִשְׁכַּן *tabernacle of* Ex 38_{21}. **2. testimony, royal protocol,** document given to king at coronation 2 K 11_{12}||2 C 23_{11}. **3. testimony, evidence,** of person's generosity Si 34_{23}, Y.'s deeds Si 36_{20}. **4. testimony, statute, law** of Y., **a.** sg. Ps 19_{8}. **b.** pl. 1 K 2_{3}. **5.** in psalm titles, **a.** שׁוּשַׁן עֵדוּת *Shushan Eduth,* perh. 'Lily of the Testimony' Ps 60_{1}. **b.** עֵדוּת לְאָסָף perh. *A Testimony of Asaph* Ps 80_{1}. → עוד I *bear witness.*

עֲדִי I 14.1.7 n.[m.]—עֶדִי; cstr. עֲדִי; sf. עֶדְיָהּ; pl. עֲדָיִים—**1. ornament(s), jewellery, adornment** of women 2 S 1_{24}, men and women Ex 33_{4}. **2. trappings** of horse Ps 32_{9}. → עדה II *adorn.*

*[**עֲדִי**] II n.[m.] **1. attack, onslaught, onset** of Y. against the wicked Ps 139_{20} (if em.), of smoke Is 14_{31} (if em.). **2. troops** Jb 10_{17} (if em.). **3. course** of horse or mule Ps 32_{9} (if em.).

*[**עֲדִי**] n.[m.] **prime, abundance,** i.e. **1. nourishment** Ps 103_{5} Si 34_{28} (both if em.). **2. sprightliness** Ps 32_{9} (if em.). **3. (menstrual) flow,** עֲדִי עִדִּים *flow of*

menstruation Ezk 16_7 (if em.).

*[עֶדִי] n.[m.] **petulance** Ps 32_9 Jb 10_{17} (both if em.).

עֲדִיא, see עֲדָיָה *Adaiah.*

עֲדִיאֵל 3.0.0.1 pr.n.m. **Adiel.**

עֲדָיָה I 10.0.0.9 pr.n.m. **Adaiah.**

*[עֲדָיָה] II n.f. **ornament, insignia (of royalty)** 2 K 11_{12}||2 C 23_{11} (if em. הָעֵדוּת *the testimony* to הָעֲדָיוֹת). → עדה II *adorn.*

עֲדָיָהוּ, see עֲדָיָה I *Adaiah.*

עִדִּים, see עִדָּה *menstrual period.*

[עָדִין] I 1 adj.—f.s. עֲדִינָה—**voluptuous,** as noun, **voluptuous one,** in ref. to Babylon Is 47_8. → עדן *be luxurious.*

עָדִין II 4 pr.n.m. **Adin.**

עֲדִינָא 1 pr.n.m. **Adina.**

עֲדִינוֹ 1 pr.n.m. **Adino.**

עֲדִיתַיִם 1 pl.n. **Adithaim.**

[עַדְלַי] 1 pr.n.m. **Adlai.**

עֲדֻלָּם 8.0.1 pl.n. **Adullam.**

עֲדֻלָּמִי 3 gent. **Adullamite.**

עדן 1 vb.—**Htp.** 1 + waw וַיִּתְעַדְּנוּ—**luxuriate, delight oneself in** (בְּ) **goodness** Ne 9_{25}. → עֵדֶן I *delight,* עֶדְנָה *(sexual) pleasure,* עָדִין I *voluptuous,* מַעֲדָן I *delicacy,* מְעֻדֶּנֶת *pampered woman.*

עֲדֶן I 2 adv.—עֲדֶנָּה—contraction of עַד־הֵנָּה, עַד־הֵן, **1. yet** Ec 4_3. **2. still** Ec 4_2.

*עֲדֶן II 2 n.m.—+ ה- of direction עֲדֶנָה—**fixed time** Ec $4_{2.3}$.

עֵדָן *Edan,* see עֵרָן *Eran.*

[עֵדֶן] I 4.0.5 n.[m.]—pl. עֲדָנִים; cstr. Q עדני; sf. עֲדָנֶיךָ—**1. luxury, finery,** of clothing or jewellery 2 S 1_{24}. **2. delicacy,** of food Jr 51_{34}. **3. delight, pleasure,** נַחַל עֲדָנֶיךָ *stream of your delights* Ps 36_9. → עדן *be luxurious.*

עֵדֶן II 14.1.7 pl.n. **Eden.**

עֵדֶן III 2 pr.n.m. **Eden.**

עֶדֶן 4 pl.n. **Eden.**

*[עִדָּן] n.m. **appointed time** Ec 4_3 (if em. עֲדֶן *yet*).

עַדְנָא 2 pr.n.m. **Adna.**

עַדְנָה 2.0.0.1 pr.n.m. **Adnah.**

עֲדֶנָה, see עֲדֶן I *yet, still;* II *fixed time.*

עֶדְנָה 1 n.f. **(sexual) pleasure** Gn 18_{12}. → עדן *be luxurious.*

עַדְנַח 1 pr.n.m. **Adnah.**

*עֶדְנִי gent. **Ednite.**

עַדְעָדָה 1 pl.n. **Adadah.**

עדף 9 vb.—**Qal** 8 Ptc. עֹדֵף, עֹדֶפֶת, עֹדְפִים—**1. be in excess, remain,** of curtain Ex 26_{12}, persons Nm 3_{46} (+ עַל *of, over and above*). **2.** ptc. as noun, **excess, surplus, remainder** of food Ex 16_{23}, money Lv 25_{27}.

Hi. 1 Pf. הֶעְדִּיף—**have a surplus** Ex 16_{18}.

עדר I 8.1.5 vb.—**Ni.** 7.1.5 Pf. נֶעְדַּר; ptc. נֶעְדֶּרֶת—**be lacking, be missing, fail,** of Y. Zp 3_5, truth Is 59_{15}, impersonal subj. 'nothing' 1 S 30_{19} (+ לְ *to*).

Pi. 1 Impf. יְעַדְּרוּ—**1. let be lacking, omit something** 1 K 5_7. **2. cause to be lacking, cause to become small,** obj. moon Jb 25_5 (if em. עַד *even* to עִדֵּר).

עדר II 2 vb.—**Ni.** 2 Impf. יֵעָדֵר—**be hoed,** of mountain Is 7_{25} (+ בְּ *with* hoe), vineyard Is 5_6. → מַעְדֵּר *hoe.*

עדר III 2 vb.—**Qal** 2 Ptc. עֹדְרֵי; inf. עֲדֹר—**1. help** 1 C 12_{34}. **2.** ptc. as noun, **helper** 1 C 12_{39}.

*עדר IV 2 vb.—**Qal** 2 Ptc. עֹדְרֵי; inf. עֲדֹר—**1. be bold** 1 C 12_{34}. **2.** ptc. as noun, **bold one** 1 C 12_{39}.

*[עֹדֵר] n.[m.] **shepherd** Gn 29_8 (if em. הָעֲדָרִים *the flocks* to הָעֹדְרִים).

עֵדֶר I 38.0.4 n.m.—cstr. עֵדֶר; sf. עֶדְרוֹ; pl. עֲדָרִים; cstr. עֶדְרֵי; sf. עֶדְרֵיהֶם—**flock, drove, herd,** usu. of sheep Gn 29_2; of goats Ca 4_1, cattle Jl 1_{18}; Israelites as flock of Y. Jr 13_{17}.

עֵדֶר II 2 pr.n.m. **Eder.**

עֵדֶר III 1 pl.n. **Eder.**

[עֵדֶר] 1 pr.n.m. **Eder.**

עַדְרִיאֵל 2 pr.n.m. **Adriel.**

[עֲדָשָׁה] 4 n.f.—pl. עֲדָשִׁים—**lentil** Gn 25_{34}.

עֲדָשִׁים, see עֲדָשָׁה *lentil.*

*[עֲדֻת] n.f. **enthronement** Ps 93_5 (if em. עֵדֹתֶיךָ *your testimonies* to עֲדֻתְךָ). → cf. עַד V *throne.*

עַוָּא 1 pl.n. **Avva.**

*עוב I 0.0.3 vb.—**Qal** 0.0.3 Ptc. עבות—**be thick,** ptc. as adj. **thick,** of fingers 4QCrypt 1.3_4. → cf. עבה I *be thick.*

עוב II 1 vb.—**Hi.** 1 Impf. יָעִיב—**cover with cloud** Lm 2_1. → עָב I *cloud.*

*עוב III 1 vb.—**Hi.** 1 Impf. יָעִיב—**scorn** Lm 2_1.

*עוב IV 1 vb.—**Hi.** 1 Impf. יָעִיב—**stain** Lm 2_1.

עוֹבֵד 10 pr.n.m. **Obed.**

עוֹבִי, see עֳבִי *thickness.*

עוֹבָל 1 pr.n.m **Obal.**

עוג I 1 vb.—**Qal** 1 Impf. תְּעֻגֶנָּה—**bake cake** (עֻגָה) of barley Ezk 4$_{12}$. → עֻגָה *cake,* מָעוֹג I *loaf,* (?) II *provisions.*

*** עוג** II vb.—**Pu., be bent,** ptc. as noun, **deformed one,** לַעֲגֵי מְעֻוָּג *mockers of a deformed one* Ps 35$_{16}$ (if em. מָעוֹג *cake*).

עוֹג 22.0.1 pr.n.m. **Og.**

עוּגָב 4.0.1 n.m.—sf. עֻגָבִי—**pipe, flute** Gn 4$_{21}$.

עוד I 40.2.9.1 vb.—**Hi.** 39.2.9.1.1 Pf. הֵעִיד, הַעִידֹתָ, הַעִדֹתָה (הַעִדֹתָה); impf. תָּעִיד; + waw וַיָּעַד, וְאָעִיד; impv. הָעֵד, הָעִידוּ; ptc. מֵעִיד; inf. abs. הָעֵד; cstr. I להעיד—**1. bear witness, testify, a. against,** with accus. 1 K 21$_{10}$, עַל CD 19$_{30}$. **b. in favour of** (accus.) Jb 29$_{11}$. **c. concerning,** with לְ 11QPs^{a} 28$_{5}$, עַל CD 9$_{20}$. **d. between** (בֵּין) Ml 2$_{14}$. **2. cause to witness,** i.e. **a. procure witness** (עֵד) Is 8$_{2}$ Jr 32$_{10}$. **b. call as witness** Dt 4$_{26}$ (+ בְּ *against*) MurEp BarC^{a}3 (+ עַל *against*). **3. warn, admonish, exhort** someone, with (usu.) בְּ of obj. Gn 43$_{3}$, also לְ of obj. Si 4$_{11}$; + (1) accus. of thing with which warned 2 K 17$_{15}$. (2) לֵאמֹר *saying,* introducing warning Gn 43$_{3}$. (3) פֶּן־ *lest* Ex 19$_{21}$. (4) כִּי *that* Dt 8$_{19}$. **4.** perh. **assure** Zc 3$_{6}$ (בְּ of obj.). **5.** ptc. as noun, **notary** MurEpBeth-Mashiko 13.

Ho. 1 Pf. הוּעַד—**be warned,** הוּעַד בִּבְעָלָיו *it has been warned,* i.e. warning has been given, *to its owner* Ex 21$_{29}$.

→ עֵד *witness,* עֵדָה II *testimony,* עֵדוּת *testimony,* תְּעוּדָה *testimony.*

עוד II 5.0.3 vb.—**Qal** 1 Ptc. עֲדֵיהֶם—**1. go round (one's course),** of moon Jb 25$_{5}$ (if em. עַד *even* to עָד). **2.** trans., **go around** Is 44$_{9}$ (unless from עֵד *witness*).

Pi. 1 Pf. עִוְּדֻנִי—**surround, embrace** Ps 119$_{61}$.

Pol. 2 Impf. יְעוֹדֵד; ptc. מְעוֹדֵד—**uphold, restore** Ps 146$_{9}$ 147$_{6}$.

Htpol. 1.0.3 Pf. Q התעודדתי; impf. Q אתעודדה; + waw וַנִּתְעוֹדָד—**hold oneself up, keep oneself upright, be restored** Ps 20$_{9}$ 1QH 12$_{22.36}$.

→ עוֹד I *still.*

*** עוד** III 0.0.1 vb.—**Qal** 1 Impf. יעודני—**be similar to** 4QHod^{a} 7.1$_{9}$.

*** עוד** IV 27.1.1.1 vb.—**Hi.** 39.2.9.1.1 Pf. הֵעִיד, הַעִידֹתָ, הַעִדֹתָה (הַעִדֹתָה); impf. תָּעִיד; + waw וַיָּעַד, וְאָעִיד; impv. הָעֵד, הָעִידוּ; ptc. מֵעִיד; inf. abs. הָעֵד; cstr. I להעיד—**adjure, admonish** someone, with (usu.) בְּ of obj. Gn 43$_{3}$, also לְ of obj. Si 4$_{11}$; + (1) accus. of thing with which admonished 2 K 17$_{15}$. (2) לֵאמֹר *saying,* introducing admonition Gn 43$_{3}$. (3) פֶּן־ *lest* Ex 19$_{21}$. (4) כִּי *that* Dt 8$_{19}$. → עֵד II *admonition.*

*** עוד** V 2 vb.—**Pol.** 2 Impf. יְעוֹדֵד; ptc. מְעוֹדֵד—**comfort, reassure** Ps 146$_{9}$ 147$_{6}$.

Htpol., rejoice Jb 31$_{29}$ (if em. הִתְרֹרַרְתִּי *I roused myself* to הִתְעֹדַדְתִּי).

*** עוד** VI vb. **Pi., protect against** (בְּ) evil Ps 141$_{5}$ (if em. עוֹד וּתְפִלָּתִי *my prayer is still* to עִוְּדוּ תְפִלֹּתַי *my prayers protect*).

*** עוד** VII 2 vb.—**Pol.** 2 Impf. יְעוֹדֵד; ptc. מְעוֹדֵד—**embolden, encourage** Ps 146$_{9}$ 147$_{6}$.

עוֹד I 491.11.67.4 adv.—עֹד; sf. עוֹדִי, עוֹדֶנּוּ, עוֹדָהּ (עוֹדֶנָּה)—**1.** expressing continuance, **still, yet** Gn 29$_{7}$ 1 K 22$_{44}$, **continually** Gn 46$_{29}$; with pronom. sf., as subj. of ptc. or nom. cl., עוֹדֶנּוּ עֹמֵד *he was still standing* Gn 18$_{22}$, עוֹדֶנּוּ נַעַר *he was still a lad* 2 C 34$_{3}$; לֹא ... עוֹד **not ... yet** 2 C 20$_{33}$. **2.** expressing addition, **a. yet, (yet) another, (any) other, (anyone, something) else, more, further,** modifying (1) noun, עוֹד נֶגַע אֶחָד *one more plague* Ex 11$_{1}$. (2) nom. cl., הַעוֹד־לִי בָנִים בְּמֵעַי *are there more sons in my womb?* Ru 1$_{11}$. (3) verb, עוֹד דִּבְּרוּ עֲבָדָיו *his servants spoke further* 2 C 32$_{16}$. **b. also, moreover** Ec 12$_{9}$ 2 C 17$_{6}$. **c.** specif. עוֹד מְעַט **(in) a little yet,** i.e. **soon** Is 10$_{25}$. **4.** expressing repetition, **again** Gn 29$_{33}$; oft. with יסף hi. *do again* as auxiliary verb, וַיֹּסֶף עוֹד לְדַבֵּר אֵלָיו *and he spoke to him again* Gn 18$_{29}$. **5.** with negation or implied negation, **a.** expressing continuance, **any more, any longer, no more, no longer** Jos 5$_{1}$ Jr 48$_{2}$. **b.** expressing repetition, **not again, no more, no longer** 1 K 10$_{10}$ Jr 3$_{16}$. **6.** כָּל־עוֹד **all the while,** i.e. **a. still** 2 S 1$_{9}$. **b. as long as** Jb 27$_{3}$. **7.** בְּעוֹד **a. while still,** modifying nom. cl., בְּעוֹד לַיְלָה *while it is still night* Pr 31$_{5}$; with pronom. sf. as subj. of nom. cl., בְּעוֹדֶנּוּ חַי *while he was still alive* Gn 25$_{6}$, בְּעוֹדִי *while I am still (alive)* Ps 104$_{33}$. **b. within,** followed by specification of time Gn 40$_{13}$. **8.** מֵעוֹד

ever since, מֵעוֹדִי עַד־הַיּוֹם הַזֶּה *ever since I was*, i.e. from my birth, *to this day* Gn 48$_{15}$. **9.** עַד עוֹד **while still,** עד עודך חי *while you are still alive* Si 30$_{29}$. → עוד II *go round*.

*עוֹד II $_{2.0.2.2}$ n.[m.]—cstr. I עוֹד; sf. עוֹדִי—**1. continuance, perpetuity,** שמחת עוד *joy of continuance*, i.e. continuous joy 4QapPsB 33$_{10}$. **2. remainder** of flour Arad ost. 1$_5$. **3. lifetime** Ps 104$_{33}$.

*עוֹד III $_1$ n.[m.] **time** Jb 34$_{23}$.

עוֹדֵד, see עֹדֵד *Oded*.

עוה I $_9$ vb.—**Qal** $_2$ Pf. עָוִינוּ—**commit iniquity, do wrong** Est 1$_{16}$ (+ עַל *to, against*) Dn 9$_5$.

Hi. $_7$ Pf. הֶעֱוִינוּ; inf. abs. הַעֲוֵה; cstr. הַעֲוֹתוֹ—**commit iniquity, do wrong** 2 S 7$_{14}$ 1 K 8$_{47}$||2 C 6$_{37}$.

→ עָוֹן *iniquity*.

עוה II $_{8.1.15}$ vb.—**Ni.** $_{4.1.15}$ Pf. נַעֲוֵיתִי; ptc. cstr. נַעֲוֵה, נַעֲוַת; pl. Q נעוות; sf. Q נעוותי—**1. be bent, bowed down** Is 21$_3$ Ps 38$_7$. **2. be wronged, suffer injustice** Si 13$_3$. **3. act perversely** 1QS 1$_{24}$. **4.** ptc. as adj., **perverse,** of spirit 1QH 5$_{21}$. **5.** ptc. as noun, **a. perverse one** 1 S 20$_{30}$ Pr 12$_8$. **b. perversity, wickedness** 4QHod^a 7.2$_4$.

Pi. $_2$ Pf. עִוָּה—**twist, distort** paths Lm 3$_9$.

Hi. $_2$ Pf. הֶעֱוִיתִי—**pervert** way Jr 3$_{21}$, right thing Jb 33$_{27}$.

→ עַוָּה I *ruin*, II *distortion*, עִי I *ruin*, מְעִי I *ruin*, עִוְעִים *distortion*.

עַוָּה I $_{3.0.1}$ n.f. **ruin** Ezk 21$_{32}$. → עוה II *bend*.

*עַוָּה II $_3$ n.f. **distortion** Ezk 21$_{32}$. → עוה II *bend*.

עַוָּה III, see עַוָּא *Avva*.

עַוָּה $_3$ pl.n. **Ivvah.**

עווה, see עַוָּה I *ruin*.

עוז $_{5.0.3}$ vb.—**Qal** $_1$ Inf. cstr. לָעוֹז—**take refuge in** (בְּ) Is 30$_2$.

Ni. $_{0.0.1}$ Ptc. Q נעוז—**seek refuge in** (בְּ) 1QH 14$_{25}$.

Hi. $_{4.0.2}$ Pf. הֵעִיזוּ; impv. הָעֵז, הָעִיזוּ; inf. Q העיז—**1. seek refuge, flee for safety,** abs. Is 10$_{31}$; + בְּ *in* 1QH 15$_{17}$, מִקֶּרֶב *from (the middle of)* Jr 6$_1$. **2. bring into safety** Ex 9$_{19}$.

→ עֹז II *refuge*, מָעוֹז I *refuge*, מָעוֹזֶן *refuge*.

עוֹז, see עֹז I *strength*.

[עַוִּי] $_4$ gent. **Avvite.**

[עֲוִיל] I $_2$ n.m.—pl. עֲוִילִים; sf. עֲוִילֵיהֶם—**young child** Jb 19$_{18}$ 21$_{11}$. → עול I *give suck*.

עֲוִיל II $_1$ n.[m] **unjust one** Jb 16$_{11}$. → עול II *act unjustly*.

עַוִּים *Avvim*, see עַוִּי *Avvite*.

עֲוִית $_2$ pl.n. **Avith.**

עול I $_{5.1}$ vb.—**Qal** $_{5.1}$ Ptc. Si עלה, עָלוֹת—**give suck,** ptc. as **1.** adj., **giving suck, milch,** of cow 1 S 6$_7$, flocks and herds Gn 33$_{13}$. **2.** noun, **one that gives suck, wet nurse,** in ref. to sheep Is 40$_{11}$, wisdom Si 51$_{17(11QPs^a)}$. → עוּל *suckling*, עֲוִיל I *young child*, עוֹלֵל *child*, עוֹלָל *child*, עִילוֹל *child*, עַל I *nourishment*.

עול II $_2$ vb.—**Pi.** $_2$ Impf. יְעַוֵּל; ptc. מְעַוֵּל—**1. act unjustly, do wrong** Is 26$_{10}$. **2.** ptc. as noun, **unjust one** Ps 71$_4$. → עָוֶל *injustice*, עַוְלָה *injustice*, עַוָּל *unjust one*.

*עול III $_5$ vb.—**Polel** $_5$ Pf. עוֹלַלְתָּ; impv. עוֹלֵל; ptc. מְעוֹלֵל—**exact unjust burdens from, exact payment from, treat extortionately** (unless עלל I poel *deal with*), with accus. Is 3$_{12}$, לְ of obj. Lm 1$_{22}$.

*עול IV vb. **Pi., howl** Ho 10$_5$ (if em. עָלָיו *over it* to עִוְּלוּ *they howled*).

עָוֶל $_{21.3.40}$ n.m.—cstr. עֶוֶל; sf. עַוְלוֹ—**injustice, wrong, evil, dishonesty, deceit,** in judgment Lv 19$_{15}$, weights and measures Lv 19$_{35}$, trade Ezk 28$_{18}$; not found with Y. Dt 32$_4$; אִישׁ עָוֶל *man of injustice* Pr 29$_{27}$, רוחות האמת והעול *spirits of truth and injustice* 1QS 3$_{19}$. → עול II *act unjustly*.

עַוָּל $_{5.2.1}$ adj. **1. unjust, evil** Si 41$_{6(B)}$. **2.** as noun, **unjust one, evildoer** Jb 18$_{21}$. → עול II *act unjustly*.

[עוּל] $_{2.0.2}$ n.m.—cstr. עוּל; sf. עוּלָהּ; pl. sf. Q עוליהן—**suckling (child), infant** Is 49$_{15}$ 1QH 17$_{36}$; עוּל יָמִים *suckling of*, i.e. who lives, *(only a few) days* Is 65$_{20}$. → עול I *give suck*.

עַוְלָה $_{34.2.48}$ n.f.—עוֹלָה, עַוְלָתָה (עֹלָתָה); pl. עוֹלֹת—**injustice, wrong, evil, dishonesty, deceit** Jb 6$_{29}$; בֶּן־עַוְלָה *son of injustice*, i.e. unjust man Ps 89$_{23}$, רוח עולה *spirit of injustice/deceit* 1QS 4$_9$. → עול II *act unjustly*.

עוֹלָה I, see עֹלָה *burnt offering*.

עוֹלָה II Is 61$_8$, see עַוְלָה *injustice*.

עוֹלוֹל, see עוֹלָל *child*.

עוֹלֵל $_{9.0.3}$ n.m.—Q עולול (Q עלול); pl. עוֹלְלִים; sf. עוֹלָלַיִךְ—**child** Jr 6$_{11}$ 1QH 15$_{21}$. → עול I *give suck*, or עלל III *act the child*; cf. עִילוֹל *child*.

עוֹלָל $_{11}$ n.m.—עֹלָל; pl. עוֹלָלִים; cstr. עֹלְלֵי; sf. עֹלְלֵיהֶם—

child 1 S 15$_{3}$. → עול I *give suck*, or עלל III *act the child*; cf. עֲוִיל *child*.

עוֹלֵלוֹת, see עֹלֵלוֹת *gleanings*.

עוֹלָם I $_{440.46.386.1}$ n.m.—עֹלָם (עֵילוֹם); sf. עוֹלָמוֹ; pl. עוֹלָמִים, Q עולמות; cstr. עוֹלְמֵי; sf. Q עלמיה—**1.** of the past, **everlastingness, eternity, ancient time, long duration,** מֵתֵי עוֹלָם *dead ones of ancient time,* i.e. those long dead Ps 143$_{3}$, גִּבְעֹת עוֹלָם *hills of everlastingness,* i.e. everlasting hills Gn 49$_{26}$, יְמֵי עוֹלָם *days of ancient time* Is 63$_{9}$, רִאשֹׁנוֹת מֵעוֹלָם *the former things of old* Is 46$_{9}$. **2.** of the future, **everlastingness,** i.e. **long duration,** for one's lifetime Ex 21$_{6}$, **perpetuity,** of permanent right Lv 25$_{32}$, institution Ps 111$_{9}$, **eternity,** of what remains for ever Is 51$_{6}$, as characteristic of Y. Is 40$_{28}$; עוֹלְמֵי עַד *everlastingness of perpetuity* Is 45$_{17}$, דֹּרֹת עוֹלָם *generations of everlastingness,* i.e. all generations Gn 9$_{12}$, עֶבֶד עוֹלָם *servant of everlastingness,* i.e. a servant for ever Dt 15$_{17}$, בְּרִית עוֹלָם *covenant of everlastingness,* i.e. everlasting covenant Gn 9$_{16}$; לְעוֹלָם *to everlastingness,* i.e. for ever Ex 3$_{15}$, לְעוֹלָם וָעֶד *to everlastingness and perpetuity,* i.e. for ever and ever Ps 9$_{6}$, לעולמי עד *to everlastingness of perpetuity,* i.e. for ever and ever 1QH 5$_{7}$, עַד־עוֹלָם *unto everlastingness,* i.e. for ever Dt 29$_{28}$. **3. age,** עולמי חושך *ages of darkness* 4QpsHodC 1$_{3}$, קץ עולמות *end of the ages* 4QCryptA 3.2$_{10}$. **4. world, creation, created order** GnzPs 1$_{4}$; perh. Ec 3$_{11}$. **5.** perh. **underworld,** עַם עוֹלָם *people of the underworld* Ezk 26$_{20}$, בֵּית עוֹלָמוֹ *house of his underworld,* i.e. his underworld house Ec 12$_{5}$. **6.** perh. **Eternal One, Ancient One,** as title for Y. זְרֹעֹת עוֹלָם *arms of the Eternal One* Dt 33$_{27}$.

*[עוֹלָם] II $_{1}$ pr.n.m. **Olam.**

*עוֹלָם III $_{3}$ n.[m.]—עֹלָם; sf. עוֹלָמוֹ—**1. darkness** Jb 22$_{15}$; בֵּית עוֹלָמוֹ *house of his darkness,* i.e. his dark house Ec 12$_{5}$. **2. ignorance** Ec 3$_{11}$. → עלם II *be dark.*

עון $_{1}$ vb.—**Qal** $_{1}$ + waw וְעָנָה—**dwell** Dt 33$_{28}$ (if em. עֵין *fountain of* to עָן or יָעוֹן *he dwelt*) Is 13$_{22}$. → מָעוֹן I *dwelling place,* מְעוֹנָה *dwelling place.*

עָוֹן I $_{233.16.97}$ n.m.—עָווֹן; cstr. עֲוֹן (עֲווֹן); sf. עֲוֹנִי; pl. עֲוֹנוֹת, cstr. עֲוֹנוֹת; sf. עֲוֹנֹתָיו, עֲוֹנֹתָם (עֲוֹנֹתֵיהֶם)—**1. iniquity, sin, fault,** עֲוֹן אָבֹת *iniquity of the fathers* Ex 20$_{5}$, עֲוֹן אַשְׁמָה *iniquity of,* i.e. resulting in, *guilt* Lv 22$_{16}$, עַם כֶּבֶד עָוֹן *a people heavy of,* i.e. full with, *iniquity* Is 1$_{4}$. **2. guilt (arising from iniquity)** Gn 44$_{16}$ 1 S 20$_{8}$. **3. punishment (for iniquity)** Gn 4$_{13}$; עֵת עֲוֹן קֵץ *time of the punishment of the end,* i.e. of the final punishment Ezk 21$_{30}$. → עוה I *commit iniquity*; cf. עָן *iniquity,* מָעוֹן III *reminder of sin.*

*[עָוֹן] II $_{1}$ n.f.—pl. sf. Qr עוֹנֹתָם—**company, group** Ho 10$_{10(Qr)}$ (Kt עינתם perh. *their eyes*).

[עוֹנָה], see עֹנָה *period.*

*[עוֹנָה] n.f. **sheath** Ezk 32$_{27}$ (if em. עֲוֹנֹתָם *their iniquities* to עוֹנֹתָם *their sheaths*); עוֹנוֹת חֶרֶב *sheath of the sword* Jb 19$_{29}$ (if em. עֲוֹנוֹת *punishment[s] of*).

*עוע $_{0.1}$ vb.—**Pi.** $_{0.1}$ + waw ועועו—perh. **die** Si 37$_{31(B)}$ (but prob. an erroneous repetition of the preceding יגועו *they expire*).

[עַוְעֻים], see עִוְעִים *distortion.*

[עַוְעִים], see עִוְעִים *distortion.*

עִוְעִים $_{1.0.2}$ n.[m.]pl. **distortion (of judgment), confusion,** רוּחַ עִוְעִים *spirit of distortion* Is 19$_{14}$, perh. *wind of distortion,* i.e. whirlwind 1QH 14$_{23}$ (עועיים). → עוה II *bend.*

עוף I $_{26.1.7}$ vb.—**Qal** $_{18.0.3}$ Impf. יָעוּף; + waw וַיָּעָף; וָעָפוּ (וַיָּעֹף); ptc. עָפָה, עָפוֹת; inf. עוּף—**1a. fly,** of bird Dt 4$_{17}$, Y. 2 S 22$_{11}$||Ps 18$_{11}$, sparks Jb 5$_{7}$, scroll Zc 5$_{1}$. **b.** perh. **hover** Is 31$_{5}$. **2.** of person, **fly away** Jb 20$_{8}$ (+ כְּ *as a dream*). **3.** of eye, **light upon** (בְּ) Pr 23$_{5(Kt)}$.

Hi. $_{1.1}$ Impf. Qr תָּעִיף; + waw Si ויעף—**1. cause** clouds **to fly** like (כְּ) birds Si 43$_{14}$. **2. cause** eye **to light upon** (בְּ) Pr 23$_{5(Qr)}$.

Ho. $_{1}$ Ptc. מֻעָף (unless from יעף I *be weary* or II *be swift* or as noun *darkness*)—**be made to fly** Dn 9$_{21}$.

Pol. $_{5.0.2}$ Impf. יְעוֹפֵף; ptc. מְעוֹפֵף; inf. עוֹפְפִי—**1. fly, soar,** of birds Gn 1$_{20}$, angel 1QH 24$_{9}$, serpent Is 14$_{29}$. **2. cause to fly, brandish** sword Ezk 32$_{10}$.

Htpol. $_{1.0.2}$ Impf. יִתְעוֹפֵף; inf. Q התעופף—**1. fly about,** of breakers 1QH 16$_{31}$. **2. fly away,** of glory Ho 9$_{11}$, arrows 1QH 11$_{27}$.

→ עוֹף *bird,* עַפְעַף *eyelid.*

עוף II $_{1}$ vb.—**Qal** $_{1}$ Impf. תָּעֻפָה—**be dark** Jb 11$_{17}$. → עֵיפָה I *darkness,* מוּעָף I *darkness,* מָעוּף *darkness.*

*[עוף] III vb. **escape,** מָעוּף צוּקָה *constraint without escape,* i.e. inescapable distress Is 8$_{22}$ (if em. מָעוּף

gloom of).

עוֹף 71.4.20 n.m.—cstr. עוֹף—**1. bird,** usu. coll., **birds, fowl** Gn 1$_{20}$; עוֹף הַשָּׁמַיִם *birds of the heavens* Gn 1$_{26}$. **2. flying things,** in general Dt 14$_{20}$. **3. flying insect,** שֶׁרֶץ הָעוֹף *swarming things (consisting) of flying insects* Lv 11$_{20}$. → עוף I *fly*.

[עוֹפַי] 1.0.0.2 pr.n.m. **Ophai,** also as עֵיפַי **Ephai.**

עוֹפֶרֶת, see עֹפֶרֶת *lead*.

עוץ I 2 vb. (byform of יעץ)—**Qal** 2 Impv. עֻצוּ—**take counsel together, devise a plan,** abs. Jg 19$_{30}$, with obj. עֵצָה *counsel* Is 8$_{10}$.

*[**עוץ**] II vb. **Qal, direct** the eye upon (עַל) someone Ps 32$_8$ (if em. אִיעָצָה *I will counsel you* [from יעץ] to אָעֻצָה *I will direct*).

עוּץ I 5.0.1 pr.n.m. **Uz.**

עוּץ II 3 pl.n. **Uz.**

עוק I 2 vb.—**Hi.** 2 Impf. תָּעִיק; ptc. מֵעִיק—**press,** of Y. Am 2$_{13}$, wagon Am 2$_{13}$. → עָקָה I *oppression,* מוּעָקָה I *distress*; cf. צוק I *oppress*.

***עוק** II 2 vb.—**Qal** 1 Impf. תָּעִיק—**be hindered** of wagon Am 2$_{13}$.

Hi. 1 ptc. מֵעִיק—**hinder, cause to sway,** of Y. Am 2$_{13}$.

***עוק** III 2 vb.—**Qal** 1 Impf. תָּעִיק—**roar,** of wagon Am 2$_{13}$.

Hi. 1 ptc. מֵעִיק—**cause a roar,** of Y. Am 2$_{13}$.

→ עָקָה II *clamour*.

***עוק** IV 2 vb.—**Hi.** 2 Impf. תָּעִיק; ptc. מֵעִיק—**split, make a furrow,** of Y. Am 2$_{13}$, wagon Am 2$_{13}$.

עור I 80.1.10 vb.—**Qal** 21.0.3 Impf. יְעוּרֶנּוּ; impv. עוּרָה (Q עוּר), עוּרִי (עוּרִי); ptc. עֵר—**1. rouse oneself, be awake,** of Y. Ps 7$_7$, arm of Y. Is 51$_9$, human Jg 5$_{12}$, sword Zc 13$_7$ (+ עַל *against*), lyre Ps 108$_3$. **2.** trans., **rouse, awaken** Jb 41$_2$ (mss hi.). **3. be watchful** Lm 4$_{14}$ (if em. עִוְרִים *blind* to עֵרֶיהָ *her watchful ones*).

Ni. 7 Pf. נֵעוֹר; impf. יֵעוֹר, יֵעֹרוּ—**rouse oneself, be roused, be awakened,** of Y. Zc 2$_{17}$ (+ מִן *from* dwelling place), human Jb 14$_{12}$ (+ מִן *from* sleep), storm Jr 25$_{32}$.

Polel 13.0.1 Pf. עוֹרֵר, עוֹרַרְתִּיךָ; impf. תְּעֹרֵר; impv. עוֹרְרָה; inf. עֹרֵר—**1. rouse, awaken, stir up** persons Zc 9$_{13}$ (+ עַל *against*) Ca 8$_5$, Leviathan Jb 3$_8$, strife Pr 10$_{12}$, love Ca 2$_7$. **2. set in motion, wield** weapon against (עַל) 2 S 23$_{18}$||1 C 11$_{20}$ Is 10$_{26}$.

Pilp. 1 יְעֹעֵרוּ—**rouse,** i.e. **raise** cry Is 15$_5$.

Hi. 33.1.5 Pf. הֵעִיר, הַעִירוֹתִי; impf. יָעִיר (יָעֵר); + waw וַיָּעַר (וַיְעִירֵנִי); impv. הָעִירוּ, הָעִירָה; ptc. מֵעִיר; inf. בְּעִיר—**1.** trans., **a. rouse, waken, stir up** person Is 41$_2$ (+ מִן *from*), spirit Jr 51$_{11}$, strength Dn 11$_{25}$ (+ עַל *against*), zeal Is 42$_{13}$, the dawn Ps 57$_9$. **b. stir,** i.e. **stoke (fire of oven)** Ho 7$_4$. **2.** reflexive, **rouse oneself,** of Y. Ps 35$_{23}$ Jb 8$_6$ (+ עַל *for*).

Htpol. 5 Impf. יִתְעֹרָר; + waw וְהִתְעֹרַרְתִּי; impv. הִתְעוֹרְרִי; ptc. מִתְעוֹרֵר—**rouse oneself, be aroused, excite oneself,** of Jerusalem Is 51$_{17}$, innocent one Jb 17$_8$ (+ עַל *against*).

→ עִיר II *agitation*, III *watcher*.

עור II 5.0.1 vb.—**Pi.** 5.0.1 Pf. עִוֵּר; impf. יְעַוֵּר—**make blind,** i.e. **put out** eyes 2 K 25$_7$||Jr 52$_{11}$; of bribe, **blind** someone Ex 23$_8$, eyes Dt 16$_{19}$. → עִוֵּר *blind*, עִוָּרוֹן *blindness*, עַוֶּרֶת *blindness*.

עור III 1 vb.—**Ni.** 1 Impf. תֵּעוֹר—**be laid bare, exposed,** עֶרְיָה תֵעוֹר קַשְׁתֶּךָ *[unto] bareness is your bow laid bare,* i.e. it is utterly made ready Hb 3$_9$ (or em. תְּעוֹרֵר *you have laid bare,* i.e. pol.).

Polel, lay bare, expose, see Ni.

→ מָעוֹר *nakedness*, מַעֲרֹם *nakedness*, עֵירֹם *naked*, עָרוֹם *naked*; cf. ערה *be bare*, ערר *strip oneself*, נער III *strip*.

***עור** IV 2 vb.—**Hi.** 2 Impf. יָעִיר—**guard, watch,** of Y. Jb 8$_6$ (+ עַל *over* Job), eagle Dt 32$_{11}$ (obj. nest).

***עור** V 1 vb.—**Qal** 1 Inf. עוּרִי—**be disgraced, abused,** אַחַר עוּרִי נִקְּפוּ־זֹאת *when (the period of) my abuse is stripped away,* i.e. at an end Jb 19$_{26}$.

עוֹר I 99.0.18 n.m.—cstr. עוֹר; sf. עוֹרִי; pl. cstr. עֹרֹת; sf. עֹרֹתָם—**1. skin** of humans Ex 34$_{29}$, as having disease Lv 13$_2$, wasting away Lm 3$_4$. **2. skin, hide** of animals Gn 27$_{16}$, for clothing Gn 3$_{21}$, constructing tabernacle Ex 25$_5$||35$_7$; as item of leather Lv 11$_{32}$.

***עוֹר** II 2 n.[m.] **pit of chin, bottom of palate, underlip** Jb 19$_{20}$.

עִוֵּר 26.0.7 adj.—m.pl. עִוְרִים, f.pl. עִוְרוֹת—**1. blind,** of man Lv 21$_{18}$, eye Is 42$_7$, animal Dt 15$_{21}$. **2.** as noun, **blind one,** of person Dt 27$_{18}$, animal Ml 1$_8$. → עור II *be* *blind.*

עוֹרֵב, see עֹרֵב I *raven*, II *Oreb*.

עִוָּרוֹן 2.0.7 n.[m.]—cstr. Q עורון; sf. עורונם—**blindness** of humans Dt 28$_{28}$, horses Zc 12$_{4}$. → עור II *be blind*.

עוֹרִים, see עַיִר *ass*.

עַוֶּרֶת 1 n.f. **blindness,** i.e. blind animal Lv 22$_{22}$. → עור II *be blind*.

עוש I 1 vb.—**Qal** 1 Impv. עוּשׁוּ—**help** Jl 4$_{11}$.

***עוש** II 1 vb.—**Qal** 1 Impv. עוּשׁוּ—**hasten** Jl 4$_{11}$.

* [**עוֹשֶׁל**] 0.0.1 pl.n. **Oshel.**

עות I 11 vb. **Ni. be deceptive, treacherous,** of kiss Pr 27$_{6}$ (if em. נַעְתָּרוֹת *abundant* [עתר ni.] to נַעֲוֹתוֹת *deceptive*).

Pi. 9 Pf. עִוְּתוּנִי; impf. יְעַוֵּת (־יְעַוֶּת); inf. עַוֵּת—**1a. bend** something Ec 7$_{13}$. **b. bring to ruin** way of wicked Ps 146$_{9}$. **2. falsify** balances Am 8$_{5}$. **3. pervert** justice Jb 34$_{12}$. **4. subvert, put someone in the wrong** Jb 19$_{6}$.

Pu. 1 Ptc. מְעֻוָּת—**be bent** Ec 1$_{15}$.

Htp. 1 + waw וְהִתְעַוְּתוּ—**be bent, stoop** Ec 12$_{3}$.

→ עַוָּתָה *wrong*.

עות II 1.0.1 vb.—**Qal** 1.0.1 Inf. עוּת (Q לעאף)—**sustain,** לָעוּת אֶת־יָעֵף דָּבָר *to sustain the weary one (with) a word* Is 50$_{4}$.

[**עַוָּתָה**] 1 n.f.—sf. עַוָּתָתִי—**wrong (done to one), subversion (of one's cause)** Lm 3$_{59}$. → עות I *be bent*.

עוּתַי 2 pr.n.m. **Uthai.**

עַז 23.3.2 adj.—עָז; cstr. עַז; f.s. עַזָּה; m.pl. עַזִּים; cstr. עַזֵּי; f. pl. עַזּוֹת—**1a. strong, mighty, fierce,** of people Is 25$_{3}$, wind Ex 14$_{21}$, water Is 43$_{16}$, love Ca 8$_{6}$, wrath Pr 21$_{14}$. **b.** cstr., עַז פָּנִים **fierce of face,** i.e. fierce looking, of nation Dt 28$_{50}$, עַזֵּי־נֶפֶשׁ **strong of appetite,** i.e. ravenous, of dogs Is 56$_{11}$. **2.** as noun, **a. strong one, mighty one, fierce one** Jg 14$_{14}$ Ezk 7$_{24}$ Ps 59$_{4}$. **b. strength, power** Gn 49$_{3}$. **3.** עַזּוֹת as adv., **harshly, fiercely** Pr 18$_{23}$. → עזז I *be strong*.

עֵז 74.0.16 n.f.—pl. עִזִּים; sf. עִזֶּיךָ—**1. she-goat** Gn 27$_{9}$. **2. goat hair,** as material for tabernacle Ex 25$_{4}$||35$_{6}$. **3.** constellation, **the She-goat,** i.e. **Capella** Am 5$_{9}$ (if em. עַז *the strong one*). → cf. עֲזָאזֵל III *scapegoat*.

עֹז I 93.5.51 n.m.—עוֹז (עָז־); cstr. עֹז; sf. עֻזִּי (עָזִּי), עֻזְּכֶם, עֻזּוֹ—**1. strength, might, power, a.** of or assoc. with Y. Ex 15$_{13}$, his arm Is 51$_{9}$, voice Ps 68$_{34}$, ark Ps 132$_{8}$. **b.** of human 2 S 6$_{14}$, lips 4QHod[a] 7.1$_{16}$, face, i.e. hardness or impudence Ec 8$_{1}$. **c.** given by Y. to humans Ps 29$_{11}$. **d.** Y. as source of strength Ex 15$_{2}$. **e.** of firmament Ps 150$_{1}$, mountains Ps 30$_{8}$, tower Jg 9$_{51}$, city Pr 10$_{15}$. **f.** of confidence Pr 14$_{26}$, judgment 1QS 10$_{25}$, praise Si 45$_{12}$. עֹז יְשׁוּעָתִי *strength of my salvation* Ps 140$_{8}$, אלוהי עוז *God of strength,* i.e. strong God 4QShirShabb[d] 1.1$_{39}$, זְרוֹעַ עֻזּוֹ *arm of his strength,* i.e. his strong arm Is 62$_{8}$, צוּר־עֻזִּי *rock of my strength,* i.e. my strong rock Ps 62$_{8}$. **2.** perh. **stronghold, fortress, bulwark** Jr 51$_{53}$ Am 3$_{11}$ Ps 8$_{3}$. **3. glory** Ps 29$_{1}$ 96$_{6}$.

→ עזז *be strong*.

***עֹז** II 13 n.m.—sf. עֻזִּי (עָזִּי), עֻזְּךָ—**refuge, protection,** given by Y. to humans Ps 21$_{2}$ 29$_{11}$, Y. as refuge of humans Ex 15$_{2}$ Is 12$_{2}$ 49$_{5}$ Jr 16$_{19}$ Ps 28$_{7}$ 46$_{2}$ 59$_{18}$ 62$_{8}$. → עוז *take refuge*.

***עֹז** III 2 n.m.—sf. עֻזּוֹ—**anger** Ezr 8$_{22}$; as changing countenance Ec 8$_{1}$ (if em. יְשֻׁנֶּא *it is changed* [pu.] to יְשַׁנֶּא *it changes*).

***עֹז** IV 3 n.[m.] **poetical and musical performance,** כָּל־עֹז *all music* 2 S 6$_{14}$ 1 C 13$_{8}$ 2 C 30$_{21}$ (if em. כְּלֵי עֹז *instruments of music*).

עֻזָּא 11.0.0.7 pr.n.m. **Uzza.**

***עֲזָאזֵל** I 4.0.3 pr.n.[m.]—Q עזזאל—**Azazel,** a demon Lv 16$_{8}$.

***עֲזָאזֵל** II 4.0.1 n.[m.]—Q עזזאל—**jagged rocks, precipice** Lv 16$_{8}$.

***עֲזָאזֵל** III 4.0.1 n.[m.]—Q עזזאל—**scapegoat** Lv 16$_{8}$. → עֵז *she-goat* + אזל *go*.

עֲזָאזֵל IV 4.0.1 n.[m.]—Q עזזאל—**entire removal** Lv 16$_{8}$.

***עֲזָאזֵל** V 4.0.1 n.[m.]—Q עזזאל—**wrath of God** Lv 16$_{8}$.

→ עֱזוּז *strength, wrath* + אֵל *God*.

עזב I 213.11.71.1 vb.—**Qal** 202.10.67 Pf. עָזַב, עֲזַבְתֶּם; impf. יַעֲזֹב (־יַעֲזָב), אֶעֱזֹב (אֶעֶזְבָה); + waw וַיַּעֲזֹב (־וַיַּעֲזָב); impv. עֲזֹב (עָזְבָה), עִזְבוּ; ptc. עֹזֵב, עֹזֶבֶת, עֹזְבִים; ptc. pass. עָזוּב, עֲזוּבָה, עֲזֻבוֹת; inf. abs. עָזוֹב; cstr. עֲזֹב (עָזְבֵךְ), עָזְבְכֶם—**1a. leave, abandon, forsake,** (1) humans leaving humans Gn 2$_{24}$, land Jr 9$_{18}$, city 1 S 31$_{7}$||1 C 10$_{7}$. (2) humans abandoning Y. Dt 28$_{28}$, his covenant Dt 29$_{24}$, law Jr 9$_{12}$. (3) Y. leaving humans Gn 28$_{15}$, the land Ezk 8$_{12}$, his house Jr 12$_{7}$. (4) humans forsaking way of life

Is 55$_7$, transgressions Pr 28$_{13}$. **b. leave behind** persons and livestock in (בְּ) field Ex 9$_{21}$, object in someone's hand Gn 39$_{12}$. **c. leave,** i.e. **give up** prostitution Ezk 23$_8$. **d. leave untouched** Jg 2$_{21}$. **e. leave (in a particular state),** a camp as it is 2 K 7$_7$, a city open Jos 8$_{17}$, a person naked Ezk 23$_{29}$. **f. leave, fail to exercise, withhold** loyalty Gn 24$_{27}$ (+ מֵעִם *from*), anger Ps 37$_8$. **g. leave for, leave to,** with לְ Lv 19$_{10}$, אֶל Jb 39$_{11}$. **h. leave (in the hand of), entrust (to)** Gn 39$_6$. **i. abandon,** i.e. **neglect** Dt 12$_{19}$. **j. let go,** in various senses: **let go of evil** Jb 20$_{13}$, **release** animal lying under load Ex 23$_5$, **cancel** debt Ne 5$_{10}$, **overlook** iniquities 4QD^f 3$_3$. **2.** pass. **a.** (1) **be abandoned, be forsaken,** of Zion Is 60$_{15}$. (2) ptc. as adj., **abandoned, forsaken,** of woman Is 54$_6$, eggs Is 10$_{14}$. (3) ptc. as noun, **forsaken (one)** Is 62$_4$, **abandoned, deserted place(s)** Is 6$_{12}$. **b. be set free,** ptc. as noun, **free (one),** עָצוּר וְעָזוּב *bond and free,* i.e. all classes of people Dt 32$_{36}$.

Ni. $_{9.1.4}$ Pf. נֶעֱזַב; impf. תֵּעָזֵב; ptc. נֶעֱזָבוֹת, נֶעֱזָב—**1. be left, be abandoned, be forsaken,** of person Ps 37$_{25}$, city Ezk 36$_4$, land Lv 26$_{43}$ (+ מִן *by*). **2. be left, be abandoned to** (לְ), of shoots to birds and beasts Is 18$_6$. **3.** perh. **let oneself loose, exclude oneself from** (מִן) wisdom 1QH 17$_{18}$.

Pu. (unless **Qal pass.**) $_2$ Pf. עֻזָּבָה, עֻזָּב—**be abandoned, be forsaken,** of city Is 32$_{14}$ Jr 49$_{25}$.

→ עֲזָב *leavings.*

עזב II $_{21.2}$ vb.—**Qal** $_{18.2}$ Impf. יַעֲזוֹב, אֶעֶזְבָה; + waw וַיַּעַזְבוּ (וַיַּעַזְב־); impv. Si עזוב; ptc. עֹזֵב; inf. abs. עָזוֹב; cstr. עֲזֹב—**1. restore,** i.e. **a. repair,** perh. **plaster** Jerusalem Ne 3$_8$ (+ עַד *as far as*). **b. resume (normal) countenance** Jb 9$_{27}$ (or §3). **2. lift (back) up, set aright** fallen ass (לְ of obj.) Ex 23$_5$. **3. arrange, set in order** countenance Jb 9$_{27}$ (or §2b), complaint Jb 10$_1$ (+ עַל *for* oneself). **4. place, set** person Ps 37$_{33}$ (+ בְּ *into* hand of) Ps 16$_{10}$ (+ לְ *into* Sheol), egg Jb 39$_{14}$ (+ לְ *on* ground). **5. commit oneself to** (עַל) Y. Ps 10$_{14}$. **6. do good, be of benefit to** (לְ) Si 3$_{13}$ 11$_{23}$. **7.** ptc. as noun, **caretaker,** עֹצֵר וְעֹזֵב *ruler and caretaker* Dt 32$_{36}$.

Ni. $_1$ תֵּעָזֵב—**be (re)arranged,** of the earth Jb 18$_4$ (+ לְמַעַן *for the sake of*).

→ עִזָּבוֹן *merchandise.*

*[עזב] III vb. **Hi. make** countenance **agreeable, pleasant** Jb 9$_{27}$ (if em. אֶעֶזְבָה *I will forsake* [עזב I] to אַעֲזִיבָה).

*עזב IV $_4$ vb.—**Qal** $_3$ Impf. תַּעֲזֹב; inf. abs. עָזֹב; cstr. עֲזֹב—**1. help** fallen ass (לְ of obj.) Ex 23$_5$. **2.** ptc. as noun, **helper** Jr 49$_{10}$ (if em. אֵינֶנּוּ׃ עִזְבָה *he is not there. Leave* to אֵינָם עזבו *there is none to help him*).

Pu. $_1$ Pf. עֻזְּבָה—**be helped,** of city Jr 49$_{25}$.

*עזב V $_5$ vb.—**Qal** $_5$ Ptc. pass. עָזוּב—**lead,** עָצוּר וְעָזוּב *ruling and leading* Dt 32$_{36}$.

*עזב VI $_{1.1}$ vb.—**Qal** $_{1.1}$ Pf. עָזַב; impf. Si תעזבהו—**grieve, harass, punish, vex** Jb 20$_{19}$ Si 3$_{12}$.

*[עֹזֶב] n.[m.] **leavings,** עֹזֵב דַּלִּים *leavings of,* i.e. what is left behind for, *the poor* Jb 20$_{19}$ (if em. עָזַב *he has abandoned*). → עזב I *leave.*

*[עֹזֶב] n.[m.] **hut, dwelling,** עֹזֵב דַּלִּים *hut of the poor* Jb 20$_{19}$ (if em. עָזַב *he has abandoned*).

[עִזָּבוֹן] $_7$ n.[m.]—pl. sf. עִזְבוֹנַיִךְ—**merchandise, wares** Ezk 27$_{12}$. → עזב II *arrange.*

עַזְבּוּק $_1$ pr.n.m. **Azbuk.**

עַזְגָּד $_4$ pr.n.m. **Azgad.**

*[עזה] vb. **be a warrior,** ptc. as noun, **warrior** Ex 15$_2$ (if em. עָזִּי *my strength* to עֹזֶה *a warrior*).

עַזָּה $_{20.0.1}$ pl.n. **Gaza.**

עֻזָּה I $_6$ pr.n.m. **Uzzah.**

*[עֻזָּה] II $_{0.0.1}$ n.f.—pl. עזות—perh. **support, clamp, holding stone in place** 3QTr 10$_9$. → עזז I *be strong.*

עֲזוּבָה $_4$ pr.n.f. **Azubah.**

[עֱזוּז] $_{3.1.1}$ n.[m.]—cstr. עֱזוּז; sf. עֱזוּזוֹ—**strength, might** Is 42$_{25}$ Ps 78$_4$ 145$_6$ Si 45$_{18}$. → עזז I *be strong.*

עִזּוּז $_{2.0.1}$ adj.—pl. cstr. Q עזוזי—**mighty,** as noun, **mighty one, powerful one,** in ref. to Y. Ps 24$_8$, warrior Is 43$_{17}$. → עזז I *be strong.*

עַזּוּר $_3$ pr.n.m. **Azzur.**

*[עֱזוּת] $_{0.1}$ n.f. **strength, harshness,** עזות אף *strength of anger,* or *harshness of countenance* Si 10$_{18}$. → עזז I *be strong;* cf. עֲזָאזֵל V *wrath of God.*

עזז I $_{11.2.2}$ vb.—**Qal** $_{9.0.2}$ Impf. יָעֹז; + waw וַתָּעָז; impv. עוּזָּה; inf. cstr. עֲזוֹז—**be strong, show oneself strong, prevail,** of Y. Ps 68$_{29}$, human Ps 9$_{20}$, hand Jg 3$_{10}$, heart CD 20$_{33}$, wisdom Ec 7$_{19}$ (+ לְ *to*).

Pi., make firm, establish, Pr 8_{29} (if em. בַּעֲזוֹז *when* the springs *became strong* to בְּעַזְּזוֹ *when he made firm*).

Hi. 2.1 Pf. הֵעַז, הֵעֵזָה; impf. Si תעיז—**1. make bold, cause to show impudence,** obj. face Pr 7_{13}, forehead Si 8_{16} (+ עִם *with*). **2. show boldness, impudence** with (בְּ) face Pr 21_{29}.

Ho. 0.1 Ptc. מוּעָז—**be impudent, defiant** Si 10_{12}.

→ עַז *strong*, עֹז I *strength*, עֱזוּז *strength*, עזוּת *strength*, עִזּוּז *mighty*, עֶזְרָה II *support*, מָעוֹז II *stronghold*.

***עזז II** 1 vb.—**Qal** 1 Inf. עֲזוֹז—**flow, burst into flood,** of spring Pr 8_{28}.

עַזָּז 1 pr.n.m. **Azaz.**

עזזאל, see עֲזָאזֵל I *Azazel.*

עֲזַזְיָהוּ 3 pr.n.m. **Azaziah.**

***עָזִי I** 1 n.[m.] **patience, endurance** Ex 15_2.

***עָזִי II** 1 n.[m.] **warrior** Ex 15_2.

עֻזִּי 11.0.0.1 pr.n.m. **Uzzi.**

עֻזִּיָּא 1 pr.n.m. **Uzzia.**

עֲזִיאֵל 1 pr.n.m. **Aziel.**

עֻזִּיאֵל 16 pr.n.m. **Uzziel.**

עָזִּיאֵלִי 2 gent. **Uzzielite.**

עֻזִּיָּה, see עֻזִּיָּהוּ *Uzziah.*

עֻזִּיָּהוּ 27.0.0.6 pr.n.m. **Uzziah.**

עזיו, see עֻזִּיָּהוּ *Uzziah.*

עֲזִיזָא 1 pr.n.m. **Aziza.**

עַזְמָוֶת I 6 pr.n.m. **Azmaveth.**

עַזְמָוֶת II 2 pl.n. **Azmaveth.**

עַזָּן 1 pr.n.m. **Azzan.**

***[עָזְנִאֵל]** 0.0.0.1 pr.n.[m.] **Ozniel.**

עָזְנִיָּה 2 n.f. **black vulture, or perh. bearded vulture (ossifrage), or osprey** Lv 11_{13} Dt 14_{12}.

עזק I 1.0.1 vb.—**Qal** 0.0.1 Inf. עזוק—**dig** ditch 1QH 16_{22}.

Pi. 1 + waw וַיְעַזְּקֵהוּ—**dig** vineyard **about** Is 5_2.

***עזק II** 1 vb.—**Pi.** 1 + waw וַיְעַזְּקֵהוּ—**surround** vineyard **with a wall, hedge** Is 5_2.

עֲזֵקָה 7.0.0.1 pl.n. **Azekah.**

עזר I 82.3.18 vb.—**Qal** 76.3.18 Pf. עֲזָרוֹ, עֲזַרְתָּ; impf. יַעֲזָר־; + waw וַיַּעֲזֹר, וַיַּעְזְרוּ; impv. עָזְרֵנִי, עִזְרֻנִי; ptc. עֹזֵר, עֹזְרֵי; ptc. pass. עָזֻר; inf. בַּעְזֹר, לַעְזֹר (לְעָזְרוֹ)—**1a. help, assist, come to the aid of,** (1) with accus. nation, people 1 S 7_{12} Ezr 8_{22} (+ מִן *from, against*), city Jos 10_{33}, individual person Is 41_6 2 C 26_7 (+ עַל *against*). (2) with לְ of obj. person 2 S 21_{17}, evil Zc 1_{15}. (3) with עִם of obj. person 1 C 12_{22} (+ עַל *against*). **b.** without obj., **give help, send help** 2 S $18_{3(Qr)}$ (+ מִן *from* city) Is 30_7 (+ הֶבֶל וָרִיק *[with] vanity and emptiness*) 2 C 25_8. **2.** ptc. as noun, **helper** Is 31_3; עֹזְרֵי רָהַב *helpers of Rahab* Jb 9_{13}, עֹזְרֵי הַמִּלְחָמָה *helpers of,* i.e. in, *war* 1 C 12_1. **3.** ptc. pass. as noun, **one who is helped** Is 31_3.

Ni. 4 Pf. נֶעֱזַרְתִּי; impf. יֵעָזְרוּ; inf. הֵעָזֵר—**be helped, receive help** Ps 28_7 1 C 5_{20} (+ עַל *against*) 2 C 26_{15}; יֵעָזְרוּ עֵזֶר מְעָט *they shall receive a little help* Dn 11_{34}.

Hi. 2 Ptc. מַעְזְרִים; inf. Kt לעזיר—**1. help** someone 2 C 28_{23}. **2.** without obj., **send help** 2 S $18_{3(Kt)}$ (+ מִן *from*).

→ עֵזֶר I *help*, עֶזְרָה I *help*.

***עזר II** 4 vb.—**Qal** 4 Pf. עָזְרוּ; + waw וַיַּעְזְרוּ—**1. be copious, abundant for** (לְ) evil, i.e. do much evil Zc 1_{15}. **2. join together, come together** 1 K 1_7 (+ אַחֲרֵי *in support of*) 1 C 12_{22} (+ עִם *with*, עַל *against*) 2 C 20_{23} (+ בְּ *with*, לְ *for* destruction).

***עזר III** 20 vb.—**Qal** 15 Pf. עָזְרוּ; impf. יַעְזְרוּ, יַעְזְרֶהָ; ptc. עֹזֵר; inf. Qr לַעְזוֹר (לְעָזְרֵנִי)—**1. be strong, valiant** 1 C 12_{22} (+ עִם *with*, עַל *against*) 2 C 20_{23} (+ בְּ *against*). **2. make valiant, strong** Ps 46_6 118_{13} Zc 1_{15} (לְ of obj.) 2 C 26_7 (+ עַל *against*). **3. deal valiantly with, show valour to** 1 C 12_{18} 2 C 32_3. **4.** ptc. as noun, **valiant one, hero, warrior, strong one** Ezk 30_8; עֹזְרֵי הַמִּלְחָמָה *valiant ones of,* i.e. in, *war* 1 C 12_1.

Ni. 4 Pf. נֶעֱזַרְתִּי; impf. יֵעָזְרוּ; inf. הֵעָזֵר—**be strengthened, made valiant** Ps 28_7 1 C 5_{20} (+ עַל *against*) 2 C 26_{15}; יֵעָזְרוּ עֵזֶר מְעָט *they shall be made a little valiant* Dn 11_{34}.

Hi. 2 Ptc. מַעְזְרִים; inf. Kt לעזיר—**1. make valiant** 2 C 28_{23}. **2. show oneself valiant** 2 S $18_{3(Kt)}$ (+ לְ *for*).

→ עֵזֶר III *strength*, עֶזְרָה II *strength*, עֵזֶר II *warrior*.

***עזר IV** 2 vb.—**Qal** 2 Impf. יַעֲזָר־—**justify,** with לְ of obj. Is $50_{7.9}$.

***עזר V** 1 vb.—**Qal** 1 Ptc. עֹזֵר—**hinder, restrain,** with לְ of obj. Jb 30_{13}.

***עזר VI** 9.1.1 vb.—**Qal** 8.1.1 Pf. עֲזָרוּ, עֲזָרָנוּ; + waw וַיַּעְזְרֵם; ptc. עוֹזֵר; inf. עָזְרֵנִי—**1. free, save** 1 S 7_{12} Ps 37_{40} Ezr 8_{22} (+ מִן *from*) Si 51_3. **2.** ptc. as noun, **saviour** Ps 22_{12}.

→ עֵזֶר V *liberation*, עֶזְרָה IV *liberation*.

עָזֶר, see עֵזֶר II *Ezer*.

עָזֻר, see עַזּוּר *Azzur*.

עֵזֶר I 21.1.13 n.m.—cstr. Q עזר; sf. עֶזְרִי—**help** Ps 20:3 Dn 11:34 1QM 4:13; i.e. **helper** Gn 2:18, in ref. to Y. Ex 18:4 Dt 33:7 (עֵזֶר מִצָּרָיו *a help[er] against his adversaries*). → עזר I *help*.

*__עֵזֶר__ II 2 n.[m.]—sf. Qr עֶזְרוֹ (Kt עזרה)—**1. lad** Ps 89:20. **2. warrior** Ezk 12:14. → עזר III *be strong*.

*__[עֵזֶר]__ III 9 n.[m.]—sf. עֶזְרָם—**1. strength, might** Dt 33:29 Ps 89:20, in ref. to Y. Ps 33:20; **valour** Dn 11:34. **2.** perh. **impetuous haste** Dt 33:26. **3. army** Ezk 12:14. → עזר III *be strong*.

*__עֵזֶר__ IV 2.0.1 n.f. **woman**, עֵזֶר כְּנֶגְדּוֹ *a woman corresponding to him* Gn 2:18.20.

*__עֵזֶר__ V 4 n.[m.]—sf. עֶזְרִי—**liberation** Ho 13:9; i.e. **liberator**, in ref. to Y. Ex 18:4 Dt 33:7 (עֵזֶר מִצָּרָיו *a liberator against his adversaries*) Ps 70:6. → עזר VI *free*.

עֵזֶר VI 5.0.0.27 pr.n.m. **Ezer**.

עֵזֶר VII, see אֶבֶן *stone*, §5c (הָ)אֶבֶן הָעֵזֶר *Ebenezer*.

עֶזֶר, see עֵזֶר II *Ezer*.

עֹזֵר I *helper*, see עזר I, qal §2.

עֹזֵר II *valiant one, warrior*, see עזר III, qal §4.

עֶזְרָא 22 pr.n.m. **Ezra**.

עֲזַרְאֵל 6.0.0.2 pr.n.m. **Azarel**.

עֲזָרָה 9.1.5 n.f.—cstr. Si, Q עזרת—**1. (surrounding) ledge, border** around altar Ezk 43:14 45:19 11QT 16:17. **2. (outer) court** of temple, as enclosed by border 2 C 4:9 6:13 Si 50:11.

עֶזְרָה I 26.0.6 n.f.—עֶזְרָת, עֶזְרָתָה; cstr. עֶזְרַת; sf. עֶזְרָתִי—**1. help** Jg 5:23 Is 10:3 Ps 60:13||108:13 (עֶזְרָת מִצָּר *help against the adversary*). **2. helper** Is 31:2, in ref. to Y. Ps 40:18. **3. acquittal** Jb 31:21. → עזר I *help*.

*__[עֶזְרָה]__ II 6 n.f.—cstr. עֶזְרַת; sf. עֶזְרָתִי—**1. strength, might** Jb 6:13. **2. battle, war** Jg 5:23 Ps 35:2. **3. young men** (coll.) Jb 31:21. → עזר III *be strong*.

עֶזְרָה III 1 pr.n.m. **Ezrah**.

*__עֶזְרָה__ IV 9 n.f.—עֶזְרָת; sf. עֶזְרָתִי—**1. liberation** Ps 22:20 60:13||108:13 (עֶזְרָת מִצָּר *liberation from the adversary*). **2. liberator** Lm 4:17 (עֶזְרָתֵנוּ הָבֶל *our liberator, vanity*, i.e. our futile liberator), in ref. to Y. Ps 46:2. → עזר VI *free*.

עֶזְרִי 1 pr.n.m. **Ezri**.

עַזְרִיאֵל 3.0.0.2 pr.n.m. **Azriel**.

עֲזַרְיָה 48.0.0.32 pr.n.m. **Azariah**.

עֲזַרְיָהוּ, see עֲזַרְיָה *Azariah*.

עזריו, see עֲזַרְיָה *Azariah*.

עַזְרִיקָם 6.0.0.6 pr.n.m. **Azrikam**.

עזרקם, see עַזְרִיקָם *Azrikam*.

עֶזְרָת, see עֶזְרָה I *help*.

עֶזְרָתָה, see עֶזְרָה I *help*.

עַזָּתִי 2 gent. **Gazite**.

*__[עַחְעָשׁ]__ 0.0.0.1 pr.n.[m.] **Ahash**.

[עֵט] 4 n.m.—cstr. עֵט—**1. stylus** Jr 17:1 Jb 19:24. **2. (reed) pen**, used by scribes Jr 8:8 Ps 45:2.

עטה I 18.7 vb.—**Qal** 15.7 Pf. Si עטו; impf. תַּעְטוּ ,יַעְטוּ ,יַעְטֶה; + waw וַיַּעַט ,וְעָטָה; ptc. עֹטְיָה ,עֹטֶה; inf. abs. עָטֹה; cstr. Si עטותו—**1.** with accus., **wrap oneself in, cover oneself with, be covered with, wear** robe 1 S 28:14, light Ps 104:2 (+ כְּ *as* garment). **2.** with עַל, **wrap, cover over** the moustache, as a sign of shame Lv 13:45, mourning Ezk 24:17.

Pu. 1 Ptc. מְעֻטָּה—**be uncovered, unsheathed,** of sword Ezk 21:20 (+ לְ *for* slaughter).

Hi. 2 Pf. הֶעֱטִיתָ; impf. יַעְטֶה—**wrap with, cover with, a.** with double accus. Is 61:10 (if em. יַעְטֵנִי *he has covered me* [from יעט] to יַעְטֵנִי *he wraps me*); first accus. elided Ps 84:7. **b.** with accus. and עַל Ps 89:46.

→ מַעֲטֶה *garment*; cf. יעט *cover*.

עטה II 5 vb.—**Qal** 4 Impf. יַעְטֶה; + waw וְעָטָה; ptc. עֹטְךָ, עֹטְיָה; inf. abs. עָטֹה—**1. grasp, seize** Is 22:17. **2. pick free of lice** Jr 43:12. **3.** without obj., **pick lice** Ca 1:7.

*__עטה__ III 1 vb.—**Hi** 1 Impf. יַעְטֶה—**give** Ps 84:7.

עָטוּף *weak one*, see עטף, qal §3.

[עֲטִין] I 1 n.[m.]—pl. sf. עֲטִינָיו—**pail, vessel** Jb 21:24.

*__[עֲטִין]__ II 1 n.[m.]—pl. sf. עֲטִינָיו—**olive** Jb 21:24.

*__[עֲטִין]__ III 1 n.[m.]—pl. sf. עֲטִינָיו—**watering place** Jb 21:24.

*__[עֲטִין]__ IV 1 n.[m.]—pl. sf. עֲטִינָיו—**breast** Jb 21:24.

*__[עֲטִין]__ V 1 n.[m.]—pl. sf. עֲטִינָיו—**side, thigh** Jb 21:24.

*__[עֲטִין]__ VI 1 n.[m.]—pl. sf. עֲטִינָיו—**body** Jb 21:24.

*__[עֲטִין]__ VII 1 n.[m.]—pl. sf. עֲטִינָיו—**trough** Jb 21:24.

[עֲטִישָׁה] 1 n.f.—pl. sf. עֲטִישֹׁתָיו—**sneezing** Jb 41:10.

עֲטַלֵּף 3 n.[m.]—pl. עֲטַלֵּפִים—**bat** Lv 11:19 Dt 14:18 Is 2:20.

→ עטף II *cover.*

*[עָטָם] n.[m.] **thigh** Jb 21$_{24}$ (if em. עֲטִינָיו *his pails* to עֲטָמָיו *his thighs*).

עטף I 13.0.2 vb.—**Qal** 5.0.1 Impf. יַעֲטֹף; ptc. pass. עֲטוּפִים; inf. עֲטֹף—**1. be faint,** of person Ps 102$_1$, heart Ps 61$_3$, spirit Is 57$_{16}$. **2.** pass. **be (made) faint,** of child Lm 2$_{19}$ (+ בְּ *with* hunger). **3.** pass. ptc. as noun, **weak one,** of sheep Gn 30$_{42}$.

Ni. 1 Inf. בֵּעָטֵף—**faint,** of child Lm 2$_{11}$.

Hi. 1 Inf. הַעֲטִיף—**show weakness,** of sheep Gn 30$_{42}$.

Htp. 6.0.1 Impf. תִּתְעַטֵּף (תִּתְעַטָּף); inf. הִתְעַטֵּף—**faint,** of child Lm 2$_{12}$ (+ כְּ *as* wounded one), spirit Ps 77$_4$, soul Jon 2$_8$ (+ עַל *within* person) Ps 107$_5$ (+ בְּ *within* person).

עטף II 2.1 vb.—**Qal** 2 Impf. יַעֲטֹף־, יַעַטְפוּ—**1.** with accus., **cover oneself with** Ps 65$_{14}$. **2. cover someone** (לְ of obj.) **with** (accus.) garment Ps 73$_6$.

Pu. 0.1 Ptc. מעוטף—**be wrapped in garments** Si 11$_{4(B)}$ (מעוטף בגדים).

→ מַעֲטֶפֶת *garment,* עֲטַלֵּף *bat.*

עטף III 1 vb.—**Qal** 1 Impf. יַעְטֹף—**turn (oneself)** Jb 23$_9$ (+ יָמִין *[to] the right*).

עטר 7.2.4 vb.—**Qal** 2 Impf. תַּעְטְרֶנּוּ; ptc. עֹטְרִים—**1.** with double accus., **surround** someone **with** Ps 5$_{13}$. **2. close in upon** (אֶל) someone 1 S 23$_{26}$.

Pi. 5.2.4 Pf. עִטַּרְתָּ; impf. תְּעַטְּרֵהוּ; ptc. מְעַטְּרֵכִי—with double accus., **1. crown someone or something with** Ps 8$_6$ 65$_{12}$ Ca 3$_{11}$. **2. wear something as a crown** Si 6$_{31}$.

Hi. 1 Ptc. מַעֲטִירָה—**bestow crowns,** or perh. **wear crowns** Is 23$_8$.

→ עֲטָרָה I *crown.*

עֲטָרָה I 23.3.4 n.f.—Q עטרת; cstr. עֲטֶרֶת; pl. עֲטָרוֹת; sf. Q עטרותיו—**1. crown, diadem, wreath** of king Ps 21$_4$, priest Zc 6$_{11}$, bridegroom Ca 3$_{11}$. **2. cornice** of wall 11QT 40$_{11}$. → עטר *surround.*

עֲטָרָה II 1 pr.n.f. **Atarah.**

עֲטָרוֹת 4 pl.n. **Ataroth.**

עַטְרוֹת אַדָּר 2 pl.n. **Ataroth-addar.**

עַטְרוֹת בֵּית יוֹאָב 1 pl.n. **Atroth-beth-joab.**

עַטְרֹת שׁוֹפָן 1 pl.n. **Atroth-shophan.**

עַי 39 pl.n. **Ai.**

עִי I 5.0.2 n.[m.] cstr. עִי; sf. Q עיכה; pl. עִיִּים (עִיִּין)—**ruin, heap of ruins** Jr 26$_{18}$ Mc 1$_6$ Jb 30$_{24}$. → עוה II *bend;* cf. מְעִי *ruin.*

*עִי II 1 adj. **weak,** as noun, **weak one** Jb 30$_{24}$.

עִיב, see עוב II *be cloudy.*

עֵיבָל I 5 pl.n. **Ebal.**

עֵיבָל II 4 pr.n.m. **Ebal.**

עַיָּה 2 pl.n. **Aija, Ayyah.**

עִיּוֹן 3 pl.n. **Ijon.**

עֵיוֹת, see עֲוִית *Avith.*

עיט 3.2 vb.—**Qal** 3.2 Impf. Si תעיט; + waw Qr וַיַּעַט (וַיַּעַט)—**1. scream, shout at** (בְּ) 1 S 25$_{14}$. **2. fly, swoop upon** (אֶל) spoil 1 S 14$_{32(Qr)}$ 15$_{19}$. **3a. look rapaciously at** (עַל) Si 14$_{10}$. **b. be rapacious** Si 34$_{16}$.

Hi. (if em. יָמִיטוּ *they let fall* to יָעִיטוּ), **scream (threats of), cry (for) trouble** Ps 55$_4$, burning coals Ps 140$_{11}$.

→ עַיִט *bird(s) of prey.*

עַיִט I 8.1 n.m.—cstr. עֵיט—**bird(s) of prey,** lit. 'screamer(s)', usu. coll. Gn 15$_{11}$ Is 18$_6$. → עיט *scream.*

*עַיִט II 1 n.[m.] **den, lair,** עֵיט צָבוּעַ *den of a hyena* Jr 12$_9$ (if em. עַיִט appar. abs.).

*עַיִט III 2 n.[m.] **massed host(s)** Is 46$_{11}$ Jr 12$_{9a}$.

עֵיטָם 5 pl.n. **Etam.**

עִיִּים 2 pl.n. **Iyim, Iim.**

עִיֵּי עֲבָרִים 2 pl.n. **Iye-abarim.**

*[עֵילוֹל] 0.0.2 n.m.—sf. עילוליו—**child** 4QpNah 3.4$_{2.4}$. → עול I *give suck* or עלל III *act the child;* cf. עוֹלֵל *child,* עוֹלָל *child.*

עֵילוֹם, see עוֹלָם *everlastingness.*

עִילַי 1 pr.n.m. **Ilay.**

עֵילָם I 13.0.1 pr.n.m. **Elam.**

עֵילָם II 15 pl.n. **Elam.**

[עָיֵם] 1 n.[m.]—cstr. בַּעְיָם—perh. **heat** Is 11$_{15}$.

*[עִים] n.[m.] **cloud,** מֵימַד עִים *measurement of cloud(s)* Jb 37$_{16}$ (if em. תְּמִים דֵּעִים *one perfect of knowledge*).

עין 1 vb.—**Qal (or Poel)** 1 Ptc. Qr, mss עוֹיֵן (Kt עון, mss עִין, mss עיין)—**eye (jealously)** 1 S 18$_9$. → עַיִן I *eye.*

עַיִן I 863.38.111 n.f.&m.—עָיִן; cstr. עֵין; sf. עֵינִי, עֵינָם (עֵינֵמוֹ); du. עֵינַיִם (עֵינָיִם); cstr. עֵינֵי; sf. עֵינַי, עֵינָיו (עֵינֵיהוּ)—**1. eye** of humans Gn 13$_{10}$, Y. Dt 11$_{12}$, images of gods Ps 115$_5$, animals Gn 30_{41}, birds Jb 28_7. **2. eye,** i.e. **sight, a.** presence, vision, witnessing, of humans Gn 23_{11}, Y. 2 S 22_{25}||Ps 18_{25}. **b.** opinion, reckoning, esteem, of humans Gn 16_4, Y. Gn 6_8. **3. surface** of land Ex 10_5. **4a. appearance, colour** of diseased area in garment Lv 13_{55}, manna, like bdellium Nm 11_7. **b. gleam, sparkle** of burnished bronze Ezk 1_7, crystal Ezk 1_{22}. → עַיִן *eye*.

עַיִן II 23.0.2 n.f.—עַיִן; cstr. עֵין; + ה- of direction הָעַיְנָה; pl. עֲיָנֹת; sf. perh. Kt עינתם; cstr. עֵינֹת—**spring, fountain,** עֵין הַמַּיִם *spring of water* Gn 16_7, pl. Ex 15_{27}, עֵין חֲרֹד *spring of Harod* Jg 7_1, שַׁעַר הָעַיִן *Fountain Gate* Ne 2_{14}. → cf. מַעְיָן *spring*.

*עַיִן III 0.0.1 n.[m.] **company, group,** עין תמימים *company of the perfect ones* 1QS 3_3.

עַיִן IV 5 pl.n. **Ain.**

עֵין אָדָם 1 pl.n. **En-adam.**

עֵין גֶּדִי 6.0.11 pl.n. **En-gedi.**

עֵין גַּנִּים 3 pl.n. **En-gannim.**

עֵין דֹּאר, see עֵין דֹּר *En-dor.*

עֵין דּוֹר, see עֵין דֹּר *En-dor.*

עֵין דֹּר 3 pl.n. **En-dor.**

עֵין הַקּוֹרֵא 1 pl.n. **En-hakkore.**

עֵין הַתַּנִּין, see עַיִן II *spring* and תַּנִּין *dragon.*

עֵינוֹן, see חֲצַר עֵינוֹן *Hazar-enon.*

עֵין חַדָּה 1 pl.n. **En-haddah.**

עֵין חָצוֹר 1 pl.n. **En-hazor.**

עֵין חֲרֹד, see עַיִן II *spring* and חֲרֹד *Harod.*

עֵינַיִם 2 pl.n. **Enaim.**

*[עֵין כּוּבָר] 0.0.1 pl.n. **En-cubar.**

עֵינָם 1 pl.n. **Enam.**

עֵין מִשְׁפָּט 1 pl.n. **En-mishpat.**

עֵינָן I 5 pr.n.m. **Enan.**

עֵינָן II, see חֲצַר עֵינוֹן *Hazar-enon.*

עֵין עֶגְלַיִם 1 pl.n. **En-eglaim.**

עֵין צִידוֹן, see עַיִן II *spring* and צִידוֹן *Sidon.*

*[עֵין קִבּוּצוֹת] 0.0.1 pl.n. **En-kibbuzoth.**

עֵין רֹגֵל 4 pl.n. **En-rogel.**

עֵין רִמּוֹן 1 pl.n. **En-rimmon.**

עֵין שֶׁמֶשׁ 2 pl.n. **En-shemesh.**

עינתם, see עַיִן I *eye.*

עֵין תַּפּוּחַ 1 pl.n. **En-tappuah.**

עיף I 5.0.1 vb. (byform of יעף I)—**Qal** 5.0.1 Pf. עָיְפָה; + waw וַיִּעַף—**be weary** Jg 4_{21} 1 S 14_{28} Jr 4_{31} (+ לְ *before*). → עָיֵף I *weary*; cf. יעף I *be weary.*

*עיף II 1 vb.—**Qal** 1 + waw וַיָּעַף—**swoon, lose consciousness** Jg 4_{21}.

עָיֵף I 17.0.3 adj.—Q עאף; f.s. עֲיֵפָה; m.pl. עֲיֵפִים (Q עפים) —**1. weary, faint,** through exhaustion, hunger or thirst, of people 2 S 17_{29}, soul (נֶפֶשׁ) Jr 31_{25}, land Is 32_2. **2.** as noun, **weary one** Is 5_{27} 28_{12}. → עיף I *be weary.*

*[עָיֵף] II 2 adj.—f.s. עֲיֵפָה; m.pl. עֲיֵפִים—**1. hungry** Jg 8_4. **2. thirsty** Pr 25_{25}.

עֵיפָה I 2 n.f.—עֵיפָתָה—**darkness, dark mist, gloom** Am 4_{13} Jb 10_{22}. → עוף II *be dark.*

*עֵיפָה II 2 n.f.—עֵיפָתָה—**light** Am 4_{13} Jb 10_{22}.

עֵיפָה III 5 pr.n.m.&f. **Ephah.**

עֵיפַי *Ephai,* see עוֹפַי *Ophai.*

*[עִיפְּרוּר] 0.0.1 n.[m.] perh. **sand** Mur 24 L 5.

עֵיפָתָה, see עֵיפָה I *darkness,* II *light.*

*עיק I 2 vb.—**Qal** 1 Impf. תָּעִיק—**creak,** of wagon Am 2_{13}.

Hi. 1 ptc. מֵעִיק—**cause to creak** Am 2_{13}.

עיק II, see עוק I *press.*

עיק III, see עוק II *be hindered.*

עיק IV, see עוק III *roar.*

עיק V, see עוק IV *split.*

*עיר I 7 vb.—**Qal** 2 Impf. יָעִיר; ptc. עָרֶךָ—**1. protect, keep,** of Y. Jb 8_6 (+ עַל of obj. Job), eagle Dt 32_{11} (accus. nest). **2. nurture** anger Ps 78_{38}. **3.** ptc. as noun, **protector** 1 S 28_{16} Is 14_{21} 33_8 Ps 139_{20}. → עֵר I *protector,* (?) עִיר I *city,* VII *protector.*

*עיר II 1 vb.—**Qal** 1 Impf. יָעִיר—**bestow (wealth)** upon (עַל) Jb 8_6.

*עיר III 2 vb.—**Polel** 1 Inf. עֹרֵר—**revile, curse** Leviathan Jb 3_8.

Hi. 1 Inf. בְּעִיר—inf. as noun, **cursing** Ps 73_{20}. → עִיר IX *reviling.*

*עיר IV 2 vb.—**Hi.** 2 Impf. יָעִיר—**bore, sharpen** the ear, i.e. provide sharp hearing Is 50_4.

*עיר V 1 vb.—**Htpol.** 1 Impf. יִתְעָרָר—**be indignant** against (עַל) Jb 17_8.

*עיר VI 3 vb.—**Qal** (unless Hi.) 3 Impf. יָעִיר; ptc. מֵעִיר —**enflame** oven Ho 7_4, anger Ps 78_{38}, zeal Is 42_{13}. →

עִיר V *fire*.

עַיִר 9 n.m.—sf. Qr עִירוֹ (Kt עירה); pl. עֲיָרִים—**(male) ass, donkey, colt** Gn 32_{16} Jg 10_{4} Zc 9_{9}.

עִיר I 1092.14.93.9 n.f. (& m.)—+ ה- of direction הָעִירָה; cstr. עִיר; sf. עִירִי; pl. עָרִים; cstr. עָרֵי; sf. עָרֵיהֶם, עָרֵי—**1.** usu. **city, town** Gn 4_{17} Jos 20_{6}; specif. of capital or royal city Nm 21_{26} 1 S 27_{5}, Jerusalem as city of Y. Is 60_{14}; pl. of towns subject to a city Jos 13_{17}. **2. city,** i.e. its inhabitants 1 S 5_{12} Jr 11_{12}. **3.** of district within a city, עִיר דּוִ(י)ד *city of David* 2 S 5_{7}||1 C 11_{5}, העיר הַתִּיכֹנָה *the middle city* 2 K 20_{4}(Kt) (Qr חָצֵר *court*). → (?) עִיר I *protect*.

עִיר II 2 n.[m.] **agitation, excitement** Jr 15_{8} Ho 11_{9}. → עור I *rouse oneself*.

*[עִיר] III 0.0.2 n.[m.]—pl. עירים; cstr. עירי—**watcher, angel** 4QpsJub^c^ 2_{4}; עירי השמים *watchers of heaven* CD 2_{18} (if em. עידי appar. *witnesses of*)=4QD^a^ 2.2_{18} ([עירי ה[שמים]). → עור I *rouse oneself*.

*עִיר IV 2 n.[m.] **invasion, raid** Jr 15_{8} Am 7_{17}.

*עִיר V 3 n.[m.] **fire** Jr 15_{8} Ho 7_{4} 11_{9}. → עִיר VI *enflame*.

*[עִיר] VI 2 n.[m.]—cstr. עִיר—**inner room** of temple 2 K 10_{25} Mc 5_{13}.

*[עִיר] VII 2 n.m.—pl. עָרִים; sf. עָרֶיךָ—**protector, god** Mc 5_{13} Ps 9_{7}. → עִיר I *protect*.

*עִיר VIII 1 n.[m.] **enemy** Am 7_{17}.

*עִיר IX 2 n.[m.] **reviling, curse** Ho 11_{9} Jr 15_{8}. → עִיר III *revile*.

*עִיר X 4 n.[m.] **little depression** Nm 22_{36} Dt 2_{36} 34_{3} 2 S 24_{5}.

עִיר XI 1 pr.n.m. **Ir.**

עִירָא 6.0.0.1 pr.n.m. **Ira.**

עִירָד 2 pr.n.m. **Irad.**

עִיר הַהֶרֶס, see עִיר I *city* and הֶרֶס *destruction*.

עִיר־הַמֶּלַח 1 pl.n. **City of Salt.**

עִיר הַתְּמָרִים, see עִיר I *city* and תָּמָר *palm*.

עִירוּ 1 pr.n.m. **Iru.**

עִירִי 1 pr.n.m. **Iri.**

עֵירֹם 10.0.1 adj.—עֵרֹם (עֵרוֹם); pl. עֵירֻמִּם—**1. naked,** of person Gn 3_{7}. **2.** as noun, **a. naked one** Ezk 18_{7}. **b. nakedness** Dt 28_{48}. → עור III *be bare*.

עִירָם 2 pr.n.m. **Iram.**

עִיר נָחָשׁ 1.0.3 pl.n. **Irnahash.**

עִיר שֶׁמֶשׁ 1 pl.n. **Ir-shemesh.**

עַיִשׁ 1 pr.n.f. **Aldebaran,** a star, or, less prob., **the Great Bear** constellation Jb 38_{32}.

עַיַּת 1 pl.n. **Aiath.**

עַכְבּוֹר 7.0.0.8 pr.n.m. **Achbor.**

עַכָּבִישׁ 2.0.1 n.[m.] **spider** Is 59_{5}=CD 5_{14} Jb 8_{14}.

עַכְבָּר 6.0.1 n.m.—pl. cstr. עַכְבְּרֵי; sf. עַכְבְּרֵיכֶם—**mouse** Lv 11_{29} 1 S 6_{5} Is 66_{17}.

עַכּוֹ 1.0.1 pl.n. **Acco.**

*[עָכוֹן] 0.0.1 pl. **Achon.**

עָכוֹר 5.0.2 pl.n. **Achor.**

עָכָן 6 pr.n.m. **Achan.**

עכס I 1 vb.—**Pi.** 1 Impf. תְּעַכַּסְנָה—**walk with jingling anklets, shake bangles** Is 3_{16} (+ בְּ *with* feet). → עֶכֶס *anklet*.

*עכס II vb. **Qal, tie** Pr 7_{22} (if em. כְּעֶכֶס אֶל־מוּסַר אֱוִיל *as [one wearing] anklets to the disciplining of a fool* to כַּעְכֹּס אֶל־מוֹסֵר אַיָּל *as one ties a deer to a trap*).

*עכס III 1.0.1 vb.—**Pi.** 1.0.1 Impf. תְּעַכַּסְנָה, Q יעכסו (or qal)—**hop, toddle,** of persons Is 3_{16} 11QPs^a^ 22_{5}, deer Pr 7_{22} (if em. כְּעֶכֶס אֶל־מוּסַר אֱוִיל *as [one wearing] anklets to the disciplining of a fool* to כַּעְכֹּס אֶל־מוֹסֵר אַיָּל *as a deer hops into a trap*).

*[עכס] IV vb. **Qal, run, hurry** Pr 7_{22} (if em. כְּעֶכֶס אֶל־מוּסַר אֱוִיל *as [one wearing] anklets to the disciplining of a fool* to כַּעְכֹּס אֶל־מוֹסֵר אַיָּל *as a deer hurries into a trap*).

עֶכֶס 2 n.[m.]—pl. עֲכָסִים—**anklet,** worn by women Is 3_{18}. → עכס I *walk with jingling anklets*.

עַכְסָה 5 pr.n.f. **Achsah.**

עכר 14.1.1 vb.—**Qal** 12 Pf. עֲכַרְתֶּם, עָכַר; impf. יַעְכָּרְךָ; ptc. עֹכֵר—**trouble, bring trouble upon** (accus.) someone Gn 34_{30}, the land 1 S 14_{29}.

Ni. 2.1.1 Pf. נֶעְכַּר; impf. Si יעכר; ptc. נֶעְכֶּרֶת—**1. be stirred up,** of people 4QM8 4_{8} (+ עַל *against*), pain Ps 39_{3}. **2. be troubled,** בִּתְבוּאַת רָשָׁע נֶעְכָּרֶת *in the income of the wicked it is troubled,* i.e. there is trouble Pr 15_{6}. → עִכְרוֹן *trouble,* עִכְרִים *trouble.*

עָכָר 1 pr.n.m. **Achar.**

*[עִכָּרוֹן] 0.1 n.m. **trouble** Si 7_{16}. → עכר *trouble.*

*[עִכְרִים] 1 n.[m.]pl.—sf. עֹכְרָי—**trouble** Jg 11_{35}. → עכר *trouble.*

עָכְרָן 5 pr.n.m. **Ochran.**

* **[עַכְשָׁו]** 0.0.1 adv. **now** 4QpsJub^a 2.2$_7$.

עַכְשׁוּב 1 n.[m.] **viper** Ps 140$_4$.

* **[עָל]** I 1 n.m. **nourishment,** עַל שְׂפָתָיו *nourishment of,* i.e. provided by, *his lips* Pr 16$_{21}$ (if em. מֶתֶק שְׂפָתַיִם *sweetness of lips*). → עול I *give suck.*

עַל II, see עַל III *High One.*

עַל I 5777.203.c.1500.25 prep.—עֲלֵי־; sf. עָלַי, עָלֶיךָ, עֲלֵיהֶם—**1.** in spatial senses, **a.** simple location, (1) **upon, on,** כַּדָּהּ עַל־שִׁכְמָהּ *her jar was upon her shoulder* Gn 24$_{15}$. (2) **in,** עַל־מְקוֹם דַּם הָאָשָׁם *in the place of the blood of the guilt offering* Lv 14$_{28}$. **b.** goal, target, direction, (1) **upon, on(to),** וַיַּעֲלוּ עַל־גַּג הַמִּגְדָּל *and they went up onto the roof of the tower* Jg 9$_{51}$. (2) **in(to),** וָאֶתֵּן אֶת־הַכּוֹס עַל־כַּף פַּרְעֹה *and I placed the cup into Pharaoh's hand* Gn 40$_{11}$. (3) **to,** as equivalent of אֶל, with הלך *go* 1 K 20$_{43}$, בוא *come* 1 C 12$_{24}$, שׁוב *go back* Pr 26$_{11}$. **c.** vicinity, (1) **beside, by, next to, near, at, in the presence of, before,** הוּא עֹמֵד עֲלֵיהֶם *he stood by them* Gn 18$_8$, עַל־פֶּתַח רֵעִי אָרָבְתִּי *at the door of my neighbour I lay in wait* Jb 31$_9$. (2) **about, around,** חוֹמָה הָיוּ עָלֵינוּ *they were a wall about us* 1 S 25$_{16}$. **d.** over, i.e. (1) **above,** בְּעַנְנִי עָנָן עַל־הָאָרֶץ *when I bring clouds over the earth* Gn 9$_{14}$. (2) **throughout, across,** פֶּן־נָפוּץ עַל־פְּנֵי כָל־הָאָרֶץ *lest we be scattered over the face of all the earth* Gn 11$_4$. **2.** location of feelings, perceptions, states, **a. upon, on,** תִּכְבַּד הָעֲבֹדָה עַל־הָאֲנָשִׁים *let the work be heavy upon the men* Ex 5$_9$. **b. within,** וַתִּתְעַטֵּף עָלַי רוּחִי *and my spirit faints within me* Ps 143$_4$. **c. to,** יֶעֱרַב עָלָיו שִׂיחִי *may my mediation be pleasing to him* Ps 104$_{34}$. **3.** direction of the mind, disposition, **a. upon, on, in,** with ראה *look* Ex 5$_{21}$, נחם ni. *have compassion* Ps 90$_{13}$, סמך ni. *rely* Ps 71$_6$, בטח *trust* Ps 31$_{15}$. **b. to,** as equivalent of אֶל, with verb דבר pi. *speak* Ho 12$_{11}$, שׁמע *listen* Jr 23$_{16}$. **4.** of hostility, opposition, **a. upon,** with שׁפך *pour* wrath Ezk 7$_8$. **b. against,** הִנְנִי עָלַיִךְ *behold, I am against you* Ezk 5$_8$. **c. at,** with חרק *gnash* teeth Ps 37$_{12}$. **5.** of culpability, moral condition, **upon,** i.e. **against, accounted to,** וְהֵבֵאתָ עָלֵינוּ אָשָׁם *and you would have brought guilt upon us* Gn 26$_{10}$, חֲמָסִי עָלֶיךָ *my wrong,* i.e. the wrong done to me, *is upon you* Gn 16$_5$. **6.** of obligation, duty, **a. upon, on,** עָלֶיךָ הַדָּבָר *the task is upon you,* i.e. your responsibility Ezr 10$_4$. **b. in the charge of, to (the keeping of),** וַיִּטֹּשׁ הַצֹּאן עַל־שֹׁמֵר *and he left the sheep in the charge of a keeper* 1 S 17$_{20}$. **7.** of addition, accompaniment, **a. (in addition) to, besides,** עַל־עֹלַת הַתָּמִיד יֵעָשֶׂה *it shall be offered in addition to the continual burnt offering* Nm 28$_{15}$. **b. (together) with,** לֹא תֹאכְלוּ עַל־הַדָּם *you shall not eat (flesh) together with the blood* Lv 19$_{26}$. **8.** of excess, comparison, **above, over, beyond, in excess of, (more) than,** הָעֹדְפִים עַל־הַלְוִיִּם *those over and above the Levites* Nm 3$_{46}$, יָמִים עַל־שָׁנָה *(in a few) days more than a year* Is 32$_{10}$. **9.** of pre-eminence, exaltation, **above,** מֶלֶךְ גָּדוֹל עַל־כָּל־אֱלֹהִים *a great king above all gods* Ps 95$_3$. **10. over,** i.e. **in charge of,** וַיַּפְקִדֵהוּ עַל־בֵּיתוֹ *and he appointed him to be in charge of his house* Gn 39$_4$. **11.** of benefit, **a. for (the sake of), to (the advantage/disadvantage of),** הִמָּלֵט עַל־נַפְשֶׁךָ *flee for your life* Gn 19$_{17}$, כָּל־תַּגְמוּלוֹהִי עָלָי *all his benefits to me* Ps 116$_{12}$. **b. for,** i.e. **on behalf of,** אֲדַבֵּר עָלֶיךָ אֶל־הַמֶּלֶךְ *I will speak on your behalf to the king* 1 K 2$_{18}$. **12.** of cause, ground, **a. on account of, because of, over,** הִנְּךָ מֵת עַל־הָאִשָּׁה *behold, you are a dead man on account of the woman* Gn 20$_3$, יָשִׂישׂ עָלַיִךְ *he will rejoice over you* Zp 3$_{17}$. **b. for,** וַיִּתְאַבֵּל עַל־בְּנוֹ *and he mourned for his son* Gn 37$_{34}$. **13. concerning, about, of, with regard to,** כֹּה־אָמַר יי׳ עַל־הַנְּבִאִים *thus says Y. concerning the prophets* Jr 14$_{15}$. **14. according to,** עַל שֵׁם אֲחֵיהֶם יִקָּרְאוּ *they shall be called according to the name of their brothers* Gn 48$_6$. **15.** of instrument, **by (means of), with, through,** עַל־חַרְבְּךָ תִחְיֶה *by your sword you shall live* Gn 27$_{40}$. **16.** as conj., **a.** עַל alone, (1) **because, for** Ps 119$_{136}$. (2) perh. **although** Is 53$_9$. **b.** עַל־דְּבַר אֲשֶׁר **because (of the fact that)** Dt 22$_{24}$. **17.** כְּעַל, **a. according to** Is 63$_7$. **b. as concerning, as of** 2 C 32$_{19}$. **18.** מֵעַל, **a. from (upon), from (within)** Gn 8$_3$ Jg 16$_{19}$. **b. from (beside), from (being with)** Gn 13$_{11}$. **c. (from) above, (from) over** Nm 12$_{10}$. **d. from (being burdensome upon)** Ex 18$_{22}$. **e. from (against)** 2 S 10$_{14}$. **f.** of excess, comparison, **above, beyond, (more) than** Ec 5$_7$. **g.** of pre-eminence, **above** Est 3$_1$. **19.** מֵעַל לְ, **a. upon** Ne 12$_{31}$. **b. (from)**

above, (from) over, Ezk 1_{25}. **c. beside, by** 2 C 26_{19}.

*עַל II 8 n.m.—עַל; sf. עָלָיו—**1. height, firmament** 1 S 2_{10} Ho 11_7 Jb 36_{33}; שָׁמַיִם מֵעַל *heaven from the height,* i.e. heaven above Gn 27_{39}. **2.** as adv., **a. on high** 2 S 23_1. **b. upwards,** i.e. to Y. Ho 7_{16}. → עלה I *go up.*

*עַל III 7 n.m.—עָל; cstr. עַל—**High One, Most High, Sublime One,** title for Y. (syn. with עֶלְיוֹן *Most High,* or a short form of it; cf. also עֵלִי II *Most High*) 2 S 23_1 Is 59_{18} Ps 7_{11} 18_{42} 68_{30} 141_3; עַל־יִשְׂרָאֵל *High One of Israel* Ps 68_{35}. → עלה I *go up.*

*[עַל] IV 6 n.[m.]—cstr. עַל; sf. עָלָיו; pl. sf. עֲלֵיהֶם—**1. deed, work** Is 59_{18} Pr 14_{14} Ezr 1_6. **2. task** Jb 37_{15} (if em. עֲלֵיהֶם *upon them* to עָלֵיהֶם *their tasks*). **3. cause** Jr $32_{31.31}$ Jb 37_{16}. → עלל I *do.*

עֹל I 40.6.6 n.m.—cstr. עֹל; sf. עֻלְּכֶם, עֻלּוֹ; pl. cstr. Si עלי—**yoke,** for cattle Dt 21_3; usu. for humans, in ref. to servitude Gn 27_{40} Lv 26_{13}.

*[עֹל] II 1 n.[m.] (byform of עָוֶל)—**iniquity, wickedness** Pr 10_{12} (if em. עַל *over*); בן על *son of iniquity* Ps $89_{23(4QPs)}$ (MT עַוְלָה *injustice*).

*[עֹל] III 1 n.[m.]—sf. עולם—**harm, injury** Mc 2_9.

עֻלָּא 1 pr.n.m. **Ulla.**

עַלְבוֹן, see אֲבִי־עַלְבוֹן *Abi-albon.*

[עִלֵּג] 1 adj.—pl. עִלְּגִים—**stammering,** as noun, **stammerer** Is 32_4.

עלה I 894.6.73.1 vb.—**Qal** 617.4.48 Pf. עָלָה, עָלִיתָ; impf. יַעֲלֶה; + waw וָאַעַל, (וַיַּעֲלֶה) וַיַּעַל (יַעַל); impv. עֲלֵה, עֲלִי, עֲלוּ; ptc. עֹלֶה, עֹלָה, עֹלִים, עֹלֹת; inf. abs. עָלֹה; cstr. עֲלוֹת—**1. go up, come up, a.** from one (lower) place to another (higher) Gn 13_1; specif. up mountain Ex 19_{12}. **b.** for specif. purpose: sexual intercourse Gn 49_4, war, conquest Jos 19_{47}, worship, sacrifice at sanctuary 1 S 1_3, officiating at altar Ex 20_{26}, to mount horse Jr 46_4. **c. go up from,** i. e. **withdraw** 1 K 15_{19}, **escape** CD 4_{18}. **2. ascend, rise,** of smoke Gn 19_{28}, fire Jg 6_{21}, cloud 1 K 18_{44}, dawn Gn 19_{15}, border following rising terrain Jos 15_3. **3. rise, spring up,** of river Is 8_7, sea Jr 51_{42}, well Nm 21_{17}. **4. spring up, grow,** of vegetation Gn 40_{10} 41_5, horn of animal Dn 8_3; of land, **be overgrown with** thorns, etc. Is 32_{13} Pr 24_{31}. **5. rise (in importance)** Dt 28_{43}, **excel** Pr 31_{29}. **6.** of battle, **increase (in intensity)** 1 K 22_{35}||2 C 18_{34}. **7.** of anger, **arise,** i.e. **be kindled** 2 S 11_{20}. **8.** of sacrifice, **be offered** Lv 2_{12}. **9.** of thoughts, **go up into, enter** one's mind 2 K 12_5. **10. be entered, be inserted** in book 1 C 27_{24}.

Preps.: (1) בְּ *in(to), on (to)* persons Ex 7_{29}, mountain Ex 19_{12}, house 1 S 1_7, land 2 K 17_5, battle 1 S 29_9; *by (means of)* steps Ex 20_{26}, way Dt 1_{22}; *with* weeping Is 15_5, shout Ps 47_6. (2) מִן *from* place Gn 13_1. (3) אֶל *to* Y. Ex 2_{23}, person 2 K 1_9, house 1 S 15_{34}, mountain Ex 19_{23}; *against* people Nm 13_{31}, land Is 36_{10}. (4) עַל *to* persons 1 S 14_{10}, altar Ex 20_{26}; *upon, onto, over* persons Ezk 44_{17}, heart 2 K 12_5, roof Jos 2_8; *against* nation 1 K 15_{17}||2 C 16_1. (5) מֵעַל *from (upon), from (beside)* person Gn 17_{22}, altar Jg 13_{20}. (6) עִם *with* Gn 50_9. (7) אֶת *with* Gn 50_7. (8) לִפְנֵי *before* Jon 1_2. (9) אַחֲרֵי *after* 1 S 14_{12}. (10) ה- of direction, *to, on to* city Jos 10_{36}, mountain Ex 24_{12}, heaven Dt 30_{12}. With accus. noun, וַיַּעֲלוּ הָעִיר *and they went up to the city* 1 S 9_{14}, וַיַּעֲלוּ דֶּרֶךְ הַבָּשָׁן *and they went up (by means of) the road to Bashan* Nm 21_{33}.

Ni. 18.0.3 Pf. נַעֲלָה, נַעֲלֵיתָ; impf. יֵעָלֶה; impv. הֵעָלוּ; inf. הֵעָלוֹת (הֵעָלֹתוֹ)—**1. be taken up, be lifted up,** of cloud Ex 40_{36} (+ מֵעַל *from over*). **2. take oneself away, remove oneself, withdraw** Nm 16_{24} (+ מִסָּבִיב לְ *from around*) 2 S 2_{27} (+ מֵאַחֲרֵי *from [following]*) Jr 37_5 (+ מֵעַל *from [beside]*). **3. be exalted,** of Y. Ps 97_9 (+ עַל *above*). **4. be taken up** upon (עַל) the tongue, i.e. **be talked about** Ezk 36_3. **5. be brought up** Ezr 1_{11} (+ מִן *from,* לְ *to*).

Pi. 0.0.2 Pf. עליה, עלו—**1. exalt** corner-stone GnzPs 1_{18}. **2. praise** words and works 11QPs^a 28_6.

Hi. 255.1.20.1 Pf. הֶעֱלָה, הֶעֱלִיתָ (הֶעֱלִיתָ); impf. יַעֲלֶה; + waw וַיַּעֲלֶה, וַיַּעַל (וַיַּעַל); impv. הַעַל, הַעֲלִי, הַעֲלוּ; ptc. מַעֲלֶה, מַעֲלָה, מַעֲלִים; inf. abs. הַעֲלֵה; cstr. הַעֲלוֹת—**1. bring up, take up, lead up, draw up, carry up** persons Ex 3_8, animals Ex 8_1, ark 1 S 7_1, chariots 2 C 1_{17}, tribute 2 K 17_4, water Is 8_7. Preps.: לְ *to* Jg 16_8; בְּ *in(to)* Ezk 32_3, *by (means of)* Hb 1_{15}, *with* 1 C 15_{28}; מִן *from* Gn 50_{24}; אֶל *to, into* Gn 50_{24} 2 K 10_{15}; עַל *upon, over* Ezk 26_{19}, *into, onto* 1 K 20_{33}, *against* Jr 50_9; ה- of direction, *to* Jos 2_6; with accus. noun, הַעַל אֹתָם הֹר הָהָר *bring them up to Mount Hor* Nm 20_{25}. **2. cause to rise, cause to ascend,** obj. mist Jr 10_{13}||51_{16} (+ מִן

from), stink Am 4_{10} (+ בְּ *into* nostrils). **3. cast up** dust on (עַל) head Jos 7_6. **4. bring upon** (עַל), i.e. **clothe with, adorn with, overlay with** 2 S 1_{24} Ezk 37_6 Am 8_{10}. **5a. bring** sickness **against** (עַל) Dt 28_{61}. **b. bring** healing **to** (לְ) Jr 33_6. **6. bring up into mind,** i.e. **set thoughts upon,** with אֶל *into* mind Ezk 14_4, var. עַל Ezk 14_3. **7. bring up,** i.e. **stir up, rouse** wrath Ezk 24_8. **8. bring up,** i.e. **rear** cub Ezk 19_3. **9. bring up,** i.e. **chew** the cud Lv 11_3||Dt 14_6. **10. cause to go up,** i.e. **offer** burnt offering Gn 8_{20} (+ בְּ *upon* altar) Ex 40_{29} (+ עַל *upon* altar), peace offerings Jg 20_{26} (+ לִפְנֵי *before* Y.), sacrifice 1 C 29_{21} (+ לְ *to* Y.); with double accus., **offer** someone or something **as a burnt offering** Jg 11_{31} 1 S 6_{14}. **11. cause to go up,** i.e. **set up,** or perh. **light lamp,** Ex 25_{37}. **12a. raise up, exalt** someone 1QH 11_{20} (+ לְ *to*) 13_{22} (+ מִן *from*). **b. promote, advance** someone 1QS 5_{24}. **13. raise,** i.e. **erect,** in building 2 C 32_5. **14a. raise,** i.e. **establish** a levy 1 K 5_{27}. **b. raise,** i.e. **establish** as (לְ) a levy 1 K 9_{21}||2 C 8_8. **15. take away, remove (from life)** Ps 102_{25}.

Ho. 3 Pf. הָעֲלָה, הָעֳלְתָה—**1. be led away** Na 2_8. **2. be entered, be inserted** in (עַל) book 2 C 20_{34}. **3.** of bull, **be offered** upon (עַל) altar Jg 6_{28}.

Htp. 1.1 Impf. יִתְעַל—**1. lift oneself up** in (בְּ) armour Jr 51_3. **2. exalt oneself** in (בְּ) folly Si $30_{13(Bmg)}$.

→ עַל I *upon,* II *height,* III *High One,* עָלֶה *leaf,* עֹלָה I *burnt offering,* II *ascent,* מַעַל II *height,* מֹעַל *raising,* מַעֲלָה I *step,* II *extolment,* מַעֲלֶה *ascent,* עֱלִי II *coming up,* עֱלִי *pestle,* עִלִּי *upper,* עֲלִיָּה I *upper chamber,* II *upper part (of thigh),* עֶלְיוֹן *high,* תְּעָלָה I *conduit,* II *healing,* עֶלִי II *Exalted One.*

*עלה II 10.0.2 vb.—**Qal** 8.0.2 Pf. עָלָה; impf. תַּעֲלֶה; + waw וַתַּעַל; ptc. עֹלֶה; inf. עֲלוֹת—**exceed all limits,** of Zion Is 57_8, king Dn 11_{23}, uproar Ps 74_{23}, anger 2 S 11_{20} Ps 78_{21} (+ בְּ *against*).

Hi. 2 Impf. יַעֲלֶה; inf. הַעֲלוֹת—**cause anger to exceed all limits** Ezk 24_8 Pr 15_1.

*עלה III 8.0.2 vb.—**Qal** 6.0.2 Pf. עָלָה; impf. תַּעֲלֶה; inf. עֲלוֹת—**boil,** of anger 2 S 11_{20} Ps 78_{21} (+ בְּ *against*), spirit, i.e. anger Ec 10_4 (+ עַל *against*).

Hi. 2 Impf. יַעֲלֶה; inf. הַעֲלוֹת—**cause anger to boil** Ezk 24_8 Pr 15_1.

עָלֶה 19.2.5 n.m.—cstr. עֲלֵה; sf. עָלֵהוּ; pl. cstr. עֲלֵי; sf. Si עליך—**leaf, leaves, foliage** Gn 3_7 8_{11} Jr 17_8. → עלה I *go up.*

*[עָלָה] n.f. **co-wife,** יְצוּעַ עָלָה *couch of a co-wife* Gn 49_4 (if em. יְצוּעִי עָלָה *my couch, he went up*).

*[עָלָה] 0.0.2 n.f.—pl. cstr. עלות—**charge, complaint,** made by husband against wife 11QT $65_{7.12}$. → עלל I *do.*

עֹלָה I 286.1.65 n.f.—cstr. עֹלַת; sf. עֹלָתוֹ; pl. עֹלוֹת; cstr. עֹלוֹת; sf. עוֹלֹתֵיהֶם, עֹלֹתֶיךָ—**burnt offering,** sacrifice entirely consumed by fire, as obj. of עלה hi. *cause to go up,* i.e. offer Gn 8_{20}, עשׂה *do,* i.e. offer Ex 10_{25}, קרב hi. *bring near,* i.e. offer Lv 7_8, קטר hi. *burn* 2 K 16_{13}; in ref. to human sacrifice Gn 22_2. → עלה I *go up.*

[עֹלָה] II 1—n.f. pl. sf. Qr עֹלוֹתָיו (Kt עלותו)—**ascent, stairway,** to gate Ezk 40_{26}. → עלה I *go up.*

[עֹלָה] III, see עַוְלָה *injustice.*

*עַלְו n.[m.] **unjust one** 1 S 2_{10} (if em. עָלָיו *against him* [Qr; Kt עלו]).

*עַלְוָה I 1 n.f. (perh. metathesis of עַוְלָה) **injustice** Ho 10_9 (mss עַוְלָה).

*עַלְוָה II 1 n.f. **hatred** Ho 10_9.

*עַלְוָה III 1 n.f. **violence** Ho 10_9.

*עַלְוָה IV 1 n.f. **rebellion** Ho 10_9.

עַלְוָה V 2 pr.n.m. **Alvah.**

[עֲלוּמִים] I 5.0.2 n.f.pl.—sf. עֲלוּמָיו—**youth, youthful vigour** Is 54_4 Ps 89_{46} Jb 20_{11} 33_{25}; perh. **youthful sins** Ps 90_8. → עלם III *be mature.*

*[עֲלוּמִים] II 1 n.[m.]pl.—sf. עֲלוּמַיִךְ—**slavery, bondage** Is 54_4.

עַלְוָן 2 pr.n.m. **Alvan.**

עֲלוּקָה I 1 n.f. **leech** Pr 30_{15}.

*עֲלוּקָה II 1 n.f. **erotic passion** Pr 30_{15}.

עלז I 16 vb. (byform of עלץ I)—**Qal** 16 Impf. יַעֲלֹז, יַעְלְזוּ (יַעֲלֹזוּ); + waw וָאֶעֱלֹז, וַיַּעֲלֹז; impv. עֲלֹזִי, עִלְזוּ; inf. לַעֲלוֹז—**exult** 2 S 1_{20} Is 23_{12} Zp 3_{14} (+ בְּ *with* heart). → עָלֵז I *exultant,* עַלִּיז *exultant,* עֲלִיזָה *exultation;* cf. עלס I *rejoice,* עלץ I *exult.*

*עלז II 1 vb.—**Qal** 1 Impf. יַעֲלֹזוּ—**suffer pangs, have colic, be feverish** Jr 51_{39}.

*עלז III 4 vb.—**Qal** 4 Impf. יַעֲלֹזוּ, Qr mss תַּעֲלֹזוּ; inf. לַעֲלוֹז—**be proud** 2 S 1_2 Is 23_{12} Jr 50_{11} Ps 94_3. → עָלֵז II *proud.*

עָלֵז I 1 adj. **exultant,** as noun, **exultant one** Is 5_{14}. → עלז I *exult.*

***עָלֵז** II 1 adj. **proud,** as noun, **proud one** Is 5_{14}. → עלז III *be proud.*

***עָלֵז** III 1 adj. **pestilent,** as noun, **pestilent one** Is 5_{14}.

*[**עֲלָזָה**] n.f. **impatience** Jb 36_{21} (if em. עַל־זֶה *this*).

עֲלָטָה 4 n.f. **darkness** Gn 15_{17} Ezk $12_{6.7.12}$.

עֵלִי I 33.0.1 pr.n.m. **Eli.**

*[**עֶלִי**] II n.m. **Exalted One, Most High,** as title for Y. (alw. if em. עַל *upon*) Dt 33_{12} 1 S 2_{10} Ps $7_{9.11}$ 13_{6} 32_{5} 57_{3} 62_{8} 86_{13} 106_{7} Jb 29_{4} Lm 3_{61}. → עלה I *go up.*

[**עִלִּי**] 2 adj.—f.s. עִלִּית; pl. עִלִּיּוֹת—**1. upper,** גֻּלֹּת עִלִּיּוֹת *upper springs* Jos 15_{19}. **2.** fem. sg. as noun, **upper place,** גֻּלֹּת עִלִּית *springs of the upper place* Jg 1_{15}. → עלה I *go up.*

***עֲלִי** I n.[m.] **pupil (of eye)** Gn 49_{22} (if em. עֲלֵי *beside* a spring).

*[**עֲלִי**] II n.[m.] **coming up,** of storm Jb 36_{33} (if em. עָלָיו *concerning it* to עֲלִיּוֹ *its coming*). → עלה I *go up.*

עֱלִי I 1 n.[m.] **pestle** Pr 27_{22}. → עלה I *go up.*

*[**עֱלִי**] II 1 n.[m.]—**1. crucible** Pr 27_{22}. **2. cauldron** Jb 30_{17} (if em. נִקַּר מֵעָלָי *bores [them] from me* to נִקְדוּ מֵעֱלִי *they are inflamed more than a cauldron*).

[**עַלְיָה**] 1 pr.n.m. **Aliah.**

עַלְיָה, see עֲלִיָּה II *upper part (of thigh).*

עֲלִיָּה I 20.0.4 n.f.—Q עליאה; cstr. עֲלִיַּת; sf. עֲלִיָּתוֹ; pl. עֲלִיּוֹת; sf. עֲלִיּוֹתָיו—**1. upper chamber, roof chamber** of Y. in heaven Ps 104_{3}, temple 1 C 28_{12}, private house 1 K 17_{19}, gate house 2 S 19_{1}; of fortress, or perh. **storey** or **staircase** 3QTr 10_{1}. **2.** appar. **ascent** 2 C 9_{4}. → עלה I *go up.*

*[**עֲלִיָּה**] II n.f. **upper part (of thigh)** 1 S 9_{24} (if em. הֶעָלֶיהָ appar. *that which was upon it* to הָעֲלִיָּה or הָעַלְיָה). → עלה I *go up.*

*[**עֲלִיָּה**] III 0.0.0.1 pr.n.f. **Alijah.**

*[**עֲלִיָּהוּ**] 0.0.0.6 pr.n.[m.] **Alijah.**

[**עֲלִיּוֹ**], see עֲלִיָּהוּ *Alijah.*

עֶלְיוֹן 53.20.39.1 adj.—f.s. עֶלְיוֹנָה; m.pl. Q עליונים; f.pl. עֶלְיוֹנֹת—**1a. high, highest, excellent,** לְתִתְּךָ עֶלְיוֹן עַל כָּל־הַגּוֹיִם *to make you high above all the nations* Dt 26_{19}, בכל מעשיך היה עליון *in all your deeds be excellent* Si 30_{31}. **b.** as noun, **highest (one),** עֶלְיוֹן לְמַלְכֵי־אָרֶץ *the highest of the kings of the earth* Ps 89_{28}. **2a. upper, uppermost,** of Beth-horon Jos 16_{5}, gate 2 K 15_{35}, house Ne 3_{25}, pool 2 K 18_{17}||Is 36_{2}. **b.** fem. sg. as noun, **upper(most) storey** Ezk 41_{7}. **3a. most high, supreme,** of Y., עֶלְיוֹן עַל־כָּל־הָאָרֶץ *most high over all the earth* Ps 83_{19}. **b.** as title for Y., **Highest, Most High** Nm 24_{16}; אֵל עֶלְיוֹן *God Most High* Gn 14_{18}, יי עֶלְיוֹן *Y. Most High* Ps 7_{18}. → עלה I *go up.*

[**עַלִּיז**] 7 adj.—f.s. עַלִּיזָה; m.pl. עַלִּיזִים; cstr. עַלִּיזֵי—**1. exultant,** or perh. **proud,** of city Is 22_{2}. **2.** as noun, **exultant one, a.** masc. Is 13_{3} 24_{8} Zp 3_{11}. **b.** fem., in ref. to city Is 23_{7}. → עלז I *exult.*

*[**עֲלִיזָה**] n.f. **exultation, carousal** Jb 36_{21} (if em. עַל־זֶה *this*). → עלז I *exult.*

עֲלִיל I 1 n.[m.] **crucible,** or less prob. **furnace,** for refining silver Ps 12_{7}. → עלל II *insert.*

***עֲלִיל** II 1 adj. **manifest,** כֶּסֶף צָרוּף בַּעֲלִיל לָאָרֶץ *refined silver, manifest to the world* Ps 12_{7}.

עֲלִילָה 24.0.13 n.f.—pl. עֲלִלוֹת; cstr. עֲלִילֹת; sf. עֲלִילוֹתָיו, עֲלִילוֹתָם (Q עלילותיהם)—**1. deed, action, a.** of Y. Is 12_{4}. **b.** of spirit of light 1QS 4_{1}. **c.** of humans 1 S 2_{3}, as evil Ezk 20_{43} 1QH 6_{9}. **2. wantonness, caprice,** עֲלִילֹת דְּבָרִים *wantonness of words,* i.e. words making (groundless) charges Dt 22_{14}. → עלל I *do.*

עֲלִילִיָּה 1.0.1 n.f.—Q העליליה—**deed** Jr 32_{19} 1QH 8_{17}. → עלל I *do.*

עליליה, see עֲלִילִיָּה *deed.*

*[**עֲלִיץ**] adj. **exultant, arrogant,** of wicked Ps 37_{35} (if em. עָרִיץ *ruthless*). → עלץ I *exult.*

*[**עֲלִיצָה**] n.f. **gullet, throat** Hb 3_{14} (if em. לַהֲפִיצֵנִי עֲלִיצֻתָם *to disperse me; their exultation* to יַפְצִין עֲלִיצָתָם *they open their gullets*).

[**עֲלִיצוּת**] 1 n.f.—sf. עֲלִיצֻתָם—**exultation** Hb 3_{14}. → עלץ I *exult.*

עַל־כֵּן *therefore,* see כֵּן I *thus.*

עלל I 16.0.1 vb.—**Qal** 0.0.1 Pf. 2mpl עללחן—**do something** (לְ of obj.) 5/6Ḥev 49_{5}.

Poel 7 Pf. עוֹלַלְתָּ; impv. עוֹלֵל; ptc. מְעוֹלֵל—**deal with, deal severely with, treat violently** (לְ of obj.) Lm $1_{22.22}$ (+ עַל *on account of*) 2_{20}.

Poal 1 Pf. עֹולַל—**be dealt out,** of pain Lm 1$_{12}$ (+ לְ *to*).

Htp. 7 Pf. הִתְעַלַּלְתִּי, הִתְעַלֵּל; + waw וַיִּתְעַלְּלוּ—**deal wantonly with, make sport of** (בְּ of obj.) Ex 10$_2$; **abuse (sexually)** Jg 19$_{25}$.

Htpo. 1 inf. הִתְעוֹלֵל—**practise, occupy oneself with, do in pretence,** obj. deeds (עֲלִלוֹת) Ps 141$_4$.

→ עֲלִילָה *deed,* עֲלִילִיָּה *deed,* מַעֲלִיל *deed,* מַעֲלָל *deed,* עַל IV *deed,* עִלָּה *charge,* תַּעֲלוּלִים *wantonness.*

עלל II 1 vb.—**Po.** 1 + waw וְעוֹלַלְתִּי—**insert, thrust** horn in (בְּ) dust Jb 16$_{15}$. → עֲלִיל I *crucible.*

עלל III 1 vb.—**Po.** 1 Ptc. מְעוֹלֵל—**act the child,** perh. ptc. as noun, **child(ren),** עַמִּי נֹגְשָׂיו מְעוֹלֵל *my people, its oppressor is acting the child* or *children are its oppressors* Is 3$_{12}$. → עוֹלֵל *child,* עוֹלָל *child,* עֲוִיל *child,* תַּעֲלוּל *child.*

עלל IV 5.1 vb.—**Qal** 0.1 Ptc. עולל—**glean** Si 30$_{25}$ (+ אח[ר] *after*).

Po. 5 Impf. תְּעוֹלֵל; + waw וַיְעֹלְלֻהוּ; inf. abs. עוֹלֵל—**glean, pick bare** vineyard Lv 19$_{10}$, remnant of Israel Jr 6$_9$ (+ כְּ *as* vine); without obj. Dt 24$_{21}$ (+ אַחֲרֵי *after*).
→ עוֹלֵלוֹת *gleanings.*

*עלל V 1 vb.—**Po.** 1 + waw וְעוֹלַלְתִּי—**sink** horn in (בְּ) dust Jb 16$_{15}$.

*עלל VI 1 vb.—**Qal** 1 Pf. עַל—**enter, come** Ho 8$_9$ (if em. עָלוּ *they have gone up* to (עָלוּ) Jb 37$_{22}$.

עֹלֵלוֹת 6.0.3 n.f.pl.—cstr. pl. עֹלְלוֹת—**gleaning(s)** of grapes Jg 8$_2$, olives Is 17$_6$. → עלל IV *glean.*

עלם I 28.7.8 vb.—**Qal** 1.1 Ptc. pass. עֲלֻמֵנוּ—**hide,** pass. ptc. as noun, **hidden thing, secret,** in ref. to sin Ps 90$_8$.

Ni. 11.2.5 Pf. נֶעְלַם, נֶעֶלְמָה; ptc. נֶעְלָם, נַעֲלָמִים—**1. be hidden, be concealed** from (מִן) Lv 4$_{13}$ 1 K 10$_3$||2 C 9$_2$. **2.** perh. **be obscured** as to one's senses, **be overcome** by intoxication, **become unconscious** Na 3$_{11}$. **3.** ptc. as noun, **a. one who hides oneself (craftily), dissembler** Ps 26$_4$. **b. hidden thing, secret** Ec 12$_{14}$. **c. secret gift** Si 46$_{19}$.

Hi. 10.2.1 Pf. הֶעְלִימוּ, הֶעְלִים; impf. תַּעְלִים (תַּעְלֵם), יַעְלִימוּ; impv. Si העלים; ptc. מַעְלִים; inf. abs. הַעְלֵם—**1. hide** the eyes Lv 20$_4$ (+ מִן *from* someone) 1 S 12$_3$ (+ בְּ *with* a bribe), the ear, i.e. close it Lm 3$_{56}$ (+ לְ *to* cry), counsel Jb 42$_3$. **2. hide oneself** Ps 10$_1$.

Htp. 6.2.2 Impf. יִתְעַלָּם, תִּתְעַלַּם־ (תִּתְעַלָּם); + waw וְהִתְעַלַּמְתָּ; inf. הִתְעַלֵּם—**hide oneself from** (מִן) Dt 22$_1$ Ps 55$_2$.

→ תַּעֲלֻמָה *hidden thing,* (?) עַלְמוּת *hiddenness,* (?) עֶלֶם II *secret,* נַעֲלָם *bribe.*

*עלם II 3 vb.—**Hi.** 1 Ptc. מַעְלִים—**make dark, obscure** counsel Jb 42$_3$.

Htp. 2 Impf. יִתְעַלָּם־, תִּתְעַלָּם—**1. be darkened, be black,** of snow Jb 6$_{16}$. **2. darken oneself, blind oneself from** (מִן), i.e. to, a needy relative Is 58$_7$.

→ עוֹלָם II *darkness,* (?) עֶלֶם II *secret, darkness,* עַלְמָה II *darkness.*

*עלם III 1 vb.—**Ni.** 1 Ptc. נַעֲלָמָה—**be deflowered,** i.e. robbed of virginity Na 3$_{11}$. → עֲלוּמִים *youth,* עֶלֶם I *young man,* עַלְמָה *young woman,* עֲלָמוֹת II *youth.*

*עלם IV 1 vb. (byform of ערם IV)—**Htp.** 1 Impf. יִתְעַלֶּם־ —**be heaped up,** of snow Jb 6$_{16}$.

עֶלֶם I 2 n.m.—עֶלֶם—**young man, lad** 1 S 17$_{56}$ 20$_{22}$. → עלם III *be mature.*

*[עֶלֶם] II n.[m.] **1. secret,** עֶלֶם פִּלְשֵׂי *secret of the poising of* the clouds Jb 37$_{16}$ (if em. עַל־מִפְלְשֵׂי *about the poising of*). **2. ignorance** Ec 3$_{11}$ (if em. הָעֹלָם *everlastingness*). **3. darkness** Jb 22$_{15}$ (if em. עוֹלָם *ancient time*). → עלם I *hide* or II *be dark.*

*[עֹלֶם] III n.[m.] **wisdom** (alw. if em. עוֹלָם *everlastingness*) Gn 31$_{33}$ Is 40$_{28}$ Jr 6$_{16}$ 10$_{10}$ Hb 3$_6$ Ps 139$_2$ Ec 3$_{11}$.

*[עֵלֶם] n.[m.] **arrow** Jb 20$_{23}$ (if em. עָלֵימוֹ *upon him* to עֲלָמָיו *his arrows*).

עַלְמָה I 9 n.f.—pl. עֲלָמוֹת—**1. young woman, girl** Gn 24$_{43}$. **2.** עַל־עֲלָמוֹת as musical term, perh. *according to (the style of) young women,* or *for sopranos* Ps 46$_1$. → עלם III *be mature.*

*עַלְמָה II 1 n.f. **darkness** Pr 30$_{19}$. → עלם II *be dark.*

עַלְמוֹן 1 pl.n. **Almon.**

*עַלְמוּת I 1 n.f.—**hiddenness,** as musical term, perh. *sotto voce* Ps 9$_1$ (mss עַל־מוּת *on the death of* Labben/the son/Ben). → (?) עלם I *hide.*

*עַלְמוּת II 1 n.f. **youth,** in psalm title Ps 9$_1$. → עלם III *be mature.*

*עַלְמוּת III 1 n.f. **musical instrument,** in psalm title

Ps 9_1.

[עַלְמֹן דִּבְלָתַיִם] 2 pl.n. **Almon-diblathaim.**

עַלֶּמֶת I 3 pr.n.m. **Alemeth.**

עַלֶּמֶת II 1 pl.n. **Alemeth.**

עלס I 3 vb.—**Qal** 1 Impf. יַעֲלֹס—**rejoice** Jb 20_{18}.

Ni. 1 Pf. נֶעֱלָסָה—**flap joyously,** of wing Jb 39_{13}.

Htp. 1 Impf. נִתְעַלְּסָה—**delight oneself with** (בְּ) love Pr 7_{18}.

→ cf. עלז *exult,* עלץ *exult.*

*** עלס** II 2 vb.—**Qal** 1 Impf. יַעֲלֹס—**taste, enjoy** Jb 20_{18}.

Htp. 1 Impf. נִתְעַלְּסָה—**taste with one another** (בְּ of obj.) love Pr 7_{18}.

*** עלס** III 1 vb.—**Ni.** 1 Pf. נֶעֱלָסָה—**be restless, flap,** of wing Jb 39_{13}.

*** עלס** IV 1 vb.—**Ni.** 1 Pf. נֶעֱלָסָה—**be weak,** of wing Jb 39_{13}.

עלע I 1 vb.—**Pi.** 1 Impf. יְעַלְעוּ—**drink, suck up** blood Jb 39_{30}.

*** עלע** II 1 vb.—**Pi.** 1 Impf. יְעַלְעוּ—**extract blood** Jb 39_{30}.

*** עלע** III 1 vb.—**Pi.** 1 Impf. יְעַלְעוּ—**enter, plunge in** blood Jb 39_{30}.

*** [עַלְעוֹל]** 0.1 n.[m.] **whirlwind** Jb 36_{33} (if em. עַל־עוֹלֶה *against what comes up* to עַלְעוֹלֹה *his whirlwind*) Si $43_{17(M)}$.

*** [עַלְעוֹלָה]** I n.f. **whirlwind** Jb 36_{33} (if em. עַל־עוֹלֶה *against what comes up*).

*** [עַלְעוֹלָה]** II n.f.—**mischief, disturbance** Jb 36_{33} (if em. עַל־עוֹלֶה *against what comes up*).

עלף I 3.0.1 vb.—**Pu.** 1.0.1 Pf. עֻלְּפוּ—**faint, swoon away** Is 51_{20}.

Htp. 2 Impf. תִּתְעַלַּפְנָה; + waw וַיִּתְעַלָּף—**faint, swoon away** Am 8_{13} (+ בְּ *on account of* thirst) Jon 4_8.

→ עֻלְפֶּה *faint.*

*** עלף** II 2.0.1 vb.—**Pu.** 1 ptc. מְעֻלֶּפֶת—**be covered,** שֵׁן מְעֻלֶּפֶת סַפִּירִים *ivory, encrusted with sapphires* Ca 5_{14}.

Htp. 1.0.1 + waw וַתִּתְעַלָּף—**wrap oneself up, veil oneself** Gn 38_{14} 4QWiles 1_{12}.

*** עלף** III 1 vb.—**Htp.** 1 + waw וַתִּתְעַלָּף—**make oneself up,** by painting the hands and feet, perh. **perfume oneself** Gn 38_{14}.

עֻלְפֶּה 1 n.m. **faint**—Ezk 31_{15} (or em. עֻלְּפוּ *they fainted,* i.e. עלף I pu.). → עלף I *faint.*

עלץ I 8.1.2 vb. (byform of עלז I)—**Qal** 8.0.2 Pf. Q עָלַץ; impf. יַעֲלֹצוּ, אֶעֶלְצָה, יַעֲלֹץ; inf. עֲלֹץ—**exult, rejoice** 1 S 2_1 (+ בְּ *in* Y.) Ps 25_2 (+ לְ *on account of*) Pr 11_{10}.

Hi. 0.1 Impf. יעליצו—**cause the heart to rejoice** Si 40_{20}.

→ עַלִּיץ *exultant,* עֲלִיצוּת *exultation;* cf. עלז *exult,* עלס I *rejoice.*

*** עלץ** II 2 vb.—**Qal** 2 Impf. יַעַלְצוּ; inf. עֲלֹץ—**prevail,** abs. Pr 28_{12}; + לְ *over* Ps 25_2.

*** עלת** 0.0.1 perh. abbrev. for על תבל **over the world** 1QS 10_2.

*** עַלַת** prep. **because of** Jb 34_{36} (if em. עַל־תְּשֻׁבֹת *because of his answering* to עַלַת שֶׁבֶת *because he sits*).

עם I 1869.34.268.2 n.m.—הָעָם, עָם; cstr. עַם; sf. עַמִּי, עַמָּם; pl. עַמִּים (עֲמָמִים); cstr. עַמֵּי (עַמְמֵי); sf. עַמֶּיךָ (עֲמָמֶיךָ), עַמָּיו—**1. people, nation** Gn 11_6 Ex 19_5; in ref. to Egyptians Gn 41_{55}, Moabites Jr 48_{42}, Israelites Ex 1_9, as people of Y. Ex 3_7. **2. people,** in general Gn 14_{16}, the common people Lv 4_{27}, inhabitants of land or city Gn 23_7 Jg 18_7, subjects of king Gn 41_{40}, army Ex 14_6, laity as distinguished from priests and Levites Dt 18_3 Ezr 2_{70} ||Ne 7_{72}. **3. people,** i.e. **compatriots** Ru 1_{10} Est 2_{10}. **4. people,** as term for ants Pr 30_{25}, rock badgers Pr 30_{26}.

עם II 36.1.1 n.[m.]—sf. עַמִּי; pl. עַמִּים; sf. עַמֶּיךָ (עֲמָמֶיךָ), עַמָּיו—**kinsman** Jg 5_{14}; וְנִכְרְתָה הַנֶּפֶשׁ הַהִוא מֵעַמֶּיהָ *and that person shall be cut off from his kinsmen* Gn 17_{14}, וַיֵּאָסֶף אֶל־עַמָּיו *and he was gathered to his kinsmen* Gn 25_8.

*** עם** III 30.1 n.m.—הָעָם, עָם; sf. עַמִּי; pl. עַמִּים—**1a. strength, power,** זְרוֹעַ עַמֶּךָ *arm of your strength,* i.e. your strong arm Ps 77_{16}. **b. hero** Is 63_{11}. **2. sagacity, wisdom** Jb 12_2 Ps 94_8 Si 10_1. **3. stronghold, fortress** Ps 62_9. **4. city,** בַּת־עַמִּי *daughter of my city* Jr 4_{11}; **Lady City,** as pl. of majesty Ezk 26_2.

*** עם** IV 17.2 adj.—עָם; sf. עַמִּי, עַמּוֹ; pl. עַמִּים—**1a. strong, powerful, vigorous,** of God Ps 47_{10}, offspring Jb 21_8 (if em. עִמָּם *with them* to עַמָּם *vigorous*). **b. wise, sagacious,** of judge Si 10_1. **2.** as noun, **a. strong one, hero, prince** Na 3_{18} Ps 89_{20} Est 1_{11}; **Strong One,** as title of Y. 2 S 22_{28}||Ps 18_{28}. **b.** perh. **wise one** Jb 12_2. → עמם II *be strong.*

*עַם V $_{1}$ n.[m.] **steppe-dweller** Ex 15$_{14}$.

*[עַם] VI n.[m.] **covering** Jb 28$_{4}$ (if em. מֵעַם־גָּר *from [being] with one who sojourns* to מֵעַם גִּר *out of a covering of chalk*). → עמם VI *cover*.

*עַם VII $_{1}$ n.m.—pl. עַמִּים—**worry** Jb 36$_{20}$. → עמם V *grieve*.

*[עַם] VIII $_{1}$ adj.—עַם—**perfect, superior** Jb 12$_{2}$.

*[עַם] IX $_{0.0.0.2}$ pr.n.[m.] **Am**.

עִם $_{1093.58.396.3}$ prep.—sf. עִמִּי (עִמָּדִי), עִמּוֹ, עִמָּם (עִמָּהֶם)—**1.** of accompaniment, **a. (in company) with, (together) with, alongside, among, in the presence of, before, by** Gn 13$_{1}$ Ex 34$_{28}$. **b.** linking nouns, **together with, as well as,** אֱלֹהֵיהֶם עִם־נְסִכֵיהֶם עִם־כְּלֵי חֶמְדָּתָם *their gods with their molten images with their precious vessels* Dn 11$_{8}$. **c. with,** of the presence or support of Y. Dt 20$_{1}$. **2.** of possession, custody, **a. with, among, in the possession of,** גַּם־תֶּבֶן גַּם־מִסְפּוֹא רַב עִמָּנוּ *we have much straw and provender* Gn 24$_{25}$, מִשְׁמֶרֶת אַתָּה עִמָּדִי *you are a (duty of) protection with me,* i.e. I promise to protect you 1 S 22$_{23}$. **b. with, having (the property of),** זְרוֹעַ עִם־גְּבוּרָה *an arm with might,* i.e. a mighty arm Ps 89$_{14}$. **3.** of benefit, **with, for, in the service of,** with עבד *serve* Gn 29$_{25}$. **4.** of dealings with or action meted out to, **with, to(wards), from, for,** with עשׂה *do* Gn 19$_{19}$, יטב hi. *do good* Gn 32$_{10}$. **5.** of dialogue, mutual agreement, **with, to,** with דבר pi. *speak* Gn 29$_{9}$, כרת *cut,* i.e. make, covenant Gn 26$_{28}$. **6.** of conflict, dispute, **with, against,** with ריב *strive* Gn 26$_{20}$, לחם ni. *fight* Ex 17$_{8}$. **7.** of thought, disposition, purpose, **with, in (the mind of), in (the estimation of), to, a.** עִם alone 1 S 2$_{26}$. **b.** עִם לֵבָב **with/in the heart/mind of** 1 K 8$_{17}$||2 C 6$_{7}$. **8. (in agreement) with, (friendly) towards, in support of, loyal to** Gn 31$_{2}$ 1 K 1$_{8}$. **9. with (the help of)** 1 S 14$_{45}$. **10.** of likeness, **(comparable) with, (likened) to, like, as,** with משׁל ni. *be comparable* Ps 28$_{1}$, חשׁב pi. *reckon* Lv 25$_{50}$; הֶחָכָם עִם־הַכְּסִיל *the wise one like the fool* Ec 2$_{16}$. **11. besides, apart from,** אֵין אֱלֹהִים עִמָּדִי *there is no god besides me* Dt 32$_{39}$. **12.** of place, **a. close to, beside, at, in** Gn 35$_{4}$ Jg 18$_{3}$. **b. with, into, among** Jg 16$_{13}$. **13.** of time, **a. with (the continuance of), as long as (there exists)** Ps 72$_{5}$. **b. (simultaneously) with, at, during, throughout** 1QM 14$_{8}$ 1QS 10$_{1}$. **14.** as conj., **when,** followed by inf. cstr. Ezr 1$_{11}$ 1QM 16$_{8}$. **16.** מֵעִם, **a.** of motion, removal, **from (being) with, from beside, from (being at)** Gn 26$_{16}$ Ex 21$_{14}$. **b.** of dealings with, **from (being) with, from (being) towards** Gn 24$_{27}$. **c.** of agency, **by (means of)** Gn 41$_{32}$ 1 S 20$_{7}$. **d.** of origin, **(from) before, in the presence of** 1 K 2$_{33}$ Ps 121$_{2}$. **e.** of request, requirement, **from, of, on the part of** Dt 10$_{12}$ 1 S 20$_{28}$.

עמד I $_{523.24.130}$ vb.—**Qal** $_{436.20.110}$ Pf. עָמַד, עָמַדְתִּי; impf. יַעֲמֹד, יַעַמְדוּ (יַעֲמֹדוּ); impv. עֲמֹד (עֲמָד־), עִמְדִי, עִמְדוּ; ptc. עֹמֵד, עֹמֶדֶת, עֹמְדִים, עֹמְדוֹת; inf. abs. עָמוֹד; cstr. עֲמֹד (עָמְדְךָ, עָמְדִי)—**1. stand, a. stand (in position), take one's stand, take position, be present,** + בְּ *in, at* Ex 32$_{26}$, *on* 1 K 19$_{11}$; אֶל *on* 1 S 17$_{3}$, *at, beside* Ezk 21$_{26}$; עַל *upon* Ne 8$_{4}$, *beside, round about* 1 K 22$_{19}$, *at* 2 C 18$_{18}$; עִם 1 S 17$_{26}$; אֵצֶל *beside* Ne 8$_{4}$; לִפְנֵי *before* Gn 18$_{22}$; בֵּין *between, among* Dt 5$_{5}$ Zc 1$_{8}$; תַּחַת *under* Gn 18$_{8}$, *in (one's) place* Jg 7$_{21}$. Sometimes with implied motion, (1) **(go in and) stand, present oneself** 2 S 20$_{4}$; + בְּ *at* Ho 13$_{13}$, לִפְנֵי *before* Gn 43$_{15}$. (2) **stand forward, stand out** Is 44$_{11}$. (3) **stand back, stand aloof** Ex 20$_{18}$ (+ מֵרָחֹק *at a distance*) Ob$_{11}$ (+ מִנֶּגֶד *aloof*) Dn 11$_{8}$ (+ מִן *from* someone). **b. stand (for service), be in attendance,** + לִפְנֵי *before* Gn 41$_{46}$, עַל *beside* Jg 3$_{19}$. **c. stand (in sacred service),** usu. + לִפְנֵי *before* Y.; of priest or Levite at sanctuary Dt 10$_{8}$ 17$_{12}$ (both + שׁרת pi. inf. *to minister*), prophet 1 K 17$_{1}$. **d. stand (for worship, prayer),** + בְּ *in* house of Y. Ps 134$_{1}$, *with* musical instruments 2 C 29$_{26}$; לִפְנֵי *before* Y. Lv 9$_{5}$, ark 1 K 3$_{15}$. **e. stand (in law court),** (1) to pass judgment Is 3$_{13}$. (2) to be judged, + לְ *for* judgment Nm 35$_{12}$, לִפְנֵי *before* Y., priests, judges Dt 19$_{17}$. (3) as accuser, + עַל *at* right hand Zc 3$_{1}$. (4) of Y. at (לְ) right hand of poor, to save from condemnation Ps 109$_{31}$. **2. stand (in authority),** + עַל *over,* i.e. in charge of Nm 7$_{2}$, נצח pi. inf. *to oversee* Ezr 3$_{9}$. **3a. make a stand, stand one's ground** Dn 11$_{15}$; + עַל *for* one's life Est 8$_{11}$. **b. stand (against), rise up (against), withstand,** + עַל *against* Jg 6$_{13}$, לִפְנֵי *against* Jg 2$_{14}$, בִּפְנֵי *against* Jos 10$_{8}$, נֶגֶד *against* Ec 4$_{12}$. **4. stand,** i.e. **rely upon** (עַל) sword

Ezk 33$_{26}$. **5a. stand,** i.e. **enter into** (בְּ) covenant) 2 K 23$_{3}$. **b. stand in** (בְּ), i.e. **participate (as member of)** council Jr 23$_{22}$. **6. remain present, stay, stay behind, wait, tarry** Gn 45$_{9}$ 2 S 17$_{17}$. **7. dwell in** (עַל) land Ex 8$_{18}$. **8a.** (1) **remain, endure, continue,** of Y. Ps 102$_{27}$, human Jb 14$_{2}$, the earth Ps 119$_{90}$, righteousness of Y. Ps 111$_{3}$ (+ לָעַד *for ever*); **survive** Ex 21$_{21}$. **b. stand fast, persist,** of person Dt 25$_{8}$, Babylon Is 47$_{12}$ (+ בְּ *in* spells), words Est 3$_{4}$, pain Si 30$_{17}$. **c. remain unchanged,** (1) of disease, i.e. **stop spreading** Lv 13$_{5}$. (2) of taste of wine Jr 48$_{11}$. **9a. stand still,** i.e. **be stationary, be inactive** Is 46$_{7}$ 2 C 20$_{17}$. **b. stand still,** i.e. **halt, stop moving,** of people 2 S 2$_{28}$, cart 1 S 6$_{14}$, sun and moon Jos 10$_{13}$; **stop flowing,** of oil 2 K 4$_{6}$. **10. stop doing, cease,** וַתַּעֲמֹד מִלֶּדֶת *and she ceased bearing* Gn 29$_{35}$, וַיַּעֲמֹד הַיָּם מִזַּעְפּוֹ *and the sea ceased from its raging* Jon 1$_{15}$. **11. stand upright,** of board Ex 26$_{15}$||36$_{20}$. **12. stand up, rise,** of person Ezk 2$_{1}$ (+ עַל *on* feet). **13. arise, come into being, appear,** of king Dn 8$_{23}$, horn Dn 8$_{22}$ (+ תַּחַת *in place of*), deliverance Est 4$_{14}$ (+ מִן *from*).

Hi. 85.4.20 Pf. הֶעֱמַדְתָּ, הֶעֱמִיד; impf. יַעֲמִיד; + waw וְהֶעֱמִיד, וְהֶעֱמַדְתָּ; וַיַּעֲמֵד ,(וַיַּעֲמֶד־) וָאַעֲמִיד; impv. הַעֲמֵד; ptc. מַעֲמִיד; inf. abs. הַעֲמֵיד; cstr. הַעֲמִיד—**1a. cause to stand, station, place** someone, + סָבִיב *round about* Nm 11$_{24}$, בְּ *in* 1 K 12$_{32}$, עַל *upon* 2 S 22$_{34}$||Ps 18$_{34}$, בַּיִת *[in] house* 2 C 29$_{25}$. **b. cause to stand, place,** i.e. **present,** someone **before** (לִפְנֵי) Y. Lv 14$_{11}$, human Gn 47$_{7}$. **c. cause to stand, place someone (in attendance) before** (לִפְנֵי) Nm 8$_{13}$. **d. cause to stand for** (לְ) **judgment** 4QpersPrayer 2$_{6}$. **2. allow to stand** next to (אֵצֶל) one Si 12$_{12}$. **3a. cause to stand up** on (עַל) feet Ezk 2$_{2}$. **b. cause oneself to stand up, prop oneself up** in (בְּ) chariot 2 C 18$_{34}$. **4. cause** face **to stand,** i.e. **fix one's gaze** 2 K 8$_{11}$. **5a. erect, raise up, repair** house of Y. Ezr 2$_{68}$, ruins Ezr 9$_{9}$. **b. set up, install** gods 2 C 25$_{14}$. **6. cause to stand firm, establish, support** Israel 2 C 9$_{8}$, name Si 40$_{19}$, heavenly bodies Ps 148$_{6}$, land Pr 29$_{4}$ (+ בְּ *with* justice). **7. confirm, fulfil** covenant Ps 105$_{10}$||1 C 16$_{17}$ (+ לְ *to*), vision Dn 11$_{14}$. **8a. issue a decree** 2 C 30$_{5}$. **b. lay obligation upon** (עַל) oneself Ne 10$_{33}$. **c. bring into covenant, impose covenant upon** (accus.) 2 C 34$_{32}$. **9. cause to remain, retain** livestock Si 7$_{22}$. **10. appoint, assign** someone as (לְ) leader 2 C 11$_{22}$, judges in (בְּ) land 2 C 19$_{5}$, Levites to oversee (לְנַצֵּחַ) work Ezr 3$_{8}$, priests for (לְ) high places 2 C 11$_{15}$, for (עַל) service 2 C 8$_{14}$, land to (לְ) fathers 2 C 33$_{8}$. **11. raise up, cause to exist** multitude Dn 11$_{11}$, wind Ps 107$_{25}$.

Ho. 2 Impf. יָעֳמַד; ptc. מָעֳמָד—**1. be caused to stand,** i.e. **be presented before** (לִפְנֵי) Y., of goat Lv 16$_{10}$. **2. be caused to stand,** i.e. **be propped up** in (בְּ) chariot 1 K 22$_{35}$.

→ עֹמֶד *standing place,* עֶמְדָּה I *standing place,* II *standard,* עַמּוּד *pillar,* מַעֲמָד *place,* מָעֳמָד *standing ground.*

*עמד II 5.1 vb.—**Qal** 3.1 Pf. עָמְדוּ (עָמֵדוּ); impf. יַעַמְדוּ; ptc. Si, Qr עֹמְדִים—**1. waver, be sore pressed** Ho 10$_{9}$ Jr 48$_{45}$ (+ מִן *for lack of* strength) Si 16$_{18(Qr)}$. **2. weigh heavily,** of water Ps 104$_{6}$ (+ עַל *upon* mountains).

Hi. 2 Pf. הֶעֱמַדְתָּה; + waw וְהַעֲמַדְתָּ—**cast down** loins Ezk 29$_{7}$, mountains Ps 30$_{8}$ (לְ of obj.).

*[עָמָד] 0.0.0.1 pr.n.f. **Amad.**

[עִמָּד], see עִם *with.*

[עֹמֶד] 9.0.9 n.[m.] (sometimes perh. עמד inf.)—sf. עָמְדִי, עָמְדָם (Q עומדם)—**1. (standing) place, post, position** Dn 8$_{17}$ Ne 8$_{7}$. **2. standing** 1QH 10$_{25}$. **3. existence** 4QapPsB 31$_{6}$. → עמד I *stand.*

[עֶמְדָּה] I 1 n.f.—sf. עֶמְדָּתוֹ—**standing place** Mc 1$_{11}$. → עמד I *stand.*

*[עֶמְדָּה] II 1 n.f.—sf. עֶמְדָּתוֹ—**(military) standard** Mc 1$_{11}$. → עמד I *stand.*

*[עֲמַדְיָהוּ] 0.0.0.7 pr.n.m.&f. **Amadiah.**

עמדיו, see עֲמַדְיָהוּ *Amadiah.*

עֻמָּה I 1 pl.n. **Ummah.**

[עֻמָּה] II, see לְעֻמַּת *close by.*

עַמּוּד 111.2.21 n.m.—עַמֻּד; cstr. עַמּוּד; sf. עַמּוּדוֹ; pl. עַמּוּדִים; cstr. עַמּוּדֵי; sf. עַמּוּדָיו—**1. pillar, column,** supporting building Jg 16$_{25}$; in palace 1 K 7$_{2}$, tabernacle Ex 26$_{32}$ ||36$_{36}$, temple Ezk 40$_{49}$; bronze pillars in front of temple 1 K 7$_{15}$; perh. feature of cave 3QTr 6$_{1}$. **2. post** of palanquin Ca 3$_{10}$. **3. (cosmic) pillar** of earth Ps 75$_{4}$, heaven Jb 26$_{11}$. **4. pillar** of wisdom Pr 9$_{1}$. **5. pillar, column** of cloud Ex 13$_{21}$, fire Ex 13$_{21}$, smoke Jg 20$_{40}$.

6. **column**, style of engraving on socket of spear 1QM 5_{10}. 7. **pillar**, in descr. of person; Jeremiah as pillar of iron Jr 1_{18}, legs as pillars of alabaster Ca 5_{15}. → עמד I *stand*.

עַמּוֹן 106.0.1 pr.n.m. **Ammon.**

עַמּוֹנִי 21.0.1 gent. **Ammonite.**

עָמוֹס 7.0.0.1 pr.n.m. **Amos.**

עָמוֹק 2 pr.n.m. **Amok.**

* **[עֲמִי]** n.[m.] **dark (of night)** Jb 34_{20} (if em. עָם וְיַעֲבֹרוּ *the people and they pass away* to עֲמִי יַעֲבֹרוּ *in the dark they pass away*) 36_{20} (if em. עַמִּים תַּחְתָּם *peoples in their place* to עֲמִי מִתַּחְתָּם *in the dark from under them*).

עַמִּיאֵל 6 pr.n.m. **Ammiel.**

עַמִּיהוּד 10 pr.n.m. **Ammihud.**

עַמִּיזָבָד 1 pr.n.m. **Ammizabad.**

עמיחוד, see עַמִּיהוּד *Ammihud.*

עַמִּינָדָב 14 pr.n.m. **Amminadab.**

עַמִּי־נָדִיב 1 pr.n.m. **Ammi-nadib.**

עָמִיר 4.0.1 n.[m.] **sheaves** Jr 9_{21} Am 2_{13}. → עמר II *bind sheaves*.

[עַמִּישַׁדָּי] 5 pr.n.m. **Ammishaddai.**

[עָמִית] 12.0.4 n.m.—sf. עֲמִיתִי—**1. neighbour, fellow** Lv 5_{21}. **2.** perh. **community, association** Zc 13_7 1QS 6_{26}.

עמל 11.0.1 vb.—**Qal** 11.0.1 Pf. עָמַל, עָמַלְתָּ; impf. יַעֲמֹל—**1a. toil, labour at**, with accus. עָמָל *toil* Ec 1_3 (+ תַּחַת *under* the sun). **b. toil, labour for**, with accus. עָמָל *(fruit of) toil* Ec 2_{19}; prep. לְ *for* wind Ec 5_{15}; בְּ *for* plant Jon 4_{10}, house Ps 127_1. **2.** perh. **have trouble in** (בְּ) life 4QInstr^c 2.1_{10}. → עָמָל I *trouble, toil*, עָמֵל *toiling*.

עָמָל I 55.3.14 n.m.—cstr. עֲמַל; sf. עֲמָלִי—**1. trouble, hardship, misfortune**, esp. as suffered by oneself Gn 41_{51} Dt 26_7. **2. harm, mischief, wrong**, esp. as done to others Is 59_4 Ps 10_7 Jb 4_8. **3a. toil, labour** Ec 1_3 6_7. **b. fruit of toil, wealth, profit, earnings** Ps 105_{44} Ec 2_{19}. → עמל *toil*.

עָמָל II 1 pr.n.m. **Amal.**

עָמֵל 9.3 adj.—pl. עֲמֵלִים—**1. toiling** Ec 2_{18} Si 34_4. **2.** as noun, **a. labourer, one who toils** Jg 5_{26} Pr 16_{26}. **b. sufferer** Jb 3_{20}. → עָמָל I *toil*.

* **[עֲמַלְיָהוּ]** 0.0.0.2 pr.n.[m.] **Amaliah.**

* **[עַמְלָץ]** n.[m.] **shark** Ps 74_{14} (if em. לְעָם לְצִיִּים *to the people, to the desert-dwellers* to לְעַמְלְצֵי יָם *to the sharks of the sea*).

עֲמָלֵק 39.0.2 pr.n.m. **Amalek.**

עֲמָלֵקִי 12 gent. **Amalekite.**

עמם I 4 vb.—**Qal** 2 Pf. עֲמָמוּךָ—**1. darken**, of cedars as casting shadow Ezk 31_8. **2.** with double accus., **darken with**, כָּל־סָתוּם לֹא עֲמָמוּךָ *they do not darken you with any secret*, i.e. no secret is hidden from you Ezk 28_3.

Ho. 1 Impf. יוּעַם—**be darkened**, of gold Lm 4_1.

Ntp. 1 Pf. נתעם—**be blackened** Is 9_{18}(1QIsa^a) (MT עתם ni.).

* **עמם** II 2 vb.—**Qal** 2 Pf. עֲמָמוּךָ—**1. be stronger than, be mightier than** Ezk 31_8. **2.** with double accus., **be too wise for, be too deep for**, thus **perplex**, of secret Ezk 28_3. → עַם IV *strong*.

* **[עמם]** III vb. **extend oneself, spread out** Jb 21_8 (if em. עִמָּם וְצֶאֱצָאֵיהֶם *with them, and their offspring* to עָמְמוּ צֶאֱצָאֵיהֶם *their offspring spread out*).

* **[עמם]** IV 2 vb.—**Qal** 2 Pf. עֲמָמוּךָ—**be like, be equal to, comparable to**, of secret Ezk 28_3, cedar Ezk 31_8.

* **[עמם]** V 1 vb.—**Qal** 1 Pf. עֲמָמוּךָ—**grieve**, of secret Ezk 28_3. → עַם VII *worry*.

* **[עמם]** VI 2 vb.—**Qal** 2 Pf. עֲמָמוּךָ—**surpass**, of secret Ezk 28_3; perh. **cover, shade**, of cedar Ezk 31_8. → עַם VI *covering*.

* **[עָמֵם]** adj. **flourishing**, of offspring Jb 21_8 (if em. עִמָּם *with them*).

עֲמָמִים, see עַם *people.*

עִמָּנוּ אֵל 2 pr.n.m. **Immanuel.**

* **[עִמָּנוּיָה]** 0.0.0.1 pr.n.f. **Immanuiah.**

עמניהו, see עמנויה *Immanuiah.*

עמס 9 vb.—**Qal** 7 Impf. יַעֲמָס־; + waw וַיַּעֲמֹס; ptc. עֹמְסִים (עֹמְשִׂים); ptc. pass. עֲמֻסִים—**1. load (a burden) on** (עַל) an ass Gn 44_{13}. **2. bear, carry** stone Zc 12_3, persons Ps 68_{20} (לְ of obj.). **3.** pass. **be borne** Is $46_{1.3}$ (+ מִן *from* womb, i.e. since birth).

Hi. 2 Pf. הֶעְמִיס—**load, impose** yoke upon (עַל) 1 K 12_{11}‖2 C 10_{11}.

→ מַעֲמָסָה *burden*, עָמָס *burden*.

* **עָמָס** n.[m.] **burden, trouble** Ps 68_{20} (if em. יַעֲמָס־לָנוּ *he bears us* to לַעֲמָסֵינוּ *in regard to our troubles*). →

עמס *load.*

עֲמָסַי, see עֲמָשַׂי *Amasai.*

עֲמַסְיָה 1.0.0.2 pr.n.m. **Amasiah.**

עמסיהו, see עֲמַסְיָה *Amasiah.*

עַמְעָד 1 pl.n. **Amad.**

עמק I 9.0.1 vb.—**Qal** 1.0.1 Pf. עָמְקוּ; + waw Q ויעמקו—**be deep,** of thoughts Ps 92$_6$.

Hi. 8 Pf. הֶעְמִיק; impv. הֶעְמִיקוּ; ptc. מַעֲמִיקִים; inf. abs. הַעֲמֵק—**make deep,** obj. rebellion Is 31$_6$, slaughter Ho 5$_2$; הֶעְמִיקוּ לָשֶׁבֶת *make deep to dwell,* i.e. dwell in the depths Jr 49$_8$, הַמַּעֲמִיקִים מֵי׳ לַסְתִּר עֵצָה *those who make deep to hide,* i.e. hide deep, *(their) counsel from Y.* Is 29$_{15}$.

→ עֵמֶק I *valley, lowland,* עֹמֶק *depth,* עָמֵק I *deep,* עָמֹק *deep,* מַעֲמָק *depth.*

***עמק** II 1 vb.—**Qal** 1 Pf. עָמְקוּ—**be strong,** of thoughts Ps 92$_6$. → עָמֵק II *strong,* עֵמֶק II *strength.*

[עָמֵק] I 3 adj. **deep,** עַם עִמְקֵי שָׂפָה *a people deep of lip,* i.e. having unintelligible speech Is 33$_{19}$. → עמק I *be deep.*

***[עָמֵק]** II 2 adj.—pl. cstr. עִמְקֵי—**1. strong,** עַם עִמְקֵי שָׂפָה *a people strong of lip,* i.e. of speech, used attrib. Ezk 3$_5$. **2.** as noun, **strong one, mighty one, hero** (alw. if em. עֵמֶק *valley)* Jg 5$_{15}$ Is 28$_{21}$ Jr 49$_4$ 1 C 12$_{16}$. → עמק II *be strong.*

עָמֹק 17.1.5 adj.—f.s. עֲמֻקָּה; m.pl. עֲמֻקִּים; f.pl. עֲמֻקּוֹת—**1. deep,** of water Pr 18$_4$, pit Pr 22$_{14}$, cup Ezk 23$_{32}$, diseased spot Lv 13$_3$ (+ מִן deeper *than),* heart (as unsearchable) Ps 64$_7$. **2.** fem. pl. as noun, **unsearchable things, mysteries** Jb 12$_{22}$ 1QM 10$_{11}$. → עמק I *be deep.*

עֵמֶק I 67.0.3.2 n.m.—cstr. עֵמֶק; sf. עִמְקָם; pl. עֲמָקִים; sf. עֲמָקַיִךְ—**1. lowland, plain,** rather than **valley** Nm 14$_{25}$ 1 S 6$_{13}$; pl. in ref. to inhabitants of plains 1 C 12$_{16}$. **2.** in place names, עֵמֶק עָכוֹר **Plain of Achor** (prob. = עכון Achon), אַיָּלוֹן **Aijalon,** הַבָּכָא **Baca,** בְּרָכָה **Beracah,** הָאֵלָה **Elah,** חֶבְרוֹן **Hebron,** יְהוֹשָׁפָט **Jehoshaphat,** יִזְרְעֶאל **Jezreel,** רְפָאִים **Rephaim,** הַשִּׂדִּים **Siddim,** שָׁוֵה **Shaveh,** סֻכּוֹת **Succoth;** see also בֵּית הָעֵמֶק **Beth-emek,** עֵמֶק קְצִיץ **Emek-keziz.** → עמק I *be deep.*

***עֵמֶק** II 6 n.m.—sf. עִמְקָם; pl. עֲמָקִים—**1. strength, power** Jr 21$_{13}$ 47$_5$ 49$_{4.4}$ Jb 39$_{21}$. **2. strong one** 1 C 12$_{16}$. → עמק II *be strong.*

עֹמֶק 2.0.3 n.[m.] **depth,** Pr 25$_3$; עִמְקֵי שְׁאוֹל *depths of Sheol* Pr 9$_{18}$, עומק רזיכה *depth of your mysteries* 1QS 11$_{19}$. → עמק I *be deep.*

עֵמֶק קְצִיץ 1 pl.n. **Emek-keziz.**

עמר I 2 vb.—**Htp.** 2 Pf. הִתְעַמֵּר־; impf. תִּתְעַמֵּר—**treat as a slave, deal tyrannically with,** with בְּ of obj. Dt 21$_{14}$ 24$_7$.

עמר II 3.0.1 vb.—**Pi.** 1.0.1 Impf. Q תעמרו; ptc. מְעַמֵּר—**1. bind sheaves** Ps 129$_7$. **2. make bales** from off (מִן) boat 5/6ḤHev 49$_7$.

Htp. 2 Pf. הִתְעַמֵּר־; impf. תִּתְעַמֵּר—**trade,** with בְּ of obj. Dt 21$_{14}$ 24$_7$.

→ עֹמֶר I *sheaf,* II *omer,* עָמִיר *sheaves.*

***עמר** III 0.0.2 vb.—**Pi.** 0.0.2 Impv. עמר; inf. עמרך—perh. **insist,** איני צריך לעמרך *I do not need to insist with regard to you* MurEpJonathan$_2$, עמר עליו שיפטר *insist concerning him that he dismisses* MurEpJonathan$_9$.

עֹמֶר I 8.0.11 n.m.—cstr. עֹמֶר; pl. עֳמָרִים—**sheaf** Lv 23$_{10}$ Dt 24$_{19}$ 11QT 18$_{10}$. → עמר II *bind sheaves.*

עֹמֶר II 6.0.4 n.m. **omer,** measure of grain, equivalent to a tenth of an ephah; the measure itself Ex 16$_{18}$, the amount measured Ex 16$_{16}$. → עמר II *bind sheaves.*

עֲמֹרָה 19.0.2 pl.n. **Gomorrah.**

עָמְרִי 18 pr.n.m. **Omri.**

עַמְרָם 14 pr.n.m. **Amram.**

עַמְרָמִי 2 gent. **Amramite.**

עמש, see עמס *load.*

עֲמָשָׂא 16.0.0.1 pr.n.m. **Amasa.**

עֲמָשַׂי 5 pr.n.m. **Amasai.**

***[עֶמְשָׁךְ]** n.m. **crocodile** Jb 40$_{15}$ (if em. בְּהֵמוֹת אֲשֶׁר עָשִׂיתִי עִמָּךְ *Behemoth, which I made like you* to רֵאשִׁית בְּהֵמוֹת עֶמְשָׁךְ *the chief of the beasts, the crocodile).*

עֲמַשְׁסַי 1 pr.n.m. **Amashsai.**

***[עָן]** n.[m.] (byform of עָוֹן) **iniquity** Ezk 18$_{17}$ (if em. מֵעָנִי *from the poor* to מֵעָן *from iniquity).*

עֲנָב 2 pl.n. **Anab.**

עֵנָב 19.2.2 n.m.—pl. עֲנָבִים; cstr. עִנְּבֵי; sf. עֲנָבֵמוֹ—**grape,** usu. fresh Gn 40$_{10}$ Lv 25$_5$; also dried Nm 6$_3$, אֲשִׁישֵׁי עֲנָבִים *raisin cakes* Ho 3$_1$.

ענג I 10.0.3 vb.—**Pu.** 1 Ptc. מְעֻנָּגָה—**be delicate,** ptc. as noun, **delicate one, pampered one** Jr 6$_{2}$.

Htp. $_{9.0.3}$ Impf. יִתְעַנָּג, תִּתְעַנַּג; + waw וְהִתְעַנְּגוּ; impv. הִתְעַנַּג; inf. הִתְעַנֵּג—**1. be delicate, be dainty,** of woman Dt 28$_{56}$. **2. delight oneself, take pleasure,** with בְּ *in* fat Is 55$_{2}$; עַל *in* Y. Is 58$_{14}$; מִן *from* teat Is 66$_{11}$. **3. make sport of, mock** (עַל of obj.) Is 57$_{4}$.

→ עָנֹג *delicate*, עֹנֶג *delight*, תַּעֲנוּג *delight*, עִנּוּג *happiness*.

*ענג II $_{4}$ vb.—**Htp.** $_{4}$ Impf. יִתְעַנָּג; impv. הִתְעַנַּג—**implore** (עַל of obj.) Y. Ps 37$_{4}$ Jb 22$_{26}$ 27$_{10}$ Is 57$_{4}$.

*ענג III $_{4}$ vb.—**Htp.** $_{4}$ Impf. יִתְעַנָּג; impv. הִתְעַנַּג—**depend on** (עַל) Y. Ps 37$_{4}$ Jb 22$_{26}$ 27$_{10}$ Is 57$_{4}$.

עָנֹג $_{4}$ adj.—sf. 1QIsa[a] ענוגו; f.s. עֲנֻגָּה—**1. delicate,** of man Dt 28$_{54}$. **2.** as noun, **a.** masc. sg., **delightful one** Is 13$_{22(1QIsa^a)}$ (MT עֹנֶג *delight*). **b.** fem. sg., **delicate one, pampered one** Dt 28$_{56}$ Is 47$_{1}$. → ענג I *be delicate*.

עֹנֶג $_{2}$ n.[m.] **delight, pleasure** Is 13$_{22}$ 58$_{13}$. → ענג I *be delicate*.

*[עֵינְגֶּדִי] $_{0.0.1}$ gent. **En-gedite.**

ענד $_{2}$ vb.—**Qal** $_{2}$ Impf. אֶעֶנְדֶנּוּ; impv. עָנְדֵם—**bind, tie** commandments and law around (עַל) throat Pr 6$_{21}$; with double accus., **bind** document to (לְ) oneself **as** a crown Jb 31$_{36}$. → מַעֲדָן II *bond*, מַעֲנָד *bond*.

ענה I $_{315.8.61.2}$ vb.—**Qal** $_{308.8.61.2}$ Pf. עָנִיתִי, עֲנִיתֶם; impf. יַעֲנֶה, תַּעֲנֶה (תַּעַן); + waw וַיַּעַן (וַיַּעֲנֶה); impv. עֲנֵה, עֲנוּ; ptc. עֹנֶה, עֹנִים; inf. עֲנוֹת—**1a.** usu. **answer, reply to,** in response to speech, whether stated or implied, (1) without obj., followed by אמר *say* Gn 18$_{27}$. (2) with accus. of person, followed by אמר *say* Gn 23$_{5}$. (3) with accus. of person and of answer: דָּבָר *word* 1 K 18$_{21}$, קָשָׁה *hard thing*, i.e. harshly 1 S 20$_{10}$. (4) with accus. only of answer: דַּעַת *(with) knowledge* Jb 15$_{2}$, עַזּוֹת *strong things*, i.e. harshly Pr 18$_{23}$. **b.** specif. of Y. responding, with help (or perh. an oracle) to one's petition or needs, with obj. of person Gn 35$_{3}$ 1 S 7$_{9}$ 2 S 22$_{42}$ ||Ps 18$_{42}$. **c. (begin to) speak, speak (up), say (to), declare solemnly,** followed by אמר *say*, in response to a situation Nm 11$_{28}$ Dt 25$_{9}$ Jg 18$_{14}$. **2. respond (as a witness), bear (witness), testify,** usu. with בְּ *against* Ex 20$_{16}$||Dt 5$_{20}$ (+ accus. עֵד שֶׁקֶר *false witness*) Dt 19$_{16}$ (+ accus. סָרָה *falsehood*) 1 S 12$_{3}$ 2 S 1$_{16}$ Is 59$_{12}$; also with בְּ *for, on behalf of* Gn 30$_{33}$, בְּפָנַי *against* Jb 16$_{8}$, לִפְנֵי *against* Dt 31$_{21}$ (+ לְעֵד *as a witness*), עַל *concerning* Ex 23$_{2}$. **3. answer,** i.e. **meet the needs of, pay for,** הַכֶּסֶף יַעֲנֶה אֶת־הַכֹּל *money answers everything* Ec 10$_{19}$. **4. answer for, be answerable for** Ho 2$_{23.24}$. **5. deliver** Ps 22$_{22}$ (+ מִן *from*) 118$_{21}$.

Ni. $_{5}$ Pf. נַעֲנֵיתִי; impf. יֵעָנֶה; ptc. נַעֲנֶה—**1. give answer** to (לְ) someone Ezk 14$_{4.7}$. **2. be answered** Jb 11$_{2}$ 19$_{7}$ Pr 21$_{13}$.

Hi. $_{2}$ Impf. יַעֲנֵנִי (or qal); ptc. מַעֲנֶה—**1. answer,** without obj. Ec 5$_{19}$ (+ בְּ *with* joy). **2. cause to answer** out of (מִן) understanding Jb 20$_{3}$ (or qal).

→ עֲנֵה *answer*, מַעֲנֶה *answer*.

ענה II $_{81.4.12}$ vb.—**Qal** $_{8}$ Pf. עָנִיתִי; impf. יַעֲנֶה; ptc. עֹנֶה—**1. be afflicted, humbled,** of people (as sheep) Zc 10$_{2}$. **2. be subdued, stilled,** of song Is 25$_{5}$. **3. be disturbed, daunted,** of lion Is 31$_{4}$ (+ מִן *on account of* tumult).

Ni. $_{4}$ Pf. נַעֲנֵיתִי; ptc. נַעֲנָה, נַעֲנֶה; inf. לֵעָנֹת—**1. humble oneself, submit** before (מִפְּנֵי) Y. Ex 10$_{3}$. **2. be afflicted, be humbled** Is 53$_{7}$ 58$_{10}$.

Pi. $_{57.3.10}$ Pf. עִנָּה, עִנִּיתָ, עִנִּיתִי; impf. יְעַנֶּה, יְעַנּוּ; + waw וַיְעַנֵּנִי; impv. עַנּוּ; ptc. מְעַנַּיִךְ; inf. abs. עַנֵּה; cstr. עַנּוֹת—**1a. afflict, oppress, mistreat** someone Gn 15$_{13}$ Ex 1$_{11}$ (+ בְּ *with* burden). **b. hurt feet with** (בְּ) fetters Ps 105$_{18}$. **2. humiliate (a woman sexually),** by rape or unlawful intercourse Gn 34$_{2}$ Dt 22$_{24}$, enforced marriage Dt 21$_{14}$. **3. humble (through discipline), afflict (as a punishment),** of Y. Dt 8$_{2}$ 2 K 17$_{20}$. **4.** ענה נֶפֶשׁ **humble oneself, afflict oneself,** by fasting Lv 16$_{29}$. **5a. overpower, weaken** someone Jg 16$_{5}$, one's strength Ps 102$_{24}$. **b. violate** justice Jb 37$_{23}$.

Pu. $_{4}$ Pf. עֻנֵּיתִי; impf. תְּעֻנֶּה; ptc. מְעֻנֶּה; inf. עֻנּוֹתוֹ—**1. be afflicted, be humbled,** by fasting Lv 23$_{29}$, the discipline of Y. Is 53$_{4}$ Ps 119$_{71}$. **2.** inf. cstr. as noun, **affliction** Ps 132$_{1}$.

Hi. $_{3}$ Impf. יַעֲנֵם—**humble, afflict,** through the discipline or punishment of Y. 1 K 8$_{35}$||2 C 6$_{26}$ Ps 55$_{20}$.

Htp. $_{6.1.2}$ Pf. הִתְעַנָּה, הִתְעַנִּיתָ; impf. יִתְעַנּוּ; impv. הִתְעַנִּי; inf. הִתְעַנּוֹת—**1. humble oneself, submit** Gn 16$_{9}$ (+ תַּחַת *under* the hand of) Dn 10$_{12}$ (+ לִפְנֵי *before* Y.). **2. be afflicted** 1 K 2$_{26}$ Ps 107$_{17}$ (+ מִן *on account of* iniquity).

→ עָנִי *poor, afflicted,* עֳנִי *affliction,* עֱנוּת I *affliction,* עָנָו *humble,* עֲנָוָה *humility,* עַנְוָנוּת *humility,* תַּעֲנִית *humiliation,* עֵת II *submission.*

ענה III 18.1 vb.—**Qal** 15.1 Impf. יַעֲנֶה, תַּעַן; + waw וְעָנָה, וַיַּעֲנוּ, וַתַּעַן; וְעָנִית; impv. עֱנוּ; inf. עֱנוֹת—**1a. sing** Ex 15$_{21}$ (+ לְ *to*) 1 S 18$_{7}$ Si 47$_{6}$ (+ לְ *concerning*); with obj., **sing** of word of Y. Ps 119$_{172}$. **b. utter** a shout (הֵידָד) Jr 25$_{30}$ (+ אֶל *against*) 51$_{14}$ (+ עַל *against*). **2.** inf. as noun, **singing, shouting** Ex 32$_{18}$.

Pi. 3 Impv. עַנּוּ; inf. עַנּוֹת—**1. sing** of (לְ) vineyard Is 27$_{2}$. **2.** inf. as noun, **singing** Ex 32$_{18}$.

→ עֱנוּת II *song.*

ענה IV 2.1 vb.—**Qal** 2.1 Ptc. Si עונה; inf. עֲנוֹת—**be occupied, be busy, be troubled with** (בְּ) business (עִנְיָן) Ec 1$_{13}$ 3$_{10}$, prostitution Si 42$_{8(Bmg, M)}$.

Hi. keep occupied Ec 5$_{19}$ (if em. מַעֲנֶה *answers* [i.e. ענה I] to מַעֲנֵהוּ *keeps him occupied*).

→ עִנְיָן *occupation,* עֲנָיָה II *care,* (?) עֹנָה *conjugal rights,* מַעֲנֶה II *purpose,* (?) מַעֲנָה *furrow,* (?) מַעֲנִית *furrow.*

*ענה V 9 vb.—**Qal** 6 Pf. עֲנִיתָנִי; impf. יַעֲנֶה; impv. Qr עֱנֵנִי—**1. triumph** Zc 9$_{9}$ (if em. עָנִי *humble* to עֹנֶה *triumphing*). **2. cause to triumph, grant victory to** Ps 20$_{2.7.10}$ 60$_{7}$ 118$_{21}$.

Pi. 3 Pf. עִנּוּ; impf. יְעַנֵּנוּ—**1. triumph against, overcome** Nm 24$_{24.24}$ Ps 89$_{23}$. **2.** ptc. as noun, **conqueror** Dt 33$_{27}$ (if em. מְעֹנָה *dwelling place*).

→ עֲנָוָה I *triumph.*

*ענה VI vb. **Pi., make into a dwelling** Dt 33$_{27}$ (if em. מְעֹנָה אֱלֹהֵי קֶדֶם *the God of old is a dwelling place* to מְעַנֶּה אָהֳלֵי קֶדֶם *who makes into dwellings the tents of old*). → עֹנָה II *dwelling.*

*ענה VII 3 vb.—**Qal** 3 + waw וְעָנָה; ptc. עֹנֶה—**dwell, stay in a place** Is 13$_{22}$ Ho 2$_{17}$ Ml 2$_{12}$. → עֳנִי III *dwelling.*

*ענה VIII 3 vb.—**Hi.** 3 Impf. תַּעֲנֶה—**cause to flow,** i.e. **1. cause heaven to drop rain** Ho 2$_{23.23}$ (if in both em. אֶעֱנֶה *I will answer for* to אַעֲנֶה *I will cause to drop rain*). **2. make fruitful,** obj. Jezreel Ho 2$_{24}$, earth Ho 2$_{23}$. **3. produce grain, wine, oil** Ho 2$_{24}$.

*ענה IX 1 vb.—**Qal** 1 Impf. יַעֲנֶה—**be disquieted,** of lion Is 31$_{4}$ (+ מִן *on account of* tumult).

*ענה X 1 vb.—**Qal** 1 Impf. אַעֲנֶה—**plough portion,** i.e. furrow Jb 32$_{17}$.

*ענה XI 1 vb.—**Pi.** 1 Pf. עִנּוּ— **imprison feet** Ps 105$_{18}$ (+ בְּ *with* fetters). → עֳנִי II *captivity.*

*ענה XII 7 vb.—**Qal** 6 Pf. עָנִיתִי; impf. תַּעֲנֶה, יַעֲנוּ—**1. attend to** Ho 2$_{23.24}$. **2.** without obj., **be attentive** Ho 2$_{17.23}$ 14$_{9}$.

Hi. 1 Ptc. מַעֲנֶה—**make attentive** Ec 5$_{19}$.

*ענה XIII 1 vb.—**Qal** 1 + waw וְעָנְתָה—**have intercourse** Ho 2$_{17}$.

*[עֲנָה] n.f. **furrow** Ps 129$_{3}$ (if em. לְמַעֲנִיתָם *their furrows* [Qr; Kt מענותם] to לָמוֹ עֲנוֹתָם *for themselves their furrows*).

*[עֲנָה] n.f. **prayer,** עֲנוֹת/עֲנַת עָנִי *prayers/prayer of the afflicted* Ps 22$_{25}$ (if em. עֱנוּת *affliction of*). → ענן *practise soothsaying.*

עֲנָה 12 pr.n.m. **Anah.**

[עֹנָה] I 1.0.7 n.f.—Q עונה; cstr. Q עונת; sf. עֹנָתָהּ; pl. cstr. Q עונות; sf. Q עונותם—**1. conjugal rights** of wife, perh. lit. 'period (of cohabitation)' Ex 21$_{10}$. **2. period,** fixed for engagement of troops in battle 4QM^{a} 1$_{15}$, office of sons of Belial 4QBer^{a} 7.2$_{6}$. → (?) ענה IV *be occupied.*

*[עֹנָה] II 1 n.f.—sf. עֹנָתָהּ—**dwelling** Ex 21$_{10}$. → ענה VI *make into a dwelling.*

*[עֹנָה] III 1 n.f.—sf. עֹנָתָהּ—**oil, ointment** Ex 21$_{10}$.

*עֹנֶה 1 n.[m.] **answer** Jg 19$_{28}$. → ענה I *answer.*

[עָנָו] 24.1.17 adj.—pl. עֲנָוִים; cstr. עַנְוֵי—**1. humble, meek, poor,** perh. **miserable,** of man Nm 12$_{3}$. **2.** as noun, **humble one, meek one, poor one,** as oppressed Is 32$_{7(Kt)}$ (Qr עֲנִיִּים, i.e. pl. of עָנִי *afflicted*) Am 2$_{7}$, devout, humble in relation to Y. Zp 2$_{3}$. → ענה II *be afflicted.*

[עֻנּוֹ] 1 pr.n.m. **Unno.**

עָנוּב 1 pr.n.m. **Anub.**

*[עִנּוּג] n.[m.]—**1. happiness** Ex 32$_{18}$ (if em. עַנּוֹת *singing* [pi. inf.] to עֱנוֹת עִנּוּג *shouting of happiness,* i.e. of happy people). **2. pampering (with cosmetics)** Ex 21$_{10}$ (if em. עֹנָתָהּ *her conjugal rights* to עִנֻּגָהּ *her pampering*). → ענג I *be delicate.*

*[עֲנָוָה] I 1 n.f.—sf. עַנְוָתְךָ—**triumph** Ps 18$_{36}$. → ענה V *triumph.*

*[עֲנָוָה] II 1 n.f.—sf. עַנְוָתְךָ—**care, providence** Ps 18$_{36}$.

עֲנָוָה III, see עֲנָוָה *humility.*

עֲנָוָה 6.6.21 n.f.—עֲנָוָה; cstr. Q ענות; sf. עַנְוַתְךָ—**1a. humility, meekness** Zp 2₃ Pr 15₃₃. **b.** concrete, **one who shows humility, one who is oppressed** 1QS 9₂₂. **2. stooping down, condescension** of Y. Ps 18₃₆. **3. humiliation, affliction** 4QMidrEschat[b] 11₁₃. → ענה II *be afflicted.*

עֲנוֹק, see עֲנָק *Anak.*

***עֲנוּשִׁים** 1 n.[m.]pl. **fines,** יֵין עֲנוּשִׁים *wine of,* i.e. bought with, *fines* Am 2₈. → ענשׁ *fine.*

עֲנוֹת, see בֵּית־עֲנוֹת *Beth-anoth.*

[עֱנוּת] I 1 n.f.—cstr. עֱנוּת—**affliction** Ps 22₂₅. → ענה II *afflict.*

***[עֱנוּת]** II 1 n.f.—cstr. עֱנוּת—**song** Ps 22₂₅. → ענה III *sing.*

***[עַנְוְתָנוּת]** 0.1 n.f.—sf. ענותנותו—**humility** Si 45₄(Bmg). → ענה II *be afflicted.*

עָנִי 80.7.17 adj.—sf. עֲנִיֵּךְ; f.s. עֲנִיָּה; m.pl. עֲנִיִּים; cstr. עֲנִיֵּי; sf. עֲנִיָּו—**1a.** of lack of wealth, **poor, needy** Dt 24₁₂. **b.** as noun, **poor one, needy one** Ex 22₂₄, as oppressed Is 3₁₄. **2a.** of general condition, **poor, afflicted, wretched,** oft. of the devout as afflicted by the wicked Ps 25₁₆ 109₁₆. **b.** as noun, **poor one, afflicted one, wretched one** Ps 10₂ 12₆. **3a. humble, lowly** Zp 3₁₂. **b.** as noun, **humble one, lowly one** Si 10₁₄. **4. subdued, gentle,** of sound of voice 4QCrypt 2.1₂. → ענה II *afflict.*

עֳנִי I 36.1.6 n.[m.]—עֳנִי (Si, Q עוני); cstr. עֳנִי; sf. עָנְיוֹ, עָנְיִי—**1. affliction, misery, hardship** Gn 16₁₁ Ex 3₇. **2. poverty** Si 13₂₄. → ענה II *afflict.*

***עֳנִי** II 3 n.[m.]—עֳנִי; cstr. עֳנִי—**captivity** Ex 3₁₇ 107₁₀ Jb 36₈. → ענה XI *imprison.*

***[עֱנִי]** III n.[m.] **dwelling** Ps 87₅ (if em. עֶלְיוֹן *the Most High* to לְעֶנְיוֹ *for his dwelling*). → ענה VII *dwell.*

עֵנִי, see עַיִן I *eye.*

***עֹנִי** 1 n.[m.] **resignation** Jb 36₂₁.

עֻנִּי 3 pr.n.m. **Unni.**

עֲנָיָה I 2 pr.n.m. **Anaiah.**

***[עֲנָיָה]** II n.f. **care, providence** 2 S 22₃₆ (if em. עֲנֹתְךָ *your answering* to עֲנָיָתְךָ *your care*) Ps 18₃₆ (if em. עַנְוַתְךָ *your stooping down* to עֲנָיָתְךָ). → ענה IV *be occupied.*

ענים Lm 4₃(Kt), see יָעֵן I *ostrich,* II *steppe-dweller.*

עָנִים 1.0.0.1 pl.n. **Anim.**

עִנְיָן 8.0.1 n.m.—cstr. עִנְיַן; sf. עִנְיָנוֹ—**occupation, task, business** Ec 1₁₃ 3₁₀. → ענה IV *be occupied.*

עָנֵם 1 pl.n. **Anem.**

[עֲנָמִי] 2 gent. **Anamite.**

עֲנַמֶּלֶךְ 1 pr.n.[m.] **Anammelech.**

***[עֲנִמֵשׁ]** 0.0.0.1 pr.n.[m.] **Animesh.**

ענן I 10.0.1 vb.—**Po.** 10.0.1 Pf. עוֹנֵן; impf. תְּעוֹנֵנוּ; ptc. מְעוֹנֵן, מְעֹנְנִים, עֹנֵנָה—**1. practise soothsaying** Lv 19₂₆. **2.** ptc. as noun, **soothsayer** Dt 18₁₀. → עֲנָה *prayer.*

ענן II 1 vb.—**Pi.** 1 Inf. עַנְנִי—**bring clouds** Gn 9₁₄. → עָנָן I *cloud,* עֲנָנָה *cloud.*

עָנָן I 87.5.10 n.m.—cstr. עֲנַן; sf. עֲנָנוֹ; pl. עֲנָנִים—**1. cloud(s), cloud mass,** in sky Gn 9₁₃, assoc. with judgment of Y. Ezk 30₃, presence of Y. Ex 19₉ Na 1₃; pillar of cloud, leading Israelites at exodus Ex 13₂₁. **2. cloud, smoke** of incense Ezk 8₁₁. → ענן II *bring clouds.*

עָנָן II 1 pr.n.m. **Anan.**

עֲנָנָה I 1 n.f. **cloud** Jb 3₅. → ענן II *bring clouds.*

***עֲנָנָה** II 1 n.f. **punishment** Jb 3₅.

עֲנָנִי 1 pr.n.m. **Anani.**

עֲנַנְיָה I 1.0.0.1 pr.n.m. **Ananiah.**

עֲנַנְיָה II 1 pl.n. **Ananiah.**

ענניהו, see עֲנַנְיָה I *Ananiah.*

עָנָף 7.2.3 n.[m.]—cstr. עֲנַף; sf. עַנְפְּכֶם; pl. cstr. Q ענפי; sf. עֲנָפֶיהָ—**branch(es), bough(s)** of trees Lv 23₄₀, vine Ezk 17₈. → cf. עָנֵף *full of branches.*

[עָנֵף] 1 adj.—f.s. עֲנֵפָה—**full of branches,** of vine Ezk 19₁₀. → cf. עָנָף *branch.*

ענק 3 vb.—**Qal** 1 Pf. עֲנָקַתְמוֹ—**serve as necklace for** (accus.), of pride Ps 73₆.

Hi. 2 Impf. תַּעֲנִיק; inf. abs. הַעֲנֵיק—**provide a necklace,** i.e. **make provision for** (לְ) someone from (מִן) one's flock, etc. Dt 15₁₄.

→ עֲנָק I *necklace.*

עֲנָק I 3 n.m.—pl. עֲנָקִים, עֲנָקוֹת—**necklace, neck-chain, bead, pendant,** for woman Ca 4₉, young person Pr 1₉, camel Jg 8₂₆. → ענק *serve as a necklace.*

עֲנָק II 9 pr.n.m. **Anak.**

[עֲנָקִי] 9 gent. **Anakite.**

עָנֵר I 2 pr.n.m. **Aner.**

עָנֵר II 1 pl.n. **Aner.**

ענשׁ 9.0.41 vb.—**Qal** 6.0.2 + waw וַיַּעֲנֹשׁ; וְעָנְשׁוּ; ptc. pass.

עֲנוּשִׁים; inf. abs. עָנוֹשׁ; cstr. עֲנוֹשׁ (עֲנֹשׁ־)—**1. fine,** with accus. of one fined and fine imposed Dt 22_{19} 2 C 36_{3}. **2. punish,** with accus. Pr 21_{11}, לְ of obj. Pr 17_{26}. **3.** pass. **be fined** Am 2_{8}.

Ni. 3.0.39 Pf. נֶעֶנְשׁוּ; impf. יֵעָנֵשׁ—**1. be fined** Ex 21_{22}; ונענשו את רביעית לחמו *and it shall be fined him a quarter of his bread (allowance)* 1QS 6_{25}. **2. be punished, suffer the consequences** Pr 22_{3} CD 3_{4} (+ לִפְנֵי *on account of* errors); perh. by being fined a proportion of food allowance (cf. §1), but without specification of the penalty 1QS 7_{4} 9_{1} (+ עַל *on account of* inadvertent sin). → עֹנֶשׁ *fine,* עֲנוּשִׁים *fines.*

עֹנֶשׁ 2.1 n.[m.]—pl. sf. Si עושניה—**fine, tribute,** imposed on Judah by Pharaoh Neco 2 K 23_{33}; **penalty,** borne by individual Pr 19_{19} Si 9_{5}. → ענשׁ *fine.*

עֲנָת I 2 pr.n.m. **Anath.**

עֲנָת II, see בֵּית עֲנָת *Beth-anath.*

עֲנָתוֹת I 13 pl.n. **Anathoth.**

עֲנָתוֹת II 2 pr.n.m. **Anathoth.**

עַנְּתֹתִי 5 gent. **Anathothite.**

עַנְתֹתִיָּה 1 pr.n.m. **Anathothijah.**

עסה, see עשׂה I *do.*

עָסִיס 5 n.m.—cstr. עֲסִיס—**sweet wine, juice** Is 49_{26} Am 9_{13}; from pomegranate Ca 8_{2}. → עסס *crush.*

עסס 1 vb.—**Qal** 1 + waw וְעַסּוֹתֶם—**crush, tread down** someone Ml 3_{21}. → עָסִיס *sweet wine.*

*עסק 0.1 vb.—**Htp.** 0.1 inf. התעשק—**busy oneself, occupy oneself with** (עם) someone Si 41_{22}. → עֵסֶק *business.*

*[עֵסֶק] 0.5 n.m.—sf. עשקך—**business, concern, toil** Si 3_{22} 7_{25} 11_{10} 38_{24} 40_{1}. → עסק *be busy.*

עסר, see עשׂר *tithe.*

[עער] Is 15_{5}, see עור I *rouse oneself,* pilp.

עפאים, see עֳפִי *foliage.*

*[עפה] vb.—**Ho., be covered over, be effaced** Ps 90_{10} (if em. וַנָּעֻפָה *and we fly away* to וְנֶעְפָּה *and it is covered over*). → עֳפִי *foliage.*

*[עָפוֹר] n.m.—**gazelle, antelope** Ca 4_{5} 7_{4} (both if em. עֳפָרִים *fawns* to עֲפֹרִים *gazelles*).

*[עֵפַי] 0.0.0.2 pr.n.m. **Ophai.**

[עֳפִי] 1.1.5 n.[m.]—cstr. Q עפי (Q עופי); pl. Qr עֳפָיִם (Kt עפאים); sf. Q עפיו—**foliage, branch(es)**—Ps 104_{12} Si 14_{26} 1QH 14_{15}. → עפה *cover.*

עפל I 2 vb.—**Pu.** 1 Pf. עֻפְּלָה—**be swelled up, puffed up** Hb 2_{4}.

Hi. 1 + waw וַיַּעְפִּלוּ—**presume, dare** Nm 14_{44} (+ לַעֲלוֹת *to go up*).

→ עֹפֶל I *mound,* II *haemorrhoid,* עַפָּל *impudent one.*

עפל II 1 vb.—**Qal, be heedless,** ptc. as noun, **heedless one** Hb 2_{4} (if em. עֻפְּלָה *it is puffed up* to הָעֹפֵל).

Hi. 1 + waw וַיַּעְפִּלוּ—**show heedlessness** Nm 14_{44} (+ לַעֲלוֹת *in going up*).

*עפל III 1 vb.—**Pu.** 1 Pf. עֻפְּלָה—**become weak, dwindle away** Hb 2_{4}.

*[עַפָּל] n.m. **impudent one** Hb 2_{4} (if em. עֻפְּלָה *it is puffed up*). → עפל I *swell.*

עֹפֶל I 8 n.[m.]—cstr. עֹפֶל—**mound, hill,** in Jerusalem Is 32_{14}, sometimes as pl.n. **Ophel** Ne 3_{26}; in Samaria 2 K 5_{24}. → עפל I *swell.*

[עֹפֶל] II 6 n.m.—(alw. as Kt for Qr טְחֹר *haemorrhoid*) pl. עפלים; cstr. עפלי—**haemorrhoid, boil** Dt 28_{27} 1 S 5_{6}; made of gold 1 S 6_{4}. → עפל I *swell.*

*[עֶפְלוּל] 0.0.1 pr.n.m. **Aphlul.**

עָפְנִי 1 pl.n. **Ophni.**

[עַפְעַף] I 10.0.1 n.m.—du. cstr. עַפְעַפֵּי; sf. עַפְעַפָּיו—**eyelid, eyelash,** of Y. Ps 11_{4}, human Jb 16_{16}, the dawn Jb 3_{9}; sometimes perh. **eyeball, pupil** Jr 9_{17}. → עוף I *fly.*

*[עַפְעַף] II 2 n.[m.] **shaft,** עַפְעַפֵּי־שָׁחַר *shafts of dawn* Jb 3_{9} 41_{10}. → עפף II *jab.*

*עפף I 1 vb.—**Po.** 1 Inf. עוֹפְפִי—**ply, wield,** perh. **double** sword before (עַל־פְּנֵי) someone Ezk 32_{10}.

*עפף II 3 vb.—**Po.** 3 Ptc. מְעוֹפֵף; inf. עוֹפְפִי—**1. jab** sword at (עַל־פְּנֵי) someone Ezk 32_{10}. **2.** without obj., **jab, prick,** i.e. **bite,** of serpent Is 14_{29} 30_{6}. → עַפְעַף II *shaft.*

עפר I 1 vb.—**Pi.** 1 Pf. עִפַּר—**throw dust** (בְּ of obj. עָפָר *dust*) 2 S 16_{13}. → עָפָר I *dust.*

*עפר II vb. **cover Qal,** Jb 7_{5} (if em. עֲפַר *dust* to עָפַר *it* [scab] *has covered* my skin).

עָפָר I 110.4.70 n.m.—cstr. עֲפַר; sf. עֲפָרוֹ; pl. cstr. עַפְרוֹת—**1. dust, (dry) earth, soil, a.** as loose on ground Ezk 24_{7}; in ref. to surface of ground Ex 8_{12}, material of the earth Is 40_{12}, gold dust Jb 28_{6}, iron ore Jb 28_{2}. **b.** as abundant Gn 13_{16}. **c.** as material of human body Gn

27 Ps 103$_{14}$. **e.** as place of grave Is 26$_{19}$. **f.** representing lowly position or humiliation 1 S 2$_{8}$. **2. plaster,** on interior walls of house Lv 14$_{41}$. **3a. dust (of pulverized material), rubble** 2 K 23$_{12}$ Ne 3$_{34}$. **b. ashes, dust (of pulverised ashes)** of sin offering Nm 19$_{17}$, image of calf Dt 9$_{21}$. **4. land, field** Mur 24 C$_{7.9}$ 5/6 ḤevBA 44$_{12.15}$. → עפר I *throw dust.*

*[עָפָר] II 1 n.[m.]—cstr. עֲפַר—**multitude** Nm 23$_{10}$.

*[עָפָר] III 1 n.[m.]—cstr. עֲפַר—**warrior** Nm 23$_{10}$.

עֵפֶר 4 pr.n.m. **Epher.**

[עֹפֶר] 5 n.m.—cstr. עֹפֶר; pl. עֳפָרִים—**young deer, fawn, stag,** or perh. **ibex** Ca 2$_{9}$ 4$_{5}$.

עַפְרָה, see בֵּית לְעַפְרָה *Beth-le-aphrah.*

עָפְרָה I 7 pl.n. **Ophrah.**

עָפְרָה II 1 pr.n.m. **Ophrah.**

עֶפְרוֹן I 12 pr.n.m. **Ephron.**

עֶפְרוֹן II 2 pl.n. **Ephron,** also as עֶפְרַיִן **Ephrain.**

עֶפְרַיִן, see עפרון II *Ephron.*

עֹפֶרֶת 9.0.2 n.m.—עוֹפֶרֶת, עֹפָרֶת—**lead** Ex 15$_{10}$ Nm 31$_{22}$.

עֵץ 329.6.52 n.m.—cstr. עֵץ; sf. עֵצוֹ; pl. עֵצִים; cstr. עֲצֵי; sf. עֵצָיו—**1. tree** Gn 18$_{4}$, perh. **shrub** Ex 15$_{25}$; sg. oft. coll., **trees** Gn 1$_{11}$; עֵץ הַשָּׂדֶה *trees of the field* Ex 9$_{25}$. **2. wood, timber, a.** sg., (1) as material of vessel Lv 11$_{32}$, image of god Dt 4$_{28}$, shaft of spear 2 S 23$_{7}$; חָרָשֵׁי עֵץ *artisans of wood,* i.e. carpenters 2 S 5$_{11}$; **woodwork** of building Hb 2$_{11}$. (2) **(piece of) wood,** for firewood Si 8$_{3}$, cedarwood used for purification Lv 14$_{4}$, **stick** 2 K 6$_{6}$. **b.** pl. (1) **(trees felled as) timber, logs** 1 K 5$_{24}$ Ezr 3$_{7}$. (2) **(pieces of) wood, timber,** for constructing tabernacle and furnishings Ex 25$_{5}$||35$_{7}$, house Lv 14$_{45}$. (3) **(pieces of) wood, sticks, (small) logs,** for firewood Gn 22$_{3}$ Ezk 24$_{10}$; as gathered Nm 15$_{32}$, cut Dt 19$_{5}$. (4) **(items made of) wood** Ex 7$_{19}$ 1 C 29$_{2}$. (5) **wood (as offering)** Ne 10$_{35}$. **3. tree (for execution by hanging), gallows** Gn 40$_{19}$ Est 5$_{14}$. **4. tree, pole,** as object in cult of Asherah Dt 16$_{21}$. **5. stalks of flax** Jos 2$_{6}$. → cf. עֵצָה II *tree.*

עצב I 15.1.1 vb.—**Qal** 3.1.1 Pf. עֲצָבוֹ; ptc. pass. עֲצוּבַת; inf. עָצְבִּי—**1. grieve, rebuke** 1 K 1$_{6}$ Si 14$_{1}$. **2. hurt** 1 C 4$_{10}$. **3.** pass. **be grieved,** עֲצוּבַת רוּחַ *grieved of,* i.e. in, *spirit* Is 54$_{6}$.

Ni. 7.1 Pf. נֶעֱצַב; impf. יֵעָצֵב, תֵּעָצְבוּ—**1. be grieved** Gn 45$_{5}$ 1 S 20$_{34}$ (+ אֶל *for*) 2 S 19$_{3}$ (+ עַל *for*). **2. be hurt** by (בְּ) stones Ec 10$_{9}$.

Pi. 2 Pf. עִצְּבוּ; impf. יְעַצֵּבוּ—**grieve, hurt** Is 63$_{10}$ Ps 56$_{6}$.

Hi. 1 יַעֲצִיבוּהוּ—**grieve, cause pain to** Ps 78$_{40}$.

Htp. 2 + waw וַיִּתְעַצֵּב—**be grieved, be filled with pain** Gn 6$_{6}$ (+ אֶל *to* one's heart) 34$_{7}$.

→ עָצֵב/עָצֵב *labourer,* עֶצֶב I *pain,* עֹצֶב I *pain,* עַצָּבָה *grief,* עִצָּבוֹן *pain,* עַצֶּבֶת *grief,* מַעֲצֵבָה *(place of) pain.*

עצב II 2 vb.—**Pi.** 1 Pf. עִצְּבוּנִי—**shape, fashion** person, of hands of Y. Jb 10$_{8}$.

Hi. 1 Inf. הַעֲצִבָה—**make an image** of the queen of heaven Jr 44$_{19}$.

→ עָצָב *image,* עֹצֶב II *image,* עֶצֶב II *pot,* עַצֶּבֶת II *image.*

*עצב III 1 vb.—**Ni** 1 Impf. יֵעָצֵב—**be cut** Ec 10$_{9}$ (+ בְּ *by* stones).

*עצב IV 1 vb.—**Qal** 1 Pf. עֲצָבוּ—**1. upbraid** 1 K 1$_{6}$. **2. revile** Ps 56$_{6}$ (if em. דְּבָרַי יְעַצֵּבוּ *they hurt my cause* to דֹּבְרַי יַעַצְבוּ *those who speak to me revile me*). → עֶצֶב III *reviling.*

[עָצָב] 17.0.2 n.[m.]—pl. עֲצַבִּים; cstr. עֲצַבֵּי; sf. עֲצַבֶּיהָ—**image (of god)** 1 S 31$_{9}$; appar. the god represented by it Ps 106$_{36}$. → עצב II *shape.*

[עָצֵב] or [עָצָב] 1 n.[m.]—pl. sf. עַצְּבֵיכֶם—**labourer** Is 58$_{3}$. → עצב I *grieve.*

עֶצֶב I 6.0.1 n.[m.]—pl. עֲצָבִים; sf. עֲצָבֶיךָ—**1. pain** of childbirth Gn 3$_{16}$, **hurt** caused by word Pr 15$_{1}$. **2. toil, labour, trouble** Pr 14$_{23}$; לֶחֶם הָעֲצָבִים *bread of,* i.e. gained by, *toil* Ps 127$_{2}$. → עצב I *grieve.*

עֶצֶב II 1 n.m. **pot** Jr 22$_{28}$. → עצב II *shape.*

*עֶצֶב III 1 n.[m.] **reviling** Pr 15$_{1}$. → עצב IV *revile.*

*עֶצֶב IV 1 n.[m.] **nerve,** יָגֹרְתִּי כָל־עַצְּבֹתַי *I shudder in my every nerve* Jb 9$_{28}$.

עֹצֶב I 3 n.[m.]—sf. עָצְבְּךָ—**pain** (perh. lit. 'toil') of childbirth 1 C 4$_{9}$, **hurt** Is 14$_{3}$ Ps 139$_{24}$. → עצב I *grieve.*

[עֹצֶב] II 2 n.m.—sf. עָצְבִּי—**image (of god)** Is 48$_{5}$ perh. Ps 139$_{24}$. → עצב II *shape.*

*[עַצָּבָה] 0.2 n.f. **grief, pain** Si 11$_{9(A)}$ 38$_{18}$. → עצב I *grieve.*

עִצָּבוֹן 3 n.[m]—cstr. עִצְּבוֹן; sf. עִצְּבוֹנֵךְ—**1. pain** (perh. lit. 'toil') of childbirth Gn 3$_{16}$. **2. toil** Gn 3$_{17}$ 5$_{29}$. → עצב I *grieve.*

[עַצֶּבֶת] I 5.1 n.f.—עַצֶּבֶת; cstr. עַצְּבַת; pl. sf. עַצְּבוֹתָם—**1. grief, sorrow, pain** Ps 16$_4$ Jb 9$_{28}$ Pr 15$_{13}$. **2. wound** Ps 147$_3$. → עצב I *grieve.*

*[עַצֶּבֶת] II 1 n.f.—pl. sf. עַצְּבוֹתָם—**image (of god)** Ps 16$_4$. → עצב II *shape.*

*[עצד] 0.0.0.1 vb.—**Qal** 1 Inf. עצד—**1. cut, forge** Is 44$_{12}$ (if em. מַעֲצָד *axe* to גֹּלֶם עָצַד *he cuts a model*). **2. pull** flax Gezer Calendar$_3$. → עֶצֶד *pulling*, מַעֲצָד *axe*, מַעֲצָדָה *axe*.

*[עֶצֶד] 0.0.0.1 n.[m.] (unless inf. of עצד)—**pulling,** ירח עצד פשת *month of flax-pulling* Gezer Calendar$_3$. → עצד *pull.*

עצה I 1 vb.—**Qal** 1 Ptc. עֹצֶה—**shut, wink the eyes** Pr 16$_{30}$.

*עצה II 0.1 vb.—**Ni.** 0.1 Impv. היעצה—**strive, struggle** for (עַל) righteousness Si 4$_{28}$. → עֵצָה III *struggle.*

*עצה III vb.—**Qal, lay (one's) eye upon** (עַל) Ps 32$_8$ (if em. אִיעֲצָה *I will counsel* to אֶעֱצֶה).

עָצֶה 1.0.2 n.[m.]—sf. Q עציהה—**sacrum, coccyx, (rear end of) spine** of sacrificial sheep Lv 3$_9$.

עֵצָה I 88.6.107 n.f.—cstr. עֲצַת; sf. עֲצָתִי; pl. עֵצוֹת; sf. עֲצָתֶיךָ —**1. counsel, advice, decision,** given by humans Jg 20$_7$ 2 S 15$_{31}$, one's heart 11QT 58$_{20}$, Y. Ezr 10$_3$; Y.'s testimonies descr. as אַנְשֵׁי עֲצָתִי *men of my counsel,* i.e. my counsellors Ps 119$_{24}$. **2. (good) counsel,** i.e. wisdom, of humans Dt 32$_{28}$ Jr 18$_{18}$, Y. Is 28$_{29}$, Wisdom Pr 1$_{25}$, the law 1QS 9$_9$. **3. counsel,** i.e. **plan, purpose, design, plot** of humans Jr 18$_{23}$ Jb 21$_{16}$; of Y. Jr 49$_{20}$, as carried out by an individual Is 46$_{11}$; of Belial 1QM 13$_{11}$. **4. council,** עצת היחד *council of the community* 1QpHab 12$_4$, אנשי עצת אל *men of the council of God* 1QSb 4$_{24}$. → יעץ *advise.*

עֵצָה II 3.0.1 n.f.—cstr. עֲצַת—**1.** coll., **trees, forest** Jr 6$_6$ 4QRitMar 8$_4$. **2a. wood,** עֲצַת־נֶפֶשׁ *wood of fragrance,* i.e. fragrant wood Pr 27$_9$. **b. (object of) wood, wooden image (of god)** Is 30$_1$. → cf. עֵץ I *tree.*

*עֵצָה III 8.2.1 n.f.—cstr. עֲצַת; sf. עֲצָתוֹ; pl. עֵצוֹת—**1. disobedience, rebellion** Ho 10$_6$ Ps 14$_6$ Jb 10$_3$. **2. firmness, endurance** Is 16$_3$ Jb 12$_{13}$. **3. hard struggle, harsh treatment, agony** Ps 13$_3$ 14$_6$. **4. constraint, compulsion** 1QS 7$_{11}$. → עצה II *strive.*

*[עֵצָה] IV 2 n.f.—pl. עֵצוֹת—**doubt** Ps 13$_3$ 106$_{43}$.

עָצוּם 31.1.4 adj.—cstr. Q עצום; m.pl. עֲצוּמִים; sf. עֲצוּמָיו; f.pl. Si עצומות—**1. mighty, powerful, numerous,** of nation Nm 14$_{12}$ (+ מִן mightier *than*), king Ps 135$_{10}$, cattle Nm 32$_1$, water Is 8$_7$, sins Am 5$_{12}$. **2.** as noun, **a. mighty one, powerful one** Is 53$_{12}$ Pr 18$_{18}$. **b.** fem. pl., **many things** Si 16$_5$. **c.** masc. sg., **might** 1QM 11$_5$. → עצם I *be mighty.*

*[עֲצוּמִים] 1 n.[m.]pl.—sf. עֲצוּמָיו—**pit** Ps 10$_{10}$.

עֶצְיוֹן־גֶּבֶר 7 pl.n. **Ezion-geber.**

עצל 1.0.3 vb.—**Ni.** 1.0.2 Impf. תֵּעָצְלוּ—**be sluggish, slow, lazy** Jg 18$_9$ 4QInstr[d] 55$_{11}$.

Htp. 0.0.1 Impf. תתעצלו—**be sluggish, slow** 11QPs[a] 18$_2$.

→ עָצֵל *sluggish*, עַצְלָה *sluggishness*, עַצְלוּת *idleness*, עֲצַלְתַּיִם *laziness.*

עָצֵל 14.0.1 adj.—**1. sluggish, lazy,** of man Pr 24$_{30}$. **2.** as noun, **sluggard, lazy one** Pr 6$_6$. → עצל *be sluggish.*

*[עַצְלָא] 0.0.1 pl.n. **Azla.**

עַצְלָה 1 n.f. **sluggishness, idleness** Pr 19$_{15}$. → עצל *be sluggish.*

עַצְלוּת 1 n.f. **idleness** Pr 31$_{27}$. → עצל *be sluggish.*

עֲצַלְתַּיִם 1 n.f.du. **laziness, double** (i.e. great) **sluggishness** Ec 10$_{18}$. → עצל *be sluggish.*

עצם I 17.0.1 vb.—**Qal** 16.0.1 Pf. עָצַמְתָּ, עָצְמוּ (עָצֵמוּ); + waw וַיַּעַצְמוּ; inf. עָצְמוֹ—**1. be mighty, powerful,** of person Gn 26$_{16}$ (+ מִן mightier *than*), he-goat Dn 8$_8$, strength Dn 8$_{24}$. **2. be numerous,** of people Ex 1$_{20}$, iniquities Ps 40$_{13}$ (+ מִן more numerous *than*).

Hi. 1 + waw וַיַּעֲצִמֵהוּ—**make people mighty** Ps 105$_{24}$ (+ מִן mightier *than* adversaries).

→ עָצוּם *mighty*, עֹצֶם I *might*, עָצְמָה *might*, תַּעֲצֻמָה *might.*

עצם II 2 vb.—**Qal** 1 Ptc. עֹצֵם—**shut (one's own) eyes** Is 33$_{15}$ (+ מֵרְאוֹת בְּרָע *from looking at evil*).

Pi. 1 + waw וַיְעַצֵּם—**shut (someone else's) eyes** Is 29$_{10}$.

*עצם III 1 vb.—**Pi.** 1 Pf. עִצְּמוֹ—**gnaw the bones of,** or perh. **break the bones of** Israel Jr 50$_{17}$. → עֶצֶם I *bone*, עֹצֶם II *bones.*

*עצם IV vb.—**Qal, go to law,** ptc. as noun, **litigant** Pr 18$_{18}$ (if em. עֲצוּמִים *the mighty* to עוֹצְמִים *litigants*). → עֲצֻמָה *argument.*

עֶצֶם I $_{126.4.22.1}$ n.f.&m.—עֶצֶם; cstr. עֶצֶם; sf. עַצְמִי; pl. (1) (usu. bones of the living) עֲצָמִים; sf. עֲצָמַי; pl. (2) (usu. bones of the dead) עֲצָמוֹת; cstr. עַצְמוֹת; sf. עַצְמוֹתַי, עַצְמוֹתֵיהֶם, עַצְמוֹתָם—**1. bone(s), bodily frame, a.** of living human Jb 19$_{20}$, as representing whole person Ps 35$_{10}$, seat of pain or feeling Jr 20$_{9}$. **b.** of the dead Gn 50$_{25}$. **c.** expression of close relationship, עֶצֶם מֵעֲצָמַי *the bone of my bones* Gn 2$_{23}$, עַצְמִי וּבְשָׂרִי *my bone and flesh* Gn 29$_{14}$. **d.** of animal Ex 12$_{46}$. **2.** perh. **(outer) body, limb** Lm 4$_{7}$. **3. self, substance, a.** עֶצֶם הַיּוֹם הַזֶּה **this selfsame day, this very day,** lit. 'bone of this day' Gn 7$_{13}$. **b.** עֶצֶם הַשָּׁמַיִם **heaven itself, the very heavens,** lit. 'bone of heaven' Ex 24$_{10}$. **c.** עֶצֶם תֻּמּוֹ **his very completeness,** lit. 'bone of his completeness' Jb 21$_{23}$. → עצם III *gnaw bones.*

עֶצֶם II $_{3}$ pl.n. **Ezem.**

[עֹצֶם] I $_{2}$ n.[m.]—cstr. עֹצֶם—**might** Dt 8$_{17}$ Jb 30$_{21}$. → עצם I *be mighty.*

***[עֹצֶם]** II $_{1}$ n.m.—sf. עָצְמִי—**bones,** skeletal frame formed in womb Ps 139$_{15}$. → עצם III *gnaw bones.*

***[עַצְמָה]** $_{4}$ n.f.—pl. cstr. עַצְמוֹת; sf. עַצְמוֹתַי—**1. misfortune, calamity, agony** Ps 22$_{18}$ Jb 4$_{14}$ 7$_{15}$. **2. wicked deed** Ps 53$_{6}$.

עָצְמָה $_{3.2}$ n.f.—cstr. עָצְמַת—**might, power** Is 40$_{29}$ 47$_{9}$ Na 3$_{9}$ Si 41$_{2}$ 46$_{9}$. → עצם I *be mighty.*

[עֲצֻמָה] $_{1}$ n.f.—pl. sf. עֲצֻמוֹתֵיכֶם—**argument,** in legal case Is 41$_{21}$. → עצם IV *go to law.*

עַצְמוֹן $_{3}$ pl.n. **Azmon.**

עצר I $_{46.2.11.1}$ vb.—**Qal** $_{36.1.11}$ Pf. עָצַר, עָצַרְתִּי; impf. יַעְצֹר (יַעֲצָר־), אֶעְצֹר; + waw וַיַּעַצְרֵהוּ; ptc. pass. עָצוּר, עֲצֻרָה; inf. abs. עָצֹר; cstr. לַעְצֹר/וְ—**1. restrain, hold back, detain, stop, prevent (from doing),** with accus. person Gn 16$_{2}$ (+ מִלֶּדֶת *from giving birth*) 1 K 18$_{44}$, drink 1QH 12$_{11}$ (+ מִן *from* someone); בְּ of obj. words Jb 4$_{2}$, water Jb 12$_{15}$; אַל־תַּעֲצָר־לִי לִרְכֹּב *do not restrain for me to ride,* i.e. slow down the riding for me 2 K 4$_{24}$. **2. rein in, rule over** (בְּ) 1 S 9$_{17}$. **3. close, shut up** heavens Dt 11$_{17}$, the womb Gn 20$_{18}$ (בְּעַד of obj.) Is 66$_{9}$ (obj. omitted). **4. confine, imprison** 2 K 17$_{4}$. **5a.** עצר כֹּחַ **retain strength** Dn 10$_{8}$. **b.** עצר כֹּחַ לְ followed by inf. cstr., **retain strength to (do),** i.e. **be able to (do)** 1 C 29$_{14}$ 2 C 2$_{5}$. **6a.** pass. (1) **be restrained, held back, kept away** 1 S 21$_{6}$ (+ לְ *from*) 1 C 12$_{1}$ (+ מִפְּנֵי *from* or *on account of*). (2) **be shut up, confined, imprisoned,** of person Jr 33$_{1}$, fire Jr 20$_{9}$ (+ בְּ *in* bones). **b.** pass. ptc. as noun, **one who is shut up, bound one,** עָצוּר וְעָזוּב *bond and free,* i.e. all classes of people Dt 32$_{36}$.

Ni. $_{10.1.0.1}$ Pf. נֶעֶצְרָה; impf. תֵּעָצַר; ptc. נֶעְצָר; inf. הֵעָצֵר—**1. be detained before** (לִפְנֵי) Y. 1 S 21$_{8}$. **2. be stopped, be stayed,** of plague Nm 17$_{13}$ 2 S 24$_{21}$ (+ מֵעַל *from* people). **3a. be shut up,** of heaven 1 K 8$_{25}$||2 C 6$_{26}$. **b. have the womb shut up,** i.e. **be barren** Si 42$_{10}$.

→ עֶצֶר *restraint,* עֹצֶר *oppression, closure,* עֲצָרָה *sacred assembly,* מַעֲצוֹר *stopping,* מַעֲצָר *stopping.*

***עצר** II $_{1}$ vb.—**Qal** $_{1}$ Impf. יַעְצֹר—**rule** over (בְּ) people 1 S 9$_{17}$. **2.** ptc. as noun, **ruler,** עֹצֵר וְעֹזֵב *ruler and caretaker* or *ruling and leading* Dt 32$_{36}$ (if em. עָצוּר וְעָזוּב *bond and free*).

***עצר** III $_{5}$ vb.—**Qal** $_{5}$ Ptc. pass. עָצוּר—**protect,** pass. ptc. as noun, **one who is protected (by the clan),** עָצוּר וְעָזוּב *protected and unprotected,* i.e. kinsman and unprotected guest, all classes of people Dt 32$_{36}$. → עֶצֶר IV *protection.*

***עצר** IV vb. **Qal, trample,** לָמָּה עָצְרוּ רְשָׁעִים קָדְשֶׁךָ *why have the wicked trampled down you holy place?* Is 63$_{18}$ (if em. לְמִצְעָר יָרְשׁוּ עַם־קָדְשֶׁךָ *your holy people have possessed for a while*).

עֶצֶר I $_{1}$ n.[m.] **restraint,** or perh. **rule, oppression** Jg 18$_{7}$. → עצר I *restrain.*

***עֶצֶר** II $_{1}$ n.[m.]—**1. abundance, fertility,** or perh **fertile land** Jg 18$_{7}$. **2. marrow** Jr 20$_{9}$ (if em. עָצֻר *shut up*).

עֹצֶר I $_{3}$ n.[m.]—cstr. עֹצֶר—**1. oppression,** or perh. **detention, imprisonment** Is 53$_{8}$ Ps 107$_{39}$. **2. closure** of womb, i.e. **barrenness** Pr 30$_{16}$. → עצר I *restrain.*

***עֹצֶר** II $_{1}$ n.[m.] **voracity,** עֹצֶר רָחָם *voracity of the carrion-vulture* Ps 30$_{16}$ (if em. רֶחֶם closure *of the womb*).

***עֹצֶר** III $_{1}$ n.[m.]—cstr. עֹצֶר—**fertility** Pr 30$_{16}$.

***עֹצֶר** IV $_{1}$ n.[m.] **protection** Is 53$_{8}$. → עצר III *protect.*

עֲצָרָה $_{11.0.1}$ n.f.—עֲצָרָה (עֲצֶרֶת); cstr. עֲצֶרֶת; pl. sf. עַצְרֹתֵיכֶם—**1. sacred assembly** Jl 1$_{14}$, perh. as closing assembly of festival Lv 23$_{36}$; for Baal 2 K 10$_{20}$. **2. assembly,**

company, band of traitors Jr 9₁. → עצר I *restrain.*

עֲצֶרֶת, see עֲצָרָה *sacred assembly.*

עקב I 5 vb.—**Qal** 4 Pf. עָקַב; impf. יַעְקֹב; + waw וַיַּעְקְבֵנִי; inf. abs. עָקוֹב—**1. supplant** Gn 27₃₆. **2. take by the heel, or perh. by the genitals** Ho 12₄.

Pi. 1 Impf. יְעַקְּבֵם—**hold back, restrain** Jb 37₄.

→ עָקֵב I *heel,* II *supplanter,* עֵקֶב *consequence,* (?) עָקֹב I *deceitful,* (?) עָקְבָּה *deceit.*

***עקב** II 3 vb.—**Qal** 3 Impf. יַעְקֹב; + waw וַיַּעְקְבֵנִי; inf. abs. עָקוֹב—**cheat** someone Gn 27₃₆; without obj. Jr 9₃. → (?) עָקֹב I *deceitful,* (?) עָקְבָּה *deceit.*

***עקב** III 1 vb.—**Pi.** 1 Impf. יְעַקְּבֵם—**delay, detain, hinder** Jb 37₄.

***עקב** IV 2 vb.—**Qal** 2 Impf. יַעְקֹב; inf. abs. עָקוֹב—**utter slander** Jr 9₃. → עָקֵב *slander.*

*[**עָקֵב**] n.[m.] **slander** Ps 41₁₀ (if em. עָקֵב *heel*). → עקב IV *slander.*

עָקֵב I 13.5.2 n.m.—cstr. עֲקֵב; sf. עֲקֵבוֹ; pl. cstr. (עִקְּבֵי) עִקְּבֵי, עִקְּבוֹת; sf. עֲקֵבָי, עִקְּבוֹתֶיךָ, עֲקֵבֶיךָ—**1a. heel** Gn 3₁₅. **b. hoof** of horse Gn 49₁₇. **2. footprint, footstep** Ps 77₂₀ 89₅₂; **mark, trace** of a good heart Si 13₂₆. **3. rear** of a troop, **rearguard** Jos 8₁₃. **4.** perh. **genitals** Jr 13₂₂. → עקב I *supplant;* cf. עָקֹב III *tracked.*

עָקֵב II 1 n.[m.]—sf. עֲקֵבַי—**supplanter** Ps 49₆. → עקב I *supplant.*

עָקֹב I 1.1.1 adj.—**deceitful,** of heart Jr 17₉. → עקב I *supplant,* or II *cheat.*

עָקֹב II 1.1 adj.—f.s. Si עקובה—**1. difficult,** of wisdom Si 6₂₀ (+ לאויל difficult *for the fool*) Si 6₂₀. **2.** as noun, **uneven ground, rugged terrain, hilly land** Is 40₄.

*[**עָקֹב**] III 1 adj.—f.s. עֲקֻבָּה—**tracked,** of city Ho 6₈ (עֲקֻבָּה מִדָּם *tracked with blood*). → cf. עָקֵב I *heel.*

עֵקֶב 14 n.[m.] —**1. reward, recompense** Ps 19₁₂. **2.** as adv. accus., **to the end** Ps 119₃₃.₁₁₂. **3.** as prep., **a.** עֵקֶב **because of, (in exchange) for** Is 5₂₃. **b.** עַל־עֵקֶב **because of** Ps 40₁₆. **4.** as conj., **because, a.** עֵקֶב Nm 14₂₄. **b.** עֵקֶב אֲשֶׁר Gn 22₁₈. **c.** עֵקֶב כִּי 2 S 12₁₀. → עקב I *supplant.*

עָקְבָּה 1 n.f. **deceit, cunning** 2 K 10₁₉. → עקב I *supplant,* or II *cheat.*

עקד 1 vb.—**Qal** 1 + waw וַיַּעֲקֹד—**bind** someone Gn 22₉. → עָקֹד *striped.*

עָקֹד 7 adj.—pl. עֲקֻדִּים—**1. striped,** of he-goat Gn 31₁₀. **2.** as noun, **striped one** Gn 30₃₉. → עקד *bind.*

עֵקֶד, see בֵּית־עֵקֶד הָרֹעִים *Beth-eked-haroim.*

[**עָקָה**] I 1 n.f.—cstr. עָקַת—**oppression** Ps 55₄. → עוק I *press.*

*[**עָקָה**] II 1 n.f.—cstr. עָקַת—**cry (of glee), clamour** Ps 55₄. → עוק III *roar.*

*[**עָקָה**] III 1 n.f.—**1. eyeball** Ps 6₈ (if em. עָתְקָה *it has grown old* to עָקָתִי *my eyeball*). **2. stare** Ps 55₄.

עַקּוּב 8 pr.n.m.—**Akkub.**

*[**עֲקִילָא**] 0.0.1 pr.n.[m.]—**Akila.**

עקל 1 vb.—**Pu.** 1 Ptc. מְעֻקָּל—**be crooked, perverted,** of justice Hb 1₄. → עֲקַלְקַל *crooked,* עֲקַלָּתוֹן *twisting.*

[**עֲקַלְקַל**] 2 adj.—f.pl. עֲקַלְקַלּוֹת; sf. עֲקַלְקַלּוֹתָם—**1. crooked, winding,** of path Jg 5₆. **2.** f.pl. as noun, **crookedness** Ps 125₅. → עקל *twist.*

עֲקַלָּתוֹן 1 adj.—**twisting,** of serpent Is 27₁. → עקל *twist.*

עָקָן 1 pr.n.m.—**Akan.**

עקר 7.0.1 vb.—**Qal** 1 Inf. עֲקוֹר—**uproot, pluck up,** without obj. Ec 3₂.

Ni. 1 Impf. תֵּעָקֵר—**be uprooted,** of Ekron Zp 2₄.

Pi. 5 Pf. עִקֵּר, עִקְּרוּ; impf. תְּעַקֵּר; + waw וַיְעַקֵּר—**hamstring,** i.e. make lame by severing the pastern, obj. ox Gn 49₆, horse Jos 11₆.

→ עִקָּר *root,* עֲקֶרֶת *root,* עָקָר *barren,* עֵקֶר I *offshoot.*

עָקָר 12.0.1 adj.—f.s. עֲקָרָה; cstr. עֲקֶרֶת—**1. barren, infertile,** of woman Gn 11₃₀. **2.** as noun, **barren one, infertile one, a.** masc. Dt 7₁₄. **b.** fem. Ex 23₂₆ 1 S 2₅. → עקר *uproot.*

[**עֵקֶר**] I 1.1 n.[m.] **offshoot, member,** עֵקֶר מִשְׁפַּחַת גֵּר *offshoot of the clan of a sojourner* Lv 25₄₇. → עקר *uproot.*

עֵקֶר II 1 pr.n.m. **Eker.**

*[**עִקָּר**] 0.1.1 n.[m.]—cstr. Q עקר—**1. root,** עקר תחבולות לבב *the root of guidance is the heart* Si 37₁₇(Bmg, D). **2.** בעקר as prep., **beside, connected to,** lit. 'at the root of', פניהם זה בעקר ז[ה] *their faces were one beside the other* 4QpsEzek[a] 6₈. → עקר *uproot.*

עַקְרָב 6.1 n.[m.]—pl. עַקְרַבִּים—**1. scorpion(s)** Dt 8₁₅ Ezk 2₆. **2. scorpion,** as descr. of scourge 1 K 12₁₁||2 C 10₁₁.

עַקְרַבִּים I 3 pl.n. **Akrabbim.**

עַקְרַבִּים II, see עַקְרָב *scorpion.*

עֶקְרוֹן 22 pl.n. **Ekron.**

עֶקְרוֹנִי 2 gent. **Ekronite.**

*[**עֵקֶרֶת**] I 0.1 n.f. **root,** עקרת תחבולות לבב *the root of guidance is the heart* Si 37$_{17(B)}$. → עקר *uproot.*

עֲקֶרֶת II, see עָקָר *barren.*

עקשׁ 5 vb.—**Ni.** 1 Ptc. cstr. נֶעְקַשׁ—ptc. as noun, **perverse, crooked one,** נֶעְקַשׁ דְּרָכַיִם *perverse one of,* i.e. in, *two ways* Pr 28$_{18}$.

Pi. 3 Pf. עִקְּשׁוּ; impf. יְעַקֵּשׁוּ; ptc. מְעַקֵּשׁ—**twist, make crooked, pervert** one's ways Pr 10$_{9}$, what is right Mc 3$_{9}$.

Hi. 1 + waw וַיַּעְקְשֵׁנִי—**declare to be perverse, prove guilty** Jb 9$_{20}$.

→ עִקֵּשׁ I *twisted,* עִקְּשׁוּת *crookedness,* עֹקֶשׁ *perfidy,* מַעֲקָשׁ *rough place.*

עִקֵּשׁ I 11 adj.—cstr. עִקֵּשׁ (עִקֶּשׁ־); pl. עִקְּשִׁים; cstr. עִקְּשֵׁי—**1. twisted, crooked, perverse,** of generation Dt 32$_{5}$, heart Ps 101$_{4}$, path Pr 2$_{15}$. **3.** as noun, **crooked one, perverse one** 2 S 22$_{27}$||Ps 18$_{27}$. → עקשׁ *twist.*

עִקֵּשׁ II 3 pr.n.m. **Ikkesh.**

*[**עֹקֶשׁ**] n.m. **perfidy** Is 59$_{13}$ (if em. עֹשֶׁק *oppression*). → עקשׁ *twist.*

[**עִקְּשׁוּת**] 2 n.f. **crookedness,** עִקְּשׁוּת פֶּה *crookedness of mouth,* i.e. crooked speech Pr 4$_{24}$ 6$_{12}$. → עקשׁ *twist.*

*[**עָר**] I 2.4 n.[m.]—sf. עָרֶךָ; pl. Si ערים; sf. עָרַיִךְ—**enemy** 1 S 28$_{16}$ Ps 139$_{20}$ Si 37$_{5}$ 47$_{7}$.

עָר II 6 pl.n. **Ar.**

*[**עָר**] III 1 n.[m.] (byform of עַרְעָר II)—pl. sf. עָרָיו—**tamarisk** Is 42$_{11}$. → cf. עַרְעָר II *juniper,* עֲרוֹעֵר I *juniper.*

*עֵר I 2 n.[m.]—pl. sf. עָרַיִךְ—**protector** Mc 5$_{13}$ Ml 2$_{12}$. → עיר I *protect.*

*עֵר II 1 n.[m.] **nomad, vagabond** Ml 2$_{12}$.

עֵר III 10 pr.n.m. **Er.**

*ערב I 5.0.21 vb.—**Qal** 0.0.4 Impf. תערוב; inf. ערב—**1. mix** something 4QInstr[d] 103.2$_{6}$. **2. share, pool wealth** 1QS 6$_{22}$.

Pi. 0.0.1 Ptc. מערבים—**mix** 11QT 35$_{12}$ (+ אלה באלה *one with another*).

Pu. 0.0.3 Ptc. מעורב—**be mixed,** perh. of field with mixed crops 4QD[f] 2$_{6}$.

Htp. 5.0.13 Pf. הִתְעָרְבוּ; impf. יִתְעָרַב; + ptc. Q מתערב—**1. associate with, mix oneself with, intermingle,** of persons, + לְ *with* Pr 20$_{19}$, בְּ *with* Ezr 9$_{2}$, עִם *with* Pr 24$_{21}$. **2. be mixed,** of blood 11QT 32$_{15}$ (+ בְּ *with*), wealth 1QS 9$_{8}$ (+ עם *with*). **3. be involved with, meddle in** (בְּ) matter 4QMMT C$_{8}$. **4. share in** (בְּ) joy Pr 14$_{10}$, wealth 1QS 6$_{17}$.

→ עֵרֶב I *woof,* עֵרֶב II *mixed peoples,* עָרֹב *swarm(s) of flies,* תַּעֲרֹבֶת *mixture.*

ערב II 17.2.7 vb.—**Qal** 15.2.7 Pf. עָרַב, עָרַבְתָּ; impf. אֶעֶרְבֶנּוּ; impv. עֲרֹב (עָרְבֵנִי); ptc. עֹרֵב, עֹרְבִים; inf. עֲרֹב—**1. stand surety for, pledge, give security,** by offering property or person as guarantee for payment of debt, with accus. person Gn 43$_{9}$ Pr 11$_{15}$, security Pr 17$_{18}$ (+ לִפְנֵי *in the presence of*), debt Pr 22$_{26}$; with לְ *for* person Pr 6$_{1}$. **2. give in pledge, mortgage** fields, etc. Ne 5$_{3}$. **3. give heart in pledge,** i.e. **dare to draw near** Jr 30$_{21}$. **4a. trade in, barter for, exchange** merchandise Ezk 27$_{9}$. **b.** ptc. as noun, **trader** Ezk 27$_{27}$.

Htp. 2 Impv. הִתְעָרֶב—**exchange pledges,** i.e. **make a wager with** (אֵת) 2 K 18$_{23}$||Is 36$_{8}$.

→ עֵרֶב II *surety,* עֲרֻבָּה *pledge,* עֵרָבוֹן *pledge,* (?) מַעֲרָב II *merchandise,* תַּעֲרֻבָה *pledge.*

ערב III 8.1.5 vb.—**Qal** 8.0.3 Pf. עָרְבָה, עָרַבְתְּ; impf. יֶעֱרַב, יֶעֶרְבוּ—**1. be pleasant, be pleasing, be sweet,** of sacrifice Jr 6$_{20}$ (+ לְ *to* Y.), sleep Jr 31$_{26}$ (+ לְ *to* person), meditation Ps 104$_{34}$ (+ עַל *to* Y.), praise 11QPs[a] 22$_{11}$ (+ בְּ *in* nose). **2. take pleasure with** (עַל) lovers Ezk 16$_{37}$.

Pu. 0.0.2 Ptc. מעורבים—perh. **be pleasing, be made pleasing** 4QCrypt 1.1$_{6}$.

Hi. 0.1 Impf. יעריבו—**make pleasant, make sweet,** obj. song Si 40$_{21}$.

→ עָרֵב *pleasant.*

ערב IV 3.1.1 vb.—**Qal** 2.1 Pf. עָרְבָה; impf. Si יערב; inf. עֲרוֹב—**be evening, become evening, grow dark,** of day Jg 19$_{9}$, joy Is 24$_{11}$.

Hi. 1.0.1 impf. Q יעריב; inf. abs. הַעֲרֵב—**1. do late in the evening,** וַיִּגַּשׁ ... הַשְׁכֵּם וְהַעֲרֵב *and he drew near ... (doing so) early in the morning and late in the evening* 1 S 17$_{16}$. **2.** of the sun, **set** 4QMMT B$_{15}$ (להערי[בו]ת). **3. wait for sunset** 4QD[d] 8.2$_{5}$.

→ עֶרֶב I *evening,* מַעֲרָב I *west,* מַעֲרָבָה *west,* מַעֲרָבִי *western.*

*ערב V 3 vb.—**Qal** 1 Impf. יֶעֶרְבוּ—**offer** heart Jr 30$_{21}$, sacrifice Ho 9$_4$ (+ לְ *to* Y.), merchandise Ezk 27$_{27}$. → (?) מַעֲרָב II *merchandise*.

*ערב VI 12.0.1 vb.—**Qal** 7.0.1 Pf. עָרְבָה, עָרַבְתְּ; יֶעֱרַב, יֶעֶרְבוּ; inf. לַעֲרֹב—**enter, go in,** with לְ *to* Jr 31$_{26}$ Ho 9$_4$, בְּ *to* 11QPs^a 22$_{11}$, עַל *to* Ezk 16$_{37}$ Ps 104$_{34}$; abs. Jg 19$_9$ Is 24$_{11}$.

Htp. 5 Pf. הִתְעָרְבוּ; impf. יִתְעָרַב, תִּתְעָרַב—**enter, go in,** with בְּ *among* Ps 106$_{35}$ Pr 14$_{10}$ Ezr 9$_2$, לְ *with* Pr 20$_{19}$, עִם *with* Pr 24$_{21}$.

עָרֵב I 2.1 adj.—**1. pleasant, sweet,** of voice Ca 2$_{14}$, bread Pr 20$_{17}$. **2.** as noun, **pleasantness, pleasant speech** Si 6$_5$. → ערב III *be pleasant*.

*[עָרֵב] II 0.0.2 n.[m.] **surety,** ערבים למרק *sureties to complete (a transaction)* Mur 30 1$_5$ 2$_{24}$. → ערב II *stand surety*.

עָרֹב 9.0.1 n.m.—Q ערוב—**swarm(s) of flies** Ex 8$_{17}$. → ערב I *mix*.

עֲרָב, see עֲרָב II *steppe*.

עֲרַב I 3.0.2 pr.n.m.—**Arabia.**

[עֲרָב] II 2 n.[m.]—בָּעְרַב (בַּעֲרָב)—**steppe, desert** Is 21$_{13}$. → cf. עֲרָבִי *dwelling in the steppe*, עֲרָבָה *steppe*.

עֵרֶב I 9 n.[m.] **woof,** alw. || שְׁתִי *warp* Lv 13$_{48-59}$. → ערב I *mix*.

עֵרֶב II, see עֶרֶב II *mixed peoples*.

עֶרֶב I 135.0.29.1 n.m. (appar. f. at 1 S 20$_5$)—עָרֶב; cstr. עֶרֶב; du. עַרְבַּיִם—**1.** usu. **evening, sunset, dusk** Gn 1$_5$; עֵת עֶרֶב *time of evening* Gn 8$_{11}$, פְּנוֹת־עֶרֶב *turning,* i.e. approach, *of evening* Dt 23$_{12}$, בֵּין הָעַרְבַּיִם *between the two evenings,* i.e. between sunset and dark, at twilight Ex 30$_8$. **2. preceding day** Dt 16$_4$. → ערב IV *be evening*.

עֶרֶב II 7 n.m.—עֵרֶב—**mixed peoples, mixed company** Ex 12$_{38}$ Jr 25$_{20}$ Ne 13$_5$. → ערב I *mix*.

עֹרֵב I 10.0.1 n.m.—pl. עֹרְבִים; cstr. עֹרְבֵי—**raven** (*Corvus corax*), or **rook** (*Corvus cornix*) Gn 8$_7$ Lv 11$_{15}$||Dt 14$_{14}$.

*עֹרֵב II 7.0.0.1 pr.n.m. **Oreb.**

עֲרָבָה I 60.0.2 n.f.—+ ה- of direction עֲרָבָתָה; sf. עַרְבָתָהּ; pl. עֲרָבוֹת; cstr. עַרְבוֹת—**1. steppe, desert,** in general Is 35$_1$. **2a. plain, the Arabah,** i.e. Jordan valley between Sea of Galilee and Dead Sea Dt 1$_1$; יָם הָעֲרָבָה *sea of the Arabah,* i.e. Dead Sea Dt 3$_{17}$. **b.** pl. **plains** of Moab Nm 22$_1$, Jericho Jos 4$_{13}$.

[עֲרָבָה] II 5.1 n.f.—pl. עֲרָבִים; cstr. עַרְבֵי—**poplar,** prob. **Euphrates poplar** (*Populus euphratica*), rather than **willow** (*Salix babylonica*) Lv 23$_{40}$ Is 44$_4$.

*[עֲרָבָה] III 1 n.f.—pl. עֲרָבוֹת—**cloud** Ps 68$_5$. → cf. ערף II *drip*.

עֲרֻבָּה 2 n.f.—עֲרֻבָּתָם—**1. pledge, security,** as guarantee Pr 17$_{18}$. **2. token,** confirming someone's welfare 1 S 17$_{18}$. → ערב II *stand surety*.

עֵרָבוֹן 3 n.[m.]—**pledge, security,** offered as guarantee Gn 38$_{17}$. → ערב II *stand surety*.

עַרְבִי 7.0.1 gent. **Arabian.**

עֲרָבִי 2 adj. **dwelling in the steppe,** as noun, **steppe dweller** Is 13$_{20}$ Jr 3$_2$. → cf. עֲרָב II *steppe*.

עַרְבָתִי 2 gent. **Arbathite.**

ערג 3 vb.—**Qal** 3 Impf. תַּעֲרֹג—**long for, pant for,** perh. **cry to,** with אֶל *for, to* Y. Jl 1$_{20}$ Ps 42$_2$; עַל *for* channels of water Ps 42$_2$. → עֲרוּגָה *garden bed*.

עֲרָד I 4.0.0.3 pl.n. **Arad.**

עֲרָד II 1 pr.n.m. **Arad.**

ערה 15.0.1 vb.—**Ni.** 1 Impf. יֵעָרֶה—**be poured out,** of spirit Is 32$_{15}$ (+ עַל *upon*).

Pi. 9.0.1 Pf. עֵרָה; impf. יְעָרֶה, תְּעַר; + waw וַתְּעַר; impv. עָרוּ; inf. abs. עָרוֹת—**1. lay bare, uncover, expose** cedarwork Zp 2$_{14}$, shield Is 22$_6$; abs. Ps 137$_7$ (+ עַד *to* foundations). **2. empty** chest 2 C 24$_{11}$, jar Gn 24$_{20}$ (+ אֶל *into*). **3. lay bare, pour out** soul, i.e. **expose life to danger** Ps 141$_8$.

Hi. 3 Pf. הֶעֱרָה—**1. lay bare, uncover, expose** Lv 20$_{18.19}$. **2. pour out** soul to (לְ) death Is 53$_{12}$.

Htp. 2 Impf. תִּתְעָרִי; ptc. מִתְעָרֶה—**1. make oneself naked** Lm 4$_{21}$. **2. spread oneself out** Ps 37$_{35}$.

→ עָרָה I *bare place*, עֶרְוָה *nakedness*, עֶרְיָה *bareness*, מַעַר *nakedness*, מַעֲרֶה I *empty space*, מְעָרָה II *empty space*, מוֹרָה *razor*, תַּעַר I *sheath*, II *razor*; cf. עור III *be naked*, ערר *strip*, נער III *strip*.

[עָרָה] I 1 n.f.—pl. עָרוֹת—**bare place** Is 19$_7$. → ערה *be bare*.

*[עָרָה] II 1 n.f.—pl. עָרוֹת—**reed** Is 19$_7$.

*[עָרֶה] 5 n.[m.]—pl. עָרִים; sf. עָרָיו—**blood-daubed stone, blood-spattered altar,** perh. **image** Ezk 6$_6$ Mc 5$_{13}$ Jr 2$_{28}$ 11$_{13}$ Ho 11$_6$.

[עֲרוּגָה] 4.0.1 n.f.—cstr. עֲרוּגַת; pl. cstr. עֲרוּגוֹת—**garden** bed Ezk 17$_{7.10}$ Ca 5$_{13}$ 6$_{2}$. → ערג *long for*.

עָרוֹד 1 n.[m.] **wild ass, onager** (*Asinus hemippus*) Jb 39$_{5}$.

עֶרְוָה 54.1.16 n.f.—cstr. עֶרְוַת; sf. עֶרְוָתָהּ; pl. Q ערוות—**1. nakedness**, i.e. genital area, of man Gn 9$_{22}$, woman Ho 2$_{11}$; usu. in connection with sexual intercourse, esp. 'uncover (גלה pi.) nakedness' as euphemism for having intercourse Lv 18$_{6}$, sim. 'see (ראה) nakedness' Lv 20$_{17}$. **2. nakedness, vulnerability** of person Si 11$_{30}$, land, i.e. its exposed, undefended parts Gn 42$_{9}$. **3. nakedness, obscenity, indecency, shame** Dt 23$_{15}$, person descr. as 'foundation of shame' 1QH 9$_{22}$. → ערה *be bare*.

ערוּל, see עָרֵל *foreskin*.

עָרוֹם 16.0.3 adj.—f.s. עֲרֻמָּה; m.pl. עֲרוּמִּים—**1. naked, stripped (of outer clothing)**, of person Gn 2$_{25}$, Sheol Jb 26$_{6}$. **2.** as noun, **a. naked one** Is 58$_{7}$. **b. nakedness** 4QpHos^{a} 2$_{12}$. → עור III *be bare*.

עָרוּם 11.0.1 adj.—m.pl. עֲרוּמִים—**1a. prudent, shrewd**, of person Pr 12$_{23}$. **b.** as noun, **prudent one, shrewd one** Pr 12$_{16}$ 13$_{16}$. **2a. crafty**, of serpent Gn 3$_{1}$. **b.** as noun, (1) **crafty one** Jb 5$_{12}$. (2) perh. **craftiness** Jb 15$_{5}$. → ערם II *be prudent*.

עֵרוֹם, see עֵירֹם *naked*.

עֲרוֹעֵר I 1 n.[m.] **juniper** (*Juniperus phoenicea* or *Juniperus oxycedrus*), or **tamarisk** (*Tamarix gallica*) Jr 48$_{6}$. → cf. עַרְעָר II *juniper* and עָר III *tamarisk*.

עֲרוֹעֵר II 16.0.1 pl.n. **Aroer**.

[עָרוּץ] I 1 adj.—cstr. עֲרוּץ—**dreadful**, as noun, **dreadful (one)** Jb 30$_{6}$. → ערץ I *be terrified*.

* **[עָרוּץ]** II 1 n.[m.]—cstr. עֲרוּץ—coll., **gullies, slopes** Jb 30$_{6}$.

עָרוֹת, see עָרָה I *bare place*, II *reed*.

עֵרִי I 2 pr.n.m. **Eri**.

עֵרִי II 1 gent. **Erite**.

עֶרְיָה 6.0.2 n.f. —pl. Q עריות—**1a. (in a state of) bareness, nakedness** Ezk 16$_{7}$. **b. (unto) bareness**, i.e. **utterly** Hb 3$_{9}$. **2.** pl. **incest** CD 5$_{9}$. → ערה *be bare*.

[עֲרִיסָה] 4 n.f.pl.—sf. עֲרִסֹתֵינוּ—**coarse meal**, perh. of barley, as whole-grain flour or dough Nm 15$_{20}$. → cf. עָרֵס *dough-maker*.

* **[עֲרִיפְיָה]** n.f. **cloud** Is 5$_{30}$ (if em. בַּעֲרִיפֶיהָ *with its clouds* to בַּעֲרִיפְיָהּ *with cloud*). → ערף II *drip*.

[עֲרִיפִים] 1 n.[m.]pl.—sf. עֲרִיפֶיהָ—**clouds** Is 5$_{30}$. → ערף II *drip*.

עָרִיץ 20.0.11 adj.—pl. עָרִיצִים; cstr. עָרִיצֵי—**1. terrifying, ruthless, violent**, of nation Is 25$_{3}$, warrior Jr 20$_{11}$. **2.** as noun, **a. terrifying one, ruthless one, tyrant** Is 13$_{11}$ 49$_{25}$; עָרִיצֵי גּוֹיִם *(most) terrifying of the nations* Ezk 28$_{7}$. **b.** perh. **rich one** Is 29$_{5}$ Pr 11$_{16}$. → ערץ *be terrified*.

עֲרִירִי 4.3.1 adj.—m.pl. עֲרִירִים—**1. childless**, as adv. Gn 15$_{2}$ Lv 20$_{20}$. **2.** as noun, **childless one** Si 16$_{4}$. → ערר *strip oneself*.

ערך I 75.3.15 vb.—**Qal** 69.1.14 Pf. עָרַךְ, עָרַכְתִּי; impf. יַעֲרֹךְ, תַּעַרְכוּ; impv. עֶרְכָה (Si ערוך), עִרְכוּ; ptc. Q עורך, עֹרְכִים; ptc. pass. עָרוּךְ, cstr. עֲרוּךְ, עֲרוּכָה, עֲרֻכוֹת; inf. abs. עָרֹךְ; cstr. עֲרֹךְ—**1. arrange, set in order, lay out** pieces of sacrificial offering upon (עַל) wood Lv 1$_{8}$, showbread upon table Ex 40$_{23}$, lamp before (לִפְנֵי) Y. Ex 27$_{21}$; **prepare, spread** table Is 21$_{5}$. **2. array oneself** for (לְ) Y. in council of holy ones 1QH 12$_{24}$. **3a. arrange battle, set battle in array, form battle-line**, with obj. מִלְחָמָה *battle* Gn 14$_{8}$ (+ אֵת *with, against*) 1 S 17$_{2}$ (+ לִקְרַאת *against*), מַעֲרָכָה *battle-line* 1 S 17$_{21}$; without obj. **array oneself for battle** 1 S 4$_{4}$ (+ לִקְרַאת *against*) Jr 50$_{9}$ (+ לְ *against*) 50$_{14}$ (+ עַל *against*). **b.** with obj. of person, **array oneself against, be arrayed against** Jb 6$_{4}$. **4. prepare, make ready** shield Jr 46$_{3}$, spear 1 C 12$_{9}$. **5a. arrange** words Jb 32$_{14}$, **set out** a (legal) case Jb 13$_{18}$ 23$_{4}$ (+ לִפְנֵי *before* Y.); without obj. Jb 37$_{19}$, **make a charge** Ps 50$_{21}$ (+ לְעֵינֵי *before*). **b. give an ordered account** of something to (לְ) Y. Is 44$_{7}$. **c.** without obj., perh. **set prayer in order**, or **prepare sacrifice** before (לְ) Y. Ps 5$_{4}$. **6a. compare likeness** with (לְ) Y. Is 40$_{18}$. **b.** intrans., **be comparable** Ps 40$_{6}$ (+ אֶל *to* Y.) 89$_{7}$ (+ לְ *to* Y.). **c. be comparable to, equal** something **(in value)** Jb 28$_{17.19}$. **7.** pass. **a. be laid out in order**, of flax Jos 2$_{6}$ (+ עַל *upon*); **be spread**, of table Ezk 23$_{41}$ (+ לִפְנֵי *before*). **b. be arranged, ordered**, of covenant 2 S 23$_{5}$ (+ בְּ *in [respect of]*). **c. be made ready, prepared**, of Topheth Is 30$_{33}$. **d. be set in array for battle**, (1) עָרוּךְ ... לַמִּלְחָמָה Jr 6$_{23}$ (+ עַל *against*). (2) עָרוּךְ מִלְחָמָה Jl 2$_{5}$.

Ni. 0.0.1 Impf. תערך—of war, **be prepared, be waged** 1QM 2_9.

Hi. 6.2 Pf. הֶעֱרִיךְ; impf. יַעֲרִיךְ—**1.** appar. **set in order, prepare** lamp Si 39_{17} 50_{18}. **2. value** person or thing vowed Lv $27_{8.12}$ (+ בֵּין *between* good and bad), **assess** land for taxation 2 K 23_{35}.

→ עֵרֶךְ *arrangement*, מַעֲרָךְ *disposition*, מַעֲרָכָה *array*, מַעֲרֶכֶת *array*.

*עָרַךְ II 1 vb.—**Qal** 1 Impf. יַעַרְכוּנִי—**wear down, wear away** person, of terror Jb 6_4.

עָרַךְ III 6 vb.—**Hi.** 6 Pf. הֶעֱרִיךְ; impf. יַעֲרִיךְ—**value, assess** person or thing vowed Lv $27_{8.12}$ (+ בֵּין *between* good and bad), land for taxation 2 K 23_{35}. → (?) עֵרֶךְ I *arrangement, valuation*.

[עֵרֶךְ] I 33.1.5 n.m.—cstr. עֵרֶךְ; sf. עֶרְכִּי—**1. arrangement, order, row** of showbread on table Ex 40_4, **suit** of garments Jg 17_{10} (or §2), **proportion, symmetry** of Leviathan Jb 41_4. **2. valuation** of ram, for guilt offering Lv 5_{15}, of persons or things vowed, for redemption Lv $27_{2\text{-}27}$, of firstborn Nm 18_{16}; אֱנוֹשׁ כְּעֶרְכִּי *a person according to my valuation*, i.e. my equal Ps 55_{14}; **assessment** for taxation purposes 2 K 23_{35}, **value** of wisdom and understanding Jb 28_{13}, **value**, i.e. **allowance** of clothing Jg 17_{10} (or §1). → ערך I *arrange*, or III *value*.

*[עֵרֶךְ] II 1 n.[m.]—sf. עֶרְכָּהּ—**house, temple** of wisdom and understanding Jb 28_{13}.

ערל 2 vb.—**Qal** 1 + waw וַעֲרַלְתֶּם—**treat** fruit **as foreskin** (עָרְלָה), thus forbidden Lv 19_{23}.

Ni. 1 Impv. הֵעָרֵל—**show the foreskin,** i.e. expose oneself, or perh. **act as one uncircumcised** Hb 2_{16} (=1QpHab הרעל *stagger*, i.e. רעל ni.).

→ עָרֵל *having foreskin*, עָרְלָה *foreskin*, עֹרֶל *foreskin*.

עָרֵל 35.1.3 adj.—cstr. עֲרַל (עֶרֶל); f.s. עֲרֵלָה; m.pl. עֲרֵלִים; cstr. עַרְלֵי—**1a. having foreskin,** i.e. **uncircumcised,** of Philistine Jg 14_3, house of Israel Jr 9_{25} (עַרְלֵי־לֵב *uncircumcised of heart*), heart Lv 26_{41}, ear Jr 6_{10}. **b. unskilled** in speech, lit. 'uncircumcised of lips' Ex 6_{12}. **c. forbidden,** of fruit Lv 19_{23}. **2.** as noun, **uncircumcised one** Gn 17_{14} Ex 12_{48}; ערל אוזן *one uncircumcised of ear* 1QH 2_{15}; perh. **weak one, strengthless one** Ezk 28_{10} 32_{19}. → ערל *regard as foreskin*.

*[עֹרֶל] 0.0.1 n.[m.]—cstr. ערול—**foreskin,** i.e. **uncircumcision** of lip, i.e. lack of ability in speech 1QH 10_{18}. → ערל *regard as foreskin*.

עָרְלָה 16.0.6 n.f.—cstr. עָרְלַת (Q עורלת); sf. עָרְלָתוֹ; pl. עֲרָלוֹת; cstr. עָרְלוֹת (Q עורלות); sf. עָרְלֹתֵיהֶם—**foreskin,** usu. of man's penis Gn 17_{11}; of heart Dt 10_{16}, inclination 1QS 5_5, fruit tree Lv 19_{23}. → ערל *regard as foreskin*.

ערם I 1 vb.—**Ni.** 1 Pf. נֶעֶרְמוּ—**be heaped up,** of water Ex 15_8. → עֲרֵמָה *heap*.

ערם II 5.1 vb.—**Qal** 4.1 Impf. יַעְרִם (unless hi.); inf. abs. עָרוֹם—**1. be prudent** Pr 15_5 19_{25} Si 6_{32}. **2. be crafty** 1 S 23_{22}.

Hi. 5.1 Impf. יַעְרִם (unless qal), יַעֲרִימוּ—**1. show prudence** Pr 15_5 19_{25} Si 6_{32}. **2. show craftiness,** עָרוֹם יַעְרִם *he shows much craftiness* 1 S 23_{22}. **3. make** counsel **crafty** against (עַל) Ps 83_4.

→ עָרוּם *prudent*, עֹרֶם *craftiness*, עָרְמָה *prudence*.

עֵרֹם, see עֵירֹם *naked*.

[עֹרֶם] 1 n.[m.]—sf. עָרְמָם (unless from עָרְמָה)—**craftiness** Jb 5_{13}. → ערם II *be prudent*.

עָרְמָה 6.0.18 n.f.—cstr. Q ערמת; sf. Q ערמתו, עָרְמָם (unless from עֹרֶם)—**1. prudence, wisdom** Pr 14 8_5 1QS 4_6 1QH 10_9. **2. craftiness, cunning** Ex 21_{14} Jos 9_4 1QS 4_{11}. → ערם II *be prudent*.

עֲרֵמָה 11 n.f.—cstr. עֲרֵמַת; pl. עֲרֵמִים, עֲרֵמוֹת; cstr. עֲרֵמוֹת—**heap** of grain Hg 2_{16}, grain and other produce 2 C 31_6, rubble Ne 3_{34}. → ערם I *heap up*.

עַרְמוֹן 2 n.[m.]—pl. עַרְמֹנִים—**plane (tree)** (*Platanus orientalis*) Gn 30_{37}.

עֵרָן 1 pr.n.m. **Eran.**

עֵרָנִי 1 gent. **Eranite.**

*[עָרָס] 0.0.0.1 pr.n.m. **Aris.**

*[עָרָס] 0.0.0.1 n.[m.] **dough-maker, baker** Judaean Hills ost. 3_6 (unless from עָרָס *Aris*). → cf. עֲרִיסָה *coarse meal*.

עֲרֹעוֹר, see עֲרוֹעֵר II *Aroer*.

עַרְעָר I 1 adj. **destitute,** as noun, **destitute one** Ps 102_{18}. → ערר *strip oneself*.

*עַרְעָר II 1 n.[m.] **juniper** (*Juniperus phoenicea* or *Juniperus oxycedrus*), or **tamarisk** (*Tamarix gallica*)

Jr 17$_6$. → cf. עֲרוֹעֵר *juniper*, עַר III *tamarisk*.

עֲרֹעֵר, see עֲרוֹעֵר II *Aroer*.

עֲרֹעֵרִי 1 gent. **Aroerite.**

ערף I 6.0.2 vb.—**Qal** 6.0.2 Impf. יַעֲרֹף; + waw וְעָרְפוֹ; ptc. עֹרֵף; ptc. pass. עֲרוּפָה—**1. break the neck of** an animal Ex 13$_{13}$. **2. break down** altar Ho 10$_2$. **3.** pass. **have one's neck broken,** of heifer Dt 21$_6$. → עֹרֶף *neck.*

ערף II 2 vb.—**Qal** 2 Impf. יַעֲרֹף, יַעַרְפוּ—**drip, drop, 1.** intrans., of teaching as (כְּ) rain Dt 32$_2$. **2.** trans., of heavens dropping dew Dt 33$_{28}$. → עֲרָפֶל *thick cloud,* עֲרִיפִיָּה *cloud,* עֲרִיפִים *clouds,* עֲרִיפִיָּה *cloud,* מַעֲרָף *drop (of rain)*; cf. עֲרָבָה III *cloud*; cf. רעף *trickle.*

עֹרֶף 33.1.18 n.m.—cstr. עֹרֶף; sf. עָרְפִּי—**neck,** esp. **back of neck, nape,** as obj. of פנה *turn* Jr 2$_{27}$, קשה hi. *stiffen* Dt 10$_{16}$; קְשֵׁה־עֹרֶף *stiff of neck,* i.e. stiff-necked Ex 32$_9$; neck of Y. Jr 18$_{17}$, bird Lv 5$_8$. → ערף I *break the neck of.*

עָרְפָּה 2 pr.n.f. **Orpah.**

עֲרָפֶל 15.1.1 n.m.—pl. cstr. Q ערפלי—**thick cloud,** perh. properly **thick darkness** Is 60$_2$; oft. as covering of Y. Ex 20$_{21}$. → ערף II *drip.*

ערץ I 15.2.3 vb.—**Qal** 11.0.3 Impf. תַּעֲרֹץ (תַּעֲרוֹץ), אֶעֱרוֹץ; inf. עֲרֹץ—**1. be terrified, in dread** Dt 1$_{29}$ 7$_{21}$ (+ מִפְּנֵי *[on account] of*). **2a. terrify** Is 2$_{19}$. **b.** abs., **cause terror** Is 47$_{12}$.

Ni. 1 Ptc. נַעֲרָץ—**be feared, inspire awe,** of Y. Ps 89$_8$.

Hi. 3.2 Impf. יַעֲרִיצוּ; ptc. מַעֲרִצְכֶם—**1a. terrify, intimidate** Si 13$_7$, **inspire with awe** Is 8$_{13}$. **b.** perh. **make an object of awe** Si 43$_{8(Bmg)}$. **2a. be in awe** of Y. Is 29$_{23}$. **b. be terrified, show dread** Is 8$_{12}$.

→ עָרִיץ *terrifying,* עָרוּץ I *dreadful,* מַעֲרָץ *terror,* מַעֲרָצָה *terror.*

***ערץ II** 1 vb.—**Qal** 1 Impf. תַּעֲרוֹץ—**follow** leaf Jb 13$_{25}$.

ערק I 2 vb.—**Qal** 2 Ptc. עֹרְקַי, עֹרְקִים—**1. gnaw** dry ground Jb 30$_3$. **2.** ptc. as noun, **gnawing pain,** or perh. **sinew** Jb 30$_{17}$.

***ערק II** 1 vb.—**Qal** 1 Ptc. עֹרְקִים—**flee** Jb 30$_3$ (+ צִיָּה *[to the] wilderness*).

***[עָרָק]** n.m. **vein** Jb 30$_{17}$ (if em. עֹרְקַי *my gnawing pains/sinews* to עֲרָקַי *my veins*).

עַרְקִי 2 gent. **Arkite.**

ערקם, see עַזְרִיקָם *Azrikam.*

ערר 4.1.2.1 vb.—**Qal** 1.0.1 Impf. Q יער; impv. עֹרָה—**strip oneself, make oneself bare** Is 32$_{11}$.

Po. 1 Pf. עֹרְרוּ—**lay bare,** i.e. **demolish** fortress Is 23$_{13}$.

Pilp. 1 Inf. abs. עַרְעֵר—**lay bare,** i.e. **demolish,** עַרְעֵר תִּתְעַרְעָר *laying bare it shall be laid bare,* i.e. be completely demolished Jr 51$_{58}$.

Htpalp. 1.1.1.1 Pf. I התערערה; impf. תִּתְעַרְעָר—**1. be stripped bare,** i.e. **be destitute** Si 19$_1$ (יתערער[ו]). **2. be laid bare,** i.e. **be destroyed, demolished,** of spirit of flesh 4QInstr^b 1$_{12}$, wall Jr 51$_{58}$.

→ עַרְעָר I *destitute,* עֲרִירִי *childless*; cf. ערה *be bare,* עור III *be bare.*

עֶרֶשׂ 10.0.3 n.f.—עֶרֶשׂ; cstr. עֶרֶשׂ; sf. עַרְשִׂי; pl. sf. עַרְשׂוֹתָם—**couch, divan** Dt 3$_{11}$ Am 3$_{12}$.

עֵשֶׂב 33.0.3 n.m.—cstr. עֵשֶׂב; sf. עֶשְׂבָּם; pl. cstr. עִשְׂבוֹת—**plant(s), herbage, grass,** as food for humans Gn 1$_{29}$, beasts Gn 1$_{30}$; representing profuseness Ps 72$_{16}$, vulnerability Ps 102$_5$; עֵשֶׂב הַשָּׂדֶה *plant(s) of the field* Gn 2$_5$.

עשׂה I 2628.41.401.8 vb.—**Qal** 2528.41.382.8 Pf. עָשָׂה, עָשִׂיתָ; impf. יַעֲשֶׂה (יַעַשׂ), אֶעֱשֶׂה; + waw וַיַּעַשׂ (וַיַּעַשׂ, וַיַּעֲשֶׂה); impv. עֲשֵׂה, עֲשִׂי, עֲשׂוּ; ptc. עֹשֶׂה, עֹשָׂה, עֹשִׂים, עֹשׂוֹת; ptc. pass. עָשׂוּי, עֲשׂוּיָה, עֲשׂוּיִם; inf. abs. עָשֹׂה (עָשׂוֹ); cstr. עֲשׂוֹת (עֲשֹׂה, עֲשׂוֹ, עֲשֹׂתִי, עֲשֹׂתָם)—**1a. do** something, **do, work, perform** deed Gn 44$_{15}$, thing Gn 19$_{22}$, word Ex 24$_3$, work Gn 2$_2$, wonder Ex 15$_{11}$, **practise, carry out, show (the practice of)** good Dt 6$_{18}$, kindness Gn 19$_{19}$, evil Nm 32$_{13}$, deceit Ps 52$_4$, **commit** sin Nm 5$_7$, abomination Lv 18$_{27}$, **maintain** cause 1 K 8$_{59}$, **observe, keep** festival Ex 12$_{47}$, sabbath Ex 31$_{16}$, **observe, perform, execute** statutes, ordinances Dt 4$_1$, justice Gn 18$_{19}$, **exercise** kingship 1 K 21$_7$, **defend** rights Ps 9$_5$, **take** vengeance Jg 11$_{36}$; perh. **do (with),** i.e. **bestow** life and kindness **upon** Jb 10$_{12}$. Preps.: לְ *to* someone Gn 20$_9$, *for* someone Ex 13$_8$; בְּ *in* place Ex 9$_5$, *by (means of), with* something Ex 4$_{17}$, *against, to* Ex 14$_{31}$; כְּ *as, like* 1 K 11$_{33}$, *according to* Nm 9$_3$; עִם *with, to(wards), for* Gn 20$_{13}$; אֵת *with, to(wards), for* Dt 1$_{30}$. **b.** without accus. (exc. as adv. obj.), **do, act, work, be active,** abs. 1 S 14$_6$ 2 S 3$_{18}$ Is 44$_{23}$, **be busy** 1 K 20$_{40}$; **do, act**

in a particular way, as indicated by (1) prep., **do according to** (כְּ) something Gn 44$_{2}$, **do as** (כְּ) someone has done Jg 9$_{48}$, **do with, in** (בְּ) faithfulness Jg 9$_{19}$, inadvertence Nm 15$_{29}$. (2) adv., **do so** (כֵּן) Gn 6$_{22}$, **do thus** Ex 5$_{15}$ (כֹּה) 29$_{35}$ (כָּכָה), **do as** (כַּאֲשֶׁר) Gn 21$_{1}$. (3) verb, הִגְדִּיל לַעֲשׂוֹת *he has acted mightily to do*, i.e. done great things Jl 2$_{20}$. **2a. make, create, build, fashion** humans Gn 1$_{26}$, animals Gn 1$_{25}$, earth and heaven Gn 2$_{4}$, bread Gn 27$_{17}$, house 1 K 7$_{8}$, altar Gn 35$_{1}$, garments Ex 28$_{2}$, vessel Jr 18$_{4}$; with accus. of material, **make (out) of, make with** wood Ex 25$_{10}$||37$_{1}$, gold Ex 25$_{18}$||37$_{7}$ (in other cases material is defined not by an accus. but by the second element in a construct chain, e.g. אֱלֹהֵי כֶסֶף *gods of silver* Ex 20$_{23}$); with accus. of style, **make (as consisting) of, make as having** cherubim Ex 26$_{1}$||36$_{8}$, hammered work Ex 25$_{18}$ ||37$_{7}$, **make as being** hollow Ex 27$_{8}$||38$_{7}$. Preps.: לְ *for* Ex 28$_{2}$; בְּ *by (means of), with* Jr 18$_{4}$; מִן *(out) of* Ex 39$_{1}$. **b. make into,** (1) with double accus., gold and silver into god Is 46$_{6}$, spices into incense Ex 30$_{35}$. (2) with accus. and prep. לְ *into*, Abram into nation Gn 12$_{2}$, ingredients into bread Ezk 4$_{9}$. **c.** ptc. as noun, **maker, creator,** alw. ref. to Y. Is 17$_{7}$ Jb 4$_{17}$. **3. produce, yield, bear fruit,** produce, etc. Gn 1$_{11}$ Lv 25$_{21}$ (+ לְ *[sufficient] for*) Is 5$_{2}$. **4a. make,** i.e. **cause, bring about** a state of affairs, event, time: salvation Ex 14$_{13}$ (+ לְ *for*), peace Jos 9$_{15}$ (+ לְ *with*), war Gn 14$_{2}$ (+ אֵת *with*), end Is 10$_{23}$. **b. make,** i.e. **cause** someone or something **to be** free 1 S 17$_{25}$, upright Ec 7$_{29}$, darkness Am 4$_{13}$. **c. bring it about that** Gn 50$_{20}$. **5a. make,** i.e. **issue, proclaim** a decree Est 1$_{20}$. **b. make,** i.e. **arrive at, conclude** an agreement with (עִם) Is 28$_{15}$. **6a. appoint** person 1 S 12$_{6}$. **b. appoint, institute** festival 1 K 12$_{32}$. **c. establish, fix, set** bounds, etc. Jb 28$_{25.26}$ Pr 22$_{28}$. **d. determine, plan** future events 2 K 19$_{25}$||Is 37$_{26}$. **7. acquire, gain, get, amass** persons Gn 12$_{5}$, cattle Ezk 38$_{12}$, wealth Dt 8$_{17}$. **8. make,** i.e. **achieve** a name, usu. for (לְ) oneself Gn 11$_{4}$. **9. make ready, prepare** provisions Ex 12$_{39}$, calf Gn 18$_{7}$, cart 1 S 6$_{7}$, chamber Ne 13$_{5}$. **10a. offer (in sacrifice), present (as offering)** bull Ex 29$_{36}$, lamb Lv 23$_{12}$ (+ לְ *as* burnt offering), sacrifices and burnt offerings Ex 10$_{25}$ (+ לְ *to* Y.), **provide** an offering Ezk 45$_{17}$; with double accus., **offer** animal **as** sacrifice Nm 6$_{17}$. **b.** without obj., (1) **sacrifice, officiate** 2 K 17$_{32}$. (2) **make provision (for offering)** Ezk 45$_{25}$. **11. attend to** feet 2 S 19$_{25}$, **pare** nails Dt 21$_{13}$, **trim** moustache 2 S 19$_{25}$. **12. use for** (לְ) Ho 2$_{10}$, **put to** (לְ) work 1 S 8$_{16}$. **13. work,** i.e. **till, cultivate** land Mur 24 C$_{10}$. **14. make** (one's) way, i.e. **journey** Jg 17$_{8}$. **15. spend** time Ec 6$_{12}$. **16.** perh. **make up, comprise** community 4QMidrEschat[b] 8$_{16}$. **17.** pass. **a. be done, be carried out,** of precepts Ps 111$_{8}$ (+ בְּ *with* faithfulness). **b. be made, be built,** of vessels 2 K 23$_{4}$ (+ לְ *for* Baal), chamber and pavement Ezk 40$_{17}$; **be artificial,** of pool Ne 3$_{16}$. **c. be appointed, be instituted,** of burnt offering Nm 28$_{6}$. **d. be prepared, be dressed,** of sheep 1 S 25$_{18}$. **e. be used for** (לְ) work, of gold Ex 38$_{24}$.

Ni. 99.0.24 Pf. נַעֲשָׂה, נַעֲשְׂתָה (נֶעֶשְׂתָה); impf. יֵעָשֶׂה; ptc. נַעֲשֶׂה, Q נעסה, נַעֲשִׂים, נַעֲשׂוֹת; inf. הֵעָשׂוֹת—**1. be done, be practised, be performed, be carried out, be accomplished,** of deed Gn 20$_{9}$, work Ex 12$_{16}$, word Ezk 12$_{25}$, request Est 5$_{6}$, honour Est 6$_{3}$, abomination Dt 13$_{15}$, evil Dn 9$_{12}$; subj. impersonal Gn 29$_{6}$ (+ כֵּן *so*) Ex 21$_{31}$ (+ לְ *to* someone); sometimes perh. equivalent to **occur** Ec 1$_{9}$; of counsel, **be acted upon** 2 S 17$_{23}$; of festival, **be observed, be kept** 2 C 35$_{18}$. **2. be made, be created, be built,** of heavens Ps 33$_{6}$ (+ בְּ *by [means of]* word), ark Jr 3$_{16}$, altar Ezk 43$_{18}$, grain offering Lv 2$_{7}$ (+ סֹלֶת בַּשֶּׁמֶן *[of] fine flour with oil*); **be produced** from (מִן) grapevine Nm 6$_{4}$. **3.** of food, **be prepared for** (לְ) someone Ne 5$_{18}$. **4. be offered (in sacrifice)** Nm 28$_{15}$. **5. be used for** (לְ) purpose Lv 7$_{24}$.

Pu. 1 Pf. עֻשֵּׂיתִי—**be made,** of person Ps 139$_{15}$ (+ בְּ *in* secret).

Hi. 0.0.1 Inf. העשות—**cause** law **to be performed** 4QZedek 1$_{4}$.

→ מַעֲשֶׂה I *deed*.

עשׂה II 4 vb.—**Qal** 1 Inf. בַּעֲשׂוֹת—**squeeze** breast Ezk 23$_{21}$ (or em. pi. בַּעֲשׂוֹת, or pu. בְּעֻשּׂוֹת).

Pi. 2 Pf. עִשּׂוּ—**squeeze** breast Ezk 23$_{3.8.21}$ (if em.; see Qal).

Pu. 1 Pf. עֻשֵּׂיתִי—**1. be squeezed,** of breast Ezk 23$_{21}$

(if em.; see Qal). **2. be plucked off,** of person Ps 139_{15}.

*עשׂה III $_{10.0.1}$ vb.—**Qal** $_{8.0.1}$ Pf. עָשׂוּ; impf. יַעֲשֶׂה; + waw וַיַּעַשׂ; inf. עֲשׂתוֹ—**1. cover** ark Gn 6_{14} (+ קִנִּים *[with] reeds;* if em. קִנִּים *nests*), fat Jb 15_{27} (+ עַל *over* thigh). **2. conceal** pit Ps 9_{16}, iniquity Is 32_6, knowledge Pr 13_{16} (בְּ of obj.). **3. cover oneself** Jb 23_9. **4. protect** with (בְּ) army Ezk 17_{17}.

Ni. $_1$ Pf. נֶעֶשְׂתָה—**be concealed** from (מִן) sight Nm 15_{24} (+ לִשְׁגָגָה *with inadvertence*).

Pu. $_1$ Pf. עֻשֵּׂיתִי—**be covered up, be concealed,** of person in womb Ps 139_{15}.

→ עָשָׂה *covering,* עֶשֶׂה *hidden thing,* מַעֲשֶׂה II *covering.*

*עשׂה IV $_6$ vb.—**Qal** $_5$ Pf. עָשִׂית; ptc. עֹשֶׂה; inf. עֲשׂתוֹ—**1. turn, turn oneself to** (לְ) Y. Ezk 29_{20}, upon (אֶל) spoil 1 S $14_{32(Kt)}$, from (מִן) evil 1 C 4_{10}; 1 K 20_{40} Jb 23_9 Ru 2_{19}. **2. turn to, go to, approach** Pr 6_{32}.

*עשׂה V $_2$ vb.—**Qal** $_2$ Pf. עָשׂוּ; ptc. עֹשִׂים—**worship** god 2 K 17_{29}, calf Ex 32_{35}.

*עשׂה VI $_1$ vb.—**Qal** $_1$ Ptc. עֹשֶׂה—**assail** oppressors Zp 3_{19}.

*עָשָׂה $_1$ n.f. **covering** Jb 23_9. → עשׂה III *cover.*

*[עֶשֶׂה] n.m.—**hidden thing,** i.e. sin Ob$_6$ (if em. עֵשָׂו *Esau* to עֲשָׂיו *his hidden things*) Jb 33_{17} (if em. מַעֲשֶׂה *[their] deed[s]* to מֵעֲשִׂים *from [their] hidden things*). → עשׂה III *cover.*

עֲשָׂהאֵל $_{18}$ pr.n.m. **Asahel.**

עֵשָׂו $_{97.0.9}$ pr.n.m. **Esau.**

עָשׂוֹר $_{16.0.1}$ n.[m.]—עָשֹׂר—**1. ten,** נֵבֶל עָשׂוֹר *harp of ten (strings)* Ps 33_2, יָמִים אוֹ עָשׂוֹר *ten days or so* Gn 24_{55}. **2.** ordinal number, **tenth,** in date, בֶּעָשׂוֹר לַחֹדֶשׁ *on the tenth of the month* Ex 12_3. → עשׂר *take a tenth part.*

*[עֲשִׂי] $_{0.0.0.2}$ pr.n.[m.] **Asi.**

עֲשִׂיאֵל $_1$ pr.n.m. **Asiel.**

עֲשָׂיָה $_{8.0.0.15}$ pr.n.m. **Asaiah.**

עשׂיהו, see עֲשָׂיָה *Asaiah.*

עֲשִׂירִי $_{29.0.13.16}$ adj.—עֲשִׂרִי, f.s. עֲשִׂירִית, עֲשִׂרִיָּה—**1. tenth,** of generation Dt 23_3, day Nm 7_{66}, month Gn 8_5, year Jr 32_1. **2.** as noun, **a. tenth (one),** in ref. to person 1 C 12_{14}, animal Lv 27_{32}, lot 1 C 24_{11}. **b.** fem. sg., (1) עֲשִׂירִית **tenth (part)** of ephah Ex 16_{36}. (2) עֲשִׂירִיָּה **a tenth (of the inhabitants)** Is 6_{13}. → עשׂר *take a tenth part.*

עשׂק I $_1$ vb.—**Htp.** $_1$ Pf. הִתְעַשְּׂקוּ—**contend** Gn 26_{20}.

עשׂק II, see עסק *be busy.*

עֵשֶׂק $_1$ pl.n. **Esek.**

עשׂר $_{9.0.3}$ vb.—**Qal** $_2$ Impf. יַעְשֹׂר—**take a tenth part of** flock 1 S 8_{17}, seed, etc. 1 S 8_{15}.

Pi. $_5$ Impf. תְּעַשֵּׂר; ptc. מְעַשְּׂרִים; inf. abs. עַשֵּׂר—**1. give a tenth part of, pay a tithe of** yield of seed Dt 14_{22}, everything Gn 28_{22} (+ לְ *to* Y.). **2. receive a tithe** Ne 10_{38}.

Pu. $_{0.0.3}$ Ptc. מעשרת (מעסרת)—**have tithe deducted, be subject to payment of tithe,** of wheat Mur 24 B_{17}.

Hi. (unless pi.) $_2$ Inf. cstr. בַּעְשֵׂר/לְ—**1. pay a tithe** Dt 26_{12}. **2. receive a tithe** Ne 10_{39}.

→ עֶשֶׂר *ten,* עָשָׂר *ten,* עָשׂוֹר *ten,* עֶשְׂרִים *twenty,* עֲשִׂירִי *tenth,* עִשָּׂרוֹן *tenth,* מַעֲשֵׂר *tenth.*

עָשָׂר $_{337.0.139.1}$ n.m.&f.—m. (with m. nouns) עָשָׂר; f. (with f. nouns) עֶשְׂרֵה (Q עסרה)—**ten,** only after units to make the numerals 11–19, both cardinal and ordinal, **1. eleven(th),** אַחַד עָשָׂר Gn 32_{23}, אַחַת עֶשְׂרֵה Jos 15_{51}, עַשְׁתֵּי עָשָׂר Nm 29_{20}, עַשְׁתֵּי עֶשְׂרֵה Ex 26_7||36_{14}. **2. twelve, twelfth,** שְׁנֵים עָשָׂר Gn 49_{28}, שְׁנֵי עָשָׂר Ex 28_{21}, שתים עשר 4QAstrCrypt 9_7, שְׁתֵּים עֶשְׂרֵה Jos 18_{24}, שְׁתֵּי עֶשְׂרֵה Jos 4_8. **3. thirteen(th),** שְׁלֹשָׁה עָשָׂר Nm 29_{13}, שְׁלֹשׁ עֶשְׂרֵה Gn 17_{25}. **4. fourteen(th),** אַרְבָּעָה עָשָׂר Nm 29_{13}, אַרְבַּע עֶשְׂרֵה Gn 31_{41}. **5. fifteen(th),** חֲמִשָּׁה עָשָׂר Lv 27_7, חֲמֵשֶׁת עָשָׂר Jg 8_{10}, חֲמֵשׁ עֶשְׂרֵה Gn 7_{20}. **6. sixteen(th),** שש עשר 4Q ShirShabb^d 1.1_{30}, שִׁשָּׁה עָשָׂר 1 C 4_{27}, שֵׁשׁ עֶשְׂרֵה Jos 15_{41}. **7. seventeen(th),** שִׁבְעָה עָשָׂר 1 C 7_{11}, שְׁבַע עֶשְׂרֵה Gn 47_{28}. **8. eighteen(th),** שְׁמֹנָה עָשָׂר Ezr 8_{18}, שְׁמֹנַת עָשָׂר Jg 20_{25}, שְׁמֹנֶה עֶשְׂרֵה Jg 3_{14}. **9. nineteen(th),** תִּשְׁעָה עָשָׂר 2 S 2_{30}, תְּשַׁע עֶשְׂרֵה Jos 19_{38}. → עשׂר *take a tenth part of;* cf. מַעֲשֵׂר *tenth.*

עֶשֶׂר $_{176.1.57.5}$ n.m.&f.—m. (with f. nouns) עֶשֶׂר (עֲשַׂר, Q עסר); cstr. עֶשֶׂר; f. (with m. nouns) עֲשָׂרָה; cstr. עֲשֶׂרֶת; pl. עֲשָׂרֹת; sf. Q עשרותיו—**1a. ten,** עֶשֶׂר נָשִׁים *ten women* Lv 26_{26}, עָרִים עֶשֶׂר *ten cities* Jos 15_{57}, עֲשָׂרָה אֲנָשִׁים *ten men* Jg 6_{27}, פָּרִים עֲשָׂרָה *ten bulls* Gn 32_{16}, עֲשֶׂרֶת הַשְּׁבָטִים *the ten tribes* 1 K 11_{35}. **b.** as constituent of a larger number, אַרְבַּע מֵאוֹת וַעֲשָׂרָה *four hundred and ten* Ezr 1_{10}, עֲשֶׂרֶת אֲלָפִים *ten thousand* Jg 1_4. **2.** עֲשָׂרָה, עֲשֶׂרֶת

with ellip. of noun, **a. ten (persons)** Gn 18$_{32}$. **b. ten (shekels)** Gn 24$_{22}$. **c. ten (measures)** Hg 2$_{16}$. **3.** עֲשָׂרֹת **tens, groups of ten** 1QS 2$_{22}$; שָׂרֵי עֲשָׂרֹת *princes of tens* Ex 18$_{21}$. **4.** as ordinal numeral, **tenth,** יום עשרה *the tenth day* 4QCommGenA 1$_{13}$; with ellip. of noun, **tenth (day)** 4QAstrCrypt 1.2$_{12}$. → עשׂר *take a tenth part of;* cf. מַעֲשֵׂר *tenth.*

עִשָּׂרוֹן 33.0.9 n.m.—עִשָּׂרֹן; pl. עֶשְׂרֹנִים—**tenth part (of ephah)** Ex 29$_{40}$. → עשׂר *take a tenth part of.*

עֶשְׂרִים 315.0.82 n.m.&f.pl.—Q עשרין, Q עסרין—both cardinal and ordinal, **1.** עֶשְׂרִים alone, **a.** as cardinal number, **twenty,** with (usu. sg.) noun, עֶשְׂרִים אִישׁ *twenty men* 1 S 14$_{14}$; with ellip. of noun, **twenty (persons)** Gn 18$_{31}$, **twenty (cubits)** Ezk 42$_{3}$, **twenty (measures)** Hg 2$_{16}$. **b.** as ordinal number, **twentieth,** שְׁנַת עֶשְׂרִים *the twentieth year* 1 K 15$_{9}$; with ellip. of noun, **twentieth (day)** Nm 10$_{11}$, **twentieth (lot)** 1 C 24$_{16}$. **2.** with unit, **a.** as cardinal number, e.g. **twenty-one,** עֶשְׂרִים וְאֶחָד Dn 10$_{13}$, עֶשְׂרִים וְאַחַת 2 K 24$_{18}$, אחת ועשרים 11QT 4$_{12}$. **b.** as ordinal number, e.g. **twenty-first,** עֶשְׂרִים וְאֶחָד Hg 2$_{1}$, אֶחָד וְעֶשְׂרִים Ex 12$_{18}$. **3.** as constituent of a larger number, מֵאָה וְעֶשְׂרִים *a hundred and twenty* Dt 34$_{7}$, אֶלֶף מָאתַיִם עֶשְׂרִים וּשְׁנָיִם *one thousand two hundred and twenty-two* Ezr 2$_{12}$. → עשׂר *take a tenth part of.*

עֲשֶׂרֶת, see עֶשֶׂר *ten.*

עָשׁ I 7.1.2 n.m. **moth,** or another cloth-eating insect Is 50$_{9}$.

עָשׁ II 1 pr.n.m. (byform of עַיִשׁ) **Aldebaran** or **Arcturus, the Great Bear** Jb 9$_{9}$.

*עָשׁ III 3 n.m. **bird's nest** Ps 39$_{12}$ Jb 4$_{19}$ 27$_{18}$.

*עָשׁ IV 1 n.m. **night watchman** Jb 27$_{18}$.

*עָשׁ V 0.0.1 n.[m.] **darkness** 1QH 17$_{5}$. → עשׁשׁ II *be dark.*

*עָשׁ VI 1 n.[m.] **pus** or **emaciating disease** Ho 5$_{12}$. → עשׁשׁ I *be diseased.*

*[עַשָּׁא] 0.0.0.1 pr.n.m. **Asha.**

עָשׁוֹק 1 n.[m.] **oppressor** Jr 22$_{3}$. → עשׁק I *oppress.*

עֲשׁוּקִים 3.0.1 n.[m.]pl. **oppressions** Ec 4$_{1}$. → עשׁק I *oppress.*

עַשְׁוָת 1 pr.n.m. **Ashvath.**

עָשׁוֹת 1 adj. **smooth,** of iron Ezk 27$_{19}$. → עשׁת I *be shiny.*

עָשִׁיר I 23.14.1.1 adj.—pl. עֲשִׁירִים; cstr. עֲשִׁירֵי; sf. עֲשִׁירֶיהָ—**1. rich** Pr 28$_{11}$. **2.** as noun, **a. rich (one)** Si 13$_{3}$. **b. ruler, authority** Ec 10$_{6}$ (unless §2a). → עשׁר I *be rich.*

*עָשִׁיר II 1 n.[m.] **refuse, rabble** Is 53$_{9}$.

*עָשִׁיר III 1 adj. **corrupt,** as noun, **corrupt one** Is 53$_{9}$.

עשׁן I 6.0.1 vb.—**Qal** 6.0.1 Pf. עָשַׁן; impf. יֶעְשַׁן, יֶעֶשְׁנוּ—**1a. smoke,** i.e. **be kindled,** of mountains Ps 104$_{32}$, anger, jealousy Dt 29$_{19}$. **b. be kindled, angry,** of Y. Ps 80$_{5}$. **2. be wrapped in smoke,** of Mt Sinai Ex 19$_{18}$. → עָשָׁן *smoke,* עָשֵׁן *smoking.*

*עשׁן II 2 vb.—**Qal** 2 Pf. עָשַׁנְתָּ; impf. יֶעְשַׁן—**be strong, heavy,** of Y. Ps 80$_{5}$, anger Ps 74$_{1}$. → עָשֵׁן II *strong.*

עָשָׁן I 25.0.4 n.m.—cstr. עֲשַׁן (עֶשֶׁן); sf. עֲשָׁנוֹ—**smoke,** from burning city Jos 8$_{20}$, nose of Y. 2 S 22$_{9}$. → עשׁן I *smoke.*

עָשָׁן II 4 pl.n. **Ashan.**

עָשֵׁן I 2.0.0.1 adj.—pl. עֲשֵׁנִים—**smoking,** of firebrand Is 7$_{4}$, mountain Ex 20$_{18}$. → עשׁן I *smoke.*

*עָשֵׁן II adj. **strong,** as noun, **strong one** Is 14$_{31}$ (if em. עָשָׁן *smoke*). → עשׁן II *be strong.*

*[עֲשַׂנְאֵל] 0.0.0.1 pr.n.m. **Ashanel.**

*[עֲשַׁנְיָהוּ] 0.0.0.1 pr.n.m. **Ashaniah.**

עשׁק I 38.0.7 vb.—**Qal** 37.0.7 Pf. עָשַׁק; impf. יַעֲשֹׁק; ptc. עוֹשֵׁק, עֹשְׁקֵי, עֹשְׁקוֹת; pass. עָשׁוּק, עֲשׁוּקִים; inf. עֲשֹׁק (עָשְׁקָם)—**1a. oppress, defraud** person financially Mc 2$_{2}$ Pr 22$_{16}$; **extort** object of financial value Lv 5$_{23}$. **b. oppress** person(s) socially or politically Ps 119$_{122}$. **2.** pass., **be oppressed, a.** socially or politically Jr 50$_{33}$. **b.** in matters of conscience Pr 28$_{17}$. **3.** ptc. as noun, **oppressor** Ec 4$_{1}$. **4.** pass. ptc. as noun, **oppressed one** CD 13$_{10}$.

Pu. 1 Ptc. מְעֻשָּׁקָה—**be oppressed,** socially or politically Is 23$_{12}$.

→ עֹשֶׁק I *oppression,* עֲשֻׁקָה *oppression,* עָשׁוֹק *oppressor,* עֲשׁוּקִים *oppressions,* מַעֲשַׁקָּה *extortion.*

*עשׁק II 1 vb.—**Qal** 1 Impf. יַעֲשֹׁק—**be turbulent,** of river Jb 40$_{23}$.

*עשׁק III 1 vb.—**Qal** 1 Impf. יַעֲשֹׁק—**come and go** Jb 40$_{23}$.

*עשׁק IV 1 vb.—**Qal** 1 Ptc. pass. עָשֻׁק—**1. busy oneself** with (בְּ) person's blood Pr 28$_{17}$. **2. cling to** (בְּ) person's blood Pr 28$_{17}$ (unless §1).

*עשׁק V 2 vb.—**Qal** 2 Ptc. עֹשֵׁק—**slander** poor Pr 14$_{31}$ perh. 22$_{16}$. → עֹשֶׁק II *calumny.*

עֵשֶׁק 1 pr.n.m. **Eshek.**

עֹשֶׁק I 15.3.3 n.m.—cstr. עֹשֶׁק; sf. Si עשקך—**1. oppression,** social or political Ps 119134. 2. **extortion, extortion money** Lv 523 Ec 77. 3. **anxiety** Si 1110. → עשׁק I *oppress.*

*עֹשֶׁק II 4 n.m. **calumny** Ec 77. → עשׁק V *slander.*

עָשְׁקָה 1 n.f. **oppression** Is 3814. → עשׁק I *oppress.*

עשׁר I 17.2.1 vb.—**Qal** 2 Pf. עָשַׁרְתִּי; impf. יֶעְשַׁר—**be rich** Jb 1525.

Hi. 14.1.1 Pf. הֶעֱשַׁרְתְּ; impf. יַעֲשִׁיר; inf. הַעֲשִׁיר—**1. be, become rich** Zc 115. **2. make rich, enrich** person Gn 1423, land Ps 6510.

Htp. 1.1 Ptc. מִתְעַשֵּׁר—**1. pretend to be rich** Pr 137. **2. make oneself rich** Si 1118.

→ עָשִׁיר I *rich,* עֹשֶׁר I *riches.*

*עשׁר II 1 vb.—**Hi.** 1 Impf. תַּעְשְׁרֶנָּה—**give drink to** land Ps 6510.

עֹשֶׁר I 37.11.3 n.m.—sf. עָשְׁרָם—**riches** 1 S 1725. → עשׁר I *be rich.*

[עֹשֶׁר] II 1 n.m.—sf. עָשְׁרָם—**insight,** of wise Pr 1424.

*[עֲשֵׁרֹת] 0.0.0.1 pl.n. **Asheroth.**

עשׁשׁ I 3.0.1 vb.—**Qal** 3.0.1 Pf. עָשְׁשָׁה, עָשְׁשׁוּ—**be diseased, deteriorate,** of eyes Ps 68, palate, belly Ps 3110. → עָשׁ VI *pus.*

*עשׁשׁ II 2 vb.—**Qal** 2 Pf. עָשְׁשָׁה—**be dark, dim,** of eyes Ps 68. → עָשׁ V *darkness.*

*עשׁשׁ III 2 vb.—**Qal** 2 Pf. עָשְׁשָׁה—**be swollen,** of eyes Ps 68, palate, belly Ps 3110.

*עשׁשׁ IV vb. **be afflicted** Ps 3110 (LXX ἐταράχθη, Vg *conturbata est*).

עשׁת I 1 vb.—**Qal** 1 Pf. עָשְׁתוּ—**be shiny,** from eating fatty food Jr 528. → עֶשֶׁת I *plaque,* עָשׁוֹת *smooth.*

עשׁת II 1 vb. **Qal, devise** Is 326 (if em. לַעֲשׂוֹת *to practise* to לַעְשֹׁת *to devise*).

Htp. 1 Impf. יִתְעַשֵּׁת—**bear in mind** Jon 16.

→ עֶשְׁתּוֹן *thought,* עַשְׁתּוּת *thought.*

[עֶשֶׁת] I 1.0.2 n.f.—cstr. עֶשֶׁת; pl. Q עשתות—**plaque, ingot** of ivory Ca 514, gold 3QTr 15. → עשׁת I *be shiny.*

*[עֶשֶׁת] II 1 n.f. **body,** עֶשֶׁת שֵׁן *body of ivory* Ca 514.

[עֶשְׁתּוֹן] 1.1 n.[m.]—pl. sf. עֶשְׁתֹּנֹתָיו—**thought** Si 324. → עשׁת II *bear in mind.*

[עַשְׁתּוּת] 1 n.f.—cstr. עַשְׁתּוּת—**thought** Jb 125. → עשׁת II *bear in mind.*

עַשְׁתֵּי 19.0.25 n.m.&f. **one,** alw. in combination with עָשָׂר/עֶשְׂרֵה/Q עשרא meaning **eleven, eleventh, 1.** as cardinal number, **eleven** Nm 2920. **2.** as ordinal number, **a. eleventh day** Nm 772, month Dt 13, year 2 K 252. **b.** as noun, **the eleventh,** i.e. commander 1 C 1214, lot 1 C 2412.

עַשְׁתָּרוֹת I 6 pl.n. **Ashtaroth.**

עַשְׁתָּרוֹת II, see עַשְׁתֹּרֶת *Ashtoreth.*

עַשְׁתָּרוֹת III, see עַשְׁתֹּרֶת *offspring.*

*[עַשְׁתְּרוֹת] 1 n.f.pl.—pl. cstr. עַשְׁתְּרֹת—**lust, sexual desire** of flock Dt 713.

עַשְׁתֹּרֶת 9.0.1 pr.n.f. **Ashtoreth** (pl. **Ashtaroth**). → cf. עַשְׁתָּרוֹת I *Ashtaroth.*

[עַשְׁתֹּרֶת] 4.0.2 n.f.—pl. cstr. עַשְׁתְּרוֹת—**offspring,** small farm animal Dt 713.

[עַשְׁתְּרָתִי] 1 gent. **Ashterathite.**

עַשְׁתְּרֹת קַרְנַיִם 1 pl.n. **Ashteroth-karnaim.**

עֵת I 296.45.114.2 n.m.&f.—cstr. עֵת (עֶת); sf. עִתּוֹ; pl. עִתִּים (עִתּוֹת); cstr. עִתּוֹת (Q עתי); sf. עִתֹּתַי—**1. recurring time** in nature, **a. time less than twenty-four hours,** evening Gn 811, day, night Jr 3320. **b. rainy season** Zc 101. **c. dry season** Jb 617. **d. spring season** 1 C 201. **e. mating season** Gn 3110. **f. harvest season** Jb 526. **g. time** of migration of birds Jr 87. **h. season** of Mazzaroth Jb 3832. **i. menstrual period** Lv 1525. **2. usual time** of habitual action, **meal-time** Ru 214, **bed-time** Si 405. **3. time** of event, birth Mc 52, death 1 S 420. **4a. due time, right moment,** for love Ezk 168, food Ec 1017. **b.** preceded by בל, **wrong time** Si 354. **5. appointed time** by Y. 2 S 2415, **hour** of doom Is 1322. **6. end-time** Dn 817. **7. person's time** to die Ec 912. **8. scheduled time** Ezr 1014. **9. turn** of a land to be subjected Jr 277. **10. situation, circumstances** Si 68. **11. opportunity** Si 1216. **12. phase in life,** old age 1 K 114. **13. age, era** CD 105. **14. calendar time** 4QCitJub 1.14.7. **15.** pl., **holy times** 1QS 114.

*עֵת II 1 n.[m.]—sf. עִתָּם—**submission, subjugation** Ps 8116. → ענה II *be afflicted.*

*עֵת III 1 n.[m.]—sf. עִתָּם—**trouble** Ps 8116.

עתד 2.0.5 vb.—**Qal** 0.0.4 Ptc. pass. עתודי, עתודים—**1.** pass., **be ready** for battle 1QM 75. **2.** ptc. pass. as noun, **one who is ready** 1QM 105.

Pi. 1 Impv. עַתְּדָהּ—**make ready, prepare** work Pr

24_{27}.

Htp. 1.0.1 Pf. הִתְעַתְּדוּ—**be destined to become** like (לְ) heap Jb 15_{28}.

→ עָתוּד *ready,* עָתִיד *ready.*

*עתה 0.0.1 vb.—**Qal** 0.0.1 Inf. cstr. עתות—appar. **be afflicted** by (מִן) terror 4Q185 1.2₅.

עַתָּה 433.7.43.25 adv.—עַתָּה (Kt, Q, I עת, Q עתהא)—**1. now, at present,** present opp. to past Gn 22_{12}, specif. **now at last** 2 K 19_{25}. **2. still now,** present continuation of past Jos 14_{11}. **3a. now, already,** present opp. to future Jg 8_6. **b.** with negation, **(not) yet** Nm 24_{17}. **4. now, soon,** imminent future Ezk 7_3. **5. now, in these circumstances, as things are,** descr. of present situation 2 C 29_{10}. **6. after all** Jg 8_2. **7. now then, now therefore,** drawing conclusion from previous statement Gn 31_{28}. **8. now, now then, now come on,** exhortation 2 K 4_{26}. **9. yet nevertheless** 1 S 15_{30}. **10.** in rhetorical questions, **now,** expecting answer 'no', **(now) not,** expecting answer 'yes', אַתָּה עַתָּה תַּעֲשֶׂה מְלוּכָה עַל־יִשְׂרָאֵל *do you yourself (now) not reign over Israel?* 1 K 21_7. **11.** idioms, **a.** עַתָּה הַפַּעַם **now at last** Gn 29_{34}. **b.** מֵעַתָּה **from now on** Mc 4_7. **c.** עַד־עַתָּה **until now** Gn 32_5. **d.** עַתָּה זֶה **just now, even at this moment** 2 K 5_{22}. **e.** עת כים **(now) even today** Lachish ost. 2_3. **f.** גַּם־עַתָּה **so now** Gn 44_{10}. **g.** עַתָּה מְהֵרָה **soon now** Jr 27_{16}. **h.** עַתָּה מִקָּרוֹב **soon now** Ezk 7_8. **i.** לֹא עַתָּה **no longer now** Is 29_{22}. **j.** עַתָּה הִנֵּה **now behold** 2 K 18_{21}. **k.** עַתָּה לָמָּה **now why?** Mc 4_9. **l.** כִּי עַתָּה **for then, surely then** Mc 5_3. **m.** אַף כִּי עַתָּה **surely then also, how much more** 2 S 16_{11}. **n.** ועת/וְעַתָּה **(1) and now, but now** Ezr 9_8. **(2) likewise now** 2 S 15_{34}. **(3) already now** Mc 4_{11}. **(4) and soon** Ne 6_7. **(5) yet in this present situation** 2 K 13_{19}. **(6) now therefore, now then** Jg 11_{23}. **o.** ועתה כיום הזה **and now on this day** 4QDibHam[a] 1.6₄. **p.** ועת הן/וְעַתָּה הִנֵּה **and now see** Jos 9_{12}. **q.** וְעַתָּה כִּי **and now indeed** Ru 3_{12}. **r.** וְעַתָּה לָכֵן **and now therefore** Jr 42_{15}. **s.** ... וְעַתָּה אֲשֶׁר ... כִּי **and now the reason that ..., is because ...** 2 S 14_{15}.

[עָתוּד] 2 adj.—pl. Kt עתודים; sf. Qr עֲתוּדֹתֵיהֶם—**1. ready,** of person Est $8_{13(Kt)}$. **2.** as pl. noun, **things prepared, provisions** Is $10_{13(Qr)}$. → עתד *be ready;* cf. עָתִיד *ready.*

[עַתּוּד] 29.0.1 n.m.—pl. עַתֻּדִים; cstr. עַתּוּדֵי—**1. male goat,** usu. as sacrifice Nm 7_{17}. **2. person depicted as male goat, esp. leader** Ezk 39_{18}.

עַתַּי 4 pr.n.m. **Attai.**

עִתִּי 1.0.2 adj. **ready,** of person 4QS[d] 8_7.

עָתִיד 6.0.1 adj.—pl. m. עֲתִידִים; f. עֲתִדֹת—**1. ready for battle** Jb 15_{24}. **2.** as pl. noun, **a. those skilled** Jb 3_8. **b. things prepared, provisions** Is $10_{13(Kt)}$. **c. imminent things** Dt 32_{35}. → עתד *be ready;* cf. עָתוּד *ready.*

עֲתָיָה 1.0.0.1 pr.n.m. **Athaiah.**

עָתִיק 1 adj. **fine,** of clothes Is 23_{18}. → עתק I *move, advance.*

[עַתִּיק] I 1 adj.—cstr. עַתִּיקֵי—**removed,** as noun, **one taken away** from (מִן) breast, i.e. weaned child Is 28_9. → עתק I *move, advance.*

*[עַתִּיק] II 1 adj.—pl. עַתִּיקִים—**old, ancient,** of records 1 C 4_{22}.

עֶתֶךְ 1 pl.n. **Athach.**

*[עָתֵל] adj. **noble** Na 2_8 (if em. הֹעֲלָתָה *she is carried off* to הָעֲתֵלָה *the noble woman*).

עַתְלָי 1 pr.n.m. **Athlai.**

עֲתַלְיָה 17 pr.n.m.&f. **Athaliah.**

עתם 1 vb.—**Ni.** 1 Pf. נֶעְתַּם—**be burned,** of earth Is 9_{18}.

עָתְנִי 1 pr.n.m. **Othni.**

עָתְנִיאֵל 7 pr.n.m. **Othniel.**

*עתף vb. **Qal, tear out** engraving Ps 74_6 (if em. וְעַתָּה [Qr; Kt ועת] *and now* to וְעָתוֹף/וְעָתְפוּ *and tearing out/ and they tear out*).

עתק I 9.1 vb.—**Qal** 4 Pf. עָתְקָה; impf. יֶעְתַּק—**1. move,** of rock Jb 14_{18}. **2a. advance in years** Jb 21_7. **b. grow old and weak** Ps 6_8.

Hi. 5.1 Pf. הֶעְתִּיקוּ; + waw וַיַּעְתֵּק; ptc. מַעְתִּיק—**1. move forward,** of person Gn 12_8. **2. be far removed, fail,** of words Jb 32_{15}. **3.** of Y., **remove** mountain Jb 9_5. **4. transcribe** proverb Pr 25_1.

→ עָתִיק *fine,* עַתִּיק I *removed,* עָתָק I *arrogant talk,* II *arrogant,* עָתֵק *enduring.*

*עתק II 1 vb.—**Qal** 1 Pf. עָתְקוּ—**thrive, prosper,** of wicked Jb 21_7.

*עָתָק I 4 n.[m.] **arrogant talk** Ps 31_{19}. → עתק I *move, advance.*

עָתָק II 1 adj. **arrogant,** of neck Ps 75_6. → עתק I *move,* *advance.*

עָתֵק I $_1$ adj. **enduring,** of wealth Pr 8_{18}. → עתק I *move, advance.*

*עָתֵק II $_1$ adj. **negotiable,** of wealth Pr 8_{18}.

[עֵת] קָצִין $_1$ pl.n. **Eth-kazin.**

עתר I $_{20.3}$ vb.—**Qal** $_{5.1}$ Impf. יֶעְתַּר—with לְ or אֶל of obj., **supplicate, entreat** Y. Gn 25_{21} Jg 13_8.

Ni. $_8$ + waw וַיֵּעָתֵר ;וְנֶעְתַּר; inf. abs. נַעְתּוֹר; cstr. הֵעָתֵר—alw. of Y., **be entreated,** perlocutionary verb, thus **be persuaded to grant an entreaty** Is 19_{22}.

Hi. $_{7.2}$ Impf. אַעְתִּיר; + waw וְהַעְתַּרְתִּי—with לְ or אֶל of obj., **supplicate, entreat** Y. Ex 10_{17} Jb 22_{27}.

→ עָתָר I *suppliant,* עָתָר II *odour,* עֲתָרָה *supplication.*

עתר II $_2$ vb.—**Ni.** $_1$ Ptc. נַעְתָּרוֹת—**be abundant, excessive,** of (false) kisses Pr 27_6.

Hi. $_1$ Pf. הַעְתַּרְתֶּם—**multiply** words Ezk 35_{13}. → עֲתֶרֶת *abundance.*

*עתר III vb. **Qal, offer sacrifice,** ptc. as noun, **one who offers sacrifice** Zp 3_{10} (if em. עֲתָרַי *my worshippers* to עֹתְרַי *those who offer sacrifice to me*). → (?) עָתָר I *suppliant,* (?) II *odour.*

[עָתָר] I $_1$ n.[m.]—pl. sf. עֲתָרַי—**suppliant** Zp 3_{10}. → עתר I *supplicate* or III *offer sacrifice.*

[עָתָר] II $_1$ n.[m.]—cstr. עֲתַר—**odour,** less prob., **sacrificial odour** Ezk 8_{11}. → עתר I *supplicate* or III *offer sacrifice.*

עֶתֶר $_2$ pl.n. **Ether.**

*[עֲתָרָה] n.f. **supplication** 4QpPs[b] 1_4 (ע]תרות]). → עתר I *supplicate.*

עֲתֶרֶת $_1$ n.f. **abundance** of peace and truth Jr 33_6. → עתר II *be abundant.*

פ

*[פְּ־] or [פַּ־] conj. **and, but, for, then** Ho 4_2 (if em. נָאוֹף פָּרָצוּ *adultery has broken out* to נָאֹף פְּ־רָצוֹ *adultery and pleasure*).

פֹּא, see פֹּה *here.*

פאה $_1$ vb.—**Hi.** $_1$ Impf. אַפְאֵיהֶם—of Y., **cut people in pieces** Dt 32_{26}. → פֵּאָה III *piece.*

פֵּאָה I $_{86.1.1}$ n.f.—cstr. פְּאַת; du. cstr. פַּאֲתֵי; pl. פֵּאֹת—**1. side, border** of field Lv 19_9, **corner** of table Ex 25_{26}, prob. **foot-board** Am 3_{12}. **2. border** of territory, followed by compass direction, זֹאת פְּאַת־יָם *this is the western border* Jos 18_{14}.

*[פֵּאָה] II $_1$ n.f.—cstr. פְּאַת—**splendour** Am 3_{12}.

*פֵּאָה III $_1$ n.f. **piece, portion** Ne 9_{22}. → פאה *cut.*

*פֵּאָה IV $_1$ n.f. **spoils of war** Ne 9_{22}.

פאר I $_{13.7.7}$ vb.—**Pi.** $_{6.1.5}$ Pf. פֵּאֲרָךְ; impf. יְפָאֵר; inf. פָּאֵר—**glorify, adorn** Y. 11QPs[a] 18_1, temple Is 60_7.

Htp. $_{7.6.2}$ Pf. Si התפאר; impf. יִתְפָּאֵר; impv. הִתְפָּאֵר; ptc. Si מתפאר; inf. הִתְפָּאֵר—**1. display one's glory** or **honour,** of Y. Is 44_{23}, priest Si 50_{20}. **2. be glorified,** of Zion 11QPs[a] 22_6, human being Si 38_6.

→ פְּאֵר *headdress,* פֹּארָה II *glory,* מִפְאָר *beauty,* תִּפְאָרָה *glory,* תִּפְאֶרֶת *glory.*

פאר II $_1$ vb.—**Pi.** $_1$ Impf. תְּפָאֵר—**beat branches** Dt 24_{20}. → פֹּארָה I *branch,* פֻּארָה *leafy branches.*

*פאר III $_1$ vb.—**Htp.** $_1$ Impv. הִתְפָּאֵר—**choose course of action for** (עַל) **person** Ex 8_5.

פְּאֵר $_{7.0.3}$ n.m.—sf. פְּאֵרְךָ; pl. פְּאֵרִים; cstr. פַּאֲרֵי (Q פרי)—**1. headdress** Is 3_{20}. **2. adornment** 4Q408 3_5. → פאר I *glorify.*

[פֹּארָה] I $_{6.0.3}$ n.f.—cstr. Q פארת; pl. פֹּארוֹת—**(leafy) branch, foliage, shoot,** of vine Ezk 17_6, cedar Ezk 31_8. → פאר II *beat branches.*

*[פֹּארָה] II $_{0.0.5}$ n.f.—sf. Q פארתכה—**1. glory, honour** CD 6_7. **2. haughtiness** 4QRebukes 2.2_4. → פאר I *glorify.*

פֻּארָה $_1$ n.f.—Qr mss פוּרָה—**(leafy) branches** Is 10_{33}. → פאר II *beat branches.*

פָּארוּר I $_2$ n.[m.] **paleness** Jl 2_6 Na 2_{11}.

*פָּארוּר II $_2$ n.[m.] **darkness** Jl 2_6 Na 2_{11}.

*פָּארוּר III $_2$ n.[m.] **redness** Jl 2_6 Na 2_{11}.

*פָּארוּר IV 2 n.[m.] **glow** Jl 2$_{6}$ Na 2$_{11}$.

*פָּארוּר V 2 n.[m.] **pot** Jl 2$_{6}$ Na 2$_{11}$.

*פָּארוּר VI 2 n.[m.] **furrow (of face)** Jl 2$_{6}$ Na 2$_{11}$. → פרר I *break*.

*פָּארוּר VII 2 n.[m.] **brightness** Jl 2$_{6}$ Na 2$_{11}$.

פָּארָן 12 pl.n. **Paran.**

*[פָּארֻר] 0.0.0.3 pr.n.m. **Parur.**

*[פְּאֹרֶת] 0.0.0.1 pr.n.[m.] **Peoreth.**

[פַּג] 1 n.[f.]—sf. פַּגֶּיהָ—**unripe fig** Ca 2$_{13}$.

פִּגּוּל 4.0.3 n.m.—pl. פִּגֻּלִים (פִּגּוּלִים); sf. Q פגוליכמה—**meat unfit for use, deconsecrated** Lv 7$_{18}$. → פגל *render unfit for use.*

*[פָּגִי] 0.0.0.1 pr.n.[m.] **Pagy.**

*פגל 0.0.1 vb.—**Pu.** 0.0.1 Ptc. מפגול—**be rendered unfit for use, deconsecrated,** of tithe 3QTr 1$_{11}$(Wolters). → פִּגּוּל *meat unfit for use.*

פגע 46.3.10 vb.—**Qal** 40.3.10 Pf. פָּגַע, פָּגַעְתָּ; impf. אֶפְגַּע; impv. פְּגַע, פִּגְעוּ; ptc. Q פוגעים; pass. Q פגועים; inf. פְּגֹעַ (פִּגְעוֹ) —**1. meet, come upon in the course of travel, a.** obj., person Ex 5$_{20}$, animal Ex 23$_{4}$. **b.** with בְּ of obj., + person Nm 35$_{19}$, place Gn 28$_{11}$. **2a.** with בְּ of obj., **meet with a request, entreat** human being Ru 1$_{16}$, Y. Jr 7$_{16}$ (‖ פלל htp. *pray*). **3. meet with hostility, attack, a.** with בְּ of obj., + person 1 K 2$_{25}$ (unless §4). **b.** obj., people with (בְּ) pestilence or sword, of Y. Ex 5$_{3}$. **4.** with בְּ of obj., **execute** person 1 K 2$_{25}$. **5.** of Y., **meet** person **with kindness** Is 47$_{3}$. **6.** of border, **reach to/as far as** (בְּ) valley Jos 19$_{27}$. **7.** of event, **happen to** (בְּ) person 1QH fr. 4$_{16}$. **8.** pass. ptc. as noun, **stricken one,** i.e. one possessed by demons 11QPs^{a} 27$_{10}$.

Hi. 6 Pf. הִפְגִּיעַ; impf. יַפְגִּיעַ; ptc. מַפְגִּיעַ—**1.** of Y., **cause** (punishment for) sin **to come upon** (בְּ) servant Is 53$_{6}$. **2. make entreaty, plead with** (בְּ) king Jr 36$_{25}$. **3.** of Y., **cause** enemy **to entreat with** (בְּ) people Jr 15$_{11}$. **4.** ptc. as noun, **assailant** Jb 36$_{32}$.

→ פֶּגַע *occurrence,* מִפְגָּע *target.*

פֶּגַע 2.0.1 n.[m.] **occurrence** 1 K 5$_{18}$. → פגע *meet.*

פַּגְעִיאֵל 5 pr.n.m. **Pagiel.**

פגר I 2 vb.—**Pi.** 2 Pf. פִּגְּרוּ—**be exhausted** 1 S 30$_{10.21}$. → (?) פֶּגֶר I *corpse.*

*פגר II 2 vb.—**Pi.** 2 Pf. פִּגְּרוּ—**be petrified** 1 S 30$_{10.21}$.

פֶּגֶר I 22.0.4 n.m.—פֶּגֶר; cstr. פֶּגֶר; pl. פְּגָרִים; cstr. פִּגְרֵי; sf. פִּגְרֵיכֶם—**1. corpse, carcass** of human Jr 33$_{5}$, animal Gn 15$_{11}$ (unless §2). **2.** perh. **piece of sacrificed animal** Gn 15$_{11}$. → (?) פגר I *be exhausted.*

*[פֶּגֶר] II 3 n.m.—pl. cstr. פִּגְרֵי—**memorial stele** Lv 26$_{30}$ Ezk 43$_{7.9}$.

*[פֶּגֶר] III 4 n.m.—pl. פְּגָרִים; cstr. פִּגְרֵי—**sacrifice for the dead** Gn 15$_{11}$ Jr 31$_{40}$ Ezk 43$_{7.9}$.

*[פֶּגֶר] IV 1 n.m.—pl. cstr. פִּגְרֵי—**broken fragment** Lv 26$_{30}$.

פגשׁ 14.0.2.1 vb.—**Qal** 10.0.2.1 Pf. פְּגָשַׁתִּי; impf. יִפְגָּשְׁךָ; inf. abs. פָּגוֹשׁ; cstr. פְּגֹשׁ—**1. meet** in course of travel, **a.** obj., human being 1 S 25$_{20}$, animal Is 34$_{14}$. **b.** בְּ of obj., human being, of bear Pr 17$_{12}$. **2.** of Y., **meet with hostility, strike** Israelites Ho 13$_{8}$.

Ni. 3 Pf. נִפְגָּשׁוּ—**meet together** Pr 22$_{2}$.

Pi. 1 Impf. יְפַגְּשׁוּ—**meet** darkness Jb 5$_{14}$.

*[פַּדָּא] 0.0.0.2 pr.n.m. **Padda.**

פדה 61.2.16 vb.—**Qal** 56.2.16 Pf. פָּדָה, פָּדִיתָ; impf. יִפְדֶּה; + waw וַיִּפְדּוּ; impv. פְּדֵה (פְּדֵנִי); ptc. פּוֹדֶה (פֹּדְךָ); ptc. pass. פְּדוּיֵי; inf. פְּדוֹת—**1. ransom** firstborn **for a price** Ex 13$_{13}$. **2.** of Y., **redeem** Israel Dt 7$_{8}$. **3. deliver oneself from obligation to, break** oath CD 16$_{8}$. **4.** pass. ptc. as a noun, **a. redeemed one** Is 35$_{10}$. **b. redemption** 4QD^{e} 2.2$_{9}$.

Ni. 3 Pf. נִפְדָּתָה; impf. יִפָּדֶה—**1. be redeemed for a price** Lv 19$_{20}$. **2. be delivered** Is 1$_{27}$.

Hi. 1 Pf. הֶפְדָּהּ—**cause** woman **to be redeemed** Ex 21$_{8}$.

Ho. 1 Inf. הָפְדֵּה—**be redeemed** Lv 19$_{20}$.

→ פִּדְיוֹם *redemption price,* פִּדְיוֹן *redemption price,* פְּדוּיִם *redemption price,* פְּדוּת *redemption.*

*[פְּדָה] 0.0.0.1 pr.n.[m.] **Padah.**

פְּדַהְאֵל 1 pr.n.m. **Pedahel.**

פְּדָהצוּר 5 pr.n.m. **Pedahzur.**

[פְּדוּיִם] 4.0.1 n.m.pl.—cstr. פְּדוּיֵי; sf. פְּדוּיָו—**redemption price** Nm 3$_{46}$. → פדה *ransom.*

פָּדוֹן 2 pr.n.m. **Padon.**

פְּדוּת I 4.0.14 n.f.—פְּדֻת; pl. sf. Q פדותיך—**1. redemption** Ps 130$_{7}$. **2. redeemed ones** 1QM 14$_{10}$. **3. division** Ex 8$_{19}$. → פדה *ransom.*

*[פְּדוּת] II 1 n.f.—פְּדֻת—**separation** Ex 8$_{19}$.

*[פָּדִי] 0.0.0.4 pr.n.[m.] **Padi.**

פְּדָיָה 8.0.0.25 pr.n.m. **Pedaiah.**

פְּדָיָהוּ, see פְּדָיָה *Pedaiah.*

*[**פְּדִיוֹ**] 0.0.0.1 pr.n.[m.] **Padiah.**

פְּדִיוֹם 1 n.m. **redemption price** Nm 3$_{49}$. → פדה *ransom.*

פִּדְיוֹן 2 n.m.—פִּדְיֹן—**redemption price** Ex 21$_{30}$ Ps 49$_{9}$. → פדה *ransom.*

פַּדָּן 1 pl.n. **Paddan.**

פַּדַּן אֲרָם *Paddan-aram,* see אֲרָם *Aram.*

פדע 1 vb.—**Qal** 1 Impv. פְּדָעֵהוּ—of Y., **deliver** human being Jb 33$_{24}$.

[**פֶּדֶר**] 3 n.[m.]—sf. פִּדְרוֹ—**suet** Lv 1$_{8}$.

*[**פה**] vb. **Qal, watch** Pr 11$_{9}$ (if em. בְּפֶה *with the mouth* to בְּפוֹה *by watching*).

פֶּה 500.25.269 n.m.—cstr. פִּי (Q פיא); sf. פִּי, פִּיךָ; pl. פִּיוֹת (פִּיפִיּוֹת, פֵּיוֹת)—**1. mouth,** of **a.** person Ex 4$_{11}$. **b.** Y. Dt 8$_{3}$. **c.** god, image Jr 51$_{44}$. **d.** Belial 4QMidrEschat[a] 2$_{15}$(Abegg). **e.** bird Gn 8$_{11}$. **f.** animal Nm 22$_{28}$. **2. opening, entrance,** of **a.** Sheol Is 5$_{14}$. **b.** cave Jos 10$_{18}$. **c.** well Gn 29$_{2}$. **d.** city Pr 8$_{3}$. **e.** sack Gn 42$_{27}$. **3. speech, a. command** Gn 41$_{40}$. **b. evidence** of witness Dt 17$_{6}$. **c. dictation** Jr 36$_{4}$. **d. guidance** of Y. Jos 9$_{14}$, priests Dt 21$_{5}$. **4. edge** of sword Gn 34$_{26}$. **5.** פִּי שְׁנַיִם lit. 'mouth of two', **a. double portion** 2 K 2$_{9}$. **b. two thirds** Zc 13$_{8}$. **6. mouth** or **bank** of Nile Is 19$_{7}$. **7. sound** of harp Am 6$_{5}$. **8. hunger** of worker Pr 16$_{26}$. **9.** adv., פֶּה אֶחָד **unanimously, with one accord** Jos 9$_{2}$. **10.** prep., **a.** כְּפִי **in accordance with** Nm 7$_{5}$. **b.** לְפִי **according to** Pr 12$_{8}$.

פֹּה 82.0.1.1 adv.—פֹּא, פּוֹ—**1. here** Jos 18$_{6}$. **2a.** מִפֹּה וּמִפֹּה **on either side** Ezk 40$_{10}$. **b.** מִפּוֹ ... מִפּוֹ **on the one side ... on the other side** Ezk 41$_{19}$. **c.** מִפֹּה **on either side** Ezk 40$_{12}$.

*__פהך__ 0.0.1 vb.—**Qal** 0.0.1 Pf. פהכו—**turn** 4QInstr[d] 34$_{3}$.

פּוּאָה 2 pr.n.m. **Puah.**

פוג 4.1 vb.—**Qal** 3 Impf. תָּפוּג; + waw וַיָּפָג—**1. turn cold,** of heart Gn 45$_{26}$. **2. be powerless,** of law Hb 1$_{4}$. **3. grow weary,** of hand Ps 77$_{3}$.

Ni. 1 Pf. נְפוּגוֹתִי—**be numb,** of human being Ps 38$_{9}$.

Pi. 0.1 Impv. פייג—**comfort** heart Si 30$_{23}$.

→ פוּגָה *rest,* הֲפֻגָה *cessation.*

[**פוּגָה**] 1 n.f.—פּוּגַת—**rest** Lm 2$_{18}$. → פוג *be numb.*

פֻּוָּה 2 pr.n.m. **Puvah.**

פוח I 11.1.1 vb.—**Qal** 2.1 Impf. יָפוּחַ—**1. blow, i.e. dishearten** soul Si 4$_{2}$. **2. breathe,** of day Ca 2$_{17}$.

Ni. with infixed-t 2 Impf. תִּפָּתַח, יִפָּתַח—**1. be blown,** of evil Jr 1$_{14}$. **2. be aerated,** of wine Jb 32$_{19}$.

Hi. 7.0.1 Impf. יָפִיחַ; impv. הָפִיחִי; inf. הָפֵחַ—**1. blow,** of Y. Ezk 21$_{36}$, wind Ca 4$_{16}$. **2. blow, puff** on, at (בְּ) adversary in scorn Ps 10$_{5}$. **3. blow, sigh** in longing Ps 12$_{6}$. **4. blow,** i.e. **hasten** vision Hb 2$_{3}$.

→ פֵּחַ *scent.*

*__פוח II__ 9 vb.—**Hi.** 9 Impf. יָפִיחַ—**testify (against), 1.** obj., city Pr 29$_{8}$. **2.** בְּ *against,* + adversary Ps 10$_{5}$. → יָפֵחַ II *witness.*

*[**פּוּחַ**] 0.0.1 adj. **1. clad in rags,** of person 1QS 7$_{14}$ (unless §2). **2. with holes,** of garment 1QS 7$_{14}$. → פחח II *have holes in one's garments.*

פּוּט 7.0.1 pr.n.m. **Put.**

פּוּטִיאֵל 1 pr.n.m. **Putiel.**

פּוֹטִיפַר 2 pr.n.m. **Potiphar.**

פּוֹטִי פֶרַע 3 pr.n.m. **Potiphera.**

פּוּךְ 4 n.[m.] **antimony,** a silver-white metalic substance, or perh. **malachite** Is 54$_{11}$.

*[**פול**] vb. **Qal, wither,** of human being Pr 11$_{28}$ (if em. יִפֹּל *he will fall* to יָפוּל).

פּוֹל 2 n.[m.] **beans** 2 S 17$_{28}$.

פּוּל I 1 pl.n. **Pul.**

פּוּל II 3 pr.n.m. **Pul.**

פּוּם *mouth,* see פֶּה *mouth.*

פון 1 vb.—**Qal** 1 Impf. אָפוּנָה—**be helpless** Ps 88$_{16}$.

פּוּנִי 1 gent. **Punite.**

פּוּנֹן 2 pl.n. **Punon.**

פּוּעָה 1 pr.n.f. **Puah.**

פוץ I 62.1.8 vb.—**Qal** 10.1.3 Impf. נָפוּץ; + waw וַיָּפֻצוּ; impv. פֻּצוּ; ptc. פוצי—**1.** intrans., **scatter** Ezk 34$_{5}$. **2.** pass. ptc. as noun, **scattered one** Zp 3$_{10}$.

Ni. 15 Pf. נָפֹצוּ; ptc. נְפוֹצִים (נְפֹצִים)—**1. be scattered** Jr 40$_{15}$. **2.** ptc. as noun, **scattered one** 4QPrFêtes[c] 3$_{4}$ (נפוצות[י]נו).

Hi. 37.0.4 Pf. הֱפִיצְךָ, הֲפִצוֹתִיךָ; impf. יָפִיץ (יָפֵץ); + waw וַיָּפֶץ; impv. הָפֵץ; ptc. מֵפִיץ, מְפִצִים; inf. cstr. הָפִיץ—**1.** oft. of Y., **cause people to scatter** Jr 9$_{15}$. **2. disperse oneself** Ex 5$_{12}$. **3.** ptc. as noun, **scatterer** Na 2$_{2}$.

Pilp. 0.0.1 Ptc. מפצפצים—**be scattered** 4QapJoseph[b] 1_{11}.

→ מֵפִיץ I *scatterer*, II *club*, פַּצִּים *scattering*, תְּפוֹצָה *dispersion*; cf. נפץ II *scatter*.

פוץ II 3.0.1 vb.—**Qal** 2.0.1 Impf. תְּפוּצֶינָה—**overflow, flow,** of city Zc 1_{17}, spring Pr 5_{16}.

Hi. 1 Impf. יָפִיץ—**cause** cloud **to overflow** Jb 37_{11} (if em. אוֹרוֹ cloud of *his light* to אֵדוֹ *his torrents*).

*פוץ III 1 vb.—**Hi.** 1 Pf. הֱפִיצָהוּ—of terror, **crush** wicked one Jb 18_{11}. → cf. פצץ *break*.

*פוץ IV 2 vb.—**Hi.** 2 Pf. הֲפִיצוֹתֶם—of sheep, **chase** weak one Ezk 34_{21}.

*פּוּצַי 1 pl.n. **Puzai.**

פוק I 2 vb.—**Qal** 1 Pf. פָּקוּ—**stumble,** of priest, prophet Is 28_7.

Hi. 1 Impf. יָפִיק—**totter,** of tree Jr 10_4.

→ פּוּקָה I *stumbling (block)*, פִּיק I *knocking*.

פוק II 7.2.3 vb.—**Hi.** 7.2.3 Impf. יָפִיק; + waw וַיָּפֶק; impv. Q הפק; ptc. מְפִיקִים—**1a. obtain favour** Pr 8_{35}, **understanding** Pr 3_{13}. **b. realize plan** Ps 140_9. **2. offer oneself** Is 58_{10}. **3.** of storehouse, **provide** Ps 144_{13}.

*פוק III 1 vb.—**Hi.** 1 Impf. יָפִיק—**awake, stand up,** of tree Jr 10_4.

*פוק IV 2 vb.—**Qal** 1 Pf. פָּקוּ—**hiccough** Is 28_7.

Hi. 1 Impf. יָפִיק—**break apart,** of tree Jr 10_4.

→ פּוּקָה II *cracking up*, פִּיק II *giving way*.

*פוק V 1 vb.—**Qal** 1 Pf. פָּקוּ—**vomit** Is 28_7.

פּוּקָה I 1 n.f. **stumbling (block)** 1 S 25_{31}. → פוק I *stumble*.

*פּוּקָה II 1 n.f. **cracking up** 1 S 25_{31}. → פוק IV *break apart*.

*פור 6.0.2 vb.—**Qal** 1 Inf. cstr. פּוֹר—**be split apart,** of earth Is 24_{19}.

Hi. 3.0.2 Pf. הֵפִיר; impf. אָפִיר; inf. cstr. Q הפיר—**break covenant** Ezk 17_{19}, **statute** CD 1_{20}.

Pol. 1 Pf. פּוֹרַרְתָּ—of Y., **split open sea** Ps 74_{13}.

Htpol. 1 Pf. הִתְפּוֹרְרָה—**be split apart,** of land Is 24_{19}.

→ cf. פרר I *break*.

פּוּר I 8 n.m.—pl. פֻּרִים—**1. lot,** equivalent to גּוֹרָל Est 3_7. **2.** pl., **Purim,** Jewish festival celebrated on 14th and 15th of Adar (March–April) Est 9_{26}.

*פּוּר II 2 n.m. **stone(s),** used in casting lots Est 3_7.

פּוּרָה I 2 n.f. **1. winepress** Is 63_3. **2. liquid from the winepress** Hg 2_{16}.

פּוּרָה II, see פֹּארָה *(leafy) branches*.

פּוּרִים *Purim*, see פּוּר I *lot*.

פּוֹרָתָא 1 pr.n.m. **Poratha.**

פוש I 3 vb.—**Qal** 3 Impf. Qr תְּפוּשׁוּ; + waw וּפָשׁוּ, וּפִשְׁתֶּם—**skip about** like (כְּ) calf Ml 3_{20}.

פוש II 1 vb.—**Ni.** 1 Pf. נָפֹשׁוּ—**be scattered,** of people Na 3_{18}.

פּוּתִי, see פֶּתִי I *simple-minded*.

פּוּתִי 1 gent. **Puthite.**

*[פּוֹתְלָאִיס] 0.0.1 pr.n.m. **Potlais.**

פָּז 9.3.5 n.m. **pure gold**—פָּז; cstr. Q פז—Ca 5_{11}. → פזז I *refine*.

פזז I 1 vb.—**Ho.** 1 Ptc. pass. מוּפָז—**be refined,** of gold 1 K 10_{18}. → פָּז *pure gold*.

פזז II 2 vb.—**Qal** 1 + waw וַיָּפֹזּוּ—**be agile,** of arm, hand Gn 49_{24}.

Pi. 1 Ptc. מְפַזֵּז—**leap before** (לִפְנֵי) Y. 2 S 6_{16}.

*[פָּזַי] 0.0.0.2 pr.n.m. **Pazai.**

פזר I 10.0.4 vb.—**Qal** 1 Ptc. pass. פְּזוּרָה—pass., **be scattered,** of sheep Jr 50_{17}.

Ni. 1 Pf. נִפְזְרוּ—**be scattered,** of bones Ps 141_7.

Pi. 7.0.2 Pf. פִּזַּר; impf. יְפַזֵּר; ptc. מְפַזֵּר—**1. scatter** people Jl 4_2, bones Ps 53_6. **2. distribute (freely)** to poor Ps 112_9.

Pu. 1 Ptc. מְפֻזָּר—**be scattered,** of people Est 3_8.

Htp. 0.0.2 Pf. התפזרו—**be scattered,** of enemies 11QPs[a] 22_{11}.

→ cf. בזר *scatter*.

*פזר II 2 vb.—**Ni.** 1 Pf. נִפְזְרוּ—**come out, arise,** of bones Ps 141_7.

Pi. 1 Pf. פִּזַּר—of Y., **bring out, raise** bones Ps 53_6.

*[פִּזְּרִי] 0.0.0.1 pr.n.m. **Pizzary.**

פַּח I 25.1.12 n.m.—cstr. פַּח; pl. פַּחִים; cstr. Q פחי; sf. Q פחיה—**trap** Ps 11_6. → פחח I *trap*.

[פַּח] II 2 n.m.—pl. פַּחִים; cstr. פַּחֵי—**sheet (of metal)** Ex 39_3.

*[פַּחַ] 0.1 n.[m.]—sf. פחה—**scent** Si 51_4. → פוח I *blow*.

*[פָּחָא] 0.0.0.2 pr.n.[m.] **Paha.**

פחד 25.7.15 vb.—**Qal** 22.5.10 Pf. פָּחַד, פָּחֲדוּ; impf. יִפְחַד; impv.

Si פחד—1. **be afraid** on account of (מִן) Y. Jb 23$_{15}$, death Si 41$_{3}$. **2. fear** Y. Si 7$_{29}$. **3. turn in fear to** (אֶל) Y. Ho 3$_{5}$. **4. be in awe before** (לִפְנֵי) Y. 4Q460 9.1$_{2}$. **5. shiver with excitement,** of heart Is 60$_{5}$.

Pi. 2.2.5 Impf. תְּפַחֵד; ptc. מְפַחֵד—**1. be (continually) afraid** Is 51$_{13}$. **2. frighten** heart 1QS 4$_{2}$. **3. be respectful** Si 42$_{14(M)}$. **4.** ptc. as noun, **one who frightens** 4QapPsB 31$_{8}$.

Hi. 1 Pf. הִפְחִיד—of dread, **cause** bones **to shake with fear** Jb 4$_{14}$.

→ פַּחַד I *fear,* פַּחְדָּה *awe.*

פַּחַד I 49.4.20 n.m.—cstr. פַּחַד; sf. פַּחְדּוֹ; pl. פְּחָדִים; cstr. Si פחדי—**1. dread** of the Jews Est 8$_{17}$, of evil Pr 1$_{33}$. **2. awe** of Y. Ps 36$_{2}$. **3. Fear of Isaac,** name for Y. Gn 31$_{42}$. → פחד *be afraid.*

[**פַּחַד**] II 1 n.m.—pl. sf. Qr פַּחֲדָיו—**thigh** of Behemoth, prob. hippopotamus Jb 40$_{17}$.

*[**פַּחַד**] III 12 n.m.—cstr. פַּחַד; pl. פְּחָדִים—**1. kinsman** Gn 31$_{42}$. **2. cabal** Ps 14$_{5}$. **3. pack (of dogs)** Jb 22$_{10}$. **4. flock (of birds)** Jb 39$_{16}$.

[**פַּחַד**] IV 1 n.m.—pl. sf. Qr פַּחֲדָיו—**penis** of Behemoth, prob. hippopotamus Jb 40$_{17}$.

[**פַּחַד**] V 1 n.m.—pl. sf. Qr פַּחֲדָיו—**testicle** of Behemoth, prob. hippopotamus Jb 40$_{17}$.

[**פַּחְדָּה**] 1 n.f.—sf. פַּחְדָּתִי—**awe** of Y. Jr 2$_{19}$. → פחד *fear.*

***פחה** 0.1 vb.—**Qal** 0.1 Ptc. פחה—**quench** flames Si 51$_{4}$.

פֶּחָה 28.1.0.2 n.m.—cstr. פַּחַת; sf. פֶּחָתְךָ, פֶּחָם; pl. פַּחוֹת; cstr. פַּחוֹת (פַּחֲווֹת); sf. פַּחוֹתֶיהָ—**governor** Ne 5$_{15}$. → cf. פַּחֲוָא *governor.*

*[**פַּחֲוָא**] I 0.0.0.7 n.m. **governor** Yehud Governor Stamp 14. → cf. פֶּחָה *governor.*

*[**פַּחֲוָא**] II 0.0.0.7 n.m. **cellerer** Yehud Governor Stamp 14.

*[**פַּחוֹז**] 0.0.1 n.[m.] **recklessness** 4QWiles 1$_{2}$. → פחז I *be reckless.*

פחז I 2.3.4 vb.—**Qal** 2.1.4 Pf. Q פחזתה; ptc. פֹּחֲזִים—**be reckless** Jg 9$_{4}$.

Hi. 0.1 Pf. הפחיז—of gold, **cause** someone **to be reckless** Si 8$_{2}$.

Htp. 0.1 Ptc. מתפחז—**allow oneself to be careless** Si 4$_{30(C)}$.

→ פַּחַז *recklessness,* פַּחֲזוּת *recklessness,* פַּחוֹז *recklessness.*

*[**פחז**] II vb. **Qal,** pass., **be scattered** Gn 49$_{4}$ (if em. פַּחַז *recklessness* to פָּחֻז *scattered*).

***פחז** III 2 vb.—**Qal** 2 Ptc. פֹּחֲזִים—**boast** Jg 9$_{4}$ Zp 3$_{4}$.

***פחז** IV 1 vb.—**Qal** 1 + waw ויפחז—**raise oneself** 1 S 20$_{34(4QSam^b)}$.

פַּחַז 1.1.6 n.[m.]—cstr. Q פחז—**recklessness** Si 41$_{17(M)}$. → פחז I *be reckless.*

[**פַּחֲזוּת**] 1 n.f.—sf. פַּחֲזוּתָם—**recklessness** Jr 23$_{32}$. → פחז I *be reckless.*

פחח I 1 vb.—**Hi.** 1 Inf. הָפֵחַ—**trap** people Is 42$_{22}$ (or em. הֻפְּחוּ *they were trapped,* i.e. Ho.). → פַּח I *trap.*

*[**פחח**] II vb. **Qal, have holes in one's garments** 1QS 7$_{14}$ (if em. פוח *clad in rags* or *ragged* to פוחח *[he] has holes in his garments*). → פּוּחַ *clad in rags, ragged.*

***פֶּחֶל** n.[m.] **he-goat** Mc 6$_{7}$ (if em. נַחֲלֵי *rivers of* to פַּחֲלֵי *he-goats of*).

*[**פֶּחָם**] n.[m.]du. (contracted) **bellows** Is 54$_{16}$ (if em. פֶּחָם *coals*).

פֶּחָם 3.0.2 n.[m.] **1. coals** Is 54$_{16}$. **2. charcoal** Pr 26$_{21}$.

*[**פֶּחָר**] n.m. **company** Is 14$_{13}$ (if em. הַר־ *mountain of*).

*[**פֶּחָרָא**] 0.0.0.5 n.m. **potter** Yehud Governor Stamp 14.

***פחת** 0.0.1 vb.—**Ni.** 0.0.1 Impf. יפחת[ו]—**be broken down,** of gates 4QHod^f 5$_{5}$ ([שערי]). → פַּחַת *pit,* פְּחֶתֶת *mildew.*

פַּחַת I 10.0.3 n.m.—pl. פְּחָתִים—**pit, ravine** Jr 48$_{28}$. → פחת *break down.*

***פַּחַת** II n.m. **awe** Lm 3$_{47}$ (LXX θάμβος).

פַּחַת מוֹאָב 6 pr.n.m. **Pahath-moab.**

פְּחֶתֶת 1 n.f. **mildew,** on garments Lv 13$_{55}$. → פחת *break down.*

פִּטְדָה 4 n.f. **peridot,** פִּטְדַת־כּוּשׁ *peridot of Ethiopia* Jb 28$_{19}$.

*[**פַּטְיָהוּ**] 0.0.0.1 pr.n.[m.] **Pattaiah.**

פַּטִּישׁ 3.0.1 n.m.—cstr. פַּטִּישׁ—**hammer** Is 41$_{7}$. → cf. פַּלְטִישׁ *hammer.*

פטר 9.1.4 vb.—**Qal** 8.1.1 Pf. פָּטַר; + waw וַיִּפְטַר; impv. Si פטר; ptc. פּוֹטֵר; ptc. pass. Qr פְּטוּרִים, פְּטוּרֵי—**1. release** water Pr 17$_{14}$. **2. dismiss (from duty)** division 2 C 23$_{8}$. **3. escape** from before (מִפְּנֵי) enemy 1 S 19$_{10}$. **4. set off to** (לְ) one's house Si 35$_{11}$. **5.** pass., **be dismissed (from duty)** 1 C 9$_{33(Qr)}$. **6.** pass. ptc. as noun, **out-**

spread, פְּטוּרֵי צִצִּים *outspreads of flowers*, i.e. open flowers 1 K 6$_{18}$.

Ni. 0.0.3 Pf. נפטר—**leave** 1QS 7$_{12}$.

Hi. 1 Impf. יַפְטִירוּ—**make an opening (of the mouth)** with (בְּ) lip Ps 22$_{8}$.

→ פֶּטֶר *firstborn*, פִּטְרָה *firstborn*.

פֶּטֶר 11.0.2 n.[m.]—cstr. פֶּטֶר—**firstborn,** lit. 'that which (first) opens' the womb, of animals Ex 13$_{12}$, humans Nm 3$_{12}$. → פטר *release*.

[פִּטְרָה] 1 n.f.—cstr. פִּטְרַת—**firstborn** of humans Nm 8$_{16}$. → פטר *release*.

[פִּי], see פִּים *pim*.

פִּיא, see פֶּה *mouth*.

פִּי־בֶסֶת 1 pl.n. **Pibeseth.**

פִּיד 4 n.[m.]—cstr. פִּיד; sf. פִּידוֹ—**misfortune** Pr 24$_{22}$.

פִּי הַחִירֹת 3 pl.n. **Pi-hahiroth.**

פִּיּוֹת, see פֶּה *mouth*.

[פִּיחַ] 2 n.[m.]—cstr. פִּיחַ—**soot** Ex 9$_{8}$.

***[פִּיךְ]** n.m. **jar** Jb 33$_{6}$ (if em. אֲנִי כְפִיךָ לָאֵל *I am as you are towards God* to אֲנִי כְּפִיךְ לָאֵל *I am like a jar from God*).

פִּיכֹל 3 pr.n.m. **Phicol.**

פִּילֶגֶשׁ 37.0.3 n.f.—פִּלֶגֶשׁ; cstr. (פִּלֶגֶשׁ) פִּילֶגֶשׁ; sf. פִּילַגְשׁוֹ; pl. (פִּלַגְשִׁים) פִּילַגְשִׁים; cstr. פִּלַגְשֵׁי; sf. פִּילַגְשָׁיו—**1. secondary wife (rather than concubine),** פִּילֶגֶשׁ אַבְרָהָם *secondary wife of Abraham* 1 C 1$_{32}$. **2. male lover** Ezk 23$_{20}$.

פִּים 1.0.0.4 n.[m.]—I פִּי—**pim,** weight 1 S 13$_{21}$; abbrev. פ Weight 22.

פִּימָה 1 n.f. **fat** Jb 15$_{27}$.

פִּינְחָס 25.2.1.1 pr.n.m. **Phinehas.**

פִּינֹן 2 pr.n.m. **Pinon.**

פִּיפִיּוֹת, see פֶּה *mouth*.

***פִּיץ** 1 vb.—**Hi.** 1 Pf. הֱפִיצָהוּ—of terror, **cause** someone **to urinate** Jb 18$_{11}$.

***פִּיק** 3 vb.—**Hi.** 3 Impf. יָפִיק, תָּפֵק—**1. acquire understanding** Pr 3$_{13}$, **purpose** Ps 140$_{9}$. **2. supply abundance to** (לְ) hungry one Is 58$_{10}$.

[פִּיק] I 1 n.m.—cstr. פִּק—**knocking,** of knees Na 2$_{11}$. → פוק I *stumble*.

***[פִּיק]** II 1 n.m.—cstr. פִּק—**giving way,** lit. 'breaking', of knees Na 2$_{11}$. → פוק IV *break apart*.

פִּירוֹת, see פְּרִי *fruit*.

פִּישׁוֹן 1 pl.n. **Pishon.**

פִּישְׁתִּי, see פֵּשֶׁת *flax*.

פִּיתוֹן 2 pr.n.m. **Pithon.**

פַּךְ 3 n.m. **flask,** פַּךְ הַשֶּׁמֶן *flask of oil* 1 S 10$_{1}$.

פכה 1 vb.—**Pi.** 1 Ptc. מְפַכִּים—**trickle,** of water Ezk 47$_{2}$.

***[פַּכְמַת]** 0.0.0.1 perh. pr.n.[m.] **Pachmath.**

פֹּכֶרֶת הַצְּבָיִים 2 pr.n.m. **Pochereth-hazzebaim.**

פלא 71.10.69 vb.—**Ni.** 56.7.43 Pf. נִפְלְאת; impf. יִפָּלֵא; ptc. Q נפלא, נִפְלָאת, נִפְלָאִים, נִפְלָאוֹת (נִפְלְאֹתָיו)—**1. be wonderful,** of Y. 4QShirShabb[f] 6$_{6}$, activity of Y. Ps 139$_{14}$, human love 2 S 1$_{26}$. **2. be too difficult,** of commandment Dt 30$_{11}$, matter Gn 18$_{14}$. **3.** ptc. pl. as noun, **wonderful deeds,** alw. performed by Y. Ex 3$_{20}$. **4.** ptc. as adv., **wondrously** Jb 37$_{5}$.

Pi. 3.0.1 Inf. פַּלֵּא—**1. fulfil** vow Lv 22$_{21}$. **2. make wonderful,** of Y. perh. 4QTwoWays 1$_{2}$.

Hi. 11.3.25 Pf. הִפְלִיא; impf. יַפְלִא; + waw וְהִפְלָא; ptc. מַפְלִא (Q מפלי); inf. abs. הַפְלֵא; cstr. הַפְלִיא—**1. do wonderful deeds,** usu. of Y. Jg 13$_{19}$, of human Si 34$_{9}$. **2.** oft. of Y., **make wonderful, extraordinary,** obj. loyalty Ps 31$_{22}$, plague Dt 28$_{59}$. **3. do wonderfully,** of Y. Jl 2$_{26}$, human 2 C 26$_{15}$. **4. be wonderful,** of temple 2 C 2$_{8}$. **5. ascribe wonder to** (לְ) Y. 4QHod[b] 20$_{3}$. **6.** פלא נֶדֶר hi. **make a difficult vow** Lv 27$_{2}$.

Htp. 1 Impf. תִּתְפַּלָּא—of Y., **display wondrous power against** (בְּ) person Jb 10$_{16}$.

→ פֶּלֶא *wonder*, פִּלְאִי *wonderful*, מִפְלָאָה *wondrous work*; cf. פלה II *amaze*.

פֶּלֶא 13.4.135 n.m.—Q פלוא; sf. פִּלְאֲךָ; pl. פְּלָאִים, פְּלָאוֹת; cstr. Q פלאי, Q פלאות; sf. Q פלאותיכה, Q פלאיו—**1. miracle,** performed by Y. Ex 15$_{11}$, **awe,** evoked by Y. 1QH 5$_{8}$, person 1QH 13$_{21}$, object 4QShirShabb[d] 1.2$_{19}$. **2. wonderful,** name of future ruler Is 9$_{5}$. **3. wonderful one** 1QH 11$_{10}$. **4.** adv., **wonderfully** Is 29$_{14}$. → פלא *be wonderful*.

פַּלֻּאִי 1 gent. **Palluite.**

פִּלְאִי I 2 adj.—f.s. Kt פלאיה, Qr פְּלִיאָה—**wonderful,** of name Jg 13$_{18}$, knowledge Ps 139$_{6(Qr)}$. → פלא *be wonderful*.

***פַּלְאִי** II 1 pr.n.[m.] **Peli.**

פְּלָאיָה 3.0.0.3 pr.n.m. **Pelaiah.**

פלג 4.0.12 vb.—**Ni.** 2 Pf. נִפְלְגָה—**be divided,** of land Gn 10_{25}.

Pi. 2.0.12 Pf. פִּלַּג; impf. Q יפלג; impv. פַּלַּג—**1. cleave** path Jb 38_{25}. **2. assign, apportion** understanding 4QMyst[a] 8_{2}, name 4QPrEnosh 1.2_{1}, service 1QH 9_{16}. **3. confound** speech Ps 55_{10}.

→ פֶּלֶג I *channel,* פְּלַגָּה *division,* פְּלֻגָּה *division,* מִפְלָג *division,* מִפְלַגָּה *division.*

פֶּלֶג I 10.0.10.1 n.m.—cstr. פֶּלֶג; pl. פְּלָגִים; cstr. פַּלְגֵי; sf. פְּלָגָיו—**1a. water-channel** Is 30_{25}. **b. stream** of water Lm 3_{48}, oil Jb 29_{6}. **2. division** of house CD 20_{22}, borders 4QTime 1.2_{9}; **half** of monetary unit Weight 51_{2}. → פלג *be divided.*

פֶּלֶג II 7 pr.n.m. **Peleg.**

[פְּלַגָּה] 3 n.f.—pl. פְּלַגּוֹת; cstr. פְּלַגּוֹת—**1. division** of tribe Jg 5_{15}. **2. stream** of honey and butter Jb 20_{17}. → פלג *be divided.*

[פְּלֻגָּה] 1 n.f.—pl. cstr. פְּלֻגּוֹת—**division** 2 C 35_{5}. → פלג *be divided.*

פִּלֶגֶשׁ, see פִּילֶגֶשׁ *secondary wife.*

[פְּלָדָה] I 1 n.f.—pl. פְּלָדוֹת—**steel fitting** Na 2_{4}.

***[פְּלָדָה]** II 1 n.f.—pl. פְּלָדוֹת—**covering** Na 2_{4}.

פִּלְדָּשׁ 1 pr.n.m. **Pildash.**

פלה I 5 vb.—**Ni.** 1 + waw וְנִפְלֵינוּ—**be separate** from (מִן) people Ex 33_{16}.

Hi. 4 Pf. הִפְלָה; impf. יַפְלֶה; + waw וְהִפְלֵיתִי—**1.** of Y., **set apart** land Ex 8_{18}, godly one Ps 4_{4}. **2.** of Y., **make a distinction** between (בֵּין) Israel and Egypt Ex 11_{7}.

→ פְּלֵת *separation.*

***פלה** II 2 vb. (byform of פלא)—**Ni.** 1 Pf. נִפְלֵיתִי—**be amazed** Ps 139_{14}.

Hi. 1 Impv. הַפְלֵה—of Y., **show loyalty wondrously** Ps 17_{7}.

→ cf. פלא *be wonderful.*

פַּלּוּא 5 pr.n.m. **Pallu.**

פלח I 5 vb.—**Qal** 1 Ptc. פֹּלֵחַ—**split,** of rock Ps 141_{7} (if ins. סֶלַע *rock*).

Pi. 4 Impf. יְפַלַּח—**1. split open** body Jb 16_{13}, herbs (implied) 2 K 4_{39}. **2. give birth to,** lit. 'open (the womb) for', offspring Jb 39_{3}.

→ פֶּלַח *slice.*

***פלח** II 1 vb.—**Pi.** 1 Impf. תְּפַלַּחְנָה—**open (the womb),** of animal Jb 39_{3}.

***פלח** III 1 vb.—**Qal** 1 Ptc. פֹּלֵחַ—**work, till** Ps 141_{7}.

פֶּלַח 6 n.f.—cstr. פֶּלַח—**1. slice** of fruit Ca 4_{3}. **2. millstone** Jg 9_{53}. → פלח *split.*

פִּלְחָא 1 pr.n.m. **Pilha.**

פלט I 27.1.11 vb.—**Qal** 1 Pf. פָּלְטוּ—**escape** Ezk 7_{16}.

Ni. 0.0.1 + waw ויפלט—**be delivered** from (מִן) breakers 1QH 11_{10}.

Pi. 24.0.10 Pf. Q פלטתה; impf. תְּפַלֵּט; impv. פַּלֵּט (פַּלְּטָה), פַּלְּטוּ; ptc. (מְפַלְּטִי) מְפַלְּטִי; inf. פַּלֵּט—**1a.** oft. of Y., **deliver** righteous from (מִן) wicked Ps 37_{40}. **b.** inf. as noun, **deliverance** Ps 56_{8}. **2. save** provisions Mc 6_{14}. **3. deliver, give birth** Jb 21_{10}. **4. be delivered from** (מִן) judge Jb 23_{7}. **5.** ptc. as noun, **deliverer,** of Y. 2 S 22_{2}.

Hi. 2.1 Impf. יַפְלִיט—**save** someone Si $51_{3(C)}$.

→ פָּלִיט *survivor,* פָּלֵיט *survivor,* פְּלֵיטָה *remnant,* מִפְלָט *refuge.*

***פלט** II 3 vb.—**Pi.** 2 Impf. תְּפַלֵּט—**give birth,** of cow Jb 21_{10}.

Hi. 1 Impf. תַּפְלִיט—**give birth,** of people Mc 6_{14}.

פֶּלֶט 2.0.0.1 pr.n.m. **Pelet.**

***[פַּלְטָה]** 0.0.0.3 pr.n.m. **Paltah.**

פַּלְטִי I 2.0.0.2 pr.n.m **Palti.**

פַּלְטִי II 1 gent. **Paltite.**

[פִּלְטַי] 1.0.0.2 pr.n.m. **Piltai.**

פַּלְטִיאֵל 2 pr.n.m. **Paltiel.**

פְּלַטְיָה 5.0.0.25 pr.n.m. **Pelatiah.**

פְּלַטְיָהוּ, see פְּלַטְיָה *Pelatiah.*

***[פַּלְטִישׁ]** 1 n[m.] **hammer** Is $41_{7(1QIsa^a)}$. → cf. פַּטִּישׁ *hammer.*

פְּלִי, see פֶּלֶאִי *wonderful.*

פְּלָיָה, see פְּלָאיָה *Pelaiah.*

[פָּלִיט] 5.0.1 n.m.—pl. פְּלִטִים—**survivor** Jr 50_{28}. → פלט I *escape.*

פָּלִיט 19.0.1 n.m.—pl. cstr. פְּלִיטֵי; sf. פְּלִיטָיו—**survivor** Jos 8_{22}. → פלט I *escape.*

פְּלֵיטָה 28.0.7 n.f.—פְּלֵטָה; cstr. פְּלֵיטַת—**1. remnant, survivors, a.** people Jg 21_{17}. **b.** produce Ex 10_{5}. **2. escape** Jr 25_{35}. → פלט I *escape.*

[פָּלִיל] I 3 n.m.—pl. פְּלִלִים (פְּלִילִים)—**judge** Ex 21_{22} Dt 32_{31} Jb 31_{11}. → פלל I *intervene.*

***[פָּלִיל]** II 1 n.m.—pl. פְּלִילִים—**fragment** Dt 32_{31}.

*[פָּלִיל] III 3 n.m.—pl. פְּלִילִים (פְּלִלִים)—**estimate** Ex 21$_{22}$ Dt 32$_{31}$ Jb 31$_{11}$. → פלל II *assess*.

*[פָּלִיל] IV 1 n.m.—pl. פְּלִילִים—**fool** Dt 32$_{31}$. → cf. פְּלִילִיָּה II *frenzy*.

*[פָּלִיל] V 2 adj.—m.pl. פְּלִילִים (פְּלִלִים)—**alone, solely responsible** Ex 21$_{22}$ Dt 32$_{31}$. → פלל III *be alone*.

פְּלִילָה I 1 n.f. **decision, intervention,** perh. **strength** Is 16$_3$. → פלל I *intervene*.

*פְּלִילָה II 1 n.f. **watchfulness** Is 16$_3$.

*פְּלִילָה III 1 n.f. **judgment, responsibility** Is 16$_3$. → פלל III *be alone*.

פְּלִילִי I 3 adj.—m.pl. פְּלִילִים—1. **requiring judgment** or **strong,** of iniquity Jb 31$_{28}$. 2. as noun, **strong one** Ex 21$_{22}$. → פלל I *intervene*.

*פְּלִילִי II 1 adj. **assessable,** of iniquity Jb 31$_{28}$. → פלל II *assess*.

*פְּלִילִי III 3 adj.—m.pl. פְּלִילִים—**alone, solely responsible** Dt 32$_{31}$ Jb 31$_{11.28}$. → פלל III *be alone*.

פְּלִילִיָּה I 1 n.f. **giving judgment, reasoning,** perh. **strength** Is 28$_7$. → פלל I *intervene*.

*פְּלִילִיָּה II 1 n.f. **frenzy** Is 28$_7$. → cf. פָּלִיל IV *fool*.

*פְּלִילִיָּה III 1 n.f. **vomit** Is 28$_7$.

*פְּלִילִיָּה IV 1 n.f. **responsibility** Is 28$_7$. → פלל III *be alone*.

*פְּלִילִיָּה V 1 n.f. **watchfulness** Is 28$_7$.

פֶּלֶךְ I 2 n.[m.]—פֶּלֶךְ—**spindle,** rather than **spindle-whorl** Pr 31$_{19}$.

*פֶּלֶךְ II 8 n.[m.]—cstr. פֶּלֶךְ; sf. פִּלְכּוֹ—**district** Ne 3$_{14}$.

*פֶּלֶךְ III 9 n.[m.]—cstr. פֶּלֶךְ; sf. פִּלְכּוֹ—**work-duty** Ne 3$_{14}$.

*פֶּלֶךְ IV 1 n.[m.] **crutch** 2 S 3$_{29}$.

פלל I 84.3.5 vb.—**Pi.** 4.1 Pf. פִּלַּלְתְּ; + waw וַיְפַלֵּל—1. **intercede for** (לְ) sister Ezk 16$_{52}$. 2. **pray to** (אֶל) Y. Si 38$_9$ (Bmg). 3. **expect** to see person Gn 48$_{11}$ (unless §4). 4. **have strength** to see person Gn 48$_{11}$.

Htp. 80.2.5 Pf. הִתְפַּלֵּל; impf. יִתְפַּלֵּל, יִתְפַּלְלוּ; impv. הִתְפַּלֵּל, הִתְפַּלְלוּ; ptc. מִתְפַּלֵּל, מִתְפַּלְלִים; inf. הִתְפַּלֵּל (הִתְפַּלְלוֹ)—1a. **pray** Ezr 10$_1$. b. with obj. תְּפִלָּה *prayer*, **offer prayer** 2 S 7$_{27}$. 2. **intercede** on behalf of (בְּעַד) person Gn 20$_7$, for (עַל) friend Jb 42$_8$.

→ פָּלִיל I *judge*, פְּלִילָה *decision*, פְּלִילִי *requiring judgment*, פְּלִילִיָּה *giving judgment*, תְּפִלָּה *prayer*.

*פלל II 2 vb.—**Pi.** 2 Pf. פִּלַּלְתְּ—1. **cause reassessment** for (לְ) sister Ezk 16$_{52}$. 2. **expect** to see person Gn 48$_{11}$. → פָּלִיל III *estimate*, פְּלִילִי II *assessable*.

*פלל III 4 vb.—**Pi.** 4 Pf. פִּלַּלְתְּ; + waw וַיְפַלֵּל—1. **take sole responsibility,** of Phinehas Ps 106$_{30}$. 2. of Y., **regard sinner as responsible** 1 S 2$_{25}$. → פָּלִיל V *alone*, פְּלִילִי III *alone*, פְּלִילָה III *judgment, responsibility*, פְּלִילִיָּה IV *responsibility*.

פָּלָל 1.0.0.2 pr.n.m. **Palal.**

פְּלַלְיָה 1 pr.n.m. **Pelaliah.**

פַּלְמוֹנִי 1 n.m. **certain one** Dn 8$_{13}$. → cf. פְּלֹנִי *such and such*.

פְּלֹנִי I 3 n.m. & adj. **such and such, so and so,** מְקוֹם פְּלֹנִי אַלְמֹנִי *such and such a place* or *the place of so and so* 1 S 21$_3$. → cf. פַּלְמוֹנִי *certain one*.

פְּלֹנִי II 3 gent. **Pelonite.**

פלס I 6.0.3 vb.—**Pi.** 6.0.3 Impf. יְפַלֵּס; impv. פַּלֵּס; ptc. מְפַלֵּס—1. **make path level, smooth** Ps 78$_{50}$. 2. **weigh out,** i.e. **deal out, recompense** violence Ps 58$_3$. → פֶּלֶס *balance*, מִפְלָשׂ *poising*, פֶּלֶשׂ *weight*.

*פלס II 6 vb.—**Pi.** 6 Impf. יְפַלֵּס; impv. פַּלֵּס; ptc. מְפַלֵּס—**examine** path Pr 4$_{26}$.

פֶּלֶס 2.1 n.[m.] **balance,** i.e. **apparatus for weighing** Pr 16$_{11}$. → פלס I *make level*.

*[פֶּלַע] I 0.0.1 n.[m.] **undergrowth** 3QTr 9$_{15}$.

*[פֶּלַע] II 0.0.0.1 pr.n.[m.] **Pela.**

[פֶּלַע] III, see גר פלע *Ger-pela*.

פלץ 1 vb.—**Htp.** 1 Impf. יִתְפַּלָּצוּן—**tremble,** of pillar Jb 9$_6$. → פַּלָּצוּת *shuddering*, מִפְלֶצֶת *horrible image*, תִּפְלֶצֶת *terror*.

פַּלָּצוּת 4.0.2 n.f. **shuddering** Is 21$_4$. → פלץ *tremble*.

*[פלשׁ] vb. **Qal, pierce,** of point of arrow Jb 20$_{25}$ (if em. שָׁלַף *he draws [it] out* to פֶּלֶשׁ *it pierces*).

*[פֶּלֶשׁ] 0.0.1 n.[m.] **weight,** perh. 4QapJoseph^a 3$_5$. → פלס *make level*.

פלשׁ I 4 vb.—**Htp.** 4 Impf. יִתְפַּלָּשׁוּ; impv. הִתְפַּלְּשִׁי, הִתְפַּלָּשׁוּ—**roll oneself (in dust),** while mourning Jr 6$_{26}$ Ezk 27$_{30}$ (both בָּאֵפֶר) Mc 1$_{10(Qr)}$ (עָפָר); abs. Jr 25$_{34}$.

*פלשׁ II 4 vb.—**Htp.** 4 Impf. יִתְפַּלָּשׁוּ; impv. הִתְפַּלְּשִׁי—1. **grovel** in dust Jr 6$_{26}$ Ezk 27$_{30}$ (both בָּאֵפֶר) Mc 1$_{10(Qr)}$ (עָפָר). 2. **beseech** Jr 25$_{34}$.

*פלשׁ III 4 vb.—**Htp.** 4 Impf. יִתְפַּלָּשׁוּ; impv. הִתְפַּלְּשִׁי—

sprinkle (dust) Jr 6:26 Ezk 27:30 (both בָּאֵפֶר) Mc 1:10(Qr) (עָפָר); abs. Jr 25:34.

*פלשׁת 1 vb.—Htp. 1 Impv. Kt התפלשתי—behave like a Philistine Mc 1:10(Kt).

פְּלֶשֶׁת 8.1.3 pl.n. Philistia.

פְּלִשְׁתִּי 287.2.3 gent. Philistine.

פֶּלֶת 2 pr.n.m. Peleth.

*[פֶּלֶת] n.m. distinction Ex 8:19 (if em. פְּדֻת *division*). → פלה I *separate*.

פְּלֵתִי 7 gent. Pelethite.

*[פָּמָן] 0.0.0.1 pr.n.[m.] Paman.

*[פָּן] I 0.0.0.1 pr.n.[m.] Pan.

[פַּן] II, see פָּ־ *and, but, for, then*.

פֶּן 133.34.40.2 conj. lest, לֹא תִגְּעוּ בּוֹ פֶּן־תְּמֻתוּן *do not touch it, lest you die* Gn 3:3; (take heed) lest, חֵמָה פֶּן־יְסִיתְךָ *take heed lest it lead you astray* Jb 36:18 (if em. חֵמָה *anger*).

*[פְּנֻאֵל], see פְּנוּאֵל *Penuel*.

פַּנַּג I 1 n.[m.] early figs Ezk 27:17.

*פַּנַּג II 1 n.[m.] pastry Ezk 27:17.

*פַּנַּג III 1 n.[m.] millet Ezk 27:17.

*פַּנַּג IV 1 n.[m.] panakes or opopanax, sweet myrrh Ezk 27:17.

פנה I 134.3.10 vb.—Qal 116.3.6 Pf. פָּנוּ ,פָּנִיתָ; impf. יִפְנֶה; + waw וַיִּפֶן; impv. פְּנוּ ,פְּנֵה; ptc. פּוֹנוֹת ,פֹּנִים ,פּוֹנֶה; inf. abs. פָּנֹה; cstr. פְּנוֹת—1a. turn to (אֶל) person Jg 6:14; to (לְ) way Is 53:6, to (עַל) side Gn 24:49. b. turn away from (מִן) place Gn 18:22. c. turn back of the neck Jos 7:12, face Jr 2:27. 2a. turn, look to (אֶל) person Jb 21:5, steppe Ex 16:10. b. oft. of Y., turn, look with regard to (אֶל) Israel 2 K 13:23, offering Nm 16:15. c. turn, look in expectation to (אֶל) increase Hg 1:9. d. turn, look in consideration upon (בְּ) one's deeds Ec 2:11. e. of Y., turn, take heed to (אֶל) sin Dt 9:27. f. of entrance, gate, border, etc., turn, face to (ה-) north Jos 15:7. 3a. turn in worship to (אֶל) Y. Is 45:22, image Lv 19:4. b. turn for guidance to (אֶל) Ben Sira Si 51:23, ghost Lv 19:31. c. turn for aid to (אֶל) people Is 13:14. d. turn to do an action Ec 2:12. 4a. turn, approach, of evening Gn 24:63, morning Jg 19:26. b. turn, decline, of day Jr 6:4.

Pi. 8.0.3 Pf. פִּנָּה ,פִּנִּיתִי; impv. פַּנּוּ—turn out, make clear, prepare house Gn 24:31, way Is 40:3.

Hi. 8.0.1 Pf. הִפְנָה ,הִפְנְתָה ,הִפְנָה; + waw וַיֶּפֶן; ptc. מַפְנֶה; inf. הַפְנוֹתוֹ—1. turn shoulder 1 S 10:9. 2. turn back Jr 46:5.

Ho. 2 Impv. הָפְנוּ; ptc. מָפְנֶה—1. be made to turn back, in flight Jr 49:8. 2. of gate, be turned, be facing (towards) (ה-) north Ezk 9:2.

→ פָּנִים *face*, פִּנָּה *corner*, פְּנִימָה *within*, פְּנִימִי *inner*.

*פנה II 3 vb.—Qal 3 Pf. פָּנָה ,פָּנוּ—pass away, come to an end, of day Jr 6:4, moon Ps 72:5.

פִּנָּה 31.1.31 n.f.—Q פנא; cstr. פִּנַּת; sf. פִּנָּתָהּ (פִּנָּה); pl. פִּנּוֹת (פִּנִּים); cstr. פִּנּוֹת; sf. פִּנֹּתָיו —1. corner of altar Ex 27:2, house Jb 1:19, street Pr 7:8. 2a. corner-stone, i.e. foundation stone, of Jerusalem Is 28:16. b. capstone, topmost stone in building Ps 118:22. c. chief, leader Jg 20:2. 3. battlement Zp 3:6. 4. Corner (Gate), in Jerusalem 2 K 14:13. → פנה I *turn*.

פְּנוּאֵל I 7 pl.n. Penuel.

פְּנוּאֵל II 2.0.0.1 pr.n.m. Penuel.

פִּנְחָס, see פִּינְחָס *Phinehas*.

פְּנִיאֵל, see פְּנוּאֵל I *Penuel*.

*[פְּנִיָּה] 0.0.0.1 pr.n.[m.] Paniah.

[פְּנִיִּים] see פְּנִינִים *rubies*.

פָּנִים 941.41.139.4 n.m.pl.—cstr. פְּנֵי; sf. פָּנַי ,פְּנֵיכֶם—1a. face of person Gn 17:3. b. appearance of person Jb 14:20. c. presence or person Gn 44:29. d. idioms, אוּלַי יִשָּׂא פָנָי *perhaps he will show me favour* Gn 32:21, וְחִלּוּ פָנֶיךָ רַבִּים *and many will entreat your favour* Jb 11:19, ויתנם פניהם לשלושת מיני הצדק *and he directed their attention to three kinds of righteousness* CD 4:16, נָתַתִּי פָנַי אַרְצָה *I looked down* Dn 10:15, אַל־תָּשֵׁבִי אֶת־פָּנָי *do not refuse me* 1 K 2:16. 2a. face of Y. Gn 33:10. b. presence of Y. 1 S 26:20. c. idioms, וְיַסְתֵּר פָּנָיו מֵהֶם *and he will hide his face*, i.e. withdraw, *from them* Mc 3:4, וַיְחַל מֹשֶׁה אֶת־פְּנֵי י״ *but Moses implored Y.* Ex 32:11, הָאִירָה פָנֶיךָ עַל־עַבְדֶּךָ *show favour to your servant* Ps 31:17. 3. face of cherubim Ezk 10:14, seraphim Is 6:2. 4. face of animal Gn 30:40. 5. of objects, a. surface of ground Gn 2:6. b. front of lampstand Ex 25:37, gate Ezk 40:6. c. top side of dish 2 K 21:13. d. edge of sword Ezk 21:21. e. entrance of cistern 2 S 17:19. f. front line of battle 2 S 10:9. 6. appearance, i.e. situation, of a matter 2 S 14:20, condition of animals Pr 27:23. 7. estimation, alw. one's own Is 5:21. 8. intellect Pr 27:17. 9. hospitality

MurEpBarC^{b}5. **10. partiality** Is 3_{9}. **11. favour** Gn 31_{2}. **12. fury** Ps 9_{4}. **13. mirror** 11QT^{c} 1_{2}. **14. region** 1 C 5_{10}. **15. prep., a.** פְּנֵי **(1) before** Is 1_{12}. **(2) (facing) towards** Ezk 40_{44}. **b.** אֶל־פְּנֵי **in front of** Ezk 44_{4}. **c.** אֶל־מוּל פְּנֵי **in front of** Ex 28_{37}. **d.** אֶל־נֹכַח פְּנֵי **toward the front of** Nm 19_{4}. **e.** אֶת־פְּנֵי **in the presence of** Ps 16_{11}. **f.** מֵאֵת פְּנֵי **(away) from the presence of** Ex 10_{11}. **g.** בִּפְנֵי **(1) against** Jos 10_{8}. **(2) in front of** Ezk 42_{12}. **h.** לִפְנֵי **before** Ex 7_{9}. **i.** מִלִּפְנֵי **from before** Lv 9_{24}. **j.** עַד לִפְנֵי **to the front of** Est 4_{2}. **k.** עַל־לִפְנֵי **to the front of** Ezk 40_{15}. **l.** מִפְּנֵי **(1) (from) before** Gn 3_{8}. **(2) away from** Jr 1_{13}. **(3) on account of** Jos 22_{4}. **m.** כְּמִפְּנֵי **as from before** Lv 26_{37}. **n.** מִמּוּל פְּנֵי **from the front of** Ex 28_{27}. **o.** עַל־פְּנֵי **(1) in front of** Zc 14_{4}. **(2) towards** 2 S 15_{23}. **(3) upon** 1 K 7_{42}. **(4) against** Na 2_{2}. **(5) equal to** 1 K 6_{3}. **p.** מֵעַל פְּנֵי **from before** Gn 23_{3}. **16. adv., a.** פָּנִים **to the front** 2 C 13_{14}. **b.** מִפָּנִים **forwards** 2 S 10_{9}. **c.** לְפָנִים **formerly** Ne 13_{5}. **d.** פָּנִים אֶל־פָּנִים **face to face** Jg 6_{22}. **17. conj.,** מִפְּנֵי אֲשֶׁר **because** Ex 19_{18}. → פנה I *turn*; cf. פְּנִימָה *within*, פְּנִימִי *inner*.

פְּנִימָה 13.0.7 adv. **1. within** 1 K 6_{18}. **2.** לִפְנִימָה **inside** Ezk 40_{16}. **3.** מִפְּנִימָה **on the inside** 2 C 3_{4}. **4.** perh. noun, **harem** Ps 45_{14}. → פנה I *turn*; cf. פָּנִים *face*, פְּנִימִי *inner*.

פְּנִימִי 32.0.4 adj.—f.s. פְּנִימִית; m.pl. פְּנִימִים; f.pl. פְּנִימִיּוֹת—**1. inner,** oft. of court Est 5_{1}. **2.** as noun, **inner one,** of court of temple Ezk 8_{3}. → פנה I *turn*; cf. פָּנִים *face*, פְּנִימָה *within*.

פְּנִינִים 6.3.1 n.[f.]pl.—Kt פניים—**rubies** Pr 8_{11}.

פְּנִנָּה 3 pr.n.f. **Peninnah.**

פנק 1.1 vb.—**Pi.** 1.1 Ptc. מְפַנֵּק—**indulge** servant Pr 29_{21}.

[פַּס] I 5 n.m.—pl. פַּסִּים—**palm, sole** Gn 37_{3}.

***[פַּס]** II 5 n.m.—pl. פַּסִּים—**variously coloured material** Gn 37_{3}.

***[פַּס]** III 5 n.m.—pl. פַּסִּים—**coloured stuff** Gn 37_{3}.

***[פַּס]** IV 0.0.1 n.m.—pl. cstr. פסי—**tax** 4Q523 3_{2}.

פסג I 1 vb.—**Pi.** 1 Impv. פַּסְּגוּ—**pass between** fortresses Ps 48_{14}.

***פסג** II 1 vb.—**Pi.** 1 Impv. פַּסְּגוּ—**consider** fortresses Ps 48_{14}.

***פסג** III 1 vb.—**Pi.** 1 Impv. פַּסְּגוּ—**stride through** fortresses Ps 48_{14}.

פִּסְגָּה 8 pl.n. **Pisgah.**

***פסד** 0.0.1 vb.—**Ni.** 0.0.1 + waw ונפסד—**lose everything** Mur 24 B_{12}.

פַּס דַּמִּים 1 pl.n. **Pas-dammim.**

[פִּסָּה] I 1 n.f.—cstr. פִּסַּת—**abundance** or **expanse,** of grain Ps 72_{16}.

***[פִּסָּה]** II 1 n.f.—cstr. פִּסַּת—**portion,** of grain Ps 72_{16}.

פסח I 4.0.2 vb.—**Qal** 4.0.2 Pf. פָּסַח; inf. abs. פָּסֹחַ—**pass over, spare** Israelites Ex 12_{13}, Jerusalem Is 31_{5}. → פֶּסַח *passover*.

***פסח** II 3 vb.—**Qal** 1 Ptc. פֹּסְחִים—**limp,** i.e. **waver upon/between** (עַל) two opinions 1 K 18_{21}.

Ni. 1 + waw וַיִּפָּסֵחַ—**become lame** 2 S 4_{4}.

Pi. 1 + waw וַיְפַסְּחוּ—**hop, leap upon** or **around** (עַל) altar, appar. as cultic dance 1 K 18_{26}.

→ (?) פֶּסַח *passover*, פִּסֵּחַ *lame*.

***פסח** III 4 vb.—**Qal** 4 Pf. פָּסַח; inf. abs. פָּסֹחַ—of Y., **protect, 1.** עַל of obj., + Israelites Ex 12_{13}, door Ex 12_{23}, house Ex 12_{27}. **2.** abs. Is 31_{5}. → (?) פֶּסַח *passover*.

***פסח** IV 1 vb.—**Pi.** 1 + waw וַיְפַסְּחוּ—**run against, strike against** (עַל) altar 1 K 18_{26}.

פָּסֵחַ 4.0.0.3 pr.n.m. **Paseah.**

פֶּסַח 49.0.21 n.m.—פֶּסַח; pl. פְּסָחִים—**1. passover festival,** in the month of Nisan (March/April) Ezr 6_{19}. **2. passover sacrifice** of lamb Ex 12_{21}. → פסח I *pass over*, (?) II *limp, leap* or (?) III *protect*.

פִּסֵּחַ 14.0.4 adj.—pl. פִּסְחִים—**1. lame,** of person 2 S 9_{13}, animal 11QT 52_{10}. **2.** as noun, **lame animal** Ml $1_{8.13}$. → פסח II *limp, leap*.

[פָּסִיל] I 23.0.4 n.m.—pl. פְּסִילִים; cstr. פְּסִילֵי; sf. פְּסִילֶיךָ—**image** of deity, sometimes specif. **carved image** Dt $7_{5.25}$. → פסל *hew*.

***[פָּסִיל]** II 2 n.m.—pl. פְּסִילִים—**quarry** Jg 3_{19}. → פסל *hew*.

***פְּסִילִים** 2 pl.n. **Pesilim.**

פָּסַךְ 1 pr.n.m. **Pasach.**

פסל 6.0.1 vb.—**Qal** 6.0.1 Pf. פָּסְלוֹ; + waw וַיִּפְסֹל; impv. פְּסָל־—**hew (stone), 1.** obj. tablet Ex 34_{1}, image Hb 2_{18}. **2.** abs. 1 K 5_{32}. → פָּסִיל I *image*, II *quarry*, פֶּסֶל *image*.

פֶּסֶל 31.0.3 n.m.—cstr. פֶּסֶל; sf. פִּסְלִי; pl. cstr. Q פסלי—**image** of deity, sometimes specif. **carved from wood** Is 44_{15}. → פסל *hew*.

פסס 1 vb.—**Qal** 1 Pf. פַּסּוּ—**vanish,** of faithful ones Ps

12₂.

פִּסְפָּה 1 pr.n.m. **Pispa.**

פעה 1 vb.—**Qal** 1 Impf. אֶפְעֶה—of Y., **groan** like (כְּ) woman in labour Is 42₁₄.

[פָּעוּ] 1 pl.n. **Pau.**

פְּעוֹר 4 pl.n. **Peor.**

[פָּעִי] 1 pl.n. **Pai.**

פעל 57.8.11 vb.—(usu. in poetic contexts) **Qal** 57.8.11 Pf. פָּעַל, פָּעֲלוּ; impf. יִפְעַל; ptc. פֹּעֵל, פֹּעֲלֵי—**1a. make** an object Is 44₁₅. **b. do** a deed Ps 44₂. **c. practise, carry out** good Si 33₁, evil Jb 34₃₂. **d. make, create** a state of affairs Ps 74₁₂. **e. work,** i.e. form, shape, metal image Is 44₁₂.₁₂. **f. make** something into something else Ex 15₁₇. **g. perform** justice Zp 2₃, **execute** instructions Jb 37₁₂. **h.** intrans., **be active, work** Is 41₄. **2.** ptc. as noun, **doer, maker, worker,** freq. of evil-doers (פֹּעֲלֵי אָוֶן) Ho 6₈ Ps 5₆, of Y. as Creator Jb 36₃.

Ni., be done, of deed Hb 1₅ (if em. qal).

Pu., be done in an extraordinary way, of deed Hb 1₅ (if em. qal).

→ פֹּעַל *act*, פְּעֻלָּה *wages*, מִפְעָל *deed*; cf. בעל II *do*.

פֹּעַל 37.6.3 n.m.—cstr. פֹּעַל; sf. פָּעֳלִי; pl. פְּעָלִים; cstr. Q פועלי; sf. Q פועליך—**1. act** Ru 2₁₂. **2. work as product** Ps 9₁₇; specif. Y.'s **creature,** מי כפועליך *who is like your creatures?* GnzPs 1₁₂. **3. daily labour** Ps 104₂₃. **4. wage** Jr 22₁₃. **5. acquisition** Pr 21₆. → פעל *do*.

[פְּעֻלָּה] 14.1.27 n.f.—cstr. פְּעֻלַּת; sf. פְּעֻלָּתִי; pl. cstr. פְּעֻלּוֹת (פְּעֻלֹּת)—**1. wages,** פְּעֻלַּת שָׂכִיר *wages of a hired servant* Lv 19₁₃. **2. recompense, reward** for actions Is 49₄. **3.** specif. **punishment** Is 65₇. **4. deed** Jr 31₁₆. **5. activity** 1QS 4₁₅. → פעל *do*.

פְּעֻלְּתַי 1 pr.n.m. **Peullethai.**

פעם 5 vb.—**Qal** 1 (unless Pi.) Inf. cstr. פַּעֲמוֹ—of spirit, **inspire** person Jg 13₂₅.

Ni. 3 Pf. נִפְעַמְתִּי; + waw וַתִּפָּעֶם—**be agitated,** of spirit Gn 41₈, person Ps 77₅.

Htp. 1 + waw וַתִּתְפָּעֶם—**be agitated,** of spirit Dn 2₁.

→ (?) פַּעַם *step, foot; set; time,* (?) פַּעֲמוֹן *bell*.

פַּעַם 118.4.35 n.f.—du. פַּעֲמַיִם; pl. פְּעָמִים; cstr. פַּעֲמֵי; sf. פְּעָמַי, פְּעָמָיו (פַּעֲמֹתָיו)—**1. foot, a.** of human being Ca 7₂. **b.** of object Ex 37₃. **2. footstep;** pl., **tread** Ps 119₁₃₃. **3. set, row, rank, tier, section** Ezk 41₆. **4. wheel** Jg 5₂₈. **5. anvil** Is 41₇. **6. stroke** 1 S 26₈. **7. battle** Jos 10₄₂. **8. time, moment, occasion,** oft. as adv., **a.** ... פַּעַם פַּעַם **one time ... another time** Pr 7₁₂. **b.** בַּפַּעַם הַהִוא **at that time** Dt 9₁₉. **c.** בַּפַּעַם הַשְּׁבִיעִית **at the seventh time** Jos 6₁₆. **d.** רַק־הַפַּעַם **just once more** Jg 6₃₉. **e.** פַּעֲמַיִם **twice** Si 45₁₄. **f.** פְּעָמִים רַבּוֹת **many times** 1QM 11₃. → (?) פעם *agitate, inspire*.

[פַּעֲמוֹן] 7.2 n.m.—cstr. פַּעֲמֹן; pl. פַּעֲמֹנִים; cstr. פַּעֲמֹנֵי—**bell,** on high-priest's robe Ex 28₃₄. → (?) פעם *agitate, inspire*.

***[פַּעֲנָה]** 0.0.1 n.f. perh. **truth** 4QapPsB 31₇.

פַּעְנֵחַ, see צָפְנַת פַּעְנֵחַ *Zaphenath-paneah*.

פער 4 vb.—**Qal** 4 Pf. פָּעֲרָה—**open wide** one's mouth Jb 29₂₃.

פַּעֲרַי 1 pr.n.m. **Paarai.**

***[פֶּפִּי]** 0.0.0.1 pr.n.[m.] **Pepi.**

***[פַּפְּיָס]** 0.0.0.1 pr.n.[m.] **Papias.**

פצה 15.1.5 vb.—**Qal** 15.1.4 Pf. פָּצוּ, פָּצִיתָה, פָּצְתָה; impf. יִפְצֶה; impv. פְּצֵה; ptc. פּוֹצֶה—**1. open mouth** 1QH 15₂₁. **2. utter vow** Ps 66₁₄. **3.** of Y., **rescue someone** Si 51₂. **4.** perh. **escape** 4QTobit[e] 6₇.

Hi. 0.0.1 Pf. הפצתיך—perh. **inform** someone, or **declare free from obligation** MurEpBeth-Mashiko₆.

פצח I 7.0.1 vb.—**Qal** 7.0.1 Pf. פָּצְחוּ; impf. יִפְצְחוּ—**be jubilant,** oft. with רִנָּה *jubilation*, רִנָּה פִּצְחִי ... עֲקָרָה *O infertile woman, ... be jubilant* Is 54₁.

***פצח II** 1 vb.—**Pi.** 1 Pf. פִּצֵּחַ—**break bones** Mc 3₃.

***פְּצִים** 1 n.m.pl.—sf. פּוּצַי—**scattering,** of people Zp 3₁₀. → פוץ I *scatter*.

פְּצִירָה I 1 n.f. **fee** of a pim 1 S 13₂₁. → פצר *urge*.

***פְּצִירָה II** 1 n.f. **sharpening** of plough shares and mattocks 1 S 13₂₁.

פצל 2.0.1 vb.—**Pi.** 2.0.1 Pf. פִּצֵּל; impf. יְפַצֵּל—**1. peel (away)** strips of bark Gn 30₃₇.₃₈. **2. divide words,** i.e. **speak clearly** 4QD[a] 5.2₂. → פְּצָלָה *peeled strip*.

[פְּצָלָה] 1 n.f.—pl. פְּצָלוֹת—**peeled strip** Gn 30₃₇. → פצל *peel*.

פצם 1 vb.—**Qal** 1 Pf. פְּצַמְתָּה—**tear** earth **open** Ps 60₄.

פצע 3.0.3 vb.—**Qal** 3.0.3 Pf. פְּצָעוּנִי; ptc. pass. פְּצוּעַ; inf. abs. פָּצֹעַ—**1. wound** someone, prob. not **lacerate** 1 K 20₃₇. **2.** pass. ptc. as noun, **one who is wounded** Dt 23₂. → פֶּצַע *wound*.

פֶּ֫צַע 8.2.1 n.m.—sf. פִּצְעִי; pl. פְּצָעִים; cstr. פִּצְעֵי; sf. פְּצָעַי—**wound** of friend Pr 27$_{6}$, of slanderer Si 11$_{29}$. → פצע *wound*.

פצץ I 3.0.2 vb.—**Po.** 1 Impf. יְפֹצֵץ—**break in pieces, shatter** rock Jr 23$_{29}$.

Htpo. 1.0.1 + waw וַיִּתְפֹּצְצוּ—of mountain, **crumble** Hb 3$_{6}$.

Pilp. 1 + waw וַיְפַצְפְּצֵנִי—of Y., **crush** human being Jb 16$_{12}$.

Polp. 0.0.1 Ptc. מפצפצים—of mountain, **be shattered** 4QapJoseph[b] 1$_{11}$.

→ cf. פוץ III *crush*.

*__פצץ__ II 1 vb.—**Pilp.** 1 + waw וַיְפַצְפְּצֵנִי—of Y., **maul** human being Jb 16$_{12}$.

פַּצֵּץ, see בֵּית פַּצֵּץ *Beth-pazzez*.

[פִּצֵּץ] 1.0.12 pr.n.m. **Pizzez**.

פצר 7 vb.—**Qal** 6 + waw וַיִּפְצַר—**1.** with בְּ of obj., **urge** someone Jg 19$_{7}$ 2 K 2$_{17}$. **2.** with בְּ of obj., **coerce** someone Gn 19$_{9}$.

Hi. 1 Inf. abs. הַפְצַר—**be stubborn** 1 S 15$_{23}$.

→ פְּצִירָה I *fee*; cf. פרץ II *urge, command*.

*__[פַּצְרִי]__ 0.0.0.1 pr.n.m. **Pazri**.

פקד 304.10.71.2 vb.—**Qal** 235.5.60.1 Pf. פָּקַד; impf. יִפְקֹד; impv. פְּקֹד (פָּקְדֵנִי), פִּקְדוּ; ptc. פֹּקֵד; pass. Q פקוד, פְּקֻדִים (פְּקֻדָיו), פְּקוּדֵי; inf. abs. פָּקֹד; cstr. פְּקֹד (פָּקְדִי)—**1a.** oft. of Y., **visit** person Gn 50$_{25}$, place Jb 5$_{24}$. **b. come for** object Jr 27$_{22}$. **2a. observe, pay attention to** thing or person 1 S 17$_{18}$, **tend** sheep Jr 23$_{2}$. **b. search for, miss** person 1 S 20$_{6}$, belongings Jr 3$_{16}$. **c. examine, review** disposition, deeds 1QS 5$_{24}$. **3a. count, register** someone into army, community, etc., Nm 1$_{3}$ CD 15$_{8}$. **b.** pass. ptc. as noun, **one who is counted, registered** Nm 14$_{29}$ 1QM 12$_{8}$. **c.** pass. ptc. pl. as noun, **things counted** Ex 38$_{21}$. **4. assign** task, object or person to (עַל) someone for attention Ezr 1$_{2}$. **5a.** usu. of Y., **assign** (punishment for) guilt to (עַל) someone, thus perh. **punish** Ex 20$_{5}$. **b. punish** (without mention of guilt) Ho 4$_{14}$. **c. punish** (without mention of person punished) Lm 4$_{22}$. **6.** with עַל of obj., **harm, hurt** vineyard Is 27$_{3}$. **7a. appoint, put** someone **in charge over** (עַל or אֶל) congregation Nm 27$_{16}$, land Jr 50$_{44}$. **b.** of Y., **appoint** a time Si 33$_{10}$. **c.** pass. ptc. as noun, **military officer** 2 C 23$_{14}$. **8a. muster** soldier 1QM 12$_{4}$. **b.** pass. ptc. as noun, **mustered soldier** 4QShirShabb[f] 20.2$_{14}$. **9a. deposit** dead body, i.e. assign it to a location 2 K 9$_{34}$ (unless §11). **b. place** storehouse, i.e. entrust it, into (בְּ) hands of person 4Q424 1$_{6}$. **10. keep** rules 1QS 5$_{22}$. **11. care for** dead body, by funerary rites 2 K 9$_{34}$.

Ni. 21.4.2 Pf. נִפְקַד; impf. תִּפָּקֵד; inf. הִפָּקֵד—**1. be visited, a.** subj. Ariel, מֵעִם י׳ צְבָאוֹת תִּפָּקֵד בְּרַעַם *you will be visited by Y. of hosts with thunder* Is 29$_{6}$. **b.** with cognate noun as subj., פְּקֻדַּת כָּל־הָאָדָם יִפָּקֵד עֲלֵיהֶם lit. *the visitation of all humanity will be visited upon them*, i.e. their lot will be the common fate of all humanity Nm 16$_{29}$. **2. be looked after,** of building Si 50$_{1}$. **3. be looked for, missed,** of person Nm 31$_{49}$, of belongings 1 S 25$_{7}$. **4. be empty,** of place 1 S 20$_{25}$. **5. be counted, registered,** of person CD 14$_{3}$. **6. be punished,** of person Is 24$_{22}$. **7. be harmed,** of leafage Is 27$_{3}$ (if em. qal). **8. be appointed,** of Levites Ne 7$_{1}$, of animals, sword as punishment Si 39$_{30}$. **9. be mustered,** of Gog Ezk 38$_{8}$. **10. be deposited, buried,** of corpse Si 49$_{15}$.

Pi. 1 Ptc. מְפַקֵּד—of Y., **muster** army Is 13$_{4}$.

Pu. 2.0.4 Pf. פֻּקַּד (Q פוקד)—**1. be counted,** of things Ex 38$_{21}$. **2. be caused to miss,** i.e. **be deprived of** remainder of years Is 38$_{10}$ (unless §4). **3. be laid as a charge,** of measure 4QInstr[d] 81$_{9}$ (פוקד[ה]). **4. be consigned** to (בְּ) gates of Sheol Is 38$_{10}$.

Hi. 29.1.3.1 Pf. הִפְקִיד; impf. יַפְקִיד; + waw וַיַּפְקֵד; impv. הַפְקֵד, הַפְקִידוּ—**1. count** number Si 42$_{7}$(M). **2a. appoint** someone **(as governor)** over (עַל) people 2 K 25$_{22}$. **b.** with double accus., **assign** a person to another, i.e. to rule over him Jr 41$_{10}$. **c. appoint, summon** wicked person against (עַל) someone Lv 26$_{16}$. **3a. place, station** person 1 S 29$_{4}$, **deposit** object Jr 36$_{20}$. **b. place, commit** shields upon/into (עַל) hands of officers 1 K 14$_{27}$, one's spirit into (בְּ) Y.'s hands Ps 31$_{6}$.

Ho. 8.0.2 Pf. הָפְקַד; ptc. מֻפְקָדִים—**1. be visited** for punishment Jr 6$_{6}$. **2. be assigned** to (אֵת) person, specif. of deposit, thus **be entrusted** Lv 5$_{23}$. **3a. be appointed** over (בְּ) temple 2 K 22$_{5}$, over (עַל) person

2 C 34$_{12}$. **b.** ptc. as noun, **overseer** 2 C 34$_{17}$.

Htp. 4 Pf. הִתְפָּקְדוּ; + waw וַיִּתְפָּקֵד—**1. be counted, registered** Jg 20$_{15}$. **2. be mustered** Jg 21$_{9}$.

Hothp. 4 Pf. הָתְפָּקְדוּ; + waw וַיִּתְפָּקֵד—**1. be counted, registered** Nm 1$_{47}$. **2. be mustered** 1 K 20$_{27}$.

→ פְּקֻדָּה *visitation, oversight; store,* פִּקָּדוֹן *store,* פְּקִדֻת *supervision,* פָּקִיד *overseer,* מִפְקָד *muster,* פִּקּוּד *precept.*

פְּקֻדָּה 32.0.35 n.f.—cstr. פְּקֻדַּת (Q פקודת); sf. פְּקֻדָּתוֹ; pl. פְּקֻדֹּת (פְּקֻדֹּת); cstr. פְּקֻדּוֹת (פְּקֻדֹּת)—**1. visitation,** usu. by Y., for favour 1QS 4$_{6}$, oft. for punishment, יְמֵי הַפְּקֻדָּה *days of (divine) visitation* Ho 9$_{7}$. **2. punishment** 4Q Instr[b] 7$_{2}$. **3a. oversight** of tabernacle Nm 3$_{36}$. **b. task, work** 1QS 3$_{26}$ ([פ]קודה). **4a. overseer** of temple 2 K 11$_{18}$, city Ezk 9$_{1}$, prison Jr 52$_{11}$. **b.** coll., **rulers, government** Is 60$_{17}$, **royal officials** 2 C 24$_{11}$. **5. reckoning** 1 C 23$_{11}$. **6. ordering** 1 C 24$_{3}$. **7. mustering** 2 C 17$_{14}$. **8. muster** 4QShirShabb[c] 4$_{9}$ (פקוד[תו]). **9. store, goods** Is 15$_{7}$. → פקד *visit, observe; assign, appoint.*

פִּקָּדוֹן 3.0.1 n.m.—Q פקדן—**1. store, reserve,** of food Gn 41$_{36}$. **2. deposit,** as pledge Lv 5$_{23}$. → פקד *visit, observe; assign, appoint.*

*[**פְּקַדְיָהוּ**] 0.0.0.2 pr.n.m. **Pekadiah.**

פְּקִדֻת 1 n.f. **supervision** Jr 37$_{13}$. → פקד *visit, observe; assign, appoint.*

[**פִּקּוּד**] 24.0.2 n.m.—pl. פִּקּוּדִים; cstr. פִּקּוּדֵי; sf. פִּקּוּדֶיךָ (פִּקֻּדֶיךָ)—**precept,** alw. pl., oft. in Psalms, of Y. Ps 19$_{9}$ GnzPs 4$_{27}$. → פקד *visit, observe; assign, appoint.*

פְּקוֹד I 1 pr.n.m. **Pekod.**

פְּקוֹד II 1 pl.n. **Pekod.**

[**פַּקֻּעַ**] 1 n.f.—pl. cstr. פַּקֻּעֹת—**gourd,** of field 2 K 4$_{39}$.

פקח 20.0.5.1 vb.—**Qal** 17.0.4 Pf. פָּקַח; impf. אֶפְקַח; impv. פְּקַח; ptc. פֹּקֵחַ; ptc. pass. פְּקֻחוֹת; inf. abs. פָּקוֹחַ; cstr. פְּקֹחַ—**1. open** eyes, of Y. Gn 21$_{19}$, of person 2 K 4$_{35}$, **open** ears, of Y. 4QBark[a] 1.1$_{3}$, of person Is 42$_{20}$; pass., **be opened,** of eyes of Y. Jr 32$_{19}$. **2.** of Y., **give sight** to blind Ps 146$_{8}$.

Ni. 3.0.1 Impf. תִּפָּקַחְנָה; + waw וְנִפְקְחוּ—**1. be opened,** of eyes by Y. Is 35$_{5}$. **2. be given sight** 4QErr 2$_{6}$.

Hi. 0.0.0.1 Impv. הפקח—**open** ear, i.e. cause to understand Lachish ost. 3$_{4}$.

→ פִּקֵּחַ *sighted,* פְּקַח־קוֹחַ *liberation.*

פֶּקַח 11.0.0.7 pr.n.m. **Pekah.**

פִּקֵּחַ 2 adj.—pl. פִּקְחִים—**1. sighted,** or perh. both **sighted and hearing** Ex 4$_{11}$. **2.** as noun, **one who sees** Ex 23$_{8}$. → פקח *open (eyes).*

*[**פִּקְחִי**] 0.0.0.1 pr.n.m. **Pikhi.**

פְּקַחְיָה 3.0.0.1 pr.n.m. **Pekahiah.**

פְּקַח־קוֹחַ 1 n.[m.] **liberation,** perh. lit. 'opening up (of eyes)' after release from prison Is 61$_{1}$. → פקח *open (eyes).*

פָּקִיד 13.0.5.1 n.m.—cstr. פְּקִיד; sf. פְּקִידוֹ; pl. פְּקִדִים—**1. cultic overseer** 2 C 24$_{11}$; at Qumran, perh. specif. **head of priests** 1QS 6$_{14}$. **2. political governor** Ne 11$_{9}$. **3. military commander** Jr 52$_{25}$. → פקד *visit, observe; assign, appoint.*

*[**פָּקָל**] 0.0.0.1 pr.n.m. **Pakal.**

*[**פַּקְלָל**] 0.0.0.1 pr.n.m. **Paklal.**

[**פֶּקַע**] I 3 n.m.—pl. פְּקָעִים—**gourd-shaped ornament,** in wood 1 K 6$_{18}$, metal 1 K 7$_{24}$.

*[**פֶּקַע**] II 0.1 n.m. **blast** Si 46$_{17}$. → cf. בקע I *split.*

*פקר 0.0.1 vb.—**Qal** 0.0.1 Pf. פקרון (unless ptc. פקרין)—perh. **inspect** ship 5/6 Ḥev 49$_{5}$.

*[**פֶּקֶר**] n.[m.] **licence** Jr 6$_{6}$ (if em. הִיא הָעִיר הָפְקַד *this is the city to be visited* to אֲהָהּ/הוֹי הָעִיר הַפֶּקֶר *Alas! city of licence*).

פַּר 133.0.24 n.m.—פָּר; cstr. פַּר; pl. פָּרִים; sf. פָּרֶיהָ—**bull,** irrespective of age, oft. for sacrifice Nm 7$_{15}$, corrupt leader Jr 50$_{27}$, personal enemy Ps 22$_{13}$.

פרא I 1 vb.—**Hi.** 1 Impf. יַפְרִיא—**flourish, prosper,** of Ephraim Ho 13$_{15}$. → cf. פרה I *be fruitful.*

*פרא II 1 vb.—**Hi.** 1 Impf. יַפְרִיא—**bring division between brothers** Ho 13$_{15}$ (if em. בֵּן *son* to בֵּין *between*).

*פרא III 1 vb.—**Hi.** 1 Impf. יַפְרִיא—**behave wilfully** among brothers Ho 13$_{15}$ (if em. בֵּן *son* to בֵּין *among*). → פֶּרֶא *wild ass.*

פֶּרֶא I 10.1.2 n.m.&f.—פֶּרֶה; cstr. פֶּרֶא; pl. פְּרָאִים—**wild ass,** less prob. **zebra,** of steppe Si 13$_{19}$. → פרא III *behave wilfully.*

*פֶּרֶא II 1 n.m. **shoot** Ho 8$_{9}$.

פֶּרֶא III 1 n.m. **chieftain** Gn 16$_{12}$.

פִּרְאָם 1 pr.n.m. **Piram.**

*[**פָּרְאָן**] 0.0.0.1 pl.n. **Paran.**

פַּרְבָּר, see פַּרְוָר I *(fore)court, porch,* II *summer house,* *treasury*, III *place of ritual separation*.

*פרג 0.2 vb.—**Hi.** 0.2 Impf. תפריג—**drive away** sleep Si 34:2.

פרד I 27.0.15 vb.—**Qal** 2 Ptc. pass. פְּרֻדוֹת—**1.** pass., **be spread out,** of wings Ezk 1:11. **2.** pass. ptc. as noun, **what is put aside, stored provision** Jl 1:17.

Ni. 12.0.7 Pf. נִפְרְדוּ; impf. יִפָּרֵד; impv. הִפָּרֶד; ptc. נִפְרָד, נִפְרָדִים; inf. הִפָּרֵד—**1a. be separated,** of people 2 S 1:23. **b. separate (oneself)** from (מֵעַל) another Gn 13:9. **c. diverge,** of river Gn 2:10. **d.** perh. **have a miscarriage,** i.e. be separated from one's child 4QInstr[a] 11:11. **2.** ptc. as noun, **one who separates himself,** perh. **recluse** Pr 18:1.

Pi. 1 Impf. יְפָרֵדוּ—**1. go off with** (עִם) prostitute, i.e. separate from wife Ho 4:14. **2. flee alone,** of camel Jr 2:24 (if em. פֶּרֶה לִמֻּד מִדְבָּר *a wild ass used to the steppe* to מְפָרֵדָה הַמִּדְבָּר *fleeing alone to the steppe*).

Pu. 1 Ptc. מְפֹרָד—**be dispersed,** of people Est 3:8.

Hi. 7.0.5 Pf. הִפְרִיד; impf. יַפְרִיד; ptc. מַפְרִיד; inf. cstr. הַפְרִיד—**1a. separate** humans, of Y. Dt 32:8, **segregate** animals Gn 30:40. **b. cause a separation** between (בֵּין) humans, of death Ru 1:17. **2.** perh. **disperse** from (מִן) a position 1QH fr. 5:2.

Htp. 4.0.3 Pf. הִתְפָּרְדוּ; impf. יִתְפָּרְדוּ—**1. be separated (from one another), a. be scattered,** of people Ps 92:10, animals Jb 4:11. **b. become dislocated,** of bones Ps 22:15. **2. be shattered,** of creature of dust 4QHod[b] 13:8 (הו[ת]פרד).

→ (?) פְּרֻדָה *grain*.

*פרד II 1 vb.—**Pi.** 1 Impf. יְפָרֵדוּ—**make offering** Ho 4:14.

פֶּרֶד 14.0.1 n.m.—sf. פִּרְדּוֹ; pl. פְּרָדִים; sf. פִּרְדֵיהֶם—**mule** 2 S 13:29.

פִּרְדָּה 3 n.f.—cstr. פִּרְדַּת—**female mule** 1 K 1:33.

[פְּרֻדָה] I 1 n.f.—pl. פְּרֻדוֹת—**grain,** of seed Jl 1:17. → (?) פרד I *separate*.

*[פְּרֻדָה] II 1 n.f.—pl. פְּרֻדוֹת—**dried figs** Jl 1:17.

פַּרְדֵּס 3 n.m.—cstr. פַּרְדֵּס; pl. פַּרְדֵּסִים—**1. orchard** Ec 2:5. **2. forest** Ne 2:8.

פרה I 29.2.5 vb.—**Qal** 22.2.3 Pf. פָּרוּ; impf. יִפְרֶה; impv. פְּרֵה, פְּרוּ; ptc. פֹּרֶה, פֹּרִיָּה (פֹּרָת); inf. Q פרות—**1.** abs., **produce (much) offspring,** of people Gn 1:28, of animals Gn 1:22. **2a.** abs., **bear fruit,** of vineyard, vine, etc. Is 32:12. **b.** ptc. as noun, **fruit-bearer, fruit-tree** Is 17:6. **3.** trans., **bring forth, give birth to offspring** 1QS 4:7, poison, wormwood Dt 29:17. **4. branch off,** of vine, shoot etc. Is 11:1 Ezk 19:10. **5.** intrans., **increase,** of salvation Is 45:8 (if em. pl. to sg.).

Hi. 7.0.2 Pf. הִפְרַנִי; impf. יַפְרְךָ; + waw וַיֶּפֶר וְהִפְרֵיתִי; ptc. מַפְרְךָ—of Y., **cause someone to have (many) descendants** Gn 17:6 Ps 105:24.

→ פְּרִי *fruit, offspring*; cf. פרא I *flourish*.

*פרה II 2 vb.—**Qal** 2 Impf. יִפְרֶה, יִפְרוּ—**come out,** of shoot Is 11:1, salvation, righteousness Is 45:8.

פָּרָה I 26.0.6 n.f.—sf. פָּרָתוֹ; pl. פָּרוֹת; cstr. פָּרוֹת—**cow, female bovine, 1.** oft. for sacrifice, פרת החטאת *cow of the sin offering* 4QMMT B13. **2.** image of stubborn Israel Ho 4:16, of upper-class women in Samaria, פָּרוֹת הַבָּשָׁן *cows of Bashan* Am 4:1.

פָּרָה II 1 pl.n. **Parah.**

פֵּרָה, see חֲפַרְפָּרָה *mole*.

פֶּרֶה, see פֶּרֶא *wild ass*.

פֻּרָה 2 pr.n.m. **Purah.**

פְּרוּדָא 1 pr.n.m. **Peruda.**

פָּרוּחַ 1 pr.n.m. **Paruah.**

*[פְּרוּט] 0.0.1 n.[m.] **inventory** 3QTr 12:12.

פַּרְוַיִם 1 pl.n. **Parvaim.**

*[פְּרוּצִים] n.m.pl. **violence,** וּפְרוּצִים תֵּצֶאנָה *and (with) violence you will go out* Am 4:3 (if em. וּפְרָצִים תֵּצֶאנָה *and [through] breaches you will go out*). → פרץ I *break through, break out*.

פָּרוּר 3.1 n.[m.] **cooking-pot,** ceramic Si 13:2, used to cook food Jg 6:19. → (?) פרר I *break*.

פַּרְוָר I 3.0.9 n.m.—פַּרְבָּר; pl. פַּרְוָרִים; sf. Q פרוריהמה—**(fore)court, porch,** of temple 2 K 23:11 1 C 26:18.18.

*פַּרְוָר II 3.0.9 n.m.—פַּרְבָּר; pl. פַּרְוָרִים; sf. Q פרוריהמה—**summer house, treasury** 2 K 23:11 1 C 26:18.18.

*פַּרְוָר III 3 n.m.—פַּרְבָּר; pl. פַּרְוָרִים—**place of ritual separation** 2 K 23:11 1 C 26:18.18. → (?) פרר I *break*.

*[פֵּרוּשׁ] 0.0.23 n.m.—cstr. פירוש; sf. פרושה; pl. sf. פרושיהם—**1. detail(s)** of times CD 2:9, names 1QM 4:6, deeds CD 4:6, document 3QTr 12:12. **2. detailed instruction, stipulation, elaboration** of law CD 4:8. ↳ פרש I *make clear*.

*[פְּרוּשָׁה] 0.0.1 n.f. **specification of contents** 3QTr 12₁₂. → פרשׁ I *make clear*.

פֵּרוֹת, see חֲפַרְפָּרָה *mole*.

[פְּרָז] 1 n.m.—sf. Kt פרזו; pl. sf. Qr פְּרָזָיו—**warrior** or **ruler** Hb 3₁₄.

[פֶּרֶז], see פְּרָז *warrior*.

[פְּרָזָה] 3 n.f.—pl. פְּרָזוֹת—**open region, unwalled town** Est 9₁₉.

פְּרָזוֹן I 2 n.[m.]—sf. פִּרְזֹנוֹ—**peasantry, dwellers in the open** Jg 5₇.₁₁.

***פְּרָזוֹן** II 2 n.[m.]—sf. פִּרְזֹנוֹ—**iron** Jg 5₇.₁₁. → cf. פַּרְזֶל *iron*, בַּרְזֶל *iron*.

***פְּרָזוֹן** III 2 n.[m.]—sf. פִּרְזֹנוֹ—**prowess, leadership; warriors** Jg 5₇.₁₁.

***פְּרָזוֹן** IV 2 n.[m.]—sf. פִּרְזֹנוֹ—**hospitality** Jg 5₇.₁₁.

פְּרָזִי 3 n.m. **inhabitant of the open country, peasant living in unwalled village** 1 S 6₁₈.

פְּרִזִּי 23.0.3 gent. **Perizzite.**

*[פַּרְזֶל] 0.0.1 n.[m.] **iron** 5/6 Ḥev 51₅ (unless פרין *fruits*). → cf. פְּרָזוֹן II *iron*, בַּרְזֶל *iron*.

פרח I 24.6.12 vb.—**Qal** 19.3.8 Pf. פָּרַח; impf. יִפְרַח; ptc. פֹּרַחַת; inf. abs. פָּרֹחַ; cstr. פְּרֹחַ—**1. sprout, blossom, flourish,** of vine Ca 6₁₁, people Ho 14₆ Ps 72₇(MT), righteousness Ps 72₇(mss). **2.** ptc. as noun, **one sprouting, one budding** Gn 40₁₀.

Hi. 5.3.4 Pf. הִפְרַחְתִּי; impf. יַפְרִיחַ; ptc. Q מפריח; inf. Q הפריח—**1.** trans., **cause to sprout, blossom, flourish,** obj. tree Ezk 17₂₄, shoot 1QH 16₆, goodness, evil Si 37₁₈. **2.** intrans., **sprout, blossom, flourish,** of tree Jb 14₉, righteous Ps 92₁₄.

→ פֶּרַח *bud, flower*, פִּרְחַח *rabble*, אֶפְרֹחַ I *nestling*.

פרח II 10.0.3 vb.—**Qal** 10.0.3 Pf. פָּרַח; impf. תִּפְרַח; ptc. פֹּרַח, פֹּרַחַת; inf. abs. פָּרוֹחַ—**1. break out,** of disease Lv 13₁₂. **2. erupt into blisters,** of inflammation Ex 9₉.

פרח III 2.1 vb.—**Qal** 2.1 Impf. Si יפרח; ptc. פורחות—**1. fly,** of snow Si 43₁₇(M). **2.** ptc. as noun, **bird** Ezk 13₂₀.

***פרח** IV 4 vb.—**Qal** 4 Impf. תִּפְרַח; inf. abs. פָּרֹחַ—**be cheerful,** of bone Is 66₁₄, desert Is 35₁.₂.₂.

[פֶּרַח], see גַּת־הַפֶּרַח *Gath-perah*.

פֶּרַח 17.2.2 n.m.—cstr. פֶּרַח; sf. פרחם; pl. sf. פְּרָחֶיהָ—**1. bud, flower** Is 18₅ Na 1₄. **2. flower-shaped decoration** of lampstand Ex 25₃₁. → פרח I *blossom*.

פִּרְחַח 1 n.m. **rabble** Jb 30₁₂. → פרח I *blossom*.

פרט I 1 vb.—**Qal** 1 Ptc. פֹּרְטִים—**sing** Am 6₅.

***פרט** II 1 vb.—**Qal** 1 Ptc. פֹּרְטִים—**improvise** Am 6₅.

***פרט** III 1 vb.—**Qal** 1 Ptc. פֹּרְטִים—**howl, bawl** Am 6₅.

פֶּרֶט 1.0.1 n.[m.]—cstr. פֶּרֶט—**fallen grapes** Lv 19₁₀.

פְּרִי 119.6.55 n.m.—פֶּרִי; cstr. פְּרִי; sf. פִּרְיִי, פֶּרְיְכֶם, פִּרְיהֶם (פִּרְיָם); pl. Q פרין (Q פירות)—**1. fruit, produce** of land Lv 25₁₉, tree Jr 17₈, vine Ho 10₁. **2. offspring** of womb, body Gn 30₂, human Lm 2₂₀, animal Dt 28₄. **3a. product, result** of thoughts Jr 6₁₉, speech Pr 12₁₄, actions GnzPs 4₂₁. **b. reward, wages** Ps 58₁₂. **4. branch** 2 K 19₃₀ (unless §1). → פרה I *be fruitful*.

פְּרִידָא 1 pr.n.m. **Perida.**

פֻּרִים *Purim*, see פּוּר I *lot*.

פָּרִיץ I 6.0.1 n.m.—cstr. פְּרִיץ; pl. פָּרִצִים; cstr. פָּרִיצֵי—**1. violent one, lawless one, criminal** Ezk 7₂₂. **2. ferocious beast** Is 35₉. → פרץ I *break through, break out* or (?) פרץ V *behave as a brigand*.

***פָּרִיץ** II 1 n.[m.] **duty, law** Ps 17₄. → פרץ III *command*.

***פְּרִיצָה** n.f. **charge** 1 S 13₂₁ (if em. פְּצִירָה). → פרץ III *command*.

פֶּרֶךְ 6 n.[m.]—פֶּרֶךְ—**ruthlessness,** alw. as adv. with prep. בְּ, i.e. 'ruthlessly' Ex 1₁₄.

פָּרֹכֶת 25.1.7 n.f.—cstr. פָּרֹכֶת; pl. Q פרכות—**curtain, separation** between the holy place and the most holy place Ex 26₃₃.

פרם 3 vb.—**Qal** 3 Impf. יִפְרֹם; ptc. pass. פְּרֻמִים—**1. tear** garment **to pieces** Lv 10₆ 21₁₀. **2.** pass., **be torn to pieces,** of garment Lv 13₄₅.

פַּרְמַשְׁתָּא 1 pr.n.m. **Parmashta.**

פַּרְנָךְ 1 pr.n.m. **Parnach.**

***פַּרְנָס** 0.0.3 n.m.—sf. פרנסו; pl. פרנסין—**administrator** 5/6Ḥev 44₆.

פרס I 16.0.2 vb.—**Qal** 4.0.2 Pf. פָּרְשׂוּ; impf. יִפְרְסוּ; ptc. פֹּרֵשׂ (Q פורס); inf. abs. פָּרֹס—**1. break (bread), a.** with obj. לֶחֶם Lm 4₄. **b.** abs. Jr 16₇(L). **2. chop** bones **in pieces** Mc 3₃. **3a. separate (oneself)** from (מִן) multitude 4QMMT C₇. **b.** ptc. as noun, perh. **separatist** 4Q424 1₂.

Hi. 12 Pf. הִפְרִיסָה; impf. יַפְרִיס; ptc. מַפְרִיס, מַפְרֶסֶת—**1. have hoofs,** perh. **have separated hoofs, a.** with obj. פַּרְסָה, of pig Lv 11₇, camel Dt 14₇, hare Lv 11₆. **b.**

abs., of ox, bull Ps 69₃₂. **2.** ptc. as noun, **animal that has hoofs (perh. separated hoofs)**, with cognate noun פַּרְסָה Lv 11₄.

→ פֶּרֶס II *piece,* פַּרְסָה *hoof.*

*פרס II 0.0.1 vb.—**Ni.** 0.0.1 Pf. נפרס—**be left, remain** 4QD^b 6₆.

*פרס III vb. (byform of פרשׂ)—**Qal, spread** clouds Jb 38₃₇ (if em. יְסַפֵּר *he counts* to יִפְרֹס *he spreads*).

פָּרַס 28.0.1 pr.n.[m.] **Persia.**

פֶּרֶס I 2 n.[m.] **ossifrage, bearded vulture** (*Gypaetus barbatus*), unclean bird Lv 11₁₃.

*[פֶּרֶס] II 1 n.[m.]—pl. sf. פְּרְסֵיהֶן—**piece** Zc 11₁₆. → פרס I *separate.*

פַּרְסָה 21 n.f.—pl. פְּרָסוֹת; cstr. פַּרְסוֹת; sf. פַּרְסֹתַיִךְ, פַּרְסֵיהֶן—**hoof,** of horse Is 5₂₈, beast Ezk 32₁₃. → פרס I *separate.*

*[פְּרַסְטְלִין] 0.0.1 n.[m.] **peristyle** 3QTr 1₇.

[פַּרְסִי] 1 gent. **Persian.**

פרע I 16.8.9 vb.—**Qal** 13.5.5 Pf. פָּרְעָה; impf. יִפְרַע; + waw וּפָרַע; impv. פְּרָעֵהוּ; ptc. פּוֹרֵעַ; pass. פָּרוּעַ; inf. פְּרֹעַ—**1a. loose, open** storehouse Si 43₁₄(M). **b. let hair hang loose** Lv 10₆; pass., **be hung loose,** of hair Lv 13₄₅. **c.** appar. **be hung loose,** of hair Jg 5₂. **2a. let free, deliver** someone Jb 33₂₄(mss). **b.** of clouds, **release** moisture Si 43₂₂. **3a. let someone go out of control** Ex 32₂₅; pass., **let oneself go out of control** Ex 32₂₅. **b. cast off restraint** Jg 5₂. **4.** of Y., **refrain from acting** Ezk 24₁₄. **5. ignore, spurn** advice Pr 1₂₅, authority 1QS 6₂₆. **6. avoid** evil way Pr 4₁₅. **7. let go of, try to forget** deceased person Si 38₂₀.

Ni. 1.0.4 Impf. יִפָּרַע—**let oneself go** Pr 29₁₈.

Hi. 2.3 Pf. הִפְרִיעַ; impf. תַּפְרִיעוּ—**1a. let lawlessness develop** 2 C 28₁₉. **b. cause someone to become lawless** Si 47₂₃. **2. cause someone to refrain from** (מִן) labour Ex 5₄. **3. make sleep disappear** Si 34₁(B).

→ פֶּרַע I *long hair.*

פרע II 1 vb.—**Qal** 1 Inf. cstr. פְּרֹעַ—**take lead** Jg 5₂. → פֶּרַע II *leader.*

*פרע III 0.0.2 vb.—**Qal** 0.0.2 Impf. אפרך, תפרען—**(re)pay** someone XḤev/Se 49₈. → פִּרְעָן *payment.*

*פרע IV 4.0.1 vb.—**Qal** 4.0.1 Impf. יִפְרַע; + waw וּפָרַע; ptc. pass. פָּרוּעַ—**shave** head Lv 10₆ 21₁₀ Nm 5₁₈ 4QD^e 4₅ ([ראש]); pass., **be shaven,** of head Lv 13₄₅.

*פרע V 1 vb.—**Qal** 1 Inf. cstr. פְּרֹעַ—**dedicate oneself** Jg 5₂.

פֶּרַע I 3.0.1 n.[m.]—cstr. פֶּרַע; pl. פְּרָעוֹת—**long hair** Nm 6₅; אוהבי פרע *lovers of long hair* 4QpPs^a 1.1₁₅. → פרע I *let go.*

[פֶּרַע] II 2 n.[m.]—pl. פְּרָעוֹת; cstr. פַּרְעוֹת—**leader** Jg 5₂. → פרע II *take lead.*

*[פֶּרַע] III 1 n.[m.]—cstr. פַּרְעוֹת—**rebel** Dt 32₄₂.

*[פֶּרַע] IV 0.0.0.1 pr.n.[m.] **Phera.**

פֶּרַע V, see פּוֹטִי פֶרַע *Potiphera.*

פַּרְעֹה 274.1.8 n.m.—Q פרעוה (פרעו)—**Pharaoh,** title of Egyptian king Gn 40₁₃ 2 K 23₃₃ Is 36₆.

*[פִּרְעָן] 0.0.1 n.[m.] **payment** Mur 22 1₂. → פרע III *repay.*

פַּרְעֹשׁ I 2 n.m. **flea** 1 S 24₁₅.

פַּרְעֹשׁ II 6.0.0.3 pr.n.m. **Parosh.**

פִּרְעָתוֹן 1 pl.n. **Pirathon.**

פִּרְעָתוֹנִי 5 gent. **Pirathonite.**

*[פַּרְפַּר] I 0.0.0.1 pr.n.[m.] **Parpar.**

פַּרְפַּר II 1 pl.n. **Pharpar.**

פרץ I 45.0.2 vb.—**Qal** 41.0.2 Pf. פָּרַץ; impf. יִפְרֹץ (יִפְרָץ); ptc. פֹּרֵץ; pass. פְּרוּצָה; inf. abs. פָּרֹץ; cstr. פְּרֹץ—**1.** with obj. פֶּרֶץ, **make (a breach)** Gn 38₂₉. **2a. break through** Mc 2₁₃. **b.** ptc. as noun, **one who breaks through,** i.e. warrior Mc 2₁₃. **3. break open** trench or shaft Jb 28₄, **break into** temple 2 C 24₇. **4a.** trans., **break down** wall Ne 3₃₅; abs. Ec 3₃; pass., **be broken down,** of wall 2 C 32₅. **b.** pass. ptc. as noun, **that which has been broken down** Ne 4₁. **5.** of wine-vat, **burst open with wine** Pr 3₁₀. **6. disperse** some of (מִן) one's sons 2 C 11₂₃. **7. spread out, increase (in size, numbers)** Gn 28₁₄. **8.** of word, **spread** 2 C 31₅. **9.** of Y., **break out in anger (upon, against),** a. בְּ *against,* + people 1 C 15₁₃. **b.** obj. human being Jb 16₁₄. **10.** of disease, **break out** Ps 106₂₉. **11a.** trans., **break, transgress** boundary CD 20₂₅. **b.** abs., **break all bounds, violate true order** Ho 4₂. **12.** perh. **penetrate (sexually)** Ho 4₁₀ (unless §7). **13. dare** 1 C 13₂.

Ni. 1 Ptc. נִפְרָץ—**1. be widespread,** of vision 1 S 3₁ (unless §2). **2. be violate,** of vision 1 S 3₁.

Pu. 2 Ptc. מְפֹרֶצֶת, Kt מפרוצים—**be broken down,**

of wall Ne 1₃.

Htp. 1 Ptc. מִתְפָּרְצִים—**break away** from (מִפְּנֵי) master 1 S 25₁₀.

→ פֶּרֶץ I *breach, outburst,* מִפְרָץ I *landing place,* (?) II *wadi,* פָּרִיץ I *violent one,* פְּרוּצִים *violence,* פְּרָצָה *violence.*

*פרץ II 4 vb.—**Qal** 4 + waw וַיִּפְרָץ—with בְּ of obj., **urge** someone 2 S 13₂₅. → cf. פצר *urge.*

*פרץ III 3 vb.—**Qal** 1 Inf. פְּרֹץ—**command, ordain** thing 2 C 31₅.

Ni. 2 Pf. נִפְרְצָה; ptc. נִפְרָץ—**be commanded, ordained,** of vision 1 S 3₁.

→ פָּרִיץ II *duty, law,* פְּרִיצָה *charge.*

*פרץ IV 1 vb.—**Qal** 1 Pf. פָּרַץ—**notch, incise shaft** Jb 28₄.

*פרץ V 1 vb.—**Htp.** 1 Ptc. מִתְפָּרְצִים—**behave as a brigand** 1 S 25₁₀. → (?) פָּרִיץ I *violent one.*

*פרץ VI 1 vb.—**Qal** 1 Pf. פָּרַצְתָּ—**come first,** of Perez Gn 38₂₉.

*פרץ VII 2 vb.—**Qal** 2 Pf. פָּרַצְתָּ; impf. יִפְרֹצוּ—**1. exceed,** of Perez Gn 38₂₉. **2. overflow,** of vat Pr 3₁₀. → פֶּרֶץ II *excess.*

*פרץ VIII 1 vb.—**Ni.** 1 Ptc. נִפְרָץ—**be false,** of vision 1 S 3₁.

פֶּרֶץ I 19.2.3 n.m.—cstr. פֶּרֶץ; pl. פְּרָצִים, פְּרָצוֹת; sf. פִּרְצֵיהֶן—**1. breach, gap,** in wall Is 30₁₃, tribes of Israel Jg 21₁₅; between Y. and Israelites Ps 106₂₃; enlargement of vagina Gn 38₂₉. **2. tear, deep scratch** upon face Jb 16₁₄ (if em. יִפְרְצֵנִי פֶּרֶץ *he breaks out in anger against me [with] outburst* [cf. §6] to יִפְרֹץ פֶּרֶץ *he makes a tear*). **3. loopholes** in law CD 1₁₉. **4. breaching** Ps 144₁₄. **5. excavation** Jb 28₄ (if em. פָּרְצוּ נַחַל מֵעִם־גָּר *they open shafts [in] a valley away from where [people] sojourn* to פֶּרֶץ נַחַל עַם גָּר *an excavation is hollowed out [by] a foreign work-force*). **6. outburst,** of water 2 S 5₂₀, anger 2 S 6₈. **7. disaster** Si 7₁₇. → פרץ I *break through, break out.*

*[פֶּרֶץ] II 1 n.m.—פֶּרֶץ—**excess** Gn 38₂₉. → פרץ VII *exceed, overflow.*

פֶּרֶץ III 15.0.1 pr.n.m. **Perez.**

פֶּרֶץ IV, see רִמֹּן פֶּרֶץ *Rimmon-perez.*

*[פְּרָצָה] 0.0.1 n.f.—pl. פרצות—**violence** CD 1₁₉. → פרץ I *break through, break out.*

פַּרְצִי 1 gent. **Perezite(s).**

פְּרָצִים I 1 pl.n. **Perazim.**

פְּרָצִים II, see בַּעַל־פְּרָצִים *Baal-perazim.*

פֶּרֶץ עֻזָּה 2 pl.n. **Perez-uzzah.**

פרק 10.0.1 vb.—**Qal** 4.0.1 + waw וַיִּפְרְקֵנוּ; וּפָרַקְתָּ; ptc. פֹּרֵק—**1. tear off** yoke Gn 27₄₀, neck Ps 7₃. **2. snatch away,** i.e. rescue, people from (מִן) enemy Ps 136₂₄. **3. tear** someone **in pieces** Ps 7₃.

Pi. 3 Impf. יְפָרֵק; impv. פָּרְקוּ; ptc. מְפָרֵק—**1. tear off** ring Ex 32₂, hoof Zc 11₁₆. **2.** of wind, **tear apart** mountain 1 K 19₁₁.

Htp. 3 Pf. הִתְפָּרְקוּ; + waw וַיִּתְפָּרְקוּ; impv. הִתְפָּרְקוּ—**1. tear** ring **off oneself** Ex 32₃. **2. be torn off,** of fruit Ezk 19₁₂.

→ פָּרָק *pieces, joint,* פֶּרֶק I *crossroads,* II *plunder,* מַפְרֶקֶת *neck.*

[פָּרָק] 1.0.2 n.[m.] **1. pieces** Is 65₄(Kt). **2. joint** 4QpsEzek[b] 1.1₅. → פרק *tear off.*

פֶּרֶק I 1 n.[m.] **crossroads** or **narrow pass** or **escape route** Ob 14. → פרק *tear off.*

*פֶּרֶק II 1 n.[m.] **plunder** Na 3₁. → פרק *tear off.*

*[פְּרָקְל] 0.0.0.1 pr.n.m. **Perakel.**

פרר I 50.1.22 vb.—**Hi.** 46.1.21 Pf. הֵפֵר (הֵפַר); impf. יָפֵר; + waw וַיָּפֶר; impv. הָפֵר (הָפֵרָה); ptc. מֵפֵר, Q מפרים; inf. abs. הָפֵר; cstr. הָפֵר—**1a.** (1) **break** covenant, of Y. Lv 26₄₄, of people Ezk 16₅₉. (2) **cause** covenant **to be broken** Jr 33₂₀. **b. break, violate** law of Y. Ps 119₁₂₆. **c. annul** vow Nm 30₉. **d. cause a rupture in** brotherhood Zc 11₁₄. **e. break down** established things 1QH 5₁₈. **f.** of caper-berry, **burst** Ec 12₅. **g.** of arrow, **burst forth** 1QH 10₂₆. **2. do away with, abandon** anger Ps 85₅, devotion toward Y. Jb 15₄. **3. discredit, impugn** judgment Jb 40₈. **4a. frustrate, baffle, foil** plan Jb 5₁₂, sign Is 44₂₅. **b.** ptc. as noun, **one who frustrates** or **foils** 4QHod[a] 7.1₂₃. **5.** of aphrodisiac, **fail, be ineffective** Ec 12₅.

Ho. 3 Impf. תֻּפַר—**1a. be broken,** of covenant Zc 11₁₁. **b. be broken down,** of caper-berry Ec 12₅ (if em. וְתֻפַר hi. to וְתֻפַר; unless §3). **2. be frustrated, foiled,** of counsel Is 8₁₀. **3. be made ineffectual,** of caper-berry Ec 12₅ (if em.; see §1; unless §1).

Htp. 0.0.1 Inf. התפרר—**be shattered,** of person 1QH fr. 3_5.

Pilp. 1 + waw וַיְפַרְפְּרֵנִי—of Y., **shatter** human being Jb 16_{12}.

→ פָּארוּר VI *furrow (of face),* (?) פָּרוּר *cooking pot,* (?) פַּרְוָר III *place of ritual separation;* cf. פור *break.*

פרר II 3 vb.—**Qal** 1 Inf. cstr. פּוֹר—**be cracked through,** of earth Is 24_{19}.

Po. 1 Pf. פּוֹרַרְתָּ—of Y., **split, divide** sea Ps 74_{13}.

Htpo. 1 Pf. הִתְפּוֹרְרָה—**be cracked through,** of earth Is 24_{19}.

***פרר** III 4 vb.—**Po.** 1 Pf. פּוֹרַרְתָּ—of Y., **make** sea **flee** Ps 74_{13}.

Hi. 3 Impf. תָּפֵר, אָפִיר—**let** mercy **depart** Ps 89_{34}, **drive away** anger Ps 85_5, fear Jb 15_4.

***פרר** IV 1 vb.—**Pilp.** 1 + waw וַיְפַרְפְּרֵנִי—of Y., **worry** person Jb 16_{12}.

פרשׂ I 66.1.20 vb.—**Qal** 55.1.15 Pf. פָּרַשׂ; impf. יִפְרֹשׂ; ptc. פֹּרֵשׂ, פֹּרְשֵׂי, פֹּרְשִׂים, פּוֹרְשׂוֹת; ptc. pass. פָּרֻשׂ, פְּרוּשָׂה, פְּרֻשׂוֹת—**1a. spread out** scroll Ezk 2_{10}, net Ps 140_6, wings Dt 32_{11}; **diffuse** light Jb 36_{30}. **b.** of wing, **spread (itself) out** 2 C 3_{13}. **c.** ptc. as noun, (1) **outspreading** of wings Ex 25_{20}. (2) **one who spreads out** net Is 19_8. **2. display** folly Pr 13_{16}. **3. spread (on top) cover over** (עַל) face 2 K 8_{15}. **4. stretch out** hand Pr 31_{20}.

Ni. 1.0.3 Pf. Q נפרשה; impf. יִפָּרְשׂוּ—**1. be spread out,** of net 1QH 11_{26}. **2. be scattered,** of people Ezk 17_{21}. **3. be spread (on top)** 4QapPsB 46_4.

Pi. 9.0.2 Pf. פֵּרְשָׂה; impf. יְפָרֵשׂ; ptc. Q מפרשי; inf. פָּרֵשׂ (פָּרִשְׂכֶם)—**1. scatter** people Zc 2_{10}. **2. stretch out, a.** obj. hands Is 1_{15}. **b.** בְּ of obj., hands Lm 1_{17}. **3.** ptc. as noun, **a.** ptc. as noun, **one who spreads out** 1QH fr. 3_4 ([מפרש[י). **b. outspreading** 4QHod[b] 13_7.

Pilel 1 with euphonic change of the first שׂ to שׁ, and the second to ז—Inf. abs. פַּרְשֵׁז—**spread (over)** cloud Jb 26_9.

→ מִפְרָשׂ *spreading;* cf. פרשׂ III *scatter.*

פרשׂ II, see פרס I *separate.*

פרשׁז, see פרשׂ I *spread out,* pilel.

פרשׁ I 3.0.6 vb.—**Qal** 1.0.4 Pf. Q פרש; inf. cstr. פְּרֹשׁ—**1. expound clearly** foundation of truth 4QInstr[c] 1.1_9. **2. record** name **precisely** 4QInstr[c] 14_4.

Ni. 0.0.1 Pf. נפרשה—**be stipulated precisely,** of purification 4QRitPurB 42.2_4.

Pu. 2.0.1 Pf. פֹּרַשׁ; ptc. מְפֹרָשׁ—**1. be explained precisely,** of law Ne 8_8. **2. be recorded precisely,** of name 4QMidrEschat[b] 10_{11}.

→ פֵּרוּשׁ *detail(s),* פְּרוּשָׁה *specification of contents,* פָּרָשָׁה *precise details.*

פרשׁ II 1 vb.—**Hi.** 1 Impf. יַפְרִשׁ—**sting,** of wine Pr 23_{32}.

***פרשׁ** III 1 vb.—**Ni.** 1 Ptc. נִפְרָשׁוֹת—**be scattered,** of sheep Ezk 34_{12}. → cf. פרשׂ I *spread out.*

***פרשׁ** IV 2 vb.—**Qal** 1 Inf. פְּרֹשׁ—**make decision** Lv 24_{12}.

Pu. 1 Pf. פֹּרַשׁ—**be decided** Nm 15_{34}.

פָּרָשׁ 57.0.8 n.m.—פָּרָשׁ; pl. פָּרָשִׁים; cstr. Q פרשי; sf. פָּרָשָׁיו—**1. horse** 1 K 1_5; בַּעֲלֵי הַפָּרָשִׁים *masters of the horses,* i.e. horsemen 2 S 1_6. **2. horseman,** usu. not as rider but as **charioteer** Gn 50_9 Ex 14_9 1QM 6_9.

פֶּרֶשׁ I 7.0.2 n.m.—cstr. פֶּרֶשׁ; sf. פִּרְשׁוֹ—**1. intestines** 11QT 16_{11}. **2. excrement** Ml 2_3.

פֶּרֶשׁ II 1 pr.n.m. **Peresh.**

פַּרְשֶׁגֶן 1.0.1 n.m. **copy,** of letter Ezr 7_{11}.

פַּרְשְׁדֹנָה I 1 n.[m] **excrement** Jg 3_{22}.

***פַּרְשְׁדֹנָה** II 1 n.[m] **vent, anus** Jg 3_{22}.

***פַּרְשְׁדֹנָה** III 1 n.[m] **place of excrement** Jg 3_{22}.

[**פָּרָשָׁה**] 2 n.f.—cstr. פָּרָשַׁת—**precise details** Est 4_7 10_2. → פרשׁ I *make clear.*

פרשׁז, see פרשׂ I *spread out,* pilel.

פַּרְשַׁנְדָּתָא 1 pr.n.m. **Parshandatha.**

***פֹּרָת** I 2 n.f. **tamarisk** Gn 49_{22}.

***פֹּרָת** II 2 n.f. **female wild ass** Gn 49_{22}.

***פֹּרָת** III 2 n.f. **cow** Gn 49_{22}.

[**פֶּרֶת**], see פֶּתֶר *interpretation.*

פְּרָת 18.0.1 pl.n. **Euphrates.**

פַּרְתְּמִים 3 n.m.pl. **nobles** Est 1_3.

פשׂה 22 vb.—**Qal** 22 Pf. פָּשָׂה, פָּשְׂתָה; impf. יִפְשֶׂה; inf. abs. פָּשֹׂה—**spread,** of plague Lv 13_5.

פשׂע 1 vb.—**Qal** 1 Impf. אֶפְשְׂעָה—**march,** of Y. Is 27_4. → פֶּשַׂע *step,* מִפְשָׂע *marching.*

פֶּשַׂע 1 n.[m.] **step** 1 S 20_3. → פשׂע *march.*

פשׂק 2 vb.—**Qal** 1 Ptc. פֹּשֵׂק—**separate** lips Pr 13_3.

Pi. 1 + waw וַתְּפַשְּׂקִי—**spread wide** legs for sexual intercourse Ezk 16_{25}.

פַּשׁ I 1 n.[m.] **folly** Jb 35_{15}.

***פַּשׁ** II 1 n.[m.] **arrogance** Jb 35_{15}.

פשח I 1 vb.—**Pi.** 1 + waw וַיְפַשְּׁחֵנִי—of Y., **tear human being in pieces** Lm 3_{11}.

***פשח** II 1 vb.—**Pi.** 1 + waw וַיְפַשְּׁחֵנִי—of Y., **leave fallow** Lm 3_{11}.

פַּשְׁחוּר 14.0.0.9 pr.n.m. **Pashhur.**

פשט 43.0.6 vb.—**Qal** 24.0.2 Pf. פָּשַׁט; impf. יִפְשֹׁטוּ (יִפְשְׁטוּ); + waw וַיִּפְשֹׁט; impv. פְּשֹׁטָה; ptc. פֹּשְׁטִים—**1a. strip off** clothes Ca 5_3, skin 11QT 34_9. **b. strip oneself** Is 32_{11}, perh. of locust casting skin Na 3_{16}. **2. raid against** (עַל or אֶל) city Jg 9_{33}, people 1 S 27_8.

Ni. 0.0.2 Ptc. נפשטים—**be deployed,** of column of troops 1QM 8_6.

Pi. 3 Inf. cstr. פַּשֵּׁט—**1. strip** slain one 1 S 31_8. **2.** abs., **take spoil** 2 S 23_{10}.

Hi. 15.0.2 Pf. הִפְשִׁיט; impf. תַּפְשִׁיט; + waw וַיַּפְשֵׁט; impv. הַפְשֵׁט; ptc. מַפְשִׁיטִים, inf. הַפְשִׁיט—**1a. strip** person Gn 37_{23}; **strip off** clothes Jb 22_6, honour from (מֵעַל) person Jb 19_9. **b.** ptc. as noun, **one who strips** 1QM 7_2. **2a. strip off** skin from (מֵעַל) people Mc 3_3. **b. flay** animal Lv 1_6.

Htp. 1 + waw וַיִּתְפַּשֵּׁט—**take off** robe 1 S 18_4.

*[**פַּשִׁיד**] 0.0.0.1 pr.n.m. **Pashid.**

פשע 41.1.10 vb.—**Qal** 40.1.9 Pf. פָּשַׁע, פָּשְׁעָה; impf. יִפְשַׁע; ptc. פֹּשֵׁעַ, פּוֹשְׁעִים; inf. abs. פָּשֹׁעַ; cstr. פְּשֹׁעַ—**1a. rebel** against (בְּ) oppressor 1 K 12_{19}. **b. break away** from under (מִתַּחַת) foreign rule 2 K 8_{22}. **2a. sin** against (בְּ) Y. Is 1_2, against (עַל) law Ho 8_1. **b.** with obj. פֶּשַׁע, **commit sins** 1 K 8_{50}. **c.** ptc. as noun, **sinner** Ho 14_{10}.

Ni. 1 Ptc. נִפְשָׁע—**be offended** Pr 18_{19}.

Hi. 0.0.1 Inf. cstr. הפשיע—**cause** someone **to break away** from (מִן) Y. 4QWiles 1_{15}.

→ פֶּשַׁע *transgression.*

פֶּשַׁע 93.7.69 n.m.—cstr. פֶּשַׁע; sf. פִּשְׁעוֹ; pl. פְּשָׁעִים; cstr. פִּשְׁעֵי; sf. פְּשָׁעָיו—**sin, transgression,** usu. against Y. Ezk 33_{10} Jb 7_{21} 1QH 6_{24}, occasionally against human being Gn 31_{36}. → פשע *rebel.*

***פשר** 0.0.2 vb.—**Qal** 0.0.2 Inf. cstr. פשור—**interpret** word 1QpHab 2_8. → פֵּשֶׁר *interpretation,* פִּשְׁרָה *diagnosis;* cf. פתר *interpret.*

פֵּשֶׁר 1.0.108 n.[m.]—cstr. פֵּשֶׁר; pl. sf. Q פשריהם—**interpretation,** of biblical text Ec 8_1 11QMelch 2_{17} CD 4_{14}. → פשר *interpret.*

*[**פִּשְׁרָה**] 0.1 n.[m.] **(medical) diagnosis** Si $38_{14(B)}$. → פשר *interpret.*

פשש vb. **Ni., be scattered,** of people (if em. נָפֹשׁוּ *they are scattered,* i.e. פוש ni., to נָפֹשׁוּ *they are scattered*).

[**פֵּשֶׁת**] 16.0.2.1 n.m.—sf. פִּשְׁתִּי; pl. פִּשְׁתִּים; cstr. פִּשְׁתֵּי—**1a. flax** (*Linum usitatissimum*) Jos 2_6. **b.** perh. **grasses** (not flax) Gezer Calendar3. **2. linen** Ho 2_{11}.

פִּשְׁתָּה 4.0.1 n.f. **1. flax,** the plant Ex 9_{31}. **2. wick** of candle Is 42_3.

פַּת 14 n.f.—cstr. פַּת; sf. פִּתִּי; pl. פִּתִּים—**piece (of bread)** Ru 2_{14}. → פתת *break up.*

פֹּת I 2 n.[m.]—sf. פָּתְהֵן; pl. פֹּתוֹת—**1. socket,** in which door-pivots turn, perh. **latch socket, key** 1 K 7_{50}. **2. secret parts, genitalia** Is 3_{17}.

***פֹּת** II 3 n.[f.]—sf. פָּתְהֵן; pl. פֹּתוֹת—**1. facade** of temple 1 K 7_{50}. **2. forehead** Is 3_{17}. **3. mind** Ps 19_8.

פִּתְאֹם 25.3.8 n.[m.]—Si, Q פתאום, Q פיתאום, Q פתאאום—**1. suddenness** Jb 22_{10}. **2.** as adv., **suddenly** Is 29_5.

[**פַּת־בַּג**] 6 n.[m.]—cstr. פַּת־בַּג (פַּתְבַּג)—**delicacies** Dn 1_5. → פתת *break up.*

פִּתְגָם 2.2.2 n.m.—cstr. פִּתְגָם—**1. prophecy** 4QpIsa[a] 2_{26}. **2. verdict** Ec 8_{11}. **3. reply** Si 8_9.

פתה I 26.7.9 vb.—**Qal** 4.4.1 Impf. יִפְתֶּה; + waw וַיִּפְתְּ; ptc. פֹּתֶה—**1a. be simple** Ho 7_{11}. **b.** ptc. as noun, **simpleton** Si 8_{17}. **2.** of heart, **be enticed** Dt 11_{16}.

Ni. 2 Pf. נִפְתָּה; + waw וָאֶפָּת—**1. be persuaded** Jr 20_7. **2.** of heart, **be seduced,** sexually Jb 31_9.

Pi. 17.1.4 Pf. פִּתִּיתַנִי; impf. יְפַתֶּה; impv. פַּתִּי; ptc. מְפַתֶּיהָ; inf. פַּתּוֹת—**1. attempt to persuade** someone Jr 20_7. **2. encourage** oneself Si 30_{23}. **3. entice** someone Jg 14_{15}. **4. allure** someone, erotically 4QWiles 1_{17}. **5. (attempt to) deceive** someone 2 S 3_{25}; abs. Pr 24_{28}.

Pu. 3.1.3 Pf. Q פותו; impf. יְפֻתֶּה; ptc. Q מפותי—**1. be persuaded** Pr 25_{15}. **2a. be enticed** 1QH 14_{19}. **b.** ptc. as noun, **one enticed** 1QH 12_{16}. **3. be seduced,** sexually Si $42_{10(B)}$. **4. be deceived** Jr 20_{10}.

Htp. 0.1.1 Impf. Q יתפתה, Si תתפתה—**1. be seduced,** sexually Si $42_{10(Bmg)}$. **2. be deceived** CD 15_{11}.

→ פֶּתִי I *simple-minded,* II *simpleness,* פְּתַיּוּת *simpleness.*

פתה II 2 vb.—**Qal** 1 Ptc. פֹּתֶה—**open** lips Pr 20_{19}.

Hi. 1 Impf. יַפְתְּ—of Y., **enlarge** Japheth Gn 9_{27}.

פְּתוּאֵל 1 pr.n.m. **Pethuel.**

פִּתּוּחַ 11.1.3 n.m.—sf. פִּתֻּחָהּ; pl. פִּתּוּחִים; cstr. פִּתּוּחֵי; sf. פִּתּוּחֶיהָ—**engraving,** of words Ex 28_{11}, image 1 K 6_{29}. → פתח II *engrave.*

*[פְּתוֹר] I 0.1 n.[m.] **interpretation** Si 50_{27}. → פתר *interpret.*

פְּתוֹר II 2 pl.n. **Pethor.**

פְּתוֹת 1 n.[m.]—pl. cstr. פְּתוֹתֵי—**crumb,** of bread Ezk 13_{19}. → פתת *break up.*

פתח I 135.7.101.3 vb.—**Qal** 97.7.71.3 Pf. פָּתַח; impf. יִפְתַּח; impv. פְּתַח, פִּתְחוּ; ptc. פּוֹתֵחַ; pass. פָּתוּחַ, פְּתוּחָה, פְּתֻחוֹת—**1a.** (1) **open (up)** gate Is 26_2, book Ne 8_5. (2) ptc. pass., **be open,** of grave Jr 5_{16}, vessel Nm 19_{15}, letter Ne 6_5. (3) ptc. as noun, **one who opens** Jr 13_{19}. (4) ptc. pass. as noun, **open vessel** 11QT 49_9. **b. open** mouth, to eat Ezk 3_2, speak Jb 11_5. **c. open** ear, to hear Is 50_5. **d. open** womb, to conceive Gn 29_{31}. **e.** ptc. pass., **be opened,** of eyes, to see 2 C 6_{40}. **f.** (1) **open** hand, i.e. to give Dt 15_8. (2) ptc. pass., **be opened,** of hand, to take Si 4_{31}. **g. open** mind, to understand 1QS 11_{15}. **h. open** kidneys, i.e. give courage 4QBark^c 1.1_6. **i. open,** i.e. cause to flow, river Is 41_{18}, sky Dt 28_{12}. **j. open** luminary, to give light 4QpsHodC 1_1. **k. open** wide space, i.e. make room 1QH 13_{33}. **2. open to** (לְ), i.e. **let in,** lover Ca 5_2, enemy Dt 20_{11}. **3a. draw** sword Ps 37_{14}. **b.** ptc. pass., **be drawn,** of sword Ezk 21_{33}. **4. release** prisoner Is 14_{17}. **5. relieve** distress 1QH 7_{16}. **6. loosen** fetter 4QBark^d 2.2_{14}. **7. lay bare** region Ezk 25_9. **8. display** item for sale Am 8_5. **9. disclose** riddle Ps 49_5. **10.** intrans., **open itself,** of earth Is 45_8. **11.** ptc. pass., **a. be open to** (אֶל) water, of root Jb 29_{19}. **b. be in bloom,** of blossom Ca 7_{13}.

Ni. 18.0.23 Pf. נִפְתַּח; impf. יִפָּתַח; ptc. נִפְתָּח; inf. הִפָּתֵחַ—**1a. be opened,** of window Gn 7_{11}, book CD 5_3. **b. be left open,** of gate Is 60_{11} (if em. pi.). **c. be opened,** of mouth, for speech Ezk 24_{27}. **d. be opened,** of ear, for hearing Is 35_5. **e. be opened, caused to flow,** of fountain Zc 13_1. **2. be unbottled,** of wine Jb 32_{19}. **3. be freed,** of captive Is 51_{14}. **4. be loosened,** of girdle Is 5_{27}. **5. be unleashed,** of calamity Jr 1_{14}. **6. be disclosed,** of word 1QH 21_5. **7. be open to** (לְ) water, of shoot 1QH 16_7, to (לְ) source of eternity, of heart 1QH 18_{31}. **8. be in bloom,** of foliage 1QH 16_{26}. **9. open itself,** of gate 1QH 11_{17}.

Pi. 19.0.6 Pf. פִּתַּח (פִּתֵּחַ); impf. יְפַתַּח, אֲפַתֵּחַ; ptc. מְפַתֵּחַ; inf. abs. פַּתֵּחַ; cstr. פַּתֵּחַ—**1a. let loose** or perh. **unburden** camel Gn 24_{32}. **b. liberate** person Ps 105_{20}. **2a. loosen,** (1) obj., sackcloth Is 20_2, tongue, for speech 1QH 13_{26}. (2) לְ of obj., bond Jb 12_{18}. **b.** ptc. as noun, **one who loosens** armour 1 K 20_{11}. **3. release** mercies 4QInstr^c 2.2_2. **4a. open** door Jb 41_6. **b. leave open** gate Is 60_{11}. **c. open** ear Is 48_8 (if em. 3fs to 1cs). **5. uncover** loins Is 45_1. **6. break open** ground Is 28_{24}. **7. be in bloom,** of blossom Ca 7_{13}.

Htp. 1.0.1 Impv. Qr הִתְפַּתְּחִי (Kt התפתחו)—**free oneself from** bonds Is 52_2.

→ פֵּתַח *opening,* פֵּתַח *unfolding,* פִּתְחָא *opening,* פִּתְחוֹן *opening,* מִפְתָּח *opening,* פְּתִיחָה *drawn sword,* מַפְתֵּחַ *key.*

פתח II 9.0.3 vb.—**Pi.** 8.0.1 Pf. פִּתַּח; impf. תְּפַתַּח; ptc. מְפַתֵּחַ; inf. פַּתֵּחַ—**1.** with double accus., **engrave** stone **with** engraving of signet Ex 28_{11}. **2.** with one obj., **engrave** cherub **on** (עַל) wall 2 C 3_7. **3.** with cognate noun פִּתּוּחַ as obj., **make engraving** Zc 3_9.

Pu. 1.0.2 Ptc. מְפֻתָּחֹת—**1. be engraved (with),** subj. object engraved Ex 39_6. **2. be engraved,** subj. engraving 1QM 5_7.

→ פִּתּוּחַ *engraving.*

*[פְּתַח] 0.0.0.2 pr.n.m. **Pathah.**

פֵּתַח 1 n.m.—cstr. פֵּתַח—**1. unfolding** of word Ps 119_{130}. **2. revelation** of vision Hb 2_3 (if em. וְיָפֵחַ *and it hastens* to וּפֵתַח). → פתח I *open.*

פֶּתַח 164.2.28 n.m.—cstr. פֶּתַח; sf. פִּתְחוֹ; pl. פְּתָחִים (Q פתחין); פִּתְחֵי; sf. פְּתָחֶיהָ—**1. opening** of tent Gn 18_2, **mouth** of cistern 3QTr 1_8. **2. entrance** of gate Jr 26_{10}. **3. entrance** to country Mc 5_5. **4. gate(way)** of town Pr 8_3, court Nm 3_{26}. **5. door(way)** of house 1 K 14_6. → פתח I *open.*

*[פִּתְחָא] 0.0.1 n.[m.] **mouth** of pit 3QTr 12_{10}. → פתח I *open.*

[פִּתְחוֹן] 2 n.[m.]—cstr. פִּתְחוֹן—**opening** of mouth, for speech Ezk 29_{21}. → פתח I *open.*

פְּתַחְיָה 4.0.10 pr.n.m. **Pethahiah.**

פֶּתִי I 17.0.22 adj.—Q פותי; pl. פְּתָיִים (פְּתָאיִם); cstr. Q פתאי; sf. Q פתאיהם—**1. simple-minded** 1QSa 1_{19}. **2.** as noun, **simple-minded person** Pr 14_{15}. → פתה I *be simple*.

פֶּתִי II 2.0.2 n.m.—Q פותי; pl. פְּתָאיִם—**simpleness, lack** of wisdom; pl. **simple ways** Pr 9_6. → פתה I *be simple*.

פְּתִיגִיל 1 n.[m.] appar. **magnificent garment** Is 3_{24}.

פְּתַיּוּת 1 n.f. **simpleness, lack of wisdom** Pr 9_{13}. → פתה I *be simple, be enticed*.

[פְּתִיחָה] 1 n.[f.]—pl. פְּתִחוֹת—**drawn sword** Ps 55_{22}. → פתח I *open*.

פְּתִיל 11.1.1 n.m.—cstr. פְּתִיל; pl. פְּתִילִים—**1. cord, string** for fastening Jg 16_9. **2. thread, fine strip** of gold in ephod Ex 39_3. → פתל *twist*.

פתל 5.0.2 vb.—**Ni.** 3.0.2 Pf. נִפְתַּלְתִּי; ptc. נִפְתָּל, נִפְתָּלִים—**1.** with נַפְתּוּלִים as obj., **wrestle with** (עִם) sister Gn 30_8. **2.** ptc. as noun, **a. tortuous person** Jb 5_{13}. **b. perverse thing** Pr 8_8.

Htp. 2 Impf. תִּתְפַּתָּל—**show oneself shrewd, crafty** 2 S 22_{27}.

→ נַפְתּוּלִים *wrestlings*, פְּתִיל *cord*, פְּתַלְתֹּל *tortuous*.

***פְּתָלְמִיס** 0.0.3 pr.n.m. **Ptolemy.**

פְּתַלְתֹּל 1 adj. **tortuous,** of generation Dt 32_5. → פתל *twist*.

פִּתֹם 1 pl.n. **Pithom.**

פֶּתֶן 6.2.8 n.m.—pl. פְּתָנִים—**venomous serpent,** perh. viper or cobra Is 11_8.

פֶּתַע 7.1.2 n.[m.] **1. instant** Nm 35_{22}. **2.** as adv., **instantly** Hb 2_7.

***פתק** vb. **Qal, form, shape,** of worm Jb 24_{20} (if em. מְתָקוֹ *it sucks him* to פְּתָקוֹ *it shapes him*).

פתר 9.1.1 vb.—**Qal** 9.1.1 Pf. פָּתַר; + waw וַיִּפְתָּר; ptc. פּוֹתֵר; inf. לִפְתֹּר—**interpret** dream Gn 40_8. → פִּתְרוֹן I *interpretation*, פֵּתֶר *interpretation*, פִּתְרוֹן *interpretation*; cf. פשׁר *interpret*.

***[פֵּתֶר]** 0.0.3 n.m. **interpretation** 4QCryptA 3.2_9. → פתר *interpret*.

פִּתְרוֹן 5 n.m.—cstr. פִּתְרוֹן; sf. פִּתְרֹנוֹ; pl. פִּתְרֹנִים—**interpretation** Gn 40_5. → פתר *interpret*.

פַּתְרוֹס 5 pl.n. **Pathros.**

פַּתְרֻסִים 2 gent. pl. **Pathrusim.**

פַּתְשֶׁגֶן 3 n.m. **copy,** of document Est 3_{14}.

פתת 1.0.0.1 vb.—**Qal** 1.0.0.1 Impf. I יפת; inf. abs. פָּתוֹת—**break up** grain offering Lv 2_6. → פַּת *piece (of bread)*, פַּת־בַּג *delicacies*, פְּתוֹת *crumb*.

צ

***צֵא** 1 n.[m.] **filth,** צֵא תֹּאמַר לוֹ *you shall say to it: '(you are) filth'* Is 30_{22} (unless *'go out!'*). → cf. צֵאָה *excrement*, צֹאָה *filth*, צוֹ *excrement*.

[צֵאָה] 2 n.f.—cstr. צֵאת; sf. צֵאָתֶךָ—**excrement** Ezk 4_{12}. → cf. צֵא *filth*, צֹאָה *filth*, צוֹ *excrement*.

צֹאָה 5.0.1 n.f.—Q צואה; cstr. צֹאַת; sf. צֹאָתוֹ—**filth,** excrement 2 K 18_{27}, vomit Is 28_8, menstrual blood Is 4_4, iniquity Pr 30_{12}. → cf. צֵא *filth*, צֵאָה *excrement*, צוֹ *excrement*.

צֹאִי 2.0.3 adj.—pl. צֹאִים (צוֹאִים)—**filthy, impure,** of water CD 10_{11}, garment Zc 3_3. → cf. צֵא *filth*, צֵאָה *excrement*, צֹאָה *filth*, צוֹ *excrement*.

צֶאֱלִים 2 n.m.pl. **lotus trees** or **lotus bush** (*Zizyphus lotus*) Jb 40_{21}.

צֹאן 274.0.33 n.f.—Q צואן (Q צאון, Q צון); cstr. צֹאן; pl. sf. Q צואניכמה—alw. sg., exc. at 4QRPa 7_7, **1a.** oft. coll., **flock(s), small livestock beasts,** i.e. **sheep and goats** Gn 30_{32}, only **sheep** 1 S 25_2, oft. ambiguous. **b. flock, sheep,** in comparison with persons Is 53_6. **2a. flock(s), sheep** representing **people** of Y. Mc 7_{14}. **b. flocks, multitude** of people Ezk 36_{37}. → cf. צֹנֶה *flock*.

צַאֲנָן 1 pl.n. **Zaanan.**

[צֶאֱצָא] 11.2.16 n.m.—pl. צֶאֱצָאִים; cstr. צֶאֱצָאֵי—alw. pl., **1. produce** of the earth Is 34_1. **2. offspring, descendant** of humans Is 48_{19}. → יצא I *go out*.

צָב I 2 n.[m.]—pl. צַבִּים—**wagon, dray,** prob. not specif.

covered wagon Nm 7₃.

צָב II 1.0.1 n.[m.] **lizard,** prob. not specif. **thorn-tailed lizard,** unclean animal 11QT 50₂₀.

צבא 14.0.1 vb.—**Qal** 12.0.1 Pf. צָבְאוּ; + waw וַיִּצְבְּאוּ—**1a. fight** against (עַל) people Nm 31₇. **b. attack** Ariel Is 29₇. **2a.** with obj. צָבָא, **perform service** Nm 4₂₃. **b.** intrans., serve 1 S 2₂₂. **3.** ptc. as noun, **cultic servant** Ex 38₈.

Hi. 2 Ptc. מַצְבִּא—**levy** people **for military service** 2 K 25₁₉.

→ צָבָא *host.*

צָבָא 486.5.59.1 n.m.&f.—cstr. צְבָא; sf. צְבָאִי; pl. צְבָאוֹת; cstr. צִבְאוֹת (Q צבי); sf. צְבָאָיו, צִבְאֹתַי—**1a. army** Jg 4₇. **b. host of Y.,** perh. army of angels Jos 5₁₄. **2. war, battle** Dn 10₁. **3. assembly, group, division** Ex 6₂₆. **4. heavenly host, angels** Ps 148₂. **5. celestial bodies** Dt 4₁₉. **6. host of clouds** Si 43₈. **7. multitude** of created things and beings Gn 2₁. **8.** pl., **hosts of the nations** Jr 3₁₉. **9. cultic service** of Levites Nm 4₂₃. **10. (term of) hard service** Is 40₂. **11.** as epithet of Y., צְבָאוֹת ״ **Y. of hosts** 1 S 1₃, connotation uncertain, proposals: a. military, b. spiritual, c. celestial, d. heavenly, e. cosmic, f. intens. abstract pl., i.e. 'Y. the Almighty (One)'. → צבא *fight, serve.*

*[צַבָּא] 0.0.0.2 pr.n.m. **Zabba.**

צִבָא, see צִיבָא *Ziba.*

צְבָאוֹת I, see צָבָא *host.*

צְבָאוֹת II, see צְבִי I *glory.*

צְבָאוֹת, see צְבִיָּה *female gazelle.*

צְבָאִים, see צְבִי II *gazelle.*

צְבֹאִים 5 pl.n. **Zeboiim.**

צֹבֵבָה 1 pr.n.m. **Zobebah.**

צבה 2 vb.—**Qal** 1 + waw וְצָבְתָה—**swell up,** of abdomen Nm 5₂₇.

Hi. 1 Inf. cstr. לַצְבּוֹת—**cause** abdomen **to swell up** Nm 5₂₂.

→ צָבֶה *swollen.*

[**צָבֶה**] 1 adj.—f.s. צָבָה—**swollen,** of body Nm 5₂₁. → צבה *swell up.*

צֹבָה, see צוֹבָה I *Zobah.*

צְבוֹיִים, see צְבֹאִים *Zeboiim.*

צְבוֹיִם, see צְבֹאִים *Zeboiim.*

צָבוּעַ 1.1 adj. **1. coloured,** of bird Jr 12₉. **2.** as noun, **coloured one, hyena (with coloured stripes)** Si 13₁₈. → צבע *dye.*

[**צָבוֹעַ**] 1.1 n.m.—pl. צְבֹעִים—**hyena** Si 13₁₈. → (?) צבע *dye.*

צִבּוּר 1 n.m.—pl. צִבֻּרִים—**heap** 2 K 10₈. → צבר *heap up.*

*[**צְבוּת**] 0.0.1 n.f.—sf. צבותכה—**desire** 1QH 18₁₈.

צבט 1 vb.—**Qal** 1 + waw וַיִּצְבָּט—**hold out** grain **to** (לְ) person Ru 2₁₄.

צְבִי I 19.0.2 n.m.—צְבִי; cstr. צְבִי; sf. Q צביו; pl. cstr. צִבְאוֹת—**glory, beauty, pride,** of branch of Y. Is 4₂, land Jr 3₁₉, city Ezk 25₉, crown Is 28₅; **honour** given to righteous Is 24₁₆.

צְבִי II 14.0.2 n.m.—pl. צְבָיִם (צְבָאִים)—**1. gazelle, deer,** permitted for food Dt 12₁₅, royal food 1 K 5₃; in analogy with humans, agile warrior 2 S 2₁₈, graceful beloved Ca 2₉. **2. gazelle** as symbolic representation of prince 2 S 1₁₉; coll., of princes, leaders Is 23₉. → cf. צְבִיָּה *female gazelle.*

*[**צְבִי**] III 0.0.0.1 pr.n.m. **Zebi.**

צִבְיָא 1 pr.n.m. **Zibia.**

צִבְיָה 2 pr.n.f. **Zibiah.**

צְבִיָּה, see צבא *fight.*

צְבִיָּה 4 n.f. **female gazelle** Ca 4₅. → cf. צְבִי II *gazelle.*

צְבִיִּים, see צְבֹאִים *Zeboiim.*

צְבִיִם, see צְבֹאִים *Zeboiim.*

*[**צְבָלִי**] 0.0.0.1 pr.n.m. **Zebali.**

***צבע** vb. **Qal, dye,** ptc. as noun, **dyer** 1 C 4₂₂ (if ins. after אַשְׁבֵּעַ [cf. 4₂₁], אֶת־בֵּית צֹבֵעַ וְרֹקֵם *together with the house of the dyer and embroiderer*).

Ni., be(come) dyed, of earth Jb 38₁₄ (if em. וְיִתְיַצְּבוּ *and they stand* to וְתִצָּבַע *and it becomes dyed*).

Htp., appear dyed, of earth Jb 38₁₄ (if em. וְיִתְיַצְּבוּ *and they stand* to וְתִצְטַבַּע *and it appears dyed*).

→ צֶבַע *colour, coloured material,* צָבוּעַ *coloured,* (?) צָבוֹעַ *hyena.*

צֶבַע 3.0.5 n.[m.]—cstr. צֶבַע; pl. צְבָעִים; cstr. Q צבעי—**1. colour, dye** 4QShirShabb[f] 20.2₁₁. **2. coloured material, dyed cloth** Jg 5₃₀. → צבע *dye.*

צִבְעוֹן 8 pr.n.m. **Zibeon.**

צְבֹעִים 2 pl.n. **Zeboim.**

צבר 7.1.1.1 vb.—**Qal** 7.1.1.1 Impf. יִצְבֹּר—**heap up** dust Hb 1₁₀, grain Gn 41₃₅, gold Si 47₁₈. → צִבּוּר *heap,* צִבְרוֹן

throngs.

*[צִבָּרוֹן] n.m. **throngs** Zc 9₁₂ (if em. לְבִצָּרוֹן *to the stronghold/Bizzaron* to לְצִבָּרוֹן *in throngs*). → צבר *heap up*.

[צֶבֶת] 1 n.[m.]—pl. צְבָתִים—**bundle** or **handful** of grain (rather than **heap**) Ru 2₁₆.

צַד I 33.0.8 n.m.—cstr. צַד; sf. צִדֵּךְ; pl. צִדִּים; cstr. צִדֵּי—**1. side of object**, grave 3QTr 6₁₁, ark Gn 6₁₆, lampstand Ex 25₃₂. **2. side of body** Nm 33₅₅, **hip** Is 60₄. **3.** with prep. מִן, **a.** מִצַּד **at the side of, beside, next to,** מִצַּד שָׁאוּל *next to Saul* 1 S 20₂₅. **b.** מצד **aside,** חיי מצד *my life (has been set) aside* 1QH 17₆.

*[צַד] II 1 n.m.—pl. צִדִּים—**trap** Jg 2₃.

[צְדָד] or [צְדָדָה] 2 pl.n. **Zedad.**

צדה I 2 vb.—**Qal** 2 Pf. צָדָה; ptc. צֹדֶה—**1.** trans., **lie in wait for** life of person 1 S 24₁₂. **2.** abs., **lie in wait** Ex 21₁₃. → צְדִיָּה *lying in wait.*

צדה II 1 vb.—**Ni.** 1 Pf. נִצְדּוּ—**be laid waste,** of city Zp 3₆.

צֵדָה I, see צֵידָה I *provision (of food).*

[צֵדָה] II, see צֵידָה II *hunting.*

צָדוֹק 53.1.14.4 pr.n.m. **Zadok.**

צְדִיָּה 2 n.f. **malicious intent, lying in wait** Nm 35₂₀. → צדה I *lie in wait.*

צִדִּים 1 pl.n. **Ziddim.**

צַדִּיק 206.6.72 adj.—pl. צַדִּיקִים (צַדִּקִם, צַדִּקִים, Q צדקם)—**1.** of human being, **righteous, just,** keeping Y.'s commandments Ezk 18₉, not involved in idolatry, sexual immorality, social injustice Ezk 18₅; of messianic ruler, reigning with wisdom and justice Jr 23₅; **innocent, blameless,** not guilty of a specific offence 2 K 10₉, **right, in the right** Pr 18₁₇; **correct, right,** having given the right information Is 41₂₆. **2.** of Y., **righteous, just,** in actions Dn 9₁₄, without iniquity, faithful Dt 32₄; juridical, **in the right** Jr 12₁. **3.** of Y.'s laws, **just, right** Dt 4₈. **4.** of Messianic king, **victorious** Zc 9₉. **5.** as noun, **a.** of human being, **righteous one, just one,** serving Y. Ml 3₁₈, not living in sin Ec 7₂₀, generous Ps 37₂₁, honest Pr 13₅, speaking wisely Pr 10₃₁; juridical, **innocent one, one who is in the right,** i.e. right according to law, not under penalty Ex 23₇. **b.** of Y., **Righteous One, Just One,** as punisher Ex 9₂₇, worthy of praise Is 24₁₆. **c.** of human being, **victor** Is 49₂₄. **6.** as adv., **a. justly, with fairness,** מוֹשֵׁל בָּאָדָם צַדִּיק *he who rules human beings justly* 2 S 23₃. **b.** as (being) righteous, **אֹתְךָ רָאִיתִי צַדִּיק לְפָנַי** *you (alone) have I seen as righteous before me* Gn 7₁. → צדק *be righteous, be justified.*

צִדְנִית, see צִידֹנִי *Sidonian.*

צדק 41.4.35 vb.—**Qal** 22.0.21 Pf. צָדְקָה; impf. יִצְדַּק—**1.** of Y., **be righteous, be just** 1QH 9₆, as judge Ps 51₆. **2.** of Y.'s laws, **be righteous, be just** Ps 19₁₀. **3.** of people, **be righteous, be innocent, be blameless, be right** Jb 9₁₅. **4.** of people, **be declared righteous, be justified, be vindicated** Is 43₉, by (מִן) God Jb 4₁₇, before (לִפְנֵי) Y. Ps 143₂.

Ni. 1 + waw וְנִצְדַּק—**be brought to its right state,** of sanctuary Dn 8₁₄.

Pi. 5.0.2 Pf. צִדְּקָה; + waw וַתְּצַדְּקִי—**1. declare righteous, declare as in the right, justify** someone, of Y. 4QBéat 10₅, of human Jb 33₃₂. **2. make someone appear upright** Ezk 16₅₁. **3.** with מִן of comparison, **show oneself more upright than** (מִן) someone else Jr 3₁₁.

Hi. 12.3.12 Impf. יַצְדִּיק; + waw וְהִצְדִּיקוּ, וְהִצְדַּקְתִּיו—**1a. declare righteous, justify, acquit, vindicate** someone, of Y. Ex 23₇, of people CD 1₁₉; **declare just** Y.'s judgment, of worshipper 1QH 17₉. **b.** ptc. as noun, **one who declares righteous, vindicator** Is 50₈. **2. admit** someone **to be right** Jb 27₅. **3. cause justice to be done to, obtain rights for** someone Ps 82₃. **4.** with לְ of obj., **cause** someone **to be acquitted** Is 53₁₁. **5a. lead** someone **to righteousness,** i.e. help him to walk in the way of Y. CD 20₁₈. **b.** ptc. as noun, **one who leads to righteousness,** מַצְדִּיקֵי הָרַבִּים *those who lead many to righteousness* Dn 12₃.

Htp. 1.1 Impf. Si חצטדק, נִצְטַדָּק—**(attempt to) prove oneself innocent** Gn 44₁₆.

→ צַדִּיק *righteous,* צֶדֶק *righteousness; vindication,* צְדָקָה *righteousness; vindication.*

צֶדֶק 119.7.220 n.m.—Q צדוק; cstr. צֶדֶק; sf. צִדְקִי—צֶדֶק may mean righteousness in general, צְדָקָה a single act of righteousness or justice; alternatively, צֶדֶק may refer to right order, צְדָקָה to right behaviour, **1a. righ-**

teousness, (moral) uprightness, right conduct, godliness, integrity, i.e. what is right in Y.'s eyes Is 51_1; ritual perfection 4QRitPurB 40_5. b. /מורה/מורי צדק or יורה הצדק Teacher of Righteousness, spiritual leader at Qumran 1QpHab 1_{13}. c. /בני צדק הצד(ו)ק sons of righteousness, ruled by Prince of Light 1QS 3_{20}. 2. of earthly ruler, justice, fairness, impartiality Dt 16_{18}; honesty in paying wages Jr 22_{13}. 3. righteous plea, just cause Ps 17_1. 4a. divine benevolence Ps 35_{28}, divine justice Ps 9_9. b. used adjectivally, oft. in cstr., just, right, righteous, מִשְׁפְּטֵי־צֶדֶק *just ordinances* Is 58_2, משפט צדק *righteous judgment* 1QSb 2_{26}. 5. righteous will of Y. GnzPs 3_5. 6. righteousness as personified divine attribute Ps 85_{12}. 7. רוחות צדק spirits of righteousness 4QShirShabb[d] 1.1_{38}. 8. justice, right ordering of the world Jb 8_3. 9. rightness, accuracy, legitimacy, i.e. what is correct, of weights Lv 19_{36}, sacrifices Dt 33_{19}. 10. truth, of words, lips, etc. Pr 16_{13}. 11a. saving righteousness, vindication, victory, deliverance, oft. accomplished by Y. Is 51_5. b. of Y., Vindicator 1QS 10_{11}. 12. as adv., a. justly, fairly, וּשְׁפַטְתֶּם צֶדֶק *and you will judge fairly* Dt 1_{16}. b. in triumph, יִלְבְּשׁוּ־צֶדֶק *they are clothed in triumph* Ps 132_9. → צדק *be righteous*.

*[צְדָקָא] 0.0.0.1 pr.n.m. Zedaka.

צְדָקָה 157.9.69 n.f.—cstr. צִדְקַת; pl. צְדָקוֹת; cstr. צִדְקוֹת—צֶדֶק may mean righteousness in general, צְדָקָה a single act of righteousness or justice; alternatively, צֶדֶק may refer to right order, צְדָקָה to right behaviour, 1a. righteousness, (moral) uprightness, right conduct, godliness, i.e. what is right in Y.'s eyes; specif. charity, almsgiving, kindness Ps 112_9; blamelessness, innocence with regard to sin or offence Jb 27_6. b. false righteousness Is 57_{12}. c. מורה הצדקה Teacher of Righteousness, spiritual leader at Qumran 1QpHab 2_2. 2. of earthly ruler, justice 1 K 10_9, specif. social justice toward poor Am 5_7. 3. merit Gn 15_6 Ps 106_{31} 4QMMT C_{31}. 4. (legal) right, entitlement, claim Ne 2_{20}. 5. divine benevolence Jl 2_{23}, divine justice, of Y. as judge, lawgiver, king Is 54_{14} Ps 99_4, divine retribution Is 10_{22}. 6. righteous will of Y. Dt 33_{21}. 7. saving righteousness, vindication, victory, deliverance, oft. accomplished by Y. for his people Is 48_{18}; prosperity, success Pr 8_{18}. 8. truthfulness in speech Jr 4_2; honesty in behaviour Gn 30_{33}. 9. justness, done according to law Ml 3_3. 10. pl., good deeds, virtues Ezk 3_{20}; charity, almsgiving 4QTobit[e] 2_6. 11. pl., of Y., righteous acts, oft. specif. saving deeds, victorious deeds Jg 5_{11}, deeds of atonement 1QS 11_3. 12. as adv., a. sg., truthfully, יָצָא מִפִּי צְדָקָה דָּבָר *a word has come out of my mouth truthfully* Is 45_{23}. b. pl., uprightly, הֹלֵךְ צְדָקוֹת *he who walks uprightly* Is 33_{15}. → צדק *be righteous*.

צִדְקִיָּה 63.0.4.5 pr.n.m. Zedekiah.

צִדְקִיָּהוּ, see צִדְקִיָּה *Zedekiah*.

צהב 1.1 vb.—Hi. 0.1 יצהיב—perh. make (someone's face) gleam Si 10_{10}.

Ho. 1 Ptc. מֻצְהָב—gleam, of copper Ezr 8_{27}.
→ צָהֹב *gleaming*.

צָהֹב 3.0.1 adj.—Q צוהב—gleaming, of hair Lv 13_{30}. → צהב *gleam*.

צהל I 8.1.3 vb.—Qal 8.1.3 Pf. צָהֲלָה; impf. יִצְהֲלוּ—1. shout (for joy) Est 8_{15}. 2. neigh like (כְּ) stallion, out of greediness Jr 50_{11}. 3. cry (shrilly), in distress Is 10_{30}. → מִצְהָלָה *neighing*.

צהל II 1 vb.—Hi. 1 Inf. cstr. הַצְהִיל—of Y., light up face Ps 104_{15}.

צהר I 1 vb.—Hi. 1 Impf. יַצְהִירוּ—press oil Jb 24_{11}. → יִצְהָר I *oil*.

*צהר II 0.1 vb.—Hi. 0.1 Inf. cstr. הצהיר—reach noontime, shine at noon, of the sun Si 43_3.

צֹהַר I 1 n.f. roof of ark Gn 6_{16}.

*צֹהַר II 1 n.f. skylight of ark Gn 6_{16}.

צָהֳרַיִם 23 n.[m.].du.—צָהֳרַיִם—1. noon, midday Ca 1_7, noonday sun Ps 37_6. 2. as adv., at noon Ps 55_{18}.

*צוֹ 0.0.1 n.[m.] excrement(s) 4QHalakhahC$_2$. → cf. צֵא *filth*, צֵאָה *excrement*, צֹאָה *filth*, צֹאִי *filthy*.

צַו I 8.0.4 n.[m.]—צָו—term of unknown meaning, perh. exclamation, *blah!* or *ho!*, *hey!*, less prob. *precept* Is 28_{10}.

צַו II 1 n.[m.] (byform of שָׁוְא)—צָו—vanity Ho 5_{11}.

צוֹא, see צוה *command*.

צוֹאִים, see צֹאִי *filthy*.

צַוָּאר 41.1.4 n.[m.]—Q צור; cstr. צַוַּאר; sf. צַוָּארָם (צַוְּרָם); pl.

cstr. צַוְּארֵי; sf. צַוְּרֹתֵיכֶם—**1. neck, nape** of human Ca 1_{10}. **2. neck** of animal Jb 39_{19}. → cf. צַוָּרוֹן *necklace.*

צוֹבָא, see צוֹבָה I *Zobah.*

צוֹבָה I $_{13}$ pl.n. **Zobah.**

צוֹבָה II, see חֲמַת צוֹבָה *Hamath-zobah.*

צוד I $_{17.0.2}$ vb.—**Qal** $_{13.0.2}$ Pf. צָדוּ; impf. תְּצוּדֵנִי, יָצוּד; impv. צוּדָה; ptc. צָד; inf. abs. צוֹד; cstr. צוּד—**hunt (and catch)** game Gn 27_3, **hunt (for), hound (and trap)** people Jr 16_{16}, **chase (after)** man, of woman Pr 6_{26}, **chase** person's steps, i.e. stalk with evil intent Lm 4_{18}.

Pol. $_4$ Impf. תְּצוֹדֵדְנָה; ptc. מְצֹדְדוֹת; inf. cstr. צוֹדֵד—**hunt for, hound** lives Ezk 13_{18}.

→ צַיִד I *hunter,* צֵידָה II *hunting,* צַיִד *hunting, game,* מָצוֹד I *net,* מְצוֹדָה I *net,* מְצוּדָה I *net, prey.*

צוד II, see ציד *take along as provision.*

צוה $_{494.5.77.3}$ vb.—**Pi.** $_{485.4.77.3}$ Pf. צִוָּה (צִוַּנִי), צִוִּתָה (צִוִּתָה), צִוִּיתָה (צִוִּיתָה) צִוִּית; impf. יְצַוֶּה (יְצַו); + waw וַיְצַוּוּ; impv. צַו (צַוֵּה), צַוּוּ; ptc. מְצַוֶּה (Q מצוא); inf. cstr. צַוּוֹת—**1. command,** with double accus. of thing and person, הַתּוֹרָה אֲשֶׁר צִוִּיתִי אֶת־אֲבֹתֵיכֶם *the law which I commanded your forefathers* 2 K 17_{13}. **2. command,** with double accus. of thing (with further addition) and person, e.g. כָּל־הַדְּבָרִים אֲשֶׁר צִוִּיתִיךָ לְדַבֵּר אֲלֵיהֶם *all the words which I commanded you to speak to them* Jr 26_2. **3. command, instruct,** with sg. accus. of person, with command expressed in following clause, וַיְצַו יוֹסֵף אֶת־עֲבָדָיו אֶת־הָרֹפְאִים לַחֲנֹט אֶת־אָבִיו *then Joseph instructed his servants who were physicians to embalm his father* Gn 50_2. **4. command, instruct,** with sg. accus. of person, in sub-clause beginning with כַּאֲשֶׁר *as,* בָּאוּ אֶל־נֹחַ ... כַּאֲשֶׁר צִוָּה אֱלֹהִים אֶת־נֹחַ *they came to Noah ... as God commanded Noah* Gn 7_9. **5. command,** with sg. accus. of person, with command expressed in previous clause, ... אִם אֶת־הַדָּבָר הַזֶּה תַּעֲשֶׂה וְצִוְּךָ אֱלֹהִים *if you do this (thing)—and God (so) commands you—then ...* Ex 18_{23}. **6. command, decree,** with sg. accus. of thing, וַיַּעֲשׂוּ כֹּל אֲשֶׁר־צִוָּה הַמֶּלֶךְ *and they did everything that the king commanded* 2 S 21_{14}. **7. command,** with sg. accus. of thing, with further addition, כול חוקיו אשר צוה לעשות *all his statutes which he commanded (them) to do* 1QS 5_{22}. **8. command, instruct,** with omission of accus. of person, with command expressed in following clause, וַיְצַו יוֹסֵף וַיְמַלְאוּ אֶת־כְּלֵיהֶם בָּר *then Joseph commanded that they fill their containers with grain* Gn 42_{25}. **9. command, instruct,** with omission of accus. of person, in sub-clause beginning with כַּאֲשֶׁר *as,* וַיּוֹשֵׁב יוֹסֵף אֶת־אָבִיו ... כַּאֲשֶׁר צִוָּה פַרְעֹה *so Joseph settled his father ... as Pharaoh had commanded* Gn 47_{11}. **10. command, instruct,** with omission of accus. of person, in sub-clause beginning with כֵּן *thus,* עַבְדֵי הַמֶּלֶךְ ... מִשְׁתַּחֲוִים לְהָמָן כִּי־כֵן צִוָּה־לוֹ הַמֶּלֶךְ *the servants of the king ... bowed down to Haman, for thus the king had commanded concerning him* Est 3_2. **11. command** (to) someone, with command expressed in following clause, וַיְצַו דָּוִיד לְכָל־שָׂרֵי יִשְׂרָאֵל לַעְזֹר לִשְׁלֹמֹה בְנוֹ *David also commanded (to) all the princes of Israel to support Solomon his son* 1 C 22_{17}. **12. command** (to) someone, in sub-clause beginning with כַּאֲשֶׁר *as,* כַּאֲשֶׁר צִוָּה י׳ אֶל־מֹשֶׁה וַיַּנִּיחֵהוּ אַהֲרֹן לִפְנֵי הָעֵדֻת *as Y. had commanded (to) Moses, (so) Aaron placed it in front of the Testimony* Ex 16_{34}. **13a. give** someone **commandments, instructions,** with sg. accus. of person, הָאֲבָנִים הָאֵלֶּה אֲשֶׁר אָנֹכִי מְצַוֶּה אֶתְכֶם הַיּוֹם *these stones concerning which I give you instructions today* Dt 27_4. **b. give** the clouds **orders,** i.e. make them give rain Ps 78_{23}, **give** the morning **orders,** i.e. cause it to break Jb 38_{12}. **14. give orders, give instructions** to someone, אֲנִי צִוֵּיתִי לִמְקֻדָּשָׁי *I have given orders to my holy ones* Is 13_3. **15. give commandments, instructions,** abs., הַיּוֹם אֲשֶׁר צִוָּה י׳ *the day on which Y. gave (the) commandments* Nm 15_{23}. **16. lay (as) a charge** upon someone or **command** + עַל introducing obj., with the command expressed in the following clause, וצוה עליו וילןמד] עד שנה תמימה *and he will lay as a charge upon him,* or *and he will command him, to study for a full year* CD 15_{14}. **17. lay as a charge** upon someone or **command** + עַל introducing obj., in sub-clause beginning with כַּאֲשֶׁר *as,* אֵין אֶסְתֵּר מַגֶּדֶת מוֹלַדְתָּהּ וְאֶת־עַמָּהּ כַּאֲשֶׁר צִוָּה עָלֶיהָ *Esther had not made known her kindred and her people, as he had laid as a charge upon her* or *as he had commanded her* Est 2_{20}. **18. lay a charge** upon lightning (or **command** + עַל introducing obj.), i.e. make it strike Jb 36_{32}. **19. enjoin, impose** upon someone commandment, oath, covenant Nm 36_{13}. **20a. order** someone **to convey a message,** i.e. send as messenger Jr 27_{4}; **b.** elliptical (with omission of obj.) Gn 50_{16}. **21. order to come, summon** someone Arad ost. 3_{2}. **22. appoint, commission** someone as leader 1 K 13_{5}. **23. ordain, determine, predestine** former event Is 48_{5}, blessing Lv 25_{21}, judgment Ps 7_{7}. **24. marshal** celestial bodies, of Y. Is 45_{12}. **25.** ptc. as noun, **commander** Is 55_{4}.

Pu. 9.1 Pf. צֻוֵּיתָה, צֻוָּה; impf. יְצֻוֶּה—**be told, commanded, instructed** Ezk 12_{7}.

→ מִצְוָה *commandment*; cf. יצה *give last injunctions*.

צוהב, see צָהֹב *gleaming*.

צוח 1 vb.—**Qal** 1 Impf. יִצְוָחוּ—**shout loudly** Jos 15_{18}. → צְוָחָה *outcry*.

צְוָחָה 4 n.f.—cstr. צִוְחַת; sf. צִוְחָתֵךְ—**outcry** Jr 14_{2}. → צוח *shout loudly*.

צוחות, see צח I *glowing, clear*.

*[**צְוָיָה**] 0.0.1 n.f. perh. **burial mark** 3QTr 8_{14}. → cf. צִיּוּן *marker*.

צול, see צלל II *sink*.

צוּלָה 1 n.f. **depths of the sea** Is 44_{27}.

צום 21.0.2 vb.—**Qal** 21.0.2 Pf. צַמְתָּ; impf. יָצֻמוּ, אָצוּם; + waw וָנָצוּמָה, וַיָּצֻמוּ, (וַיָּצוֹם) וַיָּצָם; impv. Q צוּם; ptc. צָם; inf. abs. צוֹם—**1. fast, abstain from food** 2 S 12_{21}, at times **abstain from drink** Est 4_{16}. **2.** with obj., **fast for Y.** Zc 7_{5}. **3.** with צוֹם as obj., **hold a fast** 2 S 12_{16}. → צוֹם *fast*.

צוֹם 26.0.4 n.m.—cstr. צוֹם; sf. צֹמְכֶם; pl. צֹמוֹת; cstr. Q צומי—**1. (day of) fast, period or act of fasting** Est 4_{3}. **2. restraint of pit/hell** 4QBéat 15_{7}. → צום *fast*.

צון, see צֹאן *flock*.

*[**צוֹנֶם**] 0.0.1 n.[m.] **granite** 4QCrypt 1.2_{2}.

צוּעָר 5 pr.n.m. **Zuar.**

צוֹעַר, see צֹעַר *Zoar*.

צוף 3.2.2 vb.—**Qal** 1.0.1 Pf. צָפוּ; ptc. Q צף—**flow,** of waters Lm 3_{54}.

Hi. 2.2.1 Pf. הֵצִיף; + waw וַיָּצֶף—**1. cause waters to flow** Dt 11_{4}. **2. make iron float** 2 K 6_{6}. **3. overflow,** of blessing Si 39_{22}.

צוּף I 2 n.m.—pl. צוּפִים—**(honey)comb** Pr 16_{24}.

צוּף II 2 pr.n.m. **Zuph.**

***צוּף** III 1 pl.n. **Zuph.**

צוֹפַח 2 pr.n.m. **Zophah.**

צוֹפַי 1 pr.n.m. **Zophai.**

צוֹפִים, see רָמָתַיִם צוֹפִים *Ramathaim-zophim*.

צוֹפַר 4 pr.n.m. **Zophar.**

צוץ I 8.1.1 vb.—**Qal** 7.1 Pf. צָץ; impf. יָצִיץ (unless hi.)—**1. (start to) bud, blossom,** of rod Ezk 7_{10}; **flourish, prosper,** of people Ps 92_{8}. **2. gleam,** of crown Ps 132_{18}.

Hi. 7.1.1 Impf. יָצִיץ (unless qal); + waw וַיָּצֵץ—**1a.** intrans., **flourish,** of grass Ps 90_{6}, Israel Is 27_{6}. **b.** with צִיץ as obj., **produce blossom,** of rod Nm 17_{23}. **c.** of Y., **cause plant to produce blossom** 1QH 15_{18}. **2. gleam,** of crown Ps 132_{18}.

→ צִיץ I *flower*, צִיצָה *flower*.

צוץ II 1 vb.—**Hi.** 1 Ptc. מֵצִיץ—**peep from** (מִן) lattice Ca 2_{9}.

צוק I 12.2.2 vb.—**Hi.** 11.1.2 Pf. הֱצִיקַתְנִי (הֱצִיקָתְנִי); impf. יָצִיק; + waw וְהֲצִיקוֹתִי; ptc. מֵצִיק—**1a.** with לְ of obj., **distress, oppress** someone Dt 28_{55}. **b.** ptc. as noun, **oppressor** 4QTime 1.2_{3}. **2.** with לְ of obj., **press** someone **to speak** Jg 16_{16}.

Ho. 1.1 Ptc. מוּצָק—**1. be oppressed** Is 8_{23}. **2.** ptc. as noun, **one oppressed** Si 4_{9}.

→ צוֹק I *distress*, צוּקָה *distress*, מוּצָק II *constraint, distress*, מָצוֹק *distress*, מְצוּקָה *distress*; cf. עוק I *press*.

צוק II 3 vb. (byform of יצק)—**Qal** 3 Pf. צָקוּן; impf. יָצוּק—**1a. pour out** oil Jb 29_{6}. **b. utter whisper** Is 26_{16}. **2. melt** stone/ore **into copper** Jb 28_{2}. → מָצוּק *pillar*.

צוֹק I 1 n.[m.]—cstr. צוֹק—**distress** Dn 9_{25}. → צוק I *distress*.

*[**צוֹק**] II 0.0.2 n.[m.] **gorge** 3QTr 8_{8}.

צוּקָה 3.1.7 n.f.—pl. sf. Q צוקותי—**distress** 4QBéat 2.2_{5}.

→ צוק I *distress*.

צור I 31.0.2 vb. (byform of צרר I)—**Qal** 31.0.2 Pf. צַרְתָּנִי; impf. נָצוּר; + waw וַיָּצַר, וַיָּצֻרוּ; impv. צוּרִי; ptc. צָרִים; inf. cstr. צוּר—**1. confine, secure** silver 2 K 12_{11}. **2a. encircle, besiege** city, (1) with obj. 1 C 20_{1}. (2) עַל of obj. Jr 32_{2}. (3) אֶל of obj. Dt 20_{19}. **b. encircle, hem in** person, (1) with accus. Ps 139_{5}. (2) עַל of obj. Jr 21_{4}. (3) אֶל of obj. 1 S 23_{8}.

→ מָצוֹר I *siege*, מָצוֹר II *fortification*, מְצוּרָה I *fortification*.

צור II 4.0.1 vb. (byform of צרר II)—**Qal** 4.0.1 Impf. תָּצַר (תְּצָרֵם)—**show hostility toward** enemy Ex 23_{22}.

צוּר III 4 vb. (byform of יצר)—**Qal** 4 Impf. Kt אצורך; + waw וַיָּצַר—**1. fashion, shape** metal 1 K 7_{15}. **2.** of Y., **form** embryo in (בְּ) womb Jr $1_{5(Kt)}$. → צוּר II *form,* צוּרָה *shape, design,* צִיר I *image,* מָצוֹר III *creatures.*

צַוָּר, see צַוָּאר *neck.*

צוֹר, see צֹר *Tyre.*

צוּר I 74.5.8.3 n.m.—צֻר; cstr. צוּר; sf. צוּרִי; pl. צוּרִים (צוּרוֹת); cstr. צוּרֵי—**1. rock, cliff, rocky mountain** Nm 23_{9}. **2. block of stone, boulder,** as altar Jg 6_{21}. **3. stone** as part of foundation of house Hb 3_{13} (if em. צַוָּאר *neck*). **4. stone, monument in stone,** for inscriptions Jb 19_{24}. **5.** coll., **small rocks, stones** Jb 22_{24}. **6. stumbling-block** Is 8_{14}. **7a.** of Y., **the Rock,** צוּר יִשְׁעֵנוּ *the Rock of our salvation* Ps 95_{1}. **b.** non-existence of any other **rock** beside Y. Is 44_{8}. **c.** of foreign deity, **rock** Dt 32_{31}. **8.** of Abraham as Israelite ancestor, **rock** Is 51_{1}.

*צוּר II 1.0.2 n.[m.]—sf. Qr צוּרָם; pl. cstr. Q צוּרֵי—**form** of the dead Ps $49_{15(Qr)}$, of spirits 4QShirShabb[f] 19_{4}. → צוּר III *fashion.*

*[צוּר] III 0.0.1 n.[m.] **distress** 4QJub[a] 1_{9}.

*[צוּר] IV 1 n.[m.]—cstr. צוּר—**blade** of sword Ps 89_{44}.

צוּר V 5 pr.n.m. **Zur.**

צוּר VI, see בֵּית־צוּר *Beth-zur.*

צוּר VII, see פְּדָה־צוּר *Pedahzur.*

צוּרָה 4.0.13 n.f.—cstr. צוּרַת; sf. צוּרָתוֹ; pl. Q צורות—**1. shape, figure** of angelic beings 4QShirShabb[f] $19_{5.6.7}$. **2. design** of temple Ezk 43_{11}. → צוּר III *fashion.*

[צַוְּרוֹן] 1 n.[m.]—pl. sf. צַוְּרֹנָיִךְ—**necklace** Ca 4_{9}. → צַוָּאר *neck* + וֹן־ (diminutive).

צוּרִיאֵל 1 pr.n.m. **Zuriel.**

[צוּרִישַׁדַּי] 5 pr.n.m. **Zurishaddai.**

צוֹרֶךְ, see צֹרֶךְ *necessity, need, needfulness.*

*צות I 0.1 vb.—**Pol.** 0.1 Impf. יצותת—**listen carefully** Si 14_{23}.

*צות II 1 vb. (byform of יצת)—**Hi.** 1 Impf. אֲצִיתֶנָּה—of Y., **set on fire** thorn-bush, weeds Is 27_{4}.

צַח I 4.0.1 adj.—f.pl. צַחוֹת (1QIsa[a] צוחות)—**1. glowing, scorching, searing,** of heat Is 18_{4}, wind Jr 4_{11}. **2. radiant,** of beloved Ca 5_{10}. **3.** masc. sg. as noun, **shiny, smooth rock** 3QTr 12_{10}. **4.** fem. pl. as noun, **clear words, eloquent speech** Is 32_{4}. → צחח *be dazzling.*

*[צַח] II 0.0.0.1 pr.n.[m.] **Zah,** calendar-month, prob. in summer Arad ost. 20_{2}. → צחח *be dazzling.*

צְחָא, see צִיחָא *Ziha.*

*צחה I 0.0.3 vb.—**Qal** 0.0.3 Impf. יצחה, אצחך—**scoff** 1QS 7_{4}.

*צחה II 0.0.3 vb.—**Qal** 0.0.3 Impf. יצחה—**accuse** 1QS 7_{4}.

[צִחֶה] 1.0.1 adj.—cstr. צִחֵה (Q צחי)—**parched,** of people Is 5_{13} (+ צָמָא *[with] thirst*).

צחח 1 vb.—**Qal** 1 Pf. צַחוּ—**be dazzling,** of prince Lm 4_{7}. → צַח I *glowing, clear,* II *Zah,* צְחִיחַ *shining surface,* צְחִיחָה *sun-scorched land,* צַחְצָחוֹת *sun-scorched regions.*

*[צְחִיאָה] 0.0.1 n.f.—cstr. צחיאת—**parched land** 3QTr 9_{15}.

[צְחִיחַ] 5 n.[m.]—cstr. צְחִיחַ; pl. Kt צחחיים (Qr צְחִיחִים)—**1. shining, bare surface** Ezk 24_{7}. **2.** pl., **open places,** perh. **bare rocks** Ne 4_{7}. → צחח *be dazzling.*

צְחִיחָה 1 n.f. **sun-scorched land** Ps 68_{7}. → צחח *be dazzling.*

[צַחֲנָה] 1.1 n.f.—sf. צַחֲנָתוֹ—**stink** Jl 2_{20}.

צַחְצָחוֹת 1 n.f.pl. **sun-scorched regions** Is 58_{11}. → צחח *be dazzling.*

צחק 13 vb. (byform of שׂחק, סחק)—**Qal** 6 Pf. צָחֲקָה, צָחַקְתְּ; impf. יִצְחַק—**laugh (mockingly),** in disbelief Gn 17_{17}; **laugh (with joy)** together with (לְ) someone, or perh. **laugh (mockingly)** at (לְ) someone Gn 21_{6}.

Pi. 7 + waw וַיְצַחֵק; ptc. מְצַחֵק; inf. cstr. צַחֵק (צַחֶק)—**1.** with בְּ of obj., **mock** someone Gn 39_{14}. **2. have sexual pleasure with** (אֵת or בְּ) woman Gn 26_{8} 39_{17}. **3. revel** Ex 32_{6}. **4. perform to cause amusement,** before (לִפְנֵי) people Jg 16_{25}. **5.** ptc. as noun, **one who jests** Gn 19_{14}. → צְחֹק *laughter;* cf. סחק *laugh,* שׂחק *laugh.*

צְחֹק 2 n.[m.] **1. laughter** Gn 21_{6}. **2. object of mockery** Ezk 23_{32}. → צחק *laugh.*

[צָחֹר] 1 adj.—f.pl. צְחֹרוֹת—**tawny,** of ass Jg 5_{10}.

[צַחַר] I 1 n.[m.]—צַחַר—**tawny colour,** of wool Ezk 27_{18}.

*[צַחַר] II 1 pl.n. **Zahar.**

צֹחַר 5 pr.n.m. **Zohar.**

צִי I 5 n.m.—pl. צִיִּים (צִים)—**ship** Dn 11_{30}.

[צִי] II 6.0.2 n.m.—pl. צִיִּים—**inhabitant of the desert,**

animal Is 13$_{21}$, person Ps 74$_{14}$.
ציא, see צִיָּה *dry land, dryness.*
צִיבָא 16 pr.n.m. **Ziba.**
*__צִיד__ 1 vb.—**Htp.** 1 הִצְטַיָּדְנוּ—**take bread along as provision** Jos 9$_{12}$. → צַיִד II *provision of food,* צֵידָה I *provision (of food).*
[צַיָּד] I 1.0.1 n.m.—pl. צַיָּדִים—**hunter** 1QH 13$_{8}$. → צוד I *hunt.*
*__[צַיָּד]__ II 0.0.0.1 pr.n.m. **Zayad.**
צַיִד I 14.0.1 n.m.—Qr צֵיד; cstr. צֵיד—**1. game, venison** Gn 25$_{28}$. **2. catch of game, fish** 11QT 60$_{8}$. **3. prey,** of Israel Jr 30$_{17}$ (if em. צִיּוֹן *Zion* to צֵידֵנוּ *our prey*). **4. hunting** Gn 25$_{27}$. → צוד I *hunt.*
צַיִד II 5 n.[m.]—sf. צֵידוֹ—**provision of food** Jos 9$_{5}$. → ציד *take along as provision.*
צֵידָה I 10.0.2 n.f.—צֵדָה—**provision (of food),** esp. for a journey Gn 42$_{25}$. → ציד *take along as provision.*
*__[צֵידָה]__ II 0.0.1 n.f.—cstr. צדת—**hunting** 4QTime 1.2$_{3}$. → צוד I *hunt.*
צִידוֹן I 2 pr.n.m. **Sidon.**
צִידוֹן II 20.0.5 pl.n. **Sidon.**
צִידֹנִי 16 gent. **Sidonian.**
צִיָּה 16.0.4 n.f.—Q ציא; pl. צִיּוֹת—**1. dry ground, land, region** Jr 50$_{12}$. **2. dryness** Is 41$_{18}$ (unless §1). **3. drought** Jb 24$_{19}$ (unless §1).
צָיוֹן 2 n.[m.] **dry land** Is 25$_{5}$.
צִיּוֹן 154.4.28.7 pl.n. **Zion.**
צִיּוּן 3 n.m.—pl. צִיֻּנִים—**marker,** i.e. **road marker** Jr 31$_{21}$, **signpost** Ezk 39$_{15}$; **stone as memorial, gravestone** 2 K 23$_{17}$.
צִיחָא 3 pr.n.m. **Ziha.**
צִין, see צִן *Zin.*
צִינֹק 1 n.[m.] **iron collar, neck collar** Jr 29$_{26}$.
צִיעֹר 1 pl.n. **Zior.**
צִיף, see צוּף II *Zuph.*
צִיץ I 14.4.4 n.m.—cstr. צִיץ; pl. צִצִּים (Si ציצים)—**1. flower, blossom** Is 40$_{6}$. **2. flower-shaped decoration, a. flower-ornament** of wood overlaid with gold, on temple-walls, doors 1 K 6$_{18}$. **b. rosette** of gold, on high priest's turban Lv 8$_{9}$. → צוץ I *blossom.*
צִיץ II 1 n.[m.] **wings** Jr 48$_{9}$.
*__צִיץ__ III 1 n.[m.] **salt** Jr 48$_{9}$.
צִיץ IV 1 pl.n. **Ziz.**
*__צִיצָה__ 1 n.f.—cstr. צִיצַת—**flower** Is 28$_{4}$. → צוץ I *blossom.*
צִיצִת 3 n.f.—cstr. צִיצִת—**1. tassel** Nm 15$_{38}$. **2. lock of hair** Ezk 8$_{3}$.
צִיקְלַג, see צִקְלַג *Ziklag.*
*__ציר__ 1 vb.—**Htp.** 1 + waw וַיִּצְטַיָּרוּ—**act as envoy** Jos 9$_{4}$. → צִיר II *envoy, messenger.*
[צִיר] I 2 n.m.—sf. Kt צירם; pl. צִירִים—**1. image, figure** of the dead Ps 49$_{15(Kt)}$. **2. idol** Is 45$_{16}$. → צור III *fashion.*
צִיר II 6.0.1 n.m.—pl. צִירִים; sf. צִרַיִךְ—**envoy** Ob 1$_{1}$. → ציר *act as envoy.*
[צִיר] III 5.0.3 n.[m.]—pl. צִירִים; cstr. צִירֵי; sf. צִירַי—**pang, (labour-)pain** Is 21$_{3}$.
[צִיר] IV 1 n.[m.]—sf. צִירָהּ—**hinge,** of door Pr 26$_{14}$.
צֵל 53.1.5 n.m.&f.—cstr. צֵל; sf. צִלִּי; pl. צְלָלִים; cstr. צִלְלֵי—**1a. shadow** of mountains Jg 9$_{36}$. **b. evening shadow(s),** i.e. evening darkness Jr 6$_{4}$. **c. fleeting shadow,** of transitoriness of life Ps 102$_{12}$, bodily organs Jb 17$_{7}$. **2. shadow, shade,** of tree Jon 4$_{5}$, cloud Is 4$_{6}$, **shelter** of house Gn 19$_{8}$, Y.'s wings Ps 17$_{8}$, **covering** of eggs by snake, bird Is 34$_{15}$, **protection** of money Ec 7$_{12}$, wisdom Ec 7$_{12}$, Y. Ho 14$_{8}$; appar. **protector,** יי צִלְּךָ עַל־יַד יְמִינֶךָ *Y. is your protector at your right hand* Ps 121$_{5}$. → צלל III *grow dark;* cf. צַלְמָוֶת *shadow of death.*
*__[צִלָּא]__ 0.0.0.2 pr.n.[m.] **Zalla.**
צלה 3 vb.—**Qal** 3 Impf. אֶצְלֶה, יִצְלֶה; inf. צְלוֹת—**roast** meat 1 S 2$_{15}$. → צָלִי *roasted;* cf. צלח III *set ablaze.*
*__[צִלָּה]__ I 0.0.1 n.f.—sf. צלתנו—**shelter** 4QRitMar 6$_{6}$. → צלל III *grow dark.*
צִלָּה II 3 pr.n.m. **Zillah.**
[צְלוֹל] 1 n.m.—cstr. Kt צלול (Qr צְלִיל)—**loaf** Jg 7$_{13}$.
צלח I 10 vb.—**Qal** 10 Pf. צָלְחוּ; impf. יִצְלַח; + waw וְצָלְחָה—**1a.** with obj., of Y., **rush upon place** Am 5$_{6}$. **b.** with prep., of spirit, **come in power upon** (עַל or אֶל) person Jg 14$_{6}$ 1 S 16$_{13}$. **2. rush through** river 2 S 19$_{18}$. **3. rush towards** river 2 S 19$_{18}$ (unless §2).
צלח II 55.7.8 vb.—**Qal** 15.3.3 Pf. צָלֵחָה; impf. יִצְלַח—**1. prosper, advance,** of (ways of) people Jr 12$_{1}$ Ps 45$_{5}$; **flourish,** of plant Ezk 17$_{9}$; **succeed, be successful,** of people Ezk 17$_{15}$, weapon Is 54$_{17}$, **be successfully accom-**

plished, of plan, will Is 53₁₀. **2. be useful, be good** for (לְ) work, of wood Ezk 15₄, for (לְ) anything, of girdle Jr 13₇. **3. give, bring success,** of Y.'s favour Si 11₁₇.

Hi. 40.4.5 Pf. הִצְלִיחַ; impf. יַצְלִיחַ; + waw וַיַּצְלַח;וְהִצְלַחְתָּ —**1a.** trans., **make prosper(ous), successful,** obj. person 2 C 26₅, deeds Gn 39₃, path Jos 1₈; **make prevail, prevalent,** obj. deceit Dn 8₂₅. **b. give prosperity, grant success to** (לְ) person Ne 1₁₁; abs. Ps 118₂₅. **2.** trans., **successfully accomplish** work planned 2 C 7₁₁. **3a.** intrans., **prosper, be successful,** of person 11QT 58₂₁, deeds Ps 1₃, **be successfully accomplished,** of Y.'s word Is 55₁₁, will Si 39₁₈. **b.** ptc. as noun, **successful person** Si 9₁₂.

→ מַצְלַחַת *success.*

*צלח **III** 1.1 vb.—**Qal** 1.1 Impf. יִצְלַח—**set house ablaze** Am 5₆. → צֵלָחָה *pot;* cf. צלה *roast.*

[צְלָחָה] 1 n.[f.]—pl. צְלָחוֹת—**pot for cooking** 2 C 35₁₃. → צלח III *set ablaze.*

צְלֹחִית 1 n.f. **jar** 2 K 2₂₀.

צַלַּחַת 3 n.f.—צַלַּחַת—**dish** 2 K 21₁₃.

צָלִי 3 adj.—cstr. צְלִי—**1. roasted,** of meat Ex 12₈. **2.** as noun, **roasted meat** Is 44₁₆. → צלה *roast.*

צְלִיל, see צְלוּל *loaf.*

צלל **I** 4 vb.—**Qal** 4 Pf. צָלְלוּ; impf. תְּצִלֶּינָה (תְּצִלֶּינָה)—**1. tingle,** of ear 1 S 3₁₁. **2. quiver,** of lip Hb 3₁₆. → צְלָצַל *whirring locust,* צִלְצַל I *whirring,* (?) צִלְצַל II *spear,* צֶלְצְלִים *cymbals,* מְצִלָּה *bell,* מְצִלְתַּיִם *cymbals.*

צלל **II** 1 vb.—**Qal** 1 Pf. צָלְלוּ—**sink in** (בְּ) **water** Ex 15₁₀. → מְצוֹלָה *depth.*

צלל **III** 2.0.2 vb.—**Qal** 1 Pf. צָלְלוּ—**grow dark,** of gate Ne 13₁₉.

Pu. 0.0.1 Ptc. מצולי—ptc. as noun, **shade** of forests 4QBerª 5₃.

Hi. 1.0.1 + waw Q ויצל; ptc. מֵצַל—**give shade,** with צֵל as obj. 1QH 14₁₅; abs. Ezk 31₃.

→ צֵל *shadow, protection,* צַלְמָוֶת *shadow of death,* צִלָּה I *shelter.*

*צלל **IV** 0.1 vb.—**Qal** 0.1 Ptc. צולל—**be settled,** of entrails Si 34₂₀.

*[צָלָל] 0.0.0.1 pr.n.[m.] **Zalal.**

צְלָלוֹ, see צֵל *shadow.*

צְלָלֵי, see צֵל *shadow.*

צְלָלִים, see צֵל *shadow.*

צֶלֶם 17.0.3 n.m.—sf. צַלְמוֹ; pl. Q צלמים; cstr. צַלְמֵי; sf. צְלָמָיו —**1a. image, replica** of plague, to avert divine wrath 1 S 6₅. **b. image of a deity** Nm 33₅₂. **c. sexual image** of human male or male deity, or perh. **phallus** assoc. with Canaanite fertility cult Ezk 16₁₇; **erotic painted engraving** of Babylonian men Ezk 23₁₄. **2. image, likeness** of God Gn 1₂₇, human father Gn 5₃. **3. transitory image, silhouette, semblance** Ps 73₂₀.

צַלְמוֹן **I** 1 pr.n.m. **Zalmon.**

צַלְמוֹן **II** 2 pl.n. **Zalmon.**

צַלְמָוֶת 18.0.1 n.[m.] **shadow of death,** rather than **darkness, deep darkness** Ps 23₄. → cf. צֵל *shadow* + מָוֶת *death.*

צַלְמֹנָה 2 pl.n. **Zalmonah.**

צַלְמֻנָּע 12 pr.n.m. **Zalmunna.**

צלע 4.1 vb.—**Qal** 4.1 Ptc. צֹלֵעַ—**1. limp** Gn 32₃₂. **2.** ptc. as noun, **one who is limping** Si 42₅. → צֶלַע *limping.*

צֵלָע 40.0.1 n.m.&f.—cstr. צֵלַע (צֶלַע); sf. צַלְעוֹ; pl. צְלָעִים (צְלָעוֹת); cstr. צַלְעוֹת—**1. side,** of ark Ex 25₁₂, tabernacle Ex 26₂₀, altar Ex 27₇. **2. side-chamber** of temple Ezk 41₉. **3. slope** of mountain 2 S 16₁₃. **4. compass direction, side of north** Ex 26₃₅. **5. rib** of man, ... וַיִּבֶן אֶת־הַצֵּלָע אֲשֶׁר־לָקַח מִן־הָאָדָם לְאִשָּׁה *then he made the rib that he had taken from man into a woman* Gn 2₂₂. **6. plank, board** 1 K 6₁₅. **7. beam** 1 K 7₃. **8. leaf** of door 1 K 6₃₄.

צֵלַע 2 pl.n. **Zela.**

צֶלַע 4.1 n.[m.]—sf. צַלְעִי—**limping, stumbling** Jr 20₁₀. → צלע *limp.*

צֵלַע הָאֶלֶף, see צֵלַע *Zela.*

צָלָף 1 pr.n.m. **Zalaph.**

צְלָפְחָד 11 pr.n.m. **Zelophehad.**

צֶלְצַח 1 pl.n. **Zelzah.**

[צִלְצַל] **I** 1 n.[m.]—cstr. צִלְצַל—**whirring,** of insects' wings Is 18₁. → צלל I *tingle, quiver.*

[צִלְצַל] **II** 1 n.[m.]—cstr. צִלְצַל—**spear, harpoon** Jb 40₃₁. → (?) צלל I *tingle, quiver.*

צְלָצַל 1 n.m. **cricket, whirring locust** Dt 28₄₂. → צלל I *tingle, quiver.*

צֶלְצְלִים 3 n.m.pl.—צֶלְצְלִים; cstr. צִלְצְלֵי—**cymbals** Ps 150₅. → צלל I *tingle, quiver.*

צֶ֫לֶק 2 pr.n.m. **Zelek.**

צִלְּתַי 2 pr.n.m. **Zillethai.**

צמא 10.0.1 vb.—**Qal** 10.0.1 Pf. צָמְאָה, צָמֵאתִי; impf. תִּצְמְאוּ; + waw וְצָמֵת; וַיִּצְמָא—**1a. be thirsty** Ru 2_{9}. **b. thirst for** (לְ) water Ex 17_{3}. **2. thirst, long for** (לְ) Y. Ps 63_{2}. → צָמָא *thirst,* צָמֵא *thirsty,* צִמְאָה *thirst,* צִמָּאוֹן *thirsty waterless ground, region.*

צָמָא 17.0.4 n.[m.]—sf. צְמָאִי—**thirst, 1.** physical Ex 17_{3}. **2.** spiritual, due to lack of knowledge 1QH 12_{11}. → צמא *be thirsty.*

צָמֵא 9.1.3 adj.—f.s. צְמֵאָה; m.pl. צְמֵאִים—**1. thirsty, a.** lacking fluids 2 S 17_{29}. **b.** lacking wisdom's 'nutrition' Si 51_{24}. **2.** as noun, **a. one who is thirsty** 1QH 12_{11}. **b. that which is thirsty, that which is dry,** land Is 44_{3}. → צמא *be thirsty.*

צִמְאָה 1.0.2 n.f.—Q צמה—**thirst** Jr 2_{25}. → צמא *be thirsty.*

צִמָּאוֹן 3.0.1 n.m. **thirsty waterless ground, region** Dt 8_{15}. → צמא *be thirsty.*

צמד 5.0.2 vb.—**Ni.** 3.0.2 + waw וַיִּצָּמֶד; ptc. נִצְמָדִים—**1. join, be (religiously) devoted to** (לְ) Baal-peor Ps 106_{28}. **2.** ptc. as noun, **one who joins, follower** 1QH 13_{24}.

Pu. 1 Ptc. מְצֻמֶּדֶת—of sword, **be bound on** (עַל) loins 2 S 20_{8}.

Hi. 1 Impf. תַּצְמִיד—of tongue, **frame** deceit Ps 50_{19}. → צֶמֶד *couple, pair,* צָמִיד I *bracelet, ring,* II *covering.*

צֶמֶד 15.0.0.1 n.m.—cstr. צֶמֶד; sf. צִמְדּוֹ; pl. צְמָדִים; cstr. צִמְדֵי—**1. couple, pair, yoke (of oxen)** 1 K 19_{19}. **2.** measure of land, like **acre,** orig. appar. what yoke of oxen can plough in day or season Is 5_{10}. **3.** pl. as adv., **together, side by side** 2 K 9_{25}. → צמד *join, bind.*

[צַמָּה] 4 n.f.—sf. צַמָּתֵךְ—**veil,** of woman Ca 4_{1}.

צמה, see צִמְאָה *thirst.*

[צִמּוּק] 4.0.0.1 n.m.—pl. צִמֻּקִים (צִמּוּקִים, I צמקם)—**dried grapes, raisin-cake** 1 S 25_{18}. → צמק *be dry.*

צמח 33.3.10 vb.—**Qal** 15.1.6 Pf. צָמַח; impf. יִצְמַח; ptc. צוֹמֵחַ—**1a. sprout, shoot up,** of seed Ezk 17_{6}, tree Ex 10_{5}. **b.** figuratively, **sprout, spring into being, grow up,** of people analogous to trees Is 44_{4}. **c.** figuratively, **spring up** from (מִן) the ground, of truth Ps 85_{12}, of trouble Jb 5_{6}. **2. grow,** of hair Lv 13_{37}. **3. come about, happen,** of event Is 42_{9}, of healing Is 58_{8}.

Pi. 4 Pf. צִמַּח; impf. יְצַמַּח; inf. cstr. צַמֵּחַ—**be fully grown (again), grow again,** of hair Jg 16_{22}.

Hi. 14.2.4 Pf. Q הצמחתה; impf. יַצְמִיחַ; + waw וְהִצְמִיחָהּ; וַיַּצְמַח—**1a. cause to sprout, bud, grow,** (1) obj. tree, of Y. Gn 2_{9}. (2) obj. thorns, of ground Gn 3_{18}. **b.** two objs., of Y., **cause** mountain **to grow** grass Ps 147_{8}. **2.** figuratively, **cause to sprout, spring up, blossom, bring to fruition,** (1) obj. salvation, desire, of Y. 2 S 23_{5}. (2) obj. vindication, of earth Is 45_{8}. **3.** abs., **produce, be fruitful,** of land Dt 29_{22}.

→ צֶמַח I *sprout, growth.*

צֶמַח I 12.2.6 n.m.—cstr. צֶמַח; sf. צִמְחָהּ; pl. Si צמחים; cstr. Si, Q צמחי—**1. growth, vegetation, crops** Si 40_{22}, specif. **foliage** of vine Ezk 17_{9}. **2. (process of) growth,** of vine Ezk 17_{9} (unless §1). **3. Branch, Shoot,** of future (Davidic) messiah Zc 6_{12} 4QMidrEschat^{a} 3_{11}. → צמח *sprout, grow.*

*[צֶמַח] II 0.0.0.1 pr.n.m. **Zemach.**

צָמִיד I 6.0.3 n.m.—pl. צְמִידִים (צמדים)—**1. bracelet** Gn 24_{22}. **2. (embossed) ring,** decoration on spear 1QM 5_{7}. → צמד *join.*

צָמִיד II 1 n.[m.] **covering,** of container Nm 19_{15}. → צמד *join.*

צַמִּים 2.0.2 n.m.pl.—cstr. Q צמי—**snare(s)** Jb 18_{9} 1QH fr. 3_{8}.

צְמִיתֻת 2 n.f.—צְמִתֻת—**perpetuity** Lv 25_{30}. → צמת *put an end to.*

צמק 1 vb.—**Qal** 1 Ptc. צֹמְקִים—**be dry,** of breasts not lactating Ho 9_{14}. → צִמּוּק *dried grapes.*

צֶמֶר 16.0.4 n.m.—צֶמֶר; sf. צַמְרִי—**wool** Is 1_{18}.

צְמָרִי 2 gent. **Zemarite.**

צְמָרַיִם 2 pl.n. **Zemaraim.**

[צַמֶּרֶת] 5 n.f.—sf. צַמַּרְתּוֹ—**tree-top** Ezk 17_{3}.

צמת 15 vb.—**Qal** 1 Pf. צָמְתוּ—**put an end to** life Lm 3_{53}.

Ni. 2 Pf. נִצְמַתוּ—**vanish,** of person Jb 23_{17}, river Jb 6_{17}.

Pi. 2 Pf. צִמְּתַתְנִי—of zeal, **annihilate, consume** someone Ps 119_{139}.

Pilel 1 Pf. צִמְּתוּתֻנִי—of terror, **annihilate, consume** someone Ps $88_{17(L)}$.

Hi. 10 Pf. הִצְמַתָּה; impf. אַצְמִית—**1. annihilate** someone, of Y. Ps 54_{7}, of human 2 S 22_{41}. **2.** ptc. as noun,

destroyer Ps 69_{5}.
→ צְמִיתֻת *perpetuity.*

צְמִתֻת, see צְמִיתֻת *perpetuity.*

[צֵן] 2 n.[m.]—pl. צִנִּים—**thorn** Pr 22_{5}. → cf. צָנִין *thorn.*

צִן 10.0.1 pl.n. **Zin.**

צֹנֶא, see צֹנֶה *flock.*

***צֹנָא** 1 n.[m.]—pl. צֹנִים—**basket** Pr 22_{5}.

צֹנֶה 2 n.[m.]—sf. צֹנַאֲכֶם—**flock** Nm 32_{24}. → cf. צאן *flock.*

[צִנָּה] I 1 n.f.—pl. צִנּוֹת—**hook** Am 4_{2}.

[צִנָּה] II 1.1 n.f.—cstr. צִנַּת (Si צינת)—**cold** Pr 25_{13}.

[צִנָּה] III 21.2.1 n.f.—pl. צִנּוֹת—**shield,** larger than מָגֵן 1 K 10_{17}‖2 C 9_{16} Am 4_{2}.

*** [צִנָּה]** IV 1 n.f.—pl. צִנּוֹת—**rope** Am 4_{2}.

*** [צִנָּה]** V 1 n.f.—pl. צִנּוֹת—**basket** Am 4_{2}.

צָנוּעַ 1.2 adj. **1. humble** Si 34_{22}. **2.** as noun, **humble person** Pr 11_{2}. → צנע *be humble.*

צָנוֹף, see צָנִיף *turban.*

צִנּוֹר 2 n.m.—pl. sf. צִנּוֹרֶיךָ—**water spout, channel** 2 S 5_{8}, **waterfall** Ps 42_{8}.

צנח 3 vb.—**Qal** 3 + waw וַתִּצְנַח—**1. dismount from** (מֵעַל) ass Jos 15_{18}. **2. go down into** (בְּ) ground Jg 4_{21}.

[צָנִין] 2 n.[m.]—pl. צְנִנִים (צְנִינִם)—**thorn** Nm 33_{55}. → cf. צֵן *thorn.*

צָנִיף 5.3 n.m.—cstr. Qr צְנִיף (Kt צנוף); pl. צְנִיפוֹת—**turban,** of high priest Zc 3_{5}, king Si 11_{5}, woman Is 3_{23}. → צנף *whirl around.*

צנם 1 vb.—**Qal** 1 Ptc. pass. צְנֻמוֹת—**harden,** pass., **be hardened,** of grain Gn 41_{23}.

צְנָן 1 pl.n. **Zenan.**

צנע 1.2.10 vb.—**Hi.** 1.2.10 Inf. abs. הַצְנֵעַ; cstr. Q הצניע—**1a. be modest, act with humility** Mc 6_{8}. **b. be modest about** insight Si 35_{3}. **2. be discreet about,** i.e. keep private, work 4Q424 1_{6}. → צָנוּעַ *humble.*

צנף 3 vb.—**Qal** 3 Impf. יִצְנֹף (יִצְנְפְךָ)—**1.** בְּ of obj., **wind turban around (one's head)** Lv 16_{4}. **2. whirl** person **around** Is 22_{18}. → צְנֵפָה *whirling,* צָנִיף *turban,* מִצְנֶפֶת *turban.*

צְנֵפָה 1 n.f. **whirling** Is 22_{18}. → צנף *whirl around.*

צִנְצֶנֶת 1 n.f. **jar** Ex 16_{33}.

צַנְתְּרוֹת 1 n.m.pl. **pipes,** of oil-lamps, צַנְתְּרוֹת הַזָּהָב *pipes of gold* Zc 4_{12}.

צעד 8.1.6 vb.—**Qal** 7.1.6 Pf. צָעֲדָה; impf. תִּצְעַד; inf. cstr. צַעֲדְךָ—**1a.** intrans., **march, walk** Ps 68_{8}. **b.** with צַעַד as obj., **walk, take (a step)** 2 S 6_{13}. **c.** with דֶּרֶךְ as obj., **walk, take (the road)** Pr 7_{8}. **2. climb over** (עַל) wall Gn 49_{22}. **3. stray from** (מִן) commandment 1QS 1_{13}.

Hi. 1 Impf. תַּצְעִדֵהוּ—**make** someone **march** Jb 18_{14}.

→ מִצְעָד *step,* צַעַד *step,* צְעָדָה I *marching, anklet.*

צַעַד 14.2.9 n.m.—צַעַד; sf. צַעֲדְךָ; pl. צְעָדִים—**(foot)step, tread,** almost alw. of human, oft. in ref. to course of life 1QS 11_{10}, of animal Pr 30_{29}. → צעד *march.*

צְעָדָה I 3 n.f. **1. marching** 2 S 5_{24}. **2. anklet** Is 3_{20}. → צעד *march.*

[צְעָדָה] II 1 n.f.—pl. צְעָדוֹת—**armband** Is 3_{20}.

צעה 5 vb.—**Qal** 4 Ptc. צֹעָה, צֹעִים—**1. bend** Is 63_{1}. **2. lie sprawled,** in sexual intercourse Jr 2_{20}. **3.** ptc. as noun, **a. one who is crouching,** out of fear Is 51_{14}. **b. decanter** Jr 48_{12}.

Pi. 1 + waw וְצֵעֻהוּ—**tilt** Moab Jr 48_{12}.

צָעִיף 3 n.[m.]—sf. צְעִיפָהּ—**veil,** of woman Gn 24_{65}.

צָעִיר I 22.0.5 adj.—sf. צְעִירוֹ; f.s. צְעִרָה; m.pl. צְעִירִים; sf. Kt צעוריה—**1. small, insignificant,** politically Ps 68_{28}, socially Ps 119_{141}. **b.** as noun, **insignificant one,** socially, of family 1 S 9_{21}, individual Jg 6_{15}, perh. specif. **servant** Jr 14_{3}, **shepherd-boy** Jr 49_{20}; **small one** in size, of family Is 60_{22}. **2a. young** opp. old Jb 32_{6}. **b.** as noun, **younger one,** within family Gn 19_{31}, **junior** Jb 30_{1}. **3.** as noun, **little one, child** Jr 48_{4}. → צער *be insignificant.*

[צָעִיר] II 1 pl.n. **Zair.**

צְעִירָה 2 n.f.—sf. צְעִרָתוֹ—**1. smallness** Dn 8_{9}. **2. youth** Gn 43_{33}. → צער *be insignificant.*

צען 1 vb.—**Qal** 1 Impf. יִצְעַן—**be moved,** of tent Is 33_{20}.

צֹעַן 7 pl.n. **Zoan.**

צענים, see צַעֲנַנִּים *Zaanannim.*

צַעֲנַנִּים 2 pl.n. **Zaanannim.**

צַעֲצֻעִים 1 n.[m.]pl. **images** 2 C 3_{10}.

צעק 55.1 vb.—**Qal** 47.1 Pf. צָעַק, צָעֲקָה; impf. יִצְעַק; ptc. Si צוֹעֵק, צֹעֶקֶת, צֹעֲקִים—**1. cry out, call out to** (אֶל or לְ) someone, oft. for help, to Y. Ex 8_{8} 2 C 13_{14}, to human being Nm 11_{2}. **2.** abs., **cry (out), call,** in distress Ps 34_{18}. **3.** with cognate accus. (צְעָקָה), **cry (a cry)** Gn 27_{34}. **4. cry out against** violence Jb 19_{7}.

Ni. 6 + waw וַיִּצָּעֲקוּ, וַיִּצָּעֵק—**be called together, summoned** 1 S 13$_4$.

Pi. 1 Ptc. מְצַעֵק—**1. cry loudly** 2 K 2$_{12}$ (unless §2). **2. call out repeatedly** 2 K 2$_{12}$.

Hi. 1 + waw וַיַּצְעֵק—**call together** to (אֶל) Y. 1 S 10$_{17}$.

→ צְעָקָה *cry*; cf. זעק *cry out.*

צְעָקָה 21.3.1 n.f.—cstr. צַעֲקַת; pl. sf. Si צעקתיה—**1. cry,** oft. call for divine help Ex 3$_7$. **2. outcry, indictment** against evil Gn 18$_{21}$. → צעק *cry.*

צער 3.0.1 vb.—**Qal** 3.0.1 Impf. יִצְעָרוּ; ptc. צֹעֲרִים—**1. be insignificant, be humbled** Jr 30$_{19}$. **2.** ptc. as noun, **humble one,** perh. specif. **shepherd-boy** Zc 13$_7$. → צָעִיר I *insignificant, young, little,* צְעִירָה *smallness, youth,* מִצְעָר I *small thing.*

צֹעַר 10 pl.n. **Zoar.**

* **[צַעַר]** 0.1.2 n.m.—pl. Q צערים—**trouble** Si 34$_{20}$.

* **[צָף]** adj. appar. **overlaid,** [צ]ף [זה]ב *overlaid with gold* 11QT 4$_{14}$. → צפה II *overlay.*

צפא, see צפה I *watch.*

צפד 1 vb.—**Qal** 1 Pf. צָפַד—**contract** on (עַל) bones, of skin Lm 4$_8$.

צפה I 35.5.18 vb.—**Qal** 26.4.14 Pf. Si צפתהו, Kt צפו; impf. תִּצְפֶּינָה, יִצֶף; + waw Q ויצפו; ptc. צוֹפֶה, Q צופא, צֹפִים; pass. Qr צְפוּי (Kt צפו)—**1a. keep watch on** (בְּ) nations, of Y.'s eye Ps 66$_7$. **b. oversee activity** Pr 31$_{27}$. **2a. spy on** (לְ) someone Ps 37$_{32}$. **b.** ptc. pass., **be spied out** Jb 15$_{22}$. **3a. look for** (לְ) salvation 1QH 6$_5$. **b. be on the look-out for** (לְ) loopholes in law CD 1$_{18}$. **4.** with לְ of obj., **foresee** violence CD 1$_{18}$. **5.** of building, **(over)look, face** northwards 3QTr 8$_{12}$. **6.** ptc. as noun, **watchman** Is 52$_8$.

Pi. 9.1.4 Pf. צִפִּינוּ; impf. אֲצַפֶּה, Q יצפו; impv. צַפֵּה (Q צפא); ptc. מְצַפֶּה—**1a. watch closely** by roadside Jr 48$_{19}$. **b. watch stars closely, carefully** 4QpsJub^a 2.1$_5$. **c.** with לְ of obj., **observe** ordinance **carefully** 1QS 9$_{25}$. **2. look for** supporter Si 51$_7$. **3. look (with expectation, hope) to** (בְּ or אֶל) someone, to Y. Mc 7$_7$, to nation Lm 4$_{17}$. **4. look, wait (in expectation)** Hb 2$_1$. **5.** ptc. as noun, **sentry** Is 21$_6$.

→ צְפִיָּה *outlook-post,* מִצְפֶּה I *watchtower.*

צפה II 47.0.11 vb.—**Qal** 1 Inf. abs. צָפֹה—**lay out** rug Is 21$_5$.

Pi. 44.0.1 Pf. צִפָּה; impf. תְּצַפֶּה; + waw וַיְצַף ;וְצִפִּיתָ; impv. Q צפו—**overlay** object, oft. with metal Ex 25$_{11}$, wood 1 K 6$_{15}$, **stud** with stones 2 C 3$_6$.

Pu. 2.0.10 Ptc. מְצֻפֶּה, מְצֻפִּים—**1. be overlaid** with gold, of doors 11QT 36$_{11}$. **2. be laid over** (עַל) earthenware, of silver Pr 26$_{23}$.

→ צָף *overlaid,* צִפּוּי *metal plating,* צָפִית *rug,* צֶפֶת *capital.*

[צָפָה] 1 n.f.—sf. צָפָתֵךְ—**outflow** Ezk 32$_6$. → צוף *flow.*

צְפוֹ 3 pr.n.m. **Zepho.**

צִפּוּי 5 n.[m.]—cstr. צִפּוּי—**metal plating** Ex 38$_{17}$. → צפה II *overlay.*

צָפוֹן I 153.2.36 n.f.—צָפֹן; cstr. צְפוֹן—**north, direction of north** Ezk 8$_5$, **north wind** Ca 4$_{16}$, **north-side** Ex 26$_{20}$, **northern territory** Zp 2$_{13}$. → cf. צְפוֹנִי *northern.*

צָפוֹן II 1 pl.n. **Zaphon.**

צְפוֹן I, see צִפְיוֹן *Ziphion.*

צְפוֹן II, see בַּעַל צְפוֹן *Baal-zephon.*

צְפוֹנִי I 1.0.3 adj. **1. northern,** of corner 3QTr 2$_{14}$, opening 3QTr 6$_3$. **2.** as noun, **northerner,** appar. northern army Jl 2$_{20}$ (or em. to הַצִּפְצְפוֹנִי *the chirper*). → cf. צָפוֹן *north.*

צְפוֹנִי II 1 gent. **Zephonite.**

צִפּוֹר I 40.0.6 n.m.&f.—צִפֹּר; cstr. צִפּוֹר; pl. צִפֳּרִים—**bird** Dt 22$_6$; coll., **birds** Ps 8$_9$.

צִפּוֹר II 7 pr.n.m. **Zippor.**

צִפּוֹר III, see בֵּית צִפּוֹר *Beth-zippor.*

צִפּוֹרֶן, see צִפֹּרֶן *nail, stylus-point.*

צַפַּחַת 7 n.f.—cstr. צַפַּחַת—**jug,** for water 1 S 26$_{11}$, oil 1 K 17$_{12}$.

צְפִי, see צְפוֹ *Zepho.*

[צְפִיָּה] 1 n.f.—sf. צְפִיָּתֵנוּ—**outlook-post** Lm 4$_{17}$. → צפה I *watch.*

צִפְיוֹן 2 pr.n.m. **Ziphion.**

צַפִּיחִת 1 n.f. **wafers,** with honey Ex 16$_{31}$.

[צָפִין] 1 n.[m.]—sf. Kt צפינך—**treasure** Ps 17$_{14(Kt)}$. → צפן *treasure up.*

[צָפִיעַ] 1 n.[m.]—pl. cstr. Q צְפִיעֵי (Kt צפועי)—**dung** Ezk 4$_{15}$.

[צְפִיעָה] 1 n.f.—pl. צְפִעוֹת—**offshoot** Is 22$_{24}$.

צָפִיר 6 n.m.—cstr. צְפִיר; pl. cstr. צְפִירֵי—**male goat,** sacrifice Ezr 8$_{35}$, king of Greece Dn 8$_{21}$.

צְפִירָה 3 n.f.—צְפִרָה; cstr. צְפִירַת—**1. circlet** of beauty Is 28_5. **2.** appar. **doom** Ezk 7_7.

צָפִית 1 n.f. **rug** Is 21_5. → צפה II *lay out.*

צפן 32.5.3 vb.—**Qal** 27.0.2 Pf. צָפַן; impf. יִצְפֹּן; ptc. צְפֻנֶיהָ; pass. צָפוּן—**1. save up, keep in store** fruit Ca 7_{14}, blessing Ps 31_{20}; **treasure up** plans in (בְּ) one's heart Jb 10_{13}. **2. close** mind to, lit. from (מִן), understanding Jb 17_4. **3.** perh. **restrain** wind Pr 27_{16}. **4. hide** person Ex 2_2. **5. hide oneself, lie in wait for** (לְ) someone Pr 1_{11}. **6.** of eyes, **watch in secret for** (לְ) hapless one Ps 10_8. **7.** pass., **a. be stored up,** of wealth Pr 13_{22}. **b. be kept on record,** of sin Ho 13_{12}. **c. be fixed,** of day 4QapPsB 31_6. **8.** ptc. as noun, **one who restrains** Pr 27_{16}. **9.** ptc. pass. as noun, **a. treasure** 4QInstr[b] 2.2_5. **b. treasured place,** Jerusalem Ezk 7_{22}. **c. cherished person** Ps 83_4.

Ni. 3.0.1 Pf. נִצְפַּן—**1. be stored up, set,** of time Jb 24_1. **2. be hidden,** of iniquity Jr 16_{17}.

Hi. 3.5 Impf. Si תצפין (תַּצְפִּנֵנִי); ptc. Si מצפין (Si מצפן); inf. cstr. הַצְפִּינוֹ—**1. hide** person Ex 2_3, folly Si $41_{15(B)}$. **2. hide oneself, lie in wait** Ps $56_{7(Kt)}$.

→ מַצְפּוֹן *hidden treasure.*

*[צָפָן] 0.0.0.23 pr.n.m. **Zaphan.**

צְפֹן, see בַּעַל צְפוֹן *Baal-zephon.*

צְפַנְיָה 10.0.0.17 pr.n.m. **Zephaniah.**

צָפְנַת פַּעְנֵחַ 1 pr.n.m. **Zaphenath-paneah.**

צֶפַע 1.0.1 n.m. **poisonous snake** 4QBéat 15_5.

צְפִעָה, see צְפִיעָה *offshoot.*

צִפְעוֹנִי 4.0.1 n.m.—צִפְעֹנִי; pl. צִפְעֹנִים (Q צפעונים)—**poisonous snake** Is 59_5.

צפף 4 vb.—**Pilp.** 4 Impf. אֲצַפְצֵף—**1. chirp,** of bird Is 10_{14}. **2. whisper,** of ghost Is 8_{19}.

צַפְצָפָה 1 n.f. **willow** Ezk 17_5.

צפר 1 vb.—**Qal** 1 Impf. יִצְפֹּר—**depart,** of person Jg 7_3.

צֹפַר, see צוֹפַר *Zophar.*

צִפֹּר I, see צִפּוֹר I *bird.*

צִפֹּר II, see צִפּוֹר II *Zippor.*

צְפַרְדֵּעַ 13.0.1 n.f.—pl. צְפַרְדְּעִים (צֻפַרְדְּעִים)—**frog** Ex 7_{29}.

צִפֹּרָה 3 pr.n.f. **Zipporah.**

צִפֹּרֶן 2.0.2 n.[m.]—pl. sf. צִפָּרְנֶיהָ (Q צפורניה)—**1. nail** on finger, toe Dt 21_{12}. **2. stylus-point** Jr 17_1.

צֶפֶת 1 n.f. **capital,** of pillar 2 C 3_{15}. → צפה II *lay out.*

צְפַת 1 pl.n. **Zephath.**

צְפָתָה 1 pl.n. **Zephathah.**

צִצִּים, see צִיץ I *flower.*

*[צָקוֹן] I 0.0.1 n.[m.] **oppression** 4QDibHam[a] 1.5_{17}.

*[צָקוֹן] II 0.0.1 n.[m.] **pouring out** 4QDibHam[a] 1.5_{17}.

צָקוֹן III, see צוק II *pour out, melt.*

צִקְלַג 15 pl.n. **Ziklag.**

[צִקְלוֹן] 1 n.[m.]—sf. צִקְלֹנוֹ—**sack,** to store grain 2 K 4_{42}.

צַר I 8 adj.—f. sg. צָרָה—**1. narrow, small,** of place Nm 22_{26}. **2. pent-up,** of river Is 59_{19}. **3. tight,** of seal Jb 41_7. **4. meagre, scanty,** of bread Is 30_{20}. **5. limited,** of strength Pr 24_{10}. → צרר I *bind up; be small.*

צַר II 38.0.7 n.[m.]—cstr. צַר; pl. cstr. צָרֵי—**trouble** Jg 11_7, **anguish** Jb 7_{11}; perh. **grief** 2 S 1_{26}. → צרר I *bind up; be distressful.*

צַר III 70.6.10.1 n.m.—sf. צָרִי; pl. צָרִים; cstr. צָרֵי—**enemy, 1.** of Israel Nm 10_9. **2.** of individual 1QH 17_{21}. **3.** of Y. Na 1_2. → צרר II *treat with hostility.*

צַר IV 1 n.[m.] **flint** Is $5_{28(MT)}$.

*[צַר] V 0.0.0.1 n.[m.] **bundle** Arad ost. 3_6. → צרר I *bind up.*

צֵר 1 pl.n. **Zer.**

צֹר I 4 n.[m.]—Q צור; pl. צֻרִים—**flint, sharp-edged stone,** as knife Ex 4_{25}.

צֹר II 42.0.2 pl.n. **Tyre.**

צֻר, see צוּר I *rock.*

צרב 1.0.3 vb.—**Qal** 0.0.3 Pf צרב; ptc. צורב—**burn** 4QInstr[d] 37_3.

Ni. 1 + waw וְנִצְרְבוּ—**be burned,** of face Ezk 21_3.

→ צָרָב *burning,* צָרֶבֶת *inflammation;* cf. צרף *refine.*

צָרָב 1 adj.—f. צָרֶבֶת—**burning,** of fire Pr 16_{27}. → צרב *burn.*

צָרֶבֶת 2 n.f. **inflammation** Lv 13_{23}. → צרב *burn.*

צְרֵדָה 2.0.1 pl.n. **Zeredah.**

צָרָה I 72.7.40 n.f.—poetic form, צָרָתָה; cstr. צָרַת; pl. צָרוֹת—**trouble** Is 33_2, **anguish** 1QH 7_{16}, **groan** of woman in labour Jr 4_{31}. → צרר I *be distressful.*

צָרָה II 1.1 n.f.—sf. צָרָתָהּ—**female rival,** within harem 1 S 1_6. → צרר III *be a rival(-wife).*

*[צָרָה] n.f. **pen,** for animals, of stones Mc 2_{12} (if em. בָּצְרָה *Bozrah* to בַּצָּרָה *inside the pen*).

צְרוּיָה 26 pr.n.f. **Zeruiah.**

צְרוּעָה 1 pr.n.f. **Zeruah.**

צְרוֹר I 8.1.2.1 n.m.—pl. cstr. צְרֹרוֹת—**1. bundle, bag** Gn 42$_{35}$. **2. sealed document** 1 S 25$_{29}$ (unless §1). → צרר I *bind up.*

צְרוֹר II 3 n.m. (byform of צֹר) **pebble** 2 S 17$_{13}$.

צְרוֹר III 1 pr.n.m. **Zeror.**

צרח 3.0.4 vb.—**Qal** 1.0.3 Ptc. צֹרֵחַ—**shout with** (בְּ) **joyful** voice 1QM 12$_{15}$; **scream, cry out** on account of (עַל) disaster 1QH 11$_{33}$.

Hi. 2.0.1 Impf. יַצְרִיחַ—**raise the battle-shout** Is 42$_{13}$.

→ צֶרַח *war-cry.*

*[צֶרַח] n.[m.] **(war-)cry** Jr 4$_{31}$ (if em. צָרָה *desperate cry* to צֶרַח *cry*) Ezk 21$_{27}$ Ps 42$_{11}$ (both if em. בְּרֶצַח *during murder* to בְּצֶרַח *with a cry*). → צרח *shout.*

צֹרִי 5 gent. **Tyrian.**

צֳרִי 6 n.[m.] **balm,** perh. gum of mastic-tree, medicine Jr 8$_{22}$, gift Gn 43$_{11}$.

צְרִי 1 pr.n.m. **Zeri.**

צְרֻיָה, see צְרוּיָה *Zeruiah.*

צְרִיחַ 4.0.5.1 n.m.—pl. צְרִחִים—**crypt** Jg 9$_{46}$.

*[צָרִיךְ] 0.5.5 adj. **1. needy, in want** Si 34$_{4}$. **2. needed, indispensable** Si 35$_{7(B)}$. **3.** as noun, **need, necessity** MurEpJonathan$_{2}$. → צרך *be necessary.*

*צרך 0.1 vb.—**Qal** 0.1 Pf. צרך—**be necessary, be a need** for (לְ) counsellor Si 42$_{21(Bmg)}$. → צֹרֶךְ *need, necessity,* צֹרֶךְ *need,* צָרִיךְ *necessary, needy, needed.*

[צֹרֶךְ] 1.19.1 n.m.—Si צורך, Si צריך; sf. צָרְכְּךָ; pl. sf. Q צורכיהמה—**1. need, necessity,** for sustenance Si 10$_{26}$. **2. needfulness, indispensability,** of physician Si 38$_{1(B)}$. → צרך *be necessary.*

*[צֹרֶךְ] 0.2 n.m.—צרוך—**need** Si 39$_{33(Bmg)}$. → צרך *be necessary.*

צרע 20.0.4 vb.—**Qal** 5.0.3 Ptc. pass. צָרוּעַ—**1.** pass., **be afflicted with a rash** Lv 13$_{44}$. **2.** ptc. pass. as noun, **one afflicted with a rash** 11QT 45$_{17}$.

Pu. 15.0.1 Ptc. מְצֹרָע—**1. be afflicted with a rash, skin disease** Ex 4$_{6}$. **2.** ptc. as noun, **a. one afflicted with a rash, skin disease** 2 K 7$_{3}$. **b. (rash as a result of) skin disease** 2 K 5$_{11}$.

→ צָרַעַת *skin disease.*

צָרְעָה 10 pl.n. **Zorah.**

צִרְעָה I 3 n.f. **hornets** Ex 23$_{28}$ Dt 7$_{20}$ Jos 24$_{12}$.

*צִרְעָה II 3 n.f. **terror** Ex 23$_{28}$ Dt 7$_{20}$ Jos 24$_{12}$.

*צִרְעָה III 3 n.f. **dejection, discouragement** Ex 23$_{28}$ Dt 7$_{20}$ Jos 24$_{12}$.

צָרְעִי 1 gent. **Zorite.**

צָרַעַת 35.0.7 n.f.—cstr. צָרַעַת; sf. צָרַעְתּוֹ—**skin disease,** with scaling as one of its symptoms; not **leprosy** Lv 13$_{51}$. → צרע *be afflicted with a rash.*

צָרְעָתִי 2 gent. **Zorathite.**

צרף 33.0.5.1 vb.—**Qal** 30.0.3.1 Pf. צָרַף; impf. אֶצְרֹף—**1.** of Y., **test, try** (the hearts of) humans Ps 26$_{2}$. **2. refine, purify** heart, thoughts 4QInstr[b] 2.3$_{13}$. **3.** abs., **refine, purge out the wicked** Jr 6$_{29}$. **4. refine (by smelting)** silver Zc 13$_{9}$. **5. smelt away, purge away dross** Is 1$_{25}$. **6. smelt, forge** chain of silver Is 40$_{19}$. **7.** pass., **a. be pure, flawless,** of Y.'s word Ps 18$_{31}$. **b. be refined,** of silver Ps 12$_{7}$. **8.** ptc. as noun, **metal smelter, refiner** Is 40$_{19}$.

Ni. 1.0.1 Impf. יִצָּרְפוּ (Q יצרופו)—**be refined, purified,** of people Dn 12$_{10}$.

Pi. 2 Ptc. מְצָרֵף—ptc. as noun, **smelter, refiner** Ml 3$_{2}$.

Htp. 0.0.1 Impf. יצטרפו—**refine, purify oneself,** of righteous 4QMidrEschat[a] 4$_{4}$.

→ צֹרְפִי *metal smelter(s), refiner(s),* מַצְרֵף *crucible;* cf. צרב *burn.*

צֹרְפִי 1 n.[m.]—pl. mss צרפים—**metal smelter(s), refiner(s)** Ne 3$_{31}$. → צרף *test, refine, smelt.*

צָרְפַת 3 pl.n. **Zarephath.**

צרר I 32.1.1.1 vb.—**Qal** 19.1.0.1 Pf. צָרָה, צָרַר; impf. יֵצֶר; impv. צוֹר (I צרר)—**1. bind, wrap up in** (בְּ) something, obj. Ephraim Ho 4$_{19}$, waters Jb 26$_{8}$, testimony Is 8$_{16}$. **2. be distressful, stressful for** (לְ) someone, oft. in ref. to enmity or hostility Jg 2$_{15}$; **be agitating,** in ref. to unfulfilled sexual desires 2 S 13$_{2}$. **3a. be small, narrow, scant,** of blanket Is 28$_{20}$. **b. be small, cramped,** of Zion Is 49$_{19}$. **c. be shortened, hampered,** of step Pr 4$_{12}$. **4.** pass., **a. be bound up, wrapped up,** of kneading trough Ex 12$_{34}$, life 1 S 25$_{29}$. **b. be bound up, kept on record,** of sin Ho 13$_{12}$. **c. be shut up, confined,** of wife denied sexual intercourse 2 S 20$_{3}$. **5.** ptc. as noun, **one who binds** Pr 26₈ (if em. כִּצְרוֹר *like binding* to כְּצוֹרֵר *like one who binds*). **6.** ptc. pass. as noun, **one who is closed up** of mouth, i.e. keeps it shut Si 26₁₅.

Pu. 1 Ptc. מְצֹרָרִים—**be bound, patched,** of skin bottle Jos 9₄.

Hi. 12.0.1 Pf. Q הצרה; impf. יָצֵר; + waw וְהֵצַר; ptc. מְצֵרָה; inf. cstr. הָצֵר—**1. cause distress, trouble** to (לְ) someone, of Y. Jr 10₁₈, of human enemy Ne 9₂₇. **2.** with לְ of obj., **besiege** people Dt 28₅₂. **3. suffer distress, labour pains** 1QH 11₉.

→ צַר I *narrow, limited,* II *trouble,* V *bundle,* צָרָה I *trouble,* מֵצַר *distress,* צְרוֹר I *bundle.*

צרר II 26.0.6 vb.—**Qal** 26.0.6 Pf. צְרָרוּנִי; impf. יָצֹר; + waw וְצָרְרוּ; ptc. צֹרֵר; inf. abs. צָרוֹר—**1a. treat people with hostility** Nm 10₉. **b. show hostility** toward (לְ) people Nm 25₁₈. **2.** ptc. as noun, **attacker, enemy** Est 9₂₄. → צַר III *enemy.*

צרר III 1 vb.—**Qal** 1 Inf. cstr. צְרֹר—**be a rival(-wife)** Lv 18₁₈. → צָרָה II *female rival.*

[צְרֵרָה] 1 pl.n. **Zererah.**

צֶרֶת 1 pr.n.m. **Zereth.**

צֶרֶת הַשַּׁחַר 1 pl.n. **Zereth-shahar.**

צָרְתָן 3 pl.n. **Zarethan.**

ק

[קָא] 1 n.[m.]—sf. קָאוֹ—**vomit,** of dog Pr 26₁₁. → קִיא *vomit.*

קָאַת 5.0.1 n.[f.]—קָאָת—**pelican,** prohibited as food Lv 11₁₈, perh. **hawk** or **vulture,** קְאַת מִדְבָּר *vulture of the steppe* Ps 102₇.

קַב 1 n.[m.] **kab, 1.** unit of capacity, approx. 2 litres 2 K 6₂₅. **2.** ק abbrev. of קַב City of David ost. 2₁.₂.

קבב 14.1 vb.—**Qal** 14.1 Pf. קַבֹּה; impf. יִקֳּבֶהוּ; inf. קֹב—**curse** people Nm 23₂₅, fool's dwelling Jb 5₃, night of birth Jb 3₈. → cf. נקב II *blaspheme.*

קֵבָה 2.0.3 n.f.—sf. קֵבָתָהּ; pl. Q קבאות—**stomach,** of woman Nm 25₈, animal for sacrifice Dt 18₃.

קֻבָּה 1 n.f. **large tent,** perh. **inner room** or **sanctuary** Nm 25₈.

[קִבּוּץ] 1 n.m.—pl. sf. קִבּוּצַיִךְ—**collection (of images)** Is 57₁₃. → קבץ *gather.*

קְבוּצוֹת*, see עֵין קְבוּצוֹת *En-Kibbuzoth.*

קְבוּרָה 14.0.0.1 n.f. **1. grave, tomb, burial place,** קְבֻרַת־רָחֵל *grave of Rachel* Gn 35₂₀. **2. burial** Is 14₂₀. → קבר *bury.*

קבל 13.8.16 vb.—**Pi.** 11.7.10 Pf. קִבֵּל; impf. נְקַבֵּל; impv. קַבֵּל; ptc. Q מקבל—**1a. receive** wealth Si 34₃, pleasure Si 34₃₍B₎, blessings 11QPsᵃ 22₁₃. **b. accept person** 1 C 12₁₉, instruction Pr 19₂₀ Si 6₁₈. **c. take vessel** Ezr 8₃₀, blood 2 C 29₂₂. **d.** of wisdom, **embrace** like (כְּ) a wife one who fears Y. Si 15₂. **2. undertake, decide, choose** a course of action Est 9₂₃.

Pu. 0.0.2 Impf. יקובל—**be accepted,** of witness CD 9₂₃.

Hi. 2.1.2 Ptc. מַקְבִּילֹת—**1.** of curtain-loops, **be opposite,** perh. **be interlinked,** one to (אֶל) another Ex 36₁₂. **2. be arrayed with** (בְּ) weapons against (אֶל) someone Si 12₅.

Htp. 0.0.2 Impf. יתקבל—of tie (קֶשֶׁר), i.e. receipt issued on payment of rent, **be received by** (לְ) person 5/6ḤevBA 45₂₆.

→ קֹבֶל *battering ram,* קִבְּלָן *in receipt.*

[קֹבֶל] 2 n.[m.]—sf. קָבָלוֹ—**something in front, 1. battering ram** Ezk 26₉. **2.** as prep., קֳבֵל **before,** קָבָל־עָם *before the people* 2 K 15₁₀. → קבל *receive.*

קִבְּלָן* 0.0.3 adj. **in receipt,** of person Mur 22 1₄ Mur 30 1₅ 2₂₂. → קבל *receive.*

קבע 6 vb.—**Qal** 6 Pf. קְבַעֲנוּךָ; impf. יִקְבַּע; ptc. קֹבְעִים—**1a. despoil** Y. Ml 3₈. **b. despoil of, rob of life** Pr 22₂₃. **2.** ptc. as noun, **despoiler** Pr 22₂₃.

קֻבַּעַת 2 n.f. **bowl (of a cup)** Is 51₁₇.₂₂.

קבץ 127.2.15 vb.—**Qal** 38.1.7 Pf. קָבַץ; impf. תִּקְבֹּץ; impv. קִבְצוּ, קִבְצוּ; ptc. קֹבֵץ; ptc. pass. קְבוּצִים; inf. (קָבְצִי)—**1.** trans.,

gather, assemble people, oft. to (אֶל) person or place, of human 1 K 20$_{1}$, of Y. Ezk 22$_{19}$. **2.** trans., **a. gather, collect** food Gn 41$_{35}$, wealth Pr 28$_{8}$. **b.** of heart, **gather, acquire** iniquity Ps 41$_{7}$. **3.** pass., **be gathered** for (עַל) work Ne 5$_{16}$.

Ni. 31.0.4 Pf. נִקְבְּצוּ; impf. תִּקָּבֵץ; impv. הִקָּבְצוּ; ptc. נִקְבָּצִים; inf. הִקָּבֵץ—**1.** intrans., **assemble, gather,** of people 1 S 7$_{6}$, of birds and beasts Ezk 39$_{17}$. **2. be gathered,** of people Jos 10$_{6}$, flock Is 60$_{7}$. **3.** ptc. as noun, **gathered one** Is 56$_{8}$.

Pi. 49.1.4 Pf. קִבְּצָם; impf. אֲקַבֵּץ; impv. קַבְּצֵנוּ; ptc. מְקַבֵּץ; inf. abs. קַבֵּץ; cstr. קַבֵּץ—**1.** oft. of Y., **gather** Israel from (מִן) peoples Dt 30$_{3}$, lambs in (בְּ) his arm(s) Is 40$_{11}$; abs., of Y.'s spirit Is 34$_{16}$. **2a. gather, collect** water Is 22$_{9}$. **b.** of face, **acquire** paleness Jl 2$_{6}$.

Pu. 1 Ptc. מְקֻבֶּצֶת—of land, i.e. its people, **be gathered** from (מִן) peoples Ezk 38$_{8}$.

Htp. 8 Pf. הִתְקַבְּצוּ; impf. יִתְקַבְּצוּ—**gather (together), be gathered (together),** of people Jos 9$_{2}$.

→ קֶבֶץ *gathering,* קִבּוּץ *collection (of images),* קְבֻצָה *assemblage.*

*[קֶבֶץ] 0.0.1 n.[m.] **gathering,** perh. **harvest** 4Q424 1$_{12}$. → קבץ *gather.*

קַבְצְאֵל 3 pl.n. **Kabzeel.**

[קְבֻצָה] 1 n.f. **assemblage,** קְבֻצַת כֶּסֶף *assemblage of silver* Ezk 22$_{20}$. → קבץ *gather.*

קִבְצַיִם 1 pl.n. **Kibzaim.**

קבר 133.0.11 vb.—**Qal** 87.0.11 Pf. קָבַר, קְבָרוּהוּ; impf. יִקְבְּרוּ; + waw וַיִּקְבֹּר; impv. קִבְרוּ, קְבֹר; ptc. קֹבֵר; pass. קָבוּר, קְבֻרִים; inf. abs. קָבוֹר; cstr. לִקְבֹּר (קְבֹר, קָבְרוֹ)—**bury** deceased person in (בְּ) grave with (עִם) ancestors 2 K 9$_{28}$. **2.** pass., **be buried** in (בְּ) grave 1 K 13$_{31}$.

Ni. 39 Impf. יִקָּבֵר—**be buried** with (עִם) ancestors in (בְּ) city of David 1 K 22$_{51}$.

Pi. 6 Impf. תְּקַבְּרֵם; ptc. מְקַבֵּר; inf. cstr. קַבֵּר—**1. bury** several people at once 1 K 11$_{15}$. **2.** ptc. as noun, **one who buries** Ezk 39$_{15}$.

Pu. 1 Pf. קֻבַּר—**be buried** Gn 25$_{10}$.

→ קֶבֶר *grave,* קְבוּרָה *grave.*

קֶבֶר 67.1.9.4 n.m.—cstr. קֶבֶר; sf. קִבְרוֹ; pl. קְבָרִים, קְבָרוֹת; cstr. קִבְרֵי, קִבְרוֹת; sf. קִבְרֹתָיו, קִבְרֵיהֶם—**grave, tomb, burial place,** קֶבֶר אָבִי *grave of my father* 2 S 19$_{38}$. → קבר *bury.*

קִבְרוֹת הַתַּאֲוָה 5 pl.n. **Kibroth-hattaavah.**

*קַד 1 n.[m.] **dried meat** Ps 102$_{4}$.

קדד 15.0.1 vb.—**Qal** 15.0.1 + waw וָאֶקֹּד—**bow, bow down, kneel down,** in worship of Y. Ex 4$_{31}$, in homage to human being, וַיִּקֹּד אַפַּיִם אַרְצָה *and he bowed with his face to the ground* 1 S 28$_{14}$.

*קדה 0.0.1 vb.—**Qal** 0.0.1 Pf. קדה (if not from יקד *be kindled,* or error for קדח *be kindled*)—**be burned** with (בְּ) fire 4QD^{b} 6$_{6}$.

*קְדָה 0.0.1 pl.n. **Kedah.**

קִדָּה 2 n.f. **cassia,** i.e. cinnamon blossom Ex 30$_{24}$.

קְדוּמִים 1.0.1 n.[m.]pl. **ancient ones** Jg 5$_{21}$. → קדם *be in front.*

קְדוֹרַנִּית, see קְדֹרַנִּית *as in mourning.*

קָדוֹשׁ 116.4.113.18 adj.—קָדֹשׁ; cstr. קְדוֹשׁ; sf. קְדוֹשׁוֹ; f.s. Q קדושה; m.pl. קְדוֹשִׁים; cstr. Q קדושי; sf. קְדֹשָׁיו—**1. holy, sacred,** of Y. Is 5$_{16}$, people Dt 7$_{6}$, Levites 2 C 35$_{3}$, spirit 1QS 3$_{7}$, name Si 39$_{35}$, place Lv 6$_{9}$, water Nm 5$_{17}$. **2.** as noun, **a. Holy One,** i.e. Y., קְדוֹשׁ יִשְׂרָאֵל *the Holy One of Israel* Is 12$_{6}$. **b. holy person, saint,** alw. Israelite, קדושי ברית *saints of the covenant* 1QM 10$_{10}$. **c. holy one, angel,** צבא קדושים *host of (the) holy ones* 1QH 11$_{22}$. **d. holy place,** i.e. dwelling of Y. Is 57$_{15}$, temple Ps 65$_{5}$. **e. holy day,** i.e. Sabbath, קְדוֹשׁ '' *holy day of Y.* Is 58$_{13}$. **f. holy matter, holy issue** GnzPs 2$_{28}$. **g. holiness,** as attribute of Y. 4QMidrEschat^{a} 3$_{4(Abegg)}$. **3.** קש abbrev. of קָדוֹשׁ Arad inscr. 102 (unless קֹדֶשׁ *holiness*). → קדשׁ *be holy.*

קדח 5.0.1 vb.—**Qal** 5.0.1 Pf. קָדְחָה; ptc. קֹדְחֵי; inf. קְדֹחַ—**1a.** of person, **kindle** fire Is 50$_{11}$. **b.** of fire, **kindle** wood Is 64$_{1}$. **2.** of fire, **be kindled** by (בְּ) Y.'s anger Dt 32$_{22}$. → קַדַּחַת *fever,* אֶקְדָּח *beryl.*

קַדַּחַת 2 n.f. **fever** Lv 26$_{16}$. → קדח *kindle.*

קָדִים 69 n.m.—+ ה- of direction קָדִימָה—**1. east,** פְּאַת קָדִים *eastern side* Ezk 47$_{18}$. **2. east wind,** יוֹם קָדִים *day of the east wind* Is 27$_{8}$. → קדם *be in front.*

*קדל 0.0.1 vb. (byform of [or error for] גדל)—**Hi.** 0.0.1 Impf. קדילו—with לְ of obj., **magnify** king of glory 4QShir Shabb^{d} 1.1$_{31}$.

קדם 26.2.9 vb.—**Pi.** 24.2.7 Pf. קִדַּמְתִּי; impf. יְקַדְּמֻנִי; impv. קַדְּמָה; ptc. Q מקדמים—**1. be in front, go at the head,** of singers Ps 68_{26}. **2. meet, come before, approach,** obj. Y., of worshipper Mc 6_6, obj. worshipper, of Y.'s compassion Ps 79_8. **3. come upon, attack, confront,** obj. person, of enemy 2 S 22_{19}, of days of affliction Jb 30_{27}, obj. city, of king 2 K 19_{32}. **4. meet, come before,** obj. person's face, of Y. Ps 17_{13}, obj. Y.'s face, of worshipper Ps 95_2, of truth and loyalty Ps 89_{15}. **5. hasten, advance** holy times 1QS 1_{14}, **anticipate** watches of the night Ps 119_{147}. **6. receive** infant, of knees and breasts Jb 3_{12}. **7. make progress** Si $30_{25(E)}$.

Hi. 2 Pf. הִקְדִּימַנִי; impf. תַּקְדִּים—**1. meet, reach,** לֹא־תַגִּישׁ וְתַקְדִּים בַּעֲדֵינוּ הָרָעָה *evil will not reach or overtake us* Am 9_{10}. **2. give (beforehand) to,** מִי הִקְדִּימַנִי וַאֲשַׁלֵּם *who has given to me that I should repay?* Jb 41_3. **3. confront** Jb 41_3 (unless §2).

Htp. 0.0.2 Impf. יתקדם—**go early, be early** CD 11_{23}. → קְדוּמִים *ancient ones,* קָדִים *east,* קֶדֶם *east,* קַדְמָה *origin,* קֵדְמָה *east,* קַדְמוֹן *eastern,* קַדְמֹנִי I *eastern.*

קֶדֶם 61.2.19 n.[m.]—pl. cstr. קַדְמֵי—**1a. east,** אֶרֶץ קֶדֶם *land of (the) east* Gn 25_6. **b. front,** i.e. east Is 9_{11}. **2a. antiquity, ancient times,** אֱלֹהֵי קֶדֶם *God of antiquity* Dt 33_{27}. **b. beginning,** קַדְמֵי־אֶרֶץ *beginnings of the earth* Pr 8_{23}. **3.** as adv., **a.** position, **to the front** Ps 139_5. **b.** time, **anciently, of old, before** Ps 74_2. → קדם *be in front.*

[קֵדֶם] 26 n.[m.] **east,** פְּאַת קֵדְמָה *eastern side* Ex 27_{13}. → קדם *be in front.*

[קַדְמָה] 6 n.f.—cstr. קַדְמַת; pl. sf. קַדְמוֹתֵיכֶם—**1. origin** Is 23_7. **2a. former state, former condition** Ezk 16_{55}. **b. former time** Ezk 36_{11}. **3.** as conj., **before** Ps 129_6. → קדם *be in front.*

[קִדְמָה] 4 n.f. **east,** קִדְמַת־עֵדֶן *east of Eden* Gn 4_{16}. → קדם *be in front.*

קֵדְמָה I, see קֶדֶם *east.*

קְדֵמָה II 2 pr.n.m. **Kedemah.**

קַדְמוֹן 1.1 adj.—f.s. קַדְמוֹנָה—**1. eastern,** of district Ezk 47_8. **2.** as noun, **former one** Si $41_{3(M)}$. → קדם *be in front.*

קְדֵמוֹת 4 pl.n. **Kedemoth.**

קַדְמִיאֵל 8 pr.n.m. **Kadmiel.**

קַדְמֹנִי I 10.0.5 adj.—m.pl. קַדְמֹנִים; f.pl. קַדְמֹנִיּוֹת—**1a. eastern,** of gate Ezk 11_1, sea Jl 2_{20}. **b.** as noun, **one from the east, eastern (one)** 1QM 2_{12}. **2a. former, ancient,** of days Ezk 38_{17}, proverb 1 S $24_{14(mss)}$. **b.** as noun, (1) **ancient one(s)** 1 S 24_{14}. (2) **former thing** Is 43_{18}. → קדם *be in front.*

קַדְמֹנִי II 1 gent. **Kadmonite.**

קדע, see יָקְדְעָם *Jokdeam.*

קָדְקֹד 11.0.1 n.[m.]—sf. קָדְקֳדוֹ—**head,** coll., קָדְקֹד בְּנוֹת צִיּוֹן *heads of the daughters of Zion* Is 3_{17}, **crown (of head)** Dt 28_{35}.

קדר 17.1 vb.—**Qal** 13 Pf. קָדַרְתִּי; + waw וְקָדַר; ptc. קֹדֵר—**1. be(come) dark, black,** of person Jb 30_{28}, sky Jr 4_{28}, sun and moon Jl 2_{10}. **2. be in mourning,** i.e. in dark clothes Jr 8_{21}. **3.** ptc. as noun, **mourner,** i.e. one in dark clothes Jb 5_{11}.

Hi. 3.1 Impf. אַקְדִּירֵם; + waw וְהִקְדַּרְתִּי—**1. darken,** obj. stars, of Y. Ezk 32_7, obj. face, of evil Si 25_{17}. **2.** of Y., **cause** Lebanon **to mourn** Ezk 31_{15}.

Htp. 1 Pf. הִתְקַדְּרוּ—**grow dark,** of sky 1 K 18_{45}. → קדרות *darkness,* קְדֹרַנִּית *as in mourning.*

קֵדָר 12 pr.n.m. **Kedar.**

*[קְדֵרָה] 0.0.1 n.f.—pl. קדרות—**pot** 3QTr 8_8.

קִדְרוֹן 11.0.1 pl.n. **Kidron.**

*[קְדֵרוּת] 0.0.1 n.f. **pottery** 3QTr 8_8.

קַדְרוּת 1.0.1 n.f. **darkness** Is 50_3. → קדר *be dark.*

*[קַדְרִי] 0.0.0.1 pr.n.m. **Kadri.**

קְדֹרַנִּית 1 adv. **as in mourning,** + הלך *walk* Ml 3_{14}. → קדר *be dark.*

קדשׁ 171.5.55 vb.—**Qal** 11.0.3 Pf. קָדְשׁוּ, קְדַשְׁתִּיךָ; impf. יִקְדַּשׁ—**1a. be holy, i.e. be regarded as belonging to the deity,** of priest and priestly garment Ex 29_{21}, food Hg 2_{12}. **b. be holy in comparison to** someone else Is 65_5. **2. be forfeited,** of produce, because dedicated to Y. Dt 22_9.

Ni. 11.1.3 Pf. נִקְדַּשׁ; impf. אֶקָּדֵשׁ—**1.** of Y., **show oneself to be holy,** i.e. divine, oft. specif. through (בְּ) Israel before (לְ) eyes of nations Ezk 20_{41}. **2.** of Y., **be honoured, i.e. be treated as holy,** among (בְּתוֹךְ) Israelites Lv 22_{32}. **3. be made holy,** i.e. dedicated to Y., of Moses 4QapPentB 2.2_{11}, tent of meeting Ex 29_{43}.

Pi. 75.0.23 Pf. קִדַּשׁ; impf. אֲקַדֵּשׁ; impv. קַדֵּשׁ, קַדְּשׁוּ; ptc. מְקַדֵּשׁ; inf. קַדֵּשׁ (קַדְּשׁוֹ)—**1.** of Y. and human being, **regard or tread as belonging to the deity** person

1 S 7_{1}, people Lv 20_{8}, mountain Ex 19_{23}, city 11QT 52_{19}, temple 2 C 29_{5}, tabernacle Nm 7_{1}. **2. keep as holy, observe** sabbath Ezk 20_{20}. **3. sanctify,** i.e. **prepare** war Jl 4_{9}. **4. treat, honour as holy** Y. Dt 32_{51}, priest Lv 21_{8}.

Pu. 5 Ptc. מְקֻדָּשׁ—**1. be consecrated, sanctified,** of priest 2 C 26_{18}, appointed feast Ezr 3_{5}. **2.** ptc. as noun, **a. consecrated one** Is 13_{3}. **b. consecrated place** Ezk 48_{11}.

Hi. 45.4.11 Pf. הִקְדִּישׁ; impf. יַקְדִּישׁ; impv. הַקְדִּשֵׁם; ptc. מַקְדִּישׁ, מַקְדִּשִׁים; inf. abs. הַקְדֵּשׁ; cstr. הַקְדִּישׁ—**1.** of Y. and human being, **regard or tread as belonging to the deity** passover sacrifice 2 C 30_{17}, place Jos 20_{7}, vessel 2 S 8_{11}, firstborn Nm 3_{13}, guest Zp 1_{7}. **2. regard, treat, praise** Y. **as holy** Is 8_{13}.

Ho. 0.0.1 Ptc. מוקדש[י]—**be sanctified, be consecrated** 1Q38 4_{2}.

Htp. 24.0.14 Pf. הִתְקַדְּשׁוּ; impf. יִתְקַדְּשׁוּ; impv. הִתְקַדְּשׁוּ; ptc. מִתְקַדְּשִׁים, מִתְקַדֶּשֶׁת; inf. הִתְקַדֵּשׁ—**1. dedicate oneself to the deity** Ex 19_{22} Lv 11_{44}. **2. be observed, celebrated as holy,** of festival Is 30_{29}.

→ קֹדֶשׁ *holiness,* קְדֻשָּׁה *holiness,* קָדוֹשׁ *holy,* מִקְדָּשׁ *sanctuary,* מְקֻדָּשׁ *holiest part,* קָדֵשׁ I *(male) prostitute,* קְדֵשָׁה *(female) prostitute.*

קָדֵשׁ I 6 n.m.—pl. קְדֵשִׁים—**(male) prostitute,** doubtfully **cult prostitute** 1 K 15_{12}. → קדשׁ *be holy.*

קָדֵשׁ II 17.3.1 pl.n. **Kadesh.**

קֶדֶשׁ 12 pl.n. **Kedesh.**

קֹדֶשׁ 469.13.490.8 n.m.—קוֹדֶשׁ; cstr. קֹדֶשׁ; sf. קָדְשִׁי; pl. קֳדָשִׁים (קָדָשִׁים, קֳדָשִׁים); cstr. קָדְשֵׁי; sf. קֳדָשָׁיו, קָדְשֵׁיהֶם—**1. holiness, sacredness, consecration,** through dedication to the deity, oft. as abs. noun in cstr. relationship, modifying cstr., e.g. עִיר הַקֹּדֶשׁ *holy city,* i.e. Jerusalem Is 48_{2}, **a.** of things dedicated to Y., i.e. mountain Zc 8_{3}, ground Ex 3_{5}, land Ezk 48_{14}, garment Ex 28_{2}, vessel 1 K 8_{4}, water 1QH 16_{13}, oil Nm 35_{25}, sacrificial meat Hg 2_{12}, sabbath Ex 16_{23}, path of redemption Is 35_{8}. **b.** of earthly and heavenly beings worshipping Y., i.e. humans, עדת קודש *holy congregation* 1QS 5_{20}, Messiah 1Q30 1_{2}, angels 1QSa 2_{9}. **2. holiness, sacredness, divinity** of Y., divine attribute, quality, activity, קודש מלך הכבוד *holiness of the king of glory* 11QShir Shabb 10_{5}. **3. holiness** of good spirit, 'spirit of truth', רוח קודשיו *his holy spirit* CD 7_{4}. **4. holy place, sanctuary, temple,** חַצְרוֹת קָדְשִׁי *courts of my temple* Is 62_{9}. **5. holy thing, holy offering,** צֹאן קֳדָשִׁים *flock for holy offerings,* i.e. sacrificial sheep Ezk 36_{38}; **holy bread** 1 S 21_{7}. **6. holy object, sacred object,** הַמִּזְבֵּחַ קֹדֶשׁ קָדָשִׁים *the altar is the holy object of holy objects,* i.e. most holy object Ex 29_{37}. **7. holy portion, holy area** of land Ezk 45_{4}. **8. holy regulation,** קָדְשֵׁי יי *holy regulations of Y.* Lv 5_{15}. **9a. holy one,** of Judah Ps 114_{2}; קֹדֶשׁ קָדָשִׁים **most holy one,** of Aaron as high priest 1 C 23_{13}; קודש קודשים **most holy community** 1QS 9_{6}; קדוש קודשים **most holy one,** of spiritual leader at Qumran 4QInstr^{d} 81_{4}. **b. holy one(s), angel(s),** Y.'s heavenly entourage, רִבְבֹת קֹדֶשׁ *ten thousands of holy ones* Dt 33_{2}. **c. Holy One, God,** משרתי קדש *servants of the Holy One* Si 4_{14}. **10.** קש abbrev. of קֹדֶשׁ **holiness** Arad inscr. 102 (unless קָדוֹשׁ *holy*). → קדשׁ *be holy.*

קָדֵשׁ בַּרְנֵעַ 10 pl.n. **Kadesh-barnea.**

קְדֵשָׁה 5 n.f.—pl. קְדֵשׁוֹת—**(female) prostitute,** doubtfully, **cult prostitute** Ho 4_{14}. → קדשׁ *be holy.*

*[קְדֻשָּׁה] 0.0.3 n.f.—sf. קדושתו—**holiness, sanctification** GnzPs 1_{16} 47_{25}. → קדשׁ *be holy.*

קהה 4 vb.—**Qal** 3 Impf. תִּקְהֶינָה—**1. be(come) blunt,** of teeth Jr 31_{29} (unless §2). **2. be set on edge,** i.e. be painfully sensitive, of teeth Jr 31_{29}.

Pi. 1 Pf. קֵהָה—**1. be blunt,** of iron Ec 10_{10} (unless §2). **2. make iron blunt** Ec 10_{10}.

קהל 39.0.3 vb.—**Ni.** 19.0.2 Pf. נִקְהֲלוּ; + waw וַיִּקָּהֲלוּ; ptc. נִקְהָלִים; inf. cstr. הִקָּהֵל—intrans., **assemble, gather together** to (אֶל) king at (בְּ) feast 1 K 8_{2}, against (עַל) leader Nm 16_{3}.

Hi. 20.0.1 Pf. הִקְהַלְתָּ; impf. יַקְהִיל (יַקְהֵל, יַקְהִיל); impv. הַקְהֵל, הַקְהִילוּ; inf. cstr. הַקְהִיל—**1.** trans., **assemble, gather, summon** people to (לְ or אֶל) Jerusalem 1 C 15_{3}, Y. Dt 4_{10}, against (עַל) leader Nm 16_{19}. **2.** abs., of Y., **summon to judgment, call to judgment, convene a court** Jb 11_{10}.

→ קָהָל *assembly,* קְהִלָּה *assembly,* מַקְהֵל *assembly.*

קָהָל 123.8.35 n.m.—cstr. קְהַל; sf. קְהָלָה, קְהַלְכֶם—**assembly, company, host, congregation,** קְהַל יִשְׂרָאֵל *as-*

sembly of Israel 1 K 12₃, ״ *of Y.* Nm 16₃, גּוֹיִם *of nations* Jr 50₉, קְדֹשִׁים *of holy ones,* i.e. angels Ps 89₆, רְפָאִים *of shadows,* i.e. ghosts Pr 21₁₆. → קהל *assemble.*

קְהִלָּה 2.2.2 n.f. **assembly, company, host, congregation,** קהלת אנשים *assembly of men* 1QM 1₁₀, קְהִלַּת יַעֲקֹב *congregation of Jacob* Dt 33₄. → קהל *assemble.*

קֹהֶלֶת 7 pr.n.m. **Koheleth.**

[קְהֵלָתָה] 2 pl.n. **Kehelathah.**

קְהָת 32.0.1 pr.n.m. **Kohath.**

קְהָתִי 15 gent. **Kohathite.**

קַו I 8 perh. n.m. **1. kav,** term of unknown meaning, קַו לָקָו *kav-la-kav* with צַו לָצָו, perh. mimicking sound of words of Isaiah Is 28₁₀. **2.** קַו־קָו perh. **idle chatter** Is 18₂.

קַו II 25.1.10 n.m.—קָו; sf. קַוָּם; pl. Q קוים—**1. (measuring) line, string, cord,** קו משפט *just measuring line* 1QH 14₂₆. **2. sound, music, melody, rhythm,** lit. 'chord' Ps 19₅. **3. law, precept, statute,** קַו לָקָו *statute upon statute* Is 28₁₀. → קוה *wait.*

קַו III, see קַוְקַו *might.*

קוֹבַע 2 n.[m.] **helmet,** קוֹבַע נְחֹשֶׁת *helmet of bronze* 1 S 17₃₈. → cf. כּוֹבַע *helmet.*

*__[קוֹבְעָה]__ 0.0.1 pl.n. **Kobah.**

קוה I 47.5.9 vb.—**Qal** 6.1.3 Ptc. קֹוֵי (קוֹיֵ, Q קואי)—ptc. as noun, **one who waits (for)** or **hopes (in)** Y. Ps 37₉.

Pi. 41.4.6 Pf. קִוָּה, קִוִּיתִי, קִוִּיתָה; impf. יְקַוֶּה (יְקַו), יְקַוּוּ—**1. wait, look, hope (for), a.** with obj., Y. Ps 25₅, Sheol Jb 17₁₃, wages Jb 7₂. **b.** with prep., לְ *for,* + Y. Is 8₁₇, salvation of Y. Gn 49₁₈; אֶל *for,* + Y. Is 51₅. **2. lie in wait (for), a.** with obj., life Ps 56₇. **b.** with prep., לְ *for,* + person Ps 119₉₅. **3.** of rain, dew, **wait about** for (לְ) men Mc 5₆.

→ קַו II *line,* קָוֶה I *line,* קַוְקַו *might,* מִקְוֶה I *hope,* תִּקְוָה I *cord,* II *hope.*

קוה II 2.0.1 vb.—**Ni.** 2.0.1 Impf. יִקָּווּ; + waw וְנִקְווּ—**be gathered (together), collected** to (לְ) Jerusalem, of nations Jr 3₁₇, to (אֶל) one place, of water Gn 1₉. → מִקְוֶה II *collection,* מִקְוָה *reservoir.*

[קָוֶה] I 3.0.1 n.m. **line,** קוה הַמִּדָּה *line for (the) measuring* Jr 31₃₉(Kt). → קוה I *wait.*

*__[קָוֶה]__ II 0.0.0.1 pr.n.m. **Kaveh.**

קְוֵה pl.n. **Kue.**

קוֹחַ, see פְּקַח־קוֹחַ *liberation.*

קוט I 7 vb. (byform of קוץ I)—**Qal** 1 Impf. אָקוּט—of Y., **feel loathing, disgust** for (בְּ) generation Ps 95₁₀.

Ni. 4 Pf. נָקֹטָה—**be disgusted** with (בְּ) life Jb 10₁, oneself, וּנְקֹטֹתֶם בִּפְנֵיכֶם בְּכָל־רָעוֹתֵיכֶם *and you be disgusted with yourselves on account of all your evil deeds* Ezk 20₄₃, vars. Ezk 6₉ (with אֶל) 36₃₁ (with עַל).

Htpol. 2 Impf. אֶתְקוֹטָט—**feel disgust** for (בְּ) Y.'s enemies Ps 139₂₁.

קוט II 1 vb.—**Ni** 1 Impf. יָקוֹט—**break, snap, break in pieces,** of confidence Jb 8₁₄. → יָקוֹט *gossamer.*

קוֹל 505.15.86.1 n.m.—קֹל; cstr. קוֹל (קֹל); sf. קוֹלִי; pl. קֹלוֹת (קֹלֹת, קוֹלֹת); cstr. קֹלוֹת (קלת)—**1a. voice, cry, shout** of humans, קוֹל בֹּכִים *voice of those who weep* Jb 30₃₁, מְשַׂחֲקִים *of those who make merry* Jr 30₁₉, שָׁרִים וְשָׁרוֹת *of singing men and singing women* 2 S 19₃₆, מְלַחֲשִׁים *of charmers* Ps 58₆. **b. voice** of Y., הוֹד קוֹלוֹ *his majestic voice* Is 30₃₀; perh. **the Voice** as name for Y. Nm 7₈₉. **c. voice** of heavenly host 1QH 11₃₅, seraph Is 6₄. **d. voice** of Baal 1 K 18₂₆. **e. voice, sound** of animal, (1) **bleating** of sheep 1 S 15₁₄. (2) **lowing** of cattle Jr 9₉. (3) **neighing** of horse Jr 8₁₆. (4) **roaring** of lion Jb 4₁₀. (5) **singing** of bird Ca 2₁₂. **f. voice** of personification, i.e. wisdom Pr 8₁, floods Ps 93₃, gates 4QShir Shabb[f] 23.1₈. **2. sound, a.** of humans, e.g. armies during battle Jr 6₂₃. **b.** of Y., e.g. walking in garden Gn 3₈. **c.** of divine beings, cherubim, etc., e.g. beating wings Ezk 1₂₄. **d.** of horses of advancing army 2 K 7₆. **e.** of musical instrument, e.g. trumpet 2 C 5₁₃. **f.** of things found in the natural environment, קוֹל עָלֶה *sound of leaves* Lv 26₃₆, מַיִם *of water* Ezk 1₂₄, רַעַשׁ *of an earthquake* Ezk 3₁₂. **g.** of tangible objects, קוֹל רֵחַיִם *sound of millstones* Jr 25₁₀, מַרְכָּבוֹת *of chariots* Jl 2₅, שׁוֹט *of a whip* Na 3₂. **3a. voice,** i.e. **command, instruction, word,** (1) of humans, קוֹל מוֹרָי *voice of my teachers* Pr 5₁₃. (2) of Y., קול עשיהם *voice of their maker* CD 3₈. **b. sound,** i.e. **utterance,** of something spoken by (1) humans, קול תפלתם *sound of their prayer* Si 48₂₀. (2) Y., קוֹל דְּבָרוֹ *sound of his word* Ps 103₂₀. **c. proclamation** Ezr 1₁. **d. report, news** Gn 45₁₆. **e. teaching, meaning, message** Ex 4₈. **4. thunder,** קוֹל־שַׁדַּי *thunder of the Almighty* Ezk 1₂₄. **5. hark!,** as exclamation introducing an announcement, קוֹל דּוֹדִי *hark! my beloved!* Ca 2_{8}.

קוֹלָיָה 2.0.0.3 pr.n.m. **Kolaiah.**

קוֹלָיָהוּ, see קוֹלָיָה *Kolaiah.*

קוּם 629.15.107.2 vb.—**Qal** 460.5.49.2 Pf. קָם, קָמוּ, קַמְתֶּם; impf. יָקוּם (יָקֹם, יָקוּם); + waw וַיָּקָם; impv. קוּם, קוּמִי, קוּמוּ, קֻמָה; ptc. קָמַי, קָמָה, קָמִים (קוֹמִים); inf. abs. קוֹם; cstr. קוּם—**1a. arise, make a move, start, set out, advance,** usu. for travel Jos 1_{2}, sometimes for flight Gn 27_{43}, or pursuit Gn 44_{4}; usu. of human being, וַיָּקָם יַעֲקֹב מִבְּאֵר שָׁבַע *so Jacob set out from Beer-sheba* Gn 46_{5}, of Y., קוּמָה י׳ לִמְנוּחָתֶךָ *advance, O Y., to your resting-place!* Ps 132_{8}. **b. arise (to do), get ready, act, rise** for action, **make a move** and do something, of human being, וַיָּקָם לִקְרָאתָם *then he rose to meet them* Gn 19_{1}, of Y., בְּקוּם־לַמִּשְׁפָּט אֱלֹהִים *when God rose for,* i.e. to execute, *judgment* Ps 76_{10}. **c. arise, rise up, get up, stand up,** (1) of changing position from lying down or prostrating oneself Gn 19_{33}. (2) from (מִן) ambush Jos 8_{7}. (3) from death Ps 88_{11}. (4) before (מִפְּנֵי) person, as sign of respect Gn 31_{35}; **stand, stand up,** i.e. be in a standing position, וַיָּקָם עַל־מַעֲלֵה הַלְוִיִּם יֵשׁוּעַ *and Jeshua stood upon the stair(s) of the Levites* Ne 9_{4}. **2a. arise (against), rise up (against),** in hostility, contention or rebellion, of human being Ps 124_{2}, of Y. Nm 10_{35}; against (עַל or אֶל or בְּ) person Gn 4_{8} Jg 20_{5} Mc 7_{6}, Y. 4QParGenEx 1_{11}, Y.'s covenant 1QH 12_{34}, Y.'s word 1QH 12_{34}. **b.** ptc. as noun, **one who rises up, adversary, enemy, opponent** Lm 3_{62}. **3a.** of property, i.e. field, cave, **be passed over, be transferred to** (לְ) person Gn 23_{17}. **b.** of firstborn, **succeed, be accounted to** (עַל) name of dead brother Dt 25_{6}. **4a. come on the scene, appear, arise, become powerful,** usu. of people coming into existence, or attaining or regaining a role or position, of brood of sinful men instead of (תַּחַת) ancestors Nm 32_{14}, of prophet in (בְּ) Israel Dt 34_{10}, of king over (עַל) Egypt Ex 1_{8}, of Y. Is 33_{10}. **b.** of violence, **arise, become** as (לְ) staff of wickedness Ezk 7_{11}. **c.** of event, **happen, arise, come to pass, come on the scene,** of disaster Pr 24_{22}, war against (עַל) person Ps 27_{3}. **d.** of life, **be bright(er)** than (מִן) noon Jb 11_{17}. **5a. stand, hold firm, maintain oneself,** of Israel before (לִפְנֵי) enemy Jos 7_{12}, of thing Jb 41_{18}. **b.** of continuing condition, existence, **stand, remain, endure,** of wealth Jb 15_{29}, kingdom 1 S 13_{14}, agreement Is 28_{18}, spirit Jos 2_{11}. **c.** of plan, **be fulfilled, be realized, stand** Pr 19_{21}. **d.** of legal matter, testimony, **prevail, stand, be proven** Dt 19_{15}. **e.** of vow, **stand, remain valid, need to be fulfilled** Nm 30_{5}. **f.** of price, assessment of field, **be fixed, stay fixed, be set** Lv 27_{17}. **6. take (an obligation)** upon (עַל) oneself CD 16_{1}.

Pi. 11.0.6 Pf. קִיַּם; impf. Q יקים; impv. קַיְּמֵנִי; inf. קַיֵּם—**1a. fulfil, make valid, confirm** predictions Ezk 13_{6}, promises Ps 119_{106}. **b. confirm, ratify, establish** transactions Ru 4_{7}, covenant CD 20_{12}. **2a. impose, enjoin (an obligation)** upon (עַל) another, יקים אותו עליו לשוב אל תורת משה *he shall impose it upon him to return to the law of Moses* CD 15_{12}. **b. take (an obligation)** upon (עַל) oneself 1QS 5_{8}. **3. establish, strengthen, encourage** someone Ps 119_{28}.

Pol. 4.2.1 Impf. יְקוֹמֵם—**1. raise up, erect** ruins, remains, of Y. Is 44_{26}, Israel Is 61_{4}. **2.** perh. of Y., **raise up, lift up** hand of the fallen 4QBark[c] 1.1_{2}. **3. raise oneself, rise up** as (לְ) enemy Mc 2_{8}. **4. raise oneself up,** i.e. **take part** in (בְּ) strife Si 11_{9}. **5. raise oneself up,** i.e. **be forward, make oneself equal** among (בֵּין) elders Si 35_{9}.

Hi. 146.7.48 Pf. הֵקִים, הֲקִימֹתִי; impf. יָקִים, (יָקֵם); + waw וַיָּקֶם; impv. הָקֵם, הָקִימוּ; ptc. מֵקִים; inf. abs. הָקֵם (הָקִים); cstr. הָקִים—**1a.** of Y., **establish, found, constitute** covenant with (אֵת) Noah Gn 6_{18}, decree in (בְּ) Jacob Ps 78_{5}, Israel as (לְ) holy people Dt 28_{9}. **b. carry out, give effect to, keep, uphold, fulfil** commandment Jr 35_{16}, covenant Lv 26_{9} 1QS 5_{21}, oath Gn 26_{3}. **c. make** oath **binding** Nm 30_{14}. **d. take (an obligation)** upon (עַל) oneself, הקימותי על נפשי לבלתי חטוא לך *I have taken (an obligation) upon myself that I should not sin against you* 1QH 6_{17}. **2a. raise up, bring up** son Jos 5_{7}. **b.** oft. of Y., **raise up, bring on the scene, nominate, appoint** someone to a position or role, i.e. royal offspring 2 S 7_{12}, prophet Dt 18_{15}, priest 1 S 2_{35}, deliverer Jg 3_{9}. **3. rouse, stir up, anger, incite** servants against (עַל) king 1 S 22_{8}, nation against (עַל)

Israel, of Y. Am 6$_{14}$. **4. set up, erect, build** altar 2 S 24$_{18}$, image Lv 26$_{1}$; **raise up, rebuild** ruins, of Y. Am 9$_{11}$. **5a. lift up, raise** deceased from (מִן) death, of Elijah Si 48$_{5}$; **help up** poor from (מִן) dust, of Y. GnzPs 3$_{13}$. **b.** oft. of Y., **set, set up, cause to stand, station** someone, i.e. sentry, shepherd, over (עַל) Israelites Jr 6$_{17}$ 23$_{4}$. **c.** of Y., **cause to hold firm, sustain** king in (בְּ) battle Ps 89$_{44}$. **6. raise up, provide** name in (בְּ) Israel for (לְ) brother Dt 25$_{7}$, plantation for (לְ) Israel, of Y. Ezk 34$_{29}$. **7.** of Y., **settle, calm down** storm to (לְ) whisper Ps 107$_{29}$.

Ho. 3 Pf. הוּקַם (הֻקַם)—**1. be erected, built,** of tabernacle Ex 40$_{17}$. **2. be raised up, exalted,** of man 2 S 23$_{1}$. **3. be observed, obeyed,** of command Jr 35$_{14}$.

Htp. 0.0.2 Impf. יתקים—**1. endure,** of Israelites 4QNarrC 1$_{12}$. **2.** of agreement, **be fulfilled** by (לְ) person XḤev/Se 49$_{10}$.

Htpol. 5.1.2 Impf. Q אתקומם; ptc. מִתְקוֹמְמַי; inf. cstr. Si התקומם—**1.** of earth, **raise oneself up, rise up** against (לְ) wicked Jb 20$_{27}$. **2.** ptc. as noun, **adversary, enemy** Ps 17$_{7}$.

→ יְקוּם *living form,* מָקוֹם *place,* מְקוֹמָה *opposition,* קוֹמָה *height,* קוֹמְמִיּוּת *upright,* קַיָּם *established,* קִים *adversary,* קִימָה *rising up,* קָמָה I *standing grain,* II *maturity,* תְּקוּם *power to stand,* תְּקוּמָה *standing,* תְּקוֹמֵם *one who rises up.*

קוֹמָה 45.1.9 n.f.—cstr. קוֹמַת; sf. קוֹמָתוֹ—**1. height** of temple 1 K 6$_{2}$, Noah's ark Gn 6$_{15}$. **2. (great) height, stature** of person 1 S 16$_{7}$, of tree, קוֹמַת אֲרָזָיו *stature of its cedars,* i.e. its tallest cedars 2 K 19$_{23}$. **3. length** of person lying on ground 1 S 28$_{20}$. → קום *arise.*

קוֹמְמִיּוּת 1 adv. **upright, erect,** + הלך hi. *cause to walk* Lv 26$_{13}$. → קום *arise.*

קוֹנֵן, see קין *chant.*

קוֹעַ 1 pr.n.m. **Koa.**

[קוֹף] 2 n.m.—pl. קוֹפִים (קֹפִים)—**ape, monkey** 1 K 10$_{22}$ ‖2 C 9$_{21}$.

קוץ I 9.3.1 vb. (byform of קוט I)—**Qal** 8.3.1 Pf. קָצָה; impf. תָּקֹץ; + waw וַיָּקָץ, וַיָּקֻצוּ; ptc. קָץ—**1a.** with בְּ of obj., **loathe, hate, abhor** life Gn 27$_{46}$, rebuke Pr 3$_{11}$, nations, of Y. Lv 20$_{23}$. **b. be loath (to do),** ויקוץ מעשות פקודי ישרים *and he was loath to perform the precepts of the upright* CD 20$_{2}$. **2. be in dread** on account of (מִפְּנֵי) people Ex 1$_{12}$.

Hi. 1 Impf. נְקִיצֶנָּה—**frighten, terrify** nation Is 7$_{6}$.

***קוץ** II 2.0.1 vb.—**Hi.** 2.0.1 Impf. יָקִיצוּ—**1. cut off, demolish, tear down** Judah Is 7$_{6}$, root 4QD[a] 6.1$_{8}$. **2. gape open,** of heavens Jb 14$_{12}$. → קוֹץ I *thorns,* III *wick,* קְוֻצּוֹת *locks (of hair).*

קוֹץ I 12.0.2 n.m.—pl. קוֹצִים (קֹצִים)—**thorn(s), thornbush(es),** קוֹצֵי הַמִּדְבָּר *thorns of the steppe* Jg 8$_{7}$. → קוץ II *cut off.*

קוֹץ II 1.0.3 pr.n.m. **Koz.**

***קוֹץ** III 1 n.m. **wick** 2 S 23$_{6}$. → קוץ II *cut off.*

[קְוֻצּוֹת] 2 n.f.pl.—sf. קְוֻצּוֹתַי (mss קְוֻצּוֹתַי), קְוֻצּוֹתָיו (mss קְוֻצּוֹתָיו)—**locks (of hair)** Ca 5$_{2.11}$. → קוץ II *cut off.*

[קַו־קָו] 2 n.[m.] **might,** גּוֹי קַו־קָו *nation of might* Is 18$_{2.7}$. → קוה I *wait for.*

קור 4 vb.—**Qal** 2 Pf. קַרְתִּי—**dig (a well)** 2 K 19$_{24}$‖Is 37$_{25}$.

Hi. 2 Pf. הֵקֵרָה; inf. cstr. הָקִיר—**cause to flow,** obj. water, of well Jr 6$_{7}$, obj. evil, of Jerusalem Jr 6$_{7}$.

→ מָקוֹר I *source.*

[קוּר] 2.0.2 n.m. **web, thread,** קוּרֵי עַכָּבִישׁ *webs of a spider* Is 59$_{5}$.

קוֹרֵא I 3.0.0.1 pr.n.m. **Kore.**

קוֹרֵא II, see עֵין הַקּוֹרֵא *En-hakkore.*

קוֹרֵב, see קָרֵב I *approach* and II *inner sanctuary.*

קוֹרָה 5.0.2 n.f.—sf. קֹרָתִי; pl. קֹרוֹת; cstr. קֹרוֹת—**1. log,** i.e. wood unshaped for construction 2 K 6$_{5}$. **2. beam (of the ceiling), rafter,** i.e. wood shaped for construction, קֹרוֹת בָּתֵּינוּ *beams of our houses* Ca 1$_{17}$. **3. roof,** i.e. the finished construction, צֵל קֹרָתִי *shelter of my roof* Gn 19$_{8}$. → קרה II *lay beams.*

קוש I 1 vb.—**Qal** 1 Impf. יְקֹשׁוּן—**lay a snare for** (לְ) person Is 29$_{21}$. → קוֹשׁ *snare;* cf. נקשׁ II *ensnare,* יקשׁ *set snare.*

***[קוש]** II vb. **Qal, stoop, be bent down,** הִתְקֹשְׁשׁוּ וָקוֹשׁוּ *bend your backs and stoop* Zp 2$_{1}$ (if em. הִתְקֹשְׁשׁוּ וָקֹשׁוּ *gather yourselves together and gather,* from קשׁשׁ).

Htpol., bend one's back, see Qal.

***[קוֹשׁ]** 0.0.1 n.[m.] **snare, trap** 4QBark[d] 2.1$_{4}$. → קוש *lay a trap.*

קוֹשִׁי, see קֹשִׁי *stubbornness.*

קוּשָׁיָהוּ 1 pr.n.m. **Kushaiah.**

***קָח** 1 n.[m.] **meadow** Ezk 17₅.

קַט 1 adv. **1. only,** or **2. very,** or **3. in a small (amount of time)** Ezk 16₄₇.

קֶטֶב 4 n.m.—sf. קָטָבְךָ—**destruction,** of pestilence Dt 32₂₄, storm Is 28₂.

קְטוֹרָה 1 n.m. **smoke, fumes,** perh. from incense Dt 33₁₀. → קטר I *burn a sacrifice.*

קְטוּרָה 4.0.2 pr.n.f. **Keturah.**

קטל 3 vb.—**Qal** 3 Impf. יִקְטְלֵנִי, תִּקְטֹל—**slay, kill** person, of Y. Ps 139₁₉, of human being Jb 24₁₄. → קֶטֶל *slaughter.*

[קֶטֶל] 1 n.[m.]—קָטֶל—**slaughter, murder** Ob9. → קטל *slay.*

קטן 4 vb.—**Qal** 3 Pf. קָטֹנְתִּי; + waw וַתִּקְטַן—**be small, insignificant, unworthy,** of person Gn 32₁₁, thing 2 S 7₁₉||1 C 17₁₇.

Hi. 1 Inf. cstr. הַקְטִין—**make** ephah **small** Am 8₅.

→ קָטָן I *small,* קָטֹן *small,* קְטֹן *little one,* קֹטֶן *smallness.*

קָטָן I 47.5.13 adj.—sf. קְטַנָּם; f.s. קְטַנָּה; m.pl. קְטַנִּים; cstr. קְטַנֵּי (קִטְנֵי); f.pl. קְטַנּוֹת—**1.** in ref. to size, **a. small,** of fox Ca 2₁₅, city Ec 9₁₄. **b.** as noun, **small one, small thing** Pr 30₂₄. **2.** in ref. to status, **a. modest, insignificant, unimportant, inferior,** of servant 2 K 18₂₄, request 1 K 2₂₀. **b.** as noun, **insignificant one, insignificant thing,** קְטַנֵּי שִׁבְטֵי יִשְׂרָאֵל *insignificant ones,* i.e. the least, *of the tribes of Israel* 1 S 9₂₁. **3.** in ref. to age, **a. young, little,** קטן הייתי מן אחי *I am younger than my brothers* 11QPsᵃ 28₃. **b.** as noun, **young one,** שֵׁם הַקְּטַנָּה *name of the young(er) one* Gn 29₁₆. **4.** in ref. to time, **short, brief,** of moment 4QTanḥ 8₉ ([רגע] קטנה). **5. mean, stingy,** as noun, **mean person** Si 14₃. → קטן *be small.*

[קָטָן] II, see הַקָּטָן *Hakkatan.*

קָטֹן 54 adj.—cstr. קְטֹן—**1.** in ref. to size, **small, little,** of luminary Gn 1₁₆, robe 1 S 2₁₉. **2.** in ref. to status, **a. small, insignificant, unimportant,** of person 1 S 15₁₇, thing Ex 18₂₂. **b.** as noun, **insignificant thing, insignificant one** Dt 1₁₇ (:: גָּדוֹל *great one*). **3.** in ref. to strength, **a. small, weak,** of Jacob Am 7₂. **b.** as noun, **weak one** Is 60₂₂. **4.** in ref. to age, **a. young, little,** of brother Gn 42₁₅, son Jg 9₅. **b.** as noun, **young one,** קְטֹן בָּנָיו *young(est) one of his sons* 2 C 21₁₇. **5.** in ref. to time, **short, brief,** of moment Is 54₇. → קטן *be small.*

***[קֹטֶן]** n.m. **smallness,** perh. in ref. to little finger or penis, קָטְנִי עָבָה מִמָּתְנֵי אָבִי *my smallness is thicker than the loins of my father* 1 K 12₁₀||2 C 10₁₀ (if em. קְטָנִּי *my little one,* from קְטֹן). → קטן *be small.*

[קְטֹן] 2 n.m.—sf. קָטָנִּי—**little one,** perh. in ref. to little finger or penis 1 K 12₁₀||2 C 10₁₀. → קטן *be small.*

קטף 5 vb.—**Qal** 4 Pf. קָטַף; impf. אֶקְטֹף; ptc. קֹטְפִים—**pluck, pluck off, break off,** obj. ears of corn, of human being Dt 23₂₆, obj. topmost of young twigs, of eagle Ezk 17₄.

Ni. 1 Impf. יִקָּטֵף—**be plucked, cut down,** of reed Jb 8₁₂.

קטר I 116.2.20 vb.—**Pi.** 42.0.1 Pf. קִטַּרְתֶּם; impf. יְקַטֵּר; ptc. מְקַטְּרוֹת, מְקַטְּרִים; inf. abs. קַטֵּר; cstr. קַטֵּר—**1.** without obj., **offer a sacrifice, burn incense (in smoke)** to (לְ) other gods, of Jews Jr 44₈; abs., of priests 2 K 23₈. **2.** with obj., **burn, offer (in smoke)** thank offering Am 4₅, fat 1 S 2₁₆; with cognate noun קִטֵּר *incense* Jr 44₂₁.

Pu. 1 Ptc. מְקֻטֶּרֶת—**be perfumed,** of column, מְקֻטֶּרֶת מוֹר וּלְבוֹנָה *perfumed with myrrh and frankincense* Ca 3₆.

Hi. 71.1.19 Pf. הִקְטִיר; impf. יַקְטִיר; + waw וַיַּקְטֵר; impv. הַקְטֵר; ptc. מַקְטִירִים, מַקְטִיר; inf. abs. הַקְטֵר; cstr. הַקְטִיר—**1.** with obj., **burn, offer (in smoke)** burnt offering 2 K 16₁₃, fire offering Ex 30₂₀, ram Ex 29₁₈, bird Lv 1₁₇, fat Lv 4₁₉, bread Lv 3₁₁, honey Lv 2₁₁, works of law (מעשי תורה) or works of thanksgiving (מעשי תודה) 4Q MidrEschatᵃ 3₆; with cognate noun, קְטֹרֶת *incense* Ex 40₂₇; oft. of priest Lv 1₉, also of Israelite community 4QMidrEschatᵃ 3₆; oft. to (לְ) Y. Lv 7₅; oft. upon (עַל) altar Lv 9₁₇. **2.** without obj., **burn an offering, burn incense (in smoke)** to (לְ) Y. 2 C 26₁₈, Baalim Ho 2₁₅; oft. upon (עַל) altar 1 C 6₃₄.

Ho. 2.1 Impf. תָּקְטַר; ptc. מֻקְטָר—**be burned, offered (in smoke),** of whole offering Lv 6₁₅.

→ קִיטוֹר *smoke,* קְטוֹרָה *smoke of sacrifice,* קְטֹרֶת *incense,* קִטֵּר I *incense,* מִקְטָר *place of burning,* מֻקְטָר *incense,* מִקְטֶרֶת *censer,* מִקְטֶרֶת *incense altar.*

קטר II 1 vb.—**Qal** 1 Ptc. pass. קְטֻרוֹת—**enclose,** pass. **be enclosed,** of court Ezk 46$_{22}$.

קִטֵּר I 1 n.f. **incense, smoke of sacrifice** Jr 44$_{21}$. → קטר I *smoke.*

***קִטֵּר** II 1 n.f. **flour offering** Jr 44$_{21}$.

קִטְרוֹן 1 pl.n. **Kitron.**

קְטֹרֶת 60.1.3 n.f.—cstr. קְטֹרֶת; sf. קְטָרְתִּי—**1. incense,** mixture of spices, קְטֹרֶת הַסַּמִּים *fragrant incense* Ex 25$_{6}$, מִזְבַּח הַקְּטֹרֶת *altar of incense* 1 C 6$_{34}$. **2. incense, smoke** from a sacrifice, קטורת ניחוח *soothing incense* 11QPs^a 18$_{9}$. **3. incense,** for creating a pleasant odour, **perfume** Pr 27$_{9}$. → קטר I *smoke.*

קַטָּת 1 pl.n. **Kattath.**

קיא 9.0.1 vb.—**Qal** 2.0.1 Impv. Si קוה, קִיוּ; ptc. קָאָה—**1.** abs., **vomit,** of person Jr 25$_{27}$. **2.** trans., **spew (out)** nation, of land Lv 18$_{28}$.

Hi. 7 Impf. תָּקִיא; + waw וַיָּקֵא, וְהֶקְאֹתוֹ—**vomit out, spew out,** obj. inhabitants, of land Lv 18$_{25}$, obj. Jonah, of fish Jon 2$_{11}$, obj. riches, of wicked Jb 20$_{15}$.

→ קִיא *vomit,* קָא *vomit.*

קִיא 3 n.m. **vomit** Is 28$_{8}$. → קיא *vomit.*

קיה, see קיא *be sick.*

***[קַיִט]** n.[m.] **summer,** קִשְׁרֵי קַיִט *threads of summer* Jb 8$_{14}$ (if em. אֲשֶׁר יָקוֹט כִּסְלוֹ *whose confidence will snap*). → קַיִץ *summer.*

קִיטוֹר I 4 n.m. **smoke, fog,** קִיטֹר הַכִּבְשָׁן *smoke of the furnace* Gn 19$_{28}$. → קטר I *smoke.*

***קִיטוֹר** II 1 n.m. **frost, ice** Ps 148$_{8}$.

***[קִילָה]** 0.0.1 n.f.—sf. קילתמה—**swiftness** 4QM^a 8.1$_{9}$. → קלל II *be swift.*

[קִים] 1 n.m.—sf. קִימָנוּ—**1. adversary** Jb 22$_{20}$ (unless §2). **2. rebellion** Jb 22$_{20}$. → קום *arise.*

***[קַיָּם]** 0.1.7 adj.—pl. Q קימים—**1. established, valid, legally binding,** of document, agreement Mur 24 C$_{18}$. **2.** as noun, **established thing,** קימי קדם *established things of ancient times* 1QH 5$_{18}$. → קום *arise.*

[קִימָה] 1 n.f.—sf. קִימָתָם—**rising up, standing up** Lm 3$_{63}$ (:: שֶׁבֶת *sitting down*). → קום *arise.*

קין 8.0.2 vb.—**Po.** 8.0.2 Pf. Q קונן; impf. תְּקוֹנֵנָּה; ptc. Q מקונן, מְקוֹנְנוֹת—**1. chant, sing (a lamentation), a.** with קִינָה *lamentation* as obj., over (עַל) nation Ezk 32$_{16}$, person 2 S 1$_{17}$. **b.** without obj., over (עַל or אֶל) city Ezk 27$_{32}$, person 2 S 3$_{33}$. **2.** ptc. fem. as noun, **dirge-singer** Jr 9$_{16}$. → קִינָה II *lamentation.*

[קַיִן] I 1 n.[m.] **spear, lance,** מִשְׁקַל קֵינוֹ *weight of his spear* 2 S 21$_{16}$.

קַיִן II 3 pr.n.m. **Kain.**

קַיִן III 16.0.1 pr.n.m. **Cain.**

קַיִן IV, see תּוּבַל קַיִן *Tubal-cain.*

קַיִן V 1 pl.n. **Kain.**

קִינָה I 1 pl.n. **Kinah.**

קִינָה II 18.1.4 n.f.—pl. קִנִים (קינות); sf. קִינוֹתֵיהֶם—**lamentation, elegy, dirge,** כנור קינה *lyre of lamentation* 1QH 19$_{22}$; pl. perh. Book of Lamentations 2 C 35$_{25}$. → קין *chant.*

קֵינִי 12 gent. **Kenite.**

קִינִים, see קֵינִי *Kenite.*

קֵינָן 6 pr.n.m. **Kenan.**

קיץ I 22.0.2 vb.—**Qal** 0.0.1 Impf. תקוץ—**stir up** blood 4Q D8 1.2$_{12}$ (תקוץ [דם]).

Hi. 22.0.1 Pf. הֵקִיץ, הֱקִיצוֹתִי; impf. אָקִיץ; impv. הָקִיצָה, הָקִיצוּ; ptc. מֵקִיץ; inf. cstr. הָקִיץ—**1.** of human being, **awake, wake up, rouse oneself** from sleep 1 S 26$_{12}$, death Dn 12$_{2}$, drunken state Jl 1$_{5}$. **2.** of Y., **rouse oneself, rise up,** i.e. begin course of action, הָקִיצָה לִפְקֹד כָּל־הַגּוֹיִם *rouse yourself to punish all the nations* Ps 59$_{6}$. **3.** of the end, **awake, come into being** against (אֶל) land of Israel Ezk 7$_{6}$.

קיץ II 1 vb.—**Qal** 1 + waw וְקָץ—of bird of prey, **spend summer** upon (עַל) shoots Is 18$_{6}$. → קַיִץ *summer,* קַיִץ II *summer fruit.*

קַיִץ 20.1.4 n.m.—sf. קֵיצֵךְ—**1. summer,** i.e. summer season, חַרְבֹנֵי קַיִץ *dry heat(s) of summer* Ps 32$_{4}$; perh. also summer harvest Is 28$_{4}$. **2. summer fruits, summer produce,** אָסְפֵּי־קַיִץ *pickings of summer fruits* Mc 7$_{1}$. → קיץ II *spend summer.*

קִיצוֹן 4 adj.—f.s. קִיצֹנָה—**outermost,** of curtain Ex 26$_{10}$. → קצץ *cut off.*

קִיקָיוֹן 5 n.m. **castor oil plant** or **gourd** Jon 4$_{6}$.

קִיקָלוֹן I 1 n.[m.] **disgrace** Hb 2$_{16}$. → קלל I *be despised.*

***קִיקָלוֹן** II 1 n.[m.] **dung, excrement** Hb 2$_{16}$. → קלל I *be despised.*

***קִיקָלוֹת** n.[m.] **dung-heap** Na 1$_{14}$ (if em. כִּי קַלּוֹתָ *for you are vile*). → קלל I *be despised.*

קִיר I 74.2.25 n.m.—קִר; cstr. קִיר; sf. Q קירו; pl. קִירוֹת; sf. קִירוֹתָיו—**1. wall, a.** of building, קִיר הַבַּיִת *wall of the house* 1 K 6$_{5}$, הַהֵיכָל *of the temple* Ezk 41$_{20}$. **b.** of place or area, קִיר הָעִיר *wall of the city* Nm 35$_{4}$, החצר *of the court* 11QT 37$_{9}$. **2a. side,** קִיר הַמִּזְבֵּחַ *side of the altar* Lv 1$_{15}$, הַחוֹמָה *of the wall* Jos 2$_{15}$. **b.** pl., **surface,** קִירוֹת הַסִּפֻּן *surface of the ceiling* 1 K 6$_{15}$ (unless §3). **3. rafter,** קִירוֹת הַסִּפֻּן *rafters of the ceiling* 1 K 6$_{15}$. **4a. wall** of heart, as seat of emotions Jr 4$_{19}$. **b. wall** of the body 1QH 15$_{9}$.

קִיר II 5 pl.n. **Kir.**

קִיר־חֶרֶשׂ *Kir-heres*, see קִיר־חֲרֶשֶׂת *Kir-hareseth.*

קִיר־חֲרֶשֶׂת 5 pl.n. **Kir-hareseth.**

קֵירֹס, see קֵרֹס *Keros.*

קִישׁ 21 pr.n.m. **Kish.**

קִישׁוֹן 6 pl.n. **Kishon.**

קִישִׁי 1 pr.n.m. **Kishi.**

קַל I 13.2.6 adj.—f.s. קַלָּה; m.pl. קַלִּים—**1. swift, quick,** of messenger Is 18$_{2}$, camel Jr 2$_{23}$, wheel Si 36$_{5}$, cloud Is 19$_{1}$. **2.** as noun, **swift one,** of people Jr 46$_{6}$, horse, קלי רגל *swift ones of foot*, i.e. fast moving 1QM 6$_{12}$. **3.** as adv., **swiftly, quickly,** קַל יָבוֹא *it comes swiftly* Is 5$_{26}$. → קלל II *be swift.*

* [קַל] II 0.1.1 adj. **insignificant**—m.s. Si קַל; f.pl. Q קלות—**1. insignificant,** of bloodshed Si 8$_{16}$. **2.** as noun, **worthless thing, insignificant thing** 4QpPs^{a} 1.1$_{19}$. → קלל I *be light.*

קַל I 1 n.[m.] **easiness, thoughtlessness** Jr 3$_{9}$. → קלל I *be light.*

קֹל II, see קוֹל *voice.*

* [קַלְבּוֹס] 0.0.2 pr.n.m. **Kalbos.**

קלה I 4 vb.—**Qal** 3 Pf. קָלָם; ptc. pass. קָלוּי—**1. roast** human being in (בְּ) fire Jr 29$_{22}$. **2.** pass., of ears of cereal, **be parched, roasted** in (בְּ) fire Lv 2$_{14}$. **3.** pass. ptc. as noun, **roasted grain, parched grain** Jos 5$_{11}$.

Ni. 1 Ptc. נִקְלֶה—ptc. as noun, **burning** Ps 38$_{8}$.

→ קָלִי *roasted grain.*

קלה II 7.9.1 vb.—**Ni.** 6.8 Pf. Si נקלו; + waw וְנִקְלָה; ptc. נִקְלֶה—**1. be dishonoured, degraded, despised,** of person 1 S 18$_{23}$, nation's glory Is 16$_{14}$. **2.** ptc. as noun, **a. dishonourable one** Is 3$_{5}$. **b. humble one, degraded one** Pr 12$_{9}$. **c. disgrace, dishonour** Ps 38$_{8}$.

Hi. 1.1 Ptc. מַקְלֶה—**dishonour, insult** parents Dt 27$_{16}$.

Htp. 0.0.1 Impf. אתקלה—**dishonour oneself** 11Q Ps^{a} 19$_{14}$.

→ קָלוֹן *dishonour*; cf. קלל I *be despised.*

קלה III, 2 S 20$_{14 (Kt)}$, see קהל ni. *assemble.*

קָלוֹן 17.4.3 n.m.—cstr. קְלוֹן; sf. קְלוֹנֵךְ—**1. dishonour, disgrace, shame,** קְלוֹן בֵּית אֲדֹנֶיךָ *shame of the house of your lord* Is 22$_{18}$. **2. shame, nakedness,** ערות קלן *shameful nakedness* 1QH 5$_{21}$. **3. contempt, abuse, insult** Pr 22$_{10}$. → קלה II *dishonour.*

קַלַּחַת 2 n.f. **cauldron, pot,** for cooking Mc 3$_{3}$.

קלט I 1 vb.—**Qal** 1 Ptc. pass. קָלוּט—pass., **be short, stunted, small,** perh. tail or limb of animal, or entire animal Lv 22$_{23}$.

* **קלט** II 0.1 vb.—**Pi.** 0.1 + waw ותקלט (or read as ותקלס, from קלס II *give praise*)—appar. **give praise** Si 47$_{15}$.

קָלִי 6 n.m.—קָלִיא—**1. roasted grain, parched grain** 1 S 17$_{17}$. **2.** perh. **roasted lentils** 2 S 17$_{28}$. → קלה I *roast.*

[קַלַּי] 1 pr.n.m. **Kallai.**

קָלִיא, see קָלִי *roasted grain.*

קֵלָיָה 1 pr.n.m. **Kelaiah.**

קֹלָיָהוּ, see קוֹלָיָה *Kolaiah.*

קֹלָיו, see קוֹלָיָה *Kolaiah.*

קְלִיטָא 3 pr.n.m. **Kelita.**

קלל I 73.3.12 vb.—**Qal** 7.0.1 Pf. קַלּוֹתִי, קַלּוּ; impf. יֵקַלּוּ; + waw וַתֵּקַל—**1a. be despised, lightly esteemed,** of nation Na 1$_{14}$ (unless §2b), mistress, וַתֵּקַל ... בְּעֵינֶיהָ *then she was lightly esteemed in her eyes* Gn 16$_{4}$. **b. be vile, unworthy, insignificant,** of person Jb 40$_{4}$, nation Na 1$_{14}$. **2.** of waters, **be abated, subsided** from (מֵעַל) earth Gn 8$_{11}$.

Ni. 10.0.1 Pf. נָקֵל (נָקַל); + waw וְנָקֵל, וּנְקַלֹּתִי; ptc. נְקַלָּה—**1a. be unimportant, trivial,** הֲנָקֵל לְבֵית יְהוּדָה מֵעֲשׂוֹת אֶת־הַתּוֹעֵבוֹת *is it a trivial matter for the house of Judah to commit the abominations?* Ezk 8$_{17}$. **b. be easy, be an easy matter,** נָקֵל לַצֵּל לִנְטוֹת עֶשֶׂר מַעֲלוֹת *it is an easy matter for the shadow to decline ten steps* 2 K 20$_{10}$. **2. be lightly esteemed, contemptible,** of person 2 S 6$_{22}$. **3.** עַל־נְקַלָּה as adv., **superficially, lightly,** + רפא *heal* Jr 6$_{14}$.

Pi. 40.3.7 Pf. קִלֵּל, קִלַּלְתָּ; impf. יְקַלֵּל, יְקַלְלוּ; + waw וַיְקַלְלוּ; impv. קַלֵּל; ptc. מְקַלֵּל, מְקַלְלִים; inf. cstr. קַלֵּל (קַלְלוֹ)—**1. trans., curse, declare contemptible,** obj. parent, of child Pr 20$_{20}$, obj. Y., of human being Ex 22$_{27}$, obj. day of one's birth, of ill person Jb 3$_{1}$, obj. ground, of Y. Gn 8$_{21}$. **2.** intrans., **curse (continually)** 2 S 16$_{5}$. **3. bring about a curse** upon (לְ) oneself 1 S 3$_{13}$. **4.** ptc. as noun, **one who curses** Lv 24$_{14}$.

Pu. 3.0.1 Impf. תְּקֻלַּל; ptc. מְקֻלָּלָיו—**1. be cursed,** of sinner Is 65$_{20}$, plot of land Jb 24$_{18}$. **2.** ptc. as noun, **cursed one** 11QT 64$_{12}$.

Hi. 13.0.2 Pf. הֵקַל, הֱקַלֹּתַנִי; impf. יָקֵל; impv. הָקֵל; inf. cstr. הָקֵל—**1. make light, lighten** burden from upon (מֵעַל) people, of Y. 1 S 6$_{5}$, of king 1 K 12$_{10}$. **2a. despise, dishonour** someone, of Y. Is 23$_{9}$, of human being 2 S 19$_{44}$. **b.** perh. of Y., **bring contempt,** הֵקַל אַרְצָה זְבֻלוּן *he brought contempt to the land of Zebulun* Is 8$_{23}$.

→ קַל I *swift,* II *insignificant,* קַל I *easiness,* קְלָלָה *curse,* קְלֹקֵל *contemptible,* קִיקָלוֹן I *disgrace,* II *dung,* קִיקָלוֹת *dung-heap;* cf. קלה II *dishonour.*

*קלל II 9.0.1 vb.—**Qal** 5 Pf. קַלּוּ; + waw וְקַלּוּ—**be swift, quick,** of person, מִנְּשָׁרִים קַלּוּ *they were swifter than eagles* 2 S 1$_{23}$, horse Jr 4$_{13}$, day Jb 7$_{6}$.

Ni. 1 Impf. יִקַּלּוּ—**be swift, show oneself to be quick,** of pursuer Is 30$_{16}$.

Pilp. 2.0.1 Pf. קִלְקַל—**1.** with בְּ of obj., in divination, **move quickly back and forward, shake** arrow Ezk 21$_{26}$. **2. move quickly back and forward, sharpen, whet** edge of axe Ec 10$_{10}$.

Htpalp. 1 Pf. הִתְקַלְקְלוּ—**move quickly back and forward, shake oneself,** of hills Jr 4$_{24}$.

→ קַל I *swift,* קָלָל *burnished,* קִילָה *swiftness.*

קָלָל I 2 adj. **burnished,** perh. from quick rubbing motion, of bronze Ezk 1$_{7}$. → קלל II *be swift.*

*קָלָל II 0.0.1 n.[m.]. **amphora, urn** 3QTr 6$_{4}$.

קְלָלָה 33.2.9 n.f.—cstr. קִלְלַת; sf. קִלְלָתוֹ; pl. קְלָלוֹת; sf. Q קללותם—**1. curse,** עָלַי קִלְלָתְךָ *your curse will be upon me* Gn 27$_{13}$. **2. (object of) curse** 2 K 22$_{19}$. → קלל I *be despised.*

*[קֶלֶם] 0.0.0.1 pr.n.[m.] (?) **Kelem.**

קלס I 4.3.2 vb.—**Pi** 1.3.2 Inf. cstr. קַלֵּס—**1. scorn, spurn,** a. with obj., fee Ezk 16$_{31}$. b. with בְּ of obj., people 1QpHab 4$_{3}$. **2.** intrans, **scorn, mock** Si 11$_{4(B)}$.

Htp. 3 Impf. יִתְקַלָּס—with בְּ of obj., **mock, deride** person 2 K 2$_{23}$.

→ קֶלֶס *mockery,* קַלָּסָה *mockery.*

*קלס II 0.1 vb.—**Pi.** 0.1 + waw ותקלס (or read as ותקלט, from קלט II *give praise*)—**give praise,** ותקלס ... שירה *and you gave praise ... (with) song* Si 47$_{15}$.

קֶלֶס 3.0.3 n.[m.] **1. object of mockery** Ps 79$_{4}$. **2. mockery** 1QM 12$_{8}$. → קלס I *mock.*

קַלָּסָה 1 n.f. **object of mockery** Ezk 22$_{4}$. → קלס *mock.*

קלע I 4 vb.—**Qal** 2 Ptc. קוֹלֵעַ—of Y., **sling (out), hurl (out)** inhabitants Jr 10$_{18}$.

Pi. 2 Impf. יְקַלְּעֶנָּה—**1. sling** stone 1 S 17$_{49}$. **2.** of Y., **hurl (away)** enemies' lives 1 S 25$_{29}$.

→ קֶלַע I *sling,* II *curtain,* קַלָּע *slinger.*

קלע II 3 vb.—**Qal** 3 Pf. קָלַע—**1. carve** cherub, palm-tree 1 K 6$_{35}$; with cognate accus., מִקְלַעַת *carving* 1 K 6$_{32}$. **2.** with double accus., **carve** walls **with** engravings 1 K 6$_{29}$. → מִקְלַעַת *carving.*

קֶלַע I 6.1.2 n.[m.]—sf. קַלְעוֹ—**sling,** אַבְנֵי קְלָעִים *stones of,* i.e. for, *slings* 2 C 26$_{14}$. → קלע I *sling.*

[קֶלַע] II 16 n.[m.]—pl. קְלָעִים; cstr. קַלְעֵי—**curtain, hanging,** in court of tabernacle, made with twisted linen thread Ex 38$_{16}$. → קלע I *sling.*

[קַלָּע] 1 n.m.—pl. קַלָּעִים—**slinger,** military role 2 K 3$_{25}$. → קלע I *sling.*

קְלֹקֵל I 1 adj. **contemptible, worthless,** of bread Nm 21$_{5}$. → קלל I *be despised.*

*קְלֹקֵל II 1 n.[m.] **cassia,** type of plant, לֶחֶם הַקְּלֹקֵל *bread,* i.e. food, *of the cassia* Nm 21$_{5}$.

קִלְּשׁוֹן 1 n.[f.] **fine points,** שְׁלֹשׁ קִלְּשׁוֹן *three of fine points,* i.e. fork or trident 1 S 13$_{21}$.

קָמָה I 10 n.f.—cstr. קָמַת; pl. cstr. קָמוֹת—**standing grain** Dt 23$_{26}$. → קום *arise.*

קָמָה II 2 n.f. **maturity** 2 K 19$_{26}$||Is 37$_{27}$. → קום *arise.*

קְמוּאֵל 3 pr.n.m. **Kemuel.**

קָמוֹן 1 pl.n. **Kamon.**

קִמּוֹשׁ 3 n.m.—pl. קִמְּשֹׂנִים—**thistle, nettle** Pr 24$_{31}$.

קֶמַח 14.0.0.7 n.[m.] **flour, meal,** קֶמַח שְׂעֹרִים *flour of barley* Nm 5$_{15}$.

קמט 2 vb.—**Qal** 1 + waw וַתִּקְמְטֵנִי—of Y., **1. seize some-**

one Jb 16$_8$ (unless §2). **2. shrivel up, wrinkle, wizen** someone Jb 16$_8$.

Pu. 1 Pf. קֻמְּטוּ—**be seized, snatched away,** of person Jb 22$_{16}$.

קמל I 2 vb.—**Qal** 2 Pf. קָמְלוּ, קָמַל—**be decayed, be mouldy, become black,** of Lebanon Is 33$_9$, reeds Is 19$_6$.

***קמל** II 2 vb.—**Qal** 2 Pf. קָמְלוּ—**be infested with lice,** of Lebanon Is 33$_9$, reeds Is 19$_6$.

***קמע** 0.1 vb.—**Hi.** 0.1 Impf. תקמיעהו—**cause distress** to someone Si 34$_{31}$.

קמץ 3.0.1 vb.—**Qal** 3.0.1 + waw וְקָמַץ—**grasp (a handful),** וְקָמַץ הַכֹּהֵן מִמֶּנָּה מְלוֹא קֻמְצוֹ אֶת־אַזְכָּרָתָהּ *then the priest will grasp a handful of it as its memorial portion* Lv 5$_{12}$. → קֹמֶץ *hand.*

[קֹמֶץ] 4 n.[m.]—pl. קְמָצִים—**1.** sg., **hand, fist,** מְלֹא קֻמְצוֹ *fulness of his hand,* i.e. a handful Lv 2$_2$. **2.** pl., **handfuls, fistfuls,** i.e. abundance Gn 41$_{47}$. → קמץ *grasp.*

קִמְּשֹׂנִים, see קִמּוֹשׁ *thistle.*

קֵן 13.2.3 n.m.—Si קין; sf. קִנִּי; pl. קִנִּים—**1. nest,** קַן־צִפּוֹר *nest of a bird* Dt 22$_6$. **2. nestlings, brood,** כְּנֶשֶׁר יָעִיר קִנּוֹ *like an eagle who rouses its nestlings* Dt 32$_{11}$. **3. compartments, cells,** in Noah's ark Gn 6$_{14}$. → קנן *nest.*

קנא 34.8.7 vb.—**Pi.** 30.8.6 Pf. קִנְאוּנִי, קִנֵּא; impf. יְקַנֵּא; ptc. מְקַנֵּא; inf. abs. קַנֹּא; cstr. קַנְאוֹ (קַנְאתוֹ)—**1a. be jealous, envious (of)** someone, (1) with בְּ Gn 30$_1$. (2) with לְ Ps 106$_{16}$. (3) with obj. Gn 26$_{14}$. **b.** ptc. as noun, **jealous one** Si 37$_{11(B)}$. **2. be wrought up about wife because of jealousy** Nm 5$_{14}$. **3. be zealous for** (לְ) Y., of Phinehas Nm 25$_{13}$, for (לְ) Zion, of Y. Zc 8$_2$. **4. stir Y. to jealousy,** הֵם קִנְאוּנִי בְלֹא־אֵל *they have stirred me to jealousy with what is no god* Dt 32$_{21}$.

Hi. 4.0.1 Impf. אַקְנִיאֵם; ptc. מַקְנֶה—**1. stir to jealousy,** obj. Y., of Israel Dt 32$_{16}$ (בְּזָרִים *with foreign [gods]*); obj. Israel, of Y. Dt 32$_{21}$ (בְּלֹא־עָם *with what is no people*). **2. provoke jealousy,** of image Ezk 8$_3$.

→ קִנְאָה *jealousy,* קַנָּא *jealous,* קַנּוֹא *jealous.*

קַנָּא 6.0.3 adj. **1. jealous,** of Y. Ex 20$_5$. **2. Jealous,** as name for Y. Ex 34$_{14}$. → קנא *be jealous.*

קִנְאָה 43.4.27 n.f.—cstr. קִנְאַת; sf. קִנְאָתִי; pl. קנאת—**1a. jealousy** of human being, in love for spouse, רוּחַ־קִנְאָה *spirit,* i.e. feelings, *of jealousy* Nm 5$_{14}$. **b. jealous anger** of Y., because of religious disloyalty, אֵשׁ קִנְאָתוֹ *fire of his jealous anger* Zp 1$_{18}$. **2. envy,** קִנְאַת־אִישׁ מֵרֵעֵהוּ *a man's envy of his neighbour* Ec 4$_4$. **3a. zeal,** of Y. for his people, אַיֵּה קִנְאָתְךָ וּגְבוּרֹתֶךָ *where are your zeal and your mighty deeds?* Is 63$_{15}$, of human being for Y. 2 K 10$_{16}$. **b. passion,** of lover Ca 8$_6$ (unless §1a). → קנא *be jealous.*

קנה 84.13.2.1 vb.—**Qal** 81.11.1.1 Pf. קָנְתָה, קָנָה; impf. יִקְנֶה, יִקְנוּ; + waw וַיִּקֶן; impv. קְנֵה; ptc. קוֹנֶה; inf. abs. קָנֹה (קָנוֹ); cstr. קְנֹה (קְנוֹת)—**1a. buy, purchase** lamb 2 S 12$_3$, field Gn 25$_{10}$ (מֵאֵת בְּנֵי־חֵת *from the Hittites*), poor person Am 8$_6$ (בַּכֶּסֶף *in exchange for silver*). **b.** ptc. as noun, **owner, buyer** Is 24$_2$. **2a.** of human being, **buy back, redeem** enslaved relative Ne 5$_8$. **b.** of Y., **redeem, recover** remnant Is 11$_{11}$. **3. acquire, get, gain** wisdom Pr 4$_5$, friend Si 6$_7$. **4a.** of Y., **create, form** people Dt 32$_6$, kidneys Ps 139$_{13}$, wisdom Pr 8$_{22}$. **b.** ptc. as noun, **creator,** קֹנֵה שָׁמַיִם וָאָרֶץ *creator of heaven and earth* Gn 14$_{19}$.

Ni. 2 Impf. יִקָּנוּ; + waw וְנִקְנָה—**be bought,** of house, field Jr 32$_{15}$.

Hi. 1.2.1 Pf. הִקְנַנִי; impf. Si תקנא—**1. enslave** someone Zc 13$_5$. **2. give oneself to** (לְ) a woman Si 9$_2$. **3.** ptc. as noun, **seller,** or perh. **purchaser** Si 37$_{11(B)}$.

→ קִנְיָן *acquisition,* מִקְנֶה *cattle,* מִקְנָה *purchase.*

קָנֶה 62.0.5 n.m.—cstr. קְנֵה; sf. קָנָהּ; pl. קָנִים; cstr. קְנֵי; sf. קְנֹתָם—**1a. reed,** water plant, חַיַּת קָנֶה *beast of the reeds* Ps 68$_{31}$. **b. cane,** קְנֵה־בֹשֶׂם *aromatic cane* Ex 30$_{23}$. **c. stalk** of grain Gn 41$_5$. **2a. shaft** of tabernacle lampstand Ex 25$_{31}$. **b. branch** of tabernacle lampstand Ex 25$_{32}$. **c. beam** of scales Is 46$_6$. **3a. rod,** קְנֵה הַמִּדָּה *measuring rod* Ezk 40$_3$. **b. reed,** unit of measurement Ezk 40$_5$. **4. bone of upper arm,** perh. **humerus,** or **shoulder,** or **shoulder socket** Jb 31$_{22}$.

קָנָה 3 pl.n. **Kanah.**

קַנּוֹא 2 adj. **jealous,** of Y. Jos 24$_{19}$. → קנא *be jealous.*

קְנַז 11 pr.n.m. **Kenaz.**

קְנִזִּי 4 gent. **Kenizzite.**

***[קְנִי]** 0.0.0.1 pr.n.m. **Kenni.**

***[קְנָיָהוּ]** 0.0.0.2 pr.n.m. **Kenaiah.**

קִנְיָן 10.2.1 n.m.—cstr. קִנְיַן; sf. קִנְיָנוֹ; pl. sf. mss קִנְיָנֶיךָ—**1.**

acquisition, possession, property, usu. of living property, esp. livestock Gn 34$_{23}$, also servants Lv 22$_{11}$, wife Si 36$_{29}$(B, C), wisdom personified as a woman Si 51$_{21}$. **2.** coll., **creatures** of Y., מָלְאָה הָאָרֶץ קִנְיָנֶךָ *the earth is full of your creatures* Ps 104$_{24}$. → קנה *acquire.*

קִנָּמוֹן 3 n.m. **cinnamon,** קִנְּמָן־בֶּשֶׂם *fragrant cinnamon* Ex 30$_{23}$.

קנן 5.1 vb.—**Pi.** 4.1 Pf. קִנְּנוּ, קִנְּנָה; impf. תְּקַנֵּן—**nest, make a nest,** of bird Ps 104$_{17}$, arrow snake Is 34$_{15}$.

Pu. 1 Ptc. Qr מְקֻנַּנְתְּ, Kt מקננתי—**be nested, nestled,** of inhabitant Jr 22$_{23}$.

→ קֵן *nest.*

[קֶנֶץ] I 1 n.[m.] **snare,** קִנְצֵי לְמִלִּין *snares for words* Jb 18$_{2}$.

*[קֶנֶץ] II 1 n.[m.] **end,** קִנְצֵי לְמִלִּין *ends for words,* i.e. an end of speeches Jb 18$_{2}$. → קצץ II *come to an end.*

קְנָת 2 pl.n. **Kenath.**

קְסָאוֹת, see קַשְׂוָה *jar.*

קסם 20.0.2 vb.—**Qal** 20.0.2 Impf. יִקְסֹמוּ; impv. Qr קָסֳמִי (Kt קסומי); ptc. קֹסֵם, קֹסְמִים; inf. cstr. קְסָם־ (קסם)—**1a.** without obj., **practise divination,** of prophet Mc 3$_{11}$, medium 1 S 28$_{8}$. **b.** with cognate obj., קֶסֶם, **practise divination,** of king Ezk 21$_{26}$. **c.** with obj. lying divination, of prophet Ezk 13$_{9}$. **2.** ptc. as noun, **diviner** 1 S 6$_{2}$. **3.** inf. as noun, **divination** Mc 3$_{6}$. → קֶסֶם *divination,* מִקְסָם *divination.*

קֶסֶם 11.0.1 n.[m.]—pl. קְסָמִים—**1. divination, prediction,** חַטַּאת־קֶסֶם *sin of divination* 1 S 15$_{23}$. **2. fee for divination** Nm 22$_{7}$ (unless §3). **3. instrument of divination** Nm 22$_{7}$. **4. decision,** by means of divination Pr 16$_{10}$. → קסם *practise divination.*

קסס I 1 vb.—**Po.** 1 Impf. יְקוֹסֵס—of eagle, **gather, pluck, strip off** fruit Ezk 17$_{9}$.

*קסס II 1 vb.—**Po.** 1 Impf. יְקוֹסֵס—of eagle, **make** fruit **scaly** Ezk 17$_{9}$.

*קסס III 1 vb.—**Po.** 1 Impf. יְקוֹסֵס—of eagle, **make** fruit **sour** Ezk 17$_{9}$.

*[קֶסֶר] 0.0.0.1 pr.n.m. **Keser.**

קֶסֶת 3 n.[f.] **writing case,** or perh. **inkpot,** קֶסֶת הַסֹּפֵר *writing case of the scribe* Ezk 9$_{2}$.

*קעה vb. **Qal, shout,** in mourning Moab Is 15$_{3}$ (if ins. קָעוּ *they shout* before עַל).

קְעִילָה I 17.0.1 pl.n. **Keilah.**

קְעִילָה II 1 pr.n.m. **Keilah.**

*קעע 0.1 vb.—**Pilp.** 0.1 Pf. קעקע—of Y., **tear down, destroy** root Si 10$_{16}$. → קַעֲקַע *tattoo.*

קַעֲקַע 1.0.1 n.[m.] **tattoo** Lv 19$_{28}$. → קעע *tear down.*

קְעָרָה 17 n.f.—cstr. קַעֲרַת; pl. קְעָרֹת; cstr. קַעֲרֹת; sf. קְעָרֹתָיו—**dish, platter,** קַעֲרַת־כֶּסֶף *silver dish* Nm 7$_{13}$.

*[קְעָרוּרָה] 0.0.1 n.f.—pl. קערורת—**depression,** perh. in wall of house, caused by disease 4QMSM$_{6}$. → cf. שְׁקַעֲרוּרָה *depression.*

קפא I 3.1.1 vb.—**Qal** 2.0.1 Pf. קָפְאוּ; ptc. קֹפְאִים—**1. become rigid, freeze,** of water Ex 15$_{8}$, people Zp 1$_{12}$. **2. contract, be reduced,** of precious things Zc 14$_{6}$(Kt).

Hi. 1.1 Impf. תַּקְפִּיאֵנִי—**1.** of Y., **curdle, coagulate** embryo like (כְּ) cheese Jb 10$_{10}$. **2. cause** water **to congeal, freeze** Si 43$_{20}$.

→ קִפָּאוֹן *frost.*

*קפא II 1 vb.—**Qal** 1 Pf. קָפְאוּ—of deep, **foam** in (בְּ) heart of sea Ex 15$_{8}$.

קִפָּאוֹן 1 n.[m.] **frost** Zc 14$_{6}$(Qr). → קפא I *congeal.*

קפד 1.1 vb.—**Qal** 0.1 Ptc. pass. קפודה—**roll up,** pass., **be rolled up, shut, clenched,** of hand Si 43$_{1}$(C).

Pi. 1 Pf. קִפַּדְתִּי—**roll up** life like (כְּ) a weaver Is 38$_{12}$.

→ קִפֹּד I *hedgehog,* קְפָדָה *shuddering.*

קִפֹּד I 3 n.[m.]—קִפּוֹד—**hedgehog** or **porcupine** Is 34$_{11}$.

→ קפד *roll up.*

*קִפֹּד II 3 n.[m.]—קִפּוֹד—**owl** Is 34$_{11}$.

קְפָדָה 1 n.f. **shuddering, anguish** Ezk 7$_{25}$. → קפד *roll up.*

קִפּוֹז I 1 n.f. **arrow snake,** reptile living in trees Is 34$_{15}$.

*קִפּוֹז II 1 n.f. **owl** Is 34$_{15}$.

קפץ I 7.3.4 vb.—**Qal** 5.2.4 Pf. קָפְצָה; impf. תִּקְפֹּץ; ptc. pass. Si קפוצה—**1a. draw together, shut, contract** hand Dt 15$_{7}$, mouth Is 52$_{15}$. **b.** of Y., **shut up, close off, keep away** compassion Ps 77$_{10}$. **2.** pass., of hand, **be shut, drawn together, clenched** in the midst of (בְּתוֹךְ) gifts Si 43$_{1}$(A).

Ni. 1 Impf. יִקָּפְצוּן—**1. wilt, wither,** lit. **be drawn together** like (כְּ) mallow, of wicked Jb 24$_{24}$ (unless §2). **2. be snatched away** just like (כְּ) all, of wicked Jb 24$_{24}$.

Pi. 1 Ptc. מְקַפֵּץ—**leap, bound, spring,** lit. con

tract legs Ca 2_{8}.

Htp. 0.1 Impf. תתקפץ—**have qualms, feel uncertain,** perh. lit. **leap about** Si $35_{19(E)}$.

*קפץ II 1 vb.—**Pi.** 1 Ptc. מְקַפֵּץ—**gambol** Ca 2_{8}.

קֵץ I 67.5.175 n.m.—cstr. קֵץ; sf. קִצִּי; pl. Q קצים; cstr. Q קצי; sf. Q קציך—**1. end,** of time, קֵץ הַיָּמִין *end of the days* Dn 12_{13}; **end, limit, cessation,** of existence, קֵץ כָּל־בָּשָׂר *end of all flesh,* i.e. people, creatures Gn 6_{13}. **2. time, era, age, period, moment;** sometimes specif. **appointed time, due season,** of an action or event, קץ משפט *time of judgment* 1QH 14_{29}. **3. end, extremity, utmost border, boundary,** of space, קצי שדה *ends of a field* 4QInstr[d] 243_{4}. → קצץ II *come to an end.*

*[קֵץ] II 0.0.0.1 n.[m.] **summer fruit** Gezer calendar$_{7}$. → קיץ II *spend summer.*

קצב 2 vb.—**Qal** 2 + waw וַיִּקְצָב־; ptc. pass. קְצוּבוֹת—**1. cut off, cut down** wooden stick 2 K 6_{6}. **2.** pass., **be cut, shorn,** of flock Ca 4_{2}. → קֶצֶב *shape.*

קֶצֶב 3.1 n.m. **1. shape, form,** of cherubim 1 K 6_{25}. **2. root, extremity, foundation,** קִצְבֵי הָרִים *roots of the mountains* Jon 2_{7}. → קצב *cut.*

קצה 5 vb.—**Qal** 1 Inf. cstr. קְצוֹת—**cut off,** i.e. destroy, people Hb 2_{10}.

Pi. 2 Ptc. מְקַצֶּה; inf. cstr. קַצּוֹת—**1. cut off, break off** feet Pr 26_{6}. **2.** of Y., **cut off,** i.e. destroy, some of (בְּ) Israel 2 K 10_{32}.

Hi. 2 Pf. הִקְצוֹ; inf. cstr. הַקְצוֹת—**scrape (off)** dust Lv 14_{41}, house Lv 14_{43}.

קָצָה 35.1.3 n.f.&m.—pl. cstr. קְצוֹת; sf. קְצוֹתָיו—**1. end, extremity, edge,** קְצוֹת הַכַּפֹּרֶת *ends of the mercy seat* Ex 25_{18}, הַשָּׁמַיִם *of the heavens* Jr 49_{36}. **2.** pl., **entirety, all, whole,** קְצוֹת הָעָם *all of the people* 1 K 12_{31}. **3.** pl., **outer parts, outskirts,** קְצוֹת דְּרָכָיו *outer parts of his ways* Jb 26_{14}. **4. time, age** 4QAges[b] 2_{9}. → קצץ II *come to an end.*

קָצֶה 92.1.7 n.[m.]—cstr. קְצֵה; sf. קָצֵהוּ—**1. end** of specified amount of time, מִקְצֵה שֶׁבַע שָׁנִים *at the end of seven years* 2 K 8_{3}. **2. end, extremity, edge, border, outskirts** of space, קְצֵה שָׂדֵהוּ *end of his field* Gn 23_{9}. **3. end parts, extremities, outskirts, outposts** of group of people, קְצֵה הַחֲמֻשִׁים *outposts of the armed men* Jg 7_{11}; **all, entirety, whole,** קְצֵה אֶחָיו *all of his brothers* Gn 47_{2}. **4. time** 4QAges[b] 1.2_{3}. → קצץ II *come to an end.*

קֵצֶה 5 n.[m.] **end, limit** Is 2_{7}. → קצץ II *come to an end.*

*[קֹצֶה] 0.0.0.2 pl.n. **Kozeh.**

[קָצוּ] 3 n.[m.] **end, border,** קַצְוֵי־אֶרֶץ *ends of the land* Ps 48_{11}. → קצץ II *come to an end.*

קְצוֹת, see קָצָה *end.*

קֶצַח 3 n.m. **black cumin** (*Nigella sativa*) Is 28_{25}.

קָצִין I 12.1.0.1 n.m.—pl. sf. קְצִינַיִךְ—**1. military commander,** קְצִינֵי אַנְשֵׁי הַמִּלְחָמָה *army commanders* Jos 10_{24}. **2. political leader,** קְצִין עָם *leader of the people* Is 3_{7}.

קָצִין II, see עֵת קָצִין *Eth-kazin.*

[קְצִיעָה] I 1 n.f.—pl. קְצִיעוֹת—**cassia** Ps 45_{9}.

קְצִיעָה II 1 pr.n.f. **Keziah.**

קְצִיץ, see עֵמֶק קְצִיץ *Emek-keziz.*

קָצִיר I 49.0.5.5 n.m.—I קצר—**1. harvest season,** קְצִיר־חִטִּים *harvest of wheat* Gn 30_{14}. **2. harvest crop,** לֶקֶט קְצִירְךָ *gleaning of your harvest* Lv 19_{9}. **3. (process of) harvesting** Ru 2_{21}. → קצר I *harvest.*

קָצִיר II 5.0.2 n.m.—sf. קְצִירִי; pl. sf. קְצִירֶהָ—**branch(es)** Is 27_{11}. → קצר I *harvest.*

קצע I 1 vb.—**Hi.** 1 Impf. יַקְצִעַ—**cause house to be scraped (off)** Lv 14_{41}. → מַקְצֻעָה I *knife.*

קצע II 1 vb.—**Ho.** 1 Ptc. מְהֻקְצָעוֹת—**be the same size,** of corners Ezk 46_{22}. → מִקְצֹעַ *corner,* מַקְצֻעָה II *square,* מְהֻקְצָעוֹת *corner rooms.*

קצף 34.1.3 vb.—**Qal** 28.0.3 Pf. קָצַפְתִּי; impf. יִקְצֹף; ptc. קֹצֵף; inf. cstr. קְצֹף—**1. be angry** against (almost alw. עַל, once אֶל [Jos 22_{18}]) someone, of Y. Lm 5_{22}, of human being Gn 41_{10}. **2.** trans., of Y., **bear (great) anger** against (עַל) Israelites, **a.** with obj., אַף and חֵמָה Dt 9_{19}. **b.** with cognate obj., קֶצֶף Zc 1_{2}.

Hi. 5 Pf. הִקְצַפְתָּ; + waw וַיַּקְצִיפוּ; ptc. מַקְצִפִים; inf. cstr. הַקְצִיף—**cause Y. to be angry,** of Israel Dt 9_{7}.

Htp. 1.1 + waw וְהִתְקַצֵּף—**be angry, enraged** Is 8_{21}. → קֶצֶף *anger,* קִצָּפוֹן *resentment.*

קֶצֶף I 28.0.4 n.m.—cstr. קֶצֶף; sf. קִצְפִּי—**1. anger, wrath, judgment, punishment** of Y. Is 34_{2}. **2. anger, frustration** of people Ec 5_{16}. → קצף *be angry.*

קֶצֶף II 1 n.[m.] **splinter, chip** Ho 10_{7}.

*קֶ֫צֶף III 1 n.[m.] **foam** Ho 10$_{7}$.

קְצָפָה 1 n.f. **splintering,** of tree Jl 1$_{7}$.

*קִצָּפוֹן 0.2 n.m. **resentment, anger** Si 30$_{23(B)}$. → קצף *be angry.*

קצץ I 14 vb.—**Qal** 4 + waw וְקַצֹּתָה; ptc. pass. קְצוּצֵי—**1. cut off** hand Dt 25$_{12}$. **2.** pass. ptc. as noun, **one who is cut,** קְצוּצֵי פֵאָה *ones cut of forehead,* i.e. who have the corners of their hair cut Jr 9$_{25}$.

Pi. 9 Pf. קִצֵּץ (קִצֵּץ); + waw וַיְקַצֵּץ—**1. cut up, cut down,** obj. door, of human being 2 K 18$_{16}$, obj. cords of wicked, of Y. Ps 129$_{4}$. **2. cut off** hands and feet 2 S 4$_{12}$.

Pu. 1 Ptc. מְקֻצָּצִים—of foot, hand, thumb, **be cut off, be mutilated** Jg 1$_{7}$.

*קצץ II vb.—**Qal, come to the end of** one's days Ps 55$_{24}$ (if em. יֶחֱצוּ *they will divide* to יִקְצוּ *they will come to the end of*).

Hi., come to an end Ps 139$_{18}$ (if em. הֱקִיצֹתִי *I was awake* to הֲקִצּוֹתִי *I came to an end*).

→ קֵץ *end,* קֶנֶץ II *end,* קִיצוֹן *outermost,* קָצָה *end,* קָצֶה *end,* קֵצָה *end,* קָצוּ, קְצָת *end.*

קצר I 35.2.2.3 vb.—**Qal** 35.2.2.3 Pf. קְצַרְתֶּם; impf. יִקְצוֹר; impv. קִצְרוּ; ptc. קוֹצֵר; inf. קְצֹר (קֻצְרְכֶם)—**1. harvest, reap** field Ru 2$_{9}$, ears of grain Is 17$_{5}$, iniquity Pr 22$_{8}$. **2.** ptc. as noun, **reaper** Ru 2$_{14}$.

Hi. 1 Impf. Kt יקצירו—**harvest, gather** fodder Jb 24$_{6(Kt)}$ (Qr יִקְצוֹרוּ).

→ קָצִיר I *harvest,* II *branch.*

קצר II 15.2.3 vb.—**Qal** 13.0.3 Pf. קָצְרָה; impf. תִּקְצַר; ptc. pass. קְצֻרוֹת; inf. abs. קָצוֹר—**1. be short, a.** in size, of bed Is 28$_{20}$. **b.** in time, of person's years Pr 10$_{27}$. **2. be shortened, curbed,** with regard to influence, of Y.'s hand Nm 11$_{23}$. **3. become impatient, displeased,** of human heart Nm 21$_{4}$, of Y.'s spirit Mc 2$_{7}$. **4.** pass., **be narrow,** of chamber Ezk 42$_{5}$. **5.** inf. as noun, **shortness,** קצור אפים *shortness of anger,* i.e. impatience 1QS 4$_{10}$.

Pi. 1.1 Pf. קִצַּר—**shorten** days, of Y. Ps 102$_{24}$, anger and jealousy Si 30$_{24(B)}$.

Hi. 1 Pf. הִקְצַרְתָּ—**shorten** days, of Y. Ps 89$_{46}$.

Htp. 0.1 Impf. Si תתקצר—**be brusque** during (בְּ) prayer Si 7$_{10(A)}$.

→ קֹצֶר *shortness,* קָצֵר *short.*

[קֹ֫צֶר] 1.0.1 n.m. **shortness,** קֹצֶר רוּחַ *shortness of spirit,* i.e. a broken spirit Ex 6$_{9}$, קוצר אפים *shortness of anger,* i.e. impatience 1QS 6$_{26}$. → קצר II *be short.*

[קָצֵר] 5.0.4 adj. **1. short,** in size, of toe 4QCrypt 1.3$_{5}$. **2-4,** all of human being, **2.** קְצַר יָמִים **short of days** Jb 14$_{1}$. **3a.** קְצַר־אַפַּיִם **short of anger,** i.e. impatient 4Q Rebukes 2.2$_{4}$. **b.** as noun, קְצַר רוּחַ **one short of spirit,** i.e. impatient person Pr 14$_{29}$. **4.** קִצְרֵי־יָד **short of power** 2 K 19$_{26}$. → קצר II *be short.*

קְצָת 9.0.7 n.f.—pl. קְצוֹת; cstr. Q קצוות; sf. קְצָתָם—**1. end, edge, extremity,** קצוות תבל *ends of the world* 1QM 1$_{8}$. **2.** מִקְצָת as prep., **a. some (of),** מקצת מעשי התורה *some of the works of the law* 4QMMT C$_{27}$. **b. at the end of,** מִקְצָת יָמִים עֲשָׂרָה *at the end of ten days* Dn 1$_{15}$. **3.** לְמִקְצָת as prep., **at the end of,** לְמִקְצָת הַיָּמִים *at the end of the time* Dn 1$_{18}$. → קצץ II *come to an end.*

[קַר] 3 adj.—pl. קָרִים—**1. cool,** of waters Pr 25$_{25}$. **2.** as noun, קַר־רוּחַ **cool one of spirit,** i.e. rational, calm, or perh. forbearing Pr 17$_{27(Kt)}$. → קרר I *be cold.*

*קֹר I 1 n.m. **noise, shout** Is 22$_{5}$.

קֹר II, see קִיר *wall.*

קֹר 1 n.[m.] **cold** Gn 8$_{22}$. → קרר I *be cold.*

קרא I 735.10.92.7 vb.—**Qal** 666.4.73.7 Pf. קָרָא, קְרָאתֶם; impf. יִקְרָא; impv. קְרָא, קִרְאוּ, קְרֶאן (קְרֶאןָ); ptc. קוֹרֵא, קֹרְאִים; pass. קָרוּא, קְרוּאִים; inf. cstr. קְרֹא (קְרֹאות), mss קְרָאת, קָרְאֵנוּ)—**1a. call, summon** someone Gn 47$_{29}$; **call, commission, appoint** someone Is 45$_{4}$; **invite** someone Jb 1$_{4}$; **call people together** 2 K 3$_{10}$; **call someone from the dead** 1 S 28$_{15}$, (1) obj. 1 K 1$_{10}$ Ps 50$_{1}$ Ca 5$_{6}$. (2) לְ of obj. Nm 25$_{2}$ Is 45$_{4}$ Dn 2$_{2}$ 1 C 15$_{11}$. (3) אֶל of obj. Gn 22$_{11}$ 2 K 18$_{18}$ Ps 50$_{4}$. **b.** oft. of Y., **call,** with person called implied 1 S 3$_{5}$. **c. call,** followed by name or title of person called, וַיִּקְרָא כְפַעַם־בְּפַעַם שְׁמוּאֵל שְׁמוּאֵל *and he called as at other times, 'Samuel, Samuel!'* 1 S 3$_{10}$. **d. summon** to do something, וַיִּקְרָא ... לִבְכִי וּלְמִסְפֵּד *then he summoned ... to weeping and lamenting* Is 22$_{12}$. **2a. call (on), pray (to)** Y., oft. for help 1 K 8$_{52}$; as act of adoration, i.e. **give praise (to), worship** Y. Ps 66$_{17}$, (1) obj. Ps 17$_{6}$. (2) אֶל of obj. or *to* Dt 4$_{7}$. (3) לְ of obj. or *to* 1 C 4$_{10}$. **b. pray,** with omission of addressee, implied to Y. Zc 7$_{13}$. **c. call (on), invoke** name of deity (oft. Y.) for assistance, (1) בְּ *on*, + שֵׁם, וַיִּקְרָא בְּשֵׁם י׳ *then he called on the name of* Y. Gn 12_{8}. (2) obj. שֵׁם Lm 3_{55}. **d. summon,** implied obj. Y. Jb 9_{16}. **3. call on** wisdom personified, for advice, help Pr 1_{28}. **4. call (for), ask (for)** something, **a.** obj. omen Nm 24_{1}. **b.** לְ of obj. or *for*, + beatings, of mouth of fool Pr 18_{6}. **5.** of Y., **call (for), decree, ordain** something, e.g. famine, abundance of food, **a.** obj. Hg 1_{11}. **b.** לְ of obj. or *for* 2 K 8_{1}. **c.** אֶל of obj. or *for* Ezk 36_{29}. **6. mention, list** cities by (בְּ) name Jos 21_{9}. **7a. announce, declare, tell (about)** something, specif. **preach** moral lesson Jon 3_{2}, **foretell** future event 1 K 13_{4}, (1) obj. 1 K 13_{4}. (2) cognate obj. קְרִיאָה Jon 3_{2}. (3) followed by אמר, introducing announcement made, הָלֹךְ וְקָרָאתָ בְאָזְנֵי יְרוּשָׁלַםִ לֵאמֹר כֹּה אָמַר י׳ *go and announce in the ears of Jerusalem (saying), 'Thus says Y.'* Jr 2_{2}. (4) introducing direct speech, תִּקְרָא ... מִי־פֶתִי יָסֻר *she announces ..., 'Whoever is simple-minded, let him turn aside'* Pr 9_{3-4}. (5) followed by כִּי *that*, introducing announcement made, קִרְאוּ אֵלֶיהָ כִּי מָלְאָה צְבָאָהּ *announce to her that her term of service has been accomplished* Is 40_{2}. **b.** abs., **make an announcement, make a prophetic statement, preach (to call to repentance),** of wisdom Pr 8_{1}, of Israelites Lv 23_{21}. **c. proclaim** festival Lv 23_{2}, liberty, of Y. Jr 34_{17}. **d. proclaim** name of Y., (1) obj. שֵׁם Dt 32_{3}. (2) בְּ of obj., + שֵׁם Ex 33_{19}. **e. proclaim, propose,** i.e. offer, peace Jg 21_{13}. **8. speak out,** i.e. express an accusation, indictment, to (אֶל) Y. against (עַל) person Dt 15_{9}. **9a. call out, cry out, exclaim, shout, scream,** (1) introducing direct speech, וַיִּקְרָא הוֹצִיאוּ כָל־אִישׁ מֵעָלָי *and he cried out, 'Have everyone withdraw from me!'* Gn 45_{1}. (2) followed by verb אמר, דבר pi. or נגד hi. introducing direct speech, וַיִּקְרָא וַיֹּאמֶר לָהֶם שִׁמְעוּ אֵלַי *and he cried out and said to them: 'Listen to me!'* Jg 9_{7}. (3) to (לְ or אֶל or עַל) someone Jb 17_{14} Is 6_{3} 2 C 32_{18}. (4) after (אַחֲרֵי) someone Jr 12_{6}. (5) abs. Gn 39_{18}. **b.** of bird, **cheep** Ps 147_{9}; of goat, **bleat to** (עַל) companion Is 34_{14}. **10a. read** scroll 2 K 5_{7}, law Dt 31_{11}, words of the law Jos 8_{34}. **b. read** from (בְּ) scroll Jr 36_{13}. **c. dictate** words to (אֶל) someone Jr 36_{18}. **11a. call, name,** sometimes specif. **rename** Nm 13_{16}, with appellation, (1) with accus. of appellation and לְ introducing (a) person or people named, הַמֹּאָבִים יִקְרְאוּ לָהֶם אֵמִים *the Moabites call them Emim* Dt 2_{11}. (b) geographical location or memorial object named, וַיִּקְרָא־לוֹ לָבָן יְגַר שָׂהֲדוּתָא *and Laban called it* (i.e. the heap) *Jegar-sahadutha* Gn 31_{47}. (c) ritual objects named, וְקָרָא לוֹ אֹהֶל מוֹעֵד *and he called it the tent of meeting* Ex 33_{7}. (d) created objects named, e.g. וַיִּקְרָא אֱלֹהִים לָאוֹר יוֹם *and God called the light 'day'* Gn 1_{5}. (e) festive day named, קָרְאוּ לַיָּמִים הָאֵלֶּה פוּרִים *they called these days 'Purim'* Est 9_{26}. (2) with double accus., (a) naming geographical location or memorial object, וַיִּקְרָא אֹתָהּ שִׁבְעָה *and he called it Shebah* Gn 26_{33}. (b) naming person, קרא אל את כולם שרים *God called them all princes* CD 6_{6}. (3) with שֵׁם as obj., (a) call person's name so and so, וַיִּקְרָא אֶת־שְׁמוֹ יִשְׂרָאֵל *and he called his name Israel* Gn 35_{10}. (b) call name of region, city, well, memorial object etc. so and so, וַיִּקְרָא שְׁמָהּ לוּז *and he called its name Luz* Jg 1_{26}. **b. give a name (to),** with שֵׁם as obj., וַיִּקְרָא הָאָדָם שֵׁמוֹת לְכָל־הַבְּהֵמָה וּלְעוֹף הַשָּׁמַיִם *then the man gave names to all the beasts and the birds of the sky* Gn 2_{20}. **c. make for oneself a name,** i.e. cause oneself to become renowned, with שֵׁם as obj., קְרָא־שֵׁם בְּבֵית לָחֶם *make for yourself a name in Bethlehem* Ru 4_{11}. **12.** ptc. pass., **be called (to a feast), be invited** Est 5_{12}. **13.** ptc. as noun, **herald** Hb 2_{2}. **14.** ptc. pass. as noun, **a. one who is called (to a party),** i.e. **one who is invited, guest** 1 S 9_{22}. **b. one who is commissioned, chosen one, elected one** Nm 26_{9}. **c.** angelic title, **heavenly dignitary** MasShirShabb 1_{12}. **d. person of renown** Ezk 23_{23}.

Ni. 62.6.19 Pf. נִקְרָאתִי; impf. יִקָּרֵא; ptc. נִקְרָא, נִקְרָאִים —**1a. be called, named,** with appellation, (1) with impersonal subj., with person, place or thing named introduced by לְ, and appellation quoted, לְזֹאת יִקָּרֵא אִשָּׁה *to this one it shall be called 'woman'*, i.e. she shall be called 'woman' Gn 2_{23}. (2) with person, thing or location named as subj., and appellation quoted, אַתֶּם כֹּהֲנֵי י׳ תִּקָּרֵאוּ *you shall be called 'priests of Y.'* Is 61_{6}. (3) with שֵׁם as subj., and appellation quoted, e.g. לֹא־יִקָּרֵא שִׁמְךָ עוֹד יַעֲקֹב *no longer will your name be* called 'Jacob' Gn 35$_{10}$. **b. (someone's name) be called (over), given (to), attached (to)** someone or something, denoting possession or a relationship, with שֵׁם as subj., שֵׁם י׳ נִקְרָא עָלֶיךָ *the name of Y. will be called over you,* i.e. you will be called by his name Dt 28$_{10}$. **c. be called** by (בְּ) Y.'s name Is 43$_{7}$. **d. be named, reckoned** under/among (עַל) a tribe 1 C 23$_{14}$. **e. call oneself** of (מִן) the city of holiness Is 48$_{2}$. **2a.** of person, **be mentioned** Is 14$_{20}$. **b.** of person's name, **be recalled, proclaimed, perpetuated** through (בְּ) descendants Gn 48$_{16}$, in (בְּ) Israel Ru 4$_{14}$. **c.** of name of Y., **be invoked** Jr 44$_{26}$. **3a. be called, summoned** by (בְּ) name Est 2$_{14}$. **b. be mustered, summoned** against (עַל) lion Is 31$_{4}$. **c. be appointed** to (לְ) council of Yahad 1QSa 1$_{27}$. **4.** of annals, **be read** Est 6$_{1}$.

Pu. 7 Pf. קֹרָא (קוֹרָא); ptc. מְקֹרָאִי—**1a. be called, named,** with impersonal subj., with person or thing named introduced by לְ, and appellation quoted, e.g. וְקֹרָא לְךָ גֹּדֵר פֶּרֶץ *and 'repairer of the breach' it will be called to you,* i.e. you will be called by that name Is 58$_{12}$. **b.** of name, **be called, given** to (לְ) someone Is 62$_{2}$. **c.** of nation, **be called by** (בְּ) Y.'s name Is 65$_{1}$. **2.** ptc. as noun, **one who is called,** perh. specif. **one who is elected** Is 48$_{12}$.

→ קֹרֵא *partridge,* קָרִיא *called,* קְרִיאָה *proclamation,* מִקְרָא *convocation.*

קרא II 137.2.10.1 vb. (byform of קרה I)—**Qal** 130.2.9.1 Pf. קָרָאת, קְרָאַנִי; impf. יִקְרָא; inf. cstr. לִקְרַאת (לִקְרָאתִי)—**1. meet** someone 1 K 2$_{19}$; specif. **meet in order to help,** of Y. Ps 59$_{5}$. **2.** oft. in context of battle, **meet, approach with hostility** person 1 S 17$_{48}$, nation Jos 11$_{20}$; of predatory beast, **approach aggressively** human being Jg 14$_{5}$; of Y., **oppose** worshipper's enemies Ps 35$_{3}$. **3. face** army 1 S 17$_{21}$. **4a. encounter, experience** kindness Si 3$_{31}$. **b. encounter, be faced with** obstacle, i.e. sea Ex 14$_{27}$. **5. receive** omen Nm 24$_{1}$. **6.** of Sheol, **welcome** coming of deceased Is 14$_{9}$. **7.** of oil, appar. **touch, come into contact with** right hand Pr 27$_{16}$. **8a.** trans., of disaster, **befall, happen to** Israelites Dt 31$_{29}$. **b.** intrans., of war, **come to pass, occur** Ex 1$_{10}$. **9.** of fear, **come upon** someone Jb 4$_{14}$. **10.** inf. cstr. לִקְרַאת as prep., **to,** לִקְרַאת צָמֵא הֵתָיוּ מָיִם *bring water to the thirsty!* Is 21$_{14}$.

Ni. 6.0.1 Pf. נִקְרָא; impf. יִקָּרֵא; inf. abs. נִקְרֹא—**1a. be met, found,** of person 2 S 18$_{9}$, nest Dt 22$_{6}$. **b.** of Y., **let oneself be met** by (עַל) Israelites Ex 5$_{3}$. **2. happen to be** somewhere 2 S 1$_{6}$. **3. happen,** שֶׁבֶר עַל־שֶׁבֶר נִקְרָא *disaster after disaster happens* Jr 4$_{20}$.

Hi. 1 + waw וַתַּקְרֵא—with double accus., of Y., **cause** disaster **to happen to** Israelites Jr 32$_{23}$.

קֹרֵא I 2 n.m. **partridge** Jr 17$_{11}$. → קרא I *call.*

קֹרֵא II, see קוֹרֵא II *Kore.*

קראה, see קוֹרֵא II *Kore.*

קרב 292.6.60 vb.—**Qal** 105.5.22 Pf. קָרַב, קָרַבְתָּ; impf. יִקְרַב; impv. קְרַב, קִרְבָה, קִרְבוּ; ptc. קָרֵב, קְרֵבִים; inf. abs. קָרוֹב; cstr. קְרֹב (קְרָב־, קִרְבָה, קָרְבָתָם)—**1. draw near, approach, come, a.** to (לְ or אֶל or עַל or בְּ) a place, of army, עד קורבם למערכת האויב *until they draw near to the battle line of the enemy* 1QM 8$_{7}$, of plague, נֶגַע לֹא־יִקְרַב בְּאָהֳלֶךָ *no plague will come near your tent* Ps 91$_{10}$. **b.** to (לְ or אֶל or עַל) or before (לִפְנֵי) a person, of Y. for judgment, וְקָרַבְתִּי אֲלֵיכֶם לַמִּשְׁפָּט *then I will come near to you for judgment* Ml 3$_{5}$, of man for sexual intercourse, אֶל־אִשְׁתּוֹ לֹא תִקְרָב *do not come near to his wife* Lv 18$_{14}$, of Israel for penitence, קִרְבוּ לִפְנֵי י׳ *come before Y.* Ex 16$_{9}$. **2.** of time, event, or situation, **draw near, approach, be at hand,** קָרַב קִצֵּינוּ *our end had come* Lm 4$_{18}$. **3.** of sacrificial offering, **come near,** i.e. **be offered** 11QT 20$_{9}$. **4.** of bones of skeleton, **come together, be joined** Ezk 37$_{7}$. **5.** of battle, **be joined, begin** 1 K 20$_{29}$. **6.** of horse, appar. **stay near to** (אֶל) person Ps 32$_{9}$. **7.** in phrase, קְרַב אֶל, **keep to oneself,** קְרַב אֵלֶיךָ *keep to yourself!* Is 65$_{5}$.

Ni. 2.0.1 + waw וְנִקְרַב—**come near, present oneself to** (אֶל) Y. Ex 22$_{7}$.

Pi. 9.0.8 Pf. קֵרַבְתִּי; impf. תְּקָרֵב; impv. קָרְבוּ, קַרְבוּ—**1. bring near, cause to approach, a.** in space, אַשְׁרֵי תִּבְחַר וּתְקָרֵב *blessed is the one whom you choose and bring near* Ps 65$_{5}$. **b.** in time, קֵרְבוּ לָבוֹא *they have brought near to come,* i.e. brought their coming near Ezk 36$_{8}$. **2. bring near,** i.e. **present, submit, deliver** case Is 41$_{21}$, property 1QS 6$_{19}$. **3. bring together, join** sticks Ezk 37$_{17}$. **4. approach** Y. Jb 31$_{37}$. **5. admit (as**

qualified to belong) to (לְ) community 1QS 6$_{22}$, into (בְּ) council 1QS 8$_{18}$.

Hi. 177.0.23 Pf. הִקְרִיב, הִקְרִיבָם; impf. יַקְרִיב; + waw וַיַּקְרֵב; impv. הַקְרֵב (הַקְרִיבֵהוּ); ptc. מַקְרִיב; inf. abs. הַקְרֵב; cstr. הַקְרִיב—**1a. bring near, offer, present** an offering; oft. to (לְ) Y. Lv 1$_2$, or before (לִפְנֵי) Y. Nm 3$_4$; of Israelite assembly Lv 4$_{14}$, of priest Lv 1$_5$; obj. burnt offering Lv 7$_8$, grain offering Nm 5$_{25}$, bull Ezk 43$_{23}$, ram Lv 8$_{18}$, lamb Lv 12$_7$, blood Lv 1$_5$, bread Lv 21$_6$, wine Nm 15$_7$, honey Lv 2$_{12}$, bracelet Nm 31$_{50}$. **b. bring near, present** someone before (לִפְנֵי) Y. Nm 8$_{10}$. **c. allow** someone **to come near** to (אֶל) Y. Nm 16$_9$. **2a. bring** captured king to (אֶל) Joshua Jos 8$_{23}$. **b. present** tribute to (לְ) king Jg 3$_{17}$. **3. bring together, join** field to (בְּ) field Is 5$_8$. **4. bring (for a decision), present** a case, before (לִפְנֵי) Y. Nm 27$_5$, to (אֶל) Moses Dt 1$_{17}$. **5. bring near, bring to a close** one's days Ezk 22$_4$. **6. draw near (to do),** תַּקְרִיב לָלֶדֶת *she draws near to giving birth,* i.e. is about to give birth Is 26$_{17}$.

Htp. 0.1.7 Impf. Si תתקרב; ptc. Q מתקרב—**1. draw near** for (לְ) battle 1QM 16$_{13}$ (מתקרבי[ם למ]לחמה). **2. bring oneself near, put oneself forward** Si 13$_{10}$.

→ קָרוֹב *near,* קְרָב *battle,* קֶרֶב *inner part,* קֹרֶב I *approach,* II *inner sanctuary,* קִרְבָה *approach,* קָרְבָּן *offering,* קֻרְבָּן I *offering,* II *delivery.*

קָרֵב, see קרב *draw near,* qal ptc.

קֶרֶב 227.4.34 n.[m.]—cstr. קֶרֶב; sf. קִרְבִּי; pl. Q קרבים; sf. קְרָבַי—**1. inner part** of body, **a. entrails** of sacrificial animal Lv 4$_{11}$. **b. belly** of cow Gn 41$_{21}$. **c. inner body** of human 1 K 17$_{21}$, specif. **stomach, bowels** Jb 20$_{14}$, **womb** Gn 25$_{22}$. **2. inner person, self, heart,** esp. as seat of thoughts and feelings, קֶרֶב אִישׁ *inner person* or *heart of a man* Ps 64$_7$. **3.** בְּקֶרֶב as prep., **in (the midst of), through (the midst of), within, among,** הֲיֵשׁ י׳ בְּקִרְבֵּנוּ *is Y. among us?* Ex 17$_7$. **4.** מִקֶּרֶב as prep., **from (the midst of), from (within), from (among),** לֹא־מָשׁוּ מִקֶּרֶב הַמַּחֲנֶה *they did not depart from the camp* Nm 14$_{44}$. → קרב *draw near.*

*[קֹרֶב] I 0.0.10 n.[m.]—cstr. קורב; sf. קורבו—**approach, nearness,** קורב קודש קודשים *approach of the most holy place* 4QShirShabb^a 1.1$_{19}$. → קרב *draw near.*

*[קֹרֶב] II 0.0.11 n.[m.]—cstr. קורב; sf. קורבו—**1. inner sanctuary,** כוהן קורב *priest of the inner sanctuary* 4QShirShabb^d 1.2$_{24}$. **2.** בקורב as prep., **in (the midst of), among** 11QMelch 2$_{10}$ (=Ps 82$_1$ בְּקֶרֶב). → קרב *draw near.*

קְרָב 9.1.2 n.[m.] **battle, war,** קְרָב־לִבּוֹ *his mind was on war* Ps 55$_{22}$. → קרב *draw near.*

*[קְרַבְאוּר] 0.0.0.2 pr.n.m. **Kerabur.**

[קִרְבָה] 2 n.f. **approach, proximity, closeness,** קִרְבַת אֱלֹהִים לִי־טוֹב *closeness to God is good for me* Ps 73$_{28}$. → קרב *draw near.*

קָרְבָּן 80.0.5.1 n.m.—Q קורבן; sf. קָרְבָּנִי; cstr. קָרְבַּן; pl. Q קורבנים; sf. קָרְבְּנֵיהֶם—**offering, gift, sacrifice,** animal Lv 1$_2$, cereal Lv 2$_1$, gold Nm 31$_{50}$. → קרב *draw near.*

[קֻרְבָּן] I 2 n.m. **offering,** קֻרְבַּן הָעֵצִים *wood offering* Ne 10$_{35}$. → קרב *draw near.*

*[קֻרְבָּן] II 2 n.m. **delivery,** קֻרְבַּן הָעֵצִים *delivery of the wood* Ne 10$_{35}$. → קרב *draw near.*

קַרְדֹּם I 5 n.[m.]—sf. קַרְדֻּמּוֹ; pl. קַרְדֻּמִּים, קַרְדֻּמּוֹת—**axe** 1 S 13$_{20}$.

*[קַרְדֹּם] II 0.1 n.[m.]—pl. קרדמות—**reed** Si 40$_{16(B)}$.

קרה I 22.1.3.2 vb. (byform of קרא II)—**Qal** 13.0.3.2 Pf. קָרָךְ; impf. יִקְרֶה, תִּקְרֶינָה; + waw וַיִּקֶר; ptc. קֹרֹת; inf. Q קרותנו—**1a. encounter,** וַיִּקֶר מִקְרֶהָ חֶלְקַת הַשָּׂדֶה לְבֹעַז *and her chance encountered,* i.e. she chanced upon, *the plot of land of the field of Boaz* Ru 2$_3$. **b. meet** people Dt 25$_{18}$. **2. befall, happen (to), a.** with obj., כָּל־אֲשֶׁר קָרָהוּ *everything that had happened to him* Est 4$_7$. **b.** with לְ of obj., לַהֲבִינְךָ אֵת אֲשֶׁר־יִקְרָה לְעַמְּךָ *to make you understand what is to befall your people* Dn 10$_{14}$.

Ni. 6.1 Pf. נִקְרָה, נִקְרֵיתִי; impf. יִקָּרֶה; + waw וַיִּקָּר—**1a.** of Y., **meet** person, (1) עַל of obj. Ex 3$_{18}$. (2) אֶל of obj. Nm 23$_4$. **b.** of Y., **come (to meet),** אוּלַי יִקָּרֶה י׳ לִקְרָאתִי *perhaps Y. will come to meet me* Nm 23$_3$. **2. come by chance upon** (עַל) mountain 2 S 1$_6$. **3. be encountered by** (בְּ) good deeds Si 14$_5$.

Hi. 3 Pf. הִקְרָה; + waw וְהִקְרִיתֶם; impv. הַקְרֵה—**1. grant success,** lit. 'cause (something favourable) to occur' before/to (לִפְנֵי) person Gn 24$_{12}$. **2. select** city of refuge Nm 35$_{11}$.

→ קָרֶה *occurrence,* קְרִי *opposition,* מִקְרֶה *chance.*

קרה II 5.0.4 vb.—**Pi.** 5 Pf. קֵרוּהוּ; ptc. מְקָרֶה; inf. קָרוֹת—

lay **the beams of, make beams for** house 2 C 34$_{11}$, gate Ne 3$_{3}$.

Pu. 0.0.4 Ptc. מקורה, מקורים—**be laid with beams, be roofed,** of house 11QT 46$_{14}$.

→ קוֹרָה *beam,* מְקָרֶה *beam-work,* מְקָרָה *beam-work.*

קָרָה 5 n.f.—sf. קָרָתוֹ—**cold, coldness,** יוֹם קָרָה *cold day* Na 3$_{17}$. → קרר I *be cold.*

[קָרֶה] 1 n.[m.] **occurrence,** קְרֵה־לָיְלָה *occurrence of the night* Dt 23$_{11}$. → קרה I *encounter.*

[קָרָה], see קוֹרָה *log.*

קָרוֹב I 77.2.14 adj.—קָרֹב; sf. קְרֹבוֹ; f.s. קְרוֹבָה (קְרֹבָה); m.pl. קְרוֹבִים; cstr. Q קרובי; sf. קְרֹבַי; f.pl. קְרֹבוֹת—**1. near, nearby, nearest, close, closest, next, a.** in space, of city Gn 19$_{20}$. **b.** in time, of day of disaster Dt 32$_{35}$. **c.** in relationship of kin, of man Ru 2$_{20}$. **d.** of Y. as near to humans Ps 34$_{19}$, of Y.'s salvation Ps 85$_{10}$, of Y.'s word Dt 30$_{14}$. **e.** of humans as near to Y. Ps 148$_{14}$, of words of prayer 1 K 8$_{59}$. **f.** of wisdom as near to those who seek her Si 51$_{26}$. **2.** as noun, **one who is near, one who is close** to Y. Lv 10$_{3}$, **one who is next, close advisor** to king Est 1$_{14}$, **neighbour** or **relative** Jb 19$_{14}$. **3.** as adv., **a.** קָרוֹב (1) of place, **near,** קרוב למקדשי *near to my sanctuary* 11QT 52$_{14}$. (2) of time, **near, soon** Ezk 7$_{8}$. **b.** מִקָּרוֹב (1) **at hand, nearby,** הַאֱלֹהֵי מִקָּרֹב אָנִי *am I a God at hand?* Jr 23$_{23}$. (2) **lately, recently** Dt 32$_{17}$. (3) **of short duration** Jb 20$_{5}$. **c.** בְּקָרוֹב of time, **near, soon,** לֹא בְקָרוֹב בְּנוֹת בָּתִּים *it* (the time) *is not near to build houses* Ezk 11$_{3}$. → קרב *draw near.*

***[קָרוֹב]** II 2 adj. **able to fight,** as noun, **warrior,** קְרֹבִים לְבֻשֵׁי מִכְלוֹל *warriors clothed in perfection* Ezk 23$_{12}$.

***[קָרוּת]** n.[m.] **cold, ice,** קוֹר וְקָרוּת וְקִפָּאוֹן *cold and ice and frost* Zc 14$_{6(Qr)}$ (if em. אוֹר יְקָרוֹת *light; the precious things*). → קרר I *be cold.*

קרח 5 vb.—**Qal** 2 Impf. Kt יקרחה, Qr יִקְרְחוּ; impv. קָרְחִי—**1.** with obj. קָרְחָה, **make a bald patch on** (בְּ) head Lv 21$_{5}$. **2.** abs., **shave oneself** Mc 1$_{16}$.

Ni. 1 Impf. יִקָּרֵחַ—**make oneself bald, shave oneself for** (לְ) deceased Jr 16$_{6}$.

Hi. 1 + waw וְהִקְרִיחוּ—with obj. קָרְחָה, **make a bald patch, shave for** (אֶל) Tyre Ezk 27$_{31}$.

Ho. 1 Ptc. מֻקְרָח—**be made bald, be shaved,** of head Ezk 29$_{18}$.

→ קֵרֵחַ *bald,* קָרְחָה *bald patch,* קָרַחַת *baldness of head.*

קָרֵחַ 14 pr.n.m. **Kareah.**

קֵרֵחַ 3 adj. **1. bald,** of man Lv 13$_{40}$. **2.** as noun, **bald one,** עֲלֵה קֵרֵחַ *go on up, you baldhead!* 2 K 2$_{23}$. → קרח *make bald.*

קֶרַח 7.1.2 n.m.—sf. קַרְחוֹ—**frost, ice, cold** Gn 31$_{40}$.

קֹרַח 37.1.2.1 pr.n.m. **Korah.**

קֹרַח, see קֹרַח *Korah.*

קָרְחָה 11.0.1 n.f.—sf. קָרְחָתֵךְ—**bald patch, baldness,** בְּכָל־רָאשָׁיו קָרְחָה *on all their heads is a bald patch* Is 15$_{2}$. → קרח *make bald.*

קָרְחִי 8 gent. **Korahite.**

קָרַחַת 4 n.f.—sf. קָרַחְתּוֹ—**baldness (of head)** Lv 13$_{43}$. → קרח *make bald.*

[קְרִי] 7.0.2 n.[m.] **opposition, hostility,** חֲמַת־קֶרִי *anger of opposition* Lv 26$_{28}$. → קרה I *encounter.*

קָרִיא 3.0.7 adj.—pl. Q קריאים; cstr. Qr קְרִיאֵי—**called,** as noun, **called one, summoned one,** קריאי אל *the called of God* 1QM 3$_{2}$. → קרא I *call.*

קְרִיאָה 1 n.f. **proclamation, preaching** Jon 3$_{2}$. → קרא I *call.*

קִרְיָה 29.2.2 n.f.—pl. Q קריות—**city, town,** קִרְיַת־עֹז *fortified city* Pr 18$_{19}$. → cf. קֶרֶת *city.*

קְרִיּוֹת 3 pl.n. **Kerioth.**

קְרִיּוֹת חֶצְרוֹן 1 pl.n. **Kerioth-hezron.**

קִרְיַת, see קִרְיַת יְעָרִים *Kiriath-jearim.*

קִרְיַת אַרְבַּע 9 pl.n. **Kiriath-arba.**

קִרְיַת־בַּעַל 2 pl.n. **Kiriath-baal.**

קִרְיַת חֻצוֹת 1 pl.n. **Kiriath-huzoth.**

קִרְיַת יְעָרִים 20 pl.n. **Kiriath-jearim.**

קִרְיַת־סַנָּה 1 pl.n. **Kiriath-sannah.**

קִרְיַת־סֵפֶר 4 pl.n. **Kiriath-sepher.**

קִרְיַת עָרִים, see קִרְיַת יְעָרִים *Kiriath-jearim.*

קִרְיָתַיִם I 6 pl.n. **Kiriathaim.**

[קִרְיָתַיִם] II, see שָׁוֵה קִרְיָתַיִם *Shaveh-kiriathaim.*

קרם 2.1.1 vb.—**Qal** 2.0.1 + waw וְקָרַמְתִּי; וַיִּקְרַם—**1.** trans., of Y., **spread, lay** skin **over** (עַל) bones Ezk 37$_{6}$. **2.** intrans., of skin, **spread, form a cover over** (עַל) bones Ezk 37$_{8}$.

Ni. 0.0.1 Impf. יקרמו—of bones, **be spread with, covered with skin** 4QpsEzek[a] 2₆.

Hi. 0.1 Impf. יקרים—of Y., **allow a covering to be formed over** (עַל) place of water Si 43₂₀.

*[קַרְמִית] 0.1 n.f. **cow-wheat,** a delicate plant Si 40₁₆(M).

קרן 4 vb.—**Qal** 3 Pf. קָרַן—**send out rays, shine,** of facial skin Ex 34₂₉.

Hi. 1 Ptc. מַקְרִן—**display horns, grow horns,** of ox, bull Ps 69₃₂.

→ קֶרֶן *horn.*

קֶרֶן 76.5.18 n.f.—cstr. קֶרֶן; sf. קַרְנִי; du. קַרְנַיִם; sf. קַרְנָיו (קַרְנָיו); cstr. קַרְנֵי; pl. קְרָנוֹת; cstr. קַרְנוֹת; sf. קַרְנֹתָיו—**1. horn** of animal, specif. ram Gn 22₁₃, oxen Ps 22₂₂, animal representing person or nation Dn 8₃. **b.** as musical instrument Jos 6₅. **c.** as receptacle for oil 1 S 16₁₃. **d.** as valuable object, קַרְנוֹת שֵׁן *horns of ivory* Ezk 27₁₅. **e.** as material for hilt of sword 1QM 5₁₄. **2a. horn,** on person or nation, as a symbol of **strength, might, dignity, power,** קֶרֶן יִשְׂרָאֵל *horn of Israel* Lm 2₃; also **pride, arrogance** Ps 75₅. **b. horn, powerful one,** representing person or nation Zc 2₄; as descr. of Y., קֶרֶן יִשְׁעִי *horn of my salvation* 2 S 22₃. **3. horn, projection,** at corners of altar Ex 29₁₂. **4. hill, peak** Is 5₁. **5. ray** Hb 3₄. → קרן *shine.*

קֶרֶן הַפּוּךְ 1 pr.n.f. **Keren-happuch.**

*[קַרְנוֹ] 0.0.0.1 pr.n.m. **Karno.**

[קַרְנַיִם] I 1 pl.n. **Karnaim.**

קַרְנַיִם II, see עַשְׁתְּרֹת קַרְנַיִם *Ashteroth-karnaim.*

קַרְנַיִם III, see קֶרֶן *horn.*

קרס 2 vb.—**Qal** 2 Pf. קָרְסוּ—**stoop, bend over,** of Bel, Nebo Is 46₂. → קֶרֶס *hook,* קַרְסֹל *ankle.*

[קֶרֶס] 10 n.[m.]—pl. קְרָסִים; cstr. קַרְסֵי; sf. קְרָסָיו—**hook, clasp,** for curtains of tabernacle, קַרְסֵי זָהָב *hooks of gold* Ex 26₆, נְחֹשֶׁת *of bronze* Ex 26₁₁. → קרס *stoop.*

קֵרֹס 2 pr.n.m. **Keros.**

*[קֵרֹסִי] 0.0.0.1 gent. **Kerosite.**

[קַרְסֹל] 2 n.[f.]—du. sf. קַרְסֻלָּי—**ankle** or **foot** 2 S 22₃₇ ||Ps 18₃₇. → קרס *stoop.*

קרע 63.0.4 vb.—**Qal** 58.0.2 Pf. קָרַע, קָרַעְתְּ; impf. אֶקְרַע; + waw וַיִּקְרַע; impv. קִרְעוּ; ptc. קֹרֵעַ; pass. קָרוּעַ; inf. abs. קָרֹעַ; cstr. קְרוֹעַ (קָרְעִי)—**1. tear, rend** clothing, as sign of mourning 2 S 1₁₁; heart rather than clothing Jl 2₁₃. **2. tear away** diseased spot from (מִן) garment Lv 13₅₆, kingdom from (מֵעַל) Saul, of Y. 1 S 15₂₈; **tear off** veil, of Y. Ezk 13₂₁. **3.** of Y., **tear open** membrane of heart Ho 13₈, heaven Is 63₁₉. **4. tear wide open,** i.e. **enlarge** eyes with (בְּ) antimony Jr 4₃₀. **5. cut out** windows for (לְ) house Jr 22₁₄. **6. cut up** scroll with (בְּ) knife Jr 36₂₃. **7.** perh. **tear (with words),** i.e. **utter slander, mock** Ps 35₁₅. **8.** pass., **a.** of garments, **be torn, rent,** as sign of mourning 2 S 1₂. **b.** קָרוּעַ כֻּתָּנְתּוֹ **torn in respect of his tunic, wearing a torn tunic,** as sign of mourning 2 S 15₃₂.

Ni. 5.0.1 Pf. נִקְרַע; impf. יִקָּרַע; + waw וַיִּקָּרַע; ptc. נִקְרָע—**1.** of robe, **be torn, rent** 1 S 15₂₇. **2.** of altar, **be torn apart, torn down** 1 K 13₃. **3.** of fish, **be torn open, split open** CD 12₁₃.

Htp. 0.0.1 Impf. יתקרע—of Israel, **be torn (apart)** 4QapJerC[b] 3₇.

→ קֶרַע *piece.*

[קֶרַע] 4 n.m.—pl. קְרָעִים—**1. piece,** torn from garment 1 K 11₃₁. **2. rag, tattered garment** Pr 23₂₁. → קרע *tear.*

קרץ 5.0.3 vb.—**Qal** 4 Impf. יִקְרְצוּ; ptc. קֹרֵץ—**1. pinch, compress** lips Pr 16₃₀. **2. wink (with)** the eye, lit. 'pinch' the eye shut, in malicious manner Ps 35₁₉.

Pu. 1.0.3 Pf. קֹרַצְתִּי—of person, **be nipped,** i.e. **be formed,** from (מִן) clay Jb 33₆.

→ קֶרֶץ *gadfly.*

קֶרֶץ I 1 n.m. **gadfly** Jr 46₂₀. → קרץ *pinch.*

*קֶרֶץ II 1 n.m. **destruction** Jr 46₂₀ (LXX ἀπόσπασμα).

קַרְקַע I 8.0.4 n.[m.]—sf. Q קרקעו—**1. floor** of building, קַרְקַע הַמִּשְׁכָּן *floor of the tabernacle* Nm 5₁₇, הַבַּיִת *of the house* 1 K 6₁₅. **2. floor,** i.e. **bottom** of the sea Am 9₃, **base** of cistern 3QTr 1₇.

[קַרְקַע] II 1 pl.n. **Karka.**

קַרְקֹר 1 pl.n. **Karkor.**

קרר I 2.1 vb.—**Hi.** 2.1 Pf. הֵקֵרָה; inf. cstr. הָקִיר—**keep cool, fresh,** כְּהָקִיר בַּיִר מֵימֶיהָ כֵּן הֵקֵרָה רָעָתָהּ *as a well keeps its water fresh, so it* (i.e. Jerusalem) *keeps fresh its wickedness* Jr 6₇(Qr). → קַר *cool,* קֹר *cold,* קָרָה *cold,* מְקֵרָה *coolness,* קָרוּת *cold.*

קרר II 2.0.3 vb.—**Pilp.** 2.0.3 + waw וְקַרְקַר; ptc. מְקַרְקַר—**tear down** wall or Kir Is 22₅, sons of Sheth Nm 24₁₇.

*קרר III 1 vb.—**Pilp.** 1 Ptc. מְקַרְקַר—with קַר as obj., **make a noise, raise a shout** Is 22$_5$.

*[קרשׁ] vb. **Pi., make framework for** gate Ne 3$_1$ (if em. קִדְּשׁוּהוּ *they sanctified it* to קֵרְשׁוּהוּ *they made a framework for it*). → קֶרֶשׁ *frame.*

קֶרֶשׁ 51.0.1 n.m.—sf. קַרְשֶׁךָ; pl. קְרָשִׁים; cstr. קַרְשֵׁי; sf. קְרָשָׁיו—**1. frame, board,** קַרְשֵׁי הַמִּשְׁכָּן *frames of the tabernacle* Nm 3$_{36}$. **2. deck** of ship Ezk 27$_6$. → קרשׁ *make framework.*

[קֶרֶת] 5 n.f. **city** Pr 11$_{11}$. → cf. קִרְיָה *city.*

קַרְתָּה 1 pl.n. **Kartah.**

קַרְתָּן 1 pl.n. **Kartan.**

[קַשְׂוָה] 4.0.2 n.f.—pl. קְשָׂוֹת (Q קסאות, Q קשואות)—**jar, jug,** קְשׂוֹת הַנָּסֶךְ *jugs for the libation* Nm 4$_7$.

קְשִׂיטָה 3 n.f. **kesitah,** unknown unit of money, perh. weight of silver Jb 42$_{11}$.

קַשְׂקֶשֶׂת 8 n.f.—pl. קַשְׂקַשִּׂים; sf. קַשְׂקְשֹׂתֶיךָ—**1. scale(s)** of fish Lv 11$_{12}$. **2. scale of armour** 1 S 17$_5$.

קֹשׁ, see קֹדֶשׁ *holiness*, §10.

קַשׁ 16 n.m. **stubble, chaff** Ps 83$_{14}$. → קשׁשׁ *gather.*

[קִשֻּׁאָה] 1 n.f.—pl. קִשֻּׁאִים—**cucumber** Nm 11$_5$. → cf. מִקְשָׁה II *cucumber field,* קשׁות *cucumber.*

קשׁב 46.1.9.1 vb.—**Qal** 1 Impf. תִּקְשַׁבְנָה—**be attentive, listen,** of ears Is 32$_3$.

Hi. 45.1.9.1 Pf. הִקְשִׁיב; impf. יַקְשִׁיב, נַקְשִׁיב; + waw וַיַּקְשֵׁב; impv. הַקְשֵׁב (הַקְשִׁיבָה), הַקְשִׁיבוּ; ptc. מַקְשִׁיב, Si מקשבת, מַקְשִׁיבִים; inf. הַקְשִׁיב—**1.** abs., **pay attention, listen,** of Y. Jr 8$_6$, people 2 C 33$_{10}$, earth Mc 1$_2$, ear Ps 10$_{17}$. **2. pay attention (to), listen (to),** of Y. Ps 61$_2$, human being Jr 23$_{18}$, **a.** obj. Y.'s word Jr 23$_{18}$, prayer Ps 61$_2$. **b.** with prep., to (לְ or אֶל or עַל or בְּ) Y. Zc 1$_4$, Y.'s commandments Is 48$_{18}$, wisdom Pr 2$_2$, human being Jr 18$_{19}$, wicked lips Pr 17$_4$, cry of supplication Ps 86$_6$. **3. cause** one's ears **to be attentive to** (לְ) wisdom Pr 2$_2$.

→ קֶשֶׁב *attentiveness,* קַשָּׁב *attentive,* קַשֻּׁב *attentive.*

[קַשָּׁב] 2 adj.—f.s. קַשֶּׁבֶת—**attentive,** of Y.'s ear Ne 1$_{6.11}$. → קשׁב *be attentive.*

[קַשֻּׁב] 3 adj.—f.pl. קַשֻּׁבוֹת—**attentive,** of Y.'s ears Ps 130$_2$. → קשׁב *be attentive.*

קֶשֶׁב 4 n.[m.]—קָשֶׁב—**attentiveness,** on the part of Baal 1 K 18$_{29}$, child 2 K 4$_{31}$. → קשׁב *be attentive.*

קשׁה 28.2.1 vb.—**Qal** 5 Pf. קָשְׁתָה; impf. יִקְשֶׁה; + waw וַיִּקֶשׁ—**1. be hard, severe, burdensome,** of words 2 S 19$_{44}$, of fury Gn 49$_7$, of hand of Y. on (עַל) humans and image of deity 1 S 5$_7$. **2. be hard, difficult,** of legal case Dt 1$_{17}$.

Ni. 1 Ptc. נִקְשֶׁה—**be hard pressed, severely distressed,** of Israel Is 8$_{21}$.

Pi. 1 + waw וַתְּקַשׁ—**have hardship, difficulty** giving birth Gn 35$_{16}$.

Hi. 21.2.1 Pf. הִקְשָׁה, הִקְשִׁיתָ; impf. אַקְשֶׁה; + waw וַיֶּקֶשׁ, וַיַּקְשׁוּ; ptc. מַקְשֶׁה; inf. הַקְשׁתָהּ—**1. make** people's yoke **hard, burdensome** 1 K 12$_4$||2 C 10$_4$. **2a. make** one's **neck stiff** Dt 10$_{16}$, **harden** one's **heart** Ps 95$_8$. **b.** of Y., **make** human heart or spirit **hard, stubborn** Ex 7$_3$ Dt 2$_{30}$. **3. make a difficulty, show stubbornness,** הִקְשָׁה פַרְעֹה לְשַׁלְּחֵנוּ *Pharaoh made a difficulty about letting us go* Ex 13$_{15}$. **4. do something hard, difficult,** הִקְשִׁיתָ לִשְׁאוֹל *you have done something hard in asking,* i.e. asked for a hard thing 2 K 2$_{10}$. **5. have difficulty** in giving birth Gn 35$_{17}$.

→ קָשֶׁה *hard,* קְשִׁי *stubbornness;* cf. קשׁח *make hard.*

קָשֶׁה 36.1.7 adj.—cstr. קְשֵׁה; f.s. קָשָׁה; cstr. קְשַׁת; m.pl. קָשִׁים; cstr. קְשֵׁי; f.pl. קָשׁוֹת—**1a. hard, severe, fierce, strong,** of lord Is 19$_4$, labour Ex 1$_{14}$, wind Is 27$_8$, jealousy Ca 8$_6$. **b.** קְשַׁת־רוּחַ **hard of spirit,** i.e. **troubled,** of woman 1 S 1$_{15}$. **2. hard, difficult,** of legal case Ex 18$_{26}$. **3a. hard, stiff, stubborn,** of neck 1QS 5$_5$. **b.** קְשֵׁה עֹרֶף **stiff-necked** Ex 32$_9$. **c.** קְשֵׁי לֵב **stubborn of heart** Ezk 3$_7$. **d.** קְשֵׁי פָנִים **hard of face,** i.e. **impudent** Ezk 2$_4$. **4.** as noun, קָשׁוֹת **harsh words** Gn 42$_7$. **5.** קָשָׁה as adv., **harshly,** + ענה *answer* 1 S 20$_{10}$. → קשׁה *be hard.*

*[קִשּׁוּת] 0.0.1 n.f. **cucumber** 4QTohA 3.1$_9$. → cf. קִשֻּׁאָה *cucumber,* מִקְשָׁה II *cucumber field.*

קשׁח 2.1 vb.—**Hi.** 2.1 Pf. הִקְשִׁיחַ; impf. תַּקְשִׁיחַ—**1.** of Y., **make** human heart **hard, stubborn** Is 63$_{17}$. **2.** of ostrich, **treat young harshly** Jb 39$_{16}$. **3. show stubbornness** Si 30$_{12(Bmg)}$. → cf. קשׁה *be hard.*

קֹשֶׁט 1 n.[m.] **bow** Ps 60$_6$. → cf. קֶשֶׁת *bow.*

קֹשְׁטְ 1 n.[m.] **truth** Pr 22$_{21}$.

[קְשִׁי] 1.0.4 n.[m.] **stubbornness,** קְשִׁי הָעָם *stubbornness of the people* Dt 9$_{27}$, **stiffness** of neck 1QS 4$_{11}$, **hardness** of heart 1QM 14$_7$. → קשׁה *be hard.*

קִשְׁיוֹן 2 pl.n. **Kishion.**

קשׁר 44.2.2 vb.—**Qal** 36.2 Pf. קְשַׁרְתֶּם; impf. תִּקְשֹׁר; impv. קָשְׁרֵם; ptc. Si קושר, קֹשְׁרִים; ptc. pass. קְשׁוּרָה, קְשֻׁרִים—**1. bind** animal Jb 40$_{29}$, cord in (בְּ) window Jos 2$_{21}$, loyalty around (עַל) neck Pr 3$_{3}$, law upon (עַל) heart Pr 6$_{21}$. **2a. conspire, be in league** against (עַל) king, leader 1 S 22$_{8}$. **b.** with obj. קֶשֶׁר, **make a conspiracy** against (עַל) king, leader 2 K 15$_{30}$. **3.** pass., **be bound up,** נַפְשׁוֹ קְשׁוּרָה בְנַפְשׁוֹ *his (own) life is (so) bound up with his* Gn 44$_{30}$. **4.** pass. ptc. as noun, **strong one, sturdy sheep** Gn 30$_{42}$.

Ni. 2.0.2 Pf. נִקְשְׁרָה; + waw וַתִּקָּשֵׁר—**1. be bound up,** נֶפֶשׁ יְהוֹנָתָן נִקְשְׁרָה בְּנֶפֶשׁ דָּוִד *Jonathan's soul became bound up with the soul of David* 1 S 18$_{1}$. **2. be joined together,** of wall Ne 3$_{38}$.

Pi. 2 Impf. תְּקַשֵּׁר, תְּקַשְּׁרִים—**1. bind (fast)** bonds of the Pleiades Jb 38$_{31}$. **2. bind** sons **to oneself,** of Zion Is 49$_{18}$.

Pu. 1 Ptc. מְקֻשָּׁרוֹת—**be strong, sturdy,** of sheep Gn 30$_{41}$.

Htp. 3 Pf. הִתְקַשְּׁרוּ; + waw וַיִּתְקַשֵּׁר; ptc. מִתְקַשְּׁרִים—**conspire** against (עַל) king, leader 2 C 24$_{25}$.

→ קֶשֶׁר *conspiracy,* קִשֻּׁרִים *bands.*

קֶשֶׁר 16.3.4 n.m.—cstr. קֶשֶׁר; sf. קִשְׁרוֹ; pl. Q קשרים; sf. Q קשריהם—**1. conspiracy, intrigue, treachery,** קֶשֶׁר נְבִיאֶיהָ *conspiracy of her prophets* Ezk 22$_{25}$. **2. bond,** חרצבות קשריהם *fetters of their bonds,* i.e. which bind them CD 13$_{10}$. **3. tie,** perh. receipt issued on payment of rent, to confirm the contract 5/6ḤevBA 45$_{25}$. → קשׁר *bind.*

קִשֻּׁרִים 2 n.[m.]pl. **bands, sashes,** worn by women Is 3$_{20}$ Jr 2$_{32}$. → קשׁר *bind.*

קשׁשׁ 8 vb.—**Qal** 1 Impv. קוֹשׁוּ—intrans., **gather,** of nation Zp 2$_{1}$.

Po. 6 + waw וְקֹשְׁשׁוּ; ptc. מְקֹשֶׁשֶׁת; inf. קֹשֵׁשׁ—trans., **gather** straw Ex 5$_{7}$, sticks Nm 15$_{32}$.

Htpo. 1 Impv. הִתְקוֹשְׁשׁוּ—**gather oneself together,** of nation Zp 2$_{1}$.

→ קַשׁ *stubble.*

קֶשֶׁת 76.2.7 n.f.—cstr. קֶשֶׁת; sf. קַשְׁתָּם; pl. קְשָׁתוֹת; sf. קַשְּׁתֹתָיו—**1. bow(s),** usu. as weapon of war, קֶשֶׁת יְהוֹנָתָן *bow of Jonathan* 2 S 1$_{22}$, for hunting Gn 27$_{3}$. **2.** appar. name of song, **'the bow'** 2 S 1$_{18}$. **3. rainbow** Gn 9$_{13}$. **4. bow, arc,** as name of a battle formation 1QM 9$_{11}$. → cf. קַשָּׁת *archer,* קֹשֶׁט *bow.*

קַשָּׁת 1 n.m. **archer** Gn 21$_{20}$. → cf. קֶשֶׁת *bow.*

ר

ראה 1304.24.143.3 vb.—**Qal** 1131.21.110.1 Pf. רָאָה, רָאִיתָ; impf. יִרְאֶה (יֵרֶא); + waw וַיִּרְאֶה (וַיַּרְא), וָאֶרְאֶה (וָאֵרֶא); impv. רְאֵה, רְאִי, רְאוּ, רְאֶינָה; ptc. רֹאֶה, רֹאֵה, רֹאָה, רֹאִים, רֹאוֹת; ptc. pass. Q ראוי, רְאֻיוֹת; inf. abs. רָאֹה (רָאוֹ, Qr רָאוֹת); cstr. רְאוֹת (רְאֹה, רַאֲוָה, רְאוֹתִי)—**1a.** oft. **see, look at** a person, object, etc. Gn 12$_{12}$ 24$_{30}$; also **stare at** Ca 1$_{6}$, **watch** 1 S 17$_{28}$, **observe, witness, experience** good Ps 34$_{13}$, toil and sorrow Jr 20$_{18}$, death Ps 89$_{49}$, **foresee, envisage** Gn 20$_{10}$; specif. **see face,** i.e. meet Gn 32$_{21}$, come into presence of Y. Jb 33$_{26}$, have access to Gn 43$_{3}$, 'those who see the face of the king', i.e. his councillors 2 K 25$_{19}$||Jr 52$_{25}$, **see nakedness,** appar. as euphemism for having (consensual) sexual intercourse Lv 20$_{17}$. **b.** without direct obj., **see, look,** without any implied obj. Is 6$_{9}$ Jr 6$_{16}$, omitted or implied obj. to be understood from context Gn 19$_{1}$ Ex 16$_{15}$, what is seen is indicated by וְהִנֵּה *and behold* Gn 8$_{13}$; **look on, watch,** as spectators Dt 28$_{32}$ Jg 13$_{19}$; **see,** i.e. **have prophetic vision** Is 30$_{10}$. **2a. see, look at, look upon,** i.e. **consider, take notice of, pay attention to, watch, have regard for** persons Ex 32$_{9}$, object Is 17$_{8}$, affliction Ex 3$_{7}$, word Jr 2$_{31}$. **b.** without obj., **see, take notice, pay heed** to situation or event Dt 32$_{19}$ Ezk 40$_{4}$; **see to it (that one does)** Jr 51$_{61}$. **c.** impv. as exclamation, **see!, behold! take notice!,** (1) without obj. Ex 33$_{12}$ Dt 1$_{8}$. (2) with obj., equivalent to **look**

now! 1 K 12_{16}||2 C 10_{16}, **here is!, here are!** 2 S 24_{22}. **3a. see, look at, look into,** i.e. **investigate, examine** someone's well-being Gn 37_{14}, skin disease Lv 13_{3}, **spy out** land Nm 13_{18}. **b.** without obj., **make an examination** Lv 13_{8}, **find out** 2 K 7_{13}. **4. see,** i.e. **visit, meet** someone Gn 45_{28}. **5. look out,** i.e. **a. provide** sheep as (לְ) burnt offering Gn 22_{8}. **b. find, select** someone Gn 41_{33}. **6. see,** i.e. **discern, find, encounter** good Ec 3_{13} (+ בְּ *in*), indecency Dt 23_{15} (+ בְּ *among*). **7.** with obj. introduced by prep., **a.** בְּ **see, look at, look upon** Ca 3_{11}, **watch** Jg 16_{27}, **experience** Ps 27_{13}, **gloat over** Ps 22_{18}, **visit, meet** Gn 34_{1}. **b.** לְ **see, notice** Ps 64_{6}, **look at, pay attention to** 1 S 16_{7}. **c.** אֶל **look to, have regard for** Is 17_{7}. **d.** מִן **look at, watch** Jg 7_{17}. **8. be able to see, have the power of vision** Gn 27_{1}. **9. see (in a particular way), have an outlook** 1 S 16_{7} Jb 10_{4}. **10a.** ראה כִּי **see that, observe that, perceive that** Gn 39_{3}, sometimes also with accus. Gn 12_{14}, **realize that** Gn 16_{4}, **take into account that** Ex 33_{13}, **see when** Jr 17_{6}. **b.** ראה אֲשֶׁר **see that, realize that** 1 S 18_{15}, var. ראה שֶׁ- Ec 2_{13}. **c.** with double accus., **see that someone/something is** Gn 7_{1} 2 K 3_{22}. **11. see,** i.e. **ascertain, find out, determine,** followed by indirect question Gn 2_{19} 1 S 14_{17}. **12. see,** i.e. **consider, decide,** followed by **a.** indirect question 1 S 25_{17} Lm 2_{20}. **b.** obj. אֲשֶׁר *what* 1 K 20_{22}. **13.** ראה בֵּין **see (the difference) between, distinguish between** Ml 3_{18}. **14.** pass., **a. be selected** Est 2_{9}. **b. be fit, be suitable (for marriage) to** (לְ) 11QT 66_{9}. **c. be fitting, be suitable, be proper for** (לְ) someone 5/6ḤevBA 44_{13}.

Ni. 101.2.20 Pf. נִרְאָה; impf. יֵרָאֶה (יֵרָא); + waw וַיֵּרָא, וַיֵּרָאוּ, וָאֵרָא; impv. הֵרָאֵה; ptc. נִרְאָה, נִרְאֶה; inf. הֵרָאוֹת (הֵרָאֹתוֹ, הֵרָאֹה, לֵרָאוֹת)—**1.** of divine revelation, visions, **a. appear,** of Y. Gn 12_{7} (+ אֶל *to*) 2 C 1_{7} (+ לְ *to*), glory of Y. Ex 16_{10} (+ בְּ *in* cloud) Is 60_{2} (+ עַל *over*), vision Dn 8_{1} (+ אֶל). **b. be seen, be visible,** of Y. Nm 14_{14} (+ עַיִן בְּעַיִן *eye to eye,* i.e. face to face), face of Y. Ex 33_{23}. **2a. present oneself to** (אֶל) someone Gn 46_{29}. **b. appear before, in the presence of** Y., with אֶת־פְּנֵי Ex 34_{23}, פָּנִים without preceding prep. Ex 23_{15}. **3. appear, become visible, be exposed,** of dry land Gn 1_{9}, rainbow Gn 9_{14}, sins Ezk 21_{29}. **4a. be seen,** i.e. **be observed, be witnessed,** of person 2 S 17_{17}, event Jg 19_{30}. **b. be seen,** i.e. **be present, be found,** of person Ex 34_{3} (+ בְּ *in*), leaven Ex 13_{7} (+ לְ *to,* i.e. among). **c. be seen, be visible,** of top of pole 1 K 8_{8}||2 C 5_{9}. **d. be shown, be manifested,** of works of Y. Ps 90_{16} (+ אֶל *to*). **5. be provided** Gn 22_{14}.

Pu. 1 Pf. רֻאּוּ—**be seen, be visible,** of bones Jb 33_{21}.

Hi. 62.0.13.2 Pf. הֶרְאָה (הֶרְאַנִי, הִרְאַנִי), הִרְאִיתָ; impf. יַרְאֶה; + waw וַיַּרְא, וַיַּרְאוּם; וְהֶרְאָה, וְהַרְאֵיתִי; impv. הַרְאֵנִי, הַרְאִינִי; ptc. מַרְאֶה; inf. הַרְאוֹת (הַרְאֹתְכֶם, לְרְאֹתְכֶם, הַרְאֹתָם)—**1a. cause to see, show, let see,** (1) with accus. of one to whom shown and also of thing shown Gn 12_{1} Jg 4_{22}. (2) with accus. of one to whom shown, and בְּ with obj. of thing shown Dt 13_{3} Ps 91_{16}. (3) preceded by כַּאֲשֶׁר *as,* כַּאֲשֶׁר הֶרְאָה אֹתְךָ ... כֵּן יַעֲשׂוּ *as he has shown you ... so shall they do* Ex 27_{8}. (4) with accus. of person and וְהִנֵּה *and behold* to introduce prophetic vision Jr 24_{1}. **b.** with double accus., **make see, cause to experience** loyalty Ps 85_{8}, trouble Ps 71_{20}, iniquity Hb 1_{3}. **2a.** with triple accus., **show someone** someone else **as** king 2 K 8_{13}. **b.** with כִּי *that,* **show** someone **that** 2 K 8_{10}. **3. cause to be seen, display, show,** riches Est 1_{4}.

Ho. 4.1 Pf. הָרְאֵיתָ; ptc. מָרְאֶה—**1. be shown** something, with subj. of person, and accus. of thing show Ex 25_{40}. **2. be shown to,** with subj. of thing, and accus. of person to whom shown Lv 13_{49}.

Htp. 5 Impf. נִתְרָאֶה; + waw וַיִּתְרָאוּ—**1. look at one another,** i.e. do nothing Gn 42_{1}. **2.** with accus. פָּנִים, **look one another in the face,** i.e. meet in combat 2 K 14_{8}||2 C 25_{17}.

→ רֹאֶה I *seer,* II *vision,* רָאֶה I *seeing,* רְאִי *choice,* רְאוּת *look,* רְאִי *sight,* מַרְאֶה *sight, appearance,* רְאִי *mirror,* מַרְאָה *vision, mirror.*

רָאָה, see דָּאָה *kite.*

[רָאֶה] I 1 adj. **seeing,** רְאֵה עָנְיִי *seeing of,* i.e. looking at, *my affliction* Jb 10_{15}. → ראה *see.*

*[רָאֶה] II 1 adj. (byform of רָוֶה) **satiated,** רְאֵה עָנְיִי *satiated of,* i.e. with, *my affliction* Jb 10_{15}. → רוה *be saturated.*

רֹאֶה I 12 n.[m.]—pl. רֹאִים—**seer**, term for נָבִיא *prophet* 1 S 9$_{9}$. → ראה *see*.

רֹאֶה II 1 n.[m.] **vision** Is 28$_{7}$. → ראה *see*.

רֹאֶה III 1 pr.n.m. **Haroeh** (הָרֹאֶה).

*__רֹאֶה__ IV n.[m.] **drunkenness** Is 28$_{7}$. → רוה *be saturated*.

רְאוּבֵן 72.0.11 pr.n.m. **Reuben.**

רְאוּבֵנִי 18 gent. **Reubenite.**

רַאֲוָה Ezk 28$_{17}$, see ראה *see*, qal (inf.).

רָאוּי *selected, fitting*, see ראה, qal §14.

רְאוּמָה 1 pr.n.f. **Reumah.**

[רְאוּת] 1.0.1 n.f.—Kt ראית—**1. looking, observing** Ec 5$_{10(Qr)}$. **2. sight, ability to see** 1QSa 2$_{7}$ (unless inf. cstr. of ראה). → ראה *see*.

*__[רָאִי]__ 0.1 adj. **choice,** of wine Si 34$_{28}$. → ראה *see*.

רֳאִי 4 n.[m.]—רֳאִי—**1. seeing, perception,** אֵל רֳאִי *God of seeing* Gn 16$_{13}$. **2. sight, spectacle,** in ref. to Nineveh Na 3$_{6}$. **3. visibility,** מֵרֹאִי *(it is) without visibility,* i.e. cannot be seen Jb 33$_{21}$. **4. appearance,** טוֹב רֳאִי *good of appearance,* i.e. handsome 1 S 16$_{12}$. → ראה *see*.

רֹאִי, see ראה *see*, qal (ptc.); רֳאִי *sight*; בְּאֵר לַחַי רֹאִי *Beer-lahai-roi*.

רְאִי 1 n.m. **mirror,** רְאִי מוּצָק *a cast mirror* Jb 37$_{18}$. → ראה *see*.

רְאָיָה 4.0.0.1 pr.n.m. **Reaiah.**

רְאִיהוּ, see רְאָיָה *Reaiah*.

רְאֵים, see רְאֵם *wild ox*.

רִאישׁוֹן, see רִאשׁוֹן *former*.

רְאִית, see רְאוּת *look*.

ראם 1 vb. (byform of רום)—**Qal** 1 Pf. רָאֲמָה—**rise** Zc 14$_{10}$.

רְאֵם 9.1 n.m.—רְאֵים (רֵים); pl. רְאֵמִים (רֵמִים)—**wild ox** (*Bos primigenius*) Nm 23$_{22}$ Dt 33$_{17}$.

רָאמוֹת I 2 n.[f.pl.] **(black) corals,** or perh. **sea shells, pearls** Ezk 27$_{16}$ Jb 28$_{18}$.

רָאמוֹת II 25 pl.n. **Ramoth.**

רָאמוֹת III, see רום *be high*, qal, ptc.

רָאמַת נֶגֶב 1.0.0.2 pl.n. **Ramath-negeb.**

רְאסוֹת, see רַס *stade*.

רָאשׁ, see רושׁ *be poor*.

רֵאשׁ, see רֵישׁ *poverty*.

רֹאשׁ I 599.26.133.3 n.m.—Q ראוש, Q רוש; cstr. רֹאשׁ; sf. רֹאשִׁי; pl. רָאשִׁים (Q רשים); cstr. רָאשֵׁי (Q ראושי, רשי); sf. רָאשֵׁיהֶם, רָאשָׁיו—**1. head, a.** of person Gn 48$_{14}$, sometimes perh. **hair of head** Lv 10$_{6}$; representing extremity of body, מִכַּף־רֶגֶל וְעַד־רֹאשׁ *from the sole of he foot to the head* Is 1$_{6}$; representing one's life Dn 1$_{10}$, שֹׁמֵר לְרֹאשִׁי *keeper of my head,* i.e. my bodyguard 1 S 28$_{2}$; לְרֹאשׁ גֶּבֶר *for the head of a man,* i.e. for each man, per capita Jg 5$_{30}$; specif. of lifting head (with נשׂא or רום hi.), lift (one's own) head, i.e. show defiance Jg 8$_{28}$, lift head of someone else, i.e. grant favour, exalt Gn 40$_{13}$ Ps 3$_{4}$, free from prison 2 K 25$_{27}$||Jr 52$_{31}$. **b.** of animal Ex 12$_{9}$. **c.** of Y. Is 59$_{17}$. **d.** of gates, personified Ps 24$_{7}$. **2a. head, top, summit** of mountain or hill Gn 8$_{5}$ Ex 17$_{9}$, tower Gn 11$_{4}$, pillar Ex 36$_{38}$, tree 2 S 5$_{24}$||1 C 14$_{15}$. **b. topmost (one), highest (one),** of mountains Is 2$_{2}$||Mc 4$_{1}$, stars Jb 22$_{12}$. **c. end, tip** of pole 1 K 8$_{8}$||2 C 5$_{9}$, sword 1QM 5$_{11}$. **3a. head (person), chief, leader,** רָאשֵׁי הָאָבוֹת *heads of the fathers' houses* Nm 36$_{1}$, הַמַּטּוֹת *of the tribes* Nm 30$_{2}$, הָעָם *of the people* Nm 25$_{4}$; כֹּהֵן הָרֹאשׁ *chief priest* 2 K 25$_{18}$||Jr 52$_{24}$. **b. chief (angelic being)** 4QShirShabb[d] 1.2$_{24}$. **c. chief (nation, city)** Jos 11$_{10}$ Is 7$_{8}$ Jr 31$_{7}$. **d. chief (one), choicest (one),** of spice Ex 30$_{23}$, produce Dt 33$_{15}$, joy Ps 137$_{6}$. **e. head, chief (place, position),** רֹאשׁ הָעָם *head of the people* Dt 20$_{9}$, כָּל־חוּצוֹת *of all the streets* Is 51$_{20}$, פִּנָּה *of the corner,* i.e. chief cornerstone Ps 118$_{22}$. **4.** of place, **a. front one,** in ref. to wheel Ezk 10$_{11}$. **b. head, beginning** of conduit 3QTr 5$_{1}$, **headwater, branch** of river Gn 2$_{10}$. **5.** of time, **a. beginning** of month Nm 10$_{10}$, year Ezk 40$_{1}$, watch Jg 7$_{19}$. **b. first** of the dust of the world Pr 8$_{26(mss)}$. **6. sum, full amount, total number** of people Ex 30$_{12}$, booty Nm 31$_{26}$, word of Y. Ps 119$_{160}$, **value** of expropriated object Lv 5$_{24}$. **7. company, band, column (of troops)** Jg 7$_{16}$ 1 S 11$_{11}$ 1QM 8$_{6}$.

→ cf. רֵאשָׁה *beginning,* רֵאשִׁית *beginning,* רֹאשָׁה *top,* רִאשׁוֹן *first,* רִאשֹׁנִי *first,* מְרַאֲשׁוֹת *place of head.*

רֹאשׁ II 12.0.3 n.m.—רוֹשׁ; cstr. רֹאשׁ—**1. a particular poisonous plant** Dt 29$_{17}$. **2. poison, bitterness** Dt 32$_{32}$ Jr 8$_{14}$. **3. venom** of snakes Dt 32$_{33}$.

רֹאשׁ III 1 pr.n.m. **Rosh.**

ראשׁ IV 3 pl.n. **Rosh.**

[רִאשָׁה] 1 n.f.—רִאשֹׁתֵיכֶם—**beginning, early time** Ezk 36₁₁. → cf. ראשׁ I *head.*

רֹאשָׁה 1 n.f. **top,** הָאֶבֶן הָרֹאשָׁה *the stone, the top,* i.e. the topmost stone Zc 4₇. → cf. ראשׁ I *head.*

רִאשׁוֹן 182.3.96.4 adj.—רִאשֹׁן (רִאישׁוֹן, רִישׁוֹן); f.s. רִאשֹׁנָה; m.pl. רִאשֹׁנִים; f.pl. רִאשֹׁנוֹת—**1.** of time, **first, a.** as adj. of father Is 43₂₇, sign Ex 4₈, slaughter 1 S 14₁₄, day Ex 12₁₅. **b.** as noun, **first (one),** in ref. to battalion 1QM 8₁₅, person 2 S 19₂₁, month Gn 8₁₃. **2. former, earlier, previous, a.** as adj. of generation Jb 8₈, husband Dt 24₄, loyalty Ps 89₅₀, deeds 1 C 29₂₉. **b.** as noun, (1) **former one, forebear, ancestor** Lv 26₄₅ Dt 19₁₄. (2) **older one** 2 C 22₁. (3) masc. sg., **beginning** Jr 17₁₂, **former time** Jl 2₂₃. (4) masc. pl., **former time, ancient time** Is 61₄. (5) fem. pl., **former things** Is 43₉. **3.** of position, **foremost, a.** as adj. of hand Ezr 9₂. **b.** as noun, **foremost (one),** in ref. to person Gn 32₁₈. **4.** of rank, **first, chief, a.** as adj. of prince Dn 10₁₃. **b.** as noun, **first (one), chief (one),** in ref. to official 1 C 18₁₇. **5.** as adv., **a.** רִאשׁוֹן, of time, **first** 4QSela 9.2₇. **b.** רִאשֹׁנָה **first,** of time Gn 38₂₈, rank Est 1₁₄; **first, in front,** of place Gn 33₂. **c.** בָּרִאשֹׁנָה (1) **at the first, first (of all),** usu. of time Dt 13₁₀, also of place Is 60₉. (2) **formerly, previously** 2 S 20₁₈. **d.** כָּרִאשֹׁנָה **as before, as formerly** Dt 9₁₈. **e.** כְּבָרִאשֹׁנָה **as before, as formerly** Jg 20₃₂. **f.** לָרִאשֹׁנָה, (1) **first,** of time 11QT 23₁₁, place/rank 1QS 6₈ CD 14₃. (2) **formerly, previously** Gn 28₁₉. **g.** לְמַבָּרִאשׁוֹנָה (for לְמַה־בָּרִאשׁוֹנָה) **at the first,** lit. 'for what was at the first' 1 C 15₁₃. → cf. ראשׁ I *head,* רִאשֹׁנִי *first.*

רַאֲשׁוֹת, see מְרַאֲשׁוֹת *place of head.*

רֵאשִׁית 51.3.29 n.f.—cstr. רֵאשִׁית (רֵשִׁית, Q רישית, Q רשת); sf. רֵאשִׁיתוֹ—**1. beginning** of creation Gn 1₁, person, i.e. early life Jb 8₇, reign of king Jr 26₁, fig tree, i.e. its first season Ho 9₁₀, wisdom Ps 111₁₀. **2. first (one), first (thing), firstfruits** of harvest, produce Ex 23₁₉ Lv 23₁₀, one's strength, i.e. firstborn Gn 49₃. **3. first,** i.e. **chief (one, thing, part), choice(est) (thing, part)** of the nations Am 6₁, an offering 1 S 2₂₉, oils Am 6₆. → cf. ראשׁ I *head.*

[רִאשֹׁנִי] 1 adj. **first**—f.s. רִאשֹׁנִית—of year Jr 25₁. → cf. ראשׁ I *head,* רִאשׁוֹן *first.*

רַב I 424.28.130 adj.—רָב; cstr. רַב; f.s. רַבָּה; cstr. רַבַּת (רַבָּתִי); m.pl. רַבִּים; f.pl. רַבּוֹת—**1a. much, many, numerous,** in ref. to people Gn 50₂₀, nations Dt 7₁, son 1 C 4₂₇, blood 1 C 22₈, cattle Nm 32₁, wealth Pr 13₇, days Gn 21₃₄. **b. great, mighty,** in ref. to king Ps 48₂, the deep Gn 7₁₁, water 2 S 22₁₇||Ps 18₁₇. **c.** cstr., **great of,** רַבָּתִי עָם (of city) *great,* i.e. full, *of people* Lm 1₁, רַב־חֶסֶד וֶאֱמֶת (of Y.) *great of,* i.e. abounding in, *mercy and reliability* Ex 34₆, רַב־פְּעָלִים (of person) *great of,* i.e. performing great, *deeds* 2 S 23₂₀||1 C 11₂₂. **d.** רַב מִן **greater than** Am 6₂, **more than** Is 54₁, **too great for** 1 K 19₇, **too many for** Jg 7₂. **2.** as adv., **a.** רַב **much, exceedingly** Ps 123₃. **b.** רַבָּה **much, greatly, abundantly** Ps 62₃ 78₁₅. **c.** רַבַּת (1) **much, greatly** Ps 65₁₀ 129₁. (2) of time, **long** Ps 120₆. **3.** as noun, **a. great one, mighty one,** in respect of age or seniority Gn 25₂₃, size (of tribe) Nm 26₅₄, power Jb 35₉; רַבַּת בָּנִים *(one) great (fem.) of,* i.e. who has many, *sons* 1 S 2₅, הַמְּהוּמָה *of,* i.e. with much, *discomfiture* Ezk 22₅; רבה **(the) great one,** i.e. the great deep (תְּהוֹם רַבָּה), the ocean Si 43₂₅(B). **b. enough** Gn 33₉; רַב־לָכֶם שֶׁבֶת *it is enough for you to stay,* i.e. you have stayed long enough Dt 1₆. **c. many (people),** usu. masc. pl. Ex 23₂, also masc. sg. coll. Ex 19₂₁, fem. sg. coll. 2 C 30₁₇; הרבים *the many* as technical term for full member of Qumran community 1QS 6₁; fem. pl. **many things** Is 42₂₀. **d. greatness, abundance,** (1) masc., רַב־טוּב *greatness of goodness,* i.e. great goodness Is 63₇. (2) fem., רַבַּת חֶלְאָתָהּ *greatness of its rust,* i.e. its great rust Ezk 24₁₂. → רבב I *be many.*

[רַב] II 50.1.1.1 n.m.—cstr. רַב; pl. cstr. רַבֵּי—**1. chief officer, official** of king of Babylon Jr 39₁₃, Persia Est 1₈. **2.** רַב־טַבָּחִים **captain of (the body)guard(s),** head of Babylonian forces 2 K 25₈||Jr 52₁₂. **3.** high-ranking officials of king of Assyria, **a.** רַב־שָׁקֵה **Rabshakeh,** lit. 'chief cup-bearer' 2 K 18₁₇||Is 36₂. **b.** רַב־סָרִיס **Rabsaris,** lit. 'chief official' 2 K 18₁₇. **c.** רַב־מָג **Rabmag,** perh. lit. 'chief soothsayer' Jr 39₃. **4.** רַב הַחֹבֵל **chief of the sailor(s),** i.e. **captain** Jon 1₆. → רבב I *be many;* cf. רַבִּי *rabbi.*

רַב III 3 n.m.—pl. רַבִּים; sf. רַבָּיו—**archer** Jb 16₁₃ Jr 50₂₉ Pr 26₁₀. → רבב II *shoot.*

*[רָב] IV $_1$ n.[m.] (byform of רְבִיבִים)—רָב—**showers** Jb 36$_{28}$. → רבב I *be many.*

רֹב $_{148.11.91}$ n.m.—רוֹב; cstr. רֹב (רָב־); sf. Q רובם; pl. cstr. רֻבֵּי—**1. abundance** of food Pr 13$_{23}$, wealth Ezk 27$_{12}$, mercy Ps 5$_8$, peace Ps 37$_{11}$, **multitude, great number** of people Pr 14$_{28}$, words Pr 10$_{19}$, sacrifices Is 1$_{11}$, transgressions Ps 5$_{11}$. **2. greatness** of strength Ps 33$_{16}$, glory Si 44$_2$, wisdom Ezk 28$_5$, iniquity Jr 13$_{22}$. **3.** as adv., **a.** לָרֹב **abundantly, in abundance, greatly, in great number(s), in great quantity** Gn 30$_{30}$ 1 C 12$_{41}$. **b.** עַד־לָרוֹב **in great quantity** 2 C 31$_{10}$. → רבב I *be great.*

*[רַבָּא] $_{0.0.1}$ pr.n.m. **Rabba.**

רבב I $_{26.1.3}$ vb. (byform of רבה I)—**Qal** $_{25.1.3}$ Pf. רַבּוּ (רָבּוּ); + waw וְרָבָּה; inf. cstr. רֹב (רֻבָּם)—**1. be many, multiply, abound,** of persons Gn 6$_1$ Dt 7$_7$ (+ מִן *[more] than*), beasts Ex 23$_{29}$, grain and wine Ps 4$_8$, transgressions Is 59$_{12}$. **2. be great,** of cry Gn 18$_{20}$; **be long,** of journey Jos 9$_{13}$.

Pu. $_1$ Ptc. מְרֻבָּבוֹת—**multiply ten thousand-fold,** of sheep Ps 144$_{13}$.

→ רַב I *much,* II *chief,* IV *showers,* רֹב *abundance,* רְבָבָה *ten thousand,* רִבּוֹא *ten thousand,* רְבִיבִים *showers.*

רבב II $_2$ vb.—**Qal** $_2$ Pf. רַב; + waw וָרֹבּוּ—**shoot (at)** Gn 49$_{23}$ perh. Ps 18$_{15}$. → רַב III *archer;* cf. רבה II *shoot.*

רְבָבָה $_{16.1}$ n.f.—sf. Kt רבבתו; pl. רְבָבוֹת; cstr. רִבְבוֹת, sf. Qr רִבְבֹתָיו—**ten thousand, myriad,** אַלְפֵי רְבָבָה *thousands of ten thousands* Gn 26$_{40}$, רִבְבוֹת אַלְפֵי יִשְׂרָאֵל *ten thousands of the thousands of Israel* Nm 10$_{36}$. → רבב I *be many.*

רבד $_1$ vb.—**Qal** $_1$ Pf. רָבַדְתִּי—**deck, spread** couch **with** a cover Pr 7$_1$. → רֹבֶד *terrace,* מַרְבַד *cover,* רָבִיד *necklace.*

*[רֹבֶד] $_{0.0.3}$ n.m.—רובד—**terrace, ledge,** around outer court of temple 11QT 44$_5$ 46$_5$. → רבד *deck.*

רבה I $_{230.23.39}$ vb.—**Qal** $_{60.4.7}$ Pf. רָבוּ; impf. יִרְבֶּה (יִרֶב); + waw וַיִּרְבּוּ, וַתֵּרֶב, וַיִּרֶב, וְרָבִית; impv. רְבוּ, רְבֶה; ptc. רֹבֶה; inf. רְבוֹת—**1. be many, multiply, increase,** of persons Gn 1$_{28}$, creatures Gn 1$_{22}$, thoughts Ps 139$_{18}$ (+ מִן *[more] than*), knowledge Dn 12$_4$, days Gn 38$_{12}$. **2. be great,** of Y. Jb 33$_{12}$ (+ מִן greater *than*), way, i.e. distance Dt 14$_{24}$ (+ מִן too great *for*). **3. grow up,** of person Ezk 16$_7$, beast Jb 39$_4$.

Pi. $_4$ Pf. רִבִּיתָ; impv. רַבֶּה (mss רַבָּה)—**1. make great, increase** army Jg 9$_{29}$, price Ps 44$_{13}$ (בְּ of obj.). **2. rear, bring up** children Lm 2$_{22}$.

Hi. $_{162.20.32}$ Pf. הִרְבֵּיתִי, הִרְבִּיתָ, הִרְבָּה; impf. יַרְבֶּה (יֶרֶב); + waw וַתַּרְבֶּה, וַיֶּרֶב; impv. הַרְבֵּה (הֶרֶב), הַרְבִּי, הַרְבּוּ; ptc. מַרְבֶּה, מַרְבָּה, מַרְבִּים; inf. abs. הַרְבֵּה (הַרְבָּה); cstr. הַרְבּוֹת—**1a. make much, multiply, increase** people Gn 16$_{10}$ Dt 30$_5$ (+ מִן *[more] than*), wealth Pr 28$_8$ (+ בְּ *with* interest), signs and wonders Ex 7$_3$, words Ec 10$_{14}$, might Is 40$_{29}$, pain Gn 3$_{16}$, **have many feet** Lv 11$_{42}$, **make abundant** produce Ezk 36$_{30}$. **b.** with omission of obj., **increase** sons 1 C 4$_{27}$, wealth Pr 13$_{11}$, **collect more** manna Ex 16$_{17}$, **pay more** money Ex 30$_{15}$. **2.** with inf. of other verb, **do much** 2 K 21$_6$||2 C 33$_6$, i.e. **go on doing** 1 S 1$_{12}$, **do often** Ps 78$_{38}$, **do thoroughly** Is 55$_7$, **do more** 2 S 18$_8$ (+ מֵאֲשֶׁר *than*). **3. make someone great** 2 S 22$_{36}$||Ps 18$_{36}$. **3.** inf. abs. הַרְבֵּה, **a.** as adv., (1) הַרְבֵּה alone, **much, greatly** 2 K 10$_{18}$, **overmuch** Ec 7$_{16}$. (2) הַרְבֵּה מְאֹד **very greatly, exceedingly** 1 S 26$_{21}$; **in very great abundance** Gn 41$_{49}$. (3) לְהַרְבֵּה **in abundance** Ne 5$_{18}$. (4) לְהַרְבֵּה מְאֹד **very greatly** 2 C 11$_{12}$; **in very great numbers** 2 C 16$_8$. **b.** as adj., **much, many,** of flocks and herds 2 S 12$_2$ (+ מְאֹד *very*), weeping Ezr 10$_1$, study Ec 12$_{12}$; **great,** of reward Gn 15$_1$. **c.** as noun, **much, many** 2 S 1$_4$ Hg 1$_9$; **more,** הַרְבֵּה מִזֶּה *more than this* 2 C 25$_9$. **7.** inf. cstr. הַרְבּוֹת, **a.** as adj., **much,** of honey Pr 25$_{27}$. **b.** as adv., **many times, repeatedly,** or as noun, **multitude** of gardens and vineyards Am 4$_9$.

→ מַרְבֶּה *abundance,* מִרְבָּה *much,* מַרְבִּית *increase,* תַּרְבִּית *increase,* תַּרְבּוּת *increase, brood,* אַרְבֶּה *locust.*

רבה II $_1$ vb.—**shoot Qal** $_1$ Ptc. רֹבֶה—Gn 21$_{20}$. → cf. רבב II *shoot.*

רַבָּה $_{15}$ pl.n. **Rabbah.**

רִבּוֹ, see רִבּוֹא *ten thousand.*

רִבּוֹא $_{10.0.3}$ n.f.—רִבּוֹ; du. רִבֹּתַיִם; pl. רִבֹּאוֹת (רִבּוֹת); cstr. Kt רבו; sf. Q רבאותם—**ten thousand, myriad,** שְׁתֵּים־עֶשְׂרֵה רִבּוֹ אָדָם *a hundred and twenty thousand persons* Jon 4$_{11}$, דַּרְכְּמוֹנִים שְׁתֵּי רִבּוֹת *twenty thousand darics* Ne 7$_{70}$. → רבב I *be many.*

*רבט 0.1 vb.—**Hi.** 0.1 Ptc. Si מרביט—perh. **show splendour** Si $43_{1(B)}$.

*[רַבִּי] 0.0.0.1 n.m. **rabbi**, lit. 'my chief', title of scholar Frey 14_{10}. → cf. רַב II *chief*.

*[רִבִּי] n.m. **projectile, dart** Jb 16_{13} (if em. רַבָּיו *his archers* to רִבָּיו *his projectiles*).

רְבִיבִים 6.0.3 n.m.pl.—רְבִבִים—**showers,** perh. as heavy or frequent Dt 32_{2}. → רבב I *be many*.

רָבִיד 2.1 n.m.—cstr. רְבִד—**necklace, chain** Gn 41_{42} Ezk 16_{11} Si 35_{5}. → רבד *deck*.

*[רַבְּיָהוּ] 0.0.0.1 pr.n.[m.] **Rabbiah**.

*[רְבִיעַ] I 0.0.2 adj. **fourth** CD $14_{4.6}$ (=4QD^{b} 9.5_{10} רביעי). → רבע I *be square*.

*[רְבִיעַ] II 0.0.0.1 n.[m.] **quarter (of shekel)** Jewish War Year 4 Coin 162. → רבע I *be square*.

רְבִיעִי 45.0.42.4 adj.—f.s. רְבִיעִית; m.pl. רְבִיעִים—**1. fourth,** of generation Gn 15_{16}, lot Jos 19_{17}, day Gn 1_{19}, month Jr 39_{2}, year Lv 19_{24} Jr 46_{2} (שְׁנַת הָרְבִיעִית). **2.** as noun, **fourth (one),** in ref. to cherub Ezk 10_{14}, generation 2 K 10_{30}, son 1 C 2_{14}, lot 1 C 24_{8}, month Ezk 1_{1}. → רבע I *be square*.

רְבִיעִית I, see רְבִיעִי *fourth*.

*רְבִיעִית II 11.0.2.3 n.f.—cstr. רְבִיעִית—**fourth (part), quarter** of hin of wine Ex 29_{40}, allowance of bread 1QS 6_{25}, day Ne 9_{3}. → רבע I *be square*.

רַבִּית 1 pl.n. **Rabbith**.

רבך 3 vb.—**Ho.** 3 Ptc. מֻרְבֶּכֶת (מֻרְבֶּכֶת)—**be well mixed, soaked,** of fine flour in offering Lv 6_{17} 7_{12} 1 C 23_{29}.

רִבְלָה 11 pl.n. **Riblah**.

רַב־מָג *Rabmag*, see רַב II *chief*.

רַב־סָרִיס *Rabsaris*, see רַב II *chief*.

רבע I 12.0.4 vb.—**Qal** 9 Pass. ptc. רָבוּעַ, רְבֻעָה, רְבֻעִים—**1.** pass. **be square(d),** of altar Ex 27_{1}||Ex 38_{1}, breastplate Ex 28_{16}||39_{9}. **2.** fem. sg. pass. ptc. as noun, **square,** מְזוּזַת רְבֻעָה *doorpost of a square,* i.e. square doorpost Ezk 41_{21}.

Pu. 3.0.4 Ptc. מְרֻבָּע, מְרֻבַּעַת, מְרֻבָּעוֹת—**be square(d),** of panel 1 K 7_{31}, column 11QT 30_{9}, court Ezk 40_{47}.

→ אַרְבַּע *four,* רֶבַע *fourth part,* רֹבַע *fourth part,* רְבִיעִי *fourth,* רְבִיעִית *fourth (part),* רְבִיעַ I *fourth,* II *quarter (of shekel),* רִבֵּעַ *belonging to the fourth,* אַרְבָּעִים *forty*.

רבע II 4.0.1 vb.—**Qal** 3 Inf. רִבְעָה (רִבְעִי)—**1. lie down,** for rest Ps 139_{3}. **2. copulate with** (accus.) beast Lv 18_{23}.

Hi. 1.0.1 Impf. תַּרְבִּיעַ—**cause to lie down, cross-breed** beasts of two kinds (כִּלְאַיִם) Lv 19_{19}.

[רֶבַע] I 7.0.0.3 n.m.—cstr. רֶבַע; pl. sf. רִבְעֵיהֶם, רִבְעָיו—**1. fourth part, quarter** of hin Ex 29_{40}, shekel 1 S 9_{8}. **2.** pl. **(four) sides** of creatures Ezk 1_{8}, the directions in which they moved Ezk 1_{17}; of hearth of altar Ezk 43_{16}, its ledge Ezk 43_{17}. → רבע I *be square*.

רֶבַע II 2 pr.n.m. **Reba**.

[רִבֵּעַ] 4 adj. pl. רִבֵּעִים—**belonging to the fourth,** as noun, **member of the fourth generation** Ex 20_{5}||Dt 5_{9}. → רבע I *be square*.

[רֹבַע] I 2.0.3 n.[m.]—cstr. רֹבַע; sf. Q רובעו—**fourth part, quarter** of Israel Nm 23_{10}, kab 2 K 6_{25}. → רבע I *be square*.

*[רֹבַע] II 1 n.[m.]—cstr. רֹבַע—**dust-cloud** Nm 23_{10}.

רבץ 30.1.1 vb.—**Qal** 24.1.1 Pf. רָבַץ, רָבְצָה; impf. יִרְבַּץ; + waw וַתִּרְבַּץ; ptc. רֹבֵץ, רֹבֶצֶת, רֹבְצִים—**1a. lie down, lie, rest,** usu. of animals Gn 29_{2}; also of humans Jb 11_{19}, the deep Gn 49_{25}. **b.** of bird, **sit upon** (עַל) chicks or eggs Dt 22_{6}. **c. recline,** at meal Si 35_{2}. **2. crouch, lurk, lie in wait,** appar. of sin Gn 4_{7} (+ לְ *at*). **3. descend, fall, settle,** of curse Dt 29_{19} (+ בְּ *upon*).

Hi. 6 Impf. תַּרְבִּיץ; ptc. מַרְבִּיץ, מַרְבִּצִים—**1. cause to lie down,** obj. flock Jr 33_{12}, person Jr 33_{12}; without obj. Is 13_{20}. **2. set** (precious) stones in (בְּ) antimony Is 54_{11}.

→ רֵבֶץ *place of lying down,* מַרְבֵּץ *resting place*.

[רֵבֶץ] 4 n.[m.]—cstr. רֵבֶץ; sf. רִבְצוֹ—**1. resting place, lair,** for animals Is 65_{10}. **2. dwelling place,** for humans Pr 24_{15}. → רבץ *lie down*.

רִבְקָה 30 pr.n.f. **Rebekah**.

רַב־שָׁקֵה, see רַב II *chief*.

רַבַּת, see רַב I *much*.

רַבָּתִי, see רַב I *much*.

*[רָגָא] 0.0.0.2 pr.n.[m.] **Raga**.

[רֶגֶב] 2.1.1 n.m.—pl. רְגָבִים; cstr. רִגְבֵי—**clod (of earth)** Jb 21_{33} 38_{38} Si $43_{20(M)}$.

רגז 41.1.1 vb.—**Qal** 30.1 Pf. רָגְזָה; impf. יִרְגְּזוּ; impv. רִגְזָה, רִגְזוּ—**1. tremble, shake, quake,** of earth 1 S 14_{15}, the deep Ps 77₁₇, tent curtains Hb 3₇; of people, from dread Dt 2₂₅, in awe Jr 33₉ (+ עַל *on account of*). **2. come trembling,** through fear Mc 7₁₇ (+ מִן *from*). **3. be shaken, be moved,** through grief 2 S 19₁. **4. be stirred up, be astir,** of Sheol Is 14₉ (+ לְ *on account of*). **5. quarrel** Gn 45₂₄. **6. rage,** of Y. Is 28₂₁, human Pr 29₉. **7. enrage** Ezk 16₄₃ (לְ of obj.).

Hi. 7 Pf. הִרְגַּזְתָּנִי ,הִרְגִּיז; impf. אַרְגִּיז; ptc. מַרְגִּיז ,מַרְגִּיזֵי—**1. cause to tremble, shake,** obj. heaven Is 13₁₃, earth Jb 9₆ (+ מִן *from* place), kingdoms Is 23₁₁. **2. cause disquiet, unrest for** (לְ) someone Jr 50₃₄. **3. disturb** (dead) person 1 S 28₁₅. **4. enrage, provoke** Y. Jb 12₆.

Htp. 4.0.1 Impf. Sam, Q תתרגזו; inf. הִתְרַגֶּזְךָ—**1. rage against** (אֶל) 2 K 19₂₇||Is 37₂₈. **2. quarrel** Gn 45₂₄(Sam, 4QRPb) (MT qal).

→ רֹגֶז *agitation*, רַגָּז *trembling*, רָגְזָה *trembling*.

רַגָּז 1 adj. **trembling, agitated,** of heart Dt 28₆₅. → רגז *tremble*.

רֹגֶז 7.2 n.m.—cstr. רֹגֶז; sf. רָגְזֶךָ—**1. turmoil, trouble** Is 14₃ Jb 14₁. **2. raging, wrath, excitement** of Y. Hb 3₂, the wicked Jb 3₁₇, horse Jb 39₂₄. **3. rumbling** of thunder Jb 37₂. → רגז *tremble*.

רָגְזָה 1 n.f. **trembling** Ezk 12₁₈. → רגז *tremble*.

רגל I 23.1.1 vb.—**Pi.** 23.1.1 + waw וַיְרַגְּלוּ; impv. רַגְּלוּ; ptc. מְרַגְּלִים; inf. רַגֵּל (רַגְּלָהּ)—**1. spy out, scout** land Jos 6₂₂, city 2 S 10₃. **2.** abs., **act as spy** Jos 6₂₃. **3.** ptc. as noun, **spy, scout** Gn 42₉, **secret agent** 2 S 15₁₀.

***רגל** II 2.2.1 vb.—**Qal** 1.2.1 Pf. רָגַל; impf. Si תרגל (unless pi.)—**slander** with (various preps.) tongue Ps 15₃ (עַל) Si 5₁₄ (בְּ) 5₁₄ (אֶל).

Pi. 1.2 + waw וַיְרַגֵּל—**slander** someone (בְּ of obj.) to (אֶל) someone else 2 S 19₂₈.

רגל III 1.1.1 vb.—**Pu.** 0.0.1 Ptc. מרוגלת—**be attached, be tied,** perh. lit. 'be hindered from using the foot' 1QM 5₁₃.

Hi 0.1 Impf. תרגיל—**be familiar, have friendly relations with** (עִם) Si. 8₄.

Tiphel 1 Pf. תִּרְגַּלְתִּי—**teach to walk** Ho 11₃ (לְ of obj.).

→ רֶגֶל *foot*, רַגְלִי *on foot*, מַרְגְּלוֹת *place of feet*.

***רגל** IV 0.0.1 vb.—**Qal** 1 Impf. תרגל—**be curly,** of beard 4QCrypt 2.1₂.

רֶגֶל 247.4.40 n.f.—רֶגֶל; cstr. רֶגֶל; sf. רַגְלִי; du. (רַגְלַיִם) רַגְלַיִם; cstr. רַגְלֵי; sf. רַגְלָיו ,רַגְלֵיהֶם—**1. foot,** sometimes **leg** (1 S 17₆), **a.** of human Gn 18₄; representing extremity of body, 'from the sole of the foot to the crown/head' Dt 28₃₅; perh. 'feet' as euphemism for genitals Jg 3₂₄, מֵימֵי רַגְלֵיהֶם *water of their feet* 2 K 18₂₇(Qr)||Is 36₁₂(Qr) (Kt שיניהם *their urine*). **b.** of Y. Ex 24₁₀. **c.** of animals Is 32₂₀, birds Gn 8₉, insects Lv 11₂₁. **f.** of table Ex 25₂₆ ||37₁₃. **2.** with prep. לְ or בְּ **at one's foot,** i.e. following one Ex 11₈ (בְּ) Dt 33₃ (לְ), at every step, wherever one turns Gn 30₃₀ (לְ). **3. pace** Gn 33₁₄. **4.** pl. **(number of) times** Ex 23₁₄. → רגל III *use the foot*; cf. רַגְלִי *on foot*, מַרְגְּלוֹת *place of feet*, מְרוֹגֶלֶת *clothing for legs*.

רַגְלִי 12.2 adj.—pl. רַגְלִים—**1. on foot,** of man Jg 20₂. **2.** as noun, **one who goes on foot** Jr 12₅; elsewhere alw. coll., in ref. to Israelites at Exodus Ex 12₃₇, **infantry soldiers** 1 S 4₁₀. → רגל III *use the foot*; cf. רֶגֶל *foot*.

רֹגְלִים 2 pl.n. **Rogelim.**

רגם I 16.0.1 vb.—**Qal** 16.0.1 Impf. יִרְגְּמוּ; + waw וְרָגְמוּ; inf. cstr. לִרְגּוֹם; abs. רָגוֹם—**stone** someone to death, **a.** with accus. of person Lv 20₂ (+ בָּאֶבֶן *with stones*) 24₁₄.₂₃ (+ אֶבֶן *[with] stones*) Dt 21₂₁ (+ בָּאֲבָנִים *with stones*). **b.** with עַל of obj. Ezk 23₄₇ (+ אֶבֶן *[with] stones*). → רֶגֶם II *stone*, רִגְמָה *crowd*, מַרְגֵּמָה I *sling*, II *heap of stones*.

*[רגם] II vb. **Qal, 1. speak** Ps 68₂₈ (if em. רִגְמָתָם *their crowd* to רֹגֵם תָּם *speaking honestly*). **2.** fem. sg. ptc. as coll. noun, **speakers** Ps 68₂₈ (if em. רִגְמָתָם *their crowd* to רֹגְמָתָם *their speakers*). → רִגְמָה III *command*.

רֶגֶם I 1 pr.n.m. **Regem.**

*[רֶגֶם] II 0.0.2 n.m. **stone** 3QTr 5₉ 6₈. → רגם I *stone*.

[רִגְמָה] I 1 n.f.—sf. רִגְמָתָם—**crowd (of people),** perh. viewed as heap (of stones) Ps 68₂₈ (or em. רֹגֵם תָּם *speak honestly* or רֹגְמָתָם *their speakers*). → רגם I *stone*.

*[רִגְמָה] II 1 n.f.—sf. רִגְמָתָם—**noisy throng** Ps 68₂₈.

*[רִגְמָה] III 1 n.f.—sf. רִגְמָתָם—**command,** i.e. **commander(s), leader(s)** Ps 68₂₈. → רגם II *speak*.

*[רְגָמָה] 0.0.2 n.f.—pl. רגמות—**pace,** as unit of measure 3QTr 10₆.₁₃.

רֶגֶם מֶלֶךְ 1 pr.n.m. **Regem-melech.**

רגן 7.1.2 vb.—**Qal** 1 Ptc. רוֹגְנִים—**murmur, grumble** Is 29₂₄.

Ni. 6.1.2 + waw וַיֵּרָגְנוּ; ptc. נִרְגָּן—**1. murmur, grumble** Dt 1₂₇ 1QH 17₂₂ (+ בְּ *against*). **2.** ptc. as noun, **whisperer, backbiter, gossip** Pr 16₂₈. → רֶגֶן *murmuring.*

*[**רֶגֶן**] 0.0.1 n.[m.] **murmuring, grumbling** 1QH 13₂₃. → רגן *murmur.*

רגע I 6.0.1 vb.—**Qal** 3 Pf. רָגַע; ptc. רֹגַע—**disturb, stir up** sea Is 51₁₅=Jr 31₃₅ Jb 26₁₂ (or רגע II).

Hi. 3.0.1 Impf. אַרְגִּיעָה—**1. wink the eye,** עַד־אַרְגִּיעָה *while I would wink the eye,* i.e. but for a moment Pr 12₁₉. **2. do in a moment,** אַרְגִּיעָה אֲרִיצֶנּוּ *I will do in a moment, I will cause him to run,* i.e. in a moment I will cause him to run Jr 49₁₉=50₄₄.

→ רֶגַע I *moment.*

רגע II 7.1.2 vb.—**Qal** 1 Pf. רָגַע—of sea, **become still,** or perh. **make sea still** Jb 26₁₂ (or רגע I).

Ni. 1 Impv. הֵרָגְעִי—**rest,** of sword Jr 47₆.

Hi 5.1.2 Pf. הִרְגִּיעָה; impf. תַּרְגִּיעַ; ptc. Si מרגיע; inf. הַרְגִּיעַ (הַרְגִּיעוֹ)—**1. cause to rest, give rest to** (accus.) Israel Jr 31₂, earth Jr 50₃₄. **2. place, establish justice** as (לְ) light Is 51₄. **3.** intrans., **rest** Dt 28₆₅.

→ רָגֵעַ *restful,* רֶגַע II *rest,* מַרְגּוֹעַ *(place of) rest,* מַרְגֵּעָה *(place of) rest.*

רגע III 1 vb.—**Qal** 1 Pf. רָגַע—**harden,** or perh. **crack, break,** of skin Jb 7₅.

*[**רָגַע**] 0.0.0.1 pr.n.[m.] **Raga.**

[**רָגֵעַ**] 1 adj.—pl. cstr. רִגְעֵי—**restful,** as noun, **restful one, quiet one** Ps 35₂₀. → רגע II *rest.*

רֶגַע I 22.1 n.m.—רֶגַע; pl. רְגָעִים—**1. moment, short time** Ps 30₆. **2.** adv., **a.** רֶגַע **in a moment** Is 47₉, **for a moment** Is 54₈. **b.** רֶגַע ... רֶגַע **at one moment ... at another moment** Jr 18₇-₉. **c.** רֶגַע אֶחָד **for a single moment** Ex 33₅. **d.** כִּמְעַט־רֶגַע **for a little moment** Is 26₂₀. **e.** בְּרֶגַע קָטֹן **for a little moment** Is 54₇. **f.** כְּרֶגַע **in a moment** Nm 16₂₁. **g.** לִרְגָעִים **at every moment** Is 27₃. **h.** עֲדֵי־רָגַע **for only a moment** Jb 20₅. → רגע I *disturb.*

*[**רֶגַע**] II 1 n.[m.] **rest, quietness, peace** Jb 21₁₃. → רגע II *rest.*

רגשׁ 1.1.4 vb.—**Qal** 1.1 Pf. רָגְשׁוּ; inf. Si רגשו—**be in tumult, throng tumultuously, rage,** of nations Ps 2₁.

Ni. 0.0.1 Inf. הרגש—**be turbulent, churn,** of waves 1QH 10₁₂.

Htp. 0.0.3 Impf. תתרגש; inf. התרגשם—**rage, storm, surge,** of assembly of wicked 1QH 10₁₂ (+ עַל *against*), waves 1QH 11₁₆.

→ רֶגֶשׁ *throng,* רִגְשָׁה *throng.*

[**רֶגֶשׁ**] 1 n.[m.]—רֶגֶשׁ—**throng** Ps 55₁₅. → רגשׁ *be in tumult.*

[**רִגְשָׁה**] 1 n.f.—cstr. רִגְשַׁת—**throng,** or perh. **tumult** Ps 64₃. → רגשׁ *be in tumult.*

רַד Jg 19₁₁, see ירד *go down.*

רדד 3.0.2 vb.—**Qal** 2 Ptc. רוֹדֵד; inf. לָרֹד—**beat down, subdue, subjugate** nations Is 45₁ Ps 144₂.

Pu. 0.0.2 Ptc. מרודד—**be subdued,** or perh. **be sustained,** of trumpet blast 1QM 8₅.₁₄.

Hi. 1 + waw וַיָּרֶד—**beat out** gold 1 K 6₃₂.

→ רְדִיד *veil;* cf. רדה I *rule over.*

רדה I 23.1.3 vb.—**Qal** 22.1.3 Pf. רְדִיתֶם; impf. יֵרְדְּ, תִּרְדֶּה; + waw וַיִּרְדְּ, וַיִּרְדוּ; impv. רְדֵה, רְדוּ, Q רדינה; ptc. רֹדֶה, רֹדִים; inf. רְדוֹת—**1. have dominion over, rule over,** usu. with בְּ *over* Gn 1₂₆ Lv 26₁₇; also with accus. Lv 25₅₃ (+ בְּפֶרֶךְ *with harshness*). **2.** without obj., **have dominion, rule** Ps 72₈. **3.** ptc. as noun, **ruler** Si 44₃(Bmg).

Hi. 1 Impf. יַרְדְּ—**cause to rule** Is 41₂ (or em. יָרֹד to יָרֹד תַּחְתָּיו *he beats down beneath him,* i.e. רדד qal).

→ מִרְדּוּת II *chastisement;* cf. רדד *beat down.*

רדה II 3 vb.—**Qal** 3 Pf. רָדָה; impf. יִרְדּוּ—**1. scrape out, scoop out** honey into (אֶל) hands Jg 14₉. **2. make gains, take gifts** into (עַל) hands Jr 5₃₁.

רַדַּי 1 pr.n.m. **Raddai.**

[**רְדִיד**] 2 n.[m.]—sf. רְדִידִי; pl. רְדִידִים—**veil, shawl** Is 3₂₃ Ca 5₇. → רדד *beat out.*

רדם 7.0.3 vb.—**Ni.** 7.0.3 Pf. נִרְדַּמְתִּי; + waw וַיֵּרָדַם; ptc. נִרְדָּם—**be in, or fall into, a deep sleep** Jg 4₂₁ Jon 1₅, perh. **be stunned** Ps 76₇. → תַּרְדֵּמָה *deep sleep.*

רדף 143.3.22 vb.—**Qal** 131.2.21 Pf. רָדַף; impf. יִרְדֹּף (יִרְדָּף־); + waw וַיִּרְדֹּף; impv. רְדֹף (רָדְפֵהוּ), רִדְפוּ; ptc. רֹדֵף, רֹדְפִים; inf. לִרְדֹּף, מִרְדֹּף, לִרְדֹּף (רָדְפוֹ)—**1a.** with accus., **pursue, chase** Gn 14₁₅ (+ עַד *as far as*) Lv 26₇. **b.** with אַחֲרֵי, less oft. אַחַר, **pursue, chase (after)** Gn 31₂₃ Ex 14₄ 2 K 25₅; **follow (after)** Jg 3₂₈. **c.** abs., **pursue, go in pursuit** Gn 14₁₄. **2. put to flight** Lv 26₃₆. **3. hunt** partridge 1 S 26₂₀. **4a. pursue a goal, seek (to obtain)**

righteousness Dt 16$_{20}$, wickedness Ps 119$_{150}$, strong drink Is 5$_{11}$, reward Is 1$_{23}$. **b.** with אַחֲרֵי or אַחַר, **pursue (after) a goal, seek (after)** way 4QBark^{c} 1.1$_{6}$, root of understanding 4QInstr^{d} 55$_{9}$. **c.** with inf., **press on (for a purpose)** Ho 6$_{3}$. **5. persecute** Dt 30$_{7}$ Ps 119$_{161}$ (+ חִנָּם *without cause*) Jb 19$_{28}$ (לְ of obj.). **6. pursue (at law)** 5/6ḤevBA 44$_{24}$. **7.** ptc. as noun, **a. pursuer** Jos 2$_{16}$. **b. persecutor** Jr 17$_{18}$.

Ni. 2.1.1 Pf. נִרְדָּפְנוּ; ptc. נִרְדָּף—**1. be pursued, be hard-driven** Lm 5$_{5}$. **2. be pursued, i.e. pass away, disappear** Ec 3$_{15}$. **3. be persecuted** Si 5$_{3}$.

Pi. 8 Impf. תְּרַדֵּף, יְרַדֶּף־; + waw וְרִדְּפָה; ptc. מְרַדֵּף—**1. pursue** Ho 2$_{9}$ Na 1$_{8}$ (+ חֹשֶׁךְ *[into] darkness*). **2. pursue a goal, seek (to obtain)** righteousness Pr 15$_{9}$, evil Pr 11$_{19}$.

Pu. 1 + waw וְרֻדַּף—**be chased away** Is 17$_{13}$.

Hi. 1 Pf. הִרְדִּיפֻהוּ—**pursue** Jg 20$_{43}$.

→ רֶדֶף *pursuit*, מִרְדֹּף *pursuit*, מֻרְדָּף *persecution*.

*[רֶדֶף] 0.0.2 n.[m.]—cstr. רדף—**pursuit** 1QM 9$_{6}$ 18$_{2}$. → רדף *pursue*.

רהב 4.1 vb.—**Qal** 2.1 Impf. יִרְהֲבוּ; impv. רְהַב—**1. storm, act insolently, act arrogantly** Is 3$_{5}$ (+ בְּ *against*) Si 13$_{8}$. **2. importune, plead with** (accus.) Pr 6$_{3}$.

Hi. 2 Pf. הִרְהִיבֻנִי; impf. תַּרְהִבֵנִי—**1. overwhelm, disturb** Ca 6$_{5}$. **2. make proud, make bold, encourage** Ps 138$_{3}$ (+ עֹז *[with] strength*).

→ רָהָב *proud*, רֹהַב *pride*, מַרְהֵבָה *raging*.

[רָהָב] 1 adj.—pl. רְהָבִים—**proud,** as noun, **proud one, arrogant one** Ps 40$_{5}$. → רהב *act stormily*.

רַהַב 6.1 pr.n.[m.] **Rahab.**

[רֹהַב] 1 n.[m.]—sf. רָהְבָּם—**(object of) pride,** of one's years Ps 90$_{10}$. → רהב *act stormily*.

רָהְגָּה 1 pr.n.m. **Rohgah.**

[רַהַט] I 3 n.[m.]—pl. רְהָטִים (רֲהָטִים)—**trough,** for watering cattle Gn 30$_{38.41}$ Ex 2$_{16}$.

[רַהַט] II 1 n.[m.]—pl. רְהָטִים—**lock (of hair), tress** Ca 7$_{6}$.

*[רַהַט] III 1 n.[m.]—pl. רְהָטִים—**beam (of loom)** Ca 7$_{6}$.

*[רַהַט] IV 1 n.[m.]—pl. רְהָטִים—**leather strip** Ca 7$_{6}$.

[רָהִיט] 1 n.[m.]—sf. Qr L רַהִיטֵנוּ (mss רְהִיטֵנוּ), Kt רחיטנו—**rafters** of house Ca 1$_{17}$.

רוא, see רוה *be saturated*.

רוב, see רֹב *multitude*.

רובד, see רֹבֶד *terrace*.

רוד 4 vb.—**Qal** 2 Pf רָד, רַדְנוּ—**wander, roam about freely** Jr 2$_{31}$ Ho 12$_{1}$ (+ עִם *with*).

Hi. 2 Impf. תָּרִיד—**show restlessness** Ps 55$_{3}$ (+ בְּ *on account of* complaint), perh. **break loose** Gn 27$_{40}$.

→ מָרוּד *wandering*.

רוֹדָנִים 1 pr.n.m. **Rodanim.**

רוה 15.3.5 vb.—**Qal** 3.0.1 Impf. יִרְוְיֻן, נִרְוֶה; + waw וְרָוְתָה—**1. be saturated with, drink one's fill of** (מִן) blood Jr 46$_{10}$, fat Ps 36$_{8}$. **2. drink to the full, have one's fill of** (accus.) love Pr 7$_{18}$.

Pi. 6.3.3 Pf. רִוְּתָה; impf. יְרַוֶּךְ, אֲרַיָּוֶךְ; ptc. Si מרוה; inf. cstr. (Q רוות); abs. רַוֵּה—**1. be saturated, drenched, drink one's fill** Is 34$_{5.7}$ (+ מִן *of blood*). **2. saturate, water abundantly, sate** furrow Ps 65$_{11}$, world Si 39$_{22}$, person Pr 5$_{19}$. **3. saturate, drench someone with, a.** accus. tears Is 16$_{9}$, fat Jr 31$_{14}$. **b.** מִן *with* good Si 35$_{13}$. **4.** of canal, **draw water from** (מִן) wadi 3QTr 10$_{3}$.

Hi. 5.0.1 Pf. הִרְוָה, הִרְוֵיתִי; ptc. מַרְוֶה; inf. Q הרות—**1. saturate, water** land Is 55$_{10}$. **2. give to drink, satisfy, refresh** weary Jr 31$_{25}$; abs. Pr 11$_{25}$. **3. satisfy someone with something** Is 43$_{24}$ Lm 3$_{15}$.

Ho. 1 Impf. יוֹרֶא—**be given a drink, be satisfied, be refreshed** Pr 11$_{25}$.

→ רָאֶה II *satiated,* רְאֵה IV *drunkenness,* רָוֶה *watered,* רְוָיָה *saturation,* רִי *moisture;* cf. ירה II *water.*

רָוֶה 3.0.2 adj.—Q רוי; f.s. רָוָה—**1. watered,** of garden Is 58$_{11}$, spirit 1QS 2$_{14}$. **2.** as noun, **watered one** Dt 29$_{18}$; **irrigated place** 3QTr 8$_{14}$. → רוה *saturate*.

רוהגה, see רָהְגָּה *Rohgah*.

רוח I 3.0.1 vb.—**Qal** 2 Impf. יִרְוַח; + waw וְרָוַח—**be relief, be refreshment for** (לְ) someone 1 S 16$_{23}$ Jb 32$_{20}$.

Pu. 1 Ptc. מְרֻוָּחִים—**be spacious,** of upper chamber Jr 22$_{14}$.

Hi. 0.0.1 Inf. Q הרויח—**give relief** 4QTobit^{e} 1.1$_{4}$.

→ רֶוַח *space, respite,* רְוָחָה *respite*.

רוח II, see ריח *smell*.

רֶוַח 2.0.5 n.m.—**1. space, interval** Gn 32$_{17}$ 1QM 7$_{6}$. **2. respite, relief** Est 4$_{14}$. → רוח I *be relief*.

רוּחַ 378.11.365 n.f.&m.—+ ה- of direction רוּחָה; cstr. רוּחַ; sf.

רוּחִי; pl. רוּחוֹת; cstr. רוּחוֹת, רוּחוֹת, Q רוּחֵי; sf. Q רוחיו (Q רוחותיו) —**1a. wind, breeze** Gn 8$_{1}$; רוּחַ קָדִים *east wind* Ex 10$_{13}$, רוּחַ סְעָרָה *storm wind* Ezk 1$_{4}$, רוּחַ הַיּוֹם *breeze of the day* Gn 3$_{8}$, כַּנְפֵי־רוּחַ *wings of the wind* Ps 104$_{3}$. **b. wind,** i.e. (1) **direction** Jr 49$_{32}$. (2) **side, corner** Jr 52$_{23}$; רוּחַ הַקָּדִים *the east side* Ezk 42$_{16}$. **c. wind,** i.e. **air** Is 26$_{18}$ Jb 41$_{8}$. **d. wind,** i.e. **emptiness, vanity** Is 41$_{29}$ Jr 5$_{13}$. **e. (breath of) wind, (mere) breath,** as descr. of transitoriness of life Ps 78$_{39}$ Jb 7$_{7}$. **2. breath, a. breath, blast (from nostrils or mouth)** of Y. Ex 15$_{8}$, human Is 11$_{4}$. **b. breath,** i.e. **(life-giving) spirit,** רוּחַ חַיִּים *breath/spirit of life* Gn 6$_{17}$; essential for life of all flesh Jb 34$_{14}$, departs at death Ps 146$_{4}$. **3. spirit, a.** of Y., (1) present at creation Gn 1$_{2}$. (2) inspiring ability, wisdom Gn 41$_{38}$ Ex 31$_{3}$||35$_{21}$, prophecy Nm 11$_{29}$ Mc 3$_{8}$. (3) with power of transportation 1 K 18$_{12}$ Ezk 37$_{1}$. (4) Y.'s will Is 30$_{1}$, mind Is 40$_{13}$. (5) Y. himself or his presence Is 34$_{16}$ Ps 139$_{7}$. **b.** of or in humans, (1) life force, life principle Zc 12$_{1}$, enters the foetus Ec 11$_{5}$, present in blood circulating 4QD[a] 6.1$_{6}$, departs at death Ec 12$_{7}$. (2) vigour, vitality Gn 45$_{27}$. (3) courage Jos 2$_{11}$. (4) mind, intellect Dt 34$_{9}$ Si 16$_{25}$. (5) disposition, feeling, as lowly Is 57$_{15}$, bitter Gn 26$_{35}$, troubled Gn 41$_{8}$, impatient Jb 21$_{4}$, jealous Nm 5$_{14}$, proud Pr 16$_{18}$. (6) inclination, will Ex 35$_{21}$. (7) anger Jg 8$_{3}$. (8) moral character, inward nature Ezk 11$_{19}$ Ps 32$_{2}$. (9) spiritual condition, spiritual qualities 1QS 5$_{21.24}$. (10) human being 1QH 9$_{9}$, descr. as 'spirit of flesh' 1QH 5$_{19}$, 'of error' 1QH 9$_{22}$. **c.** power of judgment Is 4$_{4}$. **d.** of destroying angels, demons and bastards 4QShir[a] 1$_{5}$. **e.** two spirits that control humans 1QS 3$_{18}$, termed 'spirits of truth and deceit' 1QS 3$_{19}$, 'of light and darkness' 1QS 3$_{25}$. **f.** personified spirits, (1) in presence of Y. 1 K 22$_{21}$||2 C 18$_{20}$. (2) angelic beings 1QH 5$_{14}$, specif. spirits of holiness 1QH 16$_{12}$, truth 1QM 13$_{10}$, righteousness 4QShirShabb[d] 1.1$_{38}$, wickedness 4QShir[b] 1$_{6}$; assoc. with Belial 1QM 13$_{2.4}$. **g.** perh. spiritual substance, i.e. as opposed to material 4QShir Shabb[f] 23.2$_{8}$.

רְוָחָה 2 n.f.—sf. רְוָחָתִי—**respite** Ex 8$_{11}$, appar. plea for respite Lm 3$_{56}$. → רוח I *be relief.*

רוחץ, see רַחַץ *washing.*

רוחק, see רֹחַק *distance.*

רְוָיָה 2.0.1 n.f.—**1. satiation** Ps 23$_{5}$. **2. drunkenness, excess** 1QpHab 11$_{14}$. → רוה *be saturated.*

רום 195.16.100 vb.—**Qal** 69.0.43 Pf. רָם, רָמוּ (רָמּוּ); impf. יָרוּם (יָרֹם, יָרֻם); + waw וַיָּרָם; impv. רוּמָה, Q רומי; ptc. רָם, רָמָה, רָמִים, רָמֵי, רָמוֹת (רָאמוֹת); inf. רוּם (רוֹמָם)—**1a. be high, be lofty, be raised up,** of stars Jb 22$_{12}$, rock Ps 61$_{3}$ (+ מִן higher *than*), highway Is 49$_{11}$. **b.** ptc. as (1) adj., **high, tall, lofty,** of people Dt 1$_{28}$ cedar Is 2$_{13}$, mountain Dt 12$_{2}$. (2) noun, **high one, tall one, lofty one,** of person 1QM 14$_{11}$, tree Is 10$_{33}$; pl. **heights (of heaven)** Ps 78$_{69}$. **2a. be high,** i.e. **be lifted up, exalted,** of Y. Ps 99$_{2}$ (+ עַל *over*), human Is 52$_{13}$, city Pr 11$_{11}$. **b.** ptc. as (1) adj., **uplifted, exalted,** of hand Ex 14$_{8}$, throne Is 6$_{1}$. (2) noun, **high one, exalted one,** of Y. Is 57$_{15}$, heavenly beings Jb 21$_{22}$. **3a. exalt oneself, be haughty, be arrogant, be triumphant,** of enemy Ps 13$_{3}$ (+ עַל *over*), eyes Ps 131$_{1}$, heart Dt 8$_{14}$ 17$_{20}$ (+ מִן *above*). **b.** ptc. as, (1) adj., **haughty,** of eyes Ps 18$_{28}$. (2) noun, **haughty one,** of person 2 S 22$_{28}$. **4.** of motion, **rise, be lifted up, go up,** of ark Gn 7$_{17}$ (+ מֵעַל *[from] above*), glory of Y. Ezk 10$_{4}$ (+ מֵעַל). **5. rise,** i.e. **grow,** of tree 1QH 16$_{9}$ (+ עַל *over*). **6.** of position in community, **move up, be promoted** 1QS 2$_{23}$ (+ מִן *from*). **7. arise, come into being,** of wickedness 1QH fr. 5$_{7}$. **8.** ptc. as adj., **loud,** of voice Dt 27$_{14}$.

Polel 25.4.27 Pf. רוֹמַמְתִּי; impf. יְרוֹמֵם, אֲרוֹמִמְךָ; impv. רוֹמְמוּ; ptc. מְרוֹמֵם; inf. רוֹמֵם—**1. lift up,** i.e. **raise** person Ps 9$_{14}$ (+ מִן *from*) 27$_{5}$ (+ בְּ *onto*), waves Ps 107$_{25}$. **2. exalt** nation Pr 14$_{34}$, person 2 S 22$_{49}$||Ps 18$_{49}$ (+ מִן *above*); without obj., 1 S 2$_{7}$. **3. exalt (in praise), extol** Y. Ex 15$_{2}$, name of Y. Ps 34$_{4}$. **4a. raise, bring up, rear** child Is 1$_{2}$. **b. cause tree to grow** Ezk 31$_{4}$. **5. erect** temple Ezr 9$_{9}$.

Polal 3.0.3 Pf. רוֹמַם; impf. תְּרוֹמַמְנָה; ptc. מְרוֹמָם—**1. be lifted up, be exalted,** of horn Ps 75$_{11}$. **2. be exalted (in praise), be extolled,** of Y. Ps 66$_{17}$ (+ תַּחַת *under* tongue), name of Y. Ne 9$_{5}$ (+ עַל *above*). **3. rise,** of wheel 4QShirShabb[f] 20.2$_{12}$.

Hi. 92.10.48 Pf. הֵרִים, הֲרִימֹתִי; impf. יָרִים (יָרֵם); + waw וַיָּרֶם; impv. הָרֵם (הָרִימִי ,הָרִימָה ,הָרֶם), הָרִימוּ; ptc. מֵרִים, מְרִימֵי; inf. הָרִים (הֲרִימִי)—**1a. lift up, raise** hand Ex 17$_{11}$, face Ezr 9$_{6}$ (+ אֶל *to*), head Ps 110$_{7}$, rod Ex 7$_{20}$ (בְּ of obj.), standard Is 62_{10} (+ עַל *over*). **b. lift up (in the hand), pick up, take up** stone Jos 4_5, ashes Lv 6_3, cloak 2 K 2_{13}. **c. set on high** throne Is 14_{13} (+ מִמַּעַל לְ *above* stars), nest Jb 39_{27}. **2.** with obj. קוֹל, **raise voice, make a loud sound** Gn 39_{15} 2 C 5_{13} (+ בְּ *with* trumpets, etc.). **3a. lift up, raise up,** i.e. **exalt** person 1 S 2_8 1 K 16_2, (+ מִן *from* dust), horn 1 S 2_{10}; perh. **heighten, increase** shame Pr 3_{35}, folly Pr 14_{29}. **b.** inf. as noun, **lifting up, exaltation** Ps 75_7. **4. raise up,** i.e. **resurrect** person 1QH 19_{12} (+ לְ *to* company). **5. raise up,** i.e. **bring about, bring on to the scene** survivors and remnant 1QH 14_8. **6. set up, erect** stone as (accus.) pillar Gn 31_{45}. **7. lift up,** i.e. **take away, remove** fat Lv 4_8 (+ מִן *from*), crown Ezk 21_{31}. **8. raise,** i.e. **offer, present, contribute** an offering Nm 15_{19} (+ לְ *to* Y.) 18_{26} (+ מִן *from* tithes); **contribute** animals for offering 2 C 30_{24} (+ לְ *to* assembly).

Ho. $_{3.2}$ Pf. הוּרַם (Qr הוּרַם); impf. יוּרַם; ptc. Si מורם—**1. be exalted** Si $10_{25(A)}$. **2. be taken away, be removed** Dn $8_{11(Qr)}$. **3. be lifted up (as offering), be offered, be presented** Ex 29_{27} (+ מִן *from*).

Htpolel $_{2.0.5}$ Impf אֲרוֹמָם, יִתְרוֹמֵם; inf. Q התרומם—**lift oneself up, exalt oneself, be lifted up, be exalted,** of Y. Is 33_{10}, king Dn 11_{36}, waves 1QH 10_{28}.

→ רוּם *height*, רָמוּת I *height*, מָרוֹם *height*, רוֹם I *on high*, II *exalted*, רוֹמָה *haughtily*, רוֹמָם *exaltation*, רוֹמֵמוּת *uplifting*, יָרוּם *elevated*, תְּרוּמָה *contribution*, תְּרוּמִיָּה *special contribution*, תְּרוּם *offering (of praise)*, רָמָה I *height*; cf. ראם *rise*, ירם *be high*.

רוֹם I $_1$ adv. **on high** Hb 3_{10}. → רום *be high*.

***[רוֹם] II** $_{0.0.1}$ adj.—cstr. pl. רומי—**exalted,** as noun, **exalted one** 4QShirShabb[f] 3.2_4. → רום *be high*.

רוּם $_{6.1.48}$ n.m.—cstr. רוּם (רֻם); sf. Q רמו; pl. Q רומים; cstr. Q רומי; sf. Si רומיה—**1. height, loftiness, exaltation,** שָׁמַיִם לָרוּם *the heavens for height* Pr 25_3, רום ארזים *height of cedars* CD 2_{19}, מרומי רום *heights of the height*, i.e. highest heights 4QShirShabb[a] 1.1_{20}, אלי רום *gods of exaltation*, i.e. exalted gods 4QShirShabb[d] 1.1_{33}. **2. haughtiness, arrogance, pride** of men Is 2_{11}, eyes Is 10_{12}, heart Jr 48_{29}. → רום *be high*.

רוֹמָה $_1$ adv. **haughtily,** or perh. **erect** Mc 2_3. → רום *be high*.

רוּמָה $_2$ pl.n. **Rumah.**

רומות 4QCrypt 1.3_3, see רמה III *protrude*.

רוֹמָם $_{2.0.7}$ n.[m.]—cstr. Q רומם; sf. Q רוממו; pl. cstr. רוֹמְמוֹת—**1. exaltation, extolling, praise** Ps 149_6 1QM 4_8. **2. exaltedness** 4QShirShabb[d] 1.1_{33}. → רום *be high*.

[רוֹמֵמוּת] $_1$ n.f.—sf. רוֹמְמֻתֵךְ—**uplifting, exaltation, majesty** Is 33_3. → רום *be high*.

רון I $_1$ vb.—**Htpol.** $_1$ Ptc. מִתְרוֹנֵן—**be overcome with** (מִן) wine Ps 78_{65}.

***רון II** $_1$ vb. (byform of רנן)—**Htpol.** $_1$ Ptc. מִתְרוֹנֵן—**shout** Ps 78_{65} (+ מִן *on account of* wine).

רונן 4QShirShabb[d] 1.1_{36}, see רֹנֵן *rejoicing*.

רוע $_{45.2.27}$ vb.—**Qal** $_{1.0.5}$ Impf. Q ירועו; impv. רֹעוּ—**1. shout, cry out,** in distress 1QH 11_{33}. **2. raise a war cry** Is 8_9.

Hi. $_{40.2.22}$ Pf. הֵרִיעוּ (הֵרֵעוּ); impf. יָרִיעַ; + waw וַהֲרֵעֹתֶם; וַיָּרִיעוּ, וַיָּרַע; impv. הָרִיעוּ, הָרִיעִי; ptc. מְרִיעִים; inf. הָרִיעַ (Q לריע)—**1a. shout, cry out,** in acclamation 1 S 10_{24}, triumph Jr 50_{15}, distress Is 15_4; as after (עַל) a thief Jb 30_5. **b.** with obj., **raise a shout** (תְּרוּעָה), for joy 1 S 4_5, **utter a cry** (רֵעַ), out of distress Mc 4_9. **2. raise a war cry** (תְּרוּעָה) Jos 6_5; without obj. 2 C 13_{15}; **shout for battle** (בַּמִּלְחָמָה) 1 S 17_{30}. **3a. give a blast on the trumpet, blow the horn, sound an alarm,** during worship Si 50_{16} (+ בְּ *with* trumpets), for day of Y. Jl 2_1, war Nm 10_9 (+ בְּ *with* trumpets); as signal during battle, with obj. קוֹל *sound* 1QM 8_8, תְּרוּעָה *alarm* 1QM 8_9. **b.** of trumpet, **sound out,** for assembly CD 11_{22}, as signal during battle 1QM 8_1. **4. shout joyfully, make a joyful noise,** in worship or praise Ps 47_2 (+ לְ *to* Y.) 98_6 (+ לִפְנֵי *before* Y., בְּ *with* trumpets).

Polal $_1$ יְרֹעַע—**be shouted,** of joy at grape harvest Is 16_{10}.

Htpol. $_3$ Impf. יִתְרוֹעֲעוּ, אֶתְרוֹעָע; impv. הִתְרֹעָעִי—**shout,** in acclamation Ps 60_{10} (+ עַל *on account of*), triumph Ps 108_{10} (+ עַל *over*), for joy Ps 65_{14}.

→ רֵעַ I *shouting*, תְּרוּעָה *shout*.

רוּץ $_{103.3.3}$ vb.—**Qal** $_{97.3}$ Pf. רַץ, רַצְתִּי; impf. יָרוּץ (יָרֻץ); + waw וַיָּרָץ (וַיָּרֹץ); impv. רוּץ; ptc. רָץ, רָצִים (רָצִין); inf. רוּץ—**1. run,** sometimes **go quickly** 2 K 4_{22}; + לְ *to* Hb 1_9, אֶל *to* Gn 24_{29}, מִן *from* Gn 18_2, לִפְנֵי *before* 2 S 15_1, אַחֲרֵי *after* 2 S 18_{22}; + noun without prep., הַמַּעֲרָכָה *(to* *the) battle-line* 1 S 17$_{22}$, דֶּרֶךְ *(by) way (of)* 2 S 18$_{23}$; וַתְּמַהֵר ... וַתָּרָץ *and she hastened ... and ran*, i.e. ran quickly Jg 13$_{10}$, לְמַעַן יָרוּץ קוֹרֵא בוֹ perh. *so that the one who reads it may run*, i.e. read it quickly, readily Hb 2$_{2}$. **2.** ptc. as noun, **a. guard, body-guard** of king 1 S 22$_{17}$. **b. runner, messenger, courier** Est 3$_{13}$.

Polel 1 יְרוֹצֵצוּ—**run, dart about,** of chariot, like (כְּ) lightning Na 2$_{5}$.

Hi. 6 Impf. תָּרִיץ; impv. הָרֵץ—**1. cause to run, drive away** from (מֵעַל) Jr 49$_{19}$||50$_{44}$(Qr). **2. bring quickly, take quickly** Gn 41$_{14}$ (+ מִן *from*) 2 C 35$_{13}$ (+ לְ *to*). **3. stretch out hand quickly** Ps 68$_{32}$.

→ מֵרוֹץ *race,* מְרוּצָה I *running;* cf. רצא I *run.*

רוש 24.4.12 vb.—**Qal** 23.3 Pf. רָשׁוּ; ptc. רָשׁ (רָאשׁ, Q רוש), רָשִׁים (רָאשִׁים)—**1. be in want,** of young lion Ps 34$_{11}$. **2.** ptc. as adj., **poor,** of man 1 S 18$_{23}$. **3.** ptc. as noun, **poor one, pauper** 2 S 12$_{3}$ Ps 82$_{3}$.

Polel 0.1 Impf. Si. ירששך—**impoverish** Si 13$_{5}$.

Hithpolel 1 Ptc. מִתְרוֹשֵׁשׁ—**pretend to be poor** Pr 13$_{7}$.

→ רוֹשׁ *poverty,* רֵישׁ *poverty;* cf. רשש III *be poor.*

רוֹשׁ I, see ראש II *poison.*

*[**רוֹשׁ**] II 0.1.1 n.[m.] **poverty** Si 34$_{29}$(F) 4QInstr^c 1.1$_{14}$. → רוש *be poor.*

רוּת 12 pr.n.f. **Ruth.**

[**רָז**] 2.2.91 n.[m.]—cstr. Q רז; sf. רָזִי, Q רזו; pl. Q רזים; cstr. Q רזי; sf. Q רזיו—**1. secret, confidential matter,** among humans perh. Is 24$_{16.16}$ (or both from רָזִי *wasting away*) Si 8$_{18}$. **2. secret, mystery,** רזי אל *mysteries of God* 1QM 3$_{9}$, דעת *of knowledge* 1QS 4$_{6}$, פלא *of wonder*, i.e. wonderful mysteries 1QH 9$_{21}$, רז נהיה *mystery of existence/the future* 1QMyst 1.1$_{3}$.

רזה 2 vb.—**Qal** 1 Pf. רָזָה—**make lean,** obj. gods Zc 2$_{11}$ (or em. pi. יְרַזֶּה, in same sense).

Ni. 1 Impf. יֵרָזֶה—**be lean, be made lean,** of fat Is 17$_{4}$.

→ רָזֶה *lean,* רָזִי *wasting away,* רָזוֹן I *leanness.*

[**רָזֶה**] 2 adj.—f.s. רָזָה—**lean,** of sheep Ezk 34$_{20}$, land Nm 13$_{20}$. → רזה *be lean.*

רָזוֹן I 3 n.[m.]—**1. leanness, emaciation, wasting disease** Is 10$_{16}$ Ps 106$_{15}$. **2. scantiness,** אֵיפַת רָזוֹן *ephah of scantiness*, i.e. scant ephah Mc 6$_{10}$. → רזה *be lean.*

רָזוֹן II 1 n.[m.]—**ruler** Pr 14$_{28}$. → רזן *be weighty.*

רְזוֹן 1 pr.n.m. **Rezon.**

רָזִי 2 n.[m.] **wasting away** Is 24$_{16.16}$. → רזה *make lean.*

*[**רְזִיל**] n.[m.] **wickedness, baseness** Is 24$_{16.16}$ (both if em. רְזִי־לִי *wasting away is to me!*).

רזם I 1 vb.—**Qal** 1 יִרְמְזוּן—**wink, flash,** of eyes Jb 15$_{12}$.

*__רזם__ II 1 vb.—**Qal** 1 יִרְמְזוּן—**fail, become weak,** of eyes Jb 15$_{12}$.

רזן 6.1.2 vb.—**Qal** 6.1.2 Ptc. רוֹזְנִים (רֹזְנִים); cstr. Q רוזני—**be weighty,** ptc. as noun, **ruler, prince** Jg 5$_{3}$. → רָזוֹן II *ruler.*

רחב 25.0.4 vb.—**Qal** 3.0.2 Pf. רָחַב; impf. Q תרחב; impv. Q רחבי—**be wide,** of mouth, in derision or gloating 1 S 2$_{1}$ (+ עַל *against* enemies); of heart, in joy Is 60$_{5}$.

Ni. 1 Ptc. נִרְחָב—ptc. as adj., **wide, spacious,** of pasture Is 30$_{23}$.

Hi. 21.0.2 Pf. הִרְחִיב, הִרְחַבְתְּ; impf. יַרְחִיב; impv. הַרְחֶב־, הַרְחִיבִי; ptc. מַרְחִיב; inf. הַרְחִיב—**1. make wide, open wide** one's mouth Is 57$_{4}$ (+עַל *against*), throat Is 5$_{14}$, **give wide space to** one's steps 2 S 22$_{37}$||Ps 18$_{37}$, **enlarge** border Ex 34$_{24}$, place of tent Is 54$_{2}$. **2.** without obj., **a. make a wide space, make room** for (לְ) someone Gn 26$_{22}$. **b. be wide, be enlarged,** of troubles Ps 25$_{17}$.

→ רָחָב I *wide,* רַחַב *broad expanse,* רֹחַב *breadth,* רְחוֹב I *broad space.* מֶרְחָב *broad place,*

רָחָב I 21.1.4 adj.—cstr. רְחַב; f.s. רְחָבָה; cstr. רַחֲבַת; m.pl. Q רחבים; cstr. רַחֲבֵי—**1.** רָחָב **wide, broad, extensive,** of land Ex 3$_{8}$, wall Ne 3$_{8}$, commandment Ps 119$_{96}$. **2.** רְחָבָה as noun, **wide place** Ps 119$_{45}$. **3.** רַחֲבֵי יָדַיִם/רְחַב/רַחֲבַת *wide of both hands*, i.e. on both sides, of land Gn 34$_{21}$, city Ne 7$_{4}$, sea Ps 104$_{25}$, river Is 33$_{21}$. **4.** רְחַב לֵבָב as noun, **one who is wide of heart,** i.e. arrogant Ps 101$_{5}$. **5.** רְחַב־נֶפֶשׁ as noun, **one wide of appetite,** i.e. greedy Pr 28$_{25}$. **6.** רחב אולת **broad of,** i.e. in, **folly,** of Rehoboam Si 47$_{23}$. → רחב *be wide.*

רָחָב II 5 pr.n.f. **Rahab.**

רַחַב 2 n.f. pl.—cstr. רַחֲבֵי—**broad place, expanse** Jb 36$_{16}$ 38$_{18}$. → רחב *be wide.*

רֹחַב 101.0.32 n.[m.]—Q רוחב (Q רחוב); cstr. רֹחַב; sf. רָחְבּוֹ—**1. breadth, width** of land Gn 13$_{17}$, water Jb 37$_{10}$; in connection with measurements, of Noah's ark Gn 6$_{15}$, temple buildings 1 K 6_{2}||2 C 3_{3}, **thickness** of wall Ezk 40_{5}. **2. breadth,** i.e. **extensiveness** of heart, i.e. understanding 1 K 5_{9}, of desire (נפש), i.e. greed 1QS 4_{9}. **3. space, expanse** 1QH 17_{27}. → רחב *be wide.*

רְחֹב, see רְחוֹב I *broad place,* II *Rehob,* III *Rehob.*

רְחֹבוֹת 4 pl.n. **Rehoboth.**

רְחַבְיָה, see רְחַבְיָהוּ *Rehabiah.*

רְחַבְיָהוּ 5 pr.n.m. **Rehabiah.**

רְחַבְעָם 50.1 pr.n.m. **Rehoboam.**

רְחוֹב I 43.0.5 n.f.—cstr. רְחוֹב; sf. רְחֹבָהּ; pl. רְחֹבוֹת; cstr. רְחֹבוֹת; sf. רְחֹבֹתֶיהָ—**broad place, square,** in city Gn 19_{2} Jg 19_{15}, usu. near gate Ne 8_{1}. → רחב *be wide.*

רְחוֹב II 7 pl.n. **Rehob.**

רְחוֹב III 3 pr.n.m. **Rehob.**

רַחוּם 13.2.2 adj.—**1. compassionate,** alw. (exc. perh. Ps 112_{4}) of Y., רַחוּם וְחַנּוּן *compassionate and gracious* Ex 34_{6}, חַנּוּן וְרַחוּם *gracious and compassionate* Jl 2_{13}. **2.** as noun, **compassionate one,** in ref. to Y. Si 50_{19}. → רחם *love.*

רְחוּם 4 pr.n.m. **Rehum.**

רָחוֹק 85.2.22 adj.—f.s. רְחוֹקָה; m.pl. רְחוֹקִים; f.pl. רְחֹקוֹת—**distant, far, 1.** of space, **a.** as adj. (oft. + מִן far *from*) of people Dt 13_{8}, city Dt 20_{15}, land Dt 29_{21}, way, i.e. journey Nm 9_{10}, salvation Ps 119_{155}. **b.** as noun, (1) **distant one, one afar off,** masc. Is 33_{13}, fem. Ezk 22_{5} (+ מִן ones far *from*). (2) **distance** Jos 3_{4}; בְּרָחוֹק *at a distance* Ps 10_{1}; מֵרָחוֹק *at a distance, afar off* Ex 20_{18}, *from a distance, from afar* Is 49_{12}, *to afar* Is 22_{3}; לְמֵרָחוֹק *from afar* Jb 36_{3}; עַד־מֵרָחֹק *far away* Is 57_{9}; עַד־לְמֵרָחוֹק *far away* 2 C 26_{15}, עַד־רָחוֹק *afar off* Mc 4_{3}. **c.** as adv., רָחוֹק מִן **at a (specified) distance away from** 11QT 52_{17}. **2.** of time, **a.** as adj. Ezk 12_{27}. **b.** as noun, **a long time, a great while,** מֵרָחוֹק *long ago* Is 22_{11}; לְמֵרָחוֹק *from of old, long ago* 2 K 19_{25}||Is 37_{26}, *for a great while to come* 2 S 7_{19}||1 C 17_{17}. **3.** of price, רָחוֹק מִן **far more than, far beyond** Pr 31_{10}. → רחק *be distant.*

[רָחִיט], see רָהִיט *rafters.*

רֵחַיִם 5.0.1 n.[m.]du. **(hand-)mill** Ex 11_{5} Nm 11_{8}.

*[רְחִיצָה] 0.0.1 n.f. **washing** 4QSh 1_{3} (=1QSh 3_{5} רחץ). → רחץ *wash.*

רָחֵל I 4 n.f.—pl. רְחֵלִים; sf. רְחֵלֶיךָ—**ewe** Gn 31_{38} 32_{15} Is 53_{7} Ca 6_{6}.

רָחֵל II 47.0.3 pr.n.f. **Rachel.**

רחם 46.3.14 vb.—**Qal** 1 Impf. אֶרְחָמְךָ—**love** Y. Ps 18_{2}.

Pi. 42.3.14 Pf. רִחַם; impf. יְרַחֵם; + waw וַיְרַחֲמֵם, וְרִחַמְתִּי; impv. Si רחם; ptc. מְרַחֵם; inf. abs. רַחֵם, cstr. רַחֵם (רַחֶמְכֶם)—**1. have compassion upon, have mercy upon, take pity upon, a.** with accus., subj. usu. Y. Ex 33_{19} Dt 13_{18}, also humans 1 K 8_{50}. **b.** with עַל *upon* Ps 103_{13}. **2.** without obj., **have compassion, be compassionate, show mercy, be merciful,** subj. Y. Jr 13_{14} Ps 116_{5}, humans Jr 6_{23}=50_{42}.

Pu. 3 Pf. רֻחָמָה; impf. יְרֻחָם—**be shown mercy, find mercy** Ho 2_{3} 14_{4} (+ בְּ *through* Y.) Pr 28_{13}.

→ רַחֲמִים *compassion,* רַחוּם *compassionate,* רַחֲמָן *compassionate,* רַחֲמָנִי *compassionate,* רַחֲמוֹן *compassionate,* רֶחֶם *womb.*

רָחָם 2 n.[m.]—רָחָמָה—**carrion-vulture,** or perh. **osprey** Lv 11_{18} Dt 14_{17}.

רַחַם I 1 pr.n.m. **Raham.**

רַחַם II, see רֶחֶם *womb.*

רֶחֶם 32.4.5 n.m. (f. at Jr 20_{17})—(רָחֶם), רַחַם (רַחַם); cstr. רֶחֶם; sf. רַחְמָהּ; du. רַחֲמָתַיִם—**1. womb** of humans and animals Ex 13_{2}, the dawn Ps 110_{3}. **2. woman, female slave** Jg 5_{30}. → רחם *love.*

רָחָמָה, see רָחָם *carrion-vulture.*

[רַחֲמָה] *woman, female slave,* see רֶחֶם *womb,* §2.

*[רַחֲמוֹן] 0.0.2 adj. **compassionate** 4QapPsB 10_{3} 47_{1}. → רחם *be compassionate.*

רַחֲמִים 39.8.75 n.m.pl.—cstr. רַחֲמֵי; sf. רַחֲמָיו—**compassion, love, mercy, pity,** usu. of Y. 2 S 24_{14}||1 C 21_{13} Is 63_{7}, also of humans Gn 43_{14}; **(object of) compassion,** וּנְתַתָּם לְרַחֲמִים לִפְנֵי שֹׁבֵיהֶם *and may you make them an object of compassion before their captors* 1 K 8_{50}. → רחם *be compassionate.*

*[רַחֲמָן] 0.0.1 adj. **compassionate,** as noun, **compassionate one, merciful one,** in ref. to Y. GnzPs 2_{3}. → רחם *be compassionate.*

[רַחֲמָנִי] 1 adj.—f.pl. רַחֲמָנִיּוֹת—**compassionate,** of woman Lm 4_{10}. → רחם *be compassionate.*

רחף I 1 vb.—**Qal** 1 Pf. רָחֲפוּ—**become soft,** of bones Jr 23_{9}.

רחף II 3.0.2 vb.—**Qal** 1 Pf. רָחֲפוּ—**tremble,** of bones Jr 23_{9}.

Pi. 2.0.2 Impf. יְרַחֵף; ptc. מְרַחֶפֶת—**hover,** of spirit of Y. Gn 1_2 (+ עַל *over* waters), eagle over its young Dt 32_{11}.

רחץ 72.0.27.10 vb.—**Qal** 69.0.26.10 Pf. רָחַצְתִּי ,רָחַץ; impf. יִרְחֲצוּ ,יִרְחַץ; impv. רַחֲצוּ ,רְחַץ; ptc. רֹחֲצוֹת ,רֹחֶצֶת; ptc. pass. I רחץ; inf. רְחֹץ (רָחְצָה)—**1.** trans., **wash** person Ex 29_4 (+ בְּ *with* water), body (בָּשָׂר) of person Lv 14_9 (+ בְּ *in* or *with* water), hands and feet Ex 30_{19}, face Gn 43_{31}, parts of sacrificial victim Ex 29_{17}. **2. wash away** filth Is 4_4. **3.** intrans., **wash, bathe oneself** 2 S 12_{20}; as ritual for purification Lv 14_8 (+ בְּ *in* or *with* water). **4.** pass. **be refined,** of oil Samaria ost. 16_3.

Pi. 0.0.1 Ptc. מרחצים—**wash** parts of sacrificial victim 11QT 34_{10}.

Pu. 2 Pf. רֻחַצְתְּ ,רֻחָץ—**be washed for** (לְ) cleansing, after being born Ezk 16_4 (+ בְּ *with* water), **be cleansed of** (מִן) filth Pr 30_{12}.

Htp. 1 Pf. הִתְרָחַצְתִּי—**wash oneself with** (בְּ) snow Jb 9_{30}.

→ רַחַץ *washing*, רֹחַץ *washing*, רְחִיצָה *washing*, רַחְצָה *washing, washing pool.*

[רַחַץ] 2.0.3 n.[m.]—sf. רַחְצִי—**washing, bathing,** for ritual purposes 1QS 3_5; סִיר רַחְצִי *pot of my washing*, i.e. my washbasin Ps 60_{10}||108_{10}. → רחץ *wash.*

*** [רֹחַץ]** 0.0.1 n.[m.]—רוחץ—**washing, bathing,** for ritual purposes 4QRitPurA 13_7. → רחץ *wash.*

רַחְצָה 2 n.f. **washing, washing pool,** for sheep Ca 4_2=6_6. → רחץ *wash.*

רחק 58.5.15 vb.—**Qal** 30.2.8 Pf. רָחֲקוּ ,רָחַק; impf. יִרְחַק; impv. Q רחק ,רַחֲקִי ,רַחֲקוּ; inf. רְחֹק (רָחֳקָה)—**1. be distant, be far,** of place Dt 12_{21} (+ מִן *from*), righteousness Is 46_{13}. **2. keep one's distance, go far,** of Y. Ps 22_{12} (+ מִן *from* person), humans Ex 23_7 (+ מִן *from* false charge) Ezk 11_{15} (+ מֵעַל *from* Y.).

Ni. 1 Impf. Kt ירחק—**be made distant, be removed,** of cord Ec $12_{6(Kt)}$ (or qal).

Piel 4.0.2 Pf. רִחַק; impf. יְרַחֲקוּ; inf. Q רחקך—**1. make distant, send far away, remove** persons Is 6_{12}, prostitution and corpses Ezk 43_9 (+ מִן *from* Y.), ends of land, i.e. **extend** its boundaries Is 26_{15}. **2. be far distant,** of heart Is 29_{13} (+ מִן *from* Y.; or §1).

Pu. 0.0.1 Ptc, מרוחקי—**be rejected** 4QLitB 2_4.

Hi. 24.2.4 Pf. הִרְחַקְתָּ ,הִרְחִיק; impf. תַּרְחִיק; impv. הַרְחֵק (הַרְחִיקֵהוּ); ptc. Q מרחיקים; inf. abs. הַרְחֵק; cstr. הַרְחִיק—**1. make, or exhibit distance, go far** Gn 44_4 Jos 8_4 (+ מִן *from*); הַרְחֵק לֹא־תַרְחִיקוּ לָלֶכֶת *you shall not go very far away* Ex 8_{24}. **2. put far away, remove** persons Jr 27_{10} (+ מֵעַל *from* land) Ezk 11_{16} (+ בְּ *among* nations), falsehood Pr 30_8 (+ מִן *from* person). **3.** inf. abs. as adv., **at a distance, far away** Gn 21_{16}.

Htp. 0.2 Impf. תתרחק—**1. keep oneself at a distance** Si 13_{10}. **2. be put at a distance, be rebuffed** Si 13_{10}.

→ רָחֵק *being far*, רָחוֹק *distant*, רֹחֶק *distance*, מֶרְחָק *distance.*

[רָחֵק] 1 adj.—pl. sf. רְחֵקֶיךָ—**being far,** ptc. as noun, **one who keeps far away** Ps 73_{27}. → רחק *be distant.*

*** [רֹחֶק]** 0.0.1 n.[m.]—רוחק—**distance** 4QapPentB 2.2_{10}. → רחק *be distant.*

רחשׁ 1 vb.—**Qal** 1 Pf. רָחַשׁ—**be astir,** of heart Ps 45_2 (+ דָּבָר טוֹב *with a good word*). → רֶחֶשׁ *worm*, מַרְחֶשֶׁת *pan.*

*** [רֶחֶשׁ]** 0.0.1 n.[m.] **worm** 4QDª 6.1_8. → רחשׁ *be astir.*

רַחַת 1 n.[f.] **winnowing shovel** Is 30_{24}.

רטב 1 vb.—**Qal** 1 Impf. יִרְטָבוּ—**be wet** Jb 24_8 (+ מִן *on account of* downpour). → רָטֹב *moist.*

רָטֹב 1.1 adj.—**1. moist, full of sap,** of person descr. as plant Jb 8_{16}. **2.** as noun, **moist ground** Si $43_{22(Bmg)}$. → רטב *be wet.*

רטה 1 vb.—**Qal** 1 Impf. יִרְטֵנִי (but prob. from ירט *push*)—**wring out** someone Jb 16_{11}.

רֶטֶט 1 n.[m.] **trembling, panic** Jr 49_{24}.

רטפשׁ 1 vb.—**Qal Pass.** 1 Pf. רֻטֲפַשׁ—**be fresh,** of flesh Jb 33_{25} (+ מִן *[more] than [in]* youth).

רטשׁ I 6.0.1 vb.—**Pi.** 2 Impf. תְּרַטֵּשׁ—**dash child in pieces** 2 K 8_{12}.

Pu. 4.0.1 Pf. רֻטָּשָׁה; impf. יְרֻטָּשׁוּ (יְרֻטָּשׁוּ)—**be dashed in pieces,** of child Is 13_{16}, mother Ho 10_{14} (+ עַל *with* children), corpse 1QM 11_1.

*** רטשׁ II** 0.1 vb.—**Htp.** 0.1 Impv. התרטש—**abandon oneself in,** i.e. **occupy oneself with** (בְּ) riddles Si 8_8.

רִי 1 n.[m.] **moisture** Jb 37_{11}. → רוה *be saturated.*

ריב 68.3.13 vb.—**Qal** 66.3.11 Pf. רַבְתָּ ,רָב (רִיבוֹתָ); impf. יָרִיב, רִיבוּ (רִיבָה), (יָרֶב ,יָרֶב); + waw וָאָרִיב ,וַיָּרֶב; impv. רִיב (רִיבָה), רִיבוּ; ptc. רָב; inf. abs. רוֹב (רִיב); cstr. רִיב (רִבָם)—**1.** physically, **strive, struggle, fight** Ex 21_{18} Jg 11_{25} (+ עִם *with*). 2. verbally, a. without obj., **strive, contend, quarrel** Gn 26_{20} (+ עִם *with*) Nm 20_{13} (+ אֵת *with*); unilaterally, **remonstrate with, plead with,** i.e. **upbraid, rebuke** Gn 31_{36} (+ בְּ *with*) Ne 5_{7} (+ אֵת *with*). b. with obj., **strive with, contend with** Dt 33_{8}. 3. mentally, **strive, struggle** 1QS 4_{23} (+ בְּ *within* heart). 4. in legal dispute, a. without obj., **contend, plead, conduct a law suit, make out a case, make a defence** Is 3_{13}; + לְ *for* Jg 6_{31}, בְּ *with* Jg 6_{32}, עִם *with* Jb 9_{3}, אֵת *with* Is 50_{8}. b. with obj. רִיב, (1) **plead cause,** usu. that of others 1 S 24_{16} Ps 43_{1} (+ מִן *against*) Pr 23_{11} (+ אֵת *with*); one's own cause Ps 74_{22}. (2) **conduct legal case** 1QSa 1_{13} (ריב ומ[ש]פט *a legal case and a trial*). c. with obj. of person, (1) **plead the cause of, plead for** Is 1_{17}. (2) **contend with, contend against** Jb 10_{2}. 5. **complain** to (אֶל) Jr 12_{1}, against (אֶל) Jr 2_{29}. 6. ptc. as noun, **defender, champion** Is 19_{20}.

Hi. 2.0.1 Ptc. מְרִיבֵי; inf. Q הריב—**1. strive, contend, quarrel** with (בְּ) 4QapJerCe 2.1$_{6}$. **2.** ptc. as noun, **contender, adversary** 1 S 2_{10}.

Htpol. 0.0.1 Impf. יתרובב; inf. התרובב—**dispute, argue with** (עִם) 1QS 9_{16}=4QSd 8_{1}.

→ רִיב *strife,* מְרִיבָה I *strife,* רִיבָה *lawsuit,* יָרִיב I *adversary.*

רִיב 62.7.36 n.m.—cstr. רִיב; sf. רִיבִי; pl. רִבֹת; cstr. רִיבֵי, רִבוֹת—**1. strife, conflict, quarrel, dispute** Gn 13_{7}, assoc. with violence Ps 55_{10}. **2. law suit, legal case, legal dispute, contention, cause,** undertaken by humans Ex 23_{3} 2 S 15_{2}, pursued by or committed to Y. 1 S 24_{16} Jr 25_{31} 50_{34}, **pleading, argument, case,** set out by legal opponents Is 41_{21} Pr 18_{17}; אִישׁ רִיבִי *man of my contention,* i.e. my adversary Jb 31_{35}, בעלי רבי *owners of my dispute,* i.e. my adversaries 1QH 15_{23}. → רִיב *strive.*

*[רִיבָה] 2 n.f.—pl. רִיבֹת; cstr. רִבוֹת—**1. lawsuit** Dt 17_{8}. **2. legal argument** Jb 13_{6}. → רִיב *strive.*

רִיבַי 2 pr.n.m. **Ribai.**

ריח 11.0.2 vb.—**Hi.** (unless רוח hi.) 11.0.2 Impf. יָרִיחַ (יָרַח); + waw וַיָּרַח; inf. הָרִיחַ (Q לריח, הֲרִיחוֹ)—**1a. smell, sense** fire Jg 16_{9}, battle Jb 39_{25}. **b. smell,** i.e. **delight in, accept,** (1) with accus. odour of offering Gn 8_{21}, offering 1 S 26_{19}. (2) with בְּ *in* or of obj. odour Lv 26_{31}, incense Ex 30_{38}, sacred assembly Am 5_{21}. **2.** abs., **(be able to) smell,** of gods Dt 4_{28}. **3.** perh. **cause to delight in** (בְּ) understanding 4QBarkc 1.1$_{i}$. → רֵיחַ *smell.*

רֵיחַ 58.1.18 n.m.—cstr. רֵיחַ; sf. רֵיחוֹ—**smell, odour, fragrance** of plants Ca 2_{13}, ointments Ca 1_{3}, water Jb 14_{9}, person Gn 27_{27}; oft. רֵיחַ נִיחֹחַ (or var.) *odour of soothing,* i.e. soothing odour, of offering Gn 8_{21}. → ריח *smell.*

*[רִיחַ] 1 n.[m.]—pl. רִיחִים—**coracle** Is 43_{14} (unless from בָּרִיחַ *fugitive*).

רִיחִים, see רִיחַ *coracle.*

רִים, see רום *be high.*

רֵים, see רְאֵם *wild ox.*

[רֵיעַ] Jb 6_{27}, see רֵעַ *friend.*

רִיפוֹת 2 n.[f.]pl.—רִפוֹת—**barley groats** 2 S 17_{19} Pr 27_{22}.

רִיפַת 1 pr.n.m. **Riphath.**

ריק 19 vb.—**Hi.** 17 Impf. יָרִיק; + waw וַיָּרֶק, וַהֲרִיקוּ, וַהֲרִיקֹתִי; impv. הָרֵק; ptc. מְרִיקִים; inf. הָרִיק—**1. empty** sack Gn 42_{35}, net Hb 1_{17}, vessel Jr 48_{12}. **2. pour out, pour down** oil Zc 4_{12}, blessing (as rain) Ml 3_{10}. **3. empty oneself,** of clouds Ec 11_{3} (+ עַל *upon* earth). **4. unsheathe, draw** sword Ex 15_{9} Lv 26_{33} (+ אַחֲרֵי *after*) Ezk 30_{11} (+ עַל *against*), spear Ps 35_{3}. **5. lead out** Gn 14_{14}. **6. leave empty, unsatisfied,** obj. throat Is 32_{6}.

Ho. 2 Pf. הוּרַק; impf. תּוּרַק—**be emptied, be poured out from** (מִן) vessel to (אֶל) vessel Jr 48_{11}.

→ רֵיק *empty,* רִיק *emptiness,* רֵיקָם *emptily.*

[רֵיק] 14.0.2 adj.—רֵק; f.s. רֵקָה; m.pl. רֵיקִים; f.pl. רֵקוֹת—**1. empty,** of jar Jg 7_{16}, pit Gn 37_{24}, throat Is 29_{8}. **2a. vain, worthless,** of man Jg 9_{4}, thing Dt 32_{47}. **b.** ptc. as noun, (1) **vain one, worthless one** 2 S 6_{20}. (2) **vanity, worthlessness** Pr 12_{11} 28_{19}. → ריק *empty.*

רִיק 12.2.3 n.[m.]—**emptiness, vanity,** כְּלִי רִיק *vessel of emptiness,* i.e. empty vessel Jr 51_{34}; לְ/לְרִיק *to, for vanity,* i.e. in vain Is 49_{4} 65_{23}; רִיק as adv., *in vain* Ps 73_{13}. → ריק *empty.*

רֵיקָם 16.0.1 adv.—**1. empty, in an empty condition, with empty hands** Gn 31_{42} Ex 23_{15}. **2. in vain, without success** 2 S 1_{22}. **3. without cause** Ps 7_{5}. → ריק *empty.*

ריקמה, see רִקְמָה *variegated material.*

ריר 1 vb.—**Qal** 1 Pf. רָר—**flow with, secrete discharge** Lv 15$_{3}$. → ריר *spittle, slime.*

ריר 2 n.[m.]—sf. רִירוֹ—**1. spittle** 1 S 21$_{14}$. **2. slime, juice** Jb 6$_{6}$. → ריר *flow.*

רֵישׁ 7.4.7 n.m.—רִישׁ, רֵאשׁ; sf. רִישׁוֹ, רֵישָׁם—**poverty** Pr 6$_{11}$ =24$_{34}$. → רושׁ *be poor.*

רִישׁ, see רֵישׁ *poverty.*

רִישׁוֹן, see ראשׁוֹן *first.*

רַךְ 16.0.3 adj.—רָךְ; cstr. רַךְ; f.s. רַכָּה; m.pl. רַכִּים; f.pl. רַכּוֹת —**1. tender, soft, delicate, weak,** of man Dt 20$_{8}$ (רַךְ הַלֵּבָב *tender of heart,* i.e. timid), child Gn 33$_{13}$, eyes Gn 29$_{17}$, tongue Pr 25$_{15}$, answer Pr 15$_{1}$. **2.** as noun, **tender one, soft one,** of twig Ezk 17$_{22}$, woman Dt 28$_{56}$; f.pl. **soft words** Jb 40$_{27}$. → רכך *be tender.*

רֹךְ 1.0.1 n.[m.] **tenderness** Dt 28$_{56}$. → רכך *be tender.*

רכב 78.1.3.1 vb.—**Qal** 58.1.2 Pf. רָכַב; impf. יִרְכַּב; impv. רְכַב; ptc. רֹכֵב, רֹכֶבֶת, רֹכְבִים; inf. לִרְכֹּב—**1a. mount** (עַל of obj.) camel Gn 24$_{6}$, ass 1 S 25$_{42}$. **b.** without obj., **mount chariot** 2 K 9$_{16}$. **2. ride, ride upon, a.** with accus. ass 2 S 16$_{2}$, heavens and clouds Dt 33$_{26}$. **b.** with בְּ *in, on,* or of obj. horse and chariot Jr 17$_{25}$, heavens Ps 68$_{34}$. **c.** with עַל *upon* or of obj. horse Jr 6$_{23}$=50$_{42}$, ass 1 S 25$_{20}$, chariot Hb 3$_{8}$, cloud Is 19$_{1}$. **d.** without obj., **ride on** Ps 45$_{5}$. **3.** ptc. as noun, **rider** Gn 49$_{17}$.

Hi. 20.0.1.1 Pf. הִרְכַּבְתָּ; impf. אַרְכִּיב; + waw וַיַּרְכֵּב (וַיַּרְכִּבֵם); impv. הַרְכֵּב—**1. cause someone to ride,** + בְּ *in* chariot Gn 41$_{43}$; אֶל *upon* wind Jb 30$_{22}$; עַל *upon* horse Est 6$_{9}$, mule 1 K 1$_{33}$, high places Dt 32$_{13}$. **2. cause to ride,** i.e. **load, carry** ark on (עַל/אֶל) cart 2 S 6$_{3}$||1 C 13$_{7}$. **3. cause hand to ride upon** (עַל), i.e. **draw** bow 2 K 13$_{16}$. **4. harness** Ho 10$_{11}$.

→ רֶכֶב *chariot,* רְכוּב *chariot,* מֶרְכָּב *means for riding,* מֶרְכָּבָה *chariot,* רַכָּב *charioteer,* רִכְבָּה *riding.*

רֶכֶב 119.0.9 n.m.—רָכֶב; cstr. רֶכֶב; sf. רִכְבּוֹ; pl. cstr. רִכְבֵי— **1.** coll., usu. **chariotry, chariots** Gn 50$_{9}$ Ex 14$_{7}$; **chariot crew** 2 S 10$_{18}$||1 C 19$_{18}$, **chariot horses** 2 S 8$_{4}$||1 C 18$_{4}$. **2. (individual) chariot** 1 K 22$_{38}$. **3.** perh. **riders, riding company, cavalry** Is 21$_{7}$; רֶכֶב סוּסִים *riders of horses* 2 K 7$_{14}$. **4. mounts** 1QM 6$_{11}$. **5. riding (of horses),** מלומדי רכב *(ones) skilled of,* i.e. in, *riding* 1QM 6$_{13}$. **6. riding (of millstone), upper millstone** Dt 24$_{6}$; פֶּלַח רֶכֶב *millstone of riding,* i.e. upper millstone Jg 9$_{53}$. → רכב *ride.*

רַכָּב 3 n.m.—sf. רַכָּבוֹ—**1. charioteer** 1 K 22$_{34}$||2 C 18$_{33}$. **2. rider** 2 K 9$_{17}$. → רכב *ride.*

רֵכָב 13 pr.n.m. **Rechab.**

רִכְבָּה 1 n.f. **riding** Ezk 27$_{20}$. → רכב *ride.*

[רֵכָבִי] 4 gent. **Rechabite.**

רֵכָה 1 pl.n. **Recah.**

[רְכוּב] 1 n.[m.]—sf. רְכוּבוֹ—**chariot** Ps 104$_{3}$. → רכב *ride.*

רכוּשׁ 28.0.1 n.m.—רְכֻשׁ; cstr. רְכוּשׁ; sf. רְכוּשׁוֹ—**possessions, property, goods, equipment,** movable possessions in general Gn 12$_{5}$ Nm 16$_{32}$, consisting of or including livestock Gn 13$_{6}$; as supplies, stores Dn 11$_{13}$. → רכשׁ *collect.*

רָכִיל 6.0.5 n.[m.]—**slander, gossip,** הלך רָכִיל *go about (for) slander,* i.e. as a slanderer Lv 19$_{16}$, *(for) gossip,* i.e. as a gossip Pr 11$_{13}$; אַנְשֵׁי רָכִיל *men of slander* Ezk 22$_{9}$. → רכל II *slander.*

רכך 8.0.2 vb.—**Qal** 6.0.1 Pf. רַךְ, רַכּוּ; impf. יֵרַךְ—**be tender, soft, weak,** of heart Dt 20$_{3}$, words Ps 55$_{22}$ (+ מִן *[more] than* oil).

Pu. 1 Pf. רֻכְּכָה—**be softened, soothed,** of wounds Is 1$_{6}$ (+ בְּ *with* oil).

Hi. 1.0.1 Pf. הֵרַךְ—**1. make heart faint, timid** Jb 23$_{16}$.

→ רַךְ *tender,* רֹךְ *tenderness,* מֹרֶךְ *faintness.*

***[רְכָכִים]** n.[m.]pl. **softening, soothing, salve** Jr 30$_{13}$ (if em. דָּן דִּינֵךְ *one who pleads your cause*).

רכל I 17.0.1 vb.—**Qal** 17.0.1 Ptc. רוֹכֵל, רֹכֶלֶת (רֹכַלְתֵּךְ), רֹכְלִים—**trade,** ptc. as noun, **trader, merchant, trafficker,** masc. 1 K 10$_{15}$, fem. Ezk 27$_{3}$. → רְכֻלָּה *trade,* מַרְכֹּלֶת *market place.*

***רכל** II 0.2 vb.—**Qal** 2 Ptc. רוכל—**slander,** ptc. as noun, **slanderer** Si 11$_{29.30}$. → רָכִיל *slander.*

רָכָל 1 pl.n. **Racal.**

[רְכֻלָּה] 4 n.f.—sf. רְכֻלָּתֵךְ—**1. trade** Ezk 28$_{5.16.18}$. **2. merchandise** Ezk 26$_{12}$. → רכל I *trade.*

***רכן** 0.0.1 vb.—**Qal** 0.0.1 Ptc. רוכנים—**murmur** (perh. error for רגן) 1QS 1$_{1}$.

רכס 2 vb.—**Qal** 2 Impf. יִרְכְּסוּ—**bind** breastpiece Ex 28$_{28}$||39$_{21}$ (+ בְּ *with* cord). → רֶכֶס *rough place,* רֹכֶס *plot,* (?) רֶכֶשׁ *steeds.*

[רֶ֫כֶס] 1 n.[m.]—pl. רְכָסִים—**rough place, uneven ground** Is 40$_{4}$. → רכס *bind.*

[רֹ֫כֶס] 1 n.[m.]—pl. cstr. רֻכְסֵי—**plot, conspiracy, intrigue** Ps 31$_{21}$. → רכס *bind.*

רכשׁ 5 vb.—**Qal** 5 Pf. רָכַשׁ, רָכְשׁוּ (רָכָשׁוּ)—**collect, acquire** possessions Gn 12$_{5}$ 31$_{18}$ 36$_{6}$ 46$_{6}$. → רְכוּשׁ *possessions.*

רֶ֫כֶשׁ 4 n.m.—רֶכֶשׁ—**steeds,** harnessed to chariot Mc 1$_{13}$, ridden Est 8$_{10}$. → (?) רכס *bind.*

רָם I 7 pr.n.m. **Ram.**

רָם II, see רום *be high.*

[רֵם], see רְאֵם *wild ox.*

רמה I 4 vb.—**Qal** 4 Pf. רָמָה; ptc. רֹמֵה, רוֹמֵי—**1. throw** horse and rider into (בְּ) sea Ex 15$_{1}$. **2.** ptc. as noun, רֹמֵה קֶשֶׁת **shooter of the bow, archer** Jr 4$_{29}$. → רְמוּת II *refuse.*

רמה II 8.0.2 vb.—**Pi.** 8 Pf. רִמָּה, רִמִּיתָנִי; inf. רַמּוֹתֵנִי—**1. deceive** someone Gn 29$_{25}$. **2. betray** someone to (לְ) adversaries 1 C 12$_{18}$.

Htp. 0.0.2 Impf. יתרמה—**act deceitfully, commit fraud,** perh. **be negligent** against (בְּ) someone 1QS 7$_{6(mg)}$, with (בְּ) wealth 1QS 7$_{6}$.

→ מִרְמָה I *deceit,* רְמִיָּה I *deceit,* תַּרְמִית *deceit,* תָּרְמָה I *deceit.*

*רמה III 0.0.1 vb.—**Qal** 0.0.1 Ptc. רומות—**protrude,** or perh. **be uneven, lie askew,** of teeth 4QCrypt 1.3$_{3}$.

רָמָה I 5.0.1 n.f.—sf. רָמָתֵךְ; pl. cstr. Q רמות; sf. רָמֹתַיִךְ—**1. height, hill** 1 S 22$_{6}$. **2. high place,** built as place of worship Ezk 16$_{24}$. **3. height, supremacy** of power 1QH 24$_{13}$. → רום *be high.*

רָמָה II 36 pl.n. **Ramah.**

רִמָּה 7.2.3 n.f. **worm(s), maggot(s),** in decaying manna Ex 16$_{24}$, corpse Jb 21$_{26}$; as descr. of person Jb 25$_{6}$, corrupt company 1QS 11$_{10}$. → רמם II *be wormy.*

רִמּוֹן I 32.1.2 n.m.—sf. רִמֹּנִי; pl. רִמּוֹנִים (Q רמנאים); cstr. רִמּוֹנֵי—**pomegranate, 1.** fruit Nm 13$_{23}$. **2.** tree 1 S 14$_{2}$. **3.** ornaments, on priestly robes Ex 28$_{33}$||39$_{24}$, capitals of columns 1 K 7$_{18}$.

רִמּוֹן II 3 pr.n.m.—רִמֹּן—**Rimmon,** Aramaean deity 2 K 5$_{18}$.

רִמּוֹן III 3 pr.n.m. **Rimmon.**

רִמּוֹן IV 5 pl.n. **Rimmon.**

רִמּוֹנוֹ 1 pl.n. **Rimmono.**

*רָמוֹת I 1 pr.n.m. **Ramoth.**

רָמוֹת II, see רָאמוֹת *Ramoth.*

רָמוֹת III, see רָמוֹת־נֶגֶב *Ramoth-negeb.*

[רָמוּת] I 1 n.f.—sf. רָמוּתֶךָ—**height, stature** Ezk 32$_{5}$. → רום *be high.*

*[רְמוּת] II 1 n.f.—sf. רָמוּתֶךָ—**refuse** Ezk 32$_{5}$. → רמה I *throw.*

רָמוֹת־נֶגֶב 1 pl.n. **Ramoth-negeb.**

*רמז 1 vb.—**Qal** 1 Impf. יִרְזְמוּן—**wink, flash,** of eyes Jb 15$_{12(mss)}$ (L יִרְזְמוּן, from רזם I *wink* or II *fail*).

רֹמַח 15.0.7 n.m.—pl. רְמָחִים; sf, רָמְחֵיהֶם—**spear, lance** Nm 25$_{7}$.

רַמְיָה 1 pr.n.m. **Ramiah.**

רְמִיָּה I 10.0.20 n.f.—**deceit, treachery** Jb 13$_{7}$; לְשׁוֹנָם רְמִיָּה *their tongue is deceit,* i.e. deceitful Mc 6$_{12}$, אנשי רמיה *men of deceit* 1QH 6$_{14}$. → רמה II *deceive.*

רְמִיָּה II 7.0.1 n.f.—**slackness, negligence** Jr 48$_{10}$; in ref. to slack person Pr 12$_{24.27}$, also as נֶפֶשׁ רְמִיָּה lit. 'soul of slackness' Pr 19$_{15}$; קֶשֶׁת רְמִיָּה *bow of slackness,* i.e. slack bow Ho 7$_{16}$.

רמיהו, see רַמְיָה *Ramiah.*

[רַמִּים], הָרַמִּים 2 C 22$_{5}$, see אֲרַמִּי *Aramaean.*

[רַמָּךְ] 1 n.[f.]—pl. רַמָּכִים—**mare** Est 8$_{10}$.

רְמַלְיָהוּ 13 pr.n.m. **Remaliah.**

רמם I 5.0.2 vb. (byform of רום)—**Qal** 1 Pf. רוֹמּוּ—**be exalted** Jb 24$_{24}$.

Ni. 4.0.2 Impf. יֵרוֹמּוּ; impv. הֵרֹמּוּ; inf. Q הרומם—**1. lift oneself up** Ezk 10$_{15.19}$ (+ מִן *from*). **2. remove oneself** Nm 17$_{10}$ (+ מִתּוֹךְ *from among*).

רמם II 1.1 vb.—**Qal** 1 + waw וַיָּרֻם—**be full of worms** (accus. תּוֹלָע), of manna Ex 16$_{20}$.

Ho. 0.1 Impf. יורם—**be wormy, decay,** of body Si 10$_{9}$.

→ רִמָּה *worm(s).*

*[רְמָמָה] n.f. **thunder, roar** Is 33$_{3}$ (if em. רוֹמְמֻתֶךָ *your uplifting* to רְמָמָתְךָ *your thunder*).

רֹמַמְתִּי עֶזֶר 2 pr.n.m. **Romamti-ezer.**

[רִמֹּן פֶּרֶץ] 2 pl.n. **Rimmon-perez.**

רמס 19.0.5 vb.—**Qal** 18.0.3 Pf. רָמַס; impf. יִרְמֹס (יִרְמָס־); impv. רִמְסִי; ptc. רֹמֵס; inf. רְמֹס—**1. trample, trample upon, trample down** person 2 K 9$_{33}$, thistle 2 K 14$_{9}$ ||2 C 25$_{18}$, streets Ezk 26$_{11}$; abs. Mc 5$_{7}$; **tread** clay for pottery Is 41$_{25}$, mortar for bricks Na 3$_{14}$ (בְּ of obj.). **2.** ptc. as noun, **one who tramples, marauder** Is 16$_4$.

Ni. 1.0.2 Impf. תֵּרָמַסְנָה—**be trampled,** of Jerusalem 4QpNah 3.1$_3$, crown Is 28$_3$ (+ בְּ *with* feet).

→ מִרְמָס *trampling place.*

*[רֶמַע] 0.0.0.1 pr.n.[m.] **Rema.**

רמשׂ 17.0.2 vb.—**Qal** 17.0.2 Impf. תִּרְמֹשׂ; ptc. רֹמֵשׂ, רֹמֶשֶׂת—**1.** of creatures, **creep, crawl, move about,** + בְּ *in* water Lv 11$_{46}$, *on* ground Dt 4$_{18}$; עַל *upon* earth Gn 1$_{26}$. **2.** of ground, **creep with, teem with** Gn 9$_2$. → רֶמֶשׂ *creeping thing,* מִרְמָשׂ *reptile.*

רֶמֶשׂ 17.1.4 n.m.—cstr. רֶמֶשׂ—usu. coll., **creeping things, moving things,** esp. (but not exclusively) **reptiles, insects,** on ground Gn 1$_{25}$, in sea Ps 104$_{25}$. → רמשׂ *creep.*

רֶמֶת 1 pl.n. **Remeth.**

***רָמַת הַמִּצְפֶּה** 1 pl.n. **Ramath-mizpeh.**

רָמָתִי 1 gent. **Ramathite.**

[רָמָתַיִם צוֹפִים] 1 pl.n. **Ramathaim-zophim.**

רָמַת לֶחִי *Ramath-Lehi,* see לְחִי *Lehi.*

רמת נגב, see רָאמַת נֶגֶב *Ramath-negeb.*

[רֹן] 1 n.[m.]—pl. cstr. רָנֵּי—**shout,** or perh. **song** Ps 32$_7$. → רנן *cry.*

רנה I 1 vb.—**Qal** 1 Impf. תִּרְנֶה—**rattle,** of quiver Jb 39$_{23}$.

*[**רנה**] II vb.—**Qal, cry,** ptc. as noun, **crier, herald** 1 K 22$_{36}$ (if em. הָרִנָּה *the cry* to הָרֹנֶה). → cf. רנן *cry.*

רִנָּה I 33.0.33 n.f.—cstr. Q רנת; sf. רִנָּתִי; pl. Q רנות; cstr. Q רנות—**1. (joyful) cry, shout, song, rejoicing** Is 14$_7$ 48$_{20}$. **2. cry,** in prayer or entreaty, **supplication** 1 K 8$_{28}$||2 C 6$_{19}$. **3. cry, shout,** in proclamation 1 K 22$_{36}$. → רנן *cry.*

רִנָּה II 1 pr.n.m. **Rinnah.**

רנן 53.4.27 vb.—**Qal** 19.3.2 Impf. יָרֹנּוּ, תָּרֹן, יָרוֹן; impv. Q רון, רָנּוּ ,(רֹנִּי) רָנִּי; inf. רָן—**1a. cry, shout, sing,** for joy, **rejoice, exult** Lv 9$_{24}$ Is 35$_6$. **b.** with obj., **rejoice in** something Is 61$_7$. **2. cry aloud, call out,** in exhortation Pr 1$_{20}$. **3. cry, call out,** in prayer Si 50$_{19}$ (+ לִפְנֵי *before*). **4. cry out, shout,** in distress Lm 2$_{19}$.

Pi. 28.0.23 Impf. תְּרַנֵּן, יְרַנְּנוּ; + waw וִירַנְּנוּ; impv. רַנְּנוּ; ptc. Q מרננים; inf. abs. רַנֵּן; cstr. רַנֵּן—**1. cry, shout, sing,** for joy, **rejoice, exult** Is 26$_{19}$ Ps 33$_1$ (+ בְּ *in* Y.) 84$_3$ (+ אֶל *to* Y.) 95$_1$ (+ לְ *to* Y.). **2.** with obj., **a. sing psalm** 1QM 14$_2$. **b. sing (of), rejoice in** something Ps 51$_{16}$. **3.** inf. cstr. as noun, **exultation** Is 35$_2$.

Pu. 1 Impf. יְרֻנַּן—**be a cry given** Is 16$_{10}$.

Hi. 5.1.2 Impf. תַּרְנִין; impv. הַרְנִינוּ—**1. cause to shout, cause to sing,** for joy Ps 65$_9$ Jb 29$_{13}$. **2. sing joyfully** of Dt 32$_{43}$. **3. shout, sing,** for joy Ps 32$_{11}$ 81$_2$ (+ לְ *to* Y.).

→ רֹן *shout,* רִנָּה I *cry,* רְנָנָה *cry,* רַנֵּן *rejoicing,* רְנָנִים *ostrich;* cf. רנה II *cry.*

*[**רֹנֶן**] 0.0.2 n.[m.]—רונן—**rejoicing** 4QShirShabb[d] 1.1$_{36}$. → רנן *cry.*

רְנָנָה 4 n.f.—cstr. רִנְנַת; pl. רְנָנוֹת—**(joyful) cry, shout, song, rejoicing** Ps 63$_5$ 100$_2$ Jb 3$_7$ Jb 20$_5$. → רנן *cry.*

רְנָנִים 1 n.[m.]pl. **ostrich** Jb 39$_{13}$. → רנן *cry.*

*[**רס**] 0.0.3 n.[m.]—pl. ראסות—**stade,** measure of length, approx. one seventh of a mile 4QSD 7$_6$ 4QapJoseph[c] 1$_5$ 11QT 52$_{17}$.

רִסָּה 2 pl.n. **Rissah.**

[רָסִיס] I 1 n.[m.]—pl. cstr. רְסִיסֵי—**drop (of dew)** Ca 5$_2$. → רסס *moisten.*

[רָסִיס] II 1 n.[m.]—pl. רְסִיסִים—**fragment** Am 6$_{11}$.

רֶסֶן I 4 n.m.—sf. רִסְנוֹ—**1. halter,** for horse or mule Ps 32$_9$. **2. jaw** of Leviathan Jb 41$_5$.

רֶסֶן II 1 pl.n. **Resen.**

רסס 1 vb.—**Qal** 1 Inf. רֹס—**moisten** flour Ezk 46$_{14}$. → רסס I *drop (of dew).*

רַע I 155.35.36 adj.—רַע; cstr. רַע; f.s. רָעָה; m.pl. רָעִים; cstr. רָעֵי; f.pl. רָעוֹת; cstr. רָעוֹת—**1. bad,** i.e. **poor (in quality), unhealthy, of little value, a.** as adj. of cow Gn 41$_3$ (רָעוֹת מַרְאֶה *bad of,* i.e. in, *appearance*), fig Jr 24$_2$, water 2 K 2$_{19}$. **b.** as noun, **bad (one),** in ref. to animal for sacrifice Lv 27$_{10}$. **2. bad, evil,** i.e. **displeasing, unpleasant, unsatisfactory, distressing,** of person Gn 28$_8$ (רַע בְּעֵינֵי *displeasing in the eyes of*), name Dt 22$_{14}$, deed Ec 4$_3$, report Jr 49$_{23}$. **3. (ethically) evil, wicked, a.** as adj. of generation Dt 1$_{35}$, person Gn 38$_7$ (רַע בְּעֵינֵי *evil in the eyes of* Y.), heart Jr 3$_{17}$, inclination 11QPs[a] 19$_{16}$, deed Ezr 9$_{13}$, way 1 K 13$_{33}$. **b.** as noun, **evil one, wicked one,** (1) masc. Jr 6$_{29}$ Jb 21$_{30}$. (2) fem. Jr 23$_3$. **4. evil,** i.e. **unkind, mean, a.** as adj. of person Pr 28$_{22}$, spirit Jg 9$_{23}$. **b.** as noun, **one who is evil,** i.e. **mean,** רע לנפשו *one who is mean to himself*

Si 14$_5$, רע על לחם *one who is mean over bread* Si 34$_{24}$. **5. evil,** i.e. **greedy, a.** as adj. of eye Si 34$_{13}$. **b.** as noun, **one who is evil of eye,** i.e. **greedy** Si 34$_{13}$. **6. evil,** i.e. **harmful, severe, grievous, awesome, a.** as adj. of beast Gn 37$_{20}$, sickness Dt 28$_{59}$, sword Ps 144$_{10}$. **b.** as noun, **awesome thing,** רעים ממך *things too awesome for you* Si 3$_{21(C)}$. **7. sad, downcast,** as adj. of heart Pr 25$_{20}$, face Gn 40$_7$. → רעע I *be bad.*

רַע II 196.19.42.1 n.m.—רָע; cstr. רַע—**1. bad (thing),** what is unpleasant or displeasing Gn 24$_{50}$ Si 13$_{25}$. **2. (ethical) evil** Gn 2$_9$; אַנְשֵׁי רָע *men of evil* Pr 28$_5$, עשׂה הָרַע בְּעֵינֵי י״ *do evil in the eyes of* Y. Nm 32$_{13}$. **3. evil,** i.e. **harm, injury, wrong** 1 K 22$_8$ Ps 7$_5$ Pr 19$_{23}$. **4. evil,** i.e. **distress, trouble, adversity, disaster** Gn 44$_{34}$ Si 12$_{17}$; יוֹם רָע *day of evil* Am 6$_3$. **5. evil,** i.e. **unpleasantness, worthlessness,** עִנְיַן רָע *occupation of evil,* i.e. worthless occupation Ec 1$_{13}$. → רעע I *be bad.*

רֵעַ I 3 n.[m.]—sf. רֵעֹה—**1. shouting, cry** of people Ex 32$_{17}$ Mc 4$_9$. **2.** perh. **roar, crash of thunder** Jb 36$_{33}$. → רוע *shout.*

רֵעַ II 187.25.64.3 n.m.—cstr. רֵעַ; sf. רֵעִי, רֵעֵהוּ (רֵעוֹ); pl. רֵעִים; cstr. רֵעֵי; sf. רֵעַי, רֵעָיו (רֵעֵהוּ)—**1. friend, companion** Gn 38$_{12}$ Jb 2$_{11}$; רֵעַ הַמֶּלֶךְ *friend,* i.e. confidant, advisor, *of the king* 1 C 27$_{33}$. **2. lover, darling, paramour** Jr 3$_1$ Ca 5$_{1.16}$. **3a. neighbour, fellow, another person** Ex 2$_{13}$ Lv 19$_{13}$; אֵשֶׁת רֵעֵהוּ *wife of his neighbour* Lv 20$_{10}$. **b.** אִישׁ ... רֵעֵהוּ **a man ... his neighbour/his fellow, one ... another, each ... the other** Gn 11$_3$ Ex 11$_2$; of goat-demon Is 34$_{14}$, parts of sacrificial animal Gn 15$_{10}$. **c.** גֶּבֶר ... רֵעֵהוּ **a man ... his neighbour/his fellow** Pr 29$_5$. → רעה II *associate with.*

רֵעַ III 2 n.[m.]—sf. רֵעִי; pl. sf. רֵעֶיךָ—**will, purpose, thought** of Y. Ps 139$_{17}$, human Ps 139$_2$. → רעה III *take delight in.*

רֹעַ 19.5.6 n.m.—cstr. רֹעַ; sf. Si רועו—**1. badness** of cattle Gn 41$_{19}$, figs Jr 24$_2$. **2. (ethical) evil** Dt 28$_{20}$. **3. sadness** of face Ec 7$_3$, heart Ne 2$_2$. **4. wilfulness** of heart 1 S 17$_{28}$. **5. meanness** Si 34$_{24(B)}$. → רעע I *be bad.*

רעב 13 vb.—**Qal** 11 Pf. רָעֵב; impf. יִרְעַב—**1. be hungry** Is 8$_{21}$. **2.** of land, **suffer famine** Gn 41$_{55}$.

Hi. 2 Impf. יַרְעִיב—let someone **hunger** Dt 8$_3$ Pr 10$_3$.

→ רָעֵב *hungry,* רָעָב *famine,* רְעָבוֹן *hunger,* רְעָבוּת *famine.*

רָעָב 101.0.9 n.m.—sf. רְעָבָם—**1. famine, hunger,** in land or city Gn 12$_{10}$ 2 K 6$_{25}$. **2. hunger,** of individual Dt 28$_{48}$ Is 5$_{13}$. → רעב *be hungry.*

רָעֵב 20.0.1 adj. —f.s. רְעֵבָה; m.pl. רְעֵבִים—**1. hungry** 2 S 17$_{29}$ Ps 107$_9$. **2.** as noun, **hungry one** 1 S 2$_5$ Is 29$_8$. → רעב *be hungry.*

רְעָבוֹן 3 n.[m.]—cstr. רַעֲבוֹן—**hunger, famine** Gn 42$_{19.33}$ Ps 37$_{19}$. → רעב *be hungry.*

[רְעָבוּת]* 0.0.1 n.f.—**famine** 1Q42 6$_1$. → רעב *be hungry.*

רעד 3.1.1 vb.—**Qal** 1.0.1 Impf. Q ירעדו; + waw וַתִּרְעַד—**tremble, quake,** of earth Ps 104$_{32}$, foundations 1QH 11$_{35}$.

Hi. 2.1 Ptc. מַרְעִיד—**1. tremble,** of persons Dn 10$_{11}$ Ezr 10$_9$. **2. wave, wield** spear Si 38$_{25}$.

→ רַעַד *trembling,* רְעָדָה *trembling.*

רַעַד 2.0.1 n.m.—רָעַד—**trembling, quaking** Ex 15$_5$ Ps 55$_6$ 1QH 12$_{33}$. → רעד *tremble.*

רְעָדָה 4.0.1 n.f. **trembling, quaking** Is 33$_{14}$ Jb 4$_{14}$ 1QH 18$_{33}$. → רעד *tremble.*

רעה I 166.0.8 vb.—**Qal** 166.0.8 Pf. רָעוּ; impf. יִרְעֶה (יֵרַע); impv. רְעֵה; ptc. רֹעֶה (רֹעִי), רֹעָה, רֹעִים (רֹעֵי), רֹעוּ, רֹעִי, רְעֵה, רֹעֵי, רֹעוֹת; inf. רְעוֹת—**1.** trans., **a. pasture, tend, feed,** animals, esp. sheep Gn 30$_{31}$. **b.** of ruler, leader, prophet, (1) **shepherd, tend, feed, lead, rule** people as flock 2 S 5$_2$||1 C 11$_2$ Ps 78$_{71}$ (בְּ of obj.). (2) with double accus., **feed** someone **with knowledge** Jr 3$_{15}$. **c.** of Y., **shepherd, tend, feed, lead** Gn 48$_{15}$ Mc 7$_{14}$ (+ בְּ *with* staff) Ezk 34$_{13}$. **d. feed, nourish, sustain,** subj. threshing floor Ho 9$_2$, lips of the righteous Pr 10$_{21}$. **2a.** intrans., **feed, graze,** of animals Gn 41$_2$, humans Is 49$_9$. **b.** with accus. of food or place, **feed on, graze on,** of animals Ps 80$_{14}$ 1QH 16$_8$ (בְּ of obj.), humans Is 44$_{20}$ Jr 50$_{19}$. **3.** ptc. as noun, **a. shepherd, herder, keeper** of sheep, cattle, (1) masc. Gn 4$_2$ Nm 14$_{33}$. (2) fem. Gn 29$_9$. **b. shepherd, ruler,** over people as flock Jr 50$_6$ Ezk 34$_2$. **c. Shepherd,** as epithet of Y. Ps 23$_1$ 80$_2$.

→ רְעִי *pasture,* מֵרֵעַ *pasture supervisor,* מִרְעֶה *pasture,* מַרְעִית *pasturing,* רֹעִי *shepherd.*

רעה II 11.3.1 vb.—**Qal** 9.3 Impf. יִרְעֵם; impv. רְעֵה; ptc. רֹעֶה

—**associate with, involve oneself with, befriend** someone Pr 13$_{20}$ 28$_{7}$ Jb 24$_{21}$, faithfulness Ps 37$_{3}$.

Pi. 1 Pf. רֵעָה—**be a special friend, best man** for (לְ) someone, at wedding Jg 14$_{20}$.

Htp. 1.0.1 Impf. תִּתְרַע (Q תתרעה)—**1. associate with, have friendship with** (אֵת) Pr 22$_{24}$. **2. associate with one another** Pr 18$_{24}$ (if em. לְהִתְרֹעֵעַ *to be broken* [רעע II htp.] to לְהִתְרָעוֹת).

→ רֵעַ I *friend,* רֵעֶה *friend,* רֵעָה *companion,* רַעְיָה *companion,* מֵרֵעַ *friend,* רְעוּת I *fellow (female).*

*רעה III 0.2 vb.—**Qal** 0.2 Impv. רעה—**take delight in, show favour to, respect** someone Si 34$_{15(Bmg)}$ 38$_{1}$. → רֵעַ III *purpose,* רְעוּת II *striving,* רַעְיוֹן *striving.*

*רעה IV 0.1 vb. (byform of ראה)—**Qal** 0.1 Ptc. רועה—**see,** ptc. as noun, **seer** Si 46$_{15}$.

רָעָה 315.31.31.1 n.f.—cstr. רָעַת; sf. רָעָתִי, רָעַתְכֶם; pl. רָעוֹת; cstr. רָעוֹת; sf. רָעוֹתֵיהֶם—**1. (ethical) evil, evil deed, wickedness** Gn 6$_{5}$, as obj. of עשׂה *do* Dt 31$_{18}$; רָעַת עַמִּי יִשְׂרָאֵל *evil of my people Israel* Jr 7$_{12}$, רָעוֹת שֹׁמְרוֹן *evil deeds of Samaria* Ho 7$_{1}$. **2. evil,** i.e. **harm, injury, wrong, mischief,** as obj. of עשׂה *do* Gn 26$_{29}$, חשׁב *plan* Gn 50$_{20}$; דֹּרְשֵׁי רָעָתִי *those who seek my harm* Ps 38$_{13}$. **3. evil,** i.e. **distress, misfortune, trouble, disaster,** as subj. of בוא *come* 2 S 19$_{8}$, דבק *overtake* Gn 19$_{19}$; as obj. of בוא hi. *bring* 2 S 17$_{14}$; עֵת־רָעָה *time of trouble* Jr 15$_{11}$. **4. displeasure** Jon 4$_{1}$. → רעע I *be bad.*

[רֵעָה] 3 n.f.—sf. רֵעוֹתֶיהָ—**companion, friend** Jg 11$_{37(Qr)}$ (Kt רעיתי, from רַעְיָה) 11$_{38}$ Ps 45$_{15}$. → רעה II *associate with.*

[רֵעֶה] 4 n.m.—cstr. רֵעֵה—**friend,** in general Pr 27$_{10}$, as confidant, advisor of king 1 K 4$_{5}$. → רעה II *associate with.*

רֹעָה, see רעע II *break.*

רֹעֶה *shepherd,* see רעה I, §3.

רְעוּ 5 pr.n.m. **Reu.**

רְעוּאֵל 11.0.2 pr.n.m. **Reuel.**

[רְעוּת] I 6 n.f. **fellow (female), (female) neighbour, companion,** אִשָּׁה ... רְעוּתָהּ *a woman,* i.e. each one ... *her fellow* Est 1$_{19}$; sim. in ref. to birds Is 34$_{15}$, sheep Zc 11$_{9}$. → רעה II *associate with.*

[רְעוּת] II 7 n.f. **striving,** רְעוּת רוּחַ *striving of,* i.e. after, *wind* Ec 1$_{14}$. → רעה III *take delight in.*

רְעִי 1 n.[m.] **pasture,** בְּקַר רְעִי *cattle (from) pasture* 1 K 5$_{3}$. → רעה I *pasture.*

רֵעִי 1 pr.n.m. **Rei.**

*רֹעִי 2.0.1 adj.—**1. belonging to a shepherd,** of tent Is 38$_{12}$. **2.** as noun, **shepherd** of worthlessness, in descr. of ruler Zc 11$_{17}$. → רעה I *pasture.*

[רַעְיָה] 10.0.1 n.f.—sf. רַעְיָתִי—**1.** coll., **(female) companions** Jg 11$_{37(Kt)}$ (Qr רֵעוֹתַי *my companions,* from רֵעָה). **2.** רַעְיָתִי **my companion, my beloved,** as term of affection for female lover Ca 1$_{9}$. → רעה II *associate with.*

[רַעְיוֹן] 3 n.[m.] **striving, longing,** רַעְיוֹן לִבּוֹ *striving of his heart* Ec 2$_{22}$, רוּחַ *of,* i.e. after, *wind* Ec 1$_{17}$. → רעה III *take delight in.*

רעל I 1.0.3 vb.—**Ni.** 0.0.1 Impv. הרעל—**stagger, reel** Hb 2$_{16(1QpHab)}$ (MT הֵעָרֵל *act as one uncircumcised,* i.e. ערל ni.).

Hi. 0.0.2 Ptc. מרעיל—**make a ripple,** אין בו די מרעיל *there is not sufficient in it* [cistern] *to make a ripple* CD 10$_{13}$.

Ho. 1 Pf. הָרְעָלוּ—**be made to quiver, be brandished,** of spear shaft Na 2$_{4}$.

→ רַעַל *reeling,* תַּרְעֵלָה *reeling.*

*רעל II 1.0.2 vb.—**Hi.** 0.0.2 Ptc. מרעיל—of water, **cover** a man CD 10$_{11}$; without obj. CD 10$_{13}$.

Ho. 1 Pf. הָרְעָלוּ—**be adorned,** of horses Na 2$_{4}$ (if em. הַבְּרֹשִׁים *the spear shafts* to הַפָּרָשִׁים *the horses*).

→ רְעָלָה *veil.*

*רעל III 1 vb.—**Ho.** 1 Pf. הָרְעָלוּ—**march in file, stand in rank and file,** of horses Na 2$_{4}$ (if em. הַבְּרֹשִׁים *the spear shafts* to הַפָּרָשִׁים *the horses*).

רַעַל 1 n.[m.] **reeling** Zc 12$_{2}$. → רעל I *quiver.*

[רְעָלָה] 1 n.f.—pl. רְעָלוֹת—**veil** Is 3$_{19}$. → רעל II *veil.*

רְעֵלָיָה 1 pr.n.m. **Reelaiah.**

רעם I 11.0.3 vb.—**Qal** 3.0.1 Impf. יִרְעַם, Q ירעמו—**thunder, roar,** of sea Ps 96$_{11}$||1 C 16$_{32}$.

Hi. 8.0.2 Pf. הִרְעִים; impf. יַרְעֵם—**thunder, cause thunder,** of Y. 1 S 2$_{10}$ 7$_{10}$ (+ בְּ *with* voice).

→ רַעַם *thunder.*

*רעם II 2 vb.—**Qal** 1 Pf. רָעֲמוּ—**be downcast, be troubled,** of face Ezk 37$_{35}$.

Hi. 1 Inf. הַרְעִמָה—**bring low, humiliate,** or perh.

appear downcast, show oneself oppressed 1 S 1₆.

רַעַם 6.1 n.[m.]—cstr. רַעַם; sf. רַעַמְךָ—**thunder** Is 29₆ Ps 77₁₉; i.e. **roar, shout** Jb 39₂₅. → רעם I *thunder*.

רַעְמָה I 1 n.f. **mane** of horse Jb 39₁₉.

רַעְמָה III 1 pl.n. **Raamah.**

*[**רַעְמָה**] IV n.[m] **uproar** Is 33₃ (if em. רוֹמְמֻתֶךָ *your uplifting* to רַעְמָתֶךָ *your uproar*).

רַעַמְיָה 1 pr.n.m. **Raamiah.**

רַעְמְסֵס 5 pl.n. **Rameses, Raamses.**

רען 1 vb.—**Pal.** 1 Pf. רַעֲנָנָה—**be luxuriant, green,** of branch Jb 15₃₂. → רַעֲנָן *luxuriant*.

רַעֲנָן 19.2 adj.—f.s. רַעֲנָנָה; m.pl. רַעֲנַנִּים—**1. luxuriant, green, leafy,** of tree Dt 12₂, leaf Jr 17₈, couch Ca 1₁₆. **2. fresh,** of oil Ps 92₁₁. → רען *be luxuriant*.

רעע I 96.5.8 vb.—**Qal** 25 Pf. רַע (רָע); impf. יֵרַע; inf. רֹעַ—**1. be bad, displeasing,** subj. דָּבָר *thing* or impersonal, + בְּעֵינֵי *in the eyes of* Gn 21₁₁, לְ *to* Ne 2₁₀, אֶל *to* Jon 4₁. **2. be ill-disposed, hostile, mean against, towards,** + בְּ Dt 15₉, לְ 2 S 20₆. **3. be sad,** of face Ne 2₃, heart Dt 15₁₀. **4. be injurious to, go ill with** (לְ) Ps 106₃₂.

Ni. 2 Impf. יֵרוֹעַ—**suffer harm** Pr 11₁₅ 13₂₀.

Hi. 69.5.8 Pf. הֵרַע, הֲרֵעֹתִי, הֵרֵעוּ; impf. יָרַע, תָּרַע; + waw וַיָּרַע, וַיָּרֵעוּ; ptc. מֵרַע, מְרֵעִים; inf. abs. הָרֵעַ; cstr. הָרַע (הָרֵעַ)—**1a. injure, harm, treat someone harshly** Dt 26₆ 1 S 25₃₄; **destroy** something Ps 74₃. **b.** without obj., (1) with prep., **do harm to, deal harshly with, deal badly with, bring trouble upon,** usu. לְ Gn 19₉; also בְּ Jr 25₂₉, עַל 1 K 17₂₀, עִם Gn 31₇. (2) abs., **do harm, cause injury** Is 11₉ 41₂₃. **2a. do evil, act wickedly, do wrong** Gn 19₇ 1 K 16₂₅ (+ מִן *[more] than*). **b.** with obj., (1) **make evil, do evil in (respect of)** deeds Mc 3₄. (2) **do evil** (רָעָה) Si 34₁₀. **3.** ptc. as noun, **evildoer** Is 1₄ Ps 22₁₇.

→ רַע I *bad, evil*, II *bad (thing), evil*, רֹעַ *badness*, רָעָה *evil*.

רעע II 10.0.5 vb. (by-form of רצץ)—**Qal** 8.0.5 Impf. יָרֹעַ; + waw וְרָעוּ; impv. רֹעוּ; ptc. רֹעָה; inf. abs. רֹעָה—**1.** trans., **break, shatter** nations Ps 2₉ (+ בְּ *with* rod), the mighty Jb 34₂₄, iron Jr 15₁₂. **2.** intrans., **break, shatter,** i.e. **be broken, be shattered,** of people Is 8₉, bones 1QH 12₃₃, branches Jr 11₁₆.

Htpo. 2 Pf. הִתְרֹעֲעָה; inf. הִתְרֹעֵעַ—**1. be broken,** of earth Is 24₁₉. **2. shatter one another,** of friends Pr 18₂₄.

רעף 5 vb.—**Qal** 4 Impf. יִרְעֲפוּ—**drip, drip with,** of tracks dripping with fat Ps 65₁₂, clouds with rain Jb 36₂₈ (+ עַל *upon*), dew Pr 3₂₀.

Hi. 1 Impv. הַרְעִיפוּ—**drip, trickle,** of heavens Is 45₈ (+ מִמַּעַל *from above*).

רעץ 2 vb.—**Qal** 2 Impf. תִּרְעַץ—**shatter, crush** persons Ex 15₆ Jg 10₈.

רעשׁ I 30.2.2 vb.—**Qal** 22.2.2 Pf. רָעֲשָׁה (רָעֲשָׁה); impf. יִרְעַשׁ; ptc. רֹעֲשִׁים; inf. abs. Si רעשׁ—**1. quake, shake, tremble,** of earth Is 13₁₃ (+ מִן *from* place) Jr 8₁₆ (+ מִן *at* sound), mountains Jr 4₂₄, humans and animals Ezk 38₂₀. **2. wave, sway,** of fruit Ps 72₁₆.

Ni. 1 Pf. נִרְעֲשָׁה—**quake,** of earth Jr 50₄₆ (+ מִן *at* sound).

Hi. 7 Pf. הִרְעַשְׁתִּי; impf. תַּרְעִישֶׁנּוּ; ptc. מַרְעִישׁ—**1. cause to quake, cause to shake,** obj. nations Ezk 31₁₆ (+ מִן *at* sound), heavens and earth Hg 2₂₁. **2. cause** horse **to leap** like (כְּ) locust Jb 39₂₀.

→ רַעַשׁ *quaking*.

*__רעשׁ__ II 1 vb.—**Qal** 1 Impf. יִרְעַשׁ—**be abundant,** of fruit Ps 72₁₆.

*__רעשׁ__ III 1 vb.—**Qal** 1 Impf. יִרְעַשׁ—**suck,** appar. of lambs Ps 72₁₆.

רַעַשׁ 17.1 n.m.—רָעַשׁ; cstr. רַעַשׁ; sf. Q רעשכה—**1. earthquake** 1 K 19₁₁ Am 1₁. **2. quaking, trembling, shaking** of person Ezk 12₁₈, horse Jb 39₂₄, perh. javelin Jb 41₂₁. **3. (clattering or rattling) noise** of wheel Na 3₂, bones Ezk 37₇; **commotion, tumult (of battle)** Jr 10₂₂. → רעשׁ I *quake*.

רפא I 67.9.17.1 vb.—**Qal** 38.7.9.1 Pf. רְפָאם; impf. אֶרְפָּא, תִּרְפֶּינָה; impv. רְפָא (רְפָאָה); ptc. רֹפֵא, רֹפְאִים; inf. abs. רָפוֹא; cstr. לִרְפֹּא (רְפָאִי)—oft. with Y. as subj., **1.** with obj. or לְ of obj., **heal, cure** person from disease, pain, infertility Gn 20₁₇, emotional suffering Jr 30₁₇, spiritual depravity Is 6₁₀. **2.** with obj., **heal** skin GnzPs 4₅. **3.** with obj. or לְ of obj., **heal, cure** wound Is 30₂₆, disease Ps 103₃. **4.** abs., **heal, bring healing** Jb 5₁₈. **5.** with obj., **repair, mend** breach Ps 60₄. **6.** inf. cstr. as noun, **healing** Ec 3₃. **7.** ptc. as noun, **physician,** human Si 381, Y. Ex 1526, **healer** of suffering Jb 134.

Ni. 17.0.4 Pf. נִרְפָּא, נִרְפְּתָה; impf. תֵּרָפֵא; + waw וַיֵּרָפוּ; inf. הֵרָפֵא—**1. be healed,** of person, from physical ailment Dt 2827, spiritual, moral ailment Jr 1714. **2. be healed,** of disease, etc. Lv 143. **3. be healing** for someone, in ref. to spiritual restoration, subj. indef. Is 535. **4. be made fresh, purified,** of water 2 K 222. **5. be repaired,** of vessel Jr 1911.

Pi. 9.2.3 Pf. רִפֵּאתֶם, Qr רִפִּינוּ; impf. יְרַפֵּא; inf. abs. רַפֹּא; cstr. Si רפאות—**1. heal** Babylon Jr 519, flock Zc 1116. **2. cause** someone **to be healed,** by paying for loss of time Ex 2119. **3. heal** wound Si 328. **4.** with לְ of obj., **purify** water 2 K 221. **5. repair** altar 1 K 1830.

Htp. 3.0.1 Inf. cstr. הִתְרַפֵּא—**have oneself healed** 2 K 829.

→ מַרְפֵּא *healing*, רִפְאוּת *remedy*, רְפוּאָה *remedy*; cf. תְּרוּפָה *healing*.

רפא II, see רפה *drop*.

רפא III, see רָפֶה *weak, slack*.

רָפָא I 1.0.0.9 pr.n.m. **Rapha.**

רָפָא II, see בֵּית רָפָא *Beth-rapha*.

רָפָא III, see רָפָה I *giants*.

רִפְאוּת 1.1.1 n.f. **healing, cure** Pr 38. → רפא *heal*.

רְפָאִים I 8 n.m.pl. the dead in the underworld Is 2614.

רְפָאִים II 19 gent. **Rephaim.** → cf. רָפָה I *giants*.

רְפָאֵל 1.0.3 pr.n.m. **Raphael, Rephael.**

רפד 3.0.1 vb.—**Qal** 1 Impf. יִרְפַּד—**spread out** threshing sledge upon (עַל) mud Jb 4122.

Pi. 2.0.1 Pf. רִפַּדְתִּי—**1. spread out** couch Jb 1713. **2. sustain** lover Ca 25.

→ רְפִידָה I *support*, II *cover*.

רפה 46.2.5.1 vb.—**Qal** 14.0.1 Pf. רָפָה, רָפְתָה, רָפוּ; impf. יִרְפֶּה; + waw וַיִּרֶף—**1. drop** out of fear, of hands 2 S 41. **2. sink down** in flames, of grass Is 524. **3. wane toward** (לְ) evening, of day Jg 199. **4a. withdraw oneself from** (מִן) someone, of Y. Ex 426. **b.** abs., **withdraw oneself in fear,** of Damascus Jr 4924. **5. withdraw away from** (מֵעַל) someone, **abate,** of temper Jg 83.

Ni. 3 Ptc. נִרְפִּים—**be idle,** of servant Ex 517.

Pi. 5.0.0.1 Pf. רִפָּה; impf. תְּרַפֶּינָה; ptc. מְרַפֵּא, מְרַפִּים; inf. cstr. I רפת—**1. make hands drop,** i.e. discourage Jr 384. **2. let wings drop** Ezk 124. **3. loosen** girdle Jb 1221.

Hi. 21.2.4 Impf. אַרְפְּךָ, תֶּרֶף, יַרְפְּךָ; impv. הֶרֶף, הַרְפּוּ—**1. abandon** people Dt 431. **2a. withdraw from** (מִן) someone Jg 1137. **b. let** someone **alone,** (1) obj. Jb 719. (2) לְ of obj. 2 K 427. **3. let go of** lover Ca 34. **4. let** hands **drop** Jos 106. **5. quit** work Ne 63. **6.** abs., **stop, desist** Ps 4611. **7. refrain from** (מִן) anger Ps 378. **8. grant a respite to** (לְ) someone 1 S 113.

Htp. 3 Pf. הִתְרַפִּיתָ; ptc. מִתְרַפֶּה—**1. show oneself slack** Jos 183. **2. show oneself without courage** Pr 2410. **3.** ptc. as noun, **one who shows himself slack** Pr 189.

→ רָפֶה *weak, slack*, מַרְפֵּא II *calmness*, מַרְפֶּה *relaxation*, רִפְיוֹן *dropping*.

רָפָה I 6 n.[m.]—רָפָא—**giants** 2 S 2116. → cf. רְפָאִים II *Rephaim*.

רָפָה II 1 pr.n.m. **Raphah.**

רָפֶה 4.2.2 adj.—Sam רפא (Si רפי); cstr. רְפֵה; pl. רָפוֹת—**1. weak** of hands 2 S 172. **2. slack, lazy** in deeds Si 429.

→ רפה *drop*.

רָפוּא 1 pr.n.m. **Raphu.**

[רְפוּאָה] 3.1.2 n.f.—pl. רְפֻאוֹת—**remedy** Jr 3013. → רפא *heal*.

רְפוֹת, see רִיפוֹת *groats*.

רֶפַח 1 pr.n.m. **Rephah.**

[רְפִידָה] I 1 n.f.—sf. רְפִידָתוֹ—**1. rest, back of chair** Ca 310 (unless §2). **2. base** Ca 310. → רפד *spread out, support*.

*[**רְפִידָה**] II 1 n.f.—sf. רְפִידָתוֹ—**cover** Ca 310. → רפד *spread out*.

רְפִידִים 5 pl.n. **Rephidim.**

רְפָיָה 5.0.1.13 pr.n.m. **Rephaiah.**

רִפְיוֹן 1.1 n.[m.] **dropping,** of hands, out of discouragement, agony Si 2523. → רפה *drop*.

רפס 5.0.1 vb.—**Qal** 2.0.1 Impf. תִּרְפְּשׂוּן; + waw וַתִּרְפֹּס; ptc. pass. Q רפוס—**1. make muddy, foul** river Ezk 322. **2.** pass., **be trampled down,** of field 4QDe 3.216.

Ni. 1 Ptc. נִרְפָּשׂ—**be muddied, befouled,** of spring Pr 2526.

Htp. 2 Impv. הִתְרַפֵּס; ptc. מִתְרַפֵּס—**1. trample upon** (בְּ) silver Ps 6831. **2. trample upon oneself,** i.e. **humble oneself** Pr 63.

→ מִרְפָּשׂ *muddied waterhole*.

[רַפְסֹדָה] 1 n.[f.]—pl. רַפְסֹדוֹת—**raft** 2 C 2$_{15}$.

רפף 1 vb.—**Po.** 1 Impf. יְרוֹפָפוּ—**shake,** of pillar of heaven Jb 26$_{11}$.

רפק 1 vb.—**Htp.** 1 Ptc. מִתְרַפֶּקֶת—**lean against** (עַל) beloved Ca 8$_5$.

רפשׂ, see רפס *trample, foul.*

רֶפֶשׁ 1.0.3 n.[m.]—sf. Q רפשם—**mire** Is 57$_{20}$.

רֶפֶת 1 n.[m.]—pl. רְפָתִים—**stable** Hb 3$_{17}$.

*[רַפְתִּי] 0.0.0.2 pr.n.m. **Raphti.**

*[רַפְתָּן] 0.0.0.1 pl.n. **Raphtan.**

רָץ, see רוץ *run.*

[רַץ] 1 n.[m.]—pl. cstr. רַצֵּי—**piece,** of silver Ps 68$_{31}$. → רצץ *crush, oppress.*

רצא I 1 vb. (byform of רוץ)—**Qal** 1 Inf. abs. רָצוֹא—**run** Ezk 1$_{14}$.

רצא II, see רצה *delight in, accept favourably.*

רצד 1.1 vb.—**Pi.** 1.1 Impf. תְּרַצְּדוּן—**watch stealthily** Si 14$_{22}$.

רצה I 57.2.41.2 vb.—**Qal** 47.2.35.2 Pf. רָצָה, רָצְתָה, רָצִית, רָצִאתִי, רָצוּ; impf. יִרְצֶה; + waw וַתֵּרֶץ; impv. רְצֵה; ptc. רוֹצֶה; ptc. pass. רָצוּי; inf. cstr. רְצוֹת—**1.** oft. of Y., **be pleased (with), accept favourably, a.** person, e.g. king 2 S 24$_{23}$, (בְּ *with*) people Ps 149$_4$. **b.** offering Am 5$_{22}$, (בְּ *with*) ram Mc 6$_7$. **2.** abs., **show one's favour,** of Y. Ps 77$_8$ (:: זנח *reject*). **3. enjoy, take pleasure (in), delight (in)** sabbath Lv 26$_{34}$, (בְּ *in*) temple 1 C 29$_3$, (אַחַר appar. *in*) truth 4Q424 1$_9$. **4. be pleased, be happy** to do something Ps 40$_{14}$. **5.** abs., **be pleased, be content** 1QS 10$_{20}$. **6. accept (humbly)** guilt caused by sin Lv 26$_{41}$, (+ בְּ of obj.) affliction 4QBéat 2.2$_4$. **7. be(come) friends** with (עִם) Y. Jb 34$_9$, thief Ps 50$_{18}$. **8.** ptc. pass., **be a favourite, be loved** Si 46$_{13}$. **9.** ptc. as noun, **one who is desirous** Ps 68$_{31}$. **10.** ptc. pass. as noun, **favourite one** Dt 33$_{24}$.

Ni. 7.0.6 Pf. נִרְצָה; impf. יֵרָצֶה, יֵרָצוּ—**1. be regarded as pleasing, be accepted as satisfactory,** of sacrifice, means of atonement Lv 1$_4$. **2. find favour, be accepted,** of person 11QPs[a] 18$_8$.

Pi. 1.0.1 Impf. יְרַצּוּ—**1. seek the favour of** poor Jb 20$_{10}$. **2. make** knowledge **acceptable** 4QShirShabb[d] 1.1$_{39}$.

Hi. 2 + waw וְהִרְצָת (Sam והרצתה)—of land, **enjoy** sabbath Lv 26$_{34}$.

Htp. 1 Impf. יִתְרַצֶּה—**make oneself acceptable** 1 S 29$_4$.

→ רָצוֹן *will, favour, delight.*

*רצה II 8.0.5 vb.—**Qal** 5.0.4 Pf. Q רצינו; impf. תִּרְצֶה; + waw Q וירצו; inf. cstr. Q לרצת—**1. pay for, make (vicarious) atonement for sin,** one's own Lv 26$_{41}$, someone else's 1QS 8$_3$. **2. restore** sabbath Lv 26$_{34}$.

Ni. 1.0.1 Pf. נִרְצָה—**be paid for, be atoned for,** of iniquity Is 40$_2$.

Pi. 1 Impf. יְרַצּוּ—**restore** poor Jb 20$_{10}$.

Hi. 2 + waw וְהִרְצָת (Sam והרצתה)—of land, **have sabbath restored** Lv 26$_{34}$.

רָצוֹן 56.16.130 n.[m.]—cstr. רְצוֹן; sf. רְצֹנוֹ—**1. divine will,** what Y. wants humans to do Ps 40$_9$, that which determines events Si 39$_{18}$, **divine agreement** with human action 1QH 18$_6$. **2. divine goodwill, favour** towards Israel Is 49$_8$, righteous Ps 5$_{13}$. **3. divine acceptance,** of sacrifice 4QPrFêtes[c] 131.2$_6$. **4. divine delight,** in faithful one Pr 12$_{22}$, in prayer Pr 15$_8$. **5. will, desire, pleasure, delight** of all living things Ps 145$_{16}$, **will** of parents 4QJub[h] 35$_{13}$, **freewill** CD 11$_4$, **self-will** CD 2$_{21}$, perh. **disposition** Si 32$_{20}$. **6. goodwill, favour** of human Pr 16$_{15}$. **7. that which is pleasing, that which is acceptable** Pr 10$_{32}$. → רצה I *delight in, accept favourably.*

*[רָצוֹץ] 0.1 n.[m.] perh. **favour** Si 35$_{14}$(Bmg).

רצח 47.0.2 vb.—**Qal** 40.0.1 Pf. רָצַחְתָּ; impf. יִרְצַח; ptc. רֹצֵחַ; inf. abs. רָצֹחַ—**1a.** trans., **murder, kill** a person unlawfully Dt 22$_{26}$. **b.** abs., **commit murder** Ex 20$_{13}$. **2.** trans., **commit manslaughter against, kill** a person unintentionally Dt 4$_{42}$. **3.** trans., **put to death, administer the death-penalty to, kill in revenge** a manslayer Nm 35$_{27}$. **4.** inf. abs. as noun, **(act of) murder** Ho 4$_2$. **5.** ptc. as noun, **murderer** Nm 35$_{18}$, **manslayer** Nm 35$_6$.

Ni. 2 Pf. נִרְצָחָה; impf. אֵרָצֵחַ—**be murdered** Jg 20$_4$.

Pi. 4.0.1 Impf. יְרַצֵּחוּ; ptc. מְרַצֵּחַ—**1.** trans., **commit murder (frequently),** obj. orphans CD 6$_{17}$. **2.** abs., **commit murder frequently** Ho 6$_9$. **3.** ptc. as noun, **murderer** Is 1$_{21}$.

Pu. 1 Impf. תְּרָצְּחוּ—**be murdered** Ps 62$_4$.

→ רֶצַח *murder.*

רֶצַח 2 n.[m.] **1. murder** Ezk 21$_{27}$. **2. murderous blow** Ps 42$_{11}$. → רצח *murder.*

רִצְיָא 1 pr.n.m. **Rizia.**

רְצִין, see רוץ *run.*

רְצִין 11.0.1 pr.n.m. **Rezin.**

רצע 1 vb.—**Qal** 1 + waw וְרָצַע—**pierce ear** Ex 21$_6$. → מַרְצֵעַ *awl.*

רצף I 1.1 vb.—**Qal** 1 ptc. pass. רָצוּף—pass., **be inlaid,** of interior of palanquin Ca 3$_{10}$.

Pi. 0.1 Ptc. מרצף—**pave** firmament, of moon Si 43$_8$ (B, M).

→ מַרְצֶפֶת *pavement,* רִצְפָּה *pavement.*

*__רצף__ II 0.1 vb.—**Pi.** 0.1 Ptc. מרצף—**set firmament aglow,** of moon Si 43$_8$(B). → רִצְפָּה I *glowing coal.*

רֶצֶף 2 pl.n. **Rezeph.**

רִצְפָּה 7 n.f.—cstr. רִצְפַת—**pavement,** in temple Ezk 40$_{17}$, palace Est 1$_6$. → רצף I *inlay, pave.*

רִצְפָּה I 2 n.f.—pl. רְצָפִים—**glowing coal** 1 K 19$_6$. → רצף II *set aglow, illuminate.*

רִצְפָּה II 4 pr.n.f. **Rizpah.**

רצץ 19.1.2 vb.—**Qal** 11.0.2 Pf. רַצּוֹתִי; impf. יָרוּץ, תָּרֻץ; ptc. רֹצְצוֹת; pass. רָצוּץ—**1. crush, oppress** the poor Am 4$_1$. **2. be crushed, broken,** of bowl Ec 12$_6$, servant of Y. Is 42$_4$. **3.** ptc. pass., **a. be crushed, oppressed** Ho 5$_{11}$. **b. be bruised, broken,** of reed 2 K 18$_{21}$. **5.** ptc. pass. as noun, **oppressed one** CD 13$_{10}$.

Ni. 2 Pf. נָרֹץ; impf. תֵּרוֹץ—**be crushed, broken,** of wheel Ec 12$_6$, Pharaoh Ezk 29$_7$.

Pi. 3.1 Pf. רִצַּץ; + waw וַיְרַצֵּץ—**1. brutally oppress** the poor Jb 20$_{19}$. **2. crush (in pieces)** head of Leviathan Ps 74$_{14}$.

Po. 1 + waw וַיְרֹצְצוּ—**oppress** Israelites Jg 10$_8$.

Hi. 1 + waw וַתָּרִץ—**crush** skull Jg 9$_{53}$.

Htpo. 1 + waw וַיִּתְרֹצְצוּ—**kick and shove one another,** of twins in womb Gn 25$_{22}$.

→ רַץ *piece,* מְרוּצָה II *extortion,* מַרְצֵעַ *awl.*

[רַק] I 3.0.1 adj.—pl. רַקּוֹת—**1. thin, lean,** of cow Gn 41$_{19}$. **2. empty, idle,** of word CD 10$_{18}$. → cf. רֵיק *empty.*

רַק II 109.0.18 adv. **1. only, merely, nothing but, (but) exclusively,** רַק רָחָב הַזּוֹנָה תִּחְיֶה *only Rahab the prostitute will live* Jos 6$_{17}$. **2. only, except, save, but,** אֵין בָּאָרוֹן רַק שְׁנֵי לֻחוֹת הָאֲבָנִים *there was nothing inside the ark, except the two stone tablets* 1 K 8$_9$. **3. only with respect to,** רַק הַכִּסֵּא אֶגְדַּל מִמֶּךָּ *only with respect to the throne shall I be superior to you* Gn 41$_{40}$. **4. only, however, nevertheless, yet,** אֲשַׁלַּח אֶתְכֶם ... רַק הַרְחֵק לֹא־תַרְחִיקוּ לָלֶכֶת *I will let you go ... only do not go very far* Ex 8$_{24}$. **5. surely,** רַק אֵין־יִרְאַת אֱלֹהִים בַּמָּקוֹם הַזֶּה *surely there is no fear of God in this place* Gn 20$_{11}$. **6.** idiomatic phrases, **a.** רַק אִם **if only** 2 K 21$_8$. **b.** רַק לְמַעַן **only so that** Jg 3$_2$. **c.** רַק אַךְ **only** (emphatic) Nm 12$_2$. **d.** רַק־הַפַּעַם **just once more** Jg 6$_{39}$.

רֵק, see רֵיק *empty, vain.*

רֹק 3 n.[m.]—sf. רֻקִּי—**spittle** Jb 7$_{19}$. → רקק *spit;* cf. מְצִירוֹק *emission of spittle.*

רקב 2.0.2 vb.—**Qal** 2.0.2 Impf. יִרְקַב; inf. abs. Si רקוב—**rot,** of tree Is 40$_{20}$, name Pr 10$_7$. → רָקָב *rottenness,* רִקָּבוֹן *rottenness.*

רָקָב I 5 n.[m.]—cstr. רְקַב—**rottenness,** oft. of bones Pr 12$_4$. → רקב *rot.*

*__רָקָב__ II 0.1 n.[m.] **solid ground** Si 43$_{20}$.

*__[רֹקֶב]__ n.[m.] **waterskin** Jb 13$_{28}$ (if em. רָקָב *rottenness*).

רִקָּבוֹן 1 n.[m.] **rottenness,** of wood Jb 41$_{19}$. → רקב *rot.*

רקד 9 vb.—**Qal** 3 Pf. רָקְדוּ; impf. תִּרְקְדוּ—**1. skip, leap (about)** like (כְּ) ram Ps 114$_4$. **2. dance** Ec 3$_4$.

Pi. 5 Impf. יְרַקְּדוּ; ptc. מְרַקֵּד, מְרַקֵּדָה—**1. skip, leap (about),** of animal Is 13$_{21}$. **2. dance,** of human being 1 C 15$_{29}$. **3. jolt,** of chariot Na 3$_2$.

Hi. 1 + waw וַיַּרְקִידֵם—**make skip, make leap (about)** Ps 29$_6$.

[רַקָּה] I 5 n.f.—sf. רַקָּתוֹ—**temple(s)** of forehead Jg 4$_{21}$ Ca 4$_3$.

*__[רַקָּה]__ II 2 n.f.—sf. רַקָּתֵךְ—**cheek(s)** Ca 4$_3$.

[רִקּוּחַ] 1 n.[m.]—pl. sf. רִקֻּחָיִךְ—**perfume** Is 57$_9$. → רקח *mix ointment.*

רַקּוֹן 1 pl.n. **Rakkon.**

רָקוּעַ 1.0.1 n.[m.] **1. beaten out object** Nm 17$_3$. **2. tract of land** 1QH 11$_{31}$. → רקע *spread out.*

רקח 8.2 vb.—**Qal** 6.2 Impf. יִרְקַח; ptc. רֹקֵחַ, רֹקְחֵי—**1. mix, compound ointment** Ex 30$_{33}$. **2.** ptc. as noun, **blender of ointment and spices,** specif. **perfumer** Ex 30$_{25}$, **apothecary** Si 38$_8$.

Pu. 1 Ptc. מְרֻקָּחִים—**be mixed as ointment** 2 C 16$_{14}$.

Hi. 1 Impv. הַרְקַח—with מֶרְקָחָה as obj., perh. **spice, add spice** Ezk 24$_{10}$.

→ רֶקַח *spice,* רֹקַח *ointment mixture,* רַקָּח *ointment-maker,* רַקָּחָה *female ointment-maker,* רִקּוּחַ *perfume,* מֶרְקָח *perfume,* מֶרְקָחָה *pot of ointment,* מִרְקַחַת *ointment mixture.*

רֹקַח 2 n.[m.] **ointment mixture** Ex 30$_{25}$. → רקח *mix ointment.*

[רַקָּח] 1 n.m.—pl. רַקָּחִים—**ointment-maker** Ne 3$_{8}$. → רקח *mix ointment.*

רֶקַח 1 n.[m.] **spice, in wine** Ca 8$_{2}$. → רקח *mix ointment.*

[רַקָּחָה] 1 n.f.—pl. רַקָּחוֹת—**female ointment-maker** 1 S 8$_{13}$. → רקח *mix ointment.*

רָקִיעַ 17.2.24 n.m.—cstr. רְקִיעַ; pl. cstr. Q רקיעי—**firmament, expanse of the sky, vault of heaven** Gn 1$_{6}$ Ps 150$_{1}$. → רקע *hammer out.*

רָקִיק 8.0.1 n.m.—cstr. רְקִיק; pl. cstr. רְקִיקֵי—**wafer, thin bread** Nm 6$_{19}$.

רקם 9 vb.—**Qal** 8 Ptc. רֹקֵם—ptc. as noun, **weaver of coloured fabric, variegator** Ex 38$_{23}$.

Pu. 1 Pf. רֻקַּמְתִּי—**be woven, formed,** of embryo Ps 139$_{15}$.

→ רִקְמָה *variegated material.*

רֶקֶם I 5 pr.n.m. **Rekem.**

רֶקֶם II 1.0.1 pl.n. **Rekem.**

*** [רָקְמָה]** 0.0.1 n.f.—רוקמה—perh. **authoritative status** 4QD^{e} 7.1$_{14}$.

רִקְמָה 12.0.16 n.f.—Q ריקמה (Q רוקמה); cstr. Q רוקמת; sf. רִקְמָתֵךְ; du. רִקְמָתַיִם; pl. רְקָמוֹת; sf. Q רוקמותם—**1. variegated material, colourfully woven cloth, embroidered work,** oft. clothes Ezk 16$_{13}$. **2. varicoloured design** of mosaic 1 C 29$_{2}$. **3. variegated pattern** of spiritual beings 4QBer^{b} 1$_{4}$. **4. colouring** of feathers of bird Ezk 17$_{3}$. → רקם *variegate.*

רקע 11.1 vb.—**Qal** 6.1 Impf. אֶרְקָעֵם; impv. רְקַע; ptc. רֹקַע; inf. רַקְעֲךָ—**1a. stamp** with (בְּ) foot Ezk 6$_{11}$. **b. trample** enemy 2 S 22$_{43}$. **2. spread out** beauty Si 43$_{1(Bmg)}$. **3.** ptc. as noun, **the one who spread(s) out the earth,** i.e. Y. as creator Is 42$_{5}$.

Pi. 3 Impf. יְרַקְּעֶנּוּ—**1. hammer out** sheets of gold Ex 39$_{3}$, censers Nm 17$_{4}$. **2. overlay** image with (בְּ) gold Is 40$_{19}$.

Pu. 1 Ptc. מְרֻקָּע—**be hammered, beaten,** of silver Jr 10$_{9}$.

Hi. 1 Impf. תַּרְקִיעַ—with לְ of obj., **spread out** clouds Jb 37$_{18}$.

→ רָקִיעַ *firmament,* רִקּוּעַ *beaten out object.*

רקק 1.0.1 vb.—**Qal** 1.0.1 Impf. יָרֹק (Q ירוק)—**spit** 1QS 7$_{13}$. → רֹק *spittle.*

רַקַּת 1 pl.n. **Rakkath.**

רָשׁ, see רושׁ *be poor.*

רשׁא, see רשׁה *have authority.*

*** [רְשָׁאוּת]** n.[m.] **authority, prestige** Gn 49$_{3}$ (if em. שְׂאֵת *dignity*). → רשׁה *have authority.*

*** רשׁה** 0.1.4 vb.—**Qal** 0.0.2 Ptc. רשׁאים; inf. cstr. רשׁות—**1. have authority, have (legal) permission** 5/6ḤevBA 44$_{24}$. **2. direct** hand 1QM 12$_{4}$.

Hi. 0.0.2 + waw וירשׁה; inf. cstr. הרשׁות—**allow** someone to defile altar CD 11$_{20}$.

Ho. 0.1 Pf. הורשׁית (הורשׁיתה)—**be given permission** Si 3$_{22}$.

→ רְשָׁאוּת *authority,* רְשׁוּת *jurisdiction,* רִשְׁיוֹן *authorization.*

רִשׁוֹן, see ראשׁון *first.*

*** [רְשׁוּת]** 0.0.6 n.f.—רשׁת; cstr. רשׁות; sf. רשׁותו—**jurisdiction** 5/6ḤevBA 45$_{8}$. → רשׁה *have authority.*

רִשְׁיוֹן 1 n.[m.] **authorization** Ezr 3$_{7}$. → רשׁה *have authority.*

*** [רָשִׁיעַ]** 0.0.1 n.[m.] **wickedness** CD 6$_{10}$. → רשׁע *act wickedly.*

*** [רָשִׁישׁ]** 0.1 adj. **slack,** in deeds Si 4$_{29}$. → רשׁשׁ II *be slow, sluggish.*

רֵשִׁית, see רֵאשִׁית *beginning.*

רשׁם 1.0.1 vb.—**Qal** 1.0.1 Pf. Q רשׁמתה; ptc. pass. רָשׁוּם—**1. inscribe** spirit of righteous 1QH 8$_{19}$. **2.** ptc. pass. as noun, **that which is inscribed, recorded** in the book of truth Dn 10$_{21}$.

רשׁע 34.2.33 vb.—**Qal** 9.0.4 Pf. רָשַׁעְתִּי; impf. תִּרְשַׁע—**act wickedly** Ec 7$_{17}$, **be guilty** Jb 10$_{7}$, **be accounted guilty** Jb 9$_{29}$.

Hi. 25.2.28 Pf. הִרְשִׁיעַ, הִרְשַׁעְנוּ; impf. יַרְשִׁיעַ; ptc. מַרְשִׁיעַ, מַרְשִׁיעֵי; inf. cstr. הַרְשִׁיעַ—**1. declare wicked or guilty, condemn** Y. Jb 40$_{8}$, wicked Dt 25$_{1}$, work 4QShir^{b} 48$_{6}$;

abs. Jb 34$_{29}$. 2. perh. **inflict punishment,** i.e. condemn by punishing 1 S 14$_{47}$. **3. act wickedly, do evil** Ne 9$_{33}$, against (עַל) chosen one 1QpHab 9$_{11}$. **4. make (oneself) guilty,** with obj. sf. in ref. to subj. Si 7$_{7}$. **5.** abs., **make wicked** or **guilty, lead astray** 1QM 13$_{11}$. **6.** ptc. as noun, **wicked one, violator** 1QM 1$_{2}$.

Htp. 0.0.1 Inf. cstr. התרשע—**condemn oneself** 4QM^{a} 8.1$_{7}$.

→ רָשָׁע *wicked,* רֶשַׁע I *wickedness,* רִשְׁעָה *wickedness,* רְשִׁיַע *wickedness,* מִרְשַׁעַת *wickedness.*

רָשָׁע 263.17.89 adj.—f. רְשָׁעָה; pl. רְשָׁעִים, רִשְׁעֵי—**1. wicked, guilty,** of human Jb 20$_{29}$, way Ezk 3$_{18}$. **2.** as noun, **wicked one, wrongdoer,** oft. specif. **guilty one** before Y. Ps 9$_{18}$, **one guilty of crime** Dt 25$_{1}$. **3.** as adv., **as (being) wicked** or **guilty** Ps 109$_{7}$. → רשׁע *act wickedly.*

רֶשַׁע I 30.1.33 n.m.—רֶשַׁע; sf. רִשְׁעוֹ—**wickedness, sin, evil** Ec 3$_{16}$, specif. **dishonesty** Pr 8$_{7}$. → רשׁע *act wickedly.*

רֶשַׁע II, see מַלְכִּי־רֶשַׁע *Melchiresha.*

רִשְׁעָה 15.0.78 n.f.—cstr. רִשְׁעַת; sf. רִשְׁעָתוֹ—**wickedness, sin** 1QS 4$_{21}$, specif. **crime, offence** Dt 25$_{2}$. → רשׁע *act wickedly.*

רִשְׁעָתַיִם, see כּוּשַׁן רִשְׁעָתַיִם *Cushan-rishathaim.*

*__רשׁף__ 0.1 vb.—**Qal** 0.1 Pf. רשפה—**burn,** of flame Si 16$_{6(B)}$. → רֶשֶׁף *plague, flame, arrow.*

רֶשֶׁף I 7.0.5 n.m.—pl. רְשָׁפִים; cstr. רִשְׁפֵי (רִשְׁפֵּי); sf. רְשָׁפֶיהָ—**1. plague, pestilence** Dt 32$_{24}$. **2. flame** Ca 8$_{6}$. **3. arrow** Ps 76$_{4}$. → רשׁף *burn.*

*__רֶשֶׁף__ II 1.1.1 n.m. **birds,** perh. **vultures** 4QInstr^{d} 127$_{3}$.

רֶשֶׁף III 1 pr.n.m. **Resheph.**

רשׁשׁ I 2.1 vb.—**Qal** 0.1 Ptc. רשש—ptc. as noun, **one crushed** Si 11$_{12}$.

Po. 1 Impf. יְרֹשֵׁשׁ—**batter down** city Jr 5$_{17}$.

Pu. 1 Pf. רֻשַּׁשְׁנוּ—**be crushed,** of Edom Ml 1$_{4}$.

→ תַּרְשִׁישׁ I *topaz.*

*__רשׁשׁ__ II 0.1 vb.—**Qal** 0.1 Ptc. רשש—**be slow, sluggish,** ptc. as noun, **sluggard** Si 11$_{12}$. → רָשִׁישׁ *negligent, slack.*

*__רשׁשׁ__ III 0.1 vb.—**Qal** 0.1 Ptc. רשש—**be poor,** ptc. as noun, **poor one** Si 11$_{12}$. → cf. רושׁ *be poor.*

רֶשֶׁת 22.2.7 n.f.—רֶשֶׁת; cstr. רֶשֶׁת; sf. רִשְׁתִּי—**1. net,** for catching **a.** birds Pr 1$_{17}$. **b.** people Ps 9$_{16}$ Si 9$_{13}$. **2. network, grid** as fixture on altar Ex 27$_{4}$. → ירשׁ *take possession.*

רַתּוֹק 2 n.[m.] **chain** Ezk 7$_{23}$. → רתק *bind.*

רתח 3.1.1 vb.—**Qal** 0.0.1 Inf. cstr. רתוח—**boil over** (עַל) springs of water, of ocean depths 1QH 11$_{15}$.

Pi. 1 Impv. רַתַּח—**(cause to) boil bones** Ezk 24$_{5}$.

Pu. 1 Pf. רֻתְּחוּ—**boil, be in turmoil,** of belly Jb 30$_{27}$.

Hi. 1.1 Impf. יַרְתִּיחַ—**1. make world swelter,** of sun Si 43$_{3}$. **2. make deep sea boil,** of Leviathan Jb 41$_{23}$.

→ רֶתַח *boiling.*

[רֶתַח] 1 n.[m.]—pl. sf. רְתָחֶיהָ—**boiling,** of bones Ezk 24$_{5(L)}$. → רתח *boil.*

רתם 1 vb.—**Qal** 1 Impv. רְתֹם—**bind** chariot to (לְ) team of horses Mc 1$_{13}$.

רֹתֶם 4 n.m.—pl. רְתָמִים—**broom-shrub** for shelter 1 K 19$_{4.5}$, **broom-wood** as fuel Ps 120$_{4}$ Jb 30$_{4}$.

רִתְמָה 2 pl.n. **Rithmah.**

רתק I 2.0.1 vb.—**Qal** 0.0.1 Inf. cstr. רתוק—prob. **bind** 2QVerdict 2$_{2}$.

Ni. 1 Impf. Qr יֵרָתֵק—perh. **be bound, joined,** of cord Ec 12$_{6(Qr)}$.

Pu. 1 Pf. רֻתְּקוּ—**be bound, chained** in (בְּ) fetters Na 3$_{10}$.

→ רַתּוֹק *chain,* רְתֻקָה *chain.*

רתק II 1 vb.—**Ni.** 1 Impf. Qr יֵרָתֵק—**be snapped,** of cord Ec 12$_{6(Qr)}$.

[רְתֻקָה] 1 n.[f.]—pl. cstr. רַתְּקוֹת—**chain** Is 40$_{19}$. → רתק *bind.*

רְתֵת 1.0.2 n.[m.]—Q רתית—**trembling,** out of intimidation, fear Ho 13$_{1}$ GnzPs 4$_{2}$.

שׂ

שְׂאֹר 5 n.m. **leaven** Ex 12$_{19}$.

שְׂאֵת 14.0.2 n.f.—cstr. שְׂאֵת; sf. שְׂאֵתוֹ (שֵׂתוֹ)—**1. swelling** in skin Lv 13_{10}. **2. exaltation, majesty,** of humans Gn 49_3, of Y. Jb 13_{11}. **3. uprising** Jb 41_{17}. **4. uplifting of** countenance, i.e. cheerfulness Gn 4_7. **5. forgiveness** Gn 4_7. **6. acceptance** Gn 4_7. → נשׂא I *lift*.

שָׁב, see שׂיב *be grey-haired*.

שְׂבָכָה 16 n.f.—pl. שְׂבָכוֹת (שְׂבָכִים)—**1. net-ornament** on pillars 1 K 7_{41}. **2. network, toils** Jb 18_8. **3. window-lattice, grid** 2 K 1_2.

שְׂבָם 1 pl.n. **Sebam.**

שִׂבְמָה 5 pl.n. **Sibmah.**

שׂבע 98.3.15.1 vb.—**Qal** 80.3.11.1 Pf. שָׂבְעָה, שָׂבַע; impf. יִשְׂבַּע; impv. שְׂבַע; inf. abs. שָׂבוֹעַ; cstr. שְׂבֹעַ (שָׂבְעָה)—**1a.** abs., (1) **be sated, have enough to eat and drink,** of person Ru 2_{14}, animal Ps 104_{28}. (2) **be sated with water,** of earth, tree Ps $104_{13.16}$. **b.** trans., (1) **have one's fill** of bread, of person Ex 16_{12}. (2) **be sated with water,** of earth Pr 30_{16}. **2a.** abs., **be satisfied, content** Pr 30_9. **b.** trans., **be satisfied with** wealth Pr 5_{10}, goodness Ps 65_5. **3. be surfeited with, have enough of, be weary of** burnt offering Is 1_{11}, poverty Pr 28_{19}. **4. be full of** days, i.e. reach a ripe old age 1 C 23_1.

Ni. 1 Ptc. נִשְׂבָּע—**be sated with** (מִן) flesh Jb 31_{31}.

Pi. 2 Impf. יְשַׂבְּעוּ; impv. שַׂבְּעֵנוּ—**1. satisfy** one's appetite Ezk 7_{19}. **2. satisfy** someone **with loving kindness** Ps 90_{14}.

Hi. 16.0.4 Pf. הִשְׂבִּיעַ ,הִשְׂבַּעְתָּ; impf. יַשְׂבִּיעֵנִי; ptc. מַשְׂבִּיעַ; inf. הַשְׂבִּיעַ—**1a. satisfy, supply needs of** person Ps 107_9. **b. cause to be sated with water, saturate** ground Jb 38_{27}. **2. satisfy** someone **with food** Ps 132_{15}. **3. satisfy** needs, desires Ps 145_{16}, **slake** thirst Is 58_{11}. **4. sate, overindulge oneself with food** 4QInstr[b] 2.2_{18}. **5.** of Y., **satisfy** someone **with a long life,** i.e. cause one to become old Ps 91_{16}. **6. fill** someone **with bitterness** Jb 9_{18}. **7. enrich** people Ezk 27_{33}.

→ שָׂבֵעַ *full,* שָׂבָע *abundance of food, satiety,* שֹׂבַע *satiety, fulness,* שָׂבְעָה *satiety.*

שָׂבֵעַ 10.0.1 adj.—cstr. שְׂבַע; f.s. שְׂבֵעָה; m.pl. שְׂבֵעִים—**1. full (of days),** i.e. old 1 C 29_{28}. **2. full of, a. abounding with divine favour** Dt 33_{23}. **b. surfeited with, weary of trouble** Jb 14_1. **3. sated** Pr 27_7. **4. satisfied** Pr 19_{23}. **5.** as noun, **one who is sated** 1 S 2_5. → שׂבע *be sated.*

שָׂבָע 8 n.m. **1. abundance of food** Gn 41_{31}. **2. satiety** Ec 5_{11}. → שׂבע *be sated.*

שֹׂבַע 8.0.1 n.[m.]—cstr. שֹׂבַע; sf. שָׂבְעָהּ—**1. satiety, satiation** Pr 13_{25}. **2. fulness, abundance,** שֹׂבַע שְׂמָחוֹת *fulness of joy* Ps 16_{11}. → שׂבע *be sated.*

שָׂבְעָה 6.0.1 n.f.—cstr. שִׂבְעַת; sf. שָׂבְעָתֵךְ—**1. satiety, satiation, surfeit** Is 23_{18}. **2. (sexual) satisfaction, gratification** Ezk 16_{28}. → שׂבע *be sated.*

שׂבר I 2 vb.—**Qal** 2 Ptc. שֹׂבֵר—with בְּ of obj., **inspect** wall Ne 2_{13}.

שׂבר II 6.0.1 vb.—**Pi.** 6.0.1 Pf. שִׂבַּרְתִּי; impf. יְשַׂבְּרוּ—**1a. hope for** (לְ or אֶל) salvation Ps 119_{166}, faithfulness Is 38_{18}. **b. hope to** (לְ) do something, with inf. Est 9_1. **2. look to** (אֶל) Y. for food Ps 104_{27}. **3. wait** Ru 1_{13}. → שֵׂבֶר *hope.*

[שֵׂבֶר] 2 n.m.—sf. שִׂבְרִי—**hope** Ps 146_5. → שׂבר II *hope.*

שׂגא 2 vb.—**Hi.** 2 Impf. תַּשְׂגִּיא; ptc. מַשְׂגִּיא—**1.** with לְ of obj., **make** nation **great** Jb 12_{23}. **2. magnify** deed Jb 36_{24}. → שַׂגִּיא *great;* cf. שׂגה *grow,* שׂגג *make grow.*

שׂגב 20.0.3 vb.—**Qal** 2 Pf. שָׂגְבָה—**1. be high,** of city Dt 2_{36}. **2. be elevated,** of person Jb 5_{11}.

Ni. 10.0.3 Pf. נִשְׂגְּבָה; ptc. נִשְׂגָּב—**1. be high,** of wall Is 30_{13}. **2. be (safely) set on high,** of righteous Pr 18_{10}. **3. be exalted,** of Y. Is 2_{11}. **4. be unattainable,** of knowledge Ps 139_6.

Pi. 6 Impf. יְשַׂגֶּבְךָ—**1. set (securely)** someone **on high** Ps 59_2. **2. raise** enemy **against** (עַל) Israel Is 9_{10}.

Pu. 1 Impf. יְשֻׂגָּב—**be set (securely) on high,** of one who trusts in Y. Pr 29_{25}.

Hi. 1 Impf. יַשְׂגִּיב—**act exaltedly,** of Y. Jb 36_{22}.

→ מִשְׂגָּב I *stronghold.*

***שׂגג** 1.0.1 vb. (byform of שׂגה)—**Pilp.** 1 Impf. תְּשַׂגְשֵׂגִי—**cause** plant **to grow** Is 17_{11}.

Htpilp. 0.0.1 Impf. יתשגשגו—**grow upwards,** of tree 1QH 16_9.

→ cf. שׂגה *make grow,* שׂגא *flourish.*

שׂגה 4 vb. (byform of שׂגג)—**Qal** 3 Impf. יִשְׂגֶּה—**1. grow, flourish,** of reed Jb 8_{11}, righteous Ps 92_{13}. **2. be prosperous,** of future Jb 8_7.

Hi. 1 Pf. הִשְׂגּוּ—**increase wealth** Ps 73_{12}.

→ cf. שׂגג *grow.*

שְׂגוּב 3 pr.n.m. **Segub.**

שַׂגִּיא 2 adj. **great,** of Y. Jb 36$_{26}$. → שׂגא *make great.*

שׂגיב, see שְׂגוּב *Segub.*

שׂדד 3.2 vb.—**Pi.** 3.2 Impf. יְשַׂדֵּד—**harrow, 1.** with obj., ground Is 28$_{24}$. **2.** without obj., Ho 10$_{11}$.

שָׂדֶה 320.1.30.4 n.m.—cstr. שְׂדֵה (שׂדו I); sf. שָׂדֵהוּ; pl. שָׂדוֹת; cstr. שְׂדֵי, שְׂדוֹת; sf. שָׂדֶיךָ, שְׂדֹתֵיהֶ—**1. portion of ground, field(s),** oft. **arable land, cultivated ground** Ne 5$_5$. **2. burial-plot** of individual, family 2 C 26$_{23}$. **3. city-land, city-fields, village-fields,** i.e. adjacent to habitation Gn 41$_{48}$. **4. country, territory** of tribe, nation Jg 20$_6$. **5. open field, country(-side), outdoors** Jos 8$_{24}$, **open country,** i.e. outside city wall Lv 25$_{31}$, **forest field** 1 S 14$_{25}$, **plateau** in mountainous region Nm 23$_{14}$, **(main)land,** contrasted to sea Ezk 26$_6$. → cf. (?) שְׁדֵמָה *field.*

שָׂדַי 13.1 n.m.—שָׂדָי—alw. in poetry, **1. cultivated field(s)** Lm 4$_9$. **2. open field** Is 56$_9$.

שִׂדִּים 3 pl.n. **Siddim.**

שְׂדֵרָה 4 n.f.—pl. שְׂדֵרוֹת—**1. row, rank** of soldiers in line 2 K 11$_8$. **2. plank** in cedar 1 K 6$_9$. → cf. סְדֵרָה *row (of beams);* סדר *arrange.*

שֶׂה 47.0.13 n.m.&f.—cstr. שֵׂה; sf. שֵׂיו (שֵׂיהוּ)—**1. small livestock beast, sheep, lamb, goat** Gn 22$_7$ Dt 14$_4$. **2. flock,** Israel Jr 50$_{17}$.

שָׂהֵד 1.0.1 n.m.—sf. שָׂהֲדִי—**witness** Jb 16$_{19}$.

שָׂהֲדוּתָא 1 n.[m.] **testimony** Gn 31$_{47}$.

שַׂהֲרֹן 3 n.[m.]—pl. שַׂהֲרֹנִים—**crescent, little moon,** as ornament Jg 8$_{26}$.

שׂוֹא, see נשׂא *lift.*

*[**שׂוֹאָה**] 0.1 n.f. perh. **acquisition** Si 42$_{7}$(Bmg). → נשׂא *lift,* i.e. take.

שׂוֹבֶךְ 1 n.[m.] **tangled branches** 2 S 18$_9$.

שׂוג, see סוג I *turn back,* II *hedge in.*

שׂוח I 1 vb.—**Qal** 1 Inf. שׂוּחַ—**meditate** Gn 24$_{63}$.

***שׂוח** II 1 vb.—**Qal** 1 Inf. שׂוּחַ—**wander about** in (בְּ) field Gn 24$_{63}$.

שׂוט 1.1 vb. (byform of שׂטה)—**Qal** 1.1 Ptc. שָׂטֵי—**fall away,** ptc. as noun, **one who falls away, goes astray** Si 51$_2$. → שֵׂט *swerver;* cf. סֵט I *apostate.*

שׂוך 2.0.6 vb.—**Qal** 2.0.6 Pf. Q שַׂךְ, שַׂכְתָּ; impf. Q 2ms תשוך; ptc. שָׂךְ—**1. fence in** (בְּעַד) (to protect) person Jb 1$_{10}$, fruit 1QH 16$_{11}$. **2. fence in** (בְּעַד) (to overpower) person 1QH 13$_{33}$. **3. hedge up, shut up,** i.e. obstruct the way Ho 2$_6$, contain water 4QapPsB 1$_4$. → מְשׂוּכָה *hedge.*

[**שׂוֹךְ**] 1 n.[m.]—sf. שׂוֹכֹה—**branch** Jg 9$_{49}$.

[**שׂוֹכָה**] 1 n.f.—cstr. שׂוֹכַת—**branch** Jg 9$_{48}$.

שׂוֹכֹה 7.0.0.5 pl.n. **Socoh.**

שׂוֹכוֹ I 1.0.0.1 pr.n.m. **Soco.**

שׂוֹכוֹ II, see שׂוֹכֹה *Socoh.*

[**שׂוּכָתִי**] 1 gent. **Sucathite.**

שׂוּם, see שׂים *set.*

שׂור I 1.0.1 vb.—**Qal** 1.0.1 Pf. Q שר; inf. שׂוּרִי—**turn away** from (מִן) Ephraim, of Y. Ho 9$_{12}$. → cf. סור *turn aside.*

***שׂור** II 1 vb.—**Qal** 1 + waw וַיָּשַׂר—**saw people apart** 1 C 20$_3$.

שׂוֹרָה 1 n.f. **row** Is 28$_{25}$.

שׂוֹרֵק I, see שֹׂרֵק I *choice vines.*

שׂוֹרֵק II, see שֹׂרֵק II *Sorek.*

שׂוּשׂ, see שׂישׂ *rejoice.*

[**שֵׂחַ**] 1 n.[m.]—sf. שֵׂחוֹ—**thought, disposition, wish** or **plan** of Y. Am 4$_{13}$.

שׂחה 3 vb.—**Qal** 2 Ptc. שֹׂחֶה; inf. שְׂחוֹת—**1. swim** Is 25$_{11}$. **2.** ptc. as noun, **swimmer** Is 25$_{11}$.

Hi. 1 Impf. אַשְׂחֶה—**make swim, flood bed** Ps 6$_7$. → שָׂחוּ *swimming.*

שָׂחוּ 1 n.[m.] **swimming** Ezk 47$_5$. → שׂחה *swim.*

שְׂחוֹק 16 n.[m.]—שְׂחֹק—**1. laughingstock, object of ridicule** Lm 3$_{14}$. **2. laughter,** שְׂחֹק הַכְּסִיל *laughter of the fool* Ec 7$_6$. **3. pleasure** Pr 10$_{23}$. → שׂחק *laugh.*

שׂחט 1 vb.—**Qal** 1 + waw וָאֶשְׂחַט—**press out** grapes Gn 40$_{11}$.

שְׂחִיף 1 adj.—cstr. שְׂחִיף—perh. **panelled,** with wood Ezk 41$_{16}$.

שׂחק 36.4.3 vb. (byform of צחק, סחק)—**Qal** 18.3.3 Pf. שָׂחַק, שָׂחֲקוּ; impf. יִשְׂחַק; ptc. Si שוחק; inf. שְׂחוֹק—**1a. laugh at** (לְ or עַל), i.e. **mock** someone, of human being Ps 52$_8$, of Y. Ps 59$_9$. **b. smile at** (לְ) hunger, i.e. be unconcerned about it Jb 5$_{22}$. **2. laugh,** joyfully Ec 3$_4$, foolishly 1QS 7$_{14}$. **3. smile at** (לְ or אֶל) someone in pleasure Jb 29$_{24}$ Si 13$_6$. **4. perform to cause amusement, entertain** Jg 16$_{27}$.

Pi. 17.1 Pf. שִׂחַקְתִּי; impf. יְשַׂחֵק; ptc. מְשַׂחֶקֶת, מְשַׂחֵק, מְשַׂחֲקִים; inf. שַׂחֵק—**1. play, celebrate,** i.e. by dancing, singing, making music 1 S 18₇. **2. play (games),** of children Zc 8₅, animals Jb 40₂₀. **3a. rejoice in** (בְּ) world, of wisdom Pr 8₃₁. **b. rejoice, be happy,** of Ben Sira Si 51₁₈₍₁₁QPsᵃ₎, wisdom Pr 8₃₀. **4. jest, joke** Pr 26₁₉. **5. provide amusement for** (לְ) people Jg 16₂₅. **6. have a contest** 2 S 2₁₄. **7.** ptc. as noun, **merrymaker, reveller** Jr 15₁₇.

Hi. 1 Ptc. מַשְׂחִיקִים—**laugh at** (עַל) someone 2 C 30₁₀.

→ שְׂחוֹק *laughingstock, laughter,* מִשְׂחָק *(object of) laughter;* cf. סחק *laugh,* צחק *laugh.*

[שֵׂט] 1 n.[m.]—pl. שֵׂטִים—**swerver** Ho 5₂. → שׂוּט *fall away.*

שׂטה 6.1 vb. (byform of שׂוּט)—**Qal** 6.1 Pf. שָׂטִית; impf. יֵשְׂטְ, תִּשְׂטֶה; impv. שְׂטֵה—**1. go astray, sin, commit adultery** Nm 5₂₀. **2a. turn aside to, go astray in** defilement Nm 5₁₉. **b. turn aside to** (אֶל) way Pr 7₂₅. **3. turn away from** (מֵעַל) way Pr 4₁₅.

שׂטם 6.0.2 vb.—**Qal** 6.0.1 Impf. יִשְׂטְמֻנוּ; + waw וַיִּשְׂטֹם—**1. harass, persecute** someone Gn 49₂₃ Ps 55₄. **2. bear a grudge against** someone Gn 27₄₁.

Hi. 0.0.1 + waw וישטים—**accuse** someone 4QpsJubᵃ 2.1₁₀.

→ מַשְׂטֵם *hostility,* מַשְׂטֵמָה *hostility,* שִׂטְמָה *hatred.*

*[שִׂטְמָה] 0.0.1 n.f.—sf. שטמתו—**hatred** 1QM 14₉. → שׂטם *harass.*

שׂטן 6 vb.—**Qal** 6 Impf. יִשְׂטְנוּנִי; ptc. שֹׂטְנַי; inf. שִׂטְנוֹ—**1. be an adversary to** someone Zc 3₁. **2.** ptc. as noun, **adversary** Ps 109₂₀. → שָׂטָן *adversary, Satan,* שִׂטְנָה I *accusation.*

שָׂטָן 27.0.5 n.m. **1. supernatural adversary,** i.e. celestial figure, **a. Satan** Jb 1₆. **b.** angel of Y. Nm 22₂₂. **2. earthly adversary,** military, political **enemy** 1 S 29₄ 1 K 5₁₈, judicial **opponent, accuser** Ps 109₆. → שׂטן *be an adversary.*

שִׂטְנָה I 1 n.f. **accusation** Ezr 4₆. → שׂטן *be an adversary.*

שִׂטְנָה II 1 pl.n. **Sitnah.**

[שִׂיא] 1 n.m.—sf. שִׂיאוֹ—**1. pride, arrogance** Jb 20₆ (unless §2). **2. majesty, excellency** Jb 20₆. → נשׂא I *lift.*

שִׂיאֹן 1 pl.n. **Siyon.**

שׂיב 2.4 vb.—**Qal** 2.4 + waw וְשַׂבְתִּי; ptc. שָׂב, Si שבים—**1. be grey-haired, old** 1 S 12₂. **2.** ptc. as noun, **grey-haired one, elder** Si 8₉. → שֵׂיב *old age,* שֵׂיבָה *grey hair.*

[שֵׂיב] 1 n.[m.]—sf. שֵׂיבוֹ—**old age** 1 K 14₄. → שׂיב *be grey-haired, old.*

שֵׂיבָה 19.2.2 n.f.—cstr. שֵׂיבַת; sf. שֵׂיבָתִי—**1. grey hair, white hair** Pr 20₂₉. **2. old age** Ru 4₁₅ Si 6₁₈. **3. grey-haired, white-haired, elderly person** Lv 19₃₂. → שׂיב *be grey-haired, old.*

שִׂיג 1 n.[m.] **withdrawal, 1.** physical 1 K 18₂₇. **2.** physical and psychological Si 13₂₆.

שׂיד 2.0.1 vb.—**Qal** 2.0.1 + waw וְשַׂדְתָּ—**whitewash** stones with (בְּ) plaster Dt 27₂. → שִׂיד *lime, whitewash, plaster.*

שִׂיד 4.0.1 n.[m.] **lime, whitewash, plaster** Dt 27₂. → שׂיד *whitewash.*

שֵׂיֵהוּ, see שֶׂה *sheep, goat, flock.*

שֵׂיוֹ, see שֶׂה *sheep, goat, flock.*

שׂיח 20.1.13 vb.—**Qal** 18.1.8 Impf. תָּשִׂיחַ, יָשִׂיחַ; impv. שִׂיחַ, שִׂיחוּ; ptc. Q שחי; inf. שִׂיחַ—**1a. meditate upon** (בְּ) Y.'s word Ps 119₁₄₈. **b. ponder** thoughts Si 13₂₆. **2. converse with** (עִם) one's heart, i.e. with oneself Ps 77₇. **3a. tell of** (בְּ) Y.'s faithfulness 4QInstrᵈ 126.2₁₀. **b. proclaim** Y.'s majestic deeds Ps 145₅. **4. lament, complain in** (בְּ) bitterness Jb 7₁₁. **5. talk, gossip about** (בְּ) someone Ps 69₁₃. **6.** of teaching, **speak to** son Pr 6₂₂. **7.** abs., **speak** Jg 5₁₀. **8.** ptc. as noun, **one who meditates** on knowledge 1QH 9₃₅.

Pol. 2.0.5 Impf. יְשׂוֹחֵחַ—**1. meditate upon** (בְּ) Y.'s deeds Ps 143₅. **2. tell of** (בְּ) Y.'s mighty deed 1QS 10₁₆ (unless §1). **3. consider** generation Is 53₈ (or em. דּוֹרוֹ *his generation* to רִיבוֹ *his case*).

→ שִׂיחַ I *lament, talk, musing,* שִׂיחָה *meditation, discourse.*

שִׂיחַ I 14.6.2 n.m.—sf. שִׂיחִי—**1. lament, complaint** Jb 21₄; **anxiety** 1 S 1₁₆. **2. talk, conversation** Si 44₄. **3. prayer** Ps 104₃₄. **4. musing** 1 K 18₂₇. → שׂיח *ponder, tell, complain.*

שִׂיחַ II 4.0.1 n.[m.]—pl. שִׂיחִים—**bush, shrub, plant** Gn 2₅.

שִׂיחָה 3.3.2 n.f.—sf. שִׂיחָתִי—**1. meditation, study** Ps 119₉₇; **prayer, devotion** Jb 15₄. **2. discourse, wise conversation** Si 8₈. → שׂיח *ponder, tell, complain.*

שׂים 586.13.95.1 vb.—**Qal** 581.12.95.1 Pf. שָׂם; impf. יָשִׂים (יָשֵׂם);

+ waw וַיָּשֶׂם, וַיָּשִׂימוּ; impv. שִׂים, שִׂימָה, שִׂימוּ; ptc. שָׂם, שָׂמִים; pass. שִׂים; inf. abs. שׂוֹם; cstr. שׂוּם (שִׂים)—at times with ellip. of object (e.g. Gn 22_{6} 1 K 18_{23}). **1. put, place, a. (up)on, on top** (אֶל, בְּ, עַל), sandals on feet Ezk 24_{17}, crown on head Est 2_{17}, person on throne, i.e. make him king 2 K 10_{3}, **lay** hands on person, i.e. seize 2 K 11_{16}, **impose** labour Ex 5_{8}, payment 2 K 18_{14}, punishment Ps 66_{11}, **impute** fault, sin 1 S 22_{15}, **bestow** honour Ezk 16_{14}, **impress** words on mind Dt 11_{18}. **b. in** (בְּ), fruit in basket Dt 26_{2}, one's life in one's hand, i.e. risk it Jg 12_{3}, words in person's mouth, i.e. tell him what to say Ezr 8_{17}, **lay, store** words in heart, i.e. remember them Jb 22_{22}. **c. before, in front of** (לִפְנֵי, נֶגֶד, נֹכַח), altar before curtain Ex 40_{26}, Ephraim before Manasseh Gn 48_{20}. **d. underneath** (תַּחַת), rags under armpit Jr 38_{12}. **e. between** (בֵּין), torch between tails Jg 15_{4}. **f. in the midst of** (קֶרֶב, בְּתוֹךְ), corpses in the midst of city Ezk 11_{7}. **g. into** (without prep.), people into (military) division 1 S 11_{11}. **h. among** (בְּ), basket among rushes Ex 2_{3}. **i. at** (without prep.), altar at the entrance Ex 40_{29}. **j. through** (בְּ), rush through nose Jb 40_{26}. **k. behind** (אַחֲרֹנִים), person in second and third place Gn 33_{2}. **l. beside** (אֵצֶל, מִצַּד), book beside ark Dt 31_{26}. **m. on the side** (עַל + יֶרֶךְ, צֶלַע), lampstand on the south side Ex 40_{24}. **n. outside** (מִחוּץ לְ), table outside curtain Ex 26_{35}. **o. above** (מֵעַל), person's seat above officials, as sign of honour Est 3_{1}. **p. on high** (בְּ, לְ + מָרוֹם), lowly on high, i.e. elevate Jb 5_{11}. **q. together** (יַחַד), remnant together like sheep Mc 2_{12}. **2. set, set up, a. set up, install, put in place, fix, mount** curtain Ex 40_{21}, stumbling block 1QS 2_{12}, **pitch** tent Ps 19_{5}. **b. plant** tree Is 41_{19}. **c. set up** ambush against (לְ) city Jos 8_{2}. **d. post, station** soldiers in ambush Jos 8_{12}. **e. set** people to work 2 S 12_{31}. **f. set oneself up, take one's position** against (עַל) city of enemy 1 K 20_{12}. **g. set, put in position** pole Nm 4_{6}, bread of display 1 S 21_{7}. **h. set, serve** food Gn 43_{31}. **3. set, direct, a. set, direct, turn** sword against (בְּ) army Jg 7_{22}. **b. set** face, i.e. fix gaze 2 K 8_{11}. **c. set, fix** eyes on (עַל) someone Gn 44_{21}. **d. set, apply** mind, i.e. consider Hg 2_{15}, **lay, take** to (אֶל) heart 2 S 13_{33}. **4. set, establish, found, determine, ordain, a. establish, found,** i.e. secure its continuity, stability, obj. foundation 1QH 14_{26}, name Dt 12_{5}, descendants Ps 89_{30}. **b. set, establish** as authoritative, law, rule Ex 15_{25}. **c. set, determine, fix (as)** bounds Ps 104_{9}. **d. set** time Ex 9_{5}. **e. appoint, designate, ordain** place Ex 21_{13}, way Ezk 21_{24}. **f. destine** nation for (לְ) judgment Hb 1_{12}. **g. order** world Jb 34_{13}. **h. commit** cause to (אֶל) Y. Jb 5_{8}. **5. appoint as, appoint over, place over, make (into), a.** two objs., Absalom as judge 2 S 15_{4}. **b.** obj. + בְּ *into*, man into leader Dt 1_{13}. **c.** obj. + בְּ *over*, Manasseh over city 2 C 33_{14}. **d.** obj. + בְּ *through*, overseer through agency of priests 2 C 23_{18}. **e.** obj. + לְ *into, as*, Solomon as king 1 K 10_{9}. **f.** obj. + לְ *over*, Samuel over Israel 1 S 8_{5}. **g.** obj. + לְ introducing obj., all into captains 1 S 22_{7}. **h.** obj. + עַל *over*, king over Israel Dt 17_{14}. **i.** obj. + אֶל *over*, Benaiah over bodyguard 2 S 23_{23}. **j.** לְ introducing obj. + בְּ *over*, keeper over sanctuary Ezk 44_{8}. **k.** obj. + תַּחַת *instead*, Amasa instead of Joab 2 S 17_{25}. **6. make, transform, a. make (into), transform (into), turn (into),** (1) two objs., Most High into safe haven Ps 91_{9}. (2) obj. + לְ *into, as*, worshipper into object of contempt 1QH 10_{33}. (3) מִן partitive + לְ *into, as*, some days as days of counting, i.e. ordinary days Si 36_{9}. **b. make** desert like (כְּ) Eden Is 51_{3}. **c. make (of),** (1) obj. + לְ *of*, gate of stone Is 54_{12}. (2) two objs., hoofs of bronze 4QapPsB 46_{7}. **d. make, create,** river in (בְּ) desert Is 43_{19}. **e. make, set, kindle** fire 1 K 18_{23}. **f. make** a distinction between (בֵּין) people Ex 8_{19}. **g. make, prepare** grave Na 1_{14}. **h. make, ratify** covenant 2 S 23_{5}. **i. make an** end to (לְ) something, e.g. darkness Jb 28_{3}. **j. form** company Jb 1_{17}. **k.** perh. **produce offspring** Ezr 10_{44}. **l. perform, bring to pass, make happen** sign Ex 10_{2}, miracle Jr 32_{20}. **7. give, a. give, grant, leave** garment to (לְ) someone Is 61_{3}. **b. endow** someone **with** humility 4QBark[c] 1.2_{2}. **c. give** sense, i.e. make clear Ne 8_{8}. **8. give a name, make a name, a. name, give a name,** (1) two objs., name to Abraham Ne 9_{7}. (2) obj. + לְ *to*, name to Daniel Dn 1_{7}. **b. make a** name for oneself, i.e. win renown 2 S 7_{23}. **9. keep, preserve** remnant Gn 45_{7}; **keep inside, harbour** resentment Jb 36_{13}. **10. shed** blood 1 K 2_{5}. **11.** pass.,

a. be set in (בְּ) rock, of nest Nm 24_{21}. **b. be determined** as decree, of person's death 2 S 13_{32}. **12.** ptc. as noun, **a. the one who puts** holy spirit among (בְּקֶרֶב) people, in ref. to Y. Is 63_{11}. **b. one who presents** darkness as (לְ) light Is 5_{20}.

Qal Pass. 1 + waw וַיִּישֶׂם—**be put, placed in** (בְּ) coffin Gn 50_{26}.

Hi. 3.1 + waw וַהֲשִׂמֹתִיהוּ; impv. הָשִׂימִי; ptc. מֵשִׂים—**1. make** someone **into** (לְ) byword Ezk 14_{8}. **2. make** cause of contention **out of** (לְ) property Si 11_{30}. **3.** perh. **pay attention to,** מִבְּלִי מֵשִׂים *without (anybody) paying attention,* i.e. unnoticed Jb 4_{20}. **4.** perh. **turn,** of sword Ezk 21_{21}.

Ho. 1 Impf. Qr יוּשַׂם—**be put, set,** of food before (לִפְנֵי) person Gn $24_{33(Qr)}$.

→ תְּשׂוּמֶת *pledge, security;* cf. סִימָה *treasure.*

*שִׂימָה, see סִימָה *treasure.*

שׂישׂ 27.1.6 vb. (byform of סיס)—**Qal** 27.1.6 Pf. שָׂשׂ; impf. יָשִׂישׂוּ (יְשִׂישׂוּם); impv. שִׂישׂוּ; ptc. שָׂשׂ; inf. abs. שׂוֹשׂ; cstr. שׂוּשׂ—**1. rejoice in, take delight in, a.** בְּ *in,* + Y. Is 61_{10}. **b.** obj. Y.'s creation Is 65_{18}. **2. rejoice over** (עַל) Y.'s word Ps 119_{162}. **3. rejoice (greatly),** with intensifying cognate noun מָשׂוֹשׂ Is 66_{10}. **4. be happy, eager** to (לְ) do something Ps 19_{6}. **5.** abs., **be joyful, delighted** CD 20_{33}. **6.** ptc. as noun, **one who is glad** Is 64_{4}.

→ מָשׂוֹשׂ *joy,* שָׂשׂוֹן *joy.*

שֵׂךְ 1 n.[m.]—pl. שִׂכִּים—**thorn,** in eye Nm 33_{55}.

[שֹׂךְ] 1 n.[m.]—sf. שֻׂכּוֹ—**booth** Lm 2_{6}.

*שׂכה vb. **Qal, look out for** (לְ) someone Ps 35_{12} (if em. שְׁכוֹל לְנַפְשִׁי *to the forlornness of my soul* to שָׂכוּ לְנַפְשִׁי *they look out for me*). → מַשְׂכִּית I *image.*

[שֻׂכָּה] 1 n.f.—pl. שֻׂכּוֹת—**harpoon** Jb 40_{31}.

שֹׂכֹה, see שׂוֹכֹה *Socoh.*

שֶׂכוּ 1 pl.n. **Secu.**

שֶׂכְוִי I 1 n.[m.] **cock, rooster** Jb 38_{36}.

*שֶׂכְוִי II 1 n.[m.] **mind** Jb 38_{36}.

שֶׂכְוִי III 1 n.[m.] **mists** Jb 38_{36}.

*[שֶׂכְוִי] IV 0.0.0.1 pr.n.m. **Sechvi.**

שָׂכְיָה 1 pr.n.m. **Sachia.**

[שְׂכִיָּה] 1 n.f.—pl. cstr. שְׂכִיּוֹת—**ship** Is 2_{16}.

שַׂכִּין 1 n.[m.] **knife** Pr 23_{2}. → cf. סכין VII *cut.*

שָׂכִיר 18.3 adj.—cstr. שְׂכִיר; sf. שְׂכִירֵךְ; f.s. שְׂכִירָה; m.pl. sf. שְׂכִרֶיהָ—**1. hired,** of worker Si 37_{11}, animal Ex 22_{14}. **2.** as noun, **a. hired labourer** Lv 19_{13}. **b. hired soldier** Jr 46_{21}. **c. mercenary** Jr 46_{21}. → שׂכר *hire.*

שְׂכִירָה 1 n.f. **hiring** or **hired object,** תַּעַר הַשְּׂכִירָה *razor of hiring* or *a razor, a hired object* Is 7_{20} (unless שָׂכִיר *hired,* fem.). → שׂכר *hire.*

שׂכך 1 vb.—**Qal** 1 + waw וְשַׂכֹּתִי—with עַל of obj., **cover someone with one's hand** Ex 33_{22}. → מְשׂוּכָה *hedge.*

שׂכל I 60.7.96 vb. (byform of סכל, שׁכל)—**Qal** 1.0.1 Pf. שָׂכַל—**1. be prudent, wise** 1 S 18_{30} (unless §2). **2. be successful** 1 S 18_{30}.

Hi. 59.7.95 Pf. הִשְׂכִּיל, הִשְׂכִּילוּ; impf. תַּשְׂכִּיל (תַּשְׂכֵּל); impv. הַשְׂכִּילוּ; ptc. מַשְׂכִּיל, מַשְׂכֶּלֶת, מַשְׂכִּילִים; inf. abs. הַשְׂכֵּל; cstr. הַשְׂכִּיל.—**1a. (1) give insight to** (לְ or בְּ) someone Pr 21_{11} 4QapPsB 69_{7}. **(2) make wise, teach** someone CD 13_{7}. **b. teach, give insight into** something, with omission of person taught 1 C 28_{19}. **c.** abs., **make wise, give insight** Gn 3_{6}. **2a. understand** something Dt 32_{29}. **b. have insight in** (בְּ) wisdom Dn 1_{4}. **c.** with שֵׂכֶל as obj., **have insight into** (לְ) (service of) Y. 2 C 30_{22}. **3. be wise, prudent** Pr 19_{14}. **4a. ponder** miracle Ps 106_{7}. **b. give thought to** (בְּ or אֶל or לְ) truth Dn 9_{13}, word Ne 8_{13}, wisdom 4QapPsB 76_{8}. **5. look (around),** of eyes 4QWiles 1_{13}. **6a. have success in, a.** obj. everything Dt 29_{8}. **b.** לְ *in,* + undertaking 1 S 18_{14}. **7.** ptc. as noun, **a. one with understanding** Dn 11_{33}. **b. one who gives heed to** (עַל) instruction Pr 16_{20}. **c.** Qumran, **sage, teacher** 1QH 20_{11}. **d. one who has regard for** (אֶל) the poor Ps 41_{2}. **8.** inf. as noun, **understanding, wisdom, wise dealing** Pr 1_{3}.

→ שֵׂכֶל *intelligence,* מַשְׂכִּיל I *maskil,* III *instructive song.*

שׂכל II 1 vb.—**Pi.** 1 Pf. שִׂכֵּל—**lay hands crosswise** Gn 48_{14}. → מַשְׂכִּיל II *responsive song.*

שׂכל III, see סכל I *be foolish,* pi.

שֵׂכֶל 16.15.58 n.m.—שֶׂכֶל (שֵׂכֶל); cstr. שֵׂכֶל; sf. שִׂכְלוֹ; pl. sf. Q שכליך—**1. intelligence, wisdom** Si 11_{15}. **2. cunning, craftiness** Dn 8_{25} Si $35_{4(F)}$. **3. sense, meaning** Ne 8_{8}. **4. mind, disposition** 4QWays[a] 1a.2_{4}. **5. approbation, approval** Pr 3_{4}. → שׂכל *be wise, successful.*

שִׂכְלוּת, see סִכְלוּת *folly*.

שׂכר 20 vb. (byform of סכר)—**Qal** 17 Pf. שָׂכַר; impf. יִשְׂכְּרוּ; + waw וַיִּשְׂכֹּר; ptc. שֹׂכֵר; ptc. pass. שָׂכוּר; inf. abs. שָׂכֹר; cstr. שְׂכֹר—**1. hire** lover Gn 30$_{16}$, chariot 1 C 19$_{6.7}$. **2. hire** warriors against (עַל) people 2 K 7$_6$. **3.** pass., **be hired** to prophesy Ne 6$_{13}$.

Ni. 1 Pf. נִשְׂכָּרוּ—**hire oneself out** for (בְּ) bread 1 S 2$_5$.

Htp. 2 Ptc. מִשְׂתַּכֵּר—**1. hire oneself out** Hg 1$_6$. **2.** ptc. as noun, **one who hires himself out** Hg 1$_6$.

→ שָׂכָר I *wages, reward, fare,* שֶׂכֶר *wages, reward,* מַשְׂכֹּרֶת *recompense,* שָׂכִיר *hired,* שְׂכִירָה *hiring.*

שָׂכָר I 28.5.2 n.m.—cstr. שְׂכַר; sf. שְׂכָרִי—**1. wages,** שְׂכַר שָׂכִיר *wages of a hired labourer* Dt 15$_{18}$; **return** Ec 4$_9$; **recompense** Ec 9$_5$. **2. reward** from Y. Si 16$_{14}$. **3. fare** Jon 1$_3$. → שׂכר *hire.*

שָׂכָר II 2 pr.n.m. **Sacar.**

שֶׂכֶר 2 n.[m.]—cstr. שֶׂכֶר—**wages** Is 19$_{10}$; **reward** Pr 11$_{18}$. → שׂכר *hire.*

*[**שִׁלְּה**] 0.0.1 n.[f.]—cstr. שלת—**insolence** 4Q468i$_5$.

שְׂלָו 4 n.f.—pl. שַׂלְוִים—**quail(s)** Ex 16$_{13}$.

שַׂלְמָא 4 pr.n.m. **Salma.**

שַׂלְמָה I 16.0.3 n.f.—cstr. שַׂלְמַת; sf. שַׂלְמָתוֹ; pl. שְׂלָמוֹת; cstr. Q שלמות; sf. שַׂלְמֹתַיִךְ—**1. clothing, garment** Ca 4$_{11}$. **2. covering, wrapper, bed-clothes** 11QT 65$_{13}$. → cf. סַלְמָה *garment;* שִׂמְלָה *garment.*

שַׂלְמָה II 1 pr.n.m. **Salmah.**

שַׂלְמוֹן 1 pr.n.m. **Salmon.**

שַׂלְמַי 2 pr.n.m. **Salmai.**

שׂלק 3.3 vb.—**Ni.** 1 Pf. נִשְּׂקָה—**be kindled,** of fire Ps 78$_{21}$.

Hi. 2.3 Impf. יַשִּׂיק (Si Bmg יסיק); + waw וְהִשִּׂיקוּ—**1. make a fire** Is 44$_{15}$. **2.** of sun, **set ablaze, burn** mountain Si 43$_{21}$. **3. kindle sexual desire** Si 34$_{19(B)}$.

*[**שְׂלֻקַּי**] 0.0.0.1 pr.n.m. **Selukkai.**

[**שֵׂם**], see סַם *spice.*

שׂמאל 5.0.1 vb.—**Hi.** 5.0.1 Impf. אַשְׂמְאִילָה; impv. הַשְׂמִילִי; ptc. מַשְׂמְאלִים; inf. הַשְׂמִיל—**1. go to the left** Gn 13$_9$. **2. use the left hand** 1 C 12$_2$. → שְׂמֹאל *left,* שְׂמָאלִי *left.*

שְׂמֹאל 54.0.17 n.[m.]—שְׂמֹאול (Q סמל, Q סמול); cstr. שְׂמֹאל (שְׂמֹאול); sf. שְׂמֹאלוֹ, שְׂמֹאולָהּ—**1. left, left side, region on the left** Gn 13$_9$. **2. left hand** Pr 3$_{16}$, perh. also **left arm** Ca 2$_6$. **3. north** Ezk 16$_{46}$. → שׂמאל *go to the left.*

שְׂמָאלִי 9.0.3 adj.—f.s. שְׂמָאלִית—**1. left,** of hand Lv 14$_{15}$. **2.** as noun, in ref. to pillar, **left one** or **northern one** 2 C 3$_{17}$. → שׂמאל *go to the left.*

שׂמח 175.10.54 vb.—**Qal** 147.7.45 Pf. שָׂמַח (שָׂמֵחַ); impf. יִשְׂמַח; impv. שְׂמַח, שִׂמְחִי; ptc. שָׂמֵחַ, שְׂמֵחָה, שְׂמֵחִים; inf. שְׂמֹחַ—**1. rejoice,** in religious context, **a.** celebrate Y.'s redemption, support, blessings, etc., (1) abs. Ps 14$_7$. (2) בְּ *in,* + salvation 1 S 2$_1$. **b.** at religious gatherings, festivals, offerings, meals etc., (1) abs. 2 C 30$_{25}$. (2) בְּ *in,* + festival Dt 16$_{14}$. **c.** 'in' or 'before' Y., (1) בְּ *in,* + Y. Jl 2$_{23}$. (2) לִפְנֵי *before,* + Y. Lv 23$_{40}$. **2. rejoice, be happy, a.** abs. Pr 23$_{25}$. **b.** בְּ *in,* + dance Jr 31$_{13}$. **c.** with cognate noun as obj., שְׂמֵחִים שִׂמְחָה גְדוֹלָה *(they) were very happy* 1 K 1$_{40}$. **3. make merry** to (לְ) sound of flute Jb 21$_{12}$. **4a. get (sexual) pleasure** from (מִן) wife Pr 5$_{18}$. **b. find (sexual) enjoyment** in (בְּ) lover Ca 1$_4$. **5. rejoice maliciously** over (לְ) someone Ps 35$_{19}$. **6. be pleased, happy** with (בְּ) son Si 16$_{1(A).2}$. **7. radiate, shine,** of light Pr 13$_9$. **8.** ptc. as noun, **a. one who rejoices,** in religious context, [ש]מחי רצון *those who rejoice in favour* 4QPrFêtes^c 32$_3$. **b. one who is merry,** כָּל־שִׂמְחֵי־לֵב *all the merry-hearted ones* Is 24$_7$. **c. one who rejoices maliciously,** שְׂמֵחֵי רָעָתִי *those who rejoice maliciously at my misfortune* Ps 35$_{26}$. **9.** ptc. as adj., **joyful,** of mother Ps 113$_9$, heart Pr 15$_{13}$.

Pi. 27.3.9 Pf. שִׂמַּחְתָּ; impf. יְשַׂמַּח; impv. שַׂמַּח (שַׂמֵּחַ); ptc. מְשַׂמֵּחַ; inf. abs. שַׂמֵּחַ—**1. make happy, bring happiness to someone,** of Y. Is 56$_7$, husband Dt 24$_5$, precepts of Y. Ps 19$_9$, wine Ps 104$_{15}$. **2.** of Y., **make someone happy again,** i.e. after sorrow Jr 31$_{13}$. **3.** of Y., **cause someone to triumph** Ps 30$_2$. **4.** of wine, **make life enjoyable** Ec 10$_{19}$.

Hi. 1 Pf. הִשְׂמַחְתָּ—of Y., **cause enemy to triumph** Ps 89$_{43}$.

→ שִׂמְחָה *joy,* מִשְׂמָחָה *celebration.*

שִׂמְחָה 94.6.63 n.f.—Q סמחה; cstr. שִׂמְחַת; sf. שִׂמְחָתִי; pl. שְׂמָחוֹת—**1a. joy, jubilation,** expressed during religious festivals, sacrifices, etc. Nm 10$_{10}$; make **sacred festivity** Ne 8$_{12}$; **inward joy** Ps 4$_8$. **b. joy, jubilation** during coronation of a king as Y.'s representative 1 K 1$_{40}$. **2.**

joy, merriness, gaiety, pleasure, with no specif. religious connotation, **a.** positive, שמחת לבב הם חיי איש *joy of heart is the (very) life of a person* Si 30_{22}, **b.** negative, אִוֶּלֶת שִׂמְחָה לַחֲסַר־לֵב *folly is merriness to the person who lacks sense* Pr 15_{21}. **3. malicious joy, (hostile) triumph** Jb 20_5. **4. imposed joy, faked merriness,** sadistically enforced by enemy on subject Ps 137_3. **5. divine joy** experienced by Y. over his people Zp 3_{17}. **6.** perh. **Joy,** i.e. the one who gives joy, in ref. to Y. Ps 43_4. → שׂמח *rejoice.*

שְׂמִיכָה 1 n.f. **covering, rug** Jg 4_{18}. → cf. סמך *support.*

שׂמל, see שׂמאל *go to the left.*

שַׂמְלָה 4 pr.n.m. **Samlah.**

שִׂמְלָה 29.1 n.f.—cstr. שִׂמְלַת; sf. שִׂמְלָתוֹ; pl. שְׂמָלֹת; sf. שִׂמְלֹתָיו—**garment, mantle, clothing** Gn 45_{22} Dt 8_4, **bed-covering** Ex 22_{26}, **wrapper** for weapon 1 S 21_{10}. → cf. שַׂלְמָה *garment.*

שׂמם 2 vb. **Qal, paint the face, colour** 2 K 9_{30} (if em. וַתָּשֶׂם *and she put* to וַתָּשֶׂם *and she coloured*).

Hi. 2 Impf. יָשֵׂם—**coat, plaster** foot with (בְּ) chalk Jb 13_{27} 33_{11}.

שְׂמָמִית 1 n.f. **lizard** Pr 30_{28}.

שׂמר, see סמר *nail.*

שׂנא 146.19.57 vb.—**Qal** 129.18.48 Pf. שָׂנֵא, שָׂנֵאתִי; impf. יִשְׂנָא; impv. שִׂנְאוּ; ptc. שֹׂנֵא, שֹׂנְאֵי (שֹׂנְאָיו); ptc. pass. שְׂנוּאָה; inf. abs. שָׂנֹא; cstr. שְׂנֹא (שִׂנְאַת)—**1.** personal, **a. hate, loathe, dislike** someone Gn 37_4; specif. in silence, **bear a grudge against** someone 2 S 13_{22}; **take an aversion** to woman after sexual intercourse 2 S 13_{15}; **despise, shun** poor man Pr 19_7; **have enough of, be weary** of frequent guest Pr 25_{17}. **b. be at enmity** with (לְ) someone Dt 4_{42}. **2.** political, **show hostility toward** nation Ps 105_{25}. **3a. lack love for** child by withholding discipline Pr 13_{24}. **b. lack self-love** Pr 29_{24}. **4. detest, loathe** something, e.g. evil Si 15_{13}, life Ec 2_{17}. **5.** abs., **hate,** עֵת לִשְׂנֹא *there is a time for hating* Ec 3_8. **6.** pass., **a. be detested, hateful,** of Zion Is 60_{15}, pride Si 10_7. **b. be unloved,** of wife Gn 29_{31}. **7.** ptc. as noun, **a. one who hates, dislikes intensely** someone, i.e. **political enemy** 11QT 59_{11}, **personal enemy** Si 6_1, **enemy** of Y. CD 8_{18}, of Y.'s people Is 66_5. **b. one who hates, spurns** something, e.g. bribes Pr 15_{27}, the law Si 36_2, peace Ps 120_6. **8.** ptc. pass. as noun, **a. enemy,** i.e. **one hated, intensely disliked** 2 S $5_{8(Qr)}$. **b.** fem., **unloved wife** Pr 30_{23}.

Ni. 2.1.1 Impf. יִשָּׂנֵא—**1. be hated, disliked,** of man of intrigues Pr 14_{17}. **2. be shunned, despised,** of poor Pr 14_{20}.

Pi. 15.0.7 Ptc. מְשַׂנְאֶיךָ (Q מסנאיך)—ptc. as noun, **one who hates,** i.e. **political enemy** 2 S 22_{41}, **personal enemy** Jb 31_{29}, **enemy** of Y. Ps 68_2, of wisdom Pr 8_{36}, of righteousness 1QM 3_5.

Pu. 0.0.1 Ptc. משונאה—ptc. as noun, **one who is (continually) unloved, unloved wife** 4QapLamA 1.2_3.

→ שִׂנְאָה *hatred,* שָׂנִיא *unloved.*

שִׂנְאָה 17.0.3 n.f.—cstr. שִׂנְאַת; sf. שִׂנְאָתוֹ—**hatred, enmity, dislike,** for human beings, of Y. Dt 1_{27}, of murderer Nm 35_{20}, of foreign nations for Israel Ezk 23_{29}, of human beings in general Ec 9_6, **repulsion** towards woman after sexual intercourse 2 S 13_{15}. → שׂנא *hate.*

[שָׂנִיא] 1 adj.—f.s. שְׂנִיאָה—**unloved,** as noun, **unloved wife** Dt 21_{15}. → שׂנא *hate.*

שְׂנִיר 4 pl.n. **Senir.**

שְׂעִיפִּים, see שְׂעִפִּים *disquieting thoughts.*

שָׂעִיר I 53.0.21 n.m.—cstr. שְׂעִיר; pl. שְׂעִירִם; cstr. שְׂעִירֵי—**male goat** 11QT 26_{13}; in ref. to absolute ruler Dn 8_{21}. → cf. שְׂעִירָה *female goat.*

שָׂעִיר II 4.0.3 n.m.—pl. שְׂעִירִים—**goat-demon, satyr,** living in desolate places Is 13_{21}, images of deities Lv 17_7.

שָׂעִיר III 1 n.m.—pl. שְׂעִירִם—**rain drop** Dt 32_2.

שֵׂעִיר I 38.1.2 pr.n.m. **Seir.**

שֵׂעִיר* II 1 pl.n. **Seir.**

[שְׂעִירָה] I 2 n.f.—cstr. שְׂעִירַת—**female goat** Lv 4_{28}. → cf. שָׂעִיר *male goat.*

[שְׂעִירָה] II 1 pl.n. **Seirah.**

שְׂעִפִּים 2 n.m.pl.—sf. שְׂעִפַּי—**disquieting thoughts** Jb 4_{13}. → cf. שַׂרְעַפִּים *disquieting thoughts.*

שׂער I 3.0.1 vb.—**Qal** 3 Pf. שָׂעֲרוּ; impf. יִשְׂעֲרוּ; impv. שַׂעֲרוּ—**bristle, shudder with horror, 1.** trans., obj. שַׂעַר Ezk 27_{35}. **2.** intrans. Jr 2_{12}.

Hi. 0.0.1 + waw וישעירו—**behave in an appalling way** 4QapJoseph[b] 1_{13}.

→ שַׂעַר I *bristling;* cf. סער II *excite.*

שׂער II 4 vb. (byform of סער)—**Qal** 1 Impf. יִשְׂעָרֶנּוּ—of

Y., **whirl away (in a storm)** wicked Ps 58$_{10}$.

Ni. 1 Pf. נִשְׂעֲרָה—pf. 3fs, **be tempestuous** Ps 50$_3$.

Pi. 1 Impf. יְשָׂעֲרֵהוּ—of wind, **whirl away** wicked Jb 27$_{21}$.

Htp. 1 Impf. יִשְׂתָּעֵר—**storm out against** (עַל) enemy Dn 11$_{40}$.

→ שַׂעַר II *storm*, שְׂעָרָה *storm*.

שׂער III 1 vb.—**Qal** 1 Pf. שְׂעָרוּם—**be acquainted with** new god Dt 32$_{17}$.

שָׂעִר 2 adj.—f.pl. שְׂעִרֹת—**hairy,** of man Gn 27$_{11}$, hand Gn 27$_{23}$. → cf. שֵׂעָר *hair*, שַׂעֲרָה *hair*.

שַׂעַר I 3 n.[m.] **bristling, horror** Ezk 27$_{35}$. → שׂער I *bristle*.

שַׂעַר II 1 n.[m.] **storm** Is 28$_2$. → שׂער II *whirl away*; cf. סַעַר *tempest*.

שֵׂעָר 28.0.4 n.m.—cstr. שְׂעַר (שַׂעַר); sf. שְׂעָרֵךְ (שַׂעֲרֵךְ), שְׂעָרוֹ—**hair, 1.** of furry animal Zc 13$_4$. **2.** of human being, i.e. of skin Lv 13$_3$, head Ca 4$_1$, head and beard Ezr 9$_3$, legs perh. Is 7$_{20}$, genitals Ezk 16$_7$. → cf. שַׂעֲרָה *hair*, שָׂעִר *hairy*.

שַׂעֲרָה 7.0.1 n.f.—cstr. שַׂעֲרַת; sf. שַׂעֲרָתוֹ; pl. cstr. שַׂעֲרוֹת—**hair** Jb 4$_{15}$. → cf. שֵׂעָר *hair*, שָׂעִר *hairy*.

שְׂעָרָה 2 n.f. **storm,** as means of divine punishment Na 1$_3$. → שׂער II *whirl away*.

שְׂעֹרָה 32.0.2 n.f.—pl. שְׂעֹרִים—**barley** Ru 2$_{17}$.

שְׂעֹרִים 1.0.10 pr.n.m. **Seorim.**

שָׂפָה 176.7.62 n.f.—cstr. שְׂפַת; sf. שְׂפָתוֹ; du. שְׂפָתַיִם; cstr. שִׂפְתֵי; sf. שְׂפָתַי, שִׂפְתֵיהֶם; pl. cstr. שִׂפְתוֹת; sf. שִׂפְתוֹתָיו—**1. lip,** oft. as organ of speech, שִׂפְתֵי־צֶדֶק *truthful lips* Pr 16$_{13}$. **2. language,** שְׂפַת כְּנַעַן *language of Canaan*, i.e. Hebrew Is 19$_{18}$. **3. edge, rim, brim, brink, bank, shore, border,** שְׂפַת־כּוֹס *brim of a cup* 1 K 7$_{26}$, שְׂפַת הַיְאֹר *river-bank* Gn 41$_3$.

שׂפח 1 vb.—**Pi.** 1 + waw וְשִׂפַּח—of Y., **smite crown of head with scab** Is 3$_{17}$. → cf. סַפַּחַת *scab*, מִסְפַּחַת *scab*.

שׂפחת, see סַפַּחַת *scab*.

שְׂפִינָה, see סְפִינָה *ship*.

שָׂפָם 5 n.[m.]—sf. שְׂפָמוֹ—**moustache** 2 S 19$_{24}$.

שִׂפְמוֹת 1 pl.n. **Siphmoth.**

שׂפן 1 vb. (byform of ספן)—**Qal** 1 Ptc. pass. שְׂפוּנֵי—**cover,** ptc. pass. as noun, **covered thing** Dt 33$_{19}$.

שׂפק I 2 vb.—**Qal** 1 Impf. יִשְׂפּוֹק—with obj., **clap (in derision)** hands Jb 27$_{23}$.

Hi. 1 Impf. יַשְׂפִּיקוּ—without obj., **clap one's hands with** (בְּ) gentiles, i.e. trade with them Is 2$_6$.

→ cf. ספק I *clap*.

שׂפק II 1 vb. (byform of ספק V)—**Qal** 1 Impf. יִשְׂפֹּק—**be sufficient** 1 K 20$_{10}$. → שֶׂפֶק *sufficiency*.

[שֶׂפֶק] 1 n.[m.]—sf. שִׂפְקוֹ—**sufficiency** Jb 20$_{22}$. → שׂפק *be sufficient*; cf. סֶפֶק II *abundance*.

שַׂק 48.0.1 n.m.—sf. שַׂקּוֹ; pl. שַׂקִּים; sf. שַׂקֵּיהֶם—**1. sackcloth** Gn 37$_{34}$; מַחֲגֹרֶת שָׂק *girding of sackcloth* Is 3$_{24}$. **2. cloth, mourning-blanket,** וַיִּשְׁכַּב בַּשָּׂק *and he lay down in a mourning-blanket* 1 K 21$_{27}$. **3. sack,** שַׂקִּים ... לַחֲמוֹרֵיהֶם *sacks ... for their asses* Jos 9$_4$.

שׂקד 1 vb.—**Ni.** 1 Pf. נִשְׂקַד—**be bound,** of yoke Lm 1$_{14}$.

שׂקר I 1 vb.—**Pi.** 1 Ptc. מְשַׂקְּרוֹת—**ogle,** of eyes Is 3$_{16}$.

***שׂקר** II 1 vb.—**Pi.** 1 Ptc. מְשַׂקְּרוֹת—**paint eyes red** Is 3$_{16}$.

שַׂר 420.8.76.19 n.m.—cstr. שַׂר; pl. שָׂרִים; cstr. שָׂרֵי; sf. שָׂרָיו, שָׂרֵיהֶם—**1a. army commander** Nm 31$_{14}$. **b. officer** of soldiers protecting palace 1 K 14$_{27}$. **c. body-guard** protecting workmen Ne 4$_{10}$. **d. captain** of fortress Ne 7$_2$. **e. heavenly captain** Jos 5$_{14}$. **2.** in general, **prince, national leader, ruler, official,** oft. under king; specif. **court official, royal ambassador** 1 K 5$_{30}$. **3. royal domestic master, courtier, steward** Dn 1$_{10}$. **4. tribal chief, leader of clan** Jg 5$_{15}$. **5. ruler of district, provincial governor** Est 1$_3$. **6a. principal city governor** Jg 9$_{30}$. **b. city official** 2 C 29$_{20}$. **7. magistrate, arbiter** Ex 18$_{21}$. **8. religious leader, cultic overseer** 1 C 15$_{22}$. **9. notable** Ps 82$_7$. **10. person of authority, elder** Si 7$_{14}$. **11. warden of prison** Gn 39$_{21}$. **12. chief herdsman** Gn 47$_6$. **13. taskmaster** Ex 1$_{11}$. **14. music-master** 1 C 15$_{27}$. **15. leader of itinerants, vagabonds** 1 S 22$_2$, **leader of raiding bands** 2 S 4$_2$. **16. messianic ruler, Prince of Peace** Is 9$_5$ (שַׂר־שָׁלוֹם). **17. angelic prince,** i.e. **archangel** Michael Dn 12$_1$ (מִיכָאֵל הַשַּׂר הַגָּדוֹל). **18.** of Y., **Divine Prince** Dn 8$_{11}$, **chief of the gods** 1QH 18$_8$ (שר אלים). **19.** Qumran, **a. Prince of Light** 1QM 13$_{10}$ (שר מאור), **Prince of Lights** 1QS 3$_{20}$ (שר האורים). **b. Wicked Prince,** שר ממשלת רשעה *prince of the realm of wickedness* 1QM 17$_5$. **c. angelic prince** 4QShirShabb^b 6$_4$.

d. eschatological prince 4QPrEnosh 1.2₇. e. prince as honorary title for one who seeks Y. CD 6₆. f. angelic captain in eschatological battle, שר מלאכיו *captain of his angels* 4QMᵃ 1₃. → שׂרר I *rule*.

שַׂרְאֶצֶר 3 pr.n.m. **Sharezer.**

שׂרג 2.0.1 vb.—**Pi.** 0.0.1 Pf. שרגו—**weave crown** 4QapPsB 31₇.

Pu. 1 Impf. יְשֹׂרָגוּ—**be intertwined,** of sinews Jb 40₁₇.

Htp. 1 Impf. יִשְׂתָּרְגוּ—**be braided together,** of transgressions Lm 1₁₄.

→ שָׂרִיג *branch*; cf. שׂרך *interlace*.

שׂרד 1 vb.—**Qal** 1 Pf. שָׂרְדוּ—**escape** from (מִן) enemy Jos 10₂₀. → שָׂרִיד I *survivor*.

שְׂרָד I 4.0.1 n.[m.] **finely woven work** Ex 39₁.

*שְׂרָד II 4.0.1 n.[m.] **service** Ex 39₁.

שֶׂרֶד 1 n.[m.] **marker, stylus** Is 44₁₃.

*[שַׂרְדִּי] 0.0.1 gent. perh. **Sardite.**

שׂרה I 3.0.1 vb.—**Qal** 3.0.1 Pf. שָׂרִיתָ, שָׂרָה; + waw וַיָּשַׂר—**strive with** (אֵת or עִם or אֶל) God Ho 12₄, God and men Gn 32₂₉, angel Ho 12₅.

שׂרה II, see שׂרר *rule*.

שָׂרָה I 5.0.1 n.f.—cstr. שָׂרָתִי; pl. שָׂרוֹת; cstr. שָׂרוֹת; sf. שָׂרוֹתֶיהָ—**princess, queen, noble woman, lady,** of Persia and Media Est 1₁₈, in ref. to Zion Lm 1₁. → שׂרר I *rule*.

שָׂרָה II 38.0.2 pr.n.f. **Sarah.**

שְׂרוּג 5 pr.n.m. **Serug.**

שְׂרוֹךְ 2 n.[m.] **thong,** of sandal Is 5₂₇. → שׂרך *entwine*.

שְׂרוּקִים, see שֹׂרֵק II *vine-tendril*.

שֶׂרַח 3.0.1 pr.n.f. **Serah.**

שׂרט 3 vb.—**Qal** 2 Impf. יִשְׂרְטוּ; inf. abs. שָׂרוֹט—**1.** with שָׂרֶטֶת as obj., **make cuttings** in (בְּ) one's body, as mourning ritual Lv 21₅. **2. inflict a wound on oneself** Zc 12₃.

Ni. 1 Impf. יִשָּׂרֵטוּ—**inflict a wound on oneself** Zc 12₃.

→ שֶׂרֶט *cuttings*, שָׂרֶטֶת *cuttings*.

שֶׂרֶט 1 n.[m.] **cuttings** Lv 19₂₈. → שׂרט *make cuttings*.

[שָׂרֶטֶת] 1.0.1 n.f.—שָׂרֶטֶת—**cuttings** Lv 21₅. → שׂרט *make cuttings*.

שָׂרַי 17 pr.n.f. **Sarai.**

*[שָׂרִיאֵל] 0.0.1 pr.n.m. **Sariel.**

[שָׂרִיג] 3.0.2 n.m.—pl. שָׂרִגִים (שָׂרִיגִם); sf. שָׂרִיגֶיהָ—**branch,** of vine Gn 40₁₀, fig-tree Jl 1₇. → שׂרג *intertwine*.

שָׂרִיד I 28.1.2 n.m.—pl. שְׂרִידִים; cstr. שְׂרִידֵי; sf. שְׂרִידָיו—**1. survivor, refugee, remnant,** יי׳ צְבָאוֹת הוֹתִיר לָנוּ שָׂרִיד כִּמְעָט *Y. of hosts left to us a small remnant* Is 1₉, לֹא הָיָה בְּיוֹם אַף־יי׳ פָּלִיט וְשָׂרִיד *there will be no fugitive or survivor in the day of Y.'s wrath* Lm 2₂₂. **2. that which escapes, is left,** שָׂרִיד בְּאָהֳלוֹ *that which is left in his tent* Jb 20₂₆. → שׂרד *escape*.

שָׂרִיד II 2 pl.n. **Sarid.**

שְׂרָיָה 20.0.1.7 pr.n.m. **Seraiah.**

שִׂרְיֹן 2 pl.n. **Sirion.**

[שָׂרִיק] 1 adj.—pl. שְׂרִיקוֹת—**combed,** of flax Is 19₉. → שׂרק I *comb*.

שׂרך 1 vb.—**Pi.** 1 Ptc. מְשָׂרֶכֶת—**interlace, entwine tracks,** בִּכְרָה קַלָּה מְשָׂרֶכֶת דְּרָכֶיהָ *a shift camel interlacing her tracks,* i.e. running aimlessly Jr 2₂₃. → שְׂרוֹךְ *thong*; cf. שׂרג *weave*.

שַׂר־סְכִים 1 pr.n.m. **Sarsechim.**

*[שַׂרְמֶלֶךְ] 0.0.0.2 pr.n.m. **Sarmelech.**

שׂרע 3 vb.—**Qal** 2 Ptc. pass. שָׂרוּעַ—**pass., be over-developed,** i.e. of limbs, members Lv 21₁₈.

Htp. 1 Inf. cstr. הִשְׂתָּרֵעַ—**stretch oneself out** Is 28₂₀.

[שַׂרְעַפִּים] 2 n.[m.]pl.—cstr. שַׂרְעַפַּי (שַׂרְעַפַּי)—**disquieting thoughts,** doubts Ps 94₁₉, secrets Ps 139₂₃. → cf. שְׂעִפִּים *disquieting thoughts*.

שׂרף 117.1.11 vb. (byform of סרף)—**Qal** 102.1.10 Pf. שָׂרַף, שְׂרַפְתִּי; impf. יִשְׂרֹף; ptc. שֹׂרֵף, שֹׂרְפִים; ptc. pass. שְׂרוּפָה, שְׂרוּפוֹת, שְׂרֻפִים; inf. abs. שָׂרוֹף; cstr. שְׂרֹף (שָׂרְפוֹ)—**1. burn objects, food, animals, usu. to destroy** Lv 13₅₂. **2. burn wood for fuel** Is 44₁₆. **3a. burn (alive)** human being Lv 20₁₄ Is 47₁₄. **b. sacrifice human being to** (לְ) a deity 2 K 17₃₁. **c. consume, destroy young man** Si 9₄ (ישׂ[ר]פך; unless §9). **4. cremate corpse, skin, flesh** 1 S 31₁₂, bones 1 K 13₂. **5. fire, bake bricks** Gn 11₃. **6a.** with שְׂרֵפָה as obj., **kindle fire** Lv 10₆. **b.** without obj., **make a fire,** perh. **burn spices, burn incense,** as funeral ritual Jr 34₅. **7.** appar. **cause city to be burned** Jr 38₂₃. **8. make young man burn with passion** Si 9₄ (ישׂ[ר]פך; unless §3c). **9.** pass., **be burned,** i.e. be destroyed, of city 1 S 30₃. **10.** ptc. as noun, **one** who burns (refuse of) animal Nm 19$_8$. 11. ptc. pass. as noun, a. **one who is burned** Nm 17$_4$. b. **flame** 4QNarrA 1$_5$.

Ni. 14.0.1 Impf. יִשָּׂרֵף—1. **be burned,** usu. in order to be destroyed, of object, food, animal 1 C 14$_{12}$. 2. **be burned (alive),** of human being Gn 38$_{24}$.

Pu. 1 Pf. שֹׂרַף—**be burned,** of goat Lv 10$_{16}$.

→ שְׂרֵפָה *incineration,* שֶׂרֶף *fire,* שָׂרָף I *venomous snake,* II *saraph,* מִשְׂרָפָה *burning.*

שָׂרָף I 4.0.3 n.m.—pl. שְׂרָפִים—**venomous snake,** perh. **cobra,** living Nm 21$_6$, in bronze Nm 21$_8$.

[שָׂרָף] II 2 n.m. **seraph,** winged supernatural being Is 6$_6$. → שׂרף *burn.*

שָׂרָף III 1 pr.n.m. **Saraph.**

*[שֶׂרֶף] 0.0.1 n.[m.] **fire** 4QD^b 6$_6$. → שׂרף *burn.*

שְׂרֵפָה 13.0.5 n.f.—cstr. שְׂרֵפַת; sf. Q שרפתה—**incineration** Gn 11$_3$, **funeral pyre** 2 C 16$_{14}$, **fire-debris, burnt place** Nm 17$_2$. → שׂרף *burn.*

שׂרק I vb. **Qal, comb** Is 19$_9$ (if em. שְׂרִיקוֹת *combed,* from שָׂרִיק, to שֹׂרְקוֹת or שֹׂרְקִים *combing*). → שָׂרִיק *combed.*

*שׂרק II 0.2 vb.—**Hi.** 0.2 Ptc. משריק, משרקת—**shine brightly, sparkle,** of moon Si 43$_{9(M)}$; perh. **shed a red glow,** of sun Si 50$_7$. → שָׂרֹק I *sorrel,* II *vine-tendril,* שֹׂרֵק I *choice vines,* שֹׂרֵקָה *choice vine.*

[שָׂרֹק] I 1 adj.—pl. שְׂרֻקִּים—**sorrel, brown,** of horse Zc 1$_8$. → שׂרק II *shine brightly.*

[שָׂרֹק] II 1 n.[m.]—pl. sf. שְׂרוּקֶּיהָ—**vine-tendril** Is 16$_8$. → שׂרק II *shine brightly.*

שֹׂרֵק I 2 n.[m.] **choice vines** Is 5$_2$. → שׂרק II *shine brightly.*

שֹׂרֵק II 1 pl.n. **Sorek.**

*שֹׂרֵק III 0.0.0.2 pr.n.m. **Sorek.**

שֹׂרֵקָה 1 n.f. **choice vine** Gn 49$_{11}$. → שׂרק II *shine brightly.*

שׂרר I 7.1.4 vb.—**Qal** 4.0.3 Pf. Q סרות; impf. יָשֹׂרוּ; + waw וַיָּשַׂר; ptc. שֹׂרֵר—**rule, reign, act as prince** Pr 8$_{16}$.

Hi. 1 Pf. הֵשִׂירוּ—abs., **appoint a ruler** Ho 8$_4$.

Htp. 2.1.1 Impf. תִּשְׂתָּרֵר, Si תסתורה—**make oneself a prince or ruler** Nm 16$_{13}$.

→ שַׂר *commander,* שָׂרָה I *princess,* מְשׂוֹרָה *government,* מִשְׂרָה *government.*

שׂרר II, see שׂור II *saw apart.*

שָׂשׂוֹן 22.3.1 n.m.—שָׂשֹׂן; cstr. שְׂשׂוֹן—**joy, gladness, happiness** Is 12$_3$; **merriment, gaiety** Is 22$_{13}$. → שׂישׂ *rejoice.*

שֵׂת, see שְׂאֵת *uprising.*

שׂתם 1 vb.—**Qal** 1 Pf. שָׂתַם—1. of Y., **shut out, silence** prayer Lm 3$_{8(MT)}$ (mss סתם). 2. of Y., **shut off (the ear) from** (מִן) prayer Lm 3$_8$ (if em. תְּפִלָּתִי *my prayer* to מִתְּפִלָּתִי *from my prayer*). → cf. סתם *stop up.*

שׂתר 1 vb.—**Ni.** 1 + waw וַיִּשָּׂתְרוּ—**burst open, break out,** of boil 1 S 5$_9$.

שׁ

שׁ I, see שֹׁמְרוֹן *Samaria.*

שׁ II, see שֶׁקֶל *shekel.*

שׁ III, see שָׁנָה *year.*

-שֶׁ 139.2.251.7 part.—שֶׁ (שָׁ, שְׁ, Q שי, Q שא, Q שה)—alternative form of אֲשֶׁר, alw. attached to following word; usu. שֶׁ or שַׁ with doubling of the following consonant, שָׁ or שֶׁ if doubling is not permitted, once שֶׁ before ה (Ec 3$_{18}$); in MT mostly used in later documents, esp. Ec (68 t) and Ca (32 t). 1. as rel. pron., a. **which, that, who,** שֶׁ subj. of rel. clause, דויד שהיא איש חסדים *David who was a man of good deeds* 4QMMT C$_{25}$, כל שבו *everything that is in it* Mur 30 1$_4$. b. **which, that, whom,** שֶׁ obj. of rel. clause, מקצת מעשי התורה שחשבנו לטוב *some of the works of the law which we consider beneficial* 4QMMT C$_{27}$. c. שֶׁ + possessive pron., **whose,** אַשְׁרֵי הָעָם שֶׁיְ׳ אֱלֹהָיו *happy are the people whose God is Y.* Ps 144$_{15}$. 2. as noun, without explicit antecedent, a. in ref. to person, **the one who(m), the one whose,**

those who(m), אשרי שימצא כבוד בחפצי רצונך *happy is the one who finds honour in the desires of your will* GnzPs 3₁; as voc., **you whom,** הַגִּידָה לִּי שֶׁאָהֲבָה נַפְשִׁי *tell me, you whom my life loves,* i.e. I love Ca 1₇. **b.** in ref. to thing, **that which,** אל תתן שלך לאחר *do not give that which belongs to you to another* Si 30₂₈. **3.** as conj., **a. that,** וְעָשִׂיתָ לִּי אוֹת שָׁאַתָּה מְדַבֵּר עִמִּי *then show me a sign that it is you who is speaking with me* Jg 6₁₇. **b. because, since,** שֶׁאֲנִי שְׁחַרְחֹרֶת do not look at me, *because I am dark of skin* Ca 1₆. **c. when,** אִי־לָךְ אֶרֶץ שֶׁמַּלְכֵּךְ נָעַר *woe to you, O land, when your king is a child* or *lackey* Ec 10₁₆. **4.** שֶׁ or שַׁ in compounds, **a.** שֶׁל **of,** אחד של אדם *one (face) of a human* 4QpsEzekª 6₉. **b.** בְּשֶׁלִּי **on my account,** בְּשֶׁלִּי הַסַּעַר הַגָּדוֹל הַזֶּה עֲלֵיכֶם I know that *on my account this great storm is upon you* Jon 1₁₂. **c.** עַד שֶׁ **until (that), while,** עַד שֶׁיְּחָנֵּנוּ our eyes look to Y. our God *until he has mercy on us* Ps 123₂, עַד־שֶׁהַמֶּלֶךְ בִּמְסִבּוֹ *while the king was at his table* Ca 1₁₂. **d.** כְּשֶׁ **as (when),** עָרוֹם יָשׁוּב לָלֶכֶת כְּשֶׁבָּא *naked will he depart again, as when he came* Ec 5₁₄. → אֲשֶׁר *which, that, who.*

שׁאב 19.0.2 vb.—**Qal** 19.0.2 Impf. אֶשְׁאָב; impv. שַׁאֲבִי; ptc. שֹׁאֵב, שֹׁאֲבֹת; inf. cstr. שְׁאֹב—**1. draw water, a.** obj. מַיִם 1 S 7₆. **b.** without obj. Gn 24₁₉. **2.** ptc. as noun, **one who draws water** Jos 9₂₁. → מַשְׁאָב perh. *watering hole.*

שׁאג 20.0.2 vb.—**Qal** 20.0.2 Pf. שָׁאַג, שָׁאֲגוּ; impf. יִשְׁאַג; ptc. שֹׁאֵג, שֹׁאֲגִים; inf. abs. שָׁאֹג—**1. roar,** of Y. Ho 11₁₀, enemy Ps 74₄, lion Jr 2₁₅ (at [עַל] Israel). **2. groan,** out of anguish Ps 38₉. → שְׁאָגָה *roaring, groaning.*

שְׁאָגָה 7 n.f.—cstr. שַׁאֲגַת; sf. שַׁאֲגָתִי; pl. sf. שַׁאֲגֹתָי—**1. roaring** of lion Zc 11₃. **2. groaning** of person feeling deserted by Y. Ps 22₂. → שׁאג *roar, groan.*

שׁאה I 4 vb.—**Qal** 1 Pf. שָׁאוּ—**be desolate,** of city Is 6₁₁.

Ni. 1 Impf. תִּשָּׁאֶה—**be ruined,** of ground Is 6₁₁.

Hi. 2 Inf. cstr. לְהַשְׁוֹת—**lay waste** city 2 K 19₂₅.

→ שְׁאִיָּה *ruin,* שׁאת *onrush, devastation,* (?) שְׁאוֹל *Sheol,* שָׁאוֹן II *wasteland,* שׁוֹא *onslaught,* שׁוֹאָה *disaster.*

שׁאה II 1 vb.—**Htp.** 1 Ptc. מִשְׁתָּאֵה—**gaze at** (לְ) someone Gn 24₂₁.

*שׁאה III 2 vb.—**Ni.** 2 Impf. יִשָּׁאוּן—**roar, rage,** of nations Is 17₁₂.₁₃. → שָׁאוֹן I *roaring, uproar,* תְּשֻׁאָה *shouting.*

שָׁאָה, see שׁוֹאָה *disaster; ruin.*

שָׁאוָה, see שׁוֹאָה *disaster; ruin.*

שְׁאוֹל 65.8.21 n.m.&f.—שְׁאֹל—**Sheol, abode of the dead,** place of peaceful rest 1 K 2₆, place without enjoyment Si 14₁₂, belly of fish Jon 2₃; **Sheol** as monster swallowing up sinful people Is 5₁₄. → (?) שׁאה I *be desolate.*

שָׁאוּל 406.0.4.5 pr.n.m. **Saul, Shaul.**

שָׁאוּלִי 1 gent. **Shaulite.**

שָׁאוֹן I 18.1.3 n.m.—cstr. שְׁאוֹן; sf. שְׁאוֹנָהּ—**1. roaring, roar** of water Is 17₁₂, **uproar, noise, tumult,** of army 1QH 10₂₇, of revellers Is 24₈. **2.** in ref. to Pharaoh Neco, **loud noise, braggart** Jr 46₁₇. → שׁאה III *roar.*

*שָׁאוֹן II 1.0.1 n.[m.] **wasteland** Ps 40₃. → שׁאה I *be desolate.*

*שָׁאוֹן III 1 pl.n. **Shaon.**

שְׁאָט 3 n.[m.]—cstr. שְׁאָט—**contempt,** בְּכָל־שָׁאטְךָ בְּנֶפֶשׁ *with every contempt in your heart* Ezk 25₆. → שׁוט II *despise.*

שְׁאִיָּה 1 n.f. **ruin** Is 24₁₂. → שׁאה I *be desolate.*

שְׁאִיהֶם, see שׁוֹא *ravage.*

שְׁאִירִית, see שְׁאֵרִית *remnant, rest.*

שׁאל 172.6.29.2 vb.—**Qal** 163.5.19.2 Pf. שָׁאַל, שְׁאִלְתִּי (שְׁאֶלְתִּיו), שְׁאֶלְתֶּם (שְׁאִלוּנוּ, שְׁאֵלוֹ) שְׁאֵלוּ; impf. יִשְׁאַל; impv. שְׁאַל, שְׁאָלוּ, שְׁאֵלָה; ptc. שֹׁאֵל, שֹׁאֶלֶת, שֹׁאֲלִים; ptc. pass. שָׁאוּל; inf. abs. שָׁאוֹל; cstr. שְׁאֹל—**1a. ask, inquire, interrogate** person, (1) two objs., שֹׁאֵל אֲנִי אֹתְךָ דָּבָר *I want to ask you something* Jr 38₁₄. (2) obj. person + עַל *about,* וָאֶשְׁאָלֵם עַל־הַיְּהוּדִים *and I asked them about the Jews* Ne 1₂. (3) לְ *regarding,* וַיִּשְׁאֲלוּ אִישׁ־לְרֵעֵהוּ לְשָׁלוֹם *then they asked each other regarding (their) welfare,* i.e. greeted each other Ex 18₇. (4) obj. thing, reply, opinion, וְנִשְׁאֲלָה אֶת־פִּיהָ *and we will ask her opinion* Gn 24₅₇. (5) abs., **make inquiries,** וַיִּשְׁאַל וַיֹּאמֶר אֵיפֹה שְׁמוּאֵל וְדָוִד *then he made inquiries and said, 'Where are Samuel and David?'* 1 S 19₂₂. **b.** with בְּ of obj., **consult deity,** idol, oracle, ghost, וַיִּשְׁאַל דָּוִד בַּי״ *then David consulted Y.* 1 S 23₂. **2a. ask for** Jos 15₁₈, **pray for** 1 S 1₂₀, **beg for** Lm 4₄, **desire** Ec 2₁₀, **require, demand** Ps 137₃, (1) obj. + מִן *of,* מֵי״ שְׁאִלְתִּיו *I have asked him of Y.* 1 S 1₂₀. (2) two objs., שְׁאֵלוּנוּ שׁוֹבֵינוּ דִּבְרֵי־שִׁיר *our captors required of us songs* Ps 137₃. (3) without obj., מִן *of,*

שָׁאַל מִמֶּנִּי וְאֶתְּנָה גוֹיִם נַחֲלָתֶךָ *ask of me and I will make the nations (into) your inheritance* Ps 2₈. (4) obj. cognate noun + מִן *of*, אֶשְׁאֲלָה מִכֶּם שְׁאֵלָה *I have a request to make of you* Jg 8₂₄. (5) abs., **make a request** or **petition** 1 K 2₂₀, **beg** Pr 20₄, **give orders,** וַיִּשְׁאַל וַיָּשִׂימוּ לוֹ לֶחֶם *then he gave orders and they set food before him* 2 S 12₂₀. **b. ask for temporary use,** i.e. **borrow,** כִּי־יִשְׁאַל אִישׁ מֵעִם רֵעֵהוּ *when a man borrows from his neighbour* Ex 22₁₃. **3. seek (for), concern oneself (with),** שאל לשלמך ״ *may Y. seek for your welfare* Arad ost. 18₂. **4.** ptc. pass., **a. be lent,** perh. **be given, be granted,** הוּא שָׁאוּל לַי״ *he* (Samuel) *will be given to* Y. 1 S 1₂₈. **b. be borrowed,** הוּא שָׁאוּל *it* (axe) *was borrowed* 2 K 6₅. **5.** ptc. as noun, **one who consults,** שֹׁאֵל אוֹב *one who consults a ghost,* i.e. necromancer Dt 18₁₁. **6.** ptc. pass. fem. as noun, **request, begging,** שאולות דל *requests of the poor* Si 4₄.

Ni. ₅.₀.₁₀ Pf. נִשְׁאַל; inf. abs. נִשְׁאֹל—**1. be questioned, interrogated,** ישאל אל המשפט *he will be interrogated concerning precept(s)* 1QS 7₂₁. **2. ask permission,** נִשְׁאֹל נִשְׁאַל *David earnestly asked permission* 1 S 20₆.

Pi. ₂ Impf. יְשָׁאֲלוּ; + waw וְשִׁאֲלוּ—**1. inquire carefully,** שָׁאוֹל יְשָׁאֲלוּ *let them inquire carefully* 2 S 20₁₈. **2. beg,** וְשִׁאֲלוּ *and may they beg!* Ps 109₁₀.

Pu. ₀.₁ Ptc. משואל—ptc. as noun, **one who is pledged, consecrated** Si 46₁₃.

Hi. ₂ Pf. הִשְׁאִלְתִּהוּ; + waw וַיַּשְׁאִלוּם—**1. give on request,** וַיַּשְׁאִלוּם *and they gave to them on request* Ex 12₃₆. **2. treat as having been requested,** perh. **consecrate,** הִשְׁאִלְתִּהוּ לַי״ *I have consecrated him to Y.* 1 S 1₂₈.

→ מִשְׁאָלָה *request,* שְׁאֵלָה I *request.*

שְׁאָל ₁.₀.₀.₅ pr.n.m. **Sheal.**

שְׁאֵלָה I ₁₄.₃.₄ n.f.—sf. שְׁאֵלָתִי (שֶׁאֱלָתִי), שְׁאֵלָתֵךְ (שֶׁלָתֵךְ)—**request, plea, petition, wish, prayer** for godliness GnzPs 3₄, atonement 11QPsª 24₄.₁₄, wife 1 K 2₁₆; **begging** Si 40₃₀. → שאל *ask.*

***[שְׁאָלָה]** II ₀.₀.₀.₂ pr.n.m. **Sheelah.**

שְׁאַלְתִּיאֵל ₉ pr.n.m. **Shealtiel.**

שאן ₅ vb.—**Pal.** ₅ Pf. שַׁאֲנַן—**be at ease** Jr 48₁₁. → שַׁאֲנָן *at ease.*

שְׁאָן, see בֵּית־שְׁאָן *Beth-shean.*

שַׁאֲנָן ₁₀ adj.—m. pl. שַׁאֲנַנִּים; f.pl. שַׁאֲנַנּוֹת—**1. at ease, carefree, complacent,** of nation Zc 1₁₅, woman Is 32₉. **2. quiet, peaceful, undisturbed,** of habitation Is 33₂₀. **3.** as noun, **a. one at ease, carefree** Jb 12₅. **b. arrogance** 2 K 19₂₈. → שאן *be at ease.*

שאף I ₁₄.₀.₂ vb.—**Qal** ₁₄.₀.₂ Pf. שָׁאֲפָה; impf. יִשְׁאַף; ptc. שׁוֹאֵף—**1a.** trans., **pant for, snuff up wind,** of ass Jr 2₂₄. **b.** intrans., **pant, gasp (for air),** like woman in labour, of Y. Is 42₁₄. **2a.** trans., **pant after, long for** shadow Jb 7₂. **b.** abs., **pant with desire** Ps 119₁₃₁. **3. swallow up** someone Ps 56₂. **4.** ptc. as noun, **a. one who pants** Am 2₇. **b. one who swallows up** Ps 57₄.

שאף II ₆.₀.₂ vb. (byform of שׁוּף I)—**Qal** ₆.₀.₂ Pf. שְׁאָפַנִי, שָׁאֲפוּ; ptc. שֹׁאֲפִי; inf. abs. שָׁאֹף—**1. trample (upon), crush** someone Ps 56₂. **2.** ptc. as noun, **one who tramples (upon)** 4QpsHodB 3₇.

שאר ₁₃₃.₁.₁₃ vb.—**Qal** ₁ Pf. שָׁאַר—**remain** at home 1 S 16₁₁.

Ni. ₉₄.₁.₁₀ Pf. נִשְׁאַר, נִשְׁאֲרָה; impf. יִשָּׁאֵר, יִשָּׁאֲרוּ; + waw וַיִּשָּׁאֵר; ptc. נִשְׁאָר, נִשְׁאֶרֶת, נִשְׁאָרִים—**1. remain (over), be left (over), escape, survive** from among (מִן) captives Ne 1₂, clan Jr 8₃, among (בְּ) nations Dt 4₂₇. **2. remain, be left behind, stay back** in (בְּ) camp Nm 11₂₆. **3.** ptc. as noun, **a. one who remains, is left, survives, escapes** Hg 2₃. **b. that which remains, is left over, has been reserved** 1 S 9₂₄.

Hi. ₃₈.₀.₃ Pf. הִשְׁאִיר; impf. יַשְׁאִיר, נַשְׁאֵר; inf. הַשְׁאִיר—**1. leave over, spare remnant,** of Y. CD 1₄, plants, of hail Ex 10₁₂. **2. preserve people alive,** of city Am 5₃. **3. leave behind** people, of king 2 K 25₂₂, gift of blessing, of Y. Jl 2₁₄. **4. keep over** from (מִן) unleavened bread Nm 9₁₂.

→ שְׁאָר *rest, remnant,* שְׁאֵרִית *remnant, rest;* cf. תְּשׁוּרָה III *residue.*

שְׁאָר ₂₆.₀.₉ n.m.—cstr. שְׁאָר—**1. remnant, those who are left,** of Israel and Judah Is 10₂₂, Moab Is 16₁₄; **rest, remainder,** of people, i.e. **the others** 1QS 6₈, of provinces Est 9₁₂, of trees Is 10₁₉; **residue of spirit** Ml 2₁₅. **2. posterity** Is 14₂₂. **3. vestige, last traces** of Baal Zp 1₄. → שאר *remain.*

שְׁאֵר ₁₆.₇.₁₀ n.m.—cstr. שְׁאֵר (Q שיר); sf. שְׁאֵרִי—**1. flesh,** in ref. to blood-relation, i.e. **(close) relative(s), (next**

of) kin, שְׁאֵר בְּשָׂרוֹ *flesh of his flesh,* i.e. his own flesh and blood Lv 18_{6}, שַׁאֲרָה הֵנָּה *they are her close relatives* Lv 18_{17} (if em. שְׁאֵרָה). **2. body** Si 7_{24}. **3. flesh** as food, i.e. **meat,** of animal Ex 21_{10}, human Mc 3_{2}. **4. self** Pr 11_{17}. → cf. שְׁאֵר II *flesh.*

שֶׁאֱרָה I 1 pr.n.f. **Sheerah.**

שֶׁאֱרָה II, see אֻזֵּן שֶׁאֱרָה *Uzzen-sheerah.*

שְׁאָר יָשׁוּב 1 pr.n.m. **Shear-jashub.**

שְׁאֵרִית 66.1.24 n.f.—cstr. שְׁאֵרִית (שֵׁרִית); sf. שְׁאֵרִיתֵךְ—**1. remnant, people who are left,** oft. specif. **survivors** Jr 44_{7}; **rest, remainder,** i.e. **the others** 1 C 12_{39}. **2. remainder, descendants, successors** 2 S 14_{7}. **3.** of things, **remainder, rest, residue,** of wood Is 44_{17}, Y.'s wrath Ps 76_{11}. → שׁאר *remain.*

שְׁאֵת 1.1 n.f. **devastation** Lm 3_{47}. → שׁאה I *be desolate.*

שְׁבָא 23 pr.n.m. **Sheba.**

שְׁבָאִים 1 gent. **Sabaeans.**

***שׁבב** vb. **Qal, cut down** pride, of Y. Na 2_{3} (if em. שָׁב *he restores* to שָׁב *he cuts down*). → שְׁבָבִים *splinters.*

שְׁבָבִים 1 n.m.pl. **splinters** Ho 8_{6}. → שׁבב *cut down.*

שׁבה 47.0.10 vb.—**Qal** 39.0.6 Pf. שָׁבָה, שָׁבִיתָ, שָׁבוּ; + waw וַיִּשְׁבְּ, וַיִּשְׁבּוּ; impv. שְׁבֵה; ptc. שֹׁבִים; ptc. pass. שְׁבוּיִם (Q שבאים); inf. שְׁבוֹת—**1a. take** people **captive** Jr 41_{10}; **carry away** property Ob $_{11}$. **b.** with שְׁבִי as obj. וְשָׁבִיתָ שִׁבְיוֹ *and you will take him captive* Dt 21_{10}. **2.** ptc. as noun, **one who takes captive, captor** Is 14_{2}. **3.** ptc. pass. as noun, **captive** 11QMelch 2_{4}.

Ni. 8.0.4 Pf. נִשְׁבָּה, נִשְׁבּוּ—**be taken captive,** of human being 1 S 30_{3}; **be appropriated, be taken away,** of animal Ex 22_{9}.

→ שְׁבִי *captivity, captives,* שִׁבְיָה *captives, captivity,* שְׁבִי *captive,* שְׁבוּת I *captivity.*

שְׁבוֹ 2 n.[f.] **agate,** a semi-precious stone Ex 28_{19}.

שְׁבוּאֵל 6.0.0.3 pr.n.m. **Shebuel, Shubael.**

שְׁבוּל, see שְׁבִיל *path.*

שָׁבוּעַ 20.0.35 n.m.—cstr. שְׁבֻעַ; du. שְׁבֻעַיִם; pl. שָׁבֻעוֹת; cstr. שְׁבֻעוֹת; sf. שָׁבֻעֹתֵיכֶם—**1. period of seven days, week,** sg. **bridal-week** Gn 29_{27}, **creation-week** 4QSD 7_{11}; pl. **weeks of impurity** Lv 12_{5}, **harvest-weeks,** i.e. season created by Y. Ezk 45_{21}, **festival-weeks,** of harvest-celebration and thanksgiving Ex 34_{22}, **weeks of mourning** Dn 10_{3}, **holy weeks** 4QBer[a] 1.2_{9}. **2. period of seven years,** i.e. seventh part of a Jubilee Dn 9_{25}.

שְׁבוּעָה 31.2.26 n.f.—שְׁבֻעָה; cstr. שְׁבֻעַת; sf. שְׁבֻעָתִי, שְׁבוּעָתוֹ; pl. שְׁבֻעוֹת—**1a. oath, swearing** of humans, oft. while invoking Y., sworn to human being Gn 24_{8}, to Y. 1QS 5_{8}. **b.** שְׁבֻעֵי שְׁבֻעוֹת *oath-takers,* i.e. confederates Ezk 21_{28} (unless §2). **2. oath, promise of Y.,** שְׁבֻעֵי שְׁבֻעוֹת *oaths of oaths,* i.e. the most sacred oaths Ezk 21_{28}, שְׁבוּעָתוֹ לְיִשְׂחָק *his promise to Isaac* Ps 105_{9}. **3. curse,** שְׁבֻעַת הָאָלָה *curse of adjuration* Nm 5_{21}. → שׁבע *swear.*

שְׁבוּת I 32.0.1 n.f.—שְׁבִית; cstr. שְׁבוּת (שְׁבִית); sf. שְׁבוּתְךָ; pl. sf. שְׁבוּתֵיכֶם, שְׁבִיתַיִךְ—**1. captivity,** alw. with verb שׁוב (qal or hi.), except at Nm 21_{29}, e.g. וְשָׁב י׳ אֱלֹהֶיךָ אֶת־שְׁבוּתְךָ *and Y. your God will turn your captivity,* i.e. will bring you back from captivity Dt 30_{3}. **2.** coll., **captives** Nm 21_{29} (|| פָּלִיט *fugitive*). → שׁבה *take captive.*

***שְׁבוּת** II 31.0.1 n.f.—שְׁבִית; cstr. שְׁבוּת (שְׁבִית); sf. שְׁבוּתְךָ; pl. sf. שְׁבוּתֵיכֶם, שְׁבִיתַיִךְ—**restoration,** alw. with שׁוב (qal or hi.), וְשָׁב י׳ אֱלֹהֶיךָ אֶת־שְׁבוּתְךָ *and Y. your God will restore your restoration,* i.e. will restore you Dt 30_{3}; of **1.** Israel or Judah Jl 4_{1}. **2.** other nations Jr 48_{47}. **3.** individual Jb 42_{10}. → שׁוב *return.*

***שְׁבוּת** III 1 n.f.—cstr. Qr שְׁבוּת (Kt שבית)—**punishment, sentence of imprisonment** Jb 42_{10}.

שׁבח I 8.1.9 vb.—**Pi.** 6.0.5 Pf. שִׁבַּחְתִּי; impf. יְשַׁבַּח; impv. שַׁבְּחִי; inf. abs. שַׁבֵּחַ—**1a. praise, laud** Y. Ps 63_{4}, Y.'s deeds Ps 145_{4}. **b. sing praises to** (לְ) Y. 4QShirShabb[d] 1.1_{2}. **2. declare** the dead **fortunate, happy** Ec 4_{2}. **3. commend** pleasure Ec 8_{15}.

Pu. 0.1.1 + waw Q ושובחה—**be praised,** of name Si 51_{30}.

Htp. 2.0.3 Ptc. Q מתשבח; inf. cstr. הִשְׁתַּבֵּחַ—**1. glory in** (בְּ) praise of Y. Ps 106_{47}. **2.** ptc. as noun, **one who glories,** perh. **braggart** 4Q185 1.2_{11}.

→ שֶׁבַח *praise, glory,* תִּשְׁבֹּחָה *praise.*

שׁבח II 3.0.1 vb.—**Pi.** 2.0.1 Pf. יְשַׁבְּחֵם; impf. תְּשַׁבְּחֵם—**1.** of Y., **still waves** Ps 89_{10}. **2. calm down, cool temper** Pr 29_{11}.

Hi. 1 Ptc. מַשְׁבִּיחַ—of Y., **still tumult** Ps 65_{8}.

***[שֶׁבַח]** 0.2.3 n.[m.]—cstr. Si שבח; sf. Q שבחי—**praise, eulogy,** to Y. GnzPs 1_{16}, humans Si 44_{1}; **divine glory** Si 16_{16}. → שׁבח I *praise.*

*שׁבט vb. **Qal, hold a sceptre,** ptc. as noun, **sceptre-holder** Dt 33_5 2 S 5_1 7_7 (all if em. שִׁבְטֵי *tribes of* to שֹׁבְטֵי *sceptre-holders of*). → שֵׁבֶט *staff.*

שֵׁבֶט 191.7.46 n.m.—cstr. שֵׁבֶט; sf. שִׁבְטוֹ; pl. שְׁבָטִים; cstr. שִׁבְטֵי; sf. שְׁבָטֶיךָ—**1. tribe,** oft. of Israel, שִׁבְטֵי יִשְׂרָאֵל שְׁנֵים עָשָׂר *the twelve tribes of Israel* Gn 49_{28}; Israel as one tribe, hence **people, nation** Jr 10_{16}; **subdivision of tribe, clan** 1 S 9_{21}. **2. rod, staff,** for beating Ex 21_{20}, **club** of shepherd Lv 27_{32}, **dart** 2 S 18_{14}, **sceptre** of authority Am 1_5, perh. **leader** Nm 24_{17}. **3.** appar. **branch** Si $37_{18(B)}$. → שׁבט *hold a sceptre.*

שְׁבָט 1.0.4 pr.n.[m.] **Shebat,** eleventh month of the post-exilic Jewish calendar, February/March Zc 1_7.

[שָׁבִי] 1.0.1 adj.—f.s. שְׁבִיָּה—**captive** Is 52_2. → שׁבה *take captive.*

[שֹׁבַי] 2.0.2.5 pr.n.m. **Shobai.**

שֹׁבִי 1 pr.n.m. **Shobi.**

שְׁבִי 50.0.20 n.m.—שֶׁבִי; cstr. שְׁבִי; sf. שִׁבְיוֹ—**1. captivity,** אֶרֶץ שִׁבְיָם *land of their captivity* Jr 30_{10}. **2. capture,** שְׁבִי סוּסֵיכֶם *capture of your horses,* i.e. your captured horses Am 4_{10}. **3.** coll., **captives, prisoners,** הַשְּׁבִי אֲשֶׁר בְּבֵית הַבּוֹר *the captives that are in the house of the pit,* i.e. prison Ex 12_{29}. → שׁבה *take captive.*

שְׁבִיב 1.2.3 n.m.—cstr. שְׁבִיב; pl. cstr. Q שביבי—**flame, spark,** שְׁבִיב אִשּׁוֹ *flame of his fire* Jb 18_5.

שִׁבְיָה 9.0.1 n.f. **1.** coll., **captives,** דַּם ... שִׁבְיָה *blood of ... the captives* Dt 32_{42}. **2. captivity,** אֶרֶץ שִׁבְיָה *land of captivity* Ne 3_{36}. → שׁבה *take captive.*

[שְׁבִיל] 2.1.6 n.m.—sf. Qr שְׁבִילֶךָ; pl. cstr. שְׁבִילֵי (mss שְׁבוּלֵי)—**1. path, way, track** Jr 18_{15}. **2. stream** 4QShir Shabb[f] 20.2$_{10}$. **3.** בִּשְׁבִיל conj. **in order that** Mur 47_4.

[שָׁבִיס] I 1 n.[m.]—pl. שְׁבִיסִים—**headband** Is 3_{18}.

*[שָׁבִיס] II 1 n.[m.]—pl. שְׁבִיסִים—**ornament,** in the shape of the sun, as jewellery or as an amulet Is 3_{18}.

שְׁבִיעִי 98.0.45.1 adj.—f.s. Q שביעית, (שְׁבִעִת, שְׁבִיעִת)—**1. seventh,** of יוֹם *day* Gn 2_2, שַׁבָּת *Sabbath* Lv 23_{16}, חֹדֶשׁ *month* Ne 7_{72}, שָׁנָה *year* 2 K 18_9. **2.** as noun, **seventh (one),** i.e. **seventh month** Ezk 45_{25}, **seventh year** 1QM 2_{12}, **seventh son** 1 C 2_{15}. → שֶׁבַע *seven.*

שְׁבִית I, see שְׁבוּת I *captivity.*

שְׁבִית II, see שְׁבוּת II *restoration.*

שְׁבִית III, see שְׁבוּת III *punishment, sentence of imprisonment.*

שֹׁבֶל 1 n.[m.] **skirt** Is 47_2.

שַׁבְּלוּל 1 n.m. **snail** Ps 58_9.

שִׁבֹּלֶת I 4.2.1 n.f.—Si שבולת—**1. flood, current,** שִׁבֹּלֶת הַנָּהָר *flood of the river* Is 27_{12}. **2. shibboleth,** the pronunciation of the term as *shibboleth* used as a test to detect Ephraimites, who said סִבֹּלֶת *sibboleth* Jg 12_6 (unless שִׁבֹּלֶת II *ear of grain*).

שִׁבֹּלֶת II 15.0.4 n.f.—Q שבולת; cstr. Q שבולת; pl. שִׁבֳּלִים; cstr. שִׁבֳּלֵי—**1a. ear of grain** Gn 41_5. **b. ears of grain ornament** 1QM 5_{11}. **2. top of tree** Zc 4_{12}. **3. shibboleth,** the pronunciation of the term as *shibboleth* used as a test to detect Ephraimites, who said סִבֹּלֶת *sibboleth* Jg 12_6 (unless שִׁבֹּלֶת I *flood*).

שֶׁבְנָא 9.0.0.18 pr.n.m. **Shebna, Shebnah.**

שֶׁבְנָה, see שֶׁבְנָא *Shebna, Shebnah.*

שְׁבַנְיָה 7.0.0.29 pr.n.m. **Shebaniah.**

*[שְׁבָנֹת] 0.0.0.1 pr.n.m. **Shebanot.**

*שׁבס vb. **Qal, exact a payment of grain, impose grain tax** Am 5_{11} (if em. בּוֹשַׁסְכֶם *your trampling,* i.e. בשׁס po., to שָׁבְסְכֶם *your imposing of grain tax*).

שׁבע 186.0.24.1 vb.—**Qal** 1 Ptc. pass. שְׁבֻעֵי—ptc. pass. as noun, **one who takes an oath,** שְׁבֻעֵי שְׁבֻעוֹת *oath-takers,* i.e. political allies Ezk 21_{28}.

Ni. 154.0.14.1 Pf. נִשְׁבַּע; impf. יִשָּׁבַע, תִּשָּׁבַע; impv. הִשָּׁבְעָה, הִשָּׁבְעוּ; ptc. נִשְׁבָּע, נִשְׁבָּעִים; inf. abs. הִשָּׁבֵעַ (הִשָּׁבַע); cstr. הִשָּׁבַע—**1.** of human being, **a. swear to** (לְ) someone Gn 47_{31}; by (בְּ) Y. Jos 2_{12}, name of Y. Jr 12_{16}. **b.** with שְׁבוּעָה as obj., **swear an oath** Jos 9_{20}. **c. swear allegiance to** (לְ) Y. 2 C 15_{14}. **d. swear by** (בְּ) Baal Jr 12_{16}. **e. swear, curse by** (בְּ) an individual, i.e. use his name as a curse Ps 102_9. **2.** of Y., **a. swear (by himself) to** (לְ) Israel Ex 13_{11}; by (בְּ) his name Jr 44_{26}. **b.** with שְׁבוּעָה as obj., **swear an oath** Gn 26_3. **c. swear covenant agreement** Dt 7_{12}. **d. promise (while taking an oath) land of Canaan** Nm 14_{16}. **3.** ni. ptc. as noun, **one who swears, takes an oath** Ec 9_2.

Hi. 31.0.10 Pf. הִשְׁבִּיעַ; + waw וַיַּשְׁבַּע; ptc. מַשְׁבִּיעֲךָ; inf. abs. הַשְׁבֵּעַ; cstr. הַשְׁבִּיעַ—**1. make someone swear** Gn 24_3; less formally, **adjure, urgently admonish, beg** someone Ca 2_7. **2. pronounce an oath** Jos 6_{26}. **3. swear by foreign gods** Jos 23_7. **4. curse with** (בְּ) an oath CD 9₁₁.

→ שְׁבוּעָה *oath.*

שֶׁבַע I 393.2.213.2 n.m.&f.—m. (with f. nouns) שֶׁבַע; cstr. שְׁבַע (שֶׁבַע); f. (with m. nouns) שִׁבְעָה; cstr. שִׁבְעַת; sf. Qr שִׁבְעָתָם—**1. seven, a.** שֶׁבַע פְּעָמִים *seven times* Gn 33₃, שִׁבְעַת לֵילוֹת *seven nights* Jb 2₁₃; as constituent of a larger number, שִׁבְעִים וְשִׁבְעָה אִישׁ *seventy-seven men* Jg 8₁₄. **b.** ellip., יָלְדָה שִׁבְעָה *she has given birth to seven (children)* 1 S 2₅. **c.** idioms, שִׁבְעָה שִׁבְעָה *seven pairs* Gn 7₂, שִׁבְעָתָם יָחַד *the seven of them together* 2 S 21₉ (Qr). **d.** as adv., שֶׁבַע בַּיּוֹם הִלַּלְתִּיךָ *I praise you seven times each day* Ps 119₁₆₄. **2.** as ordinal numeral, **seventh, a.** שְׁנַת־הַשֶּׁבַע *the seventh year* Dt 15₉; as constituent of a larger number, שִׁבְעָה וְעֶשְׂרִים יוֹם *the twenty-seventh day* Gn 8₁₄. **b.** as noun, בְּשִׁבְעָה בַחֹדֶשׁ *on the seventh (day) of the month* Ezk 45₂₀. **3.** as compound, שְׁבַע־עֶשְׂרֵה/שִׁבְעָה־עָשָׂר/שְׁבַע־עֶשְׂרֵה, **a. seventeen,** שְׁבַע־עֶשְׂרֵה שָׁנָה *seventeen years* Gn 47₂₈. **b. seventeenth,** שִׁבְעָה־עָשָׂר יוֹם *the seventeenth day* Gn 7₁₁. **c.** as noun, לְחֵזִיר שִׁבְעָה עָשָׂר *to Hezir was the seventeenth (lot)* 1 C 24₁₅.

→ שִׁבְעָנָה *seven,* שְׁבִיעִי *seventh,* שִׁבְעָתַיִם *sevenfold, seven times,* שִׁבְעִים *seventy.*

שֶׁבַע II 9.0.0.4 pr.n.m. **Sheba.**

שֶׁבַע III 1 pl.n. **Sheba.**

שֶׁבַע IV, see בְּאֵר שֶׁבַע *Beer-sheba.*

שֶׁבַע V, see בַּת־שֶׁבַע *Bathsheba.*

שִׁבְעָה 1 pl.n. **Shibah.**

שִׁבְעִים 91.1.13 n.m.pl.—Q שבעין—**1. seventy,** שִׁבְעִים שָׁנָה *seventy years* Jr 25₁₁, שָׁבֻעִים שִׁבְעִים *seventy periods of seven years* Dn 9₂₄, שבעים באמה *seventy cubits* 11QT 40₁₂. **2.** ellip., **seventy (persons),** שִׁבְעִים מִזִּקְנֵי יִשְׂרָאֵל *seventy from the elders of Israel* Ex 24₁. **3.** adv., **seventy times,** שִׁבְעִים שִׁבְעָה *seventy-seven times* Gn 4₂₄.

→ שֶׁבַע *seven.*

שִׁבְעָנָה 1 n.f. **seven,** שִׁבְעָנָה בָנִים *seven sons* Jb 42₁₃ (or em. שִׁבְעָה *seven*). → שֶׁבַע *seven.*

שִׁבְעָתַיִם 7.2.3 n.f.du. **sevenfold, seven times,** שִׁבְעָתַיִם יֻקָּם *he will be avenged sevenfold* Gn 4₁₅. → שֶׁבַע *seven.*

שבץ 2 vb.—**Pi.** 1 + waw וְשִׁבַּצְתָּ—**weave tunic with patterns** Ex 28₃₉.

Pu. 1 Ptc. מְשֻׁבָּצִים—**be inwoven, be set,** of stone Ex 28₂₀.

→ מִשְׁבְּצָה *setting,* תַּשְׁבֵּץ *chequered work.*

שָׁבָץ 1 n.m. **cramp, dizziness** or **anguish** 2 S 1₉.

שבר I 148.5.27 vb.—**Qal** 53.3.14 Pf. שָׁבַר, שָׁבַרְתִּי; impf. יִשְׁבֹּר; impv. שְׁבֹר (שִׁבְרָם); ptc. שֹׁבֵר; ptc. pass. שָׁבוּר, שְׁבוּרֵי; inf. שְׁבוֹר (שִׁבְרִי, לִשְׁבֹּר)—oft. of Y., **1. break** object, e.g. jar Jg 7₂₀, cedar Ps 29₅. **2.** of wind, **wreck** Tyre like ship Ezk 27₂₆. **3. break** limb, bodily part, e.g. bone Nm 9₁₂, arm Ezk 30₂₁. **4. crush, destroy** people Jr 19₁₁. **5.** of lion, **tear** human being 1 K 13₂₆. **6. break up** kingdom 4QapJerCc 7.2₄. **7. break, break down** pride Lv 26₁₉. **8. break, hurt** heart Ps 69₂₁. **9. banish** sword Ho 2₂₀. **10. quench** thirst Ps 104₁₁. **11.** ptc. as noun, **breaker, tearer,** i.e. wild animal 1QH 13₇. **12.** pass. ptc. as noun, **a. injured animal** Lv 22₂₂. **b. one (emotionally) broken, one hurt** Ps 147₃.

Ni. 57.1.10 Pf. נִשְׁבַּר; impf. תִּשָּׁבֵר (תִּשָּׁבַר); ptc. נִשְׁבָּר, נִשְׁבֶּרֶת (נִשְׁבָּרָה); inf. הִשָּׁבֵר—**1. be broken** or **break, a.** of object, vessel Lv 6₂₁, reed Ezk 29₇. **b.** of wickedness Jb 24₂₀. **2. be wrecked,** of ship Jon 1₄. **3. be broken, fractured,** of bodily part, neck 1 S 4₁₈. **4. be maimed, injured,** of animal Ex 22₉. **5. be injured, crushed, destroyed,** of people 2 C 14₁₂. **6. be broken down, ruined,** of city Is 24₁₀, kingdom Dn 11₄. **7. be broken, suffer emotional pain,** of heart Jr 23₉, specif. **be contrite,** of spirit Ps 51₁₉. **8.** ptc. as noun, **a.** fem., **that which is broken, injured one** Ezk 30₂₂. **b. one (emotionally) broken** Is 61₁.

Pi. 36.2 Pf. שִׁבֵּר (שִׁבַּר); impf. יְשַׁבֵּר; ptc. מְשַׁבֵּר; inf. abs. שַׁבֵּר—**1a. shatter** by throwing to the ground, obj. tablets Ex 32₁₉, **tear down completely,** obj. image Is 21₉. **b.** of Y., **break** weapons, i.e. make wars cease Ps 46₁₀. **2. break, crush** bodily parts Jb 29₁₇. **3.** in nature, **shatter, tear apart** rocks, trees, **a.** of wind, obj. rocks 1 K 19₁₁. **b.** of Y., obj. trees Ps 105₃₃. **4.** of Y., **cause ship to be wrecked** by (בְּ) wind Ps 48₈.

Pu. 1.1.2 Pf. mss שֻׁבְּרוּ—**1. be broken, loosened,** of fetters 1QH 13₃₇, **be torn down completely,** of image Is 21₉(mss). **2. be shattered,** of person Si 11₂(B).

Hi. 1.0.1 Impf. אַשְׁבִּיר—**cause to break through,** i.e. bring to the moment of birth Is 66₉.

Ho. 1 Pf. הָשְׁבַּרְתִּי—**be (emotionally) shattered,**

devastated Jr 8$_{21}$.

→ שֶׁבֶר *destruction, breach,* שִׁבָּרוֹן *breaking, destruction,* מִשְׁבָּר I *breaker,* (?) מַשְׁבֵּר *mouth of cervix.*

שׁבר II $_{21}$ vb.—**Qal** $_{16}$ Impf. תִּשְׁבְּרוּ; + waw וַיִּשְׁבֹּר; impv. שִׁבְרוּ; ptc. שֹׁבְרִים; inf. לִשְׁבֹּר—**1.** with obj., **buy grain** Gn 42$_{3}$, food Dt 2$_{6}$, wine and milk Is 55$_{1}$. **2.** without obj., **buy grain, food** Gn 41$_{57}$.

Hi. $_{5}$ Impf. נַשְׁבִּיר; + waw mss וַיַּשְׁבֵּר; ptc. מַשְׁבִּיר—**1. sell grain** Am 8$_{5}$. **2.** with double accus., **sell food to** someone Dt 2$_{28}$. **3.** without obj., **sell grain to** (לְ) someone Gn 41$_{56(mss)}$. **4.** ptc. as noun, **one who sells** or **distributes grain** Gn 42$_{6}$.

→ שֶׁבֶר I *grain.*

***שׁבר** III $_{1}$ vb.—**Qal** $_{1}$ + waw וָאֶשְׁבֹּר—**measure** boundary Jb 38$_{10}$.

שֶׁבֶר $_{45.2.2}$ n.m.—שֶׁבֶר; cstr. שֶׁבֶר (שֵׁבֶר); sf. שִׁבְרִי; pl. שְׁבָרִים—**1. destruction** Jr 48$_{3}$. **2a. bruise, emotional pain, wounding** of spirit, heart Is 65$_{14}$. **b. (sound of) anguish** Zp 1$_{10}$. **3. fracture** of member, limb Lv 21$_{19}$. **4. breach, fissure** Ps 60$_{4}$. **5. quarry** Jos 7$_{5}$. **6. breaking** of earthenware jar Is 30$_{14}$, of wall Is 30$_{13}$. **7.** perh. **splashing** of Leviathan into water Jb 41$_{17}$. **8. solution, interpretation,** i.e. 'breaking' of dream Jg 7$_{15}$.
→ שׁבר I *break, destroy.*

שֶׁבֶר I $_{9.0.0.1}$ n.[m.]—cstr. שֶׁבֶר; sf. שִׁבְרוֹ; pl. I שברם—**grain** Gn 42$_{1}$. → שׁבר II *buy grain.*

שֶׁבֶר II $_{1}$ pr.n.m. **Sheber.**

*[**שֶׁבֶר**] III $_{1}$ n.[m.]—sf. שִׁבְרוֹ—**interpretation** of dream Jg 7$_{15}$.

שִׁבָּרוֹן $_{2}$ n.[m.]—cstr. שִׁבְרוֹן—**1. breaking,** שִׁבְרוֹן מָתְנַיִם *breaking of loins,* i.e. shaking hips Ezk 21$_{11}$. **2. destruction** Jr 17$_{18}$. → שׁבר I *break, destroy.*

שְׁבָרִים $_{1}$ pl.n. **Shebarim.**

שׁבת $_{71.15.40}$ vb.—**Qal** $_{27.7.14}$ Pf. שָׁבַת, שָׁבְתָה; impf. תִּשְׁבֹּת (תִּשְׁבָּת); inf. Si שבות—**1a. cease** to exist, to happen, to come (back), to be done, **stop, be at a standstill, come to an end, disappear,** of manna Jos 5$_{12}$, work Ne 6$_{3}$, strife Pr 22$_{10}$, joy Lm 5$_{15}$. **b. be blotted out,** of memory Si 10$_{17}$. **c. be lacking,** of one of host 4QInstr[d] 126.2$_{1}$. **d. be exterminated,** of beast 11QM 1.2$_{13}$. **e.** followed by prep. מִן + inf., **cease to be** Jr 31$_{36}$, **cease, stop doing** Ho 7$_{4}$. **2. rest,** of Y. Gn 2$_{2}$ (without obj.), **rest, keep** or **observe sabbath,** of Israelites Ex 23$_{12}$ (without obj.) 23$_{32}$ (obj. שַׁבָּת), of land not in use for agriculture for one year every seventh year Lv 26$_{34}$ (without obj.) Lv 25$_{2}$ (obj. שַׁבָּת). **3.** inf. as noun, **a. disappearance** of the dead Si 38$_{23(Bmg)}$ (unless §3b). **b. resting** of the dead Si 38$_{23(Bmg)}$.

Ni. $_{4.0.2}$ + waw וְנִשְׁבַּת—**cease, come to an end, disappear,** of fortress, kingdom Is 17$_{3}$.

Hi. $_{40.7.24}$ Pf. הִשְׁבַּתִּי; impf. יַשְׁבִּית; + waw וַיַּשְׁבֵּת; impv. Si הַשְׁבִּיתוּ; ptc. מַשְׁבִּית; inf. הַשְׁבִּית—**1a. cause to cease, make disappear, put an end to** war Ps 46$_{10}$, work Ne 4$_{5}$. **b. remove** leaven Ex 12$_{15}$. **c. allow to be missing, withhold** salt Lv 2$_{13}$, redeemer Ru 4$_{14}$. **d.** leave desire **unfulfilled** Si 16$_{13}$. **e. exterminate** enemy Ps 8$_{3}$. **f. blot out** memory Dt 32$_{26}$. **g. purge, expunge** impurity 1QS 10$_{24}$. **2a. cause to desist, make discontinue, stop** someone doing something Jos 22$_{25}$. **b. cause to desist, make rest, give rest** to people Ex 5$_{5}$. **3.** inf. as noun, **ceasing,** שבת hi. inf. + לְאֵין *without ceasing, unceasingly* 1QH 19$_{24}$.

Ho. $_{0.1}$ Ptc. Si מושבת—**be put to rest,** of deceased person Si 38$_{23(B)}$.

→ מִשְׁבָּת I *cessation,* שֶׁבֶת II *desisting, cessation,* שַׁבָּת *sabbath,* שַׁבָּתוֹן *(special) sabbath (observance).*

שַׁבָּת $_{111.0.165.3}$ n.m.&f.—שַׁבָּת; cstr. שַׁבַּת; sf. שַׁבַּתּוֹ; pl. שַׁבָּתוֹת; cstr. שַׁבְּתֹת; sf. שַׁבְּתוֹתַי—**1. sabbath day, day of rest,** seventh day Ex 20$_{10}$. **2. sabbath year,** when land is not in use for agriculture for one year every seventh year Lv 25$_{4}$. **3. period of seven years** Lv 25$_{8}$. **4. produce of the sabbath year,** i.e. that which grows spontaneously Lv 25$_{6}$. → שׁבת *cease, rest.*

שֶׁבֶת I $_{8}$ n.f.—cstr. שֶׁבֶת; sf. שִׁבְתָּם—**1a. dwelling, habitation** Ob$_{3}$. **b. geographical location** Nm 21$_{15}$. **c. place, spot** 2 S 23$_{7}$. **2a. seat** 1 K 10$_{19}$. **b. throne, enthronement, reign** Am 6$_{3}$. **3a. sitting (down)** Lm 3$_{63}$. **b. sitting still,** i.e. idleness Is 30$_{7}$. → ישׁב *sit.*

שֶׁבֶת II $_{3.0.2}$ n.f.—cstr. שֶׁבֶת—**1. desisting** from strife Pr 20$_{3}$, from work Ex 21$_{19}$. **2. cessation, termination,** שֶׁבֶת חָמָס *violent termination* Am 6$_{3}$. → שׁבת *cease, rest.*

שַׁבָּתוֹן $_{11.0.6}$ n.m. **1. (special) day of sabbath (observance)** Lv 23$_{39}$. **2. (special) year of sabbath (observance),** when land is not in use for agriculture Lv

25₅. → שׁבת *cease, rest.*

שַׁבְּתַי 3 pr.n.m. **Shabbethai.**

שׁגג 4.0.4 vb. (byform of שׁגה)—**Qal** 4.0.4 Pf. שָׁגַג; impf. Q ישוגו; ptc. שֹׁגֶגֶת—**sin inadvertently, a.** without obj. Nm 15₂₈. **b.** with שְׁגָגָה as obj. Lv 5₁₈. **2.** ptc. as noun, **a. one who sins inadvertently** 1QS 9₁. **b. one who is deceived** Jb 12₁₆. → שְׁגָגָה *error.*

שְׁגָגָה 19.0.9 n.f.—sf. שִׁגְגָתוֹ—**error, inadvertent sin,** to be atoned for by sacrifice Lv 5₁₅, unintentional killing, not requiring capital punishment Jos 20₃, thoughtless words 1QS 7₃. → שׁגג *make an error.*

שׁגה 21.2.14 vb. (byform of שׁגג)—**Qal** 17.1.7 Pf. שָׁגִיתִי, שָׁגוּ; impf. תִּשְׁגּוּ, יִשְׁגֶּה; ptc. שֹׁגֶה; inf. שְׁגוֹת—**1. go astray, err, sin** Lv 4₁₃. **2. stray from** (מִן) Y.'s commandments Ps 119₂₁. **3. err mentally, misinterpret** Is 28₇ (unless §4). **4. stagger** Is 28₇. **5a. be infatuated with** (בְּ) woman Pr 5₂₀. **b. be intoxicated with** (בְּ) love Pr 5₁₉. **6.** of flock, **stray** Ezk 34₆. **7.** ptc. as noun, **a. one who strays** Ps 119₁₁₈. **b. ignoramus** 4QD^a 8.1₇. **c. one who is muddled by liquor** Pr 20₁.

Pu. 0.0.1 Ptc. משו[ו]גה—ptc. as noun, **ignoramus** CD 15₁₅.

Hi. 4.1.6 Impf. תַּשְׁגֵּנִי; ptc. מַשְׁגֶּה—**1. lead** someone **astray,** of Lady Folly 4QWiles 1₁₇, wealth Si 8₂. **2. lead astray to iniquity,** of tracks 4QWiles 1₉. **3. let someone stray** away from (מִן) commandments, of Y. Ps 119₁₀. **4.** ptc. as noun, **deceiver** Dt 27₁₈.

→ מִשְׁגֶּה *error,* מִשְׁגֶּה *mistake,* מִשְׁגָּה *error,* מְשׁוּגָה *mistake,* שְׁגִיאָה *error,* שִׁגָּיוֹן I *song of ecstasy.*

שָׁגֵה 1 pr.n.m. **Shagee.**

שׁגח 3.2 vb.—**Hi.** 3.2 Pf. הִשְׁגִּיחַ; impf. יַשְׁגִּיחוּ; ptc. מַשְׁגִּיחַ—**gaze** Ca 2₉.

[שְׁגִיאָה] 1 n.f.—pl. שְׁגִיאוֹת—**error** Ps 19₁₃. → שׁגה *go astray, err.*

שִׁגָּיוֹן I 2 n.[m.]—pl. שִׁגְיֹנוֹת—**song of ecstasy** Ps 7₁. → שׁגה *go astray, err.*

***שִׁגָּיוֹן** II 2 n.[m.]—pl. שִׁגְיֹנוֹת—**song of lamentation** Ps 7₁.

***שִׁגָּיוֹן** III 2 n.[m.]—pl. שִׁגְיֹנוֹת—**song of excitement** Ps 7₁.

שׁגל 4 vb. (perh. considered vulgar by Massoretes, Qr alw. שׁכב *lie with*)—**Qal** 1 Impf. Kt ישגלנה—**ravish** woman Dt 28₃₀.

Ni. 2 Impf. Kt תשגלנה—**be ravished, raped** Zc 14₂.

Pu. 1 Pf. Kt שגלת—**be ravished, raped** Jr 3₂.

שֵׁגָל 2 n.f. **queen** Ps 45₁₀.

שׁגע 7.0.1 vb.—**Pu.** 5.0.1 Ptc. מְשֻׁגָּע—**1. be mad** Jr 29₂₆. **2. be driven mad** Ho 9₇ (unless §3). **3. be considered a maniac** Ho 9₇. **4.** ptc. as noun, **madman** CD 15₁₅.

Htp. 2 Ptc. מִשְׁתַּגֵּעַ; inf. cstr. הִשְׁתַּגֵּעַ—**behave like a madman** 1 S 21₁₅.

→ שִׁגָּעוֹן *madness.*

שִׁגָּעוֹן 3.0.1 n.m. **madness** Dt 28₂₈. → שׁגע *be mad.*

שֶׁגֶר 5.1.1 n.[f.]—cstr. שְׁגַר (שֶׁגֶר)—**offspring, litter of farm-animals** Dt 7₁₃.

שַׁד 21.0.2 n.m.—du. שָׁדַיִם; pl. cstr. שְׁדֵי; sf. שָׁדֶיהָ—**female breast,** oft. of human, שְׁנֵי שָׁדַיִךְ כִּשְׁנֵי עֳפָרִים *your two breasts are like two fawns* Ca 4₅, of jackal Lm 4₃, of human and animal Gn 49₂₅. → cf. שֹׁד II *breast.*

[שֵׁד] 2.0.4 n.[m.]—pl. שֵׁדִים (Q שדאים)—**demon, false god** Ps 106₃₇.

שֹׁד I 25.1.3 n.m.—cstr. שֹׁד—**1. destruction, ruin,** oft. as divine punishment Is 13₆. **2. violence, oppression,** שֹׁד עֲנִיִּים *oppression of the poor* Ps 12₆. → שׁדד *devastate, destroy.*

שֹׁד II 3 n.m. **breast,** oft. coll., **breasts** Is 60₁₆. → cf. שַׁד *breast.*

שׁדא, see שָׂדָה II *chest.*

שׁדד 58.1.3 vb.—**Qal** 32.1.2 Pf. שַׁדּוּנִי; impf. יָשׁוּד, (יְשָׁדְדֵם) Qr יְשָׁדֵּם; impv. שָׁדְדוּ; ptc. שׁוֹדֵד, שֹׁדְדִים; ptc. pass. שָׁדוּד, שְׁדוּדָה; inf. abs. שָׁדוֹד; cstr. שְׁדוֹד—**1. devastate, destroy** person Ps 17₉, pasturage Jr 25₃₆, pride Ezk 32₁₂; subj. Y. Jr 25₃₆, humans Jr 49₂₈, wolf Jr 5₆, perversity Pr 11₃. **2.** ptc. pass., **be destroyed, dead,** of person Jg 5₂₇. **3.** ptc. as noun, **destroyer, marauder** Ob 5. **4.** ptc. pass. as noun, **one who has been destroyed, victim of violence** Is 33₁.

Ni. 1 Pf. נְשַׁדֻּנוּ—**be ruined,** ni. pf. with qal inf., שָׁדוֹד נְשַׁדֻּנוּ *we are utterly ruined* Mc 2₄.

Pi. 2 Impf. תְּשַׁדֵּד; ptc. מְשַׁדֶּד—**assault, do violence** to person Pr 19₂₆, **destroy** place Pr 24₁₅.

Pu. 20 Pf. שֻׁדַּד—**be destroyed, ruined,** of people Jr 4₁₃, field Jl 1₁₀.

Po. 1 Impf. יְשֹׁדַד—**violently destroy, smash pillar** Ho 10₂.

Ho. 2.0.1 (unless **Qal Pass.**) Impf. יוּשַּׁד, תּוּשַּׁד—**be destroyed,** of destroyer Is 33₁, fortress Ho 10₁₄.

→ שְׁדָדָה *destruction,* שֹׁד I *destruction, violence.*

*[שְׁדָדָה] 0.0.1 n.f. **destruction** 4QWiles 1₈. → שׁדד *devastate, destroy.*

שִׁדָּה I 2 n.f.—pl. שִׁדּוֹת—**concubine** Ec 2₈.

*[שִׁדָּה] II 0.0.2 n.f.—שדא; cstr. שדת—**chest** 3QTr 1₃.

שַׁדַּי I 48.0.4 n.m. **Shaddai, Almighty (One),** name of God of Israel Gn 17₁.

שַׁדַּי II, see צוּרִישַׁדַּי *Zurishaddai.*

שַׁדַּי III, see עַמִּישַׁדַּי *Ammishaddai.*

שְׁדֵיאוּר 5 pr.n.m. **Shedeur.**

שַׁדִּין, see שֶׁ *which, that, who.*

*[שֶׁדֶךְ] 0.0.1 n.[m.] **tranquillity** 4QpsEzek[b] 1.2₇.

שְׁדֵמָה 6 n.f.—pl. שְׁדֵמוֹת; cstr. שַׁדְמוֹת—**field,** for cultivation of food Hb 3₁₇, specif. **vineyard** Dt 32₃₂, perh. **cornfield** Is 37₂₇; burning-place for religious vessels 2 K 23₄. → cf. (?) שָׂדֶה *field.*

שׁדף 4 vb.—**Qal** 3 Ptc. pass. שְׁדֻפוֹת (שדופת)—pass., **be scorched,** of ears of grain Gn 41₆.

Ni. 1 Ptc. נשדף—**wither,** of grass Is 37₂₇(1QIsa[a]).

→ שְׁדֵפָה *blighted thing,* שִׁדָּפוֹן *blight.*

שְׁדֵפָה 1 n.f. **blighted thing** 2 K 19₂₆. → שׁדף *scorch.*

שִׁדָּפוֹן 5.0.2 n.m. **blight** Dt 28₂₂. → שׁדף *scorch.*

שַׁדְרַךְ 1 pr.n.m. **Shadrach.**

שֹׁהַם I 11.0.1 n.m. **onyx** Ex 25₇.

שֹׁהַם II 1 pr.n.m. **Shoham.**

שהתם 4QTestim10, see שׁתם I *be opened,* II *be wicked.*

שׁו, see שָׁוְא *deceit; vanity.*

שָׁוְא I 53.6.7 n.[m.]—שָׁוְא (Kt, Q שׁו, Qr שָׁיו, Q שוו)—**1. deceit, falsehood** Dt 5₂₀. **2. lies** Is 59₄, specif. **empty cry** to Y. Jb 35₁₃. **3. delusion** about other gods Jr 18₁₅. **4. delusional** or **false vision** Lm 2₁₄. **5. worthlessness,** of sinful human behaviour Si 16₁. **6. vanity, futility** Ml 3₁₄. **7. empty misery, pointless wretchedness** Si 30₁₇. **8. idleness** Si 37₁₁. **9.** adv., **in vain** Ps 127₁.

*שָׁוְא II 0.0.2 pl.n. **Shaveh.**

שְׁוָא 2 pr.n.m. **Sheva.**

[שׁוֹא] 1.0.1 n.[m.]—pl. שֹׁאֵיהֶם—**1. onslaught** Ps 35₁₇. **2. (place of) ruin** 3QTr 1₁₃. → שׁאה I *be desolate.*

שׁוֹאָה 12.1.3 n.f.—שֹׁאָה (Kt שאוה); cstr. שֹׁאַת—**1. disaster,** oft. as divine punishment, specif. **devastating storm** Ezk 38₉; **ruin of worshipper by enemies** 1QH 13₃₀. **2. (place of) ruin(s)** Jb 30₃. → שׁאה I *be desolate.*

שׁוּב 1069.32.255.5 vb.—**Qal** 689.15.162 Pf. שָׁב, שָׁבוּ; impf. יָשׁוּב (יָשֹׁב, יָשׁוּב ,יָשֻׁב); + waw וַיָּשָׁב (וַיָּשֹׁב), impv. שׁוּב, שׁוּבִי; ptc. שָׁב, שָׁבֵי (שׁוּבֵי); inf. abs. שׁוֹב; cstr. שׁוּב—**1a. return, go back, move back** to place, (1) with prep. לְ, אֶל, or עַל, Gn 18₃₃ Jr 22₂₇ 2 C 20₂₇. (2) with ה- of direction, 1 K 19₁₅. (3) without prep., מִצְרַיִם יָשׁוּבוּ *they will return to Egypt* Ho 8₁₃. **b.** process of dying, **return** to dust, ground, Sheol, (1) with prep. לְ, אֶל, or עַל, Gn 3₁₉ Ps 9₁₈ Jb 34₁₅. (2) without prep., לשוב עפר *to return to dust* Si 40₃. **c. return** to (לְ) one's home from abode of death, i.e. come back to life Jb 7₁₀. **d. go back** to (אֶל) work Ne 4₉. **2a. come back, go back** to (לְ, אֶל, or עַל) person, community Ho 2₉ Ru 1₁₀ Ne 4₆. **b. return, give allegiance** to (אֶל) king 1 K 12₂₇. **c. come back** to (אֶל) living person out of abode of dead 2 S 12₂₃. **d. return** to (אֶל) God, of spirit of the dead Ec 12₇. **e.** of judgment personified, **return** to (עַד), **accord again** with righteousness Ps 94₁₅. **3. return, go back, come back,** without mention of place or person returned to 2 S 10₅. **4. return** from (מִן) military activity, battle 1QM 4₈. **5. return, go back** to perform some activity, שׁוּב + לְ + inf., לָשׁוּב לָשֶׁבֶת בָּאָרֶץ *to return to live in the land* Nm 35₃₂; at times **revert** to activity done in past 1QS 7₂₃. **6. go back** and forth, to and fro, שׁוּב with יצא, וַיֵּצֵא יָצוֹא וָשׁוֹב *and it kept flying back and forth* Gn 8₇, שׁוּב with עבר Ex 32₂₇, הלך 1 S 17₁₅, רצא Ezk 1₁₄. **7a.** (1) **draw back, withdraw** from (מֵעַל) foreign king, i.e. leave him in peace 2 K 18₁₄, from (מֵאַחֲרֵי) soldier, i.e. leave him without protection 2 S 11₁₅. (2) **retreat** out of shame Ps 6₁₁. (3) of animal, **recoil, shy away** from (מִפְּנֵי) anyone Pr 30₃₀. **b. withdraw, escape** from (מִן) darkness, i.e. misery or death Jb 15₂₂. **c. retire** from (מִן) cultic duty Nm 8₂₅. **8. turn about, make a turn,** changing direction Nm 33₇; **turn back,** movement in opposite direction Ne 2₁₅; **turn around,** military manoeuvre to attack Jos 8₂₁. **9. turn into** (בְּ), i.e. pursue, one's course of life Jr 8₆. **10. turn, resort to**

(לְ) means of living Is 23_{17}, person Ps 119_{79}. **11a. return, turn (back), repent** to (אֶל or עַד) Y. Dt 30_{10} Lm 3_{40}. **b. turn away, repent** from (מִן) sin 1 K 8_{35}. **c. go back, return, repent** to (לְ or אֶל) covenant 1QS 5_{22}, law 1QS 5_8. **d.** abs., **repent, show repentance** Jr 8_5. **12a. turn away** from following (מֵאַחֲרֵי) Y. 1 K 9_6. **b. fall back** into (עַל) sin Jr 11_{10}. **c. return** to (לְ) former state of bondage (to sin) Ne 9_{17}. **d. turn, stray** away from (מִן) righteousness Ezk 18_{24}. **e.** abs., **stray, apostatize, become unfaithful** Jos 23_{12}. **13.** of Y., **return** to (אֶל) Israelite remnant to protect 2 C 30_6. **14.** of Y., **a. turn away** from (מֵאַחֲרֵי) humans Dt 23_{15}. **b.** abs., **withdraw protection** Jos 24_{20}. **15a. relent, turn back** from (מִן) plan of punishment Jr 4_{28}; **turn away** from (מִן) fury Ex 32_{12}. **b. turn (around), change one's mind** 2 K 24_1. **c. turn away** from (מִן) oath Ps 132_{11}, **revoke, go back on** word 1QH 5_{24}, **retract** vow Jg 11_{35}. **16a. be returned, be put back,** of ark 1 S 5_{11}. **b. be given back,** of ass Dt 28_{31}. **c. be paid back, be requited,** of evil Ps 7_{17}. **17a. be restored** to (לְ) former state, of people Ezk 16_{55}. **b. be restored** to (לְ) rest, of soul Ps 116_7. **c. be made healthy again,** of body Lv 13_{16}. **d. be made habitable again,** of city Ezk $35_{9(Qr)}$. **18. be revived,** of spirit 1 K 17_{21}. **19.** of phenomena in nature, **a.** of water, **flow back** Ex 14_{26}. **b.** of rain, **return** to sky, i.e. **evaporate** Is 55_{10}. **c.** of cloud, **be formed again** in atmosphere Ec 12_2. **d.** of wind, **return, pass again** Ec 1_6. **e.** of shadow, **recede** 2 K 20_9. **f.** of ground, **be turned, transformed** into (לְ) fruitful land Is 29_{17}. **g.** of mortal remains, **return** to (לְ) ground, i.e. **decompose** Ec 12_7. **20. roll back,** of stone Pr 26_{27}. **21. be brought in** during harvest-time, of grain Jb $39_{12(Kt)}$. **22. be put back, sheathed again,** of sword Ezk 21_{10}. **23. come back, cause affliction again,** of plague 11QPs[a] 24_{12}. **24. come back** fulfilled, of Y.'s word Is 55_{11}. **25. turn, change direction,** of border Jos 19_{12}. **26. turn away, subside, abate,** of anger Jb 14_{13}. **27. be taken back, revoked,** of word Is 45_{23}. **28. be returned (unanswered),** of prayer Ps 35_{13}. **29. end again, come to an end,** of defamation Pr 25_{10}. **30.** שׁוּב as auxiliary verb, modifying another verb, denoting repetition, renewal of action, etc., שׁוּב שְׁכַב *lie down again* 1 S 3_5. **31.** as hi., **a.** of Y., **restore** restoration, glory, וְשָׁב יי אֱלֹהֶיךָ אֶת־שְׁבוּתְךָ *and Y. your God will restore your restoration,* i.e. will restore you Dt 30_3. **b.** of Y., **restore** humility in person 1QH 4_{22}. **c.** of Y., **restore, receive back** Israelites Ps 85_5. **32.** as hi., **revive, vitalize, encourage,** לשוב כול מסי לבב *to revive all who are melting of heart,* i.e. whose courage is failing 1QM 10_5. **33.** ptc. as noun, **a. one who returns** Mc 2_8. **b. repentant one** 1QS 10_{20}.

Polel 11.1.1 Pf. שׁוֹבְבָה; impf. יְשׁוֹבֵב; + waw וְשֹׁבַבְתִּי; ptc. מְשֹׁבֵב; inf. שׁוֹבֵב—**1a.** of Y., **bring back** Israel to (לְ) Y. Is 49_5, to (אֶל) pasture Jr 50_{19}. **b.** with לְ of obj., of Y., **make** Israel **shrink back** Ps 60_3 (unless §5a or §7a). **2. lead away, astray** people Jr 50_6. **3.** of Y., **turn around** Gog Ezk 38_4. **4. urge on** (בְּ) animal Si 38_{25}. **5a.** with לְ of obj., of Y., **restore** Israel Ps 60_3. **b.** of Y., **renew** life Ps 23_3. **6. answer, reply** 4QBéat 14.2_{21}. **7a.** of Y., **turn away** from (לְ) Israel Ps 60_3. **b. apostatize** Jr 8_5. **8.** ptc. as noun, **restorer** Is 58_{12}.

Polal 1 Ptc. מְשׁוֹבֶבֶת—**be restored, recovered** from (מִן) war, of land Ezk 38_8.

Hi. 363.16.89.5 Pf. הֵשִׁיב, הֲשִׁיבוֹת; impf. יָשִׁיב, יָשֵׁב (יָשֵׁב ,יְשִׁיב); + waw וַיָּשֶׁב ;וַהֲשִׁבֹתִי; impv. הָשֵׁב (הָשִׁיבוּ ,הָשִׁיב); ptc. מֵשִׁיב, מְשִׁיבַת; inf. abs. הָשֵׁב; cstr. הָשִׁיב—**1a. bring back, take back, lead** someone to (לְ, אֶל, עַל or ־ה) a person or place, e.g. to father Gn 37_{22}, land Dt 17_{16} Jr 42_{12}, kingdom 2 C 33_{13}; specif. **bring back safely** Gn 42_{37}, **cause to come back** 1 S 29_4, **make go back** 2 K 19_{28}, **send back** Jr 37_{20}, **hurl backward,** by way of net Lm 1_{13}, **make retreat** from enemies Ps 44_{11}; **bring back** animal to stable 1 S 6_7. **b. make turn back** to (אֶל) Y., i.e. **cause to repent** Ne 9_{26}; specif. **bring back** to (אֶל) Y.'s law Ne 9_{29}. **c. make turn back** from following after (מֵאַחַר) Y., i.e. **cause to backslide** CD 6_1. **d. bring back, win back** 2 S 17_3. **e.** of Y., **bring back** humanity to (אֶל) dust Ps 90_3. **2a. bring back, take back** something to (לְ or אֶל) a person Gn 44_8 Dt 22_1, **put back** something into (לְ or אֶל) sack Gn 42_{25}, its place 1 S 5_3; specif. **carry back** 1 K 14_{28}. **b.** of Y., **make** shadow **recede** 2 K 20_{11}. **c.** of Y., **cause** water **to flow back** Ex 15_{19}. **3a. give back, return,**

restore to (לְ or אֶל) person, obj. deposit Lv 5$_{23}$, land Jg 11$_{13}$, wife Gn 20$_{7}$. **b. give in exchange** to (לְ) person, **pay** money Ex 21$_{34}$, **render** tribute 2 K 17$_{3}$, **pay** wool **as tribute** 2 K 3$_{4}$. **c. render** sacrifice to (לְ) Y. Nm 18$_{9}$. **d. make restitution for** guilt to (אֶל) close relative Nm 5$_{7}$. **e. pay back** for redemption Lv 25$_{51}$. **f. dole out** bread Lv 26$_{26}$. **g.** of Y., **bestow** blessing perh. 4QShir^b 52$_{3}$. **h.** oft. of Y., **reward** good to (לְ) David 2 S 16$_{12}$, **requite** evil to (לְ) brother Gn 50$_{15}$. **4a. report** word(s), oft. **answer** someone, **reply** to someone, specif. **return greeting** Si 4$_{8}$, (1) two objs., דָּבָר + Y. Jb 31$_{14}$, + human being 1 K 12$_{6}$, שָׁלוֹם + human being Si 4$_{8}$. (2) obj. דָּבָר + to (לְ or אֶל) Y. Ex 19$_{8}$, human being 2 C 10$_{6}$. (3) obj. human being Jb 13$_{22}$. (4) without obj., to (לְ or אֶל) Y. 4QPrFêtes^b 1$_{3}$, human being Est 4$_{13}$. **b. bring** one's knowledge, **state** one's opinion 1QS 6$_{9}$. **c.** of thoughts, **cause** someone **to reply** Jb 20$_{2}$. **5a. recover, regain, re-establish, restore** kingdom 2 C 11$_{1}$, city 2 K 13$_{25}$, boundary 2 K 14$_{25}$. **b. restore** someone to (עַל) an office, honourable position Gn 40$_{13}$. **c.** of Y., **restore** Israel after divine chastisement Ps 80$_{4}$. **d.** of Y., **restore** restoration, אָשִׁיב אֶת־שְׁבוּתָם *I will restore their restoration,* i.e. I will restore them Jr 32$_{44}$. **e. restore** one's power 2 S 8$_{3}$. **f.** abs., **restore,** of prophetic restoration Si 49$_{7}$. **6a. revive, rescue** soul Ps 19$_{8}$, weary person 4QapPentA 10.2$_{5}$. **b. recover, rescue** remnant Jr 41$_{16}$. **7a. draw back, pull back** one's hand Gn 38$_{29}$, specif. refrain from acting Lm 2$_{8}$, **withhold** one's hand from (מִן) wrongdoing Ezk 18$_{8}$, **withdraw** one's hand from (מִן) the poor, i.e. refrain from oppressing him Ezk 18$_{17}$, one's right hand, i.e. withdraw assistance Lm 2$_{3}$. **b. turn** one's hand against (עַל), i.e. assail, enemy Ps 81$_{15}$. **c. pass again** one's hand over (עַל) something Jr 6$_{9}$. **8a. turn back** one's feet, i.e. go back Ps 119$_{59}$. **b. draw back** one's foot from the sabbath, i.e. refrain from trampling, defiling it Is 58$_{13}$. **9a. turn back, turn away** a person's face, i.e. refuse request 1 K 2$_{16}$. **b. turn away** one's face from (מֵעַל) abomination Ezk 14$_{6}$. **c. turn** one's face to (לְ) stronghold Dn 11$_{19}$. **10a. lay, take to** (אֶל) heart, **bring back to** (אֶל) mind, i.e. bethink, ponder Dt 30$_{1}$. **b. set** one's heart on (אֶל) someone Si 38$_{20}$. **c. place on** (אֶל) someone's heart 4QDibHam^a 1.5$_{12}$. **d. cause** someone's heart **to turn** to (עַל) someone, i.e. reconcile them Ml 3$_{24}$. **11. regain, catch** breath Jb 9$_{18}$. **12a. turn away, placate** anger of Y. Nm 25$_{11}$, of human being Pr 29$_{8}$. **b. avert, restrain** one's own anger Ps 78$_{38}$. **c. turn away** from (מִן) anger Ps 85$_{4}$. **d. vent** anger Is 66$_{15}$. **e. take, wreak** vengeance Dt 32$_{41}$. **13a. reverse, hinder** divine plan Nm 23$_{20}$, **revoke, countermand** (order of) punishment Am 1$_{3}$. **b. remove** wages of sin, **cancel** (in mercy) deserved punishment 11QPs^a 24$_{6}$. **c.** with עַל of obj., **oppose, contest** divine counsel 1QS 11$_{18}$. **d. restrain** animal Jr 2$_{24}$. **14. turn** wheel Pr 20$_{26}$. **15.** of Y., **turn back** blade of sword, i.e. stop supporting in battle Ps 89$_{44}$. **16.** of Y., **turn** wind into (לְ) whisper 1QH 13$_{18}$. **17. turn, bend** spirit to (לְ) will 4QInstr^b 2.4$_{8}$. **18.** of Y., **bring** disease upon (בְּ) Israelite Dt 28$_{60}$. **19.** as qal, **get back, return** to (אֶל) dry land Jon 1$_{13}$. **20.** as qal, **a. turn away** from (מִן) sin Ezk 18$_{30}$. **b.** abs., **repent** Ezk 18$_{32}$. **21.** ptc. as noun, **a. one who leads back** 4QapLamB 1$_{3}$. **b. one who repels** troops Is 28$_{6}$. **c. restorer** of life Ru 4$_{15}$. **d. one who replies** Pr 26$_{16}$. **22.** inf. as noun, **a. giving** Si 4$_{31}$. **b. cease** 1QH 11$_{27}$.

Ho. 5.0.3 Pf. הוּשַׁב; + waw וַיּוּשַׁב; ptc. מוּשָׁב—**1a. be brought back,** of person Ex 10$_{8}$, vessel Jr 27$_{16}$. **b. be returned,** of money Gn 42$_{28}$. **2. be recompensed,** of guilt Nm 5$_{8}$. **3. be repudiated,** of renown CD 6$_{6}$. **4.** ptc. as noun, **one who is made repentant** 4Q ShirShabb^f 23.1$_{12}$.

→ שִׁיבָה *restoration; repentance,* שְׁבוּת II *restoration,* שׁוֹבָב I *backsliding,* שׁוּבָה I *returning,* שׁוֹבֵב *backsliding,* מָשׁוֹב *return,* מְשׁוּבָה I *going back,* תְּשׁוּבָה *return, answer.*

שׁוּבָאֵל, see שְׁבוּאֵל *Shebuel, Shubael.*

שׁוֹבָב I 4.0.1 adj.—m.pl. שׁוֹבָבִים—**1. backsliding,** of son Jr 3$_{14}$. **2.** as noun, **backsliding one** Jr 50$_{6(Kt)}$. → שׁוב *return.*

שׁוֹבָב II 4 pr.n.m. **Shobab.**

שׁוֹבֵב 3 adj.—f.s. שׁוֹבֵבָה—**1. backsliding,** of daughter Jr 31$_{22}$. **2.** as noun, **rebel** Mc 2$_{4}$. → שׁוב *return.*

שׁוּבָה I 1.0.3 n.f.—sf. Q שובתו—**1. returning** from war Is

30_{15} (unless §2). **2. repentance** Is 30_{15}. → שׁוב *return;* cf. שִׁיבָה II *repentance.*

שׁוּבָה II 1.0.1 n.f. **stillness,** i.e. sitting still Is 30_{15}. → ישׁב *sit.*

*[שׁוֹבָךְ] I 0.0.2 n.[m.] **dovecote** 3QTr $9_{1.17}$.

שׁוֹבָךְ II 2 pr.n.m. **Shobach.**

שׁוֹבָל 9 pr.n.m. **Shobal.**

שׁוֹבֵק 1 pr.n.m. **Shobek.**

שׁוה I 16.0.16 vb.—**Qal** 8.0.16 Pf. שָׁוָה; impf. יִשְׁווּ, אֶשְׁוֶה; ptc. שֹׁוֶה—**1. compare** with (בְּ) wisdom Pr 3_{15}, to (אֶל) someone Is 40_{25}, **be comparable to** (לְ) fool Pr 26_{4}. **2.** of sin, **be requited** to (לְ) human Jb 33_{27}. **3. be good, profitable** to, for (לְ) someone Est 3_{8}.

Pi. 5 Pf. שִׁוָּה, שִׁוִּיתִי; impf. יְשַׁוֶּה; ptc. מְשַׁוֶּה—**1a. make** feet like (כְּ) those of hind 2 S 22_{34}. **b.** as qal, **be comparable** to (לְ) vine Ho 10_{1}. **2a. smooth, level off, even out** surface Is 28_{25}. **b. smooth, calm** soul Ps 131_{2}.

Hi. 2 Impf. תַּשְׁווּ, אַשְׁוֶה—**compare** Y. to (לְ) someone else Is 46_{5}.

Ntp. 1 Pf. Qr נִשְׁתָּוָה—**be alike** (or em. נִשְׁתָּוָה *it is alike* to נִשְׁוְתָה ni. in same sense).

שׁוה II 5 vb.—**Pi.** 5 Pf. שִׁוִּיתִי; impf. תְּשַׁוֶּה—**1. bestow** honour upon (עַל) king Ps 21_{6}. **2. set** Y. before (לְנֶגֶד) oneself, i.e. be mindful of Y. Ps 16_{8}. **3. lie down** Is 38_{13}.

שָׁוֵה 1 pl.n. **Shaveh.**

שָׁוֵה קִרְיָתַיִם 1 pl.n. **Shaveh-kiriathaim.**

שׁוח I 3 vb. (byform of שׁחח)—**Qal** 3 Pf. שָׁחָה; impf. Qr תָּשׁוֹחַ—of house, **sink (down)** into (אֶל) death Pr 2_{18}; of soul, **be downcast** within (עַל) person Lm $3_{20(Qr)}$.

Hi. 1 Impf. Kt תשיח—of soul, **sink** within (עַל) person Lm $3_{20(Kt)}$.

→ שׁוּחַ I *pit,* שׁוּחָה *pit, pitfall,* שְׁחוּת *pit,* שִׁיחָה *pit, pitfall,* שַׁחַת *pit,* שְׁחִית *pit,* אָשִׁיחַ *reservoir.*

*שׁוח II 0.0.1 vb.—**Qal** 0.0.1 Inf. cstr. שׁוח—**gesticulate** with (בְּ) hand 1QS 7_{15}.

*[שׁוּחַ] I 0.0.1 n.[m.]—cstr. שׁוח—double entendre, **pit** of perdition, **vagina** as symbol for fornication, i.e. sexual intercourse with Lady Folly 4QWiles 1_{3}. → שׁוח *sink.*

שׁוּחַ II 2 pr.n.m. **Shuah.**

שׁוּחָה I 5.0.3 n.f. **1. pitfall** Jr 18_{20}. **2. pit, snare-pit,** licentious woman Pr 23_{27}, female mouth Pr 22_{14}, perh. vagina Pr 23_{27}. **3. ravines** in wilderness Jr 2_{6}. → שׁוח *sink.*

שׁוּחָה II 1 pr.n.m. **Shuhah.**

שׁוּחִי 5 gent. **Shuhite.**

שׁוּחָם 1 pr.n.m. **Shuham.**

שׁוּחָמִי 2 gent. **Shuhamite.**

שׁוט I 13.0.4 vb.—**Qal** 7.0.3 Pf. שָׁטוּ; + waw וַיָּשֻׁטוּ; impv. שׁוּטוּ; ptc. שָׁטִים; inf. שׁוּט—**1. go about, roam** through (בְּ) land 2 S 24_{8}. **2.** of fire, **spread** through (בְּ) flames 1QH 11_{30}. **3.** ptc. as noun, **a. wanderer** 1QDM 1.3_{9}. **b. oarsman** Ezk 27_{26}.

Pol. 5.0.1 Impf. יְשׁוֹטְטוּ; ptc. מְשׁוֹטְטִים—**1. roam, run to and fro** through (בְּ) streets Jr 5_{1}. **2.** of eye, **range** through (בְּ) earth Zc 4_{10}.

Htpol. 1 Impv. הִתְשׁוֹטַטְנָה—**run to and fro within** (בְּ) wall Jr 49_{3}.

→ מָשׁוֹט *oar,* מִשּׁוֹט *oar,* שַׁיִט *oar.*

שׁוט II 3 vb.—**Qal** 3 Ptc. שָׁאטִים—**despise** Israel Ezk 16_{57}. → שְׁאָט *contempt.*

שׁוֹט I 11.2.3 n.m.—Kt שיט; cstr. שׁוֹט; pl. שׁוֹטִים—**1. whip, scourge** Si 30_{33}. **2. lash** of tongue Jb 5_{21}.

*שׁוֹט II 3.0.1 n.m.—Kt שיט—**outburst of water, flood** Is 28_{15}.

שׁוֹטֵר 25.0.9 n.m.—שֹׁטֵר; pl. שֹׁטְרִים; cstr. שֹׁטְרֵי; sf. שֹׁטְרָיו—**1. (subordinate) officer, official, magistrate** Dt 1_{15}, serving king 1 C 27_{1}, Levites 2 C 19_{11}, **military organizer,** for recruitment, battle-preparation Dt 20_{5}, **leader** of priests and Levites 1QM 7_{14}. **2. foreman,** Israelite, working for Egyptian slave-drivers Ex 5_{14}. **3. leader** among animals Pr 6_{7}. → שׁטר *rule.*

[שׁוּל] 11.0.6 n.m.—pl. cstr. שׁוּלֵי; sf. שׁוּלַיִךְ—**1.** pl., **seams, hem** of robe Ex 28_{33}. **2. edge** of wadi 3QTr 4_{9}, conduit 3QTr 1_{11}.

שׁוּלְחָן, see שֻׁלְחָן *table.*

שׁוֹלָל 3 adj.—Kt שילל—**barefoot** Jb 12_{19}. → שׁלל *take spoil.*

שׁוּלַמִּית 2 gent. f. **Shulammite.**

[שׁוּם] I 1 n.[m.]—pl. שׁוּמִים—**garlic** Nm 11_{5}.

*[שׁוּם] II 0.0.1 n.[m.] **valuation** Mur 22 1_{2}.

שׁוּמָה, see שַׁמָּה I *desolation.*

שׁוּנִי I 2 pr.n.m. **Shuni.**

שׁוּנִי II 1 gent. **Shunite.**

שׁוּנֵם 3 pl.n. **Shunem.**

שׁוּנַמִּית 8 gent. f. **Shunammite.**

שׁוע I 21.1.1 vb.—**Pi.** 21.1.1 Pf. שִׁוַּעְתִּי; impf. תְּשַׁוַּע, אֲשַׁוַּע; ptc. מְשַׁוֵּעַ; inf. cstr. שַׁוְּעִי—**cry for help, cry out** to (אֶל) Y. Ps 22$_{25}$. → שֶׁוַע *crying out,* שׁוּעַ *cry for help,* שַׁוְעָה *cry for help,* שַׁוְעָה *cry for help.*

*__שׁוע__ II 0.1.2 vb.—**Qal** 0.0.2 Ptc. pass. שׁוע—**smear over,** ptc. pass., **be smeared over,** of eye 4Q424 3$_{3}$.

Hi. 0.1 Inf. Si השע—**besmear, seal over** mouth Si 41$_{21(Bmg)}$.

שֶׁוַע I 1 n.[m.] **crying out** Is 22$_{5}$. → שׁוע I *cry for help.*

שׁוֹעַ II 2.0.1 n.m. **noble** Jb 34$_{19}$. → ישׁע *be saved.*

שׁוֹעַ III 1 pl.n. **Shoa.**

שׁוּעַ I 2 n.m.—sf. שׁוּעֲךָ—**cry for help** Jb 36$_{19}$. → שׁוע I *cry for help.*

שׁוּעַ II 2 pr.n.m. **Shua.**

שׁוּעַ III, see בַּת־שׁוּעַ *Bath-shua.*

שׁוּעַ IV, see מַלְכִּי־שׁוּעַ *Malchishua.*

*[**שֶׁוַע**] 1 n.m.—sf. שַׁוְעִי—**cry for help,** to Y. in prayer Ps 5$_{3}$. → שׁוע I *cry for help.*

שׁוּעָא 1 pr.n.f. **Shua.**

שַׁוְעָה 11.1.4 n.f.—cstr. שַׁוְעַת; sf. שַׁוְעָתִי—**cry for help,** to Y. in prayer 2 S 22$_{7}$. → שׁוע I *cry for help.*

שׁוּעָל I 7 n.m. **1. jackal,** מְנָת שֻׁעָלִים *prey of jackals* Ps 63$_{11}$. **2. fox** Ca 2$_{15}$.

שׁוּעָל II 1 pl.n. **Shual.**

שׁוּעָל III 1.0.0.14 pr.n.m. **Shual.**

שׁוֹעֵר, see שֹׁעֵר *gatekeeper.*

שׁוף I 3.0.1 vb.—**Qal** 3.0.1 Impf. יְשׁוּפְךָ; ptc. pass. Q שופים —**1. crush** human being, of Y. Jb 9$_{17}$, head, of woman's offspring Gn 3$_{15}$, heel, of serpent Gn 3$_{15}$. **2.** pass., **be scrubbed, rubbed,** of clothes CD 11$_{4}$.

*__שׁוף__ II 1 vb.—**Qal** 1 יְשׁוּפֵנִי—of darkness, **conceal** person Ps 139$_{11}$.

שׁופחה, see שִׁפְחָה *female servant.*

שׁוֹפַךְ 2 pr.n.m. **Shophach.**

שׁוּפָם 1 pr.n.m. **Shupham.**

שׁוּפָמִי 1 gent. **Shuphamite.**

שׁוֹפָן, see עַטְרֹת שׁוֹפָן *Atroth-shophan.*

שׁוֹפָר 72.0.13 n.m.—שֹׁפָר; cstr. שׁוֹפַר; pl. שׁוֹפָרוֹת (שֹׁפָרוֹת); cstr. שׁוֹפְרוֹת; sf. שׁוֹפְרֹתֵיהֶם—**ram's horn, trumpet** Jos 6$_{16}$.

שׁוק 3 vb.—**Pol.** 1 + waw וַתְּשֹׁקְקֶהָ—of Y., **irrigate earth** Ps 65$_{10}$.

Hi. 2 Pf. הֵשִׁיקוּ—**overflow,** of wine-vat Jl 2$_{24}$.

שׁוֹק 19.0.9 n.f.—cstr. שׁוֹק; du. שֹׁקַיִם; cstr. שׁוֹקֵי; sf. שׁוֹקָיו—**thigh, leg,** of animal Lv 7$_{33}$, human Ca 5$_{15}$.

שׁוּק 4.0.1 n.m.—pl. שְׁוָקִים—**street** Ca 3$_{2}$.

שׁוּר I 2 vb.—**Qal** 2 + waw וַתָּשֻׁרִי; ptc. שָׁרוֹתַיִךְ—**1. travel** Is 57$_{9}$. **2.** ptc. as noun, **traveller, caravan** Ezk 27$_{25}$. → תְּשׁוּרָה II *provisions, sustenance (for journey).*

שׁוּר II 16.0.1 vb.—**Qal** 16.0.1 Impf. יָשׁוּר (יָשֹׁר); impv. שׁוּר—**1. behold, notice** Y. Jb 34$_{29}$, Israel Nm 23$_{9}$, cloud Jb 35$_{5}$. **2. look down** from (מִן) mountain-top Ca 4$_{8}$. **3. watch with evil intent, lurk** Jr 5$_{26}$. **4a. see** vision Nm 24$_{17}$. **b. envision** hope Jb 17$_{15}$. **c. perceive, realize** Y. speaking Jb 33$_{14}$. **d. perceive, experience** Y. Jb 35$_{14}$. **5a.** of Y., **take notice of, pay attention to** empty plea Jb 35$_{13}$. **b.** of Y., **look after,** i.e. **provide** for Ephraim Ho 14$_{9}$ (unless §6). **6. look to** Y., i.e. **trust in** Y. Ho 14$_{9}$. → שׁוּר perh. *watcher,* שׁוֹרֵר *lurking enemy.*

*__שׁוּר__ III 1 vb.—**Qal** 1 Impf. אָשׁוּר—**leap out like** (כְּ) leopard, of Y. Ho 13$_{7}$.

[**שׁוּר**] I 1 n.m.—pl. sf. שׁוּרָי—perh. **watcher** Ps 92$_{12}$. → שׁוּר II *behold.*

שׁוּר II 3 n.[m.] **wall** Gn 49$_{22}$. → cf. שׁוּרָה II *little wall.*

שׁוּר III 6.0.1 pl.n. **Shur.**

שׁוֹר 79.2.20 n.m.—cstr. שׁוֹר; sf. שׁוֹרוֹ; pl. שְׁוָרִים—**1. ox,** sacrificial animal Lv 4$_{10}$, clean animal, i.e. edible Dt 14$_{4}$, work animal Ex 23$_{12}$. **2. Taurus, Bull,** in horoscope 4QCrypt 1.2$_{9}$.

[**שׁוּרָה**] I 2.0.1 n.f.—pl. sf. שׁוּרֹתָם—**row of olives** or **row of vines** Jb 24$_{11}$.

*[**שׁוּרָה**] II 2.0.1 n.f.—שׁוּרֹתָם—**little wall, supporting wall,** for terrace in vineyard Jb 24$_{11}$. → cf. שׁוּר II *wall.*

שׁוֹרֵר 5 n.m.—pl. sf. שׁוֹרְרַי—**lurking enemy** Ps 56$_{3}$. → שׁוּר II *behold.*

שַׁוְשָׁא 1 pr.n.m. **Shavsha.**

שׁוּשַׁן I 13.1 n.m.—שׁוֹשָׁן; pl. שֹׁשַׁנִּים—**1. lily,** metaphor for sensual lips Ca 5$_{13}$, for glorious priest Si 50$_{8}$. **2. lily-shaped decoration** 1 K 7$_{19}$. **3.** titles of psalms, perh. designating the melody, שׁוּשַׁן **The Lily** Ps 60$_{1}$, שֹׁשַׁנִּים **The Lilies** Ps 45$_{1}$. → cf. שׁוֹשַׁנָּה *lily.*

שׁוּשַׁן II 21 pl.n. **Susa.**

שׁוֹשַׁנָּה 4.0.1 n.f.—cstr. שׁוֹשַׁנַּת—**1. lily,** beautiful female lover Ca 2₁. **2. lily-shaped decoration** 2 C 4₅. → cf. שׁוּשַׁן *lily.*

שׁוּשַׁק, see שִׁישַׁק *Shishak.*

***[שׁוֹשַׁרְאֶצֶר]** 0.0.0.1 pr.n.f. **Shoshsharezer.**

שׁוּתֶלַח 4 pr.n.m. **Shuthelah.**

***[שׁוּתָף]** 0.2 n.m. **partner** Si 42₃(Bmg, M).

שׁזף 3.0.1 vb.—**Qal** 3.0.1 Pf. שְׁזָפַתְנִי (שְׁזָפַתּוּ)—**1.** of eye, **catch sight of** wicked Jb 20₉. **2.** of sun, **look on,** i.e. shine on, female lover Ca 1₆. **3. look on** (עַל) Judah 4QapPsB 17₂.

שׁזר 21.0.5 vb.—**Pu.** 0.0.2 Ptc. משוזר—**be twisted,** of linen 1QM 7₁₀.

Ho. 21.0.3 Ptc. מָשְׁזָר—**be twisted,** of linen Ex 26₁.

שַׁח 1 adj. **downcast,** as noun, **one downcast** Jb 22₂₉. → שׁחח *be bowed down.*

שׁחד 2.1 vb.—**Qal** 2.1 + waw וַתִּשְׁחֲדִי; impv. שִׁחֲדוּ—**1. bribe, offer bribe** Si 32₁₄. **2. give present to** lover Ezk 16₃₃. → שֹׁחַד *bribe, gift.*

שֹׁחַד 23.1.9 n.m. **1. bribe, gift,** שֹׁחַד כֶּסֶף *gift of silver* 1 K 15₁₉. **2. bribery,** אָהֳלֵי־שֹׁחַד *tents of bribery* Jb 15₃₄. → שׁחד *bribe, give present.*

שׁחה 172.1.16 vb.—**Qal** 1 Impv. שְׁחִי—**get down** Is 51₂₃.

Hi. 1 Impf. יַשְׁחֶנָּה—**1. quash, suppress** anxiety Pr 12₂₅ (unless §2). **2.** of anxiety, **weigh down** person Pr 12₂₅.

Htpal. 170.1.16 Pf. הִשְׁתַּחֲוֵיתִי, הִשְׁתַּחֲווּ (הִשְׁתַּחֲווּ); impf. יִשְׁתַּחוּ (יִשְׁתַּחֲוֶה); impv. הִשְׁתַּחֲוִי; ptc. מִשְׁתַּחֲוֶה; inf. הִשְׁתַּחֲוֹת (הִשְׁתַּחֲוָיָתִי)—**1.** in religious context, **bow down** in reverence, **worship, a.** to (לְ) Y. 1 S 1₂₈, before (לִפְנֵי) Y. GnzPs 3₁₇. **b.** abs., implied to angel of Y. Jos 5₁₄. **c.** to (לְ) Baal 1 K 16₃₁, before (לִפְנֵי) gods 2 C 25₁₄. **2. bow down, make an obeisance,** before persons, as gesture of respect or submission, to (לְ) priest 1 S 2₃₆, before (לִפְנֵי) king 2 S 14₃₃. **3.** ptc. as noun, **one who bows down** to (לְ) foreign deities Zp 1₅.

→ cf. שׁחח *be low,* הִשְׁתַּחֲוֹת *prostration.*

שְׁחוֹר, see שִׁיחוֹר *Shihor.*

***שְׁחוֹר** 1 n.[m.] **soot** Lm 4₈. → שׁחר *be black.*

[שְׁחוּת] 1 n.f.—sf. שְׁחוּתוֹ—**pit** Pr 28₁₀. → שׁוח *sink.*

שׁחח 21.1.5 vb.—**Qal** 11.0.2 Pf. שַׁחוֹתִי, שַׁחוּ (שָׁחֲחוּ); impf. יָשֹׁחַ; + waw וַיָּשַׁח; inf. שְׁחוֹחַ—**1. be brought low, humbled, a.** of person Ps 107₃₉. **b.** of pride Is 2₁₁. **2. be bowed down,** out of sadness Ps 35₁₄. **3. bow,** in submission Pr 14₁₉. **4. crouch,** of lion Jb 38₄₀. **5. come down, collapse,** of hill Hb 3₆.

Ni. 4.1 Impf. תִּשַּׁח—**1. be brought low, humbled,** of humanity Is 2₉. **2. be bowed down,** i.e. relax guard, of star Si 43₁₀. **3. die down, grow faint,** of speech Is 29₄.

Hi. 2.0.1 Pf. הֵשַׁח—**bring down, low** people Is 26₅, fortification Is 25₁₂, pride CD 1₁₅.

Hithpoel 0.0.1 Ptc. משתוחיחי—ptc. as noun, **one who casts down, oppressor** 1QH 17₉.

Hithpoal 4.0.1 Impf. תִּשְׁתּוֹחֵחַ—of soul, **be downcast, depressed** within (עַל) worshipper Ps 42₆.

→ שַׁח *downcast;* cf. שׁחה *be low.*

שׁחט 85.0.9 vb.—**Qal** 82.0.9 Pf. שָׁחַט, שָׁחֲטוּ; impf. יִשְׁחַט; impv. שַׁחֲטוּ; ptc. שׁוֹחֵט; ptc. pass. שָׁחוּט, שְׁחוּטָה; inf. abs. שָׁחֹט; cstr. שְׁחֹט (שַׁחֲטָם)—**1.** of human being, **slaughter, kill** animal, **a.** with obj., (1) as sacrifice Ezr 6₂₀. (2) for food 1 S 14₃₂. (3) for blood Gn 37₃₁. **b.** without obj., **slaughter sacrifices on** (אֶל) table Ezk 40₄₁. **c.** appar. **offer** blood Ex 34₂₅. **2.** of human being, **slay another human being, a.** for political reasons Jg 12₆. **b.** for religious reasons 1 K 18₄₀, specif. as sacrifice to deity Gn 22₁₀. **3.** of deity, **kill people** Nm 14₁₆. **4.** of weapon, **have potential to kill, be lethal** Jr 9₇(Kt). **5.** ptc. pass., **a. be killed,** of bird Lv 14₆. **b. be beaten,** of gold 1 K 10₁₆, **be hammered,** i.e. be sharpened, of arrow Jr 9₇(Qr). **6.** inf. as noun, **slaughtering** of sheep Is 22₁₃. **7.** ptc. as noun, **a. one who slaughters** an animal Is 66₃. **b. one who slays** a child as sacrifice to deity Is 57₅.

Ni. 3 Impf. יִשָּׁחֵט—**be slaughtered,** of animal, **1.** as sacrifice Lv 6₁₈. **2.** for food Nm 11₂₂.

→ שַׁחֲטָה *slaughtering,* שְׁחִיטָה *slaughtering.*

שַׁחֲטָה 1 n.f. **slaughtering** Ho 5₂. → שׁחט *slaughter.*

[שְׁחִיטָה] 1 n.f.—cstr. שְׁחִיטַת—**slaughtering** 2 C 30₁₇. → שׁחט *slaughter.*

שֻׁחִי, see שׁוּחִי *Shuhite.*

שְׁחִין 13 n.m.—cstr. שְׁחִין—**inflammation** Lv 13₂₃.

שָׁחִיס 1 n.[m.] **self-sown grain** Is 37₃₀(MT). → cf. סָחִישׁ

self-sown grain.

[שְׁחִית] 2 n.f.—pl. sf. שְׁחִיתוֹתָם—**pit** Ps 107_{20}. → שׁוח I *sink.*

*[שְׁחִיתָה] 0.1 n.f.—pl. sf. שחיתותיו—**fault** Si 30_{11}. → שׁחת *destroy, ruin.*

שַׁחַל I 7 n.m. **lion** Ps 91_{13}.

*שַׁחַל II 1 n.m. **lizard** Ps 91_{13}.

שְׁחֵלֶת 1 n.f. perh. **onycha,** spice to make frankincense Ex 30_{34}.

[שַׁחַף] 2 n.m. **sea gull,** prohibited as food Lv 11_{16}.

שַׁחֶפֶת 2 n.f. **consumption, illness** Lv 26_{16}.

[שַׁחַץ] 2 n.[m.] **pride,** בְּנֵי־שַׁחַץ *sons of pride,* i.e. majestic wild animals Jb 28_{8}.

שׁחק 4.1.1 vb.—**Qal** 4.1.1 Pf. שָׁחֲקוּ; impf. אֶשְׁחָקֵם—**1. crush, pound** enemy 2 S 22_{43}. **2.** with partitive מִן, **grind, beat fine** spices Ex 30_{36}. **3.** of water, **wear away, erode** stone Jb 14_{19}. → שַׁחַק *cloud; dust.*

שַׁחַק 21.1.13 n.m.—pl. שְׁחָקִים—**1.** oft. pl., **clouds, rags of clouds, sky** Is 45_{8}. **2.** sg., **sky, heaven** Ps 89_{7}, **rags of clouds** Is 40_{15}(1QIsa[a]). **3.** sg., **dust,** שַׁחַק מֹאזְנַיִם *dust of,* i.e. on, *the balances* Is 40_{15}(MT). → שׁחק *crush, wear away.*

שׁחר I 1.1 vb.—**Qal** 1 Pf. שָׁחַר—**be black, darken,** of skin Jb 30_{30}.

Hi. 0.1 Impf. ישחיר—**blacken** appearance of a person Si 25_{17}.

→ שְׁחוֹר *soot,* שָׁחֹר *black, dark,* שַׁחֲרוּת I *blackness of hair,* שְׁחַרְחֹר I *dark of skin,* מִשְׁחוֹר *darkness.*

שׁחר II 12.2.16 vb.—**Qal** 1 Ptc. שֹׁחֵר—**seek,** ptc. as noun, **one who seeks** what is good Pr 11_{27}.

Pi. 11.2.16 Pf. שִׁחֲרוּ; impf. אֲשַׁחֲרֶךָּ, תְּשַׁחֵר; ptc. מְשַׁחֲרֵי—**1. seek longingly, wholeheartedly, desperately** Y. Is 26_{9}, Y.'s face 4QapJerC[a] 1.2_{4}. **2. look carefully for, seek eagerly** person Jb 7_{21}, person's face Pr 7_{15}. **3a. seek** Y.'s **favour** 4QInstr[b] 2.3_{12}. **b. search eagerly for** (לְ) food Jb 24_{5}. **4. be on the look out for** abomination, i.e. opportunity to engage in sinful activities 4QWiles 1_{1}. **5. investigate** Y.'s purpose 4QInstr[c] 1.1_{12}. **6. be eager to gain** wisdom 4QBéat 2.2_{3}. **7.** ptc. as noun, **one who seeks Y. wholeheartedly** Si 35_{14}.

*שׁחר III vb.—**Qal, bewitch,** ptc. as noun, **sorcerer** Is 47_{15} (if em. סֹחֲרַיִךְ *your merchants* to שֹׁחֲרַיִךְ *your sorcerers*). → שַׁחַר II *magic, power.*

שָׁחֹר 6.0.2.1 adj.—f.s. שְׁחוֹרָה (Q שחורא); m.pl. שְׁחֹרִים; f.pl. שְׁחֹרוֹת—**1. black,** of stone 3QTr 12_{2}, hair Lv 13_{31}, horse Zc $6_{2.6}$. **2. dark of skin,** of female lover Ca 1_{5}. → שׁחר I *be black.*

שַׁחַר I 24.0.7 n.m. **1. dawn, morning twilight, morning grey,** emphasis on its day-light Is 8_{20}, on its greyness, lack of brightness Jl 2_{2}. **2.** אַיֶּלֶת הַשַּׁחַר **Hind of the Dawn,** title of Psalm, perh. melody of a song Ps 22_{1}. **3.** Qumran, בני השחר **Sons of the Dawn** CD 13_{14}, i.e. either **a.** syn. to בני אור *Sons of Light,* hence **members of the Qumran sect,** or **b. sectarian novices, Qumran probationers.** → cf. מִשְׁחָר I *dawn.*

*שַׁחַר II 1 n.[m.] **magic, power,** to bewitch with evil intentions Is 8_{20}. → שׁחר III *bewitch.*

*שַׁחַר III 0.0.0.21 pr.n.m. **Shahar.**

שְׁחֹר, see שִׁיחוֹר *Shihor.*

שַׁחֲרוּת I 1 n.f. **blackness of hair** Ec 11_{10}. → שׁחר I *be black.*

*שַׁחֲרוּת II 1 n.f. **dawn of youth, prime of life** Ec 11_{10}.

[שְׁחַרְחֹר] I 1 adj.—f.s. שְׁחַרְחֹרֶת—**dark of skin,** of female lover Ca 1_{6}. → שׁחר I *be black.*

*[שְׁחַרְחֹר] II 0.0.0.2 pr.n.m. **Sheharhor.**

שְׁחַרְיָה 1 pr.n.m. **Shehariah.**

שַׁחֲרַיִם 1 pr.n.m. **Shaharaim.**

שׁחת 151.10.28 vb.—**Ni.** 6.0.2 Pf. נִשְׁחַת, נִשְׁחָתָה; impf. תִּשָּׁחֵת; ptc. נִשְׁחָתוֹת—**1a. be spoiled, made useless,** of vessel Jr 18_{4}. **b. be ruined, be made inhabitable,** by pests, of land Ex 8_{20}. **2. be morally corrupt,** of earth, i.e. its population Gn 6_{11}, of deed Ezk 20_{44}.

Pi. 39.0.2 Pf. שִׁחֵת, שִׁחַתָּ, שִׁחֲתוּ; impv. שַׁחֲתוּ; inf. cstr. שַׁחֵת (שַׁחֶתְכֶם)—**1. destroy, ruin** place Gn 19_{13}, **annihilate** people Ezk 20_{17}, **permanently damage** bodily part Ex 21_{26}. **2. wipe out** wickedness 1QM 3_{9}. **3. bring calamity to** (לְ) people Nm 32_{15}. **4a. spill** seed Gn 38_{9}. **b. waste** words Pr 23_{8}. **5a. corrupt, violate** covenant Ml 2_{8}. **b. pervert, debase** wisdom Ezk 28_{17}. **6. stifle, repress** compassion Am 1_{11}. **7. behave in a corrupt way, sinful way, a.** abs. Ho 9_{9}. **b.** towards (לְ) Y. Dt 32_{5}.

Pu. 0.0.1 Ptc. משוחת—ptc. as noun, **that which is blemished, blemished animal** 5QapMal 1_{1} (cf. Ml 1_{14}).

Hi. 104.9.23 Pf. הִשְׁחִית; impf. יַשְׁחִית, תַּשְׁחֵת; + waw וַיַּשְׁחֵת; impv. הַשְׁחִיתָה; ptc. מַשְׁחִית, מַשְׁחִיתִים; inf. abs. הַשְׁחֵת; cstr. הַשְׁחִית—**1. destroy** places, **annihilate** people, of Y. Gn 6$_{13}$, of angel 1 C 21$_{15}$, of people 2 C 24$_{23}$. **2. ruin** a person, i.e. reputation, by slander Pr 11$_{9}$. **3a. destroy oneself** Pr 6$_{32}$. **b.** of desire, **destroy, consume** person Si 6$_{4}$. **4. overthrow** kingdom Dn 11$_{17}$. **5. impair** one's estate Ru 4$_{6}$. **6. mar, trim** beard Lv 19$_{27}$. **7.** of Y., **spoil, make** pride **go lost** Jr 13$_{9}$. **8. make** deed **corrupt** Zp 3$_{7}$, way Gn 6$_{12}$. **9. behave in a corrupt way, sinful way** Si 51$_{5}$. **10.** of ferocious beast or poisonous animal, **devour, do harm to** people Ps 78$_{45}$; **ravage** land 1 S 6$_{5}$. **11a.** of wind, **be destructive** Jr 51$_{1}$. **b.** of downpour, **do damage to** many 1QH 10$_{27}$. **12.** ptc. as noun, **a. destroyer, executioner** Ex 12$_{23}$. **b. raiders** 1 S 14$_{15}$. **13.** אַל־תַּשְׁחֵת **Do Not Destroy,** title of certain psalms, perh. melody of a song Ps 57$_{1}$.

Ho. 2.1 Ptc. מָשְׁחָת—**1. be polluted,** of fountain Pr 25$_{26}$. **2. be (made) morally corrupt** Si 9$_{8}$ (ה[ש]חתו). **3.** ptc. as noun, **that which is blemished, blemished animal** Ml 1$_{14}$.

→ שְׁחִיתָה *fault,* מַשְׁחִית I *destruction,* מַשְׁחֵת *destruction,* מִשְׁחָת *disfigurement,* מָשְׁחָת *blemish.*

שַׁחַת 23.5.34 n.f.—cstr. שַׁחַת; sf. שַׁחְתָּם—**1. pit of death, Sheol** Ps 16$_{10}$, **pit of corruption** or **corruption** 4QWiles 1$_{5}$, **pit of perdition** or **perdition, destruction** 1QH 10$_{21}$, perh. **hell, damnation** 1QS 4$_{12}$. **2. pit, trap** Ps 94$_{13}$. **3. dirty ditch, cesspool** Jb 9$_{31}$. → שׁוח *sink.*

שִׁטָּה I 28.0.2 n.f.—pl. שִׁטִּים—**1.** sg., **acacia tree** Is 41$_{19}$. **2.** pl., **acacia wood** Ex 25$_{5}$.

שִׁטָּה II, see בֵּית הַשִּׁטָּה *Beth-shittah.*

שׁטח 6 vb.—**Qal** 5 + waw וַתִּשְׁטַח; ptc. שֹׁטֵחַ; inf. abs. שָׁטוֹחַ—**1. spread out** groats 2 S 17$_{19}$. **2.** with לְ of obj., of Y., **expand, enlarge** nations Jb 12$_{23}$.

Pi. 1 Pf. שִׁטַּחְתִּי—**stretch out** hand to (אֶל) Y. Ps 88$_{10}$.

→ מִשְׁטוֹחַ *spreading place,* מִשְׁטָח *spreading place.*

שֹׁטֵט 1 n.[m.] **scourge** Jos 23$_{13}$.

שִׁטִּים 5 pl.n. **Shittim.**

שטנז, see שַׁעַטְנֵז *mixed stuff.*

שׁטף 31.0.9 vb.—**Qal** 28.0.9 Pf. שָׁטַף, שְׁטָפוּנוּ; impf. יִשְׁטוֹף; ptc. שׁוֹטֵף—**1a. overflow, flood,** of river, stream, (1) obj. Israelites Is 43$_{2}$, land Jr 47$_{2}$. (2) abs. Ps 78$_{20}$. **b. gush down,** of rain Ezk 13$_{11}$. **c. come like a flood, be overwhelming,** of divine retribution Is 10$_{22}$. **d. sweep through like a flood,** of army Dn 11$_{26}$. **e. dash forward,** of horse Jr 8$_{6}$. **2a. wash away, rinse away** blood Ezk 16$_{9}$. **b. rinse, clean** hands Lv 15$_{11}$.

Ni. 2 Impf. יִשָּׁטֵף—**1. be swept away,** of army Dn 11$_{22}$. **2. be rinsed,** of vessel Lv 15$_{12}$.

Pu. 1 Pf. שֻׁטַּף—**be rinsed,** of vessel Lv 6$_{21}$.

→ שֶׁטֶף *flood.*

שֶׁטֶף 6 n.m. **flood,** שֶׁטֶף מַיִם *flood of waters* Ps 32$_{6}$, **overflowing,** שֶׁטֶף אַף *overflowing of anger* Pr 27$_{4}$. → שׁטף *overflow, rinse;* cf. שֶׁצֶף *flood.*

* **שׁטר** 0.0.1 vb.—**Qal, rule,** perh. Hazor bowl inscr. 2 (שטרו; others read שטרן or שמרן *Samaria*).

Ni. 0.0.1 Pf. נשטרה—perh. **be ruled,** 4QMyst[a] 1$_{4}$.

→ (?) מִשְׁטָר *writing,* שׁוֹטֵר *(subordinate) officer.*

[שִׁטְרַי] 1 pr.n.m. **Shitrai.**

שׁטרן, see שׁטר *rule.*

שַׁי 3.0.0.3 n.m. **tribute,** brought to Y. Is 18$_{7}$.

שיא, see שְׁוָא *Sheva.*

שִׁיאֹן 1 pl.n. **Shion.**

[שִׁיבָה] I 1 n.f.—sf. שִׁיבָתוֹ—**stay** 2 S 19$_{33}$. → ישׁב *dwell.*

[שִׁיבָה] II 1.0.2 n.f.—cstr. שִׁיבַת; sf. Q שיבתם—**1. restoration,** שִׁיבַת צִיּוֹן *restoration of Zion* Ps 126$_{1}$. **2. repentance** 4QNarrB 1$_{10}$. → שׁוב *return; be restored;* cf. שׁוּבָה *repentance.*

שׁיה 1 vb.—**Qal** 1 Impf. תֶּשִׁי—**neglect, be unmindful** of the Rock, i.e. Y. Dt 32$_{18}$.

שָׁיו, see שָׁוְא *deceit; vanity.*

שִׁיזָא 1 pr.n.m. **Shiza.**

שִׁיחָה 3 n.f.—pl. שִׁיחוֹת—**pit, pitfall** Ps 57$_{7}$. → שׁוח I *sink.*

שִׁיחוֹר 4 pl.n. **Shihor.**

שִׁיחוֹר לִבְנָת 1 pl.n. **Shihor-libnath.**

שׁיט I, see שׁוֹט I *whip.*

שׁיט II, see שׁוֹט II *outburst of water, flood.*

שַׁיִט 1 n.[m.] **oar** Is 33$_{21}$. → שׁוט I *roam.*

שִׁילוֹ I 1 pr.n.m. **Shiloh.**

שִׁילוֹ II 33.0.2 pl.n. **Shiloh.**

שִׁילוֹ III, see תַּאֲנַת שִׁלֹה *Taanath-shiloh.*

שִׁילוֹנִי 7.0.1 gent. **Shilonite.**

שילל, see שׁוֹלָל *barefoot*.

שִׁימוֹן 1 pr.n.m. **Shimon.**

[שַׁיִן] 2 n.m.—pl. sf. שֵׁינֵיהֶם—**urine** 2 K 18_{27}. → שׁתן *urinate*.

שִׁיר, see שְׁאֵר *flesh*.

שִׁיר 87.0.6 vb.—**Qal** 49.0.4 Pf. שָׁר; impf. יָשִׁיר; + waw וַתָּשַׁר; impv. שִׁירוּ; ptc. שָׁרִים ,שָׁר; inf. cstr. Qr שִׁיר (Kt שׁוּר)—**1. sing a song (of praise),** obj. שִׁירָה Ex 15_1, שִׁיר Ps 33_3, שִׁגָּיוֹן Ps 7_1, תְּהִלָּה Is 42_{10}; to (לְ) Y. Ex 15_1, beloved Is 5_1. **2. sing of, about** Y.'s loyalty Ps 89_2. **3. sing,** oft. to (לְ) Y. Jg 5_1. **4.** ptc. as noun, **singer** 2 S 19_{36}.

Pol. 37.0.1 Pf. שֹׁרְרוּ; impf. יְשׁוֹרֵר; ptc. מְשֹׁרְרִים ,מְשׁוֹרֵר (מְשֹׁרֲרִים); inf. cstr. Q שורר—**1. sing a song,** obj. שִׁיר 2 C 29_{28}. **2. sing of, about** Y.'s work Jb 36_{24}. **3.** of voice of bird, **sing, hoot, croak** Zp 2_{14}. **4.** ptc. as noun, **singer** Ezr 2_{65}.

Hi. 0.0.1 + waw וישרם—of Y., **make the meek sing** 4QBark^a 1.1_{10}.

Ho. or Pass. Qal 1 Impf. יוּשַׁר—**be sung,** of song Is 26_1.

→ שִׁיר *song*, שִׁירָה *song*, מְשִׁיר *song*.

שִׁיר I 77.8.22 n.m.—cstr. שִׁיר; sf. שִׁירִי; pl. שִׁירִים (שָׁרִים); cstr. Q שירי; sf. שָׁרֶיךָ—**1. song,** oft. **religious song,** assoc. with David Ps 65_1, Solomon Ps 127_1, Levites 1 C 6_{16}, specif. Asaph Ps 75_1, Korah Ps 45_1, **song of praise** to Y., esp. in the Psalms Ps 69_{31}, **dedication-song** Ps 30_1, **pilgrim-song** Ps 120_1; **victory-song** Jg 5_{12} Is 26_1, **farewell-song** Gn 31_{27}, **erotic love-song** Ca 1_1, **song of a prostitute** Is 23_{16}. **2. melody, music,** חליל ונבל יעריבו שיר *flute and harp produce a sweet melody* Si 40_{21}. → שִׁיר *sing*; cf. מְשִׁיר *song*.

*[שִׁיר] II 0.1 n.m. **ox** Si 38_{25}(Bmg).

שִׁירָה 13.4.8 n.f.—cstr. שִׁירַת; sf. Si שירתי; pl. שִׁירוֹת; sf. Q שירותיו—**song,** oft. **song of praise** to Y. 2 S 22_1, **lamentation** Am 8_3, **song of warning** for Israelites, written by Moses Dt 31_{19}, **love-song** Is 5_1, **ditty** about prostitute Is 23_{15}. → שִׁיר *sing*.

שַׁיִשׁ 1 n.[m.] **marble** 1 C 29_2.

שִׁישָׁא 1 pr.n.m. **Shisha.**

שִׁישַׁק 7 pr.n.m. **Shishak.**

שִׁית 83.6.5 vb.—**Qal** 81.6.5 Pf. שַׁתִּי ,שָׁת; impf. תָּשִׁית (תָּשֶׁת), תָּשֵׁת); + waw וַיָּשֶׁת; impv. שִׁיתוּ ,שִׁית; inf. abs. שֹׁת; cstr. שִׁית—**1a. place, lay** barley **on** (עַל) someone Ru 3_{15}. **b. put** ornaments **on** (עַל) oneself, i.e. wear Ex 33_4. **c.** of Y., **bring** punishment **on** (עַל) town Is 15_9. **d. impose** guilt **on** (עַל) someone Nm 12_{11}. **e.** of Y., **set, establish** world **on** (עַל) pillars 1 S 2_8. **2a.** of Y., **place, put, lay** someone **in** (בְּ) pit Ps 88_7. **b. harbour** deceit **within** (בְּקֶרֶב) oneself, i.e. inwardly Pr 26_{24}. **3.** of Y., **place, put** Israel **among** (בְּ) sons Jr 3_{19}. **4. place, put** people **with** (עִם) dogs Jb 30_1. **5.** of Y., **place, put** enmity **between** (בֵּין) woman, serpent and their offspring Gn 3_{15}. **6.** of Y., **place, put** everything **under** (תַּחַת) human feet Ps 8_7. **7. lay** child **at** (בְּ) one's bosom Ru 4_{16}. **8. set** vile thing **before** (לְנֶגֶד) one's eyes Ps 101_3. **9. set apart,** וַיָּשֶׁת־לוֹ עֲדָרִים לְבַדּוֹ *and he set (his) flocks apart (for himself)* Gn 30_{40}. **10.** of Y., **set** guard **over** (לְ) someone's mouth Ps 141_3. **11. set** snare **for** (לְ) someone Ps 140_6. **12.** of Y., **set, fix, establish, a.** border Ex 23_{31}. **b.** time Jb 14_{13}. **13.** with bodily parts as obj., **a.** (1) **lay** one's hand **upon** (עַל) person's head Gn 48_{14}. (2) **put out, reach out** one's hand Si 34_{14}(Bmg). (3) **join** hands **with** (עִם) the wicked Ex 23_1. **b. set, apply** one's heart or mind **to** (לְ) knowledge Pr 22_{17}. **c. set, turn** one's face **toward** (אֶל) steppe Nm 24_1. **d. set** eyes, עֵינֵיהֶם יָשִׁיתוּ לִנְטוֹת בָּאָרֶץ *they set their eyes to roam over the land* Ps 17_{11}. **14. appoint, put** person **in charge over** (עַל) land Gn 41_{33}. **15.** of Y., **grant, give, a.** two objs., blessing to king Ps 21_7. **b.** offspring to (לְ) wife Gn 4_{25}. **16.** oft. of Y., **make, a. make** one something, **cause to be** something, two objs., Solomon a leader 1 K 11_{34}. **b. make, turn** sons **into** (לְ) princes Ps 45_{17}. **c. make** one's shadow **like** (כְּ) night Is 16_3. **d. cause to be, bring** darkness **into existence** Ps 104_{20}. **e. perform** mourning ritual Si 38_{17}. **f. prepare** feast Jr 51_{39}. **17. take one's stand, take a position** Is 22_7; against (עַל) worshipper Ps 3_7.

Qal Pass. 2 Impf. יוּשַׁת—of redemption payment, **be laid, be imposed upon** (עַל) person Ex 21_{30}.

→ שִׁית I *mantle*, (?) שָׁת *foundation*.

שַׁיִת 7.0.3 n.[m.]—sf. שִׁיתוֹ—**thistles** Is 5_6.

שִׁית I 2 n.[m.]—cstr. שִׁית—**mantle** Pr 7_{10}. → שִׁית *put, set*.

[שִׁית] II 0.0.6 n.f. **ditch, dry well** 3QTr 3_8.

שׁכב 212.1.30.1 vb.—**Qal** 198.1.29.1 Pf. שָׁכַבְתָּ ,שָׁכַב; impf.

יִשְׁכַּב (Q ישכוב); impv. שְׁכַב, שִׁכְבִי; ptc. שֹׁכֵב, שֹׁכֶבֶת; inf. abs. שָׁכֹב; cstr. שְׁכַב (לִשְׁכַּב, Q לשכוב, שָׁכְבוֹ)—**1. lie down, go to bed, lie in bed,** to sleep 1 S 3_{2}, to rest Nm 23_{24}, to (attempt to) recover from illness, wounds 2 K 9_{16}, to have sexual intercourse Gn 19_{33}; **lie down** on (ה-) ground, ritual accompanying prayer for mercy 2 S 12_{16}, mourning ritual 2 S 13_{31}; **lie down** in (בְּ) shame Jr 3_{25}, **lie in** (בְּ) sackcloth 1 K 21_{27}, i.e. rituals of penitence. **2. lie in** (בְּ) someone's bosom 1 K 1_{2}. **3. lie upon** (עַל) someone, to revive him 2 K 4_{34}. **4. lie on** (עַל) one's side, symbolic ritual of vicariously bearing Israel's iniquity Ezk 4_{4}. **5. lodge, spend the night** Jos 2_{1}. **6. lie (beside), sleep (with), have sexual relations (with)** someone, sometimes specif. **rape** 2 S 13_{14}, **a.** with (עִם or אֵת) woman Gn 35_{22} 2 S 11_{4}. **b.** beside (אֵצֶל) woman Gn 39_{10}. **c.** obj. woman 2 S 13_{14}. **d.** of male, with (אֵת) male, + obj. מִשְׁכָּב or שְׁכָבָה, אֶת־זָכָר לֹא תִשְׁכַּב מִשְׁכְּבֵי אִשָּׁה *you shall not lie with a male the lying of,* i.e. as one lies with, *a woman* Lv 18_{22}. **7. lie down,** euphemism for **die, a. lie down with** (almost alw. עִם, once אֵת) ancestors, **join in the grave,** esp. of Israelite kings Gn 47_{30} (עִם) 2 S 7_{12} (אֵת). **b. lie dead** with (אֵת) the uncircumcised Ezk 32_{29}. **c. lie down, die with** (עִם) the truth 4QInstr[b] 2.3_{7}. **d. lie, sleep in** (בְּ) grave Is 14_{18}. **e. lie dead** in the streets (חוצות) Lm 2_{21}. **f. lie (to decompose)** on (עַל) dust Jb 20_{11}. **h.** abs., **lie down dead** Jg 5_{27}; with emphasis on death's peacefulness, **lie in repose** Jb 3_{13}. **8.** of mind, **rest** at (בְּ) night Ec 2_{23}. **9.** of pain, **settle down** Jb 30_{17}. **10.** ptc. as noun, **a. one who lies (down)** on (עַל) bed Am 6_{4}. **b. one who lodges** in (בְּ) house Lv 14_{47}. **c. one who lies** in one's bosom, i.e. wife Mc 7_{5}. **d. one who lies, has sexual intercourse** with (עִם) woman Dt 27_{20}. **e. one who lies (dead)** in grave Ps 88_{6}, **one who lies** in dust 1QH 14_{34}.

Ni. 2.0.1 Pf. Q ישכבה; impf. Qr תִּשָּׁכַבְנָה—**be lain with, slept with,** sexually Is $13_{16(Qr)}$.

Pu. 1 Pf. Qr שֻׁכַּבְתְּ—**be lain with, slept with,** sexually Jr $3_{2(Qr)}$.

Hi. 8 Pf. הִשְׁכִּיבָה; impf. יַשְׁכִּיב; inf. abs. הַשְׁכֵּב—**1. lay** child upon (עַל) bed 2 K 4_{21}. **2.** of Y., **let Israelites lie down in** (לְ) safety Ho 2_{20}. **3. make** or **force** people **to lie down on** (ה-) ground 2 S 8_{2}. **4. tilt, tip over** jar Jb 38_{37}.

Ho. 3 Impv. הָשְׁכְּבָה; + waw וְהָשְׁכַּב; ptc. מֻשְׁכָּב—**be laid out dead, be laid to rest** 2 K 4_{32}.

→ מִשְׁכָּב *bed,* שְׁכָבָה *lying down,* שְׁכֹבֶת *lying down.*

[שְׁכָבָה] or **[שִׁכְבָה]** 9.0.5 n.f.—cstr. שִׁכְבַת (Q שוכבת)—**1. lying down** of seed, in ref. to sexual intercourse Lv 15_{18}. **2. layer, covering** of dew Ex 16_{13}. → שׁכב *lie down.*

[שְׁכֹבֶת] 4 n.f.—sf. שְׁכָבְתּוֹ—**lying down,** sexual Lv 18_{20}. → שׁכב *lie down.*

שׁכה 1 vb.—**Hi.** 1 Ptc. מַשְׁכִּים—**have large testicles,** of horse Jr 5_{8}. → אֶשֶׁךְ *testicle.*

שַׁכּוּל 6 adj.—f.s. שַׁכֻּלָה; f.pl. שַׁכֻּלוֹת—**1. bereaved of cubs,** of bear 2 S 17_{8}. **2. bereaved of children,** of woman Is 47_{8}. **3.** as noun, **animal bereaved of her young** Ca 4_{2}. → שׁכל *be bereaved.*

שְׁכוֹל 3 n.[m.] **1. loss of children** Is $47_{8.9}$. **2. forlornness** of soul Ps 35_{12}. → שׁכל *be bereaved.*

[שָׁכוּל] 1 adj.—f. שְׁכוּלָה—**bereaved, childless,** of Zion Is 49_{21}. → שׁכל *be bereaved.*

שִׁכּוֹר 13.1.2 adj.—שִׁכֹּר; f.s. שִׁכֹּרָה; m.pl. cstr. שִׁכּוֹרֵי (שִׁכֹּרֵי)—**1. drunk** 1 S 25_{36}. **2.** ptc. as noun, **drunkard, a.** masc. Is 28_{1}. **b.** fem. 1 S 1_{13}. → שׁכר *be drunk.*

שׁכח I 102.7.17 vb.—**Qal** 86.2.16 Pf. שָׁכַח (שְׁכֵחֲנִי), שָׁכַחַתְּ; impf. יִשְׁכַּח; impv. שִׁכְחִי; inf. abs. שָׁכֹחַ—**1a. forget** (by failing to observe) precepts Ps 119_{93}. **b. forget, fail to show** kindness Si $3_{14(C)}$. **c. forget, be unfaithful** to covenant Dt 4_{23}. **d. forget** Jerusalem, i.e. its temple worship Ps 137_{5}. **2. forget** events, acts, former condition, state Is 54_{4}; sometimes **deliberately dismiss from one's mind,** hence **attempt to forget** Dt 9_{7}; **ignore** person's cry, affliction Ps 9_{13}; perh. **forgive** unkind act Gn 27_{45}. **3. forget (location of)** place Jr 50_{6}. **4. forget, be careless about** belongings Jr 23_{2}. **5. forget, leave behind** something Dt 24_{19}. **6a. forget, be unmindful of** Y., oft. by being disobedient, worshipping other gods Ho 2_{15}. **b. forget, be unmindful of, be careless about** someone Is 49_{15}; specif. **forget to mention** someone Gn 40_{23}. **7.** obj. implied, **a.** of Y., **overlook** sin Ps 10_{11}. **b.** of human being, **forget** to do something Pr 4_{5}, what Y. has done Ps 59_{12}, **be**

unmindful of someone Is 49$_{15}$. c. of hand, **forget its skill** Ps 137$_5$. 8. followed by inf., **forget,** הֲשָׁכַח חַנּוֹת אֵל *has God forgotten to be gracious?* Ps 77$_{10}$. 9. followed by כִּי, **forget,** וַתִּשְׁכַּח כִּי־רֶגֶל תְּזוּרֶהָ *and she forgets that a foot may crush them* Jb 39$_{15}$. 10. ptc. as noun, **one who forgets, one who is unmindful of** Y. Jb 8$_{13}$.

Ni. 13.2.1 Pf. נִשְׁכַּחְתִּי; impf. תִּשָּׁכַח (תִּשָּׁכֵחַ); נִשְׁכָּחָה (נִשְׁכַּחַת), נִשְׁכָּחִים—**1.** of events, acts, former condition, state, **be forgotten** Is 65$_{16}$. **2.** of remote place, **be forgotten, be unknown** Jb 28$_4$. **3.** of covenant, **be forgotten, be broken** Jr 50$_5$. **4.** of person, **be forgotten, be ignored** Ps 9$_{19}$. **5.** of memory of deceased, **be forgotten** Ec 9$_5$.

Pi. 1.3 Pf. שִׁכַּח—**cause to be forgotten, 1.** of hardship, obj. enjoyment Si 11$_{27}$. **2.** of Y., obj. festival, sabbath Lm 2$_6$.

Hi. 1 Inf. cstr. הַשְׁכִּיחַ—**cause people to forget** name of Y. Jr 23$_{27}$.

Htp. 1 Impf. יִשְׁתַּכְּחוּ—**be forgotten,** of wicked Ec 8$_{10}$.

→ שָׁכֵחַ *forgetful.*

***שׁכח** II 4 vb.—**Qal** 3 Pf. שָׁכַחְתִּי; impf. תִּשְׁכַּח—**wilt, wither,** of worshipper Ps 102$_5$, hand Ps 137$_5$.

Ni. 1 Pf. נִשְׁכַּחְתִּי—**be wilted,** of worshipper Ps 31$_{13}$.

***שׁכח** III 4 vb.—**Qal** 3 Pf. שָׁכַחְתִּי; impf. תִּשְׁכַּח—**1. sink low, be knocked down,** of worshipper Ps 102$_5$. **2. drop,** of hand Ps 137$_5$.

Ni. 1 Pf. נִשְׁכַּחְתִּי—**bow down, sink low,** of worshipper Ps 31$_{13}$.

→ cf. שׁכך *subside.*

[**שָׁכֵחַ**] 2 adj.—pl. שְׁכֵחִים; cstr. שִׁכְחֵי—**forgetful** Ps 9$_{18}$.

→ שׁכח I *forget.*

שׁכך 5 vb.—**Qal** 4 Pf. שָׁכָכָה; + waw וַיָּשֹׁכּוּ; inf. cstr. שֹׁךְ (שַׁךְ) —**1. subside, recede,** of water Gn 8$_1$. **2. subside, abate,** of wrath Est 2$_1$. **3. bend, crouch,** of hunter Jr 5$_{26}$.

Hi. 1 + waw וַהֲשִׁכֹּתִי—**get rid of murmuring,** וַהֲשִׁכֹּתִי מֵעָלַי אֶת־תְּלֻנּוֹת בְּנֵי יִשְׂרָאֵל *and I will rid myself of the murmurings of the Israelites* Nm 17$_{20}$.

→ cf. שׁכח III *be low.*

שׁכל I 23.0.2 vb.—**Qal** 4 Pf. שָׁכֹלְתִּי (שָׁכָלְתִּי); impf. תְּשַׁכֵּל—**1. be bereaved, childless,** of father Gn 43$_{14}$, mother 1 S 15$_{33}$. **2. be bereaved of** children Gn 27$_{45}$.

Pi. 18.0.2 Pf. שִׁכַּלְתִּי; impf. תְּשַׁכֵּל; ptc. מְשַׁכֵּלָה (מְשַׁכֶּלֶת); inf. שַׁכְּלָם—**1. bereave of children, make** Israelites **childless** Lv 26$_{22}$. **2. miscarry,** of animal Gn 31$_{38}$. **3. fail to bear (good) fruit,** of vine Ml 3$_{11}$. **4. be unproductive, infertile,** of land 2 K 2$_{19}$. **5.** ptc. as noun, **a. one who causes bereavement** Ezk 36$_{13}$. **b. one who is bereaved** 4QapLamA 2$_8$, **one who is barren** 11QM 1.2$_{11}$.

Hi. 1 Ptc. מַשְׁכִּיל—**miscarry,** of womb Ho 9$_{14}$.

→ שְׁכוֹל *loss of children,* שִׁכֻּלִים *bereavement,* שַׁכּוּל *bereaved of offspring,* שַׁכּוּל *bereaved, childless.*

***שׁכל** II 1 vb. (byform of שׂכל)—**Hi.** 1 Ptc. מַשְׁכִּיל—**be skilled,** of warrior Jr 50$_9$. → cf. שׂכל *be wise, successful.*

[**שִׁכֻּלִים**] 1 n.m.pl.—sf. שִׁכֻּלַיִךְ—**bereavement** Is 49$_{20}$.

→ שׁכל I *be bereaved.*

שׁכם 65.0.2 vb.—**Hi.** 65.0.2 Pf. הִשְׁכִּים; impf. אַשְׁכִּים, תַּשְׁכִּים; + waw וַיַּשְׁכֵּם; impv. הַשְׁכֵּם; ptc. מַשְׁכִּים, מַשְׁכִּימֵי; inf. abs. הַשְׁכֵּם—**1. get up early,** when followed by other verbs, perh. as auxiliary verb, **do early,** וַיַּשְׁכֵּם אַבְרָהָם בַּבֹּקֶר וַיַּחֲבֹשׁ אֶת־חֲמֹרוֹ *and Abraham saddled his donkey early in the morning* Gn 21$_{14}$ (unless *Abraham got up early in the morning and saddled his donkey*), perh. **go early** Ca 7$_{13}$. **2.** inf. used adv., modifying other verb, **a. (doing) again and again, persistently,** וָאֲדַבֵּר אֲלֵיכֶם אַשְׁכֵּים וְדַבֵּר *now I have spoken to you persistently* Jr 25$_3$. **b. (doing) early in the morning,** וַיִּגַּשׁ ... הַשְׁכֵּם וְהַעֲרֵב *and he drew near ... (doing so) early in the morning and late in the evening* 1 S 17$_{16}$. **3.** ptc. used adv., modifying other verb, **(doing) early,** כַּטַּל מַשְׁכִּים הֹלֵךְ *like the dew that goes away early* Ho 6$_4$. **4.** ptc. as noun., **one who gets up early** Is 5$_{11}$.

שֶׁכֶם 3 pr.n.m. **Shechem.**

שְׁכֶם I 22.1.7 n.m.—שֶׁכֶם; cstr. שְׁכֶם; sf. שִׁכְמִי—**1. shoulder, shoulder-blade, nape of the neck, upper part of the back,** of **a.** human being Gn 9$_{23}$. **b.** animal 11QT 60$_7$. **2. mountain-ridge, slope** Gn 48$_{22}$.

שְׁכֶם II 49.1.0.1 pl.n. **Shechem.**

שְׁכֶם III 15 pr.n.m. **Shechem.**

שִׁכְמִי 1 gent. **Shechemite.**

שׁכן 129.7.37 vb.—**Qal** 111.7.25 Pf. שָׁכַן (שָׁכֵן); impf. יִשְׁכֹּן,

תִּשְׁכֹּנָּה; impv. שִׁכְנוּ ,שְׁכֹן; ptc. שֹׁכְנִים ,שֹׁכֵן; ptc. pass. שְׁכוּנֵי; inf. cstr. לִשְׁכֹּן (לְשָׁכְנוֹ ,לְשָׁכְנֵי)—**1.** of human being, **a. dwell in** (בְּ) a place Si 14_{25}. **b. live among** (בְּ) troops Jb 29_{25}, alongside (עַל־פְּנֵי) kinsmen Gn 16_{12}. **c. live in** (לְ) solitude Nm 23_{9}. **d. live, abide, rest in** (לְ) security Dt 33_{12}. **e. lie inert, slumber** Na 3_{18}. **f. couch** like (כְּ) lion Dt 33_{20}. **g. sit upon** throne Si $40_{3(Bmg)}$. **h. dwell in silence** (דוּמָה), i.e. in place or state of death Ps 94_{17}. **2.** of animal, **dwell, nest in** (בְּ) shade Ezk 17_{23}. **3.** of Y., **a. dwell, be present** on (בְּ) Mt Zion Is 8_{18}, in the midst of (בְּתוֹךְ) Israelites Ex 25_{8}. **b. sit upon** throne Is 57_{15}. **4.** of Y.'s glory, **abide** on (עַל) mountain Ex 24_{16}. **5.** of cloud, **rest** on (עַל) tent Ex 40_{35}. **6.** of frost, **settle** Si $43_{19(B)}$. **7.** of light, **have its abode**, i.e. its source of origin Jb 38_{19}. **8.** of feet, **stay, remain in** (בְּ) house Pr 7_{11}. **9.** of land, **be inhabited, populated** Jr 46_{26}. **10.** appar. as pi., of Y., **establish** his name Dt 12_{5}. **11.** ptc. as noun, **a.** living person, **inhabitant** of the world Is 18_{3}. **b.** deceased person, **inhabitant** of the netherworld Jb 26_{5}. **c. denizen** of the deep, i.e. fish, marine monster, etc. Jb 26_{5}. **d.** Y., (1) **the One who lives** forever Is 57_{15}. (2) **the One who is present** in the bush Dt 33_{16}. **12.** ptc. pass. as noun, appar. **one who dwells** Jg 8_{11} (or em. שְׁכוּנֵי to שֹׁכְנֵי).

Pi. 12.0.3 Pf. שִׁכַּנְתִּי ,שִׁכֵּן; impf. אֲשַׁכְּנָה; inf. שַׁכֵּן—alw. of Y., **1. establish** his name Ne 1_{9}. **2. cause to dwell, make** Israelites **settle down** in (בְּ) land Nm 14_{30}. **3. set up** tent among (בְּ) people Ps 78_{60}.

Hi. 6.0.9 Pf. Q השכנתה; impf. יַשְׁכֵּן; + waw וַיַּשְׁכִּינוּ—**1.** of Y., **establish** his name 4QSela 9.2_{2}. **2.** of Y., **a. cause** tribes **to dwell** in (בְּ) tents Ps 78_{55}. **b. cause** birds **to settle** on (עַל) Pharaoh Ezk 32_{4}. **3a. set up** tent Jos 18_{1}. **b. place, station** cherub on (מִן) east side Gn 3_{24}. **c. lay** glory in (לְ) dust Ps 7_{6}.

→ מִשְׁכָּן *tabernacle*, שֶׁכֶן *dwelling place*, שָׁכֵן *neighbour*, שְׁכֵנָה *female neighbour*.

שָׁכֵן 18.0.2 n.m.—cstr. שְׁכַן; sf. שְׁכֵנוֹ; pl. sf. שְׁכֵנַיִךְ—**1. neighbouring people** Ps 79_{12}. **2. neighbour, acquaintance living nearby** Pr 27_{10}. **3. neighbour** of man of Belial, i.e. affected by his destructive influence 4QTestim$_{24}$. **4. resident** Is 33_{24}; coll., **inhabitants** Ho 10_{5}. **5. neighbouring town** Jr 49_{18}. **6. neighbouring region** Dt 1_{7}. → שכן *dwell, abide*.

[שֶׁכֶן] 1.1 n.m.—sf. שִׁכְנוֹ—**dwelling place** Si 14_{25}. → שכן *dwell, abide*.

[שְׁכֵנָה] 2 n.f.—sf. שְׁכֶנְתָּהּ; pl. שְׁכֵנוֹת—**female neighbour** Ru 4_{17}. → שכן *dwell, abide*.

שְׁכַנְיָה 10.0.37.8 pr.n.m. **Shecaniah.**

שׁכר 19.0.1 vb.—**Qal** 10.0.1 Pf. שָׁכְרוּ; impf. יִשְׁכְּרוּן; impv. שִׁכְרוּ; ptc. pass. שְׁכֻרַת; inf. שָׁכְרָה—**1a. be drunk** Lm 4_{21}, specif. with blood (דָּם) Is 49_{26}. **b. be merry as a result of drinking,** with (עִם) Benjamin Gn 43_{34}. **2. drink one's fill** Hg 1_{6}. **3.** ptc. pass. as noun, **drunkard,** i.e. one who staggers after catastrophe Is 51_{21}.

Pi. 4 + waw וַיְשַׁכְּרֵהוּ; ptc. מְשַׁכֶּרֶת; inf. abs. שַׁכֵּר—**make drunk, make** someone **lose control** 2 S 11_{13}.

Hi. 4 Impf. אַשְׁכִּיר; impv. הַשְׁכִּירֻהוּ—**1. make drunk, make** someone **lose control** Jr 51_{57}. **2. make** arrows **drunk** with (מִן) blood, i.e. use frequently as lethal weapons Dt 32_{42}.

Htp. 1 Impf. תִּשְׁתַּכָּרִין—**make oneself drunk** 1 S 1_{14}.

→ שִׁכָּרוֹן I *drunkenness*, שֵׁכָר *fermented drink*, שִׁכּוֹר *drunk*.

שֵׁכָר 23.3.1 n.[m.]—sf. Q שכרכם—**fermented drink** Si 40_{20}. → שכר *be drunk*.

שִׁכָּרוֹן I 3 n.[m.] **drunkenness** Ezk 23_{33}. → שכר *be drunk*.

[שִׁכָּרוֹן] II 1 pl.n. **Shikkeron.**

שֶׁל, see שֶׁקֶל *shekel*.

שַׁל I 1 n.[m.] **indiscretion** 2 S 6_{7}.

*שַׁל II 0.0.0.1 pr.n.m. **Shal.**

שֶׁל, see שֶׁ *which, that, who*.

שַׁלְאֲנַן 1 adj. **peaceful,** of person Jb 21_{23}.

שׁלב 2 vb.—**Pu.** 2 Ptc. מְשֻׁלָּבֹת—of tenons, **be joined,** one to (אֶל) another Ex 26_{17}. → שָׁלָב *cross-bar*.

שָׁלָב 3 n.[m.]—pl. שְׁלַבִּים—**cross-bar** 1 K 7_{28}. → שלב *join*.

שׁלג 1 vb.—**Hi.** 1 Impf. תַּשְׁלֵג—**snow** Ps 68_{15}. → שֶׁלֶג I *snow*.

שֶׁלֶג I 20.1.2 n.m.—שָׁלֶג; cstr. שֶׁלֶג; sf. Si שלגו—**snow** Ps 51_{9}. → שלג *snow*.

*[שֶׁלֶג] II 1 n.[m.]—שָׁלֶג—**soap(wort)** Jb 9_{30}.

שׁלה I 7.1.1 vb.—**Qal** 5.1 Pf. שָׁלַוְתִּי ,שָׁלוּ; impf. Si אשלה, יִשְׁלָיוּ—**be at ease, be undisturbed** Ps 122_{6}.

Ni. 1 Impf. תִּשָּׁלוּ—**be slack** 2 C 29_{11}.

Hi. 1.0.1 Impf. תַּשְׁלֶה; + waw Q והשלוני—**raise hope** of someone 2 K 4_{28}.

→ שַׁלְוָה *peace, prosperity,* שְׁלִי *quietness,* שָׁלֵו *at ease, peaceable.*

שׁלה II 1 vb.—**Qal** 1 Impf. יֵשֶׁל—of Y., **take away** life Jb 27_{8}. → שִׁלְיָה *afterbirth.*

שֵׁלָה 8 pr.n.m. **Shelah.**

שֵׁלֹה, see שִׁילוֹ *Shiloh.*

שַׁלְהֶבֶת 3.1.1 n.f.—cstr. Q שלהובת—**flame** Ezk 21_{3} Jb 15_{30}; שַׁלְהֶבֶתְיָה *flame of Y.* or *mighty flame* Ca 8_{6}.

שָׁלֵו 8.1.0.1 adj.—שְׁלֵיו (שָׁלֵיו); pl. cstr. שַׁלְוֵי; f.s. שְׁלֵוָה—**1. at ease, feeling secure, untroubled,** of people Ps 73_{12}. **2. peaceable,** of land 1 C 4_{40}. **3.** as noun, **peace, contentment** Jb 20_{20}. → שׁלה *be at ease.*

שָׁלוֹ, see שִׁילוֹ *Shiloh.*

שַׁלְוָה 9.1.3 n.f.—cstr. שַׁלְוַת; sf. שַׁלְוִי; pl. sf. שַׁלְוֹתַיִךְ—**time of peace, security, prosperity** Jr 22_{21}, **peace, tranquillity** Pr 17_{1}, **ease, confidence** Ezk 16_{49}. → שׁלה I *be at ease.*

[שְׁלוּחָה] 1 n.f.—pl. sf. שְׁלֻחוֹתֶיהָ—**shoot,** of vine Is 16_{8}. → שׁלח *send.*

*[שְׁלוֹחִי] 0.0.1 gent. **Shiloahite.**

שִׁלּוּחִים 3 n.m.pl.—שִׁלֻּחִים; sf. שִׁלּוּחֶיהָ—**1. parting gift** Mc 1_{14}, **dowry** 1 K 9_{16}. **2. dismissal** Ex 18_{2}. → שׁלח *send.*

שָׁלוֹם I 237.11.128.23 n.m.—שָׁלֹם; cstr. שְׁלוֹם; sf. שְׁלוֹמִי; pl. שְׁלוֹמִים; sf. שְׁלֹמָיו—**1a. welfare, well-being, health, prosperity,** הֲשָׁלוֹם אֲבִיכֶם *is your father well?* Gn 43_{27}, אֵין־שָׁלוֹם בַּעֲצָמַי *there is no health in my bones* Ps 38_{4}, רַב שְׁלוֹם בָּנָיִךְ *great will be the prosperity of your sons* Is 54_{13}; oft. as reflecting Y.'s favour, hence **blessing,** שָׁלוֹם עַל־יִשְׂרָאֵל *blessing be upon Israel* Ps 125_{5}; specif. **safety, security,** וְשַׁבְתִּי בְשָׁלוֹם *and I will return in safety,* i.e. safely Gn 28_{21}. **b.** as salutation in letter, שָׁלוֹם **greetings!** MurEpBeth-Mashiko$_{2}$. **2a. peace, friendship, harmony, alliance, reconciliation,** oft. between humans Gn 26_{31}, humans and Y. Nm 25_{12}, animals Si 13_{18}. **b. ally** Ps 55_{21}. **3. peace, peacetime, military reconciliation,** opp. war Jg 4_{17}; specif. **deliverance** from oppression Is 52_{7}; **military victory, triumph** Jg 8_{9}. **4. peace, tranquillity, contentment** Jr 30_{5}. **5. integrity, equity, justness, justice,** of person Zc 8_{19}, of divine law 4QBark[a] 1.1_{9}, personified divine attribute Ps 85_{11}. **6. order** Jb 25_{2}. **7. intactness,** שָׁלוֹם אָהֳלֶךָ *your dwelling* (lit. 'tent') *is intact* Jb 5_{24}. **8.** pl. noun as adv., **completely,** הָגְלַת שְׁלוֹמִים *she was exiled completely* Jr 13_{19}. → שׁלם *be complete, be at peace, be recompensed.*

*שָׁלוֹם II 0.0.3.2 pr.n.f. **Salome.**

שַׁלּוּם 27.1.0.45 pr.n.m. **Shallum.**

שִׁלּוּם 3.0.7 n.[m.]—שִׁלֻּם; pl. שִׁלּוּמִים; cstr. Q שלומי; sf. Q שלומם—**1. requital** Is 34_{8}. **2. bribe** Mc 7_{3}. → שׁלם *be complete, be at peace, be recompensed.*

שַׁלּוּן 1 pr.n.m. **Shallun.**

שָׁלוֹשׁ, see שָׁלֹשׁ *three.*

שׁלח I 847.4.102.34 vb.—**Qal** 564.3.68.34 Pf. שָׁלַח (שְׁלָחֲךָ); impf. יִשְׁלַח; impv. שְׁלַח, שִׁלְחָה, שִׁלְחוּ; ptc. שֹׁלֵחַ, שֹׁלְחִים; ptc. pass. שָׁלוּחַ, inf. abs. שָׁלֹחַ; cstr. שְׁלֹחַ (שָׁלְחִי, שְׁלֹחוֹ)—**1. send, dispatch, commission,** subj. Y. Hg 1_{12}, human Ex 24_{5}; obj. servant 1 S 25_{40}, messenger Ne 6_{3}, angel Gn 24_{7}, prophet Hg 1_{12}, saviour Is 19_{20}; prep., into (לְ) battle Nm 31_{4}, to (אֶל) Y. to make intercession Jr 37_{7}; **send** someone **off** Gn 28_{5}; **let** someone **go** Jg 11_{38}; **send** someone **away** 2 S 13_{17}, **divorce** wife 1 C 8_{8} (or em. to pi.). **2. send, dispatch, commission,** with ellip. of person or message sent, subj. Y. Jr 23_{38}, human Gn 41_{8}; prep., to (אֶל or עַל) someone Jr 23_{38} 2 C 28_{16}. **3. send for** counsellor 2 S 15_{12}. **4a. send** letters to (אֶל) people Est 1_{22}; of Y., **cause** law **to be conveyed** to (אֶל) Israelites 2 K 17_{13}. **b.** with ellip., **send (an inquiry)** concerning (לְ) person's well-being Arad ost. 16_{1}. **5. send, cause** something **to be brought** to (לְ or אֶל) someone 1 S 16_{20} 2 C 2_{14}. **6.** specif. of Y., **send (from heaven)** food Jl 2_{19}, help Ps 20_{3}, Y.'s word Is 55_{11}, light, truth Ps 43_{3}, Y.'s spirit Is 48_{16}, evil spirit Jg 9_{23}, plague Ex 9_{14}. **7a. stretch out, extend** hand, arm Gn 3_{22}; **point** finger Is 58_{9}; **stretch out** foot, i.e. take step 1QH 16_{34}. **b. (1) lay** hand **on** (בְּ) something, e.g. what one desires Si 15_{16}, someone else's property, i.e. steal Ob$_{13}$, rock, i.e. cut it Jb 28_{9}. **(2) raise** hand against (בְּ or אֶל or עַל) someone Ex 24_{11} 1 K 13_{4} Est 8_{7}. **c. set** one's hand to (בְּ) evil Ps 125_{3}. **8. bring** branch to (אֶל) one's nose Ezk 8_{17}. **9. stretch out** staff Jg 6_{21},

extend sceptre Ps 110_{2}, **put** sickle **to the harvest** Jl 4_{13}. **10. give free rein to** mouth Ps 50_{19}. **11.** of sun, **radiate (heat)** Si $43_{4(B)}$. **12.** pass., **a. be sent, commissioned,** of messenger Ezk 23_{40}. **b. be sent,** of present Gn 32_{19}. **c. be let loose,** of hind Gn 49_{21}. **d. be stretched out,** of hand Ezk 2_{9}. **13.** ptc. as noun, **a. one who sends** person 2 S 24_{13}. **b. one who stretches out, one who points** finger 1QS 11_{2}. **14.** ptc. pass. as noun, **that which is sent out, that which is radiated** by the sun Si $43_{4(Bmg)}$.

Ni. 1 Inf. abs. נִשְׁלוֹחַ—**be sent,** of letter Est 3_{13}.

Pi. 267.1.25 Pf. שִׁלַּח; impf. יְשַׁלַּח (יְשַׁלֵּחַ); impv. שַׁלַּח, שַׁלְּחוּ; ptc. מְשַׁלֵּחַ, מְשַׁלְּחִים; inf. abs. שַׁלֵּחַ (שַׁלַּח); cstr. שַׁלַּח (שַׁלֵּחַ)—**1a. let go, set free, let escape, give leave** to people Ex 3_{20}; **let** children **run loose** Jb 21_{11}. **b. let go, let loose, release** animal Gn 8_{7}. **2. send** someone **away** from (מִתּוֹךְ) dangerous place Gn 19_{29}, **cause** people **to go into exile** from (מִן) Jerusalem into (בְּ) Babylon Jr 29_{20}, **expel** Adam from (מִן) Garden of Eden Gn 3_{23}, **excommunicate** member 1QS 7_{17}, **divorce** wife Dt 22_{19}, **marry off** daughter outside (הַחוּצָה) clan Jg 12_{9}; of Y., **banish** human being from (מֵעַל) the earth, i.e. cause person to die Jr 28_{16}. **3a. send off, send** someone **on his way** Gn 12_{20}, specif. **escort** 2 S 19_{32}. **b. send (back)** to (לְ or אֶל) home 1 S 10_{25}. **4. send** with a task, **commission** someone, **a.** of Y., **send** angel, people, to execute divine punishment Gn 19_{13}. **b. send** envoy Is 57_{9}. **c. send out** troops 2 S 18_{2}. **5. let** someone **down** Jr 38_{6}. **6.** of Y., **deliver** human being into (בְּ) power of sin Jb 8_{4}. **7.** of Y., **set, turn** one person against (בְּ) another Zc 8_{10}. **8. send, cause** something **to be brought** 1 S 5_{10}. **9.** of Y., **send, shoot** arrow Ezk 5_{16}. **10.** of Y., **send** plague **as divine punishment** upon (בְּ) people Am 4_{10}. **11.** of Y., **send** spirit, i.e. to give life to creatures Ps 104_{30}. **12. send forth** lightnings Jb 38_{35}. **13. send down, cast down** bread Ec 11_{1}. **14a. let** bridle **loose** Jb 30_{11}. **b. let** hair **hang loose** Ezk 44_{20} (unless §20b). **c.** of Y., **release** water Jb 12_{15}, **make** springs **gush forth** Ps 104_{10}; of sea, **make** its channels **well up** Ezk 31_{4}. **d.** of animal, **release, give birth to** foetus Jb 39_{3}. **e.** of Y., **unleash** anger on (בְּ) Israelites Ezk 7_{3}. **15a.** of tongue, **express, convey, reveal** good, evil Si 37_{18} (Bmg, D). **b.** of Y., **cause** commandment **to be conveyed** Ml 2_{4}. **16.** of Y., **drive away, remove** stubbornness from (מִן) someone 4QBark[c] 1.2_{2}. **17.** of Y., **reject** temple from (מֵעַל) his presence 1 K 9_{7}. **18. set** city on (בְּ) fire Jg 1_{8}. **19. incite** strife Pr 6_{14}. **20a.** of tree, **shoot** roots Jr 17_{8}. **b.** of person, let hair **grow long** Ezk 44_{20} (unless §14b). **21.** as qal, **stretch out** hand Pr 31_{19}. **22.** inf. as noun, **sending away** one's wife, **divorce** Ml 2_{16}. **23.** ptc. as noun, **a. one who lets** animal **loose** Lv 16_{26}. **b. one who incites** strife Pr 6_{19}.

Pu. 10.0.4 Pf. שֻׁלַּח; impf. יְשֻׁלַּח; ptc. מְשֻׁלָּח—**1a. be sent away, be divorced** Is 50_{1}, **be excommunicated** 1QS 7_{16}. **b. be driven away, be scattered,** of nest Is 16_{2}. **2. be sent off** on journey Gn 44_{3}. **3. be sent** to convey message Ob $_{1}$. **4. be led** into (בְּ) net Jb 18_{8}. **5.** perh. **be impelled** Jg 5_{15}. **6. be unrestrained,** of Belial CD 4_{13}, lad Pr 29_{15}. **7. be deserted,** of habitation Is 27_{10}.

Hi. 5.0.1 + waw וְהִשְׁלַחְתִּי; ptc. מַשְׁלִיחַ; inf. הַשְׁלִיחַ—alw. of Y., **send** enemy **as divine punishment** against (בְּ) Judah 2 K 15_{37}.

Htp. 0.0.4 Pf. התשלחו; impf. ישתלח; ptc. משתלח—**1.** appar. **send** 5/6Ḥev 51_{2}. **2. be sent away** 4QD[a] 11_{8}. **3.** ptc. as noun, **excommunicated one** 4QD[a] 11_{14}.

→ שֶׁלַח I *missile,* שְׁלוּחָה *shoot,* שִׁלּוּחִים *parting gift,* מִשְׁלָח *extending,* מִשְׁלַח *extending,* מִשְׁלַחַת *undertaking.*

*שׁלח II 5.1.1 vb.—**Qal** 2.1 + waw וַיִּשְׁלַח—**1.** of Y., **forge** arrowhead 2 S 22_{15}. **2.** of sun, **radiate heat** Si $43_{4(B)}$.

Pi. 3.0.1 Ptc. מְשַׁלֵּחַ—**1. inflame** strife Pr 6_{14}. **2.** ptc. as noun, **one who inflames** strife Pr 6_{19}.

שֶׁלַח I 8 n.[m.] **1. missile, weapon** 2 C 23_{10}. **2. shoot** Ca 4_{13}. → שׁלח I *send.*

שֶׁלַח II 9 pr.n.m. **Shelah.**

שֶׁלַח III 1 pl.n. **Shelah.**

שִׁלֹחַ 1 pl.n. **Shiloah.**

שִׁלְחִי 2 pr.n.m. **Shilhi.**

שִׁלְחִים 1 pl.n. **Shilhim.**

שֻׁלְחָן 71.7.7 n.m.&f.—Q שולחן; cstr. שֻׁלְחַן; sf. שֻׁלְחָנִי, pl. שֻׁלְחָנוֹת; sf. Q שלחניו—**ceremonial table** for holy vessels, shewbread Nm 4$_{7}$, **table of slaughter** Ezk 40$_{39}$, **altar** Ezk 41$_{22}$, **priestly table** 11QT 37$_{8}$, **dinner-table** Si 6$_{10}$, **communal table** of sect 1QS 6$_{4}$, **bedroom-table, desk** 2 K 4$_{10}$.

שׁלט 8.1.1 vb.—**Qal** 5 Pf. שָׁלַט, שָׁלְטוּ; impf. יִשְׁלַט; inf. שְׁלוֹט —1. **domineer** over (בְּ or עַל) someone Est 9$_{1}$ Ne 5$_{15}$. 2. **have control** over (בְּ) one's fruit of toil Ec 2$_{19}$.

Hi. 3.1.1 Pf. הִשְׁלִיטוֹ; impf. יַשְׁלִיטֶנּוּ, תַּשְׁלֶט—1. of iniquity, **dominate** over (בְּ) someone Ps 119$_{133}$. 2. of Y., **empower, enable** human being Ec 5$_{18}$.

→ שִׁלְטוֹן *authority,* שַׁלִּיט *having authority.*

שֶׁלֶט 7.0.1 n.m.—pl. שְׁלָטִים; cstr. שִׁלְטֵי; sf. שִׁלְטֵיהֶם—1. traditionally **shield,** prob. **quiver** or **bow-and-arrow case** Jr 51$_{11}$. 2. **missile** 1QM 6$_{2}$.

*[שִׁלְטוֹ] 0.0.0.2 pr.n.m. **Shilto.**

שִׁלְטוֹן 2.1 n.[m.] 1. **authority** Ec 8$_{4}$. 2. **powerful one, leader** Si 4$_{7}$. → שׁלט *domineer.*

[שְׁלִי] 1.0.0.1 n.[m.]—שֶׁלִי—**quietness** 2 S 3$_{27}$. → שׁלה I *be at ease.*

[שִׁלְיָה] 1 n.f.—sf. שִׁלְיָתָהּ—**afterbirth** Dt 28$_{57}$. → שׁלה II *draw out, take away.*

שָׁלֵיו, שְׁלֵיו, see שָׁלֵו *at ease, peaceable.*

שַׁלִּיט 5.0.1 adj.—f.s. שַׁלֶּטֶת; m.pl. שַׁלִּיטִים—1. **having power** Ec 8$_{8}$. 2. **self-willed** Ezk 16$_{30}$. 3. as noun, **ruler** Gn 42$_{6}$. → שׁלט *domineer.*

*[שְׁלִים] 0.0.2 n.[m.] **completion** of age CD 4$_{8}$. → שׁלם *be complete.*

שָׁלִישׁ I 2.0.1 n.[m.]—שָׁלִשׁ—**third measure** Ps 80$_{6}$. → שׁלשׁ *divide into three parts.*

[שָׁלִישׁ] II 1 n.[m.]—pl. שָׁלִשִׁים—**sistrum,** percussion musical instrument 1 S 18$_{6}$. → שׁלשׁ *divide into three parts.*

שָׁלִישׁ III 16.0.2 n.m.—sf. שָׁלִישׁוֹ; pl. שָׁלִשִׁים; cstr. Q שלישי; sf. שָׁלִשָׁיו—**third man, officer, adjutant** 1 K 9$_{22}$. → שׁלשׁ *divide into three parts.*

[שָׁלִישׁ] IV 1 n.[m.]—pl. Qr שָׁלִישִׁים—**threefold lore** Pr 22$_{20(Qr)}$. → שׁלשׁ *divide into three parts.*

שְׁלִישִׁי 106.1.68.7 adj.—שְׁלִשִׁי; f.s. שְׁלִישִׁית; m.pl. שְׁלִשִׁים —1. **third,** of day Gn 1$_{13}$, year 1 K 18$_{1}$. 2. as noun, **third (one),** i.e. of lot 1 C 24$_{8}$, son 1 S 17$_{13}$. 3. as adv., שְׁלִשִׁים **a third time** 1 S 19$_{21}$, הַשְּׁלִשִׁית **on the third day** 1 S 20$_{12}$. → שׁלשׁ *divide into three parts.*

שׁלך I 125.2.15 vb.—**Pi.** 0.0.1 + waw ושלך—appar. **throw** 4QNarrA 1$_{8}$.

Hi. 112.2.13 Pf. הִשְׁלִיךְ; impf. יַשְׁלִיךְ; + waw וַיַּשְׁלֵךְ; impv. הַשְׁלִיכוּ, הַשְׁלֵךְ; ptc. מַשְׁלִיךְ; inf. abs. הַשְׁלֵךְ; cstr. הַשְׁלִיךְ —1. **throw, cast, lay down** thing (Ezk 7$_{19}$) or person (Ezk 28$_{17}$) somewhere, **a.** into (בְּ or אֶל) street Ezk 7$_{19}$, water Ex 15$_{25}$. **b.** upon (עַל) ground Ezk 28$_{17}$. **c.** under (תַּחַת) bush Gn 21$_{15}$. **d.** at (אֶל) entrance Jos 8$_{29}$. **e.** beside (אֵצֶל) altar Lv 1$_{16}$. **f.** beyond (מֵהָלְאָה לְ) gate Jr 22$_{19}$. **g.** outside (of) (הַחוּץ מִן or חוּצָה לְ or אֶל־מִחוּץ לְ) city Lv 14$_{40}$ 2 C 33$_{15}$, chamber Ne 13$_{8}$. **h.** from off (מִן) top of rock 2 C 25$_{12}$. **i.** out of (מִן) heaven Lm 2$_{1}$; from out of (מֵעַל) one's hands Dt 9$_{17}$. **j.** behind (אַחֲרֵי) one's back, obj. sins, i.e. forgive them Is 38$_{17}$, obj. commandments, i.e. disobey them Ps 50$_{17}$, obj. Y., i.e. cease to worship him 1 K 14$_{9}$. **k.** away from (מֵעַל) one's face/presence, i.e. cease to show concern for 2 K 13$_{23}$. **2. throw, cast** something in direction of person or animal, **a.** to, at (לְ or עַל) person Nm 35$_{22}$, dogs Ex 22$_{30}$. **b.** before (לִפְנֵי) person Ex 7$_{9}$. **c.** upon (עַל or אֶל) person 1 K 19$_{19}$, animal Ezk 43$_{24}$. **3. wrest** prey from (מִן) teeth Jb 29$_{17}$. **4a. throw away** detested things Ezk 20$_{7}$. **b. fling away, risk** one's life Jg 9$_{17}$. **5. throw out** person 2 K 10$_{25}$. **6a. throw down, hurl down** staff Ex 7$_{12}$. **b. cast** lot Jos 18$_{8}$. **c. cast down, drop, let down, abandon** person Si 4$_{19}$, discipline or wisdom Si 6$_{21}$. **7a. overthrow, demolish** place Jr 9$_{18}$. **b. overthrow, destroy** person Jb 18$_{7}$. **8. cast off, shed** blossom like (כְּ) tree Jb 15$_{33}$. **9.** of wind, **hurl at** (עַל) person Jb 27$_{22}$. **10.** ptc. as noun, **one who casts hook** Is 19$_{8}$.

Ho. 13.0.1 Pf. הָשְׁלַךְ, הָשְׁלַכְתִּי; impf. יָשְׁלָכוּ; ptc. מֻשְׁלָךְ, מֻשְׁלֶכֶת, מֻשְׁלָכִים—**1.** of person, **be thrown** somewhere, **a.** on (בְּ) road 1 K 13$_{24}$. **b.** into (אֶל) the open Ezk 16$_{5}$. **c.** over (בְּעַד) wall 2 S 20$_{21}$. **d.** from out of (מִן) grave appar. Is 14$_{19}$. **2a.** of head, **be thrown to** (אֶל) person 2 S 20$_{21}$. **b.** of worshipper, **be cast upon** (עַל) Y., i.e. become his charge Ps 22$_{11}$. **3.** of slain one, **be thrown out** Is 34$_{3}$. **4.** of place, **be overthrown** Dn 8$_{11}$. **5.** of corpse, **be left exposed to** (לְ) drought, frost Jr 36$_{30}$.

→ שָׁלָךְ *cormorant,* שַׁלֶּכֶת *felling of tree.*

***שׁלך** II 1 vb.—**Hi.** 1 Impf. אַשְׁלִיךְ—**rescue** prey from (מִן) teeth Jb 29$_{17}$.

שָׁלָךְ 2 n.[m.] **cormorant, unclean bird** Lv 11_{17}. → שׁלך I *throw.*

שַׁלֶּכֶת I 1 n.f. **felling of tree** Is 6_{13}. → שׁלך I *throw.*

שַׁלֶּכֶת II 1 pl.n. **Shallecheth.**

שׁלל I 2 vb.—**Qal** 2 Impf. תָּשֹׁלּוּ; inf. abs. שֹׁל—**draw out** from (מִן) sheaves of grain Ru 2_{16}.

שׁלל II 14.0.4 vb.—**Qal** 12.0.4 Pf. שָׁלּוֹתָ; impf. יְשָׁלּוּךָ; impv. Q שול; ptc. שֹׁלְלִים; inf. שְׁלֹל (Q שול)—**1a.** obj. שָׁלָל, **take spoil** Is 10_6. **b. take property as spoil** Ezk 26_{12}. **2. plunder** people Hb 2_8. **3.** ptc. as noun, **plunderer** 1QM 7_2.

Htpol. 2 Ptc. מִשְׁתּוֹלֵל—**be despoiled** Ps 76_6.

→ שָׁלָל *spoil,* שׁוֹלָל *barefoot.*

שָׁלָל I 75.1.17 n.m.—cstr. שְׁלַל; sf. שְׁלָלוֹ; pl. sf. Q שלליה—**1. war-spoil** Jos 22_8, **distribution of spoil** Si 37_6; nation as **prey** Ezk 7_{21}. **2. plunder,** taken from individual Is 10_2. **3. prey** of animal Gn 49_{27}. **4. gain** Pr 31_{11}. → שׁלל II *take spoil.*

שׁלם 116.6.49.2 vb.—**Qal** 8.1.6 + waw וַתִּשְׁלַם; וְשָׁלְמוּ; ptc. שׁוֹלְמִי; pass. שְׁלֻמֵי—**1. be completed, a. come to an end,** of days of mourning Is 60_{20}. **b. be finished,** of work 1 K 7_{51}. **2. be whole, unscathed,** of person Jb 9_4. **3. be at peace,** of person Jb 22_{21}. **4.** ptc. as noun, **one who is peaceful, friend** Ps 7_5. **5.** ptc. pass. as noun, appar. **one who is peaceable** 2 S 20_{19}.

Ni. 0.0.3 Inf. cstr. השלם—**be fulfilled,** of statute 1QS 10_6.

Pi. 89.4.30.2 Pf. שִׁלַּם; impf. יְשַׁלֵּם; impv. שַׁלֵּם, שַׁלְּמוּ; ptc. מְשַׁלֵּם, מְשַׁלְּמִים; inf. abs. שַׁלֵּם; cstr. שַׁלְּמִי—**1.** of Y., **repay** for deed Jb 34_{11}. **2a. make restitution for** dishonest gain Lv 5_{24}. **b. pay** debt 2 K 4_7. **c. make amends for** sin 4QapJerC[d] 8.2_5. **d. pay, fulfil** vow Dt 23_{22}. **e. pay, offer thanksgiving** Ps 56_{13}. **3. fulfil desire** Si 35_{11}. **4. complete, finish temple** 1 K 9_{25}. **5. restore, reestablish habitation** Jb 8_6. **6.** ptc. as noun, **a. one who repays** Ps 38_{21}. **b. one who must repay** Si 8_{13}.

Pu. 5 Impf. יְשֻׁלַּם; ptc. מְשֻׁלָּם—**1. be recompensed,** of righteous, wicked Pr 11_{31}. **2. be a recompense,** of evil Jr 18_{20}. **3. be paid,** of vow Ps 65_2. **4.** ptc. as noun, **dedicated one** Is 42_{19}.

Hi. 13.1.8 Pf. הִשְׁלִימוּ; impf. יַשְׁלִים; + waw וַיַּשְׁלֵם; ptc. Q משלים; inf. Q השלים—**1a. make peace with** (עִם) someone 1 C 19_{19}. **b. make** enemy **to be at peace with** (אֵת) someone Pr 16_7. **c. surrender to** (אֶל) people Jos 11_{19}. **d. make people surrender to** (לְ) a nation 11QT 64_7. **2. cause person's life to be at peace** Si 34_{10}. **3. make restitution for** sin 4QapJerC[d] 8.2_5. **4. accomplish** plan Is 44_{26}, **fulfil** desire Is 44_{28}. **5. complete, fill** battle-line 1QM 5_3. **6. complete** days of one's life CD 10_{10}. **7. make an end of, consume** person Is 38_{12}.

Ho. 1 Pf. הָשְׁלְמָה—of beast, **be an ally to** (לְ) human being Jb 5_{23}.

Htp. 0.0.2 Impf. ישתלם—**be recompensed** according to (כְּ) deeds 11QPs[a] 22_{10}.

→ שָׁלוֹם I *peace,* שִׁלּוּם *requital,* שֶׁלֶם *alliance offering,* שִׁלְּמָה *retribution,* שַׁלְמוּת *completion,* שַׁלְמֹן *bribe,* שִׁלֵּם I *recompense,* שָׁלֵם I *whole.*

שָׁלֵם I 28.0.11 adj.—pl. שְׁלֵמִים; f.s. שְׁלֵמָה; f.pl. שְׁלֵמוֹת—**1a. wholly devoted,** of heart 1 K 8_{61}. **b. whole,** i.e. not underweight, of weight Dt 25_{15}. **c. unhewn,** of stone Jos 8_{31}. **d. complete (in flesh),** of bone 4QMMT B_{74}. **e. full,** of year 4QMMT A_{20}. **f. full** (in compensation), of reward Ru 2_{12}. **2a. finished, hewn,** of stone 1 K 6_7. **b. finished, completed,** of temple 2 C 8_{16}. **c. completed, having come to an end,** of age 4QTime 1.2_4. **d. finalized,** of sentence CD 9_{20}. **3. having reached its full measure,** of iniquity Gn 15_{16}. **4. fulfilled,** of petition 11QPs[a] 24_{14}. **5.** perh. **numerous,** of people Na 1_{12}. **6. unharmed,** of person Gn 33_{18}. **7. friendly,** of person Gn 34_{21}.

→ שׁלם *be complete.*

שָׁלֵם II 2 pl.n. **Salem.**

שַׁלֻּם, see שַׁלּוּם *Shallum.*

שִׁלֵּם I 1 n.[m.] **recompense** Dt 32_{35}. → שׁלם *be complete.*

שִׁלֵּם II 2 pr.n.m. **Shillem.**

שִׁלֻּם, see שִׁלּוּם *requital.*

שֶׁלֶם 87.0.11 n.[m.]—cstr. שֶׁלֶם; pl. שְׁלָמִים; cstr. שַׁלְמֵי; sf. שְׁלָמָיו—**alliance offering,** traditionally **peace offering** Lv 3_1. → שׁלם *be complete.*

*[שַׁלְמָה] 0.0.0.3 pr.n.f. **Shalmah.**

[שִׁלְּמָה] 1 n.f.—cstr. שִׁלְּמַת—**retribution** Ps 91_8. → שׁלם *be complete.*

שְׁלֹמֹה 293.2.6 pr.n.m. **Solomon.**

***[שְׁלֻמוֹת]** 0.0.2 n.f. **1. completion** of jubilees 4QapJerC[b] 2.2_{3}. **2. retribution** 4QpsEzek[e] 62.2_{2}. → שלם *be complete.*

שְׁלֹמוֹת 5.0.0.1 pr.n.m. **Shelomoth.**

שַׁלְמַי 2 pr.n.m. **Shalmai.**

שִׁלֵּמִי 1 gent. **Shillemite.**

שְׁלֹמִי 1 pr.n.m. **Shelomi.**

שְׁלֻמִיאֵל 5 pr.n.m. **Shelumiel.**

שֶׁלֶמְיָהוּ 10.0.0.13 pr.n.m. **Shelemiah.**

שְׁלֹמִית I 6.0.0.1 pr.n.m. **Shelomith.**

שְׁלֹמִית II 2 pr.n.f. **Shelomith.**

שַׁלְמַן 1.0.0.3 pr.n.m. **Shalman.**

[שַׁלְמֹן] 1 n.[m.]—pl. שַׁלְמֹנִים—**bribe** Is 1_{23}. → שלם *be complete.*

שַׁלְמַנְאֶסֶר 2 pr.n.m, **Shalmaneser.**

***[שְׁלַמְצִיּוֹן]** 0.0.2.1 pr.n.f. **Shelomzion.**

שֵׁלָנִי 1 gent. **Shelanite.**

שְׁלֹנִי, see שִׁילוֹנִי *Shilonite.*

שלף 25.1 vb.—**Qal** 25.1 Pf. שָׁלַף; + waw וַיִּשְׁלְפָהּ; impv. שְׁלֹף; ptc. שֹׁלֵף; pass. שְׁלוּפָה—**1. draw out** sword, out of (מִן) sheath 1 S 17_{51}. **2. pull off** sandal Ru 4_{7}. **3.** perh. **shoot up,** of grass Ps 129_{6}. **4.** ptc. pass., **be drawn,** of sword Nm 22_{23}. **5.** ptc. as noun, **one who draws** sword Jg 20_{25}. → שֶׁלֶף I *fallow field.*

***[שֶׁלֶף]** n.m. **knife** Jb 20_{25} (if em. שָׁלַף *he draws*).

***[שֶׁלֶף]** I 0.0.1 n.[m.] **fallow field** 3QTr 8_{10}. → שלף *pull out.*

[שֶׁלֶף] II 2 pr.n.m. **Sheleph.**

שלשׁ 9 vb.—**Pi.** 4 + waw וְשִׁלַּשְׁתָּ; וַיְשַׁלֵּשׁוּ; impv. שַׁלֵּשׁוּ—**1. divide** border **into three parts** Dt 19_{3}. **2. do a third time** 1 K 18_{34}. **3. stay three days** 1 S 20_{19}.

Pu. 5 Ptc. מְשֻׁלָּשׁ, מְשֻׁלֶּשֶׁת, מְשֻׁלָּשׁוֹת—**1a. be divided into three, be in three tiers,** of chamber Ezk 42_{6}. **b. be threefold, consist of three strands,** of cord Ec 4_{12}. **2. be three years old,** of animal Gn 15_{9} (unless §3). **3. be of the third litter** Gn 15_{9}.

→ שָׁלֹשׁ *three,* שְׁלִישִׁי *third,* שָׁלִישׁ I *third measure,* II *sistrum,* III *third man,* IV *threefold lore,* מְשֻׁלָּשׁ *triad,* שִׁלֵּשׁ *belonging to the third,* שִׁלְשׁוֹם *three days ago, in the past,* שְׁלֹשִׁים *thirty.*

שָׁלִשׁ, see שָׁלִישׁ I *third measure,* II *sistrum,* III *third man.*

שָׁלֹשׁ 432.3.144.5 n.m.&f.—m. (with f. nouns) שָׁלוֹשׁ; cstr. שְׁלֹשׁ; f. (with m. nouns) שְׁלֹשָׁה; cstr. שְׁלֹשֶׁת; sf. שְׁלָשְׁתָּם—**1a. three,** שָׁלֹשׁ פְּעָמִים *three times* Ex 23_{17}, שְׁלֹשֶׁת שָׁבֻעִים *three weeks* Dn 10_{3}; as constituent of a larger number, שנים שלוש מאות ותשעים *three hundred and ninety years* CD 1_{5}. **b.** ellip., שָׁלֹשׁ אָנֹכִי נוֹטֵל עָלֶיךָ *three (choices of punishment) I lay upon,* i.e. offer, *you* 2 S 24_{12}. **c.** idioms, הַיּוֹם שְׁלֹשָׁה *three days ago* 1 S 30_{13}, שְׁלָשְׁתְּכֶם *you three* Nm 12_{4}. **2.** as ordinal numeral, **third,** שְׁנַת שָׁלֹשׁ *the third year* 1 K 15_{28}; as constituent of a larger number, שְׁנַת שָׁלֹשׁ וְעֶשְׂרִים *the twenty-third year* Jr 52_{30}. **b.** as noun, בשלשה בחדש *on the third (day) of the month* GnzPs 3_{11}. **3.** as compound שְׁלֹשָׁה, שְׁלֹשׁ־עֶשְׂרֵה, עָשָׂר, **a. thirteen,** שְׁלֹשׁ־עֶשְׂרֵה עִיר *thirteen cities* Jos 21_{33}. **b. thirteenth,** יוֹם־שְׁלֹשָׁה עָשָׂר *the thirteenth day* Est 9_{17}. **c.** as noun, בִּשְׁלוֹשָׁה עָשָׂר לְחֹדֶשׁ שְׁנֵים־עָשָׂר *on the thirteenth (day) of the twelfth month* Est 3_{13}. → שלשׁ *divide into three parts.*

שֶׁלֶשׁ 1 pr.n.m. **Shelesh.**

[שִׁלֵּשׁ] 5 adj.—m.pl. שִׁלֵּשִׁים—**belonging to the third,** בְּנֵי שִׁלֵּשִׁים *sons of the third generation* Gn 50_{23}. → שלשׁ *divide into three parts.*

שָׁלִשָׁה I 1 pl.n. **Shalishah.**

שָׁלִשָׁה II, see בַּעַל שָׁלִשָׁה *Baal-shalishah.*

שִׁלְשָׁה 1 pr.n.m. **Shilshah.**

שִׁלְשׁוֹם 25.0.1 adv.—שִׁלְשֹׁם—**three days ago, in the past** Ru 2_{11}. → שלשׁ *divide into three parts.*

***[שָׁלִשִׁי]** 0.0.1 gent. **Shalishite.**

שְׁלִשִׁי, see שְׁלִישִׁי *third.*

שְׁלִשִׁיָּה, see עֶגְלַת שְׁלִשִׁיָּה *Eglath-shelishiyah.*

שְׁלֹשִׁים 174.0.39 n.m.&f.pl.—שְׁלוֹשִׁים—**thirty, 1.** שְׁלֹשִׁים שָׁנָה *thirty years* Nm 4_{3}. **2.** idiom, שש ושלושים באמה *thirty-six cubits* 11QT 41_{13}. **3.** ellip., הַשְּׁלֹשִׁים *the thirty (warriors)* 1 C 27_{6}. **4.** as ordinal number, שְׁלֹשִׁים שָׁנָה *the thirtieth year* Ezk 1_{1}. → שלשׁ *divide into three parts.*

***[שַׁלְשֶׁלֶת]** 0.0.1 n.f.—pl. Q שלשלות—**chain** 11QT 34_{15}.

שַׁלְתִּיאֵל, see שְׁאַלְתִּיאֵל *Shealtiel.*

שֶׁלָתֵךְ, see שְׁאֵלָה I *request.*

שם, see שֶׁמֶן *oil,* שֹׁמְרוֹן *Samaria.*

שָׁם I 834.2.71.5 adv.—+ ה- of direction שָׁמָּה—**1a.** (1) שָׁם **there** Gn 2_{12}. (2) שָׁם ... אֲשֶׁר **where,** lit. 'which ...

there' Gn 2_{11}. **b.** (1) שָׁם **to there, thither** Dt 1_{37}. (2) אֲשֶׁר ... שָׁם **to which, whither, into which,** lit. 'which ... there' Jr 8_3. (3) שָׁמָּה **to which, whither,** lit. 'which there' Ps 122_4. **c.** שָׁם perh. of time, **then** Jb 35_{12}. **2a.** (1) שָׁמָּה **to there, thither** Gn 19_{22}. (2) אֲשֶׁר ... שָׁמָּה lit. 'which ... to there', **to which, whither, into which** Gn 20_{13}. **b.** (1) שָׁמָּה **there** Gn 43_{30}. (2) אֲשֶׁר ... שָׁמָּה lit. 'which ... there', **where** Ex 29_{42}. **3a.** (1) מִשָּׁם **from there, thence** Gn 26_{17}. (2) אֲשֶׁר ... מִשָּׁם lit. 'which ... from there', **from which, whence** Gn 10_{14}. **b.** מִשָּׁם **from it, from them, from the aforementioned** Lv 2_2. **4.** משמה **from there** 4QMidrEschat[b] 10_{13}.

***שָׁם** II 10 interj. **look!, behold!** Jg 5_{11} 1 S 7_6 Ps 145_5||53_6.

שָׁם III, see בֵּית שָׁם *Beth-Sham.*

שֵׁם I 864.33.214.2 n.m.—cstr. שֵׁם (שֶׁם־); sf. שְׁמִי, שִׁמְךָ; pl. שֵׁמוֹת; cstr. שְׁמוֹת; sf. שְׁמוֹתָם—**name, 1a.** of person or people 1 S 25_3 Ezk 48_1; as obj. of קרא *call,* i.e. name Gn 3_{20}, שׂים *place,* i.e. name Jg 8_{31}, סבב hi. *change* 2 K 23_{34}||2 C 36_4. **b.** i.e. **reputation, renown, fame** Gn 11_4 1 K 1_{47}; אַנְשֵׁי הַשֵּׁם *men of name,* i.e. renown Gn 6_4, שֵׁם גָּדוֹל *a great name* 2 S 7_9, שֵׁם רָע *a bad name* Dt 22_{14}; **byword** Ezk 23_{10}. **c.** i.e. **reputation, memory,** as continuing after death, esp. through one's descendants Dt 25_6 Is 66_{22} Ps 72_{17}. **2.** of (or assoc. with) Y., as representing Y. himself Dt 28_{58} Is 56_6 Ps 113_2, his presence Dt 12_{11}, his reputation, renown, fame Ex 9_{16} Jos 9_9; הַשֵּׁם *the Name* to refer to Y. Lv 24_{11}. **3.** of other gods Ex 23_{13}, as representing any continuing trace of their existence Dt 12_3. **4.** of animals and birds Gn 2_{19}. **5.** of places and geographical features: city Gn 4_{17}, sacred site Gn 22_{14}, valley Jos 7_{26}, river Gn 2_{11}, rocky crag 1 S 14_4. **6.** of objects: altar Ex 17_{15}, pillar 1 K 7_2||2 C 3_{17}, stars Is 40_{26}, manna Ex 16_{31}. **7. name,** i.e. **memorial, monument,** for Y. Is 55_{13}, Israelites Is 56_5 (יָד וָשֵׁם *a monument and a name*).

שֵׁם II 17.1.1.2 pr.n.m. **Shem.**

שַׁמָּא 2 pr.n.m. **Shamma.**

*[**שֶׁמְאָב**] 0.0.0.1 pr.n.[m.] **Shemab.**

***שֶׁמְאֵבֶר** 0.0.0.1 pr.n.m. **Shemeber.**

שִׁמְאָה 1 pr.n.m. **Shimeah.**

שִׁמְאָם 1 pr.n.m. **Shimeam.**

שַׁמְגַּר 2 pr.n.m. **Shamgar.**

שׁמד 90.1.14 vb.—**Ni.** 21.0.2 Pf. נִשְׁמְדָה; impf. יִשָּׁמֵד; + waw וְנִשְׁמַד; inf. abs. הִשָּׁמֵד; cstr. הִשָּׁמְדָם—**be destroyed, be exterminated,** of persons Gn 34_{30} Jr 48_{42} (+ מִן *from [being]* a people), name Is 48_{19} (+ מִלִּפְנֵי *from before*), high places Ho 10_8.

Hi. 69.1.12 Pf. הִשְׁמַדְתִּי, הִשְׁמִיד; impf. יַשְׁמִיד; + waw (וַיַּשְׁמִידֵם) וַיַּשְׁמֵד; impv. הַשְׁמֵד; inf. abs. הַשְׁמֵד; cstr. (הַשְׁמִידוֹ, הַשְׁמִידוֹ, לַשְׁמִד) הַשְׁמִיד—**1. destroy, exterminate** persons Dt 1_{27} 6_{15} (+ מֵעַל־פְּנֵי *from upon the face of* the earth) Jos 9_{24} (+ מִפְּנֵי *from before* Israel), Baal 2 K 10_{28} (+ מִן *from* Israel), high places Lv 26_{30}, strongholds Is 23_{11}, injustice 1QS 4_{19}. **2.** inf. abs. as noun, **destruction,** מַטְאֲטֵא הַשְׁמֵד *broom of destruction* Is 14_{23}.

[**שֶׁמֶד**] 1 pr.n.m. **Shemed.**

שָׁמָּה, see שָׁם *there.*

שַׁמָּה I 39.0.4 n.f.—Q שומה; pl. שַׁמּוֹת—**1. desolation, desolate place, waste** Is 5_9 (+ מֵאֵין יוֹשֵׁב *without inhabitant*) Jr 2_{15}. **2. horror, object of horror** Dt 28_{37} Jr 42_{18}. → שׁמם *be desolate.*

שַׁמָּה II 7 pr.n.m. **Shammah.**

שַׁמְהוּת 1 pr.n.m. **Shamhuth.**

שְׁמוּאֵל 140.1.4 pr.n.m. **Samuel, Shemuel.**

שַׁמּוּעַ 5 pr.n.m. **Shammua.**

שְׁמוּעָה 27.1.4.3 n.f.—שְׁמֻעָה; cstr. שְׁמֻעַת; sf. שְׁמֻעָתֵנוּ; pl. שְׁמֻעוֹת—**report, news, rumour** 1 S 2_{24} 2 K 19_7||Is 37_7, **message** Is 28_9, perh. **byword** Ezk 16_{56}. → שׁמע *hear.*

[**שָׁמוּר**] *Shamur,* see שָׁמִיר III *Shamir.*

שְׁמוּרִים, see שִׁמֻּרִים *watching.*

שַׁמּוֹת I 1 pr.n.m. **Shammoth.**

שַׁמּוֹת II, see שַׁמָּה *desolation.*

*[**שׁמח**] vb. **be merciful** Is 9_{16} (if em. לֹא־יִשְׂמַח *he does not rejoice* to לֹא־יִשְׁמַח *he is not merciful*).

שׁמט 9.0.2 vb.—**Qal** 7.0.2 Pf. שָׁמְטוּ; impf. תִּשְׁמְטֶנָּה; impv. Qr שִׁמְטוּהָ; inf. abs. שָׁמוֹט—**1. let drop, let fall, let slip,** obj. ark 2 S 6_6||1 C 13_9 (or §2). **2. stumble, fall,** of oxen 2 S 6_6||1 C 13_9 (or §1). **3. remit, release (debt)** Dt 15_2. **4. let rest, leave fallow,** obj. land Ex 23_{11}.

Ni. 1 Pf. נִשְׁמְטוּ—**be thrown down,** of judges Ps 141_6.

Hi. 1 Impf. תַּשְׁמֵט—**remit, release (debt)** Dt 15_3 (or em. qal).

→ שְׁמִטָּה *remission.*

שְׁמִטָּה 5.0.23 n.f.—pl. Q שמטים—**1. remission (of debt), release** Dt 15_{1}. **2. (year of) remission (of debt)** 4QOtot 4_{16}; ערב השמטה *eve of the remission* Mur 24 B_{14}. → שׁמט *let drop.*

שמטים, see שְׁמִטָּה *remission.*

שַׁמַּי 6 pr.n.m. **Shammai.**

שְׁמִידָע I 3 pr.n.m. **Shemida.**

*[**שְׁמִידָע**] II 0.0.0.13 pl.n. **Shemida.**

שְׁמִידָעִי 1 gent. **Shemidaite.**

*[**שְׁמִיָּה**] 0.0.0.1 pr.n.m. **Shemiah.**

שָׁמַיִם 421.7.104 n.m.pl.—שָׁמָיִם; + ה- of direction הַשָּׁמַיְמָה; cstr. שְׁמֵי; sf. שְׁמֵיכֶם, שָׁמֶיךָ—**heaven(s), sky,** as name given to firmament Gn 1_{8}, place of stars Gn 22_{17}; source of rain Gn 7_{11}, dew Gn 27_{28}, snow Is 55_{10}, frost Jb 38_{29}, hail Jos 10_{11}, manna Ps 78_{24}, fire 2 K 1_{10}; dwelling place of Y. 1 K 8_{30}||2 C 6_{21}, assoc. with angels 1QM 12_{1}.

שְׁמִינִי 31.0.15 adj.—f.s. שְׁמִינִת—**1. eighth,** of day Ex 22_{29}, month 1 K 6_{38}, year Lv 25_{22}, sabbath 4QShirShabb[d] 1.2_{18}. **2.** as noun, **a. eighth (one),** in ref. to person 1 C 12_{13}, month 1 C 27_{11}. **b.** עַל־הַשְּׁמִינִית **on/according to the sheminith,** in psalm titles, perh. for an instrument with eight strings, played in the eighth key or sung an octave lower Ps 6_{1}. → cf. שְׁמֹנֶה *eight.*

*[**שְׁמִיעָה**] 0.1 n.f. **(oral) tradition, teaching,** שמיעת שבים *tradition of the elders* Si 8_{9}. → שׁמע *hear.*

שָׁמִיר I 8.0.1 n.[m.]—sf. שְׁמִירוֹ—**thorn(s), thorn-bush(es),** שָׁמִיר וָשַׁיִת *thorns and briars* Is 5_{6}.

שָׁמִיר II 3 n.m. **adamant, diamond** Jr 17_{1} Ezk 3_{9} Zc 7_{12}.

שָׁמִיר III 1 pr.n.m. **Shamir.**

שָׁמִיר IV 3 pl.n. **Shamir.**

שְׁמִירָמוֹת 4 pr.n.m. **Shemiramoth.**

[**שַׁמְלַי**] 1 pr.n.m. **Shamlai.**

שׁמם 89.3.19 vb.—**Qal** 34.0.10 Pf. שָׁמֵם, שָׁמְמוּ; impf. יֵשַׁם, יִשֹּׁמּוּ; impv. שֹׁמּוּ; ptc. שֹׁמֵם, שֹׁמֵמָה, שֹׁמֲמִים, שֹׁמֵמוֹת (שֹׁמְמֹתַיִךְ), שֹׁמְמוֹת; inf. שַׁמּוֹת—**1a. be desolate,** of mountains Ezk 33_{28}, land CD 3_{10}, gates Lm 1_{4}. **b.** ptc. as noun, **desolate place, desolation, devastation** Is 49_{19} 61_{4}. **2a. be desolate, deserted, forlorn,** of person 2 S 13_{22}, Jerusalem Lm 1_{13}. **b.** ptc. as noun, **desolate one** Is 54_{1}. **3. be astonished, appalled,** of person Jr 18_{16} Ezk 26_{16} (+ עַל *on account of*), heavens Jr 2_{12}.

Ni. 25 Pf. נָשַׁמּוּ, נְשַׁמָּה; ptc. נְשַׁמָּה, נְשַׁמּוֹת—**1a. be desolate, be made desolate,** of land Jr 12_{11}, cities Is 54_{3}, ways Lv 26_{22}. **b.** ptc. as noun, **desolate place** Ezk 36_{36}. **2. be appalled, be dismayed,** of person Jr 4_{9} Ezk 4_{17}.

Po. 7.1 Ptc. מְשׁוֹמֵם (שֹׁמֵם [or Qal]); inf. Si שומם—**1. make desolate, devastate,** without obj.; subj. abomination Dn 11_{31}, transgression Dn 8_{13}. **2.** ptc. as noun, **desolator, devastator** Dn 9_{27}. **3. be appalled,** of person Ezr 9_{3}. **4. cause appalment,** or perh. **be desolate,** after (אַחַר) (going to) house of prostitute Si 9_{7}.

Hi. 17.1.6 Pf. הֵשַׁמּוּ, הֲשִׁמּוֹתָ; impf. יַשִּׁים; + waw וַיַּשְׁמֵם, וַנַּשִּׁים; impv. הָשַׁמּוּ; ptc. מְשִׁמִּים; inf. abs. הַשְׁמֵם; cstr. Q השם—**1. make desolate, devastate, lay waste, ravage** land Lv 26_{32}, sanctuary Lv 26_{31}, vines and fig trees Ho 2_{14}; without obj. Mc 6_{13} (+ עַל *on account of*). **2. make appalled, horrified,** obj. persons Ezk 20_{26}, pasture Jr 49_{20} (+ עַל *on account of*). **3. show horror,** of person Ezk 3_{15} Jb 21_{5}.

Ho. 4.0.3 Pf. Q השם; inf. abs. הָשַׁמָּה (בָּהְשַׁמָּה)—**1. be desolate,** of land Lv $26_{34.43}$ (+ מִן *without* people). **2. be appalled, horrified,** of heart 1QH 15_{3} (+ מִן *on account of*).

Htpo. 5.1 Impf. אֶשְׁתּוֹמֵם, תִּשׁוֹמֵם, יִשְׁתּוֹמֵם—**1. be appalled, horrified,** of Y. Is 59_{16} (+ כִּי *that*), human Dn 8_{27} (+ עַל *on account of*), heart Ps 143_{4}; **be amazed, marvel at** (לְ) Si 43_{24}. **2. ruin oneself** Ec 7_{16}.

→ שָׁמֵם *desolate,* שְׁמָמָה *desolation,* שִׁמָמָה *waste,* שִׁמָּמוֹן *appalment,* שַׁמָּה I *desolation,* מֶשַׁם *desolation,* מְשַׁמָּה *devastation;* cf. ישׁם *be desolate.*

שָׁמֵם 3 adj.—f.s. שְׁמֵמָה—**desolate, devastated,** of sanctuary Dn 9_{17}, Mount Zion Lm 5_{18}. → שׁמם *be desolate.*

שְׁמָמָה 56.0.2 n.f.—pl. cstr. שִׁמְמוֹת—**desolation, devastation, waste,** of land Ex 23_{29}, cities Jr 9_{10} (+ מִבְּלִי יוֹשֵׁב *without inhabitant*), mountains Ml 1_{3}, houses Zp 1_{13}, images of gods Mc 1_{7}. → שׁמם *be desolate.*

שִׁמָמָה 1 n.f. **waste** Ezk 35_{7}. → שׁמם *be desolate.*

שִׁמָּמוֹן 2 n.f. **appalment, horror** Ezk 4_{16} 12_{19}. → שׁמם *be desolate.*

שׁמן 5 vb.—**Qal** 3 Pf. שָׁמַנְתָּ, שָׁמְנוּ; + waw וַיִּשְׁמַן—**become fat** Dt 32_{15} Jr 5_{28}.

Hi. 2 + waw וַיַּשְׁמִינוּ—**1. make heart fat,** i.e. unreceptive Is 6$_{10}$. **2. show fatness, gain fat** Ne 9$_{25}$.
→ שָׁמֵן *fat,* שֶׁמֶן *oil, fatness,* שָׁמָן *fatness,* מַשְׁמָן *rich food,* מִשְׁמָן *fat.*

[שָׁמָן] 2 n.[m.]—pl. cstr. שְׁמַנֵּי—**fatness** (pl.) of the earth, i.e. its **choice produce** Gn 27$_{28}$, **choice parts, fertile places** Gn 27$_{39}$. → שׁמן *be fat.*

שָׁמֵן 10.0.1 adj.—f.s. שְׁמֵנָה—**1. fat, rich, fertile,** of land Ne 9$_{35}$, pasture Ezk 34$_{14}$, bread Gn 49$_{20}$. **2.** as noun, **fat one, fatling, robust one,** of person Jg 3$_{29}$, sheep Ezk 34$_{16}$. → שׁמן *be fat.*

שֶׁמֶן 193.2.24.28 n.m. (appar. f. at Ca 1$_3$)—שָׁמֶן; cstr. שֶׁמֶן; sf. שַׁמְנִי; pl. שְׁמָנִים; sf. שְׁמָנֶיךָ—**1. oil, specif. olive oil** (שֶׁמֶן זַיִת) Ex 27$_{20}$||Lv 24$_2$, **a.** in connection with olive (or perh. oleaster) tree (עֵץ שֶׁמֶן) Ne 8$_{15}$, or wood 1 K 6$_{23}$. **b.** traded as commodity 1 K 5$_{25}$. **c.** for domestic use 1 K 17$_{12}$. **d.** as fuel for lamp Ex 25$_6$||35$_8$. **e.** applied to body: for anointing Ex 25$_6$||35$_8$; in cosmetic preparation Est 2$_{12}$, for softening wound Is 1$_6$. **f.** poured on or mixed with grain offering Lv 2$_1$ 7$_{10}$. **2. fatness, fat thing, richness,** פרי שמן *fruit of fatness,* i.e. the best fruit 4QAdmonPar 2.2$_4$, קֶרֶן בֶּן־שָׁמֶן *hill of a son of fatness,* i.e. a fertile hill Is 5$_1$, גֵּיא־שְׁמָנִים *valley of fatness(es),* i.e. fertile valley Is 28$_1$. → שׁמן *be fat.*

שְׁמֹנֶה 109.0.32.1 n.m.&f.—m. (with f. nouns) שְׁמוֹנֶה; f. (with m. nouns) שְׁמֹנָה; cstr. שְׁמֹנַת—**1. eight,** שְׁמֹנֶה שָׁנִים *eight years* Jg 3$_8$, שְׁמֹנָה אֲנָשִׁים *eight men* Jr 41$_{15}$, פָּרִים שְׁמֹנָה *eight bulls* Nm 29$_{29}$, שְׁמֹנַת יָמִים *eight days* Gn 17$_{12}$. **2.** with ellip. of noun, **a. eight (persons)** 1 C 24$_4$. **b. eight (parts of moon's surface),** 4QAstrCrypt 1.2$_{21}$. **3.** as ordinal numeral, **eighth,** שְׁנַת שְׁמֹנֶה *the eighth year* 2 K 24$_{12}$, יוֹם שְׁמֹנָה *the eighth day* 2 C 29$_{17}$. **4.** as constituent of a larger number, שְׁמֹנָה עָשָׂר *eighteen* Jg 20$_{44}$, var. שְׁמֹנֶה עֶשְׂרֵה Jg 3$_{14}$; שְׁמֹנֶה וְעֶשְׂרִים *twenty-eight* Ex 26$_2$||36$_9$, var. עֶשְׂרִים וּשְׁמֹנֶה 2 K 10$_{36}$; שְׁמֹנֶה מֵאוֹת *five hundred* Gn 5$_4$, שְׁמוֹנָה אֶלֶף *eight thousand* 1 C 12$_{36}$. → cf. שְׁמִינִי *eighth,* שְׁמֹנִים *eighty.*

שְׁמַנֵּי, see שָׁמָן *fat.*

שְׁמֹנִים 38.0.7 n.m.&f.pl.—שְׁמוֹנִים—**eighty, 1.** as cardinal number, שְׁמֹנִים אִישׁ *eighty men* 2 K 10$_{24}$, שְׁמֹנִים שָׁנָה *eighty years* Ex 7$_7$. **2.** as constituent of a larger number, חָמֵשׁ וּשְׁמֹנִים *eighty-five* Jos 14$_{10}$. **3.** as ordinal number, **eightieth,** שְׁמוֹנִים שָׁנָה וְאַרְבַּע מֵאוֹת שָׁנָה *the four hundred and eightieth year* 1 K 6$_1$. → cf. שְׁמֹנֶה *eight.*

*[שִׁמְנָם] 0.0.0.1 pr.n.m. **Shimnam.**

שׁמע 1159.25.145.10 vb.—**Qal** 1051.20.108.4 Pf. שָׁמַע (שָׁמֵעַ), שָׁמַעְתִּי; impf. יִשְׁמַע, יִשְׁמְעוּ (יִשְׁמָעוּ); impv. שְׁמַע (שִׁמְעָה), שְׁמָעָה, שְׁמָעֻנִי, שִׁמְעִי, שִׁמְעוּ (שְׁמָעוּ), (שְׁמַעַן) שְׁמַעְנָה; ptc. שֹׁמֵעַ, שֹׁמַעַת, שֹׁמְעִים, שֹׁמְעֵי; inf. abs. שָׁמוֹעַ; cstr. שְׁמֹעַ (שָׁמְעוֹ, שָׁמְעִי)—**1. hear, listen to** (accus.) sound Gn 3$_8$, word Gn 24$_{30}$, person speaking Jr 20$_1$; abs. Gn 18$_{10}$. **2. hear (with attentiveness), listen to,** i.e. **pay attention to, give heed to, hear (and respond to), a.** with accus. person Gn 17$_{20}$, cry Ex 3$_7$, prayer Ps 4$_2$, word Nm 12$_6$, rebuke Pr 13$_1$. **b.** with prep., (1) לְ *to* or of obj. person Jos 24$_{10}$, voice Ex 3$_{18}$. (2) בְּ *to* or of obj. voice Gn 30$_6$. (3) אֶל *to* Y. Is 46$_3$, person Gn 30$_{17}$, prayer Dn 9$_{17}$. **3. listen,** i.e. **obey, a.** with accus. word Dt 12$_{28}$. **b.** (usu.) with prep., (1) לְ *to* or of obj. Y. Lv 26$_{14}$, voice Gn 3$_{17}$, commandment Ne 9$_{29}$. (2) בְּ *to* or of obj. voice Gn 21$_{12}$. (3) אֶל *to* or of obj. person Dt 34$_9$. **4. listen to** (אֶל), i.e. **agree terms with** Gn 23$_{16}$. **5. hear (a judicial case), dispense justice** Dt 1$_{16}$ (+ בֵּין *between*) 2 S 15$_3$ 1 K 3$_{11}$. **6. hear (as witness)** Jg 11$_{10}$ (+ בֵּין *between*) Is 43$_9$. **7. be able to hear, able to listen,** abs. Dt 4$_{28}$; with accus. Is 29$_{18}$, לְ of obj. Ps 58$_6$, בְּ *to* or of obj. 2 S 19$_{36}$. **8a. understand (a language),** with accus. Gn 11$_7$ Dt 28$_{49}$; abs. Gn 42$_{23}$. **b. be understanding, be discerning,** of mind 1 K 3$_9$. **9. hear (news), hear of (thing, event),** with accus. Gn 29$_{13}$ Ex 2$_{15}$; abs. Ex 15$_{14}$. **10.** שׁמע כִּי **hear that** Gn 14$_{14}$.

Ni. 43.3.3.8 Pf. נִשְׁמַע; impf. יִשָּׁמַע (יִשָּׁמֵעַ); + waw וַיִּשָּׁמַע; ptc. נִשְׁמָע, נִשְׁמַעַת, נִשְׁמָעִים; inf. הִשָּׁמַע—**1. be heard,** of sound Ex 28$_{35}$, report Jr 51$_{46}$, violence Is 60$_{18}$; **be overheard,** of words Jr 38$_{27}$. **2. be proclaimed,** of decree Est 1$_{20}$. **3. listened to, be heeded,** of words Ec 9$_{16}$. **4. be obedient** to (לְ) someone 2 S 22$_{45}$||Ps 18$_{45}$. **5. be heard of,** subj. impersonal Dt 4$_{32}$. **6. be reported,** subj. impersonal Ne 6$_1$ (+ לְ *to,* כִּי *that*).

Pi. 2 + waw וַיְשַׁמַּע—**summon** people 1 S 15$_4$ 23$_8$ (+ לְ *to* war).

Hi. 63.4.29.6 Pf. הִשְׁמִיעַ, הִשְׁמַעְתִּי; impf. יַשְׁמִיעַ, תַּשְׁמַע; impv. הַשְׁמִיעוּ, הַשְׁמִיעִנִי, הַשְׁמִיעֻנִי; ptc. מַשְׁמִיעַ, מַשְׁמִיעִים; inf. הַשְׁמִיעַ, לַשְׁמִעַ—**1.** with double accus., **cause some-**

one to hear, let someone hear something Dt 4₁₀ Ps 51₁₀. **2. cause to be heard, let be heard,** with accus. voice Jos 6₁₀, war-cry Jr 49₂ (+ אֶל *against*). **3.** as musical term, **make a loud sound, sing loudly** 1 C 15₂₈ (+ בְּ *with* harps and lyres) 2 C 5₁₃ (+ קוֹל אֶחָד *[with] one sound*, i.e. in unison). **4.** with double accus., **cause to hear,** i.e. **announce, make known** something **to** someone 1 S 9₂₇ Is 41₂₂. **5. cause** something **to be heard,** i.e. **announce, proclaim, make known** praise Ps 106₂, peace Is 52₇, judgment Ps 76₉, former things Is 48₃. **6. cause** someone **to hear,** i.e. **announce to, make a proclamation to** Is 44₈. **7.** without obj., **make an announcement, make a proclamation** Is 62₁₁ (+ אֶל *to*) Jr 4₅. **8. make** someone **hear, listen** CD 6₃. **9. summon** someone Jr 50₂₉ (+ אֶל *against*) 51₂₇ (+ עַל *against*).

→ שְׁמִיעָה *(oral) tradition*, שֶׁמַע I *sound*, שֵׁמַע *report*, שֹׁמַע *report*, הַשְׁמָעוּת *causing to hear*, שְׁמוּעָה *report*, מִשְׁמָע I *hearing*, מִשְׁמַעַת *hearing*.

שָׁמָע 1 pr.n.m. **Shama.**

שֵׁמַע 17.1.2 n.[m.]—cstr. שֵׁמַע; sf. שִׁמְעִי—**1. report, news, rumour, fame,** שֵׁמַע יַעֲקֹב *news of*, i.e. about, *Jacob* Gn 29₁₃, שִׁמְעֲךָ *your report*, i.e. the report about you Dt 2₂₅, שֵׁמַע שָׁוְא *report of emptiness*, i.e. false report Ex 23₁. **2. hearing,** שֵׁמַע אֹזֶן *hearing of the ear* Ps 18₄₅. → שמע *hear*.

[שֶׁמַע] I 1 n.[m.] **sound,** צִלְצְלֵי־שָׁמַע *cymbals of sound*, i.e. (loud) sounding cymbals Ps 150₅. → שמע *hear*.

[שֶׁמַע] II 5.0.0.15 pr.n.m. **Shema.**

[שֹׁמַע] 4 n.m. **report, fame,** שָׁמְעוֹ *his report*, i.e. the report about him Jos 6₂₇ 9₉ Jr 6₂₄ Est 9₄. → שמע *hear*.

שְׁמַע 1 pl.n. **Shema.**

שִׁמְעָא 5 pr.n.m. **Shimea.**

שִׁמְעָה 3 pr.n.m. **Shimeah.**

שְׁמָעָה 1.0.2 pr.n.m. **Shemaah.**

שְׁמֻעָה, see שְׁמוּעָה *report*.

שִׁמְעוֹן 44.5.41.15 pr.n.m. **Simeon, Shimeon, Simon.**

שִׁמְעוֹנִי, see שִׁמְעֹנִי *Simeonite*.

שִׁמְעִי I 44.0.0.1 pr.n.m. **Shimei.**

שִׁמְעִי II 2 gent. **Shimeite.**

שְׁמַעְיָה 41.0.0.28 pr.n.m. **Shemaiah.**

שְׁמַעְיָהוּ, see שְׁמַעְיָה *Shemaiah*.

שִׁמְעֹנִי 4 gent. **Simeonite.**

שִׁמְעַת 2 pr.n.f. **Shimeath.**

[שִׁמְעָתִי] 1 gent. **Shimeathite.**

שֶׁמֶץ 2.2 n.m.—cstr. שֶׁמֶץ—**whisper,** perh. alw. as representing **a little** Jb 4₁₂ Si 18₃₂; שֶׁמֶץ דָּבָר *whisper of a word* Jb 26₁₄, שמץ מחלה *whisper of a sickness*, i.e. a slight sickness Si 10₁₀.

שִׁמְצָה 1 n.f. **(object of) whispering, derision** Ex 32₂₅.

שמר 468.22.90.6 vb.—**Qal** 427.16.75.5 Pf. שָׁמַר; impf. יִשְׁמֹר (יִשְׁמָר); + waw וַיִּשְׁמֹר־ ,וַתִּשְׁמֹר; impv. שְׁמֹר (שְׁמָר־) ,שָׁמְרָה ,שָׁמְרָה, שָׁמְרֵנִי), שִׁמְרוּ; ptc. שֹׁמֵר ,שֹׁמְרִים ,שֹׁמְרֵי; ptc. pass. שָׁמוּר, שְׁמֻרָה; inf. abs. שָׁמוֹר; cstr. שְׁמֹר (שָׁמְרְךָ ,שָׁמְרוֹ)—**1a. keep, have charge of, mind, tend** animals Ex 22₉, garden Gn 2₁₅, property in trust Ex 22₆, ark 1 S 7₁. **b.** without obj., **keep sheep** Gn 30₃₁. **2a. keep, retain, hold on to** food in store Gn 41₃₅, lost item CD 9₁₆, words in mind Gn 37₁₁; **retain anger** Jr 3₅. **b. keep, restrain, hold back** animal (within bounds) Ex 21₂₉, one's hand from doing (מֵעֲשׂוֹת) evil Is 56₂. **3. keep watch over, keep guard over, guard,** with accus. person Jos 10₁₈, way Gn 3₂₄, gate Ne 13₂₂; אֶל *over* person 1 S 26₁₅; עַל *over* person 1 S 26₁₆. **4. keep, guard, preserve, protect, take care of,** with accus. person Gn 28₁₅ Pr 6₂₄ (+ מִן *from*), feet 1 S 2₉, knowledge Ml 2₇; בְּ of obj. person 2 S 18₁₂; עַל of obj. person Pr 2₁₁. **5a. observe, watch,** with accus. person 1 S 19₁₁, mouth 1 S 1₁₂, ways Jb 13₂₇; עַל *over* sin Jb 14₁₆. **b. watch for, wait for,** with accus. of one's life Ps 71₁₀, twilight Jb 24₁₅; אֶל *for* signal Lachish ost. 4₁₁. **6. keep, observe, perform** charge, commandments, laws Gn 26₅, covenant Gn 17₉, loyalty 1 K 3₆, sabbath Ex 31₁₃, feast Ex 23₁₅. **7.** with other verb, **be careful, take care (to do), do, act carefully,** וּשְׁמַרְתֶּם לַעֲשׂוֹת *and you shall be careful to do* Dt 5₃₂, וּשְׁמַרְתֶּם וַעֲשִׂיתֶם *and you shall take care and do*, i.e. do carefully Dt 4₆, שִׁמְרוּ וְדִרְשׁוּ *you shall take care and seek*, i.e. seek carefully 1 C 28₈. **8. give heed to, pay regard to, take note of** reproof Pr 13₁₈, iniquity Ps 130₃. **9. keep loyal to, devote oneself to** Y. CD 19₉, images Ps 31₇. **10a. keep oneself from** (מִן) something Jos 6₁₈. **b.** שמר נֶפֶשׁ מִן **keep oneself from,** i.e. **beware of** someone Si 37₂₀. **11.** ptc. as noun, **keeper, protec-**

tor, guard, sentry Jg 7₁₉; שֹׁמְרֵי הַסַּף *keepers of the threshold* 2 K 12₁₀. **12. pass. a. be kept, be reserved,** of food 1 S 9₂₄ (+ לְ *for*), riches Ec 5₁₂ (+ לְ *by*). **b. be secure,** of covenant 2 S 23₅.

Ni. 37.6.16.1 Pf. נִשְׁמַר; impf. תִּשָּׁמֵר; impv. הִשָּׁמֵר (הִשָּׁמֶר), הִשָּׁמְרוּ, הִשָּׁמְרִי; ptc. Si נשמר; inf. Si. השמר—**1. be on one's guard, beware, take heed, be careful** Gn 24₆ (+ לְ reflexive, sf. in ref. to subj.) 2 S 20₁₀ (+ בְּ *concerning*) Jr 9₃ (+ מִן *concerning*); impv. of שמר ni. followed (not alw. immediately) by פֶּן *lest* Gn 24₆, מִן + inf. cstr. *from (doing), so as not to do* Gn 31₂₉, לְ + inf. cstr. *to do, that you do* Dt 24₈, negated juss. or impf. Jg 13₄ Jb 36₂₁. **2. keep oneself, abstain** from (מִן) something Dt 23₉. **3. be kept, be guarded, be preserved** Ho 12₁₃ (+ בְּ *by*) Ps 37₂₈.

Pi. 1 Ptc. מְשַׁמְּרִים—**pay regard to, devote oneself to** vanities, i.e. images Jon 2₉.

Htp. 3 Impf. יִשְׁתַּמֵּר; + waw וָאֶשְׁתַּמֵּר (וָאֶשְׁתַּמְּרָה)—**1. keep oneself from** (מִן) iniquity 2 S 22₂₄||Ps 18₂₃. **2. be kept, be observed,** of statutes Mc 6₁₆.

→ שִׁמֻּרִים *watching,* שָׁמְרָה *guard,* אַשְׁמוּרָה *watch,* מִשְׁמָר I *guard,* II *muzzle,* III *wakefulness,* מִשְׁמָרָה *guardhouse,* מִשְׁמֶרֶת *watch,* שְׁמֻרָה *eye-lid.*

שמר׳, see שֹׁמְרוֹן *Samaria.*

שֶׁמֶר I 4 pr.n.m. **Shemer.**

[שֶׁמֶר] II 5 n.m.—pl. שְׁמָרִים; sf. שְׁמָרֶיהָ, שִׁמְרֵיהֶם—**1. lees, dregs** of wine Jr 48₁₁ Ps 75₉ Zp 1₁₂. **2. wine matured on the lees** Is 25₆.

שֹׁמֵר 2 pr.n.m. **Shomer.**

שָׁמְרָה 1 n.f. **guard, watch** Ps 141₃. → שמר *keep.*

[שְׁמֻרָה] 1 n.f. **eyelid,** שְׁמֻרוֹת עֵינָי *lids of my eyes* Ps 77₅. → שמר *keep.*

שִׁמְרוֹן I 3 pl.n. **Shimron.**

שִׁמְרוֹן II 3 pr.n.m. **Shimron.**

שֹׁמְרוֹן 109.0.1.24 pl.n. **Samaria.**

שִׁמְרִי 4 pr.n.m. **Shimri.**

שְׁמַרְיָה 4.0.0.10 pr.n.m. **Shemariah.**

שְׁמַרְיָהוּ, see שְׁמַרְיָה *Shemariah.*

שִׁמֻּרִים 2.0.1 n.m.[pl.] **watching, vigil,** in connection with Passover Ex 12₄₂. → שמר *keep.*

שמרימות, see שְׁמִירָמוֹת *Shemiramoth.*

שמרין, see שֹׁמְרוֹן *Samaria.*

שִׁמְרִית 1 pr.n.f. **Shimrith.**

שמרן, see שֹׁמְרוֹן *Samaria.*

שִׁמְרֹנִי 1 gent. **Shimronite.**

[שֹׁמְרֹנִי] 1 gent. **Samaritan.**

שִׁמְרָת 1 pr.n.f. **Shimrath.**

*שמש 0.1 vb.—**Pi.** 0.1 Impf. ישמש—perh. **hasten, depart** from (מִן) Si 38₁₂(Bmg).

שֶׁמֶשׁ 134.7.30 n.f.&m.—שָׁמֶשׁ; cstr. שֶׁמֶשׁ; sf. שִׁמְשֵׁךְ; pl. cstr. שִׁמְשֹׁתַיִךְ—**1. sun** Gn 15₁₂; as subj. of זרח *rise* Gn 32₃₂, יצא *go out,* i.e. rise Gn 19₂₃, בוא *come,* i.e. set Gn 15₁₂; מִזְרַח הַשֶּׁמֶשׁ *rising of the sun,* i.e. east Jos 13₅, מְבוֹא הַשֶּׁמֶשׁ *setting of the sun,* i.e. west Dt 11₃₀; as object of worship Dt 17₃; Y. as a sun and shield Ps 84₁₂. **2.** pl. **pinnacles, battlements** Is 54₁₂.

*[שֶׁמֶשְׁעֶזֶר] 0.0.0.1 pr.n.[m.] **Shemeshezer.**

שִׁמְשׁוֹן 38 pr.n.m. **Samson.**

שַׁמְשְׁרַי 1 pr.n.m. **Shamsherai.**

שֻׁמָתִי 1 gent. **Shumathite.**

שָׁן, שְׁן, see בֵּית־שְׁאָן *Beth-shean.*

שֵׁן I 55.4.8 n.f. (m. at 1 S 14₅)—cstr. שֵׁן (שֶׁן־); sf. שִׁנּוֹ; du. שִׁנַּיִם; cstr. שִׁנֵּי; sf. שִׁנָּיו, שִׁנֵּיהֶם (שִׁנֵּימוֹ)—**1. tooth,** of humans Gn 49₁₂ Ex 21₂₄, animals Dt 32₂₄ Jl 1₆. **2. ivory** 1 K 10₁₈||2 C 9₁₇. **3. prong,** הַמַּזְלֵג שְׁלֹשׁ־הַשִּׁנַּיִם *a three-pronged fork* 1 S 2₁₃. **4. crag** of rock 1 S 14₄. → שנן *sharpen.*

שֵׁן II 1 pl.n. **Shen.**

שן, see שֹׁמְרוֹן *Samaria.*

שנא, see שנה I *change.*

שֵׁנָא I Ps 127₂, see שֵׁנָה *sleep.*

*שֵׁנָא II 1 n.[m.] **high estate, honour** Ps 127₂.

*שֵׁנָא III 1 n.[m.] **prosperity** Ps 127₂.

שִׁנְאָב I 1 pr.n.m. **Shinab.**

*[שִׁנְאָב] II 0.0.1 n.[m.]—pl. sf. שאנביהם—perh. **channel** 1QH 11₂₉.

שִׁנְאָן I 1 n.[m.] **repetition,** אַלְפֵי שִׁנְאָן *thousands of repetition,* i.e. thousands upon thousands Ps 68₁₈. → שנה II *repeat.*

*שִׁנְאָן II 1 n.[m.] coll. **archers, warriors** Ps 68₁₈.

שֶׁנְאַצַּר 1 pr.n.m. **Shenazzar.**

שנה I 17.9.10 vb.—**Qal** 6.3.2 Pf. שָׁנִיתִי; impv. יִשְׁנֶא; ptc. Si שונה, שֹׁנִים, שֹׁנוֹת; inf. שְׁנוֹת—**1. intrans., change,** of Y. Ml 3₆, gold Lm 4₁. **2. be different from** (מִן), of vessels Est 1$_7$, law Est 3$_8$.

Pi. 9.4.3 Pf. שִׁנָּה (שִׁנָּא); impf. אֲשַׁנֶּה, וִישַׁנֶּה; + waw וַיְשַׁנּוֹ; impv. Si שַׁנֵּה; ptc. מְשַׁנֶּה; inf. שַׁנּוֹת—**1.** trans., **change** garments 2 K 25$_{29}$||Jr 52$_{33}$, order of battalions 1QM 9$_{10}$, countenance Jb 14$_{20}$, **disguise** behaviour 1 S 21$_{14}$, **pervert** judgment Pr 31$_5$. **2. change (the place of), i.e. transfer** someone to (לְ) best place Est 2$_9$.

Pu. 1.1.1 Impf. יְשֻׁנֶּא—**be changed,** of hardness of countenance Ec 8$_1$.

Hi. 0.0.4 Inf. השנות—**change** flesh 1QH 24$_8$, words 1QH 7$_{14}$; אין להשנות *one cannot change (anything)* 1QS 3$_{16}$.

Htp. 1.1 + waw וְהִשְׁתַּנִּית; inf. Si השתנותו—**1.** intrans., **change,** of new moon Si 43$_{8(B)}$. **2. disguise oneself** 1 K 14$_2$.

→ שָׁנָה *year,* שֵׁת *year.*

שׁנה II 9.6.3.2 vb.—**Qal** 8.6.2.2 Pf. שָׁנָה; impf. אֶשְׁנֶה, יִשְׁנוּ; impv. שְׁנוּ; ptc. שֹׁנֶה; inf. Si שנות—**1. repeat** something Pr 26$_{11}$ (בְּ of obj.) Si 7$_8$; by speaking about it Si 44$_{15}$, i.e. **harp upon** (בְּ) Pr 17$_9$. **2. repeat** an activity, **do again, do a second time** 1 S 26$_8$ 1 K 18$_{34}$. **3. speak again** Jb 29$_{22}$. **4. repeat oneself** in (בְּ) prayer Si 7$_{14}$.

Ni. 1.0.1 Pf. Q נשניתי; inf. הִשָּׁנוֹת—**1. be repeated,** of dream Gn 41$_{32}$ (+ אֶל *to*). **2. be taught,** of person 4QMa 11.1$_{16}$.

→ שְׁנַיִם *two,* שֵׁנִי *second,* מִשְׁנֶה I *second,* שִׁנְאָן I *repetition.*

***שׁנה III** 2 vb.—**Qal** 1 Ptc. שׁוֹנִים—**be exalted,** ptc. as noun, **exalted one, noble** Pr 24$_{21}$.

Pi. 1 + waw וַיְשַׁנֶּהָ—**advance, promote** someone to (לְ) best place Est 2$_9$.

שָׁנָה 874.5.217.37 n.f.—Q שנא; cstr. שְׁנַת; sf. שְׁנָתוֹ; du. שְׁנָתַיִם; pl. שָׁנִים; cstr. שְׁנֵי; sf. שָׁנָיו, שְׁנֵיהֶם; pl. cstr. שְׁנוֹת; sf. שְׁנוֹתָיו, שְׁנוֹתָם—**year, 1.** usu. the lunar year of 354 days Gn 1$_{14}$; שְׁנַת אַחַת *the first year* Dn 1$_{21}$, בַּשָּׁנָה הָרִאשׁוֹנָה *in the first year* 2 C 29$_3$, בֶּן־שָׁנָה *son of a year,* i.e. one year old Ex 12$_5$, בַּת־תִּשְׁעִים שָׁנָה *daughter of ninety years,* i.e. ninety years old Gn 17$_{17}$, שָׁנָה בְשָׁנָה *year by year,* lit. 'a year by a year' Lv 25$_{53}$, מִדֵּי שָׁנָה בְשָׁנָה *as often as there was a year,* i.e. from year to year 1 S 7$_{16}$, דְּבַר־שָׁנָה בְּשָׁנָה *the thing of a year for a year,* i.e. what is due each year 1 K 10$_{25}$||2 C 9$_{24}$, אַחַת בַּשָּׁנָה *once a year* Ex 30$_{10}$, הַשָּׁנָה *this year* 2 K 19$_{29}$||Is 37$_{30}$. **2.** at Qumran, the solar year of 364 days 11QPsa 27$_6$. → שָׁנָה I *change;* cf. שֵׁת *year.*

שֵׁנָה 24.3 n.f.—שֵׁנָא, שְׁנַת (Ps 132$_4$; mss שְׁנָת); cstr. שְׁנַת; sf. שְׁנָתִי; pl. שֵׁנוֹת—**sleep** Gn 28$_{16}$; מְעַט שֵׁנוֹת *a few (more of) sleeps* Pr 6$_{10}$. → ישׁן I *sleep.*

שֶׁנְהַבִּים 2 n.m.[pl.] **ivory** 1 K 10$_{22}$||2 C 9$_{21}$.

שָׁנִי I 42.1.3 n.[m.]—cstr. שְׁנִי; pl. שָׁנִים—**crimson,** less accurately **scarlet,** cloth, thread, etc., esp. in תְּכֵלֶת וְאַרְגָּמָן וְתוֹלַעַת שָׁנִי *blue and purple and crimson (material)* Ex 25$_4$||35$_6$, עֵץ אֶרֶז וּשְׁנִי תוֹלַעַת וְאֵזֹב *cedarwood and crimson (material) and hyssop* Lv 14$_4$, חוּט הַשָּׁנִי *thread of the crimson* Jos 2$_{18}$.

***[שָׁנִי] II** adj. **fully grown,** of bull Jg 6$_{25.26.28}$ (all three if em. הַשֵּׁנִי *the second*).

שֵׁנִי 156.1.219.4 adj.—f.s. שֵׁנִית (Q שניה); m.pl. שֵׁנִים (Q שניים); f.pl. Q שניות—**1. second, other (of two),** of son Gn 30$_7$, ram Ex 29$_{19}$||Lv 8$_{22}$, wing 1 K 6$_{24}$, day Gn 1$_8$, month Gn 7$_{11}$, year Gn 47$_{18}$. **2.** as noun, **second (one), other (one of two), a.** masc., in ref. to person Gn 32$_{20}$, shield 1QM 9$_{15}$, lot 1 C 25$_9$, month 4QCalMishA 1.1$_7$. **b.** fem., in ref. to wife Gn 4$_{19}$, horn Dn 8$_3$, net CD 4$_{17}$. **3.** שֵׁנִית as adv., **a second time** Gn 22$_{15}$. → שׁנה II *repeat.*

***[שְׁנִי]** n.[m.] **high rank** Pr 24$_{22}$ (if em. שְׁנֵיהֶם *of both of them* to שְׁנִיָּם *their high rank*).

***[שֶׁנְיוֹ]** 0.0.0.1 pr.n.[m.] **Shenio.**

שְׁנַיִם, שְׁתַּיִם 768.26.163.4 n.m.&f.du.—m. du. שְׁנַיִם; cstr. שְׁנֵי, שְׁנֵים עָשָׂר, שְׁנֵי עָשָׂר; sf. שְׁנֵיהֶם; f. du. שְׁתַּיִם (שְׁתָּיִם); cstr. שְׁתֵּי, שְׁתֵּים עֶשְׂרֵה, שְׁתֵּי עֶשְׂרֵה; sf. שְׁתֵּיהֶם—**1. two,** שְׁנַיִם־אֲנָשִׁים *two men* Jos 2$_1$, שְׁנֵי־אֲנָשִׁים *two men* Ex 2$_{13}$, שְׁתַּיִם נָשִׁים *two women* 1 K 3$_{16}$, שְׁתֵּי נָשִׁים *two wives* Gn 4$_{19}$. **2a.** שְׁנַיִם with ellip. of noun, **two (persons)** Am 3$_3$, **two (creatures)** Gn 6$_{20}$, **two (pieces)** 1 K 3$_{25}$. **b.** שְׁתַּיִם with ellip. of noun, **two (wings)** Is 6$_2$, **two (things)** Is 51$_{19}$, **two (cubits)** 3QTr 9$_2$. **3a.** with pronom. sf., **the two of, both of,** שְׁנֵיהֶם *both of them* Gn 2$_{25}$, שְׁתֵּיהֶן *both of them* (fem.) 1 S 25$_{43}$. **4a.** שְׁתַּיִם as ordinal numeral, **second,** שְׁנַת שְׁתַּיִם *the second year* 1 K 15$_{25}$. **b.** שְׁנַיִם as ordinal numeral with ellip. of noun, **second (day)** 4QCalMishB 1$_1$. **5a.** שְׁנַיִם **double amount** Ex 22$_3$. **b.** פִּי שְׁנַיִם lit. 'mouth of two', (1) **double portion** Dt 21$_{17}$.

(2) two thirds Zc 13_8. 6. as adv., a. שְׁתַּיִם **twice** Jb 40_5. b. שְׁנַיִם שְׁנַיִם **in twos, two by two** Gn 7_9. 7. as constituent of a larger number, שְׁנֵים עָשָׂר *twelve* Ex 24_4, vars. שְׁתֵּים עֶשְׂרֵה 4QAstrCrypt 9_7, שתים עשר Ex 28_{21}, שְׁנֵי עָשָׂר Ex 15_{27}, שְׁתֵּי־עֶשְׂרֵה Jos 4_8; שְׁנַיִם וּשְׁלֹשִׁים *thirty-two* Nm 1_{35}, vars. שְׁלֹשִׁים וּשְׁנַיִם 1 K 20_1, שְׁתַּיִם וּשְׁלֹשִׁים Gn 11_{20}, שְׁלֹשִׁים וּשְׁתַּיִם 2 C 21_{20}. → שנה II *repeat*.

שְׁנִינָה 4.0.1 n.f.—Q שנניה—**sharp word, taunt** Dt 28_{37} 1 K 9_7 11QT 59_2. → שנן I *sharpen*.

שנן I 9.1.6 vb.—**Qal** 7.0.2 Pf. שָׁנַנּוּ, שְׁנּוֹתִי; ptc. pass. שָׁנוּן, שְׁנוּנִים—**1. sharpen, whet** sword Dt 32_{41}, tongue Ps 64_4 (+ כְּ *like* sword). **2.** pass. **be sharpened,** of arrow Is 5_{28}.

Pi. 1.1.4 Pf. Q שננתה; impf. Si אשננה; + waw וְשִׁנַּנְתָּם; inf. Q שנן—**1. sharpen** words 4QWiles 1_1. **2. teach incisively,** obj. kidney, i.e. mind 4QBark[c] 1.15, words Dt 6_7 (+ לְ *to*), law 1QH 12_{10} (+ בְּ *in* heart).

Htpo. 1 Impf. אֶשְׁתּוֹנָן—**be pierced,** כִּלְיוֹתַי אֶשְׁתּוֹנָן *I was pierced (in) my kidneys* Ps 73_{21}.

→ שֵׁן I *tooth*, שְׁנִינָה *sharp word.*

***שנן** II 1.1.1 vb. (byform of שנה II)—**Pi.** 1 Pf. Q שננתה; impf. Si אשננה; + waw וְשִׁנַּנְתָּם—**repeat** words Dt 6_7 (+ לְ *to*), law 1QH 12_{10} (+ בְּ *in* heart).

שנניה, see שְׁנִינָה *sharp word.*

שנס 1 vb.—**Pi.** 1 + waw וַיְשַׁנֵּס—**gird** loins 1 K 18_{46}.

שִׁנְעָר 8 pl.n. **Shinar.**

שסה 12 vb.—**Qal** 11 Pf. שָׁסוּ; impf. יִשְׁסֶה; ptc. שֹׁסִים; ptc. pass. שְׁסוּי—**1a. plunder, spoil, loot** people Jg 2_{16}, threshing floor 1 S 23_1, treasury Ho 13_{15}. **b.** without obj., **plunder, take spoil** Ps 44_{11} (+ לְ *for* oneself). **2.** ptc. as noun, **plunderer** Jg 2_{14}. **3.** pass. **be plundered,** of people Is 42_{22}.

Po. 1 Pf. שׁוֹשֵׂתִי—**plunder** stores Is 10_{13}.

→ cf. שסס *plunder.*

שסס 5 vb. (byform of שסה)—**Qal** 3 Pf. שְׁסָהוּ; + waw וַיָּשֹׁסּוּ—**plunder** persons Jg 2_{14}, camp 1 S 17_{53}.

Ni. 2 Impf. יִשַּׁסּוּ; + waw וְנָשַׁסּוּ—**be plundered,** of house Is 13_{16}.

→ מְשִׁסָּה *plunder*, מְשׁוּסָּה *plunder*; cf. שסה *plunder.*

שסע 9 vb.—**Qal** 5 Ptc. שֹׁסַע, שֹׁסַעַת; ptc. pass. שְׁסוּעָה—**1. divide, cleave** cleft (שֶׁסַע) of hoof Lv 11_3. **2.** pass. **be divided, cloven,** of hoof Dt 14_7.

Pi. 4 + waw וַיְשַׁסַּע, וְשִׁסַּע; inf. שַׁסַּע—**1. tear apart, tear in pieces** lion Jg 14_6, bird Lv 1_{17}. **2.** perh. **restrain** someone with (בְּ) words 1 S 24_8.

→ שֶׁסַע *division.*

שֶׁסַע 4 n.[m.]—cstr. שֶׁסַע—**division, cleft** of hoof Lv 11_3.

→ שסע *divide.*

שסף 1 vb.—**Pi.** 1 + waw וַיְשַׁסֵּף—perh. **hew** person **in pieces** 1 S 15_{33}.

שעה I 15.1 vb.—**Qal** 12.1 Pf. שָׁעָה, שָׁעוּ; impf. יִשְׁעֶה; + waw וַיִּשַׁע; impv. שְׁעֵה, שְׁעוּ—**1a. look** 2 S 22_{42}. **b. look away, turn one's gaze** Is 22_4 (+ מִן *from*) Jb 14_6 (+ מֵעַל *from*). **c.** perh. **gaze about (aimlessly),** of eyes Is 32_3. **2. look towards, pay attention to, have regard for, look with favour upon,** with בְּ Ex 5_9, אֶל Gn 4_4, עַל Is 17_7.

Hi. 1 Impv. הָשַׁע—**look away, turn one's gaze from** (מִן) Ps 39_{14}.

Htp. 2 Impf. נִשְׁתָּעָה, תִּשְׁתָּע—**gaze about (anxiously), be dismayed** Is 41_{10}, perh. **look at one another** Is 41_{23}.

→ שְׁעִיָּה *anxiety.*

***שעה** II 0.1 vb.—**Ni.** 0.1 Inf. השעות—**tell, recount** Si $44_{8(Bmg)}$ (B להשענות *for support*).

Htp. 0.1 Inf. השתעות—**tell, recount** Si $44_{8(Bmg)}$.

*[שָׁעָה] 0.0.1 n.f.—pl. שעת—**smooth rock,** pl. **smooth stones** 3QTr 9_2.

[שַׁעֲטָה] 1 n.f.—cstr. שַׁעֲטַת—**stamping** of hooves Jr 47_3.

[שַׁעַטְנֵז] 2.0.2 n.m.—Q שעטנז—**mixed stuff, diverse material,** for garment Lv 19_{19} Dt 22_{11} 4QMMT B_{78} 4QT 14_5.

*[שְׁעִיָּה] 0.2 n.f.—pl. sf. שעיותיו—**anxiety, concern** Si 37_{14} 38_{25}. → שעה I *look.*

*[שְׁעַיָּהוּ] 0.0.0.1 pr.n.[m.] **Sheaiah.**

*[שָׁעִיס] 1 n.[m.] (var. form of שָׁחִיס and סָחִישׁ) **self-sown grain** Is $37_{30(1QIsa^a)}$.

[שֹׁעַל] 3.0.1 n.[m.]—cstr. Q שועל; sf. שָׁעֳלוֹ; pl. שְׁעָלִים; cstr. שַׁעֲלֵי—**1. hollow of the hand** Is 40_{12}. **2. handful of** barley Ezk 13_{19}. → cf. מִשְׁעוֹל *narrow pathway.*

[שָׁעָל], see שׁוּעָל III *Shual.*

שַׁעַלְבִים 2 pl.n. **Shaalbim.**

שַׁעֲלַבִּין 1 pl.n. **Shaalabbin.**

שַׁעַלְבֹנִי 2 gent. **Shaalbonite.**

שַׁעֲלִים 1 pl.n. **Shaalim.**

שׁען 22.3.15 vb.—**Ni.** 22.3.15 Pf. נִשְׁעַן, נִשְׁעֲנוּ, נִשְׁעָנוּ; impf. יִשָּׁעֵן; impv. Q השען, הִשָּׁעֲנוּ; ptc. נִשְׁעָן, Q נשענת; inf. הִשָּׁעֵן (הִשָּׁעֶנְךָ)—**1. support oneself, lean** upon, against (עַל) person Ezk 29₇, pillar Jg 16₂₆, spear 2 S 1₆. **2. rest oneself, recline** under (תַּחַת) tree Gn 18₄. **3.** of slopes of wadis, **lean, lie towards** (לְ) Nm 21₁₅. **4. lean,** i.e. **rely, depend,** with בְּ *upon* Y. Is 50₁₀, truth 1QH 18₁₇; אֶל *upon* understanding Pr 3₅; עַל *upon* Y. Is 10₂₀, king 2 C 16₇, horses Is 31₁, wisdom Si 15₄. **5. be supported, be upheld,** of the wicked Jb 24₂₃. → מַשְׁעֵן *support,* מִשְׁעָן I *support,* מַשְׁעֵנָה *support,* מִשְׁעֶנֶת *support,* הִשְׁתַּעֲנוּת *support.*

*[שְׁעָנָף] 0.0.0.1 pr.n.m. **Sheanaph.**

שׁעע I 3.2.2 vb.—**Qal** 1.0.2 Impv. שֹׁעוּ; inf. Q שוע—**be smeared over, be blind,** of people Is 29₉ (see Htpalp.), eyes Is 32₃ (if em. תִּשְׁעֶינָה [from שׁעה *gaze*] to תְּשֹׁעֶינָה).

Hi. 1.2 + waw Si והשיע; Q ותשע; impv. הָשַׁע; inf. Si השע—**1a. besmear, seal over** eyes Is 6₁₀. **b.** with double accus., **besmear** mouth **with** plans Si 41₂₁ (Bmg). **2. flatter** (לְ of obj.) someone Si 13₆.

Htpalp. 1 Impv. הִשְׁתַּעַשְׁעוּ—**blind oneself,** + qal, הִשְׁתַּעַשְׁעוּ וָשֹׁעוּ *blind yourselves and be blind* Is 29₉.

→ מִשְׁעִי I *cleansing,* II *rubbing,* IV *smoothness.*

שׁעע II 6.0.9 vb.—**Pilp.** 3.0.5 Pf. שִׁעֲשַׁעְתִּי; impf. יְשַׁעַשְׁעוּ; + waw שִׁעֲשַׁע; inf. Q שעשע—**1. delight, gladden** someone 1QH 17₃₂ (+ בְּ *with* spirit), one's soul Ps 94₁₉. **2. take delight in,** with accus. law Ps 119₇₀; בְּ of obj. truth 4QInstr[d] 69.2₁₂. **3. enjoy oneself, play,** of child Is 11₈.

Polp. 1 תְּשָׁעֳשָׁעוּ—**be played with, be dandled** upon (עַל) knees Is 66₁₂.

Htpalp. 2.0.4 Impf. אֶשְׁתַּעֲשָׁע (אֶשְׁתַּעֲשַׁע)—**delight oneself, take delight in** (בְּ) statutes Ps 119₁₆, forgiveness 1QH 17₁₃.

→ שַׁעֲשׁוּעִים *delight.*

שַׁעַף 2 pr.n.m. **Shaaph.**

שׁער I 1 vb.—**Qal** 1 Pf. שָׁעַר—**calculate, reckon** Pr 23₇ (+ בְּנַפְשׁוֹ *within himself*). → שַׁעַר II *measure.*

***שׁער** II 0.0.1 vb.—**Hi.** 0.0.1 + waw וישעירו—**act horribly** with (בְּ) words, i.e. speak horrifying things 4QapJoseph[b] 1₁₃. → שֹׁעָר *horrid,* שַׁעֲרוּרָה *horror,* שַׁעֲרוּרִיָּה *horror,* שַׁעֲרֻרִת *horror.*

שַׁעַר I 374.5.131 n.m.&f.—שָׁעַר; cstr. שַׁעַר; + ה- of direction שַׁעְרָה (שָׁעְרָה); pl. שְׁעָרִים; cstr. שַׁעֲרֵי; sf. שְׁעָרָיו, שַׁעֲרֵיהֶם—**1. gate, gateway, a.** of city or town Gn 19₁; specif. the gate itself 2 S 18₂₄; gateway building, **gatehouse** 2 S 19₁, area of gateway as place of meeting Ps 69₁₃, oft. for legal proceedings Dt 21₁₉. **b.** of palace or fortress 2 K 11₁₉ Est 2₁₉, temple 2 K 15₃₅, tabernacle court Ex 27₁₆, camp Ex 32₂₆, house Pr 14₁₉. **2.** pl. **gates,** i.e. **cities, towns** Ex 20₂₀. **3. gate** of river, perh. **sluice** Na 2₇. **4. gate,** as term for place of entrance, **a.** of land Na 3₁₃, heaven Gn 28₁₇, Sheol Is 38₁₀, wisdom Si 51₁₉(B), salvation 1QM 18₇. **b.** through which the sun sets CD 10₁₆; 'gates of light', the number of which corresponds to the day of the month, i.e. the number of times the sun has risen that month 4QPrQuot 29.8₁₀. **c.** in battle formation, i.e. **interval,** through which skirmishers advance 1QM 3₁.

[שַׁעַר] II 1 n.[m.] **measure** of produce of land, מֵאָה שְׁעָרִים *a hundred measures,* i.e. a hundred-fold Gn 26₁₂. → שׁער I *calculate.*

[שֹׁעָר] 1 adj.—pl. שֹׁעָרִים—**horrid, rotten,** of figs Jr 29₁₇. → שׁער II *be horrible.*

שֹׁעֵר 37.0.0.1 n.m.—שׁוֹעֵר; cstr. שֹׁעֵר; pl. שֹׁעֲרִים; cstr. שֹׁעֲרֵי—**gatekeeper, porter** of sanctuary 1 C 9₁₇, city gate 2 K 7₁₀, prison Bulla 858. → cf. שַׁעַר *gate,* שֹׁעֶרֶת *female gatekeeper.*

שַׁעֲרוּרָה 2 n.f. **horror, horrid thing** Jr 5₃₀ 23₁₄. → שׁער II *be horrible.*

[שַׁעֲרוּרִיָּה] 1.0.3 n.f.—Kt שעריריה; pl. cstr. Q שערוריות—**horror, horrid thing** Ho 6₁₀ 1QpHab 9₁ 4QTestim₂₇. → שׁער II *be horrible.*

שְׁעַרְיָה 2.0.0.2 pr.n.m. **Sheariah.**

שעריהו, see שְׁעַרְיָה *Sheariah.*

שַׁעֲרַיִם 3 pl.n. **Shaaraim.**

שעריריה, see שַׁעֲרוּרִיָּה *horror.*

שַׁעֲרֻרִת 1 n.f. **horror, horrid thing** Jr 18₁₃. → שׁער II *be horrible.*

*[שֹׁעֶרֶת] n.f. **female gatekeeper**—2 S 4₆ (if em. בָּאוּ עַד־תּוֹךְ הַבַּיִת *they went to the middle of the house* to שֹׁעֶרֶת הַבַּיִת *the gatekeeper of the house*). → cf. שֹׁעֵר

gatekeeper.

שַׁעַשְׁגַז 1 pr.n.m. **Shaashgaz.**

שַׁעֲשׁוּעִים 9.0.2 n.[m.]pl.—sf. שַׁעֲשֻׁעָי, שַׁעֲשׁוּעָיו—**delight** Pr 8₃₁; יֶלֶד שַׁעֲשֻׁעִים *child of delight*, i.e. in whom one delights Jr 31₂₀, תּוֹרָתְךָ שַׁעֲשֻׁעָי *your law is my delight* Ps 119₇₇. → שׁעע II *delight.*

*__שׁפד__ 0.0.1 vb.—**Qal** 0.0.1 Ptc. pass. שפוד—pass. **be tapered,** of blade of spear 1QM 5₁₀ (+ אֶל *towards* head, i.e. point).

שׁפה I 2.0.2 vb.—**Ni.** 1 Ptc. נִשְׁפֶּה—**be swept bare, be wind-swept,** of mountain Is 13₂.

Pi. 0.0.2 Inf. שפות—**cleanse, provide clearance** before (לִפְנֵי) someone of (מִן) claims against property being let out 5/6HevBA 45₂₇.

Pu. 1 Pf. Qr שֻׁפּוּ—**be made bare, be stripped of flesh,** of bones Jb 33₂₁(Qr) (Kt שְׁפִי *bareness*).

→ שְׁפִי I *bareness,* (?) שְׁפוֹת *cheese.*

*__שׁפה__ II 0.0.2 vb.—**Pi.** 0.0.2 Inf. שפות—**silence** (מִן of obj.) disputes (about the letting of property) before (לִפְנֵי) someone 5/6HevBA 45₂₇.

שְׁפוֹ 1 pr.n.m. **Shepho.**

שְׁפוֹט 2 n.m.—pl. שְׁפוּטִים—**judgment** Ezk 23₁₀ 2 C 20₉. → שׁפט *judge.*

שְׁפוּפָם 1 pr.n.m. **Shephupham.**

שְׁפוּפָן 1 pr.n.m. **Shephuphan.**

[שְׁפוֹת] 1 n.f.—cstr. שְׁפוֹת—**cheese** 2 S 17₂₉. → (?) שׁפה I *sweep bare.*

שִׁפְחָה 63.0.1 n.f.—Q שופחה; cstr. שִׁפְחַת; sf. שִׁפְחָתִי; pl. שְׁפָחוֹת; sf. שִׁפְחֹתָיו, שִׁפְחוֹתֵיכֶם—**1. female servant, slave, maid** of household or person Gn 12₁₆ 16₁. **2.** שִׁפְחָתְךָ **your servant,** in self-deprecatory address 1 S 1₁₈.

שׁפט 203.14.86 vb.—**Qal** 185.12.71 Pf. שָׁפַט; impf. יִשְׁפֹּט, יִשְׁפְּטוּ (יִשְׁפּוּטוּ, יִשְׁפֹּטוּ); impv. שְׁפֹט־ (Si שפוט, שָׁפְטָה, שָׁפְטֵנִי), שִׁפְטוּ (שְׁפֹטוּ); ptc. שֹׁפֵט, שֹׁפְטָה, שֹׁפְטִים; inf. abs. שָׁפוֹט; cstr. שְׁפֹט (לִשְׁפֹּט, שָׁפְטֵנוּ)—**1a. judge** someone, in judicial context Dt 16₁₈, king's court Pr 29₁₄; of Y. judging individuals Ec 3₁₇, nations Jl 4₁₂. **b. judge, decide** a legal case, **settle a dispute** Ex 18₂₂ Ezk 44₂₄. **c.** with obj. מִשְׁפָּט, **pass judgment, make decision** 1 K 3₂₈. **d.** with prep. בֵּין, **judge between, decide between** the parties to a dispute Gn 16₅ Ex 18₁₆. **e.** without obj., (1) **judge, execute justice, pronounce judgment, sit in judgment** Is 11₃ Ps 51₆. (2) **make a judgment, decision** CD 10₁₈ (+ עַל *concerning*). **2. judge,** according to desert or merit, i.e. **a. condemn, punish** someone 1 S 3₁₃ Ezk 7₃ (+ כְּ *according to* ways). **b. arraign, accuse, rebuke** someone Ezk 20₄. **c. vindicate, deliver** someone 1 S 24₁₆ (+ מִן *from*) Ps 7₉ (+ כְּ *according to* righteousness) 72₄. **d.** with obj. מִשְׁפָּט, **defend the rights, plead the cause of** Jr 5₂₈ Lm 3₅₉. **3a. judge,** i.e. **rule, govern, lead** people (prob. oft. including a judicial role) Jg 10₂ 1 S 7₆ 1 K 3₉. **b.** abs., **act as judge, ruler** Gn 19₉. **4.** ptc. as noun, **judge, ruler, a.** of Y. Gn 18₂₅ Jr 11₂₀. **b.** of humans, in judicial context Dt 16₁₈, as deliverer or ruler Jg 2₁₆.

Ni. 17.2.14 Pf. נִשְׁפַּטְתִּי; impf. אִשָּׁפֵט (אִשָּׁפְטָה), יִשָּׁפְטוּ; ptc. נִשְׁפָּט; inf. הִשָּׁפֵט (הִשָּׁפְטוֹ)—**1. enter into controversy, argue (a legal case),** of Y. Is 43₂₆, human Pr 29₉ (+ אֵת *with* someone); **plead with** (אֵת) someone **concerning** (accus.) deeds of Y. 1 S 12₇. **2. enter into judgment, execute judgment,** of Y. Is 66₁₆ (+ אֵת *with*), human 2 C 22₈ (+ עִם *with*). **3. be judged, be brought to trial** Ps 9₂₀ 37₃₃. **4. be judged,** i.e. **be ruled, be governed** 1QS 9₁₀ (+ בְּ *in accordance with* ordinances). **5.** of days, **be distinguished (from one another)** by (בְּ) wisdom of Y. Si 36₈.

Po. 1 Ptc. מְשֹׁפְטִי—ptc. as noun, **opponent at law, adversary** Jb 9₁₅.

→ מִשְׁפָּט *judgment,* שֶׁפֶט *judgment,* שְׁפוֹט *judgment.*

שָׁפָט 8.0.0.9 pr.n.m. **Shaphat.**

[שֶׁפֶט] 16.0.9 n.m.—pl. שְׁפָטִים; sf. שְׁפָטַי—alw. pl., **judgment(s), acts of judgment** Ex 6₆; oft. עָשָׂה שְׁפָטִים בְּ *execute judgment upon,* subj. Y. Ex 12₁₂, humans Ezk 16₄₁; perh. **punishment** Pr 19₂₉. → שׁפט *judge.*

שְׁפַטְיָה 13.0.0.13 pr.n.m. **Shephatiah.**

שְׁפַטְיָהוּ, see שְׁפַטְיָה *Shephatiah.*

שִׁפְטָן 1 pr.n.m. **Shiphtan.**

[שְׁפִי] I 10 n.m.—שְׁפִי; pl. שְׁפָיִם (שְׁפָיִם)—**1. bareness** Jb 33₂₁(Kt). **2. bare height,** or perh. **sand dune,** or **track** Nm 23₃ Is 41₁₈. → שׁפה I *sweep bare.*

שְׁפִי II 1 pr.n.m. **Shephi.**

שֻׁפִּים 3 pr.n.m. **Shuppim.**

שְׁפִיפֹן 1 n.[m.] **horned viper** (*Vipera cerastes*) Gn 49₁₇.

שָׁפִיר 1 pl.n. **Shaphir.**

*[**שַׁפִּירָה**] 0.0.1 pr.n.f. **Shappirah.**

שׁפך 115.7.22 vb.—**Qal** 102.6.20 Pf. שָׁפַךְ; impf. יִשְׁפֹּךְ; impv. שִׁפְכוּ ,שִׁפְכִי ,(שְׁפָךְ־) שְׁפֹךְ; ptc. שֹׁפְכוֹת ,שֹׁפְכִים ,שֹׁפֶכֶת ,שֹׁפֵךְ; ptc. pass. שְׁפוּכָה ,שָׁפוּךְ; cstr. ־שְׁפָךְ (בְּשָׁפְכָהּ/לִ)—**1. pour, pour out** blood Ex 29$_{12}$ (+ אֶל *at* base of altar) Dt 12$_{16}$ (+ עַל *upon* ground), water Ex 4$_{9}$, broth Jg 6$_{20}$, dust, i.e. plaster Lv 14$_{41}$. **2. shed** blood Gn 9$_{6}$. **3. pour out** soul 1 S 1$_{15}$ (+ לִפְנֵי *before* Y.), complaint Ps 102$_{1}$ (+ לִפְנֵי), Y.'s spirit Ezk 39$_{29}$ (+ עַל *upon* people), anger Is 42$_{25}$ (+ עַל). **4. cast up** siege mound 2 S 20$_{15}$ (+ אֶל *against*) Jr 6$_{6}$ (+ עַל *against*). **5.** intrans., **pour out, gush out,** of blood 1 K 18$_{28}$ (+ עַל *upon*). **6.** pass. **a. be poured out,** of anger Ezk 20$_{33}$. **b. be shed,** of blood Ps 79$_{10}$.

Ni. 8.0.2 Pf. נִשְׁפַּךְ; impf. יִשָּׁפֵךְ; inf. הִשָּׁפֵךְ—**1. be poured out, be spilled,** of blood Dt 12$_{27}$ (+ עַל *upon* altar), water 11QT 32$_{14}$, liver Lm 2$_{11}$ (+ לְ *upon* ground), ashes 1 K 13$_{3}$. **2. be shed,** of blood Gn 9$_{6}$.

Pu. 3.1 Pf. שֻׁפַּךְ; impf. Si תשפך—**1. be poured out, be shed,** of blood Nm 35$_{33}$. **2. slip, be caused to slip,** of person Si 37$_{29(D)}$, one's step Ps 73$_{2}$.

Htp. 3 Impf. תִּשְׁתַּפֵּךְ; inf. הִשְׁתַּפֵּךְ—**1. be poured out,** of soul, life Jb 30$_{16}$ (+ עַל *within [oneself]*) Lm 2$_{12}$ (+ אֶל *in* mother's bosom). **2. be spilled, be scattered about,** of stones Lm 4$_{1}$.

→ שֶׁפֶךְ *place of pouring,* שָׁפְכָה *penis.*

[**שֶׁפֶךְ**] 2 n.[m.]—cstr. שֶׁפֶךְ—**place of pouring,** for ashes of altar Lv 4$_{12}$. → שׁפך *pour.*

שָׁפְכָה 1.0.1 n.f.—Sam, Q שפכת—**penis** Dt 23$_{2}$. → שׁפך *pour.*

[**שָׁפְכַת**] 4QMMT B39, see שָׁפְכָה *penis.*

שׁפל 31.5.18 vb.—**Qal** 12.0.6 Pf. שָׁפֵל; impf. תִּשְׁפַּל; inf. שְׁפַל (Q שפול)—**1. be lowly** 4QShirShabb^{f} 23.1$_{12}$; שְׁפַל־רוּחַ *to be lowly of spirit* Pr 16$_{19}$. **2. be brought low, be abased,** of person Is 2$_{9}$, haughtiness Is 2$_{17}$, mountain Is 40$_{4}$. **3. move down, be demoted** from (מִן) position in community 1QS 2$_{23}$. **4.** of sound, **be low, subdued** Ec 12$_{4}$. **5.** inf. as noun, **lowness, sinking** of hands, i.e. negligence 1QS 4$_{9}$.

Hi. 19.4.12 Pf. הִשְׁפִּיל ,הִשְׁפַּלְתִּי; impf. יַשְׁפִּיל; impv. Si השפל ,הַשְׁפִּילוּ; ptc. מַשְׁפִּיל; inf. הַשְׁפִּיל—**1. bring low, abase, humiliate** person Pr 29$_{23}$, fortifications Is 25$_{12}$, tree Ezk 17$_{24}$, pride Is 13$_{11}$, darkness 1QM 13$_{15}$. **2.** with obj. נֶפֶשׁ, **humble oneself** Si 3$_{18(C)}$. **3.** as auxiliary verb, **go low down,** הַשְׁפִּילוּ שֵׁבוּ *go low down, sit,* i.e. take a lowly seat Jr 13$_{18}$, הַמַּשְׁפִּילִי לִרְאוֹת *the one who goes low down to look,* i.e. who looks low down Ps 113$_{6}$.

Ho. 0.1 Pf. Si הָשְׁפָּלוּ (Si הושפלו)—**be brought low, be abased** Si 11$_{6}$.

→ שָׁפָל *low,* שֵׁפֶל *lowliness,* שִׁפְלָה *humiliation,* שְׁפֵלָה *lowland,* שִׁפְלוּת *sinking.*

שָׁפָל I 17.1.2 adj.—f.s. שְׁפָלָה; cstr. שְׁפַלַת; m.pl. שְׁפָלִים; cstr. Si שפלי—**1. low (in height),** of tree Ezk 17$_{24}$, spot Lv 13$_{20}$ (שָׁפָל מִן־הָעוֹר *lower,* i.e. deeper, *than the skin*). **2. low (in esteem), abased,** of person 2 S 6$_{22}$. **3a. lowly, humble,** of kingdom Ezk 17$_{14}$. **b.** as noun, **lowly one, humble one** Ps 138$_{6}$; שְׁפַל־רוּחַ *lowly (one) of,* i.e. in, *spirit* Is 57$_{15}$. → שׁפל *be low.*

*__שָׁפָל__ II 0.0.0.1 pr.n.[m.] **Shaphal.**

שָׁפֵל, see שׁפל *be low.*

שֵׁפֶל 2 n.[m.]—sf. שִׁפְלֵנוּ—**lowliness, humiliation** Ps 136$_{23}$ Ec 10$_{6}$. → שׁפל *be low.*

שִׁפְלָה 1.0.1 n.f.—cstr. Q שפלת—**1. lowness** of measure 1QH 4$_{1}$. **2. humiliation** Is 32$_{19}$. → שׁפל *be low.*

שְׁפֵלָה 20 n.f.—sf. שְׁפֵלָתָהּ—**lowland, 1.** of Judah, between mountains and coastal plain, **the Shephelah,** alw. בַּ/הַשְּׁפֵלָה Dt 1$_{7}$. **2.** of Israel, perh. between hill country of Samaria and Carmel range Jos 11$_{2}$. → שׁפל *be low.*

[**שִׁפְלוּת**] 1 n.f. **lowness,** שִׁפְלוּת יָדַיִם *lowness of hands,* i.e. negligence, idleness Ec 10$_{18}$. → שׁפל *be low.*

שְׁפָם 1 pr.n.m. **Shapham.**

שְׁפָם 2 pl.n. **Shepham.**

שִׁפְמִי 1 gent. **Shiphmite.**

שָׁפָן I 4 n.m.—pl. שְׁפַנִּים—**rock badger, hyrax** (*Procavia syriaca*) Lv 11$_{5}$||Dt 14$_{7}$.

שָׁפָן II 30.0.0.8 pr.n.m. **Shaphan.**

[**שֶׁפַע**] I 1 n.[m.]—cstr. שֶׁפַע—**abundance, affluence** Dt 33$_{19}$.

*[**שֶׁפַע**] II 0.0.0.1 pr.n.[m.] **Shepha.**

[**שִׁפְעָה**] 6.0.1 n.f.—שִׁפְעַת; cstr. שִׁפְעַת—**1. multitude** of camels Is 60$_{6}$, horses Ezk 26$_{10}$; **company, troops** of Jehu 2 K 9$_{17}$. **2. mass, surfeit, torrent** of water Jb

22_{11}.

שִׁפְעִי 1 pr.n.m. **Shiphi.**

שִׁפְעַת, see שִׁפְעָה *multitude, mass.*

***שׁפף** 1 vb. (byform of שׁוף)—**Qal** 1 Pf. שפותי—**be crushed, downcast** Is $38_{13(1QIsa^a)}$.

שׁפר 1.0.1 vb.—**Qal** 1.0.1 Pf. שָׁפְרָה—**be beautiful, pleasing,** of inheritance Ps 16_6 (+ עַל *to*). → שָׁפָר *fine,* שֶׁפֶר I *beauty,* שִׁפְרָה I *beauty.*

*[**שָׁפָר**] 0.0.0.1 adj. **fine, good,** of oil Jar inscr. → שׁפר *be beautiful.*

[**שֶׁפֶר**] I 1 n.[m.]—שָׁפֶר—**beauty** Gn 49_{21}. → שׁפר *be beautiful.*

[**שֶׁפֶר**] II 2 pl.n. **Shepher.**

שֹׁפָר, see שׁוֹפָר *ram's horn.*

שִׁפְרָה I 1 n.f. **beauty, clearness,** שָׁמַיִם שִׁפְרָה *the heavens are beauty* or *clearness,* i.e. made beautiful or clear (of clouds) Jb 26_{13}. → שׁפר *be beautiful.*

שִׁפְרָה II 1 pr.n.f. **Shiphrah.**

[**שפרור**], see שַׁפְרִיר *royal canopy.*

[**שַׁפְרִיר**] I 1 n.[m.]—sf. Qr שַׁפְרִירוֹ (Kt שפרורו)—**royal canopy** Jr 43_{10}.

*[**שַׁפְרִיר**] II 1 n.[m.]—sf. Qr שַׁפְרִירוֹ (Kt שפרורו)—**carpet** Jr 43_{10}.

*[**שַׁפְרִיר**] III 1 n.[m.]—sf. Qr שַׁפְרִירוֹ (Kt שפרורו)—**sceptre** Jr 43_{10}.

שׁפת 5 vb.—**Qal** 5 Impf. תִּשְׁפֹּת; impv. שְׁפֹת—**1. set pot (on the fire)** 2 K 4_{38} Ezk 24_3. **2. set, lay** someone **down in** (לְ) the dust Ps 22_{16}. **3. ordain, establish** peace for (לְ) someone Is 26_{12}. → אַשְׁפֹּת *refuse heap,* מִשְׁפְּתַיִם I *fire-places,* שְׁפַתַּיִם I *fire-places.*

[**שְׁפַתַּיִם**] I 1 n.[m.]du.—שְׁפַתַּיִם—**fire-places, ash-heaps** Ps 68_{14}. → שׁפת *set on the fire.*

שְׁפַתַּיִם II 1 n.[m.]du. **(double-pronged) hooks, pegs,** or perh. **ledges, shelves** Ezk 40_{43}.

*[**שִׁפְתָּן**] 0.0.0.1 pl.n. **Shiphtan.**

[**שֶׁצֶף**] 1 n.[m.] (var. form of שֶׁטֶף)—**flood, overflowing,** שֶׁצֶף קֶצֶף *flood of anger* Is 54_8.

שׁקד I 12.1.7 vb.—**Qal** 12.1.7 Pf. שָׁקַד; impf. אֶשְׁקֹד, יִשְׁקוֹד; impv. שִׁקְדוּ; ptc. שֹׁקֵד, שֹׁקְדֵי; inf. שְׁקֹד—**1. keep watch, be wakeful, vigilant over** (עַל) people Jr 31_{28}, word Jr 1_{12}, calamity Dn 9_{14}; at (עַל) doors Pr 8_{34}; abs. Ps 127_1. **2.** trans., **watch for** iniquity Is 29_{20}. **3.** trans., **watch, guard** (ellip. of obj.) silver and gold Ezr 8_{29}. **4.** trans., **spend wakefully, keep vigil for** a third of each night 1QS 6_7. **5.** abs., **keep awake, lie awake** Ps 102_8.

Ni., be kept watch Lm 1_{14} (if em. נִשְׁקַד עַל פְּשָׁעַי *the yoke of my transgressions is bound* [mss נִשְׂקַד] to נִשְׁקַד עַל־פְּשָׁעַי *watch has been kept over my transgressions*).

→ שֶׁקֶד *watchfulness,* שְׁקִידָה *watchfulness.*

שׁקד II 6.0.1 vb.—**Pu.** 6.0.1 Ptc. מְשֻׁקָּדִים—**be shaped like almond blossom,** of cups on lampstand Ex 25_{33}||37_{19}. → שָׁקֵד *almond tree.*

***שׁקד** III 1 vb.—**Qal** 1 Pf. שָׁקַדְתִּי—**be emaciated** Ps 102_8.

שָׁקֵד 4 n.m.—pl. שְׁקֵדִים—**1. almond tree** (*Amygdalus communis*) Jr 1_{11} Ec 12_5. **2. almond nuts** Gn 43_{11} Nm 17_{23}. → שׁקד II *shape like almond blossom.*

*[**שֶׁקֶד**] 0.1.1 n.m.—cstr. Si שקד—**watchfulness, wakefulness, vigilance** Si $34_{1(Bmg)}$ (B שקר *falsehood*) 4Q Instr[d] 55_4. → שׁקד I *watch.*

שׁקה 62.1.8 vb.—**Ni.** 1 + waw Kt ונשקה—perh. **be watered,** of land Am $8_{8(Kt)}$ (Qr שׁקע ni. *sink*).

Hi. 60.1.8 Pf. הִשְׁקִיתָנוּ; impf. יַשְׁקֶה; + waw וְהִשְׁקָה, וַיַּשְׁקְ; וָאַשְׁקֶה; impv. הַשְׁקוּ, הַשְׁקִינִי, הַשְׁקֵהוּ; ptc. מַשְׁקֶה; inf. הַשְׁקוֹת—**1.** with accus. of recipient, **give a drink to** someone Gn 21_{19}, **water a beast** Gn 24_{14}. **2.** with accus. of recipient and of drink, **give** someone something **to drink, make** someone **drink** something Gn 19_{32} Jr 25_{15}. **3. water, irrigate** face of ground Gn 2_6, garden Gn 2_{10}, vineyard Is 27_3. **4.** without obj., **serve drinks** Est 1_7. **5.** appar. **provide drink for** (לְ), i.e. **take care of** distress (or person driven out) CD 13_9.

Pu. 1 Impf. יְשֻׁקֶּה—**be watered, moistened,** of marrow Jb 21_{24}.

→ מַשְׁקֶה I *cup-bearer,* II *drink,* שִׁקּוּי *drink,* שֹׁקֶת *trough.*

שָׁקֵה, see רַב II *chief,* §3 רַב־שָׁקֵה *Rabshakeh.*

שִׁקּוּי 3.0.2 n.[m.]—pl. sf. שִׁקּוּיַי (שִׁקּוּיִ)—**drink** Ho 2_7 Ps 102_{10}, i.e. **refreshment** Pr 3_8. → שׁקה *give to drink.*

*[**שָׁקוֹף**] 0.0.0.1 n.m. **lintel**—Kfar Baram inscr.2. → שׁקף *look out.*

[**שָׁקוּף**] 2 n.[m.]—pl. שְׁקֻפִים—**frame** of window, or perh.

lattice-work 1 K 6_4 7_4. → שׁקף *look out.*

שִׁקּוּץ $28.0.5$ n.m.—cstr. שִׁקֻּץ; pl. שִׁקּוּצִים (שִׁקֻּצִים); cstr. שִׁקּוּצֵי; sf. שִׁקּוּצֶיהָ—**detestable thing, abomination,** of images, foreign gods Dt 29_{16} 1 K 11_5, unclean food Zc 9_7, filth Na 3_6, profanity of speech 1QS 10_{22}. → שׁקץ *detest.*

שׁקט $41.3.6$ vb.—**Qal** $31.3.3$ Pf. שָׁקְטָה (שָׁקָטָה), שָׁקַטְתִּי; impf. יִשְׁקֹט; ptc. שֹׁקֵט, שֹׁקֶטֶת, שֹׁקְטִים—**1. be quiet, be at peace, have rest,** of land Jos 11_{23} (+ מִן *from* war), city 2 K 11_{20}||2 C 23_{21}, person Jb 3_{13}; of Moab, **be settled on** (אֶל) lees Jr 48_{11}. **2. be quiet (in attitude), hold one's peace, be inactive, be still,** of Y. Is 18_4, human Ru 3_{18}, sword Jr 47_6.

Hi. $10.0.3$ Impf. יַשְׁקִיט; impv. הַשְׁקֵט; inf. abs. הַשְׁקֵט; cstr. הַשְׁקִיט—**1a. show quietness, be quiet, rest,** of Y. Jb 34_{29}, human Is 7_4, earth Jb 37_{17}, sea Is 57_{20}. **b. be silent,** of voice 4QShirShabb[f] 20.2_{13}. **2. give respite** to (לְ) someone from (מִן) days of trouble Ps 94_{13}. **3. quieten, calm** strife Pr 15_{18}. **5.** inf. abs. as noun, **quietness** Is 30_{15} 32_{17}.

→ שֶׁקֶט *quietness.*

שֶׁקֶט $1.0.4$ n.[m.]—sf. Q שקטה—**quietness,** שָׁלוֹם וָשֶׁקֶט *peace and quietness* 1 C 22_9. → שׁקט *be quiet.*

*[**שְׁקִידָה**] 0.1 n.f.—sf. שקידתו—**watchfulness, carefulness** Si 38_{26}. → שׁקד I *watch.*

שׁקל $22.1.12.1$ vb.—**Qal** $19.1.12$ Pf. שָׁקַל; impf. יִשְׁקֹל; impv. Q שקול; ptc. שֹׁקֵל, Q שוקלים; inf. abs. שָׁקוֹל; cstr. לִשְׁקוֹל—**1. weigh** something 2 S 14_{26} (+ accus. specifying weight) Is 40_{12} (+ בְּ *with* scales). **2. weigh out,** i.e. **pay, hand over** (oft. + accus. specifying weight) silver Gn 23_{16} (+ לְ *to* someone), wheat Mur 24 B_{15} (+ לְ), hire Zc 11_{12}. **3. weigh,** i.e. **hold the weight of** a thousand pieces of silver in (עַל) hands 2 S 18_{12}.

Ni. 3 Pf. נִשְׁקַל; impf. יִשָּׁקֵל—**1. be weighed,** of vexation Jb 6_2 (+ qal inf. abs.). **2. be weighed out,** i.e. **be paid, handed over,** of silver., etc. Jb 28_{15} Ezr 8_{33} (+ עַל *into* hands).

→ שֶׁקֶל *shekel,* מִשְׁקָל *weight,* מִשְׁקוֹל *weight,* מִשְׁקֹלֶת *level.*

שֶׁקֶל $88.0.5.19$ n.m.—שֶׁקֶל (I שׁ, I שׁל); cstr. שֶׁקֶל; pl. שְׁקָלִים; cstr. שִׁקְלֵי—**shekel,** lit. 'weight', **1.** a particular weight of more than one standard, the shekel of the sanctuary (20 gerahs) Ex 30_{13} and the royal shekel 2 S 14_{26} were appar. distinct from that in common use; oft. specifying amount of silver used in payment Gn 23_{15}, or for valuations Lv 5_{15}. **2.** coins, שקל ישראל *shekel of Israel* Jewish War Year 1 Coin 148, חצי השקל *half a shekel* Jewish War Year 1 Coin 149. → שׁקל *weigh.*

[**שִׁקְמָה**] 7 n.f.—pl. שִׁקְמִים; sf. שִׁקְמוֹתָם—**sycamore tree** (*ficus sycomorus*) 1 K 10_{27}||2 C 9_{27}.

שׁקע 6 vb.—**Qal** 3 Impf. תִּשְׁקַע; + waw וְשָׁקְעָה; וַתִּשְׁקַע—**sink,** of Babylon Jr 51_{64}, land Am 9_5, fire, i.e. **abate, die out** Nm 11_2.

Ni. 1 + waw Qr וְנִשְׁקְעָה—**sink, sink down,** of land Am $8_{8(Qr)}$ (Kt שקה ni. perh. *be watered*).

Hi. 2 Impf. תַּשְׁקִיעַ—**1. cause water to settle,** and thus become clear Ezk 32_{14}. **2. press down** tongue with (בְּ) cord Jb 40_{25}.

→ מִשְׁקָע *what is settled.*

[**שְׁקַעֲרוּרָה**] 1 n.f.—pl. שְׁקַעֲרוּרֹת—**depression, hollow,** in wall Lv 14_{37}. → cf. קַעֲרוּרָה *depression.*

שׁקף 22.1 vb.—**Ni.** 10 Pf. נִשְׁקַף, נִשְׁקְפָה (נִשְׁקָפָה); ptc. נִשְׁקָף, נִשְׁקָפָה—**look down, look out,** of person Jg 5_{28} (+ בְּעַד *through* window), top of mountain Nm 23_{28} (+ עַל־פְּנֵי *[over] towards*).

Hi. 12.1 Pf. הִשְׁקִיף; impf. יַשְׁקִיף; + waw וַיַּשְׁקֵף; וַיַּשְׁקִיפוּ; impv. הַשְׁקִיפָה; ptc. Si משקיף—**look down, look out,** of Y. Dt 26_{15} (+ מִן *from*) Ps 14_2||53_3 (+ עַל *upon*), humans Gn 19_{28} (+ עַל־פְּנֵי *[over] towards*) 26_8 (+ בְּעַד *through* window) 2 K 9_{32} (+ אֶל *towards*).

→ מַשְׁקוֹף *lintel,* שְׁקוּף *lintel,* שֶׁקֶף *frame,* שָׁקוּף *frame.*

[**שֶׁקֶף**] 1 n.[m.]—שֶׁקֶף—**frame,** or perh. **opening,** for door or window 1 K 7_5. → שׁקף *look out.*

שְׁקֻפִים, see שָׁקוּף *frame.*

שׁקץ $7.0.5$ vb.—**Pi.** $7.0.5$ Pf. שִׁקַּץ; impf. תְּשַׁקְּצוּ (תְּשַׁקֵּצוּ); inf. abs. שַׁקֵּץ—**1. detest, abominate** something, as ritually unclean Lv 11_{11} Dt 7_{26}. **2a.** with obj. נֶפֶשׁ, **make oneself detestable, abominable** Lv 11_{43}. **b. defile** one's holy spirit CD 7_3. **3. abhor, spurn** affliction Ps 22_{25}. → שִׁקּוּץ *detestable thing,* שֶׁקֶץ I *detestable thing.*

שֶׁקֶץ I 11 n.m. **detestable thing, abomination,** of what is ritually unclean, esp. creatures prohibited as food Lv 7_{21} 11_{10} Is 66_{17}. → שׁקץ *detest.*

*[**שֶׁקֶץ**] II $0.0.0.1$ pr.n.m. **Shekez.**

שׁקק I 6 vb.—**Qal** 5 Impf. יָשֹׁקּוּ; ptc. שׁוֹקֵק, שֹׁקֵקָה—**1. rush upon** (בְּ) something Is 33₄ Jl 2₉. **2. prowl,** of bear Pr 28₁₅. **3. rush about,** i.e. **long for a drink,** subj. throat (נֶפֶשׁ) Is 29₈ Ps 107₉.

Htpalp. 1 Impf. יִשְׁתַּקְשְׁקוּן—**rush to and fro,** of chariot Na 2₅.

→ מַשָּׁק I *rushing about.*

*__שׁקק__ II 3 vb.—**Qal** 3 Ptc. שׁוֹקֵק, שֹׁקֵקָה—**be thirsty,** of throat (נֶפֶשׁ) Is 29₈ Ps 107₉, bear Pr 28₁₅.

שׁקר 6.0.2 vb.—**Qal** 1 Impf. תִּשְׁקֹר—**deal falsely with** (לְ) someone Gn 21₂₃.

Pi. 5.0.2 Pf. שִׁקַּרְנוּ; impf. יְשַׁקֵּר—**1. deal falsely, be false with** (בְּ) someone Lv 19₁₁; regarding (בְּ) covenant Ps 44₁₇, wealth 1QS 6₂₄; abs. 1 S 15₂₉. **2.** ptc. as noun, **liar, deceiver** Pr 17₄ (if em. שֶׁקֶר *falsehood* to מְשַׁקֵּר).

→ שֶׁקֶר *falsehood,* שַׁקָּר *liar.*

*__[שַׁקָּר]__ n.m. **liar, deceiver** Pr 17₄ (if em. שֶׁקֶר *falsehood*). → שׁקר *deal falsely.*

שֶׁקֶר 113.6.28 n.m.—שָׁקֶר; cstr. שֶׁקֶר; sf. Q שקרם (Q שקרמה); pl. שְׁקָרִים; sf. שִׁקְרֵיהֶם—**1. falsehood, deceit, deception, lie,** in everyday speech Ex 5₉, taking oaths Lv 5₂₂, bearing witness Ex 20₁₆, prophecy Jr 5₃₁, general conduct Ps 119₂₉; as descr. of images of gods Jr 10₁₄. **2.** as adv., **wrongfully, without cause** Ps 119₈₆; אֹיְבַי שֶׁקֶר *those who are my enemies without cause* Ps 35₁₉. **3. disappointment, futility, vanity** Ps 33₁₇; לַשֶּׁקֶר *for vanity,* i.e. in vain 1 S 25₂₁. → שׁקר *deal falsely.*

שֹׁקֶת 2.0.1 n.f.—pl. cstr. שִׁקֲתוֹת—**trough,** perh. **channel,** for watering livestock Gn 24₂₀ 30₃₈ 3QTr 10₁₆. → שׁקה *give to drink.*

[שֵׁר] I 1 n.[m.]—pl. שֵׁירוֹת—**bracelet, bangle** Is 3₁₉.

*__[שֵׁר]__ II 0.2 n.[m.] (alternative form of שְׁאֵר)—**flesh** Pr 3₈ (if em. לְשָׁרֶּךָ *for your navel* to לִשְׁאֵרֶךָ *for your flesh*); שר עצם *flesh of,* i.e. on, *the bone(s)* Si 30₁₆(B), חיי שר *life of the flesh,* i.e. body Si 30₁₅(B).

[שֹׁר] 3 n.[m.]—sf. שָׁרֵּךְ (שָׁרְרֵךְ)—**navel** Ca 7₃; **navel cord** Ezk 16₄.

שָׁרָב 2.1 n.m.—**1. scorching heat** Is 49₁₀. **2. parched ground** Is 35₇ Si 43₂₂(B).

שֵׁרֵבְיָה 8 pr.n.m. **Sherebiah.**

שַׁרְבִיט 4.1 n.m. (alternative form of שֵׁבֶט)—cstr. שַׁרְבִיט; pl. Si שרביטים—**1. sceptre** Est 4₁₁ 5₂ 8₄. **2. branch, shoot** Si 37₁₈(Bmg, D).

שָׁרָד, see שָׁרָר *Sharar.*

שׁרה 2 vb.—**Qal** 1 Impf. יִשְׁרֵהוּ—**let loose, release thunder** Jb 37₃.

Pi. 1 Pf. Qr שֵׁרִיתִךָ—**set free, release** someone 15₁₁(Qr) (Kt שרותך, from שׁרר I *be strong*).

→ (?) שִׁרְיָה *javelin.*

*__[שָׁרָה]__ 1 n.f.—pl. sf. שָׁרוֹתֶיהָ—**row of vines,** or perh. **wall** Jr 5₁₀ (or em. בְּשׁוּרֹתֶיהָ, from שׁוּרָה *wall*).

[שֵׁרָה], see שֵׁר *bracelet.*

שָׁרוּחֶן 1 pl.n. **Sharuhen.**

שָׁרוֹן 7.0.2 pl.n. **Sharon.**

שָׁרוֹנִי 1 gent. **Sharonite.**

[שרוקת] Jr 18₁₆, see שְׁרִיקָה *hissing.*

[שִׁרְטַי], see שִׁטְרַי *Shitrai.*

[שָׂרַי] 1 pr.n.m. **Sharai.**

שִׁרְיָה 1 n.f. **javelin, lance,** or **small arrow** Jb 41₁₈. → (?) שׁרה *let loose.*

שִׁרְיוֹן 8.1 n.[m.]—שִׁרְיָן; cstr. שִׁרְיוֹן; pl. שִׁרְיֹנִים, שִׁרְיֹנוֹת—**coat of armour, breastplate** 1 S 17₃₈; שִׁרְיוֹן קַשְׂקַשִּׂים *coat of scale armour* 1 S 17₅.

שִׁרְיָן, see שִׁרְיוֹן *coat of armour.*

[שְׁרִיקָה] 2 n.f.—pl. cstr. שְׁרִקוֹת (Kt שרוקת)—**1. (object of) hissing,** in derision, or perh. to avert the power of demons Jr 18₁₆. **2. whistling, piping,** as signal for flocks Jg 5₁₆. → שׁרק *hiss.*

[שָׁרִיר] 1 n.[m.]—pl. cstr. שְׁרִירֵי—**muscle, sinew** Jb 40₁₆. → שׁרר I *strengthen.*

שְׁרִירוּת, see שְׁרִרוּת *stubbornness.*

שְׁרִית, see שְׁאֵרִית *remainder.*

שרמות Jr 31₄₀, see שְׂדֵמָה *field.*

*__[שֶׁרַע]__ n.[m.] **surging, foaming,** שֶׁרְעֵי תְהוֹמוֹת *surgings of the depths* 2 S 1₂₁ (if em. שְׂדֵי תְרוּמֹת *fields of contributions*).

שׁרץ 14.0.1 vb.—**Qal** 14.0.1 Pf. שָׁרַץ; impf. יִשְׁרֹץ; impv. שִׁרְצוּ; ptc. שֹׁרֵץ, שֹׁרֶצֶת—**1. swarm, team, abound, be prolific,** of persons Gn 9₇ (+ בְּ *on* earth), swarming things Gn 7₂₁ (+ עַל *upon* earth). **2.** with accus., **swarm with, teem with,** subj. water Gn 1₂₀ (accus. swarming things), land Ps 105₃₀ (accus. frogs Ps 105₃₀. → שֶׁרֶץ *swarming things.*

שֶׁרֶץ 15.0.3 n.m.—שָׁרֶץ; cstr. שֶׁרֶץ—**swarming things,**

swarms, in water Gn 1_{20}, on land Gn 7_{21}; specif. small mammals and reptiles Lv 11_{29}, flying insects Lv 11_{20}. → שׁרץ *swarm.*

שׁרק $_{12}$ vb.—**Qal** $_1$ Pf. שָׁרְקוּ; impf. יִשְׁרֹק; + waw וְשָׁרַק (וְשָׁרֵק)—**1. hiss, whistle,** in derision, or perh. to avert the power of demons 1 K 9_8 Jr 19_8 (+ עַל *on account of*). **2. whistle for** (לְ) someone, as signal Is 5_{26}. → שְׁרֵקָה *hissing,* שְׁרִיקָה *hissing.*

שְׁרֵקָה $_{7.0.1}$ n.f. **(object) of hissing,** in derision, or perh. to avert the power of demons Jr 19_8. → שׁרק *hiss.*

***שׁרר I** $_1$ vb.—**Qal** $_1$ Pf. Kt שרותך—appar. **strengthen** someone Jr $15_{11(Kt)}$ (or em. שֵׁרַרְתִּךָ, i.e. pi., in same sense). → שָׁרִיר *muscle,* שְׁרִרוּת *stubbornness.*

***שׁרר II** $_1$ vb.—**Qal** $_1$ Pf. Kt שרותך—**make things abundant for, cause someone to prosper** Jr $15_{11(Kt)}$.

***שׁרר III** $_1$ vb.—**Qal** $_1$ Pf. Kt שרותך—**treat with hostility, vex** someone Jr $15_{11(Kt)}$.

שָׁרָר $_1$ pr.n.m. **Sharar.**

[שֹׁרֵר], see שׁוֹרֵר *lurking enemy.*

[שְׁרִרוּת] $_{10.0.22}$ n.f.—cstr. שְׁרִרוּת (שְׁרִירוּת)—**stubbornness,** alw. as cstr. with לֵב *heart* Dt 29_{18} Jr 3_{17}; at Qumran perh. **inclination, thinking,** before becoming a member of the community 1QS 2_{14}, or after leaving it 1QS 7_{19}. → שׁרר I *strengthen.*

שׁרשׁ $_{8.1.1}$ vb.—**Pi.** $_{2.1}$ impf. תְּשָׁרֵשׁ; + waw וְשֵׁרֶשְׁךָ—**uproot, burn to the root, destroy** someone Ps 52_7 (+ מִן *from* land), fruit Si 6_3, produce Jb 31_{12} (בְּ of obj.).

Pu. $_1$ Impf. יְשֹׁרָשׁוּ—**be uprooted,** of produce Jb 31_8.

Poel $_1$ Pf. שֹׁרֵשׁ—**take root,** of stem Is 40_{24}.

Poal $_1$ שֹׁרָשׁוּ—**take root,** of person Jr 12_2.

Hi. $_{3.0.1}$ Impf. יַשְׁרֵשׁ; ptc. מַשְׁרִישׁ; inf. Q השריש—**take root,** of person Jb 5_3, vine Ps 80_{10} (וַתַּשְׁרֵשׁ שָׁרָשֶׁיהָ *and it took root [with] its roots*).

→ שֹׁרֶשׁ *root.*

[שֹׁרֶשׁ] $_1$ pr.n.m. **Sheresh.**

שֹׁרֶשׁ $_{33.3.19}$ n.m.—cstr. שֹׁרֶשׁ; sf. שָׁרְשִׁי; pl. cstr. שָׁרְשֵׁי (Q שורשי); sf. שָׁרָשָׁיו (Q שורשיו)—**1. root, a.** of tree Jr 17_8, vine Ezk 17_7. **b.** of person, descr. as plant Dt 29_{17} Jb 8_{17}. **c.** of serpent, perh. representing Judah Is 14_{29}. **d.** of mountain Jb 28_9, flint 1QH 11_{31}, the sea Jb 36_{30}. **e.** of a matter Jb 19_{28}, wisdom 4QMyst[b] $1b_3$, injustice 4QInstr[b] 2.3_{14}. **2. root,** i.e. **sole,** or perh. **print** of foot Jb 13_{27}. → שׁרשׁ *take root.*

[שַׁרְשְׁרָה] or **[שַׁרְשֶׁרֶת]** $_8$ n.f.—pl. שַׁרְשְׁרוֹת; cstr. שַׁרְשְׁרֹת (שַׁרְשֹׁת)—**chain,** on robe of high priest Ex 28_{14}, pillars at porch of temple 1 K 7_{17}.

שַׁרְשְׁרוֹת, see שַׁרְשְׁרָה *chain.*

שַׁרְשֶׁרֶת, see שַׁרְשְׁרָה *chain.*

שַׁרְשֹׁת, see שַׁרְשְׁרָה *chain.*

שׁרת $_{97.9.36}$ vb.—**Pi.** $_{97.9.36}$ Impf. יְשָׁרְתֻנִי; + waw וְשֵׁרֵת; וַיְשָׁרֶת; impv. Si שָׁרְתוּ; ptc. מְשָׁרֵת, מְשָׁרֶת, מְשָׁרְתִים, מְשָׁרְתֵי; inf. שָׁרֵת (שָׁרֵת, שָׁרְתוֹ)—**1a. minister to, attend to, serve** someone, (1) as personal attendant Gn 39_4. (2) as official in king's service 1 C 27_1 22_8 (לְ of obj.). (3) obj. oneself (נֶפֶשׁ), i.e. making use of what one has Si 14_{11}. **b.** without obj., **minister, serve, be in attendance** in presence of (אֶת־פְּנֵי) king Est 1_{10}. **2.** of cultic service, **a.** without obj., **minister, serve, officiate** Ex 28_{35} 1 S 2_{18} (+ אֶת־פְּנֵי *in the presence of* Y.) 1 C 16_{37} (+ לִפְנֵי *before* ark). **b. minister to, attend to, serve** Y. Dt 10_8, Aaron Nm 3_6, congregation Nm 16_9, (images of) wood and stone Ezk 20_{32}. **c. attend to, tend, take care of** tabernacle Nm 1_{50}, temple Ezk 44_{11}, lampstand Nm 4_9 (לְ of obj.). **3.** ptc. as noun, **minister, attendant, servant, a.** in secular service, as personal attendant Ex 24_{13}, attendant of king 1 K 10_5||2 C 9_4. **b.** in cultic service Jr 33_{21}; in ref. to angels Ps 103_{21}. → שָׁרֵת *service.*

שָׁרֵת $_2$ n.[m.] **service, ministry,** in the cult Nm 4_{12} 2 C 24_{14}. → שׁרת *minister.*

שׁשׁה, see שׁסה *spoil,* po.

שֵׁשׁ I $_{216.2.66.1}$ n.m.&f.—m. (with f. nouns) שֵׁשׁ (שֶׁשׁ־); f. (with m. nouns) שִׁשָּׁה; cstr. שֵׁשֶׁת—**1. six,** שֵׁשׁ שָׁנִים *six years* Gn 31_{41}, עָרִים שֵׁשׁ *six cities* Jos 15_{59}, שִׁשָּׁה אֲנָשִׁים *six men* Ezk 9_2, שֵׁשֶׁת יָמִים *six days* Ex 16_{26}. **2.** with ellip. of noun, **a.** שֵׁשׁ, **six (things)** Pr 6_{16}, **six (parts of spirit)** 4QCrypt 1.2_7, **six (cakes)** Lv 24_6. **b.** שִׁשָּׁה, **six (sons)** 1 C 3_4. **3.** as ordinal numeral, **a. sixth,** שְׁנַת־שֵׁשׁ *the sixth year* 2 K 18_{10}. **b.** שִׁשָּׁה with ellip. of noun, **sixth (day)** 4QPrQuot 1.3_{18}. **4.** as constituent of a larger number, שִׁשָּׁה עָשָׂר *sixteen* 1 C 4_{27}, var. שֵׁשׁ עֶשְׂרֵה Jos 15_{41}; עֶשְׂרִים וְשִׁשָּׁה *twenty-six* Jg 20_{15}, vars. שש ועשרים 11QT 36_7, ששה ועשרים 1QM 2_2; שֵׁשׁ מֵאוֹת *six hundred*

Gn 7_{6}. → ששׁה *give a sixth part.*

שֵׁשׁ II 3 n.[m.] **alabaster, marble** Ca 5_{15} Est 1_{6}.

שֵׁשׁ III 38.0.2 n.m.—Kt שׁשׁי—**fine linen, byssus,** for garment Gn 41_{42}, tabernacle hangings Ex 26_{1}||36_{8}, sail Ezk 27_{7}.

שׁשׂא 1 vb.—**Pi.** 1 + waw וְשִׁשֵּׁאתִיךָ—**lead on, drive forward** Ezk 39_{2}.

שֵׁשְׁבַּצַּר 2 pr.n.m. **Sheshbazzar.**

ששׁה 1 vb.—**Pi.** 1 + waw וְשִׁשִּׁיתֶם—**give a sixth part of** an ephah Ezk 45_{13}. → שֵׁשׁ *six,* שִׁשִּׁי *sixth,* שִׁשִּׁים *sixty.*

ששׁי Ezk 16_{13}, see שֵׁשׁ III *fine linen.*

שָׁשַׁי 1 pr.n.m. **Shashai.**

שֵׁשַׁי 3 pr.n.m. **Sheshai.**

שִׁשִּׁי 28.0.29.1 adj.—f.s. שִׁשִּׁית (I ששׁת)—**1. sixth,** of son Gn 30_{19}, day Gn 1_{31}, month Hg 1_{1}, year Lv 25_{21}, lot Jos 19_{32}. **2.** as noun, **a.** שִׁשִּׁי **sixth (one),** in ref. to person 1 C 12_{12}, month Ezk 8_{1}. **b.** שִׁשִּׁית (1) **sixth one,** in ref. to standard 1QM 4_{10}, year 1QM 2_{12}. (2) **sixth part** of hin Ezk 4_{11}, ephah Ezk 45_{13}. → ששׁה *give a sixth part.*

שִׁשִּׁים 59.0.30 n.m.&f.pl.—Q ששׁין—**sixty, 1.** as cardinal number, שִׁשִּׁים אִישׁ *sixty men* 2 K 25_{19}||Jr 52_{25}, שִׁשִּׁים שָׁנָה *sixty years* Lv 27_{3}, שִׁשִּׁים עָרִים *sixty cities* 1 K 4_{13}, אַמּוֹת שִׁשִּׁים *sixty cubits* 2 C 3_{3}. **2.** as constituent of a larger number, שִׁשִּׁים וּשְׁנַיִם *sixty-two* Dn 9_{25}. → ששׁה *give a sixth part.*

שֵׁשַׁךְ 2 pl.n. **Sheshach,** cipher for בָּבֶל *Babylon.*

שֵׁשָׁן 5 pr.n.m. **Sheshan.**

שֹׁשַׁנִּים, see שׁוּשַׁן I *lily.*

שָׁשַׁק 2 pr.n.m. **Shashak.**

[שָׁשֵׁר] 2 n.[m.] שָׁשֵׁר—**vermilion,** pigment used in wall decoration Jr 22_{14} Ezk 23_{14}.

[שָׁת] 2 n.m.—pl. שָׁתוֹת; sf. שָׁתֹתֶיהָ—**foundation, pillar (of society)** Is 19_{10} Ps 11_{3}. → (?) שִׁית *place.*

*__[שַׁת]__ 0.0.0.49 n.f. (byform of שָׁנָה)—**year** Samaria ost. 1_{1}. → שָׁנָה I *change.*

שֵׁת I 9.1.4 pr.n.m. **Seth.**

שֵׁת II 2 n.[m.] **buttocks**—pl. sf. שְׁתוֹתֵיהֶם—2 S 10_{4} Is 20_{4}.

שׁתה I 217.4.23 vb.—**Qal** 216.2.23 Pf. שָׁתָה, שָׁתִיתִי; impf. יִשְׁתֶּה (יִשְׁתְּ), יִשְׁתּוּ (יִשְׁתָּיוּן); + waw וַיֵּשְׁתְּ (וַיִּשְׁתֶּה); impv. שְׁתֵה, שְׁתוּ; ptc. שֹׁתֶה, שֹׁתָה, שֹׁתִים, שֹׁתֵי; inf. abs. שָׁתֹה (שָׁתוֹ, שָׁתוֹת); cstr. לִשְׁתּוֹת (שְׁתוֹת, שְׁתוֹ, שְׁתוֹתוֹ, שְׁתוֹתָהּ)—**1. drink,** perh. also **feast** Est 7_{1}; subj. Y. Ps 50_{13}, gods Dt 32_{38}, humans Gn 9_{21} (+ מִן *of* wine) 44_{5} (+ בְּ *from* cup) Ex 15_{23} Pr 9_{5} (+ בְּ *of* wine), beasts Gn 30_{38}, land Dt 11_{11}; obj. water Ex 7_{18}, wine Lv 10_{9}, blood Nm 23_{24}, poison Jb 6_{4}, cup Is 51_{17}, derision Jb 34_{7}; obj. (clear from context) oft. omitted Gn 24_{14}; abs. Ec 2_{24}. **2.** ptc. as noun, **drinker, one who drinks** Jl 1_{5}.

Ni. 1.2 Impf. יִשָּׁתֶה; ptc. Si נשתה—**be drunk,** subj. drink Lv 11_{34} (+ בְּ *in, from* vessel), wine Si $34_{28.29}$ (+ בְּ *with* anger and strife).

→ שְׁתִי I *drunkenness,* שְׁתִיָּה *(manner of) drinking,* מִשְׁתֶּה *feast.*

*__[שׁתה]__ II vb.—**Qal, weave,** ptc. as noun, **weaver** Is 19_{10} (if em. שָׁתֹתֶיהָ *its foundations* [from שָׁת] to שֹׁתֶיהָ *its weavers*). → שְׁתִי II *warp.*

שְׁתִי I 1 n.[m.] **drunkenness** Ec 10_{17}. → שׁתה I *drink.*

שְׁתִי II 9 n.m. **warp,** in woven material, alw. || עֵרֶב *woof* Lv 13_{48}. → שׁתה II *weave.*

שְׁתִיָּה 1 n.f. **(manner of) drinking** Est 1_{8}. → שׁתה I *drink.*

[שָׁתִיל] 1.1 n.[m.]—pl. cstr. שְׁתִלֵי (Si שתילי)—**(transplanted) shoot, sapling** of olive Ps 128_{3}, cedar Si 50_{12}. → שׁתל *transplant.*

שְׁתַּיִם, see שְׁנַיִם *two.*

שׁתל 10 vb.—**Qal** 10 Impf. אֶשְׁתֳּלֶנּוּ; ptc. pass. שָׁתוּל, שְׁתוּלָה, שְׁתוּלִים; + waw וְשָׁתַלְתִּי—**1. transplant, plant tender** twig Ezk 17_{22}. **2.** pass. **be transplanted, be planted,** of tree Jr 17_{8} (+ עַל *beside* water), vine Ezk 19_{13} (+ בְּ *in* steppe). → שָׁתִיל *(transplanted) shoot.*

שֻׁתַלְחִי 1 gent. **Shuthelahite.**

שׁתם I 2 vb.—**Qal** 2 Ptc. pass. שְׁתֻם—pass. **be opened,** הַגֶּבֶר שְׁתֻם הָעָיִן *the man opened of eye,* i.e. whose eye is opened Nm $24_{3.15}$.

*__שׁתם__ II 2 vb.—**Qal** 2 Ptc. pass. שְׁתֻם—pass. **be wicked, malicious,** הַגֶּבֶר שְׁתֻם הָעָיִן *the man wicked of eye,* i.e. with a wicked expression Nm $24_{3.15}$.

שׁתן 6 vb.—**Hi.** 6 Ptc. מַשְׁתִּין—**urinate,** alw. in phrase מַשְׁתִּין בְּקִיר **one who urinates against a wall,** i.e. **male person** 1 S 25_{22}. → שַׁיִן *urine.*

*__שׁתע__ 2 vb.—**Qal** 2 (unless שׁעה I htp. *gaze about [anxiously]*) Impf. נִשְׁתָּעָה, תִּשְׁתָּע—**be afraid** Is $41_{10.23}$.

שׁתק 4 vb.—**Qal** 4 Impf. יִשְׁתֹּק—**1. become quiet, calm down,** of sea Jon 1_{11} (+ מֵעַל *from [being against]*), strife Pr 26_{20}. **2. have quietness,** of persons Ps 107_{30}.

שֵׁתָר 1 pr.n.m. **Shethar.**

שׁתת 2 vb. (byform of שׁית)—**Qal** 2 Pf. שָׁתוּ—**1. set mouth against** (בְּ) heaven Ps 73$_{9}$. **2. set oneself, head towards** (לְ) Sheol Ps 49$_{15}$.

שְׁתִתִיָּה, see שֵׁת *foundation*.

ת

ת, see אֵת object marker.

תָּא 13.0.7 n.m.—Q תאו (Q תו); cstr. תָּא; pl. תָּאִים; cstr. תָּאֵי; sf. Qr תָּאָיו (Kt תאו)—**chamber,** for guards 1 K 14$_{28}$||2 C 12$_{11}$, in temple buildings Ezk 40$_{7}$ 11QT 38$_{15}$.

תאב I 2 vb.—**Qal** 2 Pf. תָּאַבְתִּי—**long for** (לְ) precepts Ps 119$_{40}$, salvation Ps 119$_{174}$. → תַּאֲבָה *longing.*

תאב II 1 vb. (perh. byform of תעב)—**Qal** 1 Ptc. מְתָאֵב—**abhor, loathe** Am 6$_{8}$.

תַּאֲבָה 1 n.f. **longing** for (אֶל) ordinances Ps 119$_{20}$. → תאב I *long for.*

תאה 2 vb.—**Pi.** 2 Impf. תְּתָאוּ—**mark out (a boundary)** Nm 34$_{7.8}$ (+ מִן *from*). → תַּאֲוָה II *boundary.*

תאו, see תָּא *chamber.*

תְּאוֹ 2 n.[m.]—cstr. תוֹא—**antelope** Dt 14$_{5}$ Is 51$_{20}$.

תַּאֲוָה I 21.2.1 n.f.—cstr. תַּאֲוַת; sf. תַּאֲוָתִי, תַּאֲוָתָם—**1. desire,** i.e. **wish, longing** Is 26$_{8}$; תַּאֲוָה בָאָה *desire fulfilled* Pr 13$_{12}$, מַאֲכַל תַּאֲוָה *food of desire,* i.e. desirable food Jb 33$_{20}$; **craving, covetousness** Nm 11$_{4}$. **2. desire,** i.e. **thing desired** Ps 21$_{3}$, **thing craved** Ps 78$_{29}$. **3. delight,** תַּאֲוָה ... לָעֵינַיִם *a delight ... to the eyes* Gn 3$_{6}$. → אוה I *desire.*

***[תַּאֲוָה] II** 1 n.f.—cstr. תַּאֲוַת—**boundary** Gn 49$_{26}$. → תאה *mark out.*

תְּאוֹמִים, see תּוֹאָם *twin.*

[תַּאֲלָה] 1 n.f.—sf. תַּאֲלָתְךָ—**curse** Lm 3$_{65}$. → אלה *curse.*

תאם 4 vb.—**Qal** 2 Ptc. תֹּאֲמִם (תּוֹאֲמִם)—**be double,** or perh. **be alike, match** Ex 26$_{24}$||36$_{29}$.

Hi. 2 Ptc. מַתְאִימוֹת—**bear twins** Ca 4$_{2}$ 6$_{6}$.

→ תּוֹאָם *twin.*

[תַּאֲנָה] 1 n.f.—sf. תַּאֲנָתָהּ—**season (of heat)** of wild ass Jr 2$_{24}$. → אנה II *happen.*

תְּאֵנָה 39.0.3.1 n.f.—sf. תְּאֵנָתוֹ; pl. תְּאֵנִים; cstr. תְּאֵנֵי; sf. תְּאֵנֵיכֶם—**1. fig tree(s)** Dt 8$_{8}$ Jl 1$_{12}$. **2. fig,** alw. pl. Nm 13$_{23}$ Jr 24$_{1}$.

תֹּאֲנָה 1 n.f. **occasion, pretext,** for quarrel Jg 14$_{4}$. → אנה II *happen.*

תַּאֲנִיָּה 2 n.f. **mourning** Is 29$_{2}$ Lm 2$_{5}$. → אנה *mourn.*

תְּאֻנִים 1 n.[m.]pl. **toil** Ezk 24$_{12}$.

תַּאֲנַת שִׁלֹה 1 pl.n. **Taanath-shiloh.**

תאר I 6 vb.—**Qal** 5 + waw וְתָאַר—**incline, curve round, turn,** of border Jos 15$_{9}$ (+ מִן *from,* אֶל *to*).

Pu. 1 Ptc. מְתֹאָר—appar. **be inclined, curved round, turned,** of border Jos 19$_{13}$.

תאר II 2 vb.—**Pi.** 2 Impf. יְתָאֲרֵהוּ (יְתָאֳרֵהוּ; or po.)—**mark out, draw in outline** with (בְּ) stylus, compass Is 44$_{13}$. → תֹּאַר *form.*

תֹּאַר 15.10.5 n.m.—Si, Q תואר, Q תור; cstr. תֹּאַר; sf. תָּאֳרוֹ (תֹּאֲרוֹ)—**form, appearance** of woman Gn 29$_{17}$, man Gn 39$_{6}$, cow Gn 41$_{18}$; more specif. **goodly form, beautiful appearance, beauty** of woman Si 36$_{27}$, man 1 S 16$_{18}$, heavens Si 43$_{1}$, snow Si 43$_{18}$. → תאר II *mark out.*

תַּאְרֵעַ 1 pr.n.m. **Tarea.**

תְּאַשּׁוּר 2.0.1 n.[m.] **cypress,** or perh. **box tree** Is 41$_{19}$, wood Is 60$_{13}$. → (?) אשר I *go forward;* cf. מְאַשֵּׁר *evergreen tree.*

תֵּבָה 28.0.12 n.f.—cstr. תֵּבַת—**ark, chest, 1.** Noah's vessel Gn 6$_{14}$. **2.** papyrus chest in which the infant Moses was placed Ex 2$_{3}$.

תְּבוּאָה 43.2.17 n.f.—cstr. תְּבוּאַת; sf. תְּבוּאָתִי; pl. תְּבוּאוֹת; cstr. תְּבוּאֹת; sf. תְּבוּאֹתֵיכֶם—**1. produce, yield, harvest** Ex 23$_{10}$ Dt 14$_{22}$; perh. **harvest time** Gn 47$_{24}$. **2. income, profit, gain** Pr 3$_{14}$ Ec 5$_{9}$. → בוא *come.*

תְּבוּנָה 42.8.4 n.f.—cstr. mss תְּבוּנַת; sf. תְּבוּנָתִי; pl. תְּבוּנוֹת; cstr. תְּבוּנוֹת; sf. תְּבוּנֹתֵיכֶם—**understanding, 1.** of Y. Is 40$_{28}$ Ps 136$_{5}$. **2.** of humans Ezk 28$_{4}$, i.e. **a. intelligence, discernment** Dt 32$_{28}$ 1 K 5$_{9}$. **b. skill, ability**

Ex 31₃||35₃₁. c. **insight, wise saying** Jb 32₁₁. 3. **personified Understanding** Pr 8₁. → בין *understand.*

[תְּבוּסָה] 1 n.f.—cstr. תְּבוּסַת—**downfall, ruin** 2 C 22₇. → בוס *trample.*

תָּבוֹר 10 pl.n. **Tabor.**

תֵּבֵל 36.5.50 n.f. (m. at Is 14₁₇)—cstr. תֵּבֵל—**world** 1 S 2₈; מוֹסְדוֹת תֵּבֵל *foundations of the world* 2 S 22₁₆||Ps 18₁₆, יֹשְׁבֵי תֵבֵל *inhabitants of the world* Is 18₃, תֵּבֵל *(inhabitants of) the world* Is 13₁₁.

תֶּבֶל 2.0.1 n.[m.] **perversion, confusion,** in ref. to female bestiality Lv 18₂₃, incest with daughter-in-law Lv 20₁₂, wicked deeds in general 4QJub[d] 21₂₁. → בלל *mix.*

תֻּבַל 8 pr.n.m. **Tubal.**

[תַּבְלִית] 1 n.f.—sf. תַּבְלִיתָם—**destruction** Is 10₂₅. → בלה *be worn out.*

תְּבַלֻּל 1 n.[m.] **mingling,** term for specif. eye defect, perh. **white spot** Lv 21₂₀. → בלל *mix.*

תֶּבֶן 17 n.m. **straw,** as food for animals Gn 24₂₅ 1 K 5₈, used in making bricks Ex 5₇. → cf. מַתְבֵּן *heap of straw.*

תִּבְנִי 3 pr.n.m. **Tibni.**

תַּבְנִית 20.1.9 n.f.—cstr. תַּבְנִית; sf. תַּבְנִיתוֹ—**1a. construction, structure** of palace Ps 144₁₂, knowledge 4QBer[a] 1.2₆. **b. pattern (for construction), plan, design** of tabernacle and its furnishings Ex 25₉. **2. form, image, likeness** of hand Ezk 8₃, person Is 44₁₃, ox Ps 106₂₀. **3. copy, replica** of altar Jos 22₂₈. → בנה I *build.*

* תבע 0.0.1 vb. (perh. byform of בעה II *seek*)—**Qal** 1 Ptc. Q תבע—**claim,** through legal contest 5/6ḤevBA 45₂₈.

תַּבְעֵרָה 2 pl.n. **Taberah.**

תֵּבֵץ 3 pl.n. **Thebez.**

תגאולת, see תְּגְאֹלֶת *defilement.*

* [תְּגְאֹלֶת] 0.0.1 n.f.—cstr. תגאולת—**defilement, stain,** from liquids 11QT 49₁₂. → גאל II *defile.*

תִּגְלַת פִּלְאֶסֶר 6 pr.n.m. **Tiglath-pileser,** also as תִּלְגַת פִּלְנֶסֶר **Tilgath-pilneser.**

[תַּגְמוּל] 1.1 n.[m.]—cstr. Si תגמל; pl. sf. תַּגְמוּלוֹהִי—**1. recompense** perh. Si 37₁₁(B). **2. benefit** Ps 116₁₂. → גמל *repay.*

* תגר 0.1 vb.—**Htp.** 0.1 Impf. תתגר—**bargain, haggle** with (עִם) Si 37₁₁(B). → תַּגָּר *merchant.*

* [תַּגָּר] 0.1 n.[m.] **merchant** Si 42₅. → תגר *trade.*

* [תִּגָּר] 0.0.3 n.[m.] **contention, legal contest** Mur 30 2₂₅ 5/6ḤevBA 45₂₈. → גרה *contend.*

[תִּגְרָה] 1 n.f.—cstr. תִּגְרַת—**hostility, blow** Ps 39₁₁. → גרה *contend.*

תֹּגַרְמָה 4 pr.n.m. **Togarmah.**

תִּדְהָר 2.0.1 n.[m.] **pine,** or perh. **elm** or **plane tree** Is 41₁₉, wood Is 60₁₃.

תַּדְמֹר 2 pl.n. **Tadmor.**

תִּדְעָל 2 pr.n.m. **Tidal.**

תֹּהוּ 20.1.7 n.m.—pl. sf. Q תוהיה—**1. formlessness, chaos** of earth at creation Gn 1₂, ruined city Is 24₁₀, **void, empty space** Jb 26₇, **wasteland** Dt 32₁₀. **2. emptiness, vanity, nothing(ness),** of images Is 41₂₉, nations Is 40₁₇, legal argument Is 29₂₁. **3.** as adv., **emptily, in vain** Is 45₁₉.

תְּהוֹם 36.3.32 n.f.&m.—pl. תְּהֹמוֹת; cstr. תְּהֹמוֹת; sf. Q תהומיה—**1. deep, abyss** Am 7₄, assoc. with or equivalent to Sheol 1QH 18₃₃, place of subterranean waters Gn 7₁₁. **2. deep (sea)** Jon 2₆; pl. **deep waters, depths** Ps 135₆, of Reed Sea Ex 15₅, troughs of waves Ps 107₂₆. **3. deep, primaeval ocean** Gn 1₂. **4. fountain, spring** Dt 8₇.

תָּהֳלָה 1 n.f. **error**—Jb 4₁₈. → (?) הלל III *be foolish.*

תְּהִלָּה I 57.6.45 n.f.—cstr. תְּהִלַּת; sf. תְּהִלָּתִי; pl. תְּהִלֹּת, Q תהלים; cstr. תְּהִלּוֹת, Q תהלי; sf. תְּהִלֹּתֶיךָ (unless sg.), Q תהלותיהו, Q תהליהמה—**1. praise, adoration,** due or given to Y. Is 42₁₀ Ps 51₁₇. **2. (song of) praise, (offering of) praise,** to Y. Ps 22₄ 40₄. **3.** more specif. than §2, **song of praise, psalm, hymn,** תְּהִלָּה לְדָוִד *a psalm of David* in psalm title Ps 145₁, תהלת שבח *psalm of praise* 4QShirShabb[d] 1.1₂, ספר התהלים *the Book of Psalms* as title of Psalter 4QM[a] 17₄. **4. praise(s),** i.e. **praiseworthy deeds, praiseworthiness** of Y. Is 60₆, humans Si 44₁₅. **5. praise,** i.e. **renown, glory** of Y. Ps 48₁₁, people of Y. Ps 148₁₄. **6. (object of) praise, (object of) renown,** in ref. to Y. Dt 10₂₁, Jerusalem Is 62₇. → הלל I *praise.*

* תְּהִלָּה II 1 n.f.—sf. תְּהִלָּתוֹ—**radiance** of Y. Hb 3₃. → הלל II *shine.*

[תַּהֲלֻכָה] 1 n.f.—pl. תַּהֲלֻכֹת—**procession,** at dedication of wall Ne 12₃₁. → הלך *go.*

[תַּהְפֻּכָה] 10 n.f.—pl. תַּהְפֻּכוֹת; cstr. תַּהְפֻּכוֹת—**perversity, perverse thing** Pr 2₁₂; דּוֹר תַּהְפֻּכֹת *generation of per-*

versity, i.e. perverse generation Dt 32$_{30}$. → הפך *turn*.

תו, see תָּא *chamber*.

תָּו $_{3.0.1}$ n.[m.]—Q תיו; sf. תָּוִי—**mark, sign,** on forehead Ezk 9$_{4}$, as signature Jb 31$_{35}$. → תוה I *make a mark*.

תוֹא, see תְּאוֹ *antelope*.

[תּוֹאָם] $_{4}$ n.m.—pl. תּוֹמִם (תְּאוֹמִים); cstr. תְּאֳמֵי (תְּאוֹמֵי)—**twin** of humans Gn 25$_{24}$, animals Ca 4$_{5}$. → תאם *be double*.

תוֹאַר, see תֹּאַר *form*.

תּוּבַל, see תֻּבַל *Tubal*.

תּוּבַל קַיִן $_{2}$ pr.n.m. **Tubal-cain.**

תובנתו Jb 26$_{12}$, see תְּבוּנָה *understanding*.

תּוּגָה $_{4}$ n.f.—cstr. תּוּגַת—**grief** Ps 119$_{28}$ Pr 14$_{13}$, i.e. **cause of grief** Pr 10$_{1}$ 17$_{21}$. → יגה I *be grieved*.

***[תּוֹגַר]** $_{0.0.1}$ pr.n.m. **Togar.**

תּוֹגַרְמָה, see תֹּגַרְמָה *Togarmah*.

תּוֹדָה $_{32.0.4}$ n.f.—cstr. תּוֹדַת; pl. תּוֹדֹת—**1. praise,** given to Y. Jos 7$_{19}$, perh. **confession** Ezr 10$_{11}$. **2. thanksgiving (through song), praise, esp.** offered liturgically Is 51$_{3}$ Ps 100$_{4}$. **3. thanksgiving company, choir** Ne 12$_{31}$. **4. thanksgiving (through sacrifice), thank offering** Lv 7$_{12}$ Ps 50$_{14}$. → ידה I *praise*.

תוה I $_{2.1.1}$ vb.—**Pi.** $_{1}$ + waw Kt ויתו (Qr, mss וַיְתָיו)—**make marks upon** (עַל) door 1 S 21$_{14}$.

Hi. $_{1.1.1}$ + Impf. Si תתוה; waw וְהִתְוִיתָ; inf. Q התות—**1. place a mark upon** (עַל) forehead Ezk 9$_{4}$. **2. mark out** something Si 43$_{13}$.

→ תָּו *mark*.

תוה II $_{1}$ vb.—**Hi.** $_{1}$ Pf. הִתְווּ—**grieve, distress, pain** Ps 78$_{41}$.

תּוֹחַ $_{1}$ pr.n.m. **Toah.**

***[תּוֹחֲלָה]** $_{0.0.1}$ n.f. **hope, expectation** 1QH 17$_{14}$. → יחל I *wait*.

תּוֹחֶלֶת $_{6.2.3}$ n.f.—cstr. תּוֹחֶלֶת; sf. תּוֹחַלְתִּי—**hope, expectation** Ps 39$_{8}$ Jb 41$_{1}$. → יחל I *wait*.

***תוך** $_{0.0.2}$ vb.—**Hi.** $_{0.0.1}$ Inf. התיכמה—**allow to be united,** in marriage 4QMMT B$_{44}$.

Htpol. $_{0.0.1}$ Ptc. מתוככים—**become united, unite with one another,** in marriage 4QMMT B$_{81}$.

→ תָּוֶךְ *middle*, תִּיכוֹן *middle*.

תָּוֶךְ $_{418.7.137}$ n.[m.]—cstr. תּוֹךְ; sf. תּוֹכִי, תּוֹכָם, תּוֹכָהְנָה—**1.** תָּוֶךְ, **a. middle** of temple court 1 K 8$_{64}$||2 C 7$_{7}$, wadi Dt 3$_{16}$; position between troops Jos 8$_{22}$; עַמּוּדֵי הַתָּוֶךְ *pillars of the middle*, i.e. middle pillars Jg 16$_{29}$. **b. interior** of palanquin Ca 3$_{10}$, staircase 11QT 30$_{8}$. **c. inner person** Ezk 28$_{16}$. **2.** construct or suffixed form in compound prep., **a.** בְּתוֹךְ usu. of space, **in the middle of, within, in, among, between** Gn 1$_{6}$ 3$_{8}$ 18$_{24}$ Ex 28$_{33}$||39$_{25}$, with verbs of motion sometimes **into, through** Ex 14$_{29}$ 1 S 9$_{14}$; also of time, **in the middle of, in, during** 1 K 3$_{20}$ Is 16$_{3}$. **b.** מִתּוֹךְ **from the middle of, from within, from out of, from among** Gn 19$_{19}$ Ex 3$_{2}$ 7$_{5}$ Nm 16$_{21}$. **c.** אֶל־תּוֹךְ **into the middle of, into, inside, within** Ex 14$_{23}$ Lv 11$_{33}$ Dt 23$_{11}$. **d.** עַד־תּוֹךְ **into the middle of, inside** 2 S 4$_{6}$. **e.** מֵעַל תּוֹךְ **from upon the middle of, from within** Ezk 11$_{23}$. **f.** לְתוֹךְ **into, within** 11QT 50$_{13}$. → תוך *cohere*.

תּוֹךְ, see תָּוֶךְ *middle*; תֹּךְ *oppression*.

תּוֹכֵחָה $_{4}$ n.f.—pl. תּוֹכֵחוֹת—**rebuke, punishment** 2 K 19$_{3}$ ||Is 37$_{3}$ Ho 5$_{9}$ Ps 149$_{7}$. → יכח *contend*.

תּוֹכַחַת $_{24.4.14}$ n.f.—cstr. תּוֹכַחַת; sf. תּוֹכַחְתִּי; pl. תּוֹכָחוֹת; cstr. תּוֹכְחוֹת; sf. Q תוכחותיה—**1. argument, complaint, retort** Hb 2$_{1}$ Jb 13$_{6}$. **2. reproof, correction** Pr 1$_{23}$ 6$_{23}$. **3. rebuke, reprimand, punishment** of, i.e. given by Y. Ezk 5$_{15}$, Y.'s elect to the wicked 1QpHab 5$_{4}$; given in legal context 1QS 6$_{1}$. → יכח *contend*.

תּוֹלָד $_{1.0.0.1}$ pl.n. **Tolad.**

[תּוֹלֵדוֹת] $_{39.0.13}$ n.f.pl.—cstr. תּוֹלְדוֹת; sf. תֹּלְדֹתָיו, תּוֹלְדֹתָם—**1. (successive) generations, genealogies, descendants** Gn 5$_{1}$, **order of birth** Gn 25$_{13}$. **2.** perh. more generally, **history** Gn 2$_{4}$, **origins** 1QS 3$_{19}$. **3.** perh. **nature, characteristics** 1QS 3$_{13}$. → ילד *give birth*.

תּוֹלוֹן, see תִּילוֹן *Tilon*.

[תּוֹלָל] I $_{1}$ n.[m.]—pl. sf. תּוֹלָלֵינוּ—**tormentor** Ps 137$_{3}$. → (?) ילל *howl*.

***[תּוֹלָל]** II $_{1}$ n.[m.]—pl. sf. תּוֹלָלֵינוּ—**mocker** Ps 137$_{3}$. → הלל III *be foolish*.

תּוֹלָע I $_{3.0.4}$ n.[m.]—pl. תּוֹלָעִים—**1. worm** Ex 16$_{20}$. **2. crimson,** less accurately **scarlet,** colour produced by dye of *Cocus ilicis* worm Is 1$_{18}$, material dyed with it Lm 4$_{5}$. → תלע *clothe in crimson*; cf. תּוֹלֵעָה *worm, crimson*.

תּוֹלָע II $_{6}$ pr.n.m. **Tola.**

תּוֹלֵעָה 40.2.5 n.f.—תּוֹלַעַת (תּוֹלָעַת); cstr. תּוֹלַעַת; sf. תּוֹלַעְתָּם —**1. worm(s), grub(s) maggot(s),** attacking plant Jon 4₇; in connection with death Is 14₁₁, representing insignificance Is 41₁₄. **2. crimson,** less accurately **scarlet,** cloth, thread, etc., coloured with dye of *Cocus ilicis* worm Lv 14₄; תְּכֵלֶת וְאַרְגָּמָן וְתוֹלַעַת שָׁנִי *blue and purple and crimson (material)* Ex 25₄||35₆. → תלע *clothe in crimson;* cf. תּוֹלָע I *worm, crimson.*

תּוֹלָעִי 1 gent. **Tolaite.**

תולעת Si 20₃₀, see תּוֹעֶלֶת *profit, use.*

תּוֹלַעַת, see תּוֹלֵעָה *worm, crimson.*

תּוֹמִיךְ, see תמך *hold.*

תומים, see תֻּמִּים *Thummim.*

תֹּומִם, see תּוֹאָם *twin.*

תּוֹעֵבָה 117.4.34 n.f.—pl. תּוֹעֵבוֹת; cstr. תּוֹעֲבוֹת; sf. תּוֹעֲבוֹתֵיהֶם (תּוֹעֲבֹתָם)—**abomination, abominable thing** or **deed, 1.** things abominable to the Egyptians: shepherds Gn 46₃₄, eating with Hebrews Gn 43₃₂. **2.** sacrifice of animals with blemish Dt 17₁. **3.** prohibited food Dt 14₃. **4.** foreign gods and their images Dt 7₂₅ 2 K 23₁₃, practices assoc. with them Dt 18₁₂. **5.** sexual indecency Lv 18₂₂ Ezk 22₁₁. **6.** lying lips Pr 12₂₂, blasphemous speech CD 5₁₂. **7.** false weights and measures Pr 20₁₀. → תעב *abhor.*

תּוֹעָה 2.0.4 n.f.—pl. Q תועות—**1. error,** concerning Y. Is 32₆, righteous statutes CD 20₁₁; רוח התועה *spirit of error* 1QH 9₂₂. **2. confusion** Ne 4₂. → תעה *wander.*

*[**תּוֹעֵלָה**] 0.2 n.f.—תעלה—**profit, gain** Si 30₂₃ 41₁₄. → יעל *profit.*

*[**תּוֹעֶלֶת**] n.f.—**profit, use** Si 20₃₀ (if em. תולעת, appar. error; cf. 41₁₄). → יעל *profit.*

[**תּוֹעָפָה**] 4.1.1 n.f.—תּוֹעָפוֹת; cstr. תּוֹעֲפֹת—**1. eminence** of wild ox, perh. in ref. to towering horns Nm 23₂₂. **2. height, peak** of mountain Ps 95₄. **3.** perh. **heap, bar** of silver Jb 22₂₅. **4. deepest darkness, depth** of night 4QWiles 1₄.

תופלה, see תִּפְלָה *insolence.*

[**תּוֹצָאָה**] 23.0.4 n.f.—pl. תּוֹצָאוֹת; cstr. תּוֹצְאוֹת; sf. תּוֹצְאֹתָיו —**1. extremity** of border Nm 34₈. **2. exit,** i.e. gate, of city Ezk 48₃₀. **3. outcome, consequence** of righteousness 4QWays[b] 1.2₁₅, mysteries 4QInstr[c] 1.1₁₃. **4. source** of life Pr 4₂₃. **5. escape** from death Ps 68₂₁. → יצא I *go out.*

תוקהת, see תָּקְהַת *Tokhath.*

תּוֹקְעִים, see תֹּקְעִים *handshake,* תקע *thrust.*

תור 24.1.7 vb.—**Qal** 22.1.5 Pf. תַּרְתִּי, תָּרוּ, תַּרְתִּי; impf. יָתוּר, יָתֻרוּ; ptc. תָּרִים; inf. תּוּר—**1. spy out, explore** land Nm 13₂. **2a. search out, investigate, study** wisdom Ec 7₂₅, all that is done Ec 1₁₃ (עַל of obj.). **b.** with inf., **seek to, search how to do** Ec 2₃. **3. seek out, find** place for (לְ) someone Dt 1₃₃. **4a. go about,** of wild ass Jb 39₈. **b. follow after** (אַחֲרֵי) one's heart and eyes Nm 15₃₉. **c.** ptc. as noun, **one who goes about, itinerant,** אַנְשֵׁי הַתָּרִים *men of the itinerants,* i.e. traders 1 K 10₁₅||2 C 9₁₅.

Hi. 2.0.2 Impf. יָתֵר; + waw וַיָּתִירוּ; inf. Q מתיר—**1. search out** one's friend Pr 12₂₆. **2. make reconnaissance, cause reconnaissance to be made** Jg 1₂₃. **3. go about** 1QS 3₃ (+ שְׁרִירוּת *[in] stubbornness).*

→ מָתוֹר *following after.*

[**תּוֹר**] I 5.0.2 n.[m.]—cstr. תֹּר; sf. Q תרו; pl. תֹּרִים; cstr. תּוֹרֵי—**1. plait (of gold),** or perh. **earring, pendant,** in a sequence Ca 1₁₀.₁₁. **2.** one's **turn** to do something Est 2₁₂ 1QS 6₁₁.

תּוֹר II, see תֹּר *turtledove.*

[**תּוֹר**] III, see תֹּאַר *form.*

תּוֹרָה 220.12.133 n.f.—cstr. תּוֹרַת; sf. תּוֹרָתִי; pl. תּוֹרֹת; cstr. תּוֹרוֹת; sf. תּוֹרֹתָיו—**1. instruction, teaching, a.** of Y., the prophetic word Is 1₁₀, given by priests Dt 17₁₁ Jr 18₁₈, given by Y. to an individual Jb 22₂₂. **b.** of human Ps 78₁, given for education, enlightenment, wisdom Pr 1₈ 3₁. **2a. (collection, summary of) instruction, (code of) law,** expressing the will of Y., and having binding force, **the Torah** Ex 24₁₂ Dt 1₅; תּוֹרַת י׳ *law of Y.* 2 K 10₃₁, סֵפֶר הַתּוֹרָה *document of the law* Dt 28₆₁. **b.** pl. **laws,** in general Is 24₅, of Y. Gn 26₅, given at Sinai Lv 26₄₆. **c. law, regulation, rule,** governing or concerning something in particular: the burnt offering Lv 6₂, the Nazirite Nm 6₁₃, leprosy Lv 14₅₇. **3. decree, will** of Y., concerning death of humans Si. 41₄. **4.** perh. **custom, manner** of humans 2 S 7₁₉. → ירה III *teach.*

*__תּוֹרֵק__ 1 adj. **green,** i.e. fresh, of oil Ca 1₃.

תּוֹשָׁב I 14 n.m.—cstr. תּוֹשַׁב; sf. תּוֹשָׁבְךָ; pl. תּוֹשָׁבִים; cstr. תֹּשָׁבֵי—**sojourner,** i.e. **resident alien, (temporary)**

inhabitant, similar to the גֵּר but with fewer rights Lv 22$_{10}$; of Abraham among the Hittites Gn 23$_{4}$, Israelites with Y. Lv 25$_{23}$; perh. **settler** 1 K 17$_{1}$. → ישׁב *sit.*

*[תּוֹשָׁב] II 0.0.0.1 pr.n.[m.] **Toshab.**

תושבחות, see תִּשְׁבַּחָה *praise.*

תּוּשִׁיָּה 11.1.4 n.f.—תֻּשִׁיָּה (Q תושייה)—**1. sound wisdom, competence** Is 28$_{29}$ Pr 3$_{21}$. **2. success** Jb 5$_{12}$, **effective aid** Jb 6$_{13}$. **3. sound health** Si 38$_{8}$.

תּוֹתָח 1 n.[m.] **club,** or other weapon Jb 41$_{21}$.

תזז 1 vb.—**Hi.** 1 Pf. הֵתַז—**tear away, cut down tendrils** Is 18$_{5}$. → תְּזִיז *hornet.*

*[תְּזִיז] 0.0.1 n.m. **hornet,** or perh. **wasp,** as unable to make honey 4QpsEzek[b] 1.2$_{5}$. → תזז *tear away.*

תִּזָּכֵר, see זכר *remember,* ni.

[תַּזְנוּת] 20 n.f.—sf. תַּזְנוּתֵךְ; pl. תַּזְנוּתַיִךְ—**prostitution, fornication,** in ref. to religious infidelity Ezk 16$_{15}$ 23$_{7}$. → זנה I *prostitute oneself.*

[תַּחְבֻּלָה] 6.3 n.f.—**guidance, direction, counsel**—pl. תַּחְבֻּלוֹת; cstr. תַּחְבֻּלוֹת; sf. Qr תַּחְבּוּלֹתָיו (Kt תחבולתו)—of Y. Jb 37$_{12}$, humans Pr 1$_{5}$ 11$_{14}$ 20$_{18}$. → חבל IV *bind.*

תֹּחוּ 1 pr.n.m. **Tohu.**

*[תְּחוּם] 0.0.6.2 n.[m.]—cstr. I תחם; sf. Q תחומו; pl. Q תחומים; cstr. I תחומי—**boundary, limit** of city Gezer boundary inscr., plot of land Mur 30 1$_{3}$, house Kh. Qumran ost. 1$_{6}$.

תַּחְכְּמֹנִי 1 gent. **Tahchemonite.**

תַּחֲלֻאִים 5.0.1 n.m.pl.—cstr. תַּחֲלוּאֵי; sf. תַּחֲלוּאָיְכִי, תַּחֲלֻאֶיהָ—**diseases** Dt 29$_{21}$ Jr 14$_{18}$. → חלא I *be diseased.*

תְּחִלָּה 22.4.5 n.f.—cstr. תְּחִלַּת; sf. Q תחלתו—**1. beginning** of harvest 2 S 21$_{10}$, reign Ezr 4$_{6}$, wisdom Pr 9$_{10}$. **2a.** בַּתְּחִלָּה **in the beginning,** i.e. (1) **at first, the first time, previously** Gn 41$_{21}$ 43$_{18}$. (2) **at the first, first (in order)** Jg 1$_{1}$ 2 S 17$_{9}$. **b.** כְּבַתְּחִלָּה **as in the beginning, as at the first** Is 1$_{26}$. **c.** בִּתְחִלַּת **at the beginning of,** בִּתְחִלַּת שִׁבְתָּם *at the beginning of their dwelling,* i.e. when they first dwelt 2 K 17$_{25}$. **d.** תְּחִלַּת **(at the) beginning of,** תְּחִלַּת דִּבֶּר־י׳ *at the beginning of Y. spoke,* i.e. when Y. first spoke Ho. 1$_{2}$. → חלל II *begin.*

*[תַּחֲלִיף] 0.3 n.[m.] **replacement, renewal, successor** Si 44$_{17}$ 46$_{12}$ 48$_{8}$. → חלף I *pass.*

[תֹּחֶלֶת], see תּוֹחֶלֶת *hope.*

תחם, see תַּחַן *Tahan.*

תחמי, see תַּחֲנִי *Tahanite.*

תַּחְמָס 2 n.[m.] **short-eared owl,** or perh. **nighthawk,** or **male ostrich** Lv 11$_{16}$ Dt 14$_{15}$.

תַּחַן 2 pr.n.m. **Tahan.**

תחנא, see תְּחִנָּה II *Tehinnah.*

[תַּחֲנָה] 1 n.f.—sf. תַּחֲנֹתִי—**encampment** 2 K 6$_{8}$ (or em. תֵּחָבְאוּ *you shall hide yourselves* or תִּנְחָתוּ *you shall go down*). → חנה I *encamp.*

תְּחִנָּה I 25.0.3 n.f.—cstr. תְּחִנַּת; sf. תְּחִנָּתִי; pl. sf. תְּחִנֹּתֵיהֶם—**1. supplication, plea (for favour),** usu. made to Y. in prayer 1 K 8$_{38}$||2 C 6$_{29}$, also made to human Jr 37$_{20}$. **2. favour, mercy,** shown by Y. Ezr 9$_{8}$, humans Jos 11$_{20}$. → חנן I *be gracious.*

תְּחִנָּה II 1.0.4.1 pr.n.m. **Tehinnah.**

[תַּחֲנוּן] 18.2.2 n.[m.]—sf. Q תחנונו; pl. תַּחֲנוּנִים; cstr. תַּחֲנוּנֵי; sf. תַּחֲנוּנָי, תַּחֲנוּנוֹתָי—**supplication, plea (for favour),** usu. made to Y. in prayer Ps 28$_{2}$, also made to human Pr 18$_{23}$. → חנן I *be gracious.*

תַּחֲנִי 1 gent. **Tahanite.**

תחפנס, see תַּחְפַּנְחֵס *Tahpanhes.*

תַּחְפַּנְחֵס 7.0.3 pl.n. **Tahpanhes.**

תַּחְפְּנֵיס 3 pr.n.f. **Tahpenes.**

תַּחְרָא 2 n.[m.] perh. **coat of mail** Ex 28$_{32}$||39$_{23}$.

*[תַּחֲרָה] 0.2 n.f.—תחרה—**strife** Si 34$_{29}$ 40$_{5}$. → חרה I *burn.*

תַּחְרֵעַ 1 pr.n.m. **Tahrea.**

תַּחַשׁ I 14 n.[m.]—תַּחַשׁ; pl. תְּחָשִׁים—**dolphin, porpoise,** or other animal whose skin is used for leather, or perh. **tahash,** a specif. kind of leather Ex 25$_{5}$||35$_{7}$.

תַּחַשׁ II 1 pr.n.m. **Tahash.**

תַּחַת I 512.9.46.1 prep.—תַּחַת; sf. תַּחְתַּי (תַּחְתֵּנִי, תַּחְתַּי), תַּחְתָּיו, תַּחְתֶּיהָ (תַּחְתֶּנָּה), תַּחְתֵּיהֶם (תַּחְתָּם)—**1a. under, beneath, below** Gn 7$_{19}$ 18$_{4}$. **b. under (the authority of)** Nm 5$_{19}$. **c. under (the care of), at the side of** Lv 22$_{27}$. **d. under (the burden of), on account of** Pr 30$_{21}$. **2a. (1) in the place of (someone or something else)** Gn 2$_{21}$ Jb 16$_{4}$. **(2) in (one's own) place** 1 S 14$_{9}$. **b. in place of, instead of, as a substitute for** Gn 22$_{13}$ 30$_{2}$. **c. in place of, instead of, in succession to** Gn 36$_{33}$||1 C 14$_{4}$. **d. in exchange for, as payment for** Ex 21$_{23}$ 1 K 21$_{2}$. 3. in compounds, **a.** תַּחַת לְ **under**

Ca 2_6. **b.** מִתַּחַת (1) **(from) under, (from) beneath** Gn 1_9. (2) **from under (the authority of), from (being subject to)** Ho 4_{12}. (3) **from (one's own) place** Ex 10_{23}. **c.** מִתַּחַת לְ (1) **under, beneath** Gn 1_7. (2) **below** Gn 35_8. **d.** לְמִתַּחַת לְ **under, beneath** 1 K 7_{32}. **e.** עַד־מִתַּחַת לְ **as far as below** 1 S 7_{11}. **f.** אֶל־תַּחַת (1) **under** Jg 6_{19}. (2) **in replacement of** Lv 14_{42}. **g.** אֶל־תַּחַת לְ **under, beneath** Ezk 10_2. **h.** לְתַחַת **under, beneath** 3QTr 10_{15}. **4.** as adv., **a.** תַּחַת, **beneath, below** Gn 49_{25}. **b.** מִתַּחַת **beneath, below** Ex 20_4||Dt 5_8. **5.** as conj., **a.** תַּחַת (1) **because** Ps 38_{21}. (2) **whereas, although** Is 60_{15}. **b.** תַּחַת אֲשֶׁר (1) **because, since** Dt 21_{14}. (2) **whereas, although** Dt 28_{62}. **c.** תַּחַת כִּי **because** Pr 1_{29}. **6.** תַּחַת מָה as interrog., **on account of what?, why?** Jr 5_{19}. → cf. תַּחְתּוֹן *lower*, תַּחְתִּי *lower*.

תַּחַת II 4 pr.n.m. **Tahath.**

[תַּחַת] III 2 pl.n. **Tahath.**

תַּחְתּוֹן 13.0.5.1 adj.—f.s. תַּחְתּוֹנָה, m.pl. I תחתנם, f.pl. תַּחְתֹּנוֹת—**1. lower, lowest,** of storey 1 K 6_6, gate Ezk 40_{19}, pool Is 22_9. **2.** as noun, **lower one, lowest one,** in ref. to chamber Ezk 42_5, storey Ezk 41_7. → cf. תַּחַת I *under*.

[תַּחְתִּי] 19.1.6 adj.—f.s. תַּחְתִּית (תַּחְתִּיָּה), m.pl. תַּחְתִּים, f.pl. תַּחְתִּיּוֹת—**1. lower, lowest,** of Sheol Dt 32_{22}, land Ezk 31_{14}, millstone Jb 41_{16}. **2.** as noun, **a.** masc., **lower storey** or **deck** of Noah's ark Gn 6_{16}. **b.** fem., **lower part** or **place, lowest part** or **place,** תַּחְתִּיּוֹת אֶרֶץ *lowest places of the earth* Is 44_{23}, אֶרֶץ תַּחְתִּיּוֹת *land of the lowest places* Ezk 26_{20}. → cf. תַּחַת I *under*.

תַּחְתִּים חָדְשִׁי 1 pl.n. **Tahtim-hodshi.**

*[תַּחְתֹּנָה] 0.0.0.1 pr.n.[m.] **Tahtonah.**

תִיו, see תָּו *mark*.

תִּיכוֹן I 11.0.2 adj.—f.s. תִּיכוֹנָה, f.pl. תִּיכֹנוֹת—**1. middle,** of storey 1 K 6_8, gate 1QM 7_9, watch Jg 7_{19}. **2.** as noun, **middle one,** in ref. to chamber Ezk 42_5, storey Ezk 41_7. → תָּוֶךְ *middle*.

תִּיכוֹן II, see חֲצַר הַתִּיכוֹן *Hazer-hatticon*.

תִּילוֹן 1 pr.n.m. **Tilon.**

תֵּימָא I 2.0.0.1 pr.n.m. **Tema.**

תֵּימָא II 3 pl.n. **Tema.**

תֵּימָן I 23.1 n.f.—תֵּמָן; + ה- of direction תֵּימָנָה—**1. the south** Ex 26_{18}||36_{23} Zc 6_6. **2. south wind** Ps 78_{26}. → ימן *go right*.

תֵּימָן II 5 pr.n.m. **Teman.**

תֵּימָן III 6.0.0.2 pl.n. **Teman.**

תֵּימָנִי 8 gent. **Temanite.**

תֵּימְנִי 1 pr.n.m. **Temeni.**

[תִּימָרָה] 2 n.f.—pl. cstr. תִּימְרוֹת—**column** of smoke, perh. palm-shaped, spreading at the top Jl 3_3 Ca 3_6. → cf. (?) תָּמָר I *palm tree*.

תִּיצִי 1 gent. **Tizite.**

תִּירוֹשׁ 38.3.20 n.m.—תִּירֹשׁ; sf. תִּירוֹשִׁי—**new wine, must** Gn 27_{28} Dt 7_{13}, perh. **juice** Is 65_8. → ירשׁ II *press (grapes)*.

תִּירְיָא 1 pr.n.m. **Tiria.**

תִּירָס 2 pr.n.m. **Tiras.**

*[תִּירְקוֹס] 0.0.1 pr.n.[m.] **Tirkos.**

תִּירֹשׁ, see תִּירוֹשׁ *new wine*.

[תַּיִשׁ] 4 n.m.—תָּיִשׁ; pl. תְּיָשִׁים—**he-goat** Gn 30_{35}.

תֹּךְ 4 n.m.—תּוֹךְ; pl. תְּכָכִים—**oppression, injury** Ps 10_7 55_{12} 72_{14}; אִישׁ תְּכָכִים *man of oppression*, i.e. oppressor Pr 29_{13}.

תכה 1 vb.—**Pu.** 1 Pf. תֻּכּוּ—perh. **be led** Dt 33_3 (+ לְ *at feet*).

*[תְּכוֹן] 0.0.39 n.m. (unless all forms belong to תֹּכֶן)—cstr. תכון; sf. תכונו; pl. תכונים; cstr. תכוני—**1a. measure, specification** of ephah and bath 4QD[f] 2_2. **b. measure of days.** i.e. full their number or range 1QM 6_{12}. **2. regulation, norm, decision** 1QS 5_3 9_3 1QH 20_5; שמש תכון תבל *the sun, the regulation of*, i.e. which regulates, *the world* 1QMyst 1.1_6. **3. rank, proper place** of person in community 1QS 6_8 7_{21}. **4. fixed order, sequence** of holy days 1QS 10_5, end times 1QpHab 7_{13}. → תכן *measure*.

תְּכוּנָה 3 n.f.—sf. תְּכוּנָתוֹ—**1. fixed place,** as dwelling place of Y. Jb 23_3. **2. arrangement, layout** of temple Ezk 43_{11}. **3. preparation,** i.e. **store, treasure** Na 2_{10}. → כון *be upright*.

תֻּכִּיִּים 2 n.m.pl.—תּוּכִּיִּים—**peacocks,** or perh. **poultry,** or **apes** 1 K 10_{22}||2 C 9_{21}.

*[תָּכִין] 0.0.1 adj.—f.s. תכינה—**meted out,** of spirit 4QInstr[a] 1_{19}. → תכן *measure*.

תְּכָכִים, see תֹּךְ *oppression*.

*[תֶּכֶל] n.[m.] **completeness,** אַפִּי עַל־תֶּכֶל יִתַּם *my anger to completeness will be ended*, i.e. be completely end-

ed Is 10_{25} (if em. תַּבְלִיתָם *their destruction*).

תִּכְלָה 1 n.f. **perfection** Ps 119_{96}. → כלה *be complete.*

תַּכְלִית 5.0.2 n.f.—cstr. תַּכְלִית—**1. completeness, perfection** of hatred Ps 139_{22}. **2. end, extremity, limit** Jb 28_3 Ne 3_{21}; **boundary** of light with darkness Jb 26_{10}. → כלה *be complete.*

תְּכֵלֶת 49.2.4 n.f. **blue, violet** cloth, thread, etc., oft. תְּכֵלֶת וְאַרְגָּמָן וְתוֹלַעַת שָׁנִי *blue and purple and crimson (material)* Ex 25_4||35_6.

*[**תְּכֵלֶת הַשָּׁנִי**] 0.0.1 pl.n. **Techeleth-hashani.**

*[**תֻּכֶם**] 0.0.11 n.[m.]—pl. cstr. תכמי; sf. תכמיה—alw. pl., **inward parts, bowels** 1QH 15_4, perh. **blood vessels, blood** 1QS 4_{20}.

תכן 18.1.14 vb.—**Qal** 3 Ptc. תֹּכֵן—**weigh up, assess** the heart Pr 21_2, spirit Pr 16_2.

Ni. 10 Pf. נִתְכְּנוּ; impf. יִתָּכֵן—**1. be weighed up, be assessed,** of deeds 1 S $2_{3(Qr)}$ (+ לְ *by* Y.). **2. be adjusted to the standard,** i.e. **be right, just,** of one's ways Ezk 18_{25}.

Pi. 4.1.14 Pf. תִּכֵּן, תִּכַּנְתִּי; + waw Q ויתכנם; ptc. Q מתכן; inf. Q תכן—**1. measure, gauge** heaven Is 40_{12} (+ בְּ *with* span), water Jb 28_{25} (+ בְּ *by* measure), words 4QBark[a] 1.1_{10} (+ בְּ *by* weight). **2. regulate, direct, set in order** spirit of Y. Is 40_{13}, strength 1QS 1_{12}, mighty deeds of wisdom Si 42_{21}; **keep steady, make firm** pillars of the earth Ps 75_4. **3.** perh. **weigh up, assess** labour 4QMyst[a] 10_8.

Pu. 1 מְתֻכָּן—**be weighed out,** of money 1 K 12_{12}.

→ תֹּכֶן I *measurement,* תְּכוּן *measurement,* מַתְכֹּנֶת *measurement,* תָּכִין *meted out,* תָּכְנִית *measurement.*

תֹּכֶן I 2.1.5 n.m. (all refs. analysed under תְּכוּן could belong to תֹּכֶן)—Si תוכן; cstr. תֹּכֶן—**1a. measure, specification** of ephah and bath Ezk 45_{11}, **proportion** of woman's figure Si 26_{17}. **b.** בתכן אצלם **in measure next to them,** i.e. right next to them 3QTr 5_7. **2. specified number, quantity** of bricks Ex 5_{18}. → תכן *measure.*

תֹּכֶן II 1 pl.n. **Tochen.**

תָּכְנִית 2 n.f. **measurement, proportion** Ezk 28_{12} 43_{10}. → תכן I *measure.*

[**תַּכְרִיךְ**] 1 n.[m.]—cstr. תַּכְרִיךְ—**mantle** Est 8_{15}.

[**תֵּל**] 5.0.2.6 n.[m.]—cstr. תֵּל; sf. תִּלָּהּ—**mound,** on which city stood Jos 11_{13}, **heap of ruins (of city)** Dt 13_{17}.

תלא 3 vb. (byform of תלה)—**Qal** 3 Pf. Qr תְּלָאוּם; ptc. pass. תְּלוּאִים—**1. hang up** bones 2 S $21_{12(Qr)}$. **2.** pass. **a. be hung (in suspense), be suspended,** of life Dt 28_{66}. **b. be hung up to** (לְ), i.e. **bent on, attached to** apostasy Ho 11_7.

[**תַּלְאֻבָה**] I 1 n.f.—Pl. תַּלְאֻבוֹת—**drought,** or perh. **heat** Ho 13_5.

*[**תַּלְאֻבָה**] II 1 n.f.—pl. תַּלְאֻבוֹת—**fever** Ho 13_5.

תֵּל אָבִיב 1 pl.n. **Tel-abib.**

תְּלָאָה 4 n.f. **hardship** Ex 18_8 Nm 20_{14} Lm 3_5 Ne 9_{32}. → לאה *be weary;* cf. מַתְּלָאָה *what a weariness!*

תְּלַאשָּׂר 2 pl.n. **Tel-assar.**

תִּלְבֹּשֶׁת 1 n.f. **clothing** Is 59_{17}. → לבשׁ *dress.*

תִּלְגַת פִּלְנֶסֶר *Tilgath-pilneser,* see תִּגְלַת פִּלְאֶסֶר *Tiglath-pileser.*

תלה 28.1.7 vb.—**Qal** 24.1 Pf. תָּלָה, תְּלִינוּ; impf. יִתְלוּ; impv. תְּלֻהוּ; ptc. תֹּלֶה; ptc. pass. תָּלוּי, תְּלוּיִם; inf. תְּלוֹת—**1. hang** someone, in execution Gn 40_{19} (+ עַל *upon* tree). **2a. hang up** a corpse, or parts of it, to dishonour someone Dt 21_{22} (+ עַל *upon* tree) 2 S 4_{12} $21_{12(Kt)}$. **b. hang up, suspend** an object upon (עַל) someone or something Is 22_{24} Ps 137_2. **3a.** pass. **be hung up,** of person, in (בְּ) tree 2 S 18_{10}, upon (עַל) tree Jos 10_{26}; of shields upon (עַל) tower Ca 4_4. **b.** pass ptc. as noun, **one who has been hanged** Dt 21_{23}. **c.** pass. ptc. as adj., **dependent,** of brother Si 7_{18}.

Ni. 2 Pf. נִתְלוּ; + waw וַיִּתָּלוּ—**1. be hung,** in execution Est 2_{23} (+ עַל *upon* tree, i.e. gallows). **2. be hung up,** of person, in order to dishonour Lm 5_{12}.

Pi. 2 Pf. תִּלּוּ—**hang up, suspend** shields Ezk 27_{10} (+ בְּ *in*) 27_{11} (+ עַל *upon*).

→ תְּלִי *quiver.*

תָּלוּל 1 adj. **lofty,** of mountain Ezk 17_{22}.

[**תְּלוּנָה**], see תְּלֻנָּה *murmuring.*

תֶּלַח 1 pr.n.m. **Telah.**

תֵּל חַרְשָׁא 2 pl.n. **Tel-harsha.**

[**תְּלִי**] 1 n.[m.]—sf. תֶּלְיְךָ—**quiver,** used in hunting Gn 27_3. → תלה *hang.*

תלל I 9 vb.—**Hi.** 8 Pf. הֵתֵל, הֵתַלְתְּ; impf. יְהָתֵלּוּ; inf. הָתֵל—**1. mock, trifle with, deceive** someone (בְּ of obj.) Gn 31_7 Jg 16_{10} Jr 9_4. **2. act deceitfully** Ex 8_{25}.

Ho. 1 Pf. הוּתַל—**be deceived, deluded,** of mind Is 44$_{20}$.
→ מְהַתְּלָה *deception;* cf. התל *mock.*

* [תלל] II vb. **Qal, lead into slavery** Ps 137$_3$ (if em. תּוֹלָלֵינוּ *our tormentors* to תּוֹלְלֵינוּ *those who lead us into slavery*).

תֶּלֶם 5.0.1 n.m.—pl. cstr. תַּלְמֵי; sf. תְּלָמֶיהָ—**furrow** Ho 10$_4$ Ps 65$_{11}$ Jb 31$_{38}$.

* [תַּלְמוּד] 0.0.2 n.[m.]—cstr. תלמוד; sf. תלמודכה—**teaching** 4QpNah 3.2$_8$ 4QBéat 14.2$_{15}$. → למד *learn.*

תַּלְמַי 6 pr.n.m. **Talmai.**

תַּלְמִיד 1 n.[m.] **scholar** 1 C 25$_8$. → למד *learn.*

תֵּל מֶלַח 2 pl.n. **Tel-melah.**

[תְּלֻנָּה] 8.0.4 n.f.—pl. cstr. תְּלֻנּוֹת (תְּלוּנֹּת); sf. תְּלֻנֹּתֵיכֶם, תְּלוּנֹּתָם—**murmuring, grumbling, complaint** Ex 16$_7$ Nm 14$_{27}$. → לון I *murmur.*

תלע 1 vb.—**Pu.** 1 Ptc. מְתֻלָּעִים—**be clothed in crimson,** less accurately, **in scarlet** Na 2$_4$. → תּוֹלָע I *worm, crimson,* תּוֹלֵעָה *worm, crimson.*

תַּלְפִּיּוֹת I n.f.pl. **weapons** Ca 4$_4$.

*תַּלְפִּיּוֹת II n.f.pl. **courses, layers** Ca 4$_4$.

תְּלַשַּׂר, see תְּלַאשָּׂר *Tel-assar.*

*תלש 0.0.1 vb.—**Pi.** 0.0.1 Ptc. מתלש—**tear, uproot** 4Q238$_1$.

תַּלְתַּלִּים I 1 n.f.(?)pl. **waving palm branches,** descr. of locks of hair Ca 5$_{11}$.

*תַּלְתַּלִּים II 1 n.f.(?)pl. **drops (of dew),** in locks of hair Ca 5$_{11}$.

תָּם 15.1.2 adj.—f.s. sf. תַּמָּתִי; m.pl. תַּמִּים; sf. Q תמיך—**1. complete, entire,** of boards Ex 26$_{24}$||36$_{29}$. **2. simple, plain, decent,** of person Gn 25$_{27}$. **3. blameless, having integrity,** of person Jb 1$_8$. **4.** as noun, **a. blameless one, one of integrity** Jb 8$_{20}$ Pr 29$_{10}$. **b.** specif. תַּמָּתִי **my perfect one,** as term of affection for female lover Ca 5$_2$ 6$_9$. → תמם *be complete.*

תֹּם 23.0.6 n.[m.]—cstr. תֹּם (תָּם־, Q תום); sf. תֻּמִּי—**1. completeness, full measure** Is 47$_9$; עֶצֶם תֻּמּוֹ *bone of his completeness,* i.e. his very completeness Jb 21$_{23}$. **2. simplicity, innocence** 2 S 15$_{11}$; לְתֻמּוֹ *in his innocence,* i.e. at random 1 K 22$_{34}$||2 C 18$_{33}$. **3. integrity, blamelessness, perfection** Ps 7$_9$ Pr 2$_7$; of one's heart Gn 20$_5$, ways Jb 4$_6$. → תמם *be complete.*

[תֵּמָא], see תֵּימָא I *Tema,* II *Tema.*

תמה 9.2.2 vb.—**Qal** 8.1 Pf. תָּמְהוּ; impf. תִּתְמַהּ, יִתְמְהוּ; impv. תְּמָהוּ; ptc. Q תומהים—**1. be astounded, amazed** Jr 4$_9$ Jb 26$_{11}$ (+ מִן *at*) Ec 5$_7$ (+ עַל *at*), **be stupefied** Is 29$_9$. **2. look in astonishment, look aghast at** (אֶל) Gn 43$_{33}$.

Hi. 0.1 Impf. יתמיה—**be amazed, marvel at** (מִן) Si 43$_{18(M)}$.

Htp. 1 Impv. הִתַּמְּהוּ—**astonish oneself, be astounded** Hb 1$_5$.
→ תִּמָּהוֹן, תְּמַהּ *marvel,* תִּמָּהוֹן *confusion.*

* [תְּמַהּ] 0.4 n.[m.]—pl. cstr. תמהי—**marvel, wonder** Si 16$_{11}$ 33$_{6(Bmg)}$ 43$_{25}$ 48$_{14}$. → תמה *be astounded.*

[תֻּמָּה] 5 n.f.—cstr. תֻּמַּת; sf. תֻּמָּתִי—**integrity** Jb 2$_3$ Pr 11$_3$. → תמם *be complete.*

תִּמָּהוֹן 2.0.3 n.[m.]—cstr. תִּמְהוֹן—**confusion** of mind Dt 28$_{28}$; **panic,** perh. **stupefaction** Zc 12$_4$. → תמה *be astounded.*

[תְּמְהוּת], see תֶּמַח *wiping.*

תַּמּוּז 1 pr.n.m. **Tammuz,** Babylonian (orig. Sumerian) deity Ezk 8$_{14}$.

תְּמוֹל, see אֶתְמוֹל *previous time.*

תְּמוּנָה 10 n.f.—cstr. תְּמוּנַת (תְּמֻנַת); sf. תְּמוּנָתֶךָ—**form, likeness, representation of Y.** Nm 12$_8$; in ref. to cultic image Ex 20$_4$||Dt 5$_8$, nocturnal apparition Jb 4$_{16}$.

* [תְּמוּר] 0.2 prep.—**1. in exchange for, in return for** Si 3$_{14(A)}$. **2. instead of, in place of** Si 4$_{10}$. → מור I *change.*

תְּמוּרָה 6.1 n.f.—cstr. Si תמורת; sf. תְּמוּרָתָהּ, תְּמוּרָתוֹ—**1. exchange,** i.e. thing acquired by exchange Lv 27$_{10}$; **recompense** Jb 15$_{31}$. **2.** activity of **exchanging** Ru 4$_7$; **trade** Jb 20$_{18}$. → מור I *change.*

תְּמוּתָה 2 n.f. **death,** בְּנֵי־תְמוּתָה *sons of death,* i.e. those deserving of, or condemned to, death Ps 79$_{11}$ 102$_{21}$. → מות *die.*

[תֶּמַח] I 2 pr.n.m. **Temah.**

* [תֶּמַח] II 0.1 n.[m] **wiping, cleansing** of ephah and weight Si 42$_{4(M)}$. → מחה I *wipe.*

[תַּמְחוּת], see תֶּמַח *wiping.*

תָּמִיד 104.5.54 n.m.—**1. continuity,** עֹלַת תָּמִיד *burnt offering of continuity,* i.e. continual burnt offering Ex 29$_{42}$, אַנְשֵׁי תָמִיד *men of continuity,* i.e. continually employed Ezk 39$_{14}$. **2.** הַתָּמִיד **the continual burnt offering** Dn

8_{11}. **3.** as adv., **continually, always** Ex 25_{30} Nm 9_{16}.

תָּמִים 91.4.57 adj.—cstr. תְּמִים; f.s. תְּמִימָה; m.pl. תְּמִימִם; cstr. תְּמִימֵי; sf. Si תמימיך; f.pl. תְּמִימֹת (Q תמימות)—**1. complete, entire, whole,** of fat tail Lv 3_9, sabbath Lv 23_{15}, year Lv 25_{30}. **2a. blameless, having integrity, perfect,** of man Ps 18_{26}, heart Ps 119_{80}, law Ps 19_8, way Ps 101_2. **b.** used as adv., **blamelessly, with integrity, perfectly** Ps 15_2. **3. without blemish,** of sacrificial animals Ex 29_1. **4.** perh. **sound, safe,** as adv. accus. 2 S 22_{33}||Ps 18_{33}. **5.** as noun, **a.** of extent, **complete one, perfect one,** תְּמִים דֵּעִים *one perfect of,* i.e. in, *knowledge* Jb 37_{16}. **b.** of character, **blameless one, one of integrity, perfect one** Pr 11_5 28_{10}; תְּמִימֵי־דֶרֶךְ *blameless ones of way,* i.e. those whose way is blameless Ps 119_1. **c. blamelessness, integrity** 1QS 9_2 (sg.) Si 7_6 (pl.), **perfection** of holiness CD 20_2. **d. sincerity, truth** Jos 24_{14} Am 5_{10}. **e. right answer** 1 S 14_{41} (or em. תֻּמִּים *Thummim*). → תמם *be complete.*

תֻּמִּים 5.0.5 n.[m.]pl.—Q תומים; sf. תֻּמֶּיךָ—**Thummim,** sacred oracle in high priest's breastpiece, usu. + אוּרִים *Urim* Ex 28_{30} Lv 8_8. → (?) תמם *be complete.*

תמך 21.3.19 vb.—**Qal** 20.3.19 Pf. תָּמְכָה, תָּמַכְתְּ; impf. יִתְמֹךְ (יִתְמָךְ־); ptc. תּוֹמֵךְ (תוֹמִיךְ), תֹּמְכֶיהָ; inf. abs. תָּמֹךְ; cstr. תְּמֹךְ—**1. take hold of, grasp, seize,** with accus. hand Gn 48_{17}, wisdom Pr 3_{18}, riches Pr 11_{16}; בְּ of obj. bribe Is 33_{15}. **2. hold, keep hold of, hold fast (to),** with accus. sceptre Am 1_5, words Pr 4_4; בְּ of obj. way 4QBéat 2.2_1, covenant 1QH 10_{21}. **3. hold up, uphold, support,** with accus. Israel Is 41_{10} (+ בְּ *with* right hand); בְּ of obj. person Ps 41_{13}, hand Ex 17_{12}.

Ni. 1 Impf. יִתָּמֵךְ—**be caught, be held fast** with (בְּ) cords Pr 5_{22}.

*[תְּמַכְאֵל] 0.0.0.1 pr.n.m. **Temachel.**

תמם 64.4.48.1 vb.—**Qal** 54.2.38.1 Pf. תַּם, תָּמּוּ (תַּמּוּ), תַּמְנוּ (תַּמְנוּ); impf. יִתֹּם, תִּתֹּם, אִיתָּם, יִתַּמּוּ (יִתָּמּוּ); inf. תֹּם (תֹּם־), תֻּמּוֹ (תַּמּוֹ)—**1. be completed, finished,** of house 1 K 6_{22}, work 1 K 7_{22}, words Dt 31_{24}. **2. be complete, come to an end,** of year Gn 47_{18}, (number of) people 1 S 16_{11}. **3. come to an end, be gone, cease, be spent,** of blossom Is 18_5, bread Jr 37_{21} (+ מִן *from* city), strength Lv 26_{20} (+ לְרִיק *in vain*), transgression 1QS 10_{23}. **4. be consumed, be destroyed, perish, die out,** of persons Nm 14_{35} Ps 104_{35} (+ מִן *from* earth), scroll Jr 36_{23}, rust Ezk 24_{11}. **5.** as auxiliary verb, **do (something) completely, finish (doing), be wholly,** with inf. Jos 3_{17} Nm 17_{28}, fin. verb Jos 3_{16}. **6. be blameless, be perfect,** of person Ps 19_{14}, way 1QS 8_{25}.

Pi. 0.0.1 Impf. יתממ[ו]—**destroy** with (בְּ) fire 11QMelch 3_7.

Hi. 8.2.9 Pf. הֵתַמּוּ; impf. יַתֵּם; + waw וַהֲתִמֹּתִי; impv. הָתֵם; inf. abs. הָתֵם; cstr. הָתֵם (הֲתִמְּךָ)—**1. complete, accomplish** events 4QAges[a] 1_1, mourning Si 38_{17}. **2. complete (the cooking of)** flesh Ezk 24_{10}. **3. cause to cease, make an end of** strength 1QH 13_{28}, sin Dn $9_{24(Qr)}$. **4. consume, destroy** tree 1QH 11_{29}, uncleanness Ezk 22_{15} (+ מִן *from*). **5. make blameless, make perfect** heart Si 49_3, ways Jb 22_3. **6. reckon the sum of** money 2 K 22_4. **7. finish, cease doing,** with ptc. Is 33_1. **8. be complete (in number)** Dn 8_{23}. **9. settle a matter** 2 S 20_{18}.

Htp. 2 Impf. תִּתַּמָּם—**show oneself blameless, deal in integrity** with (עִם) 2 S 22_{26}||Ps 18_{26}.

→ תָּם *complete,* תֹּם *completeness,* תָּמִים *complete,* תֻּמָּה *integrity,* (?) מְתֹם *well-being,* אוֹרְתוֹם *perfect light,* (?) תֻּמִּים *Thummim.*

תֵּמָן, see תֵּימָן I *south,* III *Teman.*

תִּמְנָה 12 pl.n. **Timnah.**

*[תִּמְנוֹ] 0.0.1 pl.n. **Timno.**

תֵּמָנִי, see תֵּימָנִי *Temanite.*

תִּמְנִי 1 gent. **Timnite.**

תִּמְנָע 6.0.1 pr.n.m.&f. **Timna.**

תִּמְנַת־חֶרֶס 1 pl.n. **Timnath-heres.**

תִּמְנַת־סֶרַח 2 pl.n. **Timnath-serah.**

תֶּמֶס 1 n.[m.] **melting away, slime** of snail Ps 58_9. → מסס *melt.*

תָּמָר I 12 n.m.—pl. תְּמָרִים—**palm tree,** specif. **date-palm** (*Phoenix dactylifera*) Ex 15_{27} Lv 23_{40}. → cf. תֹּמֶר *palm tree,* תִּמֹּרָה *(decorative) palm tree,* (?) תִּימָרָה *column.*

תָּמָר II 22 pr.n.f. **Tamar.**

תָּמָר III 3 pl.n. **Tamar.**

[**תֹּמֶר**] 2 n.[m.] (byform of תָּמָר I)—cstr. תֹּמֶר—**1. palm tree** Jg 4_5. **2. post,** i.e. scarecrow Jr 10_5. → cf. תָּמָר I *palm tree.*

תִּמֹרָה 19 n.m.—pl. תִּמֹרִים, תִּמֹרֹת; sf. Qr תִּמֹרָיו (Kt תמרו)—**(decorative) palm tree,** as carving or engraving in temple 1 K 6_{29} Ezk 40_{16}. → cf. תָּמָר I *palm tree.*

תַּמְרוּק 4 n.[m.]—pl. cstr. תַּמְרוּקֵי; sf. תַּמְרוּקֶיהָ—**1. cosmetic treatment,** for women, perh. **rubbing (with oil, ointment), massage** Est $2_{3.9.12}$. **2. scouring, cleansing,** for evil Pr $20_{30(Qr)}$ (Kt תמריק *it cleanses* [מרק I hi.], or תַּמְרִיק *hurt*). → מרק I *polish.*

[תַּמְרוּר] I 3.1 n.[m.]—pl. תַּמְרוּרִים; cstr. Si תמרורי—**bitterness** Ho 12_{15} Si 32_{20}; מִסְפַּד תַּמְרוּרִים *mourning of bitterness(es),* i.e. bitter mourning Jr 6_{26}. → מרר I *be bitter.*

[תַּמְרוּר] II 1 n.[m.]—pl. תַּמְרוּרִים—**guidepost, waymark** Jr 31_{21}.

***[תַּמְרִיק]** 1 n.[m.] **hurt** Pr $20_{30(Kt)}$ (Qr תַּמְרוּק *scouring*).

[תַּן] 14 n.[m.]&f.—pl. תַּנִּים (Kt תנין); cstr. תַּנּוֹת—**jackal** (*Canis aureus*) Is 13_{22}.

תנה I 2 vb.—**Qal** 1 Impf. יִתְנוּ—**hire lovers,** i.e. recruit allies Ho 8_{10}.

Hi. 1 Pf הִתְנוּ—**hire** lovers Ho 8_{9}.

תנה II 2 vb.—**Pi.** 2 Impf. יְתַנּוּ; inf. תַּנּוֹת—**1. recount, recite** righteousness Jg 5_{11}. **2. commemorate,** perh. **lament** (לְ of obj.) someone Jg 11_{40}.

[תְּנוּאָה] 2 n.f.—sf. תְּנוּאָתִי; pl. תְּנוּאוֹת—**1. opposition** of, i.e. from, Y. Nm 14_{34}. **2.** pl. **grounds for opposition** Jb 33_{10}. → נוא *restrain.*

תְּנוּבָה 5.2.6 n.f.—cstr. תְּנוּבַת; sf. תְּנוּבָתִי; pl. Si, Q תנובות; cstr. תְּנוּבֹת—**produce, fruit** of field Dt 32_{13}, fig tree Jg 9_{11}, bee Si 11_{3}. → נוב *flow.*

[תְּנוּךְ] 8 n.[m.]—cstr. תְּנוּךְ—**lobe** of ear, alw. + בֹּהֶן *thumb, big toe* Ex 29_{20} Lv 8_{23} 14_{14}.

תְּנוּמָה 5.0.1 n.f.—pl. תְּנוּמוֹת—**slumber,** sg. Ps 132_{4}; pl., assoc. with vision Jb 33_{15}, laziness Pr 6_{10}. → נום I *be drowsy.*

תְּנוּפָה I 30.1.4 n.f.—cstr. תְּנוּפַת; pl. cstr. תְּנוּפֹת; sf. Q תנופותמה—**1. wave offering, offering (presented by waving), a.** usu. item offered in sacrifice Ex 29_{24}, portion of it as priest's due Lv 7_{34}. **b.** Levites as a wave offering Nm 8_{11}. **c.** gold and bronze for tabernacle Ex $38_{24.29}$. **d.** offering placed before image Si 30_{18}. **2. waving** of hand Is 19_{16}, perh. **brandishing (weapons)** Is 30_{32}. → נוף I *wave.*

***תְּנוּפָה** II 30.1.4 n.f.—cstr. תְּנוּפַת; pl. cstr. תְּנוּפֹת; sf. Q תנופותמה—**1. raised offering, offering (presented by raising), a.** usu. item offered in sacrifice Ex 29_{24}, portion of it as priest's due Lv 7_{34}. **b.** Levites as a raised offering Nm 8_{11}. **c.** gold and bronze for tabernacle Ex $38_{24.29}$. **d.** offering placed before image Si 30_{18}. **2. raising** of hand Is 19_{16}, perh. **brandishing (weapons)** Is 30_{32}. → נוף V *raise.*

***תְּנוּפָה** III 28.1.4 n.f.—cstr. תְּנוּפַת; pl. cstr. תְּנוּפֹת; sf. Q תנופותמה—**special contribution, additional gift, 1.** usu. item offered in sacrifice Ex 29_{24}, portion of it as priest's due Lv 7_{34}. **2.** Levites as a special contribution Nm 8_{11}. **3.** gold and bronze for tabernacle Ex $38_{24.29}$. **4.** placed before image Si 30_{18}. → נוף IV *declare superfluous.*

תַּנּוּר 15.2 n.m.—cstr. תַּנּוּר; pl. תַּנּוּרִים; sf. תַּנּוּרֶיךָ—**oven, firepot** Gn 15_{17}, for baking Ex 7_{28} Lv 2_{4}.

[תַּנְחוּם] 5.0.3 n.m.—pl. תַּנְחוּמִים; cstr. תַּנְחֻמוֹת; sf. תַּנְחוּמֶיךָ, תַּנְחוּמֹתֵיכֶם—alw. pl., **consolation(s), comfort** Is 66_{11} Jr 16_{7} Jb 15_{11}. → נחם *regret.*

תַּנְחוּמִים, see תַּנְחוּם *consolation.*

***[תַּנְחֻם]** 0.0.0.23 pr.n.m. **Tanhum.**

תַּנְחֻמוֹת, see תַּנְחוּם *consolation.*

תַּנְחֻמֶת 2 pr.n.m. **Tanhumeth.**

תַּנִּים, see תַּן *jackal,* תַּנִּין *sea monster.*

תַּנִּין I 15.0.6 n.m.—תַּנִּים; pl. תַּנִּינִם—**1. monster, dragon** Jr 51_{34}; in sea Gn 1_{21} Is 27_{1}, river Ezk 29_{3}; עֵין הַתַּנִּין *Spring of the Dragon* Ne 2_{13}. **2. serpent** Ex 7_{9} Dt 32_{33}.

[תַּנִּין] II, see תַּן *jackal.*

תִּנְשֶׁמֶת 3.0.1 n.f.—תִּנְשָׁמֶת—**1. white owl,** or perh. **little owl** or **water hen** Lv 11_{18}. **2.** perh. **chameleon** Lv 11_{30}. → נשם *pant.*

***[תְּסִבָּה]** 0.0.0.1 n.f. **going round,** תסבת הבקר *going round of the morning,* perh. morning tour, or, duration of the morning Lachish ost. 4_{9}. → סבב *surround.*

***[תְּסִבָּה]** 0.0.1 n.f. **rotation,** תסובות כלי אור *rotations of vessels of light* 4QPrQuot 1.3_{9} (corrected from תסובת *rotation of*). → סבב *surround.*

תעב 22.2.18 vb.—**Ni.** 3.0.2 Pf. נִתְעַב; ptc. נִתְעָב—**be abhorred, abhorrent, abominable,** of person Jb 15_{16}, word 1 C 21_{6} (+ אֶת *with,* i.e. to).

Pi. 15.2.15 Pf. תִּעֲבוּנִי; impf. יְתָעֵב; + waw וַיְתָעֵב, וָאֲתַעֲבָה;

ptc. מְתָעֵב, מְתַעֲבִים; inf. abs. תָּעֵב; cstr. Q תעב—**1. abhor, treat as an abomination,** obj. person Ps 5:7, image of god 1QS 4:5, food Ps 107:18, justice Mc 3:9. **2. make one's beauty abominable** Ezk 16:25.

Hi. 4.0.1 Pf. הִתְעִיבוּ, הִתְעַבְתְּ; + waw וַיַּתְעֵב—**1. act abominably** 1 K 21:26 Ezk 16:52 (+ מִן *[more] than*). **2. make abominable, do abominably,** obj. deeds Ps 14:1, injustice Ps 53:2.

→ תּוֹעֵבָה *abomination.*

תעה 50.2.30 vb. (byform of טעה)—**Qal** 27.1.15 Pf. תָּעָה, תָּעִיתִי; impf. יִתְעוּ, תֵּתַע; ptc. תֹּעֶה, Q תועים; inf. תְּעוֹת—**1. wander (about), stray,** of persons Gn 21:14 (+ בְּ *in* steppe) Is 53:6 (+ כְּ *like* sheep), animals Ex 23:4. **2. stagger, reel through** (בְּ or מִן) strong drink Is 28:7.7. **3.** ethically, **go astray, err** Ezk 14:11 (+ מֵאַחֲרֵי *from* Y.) 44:10 (+ מֵעַל *from* Y.) Pr 21:16 (+ מִן *from* way) CD 3:1 (+ בְּ *through* stubbornness); תֹּעֵי־רוּחַ *ones who err of,* i.e. in, *spirit* Is 29:24.

Ni. 2 Pf. נִתְעָה; inf. הִתָּעוֹת—**1. be made to stagger, stagger about** Is 19:14. **3. allow oneself to be led astray, deceive oneself** Jb 15:31.

Hi. 21.1.15 Pf. הִתְעָה, הִתְעוּ; impf. תַּתְעֵם; + waw וַיַּתַע (וַיַּתְעֵם), וַיַּתְעוּ; ptc. מַתְעֶה, מַתְעִים, Si מתעות; inf. Q לתעות—**1a. cause to wander** Gn 20:13 (+ מִן *from*). **b. cause to wander about, cause to stray** Ps 107:40. **2. cause to stagger about** like (כְּ) drunkard Jb 12:25. **3. lead astray, mislead, cause to err** 2 K 21:9||2 C 33:9 Is 63:17 (+ מִן *from* ways) Jr 23:32 (+ בְּ *with* falsehood). **4. go astray, err** at the cost of (בְּ) one's life Jr 42:20.

→ תּוֹעָה *error, confusion,* תְּעוּת *error.*

תֹּעוּ, 5 pr.n.m. **Tou,** also as **תֹּעִי Toi.**

תְּעוּדָה 3.0.34 n.f.—cstr. Q תעודת; sf. Q תעודתו; pl. cstr. Q תעודות; sf. Q תעודותיו—**1. testimony, command, instruction** of Y. perh. 1QM 3:4, military commander 1QM 4:5; in ref. to prophetic message Is 8:16.20. **2. (method of) attestation,** in legal transaction Ru 4:7. **3. fixed time, predetermined time or thing** 1QS 1:9 1QM 11:8 MasShirShabb 1:3, **destiny** 1QH 9:19. **4. convocation, required gathering** 1QSa 1:25.26. → עוד I *bear witness.*

*[תְּעוּפָה] I 0.1 n.f. perh. **magnificence** Si 45:7(Bmg).

[תְּעוּפָה] II, see תְּעָפָה *darkness.*

*[תָּעוּת] 0.0.8 n.f.—cstr. תעות; sf. תעותם; pl. תעואת—**error, straying** 1QH 10:14 1QS 3:21. → תעה *wander.*

תֹּעִי *Toi,* see תֹּעוּ *Tou.*

תְּעָלָה I 9.0.1 n.f.—cstr. תְּעָלַת; pl. cstr. תְּעָלֹתֶיהָ—**1. (natural) watercourse, channel, stream** Ezk 31:4. **2. (man-made) conduit, aqueduct** 2 K 20:20. **3. trench,** around altar 1 K 18:32, **channel,** around laver 11QT 32:12. → עלה I *go up.*

תְּעָלָה II 2 n.f. **healing,** growth of new flesh over wound Jr 30:13 46:11. → עלה I *go up.*

*[תַּעֲלוּל] 1 n.m.—pl. תַּעֲלוּלִים—**child** Is 3:4. → עלל III *act the child.*

תַּעֲלוּלִים 2 n.m.pl.—pl. sf. תַּעֲלֻלֵיהֶם—**1. wantonness,** i.e. wanton person Is 3:4. **2. wanton dealing, harsh treatment** Is 66:4. → עלל I *do.*

[תַּעֲלֻמָה] 3 n.f.—תַּעֲלֻמָה; pl. cstr. תַּעֲלֻמוֹת—**hidden thing, secret** Jb 28:11; of the heart Ps 44:22, of wisdom Jb 11:6. → עלם I *hide.*

תַּעֲנוּג 5.12.5 n.[m.]—cstr. Q תענוג; pl. תַּעֲנוּגִים; pl. cstr. תַּעֲנֻגוֹת; sf. תַּעֲנוּגַיִךְ—**1. delight, pleasure** Ec 2:8; בְּנֵי תַּעֲנוּגָיִךְ *sons of your delight,* i.e. in whom you delight Mc 1:16. **2. luxury** Pr 19:10. **3. delicacy, delicacies** Si 37:28(Bmg, D) 4QInstr[b] 2.2:19. → ענג I *be delicate.*

[תַּעֲנִית] 1.0.9 n.f.—sf. תַּעֲנִיתִי; pl. Q תענייות; cstr. Q תעניות—**1. humiliation, affliction** 4QShir[a] 1:7. **2. (self-) humiliation,** as act of penitence, **fasting** Ezr 9:5 CD 6:19. → ענה II *be afflicted.*

תַּעְנָךְ 7 pl.n. **Taanach.**

תעע 2.0.3 vb.—**Pilp.** 1.0.3 Pf. Q תעתעו; ptc. מְתַעְתֵּעַ—**1. mock someone** (בְּ of obj.) 4QPrFêtes[c] 16:5. **2.** ptc. as noun, **mocker** Gn 27:12.

Htpal. 1.0.1 Impf. Q יתעתעו; ptc. מִתַּעְתְּעִים—**mock** someone, with accus. 1QpHab 4:3; בְּ of obj. 2 C 36:16.

→ תַּעְתֻּעִים *mockery.*

*[תְּעָפָה] n.f. **darkness** Jb 11:17 (if em. תָּעֻפָה *it will be dark,* from עוף II).

[תַּעֲצֻמָה] 1 n.f.—pl. תַּעֲצֻמוֹת—**might** Ps 68:36. → עצם I *be mighty.*

תַּעַר I 7.0.1 n.[m.]—sf. תַּעְרָהּ—**sheath,** for sword 1 S 17:51. → ערה *be bare.*

[תַּעַר] II 6 n.m.&f.—cstr. תַּעַר—**1. razor,** for shaving Nm 6:5. **2. knife of scribe** Jr 36:23. → ערה *be bare.*

[תַּעֲרֻבָה] 2 n.f. **pledge, security,** בְּנֵי הַתַּעֲרֻבוֹת *the sons of the pledges,* i.e. hostages 2 K 14_{14}‖2 C 25_{25}. → ערב II *stand surety.*

*[תַּעֲרֹבֶת] 0.0.3 n.f.—תערובת; cstr. תערובת—**mixing, (inter)mingling** of divisions of priests and Levites 11QT 45_7; in ref. to mixed marriage 4QMMT $B_{48.50}$. → ערב I *mix.*

[תַּעֲרוֹבֶת], see תַּעֲרֹבֶת *mixture.*

תַּעְתֻּעִים 2 n.[m.]pl. **mockery** Jr 10_{15}‖51_{18}. → תעע *mock.*

תֹּף 17.0.1 n.[m.]—pl. תֻּפִּים; sf. תֻּפַּיִךְ—**1. timbrel, tambourine** Gn 31_{27} Ps 81_3. **2.** perh. **earring, pendant** Ezk 28_{13}. → תפף *play the timbrel.*

תִּפְאָרָה 2 n.f. (byform of תִּפְאֶרֶת)—**glory** Is 28_5 Jr 48_{17}. → פאר I *glorify.*

תִּפְאֶרֶת 49.12.26 n.f.—תִּפְאֶרֶת; cstr. תִּפְאֶרֶת; sf. תִּפְאַרְתִּי—**1. glory,** i.e. **a. majesty** of, or assoc. with, Y. Ps 71_8 1 C 29_{11}; בֵּית תִּפְאַרְתִּי *house of my glory,* i.e. my glorious house Is 60_7. **b. splendour, majesty** of king Est 1_4, Israel Lm 2_1, the heavenly height 4QBer[a] 1.2_4, crown Is 62_3. **c. pride, boasting** Is 10_{12}, object of pride, boasting Is 20_5 Pr 17_6. **d. honour, renown** of humans Dt 26_{19} Jg 4_9. **2. beauty, adornment** of a person Is 44_{13}; בִּגְדֵי תִּפְאַרְתֵּךְ *garments of your beauty,* i.e. your beautiful garments Is 52_1; **finery** of anklets Is 3_{18}. → פאר I *glorify;* cf. תִּפְאָרָה *glory.*

תַּפּוּחַ I 6 n.[m.]—pl. תַּפּוּחִים; cstr. תַּפּוּחֵי—**1. apple tree** Jl 1_{12}. **2. apple** Ca 2_5. **3. ornamental apple** Pr 25_{11}. → נפח I *blow.*

תַּפּוּחַ II 1 pr.n.m. **Tappuah.**

תַּפּוּחַ III 5 pl.n. **Tappuah.**

[תְּפוֹצָה] 1 n.f. pl.—sf. תְּפוֹצוֹתֵיכֶם—**dispersion** Jr 25_{34}. → פוץ I *scatter.*

[תֻּפִינִים] 1 n.[m.]pl.—cstr. תֻּפִינֵי—perh. **baked pieces** Lv 6_{14} (or em. תְּפַתֶּנָּה *you shall crumble it,* from פתת).

*תפל 1 vb.—**Htp.** 1 תִּתַּפָּל—**act stupidly with** (עִם) 2 S 22_{27} (‖Ps 18_{27} פתל htp. *deal tortuously*). → תָּפֵל I *tasteless,* תִּפְלָה *tastelessness,* תְּפִלָּה *insolence.*

תָּפֵל I 2.0.1 adj.—as noun, **1. tasteless thing** Jb 6_6. **2. stupidity, insanity** 5QCurses$_3$. **3. folly, worthlessness** Lm 2_{14}. → תפל *be stupid.*

תָּפֵל II 6.0.3 n.[m.] **whitewash, plaster** Ezk 13_{10} 22_{28}.

תֹּפֶל 1 pl.n. **Tophel.**

תִּפְלָה 3 n.f. **tastelessness, unseemliness** Jr 23_{13} Jb 1_{22} 24_{12} (mss תְּפִלָּה *prayer*). → תפל *be stupid.*

*[תְּפִלָּה] 0.0.1 n.f.—תופלה—**insolence, impertinence** 4QBéat 14.2_{28}. → תפל *be stupid.*

תְּפִלָּה 77.8.10 n.f.—cstr. תְּפִלַּת; sf. תְּפִלָּתִי; pl. cstr. תְּפִלּוֹת—**prayer,** תְּפִלַּת עַמֶּךָ *prayer of your people* Ps 80_5, תְּפִלָּה לְדָוִד *a prayer of David* Ps 17_1, תפלה ליום כפורים *a prayer for the day of atonement* 1QLitPr 1_6, תְּפִלָּתוֹ אֶל־אֱלֹהָיו *his prayer to his God* 2 C 33_{18}, בֵּית תְּפִלָּה *house of prayer* Is 56_7. → פלל I *intervene.*

[תִּפְלֶצֶת] 1 n.f.—sf. תִּפְלַצְתְּךָ—**terror** Jr 49_{16}. → פלץ *tremble.*

תִּפְסַח 2 pl.n. **Tiphsah.**

תפף 2 vb.—**Qal** 1 Ptc. תּוֹפְפוֹת—**play the timbrel** Ps 68_{26}.
Po. 1 Ptc. מְתֹפְפֹת—**beat upon** (עַל) breast Na 2_8.
→ תֹּף *timbrel.*

תפר 4 vb.—**Qal** 3 Pf. תָּפַרְתִּי; + waw וַיִּתְפְּרוּ; inf. לִתְפּוֹר—**sew, sew together** fig leaves Gn 3_7, sackcloth Jb 16_{15} (+ עַל *upon* skin); abs. Ec 3_7.

Pi. 1 Ptc. מְתַפְּרוֹת—**sew** bands **upon** (עַל) wrists Ezk 13_{18}.

תפשׂ 65.2.17 vb.—**Qal** 49.2.9 Pf. תָּפַשׂ; impf. יִתְפֹּשׂ; impv. תִּפְשׂוּ; ptc. תֹּפֵשׂ, תֹּפְשֵׂי; ptc. pass. תָּפוּשׂ; inf. abs. תָּפֹשׂ; cstr. תְּפֹשׂ (לְתָפְשׂוֹ, תָּפְשָׂה)—**1. take hold of, seize,** with accus. person Gn 39_{12} (+ בְּ *by* garment), heel Si 12_{17}; בְּ of obj. person Dt 21_{19}, garment 1 K 11_{30}. **2a. seize, capture, catch** someone, with accus. 1 S 23_{26}, בְּ of obj. CD 4_{16} (+ בְּ *with* net). **b.** תפשׂ חַי **capture, take** someone **alive** Jos 8_{23}. **3. seize possession of, capture, conquer** city Dt 20_{19}. **4. hold in possession, occupy** city Jr 40_{10}, height Jr 49_{16}. **5. handle, wield, use skilfully** lyre and pipe Gn 4_{21}, bow Am 2_{15}, sickle Jr 50_{16}. **6. handle, deal with, engage in** war Nm 31_{27}, the law Jr 2_8. **7. handle disrespectfully, profane** name of Y. Pr 30_9. **8.** pass. **be overlaid,** תָּפוּשׂ זָהָב וָכֶסֶף *overlaid with gold and silver* Hb 2_{19}.

Ni. 15.0.8 Pf. נִתְפְּשָׂה; impf. תִּתָּפֵשׂ; + waw וְנִתְפַּשׂ; ptc. Q נתפשים; inf. הִתָּפֵשׂ—**1. be caught, be captured,** of person Jr 34_3, lion Ezk 19_4 (+ בְּ *in* pit). **2. be seized, captured,** of stronghold Jr 48_{41}, fords Jr 51_{32}. **3. be caught (in the act)** Nm 5_{13} CD 4_{20} (+ בְּ *in* prostitution).

Pi. 1 Impf. תְּתַפֵּשׂ—**grasp** lizard with (בְּ) hands Pr 30₂₈.

תֹּפֶת I 1 n.f. **spitting,** תֹּפֶת לְפָנִים *a spitting in the face,* i.e. one in whose face people spit Jb 17₆.

תֹּפֶת II 9 pl.n. **Topheth.**

תָּפְתֶּה 1 pl.n. **Topheth.**

תָּקְהַת 1 pr.n.m. **Tokhath.**

[**תִּקְוָה**] I 3 n.f.—cstr. תִּקְוַת—**cord, thread** Jos 2₁₈.₂₁ perh. Jb 7₆. → קוה I *wait.*

תִּקְוָה II 32.8.11 n.f.—cstr. תִּקְוַת; sf. תִּקְוָתִי—**1. hope, expectation** Jr 31₁₇; אֲסִירֵי הַתִּקְוָה *the prisoners of hope,* i.e. with hope of deliverance Zc 9₁₂. **2. (result of) hope, hoped for outcome, prospect** Jr 29₁₁ Jb 14₁₉. **3. (grounds for) hope** Ps 71₅ Jb 4₆. → קוה I *wait.*

תִּקְוָה III 2 pr.n.m. **Tikvah.**

* [**תְּקוּם**] 0.0.1 n.m. perh. **power,** תקומי הארץ *powers of the earth,* i.e. those who exercise power in it GnzPs 3₁₇. → קום *arise.*

תְּקוּמָה 1 n.f. **power to stand** before enemies Lv 26₃₇. → קום *arise.*

[**תְּקוֹמֵם**] 1 n.[m.]—תְּקוֹמְמֶיךָ—**one who rises up** Ps 139₂₁. → קום *arise.*

* [**תִּקּוּן**] 0.0.1 n.[m.]—pl. sf. תקוניו—**base** XḤev/SeHymn 3₉. → תקן *be straight.*

תָּקוֹעַ 1 n.[m.] **horn, trumpet,** sounded for battle Ezk 7₁₄. → תקע *thrust.*

תְּקוֹעַ I 7 pl.n. **Tekoa.**

* [**תְּקוֹעַ**] II 0.0.0.1 pr.n.[m.] **Tekoa.**

תְּקוֹעִי 7 gent. **Tekoite.**

* [**תְּקוֹף**] 0.1 n.[m.] **strength** Si 6₁₄. → תקף *be strong.*

[**תְּקוּפָה**] 4.1.14 n.f.—cstr. תְּקוּפַת; sf. תְּקוּפָתוֹ; pl. cstr. תְּקֻפוֹת; sf. Q תקופותיהמה—**circuit** of the sun Ps 19₇, moon, i.e. its phases Si 43₇; **circulation, coming round, turn(ing-point)** of light, darkness, times 1QS 10₁.₂.₃, the day 1QH 20₅, days, i.e. in due time 1 S 1₂₀, the year, i.e. its end or beginning Ex 34₂₂; **cycle, period** of years 1QH 9₂₄. → נקף II *go around.*

* [**תְּקִיעָה**] 0.0.0.1 n.f. **blowing (of ram's horn)** Temple area inscr. → תקע *thrust, blow.*

תַּקִּיף 1.1.2 adj. **strong, mighty,** of angel 11QPsApᵃ 4₅, person Ec 6₁₀ (שֶׁתַּקִּיף מִמֶּנּוּ [Qr] *one who is stronger than he*), shield Si 6₁₄₍C₎. → תקף *be strong.*

* **תקל** 0.3 vb.—**Ni.** 0.2 Pf. נתקל; impf. תתקל—**stumble** Si 13₂₃; perh. **allow oneself to stumble** Si 35₂₀.

Hi. 0.1 Pf. התקילני—**cause to stumble** Si 15₁₂.

→ מִתְקָל *offence,* תַּקָּלָה *stumbling block.*

* [**תַּקָּלָה**] 0.1 n.f. **stumbling block** Si 34₇. → תקל *stumble.*

תקן 3.1.2 vb.—**Qal** 1 Inf. לִתְקֹן—**become straight** Ec 1₁₅.

Pi. 2.1.2 Pf. תִּקֵּן; impf. Q יתקן; inf. תַּקֵּן—**1. make straight** what Y. has bent Ec 7₁₃. **2a. arrange, set in order** proverbs Ec 12₉, song Si 47₉₍B₎. **b. prepare** place MurEpBarCᵇ₄.

→ תִּקּוּן *base.*

תקע 68.0.22 vb.—**Qal** 65.0.22 Pf. תָּקַע; impf. יִתְקַע; + waw וַיִּתְקַע; impv. תִּקְעוּ; ptc. תֹּקֵעַ, תּוֹקְעִים; ptc. pass. תְּקוּעָה; inf. abs. תָּקוֹעַ; cstr. תְּקֹעַ—**1. thrust, drive** sword into (בְּ) belly Jg 3₂₁, locusts into sea (יָמָּה) Ex 10₁₉. **2a. pitch** tent Gn 31₂₅. **b.** without obj., **encamp** Gn 31₂₅. **3. fasten** body to (בְּ) wall 1 S 31₁₀. **4. strike, clap** hands, in triumph Na 3₁₉, to ratify agreement Pr 6₁. **5. blow, give a blast, sound an alarm, a.** with accus. ram's horn (שׁוֹפָר) Jos 6₉, alarm (תְּרוּעָה) Nm 10₅, sound (קוֹל) 1QM 8₅ (+ בְּ *with* trumpet). **b.** with בְּ of obj. trumpet (חֲצוֹצְרָה) Nm 10₈, ram's horn (שׁוֹפָר) Jos 6₄. **c.** without obj. Nm 10₇. **6.** pass. **be fastened,** of peg, in (בְּ) place Is 22₂₅.

Ni. 3 Impf. יִתָּקַע (יִתָּקֵעַ)—**1. be struck, allow oneself to be struck,** with (לְ) the hand, to ratify agreement Jb 17₃. **2. be blown,** of ram's horn Am 3₆.

→ תֵּקַע *blast,* תָּקוֹעַ *horn,* תְּקִיעָה *blowing (of ram's horn),* תֹּקְעִים *handshake.*

[**תֵּקַע**] 1 n.[m.]—cstr. תֵּקַע—**blast** of ram's horn Ps 150₃. → תקע *thrust, blow.*

* **תֹּקְעִים** 1 n.[m.]pl. **handshake, striking of hands,** in making a bargain Pr 11₁₅. → תקע *thrust, blow.*

תקף 4.0.1 vb.—**Qal** 3.0.1 Impf. יִתְקְפוֹ, תִּתְקְפֵהוּ—**1. be strong, be courageous,** of heart 11QPsᵃ 19₁₂. **2. prevail against, overpower** someone Jb 14₂₀.

Hi. 1 Pf. Kt התקיף—**be stronger** than (מִן) Ec 6₁₀₍Kt₎.

→ תַּקִּיף *strong,* תְּקוֹף *strength,* תֹּקֶף *might.*

תֹּקֶף 3 n.[m.]—cstr. תֹּקֶף; sf. תָּקְפּוֹ—**might, power, authority** Est 9₂₉ 10₂ Dn 11₁₇. → תקף *be strong.*

תֹּר I 14.0.3 n.f.&m.—תּוֹר; sf. תּוֹרְךָ; pl. תֹּרִים—**turtledove** (*Streptopelia turtur*) Gn 15$_9$.

[תּוּר] II, see תּוֹר I *plait, turn.*

תַּרְאֲלָה 1 pl.n. **Taralah.**

[תַּרְבּוּת] 1.0.1 n.f.—cstr. תַּרְבּוּת—**1. increase** of kingdom 4QpUnid 3$_2$. **2. brood** of sinful men Nm 32$_{14}$. → רבה I *be much.*

תַּרְבִּית 6.0.2 n.f. **increase, usury, profit** Lv 25$_{36}$ Ezk 18$_8$ 22$_{12}$ Pr 28$_8$. → רבה I *be much.*

תִּרְגַּלְתִּי Ho 11$_3$, see רגל III *use the foot,* tiphel.

תרגם 1 vb.—**Pu.** 1 Ptc. מְתֻרְגָּם—**be translated,** of letter Ezr 4$_7$. → תְּרְגְּמָן *interpreter.*

* [תְּרְגְּמָן] 0.0.1 n.m. **interpreter** 4QCommGenC 16$_2$ (unless [מ]תרגמן in same sense). → תרגם *translate.*

תַּרְדֵּמָה 7.0.1 n.f.—cstr. תַּרְדֵּמַת—**deep sleep,** caused by Y. Gn 2$_{21}$ 1 S 26$_{12}$, laziness Pr 19$_{15}$. → רדם *sleep deeply.*

תִּרְהָקָה 2 pr.n.m. **Tirhakah.**

* [תְּרוֹם] 0.0.1 n.[m.] perh. **offering (of praise)** 4QShir Shabb[f] 32$_3$. → רום *be high.*

תְּרוּמָה 76.2.18 n.f.—cstr. תְּרוּמַת; sf. תְּרוּמָתִי; pl. תְּרוּמֹת; cstr. תְּרוּמֹת; sf. תְּרוּמֹתֵינוּ—**contribution, offering, 1.** of produce to Y. Nm 15$_{19}$. **2.** to Y., as contribution for priests Lv 22$_{12}$, specif. cake Lv 7$_{14}$, thigh of sacrificed animal Ex 29$_{27}$; for Levites, from tithes Nm 18$_{24}$. **3.** materials for the tabernacle and its furnishings Ex 25$_2$. **4.** half-shekel for service of sanctuary Ex 30$_{13}$. **5.** portion of land set apart for temple and priests Ezk 45$_1$. **6.** offering (of praise) 4QShirShabb[f] 23.2$_{12}$. **7.** contribution for prince Ezk 45$_{13}$. → רום *be high.*

תְּרוּמִיָּה 1 n.f. **special contribution** of land for priests Ezk 48$_{12}$. → רום *be high.*

תְּרוּעָה 36.1.19 n.f.—cstr. תְּרוּעַת—**1. (joyful) shout, shouting,** as cry of jubilation 1 S 4$_5$; in worship Ps 33$_3$. **2. blast, sounding** of horn or trumpet, on day of atonement Lv 25$_9$; as signal for beginning journey Nm 10$_5$, advance of troops 1QM 8$_7$; **clashing** of cymbals, in worship Ps 150$_5$. **3. war-cry, alarm** of war Jos 6$_5$ Jr 4$_{19}$ 1QM 1$_{11}$. → רוע *shout.*

תְּרוּפָה 1.1 n.f.—pl. Si תרופות—**healing, medicine** Ezk 47$_{12}$ Si 38$_{4(B)}$. → cf. רפא I *heal.*

תִּרְזָה 1 n.f. **holm,** or other tree Is 44$_{14}$.

תֶּרַח I 11.0.2 pr.n.m. **Terah.**

[תֶּרַח] II 2 pl.n. **Terah.**

תִּרְחֲנָה 1 pr.n.m. (or f.) **Tirhanah.**

תָּרְמָה I 1.0.1 n.f. **deceit, cunning** Jg 9$_{31}$ 1QH 4$_7$. → רמה II *deceive.*

*תָּרְמָה II 1 pl.n. **Tormah.**

תרמות, see תַּרְמִית *deceit.*

תַּרְמִית 5.1 n.f.—cstr. Qr תַּרְמִית (Kt תרמות); sf. תַּרְמִיתָם—**deceit** Jr 8$_5$ 23$_{26}$ Zp 3$_{13}$. → רמה II *deceive.*

תֹּרֶן 3.0.1 n.[m.]—sf. תָּרְנָם—**1. mast** of ship Is 33$_{23}$ Ezk 27$_5$. **2. flag pole, flag** Is 30$_{17}$ 1QH 14$_{34}$.

* [תַּרְנְגוֹל] 0.0.1 n.[m.] **cock** 11QT[c] 3$_3$.

* [תַּרְעִית] n.f. **thinking** Ps 119$_{118}$ (if em. תַּרְמִיתָם *their deceit* to תַּרְעִיתָם *their thinking*).

תַּרְעֵלָה 3 n.f. **reeling,** caused by drink Is 51$_{17.22}$ Ps 60$_5$. → רעל I *quiver.*

[תַּרְעֲלָה], see תַּרְאֲלָה *Taralah.*

[תִּרְעָתִי] 1 gent. **Tirathite.**

תְּרָפִים 15 n.m.pl. **teraphim,** image(s) as household god(s) Gn 31$_9$ Jg 17$_5$, for divination Ezk 21$_{26}$.

תִּרְצָה I 4 pr.n.f. **Tirzah.**

תִּרְצָה II 14 pl.n. **Tirzah.**

תֶּרֶשׁ 2 pr.n.m. **Teresh.**

תַּרְשִׁישׁ I 7 n.[m.] **topaz,** or perh. **beryl,** or **chrysolite** Ex 28$_{20}$||39$_{13}$ Ezk 1$_{16}$. → רשׁשׁ I *crush.*

תַּרְשִׁישׁ II 4 pr.n.m. **Tarshish.**

תַּרְשִׁישׁ III 24.0.0.1 pl.n. **Tarshish.**

תִּרְשָׁתָא 5 n.m. **Tirshatha,** title of Persian governor in Judaea Ezr 2$_{63}$||Ne 7$_{65}$.

תַּרְתָּן 2 n.m. **Tartan.**

תַּרְתָּק 1 pr.n.[m.] **Tartak.**

* [תְּשֻׁאָה] n.f. **height,** תְּשֻׁאוֹת סֻכָּתוֹ *heights of his booth* Jb 36$_{29}$ (if em. תְּשֻׁאוֹת *crashes [of thunder] of*).

[תְּשׂוּמֶת] 1 n.f. **pledge,** תְּשׂוּמֶת יָד lit. 'placing of the hand', i.e. thing placed in the hand (as security) Lv 5$_{21}$. → שׂים *place.*

[תְּשֻׁאָה] 5 n.f.—Kt תשוה; pl. תְּשֻׁאוֹת; cstr. תְּשֻׁאוֹת—**1. shouting, tumult** Is 22$_2$ Jb 39$_7$ Zc 4$_7$. **2. crash (of thunder)** Jb 36$_{29}$, **(roar of) storm** Jb 30$_{22(Kt)}$. → שׁאה III *roar.*

תִּשְׁבִּי 6 gent. **Tishbite.**

תֹּשָׁבֵי, see תּוֹשָׁב *sojourner.*

*[תִּשְׁבָּחָה] 0.1.22 n.f.—Q תשבוחת; cstr. Q תשבוחת; sf. Q תשבוחתך; pl. Q תשבוחות; cstr. Q תשבוחות; sf. Q תשבוחותו—**praise, praiseworthiness** 4QShirShabb[d] 1.2$_{25}$; תשבוחת אל *praise of God* 1QM 4$_8$, אל התשבחות *the God of praises* Si 51$_{12}$. → שׁבח I *praise.*

תשבוחת, see תִּשְׁבָּחָה *praise.*

תַּשְׁבֵּץ 1 n.[m.] **chequered work,** or perh. **plaited work** Ex 28$_4$. → שׁבץ *weave with patterns.*

[תְּשׁוּבָה] 8.2.7 n.f.—cstr. תְּשׁוּבַת; sf. תְּשֻׁבָתוֹ; pl. תְּשֻׁבֹת; sf. תְּשׁוּבֹתֵיכֶם—**1a. return** 1 S 7$_{17}$; specif. of humans to dust 1QH 18$_4$, of the year, i.e. spring 2 S 11$_1$||1 C 20$_1$. **2. answer** Jb 21$_{34}$. **3. repentance** CD 19$_{16}$. → שׁוב *go back.*

תשוה Jb 30$_{22(Kt)}$, see תְּשֻׁאָה *roar of storm.*

*[תְּשֻׁוִית] n.f. **cushioned couch, carpet** Jb 36$_{29}$ (if em. תְּשֻׁאוֹת *crashes [of thunder] of*).

תְּשׁוּעָה 34.3.1 n.f.—תְּשֻׁעָה; cstr. תְּשׁוּעַת; sf. תְּשׁוּעָתִי—**salvation, deliverance, victory, help, 1.** in war 1 C 19$_{12}$, brought about by Y. 1 S 11$_{13}$. **2.** originating from humans, as vain Ps 60$_{13}$||108$_{13}$. **3.** saving activity of Y. in general Ps 71$_{15}$ Lm 3$_{26}$. → ישׁע *save.*

[תְּשׁוּקָה] 3.0.5 n.f.—sf. תְּשׁוּקָתוֹ—**desire, longing** Gn 3$_{16}$ 4$_7$ Ca 7$_{11}$ 1QS 11$_{22}$ 1QM 17$_4$.

תְּשׁוּרָה I 1 n.f. **present, gift** 1 S 9$_7$.

*תְּשׁוּרָה II 1 n.f. **provisions, sustenance (for journey)** 1 S 9$_7$. → שׁור *travel.*

*תְּשׁוּרָה III 1 n.f. **residue, remainder** 1 S 9$_7$. → cf. שׁאר *remain.*

[תֻּשִׁיָּה] I 1 n.f. appar. **storm** Jb 30$_{22(Qr)}$ (Kt תשוה, from תְּשֻׁאָה *[roar of] storm*).

תֻּשִׁיָּה II, see תּוּשִׁיָּה *sound wisdom.*

תְּשִׁיעִי 18.0.10.9 adj.—f.s. תְּשִׁיעִית—**1. ninth,** of day Nm 7$_{60}$, month Jr 36$_9$, year Lv 25$_{22}$ 2 K 17$_6$ (שְׁנַת הַתְּשִׁיעִית). **2.** as noun, **ninth (one),** in ref. to person 1 C 12$_{13}$, lot 1 C 24$_{11}$.

תשלומת, see תַּשְׁלֻמֶת *recompense.*

*[תַּשְׁלֻם] 0.0.1 n.[m.] **payment** XḤev/Se 49$_{10}$.

*[תַּשְׁלֻמֶת] 0.4 n.f.—תשלומת; pl. תשלומות—**recompense, reward, retribution** Si 12$_2$ 14$_6$ 32$_{13}$ 48$_8$. → שׁלם *be complete.*

*[תַּשְׁנִיק] 0.1 n.[m.] **suffocation, anguish** Si 34$_{20}$.

תֵּשַׁע 58.0.26 n.m.&f.—m. (with f. nouns) תֵּשַׁע; cstr. תְּשַׁע; f. (with m. nouns) תִּשְׁעָה; cstr. תִּשְׁעַת—**1. nine,** תְּשַׁע אַמּוֹת *nine cubits* Dt 3$_{11}$, תִּשְׁעָה חֳדָשִׁים *nine months* 2 S 24$_8$. **2.** with ellip. of noun, **nine (persons)** 1 C 3$_8$. **3.** as ordinal numeral, **ninth,** שְׁנַת־תֵּשַׁע *the ninth year* 2 K 18$_{10}$, בְּתִשְׁעָה לַחֹדֶשׁ *on the ninth (day) of the month* Lv 23$_{32}$. **4.** as constituent of a larger number, תְּשַׁע־עֶשְׂרֵה *nineteen* Jos 19$_{38}$, תֵּשַׁע וְעֶשְׂרִים *twenty-nine* Gn 11$_{24}$, vars. עֶשְׂרִים וָתֵשַׁע Jos 15$_{32}$, תִּשְׁעָה וְעֶשְׂרִים Ezr 1$_9$; תְּשַׁע מֵאוֹת *nine hundred* Jg 4$_3$. → cf. תִּשְׁעִים *ninety.*

תִּשְׁעָה, see תֵּשַׁע *nine.*

תִּשְׁעִים 20.0.3 n.m.&f.pl. **ninety,** תִּשְׁעִים שָׁנָה *ninety years* Gn 5$_9$; as constituent of a larger number, תִּשְׁעִים וַחֲמִשָּׁה *ninety-five* Ezr 2$_{20}$||Ne 7$_{25}$. → cf. תֵּשַׁע *nine.*

*[תִּשְׁרִי] 0.0.1 pr.n.[m.] **Tishri,** seventh month of post-exilic calendar = September/October Mur 30 2$_8$.

תִּתַּחֲרֶה, see חרה I *burn,* Tiphel.

*[תִּתָּה] 0.1 n.f. **giving out,** in business transaction Si 42$_{7(Bmg)}$. → נתן *give.*